47th Decision Sciences Institute Annual Meeting (DSI 2016)

Austin, Texas, USA
19 - 21 November 2016

Volume 1 of 2

ISBN: 978-1-5108-4273-1

Printed from e-media with permission by:

Curran Associates, Inc.
57 Morehouse Lane
Red Hook, NY 12571

Some format issues inherent in the e-media version may also appear in this print version.

Printed by Curran Associates, Inc. (2017)

For permission requests, please contact Decision Sciences Institute
at the address below.

Decision Sciences Institute
University of Houston
C.T. Bauer College of Business
334 Melcher Hall, Suite 325
Houston, TX 77204-6021
USA

Phone: 713-743-4815
Fax: 713-743-8984

info@decisionsciences.org

Additional copies of this publication are available from:

Curran Associates, Inc.
57 Morehouse Lane
Red Hook, NY 12571 USA
Phone: 845-758-0400
Fax: 845-758-2633
Email: curran@proceedings.com
Web: www.proceedings.com

TABLE OF CONTENTS

VOLUME 1

A COMPARATIVE STUDY OF BELIEFS, ATTITUDES, AND BEHAVIOR OF CLICKING TOWARD INTERNET ADVERTISING AMONG RESPONDENTS FROM TAIWAN, AND CANADA 1
P. Wang, M. Wen, K. Wu, C. Yeh, C. Lien

A FRAMEWORK FOR DIABETES SELF-CARE EFFICACY IN EVALUATING PERSONAL HEALTH RECORD 14
E. Lin, H. Hwang, M. Sher

A FRAMEWORK FOR INDEX DEVELOPMENT FOR MEASURING THE PERFORMANCE OF TELECOM OPERATORS: A CONSENSUS-BASED APPROACH 21
A. Bhadani, R. Shankar, D. Rao

A HEURISTIC DATA SAMPLING APPROACH FOR ASSOCIATION RULE CLASSIFICATION UNDER A BIG DATA ENVIRONMENT 44
C. Chern, H. Peng, L. Kung

A LEAN HOSPITAL SUPPLY CHAIN PERSPECTIVE TO IMPROVING PATIENT CARE QUALITY 54
S. Chakraborty

A META-ANALYTICAL VIEW OF NON-TECHNICAL SKILLS FOR BUSINESS AND ENGINEERING STUDENTS 81
T. Porterfield, R. Graham, D. Nesterkin

A MULTI-METHOD INVESTIGATION OF OVERORDERING BEHAVIOR IN SUPPLY CHAINS 95
T.T. Niranjan

A MULTI-OBJECTIVE DECISION MODEL FOR SUPPLY CHAIN COLLABORATION PROGRAMS 97
P. Parsa, M. Shbool, M. Rossetti, S. Zhang, E. Pohl

A NOTE ON MODELING PRODUCT ALLOCATION BETWEEN BRICK-AND-MORTAR AND ONLINE STORES 113
H. Zhang, H. Mesak, J. Ma

A NOTE ON THE SIMPLE TRADING RANGE BREAK-OUT RULE FOR NASDAQ INDEX 124
L. Ren

A SIMULATION MODEL FOR COMPARING THE ROBUSTNESS OF ALTERNATIVE LIQUEFIED NATURAL GAS (LNG) ANNUAL DELIVERY PROGRAMS (ADPS) 125
F. Mutlu, H. Yildiz, E. Sonmez, S. Pokharel

A STUDY OF VIRTUAL PROJECT TEAM TYPES AND THEIR IMPACT ON PROJECT SUCCESS 136
P. Ludden, A. Ledwith

A SYSTEMS THEORY PERSPECTIVE OF DATA ANALYTICS IMPLEMENTATION 156
N. Gerhart

ADDING SPICE TO THE TEACHING OF QUALITY: VARIATION, POKA YOKE, AND A DEFECT COLLECTION 168
B.C. Meyer

AN ECONOMIC PRODUCTION LOT SIZE MODEL IN AN IMPERFECT PRODUCTION SYSTEM WITH A MARKOV PROCESS AND SHORTAGE BACKORDERING 180
K. Hou, L. Lin

AN EMPIRICAL INVESTIGATION OF THE BALDRIGE FRAMEWORK USING APPLICANT SCORING DATA 187
F. Mai, M. Ford, J. Evans

AN EXAMINATION OF CONSUMER ATTITUDES ON ONLINE USER REVIEWS 203
C. Changchit, T. Klaus

AN INNOVATIVE APPROACH TO PROJECT DESIGN OF SOCIAL ENTREPRENEURSHIP 215
D. Chou

AN OPTIMIZATION MODEL FOR DETERMINING BIOREFINERY SIZE AND LOCATION 223
F. Zhang, D. Johnson, M. Johnson

ANALYZING THE EFFICIENCIES OF RENEWABLE ENERGY SOURCES WITH DATA ENVELOPMENT ANALYSIS 238
U. Saglam
APPLYING LEAN MANUFACTURING PRINCIPLES TO NEW PRODUCT DEVELOPMENT 251
M. Meybodi
ARE SERVICE PRODUCTIVITY AND QUALITY IN PERMANENT CONFLICT? (THE EFFECT OF SERVICE INNOVATION AND THE ROLE OF CUSTOMER SATISFACTION) 267
D. Rew
ARTIFICIAL REEF STRUCTURE AND MATERIAL DEPLOYMENT DECISIONS: A BIG DATA ANALYTICS EXERCISE ON PRESENCE AND ABUNDANCE OF REEF FISH 281
S. Coy, M. Shipley, J. Shipley
ASSESSMENT OF TOTAL QUALITY MANAGEMENT IMPLEMENTATION IN INDIAN SERVICE INDUSTRIES 293
F. Talib, M. Faisal
ASYMMETRY, TRUST, INNOVATION, AND PERFORMANCE IN SUPPLY CHAIN MANAGEMENT - A NON-LINEAR APPROACH 309
M. Michalski, J. Botella, R. Narasimhan
BALANCE OR STABILITY: A RE-CONCEPTUALIZATION OF THE KEY ELEMENTS OF SERVICE TRIAD SUSTAINABILITY 341
S. Sengupta, M. Krishnamoorthy, T. Niranjan
BALANCING SERVICE RISK WITH TECHNOLOGY COST FOR WEB-BASED APPLICATIONS USING EMULATION DRIVEN SIMULATION 343
S. Mohan, M. Gopalakrishnan, S. Pattabhiraman, A. Feller
BERMUDAN PUT OPTION PRICING UNDER RISK AVERSION IN BILATERAL GAMMA MODELS 366
B. Fontem, H. Tibbett, R. Graefe-Anderson
BOARD COMPOSITION AND PERSISTENCE ON CAPITAL MARKETS: EMPIRICAL EVIDENCE OF COMPANIES DELISTING FROM THE ASX 376
A. Lunt, D. Bumblauskas
BOWMAN'S PARADOX REVISITED: AN INVESTIGATION OF THREE EAST ASIAN MARKETS 398
C. Nguyen, A. Alikaj, W. Ning
BUILDING EFFECTIVE ONLINE EDUCATION VIDEO LECTURES: RECOMMENDATIONS FROM RESEARCH AND PRACTICE 411
P. Van Vliet
CAN CORPORATE ENTREPRENEURSHIP ATTRIBUTES IN ACQUIRED FIRMS AVOID THEIR ACQUISITION-TURNED-DIVESTITURE FATE? 435
S. Nandi, S. Wu
CONSUMER SELF-CONFIDENCE WITH MOBILE COMMERCE 459
S. Park, S. Park, J. Smith, K. Kim
CONSUMERS' INTENTION TOWARD MOBILE BANKING: FROM PERSPECTIVE OF TRIPARTITE MODEL OF ATTITUDE 480
I. Chang, E. Lin, H. Hwang
CORPORATE SUSTAINABILITY: AN ANALYSIS OF CSR AND CSV 497
R. Behara, R. Knight, J. DiCicco
CRITICAL SUCCESS FACTORS IMPACTING CLOUD-BASED EHR SYSTEMS 505
M. Merhi, S. Patel
CROSS AISLE PLACEMENT IN ORDER PICKING OPERATIONS 511
C. Petersen, G. Aase
CSR AND EMPLOYEE SATISFACTION: MEDIATING ROLE OF MARKETING INNOVATION 524
J. Hwang, J. Jung
DOES NEGOTIATION MATTER FOR BUSINESS RELATIONSHIP? A STUDY OF CREDIBLE INFORMATION DISCLOSURE AND PERCEIVED FAIRNESS 537
B. Yu, R. Vahidov, G. Kersten
E-COMMERCE, CHALLENGES, AND DEVELOPING COUNTRIES 551
S. Uwemi, H. Khan
EFFECT OF INSTITUTIONAL HETEROGENEITY IN PARTNERSHIP CONFIGURATION ON M&A PERFORMANCE 559
A. Papadopoulos, A. Taleb
EFFECTIVENESS OF CONTROL CHARTS FOR INTERMITTENT DEMAND 576
M. Lindsey, R. Pavur

EFFICACY BELIEFS AND CUSTOMER COLLABORATION IN ONLINE COLLABORATIVE COMMUNITIES: A RELATIONSHIP MARKETING PERSPECTIVE 582
C. Hsiao

EQUILIBRIUM ANALYSIS OF AN ADVERTISING-INVENTORY-PRICING COMPETITIVE MODEL 587
H. Mesak, A. Bari, R. Blackstock

EVALUATING PERFORMANCE QUALITY OF A FIRM'S SOCIAL MEDIA ACTIVITIES 599
J. Lim, K. Lim, J. Heinrichs

EXAMINING THE RELATIONSHIP BETWEEN EXTERNAL SOFTWARE CHARACTERISTICS AND VULNERABILITIES 604
Y. Roumani, J. Nwankpa, Y. Roumani

EXPERIENTIAL LEARNING THEORY: EVIDENCE FROM A STUDY ABROAD PROGRAM 618
S. Nargundkar, M. Shrikhande

EXPLORATIVE AND EXPLOITATIVE USE OF SMART TOURISM TECHNOLOGIES IN TRAVEL PLANNING 632
C. Huang, J. Goo, K. Nam, C. Yoo

EXTRACTING LIFE SKILLS FROM AN INTRODUCTORY EXCEL PROGRAMMING CLASS 643
B. Martz, D. Manning

FACTORS THAT INFLUENCE EMPLOYEES' SECURITY POLICY COMPLIANCE BEHAVIOR: AN AWARENESS-MOTIVATION-CAPABILITY (AMC) PERSPECTIVE 659
X. Chen, L. Chen

FINANCIAL DATA ANALYTICS AND EXTRACTION FROM SECURITY EXCHANGE COMMISSION'S (SEC) EDGAR FILLINGS 670
R. Green, R. Burdwell, R. Vinaja

FIRM'S SHORT-TERM GROWTH RATE AND EARNINGS MANAGEMENT 676
Y. He

GARMENT SUPPLIERS' STRATEGIES TO MANAGE COMMERCIAL AND SOCIAL TENSIONS: AN INSTITUTIONAL LOGICS' PERSPECTIVE 689
M. Mueller, J. Hofstetter, A. Goerzen

GLOBAL GROWTH OF SERVICE INNOVATION: INFLUENCE OF NATIONAL CULTURE AND ORGANIZATIONAL STRUCTURE 698
S. Mukhopadhyay, K. Bagchi, S. Samaddar

PREPARING LEADERS TO LIVE IN A VIRTUAL WORLD: A TEMPLATE TO ENHANCE EFFECTIVENESS OF ONLINE GLOBAL SUPPLY SIMULATIONS 721
L. Taube, D. Parkes, C. Nemer

HOSPITAL UNIT UNDERSTAFFING AND MISSED TREATMENTS: THE MODERATING EFFECT OF TEAMWORK 731
A. Metcalf

IMPACT OF NEW PRODUCT DEVELOPMENT FLEXIBILITY ON PERFORMANCE 741
J. Lim, J. Heinrichs, K. Lim

IMPACT OF SUPPLY CHAIN COLLABORATION ON LOGISTICS PERFORMANCE: EVIDENCE FROM A SUB-SAHARA AFRICA NATION'S PETROLEUM DOWNSTREAM 748
B. Agyei-Owusu, D. Asamoah, F. Andoh-Baidoo, J. Akaribo

IMPROVING LEARNING OUTCOMES IN A FLIPPED SPREADSHEET-BASED GRADUATE DECISION MODELING COURSE 766
S. Coy, D. TeDuits, J. Crawford

"INTERNET OF THINGS" (IOT)-ENABLED PRODUCT MONITORING: INSIGHTS FROM SOCIO-TECHNICAL SYSTEMS THEORY, AFFORDANCES THEORY, AND STRUCTURATIONAL MODEL OF TECHNOLOGY 774
R. Angeles

IN SEARCH FOR IMPREGNABLE EXCHANGE RELATIONSHIPS WITH BUYERS: INSIGHTS FOR SUPPLIERS 809
T. Clauss, C. Tangpong

DISCRIMINATING RATED LEADERSHIP IN THE U.S PRESIDENCY FROM VALUE CONTENT AND STYLISTIC VARIABLES IN STATE OF THE UNION ADDRESSES: A DATA MINING METHODOLOGY 814
S. Silver

INDIVIDUAL ADOPTION AND USE OF HR ANALYTICS: IMPLICATIONS OF ORGANIZATIONAL ADOPTION 824
R. Vargas, Y. Yurova, C. Ruppel

INFLUENCE OF THE CEO CHARACTERISTICS IN MERGERS AND ACQUISITIONS IN THE PHARMACEUTICAL INDUSTRY 825
A. Sanchez, M. Abebe
INFORMATION EXCHANGE RESEARCH OPPORTUNITIES 839
S. Jagani, A. Kunnathur, S. Wallace
INSIDE THE BLACK BOX OF OPERATIONAL CAPABILITIES: AN EVOLUTION FROM OPERATIONAL PRACTICES 847
M. Scarpin, L. Brito, B. Flynn
INSTITUTIONAL STUDENT RETENTION INITIATIVES FOR ACCELERATED PROGRAMS 874
A. Lo, J. Reeves, P. Jenkins, R. Parkman
INTEGRATION OF TEACHING AND RESEARCH: THE ACTIVE-LEARNING AND RESEARCH-LED APPROACH IN INTEGRATING MULTI-DISCIPLINARY CONCEPTS IN OPERATIONS MANAGEMENT 896
M. Gopalakrishnan

VOLUME 2

INTERNET USE FOR E-COMMERCE IN US COUNTIES: GEOGRAPHIC PATTERNS AND SOCIO-ECONOMIC INFLUENCES 907
J. Pick, A. Sarkar, J. Rosales
INVENTORY MODELS IN A CLOSED-LOOP SUPPLY CHAIN WITH PRODUCT RETURNS AND REFURBISHMENT 931
S. Yoo, S. Joo, M. Park
INVESTIGATION INTO THE MARRIAGE PENALTY UNDER THE ALTERNATIVE MINIMUM TAX 950
M. Keane, N. Oestreich, J. Williamson
IS SOA REALLY DEAD? 956
S. Ghosh
MAXIMIZATION OF SELLER'S NET REVENUE IN DISCRETE DUTCH AUCTIONS WITH TRANSACTION COST 969
Z. Li, C. Kuo, J. Yue
MEASURING THE IMPACT OF A WEB-BASED BLENDED LEARNING PLATFORM ON STUDENT LEARNING 973
T. Bayrak, B. Akcam
MESSAGES FROM FORTUNE 500 CEOS 986
A. Papadopoulos
METHODOLOGICAL DEVELOPMENTS IN UNDERSTANDING BRAND CREATION AND BRAND IDENTITY – THE CASE OF SEVENS WELLINGTON - AN INTERNATIONAL RECURRING SPORTS EVENT 1013
S. Harrison, J. Davies
MINING FOR THE ENTREPRENEURIAL ELEMENT 1023
R. Morrison
MOBILE BANKING ADOPTION: THAI CONSUMERS' PERSPECTIVE 1042
C. Changchit, R. Lonkani, J. Sampet
MOBILE BANKING RESISTANCE IN IVORY COAST 1058
M. Merhi, P. Avoaka
MODIFYING RESOURCE ALLOCATION FOR TRANSITION OF EMERGENCY DEPARTMENT (ED) VISITS TO URGENT CARE (UC) VISITS 1064
L. Frederick, B. Park, M. Korir, M. Hysell, N. Johnson
MULTI-CRITERIA STOCK PORTFOLIO MANAGEMENT – A DISTANCE FUNCTION APPROACH 1075
D. Sharma, R. Jana, H. Sharma
OFFSHORING AND RESHORING IN THE INTERNATIONALIZATION STRATEGY: A MULTIPLE CASE STUDY APPROACH 1083
C. Di Mauro, L. Fratocchi, G. Orzes, M. Sartor
ON THE JOB TRAINING: A CASE STUDY ON USING CONSULTING EXPERIENCES TO ENHANCE STUDENTS' EMPLOYABILITY 1115
R. Graham, P. Sheff
OPEN SERVICES INNOVATION: IDENTIFYING LINKAGES BETWEEN KNOWLEDGE SOURCING AND FIRM PERFORMANCE 1128
S. Schafer, S. Powless

OPTIMAL LOCATION OF REPAIR STATIONS IN A GARMENTS PRODUCTION LINE 1138
S. Hossain, B. Sarker
ORDERING BLOOD DONATIONS UNDER UNCERTAIN ENVIRONMENT 1146
S. Fortsch, Q. Liao
OVERALL EQUIPMENT EFFECTIVENESS MEASURES OF ENGINEERING PRODUCTION SYSTEMS 1170
S. Hossain, B. Sarker
PERFORMANCE EVALUATION OF A MICRO-IRRIGATION COMPANY USING THE APC MODEL 1180
M. Rao, R. Chhabria
PERFORMANCE OF SUPERVISED ARTIFICIAL NEURAL NETWORKS FOR FOREIGN EXCHANGE RATE PREDICTION 1185
H. Sharma, D. Sharma, H. Hota
POWER AND COLLABORATIVE CLIMATE: BUILDING COMPETITIVE ADVANTAGE THROUGH FLEXIBILITIES 1192
Y. Jin, E. Marsillac
PREVENTING INFERENCE ATTACKS IN ONLINE SOCIAL NETWORKS: A DATA-DRIVEN FRAMEWORK 1206
X. He, H. Lu
PROACTIVE INCENTIVE STRATEGIES FOR QUALITY IMPROVEMENT IN A THREE-STAGE SUPPLY CHAIN 1214
S. Yoo, D. Kim, T. Choi
PROBLEM-SOLVING IS DECISION-MAKING 1239
S. Talanker
RENEWABLE TWO-DIMENSIONAL PRO-RATA WARRANTY ANALYSIS FOR REVERSE SUPPLY CHAIN 1257
A. Alqahtani, S. Gupta
RE-SLOTTING TO REDUCE WAREHOUSE OPERATING EXPENSES 1269
G. Aase, C. Petersen
RETHINKING UNDERGRADUATE BUSINESS CORE CURRICULUM: ONE SCHOOL'S EXPERIENCE OF REDESIGNED CURRICULUM WITH A HOLISTIC APPROACH 1280
A. Morton, J. Harrison, L. Re, N. Schmitt
ROLE OF PERCEIVED PLAYFULNESS/SERIOUSNESS IN LEARNING PROCESS USING BUSINESS SIMULATION GAME 1289
J. Kim, E. Watson
SHOULD BUSINESS ANALYTICS BE TAUGHT TO EVERY UNDERGRADUATE? – WE ARE ALREADY DOING IT 1318
Z. Ugray
SHOULD SUPPLIERS CHOOSE TO BE LEADING INNOVATORS? 1325
A. Mackelprang, E. Bernardes, J. Burke, C. Welter
SITUATION AWARENESS DIFFERENCES ON THE USE OF CLOUD COMPUTING 1326
S. Sun, C. Sankar, J. Song
SOCIAL CAPITAL AND KNOWLEDGE SHARING IN ORGANIZATION: AN INITIAL META-ANALYSIS 1346
Q. Ha, J. Chen
STATUS OF GREEN SUPPLY CHAIN MANAGEMENT ADOPTION IN MIDWEST MANUFACTURING: AN EMPIRICAL STUDY 1356
A. Agarwal, F. Giraud-Carrier, L. Penumatsa
STOCK TRADING DECISIONS USING ENSEMBLE-BASED FORECASTING MODELS 1365
D. Jothimani, R. Shankar, S. Yadav
STRATEGIC GLOBAL WORK-LIFE BALANCE INITIATIVES: THE ROLES OF THE EXPATIRATION CYCLE AND GENDER 1378
E. Medina
SUBJECTIVE WELL-BEING OF CHILDREN OF MIGRANT FAMILIES IN SCHOOLING ALTERNATIVES OF URBAN CHINA 1391
S. Silver
SUBSTITUTES OR COMPLEMENTS? THE IMPACT OF CONTRACTUAL AND RELATIONAL GOVERNANCE ON LOGISTICS INTEGRATION AND OPERATIONAL PERFORMANCE 1400
Q. Wang, B. Huo, X. Zhao
SUCCESS FACTORS FOR A CLASSROOM PROJECT 1409
T. Jitpaiboon, S. Smith, Q. Gu

SUPPLY CHAIN DISRUPTION HANDLING: A DYNAMIC EXTENDED RESOURCE-BASED (DE-RBV) VIEW 1416
B. Qin, P. Hong, Y. Zhang
SUPPLY CHAIN PERFORMANCE ANALYSIS BASED UPON LITTLE'S LAW 1446
S. Choi
SUPPLY CHAIN RISK NETWORK MANAGEMENT (SCRNM): A PARADIGM SHIFT TOWARDS MODELLING SYSTEMIC RISKS AND RISK APPETITE 1466
A. Qazi, A. Dickson, J. Quigley
SUSTAINABLE TOURISM DEVELOPMENT AND SERVICE OPERATIONS MANAGEMENT AT THE MISSOURI STATE PENITENTIARY (MSP) 1479
D. Bumblauskas
THE ANALYSIS OF E-PRODUCT SALES AFFECTED BY ONLINE WORKD-OF-MOUTH AND E-COMMEERCE SERVICE QUALITY BASED ON OBSERVATIONAL LEARNING 1505
M. Lei, M. Zhang, H. Deng, M. Rothenberger, N. Christodoulidou
THE EFFECT OF SOCIAL AND TEMPORAL DISTANCE ON RISK PREFERENCES: AN EXPERIMENTAL INVESTIGATION 1523
E. Demiral, U. Saglam
THE EFFECT OF SOCIAL MEDIA ON PURCHASING BEHAVIOR 1532
M. McGrath, Y. Li
THE EFFECTIVENESS OF INTENTIONAL DESIGN IN AN ONLINE INVENTORY MANAGEMENT CLASS 1540
J. Strakos
THE EFFECTS OF CONSUMER PERCEPTIONS OF ETHICS IN ONLINE GRAY MARKET SOURCING ACTIVITIES ON TRUST AND PURCHASE INTENTION 1559
N. Gudigantala, M. Abreu
THE GLOBAL APTITUDE ASSESSMENT MODEL: A CRITICAL PERSPECTIVE 1574
R. Kaushik, M. Raisinghani, S. Gibson, N. Assis
THE IMPACT OF CHOICE OF COSTING METHOD ON PROJECT/PRODUCT PROFITABILITY 1585
A. Foroughi, M. Kocakulah, L. Manyoky
THE IMPACT OF INTER-ORGANIZATIONAL INFORMATION SYSTEMS ON CAPABILITIES OF BUYER-SUPPLIER DYADS 1601
A. Radhakrishnan, D. David
THE IMPACTS OF SERVICE QUALITY ON CONTINUANCE INTENTION TO USE VIDEO SURVEILLANCE-AS-A-SERVICE 1605
J. Chen, G. Kuritsyn, Q. Ha, A. Widjaja
THE INFLUENCE OF ETHICAL RELATIVISM ON ETHICAL COMPROMISE IN BUSINESS EXCHANGES 1622
J. Li, C. Tangpong, K. Hung
THE INFLUENCE OF MANAGERIAL METACOGNITION ON QUALITY MANAGEMENT PRACTICES AND A FIRM'S SUSTAINABLE COMPETITIVE ADVANTAGES 1627
Y. Cho
THE PRIVATIZATION OF LARGE AND SMALL-SCALE FIRMS AND THEIR DIFFERENTIAL IMPACTS ON THE MACROECONOMY UNDER TRANSITION 1647
M. DelVecchio
THE PROFITABILITY OF US COMMUNITY BANKS: A CROSS-SECTIONAL AND DYNAMIC PANEL ANALYSIS 1660
R. Morrison, D. Escobari
THE RELATIONSHIP BETWEEN OBSERVED AND PUBLISHED MULTIPLE-CHOICE QUESTION DIFFICULTY MAY DEPEND ON WHAT MEANS "RELATED" 1677
J. Dickinson
THE RELATIONSHIP BETWEEN TECHNOSTRESS CREATORS AND ONLINE EDUCATION AMONG STUDENTS 1678
Q. Booker, C. Rebman
THE ROLE OF MARKETING IN REVERSE SUPPLY CHAIN 1688
S. Dowlatshahi
TOWARDS A PROCESS FRAMEWORK FOR SUB-SUPPLIER SUSTAINABILITY MANAGEMENT 1689
J. Hofstetter
TOWARDS A THEORY OF DYNAMIC INFORMATION SECURITY BEHAVIORS 1699
C. Lin, A. Kunnathur

TRAINING BEYOND JOB SKILLS TO ENHANCE PERCEIVED ORGANIZATIONAL SUPPORT AND JOB SATISFACTION IN CENTRAL AMERICAN MAQUILAS 1722
R. Morrison, J. Welbourne, C. Dole, J. Chavarria
TURNAROUND IN LARGE COMPLEX LEGACY ORGANIZATIONS 1745
D. Lehmberg, C. Tangpong
TWO OBSERVATIONS BETWEEN "TRUTH" AND MEH: A COMPLEMENT TO CROSS-TABULATION CHI-SQUARE HYPOTHESIS TESTING 1751
J. Dickinson
UNDERSTANDING THE EFFECT OF FLICKR'S SCREENSHOT ANNOTATIONS ON LEARNING EFFECTIVENESS 1752
T. Huang, S. Lin, L. Lo
UNDERSTANDING THE ORGANIZATIONAL NEEDS OF AN INTERNATIONAL SPORTS EVENT: A SYSTEMS PERSPECTIVE ON SEVENS WELLINGTON - THE WELLINGTON 7S 1762
S. Harrison, J. Davies
USE OF SOCIAL MEDIA IN TEACHING AND ITS IMPACT ON STUDENT LEARNING OUTCOMES 1772
S. Rahman, T. Ramakrishnan, L. Ngamassi
USING A SELF-MANAGED LEARNING CASE IN AN INTERMEDIATE ACCOUNTING I COURSE INCLUDING ETHICS WITH VALUE-ADDED ASSESSMENT 1780
J. Sage, L. Sage
VALIDATING REGRESSION ASSUMPTIONS THROUGH RESIDUAL PLOTS – CAN STUDENTS DO IT? 1797
H. Ravinder, M. Berenson, H. Su
WAS DEMING AGILE? LOOKING AT INFORMATION TECHNOLOGY FRAMEWORKS AND PRACTICES 1806
D. Miller, T. Krehbiel
WECHAT SHOPPING: A STUDY OF COSMETIC PRODUCT SELLING TO COLLEGE STUDENTS IN CHINA 1823
Y. Zheng, J. Wang, D. DiRusso, J. Gao
Author Index

DECISION SCIENCES INSTITUTE

A comparative study of beliefs, attitudes, and behavior of clicking toward internet advertising among respondents from Taiwan, and Canada

Ping Wang
James Madison University
Email: wangpx@jmu.edu

Miin-Jye Wen
National Cheng Kung University
Email: mjwen@mail.ncku.edu.tw

Kuo-Lung Wu
Kun Shan University
Email: klwu@mail.ksu.edu.tw

Chun-Wu Yeh
Kun Shan University
Email:davidyeh929@gmail.com

Che-Hui (Eric) Lien
Thompson Rivers University
Email: elien@tru.ca

ABSTRACT

Creative interactive multimedia advertising on internet shows its ability to entertain customers while provide product and alternatives information, thus add values to the advertised products and services. Customers' attitudes to advertising on internet are associated with beliefs of entertainment, information, irritation, and trustworthiness, and attitudes toward internet advertising, and influence customers' clicking and purchasing behavior. This study aims to find interrelationships among internet users' perception, attitudes, and behavior of clicking toward online advertising by using multiple group structural equation modeling to analyze responses from college students in Taiwan and Canada.

KEYWORDS: Internet advertising, Beliefs, Attitudes, Multiple group structural equation modeling

INTRODUCTION

The number of internet users around the globe have grown significantly. According to the statistics by(Stats 2015) Internet World Stats (2016) as of November 2015, Taiwan has close to 20 million of internet users or 84% of its 23.4 million of population and Canada has over 33 million internet users or 94.5% of its 35.7 million of population. Due to its fast delivery speed, low cost, distance-free, real-time and capability for instant and comprehensive information, internet has become a major platform for advertising. Internet have been used to carry out many activities such as searching for product and service information, watching video, shopping, chatting or job hunting, to list a few. Marketing and advertising businesses have increasingly used internet to reach their potential audience. According to PwC's global entertainment and media outlook of 2015 – 2019 (2016), by 2019, internet advertising could become the largest advertising segment with the potential for the global total internet advertising revenue to reach US$239.87 billion in 2019 for a compound annual growth rate of 12.1% over the US$ 135.42 billion in 2014 ("Global Entertainment and Media Outlook 2015-2019: Home Page: PwC" 2015).

The main objective of this study is to find if there exists cultural differences in the effect of perception toward attitudes and the behavior of clicking over internet advertising. The perceptions toward online advertising include informativeness, entertainment, irritation and trustworthiness (Ducoffe 1995; Ducoffe 1996). This study investigates the relationships among the perceptions, attitudes, and the behavior of clicking. The survey of this study was conducted in Taiwan and Canada via questionnaires to internet users, more specifically, the college students. The main contributions of this study include a conceptual framework that studies the cultural differences on internet users' perceptions, attitudes toward internet advertising, and the behavior of clicking among subjects and responses between Taiwan and Canada, two quite different East and West cultures. This study demonstrates the differences of country effects on attitude toward internet advertising through structure equation modeling.

Section 2 reviews the previous studies on internet advertising, internet users' perceptions, attitudes and the behavior of clicking toward internet advertising, and cross cultural comparisons. Section 3 outlines development of the research hypotheses to be tested in this study. Section 4 presents the survey instrument, data collected, analysis of results, and cultural comparisons. Finally, Section 5 presents the conclusions and discussions.

LITERATURE REVIEW

In his study of advertising value and advertising on the web, (Ducoffe 1996) states that, even though internet advertising and traditional advertisement share many similarities, the electronic commercial contents in internet advertising, such as corporate websites, differ quite significantly from that in the traditional advertisements. (Zeff and Aronson 1999) indicate that internet advertising enables enterprises to use banners, buttons and links to post information throughout internet. Internet advertising combines advantages of traditional advertisements and direct marketing. The Web Ad.vantage Company (2013) categorizes internet advertisements into text, display, pop-up, interstitial, video, and email advertisements. The perceptions of internet users toward online advertising refer to the organization, identification, and interpretation of sensory information that internet users received in order for them to represent and understand the advertisement (Schacter, Gilbert, and Wegner 2011).

Ducoffe (1995) believed that internet advertising provides real-time information better than a traditional advertisement. (Ducoffe 1996) described informativeness as the "the ability of advertising" that bring to consumers the available information on products and purchase alternatives in order for consumers to make satisfactory purchases decisions. Any internet user can search online for information whenever he or she wants. Ha and James (1998) considered informativeness the most widely used marketing function of the internet because there is no limit to the amount of information in websites and advertisements. Ju-Pak (1999) also pointed out that one of the roles that internet advertising plays is an information provider. The information that internet advertising provides makes the market more efficient. Though the internet advertising gives much information, what individual internet user needs are not the same. Therefore, internet users would like to choose what they need among different choices that internet advertising provides. Rodgers and Thorson (2000) believed that internet users should be more aggressive to accomplish their goals and needs. All of internet users have to do is to click the mouse to get the information which fits their requirements. According to Brackett and Carr (2001), the information immediacy is the sole reason that internet users expect the internet advertising to replace traditional television as the main resource for product and market information.

A successful internet advertisement includes not only information but also the ways to attract and entertain internet users. It has been recognized in the attitude toward advertising research that entertaining or pleasant or likeable advertising is believed to associate positively to attitude to the advert and product (MacKenzie, Lutz 1989). The advertising's entertainment function could be linked to consumers' "needs for escapism, diversion, aesthetic enjoyment, or emotional enjoyment" (McQuail 1983), be viewed as social messages to positively impress consumers (Shavitt, Lowrey, & Haefner, 1998), and be shown in an action, event or activity to entertain, satisfy and attract one or more users (Daily Heritage, 2014). Similarly, McQuail (1983) indicated entertainment derives its value from fulfilling consumers' entertaining needs. Marketers often use the ability of advertising to entertain to enhance consumers' experience of viewing advertising. Internet provides a creative interactive multimedia platform for advertising to be amusing, delightful, and entertaining, which improves the ability to attract customers' attention and therefore be more effective, thus add value to the advertised products or services. Customers view an entertaining advertising as more informative (Ducoffe 1995). Taylor et al.(2011) showed entertainment played a much stronger role to impact customers' attitude toward advertising than information in their study of advertising on social network sites. The future of internet advertising is lies on delivering the advertising information with creative, enjoyable, and interactive messages (Hoffman and Novak 1996), such as its multimedia functions, which not only entertain viewers but also increase values to the advertised products or services (Lutz 1985, Pollay and Mittal 1993). Consumers surfing commercial websites are primarily motivated by the entertainment value, personal relevance, and information involvement (Eighmey 1997). Wolin et al. (2002) considered a good looking, attractive and interesting design and an interactive presentation of products would entertain internet users and improve the internet users' attitudes toward internet advertising. However, there exists a different opinion toward the entertainment of internet advertising. Schlosser et al. (1999) found that people who enjoyed watching an internet advertisement is obviously less than who enjoyed watching a traditional advertisement.

The informativeness and entertainment are viewed as the positive factors about the internet advertising that are non-intrusive and value-based (Nutley 2004). (Schlosser et al., 1999) pointed out in their studies that internet advertising is often viewed to be not as insulting, offending, or misleading consumers as other forms of advertising. However, internet users often irritated with the commercial contents they are intruded upon their attention (Hawkins 1994), and with unfavorable banner brands (Thota et al. 2012). Irritation negatively affects consumers' attitudes toward the host website.. Irritation and deception are among the negative effects of internet advertising (Aaker and Bruzzone 1985), and still negatively impact upon the perception of internet advertising (Ducoffe 1996, and Brackett and Carr 2001).

Deceptiveness as another factor in Ducoffe (1995) revealed importance of considering trustworthiness as another significant factor that affects internet users' attitudes toward internet advertising. Even though advertising, traditional or internet, is often believed to carry only half-truths and false claims (Nadilo 1998), internet advertising is perceived to be more believable than traditional advertisement (Schlosser et al. 1999). Nevertheless, the internet users' trustworthiness toward internet advertising affects positively to their attitudes to internet advertising (Brackett and Carr 2001).

Many researches connect the internet users' perception (Ducoffe 1996)(An and Kim, 2007; Wang and Sun, 2010), and attitudes to their behavior toward internet advertising. The model that (Ducoffe 1995; Ducoffe 1996) proposed shows the entertainment and informativeness of internet advertising have positive effects on the advertising value while the irritation and deceptiveness have negative effects. The consumers perceived value of internet advertising positively affects their attitudes toward internet advertising. Wolin et al. (2002) used seven belief factors in this regard, where, product information, hedonic/pleasure, social role and image, good for the economy are assumed to positively affect internet users' attitudes toward internet advertising while materialism, falsity and value corruption are assumed to negatively affect internet users' attitudes toward internet advertising. The demographical information, such as, internet users' education, age, and income, is shown to have negatively effects on their attitudes and behavior. (Schlosser, Shavitt, and Kanfer 1999) extends Ducoffe's model (1995) with a perceiving factor, trustworthiness, the positive aspect of deceptiveness.

(An and Kim 2008) discover that there exists cultural differences from responses in South Korea and the United States. Hence, the cultural differences could also exist from responses in Taiwan and Canada, thus worth of being discussed in this study. Culture defines how people live and impact their attitudes, behavior, and material things (Hall 1976). East culture (Chinese in Taiwan) differs significantly from those West culture in Canada (Hofstede and Hofstede 2001). Culture and advertising are intrinsically linked to each other (Wang and Sun, 2010). Mueller (1992) concluded that Japanese advertising may become increasingly Japanese-culture-oriented instead of being westernized. Attitudes toward advertising have also been examined in many cross-cultural studies. For example, Singh et al. (2006) provided empirical evidence that consumers from Germany, China, and India prefer internet sites adapted to their local cultures, and that culture influences consumer beliefs, attitudes, and purchase intention on the website. An and Kim (2007) extended Ducoffe's model (1996) and made a cross-cultural comparison between South Korean and American website users' to point out the factors which affect significantly the website users' attitudes toward internet advertising. La Ferle et al. (2008) examined attitudes toward advertising across China, Taiwan, and the United States. They find that Chinese and Taiwanese exhibited more favorable attitudes toward advertising than American consumers did. Wang and Sun (2010) used five factors including entertainment, information seeking, credibility, economy, and value corruption between the Chinese and American samples and showed that all belief factors are significant predictors of web users' attitudes toward internet advertising except for credibility. They also found significant differences in information, credibility, and economy beliefs between the Chinese and American samples.

CONCEPTUAL FRAMEWORK AND RESEARCH HYPOTHESIS

The main objective of this study is to research if cultural differences exist among countries with web users' perceptions, attitudes toward internet advertising, and behavior of clicking. This research combines the concept of abovementioned models including Ducoffe (1996), Wolin et al. (2002), An and Kim (2007), and Wang and Sun (2010) to propose a conceptual framework as shown in Figure 1. An and Kim (2007) proposed a model that described the relationship between perceptions and attitudes toward internet advertising. Wolin et al. (2002) found that the internet users' attitudes toward internet advertising would positively affect their behavior of clicking. Ducoffe (1996) and Wang and Sun (2010) both mentioned that there existed correlation among informativeness, entertainment, irritation and trustworthiness. An and Kim (2007) compared the American and South Korean internet users' perception toward attitudes and found there were difference between these two countries. Wang and Sun (2010) also found some differences in Chinese and American internet users' belief and attitudes toward internet advertising.

Figure 1 The Conceptual Model Underlying the Study

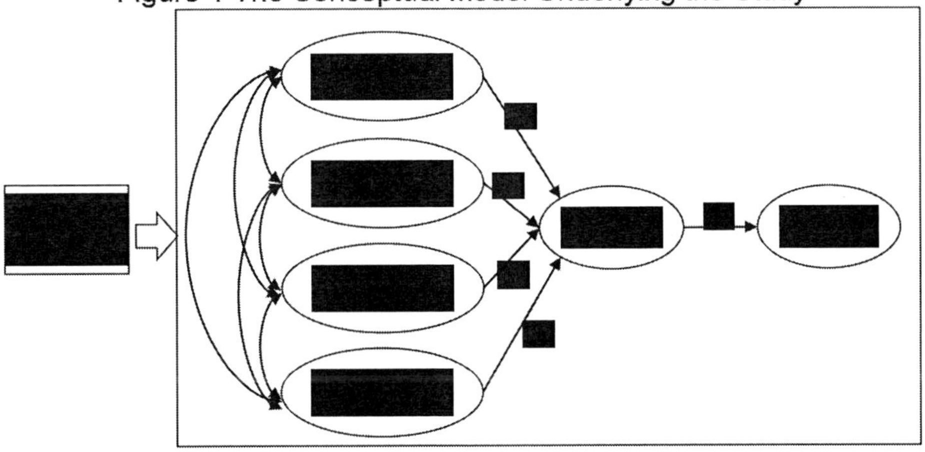

The research question related is whether or not the informativeness is related to internet users' attitude toward online advertising in the same way for both responses from Taiwan and Canada? The research hypothesis is:

H1. Informativeness positively affects the Attitudes for subjects from Taiwan and Canada, but the degree of importance may differ.

The research question related is whether or not the entertainment is related to internet users' attitude toward online advertising in the same way for both responses from Taiwan and Canada? The research hypothesis is:

H2. Entertainment positively affects the attitudes for subjects from Taiwan and Canada, but the degree of importance may differ.

The research question related is whether or not the irritation is related to internet users' attitude toward online advertising in the same way for both responses from Taiwan and Canada? The research hypothesis is:

H3. Irritation negatively affects the attitudes for subjects from Taiwan and Canada, but the degree of importance may differ.

The research question related is whether or not the trustworthiness is related to internet users' attitude toward online advertising in the same way for both responses from Taiwan and Canada? The research hypothesis is:

H4. Trustworthiness positively affects the Attitudes for subjects from Taiwan and Canada, but the degree of importance may differ.

The research question related is whether or not the users' attitude toward online advertising is related to internet users' behavior of clicking or purchasing in the same way for both responses from Taiwan and Canada? The research hypothesis is:

H5. Attitudes positively affect behavior of clicking for subjects from Taiwan and Canada, but the degree of importance may differ.
Other research hypothesis to be tested in this study include

H6. Informativeness positively and indirectly affects behavior of clicking through attitudes for subjects from Taiwan and Canada, but the degree of importance may differ.

H7. Entertainment positively and indirectly affects behavior of clicking through attitudes for subjects from Taiwan and Canada, but the degree of importance may differ.

H8. Irritation negatively and indirectly affects behavior of clicking through attitudes for subjects from Taiwan and Canada, but the degree of importance may differ.
H9. Trustworthiness positively and indirectly affects behavior of clicking through attitudes for subjects from Taiwan and Canada, but the degree of importance may differ.

METHODS

Ducoffe (1996) survey instrument with minor modifications is used in this study to investigate the perceptions, attitudes, and behavior of clicking for internet users respectively and the responses were measured on a 5-point Likert scale ranging from 1 (strongly disagree) to 5 (strongly agree). There are 20 items in Part A including the measurement in A1-A7 for informativeness, the measurement in A8-A12 for entertainment, the measurement in A13-A17 for irritation, and the measurement in A18-A20 for trustworthiness of internet users toward an internet advertisement. There are 3 items in Part B for the measurement of internet users' attitudes toward internet advertising. There are 3 items in Part C for the measurement of internet users' behavior of clicking toward internet advertising. In Part D, it records the demographic factors of the respondents.

Additionally, this study uses reliability and validity to assess the consistency and accuracy of the measurement items. The former is an assessment of the degree of consistency between multiple measurements of a variable, and Cronbach's α is a common used measure of reliability defined as Eq. (1).

$$\alpha = \frac{k}{k-1}\left[1-\frac{\Sigma V(X_i)}{V(H)}\right] \qquad (1)$$

where k is the number of items, $V(X_i)$ is the variance of each item score and $V(H)$ is the variance of total score. A low Cronbach's α (< 0.6) indicates a low consistency among items. Moreover, item-to-total correlation measures the correlation of each item to the sum of the remaining items. The high inter-item correlations explain that the items of a scale have a strong relationship to the latent construct. The latter is the extent to which a scale or set of measures accurately represents the concept of interest. Construct validity is a widely employed form of validity. The greater a construct is used by researchers in more settings with outcomes consistent with theory, the higher its construct validity. Confirmatory factor analysis (CFA) within structural equation modeling (SEM) is a common method of assessing construct validity. Discriminant validity reflects the degree to which two conceptually similar concepts are distinct, and the correlation here should be low. A rigorous SEM-based alternative approach to discriminant validity is to run the model unconstrained and also constraining the correlation between constructs to 1, namely, to test H_0: $\rho=1$ versus H_1: $\rho\neq1$, where ρ is the correlation between paired constructs. If the two models differ significantly on a Chi-squared difference test, that is $\Delta\chi^2 > \chi^2_{1,0.05}$, we can conclude that the two constructs differ (Anderson and Gerbing, 1988). Convergent validity refers to the degree to which two measures of the same concept are correlated, and the correlation here should be high. If measuring items of each construct have individual factor loadings at least 0.50 (Grandon and Pearson, 2003; Lee et al., 2004) and all measuring items are significant with t-value greater than 1.96, we can conclude that the scale has convergent validity. What is more, the composite reliability (CR), variance extracted (VE) are also considered to display reliability of a construct when assessing convergent validity (Fornell and Larcker, 1981). The commonly used threshold values are (1) CR ≥ 0.70; (2) VE ≥ 0.50 (Hair et al., 2009). The composite reliability and variance extracted of a construct are given by Eq. (2) and Eq. (3):

$$CR = \frac{(\Sigma\lambda)^2}{(\Sigma\lambda)^2 + \Sigma\theta} \quad (2)$$

$$VE = \frac{\Sigma(\lambda^2)}{\Sigma(\lambda^2) + \Sigma\theta} \quad (3)$$

where λ is the standardized loading; θ is the indicator measurement error.

For multi-group structural equation modeling, it is to analyze if there exists parameter difference in each model of different groups by constraining the parameters in each nested model. This study mainly concerns about the invariance of measurement weights, structural weights, and structural covariance. Concerning the indices of model fitting, the criteria of measurement in this study include $\chi^2/df < 3$, Goodness-of-Fit Index (GFI)>0.9, Adjusted Goodness- of-Fit Index (AGFI)>0.8, Root Mean Square Residual (RMR)<0.08, and Root Mean Square Error of Approximation (RMSEA)<0.08.

DATA COLLECTION AND RESULT

Concerning the test objects, most internet users are aged between 12 and 34, the majority of these internet users are college students. They have easy access to the internet in many countries, and hence are more likely to be exposed to online advertising. Therefore, the main objects in this study are college students. For the convenience of sampling, this study collects data from National Cheng Kung University (NCKU) in Taiwan, Thompson Rivers University (TRU) in Canada. Besides, 632 available questionnaires are collected, of which 337 were from NCKU, and 295 were from TRU. SPSS 19.0 and LISREL 9.1software were used to analyze the data.

The analysis results involve the descriptive statistics of the respondents, the reliability, the validity of measurement scales, and the analysis of difference among demographics of the sample. Finally, the multi-group structural equation modeling is to demonstrate the relationships among research constructs in different countries. Path analysis and model comparisons are subsequently discussed to validate research hypotheses.

The descriptive profiles of the collected sample (*n*=632) includes two categorical items of gender and country. The collected sample consists of 54.7% male and 45.3% female. There are 53.3% of respondents from Taiwan, and 46.7% from Canada.. The summarized demographic statistics of daily online hours, age, and years of using internet for the area (Taiwan, Canada) includes the mean of (4.58, 4.08), (20.7, 23.5), (9.2, 10.1) and the standard deviation of (2.27, 3.41), (1.35, 3.28), (2.37, 3.16), respectively. For questionnaire items of the research variables, it is shown that the final survey received high Cronbach's α (>0.7) not only in the entire questionnaire but also in each construct. In addition, the Chi-square differences ($\Delta\chi^2$) of paired constructs exceed 3.84 and thus prove discriminant validity of measurement variables. We also use the composite reliability (CR) and variance extracted (VE) for the measurement of internal consistency of the relevant items, and use a standardized factor loading for removing the item from the model. Items A7, A13, A17 and B3 will not be considered in the model. The CR and VE values of the adjusted model are shown in Table 1.

Table 1 Summarized Convergent Validities among Constructs

Construct	Item	Standardized Factor Loading	Composite Reliability	Variance Extracted
Informativeness	A1	.758	.878	.546
	A2	.728		
	A3	.730		
	A4	.758		
	A5	.684		
	A6	.744		
Entertainment	A8	.857	.938	.751
	A9	.948		
	A10	.949		
	A11	.898		
	A12	.829		
Irritation	A14	.905	.860	.678
	A15	.957		
	A16	.626		
Trustworthiness	A18	.593	.822	.612
	A19	.844		
	A20	.814		
Attitudes	B1	.811	.820	.695
	B2	.850		
Behavior	C1	.843	.824	.701
	C2	.841		

In order to know if there exists cultural difference in countries, it is a good way to check if there is difference in concepts among countries. This study checks if the means of construct score are different among countries. Table 2 shows the means, standard deviations and comparisons in constructs among countries. According to Table 2, the US respondents tend to have moderate opinions in Informativeness, Entertainment and Trustworthiness with mean scores 3.56, 2.70 and 2.67, respectively. However, Canadian respondents have higher mean score in Informativeness, Entertainment and Trustworthiness with 3.83, 3.19 and 3.01 respectively.

The primary purpose of this study is to examine the relationships among internet users' perceived informativeness, entertainment, irritation and trustworthiness to their attitudes and behavior of clicking. Structure equation modeling (SEM) was performed with using LISREL 9.1 to collectively test the hypothesized relationships. Figure 2 illustrates the complete model with all relationships.

The indices of model fit include χ^2/df =1.944, GFI=0.91, AGFI=0.882, RMSEA=0.031, and RMR=0.052. For path analysis, there are five direct paths and four indirect paths in each country, and the results are shown in Figure 3. The dotted line shows the standardized coefficient of linkage is not significant at $\alpha = 0.05$.

Table 2 Scale Means (Stdev) and Comparison among Countries

Construct	Taiwan	Canada	Tukey's Comparison	P-value
Informativeness	3.78 (.695)	3.83 (.795)	TW < CAN	<.001
Entertainment	2.96 (.839)	3.19 (1.18)	TW < CAN	<.001
Irritation	2.85 (.710)	2.97 (.877)	TW < CAN	<.001
Trustworthiness	2.76 (.656)	3.01 (.822)	TW < CAN	<.001
Attitudes	3.10 (.744)	3.36 (.919)	TW < CAN	<.001
Behavior	2.69 (.791)	2.35 (.971)	CAN < TW	<.001

The findings of this study are as follows. The effect of informativeness and entertainment toward attitudes of Canadian respondents are statistically significant. The effects of informativeness toward attitudes are different in Taiwan. Additionally, Chinese traditional culture teaches people to be cautious in general, especially toward new things and leads to a conservative view about trustworthiness toward attitudes and makes the trustworthiness an important factor to explain the attitudes toward internet advertising than Canadian do.

Irritation effect of Canada is less than that in either Taiwan. This result suggests a cultural difference in North America. The effects of attitudes toward behavior of clicking are the highest in these two countries. The result matches the fact that internet advertising in the Canada is more mature than that in Taiwan. Commercial websites in Canada are more sophisticated and serve people's information needs better, which naturally leads to Canada' strong perception of the information function of online advertising. Taiwanese consumers have lower trustworthiness toward internet advertising than Canadian do. Such a perception difference may be attributed to the fact that Taiwan is higher in the uncertainty avoidance dimension. Parents in Taiwan teach their children to be cautious in general, especially toward new things. On the other hand, the Canadian culture emphasizes risk taking and embracing new things.

For model comparison, multi-group analysis is used to check if the corresponding parameters are significantly different between among groups. This study compares different countries and test if the path coefficients are equal in different conditions. Table 3 shows the summary of the model comparison, DF is the degree of freedom of the unconstrained model minus that of the constrained model. $\Delta\chi^2$ is the χ^2 value difference between unconstrained and constrained model. P is the *p*-value of a hypothesis testing which has null hypothesis that, for instance, measurement weights among each country are equal. If *p*-value is smaller than 0.05, there is sufficient evidence to conclude that unconstrained model is better than a constrained one. In this study, an unconstrained model is a good one to tell the difference among country effects since the path coefficients are not entirely equal among countries.

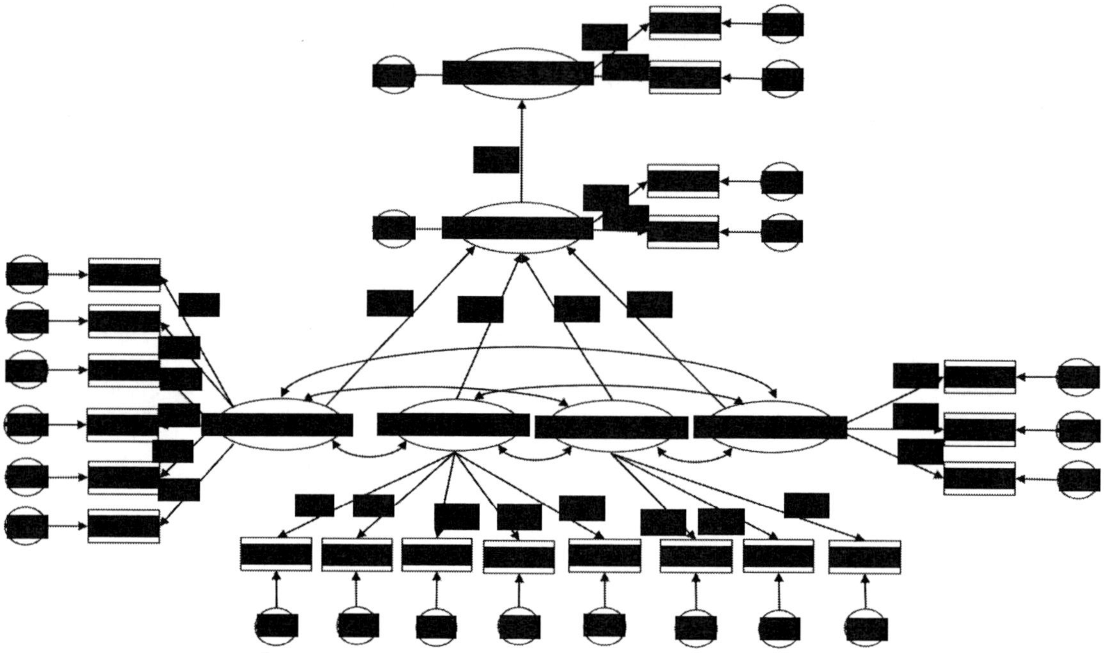

Figure 2 Adjusted Theoretical Model Diagram

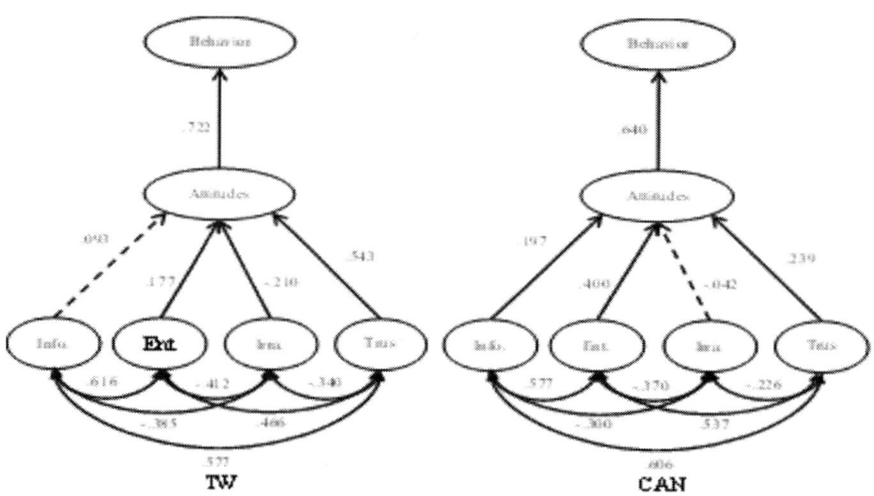

Figure 3 Path Coefficients between Countries

Table 3 Summary of Model Comparison

Unconstrained Model	DF	$\Delta\chi^2$	P
Measurement weights	30	53.730	.005
Structural weights	40	90.410	.000
Structural covariances	60	191.037	.000
Structural residuals	64	230.354	.000
Measurement residuals	110	545.907	.000

DISCUSSIONS AND CONCLUSIONS

This study aims to find if there exists cultural difference through the effect of perception toward attitudes and behavior of clicking as well. We also investigate the relationship among the perceptions, attitudes, behavior of clicking. The results of this study provide some information to an advertisement supplier or an enterprise which is interested in some local markets. For instance, if an enterprise is promoting its new product in Canada, it is recommended that an advertisement with more entertainment such as a delightful video or a fancy display or anything that can catch internet users' eyes will be effectively affect internet users' attitudes. Besides, irritation of an internet advertisement is undoubtedly to affect the internet users' attitudes in Taiwan. In this case, an advertisement supplier should have their advertisements less provocative, less annoying to reach their expected effect.

It will be interesting to explore the proposed model to gain understanding of the complex relationship among countries. The proposed study serves as a basis for more advanced study. For examples, more cultural factors can be considered in addition to the effect of countries. More factors about perceptions should be considered and the existing factors can be revised to be more specific.

ACKNOWLEDGEMENT

The authors sincerely appreciated the support from the Faculty Undergraduate Research Assistant Program in College of Business at James Madison University.

REFERENCES

Aaker, D. A. and Bruzzone, D. E. (1985), "Causes of Irritation in Advertising," *Journal of Marketing*, 49(2), pp. 47-57.

An, D. and Kim, S.H. (2007), "A First Investigation into the Cross-Cultural Perceptions of Internet Advertising : A Comparison of Korean and American Attitudes." *Journal of International Consumer Marketing,* 20(2), pp. 49-65.

Anderson, J. C. and Gerbing, D. W. (1988), "Structural Equation Modeling in Practice: A review and Recommended Two-step Approach," *Psychological Bulletin*, 103(3), pp. 411-423.

Brackett, L. K. and Carr, B. N. (2001), "Cyberspace Advertising vs. Other Media: Consumer vs. Mature Student Attitudes," *Journal of Advertising Research*, 41(5), pp. 23-32.

Ducoffe, R. H. (1995), "How Consumers Assess the Value of Advertising," *Journal of Current Issues and Research in Advertising,* 17(1), pp. 1-18.

Ducoffe, R. H. (1996), "Advertising Value and Advertising on the Web," *Journal of Advertising Research*, 36(5), pp. 21-35.

Eighmey, J. (1997), "Profiling User Responses to Commercial Web Sites," *Journal of Advertising Research*, 37(3), pp. 59-66.

Fornell, C. and Larcker, D. F. (1981), "Evaluating Structural Equation Models with Unobservable Variables and Measurement Error," *Journal of Marketing Research*, 18(1), pp. 39-50.

Grandon, E. E. and Pearson, M. J. (2003), "Perceived Strategic Value and Adoption of Electronic Commerce: An Empirical Study of Small and Medium Sized Businesses," Paper Presented at the Proceedings of the 36th Hawaii International Conference on System Sciences, Hawaii.

Ha, L. and James, E. L. (1998), "Interactivity Reexamined: a Baseline Analysis of Early Business Websites," *Journal of Broadcasting and Electronic Media*, 42(4), pp. 457-474.

Hair, J. F., Black, W. C., Babin, B. J. and Anderson, R. E, (2009), Multivariate data analysis (7th ed.), Upper Saddle River, NJ: Prentice Hall.

Hall, E. T. (1976), Beyond Cultures, Garden City, NY: Anchor Press Doubleday.

Hawkins, D. T. (1994), "Electronic Advertising: On Online Information Systems," *ONLINE,* 18(2), pp. 26-40.

Hoffman, D. L. and Novak, T. P. (1996), "Marketing in Hypermedia Computer-Mediated Environments: Conceptual Foundations," *Journal of Marketing,* 60(3), pp. 50-68.

Internet World Stats, retrieved on March 28, 2016, at http://www.internetworldstats.com/.

Ju-Pak, K. (1999), "Content Dimensions of Web Advertising：A Cross-national Comparison," *International Journal of Advertising,* 18(5), pp. 207-231.

La Ferle, C., Edwards, S. and Lee, W. (2008), "Culture, Attitudes, and Media Patterns in China, Taiwan, and the U.S.: Balancing Standardization and Localization Decisions," *Journal of Global Marketing*, 21(3), pp. 191-205.

Lee, S., Kim, B.G. and Lee, K. (2004), "Fuzzy Cognitive Map-based Approach to Evaluate EDI Performance: A Test of Causal Model," *Expert Systems with Applications*, 27(2), pp. 287-299.

Lutz, R. J. (1985), "Affective and Cognitive Antecedents of Attitude toward the Ad: A conceptual Framework. in Alwitt, L. and Mitchell, A. (Eds.)," *Psychological Processes and Advertising Effects: Theory, Research, and Application,* pp.45-63. Hillsdale, NJ: Lawrence Erlbaum.

MaCKenzie, S.B. and Lutz, R.J., 1989. An empirical examination of the structural antecedents of attitude toward the ad in an advertising pretesting context. *The Journal of Marketing,* , pp. 48-65.

McQuail, D., 1983. *McQuail's mass communication theory.* Sage publications.

Mueller, B. (1992), "Standardization vs. Specialization: An Examination of Westernization in Japanese Advertising," *Journal of Advertising Research*, 32, pp. 15-24.

Nadilo, R. (1998), "Online Research Taps Consumers who Spend,". *Marketing Research,* 32(12), p. 12.

Nutley, M. (2004). "Seeing the Full Potential of Word-of-mouth Advertising," *New Media Age*, 15 April, p. 18.

PwC, Global entertainment and media outlook 2015 – 2019, retrieved on March 28, 2016, at http://www.pwc.com/gx/en/industries/entertainment-media/outlook/segment-insights/internet-advertising.html.

Pollay, R. and B. Mittal (1993), "Here's the Beef: Factors, Determinants, and Segments in Consumer Criticism of Advertising," *Journal of Marketing*, 57(3), pp. 99-114.

Rodgers, S. and Thorson, E. (2000), "The Interactive Advertising Model: How Users Perceive and Process Online Ads," *Journal of Interactive Advertising,* 1(1), pp.42-61.

Russell, H., Staffaroni, J. and Fox, A. (1994), "The Missing Measures of Copy Testing," *Journal of Advertising Research*, 34(3), pp. 46-56.

Schacter, D. L., Gilbert, D. T. and Wegner, D. M. (2011), Psychology (2nd ed.), New York: Worth.

Schlosser, A. E., Shavitt, S. and Kanfer, A. (1999), "Survey of Internet Users' Attitudes toward Internet Advertising," *Journal of Interactive Marketing,* 13(3), pp. 34-54.

Singh, N., Fassott, G., Zhao, H. and Boughton, P. D. (2006), "A Cross-cultural analysis of German, Chinese and Indian consumers' perception of web site adaptation," *Journal of Consumer Behaviour*, 5(1), pp. 56-68.

Stats, Internet World. 2015. "Internet World Stats: Usage and Population Statistics." http://www.internetworldstats.com/.

Taylor, D.G., Lewin, J.E. and Strutton, D., 2011. Friends, fans, and followers: do ads work on social networks? *Journal of Advertising Research,* 51(1), pp. 258-275.

Thota, S. C., Song, J. H. and Biswas, A. (2012), "Is a Website Known by the Banner Ads It Hosts? Assessing forward and Reciprocal Spillover Effects of Banner Ads and Host Websites," *International Journal of Advertising*, 31(4), pp. 877-905.

Wang, Y., and Sun, S. (2010), "An Online Advertising Model: Comparing China and the U.S.," *Journal of Current Issues and Research in Advertising*, 32(2), pp. 101-115.

Web Ad.vantage Company (2013), "Types of Online Advertising," http://www.webadvantage.net/digital-marketing-services/online-media-buying-planning/types-of-online-advertising

Wolin, L. D., Korgaonkar, P. and Lund, D. (2002), "Beliefs, Attitudes, and Behavior towards Web Advertising," *International Journal of Advertising,* 21(1), pp. 87-113.

Zeff, R. and Aronson, B. (1999), Advertising on the Internet (2nd ed.), New Jersey: John Wiley & Sons, Inc.

DECISION SCIENCES INSTITUTE

A Framework for Diabetes Self-care Efficacy in Evaluating Personal Health Record

Elisa Lin
Chiao Tung University, Taiwan
Email: elisa.iim01g@nctu.edu.tw

Hsin-Ginn Hwang
Chiao Tung University, Taiwan
Email: hghmis@nctu.edu.tw

Ming-Ling Sher
Chung Cheng University, Taiwan
Email: r8843003@ms55.hinet.net

ABSTRACT

This study attempts to develop a diabetes self-efficacy conceptual model and presents the diabetes PHR self-efficacy scale (DPSES) as an assessment of using PHR application in diabetes self-care field. A convenient sampling was applied and a total of 57 valid data were collected and analyzed to yield a three-factor structure PHR diabetes self-efficacy model. The DPSES captures the diabetes self-efficacy concept as a tool for evaluating the patient-oriented benefits in using PHR for the purpose of diabetes self-management. Related findings and the results of the instrument are discussed in this study.

KEYWORDS: Diabetes self-care, Personal Health Records, and Self-efficacy

INTRODUCTION

Diabetes is a major and growing health care problem. With it accounts for a vast burden of morbidity through multiple complications. Self-care is an important mechanism by which self-efficacy influences such lifestyle choices as diet and exercise. The strength of self-efficacy belief is of importance as a diagnostic strategy for diabetes self-management education aimed at the improvement of health outcomes (Maibach & Murphy, 2001). Diabetes management depends heavily on behavioral self-regulation. Bandura's self-efficacy theory is an optimal strategy to facilitate diabetes self-care to achieve these lofty treatment goals and actualize the holistic healthcare concept.

As the dramatic information technology evolution in health care, the personal health record (PHR) is seen as a possible solution for coping with the cumbersome psycho-behavioral complexity of diabetes self care. PHR is also a new healthcare paradigm to develop the patient-centered information systems. However, there still remain few instruments available to assess the benefits of using PHR. Thus, this research serves self-efficacy viewpoint to develop an instrument for assessing PHR benefit on the diabetes self-care.

LITERATURE REVIEW

Diabetes Self-care

Diabetes is a self-care intensive illness in which patients must maintain constant vigilance for symptoms that signal hypo- or hyperglycemia, the activity daily life (e.g., nutrition, physical activity) most affecting the wellness and quality of life are controlled by the patients(Glasgow et al., 1999; Gonder-Frederick, Cox, & Ritterband, 2002; McCaul, Glasgow, & Schafer, 1987).
The major goal of contemporary diabetes treatment is to keep blood glucose levels in a normal range through the use of medication, blood glucose monitoring, diet therapy, and exercise to decrease the long-term complications of chronic hyperglycemia. Furthermore, the diabetes must perform multiple self-care behaviors such as foot-care regimen, regular aerobic exercise, and frequent medical appointments on a daily basis for the remainder of their life spans after diagnosis.
Self-care is a term generally implies an approach to acquire needed health service and refers to activities that individuals undertake in promoting their health status, preventing occurrence of disease, and adapting to their irreversible illness condition. A definition of self-care in a World Health Organization (WHO) publication emphasizes "the unorganized health activities and health-related decision-making by individuals, families, neighbors, and colleagues (Ward, 1990)". Although it is technologically possible to normalize diabetic blood glucose levels, actually seldom patients achieve this goal. Thus we need to recognize the psychological and social factors involved in the process of diabetes self-management is a critical factor in helping patients to improve their coping with the daily demands of self-regulation. The diabetes need a comprehensive approach to communicate with health-care providers regarding adherence issues and cope with emotional responses (e.g., diabetes burnout) (Frohna, Frohna, Gahagan, & Anderson, 2001; Glasgow & Eakin, 1998; Glasgow et al., 1999; Glasgow et al., 1992; Polonsky, 1999)

Self-efficacy

Self-efficacy is a construct derived from social cognitive theory (Bandura, 1986) positing a triadic reciprocal causation model in which behavior, cognitions, and the environment all influence each other in a dynamic fashion (Bandura, 1977). When applied to health, the theory suggests that patients are empowered and motivated to manage their health problems when they feel confident in their ability to achieve this goal (Maibach & Murphy, 2001). Self-efficacy has also assumed an increasingly important role in health promotion practice and researches independent of its original theoretical context (Garland, Weinberg, Bruya, & Jackson, 1988; Rosenstock, Strecher, & Becker, 1988; Strecher & DeVellis, 1986).
These studies emphasize on that patients' daily self-care regimen is more difficult than the diagnosis. Adherence to treatment is low according to data in the literature (Brownlee-Duffeck, 1987; Funnell & Anderson, 2000; Robiner & Keel, 1997) and inadequate control of the disease may lead to acute and chronic complications in several organs, such as the kidneys, eyes and heart, and in the circulation (Hayden, 1998; Shamoon et al., 1993). Therefore, with the importance of keeping good glucose control, the role self-efficacy plays in diabetes self-care is the key factor in successfully achieving behavioral goals.

Personal Health Record

There is no uniform definition of PHR (NCVHS, 2006) and the authors attempt to depict it from many studies as below. The concept of PHR includes any internet-accessible application that enables a patient to create, review, annotate or maintain a record of any aspects of their health condition, medication, medical problems, allergies, vaccination history, visit history, or communications with their healthcare providers (Markle Foundation, 2003; Sittig, 2002).

The Markle Foundation (2003) describes PHR as an electronic application through which individuals can access, manage and share their health information in a private, secure, and confidential environment. The Foundation also recommends that an ideal PHR must have the following attributes: each person controls his or her own PHR, contains information all over one's entire lifetime, accessible at any time and anywhere, private and secure, transparent, individuals can trace who accessed each piece of data, and permits easy exchange of information across the health care system (Markle Foundation, 2004).

The American Health Information Management Association (AHIMA, 2005) also describes PHR as an electronic, universally available, lifelong resource of health information needed by individuals to make health decisions, individuals own and manage their information in their own PHR which comes from both healthcare providers and the individual, the PHR is maintained in a secure and private environment, with the individual determining rights of access, and the PHR will not replace the legal record of any provider.

PHR seems to have the potential to facilitate the interaction of health care continuum, empower patients to get involved in their own health, increase the relationship between physician and patient through the integrated mechanism to tailor and canalize the information to fit personal health needs (Houston & Ehrenberger, 2001; Tang, Ash, Bates, Overhage, & Sands, 2006) With PHR, patients with chronic illnesses will be able to track their diseases in conjunction with their providers, promoting earlier interventions when they encounter a deviation or problem (Tang et al., 2006). A survey reported more than 72% respondents are eager for the new functionalities PHR offer (McInturff, 2005).

Based on several previous studies (Endsley, Kibbe, Linares, & Colorafi, 2006; Markle Foundation, 2004; Pratt, Unruh, Civan, & Skeels, 2006; Sprague, 2006; Tang et al., 2006; Ueckert, Goerz, Ataian, Tessmann, & Prokosch, 2003; Win, 2006), PHR offer a number of potential benefits to patients, primary care physicians and other healthcare providers. These benefits include: 1) Empowerment of patients; 2)Improved relationships between patients and health providers; 3) Increased patient safety; 4) Improved quality of care; 5) More efficient delivery of care; 6) Better safeguards on health information privacy; and 7)Cost saving.

HYPOTHESES/MODEL

The survey methodology was adopted in this study. The seven-factor structure derived from PHR's benefits (Markle Foundation, 2004) to this research framework and attempted to analyze what the conceptual model of diabetes self-efficacy is within PHR context. From the review of researches, the Diabetes PHR Self-Efficacy Scale (DPSES) was proposed with empowerment, patient-provider relationship, patient safety, and quality of care, efficient care, privacy, and cost saving constructs.

METHODS

Prior to the survey, an expert panel was conducted after the draft questionnaire to serve as a content validity test. For the purpose of content and preface validity, the instrument is administered on ten participants who have been involved in more than two weeks patient education and familiar with diabetes self-care context, including an with four MIS professors, five Certified Diabetes Educators (CDE), and a metabolic physician were invited to participate in panel evaluation. The expert panels were conducted to get maximum feedback for designing the scale.

Responses from all panelists are pooled and the number indicating "essential" and "useful but not essential" for each item is determined. In validating a test, a content validity ratio (CVR)

value is computed for each item. We adopted the minimum CVR (Lawshe, 1975) .62 to retain or eliminate the items for our further tests. We dropped out two constructs (patient safety and privacy safeguard) in the expert panel evaluation and yielded 23 items for the pretest.
Next, we invited five diabetes educators to participate the pretest and they confirmed all items retained by the expert panel except one item was modified for semantic confusion. Those items that fit five constructs (empowerment, patient-physician relationship, quality of care, efficiency of care, and save money) were retained, yielding 23 items for field survey
Convenient sampling method was used to recruit participants (over 18 year-old) from voluntary outpatients with diabetes and their caregivers including physicians, CDE, therapists, and the diabetes' families in the department of endocrinology and metabolism in five hospitals in south Taiwan. Structured questionnaires were administered to the participants.
A total 60 participates got involved in the study. After dropping some invalid and inadequate responses, the total valid responses were 57. The SPSS 16.0 was used for processing the data analysis. All of the respondents in the sample aged from 20 to 69. Approximately 58% of the respondents are female, and 42% are male. 31.6 % participants have experienced diabetes care for 2~5 years, and 26.3 % for 6~10 years. The diabetes patient accounts for 35.1% respondents in this survey and the rest part is diabetes care provider.

RESULTS

The questionnaire was used to capture latent variables were measured on a 7-point Likert scale anchored by 1 (absolutely disagree) to 7 (absolutely agree). Next, exploratory factor analyzed the 23-item instrument to examine the dimensionality of the construct. In the quest for a stable structure, we took an iterative procedure that began with submitting the items to a factor analysis with varimax rotation. Hair et al. (2006) suggest that item loadings above 0.30 are considered significant, over 0.40 are more important, and exceed 0.50 are considered very significant.
To examine the most significant loadings in interpreting the factor solution, the authors decided to use a cut-off point of 0.50 for item loadings. The process went on until reaching a meaningful factor structure. The factor analysis reveals three factors with eigenvalue over 1 to filter the items.
Table 1 shows that there are three factors explaining 77.89 % of the variance in diabetes PHR self-efficacy.

Table 1 Principal components analysis with varimax rotation

	Component		
	Factor 1	Factor 2	Factor 3
Q20	.825		
Q19	.785		
Q18	.782		
Q21	.770		
Q17	.742		
Q10	.733		
Q11	.725		
Q16	.671		
Q1	.598		
Q6		.864	
Q7		.784	

Q8		.722	
Q5			.842
Q4			.732
Q12			.725
Variance explained	37.916	20.879	19.096

With the result of factor analysis, the authors renamed the three factors as quality of diabetes self-care, physician-patient relationship, and empowerment respectively, and 15 items are remained in the end of factor analysis.

DISCUSSION AND CONCLUSIONS

The results of the research depict three dimensions of diabetes PHR self-efficacy (empowerment, patient-physician relationship, and quality of diabetes self-care) and provide the psychometric properties of the 15-item instrument. Coping with one's diabetes requires the specific behaviors to be carried out many times a day to achieve homeostatic metabolic control. Most of the information system evaluation researches focused on user's satisfaction, perceived usefulness, user's acceptation, ease of use, and diffusion of innovation issues to construct identification or measurement of IS efforts. In this study, we moved our strides to the nature of the diabetes' need of self-care from using PHR, and also expected the PHR will be a new paradigm of diabetes education.

A primary contribution of this study is to establish an instrument for assessing the diabetes self-efficacy by using PHR and construct the self-efficacy conceptual model by using PHR. The research adapted the benefits of PHR to quest what are the factors forming diabetes self-efficacy conceptual model by using PHR. The authors view patient's demand on HIT as an important concept for PHR's development and adoption, and this research findings create a possible strategy for healthcare industry practitioners to figure out the appropriate business model to make PHR into practice.

The nature of respondents (diabetes patients and their healthcare providers) is a limitation in this study. However, our literature review shows self-care concept involving the health-related decision-making by patients, families, neighbors, and self-care colleagues, that's the reason we combined those population as possible as we could to investigate the conceptual of diabetes self-efficacy. The DPSES measures the perceived concept of diabetes PHR self-efficacy, not the real experience of using PHR. However, it is definitely a worthwhile starting point to evaluate the PHR's benefits in diabetes education.

Nowadays the definition of PHR is still evolving. It is an exploratory study of diabetes PHR self-efficacy. Translating health knowledge into behaviors remains a challenge in health promotion domain (Rimal, 2000). There are ample studies that self-efficacy intervention can increase our perceived ability to exert health behaviors. Given that diabetes is rooted in morbid dietary habits and sedentary lifestyle, behavioral modification is useful to enhance diabetes self-care behaviors and personal health management.

PHR is perhaps the holy grail (Rissel, 2001; Tang & Lansky, 2005) in the realm of health promotion, a 2005 annual survey of the Palo Alto Medical foundation (PAMF) showed that one-fifth of respondents reported that they had changed their health behavior (Tang et al., 2003;

Tang & Lansky, 2005). This research results reveal an instrument for assessing PHR's benefits to support the diabetes for facilitating their diabetes self-efficacy to exert self-care behaviors. More related psychosocial researches upon the information technology to improve the quality of diabetes care are expected.

REFERENCES

AHIMA. (2005). The Role of the Personal Health Record in the EHR. Journal of AHIMA, 76(7), 64A-D.

Bandura, A. (1977). Self-efficacy: toward a unifying theory of behavioral change. Psychological Review, 84(2), 191-215.

Bandura, A. (1986). Social Foundations of Thought andAction: A Social Cognitive Theory. New Yersey: Prentice Hall.

Brownlee-Duffeck, M. (1987). The Role of Health Beliefs in the Regimen Adherence and Metabolic Control of Adolescents and Adults with Diabetes Mellitus. Journal of Consulting and Clinical Psychology, 55(2), 139-144.

Endsley, S., Kibbe, D. C., Linares, A., & Colorafi, K. (2006). An introduction to personal health records. Fam Pract Manag, 13(5), 57-62.

Foundation, M. (2003). Connecting for Health-A Public-Private Collaboration: The Personal Health Working Group, Executive Summary.

Foundation, M. (2004). Connecting Americans to Their Healthcare: Final Report. Connecting for Health.

Frohna, J. G., Frohna, A., Gahagan, S., & Anderson, R. M. (2001). Tips for communicating with patients in managed care. Seminars in medical practice, 4(2), 29-36.

Funnell, M. M., & Anderson, R. M. (2000). The Problem With Compliance in Diabetes (Vol. 284, pp. 1709-1709): Am Med Assoc.

Garland, H., Weinberg, R., Bruya, L., & Jackson, A. (1988). Self-efficacy and endurance performance: a longitudinal field test of cognitive mediation theory. Revue internationale de psychologie appliquee, 37(4), 381-394.

Glasgow, R. E., & Eakin, E. G. (1998). Issues in diabetes self-management. The Handbook of Health Behavior Change, 435-461.

Glasgow, R. E., Fisher, E. B., Anderson, B. J., LaGreca, A., Marrero, D., Johnson, S. B., et al. (1999). Behavioral science in diabetes. Contributions and opportunities. Diabetes Care, 22(5), 832-843.

Glasgow, R. E., Toobert, D. J., Hampson, S. E., Brown, J. E., Lewinsohn, P. M., & Donnelly, J. (1992). Improving self-care among older patients with type II diabetes: the "Sixty Something..." Study. Patient Educ Couns, 19(1), 61-74.

Gonder-Frederick, L. A., Cox, D. J., & Ritterband, L. M. (2002). Diabetes and behavioral medicine: The second decade. Journal of Consulting and Clinical Psychology, 70(3), 611-625.

Hair, J. F., Anderson, R. E., Tatham, R. L., & Black, W. C. (2006). Multivariate data analysis, (six ed.): Englewood Cliffs, NJ: Prentice-Hall.

Hayden, M. R. (1998). Intensive blood-glucose control with sulphonylureas or insulin compared with conventional treatment and risk of complications in patients with type 2 diabetes (UDPDS 33). Lancet, 352, 837-853.

Houston, T. K., & Ehrenberger, H. E. (2001). The potential of consumer health informatics. Semin Oncol Nurs, 17(1), 41-47.

Lawshe, C. H. (1975). A QUANTITATIVE APPROACH TO CONTENT VALIDITY 1. Personnel Psychology, 28(4), 563-575.

Maibach, E., & Murphy, D. A. (2001). Self-efficacy in health promotion research and practice: conceptualization and measurement. Health Education Research, 10(1), 37-50.
McCaul, K. D., Glasgow, R. E., & Schafer, L. C. (1987). Diabetes Regimen Behaviors: Predicting Adherence. Medical Care, 25(9), 868-881.
McInturff, B. (2005). Public Opinions Strategies. Key findings from focus groups and two national surveys conducted on behalf of the Markle Foundation, the Robert Wood Foundation, and Connecting for Health. Presented October, 11, 2005.
NCVHS. (2006). Personal Health Records and Personal Health Record Systems.
Norman, C. D., & Skinner, H. A. (2006). eHealth Literacy: Essential Skills for Consumer Health in a Networked World. Journal of Medical Internet Research, 8(2).
Polonsky, W. H. (1999). Diabetes Burnout: McGraw-Hill/Contemporary.
Pratt, W., Unruh, K., Civan, A., & Skeels, M. M. (2006). Personal health information management. Communications of the ACM, 49(1), 51-55.
Rimal, R. N. (2000). Closing the Knowledge-Behavior Gap in Health Promotion: The Mediating Role of Self-Efficacy. Health Communication, 12(3), 219-237.
Rissel, C. (2001). Empowerment: the holy grail of health promotion? (Vol. 9, pp. 39-47): Oxford Univ Press.
Robiner, W., & Keel, P. K. (1997). Self-Care Behaviors and Adherence in Diabetes Mellitus. Semin Clin Neuropsychiatry, 2(1), 40-56.
Rosenstock, I. M., Strecher, V. J., & Becker, M. H. (1988). Social Learning Theory and the Health Belief Model. Health Education & Behavior, 15(2), 175.
Shamoon, H., Duffy, H., Fleischer, N., Engel, S., Saeger, P., & Strelzyn, M. (1993). The Effect of Intensive Treatment of Diabetes on the Development and Progression of Long-Term Complications in Insulin-Dependent Diabetes Mellitus. The New England Journal of Medicine, 329(14), 977-986.
Sittig, D. F. (2002). Personal health records on the internet: a snapshot of the pioneers at the end of the 20th Century. International Journal of Medical Informatics, 65(1), 1-6.
Sprague, L. (2006). Personal Health Records: The People's Choice? NHPF Issue Brief, 820, 1-13.
Strecher, V. J., & DeVellis, M. E. (1986). The Role of Self-Efficacy in Achieving Health Behavior Change. Health Education & Behavior, 13(1), 73.
Tang, P. C., Ash, J. S., Bates, D. W., Overhage, J. M., & Sands, D. Z. (2006). Personal Health Records: Definitions, Benefits, and Strategies for Overcoming Barriers to Adoption (Vol. 13, pp. 121-126): Am Med Inform Assoc.
Tang, P. C., Black, W., Buchanan, J., Young, C. Y., Hooper, D., Lane, S. R., et al. (2003). PAMFOnline: Integrating EHealth with an Electronic Medical Record System. AMIA... Annual Symposium proceedings [electronic resource], 2003, 644.
Tang, P. C., & Lansky, D. (2005). The Missing Link: Bridging The Patient-Provider Health Information Gap. Health Affairs, 24(5), 1290-1295.
Ueckert, F., Goerz, M., Ataian, M., Tessmann, S., & Prokosch, H. U. (2003). Empowerment of patients and communication with health care professionals through an electronic health record. International Journal of Medical Informatics, 70(2-3), 99-108.
Ward, W. B. (1990). Advances in Health Education and Promotion: JAI Press.
Win, K. T. (2006). Web-based personal health record systems evaluation. International Journal of Healthcare Technology and Management, 7(3), 208-217.

DECISION SCIENCES INSTITUTE

A Framework for Index Development for Measuring the Performance of Telecom Operators: A Consensus-based Approach

Abhay Kumar Bhadani
Indian Institute of Technology Delhi
Email: abhay_bhadani@dbst.iitd.ac.in

Ravi Shankar
Indian Institute of Technology Delhi
Email: ravi1@dms.iitd.ac.in

D. Vijay Rao
Institute for Systems Studies and Analyses
Email: doctor.rao.cs@gmail.com

ABSTRACT

Today we observe a divide between urban and rural areas with respect to adoption of advanced mobile technologies and services. This can be attributed to various factors. We propose a framework to develop an index to measure this divide. Our two-stage method builds a consensus based on OWA operator in its first stage and uses this consensus to derive a divide measuring index using Graph Theory Matrix Approach in the second stage. The index can be used by different stakeholders such as consumers, policy makers and operators to measure the performance of the operators, which will help in their decision-making.

KEYWORDS: Consensus building, Graph Theory, Mobile Services, Index Development, Ordered Weight Aggregation, Fuzzy Preference

INTRODUCTION

In many developing countries like India, Malaysia and Bangladesh, 3G and 4G/LTE are still at their initial stage of adoption. Since, Mobile Network Operators (MNOs) are interested in quick return on investment, they primarily start targeting urban users first. This creates an information access divide among the urban and the rural users. There are several factors that play a critical role in the adoption or abandonment of advanced mobile technologies and services.

This paper first identifies few relevant factors and then derives an index, which can be used to measure this divide. Thus, this paper has primarily three contributions: first, a precise list of factors are identified; second, a consensus among the experts are formed using our proposed consensus building algorithm and finally, a systematic approach to derive an index is recommended. The index can be used to compare the performance of different operators, and thus, it can help in improving the overall experience of using the services at the desired location, help in promoting healthy competition among the operators and can help in improving the existing policies.

The flow of the paper is as follows: Section 2 presents the background for the need for such framework and related concepts are discussed; the proposed framework is presented in Section

3. An illustrative example is provided in Section 4, finally, conclusions drawn are presented in Section 5.

BACKGROUND

While solving real life problems, decision-making is not so straightforward and most of the decisions are made under uncertainty. In most of the cases, there is no direct way to take a firm decision. Hence, opinions are taken from the experts. It is a well-acknowledged fact that the ability to take a virtuous and timely decision under dubious situation helps an organization to gain competitive advantage. However, there are certain problems associated with the collection of opinion from the experts such as bringing all experts under one table, the dominance of a senior or influential person leading to a biased decision making.

In the era of Internet and social media, the traditional barrier to bringing experts' on a round table has almost become extinct as virtual meetings have become more common. There are situations when the experts have different opinions on the same subject, and decision-making becomes a difficult task, especially when there is a lack of common framework. In this situation, often, the entire process becomes disorganized resulting in a biased decision.

Normally, board members, who are usually comprised of more than one person, take decisions. Similarly, multiple factors are considered when the decision is to be taken. It may happen that the opinion on a particular note may differ. In the absence of appropriate consensus-building algorithm, decisions may be taken without much deliberation leading to bias in the decision-making. As a result, the decision may not incorporate suggestions of the expert having a different opinion. In such situations, a guided framework can assist in incorporating opinions of each expert in the decision-making process. Lack of such a framework may lead to bias in decision-making and conflict may arise among the experts involved in the process. In order to address this issue, several researchers (Herrera-Viedma et al., 2002; Chen and Lin, 2004; Choudhury et al., 2006; Singh et al., 2007) have proposed different consensus building algorithms that address this problem.

Consensus usually involves compromise, but at the same time, it is considered safe, as none of the experts are 100\% sure about the future events. Rather they share their expertise so that decisions on critical factors can be taken. It may help in being prepared for possible events that may occur in the future. It is also well acknowledged and understood that a group will lead to a better decision under uncertainty than just an individual (Herrera-Viedma et al., 2002; Choudhury et al., 2006; Singh et al., 2007). The phenomenon where more than one person participates in the decision-making process is termed as Group Decision Making (GDM). GDM is a process of converging to an agreement on a common theme when more than one person participate. It helps to minimize the decision bias, often created by an individual, in a decision-making process. A group decision is usually carried out in an unstructured manner and requires substantial time to reach a consensus. The GDM process gets complicated as multiple criteria are taken into account as it involves several subjective and qualitative factors. Further, the knowledge of the members may vary, which may lead to a conflict.

A framework that satisfies the group and is capable of eliminating the dominance of an individual such that a reliable decision can be taken by minimizing the bias is of much help. Conventional approaches such as Delphi and Nominal Group Technique normally fail to deliver a fair decision. In these approaches, often, senior member overtakes the decision-making process and individual inclination becomes quite common phenomena during consensus building process. It leads to unfair estimation about the intensity of the problem. In order to overcome some of the mentioned problems and limitations of existing consensus building approaches a guided framework that can smoothen the entire decision-making process is proposed.

Consensus Building

Consensus is typically defined as the full and unanimous harmony among all the experts regarding all the feasible alternatives (Herrera-Viedma et al., 2002). However, forming a full agreement on any issue is not possible in a complex real-life situation. In simple terms, consensus mainly refers to how any group of experts who value autonomy might work together. A decision that involves consensus might take an exceptionally longer time, and thus may be unbearable for critical matters, e.g., decisions that involve competitive advantage or strategic policy.

Before going into a detailed explanation of the consensus building process, first we define some of the commonly referred terms such as entropy, consensus measure, proximity measure, and confidence degree and consensus level. Now, we define each term one by one.

Consensus Measure has been defined as ``the measure of agreement amongst the experts involved in decision-making process". It guides experts to form an agreement, possibly over little iteration. Different distance metrics is used to evaluate the difference of opinions (Herrera-Viedma et al., 2002; Choudhary et al., 2006).

Proximity Measure is defined as ``the measure of agreement amongst the expert's opinion with the collaborative solution". The measure of proximity provides feedback to the expert so that next iteration is closer to the solution (Herrera-Viedma et al., 2002; Choudhary et al., 2006).

Consensus Level is the defined as “the agreed upon value to terminate the consensus process”. It means that all the experts have reached to the agreed upon the level and the iteration process can be terminated (Herrera-Viedma et al., 2002; Choudhary et al., 2006).

Entropy (also termed as dispersion) is one of the measures derived from Shannon entropy that calculates the variability in the opinions furnished by the experts for the considered problem (Shannon, 1948).

The entropy of the system, Ent(X) is calculated using the formula given below:

$$Ent(X) = -\sum_{i=1}^{n} p_i log_2(p_i) \tag{1}$$

Where, X is the opinion of different experts. The Shannon entropy takes into account the probabilities p_i and n, the number of opinions from different experts.

Formats for Recording Opinion

An expert can give their opinion in a format in which he/she is more comfortable. It could be possible that the experts may not be comfortable with the strict format that we might prefer to build consensus. There are different formats that can be used to record the opinion of the experts as suggested by Herrera-Viedma et al., (2002), which is discussed below. Hence, four different formats (multiplicative preference, utility values, fuzzy preference and preference ordering) are made available for the experts so that they can furnish their opinions in their preferred format.

Multiplicative Preference Structure: In multiplicative preference structure, the values are assigned with the help of pair-wise comparisons. The upper triangular matrix is the inverse of the lower triangular matrix in the multiplicative preference structure input format. The expert δ_e assign the values on a scale of 1 to 9 (Saaty, 2005). For example, if the value associated with factor $\alpha_{ij}=7$, then $\alpha_{ji}=1/7$.

Utility Values: The expert δ_e, provides his/her input based on a set of *n* factors in terms of utility value. Utility values are represented as $u^e = \{u_i^e; i=1,2,...,n\}$; $u_i^e \in [0,1]$. u_i^e represents the utility associated with the expert *e* for the factor α_i (Herrera-Viedma et al., 2002; Choudhary et al., 2006). If the value associated with the factor α_i is high then, it is considered to be more important than others.

Fuzzy Preference Relations: In this case, the expert δ_e assigns his/her preferences on a set of alternatives α using a fuzzy membership function $\mu_F{}^e$; it is stored in matrix form F^e, where, *e* is the expert. F^e is a set of all alternatives represented as $F^e \subset \alpha \ X \ \alpha$. The fuzzy membership function is represented as $\mu_F{}^e$: aXa $\rightarrow$ [0,1] where, $\mu e_F(\alpha_i,\alpha_j) = f^e_{ij}$ the preference degree or intensity of the factor α_i over α_j. f^e_{ij} is the fuzzy preference degree given by e[th] expert over alternatives α_i and α_j (Herrera-Viedma et al., 2002; Choudhary et al., 2006). In this case, it is fair to assume that $f^e_{ij} + f^e_{ji} = 1$ and $f^e_{ii} = 1/2$ in particular case.

Preference Ordering for the Factors: In preference ordering, as the name suggests, the expert δ_e decides the order among the set of factors α. The preference ordering (ρ^e) is a set of values given by e[th] expert represented as $\rho^e = \{ \rho_1{}^{(e)}, \rho_2{}^{(e)}, ..., \rho_n{}^{(e)}\}$ where, $\rho_i{}^{(e)}$ is the preference assigned for factor α_i by an expert *e* (Herrera-Viedma et al., 2002; Choudhary et al., 2006).

Graph Theoretic Approach

Graph theory is a well-established branch of mathematics and computer science. The concept was first introduced and applied to represent the Seven Bridges of Konigsberg by Euler in 1736. Since then, it has been applied in several disciplines to solve numerous problems ranging from computer science, biology to decision-making. It represents the problem in the form of vertices and edges. Sometimes, the edges are associated with weights. These weights ascertain the importance of connections among the pair of vertices.

Mathematically, a graph is represented as $G=(V,E,\lambda)$. It consists of a set of objects $V=\{v_1, v_2,..., v_n\}$ called vertices; another set $E=\{e_1, e_2, ..., e_n\}$ whose elements are called edges, such that unordered pair of (v_i, v_j, e_k) vertices identifies edges. λ maps weights associated with edge and vertex connections (Deo, 1974). A graph can be *directed* or *undirected*. For a detailed discussion on graph theory concepts, the researcher is suggested to refer the book written by Deo, (1974).

Graph Theoretic Matrix Approach (GTMA)

According to Grover et al. (2004), and Sabharwal and Garg (2013), digraph and matrix approach is used to represent the problem in the form of vertices and edges, where matrix representation of the graph helps in faster processing through computer algorithms. It takes into account structural as well as the functional interaction of the overall system. In addition, GTMA has several advantages over other approaches such as case studies, empirical studies, structural equation modeling and multi-criteria decision-making approaches. It presents a more appropriate mechanism to obtain a single score for all the factors under consideration. It follows a systematic method for conversion of qualitative variables to a quantitative value. It is based on the isomorphic properties of the two graphs. It leads to self-analysis (comparing with the best case or desired level) and comparison of a similar context within or outside the organization.

PROPOSED FRAMEWORK

As a first step, critical success factors are identified. These factors are then represented as a graph, which is stored in a matrix containing the off-diagonal elements, whereas the diagonal elements represent weights associated with the vertices. The edge weights are the visual representations of the characteristics and their inter-dependencies on other factors, whereas the weights associated with the vertex represents the importance of the factor in the overall system. These weights are obtained with the help of participating experts or from the available data, which is frozen with the help of consensus-building algorithm discusses below. These edge weights, which is stored in the matrix is used to obtain the index of the system under study. The matrix converts the graph into a mathematical form to obtain the index by calculating the permanent matrix. The obtained score is termed as Mobile Service Divide Index (MSDI). Contrary to the determinant, permanent has no negative symbol, which means there is no loss of information. Hence, application of permanent concept leads to a better estimation of the impact of the factors (Jurkat and Ryser, 1966). The abstract representation of MSDI is as follows:

$$MSDI = f(critical\ success\ factors) \tag{2}$$

MSDI is obtained by calculating the permanent value of the matrix, which consists of the diagonal and off-diagonal elements. The diagonal and off-diagonal values are obtained separately in two different separate steps. In the two-stage process, the first stage deals with forming of consensus among the diagonal elements and off-diagonal elements, whereas the second stage deals with the development of the permanent matrix by combining diagonal and off-diagonal elements. Once, MSDI is calculated, resemblance ratio can be calculated to compare two different scenarios. The proposed algorithm to obtain MSDI is pictorially shown in Figure 1.

We use Yager's neat Ordered Weighted Averaging (OWA) operators for aggregating the opinions of the experts and then apply the concepts of GTMA to obtain MSDI. The opinions for the diagonal elements (i.e., factors) are captured using the linguistic-based qualitative measure (Table 1).

The difference of opinions among the experts is measured using Entropy (Choudhury et al., 2006; Singh et al., 2007). However, Shannon's entropy measure has few limitations. First, it fails to distinguish between two different sets of opinions. Second, the entropy remains constant notwithstanding the order of the grouping of the distribution. Third, neither the mean and standard deviation nor measure of entropy is adequate to capture proximity in ordinal or fuzzy scales. Therefore, a consensus is reached for the diagonal elements using a modified Shannon's approach as suggested in Tastle and Wierman (2007).

First, it overcomes the problem associated with the entropy measure, and second, the consensus measure remains unaffected with the increase in the size of the number of participants.

The consensus for the diagonal elements is measured using the following equation:

$$Cons(X) = 1 + \sum_{i=1}^{n} p_i log_2 \left(1 - \frac{|X_i - \mu_X|}{d_X}\right) \quad (3)$$

where, X is the opinion of different decision makers, μ_X is the mean of X and d_X is the width of X; $d_X = X_{max} - X_{min}$.

Steps for Obtaining Index

In this section, we discuss the steps required to derive the index. In Stage I, helps to build consensus whereas Stage II, calculates the permanent value of the matrix, which is termed as MSDI.

Table 1: factors Importance Values

Linguistic-based qualitative measure	Value
Exceptionally Low	0.045
Extremely Low	0.135
Very Low	0.255
Low	0.335
Below Average	0.410
Average	0.500
Above Average	0.590
High	0.665
Very High	0.745
Extremely High	0.865
Exceptionally High	0.955

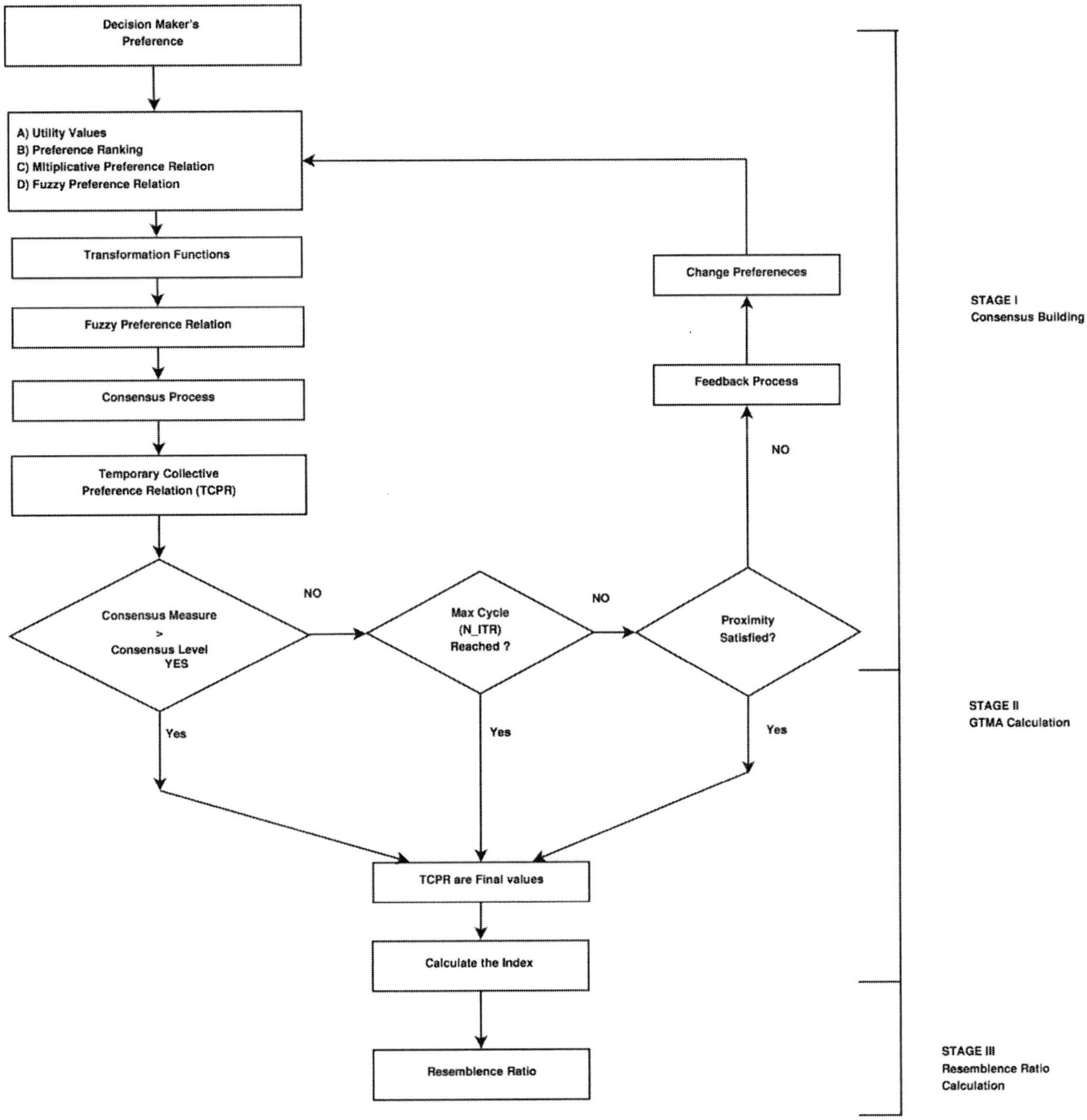

Figure 1: Flowchart for Estimating Cumulative Impact

STAGE I: Consensus Building

In this stage, several steps to reach consensus is discussed.

Step 1: Opinion Collection

Let $\alpha = \{ \alpha_1, \alpha_2, ..., \alpha_n\}$ be a set of n factors, and $\delta = \{ \delta_1, \delta_2, ..., \delta_m\}$ be m experts, where both m and n are finite. The experts are free to record their opinions in any of the specified four forms. For obtaining the importance of diagonal elements, opinions are recorded based on the linguistic quantifiers (Table 1), which are further mapped to the equivalent fuzzy number. The 11-point fuzzy scale has been used in few studies for recording the opinions of the experts (Venkatasamy and Agrawal, 1997; Rao, 2006). Figure 2 shows the 11-point fuzzy scale conversion mechanism and mapping between X and μ_X to determine equivalent fuzzy values.

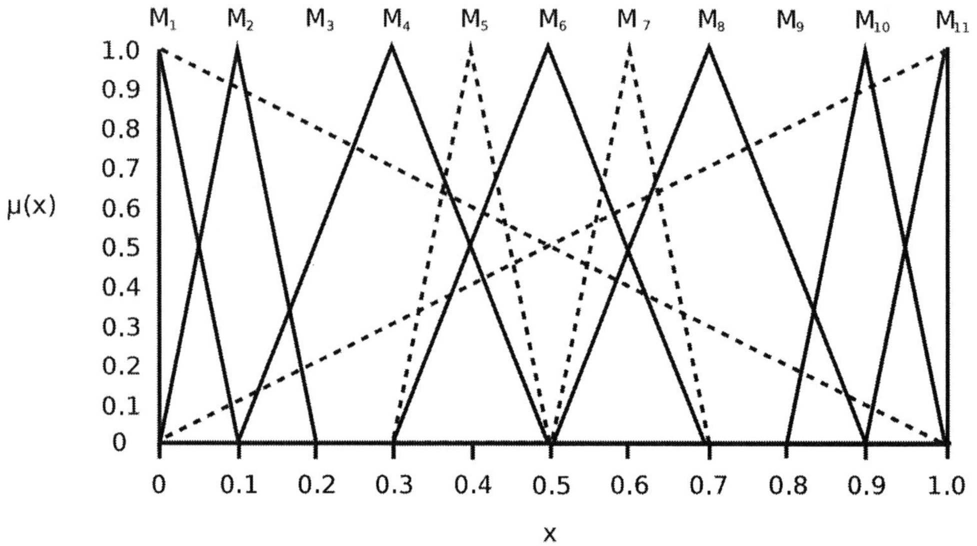

Figure 2: 11-point Linguistic Terms Scale for Conversion to Fuzzy Numbers

Step 2: Input Transformation

Initial responses are collected in various formats, which are then converted to fuzzy preference relations. It is achieved using the following transformation function: Let $\alpha = \{ \alpha_1, \alpha_2, ..., \alpha_n\}$ be the set of factors that are to be considered for decision making where, α_i is the value associated with factor i. Let χ_i^e be the evaluation associated with factor α_i for the expert δ_e. Then, the intensity of preference of alternative α_i over α_j, f^e_{ij} for δ_e is given by the following transformation function $f^e_{ij} = \phi(\chi^e_i, \chi^e_j)$

$$f^e_{ij} = \frac{1}{2}[1 + g(\chi^e_i, \chi^e_j) - g(\chi^e_i, \chi^e_j)] \quad (4)$$

where g ascertains that: $g(\chi, \chi) = \frac{1}{2} \forall \chi \in \mathbb{R}$ and, g is a non-decreasing in the first parameter and non-increasing in second parameter.

A) to bring preference ordering to fuzzy preference relations structure:

Suppose $\chi_i^e = \tau_i^e$ represents the preference ordering of factor α_i and $g(l,u) = \frac{(u-l)}{2(n-1)}$ where *g(l,u)* is a transformation function (Chiclana et al., 1998; Tanino, 1988); *u* and *l* are the upper and lower bounds and *n* is the number of alternatives. Then,

$$f_{ij}^e = h^1(\tau_i^e, \tau_j^e) = \frac{1}{2}\left[1 + \frac{(\tau_j^e - \tau_i^e)}{n-1}\right] \tag{5}$$

B) to bring utility values to fuzzy preference relations format:

In this case, if $\chi_i^e = \upsilon_i^e$ represents the utility value of the factor α_i and $g(l,u) = \frac{l^2}{l^2+u^2}$, where *g(l,u)* is a transformation function (Chiclana et al., 1998; Tanino, 1988); *u* and *l* are the upper and lower bounds and *n* is the number of alternatives. Then,

$$f_{ij}^e = h^2(\upsilon_i^e, \upsilon_j^e) = \frac{(\upsilon_i^e)^2}{(\upsilon_j^e)^2 + (\upsilon_i^e)^2} \tag{6}$$

C) to bring multiplicative preference relation to fuzzy preference relations format:

$\eta^e = (\eta_{ij}^e)$ is the association in multiplicative preference relation form. Then, the corresponding additive fuzzy preference relation $F^e = (f_{ij}^e)$ associated with η^e is given as follows (Saaty, 1980):

$$f_{ij}^e = h^3(\eta_{ij}^e) = \frac{1}{2}(1 + log_9 \eta_{ij}^e) \tag{7}$$

Step 3: Aggregation Operation

In this phase, a collective solution is obtained by using the opinions furnished by the experts after transforming them to the fuzzy preference relations format. The aggregation operation is carried out with the help of neat Ordered Weight Aggregation (OWA) operators (Yager, 1988). Fuzzy linguistic quantifiers like "majority", "at least half", "as many as possible", etc. are used. These quantifiers are defined by providing a lower and an upper bound value, for example, (l, u) can be (0, 0.5) for "at least half", (0.5, 1) for "as many as possible" and (0.3, 0.8) for representing "majority". The collective solution is found using the following equation:

$$f_{ij}^c = \Upsilon_\mu(f_{ij}^1, f_{ij}^2, ..., f_{ij}^m) = \sum_{e=1}^{n} w_e . f_{ij}^e \tag{8}$$

where, µ is a fuzzy linguistic quantifier that represents the concept of fuzzy majority (Zadeh,

1983). It is used to calculate the weights of Y_μ, w= { w1, w2, ..., wn} such that, $w_e \in [0,1]$ and $\Sigma^n_{\{e=1\}}$.

$$w_e = \mu\left(\frac{e}{n}\right) - \mu\left(\frac{e-1}{n}\right) \tag{9}$$

where, $e = 1, 2, ..., n$ and

$$\mu(t) = \begin{cases} 0, & \text{if } t < l \\ \frac{t-l}{u-l}, & \text{if } l \leq t \leq u \text{ and } (l,t,u) \in [0,1] \\ 1, & \text{if } t > u \end{cases}$$

Step 4: Estimating the Proximity

In this step, the closeness or the proximity of decisions among different experts is calculated. Thereafter, choice degrees are calculated. The quantifier guided dominance degree (QGDD) is used to quantify the dominance of α_i over all other factors, and quantifier guided non-dominance degree (QGNDD) provides the information on the non-dominance among remaining factors to calculate the priority of the factors (Orlovsky, 1978). Each choice degree is self-sufficient to rank the factors. However, when there is a difference, the maximum from both is taken to rank them.

$$QGDD_i = \Upsilon_\mu(f^e_{ij}, j = 1, 2, ..., n) \tag{10}$$

$$QGNDD_i = \Upsilon_\mu(1 - max\{f^c_{ij} - f^c_{ji}, 0\}) \tag{11}$$

The temporary result is stored in X_{tres}, where

$$X_{tres} = max\{QGDD_i, QGNDD_i\} \tag{12}$$

Step 5: Computation of Difference of Opinion

At the beginning of this process, the number of iterations (N_{ITR}) and the Consensus Level (CL) are pre-decided. The Euclidean distance measure is used to find the difference in opinion furnished by the experts. It is then used to compare with the aggregated collective solution. $d(v^i, v^c)$, is the Euclidean difference function where, $v^i = (v_1^i, v_1^i, ..., v_n^i)$ is the set of individual opinions for all the factors, and $v^c = (v_1^c, v_1^c, ..., v_n^c)$ is the set of collective opinion.

Step 6: Calculation of Consensus Degree

The consensus degree $\zeta(\alpha_j)$ of all the experts on each of the alternative α_j is calculated using:

$$\zeta(\alpha_j) = 1 - \sum_{i=1}^{m} \frac{\pi_i(\alpha_j)}{m} \tag{13}$$

where, $\pi_i(\alpha_j)$ is the proximity degree π_i of each factor α_j and m is the number of experts.

Estimation of Proximity Degree

The proximity degree $\pi_i(\alpha_j)$ of each expert is calculated for each alternative:

$$\pi_i(\alpha_j) = p(v^i, v^c)(\alpha_j) = f(|v_j^c - v_j^i|) \tag{14}$$

where, $f(x) = \left(\frac{|v_j^c - v_j^i|}{n-1}\right)^{\lambda} \in [0,1]$ and $\lambda \in [0,1]$

Different values for λ such as 1, 0.7 and 0.5, etc. can be chosen where λ controls the consensus rigorousness. If λ is close to 1, then the rigorousness process decreases.

Step 7: Calculation of Consensus Measure

The consensus measure ζ_X is calculated by applying neat OWA operator (Yager, 1988; Yager, 1994). The neat OWA operator for each factor α_i with associated weight $w_j = \frac{\alpha_j^{\beta}}{\sum_j \alpha_j^{\beta}}$, is defined as

$$\zeta_X = neatOWA_{OR-LIKE}(\zeta(\alpha_1), \zeta(\alpha_2), ..., \zeta(\alpha_n)) \tag{15}$$

$$F(\alpha_1, \alpha_2, ..., \alpha_n) = \frac{\sum \alpha_j^{\beta+1}}{\sum_j \alpha_j^{\beta}} \tag{16}$$

where, β controls the behavior of the aggregation process. Thus, by using this kind of function, the weights are directly deduced from the values to be aggregated. If β = 0.0, we get a simple average operator, and as β approaches infinity, we obtain a maximum operator. The detailed analysis for neat OWA operators and the effect of β on the optimism degree can be found in Zarghami et al. (2008). The sensitivity of neat OWA operator with the OR-LIKE feature is presented in Table 2

Table 2: Fuzzy Linguistic Quantifiers and Equivalent Optimism Degree

Fuzzy Linguistic Quantifiers	Quantifier Index β	Optimism degree, θ
At least one of them	$\beta \to 0.0$	0.999
Few of them	0.1	0.909
Some of them	0.5	0.667
Half of them	1.0	0.500
Many of them	2.0	0.333
Most of them	10.0	0.091
All of them	$\beta \to \infty$	0.001

Step 8: Calculation of Proximity Measure

The proximity measure Π_X^i of the ith decision maker is calculated using the neat $OWA_{AND\text{-}LIKE}$ operator, which is 1 - neat $OWA_{OR\text{-}LIKE}$.

$$\Pi_X^i = 1 - neatOWA_{OR-LIKE}(\pi_i(\alpha_j)) \tag{17}$$

Step 9: Re-evaluation Rules

a) If the difference in the rank of opinions between the collective solution and individual solution of the factors is positive, then the concerned expert is requested to change his opinion by lowering the previous values.

b) If it is negative, the expert is requested to increase the evaluation associated with a particular factor.

c) If there is no difference in opinion between the collective and individual solution, previous values are kept.

Step 10: Check for the number of iterations

Step 11: Calculate the fuzzy preference values of interactions among the factors for the micro variables or sub-factors, if present.

STAGE II: Estimation using Permanent Value

Step 12: Combining the Diagonal Matrix and Off-Diagonal Matrix

The permanent matrix f^c is a combination of two matrices. A diagonal matrix *I* describing the importance of individual factor I^i in the system under consideration and another off-diagonal matrix f^c_{sol}, which contains pair-wise comparison among various factors.

Step 13: Calculate the permanent matrix

Let A be an nXn matrix. S_n, is the symmetric group of degree n. If $\sigma \in S_n$, then the set $\{a_{1\sigma(1)}; a_{2\sigma(2)}; \ldots; a_{n\sigma(n)}\}$ is called a diagonal of A corresponding to the permutation σ. The product $\prod_{i=1}^{n} a_{i\sigma(i)}$ is called a diagonal product. Following equation is used to calculate the value of the matrix:

$$perm(M) = \sum_{\sigma \in S_n} \prod_{i=1}^{n} a_{i\sigma(i)} \tag{18}$$

Step 14: Calculate Resemblance Ratio, if the comparison is to be done with other scenarios

Resemblance Ratio (RR) is a measure that helps to compare two different scenarios based on the index obtained in the previous step using Equation 18. The resemblance ratio lies in between 0 to 1. If both companies have same capabilities (regarding handling factors related to mobile service adoption) then the resemblance will be 0. The closer is to 1, and then higher is the non-resemblance. RR can be calculated using the following equation:

$$RR = \frac{1}{max\left(perm(M_1), perm(M_2)\right)}\left(\left|perm(M_1) - perm(M_2)\right|\right) \qquad (19)$$

where, M_1 and M_2 are the permanent matrix for scenario 1 and scenario 2, respectively.

AN ILLUSTRATIVE EXAMPLE

Spectrum is considered as a key resource for the success of mobile services. It makes communication possible over the mobile phones at a specific frequency range. Indian government auctioned 71 blocks of 3G spectrum (1959 - 1979 MHz) in 22 service areas covering pan-India in May 2010 (DOT, 2010). 3G spectrums allow mobile phones to connect to the Internet wirelessly, and the speed of data transfer is high as compared to data speed offered through 2G spectrums.

In order to remain operational in the market, the MNOs retain existing spectrum (2G) and also obtain licenses for new spectrum (3G, 4G/LTE) to float their services. However, there are certain challenges associated with recovering the return on investment.

However, due to huge competition and government policies, basic services like voice and SMS are not able to contribute to their profitability anymore. In order to overcome this, MNOs try to invest and market in mobile services as it is considered to be one of the profitable business units. Despite their efforts, people at large are not adopting them. Several researchers (Carlsson et al., 2005; Bouwman et al., 2007; Nikou and Mezei, 2013) have discussed the possible impact of factors as well as driving forces related to usage of different mobile value added services. In order to address these issues, we have identified few factors that lead to the poor adoption of advanced mobile services. Estimating the cumulative impact of factors can help MNOs and other stakeholders to compare their performance with their previous performances and/or with their competitors.

For the purpose of illustration, we consider only five critical factors, though others can also be considered for detailed analysis. The factors are enumerated below:

1. Operational Cost
2. Low Spectrum Availability
3. Unavailability of Context-aware Services
4. Return on Investment for the operator

5. Inefficient Bundling Strategies

These five factors I_i (i.e., I_1, I_2, I_3, I_4, and I_5) were circulated to four experts (DM1, DM2, DM3 and DM4). They were requested to assign importance to each of the factors I_i on the overall system. These importance were recorded using 11-point fuzzy scale (Table 1). The weights of each element I_i were aggregated using neat OWA operator (Table3).

Table 3: Importance of factors on the Entire System

	DM1	DM2	DM3	DM4	μ_{x_i}	$Entropy(x_i)$	$Cons(x_i)$	neat OWA_Q		
								$\beta = 0.0$ *"At least one of them"*	$\beta = 1.0$ ***"Half of them"***	$\beta = 100.0$ *"All of them"*
I1	0.7450	0.6650	0.7450	0.6650	0.7050	1.0000	0.9351	0.7050	0.7073	0.7450
I2	0.3350	0.4100	0.2550	0.3350	0.3338	1.5000	0.9348	0.3338	0.3428	0.4100
I3	0.0450	0.0450	0.1350	0.0450	0.0675	0.8113	0.9451	0.0675	0.0900	0.1350
I4	0.5900	0.6650	0.7450	0.6650	0.6663	1.5000	0.9348	0.6663	0.6708	0.7450
I5	0.4100	0.3350	0.3350	0.1350	0.3038	1.5000	0.8560	0.3038	0.3381	0.4100

Aggregation operation (neat OWA_Q) was applied on the collected opinions of all elements I_i for different values of β. It helped to analyze the sensitivity of the neat OWA operator. It was observed that as the value of β increased it acted more like OR operation (termed as OR-LIKE) and if β was 0.0, it acted more like mean μ_x operation. Similarly, if β was assigned to 1.0, it meant that all participating experts agree to these values up to 50%. Further, we adopted quantifier Q "Half of them" with β = 1.0 for further processing as it acts as a mean operator. Hence, the aggregated opinion for diagonal matrix I came to be {(I_1, 0.7617), (I_2, 0.3427), (I_3, 0.5487), (I_4, 0.7307), (I_5, 0.7072)}.

In the second part, opinions were collected for the non-diagonal elements in various formats for pairwise comparison and it was then transformed using an appropriate transformation function into fuzzy preference relations' format. The values obtained from different experts (DM1 and DM3 in fuzzy preference relations format and DM2 and DM4 in multiplicative preference format) are as follows:

$$DM1 = \begin{pmatrix} - & 0.75 & 0.70 & 0.55 & 0.55 \\ 0.25 & - & 0.40 & 0.30 & 0.25 \\ 0.30 & 0.60 & - & 0.40 & 0.30 \\ 0.45 & 0.70 & 0.60 & - & 0.50 \\ 0.45 & 0.75 & 0.70 & 0.50 & - \end{pmatrix}$$

$$DM2 = \begin{pmatrix} - & 9 & 5 & 3 & 2 \\ 1/9 & - & 1/2 & 1/3 & 1/4 \\ 1/5 & 2 & - & 1/3 & 1/2 \\ 1/3 & 3 & 3 & - & 1/3 \\ 1/2 & 4 & 2 & 3 & - \end{pmatrix}$$

$$DM3 = \begin{pmatrix} - & 0.75 & 0.8 & 0.7 & 0.6 \\ 0.25 & - & 0.3 & 0.3 & 0.2 \\ 0.2 & 0.7 & - & 0.4 & 0.3 \\ 0.3 & 0.7 & 0.6 & - & 0.4 \\ 0.4 & 0.8 & 0.7 & 0.6 & - \end{pmatrix}$$

$$DM4 = \begin{pmatrix} - & 3 & 5 & 4 & 3 \\ 1/3 & - & 1/2 & 1/3 & 1/5 \\ 1/5 & 2 & - & 1/2 & 5 \\ 1/4 & 3 & 2 & - & 1/2 \\ 1/3 & 5 & 1/5 & 2 & - \end{pmatrix}$$

The initial responses of DM1, DM2 and DM4 are then converted to the fuzzy preference relations P2 and P4 using Equation 7.

$$P1 = \begin{pmatrix} - & 0.75 & 0.70 & 0.55 & 0.55 \\ 0.25 & - & 0.40 & 0.30 & 0.25 \\ 0.30 & 0.60 & - & 0.40 & 0.30 \\ 0.45 & 0.70 & 0.60 & - & 0.50 \\ 0.45 & 0.75 & 0.70 & 0.50 & - \end{pmatrix}$$

$$P2 = \begin{pmatrix} - & 1.0000 & 0.8662 & 0.7500 & 0.6577 \\ 0.0000 & - & 0.3423 & 0.2500 & 0.1845 \\ 0.1338 & 0.6577 & - & 0.2500 & 0.3423 \\ 0.2500 & 0.7500 & 0.7500 & - & 0.2500 \\ 0.3423 & 0.8155 & 0.6577 & 0.7500 & - \end{pmatrix}$$

$$P3 = \begin{pmatrix} - & 0.75 & 0.8 & 0.7 & 0.6 \\ 0.25 & - & 0.3 & 0.3 & 0.2 \\ 0.2 & 0.7 & - & 0.4 & 0.3 \\ 0.3 & 0.7 & 0.6 & - & 0.4 \\ 0.4 & 0.8 & 0.7 & 0.6 & - \end{pmatrix}$$

$$P4 = \begin{pmatrix} - & 0.7500 & 0.8662 & 0.8155 & 0.7500 \\ 0.2500 & - & 0.3423 & 0.2500 & 0.1338 \\ 0.1338 & 0.6577 & - & 0.3423 & 0.8662 \\ 0.1845 & 0.7500 & 0.6577 & - & 0.3423 \\ 0.2500 & 0.8662 & 0.1338 & 0.6577 & - \end{pmatrix}$$

Now, aggregation operation was performed as described in Step 3. Using the fuzzy majority criterion with the fuzzy quantifier "majority'", with the pair (0.3, 0.8) and the corresponding neat

OWA operator with the weighting vector W_{DM} = { 0, 0.4, 0.5, 0.1 }, the temporary collective fuzzy preference relation f_{sol}^c is

$$f_{sol}^c = \begin{pmatrix} - & 0.7500 & 0.8331 & 0.7577 & 0.6750 \\ 0.2500 & - & 0.3211 & 0.2750 & 0.1669 \\ 0.1669 & 0.6789 & - & 0.3711 & 0.5831 \\ 0.2423 & 0.7250 & 0.6289 & - & 0.3711 \\ 0.3250 & 0.8331 & 0.4169 & 0.6289 & - \end{pmatrix}$$

As discussed in Step 4, we obtain the order (Morder) based on the temporary collective solution for finding the proximity derived from QGDD and QGNDD. The order can be determined independently either by QGDD or QGNDD. However, both can also be used with a max operation to determine the order X_{sol} =max (QGDD, QGNDD).

$$\begin{array}{rcl} & & \begin{array}{ccccc} I1 & I2 & I3 & I4 & I5 \end{array} \\ QGDD_{f_{sol}^c} & = & \begin{pmatrix} 0.7713 & 0.3013 & 0.4480 & 0.5127 & 0.5466 \end{pmatrix} \\ & & \begin{array}{ccccc} I1 & I2 & I3 & I4 & I5 \end{array} \\ QGNDD_{f_{sol}^c} & = & \begin{pmatrix} 1.0 & 0.7285 & 0.7335 & 0.7938 & 0.8268 \end{pmatrix} \end{array}$$

$$X_{sol} = max\{QGDD_{f_{sol}^c}, QGNDD_{f_{sol}^c}\} \tag{20}$$

$$X_{sol} = \begin{array}{c} \begin{array}{ccccc} I1 & I2 & I3 & I4 & I5 \end{array} \\ \begin{pmatrix} 1.0 & 0.7285 & 0.7335 & 0.7938 & 0.8268 \end{pmatrix} \end{array} \tag{21}$$

However, for simplicity, we use QGDD to continue with our algorithm, hence X_{sol} will not be used. Similarly, for different factors, weights for the alternatives are determined using the fuzzy quantifier ``as many as possible'' with the pair (0, 0.5). The corresponding neat OWA operator for the alternative weighting vector is: W_{Alt} = { 0.4, 0.4, 0.2, 0, 0 }.

$$QGDD_{DM} = \begin{array}{c} \\ I1 \\ I2 \\ I3 \\ I4 \\ I5 \end{array} \begin{array}{c} \begin{array}{cccc} DM1 & DM2 & DM3 & DM4 \end{array} \\ \begin{pmatrix} 0.7447 & 0.7779 & 0.7647 & 0.7779 \\ 0.3171 & 0.3055 & 0.2971 & 0.3055 \\ 0.4700 & 0.4263 & 0.4697 & 0.4263 \\ 0.5800 & 0.5054 & 0.5200 & 0.5054 \\ 0.6200 & 0.4732 & 0.6200 & 0.4732 \end{pmatrix} \end{array}$$

Based on $QGDD_{DM}$ and QGDD)f^c_{sol}), we obtain M_{order}, which is used to find the difference of opinions of DM_i with f^c_{sol} based on Euclidean distance (V_j^c-V_j^i) as described in Step 5.

$$M_{order} = \begin{array}{c} \\ I1 \\ I2 \\ I3 \\ I4 \\ I5 \end{array} \begin{array}{c} \begin{array}{ccccc} DM1 & DM2 & DM3 & DM4 & f^c_{sol} \end{array} \\ \left[\begin{array}{cccc|c} 1 & 1 & 1 & 1 & 1 \\ 5 & 5 & 5 & 5 & 5 \\ 4 & 4 & 4 & 4 & 4 \\ 3 & 2 & 3 & 2 & 3 \\ 2 & 3 & 2 & 3 & 2 \end{array} \right] \end{array}$$

$$V_j^c - V_j^i = \begin{array}{c} \\ I1 \\ I2 \\ I3 \\ I4 \\ I5 \end{array} \begin{array}{c} \begin{array}{cccc} DM1 & DM2 & DM3 & DM4 \end{array} \\ \begin{pmatrix} 0 & 0 & 0 & 0 \\ 0 & 0 & 0 & 0 \\ 0 & 0 & 0 & 0 \\ 0 & -1 & 0 & -1 \\ 0 & 1 & 0 & 1 \end{pmatrix} \end{array}$$

Now, we calculate the consensus degree ζ (α_j) as described in Step 6 with varying λ values ranging from 0.5 to 1.

$$\zeta(\alpha_j) = \begin{array}{c} \\ \zeta(I1) \\ \zeta(I2) \\ \zeta(I3) \\ \zeta(I4) \\ \zeta(I5) \end{array} \begin{array}{c} \begin{array}{cccc} \lambda(0.5) & \lambda(0.7) & \lambda(0.9) & \lambda(1) \end{array} \\ \begin{pmatrix} 1 & 1 & 1 & 1 \\ 1 & 1 & 1 & 1 \\ 1 & 1 & 1 & 1 \\ 0.75 & 0.8105 & 0.8566 & 0.875 \\ 0.75 & 0.8105 & 0.8564 & 0.875 \end{pmatrix} \end{array}$$

Now, we estimate the consensus measure (ζ_X) with neat \$OWA$_{OR\text{-}LIKE}$ operator with β = 0.98 as described in Step 7 to find the f_{sol}^c.

$$\zeta_X = \begin{array}{c} \begin{array}{cccc} \lambda(0.5) & \lambda(0.7) & \lambda(0.9) & \lambda(1) \end{array} \\ \begin{pmatrix} 0.9163 & 0.9334 & 0.9477 & 0.9539 \end{pmatrix} \end{array}$$

The final solution f^c is obtained by combining *I* (diagonal elements) and f^c_{sol} (off-diagonal elements). It represents the adoption factors in the form of a complete graph (Figure 3), where vertices and edges are represented by the factors and weights of the collective solution (f^c), respectively. The permanent value of the graph is calculated as follows:

$$
\begin{aligned}
perm(M_{5X5}) &= \prod_i E_i + \sum_i \sum_j \sum_k \sum_l \sum_m (a_{ij}a_{ji})\, E_k E_l E_m \\
&+ \sum_i \sum_j \sum_k \sum_l \sum_m (a_{ij}a_{jk}a_{ki} + a_{ik}a_{kj}a_{ji}) E_l E_m \\
&+ \left(\begin{array}{l} \sum_i \sum_j \sum_k \sum_l \sum_m (a_{ij}a_{jk})\,(a_{kl}a_{lk}) E_m \\ + \sum_i \sum_j \sum_k \sum_l \sum_m ((a_{ij}a_{jk}a_{kl}a_{li}) + (a_{il}a_{lk}a_{kj}a_{ji})) E_m \end{array} \right) \\
&+ \left(\begin{array}{l} \sum_i \sum_j \sum_k \sum_l \sum_m (a_{ij}a_{ji})\,(a_{kl}a_{lm}a_{mk} + a_{km}a_{ml}a_{lk}) \\ + \sum_i \sum_j \sum_k \sum_l \sum_m (a_{ij}a_{jk}a_{kl}a_{lm}a_{mi} + a_{im}a_{ml}a_{lk}a_{kj}a_{ji}) \end{array} \right)
\end{aligned}
$$

where, i, j, k, l and m represents five different factors.

Hence, the final matrix obtained is : $f^c = I_i + f_{sol}^c$

$$
f^c = \begin{pmatrix} 0.7073 & - & - & - & - \\ - & 0.3428 & - & - & - \\ - & - & 0.0900 & - & - \\ - & - & - & 0.6708 & - \\ - & - & - & - & 0.3381 \end{pmatrix} + \begin{pmatrix} - & 0.7500 & 0.8331 & 0.7577 & 0.6750 \\ 0.2500 & - & 0.3211 & 0.2750 & 0.1669 \\ 0.1669 & 0.6789 & - & 0.3711 & 0.5831 \\ 0.2423 & 0.7250 & 0.6289 & - & 0.3711 \\ 0.3250 & 0.8331 & 0.4169 & 0.6289 & - \end{pmatrix}
$$

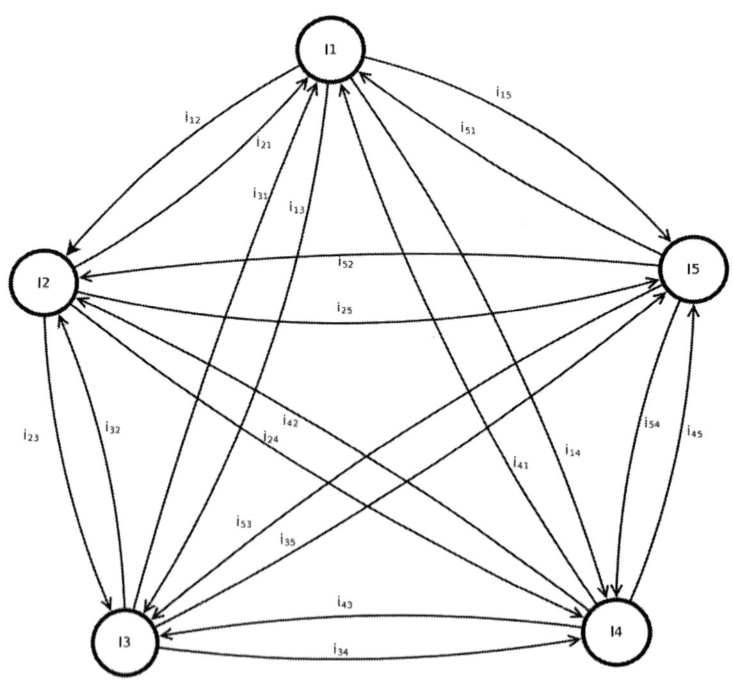

$$f^c = \begin{pmatrix} 0.7073 & 0.7500 & 0.8331 & 0.7577 & 0.6750 \\ 0.2500 & 0.3428 & 0.3211 & 0.2750 & 0.1669 \\ 0.1669 & 0.6789 & 0.0900 & 0.3711 & 0.5831 \\ 0.2423 & 0.7250 & 0.6289 & 0.6708 & 0.3711 \\ 0.3250 & 0.8331 & 0.4169 & 0.6289 & 0.3381 \end{pmatrix}$$

The mobile service adoption divide index for the MNO A (Case A) came to be: MSDI (Case A) = 2.237248

It indicates the cumulative impact of all the factors leading to poor usage of mobile services of a particular MNO. This index can be compared with other operators offering similar services, possibly facing a similar set of factors and are offering their services in the same zone. In general, two scenarios for an MNO are never identical from the service provider's perspective; a particular barrier that acts as a barrier for one particular scenario may not have any impact on the other. Similarly, another operator can also be considered for comparison purpose.

Hence, similar steps were followed to find the index for another operator (Case B) offering mobile services in the same area. The opinion of experts are given below in Table 4:

Table 4: Importance of factors on the Entire System in Case B

	DM1	DM2	DM3	DM4	μ_{x_i}	$Entropy(x_i)$	$Cons(x_i)$	neat OWA_Q		
								$\beta = 0.0$ *"At least of one them"*	$\beta = 1.0$ ***"Half of them"***	$\beta = 100.0$ *"All of them"*
I1	0.9950	0.8650	0.9550	0.7450	0.8900	1.5000	0.8564	0.8900	0.9004	0.9943
I2	0.4100	0.5000	0.5000	0.5000	0.4775	0.8113	0.9451	0.4775	0.4807	0.5000
I3	0.6650	0.5000	0.7450	0.6650	0.6438	1.5000	0.8784	0.6438	0.6561	0.7450
I4	0.7450	0.8650	0.7450	0.7450	0.7750	0.8113	0.9262	0.7750	0.7785	0.8650
I5	0.6650	0.4100	0.4100	0.5000	0.4963	1.5000	0.8527	0.4963	0.5181	0.6650

$$DM1 = \begin{pmatrix} - & 0.9500 & 0.9000 & 0.7500 & 0.9000 \\ 0.0500 & - & 0.5000 & 0.7000 & 0.7500 \\ 0.1000 & 0.5000 & - & 0.5000 & 0.3000 \\ 0.2500 & 0.3000 & 0.5000 & - & 0.3000 \\ 0.1000 & 0.2500 & 0.7000 & 0.7000 & - \end{pmatrix}$$

$$DM2 = \begin{pmatrix} - & 7 & 7 & 5 & 7 \\ 1/7 & - & 7 & 1 & 3 \\ 1/7 & 1/7 & - & 1/2 & 1/2 \\ 1/5 & 1 & 2 & - & 1/2 \\ 1/7 & 1/3 & 2 & 2 & - \end{pmatrix}$$

$$DM3 = \begin{pmatrix} - & 0.8500 & 0.8000 & 0.7000 & 0.7000 \\ 0.1500 & - & 0.4000 & 0.8000 & 0.8000 \\ 0.2000 & 0.6000 & - & 0.6500 & 0.4000 \\ 0.3000 & 0.2000 & 0.3500 & - & 0.3500 \\ 0.3000 & 0.2000 & 0.6000 & 0.6500 & - \end{pmatrix}$$

$$DM4 = \begin{pmatrix} - & 5 & 5 & 7 & 7 \\ 1/5 & - & 6 & 1 & 5 \\ 1/5 & 1/6 & - & 1/3 & 1/2 \\ 1/7 & 1 & 3 & - & 1/2 \\ 1/7 & 1/5 & 2 & 2 & - \end{pmatrix}$$

$$f^c = \begin{pmatrix} 0.9004 & 0.8887 & 0.8637 & 0.7908 & 0.8214 \\ 0.1113 & 0.4807 & 0.6679 & 0.6500 & 0.7866 \\ 0.1363 & 0.3321 & 0.6561 & 0.4869 & 0.3711 \\ 0.2092 & 0.3500 & 0.5131 & 0.7785 & 0.3461 \\ 0.1786 & 0.2134 & 0.6289 & 0.6539 & 0.5181 \end{pmatrix}$$

MSDI (Case B) = 3.267410

Now, we are ready to compare the differences in the index, which is calculated using resemblance ratio. The closer the ratio to 1, higher is the non-resemblance. In order to compare both the scenarios, we find the resemblance ratio for the obtained indices using Equation 19.

$$RR = \frac{1}{max(2.2372, 3.2674)} * (|2.2372 - 3.2674|)$$

$$RR = \frac{1}{3.2674} * 1.0302 = 0.3153$$

We observe that the scenarios are in favor of the first operator, which means that the first operator is better positioned while compared with the second operator when it comes to offering mobile services. The MSDI along with resemblance ratio would help different operators to rank their ability to overcome the factors and reduce their effect on the adoption process. It will help the customers to choose the best service providers in their area without having the knowledge of the intricacies involved in the index development process. In graph theoretical methodology, each and every characteristic is evaluated independently, which can help in overcoming the factors systematically; hence, it can be used as a tool for self-improvement on a continuous basis. Also, it allows adding new factors with ease, and it is flexible enough to incorporate such changes. Acknowledging the above benefits, this framework can also be used as an evaluation tool that may aid in decision-making for overcoming the factors to mobile service adoption.

CONCLUSION

In this paper, a framework to estimate mobile service adoption divide index is proposed. It uses the perception of telecom experts to derive an index. It helps to quantify the factors systematically with the help of consensus building algorithm. The proposed framework tries to minimize the bias involved when opinions are sought from the experts. The neat OWA helps to aggregate the opinions in a more comprehensive manner. The availability of different input mechanism puts the experts in a more comfortable position to record their opinions; the transformation functions convert them into a fuzzy preference format, which becomes easier for aggregation using the neat OWA operators.

The use of fuzzy scales offers more flexibility in deciding the importance as it becomes quite difficult to quantify the effects accurately in real situations. The final matrix is a fair representation of the problem under study and offers ease of processing with the help of computer algorithms. Application of digraph and matrix algebra makes it convenient for visual representation and processing of the matrix with the computers. A detailed analysis can be done using MSDI to overcome the factors related to the adoption of mobile services. Resemblance ratio helps to compare two or more different scenarios. The proposed methodology is illustrated with the help of a case study to compare two different MNOs so that a fair judgment can be derived for their capability to overcome the factors.

REFERENCES

Bouwman, H., Carlsson, C., Molina-Castillo, F. J., Walden, P., 2007. Barriers and drivers in the adoption of current and future mobile services in Finland. Telematics and Informatics 24 (2), 145–160.

Bouwman, H., Carlsson, C., Walden, P., Molina-Castillo, F. J., 2009. Reconsidering the actual and future use of mobile services. Information Systems & E-Business Management 7 (3), 301–317.

Carlsson, C., Hyvonen, K., Repo, P., Walden, P., January 2005. Asynchronous adoption patterns of mobile services. In: Proceedings of the 38th Annual Hawaii International Conference on System Sciences, HICSS 2005. pp. 189a: 1–10.

Chen, J., Lin, S., 2004. A neural network approach-decision neural network (DNN) for preference assessment. IEEE Transactions on Systems, Man, & Cybernetics, Part C: Applications & Reviews 34 (2), 219–225.

Chiclana, F., Herrera, F., Herrera-Viedma, E., 1998. Integrating three representation models in fuzzy multipurpose decision-making based on fuzzy preference relations. Fuzzy Sets & Systems 97 (1), 33–48.

Choudhury, A., Shankar, R., Tiwari, M., 2006. Consensus-based intelligent group decision-making model for the selection of advanced technology. Decision Support Systems 42 (3), 1776–1799.

Deo, N., 1974. Graph Theory with Applications to Engineering with Computer Science. PHI

Learning Pvt. Ltd., New Delhi, India.

DOT, May 2010. 3G auction - final results. Department Of Telecommunications, F. No. P-11014/13/2008-PP. Accessed on April 7, 2014. URL http://www.dot.gov.in/sites/default/files/3G_Auction_Final_Results_0.pdf

Gandhi, O., Agrawal, V., 1992. FMEA – a diagraph and matrix approach. Reliability Engineering & System Safety 35 (2), 147 – 158.

Grover, S., Agrawal, V. P., Khan, I. A., 2004. A digraph approach to TQM evaluation of an industry. International Journal of Production Research 42 (19), 4031–4053.

Herrera-Viedma, E., Herrera, F., Chiclana, F., 2002. A consensus model for multiperson decision making with different preference structures. IEEE Transactions On Systems, Man & Cybernetics - Part A: Systems & Hu- mans 32 (3), 394–402.

Jurkat, W. B., Ryser, H. J., 1966. Matrix factorisation of determinants and permanents. Journal of Algebra 3:1 (3), 1–11.

Muduli, K., Govindan, K., Barve, A., Geng, Y., 2013. Barriers to green supply chain management in Indian mining industries: A graph theoretic approach. Journal of Cleaner Production 47 (1), 335–344.

Nikou, S., Mezei, J., 2013. Evaluation of mobile services and substantial adoption factors with Analytic Hierarchy Process (AHP) . Telecommunications Policy 37 (10), 915 – 929.

Orlovsky, S., 1978. Decision-making with a fuzzy preference relation. Fuzzy Sets & Systems 1 (3), 155–167.

Raj, T., Shankar, R., Suhaib, M., Khan, R., 2010. A graph-theoretic approach to evaluate the intensity of barriers in the implementation of FMSs. International Journal of Services & Operations Management 7 (1), 24–52.

Rao, R. V., January 2006. A decision-making framework model for evaluating flexible manufacturing systems using digraph and matrix methods. International Journal of Advanced Manufacturing Technology 30 (11-12), 1101–1110.

Saaty, T., 1980. The Analytic Hierarchy Process. McGraw Hill Company.

Saaty, T. L., 2005. Theory and Applications of the Analytic Network Process. RWS Publications, Pittsburgh, PA.

Sabharwal, S., Garg, S., August 2013. Determining cost effectiveness index of remanufacturing: A graph theoretic approach. International Journal of Production Economics 144 (2), 521–532.

Shannon, C., 1948. The mathematical theory of communication. The Bell System Technical Journal 27 (3-4), 379–423; 623–656.

Singh, R., Choudhury, A., Tiwari, M., Shankar, R., July 2007. Improved Decision Neural Network (IDNN) based consensus method to solve a multi- objective group decision making problem. Advanced Engineering Informatics 21 (3), 335–348.

Tanino, T., 1988. Fuzzy preference relations in group decision-making. In: Kacprzyk, J., Roubens, M. (Eds.), Non-Conventional Preference Relations in Decision-Making. Springer, Berlin, pp. 54–71.

Tanino, T., 1990. On group decision-making under fuzzy preferences. Multi-person decision-making using fuzzy sets and possibility theory. Kluwer, Norwell, MA.

Tastle, W. J., Wierman, M. J., 2007. Consensus and dissention: A measure of ordinal dispersion. International Journal of Approximate Reasoning 45 (3), 531–545.

Venkatasamy, R., Agrawal, V. P., 1997. A digraph approach to quality evaluation of an automotive vehicle. Quality Engineering 9 (3), 405–417.

Yager, R. R., 1988. On ordered weighted averaging aggregation operators in multicriteria decision making. IEEE Transactions on Systems, Man & Cybernetics, Part A: Systems & Humans 18 (1), 183–190.

Yager, R. R., Filev, D. P., 1994. Parameterized and-like and or-like OWA operators. International Journal of General Systems 22 (3), 297–316.

Zadeh, L., 1983. A computational approach to fuzzy quantifiers in natural languages. Computers & Mathematics with Applications 9 (1), 149–184.

Zarghami, M., Szidarovszky, F., Ardakanian, R., April 2008. Sensitivity analysis of the OWA operator. IEEE Transactions on Systems, Man, and Cy- bernetics, Part B: Cybernetics 38 (2), 547–552.

DECISION SCIENCES INSTITUTE

A Heuristic Data Sampling Approach for Association Rule Classification under a Big Data Environment

Ching-Chin Chern
National Taiwan University
Email: cchern@ntu.edu.tw

Huai-De Peng
National Taiwan University
Email: r01725017@ntu.edu.tw

Ling-Chieh Kung
National Taiwan University
Email: lckung@ntu.edu.tw

ABSTRACT

This study proposes a heuristic data sampling approach to solve the problem of mining big data without changing the association rule classification method. The proposed heuristic data sampling approach consists of two parts. The first part is a heuristic sampling method applied in the initial phase, which samples representative data from a big data set with important, discriminative attributes. Then the second part deals with the incremental big data problem. Merging the sampled data from both the preliminary and incremental data sets and their classifiers, it is possible to apply them to verify the combined classifier.

KEYWORDS: Big Data, Incremental Algorithm, Association Rule Classification, Data Sampling, Attribute Selection

INTRODUCTION

In the past few years, a new concept, called "big data", has emerged as an important issue of business decision making. The so-called "big data" includes three special characteristics, called "3Vs": Volume, Variety and Velocity (Lamont, 2012; McAfee and Brynjolfsson, 2012; Stackpole, 2012). We need new solutions to solve the problem under the big data environment because previous ones are having troubles while facing big data problems. Techniques for reckoning with data at small scales can become insufficient or irrelevant at larger ones (McAfee and Brynjolfsson, 2012; Skinner, 2013). What make most big data big are repeated observations over time and/or space (Jacobs, 2009). Traditional data systems simply cannot handle big data very well, either because it is impossible to handle the variety of data – big data is much less structured due to the speed of evolution, or because such systems just cannot scale at the rate of ingesting data (Jackson, 2012).

The new solutions dealing with big data problems are expected to respond to three special characteristics of big data. For volume and velocity, it is no longer necessary to have a sophisticated model anymore, which may mean a shift in the way data mining is done (Collett, 2011). The solutions depend on breaking up data, sending out subsets for analysis and then regrouping the results to produce the output (Lamont, 2012). For variety, users have to put different forms of data together from many sources and make sense from them (Olavsrud, 2012).

Recently, Apache Hadoop is described as the core technology driving the adoption of big data and capable to quickly and economically process the huge datasets (Reid, 2012).

However, attributes are also dynamic in a big data problem (Jacobs, 2009). Although attributes do not change as significantly as records do most of the time, they still vary not only on values of attributes but also on the total number of attributes. Missing values of attributes in each record also need to be considered. The volume problem on records also happens on attributes. Since including all attributes into association rule classification method apparently slows down the processing speed, determining how many and which attributes should be selected are also issues in big data analytic.

To make the analysis of big data more feasible, the efficiency must be enhanced. Here, we are not focusing on the algorithm and the process of an association rule classification method but the data pre-process. By selecting proper data from a big data set and applying some treatment, the chosen data can be much more manageable than the volume of original data but still be representative of the original data. Thus, we can input these data to an association rule classification method with the expectation of generating patterns in a more efficient way.

PROBLEM DESCRIPTION

This study aims to solve the performance problem of an association rule classification method under big data environment by proposing a proper data preparation approach. Association rule classification is a popular way to extract patterns from several data records and then turn these patterns into knowledge for decision makers to support their decision (Liu et al., 1998). Though association rule classification methods have been developed for a long period, very few discussions have been focused on processing times unless the calculating of an association rule algorithm takes too much time (Thabtah, 2007). Most of the researches focus more on the accuracy and interpretation of an association rule classification method rather than the processing time issues.

A major reason of this situation is the limitation on the number of data records in the past due to data storage problem. However, by Moore's Law (Moore, 1965), the total data volume is growing at an exponential rate. The fact is that terabytes of data with different features are created every day and the rate of data generation grows steadily nowadays, which is not yet expected by authors of previous data mining methods as well as users. This situation does not cause severe accuracy problem when applying original association rule classification methods, but rather it incapacitates these methods to handle the current characteristics of big data well. Hence, this study focuses on refining input of the general association rule classification methods based on existing procedures and trying to solve the problem without any adjustment on association rule classification methods themselves.

Most mechanisms dealing with big data problems are actually developed to solve the data collecting problem of unstructured data from various sources, e.g., MapReduce and Hadoop (Reid, 2012). These methods can be used as frameworks to collect and store data in several servers and then the results from different servers are computed and compared. Although they provide some simple ways to handle big data collection problem, these methods do not perform further analyses on the collected data. Our study focuses rather on volume and velocity than variety, and thus we just assume that the data is already collected and transformed to a structured database.

To be specific, we break down the performance problem of an association rule classification method caused by big data into three dimensions. First is the perspective of data records. Given that the data not only has extreme large size but also is incremental, the size of these records increases quickly and steadily. Thus, using all data to conduct data mining is almost impossible. Second, attributes of the dataset also have the potential to grow. Because of the variety of data features, diverse sources and different types of data result in possibly changes in dimensions of the data. Finally, the dynamicity makes analyses real-time impossible to make corresponding decisions in time. In the meantime, analytical result in previous period could be infeasible for making further decisions overtime. Moreover, growths on records and attributes make dataset harder to access. The increasing amount of data and properties causes it harder to analyze. These three sub-problems consists the difficulties of using big data.

The answers to the above three sub-problems can be broken down into three parts: determining how many and what records to be selected, determining how many and what attributes to be selected and dealing with the incremental nature of a big data problem. Our approach is to alter the original data preparing process without affecting the process and algorithm being used in data mining. Under this premise, our method will focus on the substances and features, selecting them from the original dataset, and then using them as input of upcoming data mining process, which means that the proposed data preparation process will not influence the following data mining steps.

Sampling is a possible solution to deal with big data. While the size of original dataset is extremely large, sampling can choose and analyze a small subset from the dataset and then infer the results to the entire dataset. Although sampling can reduce the size of data for data mining, it creates other problem, such as determining how many and what the records should be sampled. Choosing a smaller subset will significantly decrease the processing time on data mining, but may be insufficient to represent the whole dataset. There are trade-off between processing time and coverage of data. Thus, using sampling methods in data preparation of data mining should consider about the number of records to be sampled.

The strategy of stratification sampling is a valid way to handle the problem caused by the scale of data (Cano et al., 2005). The concept of stratification is to separate initial dataset into disjoint strata with same analogy of stratifying based on the distribution of the population. Hence, the representation of stratified sampled data is higher than the data by simple random sampling.

Facing the problem that the number of attributes is large and also increasing, the dimensions of data should be degraded to make sure processing time to be short so that the analysis result can be used on time (Shannon, 1948). Attribute selection is a viable way to deal with large amount of attributes under big data. In many attribute selection methods, entropy is used as a criterion to compare and choose corresponding features (Shannon, 1948).

Since prevailing data mining methods are not designed for big data, difficulties occur while using these original analyses to handle big data. Our goal in this study is to apply association rule classification methods on big data. Currently, most mechanisms proposed to solve problems caused by big data are mainly about the variety characteristic. In the other word, these solutions focused on how the data is collected rather than analyzed. However, this study is trying to work on the volume and velocity of big data. Hence, we have to make some proper adjustment and assumption so that we can aim on our target problem more clearly.

First, we assume the data is well collected in a structured database with extremely large size and high dimension. Thus, we are able to focus on the situations that are brought by volume and velocity instead of variety. Second, we assume that classes in original data or in incoming data are known before building classifiers. To enhance the efficiency of data mining under big data environment, we have to deal with both the size and the dimension problem. The method we proposed is using modified data preparation to refine the input of data mining. Therefore, the existing association rule classification methods can be adopted on analysis. We use sampling to solve the size problem and attribute selection for the dimension problem.

Dataset under big data environment is not static because new data objects are consistently adding to the dataset. The possibilities of growth on records, attributes and classes are all expected to happen. In this way, previous classifier could be unsuitable for incoming data with new elements. Thus, the time factor is considered to decide whether the model is fit or not. We have to choose between merging the new model with previous one or simply abandon previous model to use the new one. In the meantime, the processing time of these procedures is still an important criterion.

THE HEURISTIC BIG-DATA SAMPLING ALGORITHM (HBDSA)

The heuristic data selection algorithm proposed in this study includes two different phases: initial and incremental. The initial phase refers to the initial stage, where no valid sampled data exists before or a whole new dataset is sampled to regenerate the classifier. The second phase aims to handle the problem of using incremental data to update the classifier when there are already sampled data and a classifier generated before. Under this situation, we will make proper modification to the classifier because the original classifier is incapable to classify the newly arrived (incremental) data accurately. Separating the incremental stage from the initial stage mainly focuses on solving the velocity problem caused by big data. In a general case, the frequency of initial procedure runs should be much lesser than incremental procedure since the processing time of incremental phase is significantly less than initial stage. The incremental procedure attempts to modify the existing classifier to fit newly arrived data and thus the time to build up a valid classifier can be significantly reduced.

Dividing the job of constructing a valid classifier into these two phases reduces the scale of big data while transforming a big data into smaller datasets makes it both discriminative and analyzable. The first step in the initial phase samples data from the dataset in order to diminish the extreme scale on big data. Afterward, certain attributes are sorted and selected to generate the classifier. Both steps deal with volume and variety problems of a big data. Choosing data and features reduces the scales of database in both attributes and records, which in turn significantly enhances the efficiency and effectiveness of the association rule classification method applied on these data. The problem we have to face is the tradeoff between the efficiency and the accuracy or the coverage while reducing the scale of the dataset.

At the second phase, the incremental data is sampled first as well. Then, this sampled incremental data is tested by the original classifier. If the incremental data cannot be classified accurately, it is necessary to modify the preliminary classifier. Consequently, the inapplicable rules are removed and the new rules are generated to refine and thus increase accuracy of the classifier. In the following sections, we discuss and elaborate these two phases of the Heuristic Big-Data Sampling Algorithm (HBDSA) in detail based on the situations under which these two phases may face.

Under the big data environment, the data set contains considerably numerous data records and attributes. Since the data mining techniques screen out useless data and extract the discriminative data, scaling down the dataset is very important to ensure the success of analyzing big data. In the meantime, the scaled down dataset should still be representative enough for the original dataset so that the result of association rule classification is useful to classify the entire data set. The process of the Data and Attribute Sampling Algorithm (DASA) is based on these two aforementioned principles.

DASA first samples data before selecting attributes for two reasons. First is about the feasibility. Attribute selection requires calculation, ordering and sorting, which will be largely affected by the amount of records no matter which method it takes. Sampling data can narrow down the size of data, and hence speed up the process of attribute selection. Second is to retain the characteristics of original data. By ensuring that the sampled data is approximately similarly distributes as the original big data, the results of further analyses applied on the sampled data can be inferred to the original big dataset. Hence, after sampling the data, DASA selects attributes to extract needed features for building up a classifier.

After generating the preliminary classifier, it should be available to classify data for a period of time. However, as time passes, the incoming data are possibly changed. The scope of data variation not only includes changes in value, but also affect changes in classes and attributes. These diversifications could make original classifier infeasible to classify new data inflow, which leads to a lower accuracy rate and possible misclassification risks. Hence, the preliminary classifier should be modified to adapt changes on data. We first separate the problem into two possible scale-wise problems, which are the changes on attributes and classes, and to handle them sequentially. Afterward, we use actual data to verify the combined classifier and to rank rules in the classifier to generate modified classifier.

We discuss both scale-wise problems individually and solve the problems case by case. Still, the real situation could include at most both problems, i.e. adding and removing both attributes and classes simultaneously. Thus, we only need to decide the sequential of the problems to be handled. Simplifying the problem will make the process easier to settle.

First, the characteristics of both scale-wise problems need to be clarified. Removing attributes and classes requires the removal of inappropriate rules in the preliminary classifier. This action will not influence the combination of both original and new classifier. Nevertheless, adding attributes and classes results in some specific rules that should be retained from new classifier in the final modified classifier. The procedure of addition is more complicated than removal.

In a different view, adding or removing classes may only cause removing and creating corresponding rules. However, adding or removing attributes will alter the schema of a classifier. That is, the change of attributes will possibly impact on other rules, further affects the efficiency of the process. Thus, the attribute problem should be considered before class problem.

As a result, dealing with mixed problems of attribute and class variations, we should solve these scale-wise problems by the following order: (1) removing and adding attributes; and (2) removing and adding classes. The process of verifying a modified classifier requires both previous and incremental data.

After dealing with these problems, we then combine the preliminary and incremental classifier. Since the combined classifier still needs to be ranked to establish the priority of the classification rules, it requires some data to verify the classifier. Both previous and incremental sampled data are similar to the distribution of population, so we only have to choose enough data from them, which is the minimum sample size we calculate before in order to satisfy required condition of Chi-squared goodness-of-fit test, all expected frequency is no lesser than 5. Comparing the size of original and new sampled data, we sample them again by proportions to obtain the minimum sample size of data and use them to compute support rate and confidence. For the extracted rules with new attributes or classes, we use their support rate and confidence in the incremental classifier because previous data cannot verify them. Next, we can further prune the rules that do not reach the threshold. After all, the result is the final modified classifier.

COMPUTATIONAL ANALYSIS

The dataset used in following experiments to verify the validity and efficiency of the HBDSA is originally from KDD Cup 1999, which is a competition held by SIGKDD in conjunction with the annual conference every year. This dataset, retrieved from UCI Machine Learning Repository (KDD, 1999), contains 4,898,431 connection records originally, which can be used to detect intrusion. Furthermore, the dataset includes 43 attributes of both continuous and discrete data type. These attributes represent different parameters and features of connection records, depending on various classes of data. In this study, we use FID (Fayyad and Irani, 1993) to part the values of continuous attributes into intervals, mapping these intervals to sequential integer values.

In order to demonstrate the real condition in big data, we have to consider not only increasing the number of objects but also changing in attributes and classes. Thus, we further partition the original dataset into several groups with possibly different numbers of attributes and numbers of classes. We separate the dataset into six smaller datasets, one for initial stage and other four for incremental scenarios. Hence, we divide the data with high frequency class into 4 classes so that the class distribution will be closer to uniform. Let dataset 0 be the dataset for the initial phase, dataset 1 to 4 be the datasets for the incremental phase. Moreover, the class distribution in original dataset has one extremely high and one extremely low class. The original data set will be used as a representation of long tail class distribution. Let dataset 5 be the dataset for the initial phase, dataset 6 to 9 be the datasets for the incremental phase.

For the purpose of validating the feasibility of the DASA, we separate two different types of class distributions, uniform and long tail. In each distribution, we first compare the differences between the sampled data and the population in certain criteria, including accuracy and runtime. In addition, we will discuss the misclassification cost issue in long tail class distribution and comparing the result of original classifier after sampling. Afterward, we show the effect of changing number of attributes selected on the efficiency and effectiveness of the DASA.

We use dataset 0, consisting of 1,574,501 records, 43 attributes and 11 classes, in the experiments for data with a uniform class distribution. The experiments of data with long tail distribution use dataset 5, including 1,574,501 records, 43 attributes and 8 classes. We further divide data into a training set and a test set, with the proportion of their sizes as 10:1. The accuracy is calculated by the ratio of correctness in classifying objects in the test set. All the experiments set up thresholds in CBA, with minSupp = 0.01 and minConf = 0.5. The minSupp stands for that a rule should be happened at least 1% in all training data so that it can be considered as a frequent rule. The minConf means the probability of classifying an object right when it matches a corresponding association rule, thus there is at least 50% possibility to correctly classify the object if it fits one of the rules in the classifier. We set these thresholds relatively low in order to obtain more rules in classifier.

At the beginning, we would like to verify the validity and accessibility of the sampled data comparing with population. However, the population, either dataset 0 or dataset 5, is too large in both size and number of attributes so that the CBA is unable to generate the classifier and analysis result. Since proving that the sampling method does not distort the result of building classifier is necessary, we have to use another approach instead of using original population of dataset 0 and dataset 5. We further select 20 attributes and 157,451 records by random selection from dataset 0 and dataset 5 to be populations, which is barely applicable for the CBA. Moreover, we also select 10 attributes randomly in these records from dataset 0 and dataset 5 in order to show that no matter how the number of attribute changes in the population, the sampling method is still available and representative.

After defining the populations, we further apply the DASA to sample attributes and records from these populations. The sample size is calculated by the pilot test in each population using Good-Turing estimation method, thus the size to be sampled in each population is fixed. We have to use Kolmogorov-Smirnov test to test whether difference occurs in the class distribution between every pair of sample and population. Since the populations from the same dataset have the same number of records and are only different in attributes, we need to conduct one test for each data source. The critical value of the Kolmogorov-Smirnov test, D_n, and the test values of samples from dataset 0 and dataset 5 are then computed. Because the test values are lesser than D_n, there is not enough evidence to infer that there are differences between these samples and populations.

After verifying that the class distributions are similar in sampled data and populations, we further compare the result of CBA using sampled data and populations. The number of attributes to be selected increases to show the effect. From the results we can see that the accuracies of the classifiers generated by sampled data can be close to one by population although difference happens because of sampling biases. Moreover, the more attributes selected will possibly result in a higher accuracy but also a longer runtime. Furthermore, the processing time is significantly different between sampled data and population. Hence, we are convinced that using the DASA does not sacrifice too much accuracy but rather increases the efficiency significantly.

First, we compare populations from the same class distribution. From comparing results of the CBA in populations 0 with 1 and 2 with 3, we can see that increasing the number of attributes are not necessarily lead to higher accuracy since these attributes are randomly selected. Although populations 0 and 2 have 12 attributes which is more than 7 attributes in population 1 and 3, the accuracy in population 0 is lower than population 2 while the accuracy in population 1 is higher than population 3. However, increasing the number of attributes will definitely require a longer runtime. Runtimes in populations 0 and 2 needs hours to be done while populations 1 and 3 only need several minutes.

In every population, we further compare the effect of increasing the number of attributes selected from each class. We increase the numbers of attributes through 1 to 5 to see their influences on the classification results and runtimes. Like the results in population, increasing the number of attributes will result in more processing time. CBA processes all samples that selected an attribute from each class within 1 second. As the numbers of attributes grows, the runtimes also increase. In the meantime, the accuracy has potential to be higher while more attributes are selected. In populations 0 and 2, the accuracy grows when more attributes are selected. In addition, the number of attributes selected in population 1 and 3 will not make difference on the accuracy.

At last, we can observe that the runtimes are significantly decreased after applying the DASA when comparing samples and populations. The shortest runtime of population to apply the CBA is 8 minutes and 4 seconds, but all of its samples required only 1 second. Moreover, the accuracies of the classifier built by the sampled data can still be retained around the ones built by population. The largest difference in accuracy between the population and the sample is in population 3, which is 0.6352 in population and 0.5741 in all sampled data. Although greater difference occurs in population 2 and sampled data with 1 attribute selected from a class, it can be improved by selecting more attributes.

CONCLUSIONS

This study proposes the Heuristic Big-Data Sampling Algorithm (HBDSA) to deal with the performance problem of an association rule classification method under a big data environment. The algorithm we proposed focuses mainly on refining the input and integrating the output of association rule classification methods. HBDSA is divided into two phases: the initial stage and the incremental stage. At the initial stage, we use the data and attribute sampling algorithm (DASA) to sample proper amount of data objects that still maintain the characteristics of the population. Afterward, we compute the information gain for each attribute and rank the importance of attributes based on the information gain. Extracting certain number of attributes from each class on these sampled records, the dataset we apply our association rule classification method is relatively small comparing to the population. From the related experiments, we know that with a proper number of attributes, the result of association rule classification method can be very efficient without sacrificing much on accuracy. Thus, we can infer that the DASA is an effective way to deal with the volume problem under a big data environment both in object and attribute perspectives. In addition, increasing the number of selected attributes has the chance to increase the accuracy, but definitely require more processing time.

At the incremental phase, we proposed the Incremental Classifier Modifying Algorithm (ICMA) to handle the fact that data is increasing and changing. The inflow of data has different characteristics in attributes and classes. We use the characteristics based on the incremental data in order to predict the data that will arrive in the foreseen future. Combining the sampled data by the DASA from both original and incremental datasets and retaining the size of this dataset, it will be the dataset to verify the classification rules in the original and incremental classifiers. The improper rules, which contain removed classes or attributes in the incremental data, will be deleted while the ones with newly adding attributes and classes will be preserved in the final result of the modified classifier. The validity of applying the ICMA to generate a classifier is proved when comparing with using all sampled data by the DASA. Moreover, the ICMA solved the problem that data will be incremental in both perspectives of objects and attributes. Hence, the ICMA is a proper way to deal with the variety and velocity problems of an association rule classification method under a big data environment.

Nevertheless, there are many classification techniques to be used for classification. In this study, we use the classification based on the association rule (CBA) method. We choose to use the CBA not only because it is one of the simplest method of classification, the rules is relatively observable comparing to other methods. However, there are still other classification techniques that are popular and more common in the reality like decision tree, logistic regression or neural network, etc. We believe that the concept of dealing the problem with smaller scale and representativeness can be applied to any other techniques but requires only proper transformation for input and output data. Future researches should apply the concept in different classification methods under the big data environment.

At last, more and more frameworks are provided by the public because the big data problem is recently a hot issue among academia and industries. The most two well-known frameworks to apply on big data are MapReduce and Hadoop. These frameworks are still currently focus more on collecting data rather than analyzing them. Nonetheless, we are still looking forward to developing a more effective and efficient data analyzing method especially for big data in these frameworks.

ACKNOWLEDGEMENTS

This research was sponsored by the Ministry of Science and Technology in Taiwan, project number MOST 103-2410-H-002-099-MY3.

REFERENCES

Cano, J. R., Herrera, F. & Lozano, M. (2005). Stratification for scaling up evolutionary prototype selection. *Pattern Recognition Letters,* 26(7), 953-963.

Collett, S. (2011). Why Big Data Is a Big Deal? *Computerworld.*

Fayyad, U. M. & Irani, K. B. (1993). Multi-Interval Discretization of Continuous-Valued Attributes for Classification Learning. *International Joint Conferences on Artificial Intelligence*, 1022-1029.

Jackson, J. (2012). The Big Promise of Big Data. *CIO.*

Jacobs, A. (2009). The Pathologies of Big Data. *Communication of the ACM.*

KDD. (1999). Cup 1999 Data Set UCI Machine Learning Repository. Available: http://archive.ics.uci.edu/ml/datasets/KDD+Cup+1999+Data.

Lamont, J. (2012). Big data has big implications for knowledge management. *KMWorld.*

Liu, B., Hsu, W. & Ma, Y. (1998). Integrating Classification and Association Rule Mining. *Knowledge Discovery and Data Mining*, 80-86.

McAfee, A. & Brynjolfsson, E. (2012). Big Data: the Management Revolution. *Harvard Business Review*, 90(10), 60-66.

Moore, G. E. (1965). Cramming More Components onto Integrated Circuits. *Electronics*, 38(8), 114-117.

Olavsrud, T. (2012). How to Be Ready for Big Data. *CIO.*

Reid, C. (2012). Can Big Data Fix Book Marketing. *Publishers Weekly.*

Shannon, C. E. (1948). A Mathematical Theory of Communication. *The Bell System Technical Journal*, 27(3), 379-423.

Skinner, D. (2013). Big Data: It's not Just Big. *HPC Source*, ISC'13 Special Edition.

Stackpole, B. (2012). Five things IT should do to prepare for big data. *Computerworld US*.

Thabtah, F. A. (2007). A Review of Associative Classification Mining. *Knowledge Engineering Review*, 22(1), 37-65.

DECISION SCIENCES INSTITUTE

A Lean Hospital Supply Chain Perspective to Improving Patient Care Quality

Subhajit Chakraborty
Coastal Carolina University
Email: schakrabo@coastal.edu

ABSTRACT

We apply an integrated supply chain framework to the healthcare industry in the U.S., drawing support from lean systems theory. This integrated perspective can help U.S. hospitals identify and solve issues that lie outside their current boundaries. We offer a framework to streamline the three types of flows–physical product, information and financial–in the internal supply chain integrating units with technology, and maintain collaborative relations with suppliers in the external supply chain. Our propositions highlight how hospitals could deliver high quality care using an integrated supply chain perspective, coupled with internal lean practices. We discuss implications of our research.

KEYWORDS: Lean healthcare; technology integration, supplier relationship management, internal lean practices, patient care quality

INTRODUCTION

In spite of its high cost, the quality of care in the U.S. is not among the best in the world, as is evident from the discussions in the business press and healthcare journals (Davis et al., 2007; Docteur & Berenson, 2009; PGPF, 2016; Squires & Anderson, 2015; Starfield, 2000). U.S. healthcare is one of the most expensive in the world (third after Norway and Switzerland) as per health expenditure per capita data (WorldBank, 2015). The main issue is the relatively high cost of medical care in the U.S. (NationMaster, 2003; OECD, 2010). Moreover, this high cost does not always translate to quality care. While there have been many recent improvements (Boyer & Pronovost, 2010; Pronovost, Miller, & Wachter, 2006), recent reports of the Centers for Medicare and Medicaid Services (CMS) note that the degree of patient safety, an important measure of patient care quality, is still low (Boyer, Gardner, & Schweikhart, 2012). According to the Mayo clinic, improving the quality and efficiency of healthcare services available to patients and keeping their costs under control are the two most pressing needs of the U.S. healthcare industry (Toussaint & Berry, 2013).

Many problems faced by U.S. hospitals today arise beyond its own boundaries and lie with their medicine and equipment suppliers and other supporting organizations. For example, the cost of supplies now constitutes the second major component of high healthcare costs (at 31%, after 37% for the cost of facilities) (Schneller & Smeltzer, 2006). Further, hospitals and suppliers place too much emphasis on the price of the items obtained compared to their quality and the timeliness of their delivery. Hospitals are also held to the whims of the major buyer–the Group Purchasing Organization (GPO), which leverage the purchasing power of hospitals in obtaining discounts from vendors (Handfield, 2010). GPOs such as Amerinet, Consorta, Novation, Premier and MedAssets control about 72–80% of every healthcare dollar through their acquisition of supplies (Hu & Schwarz, 2011). Given the power and importance of suppliers, a few scholars in healthcare management (Coustasse, Tomblin, & Slack, 2013; Johnston & Rooney, 2012) and operations management (OM) (Cohen et al., 2008; Handfield,

2010) , as well as medical practitioners, claim that hospital supply chain management is crucial to improve U.S. healthcare (Schneller & Smeltzer, 2006).

Lean systems theory (Monden, 1981; Ōno, 1988; Sugimori, Kusunoki, Cho, & Uchikawa, 1977), an operations management (OM) theme, highlights continuous improvement in processes by focusing on essential value-adding activities and eliminating wasteful non-value added tasks. Supply chain integration and lean systems theory tenets have increased quality and productivity in many service industries such as technology consulting, software development, banking, and financial services.

Given its promise, a few scholars have already addressed a supply chain perspective in healthcare (see Brennan, 1998; McKone-Sweet, Hamilton, & Willis, 2005; Rivard-Royer, Landry, & Beaulieu, 2002; Stevens, 1989). However, the extant literature presents a limited perspective on the hospital supply chain. Although different specific aspects of hospital supply chains have been investigated, most research has followed a silo approach, and currently there is no available framework that depicts an integrated hospital supply chain. Research employing only modeling methodologies investigate specific characteristics of the external supply chain, such as the role of and problems related to GPOs (Hu & Schwarz, 2011; Hu, Schwarz, & Uhan, 2012), failing to address the internal supply chain. On the other hand, empirical research has investigated only supplier relationships from an internal hospital supply chain viewpoint, including hospital operating efficiency and supply chain performance (D. Q. Chen, Preston, & Xia, 2013b), institutional pressures on the supply chain (Bhakoo & Choi, 2013b) and hospital storage area rearrangement and related cost savings (Rivard-Royer et al., 2002). This limited perspective and absence of an integrated approach is problematic because there could be issues that originate from within the hospital or outside that have a bearing on patient care quality (PCQ). We suggest that integrating the two perspectives present a holistic supply chain approach that can help us adequately factor in all issues related to a hospital from a macro perspective which ultimately affect PCQ delivered to patients.

The lack of a clear hospital supply chain framework in healthcare literature compounds the dilemma that hospital administrators and medical experts face while deciding how to resolve several interconnected issues to provide better quality of patient care. There is no established supply chain framework in the literature that suggests methods to improve the quality of care received by patients in hospitals. The objective of this study is therefore to advocate using an inclusive approach towards improving the quality of patient care and contribute to research positioned at the cross section of operations and healthcare literature. Specifically, we investigate the following research questions: *Which internal and external hospital supply chain factors are related to patient care quality? How are these factors related to patient care quality?*

By including variables from both the external as well as the internal supply chain of a typical U.S. hospital and using lean principles as its basic underlying philosophy, this study attempts to offer a conceptual framework to improve patient care quality thereby filling the void in the literature. Full-service U.S. hospitals could use the framework to improve the quality of care available to their patients.

The framework has several useful implications for patients and medical practitioners as well. First, patients in hospitals could greatly benefit from an integration of the various entities of the healthcare supply chain because it could bring the focus of the healthcare system on the effectiveness and efficiency of all entities and their individual processes which would ultimately improve the quality of healthcare services that they receive in the hospital. Second, the framework highlights the importance of hospital leadership and lean operations and is aligned closely with the MBNQA award criteria for healthcare (NIST, 2013). The framework also directly addresses the most strategic issue raised by The American Medical Association (AMA, 2011)– quality of care. Medical practitioners involved in all hospital supply chain entities would gain from an integrated supply chain perspective because of the importance given to continuously improve quality at hospitals, steps taken to reduce hospital inventories and further, reduce and eliminate all wastes or non value-adding activities. The framework could thus show hospitals how to use their resources better. Better quality of patient care could be provided by hospitals if they allocate the resources to support their processes that reduce medical errors and focus on overall quality of care (Byrnes, 2004; Shih, Rivers, & Soya Hsu, 2009; Singh, Rice, & Riquier, 2006). Better quality of patient care is a win-win for all stakeholders because it could improve hospitals' financial performance, benefit all intermediaries and suppliers in the chain, as well as benefit patients through better, quicker care (Lee, Lee, & Schniederjans, 2011).

Our paper is structured as follows. We first review the extant OM and healthcare literature and offer our conceptual framework of specific variables that are drawn from both the internal as well as external supply chains of a typical U.S. hospital. Next, we offer four propositions that delineate our expectations of the relationships among the variables. Finally, we discuss the implications of our research.

LITERATURE REVIEW

Supply chain management (SCM) has been defined by the Council of Supply Chain Management Professionals (CSCMP) as the "*planning and management of all activities involved in sourcing, procurement, conversion, and logistics management. It also includes the crucial components of coordination and collaboration with channel partners which can be suppliers, intermediaries, third-party service providers, and customers*" (CSCMP, 2011). In the context of a hospital, the supply chain includes all departments that are within the control of the hospital administration and also entities in the external chain (Rivard-Royer et al., 2002).

Healthcare supply chain processes are known to have three types of flows—physical product flow, information flow and financial flow (Singh, Rice, & Riquier, 2006) and it is important that all these processes are managed effectively. Physical product flow refers to the use of products, and these often vary across hospitals depending on their specialization. For example, orthopedic hospitals tend to have greater need for specialized and custom bracing for neck, back, wrist, elbow, knee, and ankle conditions, cervical pillows, Transcutaneous Electrical Nerve Stimulation (TENS) units, and custom foot orthotics for the medical treatment of patients and their special needs. Information flows consist of electronic medicine inventory information from hospital to suppliers for automatic reordering. Information flows also occur within the internal supply chain among healthcare team members. By "healthcare team" we mean the group of doctors, nurses, social workers, physical therapists, dietitians and discharge planners who work together to care for patients in most hospitals to recognize the importance of information flow among them. All members of the team who come in close contact with the patient should have the most up-to-date and accurate information on the patient's medical condition. Several articles both in healthcare literature and the business press have routinely highlighted inappropriate information flows among these team members as a source of medical errors (see Allen, 2013; Jarousse, 2016; Vest & Gamm, 2010; Waldfogel, 2013). Financial flows refer to items such as pending supplier bills for payment and pending patient bills for collection (Kowalski, 2009; Singh et al., 2006).

Next, keeping in mind patients in a typical U.S. hospital, we focus on the aspects of its supply chain that we deem to have the greatest impact on PCQ. In the remainder of this section, we discuss how an integration of all technological systems in the internal hospital supply chain, as well as how supplier relationships could be effectively managed to achieve a comprehensive lean orientation. We then describe how a comprehensive lean orientation would help hospitals deliver higher PCQ. We advance four propositions to specify our expected relationships among the variables—*technology integration, supplier relationship management, internal lean practices and patient care quality.*

Technology Integration

We define *technology integration* as the interconnectedness of the different technological systems (both software and hardware) implemented in hospitals that enables frequent and up-to-date information exchange such as hospital patient medical information, inventory data about medicine/other supplies and personnel information in electronic form between different entities within the hospital, the healthcare team and hospital management (e.g., Leidner, Preston, & Chen, 2010; Li & Lin, 2006). The tight integration present in software systems that some hospitals use reduce operational uncertainty by providing coordination, visibility, and easy information sharing across transactions (Hendricks, Singhal, & Stratman, 2007; Leidner et al., 2010). Easy access to integrated data about the latest in-house hospital stock levels may make it easier for hospital administrators to transact business with other entities, both within and outside the hospital (Huber & McDaniel, 1986; Saeed, Malhotra, & Grover, 2005). The major studies on technology integration in healthcare supply chain are presented in Table 1.

Table 1. Major Studies on Technology Integration across Healthcare Supply Chains

Study	Purpose	Research Type	Main Findings
Young and Barrett (1997)	Cross-functional-process (CFP) framework for implementing an integrated delivery system (IDS) in healthcare	Conceptual	There are ten CFPs that could be put into three categories: planning processes (strategy formulation, program adaptation, budget formulation), organizational processes (authority and influence, client management, conflict resolution, motivation, and cultural maintenance), and measurement and reporting processes (financial and programmatic). The authors suggested that senior management considers how to improve both the functioning of each CFP and the overall fit of all of them.
Devaraj and Kohli (2000)	Effect of technology and business process reengineering (BPR) on performance	Empirical	Findings support the IT-performance relationship. The authors found a positive impact of technology on performance, though the degree of impact depends on the BPR practiced by hospitals.
Sirio et al. (2003)	Pittsburgh Regional Healthcare Initiative (PRHI)'s design for change using a shared learning model	Conceptual	By linking patient outcomes data with processes of care and sharing this information widely, PRHI supported measurable improvements in region wide clinical practice and patient safety.
Ilie, Van Slyke, Parikh and Courtney (2009)	Effect of IT accessibility on adoption of electronic medical records (EMR)	Empirical	Physical accessibility is defined as the availability of computers that can be used to access EMR and logical accessibility is defined as the ease or difficulty of logging into the system. The authors found that when deciding between the paper chart and EMR, accessibility is an important consideration in a physician's decision. They concluded that accessibility limits the acceptance of IT.

Study	Purpose	Research Type	Main Findings
Korst, Aydin, Signer and Fink (2011)	Hospital readiness for health information exchange	Empirical	A tool was developed to measure hospitals' readiness for data-sharing. They found that hospital leadership is important in collaborative efforts that aim to share data for quality implementation or safety purposes.
Queenan, Angst and Devaraj (2011)	Relationship between extent of computerized physician order entry (CPOE) use and patient satisfaction	Empirical	Contrary to extant research, the authors' positive findings suggest that the relationship between the CPOE use and patient satisfaction is stronger in non-academic hospitals. They also found evidence that a hospital's IT infrastructure substitutes for CPOE use in its effect on patient satisfaction.

An examination of the research presented in Table 1 shows that scholars offering conceptual models have focused mostly on healthcare in clinical settings. The cross-functional process framework (Young & Barrett, 1997) offers an integrated delivery system model but some of the organizational processes such as client management and cultural maintenance may not apply to U.S. hospital settings. Similarly, the Pittsburg Regional healthcare initiative (Sirio et al., 2003) offers a shared learning model but some of its care processes could be local to the state of Pennsylvania. The empirical studies on the other hand, discuss several specific issues related to technology adoption and integration in hospitals, such as effect of business process reengineering (BPR) on performance (Devaraj & Kohli, 2000), technology accessibility and hospital readiness its effect on electronic medical records (EMR) (Korst, Aydin, Signer, & Fink, 2011) and the extent of using computerized physician order entry (CPOE) and its effect of patient satisfaction (Queenan, Angst, & Devaraj, 2011). Overall, many of the articles have chosen to investigate very specific and detailed issues but have ignored the systemic problems caused by lack of integrating all technology systems in the hospital.

There are several benefits of using modern technology in an integrated manner in hospitals. Technology can be used for keeping electronic patient medical records and giving e-prescriptions and other laboratory orders for patient tests directly to pharmacies or laboratories, which would ensure that medical errors due to intervention of the patient/kin are reduced (Ilie, Van Slyke, Parikh, & Courtney, 2009). Hospital information systems could provide alerts to the doctors and nurses monitoring the patient whenever any drug related complications occur (Ilie et al., 2009). Patient information systems could provide service statistics on patient occupancy rates and diagnostic tests performed in hospitals laboratories. Further, technology can support sharing the medication and other inventory information with external entities such as suppliers. Important medicinal stocks from the hospital could be automatically ordered in electronic form so as to be accurate and timely (Beier, 1995).

Accurate and useful patient information needs to flow to the healthcare team whenever needed. Similarly, hospital management needs to have access to summarized patient, hospital support systems like labs and pharmacies, accounting and financial and all other types of information when they need it to be able to make the best decisions. Therefore, it is crucial that all different software and hardware systems implemented in various departments in the hospital are able to "talk" to each other and exchange information on frequent basis (Angst, Devaraj, Queenan, & Greenwood, 2011; Devaraj & Kohli, 2000; Korst et al., 2011; Leidner et al., 2010; Queenan et al., 2011; Shin-Yuan, Chen, & Wan-Ju, 2009; Sirio et al., 2003; Teplensky, Pauly, Kimberly, Hillman, & Schwartz, 1995; Young & Barrett, 1997). In other words, the advantages of technology are realized only if all the different information technology (IT) systems in the hospital are well integrated with each other (Albani & Lee, 2007).

Supplier Relationship Management

We define *supplier relationship management* as an approach that uses social ties and interpersonal contact between a firm and its suppliers to monitor, control and encourage desirable supplier behavior (e.g., Das et al., 2006; Noordewier et al., 1990; Rivard-Royer, Landry, & Beaulieu, 2002). Using the same technology such as applications software packages and relational capital development efforts such as cross-functional involvement and joint problem solving could help both firms and their suppliers communicate inventory demand and supply position quickly (Das, Narasimhan, & Talluri, 2006; Talluri & Sarkis, 2002).

In buyer-supplier relationship literature there are two major types of classifications. The first considers the relationship as a continuous process (e.g., transformation from awareness, exploration, expansion, and commitment to dissolution) (Dwyer, Schurr, & Oh, 1987). The second classification is based on the relationships at a point in time such as relationship governance that can range from a transaction-based relationship to a strategic alliance (Cooper & Gardner, 1993; Webster, 1992), or be in the continuum between competitive and cooperative orientation (Ellram & Hendrick, 1995). A detailed review of the extant literature yielded Table 2.

Table 2. Supplier Relationship Management Characteristics Identified in Literature

Study	Noordewier et al. (1990)	Han, Wilson and Dant (1993)	Larson (1994)	Carr and Pearson (1999)	Kim (2000)	Prahinski and Benton (2004)	Ferguson, Paulin and Bergeron (2005)
Variable studied	Supplier relational governance	Buyer-supplier relationship	Supplier product quality	Buyer- supplier relationship	Dyadic relationship continuity	Buyer-supplier relationship	Relational governance
Attributes identified	Supplier flexibility	Mutual trust	Degree to which product supplies meet specifications	Special agreements with few key suppliers	Continuity expectation	Buying firm's commitment	Disagreement resolution
	Supplier assistance	Satisfactory exchange	Degree to which product supplies perform as intended	Loyalty to key suppliers		Cooperation	Mutual benefit and trust
	Supplier information exchange		Lifespan of product supplies	Frequent face to face communication		Supplier's commitment	Negotiated agreements
	Supplier monitoring		Degree to which product supplies arrive as scheduled	Direct links with key suppliers			Timely and accurate information exchange
	Continuity expectation		Degree to which product supplies are protected by packaging				Reliance in times of adversity

Table 2 Continued

Study	Wang and Wei (2007)	Tangpong, Michalisin and Melcher(2008)	Liu, Luo and Liu (2009)	Ambrose, Marshall and Lynch (2010)	Nyaga, Whipple and Lynch (2010)	Tangpong, Hung and Ro (2010)	Lumineau and Henderson (2012)
Variable studied	Relational governance	Buyer-supplier relationship	Buyer-supplier relationship governance	Buyer-supplier relationship	Buyer-supplier relationship	Buyer-supplier relationship	Supply chain governance
Attributes identified	Trust	Relational mechanisms	Relational mechanisms (relational norms and trust)	Suppliers' ability of supplier to meet accuracy expectations	Collaboration	No opportunistic behavior	Relational governance
	Commitment	Power dependence	Transactional mechanisms (jointly stipulated contractual clauses)	Suppliers' ability to meet on-time delivery standards			Contractual governance
	Coordination			Suppliers' ability to meet productivity standards			
	Joint problem solving			Ability of firm to provide timely order status to supplier			

Based on a critical review of the research summaries in Table 2, it may be noted that only a few have chosen to study different aspects of governance of the supplier relationship from a buyer's perspective, while many have focused on the buyer-relationship in general. Further, a study investigated the continuity of supplier relationships using a dyadic lens while another chose to focus on quality of supplies. A detailed review of the characteristics of each variable studied suggests that supplier relationship management is a broad construct that comprises the following six characteristics (Chung, 2012; Lumineau & Henderson, 2012; Noordewier et al., 1990): *supplier flexibility, supplier assistance, supplier information exchange, supplier monitoring, continuity expectation,* and *quality of supplies*. Unforeseen requests for adjustments in price, stock levels and emergency deliveries are opportunities for a supplier to be *flexible* to quickly change its production/delivery schedules to meet the firm's requests (Chan, Bhagwat, & Wadhwa, 2008; Noordewier et al., 1990). The extent to which suppliers are willing to help firms by going beyond the contractually bound level of conduct is defined as *supplier assistance* (Dyer, Cho, & Chu, 1998; Janda, Murray, & Burton, 2002; Noordewier et al., 1990). *Supplier information exchange* refers to the frequency and type of information provided by suppliers to the firms (Noordewier et al., 1990; Trapero, Kourentzes, & Fildes, 2012). Key information such as suppliers' long-term forecasting and future component design information could help the firms plan their own product roll-out better. The supervisory actions that firms need to take to ensure supplier performance is referred to as *supplier monitoring* (Gavronski, Klassen, Vachon, & Nascimento, 2011; Noordewier et al., 1990). *Continuity expectation* describes long term expectations of a lasting relationship between firms and their suppliers (Noordewier et al., 1990; Villena, Revilla, & Choi, 2013). *Quality of supplies* delivered by the supplier to the firm (Gunasekaran, Patel, & McGaughey, 2004; Han, Wilson, & Dant, 1993; Larson, 1994) is also important for a long term relationship because poor quality products/services could lead to rework for the supplier and loss of reputation and image. Next, the major studies on supplier relationship management in extant healthcare literature are presented in Table 3.

Table 3. Major Studies on Supplier Relationships in Healthcare

Study	Purpose	Research Type	Main Findings
Rivard-Royer et al. (2002)	Rearrangement of storage areas for supplies can generate savings for hospitals	Empirical	There are benefits for both the hospital and the supplier under a stockless replenishment method. In this method, the distributor packs and delivers hospital supplies according to needs of each hospital unit. The study also revealed that the packing format of supplies is important for distributor.
Langabeer (2005)	Current state of healthcare supply chain management technologies	Conceptual	The author opined that hospital supply chain orientation, from suppliers through the delivery of patient care is a relatively new concept in hospitals. He also suggested that in the future, predictive modeling, data mining and business intelligence will be used in healthcare like in other service industries.
Fredendall, Craig, Fowler and Damali (2009)	Internal service supply chain of the surgical services department of a non-academic community hospital	Empirical	Using the theory of swift and even flow (TSEF) for their analysis the authors' findings suggested the need to incorporate supply chain coordination into the theory.
Sinha and Kohnke (2009)	3A-framework founded on affordability, access, and awareness	Conceptual	The authors present a framework, which is applicable for implantable device-based care for cardiovascular diseases in developing countries. Their framework identifies integrated continuous improvement and innovation initiatives to bridge the gap between the demand and supply for high-quality, cost-effective and timely care.
Hu and Schwarz (2011)	Controversial role of GPOs in healthcare supply chain	Modeling	GPOs reduce manufacturers' incentives to innovate. They also examined the consequences of removing the contract administration fees (CAF) that GPOs charge manufacturers and concluded that it would not influence any stakeholder profits or costs.

Table 3 Continued

Study	Purpose	Research Type	Main Findings
Hu, Schwarz and Uhan (2012)	Impact of GPOs on healthcare product supply chains	Modeling	Although CAFs influence the distribution of profits between manufacturers and GPOs, they do not affect the providers' total purchasing costs.
Bhakoo and Choi (2013a)	How institutional pressures and heterogeneity affect different elements of the healthcare supply chain	Empirical	The authors examine how organizations in different tiers of a healthcare supply chain respond to institutional pressures when implementing inter-organizational systems for coordination. The study shows how different institutional pressures such as coercive, mimetic, and normative act across the tiers. It also demonstrates how a mix of endogenous and institutional pressures leads to organizational responses.
Chen, Preston and Xia (2013a)	Improving hospital operating efficiency to reduce costs	Empirical	The following factors affect hospital supply chain performance: trust, knowledge exchange, IT integration between the hospital and its suppliers, and hospital-supplier integration. Their results show that trust and IT integration affect knowledge exchange, knowledge exchange and IT integration affect the hospital-supplier integration, and hospital-supplier integration affects hospital supply chain performance.

The research summaries in Table 3 suggest that the studies employing modeling methodologies have chosen to investigate specific characteristics of the external hospital supply chain-the role of and problems related to GPOs (Hu & Schwarz, 2011; Hu et al., 2012). Empirical papers, on the other hand, have chosen to investigate different aspects of supplier relationships from an internal hospital supply chain viewpoint-factors that determine hospital operating efficiency and supply chain performance (D. Q. Chen et al., 2013b), effect of institutional pressures on the supply chain (Bhakoo & Choi, 2013b) and hospital storage area rearrangement and related cost savings (Rivard-Royer et al., 2002). The current study is different from the major existing studies discussed above because it uses a more comprehensive construct that comprises the following six aspects–supplier assistance, supplier flexibility, supplier information exchange, supplier monitoring, continuity expectation and quality of supplies. These six characteristics are conceptually inter-related with each other and depict an aspect of supplier behavior and the focal firm's response.

In healthcare, the degree that the supplier is able to adapt to meet hospitals' needs and changes in quantities of supplies ordered represents the *supplier flexibility*. Suppliers need to respond quickly to all hospital requests. Further, suppliers should be able to make changes in quantity delivered and schedule well on time as required by the hospitals. Suppliers must be able to adjust their inventories to meet unforeseen needs that hospitals may have; they should be able to provide emergency deliveries to the hospitals (D. Q. Chen, Preston, & Xia, 2013a; Goodman & Jones, 2013; Noordewier et al., 1990). *Supplier assistance* refers to the help that the supplier is willing to provide hospitals in all matters related to the quality and quantity of their delivered goods or supplies. Hospitals may want to involve their key suppliers in the redesign of existing products such as replacing existing equipment with better and more efficient ones and using more effective medication but suppliers would need to cooperate. Further, suppliers have to be willing to provide their detailed financial information to hospitals for their item-wise cost-value analysis (Goodman & Jones, 2013; Noordewier et al., 1990). *Supplier information exchange* refers to the dyadic exchange of daily information that takes place between the supplier and the hospital is the third dimension. Hospitals need to provide suppliers with long-range forecasts of their requirements. They need to inform suppliers in advance of impending changes in products used along with the specifications and provide specific and detailed information about the quantity of supplies that they will need in the future so that the suppliers can plan their production schedules (Goodman & Jones, 2013; Langabeer, 2005; Noordewier et al., 1990). *Supplier monitoring* refers to the degree of overseeing and supervision that is required by the hospital to ensure that the supplier is responsive and is able and willing to supply the required quality and quantity of supplies. Hospitals should assess suppliers' performance through a formal vendor evaluation program and have procedures to inspect materials from suppliers. Further, hospitals should conduct quality training for supplier personnel and advise each supplier of their performance (Goodman & Jones, 2013; Noordewier et al., 1990). *Continuity expectation* refers to both parties' long term inclination to maintain ties. Hospitals should have a mutually beneficial professional relationship with their suppliers and expect suppliers to proactively resolve issues, expecting suppliers to improve their relationship with them over time. Hospitals need to have long term supplier relationships because of the advantages of trust with long term suppliers and the high costs associated with selecting new suppliers (Goodman & Jones, 2013; Noordewier et al., 1990). The *quality of supplies* refers to whether the products and services provided by the suppliers to hospitals meet the prescribed medical standards (Gunasekaran et al., 2004; Han et al., 1993; Larson, 1994; SherwoodValve, 2011). For suppliers, a way to ensure that they are able to deliver high quality supplies is by implementing quality management in their goods production/service generation units. Supplier quality management refers to a firm's quality practices such as relying on suppliers' process control as an indication of its high quality standards and ensuring that each time only high quality products are purchased (Kaynak & Hartley, 2008). Supplier quality certification may be used by suppliers to add value to hospitals. Certified suppliers could help hospitals assure everyone about the high quality of medical supplies used. Further, in order to ensure defect free quality in all of its product supplies, suppliers need to have a manual describing their quality system that must be followed by all its employees. Suppliers need to calibrate their equipment against the product and equipment standards set by the National Institute for Standards and Technology (Goodman & Jones, 2013; SherwoodValve, 2011).

Due to the nature of many healthcare service delivery process in which suppliers may contribute directly to service delivery (e.g., outsourced ambulatory services) failures in supplier services can create life-threatening risks for patients (Baltacioglu, Ada, Kaplan, Yurt, & Kaplan, 2007). Therefore, to effectively manage their supplier relationships, hospitals need to pay attention to all the above six aspects of the relationship discussed above.

Internal Lean Practices

Lean/JIT (Monden, 1981; Ōno, 1988; Sugimori et al., 1977) is a strategy that strives to improve firms' operating performance (Azadegan, Patel, Zangoueinezhad, & Linderman, 2013) by reducing the in-process inventory and associated carrying costs. In services, lean practices can be applied to improve the quality system being followed by a firm, clarify all process flows, revise process technologies to ensure that the latest techniques are being implemented correctly, level facility load, eliminate unnecessary activities, reorganize physical configuration, introduce demand-pull scheduling and develop supplier networks (Chase, Jacobs, & Aquilano, 2006). These activities help a firm streamline its operations by ensuring supplier cooperation, reduced waste in terms of safety stocks and smooth process flow.

We define *internal lean practices* as aligned hospitals operations required to achieve the outcome of performing effective medical procedures on patients in a timely manner at a reasonable cost (e.g., Alexander, Halpern, & Lee, 1996; Butler & Leong, 2000; Cook & Rasmussen, 2005; Goldstein, Ward, Leong, & Butler, 2002; Harper, 2002; Hay, 2003; Li, Rao, Ragu-Nathan, & Ragu-Nathan, 2005; Shah & Ward, 2003). An extensive review of lean literature is presented in Table 4.

Table 4. Characteristics of Lean Operations Identified in Literature

Study	Mehra and Inman (1992)	Sakakibara et al. (1993)	Flynn et al. (1995)	Lawrence and Hottenstein (1995)	Spencer and Guide (1995)	Dean and Snell (1996)
Attributes[a]	Setup time reduction	Setup time reduction	*Kanban*	JIT deliveries from suppliers	Set-up reductions	Change in the number of suppliers in the past five years
	In-house lot sizes	Small lot sizes	Lot size reduction	Inventory reduction	Lot size reductions	Change in the size of their deliveries in the past five years
	Group technology	JIT deliveries from suppliers	Daily schedule adherence	Manufacturing strategy	Preventive maintenance	Change in the length of product runs in the past five years
	Cross-training	Supplier quality level	Setup time reduction	Employee involvement	Physical layout management	Change in the number of total parts in the past five years
	Preventative maintenance	Small-group problem solving		Employee responsibility	Plant-wide program adoption of JIT methods	Change in the amount of buffer stock in the past five years
		Training		Supplier involvement	In-house quality	
		Daily schedule adherence		Process modification		
		Preventive maintenance				
		Equipment layout				
		Product design simplicity				
		Kanban				
		Pull system support				

Table 4 Continued

Study	Forza (1996)	Jayaram and Vickery (1998)	Claycomb, Droge and Germain (1999)	Sim and Curtola (1999)	Callen, Fader and Krinsky (2000)	Fullerton and McWatters (2001)	McKone et al. (2001)
Attributes	JIT deliveries from suppliers	Reduced setup times	JIT with customers	Pull system	Inventory performance	Focused factory	JIT delivery by suppliers
	JIT link with customers	Small lot sizes		Setup time reduction	Integrated product design	Group technology	Just-in-time link with customers
		Pull system		Preventative maintenance	Integrated supplier network	Reduced setup times	Pull system support
				Repetitive nature of master schedule	Preventive maintenance programs	Productive maintenance	Repetitive nature of master schedule
					Education about JIT	Multifunction employees	Setup time reduction
					Stable cycle rates	Uniform workload	
					Market paced final assembly		
					Group technology		
					Quality improvement programs for products and processes		
					Flexibility of workers' skills		

Table 4 Continued

Study	Brox and Fader (2002)	He and Hayya (2002)	Das and Jayaram (2003)	Shah and Ward (2003)	Ketokivi and Schroeder (2004)	Nahm, Vonderembse and Koufteros (2004)
Attributes	Minimum inventory in supply chain	Setup time reduction	Setup time reduction	Reduced lot sizes	JIT deliveries from suppliers	Reengineering setups
	Production and materials control pull	Training	Kanban	Continuous flow production	Setup time reduction	Cellular manufacturing
	Employee participation/ involvement	Daily schedule adherence	Group technology	Pull system	Pull system support	Quality improvement efforts
	Reduction of wastes	Preventative maintenance	Preventative maintenance	Cellular manufacturing	Manufacturing cost performance	Preventative maintenance
			JIT supply	Reduced cycle time		Pull production
				Focused production		
				Agile manufacturing		
				Quick changeover		
				Bottlenecks removed		
				Reengineered processes		

Table 4 Continued

Study	Challis, Samson and Lawson (2005)	Li et al. (2005)	Swink, Narasimhan and Kim (2005)	Cagliano Caniato and Spina (2006)	Narasimhan, Swink and Kim (2006)	Ward and Zhou (2006)
Attributes	Preventative maintenance	Reduced set-up times	Pull system in production	TQM, six sigma quality programs	Cellular manufacturing	Lead time performance JIT has a significant and positive relationship
	Setup time reduction	Small lot sizes	Produce in small lot sizes	Pull production	Pull system	Cycle time reduction with lead time performance
	Close relationship with suppliers	Pull-production	JIT flow production methods	Cellular layout	Small lot sizes	Agile manufacturing strategies
	Production cycle time		Production flow utilizes manufacturing cells		JIT link with customers	Quick changeover techniques
	On-time delivery				JIT deliveries from suppliers	Focused factory production systems
					Daily shipments from suppliers	JIT/Continuous flow production
					Product flexibility	Cellular manufacturing
						Lot size reduction
						Pull system/Kanban
						Bottleneck removal

Table 4 Continued

Study	Avittathur and Swamidass (2007)	Matsui (2007)	Dal Pont, Furlan and Vinelli (2008)	Browning and Heath (2009)	Demeter and Matyusz (2011)	Olhager and Prajogo (2012)	Azadegan et al. (2013)
Attributes	JIT deliveries from supplier	Daily schedule adherence	Daily schedule adherence	Visual replenishment systems	JIT		Product/ process improvement efforts
		Equipment layout	Equipment layout	Non-value-adding task elimination	TQM	Processes and machines close by	Daily planned equipment maintenance
		JIT delivery by suppliers	JIT deliveries from suppliers	Balanced distribution of work	Total productive maintenance	Lower set-up times	Process variance reduction
		JIT link with customers	JIT link with customers	New technologies and tools for fabrication	HRM	Use *kanban* pull system	Low equipment set up times
		Kanban	Kanban	Standard work methods			Pull production system
		MRP adaptation to JIT	Setup time reduction	Flow shop layout			Customer feedback on quality and delivery performance
		Repetitive master schedule	Small lot sizes	Concurrent engineering			Supplier feedback on quality and delivery performance
		Setup time reduction		Design for manufacturing and assembly			Grouped equipment to produce continuous flow
		Small lot size		6S (sort, straighten, shine, standardize, safety, sustain)			Process variance reduction
		Product capability		Discontinuous improvements			
	Avittathur and Swamidass (2007)	Matsui (2007)	Dal Pont, Furlan and Vinelli (2008)	Ergonomic work stations			
	JIT deliveries from supplier	Daily schedule adherence	Daily schedule adherence	Dissemination of lean through supplier network			
		Equipment layout	Equipment layout	Work sequencing			

Notes. [a] Based on Azadegan et al. (2013) and Mackelprang and Nair (2010)

An in-depth review of 32 studies presented in Table 4 reveals that lean/JIT is being investigated in operations and strategy literature for more than two decades now. A total of 89 characteristics of lean systems have been identified, which may be broadly grouped into the following three categories–*material flow management, continuous quality improvement* and *waste management* (Azadegan et al., 2013; S. Li, Rao, Ragu-Nathan, & Ragu-Nathan, 2005; Mackelprang & Nair, 2010; Shah & Ward, 2003). *Material flow management* refers to the continuous flow of production work in process without hindrance through the production factory or service generation unit (Benton et al., 2010; Chongwatpol & Sharda, 2013; Petersen & Wohlin, 2011). *Continuous quality improvement* refers to incremental improvement in quality standards of a firm on a regular periodic basis and is one of the key pillars of lean implementation (Aravindan & Devadasan, 1995; McFadden, Jung Young, Gowen Iii, & Sharp, 2014; Moran, 1992). Wastes refer to processes that add no value to the product/service or customer. *Waste management* refers to identifying, controlling and eliminating waste (Womack & Jones, 2010). Waste can occur in areas such as transportation, inventory, motion, waiting, overproduction, over processing and defects (Waring & Bishop, 2010). Next, the major studies on lean hospital operations are identified in Table 5.

Table 5. Major Studies on Lean Healthcare Operations

Study	Purpose	Research Type	Main Findings
Pocha (2010)	The implementation challenges of lean six sigma in healthcare	Conceptual	The author highlights the important lessons that were learned from lean six sigma implementation at a tertiary care medical center. These included guidelines to follow a team approach, have the "buy in" of all the stakeholders and to have the willingness of team members to change daily practice in order to adapt new and innovative ways of delivering better quality healthcare.
Graban (2011)	Improving quality, patient safety and employee satisfaction in hospitals using lean principles	Empirical	In this book, beginning with a historical perspective of lean, the author builds a case of why hospitals need a lean outlook and how lean implementation can help hospitals achieve their goals. Among the many directly measurable advantages, reduced turnaround time for clinical laboratory results, reduced instrument decontamination time, reduced patient deaths, reduced patient waiting times, increased surgical revenue and reduced patient length of stay, are some of the common ones that some of the U.S. hospitals have experienced after becoming lean.
LaGanga (2011)	Lean service operations	Empirical	Using action research methodology this outpatient clinical field research examines appointment data. The author analyzes a lean process improvement project that was conducted to increase capacity to admit new patients. The author's findings bring several insights about effective alignment of clinical resources, how clinics develop new strategies for responding to no-shows and highlights time-related variables that have been overlooked in appointment scheduling research.
Mazur, McCreery and Rothenberg (2012)	Facilitating learning during early stage of lean implementation in hospitals	Empirical	According to the author, some healthcare organizations have successfully used lean to help solve their quality and cost related problems. Most organizations accept that the challenge to sustain the lean philosophy is in continuing to learn the behaviors that are associated with lean improvement efforts. This article examines the lean implementation process in three rural hospitals, using involved healthcare professionals as lean participants and gives recommendations for facilitating lean thinking.
Toussaint and Berry (2013)	Path to becoming lean in healthcare	Empirical	The authors suggest six principles that hospitals would need to consider in their quest to become lean: an attitude of continuous improvement, value creation, unity of purpose, respect for front-line workers, visual tracking, and flexible rules. The authors provide case studies in support of these principles. Their paper aims to provide a template for healthcare leaders to use in lean implementation.

An examination of the research summaries in Table 5 highlights some of the challenges of lean implementation in healthcare such as having all stakeholder approval and having the willingness of team members to change daily practices in order to adapt new and innovative ways (Pocha, 2010). Research has also focused on identifying steps that hospitals take to facilitate learning during their early stage of lean implementation such as using involved healthcare professionals as lean participants (Mazur, McCreery, & Rothenberg, 2012). Based on his lean consulting experience, Graban (2011) has suggested some best practices for hospitals to follow in order to improve quality, patient safety and employee satisfaction while implementing lean practices. Research has also identified some of the paths that healthcare providers may need to follow to become lean such as inculcating an attitude of continuous improvement, value creation, unity of purpose, respect for front-line workers, visual tracking and flexible rules throughout the hospital/healthcare organization (Toussaint & Berry, 2013). The studies presented in Table 5 also reveal that while lean has been related to patient care quality, only case studies and action research methods have been used and no statistical test has been demonstrated yet in the U.S. hospitals. Most healthcare studies have concentrated on two characteristics–*continuous quality improvement* and *waste management*–ignoring *patient and material flow* in hospitals.

To determine the range of lean practices to implement, hospitals should consider the concept of service packages. In the healthcare context, the hospital check-up rooms are the supporting facilities. The medical equipment like a physician's stethoscope and sphygmomanometer, a surgeon's knife and other medical technology-related items like robots are the facilitating goods. Treating the illness that the patient is suffering from by giving appropriate medicines and/or performing the required medical procedure constitute the explicit services. Implicit services comprise procedures such as checking the patient for related and even unrelated complications like allergies that the patient may already have, and/or those that may arise from the medicines/procedures, counseling and trauma therapy/services in cases of life-threatening illnesses like cancer, or in procedures like amputation of limbs. All four components of healthcare service package are taken into consideration in the subsequent discussion on how hospitals can streamline their internal operations.

Patient and material flow management imply that the hospital follows efficient patient admission and discharge procedures. It also implies that appropriate hospital facilities like ICU are available to patients when required so that their procedures are not delayed and housekeeping ensures that equipment such as drip stands are available when required (Alexander et al., 1996; Butler & Leong, 2000; Cook & Rasmussen, 2005; Devaraj, Ow, & Kohli, 2013; Goldstein et al., 2002; Harper, 2002; Hay, 2003). Hospitals could employ scheduling software that factor in the patients' medical conditions and needs along with the hospital room and equipment availability information together so that both patient and material flow within the hospital could be streamlined. *Continuous quality improvement* considers whether healthcare teams internalize the lessons learnt from past mistakes on patient safety so as not to repeat them. Hospitals could use operational data from electronic clinical information systems to plan its staffing of doctors, nurses and other employees and up-to-date advanced medical equipment and technologies while performing all medical procedures. Healthcare teams in hospitals must strive to perform the correct medical procedures the very first time that they treat a patient (Albani & Lee, 2007; Axon & Williams, 2011; Butler & Leong, 2000; Goldstein et al., 2002). Hospitals need to keep abreast of the latest technological breakthroughs in the field (Hay, 2003). Upgraded physical infrastructure of labs, operation theatres and intensive care units (ICU) and other more basic elements like hospital beds are also necessary (Butler & Leong, 2000; Goldstein et al., 2002). Hospitals need to inculcate the best equipment and medical technology and share the best practices among their employees which is consistent with one of Deming's (1993) 14 point recommendations–to encourage cooperation among all employees to improve quality and productivity. Continuous quality improvement is thus a key element of lean implementation in hospitals. *Waste management* refers to whether hospitals use a "pull" production system wherein all supplies are inventoried as and when required, and whether hospitals push suppliers to achieve shorter lead-times. It incorporates whether hospitals streamline their own ordering, receiving and other paperwork from suppliers, and whether healthcare teams optimally uses all medical consumables to eliminate wastes (Hirano, 1995; Labarere, Francois, Auquier, Robert, & Fourny, 2001; Wakefield, Uden-Holman, & Wakefield, 2005; Wearmouth, 2001). Physical environment is an important attribute of lean operations. It includes the features of surroundings in which healthcare is delivered (i.e., whether the facilities and equipment used are orderly, the degree of pleasantness of hospital room atmosphere, the clarity of signs and directions to different facilities within hospitals). Effective housekeeping is an essential method of maintaining cleanliness and removing/minimizing wastes in hospital departments and helps streamline the entry and discharge procedures in a hospital (Labarere et al., 2001; Wakefield et al., 2005; Wearmouth, 2001). A clean and organized workplace is a key component of the 5-S philosophy, an overall approach to lean systems (Hirano, 1995).

Patient Care Quality

In extant literature, many studies have focused on identifying the determinants of PCQ, but all have focused on the characteristics of either the disease or ailment, or the type of medical procedure. One of the popular definitions in the extant healthcare operations literature is the classification of all healthcare practices into two—*clinical* and *experiential quality* (Chandrasekaran, Senot, & Boyer, 2012; Nair, Nicolae, & Narasimhan, 2013), which is too simplistic. *Clinical quality* reports how well physicians/nurses in both hospitals or in their private clinics conform to standardized procedures to diagnose/medically treat patients' health problems (Cf. Nair et al, 2013; Marley, Collier, & Meyer Goldstein, 2004; Theokary & Ren, 2011; and Chandrasekaran et al., 2012). Clinical quality, in general, reflects the conformance and adherence of the physicians/nurses to standardized best practices that have been shown to result in positive patient outcomes (Cf. Nair et al, 2013; Garvin, 1987, Jha, Li, Orav & Epstein, 2005, Tucker et al., 2007, Boyer et al., 2012; Chandrasekaran et al., 2012). *Experiential quality*, on the other hand, refers to external quality capabilities that emphasize quality of the service experienced by the patient and the consequent customer satisfaction (Cf. Nair et al, 2013; Flynn et al., 1997; and Sousa, 2003).

Without delving into the detailed technical realms of each ailment and the medical procedure performed as traditionally done in most healthcare studies, we define *PCQ* in a broad and comprehensive manner to denote the excellence of the medical care received by admitted hospital patients (e.g., Chang, Ma, Chiu, Lin, & Lee, 2009; Ma, Yang, Lee, & Chang, 2009; Nelson & Niederberger, 1990; Van Ess Coeling & Cukr, 2000; Ware et al., 1983). In extant literature, a few studies, listed in Table 6, have focused on the identifying the determinants of PCQ, both in hospital and clinical settings.

Table 6. Patient Care Quality Dimensions Identified in Literature

Study	Donabedian (1968)	McFadden, Stock and Gowen (2006)	Dagger et al. (2007)	Isaac, Zaslavsky, Cleary and Landon (2010)	Boyer et al. (2012)	Chandrasekaran et al. (2012)	Nair, Nicolae and Narasimhan (2013)
Attributes	Application of modem scientific medicine	Patient safety	Interpersonal quality	Communication with nurses	Patient satisfaction data collection	Clinical quality	Clinical quality
	Emphasizes prevention		Technical quality	Communication with doctors	Quality teams of employees	Experiential quality	Experiential quality
	Requires cooperation between patients and physicians		Environmental quality	Responsiveness of hospital staff	Statistical quality (process control using control charts)		
	Considers the individual as a whole		Administrative quality	Pain management	Competitive benchmarking of best-in-class processes		
	Maintains close and continuing personal relation between physicians and patients			Communication about medicines			
	Coordinated with social welfare work			Discharge information			
	Includes all types of medical services			Cleanliness and quietness of hospital			

A review of the studies cited in Table 6 reveal that a total of 25 different characteristics related to PCQ such as cooperation between patients and physicians, cleanliness and quietness of hospital, and coordination with social welfare work have been identified. Based on an extensive search and a synthesis of the multi-dimensional nature of PCQ discussed in extant literature (Dagger, Sweeney, & Johnson, 2007; Gill & White, 2009) we suggest that PCQ has the following four dimensions: *interpersonal, technical, environmental* and *administrative quality*

Interpersonal quality reflects the relationship developed and the dyadic interplay that occurs between the healthcare team and the patient (Dagger, Sweeney, & Johnson, 2007; Gill & White, 2009). It takes into consideration issues such as whether healthcare teams treat their patients with respect, healthcare team members listen to what patients have to say, members give personalized attention to patients and whether team members are willing to answer questions that the patient or their kin may have (Dagger et al., 2007). *Technical quality* reflects the expertise, professionalism, and competency of the healthcare team in delivering the cure (Dagger et al., 2007; Gill & White, 2009). It is concerned with whether patients are administered the correct medical care that is required to cure their ailment, tests (e.g., X-rays and lab tests) are ordered on patients only when required, healthcare team members are qualified, and whether they carry out their tasks competently (Dagger et al., 2007). *Environmental quality* comprises hospital atmosphere such as cleanliness and order and tangibles like hospital bed and required equipment for patient health needs (Dagger et al., 2007; Gill & White, 2009). It takes into account whether the design of the hospital is patient friendly, the lighting at the hospital is appropriate, the temperature at the hospital is pleasant and whether the furniture at the hospital is comfortable (Dagger et al., 2007). *Administrative quality* facilitates the production of the core medical cure while adding value to the patient (Dagger et al., 2007; Gill & White, 2009). Considerations such as whether the internal hospital services (e.g., pathology) work well, waiting time at the hospital is minimum, the hospital provides patients with a range of patient support services and whether the hospital records and documentation (e.g., billing) are error free (Dagger et al., 2007) are in the domain of this dimension of quality.

Hospitals could provide high quality of admitted patient care if they give importance to all the variables and the interrelationships described in the research model which would reduce medical errors and help them operate at the highest level of efficiency (Byrnes, 2004; Shih et al., 2009; Singh et al., 2006). Hospitals delivering high quality of admitted patient care is very crucial for all stakeholders because it could improve hospitals' financials, benefit all entities in the supply chain, and help the patients directly through better and more responsive medical care that cures them of their ailments quicker and at lower cost (Lee et al., 2011).

In the next few sections, we first offer a summary of all research constructs in Table 7. Then, the framework of variables proposed in this research, is depicted in Figure 1. Finally, we discuss the specific relationships proposed among the constructs.

Table 7. Definitions of the Constructs

Constructs	Definition
Technology integration	The interconnectedness of the different technological systems (both software and hardware) implemented in hospitals that enables frequent and up-to-date information exchange such as hospital patient medical information, inventory data about medicine/other supplies and personnel information in electronic form between different entities within the hospital, the healthcare team and hospital management (e.g., Leidner, Preston, & Chen, 2010; Li & Lin, 2006).
Supplier relationship management	A relationship building approach adopted by firms that uses their social ties and interpersonal contact with their suppliers to monitor, control and encourage desirable supplier behavior (e.g., Das et al., 2006; Lumineau & Henderson, 2012; Noordewier et al., 1990; Rivard-Royer, Landry, & Beaulieu, 2002). Based on a review of the literature, it is suggested that supplier relationship management has six different aspects: (1) *flexibility* of the supplier in quickly meeting hospital needs and changes in quantities of supplies ordered; (2) *assistance* that the supplier is willing to provide the hospitals in all matters related to the quality and quantity of supplies; (3) degree and intensity of *information exchange* between the supplier and the hospitals; (4) degree of *monitoring* required by hospitals to ensure that the supplier is responsive and is able and willing to supply the required quality and quantity of supplies; (5) *continuity expectation* referring to the hospitals' long term interest and orientation to maintain ties; and (6) *quality of supplies* that the supplier provides.
Internal lean practices	Aligned internal operations that help firms to perform effective medical procedures on patients in a timely manner at a reasonable cost (e.g., Alexander, Halpern, & Lee, 1996; Butler & Leong, 2000; Cook & Rasmussen, 2005; Goldstein, Ward, Leong, & Butler, 2002; Harper, 2002; Hay, 2003). Based on literature, it is suggested that internal lean practices have three characteristics: (1) *patient and material flow management*; (2) *continuous quality improvement*; and (3) *waste management.*
Patient care quality	Excellence of the medical care received by patients in U.S. hospitals (e.g., Nelson & Niederberger, 1990; Van Ess Coeling & Cukr, 2000; Ware et al., 1983). Based on a review of the literature, it is suggested that patient care quality includes four primary dimensions: (1) *interpersonal quality* that reflects the relationship developed and the dyadic interplay that occurs between the healthcare team and patient; (2) *technical quality* that reflects the expertise, professionalism, and competency of the healthcare team in delivering the cure; (3) *environmental quality* that comprises hospital atmosphere related to cleanliness and tangibles, such as hospital bed and necessary equipment like drip stands and other required equipment for patient health needs; and (4) *administrative quality* that facilitates the production of the medical cure while adding value to the patient.

Figure 1. Conceptual Model

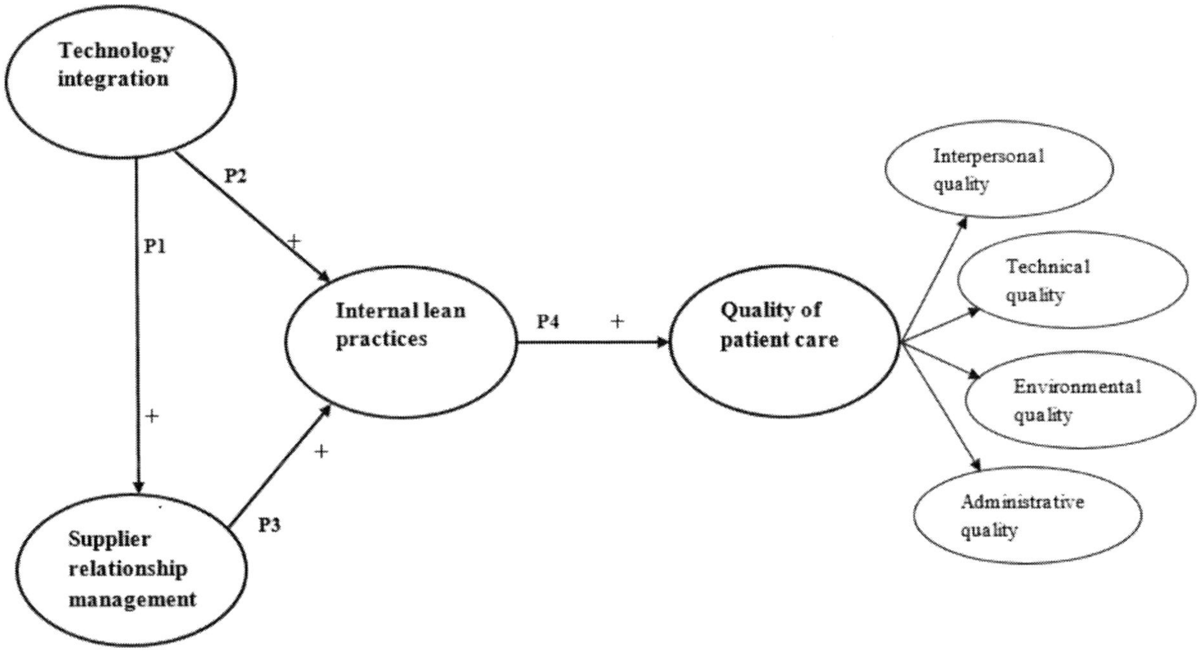

Framework of Key Relationships

Integrating the different departments and internal hospital entities would help the hospital know its stock positions and inventory requirements accurately thereby allowing the hospital to strategically source their inventory items in a planned manner from a few trusted suppliers, manage the procurement processes and govern the existing supplier relationships (Loh & Koh, 2004; Mettler & Rohner, 2009). Receiving up-to-date information on the hospital's inventory items would help the supplier increase its assistance to the hospital, which in turn would help improve its own flexibility to meet changing hospital needs for products (Coye & Kell, 2006; Wang, Tai, & Wei, 2006). It would improve the type and amount of information that the supplier could provide the hospital when requested (Pouloudi, 1999).

On the other hand, a technologically integrated hospital, like any other service firm, could become aware of the cost of purchasing items from each supplier (Das et al., 2006; Talluri & Sarkis, 2002) instantly, helping it choose its strategic suppliers for each of its products/services that are required by various departments. Collaboration between hospitals and their suppliers would increase the continuity expectations that both parties have of the relationship (Mettler & Rohner, 2009; Walshe & Smith, 2006).

In sum, a technologically integrated hospital that knows the latest information from all its internal elements would be able to manage its supplier relationships effectively (Das et al., 2006; Talluri & Sarkis, 2002) because suppliers would feel encouraged to perform better with a hospital that informs them about the required supplies quite in advance. Therefore, based on the above discussions on advantages of a technologically integrated hospital for supplier relationships, it is suggested:

***P1:** Technology integration is positively related to supplier relationship management.*

As noted earlier, technology integration in a hospital internal supply chain could focus primarily on the electronic form of data exchange adopted for all daily communication between the different entities within a hospital (S. Li & Lin, 2006). A technologically integrated hospital could spur effective inventory monitoring and control by all entities in-house in order so as to ensure that they have adequate supplies (e.g., blood units, counseling professionals, therapy professionals, medicines) at all times. In-house inventory monitoring at different supply chain entities could help reduce the hospitals' emergency buffer stocks and help them implement a lean system (Leidner et al., 2010) based on frequent but smaller delivery lots from suppliers.

Technology can help hospitals strategically plan the usage of their critical resources such as operating suites, intensive care units (ICU) and labs, various sophisticated medical equipment like magnetic resonance imaging (MRI), computed tomography (CT) scan and X-rays, considering the maximum and mean patient volumes and flow rates for each medical treatment process (Vissers & Beech, 2005). Thus technology could be used to maintain smooth patient and material flow rates in the hospital. A fundamental redesign of healthcare processes that is based on the use and integration of electronic communication across different technology platforms is now being implemented in some hospitals (Demiris et al., 2008).

Continuous quality improvement (CQI) adoption is facilitated by information systems, flexible use of personnel, and team support as well as training for managers (Lucas et al., 2005). Investing in medical technology does not automatically result in a significant improvement in patient care quality but organizational cooperation, workforce development and process analysis help improve the quality of health services (L. X. Li, 1997). Information technology such as using electronic patient record system and bar coding medicinal administration (Abrahamsen, 2005) can support all logistics and quality improvements in healthcare (Ammenwerth et al., 2002). Information technology can provide timely and accurate patient data and medical knowledge to the doctors and nurses who need it (Ammenwerth et al., 2002).

Lean philosophy strives to balance the demand for patient care with the capacity of the hospitals in order to eliminate wastes such as over-capacity or waiting times (Kollberg, Dahlgaard, & Brehmer, 2007). Healthcare requires innovation to remain competitive and cost efficient and lean implementation is a way to introduce incremental innovation in hospitals (de Koning, Verver, van den Heuvel, Bisgaard, & Does, 2006). Lean principles need to be applied to all processes to reduce all operational inefficiencies and reduce all types of wastes. Organizational information systems help in the distribution of the required information to different departments for lean implementation (de Koning et al., 2006).

Based on successful technology integration in hospitals (Stratman, 2008) and supported by IPT (Davenport, 1998; Galbraith, 1973; Tushman & Nadler, 1978), it is suggested that better information exchange would ultimately result in hospitals become lean. This is possible because better information exchange would benefit hospitals in optimizing their purchases as they can compare the product price and quality information available from each supplier and each department can buy the necessary quality products at lowest prices. In turn, it would provide the most appropriate medicines and other required supplies to the patient, keeping both the overall cost and time taken for delivery under control, helping hospitals become lean in the process. Therefore, based on the above discussions, the next hypothesis is offered:

***P2:** Technology integration is positively related to internal lean practices.*

Both the supply and demand for hospital services need to be balanced for any hospital to function well. The preparation of the initial diagnostic and consultation report by the physician, taking the patient to the emergency room (ER) department (if it is an urgent case) and transferring the patient to specialized medical suites such as the operating room (if the patient needs surgery) are some of the internal supply chain related activities. The demand related activities incorporates processes for managing the flow of patients (Heineke, 1995) with the aim of having no more than the maximum number of patients that the hospital can handle. Failures in patient and material flow in the hospital such as excessive patient wait for admission and medical procedures may have a direct negative impact on the quality and overall effectiveness of service performance (Baltacioglu et al., 2007). The strength of its supplier relationships is positively related to the patient and material flow in a hospital and its ability to serve patients.

Similarly, supplier relationship management also impacts the continuous quality improvement efforts at the hospital (McLaughlin, McLaughlin, & Kaluzny, 2004). Having structured relationships with hospital suppliers is one of the characteristics of a successful CQI implementation (LeBrasseur, Whissell, & Ojha, 2002). In addition to strong leadership support and commitment, successful and sustained CQI initiatives require hospitals to develop long term and mutually beneficial partnerships with key suppliers (LeBrasseur et al., 2002). Relationships with suppliers are necessary for hospitals to reduce their inventory and yet meet their patient care service quality standards (Dahlgaard, Pettersen, & Dahlgaard-Park, 2011).

Lean waste management can be successful only if hospitals are able to implement a "pull" system for managing their entire inventory (Womack & Jones, 2010; Zidel, 2006) which, in turn, depends upon supplier cooperation (Dahlgaard et al., 2011). Hospitals need to implement effective material restocking processes that involve more frequent but smaller batch deliveries or to rotate their supplies more quickly to reduce the amount of space used up in internal warehouses and the cash related to their tied-up in inventory (Graban, 2011), both of which could involve major supply chain improvements.

As noted earlier, lean systems theory (Flynn, Sakakibara, & Schroeder, 1995; Kaynak, 1997, 2002; Monden, 1981; Ōno, 1988; Shah & Ward, 2003; Sugimori et al., 1977) emphasizes that firms must have reduced inventory available just in time when they need it, and it requires supplier collaboration to implement such a "pull" system. Healthcare literature also supports this assertion (Dranove & White, 1987, 1989; Schneider & Mathios, 2006). Based on the above discussions, the next hypothesis suggests:

***P3:** Supplier relationship management is positively related to internal lean practices.*

One of the objectives of lean implementation in a firm is to have high product or service quality (Dean Jr & Snell, 1996; Fullerton & McWatters, 2001) that meets or exceeds the required standards of the industry. Lean systems theory (Flynn et al., 1995; Kaynak, 1997, 2002; Monden, 1981; Ōno, 1988; Shah & Ward, 2003; Sugimori et al., 1977) highlights that reducing wastes would help firms identify and eliminate scrap and rework from their goods production or service generation processes. Lean systems theory helps explain the relationship between internally implementing lean practices at hospitals and the positive effect on patient care quality.

To deliver high PCQ the practitioners, i.e., both physicians and nurses need to master two aspects of medical care. First, practitioners need to become experts in the technical quality of patient care (i.e., the medical diagnosis and cure procedures and treatments need to be accurate and most effective). Second, the healthcare team members need to learn the attributes of interpersonal quality of patient care, i.e., keeping the patient well informed about the required medical treatment and its side-effects, empathizing with patients so that they are not overly worried (Hudelson, Cleopas, Kolly, Chopard, & Perneger, 2008; Marley, Collier, & Meyer Goldstein, 2004).

Hospitals should treat only the number of patients that they can handle so that patients flow though the hospital is effectively managed (Heineke, 1995). Smooth material and patient flow in the hospital help decrease the average wait times for patients before their surgery or other medical procedures (Baltacioglu et al., 2007) by ensuring that appropriate medical equipment and supplies and suites like intensive care units (ICU)s are available when needed. Longer wait times add additional stress to patients (Paterson et al., 2006), complicate patients' ailments, cause additional medical procedures to be performed on patients, and sometimes may result in preventable outcomes like death (Derlet & Richards, 2000). Patient and material flow are related to both the interpersonal and technical aspects of PCQ.

As noted earlier, physical elements of a patient's environment such as the hospital bed, clothes and equipments must be fully clean and disinfected (Aiken, Clarke, & Sloane, 2008) in order to prevent infections (Pittet et al., 2000). Support from the administrative departments of a hospital such as billing and reception are also crucial to improving PCQ (Bokar & Perry, 2007; Conway, 1997). Implementing lean principles in a hospital encourages all practitioners to continuously develop expertise in their own areas of work, and to collaborate and share their knowledge with others in the healthcare teams (Sui-PPheng & Khoo, 2001), because value addition (Joosten, Bongers, & Janssen, 2009) and waste reduction (Toussaint & Berry, 2013) are two important concerns in a lean implementation. Thus, CQI and waste reduction, which form two pillars of a lean philosophy, are positively related to the technical, environmental and administrative dimensions of PCQ. Therefore, based on the above discussions, it is suggested that lean implementation in hospitals is positively related to all four dimensions of PCQ. Hence, the next hypothesize notes:

P4: *Internal lean practices are positively related to patient care quality.*

DISCUSSION AND CONCLUSION

In this conceptual paper, we suggested that a supply chain perspective is imperative to solving many problems U.S. hospitals face today because they arise within as well as beyond hospital boundaries. Based on tenets of lean systems theory, we offered three propositions that are concerned with the internal as well as external hospital supply chain. There are several direct and indirect implications of our conceptual framework for healthcare research and for hospitals and medical practitioners. We highlighted how a unified healthcare supply chain theory could be developed by integrating the different elements of the internal and external hospital supply chain, keeping the hospital at the center and the improvement in the quality of care received by admitted patients as the objective.

Our conceptualization targets some limitations of current conceptualization of PCQ. Most of the commonly used "hard" measures are disease or ailment-specific and reflect only specific aspects of quality of medical care administered in the hospital. Two common quality metrics available in the public domain are the 30-day risk-standardized mortality and readmission rates for ailments such as acute myocardial infarction (heart attack) and pneumonia. In addition, the Agency for Healthcare Research and Quality (AHRQ) reports patient safety indicators (PSI) for death among surgical in-patients with serious treatable complications. Many studies use CMS measures such as central line-associated bloodstream infections (CLABSI) in ICUs only or the surgical site infection from colon surgery. While using such detailed and specific measures are good to adequately know the extent of a specific outcome such as hospital-acquired infection, even a bunch of these detailed measures would not adequately reflect all dimensions of care quality, especially the interpersonal, environmental or administrative dimensions of PCQ. There are not too many healthcare studies that have considered attributes drawn from overall comprehensive and holistic consideration of both internal and external aspects of the hospital supply chain.

We believe that the broad conceptualization of a hospital supply chain offered in this paper could help spur empirical studies testing our propositions. Healthcare studies may benefit from including factors that are beyond the immediate control of the hospitals, such as their equipment and medicine suppliers and even other entities in the different layers of the external supply chain such as the insurance providers. With this paper, we have attempted to take the first step towards building a unified supply chain theory for healthcare with the research context limited to a hospital-centric view of the supply chain keeping admitted patients at the center.

Implementing lean practices in the hospital is the immediate objective while having high care quality available to admitted patients is the ultimate goal of our proposed framework

Based on several recent papers from interdisciplinary fields and status reports from the business press on the state of the U.S. healthcare referenced in this research, it is evident that poor quality of patient care is the main issue troubling U.S. healthcare. As noted by Boyer and colleagues (2012), the IOM report (Kohn, Corrigan, & Donaldson, 1999) has already prompted some corrective action in the healthcare community with many scholars working to improve various quality aspects of the system but several issues still remain unresolved. The framework presented in this paper attempts to offer a more comprehensive perspective of the patient quality issues being faced at most full-service U.S. hospitals than found in the literature. Specific propositions, supported by extant literature and theory, are advanced for relationships among the variables. This research contributes to the growing literature positioned at the cross-section of OM and health care management (HCM) fields in the following ways.

First, this research offers an integrative approach to resolving the major issues in U.S. healthcare by drawing in variables from both the internal as well as external supply chain of a typical U.S. full-service hospital. Using a lean supply chain perspective, this research offers a framework to suggest how the quality of care received by patients can be improved. It is thus an attempt to offer an integrated approach to resolving healthcare issues. The results of this study highlight relationships between the different constructs that have been overlooked in the operations and healthcare literature (such as the role of supplier relationship management on internal lean practices in healthcare or the role of healthcare team effectiveness on quality of patient care) (Bohmer, 2009; Schneller & Smeltzer, 2006; Toussaint & Berry, 2013).

Second, as discussed in SCM literature (see Caniëls & Gelderman, 2007; Das, Narasimhan, & Talluri, 2006; Goodman & Jones, 2013; Mettler & Rohner, 2009; Noordewier, John, & Nevin, 1990; Olsen & Ellram, 1997; Rivard-Royer et al., 2002; Spekman, 1988; Stuart, 1997), the framework highlights that effective supplier management is very important for hospitals, like for other service firms (Handfield, 2010). Hospitals may need to pay attention to all the six different aspects of supplier relationship suggested in this study–supplier flexibility, supplier assistance, supplier information exchange, supplier monitoring, continuity expectation, and quality of supplies–to ensure that they have the best cooperation from their suppliers.

Third, the framework being offered here integrates several constructs that have been mentioned in an isolated manner across several studies in the fields of HCM and medicine (see Bohmer, 2009; Schneller & Smeltzer, 2006; Toussaint & Berry, 2013; Weintraub, 2011). Many HCM studies do not consider all the aspects such as patient and material flow, continuous quality improvement and waste management while discussing lean implementation in hospitals. From an HCM perspective, the framework highlights that hospitals may need to consider all three characteristics of lean implementation. This study attempts to include different aspects of patient care quality in a more comprehensive manner and future HCM studies may find it beneficial to use such a measure.

Finally, our framework has several implications for U.S. hospital administrators and other medical practitioners. To maximize the positive effect of the internal implementation of lean practices on quality of care delivered (Dobrzykowski, McFadden, & Vonderembse, 2016); hospitals could focus on all three different aspects–material flow management, continuous quality improvement and waste management. Patient and material flow management refer to the hospital following efficient patient admission and discharge procedures. Although many hospitals in the U.S., especially in larger cities, may already be using emergency and operating room scheduling software, not all hospitals use such advanced scheduling systems (Bodenheimer & Pham, 2010; D. Gupta & Denton, 2008; Zaghloul & El Enein, 2010). We suggest that hospitals may need to use room scheduling systems which specifically factor in the patients' medical conditions and needs and match them with the hospital room and equipment availability information together so that both patient and material flow within the hospital are streamlined.

Continuous quality improvement considers whether healthcare teams internalize the lessons learnt from past mistakes on patient safety so as not to repeat them. Many hospitals may already be using operational data from electronic clinical information systems such as electronic health records (EHR) platform to plan its staffing of doctors, nurses and other employees. However, scholars have mentioned that the smaller and rural hospitals have still not caught up with EHR (C. Chen, Garrido, Chock, Okawa, & Liang, 2009; Graetz et al., 2014; Jha et al., 2009). Further, many hospitals are not using up-to-date advanced medical equipment and newer technologies such as using electronic aspirin, needle-free care for diabetes (MacRae, 2013) or using advanced robotics to assist the complicated surgeries even if it is justified for the patient's medical condition (Albani & Lee, 2007; Gomes, 2011).

Waste management refers to whether hospitals use a "pull" production system wherein all supplies are inventoried as and when required, and whether hospitals push suppliers to achieve shorter lead-times for delivery. Hospitals need to streamline their own ordering, receiving and other paperwork from suppliers all items, especially their emergency medicinal stocks. Hospitals may need to better train all their healthcare teams to optimally use all medical consumables so as to eliminate wastes (Hirano, 1995; Wakefield et al., 2005).

Hospitals need to ensure that both patients and the required materials and supplies flow smoothly throughout the hospital and are available when needed at the appropriate place. Sometimes patient surgeries are delayed because of lack of available operating rooms, appropriate doctors, anesthetists and even due to a lack of appropriate medicines or the correct medical equipment (B. Gupta, Agrawal, D'souza, & Soni, 2011; Kumar & Gandhi, 2012; Wong, Khu, Kaderali, & Bernstein, 2010). Further, hospitals need to use a lean orientation to identify wastes and delays that do not add value to the patient or hospital and eliminate such activities (Graban, 2011; Toussaint & Berry, 2013).

REFERENCES

References available upon request.

DECISION SCIENCES INSTITUTE

A meta-analytical view of non-technical skills for business and engineering students

Tobin Porterfield
Towson University
Email: tporterfield@towson.edu

Robert Graham
Johns Hopkins University
Email: bgraham@jhu.edu

Dmitriy Nesterkin
D# Media
Dmitriy.Nesterkin@gmail.com

ABSTRACT

Academic programs often seek methods to integrate the technical skills and non-technical skills sought by employers. A literature review explores the diverse interpretations of non-technical skills in order to build a logical and comprehensive topology. The authors then test the topology using a robust dataset of online job advertisements.

KEYWORDS: Soft skills, curriculum, content analysis

INTRODUCTION

The increasingly complex global economy, with a greater reliance on technology, flexibility and adaptability, is forcing employers, as well as colleges and universities, to develop new approaches to ensure that college graduates are best positioned to excel.

Technical skills are necessary discipline-specific knowledge, cognitive ability, proficiency, and experience (Ling, 2002). But the growing demands being placed on workers is necessitating a wider array of skills to succeed in the workplace. This additional set of skills is often described collectively as non-technical skills. These skills, including communication, leadership and teamwork, presentation, project management, and adapting to change, are not easily taught in the traditional discipline focused classroom setting. In a study of performance drivers of logisticians, Myers et al. (2004) did not find a direct relationship between performance and experience or performance and education, suggesting the need for a blend of technical and non-technical skills that directly affect job performance.

Research indicates that hiring professionals are looking beyond the discipline specific technical knowledge of recent college graduates when making hiring decisions (Salleh et al. 2015). The need for non-technical skills is being promoted based on the challenge for newly hired employees to apply their technical knowledge in a dynamic global economy (Kovacs et al. 2012; Sallah et al., 2013). Researchers suggest that these non-technical skills are important because of their role as the connective tissue between the employee's discipline specific knowledge and the workplace environment (Bennett et al. 1999).

Non-technical skills have been approached from different perspectives as: core and generic skills (Keneley & Jackling 2011; Bennett et al. 1999), collaborative capacities (Lizzio et al. 2002), generic abilities (Barrie 2006; Jones 2009), soft skills (Salleh et al. 2015; Ling 2002), professional skills (Reinig et al. 2011), personal skills and employability skills (Nunan et al. 2000) and interpersonal/managerial basic skills (Mangan & Christopher 2005). For the purposes of this study, we use the term *non-technical skills* as a generic moniker that does not understate their value in the workplace.

While it is recognized that college internship experiences can aid students in bridging the gap between academic knowledge and workplace application, universities are being called upon to provide curriculum that helps students develop non-technical skills as part of their academic program (Candy & Crebert 1991). Historically, students may have been able to focus on academic learning in college and then work out how to apply that knowledge during their early career years. But today's fast-paced and competitive work world has little time, resources or expertise to facilitate that learning process. Without workplace programs in place, newly hired graduates must self-develop or risk failure (Marsick 1988). Since universities already have learning processes in place, they are the logical place for both technical and non-technical skills to be developed.

With the wide array of perspectives on what encompasses non-technical skills, universities are left to identify their own subset to address. This study purports to provide a meta-analysis of extant empirical studies that results in a comprehensive topology of non-technical skills. A preliminary evaluation of these skills is provided using a robust dataset of online technical job advertisements.

BACKGROUND

Academic accreditation bodies, professional organizations, industry professionals, and academics all provide support for the critical role of non-technical skills. Organizational documentation and studies have drawn on these perspective from multiple disciplines to identify specific non-technical skills that new graduates should possess.

Accrediting Organizations

The Accreditation Board of Engineering and Technology (ABET) and The Institution of Engineering and Technology (IET) provide frameworks which academic engineering programs must meet in order to be accredited. The standards published by these organizations identify specific knowledge and skills that the academic programs must develop in their graduates. ABET accredits 3,600 programs at 700 colleges in 29 countries (ABET 2016). ABET's accreditation standard requires that academic programs provide traditional technical skills and integrate student outcomes related to teamwork, communication, ethics, diversity, and timeliness (ETAC 2014). By including these concepts in their accreditation standards, ABET holds accredited programs responsible for developing both technical and non-technical skills through their curriculum and ensuring that students achieve these learning outcomes. The Institution of Engineering and Technology (IET) also provides accreditation for academic programs with a focus on the UK. IET accredits bachelor- and master-level academic programs and currently accredits 1,300 undergraduate programs in the UK (IET 2016). The IET Accreditation of Higher Education Programmes (AHEP), third edition (AHEP 2014) requires academic programs to include non-technical areas such as working with information ambiguity, communication, innovation, project management, teamwork, and ethics.

The Association to Advance Collegiate Business Schools (AACSB) provides accreditation to 755 business programs in 51 countries and territories (AACSB 2016). Within the AACSB standards, programs are required to address communication skills, ethics, interpersonal skills, and teamwork within their curriculum (AACSB 2016).

Professional Organizations

The American Society of Engineering Education (ASEE), the American Society of Mechanical Engineers (ASME) and the National Academy of Engineering (NAE) all support that graduates from engineering programs need both technical and non-technical skills, thus ensuring that colleges and universities integrate these skills in their programs (Dukhan & Hassif 2014).

Business oriented professional organizations provide similar support. The Institute of Supply Management (ISM 2016) with 50,000 members provides professional certification noting the importance of ethics. The Project Management Institute (PMI) includes project management as a technical skill in their discipline along with non-technical skills related to communication and ethics (PMI 2016). The Academy of Management (AOM) with 18,000 members across 100 countries endorses the importance of ethics (AOM 2016).

Bridging the academic and employment chasm, the National Association of Colleges and Employers' (NACE) annual survey shows employers' interest in non-traditional skills. "Leadership" and "the ability to work in a team structure" (each 77.8%) were the most important traits for prospective employees, eclipsing workers' "communication skills (written)" (73.4%) and "problem-solving skills" (70.9%), according to its 2014 survey of 260 employers (NACE 2014). The 2016 survey, polling 201 employers, found respondents seeking "leadership" (80.1%), "ability to work in a team" (78.9%), "communication skills (written)" (70.2%), "problem-solving skills" (70.2%) and "communication skills (verbal)" (68.9%) as most important for applicants (NACE 2016).

Academic Research

Previous research has attempted to define non-technical skills, although the components of this list vary greatly. Goleman included several non-technical skills in his book, *Working with Emotional Intelligence*. The skills he identified included self-control, conscientiousness, trustworthiness, social skills and leveraging diversity (Goleman 1998). This list could at best be considered primitive, suggesting basic skills for successful employment.

Empirical research on the skills of architects and architectural engineers has identified important non-technical skills. In a survey of architectural firms, respondents rated the importance and their satisfaction with recent graduate's non-technical competencies (Salleh et al. 2015). Non-technical skills included teamwork, communication, managing information, conflict management, meeting management, leadership, problem-solving, and decision making. In a survey of 51 design and build contractors, performance success was positively affected by non-technical skills (decision making, enthusiasm, speed) (Ling 2002). In comparison, traditional technical skills (task proficiency, job experience, and job knowledge) were not significant contributors to performance success (Ling 2002).

In a review of job advertisements for architects, non-technical skills encompass soft skills (communication, presentation, interpersonal, leadership, and time management) and personal attributes (work independently, teamwork, flexibility, responsible, positive attitude, creativity, maturity, self-motivated, and ability to work under pressure) (Salleh et al. 2013). These skills were distinct from traditional construction technical skills, including knowledge (project management, visualization techniques, and working with construction drawings, contracts, building materials, and building codes) and hard skills (design skills and software).

Evaluations of non-technical skills for logisticians and supply chain managers provided similar results. In a triangulated multi-method study of academics, students and professionals found common expectations for the development of non-technical skills (project management, leadership, analytical thinking, and change management) (Mangan & Christopher 2005).

Kovacs and Tatham (2010) test an enhanced version of Mangan & Christopher's (2005) model of technical and non-technical skills for humanitarian logisticians. Results show strong support for problem solving (information gathering/sharing and problem analysis/identification/solving) and interpersonal skills (communication, negotiation, leadership, meeting facilitation) to be more relevant than general management (finance, accounting, information technology, project management, marketing, relationship management) or technical skills. Specifically reviewing job advertisements for humanitarian logisticians, Kovacs et al. (2012) identified general management skills (project management, relationship management, and change management), interpersonal skills (communication, negotiation, and leadership), and problem solving skills beyond the functional logistics technical skills required for the job.

Surveys of accounting students reinforce the perceived value non-technical skills. Accounting students from diverse cultural backgrounds identified that their academic programs helped them develop generic skills (behavioral and cognitive) beyond the required technical skills (Keneley & Jackling 2004). In a study of teaching effectiveness, accounting students endorsed the value of team-based learning and the development of professional skills (teamwork and interpersonal skills) in their accounting curriculum (Reinig et al. 2011).

Focusing on project managers, Cheng (2005) developed a 12 point behavioral competency model. Those qualities include achievement orientation, initiative, information seeking, focus on client's needs, impact and influence, directiveness, teamwork and cooperation, team leadership, analytical thinking, conceptual thinking, self-control, and flexibility. Seeking to quantify how managers' observations of their technical engineering project management professionals compared to test results for "soft skills quantification" (SSQ), another list of six areas of soft skills was developed. This list included results orientation, interpersonal skills, personal accountability, flexibility, problem-solving, and planning and organization (Petter et al. 2009). While these lists have some common elements, they also vary – both in the words they choose to identify specific skills and how broad the requirements of non-technical extend.

Aggregating the Breadth of Non-Technical Skills

As the NACE studies indicate, employers use their own language to specify the non-technical skill sets they are seeking in job applicants. For instance, one could easily argue that "ability to work in a team" denotes "teamwork," or vice versa. But one also could see how answering a prospective employer's request for information about when an applicant showed the "ability to work in a team" might lead to statements about the specific skills that make one able to work in a team. They might include listening, responding to different opinions, considering other points of view, communicating effectively with others, reaching a logical conclusion from all available information. Those skills could each be considered part of what makes someone skilled in non-technical areas.

Additionally, depending on the discipline, certain skills may be considered technical rather than non-technical. Skills such as project management and negotiation vary depending on discipline. Engineering and project management professionals often identify project management as a technical skill (e.g. Salleh et al. 2013; PMI 2016) and similarly, negotiation may be considered a technical skill for a supply chain manager (e.g. ISM 2016). To address this issue, this cross-disciplinary study includes skills as non-technical if they are identified as such by any discipline.

To bring greater clarity and consistency to the discussion of non-technical skills, the authors propose grouping non-technical skills into four categories (Table 1). These categories are designed to increase the specificity and clarity of those who seek to describe non-technical skills in both academic and workplace settings. These groupings also can ensure that synonyms and words that are closely aligned convey the same general ideas. Through these groupings, similar words that people may use independently, but signify the same idea, become part of the whole, adding further weight to the overall non-technical skill moniker. Furthermore, these categories can make addressing these increasingly important job qualifications easier for both employers and academic institutions.

Table 1: Non-technical Skill Categories

Skill Category	DESCRIPTION
Group Interaction	Skills that foster group success
Character/Personal	Skills and traits unique to the individual that enable that person to achieve objectives
Interpersonal	Skills that an individual employs to have positive one-on-one interactions
Tactical	Skills that applying methods and procedures to achieve results

An aggregation of the non-technical skills identified in relevant literature provides a cross-disciplinary view of what encompasses non-technical skills (Table 2). Recall that these studies represent the perspectives of faculty, students, and the professional community from various disciplines with strong technical skill requirements for their employees.

Table 2: Non-technical Skills Grouped by Category

Non-technical Skill Category	Term(s) from literature	Source
Group Interaction	Meeting facilitation, Meeting (conducting/partnering)	Kovacs & Tatham, 2010; Kovacs et al. 2012; Sallah et al. 2015
	People management	Kovacs & Tatham 2010; Kovacs et al. 2012
	Leadership, leading change	Kovacs & Tatham 2010; Salleh et al. 2013; Sallah et al. 2015; Mangan & Christopher 2005; Kovacs et al. 2012; Goleman 1995
	Change management	Mangan & Christopher 2005
Character/Personal	Analytic, Analytical	Mangan & Christopher 2005; Lizzeo et al. 2002; Sallah et al. 2015
	Persuasiveness	Goleman 1995
	Question accepted wisdom	Keneley & Jackling 2011
	Think and reason logically	Keneley & Jackling 2011
	Understand ethical implications of decisions	Keneley & Jackling 2011
	Written communication, written presentation, written skills	Kovacs & Tatham 2010, Kovacs et al. 2012, Lizzio et al. 2002; Sallah et al. 2013, Sallah et al. 2015
	Stress management	Kovacs et al. 2012; Kovacs & Tatham 2010
	Listening	Kovacs et al. 2012; Kovacs & Tatham 2010; Salleh et al. 2015
	Innovativeness	Ling 2002
	Enthusiasm in tackling a difficult assignment	Ling 2002
	Loyalty to designer/builder	Ling 2002
	Offering suggestions to improve design	Ling 2002
	Persistenct in overcoming obstacles	Ling 2002
	Respect for designer/builder as team leader	Ling 2002
	Confidence tackling unfamiliar problems	Lizzio et al. 2002
	Decision making skills, make decisions	Sallah et al. 2015; Keneley & Jackling 2011
	Able to work independently	Salleh et al. 2013
	Able to work under pressure	Salleh et al. 2013
	Matured	Salleh et al. 2013
	Proactive	Salleh et al. 2013
	Self-motivated	Salleh et al. 2013
	Willing to learn	Salleh et al. 2013
	Responsible, make and take responsibility	Salleh et al. 2013; Keneley & Jackling 2011
	Creative, think creatively, creativity	Salleh et al. 2013; Ling 2002; Keneley & Jackling 2011
	Positive attitude	Sallah et al. 2013
Interpersonal	Interpersonal	Mangan & Christopher 2005; Ling 2002; Salleh et al. 2013; Salleh et al. 2015
	Resolving conflicts	Sallah et al. 2015
	Communication, Ability to communicate at multiple levels, communication skills, oral communication	Salleh et al. 2013; Ling 2002, Kovacs et al. 2012; Kovacs & Tatham 2010; Sallah et al. 2015
	Team member, team player, teamwork, work in a team, building and leading teams, past team size	Lizzio et al. 2002; Salleh et al. 2013; Sallah et al. 2015; Keneley & Jackling 2011; Goleman 1995
Tactical	Adapt knowledge to new situations	Keneley & Jackling 2011
	Open to new possibilities	Keneley & Jackling 2011
	Work with minimum supervision	Keneley & Jackling 2011
	Human resource management	Kovacs & Tatham 2010
	Negotiation	Kovacs & Tatham 2010; Kovacs et al. 2012; Sallah et al. 2015
	Information gathering, locating information; information sharing, organizing information	Kovacs et al. 2012, Kovacs & Tatham 2010; Sallah et al. 2015
	Problem solving, problem solving skills, problem-solving, solve problems, problem identification, problem analysis	Kovacs et al. 2012; Kovacs & Tatham 2010; Salleh et al. 2015; Lizzio et al. 2002; Ling 2002; Keneley & Jackling 2011
	Attention to design and construction details	Ling 2002
	Compliance with designer/builder's instructions and orders	Ling 2002
	Preparedness to revise design to achieve higher constructability and cost and/or time savings	Ling 2002
	Speed in obtaining statutory approvals, speed in producing design drawings, speed of response to the request and instructions of the designer/builder	Ling 2002
	Project approach, project management	Ling 2002, Managan & Christopher 2005
	Planning own work	Lizzio et al. 2002
	Critical Thinking	Sallah et al. 2015
	Time management, time management skills	Salleh et al. 2013; Sallah et al. 2015
	Presentation	Salleh et al. 2013

RESEARCH DESIGN

To validate the aggregated list of non-technical skills provided in Table 2, this study applies content analysis to online job advertisements. Terms identified in the literature are matched to and abilities sought by employers as provided in the job advertisement.

Prior studies have used job advertisements to assess recruitment effectiveness (Gibson & Cook 2001), architect skills (Salleh et. al. 2013), logistician skills (Kovacs et al. 2012), as well as to identify gaps between skills needed on the job and skills advertised (Matthews & Redman 2001).

Content analysis is a range of qualitative and quantitative research methods based on the review of text or symbol-based source documents (Duriau et al. 2007). Studies also have used content analysis to explore transcripts of recorded interviews (Porterfield et al. 2012). Beyond the identification of specific terms, content analysis includes the patterns or co-occurrences of terms similar to the traditional qualitative analysis technique of correlation (Krippendorff, 2004; Weber 1990). This study proposed to use both a qualitative and quantitative content analysis.

Using content analysis for qualitative and quantitative analysis requires the development of a robust framework of appropriate terms. Existing literature provides a framework of knowledge, skills, and abilities associated with non-technical skills. The aggregated list of terms is provided in Table 2.

Data

Job advertisements were sampled from the INDEED online job database (www.indeed.com). The online service includes nearly one million job advertisements across disciplines and geography. Advertisements were sampled for a 30-day period (1FEB2016 through 1MAR2016) for jobs within 50 miles of Chicago, IL. Chicago was chosen as a sample geography based on its central location in the US. The initial sample focused on engineering jobs. Engineering job advertisements were selected based on the job title of "Engineer". In order to avoid temporary and part-time positions the query required a job type of "Full time". The engineering query was further filtered to avoid job title terms associated with short term positions, computer programming, building maintenance, and other positions that did not require a traditional engineering degree (temporary, application server, ember, java, python, linux, data, hardware, controls, developer, network, support, systems, software, service, sales, office, field, operation).

To efficiently extract the relevant job advertisements, the authors developed an application programming interface (API) that extracted the data as a comma delimited text file.

Rather than manually coding the job advertisements using multiple coders, advanced features of computer assisted qualitative data analysis software (CAQDAS) were used to identify the relevant terms in the job advertisements. Atlas.ti software provided tools to auto-code, count, and evaluate co-occurrences of the previously identified terms (see Friese 2014).

RESULTS

Descriptive Results

The API extracted 83 engineering job advertisements. Advertisements covered a range of engineering sub-disciplines (Table 3). The INDEED website requires that the organization posting the job opening select an "engineering type".

Table 3: Engineering Disciplines

	Count	Percent
Industrial/Manufacturing	20	24%
Other	18	22%
Mechanical	11	13%
Quality	10	12%
Electrical	6	7%
Civil	5	6%
Mechanical or Electrical	3	4%
Architectural or Mechanical	2	2%
Mechanical or Chemical or Electrical	2	2%
Product	2	2%
Production	2	2%
Environmental	1	1%
Mechanical or BioMed	1	1%

In the job description, the organization posting the job opening can specify any degree requirements. Forty-one percent of the jobs in the sample specify a college degree of bachelor's or higher (Table 4).

Table 4: Degrees Specified

	Count	Percent
Bachelor's	27	33%
Master's	2	2%
Either Bachelor's or Master's	5	6%
Neither Specified	49	59%

In the job description, the employer can specify whether experience is required. Eighty-eight percent of the jobs in the sample required either general experience, specific work experience, or specific experience using software tools or engineering practices (Table 5).

Table 5: Experience Requested

	Count	Percent
Experience noted	73	88%
Experience not noted	10	12%

Content Analysis

To test the non-technical skills identified from the literature, the dataset was scanned for appropriate search terms related to each skill. Preliminary results for the *interpersonal* category are provided.

Forty-eight percent of the job advertisements noted at least one of the skills identified in the *interpersonal* category (Table 6). Of the interpersonal skills, team related skills were requested most (67%), followed by communication skills (40%) and interpersonal skills (23%).

Table 6: Interpersonal Skill Category Results

	Count	Percent
interpersonal	19	23%
communicat*	33	40%
team*	56	67%

While nearly half of the job advertisements include an interpersonal skill, 14% include two of the interpersonal skills and 2% include all three (Table 7).

Table 7: Skill Concentration

	Count	Percent
Noted one interpersonal skill	26	31%
Noted two interpersonal skills	12	14%
Noted all three interpersonal skills	2	2%

Co-occurence of terms can be evaluated using a binary correlation for cases where each term is present. The correlation analysis shows a moderate positive pair-wise relationship between communication and each of the other two interpersonal skills (Table 8).

Table 8: Skill Co-occurence

	interpersonal	*communicat**	*team**
interpersonal	1		
communicat*	0.28	1	
team*	0.16	0.26	1

DISCUSSION

These results offer a new lens with which the overall preparedness of job applicants in the engineering field can be explored. Academic institutions attempt to provide employers with prospective employees whose skill sets match what those employers need. Employers, based on who they hire and interactions with academic institutions, provide feedback on the effectiveness of academic efforts to prepare these students. The results of this sampling suggest that employers in the engineering field are actively seeking workers who possess these non-technical skills, and their stating of these skills in their advertisements suggest the acute nature of this need. The sampling shows that the interest of engineering employers in non-technical skills spans a wide range of engineering disciplines. This broad appeal of job applicants with non-technical skills seems to support growing weight placed on non-technical skills by academic accrediting bodies, professional organizations, industry professionals and academics.

The Language of Non-technical Skills

All new concepts are developed through reliance on existing concepts. The effort to find a universal definition of what encompasses non-technical skills is no different. From the literature review above, it is evident that various researchers, professional associations, and industries have applied the words and characteristics they believe comprises their specific definition of non-technical skills. While literature on non-technical skills dates back several decades, this research supports the idea that definitive and universally accepted language is not established.

For instance, in looking at the literature, "non-technical skills," "behavioral skills" and "soft skills" are frequently used interchangeably, or as separate components of the first one. (For many, Goleman's use of the phrase "soft skills" carries particular weight, even though it receives passing attention in his book.) The lack of consistent language at the foundation of this area of study suggests its infancy.

This paper attempts to refine the language through its use of broader categories, giving employers, job seekers and academic institutions clearer categories under which they can group smaller components of the overall non-technical skill area. This approach could help eliminate potential confusion and redundancy in the language describing components of non-technical skills.

Driving Toward Clarity

Over time, a clearer definition of non-technical skills may emerge. At present, academic institutions, their graduates and employers also may be confronting a language barrier of sorts. This lack of clarity could be making it more complicated for employers and academic institutions to talk with each other and to properly assess the non-technical skills of job applicants. One can easily reason that "work independently" and "work with minimal supervision" are both attempting to convey the same idea. However, the difference in wording could lead to differences in how a job applicant might address a question and how a prospective employer might evaluate a response. An applicant for an engineering job might discussion in an interview a situation where she worked alone to develop a process to resolve a production problem, putting stress on the working alone aspects of the project. Asked to discuss a situation involving minimal supervision, the same applicant might discuss how once she was trained in a process, she managed the staff completing the process with weekly check-ins by her supervisor. Both answers might satisfy an employer, but at the same time, each answer might hurt the applicant's chances for that job, depending on what the employer is looking for and how he refers to it. Similar situations involving a potential lack of clarity because of differences in how the words are used can be easily identified when looking at the varied list of words used to describe non-technical skills and its components in prior literature.

The Bigger Picture

When aggregated under the broader categories this paper suggests, trends become more visible. For instance, 48 percent of job advertisements in the sampling addressed the "interpersonal" category. Recognizing the similarities of "team-related skills," the most requested among the sampling with 67 percent, followed by communication skills (40%) and the actual words themselves (23%), a more comprehensive and accurate picture of employers' needs and areas that academic institutions should focus attention becomes clearer. That 14% of the sample include two of the interpersonal skills and 2% include all three terms could suggest the need for even greater importance to be placed on the interpersonal category of non-technical skills.

Academia Needs to Dig Deeper

The results also suggest that academic institutions have more work to do. Job advertisements are a cost that employers incur to obtain qualified workers. However, employers know that the more qualifications they seek in a job posting, the word count will increase and the more it will cost. Moreover, the more qualifications they seek, the narrower the pool of applicants is likely to be. Therefore, it can be argued that because employers are taking valuable and costly space in job postings to specify the non-technical skills they seek in applicants could suggest that the applicants they are interviewing do not demonstrate these skills. The absence of the sought-after non-technical skills in graduates could suggest that academic institutions have not yet found the best ways to integrate these skills into their curriculum effectively. It also may mean that these non-technical skills, which by their own nature are not concrete, are difficult to teach in a group setting like a college classroom because each student comes to the classroom with his own strengths and weaknesses in this area, making it difficult to create a common curriculum to address identification and areas of improvement. This research does not address whether the validity of these claims, but future research should explore these areas.

Demonstration Issues

Job applicants who may have honed these non-technical skills in academic institutions may not be developing the ability to demonstrate these skills in ways that resonate with potential employers. Through examples, activities focused on real-world scenarios, internships and other efforts, academic institutions may be helping students cultivate these skills. However, students may not be as adept at describing these skills in response to employers' questions. As a result, employers may not be finding the words that applicants use or the experiences they describe matching exactly what they are looking for, thus the problem may not be in the instruction, but rather in the communication of these non-technical skills. Additional research should explore this area.

The employment advertisement pool collected for this research may not reflect the overall industry since its focus was on Chicago. Future research could use this methodology to explore employers' stated needs in their job advertisements in different geographic areas. Additional research also could focus on comparing employment advertisements among different industries to explore if the articulation of non-technical skills in these postings varies by industry.

CONCLUSION

An initial analysis of the aggregated non-technical skills list using online job advertisements for engineering positions reveals yet greater insight into how academic institutions and employers are addressing these important skills.

Developing broad categories under which the expansive list of words used to describe non-technical skills can be divided helps to improve the acceptance, clarity and usefulness of this increasingly important area of job preparation. Initial testing of one category suggest that further testing of all four categories against actual job postings yields new information on the interest employers have in finding graduates who have the appropriate non-technical skills they seek.

Armed with four important areas to address, colleges and universities can build programs more easily and efficiently. These groupings also allow employers to more effectively explore candidates and choose applicants for jobs that have the important mix of technical and non-technical skills.

References

AACSB, Association to Advance Collegiate Business Schools (2016). Retrieved 28, March, 2016 from http://aacsb.edu

ABET, Accreditation Board of Engineering and Technology (2016). Retrieved 28 March, 2016 from http://www.abet.org

AHEP, Accreditation of Higher Education Programmes, third edition. (2014). The Institute of Engineering and Technology. Retrieved 28 March, 2016, from http://www.theiet.org/academics/accreditation/policy-guidance/ahep3.cfm?type=pdf

AOM, Academy of Management (2016). Retrieved 28 March, 2016 from http://www.aom.org

Barrie, S. (2006). Understanding what we mean by generic attributes of graduates. *Higher Education*. 51(2), 215-241.

Bennett, N., Dunne, E. & Carre´ , C. (1998). Patterns of core and generic skills provision in higher education, *Higher Education*, 37, 71–93.

Candy, P. & Crebert, G. (1991). Ivory tower to concrete jungle, *Journal of Higher Education*, 62, 570–592.

Cheng, M., Dainty, A., & Moore, D. (2005). What makes a good project manager? *Human Resource Management Journal*, 15(1), 25-37.

Dukhan, N., & Hassif, R., (2014). On teaching non-technical skills for the engineers of 2020. QScience Proceedings (World Congress of Engineering Education 2013), 2014, 9.

Duriau, V. J., Reger, R. K., & Pfarrer, M. D. (2007). A content analysis of the content analysis literature in organization studies: Research themes, data sources, and methodological refinements. *Organizational Research Methods*,10(1), 5-34.

ETAC, EngineeringTechnology Accreditation Commission (2015). Criteria for accrediting engineering technology programs. Retrieved March 15, 2016, from http://www.abet.org/wp-content/uploads/2015/10/T001-16-17-ETAC-Criteria-10-16-15.pdf

Friesse, S. (2014). *Qualitative Data Analysis with ATLAS.ti*, second edition. Sage Publications, Thousand Oaks, CA.

Gibson, B. & Cook, R. (2001. Hiring practices in US third party logistics firms. *International Journal of Physical Distribution & Logistics Management*, 31(10), 714-732.

Goleman, D. (1998). *Working With Emotional Intelligence*. Bantam Dell, New York, NY.

IET, Institution of Engineering and Technology (2016). Retrieved 28 March, 2016, from http://www.theiet.org/

ISM, Institute for Supply Management (2016). Retrieved 28 March, 2016 from http://www.instituteforsupplymanagement.org

Jones, A. (2009). Generic attributes as espoused theory: The importance of context. *Higher Education,* 58:2, 175-191.

Keneley, M., & Jackling, B. (2011). The acquisition of generic skills of culturally-diverse student cohorts. *Accounting Education*, 20(6), 605-623.

Kovacs, G., Tatham, P., & Larson, P. (2012). What skills are needed to be a humanitarian logistician? *Journal of Business Logistics,* 33:3, 245-258.

Kovacs, G. & Tatham, P. (2010). What is special about a humanitarian logistician? A survey of logistic skills and performance. *Supply Chain Forum an International Journal*, 11(3), 31-41.

Krippendorff, K. (2004). *Content Analysis: An Introduction to its Methodology* (2nd edition). Sage, Thousand Oaks, CA.

Ling, Y. (2002). Model for predicting performance of architects and engineers. *Journal of Construction Engineering and Management*, 12(8), 446-455.

Lizzio, A., Wilson, K, & Wilson, R. (2002). University students' perceptions of learning environment and academic outcomes: Implications for theory and practice. *Studies in Higher Education*. 27(1), 27-52.

Mangan, J. & Christopher, M. (2005). Management development and the supply chain manager of the future. *International Journal of Logistics Management,* 16(2), 178-191.

Marsick, V.J. (1988). Learning in the workplace: The case for reflectivity and critical reflectivity. *Adult Education Quarterly*, 38, 187-198.

Matthews, B. & Redman, T. (2001). Recruiting the wrong salespeople: Are job ads to blame? *Industrial Marketing Management*, 30(7), 541- 550.

Myers, M., Griffith, D. & Daugherty, P. (2004) Maximising the human capital equation in logistics: education, experience and skills. *Journal of Business Logistics*, 25(1), 211-232.

NACE - National Association of Colleges and Employers. (2014) *Job Outlook 2015.* Retrieved November 20, 2014, from https://www.naceweb.org/s11122014/job-outlook-skills-qualities-employers-want.aspx?land-surv-lp-2-spot-joskz-11142014

NACE – National Association of Colleges and Employers (2016). *Job Outlook 2017.* Retrieved March 15, 2016, from http://www.naceweb.org/about-us/press/2016/verbal-communication-most-important-candidate-skill.aspx

Nunan, T., George, R., & McCausland, H. (2000). Implementing graduate skills at an Australian university. *Integrating Key Skills in Higher Education: Employability, Transferable Skills and Learning for Life, Kogan Page, London*, 57-66.

Petter, S., & Randolph, A. B. (2009). Developing soft skills to manage user expectations in IT projects: knowledge reuse among IT project managers. *Project Management Journal*, 40(4), 45-59.

PMI, Project Management Institute (2016). Retrieved 28 March, 2016 from http://www.pmi.org

Porterfield, T., Macdonald, J., & Griffis, S. (2012). An exploration of the relational effects of supply chain disruptions. *Transportation Journal*, 51(4), 399-427.

Reinig, B., Horowitz, I., & Whittenburg, G. (2011). The effect of team-based learning on student attitudes and satisfaction. *Decision Sciences Journal of Innovative Education,* 9(1), 27-47.

Salleh, R., Yusoff, M., Amat, S., Noor, A., & Suredah, N. (2013). Profiling industry-relevant competencies of graduate architects through online job advertisements. *International Business Research*, 6(11), 43-51.

Salleh, R., Yusoff, M., Harun, H. & Memon, M. (2015). Gauging industry's perspectives on soft skills of graduate architects: Importance v. satisfaction. *Global Business and Management Research: An International Journal,* 7(2), 95-101.

Weber, R. (1990). *Basic Content Analysis* (49). Sage Publications: Thousand Oaks, CA.

DECISION SCIENCES INSTITUTE

A Multi-Method Investigation of Overordering Behavior in Supply Chains

Tarikere T. Niranjan
Indian Institute of Technology Bombay
ttniranjan@iitb.ac.in

ABSTRACT

Misperception of feedback (MOF) hypothesis, a central theory in dynamic decision making, posits that decision makers are incapable of being cognizant of feedback delays and underweight the supply line of inventories and capacities. This paper reconsiders this assumption. Field studies of manufacturing supply chains in India revealed an alternative mechanism of overordering, which I call *supply line discounting*. The weak institutional structures, capacity shortages, and polychronic cultures that characterize emerging economies engender *deliberate* order inflation by buyers, which triggers *supply line discounting* and undersupply by suppliers. An eye tracking experiment helps flesh out and validate this behavior.

KEYWORDS: Case study; Eye tracking experiment; Misperception of feedback (MOF); Overreaction; Order inflation; Supply line discounting.

INTRODUCTION

Dynamic decision-making involves making a series of decisions under conditions in which the state of the world changes, both autonomously and as a consequence of the decision maker's actions, thereby conditioning future decisions. Feedback delays and nonlinearities make tasks dynamically complex; a long line of experimental and theoretical research highlights the challenges of learning in such settings (Sterman, 1989a; Paich & Sterman, 1993; Diehl & Sterman, 1995; Sterman, 2000; Cronin, Gonzalez, & Sterman, 2009; Rahmandad & Repenning, 2016). First, according to the *supply line underweighting* or *misperception of feedback* (MOF) hypothesis (Sterman, 1989b; a; Sterman, 2000), subjects ignore the time lag between initiation of a control action and its full effect. Second, they are overly aggressive in correcting the discrepancies between the desired and actual state of the variable of interest. "It is as if the subject purchases a car, but has to wait for delivery. The next day, the garage still empty, the subject goes to the dealer and orders another one." (Sterman, 1989a).

MOF hypothesis has found empirical support in a wide range of settings, including firefighting (Brehmer, 1992), workforce planning (Größler & Zock, 2010), management of renewable resources (Moxnes, 1998) and software development projects (Sengupta & Abdel-Hamid, 1993; Rahmandad & Repenning, 2016), capacity management (Sterman, 1989a), inventory management (Diehl & Sterman, 1995), and supply chain management (SCM) (Sterman, 1989b). Participants misperceive the supply line and "produce wildly oscillating production rates, allow their fire-fighting headquarters to burn down, and find their fleets idled after overexploiting their fisheries." (Repenning & Sterman, 2002). MOF hypothesis is thus central to dynamic decision making literature,

Despite broad agreement regarding the MOF, Niranjan, Wagner, and Bode (2011) highlight the missing link between the MOF hypothesis and its theoretical foundation viz. *anchoring & adjustment* and leave the accumulated empirical evidence open to alternative interpretations. Furthermore, the extant literature views MOF as a characteristic of individual behavior. This view rests on the empirical evidence that the *supply line underweighting* factor β, which is the relative weight of the supply line (orders already placed and yet to be delivered) relative to in-hand stock, is less than the normative value of 1 (e.g. Sterman, 1989b; Croson & Donohue, 2006; Croson, Donohue, Katok, & Sterman, 2014; Narayanan & Moritz, 2015). The evidence is potentially misleading because it is based on aggregate averages across participants, a methodological approach that Lau, Hasija, and Bearden (2014) find questionable. If a sample comprises 50% famished persons weighing 100 pounds and 50% obese persons weighing 300 pounds, the average weight is 200 pounds. However, this average is not representative of the sample and describes a type of participant that does not exist (this is derived from an example in Savage (2009) cited in Lau et al. (2014)). Niranjan et al. (2011) identified similar concerns regarding empirical support for MOF: the coefficient β held values in the hypothesized direction (positive) for only approximately half of the participants; for the rest, the values were negative. This empirical anomaly warrants further study.

Furthermore, the bulk of the empirical evidence for MOF has emanated from the SCM literature (Forrester, 1961; Sterman, 1989b), which is based on the Western context. "Most of our paradigms originated from North America in the 1950s to the 1980s, inspired by the empirical phenomena and cultural, philosophical, and research traditions of the time" (Barkema, Chen, George, Luo, & Tsui, 2015). The prevailing institutional environment fundamentally alters the way buyer-supplier transactions occur because supply chains are embedded in the macro-social context in which they operate (McFarland, Bloodgood, & Payan, 2008). One of the tenets of SCM is contracting to align conflicting goals amongst the constituent members (Lariviere, 2016). In developed countries, legal institutions operate silently and invisibly to the extent that they are seldom noticed (Meyer, Estrin, Bhaumik, & Peng, 2009; Bai, Sheng, & Li, 2016), whereas emerging economies are characterized by weak legal institutions and poor contract enforceability (Hoskisson, Eden, Lau, & Wright, 2000; Mesquita & Lazzarini, 2008; Zhou & Poppo, 2010). For example, it would take the Indian courts at least *450* years to clear the backlog of over 30 million cases (Biswas, 2013), or 35 years "if the nation's judges attacked their backlog nonstop—with no breaks for eating or sleeping—and closed 100 cases every hour, according to *Bloomberg Businessweek* calculations" (Lasseter, 2015). Despite such starkly different institutional environments, an institutional contingency perspective is missing in the literature (Bai et al., 2016).

Juxtaposition of these gaps leads to the question of *how overreaction manifests in emerging economies like India, with the concomitant legal inefficiencies and cultural issues.* In addressing this question, a case study (Study 1) uncovered an idiosyncratic *supply line discounting* behavior and the subsequent actions the firm took to mitigate it. The second case study analytically replicates that behavior (Study 2). Study 3 reports the eye tracking experiment inspired by the case studies, which explicates and validates the emergent behavior.

Note: the full, peer-reviewed paper can be obtained from the author.

DECISION SCIENCES INSTITUTE

A Multi-Objective Decision Model for Supply Chain Collaboration Programs

Payam Parsa; Mohammad Shbool; Manuel Rossetti; Shengfan Zhang; Edward Pohl
Department of Industrial Engineering,
University of Arkansas

ABSTRACT

This paper develops a multi-objective decision model that incorporates quantitative and qualitative decision objectives of two potential business partners that aim to start a supply chain collaboration program. The model enables the partners to evaluate the trade-offs between conflicting objectives of the decision. It also helps them quantify and communicate their views and preferences on key decision factors. The results of implementing the model for two major partners in health care supply chain reveal the value of different decision outcomes and the sensitivity of key decision variables from the perspective of each stakeholder.

KEYWORDS: Multi-objective decision analysis, Supply chain collaboration, Value modeling, Healthcare supply chain, Multi-criteria decision making

INTRODUCTION

The decision of entering into a supply chain collaboration program, such as Continuous Replenishment Program (CRP), or Vendor Managed Inventory (VMI), or Collaborative Planning Forecasting and Replenishment (CPFR), could be challenging. These collaboration initiatives allow the organizations to share demand, forecast, sales and policy information in order to reduce the total cost of the supply chain. The cost savings come from different cost components and with different proportion depending on various supply chain parameters. Although the expected cost savings are sometimes tempting for the involved organizations, the decision makers do not base their decisions solely on the cost savings. We call the cost related decision factors "quantitative factors" while there are other decision factors that are mostly qualitative and could have greater impacts especially among the high level decision makers. We conducted a case study in healthcare supply chain in which the process of reaching an agreement over a CRP relationship between a major manufacturer and a distributor is modeled using multi-objective decision analysis (MODA). MODA is a decision making process which inherently involves a combination of approaches to assess the candidate solutions. In this paper we present how we integrated the quantitative and qualitative decision factors of starting a CRP into a single decision making framework. The key decision factors were collected from the medium-high level managers of both organizations. Then, a comprehensive value tree that represents the views of the decision makers was created. The results provide useful insights on how close the positions of both organizations are with regard to starting a CRP relationship. The model helped both parties to engage in a constructive negotiation process towards a sustainable agreement.

The remainder of this paper is organized as follows. The next section reviews the related literature. The problem description section focuses on the problem and its challenges. Then, the methodology section explains MODA in general and how a model is developed for the problem. The outcome of the model and the perspective of stakeholders on critical decision factors are discussed in results and discussion section. Finally, conclusions and future work are addressed in the last section.

LITERATURE REVIEW

This section provides a brief overview on the history of supply chain collaboration (SCC) followed by a discussion on the relevant research articles. Table 1 provides a summarized history of SCC paradigms from when they emerged in late 80's until the last major advancements in Late 90's. SCC programs have faced various changes over time but they can be categorized into the four major paradigms presented in Table 1.

Table 1: Summary of supply chain collaboration paradigms

SCC paradigm	Emergence period	Pioneers	Relevant Papers	Motivation & Summary
Quick Response (QR)	Late 80's - Early 90's	JC Penny, Walmart	(Iyer and Bergen 1997)	Shorten the lead time in apparel industry. Retail Link platform is created in Walmart to connect the suppliers with end customer demand data
Efficient Customer Response (ECR)	Mid 90's	Grocery Industry (Spartan, HEB, Campbell Soup, P&G)	(Schiano and McKenney 1996), (Clark et al. 1994), (Keh and Park 1997), (Sahin and Robinson 2002)	The main purpose of ECR was to improve the responsiveness of SC to consumer demand in the grocery sector. CRP accounts for 38% of the total grocery industry ECR savings
Continuous Replenishment Program (CRP) & Vendor Managed Inventory (VMI)	Mid 90's	Grocery Industry	(Cachon and Fisher 1997), (Waller et al. 1999)	Since the implementation of CRP in the grocery industry, CRP has been implemented in many other SC sectors often under the name of Vendor Managed Inventory (VMI). VMI extends the collaboration area further to various supply chain functions.
Collaborative Planning, Forecasting and Replenishment (CPFR)	Late 90's	Walmart	(Sherman 1998), (Fliedner 2003) (Sari 2008)	CPFR engages all the partners of supply chain all the way from supplier to end customer in order to make the supply chain as efficient as possible by collaborating intensively. While CPFR generally results in higher benefits, the conditions that rationalize upgrading from CRP to CPFR should be justified.

Research in the area of supply chain collaboration (SCC) can be classified as either conceptual or analytical. Conceptual works mostly defined the required framework for implementing, maintaining and improving SCC initiatives (Simatupang and Sridharan 2005,Doukidis et al. 2007,Cao et al. 2010). On the other hand, analytical studies have focused on quantifying the performance of SCC programs. They mostly used simulation or mathematical modeling to evaluate the impact of supply chain parameters on the performance of SCC programs under certain assumptions (Cachon and Fisher 1997,Lee et al. 2000,Cachon and Fisher 2000,Cheung and Lee 2002,Çetinkaya and Lee 2000,Chen and Chen 2005,Yao et al. 2007,Southard and Swenseth 2008,Ramanathan 2014). Although such assumptions limit the applicability of the models, the pool of such studies has played a significant role in the advancement of SCC programs in different supply chain sectors. Parsa et al. (2016) provide a data-driven model that estimates the cost savings of CRP relationships for both partners. The application of the model in a healthcare supply chain case study is thoroughly discussed in the paper. The analytical studies that quantify the benefits of SCC programs under separate cost components are good complements to this work since they provide useful insights into the quantitative decision factors of starting a SCC program.

Multiple criteria decision making (MCDM) methodologies have been used and implemented in a variety of problem areas such as: forest management and planning (Ananda and Herath 2009), ABC inventory classification (Ramanathan 2006), selecting and evaluating suppliers in supply chain management (Zaeri et al. 2011,Vijayvagy 2012), in technology selection (Ghazinoory et al. 2012), in civil engineering problems like seismic structural retrofitting (Caterino et al. 2009), as well as healthcare: a bibliometric analysis on using Multi-criteria decision analysis techniques can be found in Diaby et al. (2013).

A problem's characteristics determine the most appropriate MCDM technique to be used, since different techniques have different capabilities. A review of MCDM techniques and classification can be found in Triantaphyllou et al. (1998). Common MCDM techniques were discussed through the literature review performed by Velasquez and Hester (2013), showing their applications, strengths and weaknesses.

The closest research stream to this paper is the supplier selection problem, which is a very common problem in the supply chain space. MCDM techniques have been used in this domain extensively. Agarwal et al. (2011) reviewed literature for most popular techniques used for this problem. They found in more than 60 articles that the most common methods are data envelopment analysis (DEA), mathematical programming (linear programming, integer-linear programming, integer-non-linear programming, goal programming, and multi-objective programming), analytical hierarchy process (AHP), case based reasoning (CBR), analytic network process (ANP), fuzzy set theory, multi-attribute rating technique (SMART), genetic algorithm, and criteria based decision making methods (ELECTREE and PROMETHEE), with DEA as the most prominent one.

According to Belton and Stewart (2002), it is not recommended to fragment methods and use them separately, instead, they recommend using more than one technique to produce a more solid framework of approaching the decision. The reason behind this is to eliminate weaknesses of techniques and benefit from their strong points. For example, goal programming does not weight coefficients, and a method like AHP does weight coefficients, and then use the goal programming to choose from a large set of alternatives (Velasquez and Hester 2013). Supplier selection is approached using a combination of AHP and Technique for Order of Preference by Similarity to Ideal Solution (TOPSIS) in a consolidated decision model by Vijayvagy (2012). The evaluation of suppliers in the auto industry using the ANP-TOPSIS approach was performed by Shahroudi and Rouydel (2012). Another combination between multi-attribute utility theory and linear programming was proposed by Sanayei et al. (2008) as an integrated group decision-making process for supplier selection and order allocation. The additive utility model was used in his research. In this work, we used multi-objective decision analysis (MODA) with an additive value model to evaluate alternatives. MODA is a decision making process which involves inherently a combination of approaches to assess the modeling elements.

Decisions can be made either individually or by a group, with the group decision making being difficult to consolidate. A study on multi-criteria group decision making based on bilateral agreements was conducted by Xia and Chen (2015). There is no right answer to the decision problem, since it is based on subjectivity (Belton and Stewart 2002). MCDM will guide the decision process, and provide a more transparent decision through focusing on trade-offs of different objectives. This paper proposes a multi-objective decision making model that integrates both the quantitative and qualitative decision factors that are involved in the decision making process from the perspective of both the manufacturer and the distributor. A range of decision factors from operational to strategic levels are identified and considered in the model.

PROBLEM DESCRIPTION

Supply chain collaboration programs such as CRP proved their capabilities in reducing the cost of operating the supply chain. However the potential partners might consider other factors that outweigh the cost savings of a CRP. Those factors are generally qualitative factors and may have considerable influence during the decision making process. Factors such as trust, team attitude, cooperation, power shift, implementation capability and shared business philosophies are all potential factors in the decision. Quantitative and qualitative decision factors cannot be combined easily from the perspective of a decision maker because some factors may conflict with others. Therefore, potential business partners often have difficulty in analyzing a potential CRP relationship considering all the positive and risky consequences. They sometimes have opposite opinions about the possibility of certain consequences. In this paper, we propose a decision model that integrates both quantitative and qualitative decision factors, prioritize them and enable the decision makers to investigate the trade-offs between conflicting objectives. The model can be used by each potential partner separately and the output is a value that reflects the preferences of each partner with regards to the decision factors. Obviously, closer numerical values mean closer perspectives from the stakeholders to the decision problem.

METHODOLOGY

In this section we first discuss the components of MODA in general and how they support the decision making process. The second part of this section is focused on applying MODA on the problem to integrate quantitative and qualitative decision factors of starting a supply chain collaboration program between two partners.

Multiple Objective Decision Analysis (MODA)

MODA is an evaluation methodology that uses the information developed from stakeholder analysis to measure how well candidate solutions satisfy the fundamental objective of the stakeholders in a decision making problem. In essence, it measures the future value of an implemented solution to the decision problem (Parnell et al. 2011). Prior to measuring the value of any candidate solution, a qualitative model must be constructed that captures the critical objectives of the stakeholders. Once the qualitative model is completed, MODA will quantify the value of each candidate solution with respect to the objectives that are identified in the qualitative model. Therefore the process can be listed as follows:

1. *Collect the views of stakeholders*
   The stakeholders of a decision problem are the parties that are influenced by the decision.
2. *Determine the fundamental objective*
   The most basic and high level objective the stakeholders are trying to achieve.
3. *Determine the objectives and sub-objectives*
   Any fundamental objective contains different aspects so it can be broken out to specific objectives that each points out to one aspect of the fundamental objective.
4. *Construct the value tree*

A pictorial representation of hierarchy of identified objectives. The fundamental objective is placed on the top of the tree while the relations between objectives and sub-objectives shape the value tree.

5. *Determine the value measures*
   Each objective at the lowest level of the value tree needs a value measure. A measure, with natural or constructed scales, assesses how well each candidate solution attains the corresponding objective.

6. *Determine the value functions*
   Each value measure has a different scale with different units. Value functions are used to convert candidate solution scores on the value measures to a standard unit.

7. *Weights*
   A value, usually between 0 and 1, that represents the importance of an objective to stakeholders. The weights of sub-objectives under one objective should sum to 1, while the weights of objectives under the fundamental objective should also sum to 1.

8. *Quantitative value model*
   This is a quantitative method for trading off conflicting objectives (Kirkwood 1996). Although different mathematical relationships can achieve this, we use the most common method called the additive value model to calculate the value of each candidate solution.

A complete review of MODA can be found at (Parnell et al. 2011) where different aspects of the methodology are investigated along with examples from various application areas.

Model Development

This section is focused on developing a MODA model by following the steps mentioned above. As stated before, this work is motivated by a disagreement that existed between two major partners in healthcare sector over the value of a continuous replenishment program (CRP). They apparently had different views on the benefits of CRP. In order to propose a constructive approach towards reaching an agreement, MODA was selected to help in this process.

After series of interviews with key decision makers at both sides, a set of questions were designed on the issues that appeared during the interviews and also discussed in the literature as critical points of agreement for future success in CRP relationships. The questions were then distributed to a wide range of responders within both organizations including middle to top-level managers. Based on the responses, the most important objectives of the stakeholders were identified, which led to determining the fundamental objective, objectives and eventually the value tree. The value tree was then slightly modified through joint discussion sessions with individuals from both organizations. The involvement of both sides in this effort is critical for making it a successful path towards a sustainable agreement. Figure 1 illustrates the final version of the value tree. Objectives 1 through 4 are focused on quantitative impacts of CRP while objectives 5 & 6 are qualitative. In this hierarchy, the sub-objectives support the objectives and objectives support the fundamental objective. In other words, each objective can be achieved if its sub-objectives are achieved and likewise, the fundamental objective would be achieved if the objectives are satisfied.

The next step is to determine value measures with appropriate scales for each sub-objective. Value measures are developed based on their alignment with the objective and their scale of measurement. Value measure scales are either natural or constructed scales (Parnell et al.

2011). For example, "days on hand" is a natural scale for sub-objective 2.1 in Figure 1. On the other hand, constructed scale is required for sub-objective 5.2 because trust cannot be naturally measured. Table 2 lists the value measures, their corresponding scales and general shape of the value functions.

Figure 1: Value tree

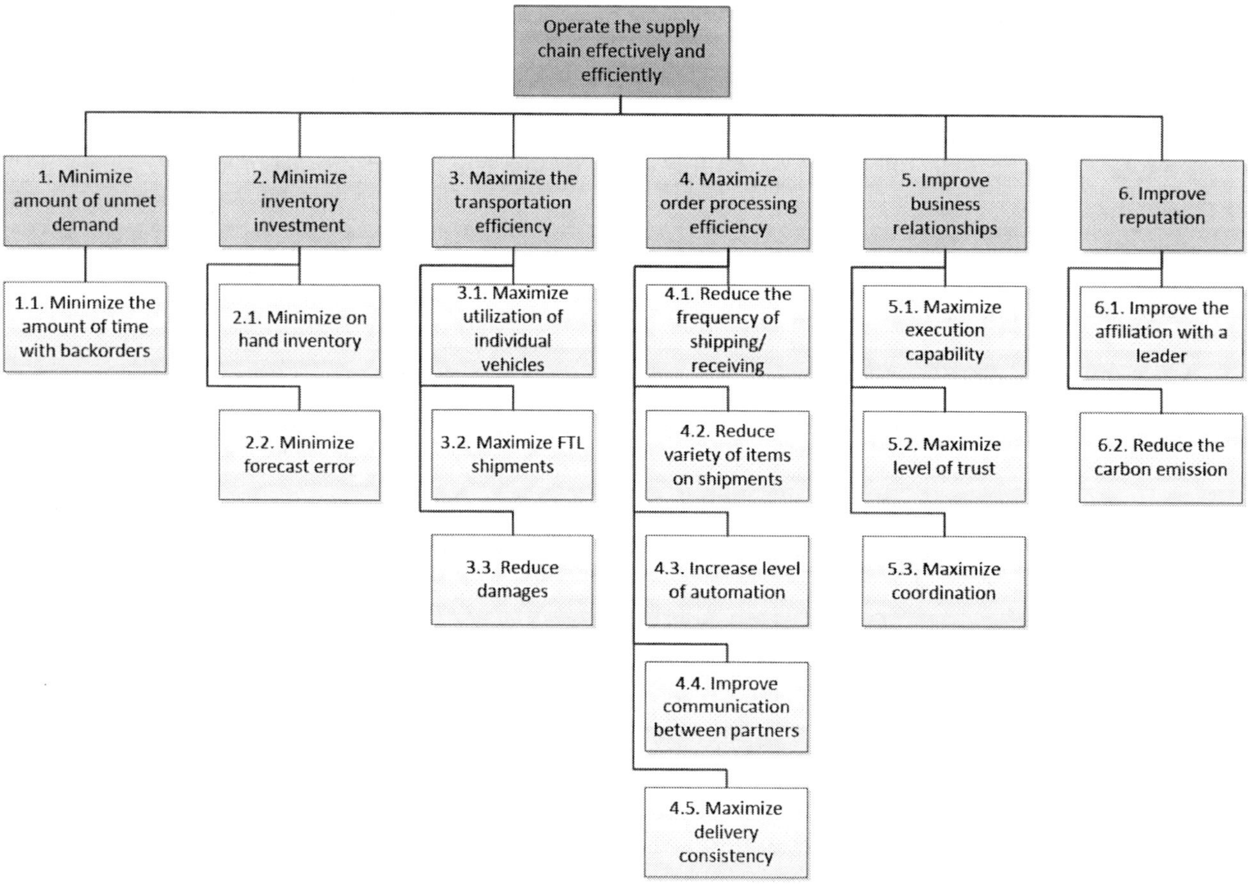

Table 2: Value measures, scales and functions

Sub-objective	Value measure	Type	Scale	Value function type
1.1	Avg back order time	Natural	[0, 30] days	Decreasing S shape
2.1	Avg days on hand	Natural	[20, 30] days	Decreasing concave
2.2	MAPE	Natural	[0%, 20%]	Decreasing linear
3.1	Avg vehicle utilization	Natural	[30%, 80%]	Increasing concave
3.2	Avg percentage of FTL shipments	Natural	[0%, 100%]	Increasing linear
3.3	Avg percentage of damaged goods	Natural	[0%, 10%]	Decreasing linear
4.1	Avg weekly order frequency	Natural	[0.5, 5]	Decreasing S shape
4.2	Avg weekly quantity per line	Natural	[1, 50] lines	Increasing linear
4.3	Automation level	Constructed	5 levels	Increasing concave
4.4	Communication level	Constructed	5 levels	Increasing linear
4.5	Percentage of delivery within the window	Natural	[60%, 100%]	Increasing convex
5.1	Execution capability level	Constructed	5 levels	Increasing linear
5.2	Trust	Constructed	5 levels	Increasing linear
5.3	Coordination	Constructed	5 levels	Increasing linear
6.1	Level of affiliation	Constructed	4 levels	Increasing linear
6.2	Avg distance traveled per ton	Natural	[250, 1000]	Decreasing linear

Once the value measures and their scales are determined, the corresponding value functions should be identified. For a single-dimensional value function, the x-axis is the scale of the value measure (e.g., days on hand) and y-axis is a standard unit of value scaled from 0 to 100. Continuous value functions typically follow four basic shapes of linear, concave, convex, and S curve (Figure 2). Depending on the impact of each value measure, value functions could be either monotonically increasing, as indicated in Figure 2, or decreasing. As suggested in (Kirkwood 1996), the shape of value functions are determined by consulting with subject experts. Once the general shape is determined, the experts should identify the increase/decrease in value from a specific incremental increase in the measure scale. Doing this multiple times up to the maximum on the measure scale will produce a piecewise linear function. The instance functions in Figure 2 are produced in linear piecewise fashion.

Figure 2: Value function types

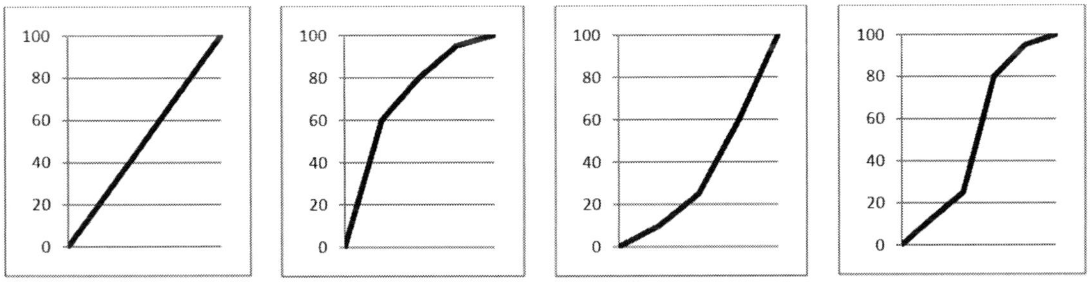

As Table 2 shows, appropriate scales must be constructed for the value measures that do not have natural scales. The scales need to be sufficiently clear and specific so the decision makers can determine the score of each candidate solution (Table 3). Constructing piecewise linear value functions for each value measure is the next step.

There are sixteen value measures in the model and each needs a value function. Although the general shapes are determined with the help of subject experts, the piecewise linear functions need to be constructed. This process is discussed in this paper for one value measure and the same approach could be used for developing similar functions for others. Note that the rest of the discussion represents ongoing work and has not been confirmed with the stakeholders.

As an example, consider the value measure of sub-objective 2.1, days on hand, from Table 2. Since the objective is to minimize days on hand, less days on hand is better. We first set the limits of the x-axis of the function for days on hand. These limits are determined based on what is expected as an ideal solution and worst feasible solution for average days of on hand inventory. Based on experts' opinions, the best we can achieve is 20 days and the maximum acceptable days of inventory is 30 days due to the distribution center capacity. Experts say the general shape of the value curve is decreasing concave. With 24 or less days, the candidate solution has a high value of 90 or above, but the value decreases rapidly beyond 24 days. The resulting value function (Figure 3) is piecewise linear, generally following the concave shape. Once this process is complete for every measure, a candidate solution's value for each measure can be derived from the constructed value functions using the candidate solution score. This process is the same for measures with constructed scales.

x_i is the score of measure i on the x-axis of value function ik

$v_i(x_i)$ is the value of measure i on the y-axis of value function ii-j

Table 3: Constructed scales for value measure with no natural scales

Automation level	
Level 0	Paper based methods for ordering, handling and receiving (OHR) activities. No telephone or fax
Level 1	Telephone and fax for ordering + paper based receiving (no scanning device)
Level 2	Email or GHX ordering and online shipment release confirmation + manual receiving (no scanning device)
Level 3	EDI ordering and ASN capability + minimal scanning in receiving (pallet level scanning)
Level 4	EDI ordering and ASN capability + full scanning capability in receiving (case level scanning)
Communication level	
Level 0	Indirect contact with customer service representatives (Email, Fax)
Level 1	Direct, real-time contact with customer service representatives (Telephone)
Level 2	Dedicated customer service representative (single point of contact)
Level 3	Highly skilled planner
Level 4	Dedicated highly skilled planner
Execution capability	
Level 0	Not capable: no experience
Level 1	Beginner: less than 1 year experience
Level 2	Intermediate: between 1 and 5 years of experience
Level 3	Good: between 5 and 10 years of experience with proven results
Level 4	Mastery: More than 10 years of experience with proven results
Trust	
Level 0	Opposite values and strong competition, Not mutual interests, One tries to have the upper hand
Level 1	Competition exists, transparency will harm, confidentiality provides an edge
Level 2	Neutral, partners are not willing to give aid to each other
Level 3	Partners are concerned about the shortcomings of each other and they are willing help sincerely
Level 4	Fully aligned goals, full transparency with minimal confidentiality
Coordination	
Level 0	No meeting and no coordination in failure occasions
Level 1	Occasional meetings for report exchange but no cooperative tactical planning
Level 2	Regular meeting to reactively tackle the problems
Level 3	Regular meeting with pro-active attitudes to avoid problems
Level 4	Regular and engaged meetings for cooperative tactical planning for production and distribution
Level of affiliation	
Level 0	No business affiliation
Level 1	Regular business relationship with no long term commitment
Level 2	Strategic business relationship with commitment
Level 3	Long term partnership agreement

Figure 3: value function for minimizing days of on hand inventory

x	$v(x)$
20	100
22	98
24	90
26	65
30	0

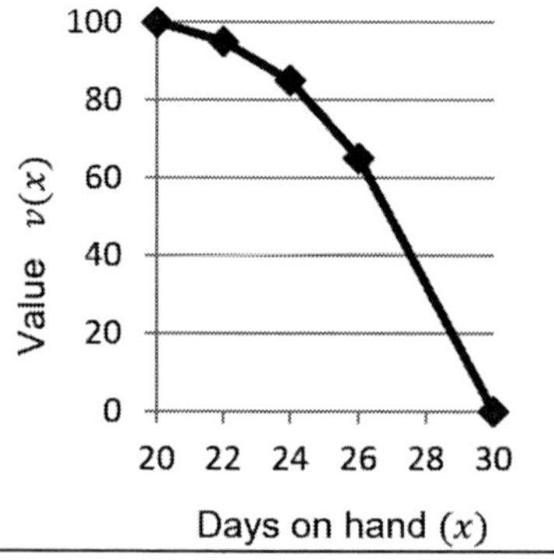

Typically, stakeholders do not view all value measures equally. In this problem, there are two stakeholders (i.e., manufacturer and distributor) and each has a different point of view and preferences towards the value measures of the model. Each stakeholder assigns different weights to the measures and also different scores to the measures which eventually produce two different overall values for each candidate solution. The weights depend on both the importance of the value measure and the impact of varying the score of value measures. We assess measure weights using the swing weight method by "swinging" the value measure score from its worst to its best. There are various ways to elicit weights from stakeholders which are discussed in (Kirkwood 1996,Clemen and Reilly 1999).

To develop weights, a matrix can be constructed in which the columns define the importance of the measures and rows define the impact of changing the value measures over their range (Table 4 and Table 5). A measure that is very important in arriving at a solution and any change across its range has a large impact on the decision should be placed on top left corner of the matrix. Also a measure with the opposite of such characteristics should be placed at the bottom right corner of the matrix. An arbitrary high number such as 100 should be assigned to the measure at the top left corner and an arbitrary low number such as 10 will be assigned to the measure at the bottom right corner. This arbitrary number is notated as f_i in the matrix. Once the measures are placed in the matrix and f_i values are determined, the measure weights (w_i), that are normalized values of f_i, can be computed using the following formula:

$$w_i = \frac{f_i}{\sum_{i=1}^{n} f_i}$$

Table 4: Swing weight matrix for determining measure weights (Manufacturer)

		Level of importance of the value measure								
		Critical			Important			Useful		
		Measure	f_i	w_i	Measure	f_i	w_i	Measure	f_i	w_i
Variation in measure range	Significant impact	3.2	100	0.10	4.3	80	0.08	5.2	65	0.07
		3.1	85	0.09	5.3	72	0.08	4.5	60	0.06
	Some impact	4.1	77	0.08	3.3	65	0.07	4.4	50	0.05
		4.2	70	0.07	1.1	55	0.06	5.1	35	0.04
	Minor impact	2.2	55	0.06	6.1	45	0.05			
					2.1	30	0.03	6.2	10	0.01

Table 5: Swing weight matrix for determining measure weights (Distributor)

		Level of importance of the value measure								
		Critical			Important			Useful		
		Measure	f_i	w_i	Measure	f_i	w_i	Measure	f_i	w_i
Variation in measure range	Significant impact	2.1	100	0.11	5.1	80	0.09	5.2	65	0.07
		4.2	85	0.09	4.5	72	0.08	4.1	60	0.06
	Some impact	1.1	77	0.08	4.4	60	0.06	3.1	35	0.04
		2.2	65	0.07	4.3	55	0.06			
	Minor impact	3.3	60	0.06	3.2	35	0.04			
		5.3	45	0.05	6.2	25	0.03	6.1	10	0.01

Once the measure weights for both stakeholders are determined, the quantitative value model can be formed for each stakeholder. The values of candidate solutions from the standpoint of each stakeholder can then be compared. The additive value model, which is the most common value model, is used here to compute the final value of the solutions. The candidate solutions that stakeholders consider in this decision making problem are two alternatives. They can either choose to start a CRP relationship or continue to have a non-CRP relationship.

RESULTS AND DISCUSSION

In this section, we compare the values of both candidate solutions (i.e., CRP and non-CRP) from the perspectives of both stakeholders (i.e., manufacturer and distributor). Table 6 shows the differences between stakeholders' views on each sub-objective with regard to both solutions. Total value of the solutions from the perspective of each stakeholder is computed in the last row of the table. Note that the total value of each solution can vary between 0 and 100.

As Figure 4 shows, the non-CRP relationship has an approximately equal overall appeal to both stakeholders. This might be the reason that they have sustained this relationship for a long time. However, the overall value of 62.04 and 64.83 are not very satisfying since there is a significant room for improvement in this business relationship. This is why they are looking for an alternative arrangement that can improve the value of their relationship. CRP as a general practice has been very appealing to many business partners in various sectors but the result of this study shows that there is a disagreement between the partners on the future value of CRP. While CRP increases the value of this business relationship for the manufacturer by 16 points ($\cong \mathbf{26\%}$), the distributor does not expect any overall increase. However, as both Figure 4 and Table 6 indicate, with the exception of a few value measures, the distributor's value on every value measure slightly increases or stays at the same level by moving from non-CRP to CRP. This means those few measures are the main reason for the slight decrease in the overall value for the distributor.

$V_m(\boldsymbol{CRP})$: is the total value of CRP from the perspective of manufacturerk
$V_m(\boldsymbol{NonCRP})$: is the total value of non-CRP from the perspective of manufacturer
$V_d(\boldsymbol{CRP})$: is the total value of CRP from the perspective of distributor
$V_d(\boldsymbol{NonCRP})$: is the total value of non-CRP from the perspective of distributor

Figure 4: Distribution of values between the value measures

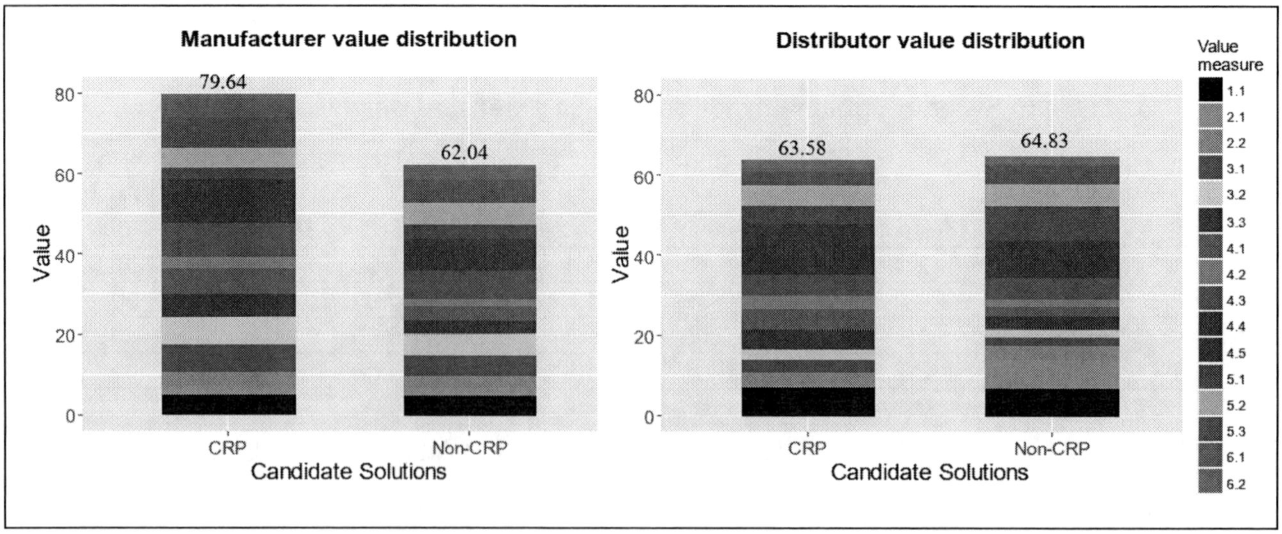

Table 6: Values of each candidate solution from the perspective of stakeholders

Stakeholder:	Manufacturer							Distributor						
Solution:		Non-CRP			CRP				Non-CRP			CRP		
Sub objective / Measure	Weight (w_i)	Score (x_i)	Value $v_i(x_i)$	$w_i v_i(x_i)$	Score (x_i)	Value $v_i(x_i)$	$w_i v_i(x_i)$	Weight (w_i)	Score (x_i)	Value $v_i(x_i)$	$w_i v_i(x_i)$	Score (x_i)	Value $v_i(x_i)$	$w_i v_i(x_i)$
1.1	.0577	10	82.5	4.76	7	90	5.19	.0829	10	82.5	6.84	9	85	7.05
2.1	.0314	26	65	2.04	26	65	2.04	.1076	26	65	7.00	30	0	0
2.2	.0577	0.1	50	2.88	0.09	55	3.17	.0700	0.1	50	3.50	0.09	55	3.85
3.1	.0891	0.5	58.34	5.20	0.65	80	7.13	.0377	0.5	58.34	2.20	0.65	80	3.01
3.2	.1048	0.51	51	5.35	0.67	67	7.02	.0377	0.51	51	1.92	0.67	67	2.52
3.3	.0681	0.05	50	3.41	0.02	80	5.45	.0646	0.05	50	3.23	0.02	80	5.17
4.1	.0807	3	42.5	3.43	2	80	6.46	.0646	3	42.5	2.74	2	80	5.17
4.2	.0734	10.5	21	1.54	18.76	37.52	2.75	.0915	10.5	21	1.92	18.76	37.52	3.43
4.3	.0839	3	85	7.13	4	100	8.39	.0592	3	85	5.03	3	85	5.03
4.4	.0524	2	50	2.62	4	100	5.24	.0646	2	50	3.23	4	100	6.46
4.5	.0629	0.85	87.5	5.50	0.9	95	5.97	.0775	0.8	80	6.20	0.8	80	6.2
5.1	.0367	4	100	3.67	3	75	2.75	.0861	4	100	8.61	2	50	4.31
5.2	.0681	3	75	5.11	3	75	5.11	.0700	3	75	5.25	3	75	5.25
5.3	.0755	3	75	5.66	4	100	7.55	.0484	4	100	4.84	3	75	3.63
6.1	.0472	2	66	3.11	3	100	4.72	.0108	2	66	0.71	2	66	0.71
6.2	.0105	550	60	0.63	500	66.67	0.70	.0269	550	60	1.61	500	66.67	1.79
		$V_m(nonCRP) =$		62.04	$V_m(CRP) =$		79.64		$V_d(nonCRP) =$		64.83	$V_d(CRP) =$		63.58

The value measures for sub-objectives 2.1 and 5.1 are negatively affected by significant margins. As Figure 1 shows, sub-objective 2.1 is minimizing on hand inventory and sub-objective 5.1 is maximizing execution capability. Apparently, the distributor believes CRP increases the inventory levels from average of 26 days of demand (current, non-CRP status) to 30 days. Also, the distributor is skeptical about the manufacturer's execution capability in CRP as opposed to non-CRP. Based on the measure weights, these two sub-objectives are the most important and the third most important objectives from the perspective of distributor therefore any change in their scores has a significant impact on the overall value. The value functions of these two measures are shown in Figure **5**.

Figure 5: Value function of average inventory days on hand (left) and execution capability (right)

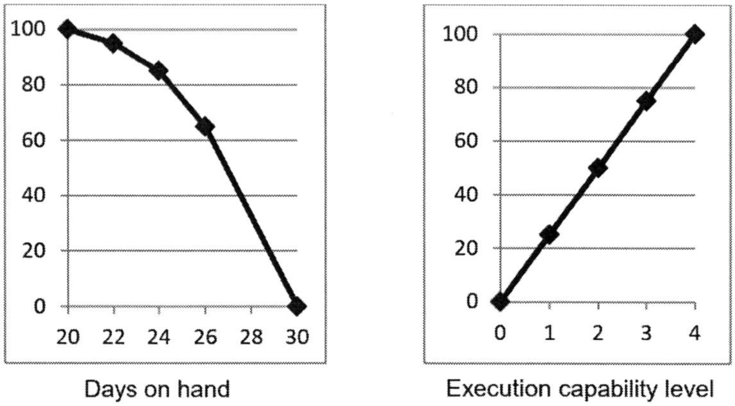

The impact of assigned weights to these measures is illustrated in Figure 6. While reducing the measure weight (f_i) of sub-objective 2.1 from 100 to zero can increase the overall value of CRP by almost 9 points, the weight of sub-objective 5.1 does not have a significant impact. The measure weights are varied one at a time assuming the weights of the other measures stay at the original level.

Figure 6: Sensitivity of CRP value to critical measure weights

Measure weight (f_i)	Obj 2.1	Obj 5.1
0	73.52	64.86
20	71.61	64.52
40	69.79	64.19
60	68.07	63.88
80	66.42	63.58
100	64.86	63.29

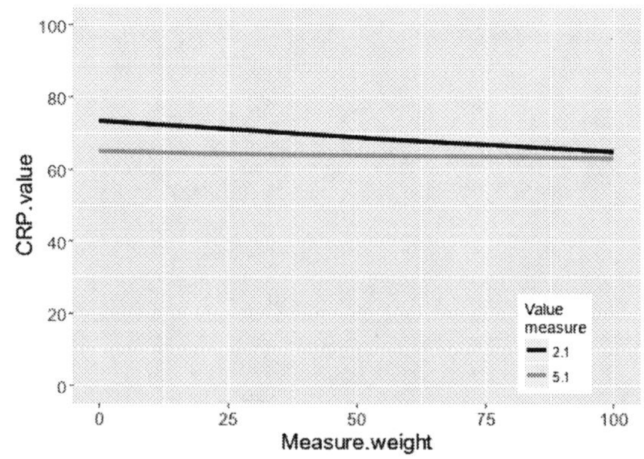

Similarly, the impact of average days of on hand inventory on the value of CRP is illustrated in Figure 7. Sub objective 2.1, minimizing on hand inventory, is the most important sub-objective for distributor (**Table 5**) and is negatively affected the most from the perspective of distributor in CRP (Figure 4.). The sensitivity analysis on this value measure shows that by reducing days of on hand inventory from 30 days, the value of CRP increases quickly until approximately 24 days where the slope of increase in value of CRP is significantly reduced. This analysis provides useful information to both partners about the difference of views on the most controversial objective. This motivates a constructive negotiation process on this objective which can lead to a guaranteed level of on hand inventory level from the manufacturer.

Figure 7: Sensitivity of CRP value to average days of on hand inventory

Measure score (x_i)	CRP value $v(x)$
30	63.58
29	65.01
28	66.72
27	68.43
26	70.14
25	71.20
24	72.25
23	72.78
22	73.30
21	73.57
20	73.83

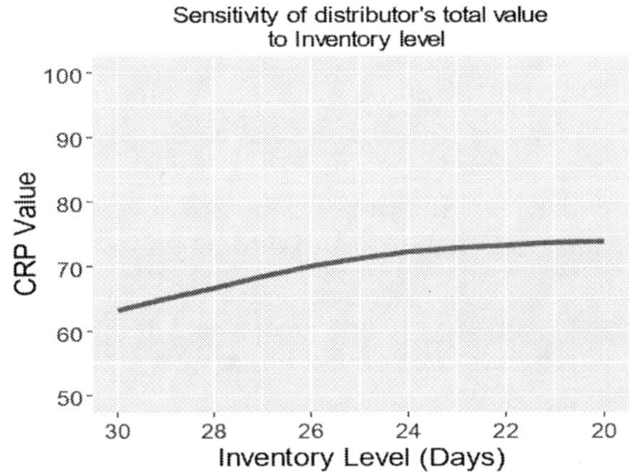

CONCLUSIONS AND FUTURE WORK

There are conflicting objectives associated with starting a supply chain collaboration program such as CRP. In addition, the stakeholders do not have the same view on the consequences of such programs. Therefore, reaching a sustainable agreement is very challenging and sometimes discourages both potential partners from the program. This paper models this decision making process by integrating the qualitative and quantitative decision factors in an framework that enables the stakeholders to quantify and communicate their views and preferences with each other. The model is in implementation process in a case study that involves a manufacturer and a distributor from healthcare sector. The preliminary results indicate that the stakeholders hold different views on each objective. The disagreement areas as well as critical sub-objectives that have significant impact on the decision outcome are identified.

One of the future research topics related to this paper is separating the analysis of quantitative (cost related) objectives and qualitative objectives. This way, the value should only represent the qualitative aspects of a candidate solution. Thus, cost of each solution will be evaluated across its value not as a part of it. Therefore, each solution will have a cost figure and a value figure and they can be different from the perspective of each stakeholder. This would enable the decision makers to evaluate the solutions and their positions on them in a two dimensional space, defined by cost and value.

REFERENCES

1. Iyer, A.V., Bergen, M.E., 1997. Quick response in manufacturer-retailer channels. Management Science, 43(4),559-70.

2. Schiano, W., McKenney, J., 1996. Spartan stores incorporated: Reengineering for efficient consumer response. HBS Case,9-396.

3. Clark, T.H., Croson, D., McKenney, J., Nolan, R., 1994. HE Butt Grocery Company: a leader in ECR implementation. HBS Case,9-195.

4. Keh, H.T., Park, S.Y., 1997. To market, to market: the changing face of grocery retailing. Long range planning, 30(6),836-46.

5. Sahin, F., Robinson, E.P., 2002. Flow coordination and information sharing in supply chains: review, implications, and directions for future research. Decision sciences, 33(4),505-36.

6. Cachon, G., Fisher, M., 1997. Campbell Soup's continuous replenishment program: evaluation and enhanced inventory decision rules. Production and Operations Management, 6(3),266-76.

7. Waller, M., Johnson, M.E., Davis, T., 1999. Vendor-managed inventory in the retail supply chain. Journal of business logistics, 20,183-204.

8. Sherman, R.J., 1998. Collaborative planning, forecasting & replenishment (CPFR): Realizing the promise of efficient consumer response through collaborative technology. Journal of Marketing Theory and Practice, 6(4),6-9.

9. Fliedner, G., 2003. CPFR: an emerging supply chain tool. Industrial Management & data systems, 103(1),14-21.

10. Sari, K., 2008. On the benefits of CPFR and VMI: A comparative simulation study. International Journal of Production Economics, 113(2),575-86.

11. Simatupang, T.M., Sridharan, R., 2005. An integrative framework for supply chain collaboration. The International Journal of Logistics Management, 16(2),257-74.

12. Doukidis, G.I., Matopoulos, A., Vlachopoulou, M., Manthou, V., Manos, B., 2007. A conceptual framework for supply chain collaboration: empirical evidence from the agri-food industry. Supply Chain Management: an international journal, 12(3),177-86.

13. Cao, M., Vonderembse, M.A., Zhang, Q., Ragu-Nathan, T., 2010. Supply chain collaboration: conceptualisation and instrument development. International Journal of Production Research, 48(22),6613-35.

14. Lee, H.L., So, K.C., Tang, C.S., 2000. The value of information sharing in a two-level supply chain. Management science, 46(5),626-43.

15. Cachon, G.P., Fisher, M., 2000. Supply chain inventory management and the value of shared information. Management science, 46(8),1032-48.

16. Cheung, K.L., Lee, H.L., 2002. The inventory benefit of shipment coordination and stock rebalancing in a supply chain. Management Science, 48(2),300-6.

17. Çetinkaya, S., Lee, C., 2000. Stock replenishment and shipment scheduling for vendor-managed inventory systems. Management Science, 46(2),217-32.

18. Chen, T., Chen, J., 2005. Optimizing supply chain collaboration based on joint replenishment and channel coordination. Transportation Research Part E: Logistics and Transportation Review, 41(4),261-85.

19. Yao, Y., Evers, P.T., Dresner, M.E., 2007. Supply chain integration in vendor-managed inventory. Decision Support Systems, 43(2),663-74.

20. Southard, P.B., Swenseth, S.R., 2008. Evaluating vendor-managed inventory (VMI) in non-traditional environments using simulation. International Journal of Production Economics, 116(2),275-87.

21. Ramanathan, U., 2014. Performance of supply chain collaboration–A simulation study. Expert Systems with Applications, 41(1),210-20.

22. Parsa, P., Rossetti, M., Zhang, S., Pohl, E., 2016. Quantifying the Benefits of Continuous Replenishment Program for Partner Selection.

23. Ananda, J., Herath, G., 2009. A critical review of multi-criteria decision making methods with special reference to forest management and planning. Ecological Economics, 68(10),2535-48.

24. Ramanathan, R., 2006. ABC inventory classification with multiple-criteria using weighted linear optimization. Computers & Operations Research, 33(3),695-700.

25. Zaeri, M.S., Sadeghi, A., Naderi, A., Kalanaki, A., Fasihy, R., Shorshani, S.M.H., Poyan, A., 2011. Application of multi criteria decision making technique to evaluation suppliers in supply chain management. African Journal of Mathematics and Computer Science Research, 4(3),100-6.

26. Vijayvagy, L., 2012. Decision framework for supplier selection through multi criteria evaluation models in supply chain. International Journal of Management and Innovation, 4(2),16.

27. Ghazinoory, S., Daneshmand-Mehr, M., Azadegan, A., 2012. Technology selection: application of the PROMETHEE in determining preferences [mdash] a real case of nanotechnology in Iran. Journal of the Operational Research Society, 64(6),884-97.

28. Caterino, N., Iervolino, I., Manfredi, G., Cosenza, E., 2009. Comparative analysis of multi-criteria decision-making methods for seismic structural retrofitting. Computer-Aided Civil and Infrastructure Engineering, 24(6),432-45.

29. Diaby, V., Campbell, K., Goeree, R., 2013. Multi-criteria decision analysis (MCDA) in health care: a bibliometric analysis. Operations Research for Health Care, 2(1),20-4.

30. Triantaphyllou, E., Shu, B., Sanchez, S.N., Ray, T., 1998. Multi-criteria decision making: an operations research approach. Encyclopedia of electrical and electronics engineering, 15,175-86.

31. Velasquez, M., Hester, P.T., 2013. An analysis of multi-criteria decision making methods. International Journal of Operations Research, 10(2),56-66.

32. Agarwal, P., Sahai, M., Mishra, V., Bag, M., Singh, V., 2011. A review of multi-criteria decision making techniques for supplier evaluation and selection. International journal of industrial engineering computations, 2(4),801-10.

33. Belton, V., Stewart, T., 2002. Multiple criteria decision analysis: an integrated approach. : Springer Science & Business Media.

34. Shahroudi, K., Rouydel, H., 2012. Using a multi-criteria decision making approach (ANP-TOPSIS) to evaluate suppliers in Iran's auto industry. International Journal of Applied Operational Research-An Open Access Journal, 2(2),0-.

35. Sanayei, A., Mousavi, S.F., Abdi, M., Mohaghar, A., 2008. An integrated group decision-making process for supplier selection and order allocation using multi-attribute utility theory and linear programming. Journal of the Franklin Institute, 345(7),731-47.

36. Xia, M., Chen, J., 2015. Multi-criteria group decision making based on bilateral agreements. European Journal of Operational Research, 240(3),756-64.

37. Parnell, G.S., Driscoll, P.J., Henderson, D.L., 2011. Decision making in systems engineering and management. : John Wiley & Sons.

38. Kirkwood, C.W., 1996. Strategic decision making. : Wadsworth Publ. Co.

39. Clemen, R.T., Reilly, T., 1999. Making hard decisions with DecisionTools Suite.

DECISION SCIENCES INSTITUTE

A Note on Modeling Product Allocation between Brick-and-Mortar and Online Stores

Hongkai Zhang
East Central University
Email: hzhang@ecok.edu

Hani I. Mesak
Louisiana Tech University
Email: mesak@cab.latech.edu

Jiehui Ma
University of Wisconsin-Whitewater
Email: maj@uww.edu

ABSTRACT

A mathematical programming model is developed and analytically solved in this study for the problem of optimally allocating a product by a monopolistic retailer to its brick-and-mortar and online stores under uncertain aggregate demand following a uniform probability distribution. Impacts of changes in six key model parameters on retailer's profitability are analytically examined.

KEYWORDS: Product allocation, Optimization, Simulation

INTRODUCTION

There has been a dramatic increase in the volume and coverage of goods and services sold online over the last two decades. While e-commerce was virtually nonexistent in the early 1990s, online sales stood at $263.3 billion and accounted for 5.6 percent of total retail sales in the U.S. economy in 2013 (Gorodnichenko et al., 2015). Major retailers such as Wal-Mart and Target currently operate not only brick-and-mortar stores but also online stores. In fact, online stores offer the convenience of consumer purchasing and allow retailers to reach those customers whom they were previously less likely to attract.

Some distinctive features of the offline and online market segments are noted in the literature. For example, Chu et al. (2007) find that across 12 vastly different product categories, consumers exhibit lower price sensitivities when they shop online than when they shop offline. Gorodnichenko et al. (2015) report that online prices are more flexible than prices charged in conventional stores. Fassnacht and Unterhuber (2016) provide experimental evidence that price differentiation with lower online prices is feasible. Because of the differences, a profit-maximizing retailer needs to resolve the strategic issue of optimally allocating a product for sale to its brick-and-mortar and online stores.

Our paper intends to tackle a problem of product allocation in a market, where a sole retailer, having achieved a monopolistic position through differentiation (Lee and Ng, 2001), sets prices in the offline and online segments and then allocates a certain quantity of a product to each segment to improve its profitability. Three notable studies are relevant to this paper. Lee and

Ng (2001) addressed the issue of optimal service capacity allocation and derived the optimal scheme of capacity allocation in a monopolistic market comprised of two segments under deterministic demand. Deng et al. (2008) studied capacity allocation in a multi-segment monopolistic market under uncertain demand following a Poisson distribution. They proposed the optimal policies of allocating capacity to the segments of higher revenue. Zeng (2013) developed multiple pricing strategies for a retailer who operates in a market composed of experienced and inexperienced consumers. Our paper, focusing on a profit-maximizing retailer under uncertain demand at the aggregate level, is significantly different from the three studies cited above in several aspects. First, a monopolistic market comprised of two segments (i.e., the offline and online segments), is incorporated in the modeling framework. Second, the quantity of a product to be allocated to each segment by the retailer is treated as a decision variable. Third, the demand in each segment is modeled as a continuous random variable. Fourth, the optimal allocation scheme is analytically determined under uncertain demand following a uniform probability distribution. Fifth, this study examines the impacts of changes in six key model parameters on retailer's profitability.

The three research questions that we attempt to address in this paper are specifically stated as follows: (i) What is the optimal scheme for a retailer to allocate K identical units of a product to the offline and online segments during a single selling season so that its expected total profit is maximized? (ii) What is the impact of changes in the unit salvage value of each segment on the retailer's profitability? (iii) What are the impacts of changes in the price sensitivities of each segment on retailer's profitability? We make the following basic assumptions while addressing these questions of strategic significance:

(i) The demand of each of the offline and online segments is affected by the prices charged in both segments. (In general, this assumption reflects the reality of consumer behavior. For example, the higher price of a textbook in a brick-and-mortar bookstore may force a student to buy a less expensive copy from an online bookstore.)

(ii) Consumers in each segment are well-informed of the prices in both segments, which are set at the beginning of the selling season.

(iii) The demand of each segment is heterogeneous and follows a continuous probability distribution conditioned by the prices charged in both segments.

The rest of the paper is organized as follows. In the next section, we develop the retailer's profit functions and then formulate a mathematical programming model to find the optimal allocation scheme for the product. The third section presents six propositions that highlight the optimal allocation scheme and the impacts of changes in six key model parameters on the retailer's profitability. The fourth section reports the computational results of a simulation experiment conducted to numerically compare nine alternative allocation schemes and examine the impacts of the six parameters mentioned above. Finally, our study concludes in its fifth section with a summary of its contributions, limitations, and directions for future research.

MODEL DEVELOPMENT

Let us consider a monopolistic retailer that has K identical units of a product to be allocated to its brick-and-mortar and online stores during a single selling season. The offline and online market segments for the product are denoted as Segments 1 and 2, respectively. Several terms are defined below in formulating the retailer's profit functions:

y_i	the quantity of the product to be allocated to Segment i (a decision variable);
P_i	the price per unit of the product charged to Segment i ($P_i > 0$);
C_i	the cost per unit of the product ($C_i > 0$);
S_i	the salvage value per unit of the product disposed of after the selling season ($S_i > 0$);
d_i	the aggregate demand for consumers of Segment i;
ω_i	the demand parameter of Segment i ($\omega_i > 0$);
$f(x\|\omega_i)$	the probability density function (p.d.f.) of d_i being a continuous random variable;
$E(d_i)$	the expected value of d_i;
π_i	the retailer's profit yielded from Segment i;
$E(\pi_i)$	the expected value of π_i;
π	the retailer's total profit yielded from the entire two-segment market;
$E(\pi)$	the expected value of π.

The aggregate demand in a market segment is usually uncertain (e.g., Deng et al., 2008). Since consumers are assumed to be well-informed of the prices charged to Segments 1 and 2, they would take the prices into consideration while making their purchases. Hence, the demand of Segment i, d_i (i = 1, 2), is modeled as a random variable following a probability distribution conditioned by P_1 and P_2. The p.d.f. of d_i takes the form of $f(x|\omega_i)$ and d_i is a continuous random variable.

For Segment i (i = 1, 2), if the demand (d_i) exceeds the quantity of the product allocated by the retailer (y_i), the profit (π_i) will equal the profit per unit multiplied by the number of units sold. On the other hand, if d_i is smaller than y_i, a portion of the allocated quantity, $y_i - d_i$, will be unsold and disposed of after the selling season at the unit salvage value, S_i. Hence, the retailer's profit yielded from segment i (i = 1, 2) is expressed as

$$\pi_i = \begin{cases} P_i d_i - C_i y_i + S_i (y_i - d_i), & d_i \le y_i, \\ (P_i - C_i) y_i, & d_i > y_i. \end{cases} \tag{1}$$

As d_i is a continuous random variable, the expected profit yielded from Segment i is derived from (1) as follows:

$$E(\pi_i) = (P_i - S_i)\int_0^{y_i} x f_i(x|\omega_i)dx - (C_i - S_i) y_i \int_0^{y_i} f_i(x|\omega_i)dx + (P_i - C_i) y_i \int_{y_i}^{\infty} f_i(x|\omega_i)dx . \tag{2}$$

Following Azoury (1985), we model the aggregate demand d_i as a uniformly distributed random variable. The p.d.f. of d_i is assumed to take the following continuous form:

$$f(x|\omega_i) = \begin{cases} 1/\omega_i, & if \;\; 0 < x < \omega_i, \\ 0, & if \;\; x \ge \omega_i, \end{cases} \tag{3}$$

where $\omega_i > 0$. The expected demand of Segment i, based on (3), is given by

$$E(d_i) = \int_0^{\omega_i} \frac{x}{\omega_i} dx = \frac{\omega_i}{2}. \qquad (4)$$

Expression (4) shows that the demand parameter, ω_i, equals twice the expected demand, $E(d_i)$, and thus serves as an indicator of the aggregate demand of Segment *i*.

Substituting (3) into (2) and carrying out the integrations yields

$$E(\pi_i) = (P_i - C_i)y_i - \frac{(P_i - S_i)}{2\omega_i} y_i^2, \quad if \;\; y_i < \omega_i; \qquad (5)$$

$$E(\pi_i) = \frac{(P_i - S_i)}{2}\omega_i - (C_i - S_i)y_i, \quad if \;\; y_i \geq \omega_i. \qquad (6)$$

The retailer's expected total profit from the entire two-segment market is expressed as

$$E(\pi) = E(\pi_1) + E(\pi_2). \qquad (7)$$

Given *K* identical units of a product, which is to be allocated by the retailer during a single selling season for sale to the offline and online segments, we aim at finding the optimal quantity to be allocated to Segment *i* (*i* = 1, 2), y_i^*, to maximize the retailer's expected total profit. The problem may, therefore, be formulated as follows:

$$\begin{aligned} & \underset{y_1, y_2}{Max} \;\; [E(\pi_1) + E(\pi_2)] \\ \text{s.t.} \quad & y_1 + y_2 \leq K, \quad y_1, \; y_2 \geq 0. \end{aligned} \qquad (8)$$

As it is assumed that the demand of each segment is dictated by both prices P_1 and P_2, a linear demand model introduced in Huang et al. (2013) is employed in this study to model the expected demand of Segment *i* (*i* = 1, 2):

$$E(d_1) = \alpha_1 - \beta_1 P_1 + \beta_{12} P_2, \qquad (9)$$

$$E(d_2) = \alpha_2 - \beta_2 P_2 + \beta_{21} P_1, \qquad (10)$$

where, $\alpha_1, \alpha_2, \beta_1, \beta_2, \beta_{12}, \beta_{21} > 0$.

For *i* = 1, 2, the constant α_i captures the part of the aggregate demand of Segment *i* that does not vary with prices; β_i measures the price sensitivity of the demand of Segment *i* to changes in the price charged in the same segment, P_i; β_{12} measures the price sensitivity of the demand of Segment 1 to changes in the price charged in Segment 2, P_2; similarly, β_{21} measures the price sensitivity of the demand of Segment 2 to changes in P_1.

OPTIMAL ALLOCATION OF PRODUCT QUANTITIES

Following the approach of Lee and Ng (2001), this study focuses on an optimal interior solution to model (8) such that $y_1^* + y_2^* < K$. In each of the following two cases, we first present a solution to model (8) and then study the impacts of changes in the unit salvage value and price sensitivities of each segment on the retailer's optimal expected total profit.

Case 1: $y_i < \omega_i$ $(i = 1, 2)$

In this case, the quantity of the product allocated to Segment i is less than ω_i. Three propositions related to this case are introduced below, for which the proofs are found in the Appendix.

Proposition 1. *Given* $\sum_{i=1}^{2} \frac{(P_i - C_i)}{(P_i - S_i)} \omega_i < K$, $P_i > C_i$ *and* $P_i > S_i$, *the retailer's expected total profit* $E(\pi)$ *reaches its maximal level* $E^*(\pi) = \sum_{i=1}^{2} E^*(\pi_i)$ *at* $y_i^* = \frac{(P_i - C_i)}{(P_i - S_i)} \omega_i$, *where* $E^*(\pi_i) = \frac{(P_i - C_i)^2}{2(P_i - S_i)} \omega_i$, $i = 1, 2$.

According to Proposition 1, the retailer can maximize its expected total profit by allocating the quantity of the product to each segment at the optimal level. The optimal quantity allocated to Segment i, y_i^*, is determined by the price charged, the unit cost, the unit salvage value, and the expected demand of the segment (see expression (4)). The conditions of $P_i > C_i$ and $P_i > S_i$ indicate $y_i^* > 0$ $(i = 1, 2)$.

Proposition 2. *Given* $P_i > C_i$ *and* $P_i > S_i$ $(i = 1, 2)$ *and all other things being equal,* $E^*(\pi)$ *is monotonically increasing in* S_i.

Proposition 3. *Given* $P_i > C_i$ *and* $P_i > S_i$ $(i = 1, 2)$ *and all other things being equal:*

(i) $E^*(\pi)$ *is monotonically decreasing in* β_i $(i = 1, 2)$.
(ii) $E^*(\pi)$ *is monotonically increasing in* β_{ij} $(i, j = 1, 2;\ i \neq j)$.

Proposition 2 shows, as expected, that profitability is enhanced as the salvage values become larger. Proposition 3 demonstrates that profitability is enhanced as the cross-price sensitivities among segments become larger and the segments' self-price sensitivities become smaller.

Case 2. $y_i \geq \omega_i$ $(i = 1, 2)$

In this case, the quantity of the product allocated to Segment i is more than or equal to ω_i. Three propositions are introduced for this case, for which the proofs are found in the Appendix.

Proposition 4. *Given* $(C_i - S_i) > 0$, $P_i + S_i - 2C_i > 0$, *and* $\sum_{i=1}^{2} \omega_i \leq K$, *the firm's expected total profit* $E(\pi)$ *reaches its maximal level* $E^*(\pi) = \sum_{i=1}^{2} E^*(\pi_i)$ *at* $y_i^* = \omega_i$ *for* $i = 1, 2$, *where*

$$E^*(\pi_i) = \frac{(P_i + S_i - 2C_i)}{2} \omega_i .$$

Proposition 4 shows that for Case 2, the retailer should allocate the quantity of the product exactly equal to twice the expected demand of each segment to maximize its expected total profit (see expression (4)).

Proposition 5. *Given all other things being equal,* $E^*(\pi)$ *is monotonically increasing in* S_i (i = 1, 2).

Proposition 6. *Given all other things being equal:*

(i) *For* $P_i + S_i - 2C_i > 0$, $E^*(\pi)$ *is monotonically decreasing in* β_i (i = 1, 2).

(ii) *For* $P_i + S_i - 2C_i > 0$, $E^*(\pi)$ *is monotonically increasing in* β_{ij} ($i, j = 1, 2;\ i \neq j$).

Proposition 5 shows, as expected, that profitability is enhanced as the salvage values become larger. Proposition 6 demonstrates that profitability is enhanced as the cross-price sensitivities among segments become larger and the segments' self-price sensitivities become smaller.

NUMERICAL ILLUSTRATIONS

This section presents a simulation experiment to (i) compare the optimal allocation scheme with other eight alternative allocation schemes and (ii) explore the impacts of six model parameters on the retailer's expected total profit. For illustrative purposes, the experiment is conducted only for Case 1 discussed in the third section. Due to the empirical evidence that consumers are less price sensitive when they shop online (see Chu et al., 2008), we particularly choose the values of β_1 and β_2 such that $\beta_1 > \beta_2$. The base values of all the model parameters chosen for the experiment are given below:

α_1 = 40000 units, α_2 = 30000 units; $\beta_1 = 45$, $\beta_2 = 35$; $\beta_{12} = 20$, $\beta_{21} = 15$;
P_1 = \$550, P_2 = \$450; C_1 = \$350, C_2 = \$200; S_1 = \$150, S_2 = \$150.

Based on Proposition 1 developed for Case 1 (see the previous section), the optimal allocation scheme (y_1^*, y_2^*) and the corresponding expected total profit $E^*(\pi)$ are calculated and reported in Table 1. The expected demands of Segments 1 and 2 (determined by expressions (9) and (10), respectively) are also shown in the table. It is found that for the selected values of model parameters, the optimal allocation scheme (y_1^*= 24250 units, y_2^* = 37500 units) yields the highest expected total profit of \$7,112,500 in comparison to the other eight allocation schemes. The expected total profit for each of the other allocation schemes are computed using expression (5) noting from expression (4) that $\omega_i = 2E(d_i)$; $i = 1,2$.

The impacts of changes in each of the six key parameters are investigated while all the other parameters are held constant at their aforementioned base values, and the computational results are reported in Table 2. As shown in the table, an increase in either of S_1, S_2, β_{12}, or β_{21} enhances retailer's profitability, whereas an increase in either β_1 or β_2 reduces the profitability. These findings are consistent with Propositions 2 and 3.

SUMMARY AND CONCLUSIONS

This paper tackles the problem of optimally allocating K identical units of a product by a monopolistic retailer to its brick-and-mortar and online stores under uncertain demand following a uniform probability distribution. A mathematical programming model is developed and then analytically solved to determine the optimal scheme of product allocation. In addition, the impacts of changes in the unit salvage value and the two types of price sensitivity for both offline and online segments are analytically investigated. A simulation experiment is conducted to

Table 1 Alternative schemes of quantity allocation and the resultant expected total profits

Prices ($/unit)		Expected Demands (in units)		Allocation Schemes (in units)		Expected Total Profit
$P_1 = \$550$	$P_2 = \$450$	$E(d_1) = 24250$	$E(d_2) = 22500$	$y_1^* = 24250$	$y_2^* = 37500$	$E^*(\pi) = \$7,112,500$
$P_1 = \$550$	$P_2 = \$450$	$E(d_1) = 24250$	$E(d_2) = 22500$	$y_1 = 20000$	$y_2 = 37500$	$E(\pi) = \$7,038,016$
$P_1 = \$550$	$P_2 = \$450$	$E(d_1) = 24250$	$E(d_2) = 22500$	$y_1 = 30000$	$y_2 = 37500$	$E(\pi) = \$6,976,160$
$P_1 = \$550$	$P_2 = \$450$	$E(d_1) = 24250$	$E(d_2) = 22500$	$y_1 = 24250$	$y_2 = 30000$	$E(\pi) = \$6,925,000$
$P_1 = \$550$	$P_2 = \$450$	$E(d_1) = 24250$	$E(d_2) = 22500$	$y_1 = 24250$	$y_2 = 40000$	$E(\pi) = \$7,091,667$
$P_1 = \$550$	$P_2 = \$450$	$E(d_1) = 24250$	$E(d_2) = 22500$	$y_1 = 20000$	$y_2 = 30000$	$E(\pi) = \$6,850,515$
$P_1 = \$550$	$P_2 = \$450$	$E(d_1) = 24250$	$E(d_2) = 22500$	$y_1 = 30000$	$y_2 = 40000$	$E(\pi) = \$6,955,326$
$P_1 = \$550$	$P_2 = \$450$	$E(d_1) = 24250$	$E(d_2) = 22500$	$y_1 = 20000$	$y_2 = 40000$	$E(\pi) = \$7,017,182$
$P_1 = \$550$	$P_2 = \$450$	$E(d_1) = 24250$	$E(d_2) = 22500$	$y_1 = 30000$	$y_2 = 30000$	$E(\pi) = \$6,788,660$

Table 2 The impacts of six key model parameters on the optimal expected total profit

Model Parameters	Expected Demands (in units)		Allocation Schemes (in units)		Expected Total Profit
$S_1 = \$130$/ unit	$E(d_1) = 24250$	$E(d_2) = 22500$	$y_1^* = 23095$	$y_2^* = 37500$	$E^*(\pi) = \$6,997,024$
$S_1 = \$170$/ unit	$E(d_1) = 24250$	$E(d_2) = 22500$	$y_1^* = 25526$	$y_2^* = 37500$	$E^*(\pi) = \$7,240,132$
$S_2 = \$130$/ unit	$E(d_1) = 24250$	$E(d_2) = 22500$	$y_1^* = 24250$	$y_2^* = 35156$	$E^*(\pi) = \$6,819,531$
$S_2 = \$170$/ unit	$E(d_1) = 24250$	$E(d_2) = 22500$	$y_1^* = 24250$	$y_2^* = 40179$	$E^*(\pi) = \$7,447,321$
$\beta_1 = 35$	$E(d_1) = 29750$	$E(d_2) = 22500$	$y_1^* = 29750$	$y_2^* = 37500$	$E^*(\pi) = \$7,662,500$
$\beta_1 = 55$	$E(d_1) = 18750$	$E(d_2) = 22500$	$y_1^* = 18750$	$y_2^* = 37500$	$E^*(\pi) = \$6,562,500$
$\beta_2 = 25$	$E(d_1) = 24250$	$E(d_2) = 27000$	$y_1^* = 24250$	$y_2^* = 45000$	$E^*(\pi) = \$8,050,000$
$\beta_2 = 45$	$E(d_1) = 24250$	$E(d_2) = 18000$	$y_1^* = 24250$	$y_2^* = 30000$	$E^*(\pi) = \$6,175,000$
$\beta_{12} = 15$	$E(d_1) = 22000$	$E(d_2) = 22500$	$y_1^* = 22000$	$y_2^* = 37500$	$E^*(\pi) = \$6,887,500$
$\beta_{12} = 25$	$E(d_1) = 26500$	$E(d_2) = 22500$	$y_1^* = 26500$	$y_2^* = 37500$	$E^*(\pi) = \$7,337,500$
$\beta_{21} = 10$	$E(d_1) = 24250$	$E(d_2) = 19750$	$y_1^* = 24250$	$y_2^* = 32917$	$E^*(\pi) = \$6,539,583$
$\beta_{21} = 20$	$E(d_1) = 24250$	$E(d_2) = 25250$	$y_1^* = 24250$	$y_2^* = 42083$	$E^*(\pi) = \$7,685,417$

numerically demonstrate the superiority of the optimal allocation scheme and the impacts of six model parameters on retailer's profitability.

Our exploratory study reveals several directions for future research. First, this study provides the analytical solutions to the problem of optimizing product allocation under uncertain demand following a uniform probability distribution. The demand following other probability distributions could be incorporated in the modeling framework. Second, in this study we focus on a retailer in a monopolistic market. Developing a model for a competitive environment would be a plausible extension. Third, while the optimal allocation scheme is determined in this study for a single product, a multiple-product scenario would be explored in the future. In addition, prices were assumed to have been determined exogenously. Treating prices as decision variables would offer an interesting direction for future research.

APPENDIX

Derivation of expression (5)

Given $y_i < \omega_i$, substituting (3) into (2) and carrying out the three integrations yield:

$$E(\pi_i) = (P_i - S_i)\int_0^{y_i}\frac{x}{\omega_i}dx - (C_i - S_i)y_i\int_0^{y_i}\frac{1}{\omega_i}dx + (P_i - C_i)y_i\int_{y_i}^{\omega_i}\frac{1}{\omega_i}dx$$

$$= \frac{(P_i - S_i)}{2\omega_i}y_i^2 - \frac{(C_i - S_i)}{\omega_i}y_i^2 + (P_i - C_i)y_i - \frac{(P_i - C_i)}{\omega_i}y_i^2$$

$$= (P_i - C_i)y_i - \frac{(P_i - S_i)}{2\omega_i}y_i^2. \qquad \text{(A.1)}$$

Derivation of expression (6)

Given $y_i \geq \omega_i$, substituting (3) into (2) and carrying out the three integrations yield:

$$E(\pi_i) = (P_i - S_i)\int_0^{\omega_i}\frac{x}{\omega_i}dx - (C_i - S_i)y_i\int_0^{\omega_i}\frac{1}{\omega_i}dx = \frac{(P_i - S_i)}{2}\omega_i - (C_i - S_i)y_i. \qquad \text{(A.2)}$$

Proof of Proposition 1

Given the objective function of model (8) where $E(\pi_i)$ takes expression (5), the first-order necessary condition for optimality implies that

$$\frac{\partial E(\pi)}{\partial y_i} = (P_i - C_i) - \frac{(P_i - S_i)}{\omega_i}y_i = 0, \quad i = 1, 2. \qquad \text{(A.3)}$$

Solving the pair of equations (A.3) simultaneously, we obtain

$$y_i^* = \frac{(P_i - C_i)}{(P_i - S_i)}\omega_i, \quad i = 1, 2. \tag{A.4}$$

The total optimal quantity of the product allocated to Segments 1 and 2 is given by

$$\sum_{i=1}^{2} y_i^* = \sum_{i=1}^{2} \frac{(P_i - C_i)}{(P_i - S_i)}\omega_i. \tag{A.5}$$

A feasible interior solution to model (8) requires $\sum_{i=1}^{2} \frac{(P_i - C_i)}{(P_i - S_i)}\omega_i < K$. Substituting y_i^* (i = 1, 2) into expressions (5) and (7) yields

$$E^*(\pi) = \sum_{i=1}^{2} \frac{(P_i - C)^2}{2(P_i - S_i)}\omega_i. \tag{A.6}$$

We now prove that the retailer's expected total profit $E(\pi)$ reaches its maximal level, $E^*(\pi)$, at y_i^* (i = 1, 2).

In our case, $\frac{\partial E^2(\pi)}{\partial y_i^2} = (-1)\frac{(P_i - S_i)}{\omega_i} < 0, \quad \frac{\partial E^2(\pi)}{\partial y_1 \partial y_2} = 0 \ \ and \ \ \frac{\partial E^2(\pi)}{\partial y_2 \partial y_1} = 0.$

Hence, $\left(\frac{\partial E^2(\pi)}{\partial y_1 \partial y_2}\right)\left(\frac{\partial E^2(\pi)}{\partial y_2 \partial y_1}\right) - \left(\frac{\partial E^2(\pi)}{\partial y_1^2}\right)\left(\frac{\partial E^2(\pi)}{\partial y_2^2}\right) < 0.$

The sufficient condition for $E(\pi)$ to reach its maximal level $E^*(\pi)$ at y_i^* (i = 1, 2) is satisfied. ■

Proof of Proposition 2

Consider $E^*(\pi) = \sum_{i=1}^{2} E^*(\pi_i)$, where $E^*(\pi_i) = \frac{(P_i - C_i)^2}{2(P_i - S_i)}\omega_i$ (see Proposition 1). We obtain the first partial derivative with respect to S_i :

$$\frac{\partial E^*(\pi)}{\partial S_i} = \frac{(P_i - C_i)^2}{2(P_i - S_i)^2}\omega_i. \tag{A.7}$$

Given $P_i > C_i$ *and* $P_i > S_i$, $\frac{\partial E^*(\pi)}{\partial S_i} > 0$ and hence, $E^*(\pi)$ is monotonically increasing in S_i. ■

Proof of Proposition 3

Consider $E^*(\pi) = \sum_{i=1}^{2} E^*(\pi_i)$, where $E^*(\pi_i) = \frac{(P_i - C_i)^2}{2(P_i - S_i)}\omega_i$ and $\omega_i = 2(\alpha_i - \beta_i P_i + \beta_{ij} P_j)$ for i, j = 1, 2; $i \neq j$. We first obtain the first partial derivative with respect to β_i:

$$\frac{\partial E^*(\pi)}{\partial \beta_i} = \frac{(P_i - C_i)^2}{(P_i - S_i)}(-P_i). \tag{A.8}$$

Given $P_i > C_i$ and $P_i > S_i$, $\frac{\partial E^*(\pi)}{\partial \beta_i} < 0$ and hence, $E^*(\pi)$ is monotonically decreasing in β_i.

We also obtain the first partial derivative with respect to β_{ij}:

$$\frac{\partial E^*(\pi)}{\partial \beta_{ij}} = \frac{(P_i - C)^2}{(P_i - S_i)} P_j .$$

Given $P_i > C_i$ and $P_i > S_i$, $\frac{\partial E^*(\pi)}{\partial \beta_{ij}} > 0$ and hence, $E^*(\pi)$ is monotonically increasing in β_{ij}. ■

Proof of Proposition 4

In Case 2, the focal firm's expected profit from segment i, $E(\pi_i)$, takes expression (6), which indicates that given $(C_i - S_i) > 0$,

$$\frac{(P_i - S_i)}{2}\omega_i - (C_i - S_i)y_i \le \frac{(P_i - S_i)}{2}\omega_i - (C_i - S_i)\omega_i \text{ holds for any } y_i \ge \omega_i \ (i = 1, 2).$$

Hence,

$$\sum_{i=1}^{2}\frac{(P_i - S_i)}{2}\omega_i - (C_i - S_i)y_i \le \sum_{i=1}^{2}\frac{(P_i - S_i)}{2}\omega_i - (C_i - S_i)\omega_i = \sum_{i=1}^{2}\frac{(P_i + S_i - 2C)_i}{2}\omega_i . \ ■$$

Proof of Proposition 5

Consider $E^*(\pi) = \sum_{i=1}^{2} E^*(\pi_i)$, where $E^*(\pi_i) = \frac{(P_i + S_i - 2C)_i}{2}\omega_i$ (see Proposition 4). We obtain the first partial derivative with respect to S_i:

$$\frac{\partial E^*(\pi)}{\partial S_i} = \frac{1}{2}\omega_i > 0. \tag{A.9}$$

Hence, $E^*(\pi)$ is monotonically increasing in S_i. ■

Proof of Proposition 6

Consider $E^*(\pi) = \sum_{i=1}^{2} E^*(\pi_i)$, where $E^*(\pi_i) = \frac{(P_i + S_i - 2C_i)}{2}\omega_i$ and $\omega_i = 2(\alpha_i - \beta_i P_i + \beta_{ij} P_j)$ for $i, j = 1, 2$; $i \neq j$. We first obtain the first partial derivative with respect to β_i:

$$\frac{\partial E^*(\pi)}{\partial \beta_i} = (P_i + S_i - 2C_i)(-P_i). \tag{A.10}$$

(i) If $P_i + S_i - 2C_i > 0$, then $\frac{\partial E^*(\pi)}{\partial \beta_i} < 0$ and hence, $E^*(\pi)$ is monotonically decreasing in β_i.

We also obtain the first partial derivative with respect to β_{ij}:

$$\frac{\partial E^*(\pi)}{\partial \beta_{ij}} = (P_i + S_i - 2C_i)P_j. \tag{A.11}$$

(ii) If $P_i + S_i - 2C_i > 0$, then $\frac{\partial E^*(\pi)}{\partial \beta_{ij}} > 0$ and hence, $E^*(\pi)$ is monotonically increasing in β_{ij}. ∎

REFERENCES

Azoury, K. S. (1985). Bayes solution to dynamic inventory models under unknown demand distribution. *Management Science*, *31*(9), 1150-1160.

Chu, J., Chintagunta, P. & Cebollada, J. (2008). A comparison of within-household price sensitivity across online and offline channels. *Marketing Science*, *27*(2), 283–299.

Deng, H., Wang, Q., Leong, G. K., & Sun, S. X. (2008). The usage of opportunity cost to maximize performance in revenue management. *Decision Sciences*, *39*(4), 737-758.

Fassnacht, M. & Unterhuber, S. (2016). Consumer response to online/offline price differentiation. *Journal of Retailing & Consumer Services*, *28*, 137-148.

Gorodnichenko, Y., Sheremirov, V., & Talavera, O. (2015). Price setting in online markets: Does it click? *Working Paper Series* (*Federal Reserve Bank of Boston*), *15*(1), 1-60.

Huang, J., Leng M., & Parlar, M. (2013). Demand functions in decision modeling: A comprehensive survey and research directions. *Decision Sciences*, *44*(3), June, 557-609.

Lee, K. S. & Ng, I. C. L. (2001). Advance sale of service capacities: Theoretical analysis of the impact of price sensitivity on pricing and capacity allocations. *Journal of Business Research*, *54*, 219-225.

Zeng, C. (2013). Optimal advance selling strategy under price commitment. *Pacific Economic Review*, *18*(2), 233–258.

DECISION SCIENCES INSTITUTE

A note on the simple trading range break-out rule for NASDAQ Index

Louie Ren
University of Houston-Victoria
Email: renl@uhv.edu

ABSTRACT

In this study, we test various simple trading range break-out rules for the NASDAQ index. Our results indicate that simple trading range break-out rules do have predictive power for profitability. It does not support the market efficiency hypothesis.

DECISION SCIENCES INSTITUTE

A Simulation Model for Comparing the Robustness of Alternative Liquefied Natural Gas (LNG) Annual Delivery Programs (ADPs)

Authors: Fatih Mutlu[*], Hakan Yildiz[+], Erkut Sonmez[#], Shaligram Pokharel[*]

[*] *Qatar University, Mechanical and Industrial Engineering Department, Doha, Qatar*
[+] *Michigan State University, Eli Broad College of Business, East Lansing, MI, USA*
[#] *Boston College, School of Management, Boston, MA, USA*

ABSTRACT

An ADP is a production and delivery plan LNG suppliers to fulfill contractual requirements. It is subject to random disturbances during the implementation, which may increase the planned costs. We develop a model simulating the ADP implementation along with contingency plans, and compare alternative ADPs using the model.

KEYWORDS: LNG supply chain, simulation, robustness, maritime logistics

INTRODUCTION

Natural gas, the source of one quarter of the global energy demand (BP Statistics, 2014), can be distributed from source to distant markets in liquid form, which is known as liquefied natural gas (LNG). Thanks to the liquefaction technology, which enables compressing the volume at an approximate ratio of 600-to-1, large volumes of natural gas can be loaded into specialized vessels in the form of LNG and sold globally. Both the liquefaction and delivery of LNG have very high capital and operational expenses. Thus LNG investments can economically be feasible with long-term sales and delivery contracts. This brings along challenging logistics problems for the LNG suppliers that necessitate an integrated plan of production, inventory, and delivery of LNG over the course of a year. Such a plan is typically referred to as the annual delivery program (ADP) in the LNG industry. In recent years, a growing body of literature focuses on preparing a cost efficient ADP has emerged (Halvorsen-Weare and Fagerholt, 2013a; Rakke et al., 2011; Stålhane et al., 2012; Goel et al., 2012, 2015; Shao et al., 2015; Mutlu et al., 2016a,b).

ADP is a tactical level plan, spanning approximately a set of year long operations, and to our knowledge, vast majority of the studies aiming at cost optimization assume deterministic problem parameters. However, there are many random elements inherent to the LNG logistics operations, the most prevalent of which is the vessel cruise times. Due to weather conditions, altering regulations for maritime transportation, and other factors such as marine pirates and breakdowns, cruise times can be longer than planned. In this case, the vessel can be late for its next delivery, which will affect the rest of the ADP including inventory levels at the liquefaction (production) port, and delivery times and volumes. This will result in increased costs as the LNG supplier has to speed-up its vessels, charter-in additional vessels, or cancel cargoes. In this regard, the robustness of a given ADP against uncertainties is an important dimension for LNG suppliers in order to keep the costs low and satisfactorily ensure delivery of customer contracts with minimal changes.

The literature that addresses the robustness of ADPs is very limited. Halvorsen-Weare et al. (2013b) consider cruise time uncertainties and modifies the ADP formulation in Halvorsen-

Weare and Fagerholt (2013a) by adding a constant slack to all of the travel times and adding penalty costs for the deviations from target inventory level at the liquefaction port and target loading berth use. They compare the solutions of pure cost minimization model to their modified formulation. Mutlu et al. (2016c) propose a multi-objective model with a second objective to improve the ADP flexibility by incorporating slackness into the model and present trade-off curves, which suggest that significant flexibility can be introduced into the plan at a relatively small incremental cost.

In this paper, we develop a simulation model that tests the robustness of a given ADP against vessel cruise time uncertainty. Several contingency actions, similar to the re-planning decisions in practice, are incorporated into the model. Our proposed model quantifies the sensitivity of the performance metrics of the ADP and the resulting penalty costs. Halvorsen-Weare et al. (2013b) also develops a simulation model, in which, rerouting decisions are made by solving the remaining subproblem as a mixed integer programming formulation. Our simulation model does not require an optimizer, and thus it has lower solution times. Moreover, our model is capable of simulating ADPs that allow for split deliveries. In a more general sense, our model simulates integrated production, inventory, and maritime routing solutions with heterogeneous vessels and delivery time windows.

Using our simulation model, we compare two alternative multi-objective ADP formulations, for which the first objective is to minimize the total operating and contractual penalty costs. The first formulation is suggested by Mutlu et al. (2016c), which aims to make the deliveries to the contracts as early as possible within the delivery time window of the contract as a second objective. This approach aims at increasing the flexibility of the plan. Flexibility and redundancy are identified as two main risk mitigation strategy types in the supply chain risk management literature (Rice and Caniato, 2003; Sheffi and Rice Jr, 2005; Talluri et al., 2013). Second multi-objective formulation we propose aims to incorporate redundancy by maximizing the idle times of the vessels between consecutive deliveries as a second objective.

The genetic algorithms-based solution approach suggested by Mutlu et al. (2016c) can effectively generate a frontier of Pareto-optimal plans. We simulate all of these plans at the optimal frontier and investigate their robustness.

The contribution of this paper is two-fold. First, we introduce a model, which is capable of simulating ADPs that are generated using various methods. The model helps LNG suppliers test the robustness of their ADPs. Second, we build several realistic recourse actions in order to relieve the side-effects of vessel delays. Delivery time of LNG using maritime transportation, especially to overseas, is highly affected by the weather and maritime traffic conditions; and without effective contingency planning, LNG supplier may fail to fulfill the his contractual requirements. Our experimental analysis indicates that the suggested recourse actions can effectively eliminate potential delays and/or cancellations in future deliveries.

The next section summarizes the model that is used in the ADP formulation. Section 2 describes the logic of the simulation model. In Section 3, we describe the problem instances for our computational study and present a comparison of alternative multi-objective formulation approaches. The paper concludes in Section 4 with the managerial takeaways derived from this study and future research directions.

THE SIMULATION MODEL

We study the integrated liquefaction, inventory, and delivery operations of An LNG supplier having one liquefaction facility accompanied by a loading port with multiple berths and delivering to a set of long-term contracted customers located around the globe. Each customer has a set of delivery requirements, which we refer to as a contract, throughout the time horizon of the ADP. Each contract has a desired volume and a time window for delivery. Typically, a contract's delivery volume would exceed the capacity of a single vessel; therefore multiple vessel deliveries have to be made to fulfill the contract requirements. Contract offers various levels of flexibility to the supplier on both delivery volume and time.

The simulation model's major input is an ADP, which includes several pieces of information such as the daily liquefaction rates, times of departure from the liquefaction port and arriving at the customer ports and delivery volumes at each visit for all the vessels. Each round trip tour of a vessel starting from the liquefaction port and delivering to a single or multiple customer ports is named as a cargo. A cargo contains the information of (i) its assigned vessel, (ii) departure time from the liquefaction port, (iii) arrival time(s) to the customer port(s), (iv) delivery volume at each visited port, and (v) return date according to the ADP. We note that a cargo may contain deliveries to multiple customer ports. Therefore, a vessel may visit several customer ports throughout its tour and deliver part of its load at each port. This phenomenon is known as ``split-deliveries." Cargo information is stored in a list of scheduled cargoes of its departure day from the liquefaction port. In the simulation, travel times of vessels between ports are assumed to be stochastic. To model the travel time uncertainty, we adopt the approach suggested in Halvorsen-Weare et al. (2013), which is discretization of a log logistic probability distribution. In this approach, the probability distribution of sailing times of LNG vessels is approximated by a log logistics distribution based on an empirical study on sailing times of vessels by Kauczynski (1994).

The simulation runs at daily steps. Each day, two stages of checks are made: First, for each cargo scheduled to be shipped on that day, whether its assigned vessel is available or not is checked. If the assigned vessels are not available, they are delayed to next day, or assigned to another available vessel, or moved to a charter vessel. In the second stage, scheduled cargoes with available vessels are checked if they can be shipped. At this stage, berth and inventory availability at the liquefaction port are checked. The cargoes that cannot be shipped are delayed or cancelled. We next present a more detailed flow of the simulation logic:

The Simulation Logic

1. For each day *t*
   1.1. For each cargo *c* in the set of *vessel waiting cargoes - t*
      - If there is an available vessel at the liquefaction port, assign an available vessel to cargo *c* and move it to the set of *scheduled cargoes – t*
      - Else:
        - If cargo *c* can be delayed by one day, move it to the set of *vessel waiting cargoes – t+1*
        - Else: assign cargo *c* to a chartered vessel and move it to *scheduled cargoes – t*

   1.2. For each cargo *c* in set of *scheduled cargoes – t*

- If the assigned vessel of cargo c is at the liquefaction port: add cargo *c* to the set of *cargoes to be shipped - t*
- Else:
  - If the cargo can be on hold till the next day without changing its assigned vessel: move cargo *c* to set of *scheduled cargoes – t+1.*
  - Else:
    - If cargo *c* can be assigned to another compatible vessel, chance its assigned vessel and add cargo *c* to the set of *cargoes to be shipped – t*
    - Else:
      - If cargo *c* can be delayed one day, move cargo *c* to the set of *vessel waiting cargoes - (t+1).*
      - Else: assign cargo *c* to a chartered vessel and move it to *scheduled cargoes – t*

1.3. Rank the cargoes in the *cargoes to be shipped – t,* according to their criticality

1.4. For each cargo *c* in the ranked list of *cargoes to be shipped – t*

- If there is a free berth and sufficient inventory: send cargo *c*
- Else:
  - If cargo *c* can be delayed by one day, move it to the set of *scheduled cargoes cargoes – t+1*
  - Else: cancel cargo *c*
  -

2. Compare the ADP and the actual deliveries and it computes the deviations from the plan. The deviations are
   i. *Delays:* the sum of the days the cargoes are delayed;
   ii. *Charters:* the total number of chartered vessels;
   iii. *Volume:* difference between the planned and actual delivery volumes. Delivery volumes to the contracts may change due to two potential reasons. If a cargo is assigned to another vessel with a different capacity than its originally assigned vessel, the delivery volume for the cargo may change. In addition, we assume that delivery volume to the intended contract is zero if a cargo is cancelled.
   iv. *Penalty Costs:* the difference between the total actual and planned contractual penalty costs.

The verification of the model is done through our discussion with the logistics planners of one of the LNG suppliers in Qatar. For the validation of the model, we ran the simulation by removing the travel time uncertainty. In this case, the actual deliveries should match the plan without any deviations. We tested over 400 different plans for various problems and obtained an exact match in each case.

The model aims to simulate a given ADP, which is a one-year long plan, and then compares the deviations from that plan. Therefore, no warm-up period is used and each simulation run spans a period of 360 days.

COMPUTATIONAL STUDY

There are two objectives of the computational study: (i) to evaluate the impact of the contingency actions, and (ii) to compare robustness of alternative ADPs using the simulation model. Adding flexibility and redundancy to the supply chain plans are identified as two main risk mitigation strategies in supply chain risk management. In the ADP preparation context, risk mitigation is very critical as the implementation of the program is subject to many disturbances. An emerging trend in the ADP literature is to employ multi-objective optimization and introduce alternative objectives that aim to maximize the flexibility and redundancy of the plan. In our study, we compare the robustness of alternative ADPs, developed by Mutlu et al (2016c).

To do so, we study five problem instances generated by Mutlu et al. (2016a). First three problems are representative of a small-to-medium scale LNG providers and the last two are representative of large scale LNG providers. The selected problems also vary according to the total annual demand to total production capacity ratio. This ratio is low in the first two problems compared to the others. In the first four problems, contractual demands are almost evenly distributed throughout the planning horizon. On the contrary, the last one has higher demand seasonality. Parameters of each problem are presented in Table 1. In this table, ρ^P is the demand to production capacity ratio and DS is the coefficient of variation of monthly demand.

Table 1: Problem Instances

Class	|V|	|P|	|C|	B	DS	ρ^P
P1	20	8	65	3	0.02	0.65
P2	20	8	65	3	0.02	0.75
P3	20	8	65	3	0.02	0.95
P4	40	16	111	5	0.05	0.95
P5	40	16	111	5	0.2	0.85

Simulation run times are rather short; thus we took a conservative approach and selected a large number of replications in order to ensure that the total simulated costs between two adjacent ADPs are different according to the one-sided hypothesis testing using 95% significance level. 100 independent simulation runs were enough for this.

RESULTS

For first objective of the computational study, we have prepared a similar version of the simulation model, which does not contain any of the contingency actions. In this version, if the assigned vessel of a scheduled cargo has not arrived on the planned day, the cargo is simply delayed until the last date it can be delivered; otherwise it is cancelled. Figure 1 displays the percentage increases from the planned costs under the absence and existence of contingency actions for alternative ADPs for P1. When there is no contingency plan, the cost increases reach above 200% but with the simple contingency plans we suggested, the increases are less than 20%. This shows the effectiveness of the simply implemented contingency plans.

Figure 1: Percentage Increase in Planned Costs for No-Action and Contingency Planning - P1

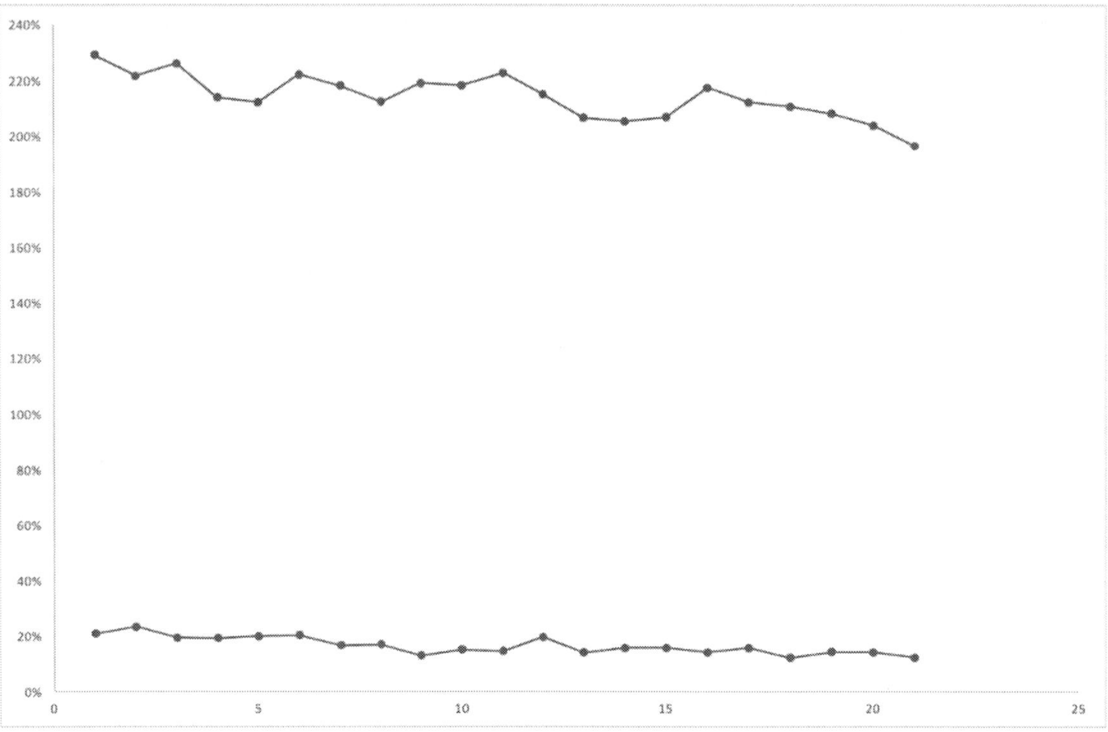

The second objective is to compare the robustness of alternative ADPs. For this purpose, we first plot the total planned and actual costs under travel time uncertainty. Figure 2 shows this comparison for P2. We note that the ADPs are ranked on the horizontal axis according to increasing order total planned cost and total planned vessel idle times. In other words, the plans on the left hand side of plot are better in terms of planned costs and the ones on the right hand side have more redundancy. We observe that, even the latter plans have higher planned costs, the actual total costs after experiencing the travel time delays and their consequences are almost the same as those of cost optimal plans. This indicates the effectiveness of vessel idle times on mitigating travel time delays. The conclusion is even stronger as the production capacity to demand ratio increases. In Figure 3, one can observe a decreasing trend in actual costs for the first 12 ADPs.

Figure 2: Planned vs. Actual Costs - P2

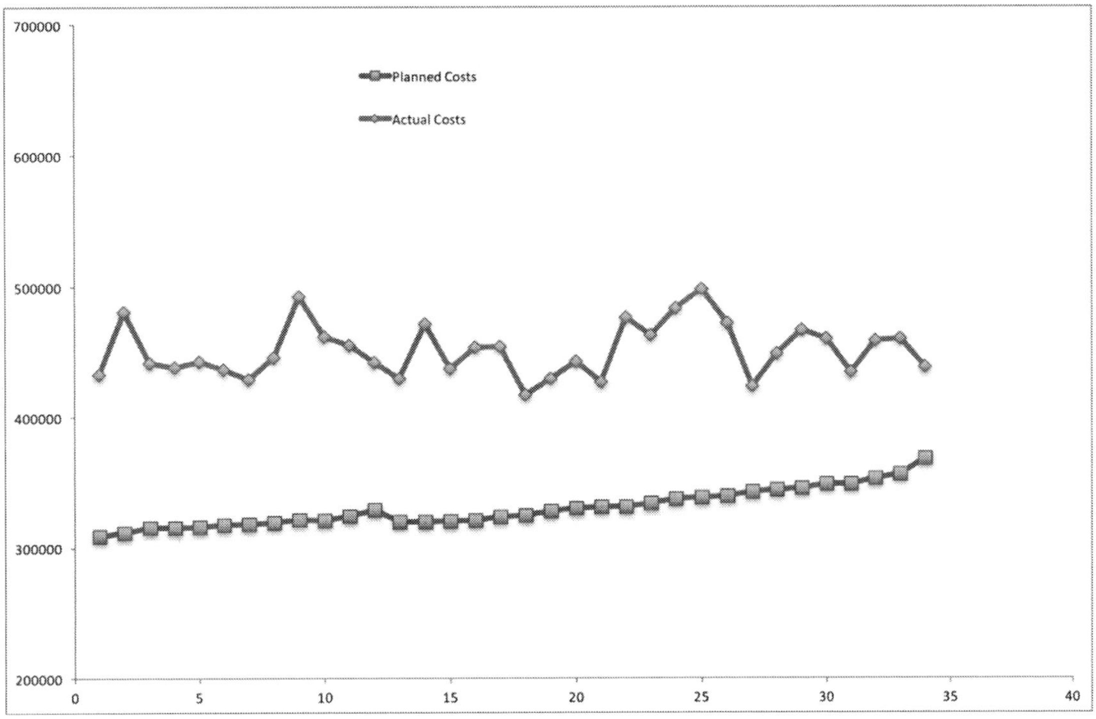

Figure 3: Planned vs. Actual Costs - P3

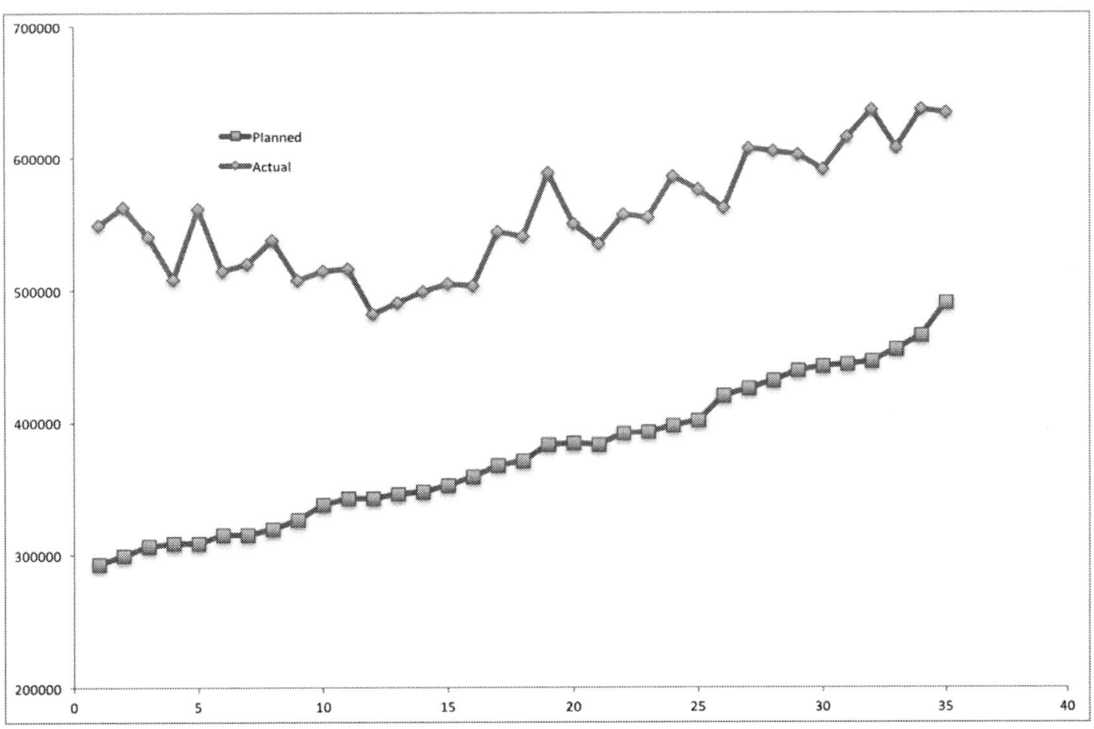

The costs show here are the summation of operating costs and penalty costs according to the contractual volumes and delivery times. Same cost parameters are also used while preparing an ADP. However, once an ADP is prepared, the supplier negotiates this plan with the customers. Intuitively, after this stage, the customers expect that the actual deliveries match the ADP. Hence, al alternative measure of robustness is the changes in delivery volumes and delivery times. By associating the same unit penalty rates for early- and late-delivery penalties, and under- and over- delivery penalties, we computed the % increases in the penalty costs. the percentage increase in the actual costs can be used as one measure of robustness. Figure 4 and Figure 5 show the percentage increases for P4 and P5, respectively. For both problems, a decreasing trend in percentage increase in penalty costs can be observed as the total vessel time of the plans increase. The trend is stronger when seasonal variation of demand is higher.

Figure 4: Percentage Increase In Penalty Costs - P4

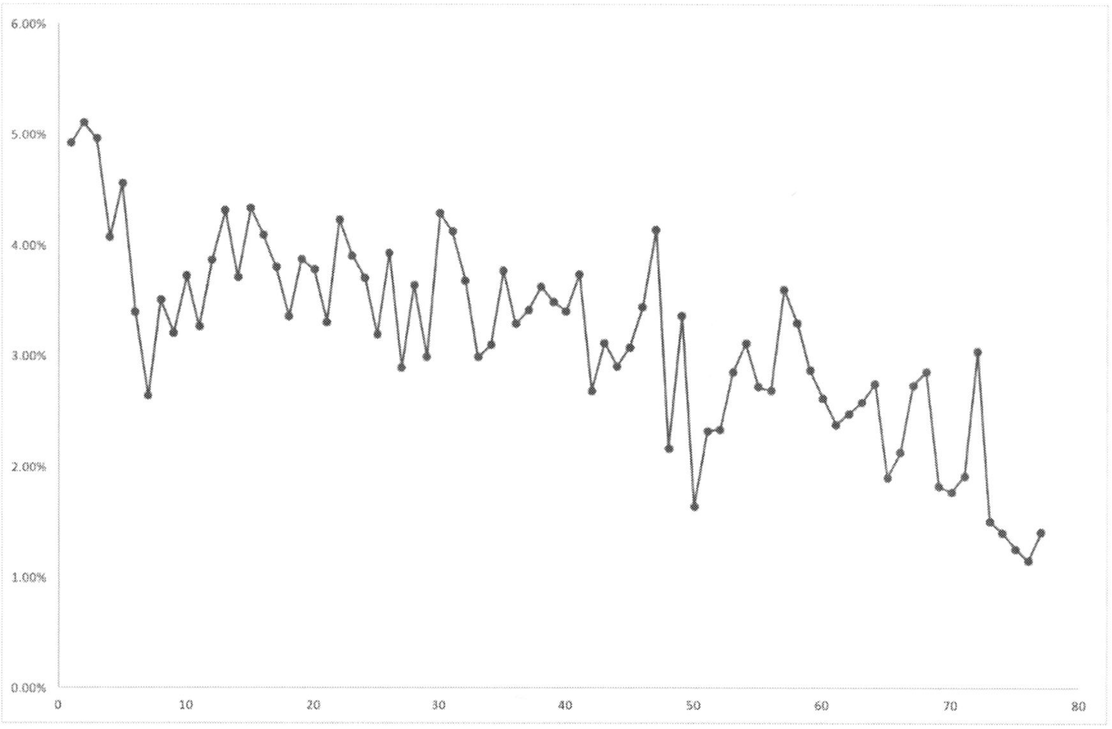

Figure 5: Percentage Increase In Penalty Costs - P5

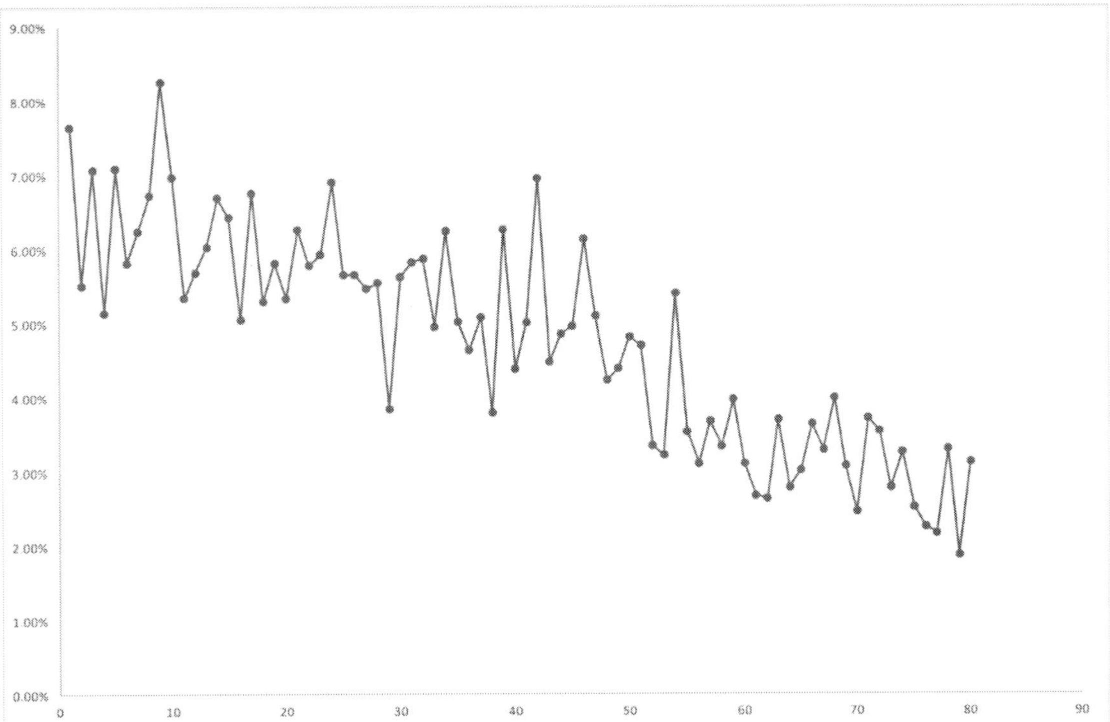

DISCUSSION AND CONCLUSIONS

In this study, we develop a novel simulation model that can simulate the implementation of an LNG ADP under various uncertainties. The simulation model is generic enough to simulate any single depot integrated production, inventory, and delivery routing plan with demand time windows. It also proposes recourse actions in case of vessel delays.
Our simulation model can be used to compare alternative ADPs. We demonstrate this by simulating Pareto-optimal solutions for a multi-objective LNG ADP formulation proposed by Mutlu et al. (2016c). Their multi-objective formulation aims to maximize vessels' idle times in between cargo delivery jobs. Our simulation results indicate that Pareto-optimal plans obtained from this formulation are highly robust against uncertainties. The model developed in this study can be utilized by LNG suppliers to test robustness of their annual delivery plans under various scenarios.

A future research avenue is to enhance the simulation model in order to make it sufficiently generic so that it can be used to compare solutions for a larger class of integrated production, inventory, and delivery routing problems.

ACKNOWLEDGEMENTS

This research was made possible by a NPRP award NPRP 4-453-5-059 from the Qatar National Research Fund (a member of The Qatar Foundation). The statements made herein are solely the responsibility of the authors.

REFERENCES

BP Statistics, D. (2014). Bp statistical review of world energy june 2014. Technical report, British Petroleum.

Goel, V., Furman, K. C., Song, J.-H., and El-Bakry, A. S. (2012). Large neighborhood search for lng inventory routing. Journal of Heuristics, 18(6), 821-848.

Goel, V., Slusky, M., van Hoeve, W.-J., Furman, K., and Shao, Y. (2015). Constraint programming for lng ship scheduling and inventory management. European Journal of Operational Research, 241(3), 662-673.

Halvorsen-Weare, E. E., & Fagerholt, K. (2013). Routing and scheduling in a liquefied natural gas shipping problem with inventory and berth constraints. *Annals of Operations Research, 203*(1), 167-186.

Halvorsen-Weare, E. E., Fagerholt, K., and R□onnqvist, M. (2013). Vessel routing and scheduling under uncertainty in the lique_ed natural gas business. Computers & Industrial Engineering, 64(1), 290-301.

Kauczynski, W. (1994). Study of the reliability of the ship transportation. In Proceeding of the international conference on ship and marine research, page 15.

Mutlu, F., Msakni, M. K., Yildiz, H., Sonmez, E., and Pokharel, S. (2016a). A comprehensive annual delivery program for upstream liquefied natural gas supply chain. European Journal of Operational Research, 250(1), 120-130.

Mutlu, F., Yildiz, H., Sonmez, E., and Pokharel, S. (2016b). A genetic algorithm based approach to the liquefied natural gas annual delivery planning problem. Manuscript Submitted for Publication.

Mutlu, F., Yildiz, H., Sonmez, E., and Pokharel, S. (2016c). Multi-objective optimization for the liquefied natural gas annual delivery problem. Working Paper.

Rakke, J. G., Stalhane, M., Moe, C. R., Christiansen, M., Andersson, H., Fagerholt, K., and Norstad, I. (2011). A rolling horizon heuristic for creating a liquefied natural gas annual delivery program. Transportation Research Part C, 19, 896-911.

Rice, J. B. and Caniato, F. (2003). Building a secure and resilient supply network. Supply Chain Management Review, 7(5), 22-30.

Shao, Y., Furman, K. C., Goel, V., and Hoda, S. (2015). A hybrid heuristic strategy for liquefied natural gas inventory routing. Transportation Research Part C: Emerging Technologies, 53, 151-171.

Sheffi, Y. and Rice Jr, J. B. (2005). A supply chain view of the resilient enterprise. MIT Sloan management review, 47(1), 41.

Stälhane, M., Rakke, J. G., Moe, C. R., Andersson, H., Christiansen, M., and Fagerholt, K.

(2012). A construction and improvement heuristic for an lng inventory routing problem. Computers & Industrial Engineering, 62, 245-255.

Talluri, S. S., Kull, T. J., Yildiz, H., and Yoon, J. (2013). Assessing the efficiency of risk mitigation strategies in supply chains. Journal of Business logistics, 34(4), 253-269.

DECISION SCIENCES INSTITUTE

A Study of Virtual Project Team Types and Their Impact on Project Success.

Padhraic Ludden
University of Limerick
Padhraic.ludden@hpe.com

Ann Ledwith
University of Limerick
Ann.ledwith@ul.ie

ABSTRACT

Based on a global survey, this paper presents empirical data to support evidence of a number of virtual team types. The study develops a simple measure of project team virtuality, which is supported by existing research and current practitioners. Based on this measure and the empirical data gathered, a number of virtual team types are defined. Using data gathered on a set of soft characteristics defined from the literature, further virtual team types are defined. The research studies the relationship of the identified team types with project success, their ability to cope with temporal dispersion and their level of usage of communication technology.

KEYWORDS: Virtual teams, Project success, Team Leadership, Team Structure

INTRODUCTION

The virtual team concept emerged in the early 1990s when U.S. multinationals and their affiliates overseas began using dispersed teams in order to integrate their work practices (Kirkman et al. 2002). Since then increased globalization and rapid improvements in communication technology have resulted in growth in the use of virtual teams, with Martin et al., (2004) contending that nearly all organizational teams are virtual to some extent. It is therefore important that the working and functioning of virtual teams is well understood.

This paper contributes to our understanding of virtual teams and project management by exploring virtual team types and their impact on project success. The team types are developed based on virtual team attributes defined from the academic literature and tested on a sample of more than 500 project managers.

The research presented here distinguishes itself from previous research on virtual project teams and adds to the body of knowledge in several ways. First, unlike previous research that has tended to focus on specific aspects or topics of virtual teams, this research provides a broad view of virtual project teams. Second, empirical data is used to define virtual team clusters. Finally, using a global study conducted across multiple companies and industry sectors, the impact of team characteristics on overall project success is analysed.

The paper is structured as follows: A review of the literature on virtual project team characteristics identifying core themes is presented, followed by a description of the research methodology employed and the development of a survey addressing these themes.

The survey results are presented and analysed. Finally a discussion of the findings and their implications for researchers concludes the paper.

LITERATURE REVIEW

Earlier research into the virtual team typology focused on defining characteristics that could be used to classify virtual teams. These characteristics include locations, number of projects, number of managers (Evaristo and Van Fenema, 1999; Cascio and Shurygailo, 2002); time, place and organisations (Lipnack and Stamps, 2000; Kimble et al., 2000; Fisher and Fisher, 2001); and people, technology and process (Bal and Grundy, 1999; Dundis and Benson, 2003). Fiol and O'Connor (2005) use the attributes of uncertainty, visibility, rich individuating cues, diversity and politeness rituals to define three virtual team types – pure, hybrid, face to face, while Bell and Kowzloski (2002) use the dimensions of member roles, lifecycle, boundaries and temporal distribution to develop a structured framework. In a meta review of academic literature on virtual teams Martins et al. (2004), identify a move away from early research of contrasting virtual teams with traditional teams, to focusing on 'virtualness' as a potential characteristic of all teams. It is noticeable that many of the structures/models proposed are based on theory and very few of the frameworks are empirically tested.

More recent publications have been based on empirical research. Gilson et al. (2015) in a review of 10 years of empirical research of virtual teams classify 10 themes – research design, team inputs, team virtuality, technology, globalisation, mediators and moderators, trust, outcomes and ways to enhance virtual team success. Many published case studies and experiments examine the cultural, communication, leadership and effectiveness of virtual teams (Han et al., 2011; Cheng et al. 2012; Domschker et al., 2009; Ocker et al., 2011; Edwards and Sridhar, 2003). Quantitative and qualitative studies explore team structure and knowledge sharing (Bal & Gundry, 1999; Klitmoller and Lauring, 2013; Reich et al., 2012). However, there is little empirical research that studies virtual teams from a general project management perspective. Some notable exceptions to this are five surveys that use project managers as their population sample (Curlee, 2008; Anantatmula and Thomas, 2010; Bourgault, Drouin, & Hamel, 2008; Henderson, 2008; Verburg et al., 2013). Most empirical research on virtual teams tends to focus on certain aspects or traits rather than actual team typologies.

Seven key themes emerge from the literature on virtual project teams, these are 1) temporal dispersion, 2) geographic dispersion, 3) culture, 4) politics, 5) social, 6) team membership and 7) communication technology. These are summarised in Table 1. Within each of these themes, virtual team attributes can be classified as either hard or soft. Hard attributes are generally used to describe a team's temporal and geographic dispersion and cannot be changed by the project manager. Soft attributes include factors such as the expertise of team members, the team's experience and reputation and the ability of the team leader.

Temporal and geographic dispersion pose many challenges for virtual teams including the difficulty of executing tasks in parallel, delayed communication, problems with developing functional working relationships, all of these have been found to impact on project success (Chudoba et al., 2005). Team dispersion also increases the cultural diversity of a project team, thus cultural experience and adaptiveness are important characteristics for virtual teams (Espinosa et al., 2006). The political standing of a virtual team's leader within an organisation plays an important role in the functioning of a virtual team (Mukherjee et al., 2012). Team leadership is critical for aligning and sharing the vision and knowledge of highly dispersed teams while the size, structure and membership of a virtual team have also been

Table 1: Seven key themes of virtual teams.

Theme	Attributes	References
1. **Temporal dispersion**	Hard Attributes: Team members in different time zones. Time difference between time zones. Extra hours worked. Soft Attributes: Difficulty of task execution. Impact on functional or workshop relationship between team members. Lack of understanding of different physiological and social habits or norms. Time delays cause confusion.	Chudoba et al., 2005; Connaughton and Shuffler, 2007; Saunders et al., 2004; Martin et al., 2004; Dundis and Benson, 2003; Sarker and Sahay, 2002; O'leary and Cummings, 2007
2. **Geographic dispersion**	Hard Attributes: Number of locations. Key location. Soft Attributes: Geographical distribution of locations. Team structures at locations.	Schweitzer and Duxbury, 2012; Hoch and Kozlowski, 2014; O'leary and Cummings, 2007; Foil and O'Connor, 2005.
3. **Culture**	Soft Attributes: Recognizing different cultural situations. Understanding different economic, social, and legal conditions. Adapting to different cultural situations. Sensitivity to cultures reflected in communication and interaction. Dominance of organizations. Use of organizational processes. Integration of functional department members and subject matter experts into the team.	Gibson and Cohen, 2003; Espinosa et al., 2006; Watson-Manheim et al., 2002; Au and Marks, 2012; Schlenkrich and Upfold, 2009; Zhang et al., 2006; Gibson and Gibbs, 2006; Kim et al; 2006
4. **Political**	Soft Attributes: Team and team leaders' political reputation and standing. Team autonomy and freedom. Team leaders' interactions with team and team organizations.	Bal and Teo, 2000; Lipnack and Stamps, 2000; Mukherjee et al., 2012; Zander et al., 2012. Harvey et al., 2005.
5. **Social**	Soft Attributes: Team vision and goals. Alignment to vision and goals. Formal job role versus expertise and knowledge. Knowledge transfer and sharing.	Bal and Teo, 2000; Geber, 1995; Moser and Axtell, 2013.
6. **Team membership**	Soft Attributes: Experience of working on virtual teams. Experience of working with other team members. Diversity of knowledge. Number of fully dedicated members. Number with dedicated roles. Number reporting directly to team leader. Number of contractors.	Staples and Cameron, 2005; Lee-kelley, 2002; Zhang et al., 2006; Nader et al., 2007; Henry and Hartzler, 1997; Connaughton and Shuffler, 2007; Wong and Burton, 2000.
7. **Communication technology**	Soft Attributes: Experience of using communication technology. Usage of communication technologies.	Nader et al., 2009; Watson-Manheim and Belanger, 2002; Domscheker et al., 2009; Webster and Wong, 2008.

related to its performance (Staples and Cameron, 2005; Wong and Burton, 2000). Finally, virtual teams rely on electronically mediated communication and the research suggests that certain types of media are more useful for knowledge sharing than others (Kiltmoller and Lauring, 2013).

In summary, while the themes identified in Table 1 have emerged from the literature as having a key impact on the functioning of virtual teams they have to date been studied in isolation rather than in the context of the overall operation and success of the project team.

The objective of this study is to take a more integrated look at the operation and success of virtual teams. Specifically, a selected range of soft attributes identified in Table 1 – culture, political, social, team membership - are used with the hard attributes relating to temporal and geographic dispersion to define virtual project team classifications. These classifications are then compared using the key themes of temporal dispersion and use of communication technology.

Project success will be defined using the factors developed by Pinto and Slevin (1988) – 1) completion on schedule, 2) within or on budget, and 3) achievement of quality and performance objectives. An additional fourth constraint, meeting client expectations, is included (Jugdev and Muller, 2005).

While the main aim of this study is to identify the virtual team types that are linked with project success there are two secondary aims. The first is to examine how virtual teams cope with the challenges posed by temporal dispersion. The second is to examine the levels of usage of communication technology by virtual teams. The next section of this paper describes the methods used to conduct this study.

METHOD

The research method used was grounded exploratory research using a quantitative survey. The survey tool was Survey Monkey and study population was a section of Project Management Institute (PMI) members with a target size of more than 5000. An original questionnaire was developed based on the frameworks outlined in the literature review. The seven data categories for the questionnaire were 1) temporal dispersion, 2) geographic dispersion, 3) culture 4) political, 5) social 6) team membership and 7) communication technology. The survey also gathered data to measure project team performance, in order to analyse the impacts of key virtual team attributes on performance. A pilot survey was distributed to 20 experienced project management professionals and based on feedback a revised questionnaire was distributed to members of the PMI, using the PMI chapter member's advisory group and PMI chapter mentors who contacted selected PMI Chapter presidents requesting them to email the survey to their membership. The survey was issued to PMI members in over 30 countries and the total number of responses collected was 521. Each respondent was asked to complete the questionnaire based on a project that was recently completed by a virtual project team of which they were a member.

In addition to the main survey described above, a further small-scale study of 50 practitioners with experience working on virtual project teams was used in order to establish a working measure of virtuality. This research found that two hard attributes are deemed to have the most impact on the level of virtuality of a team: 1) the number of hours' difference in time zones between the two locations of the virtual team; and 2) the number of team locations existing for the virtual team. This definition was used to identify the level of virtuality of teams within the study.

Using the data gathered from the two surveys, data analysis was conducted to identify virtual team types and study their impact on project success. This data analysis is described in the next section.

Data Analysis

Data analysis was conducted in four phases. First, component factor analysis was conducted on the virtual team soft attribute data to identify key factors of virtual project teams. Cluster analysis using the key factors, was then preformed to identify the teams that had positive or advanced attributes and those that had negative or basic attributes. This team type was labelled basic/advanced.

Second, based on the measure of virtuality defined in the method section above, the sample was divided into those project teams that were "highly virtual" and those that were "moderately virtual". This team type was labelled moderately virtual/highly virtual. (Note: All teams were virtual to some extent, as this was a prerequisite for participating in the study). The third phase of the data analysis, compared the project success results for each of the team types. For the final analysis phase, the challenges posed by temporal dispersion and the level of usage of communication technology for each of the team types is studied.

<u>Developing Team Types based on Soft Virtual Team Characteristics</u>

Statistical analysis was conducted using IBM SPSS Version 22 software. Component factor analysis was used on the data gathered to reduce the soft characteristic attributes of the key themes of team membership, political, social and culture to nine common factors. (Appendix 1 details the results of the factor analysis).These are

- Dedicated team members – the level of dedication to project, role and project manager.
- Virtual team experience – experience of working on virtual teams and with the other team members.
- Team leader status – team leader's achievements, recognition and interaction with team and organisation.
- Team status - teams reputation , political power and independence
- Vision and goals - clearly defined team vision and goals and aligned to them.
- Expertise and knowledge - expertise more important than role and there is strong knowledge sharing among the team.
- Common processes – one set of organisational policies, processes and methodologies.
- Cultural awareness – team members understand each other's economic, social and legal conditions
- Cultural adaptiveness – team members work hard to adapt to the different cultures within the team.

Cluster analysis was conducted on the data set with the nine soft factors identified from the component factor analysis in order to identify whether teams could be grouped based on these factors. Using K means cluster analysis, three clusters were identified (Table 2).

Table 2: Cluster Analysis Results.

Nine Common Factors	Cluster 1 (N=84)	Cluster 2 (N=232)	Cluster 3 (N=194)
Dedicated team members	-0.06	0.35	-0.39
Virtual team experience	-0.23	0.45	-0.43
Team leader status	-0.85	0.28	0.01
Team status	-0.46	0.45	-0.36
Vision and goals	-1.63	0.37	0.21
Expertise and knowledge	-0.10	0.40	-0.45
Common processes	-0.86	0.43	-0.16
Cultural awareness	-0.47	0.56	-0.47
Cultural adaptiveness	-0.79	0.24	0.04

The numbers in the columns are the mean scores for each cluster of the component factor scores for each of the nine factors. As the total sample mean component factor score for each of the factors is equal to zero, Cluster 1 (17% of the total sample) can be identified as the group with mean scores for all nine factors below the total sample mean. Thus Cluster 1 is labelled 'Basic' as teams within this cluster demonstrate below average performance in all nine virtual team characteristics. Cluster 2 (45% of the total sample) is the group in which the mean scores are above the total sample mean, and is therefore labelled 'Advanced' as teams within this cluster demonstrate above average performance for all nine virtual team characteristics. Cluster 3 (38%) is the group with a mix of mean factor scores above and below the total sample mean and is labelled 'Neutral' as teams in this group demonstrate performance both above and below average for the nine factors. This research focuses on only the basic and advanced clusters as these two clusters have the maximum differences in performance. A detailed description of the differences between basic and advanced classification is given in Table 3.

Developing Team Types based on Hard Virtual Team Characteristics

Two hard attributes relating to temporal and geographic dispersion were deemed to have the most impact on the level of virtuality of a team. The upper and lower quartile figures for these two attributes from the main data set (the 521 responses) were then used to classify teams as highly virtual or moderately virtual. These are defined as follows:

Highly virtual: The difference in time zones between two locations is greater than six hours, *and* the number of team locations is greater than four.

Moderately virtual: The difference in time zones between two locations is fewer than six hours, *and* the number of team locations is less than four.

Of the 521 survey responses, 107 (20%) of the sample can be classed as belonging to the moderately virtual typology and 134 (26%) can be classed as belonging to the highly virtual typology, see Table 3. The remaining 280 (54%) responses were in between these extremes and are omitted in the analysis that follows.

Table 3: Basic versus Advanced Team Properties

Attribute	Basic	Advanced
Dedicated team members	• The team members are **less likely to be dedicated** to the project, have a dedicated role, or report directly to the project leader.	• The team members **are dedicated** to the project, have a dedicated role, or report directly to the project leader.
Virtual team experience	• The team members **are less likely to have experience** working on virtual teams and are **unlikely to have** worked together.	• The team members **have previous experience** working on virtual teams and **have** previously worked together.
Team leader status	• The team leader or leaders **were well known**, have achieved recognition, and have a **high degree** of interaction within the team and within the organization or organizations to which the team belonged.	• The team leader or leaders **were very well known,** have achieved recognition, and have a **very high degree** of interaction within the team and within the organization or organizations to which the team belonged.
Team status	• The **team is likely to have a strong reputation** for having the political power to get things done and is likely to be allowed the freedom to run the project as it wishes.	• **The team has a strong reputation** for having the political power to get things done and is likely to be allowed the freedom to run the project as it wishes.
Vision and goals	• The team has **a clearly defined** vision, goals, and objectives, and team members are aligned to them.	• The team has **a strong and clearly defined** vision, goals, and objectives, and team members are strongly aligned to them.
Expertise and knowledge	• Team members' expertise and knowledge **is considered more** important than job title or position, and team members are encouraged to, and willingly share their knowledge with the rest of the team.	• Team members' expertise and knowledge **is considered much more** important than job title or position, and team members are strongly encouraged to, and actively share their knowledge with the rest of the team.
Common processes	• The team **is likely to have one set** of organizational policies, methodologies, and processes.	• The team **has one set** of organizational policies, methodologies, and processes.
Cultural awareness	• The team **members are likely to be good** at recognizing the different cultural situations that arise within the team **and are likely to understand** the different economic, social, and legal conditions of the various countries in which the other team members lived.	• The team **members are good at recognizing** the different cultural situations that arise within the team **and understand** the different economic, social, and legal conditions of the various countries in which the other team members lived.
Cultural adaptiveness	• Team members **are likely to work hard** to adapt to the different cultural situations that occur within the team and are likely to be sensitive to other team members' cultural behaviours. This is likely to be reflected in the way team members communicate and interact within the team.	• Team members **work hard** to adapt to the different cultural situations that occur within the team, and are sensitive to other team members' cultural behaviours. This is reflected in the way team members communicate and interact within the team.

In summary, using component factor analyse the soft attributes for cultural, political, social and team member characteristics were reduces to nine factors from which two distinct team types are identified which are labelled basic and advanced. A basic team registers below-mean responses for the nine attributes and an advanced team registers above-mean responses for the nine attributes. From a secondary survey, the greatest difference in time zones and number of locations were the two physical characteristics of virtual teams that have the most impact on the level of virtuality. Based on the quartile percentage findings for the survey questions on difference in time zones and number of locations, two further team types were identified—highly virtual and moderately virtual.

The primary aim of this research is to link virtual team types to project success. The next section will study the impact the identified team types have on project success and will then explore the challenges of temporal dispersion and the level of communication technology usage for the four team types.

RESULTS

Impact of Virtual Team Types on Project Success

Pearson's chi squared tests for difference was conducted on the data gathered from the survey questions used to study project success as the question formats used a standard 5 point likert scale ranging from 1- 'Strongly disagree', 2- 'Disagree' , 3- 'Neutral', 4- 'Agree' to 5- 'Strongly agree'. The Pearson chi-squared test for difference results indicate that there is statistically significant differences between basic and advanced teams for the four success factors (Table 4). The mean scores show that for all success factors, advanced teams perform better than basic teams.

Table 4: Project Success: Basic versus Advanced

Success factors	**Basic Mean**	**Advanced Mean**	**Pearson Chi-Squared Test for Difference**
Completed on schedule	2.86	3.73	0.000**
Completed within budget	2.84	3.72	0.000**
Achieved quality and performance objectives	3.08	4.14	0.000**
Deliverables met client expectations	3.3	4.08	0.000**

** *Statistically significant difference p<0.05*

From Table 5, Pearson's chi squared test for difference show there is no statistically significant difference between the performance of moderately virtual and highly virtual teams. Therefore, although the mean scores show that highly virtual teams perform better than moderately virtual teams, there is no statistically significant evidence that one team type out performs the other with regard to project success.

Table 5: Project Success: Moderately versus Highly Virtual.

	Moderately Virtual **Mean**	**Highly Virtual** **Mean**	**Pearson Chi-Squared Test for Difference**
Completed on schedule	3.4	3.44	0.665
Completed within budget	3.52	3.44	0.873
Achieved quality and performance objectives	3.72	3.97	0.196
Deliverables met client expectations	3.82	4	0.554

** *Statistically significant difference $p<0.05$*

Team Performance in a Temporal Dispersed Environment.

Table 6 details the results of the performance of basic and advanced teams with regard to their ability to cope with temporal dispersion. As a 5- point likert scale was used to capture information on the challenges of temporal dispersion, Pearson's chi-squared test for difference was used to compare the ability of the team types to cope with temporal dispersion. The data shows a marked difference between basic and advanced teams with all factors having statistically significant differences. The mean scores of basic teams are consistently higher than those of advanced teams. This indicates that basic teams are impacted more by time-zone dispersion than advanced teams.

The findings that emerge are:

- Basic teams find doing tasks in parallel more difficult than advanced teams.
- Basic teams experience more delays in communication than advanced teams.
- The functional and working relationship between team members is negatively impacted by time-zone difference to a greater extent on basic teams than on advanced teams.
- Basic teams experience more confusion with clock times than advanced teams, resulting in missed meetings and task deadlines.
- In basic teams, there is a greater lack of understanding of the different physiological and social norms of the team members than in advanced teams, and this causes conflict.

Table 6: Ability to Cope with Temporal Dispersion: Basic versus Advanced Teams

	Virtually Basic Mean	**Virtually Advanced Mean**	**Pearson's Chi-Squared Test for Difference**
Executing tasks in parallel is difficult	3.37	2.78	0.020**
Delays in communication	3.8	2.97	0.000**
Negatively impacted the functional working relationship	3.42	2.33	0.000**
Lack of understanding of the different physiological and social norms	3.41	2.35	0.000**
Lack of understanding of the different physiological and social norms caused conflict	3	2.16	0.000**
Confusion over clock times caused missed scheduled meetings	2.34	1.87	0.003**
Confusion over clock times caused missed task deadlines	2.36	1.73	0.000**

** *Statistically significant difference p<0.05*

Comparison of the differences between moderately and highly virtual team structures for temporal dispersion factors show that the differences are not as striking as the differences between basic and advanced virtual teams (Table 7). Only one factor - executing tasks in parallel is difficult - has a significantly statistical difference between low and highly virtual teams. The mean scores for most of the factors for moderately virtual teams are consistently lower than those of highly virtual teams.

Level of use of Communication Technology

To capture information on communication media usage, the Webster and Wong (2008) 7 point likert scale for communication media usage, was adapted to a 6 point likert scale ranging from 1- 'Never', 2- 'A number of times in a 6 month period', 3- 'A number of times a month', 4- 'A number of times a week', 5- 'A number of times a day', to 6-'Almost continuously'. The question on experience of using communication technology used a standard 5 point likert scale. A comparison of the level of usage of communication technology for basic and advanced team structures shows that one technology type has a statistically significant different level of usage- team and organisation web portals (Table 8). Also the level of experience of using communication technology is also different with advanced teams members have more experience than basic team members. Apart from fixed line phones, the mean level of usage by advanced teams for all other technologies is higher than that of basic teams. We can therefore suggest there is no statistically significant difference between basic teams and advanced teams in their usage of communication technology, apart from team and organisation web portals. Also advanced teams are more experienced in using communication technology.

Table 7: Ability to Cope with Temporal Dispersion: Highly versus Moderately Virtual Teams

Temporal Dispersion challenges	Moderately Virtual Mean	Highly-Virtual Mean	Pearson Chi-Squared Test for Difference
Executing tasks in parallel is difficult	2.59	3.26	0.004**
Delays in communication	2.96	3.41	0.101
Negatively impacted the working relationship	2.39	2.69	0.256
Lack of understanding of the different physiological and social norms	2.80	2.65	0.129
Lack of understanding of the different physiological and social norms caused conflict	2.69	2.37	0.358
Confusion over clock times caused missed scheduled meetings	1.86	2.10	0.109
Confusion over clock times caused missed task deadlines	1.78	2	0.315

*** Statistically significant difference p<0.05*

The study of the comparisons between moderately and highly virtual teams for the level of usage of communication technology is outlined in Table 9. Analysis of the data shows that there is little difference between moderately and highly virtual teams in the experience of and use of communication technology. Only the usage of web conferencing tools, instant

Table 8: Use of Communication Technology: Basic versus Advanced Teams

Usage of Communication Technology	Basic Mean	Advanced Mean	Pearson's Chi-Squared Test
Experience of using communication technology	3.92	4.4	0.000**
Stand-alone video conferencing	1.92	2.05	0.776
Web conferencing	3.24	3.76	0.217
Instant messaging	3.64	4.32	0.152
Remote access and control tool	2.38	2.88	0.250
Email	5.51	5.57	0.656
Fixed telephone	4.5	4.45	0.682
Mobile phone	4.08	4.27	0.351
Letter/Fax	1.51	1.53	0.825
Social networks	1.15	1.54	0.106
Data-sharing repositories	3.7	3.92	0.484
Team and organization web portals	2.59	3.62	0.001**

*** Statistically significant difference p<0.05*

messaging tools, and data-sharing repositories have statistically significant differences. Thus we can conclude that there is no statistically significant difference between moderately virtual and highly virtual teams in the usage of communication technology, apart from the use of web conferencing, instant messaging and data sharing repositories portals.

Table 9: Use of Communication Technology: Highly versus Moderately Virtual Teams

Usage of communication technology	Moderately-Virtual Mean	Highly-Virtual Mean	Pearson chi squared test for difference
Experience of using communication technology	4.20	4.40	0.058
Standalone video conferencing	2.00	1.94	0.054
Web conferencing	3.13	3.95	0.003**
Instant messaging	3.89	4.60	0.044**
Remote access & control tool	3.01	2.80	0.464
Email	5.49	5.63	0.314
Fixed telephone	4.49	4.47	0.54
Mobile phone	4.11	4.02	0.127
Letter /Fax	1.58	1.35	0.211
Social networks	1.42	1.36	0.881
Data sharing repositories	3.45	4.35	0.002**
Team and organisation web portals	3.18	3.46	0.601

*** Statistically significant difference p<0.05*

DISCUSSION

This research into virtual project team types provides three contributions to the body of knowledge of virtual project teams.

First, a clear definition of virtuality is provided, that will prove useful to virtual team researchers and practitioners. Virtual teams that have more than four team locations and a time difference of more than six hours between locations are classified as highly virtual, while those with fewer than four team locations and a time difference of less than six hours are moderately virtual. Teams in between these two extremes can be simply classified as virtual. While earlier researchers have used various definitions of team virtuality (Bell and Kozlowski, 2002; Fiol and O'Connor, 2005; Griffith and Neal, 2001), none have produced a simple, easy-to-operationalize measure.

The second contribution is the identification of a basic / advanced typology for virtual teams based on key soft characteristics of virtual teams. The characteristics are developed from the literature and have a sound theoretical basis. Using data gathered from a large scale survey of virtual teams working in a wide range of industry sectors the following traits were identified for advanced virtual teams:

- Team members are dedicated to the project and have fully dedicated team roles.
- Team members have previous experience of working on virtual project teams.
- Team members have previously worked other team members.
- The team leaders are very well known and have a high degree of interaction within the organisation and the virtual team.
- Advanced teams have a strong reputation within their organisation.
- Advanced teams have very clearly defined vision and goals and are strongly aligned to them.
- The level of expertise and knowledge of team members is considered more important than the role/position of team member.
- Advanced team members willingly share their knowledge amongst the team.
- Advanced teams use one set of organisational policies, methodologies and processes.

- Advanced team members are culturally aware and are adaptive to other cultures.

The third contribution provides evidence of the project success rates of virtual teams, the functional performance of teams in a dispersed time zone environment and their level of usage of communication technology.

The basic /advanced team type which is based on the soft characteristics of culture, team member traits, team social and political aspects, have a significant impact on project success. Advanced teams outperform basic teams in all project success factors – on schedule, on/ within budget, achievement of quality objectives and meeting client expectations. There is no difference between moderately virtual teams and highly virtual teams – a typology derived from physical virtuality factors of level of times zones dispersion and number of team locations – in the success of projects performed. Advanced teams have the best project success rate and basic teams have the worst project success rate. The project success rates of moderately and highly virtual teams' lies between basic and advanced teams, with highly virtual teams slightly outperforming moderately virtual teams.

Temporal dispersion has a greater negative impact on the workings of basic teams. Advanced teams are not as impacted and they outperform basic teams in executing tasks in parallel across time zones, have better working relationships with team members that are dispersed across time zones, demonstrate a better understanding of the different physiological and social norms of team members in different time zones and are less likely to miss deliverable deadlines as a result of confusion over times. There is no real difference in the impact temporal dispersion has on the team performance of moderate virtual and highly virtual teams. The only factor where temporal dispersion has differing impacts is executing tasks parallel, with highly virtual teams having greater difficulty than moderately virtual teams.

Advanced virtual teams are more experienced than basic teams in the use of communication technology. They differ significantly with basic teams with a higher level of usage of team and organisation websites, and show slightly higher usage of email, phone, and web conferencing. While team members of moderately virtual and highly virtual teams show no difference in their level of experience of using communication technologies, there is significant differences between the team types in their use of web conferencing, instant messaging and data sharing repositories, with virtually advanced teams demonstrating higher level of usage than virtually basic teams for all three. Moderately virtual teams show slightly higher level of usage of phones than highly virtual teams.

CONCLUSION

This research is based on a detailed global study of 521 virtual teams. It shows that virtual teams have been adopted globally as a standard way of managing projects.

The study has developed a simple measure of project virtuality - using the two physical measures of largest time zone difference and number of team locations- that is supported by existing research and current practitioners. Analysis of teams classified as moderately virtual and highly virtual by this measure of virtuality, shows that there is no difference in the success of projects performed by moderately virtual teams and the success of projects performed by highly virtual teams.

Using a set of soft characteristics defined from the literature, this research developed two further virtual team types – basic and advanced. Teams classed as basic, have performance factors scores below the mean average for the soft attributes of dedicated team members, virtual team experience, team leader status, team status, vision and goals, expertise and knowledge, common processes, cultural awareness and cultural adaptiveness. Advanced teams have performance factor scores above the mean for all the above. Significantly this research shows that advanced teams have a higher level of project success than basic teams. It is worth noting that apart from the soft characteristics of virtual team experience, cultural awareness and adaptiveness, the other characteristics apply equally to traditional co located project teams. This highlights that the team characteristics to focus on when developing successful virtual projects teams are very similar to the team characteristics focused on in the development of successful traditional co located project teams.

For researchers, this study addresses some of the limitations of previous research (Martin et al., 2004; Nader et al., 2009; Powell et al., 2006) by providing a better understanding of how virtual teams operate and the patterns and practices that they must adopt in order to perform effectively. The measure of virtuality developed can be adopted in future work to improve consistency between studies. The characteristics of advanced virtual teams can also be built on to deepen our understanding of how project team characteristics have an impact on successful outcomes.

Future research on this topic could focus on some of the issues and limitations of this paper. The survey only gathered information from a single member of the virtual team, in most cases the project manager. The study was based on only one project performed by the virtual teams and there was no examination of the project methodologies being used by the teams. Finally, the demographic data also gathered, but not discussed in this paper suggests a high level of usage of virtual teams to execute projects; thus the need for further research.

APPENDIX 1

Component Factor Analysis

Principle component factors analysis (Varimax rotation) was conducted for each of the themes. The table below details the themes, the number of survey questions associated with each theme and the resulting component factors. In all cases the Kaiser Meyer Olkin measure of sampling adequacy (KMO) was greater than 0.5, which is acceptable. Also the Bartlett's test of sphericity was significant at p =0.000 for all cases. A factor loading of > 0.5 was accepted.

Nine soft factors of virtual teams.

Key Themes	No. of Questions	Factors	Meaning
Team Membership KMO = 0.55 FL > 0.7	5	• **Dedicated team members** E=1.6, %V=33	The level of dedication of team members: Dedication-measuring factors are: dedicated to the project, dedicated roles, and reporting directly to the project manager.
		• **Virtual team experience** E= 1.3, %V=27	The team members were experienced with working on virtual teams and also had previous experiences working with other team members.
Political KMO = 0.73 FL > 0.6	5	• **Team leader status** E= 2, %V= 39	The team leader or leaders were well-known, had achieved recognition, and had a high degree of interaction within the team and within the organization or organizations to which the team belonged.
		• **Team status** E=1.4, %V=28	The team had a strong reputation for having the political power to get things done and was allowed the freedom to run the project as it wished.
Social KMO= 0.83 FL > 0.6	7	• **Vision and goals** E= 3, %V= 43	The team had a clearly defined vision, goals, and objectives and team members were aligned to them.
		• **Expertise and knowledge** E= 2, %V=28	Team members' expertise was considered more important than job title or position, and team members were encouraged to share their knowledge with the rest of the team.
Organizational Culture KMO = 0.68 FL> 0.7	4	• **Common processes** E=2.4, %V=59	The team had one set of organizational policies, methodologies, and processes.
National Culture KMO = 0.87 FL> 0.5	7	• **Cultural awareness** E=2.6, %V=37	The team members were good at recognizing the different cultural situations that arose within the team and understood the different economic, social, and legal conditions of the various countries in which the other team members lived.
		• **Cultural adaptiveness** E=2, %V=30%	Team members worked hard to adapt to the different cultural situations that occurred within the team and were sensitive to other team members' cultural behavior. This was reflected in the way team members communicated and interacted within the team.

Note 1: Extraction method: Principle component analysis and rotation method: Varimax with Kaiser Normalization.

Note 2: KMO = Kaiser Meyer Olkin measure of sampling adequacy; E = eigenvalue: % V = percentage of variance; FL = Factor loadings

REFERENCES

Anantatmula, V., & Thomas, M. (2010). Managing global projects: A structured approach for better performance. *Project Management Journal, 41*(2), 60–72.

Andriessen, J.H.E., Verburg, R.M., (2004). A model for the analysis of virtual teams. Virtual and collaborative teams: process, technologies and practices: edited by Susan Hayes Godar, Shamila Pixy Ferris, Idea Group publishing, UK, Chapter XV, Page 269

Au, Y., & Marks, A. (2012). Virtual teams are literally and metaphorically invisible: Forging identity in culturally diverse virtual teams. *Employee Relations*, *34*, 271–287.

Bal, J., & Gundy, J. (1999). Virtual teaming in the automotive supply chain. *Team Performance Management*, *5*(6), 174–193.

Bal. J., & Teo, P. K. (2000). Implementing virtual team working. Part 1: A literature review of best practice. *Logistic Information Management, 13*(6), 346–352.

Belanger, F., & Watson-Manheim, M. B. (2006). Virtual teams and multiple media: Structuring media use to attain strategic goals. *Group Decision and Negotiation*, *15*, 299–321.

Bell, B. S., & Kozlowski, S. W. J. (2002). A typology of virtual teams: Implications for effective leadership. *Group and Organization Management, 27*(1), 14–49.

Berry, G. (2011). Enhancing effectiveness on virtual teams: Understanding why traditional teams' skills are insufficient. *Journal of Business Communication*, *48*(2), 186–206.

Bourgault, M., Drouin, N., & Hamel, É. (2008). Decision making within distributed project teams: An exploration of formalization and autonomy as determinants of success. *Project Management Journal*, *39*, S97–S110.

Cascio, W.F., Shurygailo, S., (2003), E-Leadership and Virtual teams, *Organisational Dynamics* , Volume 31, Issue 4, Jan 2003, Pages 362-376.

Cheng, C., Chua, R., Morris, M., & Lee, L., (2012). Finding the right mix: How the composition of self-managing multicultural teams' cultural value orientation influences performance over time. *Journal of Organisational Behaviour*. *33*, 389–411.

Chudoba, K. M., Wynn, E., Lu, M., & Watson-Manheim, M. B. (2005). How virtual are we? Measuring virtuality and understanding its impacts in a global organisation. *Information Systems Journal, 15*(4), 279–306.

Cummings, J., & Haas, M. (2012). So many teams, so little time: Time allocation matter in geographically dispersed teams. *Journal of Organisational Behavior*, *33*, 316–341.

Curlee, W. (2008). Modern virtual project management: The effects of a centralized and decentralized project management office. *Project Management Journal*, *39*, Supplement S83–S96.

Dekker, D. M., Rutte, C. G., & Van den Berg, P. T. (2008). Cultural differences in the perception of critical interaction behaviors in global virtual teams. *International Journal of Intercultural Relations*, *32*, 441–452.

Domchke, M., Bog, A., Uflacker, M., & Zeier, A. (2009). Managing globally distributes engineering teams: A case study on virtual industrial engineering. *Industrial Engineering and Engineering Management*, 2009, 16th International Conference. 21-23 October, Beijing.

Dube, L., Bourhis, A., & Jacob, R. (2006). Towards a typology of virtual communities of practice. *Interdisciplinary Journal of Information, Knowledge, and Management, 1*, 69–93.

Dundis, S., Benson, S., (2003). Making virtual work teams successful: Measuring the 'Interactive Demand' of tasks and fitting it to the demands of technology, people and structure, Proceedings of the 3ed IEEE International Conference on Advanced Learning Technologies. (ICALT'03)

Duranti, C. M., & de Almeida, F. C. (2012). Is more technology better for communication in international virtual teams? *International Journal of e-Collaboration, 8*, 36–52.

Edwards, H., & Sridhar, V. (2003). Analysis of the effectiveness of global virtual teams in software engineering projects, *36th Hawaii International Conference on System Sciences* (HICSS'03), Hawaii, 6-9th Jan.

Espinosa, J. A., DeLone, W., & Lee, G. (2006). Global boundaries, task processes, and IS project success: A field study. *Information Technology & People, 19*(4), 345–370.

Evaristo, R., Van Fenema, P.C., (1999). A typology pf project management: emergence and evolution of new forms, *International Journal of Project Management*, Volume 17, Issue 5, October 1999, pages 275-281

Fiol, C. M., & O'Connor, E. J. (2005). Identification in face-to-face, hybrid, and pure virtual teams: Untangling the contradictions. *Organization Science, 16*(1), 19–32.

Fisher, K., Fisher, M., (2000). The distance manager: A hands on guide to managing off-site employees and virtual teams, McGraw-Hill, Inc. New York, NY, ISBN: 1589453700

Geber, B. (1995, April). Virtual teams. *Training, 32*, 36–40.

Gibson, C. B., & Cohen, S. G. (2003). *Virtual teams that work: Creating conditions for virtual team effectiveness.* San Francisco, CA: Jossey-Bass.

Gibson, C. B., & Gibbs, J. L. (2006). Unpacking the concept of virtuality: The effects of geographic dispersion, electronic dependence, dynamic structure, and national diversity on team innovation. *Administrative Science Quarterly, 51,* 451–495.

Gilson, L., Maynard, M. T., Jones Young, N. C., Vartiainen, M., & Hakonen, M. A. (2015). Virtual teams research: 10 years, 10 themes, and 10 opportunities. *Journal of Management, 41*(5), 1313–1337.

Griffith, T. L., & Neale, M. A. (2001). Information processing in traditional, hybrid, and virtual teams: From nascent knowledge to transactive memory. *Research in Organizational Behavior, 23*, 379–421.

Griffith, T. L., & Sawyer, J. E. (2006). Supporting technologies and organisational practices for the transfer of knowledge in virtual environments. *Group Decision and Negotiation, 15,* 407–423.

Han, H., Hiltz, S., Fjermstad, J., & Wang, Y. (2011). Does medium matter? A comparison of initial meeting modes for virtual teams, *IEEE Transactions on Professional Communication, 54*, 376–391.

Henderson, L. S. (2008). The impact of project managers' communication competencies: Validation and extension of a research model of virtuality, satisfaction, and productivity on project teams. *Project Management Journal, 39*, 48–59.

Henry, J. E., & Hartzler, M. (1997). Virtual teams: Today's reality, today's challenge. *Quality Progress, 30*, 108–109.

Jugdev, K., & Muller, R. (2005). A retrospective look at our evolving understanding of project success. *Project Management Journal, 36*(4), 19–31.

Kim, K., Kirkman, B.L., Chen, G., (2006). Cultural Intelligence and International Assignment Effectiveness: A conceptual model and preliminary findings. In Ang, S., Van Dyne L., (Eds.), *Handbook of Cultural Intelligence: Theory, Measurement and Application*, (p 71), Armonk NY, ME Sharpe.

Kimble, C., Li, F., & Barlow, A. (2000). Effective virtual teams through communities of practice. *Management Science Theory, Method, and Practice*, Strathclyde Business School, Research Paper 2000/9.

Kirkman, B. L., Rosen, B., Gibson, C., Tesluk, P., & McPherson, S. (2002). Five challenges to virtual team success: Lessons from Sabre, Inc. *Academy of Management Executive, 16*(3), 67-79.

Klitmoller, A., & Lauring, L. (2013). When global virtual teams share knowledge: Media richness, cultural difference, and language commonality. *Journal of World Business, 48*, 398–406.

Krumm, S., Terwiel, K., & Hertel, G. (2013). Challenges in norm formation and adherence: The knowledge, skills, and ability requirements of virtual and traditional cross-cultural teams. *Journal of Personnel Psychology, 12*(1), 33–44.

Lee-Kelley, L. (2002). Situational leadership: Managing the virtual project team. *Journal of Management Development, 21*(6), 461–476.

Lipnack, J., & Stamps, J. (2000). *Virtual teams: People working across boundaries with technology*. (2nd Ed.). New York, NY: John Wiley & Sons.

Martin, L. L., Gilson, L. L., & Maynard, M. T. (2004). Virtual teams: What do we know and where do we go from here? *Journal of Management, 30*(6), 805–835.

Maynard, M. T., Mathieu, J. E., Rapp, T. L, & Gilson, L. L. (2012). Something(s) old and something(s) new: Modeling drivers of global virtual team effectiveness. *Journal of Organisational Behaviour*, 33, 342–365.

Mockaitis, A. I., Rose, E. L., & Zettinig, P. (2012). The power of individual cultural values in global virtual teams. *International Journal of Cross-Cultural Management, 12*, 193–210.

Mohammed, S., & Nadkarni, S. (2011). Temporal diversity and team performance: The moderating role of team temporal leadership. *Academy of Management Journal, 54*(3), 489–508.

Moser, K., & Axtell, C. (2013). The role of norms in virtual work: A review and agenda for future research. *Journal of Personnel Psychology, 12*(1), 1–6.

Mukherjee, D., Lahiri, S., Mukherjee, D., & Billing, T. (2012). Leading virtual teams: how do social, cognitive, and behavioral capabilities matter? *Management Decision, 50*(2), 273–290.

Nader, A. E, Shamsuddin, A., & Zahari, T. (2009). Virtual teams: A literature review. *Australian Journal of Basic and Applied Sciences, 3*(3), 2653–2669.

Ocker, R. J., Huang, H., Benbunan-Fich, R., & Hiltz, S. R. (2011). *Group Decision & Negotiation, 20*, 273–292.

Orlikowski, W. J. (2002). Knowing in practice: Enacting a collective capability in distributed organizing. *Organization Science, 13*(3), 249–273.

Pinjani, P., & Palvia, P. (2013). Trust and knowledge sharing in diverse global virtual teams. *Information and Management, 50*, 144–153.

Pinto, J. K., & Slevin, D. P. (1988). Critical success factors in successful project management. *IEEE Transactions on Engineering Management, 34*(1), 22–27.

Powell, A., Galvin, J., & Piccoli, G. (2006). Antecedents to team member's commitment from near and far: A comparison between co-located and virtual teams. *Information Technology & People, 19*(4), 299–322.

Reich, B., Gemino, A., & Sauer, C. (2012). Knowledge management and project-based knowledge in IT projects: A model and preliminary empirical results. *International Journal of Project Management, 30*(6), 663–674.

Robert, L. (2013). *A multilevel analysis of the impact of shared leadership in diverse virtual teams.* Research Gate, 23–27 February, San Antonio, TX, USA.

Schlenkrich, L., & Upfold, C. (2009). A guideline for virtual team managers: The key to effective social interaction and communication. *The Electronic Journal Information Systems Evaluation, 12(*1), 109–118.

Schweitzer, L., & Duxbury, L. (2010). Conceptualizing and measuring the virtuality of teams. *Information Systems Journal, 20*, 267–295.

Staples, D. S., & Cameron, A. F. (2005). *The effect of task design, team characteristics, organizational context, and team processes on the performance and attitudes of virtual team members.* Proceedings of the 38th Hawaii International Conference on System Sciences, Hawaii, 6-9th January.

Staples D. S., & Zhao, L., (2006). The effects of cultural diversity in virtual teams versus face to face teams. *Group Decision and Negotiation*, 15, 389–406.

Timmerman, C., & Scott, C. (2006). Virtually working: Communicative and structural predictors of media use and key outcomes in virtual work teams, *Communication monographs,* 73(1), 108—136.

Verburg, R., Bosch-Sijtsema, P., & Vartiainen, P. (2013). Getting it done: Critical success factors for project managers in virtual work settings. *International Journal of Project Management, 31*, 68–79.

Webster, J., Wong, W. K. P. (2008). Comparing traditional and virtual group forms: Identity, communication, and trust in naturally occurring project teams. *The International Journal of Human Resource Management*, *19*(1), 41–62.

Wang, D., Waldman, D., & Zhang, Z. (2014). A meta-analysis of shared leadership and team

Watson-Manheim, M. B., Chudoba, K. M., & Crowston, K. (2002). Discontinuities and continuities: A new way to understand virtual work. *Information, Technology & People, 15*(3), 191–209.

Wong, S., & Burton, R. M. (2000). Virtual teams: What are their characteristics and impact on team performance? *Computational & Mathematical Organization Theory*, 6, 339–360.

Zander, L., Mockaitis, A., & Butler, C. (2012). Leading global teams. *Journal of World Business*, *47*, 592–603.

Zhang, S., Tremaine, M., Fjermstad, J., Milewski, A., & O'Sullivan, P. (2006). Delegation in virtual teams: The moderating effects of team maturity and team distance. *IEEE International Conference on Global Software Engineering* (ICGSE'06), Florianopolis, Oct 2006, 3-11.

DECISION SCIENCES INSTITUTE

A systems theory perspective of data analytics implementation

Natalie Gerhart
University of North Texas
Email: natalie.gerhart@unt.edu

ABSTRACT

Big data is often seen as a silver bullet when applied with the appropriate data analytics tools; however, there is a downside: dependence. Over time, data analytics users begin to apply less cognitive effort or apply data analytics in the wrong scenario, which can have a long-term negative effect on firms. The limits to the applicability of big data has not been vetted in data analytics research. Through General Systems Theory and causal map modeling, this work provides a perspective on a negative of big data analytics and conceptually adds to the practical and theoretical understanding of big data analytics.

KEYWORDS: Data Analytics, General Systems Theory, Technology Dependence, Cognitive Effort

INTRODUCTION

The potential of big data and business analytics is seemingly limitless. Since entering the list, big data is consistently in the top ten of most significant investments by Information Technology leaders (Kappelman, McLean, Johnson, & Gerhart, 2014). While most companies see big data as an opportunity, it does not instantly and easily solve business problems unless properly handled. By one estimate, the amount of data doubles every year (Helbing, 2014). While big data is leveraged in many businesses, the research on how analysts are actually using big data and improving strategy is lagging.

Big data is not just a large quantity of data, instead it incorporates the 3Vs: volume, velocity, and variety (Gartner Inc., 2013). The combination addresses the amount, the speed it is collected, and the many sources and structures of the data. Big data alone can be a problem more than a solution from a strategic perspective; creating value out of big data requires big data analytics. Big data analytics has been defined to include advanced analytic techniques as well as the actual big data (Russom, 2011). Common software packages, such as SAS Enterprise Miner and IBM SPSS Modeler, allow more data scientists access to the power of big data analytics by simplifying the analytics.

Organizations are seeking employees with greater analytical and technical skills than previous generations. The modern employee, many of whom are digital natives, or those born into a world with ubiquitous computing, have a changing view of technology (Prensky, 2001). The connected nature of digital natives both fuels the amount of data available for a business, but also changes how strategic decisions are made for an organization.

The combination of big data and digital natives in the workforce presents an interesting paradox for businesses. There is a new abundance of information to be gained and a new reliance on technology for decision making. In the short-term, these seem to align, however in the long-term, there will be a side effect of technology dependence that makes decision makers unable to use intuition or common sense. Cognitive effort theories indicate that a reliance on previous technologies results in reduced effort instead of increased quality of outcomes on the part of the employee (Todd & Benbasat, 1992).

Through the lens of General Systems Theory (GST), this research addresses a gap in the literature concerning the impacts of big data and technology dependence on long-term business strategy. Generally, GST seeks to address problems from a holistic perspective to better understand the relationships between the parts of a system (von Bertalanffy, 1972). More specifically, causal maps allow representation of these relationships in a meaningful way that help draw attention to discrepancies that are not intuitive. Combining these tools with a cognitive effort perspective and the theory of technology dominance, this research proposes that big data use follows the "shifting the burden" archetype to show that big data analytics might not always be the best solution to decision making.

This research outlines a clear concern for companies as we move forward with big data analytics: what is the appropriate balance of big data analytics strategies? Organizations are encouraged to pursue big data analytics, even if they are not yet capable of handling the behemoth that is big data. Current research in the area of big data analytics simplifies the contribution of big data, which this research expands.

LITERATURE REVIEW

An Overview of General Systems Theory

The founding of GST is historically credited to Ludwig von Bertalanffy whose academic pursuits were in biology (von Bertalanffy, 1972). In his work, he cites the ideas to ancient times when Aristotle propositioned that a whole could be greater than the sum of its parts (von Bertalanffy, 1972). Despite his biological sciences background, a key focus of GST is the interdisciplinary nature of all problems (Boulding, 1956). In practice, GST research not only spans several disciplines, it attempts to bridge the differences into a common language and develop models of behavior and structure that can be used to explain phenomena on a macro level (Wilby, 2006).

One available output of GST is a causal map. A causal map seeks to show relationships between variables in a given context (Burgess, Clark, Hauser, & Zmud, 1992). Causal maps are an ideal tool for explaining complex organizational behaviors to participants in an organization that might not be able to overcome their own innate human biases (Burgess et al., 1992). While very useful, they do lack some detail and explanation of how the system behaves over time (Lane, 2008). Often, users that are unfamiliar with causal maps will find them difficult to understand, so to provide practical value it is good to use a cyclical process and several participants to help develop and explain the maps iteratively (Burgess et al., 1992).

Some researchers use causal maps as a starting place for understanding a complex situation, and then later develop them into stock and flow diagrams (Homer & Oliva, 2001). Stock and flow diagrams depict the same concepts as causal maps, however they clearly indicate where variables accumulate over time and how the detailed dynamics of the system evolve (Lane, 2008). These diagrams can be created with complex mathematical equations underlying the relationships and then simulated to show how the system may behave (Forrester, 2003). Because research on the intricacies of the impact of big data on organizational behaviors has not been heavily developed, a causal map is used to fill the gap in current research, with the potential for later development of stock and flow diagrams.

Big Data

The problem of big data is not new; however, the extent to which this data is captured and stored is increasing constantly, thanks to ubiquitous computing. As previously stated, big data is not just volume but includes the 3Vs (Gartner Inc., 2013). While the 3Vs describe what big data is, big data is not inherently useful based on this definition. Value is sometimes considered a fourth "V" of big data, because it is an essential part of why big data should be used by organizations (Watson, 2014). For big data to be useful, analytics must be performed to discern information from the data.

The insights possible from big data are seemingly endless if the proper tools and people are able to translate the data into information. Technology is the only solution for handling big data, as it is too massive to be valuable without the assistance of computers. Technology has a legacy of making complicated situations manageable. As an example, Decision Support Systems (DSSs) were developed in the 1970s as tools to help users make better decisions (Watson & Wixom, 2007). Organizational decisions are often complicated with many different factors to consider at once, and big data is a prime example of aggregating many variables. Paradoxically, the technology that allows for big data might allow for both insights as well as overload (Clark, Jones, & Armstrong, 2007). Analytical decision making involves using analytics instead of intuitions to make decisions (Davenport, Harris, & Morison, 2010). Usually these decisions are judged based on the quality of the decision. Decision quality is not objective and can be the outcomes of the decision, the satisfaction of the decision maker (Lilien, Rangaswamy, Van Bruggen, & Starke, 2004), or the efficiency of the decision (Speier & Morris, 2003).

In the 1990s, DSS focus turned towards Business Intelligence (BI) (Watson, 2014). DSSs have similar traits to BI, and BI is sometimes considered a subfield of DSSs (Kowalczyk, Buxmann, & Besier, 2013). BI is a term that describes a large set of tools used for statistical analysis, data storage techniques, and modeling techniques (Seddon, Constantinidis, & Dod, 2012). BI is important in understanding big data because often BI uses big data to draw insights for the business environment.

The term big data was solidified in BI publications around the year 2011 (Wixom et al., 2014). Some argue that big data analytics is the second half of the BI process; while BI is getting data in, big data analytics is getting information out (Watson, 2014). Others see the two terms as interchangeable. While the two are certainly related, big data presents separate problems from general BI. One of the most significant concerns with big data is the inability to hire enough people that can handle the 3Vs properly (Wixom et al., 2014). The amount of classes and programs to educate students about BI and big data tools are increasing, but practitioners still report a shortage of knowledgeable people to provide business value from big data (Wixom et al., 2014).

A Reliant Workforce

Big data continues to grow in importance, and simultaneously the workforce is fundamentally changing. Many students today, and therefore future employees, are termed digital natives. This generation of people were raised completely engrossed in the use of technology (Prensky, 2001). In contrast, people who might be just as proficient at using technology, but had to learn how to use it manually are digital immigrants (Prensky, 2001). Brains of digital natives develop differently than digital immigrants (Prensky, 2001). Arguably, digital natives see no need to memorize any basic information, because a person can always look up any information on a nearby smartphone (Pogue, 2013). Because of the changing workforce, business operations are evolving because these users are comfortable with relying on modern technology and they make up the bulk of the upcoming workforce.

The use of technology can be a blessing and a burden. Technology can improve decision quality, in fact decision aids should be used to assist professionals with complex tasks (Arnold, Collier, Leech, & Sutton, 2004). For instance, DSSs improve decision quality compared to using unsophisticated tools (Lilien et al., 2004). Others argue that for the technology to truly be effective, it should reduce effort and increase accuracy of decision makers (Todd & Benbasat, 1992). If it does not meet one of these two goals, it will not create value for the company.

Contrastingly, technology might also decrease the drive of the user, particularly if the user does not understand how the technology works. Prior research on cognitive effort theory indicates that technology is often designed to reduce cognitive effort, which is desirable to the brain. Despite technology assistance, analysis of big data is complex because of the 3Vs. The decision situation is constantly changing and growing. The cognitive effort perspective, first argued by Payne (1982), claims there is a cost and benefit to every cognitive task. Just as with purchases, thinkers must make a tradeoff between effort and quality of the outcome (Payne, 1982). Using big data analytical technology, a user should be able to reduce cognitive load, which leaves energy to be absorbed somewhere: either reinvested into more analysis, possibly with more variables, or saved by the analyst. DSS research shows people do not reinvest effort saved by the benefits of technology, but just finding a satisfactory answer instead (Todd & Benbasat, 1992). With search technologies, research shows, those who are given a query as a starting search line resulted in more errors, less time, and more confidence in the query than those without a starting point (Allen & Parsons, 2006). Put simply, those who put forth less effort did not have as good of results as those who started from nothing. By not reapplying the effort to handle more complex problems, the employee is in effect depending on the technology for future solutions as well.

The dependence that is created through a lack of reinvested effort can be partially explained by the theory of technology dominance (TTD). TTD recognizes an incongruence between a user's skillset and the complexity of tasks which impacts reliance on technology (Arnold & Sutton, 1998). The key ideas in this theory center on experience with a task and a decision aid, complexity of the task, and the cognitive fit between the user and the decision aid (Arnold & Sutton, 1998). If a person begins to form a reliance on a decision aid, this will cause deskilling (Arnold & Sutton, 1998). Deskilling is a term to describe a growing dependence on technology that results in the decision maker losing understanding of the decision process, which ultimately results in an inability to make a quality decision in the future (Mascha & Smedley, 2007).

TTD has been researched in many decision aid contexts, but not in regards to big data analytics specifically. Research indicates that decision aids might negatively impact inexperienced decision makers (Arnold et al., 2004). Some researchers find that providing feedback on the decision aids functionality can mitigate some of the concern with deskilling (Mascha & Smedley, 2007). Contrastingly, some find that experience does not impact decision quality, however inexperienced users are more reliant on the decision aid (Jensen, Lowry, Burgoon, & Nunamaker, 2010). These studies indicate using technology might debilitate a user from making a quality decision without the aid.

The effect of technology dependence is a heavily debated topic in Information Systems research, and often a poorly defined concept. Some use the term technology dependence, while others use addiction, excessive use, problematic use, and some stop at habit; the consensus is only that there is not one definition (Vaghefi & Lapointe, 2014). Despite a debate in terminology, there is generally an idea that it is a problem if overuse of technology cripples a user's ability to function without the technology. For this research, this concept is the definition for technology dependence.

A logical assumption is, if there are more inputs, and better processes, outcomes will improve for a given situation. Despite the increase of the data (input), and the increasing sophistication of analytical tools (process), there is still little research into if and how users are gaining benefits (outcomes) from big data analytics.

A CAUSAL MODEL OF DECISION MAKING WITH BIG DATA ANALYTICS

Peter Senge (1990) is often credited with promoting causal maps developed out of archetype structures. An archetype is a pattern of system structure that occurs repeatedly across different situations (Wolstenholme, 2003). Complex systems result in poor mental models, often because of counterintuitive behavior. By using an archetype as a frame of reference to begin to shape the situation, the system structure may become clearer. To better understand this structure, the "shifting the burden" archetype is applied to using big data analytics to improve decision making (see Figure 1).

Figure 1: Shifting the Burden Archetype

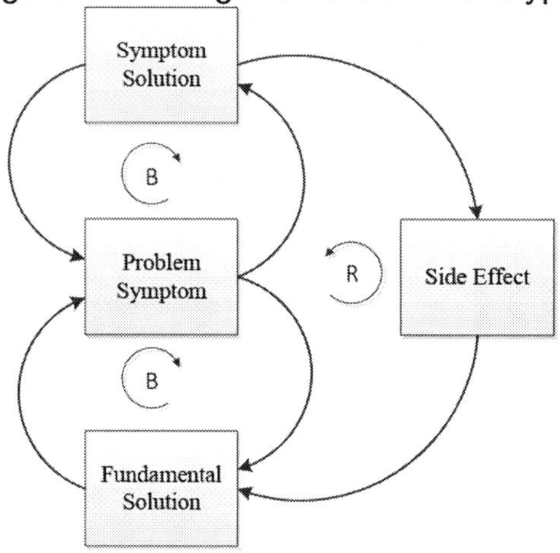

The "shifting the burden" archetype, put simply, proposes there is a problem for which a solution is developed to treat the symptoms, which creates a side effect and ultimately has a negative impact on the fundamental solution to the problem (Senge, 1990). In this context, the problem is poor decision quality and the symptom solution is analytical decision making. This could be a reasonable solution, although it creates a side effect that makes it harder to resort back to the original long-term treatment that should have been applied originally (Senge, 1990). In this case, relying only on analytical decision making creates a side effect of big data dependence, which makes it harder to ultimately make independent decisions. Through this archetype, I will discuss the role of big data in organizations (see Figure 2).

Figure 2: Big Data Analytics Archetype

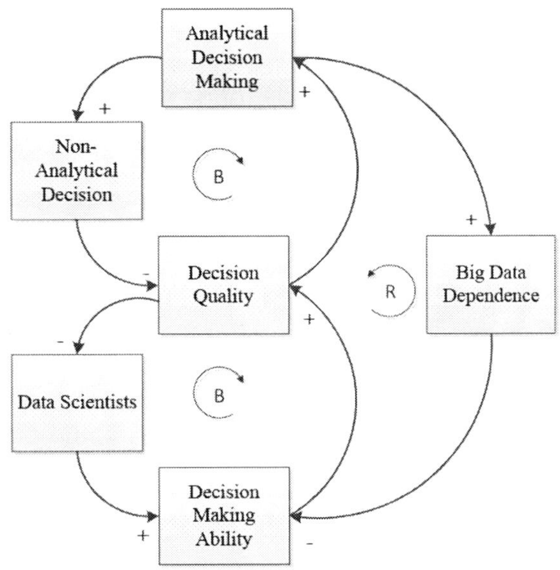

Figure 3: Analytical Decision Making

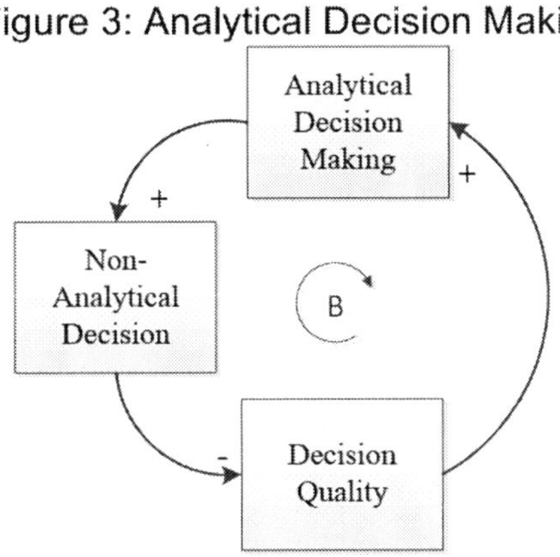

To better understand this archetype from a GST perspective, individual loops are explained in detail. First, "shifting the burden" revolves around a problem behavior: the need for a higher decision quality (see Figure 3). Organizations might have a poor decision quality, or might have a poor *perceived* decision quality because competitors are using cutting edge decision tools. Currently, there is a significant push for more analytical decision making to improve decision quality (Davenport, 2006). When applied appropriately, analytical decision making can be a huge benefit resulting in better decisions (Davenport, 2006). Big data innately requires technology, however big data analytics is treated as somewhat of a golden ticket to problem solving. Using big data analytics allows for new insights that otherwise might not be intuitive for a decision maker. The benefits of big data analytics are obvious and most companies see big data analytics as an opportunity for the future (Russom, 2011). As decision quality of the firm increases, the organization will begin to use more analytical decision making. Discovering these new insights increases the perceived value of big data analytics, and thus the organization will want to do more big data analytics.

The downside of analytical decision making is that not all decisions should be made using big data, such as non-routine decisions (Kowalczyk & Buxmann, 2014). Data analytics relies on past occurrences, and as a result, if a situation is an anomaly, it would not be wise to try to use past data analysis to arrive at a solution. Analytics provide sound reasons for making decisions, but not all companies are able to continuously gain benefits from big data analytics given the current state of their business. Presumably, more analytical decisions should positively impact the decision quality, however this is not always the case. Part of decision quality includes the financial cost of the decision and the time it takes to make the decision. The use of big data analytics for simple decision tasks would also hurt decision quality if the decision could have been reached by cheaper, faster, and simpler means. Instead, big data should be used in appropriate decision tasks that relevant data is available to determine factors that are important for a problem that has happened before (Kowalczyk & Buxmann, 2014). Another primary concern with big data comes from making decisions using dirty data (Kopytoff, 2014). If the data is not cleaned properly, there is a high potential for misleading information, and data cleaning can be time consuming and costly (Li & Joshi, 2012). Making decisions with analytics when it is not appropriate can have a negative impact on decision quality. As a result, this creates a balancing loop as pictured in Figure 3.

Analytical decision making can certainly be used only in appropriate situations, however, even in this case it creates a side effect (see Figure 4). The side effect is a dependence on big data. Companies are facing a shortage of people able to perform the required analytical tasks, and as a result, they are trying to replace the people with automated statistical tools (Fitzgerald, 2014). Because there is a shortage of people who can effectively make analytical decisions, the tools might be used by inexperienced decision makers. This idea is addressed in the TTD and suggests that this will create a reliance on the tool (Arnold et al., 2004).

Figure 4: A Side Effect of Dependence

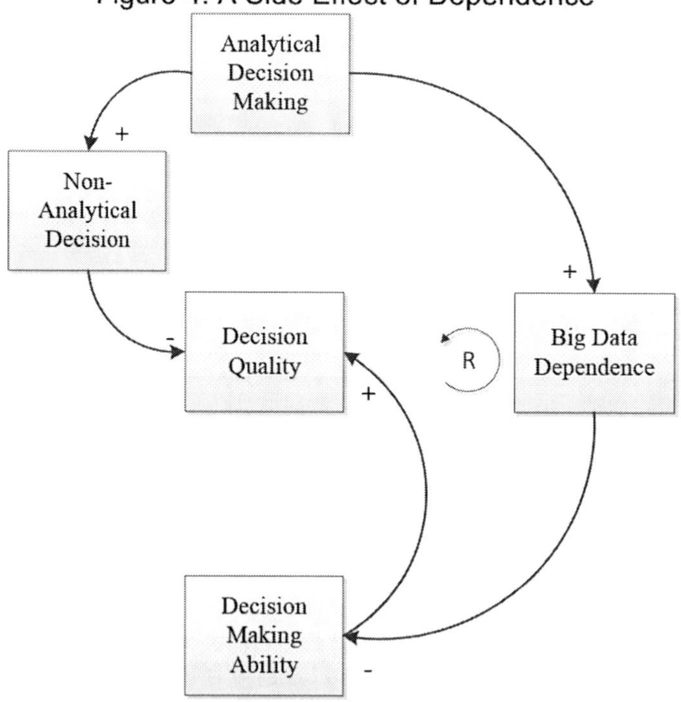

For the organizations that have high quality data scientists who can perform appropriate analytics, there is still a concern. As long as the data scientist constantly reinvests the effort that is saved from using the technology back into using more data or making more complex decisions, then the result will be good. Unfortunately, as prior research suggests, saved effort from technology use is often not reinvested to improve decision quality (Todd & Benbasat, 1992). Instead, the user just becomes more dependent on the technology.

People are relying on technology at the individual level as a cognitive crutch that no longer requires effort (Pogue, 2013). When people rely on technology, they no longer exercise their brains and lose some ability to process complex problems, or deskill (Mascha & Smedley, 2007). At the organizational level, some companies are relying heavily on analytics to make decisions (Davenport et al., 2010). Using System Dynamics, deskilling was effectively shown as a concern in IT outsourcing in prior research (McCray & Clark, 1999). Instead of outsourcing to another company, big data analytics are being "outsourced" to automated tools that can also hurt the users knowledge (Fitzgerald, 2014). While big data can improve decision making, there is still a need to have quality decision makers that know how to make a quality decision with the aid of data (McAfee & Brynjolfsson, 2012). A shortage of people, as well as a lack of understanding and effort by current decision makers, creates a dependence on big data that further creates a problem for a company.

The dependence on big data results in a negated ability to make decision appropriately. If people are reliant on the big data analytics and not reinvesting effort, or if there are not proper data scientists performing the analysis, the ability to make decisions without analytics will suffer. As the company grows in dependence, big data analytics will become the default option, even when it is not the proper solution to a decision making task. The more dependent a company is on big data analytics, the harder it will be to correct the behavior of misusing big data analytics. This problem continues to perpetuate as a greater need for increased decision quality leads to more analytical decision making, which in turn creates greater dependence on big data.

Figure 5: The Solution

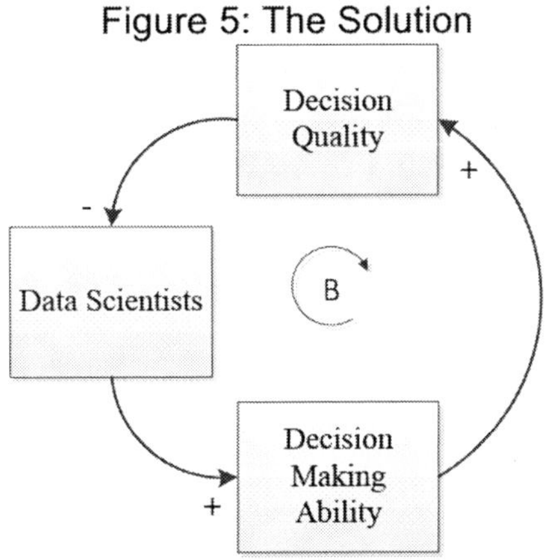

The solution to the problem is to apply the appropriate decision making techniques with the appropriate amount of resources that fit the task (see Figure 5). Put simply, hiring data scientists that can properly reinvest effort to increase decision quality. The primary reason this is not the chosen solution for some organizations is because it can be a delayed effect. For instance, hiring sophisticated data scientists that can properly turn big data into a valuable resource might take significant time, money, and training.

Using big data analytics will likely appear to improve perceived decision quality in the beginning, even if it is misapplied or handled by unskilled statisticians. The belief that the decision is better will send the organization spiraling into the loop pictured in figure 3. However, hiring the appropriate data scientists will more accurately provide a long-term solution. If an organization is experiencing a high decision quality at the moment, the relationship to hiring high quality data scientists will be negative. There is no need to hire data scientists if there is a perceived high decision quality.

Overall, data scientists improve decision making ability in the long-term. Because these employees are sophisticated at handling big data analytics, they are more likely to use the conserved effort and reapply it into decision-making. Further, only using big data for tasks that big data can supply answers to will reduce dependence on big data. Using the most appropriate decision making task would reduce the big data dependence, and instead only encourage it when it is an appropriate tool for a decision. This creates a balancing loop that keeps decision making and decision quality in an optimal balance.

DISCUSSION

The causal map presented in this research explains how big data analytics might not always be the best solution, and instead it might create a dependence on big data technology that is not necessary for simple decisions. The implications of these ideas are two-fold. First, practitioners should take caution in dependence on big data to make decisions. As illustrated, this can lead to a vicious cycle of dependence that begins to inhibit quality decision making. Instead, big data should be used in tasks that are appropriate and some decisions should still be made on intuition and available information.

Secondly, research can benefit from this analysis. This work suggests there are boundary conditions for when big data analytics is the optimal solution. Research should further investigate what are the prime situations for big data analytics, and what simply further perpetuates a dependence that is unnecessary. This should be analyzed in two ways; first a simulation model might further indicate counterintuitive behaviors of the behaviors presented that might result in bigger problems that it is hard to foresee using only mental models (Sterman, 2001). Secondly, reductionist research might provide other insights into these relationships. Using other methodologies, such as empirical analysis of practitioner data, would be a useful way to validate these ideas. Further research into the relationship between big data and decision-making could shed new light on the use of technology as a decision aid. Specifically a few research questions might include:

What are the limits of big data analytics?

In what contexts is big data analytics most efficient at creating value for an organization?

How can organizations encourage reapplication of conserved effort in big data contexts?

By exploring some of these questions, new ideas will likely arise that will make big data analytics more valuable to companies, and thus make an impact on determining what is the best solution for an individual context.

LIMITATIONS

All systems theory models are subject to boundary conditions that can be just as important as the causal map itself (Wolstenholme, 2004). The model presented here is no exception and was designed with boundary conditions in mind. First, this work assumes that there are not an adequate number of data scientists available and that there is a delay before future scientists can be integrated into an organization. Second, not all individuals behave in the same way, and some employees will reinvest effort appropriately instead of conserving. This would make the dependence on big data less of a concern if the energy is reinvested appropriately. Third, this model is bounded by the investment capabilities of the organization. Big data analytics is not applicable for every organization, as it can be costly and too sophisticated for some smaller organizations. Finally, decision-making is a complex task in itself, and as a result there are several outside factors that go beyond the scope of this research that might play a significant role in big data dependence.

Further, without simulation, causal maps are arguably untested. Many systems theorists believe that the true nature of the system can only be understood with simulation, and thus a causal map would not accurately portray the complex dynamics (Homer & Oliva, 2001). Despite the concern, causal maps are a useful place to begin to understand complex situations, particularly with behaviors that are not easily measured, such as decision making (Coyle, 2001). As a result, the causal map presented here provides a good background structure for understanding the problem and furthering the ideas in this area. More traditional empirical research in this area, with the consideration of the issues brought out by the causal map presented, would likely provide valuable insights to business practitioners.

CONCLUSION

The causal map presented in this research attempts to explain the role big data can play in an organization and the counterintuitive behavior it might cause. Primarily, the nature of big data might lend itself to creating a dependence that can ultimately have a negative impact on decision making within an organization. This work fills a gap in big data research by considering the limits to the value of big data analytics and considering inappropriate contexts to use big data. While the opportunities big data presents can be limitless, like all good tools it should be used within the contexts that it is most suited for.

REFERENCES

Allen, G., & Parsons, B. J. (2006). A Little Help can Be A Bad Thing: Anchoring and Adjustment in Adaptive Query Reuse. In *ICIS 2006 Proceedings* (p. Paper 45).

Arnold, V., Collier, P. A., Leech, S. A., & Sutton, S. G. (2004). Impact of intelligent decision aids on expert and novice decision-makers' judgments. *Accounting and Finance*, *44*(1), 1–26. doi:10.1111/j.1467-629x.2004.00099.x

Arnold, V., & Sutton, S. G. (1998). The Theory of Technology Dominance: Understanding the Impact of Intelligent Decision Aids on Decision Makers' Judgments. *Advances in Accounting Behavioral Research*, *1*, 175–194.

Boulding, K. E. (1956). General Systems Theory - The Skeleton of Science. *Management Science*, *2*(3), 197–208.

Burgess, G. M., Clark, T. D. J., Hauser, R. D. J., & Zmud, R. W. (1992). The Application of Causal Maps to Develop a Collective Understanding of Complex Organizational Contexts in Requirements Analysis. *Accounting, Management and Information Technologies*, *2*(3), 143–164.

Clark, T. D. J., Jones, M. C., & Armstrong, C. P. (2007). The Dynamic Structure of Management Support Systems: Theory Development, Research Focus, and Direction. *MIS Quarterly*, *31*(3), 579–615.

Coyle, G. (2001). Rejoinder to Homer and Oliva. *System Dynamics Review*, *17*(4), 357–363. doi:10.1002/sdr.223

Davenport, T. H. (2006). Competing on Analytics. *Harvard Business Review*, *84*(1), 1–11.

Davenport, T. H., Harris, J. G., & Morison, R. (2010). *Analytics at Work: Smarter Decisions, Better Results*. Harvard Business Press.

Fitzgerald, M. (2014). Data Scientist In a Can? Retrieved April 6, 2015, from http://sloanreview.mit.edu/article/data-scientist-in-a-can/

Forrester, J. W. (2003). Dynamic models of economic systems and industrial organizations. *System Dynamics Review*, *19*(4), 329–345. doi:10.1002/sdr.284

Gartner Inc. (2013). IT Glossary Big Data. Retrieved May 7, 2014, from http://www.gartner.com/it-glossary/big-data

Helbing, D. (2014). What the digital revolution means for us. Retrieved August 7, 2014, from http://www.sciencebusiness.net/news/76591/What-the-digital-revolution-means-for-us

Homer, J., & Oliva, R. (2001). Maps and models in system dynamics: A response to Coyle. *System Dynamics Review*, *17*(4), 347–355. doi:10.1002/sdr.224

Jensen, M. L., Lowry, P. B., Burgoon, J. K., & Nunamaker, J. F. (2010). Technology Dominance in Complex Decision Making: The Case of Aided Credibility Assessment. *Journal of Management Information Systems*, *27*(1), 175–202. doi:10.2753/MIS0742-1222270108

Kappelman, L., McLean, E. R., Johnson, V. L., & Gerhart, N. (2014). The 2014 SIM IT Key Issues and Trends Study. *MIS Quarterly Executive*, *13*(4), 237–263.

Kopytoff, V. (2014). Big data's dirty problem. Retrieved from http://fortune.com/2014/06/30/big-data-dirty-problem/

Kowalczyk, M., & Buxmann, P. (2014). Big Data and Information Processing in Organizational Decision Processes. *Business & Information Systems Engineering*, *6*(5), 267–278. doi:10.1007/s12599-014-0341-5

Kowalczyk, M., Buxmann, P., & Besier, J. (2013). Investigating Business Intelligence and Analytics from a Decision Process Perspective: A Structured Literature Review. In *European Conference on Information Systems* (pp. 1–14).

Lane, D. C. (2008). The Emergence and Use of Diagramming in System Dynamics: A Critical Account. *Systems Research and Behavioral Science*, *25*, 3–23.

Li, Y., & Joshi, K. D. (2012). Data Cleansing Decisions: Insights from Discrete-Event Simulations of Firm Resources and Data Quality. *Journal of Organizational Computing and Electronic Commerce*, *22*(4), 361–393. doi:10.1080/10919392.2012.723588

Lilien, G. L., Rangaswamy, A., Van Bruggen, G. H., & Starke, K. (2004). DSS Effectiveness in Marketing Resource Allocation Decisions: Reality vs. Perception. *Information Systems Research*, *15*(3), 216–235. doi:10.1287/isre.1040.0026

Mascha, M. F., & Smedley, G. (2007). Can computerized decision aids do "damage"? A case for tailoring feedback and task complexity based on task experience. *International Journal of Accounting Information Systems*, *8*(2), 73–91. doi:10.1016/j.accinf.2007.03.001

McAfee, A., & Brynjolfsson, E. (2012). Big Data: The Management Revolution. *Harverd Business Review*, *90*(10), 61–68.

McCray, G. E., & Clark, T. D. J. (1999). Using system dynamics to anticipate the organizational impacts of outsourcing. *System Dynamics Review*, *15*(4), 345–373. doi:10.1002/(SICI)1099-1727(199924)15:4<345::AID-SDR177>3.0.CO;2-Z

Payne, J. W. (1982). Contingent decision behavior. *Psychological Bulletin*, *92*(2), 382–402. doi:10.1037//0033-2909.92.2.382

Pogue, D. (2013, July). Smartphones Mean You Will No Longer Have to Memorize Facts. Retrieved October 28, 2014, from http://www.scientificamerican.com/article/smartphones-mean-no-longer-memorize-facts/

Prensky, M. (2001). Digital Natives, Digital Immigrants. *On the Horizon*, *9*(5), 1–6.

Russom, P. (2011). *Big Data Analytics. TDWI Best Practices Report, Fourth Quarter*. Retrieved from http://public.dhe.ibm.com/common/ssi/ecm/en/iml14293usen/IML14293USEN.PDF

Seddon, P. B., Constantinidis, D., & Dod, H. (2012). How Does Business Analytics Contribute to Business Value? In *Thirty Third International Conference on Information Systems* (pp. 1–17). Orlando.

Senge, P. M. (1990). *The Fifth Discipline: The Art and Practice of the Learning Organization*. New York, NY: Currency Doubleday.

Speier, C., & Morris, M. G. (2003). The Influence of Query Interface Design on Decision-Making Performance. *MIS Quarterly*, *27*(3), 397–423.

Sterman, J. D. (2001). System Dynamics Modeling: Tools for Learning in a Complex World. *California Management Review*, *43*(4), 8–25.
Todd, P., & Benbasat, I. (1992). The Use of Information in Decision Making: An Experimental Investigation of the Impact of Computer-Based Decision Aids. *MIS Quarterly*, *16*(3), 373–393.
Vaghefi, I., & Lapointe, L. (2014). When Too Much Usage is Too Much: Exploring the Process of IT Addiction. In *47th Hawaii International Conference on System Sciences* (pp. 4494–4503). Ieee. doi:10.1109/HICSS.2014.553
von Bertalanffy, L. (1972). The History and Status of General Systems Theory. *The Academy of Management Journal*, *15*(4), 407–426.
Watson, H. J. (2014). Tutorial: Big Data Analytics: Concepts, Technologies, and Applications. *Communications of the Association for Information Systems*, *34*(2), 1247–1268.
Watson, H. J., & Wixom, B. H. (2007). The Current State of Business Intelligence. *Computer*, *40*(9), 96–99.
Wilby, J. (2006). An Essay on Kenneth E. Boulding's General Systems Theory: The Skeleton of Science. *Systems Research and Behavioral Science*, *23*, 695–699.
Wixom, B. H., Ariyachandra, T., Douglas, D., Goul, M., Gupta, B., Iyer, L., ... Turetken, O. (2014). The Current State of Business Intelligence in Academia: The Arrival of Big Data. *Communications of the Association for Information Systems*, *34*(1), 1–13.
Wolstenholme, E. F. (2003). Towards the definition and use of a core set of archetypal structures in system dynamics. *System Dynamics Review*, *19*(1), 7–26. doi:10.1002/sdr.259
Wolstenholme, E. F. (2004). Using generic system archetypes to support thinking and modelling. *System Dynamics Review*, *20*(4), 341–356. doi:10.1002/sdr.302

DECISION SCIENCES INSTITUTE
Adding Spice to the Teaching of Quality:
Variation, Poka Yoke, and a Defect Collection

Brad C. Meyer
Drake University

ABSTRACT

This paper presents several ideas for teaching quality in an introduction to operations management class. Contained is a teaching outline for the subject of poka yoke along with both a short and a longer assignment for students. Then the paper describes a defect collection and discusses its usefulness in adding interest to the subject of quality.

KEYWORDS: innovative education, quality, poka yoke, defects

INTRODUCTION

Although we are past the heyday of the quality management movement, the subject of quality is still a critical one for students in an introduction to operations course. Product and service quality are subjects all students are painfully aware of through personal experience, but insuring that goods and services meet customer requirements and are free of defects requires skills that are not natural to most people and a background in quality principles can go along way even for students who are not officially management majors. Coverage of quality commonly includes a history of managing quality, variation, statistical process control, acceptance sampling, control charts, Deming method, DMAIC, quality function deployment, Six Sigma, quality mindset as a strategic and cultural phenomenon, PDCA cycles, cost of quality, quality certifications and awards, and other related concepts.

The purpose of this paper is to present a few ideas useful to the teaching of quality. I will first present a context for teaching a major portion of the unit on quality and then will provide more detail on the area of poka yoke, including a short and a longer assignment. Then I will discuss the power of a defect collection to stir student interest in the material.

THE THREE KINDS OF DEFECTS

My presentation on quality generally begins with definitions of quality (manufacturing and service), cost of quality, and the impact of defects on production rate and capacity. After that I organize tools for improving quality around three kinds of defects. The three kinds stemming from three causes. These are degradation errors, careless errors, and lack of training errors. See table 1. Each type of defect can be addressed with a different type of management action.

This organizational structure allows me to first discuss variation and control charts. My coverage of those subjects in not particularly novel. If you are not familiar with Deming's Red Bead Experiment or the Funnel Experiment, I recommend that you explore those as options for adding interest and engagement to this subject. (Deming, 1982, Turner, 1998, Wright & Smith, 2003)

Table 1: Three types of defects/errors

degradation defects/errors	**random/careless defects/errors**	**lack of training defects/errors**
caused by a slow decline in system performance or materials	caused by human inconsistency or interruptions	caused by workers who do not know the proper methods.
prevented by use of control charts and variance reduction	prevented by poka yoke devices	prevented by better training
example: you go to cut some paper on a paper cutter at the office, but the blade is so dull it frays the edges and you have to do it over.	example: you assemble the report containing your budget request and you forget the appendix that details your cost assumptions.	example: new person doesn't know what to do when insured had a pre-existing condition.

POKA YOKE

The concept of poka yoke is not given much coverage in typical operations management textbooks. This is unfortunate because the concept is very powerful, even if simple (Shingo, 1986). Appendix 1 shows the outline I use to introduce poka yoke. My main points are the psychological difference between "fool-proofing" and "mistake-proofing", the 3 levels of poka yoke, the difference between poka yoke and automation or better training, and examples of poka yoke devices. I have two exercises I have used when teaching poka yoke. The first is a simple exercise appropriate for undergraduates (works best with students who have internships or part time jobs.) or graduate students with work experience. This activity takes 10 to 20 minutes and is done in class.

> Poka Yoke Activity: in groups, pick an example of a service failure that occurred recently to one of the members of your group. Answer the following questions.
> a. how likely was this failure to cause lost business for the service provider?
> b. was any service recovery action taken? Explain.
> c. how could this failure have been prevented?
> -make the error impossible?
> -make the error immediately visible
> -create a self-check so the error won't reach the next process step
> Prepare to share briefly with rest of class

The second exercise I have used with poka yoke is best for MBA students, especially those in a part time program who are also in the workplace 8 hours a day, 5 days a week. This assignment asks them to find a commonly occurring error at their place of work, estimate the impact, and design a poka yoke. There is also a substantive write up to go along with exercise, which can be done individually or in small groups. The entire assignment write-up and a grading rubric can be found in Appendix 2. I have had some very useful applications among MBA students who can often save their company significant amounts of money by putting poka yoke into place.

THE DEFECT COLLECTION

To introduce the subject of defects, I bring to my class my defect collection. This is a set of items and stories of defects. I have collected these over several years and after showing them to my class, I often find students are willing to expand my collection by bringing in defects that they have encountered. I have used the collection in two different ways. At times, I simply show the items and pose questions as to how they occurred, how much expense they caused to the organization, and how they could have been prevented. The other approach I have is to divide the class into groups and hand one example to each group and ask them to determine the error, make a best guess as to how it was caused, and then think of ways that such an error could be prevented using the principles of poka yoke.

My inspiration for a defect collection began when I purchased a quart of Havoline motor oil at a Walmart. I selected the item off the shelf as SAE 30 weight oil. See Figure 1. When the item was rung up at the cashier, the register displayed an "item not found" message, meaning it was an item that the store did not carry. I checked the shelf label and it seemed clear that the store did carry Havoline SAE 30 oil. After some time of examining the container, I finally discovered that the label on the back of the container was for SAE 5W-20, an uncommon oil weight not sold at this Walmart. See Figure 2. The back label was the one that contained the scanable UPC code, and thus the item not found message. I was able to talk the cashier into letting me purchase the item, which I thought would be a good classroom prop and my defect collection was born.

Figure 1 – Front of Havoline SAE 30 oil container

Figure 2. Back sine of Havoline oil container

Figure 3 shows the correct look of Brach's mint filled straws, a classic holiday candy. Figure 4 shows a bag also labeled as mint filled straws, but it is clearly not the same candy.

Figure 3. Brach's mint filled straws

Figure 4. Bag of holiday candy that is not mint filled straws

Mislabeling of products is not be a significant problem in many cases. Figure 5 shows one example, however, where a lawsuit claimed a serious result from purported mislabeling.

Figure 5. Lawsuit resulting from mislabeled product

Judge Tosses Hair Dye Lawsuit for Blonde Who Had Less Fun as Brunette

Wednesday, October 08, 2008

Associated Press

BRIDGEPORT, Conn. –

A judge has brushed off a Connecticut woman's claim that L;Oreal Inc. ruined her social life when she accidentally dyed her hair brunette with one of its products.

Charlotte Feeney of Stratford said she can never return to her natural hue, a shock that left her so traumatized she needed anti-depressants.

She says she suffered headaches and anxiety, missed the attention that blondes received and had to stay home and wear hats most of the time.

A Superior Court judge dismissed Feeney's 2005 lawsuit Monday, saying she never proved her allegation that L'Oreal put brown hair dye in a box labeled as blonde. The company also had disputed the claim.

Feeney's attorney, David Laudano, declined to comment and she could not be reached after the judge's decision.

It is not uncommon to find errors in print, such as the pizza coupon in Figure 6.

Figure 6. Pizza coupon

Websites also have their analog of the misprint. Figure 7 shows how mistyped information might interact with algorithms that create the text for webpages.

Figure 7. Amazon listing of the Arab Studies Quarterly Journal.

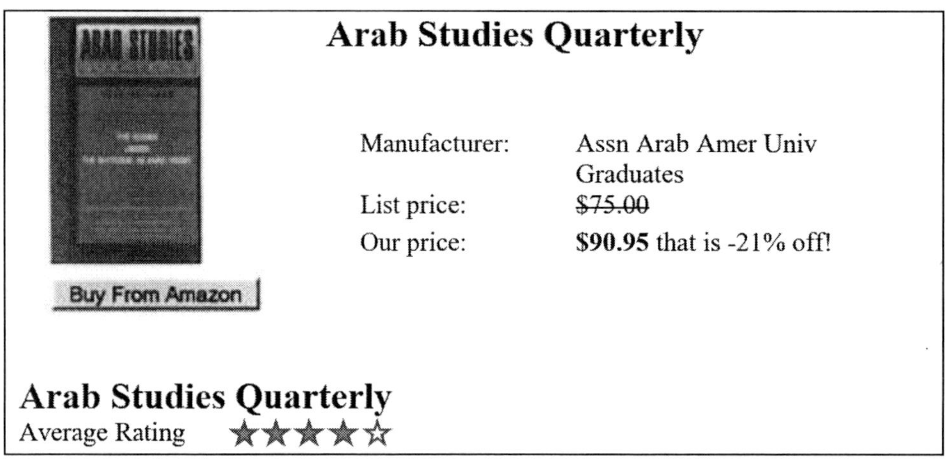

More serious are cases where prices are mistakenly listed far below the actual price. Occasionally this happens with airline prices and show in Figure 8.

Figure 8. News article about an error in airline prices

When Airline Fares Are Too Good To Be True

By Scott McCartney

It's a sport among many hardcore travelers: trying to spot ridiculously low fares that airlines post by mistake—a %5,000 ticket offered for say, $500.

Airlines, once the realize their mistake, often try to wriggle out of honoring the deal—even though they typically charge heavy fees to customers who want to make changes after a ticket is purchased.

Now, armed with a government opinion in their favor, carriers have gotten even stingier. British Airways, PLC canceled 1,200 reservations for 2,200 passengers from the U.S. to India last fall when it mistakenly offered tickets for $40 on Oct. 2. The airline had been trying to raise prices by $40, but that increase mistakenly became the full coach fare when sent to reservation systems by a British Airways office in India, according to a company spokesman. In a letter to customers who complaint, the DOT said it believed airlines should accept "some responsibility: for erroneous fares and should make customers "whole" when tickets are rescinded.

Siddharth Dutta wanted more than just a refund from British Airways and sued the airline in small claims court in Santa Clara County Calif. Last month, a judge ordered British Airways to cover the higher cost of a replacement ticket because the airline entered into a contract when it charged Mr. Dutta's credit card and gave…

An important class of defects are those that occur when changes are made in systems and there is no process to insure that everything affected by the change is updated. This can lead to inconsistency in the process, or even contradictions in a product, document or label. Figure 9 shows the label from a child's stackable donuts toy. The customer is told that the toy is for children 3 to 18 months. At the same time, the toy is a choking hazard and is not for children under 3 years of age.

Figure 9. Label for child's stackable donuts toy.

As a manufacturing example, I show the class a pen cap. Figure 10 shows a non-defective classic Bic pen cap.

Figure 10. Classic Bic pen cap.

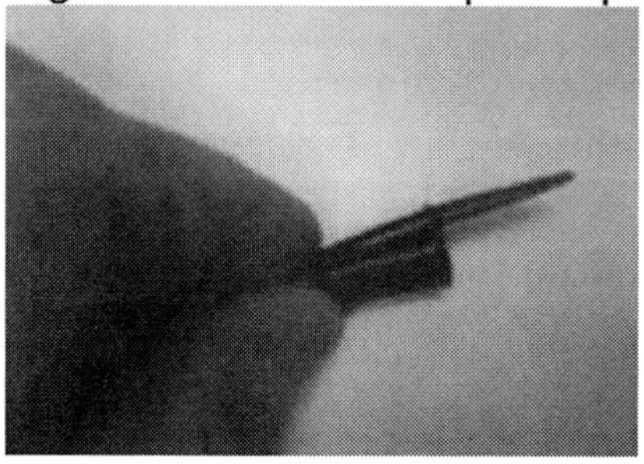

Then I ask the students to compare that to a defective pen cap I acquired as a young boy. The cap is shown in Figure 11. While I am not 100% sure of the cause of the error, it does provide an opportunity to discuss the danger of tools or fixtures that can be aligned either correctly or with a turn of 180%. This pen cap could have been produced with an injection mold where the top was turned 180% from the correct orientation.

Figure 11. Defective Bic pen cap.

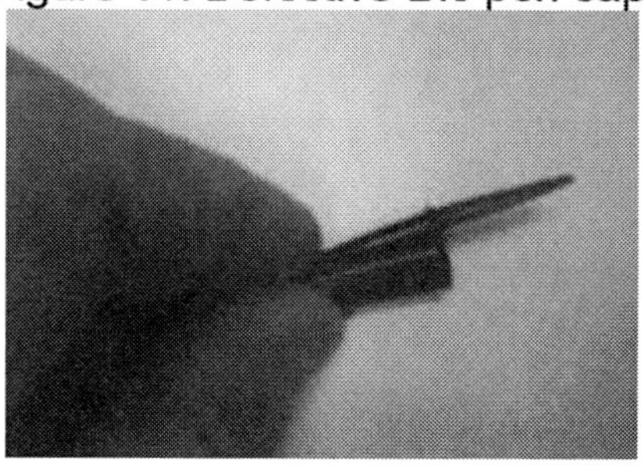

Other examples in the collection are sealed retail packages with no product or with fewer items than the package is supposed to have, misprinted books, and products with missing parts. I also discuss more serious cases such as Toyota accelerators, peanut products with salmonella, and exploding batteries in cell phones.

These examples of errors have left such an impression on my students that I think I have won at least one teaching award based primarily on my defect collection. I believe this is a transferable classroom prop, meaning that it is something most professors could create by keeping a watchful eye out for examples.

CONCLUSION

This paper provides some tangible examples for adding color to the teaching of quality. Poka yoke is a topic that is easy to understand and apply and students can leverage it immediately if they are working at the time of their schooling. A defect collection can add interest to the teaching of quality as well by providing students with interesting, if not entertaining, examples of defects and helping them to ponder how such defects can be prevented.

APPENDIX 1 – Poka Yoke teaching outline

Poka Yoke (*mistake* proofing – not *fool* proofing)

1. Shigeo Shingo – working with Toyota and other Japanese companies
2. Add process elements to prevent a defect from passing to the next step in the process. Such process elements are called "poka yokes" or "poka yoke devices"
3. Three levels of mistake proofing
   i). make the error impossible
   ii). make the error visible so it can be corrected right away
   iii). require the operation to perform a self-check so errors will not pass to next step
4. Try to effect level i, if that is not possible, then level ii, if that is not possible, level iii.

5. Examples
   a. Shigeo Shingo's fix for keeping manuals in alphabetical order
   b. insert for car gas tank that will not allow a leaded fuel pump to be used to fill a car requiring unleaded fuel
   c. small wires connecting the gas cap to the car that will not allow the mistake of leaving the gas cap at the pump
   d. waste receptacles at McDonalds with an oval hole for waste that will not allow a tray to be thrown away
   e. MS Word underlining of misspelled words
   f. a check list for a mortgage document, detailing all signatures and addendums that must be present.

6. What poka yoke is not:
   - simply making something more efficient is not poka yoke. Poka Yoke reduces mistakes or defects.
   - poka yoke is not training or some behavioral modification technique to change the worker behavior. The idea is to find ways to prevent mistakes without depending on the attentiveness or skill of the person.
   - poka yoke is not the same as automation.
     a. poka yoke seeks for small expenditures and simple fixes. They are generally add-ons to the process or product design.
     b. however, automation does take out the human element that causes mistakes

7. Some approaches of poka yoke
   - redesign the product (good or service) to eliminate the process mistake
   - add a device that forces the correct execution of the step
   - add limiters that allow only correct actions (menu instead if command line)
   - add a sensing device that detects the mistake and alerts the operator
   - add a software check that detects an error and alerts the user
   - require workers to perform a self-check
   - use visuals to direct worker actions and reveal errors

For more examples see: http://www.mistakeproofing.com

8. Do poka yokes always accomplish their goal? Here is a portion of a student's paper submitted for the poka yoke assignment in this class. (Marsha Weber, Fall 05)

A huge benefit to a pharmacist is the software that the company utilizes in the filling of prescriptions. These pharmaceutical systems have been designed to detect drug/drug interactions, drug/disease state interactions, overusage/underusage of medications, and various insurance problems. These problems are presented to the user as a Drug Utilization Review (DUR). When the computer system detects an interaction or a problem of some sort with the prescription being entered, it presents the user with a "hard-halt error". It forces the user to read and acknowledge the error that has been detected, and to enter in a password or otherwise physically override the problem before moving on to the next screen. This is an area where a pharmacist is able to utilize their expertise for the benefit of the patients.

While the DUR process is a great mechanism for detecting problems with medications, it is often overlooked and ignored. Pharmacy Technicians are often the ones responsible for inputting prescriptions into the computer and for filling them once they are completed. The pharmacist spends little time in front of the computer, and is mainly responsible for just performing the final check on the prescription. This allows them a great deal of time to spend with patients who need prescription counseling or have questions on their medications. While it is beneficial for the pharmacists to be interacting directly with the patients, it leaves the technicians with a lot of responsibility for filling prescriptions correctly and for attending to these DURs.

Because technicians are used to entering prescriptions into the computer, they often operate on "autopilot", and this is where many mistakes are made. When they learn of a pharmacist's override password (which is generally common knowledge amongst the pharmacy employees), they tend to enter it in automatically when prompted, often without even reading the problem that the computer system has detected. This leaves the pharmacist unaware of the problem and can lead to complications for the patient ranging anywhere from minor to severe to fatal.

APPENDIX 2 - Error Elimination Assignment

This assignment should be emailed to bradley.meyer@drake.edu as a Word document.

Select a commonly occurring and economically significant error that occurs in a process of your company or of some other company with which you do business. Use the principles/ideas discussed in class to invent a process change that will eliminate this error, or greatly reduce its occurrence. Do not simply report on an idea that has already been implemented or is already under consideration. You must come up with an original idea.

Note, on John Grout's mistakeproofing site (http://www.mistakeproofing.com) , most of the everyday examples are presented in the context of a consumer product, like an automobile, or a filing cabinet. I am asking you to think in terms of error proofing a process, not a product. So, don't give me a paper that describes some consumer **product** and an error that can occur in using the **product** and how the company can redesign the **product** to prevent the customer from making this error. I want a recommendation for an error prevention process change that will prevent an **employee** from making an error when carrying out a **process** of the company.

Your report must contain the following:

1. Describe the process and the error that occurs.

2. Estimate how much this error costs the company who owns the process.

3. Describe a process change that would eliminate or greatly reduce the occurrence of this error.

4. Categorize this process change as

- poka yoke – prevent
- poka yoke – make visible
- poka yoke – self inspection

5. Estimate how much it would cost to implement your ideas.

6. Compare the cost of changes with the cost of the error and recommend a course of action for the organization.

You will be graded both on the presentation of your report (grammar, spelling, clarity, format) and on how useful the content of your report would be to the organization. Strive for brevity in this assignment. Make your information clear and concise and avoid extra fluff. For example, don't include an explanation of the concept of poka yoke, assume the reader knows that. A typical paper will be 1 to 3 pages in length.

Error Elimination Grading Form

Name ____________________

Content (12)

_____ product error (should be process)

_____ not a costly error

Device is

    _____ prevention

    _____ make visible

    _____ stop before passed on

_____ left out cost of poka yoke

_____ no course of action recommended

_____ report not useful to organization

Quality of Idea (4)

_____ still allows errors

_____ depends on the person

_____ probably an irritation to the worker

Mechanics (3)

_____ grammar problems

_____ spelling problems

_____ expression problems

Organization (1)

_____ grouping problems

_____ sequencing problems

_____ transitions problems

Total Score _________

REFERENCES

Deming, W. E. (1982). *Out of the crisis.* Cambridge , MA : Massachusetts Institute of Technology, Center for Advanced Engineering Study.

Shingo, S. (1986). *Zero quality control: Source inspection and the poka-yoke system.* Productivity Press.

Turner, R. (1998). The red bead experiment for educators. *Quality progress*, *31*(6), 69.

Wright, C. M., & Smith, M. E. (2003). Serving Up the Red Beads Experience. *Decision Sciences Journal of Innovative Education*, *1*(1), 127-131.

DECISION SCIENCES INSTITUTE

An economic production lot size model in an imperfect production system with a Markov process and shortage backordering

Kuo-Lung Hou
Overseas Chinese University, Taiwan
Email: klhou@ocu.edu.tw

Li-Chiao Lin
National Chinyi University of Technology, Taiwan
Email: chiao@ncut.edu.tw

ABSTRACT

This paper studies optimal lot size for an imperfect production system in which the shortages are allowed and the deterioration process is characterized by a two-state discrete-time Markov chain. We show that there exists a unique optimal lot size to minimize the expected total relevant cost. In addition, bounds for the optimal lot size are provided to develop the solution procedure. Finally, a numerical example is given to illustrate the results. Sensitivity analysis and managerial insights are also provided.

KEYWORDS: Lot sizing, Imperfect production system, Markov chain; Shortages

INTRODUCTION

Considerable attention has also been paid to EPQ model in the presence of deteriorating production process. The effect of process deterioration on the lot size was initially studied by Rosenblatt & Lee (1986) and Porteus (1986). Specifically, Porteus (1986) considered an EOQ model with deteriorating process and assume that all items produced are defective when the system is out-of-control. However, Rosenblatt & Lee (1986) assumed that a proportion of the items produced are defective once the production process is out-of-control. In addition, Porteus (1986) showed that the optimal lot size is smaller than that of the traditional EOQ model. However, as we will see later on, this result may not be true when the maintenance cost is high as compared to the rework cost incurred by defective items. More recently, Hou et al. (2015) extended Porteus (1986) to present the optimal lot size model for defective items with a constant probability when the system is out-of control and taking maintenance cost into account. Maddah et al. (2010) considered an inventory system within the economic order quantity model framework under random supply where imperfect items are removed from inventory. Sana (2010) considered an economic production lot size model in an imperfect production system and assumed that a certain percent of total product is defective in the out-of-control state. Yoo et al. (2012) examined an imperfect production and inspection system with customer return and defective disposal. Other related studies considering imperfect quality production process include Chen & Kang (2010), Goyal & Cárdenas-Barrón (2002), Khan et al. (2011), Lee and Kim (2014), Maddah & Jaber (2008), Pal et al. (2012-2013), Papachristors & Konstantaras (2006), Salameh & Jaber (2000), and Sarkar (2012).

All of the above-mentioned models assume that shortages are not permitted to occur. However, in many practical situations, stockout is unavoidable due to various uncertainties. Therefore, the main purpose of this paper is to generalize the traditional EPQ model to assume that shortages are allowed in an imperfect production system with a Markov process. In addition, we focus on investigating the effects of system deterioration on the optimal lot size with maintenance actions when the defective items can be reworked and shortages are completely backlogged. We show that there exists a unique optimal lot size such that the expected total relevant cost is minimized. Bounds for the optimal lot size are also provided to develop the solution procedure. The analyses show that our model is a generalization of the models in current literatures. Specifically, the numerical results in this paper show that our model always results in better performance.

NOTATION AND ASSUMPTIONS

To develop an EPQ model for the deteriorating production system, the following notation and assumptions are adopted:

Notation

d demand rate,
p production rate, $p > m$,
K setup cost for each production run,
h holding cost per unit per unit time,
c_r rework cost for a defective item,
R maintenance cost for restoring the system from out-of-control back to in-control,
π the backordering cost per unit
q the probability that the system from in-control state shifts to out-of-control state,
$\bar{q}$ the probability that the system stays in-control state during the production of an item and $\bar{q}$ =1-q,
θ the percentage of defective items when the process is in the out-of-control state,
$I_{\max}$ the maximum on-hand inventory level,
b the maximum backordering quantity in units,
N number of defective items produced in a production run,
T cycle time of a production run,
Q lot size for each production run,
$TC(Q,b)$ the expected total relevant cost per unit time for lot size Q and maximum backordering quantity b,

Assumptions

We develop the model with the following assumptions:

1. We suppose that the operating condition of the production system at any time can be classified into one of the two states, i.e., in-control and out-of-control.
2. When the system is in the in-control state, it may either shift to the out-of-control state with probability q or stay in the in-control state with probability $1\text{-}q$ during the production of an item. Once the system shifts to the out-of-control state, it remains in this state until the end of a production run. That is, the deteriorating process can be modeled by a two-state discrete-time Markov chain.
3. After the production of a lot of size Q, the production process is inspected to reveal the state of the process. If the process is out-of-control then it is restored to the in-control state with restoration cost R for the next production run.

4. Due to manufacturing variability, if the production process is out-of-control, then it will lead to an item produced is defective with a fixed proportion θ not rather than all items produced are defective as in Porteus (1986).
5. The defective items will eventually be reworked with cost c_r such that the capacity of the production system is not affected.
6. Shortages are allowed and are completely backlogged.

THEORETICAL MODEL

The expected total relevant cost per unit time composed of setup costs, holding costs, backorder costs, restoration cost, and rework costs. These costs are evaluated as follows.

(1) Setup cost: the setup cost per unit time is given by

$$\frac{K}{T}=\frac{Kd}{Q} \tag{1}$$

(2) Holding cost: During each cycle, holding cost will occur during T_2 and T_3. Note that $T_2 = I_{max}/(p-d)$ and $T_3 = I_{max}/d$. So the average inventory over the cycle is the area under the inventory triangle, divided by T. Denoting this by $\bar{I}$, we have

$$\bar{I}=\frac{1}{T}\left\{\frac{[Q(1-d/p)-b]^2}{2d(1-d/p)}\right\}$$
$$=\frac{[Q(1-d/p)-b]^2}{2Q(1-d/p)} \tag{2}$$

Thus, according to Eq. (2), the holding cost per unit time is given by

$$h\bar{I}=\frac{h[Q(1-d/p)-b]^2}{2Q(1-d/p)} \tag{3}$$

(3) Backordering cost: The backordering cost will occur during T_1 and T_4. Note that $T_1=b/(p-d)$ and $T_4=b/d$. So that the average backorder level is given by

$$\bar{B}=\frac{1}{T}\left[\frac{b^2}{2d(1-d/p)}\right]$$
$$=\frac{b^2}{2Q(1-d/p)} \tag{4}$$

Thus, according to Eq. (4), the backordering cost per unit time is given by

$$\pi\bar{B}=\frac{\pi b^2}{2Q(1-d/p)} \tag{5}$$

(4) Restoration cost: The restoration cost occurs only when the production process is out-of-control at the end of a production run for lot size Q. Thus, the expected restoration cost becomes $R(1-\bar{q}^Q)$. Hence, the restoration cost per unit time is given by

$$\frac{R(1-\bar{q}^Q)}{T}=\frac{dR(1-\bar{q}^Q)}{Q} \tag{6}$$

(5) Rework cost: To obtain the expected rework cost, we need to compute the expected number of defective items in a lot. Let $\bar{q}=1-q$ and in a lot of size Q, the probability distribution of number of items produced in the in-control state, X, is

$$\Pr\{X=j\}=\begin{cases}\bar{q}^j q, & 0\le j<Q\\ \bar{q}^Q, & j=Q\end{cases} \tag{7}$$

Then, the expected value of X is given by

$$E(X)=q\sum_{j=1}^{Q-1} j\bar{q}^j+Q\bar{q}^Q$$
$$=\sum_{j=1}^{Q}\bar{q}^j \tag{8}$$

So that the number of defective items in a lot of size Q becomes $N=\theta(Q-X)$. Hence, the expected value of N is

$$E(N)=\theta\left(Q-\sum_{j=1}^{Q}\bar{q}^j\right) \tag{9}$$

Thus, according to Eq. (9), the expected rework cost per unit time is given by

$$\frac{c_r E(N)}{T} = c_r d\theta - \frac{d}{Q}\left(c_r \theta \sum_{j=1}^{Q} \bar{q}^j\right) \quad (10)$$

Let *TC*(*Q*,*b*) be the expected total relevant cost per unit time composed of setup cost, inventory holding cost, backordering cost, restoration cost, and rework cost. Then *TC*(*Q*,*b*) is given as follows.

$$TC(Q,b) = \frac{dK}{Q} + \frac{h[Q(1-d/p)-b]^2}{2Q(1-d/p)} + \frac{\pi b^2}{2Q(1-d/p)} + c_r d\theta + \frac{d}{Q}\left[R(1-\bar{q}^Q) - c_r \theta \sum_{j=1}^{Q} \bar{q}^j\right] \quad (11)$$

Notice that the *TC*(*Q*,*b*) is convex with respect to *b*. Thus, taking the first derivate of the *TC*(*Q*,*b*) with respect to *b* and equating it to zero will yield the optimal backordering quantity as follows.

$$b^* = \frac{hQ(1-d/p)}{h+\pi} \quad (12)$$

Substituting Eq. (12) unto Eq. (11) yields the following expression of *C*(*Q*).

$$C(Q) = \frac{dK}{Q} + \frac{hQ(1-d/p)}{2}\left(\frac{\pi}{h+\pi}\right) + c_r d\theta + \frac{d}{Q}\left[R(1-\bar{q}^Q) - c_r \theta \sum_{j=1}^{Q} \bar{q}^j\right] \quad (13)$$

So far, we have appropriately established mathematical model to investigate the lot size for a deteriorating production system. The problem is then to find the optimal lot size Q^* that leads to the minimum of $C(Q)$. In addition, based on Eq. (13), following observations should be mentioned:

(1) When q = 0, Eq. (13) reduces to the case that the production system does not deteriorate and is always in the in-control state and items produced are perfect quality.

(2) If π approaches to infinity, Eq. (13) becomes the expected total relevant cost of no-shortage-allowed case. Thus, Eq. (13) will reduce to Eq. (8) in Hou et al. (2015). Therefore, the model in this paper is an extension of Hou et al. (2015).

(3) Combining the arguments of (1) and (2), Eq. (13) will reduce to the traditional EPQ model. In other words, the traditional EPQ model is a special case of the model proposed in this paper when the system deterioration, defective items, and shortages are all not considered.

(4) Note that as π approaches to infinity, it is equivalent to instantaneous production of the entire lot, the Eq. (13) reduces to the EOQ model with an imperfect production process.

(5) When R = 0, Eq. (13) reduces to the case that the restoration cost is not considered.

(6) When θ=1, Eq. (13) reduces to the case that all items produced are defective as the production process is in an out-of-control state.

Combining the arguments of (2) and (4)–(6), Eq. (13) will reduce to the model in Porteus (1986). Therefore, the proposed model in this paper is also an extension of Porteus (1986).

NUMERICAL RESULTS

In order to illustrate the performance of our proposal model, let us consider an imperfect production system with the following data: p = 1500 units/year, d = 1000 units/year, K = \$600/cycle, h = \$8/unit/year, π = \$10/unit/year, c_r = \$5/unit, R = \$200/cycle, θ = 0.75, and q = 0.1. Using the above parameters, it can be verified that β is positive (β=166.25). Applying the algorithm described above, we find that optimal lot size Q^* = 1017.07, b^* =150.677, and expected total relevant cost per unit time $TC(Q^*,b^*)$ = \$5256.775. In addition, we show that optimal lot size Q^* is larger than the traditional EPQ model (that is, $Q^* > Q_{tr}$ = 670.82) for the case of $\beta > 0$. It is unlike the results in previous works, e,g, see Maddah et al. (2010), Porteus (1986), and Rosenblatt & Lee (1986). The reason is that they only derive an approximately optimal lot size and do not take the restoration cost into account properly. However, the optimal lot size Q* may be larger than the traditional EPQ when the restoration cost is considered and relatively high as compared to the rework cost incurred by defective items.

CONCLUSIONS

In this paper, we propose a generalized production lot size model with system deterioration, imperfect quality and shortage backordering. The proposed model can be considered as a good extension of the previous literatures. We show that there exists a unique optimal lot size such that the expected total relevant cost is minimized no matter whether q is small or not. In addition, the bounds of optimal lot size are provided so that the bisection method can be used to locate optimal lot size easily. The analyses show that our model is a generalization of the models in current literatures. The numerical results in this paper show that our model always results in better performance. Specifically, significant cost savings can be achieved by considering shortages backordered in our proposed model.

REFERENCES

Chen, L.H., Kang, F.S. (2010). Coordination between vendor and buyer considering trade credit and items of imperfect quality. *International Journal of Production Economic*, 123, 52-61.

Goyal, S.K., Cárdenas-Barrón L.E. (2002). Note on: economic production quantity model for items with imperfect quality-a practical approach. *International Journal of Production Economic*, 77, 85-87.

Hou, K.L., Lin, L.C., Lin, T.Y. (2015). Optimal lot sizing with maintenance actions and imperfect production processes. International Journal of System Sciences,.

Khan, M., Jaber, M.Y., Bonney, M. (2011). An economic order quantity (EOQ) for items with imperfect quality and inspection errors. *International Journal of Production Economic*, 133, 113-118.

Lee, S., Kim, D. (2014). An optimal policy for a single-vendor single-buyer integrated production–distribution model with both deteriorating and defective items. *International Journal of Production Economic*, 147, 161–170.

Maddah, B., Jaber, M.Y. (2008). Economic order quantity for items with imperfect quantity: revisited. *International Journal of Production Economic*, 112, 808-815.

Maddah, B., Moussawi, L., Jaber, M.Y. (2010). Lot sizing with a Markov production process and imperfect items scrapped. *International Journal of Production Economic*, 124, 340–347.

Pal, B., Sana, S.S., Chaudhuri, K. (2012). Three-layer Supply Chain - a Production-inventory model for reworkable items. *Applied Mathematical* Computation, 219, 530–543.

Pal, B., Sana, S.S., Chaudhuri, K. (2013). Maximizing profits for an EPQ model with unreliable machine and rework of random defective items. International Journal of System Sciences, 44, 582-594.

Pal, B, Sana, S.S., Chaudhuri, K. (2013). A mathematical model on EPQ for stochastic demand in an imperfect production system. Journal of Manufacturing Systems, 32, 260–270.

Papachristors, S., Konstantaras, I. (2006). Economic ordering quantity models for items with imperfect quality. *International Journal of Production Economic*, 100, 148-154.

Porteus, E.L. (1986). Optimal lot sizing, process quality improvement and setup cost reduction. Operations Research, 34, 137-144.

Rosenblatt, M.J., Lee, H.L. (1986). Economic production cycle with imperfect production processes. *IIE Transitions*, 18, 48-55.

Salameh, M.K., Jaber, M.Y. (2000). Economic production quantity model for items with imperfect quality. *International Journal of Production Economic*, 64, 59-64.

Sana, S.S. (2010). An economic production lot size model in an imperfect production system. *European Journal of Operational Research*, 201, 158 - 170.

Sarkar, B. (2012). An inventory model with reliability in an imperfect production process. Applied Math Comput, 218, 4881 - 4891.

Yoo, S.H., Kim, D.S., Park, M.S. (2012). Lot sizing and quality investment with quality cost analyses for imperfect production and inspection processes with commercial return. *International Journal of Production Economic*, 140, 922–933.

DECISION SCIENCES INSTITUTE

An Empirical Investigation of the Baldrige Framework Using Applicant Scoring Data

Feng Mai
Stevens Institute of Technology
fmai@stevens.edu

Matthew W. Ford
Northern Kentucky University
fordmw@nku.edu

James R. Evans
University of Cincinnati
evansjr@ucmail.uc.edu

ABSTRACT

This paper seeks to overcome evaluative limitations of previous studies to provide a more decisive test of the causal relationships implied in the Baldrige Criteria for Performance Excellence (CPE). Path analysis of blinded applicant scoring data from 500 Baldrige Award applicants provided strong support for the CPE framework in its entirety, with all hypothesized relationships between constructs confirmed. However, analysis of sector-specific subsets of the data did not confirm all relationships, suggesting the possibility of industry-dependent performance excellence frameworks and raising new research questions to be explored.

KEYWORDS: Quality management and systems, Process improvement, Performance measurement, Path analysis, Structural equations modeling

INTRODUCTION

Since its inception in 1988, the Malcolm Baldrige National Quality Award Criteria for Performance Excellence (CPE) have evolved from a narrow focus on quality management practices to a broad framework for organizational performance excellence (Evans et al., 2012). Its broad scope and acceptance among manufacturing, service, and non-profit organizations suggests that the CPE framework is an effective standard for promoting performance excellence among organizations operating in various internal and external contexts (Bemowski & Stratton, 1995; Ettorre, 1996; Flynn & Saladin, 2006; Steeples, 1992). As the CPE have increased in prominence, scholars have sought to empirically validate the underlying conceptual models.

Revisions to the CPE during the course of the criteria's evolution have resulted in three generations of conceptually distinct frameworks (Flynn & Saladin, 2001): a first generation framework in place during the 1988 to 1991 Baldrige Award cycles, a second generation framework in place from 1992 to 1996, and a third generation framework introduced in 1997, which is still in place. Several studies aimed at validating the CPE framework were based on earlier generation frameworks (e.g., Meyer & Collier, 2001; Pannirselvam & Ferguson, 2001; Wilson & Collier, 2000), thereby limiting the relevance of a significant portion of research findings to the current CPE structure. Moreover, studies that have investigated the validity of the third generation framework have been unable to statistically confirm all hypothesized links between CPE constructs on a consistent basis, with non-significant paths sometimes amounting to 20% or more of total paths tested (e.g., Flynn & Saladin, 2001; Lee et al., 2003). While a review of the research by Bou-Llusar et al. (2009) found that empirical studies generally support the conceptual framework of the CPE, the general support that flows from extant empirical work has not translated into confirmation of the CPE model in its entirety. Thus, although general support for the framework's validity is evident, specific issues remain that merit additional research.

Confirmation of relationships between constructs of the CPE framework has been hindered in part by the latitude that researchers have taken in interpreting the conceptual framework of the CPE. This has resulted in a plethora of model configurations and a variety of constructs and relationships proposed for testing (e.g., Curkovic et al., 2000; Flynn & Saladin, 2001; He et al., 2011; Jayamaha et al., 2008; Karimi. et al., 2014; Lee et al., 2003). Studies attempting to replicate or extend the validity of previously tested models have been rare. Methodological limitations are also evident. Data have commonly been collected using survey questionnaires that have varied considerably in design (e.g., Curkovic et al., 2000; Ghosh et al., 2003; Goldstein & Schweikhart, 2002; Lee et al., 2003; Wilson & Collier, 2000). Some instruments have contained items specifically developed to reflect the CPE framework while others include questions sourced from other studies. Sample domains have usually been limited to industry-specific sectors such as manufacturing, healthcare, or education, thereby constraining assessment to narrow sets of evaluative conditions. Respondents have been sourced from various organizational groups ranging from senior executives to quality managers to line personnel which, given well-known attribution biases and errors associated with group sampling (Dearborn & Simon, 1958; Hambrick, 1981; Nisbett & Wilson, 1977) casts some doubt on the capability of respondents from different departments or hierarchical organizational levels to accurately assess the state of far reaching, complex organizational systems such as those represented in the CPE.

Because the CPE is employed both by managers as a means for self-assessment and performance improvement (Ford & Evans, 2001) and by researchers as an operationalization of theoretical total quality management (TQM) concepts (Bou-Llusar et al., 2009), it is important that the validity of all constructs and linkages proposed by the CPE framework be thoroughly examined. The limitations associated with past studies suggest that further that work is necessary in order to more fully understand and validate the framework.

This paper seeks to address past limitations to provide a more decisive empirical test of the CPE framework. We employ Flynn and Saladin's (2001) representation of the current (third generation) CPE framework for our test. In addition to offering a carefully developed representation of the CPE framework as a basis for evaluation, use of Flynn and Saladin's (2001) model enriches opportunity for cross study comparison that has eluded previous investigations. We test the model by analyzing primary scoring data from 500 organizations that applied for the Malcolm Baldrige National Quality Award since 1999 that were compiled and released by the Baldrige Program. Because these data span multiple industrial sectors and reflect ratings of expert observers with extensive skill in assessing organizational activities in light of the CPE framework, use of Baldrige applicant scoring data overcomes many methodological limitations of past studies and allows us to investigate the universal applicability of the framework across industries. The primary contribution of this research is an improved analytical backdrop that provides more favorable conditions for thorough empirical testing of the CPE framework.

LITERATURE REVIEW

As noted above, Flynn and Saladin (2001) separated the conceptual evolution of the CPE framework into three generations. Although its content and terminology have undergone minor revision since then, the third generation framework enacted in 1997 remains in effect today. As shown in Figure 1 (based on the 2013-2014 Criteria), the framework proposes six categories of interlinked organizational processes related to leadership, strategy development and implementation, customer focus, information and analysis, workforce focus, and operations focus (process management). Each category is subdivided into several items that focus on factors that organizations should address to function effectively in competitive environments. The six process categories are posited to influence a seventh multidimensional results category. We note that the current 2015-2016 version of the framework has not changed substantially, except for minor category title wording changes such as “Strategy,” “Customers”, “Workforce,” and “Operations.” Detailed scholarly reviews of the conceptual CPE framework have appeared on numerous occasions; readers are referred to Evans and Mai (2014) for a recent review.

Figure 1 Third Generation Baldrige framework

Several empirical studies have investigated the validity of the third generation CPE framework indirectly by examining novel combinations of the categorical constructs (Table 1). For example, Curkovic et al., (2002) and Jayamaha et al., (2011) reconfigured the seven categorical constructs into several second order factor models to evaluate the extent to which the CPE framework reflected theoretical TQM and business excellence constructs. Goldstein and Schweikhart (2002) assessed the predictive validity of the six CPE process categories relative to various outcome dimensions specified by the seventh results category. Although findings from these studies favor the validity of the CPE framework, support for the particular configuration of the seven CPE constructs as proposed by the CPE developers in Figure 1 is limited due to the scopes of the investigations. Confirming the complete arrangement of proposed constructs and relationships, sometimes called a “nomological network,” is critical to assessing total validity of a theoretical framework (Cronbach & Meehl, 1955).

The remaining studies in Table 1 constitute direct examinations of the causal network of constructs and relationships expressed by the third generation CPE framework in. In each of these studies, the conceptual framework in Figure 1 was converted into a measurement model consisting of the seven interlinked CPE categorical constructs arranged in causal order. Model fit and significance were then usually tested using path analytical techniques and empirical data samples. However, model specification has varied between studies with no two investigations testing identical representations of the CPE framework pictured in Figure 1. Causal order of the CPE constructs has also differed between studies. For example, while the leadership construct has been positioned as the sole exogenous "driver" construct in several measurement models (e.g., Flynn & Saladin, 2001; Jayamaha et al., 2008; He et al., 2011), leadership has shared this position with the information and analysis construct in other studies (e.g., Lee et al., 2003).

Table 1: Empirical Studies Employing Third Generation CPE Framework

Study	CPE Basis	Sample	Analytical Approach	Linkages Confirmed/Proposed
Curkovic et al., (2000)	1997	Single respondent survey of 269 plant managers in US automotive industry	CPE in second order factor structural equation modeling (SEM) analysis of TQM	N.A.
Flynn & Saladin (2001)	1997	Multi-respondent survey of 164 manufacturing plants in Germany, Italy, Spain, UK, US	Path analysis of CPE causal model	12/15
Goldstein & Schweikhart (2002)	1999	Single respondent survey of quality managers at 220 US hospitals	Regression analysis of CPE process categories and results category	6/6
Ghosh et al. (2003)	2000	Single respondent survey of quality managers in 313 US manufacturing firms.	SEM analysis of CPE causal model	5/10
Lee et al., (2003)	2001	Single respondent survey of 109 Korean mid-upper level mfg mgrs	SEM analysis of CPE causal model	8/12
Badri et al., (2006)	2004	Multi-respondent survey of 224 administrators from 15 UAE colleges and universities	SEM analysis of CPE causal model	21/21
Jayamaha et al., (2008)	2005	Single respondent survey of 91 New Zealand organizations	SEM (PLS) analysis of CPE causal model	11/13
He et al., (2011)	2006	Single respondent survey from 2302 Chinese manufacturers and service firms	SEM analysis of CPE causal model	19/19
Jayamaha et al., (2011)	2009	Single respondent survey of 118 New Zealand organizations	CPE in second order factor SEM (PLS) model of business excellence	N.A.
Karimi et al., (2014)	2006	Applicant scoring data from 277 Baldrige Award applicants 2003-2006	Canonical correlation analysis of Baldrige drivers, systems, results	N.A.

The two-headed arrows shown to connect various CPE categories and groups of constructs in Figure 1 have been a source of confusion for researchers. Investigators have generally assumed the two-headed arrows to mean that the CPE developers were unsure of the direction of true causation between the constructs, leading the developers to default to the premise that all CPE categories were related (e.g., Meyer & Collier, 2001; Wilson & Collier, 2000). However, two-headed arrows and the non-causality that they imply create significant problems for path analytical methodology, and have lead researchers to specify nomological networks with directional causal order. When modeling the CPE framework, researchers have argued that the long articulated CPE proposition that "leadership drives the system that leads to results" justifies arranging the model in recursive, unidirectional order that proceeds through some configuration of the six organizational process constructs and ends with the seventh results construct. These model configurations contain no reciprocal causation or feedback loops. All path coefficients between constructs are hypothesized as positive. As demonstrated by Flynn and Saladin's (2001) model (Figure 2), researchers have redrawn the third generation CPE to conform to the conventions of path analysis. All arrows are unidirectional and point toward the results end of the model. (The 2015-2016 version of the framework replaced the multiple arrows in the figure with a central theme of "integration" that implies that all the elements of the system are interrelated, leaving the causal paths open to interpretation.) The Baldrige categories have undergone some title revisions since 1997 (on which Figure 2 is based); thus, in our investigation, we will use the category names from Figure 1; that is, Leadership; Measurement, Analysis, and Knowledge Management; Strategy; Customer Focus; Workforce Focus (for HR Development & Management); Operations Focus (for Process Management); and Results (for Business Results).

Figure 2 Flynn and Saladin's (2001) Path Model Based on 1997 Baldrige Framework

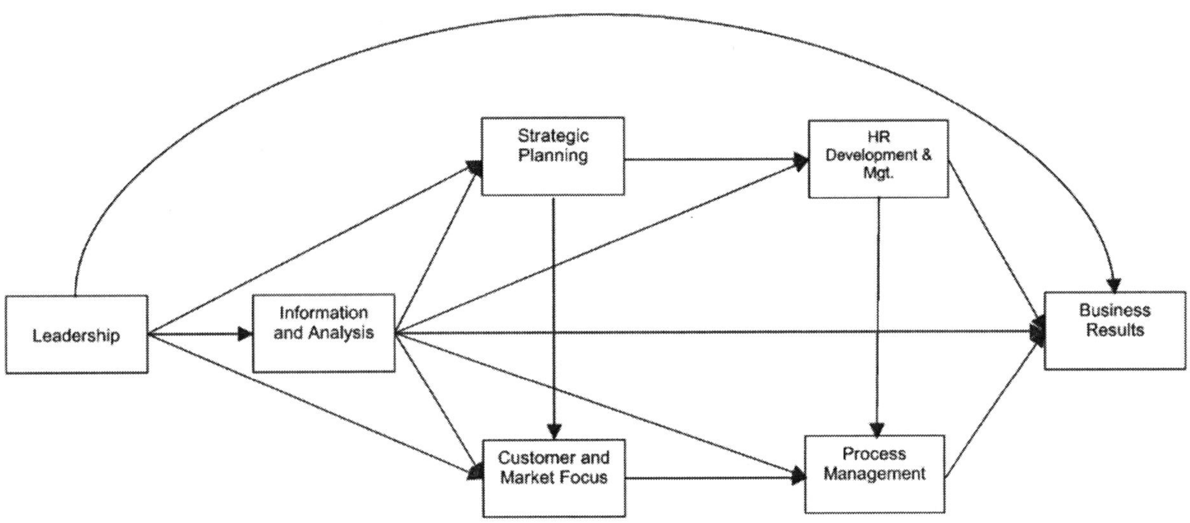

A primary source of variation in model specification between studies has been the number of relationships hypothesized between the seven categorical CPE constructs. Number of proposed paths between constructs has varied from 10 (Ghosh et al., 2000) to 21 (Badri et al., 2006), with no two studies examining the same number of linkages. Once again, Figure 1 is a source of confusion. For example, Figure 1 joins the leadership, strategy-making, and customer focus constructs in a cluster with small two-headed arrows, and relates this cluster to other parts of the model with large two-headed arrows. Do the large arrows imply that the leadership, strategy, and customer constructs are each related to all of the other constructs, or are smaller numbers of more selective relationships involved? In some cases, researchers have liberally interpreted the number of linkages embedded in the CPE framework (e.g., Badri et al., 2006; He et al., 2011) while others have been more conservative (e.g., Ghosh et al., 2000; Lee et al., 2003).

Regardless of number of paths hypothesized, measurement models across all studies in Table 1 have generally exhibited acceptable overall levels of statistical fit and significance, thus prompting conclusions that empirical studies generally support the validity of the CPE framework (e.g., Bou-Llusar et al., 2009). However, investigations have generally been unable to confirm all hypothesized linkages, with non-significant paths often amounting to 20% or more of total paths proposed. Comparing results across studies reveals no common non-significant paths. Two studies that did find all paths significant (Badri et al., 2006; He et al., 2011) also happen to propose the most relationships between constructs. This is counterintuitive from a statistical standpoint, and suggests that issues associated with model development and testing in these studies may limit the generalizeability of the findings from these two studies.

MODEL AND HYPOTHESES

Rather than adding to the model proliferation of past studies, we reviewed the studies in Table 1 for a previously developed model of the CPE framework that could provide a useful basis for a follow-up empirical test, and selected Flynn & Saladin's (2001) model shown in Figure 2. We found this model attractive for a number of reasons. In addition to being firmly grounded in previous research, Flynn and Saladin's (2001) model is unique in that researchers were careful to conceptually link it to previous generations of CPE frameworks, thereby strengthening the logic of the researchers' causal model as an accurate representation of the nomological network intended by the CPE developers. Although three of the fifteen hypothesized paths between the seven CPE constructs were found to be non-significant, it is unclear as to whether this was due to possible model misspecification, the possibility of which the authors did not rule out in their discussion of results, or due to methodological limitations. Regardless, Flynn and Saladin's (2001) analysis of overall model fit and strength of measured relationships produced statistical results consistent with standards for well-performing measurement models. Flynn & Saladin's (2001) model is also attractive because it is a prominent one. It is well cited, and is used as a basis for discussion in several subsequent empirical studies listed in Table 1. As such, this model provides a solid foundation for a more decisive empirical test of the CPE framework's validity.

The Flynn and Saladin (2001) model (Figure 2) begins with leadership as the "driver." Leadership is proposed to directly influence downstream organizational process constructs related to information and analysis, strategy-making, and customer focus. Stated more formally using CPE category language:

Hypothesis 1a: Leadership has a direct, positive influence on Measurement, Information, and Analysis.
Hypothesis 1b: Leadership has a direct, positive influence on Strategic Planning.
Hypothesis 1c: Leadership has a direct, positive influence on Customer Focus.
Hypothesis 1d: Leadership has a direct, positive influence on Results.

The position of the information and analysis construct to the right of leadership in Flynn and Saladin's (2001) model reflects its broad influence on other organizational processes as depicted by the CPE developers in Figure 1. Information is proposed to directly influence thefour downstream organizational process constructs as well as the results construct:

Hypothesis 2a: Measurement, Information, and Analysis has a direct, positive influence on Strategic Planning.
Hypothesis 2b: Measurement, Information, and Analysis has a direct, positive influence on

Customer Focus.
Hypothesis 2c: Measurement, Information, and Analysis has a direct, positive influence on Workforce Focus.
Hypothesis 2d: Measurement, Information, and Analysis has a direct, positive influence on Operations Focus.
Hypothesis 2e: Measurement, Information, and Analysis has a direct, positive influence on Results.

The strategy making and customer focus constructs are positioned equidistantly and to the right of information and analysis. Strategy-making is proposed to influence customer focus as well as workforce focus. Customer focus is seen as influencing process management. Neither strategy-making nor customer focus processes are proposed to directly influence results:

Hypothesis 3a: Strategic Planning has a direct, positive influence on Customer Focus.
Hypothesis 3b: Strategic Planning has a direct, positive influence on Workforce Focus.
Hypothesis 4: Customer Focus has a direct, positive influence on Operations Focus.

The final two organizational processes related to workforce focus and process management are positioned equidistantly and to the right of strategy making and customer focus. These two processes also directly precede the results construct in the nomological network. Workforce focus is proposed to influence both process management and downstream results. Process management, being the operational instrument of all other organizational process activities, is proposed to influence only downstream results:

Hypothesis 5a: Workforce Focus has a direct, positive influence on Operations Focus.
Hypothesis 5b: Workforce Focus has a direct, positive influence on Results.
Hypothesis 6: Operations Focus has a direct, positive influence on Results.

Since the framework's establishment, a central proposition of the CPE is that it is applicable to organizations regardless of sector (Bell & Keys, 1998; Douglas & Fredendall, 2004). As suggested by Table 1 above, empirically testing the robustness of this proposition has been problematic due to the inherent difficulty of obtaining cross industry samples that adequately represent, for example, the manufacturing, service, healthcare, education, and non-profit sectors for which the CPE have been categorically developed. The literature provides conflicting perspectives regarding the applicability of Baldrige framework across industries. Studies of total quality management frameworks have sometimes suggested universal orientation across product-based and service-based sectors (e.g., Douglas & Fredendall, 2004; Prajogo, 2005). On the other hand, many studies highlight the differences between quality management across industries, particularly between manufacturing and service organizations (e.g., Huq & Stolen, 1998; Ronnback & Witell, 2008; Woon, 2000). To investigate this issue in the context of this study, we formulate the following hypothesis:

Hypothesis 7: The same Baldrige path model is applicable across the various categorical sectors of the CPE.

DATA AND METHOD

Data

The Baldrige Award review process consists of three stages. The first stage is the Independent Review, during which all applicants gets itemized numerical scores from a panel of examiners working independently based on the written application. Selected applicants will then advance to the second stage, the Consensus Review. At this stage the examiner team will discuss variation in the individual scoring process and reach consensus on the itemized scores. Lastly, the examiner teams visit highest-scoring applicants to interview personnel and verify information contained in written applications. During the site visit review only site visit reports are written but the applicants are not scored.

In 2009, the National Institute of Standards and Technology (NIST) and the Baldrige program prepared and released a set of blinded applicant scoring data covering 17 years from 1990 to 2006. The data were made public in response to many requests and to facilitate further analysis by interested researchers. The 2009 data set includes the application year, sector, applicant number, Independent Review median score by category, and Consensus Review score by category if applicable. In 2011, Baldrige released a second version of the blinded data, which included more detailed item scores. The data sets are publicly available and can be obtained from the Baldrige website (www.nist.gov/baldrige).

The Baldrige evaluation process at the national level is designed to be rigorous and objective, and examiners are carefully chosen and more experienced than state-level examiners, providing data having higher integrity and reliability. The Baldrige standard has been adopted in the U.S as well as around the world. The former director of the Baldrige program has suggested that the greatest success of the award is in the area of assessment (Bell and Keys 1998). Evans and Mai (2014) reported that using confirmatory factor analysis on the NIST applicant scoring dataset, there is strong evidence of reliability, convergent and discriminant validity in the Baldrige framework, which is consistent with other research that used survey or state-level data. Compared with state-level data and self-reported surveys, the use of objective and reliable applicant data allows us to make more generalizable conclusions.

There are several hurdles that discourage us from analyzing the released itemized scoring data set directly. First of all, the Baldrige framework has gone through several revisions since 1988, most notably in 1992 and 1997. In these revisions, new items have been added in the framework and the conceptual relationships between the core categories have been reorganized. Flynn and Saladin (2001) demonstrate that the newer framework offers a better fit for empirical survey data and therefore concluded that the revisions made to the Baldrige framework are beneficial. Second, trends can be observed in the applicant scoring data for several industry sectors. For instance, manufacturing applicants' scores in many categories show a declining trend during the years in the data set. Hence, analyzing the relationship between the categories without considering the time trends can produce spurious results.

In light of these challenges, we used the Independent Review scores from the applicants after 1999 in our study. The main reason for only including applicants in post-1999 period is that no significant change has been made to the framework. In addition, the number of Baldrige scoring items were abridged after 1999, each corresponding to a clear and well-defined construct under a category. Each item's raw score was converted to a percentage score, which was done by dividing it by the maximum possible score for that item. Only a small number of aggregations was needed for consistency. For instance, in Baldrige Criteria after 2003, item 6.2 and 6.3 were combined to a single item 6.2 to measure the relationship of work processes to work systems. We aggregated items 6.2 and 6.3 from 1999-2002 in a similar way. Lastly, we adjusted each item score by subtracting the mean item score of that year. Adjusting the yearly mean for each item can de-trend the time series and make the spurious regression less likely. We were left with 500 observations across five industry sectors. Table 2 shows the industry sector distribution of our sample.

Table 2: Industry Distribution of Sample

Industry Sector	*N*	Percent (%)
Manufacturing	78	15.6%
Service	58	11.6%
Small Business	103	20.6%
Education	99	19.8%
Healthcare	152	30.4%
Nonprofit	10	2.0%

Method

As discussed above, we adopt a structural model similar to Flynn and Saladin (2001) for our analysis (Figure 2). We used partial least squares (PLS) structural equation modeling to analyze the data. Traditionally, hypotheses regarding the Baldrige framework have been tested using covariance-based SEM (CBSEM). Our rationale for using PLS is as follows. First, although the overall sample size ($N = 500$) is rather large, a causal model built upon the Baldrige framework combined with all the measurement items can have many parameters. When we make comparison across industry sectors the statistical power of CBSEM can be affected, since the sample size within each group is less than the rule of thumb of 5 observations per parameter estimated (Shah & Goldstein, 2006). PLS is more flexible in this regard. It only requires a sample size of 10 times the most complex relationship in the research model (Peng & Lai, 2012). Second, many of theoretical models on quality management involve relative large number of paths between categories. PLS uses iterative method to estimates the factor loadings and structural paths in models and therefore is more appropriate to assess the predictive power in complex models (Peng & Lai, 2012). Third, many of the items scores are non-normal and PLS provides more robust estimates in the presence of non-normality (Cassel et al., 1999). We use *plspm* library in R 2.13.1 to estimate our research model.

MODEL EVALUATION AND RESULTS

Measurement Model

The measurement quality of our PLS structural equation model can be validated through internal reliability, convergent, and discriminant validities. Table 3 shows that all measurement item loadings are greater than 0.70, indicating convergent validity at indicator level. The convergent validity is also satisfactory at construct level since the average variance extracted (AVE) values are greater than 0.50 (Peng & Lai, 2012). The composite reliabilities are greater than 0.70, exceeding the recommended values (Hair et al., 2011). Evidence of discriminant validity is obtained by examining the diagonal elements (the square root of AVE) of the correlation matrix shown in Table 4. The square root of the average variance explained by each latent variable is greater than the correlations between that latent variable and other latent variables in the model, demonstrating discriminant validity (Chin, 1998). In addition, we also confirmed that an item's loading with its associated latent construct is higher than its loadings with all the remaining constructs (i.e., the cross loadings) (Hair et al., 2011). Collectively, the evidence suggests that the Baldrige constructs have adequate measurement properties.

Table 3 Measurement Properties of Baldrige Categories

Construct	**Item**	**Item loading**	**Composite reliability**	**AVE**
Leadership	Leadership approach and deployment (1.1)	0.948	0.941	0.888
	Societal Responsibility (1.2)	0.936		
Strategic Planning	Strategy development (2.1)	0.963	0.920	0.926
	Strategy deployment (2.2)	0.961		
Measurement, Information, and Analysis	Measurement and analysis (4.1)	0.942	0.936	0.880
	Information Management (4.2)	0.934		
Customer Focus	Customer and market knowledge (3.1)	0.951	0.947	0.898
	Customer relationship building and satisfaction determination (3.2)	0.944		
Workforce Focus	Work Systems (5.1)	0.894	0.872	0.797
	Education, Training, and Development (5.2)	0.899		
	Employee well-being and satisfaction (5.3)	0.885		
Operations Focus	Value creation processes (6.1)	0.943	0.881	0.894
	Support processes (incl. business and supplier) (6.2)	0.947		
Results	Customer and product results (7.1, 7.2)	0.909	0.932	0.831
	Process/operational results (7.5)	0.929		
	Financial and market results (7.3)	0.896		
	Human resource results (7.4)	0.912		

Table 4 Correlations of Latent Constructs

	L	SP	MIA	CF	WF	OF	R
L	**0.942**						
SP	0.826	**0.962**					
MIA	0.847	0.831	**0.938**				
CF	0.830	0.804	0.790	**0.948**			
WF	0.812	0.764	0.761	0.777	**0.893**		
OF	0.801	0.820	0.797	0.775	0.736	**0.946**	
R	0.792	0.772	0.790	0.762	0.746	0.762	**0.912**

Note: Values on diagonal are the square root of construct's average variance extracted (AVE)

Structural Model

We first used the entire data set to fit the model using PLS analysis. The overall quality of the research model can be assessed using Goodness of Fit (GoF) following Tenenhaus et al., (2005). The Flynn and Saladin (2001) model result in a Gof of 0.782, which is well above the suggested cut-off value of 0.36. The Stone-Geisser's Q^2 (Geisser, 1975; Stone, 1974) was used to assess the predictive relevance for endogenous variables using a blindfold procedure. With Q^2 greater than 0 (ranging from 0.42 to 0.64) for all the six endogenous variables, we can conclude that the model has considerable predictive power.

Table 5 reports the path coefficients of the CPE model estimated for the entire data set. The explanatory power of the structural model can be evaluated by looking at the R^2 value in the dependent constructs. The R^2 values for the CPE constructs are reported in Table 6. With fairly high values for all endogenous variables, especially with the R^2 being 0.699 for the Results category, we can conclude that the model has substantial explanatory power for quality management actions and outcomes. The 95% confidence intervals are estimated using 500 bootstrapped samples. We confirmed the consistency of this result by running the structural model's bootstrap procedure with 200 and 1000 times of resampling.

Table 5 Structural Estimates of PLS analysis

Path	PLS result		
	Coefficient	Std. Error	95% CI
Leadership -> Measurement, Information, and Analysis	0.825	0.0131	(0.800, 0.849)
Leadership -> Strategic Planning	0.506	0.0447	(0.412, 0.589)
Leadership -> Customer Focus	0.438	0.0537	(0.332, 0.541)
Leadership -> Results	0.294	0.0518	(0.192, 0.389)
Measurement, Information, and Analysis -> Strategic Planning	0.414	0.0426	(0.334, 0.497)
Measurement, Information, and Analysis -> Customer Focus	0.304	0.0433	(0.222, 0.389)
Measurement, Information, and Analysis -> Workforce Focus	0.424	0.0478	(0.324, 0.516)
Measurement, Information, and Analysis -> Operations Focus	0.492	0.0395	(0.412, 0.565)
Measurement, Information, and Analysis -> Results	0.204	0.0509	(0.103, 0.297)
Strategic Planning -> Customer Focus	0.167	0.0539	(0.067, 0.268)
Strategic Planning -> Workforce Focus	0.409	0.0484	(0.319, 0.511)
Customer Focus -> Operations Focus	0.252	0.0445	(0.165, 0.339)
Workforce Focus -> Operations Focus	0.164	0.0385	(0.088, 0.240)
Workforce Focus -> Results	0.191	0.0421	(0.109, 0.273)
Operations Focus -> Results	0.218	0.0505	(0.118, 0.314)

Table 6 R^2 for Endogenous Variables in PLS Model

Endogenous variables	R^2	95% CI for R^2
Strategic Planning	0.681	(0.640, 0.721)
Measurement, Information, and Analysis	0.772	(0.734, 0.804)
Customer Focus	0.739	(0.695, 0.776)
Workforce Focus	0.635	(0.588, 0.684)
Operations Focus	0.720	(0.673, 0.758)
Results	0.699	(0.658, 0.740)

We tested H1a - H1d by examining the structural model's coefficients for Leadership to other constructs. As seen in Table 5, the coefficients vary from 0.294 0.825, all of which are significant at α = 0.05 level. The results support the hypothesis H1a - H1d that senior leadership should have direct, positive impact on Measurement, Information and Analysis, Strategic Planning, Customer Focus, and Results. The magnitude of the direct linkage coefficient from Leadership to Results, however, is not strong (0.294). This suggests that results of the performance excellence system hinge on strong commitments from other parts of the organization besides leadership.

To test H2a - H2e, we first note that in the Flynn and Saladin (2001) model, Measurement, Information, and Analysis serves as a critical role in the system. It is considered the most important endogenous variable in the causal model and is the linkage between management effort and other components in the system. The PLS analysis confirms this role, as its path coefficients to Strategic Planning, Customer Focus, Workforce Focus, Operations Focus and Results are all positive and statistically significant. In addition, we fit a PLS model without the Measurement, Information and Analysis construct included. The reduced model has smaller goodness of fit measure and other endogenous variables have Stone-Geisser's Q^2 measures. This indicates that an organization's performance in Measurement, Information and Analysis is important in predicting the overall quality management outcome. Overall the evidence supports H2a - H2e.

To test H3a, H3b, and H4, we examined the structural model's path coefficients from Strategic Planning to Customer Focus and Workforce Focus, as well the path coefficient from Customer Focus to Operations Focus. Once again, the path coefficients are all positive and statistically significant. The magnitude of the coefficient between Strategic Planning and Customer Focus, estimated at 0.167, is relatively low, suggesting a reduced role of strategic planning on customer and market processes compared to other categorical constructs such as those related to leadership and information and analysis. Overall, however, the evidence supports H3a, H3b, and H4.

Table 7 Structural Estimates by Industry Sector

	Manufacturing		**Service**		**Small Business**		**Education**		**Healthcare**	
	Coefficient	Std. Error	Coefficient	Std. Error	Coefficient	Std. Error	Coefficient	Std. Error	Coefficient	Std. Error
L -> MIA	**0.77***	0.05	**0.89***	0.03	**0.85***	0.02	**0.80***	0.03	**0.80***	0.02
L -> SP	**0.63***	0.08	**0.57***	0.12	**0.38***	0.11	**0.43***	0.07	**0.59***	0.08
L -> CF	**0.46***	0.14	**0.41***	0.19	**0.36***	0.11	**0.51***	0.10	**0.42***	0.09
L -> R	0.03	0.12	0.27	0.20	**0.47***	0.10	0.17	0.13	**0.32***	0.11
MIA -> SP	**0.27***	0.09	**0.36***	0.11	**0.53***	0.10	**0.51***	0.07	**0.30***	0.08
MIA -> CF	**0.28***	0.09	0.00	0.13	**0.50***	0.11	**0.30***	0.09	**0.24***	0.09
MIA -> WF	**0.33***	0.14	0.27	0.17	**0.51***	0.10	**0.28***	0.12	**0.43***	0.08
MIA -> OF	**0.44***	0.11	**0.51***	0.10	**0.50***	0.09	**0.50***	0.10	**0.38***	0.09
MIA -> R	0.20	0.13	0.02	0.13	**0.33***	0.11	0.18	0.11	**0.21***	0.09
SP -> CF	0.14	0.13	**0.47***	0.14	0.05	0.14	0.13	0.11	**0.24***	0.09
SP -> WF	**0.37***	0.12	**0.57***	0.16	**0.38***	0.10	**0.57***	0.11	**0.38***	0.09
CF -> OF	**0.38***	0.11	**0.32***	0.13	**0.26***	0.09	0.18	0.11	**0.19***	0.09
WF -> OF	0.08	0.09	0.09	0.12	0.15	0.09	**0.25***	0.09	**0.27***	0.07
WF -> R	**0.36***	0.09	**0.27***	0.14	-0.04	0.08	**0.17***	0.09	**0.24***	0.08
OF -> R	**0.34***	0.12	**0.35***	0.14	**0.18***	0.09	**0.37***	0.12	0.09	0.10

*: significant at the $p < 0.05$ level

To test H5a, H5b, and H6, the path coefficient from Workforce Focus to Operations Focus was examined, as well as the coefficients from Workforce Focus and Operations Focus to Results. All path coefficients are positive and significant at the $\alpha = 0.05$ level. However, ranging from 0.164 to 0.218, the magnitudes of these coefficients are among the weakest in the model. These results are consistent with Flynn and Saladin's (2001) analysis that found generally weakening relationships in the model's downstream paths involving Workforce Focus, Process Management, and Results. Evidence presented here supports H5a, H5b, and H6 nonetheless.

Lastly, we conducted multiple-group analyses to examine whether the relationships between the categories are moderated by industries (H7). We omitted the nonprofit sector due to its small sample size in the data set. We conducted the group comparison at both the measurement level and structural level. We first confirmed that the measurement model is indeed adequate and similar for all groups. Then we focused on the structural level differences. That is, we wanted to test whether the magnitude of the structural coefficients (i.e., the path coefficients) are the same for all industry sectors. We used the Chin/Keil approach (Keil et al., 2000) to conduct the analysis. More specifically, for each for the industry sectors the path coefficients were estimated separately, and the standard errors and non-parametric confidence intervals of the coefficients were computed from bootstrapping observations in each group. Table 7 displays the group-specific path coefficient estimates. H7 is clearly rejected, since for all but the first three paths only a subset of industry sectors have significant coefficients.

DISCUSSION

The primary objective of this investigation was to provide a more decisive test of the CPE framework by addressing several shortcomings of previous studies. Use of Flynn and Saladin's (2001) representation of the third generation CPE framework offered a prominent, well-cited model firmly anchored in theory that provided a basis for comparative evaluation. Use of Baldrige applicant scoring data offered both a large, cross sectional sample pool and a primary data source of expert observers with extensive skill in assessing organizational activities in light of the CPE framework to overcome methodological limitations of past studies.

Findings from our analysis stemming from this approach found strong support for the third generation CPE framework as modeled by Flynn and Saladin (2001). When the entire 500 sample cross industry data set was used to estimate the structural model pictured in Figure 2, all hypothesized relationships between CPE constructs were found significant. Similar to Flynn and Saladin's (2001) analysis, the strength of those relationships as reflected by the structural model's path coefficients was found to decline among the "downstream" constructs of Workforce Focus, Process Focus, and Business Results. When discussing their results, Flynn and Saladin (2001) suggested that this might reflect failure to account for some important relationships not included in the third generation CPE framework. However, several of the relationships found to be non-significant in Flynn and Saladin's (2001) model were found significant here, suggesting that methodological differences such as sample size and composition—issues that Flynn and Saladin (2001) discussed as potential limitations of their study—may help explain findings in this context. Providing a more favorable backdrop for evaluating the third generation CPE framework's general validity, as well as associated evidence that supports the framework in its entirety, constitute the primary contributions of this study.

Although analysis based on the entire cross industry sample afforded strong support for the CPE framework in its entirety, that support did not transfer to analysis of the framework on a sector-by-sector basis. As Table 7 indicates, path coefficients between CPE constructs were found non-significant in all sector models, ranging from 1 in 15 non-significant for the health care sector structural model to 5 in 15 non-significant for the service sector structural model. Differences in sector sample size might contribute to these results. Matching the sector sample sizes appearing in Table 2 to the number of non-significant paths in Table 7 does suggest some degree of relationship. Because overcoming small, homogenous sector samples of previous studies was a primary methodological limitation that the present investigation sought to overcome when evaluating the CPE framework's general validity, then perhaps the findings in Table 7 should not be surprising. However, explanations in terms of sample issues alone are not completely satisfactory. As shown in Table 7, only 4 of the 15 path coefficients were significant across all sectors, and no discernable pattern of non-significance is evident. Moreover, low values associated with many of the non-significant path coefficients suggest lack of relationship between particular constructs regardless of sample size. Coupling historical arguments for sector-dependent quality system designs (e.g., Huq and Stolen 1998; Ronnback and Witell 2008; Woon 2000) with results reported here raises questions as to whether the performance excellence frameworks are structured differently between sectors. Investigations that assume a contingency-based stance to explore such inter-sector differences seems an interesting future research opportunity.

REFERENCES

Badri, M.A., Selim, H., Alshare, K., Grandon, E.E., Younis, H., & Abdulla, M. (2006). The Baldrige Education Criteria for performance excellence framework: Empirical test and validation. *International Journal of Quality & Reliability Management, 23,* 1118-1157.

Bell, R. & Keys, B. (1998). A conversation with Curt W. Reimann on the background and future of the Baldrige award. *Organizational Dynamics, 26*(4), 51-61.

Bemowski, K. & Stratton, B. (1995). How do people use the Baldrige award criteria? *Quality Progress, 28*(5), 43-48.

Bou-Llusar, J.C., Escrig-Tena, A.B., Roca-Puig, V., & Beltrán-Martín, I. (2009). An empirical assessment of the EFQM Excellence Model: Evaluation as a TQM framework relative to the MBNQA Model. *Journal of Operations Management, 27*, 1-22.

Cassel, C., Hackl, P., & Westlund, A.H. (1999). Robustness of partial least-squares method for estimating latent variable quality structures. *Journal of Applied Statistics,26*, 435-446.

Chin, W.W. (1998). The partial least squares approach to structural equation modeling. In G.A. Marcoulides (ed.), *Modern methods for business research*, Hillsdale, NJ: Lawrence Earlbaum Associates, 294-336.

Cronbach, L.J., & Meehl, P.E. (1955). Construct validity in psychological tests. *Psychological Bulletin, 52*(4), 281-302.

Curkovic, S., Melnyk, S., Calantone, R., & Handfield, R. (2000). Validating the Malcolm Baldrige National Quality Award framework through structural equation modelling. *International Journal of Production Research, 38*, 765-791.

Dearborn, D.C., & Simon, H.A. (1958). Selective perception: A note on the departmental identifications of executives. *Sociometry, 21*, 140-144.

Douglas, T.J., & Fredendall, L.D. (2004). Evaluating the Deming management model of total quality in services. *Decision Sciences, 35*, 393-422.

Ettorre, B. (1996). Is the Baldrige still meaningful? *Management Review, 85*, 28-43.

Evans, J.R, Ford, M.W., Masterson, S.S., & Hertz H.S. (2012). Beyond performance excellence: research insights from Baldrige recipient feedback. *Total Quality Management & Business Excellence, 23*, 489-506.

Evans, J.R., & Mai, F. (2014). Insights from the Baldrige Award item-level blinded applicant scoring data. *Quality Management Journal, 21*(2), 45-64.

Flynn, B.B., & Saladin, B. (2001). Further evidence on the validity of the theoretical models underlying the Baldrige criteria. *Journal of Operations Management, 19*, 617-652.

Flynn, B.B., & Saladin, B. (2006). Relevance of Baldrige constructs in an international context: a study of national culture. *Journal of Operations Management, 24*, 583-603.

Ford, M.W., & Evans, J.R. (2001). Baldrige assessment and organizational learning: The need for change management. *Quality Management Journal, 8*(3), 6-22.

Geisser, S. (1975). The predictive sample reuse method with applications. *Journal of the American Statistical Association, 70*, 320-328.

Ghosh, S., Handfield, R.B., Kannan, V.R., & Tan, K.C. (2003). A structural model analysis of the Malcolm Baldrige National Quality Award framework. *International Journal of Management and Decision Making, 4*(4), 289-311.

Goldstein, S.M., & Schweikhart, S.B. (2002). Empirical support for the Baldrige Award framework in US hospitals. *Health Care Management Review, 27*(1), 62-75.

Hair, J.F., Ringle, C.M., & Sarstedt, M. (2011). PLS-SEM: Indeed a silver bullet. *Journal of Marketing Theory and Practice, 19*(2), 139-52.

Hambrick, D.C. (1981). Strategic awareness within top management teams. *Strategic Management Journal, 13*, 145-158.

He, Z., Hill, J., Wang, P., & Yue, G. (2011). Validation of the theoretical model underlying the Baldrige criteria: Evidence from China. *Total Quality Management, 22*(2), 243-263.

Huq, Z., & Stolen, J.D. (1998). Total quality management contrasts in manufacturing and service industries. *International Journal of Quality & Reliability Management, 15*, 138-161.

Jayamaha, N.P, Grigg, N.P., & Mann, R.S. (2008). Empirical validity of Baldrige criteria: New Zealand evidence. *International Journal of Quality & Reliability Management, 25*, 477-93.

Jayamaha, N.P., Palitha, N., Grigg, N.P., & Mann, R.S. (2011). Empirical analysis of the Baldrige Criteria as both an organisational performance measure and a theoretical model. *Measuring Business Excellence, 15*(1), 20-33.

Karimi, A., Safari, H., Hashemi, S.H., and Kalantar, P. (2014). A study of the Baldrige Award framework using the applicant scoring data. *Total Quality Management, 25*, 461-477.

Keil, M., Tan, B.C.Y., Wei, K.K., Saarinen, T., Tuunainen, V. & Wassenaar, A. (2000). A cross-cultural study on escalation of commitment behavior in software projects. *MIS Quarterly, 24*,

299-325.

Lee, S.M., Rho, B.H., & Lee, S.G. (2003). Impact of Malcolm Baldrige National Quality Award Criteria on organizational quality performance. *International Journal of Production Research, 41*, 2003-2020.

Meyer, S.M., & Collier, D.A. (2001). An empirical test of the causal relationships in the Baldrige Health Care Pilot Criteria. *Journal of Operations Management, 19*, 403-425.

Nisbett, R.E., & Wilson, T.D. (1977). Telling more than we can know: Verbal reports on mental processes. *Psychological Review, 84*(3), 231-259.

Pannirselvam, G.P. & Ferguson, L.A. (2001). A study of the relationships between the Baldrige categories. *International Journal of Quality & Reliability Management, 18*, 14-37.

Peng, D.X., & Lai, F. (2012). Using partial least squares in operations management research: A practical guideline and summary of past research. *Journal of Operations Management, 30*, 467-480.

Prajogo, D.I. (2005). The comparative analysis of TQM practices and quality performance between manufacturing and service firms. *International Journal of Service Industry Management, 16*(3), 217-228.

Ronnback, A., & Witell, L. (2008). A review of empirical investigations comparing quality initiatives in manufacturing and service organizations. *Managing Service Quality, 18*, 577-93.

Shah, R., & Goldstein, S.M. (2006). Use of structural equation modeling in operations management research: Looking back and forward. *Journal of Operations Management, 24*, 148-169.

Steeples, M.M. (1992). *The corporate guide to the Malcolm Baldrige national quality award: Proven strategies for building quality into your organization*. Milwaukee: ASQ Quality Press.

Stone, M. (1974). Cross-validatory choice and assessment of statistical predictions. *Journal of the Royal Statistical Society, 36*(2), 111-147.

Tenenhaus, M., Vinzi, V.E., Chatelin, Y.M., & Lauro, C. (2005). PLS path modeling. *Computational Statistics & Data Analysis, 48*(1), 159-205.

Wilson, D.D., & Collier, D.A. (2000). An empirical investigation of the Malcolm Baldrige National Quality Award causal model. *Decision Sciences, 31*, 361-383.

Woon, K.C. (2000). TQM implementation: Comparing Singapore's service and manufacturing leaders. *Managing Service Quality, 10*(5), 318-331.

DECISION SCIENCES INSTITUTE

An Examination of Consumer Attitudes on Online User Reviews

Chuleeporn Changchit
Texas A&M University-Corpus Christi
Email: chuleeporn.changchit@tamucc.edu

Tim Klaus
Texas A&M University-Corpus Christi
Email: tim.klaus@tamucc.edu

ABSTRACT

With increasing numbers of Internet shoppers, many product review websites have been established to collect consumer opinions about a variety of products. However, many aspects of user behavior towards the usage of online reviews are still not well understood. This study aims at exploring factors underlying the acceptance of consumers' online review usage when considering purchasing an item. The study results provide insight into the factors that affect online customers' use of online reviews prior to a purchase. It furthers the online reviews body of knowledge and provides results that can allow e-businesses to adapt their business model to better fit consumers' expectations.

KEYWORDS: Online Reviews, Ecommerce, Review Usage

INTRODUCTION

With the rapid expansion and proliferation of e-commerce innovations, consumers are now able to use the Internet for a variety of purposes such as research, communication, online banking, and shopping. Many online shoppers are attracted to the ease and convenience that shopping via the Internet can provide (Shang, Chen, & Shen, 2005). Pew Internet, Inc. (2014) reported that 86% of American adults used the Internet in 2013, up from 14% in 1995.

With increasing numbers of Internet shoppers, many product review websites (e.g., epinions.com, Rateitall.com, cnet.com) have been established to collect consumer opinions about a variety of products Wei et al. 2010). Also, many ecommerce websites have included product reviews on the same page of the products that sell. The availability of many perspectives can benefit customers' decision-making regarding product purchases. In the past, critics generally reviewed popular products that had wide-spread interest. Currently, online product reviews not only allows for niche products to be reviewed, but also allows for many more perspectives to be expressed. Online product reviews have emerged as influential sources of information which affect customers' pre-purchase perspectives of a product. Since online shopping does not allow for the level of touch and interaction with a product which may be present in traditional retail outlets, online retailers seek to provide product evaluations online as an alternative to physically interacting with a product.

Although consumers have become familiar with the use of online product reviews, many aspects of user behavior towards the usage of online reviews are still not well understood. This study, therefore, aims at exploring the factors underlying the usage of online reviews systems in pre-purchase decision-making. The study results should provide insight into what factors encourage or discourage users from using online reviews. This study should further the body of knowledge that deals with online reviews and thus allow e-businesses to adapt their business model to better fit consumers' expectations. Also, since the use of online reviews affects purchasing behavior (Mo et al., 2015), it is important to understand what factors affect the use of online reviews.

LITERATURE REVIEW

There are various aspects of product reviews that affect the level of sales. Some studies found that the volume of user reviews positively affects sales (Duan et al., 2008; Liu, 2006). Another study found that higher quality online reviews are positively related to buying intentions (Obiedat, 2013). Similarly, the perceived quality of online reviews as well as the quantity positively affects purchasing intention (Park et al., 2007). One report found that 88% of customers who read reviews were influenced by reviews in their buying decisions (Dimensional Research, 2013). Also, a study examining hotel reviews, found that the average price difference was $45 higher for hotels that were rated one rating unit higher, and the number of reviews was less important than the actual rating (Jang et al., 2012). Thus, a financial incentive exists for companies to have products with high ratings.

Because of these financial incentives, sometimes reviews have been written by the manufacturer of a product and related third parties, such as contracted marketing firms. Thus, customers are faced with determining if reviews are trustworthy. Previous research has found that people find it difficult to identify fraudulent reviews (Ott et al., 2011) as customers do not know if a review was written by an altruistic reviewer wishing to share experiences. Indeed, quite a few companies have been caught trying to manipulate potential customers' perspectives by paying to have positive reviews written (Jansen et al., 2013). Some companies have been fined by government regulators for posting phony reviews as it is false advertising (Streitfeld, 2013). Thus, potential buyers experience the daunting task of separating the credible reviews from those that are not in order to avoid manipulative reviews or reviews with incorrect information. This causes a wide variety of perspectives regarding the helpfulness of reviews.

While some reviews are fraudulently written by people who have never used the product, other reviews are written by people who have received some form of benefit. For example, some reviewers receive a small payment for their review while others will give discounts on future purchases, free products, partial refunds, and other incentives (Streitfeld 2012). Providing incentives to potential reviewers has led to more helpful reviews, but not necessarily objective feedback (Stephen et al., 2012). Disclosing the incentive made customers doubt product quality and post-experience product evaluations (Stephen et al., 2012).

The possibility of fraudulent or misleading reviews as well as reviewers receiving something in exchange for writing a review makes users question their trust in reviews. One report studying various sources of trust found that 92% of consumers trust recommendations from people they know, followed by 70% of consumers trusting opinions posted online. The level of trust on paid advertisements was quite lower with only 47% of consumers trusting TV ads and 29% of consumers trusting text ads on mobile phones (Nielsen, 2012). However, even though consumers tend to trust opinions posted online, 40% of online customers did not trust most or all of reviewers' comments as accurate (Sterling, 2013), implying that many consumers do not naively believe all reviews. Reviewer credibility affects perceptions of quality more than purchase intention. The purchase intention seemed to be affected more by perceived importance of owning a product rather than online reviews (Jensen et al., 2013).

There also are varying perspectives on the helpfulness of reviews. The review rating, the content of reviews, and the reviewer's credibility affect the perceived helpfulness of a review (Baek, et al., 2013). In addition, if a reviewer is shown as a top-ranked reviewer or if the website indicates that the real name of the reviewer is shown, the review is perceived as more helpful (Baek et al., 2013). Furthermore, the greater the difference between the average rating of the product and the actual review rating, the less helpful a review becomes (Baek et al., 2013). Most reviews are unidimensional ratings on a scale of one to five. However, it has been found that unidimensional ratings are biased by price and correlated more with product value then with product quality (Li, 2010). Multidimensional ratings are perceived as less-biased, but take more effort for both the reviewer to assess and the reader to sort through (Li, 2010).

Research has shown that there are ways to increase and decrease the perceived credibility of a review. If a review is two-sided (addressing both positive and negative issues), reviewer credibility increases (Jensen et al., 2013). However, reviewer credibility decreases when there is higher affect intensity (emotion) in the review. Also, when a review uses language that violates sociological and cultural expectations, such as being too aggressive, the review is perceived as less credible (Jensen et al., 2013). As this was studied in anonymous reviews, however, it is possible that online vendors creating categories of reviewers ("Top 100 Reviewer", etc.), would not be discredited for using higher affect intensity (Jensen et al., 2013).

Consumers are more likely to read reviews if the price of an item is higher and these reviews are read in greater detail (Baek et al., 2013). For online customers which don't desire to read reviews are affected by the quantity rather than quality of reviews while high-involvement customers are affected by quantity only when the quality is high (Park et al., 2007).

THEORETICAL DEVELOPMENT

The Technology Acceptance Model (TAM) has been widely used to study users' acceptance of a new technology and is the most cited theory for modeling user acceptance of information systems (Bagozzi 2007; Davis et al., 1989). In regards to online user review systems, we propose that Perceived Usefulness and Perceived Ease of Use from TAM will help explain the intention to use online review systems. However, we also propose that trust is very important to consider. Even though a system may work great, the quality of the reviews and the reputation of the ecommerce company likely will impact whether people want to use the reviews. Thus we add Perceived Credibility of Online Review and Perceived Credibility to our model. In addition, we propose that the perceived Technology Competency of the individual who is using the online review system will likely impact the decision an individual makes on whether to use an online review system. The proposed research model is shown in Figure 1 below.

Figure 1. Research model

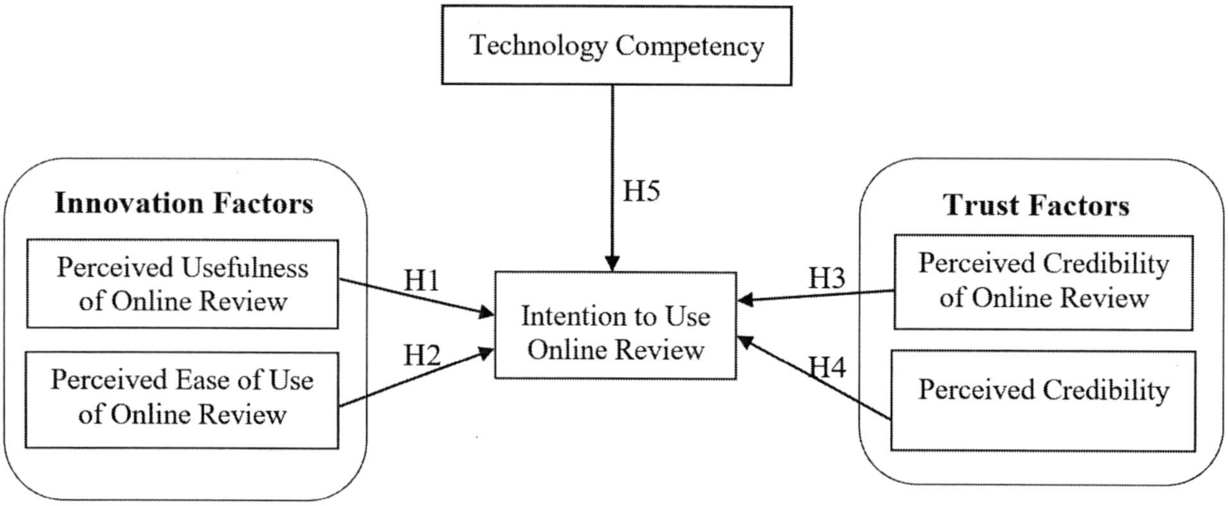

Perceived Usefulness of Online Review (PUOR)

The construct perceived usefulness is defined as the prospective users' subjective probability that using a specific application system will increase his or her job performance within an organizational context (Davis et al., 1989). This factor has a significant effect on usage intention (Agarwal & Prasad 1999; Davis et al., 1989; Venkatesh & Davis, 2000). We define PUOR as the users' subjective probability that using the online review will be valuable for his or her online purchase decision making. Perceived usefulness is, thus, predicted to be a positive driver for the online review usage. We thus propose the following hypothesis:

H1: Perceived usefulness of online review (PUOR) positively affects customers' intention to use online reviews.

Perceived Ease of Use of Online Review (PEUOR)

The construct perceived ease of use is defined as the degree to which the prospective user expects the target system to be free of effort (Davis et al., 1989). This factor plays a crucial role in understanding individual response to information technology (Agarwal & Karahanna, 2000; Chau & Hu, 2001; Hong et al., 2001). Research over the past decade provides evidence of the significant effect perceived ease of use has had on usage intention (Agarwal & Prasad 1999; Venkatesh & Davis, 2000). We therefore posit:

H2: Perceived ease of use of online review (PEUOR) positively affects subjects' intention to use online review.

Perceived Credibility of Online Review (PCOR)

Credibility has been defined and examined in prior studies. However, very few studies have examined the credibility of online reviews. One study looked at several different aspects of reviews and found that a review that is two-sided affects perceived credibility to the greatest extent (Jensen et al, 2013). As it appears that a user has considered both positive and negatives aspects of a product, a two-sided review appears to have greater credibility. In this paper, we are not seeking to determine what affects perceived credibility, but rather we seek to understand the impact that perceived credibility has on the intention to use online reviews. Thus our third hypothesis is:

H3: Perceived credibility of online review (PCOR) positively affects subjects' intention to use online review.

Perceived Credibility (PC)

Some ecommerce companies are in the news because of the decisions they make on their online reviews systems. For example, Amazon.com deletes reviews that they believe are fake or written by those with a financial interest in the item (Charman-Anderson 2012) and Amazon.com has sued people that create fake reviews of products (Roberts 2015). The perceived credibility of the company is likely affected by news about a company, information from friends, and prior experience with the company. We propose that customers that think that a company is credible will also more likely choose to use the online reviews systems of the company. Thus hypothesis 4 is:

H4: Perceived credibility (PC) of the company positively affects subjects' intention to use online review.

Technology Competency (TC)

Technology Competency is defined as the extent to which an individual is knowledgeable about and effectively utilizes Information Technology to manage information (Tippins & Sohi, 2003). Typically, consumers with a high level of self-efficacy are more motivated to use technology-based services. Moreover, they have a more positive attitude and intent to use technology-based services than consumers with a low level of technology self-efficacy. High technology competence consumers are more likely to use a system than low technology competence consumers (Yang, 2010). Therefore, consumers with a high technology self-efficacy are expected to have positive attitude and behavioral intentions to using online review systems. We, therefore posit:

H5: Technology competency (TC) of subjects positively affects intention to use online review.

RESEARCH METHODOLOGY

A questionnaire was designed for this study based on instruments and scales developed from previous studies. The TAM questions were adapted from two TAM studies (Venkatesh and Davis, 2000; Venkatesh et al., 2003). The questions used to measure the other additional constructs were adapted from other studies (Intana et al., 2013; Pikkarainen et al., 2004; Vijayasarathy, 2004; Wong and Hsu, 2008). The questionnaire consisted of thirty-seven (37) questions. Twenty-six (26) questions with a six point Likert scale were designed to measure subjects' perceptions and the usage of online review. The remaining eleven (11) questions were asked to gather some demographic data of the subjects. To validate the clarity of these questions, three professors and three research assistants were asked to read through the survey questions. Revisions to the survey were made based on the feedback received.

Three hundred and eighty (380) subjects participated in this study. The data were collected from a direct survey administered to students in a university in the U.S. Of the three hundred and eighty (380) subjects, three hundred and sixty-six (366) responses were valid. Subjects' demographics are shown in Table 1 below.

Table 1. Subject Demographics

Gender						
Male: 166 (45.36%)			Female: 200 (54.64%)		No Answer: 0 (0%)	
Age						
Under 18: 0 (0.00%)	18-25: 325 (88.80%)	26-35: 31 (8.47%)	36-45: 8 (2.19%)	46 and up: 2 (0.55%)	No Answer: 0 (0%)	
Highest Education						
High School: 4 (1.09%)	Associate's Degree: 46 (12.57%)		Bachelors: 41 (11.20%)	Master's & up: 10 (2.73%)	No answer: 3 (0.82%)	
Age (in years)						
Full-time: 54 (14.75%)	Part-time: 159 (43.44%)		Not-employed: 152 (41.53%)		No Answer: 1 (0.27%)	
Ethnicity						
Anglo: 35 (9.56%)	Hispanic 143 (39.07%)	Asian 32 (8.74%)	African American 28 (7.65%)	Other 21 (5.74%)	No Answer: 4 (1.09%)	
Have Credit or Debit Card						
Yes: 355 (96.99%)		No: 10 (2.73%)		No Answer: 1 (0.27%)		
Annual Income						
Under $20000 307 (83.88%)	$20000-$40000 38 (10.38%)	$40000-$60000 4 (1.09%)	$60000-$80000 9 (2.46%)	$80000-$100000 5 (1.37%)	Over $100,000 0 (0.00%)	No Answer: 3 (0.82%)
Average Amount of Online Order per Order						
$1-$20 43 (11.75%)	$21-$40 111 (30.33%)	$41-$60 102 (27.87%)	$61-$100 55 (15.03%)	$101-$200 35 (9.56%)	More than $200 19 (5.19%)	No Answer: 1 (0.27%)
Number of Online Orders per Month						
0 79 (21.58%)	1-2: 161 (43.99%)	3-5: 87 (23.77%)	6-9: 24 (6.56%)	10-20: 5 (1.37%)	More than 20: 7 (1.91%)	No Answer: 3 (0.82%)

Number of Online Orders per Year						
0 9 (2.46%)	1-2: 44 (12.02%)	3-5: 79 (21.58%)	6-9: 74 (20.22%)	10-20: 87 (23.77%)	More than 20: 73 (19.95%)	No Answer: 0 (0.00%)
Return						
Yes: 169 (46.17%)		No: 194 (53.01%)			No Answer: 3 (0.82%)	
Student						
Undergraduate 337 (92.08%)		Graduate 26 (7.10%)		Not a Student 1 (0.27%)		No Answer: 1 (0.27%)

DATA ANALYSIS AND DISCUSSION

In order to examine the internal consistency of the research instrument, a reliability test was conducted. The test confirms the reliability of the research items with Cronbach's alpha coefficient of 0.922.

The measurement model for the five constructs was assessed by a confirmatory factor analysis with Varimax rotation in order to test whether the questionnaire items produced the expected number of factors and whether each item was loaded on their appropriated factor. As shown in Table 2 below, results from the factor analysis indicates that all items are loaded into six (6) factors. The minimum loading factor from the result is at 0.565 which meets the minimum acceptance threshold of 0.5 (Hair et al., 1998).

The measurement model was further assessed for construct reliability. The composite reliability for all the constructs was above 0.7, conforming to an acceptable threshold suggested by Nunnally and Bernstein (1994). Table 2 below presents the mean, standard deviation, factor loading, and composite reliability of all items assessed in this study.

Table 2. Summary of Measurement Scales

Constructs	M	SD	Factor Loading*	Reliability
Perceived Usefulness of Online Review				0.945
PUOR1	4.81	1.09	0.565	
PUOR2	4.73	1.09	0.571	
PUOR3	4.64	1.15	0.597	
PUOR4	4.71	1.10	0.567	
Perceived Ease of Use of Online Review				0.915
PEUOR1	4.61	1.06	0.741	
PEUOR2	4.75	1.10	0.764	
PEUOR3	4.97	1.00	0.800	
PEUOR4	4.84	1.08	0.784	
Perceived Credibility of Online Review				0.982
PCOR1	3.77	1.15	0.855	
PCOR2	4.03	1.07	0.786	
PCOR3	3.99	1.12	0.810	
PCOR4	3.83	1.09	0.753	
Perceived Credibility				0.938
PC1	5.12	1.89	0.860	
PC2	5.04	1.06	0.886	
PC3	5.10	1.02	0.894	
PC4	5.13	1.00	0.867	
PC5	5.04	1.08	0.812	
Technology Competency				0.882
TC1	5.39	0.89	0.826	
TC2	5.17	0.96	0.868	
TC3	5.40	0.82	0.815	
TC4	5.37	0.91	0.635	
TC5	4.90	1.11	0.770	
Intention to Use Online Reviews				0.960
INT1	5.08	1.39	0.871	
INT2	5.06	2.55	0.887	
INT3	4.29	1.31	0.879	
INT4	4.42	1.32	0.905	

* Rotation Method: Varimax with Kaiser Normalization

A multiple regression analysis was conducted to test the five (5) hypotheses. The independent variables are perceived usefulness of online review (PUOR), perceived ease of use of online review (PEUOR), perceived credibility of online review (PCOR), Perceived credibility (PC) and technology competency (TC). The dependent variable is the intention to use online review (INT).

The results from Table 3 show the R2 and Adjusted R2 of 46.2% and 45.5% respectively, indicating that the factors investigated are suitable to explain the attitude towards the usage of online review systems. The F-stat was reported to be at 62.116 and was significant at 0.1% significant level. This also indicates that the combined factors are able to simultaneously explain the attitude quite well.

Table 3: Multiple Regression Analysis

Hypotheses	Unstandardized Coefficients		Standardized Coefficients	t	Sig.	Collinearity Statistics	
	β	Std. Error	Beta			Tolerance	VIF
(Constant)	.098	.396		-.247	.805		
H1: PUOR	.759	.075	.617	10.147	.000	.403	2.479
H2: PEUOR	-.215	.071	-.161	-2.792	.006	.447	2.236
H3: PCOR	.181	.071	.140	2.568	.011	.502	1.992
H4: PC	.186	.057	.414	3.257	.001	.791	1.265
H5: TC	.064	.073	.038	0.884	.377	.786	1.272

R-Square = 0.462

Adj. R-Square =0.455

F-stat = 62.116*

* Significance at p-value <0.001

Regarding each factor, the results from the multiple regression analysis demonstrates that four out of the five factors are significant determinants on whether subjects intend to use online review. These factors are perceived usefulness of online review (PUOR; β = 0.759, perceived ease of use of online review (PEUOR; β = -0.215), perceived credibility of online review (PCOR; β =0.181), and perceived credibility (PC; β=0.186). In contrast, the results show that the factors technological competency (TC; β = 0.064) does not significantly affect subjects' intention to use online review.

The Variance Inflation Factors (VIF) for all factors range between 1.265 and 2.479, which are not greater than 10, indicating that there is no problem of multicollinearity (Hair et al., 2006; Diamantopoulos et al. 2008).

DISCUSSION AND CONCLUSION

In this study, five factors are predicted to influence the intention towards the usage of online reviews. Besides the two factors (perceived usefulness and perceive ease of use) included in the original TAM model, the proposed model of this paper included three (3) additional factors as determinants of subjects' intention to use online reviews. These factors are perceived credibility of online review (PCOR), perceived credibility (PC), and subjects' technology competency (TC).

The results of this study reveal that four out of five factors examined in the proposed research model play an important role in explaining users' intention to use online reviews. The first factor is "perceived usefulness of online review". It is clear from the result that if subjects perceive online reviews as providing beneficial information, there is a high likelihood that they will use the online review system.

The second factor is "perceived ease of use of online review". It is interesting to find that although this factor significantly impacts subjects' intention to use online reviews, the beta is negative. In examining the data further, it was found that there is a significantly positive correlation between perceived ease of use of online review and the intention to use the online reviews. However, multiple regression gives coefficients while controlling for the rest of the variables. Thus if all of the remaining constructs are held constant, then there is a slight negative relationship between the perceived ease of use of online reviews.
Both the third hypothesis examining Perceived Credibility of Online Review and the fourth hypothesis examining Perceived Credibility both had significant results. This indicates that trust is important to consider as both the credibility of the online reviews as well as the credibility of the company impacts whether customers want to use an online review system. This finding expands on previous literature by establishing that trust is important to consider in the use of online review systems.

The result of the final hypothesis regarding technology competency did not show significant results. Thus there is no support for the technology competency of a customer impacting the use of online review systems. Thus even though a customer may be technologically competent with using computers and the internet, this is not an important consideration for whether the customer will use online review systems. While this may impact whether or not a customer decides to purchase online, there is no support for it affecting whether or not a customer uses the online review system when purchasing online.

As with many empirical studies, there is an inherent limitation due to the sample. The sample in this research was limited to subjects in one university. As students tend to be heavy users of the Internet for shopping and thus appropriate as subjects in this research, future research should consider expanding demographics to include non-student subjects as well as users in countries beyond the U.S.. A future study may examine these factors in a cross cultural context. In addition, further investigation may be conducted in more detail regarding which features of online review systems can encourage users to use the reviews.

REFERENCES

Baek, H., Ahn, J., and Choi, Y. (2013). Helpfulness of Online Consumer Reviews: Readers' Objectives and Review Cues. *International Journal of Electronic Commerce,* 17(2), 99–126.

Charman-Anderson, S. (November 7, 2012). Amazon Tackles Review Problem, Deletes Wrong Reviews. *Forbes.* http://www.forbes.com/sites/suwcharmananderson/2012/11/07/amazon-tackles-review-problem-deletes-wrong-reviews/#34df25801cdf, accessed February 28, 2015.

Dichter, E. (1966). How Word-of-mouth Advertising Works. *Harvard Business Review,* 44(6), 147–160.

Dimensional Research. (April 2013). Customer Service and Business Results: A Survey of Customer Service from Mid-size Companies. Sunnyvale, CA.

Duan, W., B. Gu, and A. B. Whinston. (2008). Do Online Reviews Matter? An Empirical Investigation of Panel Data. *Decision Support Systems*, 45(4), 1007–1016.
Jensen, M., Averbeck, J., Zhang, Z., and Wright, K. (2013). Credibility of Anonymous Online Product Reviews: A Language Expectancy Perspective, *Journal of Management Information Systems* 30(1), 293–323.
Li, X., and Hitt, L. (2010). Price Effects in Online Product Reviews: An Analytical Model and Empirical Analysis, *MIS Quarterly,* 34(4), 809-831.
Liu, Y. (2006). Word-of-mouth for Movies: Its Dynamics and Impact on Box Office Receipts, *Journal of Marketing.* 70(3), 74–89.
Mo, Zan, Yan-Fei Li, and Peng Fan. (2015). Effect of Online Reviews on Consumer Purchase Behavior, *Journal of Service Science and Management,* 8, 419-424.
Nielsen. (2012). A Nielsen Report: Global Trust in Advertising and Brand Messages, 1-10.
Obiedat, R. (2013). Impact of Online Consumer Reviews on Buying Intention of Consumers in UK: Need for Cognition as Mediating Role, *International Journal of Advanced Corporate Learning* 6(2), 16-21
Ott, M., Y. Choi, C. Cardie, and J. Hancock. (June 19–24, 2011). Finding Deceptive Opinion Spam by Any Stretch of the Imagination. *49th Annual Meeting of the Association for Computational Linguistics*, Portland, OR.
Park, Do-Hyung, Jumin Lee, and Ingoo Han. (Summer 2007). The Effect of On-Line Consumer Reviews on Consumer Purchasing Intention: The Moderating Role of Involvement. *International Journal of Electronic Commerce*, 11(4), 125–148.
Pew Internet, Inc. (2014). Internet Activities. Available at: http://www.pewinternet.org/data-trend/internet-use/internet-use-over-time/ (Retrieved March 2014).
Roberts, J. J. (October 19, 2015). Amazon Sues People who Charge $5 for Fake Reviews. *Forbes*. http://fortune.com/2015/10/19/amazon-fake-reviews/, accessed February 29, 2016.
Shang, R., Chen, Y., & Shen, L. (2005). Extrinsic versus Intrinsic Motivations for Consumers to Shop On-Line. *Information & Management*, 42(3), pp. 401-413.
Stephen, Andrew T., Yakov Bart, Christilene Du Plessis, and Dilney Goncalves. (2012). "Does Paying for Online Product Reviews Pay Off? The Effects of Monetary Incentives on Consumers' Product Evaluations." Faculty & Research Working Paper. Insead.
Sterling, Greg. (Sep 24, 2013). Confidence Crisis: 40 Percent Don't Trust Online Reviews. http://marketingland.com/confidence-crisis-40-percent-dont-trust-online-reviews-59822, accessed November 19, 2015.
Streitfeld, D. January 27, 2012. For $2 a Star, an Online Retailer Gets 5-Star Product Reviews, *The New York Times*.
Streitfeld, D. September 23, 2013, Give Yourself 5 Stars? Online, It Might Cost You. *New York Times*, http://www.nytimes.com/2013/09/23/technology/give-yourself-4-stars-online-it-might-cost-you.html?_r=2&, accessed December 7, 2015.
Wei, C., Chen, Y., Yang, C., and Yang, C. 2010. Understanding what Concerns Consumers: a Semantic Approach to Product Feature Extraction from Consumer Reviews, Information System E-Business Management 8(149), 167.

Appendix 1. Research Questionnaire

Perceived Usefulness of Online Review (PUOR)

Online consumer reviews are a useful tool for online shopping

Online reviews provide useful information

I find that online reviews are valuable for my online purchase decisions

The online consumer review systems are useful

Perceived Ease of Use of Online Review (PEUOR)

Overall, online consumer review systems are easy to use

It is not difficult to figure out how to use online reviews

It is easy to read online reviews about a product

It is very simple for me to use online review systems

Perceived Credibility of Online Review (PCOR)

Online consumer reviews overall are trustworthy

Most of the time, online consumer reviews seem credible to me

Overall, I believe I can trust the online reviews

Online reviews are written by people who honestly state their product views

Perceived Credibility (PC)

I can trust the company from which I purchased the product

I don't have any concern about the credibility of the company I purchased the product from

The company that I purchased the product from has a good reputation

I am satisfied with the level of service I received by the ecommerce company

I am satisfied with the speed by which the ecommerce company shipped out the product

Technology Competency (TC)

I like using a computer

I feel confident with my ability to use computers

I am confident with my ability to find information on the Internet

I am confident in my ability to purchase items online

I enjoy working with computers

Intention to Use Online Reviews (ATT)

I definitely will use online reviews for future purchases

I intend to use online reviews to help guide my purchases

I will use online reviews again

I think that it's worth the effort to read online reviews prior to purchasing

DECISION SCIENCES INSTITUTE

An Innovative Approach to Project Design of Social Entrepreneurship

David Chou
Eastern Michigan University
Email: dchou@emich.edu

ABSTRACT

In order to generate an optimal outcome of implementing social entrepreneurship, this study applied a new approach - design thinking - to build up valuable implementation mechanism for social entrepreneurship projects.

KEYWORDS: Social entrepreneurship, Design thinking, Social enterprise, Innovation

INTRODUCTION

Social entrepreneurship is a newly developed research field. A successful social entrepreneurship would make a positive contribution to the society. A valuable social entrepreneurship could provide constructive thoughts and motives that moves the society onto the right track and arrives at a harmony state. For this reason, it is worthwhile to seek a method of achieving successful social entrepreneurship. Social entrepreneurs usually desire to solve a social problem or need, which is similar to those entrepreneurs who create non-profit and charity organizations. The main difference between traditional business and social entrepreneurship is their motivation of solving social problem and needs.

In order to generate an optimal outcome of social entrepreneurship implementation, this study applies a new approach of building up valuable implementation mechanism for social entrepreneurship projects. This new approach is the design thinking approach. Design thinking is "a methodology that imbues the full spectrum of innovation activities with a human-centered design ethos." (Brown, 2008, p. 1). It is different from traditional way of handling processes in social entrepreneurship, in which social entrepreneurs could decide the way they would do.

This paper starts with literature and issues of social entrepreneurship. It then discusses the implication of design thinking methodology. A new way of building up social entrepreneurship is then proposed. After that, a case study is presented to illustrate the new social entrepreneurship approach. A conclusion is provided at the end of this paper.

LITERATURE REVIEW

Social Entrepreneurship and Its Development

Social entrepreneurship is a young research area. Researchers in the field of social entrepreneurship showed diversified focuses and a unified definition was not found (Pless 2012, p. 317; Short et al. 2009, p. 161; Dacin et al. 2011; Dacin et al., 2010).

The development of social entrepreneurship includes a series of research streams. At early stage, the dominant research was focused on "social entrepreneurs and the personalities, qualities, values and visions of individual change agents" (Pless, 2012, p. 317; Bornstein, 2007).

Another research stream was on the process mechanism. In this research path, social entrepreneurship was based on "a process involving the innovative use and combination of resources to pursue opportunities to catalyze social change and/or address social needs." (Mair and Marti, 2006, p. 37). Short et al. (2009) suggested that social entrepreneurship should focus on the strategic issues, based on the principles such as contingency theory, discovery theory and resource dependency theory.

Mort, et al. (2003) illustrated social entrepreneurship through a multidimensional construct, which included the following components: entrepreneurially virtuous, social opportunity recognition, risk tolerance, proactive-ness, innovativeness, and judgment capacity.

Another scholar, Light (2006), argued that social entrepreneurship should not just be focused on individual entrepreneur's vision and activity (such as starting a new organization to create dramatic social change), but also it needs to recognize "thousands of other individuals, groups, and organizations that are crafting solutions to troubles around the globe." (Light 2006, p. 47). Light (2006) defined a social entrepreneur as '"an individual, group, network, organization, or alliance of organizations that seeks sustainable, large-scale change through pattern-breaking ideas in what or how governments, nonprofits, and businesses do to address significant social problems." (Light 2006, p. 50).

Lately, Dacin et al. (2011, p. 1211) pinpointed the importance of social processes in the pursuit of social entrepreneurship. They also indicated that social entrepreneurship theory should be constructed based on the following disciplines: institutions and social movements, networks, culture, identity and image cognition. A successful social entrepreneurship would contribute positively to the society. A valuable social entrepreneurship could provide constructive thoughts and motives that move the society onto the right track and arrive at a harmony state. Social entrepreneurship should broad social, cultural, and environmental goals, reach a high social satisfaction, and enhance social innovation. Social entrepreneurs would seek to transform societies at large. In order to reach a maximum outcome, social entrepreneurship must utilize information technology such as the Internet for facilitating communication capability. For these reasons, it is worthwhile to seek agreeable methodology of building social entrepreneurship projects.

STAKEHOLDERS OF SOCIAL ENTREPRENEURSHIP

A major stakeholder of social entrepreneurship is social entrepreneur. Social entrepreneurs are those persons who have interests in solving social problems. For this reason, social activists, philanthropists, environmentalists, and other socially oriented practitioners belong to this group. Social entrepreneurs are also called social innovators by Bornstein (2007) since they are creative while solving social problems.

Other stakeholders of social entrepreneurships may include citizens in society, their roles consist of customers, users, clients, and others who are working closely with social entrepreneurs. Governments in different levels, communities, corporations, and non-profit organizations also interact with social entrepreneurs while performing social entrepreneurship projects.

An exemplary non-profit organization that work closely with social entrepreneurs is thesedge.org. The mission of thesedge.org is to "help organizational and individual social innovators connect with each other to access education and community" (thesedge.org, 2016). Thesedge.org serves as agent's role to "bring together the global community of change makers who are embracing a socially entrepreneurial mindset and using social enterprise to advance their social missions." (thesedge.org, 2016). They use collaboration network to educate their members how to access to the resources to build successful social entrepreneurship projects.

DESIGNING SOCIAL ENTREPRENEURSHIP PROJECT

Social design is defined as a design process that contributes to human well-being and livelihood's improvement (Holm, 2006). It is clear to see that social design is a way to move the society into a positive direction with needed changes. The main purpose of social design thinking is to create a better society and improved the life quality of the human-beings in the world. Social entrepreneurs hold the same ideology with the effort on improving the human life through social development activities. For this reason, social entrepreneurs are always called social innovators. The process of transforming societies at large rather than focusing on profit boundary is the project that social entrepreneurs intend to do. Social entrepreneurs utilize a variety of components in the environments of social entrepreneurship to create projects that could bring societies into a better state of comfort, including life quality, community development, environmental quality, social justice and equality, etc.

Three types of business models of social enterprise have been identified by Elkington and Hartigan (2008), they are:

1. The Leveraged Non-Profit: This social enterprise model leverages resources in order to respond to social needs.
2. The Hybrid Non-Profit: This social enterprise model is distinctive because it is willing to use profit to sustain its operations.
3. The Social Business Venture: This type of social enterprise model is taking business form that is designed to create change through social means.

Social entrepreneurship's business models have been implemented in a variety of formats within different industries that intend to meet diverse purposes and the needs in societies. For example, social entrepreneurship projects can be created to solve social problems in environmental, foods distribution, water safety and distribution, textbook allocation, cooking, job creation, etc.

CONCERNS AND DRAWBACKS OF TRADITIONAL SOCIAL ENTREPRENEURSHIP DESIGN

Social entrepreneurship projects can be fulfilled through the following enterprises forms: community-based enterprises, socially responsible enterprises, social services industry professionals, and socio-economic enterprises. Although these projects and created enterprises can contribute to societies with good intention, they benefit only to a specific sector in society. A more comprehensive design process to solve social problems would result in a better project outcome.

It can be inferred that a project design process should involve more participants who have diverse backgrounds, knowledge, and expertise to solve a social problem. Since social entrepreneurship projects involve social change as a needed part of their design process, the new and innovative thinking becomes one of its success factors. Most social problems are people based, therefore, human centric design approach would strengthen the quality of such projects.

A new approach to design social entrepreneurship projects is through the "design thinking" methodology. This paper intends to integrate design thinking methodology into social entrepreneurship project's design process to make the project a better solution.

DESIGN THINKING METHODOLOGY

Brown (2008) is a known practitioner of design thinking methodology. He is the CEO and President of IDEO, an innovation and design firm located in Palo Alto, California. His company promotes and utilizes the idea of design thinking to all corporate projects.

Lockwood (2010) proposed a similar definition to design thinking as "essentially a human-centered innovation process that emphasizes observation, collaboration, fast learning, visualization of ideas, rapid concept prototyping, and concurrent business analysis, which ultimately influences innovation and business strategy." (Lockwood, 2010, p. xi). Design thinking is a methodology that has been used in product design, branding design, service design (IDEO, 2016; Lockwood, 2010) and other areas such as information systems design (Vetterli et al., 2016). Based on these studies, it shown that design thinking methodology can be used to generate new and innovative products and systems.

IDEO (2016) described the design thinking process as a system of overlapping spaces rather than a sequence of steps. Brown (2008) defined the design thinking process through three spaces, they are inspiration, ideation, and implementation. Inspiration is the cause of searching for solutions, such as social problems or possible opportunities appeared to surface. The second space is ideation that is the process of identifying ideas, developing and deepening targeted ideas and then testing them through experimentation or simulation means. The final space is implementation, which puts selected project into the realization stage. Individual projects will loop back through these spaces; particularly the first two spaces, more than once as ideas are refined and new directions will be taken and refilled after debates.

Design thinking methodology is "scalable and can be applied incrementally to improve existing ideas or it can be applied radically to create disruptive solutions that meet the needs of people in entirely new ways" (Brown, 2016). Design thinking methodology can integrate technologies, innovative thinking, design process, and available resources into human's desire to build up a new and innovative product. Design thinking is a deeply human process that taps into abilities we all have but get overlooked by more conventional problem-solving practices. It relies on our ability to be intuitive, to recognize patterns, to construct ideas that are emotionally meaningful as well as functional, and to express ourselves through means beyond words or symbols.

BUILDING SOCIAL ENTREPRENEURSHIP PROJECTS THROUGH DESIGN THINKING

Social entrepreneurship's building structure contains the features of social collaboration, human-centered innovative activities, visualized idea, and social strategy determination. The features of these building structure matches design thinking's development process. This study intends to identify such a new methodology for building social entrepreneurship projects.

Social entrepreneurs seek to create innovative projects and to incorporate transformational changes into under-represented and under-served communities. Based on social entrepreneurs' desire, the project team must fully understands the lives of people who needs such help. It also involves the knowledge of culture and socio-economic conditions. We can compare the attributes between social entrepreneurship and design thinking methodology and then decide the fitness of adopting such an integrated project design approach. Possible attributes are:

1. Human-centered focus:
   Social entrepreneurship deals with social problems, therefore, it is always related to people's lives. As indicated in the earlier section, design thinking is a methodology of human-centered practice.
2. Strategy and goals:
   Social entrepreneurship seeks specific goals to be achieved and its solution should apply to specific strategies. Design thinking also seeks social entrepreneurs' goals with specific design strategy in the process.
3. Innovation approach:
   Social entrepreneurs are always described as social innovators since they pursue innovative idea and venture for social development. Design thinking methodology also applies innovative approach into its design process.
4. Altruism:
   Social entrepreneurs, in their deep mind, are to solve social problem and to improve the life of human-being. Design thinking methodology applies new idea to create new product in society.
5. Collaboration approach and brainstorming:
   Social entrepreneurship involves a variety of stakeholders such as social entrepreneurs, users, citizens, governments, communities, etc. to collaborate together to solve the social problems. Design thinking methodology also needs project team members from diversified backgrounds to collaboratively solve the design concerns.
6. Technology usage:
   Social entrepreneurs use technologies such as the Internet, social networks, and mobile devices to promote and communicate their idea and philosophy with users and the general public in societies. Design thinking methodology also needs computer technologies and tools for carrying out its design process.
7. User involvement:
   Social entrepreneurship's projects success is based on the amount of user adoption in the society. More user involvement means better success of the social entrepreneurship project. Design thinking methodology also seeks users' involvement to design a product that will meet users' desire and need.
8. Prototype usage:
   Social entrepreneurship's project may start with an initial plan or prototype for seeking further project's improvement. Therefore, continued development will enhance the quality of social entrepreneurship's project. Design thinking methodology also emphasizes the process of experimentation and prototyping process in order to identifying the opportunities of improvement.
9. Test:
   In order to seek a better social entrepreneurship plan and project, test or assessment to such plan and project is needed. Design thinking methodology also applies test stage to assess the quality of designed product for approval purpose.
10. Experimentation:

While social entrepreneurs are not sure about their desire for solving social problems, the practice of experimentation is always implemented. Social entrepreneurship's project experimentation allows such project to be accurately identified.

11. Resources need:
    Social entrepreneurship's project consumes a variety of resources such as social capital, funding, human resources, and others. Some social entrepreneurship costs a tremendous amount of resources to make it comes true.

CASE OF BUILDING SOCIAL ENTREPRENEURSHIP PROJECT THROUGH DESIGN THINKING

In 2007, a team of Stanford University used design thinking approach to design a simple and portable device (that is, sleeping bag for newborns) to help 22,000 low-birth-weight babies around the world to stay warm (Soule, 2013). The project of "The Embrace Baby Warmer" adopted an innovative phase-change material to maintain its temperature for six hours after heating for new born babies.

This social entrepreneurship project started by a group of Standard students who had been building a low-cost incubator for their class project. Later on, while this group of students visited Nepal to present their project outcome, they figured out that their project outcome wouldn't help Nepal's residents. During their visitation in Nepal, this group of students observed the need in the community, that is, "low-birth-weight babies often develop fatal hypothermia in homes, many of which lack electricity." (Soule, 2013).

Students then applied "Design Thinking" method to develop an innovative product, The Embrace Baby Warmer, to help needed families in the world (Soule, 2013).

The process of designing such product was complicated. At first, their ambitious goal of helping low-income resident's baby captured everyone's heart and mind in the project team. The team applied rapid prototyping process to create prototypes and then seeking feedback from the users quickly. The new prototypes have been created to respond to the feedback from the users. This approach made a better version of the product.

The prototype finally went through the test stage. The project team brainstormed after receiving the outcomes and feedback from the test. The designed project went through readjustment again to refine the product. This process went on again and again until the test result approved their ultimate goals.

CONCLUSION

A successful social entrepreneurship would make a positive contribution to the society. In order to generate an optimal outcome of implementing social entrepreneurship, this study applied a new approach, that is, design thinking, to build up valuable implementation mechanism for social entrepreneurship projects.

Design thinking is a human-centered innovation process that emphasizes observation, collaboration, fast learning, visualization of ideas, rapid concept prototyping, and concurrent business analysis, which ultimately influences innovation and strategy. Social entrepreneurship project and design thinking methodology are highly related to their attributes and therefore can be proved to be integrated together.

A Stanford University's case study fully exhibited the use of design thinking to implement social entrepreneurship project by creating an innovative product – the Embrace Baby Warmer – to help needed babies in the world. We expect more social entrepreneurs to use design thinking methodology to build their comprehensive, human-centered, and innovative products or projects to improve the life of human-being.

References

Bornstein, D. (2007). *How to Change the World: Social Entrepreneurs and the Power of New Ideas.* New York: Oxford University Press.

Brown, T. (2008). Design thinking. *Harvard Business Review*, June, 1-9.

Dacin, P. A., Dacin, M. T. and Matear, M. (2010). Social entrepreneurship: Why we don't need a new theory and how we move forward from here. *Academy of Management Perspectives*, 24(3), August, 37-57.

Dacin, M. T., Dacin, P. A., and Tracey P. (2011). Social entrepreneurship: A critique and future directions. *Organization Science*, 22(5), 1203-1213.

Elkington J. and Hartigan P. (2008). *The Power of Unreasonable People*. Boston, MA: Harvard Business School Publishing.

IDEO (2016). Our approach: Design thinking. Retrieved from https://www.ideo.com/about/ March 10.

Holm, Ivar (2006). *Ideas and Beliefs in Architecture and Industrial design: How attitudes, orientations, and underlying assumptions shape the built environment.* Arkitektur- og designhøgskolen i. Oslo. (Oslo School of Architecture and Design)

Mort, G.S., Weerawardena, J. and Carnegie, K. (2003). Social entrepreneurship: towards conceptualization. *International Journal of Nonprofit and Voluntary Sector Marketing*, 8(1), 76-88.

Light, P. (2006). Reshaping social entrepreneurship. *Stanford Social Innovation Review*, 4(3), Fall, 47-51.

Lockwood, T. (2010). *Design Thinking*, New York, NY: Allworth Press.

Mair, J., and Marti, I. (2006). Entrepreneurship in and around institutional voids: A case study from Bangladesh. *Journal of World Business*, 41, 36-44.

Pless, N. M. (2012). Social entrepreneurship in theory and practice – An introduction. *Journal of Business Ethics*, 111, 317-320.

Short, J. C., Moss, T. W., & Lumpkin, G. T. (2009). Research in social entrepreneurship: Past contributions and future opportunities. *Strategic Entrepreneurship Journal*, 3, 161-194.

Soule, S. (2013). Sarah Soule: How design thinking can help social entrepreneurs. Retrieved from https://www.gsb.stanford.edu/insights/sarah-soule-how-design-thinking-can-help-social-entrepreneurs.

Thesedge (2016). ehesedge website. Retrieved from http://www.thesedge.org/whats-new/22-awesome-social-enterprise-business-ideas.

Vetterli, C., Uebernickel F., Brenner W., and Petrie C. (2016). How Deutsche Bank's IT division used design thinking to achieve customer proximity. *MIS Quarterly Executive*, 15(1), 37-53.

DECISION SCIENCES INSTITUTE

An Optimization Model for Determining Biorefinery Size and Location

Fengli Zhang[a], Dana M. Johnson[b,1], Mark A. Johnson[c]

[a]*Dept of Mechanical and Transportation Engineering, China University of Petroleum, Beijing, 102249, China*

[b]*School of Business and Economics, Michigan Technological University, Houghton, MI 49931, USA*

[c]*School of Technology, Michigan Technological University, Houghton, MI 49931, USA*

ABSTRACT

Societal pressure and government mandates for reducing GHG emissions along with the need for increased energy security have fostered research to increase biofuel production from renewable biomass. Production efficiency, economic viability, and potential environmental concerns have hindered an increase in biofuel production from renewable biomass. This research developed an optimization model for biofuel facility size and location, biomass harvesting/forwarding, and transportation. The model was applied to the northern portion of the Lower Peninsula of Michigan, USA. The optimization model, selected locations, and results provide one tool to determine the optimal delivered cost, energy consumption, and GHG emissions for candidate locations.

KEYWORDS: Optimization, biofuel facility size and location, delivered feedstock cost, energy consumption, greenhouse gas emissions

INTRODUCTION

Because of high demand for oil in the United States (U.S.) to fuel the transportation industry, an array of societal issues, including climate change, air pollution, dependence on imports, and security concerns have driven the need to evaluate alternatives (Greene & Plotkin, 2011). In 2009, the transportation sector consumed over 27% of total U.S. energy and 72% of the nation's oil (US EIA, 2010). As a result, carbon emissions from transportation fuel consumption were almost one-third of the U.S. total (Greene & Plotkin, 2011; Davis, 2000). Furthermore, the forecast growth in transportation energy consumption is 1.7% per year between 1999 and 2020 (US DOE/EIA, 1999). If this growth rate materializes, U.S. transportation energy and greenhouse gas (GHG) emissions are estimated to increase by 46% above current levels by 2020 (Greene & Plotkin, 2011). U.S. oil production peaked in 1970. The U.S. has become highly dependent on foreign oil more than any other time in history, importing 60% of its supplies in 2006 (Gallagher et al, 2007).

There is increased concern about economic and security vulnerabilities that may result from heavy U.S. dependence on foreign oil (Gallagher et al, 2007). Biofuels production from lignocellulosic biomass such as wood, agriculture residues, and forest residues have the potential to be a partial substitute for, or complement to, gasoline (Kumar et al, 2009). Currently, ethanol from corn is used as a blending agent with gasoline to reduce GHG. Our research focuses on biofuel production from forest-based woody biomass feedstock, including forest residues and low value pulpwood.

This paper is organized as follows. In Section 2, a brief literature review describes prior research related to biofuel supply chains. The mathematical notation and model formulation are described in Section 3. In section 4, a case study of identifying biofuel facility size and locations

[1] Corresponding author. Email: dana@mtu.edu

in Michigan's Lower Peninsula (or the L.P. of Michigan) is presented. The results are discussed in Section 5. Section 6 concludes the paper with discussions on research findings, major contribution, and potential future research.

LITERATURE REVIEW

There is an extensive body of research focused on models and solutions as decision support tools for strategic analysis and tactical planning for biofuel systems. A biofuel system represents a typical biofuel supply chain, including location setup, procurement, production, storage and distribution. The literature review here is based on a variety of articles/reports relevant to this research. Huang et al. (2010) proposed a mathematical model to integrate spatial and temporal dimensions for strategic planning of ethanol supply chain systems. This model incorporates dynamics issues for long-term strategic planning of biofuel systems, which have been rarely considered in past studies (Huang et al, 2010). Eksioglu et al. (2009) developed a mathematical model to design a biomass-to-biorefinery supply chain and manage the logistics of a biorefinery. This model applied an integrated view of biomass harvesting, inventory, transportation processes, and biorefinery location selection. Parker et al. (2007) built an integrated model based on geographic information system (GIS) and mathematical programming to evaluate the economic potential and infrastructure requirements for hydrogen production from agricultural residues. Rentizelas et al. (2009) developed and optimized a multi-biomass supply chain model for tri-generation energy (electricity, heating and cooling) production to maximize the financial yield on investments. Luo et al. (2010) proposed a detailed technical design combined with economic and environmental analysis for a lignocellulosic feedstock (LCF) biorefinery producing ethanol, power, and high-value chemicals (succinic acid and acetic acid).

A new decision support systems tool that integrates cost, energy savings, GHG considerations, scenario analysis and a GIS was developed to provide all-inclusive analysis of alternative systems for optimizing biomass energy production (Chiew et al, 2011). A two-stage mixed integer mathematical model was developed to optimize biomass supply chain networks under uncertainty, such as supply amounts, market demand, market price, and processing technologies (Kim, Realff & Lee, 2011). The logistics of supplying forest biomass to a potential power plant was investigated using a simulation model developed by extending the Integrated Biomass Supply Analysis and Logistics (IBSAL) model (Mobini et al, 2011). The IBSAL model was used to evaluate the delivered feedstock cost, the equilibrium moisture content, and carbon emission from the logistic operations (Mobini et al, 2011). A mixed integer linear programming (MILP) model was created to optimize ethanol supply chain configuration in terms of profitability and financial risk on investment (Dal-Mas et al, 2011). This biofuel supply includes upstream fuel production, such as biomass cultivation, biomass delivery, and fuel production, to downstream, such as biofuel distribution to demand centers (Dal-Mas et al, 2011).

The optimal design and planning of corn grain- and stover-based bioethanol supply chains through first and second generation technologies were addressed (Giarola et al, 2011). A MILP model was designed to optimize environmental (in terms of overall GHG emissions) and financial (Net Present Value, NPV) performance variables simultaneously (Giarola et al, 2011). Another MILP model was created to optimize a biomass-to-ethanol supply chain in terms of NPV in a 9-state the Midwest region of the U.S. (Marvin et al, 2012). Perimenis et al. (2011) proposed a basic framework for a decision support tool to assess biofuel pathways and supply chain from biomass production to biofuel end-use. This tool integrated technical, economic, environmental, and societal dimensions with the primary objective of identifying an alternative solution by applying multi-objective optimization (Perimenis et al, 2011).

Another MILP was developed and implemented to assess potential biofuel supply across the Western region of the U.S. to include agricultural, forest, urban waste, and energy crop biomass

(Parker et al, 2010). This model determined the optimal locations, technology types, and sizes of biorefineries to satisfy a maximum profit objective function applied across the biofuel supply chain (Parker et al, 2010). Each technology type and biofuel demand chain was beyond the scope of this present study. BioFeed, A MIPL model, was developed (Shastri et al, 2010). BioFeed focused on feedstock production and related activities between farms growing energy crops and the biorefinery, such as harvesting, raking, baling, storage, handling, and transportation (Shastri et al, 2010). Kim, Realff, Lee, Whittaker et al. (2011) formulated and implemented a MIPL model to determine: (1) number, location, and size of two types of processing facilities, and (2) the quantities of biomass, intermediate products, and final products to be transported between selected locations over a specific period of time (Kim, Realff, Lee, Whittaker et al, 2011). A combined life cycle analysis (LCA) and supply chain optimization approach were proposed to access the environmental sustainability and economic viability of ethanol production systems (Zamboni et al, 2011). For the combined approach, the multi-objective function included maximizing net present value and minimizing total daily GHG impact (Zamboni et al, 2011).

As a result of the literature review, there was limited work in the area of modeling woody biomass supply chains. Past studies have primarily focused on other forms of biomass. The potential utilization of low value pulpwood, primarily used by paper mills, as biomass feedstock for biofuel production has been minimally explored. Additionally as a precursor to optimization, GIS has been used as a determinant of specific multiple locations. This study fills the gaps of previous research.

MATHEMATICAL MODEL DESIGN

The biofuel supply chain was structured around four components: biofuel facility locations and sizes, biomass harvesting/forwarding, transportation, and storage. The proposed optimization model enables the selection of biomass locations, biorefinery capacity, and logistics of transportation from woody biomass locations to the biorefinery. A linear programming model was formulated and implemented using Microsoft Excel (Johnson et al, 2011). The model represents decisions regarding (1) optimal locations and sizes of the biofuel facilities, (2) quantity of biomass to be delivered from harvesting areas to biofuel facilities over a selected period, and (3) minimize one of the three objective functions of the delivered feedstock cost, energy consumption, and GHG emissions.

Indices

- I Set of harvesting sites, indexed by i
- J Set of potential locations for biorefineries, indexed by j

Model Parameters

- s Unit stumpage price ($/ton) of biomass
- h Unit harvesting cost ($/ton) of biomass
- t_d Truck variable mileage cost ($/ton-mile)
- t_{lu} Truck fixed cost ($/ton), includes one loading and unloading routine
- d_{ij} Distance (miles) between harvesting site i and biorefinery j
- Q_i Amount of biomass available at harvesting area i
- γ Conversion rate (gallons/green ton) of biomass to ethanol

- w_h GHG emissions (lbs/green ton biomass) for harvesting/forwarding feedstock
- f_h Energy consumption (Btu/green ton biomass) for harvesting/forwarding feedstock
- w_{tr} GHG emissions (lbs/ton-mile) for truck transportation
- f_{tr} Energy consumption (Btu/ton-mile) for truck transportation
- CAP_j Capacity (gallons of ethanol per year) of biorefinery j

Decision Variables

- q_{ij} Amount (tons) of biomass transported from harvesting site i to biorefinery j

Objective Functions

The three objective functions were to: (1) minimize annual supply chain system cost of: stumpage, harvesting, and transportation (C_{tot}), (2) minimize energy consumption across the supply chain, (F_{tot}), and (3) minimize GHG emissions (W_{tot}) across the supply chain. The mathematical model is based on one year operation for a single biorefinery.

$$C_{tot} = \sum_{j=1}^{J}\sum_{i=1}^{I}(s + h + t_{lu} + t_d \times d_{ij}) \cdot q_{ij} \quad (1)$$

$$F_{tot} = \sum_{j=1}^{J}\sum_{i=1}^{I}(f_h + f_{tr} \times d_{ij}) \times q_{ij} \quad (2)$$

$$W_{tot} = \sum_{j=1}^{J}\sum_{i=1}^{I}(w_h + w_{tr} \times d_{ij}) \times q_{ij} \quad (3)$$

Constraints/Limitations

- The total amount of biomass delivered from a harvesting site i to all the biorefineries j cannot exceed the amount of biomass available for biofuel production at harvesting site i

$$\sum_{j=1}^{J} q_{ij} \le Q_i,\ i \in I \quad (4)$$

- Total amount of biomass delivered from all the harvesting sites to a biorefinery j meets the demand for biomass feedstock at the biorefinery j

$$\sum_{i}^{I} q_{ij} \ge \frac{CAP_j}{\gamma},\ j \in J \quad (5)$$

- Amount (tons) of biomass transported from harvesting area i to biorefinery j is nonnegative

$$q_{ij} \ge 0,\ i \in I\ j \in J \quad (6)$$

CASE STUDIES

The utility of the supply chain optimization model may be demonstrated by considering the location of a biofuel facility in the L.P. of Michigan. Nine potential biofuel facility sites in the L.P.

were preselected by employing the first stage of the GIS-based method (Zhang et al, 2010) combined with additional criteria. This analysis was based on the following criteria:

- Location within one mile of a major state road (Zhang et al, 2010),
- Location within one mile of railway (Zhang et al, 2010),
- Location within a community size of at least 1,000 (Zhang et al, 2010),
- Location within ¼ mile of a water body (rivers, lakes, etc.) (Johnson et al, 2011),
- The minimum residues within a 100 mile (161 km) radius of any select community have to be at least 0.7 million dry tons / 1.4 million green tons (a rough estimate of the ratio between green tons and dry tons is 2:1 (Minnesota Department of Natural Resources, 2008)) to support a facility producing 50 million gallons of fuel each year (Johnson et al, 2011), and
- Location does not have a co-fired power plant nearby. No co-location with any other competitors for biomass feedstock is considered (Johnson et al, 2011).

The nine potential locations preselected for a biofuel facility in the L.P., as well as the distance (miles) to a closest co-fired power plant are shown in Table 1. The geographical distribution of the nine potential biofuel facility locations is illustrated in the map in Figure 1. Only harvesting areas within a 100-mile (161 km) radius of a facility location were considered, because the cost of transportation per ton grows as distance increases.

Table 1: Potential site for biorefinery in the L.P. (Johnson et al, 2011)

City / Village	Distance to Closest Biomass-Cofired Power Plant (miles)
Manton city	11.19
Roscommon village	12.81
Kingsley village	23.86
Kalkaska village	23.94
Gaylord city	25.49
Clare city	33.97
West Branch city	35.29
Traverse City city	36.03
Boyne City city	41.24

Figure 1: Biomass feedstock demand locations in the L.P. (Johnson et al, 2011)

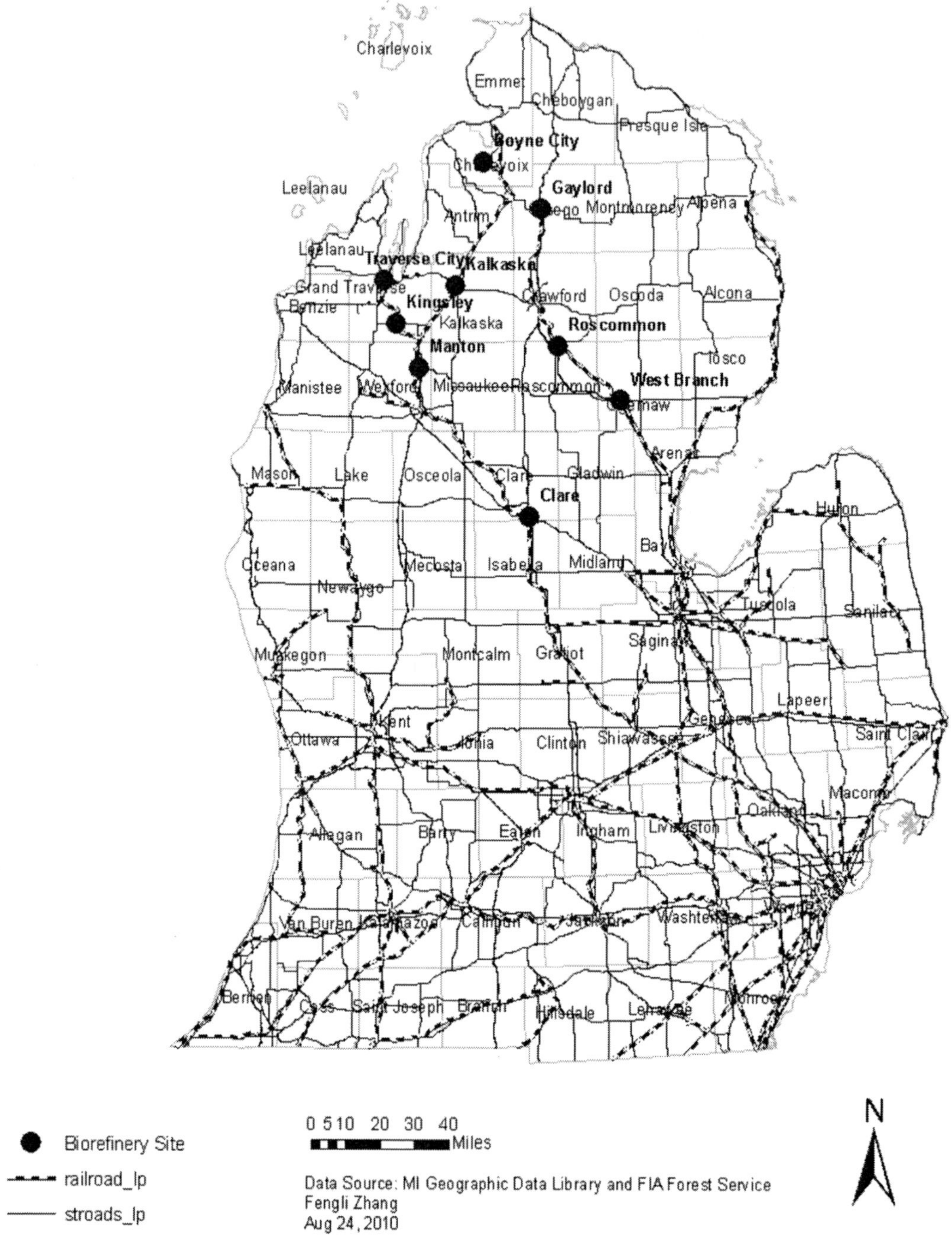

Model Assumptions

In the application of the optimization model, several assumptions were made. These include:
(1) Harvesting

- Harvesting areas are defined on a county-basis. The biomass was assumed to be uniformly distributed across a county (Zhang, Johnson et al, 2011). The centroid of each county was the starting point of transportation;
- No feedstock was transported over the Mackinac Bridge (hereafter referred to as the Bridge) from the Upper Peninsula of Michigan (hereafter referred to as the U.P.). It is assumed that all feedstock in the U.P. was not available for transport over the Bridge and was consumed by others in the U.P.;

(2) Biofuel facility

- For a biofuel facility that produces 30 million gallons per year (MGY), biomass feedstock required was 750,000 green tons with a conversion factor of 40 gallons of biofuel per green ton of biomass;
- For a biofuel facility that produces 40 million gallons per year (MGY), biomass feedstock required was 1,000,000 green tons with a conversion factor of 40 gallons of biofuel per green ton of biomass;
- For a biofuel facility that produces 50 million gallons per year (MGY), biomass feedstock required was 1,250,000 green tons with a conversion factor of 40 gallons of biofuel per green ton of biomass;

(3) Transportation

- The transportation radius was assumed to be less than 100 miles;
- Biomass feedstock was delivered by diesel truck. This is important in order to estimate energy consumption and GHG emissions associated with biomass transportation;
- No rail transportation was considered;
- The truck transportation operator provides loading and unloading. No additional/independent loaders/unloaders were necessary;

(4) Others

- The moisture content was assumed to be constant throughout the supply chain (50%); therefore, biomass weight delivered from harvesting areas to the biofuel facility remains the same;
- No dry matter loss is taken into account through the supply chain, for example, weight loss during storage due to decomposition.

Model Input

An easy-to-use input screen has been developed for the model. The input screen allows users to enter data into one or more of the model parameters before running the model. As mentioned in previous sections, the biofuel supply chain will be evaluated using three system performance indicators: the delivered feedstock cost, energy consumption and GHG emissions. Therefore information for cost, energy, and emissions are defined as the first category of model input. The delivered cost is broken down into three components: stumpage price, harvesting cost, and transportation cost. The transportation cost consists of two parts: fixed cost ($/ton, including loading and unloading cost) and distance-dependent variable cost ($/ton-mile). Information for energy and emissions are only related to harvesting and transport activities. The detailed first category data collection is illustrated in Table 2.

Table 2: First category of model input			
First category of model input	Stumpage	Harvesting	Transport
Cost	9.40 $/ton (Prentiss & Carlisle Management Company, 2008)	14 $/ton (Prentiss & Carlisle Management Company, 2008)	Fixed: 3.72 $/ton (Johnson et al, 2011) Variable: 0.074 $/ton-mile (Johnson et al, 2011)
Energy	N/A	137,433 Btu/ton (Zhang, Handler et al, 2011)	1,592 Btu/ton-mile (Zhang, Handler et al, 2011)
Emissions	N/A	25.6 lb GHG/ton (Zhang, Handler et al, 2011)	0.377 lb GHG/ton-mile (Zhang, Handler et al, 2011)

The second category of model input is defined as biomass feedstock availability, including feedstock availability factors, percentages of residue and roundwood, and adjustments for Frontier Renewable Resources (FRR) as well as other adjustments (i.e., biomass fired power plant in Mancelona). The forest biomass data were derived from the Forest Service Inventory EVALIDator web application version 4.01 (Miles, 2011). Net growth after removals was calculated. In other words, the net growth accumulating in the forest on an annual basis, after accounting for losses to mortality, existing rates of timber harvest, reversion (land becoming forest) and conversion (land becoming nonforest). This is a straightforward query using the EVALIDATOR interface. The forest biomass data were further characterized by ownership type, softwood and hardwood, and availability factors (Johnson et al, 2011). In addition, the input screen also allow users to select any location from the nine potential biofuel facility sites, and then select a plant size of 30 MGY, 40 MGY, or 50 MGY.

Excel based Model Design

Microsoft Excel™ using Excel Solver was the software employed to develop and solve the optimization models. Solver has size limitations regarding the numbers of changing cells and decisions (Johnson et al, 2011). Solver applies the simplex method to rapidly solve larger scale problems. This problem was characterized as a minimization problem because it minimized cost, energy, or emissions. Sensitivity and "what-if" scenario analysis can be easily conducted with this model (Johnson et al, 2011).

RESULTS AND DISCUSSION

The results for each of the nine candidate locations are summarized in this section. Each of the different variables, transportation cost, energy, and emissions are summarized and include individual as well as combined rankings.

Transportation Cost

The transportation cost per green ton delivered by each candidate location by size is shown in Table 3.

Table 3 Transportation Cost Per Green Ton Delivered by Candidate Location by Size									
Facility Size (MGY)	Transportation Cost ($/green ton)								
	Manton	Roscommon	Kingsley	Kalkaska	Gaylord	Clare	West Branch	Traverse City	Boyne City
30	$ 30.35	$ 31.10	$ 30.50	$ 30.44	$ 29.79	$ 31.16	$ 30.91	$ 30.98	$ 31.31
40	$ 30.86	$ 31.47	$ 31.14	$ 31.21	$ 30.51	$ 31.70	$ 31.37	$ 31.74	$ 32.53
50	$ 31.33	$ 31.72	$ 31.68	$ 31.78	$ 31.09	$ 32.25	$ 31.90	$ 32.38	$ 33.77

In reviewing the transportation costs, as the plant size grows, the cost per ton increases. This is because a larger scale biorefinery requires a larger supply of biomass. This results in a longer distance hauling of the feedstock to the biorefinery. Cost per ton by plant size was ranked from lowest to highest cost, with the lowest cost receiving a ranking of "1" and the highest cost receiving a ranking of "9" (Johnson et al, 2011). The rankings are shown in Table 4. The rankings were summed and an overall cost ranking was developed. The best location with the minimum delivered feedstock cost overall is Gaylord. The worst location (in terms of highest delivered cost per ton) is Boyne City. This in part can be attributed to the fact that feedstock is assumed to not be transported over the Bridge, even though counties in the U.P. are within the 100 mile radius of this location. This limitation likely added to the increased costs (Johnson et al, 2011).

Table 4 Ranking by Transportation Cost Per Green Ton Delivered by Candidate Location by Size and Overall Ranking									
Facility Size (MGY)	Rank by Lowest to Highest - Transportation Cost Per Green Ton								
	Manton	Roscommon	Kingsley	Kalkaska	Gaylord	Clare	West Branch	Traverse City	Boyne City
30	2	7	4	3	1	8	5	6	9
40	2	6	3	4	1	7	5	8	9
50	2	4	3	5	1	7	6	8	9
SUM	6	17	10	12	3	22	16	22	27
Overall Rank	2	6	3	4	1	7	5	8	9

Energy Consumption

The energy consumption per green ton of biomass feedstock delivered (1000 Btu) by each candidate location by size is shown in Table 5. This system performance indicator helps to identify energy efficiency of forest biofuel production.

Table 5 Energy Per Green Ton Harvested/Processed and Delivered (1000 Btu) by Candidate Location by Size									
Facility Size (MGY)	Energy Per Green Ton Harvested/Processed and Delivered (1000 Btu)								
	Manton	Roscommon	Kingsley	Kalkaska	Gaylord	Clare	West Branch	Traverse City	Boyne City
30	206.95	223.02	210.07	208.90	194.97	224.40	218.91	220.50	226.69
40	217.91	231.05	223.97	225.49	210.30	235.98	228.87	236.92	236.90
50	227.97	236.33	235.64	237.74	222.94	247.84	240.27	250.73	250.88

In reviewing the energy consumption data, as the plant size grows, the energy consumed per ton increases. This is because a larger biorefinery requires more feedstock drawn from a large area. This results in longer transport distances. Energy per ton by plant size was ranked from lowest to highest energy consumption, with the lowest energy consumption receiving a ranking of "1" and the highest energy consumption receiving a ranking of "9" (Johnson et al, 2011). The rankings are shown in Table 6. The rankings were summed and an overall energy ranking was developed. The best location overall is Gaylord. The worst location (in terms of highest energy consumption per ton) is Boyne City. This in part can be attributed to the fact that feedstock will not be transported over the Bridge, even though counties in the U.P. are within the 100 mile radius of this location. This limitation likely added to the increased energy consumption due to longer transport distances. Traverse City is a close 8 and likely experiences the same issues as Boyne City, with an additional factor of being positioned close to water. If marine transportation is considered at some point in time to transport biomass from the U.P. to the L.P., this alternatives ranking would like be more favorable (Johnson et al, 2011).

Table 6 Ranking Energy Per Green Ton Harvested/Processed and Delivered (1000 Btu) by Candidate Location by Size and Overall Ranking

Rank Lowest to Highest - Energy Per Green Ton Harvested/Processed and Delivered (1000 Btu)									
Facility Size (MGY)	Manton	Roscommon	Kingsley	Kalkaska	Gaylord	Clare	West Branch	Traverse City	Boyne City
30	2	7	4	3	1	8	5	6	9
40	2	6	3	4	1	7	5	9	8
50	2	4	3	5	1	7	6	8	9
SUM	6	17	10	12	3	22	16	23	26
Overall Rank	2	6	3	4	1	7	5	8	9

GHG Emissions

The GHG emissions per green ton of forest biomass feedstock delivered (in pounds) by each candidate location by size is shown in Table 7. This system performance indicator helps to determine the environmental impact of forest biofuel production.

Table 7 Emissions Per Green Ton Harvested/Processed and Delivered in Pounds by Candidate Location by Size

Facility Size (MGY)	Emissions Per Green Ton Harvested/Processed and Delivered in Pounds								
	Manton	Roscommon	Kingsley	Kalkaska	Gaylord	Clare	West Branch	Traverse City	Boyne City
30	42.06	45.86	42.80	42.52	39.22	46.19	44.89	45.26	46.73
40	44.65	47.76	46.09	46.45	42.85	48.93	47.25	49.15	49.15
50	47.04	49.01	48.85	49.35	45.84	51.74	49.95	52.42	52.46

In reviewing the emissions data, as the plant size grows, the emissions generated per ton increases. This is because a larger scale biorefinery requires more feedstock transported over longer distances. Emissions per ton by plant size was ranked from lowest to highest emissions, with the lowest emissions receiving a ranking of "1" and the highest emissions receiving a ranking of "9" (Johnson et al, 2011). The rankings are shown in Table 8. The rankings were summed and an overall emissions ranking was developed. The best location overall is Gaylord. The worst location (in terms of highest GHG emissions per ton) is Boyne City. This in part can be attributed to the fact that feedstock will be transported over the Bridge, even though counties in the U.P. are within the 100 mile radius of this location. This limitation likely added to the increased GHG emissions due to longer distance traveled. Traverse City is a close 8 and likely experiences the same issues as Boyne City, with an additional factor of being positioned close to water. If marine transportation is considered at some point in time to transport biomass from the U.P. to the L.P., this alternatives ranking would like be more favorable (Johnson et al, 2011).

Table 8 Ranking Emissions Per Green Ton Harvested/Processed and Delivered in Pounds by Candidate Location by Size and Overall Ranking

Rank Lowest to Highest - Emissions Per Green Ton Harvested/Processed and Delivered in Pounds

Facility Size (MGY)	Manton	Roscommon	Kingsley	Kalkaska	Gaylord	Clare	West Branch	Traverse City	Boyne City
30	2	7	4	3	1	8	5	6	9
40	2	6	3	4	1	7	5	9	8
50	2	4	3	5	1	7	6	8	9
SUM	6	17	10	12	3	22	16	23	26
Overall Rank	2	6	3	4	1	7	5	8	9

Comparative Table - Overall Rank

Because the overall rankings for each of the locations came up to be the same, there is no real need at this point to change the weighting factors for each of the three variables. However, this option is available. In this case, weights of 70%, 15% and 15% were used for cost, energy, and emissions respectively. Table 9 shows the comparative analysis. The best location choice is Gaylord with the least desirable location identified as Boyne City.

Table 9 Comparative Overall Ranking

		Manton	Roscommon	Kingsley	Kalkaska	Gaylord	Clare	West Branch	Traverse City	Boyne City
Overall Rank - Cost		2	6	3	4	1	7	5	8	9
Overall Rank-Energy		2	6	3	4	1	7	5	8	9
Overall Rank-Emissions		2	6	3	4	1	7	5	8	9
Total Average		2.0	6.0	3.0	4.0	1.0	7.0	5.0	8.0	9.0
Total Ranking		2	6	3	4	1	7	5	8	9
Cost Weight	70%									
Energy Weight	15%									
Emission Weight	15%									
Total Weighted		0.6	1.8	0.9	1.2	0.3	2.1	1.5	2.4	2.7
Total Weighted Ranking		2	6	3	4	1	7	5	8	9

Maps Showing Feedstock Requirements for 50 MGY Facility

As indicated in earlier discussion of results, individual plants indicate there is sufficient feedstock to supply candidate biorefineries within a 100-mile radius. In this case the Gaylord facility is taken as an example. The seven counties (including county name, supply amount in tons and rectilinear distance to the Gaylord facility in miles) to supply the Gaylord candidate location sufficient feedstock for a 50 MGY facility are listed in Table 10. The geographical distribution of the suppliers is shown in Figure 2. In most cases it would appear that the feedstock is readily available in somewhere between 50-75 mile radiuses of a candidate facility.

Table 10: Seven supply counties to support a 50 MGY facility at Gaylord

Supply County	Supply Amount (tons)	Rectilinear Distance (miles)
Antrim	136,929	24.75
Charlevoix	97,725	40.75
Cheboygan	232,776	37.36
Crawford	126,308	27.20
Kalkaska	164,451	43.74
Montmorency	207,182	27.61
Otsego	284,629	4.02
Total	1,250,000	N/A

Figure 2: The geographical distribution of the suppliers

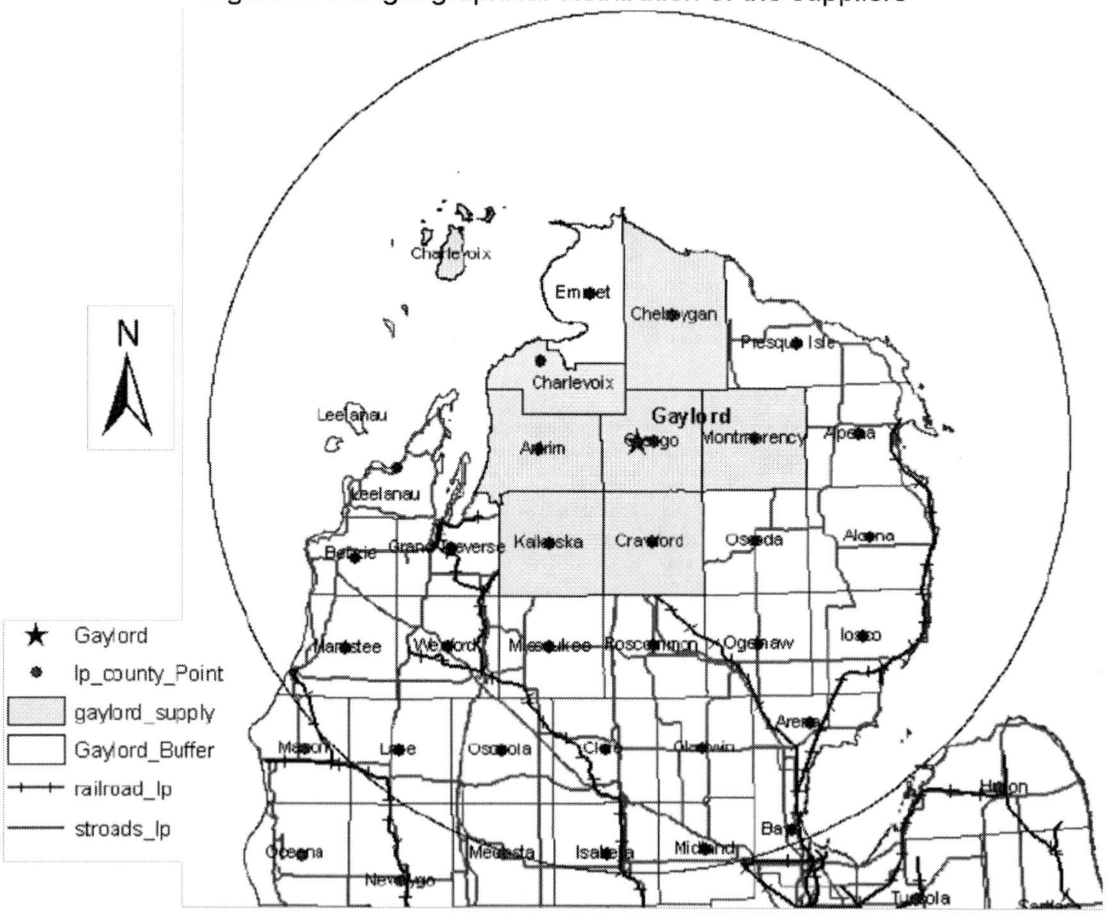

SUMMARY AND CONCLUSIONS

Government pressure and mandates for reducing GHG emissions along with the need for increased energy security have fostered research to increase biofuel production from renewable biomass. Economic viability, production efficiency, and potential environmental/sustainability concerns are common problems associated with the hindrance to increase utilization of renewable woody biomass for biofuel production. In this paper an optimization model is presented for the biomass feedstock supply chain system for biofuel production, with activities including biomass feedstock harvesting/processing, transportation, and storage. The objectives are to minimize the delivered feedstock cost, energy consumption and GHG emissions. The optimization model was applied to the L.P., Michigan. The optimization model, selected locations, and results of study provide one tool for a decision maker to determine the optimal cost, energy consumption, and emissions for candidate locations. The model developed from this case study can be extended nationwide and to other countries and regions for two main reasons. First, the model input is in standard format. For example, the county-based biomass availability can be derived from the US Forest Service Inventory EVALIDator web application (Miles, 2011). Second, the model is available to the general public via the Department of Energy website in the future, as well as a user guide and a tutorial.

Because the optimization model is a static look for a single period of time, it should be utilized in conjunction with a simulation model. Future work will focus on the development of a simulation model that will extend the analysis to consider multiple years of operations. A more complicated optimization model will also be developed using the Mathematical Programming Language. The complicated optimization model will consider multiple location configurations across multiple time periods combing with inventory management. More extensive sensitivity analysis will also be conducted by varying the model inputs, allowing for many different variants on the variables that were presented in this paper. The possibility of applying the model (subject to minor revisions) to other states in the United States and other countries and regions may be investigated.

ACKNOWLEDGEMENTS

This research was supported by National Natural Science Foundation of China (No. 71502173). The Project-sponsored by SRF for ROCS, SEM. This research was also supported by Science Foundation of China University of Petroleum, Beijing (No. 2462014YJRC040).

REFERENCES

Chiew, Y. L., Iwata, T., & Shimada, S. (2011). System analysis for effective use of palm oil waste as energy resources. *Biomass Bioenerg,* 35(7), 2925-2935.

Dal-Mas, M., Giarola, S., Zamboni, A., & Bezzo, F. (2011). Strategic design and investment capacity planning of the ethanol supply chain under price uncertainty. *Biomass Bioenerg,* 35(5), 2059-2071.

Davis, S. C. (2000). Transportation Energy Data Book, 20th Edition. ORNL-6959, Oak Ridge National Laboratory, Oak Ridge, Tennessee.

Eksioglu, S. D., Acharya, A., Leightley, L. E., & Arora, S. (2009). Analyzing the design and management of biomass-to-biorefinery supply chain. *Comput Ind Eng,* 57, 1342-1352.

Gallagher, K. S., Collantes, G., Holdren, J. P., Lee, H., & Frosch, R. (2007). Policy Options for Reducing Oil Consumption and Greenhouse-Gas Emissions from the U.S. Transportation Sector. Available at: http://environment.harvard.edu/docs/faculty_pubs/lee_policy.pdf.

Giarola, S., Zamboni, A., & Bezzo, F. (2011). Spatially explicit multi-objective optimization for design and planning of hybrid first and second generation biorefineries. *Comput Chem Eng,* 35(9), 1782-1797.

Greene, D. L. & Plotkin, S. E. (2011). Energy futures for the US transport sector. *Energ Policy,* 29, 1255-1270.

Huang, Y., Chen, C.-W., & Fan, Y. (2010). Multistage optimization of the supply chains of biofuels. *Transportation Research Part E: Logistics and Transportation Review*, 46(6), 820-830.

Johnson, D. M., Zhang, F., & Johnson, M. A. (2011). Forestry Biofuel Statewide Collaboration Center (FBSCC) Task B4 Final Report. Michigan Technological University.

Kim, J., Realff, M. J., & Lee, J. H. (2011). Optimal design and global sensitivity analysis of biomass supply chain networks for biofuels under uncertainty. *Comput Chem Eng,* 35(9), 1738-1751.

Kim, J., Realff, M. J., Lee, J. H., Whittaker, C., & Furtner, L. (2011). Design of biomass processing network for biofuel production using an MIPL model. *Biomass Bioenerg,* 35, 853-871.

Kumar, P., Barrett, D. M., Delwiche, M. J., & Stroeve, P. (2009). Methods for Pretreatment of Lignocellulosic Biomass for Efficient Hydrolysis and Biofuel Production. *Ind. Eng. Chem. Res.,* 48, 3713-3729.

Luo, L., Van der Voet, E., & Huppes, G. (2010). Biorefining of lignocellulosic feedstock - Technical, economic and environmental considerations. *Bioresource Technol,* 101(13), 5023-5032.

Marvin, A. W., Schmidt, L. D., Benjaafar, S., Tiffany, D. G., Daoutidis, P. (2012). Economic optimization of a lignocellulosic biomass-to-ethanol supply chain in the Midwest. *Chem Eng Sci,* 67(1), 68-79.

Miles, P. D. (2011). Forest Inventory EVALIDator web-application version 4.01. St.Paul, MN: U.S. Department of Agriculture, Forest Service, Northern Research Station. EVALID=260903; downloaded 03 March 2015, Available at: http://fiatools.fs.fed.us/Evalidator401/tmattribute.jsp.

Minnesota Department of Natural Resources, Division of Forestry, Forest Products Utilization & Marketing Program (October 2008). Minnesota Woody Biomass Facility Survey. Available at: http://files.dnr.state.mn.us/forestry/biomass/minnesotawoodybiomassutilization_report.pdf.

Mobini, M., Sowlati, T., & Sokhansanj, S. (2011). Forest biomass supply logistics for a power plant using the discrete-event simulation approach. *Appl Energ*, 88(4), 1241-1250.

Parker, N., Fan, Y., & Ogden, J. (2007). From waste to hydrogen: An optimal design of energy production and distribution network. *Transportation Research Part E: Logistics and Transportation Review,* 46, 534-545.

Parker, N., Tittmann, P., Hart, Q., Nelson, R., Skog, K., Schmidt, A., Gray, E., & Jenkins, B. (2010). Development of a biorefinery optimized biofuel supply curve for the Western United States. *Biomass Bioenerg,* 34(11), 1597-1607.

Perimenis, A., Walimwipi, H., Zinoviev, S., Müller-Langer, F., & Miertus, S. (2011). Development of a decision support tool for the assessment of biofuels. *Energ Policy*, 39(3), 1782-1793.

Prentiss & Carlisle Management Company (2008). Michigan Timber Market Analysis, Prepared for Michigan Department of Natural Resources. Available at: http://michigansaf.org/forestinfo/Market-2008.pdf.

Rentizelas, A. A., Tatsiopoulos, I. P., & Tolis, A. (2009). An optimization model for multi-biomass tri-generation energy supply. *Biomass Bioenerg,* 33, 223-233.

Shastri, Y., Hansen, A., Rodríguez, L., &Ting, K. C. (2010). Development and application of BioFeed model for optimization of herbaceous biomass feedstock production. *Biomass Bioenerg,* 35(7), 2961-2974.

US Department of Energy, Energy Information Administration (US DOE/EIA) (1999). Annual Energy Outlook 1999, DOE/EIA-0383, Washington, DC.

U.S. Energy Information Administration (US EIA) (2010). Annual Energy Review 2009. Available at www.eia.gov/aer.

Zamboni, A., Murphy, R. J., Woods, J., Bezzo, F., & Shah, N. (2011). Biofuels carbon footprints: whole-system optimization for GHG emissions reduction. *Bioresource Technol,* 102(16), 7457-7465.

Zhang, F., Handler, R., Johnson, D. M., & Shonnard, D. R. (2011). Comparative Analysis of Life Cycle Greenhouse Gas Emissions of Supply Chains for Biofuel and Fossil Fuel Production. 22nd Annual POMS Conference, Reno, Nevada.

Zhang, F., Johnson, D. M., & Sutherland, J. W. (2010). GIS-based Approach of Identification of the Optimal Pulpwood-to-Biofuel Facility Location in Michigan's Upper Peninsula. POMS 21st Annual Conference, Vancouver Canada.

Zhang, F., Johnson, D. M., & Sutherland, J. W. (2011). A GIS-Based Method for Identifying the Optimal Location for a Facility to Convert Forest Biomass to Biofuel. *Biomass Bioenerg,* 35, 3951-3961.

DECISION SCIENCES INSTITUTE

Analyzing the Efficiencies of Renewable Energy Sources with Data Envelopment Analysis

Umit Saglam
East Tennessee State University
Email: saglam@etsu.edu

ABSTRACT

In this paper, we compare the efficiencies of the eight major renewable energy sources that generate electricity. We use Data Envelopment Analysis (DEA) to determine the most efficient renewable energy source. We apply four different analytical approaches to rank these energy sources with respect to their efficiency scores. According to our DEA analysis, biomass and geothermal are the most efficient and solar technologies (photovoltaics technologies and solar thermal) are the least efficient renewable energy sources. We also find out land requirement is very important input to determine the efficiency scores of these technologies.

KEYWORDS: Data Envelopment Analysis (DEA), Multi-Criteria Decision Making, Renewable Energy, Efficiency

INTRODUCTION

During the Industrial Revolution, there were fundamental changes occurred in agriculture, textile, metal manufacture, and transportation besides economic and social structure of Europe. The invention of the steam engine increased the labor efficiency, and it provided an opportunity for the mass production that has important socio-economic effects: Urbanization (Vries, 1984), child labor (Nardinelli, 1990), economic growth (Jones, 2001).

During the last two decades, we have been realized that industrial revolution has also significant effects on the environmental issues that we are highly concerned (Clapp, 2014). According to Houghton (2005), human activities like large-scale deforestation and burning of fossil fuels (coal, oil, and gas) starting with the industrial revolution, are the most important causes of global warming which is the average temperature increase of Earth's surface, air and oceans. Global warming was first recognized by Fourier (1827), and Arrhenius (1896) developed the earliest model for the relationship between carbon dioxide concentration and the temperature of the ground. However, its perceived effects on human beings become more detectable and measurable last fifty years.

According to the IPCC the Fourth Assessment Report of the Intergovernmental Panel on Climate Change, the average global surface temperature is increased 0.74±0.18^{0}C (1.33±0.32^{0}F) because of irrepressible increase of the concentration of greenhouse gases such as carbon dioxide, methane, nitrous oxide, and chlorofluorocarbons. According to this report, if we will be successful to keep the level of the concentration of the greenhouses gases constant, the global average surface warming would be about 0.2^{0}C for a decade which may lead very serious problems on ecosystems all over the world. According to the scenario projections in this report, when the warming exceeds 2^{0}C increase, approximately 25% of the plant and animal species will be in danger of extinction. In addition, crop productivity will be decreased, and it leads to having food scarcity in many regions of the world. Millions of people will have health problems because of increase in malnutrition. In addition deaths, diseases and injuries will increase due to severe weather conditions. Climate change leads to rising on sea level significantly, which leads small islands in Asia, Africa and Caribbean will become vulnerable to storms surge, inundation, and erosion. This will also cause of some island will be vanished. According to this report, by 2020, climate change will cause of between 75 and 250 millions of people will have a fresh water problem in Africa. Shortly, climate change would cause many severe problems if the global warming is not restrained. Therefore global warming and climate change becomes the most important environmental and political issue between the countries. A total of 192 countries have signed and ratified the Kyoto Protocol which delimits the production of greenhouses gas (GHG) emissions to fight global warming and climate change.

According to the United States Environmental Protections Agency (EPA) data, there are five main sources of GHG emissions in the United States: electricity production 31%, transportation 27%, industry 21%, commercial and residential 12%, and agriculture 9%. These values are consistent with the worldwide data of IPCC, where the electricity production has the highest contribution to the total of GHG emissions. The U.S. Energy Information Administration data shows that in 2015, 67% of electricity was generated by burning of fossil fuels (coal 33%, natural gas 33%, and petroleum 1%) which are the primary sources of GHG emissions for the electricity production, and only 13% of electricity is generated by renewable energy sources, which produce negligible amount of GHG emissions, in the United States.

Renewable energy is a kind of energy which is produced and replenished by natural resources such as sunlight, wind, tides, and rain. There are five primary sources of renewable energy: wind power, solar, geothermal, biomass, and hydropower. Approximately, twenty percent of the total energy consumption is produced by these renewable energy sources which have positive effect on global warming with reduction of GHG emissions. According to Owen (2004), the annual growth rate of the market share of the renewable energy is about two percent, during the last two decades. According to Prindle et al. (2007), the synergies between energy efficiency and renewable energy sources are the twin pillars of sustainable energy policy that reduce GHG emissions which show us the importance of these technologies. However, each renewable energy source has significant advantages and disadvantages. Therefore how we are going to decide, which renewable energy source is the most efficient one? In this study, we model a linear programming model to compare the efficiencies of these eight major renewable energy sources that generate electricity. We evaluate the efficiency scores of each renewable energy source with Data Envelopment Analysis (DEA), which is multi-criteria decision-making tool, to determine the most efficient renewable energy source.

The remainder of this paper is organized as follows: Section 2, provides detailed literature review for DEA-related articles for the energy sectors. The third section of this paper provides an overview of the DEA framework with the four different ranking approaches that we use in this paper. Section 4, describes the model in detail with input and output variables. We also present each one of the renewable energy sources in detail in this section. Section 5, reports the results of each approaches that we consider in DEA framework; while concluding remarks and research agenda are discussed in Section 6.

LITERATURE REVIEW

Data Envelopment Analysis (DEA), which was developed by Charnes et al. (1978), is a very popular management tool for evaluating and improving the efficiency of both manufacturing and service operations. The DEA has been studied by a large number of researchers for more than four decades. According to Emrouznejad et al. (2008), there is an exponential growth in DEA –

related articles that published over the past two decades. Moreover each year more than 300 DEA – related articles are published in various journals with various applications such as education (Bessent and Bessent, 1980), bank (Favero and Papi, 1995), transport (Gillen and Lall, 1997), health (Grosskopf Valdmanis, 1987), and environment (Kao et al. 1993).
In the literature, there are more than thirty DEA – related articles for the energy sectors. Bagdadioglu et al. (1996) applied DEA to discover the relationship between privatization and ownership on the efficiency of Turkish electricity supply industry. Sueyoshi and Goto (2001) studied the performance of the electric power in Japan. Many researchers applied DEA to find out the efficiency of electricity distribution of various countries. For example, Miliotis (1992) looked at Greece electricity distribution districts, Forsund and Kittelsen (1998) compared electricity distribution companies in Norway, with using DEA efficiency scores. Chen (2002) studied the cross efficiency of the electricity distribution sector in Taiwan, Pacudan and Guzman (2002) looked at the efficiency of electricity distribution in the Philippines. Resende (2002) studied Brazilian electricity companies, and Korhonen and Syrjanen (2003) studied the efficiency of electricity distribution in Finland. Although there are established literature on the efficiency of electricity distribution, there are only a few articles that aim to determine the most efficient energy source with DEA framework.

Boyd and Pang (2000) studied the linkage between energy efficiency and productivity in two segments of the glass industry. They compared the level of electricity and fossil fuel intensity by using regression analysis. They also showed that there is a strong correlation between energy intensity and productivity. Ramanathan (2001) applied DEA to the comparative risk assessment of eight different energy supply technologies. He concludes that solar photovoltaic and nuclear power are the most efficient energy sources. After he excludes these two energy sources, windmill becomes the most efficient energy source according to his analysis. Jha and Shrestha (2006) used DEA to measure the efficiency of hydroelectric plants in Nepal. Chien and Hu (2007) apply DEA to the 45 OECD and non-OECD economies to determine the effects of renewable energy sources on the technical efficiency. They used macroeconomic data such as labor, capital stock, and energy consumption for the input variables where the real GDP is the only output variable. They concluded that there is a positive correlation between use of renewable energy and technical efficiency and there is a negative correlation with the traditional energy. Jayanthi et. al. (2009) applied DEA to U.S. photovoltaic industry. More recently, Cristobal (2011) applied DEA to evaluate the efficiency of the renewable energy sources in Spain.

DATA ENVELOPMENT ANALYSIS (DEA)

Charnes et al. (1978) introduced the DEA framework, which is a very powerful technique for the evaluating and improving the efficiency of both manufacturing and service operations. It is a non-parametric, multi-factor relative efficiency measure which is based on linear programming procedure. Charnes et al. (1978) calculated the relative efficiency score with the division of the weighted sum of outputs and weighted sum of inputs to obtain decision-making units (DMU). Equation 1 formulates the scenario where we have *N* number of maximized DMUs, which are obtained by *s* number of output and *m* number of input variables.

$$
\begin{aligned}
& max \quad E_e = \frac{\sum_{k=1}^{s} v_{ke} y_{ke}}{\sum_{i=1}^{m} u_{ie} x_{ie}} \\
& s.t. \quad \frac{\sum_{k=1}^{s} v_{ke} y_{kj}}{\sum_{i=1}^{m} u_{ie} x_{ij}} \le 1; \quad j = 1, 2, 3, \dots, n \\
& v_{ke}, u_{ie} \ge 0; \quad k = 1, 2, 3, \dots, s; \quad i = 1, 2, 3, \dots, m
\end{aligned} \tag{1}
$$

where, E_e is the maximized efficiency score which belongs to the eth DMU. Hence this set of equations can be easily converted to a linear programming problem by fixing the denominator equals to one:

$$\begin{aligned} & max\ E_e = \sum_{k=1}^{s} v_{ke} y_{ke} \\ & s.t.\ \ \sum_{k=1}^{s} v_{ke} y_{kj} - \sum_{i=1}^{m} u_{ie} x_{ij} \leq 0;\ \ j = 1, 2, 3, \dots, n \\ & \sum_{i=1}^{m} u_{ie} x_{ie} = 1 \\ & v_{ke}, u_{ie} \geq 0;\ k = 1, 2, 3, \dots, s;\ \ i = 1, 2, 3, \dots, m \end{aligned} \tag{2}$$

This formulation provides only two groups of results, efficient DMUs, and inefficient DMUs. However, this formulation doesn't provide any ranking information besides of these two groups. Therefore we use different approaches to find out the most efficient renewable energy source. In addition, we rank all of them according to their total efficiency scores which will be obtained by these different approaches. In this paper, we apply following ranking methods to determine the most efficient power plant: (1) the benchmark ranking model, (2) the super efficiency model, (3) the cross-efficiency model, and (4) the virtual model.

Benchmark Ranking Approach

One of the most popular ranking methods is benchmark ranking method which focuses on inefficient DMUs. This approach has been used in the DEA framework to rank the DMUs (e.g. Torgersen et al. 1996). This ranking method aims to improve inefficient DMUs with benchmarking of the efficient DMUs. The benchmarks are obtained by dual problem of the linear programming problem. The total number of benchmarks determine the rank of efficient DMUs, and the most referenced efficient DMU ranks first, and inefficient DMUs rank equally.

Super-Efficiency Approach

Super-efficiency approach was developed by Andersen and Petersen (1993) for ranking efficient DMUs. In this approach, linear programming problem is relaxed with omitting the unity constraint. This relaxation creates inefficient DMUs which are greater than 1, for originally efficient DMUs. Then the ranking is obtained by ordering of these inefficient DMUs.

Cross-Efficiency Approach

Another popular ranking method is the cross-efficiency approach which was developed by Sexton et al. (1986). The cross-efficiency method evaluates the performance of each DMU with respect to the optimal input and output weights of other DMUs. The cross efficiency matrix is constructed by peer evaluation, and then the ranking is obtained by the simple average of each DMUs' efficiency score.

Virtual DMU Approach

Golany and Roll (1994) developed the virtual DMU approach by selecting the best values of each input and output variables. The original model run one more time for each DMU with including new virtual DMU. After this process, virtual DMU becomes only efficient one, and the ranking is obtained by descending order of inefficient DMUs.

THE MODEL

In this study, we want to determine the most efficient renewable energy source(s) by using pre-determined input and output variables. This paper evaluates 8 major renewable energy sources: Wind Power (both onshore and offshore), Photovoltaic (both crystalline and thin film), Solar Thermal, Geothermal, Biomass, and Hydropower. In the next subsection, we look at each one of the renewable energy sources in detail. We also provide detailed information for each input and output variables in this section. The data is presented at the end of this section.

DEA Evaluations

Wind Power:

Wind power is one of the most expanded renewable and sustainable energy source in worldwide. Electricity is generated by the conversion of kinetic energy of wind by using a wind generator. According to the World Wind Energy Association data, over 300 GW of wind power would have been installed worldwide. There are two types of wind farms that we consider in this study: An onshore wind farm is located on a land, where an offshore wind farm is located in the water. We consider both of these two wind farms in our analysis because of the fact that both of them has comparative advantages. Although onshore wind farms have much cheaper total system levelized cost with respect to the offshore wind farms, they need very large areas for construction where offshore wind farms has no actual land requirements. That's why we include both of these two technologies into our DEA analysis.

Solar Photovoltaic:

The solar photovoltaic technology generates electrical power by converting sunlight into direct current electricity. Photovoltaic is one of the fastest growing power-generation technology that reaches about 200 GW total installation in the world. In this study, we consider two different types of photovoltaic technology because of the tradeoff between total levelized cost and land requirements: (1) solar photovoltaic crystalline and (2) solar photovoltaic thin film. One of the most important advantages of solar photovoltaic crystalline technology is lack of land requirements because they can easily install to rooftops of the buildings.

Solar Thermal:

Solar thermal technology is a renewable energy source, which generates solar power from solar energy by using solar thermal collectors. There are three major categories of solar thermal technology: (1) low-temperature collectors for heating and cooling systems; (2) medium temperature collector provides hot water for both residential and commercial areas, and (3) high-temperature collectors to generate electricity. Although it creates high construction and installation costs, the efficiency of these technologies is very high also.

Geothermal:

Geothermal energy is one the oldest renewable energy source which is almost emission free. Geothermal energy is generated and stored in the Earth, and it has been used for residential needs for thousands of years. Although the amount of geothermal energy is enormous but only a very small fraction may be profitably exploited. Therefore the total installation of geothermal power is about 10,715 megawatts.

Biomass:

Biomass is widely available and naturally distributed renewable energy source which is derived from distinct energy sources like garbage, wood, waste, landfill gases, and alcohol fuels. There are various different applications of biomass energy such as direct burning, electricity generation, gasification, biofuels and anaerobic digestions to obtain heat, electricity, or another form (bio-fuel, bio-gas). Total installation of biomass power is about 5 percent of the U.S. electricity supply.

Hydropower:

Hydropower is both renewable and sustainable energy source. It is derived from the force of falling or fast moving water which produces electrical power. Hydroelectricity and marine energy are the two main component of hydropower which is one of the most major renewable energy sources of the U.S. electricity supply.

The Inputs

In this study, we consider two input variables for the DEA analysis: (1) the total system levelized cost (TSLC), and (2) land requirements. Table 1 presents the related data for these input variables.

Total System Levelized Cost (TSLC):

Total system levelized cost is one of the most important input variables which combines different cost values, with electricity generation capacity, and life cycle of the system as well. The total system levelized cost has four components: (1) the total investment expenditures, (2) total operations and maintenance expenditures, (3) total fuel expenditures, (4) total amount of electricity generation. We also take into account discount rate which is associated with inflation estimates, and life cycle of the system. Therefore the total system levelized cost is calculated as follow:

$$TSLC = \frac{\sum_{t=1}^{n} \frac{I_t + M_t + F_t}{(1+r)^t}}{\sum_{t=1}^{n} \frac{E_t}{(1+r)^t}} \tag{3}$$

where;

I_t: Investment expenditures in the year t
M_t: Operations and maintenance expenditures in the year t
F_t: Fuel expenditures in the year t
E_t: Electricity generation in the year t
r: Discount rate
n: Life cycle of the system

Land Requirement:

Land requirement is another critical input variable for this DEA analysis because of the fact that some power plant requires extensive land area, and some of them require none. That's why it is very critical input to calculate the efficiency scores of renewable energy sources. The unit of this input variable is measured by hectare per megawatt.

The Outputs

In this study, we consider three output variables for the DEA analysis: (1) the plant size, (2) the capacity factor of each power plant, and (3) greenhouse gas (GHG) emissions. Table 1 presents the related data for these output variables.

Plant Size:

In this DEA framework, we use unit values for each power plant when we are calculating the total levelized system cost and land requirements to produce 1-megawatt electricity. That's why plant sizes are constant, and they are all equal to 1 for each energy source. The plants size unit is measured by megawatt.

Capacity Factor:

In this DEA analysis, capacity factor is very important output variable, which is the ratio of the actual output of a power plant and the total energy that plant would have produced at full capacity.

Greenhouse Gas (GHG) Emissions:

Greenhouse gas (GHG) emissions are the most important output variable to find out the most efficient renewable energy source due to the fact that they are the main source of global warming and climate change. The unit is measured by kilogram per megawatt.

The Data

Table 1 presents all of the input and output variables for DEA analysis. According to the U.S Energy Information Association Annual Energy Outlook 2011 data set, we construct TSCL and capacity factor columns. The land requirements and GHG emissions of each power plant are obtained by the U.S. Department of Energy.

Table 1: Power Plants Data with Input and Output Variables

Power Plant	Inputs		Outputs		
	TSLC ($/MW)	Land Req. (ha/MW)	Plant Size (MW)	Capacity Factor (%)	GHG Emissions (kg/MW)
Wind-Onshore	97.0	18.0	1.0	34.0	19.0
Wind-Offshore	243.2	0.0	1.0	34.0	14.0
Solar PV-Crystalline	291.0	0.0	1.0	25.0	53.0
Solar PV-Thin Film	254.0	2.5	1.0	25.0	62.0
Solar thermal	311.8	3.7	1.0	18.0	58.0
Geothermal	101.7	3.2	1.0	92.0	12.0
Biomass	112.5	0.7	1.0	83.0	72.0
Hydropower	86.4	6.6	1.0	52.0	5.0

DEA RESULTS

We model the linear programming problem for each one of the renewable energy sources by using the coefficients of input and output variables that are presented in Table 1. We run these models with LINDO 10 which is a comprehensive software that is designed to build and solve linear optimization models quickly and efficiently.

Table 2 presents the DMU values of each renewable energy sources. According to the Table 2, wind-offshore, geothermal, biomass and hydropower are efficient energy sources because they reached the maximum efficiency score, 1.0. On the other hand, wind-onshore, solar pv-crystalline, solar pv-thin film and solar thermal plant are inefficient renewable energy sources because their efficiency scores are less than one. According to these results, land requirement is very important input variable for the efficiency scores of these power plants. Although wind-onshore plant's TSLC is much less than wind-offshores', because of land requirements, wind-offshore reached the maximum efficiency score where wind-onshore has an inefficient score.

Table 2 also includes the reference sets of the benchmark ranking approach. According to these results, wind-offshore and geothermal energy sources have the highest reference score because of the fact that inefficient energy sources benchmarked these two power plants three times. According to this approach, wind-offshore and geothermal energy share the highest rank, and then biomass and hydropower follow them. Inefficient DMUs share the lowest rank according to the benchmark ranking method.

Table 3 shows the cross-efficiency matrix of these 8 power plants. This is an *nxn* matrix where *ij* represents the efficiency score of jth power plant with the weights of ith power plant. The highest average efficiency score represents the most efficient power plant with respect to its peers. According to these averages of these cross-efficiency scores, biomass has the highest average efficiency score, which refers to the most efficient renewable energy source. The solar thermal energy source has the lowest average efficient score which refers to the least efficient (or inefficient) renewable energy source according to the cross-efficiency method.

Table 2: Efficiencies Index of 8 Power Plants and their reference sets.

No	Power Plants	Efficiency Score	Efficiency	Inefficiency	References
1	Wind-onshore	0.4309		×	6,8
2	Wind-offshore	1.0000	×		*
3	Solar PV-Crystalline	0.6145		×	2
4	Solar PV-Thin Film	0.1778		×	2,6,7
5	Solar thermal	0.1193		×	2,6,7
6	Geothermal	1.0000	×		*
7	Biomass	1.0000	×		*
8	Hydropower	1.0000	×		*

Table 4 shows the super efficiency and virtual efficiency score of these 8 different power plants. According to the super efficiency approach, biomass has the highest efficiency score, which refers to the most efficient renewable energy source. Therefore the ranking is (1) biomass, (2) wind-offshore, (3) geothermal, (4) hydropower and (5) the rest of the other power plants.

Table 3: Cross-Efficiency Values of 8 Power Plants

Power Plants	Wind-onshore	Wind-offshore	SPV-Crystalline	SPV-Thin Film	Solar thermal	Geo-thermal	Bio-mass	Hydro-power
Wind-onshore	0.8907	0.3553	0.2969	0.3402	0.2771	0.8496	0.7680	1.0000
Wind-offshore	0.0664	1.0000	0.8357	0.3247	0.2328	0.3307	1.0000	0.1745
Solar PV-Crystalline	0.0664	1.0001	0.8358	0.3247	0.2328	0.3307	1.0001	0.1745
Solar PV-Thin Film	0.6553	0.4745	0.3965	0.4355	0.3518	0.9968	0.9999	1.0000
Solar thermal	0.6553	0.4745	0.3965	0.4355	0.3517	0.9968	0.9999	0.9999
Geothermal	0.8197	0.3269	0.2614	0.2995	0.2354	1.0000	0.8734	1.0000
Biomass	0.6562	0.4710	0.3931	0.4321	0.3487	0.9999	0.9999	1.0000
Hydropower	0.6562	0.4710	0.3931	0.4321	0.3487	1.0000	1.0000	1.0000
Average	**0.5583**	**0.5717**	**0.4761**	**0.3780**	**0.2974**	**0.8131**	**0.9551**	**0.7936**

According to the virtual efficiency approach, hydropower is the most efficient power plant because it has the highest virtual efficiency score. In general, we expect that all efficiency scores are less than 1 for the virtual efficiency method. However, Table 4 shows that the virtual efficiency score of hydropower is equal to 1 because of the fact that the constraint of virtual DMU is not binding. Therefore the ranking of the power plants should be as follow: (1) hydropower, (2) wind-onshore, (3) geothermal, (4) biomass, (5), wind-offshore, (6) solar photovoltaics-thin film, (7) solar photovoltaics-crystalline, and (8) solar thermal plant.

Table 4: Super Efficiency and Virtual Efficiency Scores for Power Plants.

Power Plants	Super Efficiency	Virtual Efficiency
Wind-onshore	*	0.8907
Wind-offshore	1.6273	0.3553
Solar PV-Crystalline	*	0.2969
Solar PV-Thin Film	*	0.3402
Solar thermal	*	0.2771
Geothermal	1.2261	0.8496
Biomass	2.6125	0.7680
Hydropower	1.1607	1.0000

Table 5 shows the summary of the ranking of power plants with respect to benchmark ranking, super efficiency, cross efficiency and virtual efficiency approaches. The final ranking is obtained by the cumulative scores of each power plant.

Table 5: Comparison of Various Approaches

Power Plants	Benchmark Ranking	Cross Efficiency	Super Efficiency	Virtual Efficiency	Cumulative Score	Ranking
Wind-onshore	5	5	5	2	17	5
Wind-offshore	1	4	2	5	12	3
Solar PV-Crystalline	5	6	5	7	23	6
Solar PV-Thin Film	5	7	5	6	23	6
Solar thermal	5	8	5	8	26	8
Geothermal	1	2	3	3	9	1
Biomass	3	1	1	4	9	1
Hydropower	4	3	4	1	12	3

SUMMARY AND CONCLUSION

In this paper, we want to determine the most efficient renewable energy source(s), with pre-determined input and output variables. We construct DEA framework to find efficient scores of each power plant. We apply four different analytic approaches, benchmark ranking, cross-efficiency, super efficiency and virtual efficiency. We rank each power plant by using these approaches, and then we calculate the cumulative scores. Therefore we rank these power plants according to their cumulative scores. Figure 1 and Table 5 summarizes the results.

Figure 1: Summary of Results

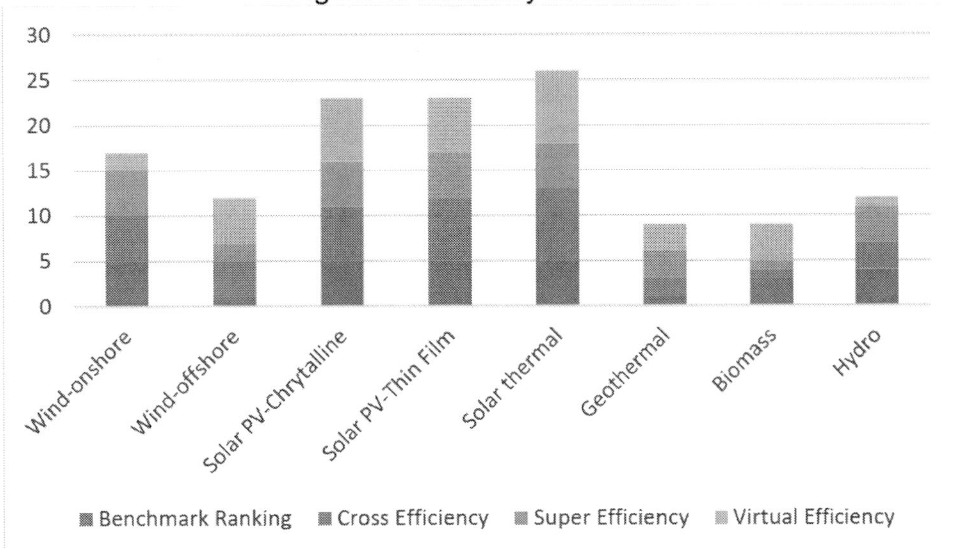

According to the results, biomass and geothermal are the most efficient renewable energy sources, where wind-offshore plant and hydropower follow these two plants. According to the DEA framework, they are all labelled as efficient renewable energy sources. Wind-onshore is ranked 5, where solar photovoltaics technologies share the sixth place, and solar thermal is the most inefficient renewable energy source. Figure 1 summarizes the contribution of each analytic techniques to the cumulative scores of each plant.

This study also shows that land availability has a really key role in this ranking and the efficiency scores of these renewable energy sources as well. Wind-offshore technology, which doesn't require any land, performs much better than wind-onshore technology, even though TLSC of wind-onshore is about 40% of TLSC of wind-offshore. These findings suggest that offshore wind farms should be more preferable because they don't have any land requirement. In addition, biomass, which requires a very small land for its operation, is one the most efficient renewable energy source as well according to our DEA analysis.

Another important finding of our DEA analysis is; although photovoltaic technology is one of the fastest growing power-generation, they are the least efficient technologies with solar thermal technology with respect to the other renewable energy sources. However in the future, the advancements in these technologies, may make them more preferable with the reduction of cost functions.

Lastly, policymakers should encourage and subsidy these technologies to reduce greenhouses gas (GHG) emissions which are it the main source of global warming and climate change. According to the EIA data, with the expansion of these renewable energy sources, GHG emissions started to decline in the United States in last five years.

REFERENCES

Andersen, P., & Petersen, N. C. (1993). A procedure for ranking efficient units in data envelopment analysis. *Management science*, *39*(10), 1261-1264.

Arrhenius, S. (1896). XXXI. On the influence of carbonic acid in the air upon the temperature of the ground. *The London, Edinburgh, and Dublin Philosophical Magazine and Journal of Science*, *41*(251), 237-276.

Bagdadioglu, N. (1996). Privatization, ownership, and technical efficiency in the Turkish electricity supply industry. *Pacific and Asian Journal of Energy*, *6*(1), 25-37.

Bessent, A. M., & Bessent, E. W. (1980). Determining the comparative efficiency of schools through data envelopment analysis. *Educational Administration Quarterly*, *16*(2), 57-75.

Boyd, G. A., & Pang, J. X. (2000). Estimating the linkage between energy efficiency and productivity. *Energy policy*, *28*(5), 289-296.

Charnes, A., Cooper, W. W., & Rhodes, E. (1978). Measuring the efficiency of decision making units. *European journal of operational research*, *2*(6), 429-444.

Chen, T. Y. (2002). An assessment of technical efficiency and cross-efficiency in Taiwan's electricity distribution sector. *European Journal of Operational Research*, *137*(2), 421-433.

Chien, T., & Hu, J. L. (2007). Renewable energy and macroeconomic efficiency of OECD and non-OECD economies. *Energy Policy*, *35*(7), 3606-3615.

Clapp, B. W. (2014). *An environmental history of Britain since the industrial revolution*. Routledge.

San Cristobal, J. R. (2011). Multi-criteria decision-making in the selection of a renewable energy project in Spain: the Vikor method. *Renewable energy*,*36*(2), 498-502.
De Vries, J. (2006). *European Urbanization, 1500-1800* (Vol. 4). Routledge.

Emrouznejad, A., Parker, B. R., & Tavares, G. (2008). Evaluation of research in efficiency and productivity: A survey and analysis of the first 30 years of scholarly literature in DEA. *Socio-economic planning sciences*, *42*(3), 151-157.

Favero, C. A., & Papi, L. (1995). Technical efficiency and scale efficiency in the Italian banking sector: a non-parametric approach. *Applied economics*,*27* (4), 385-395.

Forsund, F. R., & Kittelsen, S. A. (1998). Productivity development of Norwegian electricity distribution utilities. *Resource and Energy Economics*, *20*(3), 207-224.

Fourier, M. (1827). Les temperatures du globe terrestre et des espaces planetaires. *Memoires de l'Academie Royale des Sciences de l'Institut de France, 7.*

Gillen, D., & Lall, A. (1997). Developing measures of airport productivity and performance: an application of data envelopment analysis. *Transportation Research Part E: Logistics and Transportation Review*, *33*(4), 261-273.

Golany, B., & Roll, Y. (1994). Incorporating standards via DEA. In *Data envelopment analysis: Theory, methodology, and applications* (pp. 313-328). Springer Netherlands.

Grosskopf, S., & Valdmanis, V. (1987). Measuring hospital performance: A non-parametric approach. *Journal of Health Economics*, *6*(2), 89-107.

Houghton, J. (2005). Global warming. *Reports on Progress in Physics*, *68*(6), 1343.

Jayanthi, S., Witt, E. C., & Singh, V. (2009). Evaluation of potential of innovations: a DEA-based application to US photovoltaic industry. *Engineering Management, IEEE Transactions on*, *56*(3), 478-493.

Jha, D. K., & Shrestha, R. (2006). Measuring efficiency of hydropower plants in Nepal using data envelopment analysis. *Power Systems, IEEE Transactions on*, *21*(4), 1502-1511.

Jones, C. I. (2001). Was an industrial revolution inevitable? Economic growth over the very long run. *Advances in macroeconomics*, *1*(2).

Kao, C., Chang, P. L., & Hwang, S. N. (1993). Data envelopment analysis in measuring the efficiency of forest management. *Journal of Environmental Management*, *38*(1), 73-83.

Korhonen, P. J., & Syrjanen, M. J. (2003). Evaluation of cost efficiency in Finnish electricity distribution. *Annals of Operations Research*, *121*(1-4), 105-122.

Miliotis, P. A. (1992). Data envelopment analysis applied to electricity distribution districts. *Journal of the Operational Research Society*, 549-555

Nardinelli, C. (1990). *Child labor and the Industrial Revolution* (p. 155266). Bloomington: Indiana University Press.

Owen, A. D. (2004). Environmental externalities, market distortions and the economics of renewable energy technologies. *The Energy Journal*, 127-156

Pacudan, R., & de Guzman, E. (2002). Impact of energy efficiency policy to productive efficiency of electricity distribution industry in the Philippines. *Energy Economics*, *24*(1), 41-54.

Prindle, B., Eldridge, M., Eckhardt, M., & Frederick, A. (2007). The twin pillars of sustainable energy: synergies between energy efficiency and renewable energy technology and policy. *Washington, DC: American Council for an Energy-Efficient Economy.*

Ramanathan, R. (2001). Comparative risk assessment of energy supply technologies: a data envelopment analysis approach. *Energy*, *26*(2), 197-203.

Resende, M. (2002). Relative efficiency measurement and prospects for yardstick competition in Brazilian electricity distribution. *Energy Policy*, *30* (8), 637-647.

Sexton, T. R., Silkman, R. H., & Hogan, A. J. (1986). Data envelopment analysis: Critique and extensions. *New Directions for Program Evaluation*, *1986* (32), 73-105.

Solomon, S., D. Qin, M. Manning, Z. Chen, M. Marquis, K.B. Averyt, M. Tignor and H.L. Miller (eds.) (2007). IPCC the Fourth Assessment Report of the Intergovernmental Panel on Climate Change, Cambridge University Press, Cambridge, United Kingdom and New York, NY, USA.

Sueyoshi, T., & Goto, M. (2001). Slack-adjusted DEA for time series analysis: performance measurement of Japanese electric power generation industry in 1984–1993. *European Journal of Operational Research*, *133*(2), 232-259.

Torgersen, A. M., Førsund, F. R., & Kittelsen, S. A. (1996). Slack-adjusted efficiency measures and ranking of efficient units. *Journal of Productivity Analysis*, *7*(4), 379-398.

U.S. Energy Information Administration - EIA - Independent Statistics and Analysis. Retrieved April 1, 2016, from http://www.eia.gov/

US Environmental Protection Agency. Retrieved April 1, 2016, from https://www.epa.gov/

DECISION SCIENCES INSTITUTE

Applying Lean Manufacturing Principles to New Product Development

(Full Paper Submission)

Mohammad Z. Meybodi
Indiana University Kokomo
mmeybodi@iuk.edu

ABSTRACT

The focus of this article is to demonstrate the relationships between lean manufacturing (LM) principles and integrated new product development (INPD) method. Comparison and analysis of several critical factors show high degree of resemblances between the two sets of factors. A number of hypotheses regarding similarities between LM and INPD factors were developed and tested. Survey data strongly supports the hypotheses regarding similarities between the two methods. Statistical results also indicate compared with conventional companies, by utilizing INPD, lean manufacturing organizations are able to develop new products with 63% better quality, 52% less development time, 45% less development cost, and 36% less manufacturing cost.

KEY WORDS: Lean Manufacturing, Integrated New Product Development

INTRODUCTION

Innovation and speedy new product development is crucial for companies to gain competitive advantage in a global market. Creating new product ideas that are consistent with organizational strategy and moving these ideas through the stages of design, development, and introduction quickly has been the hallmark of successful world class organizations (Jacobs and Chase, 2014; Ferioli et al. 2010; Roulet et al. 2010; Towner, 1994; Beauregard et al. 2014). Introducing new products to the market early has several strategic and operational advantages. It often means premium prices, building name recognition, controlling a large market share, and enjoying the bottom line profits. Better competitive position in the market makes it also difficult for competition to enter the market (Blackburn, 1991; Cooper and Kleinschmidt, 1994; Lofstrand, 2010; Zahra and Ellor, 1993).

Despite its well-known strategic role, for large number of manufacturing organizations innovation, design, and successful management of new product development (NPD) has often been a major challenge. Long development time, prohibitive development and manufacturing costs, and questionable quality have been the common result for many of these organizations. The primary factor contributing to such unsuccessful result is perhaps the use conventional sequential method of NPD by these organizations (Blackburn, 1991; Morgan and Liker, 2006). In contrast, manufacturing literature for the past two decades clearly shows that through their lean manufacturing practices, world class organizations such as Toyota have dominated competition not only in the area of manufacturing but also in the area of innovation, design, development, and quick commercialization of new technologies (Marisa et al. 2008; Blackburn, 1991; Clark and Fujimoto, 1991; Ulrich and Eppinger, 2004; Michael, 2008; Unger and Eppinger 2009). Instead of traditional sequential approach to NPD, a successful strategy employed by these world class organizations is INPD. The question of interest in this article is: Are there relationships between success in lean manufacturing (LM) practices and success in INPD?

LITERATURE REVIEW

Lean manufacturing has been a great force in the world of manufacturing since mid 1980's. Some of the main benefits of LM such as lower inventory, quicker delivery, and lower cost have been well documented (Cook and Rogowski, 1996; Hobbs, 1994; Payne, 1993; Temponi and Pandya, 1995; Deshpande and Golhar, 1995; Billesbach, 1991; Handfield, 1993; Lawrence and Hottenstein, 1995; Golhar, Stamm, and Smith, 1990; Moras and Dieck, 1992). In the simplest form, LM requires maximizing value added production activities by removing unnecessary wastes. Identification and elimination of waste and respectful treatment of employee are the two fundamental principles of a LM system (Hobbs, 1994; Payne, 1993; Wantuck, 1983; Womack and Jones, 2003). Elimination of waste is achieved by adopting practices such as continuous quality improvement, setup time reduction, utilizing flexible resources, group technology layout, and pull production system (Gargeya, and Thompson, 1994; Sohal, Ramsay, and Samson, 1993; Suzaki, 1987)). Respectful treatment of people often means employee empowerment; it includes elements such as team work, fair compensation, employee training and new positive attitude toward suppliers (Sohal, Ramsay, and Samson, 1993; Wantuck, 1983). Looking at LM as a process of eliminating waste and respectful treatment of employee, its principles can be applied to other areas including service areas such as healthcare, education, government, and NPD (Womack and Jones, 2003; Gilbert, 1994; Towner, 1994). Application of lean principles to NPD has great opportunity to shorten product development time, improve design quality, and reduce product development and manufacturing costs (Anand and Kodali, 2008). The company that originated famous LM system, TPS, also developed Toyota Product Development System (TPDS). TPDS employs LM principles and tools such as value stream mapping, Kanban, 5S system, and continuous improvement to eliminate waste from product development activities and bring quality products to market faster than their leading competition (Morgan and Liker, 2006; Ward, 2007). However, TPDS is a comprehensive strategy that involves various approaches to eliminate waste from NPD activities. The focus of this article is on special case of TPDS called integrated method of new product development (INPD). With regard to the question stated earlier, the objective of the article is to answer the following questions:

1. Are there similarities between LM and INPD practices?
2. Are there differences between NPD performances for LM companies using INPD and conventional companies?

SEQUESNTIAL AND INTEGRATED METHODS OF NPD

NPD process is a sequence of inter-connected activities in which information regarding customer needs is translated into final product design. In a sequential NPD method, the process typically involves phases such as idea generation and validation, preliminary design, final design and prototyping, and pilot production and ramp-up (Wheelwright and Clark, 1992; Russell, and Taylor, 1998). Traditionally, this design process is managed sequentially by personnel from various functions of the organization. A major drawback of this approach is that the output from one design stage is passed to the next stage with little or no communication. Lack of communication and feedback among sequential stage causes the process to require too many design changes which causes the process to require longer development time which indeed causes the process to be too slow, too costly, and often of poor quality. The final result is that the designs are often rejected because the design is either outdated due to long development time or it is infeasible in term of manufacturing capability (Blackburn, 1991; Ulrich and Eppinger, 2000).

Unlike traditional method where functional units work sequentially and downstream functions are not involved until late in the process, INPD requires early involvement of cross functional teams. It requires that designers, manufacturers, marketers, suppliers, and customers work jointly as a team in an integrated manner (Albers and Braun, 2011; Liang, 2009; Anderson, 2008; Clark and Fujimoto, 1991; Donnellon, 1993; Millson, Ranj, and Wilemon, 1992; Shunk, 1992). Application of INPD under various manufacturing environments in order to shorten development time, improve quality, reduce risks, and reduce development cost is reported by these researchers (Anderson, 2008; Skalak, 2002; Kowang and Rasli, 2011; Lofstrand, 2010; Moges, 2009; Kerga et.al, 2014). Due to early cross-functional communication, INPD approach enables an organization to be more innovative in terms of improving design quality, shortening development time, reducing design risks, and reducing development and manufacturing costs (Blackburn, 1991; Ulrich, and Eppinger, 2000; Arora and Mital, 2012; Katzy et.al, 2012; Zirger and Hartley, 1996).

COMPARISON OF LEAN MANUFACTURING AND CENPD FACTORS

For the past few decades, there has been an extensive volume of research in the area of LM. As a result, there is a set of generally accepted guidelines that organizations can follow to achieve manufacturing success. However, there has been limited research on the application of LM principles to NPD and there is no comparable set of guidelines for successful management of NPD process. Recently, a number of world class NPD companies have attempted to apply the principles of lean manufacturing to NPD activities. The company that started the most famous LM system, Toyota Production System (TPS) is also started Toyota Product Development System (TPDS). TPDS employs lean principles and enable the company to bring the highest quality products to market faster than their leading competition. Similarities between LM and INPD for a number of critical factors are shown in Table 1, (Blackburn, 1991; Spencer and Guide, 1995). Following is a brief comparison and analysis of selected factors in Table 1:

Layout

Layout in LM environment is often in the form of product focus and manufacturing cells. This type of layout is necessary because small lot size production requires that the layout to be compact and efficient to ensure smooth flow of materials and close communication between work stations. Unlike conventional manufacturing, where material is pushed forward, the flow in a LM environment is in two directions; material is pulled forward, but information flows backward to provide feedback on performance and material requirements.

In INPD, overlapping of a large number of activities requires a complete change in layout that facilitates communication and encourages team work. Instead of organizing by sequential functions, INPD emphasizes on cross-functional integration and the formation of a design team. The design team sits together in one location, creating a type of project layout. A project layout creates an environment for frequent, two-way communication between team members, which encourages concurrent development of a product and its associated processes.

Table 1. Comparison of LM and INPD Factors

Factor	LM	INPD
Layout	GT/Cellular manufacturing	Project/Design teams
Process and information flow	Two way flow: material downward, information backward	Parallel activities: Two way flow of information among team members
Bottleneck	Focus is on elimination of bottleneck to shorten lead time.	Focus is on elimination of bottleneck to shorten NPD time.
Set-up/Transition time	Short	Short
Lot size	Small	Small (batches of information)
Quality	Quality at the source, continuous quality improvement, low rework activities	Early detection of design quality problems, continuous design improvement, low redesign activities
Inventory	Low	Low
Manufact./Develop. Cost	Reduced	Reduced
Lead time	Fast delivery	Short development time
Customer focus/Market responsiveness	More responsive to changes in customer demand	More responsive to product design changes
Workforce empowerment and teamwork	High	High
Workforce flexibility	High	High
Scheduling	Localized team control, team responsibility	Localized team control, team responsibility
Decision making	Manufacturing team	Design team
Supplier involvement	High level of sharing information, quality partners	High level of involvement in product development
Technology	Integrated systems, new technology after process simplification	Integrated CAD, CAE, CAM
Workplace organization	Utilizes 5S practices to organize, clean, and sustain the workplaces	Utilizes 5S practices to organize design team and data for easy access to information to conduct NPD activities
Standardization	Standardization of parts and components is a critical component of LM	Creates a standard method of doing activities (i.e. data collection, flow charting, blue prints, etc.)
Value added	High	High

Lot Size

In contrast to conventional manufacturing, lean manufacturing requires production of small lot-sizes. Production of small lot-sizes is possible by drastically reducing set-up times. It is well documented that production of small lot-sizes in LM is closely associated with improved quality, reduced inventory, faster delivery, and more responsive to market demands.

Similar to LM, INPD also utilizes small lot-sizes; the only difference is that in LM small lot sizes of goods are processed but INPD requires small lot-sizes of information. That is, continuous two way communication in INPD is similar to early release of small batches of information (Blackburn, 1991; White, 1993). With the early release of small batches of information, downstream constituents can begin working on different phases of the design while final design is evolving. The early release of information reduces uncertainty and encourages early detection of problems, which enables organizations to avoid costly, time-consuming changes.

Employee and Supplier Involvement

In LM environment, management encourages employee involvement and team work. The responsibility for job scheduling and quality are often passed to the teams at the shop floor. Due to small lot size production, delegation of authority to the teams at the shop floor is essential for smooth production flow. Also, in LM suppliers work closely with manufacturing organization to improve quality and shorten delivery time.

Similar to LM, in INPD the responsibility for scheduling of the activities pushed down to product development team at the lowest level. Passing responsibility down to the team is essential to achieve a high level of activity coordination and information sharing among team members. Also, in INPD suppliers work closely with the design team to reduce development costs, shorten development time, and offer ideas toward improving the quality of the design.

Quality

In LM and INPD environments, organizations are often proactive and quality means getting it right the first time. In LM, since batch sizes are small quality at the source and continuous quality improvement are the main foundations. Shop floor workers are empowered to become their own inspectors responsible for the quality of their output. In INPD, because of the teamwork and two-way flow of information between team members and utilization of quality improvement tool such as six sigma process quality problems are detected earlier and solved before they have a cumulative impact on the rest of the project (Chakravorty and Franza, 2009).

Technology

In a LM system, technology is not viewed as a substitute, or shortcut to process improvement. Rather, technology has been utilized after process analysis and simplification has been performed. The role of technology in INPD is also enormous; it requires that the design team with diverse expertise makes a large number of interrelated decisions regarding the form, fit, function, cost, quality, and other aspects of the design (Karagozoglu and Brown, 1993). This requires supply and processing of relevant information from multiple sources in a coordinated manner. Successful organizations use technology in their NPD process similarly to the way they use technology in their LM system. In INPD, the design team utilizes appropriate technologies and tools at various stages of NPD process. Effective use of technologies and tools can dramatically shorten NPD time, reduce number of prototypes, cut costs, and improve quality of the design (McKay et al. 2011; Yamamoto and Abu Qudiri 2011; Roulet et.al (2010). The key to the success of technology in INPD is building an effective design team with open cross-functional communication lines.

FACTOR HYPOTHESES

Comparison and analysis of factors in Table 1 show a high degree of similarities between LM and INPD. To study further, a set of twenty four hypotheses (H1-H24) that statistically test similarities between LM and INPD will be presented. The questionnaire items for the hypotheses are shown in Table 2. Each questionnaire item in Table 2 consists of two parts. In part a, the item makes a statement regarding LM factor and the corresponding statement regarding INPD factor is made in part b. The last hypothesis examines the overall impact of LM principles on INPD.

Hypotheses (H1-H24):
There is a high degree of similarities between LM and INPD factors.

NEW PRODUCT DEVELOPMENT PERFORMANCES

The following dimensions of quality, time, competency, development cost, and manufacturing cost are used to measure the performance of NPD (Ulrich and Eppinger, 2000; Wheelwright and Clark, 1992):

Quality

Quality is ultimately reflected in the price customers are willing to pay, the market share, and the bottom line profit. In NPD, quality problems are often the results of incomplete information and miscommunication among various functions. Quality often means a minimal number of redesign or rework. In this article, number of design changes during the development process and early manufacturing phase is used as a measure of design quality.

Development time

Development time is the length of time between initial idea generation until new product is ready for introduction to the market. Shorter development time raises the competitive value of new product in terms of premium price, larger market share, and higher profit margin.

Development competency

Development competency is the ability of the organization to develop future products better, faster, and cheaper. Competent workforce and effective use of technologies are important elements of organizational NPD competency. Frequency of new product introduction to the market is used as a measure of development competency.

Development cost

This is the total cost from the early idea generation until the product is ready for manufacturing. For most organizations, development cost is usually a significant portion of the budget and must be considered in light of budget realities and the timing of budget allocations.

Table 2. Survey Items for Comparison of LM and INPD Factors
(1=strongly disagree, 5=strongly agree)

1a. In LM, layout is often in form of group technology (GT) or cellular manufacturing (CM).	1b. In INPD, the layout emphasizes is on cross-functional integration and formation of project or design team.
2a. In LM, GT or cellular manufacturing layout allows smooth flow of materials downward and information flow backward.	2b. In INPD, project layout formed by the design team allows frequent and two way flow of information among team members.
3a. In LM, the focus is on identification and elimination of bottleneck to shorten manufacturing lead time.	3b. In INPD, the focus is on identification and elimination of bottleneck to shorten NPD time.
4a. LM system requires short set-up time.	4b. INPD requires fast transition (i.e. short set-up time) from one part of the design to another.
5a. LM system requires production of small lot-sizes.	5b. In INPD, continuous and two-way flow of information among team members is equivalent to releasing small batches of information.
6a. In LM, due to production of small lot-size, quality at the source and continuous quality improvement are essential to the success of the system.	6b. In INPD, due to simultaneous development of product and process, early detection of design quality problems and continuous improvement of the design are essential to the success of NPD process.
7a. In LM, production of small lot-size is associated with improving quality.	7b. In INPD, continuous and two-way communication among team members encourages early detection of the design problems, which is associated with improving design quality.
8a. In LM, production of small lot-size is associated with reducing inventory.	8b. In INPD, continuous and two-way communication among team members associated with reducing unnecessary amount of information among team members.
9a. In LM, production of small lot-size is associated with reducing manufacturing cost.	9b. In INPD, continuous and two-way communication among team members encourages early detection of the design problems, avoids costly design changes, which is associated with reducing development cost.
10a. In LM, production of small lot-size and smooth flow of materials downward and information flow backward is associated with reducing delivery time.	10b. In INPD, continuous and two-way communication among team members encourages early detection of the design problems, avoids time consuming design changes, which is associated with reducing NPD time.
11a. In LM, organizations are more responsive to the changes in customer demand.	11b. In INPD, the design teams are more responsive to the changes in product design.
12a. In LM, management encourages workforce empowerment and teamwork.	12b. In INPD, management encourages employee empowerment and teamwork.
13a. LM requires high level of workforce flexibility.	13b. INPD requires high level of design team flexibility.

Table 2. Survey Items for Comparison of LM and CENPD Factors
(1=strongly disagree, 5=strongly agree) (Continue)

14a. In LM, detailed shop floor responsibilities such as job and employee scheduling are passed to the local teams.	14b. In INPD, detailed design responsibilities such as development activities and employee scheduling are passed to the design teams.
15a. In LM, suppliers work closely with manufacturing teams.	15b. In INPD, suppliers work closely with the design and development teams.
16a. In LM, close relationship between suppliers and manufacturing teams is essential in improving quality, reducing manufacturing cost, and shortening delivery time.	16b. In INPD, close relationship between suppliers and design and development teams is essential in improving design quality, reducing design and development cost, and shortening design and development time.
17a. In LM, new technologies such as robots are integrated into manufacturing system after process analysis and simplification has been performed.	17b. In INPD, new technologies such as IT and CAD are integrated into the design and development process after process analysis and simplification has been performed.
18a. LM utilizes 5S practices to organize, clean, and sustain the workplaces.	18b. INPD utilizes 5S practices to organize data and design team members for easy access to timely information to conduct NPD activities.
19a. LM utilizes tools such as flow charts and VSM to eliminate wastes throughout manufacturing and supply chain process.	19b. INPD utilizes tools such as QFD and VSM to eliminate wastes during design and development process.
20a. LM utilizes manufacturing fail safing to minimize defects throughout manufacturing process.	20b. INPD utilizes NPD fail safing approach to minimize defects design and development process
21a. In LM, standardization of parts and components is a critical component of the system.	21b. In INPD, standard method of doing activities such as data collection and organization is a critical component of the process.
22a. In LM, due to the principles of elimination of wastes, process activities contain high value added content	22b. In INPD, simultaneous communication among team members, NPD process contain high value added content.
23a. As compared with traditional organizations, LM companies are generally better in the alignment of their manufacturing strategy and tactics.	23b. As compared with traditional NPD, INPD teams are generally better in the alignment of their NPD strategy and tactics.
24a. In LM, elimination of wastes and respectful treatment of people are the two main principles.	24b. Similar to LM, the main principles of elimination of wastes and respectful treatment of people are applicable to INPD.

FACTOR HYPOTHESES

To study further, a set of twenty hypotheses (H1-H20) that statistically test similarities between LM and CENPD will be presented. The questionnaire items for the hypotheses are shown in Table 2. Each questionnaire item in Table 2 consists of two parts. In part a, the item makes a statement regarding LM factor and the corresponding statement regarding CENPD factor is made in part b. The last hypothesis examines the overall impact of LM principles on CENPD.

Manufacturing cost

Manufacturing cost includes initial investment on equipments and tools as well as the incremental cost of manufacturing the product. There is a close relationship between manufacturing cost and the type of decisions made during the early design stage. Although early design decisions determine about 70 percent of future manufacturing cost, organizations often spend far too little time and resources during this stage (Huthwaite, B. 1991). To save future manufacturing cost, it is prudent for the companies to spend more time and resources during the early design phases of NPD process where critical design decisions are made.

PERFORMANCE HYPOTHESES

In the second set of hypotheses (H25-H29), the differences between NPD performances for lean manufacturing companies and conventional companies are tested.

Hypotheses (H25-H29):

H25: By utilizing INPD method, LM companies are able to design new products with fewer design changes than conventional companies (better quality).

H26: By utilizing INPD method, LM companies are able to design new products faster than conventional companies.

H27: By utilizing INPD method, LM companies are able to design new products more often than conventional companies.

H28: By utilizing INPD method, LM companies are able to design new products with less development cost than conventional companies.

H29: By utilizing INPD method, LM companies are able to design new products with less manufacturing cost than conventional companies.

RESEARCH METHODOLOGY

The target population for this study consisted of manufacturing firms in the states of Illinois, Indiana, Ohio, Michigan, and Wisconsin. A sample of 500 manufacturing firms with more than 50 employees was chosen from manufacturers' directories of those states. The sample covers organizations in variety of industries ranging from fabricated metal, communication, electronics, automotive, toots, chemicals, rubber, and paper products. A comprehensive survey instrument based on examination of the literature and critical factors listed in Table 1 was developed. A panel of practitioners and researchers with experience in LM and NPD was used to validate the survey. In addition to general organization and managerial profile items, the survey contained 48 items (24 paired) regarding similarities between LM and INPD factors.

Also, the survey instrument contained a number of questionnaire items on NPD performances for LM companies using INPD and conventional companies. Out of 91 completed surveys received, 84 surveys were usable resulting in a response rate of 17%. Based on a number of questionnaire items on the principles of LM practices, 33 organizations were grouped as LM companies and 51 organizations were categorized as conventional companies.

The survey data indicates that majority of respondents had various high level managerial positions from organization with less than 500 employees. Presidents and vice presidents accounted for 29% and plant managers accounted for 30% of the sample. About 35% of the sample had other managerial positions such as operations/production managers, quality managers, and the remaining 6% were production line supervisors. In terms of manufacturing and NPD experience, about 28% of the respondents had between 10 to 20 years and 60% had more than 20 years of manufacturing experience. About 72% of the sample had more than 10 years of LM experience and close to 65% of the sample had more than 10 years of NPD experience.

RESEARCH RESULTS

As stated earlier, in the first set of hypotheses the objective was to examine similarities between LM and INPD for a set of paired factors shown in Table 2. For each item, the null hypothesis was that the mean response for LM is equal to the mean response for INPD. The differences

Table 3. Statistical Result of Comparison of LM and INPD Factors
(1=strongly disagree, 5=strongly agree)

	LM		INPD			
Factor	**Mean**	**SD***	**Mean**	**SD***	**P-Value**	**Correlation**
1. Layout	3.92	0.85	3.62	1.08	0.140	0.74
2. Flow	4.08	1.03	4.06	0.96	0.640	0.83
3. Bottleneck	4.27	1.33	4.15	1.12	0.540	0.71
4. Set-up	4.34	0.70	3.81	0.96	0.003	0.47
5. Lot-size	3.85	0.88	3.55	1.03	0.100	0.65
6. Quality at source	4.23	0.77	4.28	0.74	0.300	0.69
7. Quality Improv.	3.43	0.90	3.89	0.85	0.000	0.32
8. Inventory	4.22	0.80	3.96	0.85	0.150	0.62
9. Manufacturing cost	3.58	0.80	3.94	0.67	0.001	0.45
10. Delivery	4.26	0.75	4.31	0.72	0.280	0.75
11. Customer respons.	4.22	0.73	4.24	0.70	0.480	0.79
12. Teamwork	3.98	0.81	3.83	0.90	0.360	0.76
13. Flexibility	3.86	0.93	3.72	0.96	0.330	0.65
14. Team scheduling	3.72	0.78	3.76	0.78	0.240	0.82
15. Suppliers	3.77	0.79	3.82	0.83	0.350	0.77
16. Suppliers & teams	4.23	0.72	4.02	0.70	0.390	0.73
17. Technology	3.53	0.96	3.68	0.94	0.072	0.69
18. 5S Practices	4.30	0.92	4.12	0.84	0.310	0.71
19. Flowcharts/VSM	4.11	1.12	3.88	1.18	0.281	0.75
20. Fail-safing	4.23	1.31	4.06	1.42	0.352	0.81
21. Standardization	4.22	0.87	3.84	0.88	0.320	0.67
22. Value added	4.28	1.12	4.13	0.98	0.160	0.72
23. Alignment	4.36	1.25	4.17	1.17	0.210	0.76
24. Overall	4.56	0.93	4.29	0.96	0.140	0.73

* SD = Standard deviation

between the mean responses for LM and INPD were compared using the statistical t-test. The respondents were asked to rate each element of Table 2 based on the degree of their agreement (1=strongly disagree, 5=strongly agree) to the question. Table 3 shows the statistical results of the similarities between LM and INPD factors.

As shown in this table, overall the respondents strongly agreed with the statements regarding similarities between LM and INPD factors. The mean ratings for about 70% of the factors for both LM and INPD are above 3.80. Specifically, out of twenty four hypotheses, the respondents agreed that there is a high degree of similarities between LM and INPD for all except three hypotheses H4, H7, and H9.

For H4, the mean ratings for LM and INPD are respectively 4.34 and 3.81. This means although the respondents understood that short set-up and fast transition time are the main requirements of successful LM and INPD, the relationship between short set-up and LM was much stronger. This is a reasonable result because an average manufacturing manager has longer experience with LM than INPD. They clearly understood that successful LM requires small lot-size and small lot-size requires short set-up time. However, due to their shorter experience with INPD and because INPD is primarily an information processing process, the links between small batches of information and fast transition time is not clear. H7 hypothesizes the relationships between small lot-sizes and quality improvement for both LM and INPD. For this test, the mean ratings for LM and INPD are respectively 3.43 and 3.89. This indicates for an average manager it is easier to recognize the relationship between INPD and quality improvement than the relationship between LM and quality improvement. The higher rating for INPD is perhaps due to continuous and two way communications among design team members, which encourages early detection of the design problem. The LM result is also consistent with the literature because although total quality management and quality improvement are fundamental requirements of successful LM, an average manufacturing manager has difficulty to understand this relationship. The relationships between small lot-size and reduced manufacturing cost in LM and the relationship between small batches of information and reduced development cost in INPD are examined in H9. The mean ratings for LM and INPD are respectively 3.58 and 3.94. For the same reasons as H7, this means for an average manager it is easier to understand this relationship in INPD than LM. The LM result is interesting and also consistent with the literature because reduced manufacturing cost in LM is primarily due to elimination of wastes, a fundamental principle of LM, and an average manufacturing manager has difficulty to see this relationship. The overall impact of lean principles on LM and INPD is examined in H24. It is obvious that the data supports the hypothesis as the mean ratings for LM and INPD are respectively 4.56 and 4.29 indicating strong agreement with the statements that the main principles of waste elimination and respectful treatment of people in LM can also be applied in INPD.

The last column of Table 3 shows correlation coefficients between LM and corresponding INPD factors. The correlation coefficients in Table 3 strongly support the above analysis. With the exception of three hypotheses H4, H7, and H9 other coefficients are greater than 0.60 indicating a high degree of linear association between LM and INPD factors.

The performance hypotheses (H25-H29) state that by utilizing INPD approach, LM companies are able to design new products with fewer design changes, faster, more often, with less development cost, and less manufacturing cost than conventional companies.

Table 4. NPD Performances for Conventional and LM Companies using INPD

Factor	Mean Conventional	Mean LM	p-value
Number of design changes	5.36	3.28	0.004
Development time (Months)	37.22	24.73	0.003
Development competency (Months)	49.46	32.72	0.005
Development cost	144.60*	100*	0.005
Manufacturing cost	135.75*	100*	0.005

* data reported in terms of percent improvement

Table 4 provides useful statistical information regarding NPD performances for LM companies using INPD and conventional companies using sequential method of NPD. The average number of design changes for conventional and LM companies are respectively 5.36 and 3.28, a quality improvement of 63%. The average development time for conventional and LM companies are respectively 37.52 and 24.73 months, an improvement of 52%. For development competency, the average time between introduction of new products for conventional companies is 49.46 months and 32.72 months for LM companies, an improvement of 51%. Table 4 also indicates that LM organizations enjoy a 45% reduction in NPD cost and 36% reduction in manufacturing cost. From the last column of Table 4, it is clear that the hypotheses are strongly supported by the data as the p-value for all five hypotheses is less than 0.005.

CONCLUSION

The focus of this article was to demonstrate possible links between LM practices and INPD. First, comparison and analysis of a number of factors showed remarkable similarities between LM practices and INPD. Second, a set of paired hypotheses was used to test similarities between LM practices and INPD factors. Statistical results clearly support the hypotheses regarding similarities between LM and INPD for majority of factors. Specifically, out of twenty hypotheses, the respondents agreed that there is a high degree of similarities between LM and INPD for all but three hypotheses. The last pair of hypotheses that examines the overall impact of LM principles is especially important. Statistical results strongly agreed that the main principles of waste elimination and respectful treatment of people in LM is also applicable to INPD. The correlation coefficients between LM and INPD factors also supported the same result. Third, statistical results also indicate that compared with conventional companies, LM companies are able to develop new products with 63% better quality, 52% less development time, 45% less development cost, and 36% less manufacturing cost. Also frequency of new product introduction is 51% faster than conventional companies.

REFERENCES

Anand, G. and Kodali, R. (2008), "Development of a conceptual framework for lean new product development process", *International Journal of Product Development*, Vol. 6 No. 2, pp.190-224.

Anderson, D. M. (2008), *Design for Manufacturability & Concurrent Engineering, How to Design for Low Cost, Design in High quality, Design for Lean Manufacture, and Design Quickly for Fast Production*, CIM Press, CA.

Albers, A. and Braun, A. (2011). "A generalized framework to compass and to support complex product engineering processes", *International Journal of Product Development*, Vol. 15 No 1/2/3, pp. 6-25.

Arora, A. and Mital, A. (2012). "Concurrent consideration of product usability and functionality: Part II - customizing and validating design guidelines for a consumer product (Mountain Touring Bike)", *International Journal of Product Development*, Vol. 16 No 1, pp. 1-16.

Beauregard, Y., Bhuiyan, N., and Thomson, V. (2014), "Lean engineering performance analysis", *International Jounal of Product Development*, Vol. 19, No.5/6, pp. 366 – 387.

Billesbach, T. J. (1991) "A Study of Implementation of Just-In-Time in the United States", *Production and Inventory Management Journal*, Vol. 32 No 3, 1-4.

Blackburn, J. D. (1991). *Time-Based Competition, The next Battleground in American Manufacturing,* Business one Irwin, Homewood, Illinois

Chakravorty, S. S. and Franza, R. M. (2009). "The implementation of design for Six Sigma; A development experience", *International Journal of Product Development*, Vol. 9 No 4, pp. 329-342.

Clark, K. B. and Fujimoto, T. (1991). *Product Development Performance*, Harvard Business School Press, Boston, MA.

Cook, R. L. and Rogowski, R. A. (1996). "Applying JIT principles to process manufacturing supply chains", *Production and Inventory Management*, 1st Quarter, pp. 12-17.

Cooper, R. G., and Kleinschmidt, E. J. (1994). "Determinants of timeliness in product development", *Journal of Product Innovation Management*, Vol. 11, pp. 381-396.

Deshpande, S. P., and Golhar, D. Y. (1995). "HRM practices in unionized and non-unionized Canadian JIT manufacturing firms", *Production and Inventory Management Journal*, 1st Quarter, pp. 15-19.

Donnellon, A. (1993). "Cross functional teams in product development: Accommodating the structure to the process", *Journal of Product Innovation Management*, Vol. 10, pp. 377-392.

Ferioli, M., Dekoninck, E., Culley, S., Roussel, B., and Renaud, J. (2010), "Understanding the rapid evaluation of innovative ideas in the early stages of design", *International Journal of Product Development*, Vol. 12 No 1, pp. 67-83.

Gargeya, V. B., and Thompson, J. P. (1994). " Just-in-Time production in small job shops", *Industrial Management*, July/August, pp. 23-26.

Gilbert, J. T. (Aug. 1994). "Faster! Newer! Is Not a Strategy", *Advanced Management Journal.*

Golhar, D. Y., Stamm, C. L., and Smith, W. P. (1990). "JIT implementation in manufacturing firms", *Production and Inventory Management Journal*, Vol. 31 No. 2, pp. 44-48.

Handfield, R. (1993). "Distinguishing features of Just-in-Time systems in the make-to-order/assemble to order environment", *Decision Sciences*, Vol. 24 No. 3, pp. 581-602.

Hobbs, O. K. (1994). "Application of JIT techniques in a discrete batch job shop", *Production and Inventory Management*, 1st Quarter, pp. 43-47.

Huthwaite, B. (1991). "Managing at the starting line: How to design competitive products", *Workshop at the University/Southern Claifornia-Los Angeles*, January 14, p. 3.

Jacobs, F. R., and Chase, R. B. (2014), *Operations and Supply Chain Management, 14th* edition, McGraw-Hill/Irwin.

Karagozoglu, N., and Brown, W. B. (1993). "Time-based management of the new product development process", *Journal of Product Innovation Management*, Vol. 10, pp. 204-215.

Katzy, B. R., Baltes, G. H., and Gard, J. (2012), "Concurrent process coordination of new product development by Living Labs - an exploratory case study", *International Journal of Product Development*, Vol. 17 No 1/2, pp. 23-42.

Kerga, E., Rossi, M., Terzi, S., Taisch, M., Bessega, W. and Rosso, A. (2014), "Teaching set-based concurrent engineering to practitioners through gaming", *International Jounal of Product Development*, Vol. 19, No.5/6, pp.348 – 365.

Kowang, T. O. and Rasli, A. (2011), "New product development in multi-location R& D organization: A concurrent engineering approach", *African Journal of Business Management*, Vol. 5, No 6, pp. 2264-2275.

Lawrence, J. J., and Hottenstein, M. P.(1995). "The relationship between JIT manufacturing and performance in Mexican plants affiliated U.S. companies", *Journal of Operations Management*, Vol. 13, pp. 3-18.

Liang, J. C. (2009). "An integrated product development process in automotive industry", *International Journal of Product Development*, Vol. 8 No 1, pp. 80-105.

Lofstrand, M. (2010), "Linking design process activities to the business decisions of the firm: An example from the aerospace industry", *International Journal of Product Development*, Vol. 12 No 2, pp. 141-157.

Marisa, S. Marco, B. Peter, B. and Robert, V.D.M. (2008), "Factors influencing an organization's ability to manage innovation: A structure literature review and conceptual model", *International Journal of Innovation Management*, Vol. 12, No. 4, pp. 655-676.

McKay, A., Jowers, L., Chau, H. H., Pennigton, A. D., and Hogg, D. C. (2011). "Computer-aided design synthesis: An application of shape grammars", *International Journal of Product Development*, Vol. 13 No 1, pp. 4-15.

Michael, L. (2008), "Introduction of an evaluation tool to predict the probability of success of companies: the innovativeness, capabilities and potential model", *Journal of Technology* Management and Innovations, Vol. 4 No. 1, pp. 33-47.

Millson, M. R., Ranj, S. P., and Wireman, D. A. (1992). "A survey of major approaches for accelerating new product development", *Journal of Product Innovation Management*, Vol. 9 No. 1, pp. 53-69.

Moges, A. B. (2009), "Design for Manufacturability and Concurrent Engineering for Product Development", *World Academy of Science, Engineering and Technology*, Vol. 49, pp. 240-246.

Moras, R. G., and Dieck, A. J.(1992). "Industrial applications of Just-in-Time: Lessons to be Learned", *Production and Inventory Management*, 3rd Quarter, pp. 25-29.

Morgan, J. M. and Liker, J.K. (2006), *The Toyota Product Development System: Integrating People, Process and Technology*, Productivity Press, New York, NY.

Payne, T. E. (1993). "Acme Manufacturing: A case study in JIT implementation", *Production and Inventory Management*, 2nd Quarter, pp. 82-86.

Roulet, N. Dubois, P. and Aoussat, A. (2010), "The integration of new technologies: the stakes of knowledge", *International Journal of Product Development*, Vol. 12 No. 2, pp. 126-140.

Russell, R. S. and Taylor, B. W. (1998). *Production and Operations Management, Focusing on Quality and Competitiveness*, Prentice Hall.

Shunk, D. L. (1992). *Integrated Process Design and Development*, Irwin.

Skalak, S. C (2002), *Implementing Concurrent Engineering in Small Companies,* Marcel Dekker, New York, NY.

Skalak, S. C (2002), *Implementing Concurrent Engineering in Small Companies,* Marcel Dekker, New York, NY.

Sohal, A. S., Ramsay, L., and Samson, D. (1993). "JIT manufacturing: Industry analysis and a methodology for implementation", *International Journal of Operations and Production Management*, Vol. 13 No 7, pp. 22-56.

Spencer, M. S., and Guide, V. D. (1995). "An exploration of the components of JIT, case study and survey results", *International Journal of Operations and Production Management*, Vol. 15 No. 5, pp. 72-83.

Suzaki, K. (1987). *The New Manufacturing Challenge: Techniques for Continuous Improvement*, Free Press, New York.

Temponi, C., and Pandya, S. Y. (1995). "Implementation of two JIT elements in small-sized manufacturing firms", *Production and Inventory Management Journal,* 3rd Quarter, pp. 23-29.

Towner, S. J. (1994), "Four ways to accelerate new product development", *Long Range Planning*, April.

Ulrich, K. T. and Eppinger, S. D. (2000). *Product Design and development*, McGraw Hill.

Unger, D. W. and Eppinger, S. D. (2009). "Comparing product development processes and managing risk", *International Journal of Product Development,* Vol. 8 No. 4, pp.382-402.

Wantuck, K. A. (1983). *The Japanese Approach to Productivity*, Bendix Corporation, Southfield, MI.

Ward, A. C. (2007), *Lean Product and Process Development*, Lean Enterprise Institute, Cambridge, Mass.

Wheelwright, S.C., and Clark, K. B., (1992). *Revolutionizing Product Development*, Free Press, New York.

White, R. E. (1993). "An empirical assessment of JIT in U.S. manufacturers", *Production and Inventory Management*, 2nd Quarter, pp. 38-42.

Womack, J. P. and Jones, D. T. (2003), *Lean Thinking: Banish Waste and Create Wealth in your Corporation*, Free Press, New York, NY.

Yamamoto, H. and Abu Qudeiri, J. (2010). "A concurrent engineering system to integrate a production simulation and CAD system for FTL layout design", *International Journal of Product Development*, Vol. 10 No 1/2/3, pp. 101-122.

Zahra, S. A. and Ellor, D. (1993). "Accelerating new product development and successful market introduction", *SAM Advanced Management Journal*, Winter, pp. 9-15.

Zirger, B. J. and Hartley, L. (1996). "The effect of acceleration techniques on product development time", *IEEE Transactions on Engineering Management*, Vol. 43 No. 2, pp. 143-152.

DECISION SCIENCES INSTITUTE

Are service productivity and quality in permanent conflict? (The effect of service innovation and the role of customer satisfaction)

DongJun Rew
The University of Texas Rio Grande Valley
Email: dongjun.rew01@utrgv.edu

ABSTRACT

The purpose of this study is to explore the roles of service productivity and service innovation, the relationships of service productivity and innovation with customer satisfaction, and the effects on firm performance. However, there is not much research developed in marketing literature, even though it is the important concept for both practitioners and scholars to explain important issues of marketing, such as strategical competitiveness and sustainable service providing in the market. Thus, this study verifies and demonstrates that there are positive relationships among each variable through a simple classification analysis. Therefore, this study has several theoretical and practical contributions.

KEYWORDS: Service innovation, Service productivity, Service quality, Customer satisfaction, and Firm performance

INTRODUCTION

Is there always conflict between service quality and service productivity? The purpose of this study is to re-explore the relationships among customer satisfaction, service quality and service productivity. In marketing literature, the relationship between service quality (hereafter SQ) and service productivity (hereafter SP) has been in conflict to firm's profitability, because both concepts have had intercontradictional impact on customer's satisfaction (Anderson et al., 1997). Especially, according to Anderson et al (1997), productivity has different impacts on customer satisfaction for goods and services. In detail, in the service industry, productivity is negatively related to customer satisfaction, whereas in the manufacturing industry, the productivity is positively related to the customer satisfaction. It is also true that both SP and SQ have impacted on customer satisfaction, where customer satisfaction is defined as an overall evaluation of firm's products and/or services (Anderson et al., 1997). However, these relationships had been examined at the point of operational costs, in terms of labor cost that have direct impact on firm's profit.

After the revolution of S-D logic (Vargo and Lusch, 2004; 2008), the point of view that SQ and SP are sources of operational costs has changed. Especially, advanced technology has radically changed the economic environment in the world. For example, technology can help customers and firms to interact actively with each other, even in the process of producing products/services (Sorescu and Spanjol, 2008; Vivek et al., 2012). Therefore, in service industry it is hard to believe that SP is negatively related to customer satisfaction. In other words, SP is a sources of firm's competitive advantages in the competitive service market. In short, under the SD logic the concept of SP has to be considered coincidently with the effect of technology as the way of interaction with customers.

In fact, SP in marketing literature has been still used with the definition as the ratio of outcomes over inputs (Mark, 1982; Anderson et al., 1997; Filiatrault et al., 1996; Looy et al., 1998). However, the traditional definition of SP did not consider the effect of advanced technology on SP. Thus, Grönroos and Ojasalo (2004) assert that SP must be considered and measured by three components, such as effectiveness, efficiency, and capacity. With this point of view, Rust and Huang (2012) theoretically develop and empirically test the optimizing level of SP to maximize the firm's profitability. In the study they argue that SP must be considered with customer engagement through customer's usage of technology. It indicates that SP does not need to be negatively related to customers.

This argument is based on the service innovation, because services need clients and providers to make a value by working together (Sophrer and Maglio, 2008). As one of strategies to be close to customers, companies have developed a tactic by innovating their production process and communicating with their customers, which indicates service innovation (hereafter SI) (Schumpeter, 1934; Spohrer and Maglio, 2008; Dotzel et al., 2013; Snyder et al., 2016). This challenge from SI is caused by the rapid change in the map of entire market and the characteristics of service (Spohrer and Maglio, 2008). Thus, to create a larger value for both participants companies in the service sector move their concentration to their customers by SI, including three dimensions: assimilation, demarcation and synthesis perspectives (Witell et al., 2016). Therefore, it is necessary to investigate the relationship between SP and SI, because SI is able to optimize the effect of SP. This investigation also includes the relationship between SI and firm value by Dotzel, Shankar, and Berry (2013).

Under this point of view, this study theoretically agrees with Grönroos & Ojasalo (2004) and Rust & Huang (2012), which is fundamentally that there is no contradiction between the effects of SP and SQ on firm's profit as the consequence of customer satisfaction. In fact, there is much research on the relations between SQ, SP and firm's profit to customer satisfaction (Anderson et al., 1997; Boulding t al., 1993; Choi et al., 2015). However, they have fragmentarily focused on each effect of SQ and SP on firm's profit and customer satisfaction, and there are a very limited number of studies on the effect of new conceptualized SP in marketing literature. Thus, this is the first empirical study to investigate the entire theoretical frame of relationship between SP, SQ, customer satisfaction, and profit in service industry. Additionally, through this investigation, the study will explore the role and effect of service innovation as a common antecedent of both SP and SQ. I will also verify the role and effect of customer satisfaction in the relationships of each construct. To achieve the purpose of this study as mentioned above, there are several research questions as follows;

- What are the relationships between firm performance and each SQ (CS) and SP?
- What is the role of service innovation?
- What is the role of customer satisfaction (CS) in the relationship between SP and firm's performance?

Therefore, this study will have a couple of contributions to both marketing practitioners and scholars. Theoretically this study will provide a new insight of SP and SQ impacts and the role of service innovation (hereafter SI) and CS on measuring firm's profitability, and practically it will suggest some important messages to marketing practitioners. For the remainder of this study, it will be organized with the related literature review and developed research hypotheses with theoretical research framework. It will also be concluded with results from methodological approach. Lastly, this study will deliver meaningful messages to both marketing practitioners and scholars.

LITERATURE REVIEW

Relationships among SP, CS and firm value

Up to until present, there has been still argument about effects of SP and SQ on firm profit and the relationship with the profit. The argument of productivity would start with the industrial revolution. Since the principle of scientific management (Taylor, 1998), the argument has been intensified. Then, the productivity in service industry has been discussed by other disciplines, such as economics and finance, as well as marketing (Mark, 1982; McLaughlin and Coffey, 1990). Although, in fact, there are different types of productivity between manufacturing industry point of view and service industry point of view, service productivity has been defined as operational efficiency and it has been measured as output divided by input (Anderson et al., 1997; Donbi et al., 2000). Therefore, SP has been always negative related to customer satisfaction (hereafter CS) in marketing literature (Cosby, 1979; Deming, 1982; Johnson and Fornell, 1991), because to increase productivity companies need to choose the managerial decision of decreasing input, in terms of labor resources.

However, the new discussion of SP recommences, because of the measurement, even though it is recognized that SP is considered with both effectiveness and efficiency (Donbi et al., 2000; Grönroos and Ojasalo, 2004; Johnston and Jones, 2004; Schmenner, 2004). The newly defined SP includes both concepts of effectiveness, which can directly affect customer's attitude, and efficiency, which indicates the cost reduction (Grönroos and Ojasalo, 2004). It is called, "optimal level of SP", and it can be calculated with managerial decision variables as the function of price per unit, margin of profit, market concentration, and wages (Rust and Huang, 2012).

Based on this new definition of SP and the measurement, SP can chase two hares at once, customer satisfaction and operational cost reduction, because the newly defined SP considers both key concepts. Theoretically, when waiting time of services decreases, customers recognize that they are satisfied by the decrease in waiting time (Johnston, 1995; Rust and Huang, 2012). In other words, through customers' participation using various technology, such as ticketing machine, ATM, self-service checkout system, and kiosks, etc., companies achieve both cost reduction by standardization from the technology and customer satisfaction by decrease in waiting time from their participation in using technology (Rust and Huang, 2012). Therefore, it is hypothesized that;

H1 (a): SP positively affects firm value as BE.

H1 (b): SP positively affects customer satisfaction (CS).

Relationships among SI, SP, SQ, and firm value

Despite the importance of service industry in the economy, research on the effect of service innovation on the newly defined service productivity and service quality is relatively underdeveloped. Before concerned productivity in service industry, the concept of productivity was positively influenced by innovation, measured as R&D expenditure (Wakelin, 2001). For any set of service characteristics, innovation improves operational productivity. Peterson and Jeong (2010) argue that the investment in R&D leads firm's financial performance, especially brand value and firm performance. Therefore, company investment in R&D results in positive financial performance, which means financial profit or surplus.

There is another type of research on the relationship between SI and SQ. In this type of study, it indicates that SQ is significantly related to the degree of customer satisfaction (Helms and Mayo, 2008). Thus, when SQ is improved, the degree of CS is also enhanced. In a study on service innovativeness, Dotzel et al. (2013) introduce the concept of service innovativeness, defined as "a new or enhanced intangible offering that involves the firm's performance of a task/activity intended to benefit customers". It means that service innovation has to lead positive financial performance for both customer and firm as the result of investment. In other words, the investment action for service innovativeness can also have positive relationships with SQ and SP.

Kibbeling et al. (2013) argue that there is a positive relationship between innovativeness and CS. It is fundamentally derived from the statement of the theoretical argument by Rust et al. (1995), which is that CS can be measured instated of SQ. This will be explained later in the relationship between CS and SQ. Therefore, it is assumed that there is still a positive relationship between SI and SP.

H2 (a): Service innovation (SI) positively affects frim value (BE).
H2 (b): Service innovation (SI) positively affects service productivity (SP).
H2 (b): Service innovation (SI) positively affects customer satisfaction (CS).

Relationship between SQ and CS

Service quality (SQ) has led to innovative thinking in the services industry (Rust et al., 1995). Through SQ, companies can have a chance to match with more customers' demand and better level of both firm and service performance (Aaker and Jacobson, 1994; Rice, 1990). The literature of SQ has been with the history of service marketing. As the cognitive concept, SQ has been measured from customers' perception (Parasuraman et al., 1985; 1988; 1991; 1993) as a function of expectations and performance. Thus, to reach the highest level of SQ, service companies need to deal with the gap between expectations and performance as much as it can be reduced.

Through controlling SQ, companies in services accomplish more and better in both customer satisfaction (hereafter CS) and firm/services performance, because theoretically SQ consisted of expectations and performance affects CS by influencing customers' cognition and attitude toward the service (Zeithaml, 2000). Especially, Rust et al. (1995) propose CS as an alternative way of measuring SQ, because it can be theoretically expressed that CS is explained by the perceived SQ which expressively influences CS. Also Rust and Zahorik (1993) insist that statistically customer's retention behaviors, which are affected by SQ, are expressed in a logistic regression, which ranges from 0 to 1. The changes in the regression are typically small, which ensures that changes in SQ are also small. Rust et al. (1995), therefore, argue that methodologically it is reasonable to use CS for measuring SQ, rather than to directly evaluate SQ by measurements of SQ as proposed by Parasuraman et al. (1985 & 1988) and Cronin & Taylor (1992).

Thus, once quality of service improves or increases, theoretically CS is increased as much as SQ is increased (Fornell et al., 1996). With respect to this argument, Rust et al. (2002) support the theoretical argument by extension of the effect of SQ on firm performance, even though they did not pay attention to the role of customer, which means CS. The study of relationship between SQ and CS by Anderson et al. (1997), therefore, demonstrates that CS is directly related to the quality and productivity of service even though there are contradictable relationships of CS with SQ and SP as noted above.

Relationship between CS and firm value

In market, customers always have taken a leading actor, thus companies aim to satisfy their customers to provide what they want to have from the provided services and products (Syzmanski and Henard, 2001). Drucker (1951) points that the reason of why companies exist is to satisfy their customers. Increase in CS leads firm's portability as performance, and CS indicates the level of service performance (Kotler, 1991). Thus, the goal of business is moved from maximizing profit to maximizing customer satisfaction (Anderson and Sullivan, 1993). This point of view has been supported by many studies in marketing literature. Luo and Bhattacharya (2006) insist that customers play an important role between marketing action, which is CSR, and firm's market value, which is stock return, as a mediator.

In the cognitive behavioral study, Anderson and Swaminathan (2011) identify key factors that lead to customer satisfaction in e-businesses, such as adaptation, commitment, network, assortment, transaction ease, and engagement, investigate the positive effect of CS on customer's loyalty moderated by customer trust and inertia. Thus, it can be theoretically assumed that when customers are satisfied by some factors, CS has a greater effect on

cognitive behavioral performance and firm financial performance. Therefore, it is hypothesized as follows;
H3: CS positively affects firm value (BE).

Conceptual framework

Based on the literature review, this study proposes a theoretical research framework as follows. Fundamentally, this study investigates the effect of each variable on firm performance. More importantly, the current study examines the role of service productivity in the research framework and the relationship with CS and firm performance. To verify the roles of CS and SP, this study employs the method of verifying mediating effects suggested by Baron and Kenny (1986).

Figure 1. Conceptual framework

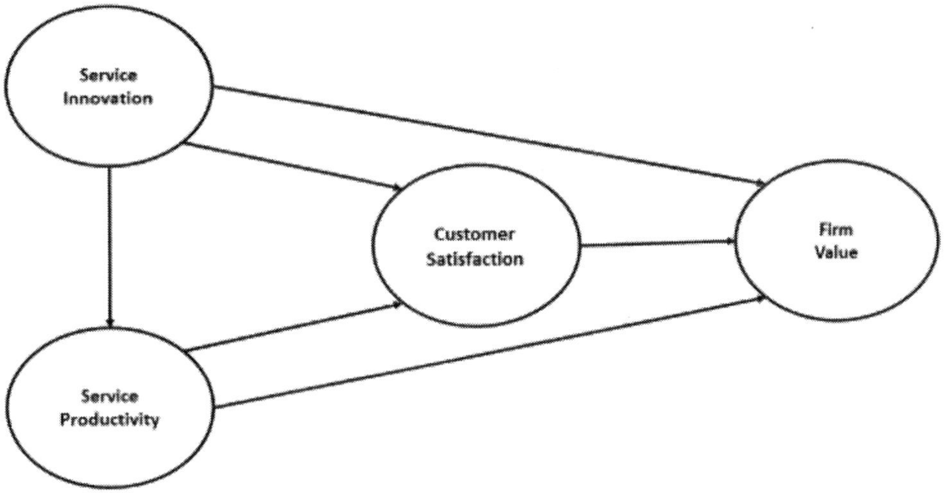

METHODS

Data

For testing the research hypotheses, this study employed secondary data, from COMPUSTAT and the American Customer Satisfaction Index (hereafter ACSI). COMPUSTAT data is about over 30,000 public companies working in the United States and Canada. It is based on the companies' accounting information. ACSI is provided by the University of Michigan, publicly. This index is intended to be representative of the nation's economy as a whole (Fornell et al. 1996). Based on the SIC codes system, the index includes seven major economic sectors, which are manufacturing/non-durable, manufacturing/durables, transportation/communication/utilities, retail, finance/insurance, services, and public administration/government. According to Fornell et al. (1996), each company in the sectors randomly interviews approximately 250 current customers, who already purchased and experienced a product/service of each company. Interviews derive from 48 duplicate national probability samples of households in the U.S. with telephones. There are customer satisfaction evaluations to publicly over 400 companies as the index. With these data sets, therefore, this study started with collecting ACSI, which is 2012 fiscal year data. Then, I matched ACSI with COMPUSTAT to get the sample for this study. After the process of matching data, this study had 127 companies in 2012.

Measurement

To estimate SP, I controlled outliers by winsorizing, which takes care of 1% and 99% outliers of each variable to reduce the impact of extreme values. I also did standardize all variables in the equations to have a mean of 0 and a standard deviation of 1 to ensure direct comparability, following studies by Rao et al. (2004) and Rust & Huang (2012). I first explored possible multicollinearity using ordinal least squares regression analysis (OLS) with return on asset (ROA) as the dependent variable. The VIF statistics are acceptable (see table 1), with a majority of them below 10. Based on the literature reviews of the construct, this study employed the way of Rust and Huang (2012). They suggest the optimal level of SP to investigate the construct under the new trend of technology (automation) in service sectors. The measurement of SP includes four main factors, such as labor wage, profit margin, market concentration, and price per unit. Each indicator has different signs to consist of optimal service productivity (see Rust and Huang, 2012, p.53).

Table 1: The result of SP measurement

Model	Unstd. Coef.		Std. Coef.	t	Sig.	95% conf. int.		Correlations			Collinearity Statistics	
	B	Std.Err.	Beta			Lower Bound	Upper Bound	Zero-order	Partial	Part	Tolerance	VIF
Constant	.120	.001		169.313	0.000	.118	.121					
HHI	.006	.003	.278	2.147	.032	.000	.011	.037	.076	.073	.222	4.532
PROFIT	-.014	.002	-.651	-7.326	.000	-.017	-.010	-.227	-.252	-.249	.146	6.845
WAGE	.006	.001	.266	3.842	.000	.003	.008	-.154	.135	.130	.241	4.151
PRICE	-.011	.003	-.550	-3.724	.000	-.017	-.005	.057	-.131	-.126	.111	8.943

Dependent variable: ROA

To measure SI, this study used the definition of innovation suggested by Hurley and Hult (1998), which is the ability of the organization to adopt or implement new ideas, processes, or products successfully. Many studies in marketing literature are using research and development expenditure of organizations as the indicator of innovation and the effect of innovation (Hurley and Hult, 1998; Kibbeling et al., 2013; Peterson and Jeong, 2010; Padgett and Galan, 2010). Therefore, in this study, innovation is calculated as the expenditure for research and development of each company as presented in COMPUSTAT.

For measuring CS, this study employs ACSI provided by consumer research institute in University of Michigan (Fornell, 1994). The data aims to study the science of customer satisfaction, and includes over 400 companies in the U.S. stock market publicly. By using phone interview with over 70,000 customers who already experienced the product/services for every year, it reports on a 0 to 100 scale. Especially, the stability of this data has been confirmed by using in various studies on CS in marketing disciplines (Anderson et al., 1997; Angelova and Zekiri, 2011; Fornell et al., 1996).

To investigate firm performance, this study follows one of ways to estimate firm performance, which is the way of measuring BE suggested by Simon and Sullivan (1993). Because as the study of Peterson and Jeong (2010), firms' innovation investment directly affects brand value, which is based on brand equity as the knowledge of the customer toward the brand/company. Even though it has been still discussed the suitability of BE to evaluate the ability as BV (Mizik, 2014), many of studies are still using the way of measuring BE with financial data, which is

Tobin's Q ratio (Simon and Sullivan, 1993; Chung and Pruitt, 1994; Torres and Tribo, 2011). Thus, this study employs Tobin's Q to measure BE.

RESULTS

All research hypotheses are supported. The results of the empirical analyses are described as follows, and the findings are summarized in table 2.

SP positively affects firm performance as BE (H1a). This test is about effects and the roles of newly determined service productivity by Rust and Huang (2012). Before their investigation of the new measured SP, SP had negative relationship with customer's attitude and their behavioral variables, such as purchase and satisfaction. Fundamentally even though their finding is limited in the positive relationship between SP and firm performance, the measurement of SP has included service quality and customer participation to increase customers' satisfaction. Thus, this hypothesis is supported by the statistical analysis ($t > 2.515$, $p^* < .013$).

SP positively affects CS (H1b). As noted above, there was negative relationship between SP and CS, because before Rust and Huang's study (2012), SP was estimated by the traditional way of measurement, which is the ratio of output over input (Anderson, Eugene W., Claes Fornell, and Roland T. Rust, 1997). This study initially tested the relationship between CS and the newly defined SP. Thus, the result shows that there is a positive relationship between them, which means the hypothesis is supported ($t > 2.130$, $p^* < .035$).

SI positively affects firm value (BE) (H2a). This investigation strongly supports the study of Dotzel et al. (2013), which argues that SI has a strong positive effect of SI on firm value, or firm performance. The statistical result also advocated by supporting the research hypothesis ($t > 46.122$, $p^* < .000$).

SI positively affects SP (H2b). According to the study of Wakelin (2001), there is a positive relationship between SI and productivity. However, the productivity used in Wakelin' study is examined by the traditional way of measuring SP. Thus, this study initially investigated the relationship between two variables, SI and SP. The statistical result supported the hypothesis ($t > 2.358$, $p^* < .020$).

SI positively affects CS (H2c). Based on the argument of Kibbeling et al. (2013), this hypothesis verified there is a positive relationship between SI and CS ($t > 8.091$, $p^* < .000$). It indicates that the degree of customer satisfaction will be increasing as much as increase in innovativeness of companies in service industry. This result is in the same vail of Menguc and Auh's study (2006) showing that innovativeness contributes to a firm's positional advantage and the competitive advantage as the result, which is positioned by customers.

CS positively affects BE (H3). Customers have played an important role for companies. Keller (1993) insists that knowledge of brand is accumulative and it is evaluated by customers. Therefore, customer who experienced satisfaction in using the brand can build a good image of the brand as one of the important indicators of brand knowledge (Keller, 2003). Thus, this result supports the arguments of previous studies, which is there is a positive relationship between CS and BE with statistical outcomes ($t > 7.897$, $p^* < .000$).

Table 2: Summary of findings

Hypothesis	t-value	p-value	Supported? (Y/N)
H1a: SP → (+) BE	2.515	.013*	Y
H1b: SP → (+) CS	2.130	.035*	Y
H2a: SI → (+) BE	46.122	.000*	Y
H2b: SI → (+) SP	2.538	.020*	Y

H2b: SI → (+) CS	8.091	.000*	Y
H3: CS → (+) BE	7.897	.000*	Y

Note: Sig.* at p < .05

Additional analyses

This study investigates the mediating effects of SP and CS, respectively. To investigate mediating effects of two variables, the study by Baron and Kenny (1986) uses three regression equations, which are from independent variable to mediator, from independent variable to dependent variable, and from mediator to dependent variable. It assumes that there is a significant relation between each variable used in each equation. As the results of table 2, each relation is significant among variables.
SP mediates the relationship between SI and BE. As shown in the table 3, there is still significantly positive relationship between SI and BE. Thus, by the explanation of Baron and Kenny (1986), there is not a mediating effect of SP in the relationship between SI and BE as the results in table 3.
CS mediates the relationship between SI and BE. As Baron and Kenny suggest (1986), to fill with the condition for mediating effect of a variable, all relationships among each variable must be satisfied; it is necessary that there is a statistically significant relationship between variable A (IV) and variable B (DV), variable C (mediator) and variable B (DV), and variable A (IV) and variable C (mediator). Then, when variable C fully mediates between variable A and variable B, it is not statistically significant in the relationship between variable A and variable B. On the other hands, if there is a partially mediating effect of variable C on the relationship between variable A and variable C, there is still a significant relationship between variable A and variable B. Thus, as CS and SI coincidently enter in the multiple regression analysis, CS is not significant any more in the relationship with BE. Thus, it is insisted that CS does not have a mediating effect on the relationship between SI and BE.
CS mediates the relationship between SP and BE. Based on the assumption to examine the mediating effect, this study shows that CS fully mediates the relationship between SI and BE. Because there is still significantly positive relationship between CS and BE, even though it turns in that there is not significant relationship between SP and BE, as the result in table 3.

Table 3: Results of mediating effect test

	β	Std. Error	t-Value	p-Value	Results
SP → BE	.134	.053	2.515	.013*	
SP → CS	.514	.241	2.130	.035*	
CS → BE	.132	.017	7.897	.000*	
CS → (SP & BE)	.115 (CS)	.018	6.432	.000*	CS fully mediated
	.070 (SP)	.046	1.523	.131	
SI → BE	1.049	.023	46.122	.000*	
SI → CS	3.040	.376	8.091	.000*	
CS → BE	.132	.017	7.897	.000*	
CS → (SI & BE)	-.006 (CS)	.007	-.800	.426	CS not mediated
	1.055 (SI)	.035	30.399	.000*	
SI → BE	1.049	.023	46.122	.000*	
SI → SP	.421	.179	2.358	.020*	
SP → BE	.134	.053	2.515	.013*	
SP → (SI & BE)	.012 (SP)	.015	.767	.445	

	1.034 (SI)	.029	35.941	.000*	SP not mediated

Notes: Sig.* at p < .05

DISCUSSIONS AND CONCLUSIONS

This study initially investigated the role of service productivity (SP) and the relationship of SP with customer satisfaction (CS), service innovation (SI), and firm performance (BE). These concepts are important factors in service operation. In particular, to sustainably improve a firm's competiveness and the ability of creating a value with customers, each factor, especially SI and SP, and the effects are very important (Jayaram and Xu, 2015). Traditionally, in marketing literature SP had a negative relationship with CS, because of the measurement issue, which is the ratio of output over input. I has been hard to look for an acute relationship between SP and CS. However, as the arguments of Rust & Huang (2012) and Grönroos & Ojasalo (2004), the concept of SP has to include not only efficiency (operational cost reduction), but also effectiveness (quality of service and the effect on customers). Therefore, this study theoretically contributes to verifying the role of SP and the relationship with CS.

Also, in this study, it is verified that CS has played an important role as a mediator in the relationship between SP and BE. Up to current, the marketing literature has limitedly stated the role of SI and the effect on customers. Peterson and Jeong (2010) argue that companies' marketing action, such as R&D investment, has direct impact on the evaluation of companies' brand. As another point of view, Menguc and Auh (2006) claim that it is possible to increase the effect of innovativeness when firms focus on market orientation, which means "into customers" as a firm's strategy. Thus, this study stands on comprehensive argument because of the findings of this study. In other words, it is that customers play a key role as the results of this study to perform brand equity, even though SI has strongly direct relationship with firm performance, especially brand equity.

As another theoretical contribution, this study arguably and empirically reveals that there is no direct relationship between SP and BE, because CS fully mediates the relationship. In other words, as noted above, customers are the key player or a group who responds and behaves toward marketing actions in market. Thus, it is not viable to obtain the effect of marketing action without any interactions with customers in market (Homburg et al., 2000). Therefore, it is necessary to reestablish the relationship between SP and BE as there is a significant relationship, because the newly defined concept of SP includes both efficiency, which is traditional concept of SP, and effectiveness, which means interactions between companies and customers.

Managerial implications

Firm value would be a central issue or goal among managers who want to increase and improve the performance of companies. Based on the results, this study suggests several managerial ideas or information about the issue, which is to increase and improve firm performance as follows.

- There are many ways to improve firm performance. One of them would be to reduce marketing expenditure (MarketingLeadershipCouncil, 2001). However, as confirmed in this study, marketing expenditure such as innovation has a strongly positive relationship to brand equity as estimated by customers. Thus, reducing an amount of the expenditure for the marketing action would lead to a negative impact on firm performance as evaluated by customers. Therefore, companies need to change their mindset from innovation expenditure to investment. As discussed by Peterson and Jeong (2010), innovation increases the firm's brand value and finally its financial performance.

- Customers are always important for firms, even the firms do focus on B-to-B business platform. The market fundamentally consists of many customers and providers (Hunt, 1976). Therefore, it is not meaningful and impossible to evaluate or estimate firm value and the performance without customers (Keller, 1993). This study shows that customers counteract the effect of operational action or marketing action, such as service productivity. Thus, firms and the managers need to remind themselves of Drucker's statement (1954), "The purpose of business is to create the customer who determines what the business is".
- Finally, both firms and managers must consider how to improve service productivity. As noted above, the concept of SP is not only efficiency, but also effectiveness. These concepts play an important role in service operation. The traditional way of thinking on this concept only focused on efficiency, which means how to produce products without any waste of time and resources (Taylor F. W., 1988). However, service means utility that is from consumption of product/service and interaction between users (clients) and providers. Thus, it is essential for firms and managers in service sectors to increase the level of customer satisfaction, or customer's utility through optimizing SP.

Limitations and further research

This study has several limitations. First of all, it would have needed to see the difference between service and non-service, in terms of how each variable works in the research model. Thus, for the future research, it would be recommended that one intends to find the difference between service companies and non-service companies. Another limitation is that this study should have investigated the timely effect of each variable. This study used one-year data. Thus, if one is interested, it is another recommendation to examine the time effect or changes in each variable by using time series analysis. Lastly, this study only focused on secondary data to analyze the role and effects of each variable. However, if this study looked at the role and effects by using another type of data, primary data, it would have been more fruitful and meaningful research for service marketing literature.

REFERENCES

Aaker, David A. & Robert Jacobson. (1994). The financial information content of percevied quality. *Journal of Marketing*, 191-204.

Anderson, Eugen W. & Mary W. Sullivan. (1993). The antecedents and consequences of customer satisfaction for firms. *Marketing Science*, 125-143.

Anderson, Eugene W., Claes Fornell, & Roland T. Rust. (1997). Customer satisfaction, productivity, and profitbaility: Differences between goods and services. *Marketing Science*, 129-145.

Anderson, Rolph E. & Srinivasan Swaminathan. (2011). Customer satisfaction and loylaty in e-markets: a PLS path modeling approach. *Journal of Marketing Theory and Practice*, 221-234.

Angelova, Biljana & Jusuf Zekiri. (2011). Meassuring customer satisfaction with service quality using American Customer Satisfaction Model (ACSI model). *Interntional Journal of Academic Research in Business and Social Sciences*, 232-258.

Baron, Rueben M. & David A. Kenny. (1986). the moderator-mediator variable distinction in social pyschological research: concpetual, strategic, and statistical considerations. *Journal of Personality and Social Psychology*, 1173-1182.

Boulding, William, Ajay Kalra, Richard Staelin, & Valarie A. Zeithaml. (1993). A dynamic process model of service qaulity: from expectations to behvaioral intention. *Journal of Marketing Research*, 7-27.

Choi, K., D. Lee, & D.L. Olson. (2015). Service quality and productivity in the U.S. airline industry: a service quality-adjusted DEA model. *Service Business*, 137-160.

Chung, Kee H., & Stephen W. Pruitt. (1994). A simple approximation of Tobin'q. *Financial Management*, 70-74.

Cronin, J. Joseph & Steven A. Taylor. (1992). Measuring service quality: A reexamination and extension. *Journal of Marketing*, 55-68.

Crosby, P. (1979). *Quality is free.* New York, NY: McGraw-Hill.

Deming, W. (1982). *Quality, prodcutivity, and competitive position.* Cambridge, MA: MIT Center for Advanced Engineering Study.

Donbi, Dawn, J.R. Brent Ritchie, & Wilf Zebre. (2000). Organizational values: the inside view of service prodcutivity. *Journal of Buseinss Research*, 91-107.

Dotzel, Thomas, Venkatesh Shankar, & Leonard Berry. (2013). Service innovativeness and firm value. *Journal of Marketing Science*, 259-276.

Drucker, P. (1954). *The practice of management.* New York, NY: Harper & Row Publishers.

Fililatrault, Pierre, Jean Harvey, & Jean-Charles Chebat. (1996). Service quality and service prodcutivity management practices. *Industrial Marketing Management*, 243-255.

Fornell, Claes, Michael D. Johnson, Eugene W. Anderson, Jaesung Cha, & Barbara Everitt Bryant. (1996). The American Customer Satisfaction Index: Nature, Purpose, and Findings. *Journal of Marketing*, 7-18.

Grönroos, Christtian & Katri Ojasalo. (2004). Service prodcutivity towards a conceptualization of the tansformation of inputs into economic results in services. *Journal of Business Research*, 414-423.

Hair, Joseph. G. Tomas M. Hult, Christian M. Rngle, & Marko Sarstedt. (2014). *A primer on partial least squares structural equation modeling (PLS-SEM).* Thousand Oaks, CA: SAGE Publications, Inc.

Helms, Marilyn M. & Donna T. Mayo. (2008). Assessing poor quality service: perceptions of customer serivce representatives. *Managing Service Quality*, 610-622.

Homburg, Christian, John P. Workman, & Ove Jensen. (2000). Fundamental changes in marketing organization: The movement towrad a customer-focused organizational structure. *Journal of the Academy of Marketing Science*, 459-478.

Hunt, S. D. (1976). The nature and scope of marketing. *Journal of Marketing*, 17-28.

Hurley, R.F. & G. T. M. Hult. (1998). Innovation, market orientation, and organizational learning: an integration and empricial exmamination. *Journal of Marketing*, 42-54.

Jayaram, Jayanth & Kefeng Xu . (2015). Determinants of quality and efficiency performance in service operations. *International Journal of Operations & Prodcution Management*, 265-285.

Johnson, Michael D. & Claes Fornell. (1991). A framework for comparing customer satisfaction across individuals and product categories. *Journal of Economic Psychology*, 267-286.

Johnston, R. (1995). The zone of tolerance: exploring the relationship between service transactions and satisfaction with the overall service. *International Jouranl of Service Industry Management*, 46-61.

Johnston, Robert & Peter Jones. (2004). Service Productivity: towards understanding the relatoinship between operational and customer prodcutivity. *International Jouranl of Productivity and Performance Management*, 201-213.

Keller, K. L. (1993). Conceptualizing, measuring, and managing customer-based brand equity. *Journal of Marketing*, 1-22.

Keller, K. L. (2003). Brand synthesis: The multidimensionality of brand knowledge. *Journal of Consumer Research*, 595-600.

Kibbeling, Mirjam, Hans van der Bij, & Arjan van Weele. (2013). Market orientation and innovativeness in supply chaines: Supplier's impact on customer satisfaction. *Journal of Product Innovation Management*, 500-515.

Kotler, P. (1991). *Marketing management - analysis, planning, implementation and contorl.* Englewood Cliffs, NJ: Prentice-Hall, Inc.

Looy, Bart Van, Paul Gemmel, Steven Desmet, Roland Van Dierdonck, & Steven Serneels. (1998). Dealinig with prodcutivity and quality indicators in a service environment: some field experiences. *International Journal of Service Industry Management*, 359-376.

Luo, Xueming & C.B. Bhattacharya. (2006). Corporate social responsibility, customer satisfaction, and market value. *Journal of Marketing* , 1-18.

Mark, J. A. (1982). Measuring prodcutivity in service industries. *Monthly Labor Review*, 3-8.

MarketingLeadershipCouncil. (2001). *Stwerading the brand for profitable growth.* Washinton DC: Corporate Executive Board, Marketing Leadership Council.

McLaughlin, Curtis P. & Sydney Coffey. (1990). Measuring prodcutivity in services. *International Journal of Service Industry Management*, 46-64.

Menguc, Bulent & Seigyung Auh. (2006). Creating a firm-level dynamic capability through capitalizing on market orientation and innovativeness. *Journal of the Academy of Marketing Science*, 63-73.

Mizik, N. (2014). Assessing the total financial performance impact of brand equity with limited time series data. *Journal of Marketing Research*, 691-706.

Padgett, Robert C. & Jose I. Galan. (2010). The effect of R&D intensity on corporate social responsibility. *Jounral of Business Ethics*, 407-418.

Parasuraman, A., Leonard L. Berry, & Valarie A. Zeithaml. (1991). Refinement and reassessment of the SERVQUAL scale. *Journal of Retailing*, 420-450.

Parasuraman, A., Leonard L. Berry, & Valarie A. Zeithaml. (1993). More on improving service quality measurment. *Journal of Retailing*, 140-147.

Parasuraman, A., Leonard L. Berry, & Valarie A. Zeithaml. (1988). SERVQUAL: a multiple-item scale for measuring customer perceptoins of service quality. *Journal of Retailing*, 12-40.

Parasuraman, A., Valarie L. Zeithaml, & Leonard L. Berry. (1985). A conceptual model of service quality and its implications for future research. *Journal of Marketing*, 41-50.

Peterson, Robert A. & Jaeseok Jeong. (2010). Exploring the impact of advertising and R&D expenditures on corporate brand value and firm-level financial performance. *Journal of the Academy of Marketing Science*, 677-690.

Rao, Vithala R., Manoj K. Agarwal, & Denise Dahlhoff . (2004). How is manifest branding strategy related to the intangible value of a corporation? *Journal of Marketing*, 126-141.

Rice, F. (1990). How to deal with tougher customers. *fortune*, 38-48.

Rust, Roland T. & Ming-Hui Huang. (2012). Optimizing service productivity. *Journal of Marketing* , 47-66.

Rust, Roland T., Anthony J. Zahoirk, & Timoty L. Keiningham . (1995). Return on Quality (ROQ): making service quality financially accountable. *Journal of Marketing*, 58-70.

Rust, Roland T., Crhistine Moorman, & Peter R. Dickson. (2002). Getting return of quality: revenue expansion, csot reduction, or both? *Journal of Marketing*, 7-24.

Rust, Ronlad T. & Anthony J. Zahorik. (1993). Customer satisfaction, customer retention and market share. *Journal of Retialing*, 193-215.

Schmenner, R. W. (2004). Service business and productivity. *Decision Sciences*, 333-347.

Simon, Carol J. & Mary W. Sullivan. (1993). The measurment and dterminants of brand equity: A financial approach. *Marketing Science*, 28-52.

Sorescu, Alina B. & Jelena Spanjol. (2008). Innovation's effect on firm value and risk: Insights from customer packaged goods. *Journal of Marketing*, 114-132.

Szymanski, David M. & David H. Henard. (2001). A meta-analysis of the empirical evidence. *Journal of the Academy of Marketing Science*, 16-35.

Taylor, F. W. (1988). *The principles of scientific management.* Mineola, NY: Dover Publicaitons, Inc.

Torres, Anna & Josep A. Tribo. (2011). Customer satisfaction and brand equity. *Journal of Busienss Research*, 1089-1096.

Vargo, Stephen L. & Robert F. Lusch. (2004). Evolving to a new dominant logic for marketing. *Journal of Marketing* , 1-17.

Vargo, Stephen L. & Robert F. Lusch. (2008). Service-dominant logic: continuing the evolution. *Journal of the Academic of Marketing Science*, 1-10.

Vivek, Shiri D., Sharon E. Beatty, & Robert M. Morgan. (2012). Customer engagement: exploring customer relatoinships beyond purchase. *Journal of Marekting Theory and Practice*, 127-145.

Wakelin, K. (2001). Prodcutivity growth and R&D expenditure in UK manufacturing firms. *Research Policy*, 1079-1090.

Zeithaml, V. A. (2000). Service quality, profitability, and the economic worth of customers: what we know and what we need to learn. *Journal of the Academy of Marketing Science*, 67-85.

DECISION SCIENCES INSTITUTE

Artificial reef structure and material deployment decisions: A big data analytics exercise on presence and abundance of reef fish

Steven P. Coy, Ph.D.
Department of Management, Marketing and Business Administration
University of Houston-Downtown
326 N. Main Street
Houston, Texas 77002, USA
coys@uhd.edu
01+ 713-222-5358

Margaret F. Shipley, Ph.D.
Department of Management, Marketing and Business Administration
University of Houston-Downtown
326 N. Main Street
Houston, Texas 77002, USA
shipleym@uhd.edu
01+ 713-221-8571

J. Brooke Shipley, Ph.D.
Texas Parks and Wildlife Department
Coastal Fisheries - Artificial Reef Program
1502 F.M. 517 East
Dickinson, Texas 77539, USA
Brooke.Shipley@tpwd.texas.gov
01+ 281-534-0100

ABSTRACT

The benefit of artificial reefs appears to be accepted. Yet the benefit of differing structures to fish populations remains unknown. Accepting that uncertainty exits in the accumulation of data by visual monitoring, researchers have amassed a large database on species and abundance of fish at artificial reefs in the Northwestern Gulf of Mexico shelf. Big data analytics techniques were employed across this lengthy study with preliminary results suggesting that artificial reef structure impacts the presence of different fish species. This analysis addresses the decisions of the Texas artificial reef program and informs the larger debate on productivity of artificial reefs.

KEYWORDS: Business Analytics, Ecological Decision Making, Artificial Reefs, Fisheries Management

INTRODUCTION

Given continuing discussion regarding the location and optimal spacing of artificial reefs, the research objective was to analyze the Northwestern Gulf of Mexico (GOM) Shelf off the Texas Coast using data on fish abundance on differing artificial reef structures to suggest whether reef structure impacted the presence of individual species and, by extension, fish biomass. If indeed, some artificial reef structures were more likely to be associated with fish populations, other variables such as water depth associated with certain structures might be contributory. The results of this analysis can both aid decision making in a fisheries context and inform the discussion on artificial reef habitats.

Though artificial reef deployment continues in the GOM and indeed, worldwide in an effort to sustain reef fish, only recently has research been conducted to determine the program's success. Prior to this, it was generally determined that while artificial reefs had the potential to meet the program's objectives for presence of fish at structures used as artificial reefs, ongoing monitoring and management were paramount to determination of success (Baine, 2001). The study presented herein attempts to more quantitatively analyze the large monitoring dataset to enhance better fisheries management decisions with respect to artificial reef deployment.

LITERATURE REVIEW

Literature Review of Artificial Reefs to Fish Populations

The Goal and Objectives for the Artificial Reef Plan G sets forth the directive of the Seventy-first Texas Legislature to The Texas Parks and Wildlife Department (TPWD) to "promote, develop, maintain, monitor, and enhance the artificial reef potential in state waters and federal waters adjacent to Texas to enhance fishery resources and commercial and recreational fishing opportunities." Enhancement of fishery resources is considered to be the restoration or creation of habitat to improve recruitment and spawning potential of reef associated species. "An artificial reef covered under this Plan must be sited, constructed, maintained, monitored, and managed in a manner that uses the best scientific information available" (Stephan et al., 1990).

The Texas Parks and Wildlife Department in its TPW magazine (June 2014) reported that through its funding, divers from the Harte Research Institute (HRI) conducted a two-year study to address the ongoing debate of whether artificial reefs increase productivity in terms of the number of fish or serve merely as gathering points for existing fish and other species. The premise was that since the seafloor along the Texas coast has very little natural structure habitat, then if artificial reefs increase production, Gulf fisheries will be healthier. Results thus far show biodiversity on artificial reefs equal to or exceeding that on natural banks. Specific results for red snapper show that fish on natural and artificial reefs are larger than those on standing platforms and that snapper species accounted for 26 percent of the total fish abundance at sites surveyed in 2012. (http://tpwmagazine.com/archive/2014/jun/ed_2_reefs/)

Artificial reefs have been attributed to improved sport and commercial fisheries (Gallway et al., and 2009; Bohnsack & Sutherland, 1985) and since anglers typically desire larger fishes, information is needed because of current debates regarding the role of artificial reefs in the life cycle of red snapper (*Lutjanus campechanus*), especially considering its overfished status in the Gulf of Mexico (GOM) since the 1980s (Cowan et al., 2010; Diamond et al., 2007). Early in life, red snapper utilize low-relief, rubble-shell habitats moving to nearshore reefs (Gallaway et al., 2009), and later to deeper reefs, such as oil platforms, rock outcroppings and larger artificial reefs (Gallaway et al., 2009; Gazey et al., 2008). Thus, artificial reef complexity and size may be important factors influencing the age and size of red snapper over different reef structures.

The impact of different artificial reef structures raises the important decision of rigs-to-reefs (RTR) in the dialog of artificial reef deployment. Uncertainty has surrounded the use of decommissioned oil rigs as a tool to offset declines in fish populations, including the commercially valuable, but overfished red snapper. The National Fishing Enhancement Act (NFEA), that authorized this program requires the "best scientific information available" (BS IA), which according to one law review will be sufficient such that it will be unlikely for a court to provide pressure on agencies accumulating such information (McQueen-Borden, 2013). A very recent study continues the gathering of information and scientific data on offshore platforms as artificial reefs regarding the effect of depth and distance from shore environmental variables which are concluded to influence species assemblages significantly (van der Stap et al., 2016).

In line with consideration of concrete reef structures and rigs-to-reefs, sunken vessels have been used as artificial reef structures, but again, the effect of the latter in reef fish communities remains unknown. Though, the results of one study indicate that increases in vessels as artificial reef habitats may affect the relative abundances of particular species (Fowler & Booth, 2012b). Unlike the RTR program where structures are in place, concrete reefs hold high fish diversity (Moffitt et al., 1989) and allow different patterns or random deployment in an area (Lukens et al, 2004; Baine, 2001).

Again, considering the bioenergetics of red snapper, it has been determined that optimal artificial reef spacing should be between 0.50 and 0.95 km such that no more than 2 fit within a 1 km^2 area (Shipley & Cowan, 2010; Shipley & Shipley, 2009), based on artificial reef clumping or blocking for optimal fish foraging and consumption. Yet, a more recent study investigated fish population dynamics on natural reefs, bare areas and varying culvert patch density of 1-190 culverts in an artificial reef system. Using the same economically valuable, red snapper studied off the Texas Coast at Port Mansfield, it was noted that though abundance did not differ according to density categories, mean total lengths were greatest at lower density suggesting that 71-120 culverts be deployed in a 30-m radius (Froehlich & Kline, 2015).

Size and age of red snapper with age of artificial reefs in the Alabama Gulf of Mexico waters south of Mobile Bay showed that the mean age of red snapper at a particular reef was not related to depth or distance to other reefs. With a positive correlation between mean age of red snapper and age of the reef, it was estimated that artificial reefs enhance production of red snapper (Syc & Szedlmayer, 2012). Furthermore, young (age 2) red snapper appear to dominate artificial reef populations suggesting the positive aspect to fisheries through the establishment of significant numbers of artificial reefs (Gallaway et al., 2009).

Thus with differing results and conclusions, artificial reef placement at varying depths may or may not affect production of fish species when considering naturally wide depth ranges. Indeed, even when artificial reefs are of similar size and shape, populations can develop with different demographics. While the majority of the studies are concerned with the overfished red snapper albeit at differing life stages, the fact that small reef fish can be sustained on artificial reefs is conclusive (Fowler & Booth, 2012a).

Given the data accumulated by TPWD and HRI by surveys conducted between 2012 and 2013 with data on hydrographic variables and type of reef structure in the same artificial reef environment of the Northwestern Gulf of Mexico Shelf a recent study compiled the data from 59 fish species into 19 family groupings at 12 artificial reef sites and 2 platforms plus a vessel (Ajemian et al., 2015). Mean species richness showed more representation on toppled and cutoff rigs. This study then focused its analysis to the five federally managed fisheries species in the GOM, snapper, triggerfish and amberjack, where like the literature cited above, red snapper was used to determine that while there was no significant differences in red snapper catch per unit effort (CPUE) among the different structures at the different sites, structure type did influence mean total length and biomass. It was suggested that the conversion of standing platforms into artificial reefs could significantly alter fish community structure with standing platforms that should be retained by the upright orientation and relatively vertical relief of the structure. For the frequently studied red snapper, no strong evidence was discovered that structure type affects abundance, biomass or mean total length on the rigs-to-reefs structures. Bottom depth, though recognized as having a role in fish assemblages in natural habitats continues to be less known as to impact on artificial reef assemblages (Ajemian et al., 2015). Of importance, is the call for further investigation of this region which is supported by the considerably large dataset accumulated by TPWD and which could provide evidence of reef structure impact on multiple fish species more so than artificial reef data examined in previous studies.

Literature Review of Knowledge and Data

Previously, knowledge-based systems and uncertainty problems in ecological research have been limited due to the difficulty in acquiring knowledge that can be suitably structured and formalized as well as the essential problem that uncertainty exists in expert knowledge and ecological data. Such uncertainty stems from inaccuracy of data, inaccuracy of interpolation methods and unreliability of measurement tools as well as the fact that some measurements are not possible. For example, the number of fish in a lake can be approximated, but is not quantifiable without allowances for error (Salski, 1992). In an ecological investigation, perfect knowledge is rarely, if ever, available since natural systems do not conform to crisp definitions (Mackinson et al., 1999; Mackinson, 2000). As detailed in the studies conducted, primarily on red snapper in GOM waters, the benefit of artificial reefs appears to be agreed upon, yet the benefit of differing structures to fish populations is still unknown as is distances and depths of the structures.

THEORETICAL DEVELOPMENT/MODEL

Accepting that uncertainty does exist in the accumulation of data gathered by visual monitoring and that further investigation of reef structure to fish populations based on environmental aspects, including, depth, remains a point for discussion in fisheries management, the following methods were utilized to address this big data analytics problem.

Data Accumulation Methods

The TPWD biological monitoring program seeks to establish baseline data and fish community composition at each artificial reef site using standard fish census methods. Each site is evaluated post-deployment for fish species, abundance at predetermined depths, and total abundance. Every attempt is made to survey the reef sites quarterly if possible with fish species, abundance, and size evaluated to determine seasonal changes in fish use at each site. A variety of gears have been used for sampling reef systems and include submersibles (Barans, 1982; Shipp et al., 1986), remotely operated vehicles (ROV; Barans, 1982), fisheries acoustics (FAS; Barans, 1982; Gledhill et al., 1996; Gledhill, 2001), fish traps, long-lines, trawls, gill nets, and hook-and-line (Barans, 1982; Haynes, 1990). Each gear has some advantages and disadvantages in terms of selectivity, sampling bias, logistics and cost. However, most surveys of reef fishes employ some visual technique using divers, cameras, submersibles or ROVs (Jones & Thompson, 1978; Sale & Douglas, 1981; Kimmel, 1985; Bohnsack & Bannerot,1986; Bortone et al., 1986; Shipp et al., 1986; Thresher & Gunn, 1986; McCormick & Choat, 1987; Bortone et al., 1989; Bortone et al., 1991; Ellis & DeMartini, 1994; Parker et al. 1994).
SCUBA diving has been the primary method of conducting research within the Artificial Reef Program. Diving projects have been executed by a core team comprised of TPWD staff with the assistance of volunteer divers from universities and other agencies. Diving conditions have varied greatly within the reef site with visibility ranging from zero to over 150 ft.

For each survey conducted, divers swam randomly around the dive location within the reef site and recorded the species present and their relative abundance at each reef site or individual structure within a reef site. Fish were accurately identified to their lowest taxonomic division. Fish were not identified to species unless the fish could be identified accurately. Juvenile fish of a species were designated as such. Fry or fish too small to be identified were recorded under a generic juvenile fish heading. Fish abundance was recorded as: Single(S) =1; Few (F) = 2-10; Many (M) = 11-100 and Abundant (A) = 100+. Environmental characteristics of the water column were conducted to examine any connection between water quality and the biotic that exist in the regions. At each sampling site, a Data Sonde was lowered into the water column and collected data related to dissolved oxygen, pH, salinity, conductivity, water depth, and water temperature.

The structures by which each fish sighting was evaluated were categorized into different reef materials including: Fly-ash blocks, Vessels, Concrete utility poles, concrete culverts, wellheads, reef balls, oil and gas jackets, and fabricated structures. The Reef Site Aliases yielded the types of structures being deployed as artificial reefs in the Texas Coast GOM: Liberty Ship, Standing, Base, Toppled, Top, Reef Balls, Navy Barge, Base and Top, Top, Towed and Toppled, Pile-Based, Texas Clipper, Deck (oil Rig), Culverts (as of 2007) and Oil and Gas Jackets (as of 2013). These were then combined into general structure materials and deployment methods as: Concrete, Culverts, Fabricated, Oil-Gas Component, Oil-Gas Jacket, Reef Balls, Vessel, Accidental Sinking, Partial Removal, Surface Deployed, Toppled, Towed and Towed then Sunk. Data categories of sightings and type of structure are in Table 1 below.
While water depths (ft.) were noted for each sighting, these ranged from a minimum of 10 feet to a maximum of 180 feet with the majority of those beyond 120 being observed in July and August 2013. The mode of recording sightings was stated as Roving (roving diver) except for May through September 2012 when the method was stated as Stationary (as given in Bohnsack & Bannerot, 1986).

The database for consideration in the study reported herein, thus, included 1248 surveys from 1993 to 2014 although sighting numbers varied. Overall, the dataset included a total of over 240 thousand observations.

ANALYSIS & RESULTS

The presence and abundance of 193 different species or groups of species of fish were recorded in each survey. Variables relevant for this analysis were survey number, survey date, site, structure material type, survey depth, water clarity, species or species grouping, and abundance. Abundance was estimated according to several categories: zero, one, few (2-10), many 11-99, and abundant (100+).Two dependent variables were explored in the first stage of this big data analytics problem: Abundance recorded as an ordinal from 0 – 4 with 0 = zero to 4 = abundant, and Presence recorded as a binary variable with 0 = zero and 1 = one or more sighted. The data were particularly sparse. Nearly 210 thousand of these observations (87%) were zero.

Correlation Analysis

Several rounds of correlation analysis were conducted. For this analysis, structure material type was represented as a group of indicator variables. These variables were correlated with Species Abundance and Presence. In addition, partial correlations were conducted using depth and water clarity as control variables.

Table 1: Surveys by Years, Months, Sightings and Structure(s)

Year	Months	No. of sightings	Structure
1993	July	1	Liberty Ship and Ash blocks
1995	June-Sept.	10	Liberty Ship
1996	Aug.-Oct.	5	Mixed
1997	May-Sept.	5	Mostly vessels
1998	Aug.	14	Base, Toppled, Top and Standing
1999	July-Sept.	14	Liberty Ship, Barge, Reef balls, Base, Base + Top, Top, Standing
2000	June-Oct.	29	Liberty Ship, Barge, Base, Base + Top
2001	Feb.-Nov.	146	Base, Base + Top, Top, Standing, Liberty Ship, Coal-ash blocks, Deck, Barge
2002	April-Oct.	91	Standing, Base, Liberty Ship (Star Reef), Toppled, Towed and Toppled
2003	June-Oct.	66	Standing, Base, Base + Top, Towed and Toppled, Base, Top,
2004	Feb.-Sept.	84	Texas Clipper, Standing, Base, Deck, Barge, Liberty Ship,
2005	May-Sept.	47	Standing, Toppled, Base + Top, Top, Base,
2006	June	62	Standing, Base, Toppled, Liberty Ship (Star Reef),
2007	Aug.-Sept.	7	Texas Clipper and Culverts
2008	Jan.-Nov.	9	Vessels
2009	May- Nov.	11	Vessels
2011	June- Oct.	186	Mostly Standing or Base; vessel in Sept.
2012	Mar.-Sept.	145	Texas Clipper, Liberty Ship, -- mostly Base or Standing
2013	June-Dec.	164	Oil and Gas Jacket, Culverts, Texas Clipper—mostly Base, Toppled and Standing
2014	June-Oct.	209	Oil and Gas Jacket, Toppled, Texas Clipper, Liberty Ship, Base, Standing

The results of the correlation analysis were inconclusive. Although a few species had modest significant correlation with one or the other of the dependent variables, there was not enough consistency across species to conclude that Abundance or Presence of species in general were highly correlated with structure material type. Furthermore, partial correlations were not helpful in this analysis. No conclusion could be reached as to the correlation of water depth to Abundance and Presence.

Cross Tabulation Analysis

Given the failure of the correlation analysis, other data analytics tools were used to try to explain the relationship of species and reef structure. Since the abundance measures are categories, cross tabulations were created to learn more about these relationships. This analysis is ongoing as of the writing of this paper, but some encouraging preliminary results suggest that there is a relationship between species and reef structure type.

Crosstab analysis and Chi -square tests of significance are hampered by sparsity. So, the data were partitioned by narrowing the list of species to the top 30 in terms of sighting frequency and by combining related structure material types to a manageable five categories. Fabricated material was combined with reef balls, and groups of concrete utility poles, concrete culverts and various discarded oil and gas components were combined into the Other category.

Table 2: Chi-squared tests of significance

Chi-Square Tests

	Value	df	Asymp. Sig. (2-sided)
Pearson Chi-Square	807.509[a]	116	.000
Likelihood Ratio	795.660	116	.000
N of Valid Cases	12836		

a. 11 cells (7.3%) have expected count less than 5. The minimum expected count is 3.17.

Similarly, a simple species presence variable for the dependent variable rather than abundance, avoided the usage of multi-level crosstabs.

Cell counts, expected counts and adjusted standardized residuals were recorded for each species and structure type. For this analysis, adjusted standardized residuals were assumed to be asymptotically normal with mean equal to zero and variance equal to one. If the absolute value of this measure was greater than or equal to two, the null hypothesis that the observed and expected count were equal was rejected (at $\alpha = 0.05$, an adjusted standardized residual greater than or equal to two is significant; see Agresti (1984) for details).

The results of the Chi-square significance test are shown below. The p-value was zero at three decimal places, which suggests that at least some fish are more likely than expected to frequent one type of reef structure more than another.

The Chi-square statics provided support to this study's objective of whether particular reef structures contributed to fish presence according to the partitioned species and structure categories for which sufficient data were available. (Results of the cross-tabulations are shown in Table 3.) The observed counts of most species were significantly different than their corresponding expected counts on at least one of the structure types. Fabricated and reef balls has a higher significant amount of shark species present; oil and gas jackets of 3-4 piles also had shark species likely but also Atlantic Spadefish; oil and gas jackets of 6-12 piles had more likelihood of Bermuda Chub being present and vessels, though not as strongly supported, showed Crevalle Jack as most abundant. The Other category had no such significant presence on any of the 30 species reported most often in the surveys. In addition, over half of the species have significantly different observed counts on two or more categories. For example, Almaco Jack was more likely to frequent large oil and gas jackets than fabricated reefs or sunken vessels. Atlantic Spadefish, on the other hand, was more likely around fabricated or smaller oil and gas jackets rather than larger oil and gas jackets. Shark species greatly preferred the fabricated and reef balls as well as the oil and gas jackets containing 3-4 piles and were significantly unlikely to be at the 6-12 pile oil and gas jackets. Similarly, though Trumpetfish preferred the oil and gas jackets of 3-4 piles, they were highly unlikely to be present at oil and gas jackets of 6-12 piles. Goldentail Moray also showed the preference for the smaller oil and gas jackets as did the Redband Parrotfish and Spanish Mackerel, while Gray Angelfish and the Hawksbill Sea Turtle had the reverse preferences.

.

Table 3: Cross tabulation of top 30 species to general reef structure. O is observed count, E is expected count, and R is the adjusted standardized residual.

	Fabricated & Reef Balls			Oil & Gas Jacket (3-4 Piles)			Oil & Gas Jacket (6-12 Piles)			Vessel			Other			
Species/groups	**O**	**E**	**R**	**O**	**E**	**R**	**O**	**E**	**R**	**O**	**E**	**R**	**O**	**E**	**R**	**Total**
Almaco Jack	2	8.8	-2.4*	125	140.0	-1.5	308	278.9	2.8*	19	28.0	-1.8	17	15.3	0.5	471
Atlantic Creolefish	2	12.0	-3.0*	150	191.7	-3.7*	422	382.0	3.3*	47	38.4	1.5	24	20.9	0.7	645
Atlantic Spadefish	17	7.3	3.7*	173	116.8	6.3*	166	232.8	-7.0*	26	23.4	0.6	11	12.7	-0.5	393
Bermuda Chub	1	7.8	-2.5*	80	124.5	-4.8*	319	248.1	7.2*	16	24.9	-1.9	3	13.6	-3.0*	419
Bicolor Damselfish	0	3.2	-1.8	31	50.5	-3.3*	125	100.7	3.8*	9	10.1	-0.4	5	5.5	-0.2	170
Blue Angelfish	15	11.7	1.0	214	187.5	2.4*	339	373.7	-2.9*	44	37.6	1.1	19	20.4	-0.3	631
Bluehead	13	11.5	0.5	177	182.8	-0.5	371	364.2	0.6	37	36.6	0.1	17	19.9	-0.7	615
Blue Tang	4	9.7	-1.9	119	154.3	-3.5*	356	307.4	4.4*	25	30.9	-1.1	15	16.8	-0.5	519
Brown Chromis	0	3.2	-1.8	30	51.1	-3.5*	135	101.9	5.2*	6	10.2	-1.4	1	5.6	-2.0*	172
Cobia	2	3.2	-0.7	58	51.4	1.1	102	102.5	-0.1	6	10.3	-1.4	5	5.6	-0.3	173
Cocoa Damselfish	14	11.8	0.6	163	189.0	-2.3*	415	376.7	3.2*	29	37.9	-1.5	15	20.6	-1.3	636
Crevalle Jack	4	7.2	-1.2	105	114.7	-1.1	212	228.6	-1.7	47	23.0	5.2*	18	12.5	1.6	386
Goldentail Moray	13	12.3	0.2	238	197.1	3.6*	332	392.7	-4.9*	55	39.5	2.6*	25	21.5	0.8	663
Goldface Toby	17	8.7	2.9*	185	138.2	4.8*	236	275.4	-3.8*	13	27.7	-2.9*	14	15.1	-0.3	465
Gray Angelfish	1	4.0	-1.5	45	64.2	-2.9*	154	127.9	3.6*	11	12.9	-0.5	5	7.0	-0.8	216
Graysby	9	10.5	-0.5	174	167.0	0.7	339	332.8	0.5	25	33.5	-1.5	15	18.2	-0.8	562
Gray Triggerfish	12	11.3	0.2	189	180.1	0.8	337	358.9	-1.9	48	36.1	2.1*	20	19.6	0.1	606
Hawksbill Sea Turtle	0	4.4	-2.1*	35	70.7	-5.1*	166	141.0	3.3*	20	14.2	1.6	17	7.7	3.4*	238
Porkfish	4	3.5	0.3	65	55.9	1.5	106	111.3	-0.8	8	11.2	-1.0	5	6.1	-0.5	188
Queen Angelfish	0	3.3	-1.8	43	52.6	-1.6	107	104.8	0.3	20	10.5	3.0*	7	5.7	0.5	177
Redband Parrotfish	17	11.0	1.9	223	175.4	4.4*	298	349.4	-4.4*	25	35.1	-1.8	27	19.1	1.9	590
Reef Butterflyfish	14	14.4	-0.1	236	229.4	0.5	459	457.2	0.1	35	45.9	-1.7	28	25.0	0.6	772
Scamp	9	9.0	0.0	144	143.3	0.1	293	285.5	0.7	21	28.7	-1.5	15	15.6	-0.2	482
Schoolmaster	1	7.6	-2.5*	69	121.9	-5.8*	299	242.8	5.7*	25	24.4	0.1	16	13.3	0.8	410
Shark Species	17	3.2	7.8*	97	51.7	7.6*	38	103.0	-10.1*	14	10.4	1.2	8	5.6	1.0	174
Slippery Dick	12	3.3	4.9*	34	52.6	-3.1*	115	104.8	1.6	7	10.5	-1.1	9	5.7	1.4	177
Soapfish	10	15.5	-1.5	234	247.0	-1.0	516	492.2	1.7	54	49.5	0.7	17	26.9	-2.0*	831
Spanish Mackerel	13	4.2	4.4*	100	67.2	4.8*	98	133.8	-4.9*	9	13.5	-1.3	6	7.3	-0.5	226
Spanish Sardine	1	10.6	-3.1*	162	169.7	-0.7	350	338.2	1.0	40	34.0	1.1	18	18.5	-0.1	571
Trumpetfish	15	4.8	4.7*	117	76.7	5.5*	89	152.8	-8.2*	23	15.4	2.0*	14	8.4	2.0*	258
Total	239	239		3815	3815		7602	7602		764	764		416	416		12,836

*Significant at the 0.05 level or better

DISCUSSION AND DIRECTIONS FOR FUTURE RESEARCH

Some of these results (see Table 3) could certainly be based on the hydrographic variables including water depth. At this time, the big data analytics problem investigated in this study can neither prove nor disprove the effects of the variables at each of the structures. What these results do provide, however, are conclusive evidence to inform the discussion of reef structure materials and the Rigs-to-Reefs initiatives using the "best scientific information available" at this time over the 20-year range of the TPWD's dataset.

While particularly challenging analytically, the data from this survey have many unique attributes that will provide material for several forthcoming articles. The summary data in Table 3, for example, are particularly rich. The results of this analysis suggest that type of reef structure does have an impact on fish presence. Furthermore, it is clear that some species prefer larger structures over smaller ones, which should be particularly valuable to fisheries managers. What is unclear from this research, thus far, is how reef structures affect the five managed species, including the commercially and recreational valuable, though overfished, red snapper so prevalent in fisheries management studies especially those related to artificial reef deployments, which are less frequently sighted than the top 30 sighted species shown here.

In future research by these authors, focus will be upon (1) identifying the impact of structure on managed species abundance, (2) assessing the impact of proximity of reef structures on abundance of top species, and (3) building longitudinal models that highlight changes in species presence and abundance over time

REFERENCES

Agresti, A. (1984). *Analysis of Ordinal Categorical Data*. New York: John Wiley and Sons.

Aljemian, M.J., Wetz, J.J., Shipley-Lozano, B., Shively, J.D. & Stunz, G.W. (2015). An analysis of artificial reef fish community structure along the Northwestern Gulf of Mexico shelf: Potential impacts of "Rigs-to-Reefs" programs. *PLOS One,* May, 22 pgs. doi:10:1371/journal.pone.0126354,

Baine, M. (2001). Artificial reefs: a review of their design, application, management and performance. *Ocean and Coastal Management*, 44(3-4), 241-259.

Barans. C. 1982. Methods for assessing reef fish stocks. Pages 105-123. In G. R. Huntsman, W. R. Nicholson, and W. W. Fox, Jr. (editors), *Proceedings of a workshop held October 7-10, 1980 at St. Thomas, Virgin Islands of the United States, U.S. Dep. Commer., NOAA Tech. Memo. NMFS-SEFC-80.*

Bohnsack, J.A. & Sutherland, D.L. (1985). Artificial reef research: a review with recommendations for future priorities. *Bulletin of Marine Science,* 37, 11-39.

Bohnsack, J.A. &. Bannerot, S.P. (1986). A stationary visual census technique for quantitatively assessing community structure of coral reef fishes. *U.S. Department of Commerce. NOAA Tech. Report NMFS 41,* 15p.

Bortone, S. A., Kimmel, J.J. &. Brundrick. C.M. (1989). A comparison of three methods for visually assessing reef fish communities: time and area compensated. *Northeast Gulf Science*, 10, 85–96.

Bortone, S.A., Hastings, R.W. & Oglesby, J.L. (1986). Quantification of reef fish assemblages: A comparison of several *in situ* methods. *Northeast Gulf Science*, 8(1),1-22.

Bortone, S.A., Martin, T.M. & Bundrick, C.M. (1991). Visual census of reef fish assemblages: A comparison of slate, audio, and video recording devices. Northeast Gulf Science, 12(1),17-23.

Cowen, J.H., Grimes, C.B., Patterson, W.F., Walters, C.J., Jones, A.C. & Lindberg, W.J. et al. (2010). Red snapper management in the Gulf of Mexico: science-or-faith-based? *Reviews in Fish Biology and Fisheries*. 21 (2), 187-204. doi:10.1007/s11160-010-9165-7

Coy, S.P., Shipley, M.F. & Shipley-Lozano, J.B. (2014) Toward a sustainable fishery management policy: An artificial neural network model for predicting Bull Shark (*Carcharhinus leucas*) presence. *International Journal of Applied Decision Sciences,* 5(2), April-June,1-20.

Diamond, S.L., Campbell, M.D., Olsen, D., Wang, Y., Zeplin, J. & Qualia, S. (2007). Movers and stayers: individual variability in site fidelity and movements of red snapper off Texas. In: Patterson, W.F., Cowan, J.H. Jr., Fitzhugh, G.R., Nieland, D.L. (eds.) *Red Snapper ecology and fisheries in the U.S. Gulf of Mexico*. American fisheries society, symposium 60, Bethesda, Maryland, 163-188.

Ellis, D.M. & DeMartini, E.E. (1994). Evaluation of a video camera technique for indexing abundances of juvenile pink snapper, *Pristipomoides filamentosus*, and other Hawaiian insular shelf fishes. Fishery Bulletin, 93, 67-77.

Fowler, A. & Booth, D. (2012b). How well do sunken vessels approximate fish assemblages on coral reefs? Conservation implications of vessel-reef deployments. *Marine Biology*, 159 (12), 2787-2796.

Fowler, A. M. & Booth, D.J. (2012a). Evidence of sustained populations of a small reef fish on artificial structures. Does depth affect production on artificial reefs? *Journal of Fish Biology*, 80, 613-629. doi:10,1111/j.1095-8649.2011.03201.x

Froehlich, C.Y.M. & Kline, R.J. (2015). Using fish population metrics to compare the effects of artificial reef density, *PLOS One*, September 30, 16 pages. doi: 10.1371/journal.pone.0139444.

Gallway, B.J., Szedlmayer, S.T. & Gazey, W.J. (2009). A life history review for red snapper in the Gulf of Mexico with an evaluation of the importance of offshore petroleum platforms and other artificial reefs. *Reviews in Fisheries Science*, 17(1), 48-67. doi: 10.1080/10641260802160717

Gazey,W.J., Gallaway, B.J., Cole, J.G. & Fournier, D.A.(2008). Age composition, growth, and density-dependent mortality in juvenile red snapper estimated from observer data from the Gulf of Mexico penaeid shrimp fishery. *North American Journal of Fisheries Management*, 28, 1828-1842.

Gledhill, C.T. (2001). Reef fish assemblages on Gulf of Mexico shelf-edge banks. University of South Alabama. August 2001. 193 p.

Gledhill, C.T., Lyczkowski-Shultz, J., Rademacher, K., Kargard, E., Crist, G. & Grace, M.A. (1996). Evaluation of video and acoustic index methods for assessing reef-fish populations. *ICES Journal of Marine Science*. 53(2): 483-485.

Haynes, J.M. (1990). Methods for sampling reef fishes, with emphasis on the red snapper (Lutjanus J.M. Haynes 7 June 2010 campechanus), in the Gulf of Mexico: is stock assessment feasible? *NOAA/NMFS/SEFC* Mississippi Laboratories. Pascagoula, MS. 66 p.

Jones, R.S. & Thompson, M.J. (1978). Comparison of Florida reef fish assemblages using a rapid visual technique. *Bulletin of Marine Science*. 28(1):159-172.

Kimmel, J.J. (1985). A new species-time method for visual assessment of fishes and its comparison with established methods. *Environmental Biology of Fishes*. 12(1):23-32.

Lukens, R.R., Selberg, C., Ansley, H., Bailey, C.M., Bedford, D. & Bell, M. (2004) *Guidelines for marine artificial reef materials*. 2nd ed. Gulf of Mexico Fisheries Management Council 121.

Mackinson, S. (2000). An adaptive fuzzy experts system for predicting structure, dynamics and distribution of herring shoals. *Ecological Modelling,* 126, 155-178.

Mackinson, S., Vasconcellos, M. & Newlands, N. (1999). A new approach to the analysis of stock-recruitment relationships: "model-free estimation" using fuzzy logic. *Canadian Journal of Fisheries and Aquatic Sciences,* 56, 686-699.

McCormick, M.I.& Choat, J.H. (1987). Estimating total abundance of a large temperate-reef fish using visual strip-transects. *Marine Biology*. 96, 469-478.

McQueen-Borden, K.K. (2013). Will the Rigs-to-Reefs experiment be based on the "best scientific information available"? *Tulane Law Review*, 87(5/6), 1281-1310.

Moffitt, R.B., Parrish, F.A. & Polovina, J.J. (1989). Community structure, biomass and productivity of deepwater artificial reefs in Hawaii. *Bulletin of Marine Science*, 44, 616-630.

Olden, J. D. & Jackson, D. A. (2002). Illuminating the "black box": a randomization approach for understanding variable contributions in artificial neural networks. *Ecological Modelling, 154*, 135–150.

Parker, R.O. Jr., Chester, A.J. & Nelson, R.S. (1994). A video transect method for estimating reef fish abundance, composition, and habitat utilization at Gray's Reef National Marine Sanctuary, Georgia. *Fishery Bulletin*, 92, 787-799.

Sale, P.F. & Douglas, W.A. (1981). Precision and accuracy of visual census technique for fish assemblages on coral patch reefs. *Environmental Biology of Fishes,* 6(3/4, 333-339.

Salski, A. (1992). Fuzzy knowledge-based models in ecological research. *Ecological Modelling*, 63, 103-112.

Seaman, W., Jr.& Sprague,L.M. (1991). *Artificial Habitats for Marine and Freshwater Fisheries*. Academic Press. San Diego, CA., 285 p.

Shipley, J.B. &Cowan, Jr, J.H. (2010). Artificial Reef Placement: A Red Snapper (*Lutjanus campechanus*) Ecosystem and Fuzzy Rule-Based Model. *Fisheries Management and Ecology,* 14 pages.

Shipley, J.B. & Shipley, M.F. (2009). A Fuzzy Rule-Based Model for Artificial Reef Placement Related to Managing Red Snapper (*Lutjanus campechanus*) Ecosystems in Alabama Waters. *Journal of Information and Knowledge Management*, 8(2), 175-188.

Shipp, R.L.,Tyler III,W.A. & Jones,R.S. (1986). Point count censusing from a submersible to estimate reef fish abundance over large areas. *Northeast Gulf Science,* 8(1), 83-89.

Stephan, C.D., Dansbury,B.G., Osburn, H.R., Matlock, G.C., Riechers, R.K. & Rayburn, R. (1990) *Texas Artificial Reef Fishery Management Plan Fishery Management Plan Series Number 3* Texas Parks and Wildlife Department Coastal Fisheries Branch 4200 Smith School Road Austin, Texas 78744, 26 pages. https://tpwd.texas.gov/publications/pwdpubs/media/pwd_pl_v3400_0332.pdf

Syc, T.S. & Szedlmayer, S.T. (2012). A comparison of size and age of red snapper (Lutjanus campechanus) with the age of artificial reefs in the northern Gulf of Mexico. *Fishery Bulletin,* 110(4), 458-469.

Thresher, R.E. & Gunn, J.S. (1986). Comparative analysis of visual census techniques for highly mobile, reef-associated piscivores (Carangidae). *Environmental Biology of Fishes*, 17(2), 93-116.

van der Stap, T., Coolen, J.W.P. & Lindeboo, H.J. (2016). Marine fouling assemblages on offshore gas platforms in the southern North Sea: Effects of depth and distance from shore on biodiversity. *PLoS ONE*. 11(1), 1-16, 16 pages. DOI: 10.1371/journal.pone.0146324

DECISION SCIENCES INSTITUTE

Assessment of total quality management implementation in Indian service industries

Faisal Talib
Department of Mechanical Engineering
Aligarh Muslim University, Aligarh, India
Email: ftalib77@gmail.com

Mohd. Nishat Faisal
Department of Management & Marketing
College of Business & Economics
Qatar University, Doha, Qatar
Email: nishat786@qu.edu.qa

ABSTRACT

The purpose of this paper is to examine the extent to which total quality management (TQM) practices have been implemented in Indian service industries. The research reports the findings of an empirical study conducted with a sample of 172 top and middle managers in Indian service industries. The results reveals that six TQM practices i.e. top-management commitment; customer focus; process management; quality systems; teamwork; and communication are effectively implemented across the Indian service industries while eleven practices are partially implemented. The proposed framework would be helpful for the managers and practitioners in implementing an effective TQM program.

KEYWORDS: Total quality management (TQM), TQM practices, service industries, performance, India.

INTRODUCTION

In the present era of global and increased competitive environment, industries have been experiencing rapid changes in the business performance propelled by phenomena like increased customer awareness of quality, adoption of new and advanced technology, globalization, cost effectiveness, efficient utilization of resources and achieving customer satisfaction (Kristianto *et al.*, 2012; Psomas *et al.*, 2014; Kumar *et al.*, 2011). In response to these challenges, many business practitioners and industry managers have started to adopt different quality improvement approaches for enhance competitiveness and sustainable business performance (Arumugam *et al.*, 2009) such as total quality management (TQM), Six Sigma, ISO 9000 and Quality Models (EFQM, MBNQA, Deming Award) (Talib *et al.*, 2011a,b&c; Talib *et al.*, 2013a). Among them, TQM is widely accepted approach that uses a set of management practices focusing on customer satisfaction, industry development, product and service quality and continuous improved performance (Kristianto *et al.*, 2012; Yusof and Aspinwal, 2000; Talib *et al.*, 2011c; Talib *et al.*, 2013b, Talib and Rahman, 2010).
Through TQM practices, both the industries i.e. manufacturing and service have been trying to upgrade their quality standards and improve product and service design to fulfill customer expectations along with overall business performance (Bhat and Rajashekhar, 2009). Further, for successful implementation of TQM, there is a need to identify a set of TQM practices applicable to service industry (Talib *et al.*, 2011c) and make assure the proper implementation of the same for earning maximum benefits. A considerable amount of literature is present on the implementation of TQM program in manufacturing industries. These studies have showed

several benefits of successful implementation of TQM and still they are being benefited in some way (Mahmood *et al.*, 2014; Belay *et al.*, 2014; Talib and Rahman, 2012; Abusa and Gibson, 2013).

Following the success of TQM in manufacturing industry, practitioners and managers have started to explore the potential of transferring and applying the TQM principles and practices to the service industries and suggested its applicability as there are not enough studies conducted in this sector especially in Indian context (Talib and Rahman, 2012; Prajogo, 2005). Based on this, the present research study tries to fill this gap by reviewing the literature on TQM implementation in the service sector and conducting a survey based research for implementing the previously identified and validated set of TQM practices in Indian service industries (Talib *et al.*, 2011a,b,c; Talib *et al.*, 2013b). Considering the benefits of TQM in manufacturing industries and lack of research studies on implementation of TQM in service industries, the present study aims:

- To examine the extent or degree to which TQM practices are practiced or implemented in Indian service industries.

This study involves a survey-based empirical research on assessment of TQM implementation program in Indian service industries with the aim of achieving greater benefits and performance. The scope of the study will focus on four service industries chosen namely healthcare, banking, hospitality, and information and communication technology (ICT). Reliability and validity tests, and One-way analysis of variance (ANOVA) has been used to empirically investigate the TQM implementation in these industries. After successfully implementing the TQM program using the identified set of TQM practices, the Indian service managers and practitioners would be able to achieve enhanced business performance and increased competitiveness in the marketplace.

The rest of the paper has been structured as follows: It begins with a review of the existing literature on TQM implementation. Next section describes the research framework, question and hypothesis formulation followed by detailed research methodology used in the study. In the subsequent section, results and discussion were presented. Finally, last section highlights the main conclusions of the research study along with some managerial implications and scope for future research.

LITERATURE REVIEW

TQM implementation

Despite the growing body of literature concerning issues with TQM implementation, there are some mixed studies that have examined the structure, impact and organization performance of TQM implementation in different organizations either theoretically or empirically or through case studies (Nasim *et al.*, 2014; Boateng-Okrah and Fening, 2012; Mahmood *et al.*, 2014; Talib, 2013; Abusa and Gibson, 2013). The implementation of TQM in organizations has a positive impact on organization's customer satisfaction, employee satisfaction and quality performance (Kristianto *et al.*, 2012; Jayaram *et al.*, 2010; Andrews *et al.*, 2011; Talib *et al.*, 2010; Talib *et al.*, 2013b; Mahmood *et al.*, 2014). Similarly, many studies have looked other issues of TQM like human resource management, supplier relationship, strategic planning, leadership, quality culture and have concluded with a positive outcome in the form of business performance. TQM also contributes to benchmarking of critical success factors for an organization (Ahmad and Elhuni, 2014).

In a study by Martinez-Costa and Jimenez-Jimenez (2008), presented evidence about TQM which promotes organization learning and improves performance in the form of profitability, customer satisfaction and product/services quality. Boateng-Okrah and Fening (2012) examines the level of TQM implementation in a mining sector and revealed positive outcome. Abusa and Gibson (2013) conducted a case study in Libyan industrial sector and found that there were no differences between TQM elements across ISO and non-ISO certified companies as well as in case of small and medium enterprises (SMEs), and large companies. Mahmood *et al.* (2014) measured the performance of Pakistan aviation manufacturing industry (PAMI) empirically and observed that the proposed model of measuring organizational performance in PAMI was in general agreement with the TQM model of renowned researchers. A study by Yapa (2012) reported the results of an investigation on the use of TQM tools, techniques and concept among Sri Lankan service organizations and found the positive response of adopting TQM by managers in their organizations. Kristianto *et al.* (2012) presented the results of a survey of customer satisfaction after adopting TQM in a wheat flour milling company. The findings supported the company to achieve customer satisfaction by focusing on TQM implementation efforts.

Past studies on TQM literature suggest that different TQM practices are identified and used in the literature by the researchers and academicians. It was observed that these studies have provided different sets of TQM practices but no common set of practices were identified, though identification of a set of TQM practices should be given special consideration for ensuring successful implementation of TQM program in any industry (Talib *et al.*, 2011c; Jha and Kumar, 2010). Until recently, Talib *et al.* (2011a,b&c) in their studies on the identification of TQM practices in the service industries, their frequency of occurrence in the TQM literature and developing contextual relationship between them, on their implementation have been published. Hence, present study utilizes a set of 17 TQM practices as identified and proposed by Talib *et al.* (2011a,b&c) for service industries and through a comprehensive review of TQM literature. These practices are depicted in Table 1. The detailed description of each TQM practice can be found in Talib *et al.* (2011a).

Table 1: Set of TQM Practices for Service Industries

TQM PRACTICE NO.	TQM PRACTICE
1.	Top-management commitment
2.	Customer focus
3.	Training and education
4.	Continuous improvement and innovation
5.	Supplier management
6.	Employee involvement
7.	Information and analysis
8.	Process management
9.	Quality systems
10.	Benchmarking
11.	Quality culture
12.	Human resource management
13.	Strategic planning
14.	Employee encouragement
15.	Teamwork
16.	Product and service design
17.	Communication

(Source: Talib *et al.*, 2011a,b&c)

RESEARCH FRAMEWORK, QUESTION AND HYPOTHESIS FORMULATION

Based on the above literature review, a conceptual framework is developed and a research model has been proposed 'to examine the extent or degree to which TQM practices are practiced or implemented in Indian service industries'. The proposed TQM research framework is depicted in Figure 1. This research model suggests that the greater the extent to which these TQM practices are present, the better the quality oriented results are achieved in Indian service industries. To carry out work to achieve the study objective as presented in the introduction section, a research question (RQ1) was articulated as follows:

RQ1: To what extent the TQM practices are practiced or implemented in the Indian service companies?

The main purpose of this study is to examine the extent or degree to which TQM practices are practiced or implemented in Indian service industries. Based on extensive literature review on TQM by Talib *et al.* (2010); Talib *et al.* (2011a,b,c); Talib *et al.* (2013b), this research utilizes 17 TQM practices that are necessary for successful TQM implementation in the Indian service industries. Further, the literature review indicated that these TQM practices are frequently used by majority of the service industries. This lead to the following hypothesis:

H1: There should not be any significant difference in the 17 TQM practices as practiced or implemented by Indian service industries.

RESEARCH METHODOLOGY

To accomplish the present research objective, a survey of select Indian service industries was conducted using self-administered questionnaire. The research methodology used in this study is discussed as follows.

Research Design

A descriptive cross-sectional study design was adopted. It is in line with the studies on TQM performed by Salaheldin (2009); Wardhani *et al.*, (2009); Ooi *et al.* (2012). In this study, electronic mail (e-mail) survey method was adopted as the means of data collection which is commonly used in similar kind of research (Talib *et al.*, 2013b; Kureshi *et al.*, 2010; Zu, 2009).

Research Instrument

A self-administered structured instrument was designed in this research based on the works of Antony *et al.* (2002); Brah *et al.* (2000); Sureshchandar *et al.* (2001); Issac *et al.* (2004). The instrument was initially validated through a pilot survey before it was actually used for primary data collection. The instrument developed was divided into two sections. The first section comprises the demographic information of the respondents including profession, gender, years of experience as well as the general background of the company and the second section collects information on implementation of TQM practices in the industry by listing 17 TQM practices measured by 110 items. The instrument used a 5-point Likert scale, with 1= very low, 3= moderate, and 5= very high. This is in line with those suggested by Brah *et al.* (2000); Salaheldin (2009).

Sampling Method and Data Collection Procedure

The target population of this study is the list of select Indian service industries published by the i^3 (i-cube, Information Infrastructure for Institutions), Centre for Monitoring Indian Economy Private Limited, India (i^3, CMIE, 2010). The four service industries mainly included in this study are healthcare, banking, hospitality (hotel and tourism), and information and communication technology (ICT) which includes telecommunication services, information technology enabled services (ITeS) and computer software services. The reasons for choosing these four sectors are their high Gross Domestic Product (GDP) share in Indian economy (about 56 percent) (i^3, CMIE, 2010); highly labor intensive industries and provides substantial employment (MoL&E, 2010); and there ever increasing net annual income to the Indian service sector. (i^3, CMIE, 2010). The list contains a total of 1781 industries at the time of research period covering all the four categories.

A stratified sampling method (a probability sampling technique) was chosen for this study. This method was thought to be appropriate to collect sufficient information from the total population to make statistical inferences. A minimum sample size was calculated according to the GDP contribution of each service industry from the total contribution of GDP in the service sector. The minimum sample size needed for this study comes out to be 591. This sample was increased to 600 to reduce the probability of Type II error (Burgess *et al.*, 2006). This minimum sample size was stratified into four strata. The sample size drawn from each stratum i.e. healthcare, banking, hospitality, and ICT industries based on proportionate stratified sampling technique were found to be 40, 67, 118, and 375 respectively. These samples were drawn using a simple random sample approach.

Instrument Administration

The target respondents for this study were top and middle level administrators/managers who have sufficient level of experience and qualification and therefore, they will be aware of the TQM practices and their implementation in respective service industries. Addressed to the top and middle level administrators/managers of the industries, the survey instruments were e-mailed to 600 industries. After several follow-ups and personal contacts, a total of 211 companies responded which are approximately 35.1 percent of the sample size, were selected for the study, however, only 172 useable survey instruments were included for the data analysis as 39 instruments were unusable, yielding a response rate of 28.6 percent. The main reasons for this are: 33 respondents (84.6 percent) did not complete the instrument or having the missing data and 6 instruments (15.4 percent) were undelivered.

RESULTS AND DISCUSSION

To accomplish the research objective, a research instrument was framed comprising of 17 TQM practices measured by 110 items. Reliability and validity tests were deployed to check the internal consistency of the measuring items and the degree to which the instrument measures the constructs that the items are intended to measure, through the various validity tests like face validity and content validity. These validity tests were conducted to ensure the data collected was valid for further analysis. One-way Analysis of Variance (ANOVA) was performed to test the proposed hypothesis (H1) through SPSS 20.0 software.

Figure 1: A research model of successful TQM implementation in Indian service industries

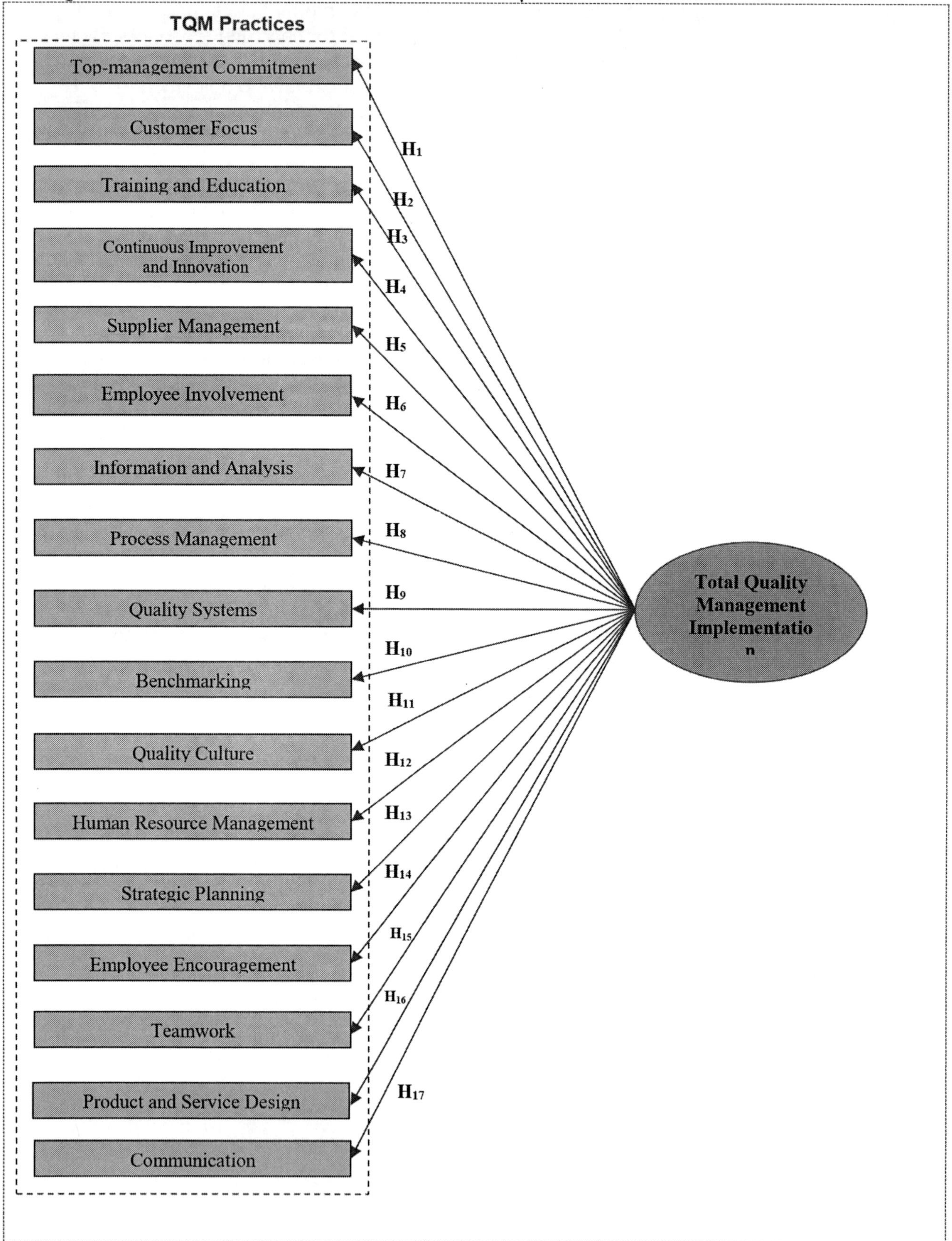

Table 2: Profile of Respondents		
POSITION/ROLE OF THE RESPONDENT	FREQUENCY	PERCENTAGE
Director/Managing Director/Executive Director/CEO/General Manager	8	4.7
Project Manager/Senior Engineer Manager/Senior Manager	32	18.6
Manager/Technical Manager/Operations Manager	38	22.1
Quality Manager/Human Resource Manager/Quality Engineer/Market Manager/Executive Manager	40	23.3
CMO/Medical Superintendent/Medical officer/Physicians	17	9.9
Others (Like Project Architect, Consultant; Customer Relation Officer; Service Manager; Assistant Manager)	37	21.5
Total	**n=172**	**100**
Years of experience	**Frequency**	**Percentage**
Less than 5 years	61	35.5
More than 5 years	111	64.5
Total	**n=172**	**100**
Gender	**Frequency**	**Percentage**
Male	144	83.7
Female	28	16.3
Total	**n=172**	**100**
Department/Section	**Frequency**	**Percentage**
Quality	16	9.3
Product and Services	35	20.3
Customer Relation	24	14.0
Marketing	34	19.8
Information Management Services	19	11.0
Others	44	25.6
Total	**n=172**	**100**
Type of industry	**Frequency**	**Percentage**
Healthcare	17	9.9
Banking	37	21.5
Hospitality (Tourism and Hotels)	34	19.8
ICT(Including ITeS and Computer Software Services)	84	48.8
Total	**n=172**	**100**

Profile of respondents

The profile of the respondents can be clearly understood through Table 2. The industry variables consisted of position of respondent, years of experience, gender, department/section, and type of industry which are self explanatory as can be seen from Table 2.

Reliability test

Reliability is the most commonly followed technique to measures internal consistency among a group of items combined to form a single scale and reflects the homogeneity of the scale. Using the SPSS 20.0 reliability analysis program software, an internal consistency analysis was performed separately for the items of each TQM practice. The alpha values of the study variables are summarized in Table 3. The reliability coefficients of the study variables exceeded the minimum acceptable level of 0.70 (Nunnally and Bernstein, 1994). Further, after performing reliability test, 10 items were deleted to increase the reliability of the scale. Hence, the total items covering 17 TQM practices were reduced from 110 to 100. As can be seen in Table 3, the alpha values range from 0.784 to 0.932, thus, provides strong evidence that the scales developed are judged to be reliable.

Table 3: Internal Consistency (Scale Reliabilities) for 17 TQM Practices

MEASURE	ORIGINAL NUMBER OF ITEMS	ORIGINAL ALPHA (RELIABILITY)	ITEMS DELETED	FINAL NUMBER OF ITEMS	FINAL ALPHA (RELIABILITY)
Top-management commitment	9	0.865	2	7	0.932
Customer focus	9	0.876	1	8	0.902
Training and education	6	0.860	1	5	0.902
Continuous improvement and innovation	7	0.793	1	6	0.882
Supplier management	8	0.910	None	8	0.910
Employee involvement	6	0.883	None	6	0.883
Information and analysis	5	0.874	None	5	0.874
Process management	6	0.775	1	5	0.833
Quality systems	5	0.667	1	4	0.784
Benchmarking	5	0.891	None	5	0.891
Quality culture	8	0.843	1	7	0.891
Human resource management	7	0.902	None	7	0.902
Strategic planning	6	0.821	1	5	0.866
Employee encouragement	6	0.904	None	6	0.904
Teamwork	4	0.871	None	4	0.871
Product and service design	8	0.874	1	7	0.902
Communication	5	0.900	None	5	0.900
Total	**110**		**10**	**100**	

Note: n=172

Face and content validity

In this research, it was argued that the 17 TQM practices for measuring TQM implementation practices had face and content validity since the majority of scales/items used in this study are borrowed from established scales that have already been subjected to tests of face and content validity. Moreover, the content validity of the instrument was also ensured through an extensive review of the literature and detailed evaluation by academicians and practitioners. Items were deleted, added, or modified based on their reviews prior to the analysis.

Implementation of TQM practices across Indian service industries

With regard to the implementation level of each TQM practice across the Indian service industries, the significant differences between each of the four categories of service industries have been examined with the help of one-way ANOVA (Mady, 2009; Selvaraj, 2009). Nevertheless, before conducting the ANOVA, the necessary assumptions must be met. The two assumptions of concern are population normality and homogeneity of variance (Coakes *et al.*, 2006). The population from which the samples have been drawn should be normal and this can be checked by using normality statistics such as skewness. On the other hand, the scores in each group should have homogeneous variance which is checked by Levene's test that determines whether variances are equal or unequal. Table 4 presents the skewness statistics, Levene statistics, and significance results of each TQM practice. From Table 4, the skewness values are generally close to zero indicating that the assumption of population normality appears not to be violated. Also, Levene's test for homogeneity of variances is not significant ($p>0.05$) and therefore, one can be confident that the population variances for each TQM practice are approximately equal. Accordingly, it is concluded that the ANOVA can be performed for further analysis.
The extent of implementation of TQM practices across Indian service industries has been computed by the mean score of each TQM practice across each service industry as well as total mean score across overall Indian service industries separately. Table 5 reports the mean scores for 17 TQM practices in four categories of service industries as well as total mean score across the Indian service industries for each TQM practice. It also includes the ANOVA results.

Table 4: Tests of Population Normality and Homogeneity of Variance (Levene's Test)

TQM PRACTICE	SKEWNESS STATISTIC	LEVENE STATISTIC	SIGNIFICANCE (p-VALUE)
Top-management commitment (TMC)	-0.695	1.504	0.215
Customer focus (CF)	-0.314	0.290	0.832
Training and education (TE)	-0.288	2.466	0.064
Continuous improvement and innovation (CII)	-0.283	0.679	0.566
Supplier management (SM)	0.466	0.421	0.738
Employee involvement (EI)	0.443	0.481	0.696
Information and analysis (IA)	-0.077	2.380	0.071
Process management (PM)	-0.124	0.553	0.647
Quality systems (QS)	-0.397	1.394	0.246
Benchmarking (BM)	-0.436	1.441	0.233
Quality culture (QC)	-0.320	2.453	0.065
Human resource management (HRM)	0.576	2.535	0.055
Strategic planning (SP)	0.000	0.737	0.531
Employee encouragement (EE)	0.564	0.198	0.898
Teamwork (TW)	-0.009	1.100	0.351
Product and service design (PSD)	0.037	0.285	0.836
Communication (COM)	-0.083	2.641	0.053

$n=172$; $^*p<0.05$; $df1=3$; $df2=168$.

Table 5: ANOVA Results of TQM Practices Implementation Across Indian Service Industries (Mean and F-Test Results)								
HYPOTHESIS	TQM PRACTICE	MEAN SCORE IN					ANOVA TEST RESULTS	
		HEALTHCARE	BANKS	HOSPITALITY	ICT	TOTAL	'F' VALUE	SIGNIFICANCE (P-VALUE)
H_1	Top-management commitment	3.77	3.55	4.04	3.70	3.74	2.062	0.107(NS)
H_2	Customer focus	3.35	3.56	3.92	3.58	3.62	2.284	0.081(NS)
H_3	Training and education	3.11	3.50	3.88	3.69	3.63	3.710	0.013*
H_4	Continuous improvement and innovation	3.56	3.60	4.09	3.75	3.77	3.181	0.025*
H_5	Supplier management	2.31	2.82	2.88	3.04	2.89	4.342	0.006**
H_6	Employee involvement	2.48	3.06	2.97	3.12	3.01	3.617	0.014*
H_7	Information and analysis	2.87	3.49	2.99	3.34	3.25	4.809	0.003**
H_8	Process management	2.96	3.44	3.31	3.47	3.38	2.428	0.067(NS)
H_9	Quality systems	3.73	3.60	3.94	3.66	3.71	1.107	0.348(NS)
H_{10}	Benchmarking	2.94	3.48	3.49	3.15	3.27	3.615	0.014*
H_{11}	Quality culture	3.55	3.61	4.10	3.61	3.70	4.423	0.005**
H_{12}	Human resource management	2.20	2.81	2.73	3.01	2.83	5.578	0.001**
H_{13}	Strategic planning	2.90	3.37	3.61	3.38	3.38	3.352	0.020*
H_{14}	Employee encouragement	2.35	2.84	2.85	3.04	2.89	3.696	0.013*
H_{15}	Teamwork	3.13	3.37	3.72	3.38	3.42	2.505	0.061(NS)

H_{16}	Product and service design	3.03	3.50	3.72	3.42	3.46	3.331	0.021*
H_{17}	Communication	2.77	3.16	3.35	3.24	3.20	1.998	0.116(NS)

Significant at $*p<0.05$; $**p<0.01$; df1=3; df2=168; NS=No Significant Difference.

Through the initial investigation of all the 17 TQM practices with respect to F-value, it can be seen that a significant difference was not found among the six TQM practices (top-management commitment, customer focus, process management, quality systems, teamwork, and communication) in the study. Seven practices (training and education, continuous improvement and innovation, employee involvement, benchmarking, strategic planning, employee encouragement, and product and service design) showed significant difference at the 0.05 level while the remaining four practices (supplier management, information and analysis, quality culture, and human resource management) showed significant difference at the 0.01 level. From these results it can be concluded that top-management commitment, customer focus, process management, quality systems, teamwork, and communication are not significantly different across Indian service industries. However, Indian service industries have better training and education, continuous improvement and innovation, and quality culture practices, as indicated by their total mean scores (>3.50). It can be further concluded that Indian service industries have better implementation of these TQM practices to improve continuous improvement culture, training and education program and emphasize the development of quality culture across the industry to enhance quality performance besides the implementation of top-management commitment, customer focus, process management, quality systems, teamwork, and communication. This in turn, will help service industries to achieve better quality over time.
When comparing the implementation of different TQM practices across Indian service industries, the significant values of the ANOVA test statistics for 'training and education' {$F(3,168)=2.062$, $p<0.05$}; 'continuous improvement and innovation' {$F(3,168)=3.71$, $p<0.05$; 'supplier management' {$F(3,168)=4.342$, $p<0.01$}; 'employee involvement' {$F(3,168)=3.617$, $p<0.05$}; 'information and analysis' {$F(3,168)=4.809$, $p<0.01$}; 'benchmarking' {$F(3,168)=3.615$, $p<0.05$}; 'quality culture' {$F(3,168)=4.423$, $p<0.01$}; 'human resource management' {$F(3,168)=5.578$, $p<0.01$}; 'strategic planning' {$F(3,168)=3.352$, $p<0.05$}; 'employee encouragement' {$F(3,168)=3.696$, $p<0.05$}; and 'product and service design' {$F(3,168)=3.331$, $p<0.05$} practices in Table 5 supported the rejection of the hypothesis that level of implementation of these 11 TQM practices are equal across Indian service industries or in other words it can be concluded that significant differences exist amongst these 11 TQM practices across the Indian service industries. Thus, hypothesis H1 was rejected for these 11 TQM practices (i.e. H_3; H_4; H_5; H_6; H_7; H_{10}; H_{11}; H_{12}; H_{13}; H_{14}; and H_{16}).
A close investigation of these 11 TQM practices with respect to their mean scores in each category of service industry and overall mean of each practice provides a better understanding of these reported significant differences at the two levels. For instance, concerning the 'supplier management' practice, the mean score obtained by ICT is 3.04 which indicates moderate implementation of supplier management practice while the same for healthcare (2.31), banking (2.82), and hospitality (2.88) indicate low implementation of supplier management practice. The overall mean score of 2.89 further supports the above argument that the level of implementation of supplier management across Indian service industries is low. This was also reported by Al-Khalifa and Aspinwall (2000); Tsang and Antony (2001); Talib and Rahman (2012). Similarly, the significant difference in the level of use of 'human resource management' practice was also found to be existing. The mean score obtained by ICT is 3.01 which again indicates moderate usage of human resource management practice while in healthcare, human resource

management is least practiced or implemented (mean score=2.20). Further, banks (2.81) and hospitals (2.73) also show low implementation of human resource management practice in these industries. The overall mean score of 2.83 further supports the above statement. This was also claimed by Issac *et al.* (2004). Similarly, other practices also showed wide variation in their mean scores across different service industries and hence, significant differences were found in these practices as can be seen from Table 5.

Further, rejecting the overall hypothesis of equal implementation level by the ANOVA does not indicate that every TQM practice mean differs significantly from every other industry mean as in case of training and education; employee involvement; quality culture; strategic planning; and product and service design. For that, Roscoe (1969) and Mady (2009) recommended the use of *Post-Hoc* Scheffe multiple comparison tests which can be utilized to test this proposition, which is beyond the scope of the present research study as it is confined to Indian service industries as a whole and not for a specific service industry.

In contrast to the above analysis, the implementation level of 'top-management commitment' {$F(3,168)=2.062$, $p=0.107>0.05$}; 'customer focus' {$F(3,168)=2.284$, $p=0.081>0.05$}; 'process management' {$F(3,168)=2.428$, $p=0.067>0.05$}; 'quality systems' {$F(3,168)=1.107$, $p=0.348>0.05$}; 'teamwork' {$F(3,168)=2.505$, $p=0.061>0.05$}; and 'communication' {$F(3,168)=1.998$, $p=0.116>0.05$} practices in Table 5 do not differ significantly. Accordingly, hypothesis H1 was not rejected for these six TQM practices (i.e. H_1; H_2; H_8; H_9; H_{15}; and H_{17}). For better understanding of the above reported results, again all these six practices were verified with respect to their mean scores in each category of service industry and with the overall mean score. For instance, concerning the 'top-management commitment' practice, the mean score obtained by hospitality is 4.04 which indicated the high implementation of top-management commitment practice. Similarly, in other three industries the levels of implementation of top-management commitment practice were found to be moderately high to high (healthcare=3.77; banks=3.55; and ICT=3.70). The overall mean score of 3.74 further supports the above claim and hence, it can be argued that top-management commitment as a TQM practice is highly implemented across Indian service industries. Majority of the studies have supported this argument and claimed that top-management commitment is the key TQM practice for successful implementation of TQM (Issac *et al.*, 2004; Al-Khalifa and Aspinwall, 2000; Yusuf *et al.*, 2007; Lee *et al.*, 2001).

Similarly, a significant difference was not found among the various levels of use of 'customer focus' as a TQM practice. The mean score obtained by hospitality is 3.92 while for ICT, healthcare, and banks it is 3.58, 3.56, and 3.35 respectively, which are all above the moderate level of implementation. This means 'customer focus' is implemented equally across all the four categories of service industries. This was also true for 'process management'; 'quality systems'; 'teamwork'; and 'communication' as depicted in Table 5.

It is finally concluded that, out of the 17 TQM practices identified in the present research study, only six practices (top-management commitment; customer focus; process management; quality systems; teamwork; and communication) are effectively implemented in Indian service industries, while the remaining 11 are partially implemented and considered in different categories of service industries. Emphasis is to be given to other important TQM practices particularly to quality culture, benchmarking, continuous improvement and innovation, training and education, and strategic planning which can enhance the quality performance of the service industries and efforts should be made to properly implement these TQM practices for steady growth and in achieving sustainability in the organization.

CONCLUSIONS

This research paper successfully accomplishes the objective of the study and assess the degree to which TQM practices are implemented in Indian service industries. It was hypothesized that there is no significant difference in the 17 TQM practices as practiced or implemented by Indian service industries. The purpose of this hypothesis was to examine the extent to which TQM practices are implemented in Indian service industries. Based on the empirical evidence obtained from one-way ANOVA, the results showed that only six practices i.e. top-management commitment; customer focus; process management; quality systems; teamwork; and communication are effectively implemented across the Indian service industries, while the remaining 11 are partially implemented and considered in different categories of service industries. Thus, no significant difference was found in above six practices while there was a significant difference observed among the remaining 11 practices across Indian service industries for their implementation potential. Thus, hypothesis H1 was accepted for top-management commitment, customer focus, process management, quality systems, teamwork, and communication, thereby meaning that these practices are significantly practiced or implemented in Indian service industries while the practices of training and education, continuous improvement and innovation, supplier management, employee involvement, information and analysis, benchmarking, strategic planning, employee encouragement, quality culture, human resource management, and product and service design are insignificant or there exists a significant difference among these 11 TQM practices. Thus, hypothesis H1 was rejected for these 11 practices. The uniqueness of this research work is that it provides a useful framework and research model for implementation of TQM program in Indian service industries. This kind of study has not been undertaken before in previous researches in Indian context. This work not only confirms that service industries can implement TQM program successfully but also suggests that it has a positive and significant impact on a industry performance. The findings of the present study provide some insights as to how the managers and practitioners of the service industries can improve their performance and how they can implement TQM program successfully in their industries. Researchers can adopt the present TQM model in their future work that can improve their research and academic performance significantly. Additionally, the proposed research model will allow managers to assess the level of industry quality management against other models proposed by various researchers. Furthermore, this paper focused particularly to four service industries namely healthcare; ICT; banking; and hospitality. The research can be extended to some emerging Indian service industries like aquaculture, airline, e-purchase, m-government, halal foods and many others. Finally, study can be extended to assess the impact of identified set of TQM practices on measures of sustainability such as business growth, competitive advantage and change management.

REFERENCES

Abusa, F.M., & Gibson, P. (2013). TQM implementation in developing countries. *Benchmarking: An International Journal*, *20*(5), 693-711.

Ahmad, M.M., & Elhuni, R. (2014). Critical quality factors for successful TQM implementation in Libyan oil and gas sector. *Benchmarking: An International Journal*, *21*(5), 713 - 733.

Al-Khalifa, K.N., & Aspinwall, E.M. (2000). The development of total quality management in Qatar. *The TQM Magazine*, *12*(3), 194-204.

Andrews, M.C., Baker, T., & Hunt, T.G. (2011). Values and person–organization fit: Does moral intensity strengthen outcomes? *Leadership and Organization Development Journal*, *32*(1), 5–9.

Antony, J., Leung, K., Knowles, G., & Gosh, S. (2002). Critical success factors of TQM implementation in Hong Kong industries. *International Journal of Quality and Reliability Management*, *19*(5), 551-566.

Arumugam, V., Chang, H.W., Ooi, K.-B., & Teh, P.-L. (2009). Self-assessment of TQM practices: a case analysis. *The TQM Journal*, *21*(1), 46-58.

Belay, A.M., Kasie, F.M., Helo, P., Takala, J., & Powell, D.J. (2014). Adoption of quality management practices. *Benchmarking: An International Journal*, *21*(1), 77-100.

Bhat, K.S., & Rajashekhar, J. (2009). An empirical study of barriers to TQM implementation in Indian industries. *The TQM Magazine*, *21*(3), 261-272.

Boateng-Okrah, E., & Fening, F.A. (2012). TQM implementation: a case of a mining company in Ghana. *Benchmarking: An International Journal*, *19*(6), 743-759.

Brah, S. A., Wong, J. L., & Rao, B. M. (2000). TQM and business performance in the service sector: a Singapore study. *International Journal of Operations and Production Management*, *20*(11), 1293-1312.

Burgess, K., Singh, P.J., & Koroglu, R. (2006). SCM: a structured literature review and implications for future research. *International Journal of Operations and Production Management*, *26*(7), 703-729.

Coakes, S.J., Steed, L., & Dzidic, P. (2006). *SPSS: Analysis without Anguish: Version 20 for Windows*, John-Wiley, India.

i^3, CMIE (2010). *i-cube, Information Infrastructure for Institutions, Centre for Monitoring Indian Economy Private Limited, India*, Website: http://www.cmie.com/database/?service=database-products/customised-solutions/information-infrastructure-for-institutions.htm [Assessed 20 May 2010].

Issac, G., Rajendran, C., & Anantharaman, R.N. (2004). A holistic framework for TQM in the software industry: a confirmatory factor analysis approach. *The Quality Management Journal*, 11(3), 35-60.

Jayaram, J., Ahire, S.L., & Dreyfus, P. (2010). Contingency relationships of firm size, TQM duration, unionization, and industry context on TQM implementation-A focus on total effects. *Journal of Operations Management*, *28*(4), 345–356.

Jha, U.C., & Kumar, S. (2010). Critical success factors (CSFs) of TQM: a literature review and analysis", paper presented at Oxford Business and Economics Conference Program, Hugh's College, Oxford University, Oxford.

Kristianto, Y., Ajmal, M.M., & Sandhu, M. (2012). Adopting TQM approach to achieve customer satisfaction. *The TQM Journal*, *24*(1), 29-46.

Kumar, R., Garg, D., & Garg, T.K. (2011). TQM success factors in north Indian manufacturing and service industries. *The TQM Journal*, *23*(1), 36-46.

Kureshi, N., Qureshi, F., & Sajid, A. (2010). Current health of quality management practices in service sector SME- a case study of Pakistan. *The TQM Journal*, *22*(3), 317-329.

Lee, C., Lee, T., & Chang, C. (2001). Quality/productivity practices and company performance in China. *International Journal of Quality and Reliability Management*, *18*(6), 604-625.

Mady, M.T. (2009). Quality management practices-an empirical investigation of associated constructs in two Kuwaiti industries. *International Journal of Quality and Reliability Management*, *26*(3), 214-233.

Mahmood, K., Ahmad, I.M.A, & Nisar, Q. (2014). An empirical study on measurement of performance through TQM in Pakistani aviation manufacturing industry. *International Journal of Quality & Reliability Management*, *31*(6), 665-680.

Martinez-Costa, M., & Jimenez-Jimenez, D. (2008). Are companies that implement TQM better learning organizations? *Total Quality Management*, *19*(11), 1101-1115.

MoL&E, GOI (2010). *Ministry of Labor and Employment*, Government of India. Website: http://labour.nic.in/. [Assessed 01 August 2010].

Nasim, K., Iqbal, M.Z., & Khan, I.A. (2014). Antecedents of TQM implementation capability: a review with a conceptual model. *Total Quality Management & Business Excellence*, *25*(12), 1395-1409.

Nunnally, J.C., & Bernstein, I.H. (1994). *Psychometric Theory*, McGraw-Hill, New York, NY.

Ooi, K.-B., Cheah, W.-C, Lin,B., & Teh, P.-L. (2012). Total quality management practices and knowledge sharing: an empirical study of Malaysia's manufacturing organizations. *Asia Pacific Journal of Management*, *29*(1), 59-78.

Psomas, E., Vouzas, F., & Kafetzopoulos, D. (2014). Quality management benefits through the "soft" and "hard" aspect of TQM in food companies. *The TQM Journal*, *26*(5), 431-444.

Roscoe, J. (1969). *Fundamental Research Statistics for Behavioral Sciences*, Holt, Rinehart and Winston, Austin, TX, p.239.

Salaheldin, S.I. (2009). Critical success factors for total quality management implementation and their impact on performance of SMEs. *International Journal of Productivity and Quality Management, 58*(3), 215-237.

Selvaraj, M. (2009). TQM in Indian commercial banks: a comparative study. *Journal of Marketing and Communication*, *4*(3), 59-70.

Sureshchandar, G. S., Rajendran, C., & Anantharaman, R.N. (2001). A holistic model for total quality service. *International Journal of Service Industry Management*, *12*, 378-412.

Talib, F. (2013), "An overview of total quality management: understanding the fundamentals in service organization", *International Journal of Advanced Quality Management, 1*(1), 1-20.

Talib, F., & Rahman, Z. (2010). Critical success factors of TQM in service organizations: a proposed model. *Services Marketing Quarterly*, *31*(3), 363-380.

Talib, F., & Rahman, Z. (2012). Total quality management practices in manufacturing and service industries: A comparative study. *International Journal of Advanced Operations Management*, *4*(3), 155-176.

Talib, F., Rahman, Z., & Qureshi, M.N. (2010). The relationship between total quality management and quality performance in the service industry: a theoretical model. *International Journal of Business, Management and Social Sciences*, *1*(1), 113-128.

Talib, F., Rahman, Z., & Qureshi, M.N. (2011b*)*. An interpretive structural modeling (ISM) approach for modeling the practices of total quality management in service sector. *International Journal of Modeling in Operations Management*, *1*(3), 223-250.

Talib, F., Rahman, Z., & Qureshi, M.N. (2011c). Identifying the Key Practices of TQM in Indian Service Industries: An Empirical Analysis. *Proceedings of International Conference on Advances in Supply Chain and Manufacturing Management (ASCMM 2011),* organized by Department of Industrial Engineering and Management, Indian Institute of Technology Kharagpur (IITKhg), West Bengal, India during December 16-18.

Talib, F., Rahman, Z., & Qureshi, M.N. (2013a). Survey on the usage of total quality management tools and techniques in Indian service industries: an empirical analysis. *International Journal of Quality and Innovation*, *2(*2), 105–119.

Talib, F., Rahman, Z., & Qureshi, M.N. (2013b). An empirical investigation of relationship between total quality management practices and quality performance in Indian service companies. *International Journal of Quality and Reliability Management*, *30*(3), 280-318.

Talib, F., Rahman, Z., Quershi, M.N., & Siddique, J. (2011a). Total quality management and service quality: an exploratory study of management practices and barriers in service industries. *International Journal of Services and Operations Management*, *10*(1), 94-118.

Tsang, J.H.Y., & Antony, J. (2001). TQM in UK service organizations: some key findings from a survey. *Managing Service Quality*, *11*(2), 132-141.

Wardhani, V., Utarini, A., van Dijk, J.P., & Post, D. (2009). Determinants of Quality Management Systems Implementation in Hospitals. *Health Policy*, *89*, 239-251.

Yapa, S. (2012). Total quality management in Sri Lankan service organizations. *The TQM Journal*, *24*(6), 505-517.

Yusof, S.M., & Aspinwall, E. (2000). TQM implementation frameworks: comparison and review. *Total Quality Management*, *11*(3), 281-294.
Yusuf, Y., Gunasekaran, A., & Dan, G. (2007). Implementation of TQM in China and organizational performance: an empirical investigation. *Total Quality Management, 18*(5), 509-530
Zu, X. (2009). Infrastructure and core quality management practices: how do they affect quality? *International Journal of Quality and Reliability Management*, *26*(2), 129-149.

DECISION SCIENCES INSTITUTE

Asymmetry, trust, innovation, and performance in supply chain management - a non-linear approach

Marek Michalski
San Francisco de Quito University
mmichalski@usfq.edu.ec

José Luis Montes Botella
Rey Juan Carlos University
joseluis.montes@urjc.es

Ram Narasimhan
Michigan State University
narasimh@broad.msu.edu

ABSTRACT

The purpose of this paper is to examine non-linear aspects of the asymmetry-performance relationship under varying conditions of trust and innovation. The paper offers a new approach that is useful for addressing strategic elements of supply chain management (SCM) relationships based on trust and innovation decisions.

The principal finding is that the influences of asymmetry on performance, in varying trust and innovation contexts, have unstable characteristics and have non-linear paths. Findings of the study provide rational insights to managers regarding when it is adequate to reduce (or not) asymmetric relationships with partners.

KEYWORDS: Supply chain management, Asymmetry, Trust, Innovation, Performance

INTRODUCTION

Supply chain (SC) is a network constructed to realize the goal of performance maximization through increasing the value and reducing the cost associated with the SC as a whole (Jüttner, Christopher and Baker, 2007).This network paradigm requires, especially today, the existence of trust and innovation in relationships among involved parties. Trust and Innovation are complex concepts, which play a key role in SC relationships. In order to develop better understanding of both concepts, we describe Trust as an expectancy of appropriate behaviors from partners and Innovation as an opportunity to create new products and/or services for customers utilizing SC relationships.

SC relationships can reduce transaction costs (Madhok, 2006), reduce risk and uncertainty (Gao et al., 2005; Spekman and Davies, 2004), increase or maintain the firm's position in the market (Pavlou and Gefen, 2004), moderate organizational and managerial behaviors (Atkinson and Butcher, 2003), obtain required resources and technologies (Cao and Zhang, 2011; Davies and Prince, 2005), and render the network more efficient (Miles and Snow, 2007). With these perspectives and possibilities, it becomes difficult to get alignment of objectives between the SC partners (Sridharan and Simatupang, 2005) and reduce the threats of opportunism (Heide and John, 1990). Given this situation, the most inter-organizational relationships are often described as asymmetric.

The concept of asymmetric relationships generally refers to imbalance in different relationship dimensions such as size, power, resources, and competencies. Imbalance in relationship dimensions could be a barrier to SC collaboration processes because in such situations relationships are often dominated by formal agreements more than by trust. They don't motivate SC collaboration leading to innovation but simply ensure access to resources (Colurcio and Russo-Spena, 2013).

Such relationships are considered inherently unstable and likely to dissolve (Kumar et al., 1995) with differential impacts on SC structures and performance. Therefore, asymmetry, trust and innovation are not only the core, essential factors of relational management, but also the basics elements of network organization formation and operations (La Londe, 2002; Varma et al., 2006).

The SC itself is a kind of network system or network structure. As such, it is a complex non-linear system, which is co-influenced by various independent but related elements. Innovation, trust and asymmetry have been suggested in the literature as the key factors in a supply chain network that impact competitive advantage and successful performance (Hult, 2004; Laeequddin et al., 2011; Thomas and Esper, 2010; Colurcio and Russo-Spena, 2013). Despite the assertion of their importance, the relationships among them are still unclear.

Research on asymmetry in relationships is limited. The asymmetries become evident when the relationships involve actors with different positioning (Johnson and Ford, 2007). Asymmetries in SC network relationships have been analyzed from different perspectives. Most studies have focused on potentially negative *linear* effects of asymmetry on relationship stability, dissatisfaction, opportunistic behavior, network development or performance (Johnsen and Ford 2001; 2006; Thomas and Skinner, 2010). Although some research on the impact of asymmetry on innovation and trust exists (Michalski et al., 2013; Colurcio and Russo-Spena, 2013; Thomas and Skinner, 2010), a more thorough analysis is noticeably lacking and this omission creates a gap in the current literature. We suggest that focusing on a linear relationship is insufficient to ensure that managerial decisions would produce the desired effects.

In the present business environments SCM has a significant role in improving the performance of each participating organization in the SC. Information sharing, collaboration, cost reduction, flexibility, delivery, integration and resource utilization have been considered in literature as key drivers of supply chain performance (Singh and Pandey, 2013). However, there is growing need to improve the quality of knowledge in this area. Given evidence indicating that SC performance is also influenced by its environmental context, we suggest that is necessary to consider asymmetry in relationships as a new and important factor that influences SC performance and explore its effects. Exploring the influence of asymmetry on SC performance under different level of trust and innovation is also interesting from a strategic viewpoint. The strategic implications of asymmetry on performance may offer additional insights into why SC relationships succeed or fail.

Collaboration and interaction between firms are recognized as requirements for a firm to create value and to realize high-quality relationship performance (Johnson and Ford, 2006). High trust decreases uncertainty and opportunism and encourages higher commitment to the SC relationships (Wu, 2011). At the same time, high level of trust and commitment reinforce strongly inter-organizational ties that can be an obstacle for innovation. The main reason for this is that strong relationships lock firms into a narrow (tightly connected) network, making them dependent on a small number of sources of creativity and innovation (Capaldo, 2007). This situation reduce the likelihood that new ideas and opportunities will be explored more broadly. Investigating these issues would be very helpful to improve our knowledge and understanding about the role of trust and innovation as the mechanisms by which relationships are established and maintained between firms in SC.

The purpose of this study is to address the gaps identified above. Specifically, we aim to extend research by investigating following research questions:

1. How does asymmetry influence the true nature of SC performance?
2. To what extent do trust and innovation mechanisms exist across the supply chain?
3. What is effect of different levels of trust and innovation on performance in asymmetric SC relationships?

This paper delivers new insights concerning these important questions. The rest of the paper is organized as follows: We first review the recent theoretical and empirical research literatures on trust, innovation and asymmetry, and propose a research model. Then we describe the methodology used to test the research model, followed by a discussion of the findings, and the implications for research and practice. Finally, we end with conclusions and areas for future research.

LITERATURE REVIEW

The performance of a SC depends on not only how efficiently the buyer and tier 1 partners cooperate with each other, but also on how well these partners cooperate with their own business partners (Halldorsson et al., 2007). Network Theory (NT) can be a basis for analyzing cooperative relationships for achieving greater performance than through individual efforts. The firm's continuous interaction with other members of a network is an important factor in the development of new resources (Haakansson and Ford, 2002). Thus, the possibility of advantageous interchange of resources helps firms to change the SC structure and motivate their members to pursue innovation.

Network Theory contributes profoundly to an understanding of the dynamics of inter-organizational relations by emphasizing the importance of trust, innovation and integration processes between partners (Halldorsson et al., 2007).The parties in a supply network gradually develop mutual trust through the exchange processes. In these activities, innovation helps organizations achieve efficiency; especially, innovative applications of information technology. Innovation leads to value creation for customers and improves the quality of processes and products (Lin, 2008).From a network perspective, trust and innovation helps partners to build an "exchange platform," continually negotiating for exchanges of resources that are needed as resource requirements change. Consequently, a network does not seek an optimal equilibrium, but is in a constant state of dynamic change.

Role of Trust in SC Relationships

Despite the vast literature on trust, there is no clear understanding of concept of trust in the context of SC partner's relationship (Laeequddin, 2011). Researchers in different disciplines have interpreted trust in different ways and assigned it different values by focusing on specific aspects. The trust definitions spans the continuum from a predisposition to a set of beliefs about the (supplier) partner to an intention to engage in a set of behaviors. In each research context, trust has been viewed differently. Table 1 presents different definitions of trust.

Table 1. Concepts of Trust

Authors	Definitions
Barney and Hansen (1994)	Trust is the **mutual confidence**[1] that no party to an exchange will exploit another's vulnerabilities.
Mayer et al. (1995)	Trust is **willingness of a party** based on the expectations

1 We mark in bold the key concept of each definition

	that the other party will perform a particular action important to the trustor, irrespective of the ability to monitor or control the party
Lippert (2001)	Technology trust is **an individual's willingness to be vulnerable** to the technology based on expectations of predictability, reliability, and utility and influenced by an individual's predisposition to trust technology.
Riegelsberger et al. (2003)	Trust is a device to reduce complexity, a shortcut to **avoid complex decision processes** when facing decisions that carry risk.
Chen and Barnes (2007)	Trust is **perceived usefulness**, perceived security, perceived privacy, perceived good reputation, and willingness to customize are the important antecedents to online initial trust.
Kim et al. (2009)	Trust is a **complex and multifaceted construct.**
Laeequddin et al. (2009)	Trust is **a threshold level of a supply chain member's** (trustor's) risk-bearing capacity related to trustee.
Thomas and Skinner (2010)	Trust exists when one firm in a cooperative relationship has **confidence in the other firm's reliability and integrity**.
Wu (2011)	Confidence or **predictive ability of client** to group behavior expectation.

For our study, the concept of trust as a set of managerial beliefs is particularly relevant. We assume that beliefs motivate appropriate managerial behaviors, especially during collaboration processes in a SC. Based on the key concepts of the definitions presented above, we define trust in SC as: a complex and multifaceted construct centered on beliefs, in which predictive ability, reliability, mutual confidence and honesty in behaviors of an organization to its SC partners help avoid complex decision processes. These beliefs are reflected in the willingness to share information and knowledge, security and privacy in SC network relations. Thus, trust in SC is determined by the partner's propensity to trust in general and their ability, benevolence and the integrity of their beliefs (Mayer et al., 1995). Trust in inter-organizational relationships has been associated with positive outcomes, such as enterprise achievements, reduction of opportunism, long-term relationships and higher performance (Wu, 2011).

Several findings regarding trust also support the central role of trust as a key managerial concept. The importance of trust arises from the fact that it is regarded as an important contributor to the strength of different relationships (Grönroos, 2000). It is widely accepted that trust is an important factor in dyadic business relations and an essential element for successful SC network interactions (Gounaris, 2005; Svensson, 2004). This suggests that in low-trust relationships managers would protect knowledge and commitment more by spending additional time and effort to improve the security of network relations. In contrast, if network relations are developed in high-trust environments the partners will be willing to share risk, resources and information much more freely. When the level of mutual trust is high, SC performance increases (Thomas and Skinner, 2010).

The concept of asymmetric relationships generally refers to imbalance in different relationship dimensions such as size, power, *trust*, resources, and competencies. Imbalance in relationship dimensions could be a barrier to SC collaboration processes because in such situations relationships are often dominated by formal agreements more than by trust. They don't motivate SC collaboration leading to innovation but simply ensure access to resources (Colurcio and Russo-Spena, 2013). In asymmetric trust environments the degree of interdependence between the partners in SC can be affected. La Londe (2002, p.10) argued that "issues of trust and risk can be significantly more important in supply chain relationships, because supply chain relationships often involve a higher degree of interdependency." According to this, it could be an advantage for each partner in SC to increase their dependency on exchange relationships. It does, however, raises the question: to what extent interdependency is mutually beneficial? It also makes it necessary to consider whether trust levels influence interdependency and consequently, performance in SC relationships.

Many scholars have suggested that relationships based on trust need to be reinforced by commitment to be successful (Gao and Bird, 2005; Gounaris, 2005; Morgan and Hunt, 1994). Both trust and commitment stimulate and facilitate the establishment of collaboration, especially in innovative activities. Thus, commitment is necessary to maintain a valuable relationship in SC collaboration agreements. Without trust and commitment, SC relationships become risky and vulnerable (Chu and Fang, 2006). Therefore, the success of supply chain management (SCM) requires a high degree of trust among SC partners (Hanfield, 2002). Based on these arguments, we hypothesize:

H1. The intensity of trust moderates the influence of asymmetry on the SC performance.

Role of Innovation in SC Relationships

The introduction of new products and services, or the entry into new markets, is likely to be more successful if accompanied by innovative SC designs, management practices, and technology (Arlbjørn et al., 2011). Innovation through SCM is becoming more prevalent and important as SC relationships become more strategic (Barret, 2000). Chen and Paulraj (2004) argue that SC network must be composed through a chain of interdependent strategic and collaborative relationships among the SC partners.

From this perspective, a SC relationship's principal objective needs to be the pursuit of mutual benefits through collaboration. Walters and Rainbird (2007), in their research, state that collaborative innovation combines elements of process innovation and product innovation within a network structure. Tether (2002) adds that collaborative efforts have been focusing on managing technological innovation and the complexity of engaging in collaborative arrangements for innovation. However, it is not understood whether collaborative innovation is possible in the presence of asymmetries in SC relationships.

Extant studies provide different definitions of SC innovation. We pointed out in Table 2, the substantial variation in the scope of innovation definitions in existing studies.

Table 2. Concepts of Innovation

Authors	Definitions
Porter (1990)	Innovation refers to **a complex process** which deals with uncertainty in the environment, so as to provide solutions for customer needs and find new ways to better organizational processes using new technologies
Garcia and Calantone (2002)	Innovation is an iterative process initiated by the perception of a new market and/or new service opportunity for a technology based invention, which **leads to development, production, and marketing tasks** striving for the commercial success of the invention.
Roy et al., (2004)	Innovation generation in a supply chain landscape involves **changes in product, process, or service** for the commercial success of the invention.
Walters and Rainbird (2007)	Innovation combines elements of process innovation management and product innovation management within a network structure that neither partner can create using its own resources to meet **customer or market-determined expectations** for product and/or service performance at an economic (viable) cost.
Arlbjørn et al., (2011)	Supply chain innovations are **not static elements** but will typically be triggered by the companies' dynamic interaction with their business environments.
Colurcio and Russo Spena (2013)	Collaborative innovation **creates challenges** to SME resulting from the inability to nurture and maintain the necessary resources and capabilities for growing to **build a competitive positioning and to create value** for the own company and for the network.

Using the key elements of each of these definitions (in Table 2), we define SC innovation as a complex and non-static process, which involves changes in product, process, or service and leads to development, production, and marketing within a network structure. SC innovation creates challenges for meeting customer or market-determined expectations, building competitive positioning and creating value for the firm and for its SC network.

In asymmetric environments, innovation is a dynamic and uncertain process, which involves deficiencies in reliable information about a partner's needs. Moreover, in asymmetric environments deficiencies of information in relationships between SC partners reduces their innovation capability, because lack of information sharing affects internal information processing (Berghman et al., 2012). Thus, one part of SC cannot use the information and knowledge related to other partners to facilitate the creation of new ideas early in the innovation process (Noordhoff et al., 2011). This condition increases the uncertainty in the relationships between SC partners. This occurs most frequently in environments with low level of trust and collaboration.

High level of trust and collaboration can help transfer of knowledge and information among SC partners, encourage innovation and overcome the impact of uncertainty. However, trust and collaboration would be insufficient for innovation success, because innovation also requires complementary activities from different knowledge domains (Anand et al., 2010).

Exchanging knowledge and human resources have been identified as key activities in managing collaborative innovation (Johnsen and Ford, 2000). In order to develop new technologies, products or services more efficiently, firms generally require extensive use of resources and collaborative R&D relationships (Liu and Chen, 2004).

Superior performance is more typical in SC networks formed by technologically advanced organizations (Jonsson et al., 2007; Sebastiao and Golicic, 2008; Skjøtt-Larsen et al., 2007). Performance is better in SCs where the focal firm is relatively stronger in its technological capabilities (Herzlinger, 2006) compared to its network partners. In this case, asymmetrical relations positively influence SC performance. However, even technologically advanced firms typically focus more on acquiring peripheral technologies than cutting-edge technologies (Liu and Chen, 2004). Furthermore, these firms often limit their transfer of new technologies to less advanced SC partners. In this manner, they restrict leakage of their innovative technologies and capabilities through their network.

This has two implications. First, the potential risk that the firm's technology will fall into the hands of its competitors (Sanna- Randaccio and Veugelers, 2007) leads to lack of trust. Second, this behavior complicates co-designing new processes, exploring new technologies, developing new product and consequently innovation level decreases across the SC. In fact, some firms see their SC partners more as potential competitors than collaborators (Alcacer and Chung, 2007). Based on these arguments, the following hypothesis is proposed:

H2. The intensity of innovation moderates the influence of asymmetry on SC performance.

Asymmetry and SC Performance

Moberg, et al. (2003) define seven constraints that block SC collaboration, including lack of trust, different goals, and lack of transparency in information systems. Lambert (2008) presents similar viewpoints, affirming that development of the right types of relationships, without constraints and limitations, and the creation of value propositions for customers are critical for SC. Limitations and constraints increase complexities in SCM processes and motivate organizations to introduce new tools and forms of inter-organization relationships. Recent research suggests that one of the causes of such varying behaviors and constraints is the presence of asymmetry in SCM process (Chen and Chen, 2002; Johnsen and Ford, 2008; Thomas and Esper, 2010).

There is disagreement in the literature regarding the manner in which asymmetry impacts SC relationships (Johnsen and Ford, 2008; Sun and Collins, 2009; Thomas and Esper, 2010). Such conceptual disagreements call for further exploration of the multi-dimensional and complex nature of asymmetry (Thomas and Esper, 2010). Table 3 shows the substantial variations in the scope of asymmetry definition in existing studies.

Table 3. Concepts of Asymmetry

Authors	Definitions
Chen and Chen (2002, p.1013)	"...asymmetric strategic alliances as an

	investment by firms from developing countries to gain access to new network opportunities, or to **enhance their power in other network relationships**."
Johnsen and Ford (2008, p.472)	"...**imbalance in size and other single relationship dimension**... as power, commitment, dependence, knowledge or the initiation of change"
Sun and Colins (2009, p.2)	"...an "**uncertainty area**" between firms in information sharing, which makes it difficult for a firm to obtain full sets of reliable, accurate and timely information."
Thomas and Esper (2010, p.476)	"...relationship asymmetry refers to a **lack of perceived dyadic balance or proportionality of relationship** attributes and/or behaviors"
Nyaga et al. (2013, p.34)	"... **distribution of power among partners** because of differences in expertise, size, switching costs, dependence, contract structure, etc."

Using the key elements of each asymmetry definitions (Table 3), we define asymmetry as imbalance in size, power, dependence or other dimensions of dyadic or SC relationships in general. Following Thomas and Esper (2010), we suggest that relationships between SC partners become asymmetric when there is disequilibrium in the dimensions that influence these relationships over time. In particular, in such dimensions as conflict, cooperation, communication quality or relational leadership.

The concept of asymmetry is important to understanding SC relationships because it significantly affects performance (Michalski et al., 2013). We view performance as a multidimensional concept that includes four outcomes: growth and diversification of incomes, profit improvements, market participation and customer satisfaction. Empirical SC research uses various frameworks to explain the nature of SC performance. Some researchers suggest SC practices based on trust and innovation influence performance positively. Narasimhan and Nair (2005) suggest performance objectives of a firm can be positively affected (directly or indirectly) by the willingness to share confidential information, which supports trustworthiness between partners. Tan et al. (2002) found that information sharing and cooperation had a positive effect on performance. Fynes et al. (2005) confirm that SC relationship quality has a positive impact on SC performance and Hsu (2005) suggests trust, transparency, and visibility in SC relationships allow unexpected actions and negative outcomes. Firms' innovation processes and activities normally involve interaction and collaboration with other SC members. It has many potential benefits, such as idea generation, cost reduction, increasing flexibility, improving development, testing and diffusion, and shortening the time-to-market (Chen et al., 2013). Narasimhan and Narayanan (2013) argue that firms can effectively align internal innovation activities and knowledge available in the supply network to gain superior performance. Sisodiya et al. (2013) found that the ability to build interfirm relationships in innovation is essential for gaining superior financial performance.

Other researchers have showed negatively influence of asymmetry: Kim et al. (2010) suggest uncertainty produces a negative effect on operation performance, product cost, and quality; Gulati et al. (2012) confirm that rising demand instabilities and high manufacturing specializations produce increased costs and affect SC performance negatively; Swink et al. (2007) report that manufacturers with supplier integration have poorer quality and potentially poorer new product flexibility. However, Swink and Song (2007) explained that cost coordination and increasing stakeholder integration in new product development efforts have both positive and negative effects on new product success.

Asymmetry in SC relationships exists not only in the aggregate form but also in a large majority of individual firms. From an individual firm perspective, suboptimal resource allocation, non-alignment of objectives and goals or asynchronous decision making process could reduce long-term performance and competitive advantage (Kearns and Lederer, 2003; Terjensen et al. 2012).

A review of the extant literature shows differing influence of trust and innovation intensity on the relationship between asymmetric relationships and SC performance. Thus, we propose:

H3. Asymmetry has a non-linear relationship with SC performance under different intensities of Trust and Innovation.

In order to validate these views, this study examines how asymmetry influences SC performance under different levels of intensity of trust and innovation processes.

METHODOLOGY

To test these hypotheses, a survey was developed and administered. Data collection was carried out in Poland and Spain, regions that are important to global supply networks. Polish market has been least affected by the financial crisis in Europe in recent years and managerial behaviors have been stable affording a suitable environment to study trust and innovation.

During the last few years, Spanish companies' interests have grown to establish businesses in emerging markets such as Poland. Several Spanish companies have adapted practices, procedures, and management tools they used in Spanish markets to new business environments such as Poland. Spanish firms have had to adapt their SCM practices, especially with respect to trust and innovation. These implementations have been made within their SCs that have disparate structures in comparison to those found in their home country. As such, the authors had access to firms in these markets assuring a high level of interest in the study. Therefore, the sampling frame consisted of firms from Spain and Poland.

Sample and survey instrument.

To test the presented theoretical model and describe the relationships among asymmetry, performance, trust and innovation we gathered primary survey data using a questionnaire. The questionnaire was electronically sent to 545 SC organizations in Spain and Poland (279 Spanish firms and 266 Polish firms). Electronic surveys present certain advantages, such as faster data collection and higher response rates (Griffis et al., 2003). The firms were selected randomly and operate in various industries (e.g., electronics, metal, mining, auto, food, construction, logistics services, electric materials, pharmaceutics, cosmetics, energy, textiles, and others; see tables 4 and 5). We selected from those firms with annual sales ranging from $15 million to $100 million. The sampling frame represented a mixed structure of capital ownership and multiple sector.

As control variables, we collected data on characteristics of the supply chains that reflect market maturity. Emerging markets require large investments to cover customer needs, distribution infrastructures, brand adaptations, and development of specific knowledge (Porter, 1990). These requirements are difficult to meet with supply chains made up of few partners. In the Polish market, for example, a majority of supply chains include more than three partners, which confirms previous observations (Tab.4).

Table. 4 Supply Chain structure and research sectors in Poland

NUMBER OF PARTNERS IN SUPPLY CHAIN	N	%
more than 6	44	86.4%
3 to 6	29	11.1%
3 or fewer	6	2.5%
TOTAL	79	100%
SECTORS		
Logistics	10	
Construction	10	
Electronics & IT Hardware	8	
Metal	8	
Clothing, Footwear, & Fashion	7	
Food Industries	7	
Mining	5	
Cosmetics	5	
Automotive	5	
Electric material	5	
Pharmaceutic	3	
Energy	2	
Other	4	
TOTAL	79	

Table. 5 Supply Chain structure and research sectors in Spain

NUMBER OF PARTNERS IN SUPPLY CHAIN	N	%
more than 6	29	23.07%
3 to 6	19	19.23%
3 or fewer	42	57.69%
TOTAL	90	100%
SECTORS		
Logistics	12	
Electronics & IT Hardware	10	
Clothing, Footwear, & Fashion	10	
Construction	10	
Metal	10	
Food Industries	9	

Energy	8	
Mining	0	
Cosmetics	5	
Pharmaceutic	4	
Automotive	7	
Electric material	4	
Other	1	
TOTAL	90	

Maturity of market with well-established market mechanisms, systematically increases capabilities of a business process and an organization's ability to deliver higher performance over time (Rosemann and de Bruin, 2005). In a mature market, domestic and global suppliers compete intensely for market share and customer satisfaction (Johnson, 2000).

Before sending of questionnaires, we pre-tested their content in a pilot study to ensure the reliability and validity of our constructs. In the first step we relied primarily on items used in prior research and subjected them to a thorough pretest. We eliminated items that were unclear, ambiguous, or led to perceived over- laps in constructs. In the second step, the initial questionnaire was presented to selected managers of Spanish and Polish firms. Several of the questions were re-worded in order to improve their clarity in the pretest stage. The questionnaire was translated into Polish and Spanish to ensure that the respondents had a good understanding and comprehension of the issues addressed. In each case, the firm was invited to participate in the study through a letter addressed to the respondent (usually the manager) of the SCM or Procurement department.

Data were collected through a two-part survey in order to minimize the problems associated with common methods bias. The first part consisted of questions on the firm's general characteristics. The second part included a set of closed and open-ended questions dealing with specific issues of inter-organizational relationships in the SC process (Appendix A). We used the literature to identify valid measures for related constructs and adapted existing scales to measure trust (Svensson, 2001 and Ryu et al., 2008), innovation (Colurcio and Russo-Spena, 2013; Gilley and Rasheed, 2000 and Spekman, et al., 1998) and performance (Germain, Dröge and Spears, 1996; and Dröge and Germain, 2000). In the case of asymmetry, we developed our own measures based on our understanding of this construct. All items were scored on a seven-point, Likert-type scales. A Chow breakpoint test on the dependent variable (Armstrong and Overton, 1977) confirmed that there were no significant differences and there was no evidence of non-response bias in the sample.

The survey's single respondent nature may be susceptible to common method bias. Based on survey design guidelines for limiting common method bias recommended by Podsakoff et al. (2003), in first step, we follow suggestions related to questionnaire, we incorporated clear guidelines for the survey, used multiple questions for each construct for increases the precision of the estimate and introduced a cover letter with briefly introducing and promising that the answers would be kept confidential. In second step, we performed Harman's single-factor test, to check the existence of common method bias. The common variance results were 39.81% for Spain and 24.14% for Poland. Both below the commonly recommended 50% threshold, therefore suggesting common method bias is not a problem.

<u>Validity and reliability</u>

We used a confirmatory factor analysis (CFA) with maximum likelihood estimation to establish the construct validity of our measurements. The factor analysis supported the expected structure because the fit indices reflected an acceptable model fit. Internal consistency was measured by

Cronbach's alpha, composite reliability and the average variance extracted (AVE) (see Tables 7 and 8).

Table 7. Latent variables coefficients. Spain

	Sym	Trust	Perform	Innov	Trust*Sym	Innov*Sym
R-Squared		0.637	0.475	0.308		
Adj. R-Squared		0.630	0.463	0.294		
Composite Reliability	0.872	0.880	0.819	0.847	0.945	0.944
Cronbach's alpha	0.803	0.828	0.720	0.772	0.938	0.937
Avg. Var. Extracted	0.631	0.596	0.483	0.532	0.471	0.463
Full Collin. VIF	3.011	3.126	2.043	2.082	2.728	2.734
Q-Squared		0.639	0.496	0.303		

Table 8. Latent variables coefficients. Poland

	Sym	Perform	Trust	Innov	Trust*Sym	Innov*Sym
R-Squared		0.292	0.438	0.195		
Adj. R-Squared		0.266	0.430	0.194		
Composite Reliability	0.823	0.794	0.769	0.770	0.852	0.834
Cronbach's alpha	0.710	0.775	0.823	0.725	0.819	0.793
Avg. Var. Extracted	0.540	0.445	0.401	0.403	0.237	0.221
Full Collin. VIF	1.977	1.155	1.927	1.283	1.418	1.158
Q-Squared		0.337	0.436	0.178		

In the two countries, Cronbach´s alpha measurements values exceed the recommended threshold of 0.700, for exploratory research. Our composite reliability values, ranged from 0.82 to 0.94 in the case of Spain and from 0.77 to 0.85 in the case of Poland. All of the CR values were greater than 0.60 thus, the values of these metrics were generally greater than the cut-off values suggested by Bagozzi and Yi (1988). As suggested by Fornell and Larcker (1981), to assess discriminant validity, we compared the average variance that was extracted and the variance that was shared between pairs of constructs. The results indicates that the square root of each average variance extracted was greater than the correlation coefficient in the corresponding columns and rows. This confirmed adequate discriminant validity for our measurements (Tables 9 and 10, on diagonal).

Table 9. Spain. Discriminant Validity. Fornell-Larcker Criterion. Square roots of variance extracted (AVEs) on main diagonal

	Sym	Trust	Innov.	Performance	Trust*Sym	Innov*Sym
Symmetry	(0.794)	0.796	0.437	0.479	-0.389	-0.437
Trust	0.796	(0.772)	0.500	0.431	-0.341	-0.416
Innovation	0.437	0.500	(0.695)	0.639	-0.269	-0.081
Performance	0.479	0.431	0.639	(0.729)	-0.451	-0.249
Trust*Sym	-0.389	-0.341	-0.269	-0.451	(0.686)	0.739
Innov*Sym	-0.437	-0.416	-0.081	-0.249	0.739	(0.681)

Table 10. Poland. Discriminant Validity. Fornell-Larcker Criterion. Square roots of variance extracted (AVEs) on main diagonal

	Sym	Trust	Innov.	Performance	Trust*Sym	Innov*Sym
Symmetry	(0.735)	0.293	0.655	0.385	-0.377	-0.007
Trust	0.293	(0.667)	0.312	0.211	-0.181	-0.119
Innovation	0.655	0.312	(0.634)	0.365	-0.346	0.035
Performance	0.385	0.211	0.365	(0.635)	0.008	-0.014
Trust*Sym	-0.377	-0.181	-0.346	0.008	(0.487)	0.305
Innov*Sym	-0.007	-0.119	0.035	-0.014	0.305	(0.470)

Latent variable correlations for both countries show moderate to high values, indicating a good convergent validity of the measures used for each construct in the model.

Once the measurement model was validated, we assessed the validity of the structural model (Tables 7 and 8). In both cases, the models' coefficients of determination R2 take values above the lower weak threshold limit of 0.190. Variance inflation factors (VIF values) were appreciably lower than the commonly admitted threshold value of 5. Therefore, we deemed multicollinearity was not a problem.

We received 169 completed surveys (90 from Spanish and 79 from Polish firms respectively), which represented a 32.24% of response rate in the case of Spain and 29.69% in the case of Poland. These response rates are sufficiently high and comparable to other studies in SCM literature (Chen and Paulraj, 2004; Lee, et al., 2011; Terjesen, et al., 2012)

Research Framework and Measures

The majority of the empirical research in SCM literature has used only linear models, which assume that there is a linear effect for asymmetry, trust, innovation and others factors on performance. Therefore, even if relationship between asymmetry and performance is curvilinear, linear models would simplify the relationship and mask the true relationships among the variables (Edwards 2002). However, Terjesen, et al. (2012) recently have showed an inverse U-shaped relationship between SC integration and performance. They found significant curvilinear relationships that indicated that integration contributed positively to performance up to a certain point, after which a negative relationship was observed. Therefore, complex congruence hypotheses using curvilinear effects are required to test the full range of component measures (Venkatesh and Goyal, 2010).

The examination of complex relationships among constructs and an outcome variable requires two step hierarchical analysis to detect accurately their relationships (Edwards 1994, 2002). Following Venkatesh and Goyal (2010) and Terjesen et al. (2012), we used Polynomial modeling in our analysis that permits examination of curvilinear relationships between constructs. Polynomial regression is a stepwise model. First step of the analysis was testing the linear relationship of components (asymmetry, trust and innovation) with outcome variable (Performance). If the direct effects are significant, nonlinear effects are introduced in the next step (for a detailed discussion, see Edwards, 2002; Edwards and Harrison, 1993). In order to corroborate the hypothesized curvilinear relationship among asymmetry and performance, previously detected in the model (Chatelain et al., 2002; Temme et al., 2006), we estimated two polynomial regressions, one for Spain and one for Poland (see tables 11 and 12) relating asymmetry and performance. In the equation for Spain, p-values of the quadratic and cubic terms are above the common threshold $p <= 0.05$ reflecting the dominance of the linear component (see table 12). On the contrary, no linear effects have a strong significance ($p<= 0.05$) in the equation for Poland (see table 11).

Table 11. Poland. Polynomial Regression Results.

Dependent Variable: PERFORM				
Independient Variables	Coefficient	Std. Error	t-Statistic	Prob.
C	0.142118	0.142133	0.999888	0.3205
ASYM	0.625807	0.189602	3.300631	0.0015
(ASYM)^2	-0.239306	0.117303	-2.040073	0.0448
(ASYM)^3	-0.179643	0.073785	-2.434697	0.0172

Table 12. Spain. Polynomial Regression Results.

Dependent Variable: PERFORM				
Independient Variables	Coefficient	Std. Error	t-Statistic	Prob.
C	0.141497	0.183857	0.769605	0.4453
ASYM	0.573735	0.214565	2.673945	0.0102
(ASYM)^2	-0.191546	0.165664	-1.156227	0.2533
(ASYM)^3	-0.089739	0.081133	-1.106074	0.2742

During the second step of analysis, we used the Warp 3 algorithm (Chatelain et al., 2002; Temme et al., 2006) to test for the presence of non-linear relationships. We have used this type of modelling and algorithm as a means to explore simultaneously the complex causal, mediation and moderation relationships arising among Trust, Innovation, Asymmetry and Performance (Figure 1). This analysis allowed us to test, simultaneously, for performance variations, for various levels of Trust and Innovation in the presence of asymmetries. To corroborate the results, we tested the extent to which the non-linear relationship is valid in the context of the current data. In order to assess the postulated hypotheses, we propose a non-linear model (Figure 1) with statistical estimates derived from Partial Least Squares (PLS) regression analysis using WarpPLS 5.0 (Kock, 2015). Originally developed for econometrics, PLS has more recently been adopted in research in business, education, and social sciences. The decision to estimate the model using the Partial Least Squares (PLS) regression method was made according to the following criteria: the phenomenon investigated is relativity new and its modeling is in a developing stage; minimal recommendations exist concerning sample size, prediction accuracy;

and non-data multi-normality requirements. PLS is the preferred choice for research models which incorporate both reflective and formative constructs (Lehner and Haas, 2010; Wetzels et al., 2009). PLS regression aims to produce a model that transforms a set of correlated explanatory variables into a new set of uncorrelated variables (Tenenhaus, 1998). The parameter estimates in a PLS regression are derived from the direct correlations between the predictor variables and the criterion variable. This procedure uses two-stage estimation algorithms to obtain weights, loadings, and path estimates (Wold, 1985). The constructs of the model are unobservable (latent) variables indirectly described by a set of observable variables, which are denominated indicators. The use of multiple questions for each construct increases the precision of the estimate.

This paper applied, Warp 3 algorithm tries to identify nonlinear functions between pairs of latent variables in structural equations models and calculate their association coefficients accordingly (Kock, 2015). The Warp 3 algorithm (Kock, 2015) identifies a set of functions:

F1(LVp1), F2(LVp2) relating blocks of latent variable predictors (LVp1, LVp2 ...) to a criterion latent variable (LVc), as in

LVc = p1*F1(LVp1) + p2*F2(LVp2) + … + e

where p1, p2 ... are path coefficients, and e is the equation error term.

All variables are standardized. The more curvilinear the functions F1(LVp1), F2(LVp2) ...are curved the greater will be the difference between the path coefficients p1, p2 ... and those that would have been obtained via a linear analysis. This is done for a wide range of functions, with modification constants included. Simple graphical inspection (see figures 2, 3, 4, 5, 7, 8, 9 and 10), later formally tested, permitted assessment of whether the functions fitted by the algorithm are a good fit to the data.

Although 100 bootstrapping resamples is said to be sufficient (Efron et al. 2004) for the PLS analysis, 5000 resamples were performed (Hair et al., 2011). The decision to estimate the model using PLS was made according to the following criteria: The phenomenon investigated is relativity new and its modeling is in a developing stage, minimal recommendations exist concerning sample size, prediction accuracy and strict multinormality requirements (Henseler et al., 2009; Joreskög and Wold, 1982).

We interpret negative symmetry values as asymmetry indication. The model shows direct and indirect influence of asymmetries (Asym) and direct influence of trust (Trust) and innovation (Innov), on performance (Results). In addition, we tested for the presence of moderation (dashed lines), enhancing or constraining the direct effect of Asymmetry on Performance. Table 6 summarizes model fit and quality indices for both countries. The following indices were used to test hypotheses and model fit (Kock, 2013): average path coefficient (APC), average R-squared (ARS), average adjusted R-squared (AARS), average block variance inflation factor (AVIF), average full collinearity VIF (AFVIF), Tenenhaus goodness-of-fit index (GoF), Sympson's paradox ratio (SPR), R-squared contribution ratio (RSCR), statistical suppression ratio (SSR), and non-linear bivariate causality direction ratio (NLBCDR).

Table 6. Model Fit and Quality Indices Overview

Index	Value (Spain)	Value (Poland)	Value Interpretation
Average path coefficient (APC)	0.338, P=0.002	0.290, P=0.001	Significant if p<0.01
Average R-squared (ARS)	0.487, P<0.001	0.308, P<0.001	Significant if p<0.01
Average adjusted R-squared (AARS)	0.462, P<0.001	0.287, P<0.001	Significant if p<0.01
Average block VIF (AVIF)	2.269	1.524	Acceptable if <= 5, ideally <= 3.3
Average full	2.620	1.486	Acceptable if <= 5,

collinearity VIF (AFVIF)			ideally <= 3.3
Tenenhaus GoF (GoF)	0.508	0.340	Small >= 0.1, medium >= 0.25; large >= 0.36
Sympson's paradox ratio (SPR)	0.857	0.857	acceptable if >= 0.7, ideally = 1
R-squared contribution ratio (RSCR)	0.984	0.985	Acceptable if >= 0.9, ideally = 1
Statistical suppression ratio (SSR)	1.000	1.000	Acceptable if >= 0.7
Non-linear bivariate causality direction ratio (NLBCDR)	0.857	0.714	Acceptable if >= 0.7

The Tennenhaus GoF index (Tenenhaus et al., 2005) is a measure of a model's explanatory power, defined as the square root of the product between the average communality index and ARS. The communality index for a latent variable is defined as the sum of squared, un-rotated loadings with each loading associated with an indicator, divided by the number of indicators. The average communality index for a model is defined similarly, and considers all latent variables in the calculation. The SPR index is a measure of the extent to which a model is free from instances of Simpson's paradox. A Simpson's paradox indicates a causality problem, suggesting that a hypothesized path is either implausible or reversed (Pearl, 2009; Wagner, 1982). The RSCR index is a measure of the extent to which a model is free from negative R-squared contributions, which occur with Simpson's paradox instances (Pearl, 2009; Wagner, 1982). The SSR index is a measure of the extent to which a model is free from statistical suppression instances (MacKinnon et al., 2000). A statistical suppression instance indicates a causality problem, suggesting a hypothesized path is either implausible or reversed. The NLBCDR index is a measure of the extent to which bivariate, non-linear coefficients of association support the hypothesized directions of causal links in a model. All fit and quality indices discussed above met recommended thresholds (Table 6).

Regarding the hypothesis, hypothesis 3 proposed a non-linear relationship between Asymmetry and Performance, testing the assumption of a relationship between the two variables. As shown in our results H3 is supported (β =.12; β =.36 with $p<0.01$, fig. 1 and 6). Although not hypothesized, drawing on different intensity of Trust and Innovation could also have a non-linear relationship to Performance. The findings suggest that separately both Trust and Innovation have a relationship with Performance, which support H1 (β =.33; β =.09 with $p<0.01$, fig. 1 and 6) and H2 (β =.35; β =.35 with $p<0.01$, fig. 1 and 6). This is consistent with the literature that argues that Asymmetry has a limited effect on Performance when Trust and Innovation are present in the model (Michalski et al., 2013). For many managers in asymmetric business environments, a high level of trust or innovation seems to be excessive interdependence of SC partners. In the case of small and medium firms, the managers can avoid increasing the level of trust or innovation, because benefits do not evolve automatically from this decision. In this situation, they prefer maintenance of asymmetric relationships, although this could lead to reduction of performance.

Overall, structural model findings support all three hypotheses.

FINDINGS

We explore whether the changes in asymmetry levels have an impact on performance, under different intensities of trust and innovation in SC relationships. We also explore these relationships in different markets, in order to be sure that the results of these relationships do not depend on market development. It is interesting to examine how the intensity of trust and innovation in symmetric relationships differs from asymmetric relationships with respect to SC performance. Figure 1 shows model hypotheses, with corresponding p-values for the Spanish sample. Solid lines indicate causal relationships; dashed lines indicate moderation path and dotted lines show insignificant relationships. Beta coefficients were normalized, taking values between zero and one, and measuring the strength and direction of the relationships.

Figure 1. Research Model and Primary Results for Spain

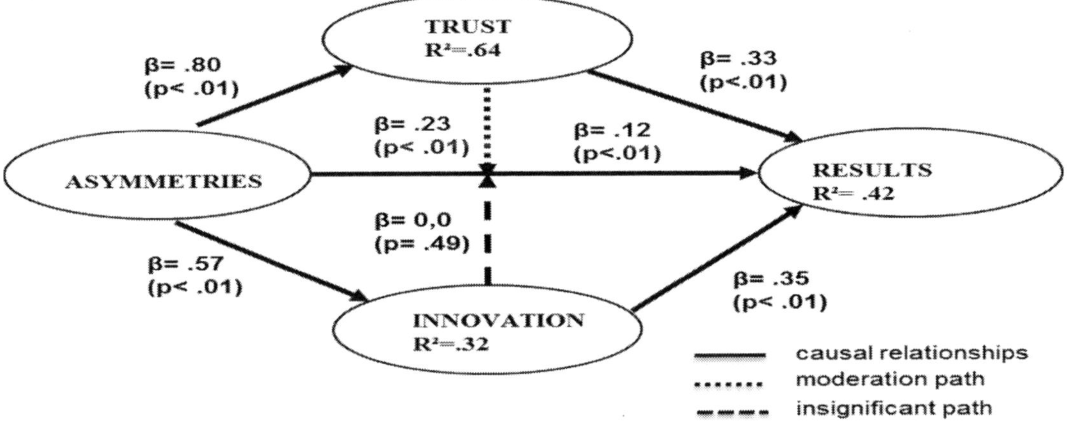

All relationships were significant (p<0.01), including the direct relationship between asymmetry and performance, with one exception. The indirect effects of innovation on performance were not significant. In the curve that reflects the relationship between asymmetry and results in the low-trust context in Spain, two inflection points are evident (Figure 2). These two turning points are at both ends of the curve, although for the most part, its path shows a steady growth tendency. In mature markets, reduction of high level of asymmetry is beneficial to SC performance, allowing its improvement. However, a small amount of asymmetry can help maintain this improvement.

At the other end of the curvilinear, relationship an increase of symmetry in relationships does not produce the same effect on performance, instead the performance begins to diminish. This situation allows us to suggest that in the case of low trust environments, SC partners must avoid highly asymmetric or highly symmetric relationships, if they want to improve their performance. The curvilinear relationship explains some of the conflicting findings in the literature. When there is asymmetry, under conditions of low trust, it can be conjectured that relational friction might lead to low collaboration and opportunism degrading performance. Similarly, when symmetry is high, network perspective would suggest that firms would have high level of connectedness with their network partners and such closure might not be conducive to knowledge exploitation and innovation (Narasimhan and Narayanan, 2013; Noordhoff et al., 2011). Our findings support Ramsay (2001) and Schoenher and Mabert (2006), who suggested that relationships among organizations of similar size, strength, and power are highly recommended.

In Spanish SCs characterized by high levels of trust, the relationship between asymmetry and performance is slightly different (see Figure. 2). Regarding the influence of asymmetry on performance in the high trust level context, the curvilinear relationship has a U shape. Decrease in the level of asymmetry (and even slight increase in symmetry) in relations between partners diminished the collaboration performance. We argue that the decrease of asymmetry may be associated with reduction of dependence on dominant partner due to attempts by dependent firms to modify the trading conditions, especially in terms of price, quality and delivery, without fear of breaking the contract. The U shape relationship between asymmetry and performance also suggests that high level of trust can be costly for the firms. In this situation, managers try to balance the level of trust with anticipated superior performance. However, tendency to increase collaboration leads to performance decreases.

High trust levels removes the threat of opportunism allowing the partners to act somewhat independently. This effect is manifested until a threshold value of symmetry is reached. Beyond this value, symmetry in the presence of high levels of trust allows firms to commit resources to the relationship enhancing collaboration and innovation.

Figure 2. Asymmetry, Trust and Performance Relationships in Spain (Standardized Scales)

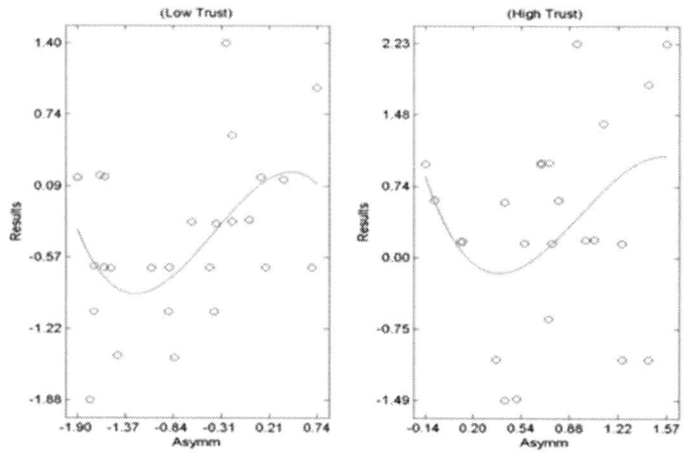

Performance was strong and positively influenced by growing of symmetry. The increasing portion of the U-shaped curve relates to this situation. In environments with high level of trust, the SC partners will be willing to communicate openly, accept sharing of information at all levels and bear risk jointly. Its influence is very positive for performance. According to this, we suggest that in the case of mature markets with high level of trust, the dependent companies should try to keep relative symmetry in their collaborative relationships as long as possible. This finding supports Feldman (1998), who argued that mutual interests are at play as long as a company can keep up their partner's perception that their relationship is still symmetric.

In Spanish SC characterized by low levels of innovation, the relationship between asymmetry and performance followed again a different curvilinear path (see Figure 3). For much of the asymmetry range, performance is negative. It seems that managers' belief that increased costs associated with innovationsare not absorbed by the entire supply chain but by each participant in asymmetric environment. Innovations lead only to the trade-offs between operating costs and changes in unit costs in the supply chain, which are not necessarily evident at the same time. In this situation the reduction of asymmetry does not produce significant change in performance degradation.

Figure 3. Asymmetry, Innovation and Performance Relationships in Spain (Standardized Scales)

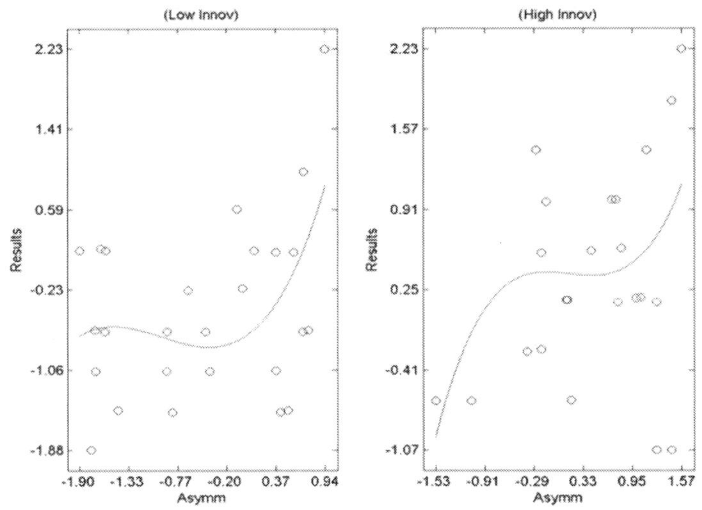

From other view point, asymmetry is not a problem for the development of collaborative innovation. Firms have a wide range of possibilities to search for larger partners to make investments in innovation. Differences in size, power, structure or resources between partners, so typical for asymmetric relations, will not affect and will not create barriers to this search.

The situation changes with the growth of symmetry in relations between partners in the SC; performance begins to grow quickly. This suggests that symmetry is necessary for driving differences in performance. Like Colurcio and Russo-Spena (2013), we reason that in mature environments with low innovation level, small firms need to work closely with other small firms, which are similar in their background of knowledge and routines whereas medium companies are searching to gain access to specific technological know-how.

In the case of high innovation, the path of performance again changes (see Figure.3). Decreased asymmetry, increasing degree of symmetry, produces rapid performance growth. In the middle part of the curve, where low levels of asymmetry or symmetry can be observed, the value of performance does not seem to be affected by these changes. The curvilinear relationship shows in an environment of high innovation intensity higher levels of asymmetry and symmetry are beneficial. This is characterized by situations where a focal firm might engage with a number of smaller but innovative firms to increase SC performance. In contrast, when innovation intensity is high, firms can also engage with supplier partners who themselves are large, have high resource endowments and similar in size, power and innovative ability in order to increase SC performance. Such situations can be observed in the behavior of firms in industries such as furniture and tiles in Spain. Companies in these sectors have begun working more closely with similar and highly innovative suppliers from other sectors such as construction, textile and lighting. The offer of innovative products produced collaboratively has increased performance and has created a new opportunity for growth.

The joint effects of asymmetry, trust and innovation on performance are shown in Figure 4 and 5 for Spain and 9 and 10 for Poland. The three-dimensional analysis facilitated by curvilinear modeling allows us to maintain distinction throughout the analysis and test complex congruence hypotheses, such as the difference in the absolute level of performance when the values of both trust and innovation are high compared to when both are low. This distinction is not possible to assess using direct measures (Venkatesh and Goyal, 2010). Positive effects on the performance from coordinated decreases in asymmetry (i.e. increasing level of symmetry) and increases in trust are evident. Even only one of these variables, if acted upon, increases Results. The same is evident when considering the joint effects of asymmetry and innovation on performance (Figure 5). A coordinated decrease of asymmetry and increase in innovation had notably positive effects on results. An effect is evident, though more slowly, when acting predominantly or exclusively on only one of these variables.

Figure 4. Simultaneous Effects of Trust and Asymmetry on Firm Performance in Spain

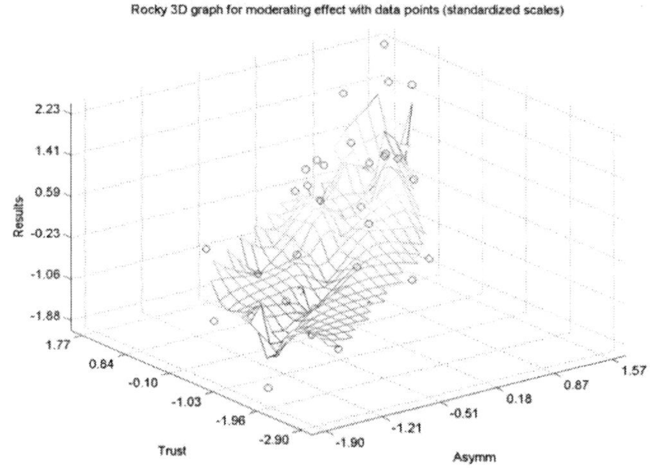

Figure 5. Simultaneous Effects of Innovation and Asymmetry on Firm Performance in Spain

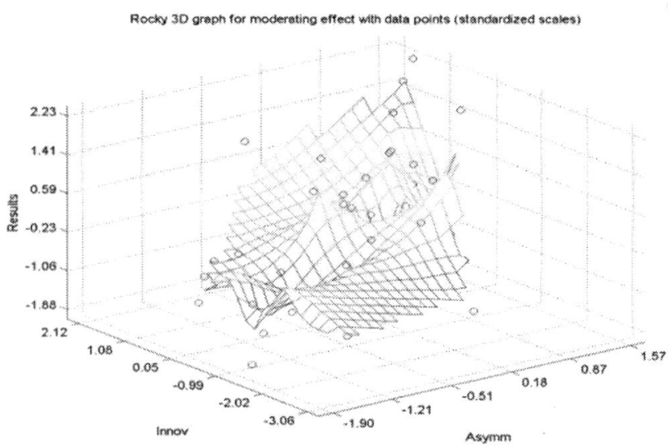

Considering the Polish sample, Figure 6 presents the results, with corresponding p-values. Most relationships were significant ($p<0.01$), with two exceptions, the indirect effects of trust and innovation on Results were not statistically significant.

Figure 6. Research Model and Primary Results for Poland

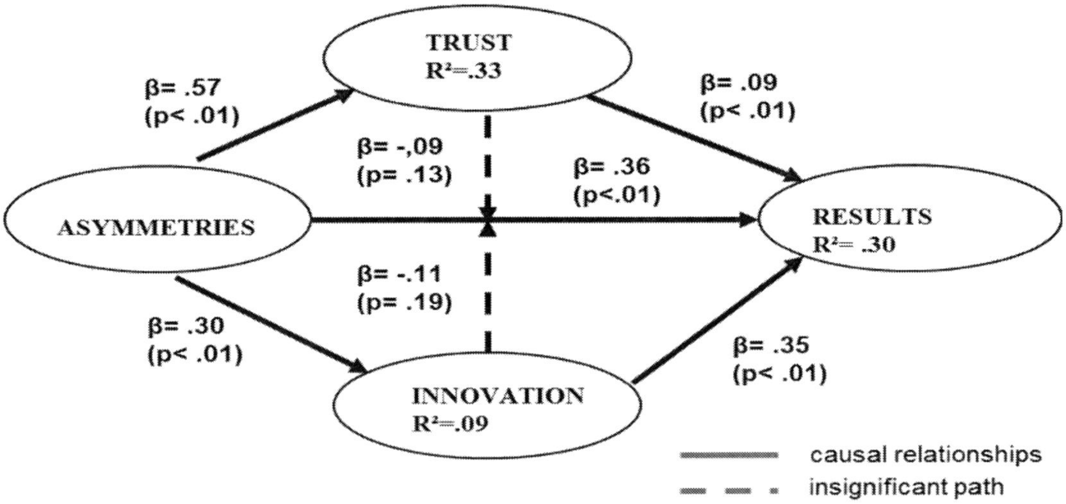

The curvilinear response functions for Poland show interesting relationships between asymmetry and performance in low and high trust context. They have a similar, although inverse path. Regarding the influence of asymmetry on performance in low trust environments, the curve had a classic-U shape. Although with a substantial spread, in high trust environments, we observed an inverted-U shape (Figure 7). A clearer picture emerges in figure 9, where it can be seen how increasing levels of symmetry and trust lead to higher performance.

In emerging markets with low levels of trust, in order to increase the performance, it is appropriate to establish highly asymmetrical or symmetrical relations between partners. In this type of relationships the safeguarding effect of collaboration is stronger, especially when risks of opportunism due to low level of trust are high (Corsten and Felde, 2004).

All intermediate solutions bring about the opposite effect (i.e. decrease performance). These findings are opposite to Johnsen and Ford's (2001) suggestions that to improve benefits from collaborative dyadic relationships it is necessary to change from asymmetrical to symmetrical relationships. We suggest that the cost and requirements of this change, especially in areas of organizational capacity and culture, in the short or medium term, do not justify it. If firms are seeking stability in relationships, the high level of asymmetry, which is reflected by the clear dominance of one party over another, could be acceptable and even beneficial.

Interestingly, the increase of trust reverses the nature of the relationship. In emerging environments, with high levels of trust, a slight asymmetry or symmetry creates the best conditions for growth of performance. High levels of symmetry and asymmetry drastically reduce performance. This suggests that it is not necessarily asymmetry or symmetry driving variations in performance, but rather the level of trust. This implies that in markets that are at a lower level of maturity in SCM, trust is much more important than symmetry in SC relationships. This finding deserves further investigation.

Figure 7. Asymmetry, Trust and Performance Relationships in Poland (Standardized Scales)

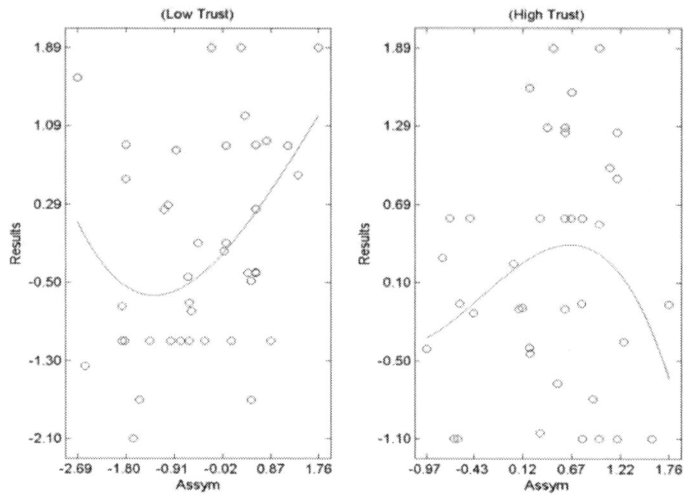

Regarding innovation, in the low-innovation context, the curvilinear relationship is very similar to that observed in the case of trust in the same environment (see Figure 8). Performance is severely affected in conditions of high degree of asymmetry and symmetry, although in the case of high symmetry environments growth of performance is limited. These findings support Noordhoff et al. (2011), who argue that one part of SC can use the innovation knowledge related to other partners to facilitate the creation of new ideas early in the innovation process. This behavior increases the uncertainty in the relationships between SC partners and could slow down performance.

If the level of innovation changes from low to high, the figure shows two breakpoints (see Figure 8). At these points, a change in the development trend occurs. In SCs with high innovation levels, in the first stages for high asymmetry, the effect on results was negative until the breakpoint, after which there was a change in benefits that turns positive until moderate symmetry is achieved. If values for symmetry continue to expand, the influence on performance becomes again negative.

As expected, the reduction of asymmetry in these environments produces improved performance (Wang, 2011), but the influence of symmetry on performance was a surprise. The results suggest that after getting by firms a high degree of symmetry, especially related to knowledge, information and power, can increase the risk of demotivation, lack of risk-taking in new projects and even lack of ambition in the relationships between the parties. This could lead directly to reduction of SC performance.

Considering the simultaneous effects of trust and asymmetry on performance (Figure 9), the results are clear in Poland, the emerging market. We detected a similar trend - increased trust and symmetry being associated with higher performance. It suggests that firms should not rely on asymmetry or trust to obtain substantial growth in performance, but the simultaneous application of both of them.

Figure 8. Asymmetry, Innovation and Performance Relationships in Poland (Standardized Scales)

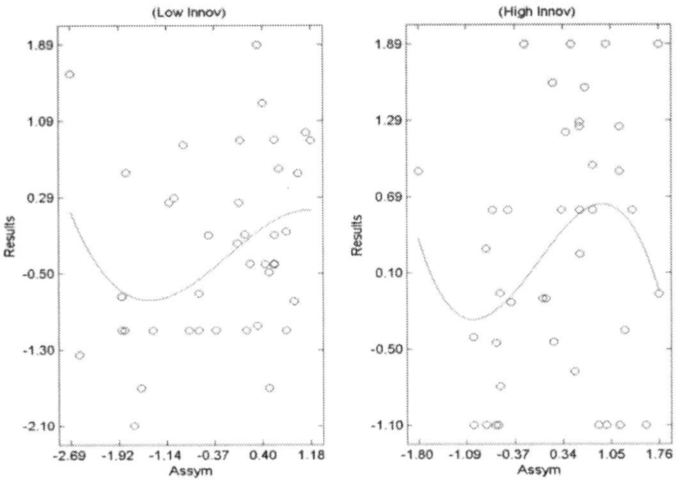

The simultaneous effects of innovation and asymmetry (Figure 10) in this market, results are similar. Although we detected a similar trend related to symmetry—increased innovation and symmetry accompanying higher results—the increase appears limited for the majority of firms in the case of high level of innovation.

Figure 9. Simultaneous Effects of Trust and Asymmetry on Firm Performance in Poland

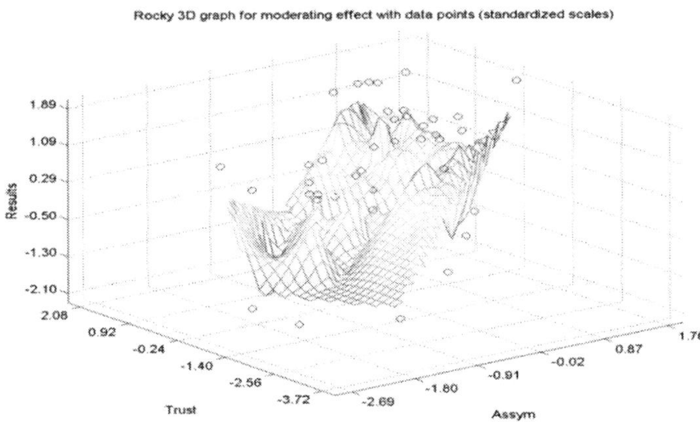

Figure 10. Simultaneous Effects of Innovation and Asymmetries on Firm Performance in Poland

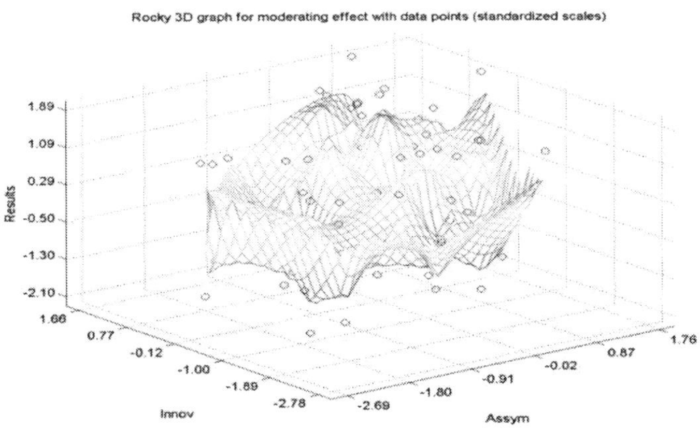

DISCUSSION

In extant literature that has investigated collaborative agreements, researchers agree that asymmetry is important and can significantly impact relationship performance. This exploratory research has uncovered some new and interesting findings relative to the nature of asymmetry's influence on performance in SC relationships. Our findings extend research that addresses asymmetry influences on performance under varying trust and innovation contexts in SCM. The findings also provide insights to practicing managers regarding how to more effectively approach their collaborative relationships.

SCM leads to greater interdependence between partners and has required monitoring and managing performance for mutual benefits. Critical issues for SCM systems are primarily concerned with trust and innovation. According to Laeequddin et al. (2012) trust is context-dependent phenomenon related to rationality, economic relationship, and dynamic capabilities of partners and adoption of technology. Mohd Noor and Pitt (2009) add that to ensure the success of collaboration, it must be founded with a high level of commitment among all parties in the SC. Maheshwari et al. (2006) observed that SC partners must focus on innovation, once they are stabilized and normal operations are achieved. Bouncken (2011) suggests that firms should invest resources in innovation, hoping that their partners will continue to offer future business once the innovation proves fruitful. We would add to these concepts the asymmetry and symmetry, context that affect and are affected by different intensity of trust and innovation. However, the effects of asymmetry or symmetry on performance are still not well understood. This research sought to shed some light upon this important issue.

From a theoretical perspective, it is apparent that relationships between asymmetry, performance, and SC trust and innovation are ambiguous depending on context. Current research, however, does not offer clear answers, but instead focuses on linear relationships among these variables. Perhaps the most significant findings are that the influences of asymmetry and symmetry on performance in varying trust and innovation contexts have varying effects (unstable character) and non-linear paths, a notion supported by Thomas and Esper (2010) who find that asymmetry is a complex and not a static issue, has a temporal character, although structural asymmetry may be constant.

The non-linearity regarding these relationships complicates the already complex and dynamic SCM processes. Temporal and unstable relationships in SC accord well with NT theoretical research (Lam, 2008; Miles and Snow, 2007; Skjoett-Larsen, 1999). Our findings confirm that managers do not seek an optimal equilibrium (i.e. stable relationship), but their management strategies rely on trust and innovation due to a constant state of dynamic movement.

Findings also indicate other suggestions for managers related to strategic decisions. Asymmetry, trust, innovation and performance relationship can take many forms. Managers operating in different environments, within varying contexts of trust and innovation, must recognize their specific contexts when making decisions since no two SCs are the same. In environments with low intensity of innovation in both contexts studied, the managers of small and medium firms are accepting asymmetric relationships over long periods of time more frequently, without suspecting that this may harm them greatly. Surprisingly, for small and medium firms, unbalanced relationships do not seem to be so critical. This is close to Colurcio and Russo-Spena (2013) line of thinking, who find that in asymmetric relationship, involvement in the innovation network of firms with different size is of mutual benefit for both partners. The larger partner offers marketing and technological input for improvement of products for small firms, which operate in a niche; thanks to this small firms can grow together with their small clients and suppliers; and Johnsen and Ford (2008) who suggest that small firms frequently accept asymmetric relationships as a method of attempting to secure their relations with important large companies and when participation in their network is more attractive than other opportunities. The smaller size of some firms gives them flexibility, agility and the advantage of early involvement in new developments. . It promotes innovations and permits them freedom to make decisions related to selection of partners.

We argue that it is important for managers to recognize that in this case, too symmetric relationships might not return as much as asymmetric relations do. Managers can see trust as a mechanism for achieving coordination among SC partners. Despite some views of trust in literature, Kumar (1996) suggests that trust in SC relationships can be built between unequal entities, but only if there is fair play. This does not mean that such asymmetry relationships are not workable or enduring. Moreover, especially in low trust intensity environments, asymmetry may also have a positive effect, improving the performance level and bringing together firms with varied viewpoints, cultures and strategies. Thomas and Esper (2010) suggest that small firms accept the differences in the levels of commitment between themselves and a large retail chain if this allows them to maintain the present status quo. However, even in such a situation the involvement in the SC network must produce mutual benefit for all partners.

CONCLUSION, LIMITATIONS AND FUTURE RESEARCH

This exploration of asymmetry in inter-firm SC relationships makes several meaningful contributions to literature on buyer-supplier relationships. First, it provides greater understanding of a neglected area of SC relationship research, that of asymmetry in relationships. Empirical research, however, does not offer clear solutions, but instead focuses on linear relationships among variables chosen for investigation. Exploration utilizing non-linear relationships involving asymmetry has been lacking. This omission is especially noticeable given that some level of asymmetry is common in many interfirm relationships. This study adds a new point of view to SCM theory by suggesting that not all trust and innovation environments always and directly lead to performance improvements. Explication of non-linear paths and unstable nature of the influences of asymmetry and symmetry on performance in varying trust and innovation contexts is the principal contribution of this study.

The second contribution to the body of knowledge is that our findings offer suggestions for managers regarding strategic decisions. Some businesses do not enter high trust or innovation environment, because benefits do not evolve automatically by changing from asymmetric to symmetric partnerships. For many managers, a high level of symmetry together with high intensity of trust or innovation leads to excessive interdependence with SC partners, especially in the case of small and medium firms. It could limit La Londe's (2002) suggestion - that it is advantageous for each partner in a SC to increase the degree of interdependence - to large firms. Findings from this study provide guidance to managers regarding when it is appropriate to reduce asymmetric relationships with partners while considering varying trust and innovation contexts.

The third contribution of this research is that the development of symmetric relationship to improve SC performance under different trust and innovation contexts has limits. Managers must be careful when making the decision to replace an asymmetric relationship with a symmetric relationship even if it seems to be necessary to achieve rapid growth in performance, because expectations can be wrong.

Fourth, previous research suggests that trust and, recently, innovation are so important that any relationship is destined to fail without them. However, these suggestions are often unclear and too simple. Findings from this study provide guidelines for managers regarding when it is appropriate to invest in trust and innovation under asymmetrical/symmetrical relationships. This becomes even more critical in multi-partner supply chain relationships. We suggest when multiple firms are involved in an asymmetrical SC network, the need to identify the magnitude of trust and innovation capabilities across all parties is essential. Our results suggest that firms should engage in “supply network mapping” to better understand relationships in supply networks. Our findings offer some initial insights that should be investigated deeply.

Limitations and future directions

This paper has some theoretical and methodological limitations. Our study focuses only on one particular business environment in two countries. Dyer and Chu (2003) suggest that cultural differences between institutional environments may influence the development of interfirm relationships. In this context, it is possible that potential contextual variables such as national culture may have influenced the relationships observed. Another limitation of this study is the issue of generalizability since our sample was drawn from two European countries. Consequently, future research could explore validation of the results of this study in other countries

We analyzed asymmetry's influence on performance from a conventional dyadic perspective of SC relationship. Multi-firms (network) analysis perspective would enhance the practical utility of this study for managerial application. Research may clearly identify the concept and roles of trust, innovation and other critical factors in asymmetrical inter-firm SC relationships.

The conceptual and empirical approach used in this study considers the non-linear effects of the relationship between asymmetry and performance in the presence of varying trust and innovation levels, an approach that needs special attention. The approach provides a point of departure for future research that could address other moderating variables that affect the high power and low power firms in supply networks. It would be interesting to test whether the high power and low power firms experience different performance effects in asymmetrical relationships.

Our research focused on relationship in industrial sectors. Future research could examine the asymmetry-performance relationship in other sectors; for example, the retail sector. Asymmetry in trust, innovation, power, collaboration or integration efforts within a retail network may have different influence on performance.

This research highlights the importance of how firms should manage potential negative or positive consequences of asymmetry in multi-tier relationships; but much more research is needed to clarify the true role of asymmetry in SC relationships.

REFERENCES

Alcacer, J., & Chung, W. (2007). Location strategies and knowledge Spillovers. *Management Science,* 53(5), 760–76.

Armstrong, J.S. & Overton, T.S. (1977).Estimating nonresponse bias in mail surveys. *Journal of Marketing Research,* 16: 396-402.

Arlbjørn, J.S., de Haas, H., & Munksgaard, K.B. (2011). Exploring supply chain innovation. *Logistics Research,* 3(1):3-18.

Atkinson, S. & Butcher, D. (2003). Trust in managerial relationships. *Journal of Managerial Psychology,* 18(4): 282-304.

Bagozzi, R.P. & Yi, Y. (1988). On the evaluation of structural equation models. *Journal of the Academy of Marketing Science,* 16(1): 74-94.

Barney, J.B. & Hansen, M.H. (1994). Trustworthiness as a Source of Competitive Advantage. *Strategic Management Journal*, 15 (Special Issue): 175-190.

Barret, P. (2000). Achieving strategic facilities management through strong relationships. *Facilities,* 18 (10/11/12): 421-6.

Basnet, C., Corner, J., Wisner, J., & Tan, K. (2003). Benchmarking supply chain Management practice in New Zealand. *Supply Chain Management: An International Journal,* 8(1): 57-64.

Bouncken, R.B. (2011).Supply Chain Contingencies: The Effects of Up-Stream Directives on Supplier's Innovation Performance. *Engineering Management Journal,* 23(4): 36-46.

Cao, M. &Zhang, Q.Y. (2011). Supply Chain Collaboration: Impact on Collaborative

Advantage and Firm Performance. *Journal of Operations Management,* 29:163–80.
Capaldo, A. (2007). Network structure and innovation. The leveraging of a dual network as a distinctive relational capability. *Strategic Management Journal,* 28: 585-608.
Chatelin, Y.M., Vinzi, V.E., & Tenenhaus, M. (2002), State-of-art on PLS path modeling through the available software. Storrs, CT: Department of Economics, University of Connecticut.
Chen, Y-H. & Barnes, S. (2007). Initial trust and online buyer behavior. *Industrial Management & Data Systems,* 107 (1): 21 – 36.
Chen, I. & Paulraj, A. (2004). Understanding supply chain management: critical research and a theoretical framework. *International Journal of Production Research,* 42(1):131-63.
Chen, W., Brennan, L. & Zeng, D. (2013). Exploring Supply Chain Collaborative Innovation: Evidence from China. *Irish Journal of Management*, 32(2): 5-27.
Chu, S-Y. & Fang, W-Ch. (2006). Exploring the Relationships of Trust and Commitment in Supply Chain Management. *Journal of American Academy of Business,* 9(1):224-28.
Colurcio, M. & Russo-Spena, T. (2013). Collaborative Innovation — A Focus on Food SMES.In I. Muzzalupo (Ed.). *Food Industry*: 647-668.
Corsten, D. & Felde, J. (2004). "Exploring the performance effects of key-supplier collaboration. *International Journal of Physical Distribution and Logistics Management*, 35(6): 445-461.
Dyer, J. & Chu, W. (2003). The role of trustworthiness in reducing transaction costs and improving performance: empirical evidence from the United States, Japan, and Korea. *Organization Science,* 14(1): 57-68.
Edwards, J. R., & Harrison, R. V. (1993). Job Demands and Worker Health: Three-Dimensional Reexamination of the Relationship Between Person–Environment Fit and Strain. *Journal of Applied Psychology* 78(4): 628-648.
Edwards, J. R. (1994). The Study of Congruence in Organizational Behavior Research: Critique and a Proposed Alternative. *Organizational Behavior and Human Decision Processes*, 58(1): 51-101.
Edwards, J. R. (2002). Alternatives to Difference Scores: Polynomial Regression Analysis and Response Surface Methodology, in Measuring and Analyzing Behavior in Organizations: Advances in Measurement and Data Analysis, F. Drasgow and N. Schmidt (eds.), San Francisco: Jossey-Bass/Pfeiffer: 350-400.
Feldman, L.J. (1998). Industry viewpoint: relational interdependency and punctuated equilibrium. *The Journal of Business and Industrial Marketing,* 13(3): 288-93
Fynes, B., S. Búrca, & C. Voss. 2005. Supply Chain Relationship Quality, the Competitive Environment and Performance. *International Journal of Production Research* 43(16): 3303-3320.
Gao, T.S.M.J., & Bird, M.M. (2005). Reducing buyer decision-making uncertainty in organizational purchasing: can supplier trust, commitment and dependence help. *Journal of Business Research,* 58: 397-405.
Garcia, R. & Calantone, R. (2002). A Critical Look at Technological Innovation Typology and Innovativeness Terminology: A Literature Review. *Journal of Product Innovation Management*, 19(2): 110-132.
Gilley, K.M., & Rasheed, A. (2000). Making more by doing less: an analysis of outsourcing and its effects on firm performance. *Journal of Management* 26(4): 763-90.
Griffis, S.E., Goldsby, T.J., & Cooper, M. (2003). Web-based and mail surveys: comparison of response, data and cost. *Journal of Business Logistics,* 24(2): 237-58.
Gounaris, S.P. (2005). Trust and commitment influences on customer retention: insights from business-to-business services. *Journal of Business Research,* 58: 126-40.
Grönroos, C. (2000).Service Management and Marketing: A Customer Relationship

Management Approach. New York, NY: John Wiley & Sons.
Gulati, R., P. Puranam, & M. Tushman. (2012). Meta-organization Design: Rethinking Design in Interorganizational and Community Contexts. *Strategic Management Journal,* 33 (6): 571-586.
Hair, J. F., Ringle, C. M., & Sarstedt, M. (2011). PLS-SEM: Indeed a silver bullet. *Journal of Marketing Theory and Practice* 19 (2): 139–151.
Håkansson, H. & Ford, D. (2002). How should companies interact in business networks? *Journal of Business Research*, 55(2):133-39.
Handfield, R.B. (2002). The new supply chain model. *APICS* January: 24.
Halldorsson, A., Kotzab, H., Mikkola, J.M. & Skjøtt-Larsen, T. (2007). Complementary theories to supply chain management. *Supply Chain Management: An International Journal*12 (4): 284–296.
Harman, H. H. (1967). Modern Factor Analysis. 2d ed. Chicago: University of Chicago Press.
Heide, J.B. & John, G. (1990). Alliances in industrial purchasing: the determinants of joint action in buyer-supplier relationships. *Journal of Marketing Research,* 27(1): 24-36.
Herzlinger, R. (2006). Innovating in Health Care-framework. Boston, MA: Harvard Business School Publishing.
Hingley, M.K. (2005), "Power to all our friends? Living with imbalance in supplier-retailer relationships", Industrial Marketing Management, Vol. 34, pp. 848-58.
Hsu, L-L. (2005). SCM System Effects on Performance for Interactions between Suppliers and Buyers. *Industrial Management & Data Systems,* 105(7): 857-875.
Johnson, J.K. 2000. *Global Marketing* (Second edition). Irwin McGraw-Hill. New York.
Johnsen, T.E. & Ford, D. (2000). Managing Collaborative Innovation in Complex Networks: Findings from Exploratory Interviews. Paper presented at the Sixteenth Annual Industrial Marketing and Purchasing Conference, 7–9 September, Bath.
Johnsen, R. & Ford, D. (2001). Asymmetrical and symmetrical customer-supplier relationships: contrasts, evolution and strategy. Paper presented at IMP Conference, Oslo, September, 9-11.
Johnsen, R. & Ford, D. (2008).Exploring the concept of asymmetry: A typology for analyzing customer-supplier relationships. *Industrial Marketing Management* 7(4):471-483.
Jones, S., Wilikens, M., Morris, P. & Masera, M. (2000). Trust requirements in e-business. *Communications of the ACM* 43 (2): 81-7.
Jonsson P, Kjellsdotter L, & Rudberg M. (2007). Applying advanced planning systems for supply chain planning: three case studies. *International Journal of Physical Distribution and Logistics Management,* 37(10):816–34.
Jüttner, U., Christopher, M. & Baker, S. (2007). Demand Chain Management-Integrating Marketing and Supply Chain Management. *Industrial Marketing Management,* 36 (3):377-92.
Kearns, G. S., & Lederer, A. L. (2003). A resource-based view of strategic IT alignment: How knowledge sharing creates competitive advantage. *Decision Sciences*, 34(1): 1–29.
Kim, D. J., Ferrin, D. L. and Rao, H. R. (2009). Trust and satisfaction, two stepping stones for successful e-Commerce relationships: A longitudinal exploration. *Information Systems Research,* 20(2): 237-257.
Kim, K. K., S-H Park, S. Y. Ryoo, and S. K. Park. (2010). Inter-organizational Cooperation in Buyer-supplier Relationships: Both Perspectives. *Journal of Business Research,* 63: 863-869.
Krishnan, R., Martin, X., & Noorderhaven, N.G. (2006). When does trust matter to alliance performance? *Academy of Management Journal*, 49: 894–917.
Kock, N. (2015). Warp PLS 5.0. Laredo, TX: ScriptWarp Systems.

Kumar, N., Scheer, L.K. & Steenkamp, J.B. (1995). The effects of perceived interdependence on dealer attitudes. *Journal of Marketing Research,* 32(3): 348-57.
Kumar, N. (1996). The power of trust in manufacturer–retailer relationships. *Harvard Business Review,* 74: 92–110.
Laeequddin, M., Sardana, G.D., Sahay, B.S., Waheed, K.A. & Sahay, V. (2009). Supply chain partners' trust building through risk evaluation: the perspectives of UAE packaged food industry. *Supply Chain Management: An International Journal,* 14(4), 280-90.
Laeequddin, M., Sahay, B.S., Sahay, V., & Waheed, K.A. (2010). Measuring trust in supply chain partners' relationships. *Measuring Business Excellence,* 14(3), 53-69.
Laeequddin, M., Sahay, B.S., Sahay, V., & Waheed, K.A. (2012).Trust building in supply chain Partners relationship: an integrated conceptual model. *Journal of Management Development,* 31(6), 550-64.
La Londe, B.J. (2002). Who Can You Trust These Days? *Supply Chain Management Review*, May-June: 9-10.
Lam, C.Y. (2008). Collaborative supply chain network using embedded genetic algorithms. *Industrial Management and Data Systems,* 108(8): 1101–10.
Lambert, D.M. (2008). Supply Chain Management: Processes, Partnerships, and Performance: Supply Chain Management Institute, 3rd edition, Sarasota, FL.
Lee, S.M, Lee, D.H., and Schniederjans, M.J. (2008). Supply chain innovation and organizational performance in the healthcare industry. *International Journal of Operations and Production Management,* 31(11): 1193-1214.
Lin, C. (2008). Determinants of the adoption of technological innovations by logistics service providers in China. *International Journal of Technology Management and Sustainable Development,* 7(1):19-38.
Liu, W.M. & Chen, J.X. (2004). A Study on Innovation Network, Complex Technology and it's Policy. *Forum on Science and Technology in China,* 5:56–9.
Madhok, A. (2006). How much does ownership really matter? Equity and trust relations in joint venture relationships. *Journal of International Business Studies,* 37(1):4-11.
Maheshwari, B., Kumar, V. & Kumar, U. (2006). Optimizing success in supply chain partnerships. *Journal of Enterprise Information Management,* 19(3): 277-91.
Mayer, R.C., Davis, J.H. and F. David Schoorman, F.D. (1995). An Integrative Model of Organizational Trust. *The Academy of Management Review,* 20(3): 709-734.
Michalski, M., Afifi, R., Montes, J.L., & Burns, R. 2013. "Asymmetries in Supply Chain Management: Differences between Poland and Spain." *The Journal of Management Policy and Practice*, 14 (6): 42-72.
Miles, R. & Snow, C. (2007). Organization Theory and Supply Chain Management: An Evolving Research Perspective. *Journal of Operations Management,* 25:459–63.
Moberg, C.R., Spey, T.W., & Freeze, T.L. 2003. SCM: Making the vision a reality. *Supply Chain Management Review* 7(5): 34-9.
Mohd Noor, M.N. & Pitt, M. (2009).The application of supply chain management and collaborative innovation in the delivery of facilities management services. *Journal of Facilities Management*, 7(4): 283-97.
Morgan, R.B, & Hunt, S.D. (1994). The Commitment-Trust Theory of Relationship Marketing. *Journal of Marketing,* 58(3):20-38.
Narasimhan R. & Nair A. (2005). The Antecedent role of quality, information sharing and supply chain proximity on strategic alliance formation and performance. *International Journal of Production Economics,* 96(3): 301-313.
Narasimhan, R. & Narayanan, S. (2013). Perspectives on Supply Network–Enabled Innovations. *Journal of Supply Chain Management,* 49(4): 27-42.
Noordhoff, C.S., Kyriakopoulos, K., Moorman, C., Pauwels, P. & Dellaertet, B.G.C. (2011).

The Bright Side and Dark Side of Embedded Ties in Business-to-Business Innovation. *Journal of Marketing,* 75(5): 34-52.

Pavlou, P., A. & Gefen, D. (2004). Building effective online marketplaces with institution based trust. *Information Systems Research,* 15(1):37-59.

Porter, M.E. 1990. *The Competitive Advantage of Nations*. The Free Press. New York.

Ramsay, J. (2001). The resource based perspective, rents, and purchasing contribution to sustainable competitive advantage. *The Journal of Supply Chain Management,* 37 (3): 38-47.

Riegelsberger, J. M., Sasse, A. & McCarthy, J.D. (2003). The researcher's dilemma: evaluating trust in computer-mediated communication. *International Journal of Human-Computer Studies,* 58 (6): 759-781,

Rosemann, M., & de Bruin, T. 2005. Application of a holistic model for determining BPM maturity. *BP Trends*, February: 1-21.

Ryu, S., Min, S. and Zushi, N. (2008). The moderating role of trust in manufacturer-supplier relationships. *Journal of Business & Industrial Marketing* 23 (1): 48-58.

Sanna-Randaccio, F. & Veugelers, R. (2007). Multinational knowledge spillovers with decentralized R&D: a game- theoretic approach. *Journal of International Business Studies,* 38(1):47–63.

Schoenherr, T., & Mabert, V.A. (2006). Bundling for B2B procurement auctions: Current state and best practices. *International Journal of Integrated Supply Management,* 2 (3):189-213.

Sebastiao, H.J., & Golicic. S. (2008). Supply chain strategy for nascent firms in emerging technology markets. *Journal of Business Logistics,* 29(1): 75–91.

Singh, S.Ch. & Pandey, S.K. (2013). Supply Chain Performance: A Review of Literature. *Journal of Supply Chain Management Systems*, 2(4): 1-12.

Sisodiya, S.R., Johnson, J.L & Grégoirec, Y. (2013). Inbound open innovation for enhanced performance: Enablers and opportunities. *Industrial Marketing Management,* 42(5): 836–849.

Skjøtt-Larsen, T. (1999). Supply Chain Management: A New Challenge for Researchers and Managers in Logistics. *International Journal of Logistics Management,* 10(2):41–54.

Skjøtt-Larsen, T., Schary, P.B., Mikkola, J.H., & Kotzab, H. (2007).Managing the global supply chain. Copenhagen, Denmark: Copenhagen Business School Press.

Spekman, R.E., Kamauff, Jr., J.W., & Myhr, N. (1998). An empirical investigation into supply chain management: A perspective on partnerships. *Supply Chain Management* 3(2): 53-67.

Spekman, R.E. & Davis, E.W. (2004). Risky business: expanding the discussions on risk and the extended enterprise. *International Journal of Physical Distribution & Logistics Management,* 34(5):414-33.

Sridharan, R. & Simatupang, T. (2005). Supply Chain Discontent. *Business Process Management Journal,* 11(4): 349-69.

Swink, M., R. Narasimhan, & C. Wang. (2007). Managing beyond the Factory Walls: effects of Four Types of Strategic Integration on Manufacturing Plant Performance. *Journal of Operations Management,* 25(1): 148-164.

Swink, M., & Song, M. (2007). Effects of marketing-manufacturing integration on new product development time and competitive advantage. *Journal of Operations Management*, 25(1), 203–217.

Svensson, G. (2001). Perceived trust towards suppliers and customers in supply chains of the Swedish automotive industry. *International Journal of Physical Distribution & Logistics Management*, 31 (9): 647-62.

Svensson, G. (2004). Vulnerability in business relationships: the gap between dependence

and trust. *Journal of Business & Industrial Marketing,* 19(7):469-83.
Tan, K. C., Lyman, S.B. & J. D. Wisner. (2002). Supply Chain Management: A Strategic Perspective. *International Journal of Operation & Production Management* 22: 614-631.
Tenenhaus, M. (1998). La regression PLS. Paris, France: Publi-Union.
Terjesen, S., Patel, P.C. & Sanders, N.R. (2012). Managing differentiation-integration duality in supply chain integration. *Decision Sciences* 43 (2): 303-339.
Tether, B. (2002). Who co-operates for innovation, and why? An empirical analysis. *Research Policy* 31:947-67.
Thomas, R. & Esper, T. (2010). Exploring relational asymmetry in supply chains: the retailer´s perspective. *International Journal of Physical Distribution & Logistics Management* 40(6): 475-94
Thomas, R. & Skinner, L. (2010). Total Trust and Trust Asymmetry: Does Trust Need to Be Equally Distributed in Interfirm Relationships? *Journal of Relationship Marketing* 9:43–53.
Temme, D., Kreis, H., & Hildebrandt, L. (2006). PLS path modeling – A software review. Berlin, Germany: Institute of Marketing, Humboldt University Berlin.
Venkatesh, V. & Goyal, S. (2010). Expectation disconfirmation and technology adoption: polynomial modeling and response surface analysis. *MIS Quarterly* 34(2): 281-303.
Walters, D., & Rainbird, M. (2007). Collaborative innovation: a value chain approach. *Journal of Enterprise Information Management* 20(5):595-607.
Wang, Ch-H. (2011). The moderating role of power asymmetry on the relationships between alliance and innovative performance in the high-tech industry. *Technological Forecasting & Social Change* 78: 1268–79.
Wold, H. (1985). Partial least squares. In S. Kotz & N.L. Johnson (Eds.), *Encyclopedia of Statistical Sciences Vol. 6.* New York, NY: Wiley: 581-91.
Wu, Z. (2011). A Model of Trust Governance on Partnership in Knowledge Supply Chain. *Contemporary Logistics* 4:61-5.

Appendix A

VARIABLE - ASYMMETRY – items
(Is the act considered as a sign of differences in behaviours of the supply chain partners? Completely disagree = 1; Completely agree =7)

Lack of communication quality between supply chain partners
Lack of cooperation in partnership relations in supply chain
Easy acceptation of leadership position
Different level of commitment

VARIABLE - PERFORMANCE – items
(Could you evaluate your firm performance in the following areas? –
We are worst = 1; we are better than last period = 7)

Growth and diversification of incomes
Productivity improvement
Profits improvements
Market participation

VARIABLE - TRUST- items
(Is the act considered a sign of trust in supply chain relationships? Completely agree =7; Completely disagree = 1)

Willingness to inform about cost and profit
We shared our knowledge with partners
Confidence partners reliability and integrity
We solve the problems through mutual agreements
The partners' suggestions are honest and true

VARIABLE - INNOVATION - items
(Could you indicate the extent of innovation in your supply chain relationships? Not at all = 1; Large =7)

Information technology improve our market position
Our partners are interested in product innovation
Some of our partners are more interested in process innovation
We pursue continuous innovation in core processes
We improved trust due to innovation

DECISION SCIENCES INSTITUTE

Balance or Stability: A Re-conceptualization of the Key Elements of Service Triad Sustainability

Sourav Sengupta
IITB-Monash Research Academy
Email: sengupta.sourav@iitb.ac.in

Mohan Krishnamoorthy
Monash University
Email: mohan.krishnamoorthy@monash.edu

Tarikere T. Niranjan
Indian Institute of Technology Bombay
Email: ttniranjan@iitb.ac.in

ABSTRACT

A service triad comprises a client organization, its customers, and a third-party vendor that serves the customers (Niranjan & Metri, 2008). In this study, we conceptualize the meaning of stability of service triads and explain how relationships in a triad develop or deteriorate. We develop our study on the foundations of balance theory. Balance theory (Heider, 1958) advocates that in interpersonal triadic relationships, individuals seek cognitive consistency and emotional harmony. A triad is balanced when (i) the three individuals have positive relationships among them or (ii) any two relationships are negative and the third is positive. *Balanced state* is characterized by cognitive consistency and harmony and is free of tension. Although balance theory was conceptualized at the interpersonal level, it has been used to explain interorganizational triads (Andersson-Cederholm & Gyimóthy, 2010; Choi & Wu, 2009). While a balanced state indicate a harmonious and stable triadic relationship, in which there is no stress towards change, unbalanced state produce tension and forces the triad towards balance.

We argue that a balanced state does not necessarily mean that the triad is stable. From the example of Harry Potter (Choi & Wu, 2009), the triadic relationship among Harry Potter, his uncle and his aunt is in a balanced state because his uncle and aunt share a positive relationship, while they share a negative relationship with Harry Potter. However, even in a balanced state, due to the unpleasantness, which brings instability in the triad, Harry Potter breaks the triad and escapes. This is even more observable in interorganizational relationships. Even when the triad is balanced, it can be unstable with high chances of the unsatisfied partner attempting to break free. We find a direct reapplication of balance theory to interorganizational studies questionable. In this study, we illustrate the key distinctions between balance and stability and explain stability of service triads. We explore the nature of the eight possible states of triads, from perfectly stable to unstable. Further, we identify three key drivers, namely, trust, dominance, and divvy that assist in developing a workable stability. These prevent degradation of a service triad to a lower state. Trust in triads improves relationship commitments and establishes loyalty. It also reduces opportunism. However, not all entities can be trusted. Dominance has a prominent role in triads in which the power divide is high and one entity depends on the other(s). Dominating entities can infuse coordination within business relationships and force its vendor (partner) to improve performance. However, without divvy, dominance and trust might not be effective in the long run. We believe that the drivers are not mutually exclusive. The importance of one driver over the other(s) varies depending on the nature of the bonding among the entities in the triad. An understanding of the appropriate driver(s) might be utilized to enforce a workable stability when the relationships are tension-filled and less harmonious. The drivers enforce a stable and sustainable triad, even when there are tension-filled negative relationships among the entities.

KEYWORDS: Service triad, stability, balance theory

REFERENCES

References available upon request.

*** Formatting Issue - Best Available Paper/Graphic ***

DECISION SCIENCES INSTITUTE

Balancing Service Risk with Technology Cost for Web-based Applications using Emulation Driven Simulation

Srimathy Mohan

Arizona State University

Email: srimathy@asu.edu

Mohan Gopalakrishnan

Arizona State University

Email: mohan@asu.edu

Sreenivas Pattabhiraman

Arizona State University

Email: 2sreeni@gmail.com

Andrew Feller

Deloitte Corporation

Email: andrfeller@deloitte.com

ABSTRACT

Organizations that operate in the e-commerce domain typically have hundreds of web-based applications that have to be updated when new software or stacks are launched. This requires extensive testing to maintain quality of service, while minimizing downtime. In this research, we propose a structured method for classifying applications and testing new stacks for each type of application thoroughly before deploying all applications on the new stack. The method uses an emulation-simulation approach and would contribute to the organization's leadership in providing high quality service to its customers while eliminating unnecessary expenditure on excess testing and maintaining multiple stacks, resulting in significant cost savings.

KEYWORDS: Web-based applications, software updates, reference architecture, service risk, emulation-simulation framework

INTRODUCTION

Web-based applications are central to delivering services at many small and large organizations. They provide a window through which customers can connect with organizations online, to take care of various needs, such as paying bills, managing accounts, and booking tickets. At the organizational level, there are typically several individual web-based applications. A medium size company can have more than 250 applications while large companies can have upwards of 3000-5000. Multiple applications are needed to perform a business transaction like paying your bill, setting up a registration, creating a travel itinerary. These transactions can range from less than one second to days with multiple batch, online or manual activities. Organizations deal with the task of managing Enterprise systems, which are complex interconnected set of individual applications sitting on myriad set of infrastructure. The infrastructure has multiple components like operating system, system utilities, application utilities and connectivity programs. During each application performing its part in a transaction, these components can be called up to support the application's activity. These components are usually made by different vendors and could have compatibility issues. These components are upgraded from time to time and these upgrades might also cause compatibility issues, since all components do not have the same upgrade cycle.

Organizations have reference architectures (or stacks) that are put together by the IT departments to standardize the components into a few bundles for application development teams to use in their applications. This leads to standardization and a level of abstraction for development teams. Once a stack is created with a version of components then applications start to consume the stack or reference model. Over time, the components will be upgraded or patches provided, which will lead to newer versions of the stack needing to be created. There are usually major and minor releases of the stack and usually can follow a 1-3 year cycle for a major release and a 3-6 month cycle for a minor release.

When one or more components in a stack are upgraded, the current practice involves testing the stacks at a high level leading to some risk being passed onto the applications. This is due to testing done with very highly simplistic or unreal code samples or snippets. Reference architecture teams do not have the time or the wherewithal to test all possible applications on the new stack. They might not even choose a set of real applications as due to the interdependencies the applications they have to setup all other system dependent applications with their corresponding stacks and data. So they setup some simplistic code or applications that might not have any relation to the real-world behavior of applications. So when application teams put their applications on these stacks, there are usually issues that slowly reduce over time but significant amount of time is lost. Hence, application teams do not want to take the risk and sometimes wait to upgrade their applications to the newer stack. Also applications want to perform more detailed regression testing of their application with the new stack to reduce the risk.

As applications teams do not want to upgrade frequently and are not comfortable with the risk associated with automatically upgrading the applications to the new reference models, there could be multiple versions of the stacks in the environment causing many different variations. This causes additional issues since support teams have to be aware of many different versions and patch levels before identifying and resolving customer complaints. It could also cause applications on older versions to not being able to leverage newer versions of the methods with additional functionality. Application upgrade cycles are sometimes expensive and cannot be done with other application changes, as the degree of change could be significant due to the infrequency of upgrades. It goes from standard upgrade to a major revision or in some cases a redesign.

The presence of multiple versions of the stack and the need to support all versions causes cost overruns and potentially, a lower service quality since older versions of the reference architecture cannot leverage all the advantages of the new reference architectures. The purpose of this research is to develop a method to deploy the applications on the new stacks in an efficient manner. This research was motivated by the presence of this problem in the technology division of a Fortune 100 financial services firm. Hatzakis et al. (2010) point out the increased use of online transactions in the financial services industry and explain how quality of service, measured by response time as well as correctness of retrieved information, is a very important aspect of service delivery. Quality of service depends on several factors, including, capacity of resources (servers in this case) and the correctness and compatibility of content available on the servers. A typical Web-based application system consists of Web servers, application servers, various external servers (for example, databases and mainframe computers) and Web-application logic that controls the flow and sequence of customer requests through all the elements of the system. The application server is central to any Web-based application as it serves as the traffic controller and controls the flow of information between the end user and across the several tiers in the network. The different kinds of applications reside on the application server. At the financial services firm we were studying, since the majority of applications were financial applications, the application teams did not want to risk automatic upgrades of the applications to the new reference models without extensive testing. Hence there were multiple versions of the stacks in the environment, causing several different variations.

We propose a robust method where real applications are tested on the new stacks. At the same time, we do not recommend exhaustive testing. We recommend an initial analysis of existing applications to classify them into broad groups based on system behavior. Research (Malek et al., 2012; Aleti et al., 2013) suggests that applications behave differently and their behavior depends on several factors such as heap size, connectivity, cpu, wait times, and memory, to name a few. Our early data analysis (data from the financial services company) showed that the behavior of an application can be characterized based on whether the application is memory intensive, CPU intensive or a combination (memory and CPU intensive) and other individual parameters play a much less important role in characterizing it's behavior. If we can test 2-3 applications of each type extensively under various scenarios (slowdowns, high demand, breakdowns, etc.), we would have a clear picture of system behavior for each type of application. With this initial testing, we can establish baseline standards for performance on the existing stacks.

When new stacks are brought online by the reference architecture teams, we can now test only one or two applications of each type. If the performance metrics with the new stacks match the ones established with the old stack with an acceptable confidence level, all applications below a pre-determined criticality level can be automatically upgraded to the latest stack. The applications that have been tagged as "critical" during the initial calibration phase can be tested individually before deployment on the new stacks. This method would significantly reduce cost of deployment on the new stacks, and the downtime as well. A key component of the proposed method is an emulation-simulation framework to establish baseline performance standards on existing stacks for all the applications and classify them into broad categories.

The rest of the paper is organized as follows. First, we present an overview of the related literature and identify the gap in the literature addressed by this research. We next provide a detailed description of the application mapping and emulation testing procedure. The following section describes the discrete event simulation model in detail, presents results, validates our model, and discusses the managerial implications. The final section concludes with directions for future research.

LITERATURE REVIEW

There are two classes of research on performance modeling for Web-based services. One stream of research focuses on maintaining the hardware and software required to keep the Web-based services updated, while the other focuses on Web-server performance from a capacity planning perspective. The first stream of research usually is focused more on Computer Science. Miedes and Munoz-Escoi (2012) present a survey about automatic software updating. This stream of research focuses on tools developed to automatically update software on distributed systems. Our research moves a step back in the chain of decision making and helps to decide which class of applications should be updated together.

The second stream of research presents a class of management science models for studying the performance of web-based applications. One class of models (Menascé, 2002; Cao, Anderson, Nyberg, & Kihl, 2003; Liu, Heo, Sha, & Zhu, 2006) describes Web-based applications as a single tier architecture. They model the Web server performance at a high level, and are useful for identifying performance trade-offs making higher level server sizing and allocation decisions. A second class of models model Web-based systems on a lower level and address many of the system interactions directly. One important system interaction is called resource locking. Resource locking occurs in multi-tier architectures. When an upstream server resource is kept occupied and waiting while it is waiting for a response from a downstream resource, it is referred to as resource locking. It is quite different from blocking and has a big impact on system performance and hence several aspects such as capacity planning. Reeser and Hariharan (2002), Urgoankar et al. (2005), Ramesh and Perros (2000a, 2000b) and Mohan et al. (2014) have addressed resource locking directly while modeling the performance of Web-based systems.

This research builds on some of the work from the second stream of research. We are utilizing a simulation model to replicate the performance of a Web-based application under several scenarios in order to characterize its performance. This characterization helps determine an efficient procedure for deploying applications on new software stacks.

APPLICATION MAPPING AND EMULATION TESTING

The initial challenge in developing a re-usable model of application server performance is the need for empirical data on how this central tier in the architecture performs when upstream loads and downstream delays vary under different patterns. To address this challenge the team developed a two-step approach (Figure 4) using emulation to first characterize application server behavior under production-like conditions followed by development of a general purpose simulation that could determine resource requirements and performance impacts without the excessive cost and time required for emulation testing.

A typical web-based application consists of web servers (WS), application servers (AS), and various external servers (ES, for example, databases and mainframe computers) and application logic that controls the flow of customers' requests through all the elements of the system. Web servers transmit user requests to the application servers where the application software translates each request into transactions, transmits the transactions, collects responses and adds promotion or personalization to complete the overall eBusiness request. This requires memory caching, parallel and sequential operations, and resource locking. A representative application architecture is shown in Figure 5.

***** Formatting Issue - Best Available Paper/Graphic *****

Figure 4: Emulation-Simulation framework

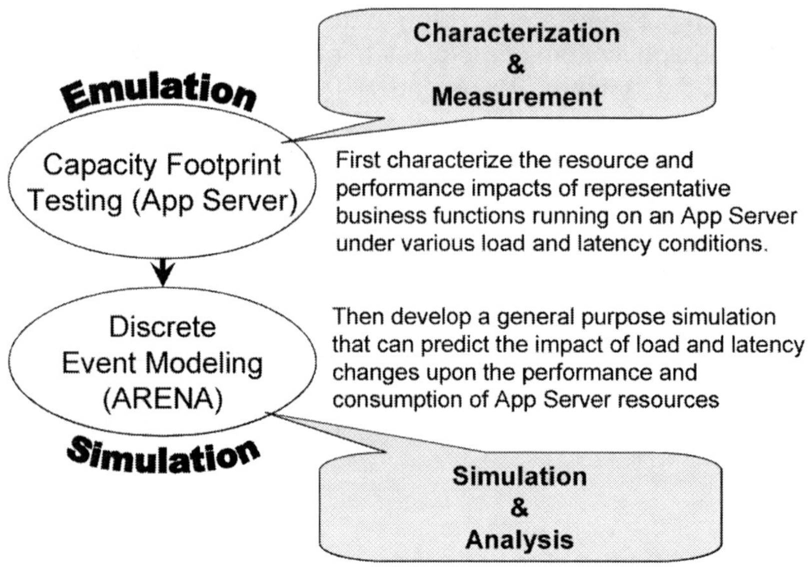

Figure 5: Architecture of a typical web-based application

*** **Formatting Issue - Best Available Paper/Graphic** ***

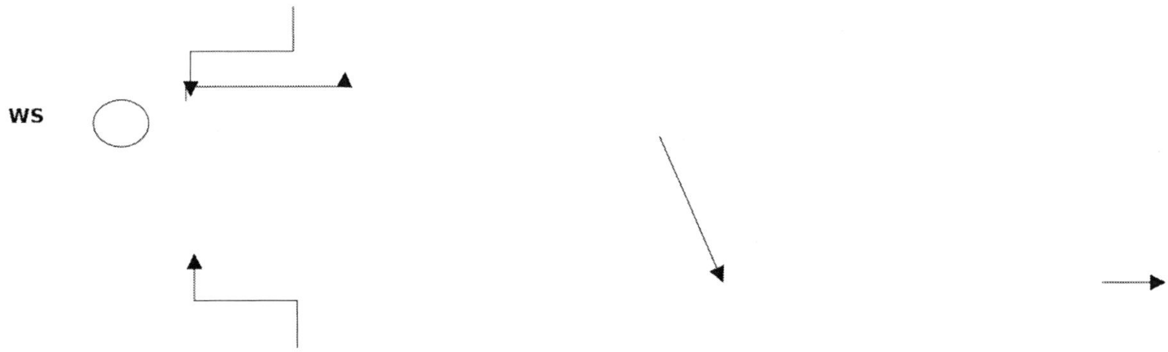

Resource locking is a unique behavior that occurs in this middle tier of multi-tiered service oriented architectures – the application server must consume and hold resources such as memory and connections when requests arrive and while waiting for external services to complete processing and respond. This introduces interaction and queuing effects resulting in non-linear consumption patterns of computing resources that are not readily characterized (Mohan et al. 2010, 2014). To gather empirical data on how application servers behave when loads and service delays vary, the team developed a portable emulation testing capability that relied on two key elements: 1) a load server that could generate controlled, statistically varying user loads at increasing stress levels, and 2) a stub server that could emulate external service responses with controlled delays. These areas are depicted graphically in Figure 6 as shaded overlays on a typical call flow between the tiers for a single business function. The reusable, object-oriented load generator and stub server software we developed to perform emulation testing could support multiple test threads and the scheduling of loads and external service delays based on arrival and delay patterns that mirror a production environment.

Configuring this testing environment and subsequent simulation model required a representative sequence of calls to the external services to be mapped. Application mapping included: 1) identification of representative business functions to be modeled, 2) mapping the sequence of services required for completion of each business function and 3) identification of the corresponding external servers for each of these services. The numbered background in Figure 6 shows a typical service-call map that sequences how the emulation environment will operate using actual logic from the live application software. This figure shows the specific sequence of steps that occur when a user interacts with the application via the browser and web-server, and in turn how the application server interacts with the external services that retrieve information and interact with systems of record for service transaction processing. The square blocks surrounding each system element organize the input and output arrows for graphical clarity. Even a very simple use-case including a field entry and mouse click to look up customer data generates this type of complex calling sequence. The mappings were derived based on expert knowledge of the particular application under study and provided the blueprint for structuring a discrete event simulation.

Figure 6: Emulation testing framework

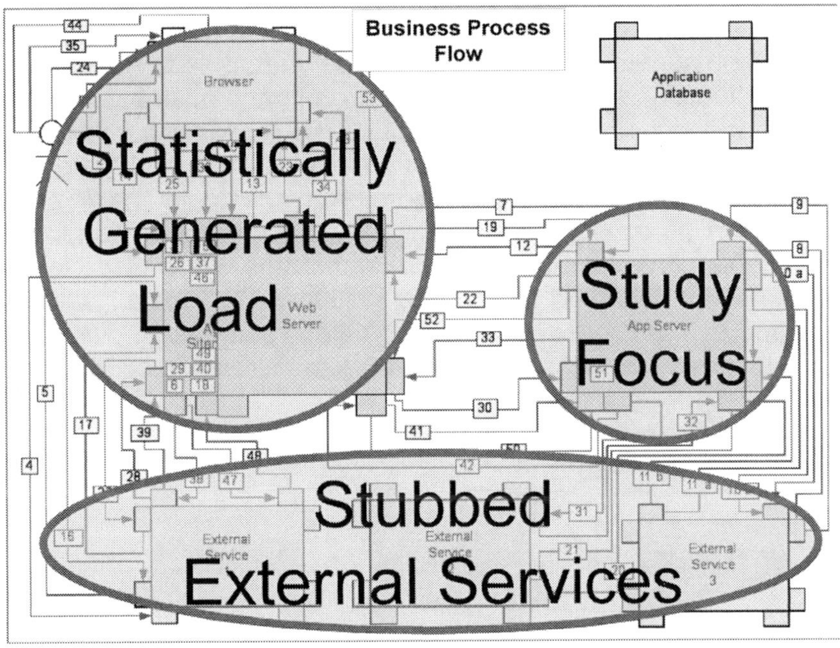

The input data necessary for emulation tests and simulation modeling are the response times and success rates for the different external servers and the demand arrival pattern at the application server. To characterize these factors, production logs from the live application were obtained providing sufficient data to develop statistically valid representations of system behavior. An example analysis for characterizing one external service is provided in the appendix. Similar analyses were performed for each external service and for the user load on the production system to identify the delay and load patterns and their current nominal levels. Next the team scaled up the loads and delays for a designed set of experiments to characterize server consumption under varying environmental conditions. Initial stress tests were conducted to characterize the maximum load and service delay levels that the test server could handle before becoming critically overloaded. Then full factorial experiments were performed over a range of operating levels to characterize the performance and consumption footprint of representative business functions under varying conditions.

The emulation environment was able to provide representative measurements of application server performance under controlled conditions because the actual production application server software was running on a complete production software and representative hardware stack. Only the loads coming from the web server and the external service responses were emulated; duplicate production http:// calls and .xml files were sent and received respectively by the load and stub servers – to the application server they looked exactly like production interactions. Network bandwidth and delays were also tested and found to have negligible impact on the time to respond. There was one factor that we could not entirely control, and that was the time delay for authentication of a valid user account at each user transaction. For security reasons this authentication could not be bypassed, adding a potential source of error for our testing, but coordination with the owners of the authentication servers allowed the team to test during periods of light use, minimizing errors from this effect.

Emulation Testing Results

To evaluate the emulation test results, data was captured both at the test load generating server and at the target application server. At the load server we were able to observe the load level over time, response durations, and the success or failure of each business function. At the application server we used monitoring agents to capture the processing levels and consumption of key server resources including the percentage of consumed CPU and the consumption of heap memory. Correlating the data from both servers on a time scale enabled empirical correlation between the varying consumption levels and response times with loads and latencies. This provided benchmarks that we would later match with a discrete event simulation. An example of the observed performance is shown in Figure 7 where the response durations are seen to improve as the external service delays decrease; however as loads increase to critical levels the system stability degrades with increasing service time variability and service failures.

Figure 7: Load server sees improving response times as external service delays shorten, yet failures (seen in red) increase as loads reach critical levels

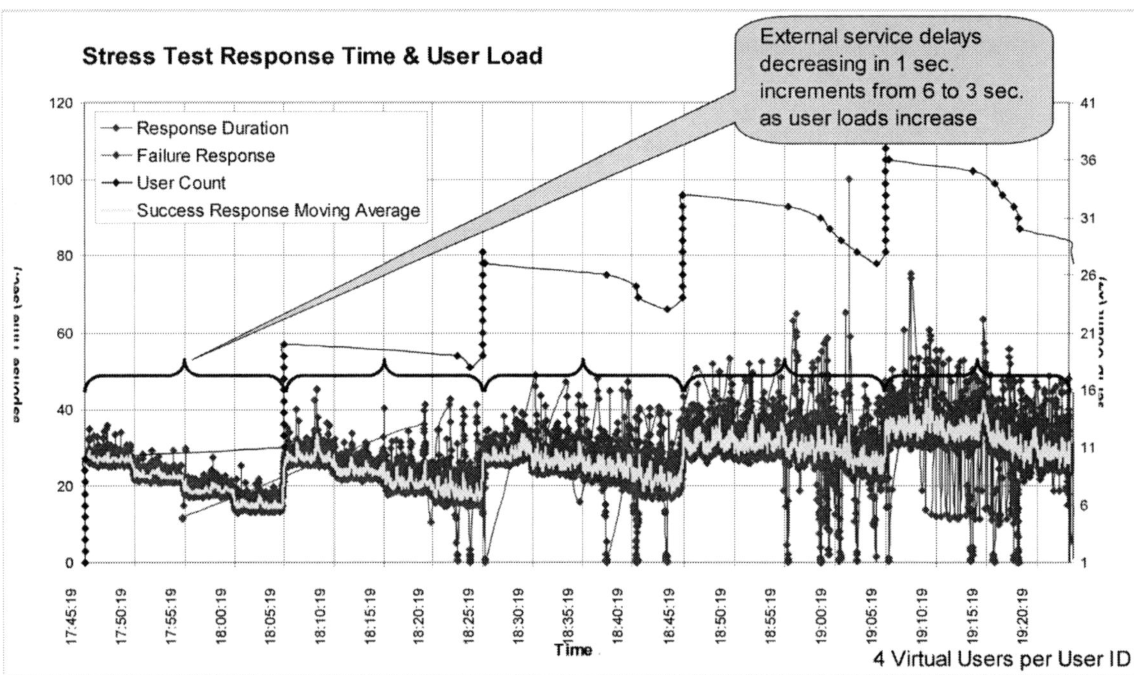

Results from the initial tests determined loading levels that stress the system and degrade performance, and identified boundary conditions for sizing. These tests increased user counts with each user generating sequential requests at 100 millisecond intervals as soon as the prior request is complete. The 100 ms interval is necessary to allow resources to recycle, avoiding a race condition. The effective user count was increased in increments of 80 until the load was sufficient to cause significant service outages. This occurred at the 240 user-thread level. The test results shown in Figures 5 used fixed delays for the stubbed services to more clearly discern the impact of increasing the external service delays. These fixed delays decrease at 1 second intervals from 6 seconds to 3 seconds for all external services.

Identification of the Bottleneck Resource

The potential resource bottleneck parameters tracked at the application server level included CPU, Java Virtual Machine (JVM) heap memory, swap space, and free memory. For the particular application functionality being tested, CPU was identified as the bottleneck resource (See Figure 8). The application under study was not very memory intensive because the application returns only small amounts of data to the user. Heap memory was also significantly consumed but was not a bottleneck, reaching a peak of 50 – 60% of the configured memory allotment. It was important to understand this result in the context of the test server configuration so that simulation results could be scaled for a production environment.

Figure 8: Application server CPU consumption reaches 100% causing increasing service failures. This was the bottleneck resource for the application under study

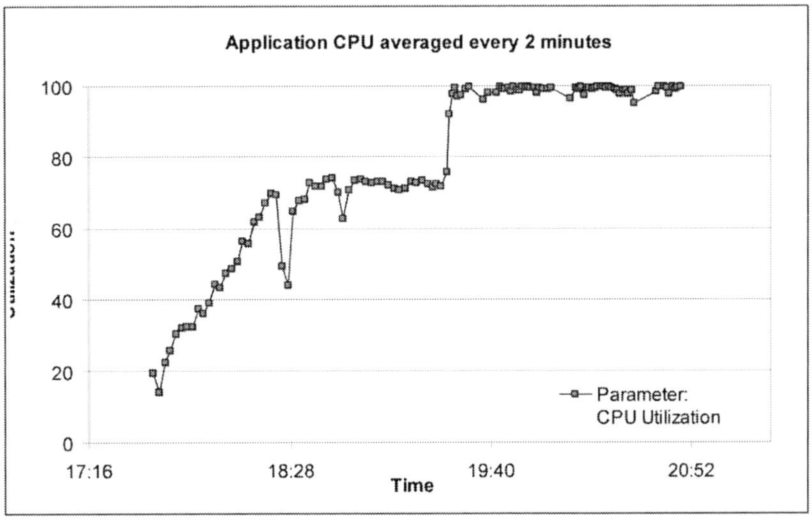

Tests with Distributed Loads and Latencies

Once initial stress tests were complete, tests were run with statistically distributed loads and both fixed and exponentially distributed external latencies. Because of the emulation testing approach, the load on the server is a function of both the request arrival rate and the number of pooled user accounts available to execute the requests. The tested application is used in call centers so users typically log in once at the beginning of their shift and are ready to handle incoming calls. For this reason the emulation load server first initialized a set of accounts to eliminate log-in processing as a part of the test, allowing the system to equilibrate to a production like state. A boundary setting was established for the requisite number of user accounts at which the test server could be crashed and tests were run with a user pool at this

*** **Formatting Issue - Best Available Paper/Graphic** ***

level. From the production log data we characterized the nominal production load level currently on the system using a Weibull distribution that best fit the observed data. There were a small number of initial beta users in the call center using the new system; however it was scheduled to be rolled out to at least a thousand more. Statistical loads were generated at 500, 1000, and 1500 times the current nominal level, allowing us to capture the effect of projected loads on the system. Examples of critical resource consumption for 1500 times the nominal load and 8 second fixed delays for each service is shown in Figure 9 which includes CPU and JVM heap utilization, the two system resources determined to be critical for evaluating server requirements for the target application. At these heavily loaded settings the test server settled into a steady response pattern averaging around 40 seconds with occasional peak times between 80 and 100 seconds. Similar utilization curves for these key resources along with response time patterns were obtained for each experimental level of load and delay.

Figure 9: CPU and JVM heap consumption and total process response times at 1500 times nominal load and 8 second service delays shows how critical resources are consumed under stress and the resulting impact on performance

CPU UTILIZATION

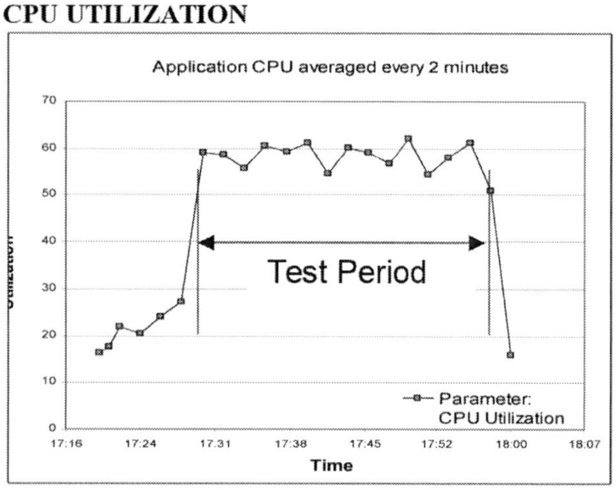

JVM HEAP UTILIZATION

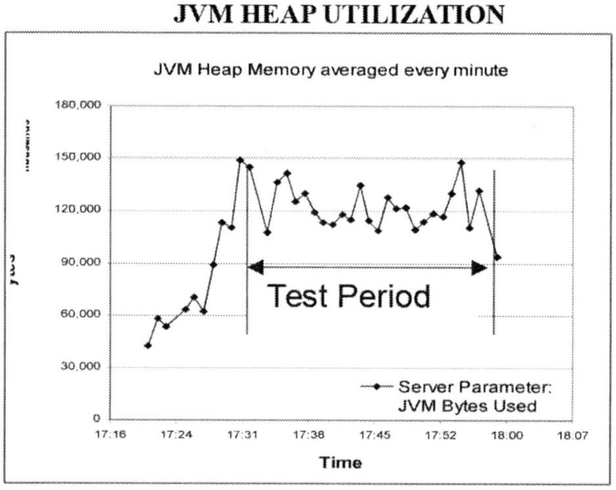

RESPONSE TIMES

*** Formatting Issue - Best Available Paper/Graphic ***

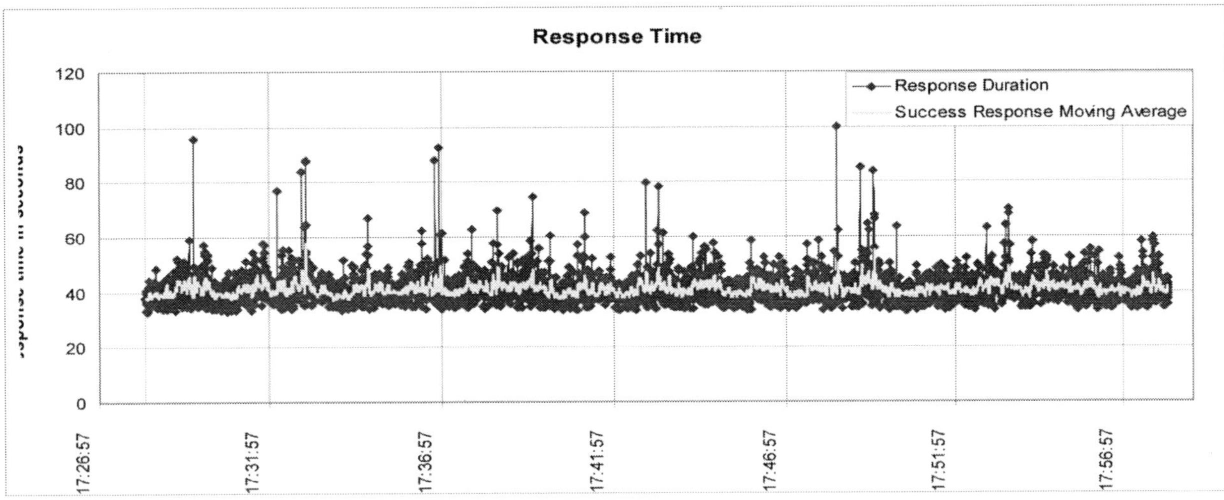

Patterns of Resource Consumption

One chief benefit from using the emulation / simulation approach is the learning it affords for determining how resources are consumed by different types of applications and how this impacts server performance. Observing actual resource consumption and performance on a test server over a range of loads and latencies, and then simulating the application server at the same loads and latencies using different patterns for consuming resources and generating delays allowed us to test a number of different simulation approaches for their representational accuracy. This provided a powerful, empirical approach for developing and validating simulation models to predict application server performance for different types of web-based applications. Some applications are CPU intensive and others which return large data-sets, graphics or multi-media files are more memory intensive. For the call-center application in our work we were able to observe patterns exhibited by a lightweight application that processes transactions that return relatively small data-sets. This type of application was found to be CPU resource constrained and observed to consume resources in specific ways.

From the designed emulation experiments we observed the following consumption trends with increasing loads and latencies: 1) increased utilization of CPU and heap memory with increased load, and 2) increased utilization of heap memory with increased delays for external services to respond. The heap memory results confirmed trends predicted by the earlier resource locking analytical model (Mohan et al. 2009) indicating that some memory is consumed and held while waiting for external services to respond; however CPU resources appear to be seized and released more immediately at the point in time when request information is being processed. Based on the observed behavior we determined that resource consumption for our test application could be simulated using two primary consumption patterns: 1) a resource locking pattern that captures and holds resources while waiting for subsequent downstream activities to occur, and 2) an instantaneous use consumption pattern that consumes and almost immediately releases resources. These two consumption patterns are depicted in the first two rows of Figure 10. These patterns occurred in combination such that a portion of required resources are consumed and released instantaneously while additional portions are locked and unavailable until the external call or the entire service process is complete.

***** Formatting Issue - Best Available Paper/Graphic *****

We also postulate that memory intensive applications that display large volumes of information or media files, or are used to upload large amounts of data will need resource consumption patterns that seize and release resources in the two patterns shown at the bottom of Figure 8. The large data return pattern would seize significant resources such as memory when the external service returns a large file, while the large data upload pattern would consume significant CPU and memory resources while streaming a large file to an external server. This second set of patterns was not applicable to our initial pilot but is planned for incorporation in the capacity planning methodology for further testing and use on memory intensive applications.

DISCRETE EVENT SIMULATION

A discrete event simulation model for analyzing the resource loading and performance of an application server was developed that mapped the application calling sequence and consumed application server resources using a blend of the resource locking and instantaneous consumption patterns outlined in Figure 10. An example of the simulated entity flow for resource locking consumption is provided in Figure 11.

Figure 8: Resource consumption patterns observed and postulated

***** Formatting Issue - Best Available Paper/Graphic *****

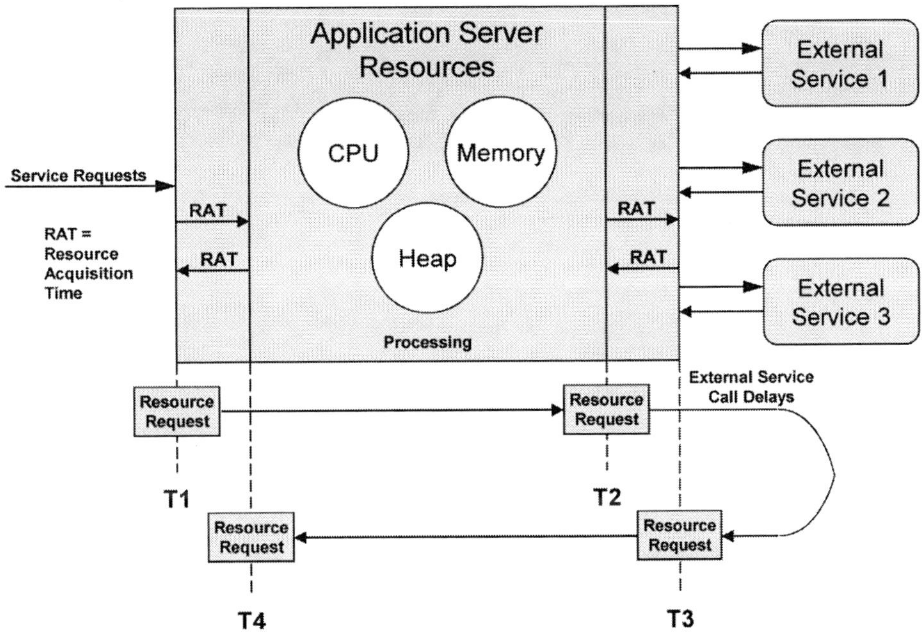

A, B, C, and D represent discrete amounts of resource consumption

	Resource Seize/Release Time			
Consumption Pattern	T1 – Service Request Arrives	T2 – External Service Call	T3 – Return from External Call	T4 – Calls Completed, Process & Return Results
Resource Locking	Seize A →	Seize B →	Release B →	Release A
Instantaneous Use	Seize A Release A →	Seize B Release B →	Seize C Release C →	Seize D Release D
Large Data Returned by External Server	Seize A →	Seize B →	Release B Seize Large C →	Release Large C Release A
Large Data Upload to External Server	Seize Large A →	Seize B →	Release B Release Large A →	Seize C Release C

Figure 11: Resource locking logic is used to simulate a portion of total resource consumption. This pattern was found useful to generate consumption levels that closely match test data for heap memory across varying loads and service delays.

***** Formatting Issue - Best Available Paper/Graphic *****

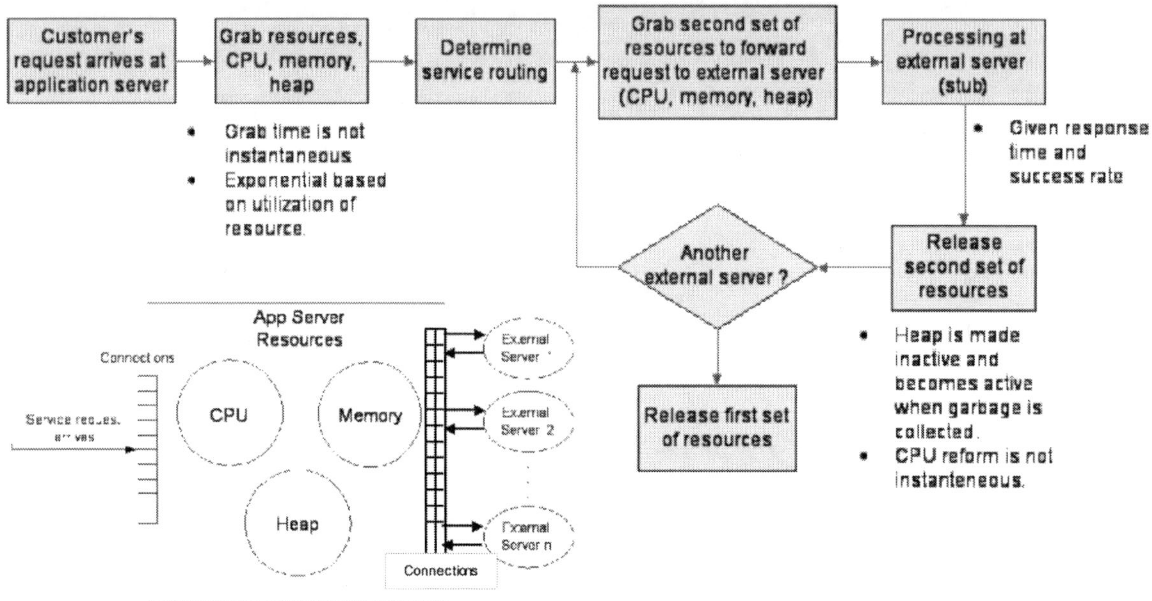

This pattern seizes resources when a request arrives, and again when external service calls are made. Then it releases resources when the external services respond, and again when the original request is complete. This generates resource consumption levels that increase both with loads and with increased external service delay times, but with increasing delay times the pattern created too steep a consumption curve to match the observed resource consumption behavior for heap memory. We found that a pure resource locking or instantaneous use model could not replicate the memory consumption observed in the test server, but that by blending the two models with a percentage of each we could tune the simulation to match the observed levels of resource consumption across the test range of loads and delays. This approach had face validity with the software engineers familiar with the application because when a request or external service call is processed some objects are persistent, while others are used briefly and destroyed, allowing garbage collection to quickly recover the memory resources. In support of this, we observed that garbage collection activity was quite high, for example averaging between 40 and 50 garbage collections per minute during the test run depicted in Figure 9. Once the correct percentage of persistent locking was determined, the simulation model consumption levels were self-tuning to the test results over the full range of loads and latencies observed in the designed emulation experiments.

The simulation approach relies on mapping an application's call flow to develop a routing for each business function to be simulated, so we developed a general purpose capability to map and load application call routings into the simulation through a spreadsheet interface. Then the resource consumption patterns were applied and tuned to characterize the impact of loads and latencies on the consumption of CPU and memory resources. Finally the timing and performance of the simulated server was tuned to match the observed performance of the application server by running it under identical loads and latencies and adjusting the time required to acquire system resources as a function of the utilization level of CPU resources. This approach generated overall resource consumption and processing time distributions that closely matched the performance observed during testing over a range of loads and latencies, and was a reasonable abstraction of the processing dependencies known to take place in the Java operating environment.

Refining the Simulation Model

Comparisons of initial simulation runs with the test data helped identify additional factors that were important for a simulation model to accurately represent server performance. For example, viewing the application server logs for each test showed that there is a baseline level of resource consumption occurring prior to applying any test loads. This baseline level of overhead is needed to support the application server operating system and other application and networking services. This overhead was represented in the simulation by using a disjoint network in the model that would seize resources at the start of the simulation and hold them for the duration of the run. Consumption of these baseline resources was analogous to "booting up" the server operating system, web-server and application software, and then logging in the call center users to be ready to accept customer calls.

We also noted that observed delays for end-to-end business functions were longer and more variable than could be accounted for if we considered only external service delays and nominal processing times within the application server. Application servers have to maintain a number of other processes that consume resources in addition to the specific processing of customer requests and external service calls. This requires additional mechanisms for incurring resource consumption beyond the instantaneous use and resource locking patterns derived from our initial analysis of the test data. Comparing test data to the simulation helped the team identify and model the fixed and variable processing overhead delays that need to be considered. In particular the team was able to develop and refine a dynamic mechanism to represent processing overhead that is load dependent. This was achieved by adding a dynamic resource acquisition timing delay to the model that is consumption dependent.

Modeling Resource Acquisition Time

The total turnaround time for a business function is dependent on the external service response times as well as the internal processing time for the application server to execute the external service calls and process their results. Each simulated external service request is assigned a success rate and response time the same as in the emulation stub server. An additional wait time is also imposed for simulated resource acquisition that is a function of the current utilization level of CPU resources in the system. A dynamic "Resource Acquisition Time" (RAT) was added to the model to provide a mechanism for adjusting the simulation to generate total delays that correspond to observed behavior. The RAT delay is an abstraction of resource processing delays caused by load-dependent processes such as garbage collection, memory management, connection pooling, and connection pool maintenance.

A RAT equation was used to tune the time taken for internal processing that the application server requires for the allocation of CPU and memory resources. Because the observed time taken by the application server to acquire resources at each stage appeared non-linearly dependent on how busy the server is we fit an exponential function of the CPU utilization level to define the average time required to acquire resources as shown in Equation (1).

$$AverageRAT_{Sim} = (RATParm1)\left(e^{(RATParm2)(CPUUtilization\%)}\right) \quad (1)$$

The RAT parameters A and B are used to tune the simulation model to generate characteristic application server processing delay patterns relating the server's average Resource Acquisition Time (RAT) to the current level of CPU utilization. This equation and values for the tuning parameters A & B were arrived at empirically to enable the simulation to closely match observed test server performance. Empirical tuning was necessary because the complexity of the internal operating system and Java Virtual Machine software precludes a purely analytical solution. Tuning starts with a best-fit curve using low and high utilization tests with fixed latencies to match the simulated total response time to observed performance. Exponentially distributed processing times for each of ten service calls and returns averaging 100 milliseconds were used at each call or return to match the minimum observed delay of one second. Since there are multiple service calls, RAT tuning requires subtracting out the summed processing and external delay times. Because there are four resource acquisitions, tuning equation (2) is used to fit the curve in Figure 12 to the observed data by adjusting A and B in equation (1).

$$AverageRAT_{Observed} = \left(ObservedDelay - \sum ProcessTime - \sum ExtServiceDelay\right) \div 4 \qquad (2)$$

Figure 12: Acquisition time for server resources is dependent on the CPU because processing time is required to make resources available. An exponential tuning equation fits the curve to observed levels of CPU utilization and response time.

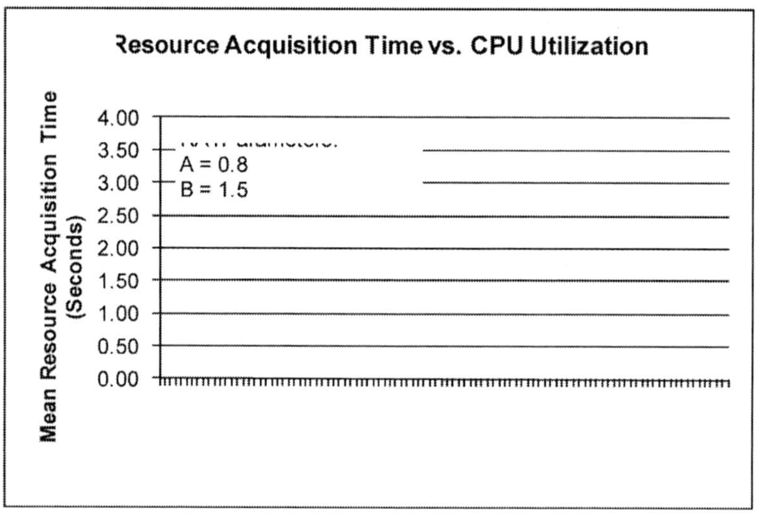

Analysis of observed total response times from the tests showed them to be Gamma distributed which led us to use summed exponential distributions to generate the total delays. The RAT at each of four resource acquisition events is sampled from an exponential distribution with a fluctuating mean that is pegged to the current level of CPU utilization using the exponential tuning equation in equation (1). Using CPU consumption and response time patterns observed during emulation testing to calculate the RAT parameter values allowed us to tune the simulation model for the particular server and application functionality being tested, enabling an accurate, valid simulation of the impact of load and external latency conditions on server performance. Using four distinct stages for resource acquisition as shown in Figure 10, and sampling the RAT from an exponential distribution centered on the Average RAT calculated with equation (1) produced total response time delay distributions that closely matched observed

***** Formatting Issue - Best Available Paper/Graphic *****

results. Statistical tests for difference between means and examination of the response time distributions provided validation that the simulation was a reasonable abstraction for predicting system behavior. Figure 13 provides comparisons between tested vs. simulated utilization of CPU, the bottleneck resource and between the total response time distributions whose means and standard deviations vary by a second or less over the tested range of loads and latencies. Sample t-tests for difference between means at 1000x are provided in the appendix.

Figure 13: Comparisons between simulated and tested performance validate that the simulation provides an adequate abstraction of system behavior. The results for simulated vs. tested CPU utilization fall within a few percent and total response times have means and standard deviations that differ by a second or less.

		Average CPU Utilization		Maximum CPU Utilization	
	Load	Latency		Latency	
		Nominal	Double	Nominal	Double
Simulation	1000x	40.3%	40.6%	45.6%	47.6%
Test	1000x	40.4%	38.6%	46.4%	42.3%
Difference		-0.1%	2.0%	-0.8%	5.3%
Simulation	1500x	58.5%	58.4%	67.1%	66.2%
Test	1500x	57.2%	55.4%	64.1%	64.0%
Difference		1.3%	3.0%	2.9%	2.2%
Times in Seconds		Mean Response Times		Response Std. Dev.	
	Load	Latency		Latency	
		Nominal	Double	Nominal	Double
Simulation	1000x	17.13	27.10	5.90	10.80
Test	1000x	17.17	26.90	5.84	10.20
Difference	*	-0.04	0.20	0.06	0.60
Simulation	1500x	19.20	28.99	6.48	10.80
Test	1500x	19.41	28.00	6.70	10.40
Difference	**	-0.21	0.99	-0.22	0.40

* Difference between mean tests not significant at 5% level
** Difference between mean tests not significant at 1% level

SIMULATION RESULTS

Initial runs with the simulation were used to refine and tune the model leading to a representation that generated simulation results that are consistent with the testing data. In particular, we learned that CPU consumption could be modeled by combining the instantaneous consumption pattern with initial and dynamic overhead processing patterns. For heap memory, however, it was necessary to combine the resource locking and instantaneous use consumption patterns to generate consumption behavior that matched the test data. These pattern combinations were reviewed with systems engineers and determined to be reasonable, and generated patterns of resource consumption that closely match the test data without having to tune the model for each level of load and external delay.

A disjoint network is used to collect data from the simulation, averaging the consumption levels over one or two minute intervals in the same fashion as the monitoring agents running on the application server that generated the test data. After tuning the simulation, the model results are within ~5% of the test system results for both average and peak CPU and heap memory utilization at high loads of 1,000 to 1,500 times the nominal level (x) and external service delays that vary up to double their nominal levels. Additional experimentation validated that the simulation could accurately predict the impact of spikes in load and external service slow-downs. Of particular interest was the peak utilization of the bottleneck resource, CPU. Comparison data for the maximum utilization of this constraining resource was presented in Figure 13 for load and latency levels of interest for sizing the application's projected growth.

All of the data was collected at the financial services firm and the emulation-simulation framework was built and validated with data from the firm. The framework has since been used for making decision for deploying applications on new stacks successfully. Subsequently, the simulation model ahs also been used for making capacity allocation decisions at the firm. The research was a mutually beneficial effort, in that the firm now has a useable framework for making decisions. The authors were able to understand several aspects of performance modeling of Web-based applications and utilize discrete event simulation to significantly reduce cost of upgrades and maintenance of Web-based applications.

CONCLUSION

The development of a valid model for the analysis of application server resource consumption and performance was achieved using an approach that included emulation testing and experimentation with alternative simulation constructs to arrive at a model that closely mimics real server performance. With this emulation-simulation framework, existing applications can be tested and classified as memory intensive, CPU intensive, or any other important characteristic. This classification of applications aids in automatic updates when new stacks are introduced. It would suffice to test one or a very small number of applications from each set, and fine tune stack parameters, if necessary, and upgrade all applications in the set to the new stack. Prior theoretical work had developed algorithms for analyzing and simulating resource locking but without empirical data it was not clear which resources exhibited locking behavior and what percentage of these resources was locked during external service calls versus what percentage would be recovered more immediately. We learned through this approach that for light-weight applications that return small amounts of data, CPU and a majority of heap memory resources are consumed and recovered very quickly, while a small portion (4%) of heap memory resources exhibit resource locking. The emulation/simulation approach enabled discovery of these patterns and provides a means for ongoing discovery and refinement of consumption patterns for other types of applications. The approach also provides a path for wider application in areas such as capacity planning and performance monitoring.

Our focus for continuing research is to apply this methodology across the organization to classify all the applications and develop a mapping for developing clusters of similar applications. and just as better information enables efficient supply chains to reduce unnecessary inventories; better knowledge of technology behavior will enable more efficient data centers. Based on the team's success with developing and testing the approach, the organization has decided to formalize the process for use across a broader range of applications and technology architectures. Future work will focus on virtual server environments and further optimization of reference architectures for web-based applications.

REFERENCES

*** Formatting Issue - Best Available Paper/Graphic ***

Alam, M., S. Mohan, J. W. Fowler, and M. Gopalakrishnan. 2011 (in press). A discrete event simulation tool for performance management of web-based application systems", *Journal of Simulation*, 6, 21-32.

Aleti, A., Buhnova, B., Grunske, L., Koziolek, A., and Meedeniya, I. (2013). Software architecture optimization methods: A systematic literature review, *IEEE Transactions on Software Engineering*, 39 (5), 658-683.

Bartolini, C., Bertolino, A., Elbaum, S., and Marchetti, E. (2011). Bringing white-box testing to service oriented architecures through a service priented approach. *The journal of Systems and Software*, 84, 655-668.

Cao, J., Andersson, M., Nyberg, C., & Kihl, M. (2003). Web server performance modeling using an M/G/1/K*PS queue. Proceedings of the 10th International Conference on Telecommunications, Papeete, Tahiti: IEEE, 1501–1506.

Freund, D. J., J.N. Bexfield. (1983). A new aggregation approximation procedure for solving closed queueing networks with simultaneous resource possession. *Journal of the ACM*, 25(1), 214-223.

Hatzakis, E.D., S.K. Nair, M.L. Pinedo. (2010). Operations in financial services – An overview. *Production and Operations Management,* 19(5), 633-664.

Jacobson, P. A., E.D. Lazowaska. (1982). Analyzing queueing networks with simultaneous resource possession. *Communications of the ACM.* 25(2), 142-151.

Liu, X., Heo, J., Sha, L., & Zhu, X. (2006). Adaptive control of multi-tiered Web applications using queueing predictor. Proceedings of the 10th IEEE/IFIP Network Operations and Management Symposium, Vancouver, Canada: IEEE, 106–114.

Menascé, D. (2002). Trade-offs in designing Web clusters. IEEE internet computing, 6(5), 76–80.

Malek, S., Medvidovic, N., Mikic-Rakic, M. (2012). An extensible framework for improving a distributed software system's deployment architecture. *IEEE Transactions on Software Engineering*, 38 (1), 73-100.

Miedes, E. and F. D. Munoz-Escoi. (2012). A survey about dynamic software updating. Technical Report ITI-SIDI-2012/003, Instituto Universitario Mixto Tecnologico de Informatica, Universitat Polytecnica de Valencia, Valencia, Spain.

Mohan, S., A. Printezis, and M. F. Alam. (2010). Impact of resource locking on performance of web-based applications. *International Journal of Operational Research.* 8(3), 355-378.

Mohan, S., Printezis, A., and Alam, M. 2009. A framework for modeling web-based applications with resource locking. *International(Jou)rnal of Operational Research.* 6(3), 289-303.

Mohan, S., Alam, F. M., Fowler, J. W., Gopalakrishnan, M. and Printezis, A. (2014). Capacity planning and allocation for Web-based applications. *Decision Sciences*, 45 (3), 535-567.

Office of Government Commerce. (2007). Information Technology Infrastructure Library Service Management Best Practices v3 – Service Design Book. The Stationary Office, London, England.

Ramesh, S., H.G. Perros. (2000a). A two-level queueing network model with blocking and non-blocking messages. *Annals of Operations Research*. 93(1), 357-372.

Ramesh, S., H.G. Perros. (2000b). A multi-layer client-server queueing network model with synchronous and asynchronous messages. *IEEE Transactions on Software Engineering*. 26(11), 1086-1100.

Reeser, P., & Hariharan, R. (2002). An analytic model of Web servers in distributed computing environments. Telecommunication Systems, 21(2), 283–299.

Rolia, J. A., K.C. Sevcik. (1995). The Method of Layers. *IEEE Transactions on Software Engineering*, 21(8), 689-700.

Urgaonkar, B., Pacifici, G., Shenoy, P., Spreitzer, M., & Tantawi, A. (2005). An analytical model for multi-tier internet services and its applications. Proceedings of the 2005 ACM SIGMETRICS International Conference on Measurement and Modeling of Computer Systems, Banff, Alberta, Canada: ACM, 291–302.

APPENDIX

Example analysis for one external service is provided showing that an exponential distribution can adequately represent the response times for the stubbed as well as the simulated external service. The input analyzer in Arena, a commercially available discrete event simulator was used to fit distributions to the data.

Example analysis of service execution time distribution (Validation Service)

Data Summary

Number of Data Points	1382
Min Data Value	209
Max Data Value	45700
Sample Mean	2640
Sample Std Dev	3220

Distribution fit summary

Function	Parameter	Sq Error	p-value of Chi-squre test	p-value of K-S test
Exponential	2430	0.0385	< 0.005	< 0.01

Similar analyses were performed for each external service and for the user load on the current production system to identify the delay and load patterns and their current nominal levels.

t Tests for Test Response Times vs Simulation Response Times
1500x nominal latency

	N	Mean	StDev	SE Mean
Test_Response_Times	9999	19.41	6.74	0.067
Simulation_Response_Time	12000	19.2	6.48	0.059
Estimate for difference:	0.2108			
95% CI for difference:	(0.0357, 0.3860)			
t-Test of difference = 0	(vs not =):			

t-Value = 2.36
p-Value = 0.018
DF = 21997

1000x nominal latency

	N	Mean	StDev	SE Mean
Test_Response_Times	10000	17.17	5.84	0.058
Simulation_Response_Time	10000	17.13	5.9	0.059
Estimate for difference:	0.0431			
95% CI for difference:	(-0.1195, 0.2058)			
t-Test of difference = 0	(vs not =):			

t-Value = 0.52
p-Value = 0.603
DF = 19998

* Both tests use Pooled Standard Deviation = 6.5997

DECISION SCIENCES INSTITUTE

Bermudan put option pricing under risk aversion in bilateral gamma models

Belleh Fontem
University of Mary Washington
Email: bfontem@umw.edu

Hannah Tibbett
University of Mary Washington
Email: htibbett@umw.edu

Rachel Graefe-Anderson
University of Mary Washington
Email: rgraefea@umw.edu

ABSTRACT

We consider a Bermudan put option holder seeking to maximize her discounted expected payoff subject to a maximum allowable payoff variance. Under a bilateral gamma asset price model, we show that the option's price is the optimal value for a linear maximization problem for which we establish a lower bound.

KEYWORDS: Bermudan put options, exercise policy, option pricing, payoff variance, bilateral gamma processes

1 INTRODUCTION

Research in American or Bermudan financial options has as its principal goal, to determine the exercise strategy (policy) which maximizes that sort of option's expected discounted payoff (under an explicit model for how the price of a primary asset evolves). Usually, the optimal exercise strategy is such that one should exercise the option as soon as the asset's price crosses a threshold to enter a special subset of the state space called the *optimal exercise region*. The value function of the optimal exercise policy-in a frictionless market without the possibility of arbitrage-corresponds to that option's price. In other words, by evaluating an option's optimal exercise policy, we effectively price the option.

The *payoff uncertainty* associated with an exercise policy is measured as the variance of the payoff yielded by that policy, and is a reflection of the risk associated with the exercise policy. By focusing only on how to maximize an option's expected payoff, state-of-the-art option pricing models implicitly assume that that option holders do not care about payoff uncertainty. That is, option holders are typically considered to be risk-neutral. For a sample of recent articles on risk neutral pricing procedures for a variety of financial options, we point the reader to Hurd and Zhou (2010), Bjerksund and Stensland (2014), Mariani et al. (2015), and Leccadito et al. (2016). However, in practice, option holders do not unconditionally seek to maximize expected payoff, but also pay attention to the uncertainty surrounding the expected payoff linked to any exercise policy under consideration. Put simply, option holders have finite payoff risk tolerance. In this paper, we attempt to price a Bermudan put option without the idealistic assumption that option holders have no sensitivity to payoff risk. A Bermudan put option offers the holder the right (without the obligation) to sell an asset for a deterministic strike price at any one of equally-spaced preselected dates within a certain time horizon. Hence, our problem setting is such that the option holder seeks a payoff-maximizing exercise policy for her option, but is only willing to search among the class of policies whose members have a payoff variance that does not exceed a pre-specified value of her choice. We call this pre-specified variance upper bound the option holder's *payoff uncertainty budget*.

The rest of the paper is organized as follows. Section 2 lays the foundation of our asset price model principally by spelling out important features of the probability distribution which characterizes our asset's random price fluctuations. In Section, 3 we solve the pricing problem via linear programming, and approximate a lower bound. Section 4 shows the results of a numerical study on some problems and Section 5 concludes the paper and suggests avenues for further exploration.

2 ANALYTICAL MODEL

2.1 Asset price models

As a basis for modeling randomly-evolving returns of asset prices, the normal distribution is widespread. Indeed, academic research on financial options took off with the analysis of European options by Black and Scholes (1973) who used geometric Brownian motion (GBM) as a model for their underlying asset. In the GBM model, the natural logarithm of an asset's infinitesimal random price increments follows a normal distribution. However, the light-tailed structure of the normal distribution usually makes GBM a poor modeling distribution for empirical financial data. To this effect, researchers have advanced new processes based on alternative distributions. See for instance discrete mixtures of normal distributions (Kon, 1984), the variance gamma distribution (Madan and Seneta, 1990), the truncated Lévy flight (Mantegna and Stanley, 1994), and the CGMY distribution (Carr et al., 2002).

More recently, Küchler and Tappe (2008) have proposed and empirically studied the bilateral gamma (BG) distribution (i.e., difference of two identical gamma distributions) as the basis for asset price fluctuations. Based on this price evolution model, they proposed a method to price the European call option. To justify their entire framework, they advanced the following three arguments for the attractiveness of the BG distribution. First, the BG distribution can be tuned by up to four parameters thereby making it highly amenable to empirical data fitting. Second, path trajectories from processes based on the BG distribution possess a higher level of realism because they have an infinite number of jumps on any time interval. Finally, the BG distribution has analytically simple Lévy characteristics. For these reasons, we also adopt the BG distribution as the modeling distribution for our asset price movements.

2.2 Moment-generating function of the sum of increments of bilateral gamma processes

Suppose we have a Poisson counting process where given some constant $\lambda > 0$, the value $\lambda \Delta t$ designates the number of new events that we can expect to observe in $\Delta t > 0$ time units. The probability distribution of the time that will elapse until we observe the next $\alpha > 0$ Poisson events is described by the gamma distribution $\Gamma(\alpha;\lambda\, \Delta t)$ with shape parameter α and rate parameter $\lambda\, \Delta t$. Define U^+ to be a $\Gamma(\alpha^+; \lambda^+)$ distribution, and U^- to be a $\Gamma(\alpha^-, \lambda^-)$ distribution where $\alpha^+ > 0$, $\alpha^- > 0$, $\lambda^+ > 0$, $\lambda^- > 0$. The random variable $X = U^+ - U^-$ follows a BG distribution described by $\Gamma(\alpha^+, \lambda^+; \alpha^-, \lambda^-) \equiv \Gamma(\alpha^+, \lambda^+) * \Gamma(\alpha^-, -\lambda^-)$. To model the randomness of the logarithm of stock prices, Küchler and Tappe (2008) introduced a continuous-time process $X_t \colon t \geq 0$ whose infinitesimal increments are drawn from identical BG distributions. They called this process the bilateral gamma process, and proved that it an infinitely divisible Lévy process. That is, if $X_t$is a continuous-time BG process, for $t \in [0,T]$, and $0 \leq \tau_1 < t_1 < \tau_2 < t_2 \leq T$, then $X_{t_1} - X_{\tau_1}$ and $X_{t_2} - X_{\tau_2}$are independent BG random variables where $X_{t_1} - X_{\tau_1} \sim \Gamma(\alpha^+(t_1 - \tau_1), \lambda^+; \alpha^-(t_1 - \tau_1), \lambda^-)$ and $X_{t_2} - X_{\tau_2} \sim \Gamma(\alpha^+(t_2 - \tau_2), \lambda^+; \alpha^-(t_2 - \tau_2), \lambda^-)$. In other words, non-overlapping increments of BG processes are independent BG random variables.

Now, let $N \in \aleph^+$ such that $n \in \{0, \dots, N\}$, and suppose we also have a continuous time horizon $[0,T]$, that is split into N equal periods with demarcation dates labeled $n = 0, n = \Delta t, n = 2\Delta t, \dots, n = N\Delta t = T$. Due to the Lévy property, we obtain$\sum_{i=1}^{n} X_{i\Delta t} - X_{(i-1)\Delta t} = X_{n\Delta t} = X_{n\Delta t} - X_0 = n\Delta t X \sim \Gamma\ (\alpha^+ n\Delta t, \lambda^+; \alpha^- n\Delta t, \lambda^-)$ for $n \in \{1, \dots, N\}$, and $X_0 \equiv 0$. The parameters $\lambda^+$and λ^- can be interpreted as Δt intensities of two independent Poisson processes that collectively determine the structure of the density function of $X_{n\Delta t}$. By scaling λ^+, λ^- such that $\Delta t = 1$, we notice that the moment-generating function (MGF) of $X\Delta t$ is $\mathbf{E}[e^{\theta X \Delta t}] = \left(\frac{\lambda^+}{\lambda^+ - \theta}\right)^{\alpha^+ \Delta t} \left(\frac{\lambda^-}{\lambda^- + \theta}\right)^{\alpha^- \Delta t} = \left(\frac{\lambda^+}{\lambda^+ - \theta}\right)^{\alpha^+} \left(\frac{\lambda^-}{\lambda^- + \theta}\right)^{\alpha^-}$ for $\theta \in \Re$ and$\lambda^+ > \theta$. Therefore, we obtain

$$\mathbf{E}[e^{\theta \sum_{i=1}^{n} X_i - X_{i-1}}] = \mathbf{E}[e^{\theta X_n}] = \mathbf{E}[e^{\theta n X}] = \left(\left(\frac{\lambda^+}{\lambda^+ - \theta}\right)^{\alpha^+} \left(\frac{\lambda^-}{\lambda^- + \theta}\right)^{\alpha^-}\right)^n \quad (1)$$

as the MGF of $\sum_{i=1}^{n} X_i - X_{i-1} = X_n$. Equation (1) is directly relevant to the option pricing problem especially for the case where $\theta = 1$.

2.3 Problem setup

Consider a non-dividend-paying asset whose price is modeled as a real-valued *exponential bilateral gamma process* $Y_t = y_0 e^{X_t}$ on a stochastic basis $(\Omega, F, \{F\}_{t \geq 0}, \mathbf{P})$ satisfying the usual conditions where $X_t : t \in [0,T]$ is a bilateral gamma process with initial value $X_0 = x_0 = 0$, and $y_0 > 0$ is the (deterministic) initial value of Y_t. To keep our model tractable, we impose the restriction $\alpha^+ = \alpha^- = 1$. The asset's price $Y_t : t \in [0,T]$ is observable in real time but the holder owns a (Bermudan) put option which can only be exercised at equally-spaced dates $n \in \{0, \dots, N\}$.

Date N is the option's maturity (expiration) date, and Y_t is totally adapted to F_n such that at any exercisable date $n \in \{0, \dots, N\}$, the holder has an observed sequence of price realizations represented by $y_1, \dots, y_n$ and another sequence of unobserved random prices $Y_{n+1}, \dots, Y_N$. An exercise policy π is a control rule encoded as a function of the form $a_n^\pi : \Re \to \{0,1\}$ for $n \in \{0, \dots, N\}$ such that

$$a_n^\pi(y_n) = \begin{cases} 1, & \textit{if based on the asset price } y_n \textit{ at date } n, \textit{one should immediately exercise} \\ 0, & \textit{if based on the asset price } y_n \textit{ at date } n, \textit{one should not exercise} \end{cases}$$

The holder makes the decision to exercise the option based only on asset price information y_n that is available up to and including date n. Hence, the stochastic evolution of Y_t means that to each arbitrary exercise policy π is associated a discrete random variable $\tilde{n}$ distributed on the support $\{0,\ldots,N\}$ such that $\Pr(\tilde{n}=n)$ represents the probability of exercising the option exactly at date $n \in \{0,\ldots,N\}$. If the option is exercised at date n, then $a_n^{\pi}(y_n)=1$ and the holder receives an immediate payoff exercise value of

$$g(n) \equiv (k(n) - y_n)^+ \equiv max\{k(n) - y_n, 0\} \text{ for } n \in \{0,\ldots,N\} \tag{2}$$

where $k(n) \equiv k_0(1-e^{wn}) + mn \geq 0$ is the strike price at date $n \in \{0,\ldots,N\}$ and $k_0 > 0, m \geq 0, w \leq \frac{1}{N}\ln\left(1+\frac{mN}{k_0}\right)$ are constants. The benefit of designing $k(n)$ in the above manner is that we can change its structure by appropriately selecting m and w. For instance $k(n)$ is; (i) k_0 for $n \geq 1$ if $m=0, w=-\infty$, (ii) nondecreasing if $m \geq 0, w \leq 0$, (iii) concave parabolic if $m > 0, 0 < w \leq \frac{1}{N}\ln\left(1+\frac{mN}{k_0}\right)$, and (iv) zero if $m = 0, 0 \leq w \leq \frac{1}{N}\ln\left(1+\frac{mN}{k_0}\right)$.

At the terminal date $n=N$, the option expires (matures) and there is no reason to postpone exercising. Hence, the exercise decision takes place before, or at the terminal date i.e., $\sum_{i=1}^{N} a_i^{\pi}(y_i)=1$. Define $\mathbf{E}[G^{\pi}(y_0)]$ to be the discounted expected payoff that the holder will receive by pursuing some arbitrary exercise policy π inducing a *random* exercise date $\tilde{n} \in \{0,\ldots,N\}$ given an initial stock price of y_0. The holder's problem is to select π such that she maximizes $\mathbf{E}[G^{\pi}(y_0)]$ without letting the variance of $G^{\pi}(y_0)$ (which we denote by $\mathbf{V}[G^{\pi}(y_0)]$) exceed a pre-specified payoff uncertainty budget $\sigma_{max}^2 > 0$. Of course, the market should be efficient enough such that arbitrage opportunities are non-existent otherwise the holder has a structural advantage over the other market participants. To summarize, the option holder is looking for an exercise policy π^* to solve

$$G^{\pi^*}(y_0) \equiv max_{\mathbf{V}[G^{\pi}(y_0)] \leq \sigma_{max}^2} \mathbf{E}[G^{\pi}(y_0)] \tag{3}$$

where $G^{\pi^*}(y_0)$ is the option's price from the standpoint of date $n=0$. In the next section, we determine the optimal exercise policy for Problem (3) (as well as the option's price) via the solution to a linear optimization problem.

3 DETERMINING THE OPTIMAL EXERCISE POLICY AND THE OPTION'S PRICE

We begin with the following restriction so as to ensure an arbitrage-free market.

Proposition 1. *To guarantee the condition of zero market arbitrage (i.e., to ensure that Y_t is a local $\mathbf{P}$-martingale), it is necessary that for $n \in \{0,\ldots,N\}$*

$$\mathbf{E}[e^{X_n}] = \left(\left(\frac{\lambda^+}{\lambda^+-1}\right)^{\alpha^+}\left(\frac{\lambda^-}{\lambda^-+1}\right)^{\alpha^-}\right)^n = 1 \tag{4}$$

where $\lambda^+ > 1$.

Proof. See Appendix A.

Given a discount factor $0 < \beta \leq 1$, the value

$$\mathbf{E}[u_n] \equiv \beta^n \mathbf{E}[(k(n) - Y_n)^+] = \begin{cases} \beta^n (k_0(1-e^{wn}) + mn - y_0 \mathbf{E}[e^{X_n}]), & if\ k_0(1-e^{wn}) + mn > y_0 \mathbf{E}[e^{X_n}] \\ 0, & otherwise \end{cases} \quad (5)$$

represents (from the standpoint of date $n = 0$) the discounted expected value of the option's payoff if exercised specifically at future date $n \in \{0, \dots, N\}$. Combining Equations (4) and (5), we obtain for an arbitrage-free market

$$\begin{aligned} \mathbf{E}[u_n] &\equiv \beta^n \mathbf{E}[(k(n) - Y_n)^+] = \begin{cases} \beta^n (k_0(1-e^{wn}) + mn - y_0), & if\ k_0(1-e^{wn}) + mn > y_0 \\ 0, & otherwise \end{cases} \\ &= \beta^n \Pr(k_0(1-e^{wn}) + mn > y_0)(k_0(1-e^{wn}) + mn - y_0)^+ \\ &= \beta^n F_{X_n}\left(\ln\left(\frac{k_0(1-e^{wn})+mn}{y_0}\right)\right)(k_0(1-e^{wn}) + mn - y_0)^+ \text{ where } F_{X_n}(z) \equiv \Pr(X_n < z) \text{ for } z \in \Re \\ &= \beta^n F_X\left(\frac{1}{n}\ln\left(\frac{k_0(1-e^{wn})+mn}{y_0}\right)\right)(k_0(1-e^{wn}) + mn - y_0)^+ \end{aligned} \quad (6)$$

For a BG random variable X with $\alpha^+ = \alpha^- = 1$, we obtain from Küchler and Tappe (2008)

$$F_X(x) = \begin{cases} \frac{\lambda^+}{\lambda^+ + \lambda^-} e^{\lambda^- x}, & if\ x < 0 \\ \frac{\lambda^+}{\lambda^+ + \lambda^-} + \frac{\lambda^-}{\lambda^+ + \lambda^-}\left(1 - e^{-\lambda^+ x}\right), & if\ 0 \le x \le \infty \end{cases} \quad (7)$$

and since $\mathbf{E}[u_n] > 0 \Leftrightarrow \frac{1}{n}\ln\left(\frac{k_0(1-e^{wn})+mn}{y_0}\right) > 0$ it follows that Equations (6) and (7) yield

$$\begin{aligned} \mathbf{E}[u_n] &= \beta^n \left(\frac{\lambda^+}{\lambda^+ + \lambda^-} + \frac{\lambda^-}{\lambda^+ + \lambda^-}\left(1 - e^{\left(-\frac{\lambda^+}{n}\ln\left(\frac{k_0(1-e^{wn})+mn}{y_0}\right)\right)}\right)\right)(k_0(1-e^{wn}) + mn - y_0)^+ \\ &= \beta^n \left(\frac{\lambda^+}{\lambda^+ + \lambda^-} + \frac{\lambda^-}{\lambda^+ + \lambda^-}\left(1 - \left(\frac{y_0}{k_0(1-e^{wn})+mn}\right)^{\frac{\lambda^+}{n}}\right)\right)(k_0(1-e^{wn}) + mn - y_0)^+ \end{aligned} \quad (8)$$

Recall that π is some arbitrary exercise policy associated with a random exercise date $\tilde{n} \in \{0, \dots, N\}$. Hence, $\mathbf{E}[G^\pi(y_0)] = \mathbf{E}[u_{\tilde{n}}]$ and we can rewrite Problem (3) as

$$G^{\pi^*}(y_0) = max_{\mathbf{V}[u_{\tilde{n}}] \le \sigma^2_{max}} \mathbf{E}[u_{\tilde{n}}] = max_{\mathbf{V}[u_{\tilde{n}}] \le \sigma^2_{max}} \sum_{n=0}^{N} \Pr(\tilde{n} = n)\mathbf{E}[u_n] \quad (9)$$

Note that from the vantage point of date $= 0$, the value u_n is only strictly positive when y_0 lies strictly below the threshold $k_0(1-e^{wn}) + mn$. Hence, for each date $n \in \{0, \dots, N-1\}$ there should exist an optimal threshold price $b_n^* < \infty$ and $b_N^* = \infty$ such that it is optimal to exercise the option if the prevailing asset price $y_n < b_n^*$. That is, the optimal policy π^* must dictate that

$$a_n^{\pi^*}(y_n) = \begin{cases} 1, & if\ y_n < b_n^*\ \ for\ n \in \{0, \dots, N\} \\ 0, & otherwise \end{cases}$$

where the condition $b_N^* = \infty$ compels the option to be exercised by date N. The challenge therefore lies in computing the sequence of values $b_0^*, \ldots, b_{N-1}^*$ associated with the optimal policy π^*. From the perspective of date $n = 0$, let $\Pr(a_n^\pi(Y_n) = 1)$ represent the probability of exercising the option *specifically* at future date $n \in \{0, \ldots, N\}$. In the same vein, denote $p_n \equiv \Pr(\sum_{i=0}^n a_i^\pi(Y_i) = 1)$ as the probability of exercising before, or on date $n \in \{0, \ldots, N\}$. By the independence of increments of Y_n, it follows that for $n \in \{1, \ldots, N\}$, the probability $\Pr(a_n^\pi(Y_n) = 1)$ is connected to $p_n = \Pr(\sum_{i=0}^n a_i^\pi(Y_i) = 1)$ in the following manner.

$$\Pr(a_n^\pi(Y_n) = 1) = \Pr(\tilde{n} = n) = p_n - p_{n-1}$$
$$= \overbrace{\Pr(a_1^\pi(Y_1) = 1)}^{p_1} + \prod_{i=1}^{n-1}(1 - \Pr(a_i^\pi(Y_i) = 1))\overbrace{\Pr(\textstyle\sum_{i=0}^n a_i^\pi(Y_i) = 1)}^{p_n} \tag{10}$$

where $p_0 \leq p_1 \leq \cdots \leq p_N$ and the initial and terminal boundary conditions are

$p_0 \equiv 0$ because $k(0) = 0$ and $y_n < 0$ imply that $u_0 = 0$
$p_N \equiv 1$ because there is no reason not to exercise the option at its maturity date $n = N$

Remark 1. *As a result of Equation (10) and its boundary conditions, Problem (9)* is equivalently

$$G^{\pi^*}(y_0) = max_{\mathbf{V}[u_{\tilde{n}}] \leq \sigma_{max}^2} \sum_{n=1}^N (p_n - p_{n-1})\mathbf{E}[u_n] \ given \ p_0 = 0, p_0 = 1, p_0 \leq p_1 \leq \cdots \leq p_N \tag{11}$$

Furthermore,

$$\sum_{n=0}^N \Pr(a_n^\pi(Y_n) = 1) = p_1 + \sum_{n=2}^N \left(\prod_{i=1}^{n-1}(1 - \Pr(a_i^\pi(Y_i) = 1))\, p_n\right) = \sum_{n=1}^N p_n - p_{n-1} = 1$$

and

$$p_n^* \equiv \Pr(\textstyle\sum_{i=0}^n a_i^{\pi^*}(Y_i) = 1) = \Pr(Y_n < b_n^*) = \Pr(y_0 e^{X_n} < b_n^*)$$
$$= \Pr\left(X_n < \ln\left(\frac{b_n^*}{y_0}\right)\right) = F_{X_n}\left(\ln\left(\frac{b_n^*}{y_0}\right)\right) = F_X\left(\frac{1}{n}\ln\left(\frac{b_n^*}{y_0}\right)\right) \Leftrightarrow b_n^* = y_0 e^{nF_X^{-1}(p_n^*)} \tag{12}$$

where $F_X^{-1}(p) = \begin{cases} -\infty, & if\ p = 0 \\ \infty, & if\ p = 1 \end{cases}$ *and*

$$F_X^{-1}(p) = \begin{cases} \frac{1}{\lambda^-}\ln\left(p\left(1 + \frac{\lambda^-}{\lambda^+}\right)\right), & if\ 0 < p < \frac{\lambda^+}{\lambda^- + \lambda^+} \\ -\frac{1}{\lambda^+}\ln\left((1-p)\left(1 + \frac{\lambda^+}{\lambda^-}\right)\right), & if\ \frac{\lambda^+}{\lambda^- + \lambda^+} \leq p < 1 \end{cases} \tag{13}$$

is the quantile function of X for any probability $p \in [0,1]$.

From Equations (12) and (13), the threshold price for date $n \in \{0, \ldots, N\}$ under the optimal exercise policy π^* is

$$b_n^* = \begin{cases} y_0 e^{n\left(\frac{1}{\lambda^-}\ln\left(p_n^*\left(1+\frac{\lambda^-}{\lambda^+}\right)\right)\right)} = y_0\left(p_n^*\left(1+\frac{\lambda^-}{\lambda^+}\right)\right)^{\frac{n}{\lambda^-}}, \; if\; 0 < p_n^* < \frac{\lambda^+}{\lambda^- + \lambda^+} \\ y_0 e^{n\left(-\frac{1}{\lambda^+}\ln\left((1-p_n^*)\left(1+\frac{\lambda^+}{\lambda^-}\right)\right)\right)} = y_0\left((1-p_n^*)\left(1+\frac{\lambda^+}{\lambda^-}\right)\right)^{-\frac{n}{\lambda^+}}, \; if\; \frac{\lambda^+}{\lambda^- + \lambda^+} \le p_n^* < 1 \end{cases} \tag{14}$$

and $b_n^* = \begin{cases} -\infty, \; if p_n^* = 0 \\ \infty, \; if\; p_n^* = 1 \end{cases}$. The nondecreasing sequence $p_0^* = 0, p_1^*, \ldots, p_{N-1,}^* p_N^* = 1$ is obtained from the optimal solution vector for Problem (11). Lemma 2.3 of Cacoullos (1982) gives an upper bound for the variance of a function of a discrete random variable. Applying that lemma to $\mathbf{V}[u_{\tilde{n}}]$ we obtain

$$\mathbf{V}[u_{\tilde{n}}] \le \sum_{i=0}^{N-1}(\Delta\mathbf{E}[u_i])^2 \sum_{n=i+1}^{N} n(p_n - p_{n-1}) = \sum_{n=1}^{N} n(p_n - p_{n-1})\left(\sum_{i=0}^{n-1}(\Delta\mathbf{E}[u_i])^2\right)$$

where $\Delta\mathbf{E}[u_i] \equiv \mathbf{E}[u_{i+1}] - \mathbf{E}[u_i]$ and $\Delta\mathbf{E}[u_0] = \mathbf{E}[u_1] - \mathbf{E}[u_0] = \mathbf{E}[u_1]$ since $\mathbf{E}[u_0] = 0$. Hence, using Remark 1 we can express Problem (5) as the following linear optimization problem

$$G^{\pi^*}(y_0) = max_{p,p_0=0,p_N=1} \sum_{n=1}^{N}(p_n - p_{n-1})\mathbf{E}[u_n] \tag{15}$$

subject to

$$\sum_{n=1}^{N} n(p_n - p_{n-1})\left(\sum_{i=0}^{n-1}(\Delta\mathbf{E}[u_i])^2\right) \le \sigma_{max}^2 \tag{16}$$

$$p_{n-1} \le p_n \text{ for all } n \in \{1, \ldots, N\} \tag{17}$$

$$0 \le p_n \le 1 \text{ for all } n \in \{1, \ldots, N\} \tag{18}$$

Proposition 2. *Suppose*

$$\hat{N} \equiv argmax_{n\in\{1,\ldots,N\}}\, n\left(\sum_{i=0}^{n-1}(\Delta\mathbf{E}[u_i])^2\right) \le \sigma_{max}^2$$
$$N' \equiv argmax_{n\in\{1,\ldots,N\}}\, \mathbf{E}[u_n]$$
$$N^* \equiv min\{\hat{N}, N'\}$$

Then a lower bound on the Bermudan put option's price is

$$\underline{G^{\pi}}(y_0) \equiv \sum_{n=1}^{N^*}\left(\frac{\frac{(N^*)^{2n}}{n!}}{\sum_{i=1}^{N^*}\frac{(N^*)^{2i}}{i!}}\right)\mathbf{E}[u_n] \tag{19}$$

Proof. See Appendix B.

The next section is an experimental investigation of the quality of our price bound.

4 NUMERICAL STUDY

To measure how good our price bound is, we choose two different strike price functions, and then compare $G^{\pi^*}(y_0)$(from Problem (15)) with $\underline{G}^{\pi}(y_0)$ (from Equation (19)) for various values of w and σ^2_{max}(see Figure 1). We experiment on the following dataset: $m = \$10, \beta = 1, y_0 = \$5, k_0 = \$25, N = 24, \lambda^+ = 20, \lambda^- = 19$, and define the following *price difference functions*

$$\Delta^*_{12} \equiv \left(G^{\pi^*}(y_0)\, for\, w = -0.025\right) - \left(G^{\pi^*}(y_0)\, for\, w = -0\right)$$

$$\Delta^*_{23} \equiv \left(G^{\pi^*}(y_0)\, for\, w = 0\right) - \left(G^{\pi^*}(y_0)\, for\, w = 0.025\right)$$

Figure 1: Effect of σ^2_{max} on $G^{\pi^*}(y_0), \underline{G}^{\pi}(y_0), |\Delta^*_{12}|$, and $|\Delta^*_{23}|$

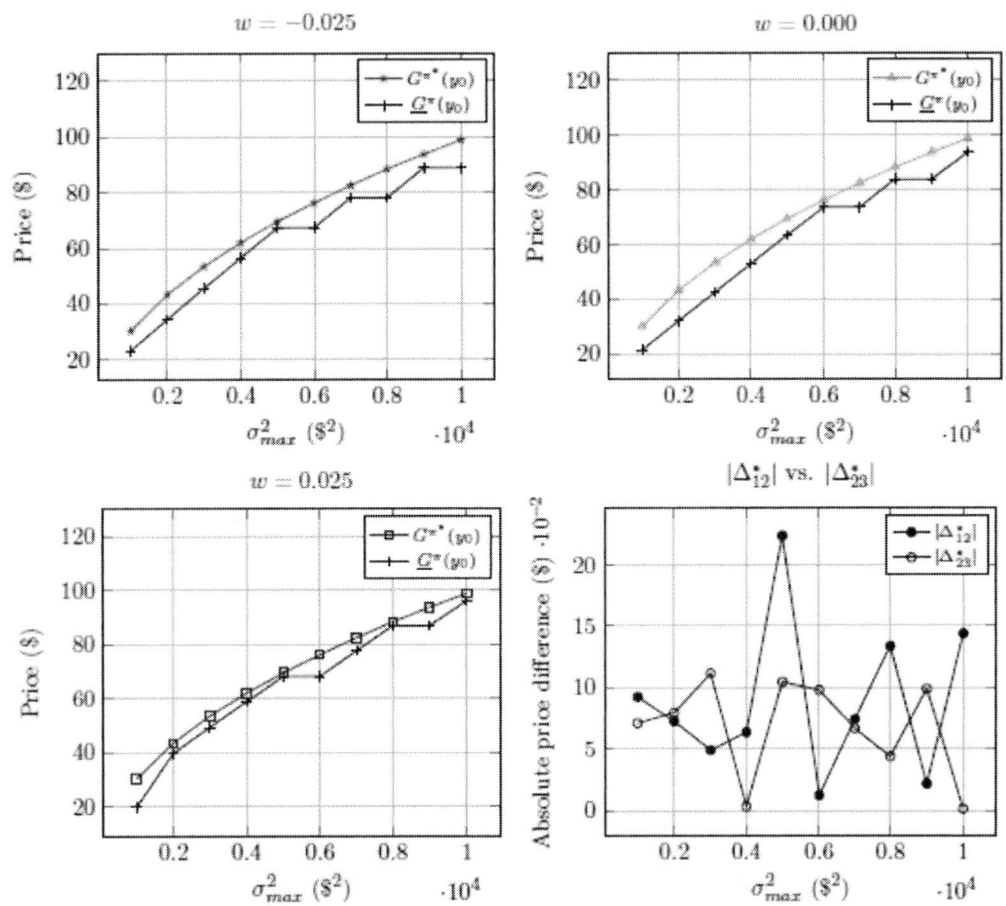

The experimentation suggests that the price lower bound ($\underline{G}^{\pi}(y_0)$) given by Equation (19) is relatively tight. In fact, in all test cases ($w = -0.025, w = 0$ and $w = 0.025$) the maximum percentage optimality gap is 26 percent. As expected, the option's price is a nondecreasing concave function of the payoff uncertainty budget, σ^2_{max}. This is consistent with the intuition that the expected payoff from exercising the option should increase as one's tolerance for payoff uncertainty increases. Alternatively stated, highly risk-averse prospective option buyers (i.e., those with low σ^2_{max}) should also be willing to pay little to own the option. Finally, the results suggest that the effect of σ_{max}^2 on the option's absolute price difference functions (i.e., $|\Delta_{12}^*|$, and $|\Delta_{23}^*|$) is neither significant nor is indicative of a consistent relationship. This implies that the option's price dependence on σ_{max}^2 is relatively insensitive to the sign of w which in turn plays an important role in governing the (deterministic) trajectory of the strike price over the time horizon.

5 CONCLUSION

In this paper, we considered the valuation of a Bermudan put option on an asset whose price fluctuations obey a simple version of a new model proposed by Küchler and Tappe (2008). We showed that the optimal exercise strategy dictates that the holder exercise the option as soon as the asset price drops below a certain threshold whose value (at every exercisable date) is efficiently computable from the vector solving a certain linear optimization problem. We characterized the option's price as the value associated to that solution vector, and heuristically established its lower bound. A numerical study confirmed the intuitive inverse relationship between risk-aversion and price, but also revealed that the aforementioned relationship is quite robust to changes in the nature of the strike price function.

We suggest two directions for further investigation. The obvious one would be to price the option for the general case when $\alpha^+ \neq 1$ and $\alpha^- \neq 1$. The other avenue would be to allow for situations in which the opportunity to exercise is modulated by some exogenous stochastic process. This would model the fact that sometimes option holders only have partial freedom to exercise their options (for instance, in situations where the right to exercise could be vetoed by some third party authority).

APPENDIX

A Proof of Proposition 1

Lemma 8.1 of Küchler and Tappe (2008) asserts that if unit time increments of X_t (under the measure **P**) follow a $\Gamma\ (\alpha^+, \lambda^+; \alpha^-, \lambda^-)$ distribution, then assuming $\lambda^+ > 1$ and that $y_0 > 0$ is deterministic, the process $Y_t = y_0 e^{X_t}$ is a local **P**-martingale if and only if $\left(\frac{\lambda^+}{\lambda^+ - 1}\right)^{\alpha^+} = \left(\frac{\lambda^- + 1}{\lambda^-}\right)^{\alpha^-} \Rightarrow \left(\frac{\lambda^+}{\lambda^+ - 1}\right)^{\alpha^+} \left(\frac{\lambda^-}{\lambda^- + 1}\right)^{\alpha^-} = 1$. By Equation (1),

$$\mathbf{E}\left[e^{\theta X_n}\right] = \mathbf{E}\left[e^{\theta \sum_{i=1}^{n} X_i - X_{i-1}}\right] = \left(\left(\frac{\lambda^+}{\lambda^+ - \theta}\right)^{\alpha^+} \left(\frac{\lambda^-}{\lambda^- + \theta}\right)^{\alpha^-}\right)^n \text{ for } \theta \in \Re,\ \lambda^+ > \theta \text{ and } n \in \{0, \ldots, N\}.$$

Therefore, for $\theta = 1$, $\mathbf{E}\left[e^{X_n}\right] = \mathbf{E}\left[e^{\sum_{i=1}^{n} X_i - X_{i-1}}\right] = \left(\left(\frac{\lambda^+}{\lambda^+ - \theta}\right)^{\alpha^+} \left(\frac{\lambda^-}{\lambda^- + \theta}\right)^{\alpha^-}\right)^n = 1^n = 1$ assuming $\lambda^+ > 1$.

B Proof of Proposition 2

By Constraint (16) $\sum_{n=1}^{N} n(p_n - p_{n-1})\left(\sum_{i=0}^{n-1}(\Delta \mathbf{E}[u_i])^2\right) \leq \sigma_{max}^2 \Rightarrow \hat{N}\left(\sum_{i=0}^{n-1}(\Delta \mathbf{E}[u_i])^2\right) \leq \sigma_{max}^2$ where $\hat{N} \equiv argmax_{n \in \{1,\ldots,N\}}\, n\left(\sum_{i=0}^{n-1}(\Delta \mathbf{E}[u_i])^2\right) \leq \sigma_{max}^2$. Now, for $n = 1$ to $n = N$ consider the sequence of probabilities $\{p_n - p_{n-1}\}_{n=1}^{\hat{N}} = \left\{\frac{\frac{(\hat{N})^{2n}}{n!}}{\sum_{i=1}^{N^*} \frac{(\hat{N})^{2i}}{i!}}\right\}_{n=1}^{\hat{N}}$ where $p_0 = 0$ and $p_{\hat{N}} = p_{\hat{N}+1} = \cdots = p_N = 1$.

Since $\sum_{n=1}^{N} p_n - p_{n-1} = \sum_{n=1}^{N} \frac{\frac{(\hat{N})^{2n}}{n!}}{\sum_{i=1}^{N^*} \frac{(\hat{N})^{2i}}{i!}} = 1$, it follows that $p_0 = 0$ and $p_{\hat{N}} = p_{\hat{N}+1} = \cdots = p_N = 1$, the sequence $\{p_n - p_{n-1}\}_{n=1}^{\hat{N}} = \left\{ \frac{\frac{(\hat{N})^{2n}}{n!}}{\sum_{i=1}^{N^*} \frac{(\hat{N})^{2i}}{i!}} \right\}_{n=1}^{\hat{N}}$ is a feasible solution for Problem (15) yielding $\sum_{n=1}^{\hat{N}} \frac{\frac{(\hat{N})^{2n}}{n!}}{\sum_{i=1}^{N^*} \frac{(\hat{N})^{2i}}{i!}} \mathbf{E}[u_n]$ as a lower bound on the option's price. However, by defining $N' \equiv argmax_{n \in \{1,\ldots,N\}} \mathbf{E}[u_n]$, $N^* \equiv min\{\hat{N}, N'\}$ and noticing that $\mathbf{E}[u_n]$ is either concave or monotonically increasing in n, we can obtain an improved lower bound if we replace $\hat{N}$ by N^*. Hence, $\underline{G^\pi}(y_0) \equiv \sum_{n=1}^{N^*} \left(\frac{\frac{(N^*)^{2n}}{n!}}{\sum_{i=1}^{N^*} \frac{(N^*)^{2i}}{i!}} \right) \mathbf{E}[u_n] \le G^{\pi^*}(y_0)$.

REFERENCES

Bjerksund P., Stensland G. (2014). Closed form spread option valuation. *Quantitative Finance, 14*(10), 1785-1794.

Black F., Scholes M. (1973). The pricing of options and corporate liabilities. *Journal of Political Economy, 81*(3), 637-654.

Cacoullos T. (1982). On upper and lower bounds for the variance of a function of a random variable. *The Annals of Probability, 10*(3), 799-809.

Carr P., Geman H., Madan D. B., Yor M. (2002). The fine structure of asset returns: an empirical investigation. *The Journal of Business, 75*(2), 305-332.

Hurd T. R., Zhuowei Z. (2010). A fourier transform method for spread option pricing. *SIAM Journal on Financial Mathematics, 1*(1), 142-157.

Kon S. J. (1973). Models of stock returns-a comparison. *The Journal of Finance, 39*(1) 147-165.

Küchler U., Tappe S. (2008). Bilateral gamma distributions and processes in financial mathematics. *Stochastic Processes and their Applications, 118*(2), 261-283.

Leccadito A., Paletta T., Tunaru R. (2016). Pricing and hedging basket options with exact moment matching. *Insurance: Mathematics and Economics*

Madan D. B., Seneta E. (1990). The variance gamma (V.G.) model for share market returns. *The Journal of Business 63*(4), 511-524.

Mantegna R. N., Stanley H. E. (1994). Stochastic process with ultraslow convergence to a Gaussian: The Truncated Lévy Flight. *Physical Review Letters, 73*(22), 2946-2949.

Sewell M. C., SenGupta I., Sewell G. (2015). Numerical methods applied to option pricing models with transaction costs and stochastic volatility. *Quantitative Finance, 15*(8), 1417-1424.

DECISION SCIENCES INSTITUTE

Board Composition and Persistence on Capital Markets: Empirical Evidence of Companies Delisting from the ASX

Amanda Lunt
University of Tasmania
Email: amanda.lunt@utas.edu.au

Dan Bumblauskas, Ph.D.
University of Northern Iowa
Email: daniel.bumblauskas@uni.edu

ABSTRACT

This article explores board composition in relation to the persistence of companies as listed entities on the Australian Securities Exchange (ASX) between 1990 and 2015. A data-driven investigation into existing theory of board heterogeneity evidences relationships between the proportion of non-executive directors, listing length and delisting likelihood.

KEYWORDS: Capital Markets, Analytics Approaches & Methods, Organizational Theory, Corporate Governance

INTRODUCTION

With an intention to extend the discussion of persistence of companies in terms of resilience as it relates to corporate governance, we began a data-driven investigation into Australian companies transitioning between listing states. In this paper we focus on delisting, which is a relatively uncommon event. The literature exploring reasons for companies' delisting is limited (Bortolon & da Silva Jr 2015). We report empirical findings of the relationship between board independence, company age and the likelihood of a company delisting from the ASX. This article therefore commences with an exploration of some of the background theory into capital market participation and board composition within an Australian corporate governance context, developing notions of persistence in the context of resilience theory.

BACKGROUND

Companies that raise equity capital by listing their securities may have a variety of underlying motivations. Research indicates these motivations vary between countries (Bird, 1995; Bebchuck & Roe, 1999). Delisting is the withdrawing of quoted company securities from a capital market. The next section considers delisting processes and literature on reasons for delisting. Relevant implications of studies on board composition and independence are proposed, and company persistence is linked to its resilience.

Delisting process in Australia

Delisting is a transition that comes in response to changed circumstances. Listing imposes certain requirements on companies that ensures delisting is not an overnight process and may be a departure from longer-term strategy. It can be considered a change in strategic direction for a company, generally accompanied by a restructuring of capital (Cohn, Mills, & Towery, 2014) and control (Cumming, Siegel, & Wright, 2007). As the company board of directors is responsible for providing strategic direction for the company (Baysinger & Hoskisson, 1990), the impetus for such a change falls within the board of directors' jurisdiction.

Under Australian corporations law, a company with "enhanced disclosure" securities included in a licensed financial market's official list is subject to specified disclosure requirements and the market's listing rules (*Corporations Act 2001* (Cth), s 111). Australia's official list is the Australian Securities Exchange (ASX) with some 2,182 listed disclosing entities on list at the time of writing (ASX, 2015b). Enhanced disclosure requires companies to prepare and lodge independently audited half-year and annual financial reports as well as to meet continuous disclosure requirements (*Corporations Act 2001* (Cth), Ch 6CA). Under continuous disclosure, a company is required to immediately release any information that could materially affect the price or value of company securities (ASX, 2014, Listing Rule 3.1). Listed disclosing entities must also report on the extent to which they have complied with ASX Corporate Governance Principles and Recommendations (ASX Corporate Governance Council, 2014) in accordance with Listing Rule 4.10.3.

Action to delist results in a change in status under the *Corporations Act* with corresponding changes to reporting requirements. In general, a public company may to continue to raise funds by offering securities to large numbers of people. Where prospectus requirements are relaxed for listed disclosing entities (*Corporations Act 2001* (Cth) s 713) in an acknowledgement of continuous disclosure activity, a public company that is not a listed disclosing entity must comply with Ch 6D's disclosure requirements when seeking to raise funds through an offer of securities. A company with no more than 50 members may apply to convert to a proprietary company, which minimises the company's financial reporting obligations. Movement away from continuous disclosure requirements is sometimes referred to as "going dark" (Campbell, Knowles, & Martin, 2014). Evidence suggests this process is likely to result in a restructuring, reconfiguring separation between management and ownership so their interests are much less differentiated (Cumming et al., 2007).

Delisting may be as an active or a passive process from a company's perspective. ASX acceptance of a company's request for removal from the official list is often termed voluntary, regardless of the circumstances of the request. A passive delisting process stems from an ASX decision and is imposed upon the company. On-going requirements are in areas such as level of operations, financial condition, proportion of assets in cash and level of spread of security holdings. ASX may suspend or remove a company if listing rules are not complied with, following a compulsory acquisition, upon failure to lodge documents or pay annual listing fees, if the company has no quoted securities, or for other reasons deemed appropriate to the circumstance (ASX, 2014).

Perhaps due to a notion of a company's "coming of age", as a company meets listing requirements before an initial public offering, IPO, (Pagano, Panetta, & Zingales, 1998) and subsequently maintains performance for continued listing, some authors present delisting as a "death" (Reeves, Levin, & Ueda, 2016), while others present it as a "momentous" event in a company's life (Mehran & Peristiani, 2009). It is surprising that such an important event is so underreported that commentators note the infrequency with which aggregation of delisting data is found in published empirical research (Bortolon & da Silva Junior, 2015). The research upon which this paper is based does take an approach to aggregating delisting data. In an email from a past legal practitioner of Australian corporate law, we have been advised that delisting is treated as a matter of responding appropriately to changed circumstances (J Streeter 2016, pers. comm., 9 January). Delisting may not always be as dramatic an occurrence as some theorists suggest, however the dataset compiled for this research article indicates delisting is a relatively rare occurrence.

Why delist?

As noted by Campbell et al. (2014), "the reasons why companies might delist from a major stock exchange are controversial, as is whether delisting sends a positive, neutral, or negative signal to markets and investors" (Campbell et al., 2014: 22). The significance of the delisting gatepost is downplayed, or ignored, in the literature on firm failure, possibly as a result of this ambiguity. Studies on delisting tend to focus on a particular scenario. In collecting data for a bankruptcy forecasting model, Shumway (2001) searched for delisted firms, ultimately including companies that filed for bankruptcy within 5 years of delisting (Shumway, 2001). Balios, Eriotis, Missiakoulis, and Vasiliou (2015) investigated the probability of delisting from the Athens Exchange, finding companies with performance issues such as poor liquidity, high leverage, low trading activity and big stock price decline are more likely to delist, voluntarily or not. A recent multivariate analysis into voluntarily delisting companies indicated five predictors of delisting in the Brazilian context: greater concentration of ownership and control; lower free float; lower liquidity of shares (particularly when majority of shareholdings are privately owned); greater availability of cash (particularly when main shareholders are public companies); and larger size (Bortolon & da Silva Junior, 2015).

A common difficulty researchers encounter in this domain is in obtaining post-delisting data (Campbell et al., 2014). Cohn et al. (2014) overcame this by accessing U.S. corporate tax returns. They concluded the delisting of the majority of companies in their study of leveraged buyouts, LBO's, was motivated in order to effect a sustained change in capital structure. Circumstances leading to delisting decisions are likely to be as varied as the number of companies who actually delist, returning us to the research problems inherent in the domain.

Conflicting results are not uncommon. Bharath and Dittmar (2010) consider the decision for delisting as the result of a trade-off, a reversal of decision to go public. Their research suggests that informed insiders (controlling shareholders) use private information to take their companies private before periods of unexpected good performance to avoid sharing the performance improvements with other shareholders. However, in their investigation into delistings by controlling shareholders in Europe, Croci and Giudice (2014) found no evidence of a change in operating performance before and up to 3 years after delisting, with minority investors benefiting from the premium on the market price of their shares at the point of delisting offer (see also Cohn et al. (2014) for a similar result from U.S. data).

According to Ferreira, Manso, and Silva (2012), a listing strategy is optimal for the exploitation of existing ideas, where transparency to market rivals is less of a concern. They observed a tendency to delist prior to pursuing an innovation strategy, with private investors being considered more tolerant of failures. A different strategic example is of relocation to another exchange in an attempt to increase company value, demonstrated in Singtel's recent delisting announcement (Singapore Telecommunications Limited, 2015). A multinational company, Singtel's shares had been traded simultaneously on two exchanges. As the ASX-quoted shares have performed poorly the company recently decided to consolidate all shares onto a single exchange. This appears to be a common event. In a study of both voluntary and involuntary delistings from prominent U.S. exchanges in 2008 and 2009 (of which involuntary delistings constituted over 60 percent), Campbell et al. (2014) found 69 percent immediately switched to an alternate exchange. However, as Australia has only the one major exchange, geographical barriers would seem to make this a less likely proposition, certainly for those companies that do not have multinational operations.

Board composition and independence

Cai, Garner, and Walkling (2009) suggest board independence is a measure of the degree to which managers entrench themselves in a company. Management entrenchment describes individual manager actions and decisions taken to increase their value to shareholders and making them costly to replace (Shleifer & Vishny, 1989). Understanding management's incentives is a long-standing central theme of organisation theory (Watts & Zimmerman, 1978). Where there is a higher degree of entrenchment, shareholders have less control over management (Cai et al., 2009). The ASX Corporate Governance Principles and Recommendations document states the "board needs to have an appropriate number of independent, non-executive directors who can challenge management and hold them to account, and also represent the best interests of the listed entity and its security holders as a whole rather than those of individual security holders or interest groups" (ASX Corporate Governance Council, 2014).

Corporate governance develops along country-specific paths (Bird, 1995). The 'if not, why not' Australian approach requires listed disclosing entities to specifically address the ASX Corporate Governance Council's Principles and Recommendations in annual reporting. Directors' duties are presented in Section 181(1) of the *Corporations Act 2001* (Cth) whereby "A director or other officer of a corporation must exercise their powers and discharge their duties: (a) in good faith in the best interests of the corporation; and (b) for a proper purpose." The oversight role of board members is associated with "legitimate authority and power to hire, fire, and compensate, provide advice, and monitor top managers" (Lim & McCann, 2013: 1568). It is argued that a company with an independent board can consider options and exert control over important decisions that are not necessarily in management's interest (Salancik & Pfeffer, 1980; Baysinger & Hoskisson, 1990).

Westphal (1998) notes an offsetting effect of increased board independence with subsequent CEO ingratiating and persuasion behaviour, or "managerial influence tactics". Increased independence is considered to come with greater control over top management, although Zajac and Westphal (1996) noted both board-controlled and CEO-controlled firms coexist and persist.

Along with reducing agency costs that arise through divergence of shareholder and manager interests (Jensen & Meckling, 1976), board independence is linked with more diverse input into decision-making (Dalton, Daily, Johnson, & Ellstrand, 1999), enhancing the board's ability to think strategically and see things differently (Roberts, McNulty, & Stiles, 2005), improved unbiased oversight of management by representing shareholders' interests (Fama & Jensen, 1983) and improved credibility in financial markets (Kroszner & Rajan, 1997). Recent work focuses on board heterogeneity "beyond independence" (Johnson, Schnatterly, & Hill, 2013). The ASX Corporate Governance Principles and Recommendations suggest a diversity policy would include gender, but also extend to "matters of age, disability, ethnicity, marital or family status, religious or cultural background, sexual orientation and gender identity" (ASX Corporate Governance Council, 2014).

When considering claims of representation of a diverse range of shareholder interests, it is interesting to note the influence of institutional investors. In Australia, New Zealand and the U.S., institutional investors hold more than 50% of all equities (Farrar, 1999). Schnatterly and Johnson (2014) find institutional investors are more likely to choose to invest in companies with a greater level of board independence over those predominantly made up of executive directors. As Lawrence and Stapledon (1999) point out, "even if independent directors do not add value, companies should still engage them because investors and potential investors believe they add value" (Lawrence & Stapledon, 1999: 5).

Linking persistence and resilience

Using performance of the organisation to indicate the adequacy of board oversight is a focus of existing literature. Investigating the longevity of public firms in the United States, Reeves et al. (2016) observe a market-wide emphasis on maximising short-term performance rather than long-term robustness. In contrast, Mitchell (1991) employs company survival itself as a measure of performance. Theory of resilience of organisations is a platform to develop understanding as to how companies persist in particular operating states.

Examining companies as complex dynamic self-adaptive systems (e.g. Levin, Xepapadeas, Crépin, Norberg, de Zeeuw, Folke, Hughes, Arrow, Barrett, Daily, Ehrlich, Kautsky, Mäler, Polasky, Troell, Vincent, & Walker, 2013) provides a useful frame for the context of strategy research into company transitions, such as those associated with delisting. Engle (2011) defines resilience as "achieving desirable states in the face of change".

The notion of survival is employed to examine company persistence in the face of challenging circumstances (Mitchell & Singh, 1996; Reeves et al., 2016). By incorporating investigation into companies "thriving", resilience theory expands on this substantively. Vogus and Sutcliffe (2007) articulate two focal questions for organisational resilience research: "Why are some organizations and institutions capable of maintaining function and structure in the face of environmental jolts and other large disruptions? Why do some organizations crumble in the face of high levels of ongoing strain while others thrive and grow more resourceful and poised to tackle future challenges?" (Vogus et al., 2007: 3418).

A variety of factors have been identified and investigated. Flexibility is considered in resilience research. Adaptive capacity covers the idea that the more successful entities not only have a capacity to adapt in response to external threats and opportunities, but can also influence the environment within which they exist (Folke, 2006). Dependability is argued to hinge on available slack (Schulman, 1993), emphasising redundancy (Haimes, 2009).

As noted by Goodstein and Boeker (1991), strategic changes may be implemented in response to changes in a company's circumstances. These changes may be exogenous such as regulatory or technological environment changes, as well as a change in tracked performance. The authors suggest an organisation's flexibility in implementing responsive changes may be constrained by an existing political or power structure. The finding that stability in ownership and board interests tends toward resistance of CEO-proposed strategic changes, suggests the lower the level of board independence, the more dynamic and responsive an organisation may be.

Researchers have noted a weak correlation with company survival and traditional performance measures (e.g. Shumway, 2001). According to Mitchell (1991), "[c]orporate strategists… have recognised survival as one organizational goal. Survival potential also is of interest to a firm's employees, the community in which it is based, and its competitors. The comparative investigation is particularly important given the potential for trade-offs between market share and survival" (Mitchell, 1991: 89).

RESEARCH HYPOTHESES

We initially set out to test for relationships between the lengths of company listing, board composition and delisting. A corollary with identified higher likelihood of delisting in years just following IPO's (Mehran & Peristiani, 2009) leads us to investigate persistence in our first hypothesis.

Hypothesis 1: The longer a company is listed on the ASX, the less likely it is to delist.

Due to earlier discussed findings, we wanted to investigate the idea that the level of board independence influences the likelihood of a company choosing to delist. The second hypothesis was developed to capture this tension.

Hypothesis 2: The greater the proportion of non-executive directors on the board, the less likely the company is to delist.

We also were interested in investigating the interaction between age and proportion of non-executive directors, and developed a third hypothesis to this end.

Hypothesis 3: The longer a company is listed and the greater the proportion of non-executive directors on the board, the less likely a company is to delist.

METHODOLOGY

We applied a Cox proportional hazards approach to the three hypotheses. A hazard model allows for an estimation of risk of an event over time. Cox's (1972) extension allows for a changing risk of an event over a predefined time function with covariation. The Cox proportional hazards (*coxph*) model is widely used for analysing survival data (Harrell Jr., 2001). Observations of each individual in a population are taken until the event or censoring. In the case of censored data, records for which an event has not been observed during the period of study, we know that the time to the event is beyond the censoring time (Cox, 1972). T is a random variable representing time to the event with a survivor function represented as, $F(t) = pr(T \geq t)$. A semiparametric model, the predictors are assumed to have a parametric relationship with the hazard function, but there are no assumptions about the form of the hazard function itself (Harrell Jr., 2001). The hazard rate, or intensity of failure, is specified as a function of time $\lambda(t) = lim_{h\downarrow 0} pr[T \leq t + h | T > t]$ (Andersen & Gill, 1982) for time listed T of an individual company with a covariate vector X which may depend on time t as follows: $\lambda(t|\mathrm{X}) = \lambda(t)\exp(X\beta), t \geq 0$. (Harrell Jr., 2001)

Cox's approach has been shown to have wider application apart from medical survival data. Mehran and Peristiani (2009) use hazard modelling in testing their financial visibility hypothesis whereby "young firms are choosing to exit the public market because they have failed to attract an adequate level of investor recognition" (Mehran & Peristiani, 2009: 3). Henebry (1996) and Shumway (2001) use Cox proportional hazards to build predictive models of company failure. Mitchell (1991) considers companies' survival in industry subfields. Tran, Thom Pham, Yang, and Tien Nguyen (2012) seek to predict the remaining useful life of a machine by modelling machine failure. Settanni, Newnes, Thenent, Bumblauskas, Parry, and Goh (2015) apply Cox proportional hazards to recurrent failure events (see also Settanni, Newnes, Thenent, Bumblauskas, Parry, & Goh, 2016).

There are various trade-offs involved in our analytical modelling decisions. Board composition and length of listing are modelled as independent variables. We are interested in the separation between management and shareholders and have defined independence through the proportion of non-executive directors. As previously mentioned, independence is frequently defined more rigorously with the meaning of independence of non-executive directors differing widely between countries (Zattoni & Cuomo, 2010). Williams, Bingham, and Shimeld (2015), for example, define independence requiring no affiliations to the company other than a role on the board. An Australian study into the top 100 largest listed companies of 1995 identified a proportion of 41% of non-executive directorships were affiliated with the company (Stapledon & Lawrence, 1997).

We retained the executive/ non-executive distinction as our measure of board composition in order to investigate a larger sample. The large number of observations within the scope of this initial investigation made it impractical to access individual companies' annual reports and incorporate this data. In an investigation into 69 commercial banks from six OECD countries for the 1996-2006 period, de Andres and Vallelado (2008) also define their proportion of outside directors as the number of non-executives out of the total. They also faced a limitation from their data source.

Apart from the incorporation of time into our dataset for Cox proportional hazards processing, our model is constrained from recognising that director selection doesn't occur in a vacuum (Zajac & Westphal, 1996). We also have not controlled for sector- or industry-specific effects. It is a market-wide investigation into delisting for any reason.

Data structure

We compiled secondary data from the DatAnalysis database (Morningstar Inc., 2015). All companies that had board membership data were included. Observations were obtained in October 2015, constraining the time series to the 25 years from 1990 to 2015 (September). DatAnalysis records commence in 1990. We have not categorised companies in any way, such as by GICS sector.

In order to prepare for the modelling process, the observations were structured with one record per interval between each event time per company. This allows for the partial-likelihood including a contribution at each event time (Thomas & Reyes, 2014). Table 1 depicts the simple structure of our dataset.

Table 1: Structure of Input Data (*inputs.dat*)

timeperiod	listing_age	director_ratio	delisted
0	5	1	0
0	29	0.5	0
...			
24	21	0.86	1
....			
25	8	0.83	0

We used the same dataset for both investigations, only using complete observations. Financial time-series data from DatAnalysis prior to 2000 is patchy on account of the introduction of GICS in Australia in that year leading to reclassification of industries. Further, comprehensive director data is not available until early 2000s. Figure **1** demonstrates the distribution of the total 28,185 observations over the 25-year period and Figure **2** shows the delistings.

Figure 1: Number of observations for each year of the dataset. Timeperiod 0 corresponds with 1990, timeperiod 25 corresponds with 2015. Observations for 2015 are complete to September 30.

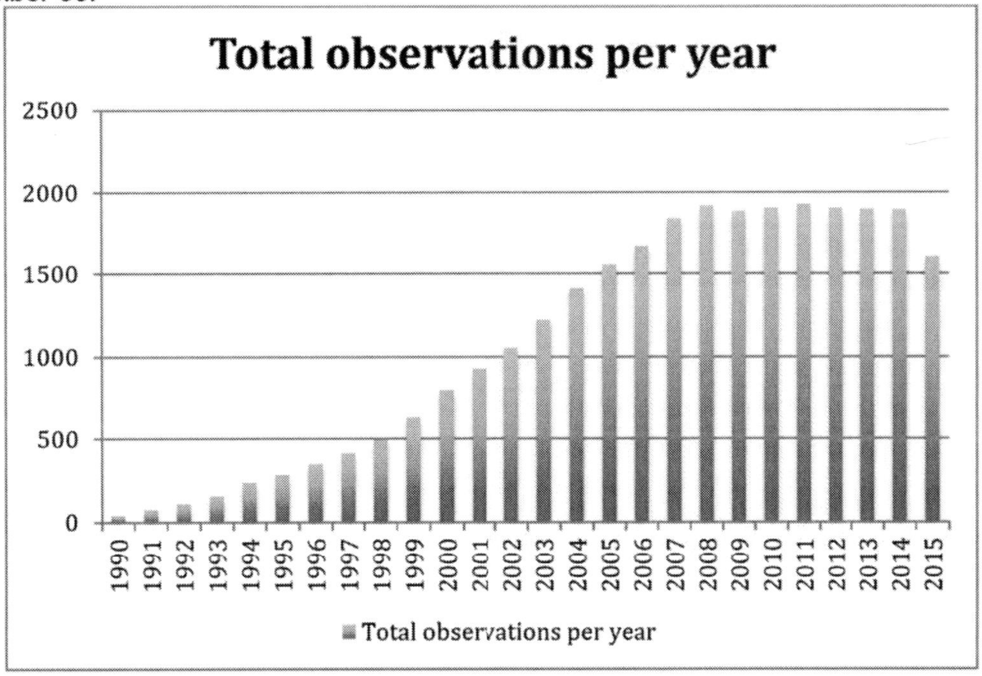

Figure 2: Number of delistings for each year of the dataset. A delisting event is recorded in the previous timeperiod. The single delisting of 2002 occurs in timeperiod 10, the 34 delistings of 2015 (to September) occur in timeperiod 24 of the dataset.

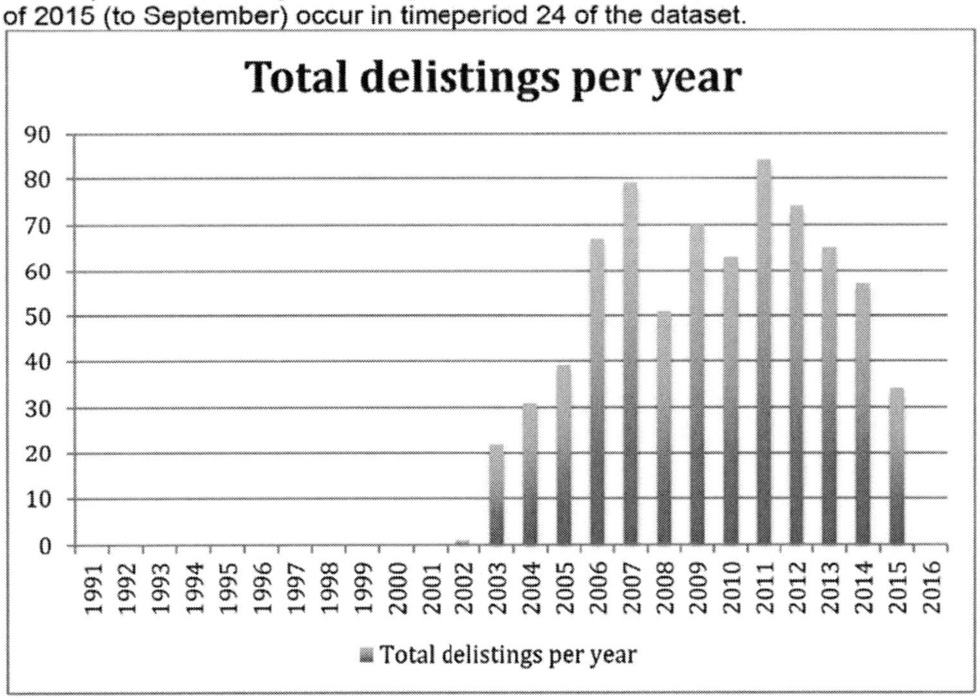

The dramatic rise in total observations from only 39 in 1990 to over 1,800 in 2007 (from which point it appears to remain fairly stable) and the lack of delisting records until 2002 is due to incomplete board composition data. Previous director data has only been captured by

DatAnalysis since November 2001 (Morningstar Inc., 2015), from which point the totals in our dataset have slight disparities with ASX-reported listing numbers (ASX, 2015a). This may be attributable to the fact that the ASX count includes listed managed investment funds, which may not have been accessed through the DatAnalysis search interface.

Records prior to 2001 are only of those companies that had a director still serving that was appointed prior to 2001. The dataset is not representative of the number of actual listings and delistings over that period. The Cox proportional hazards model allows us to incorporate what data we do have from the long early period with few recorded delisting events (Harrell Jr., 2001). Figure **2** illustrates a jump in delistings during the 2006 – 2007 onset of the global financial crisis (Williams et al., 2015) and an interesting sharp drop during 2008. The highest point at 2011 has been followed by a fall in each subsequent year.

Time period

The time period is a discrete value, representing events in each calendar year 1 January to 31 December. Observations for the year 1990 were attributed to time period 0, observations for the year 2015 to time period 25. Our total number of observations for the period is 28,185, with 737 delisting events.

Delisting year

The delisted event is recorded as a binary attribute, where 1 indicates a delisting event occurred in that time period. Due to the relationship between delisting and reporting requirements, data is not available in the actual year of delisting for the majority of the delisted companies (only about 150 of the 737 records). To incorporate all events, delisting has been associated with the year prior. A recorded delisting event therefore actually took place in the subsequent time period. This approach was taken for all companies, including those that have data associated with their delisting year. As a result, the observed data for delisted companies in the actual year of delisting has not been included in the dataset.

Company age

Following Shumway (2001), company age represents the number of years the company has traded shares on the Australian capital market. Age was calculated as the year of the observation, less the original year of listing plus one. Therefore, if the year of the current observation is the same as the year the company first listed, the value of the age variable is 1 and not 0. Figure **3** gives an overview of the average age of companies in the dataset.

Figure 3: Average age (number of years of listing) of companies observed for each year of the dataset

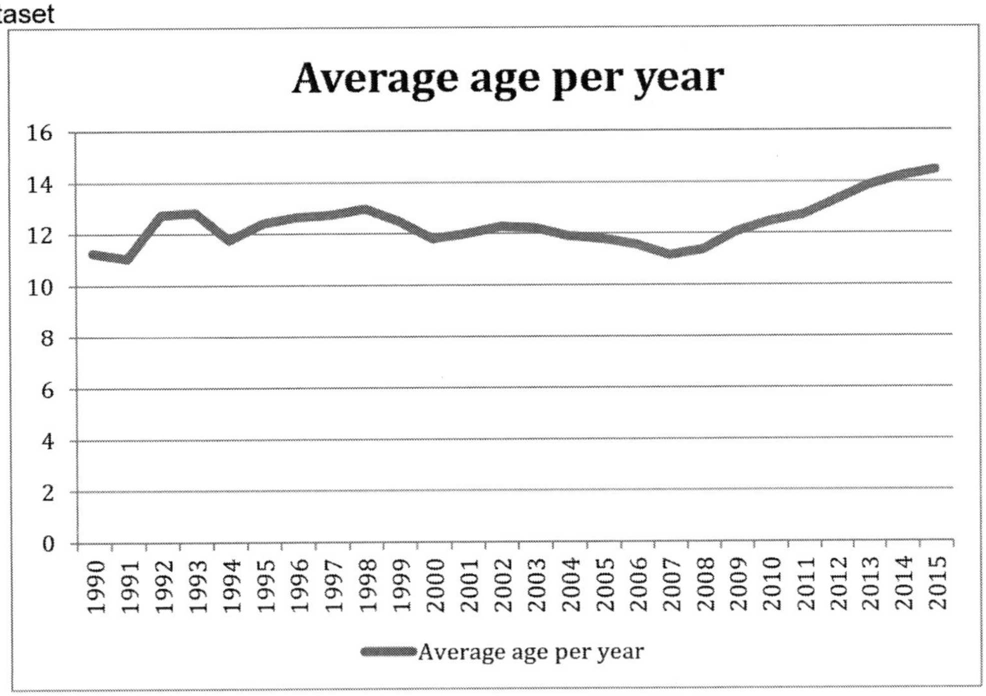

Board composition

Figure **4** demonstrates the increase in both average board size and average non-executive directors over the observation period. Clearly average board size is increasing.

Figure 4: Average board size and average number of non-executive directors has increased steadily since 2001. Average proportion of non-executive directors is also at an all-time high.

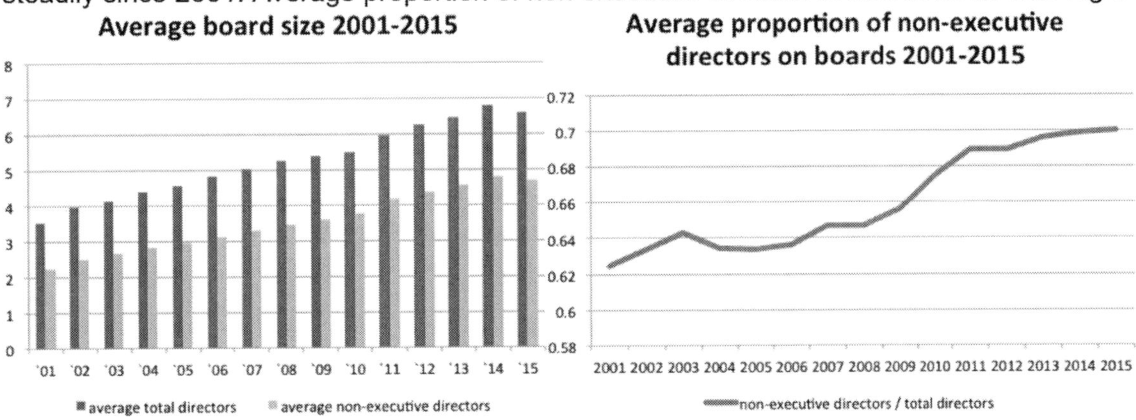

Discretisation of the proportion of non-executive directors

We chose to investigate the non-executive director ratio as both a continuous variable and a discrete variable. For purposes of Cox proportional hazards modelling, we divided the total observations into the categories shown in Table 2. These ranges were chosen in order to keep a sizeable proportion of the observations in each division, while retaining some domain meaningfulness and enhancing interpretability. Conheady, McIlkenny, Opong, and Pignatel

(2015) and Puterman (2005) also use this approach, albeit with slightly different divisions and application.

Table 2: Number of observations in each category after discretising the proportion of non-executive directors

Proportion of non-executive directors (inclusive ranges)	Number of observations
0 – 40%	4,523
40.01% – 50%	4,117
50.01 – 67%	6,047
67.01 – 80%	5,582
80.01 – 100%	7,916

Procedures In R

The *coxph* method from the survival package for R was used (Therneau & Lumley, 2015) with the exact partial likelihood method for handling tied event times.

Our code for approximation of the age hazard function for hypothesis 1 is,

$$result \leftarrow coxph(formula = Surv(timeperiod, delisted) \sim listing\_age, data = inputs.dat, method = "exact")$$

Our code for testing of the non-executive director ratio as a continuous variable is,

$$result \leftarrow coxph(formula = Surv(timeperiod, delisted) \sim director\_ratio, data = inputs.dat, method = "exact")$$

Our code for dividing the director ratio into five discrete categories is,

$$independence.dat \leftarrow cut(inputs.dat\$director\_ratio, br = c(-1,0.4,0.5,0.67,0.8,1.01), labels = c([0\text{-}0.4],[0.4001\text{-}0.5],[0.5001\text{-}0.67],[0.6701\text{-}0.8],[0.8001\text{-}1]))$$

Then we run the *coxph* method as follows,

$$result \leftarrow coxph(Surv(timeperiod, delisted) \sim independence.dat, data = inputs.dat, method = "exact")$$

The code for testing the interactive effects of age and proportion of non-executive directors is for the third hypothesis is,

$$result.interaction < -coxph(formula = Surv(timeperiod, delisted) \sim listing\_age * director\_ratio, data = inputs.dat, method = "exact")$$

RESULTS

The results from this process are presented below.

Hypothesis 1

The results of the *coxph* function for hypothesis 1 are presented in the following table. We were testing

$$\lambda\left(t, x_i^{listing\_age}\right) = \lambda(0, \alpha)\exp\left(\beta x_i^{listing_{age}}\right) \quad (1)$$

Table 3: Results of the Cox model of the first hypothesis, concerning delisting hazard and age

variable	coefficient, β	exponent of the coefficient, exp (β)	standard error of the coefficient, se (β)	z	p	lower .95	upper .95
age	-0.004127	0.995882	0.003388	-1.218	0.223	0.989	1.003

This gives us a hazard rate of (1 – 0.995882)*100 = 0.4118% decrease per additional year of listing. Our p-value is greater than 0.05.

Hypothesis 2

In hypothesis 2, we were testing

$$\lambda\left(t, x_i^{director\_ratio}\right) = \lambda(0, \alpha)\exp\left(\beta x_i^{director\_ratio}\right) \quad (2)$$

a) The results of the non-executive director ratio as a continuous variable are shown in Table 4.

Table 4: Results of the Cox model of the second hypothesis, with proportion of non-executive directors as a continuous variable

variable	β	exp (β)	se (β)	z	p	lower .95	upper .95
ratio	-0.9156	0.4003	0.1621	-5.648	1.62e-08	0.2913	0.55

The exponent of the coefficient 0.4003 gives us a 60% less hazard of delisting with 100% independent directors than with 0% independent directors. The p-value is less than 0.05, indicating a statistically significant result.

b) The results of the independent director ratio as a discrete variable are shown in Table 5.

Table 5: Results of the Cox model of the second hypothesis, with proportion of non-executive directors as a discrete variable. Each category was tested against a proportion of non-executive directors between 0% and 40% (inclusive)

categories	β	exp (β)	se (β)	z	Pr (> |z|)	lower .95	upper .95
40.01 – 50%	-0.550	0.577	0.140	-3.92	8.9e-05	0.4382	0.7597
50.01 – 67%	-0.325	0.723	0.115	-2.82	4.8e-03	0.5769	0.9055
67.01 – 80%	-0.621	0.537	0.121	-5.12	3.1e-07	0.4236	0.6817
80.01 – 100%	-0.612	0.542	0.120	-5.10	3.5e-07	0.4286	0.6863

The *coxph* function compares each of these with the delistings of the category with the lowest proportion of non-executive directors, 0 to 40% inclusive, as the base case. All exponents of the coefficients depict lower hazard rates than the base case with $p < 0.05$. The p-value of less than 0.05 for each category shows statistically significant results. Figure **5** illustrates the relative proportions for each category.

The relative risk of delisting of a company that hasn't yet delisted in the 40.01 – 50% range is 58% of the hazard of delisting for a company in the 0 – 40% range. A company with board composition in the range 50.01 – 67% range is 72% as likely to delist and in the two ranges encompassing 67.01 –100% is 54% as likely to delist than the base case.

Figure 5: Hazard rate of delisting for each category of the non-executive director ratio, as a proportion of the hazard rate for delisting for any reason, of a company with 40% or less non-executive directors

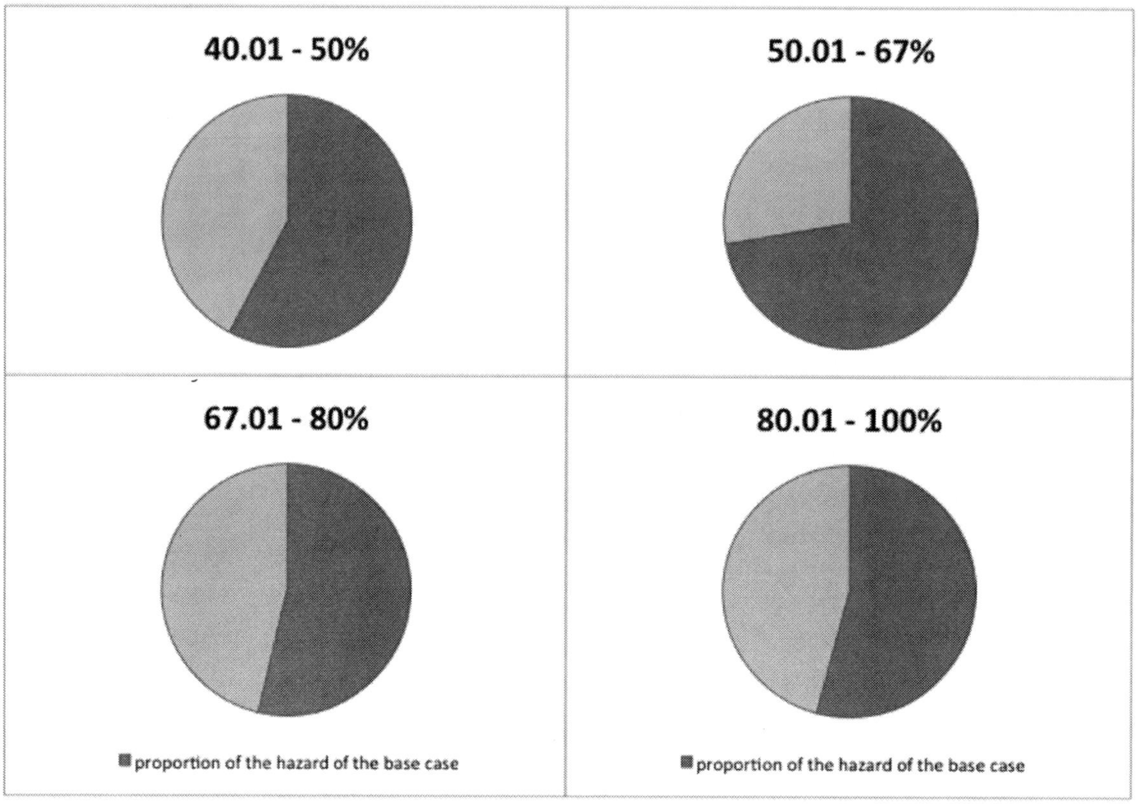

Hypothesis 3

For hypothesis 3, we are testing the proposition,

$$\lambda(t, x_i^{list\_age}, x_i^{dir\_ratio}) = \lambda(0,\alpha)\exp\left(\beta_{dir_{ratio}} x_i^{dir_{ratio}} + \beta_{list_{age}:dir_{ratio}} x_i^{list_{age}} x_i^{dir_{ratio}}\right) \quad (3)$$

We already know from hypothesis 1 that the effect of listing_age is not statistically significant on its own, hence its exclusion. The result of the test for interaction is shown in Table 6.

Table 6: Results of the Cox model of the third hypothesis, testing for interaction between company length of listing and proportion of non-executive directors, with both as continuous variables

variable	β	exp (β)	se (β)	z	p	lower .95	upper .95
age	0.01792	1.01809	0.01022	1.754	0.0795	0.9979	1.0387
ratio	-0.53336	0.58663	0.24552	-2.172	0.0298	0.3626	0.9492
age:ratio	-0.03036	0.97010	0.01466	-2.070	0.0384	0.9426	0.9984

The hazard rate for the interaction coefficient is (1 – 0.97) * 100 = 3% decrease per additional year of listing. The p-value is < 0.05.

DISCUSSION

The length of time a company has had shares quoted on the ASX does not have a statistically significant relationship to delisting on its own. However, when interacting with the director ratio, the risk of delisting decreases 3% for each additional year of listing. This is in keeping with resilience theories that emphasise experience as an important predictor of persistence.

Increasing average size of boards and the average proportion of non-executive directors may be attributable to an attempt by listed disclosing entities to "regain investor confidence through strengthening their corporate governance practices and disclosure practices" (Williams et al., 2015: 341). ASX recommends in Principle 2, 'Structure the board to add value', that the board "should be of sufficient size so that the requirements of the business can be met and changes to the composition of the board and its committees can be managed without undue disruption. However, it should not be so large as to be unwieldy." (ASX Corporate Governance Council, 2014: 14). Williams et al. (2015) raise the question whether recent series of board changes add value to a company's governance structure or are designed merely to create an impression of good governance. Schnatterly and Johnson (2014) suggest increasing board independence would make a company's securities more attractive to institutional investors. They found evidence that this preference is a result of institutional pressure rather than performance benefit.

Our results indicate companies' persistence in terms of length of listing on the ASX is related to our measure of board composition. Particularly for investors seeking longer-term investment, a company more likely to persist is a more attractive investment prospect. Although Cox's proportional hazards modelling does not provide information about the nature of the relationship between persistence and board composition (e.g. causality), we can recognise the strength of the association.

The results from evaluating board representation in isolation show that companies with non-executive director representation exceeding 40% are much less likely to delist, for any reason, than those with at least a 60% majority of executive directors. This result is statistically significant ($p < 0.05$), permitting us to generalise about our findings, keeping in mind the limitations of the dataset. In the context of previously introduced theory, the higher likelihood of delisting for companies with a very low proportion of non-executive director representation on the board is not surprising, with CEO-driven firms more likely to take advantage of opportunities to innovate afforded by that going dark. They were also seen to be more able to adapt quickly to changed circumstances and choose options that are in the interests of a less diverse range of shareholders.

The result for the category for between 40 and 50% non-executive director was surprising given that these boards are dominated by management, only 58% of the likelihood of delisting of those in the lowest range. In this case, the management oversight function is being performed by a board that is somewhat independent, but with no clear majority. The result may be explained by theory presented earlier concerning barriers to change that stem from inner political tension and corresponding inertia in such a circumstance.

The 72% proportional hazard for companies with a non-executive director ratio between 50 and 67% is also unexpected. This higher likelihood of delisting may be attributable to increased internal turmoil. As apparent control of the board is no longer with the executive, focus may be on inside political negotiating rather than on operational and strategic direction. Delisting may seem a viable option at this point if negotiations are not effective.

The final result, testing for the interaction between length of listing and the proportion of non-executive directors, both as continuous variables, reiterated our finding from investigating the director ratio in isolation. That is, the proportion of non-executive directors on the board has a significant effect on delisting ($p < 0.05$), that the effect of age as an additive variable is not significant ($p > 0.05$), but that age has an interactive relationship with the ratio of non-executive directors that is also statistically significant. This gives us the final model,

$$\lambda\left(t, x_i^{list\_age}, x_i^{dir\_ratio}\right) = \lambda(0, \alpha) \exp\left(-0.53 x_i^{dir_{ratio}} - 0.03 x_i^{list_{age}} x_i^{dir_{ratio}}\right) \tag{4}$$

CONCLUSION

Whether the delisting process is instigated from within a company's governance structure or imposed externally, it is a transition that is associated with strategic change, restructuring and sometimes company failure. Delisting decisions are in the domain of the board of directors. Amidst a trend of increasing average board size and non-executive representation on the boards of Australian listed disclosing entities, our investigation into the relationship between board composition and a proportional likelihood of delisting is suggestive of the following story. As the proportion of non-executive directors on a board heads beyond 40%, while management still holds control, board politics are fairly stable. Where the composition is such that non-executive members are only just in the majority, managerial influence tactics may cause the board's focus to turn inwards, detracting from the type of informed decision-making envisioned by the authors of corporate governance principles to come about through diversity amongst the decision-makers. This phase is associated with relatively high likelihood of delisting. As the proportion of non-executive directors reaches more than two-thirds of total representation, the executive directors are in a clear minority and management structures take on a different rhythm. Increasingly diverse board heterogeneity enables representation of a more diverse ownership group. Our findings suggest that this leads to a tendency for a company to persist in capital markets.

FURTHER WORK

Further investigation into the delisting transition could be extended by controlling for sector- or industry-specific effects and incorporating more complex definitions of board composition as suggested by the work of Atinc, Simmering, and Kroll (2011), Gertner and Kaplan (1996) and Johnson et al. (2013). Also of interest is the retention of the non-executive director ratio categories and widening the investigation to differentiate between official reasons for delisting.

REFERENCES

Andersen, P. K., & Gill, R. D. (1982). Cox's regression model for counting processes: a large sample study. *The Annals of Statistics*, 10(4), 1100-1120.

ASX (2014). ASX Listing Rules. ASX Limited. http://www.asx.com.au/regulation/rules/asx-listing-rules.htm. Accessed January 2016.

ASX (2015a). Historical Market Statistics. ASX Limited. http://www.asx.com.au/about/historical-market-statistics.htm . Accessed January 2016.

ASX (2015b). The Official List (Listed Companies). http://www.asx.com.au/asx/research/listedCompanies.do . Accessed January 2016.

ASX Corporate Governance Council (2014). Corporate Governance Principles and Recommendations. Sydney: Australian Securities Exchange.

Atinc, G., Simmering, M. J., & Kroll, M. J. (2011). Control variable use and reporting in macro and micro management research. *Organizational Research Methods*, 15(1), 57-74, DOI: 10.1177/1094428110397773.

Balios, D., Eriotis, N., Missiakoulis, S., & Vasiliou, D. (2015). Delisted versus voluntary delisted versus remain listed: an ordered analysis. *Applied Economics Letters*, 22(1), 66-70.

Baysinger, B., & Hoskisson, R. E. (1990). The composition of boards of directors and strategic control: effects on corporate strategy. *Academy of Management Review*, 15(1), 72-87.

Bebchuck, L. A., & Roe, M. J. (1999). A theory of path dependence in corporate ownership and governance. *Stanford Law Review*, 52, 127.

Bharath, S. T., & Dittmar, A. K. (2010). Why do firms use private equity to opt out of public markets? *Review of Financial Studies*, 23(5), 1771-1818.

Bird, H. (1995). Rise and fall of the independent director. *Australian Journal of Corporate Law*, 5, 235-258.

Bortolon, P. M., & da Silva Junior, A. (2015). Determining factors for delisting of companies listed on BM&FBOVESPA. *Revista Contabilidade & Finanças - USP*, 26(68), 140-153.

Cai, J. I. E., Garner, J. L., & Walkling, R. A. (2009). Electing directors. *The Journal of Finance*, 64(5), 2389-2421.

Campbell, L., Knowles, R., & Martin, K. (2014). Disappearing Act: Insight for the Management Accountant on Recently Delisted U.S. Companies. *Management Accounting Quarterly*, 15(2), 21-30.

Cohn, J. B., Mills, L. F., & Towery, E. M. (2014). The evolution of capital structure and operating performance after leveraged buyouts: evidence from U.S. corporate tax returns. *Journal of Financial Economics*, 111(2), 469-494.

Conheady, B., McIlkenny, P., Opong, K. K., & Pignatel, I. (2015). Board effectiveness and firm performance of Canadian listed firms. *The British Accounting Review*, 47(3), 290-303.

Corporations Act 2001 (Cth). https://www.comlaw.gov.au/Details/C2015C00003. Accessed January 2015.

Cox, D. R. (1972). Regression models and life-tables. *Journal of the Royal Statistical Society. Series B (Methodological)*, 34(2), 187-220.

Croci, E., & Giudice, A. D. (2014). Delistings, controlling shareholders and firm performance in Europe. *European Financial Management*, 20(2), 374-405.

Cumming, D., Siegel, D. S., & Wright, M. (2007). Private equity, leveraged buyouts and governance. *Journal of Corporate Finance*, 13(4), 439-460.

Dalton, D. R., Daily, C. M., Johnson, J. L., & Ellstrand, A. E. (1999). Number of directors and financial performance: a meta-analysis. *Academy of Management Journal*, 42(6), 674-686.

de Andres, P., & Vallelado, E. (2008). Corporate governance in banking: the role of the board of directors. *Journal of Banking & Finance*, 32(12), 2570-2580.

Engle, N. L. (2011). Adaptive capacity and its assessment. *Global Environmental Change*, 21(2), 647-656.

Fama, E. F., & Jensen, M. C. (1983). Separation of ownership and control. *The Journal of Law & Economics*, 26(2), 301-325.

Farrar, J. H. (1999). A brief thematic history of corporate governance. *Bond Law Review*, 11(2), 259-276.

Ferreira, D., Manso, G., & Silva, A. C. (2012). Incentives to innovate and the decision to go public or private. *Review of Financial Studies*, 27(1), 256-300.

Folke, C. (2006). Resilience: the emergence of a perspective for social–ecological systems analyses. *Global Environmental Change*, 16(3), 253-267.

Gertner, R., & Kaplan, S. N. (1996). The value-maximising board. Working Paper, University of Chicago and NBER.

Goodstein, J., & Boeker, W. (1991). Turbulence at the top: a new perspective on governance structure changes and strategic change. *Academy of Management Journal*, 34(2), 306-330.

Haimes, Y. Y. (2009). On the definition of resilience in systems. *Risk Analysis*, 29(4), 498-501.

Harrell Jr., F. E. (2001). *Regression modeling strategies: With applications to linear models, logistic regression, and survival analysis*. New York: Springer.

Henebry, K. L. (1996). Do cash flow variables improve the predictive accuracy of a Cox Proportional Hazards model for bank failure? *Quarterly Review of Economics & Finance*, 36(3), 395.

Holling, C. S. (1973). Resilience and stability of ecological systems. *Annual Review of Ecology and Systematics*, 4(1), 1-23.

Jensen, M. C., & Meckling, W. H. (1976). Theory of the firm: managerial behavior, agency costs and ownership structure. *Journal of Financial Economics*, 3(4), 305-360.

Johnson, S. G., Schnatterly, K., & Hill, A. D. (2013). Board composition beyond independence: social capital, human capital, and demographics. *Journal of Management*, 39(1), 232-262.

Kroszner, R. S., & Rajan, R. G. (1997). Organization structure and credibility: evidence from commercial bank securities activities before the Glass-Steagall Act. *Journal of Monetary Economics*, 39(3), 475-516.

Lawrence, J. J., & Stapledon, G. P. (1999). Is board composition important? A study of listed Australian companies. Social Science Research Network. http://ssrn.com/abstract=193528. Accessed January 2016.

Lim, E. N. K., & McCann, B. T. (2013). The influence of relative values of outside director stock options on firm strategic risk from a multiagent perspective. *Strategic Management Journal*, 34(13), 1568-1590.

Mehran, H., & Peristiani, S. (2009). Financial visibility and the decision to go private. *Staff Reports*: Federal Reserve Bank of New York.

Mitchell, W. (1991). Dual clocks: entry order influences on incumbent and newcomer market share and survival when specialized assets retain their value. *Strategic Management Journal*, 12(2), 85-100.

Mitchell, W., & Singh, K. (1996). Survival of businesses using collaborative relationships to commercialize complex goods. *Strategic Management Journal*, 17(3), 169-195.

Morningstar Inc. (2015). DatAnalysis Premium. http://datanalysis.morningstar.com.au. Accessed October 2015.

Pagano, M., Panetta, F., & Zingales, L. (1998). Why do companies go public? An empirical analysis. *The Journal of Finance*, 53(1), 27-64.

Prigogine, I., & Allen, P. M. (1982). The challenge of complexity. In W. C. Schieve, & P. M. Allen (Eds.), *Self-Organization and Dissipative Structures: Applications in the Physical and Social Sciences*. Austin, Texas: University of Texas Press, 3-39.

Puterman, M. (2005). *Markov decision processes: Discrete stochastic dynamic programming (2nd ed.)*. New York: John Wiley and Sons.

Reeves, M., Levin, S., & Ueda, D. (2016). The biology of corporate survival. *Harvard Business Review*, 94(1), 46-55.

Reid, J. (2012). The Neoliberal subject: resilience and the art of living dangerously. *Revista Pleyade*, 10(July-December), 143-165.

Roberts, J., McNulty, T., & Stiles, P. (2005). Beyond agency conceptions of the work of the non-executive director: creating accountability in the boardroom. *British Journal of Management*, 16, S5-S26.

Salancik, G. R., & Pfeffer, J. (1980). Effects of ownership and performance on executive tenure in U.S. corporations. *Academy of Management Journal*, 23(4), 653-664.

Schnatterly, K., & Johnson, S. G. (2014). Independent boards and the institutional investors that prefer them: drivers of institutional investor heterogeneity in governance preferences. *Strategic Management Journal*, 35(10), 1552-1563.

Schulman, P. R. (1993). The negotiated order of organizational reliability. *Administration & Society*, 25(3), 353-372.

Settanni, E., Newnes, L. B., Thenent, N. E., Bumblauskas, D., Parry, G., & Goh, Y. M. (2015). A case study in estimating avionics availability from field reliability data. *Quality and Reliability Engineering International.*

Settanni, E., Newnes, L. B., Thenent, N. E., Bumblauskas, D., Parry, G., & Goh, Y. M. (2016). Applying forgotten lessons in field reliability data analysis to performance-based support contracts. *Engineering Management Journal*, (In Press).

Shleifer, A., & Vishny, R. W. (1989). Management entrenchment. *Journal of Financial Economics*, 25(1), 123-139.

Shumway, T. (2001). Forecasting bankruptcy more accurately: a simple hazard model. *The Journal of Business*, 74(1), 101-124.

Singapore Telecommunications Limited (2015). General Announcement: Singtel seeks delisting from ASX. ASX Limited. http://www.asx.com.au/asxpdf/20150421/pdf/42y06805t028gp.pdf. Accessed December 2015.

Stapledon, G. P., & Lawrence, J. J. (1997). Board composition, structure and independence in Australia's largest listed companies. *Melbourne University Law Review*, 21(1), 150.

Therneau, T. M., & Lumley, T. (2015). survival: Survival Analysis package for R. Version 2.38-3. https://cran.r-project.org/web/packages/survival/index.html. Accessed November 2105.

Thomas, L., & Reyes, E. M. (2014). Tutorial: survival estimation for Cox regression models with time-varying coefficients using SAS and R. *Journal of Statistical Software*, 61(Code Snippet 1), 23.

Tran, V. T., Thom Pham, H., Yang, B.-S., & Tien Nguyen, T. (2012). Machine performance degradation assessment and remaining useful life prediction using proportional hazard model and support vector machine. *Mechanical Systems and Signal Processing*, 32(0), 320-330.

Vogus, T. J., & Sutcliffe, K. M. (2007). Organizational resilience: towards a theory and research agenda. *IEEE International Conference on Systems, Man and Cybernetics, 2007. ISIC.* 3418-3422.

Watts, R. L., & Zimmerman, J. L. (1978). Towards a positive theory of the determination of accounting standards. *Accounting Review*, 53(1), 112.

Westphal, J. D. (1998). Board games: how CEOs adapt to increases in structural board independence from management. *Administrative Science Quarterly*, 43(3), 511-537.

Williams, B. R., Bingham, S., & Shimeld, S. (2015). Corporate governance, the GFC and independent directors. *Managerial Auditing Journal*, 30(4/5), 324-346.

Zajac, E. J., & Westphal, J. D. (1996). Director reputation, CEO-board power, and the dynamics of board interlocks. *Administrative Science Quarterly*, 41(3), 507-529.

Zattoni, A., & Cuomo, F. (2010). How independent, competent and incentivized should non-executive directors be? An empirical investigation of good governance codes. *British Journal of Management*, 21(1), 63-79.

DECISION SCIENCES INSTITUTE

Bowman's Paradox Revisited: An Investigation of Three East Asian Markets

(Full Paper Submission)

Cau Ngoc Nguyen
Texas A&M International University
caunguyen@dusty.tamiu.edu

Albi Alikaj
Texas A&M International University
albialikaj@dusty.tamiu.edu

Wei Ning
Texas A&M International University
weining@dusty.tamiu.edu

ABSTRACT

One of the most puzzling phenomenons in the strategy literature is the observed inverse risk-return association known as Bowman's Paradox. This paper examines a recent five-year dataset for organizations headquartered in China, Japan, and Vietnam to investigate if such paradoxical relationship exists in the East Asian markets. Analyses from 10,623 annual firm observations across 28 industries show support for the negative relationship between organizational risk and return across the three countries. We also borrow insights from prospect theory and find that firms performing below their industry median tend to be more risk-seeking than those firms who outperform the industry median.

KEYWORDS: Risk-return association, Bowman's paradox, Prospect theory, East Asian markets

INTRODUCTION

For years, economic conventional wisdom has asserted that risk is positively associated with return. Nevertheless, a plethora of evidence has suggested otherwise. Namely, evidence have shown results of a negative risk-return association for firms when performance is measured in terms of accounting indicators (e.g. Bowman, 1982; Chang & Thomas, 1989; Chou, Chou, & Ko, 2009; Fiegenbaum, 1990; Gooding, Goel, & Wiseman, 1996; Jegers, 1991; Sinha, 1994){e.g. \Jegers, 1991 #3;Fiegenbaum, 1990 #2;Bromiley, 1991 #5;Chou, 2009 #112}. That is, the higher the risk, the lower the return on equity (ROE), return on asset (ROA), cash flows, etc. Bowman's (1980) findings were the first to document this anomaly at the firm and industry level, and it led him to label the negative association between risk and return as a paradox as he challenged future researchers for further investigations.

In his later work, Bowman (1982) offered a possible explanation for the risk-return paradox. Through a content analysis of firms' annual reports, he concluded by stating that "troubled firms take more risk." This is consistent with prospect theory (Kahneman & Tversky, 1979) which posits that people have a tendency to exhibit risk averse behaviors in situations involving sure gains; whereas in circumstances involving sure losses, people are more risk seeking. In addition, prospect theory predicts that risk attitudes are determined by the outcome's relation to some reference point. Those below a reference point tend to be more risk seeking, while those that are above, more often than not, are more risk averse.

The empirical support for prospect theory has been innumerable (e.g. Bromiley, 1991; Chang & Thomas, 1989; Chou et al., 2009; Fiegenbaum, 1990; Fiegenbaum & Thomas, 1988; Jegers, 1991). However, most of the studies have been conducted in the western-country context. This leaves many to question if the risk-return relation holds true across nations and whether or not prospect theory and can be applied to all countries and cultures (Arkes, Hirshleifer, Jiang, & Lim, 2007; Barberis, Mukherjee, & Wang, 2014). Therefore, the purpose of this paper is to address these concerns by providing a preliminary macro-level analysis on a number of Eastern countries.

This investigation seeks to answer an important research question: Will prospect theory hold in the context of eastern countries? To answer this question, data is collected from China, Japan and Vietnam. The cultural differences in sensitivities to risk have been duly noted in the literature; however, a number of studies (e.g. Park & Jun, 2003; Weber & Hsee, 1998) have found no significant differences in behaviors toward risk across countries. Thus, this study makes a contribution to the literature by examining aggregated firm data from China, Japan and Vietnam in an attempt to provide additional insights into the risk-return paradoxical relationship as well as to prospect theory.

The organization of this paper is as follows. The next section will highlight a selected literature review. The sample, data and measurements will be discussed in the third section, with the following section devoted to the statistical methods and empirical results. Finally, the last section will include the discussion, conclusion and limitations of the research.

LITERATURE REVIEW

Bowman's Paradox

Despite general consensus in economic and financial theory that risk and return are positively correlated, Bowman (1980) conducted an exploratory study on this relationship and investigated at the firm and industry level, rather than the more widely-used context of the stock market domain. Data from 85 U.S. industries for the period of 1968-1976 was examined and he found that in the majority of the industries in his sample, the relationship between risk and return was negative. More precisely, higher-average-profit companies in terms of return on equity (ROE) tended to have lower variance and risk over time. Further analysis and results showed that neither the companies within industries nor the industries themselves showed a positive correlation between risk and return.

His research was the first to report this incongruity at the organizational level and he coined his findings a "paradox" because it contradicted the common belief of a positive association between the two variables by economists. A new research stream emerged from this paradox as scholars investigated the risk-return relationship by integrating accounting data and behavioral decision theories, namely prospect theory.

Prospect Theory

In an article published in Econometrica, Kahneman and Tversky (1979) introduced an alternative model to the expected utility theory called prospect theory. In short, the theory predicts that given a choice between risky prospects, people will underweight outcomes that are probable relative to those that are definite. This indicates that people exhibit risk aversion in options involving sure gains and risk seeking behaviors in options involving sure losses. Moreover, the theory emphasizes the role of a target, or reference point. The reference point is considered to be a point of neutrality, and outcomes above the reference are considered to be gains, whereas, outcomes below a reference point are considered losses. It assumes that people are naturally risk-averse, but it also predicts that if people are below their reference point, they will engage in risk seeking behaviors.

In subsequent work, Bowman (1982) used insights from prospect theory as a theoretical foundation for his research. Bowman employed a content analysis of firm annual reports for three industries (food processing, computer/peripheral, and container) and found support for the prospect theory. Through a chi-square analysis, he found that troubled firms, or firms that are less profitable in terms of ROE, take more risks. Fiegenbaum and Thomas (1988) extended Bowman's research by using a 20-year period (1960-1979) and a more comprehensive dataset and found that similar results hold across different time periods and industries.

There have been other studies that have shown evidence that support the prospect theory on organizational and industry level investigations. In another analysis, Fiegenbaum (1990) examined 85 industries totaling about 3,300 firms for the time period of 1977-1984, showed that firms below their reference point were found to exhibit greater risk-taking behaviors while firms above the reference point were more risk-averse. He used secondary accounting measures for his study. The rate of return was measured using a firm segment's average ROA for the time period examined and risk was computed as the variance of the segment's ROA for the same period. The target level was calculated using the industry's median ROA.

Jeger (1991) extended Fiegenbaum's (1990) work with the use of Belgian accounting data. To further test the robustness of Fiegenbaum's findings and the prospect theory on firm-level analysis, Jeger also included three additional measures of returns (return on equity (ROE), cash flow on equity, cash flow plus financial outlays on total assets) as well as one additional measure of risk (coefficient of variation, measured as standard deviation of returns divided by average returns). His results also showed support for prospect theory as he concluded that inevitably, prospect theory "potentially extremely useful for the explanation of observed risk-return relations at the firm level." Nevertheless, he admitted that two confirming studies is not enough evidence for general acceptance of prospect theory.

Relatedly, Chou et al. (2009) provided a more recent sample of 27,416 U.S. firms and examined data for a period of 20 years (1984-2003). They argued that, at the time, most of the analyses have used early data from the COMPUSTAT database, which could potentially lead to biased results. They asserted that in 1978, the COMPUSTAT database was drastically updated to include over 6000 firms. The historical data of organizations were backfilled; however, no organizations that failed to survive through 1978 were added to the database. Therefore, they wanted to remove the "survivorship bias" by presenting a more current data set. In addition, they divided their sample into two ten-year time periods to further test robustness the findings. The two sub-periods examined were 1984-1993 and 1994-2003.

Interestingly, Chou and colleagues documented even stronger evidence in support of prospect theory relative to Fiegenbaum (1990). For both periods examined, they found that firms under the industry median show a strong negative risk-return relation, whereas firms performing above the industry median exhibited a positive, but weaker risk-return relationship. In their industry level analysis, they found similar results which show support for the risk adverse behaviors proposed by prospect theory.

Additional literature and empirical evidence in support for prospect theory and the risk-return relation has been well documented in literature (e.g. Chang & Thomas, 1989; Gooding et al., 1996; Sinha, 1994). The robustness of these findings have been tested with different sub-periods (e.g. Chou et al., 2009; Fiegenbaum & Thomas, 1988), multiple measures for risk and return (Jegers, 1991), and across various industries, among others. However, the majority of these studies have examined western countries, specifically in the U.S. As one of the scarce studies to employ international data to test prospect theory, Jegers (1991) asserted that additional development and evidence such as different data sources and data from other countries are imperative to fully understand the essence of economic decision making.

Cross-Cultural Differences in Risk Perceptions

There has been evidence suggesting that the perceptions of risks vary across different countries and cultures. Bontempo, Bottom, and Weber (1997) study of students from Hong Kong, Taiwan, the Netherlands, and the U.S indicated that differences of risk judgment between respondents from the two western countries and the two eastern countries exist. Respondents from Taiwan and Hong Kong were generally more sensitive to potential negative outcomes and less mitigated by the probability of gains in terms of financial risks.

Similarly, Schroeder, Tonsor, Pennings, and Mintert (2007) collected data from 4,005 beef consumers in the U.S., Canada, Mexico and Japan, and found glaring differences in risk aversion, risk perceptions, and risk behaviors in terms of food safety and consumption among the four countries. Relative to the U.S. and Canadian consumers, Mexican and Japanese consumers generally perceived risk to be higher and responded by being more risk averse and not consuming as much beef.

Although the differences in risk perceptions across countries have been empirically supported and acknowledged, there has been some evidence that suggests that these differences in risk perceptions do not necessarily altar risk behaviors. In a cross-cultural investigation of four countries that included China, Germany, Poland and the U.S., Weber and Hsee (1998) found that risk preference, measured as the buying price for risky financial options, varied across countries. But, these differences were attributed to the *perceived risk* rather than the *attitudes toward risk perceptions*. In all four cultures, the majority of respondents showed risk-aversion behaviors presented by their willingness to pay a premium price for less-risky financial options. Park and Jun (2003) found similar results in a study of Korean and American consumer internet buying behavior. They noted differences between the risk perceptions towards online shopping, but no significant differences were shown for online purchase intentions.

These findings suggest that prospect theory will hold across different cultures. Seemingly, the evidence supports the notion that people are indeed risk-averse and that the attitudes and behaviors toward risk is standard. This would suggest that there are cultural differences in reference points, but that the behaviors toward perceived risk will be in accordance with previous findings.

This paper is an exploratory investigation to examine whether or not China, Japan, and Vietnam will show behaviors toward risk that are consistent with predictions of prospect theory. Therefore, consistent with the literature, we test the following competing hypotheses[1]:

Hypothesis 1a: The relationship between risk and return is negative for firms that are low performers, such that, firms performing below the industry median will be associated with greater risk taking behaviors.

Hypothesis 1b: The relationship between risk and return is positive for firms that are low performers, such that, firms performing below the industry median will be associated with lower risk taking behaviors.

Hypothesis 2a: The relationship between risk and return is negative for firms that are high performers, such that, firms performing above the industry median will be associated with lower risk taking behaviors.

Hypothesis 2b: The relationship between risk and return is positive for firms that are high performers, such that, firms performing above the industry median will be associated with higher risk taking behaviors.

SAMPLE, DATA AND MEASUREMENTS

Sample and Data

The sample of this investigation included firm-level data from China, Japan and Vietnam. Accounting data was obtained from the COMPUSTAT database for the period of 2009-2014. Industries were distinguished using a two-digit SIC code. The original sample included 32,169 firms across 180 industries, aggregately. But, only firms with complete annual data necessary to calculate the variables were included. After elimination of firms with incomplete data, the final sample yielded 10,623 firms across 128 industries among the three countries. Table 1 presents a summary of the number of firm and industry observations for each of the countries. For a detailed list of the two-digit SIC code industry that was included for each of the countries, refer to Appendixes A-C.

Table 1: Summary of Sample

Country	Firm observations	Industries by 2-digit SIC
China	4,411	47
Japan	5,156	45
Vietnam	1,056	36
Total	10,623	128

Measurements

The two main variables of interest are return and risk. Return is represented with return on asset (ROA) for the firm segment, calculated as net income divided by total assets for the time period

1 Hypotheses 1a and 2a are consistent with Prospect Theory's assertions

(2009-2014). To operationalize risk, we calculated the variance of the return from the segment's ROA for the same time period. This approach is comparable to many of the previous studies that have examined this relationship (e.g. Bowman, 1980, 1982; Chou et al., 2009; Fiegenbaum, 1990; Fiegenbaum & Thomas, 1988).

Fiegenbaum (1990) listed several reasons why accounting measures are more relevant to organizational theorists and strategic management scholars, rather than market measures as suggested by others (e.g. Bettis & Mahajan, 1985; Laitner & Stolyarov, 2004): 1) regardless of level analysis, managers have more control over accounting data, 2) accounting data for public firms is utilized and controlled by regulatory agencies, 3) in any business, firms have only accounting measures of performance, and 4) only accounting measures are relevant for the division of firms.

Reference Point

Prospect theory does not clearly identify a measure for the point of reference. Instead, Kahneman and Tversky (1979) stated there is no universal rule to determine a reference point and that the reference point depends on the specific circumstance. Fiegenbaum and Thomas (1988) developed a procedure to determine the reference point according industrial organization economics. Industrial organization economics (Caves & Porter, 1977; Porter, 1980) is focused on the nature of competition in the industry. Firms act and react based on the decisions of other industrial firms. Moreover, potential entrants' observations of the industry as a whole and inclusive performance of the industry would either encourage or discourage them from entering.

Fiegenbaum (1990) explained that the industry average would be a good measure to indicate the reference point. Lev (1969) showed empirical results that supported the notion that firms alter their levels of performance to the industry mean. This supported his hypothesis that the industry mean is a good reference point. Drawing data from a different source, Frecka and Lee (1983) confirmed that industry average was a good reference point for firm and industry analysis.

However, the industry median return and risk have been widely used and accepted to calculate the reference point (e.g. Bowman, 1980; Bowman, 1982; Fiegenbaum, 1990; Fiegenbaum & Thomas, 1988; Jegers, 1991). Also, to evenly divide the sample into "low" and "high" risk and return, the industry median of each as the reference point is the more appropriate measure for this study.

A dummy variable was created to code whether the firm was at/above or below the reference point, *1* if at or above and *0* if below. The same procedure was used to calculate both the reference points of return and risk.

STATISTICAL METHODS AND RESULTS

This research replicates (Bowman (1980), 1982)), but does so on a more macro-level. Instead of looking at each of the industry separately for a country, data is aggregated for all of the industries to examine the cross-country differences on a more general level. This holistic approach to the investigation makes it easier to compare the three countries and it also provides a great overview to explore how the different countries behave to risk.

The analysis is split into two parts. In the first part, we use STATA 13.1 to do a chi square analysis. Chi square is used to determine if a certain distribution differs from some predetermined theoretical distribution. One of the applications of this test is to test the null hypothesis that there are no significant differences among or between the responses of individuals or groups (Downie & Heath, 1970). A two by two contingency table is created to examine the number of firms that are above or below the reference points of risk and return, shown in Figures 1-3.

In the second part of the analysis, we conduct a more complete test to confirm or refute the findings in part 1. In line with (Bowman (1980), 1982)), I calculated the negative association as "High/Low plus Low/High divided by High/High plus Low/Low." If the coefficient is less than 1, the association is indicated as a positive association. The results from these calculations are shown on Table 2.

Figure 1: China
Pearson chi-square= 2300 $p<.001$

	Low Risk	High Risk
High Return	1898	309
Low Return	319	1885

Figure 2: Japan
Pearson chi-square= 3300 $p<.001$

	Low Risk	High Risk
High Return	2324	257
Low Return	265	2320

Figure 3: Vietnam
Pearson chi-square= 3.8715 $p<.05$

	Low Risk	High Risk
High Return	365	139
Low Return	176	376

The values shown in each of the quadrants on the contingency tables shown in Figures 1-3 is based on a firm's average profit and the variability of its profit over the period of 2009-2014. The tables are split into "Low" and "High" in order to divide the firms in half within a given industry. For example, if the firm's profit and risk are below the industry's average, the firm would be put into the "Low-Low" quadrant.

The results of the first analysis show evidence that supports prospect theory's assertions for all of the three countries. Higher performing companies tended to be associated with lower risk over time. Figures 1, 2, and 3 show the two by two tables along with the results of the chi-square analysis for each of the countries examined. The results show significance for China, Japan, and Vietnam at the 1%, 1%, and 5%, respectively. Thus, the null hypothesis that there is no significant difference between risk and return is rejected.

Table 2: Countries Ranked by Negative Association Ratio[2] Based on 2009-2014 ROA and Variance

Country	Firm observations	Negative Association Ratio
Japan	5156	8.9
China	4411	6.0
Vietnam	1,056	2.4

The results in Table 2 confirm the results from Figures 1-3. A more detailed analysis shows that Japan shows a higher negative association ratio than China and Vietnam. But, across all three countries the calculations show a strong negative association ratio. Taken all together, the empirical results from both analyses show that China, Japan, nor Vietnam showed a positive relationship for risk and return. These results support hypotheses 1a and 2a, showing evidence that suggests that prospect theory holds across other nations.

DISCUSSION AND CONCLUSIONS

Against the general belief that risk and return are positively associated, (Bowman, 1980) recorded evidence of a negative relation on a firm and industry level analysis. This paradoxical relationship provided a new line of investigations in order to provide insight as to why this negative relationship exists. This led to many researchers to turn to the behavioral decisions literature in an attempt provide an explanation.

Prospect theory (Kahneman & Tversky, 1979) has served as a powerful theoretical tool to explain the relationship. A plethora of studies have tested its assertions with different time periods and sub-periods, data sources, and additional measurements of risk and return. However, the international evidence of prospect theory is scarce, especially for firms located in the eastern part of the world.

This preliminary study replicated Bowman's work on a country level analysis to test prospect theory and contributed to the literature by examining three eastern countries (China, Japan, and Vietnam) to explore whether the negative association between risk and return exists and if prospect theory can be applied to explain the negative relationship. Using a recent five-year data set (2009-2014) including observations from 10,623 firms and 28 industries across the three countries, empirical evidence show support for prospect theory and the paradoxical relationship that Bowman recorded.

A chi-square analysis of each country shows that high performing firms are associated with lower risk, whereas the underperforming firms tend to exhibit riskier behaviors. Further analysis indicates that among the three countries, Japanese firms show a stronger negative association between risk and return, followed by China and Vietnam.

Limitations and Avenues for Further Investigations

This study is a preliminary study and therefore, is not without limitations. However, these limitations offer opportunities for further investigations to provide additional insights to the literature. The first limitation is the lack of generalizability. The sample only included three

2 Consistent with Bowman (1982) "Two by two contingency table: High/Low plus Low/High divided by High/High plus Low/Low. Less than 1.0 indicates a positive association"

eastern countries. Moreover, data was only examined for five years. Future research should include other eastern countries as well as examine data for a longer period of time and for different sub periods.

Another limitation of this research is that it used the median return and risk as the reference point for analysis. This study used the same reference points as the previous investigations on western countries. However, previous literature on risk and behaviors suggest that cultural differences lie in the perceptions of risk and not in the behaviors toward risk. Subsequent studies can use different methods to indicate the reference point in order to test the robustness of the findings.

In addition, this study only used ROA when accounting for risk and return. Although previous empirical work have shown other accounting measures such as ROE and cash flows provide similar results, future work should incorporate different and multiple measurements of risk and return.

Furthermore, this investigation aggregated the industries for each country in its analysis to compare results on a macro-level. A rich avenue for further studies is to investigate with a more detailed examination and analyze on an industry level for each country, just as Bowman (1982) and others (Chou et al., 2009; Fiegenbaum, 1990; Jegers, 1991). This can potentially provide even a stronger support for the inevitable inference that Kahneman and Tversky's (1979) prospect theory is particularly useful for explaining the paradoxical relationship of risk-return on the firm and industry level.

REFERENCES

Arkes, H., Hirshleifer, D., Jiang, D., & Lim, S. (2007). Prospect theory and reference point adaptation: evidence from the US, China, and Korea: University Library of Munich, Germany.

Barberis, N., Mukherjee, A., & Wang, B. (2014). Prospect Theory and Stock Returns: An Empirical Test. *Available at SSRN 2528149*.

Bettis, R. A., & Mahajan, V. (1985). Risk/return performance of diversified firms. *Management science, 31*(7), 785-799.

Bontempo, R. N., Bottom, W. P., & Weber, E. U. (1997). Cross-Cultural differences in risk perception: A Model-Based approach. *Risk analysis, 17*(4), 479-488.

Bowman, E. H. (1980). A risk/return paradox for strategic management. *Sloan Management Review, 21*(3), 17-31.

Bowman, E. H. (1982). Risk seeking by troubled firms. *Sloan management review, 23*(4), 33-42.

Bromiley, P. (1991). Testing a causal model of corporate risk taking and performance. *Academy of Management Journal, 34*(1), 37-59.

Caves, R. E., & Porter, M. E. (1977). From entry barriers to mobility barriers: Conjectural decisions and contrived deterrence to new competition*. *The Quarterly Journal of Economics*, 241-261.

Chang, Y., & Thomas, H. (1989). The impact of diversification strategy on risk-return performance. *Strategic Management Journal, 10*(3), 271-284.

Chou, P.-H., Chou, R. K., & Ko, K.-C. (2009). Prospect theory and the risk-return paradox: some recent evidence. *Review of Quantitative Finance and Accounting, 33*(3), 193-208.

Downie, N. M., & Heath, R. W. (1970). Basic statistical methods.

Edwards, K. D. (1996). Prospect theory: A literature review. *International Review of Financial Analysis, 5*(1), 19-38.

Fiegenbaum, A. (1990). Prospect theory and the risk-return association: An empirical examination in 85 industries. *Journal of Economic Behavior & Organization, 14*(2), 187-203.

Fiegenbaum, A., & Thomas, H. (1988). Attitudes toward risk and the risk–return paradox: prospect theory explanations. *Academy of Management journal, 31*(1), 85-106.

Frecka, T. J., & Lee, C. F. (1983). Generalized financial ratio adjustment processes and their implications. *Journal of Accounting Research*, 308-316.

Gooding, R. Z., Goel, S., & Wiseman, R. M. (1996). Fixed versus variable reference points in the risk-return relationship. *Journal of Economic Behavior & Organization, 29*(2), 331-350.

Jegers, M. (1991). Prospect theory and the risk-return relation: Some Belgian evidence. *Academy of Management Journal, 34*(1), 215-225.

Kahneman, D., & Tversky, A. (1979). Prospect theory: An analysis of decision under risk. *Econometrica: Journal of the Econometric Society*, 263-291.

Laitner, J., & Stolyarov, D. (2004). Aggregate returns to scale and embodied technical change: Theory and measurement using stock market data. *Journal of Monetary Economics, 51*(1), 191-233.

Lev, B. (1969). Industry averages as targets for financial ratios. *Journal of Accounting Research*, 290-299.

Nickel, M. N., & Rodriguez, M. C. (2002). A review of research on the negative accounting relationship between risk and return: Bowman's paradox. *Omega, 30*(1), 1-18.

Park, C., & Jun, J.-K. (2003). A cross-cultural comparison of Internet buying behavior: Effects of Internet usage, perceived risks, and innovativeness. *International Marketing Review, 20*(5), 534-553.

Porter, M. E. (1980). Industry structure and competitive strategy: Keys to profitability. *Financial Analysts Journal, 36*(4), 30-41.

Schroeder, T. C., Tonsor, G. T., Pennings, J. M., & Mintert, J. (2007). Consumer food safety risk perceptions and attitudes: impacts on beef consumption across countries. *The BE Journal of Economic Analysis & Policy, 7*(1).

Sinha, T. (1994). Prospect theory and the risk return association: another look. *Journal of Economic Behavior & Organization, 24*(2), 225-231.

Weber, E. U., & Hsee, C. (1998). Cross-cultural differences in risk perception, but cross-cultural similarities in attitudes towards perceived risk. *Management science, 44*(9), 1205-1217.

APPENDIX A

China Industries by 2-digit SIC

China		China	
1	Agricultural Production - Crops	47	Transportation Services
2	Agricultural Production - Livestock	48	Communications
7	Agricultural Services	50	Wholesale Trade - Durable Goods
8	Forestry	53	General Merchandise Stores
9	Fishing, Hunting, & Trapping	54	Food Stores
12	Coal Mining	55	Automative Dealers & Service Stations
13	Oil & Gas Extraction	56	Apparel & Accessory Stores
15	General Building Contractors	57	Furniture & Homefurnishings Stores
16	Heavy Construction, Except Building	58	Eating & Drinking Places
22	Textile Mill Products	59	Miscellaneous Retail
23	Apparel & Other Textile Products	60	Depository Institutions
25	Furniture & Fixtures	61	Nondepository Institutions
26	Paper & Allied Products	62	Security & Commodity Brokers
27	Printing & Publishing	63	Insurance Carriers
29	Petroleum & Coal Products	65	Real Estate
30	Rubber & Miscellaneous Plastics Products	67	Holding & Other Investment Offices
31	Leather & Leather Products	70	Hotels & Other Lodging Places
39	Miscellaneous Manufacturing Industries	78	Motion Pictures
40	Railroad Transportation	79	Amusement & Recreation Services
41	Local & Interurban Passenger Transit	80	Health Services
42	Trucking & Warehousing	82	Educational Services
44	Water Transportation	84	Museums, Botanical, Zoological Gardens
45	Transportation by Air	87	Engineering & Management Services
		99	Non-Classifiable Establishments

APPENDIX B

Japan Industries by 2-digit SIC

Japan		Japan	
1	Agricultural Production - Crops	41	Local & Interurban Passenger Transit
2	Agricultural Production - Livestock	42	Trucking & Warehousing
7	Agricultural Services	44	Water Transportation
9	Fishing, Hunting, & Trapping	45	Transportation by Air
10	Metal, Mining	47	Transportation Services
12	Coal Mining	54	Food Stores
13	Oil & Gas Extraction	55	Automative Dealers & Service Stations
14	Nonmetallic Minerals, Except Fuels	56	Apparel & Accessory Stores
16	Heavy Construction, Except Building	60	Depository Institutions
17	Special Trade Contractors	63	Insurance Carriers
21	Tobacco Products	64	Insurance Agents, Brokers, & Service
22	Textile Mill Products	70	Hotels & Other Lodging Places
23	Apparel & Other Textile Products	72	Personal Services
25	Furniture & Fixtures	75	Auto Repair, Services, & Parking
26	Paper & Allied Products	76	Miscellaneous Repair Services
29	Petroleum & Coal Products	78	Motion Pictures
30	Rubber & Miscellaneous Plastics Products	79	Amusement & Recreation Services
31	Leather & Leather Products	80	Health Services
33	Primary Metal Industries	82	Educational Services
34	Fabricated Metal Products	83	Social Services
37	Transportation Equipment	86	Membership Organizations
39	Miscellaneous Manufacturing Industries	89	Services, Not Elsewhere Classified
40	Railroad Transportation	99	Non-Classifiable Establishments

APPENDIX C

Vietnam Industries by 2-digit SIC

Vietnam		Vietnam	
1	Agricultural Production - Crops	41	Local & Interurban Passenger Transit
10	Metal, Mining	42	Trucking & Warehousing
12	Coal Mining	47	Transportation Services
13	Oil & Gas Extraction	49	Electric, Gas, & Sanitary Services
14	Nonmetallic Minerals, Except Fuels	50	Wholesale Trade - Durable Goods
15	General Building Contractors	51	Wholesale Trade - Nondurable Goods
16	Heavy Construction, Except Building	55	Automative Dealers & Service Stations
17	Special Trade Contractors	59	Miscellaneous Retail
21	Tobacco Products	60	Depository Institutions
22	Textile Mill Products	62	Security & Commodity Brokers
27	Printing & Publishing	63	Insurance Carriers
29	Petroleum & Coal Products	65	Real Estate
30	Rubber & Miscellaneous Plastics Products	67	Holding & Other Investment Offices
32	Stone, Clay, & Glass Products	70	Hotels & Other Lodging Places
34	Fabricated Metal Products	73	Business Services
35	Industrial Machinery & Equipment	79	Amusement & Recreation Services
36	Electronic & Other Electric Equipment	87	Engineering & Management Services
39	Miscellaneous Manufacturing Industries	99	Non-Classifiable Establishments

DECISION SCIENCES INSTITUTE

Building Effective Online Education Video Lectures: Recommendations from Research and Practice

Paul J.A. van Vliet
University of Nebraska at Omaha
Email: pvvliet@unomaha.edu

ABSTRACT

As universities continue to increase their online course offerings, faculty developing online course content may find that in-class practices do not always transfer effectively to the online environment. This paper focuses on how instructors can better design and develop video lectures to improve student learning outcomes. Incorporating multimedia principles as well as lessons from practice, it is shown that effective video lecture development requires the consideration of length, structure, interactivity, accessibility, and personalization.

KEYWORDS: Online Education, Video, Educational Design

INTRODUCTION

Universities face an increasing demand for online courses, a shift driven not only by technological developments but also by the changing nature of the student population and by the universities' aim to expand their enrollment by serving out-of-state and overseas students. (Eduventures, LLC., 2006) In addition to providing educational opportunities to remote students, online courses are also valuable to local students whose schedules do not accommodate regular class sessions. (Preston et al, 2010)

The development of online courses may require educators to rethink their approaches to educational design and development. The education community's early attempts at developing pedagogy for online education have proved "daunting," as existing educational theories needed to be applied to a broad variety of new and often untested teaching practices and tools. In addition, educators' initial online education efforts were commonly based on assumptions from the traditional classroom environment, resulting in limited pedagogical insights. (Knowlton, 2000) Since then, we have learned that both teaching and studying in a distance education environment can be more difficult than in a classroom setting. (Geri, 2012)

A common aspect of online course development is the creation of video content, often in the form of video lectures. Video lectures can be defined as "CD and web viewable files that present lecture materials and narrative instruction from a course's instructor." (Brecht & Ogilby, 2008) Research has not only shown that students prefer video lectures over text, but also that the combination of auditory and visual information is superior to text in enhancing the conceptual understanding of educational content. (Ibrahim et al., 2012)

The author has taught online courses for more than 10 years and in the process realized that the transition from delivering in-class lectures to developing online lectures requires an educator to consider both pedagogical modifications and technical solutions.

From a pedagogy standpoint, the author has found that the dynamics of an online lecture differ greatly from a traditional in-class lecture. In online lectures, which tend to be recorded as a narration, direct interaction with students is absent: the students can't be queried about how well they've understood a particular concept, there are no student questions or requests for clarification, and the instructor can't work out a problem on the class whiteboard in real time. In online education, such direct interactions with students usually take place outside of the lecture. Due to the absence of this interaction, it often becomes necessary for the lectures to be rewritten before they are recorded. Based on in-class experience, clarifications and examples can be added to the lecture itself, as these can't be extemporaneously added as one might during an in-class lecture. The question arises whether these changes are all that is needed to create effective video lectures.

The objective of this paper therefore is to examine current state of research and development of video lecture development, particularly in higher education. What practices are most effective for engaging students and promoting learning? What does current research recommend regarding the design and development of online video content? What level of digital literacy should university faculty attain to develop effective lecture videos?

The technology to produce lecture videos is now affordable and quite easy to use. Using a web-cam and a microphone, faculty members can now record online lectures at their desks. A variety of software packages - such as Camtasia Studio (www.techsmith.com/camtasia.html) or Adobe Presenter (www.adobe.com/Presenter) - are available to capture the visuals and narration of a lecture and subsequently edit these into a complete online lecture.

Given the increasingly sophisticated features of these software tools, the challenge to instructors is to develop instructional videos which direct student attention to the relevant content in the most effective manner, while avoiding cognitive overload brought on by presenting too much complex information too quickly. (Ibrahim et al., 2012) This, then, requires instructors who develop lecture videos to comprehend what design characteristics will result in videos that are engaging, effective, and likely to be viewed by students. (Kim et al., 2014b) Such comprehension is at times lacking. For example, a study by (Preston et al, 2010) found that a substantial portion of faculty who had developed lecture videos often would not change their in-class lecture style, content, or structure. Yet what may be effective for in-class lectures may not necessarily be as effective in a video format. Indeed, (Koumi, 2015) argues that the requirements for the design of videos which both engage students and support student learning are greatly underestimated.

A better understanding of the use and effectiveness of online video lectures is now possible through the use of sophisticated tracking tools. Using video server logs which trace viewer activity, student viewing patterns and their interactions with the video content can now be analyzed in great detail, resulting in fresh insights for instructors and educational designers. (Guo et al, 2014; Kim et al., 2014a; Kim et al., 2014b) Tracking of student performance on quizzes and exercises which follow video lectures provides greater insights in the learning outcomes of various approaches to video lecture development. (Brecht & Ogilby, 2008; Merkt et al, 2011) When these insights are combined with educational theory developed to specifically address online lecture content, it becomes possible to provide specific and actionable recommendations for educators seeking to effectively deploy available technologies in order to transform their courses and create new learning opportunities for their students. (Chorianopoulos & Giannakos, 2013)

This paper will first examine the properties of video lectures, as well as the role of instructors developing these videos. A review of the principles of multimedia learning will provide a theoretical foundation for lecture video design. This is followed by an overview of video lecture development practices, with a specific focus on ensuring video accessibility, examining proper video length, applying structure to a video's content, and incorporating interactive features. The paper will then review current research which examine these development features and finally concludes with some specific recommendations for lecture video development.

USES, BENEFITS, AND DRAWBACKS OF VIDEO LECTURES

The initial development of video lectures in higher education targeted their deployment in online education courses. As mentioned earlier, these courses no longer focus solely on attracting remotely located students, but are now also recognized as a convenient and flexible learning option for local and on-campus students who face other work and family commitments (Green et al., 2008; Preston et al, 2010)

Once a course's lectures have been recorded, their availability provides for some additional uses as digital course content can easily be distributed and shared. An instructor may provide these recordings to in-class students in case class-time has been cancelled or when individual students have been unable to attend. Recorded lectures can also be provided to students in other courses who need an introduction to or a review of a topic. An instructor can easily create a small set of lectures designed to bring auxiliary content to a course (such as a software tutorial), or to provide remedial instruction for students lacking some prerequisite knowledge. (Brecht & Ogilby, 2008; Pavel et al., 2014)

Video lectures also allow an instructor to redesign the overall educational process of a course and present it in a flipped-class format. In this design, the students watch the online lectures as homework so that limited in-class time can be used for active learning practices such as interactive tutorials, hands-on workshops, problem-solving sessions, class discussion, or answering student questions. (Brecht & Ogilby, 2008; Preston et al, 2010)

In addition to the above uses, the availability of soundly developed lecture videos provides some clear benefits to educational institutions, educators, and students. For an educational institution offering online courses and the instructors teaching these, the availability of lecture videos permits their use in multiples sections of a given course. Instructors other than the person who developed the lecture videos can more easily administer an online course section without having to invest additional development time and effort. Use of existing lecture videos in this way also ensures that all students enrolled in the various course sections receive consistent content of a known level of quality. (Green et al., 2008; Preston et al, 2010) The more existing course content is utilized in these ways, the more appealing it becomes to the educational institution to invest in its continued development.

The use of lecture videos also provides great potential benefits for students. A collection of lecture videos provides students with a digital vending machine of knowledge which students can access anytime and anywhere. (Brecht & Ogilby, 2008; Pavel et al., 2014) Students who lack some prerequisite knowledge for a course can fill this need outside of the classroom, studying at their own pace.

For complex course content, students are able to view digital lectures multiple times in order to help comprehend the material in order to prepare for assignments or exams. These videos can be paused and repeated as will, providing the student with substantial control over the learning process. When students assert greater control over their own learning, this has been found to improve both student engagement and learning outcomes (Brecht & Ogilby, 2008; Brecht, 2012)

Video lectures also appear to appeal to student learning preferences in today's media culture, which is substantially video-based rather than text-based. As such, students may learn more effectively. (Brecht & Ogilby, 2008; O'Rourke et al, 2014; Preston et al, 2010) Moreover, (Geri, 2012) argues that video lectures may engage online education students better by enhancing social interaction in an online course. Video is a richer medium than written text for establishing a social connection between instructor and student, especially when the video lecture permits the instructor to include non-verbal cues such as tone of voice or facial expressions. (Jadin et al., 2009) In this way, the instructor's presence "resonates" more clearly than it could in text, which in turn may enhance both student learning outcomes and student retention. (Geri, 2012) An interesting example of this resonance was provided by (Green et al., 2008) who described how some lecturers would actually directly ask questions to students watching an online lecture, only to see students subsequently post answers to those questions on an online discussion forum.

Some drawbacks to the use of video lectures have been observed. First, (Preston et al, 2010) cite the concern of faculty that the availability of lecture videos for students enrolled in a traditional course may reduce student attendance at in-class lectures. Students were found to perceive this differently. They viewed lecture video availability as a positive to help them better comprehend complex content that was discussed in class and to help them study for examinations.

A more serious drawback is that in an online learning environment, lecture videos are not a complete replacement for the direct teacher-to-student and student-to-student interactions that occur in the classroom. Online students can't ask a lecture video to clarify a confusing explanation, which requires these students to have higher levels of intrinsic motivation and greater self-discipline when it comes to learning course content in order to be successful. (Jadin et al., 2009) While this drawback applies to online education in general rather than to lecture videos per se, it should encourage educators to not only develop lecture videos which provide clear and comprehensible explanations, but also to provide for effective communications options in online courses, such as e-mail, web-chats, or online forums.

ONLINE LECTURES AND THE CHANGING ROLE OF EDUCATORS

The increased usage of digital technology for both in-class and online education requires new layers of technical skills from educators. (Green et al., 2008) state that the popularity of online lecture videos in particular has changed the roles of educators to instructional designers, complicating the existing teaching efforts within this "technology rich environment." A study by Easton (2003) confirms that the skills and processes involved in teaching online courses are similar to teaching in-class courses, but stresses that the traditional approach to instructional design requires a fresh perspective. Instructional design requires not only the development of course content (such as lectures and readings) for online distribution, but must also consider the means by which other course mechanics (exams and quizzes, student presentations, responding to student questions about course content, etc.) are to be executed in the online environment.

(Berge, 1995) insists that "the ultimate technical goal for the instructor is to make the technology transparent" so that "the learner may concentrate on the academic task at hand." Two decades' worth of progress and innovation in online communication and collaboration technologies have brought educators closer to achieving this transparency. These technologies are now more affordable, reliable, powerful, and usable than ever before, permitting educators to select those specific applications and platforms that will help them meet educational objectives. Moreover, these technologies are becoming ubiquitous in education, rather than being limited to online education efforts. As these technologies are being embedded in existing educational processes, technology usage is likely to disappear as a separate role altogether. Instead the focus of educators will be on the effective implementation of available technology options in various educational settings. (Van Vliet, 2015)

For many educators, this wave of technology-driven change has resulted in new and ongoing requirements for professional development. A survey by (Kaltura, Inc., 2015) found a clear need for educator training on the tools that permit them to independently create and edit video content. (Green et al., 2008) advocate that educators take a broader perspective in their development. Educators should obtain insights on how students use online learning technologies and how both broad curricula and individual units of study can be optimized to take advantage of these technologies. This paper aims to provide instructors with current insights in the most effective design of video lectures.

PRINCIPLES OF MULTIMEDIA LEARNING

The current research and development efforts in educational media have been greatly influenced by the work of Richard E. Mayer. Mayer's work focuses on connecting the science of learning (which is student-focused) with the science of instruction (which is educator-focused) as it relates to multimedia-based education. (Mayer, 2008) Based on extensive research, Mayer summarized his findings as a series of principles for educational multimedia development in his influential 2001 text "Multimedia Learning" (Mayer, 2001)

At the heart of Mayer's work is what he calls the **Multimedia Principle**, which states that "students learn better from words and pictures than from words alone." (Mayer, 2001) Mayer asserts that even when the information contained in an image and in a piece of text are practically identical, this information is represented in two different formats, resulting in two distinct mental representations. Mayer bases this on a key notion from the science of learning, which is that humans possess two distinct channels for processing verbal and visual information. Consequently, Mayer developed a cognitive theory of multimedia learning which posits that when students experience a multimedia presentation, the words and images of that presentation are processed into both a verbal model and a pictorial model in working memory. These models are subsequently integrated using the prior knowledge drawn from the student's long-term memory. The effectiveness of multimedia learning, then, is based on the appropriate balance of verbal and visual information presented to the student in a way that does not exceed the student's cognitive capacity. (Mayer, 2008; Mayer & Fiorella, 2014) This can most easily be achieved when the narration specifically supports the graphic that is on screen, so that concurrent learning can occur. The combination of on-screen graphics and a spoken narration permits students to effectively connect them. (Moreno, 2006)

Mayer subsequently organizes his theory into three categories of principles: those which reduce the inclusion of extraneous information, those which address the proper presentation of essential content, and those which address student comprehension of the content.

Mayer considers the inclusion of unnecessary or extraneous information to be one of the most important flaws of ineffective multimedia content. The extraneous content requires the student to process more information than is necessary – referred to as extraneous cognitive processing – which places an unnecessary burden on the student's cognitive capacity. (Mayer, 2008; Mayer & Fiorella, 2014) Mayer articulated five principles which aim to reduce extraneous processing: (Mayer & Fiorella, 2014)

- **Coherence Principle:** Learning improves when extraneous words, pictures and sounds are excluded. While the inclusion of embellishments or so-called "seductive details" may appear to spice up a presentation, this information places a needless burden on the student.
- **Signaling Principle:** Learning improves when the presentation includes cues about its organization. For example, a text may start with an organizational sentence which lists five main items, which is then followed with numbered descriptions of each item.
- **Redundancy Principle:** The combination of animation and narration is more effective than the combination of animation, narration, and on-screen text. The student will obtain the textual information from the narration so that the visual component of the presentation can focus on imagery alone.
- **Spatial Contiguity Principle:** Learning improves when related words and pictures are shown adjacent rather than apart. The student does not have to scan the entire display to make this connection.
- **Temporal Contiguity Principle:** Learning improves when related words and pictures are presented simultaneously rather than in succession. If the student needs to keep information from a previous display in working memory in order to relate it to a subsequent display, the student's cognitive capacity is needlessly taxed.

Once extraneous information has been removed from a multimedia presentation, the focus should shift to the proper presentation of the essential learning content. When this content is more complex than it needs to be or is presented too fast for the learner to absorb, the amount of essential cognitive processing required to understand the instruction exceeds the cognitive capacity of the Student. Reducing this essential cognitive overload should be a key activity in the instructional design of multimedia content. (Mayer, 2008; Mayer & Pilegard, 2014) Mayer articulated three principles which address the management of essential processing: (Mayer & Pilegard, 2014)

- **Segmenting Principle:** Learning improves when content is presented in learner-paced segments rather than a single continuous unit. Segmenting slows the pace of the presentation of materials, thereby enabling the learner to carry out essential processing. Segmenting is most effective when the student controls the pace at which these segments are presented.
- **Pre-Training Principle:** Learning improves when the names and characteristics of the main concepts are known. Pre-training equips the student with prior knowledge so that the student can process the subsequent lesson with less cognitive effort. For example, when discussing a complex model, a student should first be taught about its individual components, before these are subsequently integrated into the larger model. Without such pre-training, the student would need to comprehend each component and the connections among them simultaneously.
- **Modality Principle:** The combination of graphics and narration is more effective than the combination of graphics and on-screen text. The combination of graphics and on-screen text may overload the student's visual channel; providing the text as audio reduces the load on the student's visual processing. This principle reinforces the earlier stated Redundancy Principle

Once the multimedia content has been presented, students engage in generative processing, which is a cognitive process aimed at making sense of the content, organizing it, and integrating it with the student's existing knowledge. Such generative processing is strengthened when the multimedia presentation includes social cues for the student to respond to, as these tend to increase the student's motivational commitment to the learning process. (Mayer, 2008; Mayer, 2014) Mayer articulated four principles which aim to enhance generative processing: (Mayer, 2014)

- **Personalization Principle:** Learning improves when the narration is conversational rather than formal. The personalization of a narration creates what Mayer refers to a "social partnership" of the student with the narrator, in which the student makes a greater effort to comprehend the narrator.
- **Voice Principle:** Learning improves when the narration is in a standard-accented voice, rather than in a machine-generated voice or a voice with a strong foreign accent.
- **Image Principle:** Learning does not necessarily improve when the speaker's image is included in the video, especially when the image is of an animated character. Still images or animated characters generate few, if any, social cues for the students to interpret.
- **Embodiment Principle:** Learning improves when an on-screen narrator displays humanlike gestures, movement, eye contact, and facial expressions. While animated characters could be developed for this purpose, the inclusion of video of the actual instructor is the easiest way to accomplish this.

Mayer's multimedia principles have clear practical implications for educational designers. It must be kept in mind, of course, that Mayer's principles apply to multimedia presentations in general, not to lecture videos in particular. However, there is an obvious and intuitive overlap of these two areas of digital educational content. Subsequent sections will demonstrate how these multimedia principles have been incorporated into lecture video design, following an examination of the general video lecture development process.

DEVELOPMENT OPTIONS FOR VIDEO LECTURES

Video lectures were previously defined as "CD and web viewable files that present lecture materials and narrative instruction from a course's instructor." (Brecht & Ogilby, 2008) This makes video lectures a subset of a broader range of educational video content available to instructors. Video options for instructors also include commercially developed training videos, free online content such as open courseware and creative commons stock video, documentaries, feature films, television programs, and more. This paper, however, limits its discussion to the types of educational video which instructors can develop themselves, usually referred to as lecture videos.

There is not a single type or format for lecture videos; instructors can consider quite a variety from which to choose the most appropriate format for a specific course or educational objective. (Caspi et al., 2005; Chorianopoulos & Giannakos, 2013; Guo et al, 2014; Ilioudi et al., 2013 Tunku Ahmad & Doheny, 2014), mention the following lecture video format options:

- **Capture of classroom lecture**: This requires that a camera pointed be at the blackboard or whiteboard in a classroom and that the instructor wear a microphone. This option removes the need for the instructor to spend time recording a separate narration for the lecture video.

- **Talking head lecture:** This is a video in which an instructor recites a lecture directly to the camera. These recordings can be made in the instructor's office or in a specific recording studio.
- **Voice-over-PowerPoint**: This is the common term for a video produced from presentation slides accompanied by an instructor voice-over. The Microsoft PowerPoint application permits users to record a narration for each presentation slide and export the full presentation as a video file. For instructors who already use PowerPoint to produce in-class lecture slides, this is a simple and affordable option.
- **Screencast:** This refers to a video tutorial which captures an instructor's on-screen activity, accompanied by an instructor voice-over or other audio commentary. Screencasts are quite effective for demonstrations of software usage.
- **Digital tablet drawing:** This format captures the instructor's notes or drawings on a digital tablet, resulting in an on-screen animation, and is often accompanied by an instructor voice-over. Khan Academy videos popularized this format.
- **Hybrid Format:** This combines the voice-over-PowerPoint, screencast, or digital tablet drawing formats with a video insert of the instructor providing the narration. This permits the students to see the instructor, which adds personalization to the lecture video. It is also possible to combine presentation slides, screencasts, and digital tablet usage within a single lecture video if the subject matter calls for it.

The development for any of the above lecture video formats consists of four key phases: planning, recording, editing, (Pappas, 2015b) and distribution (Green et al., 2008).

During the planning phase, the instructor designs the online lecture, based on the learning objectives it needs to achieve. The instructor may gather existing content (such as images and diagrams) or develop original content to include in the video lecture. The content of the video lecture should also be considered from the perspective of the assignments or assessments it needs to support: what specific learning needs should be addressed? (Koumi, 2015) recommends that educational videos are most effective when they have a clear narrative structure; the video's story should capture the student's attention, continuously engage the student, enable the construction of knowledge, reinforce its main concepts throughout, and conclude with a summary of key ideas. This is most readily achieved with a carefully designed, planned, and scripted video lecture. (Pappas, 2015b)

The second phase is the recording of the lecture video's original content. Current software options permit instructors to do this with a minimal investment in resources. To record a Voice-over-PowerPoint style video lecture, an instructor only needs a copy of the presentation software and a microphone to record the lecture. An investment in more fully featured recording software (such as Camtasia Studio or Adobe Presenter) allows an instructor to easily manage a greater set of recording features - such as the combination of images, video, and audio which permit the narrative to be paired with appropriate visual elements. (Guo et al, 2014; Pappas, 2015b; Sanchez-Gonzalez et al., 2013) In addition to these general development environment, specialized tools are being developed, such as the AMELIE authoring tool for the creation of multimedia educational content in medical areas such as nursing and surgery. (Sanchez-Gonzalez et al., 2013)

The use of fully featured recording software usually also permits the instructor to subsequently edit the video recordings. (Pappas, 2015b) Such editing operations could include:

- Correcting errors in narration or presentation, without having to re-record the full lecture video.

- Adjusting audio levels to provide a consistent volume-level throughout.
- Adding captions to portions of the video.
- Including break-points or interactive exercises.
- Closed-captioning the video for accessibility purposes.
- Rearranging content to produce a more effective narrative sequence.

Once the editing is complete, the final video file needs to be produced for students to see. Most video recording software applications allow the instructor to produce the video lecture in a variety of formats and compression sizes in order to serve multiple viewing platforms. For students watching the lecture video on a desktop or laptop computer, a high-resolution video file is commonly produced, while for efficient access on mobile devices – a platform which has recently experienced rapid growth in video distribution and viewing – a lower-quality version can be provided. (Clothier, 2013; Pappas, 2015b)

Finally, the lecture videos need to be made available to the students. Distribution options include the use of a university's learning management system (Van Vliet, 2015), a commercial video distribution platform (Kaltura, Inc., 2015), or the use of a dedicated web server for streaming, podcasting, or download purposes. (Green et al., 2008) The choice among these options are usually made at an institutional level, not by individual instructors.

The following sections examine lecture video development in more detail regarding four significant video characteristics: accessibility, length, structure, and interactivity.

LECTURE VIDEO ACCESSIBILITY CONSIDERATIONS – PROVIDING ACCESS FOR ALL

Lecture video development should address the inclusion of accessibility features for students with disabilities. Disabled students are those who have a sensory, cognitive, physical or psychological impairment and hence may experience difficulties in accessing educational experiences. Such difficulties may be overcome through the application of assistive technologies and services, such as adapted keyboards, Braille embossers, screen magnification applications, screen reading software, transcription services, interpreters, etc. (Seale, 2014)

Within the United States, legal requirements for accessibility come from two distinct pieces of legislation. First, Sections 504 and 508 of the Rehabilitation Act require that federal agencies ensure all electronic information is accessible to people with disabilities and that individual accommodations are provided as needed. Universities receiving federal funding are covered by this act. Second, the Americans with Disabilities Act (ADA) prohibits any discrimination against people with disabilities by either public entities, commercial entities, or public accommodations. Initially, "public accommodations" referred to public buildings such as hotels, entertainment venues, and hospitals for which physical accessibility features were required. In recent years, any organization's web-based content and processes have gained consideration as "places of public accommodation." (3PlayMedia, 2106) That this includes online education programs was made clear when in early 2015 both Harvard University and the Massachusetts Institute of Technology were sued by advocates for the deaf for failing to provide closed-captioning for online course materials such as lecture videos and podcasts. (Lewin, 2105)

Online education requires that universities take a fundamentally different approach to dealing with accessibility issues than they have in the past. For many years, accessibility issues were mostly handled by a university's disability services office, which would provide disabled students with services and equipment as needed. However, the growth of online education has moved quite a few accessibility responsibilities to the educators themselves. Faculty developing online courses are now obligated to make these courses and their content fully accessible to all students. (Ingeno, 2013)

Moreover, online education expands the availability requirements for accessibility accommodations. In traditional classroom settings, some student accommodations - such as a sign language interpreter - are only needed at the moment a lecture occurs. In online education, disabled students should have access to educational content at any time and any location, just as all other students have, requiring the continuous availability of accommodations. (Rose, 2014) This would suggest that accessibility features should be fully incorporated in all online education development efforts as part of the original development process, rather than be added later when doing so requires additional effort and expense. (Moore, 2014)

Accessibility needs in online education cover both the online learning environment which students navigate and the educational content itself. Within a learning environment, educational developers must ensure that disabled students have the ability to navigate its interface in order to access course materials online, participate in online discussions, and complete exams and assignments. (Kelly, 2008) Web Content Accessibility Guidelines play a big role here, and recommendations include the use of text alternatives for graphical elements, providing clear and simple navigation through the content, ensuring proper contrast in text and diagrams, and setting clear standards which make use of online resources more predictable. (3PlayMedia, 2106) In addition, the learning environment should support alternative modes of input and interaction to accommodate students with mobility impairments who may have difficulty operating input devices such as a computer keyboard, mouse, or touchpad. Assistive technologies such as adaptive keyboards and screen-reading software are available for these students but these require that the learning environment supports their usage. (Phipps et al, 2002)

The educational content itself, both video lectures and other types of multimedia content, presents an additional set of accessibility challenges. The controls of on-screen audio and video players may be inaccessible to blind or mobility-impaired students. Poorly tagged or titled multimedia content may be difficult to specifically identify and locate by screen-reading software. Deaf or hard-of-hearing students may be unable to access audio content. Finally, blind and visually-impaired students may be unable to access visual content. (CANnect, 2016; Moore, 2014; Phipps et al, 2002; Rose, 2014)

Each of these accessibility challenges should be addressed as part of the educational design process. The controls for on-screen audio and video should be made accessible through keyboard interaction or by screen readers. This permits students with mobility or visual impairments with playability, the first step in access to the content. (CANnect, 2016)

The proper identification of lecture videos within a learning environment can easily be improved by providing them with clear titles that reflect their content, rather than a nondescript title such as "Week 12 video," as well as representative tags if needed. (Moore, 2014)

Accessibility to audio and video files is provided by including additional representations of their educational content, which can be achieved through transcriptions of audio files and closed-captioning of video files. Transcription is word-for-word translation of audio content into a text file. Transcripts permit deaf students to read a lecture and enable blind students to access the content using a braille printer or screen reader. Closed-captioning involves the synchronization of text captions with the audio content of a video presentation. (3PlayMedia, 2106; Burgstahler, 2014; Rose, 2014)

The time and effort required to closed-caption a lecture video is usually substantial, especially considering the total amount of video a university-level course can contain. Consequently it is usually infeasible to quickly add captions to a course's video content when a disabled student requires it. It is for this reason that (Ingeno, 2013) recommends that this accessibility feature be included in the original video development process.

The closed-captioning effort can be eased somewhat by deploying additional technology. First, common digital video formats increasingly permit the easy insertion of captions. While these captioning features were originally intended to display foreign language subtitles, they can also be used for closed-captioning. (CANnect, 2016) In addition, captioning features are now included in video recording applications such as Camtasia and Captivate. The video hosting site YouTube has introduced an automatic video captioning feature which relies on speech recognition technology to caption its videos. (Moore, 2014)

In addition to captions of the instructor's audio, online lectures should also make available spoken descriptions (with closed-captioning) of important visual content that is not included in the instructor's main narration. This may include titles, diagrams, images, scenery, objects, and any other visual information. (3PlayMedia, 2106; Burgstahler, 2014; CANnect, 2016; Phipps et al, 2002)

By incorporating these accommodations in all aspects of online course development, educators can apply the concept of "universal design" into their course materials. Universal design refers to the design of products and environments which are "usable by all people, to the greatest extent possible, without the need for adaptation or specialized design," thereby removing or at least minimizing the need for special assistive technologies. (Burgstahler, 2014) For lecture videos, a universal design approach would mean that when retrieving a specific video, a student could enable or disable any of the above accessibility features as needed, rather than the instructor having to provide multiple versions of each lecture video and a student having to decide which version to retrieve. (3PlayMedia, 2106)

Finally, the inclusion of accessibility features – particularly the use of closed-captioning and transcripts – provides some interesting benefits beyond the accommodation of hearing-impaired students. Non-native English speakers may benefit from seeing the narrative in writing; students whose learning preferences tend towards text can read the captions or full transcripts; captions of full names, complex terms, and technical terms provide greater clarity; and students can access the content when an audio narration is not as useful, such as in noisy environments like buses and trains or quiet environments like libraries and offices. (3PlayMedia, 2106; Pappas, 2015a)

LECTURE VIDEO LENGTH – DOES BREVITY MATTER?

An interesting discussion among educators and educational designers concerns the recommended length of video lectures. When classroom lectures were filmed to be used of early online education efforts, the video lecture would be the length of the original lecture, which could be up to 60 or 90 minutes. (Caspi et al., 2005) The subsequent availability of affordable personal computer-based video capture and editing tools permitted experimentation with video lectures of varying lengths, and arguments were made that video lectures needed to be shorter.

Many educational designers point to a study by (Ruedlinger, 2012) which shows a drop-off in viewing as videos lengthen. The study recommends that shorter videos encourage viewers to watch the complete video. However, this study did not specifically address educational content; instead it examined viewership of business videos, mostly for the purposes of promotion. One might argue there is a substantial difference between the attention span of a motivated audience (such as online students) and the general audience for Internet-based videos. Nevertheless, proponents of short lecture videos argue that student attention will wane after 10 or 15 minutes, and hence video lectures ought to be kept short. (Linden, 2012) This stance was supported in a study on student viewing behavior by (Guo et al, 2014), who found video length to be the greatest indicator of student engagement.

Similar results were obtained by (Kim et al., 2014b), who found that students are more likely to stop watching video lectures as the videos become longer, possibly because they become bored or due to interruptions. Quitting rates went up even more when students re-watched a previously seen video, possibly because they were looking for very specific information in the video and stopped watching once that information was obtained.

Finally, (Ibrahim et al., 2012) make the argument that presenting longer videos to students requires them to process the educational content for longer periods of time, which may tax the limits of the student's working memory, resulting in cognitive overload.

The notion that educational videos should be kept short appears to be widely accepted by educators. A survey performed by video platform provider Kaltura generally found that a majority of respondents felt that video lectures should be no longer than 10 minutes. However, the study did find a distinction between instructional designers and educators: instructional designers strongly agreed video lectures should be kept under 10 minutes while a substantial portion of educators felt videos lectures could be up to 30 minutes in length. (Kaltura, Inc., 2015)

The educators' most common argument is that the additional time is needed to convey the complete content of a particular lesson, as they are used to doing in a classroom setting. (Guo et al, 2014) counter this by insisting that when video lectures are carefully planned and scripted, the result should be a concise, high-quality deliverable which more consistently engages students in a short amount of time. (Gallo, 2014) notes that the same motivation is behind the 18 minute limit for TED talks: when speakers have to pare down a longer presentation to fit a shorter time slot, they have to carefully consider what key ideas to communicate and how to present them. This application of discipline to overall content is expected to result in an improved presentation and greater impact on the audience.

A strong case for longer lecture videos was made by (Reich, 2014), who argues that studies which focus on student attention or student engagement are measuring the wrong outcome, they should be considering student learning outcomes instead. This view echoes an analysis by (Wilson & Korn, 2007) which examined a series of studies that evaluated student attention during in-class lectures. It found that while many such studies argue that student attention wanes after 10 or 15 minutes (usually as evidenced by a decline in student note-taking activity), the length of the lectures did not actually affect student retention of the educational content. Observed student attention, therefore, is not necessarily an indicator of learning achievement.

The case for longer video lectures is also supported by a study which examined the effectiveness of full video lectures – up to 75 minutes in length – on student comprehension of complex course content. (Brecht & Ogilby, 2008) The study particularly credited the video lectures with giving instructors the opportunity to present complex course content using clear and unhurried step-by-step explanations.

Brecht & Ogilby (2008) make a strong argument that students can obtain a tremendous benefit from the availability of longer online lecture videos. Complex subject matter, which is often found in higher education courses, benefits from calm, clear, precise, and comprehensive explanations. Online lecture videos provide a good opportunity for instructors to develop, capture and distribute such explanations, without having to worry about time limitations that may be imposed by classroom schedules. Students can then access these videos, review them as needed to build their comprehension of the subject matter, and master the contents at their own pace. Challenging university courses may cause students to experience great difficulty in integrating complex concepts and methods. This in turn may increase student frustration and result in reduced learning outcomes. The availability of lecture videos is one way by which these students can be supported in their learning process. (Brecht, 2012)

(Brecht, 2012) recommends that in longer lecture videos, the instructor includes graphics and sounds that liven up the video, and introduces occasional change-of-pace elements to help keep a student's attention. However, such elements may run counter to Mayer's recommendation to avoid the inclusion of extraneous content. (Mayer & Fiorella, 2014)

When the nature of a video lecture's subject matter requires a lengthy explanation of the material, greater student engagement may be obtained through the application of some of the multimedia learning principles expressed by Mayer (2008). The subsequent section examines the use of two key principles which might be quite useful in this context: signaling and segmenting.

APPLYING STRUCTURE TO LECTURE VIDEOS – SIGNALING & SEGMENTING

As discussed earlier, Mayer's Principles of Multimedia Learning recommend the clear and careful organization of educational content. Two key methods suggested here are Signaling and Segmenting. Signaling occurs when a presentation includes cues about its structure or organization, such as when an outline or list if key items is provided at the outset. (Mayer, 2001) Signaling identifies for a student the main ideas within a lesson. (Ibrahim et al., 2012) argue that signaling helps focus student attention and reduces the likelihood of students paying attention to extraneous or irrelevant information.

Segmenting is the process of subdividing content into distinct segments rather than a single continuous unit. This principle is further strengthened by the use of Mayer's Pre-Training principle, which suggests the deliberate sequencing of content by introducing individual components first before combining these into a more complex configuration. (Mayer, 2001) In practice, signaling and segmenting are commonly applied together; the structure that is signaled at the outset of a lesson is reflected in the segments that make up its full educational content.

Used this way, signaling and segmenting can actually provide an effective solution to a practical problem with lecture videos: the efficient locating of specific content a student wishes to see. (Pavel et al., 2014) point out that as a format, video itself provides viewers with little help to browse or skim the content. To navigate through a video, viewers must "scrub" back and forth through the video presentation to get an idea of the overall content or to locate a specific section. This can be especially annoying or time-consuming when students want to re-watch a relevant portion of a lecture video in order to complete a specific assignment. (Kim et al., 2014b) found that students tend to be quite selective which videos (or portions of videos) they watch and re-watch. They encourage the inclusion of easy in-video navigation so that students can find the content they wish to watch more quickly and accurately.

Signaling can be deployed in lecture video development in multiple ways. (Ibrahim et al., 2012) suggest that the instructor verbally establishes the main structure of a lesson at the outset of the video and subsequently reinforces this structure through reiteration of key ideas at the lesson's conclusion. Even more effective, however, is the display of a video lecture's structure as a navigable table of contents, which would permit the student to select a specific topic and navigate to it directly. (Jadin et al., 2009) For example, the video capture and editing software package Camtasia Studio allows for specific points in a video to be marked and named, which then automatically produces a table of contents in the resulting lecture video. The screen-capture shown in Figure 1 shows a Camtasia Studio video as presented to students. On the left of the screen is the table of contents.

Figure 1. Table of Contents in Lecture Video Developed Using Camtasia Studio Software.

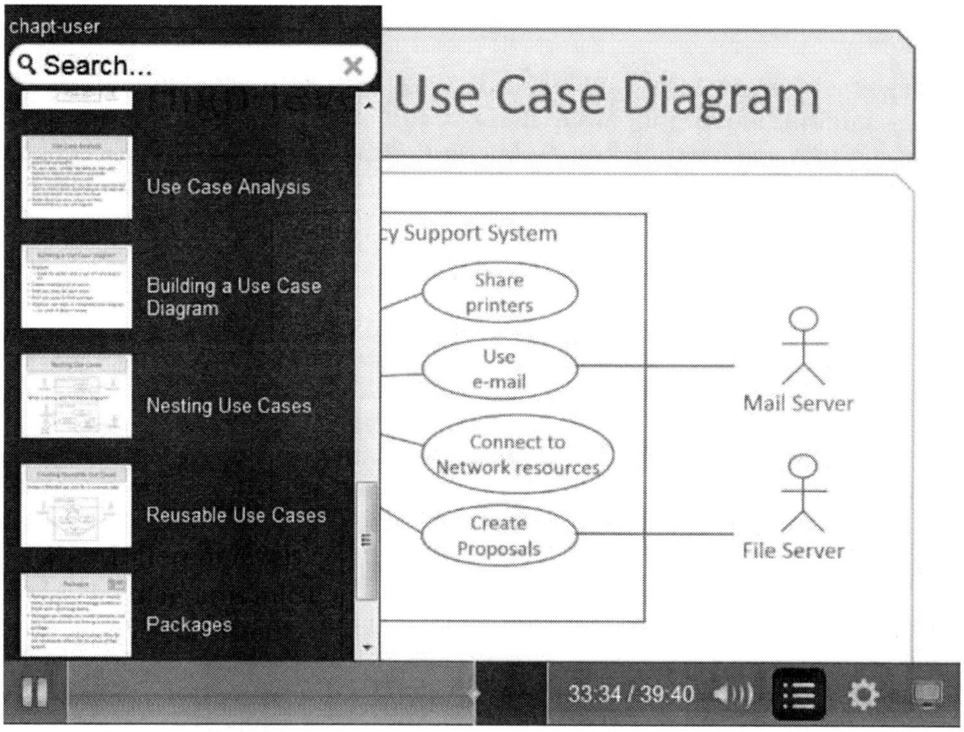

As seen in Figure 1, signaling practices need not be purely text-based. (Kim et al., 2014a) recommend the use of clear and well-chosen thumbnail images which students can navigate to easily in addition to clear and searchable section titles for video portions.

Finally, (Pavel et al., 2014) suggest the inclusion of more detailed information in a signaling approach referred to as a "video digest." In this approach, a clickable table of contents is augmented with a summarization of each video section's content or basic idea. In addition to direct section access, these section summaries provide the student with the basic ideas of the overall video lecture before it is even watched. Developing such summaries does require additional development effort, and care must be taken that the summaries are accurate and appropriately representative of the video content.

The inclusion of a clickable table of contents for signaling purposes has the additional benefit of also effectively segmenting the video lecture from a student's point of view, even if the video itself is only a single file. However, additional segmenting approaches have been proposed. For example, (Breslow et al., 2013) subdivided a long lesson into a sequence of multiple 10-minute videos. These segments were interspersed with online exercises designed to permit students to put concepts from the videos into practice. Developing these shorter videos may make the content more readily reusable across multiple courses and disciplines, especially for tutoring purposes.

(Mayer & Pilegard, 2014) mention that segmenting is most effective when the student controls the pace at which video segments are presented. The signaling techniques described above are an effective implementation of this concept, especially given that the video lecture controls also permit students to pause, re-view, or fast-forward through the video.

INTERACTIVITY AND THE PROMOTION OF ACTIVE LEARNING

It has been mentioned several times now that the on-screen buttons on video players permit the students watching an online lecture an affordance of control over the learning process. Students can use these controls to pause, repeat, or fast-forward through a lecture video in order to personalize the pace of their learning. In addition, when the practices of signaling and segmenting are incorporated in a video lecture, the students can quickly identify and navigate to a specific portion of content. Such learner control is an essential component of effective learning. It allows a student to take the initiative in viewing and reviewing course materials, which more actively engages them with the course content rather than when they passively observe it. (Moreno, 2006; Nicholson et al, 2008)

Watching lecture videos without any control or interactivity was found to be less cognitively captivating or challenging, and is therefore less effective for learning. (Geri, 2012) This realization has encouraged educational designers to add additional interactive features to lecture videos. Some interactive ideas require very little technology: (Green et al., 2008) describe how an instructor inserted direct questions to students in an online lecture's narration, which students subsequently answered in an online discussion forum. Other easily included interactive features may include encouraging students to take notes, inserting online quizzes, relating a narration directly to an assignment, or providing suggestions for additional content students may seek out if interested. (Chorianopoulos & Giannakos, 2013; Geri, 2012)

New approaches to enhancing the interactivity of lecture videos are now being explored. (Kim et al., 2014a) suggest that lecture video navigation can be enhanced by examining student viewing behavior. First, based on video server logs, analysis of previous students' viewing activities can highlight those sections of a video that were most often watched and re-watched; such sections can be highlighted as being most useful to new students. Second, if the lecture video environment permits individual students to place personal bookmarks to mark video portions of special interest, the most commonly bookmarked portions can subsequently be shared with new students.

Until recently, interactivity options such as quizzes or connections to additional content required a student to navigate through multiple videos and applications in the online learning environment. This may soon be a thing of the past. (Clothier, 2013) shows the increasing use of interactive video technologies which use in-video buttons to steer the video narrative to related content, to an in-depth feature, or a simpler explanation. The inclusion of in-video quizzes and questions – the results of which can be made available to the instructor – provide an additional layer of in-video interactivity. (Meyer, 2015) The result of these developments is not only an efficient and continuous viewing experience, but also an opportunity for the viewer to engage with and explore the content in a more immersive way. (Zhang et al, 2006) view the emergence of this type of non-linear, interactive digital video technology as a key development in building learner engagement and learning effectiveness.

VIDEO LECTURES AND STUDENT LEARNING – SOME EVIDENCE

Lecture video development takes a considerable amount of time, effort, and money, especially when sophisticated video capture, custom animation, and interactive features are to be included. (O'Rourke et al, 2014) The question then becomes whether all this effort is actually worth it. (Moreno, 2006) notes that educators tend to assume that the use of new technologies will enhance student learning, even though only limited research exists that proves this is so. She also notes that educators often assume that embedding proven teaching methods in new media technologies will not affect the effectiveness of these methods.

Early studies which compared the effectiveness of video versus print for educational purposes found print materials to better support student learning. However, these studies focused on the use of broadcast video, in which the students had no control over the video stream. (Merkt et al, 2011) More recent studies on the efficacy of lecture videos show that these videos have greater promise to support student learning objectives; however this evidence is quite fragmentary and at times anecdotal. Many of these studies focus on the use of one or a few lecture videos in a short term-setting. Large-scale longitudinal studies which cover a complete online curriculum as completed by a body of students are not yet available. Still, an examination of the more limited research currently available does offer some evidence for the previously discussed principles and guidelines for more effective lecture video development.

General Reviews of Lecture Video Usage

In the most general terms, students appear to be quite receptive to the usage of video lectures as an educational strategy for universities. (Brecht & Ogilby, 2008) Results by (Jadin et al., 2009) indicate that students primarily use video lectures for knowledge acquisition purposes and that the subsequent phase of knowledge construction derives mainly from the students interacting with the course content in order to complete assignments.

As mentioned earlier, the use of lecture videos need not be limited to online education. (Preston et al., 2010) found that students respond positively to the availability of lecture videos as an augmentation to and reinforcement of in-class lectures. Moreover, (Brecht & Ogilby, 2008) found that the use of supplemental video lectures in an in-class course enhanced student performance on exams. In a more detailed study, (Woo et al., 2008) examined the usefulness of video lectures for both in-class students (for whom the video lectures were an accompaniment to classroom lectures) and online-only students enrolled in online courses. The usage patterns of the two student groups differed significantly, with the online-only students using the video lectures more often and more extensively. However, the in-class students found the video lectures quite useful for learning content they missed in class, preparing for exams, and revisiting complex course content at their own pace.

Examining the Multimedia Principle

Mayer based his Multimedia Principle - "students learn better from words and pictures than from words alone" - on a substantial amount of early research in educational media. (Mayer, 2001) More recent studies have found continued support for this principle. (Nicholson et al, 2008) note that students learn from both visual and verbal stimuli, and that they readily connect these mentally. Consequently when educational material includes both visual and verbal information, the material increases student interest and hence will have greater impact. However, both (Caspi et al., 2005) and (Nicholson et al, 2008) note the potential for cognitive overload when the audio and visual portions of an educational video present too much simultaneous information. (Moreno, 2006) agrees that a common pitfall of online lecture design is to present too much simultaneous information, some extraneous, which results in students not being able to properly process all the information provided. (Jadin et al., 2009) recommend that online lectures carefully balance audio and visual information provided to students. For example, when in a lecture the on-screen text is also spoken verbatim by the instructor, the resulting redundancy (with the same information provided visually and via audio) needlessly taxes the student's cognitive capacity. These recommendations clearly echo Mayer's principles aimed at reducing extraneous cognitive processing, as well as the Modality Principle. (Mayer & Fiorella, 2014; Mayer & Pilegard, 2014)

Examining Lecture Video Types

It was mentioned earlier that instructors can consider from a variety of lecture video formats. Some researchers have examined the effectiveness of some of the most popular lecture video formats.

A key finding is the importance of students being able to see the video's instructor. A study by (Wang et al, 2015) compared the effectiveness of three video lecture formats: the capture of an in-class lecture, a voice-over-presentation slides video, and a voice-over-presentation slides video with an additional video insert of the instructor providing the narration. The researchers studied student attention, cognitive load, and learning outcomes. They found that while the simple voice-over-presentation slides video generated the highest level of sustained student attention, the other two video types (which both showed the instructor) resulted in both a reduced cognitive load and greater learning for the students. While these two types of lecture videos can be more expensive and time-consuming to produce, they are recommended for improved learning outcomes. A study by (Guo et al, 2014) examined the difference between video lectures specifically recorded by instructors for online delivery and those which mostly show a recording of an in-class lecture by an instructor. It was found that students were more engaged by the video lectures specifically prepared for online delivery, especially once these lectures lasted longer than 6 minutes.

Adding additional video features generally was found to have a positive effect on student learning. (Guo et al, 2014) found that providing students with more diverse video productions – those which mix video of the instructor with images, slides, animations, and video – tend engage students more effectively. (Tunku Ahmad & Doheny, 2014) studied the use of screencasts, which display the instructor's computer screen activity accompanied by a voice-over narration, and found this dynamic display to be more effective than written materials covering the same content. Finally, as suggested by the Redundancy Principle (Mayer & Fiorella, 2014), a study by (Jadin et al., 2009) found that the addition of an on-screen text transcript of the narration does not improve the effectiveness of a lecture video.

Examining Lecture Video Personalization

The previous section showed that a strong instructor presence in lecture videos has a positive effect on student learning. This conforms with Mayer's argument that a student's motivation to learn can be strengthened through the use of social cues in a lecture video, particularly when the instructor narrating the video adopts a conversational rather than formal tone. (Mayer 2014; Nielsen, 2014) (Moreno, 2006) adds that adopting this Personalization Principle may heighten student attention and thus promote greater learning. This notion was supported in studies by (Ilioudi et al., 2013) and (Wang et al, 2015), who found that a video recording of the instructor (either recorded in-class or specifically for the online lecture) provided greater student learning outcomes than presentations which merely featured a voice-over narration. (Ilioudi et al., 2013) hypothesize that having grown up with in-class instruction, students are simply used to being able to see and hear an instructor explain course content.

Examining Signaling and Segmentation

Student navigation of lecture video content can be further enhanced through the principles of signaling and segmentation. As discussed above, signaling displays the structure or key points of a lesson. Segmentation divides a large lesson into short, distinct portions. The application of these two principles in lecture videos usually results in a navigable table of contents from which students can directly access specific video segments. (Zhang et al, 2006) specifically noted the benefits of signaling when students are provided with direct access to content using a clickable table-of-contents feature. Looking specifically at segmentation, (Ibrahim et al., 2012) found that subdividing a longer video lesson into shorter segments (approximately 6 minutes long) helped reduce students' perception of the difficulty of the content. A study by (Mayer & Pilegard, 2014) found the combination of signaling and segmentation to be quite effective as the direct access to the video segments allows the student control over the pace at which video segments are presented. This combination was also examined by (O'Rourke et al, 2014), who built an "interactive wall" of on-screen clickable tiles. Each tile provided access to some form of course content: a video lecture, an image, an internet link, etc. Students consistently found this interactive online learning environment more engaging than a traditional in-class lecture. Key to the students' preference once again turned out to be self-paced learning: in the interactive environment students were able to absorb the content at their own pace, pausing or re-watching content at will.

Examining Control and Interactivity

It was mentioned above that digital video permits a student to exert some control over the medium Video lectures can be paused and sections can be directly accessed, skipped, or re-watched at will, allowing a student to learn the material at his or her own pace. (Caspi et al., 2005) found that students watching lecture videos did indeed attempt to transfer existing learning strategies from reading textbooks to watching video. The students would go forward and backward through the videos as if using a textbook, although this is sometimes more difficult in practice as videos do not always have clear markers to jump to. Studies which examined the use of video controls found that students not only preferred this type of video environment, but also that it resulted in higher levels of learning achievement when compared to videos over which students had no control. (Merkt et al, 2011; Zhang et al, 2006)

CONCLUSION – RECOMMENDATIONS FOR ONLINE LECTURE DEVELOPMENT

Instructors planning to develop video lectures may be disheartened when they consider the well-published video development efforts for Massive Open Online Courses (MOOCs). The creation of video content for MOOCs is commonly reported to require tens of thousands of dollars, with much of it spent on recording studios, audiovisual equipment, graphics and animation development, and a video production team, in addition to actual curriculum design. (Hollands & Tirthali, 2014) The recommendations and findings discussed in this paper demonstrate that effective lecture video development can actually be achieved by individual instructors, even on a limited budget. As (Nielsen, 2014) points out, "you don't need a full movie studio and video editing team to create great educational content." What is needed instead is a careful and methodical approach to video lecture design.

A key responsibility for the instructor is the organization of the video content. Extraneous materials should be removed, and the remaining content should be carefully organized, structured, and sequenced. Of course, curriculum design and educational development are not new; instructors have long performed these tasks for in-class courses. However, online lectures do require some adaptations. In particular, the instructor should take the time to develop clear and careful explanations which permit the students to more easily understand the material, a requirement that is vital outside of the immediacy of an interactive classroom setting. Then, applying the principles of signaling and segmenting, the instructor should provide the video lecture content in a structured and easily navigable format which permits students to quickly locate specific content and thereby encourages multiple viewings of complex or important portions. Finally, the instructor should ensure that the lecture videos are accessible to all potential students that might enroll in a course.

The inclusion of multimedia materials – diagrams, photographs, animations, video, etc. – was shown to engage students and positively affect the learning effects of a lecture video. Fortunately video capture, drawing, and screen-casting software packages has become more affordable even as their feature set and ease of use have increased. (Marquis, 2012) However, just as significant as the on-screen visuals is the instructor's presence. A lively and enthusiastic narration by the instructor – especially when augmented with video – can provide students with social cues, personalize the instruction for the students, and strengthen the student-instructor relationship, even in fully online courses. The ubiquity of webcams enables instructors to accomplish this at relatively low cost.

An important finding in the study of lecture video usage is the importance of a student being able to affect the manner in which the educational content is viewed and learned. Video player controls which permit students to pause, repeat, and forward a video permit a student to personalize the pace of learning. When the lecture video includes a clickable table of contents which provides direct access to specific video segments, students are able to actively seek out specific content quickly. This level of interactivity resembles the online experience in general and should therefore be easy to grasp by students.

As mentioned early in this paper, once they have been carefully developed, online lectures have multiple uses outside of a single, specific course. An investment in the development of high-quality lecture videos can therefore pay off in many ways for both individual instructors and the educational institution as a whole. While there is still a lack of large-scale longitudinal research on the learning outcomes of lecture videos, the principles and findings stated in this paper can inform instructors as they aim to improve the quality and effectiveness of their online teaching efforts.

REFERENCES

3PlayMedia. (2106). 2016 Roadmap to Web Accessibility in Higher Education. Retrieved on March 18, 2016 from http://info.3playmedia.com/wp-web-accessibility.html

Berge, Z.L. (1995). The Role of the Online Instructor/Facilitator. Retrieved March 5, 2016 from http://emoderators.com/wp-content/uploads/teach_online.html

Brecht, H.D. (2012). Learning from Online Video Lectures. *Journal of Information Technology Education: Innovations in Practice*, Volume 11, pp. 227-250.

Brecht, H.D. & Ogilby, S.M. (2008). Enabling a Comprehensive Teaching Strategy: Video Lectures. *Journal of Information Technology Education Innovations in Practice*, Volume 7, pp. 71-86.

Breslow, L., Pritchard, D.E., DeBoer, J., Stmp, G.S., Ho, A.D., & Seaton, D.T. (2013). Studying Learning in the Worldwide Clssroom; Reserach into edX's First MOOC. *Research & Practice in Assessment*, Volume 8, pp. 13-25.

Burgstahler, S. (2014). Creating Video and Multimedia Products That Are Accessible to People with Sensory Impairments. Retrieved on March 18, 2016, from http://www.washington.edu/doit/creating-video-and-multimedia-products-are-accessible-people-sensory-impairments

CANnect. (2016). Accessible Video and Audio. Retrieved on March 18, 2016 from http://projectone.cannect.org/advice/video-audio.php

Caspi, A., Gorsky, P., & Privman, M. (2005). Viewing comprehension: Students' learning preferences and strategies when studying from video. Instructional Science, Volume 33, pp. 31-47.

Chorianopoulos, K. & Giannakos, M.N. (2013). Usability design for video lectures. *11th European Conference on Interactive TV and Video*, Como. Italy, June 2013, pp. 163-164.

Clothier, P. (2013). Interactive Video: The Next Big Thing in Mobile. *Learning Solutions Magazine*, October 28, 2013. Retrieved on March 5, 2016 from http://www.learningsolutionsmag.com/articles/1292/interactive-video-the-next-big-thing-in-mobile

Easton, S.S. (2003). Clarifying the Instructor's Role in Online Distance Learning. *Communication Education*, 52(2), 87-105.

Eduventures, LLC. (2006). Traditional Universities' Continuing and Professional Education Units Position to Win in the Online Education Market. Retrieved March 5, 2016 from http://www.prweb.com/releases/2006/8/prweb430678.htm

Gallo, C. (2014). The Science Behind TED's 18-Minute Rule. Retrieved on March 12, 2016 from https://www.linkedin.com/pulse/20140313205730-5711504-the-science-behind-ted-s-18-minute-rule

Geri, N. (2012). The Resonance Factor: Probing the Impact of Video on Student Retention in Distance Learning. *Interdisciplinary Journal of E-Learning and Learning Objects*, Volume 8, pp. 1-13.

Green, D., Mcneill, M., Gosper, M., Woo, K., Phillips, R. & Preston, G. (2008). Web Based Lecture Technologies: A Lens Intensifying the Changing Roles of Learners and Lecturers. In J. Luca & E. Weippl (Eds.), *Proceedings of EdMedia: World Conference on Educational Media and Technology 2008* (pp. 3733-3750). Association for the Advancement of Computing in Education (AACE).

Guo, P.J., Kim, J. Rubin, R. (2014). How Video Production Affects Student Engagement: An Empirical Study of MOOC Videos. *Proceedings of the first ACM conference on Learning @ scale conference*, Atlanta, GA, March 4-5, 2014, pp. 41-50.

Hibbert, M. (2014). What Makes an Online Instructional Video Compelling? Retrieved on March 14, 2016 from http://er.educause.edu/articles/2014/4/what-makes-an-online-instructional-video-compelling

Hollands, F. M., & Tirthali, D. (2014). MOOCs: expectations and reality. Full report. *Center for Benefit-Cost Studies of Education, Teachers College, Columbia University, NY.* Retrieved on March 23, 2016, from http://cbcse.org/wordpress/wp-content/uploads/2014/05/MOOCs_Expectations_and_Reality.pdf

Ibrahim, M., Antonenko, P.D., Greenwood, C.M., & Wheeler, D. (2012). Effects of segmenting, signalling, and weeding on learning from educational video, *Learning, Media and Technology*, Volume 37:3, pp. 220-235.

Ilioudi, C., Giannakos, M.N., & Chorianopoulos, K. (2013). Investigating Differences among the Commonly Used Video Lecture Styles. *WAVe 2013 Workshop on Analytics on Video-based Learning*, Volume 1, pp. 21-26.

Ingeno, L. (2013). Online Accessibility a Faculty Duty. *Inside Higher Ed*. Retrieved on March 18, 2016 from https://www.insidehighered.com/news/2013/06/24/faculty-responsible-making-online-materials-accessible-disabled-students

Jadin, T., Gruber, A., & Batinic, B. (2009). Learning with E-lectures: The Meaning of Learning Strategies. *Educational Technology & Society*, Volume 12(3), pp. 282–288.

Kaltura, Inc. (2015). The state of video in education 2015: A Kaltura Report. Retrieved March 12, 2016, from http://site.kaltura.com/rs/984-SDM-859/images/The_State_of_Video_in_Education_2015_a_Kaltura_Report.pdf

Kelly, S. (2008). Distance Learning: How Accessible are Online Educational Tools. *American Foundation for the Blind*. Retrieved on March 18, 2016 from http://www.afb.org/info/programs-

and-services/public-policy-center/technology-and-information-accessibility/distance-learning-how-accessible-are-online-educational-tools-4492/1235

Kim, J., Guo, P.J., Cai, C.J., Li, S., Gajos, K.Z., & Miller, R.C. (2014a). Data-driven interaction techniques for improving navigation of educational videos. *Proceedings of the 27th annual ACM symposium on User Interface Software and Technology*, Honolulu, HI, October 5-8, 2014, pp. 563-572.

Kim, J., Guo, P.J., Seaton, D.T., Mitros, P., Gajos, K.Z., & Miller, R.C. (2014b). Understanding in-video dropouts and interaction peaks inonline lecture videos. *Proceedings of the first ACM conference on Learning @ scale conference*, Atlanta, GA, March 4-5, 2014, pp. 31-40

Knowlton, D.S. (2000). A Theoretical Framework for the Online Classroom: A Defense and Delineation of a Student-Centered Pedagogy. *New Directions for Teaching and Learning*, Vol. 84, 5-14.

Koumi, J. (2015). Learning outcomes afforded by self-assessed, segmented video-print combinations. *Cogent Education*, Volume 2(1).

Lewin, T., (2105). Harvard and M.I.T. Are Sued Over Lack of Closed Captions. *The New York Times*, February 12, 2015.

Linden, S. (2012). Why Video Length Matters. Retrieved March 12, 2016 from http://facultyecommons.org/why-video-length-matters/

Marquis, J. (2012). How To Screencast Like The Khan Academy. Retrieved on March 23, 2016, from http://www.teachthought.com/uncategorized/how-to-screencast-like-the-khan-academy/

Mayer, R.E. (2001). *Multimedia Learning*. New York, NY, Cambridge University Press.

Mayer, R.E. (2008). Applying the science of learning: Evidence-based principles for the design of multimedia instruction. *American Psychologist*, Volume 63(8), pp. 760-769.

Mayer, R.E. (2014). Principles based on Social Cues in Multimedia Learning: Personalization, Voice, Image, and Embodiment Principles. In *The Cambridge Handbook of Multimedia Learning, Second Edition*. New York, NY, Cambridge University Press.

Mayer, R.E. & Fiorella, L. (2014). Principles for Reducing Extraneous Processing in Multimedia Learning: Coherence, Signaling, Redundancy, Spatial Contiguity, and Temporal Contiguity Principles. In *The Cambridge Handbook of Multimedia Learning, Second Edition*. New York, NY, Cambridge University Press.

Mayer, R.E. & Pilegard, C. (2014). Principles for Managing Essential Processing in Multimedia Learning: Segmenting, Pre-training, and Modality Principles. In *The Cambridge Handbook of Multimedia Learning, Second Edition*. New York, NY, Cambridge University Press.

Merkt, M., Weigand, S., Heier, A., & Schwan, S. (2011). Learning with videos vs. learning with print: The role of interactive features. *Learning and Instruction*, Volume 21, pp. 687-704.

Meyer, L. (2015). 5 Lecture Capture Hacks for More Engaging Videos. *Campus Technology*. Retrieved on March 21, 2016 from https://campustechnology.com/articles/2015/04/08/5-lecture-capture-hacks-for-more-engaging-videos.aspx

Moore, E.A. (2014). Improve Accessibility in Tomorrow's Online Courses by Leveraging Yesterday's Techniques. *Faculty Focus*, Retrieved on March 18, 2016, from http://www.facultyfocus.com/articles/online-education/improve-accessibility-tomorrows-online-courses-leveraging-yesterdays-techniques/

Moreno, R. (2006). Learning in High-Tech and Multimedia Environments. *Current Directions in Psychological Science*, Volume 15(2), pp. 63-67.

Nicholson, J., Nicholson, D., & Valachich, J.S. (2008). Examining the Effects of Technology Attributes on Learning: A Contingency Perspective. *Journal of Information Technology Education*, Volume 7, pp. 185-204.

Nielsen, B. (2014). Video Production and Learner Engagement in MOOCs. Retrieved on March 12, 2016 from http://www.yourtrainingedge.com/video-production-and-learner-engagement-in-moocs/

O'Rourke, J., Main, S., & Cooper, M. (2014). Student Perceptions of Online Interactive Versus Traditional Lectures; Or How I ManagedNot To Fall Asleep With My Eyes Open. *MERLOT Journal of Online Learning and Teaching*, Volume 10(3), pp. 405-419.

Pavel, A., Reed, C., Hartmann, B., & Agrawala, M. (2014). Video digests: a browsable, skimmable format for informational lecture videos. *Proceedings of the 27th annual ACM symposium on User Interface Software and Technology*, Honolulu, HI, October 5-8, 2014, pp. 573-582.

Pappas, C. (2015a). The Top 6 Benefits Of Closed Captioning eLearning Courses. Retrieved on March 16, 2016, from http://elearningindustry.com/top-6-benefits-of-closed-captioning-elearning-courses

Pappas, C. (2015b). Producing High Quality eLearning Videos: The Ultimate Guide. Retrieved on March 16, 2016, from http://elearningindustry.com/producing-high-quality-elearning-videos-ultimate-guide

Phipps, L., Sutherland, A., & Seale, J. (2002). *Access All Areas: Disability, technology and Learning*. TechDis. Retrieved on March 18, 2016 from https://www.alt.ac.uk/sites/default/files/assets_editor_uploads/documents/accessallareaslow.pdf

Preston, G., Phillips, R., Gosper, M., McNeill, M., Woo, K., & Green, D. (2010). Web-based lecture technologies: Highlighting the changing nature of teaching and learning. *Australasian Journal of Educational Technology*, Volume 26(6), pp. 717-728.

Reich, J. (2014). Short Videos are better for Learning, Right? Maybe Not. Retrieved on March 12, 2016, from http://blogs.edweek.org/edweek/edtechresearcher/2014/03/short_videos_are_better_for_learning_right_maybe_not.html

Rose, R. (2014). Access and Equity for All Learners in Blended and Online Education. *iNACOL*. Retrieved on March 18, 2016 from http://www.inacol.org/wp-content/uploads/2015/02/iNACOL-Access-and-Equity-for-All-Learners-in-Blended-and-Online-Education-Oct2014.pdf

Ruedlinger, B. (2012). Does Length Matter? Retrieved March 5, 2016 from http://wistia.com/blog/does-length-matter-it-does-for-video-2k12-edition

Sánchez-González, P., Oropesa, I., García-Novoa, J., & Gómez, E.J. (2013). AMELIE: Authoring Multimedia-Enhanced Learning Interactive Environment for medical contents. *Studies in health technology and informatics*, Volume 190, pp. 68-70.

Seale, J.K. (2014). *E-Learning and Disability in Higher Education - Accessibility Research and Practice*, 2nd Edition. New York, NY, Routledge Publishing.

Tibus, M., Heier, A., & Schwan, S. (2013). Do Films Make You Learn? Inference Processes in Expository Film Comprehension. *Journal of Educational Psychology*, Volume 105, pp. 329-340.

Tunku Ahmad, T.B., & Doheny, F. (2014). Six key benefits of screencasts in learning Maths: An Irish case study. In *Recent Trends in Social and Behaviour Sciences: Proceedings of the International Congress on Interdisciplinary Behaviour and Social Sciences*, November 4-5, 2013, Jakarta, Indonesia, pp. 283-288.

Van Vliet, P.J.A. (2015). Building an Online Systems Development Course – Experiences with Content and Interaction Design. In D. Conway, S. A. Hillen, M. Landis, M. T. Schlegelmilch, & P. Wolcott (Eds.), *Digital Media in Teaching and its Added Value* (pp. 142-158). Germany: Waxmann Verlag GmbH.

Wang, W., Chen, C., & Wu, C. (2015). Effects of Different Video Lecture Types on Sustained Attention, Emotion, Cognitive Load, and Learning Performance. *4th International Congress on Advanced Applied Informatics*, July 12-16, 2015, Okayama, Japan, pp. 385-390.

Wilson, K. & Korn, J.H. (2007). Attention during Lectures: Beyond Ten Minutes. *Teaching of Psychology*, Volume 34(2), pp. 85-89.

Woo, K., Gosper, M., McNeill, M., Preston, G., Green, D. & Phillips, R. (2008). Web-based lecture technologies: blurring the boundaries between face-to-face and distance learning. *Research in Learning Technology*, Volume 16(2), pp. 81-92.

Zhang, D., Zhou, L., Briggs, R.O, Nunamaker Jr., J.F. (2006). Instructional video in e-learning: Assessing the impact of interactive video on learning effectiveness. *Information & Management*, Volume 43, pp. 15-27.

DECISION SCIENCES INSTITUTE

Can corporate entrepreneurship attributes in acquired firms avoid their acquisition-turned-divestiture fate?

Santosh Nandi
College of Business & Entrepreneurship
University of Texas-Rio Grande Valley
Email: santosh.nandi@utrgv.edu

Dr. Sibin Wu
College of Business & Entrepreneurship
University of Texas-Rio Grande Valley
Email: sibin.wu@utrgv.edu

ABSTRACT

More than 50% acquisitions are divested within the first year of operation. Data shows that the divestitures lacked adequate level of corporate entrepreneurship, hence, faced significant hurdles in getting integrated. We argue that presence of corporate entrepreneurship attributes in acquired firms is vital for their successful integration with their acquirers. The acquirers are less likely to divest such acquisitions that continue to demonstrate the culture of corporate entrepreneurship even after getting acquired, more specifically, during their post-acquisition integration stages. While most studies have focused on the 'process' dimension of managing post-acquisition integration, we intend to explore this largely unattended dimension, namely, 'corporate entrepreneurship level' of acquired entrepreneurial firms. In this study, we used Stopford & Baden-Fuller's (1994) two of the five 'bundles' of attributes for creating corporate entrepreneurship to explore how these attributes impact the overall efficiency of integration, and therefore, predict the likely status during post-acquisition integration stages. Connecting corporate entrepreneurship literature with M&A literature will be our contribution toward developing practical implication for entrepreneurial firms who are in the process of preparing themselves for a successful continuity or exit through M&A route, and also, for acquirers who are on the lookout for complimentary targets.

KEYWORDS: Corporate entrepreneurship, Post acquisition integration, Divestiture

INTRODUCTION

In the start of this millennium, Marconi, a UK based telecom solution provider, was well regarded in the telecom business circle for its highly innovative telecom products. Marconi's optical networking equipment, broadband access products, soft-switch products and R&D operations were considered as one of the most innovative and efficient telecom solutions available. In 2005, when Marconi started struggling to execute the multi-billion dollar British Telecom network upgrade project, it found its strategic fit in Ericsson, a Swedish telecom network service major. Ericsson acquired Marconi for $2.1 billion (Ericsson News Center, 2005). Subsequently, Ericsson renamed the acquired part as Tenet and extensively used it as a strategic tool to expand into North and Latin America. As a result, Tenet's capabilities helped Ericsson won several major telecom contracts with regional operators like AT&T (US), Vivo (Brazil), Ento (Chile) and similar others (Ericsson Publications, 2015). In a similar setting, Palm – the first generation smartphone makers got acquired by HP as a strategic-fit deal for $1.2

billion in 2010, when it started losing ground to Blackberry, Apple, Samsung, HTC, Motorola and others (HP Press, 2010). HP assumed that the combination of its financial muscle and global reach with Palm's proprietary smartphone devices and unique webOS platform will enable HP to successfully enter into the fast-growing and highly profitable smartphone and connected mobile device markets. However, HP failed to find any strategic fit due to Palm's relatively poorer hardware and OS capabilities than the existing competition. HP took less than a year to, not even divest, but, close-down the entire Palm division (The Verge, 2012). Why did Ericsson succeed, and HP failed in integrating their respective acquired firms?

The tales of these two post-acquisition outcomes prompt to reason out the causes that allow one kind of target firms to get integrated successfully while the other kind to get divested. M&A literature (Kohers and Kohers, 2001) has shown that both acquirers and target firms have different expectations from each other, and therefore, face several challenges in the wake of a takeover. While acquirers' challenge is to successfully integrate the new asset in order to meet their expectations, the acquired firms' challenge lies in establishing their identity within their acquirers. Among several challenges, one of the most common challenges that acquirers and their respective targets face is about intense organization-culture clashes (Weber et al., 2009). Another pertinent challenge surfaces when acquirers' tend to control their targets while undermining their targets' innovative creations, which leads to potential shake-ups, conflicts and poor integration (Sudarsanam, 2003). We argue that some of these challenges are related to the existence and non-existence of corporate entrepreneurial culture within the target firms, which influences acquirers to commit superior attention and effort for successful integration. We found that M&A researchers have largely not attended such an important aspect of post-acquisition integration success. As such, corporate entrepreneurial activities help the acquisitions to add value to the corporations as a whole (Thomson & Mcnamara, 2002). We, further, argue that lack of corporate entrepreneurship in target firms' culture can also be a strong determinant that leads to acquisition-turned-divestiture when acquirers' initial expectations are not met or partially met. As a result, acquirers decide not to invest further time and cost in integration, and instead they choose for alternate strategic choices such as, divestiture, hold-up or close-down. Our study focuses on establishing linkage between lack of corporate entrepreneurship in the acquired firms and the acquisition-turned-divestiture outcome.

In this paper, we use Stopford & Baden-Fuller's (1994) five 'bundles' of attributes (namely, pro-activeness, aspirations beyond current capability, team orientation, capability to resolve dilemmas, and learning capability), responsible for demonstrating the influencing role corporate entrepreneurship (CE) capability. In doing so, we qualify our rationale to use only the two "team-level" attributes, namely learning capability and team orientation, over the other three arguably "strategic-level" attributes, namely, pro-activeness, aspirations beyond current capability, and capability to resolve dilemmas. Next, we illustrate how these two "team-level" CE attributes, namely different degrees of both learning capability and team orientation with the acquired firms, have a two-fold influence. First, how do these CE two attributes influence their acquirers to consider different strategic actions, such as integration, divestiture, hold-up, or close-down. Second, how do these two attributes also influence acquired firms' organizational behaviors in their structures. Thus, we attempt to establish the role of corporate entrepreneurship within acquired firms as a vital factor for successful integration of acquisitions. More specifically, our study is aimed at conceptualizing the significance of corporate entrepreneurship in target firms (acquired firms) during post-acquisition integration phase, rather than focusing upon broader understanding of corporate entrepreneurship.

To elaborate the scope of our research, first, we attempt to understand and elaborate upon determinants (or contingencies) that trigger divestiture decisions using past studies. Second, we explore the concept of corporate entrepreneurship by using appropriate past studies and explain our rationale to use two of five 'bundles' of attributes of corporate entrepreneurship, namely, learning capabilities and team orientation, proposed by Stopford & Baden-Fuller (1994). Third, we develop our set of eight propositions related to the strategic actions by acquirers and acquired firms' organizational behaviors towards their acquirers based on different levels of acquired firms' learning capabilities and team orientation attributes. At the end, we attempt to contribute by discussing upon its managerial implications, limitation and future research scope.

LITERATURE REVIEW

DETERMINANTS AND THEORETICAL PERSPECTIVES OF DIVESTITURE DECISION

Corporate strategy scholars have conducted extensive research on divestitures and shown that divestitures attempt to change the configuration of a firm's business portfolio and thus directly affect the question of "What businesses are we in?" (Andrews, 1971; Ansoff, 1965). Brauer's (2006) review on divestiture literature has classified it into three major streams: research on the antecedents, on the outcomes of divestitures, and on the actual process of divesting. In the context of our study, we are interested to understand the determinants (antecedents) of divestitures. Using and updating his well-conducted and systematically reviewed study, we identified that the determinants (contingencies triggering divestitures) of divestiture can be simplistically classified into two categories: inter-firm related determinants and intra-firm related determinants. Brauer's (2006) study refers inter-firm related determinants as 'industry-specific contingencies' and intra-firm determinants as 'firm-specific contingencies'.

Inter-firm related determinants of divestitures

In Appendix table A-1, we present the summary of extant research for last three decades (in chronological order) that focused on the inter-firm determinants of divestiture decisions. The major triggers for divestitures have been argued as industry growth, industry concentration, environmental uncertainty, technological change, and institutional policy changes. One strong observation is that most of the studies have consistently applied an industrial economics perspective to explain their theoretical concepts. (e.g., Harrigan, 1981; Ilmakunnas & Topi, 1999; Chang & Singh, 1999; Van Kranenburg et al., 2002) with one exception of using resource-dependence perspective to explain the mutual dependence and sub-unit power concepts between firms within an industry (Xia & L1, 2013).

Intra-firm related determinants of divestitures

In Appendix table A-2, we present the summary of extant research for last three decades (in chronological order) that focused on the intra-firm determinants of divestiture decisions. The major triggers for divestitures have been argued as poor performance, internal governance, excessive diversification, firm's business age and business size. Researchers have applied a wide variety of organizational theories to build their argument about inter-firm related determinants that triggers divestiture decisions. The most commonly applied theoretical perspectives include portfolio theory (Duhaime & Grant, 1984; Montgomery & Thomas, 1988; Mata & Portugal, 2000), agency theory (Hoskisson et al., 1994; Bergh, 1995; Zuckerman, 2000; Sanders, 2001; Chatterjee et al., 2003; Bergh & Sharp, 2015), efficiency theory (Bergh, 1997;

Bushnell & Wolfram, 2005), and resource based perspective (Hoskisson & Johnson, 1992; Bergh, 1995; Chang, 1996; Bergh, 1998).

Based on the summaries presented in Appendix tables A-1 and A-2, we present our theoretical perspective wise elaboration of studies that explain the influencing factors of divestiture decisions closely related to the overall context of our study.

Industrial economics perspective

IE is the most dominant industry-specific theory being applied by researchers to explain inter-firm determinants that trigger divestiture decisions. In general, acquired units are more likely to be sold off than internally developed units (Chang & Singh, 1999). However, during times of technological change in an industry, firms are found to increase their divestiture activities (Harrigan, 1982). During increased levels of environmental uncertainty, inside directors of intermediate and highly diversified firms holding higher stock ownership push their firms for increased divestiture activities (Chatterjee et al., 2003). During such times, larger firms opt to divest their smaller units with marginal activities or insignificant market share as a corporate strategy to focus on their core businesses (Sembenelli & Vannoni, 2003). This reveals the fact that the costs of managing diverse portfolios increases during uncertain times. Furthermore, Bergh (1998) found that firms pursuing refocusing strategy are more likely to divest than firms following portfolio management strategy during high uncertainty. In addition to it, changes in the institutional setting of the firm (i.e., changes in taxes, policies, de-regulation) are triggers for realignment of firms' portfolios (Hoskisson & Hitt, 1990). Given the choice between divestiture and closure, ownership and organizational structure plays the main role on the likelihood of divestitures but not closures (Mata & Portugal, 2000).

Contrasting IE theory, Ilmakunnas & Topi (1999) found that industry size doesn't affect divestiture rates whereas industry growth reduces the likelihood of divestiture. However, low industry concentrations do not trigger for divestiture activity (Hopkins, 1991). This suggests that acquired firms are more likely to get divested when the market slows down. Interestingly, Harrigan's (1981, 1982, 1985) studies collectively suggested that the degree of product differentiation, firms' strategic flexibility (such as internal transfers between units), and industry fragmentation act as barriers towards divestiture decisions.

Agency theory perspective

Agency theory is directed as the ubiquitous agency relationship, in which one party (the principal) delegates work to another party (the agent), who performs that work. It is concerned with resolving two problems that arises when (a) the desires or goals of the principal and agent conflict and (b) it is difficult or expensive for the principal to verify what the agent is actually doing (Eisenhardt, 1989). Accordingly, agency theory perspective suggests that weak internal governance and related agency problems lead to increased levels of divestiture decisions. For example, higher outside block-holder equity (e.g., investment banks) positively influences divestiture intensity, whereas higher outside-director equity negatively influences divestiture intensity (Hoskisson, Johnson, & Moesel, 1994; Bergh & Sharp, 2015). Other the other hand, high ratio of inside director stock ownership than that of outside director increase the likelihood of divestiture during higher business turbulence (Chatterjee, Harrison, & Bergh, 2003). Additionally, both relative debt and the degree of diversification have a positive influence on divestiture intensity. Bergh (1995) showed that companies are more likely to sell unrelated and small units when owner influence is high, and vice-versa. Zuckerman (2000) found that divestitures are more likely to occur when a mismatch between the firm's corporate strategy and its identity occurs. For example, Google acquired Motorola in 2013 for $12.5 billion, but, sold Motorola's hardware division to Lenovo for $2.9 billion in less than 12 months when it realized that Motorola's hardware intense image was affecting its long-term strategy as Android OS player. Interestingly, Sanders (2001) found that firms are more likely to engage in divestitures when their CEOs are compensated with stock option pay, but less likely when their CEOs owned stock. Contrastingly, in times of high business turbulence, high levels of inside director stock ownership and relatively low levels of outside director stock ownership increase the likelihood of divestiture (Chatterjee, Harrison, & Bergh, 2003).

Efficiency and Portfolio theory perspective

The likelihood of divestiture of an acquired firm depends on motives, expectations, and initial conditions at the time of acquisition (Bergh, 1997). Perhaps, situations of weaker financial position of the divesting firm (acquirer), low competitive and financial strength of the acquired business unit relative to industry peers, and its higher interdependency with other units triggers the divestiture decisions (Duhaime & Grant, 1984). Additionally, Pashley & Philippatos (1990) argued that firms also divest for different motives, such as to reduce debt levels, to increase liquidity, and to earn higher profits, depending on their life-cycle stage. In essence, acquirers are more likely to divest their acquired units if they already have a high degree of diversification, declining performance, and/or an attractive core business in terms of profitability and size relative to industry counterparts (Montgomery & Thomas, 1988; Hoskisson & Johnson, 1992; Markides, 1992). Interestingly, Mata & Portugal (2000) argued that during business turbulence, large-firms are more inclined to divest their acquired firms which they purchased for the purpose of market entry than their green-field entries which are more likely to closures. In sum, unprofitability, focus on core activities, and need to meet corporate requirements are the three most common triggers of divestiture of acquired firms (Hamilton & Chow, 1993).

Resource-based-view and Transaction-cost-economy perspective

A substantial amount of studies have applied Resource-based-view and Transaction-cost-economy perspectives to explain various determinants of divestiture decision. Chang (1996) argued that the lines of business characteristics (such as market share, resource profiles, etc.) are strong predictors for de-selection (divestiture) of units. As such, large firms are likely to divest not as often as smaller firms when faced with the same performance gap or negative demand shock. Also, divestiture of units with dissimilar human resource profiles leads to increased profitability, as anticipated from a Resource-based perspective (Barney, 1991). Interestingly, when uncertainty increases, firms pursuing refocusing strategy (such as divestiture) outperform others following portfolio management strategy; and vice-versa applies when uncertainty decreases (Bergh, 1998). Bergh & Lawless (1998) applied transaction-cost-economics (TCE) to explain how changes in environmental uncertainty would affect divestiture intensity. They argued that highly diversified firms divest when environmental uncertainty increases, and they acquire when environmental uncertainty decreases. In contrary, firms with lower levels of diversification act oppositely.

The central argument of this study is to emphasize upon the role of corporate entrepreneurship (CE) attributes of target firms, which influences inter- and intra-firm divestiture triggers of their acquisition-turned-divestiture fate. Accordingly, the next section of this paper explores the concept, forms, and attributes of corporate entrepreneurship that target firms may possess. As such, these CE capabilities are likely to influence the acquirers' strategic actions during integration phase. For instance, from an industrial organization (IO) economics perspective of divestiture, Bergh's (1998) study indicates that acquirer's corporate strategy (e.g., refocusing vs. portfolio management) is linked to higher rates of divestiture under conditions of high uncertainty. However, a deeper consideration of acquirer's corporate strategy might explain that the acquirer might intend to retain a portion of the target firm (such as, set of high-profile managers, key assets, etc.) and sell-off assets that hold lesser value. Correspondingly, the acquirer might consider an RBV or TCE based approach to retain and/or divest their target firm (in part or full) based on their overall perception of the target firm's prevailing corporate entrepreneurship capabilities. As a demonstrative example, when Google sold Motorola to Lenovo in 2014, it retained a vast majority of Motorola's promising patents (and key high-profile talented engineers) that were related to new technology innovations – wearable computing and home markets, and divested about 2,000 patents that were related to mobile phones and cable box industry, and Motorola brand and trademark portfolio (TechCrunch, 2014).

CONCEPT OF CORPORATE ENTREPRENEURSHIP

Corporate entrepreneurship has been widely used by corporations as a deliberate and intentional means to bring in different forms of newness (such as organizational renewal, innovation, and establishing new ventures) to promote and sustain their corporate competitiveness (Dess et al., 2003). Several studies have highlighted and empirically supported that corporate entrepreneurship can provide competitive advantage to corporations in their respective markets by nurturing value-creating innovations (Guth & Ginsberg, 1990; Naman & Slevin, 1993; Lumpkin & Dess, 1996). One of the most cited studies was conducted by Zahra & Covin (1995) which examined a longitudinal impact of corporate entrepreneurship on growth and profitability based financial performance index and found a strong positive linkage between corporate entrepreneurial behavior and subsequent financial performance.

Although the concept of corporate entrepreneurship may appear straightforward, it has been studied from different perspectives. For example, Schollhammer (1982) suggested corporate entrepreneurial activities as administrative, opportunistic, imitative, acquisitive, and incubative in nature. Vesper (1984) advocated corporate entrepreneurship can be one or any possible combination of the following three kinds, namely, (a) new strategic direction, (b) initiative from lower in hierarchy structures, and (c) self-governing business creation. Vesper's study shows that corporate entrepreneurship could be any of these individual types, as well as any or all-possible combinations. From a resource-based perspective, it is a source for accruing, translating, and leveraging resources for developing new products, processes, and administrative innovations to rejuvenate and redefine the firm and its markets or industries (Floyd & Wooldridge, 1999). A handful of studies have also suggested corporate entrepreneurship as a means to create different types of new knowledge (i.e., technical, integrative, and exploitative) formally or informally (Zahra, 1999; Kuratko et al., 2001; Hitt & Ireland, 2002); however, knowledge can be either explicit or tacit in nature. Despite multi-dimensional approach to corporate entrepreneurship, its centrality exists in forming competitive advantages for firms that helps them to outperform their rivals (Coff, 2002; Grant, 1996) by facilitating development and management of knowledge stocks and flows between people and organizational units (Ireland, Hitt, Camp & Sexton, 2001).

Forms of Corporate Entrepreneurship

Having conceptualized corporate entrepreneurship as deliberate and purposeful efforts of renewal of organizations, markets, or industries in order to create or sustain competitive superiority, it may be possible to visualize the plausible forms of corporate entrepreneurship phenomenon. Our review of extant literature found that the Covin & Miles (1999) conceptualization of four forms of corporate entrepreneurship (namely, (a) sustained regeneration, (b) organizational rejuvenation, (c) strategic renewal, and (d) domain redefinition) is the most cited and consistently used typology on forms of corporate entrepreneurship. Each one of the forms is concerned with either rejuvenating or intentionally redefining the organization or establishing innovation. Largely complex firms (i.e., firms with diversified product portfolio or over-diversified firms) simultaneous apply one or more forms in different parts and processes within their structure.

Sustained regeneration

The first form, sustained regeneration, is the most commonly applied form as it is concerned primarily with continuous improvement. It enables firms to develop cultures, processes, and structures in order to support and encourage introduction of continuous stream of new products in their respective markets as well as venturing into new markets with existing products (Covin & Miles, 1999). By applying this form, firms, such as AT&T, have continuously been able to capitalize on emerging product-market opportunities unseen or underappreciated by competitors in their core industry segment.

Organizational rejuvenation

The second form, organizational rejuvenation, is concerned with the firm's internal processes, structures, and capabilities. It enables process and administrative innovations rather than product innovations. Since its primary focus is towards improving the firm's ability to execute strategies, it necessitates alteration in the value chain-map of the firm's several activities. Using organizational rejuvenation, firms are able to gain higher entrepreneurial levels by enriching its capabilities on varying the processes, structures and support activities (e.g., procurement and human resource management), apart from gaining abilities to introducing new product and/or entering new markets with existing products (Covin & Miles, 1999). Firms, such as GE, have demonstrated successful rejuvenation of one or several aspects of their firm's operations for past several years.

Strategic renewal

The third form, strategic renewal, is concerned with the "organization-environment" interface. It enables the firm to renew strategies to compete with its competitors by seeking better alignment with external environment, such as changing the nature of rivalry with competitors. In organizational rejuvenation, the organization itself sits in the center (Covin & Miles, 1999). Strategic renewal allows the firm to become more profitable by exploiting product-market opportunities through strategic moves such as strategic repositioning (i.e., reposition itself to exploit current competitive advantages and explore future advantages (Ireland et al., 2002). Firms, such as Harley-Davidson and Cisco Systems, have constantly attempted to strategic renewal by partially altering its competition strategies in their respective competitive environments and successfully demonstrated internal growth, instead of acquisition growths.

Domain redefinition

The fourth form, domain redefinition, is concerned with the firm's pro-activeness to create a new product market position against and ahead of their rivals (Covin & Miles, 1999). It focuses on exploring for possibilities, instead of exploiting the currently available one. This re-energized move allows firms to redefine their domains with an intention to gain the first-mover advantages. Being the first firm to sell a new product in their respective domains requires high level of pro-activeness and demonstration of strong entrepreneurial orientation (Lumpkin & Dess, 1996). One of the closest examples of domain redefinition was Sony's illustrated first mover actions of introducing the innovative Walkman in the eighties.

The four forms can be further re-classified based on their corporate entrepreneurial actions. Sustained regeneration and organizational regeneration activities deals at within-the-organization levels, whereas, strategic renewal and domain redefinition deals at organization-environment levels.

Attributes of Corporate Entrepreneurship

The diverse literature on corporate entrepreneurship suggests that, at the least, entrepreneurial activities create capabilities within firms to offset their structural inertia. Moreover, Covin & Miles' (1999) each of the four forms of corporate entrepreneurship share the commonality of innovations. Entrepreneurial firms must be able to cope with changes in the pattern of resource deployment in order to create newer innovative capabilities (such as new product, new strategy, new market, new positioning). However, each form of corporate entrepreneurship (namely, regeneration, rejuvenation, renewal, and redefinition) has unique characteristics, and therefore, need separate consideration (Guth & Ginsberg, 1990). The next challenge, therefore, is to explore the processes by which each of the alternate forms of corporate entrepreneurship can linked together. We identified Stopford & Baden-Fuller (1994) study that successfully identified the linkage between different forms and different attributes of corporate entrepreneurship. According to their study, the diverse literature on entrepreneurship suggests that there are three established 'bundles' of attributes (namely, pro-activeness (freedom to conduct experiments), aspirations beyond current capability, and team-orientation) common to all types of entrepreneurship. They added another two attributes (namely, capability to resolve dilemmas and learning capability), which they derived from the literatures on innovation and change and from their own observations. Together, these five 'bundles' of attributes provide indicators of managerial orientations and organizational capabilities (Stopford & Baden-Fuller, 1994).

<u>Pro-activeness</u>

The first attribute, 'pro-activeness' (Miller & Friesen, 1978; Mintzberg, 1973), is a multi-dimensional concept. According to Stopford & Baden-Fuller (1994), pro-activeness does not necessarily imply to be the first in an industry to do something. As such, entrepreneurial firms pro-actively initiate multiple projects at the same time to establish their innovation capabilities, but also, to spread their financial risks (Stevenson & Gumpert, 1985). Therefore, to gain leverage (first mover advantages) over their rivals, entrepreneurial firms must demonstrate pro-activeness, although, such pro-activeness is notionally different from taking high risks.

<u>Aspirations beyond current capability</u>

The second attribute, 'aspirations beyond current capability' captures firms' progress and continuous improvement related attributes by encouraging firms to find superior combinations of resources. Both entrepreneurial individuals and firms organizations do not limit their beliefs about opportunities within the currently available resources (Stevenson & Jarillo, 1990). This attribute is extremely important for firms that aspire to become industry leaders and to bring frame-breaking changes (Hamel & Prahalad, 1989). According to Stopford & Baden-Fuller (1994), aspirations must exceed resources to drive processes of entrepreneurship and to foster high energy levels.

Team orientation

The third attribute, 'team orientation' emphasizes upon the top and middle managers critical role in developing strong associations within team to nurture and sustain new innovative ideas as well as creative individuals (Bantel & Jackson, 1989). Social contracting is considered as an important factor for strong team orientation (Starr & MacMillan, 1990). By demonstrating strong team orientation even at lower levels, firms are maintain momentum for growth which assists managers to work across traditional organizational boundaries and keep adding value (Kanter, 1983). According to Stopford & Baden-Fuller (1994), firms must assess the conditions that encourage effective teamwork and the interaction between teams and individuals. As such, over-stress on teamwork can create group-behaviorism and that can suppress innovation (Janis, 1982). Contrastingly, bureaucracy can foster new product introduction rates (Sathe, 1985) and centralization can enable innovation (Burns & Stalker, 1962; Thompson, 1961).

Capability to resolve dilemmas

The fourth attribute, firms' 'capability to resolve dilemmas' (identified from Hampden-Turner, 1990) enables firms to overcome several challenges of organizational renewal. As observed by Stopford & Baden-Fuller (1994), it is viewed as firms' creative practice for resolving internal dilemmas and for converting the outcomes into new innovations in their respective markets.

Learning capability

The fifth and final attribute, 'learning capability' allows firms to innovate and make significant change in their domain (Schein, 1985). According to Stopford & Baden-Fuller (1994), this attribute enables firms to either formulate renewals or frame-breaking changes in their respective markets. It enables managers to call for new possibilities and create new options without worrying about the outcomes. Firms that practice corporate entrepreneurship continue to build sustained investments by facilitating suitable learning environments.

Linking CE Forms with CE Attributes

Covin & Miles (1999) conceptualization of each of the four forms of corporate entrepreneurship (namely, (a) sustained regeneration, (b) organizational rejuvenation, (c) strategic renewal, and (d) domain redefinition) is concerned with either rejuvenating or intentionally redefining the organization or establishing innovation. We argue that certain level of each of the five CE attributes is required for each of these four CE forms. However, not all CE attributes are required to be maintained at high levels for each of the four forms of corporate entrepreneurship. For example, pro-activeness levels are important for individuals, teams and managers, and therefore, it must be maintained at highest possible levels in each of the four forms. On the other hand, organizational rejuvenation deals with processes of the firms, and therefore, doesn't require high levels of learning capabilities for its associated individuals, teams and managers. Similarly, strategic renewal and domain redefinition are concerned with strategic choices and manager's decision such as positioning and competition, and therefore, firms' do not require high levels of team orientation to pursue this form of corporate entrepreneurship. In aggregating Stopford & Baden-Fuller's (1994) five CE attributes, three attributes, (namely, pro-activeness, aspirations beyond current capability, and capability to resolve dilemmas) may be grouped as "strategic-level" concepts, whereas, remaining two attributes (namely, team orientation and learning capability) may be grouped as "team-level" concepts. Since our study deals with the perception of the available CE attributes in target firms in the eyes of the acquirer, we are primarily concerned with the "team-level" concepts in influencing the acquirer's best interest. For example, if the acquirer is attempting to integrate its target that allows the acquirer to redefine its domain (such as HP-Palm acquisition, 2010), the target team must show medium to high levels of two team-level attributes (namely, team orientation and learning capability), whereas, the other CE attributes are expected to exist at higher levels with the acquirer. Likewise, if the acquirer is focusing to strategically integrate the target to achieve strategic renewal for better alignment with external environment (such as Google's selective retention and divestment of Motorola assets to Lenovo, 2014), the target firm is expected to high levels of one of the "team-level" CE attributes (i.e., learning capability as that would allow acquirer to be contingent on the target firm to learn and formulate renewals in their respective markets. On the other hand, higher levels of team orientation within the target firm may not be a contingent condition due the substantial team re-organization needed in the wake of successful post-acquisition integration. In the table 1 below, we anticipate the required levels (high-medium-low) of CE attributes for each of the four CE forms and call for future research to establish the correlation between forms and attributes of corporate entrepreneurship.

Table 1: Levels of CE attributes on CE forms

	Sustained regeneration	Organizational rejuvenation	Strategic renewal	Domain redefinition
Pro-activeness	High	High	High	High
Aspirations beyond current capability	Low	Medium	High	High
Team orientation	High	High	Low	Medium
Capability to resolve dilemmas	Low	High	Medium	High
Learning capability	High	Low	High	High

THEORY DEVELOPMENT AND PROPOSITIONS

Our study attempts to measure the impact of variations of the attributes of corporate entrepreneurship on post-acquisition integration decisions. We argue that these attributes are broad, complex, and significantly interdependent. We do not challenge their applicability, but, argue that they have been understudied and can provide interesting insights about the concept of corporate entrepreneurship in the context of mergers and acquisitions, especially, during post-acquisition integration phases. Additionally, three of Stopford & Baden-Fuller's (1994) five CE attributes, (namely, pro-activeness, aspirations beyond current capability, and capability to resolve dilemmas) may be grouped as strategic-level concepts, whereas, remaining two attributes (namely, team orientation and learning capability) may be grouped as "team-level" concepts. We argue that the "team-level" CE attributes of target are the key influential factors on acquirer's post-acquisition strategic decision, whereas, the "strategic-level" CE attributes of target are unrelated to the acquirer's post-acquisition strategic choices. Therefore, we analyzed the characteristics of only two of the five CE attributes, namely, team orientation and learning capability, and their influence on post-acquisition integration outcomes.

Team orientation and Learning capability

Organizations are inorganic constructs and therefore, they do not learn themselves. Rather, knowledge creation is an individual activity (Grant, 1996; March, 1991). The key role of a firm in the process of knowledge creation is to act as a platform for the teams to nurture its creativity, and harness that creative energy in team activities. Teams experiment with newer ideas to create innovative processes and products that isolated individuals could rarely conceptualize single handedly.

Organizational learning capability is related to team orientation. (Nonaka et al., 2000) argued that the process of innovation (i.e., organization learning) by teams requires dialogue between team members and conversations across functional boundaries to facilitate productive exploitation of new product and process concepts. As such, entrepreneurial teams require a common language to communicate their ideas and mutual trust among individuals and the firm to share their insights without fear of alienation or personal loss, in order to operate successfully. For example, an indication that team orientation has broken down is when individuals within a team hoard important information and are unwilling to pool it with others in the team (Jones & George, 1998). Essentially, lack of team orientation implies that corporate entrepreneurial activities have failed.

Post-acquisition Integration outcomes

From past literature on mergers and acquisitions, we identified four possible outcomes of post-acquisition integration efforts, namely, successful integration, hold-up, divestment, and close-down. The acquirer considers each of the four outcomes based on the combination of one or more perceived triggers. The first construct of "Successful integration" of the target firm broadly reflects a constructive post-acquisition outcome which is in alignment with the acquirer's strategic intent for acquiring the target firm. "Hold-up" reflects an unclear status of the target firm when the acquirer has asymmetric (insufficient) information about their target price prior to the sale (Schweizer, 2013). In this study, we have conceptualized the second construct of "Hold-up" as an unclear status of the target during post-acquisition integration stage due to asymmetric (insufficient) information related to the target firm or other strategic fit reasons. For example, the acquirer might put the target's integration on-hold during abrupt market conditions. The third construct of "Divestment" reflects an interesting situation when the acquirer is interested to sell-off the target's assets in full or part, instead of integrating, for strategic or liquidity reasons. The fourth construct of "Close-down" explains an extreme situation when the acquirer decides not to invest any further resource upon their target as it sees zero to little value in pursing any further integration effort.

Having conceptualized about the four probable post-acquisition integration outcomes and the two related "team-level" CE attributes, we would elucidate the inter-relationship between these two concepts. First, we argue that corporate entrepreneurship activities within the acquired firms influence their team orientation and learning capability levels to pursue new initiatives (such as both new products and new geographies). Contrastingly, when acquirers observe lack of corporate entrepreneurship activities within the newly acquired firms, they tend to re-evaluate their acquisition logic (such as their initial motives, expectations, and initial market conditions) at the time of acquisition (Bergh, 1997). For example, acquirers may chose either to fully integrate or not integrate (such as hold-up, divest, or close-down) the acquired firms when they observe that acquired firms can't demonstrate sufficient levels of required CE attributes to create new products on their behalf.

Second, we also argue that different degrees of team orientation and learning capability of target firms can explain their overall firm behavior, which becomes crucial towards their acquirers to consider actions to fully integrate or not integrate them. In table 2, we have summarized our understanding about (a) the acquired firms' observed behavior, and (b) their post-acquisition integration outcomes due to such behavior, by comparing high and low degrees of team orientation against high and low degrees of learning capability.

Table 2: Acquired firms' behavior and post-acquisition outcome based on their degrees of Team Orientation and Learning Capability during post-acquisition phase

		LEARNING CAPABILITY	
		HIGH	LOW
TEAM ORIENTATION	HIGH	INTEGRATION SUCCESS <u>Firm's behavior</u> • Trust • Knowledge sharing • Innovation	HOLD-UP <u>Firm's behavior</u> • Socialization • Group behavior • Resource wastefulness
	LOW	DIVESTMENT <u>Firm's behavior</u> • Staff turnover • Information hoarding • Resource stretch	CLOSE-DOWN <u>Firm's behavior</u> • Inertia • Fear of alienation • Low staff motivation

Research shows that learning individuals in a team oriented environment tend to perform well is illustrated by their display of higher creativity and team coherence, which in turn enhances the overall team productivity (Hirst et al., 2009). When team members are learning individuals, they tend to participate more in decision making (Converse, 1993). Research has also indicated that individuals with high team orientations tend to trust each other and are willing to take more risks to achieve innovativeness. Acquired firms that show high levels of both team orientation and learning capability during their post-acquisition integration phases are likely to get successfully integrated with their acquirers. This is likely to occur despite negative business environment because the acquirers consider the future potential aspects of such innovativeness. Accordingly, we propose:

P1: Acquired firm that displays strong trust and loyalty, participatory decision making, knowledge sharing, and innovativeness behaviors is likely to display both high degrees of team orientation and high degrees of learning capabilities.

P2: High degrees of team orientation and high degrees of learning capabilities of acquired firm positively moderates the association between determinants of post-acquisition divestiture decision and post-acquisition integration success.

On the contrary, when individuals within coherent team do not focus on higher learning activities, instead they consider the coherence as a platform to socialize and show group behavior, it leads to considerable wastage of resources. Such behavior by the acquired firms' teams is likely to cause serious challenges for managers of acquiring firms on the rate of post-acquisition integration and increases the likeness of post-acquisition hold-up status. Accordingly, we propose:

P3: Acquired firm that displays behaviors of greater socialization, group behavior, and wastage of resources is likely to display high degrees of team orientation but low degrees of learning capabilities.

P4: High degrees of team orientation and low degrees of learning capabilities of acquired firm positively moderates the association between determinants of post-acquisition divestiture decision and post-acquisition hold-up outcome.

When acquired firms show low levels of team orientation, it reflects the lack of shared language. This results into internal turbulence because only few individuals are forced to overwork (resource stretch). As a result, individuals with high learning capability tend to act opportunistically by hoarding information and by acting upon self-benefiting tasks. Acquired firms whose individual show such opportunistic behavior are less likely to survive during their post-acquisition integration phases. This phenomenon increases their acquirers to sell-off the assets of the acquired firms in full or part. Accordingly, we propose:

P5: Acquired firm that displays behaviors of opportunism, high staff turnover, information hoarding by individuals, and resource stretch is likely to display low degrees of team orientation but high degrees of learning capabilities.

P6: Low degrees of team orientation and high degrees of learning capabilities of acquired firm positively moderates the association between determinants of post-acquisition divestiture decision and post-acquisition divestment outcome.

Team motivation is an important aspect of corporate entrepreneurship. During high environmental turbulence or unfavorable conditions, the acquirer firms tend to apply cost-cutting measures. As a result, this reflects upon the behaviors of individuals of acquired firms. As such, their individuals are way out to show lower levels of both team orientation and learning capability, which in turn shapes into behaviors of high structural inertia, fear of job-loss, and alienation. Such behaviors of acquired firms question their acquirers' initial motives for acquisition. Accordingly, we propose:

P7: Acquired firm that displays behaviors of greater structural inertia, fear of alienation, and low staff motivation is likely to display both low degrees of team orientation and low degrees of learning capabilities.

P8: Low degrees of team orientation and low degrees of learning capabilities of acquired firm positively moderates the association between determinants of post-acquisition divestiture decision and post-acquisition close-down outcome.

Additionally, we propose a research framework as shown in Figure 1 to suggest how corporate entrepreneurship attributes of acquired firms strengthens and/or weakens the relationship between acquirers' strategic (integration) intent and their likely actions (considerations) in favor of their acquired firms during the post-acquisition integration stages. We propose that the constructs of this research model be operationalized and tested upon using appropriate data sample and statistical techniques.

Figure 1: Research model showing the Moderation effect of corporate entrepreneurship attributes on *associations between determinants of post-acquisition divestiture decision and post-acquisition integration outcomes.*

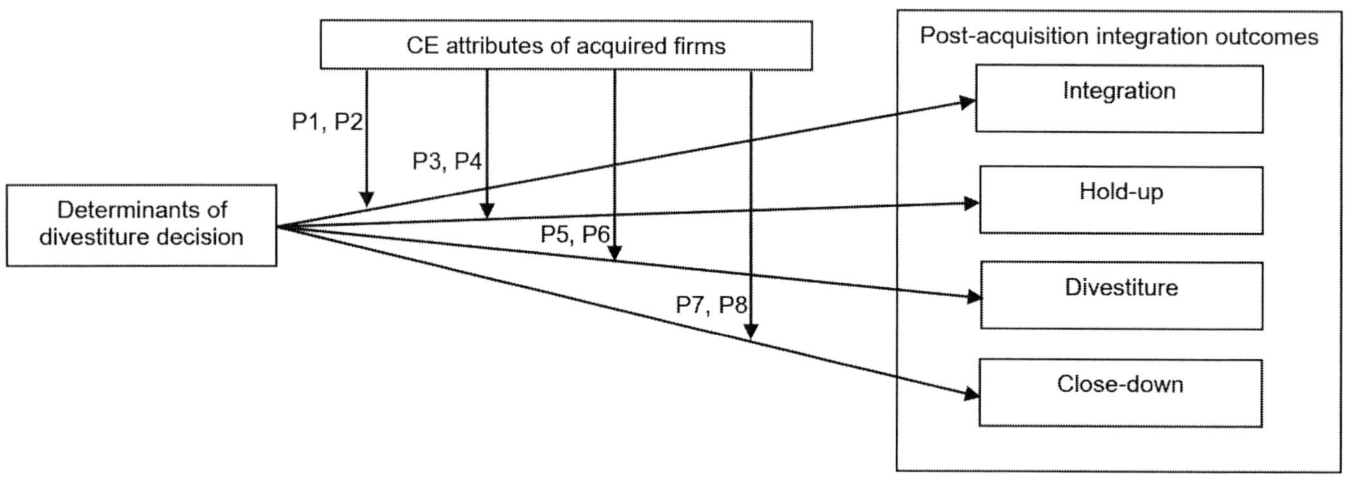

DISCUSSION, IMPLICATIONS, LIMITATIONS, & FUTURE RESEARCH DIRECTIONS

The objective our study is to stress upon the importance of corporate entrepreneurial environment as it allows firms to develop a stream of innovations in terms of organizational capabilities (novel and effective organizational systems, processes, routines) and products over a period of time. Such innovations act as influencers to prove their value when those firms get acquired. As an extension, we suggest that the stronger the presence of the various attributes of corporate entrepreneurship inside a given firm, the more likely it is to be successful at the generation of new capabilities or products. However, it solely falls upon managers to identify the key attributes of corporate entrepreneurship in a new acquisition. It creates a stimulating opportunity to nurture those factors during the early post-acquisition stage. Once these attributes are identified and preserved, their importance can be determined after integration, managers can utilize those factors to a greater degree in creating innovation culture across the wider scope of their organizations. In this study, we restrict our discussion upon the strengths of two of five attributes (namely, learning capability and team orientation) adopted from Stopford & Baden-Fuller's (1994) work and extensively used in our study.

We observed that the Argyris & Schon (1995) concepts of organizational learning and knowledge management, gained popularity in the last two decades and started competing with concepts such as corporate entrepreneurship for management attention (Argyris & Schon, 1995). Therefore, theory suggests that the core concepts of knowledge creation and organization learning form the foundation for corporate entrepreneurship (Zahra et al., 1999). However, in our perspective, corporate entrepreneurship complements and co-exists with knowledge creation and organization learning. Therefore, we assume that modern day managers are more likely to be recognizable with the both knowledge creation and organization learning aspects as a default quality of their individual and collective performance, than corporate entrepreneurship, per se. This makes our study to be highly useful for managers as it would compel them to understand the importance and practicality of corporate entrepreneurship. We believe that it is the managers who would be able to influence the two highlighted attributes of corporate entrepreneurship, which would make the management of mergers and acquisition lot easier to predict and perform.

Our study attempts for making three important contributions to literature. First, it attempted to link corporate entrepreneurship to post-acquisition success. Although, there are several studies about the relevance of corporate entrepreneurship on the renewal of mature organizations, and the creation of new, innovative businesses within large firms, the role of corporate entrepreneurship in post-acquisition integration and survival has been understudied. Through this study, we attempt to partially fill this gap. We argued that nurturing corporate entrepreneurship environments within forms play an important role in their long-term success before and after getting acquired.

Second, our study attempts to induce more scholarly works using longitudinal data sample and appropriate statistical techniques. Here, we attempt to make eight propositions that may happen to be inferentially useful for managers to make predictions about their acquisition targets based on their existence or non-existence of the two highlighted attributes of corporate entrepreneurship (team-orientation and learning capability).

Third, we restricted our study upon the two highlighted attributes of corporate entrepreneurship. This however may be a compelling reason for more scholarly work to find more useful attributes that may supersede the importance our suggested attributes. For example, we didn't study on the other three attributes (Pro-activeness, Aspirations, and Manager's dilemma) as suggested by Stopford & Baden-Fuller's (1994) work. Scholarly research must be attempted to understand its relation in the context of mergers and acquisitions, especially, how it influences strategic intents of acquirers during post-acquisition integration stage.

Like any study, our study also has certain limitations such, use of limited attributes and lack of dataset and statistical evidence on our propositions. However, we believe that these limitations are not erroneous considering the scope of our efforts to initiate the thought of linking two streams, namely, corporate entrepreneurship with merger and acquisition literature.

As a concluding note, we want scholars to follow up with an intriguing question. In the setting of post-acquisition stages, does corporate entrepreneurship attributes matter to the acquired firms only? Or, should the acquirers also attempt to initiate the corporate entrepreneurship culture within their acquisitions to bring out the value of their strategic acquisition intent? If so, under what external and internal structural situations, and at what cost and time-limits?

APPENDICES

Appendix table A-1: Overview of studies on "Inter-firm related determinants" of Divestiture decisions in chronological order (adapted from Brauer, 2006 and updated till 2015)

Studies (Year)	Applied Theory	Factors that trigger divestiture decisions (or, do not trigger)
Harrigan (1981); Harrigan (1982);	Industrial economics	• Degree of product differentiation, firms' strategic flexibility (such as internal transfers

Harrigan (1985)		between units), and industry fragmentation influence divestiture decisions
Hopkins (1991)	Industrial economics	• Low industry concentrations are not support as trigger for divestiture activity
Bergh & Lawless (1998)	Transaction cost economics	• Environmental uncertainty triggers divestiture • Firms with higher levels of diversification divest when environmental uncertainty increases and acquire when environmental uncertainty decreases. • However, firms with lower levels of diversification act in opposition
Ilmakunnas & Topi (1999)	Industrial economics; Population ecology	• Economies of scale are found to be weaker triggers for divestiture • Industry size is found not to affect divestiture rates • Industry growth is found to reduce the likelihood of divestiture
Chang & Singh (1999)	Industrial economics; Population ecology	• Acquired units are more likely to be sold off than internally developed units • Market share, business size, and industry attractiveness turned out as insignificant determinants for exit decisions • Having dissimilar market-specific resources in acquired business unit act as triggers for their divestiture • Having fewer firm-specific distinctive assets acts as trigger for divestiture of acquired units
Van Kranenburg, Palm, & Pfann (2002)	Macroeconomics	• Aggregate macroeconomic factors (real income) do not influence divestiture rates • Industry concentration is found to have a significant effect on divestiture rates
Brauer & Wiersema (2012)	Industrial economics	• Firm's position in an industry divestiture wave (i.e., imitating their industry peers) influence divestitures
Xia & L1 (2013)	Resource dependence theory	• Mutual dependence and increased subunit power reduce the likelihood of divestiture of inter-industry subunits of respective firms

Appendix table A-2: Overview of studies on "Intra-firm related determinants" of Divestiture decisions in chronological order (adapted from Brauer, 2006 and updated till 2015)

Studies (Year)	Applied Theory	Factors that trigger divestiture decisions (or, do not trigger)
Duhaime & Grant (1984)	Portfolio theory; Life-cycle theory	• Weak financial position of parent firm • Low competitive and financial strength of the target unit/firm against their industry peers • High interdependency of the target unit with

		other units • Low managerial attachment and the general economic cycle are not supported as trigger of divestiture decision
Montgomery & Thomas (1988)	Portfolio theory	• Low-performing firms • Parent firms may turn profitable after initial divestment but still under-perform when compared with similar non-divesting firms
Pashley & Philippatos (1990)	Life-cycle theory	• Strategic reasons depending on parent or target firm's life-cycle stage • Financial reasons different from divestitures (such as reduction in debt levels, increases in liquidity, and overall profitability)
Hoskisson & Johnson (1992)	Diversification perspective; resource-based view	• Restructuring (reduction of corporate scope) of mixed diversified firms (related-linked) leads to divestiture. After divestiture, firms adopt either a highly related (lean) or highly unrelated portfolio. R&D intensity and accounting performance increases as an after-effect
Markides (1992)	Portfolio theory	• High degree of diversification coupled with overall poor performance • An industry-wise attractive core business by profitability and size
Hamilton & Chow (1993)	Decision-making theory	• The triggers of divestiture (in priority order) are unprofitability, the focus on core activities, and the need to meet corporate requirements
Hoskisson, Johnson, & Moesel (1994)	Agency theory	• Higher block-holder equity supports divestiture intensity • Outside director equity do not support divestiture intensity • Both relative debt and the degree of diversification are found to be related triggers for divestiture intensity. • Higher accounting and market performance do not support (reduce) divestiture intensity
Bergh (1995)	Agency theory; Resource-based view	• Companies are more likely to sell unrelated and small units when owner influence is high. When ownership influence is lower, more related and larger units are sold. The post-sell-off performance of the parent is found to be negatively associated with the relatedness of the unit sold
Chang (1996)	Resource-based view; Evolutionary perspective	• Line of business characteristics (e.g., market share, resource profiles) are strong indicators for divestiture of business units. • Large firms are found not to divest not as often as smaller firms for similar performance parameters

		• Intent of higher profitability by divesting units with dissimilar human resource profiles
Bergh (1997)	Efficiency theory; Managerial perspective	• Motives, expectations, and initial conditions at the time of acquisition trigger acquisition-turned-divestiture • Business unit's relative smallness and unrelatedness (i.e., units that neither contribute significantly to cash flow nor reduce any variability in the acquirer's sales) are more likely to be divested • Unrelated acquired units that did not contribute significantly to the acquirer's financial synergies are more likely to be divested • Units (bought by an acquirer) with low diversity are most likely to be divested
Bergh (1998)	Information processing theory; Resource-based view	• Firms pursuing refocusing strategy coupled with increased environmental uncertainty trigger divestiture decisions • Firms following portfolio management strategy are less likely to divest
Chang & Singh (1999)	Industrial economics; Population ecology	• Acquired units are more likely to be sold off than internally developed units • Market share, business size, and industry attractiveness turned out as insignificant determinants for exit decisions • Having dissimilar market-specific resources in acquired business unit act as triggers for their divestiture • Having fewer firm-specific distinctive assets acts as trigger for divestiture of acquired units
Mata & Portugal (2000)	Portfolio theory	• Ownership and organizational structure are found to affect the likelihood of divestitures (but not closures) • Acquired firms for the purpose of market entry are more likely to divested than green-field entries that are more likely to closures
Zuckerman (2000)	Institutional theory; Agency theory	• Misalignment between the parent firm's corporate strategy and the acquired firm's attributed identity triggers divestiture • Inter-unit relatedness, past investments in a unit, and unit profitability holds up divestiture.
Sanders (2001)	Agency theory; Behavioral decision theory	• Firms with CEOs compensated with stock options (external CEOs) are more likely to consider divestitures than those with CEOs owning stock (internal CEOs)
Chatterjee, Harrison, & Bergh (2003)	Agency theory	• High ratio of inside director stock ownership than that of outside director increase the likelihood of divestiture

		• High business turbulence triggers divestitures
Sembenelli & Vannoni (2003)	Industrial economics; Population ecology	• Larger firms opt to divest their smaller units with marginal activities or insignificant market share as a corporate strategy to focus on their core businesses
Reuer & Shen (2004)	Transaction cost economics	• Geographically dispersed firms choose to sequentially divest (through IPO route) their units with significant intangible resources
Bushnell & Wolfram (2005)	Efficiency theory	• Ownership change triggers divestiture as new owners create different incentives and performance considerations
Hayward & Shimizu (2006)	Mental accounting theory (Behavioral finance)	• CEO's de-commit to poorly performing acquisitions trigger divestiture.
Lee & Madhavan (2010)	Meta-analysis	• Firm's performance measure, transaction format, transaction intent, and resource level are found to be the key indicators of divestiture decisions
Bergh & Sharp (2015)	Agency theory	• Outside block-holders pressure triggers divestiture decision • Spin-offs is preferred when divesting unit size is larger, while sell-offs is selected when divesting unit size is small or the outside block-holding percentage is less • Spin-offs allow block-holders to decide whether to hold or sell their interests in the divested firm based on their individual portfolio risks. On the other hand, sell-offs of small units is used to preserve organizational diversity and enhance liquidity to help the divesting firm's managers pursue their self-interests.

REFERENCES

Andrews, K. R. (1997). 5 The Concept of Corporate Strategy. *Resources, firms, and strategies: a reader in the resource-based perspective*, 52.

Ansoff, H. I. (1965). *Corporate strategy: business policy for growth and expansion*. McGraw-Hill Book

Argyris, C., & Schon, D. (1995). Organizational learning: A theory of action perspective, 1978. *Massachusetts: Addison-Wesley Publishing Company.*

Bantel, K. A., & Jackson, S. E. (1989). Top management and innovations in banking: Does the composition of the top team make a difference?. *Strategic Management Journal*, *10*(S1), 107-124.

Barney, J. (1991). Firm resources and sustained competitive advantage.*Journal of management*, *17*(1), 99-120.

Barrett, H., & Weinstein, A. (1998). The effect of market orientation and organizational flexibility on corporate entrepreneurship. *Entrepreneurship: Theory and Practice*, *23*(1), 57-58.

Bergh, D. 1995. Size and relatedness of units sold: An agency theory and resource-based perspective. *Strategic Management Journal*, 16: 221-239.

Bergh, D. 1997. Predicting divestiture of unrelated acquisitions: An integrative model of ex ante conditions. *Strategic Management Journal*, 18(9): 715-731.

Bergh, D. 1998. Product-market uncertainty, portfolio restructuring, and performance: An information-processing and resource-based view. *Journal of Management*, 24(2): 135-155.

Bergh, D., & Lawless, M. 1998. Portfolio restructuring and limits to hierarchical governance: The effects of environmental uncertainty and diversification strategy. *Organization Science*, 9(1): 87-102.

Burns, T., & Stalker, G. M. (1962). The Management of Innovation (London: Tavistock, 1961). *BurnsThe Management of Innovation1961*.

Bushnell, J. B., & Wolfram, C. (2005). Ownership change, incentives and plant efficiency: The divestiture of US electric generation plants. *Center for the Study of Energy Markets*.

Brauer, M. (2006). What have we acquired and what should we acquire in divestiture research? A review and research agenda. *Journal of Management*, *32*(6), 751-785.

Brauer, M. F., & Wiersema, M. F. (2012). Industry divestiture waves: How a firm's position influences investor returns. *Academy of Management Journal*,*55*(6), 1472-1492.

Chang, S. J. 1996. An evolutionary perspective on diversification and corporate restructuring: Entry, exit, and economic performance during 1981-1989. *Strategic Management Journal*, 17: 587-611.

Chang, S. J., & Singh, H. (1999). The impact of modes of entry and resource fit on modes of exit by multibusiness firms. *Strategic Management Journal*, *20*(11), 1019-1035.

Chatterjee, S., Harrison, J. S., & Bergh, D. D. (2003). Failed takeover attempts, corporate governance and refocusing. *Strategic Management Journal*, *24*(1), 87-96.

Coff, R. W. (2002). Human capital, shared expertise, and the likelihood of impasse in corporate acquisitions. *Journal of Management*, *28*(1), 107-128.

Converse, S. (1993). Shared mental models in expert team decision making. *Individual and group decision making: Current*, (1993), 221.

Covin, J. G., & Miles, M. P. (1999). Corporate entrepreneurship and the pursuit of competitive advantage. *Entrepreneurship: Theory and practice*,*23*(3), 47-47.

Dess, G. G., Ireland, R. D., Zahra, S. A., Floyd, S. W., Janney, J. J., & Lane, P. J. (2003). Emerging issues in corporate entrepreneurship. *Journal of management*, *29*(3), 351-378.

Duhaime, I. M., & Grant, J. H. (1984). Factors influencing divestment decision-making: Evidence from a field study. *Strategic Management Journal*, *5*(4), 301-318.

Ericsson News Center (2005). http://www.ericsson.com/news/1017515

Ericsson Publications (2015). http://www.ericsson.com/thecompany/our_publications/reference-stories-a-z

Floyd, S. W., & Wooldridge, B. (1999). Knowledge creation and social networks in corporate entrepreneurship: The renewal of organizational capability. *Entrepreneurship: Theory and Practice*, *23*(3), 123-123.

Grant, R. M. (1996). Toward a knowledge-based theory of the firm. *Strategic management journal*, *17*(S2), 109-122.

Guth, W. D., & Ginsberg, A. (1990). Guest editors' introduction: Corporate entrepreneurship. *Strategic management journal*, *11*(4), 5-15.

Hamel, G., Doz, Y. L., & Prahalad, C. K. (1989). Collaborate with your competitors and win. *Harvard business review*, *67*(1), 133-139.

Hampden-Turner, C. (1990). *Charting the corporate mind: graphic solutions to business conflicts*. The Free Press.

Hamilton, R. T., & Chow, Y. K. (1993). Why managers divest-Evidence from New Zealand's largest companies. *Strategic Management Journal*, *14*(6), 479.

Harrigan, K. R. 1981. Deterrents to divestiture. *Academy of Management Journal*, 24: 306-323.

Harrigan, K. R. 1982. Exit decisions in mature industries. *Academy of Management Journal*, 25(4): 707-732.

Harrigan, K. R. 1985. Exit barriers and vertical integration. *Academy of Management Journal*, 28: 686-697.

Hayward, M. L., & Shimizu, K. (2006). De-commitment to losing strategic action: evidence from the divestiture of poorly performing acquisitions.*Strategic Management Journal*, *27*(6), 541-557.

Hoskisson, R., & Hitt, M. 1994. *Downscoping: How to tame the diversified firm*. New York: Oxford University Press.

Hopkins, D. 1991. Acquisition and divestiture as a response to competitive position and market structure. *Journal of Management Studies*, 28(6): 665-677.

Hoskisson, R. O., & Johnson, R. A. (1992). Research notes and communications corporate restructuring and strategic change: The effect on diversification strategy and R & D intensity. *Strategic Management Journal*,*13*(8), 625-634.

Hoskisson, R. E., Johnson, R. A., & Moesel, D. D. (1994). Corporate divestiture intensity in restructuring firms: Effects of governance, strategy, and performance. *Academy of Management journal*, *37*(5), 1207-1251.

Hoskisson, R. E., Johnson, R. A., Tihanyi, L., & White, R. E. (2005). Diversified business groups and corporate refocusing in emerging economies. *Journal of Management*, *31*(6), 941-965.

HP Press (2010). http://www8.hp.com/us/en/hp-news/press-release.html?id=416441#.VurnOelrK70

Huber, G. P. (1991). Organizational learning: The contributing processes and the literatures. *Organization science*, *2*(1), 88-115.

Hirst, Giles, Daan Van Knippenberg, and Jing Zhou. "A cross-level perspective on employee creativity: Goal orientation, team learning behavior, and individual creativity." *Academy of Management Journal* 52.2 (2009): 280-293.

Hitt, M.A., & Ireland, R.D. (2002). The essence of strategic leadership: Managing human and social capital. *Journal of Leadership & Organizational Studies*, *9*(1), 3-14.

Ilmakunnas, P., & Topi, J. (1999). Microeconomic and macroeconomic influences on entry and exit of firms. *Review of Industrial Organization*, *15*(3), 283-301.
Ireland, R. D., Hitt, M. A., Camp, S. M., & Sexton, D. L. (2001). Integrating entrepreneurship and strategic management actions to create firm wealth.*The Academy of Management Executive*, *15*(1), 49-63.

Ireland, R. D., Hitt, M. A., & Vaidyanath, D. (2002). Alliance management as a source of competitive advantage. *Journal of management*, *28*(3), 413-446.

Janis, I. L. (1982). *Groupthink: Psychological studies of policy decisions and fiascoes* (Vol. 349). Boston: Houghton Mifflin.

Jones, G. R., & George, J. M. (1998). The experience and evolution of trust: Implications for cooperation and teamwork. *Academy of management review*, *23*(3), 531-546.

Kohers, N., & Kohers, T. (2001). Takeovers of technology firms: Expectations vs. reality. *Financial management*, 35-54.

Kuratko, D. F., Ireland, R. D., & Hornsby, J. S. (2001). The power of entrepreneurial outcomes: Insights from Acordia. *Academy of Management Executive*, *15*(4), 60-71.

Lee, D., & Madhavan, R. (2010). Divestiture and firm performance: A meta-analysis. *Journal of Management*, *36*(6), 1345-1371.

Lumpkin, G. T., & Dess, G. G. (1996). Clarifying the entrepreneurial orientation construct and linking it to performance. *Academy of management Review*, *21*(1), 135-172.

March, J. G. (1991). Exploration and exploitation in organizational learning. *Organization science*, *2*(1), 71-87.

Markides, C. C. (1992). Consequences of corporate refocusing: Ex ante evidence. *Academy of Management Journal*, 35(2), 398–412.

Mata, J., & Portugal, P. (2000). Closure and divestiture by foreign entrants: The impact of entry and post-entry strategies. *Strategic Management Journal*, *21*(5), 549-562.

Montgomery, C. A., & Thomas, A. R. (1988). Divestment: Motives and gains. *Strategic Management Journal*, *9*(1), 93-97.

Moss Kanter, R. (1983). The change masters. *New York [etc.]: Simon & Schuster Moss.*

Miller, D., & Friesen, P. H. (1978). Archetypes of strategy formulation.*Management science*, *24*(9), 921-933.

Mintzberg, H. (1973). Strategy-making in three modes. *California management review*, *16*(2), 44-53.

Naman, J. L., & Slevin, D. P. (1993). Entrepreneurship and the concept of fit: A model and empirical tests. *Strategic management journal*, *14*(2), 137-153.

Nonaka, I., Toyama, R., & Konno, N. (2000). SECI, Ba and leadership: a unified model of dynamic knowledge creation. *Long range planning*, *33*(1), 5-34.

Pashley, M. M., & Philippatos, G. C. (1990). Voluntary divestitures and corporate life-cycle: some empirical evidence. *Applied Economics*, *22*(9), 1181-1196.

Reuer, J. J., & Shen, J. C. (2004). Sequential divestiture through initial public offerings. *Journal of Economic Behavior & Organization*, *54*(2), 249-266.

Sanders, W. G. (2001). Behavioral responses of CEOs to stock ownership and stock option pay. *Academy of Management journal*, *44*(3), 477-492.

Sathe, V. (1985). *Culture and related corporate realities: Text, cases, and readings on organizational entry, establishment, and change*. Richard D Irwin.

Schein, E. H. (1985). Defining organizational culture. *Classics of organization theory*, *3*, 490-502.

Starr, J. A., & MacMillan, I. C. (1990). Resource cooptation via social contracting: Resource acquisition strategies for new ventures. *Strategic Management Journal*, *11*(4), 79-92.

Sembenelli, A., & Vannoni, D. 2003. Why do established firms enter some industries and exit others? Empirical evidence
on Italian business groups. *Review of Industrial Organization*, 17: 441-456.

Schollhammer, Hans (1982): "Internal Corporate Entrepreneurship", In C. Kent, D. Sexton and K. Vesper (eds.), Encyclopaedia of Entrepreneurship, Prentice Hall, Englewood Clipp, NJ.

Stevenson, H. H. and D. Gumpert (1985). 'The heart of entrepreneurship', *Harvard Business Review*, 85, pp. 85- 94

Stevenson, H. H. and J. C. Jarillo (1990). 'A paradigm of entrepreneurship: Entrepreneurial management', *Strategic Management Journal*, 11, pp. 17-27.

Stopford, J. M., & Baden-Fuller, C. W. (1994). Creating corporate entrepreneurship. *Strategic management journal*, 15(7), 521-536.

Sudarsanam, S. (2003). *Creating value from mergers and acquisitions: The challenges: An integrated and international perspective*. Pearson Education.

TechCrunch (2014). https://techcrunch.com/2014/01/29/google-keeps-vast-majority-of-motorola-mobility-patents-in-sale-to-lenovo

The Verge (2012). http://www.theverge.com/2012/6/5/3062611/palm-webos-hp-inside-story-pre-postmortem

Thompson, J. D. 1960 "Organizational management of conflict." Administrative Science Quarterly, 4: 389- 409.

Thomson, N., & McNamara, P. (2001). Achieving post-acquisition success: the role of corporate entrepreneurship. *Long Range Planning*, *34*(6), 669-697.

Van Kranenburg, H. L., Palm, F. C., & Pfann, G. A. 2002. Exit and survival in a concentrating industry: The case of daily newspapers in the Netherlands. *Review of Industrial Organization*, 21: 283-303.

Vesper, K. H. (1984). *Entrepreneurship: A new direction, or just a new label?*. Division of Research, Harvard Business School.

Weber, Y., Tarba, S. Y., & Reichel, A. (2009). International mergers and acquisitions performance revisited–the role of cultural distance and post. *Advances in mergers and acquisitions*, *8*, 1-17.

Xia, J., & Li, S. (2013). The divestiture of acquired subunits: a resource dependence approach. *Strategic Management Journal*, *34*(2), 131-148.

Zahra, S. A., Nielsen, A. P., & Bogner, W. C. (1999). Corporate entrepreneurship, knowledge, and competence development.*Entrepreneurship: Theory and Practice*, *23*(3), 169-169.

Zahra, S. A., & Covin, J. G. (1995). Contextual influences on the corporate entrepreneurship-performance relationship: A longitudinal analysis. *Journal of business venturing*, *10*(1), 43-58.

Zahra, S. A., Nielsen, A. P., & Bogner, W. C. (1998). Corporate entrepreneurship, knowledge, and competence development. *AUBret*.

Zuckerman, E. W. (2000). Focusing the corporate product: Securities analysts and de-diversification. *Administrative Science Quarterly*, *45*(3), 591-619.

DECISION SCIENCES INSTITUTE

CONSUMER SELF-CONFIDENCE WITH MOBILE COMMERCE

Sung-Hee Park
University of South Carolina
Email: sunny.park@moore.sc.edu

Soohoon Park
University of South Carolina
Email: soohoon.park@moore.sc.edu

Jeffery Smith
Florida State University
Email: jssmith@cob.fsu.edu

Kwanghyun Kim
Korea national University of Transportation
Email: khkim@ut.ac.kr

ABSTRACT

IS researchers and practitioners want to improve consumer acceptance of mobile commerce (MC) as MC can potentially enable new business models and provide tremendous power to marketers with its much broader reach. While consumers' individual differences have been frequently cited as important constructs in marketing much of the IS research has mainly focused on examining the technological aspects of MC systems. Recognizing the need to improve existing IS measures for individual differences in consumer acceptance of MC, this study adapts Consumer Self-Confidence (CSC) from marketing. Results demonstrate the validities of the measures and the role of CSC as a moderator.

KEYWORDS: Consumer self-confidence, Mobile commerce, Acceptance model, MGSEM

INTRODUCTION

Mobile commerce (MC), the use of mobile communication technologies between transacting partners for service initiation, agreement, or fulfillment from any location, has already taken off (Pousttchi et al., 2015). MC is the fastest growing form of electronic commerce (eMarketer, 2013) and it will make up 45 percent of total electronic commerce (i.e., $284 billion) in sales by 2020 (BI Intelligence, 2016). We can easily find its emerging relevance to our daily life. MC provides a broad range of services including buying a coffee at a café by scanning a mobile wallet, downloading digital music to a smartphone wirelessly, depositing checks into mobile bank accounts, and paying bills on mobile trading portals.

Due to the natures of mobile devices, wireless technologies, and location-based applications, MC can provide consumers many benefits, such as efficiency, spontaneousness, and ease of use (Anckar & D'Incau, 2002). From a marketer's perspective, MC can potentially enable a new business model because mobile devices can capture what consumers do in every second and also can control in very sophisticated way which marketing messages consumers are exposed to. MC also provides tremendous power to marketers because mobile devices have a much broader reach in terms of possible customers.

Consequently, using MC systems such as B2C applications and services is mutually beneficial to both consumers and marketers. However, actual acceptance of MC systems from consumers' side has not been satisfactory, especially considering how much efforts had been put to implement MC systems from the marketers' perspective. According to a Shop.org study, majority (i.e., 56%) of online retailers reported that mobile apps would not play a major part in their mobile strategy due to the low acceptance rate of their mobile apps (Forrester Research, 2015). It is not only difficult to motivate consumers to download marketers' apps but also problematical to ensure that consumers continue using apps until they fully adopt because consumers aren't shy about deleting apps they don't use regularly.

The gap between the marketers' efforts in implementing MC systems and the consumers' actual acceptance of MC systems implies there is a great need for us to research why many consumers have demonstrated reluctant behaviors in acceptance of MC systems while focusing more on consumers' individual dispositional differences. It is because explaining human behavior could not be completed without explanation of individual dispositional differences such as consumer self-confidence (Ajzen, 1988). However, much of the extant IS research regarding consumer acceptance of MC has mainly focused on examining the technological aspects of MC system that potentially enable and inhibit the utilization of MC systems. According to an extensive review of the MC literature (a total of 1,613 papers from 2002 through 2013), the vast majority of empirical research cover customer acceptance issues while focusing on technical aspects (e.g., perceived usefulness) of specific B2C applications.

Recognizing the need to improve existing IS measures for individual differences in consumer acceptance of MC, this study adapts the consumer self-confidence (CSC) measure by Bearden et al. (2001) from marketing. CSC, which reflects subjective evaluations of one's ability to generate positive experiences as a consumer in the marketplace (Adelman, 1987) , could be critical in consumers' acceptance of MC because consumer self-confidence is key to understand consumer behaviors on mobile marketplace where emerging technologies are altering traditional consumer behavior frameworks. For example, under the traditional consumer behavior frameworks, consumers with high self-confidence could show less external information search activities because consumers with high self-confidence are thought to be more confident of their own judgments and consequently less influenced by external information (Wood and Stagner, 1994). Under MC, however, consumers, who constantly access external information from their mobile devices, might show different information search activities to solve immediate buying problems.

The objective of this article is twofold. First, we looks to the marketing field where extensive research has focused on individual differences and consumer behaviors. A measurement of CSC is adapted to the MC context along with refinement and validation of scales to measure the various dimensions that underlie consumer self-confidence in MC context. Second, we offer a description of a technology acceptance model as a nomological network in which CSC is embedded. We attempt to understand the role of CSC on the nomological network.

The remainder of the paper is organized as follows: first, in the literature review section, we discuss CSC concept in consumer behaviors and CSC related constructs with CSC measures development. Then, in the methodology section, our research model are presented followed by discussions of sample data descriptions. In the analyses and results section, a series of analyses are presented to demonstrate the reliability and validities of the measures and then to test the role of CSC as a moderator, which moderate relationships among other important factors in the nomological network of consumer acceptance of MC. Concluding remarks are made in the final section.

LITERATURE REVIEW

Understanding consumer behavior is critical to marketers. Many factors, including demographics and prior product class experience, have been studied in an attempt to understand consumer behaviors. Among the factors, consumer self-confidence has been considered a crucial element to understanding consumer behaviors (Bearden et al, 2001).

The advantages of using MC systems to consumers are well known including efficiency, convenience, broader selections, competitive pricing, rich information, and diversity (Wu and Wang, 2004). However, due to the natures of MC, consumers are also faced with new challenges at the same time, which range extend from personalized location-based marketing messages to targeted threats of mobile devices' security breach. The former could cause severity of information overload and interruptions of decision making to consumers. The latter could lead identity theft and severe financial losses. MC is changing the way consumers gather, process, and interact with information. Consequently, consumers often feel less-confident with to their decisions and behaviors on mobile marketplace.

Thus, we look to marketing literature if CSC has been used to improve our understanding why consumers with high-confidence behave different in MC context than consumers with low-confidence. CSC in the consumer behavior research has been used as a distinguishing characteristic of market-segment profiles (Darden and Ashton, 1974). Marketing managers, who would like to utilize these incredible expansion opportunities and need to know how to keep a diffident and picky customer with substantial discretion (it is generally much easier for mobile consumers to find alternatives on their mobile devices than for regular customers to go to the next stores physically in traditional marketplace) in their mobile marketplace, want to know how consumer self-confidences are different among consumers on mobile marketplace

Consumer Self-Confidence

Researchers have defined CSC 1) as the extent to which an individual feels capable and assured with respect to his or her marketplace decisions and behaviors, and 2) as a relatively stable self-appraisal that is assumed to be readily accessible to the individual because of the pervasiveness of consumer activity in everyday life (Bearden et al, 2001).

Although there are slight disagreements among the definitions, consumer behavior studies seem to agree upon that CSC is a trait as an individual difference, but it is derived from more basic traits. Basic traits and CSC are different since a trait is seen more from other person's viewpoint (e.g., psychologist's observation) while CSC are formulated from an internal standpoint. Each trait should be conceptualized as a facet of a person. So, it is difficult to see as a combined system. In the other hand, CSC is viewed as a multifaceted disposition (Adelman, 1987). Moreover, while basic traits (e.g., self-esteem, perceived control, and dominance) are more global and central dispositions, which are enduring across-situational individual differences, CSC is considered as a secondary disposition that is more closely related to consumer phenomena. In other words, CSC represents product- or situation-specific confidence (Bearden et al, 2001).

Bearden et al (2001) argued that CSC results not only from more basic traits but also from the collection of the individual's prior marketplace experiences. They called this type of CSC (from the collection of the individual's prior marketplace experiences) as general CSC. General CSC could differentiate individuals within product-decision categories and purchase experiences. Consequently, general CSC could predict individual tendencies across product- or situation-specific conditions. And, even in instances where the level of product- or situation-specific confidence may be low for most consumers, general consumer self-confidence will still vary across individuals.

Gerbing, Hamilton, and Freeman (1994) also conceptualized CSC as a multidimensional concept consisting initially of two higher-order factors. The two higher-order factors are CSC (1) to make effective decisions; and (2) to protect himself or herself from marketing tactics. These two higher-order factors are also consistent with the most frequently studied roles of consumer self-confidence in the consumer behavior and marketing literature. For example, Park et al. (1994) and Wright (1975) propose that CSC operates as ah antecedent to marketplace choices and subjective knowledge perceptions. Likewise, Luce (1994) and others relate self-confidence to the individual's ability to protect himself or herself from harm under emotional strain and to resist persuasive attempts emanating from others in the marketplace.

Constructs Related to Consumer Self-Confidence

Computer Self-Efficacy: From the IS perspective, using mobile devices to buy a product or service by itself is an effort involving operating mobile technology. So the mobile consumer's computer self-efficacy might be an important factor. The construct self-efficacy from the psychology literature in general, and computer self-efficacy (Compeau and Higgins, 1995) in particular may explain the mobile consumer's intension and behavior. Generally, self-efficacy is assumed to represent the evaluative component of one's self- evaluation of one's abilities and performance in the marketplace. In general, high self-efficacy should enhance consumer self-confidence, and thus self-efficacy scales should have a modest, positive relationship with measures of consumer self-confidence.

The construct computer self-efficacy (CSE) denotes people's overall judgment of their abilities of operating computers for different tasks (Compeau and Higgins, 1995; Marakas et al, 1998). CSE has been examined as an antecedent for dependent variables such as computer performance and outcome expectation. Some factors that affect CSE include task complexity, personal innovativeness in IT, computer anxiety, and prior experience. CSE has been investigated for its effect on computer training and education (Gallivan et al, 2005). CSE is also studied as a factor in an integrated theoretical model to forecast whether users will continue using World Wide Web (Hsu et al, 2004). In the context of online electronic service, Internet self-efficacy has been examined for its impact on user acceptance (Hsu and Chiu, 2004a). Integrated with a decomposed theory of planned behavior, another study evaluates the role of CSE for predicting users' continued usage of electronic service (Hsu and Chiu, 2004b).

E-Commerce consumers have duo roles of both shoppers and information technology users (Cho and Park,2001). Therefore, we argue that computer self-efficacy affects mobile consumers' online purchase intention and behavior. In the E-Commerce context, previous research found constructs similar to Internet self-efficacy play important roles. For example, general web apprehensiveness is negatively correlated with the amount of time spent online (Susskind, 2004). Moreover, comfort level with the web has a positive correlation with Internet shopping tendency (Mauldin and Arunachalam, 2002).

One factor closely related to the Internet self-efficacy construct is users' web experiences. Internet users' web experiences affect their trust in E-Commerce (Corbitt et al., 2003) Compared to the traditional shopping experience at physical stores, online shopping experience is more complex (Constantinides, 2004). Online shopping process involves various tasks such as browsing, searching, selecting, comparing and evaluating information (Constantinides, 2004). Thus, mobile consumers with different levels of technology experiences may exhibit different patterns of behavior.

Perceived Risks: In the recent years, as the Mobile Technology becomes easier to use and broadband Internet is more readily accessible, many individuals and businesses move their transactions on mobile devices. The past decade witnessed the tremendous development of Internet and mobile technology, the steady growth of e-commerce and mobile-commerce adoption, and the creation of various innovative business models exploiting the potentials of this technology advancement. Online consumer behavior and e-commerce adoption became important research topics. Technology acceptance model (Davis, 1989) has been applied to the E-Commerce context.

To predict the intention to purchase physical item online, the perceived benefits and perceived risks were found to be significant factors (Cha, 2011). In a study examining the antecedents of the amount spent online, both the consumers experience with online shopping and the comfort level of providing personal information online (privacy concern) were found significant (Spake et al., 2011). However, surprisingly privacy concerns were not significant in predicting online spending (Spake et al., 2011). In another study investigating expert household end users' online behavior, the privacy-active behavior was found not significant in increasing the likelihood of online purchase or subscription (Drennan et al., 2006). However, perceived online risk did have a significantly negative impact (Drennan et al., 2006). In another empirical study, in addition to perceived risk, computer self-efficacy and personal innovativeness were found as significant predictors for the intension to shopping online (Boyle and Ruppel, 2004).

Consumer Knowledge: Alba and Hutchinson (1987) define consumer knowledge as having two major components: familiarity and expertise. Familiarity, in this case, is the number of product-related experiences that have been accumulated by the consumer. Expertise is defined as the ability to perform product-related tasks successfully. They also identify five dimensions of expertise: (1) automaticity that reduces the cognitive effort; (2) the cognitive structure categorization, used to differentiate products, becomes richer, more complete, and more accurate; (3) the ability to analyze information by separating the important and relevant from unimportant and irrelevant; (4) the ability to elaborate and make accurate inferences from limited information; (5) the ability to remember product information (memory).

Consumer expertise represents the individual's ability to perform product-related tasks successfully (Wood and Stagner, 1994). Product expertise includes both the cognitive structure and the processes required to effectively use product information and beliefs stored in memory. As such, expertise, which typically increases as product-related experiences accumulate, reflects product-specific issues (Wood and Stagner, 1994).

Consumer Self-Confidence Measure Development

Researchers have been developed and validated measures to assess consumer self-confidence. Preeminent in this stream of research is the work in marketing of Bearden et al (2001). While empirically establishing a measure of consumer self-confidence, Bearden et al (2001) found that the two-factor higher-order model and the six-factor correlated model provided the best fit to the data when compared with the other models investigated. The two higher-order constructs are Decision-Making Self-Confidence and Protection. The six-dimensions are:

- Information Acquisition (IA): consumer confidence in his or her ability to obtain needed marketplace information
- Consideration-Set Formation (CSF): consumer confidence in one's ability to identify acceptable choice alternatives, including products, brands, and shopping venues.
- Personal Outcomes (PO): consumer confidence in one's ability to meet purchase objectives such that choices are personally satisfying
- Social Outcomes (SO): consumer confidence in one's ability to meet purchase objectives such that choices generate positive outcomes in the form of the reactions of others
- Persuasion Knowledge (PK): consumer confidence in his or her knowledge regarding the tactics used by marketers in efforts to persuade consumers
- Marketplace Interfaces (MI): consumer confidence in the ability to stand up for one's rights and to express one's opinion when dealing with others in the marketplace

Bearden et al (2001) initially identified seven conceptual dimensions (six dimensions above + Information Processing dimension) but Information Processing factor and its items cross-loaded with the IA items and CSF items. The model was revised and then resulted in six factors. The final set of confidence items is depicted in Appendix A along with their dimension labels and factor loadings from Bearden et al (2001)'s Study 3.

METHODOLOGY

The research model is shown in Figure 1. The phenomenon of interest that we intend to investigate is the role of CSC in consumer acceptance of MC system. Instead of developing a new model, we adapted a pre-validated model from Smith et al. (2014) paper. Smith et al. (2014) developed a RFID adoption model based on Regulatory Focus Theory (RFT) by Higgins (1997). RFT centers on two self-regulation mechanisms toward a desired end state, namely promotion and prevention focus. Promotion focus is centered on the premise that individuals possess an orientation where the end goal is attained through positive mechanisms. In contrast, prevention focus centers on the need to minimize the potential negatives associated with a decision. In the conceptualization of their model, Smith et al. (2014) plugged perceived usefulness and perceived ease of use from the technology acceptance literature into a promotion focus as the variables, which are presented in a positive fashion while adopting trust and privacy concern constructs from IS research, which are associated with potential negatives, and in turns represent the prevention focus.

The research model proposes that individual attitudes toward the technology and subsequent behavioral intentions to accept MC systems can originate from a motivation toward finding more effective and/or efficient ways to move through business processes. Namely, the promotion focused path will lead individuals to pursue positive aspects such as efficiency, convenience, and broader selections. Perceived usefulness and perceived ease of use are two salient technological characteristics which are conceptualized as consumers' evaluations and as the main antecedents to consumers' attitude toward MC systems. Perceived usefulness and attitude, in turn, can contribute towards IS acceptance outcomes such as behavioral intentions.

Prevention focused path will follow a similar logic with the promotion focused path while it is expected to be governed by the personal safety and security concerns. The research model posits that the attitude toward MC systems will be significantly impacted by both the concern for privacy and the trust that an organization will act in a responsible manner regarding the utilization of the capabilities of the MC system. We also believe that the effect of trust on attitude will be mediated by privacy concern in that the higher the trust component, the lower the concern. Thus, we offer the following hypotheses collectively, which address our two paths (promotion-seeking and prevention-seeking) research model.

- H1: Perceived ease of use will positively affect perceived usefulness of MC systems
- H2: Perceived ease of use will positively affect attitude toward MC systems
- H3: Perceived usefulness will positively affect attitude toward MC systems
- H4: Organizational trust will negatively affect concerns for privacy in using MC systems
- H5: Organizational trust will positively affect attitude toward MC systems
- H6: Concerns for privacy will negatively affect attitude toward MC systems
- H7: Perceived usefulness will positively affect intentions to use MC systems
- H8: Attitude toward MC systems will positively affect intentions to use MC systems
- H9: Privacy concerns will negatively affect intentions to use MC systems

The general research model depicted in Figure 1 also argues that the moderating roles of CSC on the relationship between perceived technological characteristics and the consumer's attitude, as well as on the relationships between the consumer's attitude and the MC acceptance outcomes. Thus, CSC moderate all of the paths in our research model. In Figure 1, the moderating roles of CSC are depicted as dotted lines. Collectively, we offer the following hypotheses.

- H10: CSC will moderate the relationships posited in Figure 1, thereby suggesting that the positive relationships among technological characteristics, mediating evaluation variables, and acceptance outcomes will be different between the low in CSC group and the high in CSC group

This research employs survey methodology. The survey that this research uses is shown in Appendix B. In terms of measures, we adapted scales on CSC (Bearden et al. 2001), perceived usefulness and ease of use (Davis 1989), attitude toward the technology (Taylor and Todd 1995), organizational trust (Malhotra et al. 2004), and privacy concerns (Lwin et al. 2007). We used the procedures recommended by Ajzen and Fishbein (1980) and Ajzen (1991) to generate a scale to assess the intentions to use MC systems.

The data were collected using a standard survey administration technique (Dillman 1978) while incorporating practices that have been noted as being beneficial to increasing the effective response rate. The decision to collect the data through a web-based survey was taken after an extensive discussion with a panel of experienced mobile consumers. A web survey was administered to 1000 potential respondents via an email link with 246 being returned (24.6% response rate). Characteristics of the subjects are reported in Table 1.

Figure 1. Research Model

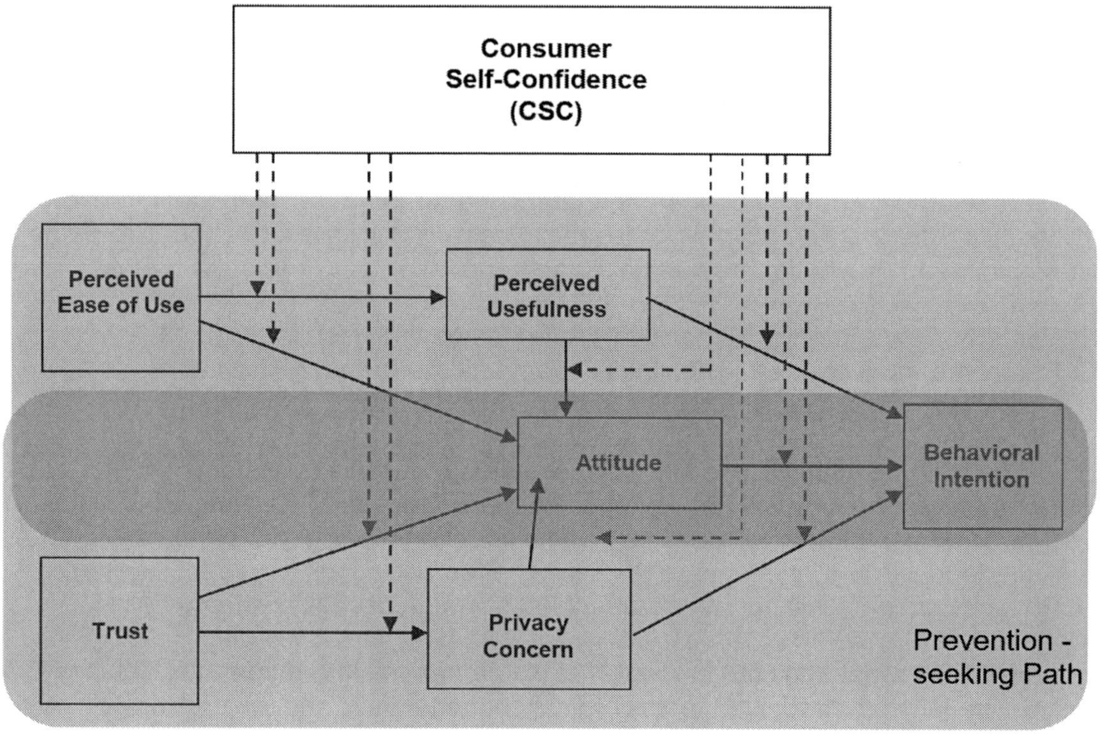

Table 1. Respondent Profiles

Metric	Number	Percentage
Gender		
Male	117	47.6%
Female	129	52.4%
Education		
No High School Diploma	4	1.6%
High School Diploma	113	45.9%
Associate's Degree	14	5.7%
Bachelor's Degree	82	33.3%
Master's Degree	7	2.8%
Professional or Doctorate Degree	25	10.2%
Not Answer	1	0.4%
Age (years)	36.7	
Work Experience (years)	12.9	
Mobile Device Usage (hour / week)	27.4	
Mobile Device Usage frequency (time(s) / week)	8.6	

ANALYSES AND RESULTS

As all constructs were modified from existing scales, the psychometric properties were analyzed through two confirmatory factor analyses (CFA) followed by the estimation of the associated structural model (Anderson and Gerbing 1988). The first CFA was performed to analyze CSC as a second-order construct. Six first-order constructs are introduced for CSC: information acquisition (IA), consideration-set formation (CSF), personal outcomes (PO), social outcomes (SO), persuasion knowledge (PK), and marketplace interfaces (MI). Among the CSC items adapted from Bearden et al. (2001), reverse coding is performed for PO and MI items because they are asked negatively. As we perform the second order CFA, the composite scores of CSC constructs are calculated (see Table 2). The results from the Second Order CFA indicate that the model fits well as observed by the fit indices, $\chi 2$ = 521.78 (d.f. = 246), Tucker-Lewis index (TLI) = 0.93, Comparative Fit index (CFI) = 0.92, Root Mean Square Error of Approximation (RMSEA) = 0.07, Standardized Root Mean Square Residual (SRMR) = 0.08.

Evidence of discriminant validity was also provided from the composite scores of CSC constructs and computer self-efficacy (CSE) (Fornell and Larcker 1981). Evidence of discriminant validity occurs when AVE in the Table 2 exceed the square of the correlation between the six factors of CSC and CSE making up each pair except correlation between IA and CSE.

Table 2. Construct Reliability of Consumer Self-Confidence

	IA	CSF	PO	SO	PK	MI	MCSE	Composite Reliability
IA	**0.73**	0.62	0.16	0.29	0.44	0.02	0.39	0.92
CSF	0.79	**0.65**	0.13	0.23	0.54	0.03	0.30	0.90
PO	0.40	0.36	**0.55**	0.01	0.08	0.19	0.02	0.83
SO	0.54	0.48	0.09	**0.69**	0.20	0.00	0.29	0.90
PK	0.66	0.73	0.29	0.45	**0.66**	0.02	0.29	0.89
MI	0.15	0.16	0.44	-0.04	0.13	**0.58**	0.01	0.80
CSE	0.63	0.54	0.16	0.54	0.54	-0.08	**0.63**	0.87

Note. Items in boldface on the diagonal are the average variance extracted (AVE) figures, the lower left triangle contains the construct correlations, and the upper right triangle contains the shared variance between constructs.

The second CFA was performed to assess the measurement model with all other constructs. The results from the CFA report that the data fit the model well as witnessed by the relevant statistics, $\chi 2$ = 484.5 (d.f. = 231), Tucker-Lewis index (TLI) = 0.94, Comparative Fit index (CFI) = 0.95, Root Mean Square Error of Approximation (RMSEA) = 0.07, Standardized Root Mean Square Residual (SRMR) = 0.05. Composite reliability (CR) measures for reliability (Fornell and Larcker, 1981). Minimum value of CR is 0.78. All of values exceed the recommended cutoff, 0.70 (Nunnally, 1978). Convergent validity is evaluated via the CFA results where the average variance extracted (AVE) is calculated and compared to the standard criteria of 0.5 (Fornell and Larcker, 1981). Minimum value of AVE is 0.57, thus convergent validity is assured. Note that two square of the correlations (i.e., ATT-INT and PRIVACY-RISK) exceed AVEs in the Table 3.

Table 3. Construct Reliability of Measurement Model

	PU	PES	ATT	INT	PRIVACY	RISK	TRUST	Composite Reliability
PU	**0.79**	0.45	0.56	0.49	0.06	0.01	0.09	0.92
PES	0.67	**0.75**	0.63	0.56	0.05	0.00	0.07	0.92
ATT	0.75	0.80	**0.69**	0.70	0.04	0.00	0.19	0.90
INT	0.70	0.75	0.84	**0.87**	0.01	0.00	0.11	0.95
PRIVACY	0.25	0.23	0.19	0.10	**0.57**	0.63	0.00	0.80
RISK	0.12	0.06	0.02	-0.03	0.79	**0.66**	0.00	0.88
TRUST	0.29	0.27	0.43	0.34	0.05	0.04	**0.59**	0.82

Note. Items in boldface on the diagonal are the average variance extracted (AVE) figures, the lower left triangle contains the construct correlations, and the upper right triangle contains the shared variance between constructs.

To evaluate structure equation model and model invariance, we perform a sequence of model comparisons and the results are shown in Table 4. In first step, we divided the sample into two groups based on the CSC and we performed Multi-Group CFA (MGCFA) with high and low self-confidence groups without constraints across two groups. Second, we constrain factor loadings to be equal across two groups. Third, item means are set invariant across two groups. Fourth, error variances are constrained to be invariant across two groups. Fifth, factor variances are constrained invariant across two groups. Finally, factor covariances are constrained to be equal across two groups. In each comparison, we test the differences in the fit between the two models using the change in chi-square. In each step, if we do not have invariance, we consider partial invariance until the two models fit equivalently. If we must meet full factorial invariance, or cannot find partial invariance, then the process stops.

Table 4. Multiple group CFA

	BS[1]	FL[2]		FI[3]	EV[4]		FV[5]		FC[6]	
		Full	Partial		Full	Partial	Full	Partial	Full	Partial
χ^2 -statistic	839.04	870.37	860.64	884.22	1038.4	902.48	935.55	910.68	970.13	931.54
d.f.	462	479	478	495	519	509	516	513	534	528
RMSEA	0.08	0.08	0.08	0.08	0.09	0.08	0.08	0.08	0.08	0.08
CFI	0.91	0.91	0.91	0.91	0.88	0.91	0.90	0.91	0.90	0.91
TLI	0.90	0.90	0.90	0.90	0.87	0.90	0.90	0.90	0.90	0.90
SRMR	0.06	0.07	0.07	0.07	0.07	0.07	0.10	0.08	0.13	0.10
$\Delta\chi2$ -statistic	-	31.33	21.61	23.57	154.19	18.26	33.07	8.20	59.46	20.87
Δ*d.f.*	-	17	16	17	24	14	7	4	21	15
Critical value : $\chi^2(0.95, \Delta d.f.)$	-	27.59	26.3	27.59	36.42	23.68	14.07	9.49	32.67	25
p-value ($\Delta\chi^2$)	-	0.02*	0.16	0.13	0.00*	0.20	0.00*	0.085	0.00*	0.14

* $p < 0.05$, 1 baseline model, 2 factor load invariant, 3 factor intercept invariant, 4 error variance invariant, 5 factor variance invariant, 6 factor covariance invariant

Once we decide the final model from the MGCFA, we test the conceptual model for the proposed relations using entire sample. The relevant fit indices are reported as $\chi2$ = 1082.43 (d.f. = 533), Tucker-Lewis index (TLI) = 0.87, Comparative Fit index (CFI) = 0.87, Root Mean Square Error of Approximation (RMSEA) = 0.131. The results of the final model from the MGCFA are shown in Table 5 and demonstrate that every path, except two (PRIVACY-ATT and PRIVACY-INT), remains significant, which support H1~H9 except H6 and H9. The results would seem to indicate that promotion-seeking path is more salient than prevention-seeking path.

Table 5. Structural Model Modeling Results

Path	High CSC			Low CSC		
	β	S.E.	z	β	S.E.	z
INT ~PU	0.270	0.093	2.883	0.030	0.114	0.261
INT ~ATT	0.988	0.117	8.464	0.886	0.126	7.032
INT ~PRIVACY	-0.086	0.080	-1.074	-0.089	0.083	-1.069
ATT ~PU	0.254	0.075	3.379	0.393	0.081	4.870
ATT ~PRIVACY	-0.081	0.066	-1.214	0.017	0.070	0.240
ATT ~PES	0.715	0.127	5.625	0.461	0.090	5.134
ATT ~TRUST	0.138	0.055	2.487	0.236	0.074	3.186
PU ~PES	0.965	0.140	6.902	0.613	0.098	6.246
PRIVACY ~TRUST	-0.047	0.086	-0.547	0.208	0.109	1.912

Note. INT = Usage intension, PU = Perceived usefulness, ATT = Attitude, PRIVACY = Privacy concern, PES = Perceived easy of usage, TRUST = Trust

When comparing the two groups, it can be seen that consumers do, in fact, perceive and behave differently based on their CSC levels (see Figures 2 and 3) while partially support H10. It is suggested that consumers with high CSC show much stronger relationships among the variables in the promotion-seeking whereby they more clearly see the tangible benefits of the MC system. Especially, the PU-INT link became significant for the consumers with high CSC group. Additionally, the TRUST-PRIVACY link became significant for the consumers with low CSC group, which suggests the key variables (e.g., Trust and Privacy) in the prevention-seeking path would have a much bigger effect on behaviors of the consumers with low CSC.

Figure 2. Path diagram of High CSC

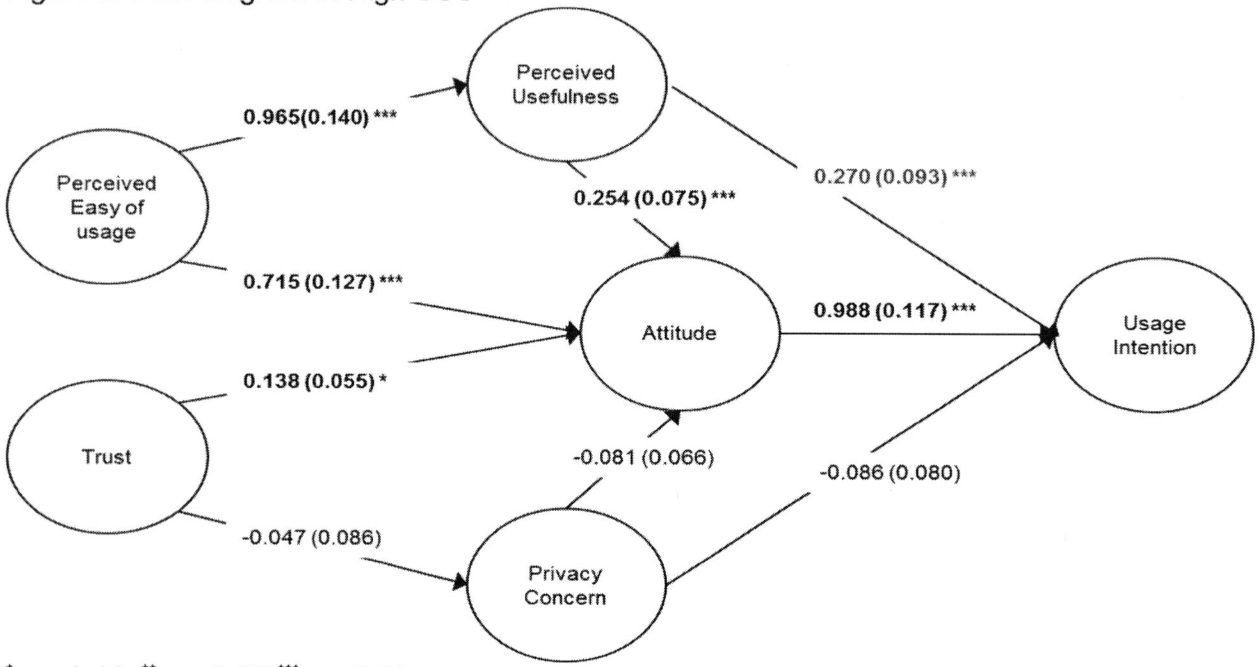

$^{*}p < 0.10$, $^{**}p < 0.05$, $^{***}p < 0.01$

Figure 3. Path diagram of Low CSC

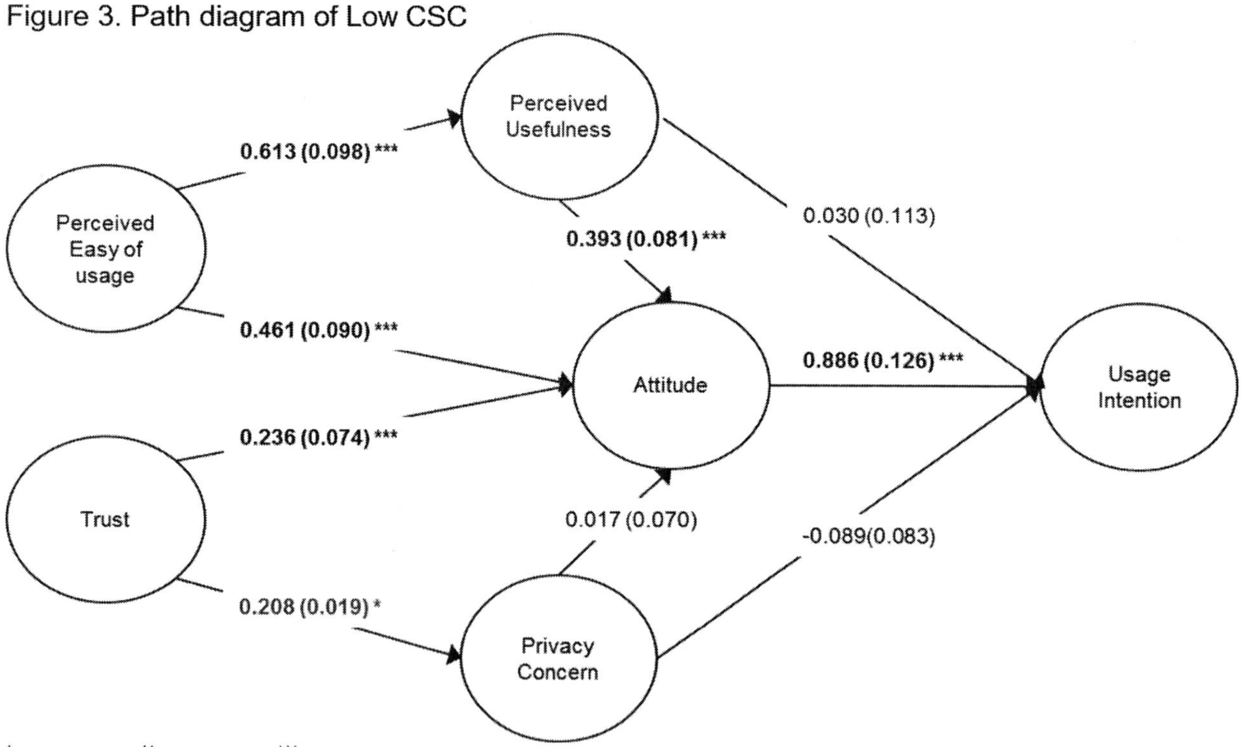

$^{*}p < 0.10$, $^{**}p < 0.05$, $^{***}p < 0.01$

CONCLUSIONS AND DISCUSSION

Evidence regarding the dimensionality, reliability, and validity of the CSC measures was provided. The results suggest that the adapted CSC measures may provide more comprehensive information about consumers' individual differences than the traditional IS measures like computer self-efficacy in MC context. CSC may also be related in predictable ways to other mobile consumer-related phenomena, and these potential relationships offer additional suggestions for future research. For example, consumer self-confidence should be positively correlated with consumer knowledge.

It is also suggested that IS researchers and practitioners may need to focus more on managing the six dimensions of CSC while facilitating its moderating role between mobile consumers' perceptions about MC systems and consumer acceptance of MC. For example, the acceptance of a new MC system may not simply rely on its technological characteristics such as easy of use. Instead, it may largely depend on the system's capability of customization to attract consumers' attention and to motivate consumers sufficiently. When a new MC app is presented at a non-trustworthy app-store, low-CSC consumers may avoid trying the new app at all or they may be less motivated to download the app than high CSC consumers. For those low-CSC consumers, benefits and usefulness of the app may not matter unless they find out how safe it would be.

REFERENCES

Adelman, Pamela K. (1987), "Occupational Complexity, Control, and Personal Income: Their Relation to Psychological Well-Being in Men and Women," Journal of Applied Psychology, 72 (November), 529-537.

Ajzen, I. (1988). Attitudes, personality, and behavior. Milton-Keynes, England: Open University Press

Ajzen, I. (1991). The theory of planned behavior. Organizational Behavior and Human Decision Processes, 50: 179-211.

Anckar B., & D'Incau D. (2002), Value Creation in Mobile Commerce: Findings from a Consumer Survey, Journal of Information Technology Theory and Application, 4 (1), 43-64.

Bearden, W. O., Hardesty, D. M., & Rose, R. L. (2001). Consumer Self-Confidence: Refinements in Conceptualization and Measurement. Journal of Consumer Research, 28(1), 121-134.

Boyle, R., & Ruppel, C. (2004). On-Line purchasing intent: The effect of personal innovativeness, perceived risk, and computer self-efficacy. Proceedings of the 7th Annual Conference of the Southern Association for Information Systems (pp. 131-137). Association for Information Systems.

Cha, J. (2011). Exploring the internet as a unique shopping channel to sell both real and virtual items: A comparison of factors affecting purchase intention and consumer characteristics. Journal of Electronic Commerce Research, 12(2), 115-132.

Cho, N., & Park, S. (2001). Development of Electronic Commerce User-consumer Satisfaction Index (ECUSI) for Internet Shopping. Industrial Management & Data Systems, 101(8), 400-406.

Compeau, D. R., & Higgins, C. A. (1995). Computer Self-efficacy: Development of a Measure and Initial Test. MIS Quarterly, 19(2), 189-211.

Constantinides, E. (2004). Influencing the Online Consumer's Behavior: The Web Experience. Internet Research, 14(2), 111-126.

Corbitt, B. J., Thanasankit, T., & Yi, H. (2003). Trust and E-commerce: A Study of Consumer Perceptions. Electronic Commerce Research & Applications, 2(3), 203-215.

Darden, William R. and Dub Ashton (1974), "Psychographic Profiles of Patronage Preference Groups," Journal of Retailing, 50 (Winter), 99-112.

Davis, F. (1989). Perceived Usefulness, Perceived Ease of Use, and User Acceptance of Information Technology. MIS Quarterly, 13(3), 319-340.

Drennan, J., Mort, G. S., & Previte, J. (2006, Jan-Mar). Privacy, risk perception, and expert online behavior: An exploratory study of household end users. Journal of Organizational and End User Computing, 18(1), 1-22.

eMarketer, Inc. “Mobile Devices to Boost US Holiday Ecommerce Sales Growth” (September 5, 2013) retrieved from http://www.emarketer.com/Article/Mobile-Devices-Boost-US-Holiday-Ecommerce-Sales-Growth/1010189#S4PGgvU8g7syyBM4.99

Forrester Research. "The State of Retailing Online series" (2015) retrieved from https://nrf.com/resources/retail-library/the-state-of-retailing-online-2015-key-metrics-initiatives-and-mobile#sthash.gE8XzRgE.dpuf

Fornell, C. & Larcker, D. F. (1981). Evaluating structural equation models with unobservable variables and measurement error. Journal of Marketing Research, 18(1), 39–50.

Gallivan, M. J., Spitler, V. K., & Koufaris, M. (2005). Does Information Technology Training Really Matter? A Social Information Processing Analysis of Coworkers' Influence on IT Usage in the Workplace. Journal of Management Information Systems, 22(1), 153-192.

Hsu, M. H., Ghiu, G. M., & Ju, T. L. (2004). Determinants of Continued Use of the WWW: An Integration of Two Theoretical Models. Industrial Management & Data Systems, 104(9), 766-775.

Hsu, M.-H., & Chiu, C.-M. (2004). Internet Self-efficacy and Electronic Service Acceptance. Decision Support Systems, 38(3), 369-381.

Hsu, M.-H., & Chiu, C.-M. (2004). Predicting Electronic Service Continuance with a Decomposed Theory of Planned Behaviour. Behaviour & Information Technology, 23(5), 359-373.

Loibl, C., Cho, S. H., Diekmann, F., & Batte, M. T. (2009, Spring). Consumer Self-Confidence in Searching for Information. The Journal of Consumer Affairs, 43(1), 26-55.

Marakas, G. M., Yi, M. Y., & Johnson, R. D. (1998). The Multilevel and Multifaceted Character of Computer self-efficacy: Toward Clarification of the Construct and an Integrative Framework for Research. Information Systems Research, 9(2), 126-163.

Mauldin, E., & Arunachalam, V. (2002). An Experimental Examination of Alternative Forms of Web Assurance for Business-To-Consumer E-Commerce. Journal of Information Systems, 16(1), 33-55.

Nunnally, Jum C. (1987), Psychomeric Theory (2nd ed.) New York, NY: McGraw-Hill.

Spake, D. F., Finney, R. Z., & Joseph, M. (2011). Experience, comfort, and privacy concerns: Antecedents of online spending. Journal of Research in Interactive Marketing, 5(1), 5-28.

Susskind, A. (2004). Electronic Commerce and World Wide Web Apprehensiveness: An Examination of Consumers' Perceptions of the World Wide Web. Journal of Computer-Mediated Communication, 9(3).

Wood, Wendy and Brian Stagner (1994), "Why Are Some People Easier to Influence than Others?" in Persuasion: Psychological Insights and Perspectives, ed. Sharon Shavitt and Timothy C. Brock, Boston: Allyn & Bacon, 149-174.

APPENDIX 1

Factor item	Factor loading
Information Acquisition (IA):	
I know where to find the information I need prior to making a purchase	0.80
I know where to look to find the product information I need product information I need	0.82
I am confident in my ability to research important purchases	0.62
I know the right questions to ask when shopping	0.60
I have the skills required to obtain needed information before making important purchases	0.64
Consideration-Set Formation (CSF):	
I am confident in my ability to recognize a brand worth considering	0.85
I can tell which brands meet my expectations	0.64
I trust my own judgment when deciding which brands to consider	0.72
I know which stores to shop	0.55
I can focus easily on a few good brands when making a decision	0.60
Personal Outcomes Decision Making (PO):	
I often have doubts about the purchase decisions I make	0.81
I frequently agonize over what to buy	0.67
I often wonder if I've made the right purchase selection	0.73
I never seem to buy the right thing for me	0.50
Too often the things I buy are not satisfying	0.65
Social Outcomes Decision Making (SO):	
My friends are impressed with my ability to make satisfying purchases	0.89
I impress people with the purchases I make	0.89
My neighbors admire my decorating ability	0.53
I have the ability to give good presents	0.53
I get compliments from others on my purchase decisions	0.68
Persuasion Knowledge (PK):	
I know when an offer is "too good to be true"	0.70

I can tell when an offer has strings attached	0.73
I have no trouble understanding the bargaining tactics used by salespersons	0.62
I know when a marketer is pressuring me to buy	0.68
I can see through sales gimmicks used to get consumers to buy	0.74
I can separate fact from fantasy in advertising	0.61
Marketplace Interfaces (MI):	
I am afraid to "ask to speak to the manager" is wrong in the store	0.79
I have a hard time saying no to a salesperson	0.59
I am too timid when problems arise while shopping	0.67
I am hesitant to complain when shopping	0.77

APPENDIX 2.

Section 1 (Self-Confidence) DIRECTIONS: Based on your mobile commerce experience, please indicate how much you agree or disagree with the following statements by circling the number. 1 is Strongly Disagree and 7 is Strongly Agree.							
Information Acquisition (IA)							
I know where to find the information I need prior to making a purchase on my mobile device	1	2	3	4	5	6	7
I know where to look to find the product information I need in an m-commerce situation	1	2	3	4	5	6	7
I am confident in my ability to research important mobile purchases	1	2	3	4	5	6	7
I have the skills required to obtain the needed information before making important mobile purchases.	1	2	3	4	5	6	7
Consideration-Set Formation (CSF)							
I am confident in my ability to recognize a brand worth considering for my mobile purchases	1	2	3	4	5	6	7
I can tell which brands meet my mobile purchase expectations	1	2	3	4	5	6	7
I trust my own judgment when deciding which brands to consider for my mobile purchases	1	2	3	4	5	6	7
I know which stores to shop for my mobile purchases	1	2	3	4	5	6	7
I can focus easily on a few good brands when making a mobile purchase decision	1	2	3	4	5	6	7
Personal Outcomes Decision Making (PO)	1	2	3	4	5	6	7
I often have doubts about the mobile purchase decisions I make	1	2	3	4	5	6	7
I frequently agonize over what to buy in a mobile setting	1	2	3	4	5	6	7
I often wonder if I've made the right mobile purchase selection	1	2	3	4	5	6	7
Too often the things I buy via my mobile devices are not satisfying.	1	2	3	4	5	6	7
Social Outcomes Decision Making (SO)							
My friends are impressed with my ability to make satisfying purchases on my mobile device.	1	2	3	4	5	6	7
I impress people with the mobile purchases I make.	1	2	3	4	5	6	7
I get compliments from others on my mobile purchase decisions	1	2	3	4	5	6	7
My neighbors admire my mobile ability.	1	2	3	4	5	6	7
Persuasion Knowledge (PK)	1	2	3	4	5	6	7

I know when a mobile offer is "too good to be true"	1	2	3	4	5	6	7
I can tell when a mobile offer has strings attached	1	2	3	4	5	6	7
I know when a mobile marketer is pressuring me to buy	1	2	3	4	5	6	7
I can see through mobile sales gimmicks used to get consumers to buy	1	2	3	4	5	6	7
Marketplace Interfaces (MI)	1	2	3	4	5	6	7
I am too timid when problems arise while mobile shopping	1	2	3	4	5	6	7
.I am hesitant to complain when mobile shopping	1	2	3	4	5	6	7
I don't like to comment when something is wrong in a mobile store.	1	2	3	4	5	6	7
I have a hard time saying no to a mobile salesperson.	1	2	3	4	5	6	7

<u>Section 2 (Beliefs, Attitude & Intention toward Mobile Commerce Systems)</u>

DIRECTIONS: Please focus on mobile commerce systems such as online shopping malls, iPhone applications, and auction websites available to your recent mobile purchasing experience. Indicate your response by circling the appropriate number next to the correct answer from 1 to 7, where 1 indicates "Completely Disagree," 4 indicates "Neither Agree nor Disagree," and 7 indicates "Completely Agree."

Using the m-commerce system improves my performance in shopping	1	2	3	4	5	6	7
Using the m-commerce system increases my productivity in shopping	1	2	3	4	5	6	7
Using the m-commerce system enhances my effectiveness in shopping	1	2	3	4	5	6	7
Overall, m-commerce system is useful	1	2	3	4	5	6	7
My interaction with the m-commerce system is clear and understandable.	1	2	3	4	5	6	7
It is easy for me to become skillful at using the m-commerce system.	1	2	3	4	5	6	7
I find the m-commerce system easy to use.	1	2	3	4	5	6	7
Learning to use the m-commerce system is easy for me.	1	2	3	4	5	6	7
Using the m-commerce system is a good idea	1	2	3	4	5	6	7
Using the m-commerce system is a wise idea	1	2	3	4	5	6	7
I like the idea using the m-commerce system	1	2	3	4	5	6	7
Using the m-commerce system is pleasant	1	2	3	4	5	6	7
I plan to use the m-commerce system frequently.	1	2	3	4	5	6	7
I predict I would use the m-commerce system frequently.	1	2	3	4	5	6	7

I intend to use the m-commerce system frequently.	1	2	3	4	5	6	7
I intend to spend considerable time and effort to learn to use the m-commerce system for enhancing my effectiveness.	1	2	3	4	5	6	7

Section 3 (Global Information Privacy Concern & Risk Beliefs)

DIRECTIONS: Please focus on your personal concern during your recent mobile purchasing experience. Indicate your response by circling the appropriate number next to the correct answer from 1 to 7, where 1 indicates "Completely Disagree," 4 indicates "Neither Agree nor Disagree," and 7 indicates "Completely Agree."

All things considered, mobile commerce would cause serious privacy problems.	1	2	3	4	5	6	7
Compared to others, I am more sensitive about the way m-commerce companies handle my personal information	1	2	3	4	5	6	7
To me, it is the most important thing to keep my privacy intact from m-commerce companies	1	2	3	4	5	6	7
I am concerned about threats to my personal privacy today.	1	2	3	4	5	6	7
In general, it would be risky to give (the information) to m-commerce companies.	1	2	3	4	5	6	7
There would be high potential for loss associated with giving (the information) to m-commerce firms.	1	2	3	4	5	6	7
There would be too much uncertainty associated with giving (the information) to m-commerce firms	1	2	3	4	5	6	7
Providing m-commerce firms with (the information) would involve many unexpected problems	1	2	3	4	5	6	7

Section 4 (Trust & MCSE)

DIRECTIONS: Please focus on your personal beliefs during your recent mobile purchasing experience. Indicate your response by circling the appropriate number next to the correct answer from 1 to 7, where 1 indicates "Completely Disagree," 4 indicates "Neither Agree nor Disagree," and 7 indicates "Completely Agree."

M-commerce companies would be trustworthy in handling my information.	1	2	3	4	5	6	7
I trust that m-commerce companies would keep my best interests in mind when dealing with (the information).	1	2	3	4	5	6	7

M-commerce companies are in general predictable and consistent regarding the usage of (the information).	1	2	3	4	5	6	7
M-commerce companies are always honest with customers when it comes to using (the information) that I would provide.	1	2	3	4	5	6	7
I feel confident understanding terms relating to m-commerce systems	1	2	3	4	5	6	7
I feel confident describing functions of m-commerce systems.	1	2	3	4	5	6	7
I feel confident trouble shooting m-commerce problems	1	2	3	4	5	6	7
I feel confident explaining why a task will not run on my mobile device	1	2	3	4	5	6	7

DECISION SCIENCES INSTITUTE

Consumers' Intention toward Mobile Banking: From Perspective of Tripartite Model of Attitude

I-Chiu Chang
Chiao-Tung University, Taiwan
Email: michaelrevlis@gmail.com

Elisa Lin
Chiao-Tung University, Taiwan
Email: elisa.iim01g@nctu.edu.tw

Hsin-Ginn Hwang
Chiao-Tung University, Taiwan
Email: hghmis@nctu.edu.tw

ABSTRACT

The purpose of this study is to develop a theoretical model based on the tripartite model of attitude to examine consumers' intention to use mobile banking. The proposed model was empirically validated by survey method that collected 262 valid data in this study. The results of the analysis show that relative advantage, personal innovativeness, and compatibility have a positive relationship with consumer's intention, and switching cost has the negative impact on consumer's intention.

KEYWORDS: Compatibility; Complexity; Habit; Mobile Banking; Personal Innovativeness; Relative Advantage; Switching Cost and Tripartite Model of Attitude

INTRODUCTION

Mobile banking is not a new IT application. Mobile banking was first introduced as a banking channel in early 2000s in form of short messaging service (SMS), and later via wireless access protocol (WAP). Recently, with the advancement of information and communication technology (ICT) and the popularity of M-commerce, the environment for mobile banking nowadays is different from the time when the concept of mobile banking was first announced. In general, mobile banking can be defined as a banking service that enables consumers to access various banking services via mobile devices (such as smart phone, tablets or PDA) (Laukkanen & Lauronen, 2005). Mobile banking is a value-added service which enables customers to have banking services at anytime and anywhere, and brings great convenience to consumers (Zhou, 2012a; Zhou, 2011; Riivari, 2005; Mallat et al., 2004) compared with traditional banking services (such as ATM, telephone banking, and non-mobile Internet banking. Since mobile banking is conducted through mobile devices, users can access banking services anywhere they want, that is, a real always-on banking service. This feature, a real always-on banking service, is especially important for time-critical consumers (Singh et al., 2010), making mobile banking being the cheapest banking services delivery channel (Koenig-Lewis et al., 2010).

Both mobile banking and Internet banking are classified as electronic banking (Laforet & Li, 2005; Laukkanen, 2007; Sripalawat et al., 2011) and are two alternative channels for banks to provide their services (Scornavacca & Hoehle, 2007). Technically, mobile banking is conducted on mobile devices and wireless network connection. Whereas, Internet banking service is simply referred as online banking services. From users" point of view, the main difference between mobile banking and Internet banking is mobility (Suoranta & Mattila, 2004). Mobile banking are much more welcomed by people living in remote villages where Internet is hard to access (Cruz et al., 2010), where communication infrastructures are not well constructed and the density of branches of banks are low.

Several surveys (Flurry, 2014; Google, 2013) indicated that browsing Internet, playing games, using social network applications, and other entertainment are the four main activities users doing with their mobile devices. Mobile banking is barely adopted by 8.2% of customers (CNNIC, 2012). Moreover, there was no more than 2.3% of banking transaction conducted on mobile devices in Taiwan (Market Intelligence Center of Taiwan, MIC, 2009). Despite the popularity of mobile devices used, the usage rate of mobile banking remains much lower than expected (Yu, 2012; Cruz et al., 2010; Datamonitor, 2009).

Banks expect to gain more competitive advantages than other competitors by having a large number of customers' adoption of mobile banking (Zhou, 2012b). Two corporations, Taiwan Mobile and Taipei Fubon Bank first adopted short message service (SMS) as the mobile banking service in Taiwan in 1999. Wireless application protocol (WAP) was then introduced into Taiwan in 2000. By 2010, mobile banking was performed on smart phone application including iOS and Android OS. Four banks (CTBC Bank, Cathay United Bank, E.SUN Bank and Citibank Taiwan) proposed their mobile banking applications for mobile devices. Nowadays, there are fourteen banks that have released their own mobile banking service applications. Each of these banks also provides Internet banking service. These mobile banking applications are better in usability, functionality and user interface than ever.

Although there are many advantages of using mobile banking, but mobile banking still suffers from the problems that e-commerce and M-commerce encounter such as great uncertainty and risk (Zhou, 2011). The user interface is limited due to the small screen and keypad compared with PC (Lee & Chung, 2009), which enhances the barriers for consumers to switch from Internet banking to mobile banking. Without a specific encryption standard, customers worry that their personal information might be accessed illegally (Lin, 2011). To have further understanding of prior researches in the adoption of mobile banking, related literatures were reviewed.

First, perceived cost plays an essential role in the adoption of mobile banking and its contribution is empirically validated (Hanafizadeh et al., 2014; Yu, 2012; Luarn & Lin, 2005; Ha et al., 2012). However, the previous studies mainly focused on the aspect of perceived financial cost (Chen, 2013; Yu, 2012; Luarn & Lin, 2005). Ha et al. (2012) called for more researches on indirect costs. Since financial cost is part of switching cost (Burnham et al., 2003) and the effect of switching cost is not yet confirmed in the context of the adoption of mobile banking (Zhou, 2012a), this study discussed the effect of switching cost instead of purely perceived financial cost. Moreover, from the point of view of status quo bias, the concept of switching cost provides a comparison between current status and changed status. Lin (2011) indicates that more comparisons of users' previous experience are needed to provide further understanding of users' intention on adopting mobile banking. Along with switching cost, habit is also considered as a critical factor to represent the attitude of past behavior (Hong et al., 2011). Thus, this study adopted switching cost and habit to conduct experiential comparison.

Secondly, self-efficacy is a common factor that influences users' intention directly and indirectly in the study of adoption of mobile banking (Zhou, 2012a; Luo et al., 2010; Gu et al., 2009; Luarn & Lin, 2005). According to Luo et al. (2010) self-efficacy is one of the important factors that can reflect personal traits. Not only self-efficacy, there are merely few factors that reflect personal differences. Ha et al. (2012) collected more researches on personal characteristics in the context of mobile banking. Although, in recent years, trust is empirically validated as a critical factor to the adoption of mobile banking, Zhou (2012a) argued that the building of initial trust might be different for any potential individual. Since personal innovativeness is an important factor that can express individual differences (Bhattacherjee et al., 2012), this study adopted personal innovativeness as a tool to investigate the personal psychological aspect.

Thirdly, innovation attributes proposed by Rogers (1995) are good drivers in the study of users' adoption of mobile banking (Chen, 2013; Lin, 2011). Among these five attributes, relative advantage, compatibility and complexity are found to be the most important factors (Lin, 2011; Hanafizadeh et al., 2014; Chen, 2013; Ha et al., 2012). The validity of relative advantage in Lin's research (2011) was validated Chen (2013). Compatibility performs as an influential factor in many researches (Hanafizadeh et al., 2014; Chen, 2013; Lin, 2011; Ha et al., 2012). The role of compatibility for adoptions of mobile banking can't be underestimated.

Last but not the least, to have further understanding of users' adoption of mobile banking, the overall evaluation is essential (Luo et al., 2010; Zhou, 2012b). Luo et al. (2010) also argues that studies that simply focus on either cost or benefit aspect will yield incomplete or contradictory findings. Since the previous researches of attitude tend to focus on cognitive dimension of attitude (Hong et al., 2011), this study investigated the attitude in a more complete way. Bizer (2004) argued that attitude is the overall evaluation of cognitive, affective and behavior dimensions. Thus, this study adopted the tripartite model of attitude from psychology literature to investigate attitudes in a more comprehensive way.

LITERATURE REVIEW

Tripartite Model of Attitude

In the psychology literature, the tripartite model of attitude is a classic model that suggests that attitude comes from different sources including affective, behavioral, and cognitive (Bizer, 2004; Breckler, 1984). According to the tripartite model of attitude, attitude is the overall evaluation of these three components (Bizer, 2004; Eagly & Chaiken, 1993). The cognitive component refers to an individual's thoughts, beliefs, and perceptual responses about the attitude object; the affective component refers to an individual's feelings, moods, emotional responses, or gut reactions engendered by the attitude of an object; the behavioral component refers to an individual's evaluations of the attitude of an object based on their past behaviors (Hong et al., 2011; Bizer, 2004; Piderit, 2000; Breckler, 1984). These three components are hypothetical and unobservable constructs and are represented by observable measures (Breckler, 1984). A person may be addicted to online games (behavior) and may think that playing online game is enjoyable (affective) but may also think that online game takes him/her too much time and money.

The tripartite model of attitude provides researchers a further understanding of IS adoption (Hong et al., 2011). Hong et al. (2011) has adopted tripartite model of attitude to investigate users' attitude of agile IS. According to Hong et al. (2011)'s definition, agile is characterized by frequent upgrades with a small number of new features released such as iPhone apps and web-based systems. Since mobile banking includes smart phone apps and Internet banking (have to be conducted via mobile devices), mobile banking can be viewed as an agile IS. Thus, the tripartite model of attitude fits the context of mobile banking.

Status Quo Bias and Omission Bias

Samuelson and Zeckhauser (1988) argued that status quo bias is the behavior that humans have a tendency to prefer options that cause no change to the state of the world. Status quo bias increases people's intention to resist any change. That is, people prefer to stay the way they are rather than altering their behavior. It is assumed that people would prefer keep using Internet banking on PCs or going to the bank counter in person even they know mobile banking are more convenient and effort-saving. Another theory named omission bias that refers to humans' tendency to require no action on their part (Ritov & Baron, 1992). This means that the few efforts needed the more preference people will have in using mobile banking. These efforts may include learning how to use mobile banking and altering their old way to access banking services.

Innovation Attributes in M-banking

In innovation diffusion theory, Rogers (1995) proposes a set of innovation attributes that may affect adoption decisions. This set of innovation attributes contains five attributes: relative advantage, compatibility, complexity, trialability and observability. In the context of Internet-based technology adoption, relative advantage, compatibility and complexity are found to be the most frequently identified factors (Papies & Clement, 2008; Vijayasarathy, 2004). Laukkanen (2007) recognizes mobile banking as a technological innovation because of the ubiquity, ease of use and fast of speed that mobile banking has. Innovation attributes were found to be vital drivers in the context of mobile banking by researchers (Lin, 2011; Chen, 2013).

Because the mobile banking application is a new banking service, different benefits may be expected from switching from an existing one to a new one. The benefits that mobile banking provides to users may include productivity gains, better access to information, and better information quality available. Relative advantage plays an important role in switching since there will be no reason to switch to a new IT if it does not have some incremental benefit over the old IT (Bhattacherjee et al., 2012). Furthermore, customers are more likely to generate positive attitude toward adopting mobile banking when they perceive clear relative advantages offered by mobile banking (Lin, 2011).

Tsai et al. (2010) pointed out that complexity is a good predictor when evaluating the changes that a technological innovation could bring. The predictability of complexity toward attitude is supported in the context of mobile banking (Chen, 2013). The compatibility of a new IT services has been proved that it has a positive effect on attitudes towards adoption (Mallat et al., 2004). Compatibility was also found to have strong positive effect toward users' intention to adopt mobile banking (Hanafizadeh et al., 2014; Koenig-Lewis et al., 2010; Wessels & Drennan, 2010).

Switching Cost in M-banking

The concept of switching costs has often been adopted in many researches to investigate the idea of losing existing benefits or incurred extra efforts when accepting a new product or services (Burnham et al., 2003). Switching cost plays an important operational measurement that is monitored regularly by service providers in e-banking environment (Huang & Hsieh, 2012). Switching cost could be an inhibitor of user behavior, and more studies related to their relationship were expected (Zhou, 2012b; Zhou, 2011).

Among the plenty literature, Burnham et al. (2003) proposed a clear concept of switching costs and identifies eight facts for switching cost: 1) economic risk cost; 2) evaluation cost; 3) learning cost; 4) setup cost; 5) benefit loss cost; 6) monetary loss cost; 7) personal relationship loss cost, and 8) brand relationship loss cost. Nevertheless, Burnham et al. (2003) also classified these eight facts into three categories named: 1) procedural switching cost, 2) financial switching cost, and 3) relational switching costs. The procedural switching costs consider the time a customer spends. Procedural switching costs contain economic risk costs, evaluation costs, setup costs and learning costs. The financial switching costs refer to the monetary aspect for the customer. Financial switching costs contain benefit loss costs and monetary loss costs. The relational switching costs pertain to the emotional aspects of the customer. Relational switching costs contain personal relationship loss costs and brand relationship loss costs.

To adopt mobile banking, individuals may have to spend more efforts and costs. These costs include extra communication fees and transaction fees due to the mobile network usage. Perceived financial cost was found to be a significant barrier for users to adopt mobile banking (Luarn & Lin, 2005). Ha et al. (2012) indicate that further research on the impact of indirect costs in mobile banking literature is required. Base on status quo bias and omission bias, this study investigates the concept of cost via switching cost.

Personal Innovativeness in M-banking

Nelson (1990) emphasized that individual difference is an important variable in new technology acceptance. High innovative people are active information seekers about new ideas (Tariq, 2007). In another word, innovative people are more likely to accept new IT and try to use it. Moreover, in marketing, research suggests that a user population faced with common incumbent and substitute technologies may exhibit differential patterns of switching based on individual differences. Personal innovativeness appeared to be the most important one (Bhattacherjee et al., 2012) and can explain why some people are early innovators while others are laggards in adopting new IT. Luo et al. (2010) recognizes personal trait factors as the major levers that override the effect of perceived risks and directly influence the intention to adopt mobile banking. Zhou (2012a) also indicated that user motivations such as personal involvement might affect initial trust building and could become indirect factors toward users' adoption of mobile banking.

Since the predictability of personal innovativeness on flow experience was found to be significant (Zhou, 2012b) and one of the characteristics of flow experience was intrinsic enjoyment (Novak et al., 2000), it is reasonable to conclude that personal innovativeness has emotional effects toward people's evaluation. Moreover, personal innovativeness revealed people's natural propensity toward a new thing that is parallel to the gut reaction mentioned in the definition of affective component. Thus, this study adopted personal innovativeness as the factor of affective attitude.

Habit

Habit could be referred as a phenomenon that IT users who have been using a certain technology for some time are predisposed to continue using it in an automatic and unknowing manner (Limayem et al., 2007). For some unknowing reasons, people prefer to stay the way they used to be. These reasons might be status quo bias or omission bias or even something else. Bhattacherjee et al. (2012) argued that there're effects between habit and IT switching behavior. Obviously, habit is an effect that prevents people from accepting new things. People are less likely to switch to a new IT because of their habit (Bhattacherjee et al., 2012). The results of Limayem et al. (2007)'s research also showed that people who have habit in using certain IT are less likely to switch to a new IT.

HYPOTHESES/MODEL

Prior study (Breckler, 1984) adopted the three-component view of attitude to analyze the tripartite model and dentify appropriate variables and represent these three components by observable measures.

Cognitive Component

Relative advantage is referred to the extent to which mobile banking is perceived as being beneficial over the preceding banking services (Bhattacherjee et al., 2012). Because mobile banking can be viewed as a new banking service channel, additional benefits are expected. The benefits may include productivity gains, better access to information, and better information quality available. Relative advantage plays an important role in switching since there would be no reason to switch to a new IT if the new IT did not have any incremental benefit over the old IT (Bhattacherjee et al., 2012). The relationship between relative advantage and intention are found to be positive in prior researches. Thus, this study proposed the following hypothesis:
H_1: Relative advantage is positively correlated with consumer's intention to use mobile banking

Complexity is referred as the degree to which mobile banking is perceived as relatively difficult to understand and use (Tsai et al., 2010; Bhattacherjee et al., 2012). Tsai et al. (2010) pointed out that complexity is a good predictor when evaluating the changes that a technology innovation could bring. The predictability of complexity toward consumer's intention is supported in the context of mobile banking (Tsai et al., 2010). This means that if people find the use of mobile banking more complexity than the way they used to access banking service, their intention to use mobile banking will be lower. Thus, this study proposed the following hypothesis:
H_2: Complexity is negatively correlated with consumer's intention to use mobile banking

In this study, switching cost refers to the one-time perceived loss and transition cost a user would incur in the process switching from current banking channel to mobile banking (Polites & Karahanna, 2012; Hong et al., 2011; Kim et al., 2009; Burnham et al., 2003). The concept of switching cost is broad including financial aspect, procedural aspect, and relational aspect (Burnham et al., 2003). Furthermore, switching cost is an inhibitor of user behavior and plays as a barrier of users' adoption of a new IT (Zhou, 2012a; Luarn & Lin, 2005). When an individual adopts mobile banking, the individual may need to spend extra efforts to get used to it and additional costs may be needed. Switching cost of adopting mobile banking may include financial cost such as purchasing a mobile device or paying mobile network fee, relational cost such as losing a clerk who is familiar with your special needs, and procedural cost such as spending time and efforts getting used to it. Thus, this study proposed the following hypotheses:
H_3: Switching cost is negatively correlated with consumer's intention to use mobile banking.

Affective Component

In elaboration likelihood model, when an individual has no ability or motivation to face a complex situation, he or she will tend to rely on the peripheral route to assist him or her to make the decision. Sometimes the reliance on affection and emotion is a quicker, easier, and more efficient way to deal with changing environment (Chaiken & Trope, 1999). Thus, the investigation on affective component of attitude is essential. In this study, effective component refers to an individual's feelings, moods, emotional responses, or gut reactions engendered by mobile banking (Hong et al., 2011; Bizer, 2004; Piderit, 2000; Breckler, 1984).

The definition of personal innovativeness is the propensity and inclination of an individual to try out or experiment with any new information systems (Bhattacherjee et al., 2012). Tariq (2007) argued that high innovative people are active information seekers about new ideas. In another word, people with more innovativeness are more likely to accept new IT and try to use it. Personal innovativeness appeared to be the most important factor to explain why some people are early innovators while others are laggards in adopting new IT (Bhattacherjee et al., 2012). This study proposed the 4th hypothesis as below.
H_4: Personal innovativeness is positively correlated with consumer's intention to use mobile banking.

Past Behavior Component

Behavior is the third component in the tripartite model of attitude. According to status quo bias, people are usually reluctant to change. Bizer (2004) also argued behavior refers to how a person has acted in the past or would act in the future. Compatibility of a new IT services has been proved to have a positive effect on consumer's intention (Lu et al., 2011; Schierz et al., 2010) in the context of E-commerce and mobile payment. The more compatible an individual perceived, the less efforts needed for the changing and the less influential status quo bias can be. Compatibility replies the consistence between adopting mobile banking and an individual's current behavioral patterns. Compatibility in this study is referred as the extent to which using mobile banking is viewed as being compatible with user's current or future needs, lifestyles and work patterns (Bhattacherjee et al., 2012). Thus, the following hypothesis was proposed:
H_5: Compatibility is positively correlated with consumer's intention to use mobile banking.

Status quo bias argues that people prefer no change against current situation. People may evaluate a new IT based on their past behavior. Since habit is referred as a phenomenon that IT users who have been using a certain technology for a period of time are predisposed to continue using it in an automatic and unknowing manner (Limayem et al., 2007). That is, the habit a person has will somehow influence his or her preference on the new IT. Limayem et al. (2007) concluded that people who have habit in using certain IT are less likely to switch to a new IT. Also, habit is found to have positive effect on people's intention to adopt a new IT (Venkatesh et al., 2012; Hong et al., 2011). Thus, this study adopted habit as the factor in past behavior component of attitude. And the following hypothesis was proposed:
H_6: Habit is negatively correlated with consumer's intention to use mobile banking.

Thus, this study identifies relevant variables for each component in order to determine attitude. There are three components to determine the attitude, and they are cognitive component, affective component, and past behavior component. In this study, the variables of cognitive component are relative advantage, complexity, and switching cost; the variables of affective component is personal innovativeness; the variables of past behavioral component are compatibility and habit. Figure 1 illustrates the initial research framework of this study.

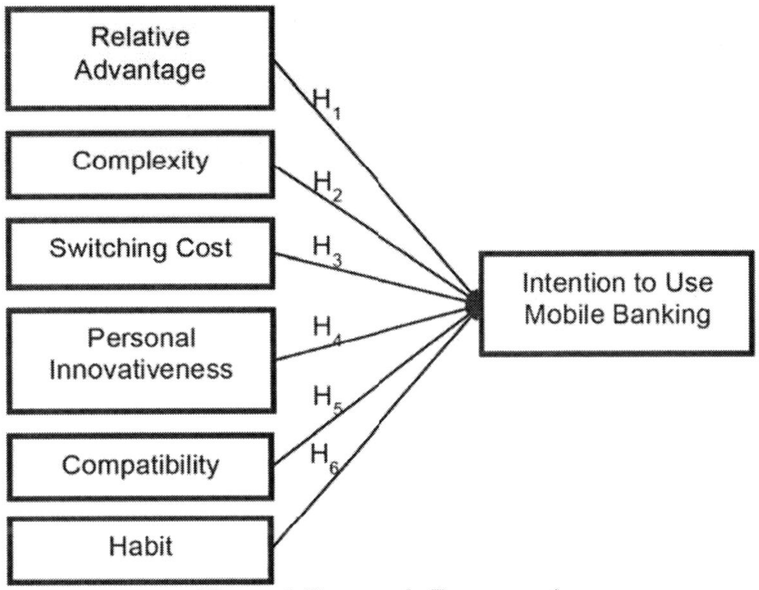

Figure 1 Research Framework

METHODS

Instrument Development

To develop the multi-item measures for each construct, this study reviewed the literature regarding IT adoption and mobile commerce, especially mobile banking, and collected the items they used. All constructs were measured using existing validated scales from prior literatures (see Table 1). After that, redundant items with similar wording were deleted. The rest items were translated into Chinese from English and were slightly adapted to fit the specific context of mobile banking.

Expert Panels and Pilot Test

After developing the instrument, the expert panels were held to validate the initial questionnaire and the initial research framework. The expert panel consisted of one associate professor and one assistant professor who were specialized in information management in academic researches, and one professional who was a vice general manager specializing in information management in financial industry. The experts validated the initial research framework for mobile banking context and the appropriateness of measurement.

After the expert panel, the revised instrument has been tested by a pilot study. The pilot study recruited Master degree students in Institute of Information Management at a university in Northern Taiwan. Some modifications were made based on the feedback of pilot study such as noting the explanation of non-mobile online banking at the end of item statement to ensure respondents' comprehension. Some items' wording was modified to fit the specific context of mobile banking usage. All items were measured by seven-point Likert scale. The working definitions of all variables in this study are exhibited in Table 1 below. None of the Cronbach's α of each scale of the measurement was lower than the cut-off value 0.7. Two items with factor loadings lower than 0.5 were dropped from the scale. Another two items were removed based on the result of pilot test and expert panel, that is, they had the same opinion about these two could be removed from the measurement.

Table 1 Operationalization of Variables

Variable	Working Definition	References
Relative Advantage	Relative advantage is referred to the extent to which mobile banking is perceived as being beneficial over the preceding banking services	Rogers, 1995; Bhattacherjee et al., 2012
Complexity	The degree to which mobile banking is perceived as relatively difficult to understand and use	Rogers, 1995; Bhattacherjee et al., 2012; Tsai et al., 2010
Switching Costs	The one-time perceived loss and extra cost a user would incur in the process switching from current banking channel to mobile banking	Polites & Karahanna, 2012; Hong et al., 2011; Kim et al., 2009; Burnham et al., 2003;
Personal Innovativenes s	The propensity and inclination of an individual to try out or experiment with any new information systems	Bhattacherjee et al., 2012; Crespo & del Bosque, 2008; Tariq, 2007
Compatibility	The extent to which using mobile banking is viewed as being compatible with user's current or future needs, lifestyles and work patterns	Rogers, 1995; Bhattacherjee et al., 2012
Habit	The extent to which using the preceding banking service, except for mobile banking, has become automatic for an individual in response to banking activities	Limayem et al., 2007
Intention to adopt mobile banking	The degree to which a person perceives his/her willingness to use mobile banking	Yu, 2012

Data Collection

The subjects of formal survey procedure were undergraduate students and graduate students, with two conditions: 1) own at least one smart phone and; 2) own at least one active bank account. For undergraduate students and graduate students are considered as the potential mobile banking users in previous studies (Zhou, 2012a; Luo et al., 2010).
To ensure that the respondents possess the abilities to become future users of mobile banking, the respondents must be available to access banking services and equipped with necessary mobile technology infrastructure. The data was collected during the period from May 26th to June 9th in 2014. A total of 300 questionnaires were distributed and 276 data were collected. 262 valid data were collected.

RESULTS

Demographic Data of Respondents

Among the 262 respondents, 50.4% were male and 49.6% were female. The age range of the respondents was mainly distributed from 20 to 24 years old (60.3%). 62.2% of the respondents were graduate students and 21.4% of the respondents were graduate degree program students. For monthly income, 31.7% of the respondents had no any income, 42.4% of the respondents had less than 20,000 NTD, and 11.5% of the respondents had their monthly income ranged from 40,001 to 70,000 NTD. Among all the respondents, 66.8% of them never used mobile banking before. For those who have mobile banking usage experience, only 27.6% of them use mobile banking at least once per week being recognized as regular users, 10.3% of them use mobile banking about once every two weeks being recognized as occasional users, and there were 62.1% of them use mobile banking about once or even less per month being recognized as rare users. All the descriptive statistics of respondents were listed in Table 2.

Table 2 Descriptive Statistics of Respondents (N=262)

Measure	Categories	Frequency	Percentage
Gender	Male	132	50.4
	Female	130	49.6
Age	< 20	11	4.2
	20-24	158	60.3
	25-29	42	16.0
	30-34	19	7.3
	35-39	12	4.6
	40-44	14	5.3
	45-49	3	1.1
	50-54	3	1.1
Occupation	Undergraduate Student	35	13.4
	Graduate Student	163	62.2
	Ph.D. Student	5	1.9
	Graduate Degree Program Student	56	21.4
	Ph.D. Degree Program Student	3	1.1
Monthly Income (NTD)	None	83	31.7
	1-20,000	111	42.4
	20,001-40,000	14	5.3
	40,001-70,000	30	11.5
	70,001-100,000	19	7.2
	>100,000	5	1.9
M-banking Experience	None	175	66.8
	Have Used It Before	87	33.2
M-banking Usage	Use It Everyday	4	4.6

Frequency (87 respondents)	About once per week	20	23.0
	About once every 2 weeks	9	10.3
	About once per month	24	27.6
	Less than once per month	30	34.5

Exploratory Factor Analysis and Confirmatory Factor Analysis

To test construct validity, factor analysis, such as exploratory factor analysis (EFA) and confirmatory factor analysis (CFA), is a common used methodology (Gefen & Straub, 2005). Kaiser-Meyer-Olkin (KMO) and Bartlett test of sphericity were conducted to ensure the data collected were appropriate for EFA. The principal component factor analysis and the Varimax rotation were conducted. The suggested criteria of extracting factors are eigenvalue greater than 1.0 and no factor loading less than 0.5. In the first round of EFA, we found that 3 items (PI1, HA4, and HA5) had its factor loading less than 0.5 and therefore we removed them from the instrument. After removing these three items, EFA was conducted again. In the second EFA process, a total of seven constructs were extracted, all the items were loaded on the construct as hypothesized, and no factor loading were less than 0.5 (See Table 3). The above results imply that there is sufficient construct validity of the items. There is a total of three scales of Cronbach's α above 0.9, three scales of Cronbach's α are above 0.8, and 1 scale of Cronbach's α is above 0.6. Thus, all the constructs of this study can be considered to be reliable (see Table 3). Except for Cronbach's α, composite reliability (CR) was another common measure of reliability. It is considered acceptable to have the value above 0.7, whereas a value below 0.6 indicates a lack of reliability. There's one scale of CR in this study above 0.9, five scales of CR above 0.8 indicating that all the constructs in this study have enough reliability. However, there's one scale of CR nearly reached the recommended value of 0.6. The value of AVE of six constructs are higher than 0.5. Only one construct fails to pass the recommended value of CR and AVE but other results of convergent validity tests of this construct are still qualified. As a result, this study recognized construct "switching cost" as lack of high convergent validity but still considerable. The above results indicate that all the constructs in this study are considered to have convergent validity.

The correlations between latent variables of this study are illustrated in Table 4 and the values in diagonal line are replaced by the square root of AVE of each construct. All the correlation coefficients among dimensions in this study are lower than 0.85. The square root of each construct is higher than its correlations between other constructs except for relative advantage and intention, complexity and switching cost, switching cost and intention, complexity and intention.

Table 3 The Results of EFA and Convergent Validity

Construct	Item	Factor Loading	Cronbach's α	CR	AVE	Squired Multiple Correlations
Relative Advantage	RA1	0.800	0.824	0.8242	0.5409	0.67
	RA2	0.820				0.77
	RA3	0.687				0.40
	RA4	0.716				0.39
Complexity	CX1	0.857	0.886	0.8323	0.5554	0.62
	CX2	0.868				0.74
	CX3	0.846				0.80
	CX4	0.704				0.52

Switching Cost	SC5	0.744	0.674	0.5736	0.2198	0.21
	SC6	0.746				0.24
	SC7	0.465				0.25
	SC8	0.497				0.35
	SC9	0.495				0.42
Personal Innovativeness	PI2	0.836	0.911	0.8518	0.6571	0.72
	PI3	0.863				0.85
	PI4	0.872				0.76
Compatibility	CP1	0.806	0.900	0.8560	0.5979	0.69
	CP2	0.819				0.81
	CP3	0.802				0.73
	CP4	0.798				0.56
Habit	HA1	0.905	0.881	0.8558	0.6642	0.73
	HA2	0.899				0.81
	HA3	0.876				0.62
Intention	IN1	0.808	0.932	0.9056	0.7063	0.76
	IN2	0.708				0.76
	IN3	0.789				0.79
	IN4	0.783				0.81

Table 4 Correlations between Latent Variables

	RA	CX	SC	PI	CP	HA	IN
RA	0.54						
CX	-0.34	0.55					
SC	-0.24	0.64	0.21				
PI	0.23	-0.23	-0.09	0.66			
CP	0.48	-0.36	-0.14	0.52	0.60		
HA	0.18	0.04	0.02	-0.09	-0.06	0.66	
IN	0.55	-0.35	-0.30	0.55	0.66	-0.01	0.71

*The vales in diagonal line are the square roots of AVE of each construct

Hypotheses Testing

We examined the structural model using LISREL 8.7. The results of testing the structural model are shown in Figure 2.

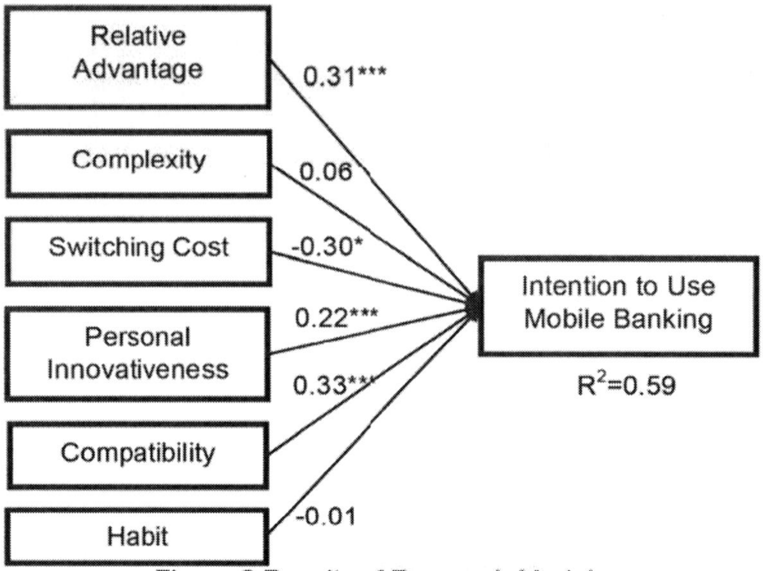

Figure 2 Results of Research Model

***$p<0.001$ **$p<0.01$ *$p<0.05$

Four out of six hypotheses in this study are supported. The results indicate that relative advantage (H_1, t-value=4.43, $p<0.001$, β=0.31), personal innovativeness (H_4, t-value=4.88, $p<0.001$, β=0.22), and compatibility (H_6, t-value=5.45, $p<0.001$, β=0.33) have significant positive effect on consumers' intention. And switching cost (H_4, t-value=-2.30, $p<0.05$, β=-0.30) has significant negative effect on consumers' intention. These four variables explain 59 percent of variance of attitude, supporting H_1, H_3, H_4, and H_5. However, complexity (H_2) and habit (H_6) have no significant negative effects on consumers' intention to use mobile banking.

DISCUSSION AND CONCLUSIONS

There are three main findings from this study. First, the tripartite model of attitude is empirically validated by the data collected with cognitive variables of relative advantage and switching cost, affective variable of personal innovativeness, and past behavior variables of compatibility. This study integrated innovation attributes, switching cost, and personal innovativeness into the tripartite model of attitude to investigate consumers' intention to adoption of mobile banking. Second, the role of personal innovativeness in the context of mobile banking is established empirically. This study shows personal innovativeness as the predictor of consumer's intention. Third, relative advantage and compatibility factor show the same relationship to intention to mobile banking as previous studies (Chen, 2013; Yang et al., 2012; Mallat et al., 2009).

REFERENCES

Ajzen, I. (2001). Nature and operation of attitudes. Annual review of psychology, 52(1), 27-58.

Bhattacherjee, A., Limayem, M., & Cheung, C. M.K. (2012). User switching of information technology: A theoretical synthesis and empirical test. Information & Management, 40, 327-333.

Bizer, G. Y. (2004). Attitudes. Encyclopedia of Applied Psychology, 1.

Boudreau, M. C., Gefen, D., & Straub, D. W. (2001). Validation in information systems research: A state-of-the-art assessment. Management Information Systems Quarterly, 1-16.

Breckler, S. J. (1984). Empirical Validation of Affect, Behavior, and Cognitive as Distinct Components of Attitude. Journal Personality and Social Psychology, 47(6), 1191-1205.

Burnham, T. A., Frels, J. K., and Mahajan, V. (2003). Consumer switching costs: a typology, antecedents, and consequences. Journal of the Academy of Marketing Science, 31(2), 109-126.

Chen, C. (2013). Perceived risk, usage frequency of mobile banking services. Managing Service Quality, 23(5), 410-436. doi: 10.1108/MSQ-10-2012-0137.

Chaiken, S., & Trope, Y. (Eds.). (1999). Dual-process theories in social psychology. Guilford Press.

CNNIC (2012). 29th Statistical survey report on the internet development in China. China Internet Network Information Center.

Cruz, P., L. B. F. Neto, P. Munoz-Gallego, and T. Laukkanen. (2010). Mobile banking rollout in emerging markets: Evidence from Brazil. International Journal of Bank Marketing, 28(5), 342-371.

Herrero Crespo, Á., & Rodríguez del Bosque, I. (2008). The effect of innovativeness on the adoption of B2C e-commerce: a model based on the theory of planned behaviour. Computers in Human Behavior, 24(6), 2830-2847.

Datamonitor. (2009). Mobile banking: Over-hyped gimmick or credible 21st century banking channel? New York: Datamonitor.

Diamantopoulos, A., Siguaw, J. A., & Siguaw, J. A. (2000). Introducing LISREL: A guide for the uninitiated. Sage.

Eagly, A. H., & Chaiken, S. (1993). The psychology of attitudes. Fort Worth, TX: Harcourt Brace Jovanovich.

Flurry. (2014). Mobile Use Grows 115% in 2013, Propelled by Messaging Apps, available at (2014.1.13): http://www.flurry.com/bid/103601/Mobile-Use-Grows-115-in-2013-Propelled-by-Messaging-Apps#.U5fBUHKSzal

Google. (2013) Our Mobile Planet: Australia – Understanding the Mobile Consumer, available at: http://services.google.com/fh/files/misc/omp-2013-au-en.pdf

Gu, J. C., Lee, S. C., & Suh, Y. H. (2009). Determinants of behavioral intention to mobile banking. Expert Systems with Applications, 36(9), 11605-11616. doi: 10.1016/j.eswa.2009.03.024

Gefen, D., & Straub, D. (2005). A practical guide to factorial validity using PLS-Graph: Tutorial and annotated example. Communications of the Association for Information systems, 16(1), 5.

Hartwick, J., & Barki, H. (1994). Explaining the role of user participation in information system use. Management science, 40(4), 440-465.

Ha, K. H., Canedoli, A., Baur, A. W., & Bick, M. (2012). Mobile banking - insights on its increasing relevance and most common drivers of adoption. Electronic Markets, 22(4), 217-227. doi: 10.1007/s12525-012-0107-1.

Hanafizadeh, P., Behboudi, M., Abedini Koshksaray, A., & Jalilvand Shirkhani Tabar, M. (2014). Mobile-banking adoption by Iranian bank clients. Telematics and Informatics, 31(1), 62-78. doi: http://dx.doi.org/10.1016/j.tele.2012.11.001.

Hoehle, H., Scornavacca, E., & Huff, S. (2012). Three Decades of Research on Consumer Adoption and Utilization of Electronic Banking Channels: A Literature Analysis. Decision Support Systems.

Hooper, D., Coughlan, J., & Mullen, M. (2008). Structural equation modelling: guidelines for determining model fit. Articles, 2.

Hong, W., Thong, J. Y.L., Chasalow, L. C., & Dhillon, G. (2011). User Acceptance of Agile Information Systems: A Model and Empirical Test. Journal of Management Information Sciences, 29(1), 235-272.

Huang L-Y & Hsieh. Y-J. (2012). Consumer electronics acceptance based on innovation attributes and switching costs: The case of e-book readers. Electronic Commerce Research and Applications, 11, 218-228.

Hu, L. T., & Bentler, P. M. (1999). Cutoff criteria for fit indexes in covariance structure analysis: Conventional criteria versus new alternatives. Structural Equation Modeling: A Multidisciplinary Journal, 6(1), 1-55.

Ilie, V., van Slyke, C., Green, G., & Lou, H. (2005). Gender differences in perceptions and use communication technologies: A diffusion of innovation approach. Information Resources Management Journal, 18(3), 13-31.

Kim, G., Shin, B., & Lee, H. G. (2009). Understanding Dynamics between Initial Trust and Usage Intentions of Mobile Banking. Information Systems Journal, 19(3), 283-311.

Kim, H. W., & Kankanhalli, A. (2009). Investigating user resistance to information systems implementation: a status quo bias perspective. Management Information Systems Quarterly, 33(3), 9.

Koenig-Lewis, N., A. Palmer, and A. Moll. (2010). Predicting young consumers' take up of mobile banking services. International Journal of Banking Marketing, 28(5), 410-432.

Koenig-Lewis, N., Palmer, A., Moll, A., 2010. Predicting young consumers' take up of mobile banking services. International Journal of Bank Marketing, 28(5), 410-432.

Laforet, S., & Li, X. (2005). Consumers' attitudes towards online and mobile banking in China. International Journal of Bank Marketing, 23(5), 362-380. doi: 10.1108/02652320510629250.

Laukkanen, T. (2007). Internet vs Mobile Banking: Comparing Customer Value Perceptions. Business Process Management Journal, 13(6), 788-797.

Laukkanen, T., & Lauronen, J. (2005). Consumer Value Creation in Mobile Banking Services. International Journal of Mobile Communications, 3(4), 325-338.

Lee, K. C., & Chung, N. (2009). Understanding Factors Affecting Trust in and Satisfaction with Mobile Banking in Korea: A Modified DeLone and McLean's Model Perspective. Interacting with Computers, 21(5-6), 385-392.

Limayem, M., Hirt, S. G., and Cheung, C. M. K. (2007). "How Habit Limits the Predictive Power of Intentions: The Case of IS Continuance," MIS Quarterly, 31(4), 705-737.

Lin, H. F. (2011). An empirical investigation of mobile banking adoption: The effect of innovation attributes and knowledge-based trust. International Journal of Information Management, 31(3), 252-260. doi: 10.1016/j.ijinfomgt.2010.07.006.

Luarn, P., & Lin, H.-H. (2005). Toward an Understanding of the Behavioral Intention to Use Mobile Banking. Computers in Human Behavior, 21(6), 873-891.

Luo, X., Li, H., Zhang, J., & Shim, J. P. (2010). Examining Multi-dimensional Trust and Multi-faceted Risk in Initial Acceptance of Emerging Technologies: An Empirical Study of Mobile Banking Services. Decision Support Systems, 49(2), 222-234.

Marsh, H. W., & Hocevar, D. (1985). Application of confirmatory factor analysis to the study of self-concept: First-and higher order factor models and their invariance across groups. Psychological bulletin, 97(3), 562.

Mallat, N., Rossi, M., & Tuunainen, V. K. (2004). Mobile Banking Services. Communications of the ACM, 47(5), 42-46.

MIC. (2009). Taiwan mobile Internet survey. Available at: http://www.find.org.tw/find/home.aspx?page=many&id=234

Moore, R. (2000). The revival of creationism in the United States. Journal of Biological Education, 35(1), 17-21.

Moore, G. C., & Benbasat, I. (1991). Development of an Instrument to Measure the Perceptions of Adopting an Information Technology Innovation. Information Systems Research, 2(3), 222.

Nelson, L. L. (1990). Individual adjustment to information driven technologies: A critical review. MIS Quarterly, 14(1), 79-100.

Ngai, E. W. T., & Gunasekaran, A. (2007). A Review for Mobile Commerce Research and Applications. Decision Support Systems, 43(1), 3-15.

Novak TP, Hoffman DL, Yung Y-F. (2000). Measuring the customer experience in online environments: a structural modeling approach. Market Sciences, 19(1), 22-42.

Papies, D., & Clement, M. (2008). Adoption of new movie distribution services on the Internet. Journal of Media Economics, 21(3), 131-157.

Piderit, S.K. (2000). Rethinking resistance and recognizing ambivalence: A multidimensional view of attitudes toward an organizational change. Academy of Management Review, 25(4), 783-794.

Polites, G. L., and Karahanna, E. (2012). Shackled to the Status Quo: The Inhibiting Effects of Incumbent System Habit, Switching Costs, and Inertia on New System Acceptance. MIS Quarterly, 36(1), 21-42.

Porter, M. E. (1998). Competitive Strategy: Techniques for Analyzing Industries and Competitors. Free Press, New York, NY.

Riivari, J. (2005). Mobile banking: A powerful new marketing and CRM tool for financial services companies all over Europe. Journal of Financial Services Marketing, 10(1), 11-20.

Ritov, I., and Baron, J. (1992). Status quo and omission biases. Journal of Risk and Uncertainty, 5(1), 49-61.

Rogers, E. M. (1995). Diffusion of Innovation (5th ed.). New York: Free Press.

Samuelson, W., and Zeckhauser, R. (1988). Status quo bias in decision making. Journal of Risk and Uncertainty, 1(1), 7-59.

Scornavacca, E. and H. Hoehle. (2007). Mobile banking in Germany: A strategic perspective. International Journal of Electronic Finance, 1(3), 304-320.

Schierz, P. G., Schilke, O., & Wirtz, B. W. (2010). Understanding consumer acceptance of mobile payment services: An empirical analysis. Electronic Commerce Research and Applications, 9(3), 209-216.

Singh, S., Srivastava, V., and R. K. Srivastava. (2010). Customer acceptance of mobile banking: A conceptual framework. SIES Journal of Management, 7(1), 55-64.

Sripalawat, J., M. Thongmak, and A. Ngramyarn, (2011). M-banking in metropolitan Bangkok and a comparison with other countries. The Journal of Computer Information Systems, 51(3), 67-76.

Suoranta, M. and M. Mattila. (2004). Mobile banking and consumer behavior: New insights into the diffusion pattern. Journal of Financial Services Marketing, 8(4), 354-366.

Tariq, B. (2007). Exploring Factors Influencing the Adoption of Mobile Commerce. Journal of Internet Banking and Commerce, 12(3).

Tsai, M-C., Lee, W., & Wu, H-C. (2010). Determinants of RFID adoption intention: Evidence from Taiwanese retail chains. Information & Management, 47, 255-261.

Venkatesh, V., & Zhang, X. (2010). Unified Theory of Acceptance and Use of Technology: US Vs. China. Journal of Global Information Technology Management, 13(1).

Venkatesh, V., Thong, J. Y., & Xu, X. (2012). Consumer acceptance and use of information technology: extending the unified theory of acceptance and use of technology. MIS quarterly, 36(1), 157-178.

Vijayasarathy, L. R. (2004). Predicting consumer intentions to use on-line shopping: The case for an augmented technology acceptance model. Information and Management, 41(6), 747-762.

Wessels, L., & Drennan, J. (2010). An Investigation of Consumer Acceptance of M-banking. International Journal of Bank Marketing, 28(7), 547-568.

Yeh, Y. S., & Li, Y.-M. (2009). Building trust in m-commerce: contributions from quality and satisfaction. Online Information Review, 33(6), 1066-1086.

Yu, C. S. (2012). Factors Affecting Individuals to Adopt Mobile Banking: Empirical Evidence from the UTAUT Model. Journal of Electronic Commerce Research, 13(2), 104-121.

Zhou, T. (2011). An Empirical Examination of Initial Trust in Mobile Banking. Internet Research, 21(5), 527-540.

Zhou, T. (2012a). Understanding users' initial trust in mobile banking: An elaboration likelihood perspective. Computers in Human Behavior, 28, 1518-1525.

Zhou, T. (2012b). Examining mobile banking user adoption from the perspectives of trust and flow experience. Information Technology & Management, 13, 27-37.

Zhou, T., Lu, Y., & Wang, B. (2010). Integrating TTF and UTAUT to explain mobile banking user adoption. Computers in Human Behavior, 26(4), 760-767. doi: http://dx.doi.org/10.1016/j.chb.2010.01.013

DECISION SCIENCES INSTITUTE

Corporate Sustainability: An Analysis of CSR and CSV

(Full Paper Submission)

Ravi S. Behara
Florida Atlantic University
rbehara@fau.edu

Rainford M. Knight
Florida Atlantic University
rknight2@fau.edu

Joel M. DiCicco
Florida Atlantic University
jdicicco@fau.edu

ABSTRACT

This study explores the reporting Corporate Social Responsibility (CSR) and Creating Shared Value (CSV) programs in organizations. We analyze Bloomberg data that is based on publicly disclosed information. Currently companies are measuring their own progress on their social benefit and business value with significantly different reporting formats. Our study explores these issues through two case studies profiling Nestlé and PepsiCo, and comparing their programs. We find that CSR and CSV program metrics are not standard across the industry, companies can select and exclude metrics to represent and best support their programs. We recommend that companies create or maintain accurate reporting and tracking for their CSR and CSV programs until standard guidelines are implemented within their industries. Standard and consistent metrics will help companies attain effective sustainable practices throughout their supply chain, and thereby contribute to improved performance and enhanced brand image.

KEYWORDS: Corporate Sustainability, Corporate Social Responsibility, Creating Shared Value

INTRODUCTION

Corporate Sustainability is a mix corporate social responsibility, creating shared value, stakeholder theory and accountability. It's an emerging concept that leaders are adopting as an alternative to the conventional growth and profit-maximization model. It takes into account that corporate growth and profitability are essential, but there also should be a focus on pursuing societal goals, relating to sustainable development, environmental protection, social justice and equity, and economic development. Corporate sustainability also creates long-term consumer and employee value by implementing green initiatives that take into consideration how a business operates in the social, cultural, and economic environment. The Institute of Supply Management defines sustainability as "Sustainability is the ability to meet current needs without hindering the ability to meet the needs of future generations in terms of economic, environmental and social challenges."

Corporate Social Responsibility (CSR) and Creating Shared Value (CSV) programs complement each but are not composed of all of the same concepts. CSR is focused on philanthropy and improving the brand image by giving back. CSV, on the other hand helps businesses to prosper over the long term, so that the communities they serve also prosper. It explains how businesses can create competitive advantage, which in turn will deliver better returns for shareholders, through actions that substantially address a social or environmental challenge. It is important for MNCs to implement these programs for brand favorability and long term sustainability.

The Sustainability Accounting Standards Board is working on creating industry standards for investors and stakeholders to compare and evaluate companies based on their social impact. The International Integrated Reporting Council is developing a process to submit integrated financial, environmental, social and governance reporting. Finally, the most important factor in establishing a corporate social responsibility program is to conduct extensive research to define a social problem that fits well within the company structure and culture.

The Institute for Supply Management (ISM) has created 10 primary Principles of Sustainability through Corporate Social Responsibility and Creating Shared Value: (1) Anti-corruption (2) Diversity (3) Environment (4) Ethics (5) Financial Integrity & transparency (6) Global citizenship (7) Human Rights (8) Labor rights and (9) Sustainability. They measure their best-in-class practices by sustainability/CSR Initiatives, committing resources to CSR, organization wide program integration in supply chain, engagement by executive management and sharing strategies internally and with suppliers. ISM recommendations to ensure Sustainability: (1) select sustainable suppliers, (2) measure supplier performance, (3) track supplier compliance, (4) establish processes for supplier sourcing, (5) manage risk and contingency plans to ensure uninterrupted supply (business continuity), (6) develop sustainability strategies, goals and objectives, establish policies and procedures and (7) publish results and accomplishments.

LITERATURE REVIEW

This literature review will begin by addressing the essence of Corporate Social Responsibility ("CSR") and its basic working definition. Some have suggested that CSR laid the foundation for the Creating Shared Value ("CSV") concept. However, not all in academia agree that CSV is a brand new concept. Therefore, the counter-argument then will be presented. Finally, an emerging concept blending both the CSR and the CSV concepts into a macro-framework, Integrated Value Creation ("IVC"), will be discussed.

Citing Carroll, Nalband and Al-Amri (2013) explained that there are "...four faces of corporate citizenship": 1) economic responsibilities to the corporation, 2) legal responsibilities to operate within the boundaries of law and policy, 3) ethical responsibilities to act morally and ethically, and 4) philanthropic responsibilities to benefit society as a whole. They then elaborated by citing Lawrence, Weber, et al who approached CSR from a slightly different perspective identifying charity and stewardship as the core elements. According to Nalband and Am-Amri, the challenge for organizations is not so much the charity, as many corporations donate to worthy causes; rather it is the stewardship component that poses difficulty because "it compels business to be 'trustees,' an obligation to function in the general interest of the public." Authors Ghasemi, Nazemi, & Hajirahimian (2014), on the other hand, opted to adopt the definition of CSR established by the World Business Council for Sustainable Development (WBCSD): "...[A] business commitment which contributes to sustainable economic development through team work with employees and their representatives, their families, and local and public communities, to improve the quality of life by means of beneficial ways both for the business itself and for development".

Orr and Sarni (2015) define CSV as: ". . . policies and operating practices that enhance the competitiveness of a company while simultaneously advancing the economic and social conditions in which it operates. Shared value creation focuses on identifying and expanding the connections between societal and economic progress". Authors Ghasemi, Nazemi, & Hajirahimian (2014) discussed how companies can morph from being a CSR to CSV using a case study of an Iranian Steel company. The Mobarakeh Steel Company believed in CSR for purposes of gaining a competitive advantage in the world marketplace but decided to progress forward with a CSV approach to improve upon its current successes. They sought a win-win through the application of a formulated set of detailed tasks. These tasks included: 1) disclosing CSR in annual reports, 2) promoting the use of CSR indicators nationally and internationally, 3) aligning synergistic goals, 4) using expert opinions with regards to social impacts of decisions made, and 5) benchmarking to competitors.

Numerous companies exhort the benefits of CSV. For example, in an interview by Nina Kruschwitz of the MIT Sloan Management Review (2013), Hans Joehr, corporate head of agriculture at Nestlé, stated that Nestlé provides "people with the access to knowledge and information they need to increase productivity and establish sustainable production systems. It's all part of the company's Creating Shared Value (CSV) approach to business, a process that requires us to look for ways to create value for our shareholders while also ensuring we create value for the communities in which we operate". He also stated that, unlike many companies, Nestlé doesn't need to use sustainability officers because CSV is built into all their operations.

Orr and Sarni (2015) stated that what delineates the CSV from CSR is that companies using CSV "embrace longer-term, more environmentally and socially inclusive strategies as opposed to *ad hoc* forays into sustainability initiatives". Glaringly missing from both models, according to Orr and Sarni, however, is the presence of personal values in the equation. Echoing the sentiment of authors Nalband and Am-Amri, Orr and Sarni also concluded that even CSV is lacking an overall stewardship of the mission. Collective action and governance seem omitted from CSV.

Orr and Sarni are not the only detractors of CSV. In a scathing critique of CSV, Crane, Palazzo, Spence and Matten (2014), argued that "...it is unoriginal, it ignores the tensions between social and economic goals, it is naïve about the challenges of business compliance, and it is based on a shallow conception of the role of the corporation in society". One of these authors' major concerns is the lack of a universal alignment for all stakeholders. Satisfying one group might not be satisfying another. They used Nestle to illustrate that in "...the processed food industry,... [companies such as Nestlé] have been lauded as pioneers of shared value in some aspects of their operations while simultaneously castigated for deliberately addicting consumers to high contents of sugar, salt, and fat in their main business". The authors continued with their arguments also pointing out that CSV is unrealistic in terms of corporate compliance with government regulations and the monitoring of its supply chains.

Recently, authors Visser and Kymal (2015) introduced yet another concept, Integrated Value Creation (IVC), which extends CSR and CSV. IVC "...combines many of the ideas and practices already in circulation, like corporate social responsibility (CSR), sustainability and creating shared values (CSV), but signals some important shifts, especially by focusing on integration and value creation". According to the authors, most organizations respond piecemeal to: 1) safety and social issues, 2) quality issues, 3) environmental, economic, and ethical issues, 4) labor issues, 5) carbon or climate issues, and 6) health and human rights issues. The authors suggested a seven step process for the integration of the goals and concepts promulgated by CSR and CSV. The steps to be taken in order are as follows: 1) Context Analysis, 2) Stakeholder Assessment, 3) Leadership Review, 4) Risk Assessment, 5) Opportunity Analysis, 6) Process Redesign, and 7) Systems Integration. The authors concluded that the most important item in this entire process of IVC is the implementation and delineated in detail the processes needed to reach the next steps.

This study explores the reporting Corporate Social Responsibility (CSR) and Creating Shared Value (CSV) programs in organizations as they relate to their supply chains. Since there are no standardized guidelines for reporting CSR and CSV programs, we analyze data from company profiles and reports with the financial and environmental data extracted from the Bloomberg terminal that is based on publicly disclosed regulatory compliance information. Currently companies are measuring their own progress on their social benefit and business value with significantly different reporting formats. Our study explores these issues through comparing two programs at Nestlé and PepsiCo.

CASE STUDY: COMPARING Nestle` and PepsiCo

PepsiCo's sustainability program "Performance with a Purpose", main goal is to deliver top-tier financial performance while creating sustainable value for all stakeholders. PepsiCo's 2013 Sustainability report, they state that they conserved water in internal operations and throughout their supply chain, respect shared users of water and work with partners to help provide access to safe water. In 2013 alone, their operational water efficiency programs achieved estimated water-flow savings of more than 14 billion liters. In 2013, their packaging, recycling and waste reduction included Frito-Lay North America eliminating more than 11 million pounds of flexible film packaging and PepsiCo recycled and/or reused nearly 93% of total waste generated at their company-owned manufacturing facilities. PepsiCo's Greenhouse Gas (GHG) Emissions program has a goal of achieving total reduction in GHG emissions by reducing energy use in their manufacturing operations, exploring renewable alternatives, and improving the efficiency of their fleet and suppliers. Sustainable agriculture helps secure their supply chain, drive productivity and enable future growth. Focus areas include responsible sourcing, sustainable certification for ingredients and sustainable palm oil sourcing.

We compared Bloomberg data by segment for Nestlé and Pepsi which are both in the food and beverage industry. The data for both companies is categorized by (1) Social; (2) Environmental; (3) Environmental Social and Governance (ESG) ratios; (4) Carbon Dioxide Project (CDP) Climate Change; (5) Executive and Director Compensation; and (5) Governance. However, key performance metrics within each of these categories are not standard across both companies. Nestlé and Pepsi report different data sets within each category. Despite the differences with metrics, there are enough comparisons across categories to compare company performance. Nestlé outperforms Pepsi in the Bloomberg data analyzed within the categories.

Social: Both Pepsi and Nestlé reported social disclosure scores from 2006 – 2013. Nestlé had higher social disclosure scores each year, except in 2010, where both companies scored the same (38.60). Nestlé shows an upward trend in scores during this time period which implies a relationship with their CSV programs. Pepsi remains flat from 2010 to 2013. Pepsi reported CSR employee training in 2009. Nestlé did not report any CSR employee training from 2006 – 2013.

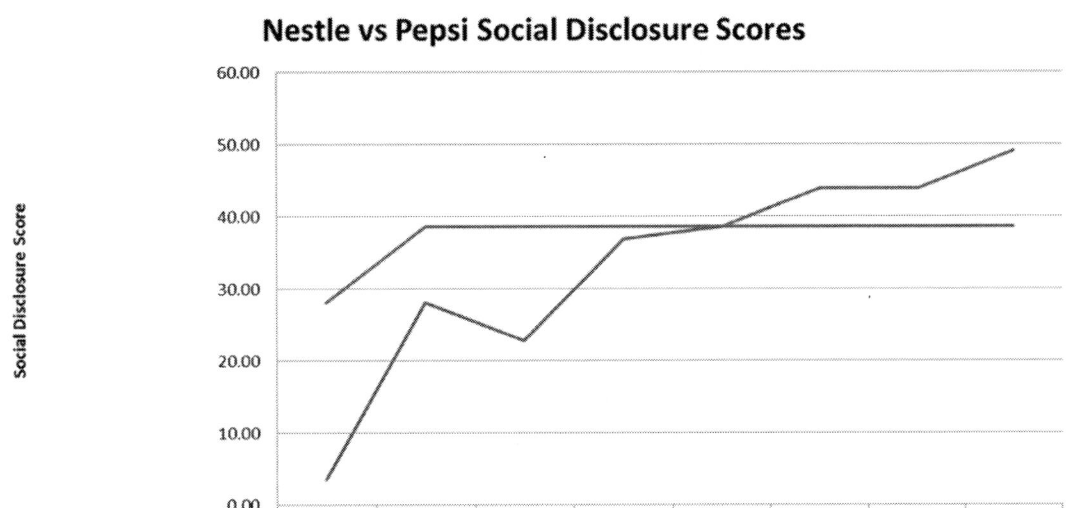

	2006	2007	2008	2009	2010	2011	2012	2013
Nestle SA (NESN VX) - Social	28.07	38.60	38.60	38.60	38.60	43.86	43.86	49.12
PepsiCo Inc (PEP US) - Social	3.51	28.07	22.81	36.84	38.60	38.60	38.60	38.60

Bloomberg reports social metrics beyond the social disclosure scores including employee related metrics. We selected the disclosure score as a metric that tied most directly to CSV programs rather than other metrics such as employee turnover and % women in management metrics. Although the employee components are important measures within a multinational company, the social disclosure score is a method to compare and contrast companies. Other metrics within this category are not reported across companies.

Environmental: Bloomberg reports several metrics within the environmental category (1) environmental disclosure score; (2) greenhouse gasses; (3) emissions; (4) energy consumption; (5) water use, and (6) waste. Nestlé and Pepsi report different metrics within the environmental category. Nestlé reports more comprehensive data than Pepsi which implies attention to detailed environmental operations, transparency and a continuous improvement culture.

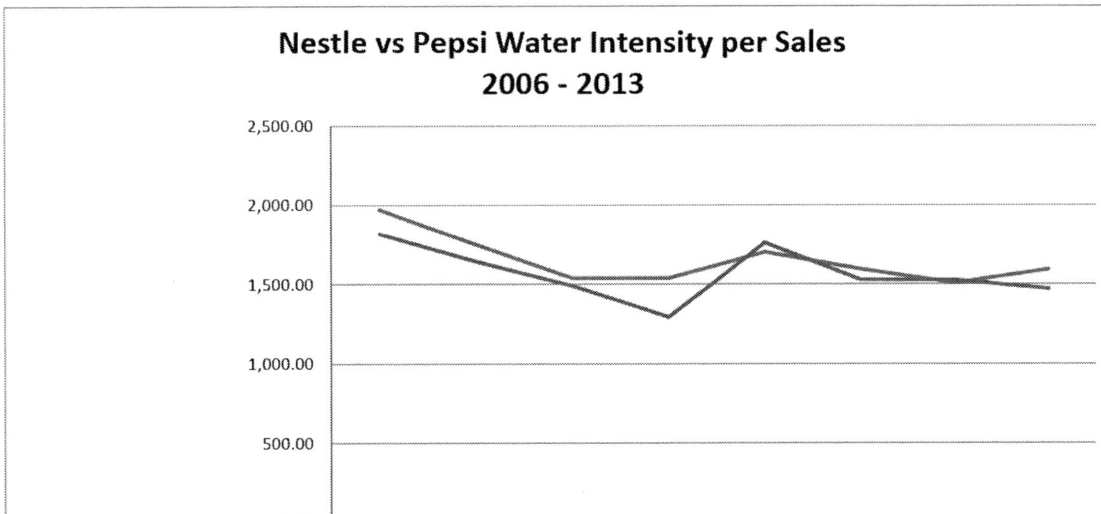

	2006	2007	2008	2009	2010	2011	2012	2013
Nestle Water Intensity per Sales	1,971.27	1,750.11	1,539.42	1,539.14	1,701.78	1,595.25	1,508.09	1,592.27
Pepsi Water Intensity per Sales	1,818.60	1,644.68	1,490.05	1,293.02	1,761.82	1,529.23	1,526.90	1,471.05

Nestlé and Pepsi both report water intensity which is a component related to operations and manufacturing processes. Water consumption is a factor for some companies to measure and market sustainability. Nestlé water intensity trends downward from 2006 – 2013 compared to Nestlé which shows a spike from 2009 to 2010 and then a decline.

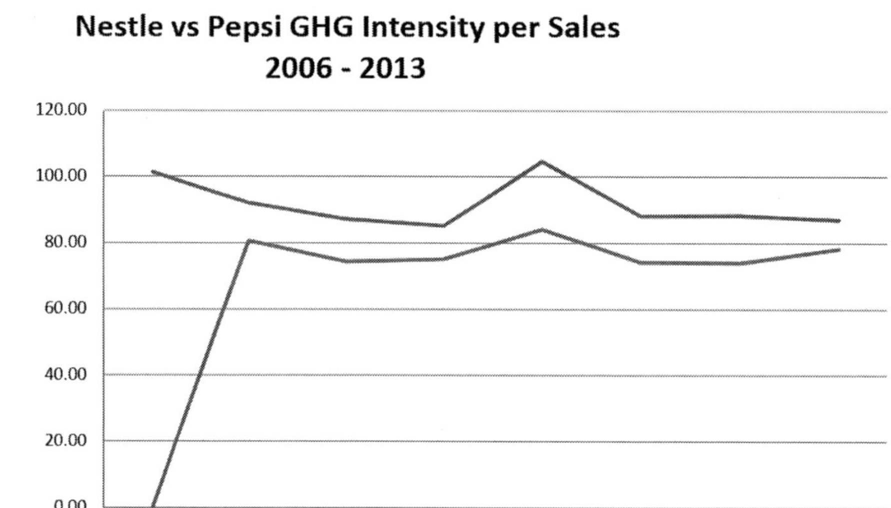

	2006	2007	2008	2009	2010	2011	2012	2013
Nestle GHG Intensity per Sales	0.00	80.59	74.35	75.13	84.09	74.23	74.00	78.23
Pepsi GHG Intensity per Sales	101.32	92.09	87.14	85.19	104.57	88.19	88.30	87.04

Nestlé and Pepsi both measure greenhouse gas intensity per Sales. Nestlé did not report this data in 2006. Both companies experienced an increase in 2010 and relatively flat performance for the time period 2006 – 2013. Pepsi has a higher intensity compared to Nestlé.

We analyzed the environmental data set and combined the most relevant operational metrics to compare Nestlé and Pepsi's performance. We selected greenhouse gas emissions, total energy consumption, total water use and total waste. During 2006 – 2013, Nestlé's total energy consumption increased while the water and waste remained flat. Total greenhouse gasses remained relatively flat with only a slight uptick from 2012 to 2013.

During the same time period, Pepsi's total water use increased from 2009 to 2010. Greenhouse gas emissions, total energy consumption and total waste increased slightly during when water use increased from 2009 to 2010. All metrics remained relatively flat from 2010 to 2013.

Nestlé and Pepsi also reported environmental scores and ISO certified sites. Nestlé reported higher environmental scores compared to Pepsi. Nestlé also had 5 to 6 times the number of ISO certified sites compared to Pepsi during 2013.

Nestle Environmental
GHG Emissions, Energy Consumption, Water and Waste
2006 - 2013

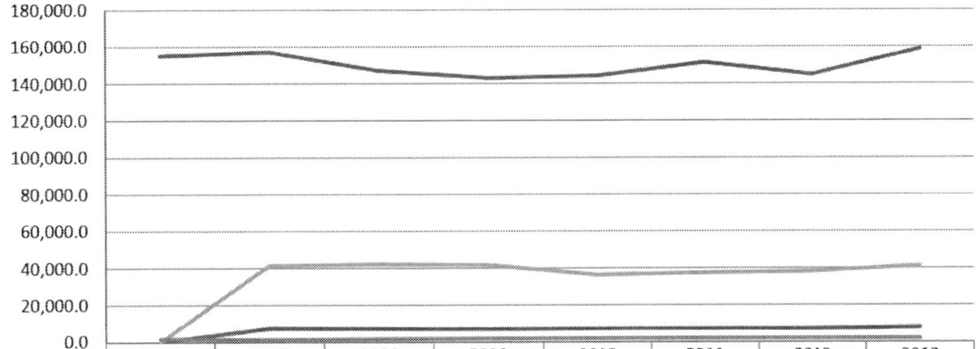

	2006	2007	2008	2009	2010	2011	2012	2013
Total GHG Emissions	0.0	7,230.0	7,100.0	6,980.0	7,120.0	7,040.0	7,100.0	7,800.0
Total Energy Consumption	0.0	41,388.9	42,275.0	41,750.0	36,277.8	37,333.3	38,111.1	41,277.8
Total Water Use	155,000.0	157,000.0	147,000.0	143,000.0	144,100.0	151,300.0	144,700.0	158,765.0
Total Waste	1,600.0	1,070.0	1,520.0	1,800.0	1,800.0	1,763.0	1,745.0	1,777.0

Pepsi Environmental
GHG Emissions, Energy Consumption, Water and Waste
2006 - 2013

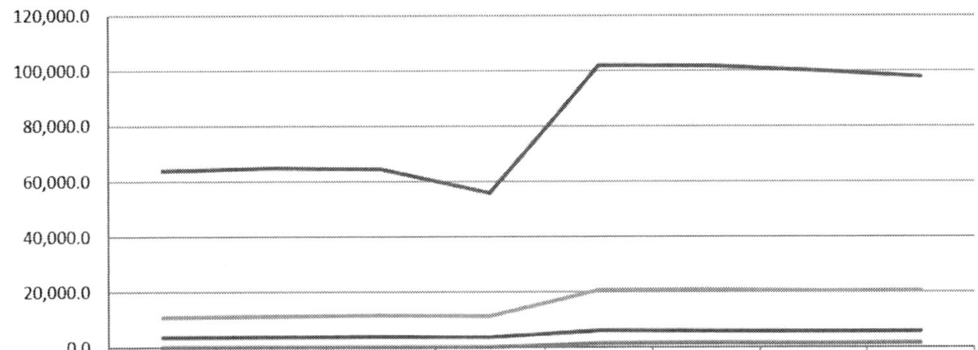

	2006	2007	2008	2009	2010	2011	2012	2013
Total GHG Emissions	3,560.0	3,635.0	3,769.0	3,683.0	6,048.0	5,865.0	5,783.0	5,781.0
Total Energy Consumption	10,900.0	11,298.0	11,600.0	11,350.0	20,655.0	20,806.0	20,405.0	20,430.0
Total Water Use	63,900.0	64,922.0	64,446.0	55,900.0	101,900.0	101,700.0	100,000.0	97,700.0
Total Waste	0.0	0.0	0.0	0.0	1,343.0	1,406.0	1,360.0	1,393.0

Environmental Social and Governance (ESG) ratios: Bloomberg reports ESG ratios which are useful to compare the relationship with the environmental metrics and the financials. Further research is necessary in order to properly interpret and derive conclusions about each metric. For example, Nestlé improved with GHG intensity per sales but increased with GHG intensity per energy. Pepsi reports improvements with GHG intensity per sales and has improved since 2006 with GHG intensity per energy. The next step in the research is to better understand the calculations and drivers of these metrics and how these associate to the operational processes with energy efficiency.

Carbon Dioxide Project (CDP): The Bloomberg category for CDP disclosure reports the same categories for both companies however the metrics within each category are different for each company. This supports the hypothesis that companies do not measure sustainability performance consistently. The differences within the CDP category are enough that conclusions cannot be drawn without further research. It is worth noting that both companies have reductions in place.

Executive and Director Compensation: Bloomberg reports executive and director compensation as part of the sustainability reporting. Both companies report essentially the same metrics. It is worth noting that Pepsi had more executive changes reported than Nestlé.

Governance: The final category of Bloomberg sustainability reporting is related to governance. Both companies report governance disclosure scores of 66 and measure similar characteristics of board diversity and structure. The governance section has the least variation with metrics and reporting. From the initial research, there do not appear to be any notable factors between the two companies that would likely contribute to sustainability differences.

CONCLUSIONS

Nestlé has more comprehensive reporting with metrics that pertain to sustainability and CSV programs compared to Pepsi. The first tier suppliers and many of the secondary suppliers seem to contribute to a “green” supply chain from the reported metrics. Since the metrics are not standard across the industry, companies can select and exclude metrics to represent and best support their CSV programs. Our recommendation is for corporations to create standardized metrics until there is an industry standard is established. Despite this it is interesting to note that Nestlé had significant food safety issues with their major brand Maggie Noodles in India in 2015.

Many companies are still trying to clarify what is a good sustainability strategy is and what does it mean to be “green”? This means different things to companies depending on their industry. Overall it means giving back to communities and creating a strategy that solves a social and/or economic problem that will in turn increase profits. CSR and CSV is still an emerging concept that varies greatly from company to company in every aspect. CSR is about “doing good” through philanthropy while CSV is focused on profit maximization while solving an economic, social problem. Both of these are essential in maintaining corporate sustainability. We found that Nestlé has done extensive reporting on their CSV program since 2005. The Bloomberg portal data varied greatly by company, and had a lot of detail on company segments, their suppliers and their customers. Our recommendation is for companies to create or maintain accurate reporting and tracking for their Corporate Social Responsibility (CSR) and Creating Shared Value (CSV) programs until standard guidelines are implemented. Standard and consistent metrics will help companies maximize profits and drive down their operational costs through supplier collaboration and efficiency. The operational improvements toward sustainability will improve the overall brand image.

REFERENCES

References available upon request.

DECISION SCIENCES INSTITUTE

Critical Success Factors Impacting Cloud-Based EHR Systems

Mohammad I. Merhi
Department of Decision Sciences
Judd Leighton School of Business & Economics
Indiana University South Bend
mmerhi@iusb.edu

Sheel Patel
Department of Decision Sciences
Judd Leighton School of Business & Economics
Indiana University South Bend
shapate@iusb.edu

ABSTRACT

The implementation of Electronic Health Record (EHR) systems continues to generate a lot of interest among researchers and practitioners. During implementation many organizations run into problems that affect the success of the project. Cloud-based EHR is a substitute system that solve some of the technical issues that organizations face. Studies on cloud-based EHR systems are scarce. This research in progress investigates the critical success factors impacting the implementation of cloud-based EHR systems. We plan to assess the significance of these factors on implementation and present our results at the conference.

KEYWORDS: Electronic Health Record, Cloud Computing, Success Factors, EHR Implementation, and Could EHR.

INTRODUCTION

Over the last decade, many countries' governments, including the U.S., are investing billions of dollars in the digitalization of the hospital legacy system of recording patient information into Electronic Health Record (EHR) (Hayrinen et al., 2008; Merhi, 2015). According to the International Organization of Standardization (ISO), EHR is defined as "a repository of patient data in digital form, stored and exchanged securely, and accessible by multiple authorized users. It contains retrospective, concurrent, and prospective information and its primary purpose is to support continuing, efficient and quality integrated health care" (ISO, 2004). In general, EHR systems contain patients' medical history, diagnoses, medications, treatment plans, immunization dates, allergies, radiology images, laboratory test results among others (Hayrinen et al., 2008). This information is securely stored and only made accessible to authorized users when needed. Authorized users are not only limited to patients, doctors, nurses and laboratories but can also be shared with pharmacies, emergency facilities, specialists and other areas where it is required (Menachemi & Collum, 2011). EHR systems not only share the information between various medical institutions to provide better care but also to help improve the safety, efficiency and quality of care and to reduce the cost of healthcare (Blumenthal & Tavenner, 2010; McClellan, 2011).

A report from Healthcare IT News states that 96% of the providers say that their infrastructure is not ready for full integration of EHR technologies in their workflow (Rossi, 2015). Over 90% of regional extension centers registered physicians are currently using EHR systems and 75.5% of the hospitals in the U.S. have basic EHR systems (Health IT, 2015; Charles et al., 2015). With all these physicians who are using and recording data in EHR systems, the data will keep on significantly increasing. The health care sector is planning to increase their spending by 65% on analytics in order to analyze the EHR data and make decisions in coming years (Rossi, 2015). Some of the areas where the healthcare sector will be spending the most are data warehouse and data models, real time data analytics applications, data security, IT systems for optimizing data processing and IT infrastructure to optimize data storage (Rossi, 2015). We argue that cloud computing can easily eliminate most of this spending especially those related to storage and infrastructure. Due to limited knowledge about Cloud and many misconceptions, clinics ignore the option of the Cloud based EHR system. In this paper we present the critical success factors that affect the implementation of Cloud based EHR systems and make it a successful project. Current studies in the literature have not explored this area. We thus aim to contribute to the body of the knowledge on EHR systems implementation and Cloud computing.

CLOUD COMPUTING

Cloud computing is made up of hardware and software through networks which are elastic, resourced pooled within an infrastructure to meet the on-time demand services (Armbrust, 2010; Bhatt, 2011; Srinivas, et al., 2012). Cloud computing provides three types of services:

- Software as a service (SaaS): It is software or applications distribution model which are hosted by the vendors or service providers and made available to customers through the network, mostly through the Internet.
- Platform as a Service (PaaS): provides a platform to the customers to run, manage and deploy application and software on Cloud without building or managing the infrastructure for Cloud computing.
- Infrastructure as a Service (IaaS): provides the basic infrastructure of the virtualized pool of outsourced services. Users are provided with the hardware, network connectivity, bandwidth and IP addresses with which the users can develop their own applications and systems. Users have flexibility of choosing their own operating system, applications and software (Armbrust, 2010; Bhatt, 2011; Srinivas, et al., 2012).

Cloud computing offers a wide range of choice and agility to the users; it is built to best suit their needs and the latest trends. The cost of implementing cloud computing is very low as the users does not have to setup new infrastructure, buy new hardware, license software or hire new personnel. Cloud computing provides encapsulated change management, that is a user can integrate his current infrastructure and technology with Cloud computing without making any major modifications in system configuration. Clouds are very compatible with next generation architecture so the new innovation and advancement in technology can be easily integrated Cloud computing, which helps to enhance the performance of the operations. Many businesses as well as organizations which lack the basic infrastructure for implementing information system can take the advantage of the cloud computing to implement information system with lowest cost and latest technology (Daley, 2008; Chao et al. 2014).

CRITICAL SUCCESS FACTORS OF CLOUD BASED EHR SYSTEM

Implementing Cloud based EHR systems is not an easy task. Below, we discuss major critical factors that organizations face and need to take care of when implementing Cloud based EHR systems. Avoiding and solving these problems will eventually lead to success in the Cloud based EHR systems implementation. The critical success factors are:

Change management

Implementation of EHR system would lead to a tremendous amount of change in the workflow of clinic and many people resist it (Chao et al., 2014). The reasons behind resistance include perceived risk and habits. The consequences of resistance can lead to delay in implementation time, decrease in efficiency, increase in cost and less chance of success in the implementation (Chao et al., 2014; Boonstra & Broekhuis, 2010). Aladwani (2001) proposed a process oriented conceptual framework that effectively deals with the change management. The framework has three phases:

- Knowledge gathering, which includes gathering as much information as possible about the resisting groups.
- Strategy implementation which includes creating strategies to communicate with the resisting groups and finding solutions.
- Status evaluation, which requires constant feedback and evaluations of the strategies implemented to make necessary changes, if required.

In addition to the conceptual framework, motivation and incentives are major factors during change management process. (Aladwani, 2001)

Data security

According to a 2014 report from the nonprofit group Identity Theft Resource Center, the Healthcare Sector accounts for 42.5% of all security breaches (Rossi, 2015). The confidential information stored in the EHR systems must be protected from entering the data into storing and retrieving. Storing information in the Cloud requires even extra security. With the Cryptographic approach, the information stored in the Cloud servers as well as the information that is being transferred from the Cloud to the application and from the application to the Cloud are all in the form of encrypted data. Only authorized users of the application can decrypt the information with the help of encryption key, which makes it safe and secure for storing and transferring information in the Cloud (Ali et al., 2015; Hoang & Dat, 2015).

Government policies

When using Cloud based EHR systems, data are stored in cloud servers which are located at different geographical sites from the clinic. Many major Cloud providers have more than one data center in the country as well as in foreign countries. Cloud providers often move their data to different locations. There are legal jurisdictions that restrict this transfer of EHR data. To comply with the national and international jurisdictions, the EHR selection team should discuss all these clauses with the Cloud based EHR system provider before selecting it (Ali et al., 2015; Schweitzer, 2012; Boonstra & Broekhuis, 2010).

Cost

High investment, lack of capital, low return on investment, lack of cost to benefit analysis are some of the major concerns about cost during implementation of EHR system (Boonstra & Broekhuis, 2010). Cloud EHR comes with the major cost saving to EHR implementation. One third of the cost of EHR system implementation is for hardware purchase and Cloud use can eliminate that cost. The U.S. government provides various incentives to the clinics for implementing EHR system and also covers the losses that occurs due to EHR system for a certain time period. It is estimated that Cloud computing can save up to 20% of the cost which is estimated to nearly $7 billion (Boonstra & Broekhuis, 2010). It is expected that the ROI to be high in the long run and have other non-monetary benefits, like satisfaction from the patient and clinic staff, reduction in errors, and many more which cannot be measured (Aita, 2008; Ambinder, 2005; Boonstra & Broekhuis, 2010).

Customization

Customizing the EHR systems based on the needs of the user is very important to increase user productivity and satisfaction. Customization process comes with a great cost as EHR system processes are developed based upon industry standards and best practices. Cloud based EHR system provides certain flexibility for customization, but this is something that EHR selection team should consult and discuss with the Cloud based EHR system provider before selecting EHR system. Many EHR systems do not allow any customizations by the users and so the user has to change the way they do business to be compatible to the new system (Ludwick & Doucette, 2008; Boonstra & Broekhuis, 2010).

User friendly application

User friendliness is a very important characteristic of computer applications because those applications containing more graphics are easier to remember, as well as to use (Ludwick, & Doucette, 2008). While selecting an EHR system for the clinic, the EHR selection team should consider the user friendliness of the application, simplicity of using application, easy to access and navigate, and how it is interacting with the user. If the application is difficult to use, users will resist it or will be frustrated and chance of error increases, leading to quitting the job. (Huser et al., 2010; Nasserh et al., 2015)

Interoperability and compatibility with other systems

EHR systems are implemented to easily maintain and transfer patient records whenever required. But due to the complexity of the structure of the system and database, it is becoming challenging to transfer EHR between different systems. Creating interfaces that are compatible with other systems can help to transfer and read the data, but the cost of developing interfaces are very high and there will be less freedom and right to customize EHR system (Chao et al., 2014).The government can play a major role in solving this problem by providing rules and guidelines for the format of data as well as storage of data. This will create a uniform structure of the data that becomes easily compatible with all the systems (Boonstra & Broekhuis, 2010; Schweitzer, 2012; Boland, 2016).

CONCLUSION

Huge spending in technology by the health care sector will move the EHR system to the Cloud computing platform. In the coming decade, more and more EHR systems will migrate towards

Cloud based EHR systems for compatibility with other systems as well as data analytics. The future of Cloud based EHR system is immeasurable. However, current research on EHR cloud based is still scarce. This research in progress extends the current literature by presenting critical factors that lead to success in Cloud-based EHR system.

After identifying the critical success factors, we aim to quantitatively assess the significance of these factors on implementation. We will happy to share any results we may have when attending the conference in November.

References

Aita, S. (2008). Implementing an EHR with ROI in mind. *Journal of Medical Practice Management*, *23*(4), 244-246.

Aladwani, A. M. (2001). Change management strategies for successful ERP implementation. *Business Process Management Journal*, *7*(3), 266-275.

Ali, M., Khan, S., & Vasilakos, A. (2015). Security in Cloud Computing. *Information Science*, *305*, 357-383.

Ambinder, E. P. (2005). Electronic Health Records. *Journal of Oncology Practice*, *1*(2), 57–63.

Armbrust, M. (2010). A view of cloud computing. *Communications of the ACM*, *53*(4), 50-58.

Bhatt, D. (2011). A Revolution in Information Technology - Cloud Computing. *Journal of Science and Technology*, *9*(2), 107-113.

Blumenthal, D. & Tavenner, M. (2010). The "Meaningful Use" Regulation for Electronic Health Records. *New England Journal of Medicine*, *363*(6), 501-504.

Boland, M. (2016). Big Data, Big Challenges. *Ophthalmology*, *123*(1), 7-8.

Boonstra, A. & Broekhuis, M. (2010). Barriers to the acceptance of electronic medical records by physicians from systematic review to taxonomy and interventions. *BMC Health Services Research*, *10*(1), 231.

Chao, G., Peng, A., & Gala, C. (2014). Cloud ERP: A new dilemma to modern organisations? *Journal of Computer Information Systems*, *54*(4), 22-30.

Charles, D., Gabriel, M., & Searcy, T. (2015). Adoption of Electronic Health Record Systems among U.S. Non Federal Acute Care Hospitals: 2008-2014. Available online at: https://www.healthit.gov/sites/default/files/data-brief/2014HospitalAdoptionDataBrief.pdf. Accessed on February 29, 2016.

Daley, W. (2008). *Computers are your future*. Upper Saddle River, NJ: Pearson/Prentice Hall.

Hayrinen, K., Saranto, K., & Nykanen, P. (2008). Definition, Structure, Content, Use and Impacts of Electronic Health Records: A Review of the Research Literature. *International Journal of Medical Informatics*, *77*(5), 291-304.

Health IT Quick Stats (2015). Health IT Quick Stats. Available online at: http://dashboard.healthit.gov/quickstats/quickstats.php. Accessed on January 23, 2016.

Hoang, D., Australia, D., & Dat, D. T. (2015). Health Data in Cloud Environments, *Proceedings of the Pacific Asia Conference on Information Systems.*

Huser, V., Narus, S., & Rocha, R. (2010). Evaluation of a flowchart-based EHR query system: A case study of RetroGuide. *Journal of Biomedical Informatics*, *43*(1), 41-50.

ISO/DTR (2014). Health Informatics – Electronic Health Record – Definition, Scope, and Context. Available online at: http://www.iso.org/iso/iso_catalogue/catalogue_tc/catalogue_detail.htm?csnumber=39525

Ludwick, D. & Doucette, J. (2008). Adopting electronic medical records in primary care: Lessons learned from health information systems implementation experience in seven countries. *International Journal of Medical Informatics*, *78*(1), 22-31.
McClellan, M. (2011). Reforming Payments to Healthcare Providers: The Key to Slowing Healthcare Cost Growth While Improving Quality? *Journal of Economic Perspectives*, *25*(2), 69-92.
Menachemi, N. & Collum, T. H. (2011). Benefits and drawbacks of electronic health record systems. *Risk Management and Healthcare Policy*, *4*, 47-55.
Merhi, M. I. (2015). A process model leading to successful implementation of electronic health record systems. *International Journal of Electronic Healthcare*, *8*(2-4), 185-201.
Nasserh Z., A., Elmogy, M., & Elkader, S. (2015). Electronic Health Records: Applications, Techniques and Challenges. *International Journal of Computer Applications*, *119*(4), 38-49.
Rose, D., Richter, L. T., & Kapustin, J. (2014). Patient experiences with electronic medical records: Lessons learned. *Journal of the American Association of Nurse Practitioners*, *26*(12), 674-680.
Rossi, B. (2015). An Inside Look at IT Trends for the Healthcare Market. Available online at: http://www.cdwcommunit.com/wp-content/uploads/2015/06/HealthTechReport_Summer2015.pdf. Accessed on January 20, 2016.
Schweitzer, E. J. (2012). Reconciliation of the cloud computing model with US federal electronic health record regulations. *Journal of the American Medical Informatics Association*, *19*(2), 161-165.
Srinivas, J., Reddy, K. V. S., & Qyser, A. M. (2012). Cloud Computing Basics. *International Journal of Advanced Research in Computer and Communication Engineering*, *1*(5), 343-347.
Thakkar, M. & Davis, D. C. (2006). Risks, Barriers, and Benefits of EHR Systems: A Comparative Study Based on Size of Hospital. *Perspectives in Health Information Management*, *3*(5), 1-19.

DECISION SCIENCES INSTITUTE
Cross aisle placement in order picking operations

Charles Petersen
Northern Illinois University
Email: cpetersen@niu.edu

Gerald Aase
Northern Illinois University
Email: gaase@niu.edu

ABSTRACT

Order picking operations need to efficiently process order in today's competitive environment. Previous research generally assumed on even placement of the cross aisles. This research examines the placement of cross aisles in order picking operations and the use of various storage policies. While previous research has examined cross aisles and storage policies, this research looks at them simultaneously. The results showed no difference between even and uneven placement of cross aisles and that within-aisle storage is better than across-aisle and random storage.

KEYWORDS: Distribution Warehousing, Order Picking, Cross Aisles, Storage Policies, Supply Chain

INTRODUCTION

Order picking is a process of retrieving items or stock-keeping units (SKU) from warehouse storage locations to satisfy customer orders and this process plays an important part in reducing warehousing and supply chain costs. Order picking constitutes 50 - 75% of the total operating costs for a typical warehouse (Bozer et al, 2010, Coyle et al, 2003). Today's warehouse managers are under a lot of pressure due to the global competition and supply chain integration initiatives to decrease order picking time in order to increase the throughput rate and lower operating costs of their operations (Frazelle, 2002).

Previous order picking research generally focuses on one of three main operating policies to improve the performance of the system: picking, routing, storage, and layout. Picking policies involve assigning items or orders to picking tours and include strict-order, batching, and zoning. Routing policies determine the route of a picker for a picking tour and range from simple heuristics to optimal procedures. Storage policies assign SKUs to storage locations. Commonly used storage policies are random storage and class-based storage where SKUs are sorted by ABC analysis into storage classes. Layout considerations are the orientation and position of picking and cross aisles.

The focus of this research is to examine the placement of a cross aisles. Previous research generally assumes an equal spacing of cross aisles, but have ignored whether unequal placement might reduce picker travel even more. In addition, the authors will evaluate the performance of class-based storage policies relative to random storage with both equally spaced and unequally spaced cross aisles in a manual picking warehouse where order size varies from only a few SKUs to many SKUs.

LITERATURE REVIEW

Order picking has been the topic of much research over the past several decades. The primary focus for most of this research has been identifying more effective picking, storage, routing, and layout policies.

Picking

Picking policies determine which SKUs are placed on a pick list and subsequently retrieved from their storage locations by a single picker. Strict-order picking is a common policy where pickers complete a tour through the warehouse to pick all SKUs for a single order. This policy is often preferred because it is easily implemented and order integrity is always maintained. Combining several orders into batches is an alternative policy that has been shown to reduce total picking time significantly (Gibson & Sharp, 1992; Rosenwein, 1996; De Koster et al, 1999; Petersen, 2000). Zone picking is another policy that divides the warehouse into zones and allows pickers to retrieve SKUs from within a single zone. Some firms have combined batching and zoning into "wave" picking where each picker is responsible for SKUs in their zone for numerous orders. The benefit for these types of policies become apparent as the size of the warehouse increases, but zone picking requires secondary operations to consolidate orders from the different zones (Petersen, 2000). For this study we will assume that orders are batched and that no picking zones are used.

Storage

Storage policies assign SKUs to storage locations. The most common policy is random storage where SKUs are assigned randomly throughout the warehouse. It is easy to administer and may ease picker congestion. Volume-based storage (VBS) policies where SKUs with the most requests or pick activity are assigned to locations near the Pick-up/Drop-off (P/D) point based on their picking volume (Jarvis & McDowell, 1991; Caron et al, 1998; Petersen & Schmenner, 1999; Jane, 2000). They are generally most effective at improving performance, but are information intensive and far more difficult to administer than a random storage policy (Petersen & Schmenner, 1999). Similar to the VBS policy, CBS ranks SKUs according to pick activity then partitions the SKUs into several storage classes and randomly assigned warehouse locations within their respective storage class area. The storage class containing the highest volume SKUs is located nearest to the P/D point. The impetus of a CBS policy is to capitalize on the logic of the VBS policy, while eliminating the considerable administrative overhead (Larson et al, 1997). Class-based storage with as few as three storage classes provides nearly the same savings as volume-based storage in an automated storage and retrieval systems (Hausman et al, 1976; Rosenblatt & Eynan, 1989; Eynan & Rosenblatt, 1994) and in manual warehouses while requiring less data processing (Petersen et al, 2004). For this study class-based storage will be used.

Routing

Routing policies determine the picking sequence of SKUs on the pick list. Using simple heuristics or optimal procedures, the goal of routing policies is to minimize the distance traveled by the picker. Optimal procedures offer the best solution, but may result in confusing routes (Ratliff & Rosenthal, 1983). Heuristics often yield near-optimal solutions while being easy to use (Hall, 1993; Petersen, 1997). Traversal routing, which is widely used in many warehouses because of its simplicity, provides good results when the pick density per picking aisle is large.

When using a traversal policy, pickers must completely traverse the entire aisle once it is entered. The combined heuristic combines traversal and return routes to further reduce picker travel to produce near-optimal solutions (De Koster & Van der Poort, 1998; Petersen, 1999; Roodbergen & De Koster, 2001a). Vaughan and Petersen (1999) developed a dynamic programming shortest path routing method to minimize the total picking distance in warehouses with multiple cross aisles. For this study we will use the combined heuristic as it has the advantage of near optimal results and requires less computational effort.

Layout

The layout of the warehouse has been considered as a factor affecting the order picking efficiency. Several issues have been researched from the alignment of the picking aisles with respect to the P/D point, the location of the P/D point, and the overall shape has also been taken into consideration as factors effecting order picking efficiency (Bassan et al, 1980; Petersen, 2002; Gue & Meller, 2009; Pohl et al, 2011). Adding cross aisles to a warehouse layout allows greater flexibility in order picking routing and therefore provides shorter order picking travel distances (Ben-Mahmud, 1987; Vaughan & Petersen, 1999; Caron et al, 2000; Roodbergen & De Koster, 2001b).

There has been research on the use of class-based storage and the placement of cross aisles. Rao and Adil (2013) investigate class based storage and the number of aisles for a variety of pick list sizes, however, their work considers only a return routing policy via the use of a center cross aisle. Berglund & Batta (2012) show analytical results that unequal cross aisles are superior to equally-spaced cross aisles. However, their results assume a center P/D point and use pick list sizes of only two to ten SKUs. In this paper, the authors use a corner P/D point, a combined routing heuristic, and use larger pick list sizes as many firms process batch orders and/or have larger orders.

This study addresses several of these outstanding items. First, this study evaluates the even and uneven placement of cross aisles with a corner P/D point in a manual order picking environment that uses bin shelving. Second, this research compares class-based storage to random storage in a warehouse with no or two cross aisles. Lastly, this research examines the effect of order pick size on the performance of cross aisle placement and storage polices.

EXPERIMENTAL DESIGN

The warehouse layout examined has ten picking aisles with front and back cross aisles. The pick-up and drop-off (P/D) point is located in the left side of the front aisle as shown in Figure 1. This model replicates a manual-picking environment where picking carts are used to transport the picked SKUs. The picking aisles are two-sided and are wide enough to allow two-way travel of picking carts. Picking can be done from both sides of the aisle without a significant change in position. The capacity of the bin shelving is 1,200 SKUs and each SKU is assigned to a single storage location. There are twelve bin facings on each side of the picking aisles and there are five storage slots per bin facing. Strict-order/batch picking is used where a picker departs the P/D point to retrieve SKUs on the pick list and transports the SKUs back to the P/D point for order consolidation, packaging, and shipment. The picking carts are designed in a manner that maintains order integrity while minimizing downstream sorting. This is commonly referred to as sort-while-pick picking. Total travel distance is collected for each simulation trial. Travel distance consists of travel along the front and back aisles and travel within the picking aisles. Because the aisle width is relatively small, we assume the operator can reach shelves on either side of the aisle without an increase in travel distance. Therefore, the composite routing heuristic is used for this experiment. This routing procedure can achieve close to optimal results when the pick density is high (Petersen & Schmenner, 1999; Petersen & Aase, 2004).

Figure 1: Basic layout

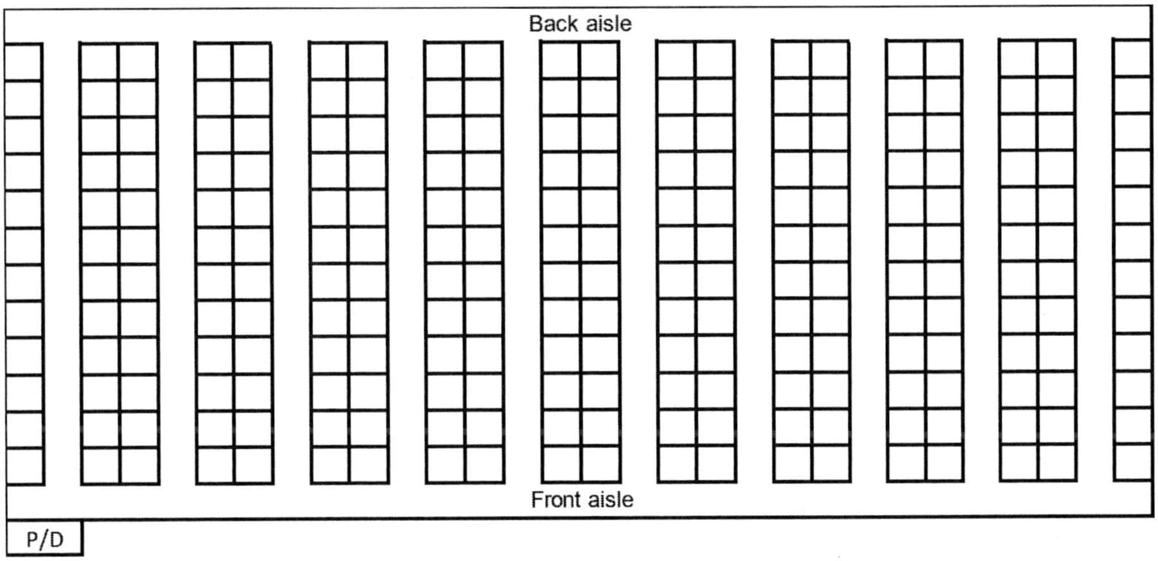

When using a class-based storage policy, SKUs are ranked according to their total volume. The ranked SKU list is partitioned into several classes, where the high volume SKUs are placed in one class and the lower volume SKUs are placed in additional classes. SKUs are then randomly assigned to storage locations within their respective class storage area (Petersen et al, 2004). For this experiment, a class partition strategy of 20/30/50 was utilized representing the ABC classes. One design parameter that a warehouse manager must select when using class-based storage policies entails the selection of the class partition strategy. Partition strategy of 20-30-50 are used for the three class system in this experiment (Petersen et al, 2004).

The other factor to consider is the number of SKUs to be picked in a picking tour. Petersen and Schmenner (1999) showed that pick list size affects the performance of storage and routing policies. Therefore, three levels of pick list sizes are considered: 5 SKUs, 15 SKUs, and 25 SKUs. Results for additional pick list sizes can be easily extrapolated from the results presented.

The purpose of this research is to examine effects of a combination of three of the factors that affect order picking efficiency is shown in the experimental design (Table 1). For the cross aisle placement Figure 2 shows an even cross aisle placement of four facings between each cross aisle. Figure 3 shows an uneven cross aisle placement of three facings between the first three cross aisles and six facings between the last two cross aisles. Figures 4 and 5 show across-aisle and within-aisle storage policies.

Table 1: Experimental design

Level	Layout	Storage Policy	Pick List Size (SKUs)
1	Basic (B)	Random (R)	5
2	Even Cross aisles (E)	Within-aisle (W)	15
3	Uneven Cross aisles (U)	Across-aisle (A)	25

There are 30 replications or pick lists generated for each pick list size. For a given pick list, SKUs are randomly generated using an 80/20 SKU demand distribution where the top 20% of the SKUs account for 80% of the demand by volume. The performance is measured by calculating the total travel distance for the order picker to complete an order. C coding has been used to simulate the warehouse model with the each of the different factors individually.

Figure 2: Even cross-aisle placement layout

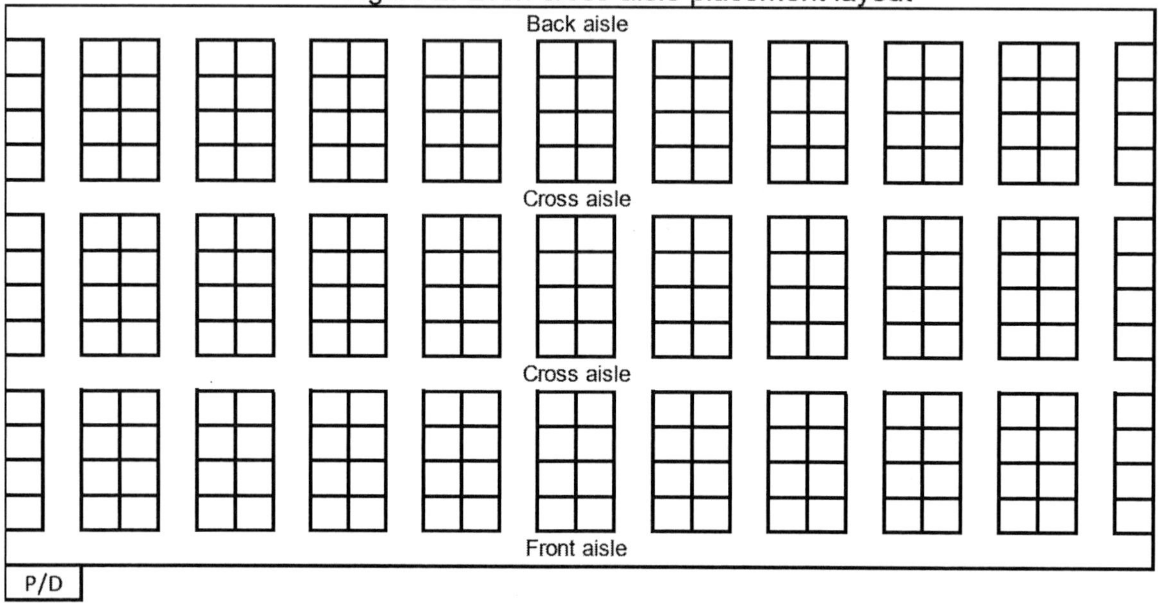

Figure 3: Uneven cross-aisle placement layout

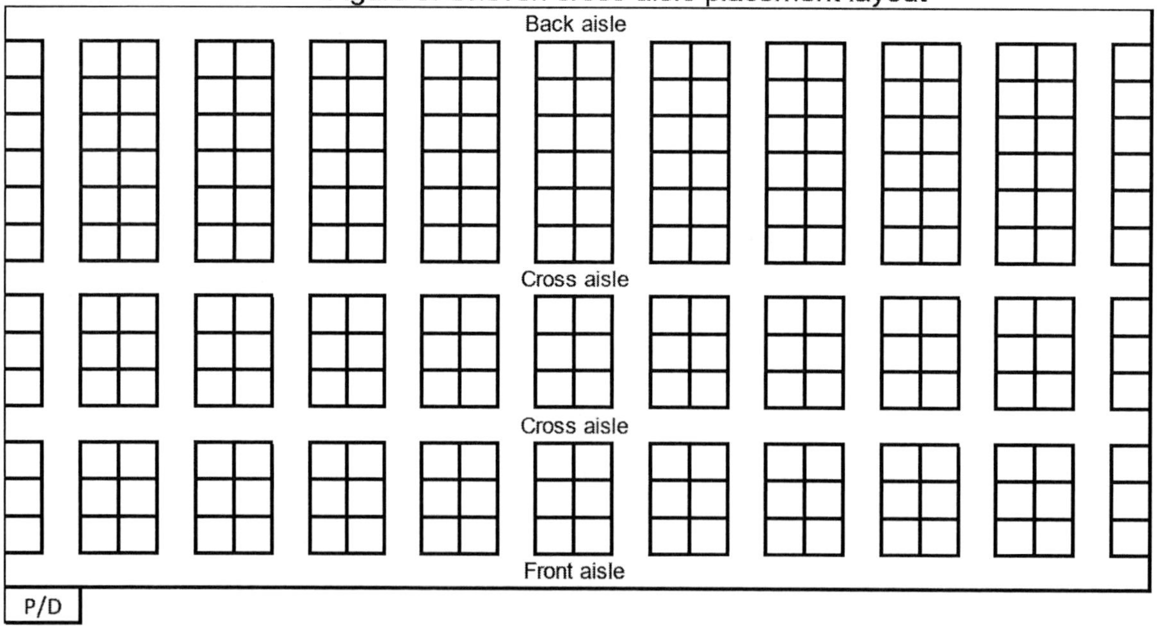

Figure 4: Across-aisle layout

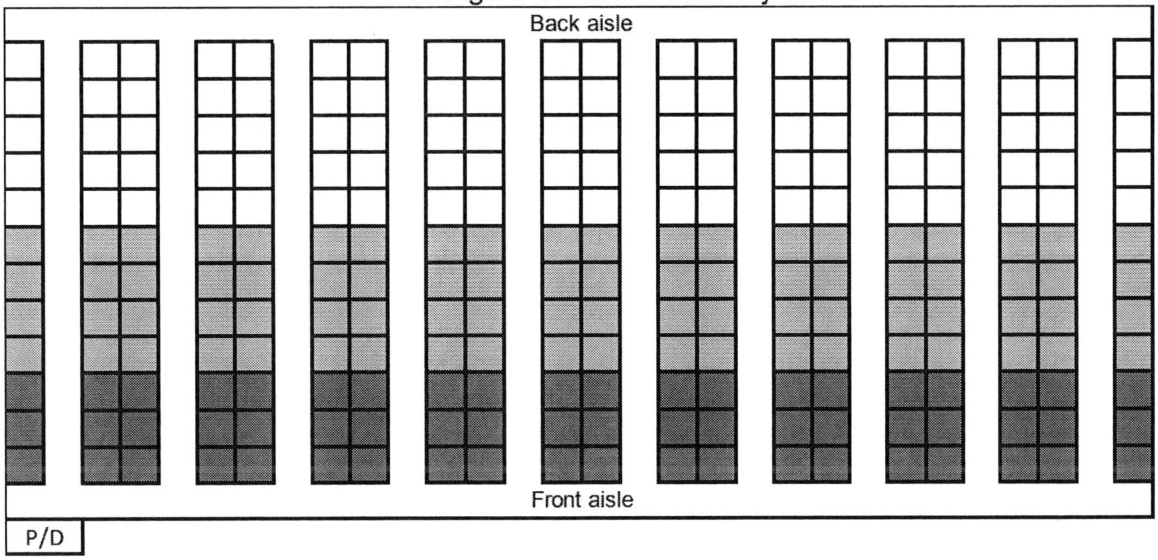

Figure 5: Within-aisle layout

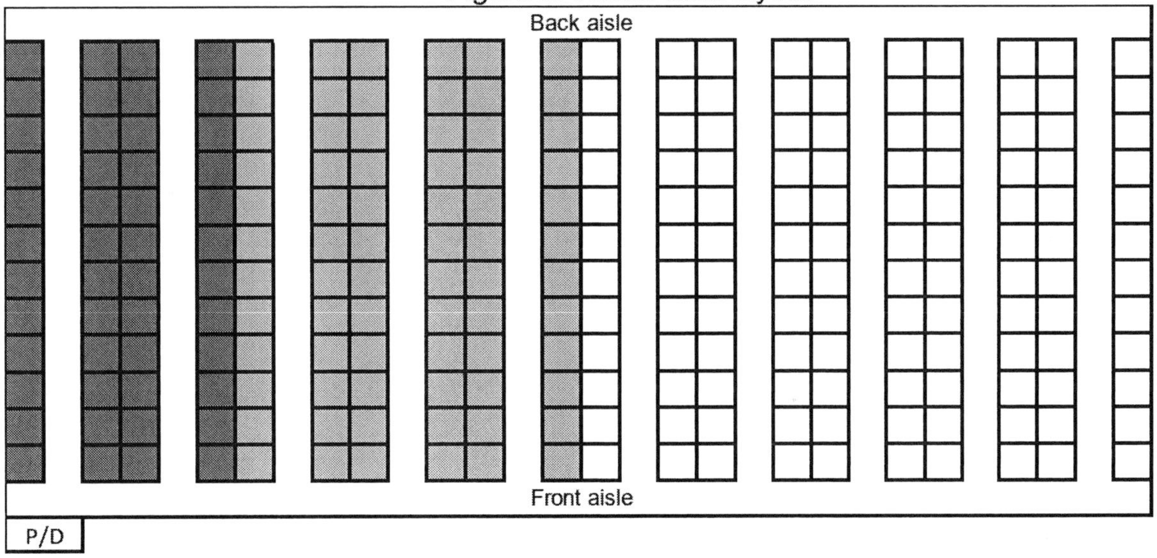

RESEARCH HYPOTHESES

The authors generated the following research hypotheses based on previous research.

Hypothesis 1

H_A: Layout with even cross aisles ≠ Layout with uneven cross aisles

Hypothesis 2

H_A: Layout with even cross aisles < Basic layout

Hypothesis 3

H_A: Layout with uneven cross aisles < Basic layout

Hypothesis 4

H_A: Layout with across-aisle storage < Layout with random storage

Hypothesis 5

H_A: Layout with within-aisle storage < Layout with random storage

Hypothesis 6

H_A: Layout with within-aisle storage < Layout with across-aisle storage

RESULTS

The results of the simulation experiment are presented in Table 2. A full-factorial analysis of variance (ANOVA) is in Table 3. The model F-value of 93.20 implies the model is significant and is statistically significance for all factors (A = Layout, B = Storage, C = SKUs) and interactions.

Table 2: Simulation results (picker travel in feet)

	Basic Layout			Even Cross Aisles			Uneven Cross Aisles		
	Random Storage	Across-aisle Storage	Within-aisle Storage	Random Storage	Across-aisle Storage	Within-aisle Storage	Random Storage	Across-aisle Storage	Within-aisle Storage
5	346.2	338.9	192.8	270.1	208.7	153.9	272.0	206.2	155.4
15	537.3	532.5	274.8	476.8	332.1	258.3	478.1	328.8	258.4
25	598.0	594.5	316.4	600.4	391.4	309.4	600.1	391.3	308.6
Overall	493.8	488.7	261.3	449.1	310.8	240.6	450.1	308.7	240.8

Table 3: Analysis of variance

Source	Sum of squares	df	Mean square	F value	Prob > F
Model	525,069	14	37,505	93.2	< 0.0001
A	39,626	2	19,813	49.2	< 0.0001
B	212,549	2	106,275	264.1	< 0.0001
C	223,780	2	111,890	278.0	< 0.0001
AB	29,150	4	7,288	18.1	< 0.0001
BC	19,963	4	4,991	12.4	0.0003
Residual	4,829	12	402		
Total	529,898	26			

The research hypothesis tests results are shown in Table 4.

Hypothesis 1

Even and uneven cross aisles perform statistically the same regardless of storage policy. This result requires further investigation as is there no difference or does it depend on the placement of uneven cross aisles.

Hypothesis 2

Layouts with even cross aisles perform statistically better than the Basic Layouts. This follows the results of Vaughan and Petersen (1999) that cross aisles can reduce picker travel.

Hypothesis 3

Layouts with Uneven cross aisles statistically perform better than the Basic Layouts. A cross aisle regardless of its location does reduce picker travel. Again this result requires further investigation that is beyond the scope of this paper.

Hypothesis 4

Across-aisle storage performs statistically better than Random storage except in the absence of cross aisles. Previous research has found that Across-aisle storage reduces picker travel compared to random storage but most of that research used optimal routing (Petersen et al, 2004). In this paper using traversal routing each aisle must be completely traversed unless there is a cross aisle that allows access to the next picking aisle.

Hypothesis 5

Within-aisle storage performs statistically better than random storage. This goes in line with the findings of (Petersen & Schmenner, 1999; Petersen & Aase, 2004).

Hypothesis 6

Within-aisle storage performs statistically better than across-aisle storage. This goes in line with the findings of (Petersen et al, 2004).

Table 4: Hypothesis test results

	Hypothesis	*t*	*p*-value
	ER≠UR	-0.048	0.9621
1	EA≠UA	0.176	0.8606
	EW≠UW	-0.025	0.9803
	ER<BR	2.433	0.0080
2	EA<BA	12.634	<0.0001
	EW<BW	2.366	0.0095
	UR<BR	2.390	0.0089
3	UA<BA	12.734	<0.0001
	UW<BW	2.359	0.00967
	BA<BR	0.320	0.3746
4	EA<ER	8.361	<0.0001
	UA<UR	8.562	<0.0001
	BW<BR	18.437	<0.0001
5	EW<ER	13.039	<0.0001
	UW<UR	13.188	<0.0001
	BW<BA	17.814	<0.0001
6	EW<EA	6.626	<0.0001
	UW<UA	6.413	<0.0001

From the results it has also been observed that a basic layout with within-aisle storage is better than layouts with even or uneven cross aisles with random or across-aisle storage. Table 5 shows that the results of some post-hoc t-tests show that within-aisle storage in a basic layout is statistically better than the addition of cross aisles with random or across-aisle storage.

Table 5: Post-hoc test results

Hypothesis	*t*	*p*-value
BW<ER	12.163	<0.0001
BW<EA	5.079	<0.0001
BW<UR	12.294	<0.0001
BW<UA	4.838	<0.0001
BW<BR	18.437	<0.0001
BW<BA	17.814	<0.0001

CONCLUSIONS

This paper evaluated cross-aisle placement in a manual warehouse with class-based storage. The results show that even and uneven cross-aisle placement does not statistically differ and that the addition of cross aisles did significantly reduce picker travel as had been shown in previous research. As in warehouses without cross aisles, within-aisle storage results in significantly less picker travel than across-aisle and random storage in a warehouse with cross aisles. In fact, within-aisle storage resulted in less picker travel than the addition of cross aisles in a random or across-aisle storage warehouse. All of these results held for small, medium, and large pick list sizes.

There are drawbacks to class-based storage in that in can result in increased picker congestion which may offset some of the picker time savings. Also the use of cross aisles could increase the possibility of picker accidents if pickers are not careful at cross and picking aisle intersections. A limitation of this research is that only one uneven cross-aisle placement strategy was considered, but this provides an avenue for future research to evaluate other uneven cross-aisle placement strategies in manual warehouses.

REFERENCES

Bassan, Y., Roll, Y., & Rosenblatt, M. J. (1980). Internal layout design of a warehouse, *AIIE Transactions*, 12(4), 317-322.

Ben-Mahmud, Y. (1987). The effect of warehouse layout on order picking efficiency. Unpublished M.S. thesis, Oregon State University, Corvallis, OR.

Berglund, P., & Batta, R. (2012). Optimal placement of warehouse cross aisles in a picker-to-part warehouse with class-based storage, *IIE Transactions*, 44(2):107-120.

Bozer, Y.A., Tanchoco, J., Tompkins, J.A., & White, J.A. (2010) Facilities planning. Hoboken: John Wiley & Sons, Inc.

Caron, F., Marchet, G., & Perego, A. (1998). Routing policies and COI-based storage policies in picker-to-part systems. *International Journal of Production Research*, 36(3), 713-732.

Caron, F., Marchet, G. and Perego, A. (2000). Optimal layout in low-level picker-to-part systems. *International Journal of Production Research,* 38(1), 101-117.

Coyle, J.J., Bardi, E.J., & Langley, C.J. (2003). *The Management of business logistics: A supply chain perspective*, 7th edition, South-Western, Mason, Ohio.

De Koster, R., & Van der Poort, E. (1998). Routing orderpickers in a warehouse: a comparison between optimal and heuristics solutions. *IIE Transactions*, 30, 469-480.

De Koster, M.B.M., Van der Poort, E.S. & Wolters, M. (1999). Efficient order batching methods in warehouses. *International Journal of Production Research*, 37(7), 1479-1504.

Eynan, A., & Rosenblatt, M.J. (1994). Establishing zones in single-command class-based rectangular AS/RS. *IIE Transactions*, 26(1), 38-46.

Frazelle, E., (2002). *World-class warehousing and material handling*, McGraw-Hill, New York.

Gibson, D.R., & Sharp, G.P. (1992). Order batching procedures. *European Journal of Operational Research*, 58, 57-67.

Gue, K.R., & Meller, R.D. (2009). Aisle configurations for unit-load warehouses, *IIE Transactions*, 41(3), 171-182.

Hall, R.W. (1993). Distance approximations for routing manual pickers in a warehouse. *IIE Transactions*, 25(4), 76-87.

Hausman, W.H., Schwarz, L.B., & Graves, S.C. (1976). Optimal storage assignment in automatic warehousing systems. *Management Science*, 22(6), 629-638.

Jane, C.C. (2000). Storage location assignment in a distribution center. *International Journal of Physical Distribution & Logistics Management*, 30(1), 55-71.

Jarvis, J. M., & McDowell, E. D. (1991). Optimal product layout in an order picking warehouse. *IIE Transactions*, 23(1), 93-102.

Larson, T.N., March, H., & Kusiak, A. (1997). A heuristic approach to warehouse layout with class-based storage. *IIE Transactions*, 29(4), 337-348.

Petersen, C.G (1997). An evaluation of order picking routing policies. *International Journal of Operations & Production Management*, 17(1), 1096-1111.

Petersen, C.G. (1999). The impact of routing and storage policies on warehouse efficiency. *International Journal of Operations & Production Management*, 19(10), 1053 -1064.

Petersen, C.G., & Schmenner, R.W. (1999). An evaluation of routing and volume-based storage policies in an order picking operation. *Decision Sciences*, 30(2), 481-501.

Petersen, C.G. (2000). An evaluation of order picking policies for mail order companies. *Production and Operations Management*, 9(4), 319-335.

Petersen, C.G. (2002). Considerations in Order Picking Zone Configuration. *International Journal of Operations & Production Management*, 22(7), 793-805.

Petersen, C.G., & Aase, G.R. (2004) A comparison of picking, storage, and routing policies in manual order picking. *International Journal of Production Economics*, 92(1), 11-19.

Petersen, C.G., Aase, G.R., & Heiser, D.R. (2004). Improving order picking performance through the implementation of class-based storage. *International Journal of Physical Distribution and Logistics Management*, 34(7), 534-544.

Pohl, L.M., Meller, R.D., & Gue, K.R. (2011). Turnover-based storage in non-traditional unit-load warehouse designs, *IIE Transactions*, 43(10), 703-721.

Rao, S., & Adil, G.K. (2013). Optimal class boundaries, number of aisles, and pick list size for low-level order picking systems. *IIE Transactions*, 45, 1309-1332.

Ratliff, H.D., & Rosenthal, A.S. (1983). Order-picking in a rectangular warehouse: A solvable case of the traveling salesman problem. *Operations Research*, 31(3), 507-521.

Roodbergen, K.J. & De Koster, R.A. (2001a). Routing order pickers in a warehouse with a middle aisle. *European Journal of Operational Research*, 133, 32-43.

Roodbergen, K.J. & De Koster, R.A. (2001b). Routing methods for warehouses with multiple cross aisles. *International Journal of Production Research*, 39(9), 1865-1883.

Rosenblatt, M.J., & Eynan, A. (1989). Deriving the optimal boundaries for class-based automatic storage/retrieval systems. *Management Science*, 35(12), 1519-1524.

Rosenwein, M.B. (1996). A comparison of heuristics for the problem of batching orders for warehouse selection. *International Journal of Production Research*, 34(3), 657-664.

Vaughan, T.S., & Petersen, C.G. (1999). The effect of warehouse cross aisles on order picking efficiency. *International Journal of Operations Research*, 37(4), 881 -897.

DECISION SCIENCES INSTITUTE

CSR and Employee Satisfaction: Mediating Role of Marketing Innovation

Jae Young Hwang
University of Texas Rio Grande Valley
Email: jaeyoung.hwang01@utrgv.edu

Joo Y. Jung
University of Texas Rio Grande Valley
Email: joo.jung@utrgv.edu

ABSTRACT

In spite of the prevailing discourse on the importance of the CSR on employee satisfaction, mediating effect related to empirical and theoretical developments are scarce. We propose that CSR contributes to employee satisfaction by marketing innovation. The theoretical framework was empirically tested using multi-source data obtained from 303 observations of 101 Korean companies from 2008 to 2010. This study finds that marketing innovation fully mediates the effects of CSR on employee satisfaction. This study provides a plausible the theoretical account and empirical validation of a mechanism through which CSR impacts on employee satisfaction.

KEYWORDS: Corporate social responsibility (CSR), Corporate fairness, Marketing innovation, and Employee satisfaction, SEM

INTRODUCTION

Corporate social responsibility (CSR) has received many spotlights from academicians and practitioners in the past several decades (Weber, 2008). In today's competitive market environment, CSR represents conspicuous notion which may become a strategic driver of a company (Luo and Bhattacharya, 2006). In the previous paper, Murray and Vogel (1997) insist that CSR refers to as prosocial corporate efforts, which has traditionally been the managerial obligation of taking action to conserve both the welfare of the society and the interest of organizations (Davis and Blomstrom, 1975). On the other hand, a company may have utilized the strategic CSR within the face of increased competition. Therefore, a company may maintain the sustainability through strategic CSR. However, does it really tell the result of strategic CSR marketing innovation?

Within the marketing literature, CSR is closely related to strategic management perspectives (Van de Ven and Jeurissen, 2005). Husted and Allen (2007) assert that firms can take in their profits through differentiation strategy from competitors such as CSR advertising, recycling, "green polis" which is an educational tool to teach people how to be more environmentally sound, and so on. Luo and Bhattacharya (2006) insist that CSR of a company result in diverse benefits such as enhancing both the brand innovation and firm value. Therefore, CSR have been used as a strategically innovative tool for winning the competition in a company.

Innovation may be one of the most important impetuses in sustaining a company that promotes

the company's competitiveness (Sood and Tellis, 2009). Marketing innovation can be predicted a degree on a firm's capacity to employ sustainable resources (Yalcinkaya, Calantone and Griffith, 2007). Marketing innovation will also be allowed to create value that connects to a firm's performance. Coca Cola has changed bottling partners to "light weight" consistently, which result in reducing greenhouse gas emissions and inducing savings in several thousands of dollars (Lubin and Esty, 2010). There is a little research to study the relationship between CSR and marketing innovation on employee satisfaction.
The purpose of this study is to investigate the effect of the CSR and marketing innovation on employee satisfaction. A theoretical background of the tendencies related in our purpose is first presented by an empirical research for CSR together with the marketing innovation as well as employee satisfaction. CSR is defined as corporate fairness, which means employees' perception between the input and the outcome. Marketing innovation is designated in terms of two components, competitive promotional support and competitive advertising support. Then the concept of employee satisfaction is considered in detail by debate of how it can be built and managed. After the conceptual framework is summarized, research methods are described and the model based on the variables to test the hypotheses are defined. Lastly, this paper summarizes the main findings and areas which have been identified for future research.

LITERATURE REVIEW AND HYPOTHESES/MODEL

CSR is "a strategy of corporations that affect a various range of organizational attitudes and behaviors beyond organization commitment" (Husted, 2000). When a company builds CSR initiatives as a marketing strategy, employees pride themselves in a company's policy and dedicate to the organization (Stawiski, Deal and Gentry, 2010). Drawing on prior research (Adams and Zutshi, 2004), we define CSR as a moral responsibility related to the corporate fairness (e.g., transparency, cooperation relationship of a company).
Our research model focuses on employee satisfaction. Employee satisfaction is defined as providing better pay, ongoing training, and making employee feel secure (Koy, 2003; Gursoy and Swanger, 2007). Employee satisfaction plays a pivotal role in making companies attain financial goals because higher level of employee satisfaction allows employees to be motivated and more diligent than unsatisfied employees (Koys, 2003; Chi and Gursoy, 2009). A company provides the customers with marketing innovation which is new or modified products/processes aimed at increasing firm performance (Naidoo, 2010). Therefore, we suggest that the logic for this argument is when a company gives employees satisfaction then the employees will take care of the customers.
As summarized in Fig. 1, we identify marketing innovation as firm-level intervening mechanism between CSR and employee satisfaction. Through stakeholder theory (Freeman, 1983), CSR is a formation of marketing strategy which is characterized by a double orientation toward the social improvement as well as stakeholders' profit (Barnett, 2007). Employees as a stakeholder group can perceive CSR programs and actions, and they evaluate them (Rowley and Berman, 2000; Rupp et al., 2006). We contend that the support of CSR on employee satisfaction is possible to secure effective business strategies (Ramus and Steger, 2000). We explain below each of the hypotheses in detail.

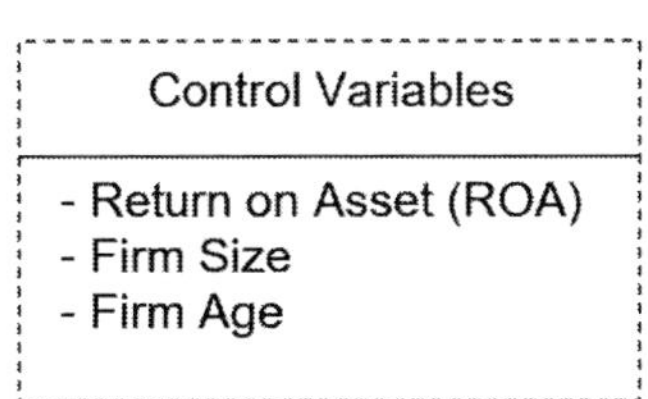

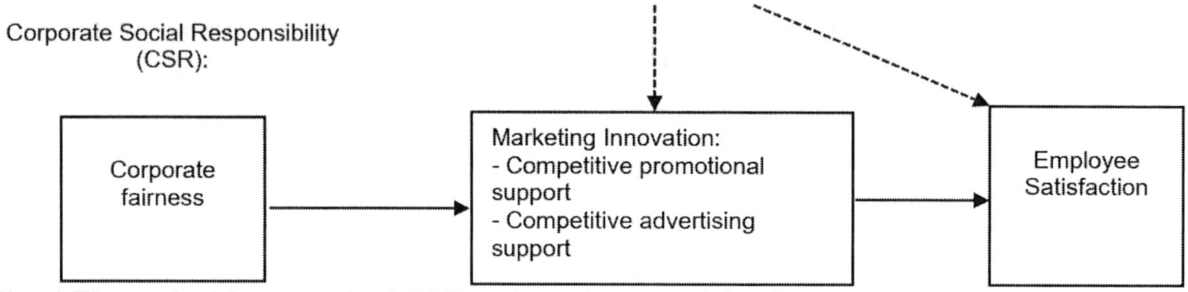

Fig. 1 Theoretical framework of CSR and employee satisfaction

Relationship of CSR and Employee Satisfaction

Research on CSR supports the idea that fairness is related to favorable employee satisfaction. Collier and Esteban (2007) argue that CSR responses on employees can try approaching to stakeholder theory because employees are a pivotal element in having an influence on the firm value. Stawiski, Deal and Gentry (2010) recommend that our personal identities are connected as the member of a company, and feel that company work for the public. For instance, employees' perceptions of their organizations' strategy for the public may be linked to their level of organizational commitment. In line with these findings, we anticipate a positive relationship between the CSR and employee satisfaction.
Social identity theory (Akremi, Gond, and Swaen, 2015) comprehends why practical employees care about CSR initiatives evolved by the companies. CSR activities are more distinctive as well as fundamental and relatively enduring than other corporate activities (Sen and Bhattacharya, 2001). That means, employees can feel more fellowship through CSR activities. Fombrun and Shanley (1990) insist that firms focused on CSR tend to achieve positive public reputations. Employees may want to work for an ethical citizen like those volunteers for the public, who not only cares about the work itself but also takes after themselves and himself, respectively. Grounded on these theories, we predict that the CSR will be positively associated with employee satisfaction.

H1: CSR is positively related to employee satisfaction.

CSR and Marketing Innovation as Intermediate Process

The dominant theoretical perspective employed to explain the increased interest on CSR is driven by moral responsibility (Adams and Zutshi, 2004). It is related to the fairness, suggesting that companies acting morally responsible have a wide morality to their circumstance, workforce, and local communities. Fairness may be referred to as the degree to which an employee perceives proportion between the input and the outcome (Adam, 1965), which stems from fairness theory. If employees recognize that they have contributed abundant inputs in their jobs, they have a tendency to seek corporate fairness in rewards (Oliver and Swan, 1989). Moreover, Clemmer (1993) insists that corporate fairness is positively related to job satisfaction. For example, if a company evaluates its employees fairly, the employees may consent on the results of their evaluation and continue to exhibit commitment and satisfactory job performance even when they accept that the company seeks to ethical values below what the employees anticipate. Therefore, corporate fairness of a company can enhance employees' perception positively and heighten employee satisfaction.
Such positive relationships between corporate fairness and employee satisfaction are likely to be realized through various intermediate processes involving the internal and external dynamics

of the firm. We employ marketing innovation as intermediary mechanisms that translate the effect of CSR on employee satisfaction. CSR initiatives can cause innovations through the use of social, environmental, or sustainability drivers to create new products and services (Mahlouji and Anaraki, 2009). Hockerts and Morsing (2008) introduce CSR on the firm's strategy that results from promoting social goods and services. Such activities may cause a firm embodying socially responsible attributes in a product or service. Mahlouji and Anaraki (2009) also explain marketing innovation and CSR as the cues of dynamic capability approach for providing a source of competitive advantage. Therefore, we propose the following hypotheses:

H2: Corporate fairness is positively related to marketing innovation.

Relationship of Marketing Innovation and Employee Satisfaction

Marketing innovation is a strategy of corporations that improve in the marketing mix to obtain a prevailing position in a highly competitive environment. It is able to reinvigorate a company that it requires exploiting the firm's resource based theory (Hu and Hsu, 2008; Kaminski et al., 2008). The pivotal factors of marketing innovation are promotional support and advertising strategy (Nystrom and Starbuck, 1981). They are focus on generating superior capabilities from a common circumstance of company capabilities as resulting in the development of the supply chain (Holland, Light and Kawaleki, 1999). Especially, marketing innovation can effect on the sustainable profitability when a company repeatedly develops valuable innovations for marketing innovation (Wuyts, Dutta, and Stremersch, 2004). For example, the exposure of a product or a service through a promotional activity or an advertisement can affect a firm value so that employees will take the future financial reward (Boles, Wood, Johnson, 2003). Thus, such marketing innovation is likely to increase positive work attitudes of employees, which improve their job satisfaction.

H3: Marketing innovation is positively related to employee satisfaction.

Mediating Effects of Marketing Innovation

By integrating the aforementioned hypotheses of the direct effects among constructs, we propose that marketing innovation mediate the relationship between CSR and employee satisfaction. The overall structure of this mediated relationship is based on competitive strategy (Weerawardena, 2003) in that CSR activities increase marketing innovation (i.e., competitive promotional support and competitive advertising support), which in turn promote employee satisfaction.

A similar process is endorsed by the CSR-marketing innovation-employee satisfaction framework, which postulates that CSR activities form a pervasive social issue that cause the public welfare as well as a stakeholders' profit (Dawkins and Lewis, 2003). Freeman (1983) suggests a companies' action spending time and other resources in addressing stakeholders' interests is a justifiable managerial activity. Furthermore, Friedman (2002) argues that CSR activity is a means to a firm's social, political, or career agenda at the expense of stakeholder. Wherein, resources used to CSR would be more carefully spent on increasing the efficiency of the firm. Based on previous papers (Freeman, 1983; Friedman, 2002; Weerawardena, 2003), we posit that, rather exerting a direct effect on employee satisfaction, CSR is linked to it by forming marketing innovation.

Hypothesis 4. Marketing innovation mediates the relationship between CSR and employee satisfaction.

METHODS

Sample

We employed a sample of large, public firms in Korea. Since 1990s, Korean companies have adjusted with the management style of the developed countries, in order to cope up with the global competency at that time. In particular, Korean firms have been increasing the investment for their stakeholder-oriented strategies to protect their own interests after the Asian financial crisis in the late 1990s. First, we used the components of Korea Economic Justice Institute (KEJI) index, from 2008 to 2010 that is period in the global financial crisis, as CSR and employee satisfaction. Second, as we mentioned, marketing innovation comprises of competitive promotional support and competitive advertising support. Bansal (2005) insists that companies have to strategize CSR on their products that require changes in the technology which will be involving the Research & Development (R&D) expenditure. To measure the marketing innovation, we collected firm-level innovation data disclosed in the Data Analysis, Retrieval and Transfer System (DART). The DART is an electronic disclosure system that collects firm information including audit and annual reports operated by the Financial Supervisory Service (FSS) in Korea that since 1997, the year when the Asian financial crisis occurred. Therefore, as our data were made from KEJI index data and DART system, some of the companies in total sample not only failed to enter the list of KEJI index for 3 consecutive years, but also missed out some information of marketing innovation. Due to the lack of total data availability, our final sample size is 101 firms, 303 observations.

Variable

We investigated the employee satisfaction to CSR by mediating the marketing innovation. In this study, CSR variables and employee satisfaction measure among the KEJI index, published by the Institute of Korea Economy, was used as a proxy to measure CSR and to measure employee satisfaction activities from 2008 to 2010. KEJI has been made the basis on the annual business performance; it is used for variables for the CSR and employee satisfaction because KEJI represents the most comprehensive and extensive quality assessments for fairness of business performance (Gilbert et al., 2014). Korean firms have acknowledged and accepted the U.S management practices (Cho and Kim, 2007), and the KEJI has ensured its reliability as a scientific method. This is because it has been consistently used since it had been made in 1991. Korean companies, listed on the Korea Exchange (KRX) on the basis of annual reports, had been evaluated by both quantitative and qualitative measures through seventeen analysts, 11 distinguished faculty members and 6 KEJI senior analysts in business or economics discipline. The KEJI index is comparable to Kinder, Lydenberg, Domini Research & Analytics (KLD) ratings in the U.S. First of all, corporate fairness evaluated fairness, transparency, and cooperation relationship of a company.

First, corporate fairness measures fair trade through a quantitative methodology and economic concentration through a qualitative methodology. Transparency includes propriety analysis for unfaithful disclosure and business report, and outside director activity, which all are measured by a quantitative methodology. We used a qualitative methodology to investigate the relationship between the subcontractors. Second, employee satisfaction evaluated safety at a workplace, human resource investment, and welfare, which all are calculated by a quantitative methodology. It employed a qualitative methodology to look into management-union relation, and gender equality.

Marketing innovation

We took balance sheet, income statement, and industry data from the DART system. It exists R&D expenditure, advertising expense, and sales promotion cost on the business report of a company. Srinivasan and Hanssens (2009) suggest that new product innovation is backed by substantial advertising. Chung (2002) insists that innovation activity is systematical promotion. Therefore, among innovation items on the financial statement, we focused on advertising expense and sales promotion cost to investigate the marketing innovation outlined by Bresser (1988). We calculated (advertising expense + sales promotion cost) / sales like as previous paper (Jiraporn et al., 2008). It was transformed logarithmically owing to the positively skewed distribution.

Control variable

We included company age, firm size, and return on assets (ROA) as control variables in this paper. First of all, we included company age because it is associated with CSR (Moore, 2001). Second, we used firm size, calculated by a measurement of total sales as control variable. It was transformed logarithmically owing to the positively skewed distribution. Lastly, ROA was measured by net income divided by total assets.

Analysis

We investigated an empirical analysis on the effect of the CSR and marketing innovation on employee satisfaction as the following research model. We employed ordinary least squares (OLS) regression. To test Hypotheses 1a and 1b, which CSR is positively related to marketing innovation, we conducted the regression; marketing innovation on the control variable, and then CSR in sequential steps. To test Hypotheses 2, which marketing innovation is positively related to employee satisfaction, we conducted the regression; marketing innovation on the control variable.

RESULTS

The descriptive statistics and correlations among study variables are reported in Table 1. There were no correlations between main variables with a magnitude greater than 0.40, which suggests that multicollinearity was not a problem (Miller and Triana, 2009). To validate our theoretical framework empirically, we conducted structural equation modeling (SEM) analyses as described below.

Table 1. Means, standard deviations, and pairwise correlations

Variable	Mean	*s.d.*	1	2	3	4	5	6
1. Employee Satisfaction	5.66	1.21						
2. Fairness	8.52	0.76	-0.10*					
3. Marketing Innovation	21.89	2.74	0.25***	-0.19***				
4. ROA	0.08	0.07	-0.03	-0.03	0.08			
5. Size	27.02	1.65	-0.26***	-0.04	0.57***	-0.10*		
6. Age	39.70	15.28	0.19***	-0.15***	0.29***	-0.13**	0.08	

Notes: N=303 for all variables.
* P < 0.10; ** p<0.05; *** p<0.001.

Hypothesized Model and Plausible Alternative Models

We first tested the hypothesized model, as shown in Fig. 1. The hypothesized structural model produced a good fit to the observed relations among variables (Hu and Bentler, 1999): $\chi 2$ (*df* = 7) = 16.84, *p* = .018; CFI = .965; GFI = 0.982; RMSEA = .068; AIC = 44.843. Hair et al. (1998) insists that if the GFI are closer to 1, the result would be better. Still, it is possible that the mediating roles of marketing innovation are only partial rather than complete. Therefore, we tested the possibility of partial mediation by adding the following direct effect paths: (a) direct effect of CSR on marketing innovation; (b) direct effects of CSR on employee satisfaction; and (c) direct effects of marketing innovation on employee satisfaction.

Results and discussion on hypothesis Testing

Results of the best-fitting, hypothesized model are presented in Fig. 2. Among the control variables, ROA and size was significant predictors of marketing innovation and employee satisfaction (ROA: β = 6.87, $p < .01$ and β = -2.30, $p < .05$; Size: β = 0.93, $p < .01$ and β = -0.44, $p < .01$, respectively). Age was significantly associated with marketing innovation (β = 0.05, $p < .01$). After controlling for its indirect effects through marketing innovation, the SEM results revealed that CSR fairness was significantly related to employee satisfaction (β = -0.01, $p < .1$), which confirmed Hypothesis 1. CSR variable were positively associated with marketing innovation ((β = -0.46, $p < .01$). Therefore, Hypothesis 2 was confirmed. Our analysis likewise supported Hypothesis 3 in that marketing innovation was significantly related to employee satisfaction (β = 0.25, $p < .01$).

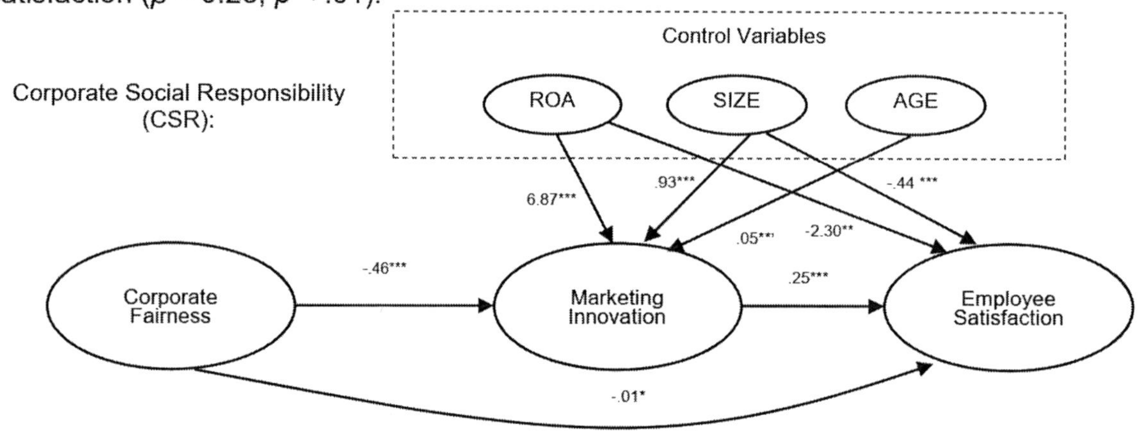

Fig. 2 Final structural model predicting employee satisfaction

Hypothesis 4 further suggested that marketing innovation mediate the effects of CSR on employee satisfaction. We tested the mediating effects through SEM as suggested by Baron and Kenny (1986) and Williams et al. (2003), to respectively take appropriate models to conduct the following four conditions: (1) the relationship between the independent variable (CSR) and the mediating variable (marketing innovation) need to be significant; (2) the relationship between the independent variable (CSR) and the dependent variable (employee satisfaction); (3) the relationship between the mediating variable (marketing innovation and the dependent variable (employee satisfaction) need to be significant; (4) simultaneously, the independent variable (corporate fairness) with the mediating variable (marketing innovation) to the dependent

variable (employee satisfaction) need to have insignificant correlation, which means independent variable effect needs to be more weakened than the second group.
We tested the statistical analysis to satisfy these four condition as shown Figure 3. "Corporate fairness" to "employee satisfaction" reach the significant level of $p < 0.1$ under the second condition. However, under the fourth condition, "corporate fairness" to "employee satisfaction" does not reach the significant level of $p < 0.1$ even though "marketing innovation" to "employee satisfaction" reach the significant level of $p < 0.01$. Consequently, marketing innovation has a full mediating effect on the relationship between CSR and employee satisfaction.

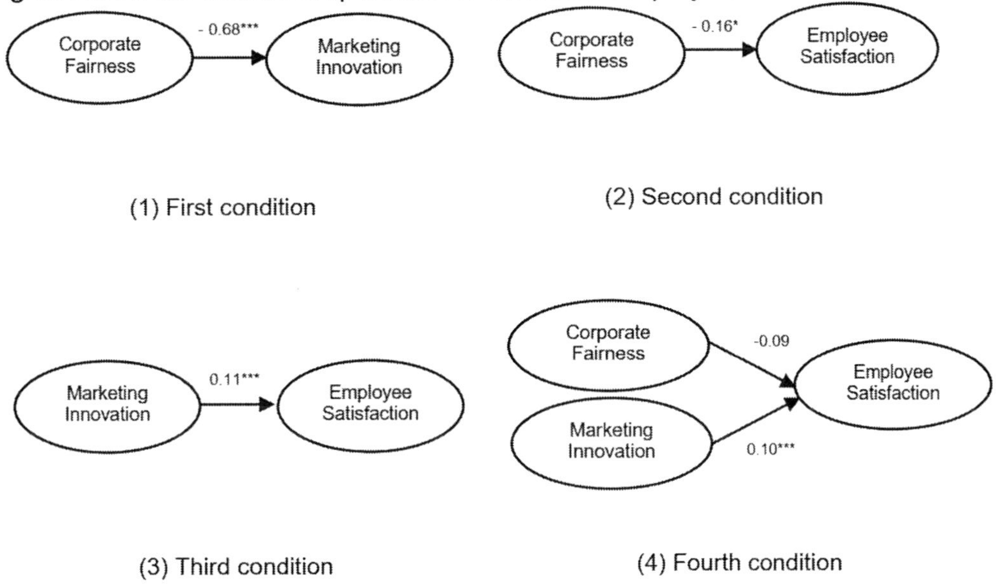

*p<0.1, **<0.05, ***<0.01

Fig. 3 The appropriate models of CSR, marketing innovation, and employee satisfaction

DISCUSSION AND CONCLUSIONS

A substantial challenge of emerging marketing agenda related to CSR is whether the CSR can be directly affected by employee satisfaction. CSR is also currently connected to the social effects of business so that it can lessen the negative effects while augmenting the positive effects of the business (Marquina and Vasquez, 2013). Luo and Bhattacharya (2006) insist that CSR of a company results in diverse benefits such as enhancing both the brand innovation and firm's value. Geyskens et al. (1999) argue that the influence of innovation strategy on employees' satisfaction should be considered. The present study provides several answers to such a dilemma by demonstrating whether marketing innovation is valuable to employee satisfaction.
Departing from existing studies that focus on managers and theirs effects on employee satisfaction in individual or group levels of analysis, the present research is one of the very few attempts to empirically test the effects of CSR on employee satisfaction. Moreover, by examining the mediating processes involving firm-level marketing innovation, we identify potential internal mechanisms through which CSR can have an impact on employee satisfaction. In this section, we highlight theoretical and practical implications of the study as well as its limitations for future research.

Theoretical Implication

The pivotal proposition of the present study is that the CSR activities are critical for employee satisfaction. Our data suggests that CSR and marketing innovation can be conflicted (See Table 2). For example, corporate fairness includes transparency and cooperation relationship of a company, which they are mainly in charge of general affairs team. While a company uses marketing innovation at a sales team. In other words, marketing components using at a company may conflict to each other due to limited resources. Therefore, a company strategically may decrease the effort for marketing innovation to enhance fairness. This pattern also endorses the proposition of moral responsibility (Adams and Zutshi 2004), which suggests that a company tends to build moral responsibility as part of CSR.
As the direct effects of CSR variable on employee satisfaction were insignificant after corporate fairness with marketing innovation to the dependent variable, our mediation analysis clearly recommended that they impact on employee satisfaction via marketing innovation (See Fig. 3). The lack of a direct relationship between CSR and employee satisfaction under conducting marketing innovation can be explained by the potential delayed effects of CSR on employee satisfaction (Jacobson 1990). The overall mediation patterns depicted in Fig. 3 provide support for the basic tenet of business interest (Adams and Zutshi, 2004), which posits that CSR affects employee satisfaction by shaping internal marketing processes that involve employee perceptions (Chi and Gursoy, 2009). These findings also endorse the validity of the CSR-marketing innovation-employee satisfaction framework (Husted, 2000; Rupp et al., 2006; Naidoo, 2010).

Practical Implications

The present findings offer several implications for marketers. First, our analysis clearly demonstrates that fulfilling the increasing social expectations and standards for CSR and achieving employee satisfaction are mutually exclusive. That is, employees negatively feel a firm's CSR policy, while they want the incentives or welfare benefit for employee satisfaction (Naidoo, 2010). In pursuit of marketing innovation, marketing managers should pay attention to CSR activities and invest on marketing resources in CSR activities. Employees tend to feel that more socially responsible companies may impact on Corporate Social Performance (CSP) and can receive the rewards for their hard work (Chi and Gursoy, 2009).
Second, firms pay attention to marketing innovation for strategic employee management because the importance of marketing innovation is recently being emphasized. Many firms already recognize a critical role of marketing innovation and are ploughing much money into innovation initiatives to enhance positive, competitive and differentiated marketing innovation (Wuyts, Dutta, and Stremersch, 2004). In the competitive market situation, diversified marketing innovation activities, such as competitive promotional support and competitive advertising support, are implemented. Such activities can create positive employee satisfaction.
Lastly, one caveat of the current study is that the link between the CSR and employee satisfaction is negative correlation. Specially, our analysis showed that unless CSR affects the marketing innovation, its influence on the employee satisfaction can be limited. In a sense, this entire process emulates an organizational change process driven by CSR and marketing innovation. Changing employee attitudes for the strategic marketing plans take longer to increase employee satisfaction from such changes. Therefore, companies need to recognize that CSR activities through marketing innovation should be regarded as a managerial agenda, and to strive effort in conducting marketing innovation within their firms as a way to increase employee satisfaction.

Limitation and Direction for future research suggestions

The present study expands the CSR literature by rendering both conceptual and empirical contributions. The present findings, however, should be interpreted with caution by considering a few limitations. First, we do not address the concern for a possible bias to select samples. Our sample is drawn from a population of firms selected by construction of its KEJI index. However, this limitation is unavoidable because the KEJI index is the only reliable CSR measure to represent comprehensive and extensive quality assessments for corporate fairness. Second, we employed samples in a single country, Korea so that specific characteristics of Korea maybe evident in our result. Therefore, our results should be carefully interpreted before generalizing them. Lastly, even though the KEJI index is considered to be the most reliable CSR measure in KOREA, it has a slot for reasonable improvement to construct CSR measurement. For future research, we are expecting to extend the coverage of sample firms both by employing improved data sets on CSR and by using alternative model specifications.

REFERENCES

Adam, H. (1965). *Adenosine-5'-diphosphate and adenosine-5'-monophosphate: In methods of enzymatic analysis*. Academic Press New York, 2, 53-577.

Adams, C., & Zutshi, A. (2004). Corporate social responsibility: why business should act responsibly and be accountable. *Australian Accounting Review*, 14(34), 31-39.

Adner, R., & Zemsky, P. (2006). A demand-based perspective on sustainable competitive advantage. *Strategic Management Journal*, 27(3), 215-239.

Barnett, S. A. (2007). *The rat: A study in behavior*. Transaction Publishers.

Boles, J. S., Wood, J. A., & Johnson, J. (2003). Interrelationships of role conflict, role ambiguity, and work–family conflict with different facets of job satisfaction and the moderating effects of gender. *Journal of Personal Selling & Sales Management*, 23(2), 99-113.

Caves, R. E., & Porter, M. E. (1977). From entry barriers to mobility barriers: Conjectural decisions and contrived deterrence to new competition*. *The Quarterly Journal of Economics*, 241-261.

Chang, Y. K., Oh, W. Y., Park, J. H., & Jang, M. G. (2015). Exploring the relationship between board characteristics and CSR: Empirical evidence from Korea. *Journal of Business Ethics*, 1-18.

Chi, C. G., & Gursoy, D. (2009). Employee satisfaction, customer satisfaction, and financial performance: An empirical examination. *International Journal of Hospitality Management*, 28(2), 245-253.

Cho, D. S., & Kim, J. (2007). Outside directors, ownership structure and firm profitability in Korea. *Corporate Governance: An International Review*, 15(2), 239-250.

Clemmer, E. C. (1993). An investigation into the relationship of fairness and customer satisfaction with services. *Justice in the Workplace: Approaching Fairness in Human Resource Management*, 193-207.

Collier, J., & Esteban, R. (2007). Corporate social responsibility and employee commitment. *Business Ethics: A European Review*, 16(1), 19-33.

Davis, K., & Bromstrom, R. L. (1975). Implementing the social audit in an organization. *Business and Society*, 16(1), 13.

Dawkins, J., & Lewis, S. (2003). CSR in stakeholde expectations: And their Implication for company strategy. *Journal of Business Ethics*, 44(2-3), 185-193.

Edmans, A. (2011). Does the stock market fully value intangibles? Employee satisfaction and equity prices. *Journal of Financial Economics*, 101(3), 621-640.

El Akremi, A., Gond, J. P., Swaen, V., De Roeck, K., & Igalens, J. (2015). How do employees perceive corporate responsibility? Development and validation of a

multidimensional corporate stakeholder responsibility scale. *Journal of Management*, 1-39.
Folger, R., Cropanzano, R., & Goldman, B. (2005). *What is the relationship between justice and morality?* Handbook of Organizational Justice, 215-245.
Fombrun, C., & Shanley, M. (1990). What's in a name? Reputation building and corporate strategy. *Academy of Management Journal*, 33(2), 233-258.
Freeman, R. E. (1983). Strategic management: A stakeholder approach. *Advances in Strategic Management*, 1(1), 31-60.
Friedman, M. (2002). *The social responsibility of business is to increase its profits.* New York: Applied Ethics: Critical Concepts in Philosophy, 5.
Grewal, R., & Tansuhaj, P. (2001). Building organizational capabilities for managing economic crisis: The role of market orientation and strategic flexibility. *Journal of Marketing*, 65(2), 67-80.
Gursoy, D., & Swanger, N. (2007). Performance-enhancing internal strategic factors and competencies: Impacts on financial success. *International Journal of Hospitality Management*, 26(1), 213-227.
Hockerts, K., & Morsing, M. (2008). *A literature review on corporate social responsibility in the innovation process.* Copenhagen Business School (CBS), Center for Corporate Social Responsibility, 1-28.
Holland C. Light B. and Kawalek P. (1999). *Beyond enterprise resource planning projects: innovative strategies for competitive advantage.* In: proceedings of the 7th European conference on information systems, 1, 288-301.
Hsu, C. W., & Hu, A. H. (2008). Green supply chain management in the electronic industry. *International Journal of Environmental Science & Technology*, 5(2), 205-216.
Husted, B. W. (2000). A contingency theory of corporate social performance. *Business & Society*, 39(1), 24-48.
Husted, B. W., & Allen, D. B. (2007). Corporate social strategy in multinational enterprises: Antecedents and value creation. *Journal of Business Ethics*, 74(4), 345-361.
Jacobson, R. (1990). Unobservable effects and business performance. *Marketing Science*, 9(1), 74-85.
Janssen, O. (2001). Fairness perceptions as a moderator in the curvilinear relationships between job demands, and job performance and job satisfaction. *Academy of Management Journal*, 44(5), 1039-1050.
Jones, T. M., & Wicks, A. C. (1999). Convergent stakeholder theory. *Academy of Management Review*, 24(2), 206-221.
Jung, H. J., & Kim, D. O. (2015). Good Neighbors but Bad Employers: Two Faces of Corporate Social Responsibility Programs. *Journal of Business Ethics*, 1-16.
Kaminski, J. W., Valle, L. A., Filene, J. H., & Boyle, C. L. (2008). A meta-analytic review of components associated with parent training program effectiveness. *Journal of Abnormal Child Psychology*, 36(4), 567-589.
Koys, D. J. (2003). How the achievement of human-resources goals drives restaurant performance? *Cornell Hospitality Quarterly*, 44(1), 17-24.
Lubin, D. A., & Esty, D. C. (2010). The sustainability imperative. *Harvard Business Review*, 88(5), 42-50.
Luo, X., & Bhattacharya, C. B. (2006). Corporate social responsibility, customer satisfaction, and market value. *Journal of Marketing*, 70(4), 1-18.
Mahlouji, H., & Anaraki, N. K. (2009). Corporate social responsibility towards social responsible innovation: A dynamic capability approach. *International Review of Business Research Papers*, 5(6), 185-194.
Maslow, A. H. (1943). A theory of human motivation. *Psychological review*, 50(4), 370.

McGregor, D. (1960). *The human side of enterprise*. New York, 21.
McWilliams, A., Siegel, D. S., & Wright, P. M. (2006). Corporate social responsibility: Strategic implications*. *Journal of Management Studies*, 43(1), 1-18.
Murray, K. B., & Vogel, C. M. (1997). Using a hierarchy-of-effects approach to gauge the effectiveness of corporate social responsibility to generate goodwill toward the firm: Financial versus nonfinancial impacts. *Journal of Business Research*, 38(2), 141-159.
Naidoo, V. (2010). Firm survival through a crisis: The influence of market orientation, marketing innovation and business strategy. *Industrial Marketing Management*, 39(8), 1311-1320.
Newbert, S. L. (2008). Value, rareness, competitive advantage, and performance: a conceptual-level empirical investigation of the resource-based view of the firm. *Strategic Management Journal*, 29(7), 745-768.
Nystrom, P. C., & Starbuck, W. H. (Eds.). (1981). *Handbook of organizational design*. Oxford University Press, 1, 409-432.
Oh, W. Y., Chang, Y. K., & Martynov, A. (2011). The effect of ownership structure on corporate social responsibility: Empirical evidence from Korea. *Journal of Business Ethics*, 104(2), 283-297.
Oliver, R. L., & Swan, J. E. (1989). Equity and disconfirmation perceptions as influences on merchant and product satisfaction. *Journal of Consumer Research*, 372-383.
Ramus, C. A., & Steger, U. (2000). The Roles of supervisory support behaviors and environmental policy in employee "Ecoinitiatives" at leading-edge European companies. *Academy of Management journal*, 43(4), 605-626.
Rowley, T., & Berman, S. (2000). A brand new brand of corporate social performance. *Business & Society*, 39(4), 397-418.
Rupp, D. E., Ganapathi, J., Aguilera, R. V., & Williams, C. A. (2006). Employee reactions to corporate social responsibility: An organizational justice framework. *Journal of Organizational Behavior*, 27(4), 537-543.
Sen, S., & Bhattacharya, C. B. (2001). Does doing good always lead to doing better? Consumer reactions to corporate social responsibility. *Journal of Marketing Research*, 38(2), 225-243.
Sood, A., & Tellis, G. J. (2009). Do innovations really pay off? Total stock market returns to innovation. *Marketing Science*, 28(3), 442-456.
Stawiski, S., Deal, J. J., Gentry, W., & Rweyongoza, S. (2010). *Employee perceptions of corporate social responsibility*. Center for Creative Leadership, Greensboro, NC, 1-12.
Turban, D. B., & Greening, D. W. (1997). Corporate social performance and organizational attractiveness to prospective employees. *Academy of Management Journal*, 40(3), 658-672.
Van de Ven, B., & Jeurissen, R. (2005). Competing responsibly. *Business Ethics Quarterly*, 15(02), 299-317.
Weber, M. (2008). The business case for corporate social responsibility: A company-level measurement approach for CSR. *European Management Journal*, 26(4), 247-261.
Weerawardena, J. (2003). The role of marketing capability in innovation-based competitive strategy. *Journal of Strategic Marketing*, 11(1), 15-35.
Williams, L. J., Edwards, J. R., & Vandenberg, R. J. (2003). Recent advances in causal modeling methods for organizational and management research. *Journal of Management*, 29(6), 903-936.
Wuyts, S., Dutta, S., & Stremersch, S. (2004). Portfolios of interfirm agreements in technology-intensive markets: Consequences for innovation and profitability. *Journal of Marketing*, 68(2), 88-100.

Yalcinkaya, G., Calantone, R. J., & Griffith, D. A. (2007). An examination of exploration and exploitation capabilities: Implications for product innovation and market performance. *Journal of International Marketing*, 15(4), 63-93.

Zhang, J., Reithel, B. J., & Li, H. (2009). Impact of perceived technical protection on security behaviors. *Information Management & Computer Security*, 17(4), 330-340.

DECISION SCIENCES INSTITUTE

Does Negotiation Matter for Business Relationship? A Study of Credible Information Disclosure and Perceived Fairness

Bo Yu
Concordia University
Email: bo.yu@concordia.ca

Rustam Vahidov
Concordia University
Email: rustam.vahidov@concordia.ca

Gregory E. Kersten
Concordia University
Email: gregory.kersten@concordia.ca

ABSTRACT

Negotiations tend to influence long-term business relationships. This paper investigates the role of perceived fairness of the exchange in forming these relationships. The impacts of fairness have been under-investigated in business exchanges. The paper proposes a research model that has perceived fairness at its core. Experiments were conducted in two multi-bilateral negotiation settings with different information disclosure strategies. The results suggest that the decision to reveal the best offer to participants affects perceived fairness. Furthermore, the perceived fairness has a positive impact on business relationships. The findings suggest important implications for the strategic role of information revelation by businesses.

KEYWORDS: perceived fairness, electronic negotiations, multi-bilateral negotiations, experimental studies

INTRODUCTION

Electronic markets are complex economic, social, and technological aggregates, which connect industrial buyers and sellers globally. As economic aggregates, they may implement such market mechanisms as catalogues, auctions and negotiations. These mechanisms control access to and regulate the execution of transactions and allocate welfare. E-markets are socio-economic institutions providing places where traders meet, interact, establish relationships, and engage in transactions (Wang & Archer, 2007). They are also technological constructs that connect different organizations and individuals (Bakos, 1991). They integrate many components in order to implement a technological infrastructure and provide information and functional services (Choudhury, Hartzel, & Konsynski, 1998).

The activities within the e-markets are organized around exchange, e.g., in form of goods, information, or services (Grieger, 2003). The operation of e-markets requires institutional infrastructures, including law, regulation, and dispute resolution (Bakos, 1991). E-markets allocate welfare and produce social outcomes. Each exchange episode can influence the relationship between participating businesses (Håkansson, 1982). Thereby, solely focusing on their economic aspects would be insufficient for guiding system design and business practices.

Focusing on B2B relationships, this study argues that fairness is a critical aspect for assessing allocation of welfare by the participants of exchange. It suggests that the perception of fairness resulting from negotiations will influence business relationships. The implementation of fairness principles in e-market and mechanism design can enhance participants' fairness perceptions. Although fairness has been intensively investigated in organizational studies, it is rarely examined in the context of business negotiations (Diekmann, Soderberg, & Tenbrunsel, 2013).

The current study conducted an enriched economic experiment involving e-procurement. The experiment used a business procurement scenario, in which one buyer would negotiate with several sellers. A contract would be assigned to one of the sellers. In the experiment, two types of multi-bilateral negotiations were implemented. The first type included non-verifiable negotiations, where participants exchanged messages and offers. The second type featured verifiable negotiations, where the current best offer received by the negotiation host was automatically revealed to all participants. The experimental results show that sellers' fairness perceptions indeed have impact on business relationships. Verifiable negotiation helps to enhance non-winners' fairness perceptions, when the disclosure of current best offer does not result in significant difference of buyers' revenues. The findings of the current study have important implications to both system designers, as well as business practitioners.

RESEARCH BACKGROUND

Exchange and Business Relationship

Exchange is an essential part of the relationships between industrial buyers and suppliers. Early view about business relationships heavily drew on Economics. It was assumed that independent firms conducted discrete transactions in impersonal markets. From this perspective, firms have two main tasks, i.e., organize production within hierarchies and obtain value by exchanging goods and money in markets (e.g.,Coase, 1937). Williamson (1979) espoused this stream of thought by pointing out that transaction cost determines the boundary of firms.

Exchange is a critical activity not only in Economics, but also in social life. Social exchange theory places exchange in a social psychology context and recognizes more resources (e.g., status, information, money, goods, and services) that are exchanged in social relationships (Cropanzano & Mitchell, 2005). Adopting a process view, the Industrial Marketing and Purchasing (IMP) group developed an interactive model describing business relationships. The relationship between two firms can be characterized by a series of exchange episodes. Four elements are involved in each episode: product/service exchange, information exchange, financial exchange and social exchange. In their view, the economic exchange in industrial market is barely an isolated activity. Repeated exchange episodes may trigger institutionalization and adaptations that characterize long-term relationships (Håkansson, 1982). The interactive model of IMP group was further extended to Actor-Resource-Activity model, which can be applied to analyze network effects (Håkansson & Snehota, 1995). The IMP approach highlights the dynamic processes of learning and value creation. At the same time, it introduces and acknowledges the importance of individuals in forming and managing business relationships.

Fairness and Negotiation

Although fairness is important for both individuals and society, the systematic development of this concept did not start until the mid-20th century. Homans (1961) laid out the theoretical foundation of social exchange theory by drawing on the economic notion of exchange and operant psychology. He argued that fairness is the instrumental motive that drives exchange. Adams (1965) further developed the notion of distributive fairness and proposed the equity principle (i.e., the comparison of input-outcome ratios of each exchange participant). Later, alternative principles were proposed including equality, need, and generosity. Studies have shown that people adopt different principles in fairness judgements. The adoption is often contingent on factors such as self-interest, social relationships, culture, and situational needs (Welsh, 2003).Thibaut and Walker (1975) highlighted procedural fairness by examining third-party dispute resolutions (e.g., mediation and arbitration), which in general have two stages: a process stage and a decision stage. They found that disputants were willing to give up some control in the decision stage, which produced the outcomes, if they retained control in the process stage, in which they had chances to voice their issues and concerns. This finding suggests that disputants see a resolution as a fair one if they perceive that they had been in control of the process. Leventhal (1980) introduced procedural fairness into organizational research and proposed normative principles. Bies and Moag (1986) enriched the fairness notion by introducing interactional fairness. They pointed out the importance of interpersonal treatments in the implementation of procedures that produce fairness perceptions. Greenberg (1993) continued along the similar lines, while suggesting separation between informational and interactional fairness. He argued that these two classes represent the social aspects of fairness that correspond to distributive and procedural fairness respectively.

Negotiation and bargaining have been used to study fairness in the participants' behaviors. Ultimatum and dictator games are frequently used in this respect (Diekmann, et al., 2013). Studies of ultimatum and dictator games revealed a weakness of the rational behavior model by showing that people, as social animals, are not as highly selfish as to claim excessive surplus. Fairness is an important element influencing both people's behaviors and judgement.

It has been found that fairness plays an important role not only in distributive but also in integrative negotiations. Albin (1993) showed that negotiators often referred to fairness when evaluating alternatives for a solution, coordinating expectations, and making consensus regarding an agreement. The adoption of fairness principles enhanced mutual responsiveness and thereby facilitated negotiation processes. Empirical results also show that fairness helps to increase the chances for mutually beneficial agreements, enhances durability of agreement, and promotes sound interpersonal relationships (Albin & Druckman, 2010). Procedural fairness enhances the acceptance of negotiated agreements and increases the potential for better negotiation outcomes in dispute resolution (Hollander-Blumoff & Tyler, 2008). It also contributes to more constructive problem-solving and integrative outcomes (Wagner & Druckman, 2012).

Challenges and Opportunities

Exchange episodes join industrial buyers and sellers in both discrete transactions and long-term partnerships (Håkansson, 1982). Economics provides model and instruments that help understand and examine exchange and related results. In practice, industrial buyers and sellers need to balance between two concerns: economic results and relational impacts. Solely focusing on economic results may not be sufficient to guide business practice. Recently, there has been growing interest in developing socio-economic exchange theories that can better satisfy business needs (e.g.,Bunduchi, 2008). Economics community also actively integrates social and behavioral findings to develop more robust models that can better explain economic phenomena. Despite these movements, the joint-venture of economics, behavioral science, and social science is undoubtedly challenging.

One of the hindrances preventing the joint-venture is lack of contextual richness in economic studies. For instance, abstract goods or services are often used in these studies. Market participants are expected or incepted to be self-interested and fully rational. The current study attempts to add the concept of fairness on top of economic theory of market exchange, in order to explore the possibility that the "socio-economic" exchange approach can better address business concerns.

Despite the importance of fairness, understanding of the roles of fairness in business negotiations is quite limited (Diekmann, et al., 2013). Most studies of fairness in negotiations focused on bargaining in games (Engel, 2011; Güth & Tietz, 1990), dispute resolution (Hollander-Blumoff & Tyler, 2008), international trade (Albin & Druckman, 2014), and political negotiations (Wagner & Druckman, 2012). In business negotiations, fairness may not only influence process and outcomes, but also have an effect on the business relationships. Therefore, studying fairness in business negotiations will have both practical, as well as theoretical implications.

RESEARCH MODEL AND HYPOTHESES

The current study aims to investigate the impact of fairness on business relationships in procurement negotiations. Negotiations enable rich social interaction between the parties involved. However, research of the effect of information disclosure in negotiations is scarce. To the best knowledge of the authors, Thomas & Wilson (2002, 2005) conducted two procurement experiments comparing four exchange mechanisms, including two negotiations (i.e., multi-bilateral negotiation and verifiable multi-bilateral negotiation) and two auctions (i.e., reverse first-price and second-price auctions). They found that verifiable negotiations generated higher price (or lower revenue to the buyer) than non-verifiable ones, although the difference was insignificant.

The above study shows that credible information disclosure may influence negotiation processes and outcomes. Credible disclosure of the current best offer can be regarded as an implemented condition of procedural or informational fairness in negotiations, if the information reflects facts and is revealed in an appropriate, accurate and unbiased manner. The disclosure of current best offer in negotiation is comparable to English auction or the "known-pie" ultimatum game with full division message.

Figure 1: The research model

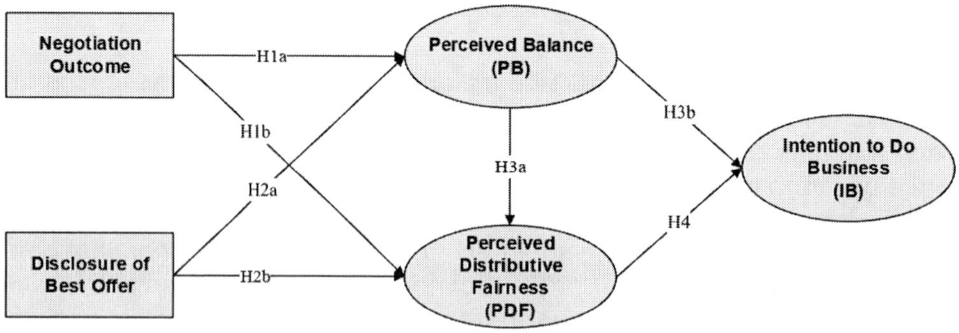

Drawing on multiple streams of literature, a research model has been constructed (Figure 1). The model has two independent variables and three subjective constructs. Disclosure of the best offer and negotiation outcome are the independent variables. Participants' fairness perceptions are restricted to distributive fairness since obtaining value is the key objective of businesses. Perceived distributive fairness (PDF) is adopted to capture participants' perceptions of distributive fairness. Perceived balance (PB) is adopted to capture negotiators' perceptions of negotiation outcomes. Four principles (i.e., equity, equality, need, and generosity) used for judging distributive fairness were identified. In market encounters, the last two are not much applicable. When key information (e.g., cost or reservations) is kept private in market encounters, equality principle would be appropriate to use. Intention to do business (IB) is adopted as an indicator of the impact on business relationship. Behavioral intention has been shown as a very strong predictor of actual action (Fishbein, 1979).

Economics theories, game theory, and negotiation analysis often expect that market participants are driven by their goals of achieving the best individual outcomes. The expectation has been empirically confirmed, while deviations may systematically take place. Studies of ultimatum game found similar results. Empirical study comparing negotiations and auctions also show that market participants are indeed motivated to obtain better outcomes (Yu, Kersten, & Vahidov, 2015). Two hypotheses regarding the impact of negotiation outcome are stated as follows.

H1a: Better negotiation outcome leads to increased perceived balance.
H1b: Better negotiation outcome leads to increased perceived distributive fairness.

By the negotiation outcome here we mean the utility of the achieved agreement to the individual negotiator if such agreement is reached. The outcome will be equal to zero if the agreement is not made. The details are discussed in the "measurements" section. The disclosure of best offer in negotiation is an implemented fairness condition. Economic theories posit that competition and self-interest behavior will drive exchange results to the equilibrium in a market. However, studies of ultimatum games show that people are not solely self-interested. Fairness motives may influence their decisions. Some studies suggest that the allocation of the pies will be more balanced between proposers and responders when more information is disclosed (Roth, Prasnikar, Okuno-Fujiwara, & Zamir, 1991; Straub & Murnighan, 1995). Similarly, other findings suggest that price is more favorable to competing sellers in verifiable negotiations compared to non-verifiable negotiations (Thomas & Wilson, 2002, 2005). Thus, we propose the following hypotheses.

H2a: Disclosure of best offer leads to increased perceived balance.
H2b: Disclosure of best offer leads to increased perceived distributive fairness.

Perceived balance is adopted to capture participants' assessment of the allocation, because equality principle will have stronger effect in market encounters. When participants perceive the allocation as more balanced, they will feel the distribution of value is fairer (and less unfair). In turn, these perceptions will influence participants' behavioral intention to do business with the counterpart in the future.

H3a: Perceived balance positively influences perceived distributive fairness.
H3b: Perceived balance positively influences intention to do business.

H4: Perceived distributive fairness positively influences intention to do business.

METHODOLOGY

Experiment and Data Collection

An experiment was conducted to test the hypotheses. The study is based on the economic experiments of (Thomas & Wilson, 2002, 2005) and focuses on only two mechanisms, i.e., multi-bilateral negotiation and multi-bilateral verifiable negotiation. The experiment enriches the economic experimental settings in several aspects. First, the negotiations involve multiple issues. Second, a business case was provided to participants. The case contains rich information about the negotiation issues, business objectives, and context. Third, the valuation between the buyer and sellers on some issues are not fully opposite, which opens a possibility of improving joint gain between the buyer and sellers.

A procurement case involving one buyer and multiple sellers was used in the experiment. The case describes a milk producing company (buyer) that requires a logistics provider (seller) to sign a contract for transportation services. The company approached several providers and invited them to participate in a negotiation. The conditions for three issues need to be established in a contract, including standard rate of transportation, rush rate for unexpected delivery, and penalty for non-delivery or delivery of spoiled goods. Each party was given a set of value schemas, representing individual private preferences. Each party was given a reservation condition, indicating the minimum value at which a party can make an agreement. The reservation conditions of sellers jointly determine the winner of a negotiation from the economic aspect (it is the one that has the lowest reservation condition). The quasi-linear scoring function was interpreted as revenue.

An e-negotiation system was used in the experiment. The system supports web-based multi-bilateral negotiations, where users can exchange messages and offers. The experiment had two treatments. One treatment included regular multi-bilateral negotiations without revealing current best offer received by the buyer (non-verifiable negotiation). The other one used the same mechanism plus an extra feature of revealing current bester offer (verifiable negotiation). Undergraduate students from four countries (Canada, Poland, Taiwan, and China) were recruited as participants, and they had to conclude their negotiations in ten days.

Measurements

Let's assume a contract contains M (non-zero) attributes. Let X_j denote the set of all possible values of attribute $j \in \{1,\dots,M\}$. An offer can be described as an M-dimensional vector $x=(x_1,\dots,x_m)$, while $x_1 \in X_1, \dots, x_m \in X_m$. Each negotiation instance will be conducted bilaterally between a buyer and multiple sellers. Suppose there is one buyer b and I sellers ($I>0$; $i \in (1,\dots,I)$). Let θ_b denote the value schema of buyer b, while θ_i denote the value schema of the seller i. The value schemas of the buyer and sellers can be mapped to a specific value function (or scoring rule): $V(x,\theta)$, $\theta \in (\theta_1, \dots \theta_I, \theta_b)$. Only one seller can be chosen as the winner at the end of each negotiation. The achievable outcome (or revenue) of the sellers and the buyer can be presented in this formula:

$$u_i(x, \theta_i) = \begin{cases} v(x, \theta_i), & \text{if an agreement is reached;} \\ 0 & \text{, if no agreement is reached.} \end{cases} \quad i \in \{1, \dots, I, b\}$$

A questionnaire was administrated to the participants after they concluded their negotiations. Four constructs were operationalized with self-reported survey questions in the form of seven-point Likert scales that had anchors varying from "Strongly disagree" to "Strongly agree". In total eight questions were used. The instruments measuring PDF were adapted from (Kim & Leung, 2007). The instrument for PB and IB were newly developed. The whole set of questions can be found in Table 2.

RESULTS

Descriptive Statistics

In total, 553 participants registered for the negotiation experiment. Before the registration, a number of potential participants from multiple groups was estimated. According to the estimation, two small groups were selected to take the role of buyers. The other groups would be the sellers. After the registration, these participants were randomly matched up into 109 negotiation instances according to the pre-selected role for each group. The negotiation instances included 54 non-verifiable negotiations and 55 verifiable negotiations. Each participant could participate in the experiment once. Within each negotiation instance, one buyer negotiated with several sellers. Most negotiation instances had four or five sellers. Only few had six sellers. Most of the participants were between 20 and 30 years old. A data screening has been conducted. Instances and related data were removed if any of three problems had been detected: 1) technological errors had been reported; 2) instance had inactive sellers; and 3) instance had unusual outcomes (i.e., the seller obtained 100% of achievable value and the instance ended in the first two days).

Table 1: The descriptive statistics of samples

Treatment		Non-verifiable Negotiations	Verifiable Negotiations	Overall
Number of instances		47	48	95
Female		113	94	207
Male		94	108	202
Number of participants		207	202	409
Seller's revenue	Mean	29.96	33.98	31.99
	Median	28	32	30
	Maximum	71	66	71
	Minimum	10	10	10
	Standard deviation	13.421	14.195	13.89
Buyer's revenue	Mean	77.15	75.74	76.44
	Median	77.50	80	79
	Maximum	93	94	94
	Minimum	50	50	50
	Standard deviation	12.165	12.068	12.071

After cleaning, 96 negotiation instances were left: 47 non-verifiable negotiation and 48 verifiable negotiations. The participants included 95 sellers and 409 buyers. The effect of the number of sellers was examined by checking correlations between the number of sellers in each negotiation instance and revenues on both seller and buyer sides. No significant effect was found. The current data analysis focused on the seller side. Among the 409 sellers, 245 completed the questionnaires. Table 1 shows the descriptive analysis of the effective samples for this study.

Refining Subjective Instruments

Before refining the instruments, MANOVA tests were conducted to test the group homogeneity of subjective variables against a set of control variables, such as gender, age, English proficiency, and experiences with similar systems. No significant effect was found to be related with these variables.

A confirmatory factor analysis, using EQS 6.1, was carried out with the maximum likelihood method. The factor model has an appropriate goodness of fit (NFI=.990, GFI=.979, AGFI=.956, CFI=.998, IFI=.998, SRMR=.016, and RMSEA=.034). The normality of the measurement, factor loadings, and largest standardized residuals had been checked. No item was eliminated. Thus, the model was accepted as the final factor model.

Table 2: The factors, items, and reliability of subjective measures.

Items	Factor Loading	Cronbach's Alpha	Rho
Intention to do business (IB):		0.972	0.973
I intend to do business with the buyer.	0.961		
I predict that I will do business with the buyer.	0.940		
I plan to do business with the buyer.	0.981		
Perceived balance (PB):		0.939	0.939
I believe that the achieved revenues were balanced between the buyer and seller sides.	0.901		
I believe that the achieved revenues were evenly allocated between the buyer and seller sides.	0.940		
I believe that the achieved revenues were symmetrically distributed between the buyer and seller sides.	0.903		
Perceived distributive fairness (PDF)		0.919	0.925
The achieved results were fair to sellers.	0.920		
As sellers, we obtained what we should get.	0.925		

Table 3: The AVEs and shared variances of factors.

Factors	IB	PB	PUF
IB	**0.923**		
PB	0.270	**0.837**	
PDF	0.367	0.514	**0.851**

The measurement reliability has also been tested. The factor loadings, Cronbach's alpha and reliability coefficient Rho are reported in Table 2. All the indices of each factor were greater than 0.7. The discriminant validity of the subjective measures was examined by following the recommendation of Fornell (1981). Comparisons between shared variance of factors and AVE (Average Variance Extracted) were conducted. The values of AVE and shared variance are reported in Table 3. All the values of AVE are above 0.8.

We noticed that PB and PDF are highly correlated and share high covariance. However, we accepted PB and PDF as two separate factors for several reasons. First, this result is in line with the theoretical prediction that PB and PDF should strongly correlate with each other. Second, their shared covariance (i.e., 0.514) is just marginally greater than the recommended value of 0.5. Second, the AVE of each factor is much higher than the shared covariance.

Research Model Testing

The testing of the research model has been conducted using the data collected from the seller side (i.e., the multiparty side). In the current study, the differences of reservation conditions of sellers were set to be small, which was expected to reduce the direct impacts of relative market positions. Before testing the research model, examination on achievable revenue on both buyer and seller sides have been conducted. A Mann-Whitney U test was conducted to compare buyer and seller revenues between treatments. The results showed that verifiable negotiations lead to insignificantly lower revenue on buyer side (1-tailed $p = 0.243$), which is consistent with past studies (Thomas & Wilson, 2002, 2005). The effect of treatment on sellers' revenues is marginally significant (1-tailed $p=0.074$).

Exchange episodes produce discrete revenues for participants. Thus, the effect of negotiation outcome needs to be examined in several tests. Empirical results show that participants of exchange episodes strongly responded to the contingency of whether they had won the contract (Yu, et al., 2015). Three tests have been conducted. The first test included all sellers (test 1). The independent variables in the first test were two coded categorical variables: disclosure of best offer and winner. The variable of disclosure of best offer was coded to be 1 for verifiable negotiations and 0 for non-verifiable negotiations. The variable of winner was coded to be 1 for winners and 0 for non-winners. The second test (test 2) was conducted among winners, in which sellers' revenues could be treated as a continuous variable. The third test (test 3) was conducted among non-winners, whose revenues were all zero.

A structural equation model was specified in accordance with the research model in test 1 (see figure 2). A MIMIC method was adopted. The testing results showed a good fit of the model (NFI=.986, GFI=.975, AGFI=.954, CFI=.999, IFI=.999, SRMR=.038, and RMSEA=.018). Significant paths and related testing results are presented in Figure 2.

The results show that the variable winner has significant effects on PB and PDF. Thus, win-or-loss contingency indeed has strong impacts on negotiators' subjective responses. The coefficient of the path from winner to PDF is positive. Thus, the hypotheses of group H1 were all supported. The variable disclosure of best offer has significant effect on PB and non-significant effects on PDF. These results indicate that disclosure of credible information will enhance sellers' perceived balance. The hypothesis H2a was supported. PB has significant effect on PDF and IB. The hypotheses of group H3 were all supported. PDF has positive effect on IB, i.e., the hypothesis H4 was supported.

Figure 2: Research model testing results

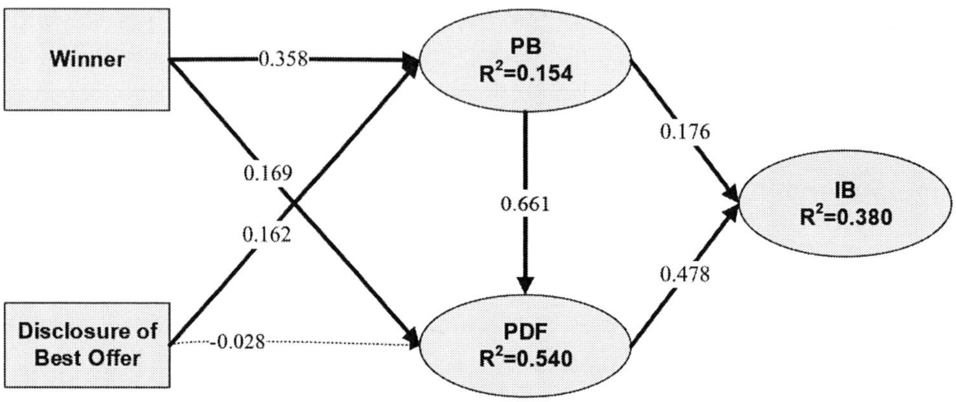

Test 2 used a path analysis among winners because it helps to increase the statistical power and reduce the overall number of paths. In this test, the sums of the values of items representing each factor were used. In variance analysis, the use of sum score to represent factors is deemed an appropriate, or even a preferred technique (DiStefano, Zhu, & Mîndrilă, 2009). Among winners, achieved revenue can be treated as a continuous variable. Thus, variable of the negotiation outcome in this test is replaced with revenue. An extra path between disclosure of best offer and revenue was added in order to test whether disclosure of credible information may help sellers obtain better outcome.

The results showed a very good fit (Chi-square = 1.217 with 2 degree of freedom, probability value for chi-square = 0.54417, NFI = 0.983, CFI = 1, GFI= 0.992, AGFI=0.941, IFI = 1.011, RMSEA =0, and 90% confidence interval of RMSEA was between 0 and 0.218). The coefficients for the paths contained in the model are presented in Figure 5. The significant paths (at 5% significant level) are highlighted.

The results of the path analysis show that disclosure of best offer slightly helps to increase sellers' revenues. However, both disclosure of best offer and revenue have no significant effects on PDF and PB. Thus, among winners, the hypotheses of group H1 and H2 were not supported. PB has a significant effect, which supports H3a. PDF has a significant effect on IB, which supports H4a.

Test 3 used another path analysis conducted among non-winners. A similar model is fit in order to compare the results with those of test 2. The model also used the sum score of factors. Among non-winners, achieved revenues were all zero. Thus, the variable of the negotiation outcome in this test was removed. The maximum-likelihood method was used as well. The results showed a very good fit (Chi-square = 0.131 with 1 degree of freedom, probability value for chi-square = 0.71735, NFI = 0.999, CFI = 1, GFI= 1, AGFI=0.996, IFI = 1.006, RMSEA =0, and 90% confidence interval of RMSEA is between 0 and 0.141). The coefficients for the paths contained in the model are presented in Figure 3. A significant effect of disclosure of current best offer on PB was found, which supports hypothesis H2a. PB had significant effect on both PDF and IB, which support H3a and H3c. PDF has a significant effect on IB, which supports hypothesis H4a.

Figure 3: Path analyses among winners and non-winners

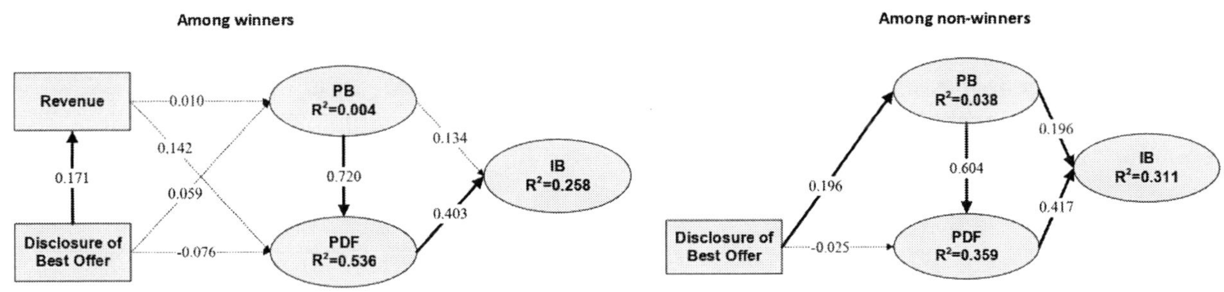

CONCLUSION

The current paper discusses the role of perceived fairness in business negotiations. Research model was introduced with two independent variables, including negotiation outcome and disclosure of the best offer. The testing results of the research model showed several interesting findings. First, the relationships between PB, PDF, and IB are consistent with the theoretical analysis of negotiator's fairness perception. In market exchange, the allocation of values of buyers and sellers is substantive. Particularly, equality principle seems to be the main principle adopted by negotiators. Therefore, PB is the key construct that influences negotiators' fairness perception (i.e., PDF).

Second, the results of test 1 showed that win-or-lose contingency have a strong impact on negotiators' fairness perception. This result is consistent with the findings of (Yu, et al., 2015). The results of test 2 show that revenue has no significant effect on PB or PDF. Combined with the results of test 1, this finding shows that winners' fairness perceptions heavily depends on the win-or-lose contingency. The actual achieved revenue may not be a fundamental factor shaping the negotiators' perceptions of fairness. These findings highlight a possibility that winners may not reasonably assess fairness in negotiations.

Third, the disclosure of current best offer in negotiations indeed has an impact on negotiators' fairness perceptions. The results of test 1 show that the disclosure of current best offer influences negotiators' perceived balance. The results of test 3 show a similar relationship among non-winners. These results are useful for both system design and strategy management. They indicate that implementing fairness in negotiation can help enhance business relationships.

Fourth, the disclosure of current best offer in negotiations has limited effect, although it significantly affects negotiators' fairness perceptions. Test 3 shows that the explained R-square of PB is 0.038, which is very marginal. Test 2 shows that explained R-square of PB is 0.004. In these two tests, the explained R-squares of PB are much lower than that of test 1 (i.e., 0.154). Similarly, the explained R-squares of PDF in both test 2 (i.e., 0.536) and test 3 (i.e., 0.359) are lower than that in test 1 (i.e., 0.540). In both test 2 and test 3, negotiation outcome either has no significant effect or is not relevant. In contrast, the variable of winner in test 1 has stronger effects than disclosure of current best offer (please check the path coefficients in test 1). These results suggest that the effect of win-or-lost contingency on negotiators' fairness perception dominates the effect of the disclosure of current best offer. This finding has an important implication to business practices. Revealing credible information during negotiation helps to enhance business relationship. At the same time, the potential benefits may be overridden by the win-or-lose contingency. Thereby, negotiation hosts may benefit more if they organized their negotiations in a way that other participants do not know that they are competing with each other. However, the achievable effect is also questionable if competition is removed from negotiations. These and other related questions need further investigation in future research.

REFERENCES

Adams, J. S. (1965). Inequity in social exchange. *Advances in experimental social psychology, 2*(267-299).

Albin, C. (1993). The role of fairness in negotiation. *Negotiation Journal, 9*(3), 223-244.

Albin, C., & Druckman, D. (2010). The role of justice in negotiation *Handbook of Group Decision and Negotiation* (pp. 109-119): Springer.

Albin, C., & Druckman, D. (2014). Procedures matter: Justice and effectiveness in international trade negotiations. *European Journal of International Relations, 20*(4), 1014-1042.

Bakos, J. Y. (1991). A Strategic Analysis of Electronic Marketplaces. *MIS Quarterly, 15*(3), 295-310.

Bies, R. J., & Moag, J. S. (1986). Interactional justice: Communication criteria of fairness. *Research on negotiation in organizations, 1*(1), 43-55.

Bunduchi, R. (2008). Trust, power and transaction costs in B2B exchanges—A socio-economic approach. *Industrial Marketing Management, 37*(5), 610-622.

Choudhury, V., Hartzel, K. S., & Konsynski, B. R. (1998). Uses and Consequences of Electronic Markets: An Empirical Investigation in the Aircraft Parts Industry. *MIS Quarterly, 22*(4), 471-507.

Coase, R. H. (1937). The Nature of the Firm. *Economica, 4*(16), 386-405. doi: 10.2307/2626876

Cropanzano, R., & Mitchell, M. S. (2005). Social Exchange Theory: An Interdisciplinary Review. *Journal of management, 31*(6), 874-900. doi: 10.1177/0149206305279602

Diekmann, K. A., Soderberg, A. T., & Tenbrunsel, A. E. (2013). Fairness and ethics in bargaining and negotiation. In M. Olekalns & W. L. Adair (Eds.), *Handbook of Research on Negotiation* (pp. 191-220). Cheltenham, UK; Northampton, MA, USA: Edward Elgar.

DiStefano, C., Zhu, M., & Mîndrilă, D. (2009). Understanding and using factor scores: Considerations for the applied researcher. *Practical Assessment Research and Evaluation, 14*(20), 1-11.

Engel, C. (2011). Dictator games: a meta study. *Experimental Economics, 14*(4), 583-610. doi: 10.1007/s10683-011-9283-7

Fishbein, M. (1979). A Theory of Reasoned Action: Some Applications and Implications *Nebraska Symposium on Motivation* (pp. 65). Lincoln, Nebraska.: University of Nebraska Press.

Fornell, C., & Larcker, D. F. (1981). Evaluating Structural Equation Models with Unobservable Variables and Measurement Error. *Journal of Marketing Research, 18*(1), 39-50.

Greenberg, J. (1993). The social side of fairness: Interpersonal and informational classes of organizational justice. In R. Cropanzano (Ed.), *Justice in the workplace: Approaching fairness in human resource management* (pp. 70-103). Hillsdale, NJ: Lawrence Erlbaum Associates, Inc.

Grieger, M. (2003). Electronic marketplaces: A literature review and a call for supply chain management research. *European Journal of Operational Research, 144*(2), 280.

Güth, W., & Tietz, R. (1990). Ultimatum bargaining behavior: A survey and comparison of experimental results. *Journal of economic psychology, 11*(3), 417-449.

Håkansson, H. (Ed.). (1982). *International Marketing and Purchasing of Industrial Goods, An Interaction Approach (By IMP Project Group)*. Chichester, New York, Brisbane, Toronto, Singapore: John Wiley & Sons, Ltd.

Håkansson, H., & Snehota, I. (1995). *Developing relationships in business networks*. London and New York: Routledge Londres.

Hollander-Blumoff, R., & Tyler, T. R. (2008). Procedural justice in negotiation: Procedural fairness, outcome acceptance, and integrative potential. *Law & Social Inquiry, 33*(2), 473-500.

Homans, G. C. (1961). *Social behavior: Its elementary forms*. New York: Harcourt, Brace and World, Inc.

Kim, T.-Y., & Leung, K. (2007). Forming and reacting to overall fairness: A cross-cultural comparison. *Organizational Behavior and Human Decision Processes, 104*(1), 83-95.

Leventhal, G. S. (1980). *What should be done with equity theory? New approaches to the study of justice in social relationships* (Vol. 9). New York: Springer Science & Business Media.

Roth, A. E., Prasnikar, V., Okuno-Fujiwara, M., & Zamir, S. (1991). Bargaining and Market Behavior in Jerusalem, Ljubljana, Pittsburgh, and Tokyo: An Experimental Study. *The American Economic Review, 81*(5), 1068-1095.

Straub, P. G., & Murnighan, J. K. (1995). An experimental investigation of ultimatum games: Information, fairness, expectations, and lowest acceptable offers. *Journal of Economic Behavior & Organization, 27*(3), 345-364.

Thibaut, J. W., & Walker, L. (1975). *Procedural justice: A psychological analysis*: L. Erlbaum Associates.

Thomas, C. J., & Wilson, B. J. (2002). A comparison of auctions and multilateral negotiations. *The Rand Journal of Economics, 33*(1), 140-155.

Thomas, C. J., & Wilson, B. J. (2005). Verifiable Offers and the Relationship between Auctions and Multilateral Negotiations. *The Economic Journal, 115*(506), 1016-1031.

Wagner, L., & Druckman, D. (2012). The role of justice in historical negotiations. *Negotiation and Conflict Management Research, 5*(1), 49-71.

Wang, S., & Archer, N. P. (2007). Electronic marketplace definition and classification: literature review and clarifications. *Enterprise Information Systems, 1*(1), 89-112.

Welsh, N. A. (2003). Perceptions of fairness in negotiation. *Marquette Law Review, 87*, 753.

Williamson, O. E. (1979). Transaction-Cost Economics: The Governance of Contractual Relations. *Journal of Law and Economics, 22*(2), 233-261.

Yu, B., Kersten, G. E., & Vahidov, R. (2015). Traders' Subjective Appraisals: Comparison of Negotiations and Auctions. *Journal of Organizational Computing and Electronic Commerce, 25*(3), 233-261.

E-commerce, challenges, and developing countries

STELLAMARIS UWEMI
Department of Computer Science, University of Liverpool, UK.
Email: stellauwemi@gmail.com

Habib Ullah Khan* (Corresponding Author)
College of Business & Economics, Qatar University, Doha, Qatar
Email: habib.khan@qu.edu.qa

ABSTRACT

The number of businesses embracing e-commerce technologies in developing countries has risen dramatically in recent years, as well as the volume of e-commerce transactions. However, this cannot yet compare with what entails in developed nations. This project examined the peculiar challenges of the growth of e-commerce in developing countries (using Nigeria as a case study). An Interpretivism research philosophy was employed for this research and qualitative and quantitative techniques were used for data collection. The study was carried out on both consumers and e-commerce operators. In the research study, a total number of 225 questionnaires were distributed to consumers, of which 200 responded adequately. A total of 10 e-commerce operators were interviewed to gain the perspective of operators.

Results of the research showed that end-users of e-commerce portals highlighted issues of security, trust and low quality of e-commerce services. Operators, however, believed that government intervention in the promotion of e-commerce could be more decisive, which would contribute to economic development. The study also revealed that e-commerce operators influenced the promotion and use of ecommerce in the developing countries, and strategies they put in place influenced the awareness of product and services.

KEYWORDS. E-commerce, Challenges, Developing countries, Case study

---

INTRODUCTION

The internet has brought about the tremendous growth of e-commerce in developed and developing countries. Meharia (2012) explains that 'The dawn of e-commerce in the mid-1990s was seen by many as the beginning of an entirely radical way of buying goods and services'. The definition of e-commerce differs among academics and scholars. Jobodwana (2009) explains e-commerce to be 'the method of doing transaction across the internet.' The use of e-commerce facilitates the transaction of business between different parties over the internet in a quick and efficient way. This has given market entry strategies to those companies whose presence is not physical. The effect of e-commerce has greatly affected the global economy in various ways. It has affected the information technology, economic sectors, and enhanced productivity. When buying and selling of products and services through the networks is known as e-commerce (Nahari & Krutz, 2011). E-commerce is about selling products and services through the means of internet communications. Before the advent of e-commerce, most business transactions were done in the traditional way in physical locations. With e-commerce, people are now able to exchange goods and services through the internet without travelling and wasting time. E-commerce transactions have encouraged the growth of businesses in different forms (Burinskienė,2012).

The emergence of e-commerce in the business sector of developed countries has brought about tremendous growth to the global economy. Measuring the strength, coverage and utilisation of e-commerce operations in developing countries requires an assessment of two views: consumers' and operators'. This research covered the consumers who patronise online businesses, and the operators who provide e-commerce services. Due to the objective of this project, consumers who have not considered patronising online businesses were not consulted. Also, companies that do not operate online businesses were not involved in this study.

E-commerce has been successfully implemented and utilised in developed countries with huge economic and social benefits. But the same cannot be said of developing countries. Several challenges have been suggested as to why e-commerce has not been a success in developing countries as recorded in the developed countries. This research will identify these challenges and also investigate the impact of e-commerce on economic growth of developing countries. These challenges will be investigated from the view point of both consumers and operators, and appropriate solutions will be proposed to address the identified challenges.

LITERATURE REVIEW

Several researches have been carried out on how e-commerce has improved business transactions globally and also the barriers that are affecting e-commerce in developing countries. E-commerce has been able to remove the duration of time in ordering, invoicing, making payment and delivery. E-commerce has greatly impacted the economy globally and this as changed the old-style of doing business transactions, service delivery etc. (Jobodwana, 2009). Makame et al., (2014), states that 'e-commerce is changing the traditional way of doing businesses at a fast rate'. It has also transformed the marketplace by changing business models, shaping between market relations and making changes to market structures. Also, it has given companies a global view of how users can relate with their products online, showing how they can engage and reward their consumers. With this, companies are able to reach targeted consumers, analyse consumer behaviour and this will enable them meet their needs and expectations, etc. Also, it will give enormous potential that will empower the people in developing countries to be able to overcome obstacles and achieve a viable economy (Oreku et al., 2009).

Factors Affecting Adoption and Utilisation of E-Commerce

Numerous factors have contributed to the slow growth of e-commerce in developing countries especially in Africa. Many of the studies that have been carried out on the adoption of e-commerce in the developing countries have highlighted some of the problems, including consumer attitudes, infrastructure, political issues, socio-economic issues, language barriers, computer illiteracy etc. Developing countries are facing a lot of technical, legal, societal and financial problems in their adoption of e-commerce (Aleid, 2012). Most Africans have not really known the essence of e-commerce and even consumers are hesitant in giving out their personal information as a result of online fraud (Anzaki, 2014). Factors that are affecting the adoption of e-commerce are socio-economic, technological infrastructure, political, cultural and legal and regulatory (Olatokun & Bankole, 2011). There are different issues hindering e-commerce such as consumer attitudes towards e-commerce systems, privacy, security of consumers' information and trust (Wei et al., 2010)

Economic and Socio-Political

The issues of e-commerce adoption in Nigeria are centred on economic, social-political and cognitive issues. The economic issues are centred on slow internet diffusion with unavailability of credit cards and logistics. Socio-political issues are into formal and informal institution which includes legal, environmental issues and policy. Cognitive issues are the lack of awareness, language barrier and computer illiteracy (Egbokhare et al., 2011). Olusegun et al., (2006) explains that 'Some of the issues affecting the adoption of e-commerce in Nigeria are mainly security and citizen's income.' In most developing countries, consumers are bent on using the traditional e-commerce transaction because of different issue and consumers' readiness is a key factor (Awa et al., 2010).

The issues of policy initiatives, economic, social, or technological context needs to be addressed in the developing countries since e-commerce has been proven to improve the economy of countries that have adopted it (Makame et al., 2014). The poor quality of internet access, high cost of accessing the internet, and cost of personal computers are issues affecting e-commerce businesses (Rajmohan et al., 2010).

Government Policies

Many studies show that right governmental policies influence the growth of e-commerce (Burinskienė, 2012). A lot of developing countries are facing different economic challenges, such as poor governance i.e. they lack efficient leaders and government that lack knowledge and willingness to address the various economic problems. Some of the issues facing Africa are multi-varied such as political uncertainty, economic mismanagement, and poverty among others (Jobodwana, 2009). Although, a number of e-commerce activities are evolving in most developing countries, the growth has been very slow because of lack of appropriate government policies (Anzaki, 2014). Government policy is one of the issue facing developing countries.

Trust of E-Commerce System

Several works have been carried out about the issue of trust which has been a concern on e-commerce and one of the most researched aspects of e-commerce from users' perceptions. Trust has a major role to play when it comes to e-commerce because it is one of the key drivers for customers concerning their transactions (Kobayashi et al., 2013). Huamei (2013) pointed out that 'one of the main issues to online shopping is lack of trust in online purchase.' Trust is very crucial in a large community of unidentified merchants (Bazdan, 2011). Trust has a way of motivating consumers to purchase products and services which in turn will make them to go online for these purchases. The ultimate issue of both consumers and the operators is that of trust.

Trust has been one of the issues affecting the adoption of e-commerce in developing countries. It has a major role to play on the growth of e-commerce due to the risk and uncertainty of cyber transactions (Nahari & Krutz, 2011). With the fast growth of e-commerce, the need for trust has to be addressed because of the increase of fraud which creates doubts in the mind of consumers. Hence, this factor is very necessary in building e-commerce in developing countries. Meanwhile, developed nations have been able to address the issue.

Trust is dependent on different factors as the two parties involved in a transaction, the trustor and trustee, need to have the necessary details that will show the transaction can be done; the products or services made by trustor must be delivered by the trustee through a reliable and well-secured system (Muhammad,2013). Shaozhong et.al (2012) stated that 'Trust has become an important issue on e-commerce application'. But in developing countries, many consumers find it difficult to trust e-commerce transactions.

Security and Privacy

The convenience of e-commerce has enabled consumers to access products and services remotely 24-hours round the clock, which has made e-commerce to become more popular. Although, some researchers have argued that security and privacy has restricted the full potential of e-commerce. Many customers have genuine fears on providing their private information to an unknown body over the internet, and they do not know the way their information will be handled. This attitude of consumers toward e-commerce is because of fear, fraud and online crime. In developing countries, security and privacy are serious issues on e-commerce services. (Ibikunle, 2013). Security and privacy seems to be the most significant factors in influencing the trust on e-commerce. Protecting consumers' data from online fraud can be achieved by proper security. The issue is critical to the consumers as a result they are hesitant towards giving out their personal information on the internet because of fraud (Mandić, 2009). Security and privacy has been a fundamental subject in the academic of computer science for over 30 years now (Feigenbaum et al., 2009). The issue of security and privacy has led to negative effects on the growth of e-commerce in developing countries. This has been a major concern for e-commerce operators because it is critical to the success of their online business (Antoniou & Batten, 2011).

Impacts of E-Commerce on Economy

Internet and e-commerce have brought different countries together to build a worldwide networked economy and this growth and integration of ICT has changed economies and societies. The economic importance of e-commerce is well-pronounced in changes that are created in the activities of enterprises and these changes result in an increase in productivity (Minculete & Minculete, 2013). This will impact on the people, organisations, industry and the country as a whole, which increases trading with other countries and greater opportunities for global information-sharing and marketing (Weber & Kauffman, 2011). E-commerce will allow firms to have the ability to become virtual businesses which will increase productivity (Smith, 2011).

(Research under progress)

REFERENCES

Askoul, R., Khan, H.U. and Madhavi Lalitha, V.V. (2016) 'Cross-functional integration of marketing and information services in banking: a cross-industry comparison', International. Journal of Process Management and Benchmarking, Vol. 6. No. 1. pp. 57-78

Adepetun, A. (2014), 'Nigeria controls 29% of Africa's Internet users' population' [Online] Available from:http://barasolutions.com/mainGuardian/compulife/55-compulife/159707-nigeria-controls-29-of-africa-s-internet-users-population (Accessed 6 June 2014).

Agwu, E. (2012), 'A Qualitative Study of the Problems and Prospects of Online Banking in Developing Economies Case of Nigeria', Journal Of Internet Banking & Commerce, Vol. 17(3) pp. 1-20 [Online] Available from: http://eds.a.ebscohost.com. ezproxy.liv.ac.uk/eds/pdfviewer/pdfviewer?sid=04684d14-52f6-4151-82eb-8a2ee53202a2%40sessionmgr4005&vid=1&hid=4211 (Accessed 6 June 2014).

Akintola K. G., Akinyede, R. O. and Agbonifo C. O. (2011), 'IJCSI International Journal of Computer Science Issues', Vol. 9 (2), No 1, Appraising Nigeria Readiness For Ecommerce Towards: Achieving Vision [Online] Available from: http://www.arpapress.com/volumes/vol9issue2/ijrras_9_2_ 18.pdf (Accessed 6 June 2014).

Aleid, E. (2012), 'Delivery Issues in E-Commerce: The Case of Saudi Arabia'. [Online] Available from: http://researchcommons.waikato.ac.nz/bitstream/handle/10289/6464/ thesis.pdf?sequence=3&isAllowed=y (Accessed 6 June 2014).

Amaefule, E. (2013), '32.5 million Nigerians access Internet via telecoms networks' [Online] Available from: http://www.punchng.com/business/32-5-million-nigerians-access-internet-via-telecoms-networks/ (Accessed 6 June 2014).

Anderson, J. D. (2006), Qualitative and Quantitative research Superintendent of Schools [Online] Available from: https://www.icoe.org/webfm_send/1936 (Accessed 6 June 2014).

Antoniou, G, and Batten, L (2011), 'E-commerce: protecting purchaser privacy to enforce trust', Electronic Commerce Research, Vol.11 (4) pp. 421-456 [Online] Available from:http://eds.b.ebscohost.com.ezproxy.liv.ac.uk/eds/pdfviewer/pdfviewer?sid=40348e98-db85-435a-9cc1-e874b0b39d7c%40sessionmgr112&vid=1&hid=109A (Accessed 7 June 2014).

Anyanwu, A. C., Ezugwu, A. E. and Abdullahi S. E. (2012), Electronic Payment System (EPS): Facilitating the Development and Adoption in Nigeria IJCSI International Journal of Computer Science Issues, Vol. 9 (2) pp. 1694-0814 [Online] Available from: https://www.academia.edu/1595264/Electronic_Payment_System_EPS_Facilitating_the_Development_and_Adoption_in_Nigeria (Accessed: 17 November 2014).

Anzaki, M. (2014), 'E-commerce in Africa: Trends and Laws' [Online] Available from: http://thelawyerschronicle.com/e-commerce-in-africa-trends-and-laws/ (Accessed: 8 May 2014).

Apulu, I. and Ige, E.O., (2011), 'Are Nigeria SMEs Effectively Utilising ICT?.' International Journal of Business and Management, 6 (6), pp. 207-215 [Online] Available from: file:///C:/Users/esteluw/Downloads/10841-32519-1-PB.pdf (Accessed: 10 May 2014)

Awa, H. O., Nwibere, B. M. and Inyang, B. J. (2010), 'The Uptake of Electronic Commerce by SMES: A Meta Theoretical Framework Expanding The Determining Constructions Of Tan And Toe Frameworks', Journal Of Global Business & Technology, vol. 6(1) pp. 1-27, [Online] Available from http://eds.a.ebscohost.com.ezproxy.liv.ac.uk/eds/pdfviewer/pdf viewer?sid=a133d3f5-8fcb-4321-ad63-9b73fe86f742%40sessionmgr4001&vid=0&hid=4205 (Accessed 30 October 2014).

Azeez, K. (2013) 'E-commerce transactions' p.1 [Online] Available from: http://national mirroronline.net/new/e-commerce-transactions-may-hit-n100bn-mark/ (Accessed: 14 November 2104).

Bangkok Post, (2006) 'Lack of Internet-awareness hampers development of e-commerce', Bangkok Post (Thailand), Regional Business News, http://eds.a.ebscohost.com.ezproxy.liv.ac.uk/eds/detail/detail?sid=754e6dc1-b892-47c5-81aa-6e99cda2fc00%40sessionmgr4003&vid=0&hid=4102&bdata=JnNpdGU9ZWRzLWxpdmUmc2NvcGU9c2l0ZQ%3d%3d#db=bwh&AN=2W62W64189123362 (Accessed: 21 November 2014.

Bansal, S. and Sharma, L. (2009), 'New Challenges Of Accounting And Auditing In E-Environment In India', Revista Universo Contábil, Vol.5 (1), pp. 88-99, [Online] Available from: http://eds.a.ebscohost.com.ezproxy.liv.ac.uk/eds/pdfviewer/pdfviewer?sid=bdde383d-42d1-46bf-82c4-04c47ff6d4a4%40sessionmgr4004&vid=1&hid=4210 (Accessed 11 June 2014).

Bazdan, Z (2011), 'An International Economy and E-commerce Case Study', Our Economy Case Study: Ebay Vol. 57(3/4) pp. 44-50 [Online] Available from: http://eds.b.ebscohost.com.ezproxy.liv.ac.uk/eds/pdfviewer/pdfviewer?sid=0a8a087b-b5eb-4f1a-b65b-86619a77716f%40sessionmgr113&vid=1&hid=105 (Accessed 11 June 2014).

Beiske, B. (2007), Research Methods: Uses and Limitations of Questionnaires, Interviews and Case Studies, GRIN.

Blumberg, B., Cooper, D. R., & Schindler, P. S. (2005), Business research methods. London: McGraw-Hill.

Blanche, M.T.,Durrheim, K. and Painter, D. (2006), Research in Practice (2nd Ed), Cape Town, UTC Press.

Brace, I. (2008), Questionnaire Design: How to Plan, Structure and Write Survey Material for Effective Second Edition [Online] Available from: http://samples.sainsburysebooks.co.uk/9780749454999_sample_128907.pdf (Accessed 12 June 2014).

Awan, M. A., Khan H.U. and Zhang, W. (2012) 'A comparative study on Online Service Quality Perception of two Major Regional Economies', *International Journal of e-Education, e-Business, e-Management and e-Learning(IJEEEE)*, Vol. 2, No.6, P.529-551.

Awan, M.A., and Khan, H.U. (2016), "Status of Internet Addiction among College Students:A Case of South Korea", First American Academic Research Conference on Global Business, Economics, Finance and Social Sciences (AAR16 New York Conference), New York, USA, May 25- May 28, 2016. (Conference Proceeding).

Brock V.F., Khan H.U.(2017), "ARE ENTERPRISES READY FOR BIG DATA ANALYTICS? A SURVEY BASED APPROACH", Int. J. of Business Information Systems (IJBIS), Forthcoming.

Das, A. and Khan, H.U. (2016) "Security behaviors of smartphone users", Information and Computer Security, Information and Computer Security, Vol. 24, No.1, pp. 116-134

Heang, J.F., and Khan, H.U. (2015), "The Role of Internet Marketing in the Development of Agricultural Industry: A Case Study of China",Vol. 14, Issue.1 , pp. 1-49.

Halabi A. E., Hachem A., Al-Akhrass L., Artail H., Khan H.U. (2014), "Identifying the linkability between Web servers for Enhanced Internet Computing", 17th IEEE Mediterranean Electrotechnical Conference MELECON 2014, 13-16 April, Beirut, Lebanon. (Conference Proceeding)

Hassan, I. M., Khan, H. U. and Lalitha, M. (2016) 'Pedagogical Potentials of IEEE 802.11 WLAN to Nigerian Universities: A Case Study of the University of Uyo', *International Journal of Information and Education Technology*, Vol. 6, No. 4, pp. 256-261.

Ho, C. H., Awan, M.A., and Khan H.U. (2016), "LUXURY BRANDS AND CORPORATE SOCIAL RESPONSIBILITY: A PERSPECTIVE ON CONSUMERS' PREFERENCES", Journal of International Management Studies, Vol. 16, No. 1, pp 77-81.

Khan, H.U., Talib, F., Nishat M.F. (2015),'An analysis of the barriers to the proliferation of M-Commerce in Qatar: A relationship modeling approach', Journal of Systems and Information Technology, Vol. 17, Issue. 1, pp. 54-81.

Khan, H.U. (2013a) 'Use of e-learning tools to solve group work problems in higher education: A Case study of gulf countries', *The Advances in Computer Science: an International Journal*, Vol. 2, No. 3, pp.90-96.

Khan, H.U. (2016), "Possible effect of video lecture capture technology on the cognitive Empowerment of higher education students: a case study of gulf-based university", International Journal of Innovation and Learning, Vol.20, No. 1, pp. 68: 84.

Khan, H.U. (2013b) 'Role of Computer Mediated Communication in Affect Empowerment and Performance Improvement', *IFRSA's International Journal of Computing*, Vol.3, No.3, P.165-171.

Khan, H.U. (2012) 'Computer Mediated Communication, Quality of Learning, and Performance', *Journal of GSTF Business Review*, Vol. 1, No. 3, pp. 81-88.

Khan, H.U., Artail, H., Malik, Z., Niazi, M.(2014a) 'Information Technology Adoption, possible challenges, and Framework of Supply Chain Management: A Case Study of a Leading Gulf Economy', *4th International Conference on International Conference on International Conference on Engineering Technology and Technopreneurship*, Kuala Lumpur, Malaysia.

Khan, H.U., Ahmed, S., Abdollahian, M. (2013) 'Supply chain technology acceptance, adoption, and possible challenges: A case study of service organizations of Saudi Arabia', *10th International Conference on Information Technology: New Generations (ITNG 2013)*, Las Vegas, Nevada, USA.

Khan, H.U., Awan, M.A., Ho. H.C. (2014b), "How do Chinese and Saudi Customers Perceive Online Service Quality? A Comparative Study", The Journal of Business Inquiry, Vol. 13, No. 2.pp.142-157.

Khan H.U., Awan M.A.(2017), "Possible Factors Affecting Internet Addiction: A Case Study of Higher Education Students of Qatar", Int. J. of Business Information Systems (IJBIS), Forthcoming.

Musa A., Khan, H.U., Alshare, K. (2015), "Factors influence consumers' adoption of mobile payment devices in Qatar", International Journal of Mobile Communications, Vol. 13, No. 6. pp. 670-689

Najmi, E., Hashmi, K., Malik, Z., Rezgui, A., Khan, H.U. (2015), 'CAPRA: a comprehensive approach to product ranking using customer reviews", Computing, Springer, DOI 10.1007/s00607-0 15-0439-8.

DECISION SCIENCES INSTITUTE

Effect of institutional heterogeneity in partnership configuration on M&A performance

Andrew Papadopoulos
Université du Québec à Montréal
Email: papadopoulos.andrew@uqam.ca

Ali Taleb
MacEwan University
Email: TalebA@macewan.ca

ABSTRACT

Developing countries' importance as national economies and as actors in foreign direct investment (FDI) has increased over the past decade. Concepts and models of international business have focused on developed-nation firms moving to developing nations. One such mode is through mergers and acquisitions that lead to the developed firm governing the developing acquisition. However, with the FDI trend reversing, there is a need to better understand how developing nations may use corporate governance, with all its institutional trappings, in developing-developing and developing-developed relationships. Our paper offers four propositions to better conceptualize these relationships.

KEYWORDS: Conceptual, Corporate governance, Mergers & acquisitions, International

INTRODUCTION

Liberalization of trade and investment coupled with economic growth of many emerging market economies has created opportunities for firms to engage in greater foreign direct investment (FDI) through mergers and acquisitions. In 2012, the United Nations Conference on Trade and Development (UNCTAD) reported in their World Investment Report (WIR) that developing countries accounted for 52% of all FDI flows – surpassing developed nations for the first time - while in 2013 that number rose to 54% of total flows. Developed nation total flows fell from 42% to 39% over the same period. Transitioning economies (South-East Europe, the Commonwealth of Independent States and Georgia) accounted for about 6% and 7% of flows, in 2012 and 2013, respectively. The role of developed-country multinationals in FDI is beginning to take a back seat to developing nations.

However, while developed nations still dominate merger and acquisition (M&A) activity, a major component of FDI, one of the important trends to emerge is the FDI outflows from developing countries towards developed and developing countries. These transnational corporations from developing economies have become important regional acquirers. In 2013, developed countries accounted for 69% of net M&A cross-border sales and 44% of net purchases, down from 88% and 83% in 2007, respectively. Over the same period, developing economies increased their share of M&A activity from 9% to 32% from 2007 to 2013 of net sales and from 14% to 37% of net purchases. The message is clear: development economies are playing a greater role in global cross-border M&A activity, either as a target nation or as the acquiring nation.

When the decision to undertake a cross-border acquisition is made, the interaction between the parties leads to an additional level of complexity with respect to performance that begins with the negotiation of the price, the future employment and roles, if any, of executives, and the integration of the target firm within the acquiring firm. The success or failure of an M&A can be linked to the degrees to which the two organizations were integrated and their resources were optimally leveraged. In a cross-border deal, the difference in institutional contexts between transacting parties may facilitate or hinder fruitful interaction (Dikova, Sahib et al. 2010, Mtar 2010) and thus determine the ultimate success or failure of the venture The institutional distance between head-office and subsidiaries is a major determinant of performance (Berry, Guillén et al. 2010) stemming from the ability of employees of two companies to share knowledge and interact effectively (Kostova & Kendall 2002). Since the institutions of developing and advanced economies are embedded in dissimilar contexts and entail different dominant logics of decision-making (Taleb 2010), it would be interesting to focus on the study of M&A ventures that involve partners from both developing and developed economies.

While M&As have been found to at best have an insignificant short-term effect on value creation for the acquiring firm, and a negative impact over longer-term (Aybar & Ficici, 2009; Fuller, Netter, & Stegemoller, 2002; King, Dalton, Daily, & Covin, 2004), their persistent use as a strategic growth instrument continues to intrigue researchers and raises fundamental questions such as why executives continue to seek them, why corporate governors approve them, and why they fail to generate promised value.

With respect to success, the board has an important role to play in the decision, execution, and possibly integration aspects of M&A transactions. The constraints and incentives put in place to shape and guide executive decisions, namely corporate governance mechanisms represent an external contingency upon executives and the board. Second, individuals' personal and professional experiences shape their preferences and motivations that represent an internal force upon decision-makers – the strategic value of the board. Thus, on one hand there are control mechanisms, structural and institutional, that constrain board action, while on the other there are directors' personal experiences and motivations that may provide strategic advice to corporate executive.

Moreover, firms from developing markets may use different governance mechanisms which do not even exist in more advanced economies. For instance, local firms in certain emerging markets relied on the formation of "business groups" to deal with institutional voids and imperfections in their home markets. This type of partnerships is unique to developing countries and entails specific governance mechanisms as well as it affects the financial performance of its members (Carney et al. 2011). Therefore, a partnership involving partners using different governance mechanisms – due to differences in their respective institutional contexts – may be of great interest to study.

Firms from emerging markets (EMNEs) may behave differently from their counterparts from more developed economies (DMNEs) owing to the distinctive institutional conditions of their home markets (Ramamurti 2012). This conferred them comparative advantages (Taleb 2010) which allow them to redraw the picture of international trade (Inkpen & Ramaswamy 2007) as their home-grown E-MNEs outperform D-MNEs both at home (Bhattacharya & Michael 2008) and abroad (Cuervo-Cazurra & Genc 2008). In fact, a quick look at the recent evolution of the Global Fortune 500 or Financial Times 500 lists of the most powerful global companies suffices to realize that E-MNEs are steadily gaining a strong and unprecedented foothold in the global economy. While some scholars suggest that E-MNEs may not represent a homogeneous population (Ramamurti 2009), we argue that they do share comparable experiences as they grew up in institutional environments that exhibit a number of similarities from poor physical infrastructure and regulatory apparatus (Khanna & Palepu (2006) to unpredictable "mood" of government officials (Wells, 1983) to highly informal institutions (Jütting, Drechsler et al. 2007).

Given the phenomenon at hand, the explicit separation of institutional effects from other influences may be fruitful (Dunning & Lundan 2008) especially because institutional diversity calls for both strategic adaptability and managerial versatility (Taleb 2010).

These realities have significant implications for research dealing with developed-developing nation firm interactions, governance perspectives, and performance. We believe, therefore, that focusing on M&As involving partners from both developing and developed economies has several theoretical merits. The primary theoretical frameworks for this research are agency theory (Jensen & Meckling 1976, Fama & Jensen 1983), and resource-based theory with a particular focus on learning (Kogut & Zander, 1992, 1993, 1996) and competencies (Hamel & Prahalad, 1994).

Our research suggests a paucity of interest in this area. From September 2002 to September 2014, 106 journal articles in ABI/Inform were found where the terms governance and merger or M&A appeared in the abstract (14 articles where the terms appear in the title) compared to 1672 results where governance and performance are in the abstract (282 articles where the terms appear in the title) and this for all of finance, management, strategy, and accounting fields, suggesting a limited understanding of how governance impacts performance in M&A transactions. When we then look at a cross-border context to contemplate institutional differences in an international context, we find that the institutional perspective to governance and cross-border M&A is very limited. Investigating contexts that are not necessarily inspired by Anglo-American governance regimes as we may find in many developing nations leads is an unexplored area as we only found, using the same abstract research approach as above, 11 articles dealing with institutional issues in M&A of which only five investigated corporate governance issues and none performance. Similarly, we found 21 articles where resource-based theories, including learning/knowledge, competencies and capabilities, were found in the abstract along with merger or acquisition and the board in the whole document; only two are international in flavour. Nevertheless, most research in the domain tend to focus on developed markets (Graham, Martey, & Yawson, 2008). Accordingly, our primary research question is:

> *How does corporate board supervisory and strategic strength impact acquirer financial performance in acquisitions involving emerging markets?*

LITERATURE REVIEW

Cross-border M&A and Performance

Performance in M&A transactions has been studied from two broad perspectives: performance at the time of announcement (event study) and performance sometime in the short, medium and/or long term at a point after the announcement, the completion of the transaction or at some other point in the future. Performance upon announcement captures the anticipated performance as determined by market agents based on characteristics of the acquirer, target, and the transaction details, among others. Other approaches to performance seek to capture performance based on the acquirer's ability to integrate the target and realize the expected cost or revenue synergies.

Bratianu & Anagnoste (2011) show that acquirers in emergent countries primarily undertake a merger to cut costs and create growth opportunities whereas acquirers from developing countries focus more on gaining access to production and new technology; the stakes are not similar. Regardless, foreign acquisitions improve shareholder value (Gregory & McCorriston,

2005; Seth, Song, & Pettit, 2002), especially in emerging markets (Chari, Chen, & Dominguez, 2012). In another study, US firms acquiring overseas businesses in developing countries are considerably better compared to those that acquire overseas businesses in developed market (Liu & Qiu, 2013).

One of the dominant perspectives that underpins performance in M&A transactions is organizational fit (Capron & Pistre, 2002, Cartwright & Cooper, 1993) in facilitating cooperation and integration. Sirmon and Lane (2004) outline national, organizational, and professional differences as the relevant levels of to consider in inter-firm relations. However, the literature, both alliance and M&A streams, has predominantly focused on national considerations given various well-established and readily available measures. Hofstede (1991) suggests that culture is a programmed mental model of a collective in a specific environment that conditions and guides processes, behaviors, and actions. This translates to unique organizations, practices, and coordination mechanisms that managers need to address. However, geo-political change has influenced many nations challenging the ongoing relevance of culture in international business. Homogenizing influence of information technologies, international tourism, financial institutions, market philosophy, IMF/World Bank activism combined with better education and informed managers have all led to a gradual narrowing of perceived cultural differences. (Menon, 2004, Micklethwait & Wooldridge, 2000, Stiglitz, 2002). Various studies have suggested a certain amount of cultural convergence (Levitt, 1983, O'Reilly, 1991) as a result of these effects.

Corporate Governance & Mergers and Acquisition

Rooted in agency theory (Jensen & Meckling, 1976), corporate governance frames the relationships among investors, the board and management as a mechanism to limit and check managerial action. This mechanism has taken various forms, including, chairman and CEO duality, remuneration, board size, importance of outside directors, and shareholder structure, among others. One such managerial action with strategic and operational consequences is the mergers and acquisition (M&A). The M&A has often been seen as mechanisms to increase market share, enter into new product and geographic market, acquire from and deploy to the target resources, capabilities and competences of both a tangible and intangible nature with the expectation to create value for the acquirer. However, others see M&A transactions as conduits for managerial opportunism (Chatterjee & Hambrick, 2007). Chief executives seek to minimize business and thus unemployment risk (Amihud & Lev, 1981) or to increase their own finances and power (Kroll, Wright, Toombs, & Leavell, 1997) through such transactions because of legitimacy-seeking isomorphism (DiMaggio & Powell 1983) or hubris (Hayward & Hambrick, 1997; Roll, 1986).

Corporate governance structures seeks to limit such behaviors and is thus seen as playing an important role in M&A outcomes (Wright, Kroll, & Elenkov, 2002) by minimizing the potential for overbidding through its structural composition (Rani, Yadav, & Jain, 2014) in the exercise of its fiduciary duty and by mitigating information asymmetries for investors of an acquiring firm's external environment (Kang, 2006). Failure to generate value for M&A transactions may be attributed to poor governance from the moment of target identification to integration an area lacking particular focus in the literature (Gaughan, 2005).

More recently, the role of boards has expanded to include a more strategic function. They are seen as offering operational (Krause, Semadeni, & Cannella, 2013) and strategic advice (Bouzinab, 2013), being a conduit for information for their firm's benefit through their networks (Carpenter & Westphal, 2001)or even signaling firm quality (Certo, 2003). However, in the context of the M&A this aspect has garnered limited attention (Bouzinab, 2013), particularly in emerging markets.

When undertaking an M&A transaction in complex or turbulent environments, boards may be able to provide an additional level of comfort to investors than weaker boards (Kang, 2006). As board members are closer to management and privy to information about the transaction, they are able to better assess the context and the target. Similarly, institutional investors – the buy side – are not only more sophisticated than non-institutional investors but also dispose of resources and employ professional that would be able to provide sufficient analysis as to evaluate the benefits and risks of an M&A transaction.

If we are were to juxtapose the concept of complexity and turbulence at an industry level to a country level, we are able to appreciate how boards and investors may provide similar advantage when a firm decides to engage in a cross-border transaction, specifically with a firm that finds itself in an environment deemed complex or turbulent by the acquirer. Sources of complexity may include geographic separation (Ghemawat, 2001), cultural differences (Kogut & Singh, 1988) and other institutional differences (Kostova & Zaheer, 1999). We develop below a series of propositions based on agency and resources arguments below.

PROPOSITION DEVELOPMENT

Corporate Governance Mechanisms

The board's role is to act as the representatives of ownership with management. This supervisory capacity takes the forms of periodic board meetings and committees. The effectiveness of such oversight has been linked to a number of factors that lead some boards to provide stronger governance, including having a separate chair and CEO (the duality argument), greater representation on the board from individuals not executives of the firm (outside directors), and a board whose size is commensurate with the business that it is overseeing. Reinforcing these mechanisms is also the structure of ownership: manager-owners and block holders. Below we discuss each in turn.

The importance of holding simultaneously the dual role of CEO and chair in the finance and strategy literature upon performance is well documented. From an agency perspective, the additional power that a CEO gains by also holding the chair role translates into greater control over the board and an ease to pursue self-interested goals rather than to make decisions privileging shareholders (Amihud & Lev, 1981). Given that M&A activity has been viewed, as a mechanism for CEO's to pursue their personal interests, holding onto both positions would facilitate such actions while a separation of such tasks would minimize the risk for opportunism. However, opposing this view, stewardship theory argues that the duality role allows for a better functioning organization as the CEO is seen as acting out in the best interest of the firm and stakeholders (Davis, Schoorman, & Donaldson, 1997). Research looking specifically into the M&A context and evaluating competing hypothesis under both theoretical lenses (Desai, Kroll, & Wright, 2003) found evidence that duality negatively impacts the performance of acquirers.

Moving beyond the CEO's role, in cases where boards are populated primarily by executives of the firm that have been hired by the CEO or their predecessor, we may expect for the CEO to exercise additional control over such members because of their structural and prestige power that they may have within the organization. Consequently, given this relationship, these internal directors, given the power that the CEO has over them with respect to hierarchy and employment, are likely to behave in a manner consistent with the CEO's desires. On the other hand, as stewards of the firm, we may expect that cohesion and intimate knowledge of the firm may enhance their oversight role. Similarly, their future prospects on the labour market (Cannella Jr. & Hambrick, 1993; Fama & Jensen, 1983) may mitigate poor decision making and execution by such insiders. The presence of outside directors – a hallmark of good governance (Geletkanycz, Boyd, & Finklestein, 2001) - would minimize the aforementioned effects from a structural perspective, leading to higher returns. There is also evidence to suggest that outside directors are more likely to fire a CEO for poor performance. Moreover, as discussed further below, outside directors may also provide strategic qualities.

The final structural aspect of the board relates to its size. The impact of any one director's ambivalence or reticence to challenge management would increase as the board size increases as the individual's impact is diluted over a larger number of individuals sitting on the board. Moreover, the cohesion of board members is more likely to decrease as board size increases as each director would have less time to interact with other members and the cost of establishing and maintaining ties in a bilateral or multilateral basis would increase geometrically as each additional board member increases the number of ties in an exponential form. While this is a desirable outcome from a connectivity perspective with respect to network ties and thus possibilities for greater information transfers, under a strategic perspective, it poses a challenge with respect to structural coordination. Under such circumstances, we may expect the CEO to take on a more dominant role (Jensen & Zajac, 2004), again increasing agency issues and leading to lower performance (Eisenberg, Sundgren, & Wells, 1998; Xie & Fukumoto, 2013; Yermack, 1996). However, the caveat being that large boards may seek more consensual or middle-of-the-road positions, their actions lead to less performance variability (Cheng, 2008).

As we have worked from management and the CEO to the board, the missing piece in the agency construct are shareholders: the beneficiaries of the board's fiduciary duties and of management's strategic and operational efforts. From this perspective there are two qualities that are important to discuss: significant controlling interest and alignment of purpose.

In the first case, the underlying argument supporting the relationship between increasing block shareholdings and performance rests with the power that such shareholder can wield on the board through direct representation, voting power or by pressure on management to align managerial and ownership interests (Shleifer & Vishny, 1998). However, once ownership reaches a certain threshold, significant positions lead to lower returns as entrenchment may set in (Shleifer & Vishny, 1998; Thomsen & Pedersen, 2000). Moreover, the nature of block holders needs to be considered as the implication for strategy varies among them (Thomsen & Pedersen, 2000). Such block holders may include other firms, financial investors (e.g. mutual funds, pension funds) or families owning a significant position in a firm.

In the case of firms, there are a few contextual distinctions. There are situations where a firm will own a minority or a majority stake in another firm through a partial acquisition or spin-off and circumstances where a network of firms is intertwined through conglomerate structures, cross-holdings or business groups. In the former case, equity ownership in another firm for the purposes of closer integration for development or resource reasons differs in nature than the conglomerate structure in a number of ways. First, the purpose of the relationship is to seek operational efficiencies in a related, vertical or horizontal manner. Second, ownership and management structures of each firm differ providing multiple instances for oversight. Generally speaking, these latter structures often lead to lower financial performance because of conglomerate discounts, cross-subsidization or dominant logic failures.

When family-owned firm are on equal footing with other shareholders, in single share class structures outperform dual-class firm market valuations by 17% on average relative to widely held firms, despite having similar returns on assets (King & Santor, 2008) – families may run firms for their private benefits in detriment of other shareholders (Fama & Jensen, 1983). Arbitrage opportunities arise where family members may prefer to increase their personal wealth at the detriment of other stakeholders. One such example is Frank Stronach, leading shareholder of Magna, a car parts manufacturer that used the firm as a vehicle to purchase racehorse tracks in the late 1990's (Cowan, 2012).

For institutional investors, they are primarily focused on financial returns their singular focus. While they may not be able to exact direct and timely control in sharping managerial decisions, they may be able to exercise latent power on strategic decisions but this power is moderated by the interaction of other shareholders in the structure (Chaganti & Damanpour, 1991) and on the country's legal traditions (Jara-Bertin, López-Iturriaga, & López-de-Foronda, 2012). In the case of differing legal tradition, the inverted-U relationship found between increasing ownership levels and firm performance is also confirmed for institutional investors.

It is also not surprising that privately owned enterprises outperform state-owned firms (Goldeng, Grünfeld, & Benito, 2008). Moreover, when dealing with emerging markets, state-owned shareholdings may also play an important role. In many cases, governments will use corporations to achieve political goals (e.g. employment, national security) that would not necessarily reflect shareholder maximizing actions. In many cases, governments have invested in organizations that would otherwise be insolvent or consistently unprofitable – permanently failing organizations - to fulfill their goals (Meyer & Zucker, 1989). However, a more recent yet subtle phenomenon has begun to emerge over the past decades where government ownership has bifurcated into direct ownership of state-owned enterprises and sovereign fund ownership of corporations. The latter case being investment and pensions funds that manage assets in the name of their respective governments but generally operate at arm's length but not always (Bernstein, Lerner, & Schoar, 2013) – operating like institutional investors most of the time.

The second aspect of ownership relevant to firm performance is that of insiders. In an effort to enhance the alignment of executives and directors with those of shareholders, remuneration in the form of stock and stock options has been used. These forms of pay vest the interest of such insiders to the market performance of the firm – the performance that shareholders are concerned most about. In seminal work, Morck et al. (1988) found that there is a convergence of interests at middle-range levels of ownership, particularly in the 5-25% range but not at lower levels or higher levels (they empirically determine this to be about 25%). They argue that inconsequential ownership levels do not offset the potential for private benefits at low levels while entrenchment effects on managers outweigh the convergence of interest effects at higher levels.

There is also a distinction to be made between insider and outside directors who both may be offered partial ownership in an effort to align interests. It is important to distinguish the interests of each type. While ownership for insiders, at certain levels, may provide for interest alignments, competing factors may mitigate those effects, including the potential for managers to find other employment outside their firm – the labour market effect – or that social or pecuniary benefits may outweigh the value of ownership offered. For external board members, the ownership that they may own may not be sufficient to dampen any status-seeking effects (Khan, Mather, & Balachandran, 2014).

Based on the existing literature and research, the preponderance of the evidence suggests that stronger mechanisms will support higher returns in general because of the constraining effects on managerial opportunism. In the specific case of mergers and acquisitions, stronger corporate governance mechanisms should also diminish the effects of managerial opportunism, constraining firms to undertake transactions that are most likely to benefit shareholders. Consequently, stronger overall governance will result in better monitoring and decision making leading to superior outcomes for the acquirer firm from the agency theory perspective (Kroll et al., 1997; Wright et al., 2002).

> *Proposition 1: Stronger corporate governance mechanisms will be positively associated with acquisition financial performance.*

Strategic Corporate Governance

As many researchers looking at agency theory noted, board members can also facilitate transactions through their competencies. Directors engage in a strategic function through their ability to increase access to resources and to leverage competencies in increasing firm performance. While insiders play an important role in the daily operations of the firm than external directors, outsiders can have important roles to play providing strategic and operational guidance on a variety of issues. These abilities come in the form of various competencies that have been developed over time. International and M&A experiences appear to be the most relevant as the M&A context has the potential for a transformational impact on the firm (Miletkov, Moskalev, & Wintoki, 2015) and is thus of great consequence.

While some have drawn on the psychological literature on expertise (McDonald, Westphal, & Graebner, 2008), others have used upper echelon theories to evaluate board M&A performance finding mixed results depending on the characteristic studied. Hagendorf and Keasey (Hagendorff, 2012) found that occupational diversity had a positive impact, age and tenure a negative one, and gender no impact on acquirer performance; same industry experience was not a factor in explaining performance. This might arise for two reasons. First, having different dominant logics may be useful in board settings (Bettis, 1986) as it may provide unconventional views to the prevailing wisdom for a particular industry (DiMaggio & Powell 1983). The fact that industry-specific experience is a non-factor lends support to this explanation. Furthermore, having different industry experience may provide complementary skills that would not be otherwise available from same industry directors.

The discussion below will develop a theoretical justification for considering a resource-based perspective for the value that directors bring to firms. Before embarking on the development, it is important to establish our theoretical posture of what the resource-based view. It is our contention that the resource-based view is a general perspective that captures the resources that a firm has at its disposal and that may provide it with a competitive advantage. It is our view that a resource may be tangible or intangible as long as it meets the conditions of it being valuable, rare, inimitable and non-substitutable (Helfat, 2003). The notion of intangibility encompasses far more than what may be contemplated by accountants (e.g. brand) or measured by financiers (e.g. Tobin's Q). In a strategic sense, we consider capabilities and knowledge to be specific cases of the resource-based view and not mutually exclusive theories – experience leads to valuable expertise (McDonald et al., 2008).

While reflecting an industry dominant logic (Bettis & Prahalad, 1986; DiMaggio & Powell 1983) may be considered as providing legitimacy, it is worthwhile to consider when board members that do not have this baggage. In order for this situation to arise, the experiential component provides competencies rooted in *extra-industry* experiences (Krause et al., 2013). While the development of this expertise may rest in psychological or learning perspectives, the use of that expertise to provide value to the acquiring firm is rooted in the resource-based view. There are two reasons why this may be beneficial in a cross-border merger: expertise and networks.

First, operational diversity provides focal firm managers with access to a broader set of resources and skills in a variety of functional areas (Hagendorff & Keasey, 2012). More specifically, acquisition experience provides important skills for target selection, evaluation, valuation and integration (Haleblian, Kim, & Rajagopalan, 2006) and the propensity to make acquisitions (Peng & Fang, 2010). While the relationship with performance is subject to various contextual factors, including size and timing (Hayward, 2002), as well as strategic factors, including relatedness (McDonald et al., 2008), the experiences that directors have leads them to develop a competency that can be leveraged for the focal firm (McDonald et al., 2008). In the same vein as above, international experience, in the context of cross-border acquisitions, provides a third experiential pillar of expertise. Transactions involving firms from different contexts adds an institutional layer of complexity, often absent in domestic acquisitions. Such complexity may arise because of cultural barriers – an often studied concept in M&A research (Berry, Guillén, & Zhou, 2010). However, these challenges go beyond culture to include other institutional, economic and geographic disparities, often referred to as distances (Mtar, 2010) that experienced directors may help focal firms navigate. Thus, the combination of experience provides both general and specific expertise in providing needed competencies to acquiring firms.

Finally, the external ties that directors have boards - networks – may provide access to key resources (Carpenter & Westphal, 2001; Hillman & Dalziel, 2003). These are two key concepts that emerge from networks: centrality and network participation. Centrality would advance that the director is at the center of a network where information passes through the director with the amount of information, and thus value, increasing with the number of ties. Moreover, being a central figure may allow the director to exert influence over their ties (Astley & Sachdeva, 1984). In the second perspective, connectedness suggests that the variety of networks that a director participates in, for example through multiple board appointments, would provide that director to multiple and heterogeneous sources of possibly valuable information (Harris & Shimizu, 2004). In the context of an M&A transaction, this phenomenon may allow the focal firm to benefit from minimizing information asymmetries. In a cross-border or increasingly complex environment, such benefits may allow the focal firm greater returns (Kang, 2006),

> <u>Proposition 2</u>: *Stronger corporate board strategic capability will be positively associated with acquisition financial performance.*

However, there are some conflicting results with respect to M&A performance that would suggest that the agency theory argument is not supported unequivocally and in all circumstances. Environmental complexity (Kang, 2006) seems to play an important role in moderating outcomes. Kang (Kang, 2006) found that for domestic acquisitions under high environmental complexity or industry dynamism monitoring plays a greater role as boards are able to bridge information asymmetries for investors more so than in stable environments. Moreover, an important consideration in mitigating this complexity comes from the M&A and international experience of board member in helping firms navigate this complexity. This notion of environmental complexity and dynamism parallels well to transactions involving firms that are embedded in complex environments.

Effect of institutional heterogeneity in partnership configuration on M&A performance

Governance structures of firms are embedded in their institutional context (Capron & Guillén, 2009). For this reason, atypical forms of governance emerge in particular settings. For instance, strategic groups are specifically designed to fill in gaps that result from institutional voids which are common in developing markets (Khanna & Palepu, 2006). Similarly, more advanced economies have strong formal institutions (Jütting et al., 2007) such as laws which shape governance systems of indigenous organizations.

The strategic ability of a board of directors to foster access to resources and leverage the capabilities and competencies of its members is also essential to corporate performance (Leiblein, M., 2003). However, not all capabilities are deemed equal. Relationship networks and context-specific knowledge are less mobile than more generic technical skills. This is particularly true in the context of developing markets where informal institutions prevail (Jütting et al., 2007) and where trust-based relationships matter more than contracts.

Several comparative studies have contrasted the strategies and performance levels of multinational enterprises from emerging markets (EMNEs) and their counterparts from developed markets (DMNEs) (e.g., Ramamurti, 2012). While significant work has been done on the drivers behind the performance of M&As, very little attention has been paid to whether the fact that one or both partners is/are from emerging markets affects the performance of the acquirer. Indeed, the comparison of governance mechanisms and board strategic capabilities of firms from developing and developing markets are likely to differ due to the significant differences in the institutional conditions in which they are embedded (Uzzi, 1996). Accordingly, two configurations of partnerships may be worth comparing. We will call the first type "institutionally homogeneous partnerships" because both partners are from emerging markets. In contrast, the second type will be called "institutionally heterogeneous partnerships" as one the partners is from emerging markets and the other partner is from developed markets.

The corporate board of a company resulting from a merger between partners from developed and developing markets is expected to include directors from both companies. Such diversity would bring varied institutional norms into the boardroom which may mitigate the self-interest temptations of board members. In the same vein, diversity in the institutional backgrounds of board members will likely increase the range of the firm's strategic capabilities. This is likely to improve the performance of the acquirer compared to a more homogeneous institutional background of board members that would result from a merger between partners that are both from emerging markets. Therefore, we propose:

> *<u>Proposition 3</u>: Overall, the performance of institutionally heterogeneous partnerships (one partner firm is from developing markets and the other is from developed markets) will be lower than the performance of institutionally homogeneous partnerships (both partnering firms from developing markets only).*

In the case of heterogeneous partnerships, the dynamics may vary within the board of directors depending on whether the acquirer is from developed or developing markets. The assumption is that dominant management logics that prevail within a firm mirror the institutional settings of its home country. For this reason, emerging and developed markets nurture different logics of thinking and operating (Khanna & Palepu 1997). EMNEs, for instance, tend to venture into other developing markets with institutional conditions that are similar to – or less developed than – the ones they are used to in their home markets (Cuervo-Cazurra & Genc, 2008). When they make acquisitions in more developed markets, they usually seek to boost their image by association.

In this paper, we are interested in what happened when the partners are driven by different and sometimes opposing logics. As suggested earlier, heterogeneous partnerships are likely to outperform homogeneous partnerships thanks to the wider span of capabilities and skills resulting from such diversity. Operating in unfamiliar institutional conditions often requires significant learning. While this this principle applies to all firms regardless of their market of origin, EMNEs may have an advantage over DMNEs. The literature has distinguished between developed, developing and least-developed countries (World Bank, 2007). Moving from one of these markets to another requires significant learning. DMNEs have been successful in bridging their "learning gap" between developed and emerging markets and EMNEs can outperform DMNEs in least developed markets. For this reason, EMNEs have more incremental value to add – in terms of institutional learning – to a heterogeneous partnership between firms developed and developing markets. As a result, we suggest that mergers where EMNEs are the acquirer are likely to perform better than those involving DMNEs as acquirer. More formally:

> *Proposition 4: All being equal, the performance of institutionally heterogeneous [developing-developed] partnerships will be higher when the acquirer is from emerging markets and the acquired is from developed markets.*

CONCLUSION

The theories developed in this paper advance our understanding of the performance of M&As depending on how the post-merger organization is governed and on how the pre-merger partnership was configured in the first place. On the one hand, the first two propositions contribute to the debate on the determinants of post-merger performance through a governance lens. Both strong governance mechanisms and board strategic capabilities are suggested to affect the financial performance in a positive way. On the other hand, the last two propositions extend and deepen the debate by submitting that partnerships should not be viewed as a rigid black box that fits it all. Instead, we suggest that configuration of the partnership matters to the performance. Specifically, we used extent comparative literature suggesting that multinationals from emerging markets (EMNEs) may behave differently from their counterparts from developed markets (DMNEs) to discuss the nature of partnerships from an institutional perspective. While unwrapping the black box of partnerships, we categorized them into institutionally homogeneous and institutionally heterogeneous which we hope will incite other scholars to take a more fine-grained approach to the analysis of partnerships in general. Another close but different contribution resides in recognizing that the differences in the institutional environments in which EMNEs and DMNEs have grown will affect the performance of mergers in which they are the acquirer positively. Researchers may find such market of origin perspective of diversity in board of directors more useful than the traditional country of origin. Practitioners may also find our findings especially the partnership configuration of interest. Diversity has traditionally been considered in M&A from an organizational fit perspective. In contrast, this paper takes a dominant logic and capability centric approach.

This paper has limitations. We elected to focus on partnerships that have at least one partner from emerging markets. The performance of institutionally homogeneous partnerships involving partners from developed economies only may be worth studying from a governance structure and strategic capabilities perspectives. However, future research may wish to explore the performance of partnerships involving EMNEs using different predictors than those here. Finally, emerging markets are not homogeneous either. Looking at subsets of countries within emerging markets would be insightful. A regional perspective may help distinguish between Latina American, African, Asian, and East-European countries for instance. And, of course, testing and refining our propositions would constitute a tangible contribution in its own right.

APPENDIX

Figure 1: Proposed model

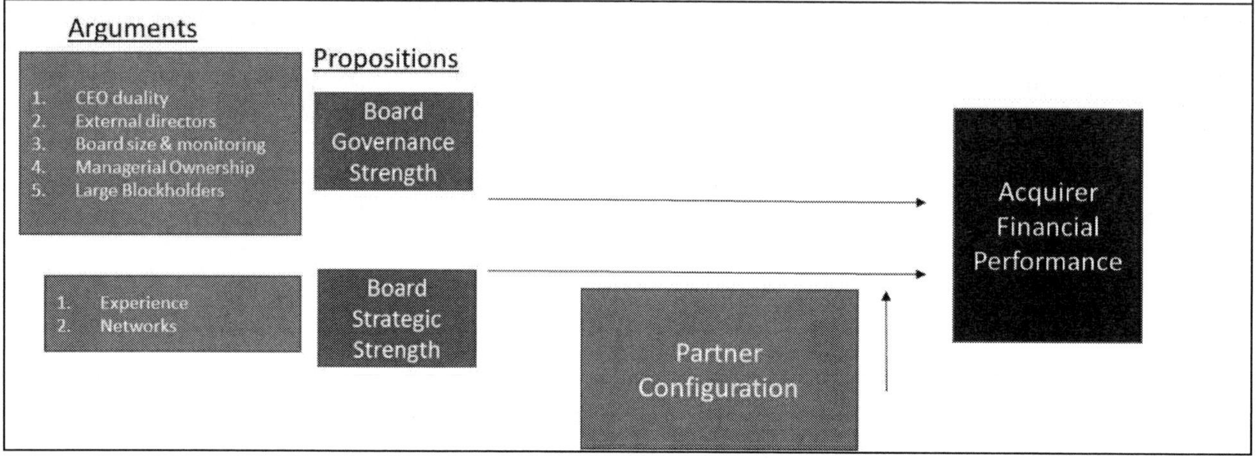

REFERENCES

Amihud, Y., & Lev, B. (1981). Risk reduction as a managerial motive for conglomerate mergers. *Bell Journal of Economics*, 12(2): 605-617.

Astley, W. G., & Sachdeva, P. S. (1984). Structural sources of intraorganizational power: A theoretical synthesis. *Academy of Management Review*, 9(1): 104-113.

Aybar, B., & Ficici, A. (2009). Cross-border acquisitions and firm value: An analysis of emerging-market multinationals. *Journal of International Business Studies*, 40(8): 1317-1338.

Bernstein, S., Lerner, J., & Schoar, A. (2013). The Investment Strategies of Sovereign Wealth Funds. *Journal of Economic Perspectives*, 27(2): 219-238.

Berry, H., Guillén, M. F., & Zhou, N. (2010). An institutional approach to cross-national distance. *Journal of International Business Studies*, 41(9): 1460-1480.

Bettis, R. A., & Prahalad, C. K. (1986). The dominant logic: A new linkage between diversity and performance. *Strategic Management Journal*, 7(6): 485-501.

Bouzinab, K. (2013). *Corporate governance, strategic capabilities of boards of directors and firm performance : the case of mergers and acquisitions*. Université du Québec à Montréal, Montreal.

Cannella Jr., A. A., & Hambrick, D. C. (1993). Effects of executive departures on the performance of acquired firms. *Strategic Management Journal*, 14(4): 137-152.

Capron, L., & Guillén, M. (2009). National corporate governance institutions and post-acquisition target reorganization. *Strategic Management Journal*, 30(8): 803-833.

Carpenter, M. A., & Westphal, J. D. (2001). The strategic context of external network ties: examining the impact of director appointments on board involvement in strategic decision making. *Academy of Management Journal*, 44(4): 639-660.

Certo, S. T. (2003). Influencing Initial Public Offering Investors With Prestige: Signaling With Board Structures. *Academy of Management Review*, 28(3): 432-446.

Chaganti, R., & Damanpour, F. (1991). Institutional ownership, capital structure, and firm performance. *Strategic Management Journal*, 12(7): 479-491.

Chari, A., Chen, W., & Dominguez, K. M. E. (2012). Foreign Ownership and Firm Performance: Emerging Market Acquisitions in the United States. *IMF Economic Review*, 60(1): 1-42.

Chatterjee, A., & Hambrick, D. C. (2007). It's all about me: Narcissistic chief executive officers and their effects on company strategy and performance. *Administrative Science Quarterly*, 52(3): 351-386.

Cheng, S. (2008). Board size and the variability of corporate performance. *Journal of Financial Economics*, 87(1): 157-176.

Cowan, L. (2012). A 'Neigh' to IPOs on Horses. *Wall Street Journal - Eastern Edition*, 259(23): B4.

Cuervo-cazurra, A., & Genc, M. (2008). Transforming disadvantages into advantages: developing-country MNEs in the least developed countries. *Journal of International Business Studies*, 39(6): 957-979.

Davis, J. H., Schoorman, F. D., & Donaldson, L. (1997). Toward a stewardship theory of management. *Academy of Management Review*, 22(1): 20-47.

Desai, A., Kroll, M., & Wright, P. (2003). CEO duality, board monitoring, and acquisition performance: a test of competing theories. *Journal of Business Strategies*, 20(2): 137-156.

DiMaggio, P. J., & Powell , W. W. (1983). The iron cage revisited: Institutional isomorphism and collective rationality in organizational fields. *American Sociological Review*, 48(2): 147-160.

Eisenberg, T., Sundgren, S., & Wells, M. T. (1998). Larger board size and decreasing firm value in small firms. *Journal of Financial Economics*, 48(1): 35-54.

Fama, E. F., & Jensen, M. C. (1983). Separation of ownership and control. *Journal of Law and Economics*, 26(2): 301-325.

Fuller, K., Netter, J., & Stegemoller, M. (2002). What do returns to acquiring firms tell us? Evidence from firms that make many acquisitions. *Journal of Finance*, 57(4): 1763-1793.

Gaughan, P. A. (2005). Failed merger: Failed corporate governance? *Journal of Corporate Accounting & Finance (Wiley)*, 16(2): 3-7.

Geletkanycz, M. A., Boyd, B. K., & Finklestein, S. (2001). The strategic value of CEO external directorate networks: Implications for CEO compensation. *Strategic Management Journal*, 22(9): 889-898.

Ghemawat, P. (2001). Distance still matters, *Harvard Business Review*, Vol. 79: 137-147.

Goldeng, E., Grünfeld, L. A., & Benito, G. R. G. (2008). The Performance Differential between Private and State Owned Enterprises: The Roles of Ownership, Management and Market Structure. *Journal of Management Studies*, 45(7): 1244-1273.

Graham, M., Martey, E., & Yawson, A. (2008). Acquisitions from UK firms into emerging markets. *Global Finance Journal*, 19(1): 56-71.

Gregory, A., & McCorriston, S. (2005). Foreign acquisitions by UK limited companies: short- and long-run performance. *Journal of Empirical Finance*, 12(1): 99-125.

Hagendorff, J., & Keasey, K. (2012). The value of board diversity in banking: evidence from the market for corporate control. *The European Journal of Finance*, 18(1): 41-58.

Haleblian, J., Kim, J.-Y., & Rajagopalan, N. (2006). The influence of acquisition experience and performance on acquisition behavior: evidence from the u.s. commercial banking industry. *Academy of Management Journal*, 49(2): 357-370.

Hamel, G., & Prahalad, C. K. (1994). *Competing for the future*. Boston, Mass.: Harvard Business School Press.

Harris, I. C., & Shimizu, K. (2004). Too Busy to Serve? An Examination of the Influence of Overboarded Directors. *The Journal of Management Studies*, 41(5): 775-798.

Hayward, M. L. A. (2002). When do firms learn from their acquisition experience? Evidence from 1990-1995. *Strategic Management Journal*, 23(1): 21-39.

Hayward, M. L. A., & Hambrick, D. C. (1997). Explaining the Premiums Paid for Large Acquisitions: Evidence of CEO Hubris. *Administrative Science Quarterly*, 42(1): 103-127.

Hillman, A. J., & Dalziel, T. (2003). Boards of directors and firm performance: integrating agency and resource dependence perspectives. *Academy of Management Review*, 28(3): 383-396.

Jara-Bertin, M., López-Iturriaga, F. J., & López-de-Foronda, Ó. (2012). Does the influence of institutional investors depend on the institutional framework? An international analysis. *Applied Economics*, 44(3): 265-278.

Jensen, M. C., & Meckling, W. H. (1976). Theory of the firm: managerial behavior, agency costs and ownership structure. *Journal of Financial Economics*, 3(4): 305-360.

Jensen, M. C., & Zajac, E. J. (2004). Corporate Elites and Corporate Strategy: How Demographic Preferences and Structural Position Shape the Scope of the Firm. *Strategic Management Journal*, 25(6): 507-524.

Jütting, J., Drechsler, D., Bartsch, S., & de Soysa, I. (2007). Informal Institutions: How Social Norms Help or Hinder Development. Development Centre Studies, OECD Publishing, Paris.

Kang, E. (2006). Investors' Perceptions of Managerial Opportunism in Corporate Acquisitions: the moderating role of environmental conditions. *Corporate Governance : An International Review*, 14(5): 377-387.

Khan, A., Mather, P., & Balachandran, B. (2014). Managerial share ownership and operating performance: Do independent and executive directors have different incentives? *Australian Journal of Management (Sage Publications Ltd.)*, 39(1): 47-71.

Khanna, T., & Palepu, K. (1997). Why focused strategies may be wrong for emerging markets, *Harvard Business Review*, Vol. 75: 41-51.

Khanna, T., & Palepu, K. G. (2006). Emerging Giants: Building World-Class Companies in Developing Countries, *Harvard Business Review*, Vol. 84: 60-69.

King, D. R., Dalton, D. R., Daily, C. M., & Covin, J. G. (2004). Meta-Analyses of Post-Acquisition Performance: Indications of Unidentified Moderators *Strategic Management Journal*, 25(2): 187-200.

King, M. R., & Santor, E. (2008). Family values: Ownership structure, performance and capital structure of Canadian firms. *Journal of Banking & Finance*, 32(11): 2423-2432.

Kogut, B., & Singh, H. (1988). The effect of national culture on the choice of entry mode. *Journal of International Business Studies*, 19(3): 411-432.

Kogut, B., & Zander, U. (1992). Knowledge of the firm, combinative capabilities, and the replication of technology. *Organization Science*, 3(3): 383-397.

Kogut, B., & Zander, U. (1993). Knowledge of the firm and the evolutionary theory of the multinational corporation. *Journal of International Business Studies*, 24(4): 625-645.

Kogut, B., & Zander, U. (1996). What firms do? Coordination, identity, and learning. *Organization Science*, 7(5) 502-518.

Kostova, T., & Zaheer, S. (1999). Organizational legitimacy under conditions of complexity: The case of the multinational enterprise. *The Academy of Management Review*, 24(1): 64-81.

Krause, R., Semadeni, M., & Cannella, A. A. (2013). External COO/presidents as expert directors: A new look at the service role of boards. *Strategic Management Journal*, 34(13): 1628-1641.

Kroll, M., Wright, P., Toombs, L., & Leavell, H. (1997). Form of control: a critical determinant of acquisition performance and ceo rewards. *Strategic Management Journal*, 18(2): 85-96.

Leiblein, M. J. (2003). The Choice of Organizational Governance Form and Performance: Predictions from Transaction Cost, Resource-based, and Real Options Theories. *Journal of Management*, 29(6): 937-961.

Liu, Q., & Qiu, L. D. (2013). Characteristics of Acquirers and Targets in Domestic and Cross-border Mergers and Aquisitions. *Review of Development Economics*, 17(3): 474-493.

McDonald, M. L., Westphal, J. D., & Graebner, M. E. (2008). What do they know? The effects of outside director acquisition experience on firm acquisition performance. *Strategic Management Journal*, 29(11): 1155-1177.

Meyer, M. W., & Zucker, L. (1989). *Permanently Failing Organizations*. Newbury Park, CA: Sage Publications.

Miletkov, M., Moskalev, S., & Wintoki, M. B. (2015). Corporate boards and acquirer returns: international evidence. *Managerial Finance*, 41(3): 244-266.

Morck, R., Shleifer, A., & Vishny, R. W. (1988). Management ownership and market valuation: An empirical analysis. *Journal of Financial Economics*, 20(1,2): 293-315.

Mtar, M. (2010). Institutional, Industry and Power Effects on Integration in Cross-border Acquisitions. *Organization Studies*, 31(8): 1099-1027.

Peng, Y.-S., & Fang, C.-P. (2010). Acquisition experience, board characteristics, and acquisition behavior. *Journal of Business Research*, 63(5): 502-509.

Ramamurti, R. (2012). What is really different about emerging market multinationals? *Global Strategy Journal*, 2(1): 41-47.

Rani, N., Yadav, S., & Jain, P. (2014). Impact of corporate governance score on abnormal returns and financial performance of mergers and acquisitions. *Decision (0304-0941)*, 41(4): 371-398.

Roll, R. (1986). The Hubris Hypothesis of Corporate Takeovers. *Journal of Business*, 59(2): 197-216.

Seth, A., Song, K. P., & Pettit, R. R. (2002). Value creation and destruction in cross-border acquisitions: An empirical analysis of foreign acquisitions of U.S. firms. *Strategic Management Journal*, 23(10): 921-940.

Shleifer, A., & Vishny, R. W. (1998). Value Maximization and the Acquisition Process. *Journal of Economic Perspectives*, 2(1): 7-20.

Thomsen, S., & Pedersen, T. (2000). Ownership structure and economic performance in the largest European companies. *Strategic Management Journal*, 21(6): 689-705.

Uzzi, B. (1996). The sources and consequences of embeddedness for the economic performance of organizations: The network effect. *American Sociological Review*, 61(4): 674-698.

Wright, P., Kroll, M., & Elenkov, D. (2002). Acquisition Returns, Increase in Firm Size, and Chief Executive Officer Compensation: The Moderating Effect of Monitoring. *Academy of Management Journal*, 45(3): 599-608.

Xie, J., & Fukumoto, Y. (2013). A new finding for corporate board size effects: evidence from Japan. *The Singapore Economic Review*, 58(4): 1-12.

Yermack, D. (1996). Higher market valuation of companies with a small board of directors. *Journal of Financial Economics*, 40(2): 185-211.

DECISION SCIENCES INSTITUTE

Effectiveness of Control Charts for Intermittent Demand

Matthew Lindsey
Stephen F. Austin State University
lindseymd@sfasu.edu

Robert Pavur
The University of North Texas
pavur@unt.edu

ABSTRACT

Modeling demand for retail items that occur intermittently with possible shifts to periods of high or regular demand and constructing reliable confidence intervals has challenged forecasting researchers. This paper uses a simulation to test the suitability of adapting control charts for intermittent data.

KEYWORDS: Croston's Method, Forecasting, Slow-moving Inventory, Control Chart

INTRODUCTION

Forecasting techniques for slow-moving inventory have been extensively explored broadening the base of knowledge related to forecasting demand for inventory items. (Syntetos and Boylan, 2001, 2005, 2011; Willemain, Smart, and Schwarz, 2004) Many of the characteristics of forecasting items with regular demand are now being applied to items with intermittent or slow-moving demand, including trends, correlated demand, seasonality and other conditions (Altay, Litteral and Rudisill, 2012). Croston's method (1972) has established itself as one of the principal procedures for forecasting items with slow or intermittent demand.

The literature promotes identifying and categorizing demand patterns so the proper forecasting method can be selected (Syntetos, Boylan, and Croston, 2005; Boylan and Syntetos, 2007). In the situation of shifting demand levels, a signal is required to know when to change from one forecasting methodology to another. The literature indicates that control charts can provide a signal in a switching rule. The literature identifies many complex systems that utilize control charts to identify changes and apply the appropriate forecasting techniques (Kadri, Harrou, Chaabane, Sun, and Tahon, 2016; Wang, Liu, and Ji, 2016; and Tan, Lee and Lam, 2015).

This paper utilizes control charts to provide a signal to indicate the switching rule for the proper forecasting technique. A similar process will be applied to control charts as the authors used in previously proposed switching rules. The procedure is tested on concatenated real date to create a demand pattern with multiple shifts in demand.

LITERATURE REVIEW

A motivation of considering control charts for intermittent data are applications such as manufacturing in which small variations occur infrequently. An application can be found in the health care industry. Control charts are useful in monitoring changes in one's health. These changes may be occurring on an intermittent basis (Albers, 2011).

The forecasting methodology proposed by Croston (1972) has evolved into the applied standard for inventory models (Teunter, Syntetos and Babai, 2010; Xu, Wang, & Shi, 2012; Ramaekers and Janssens, 2014). Croston's method has yielded well accepted benefits by Willemain, Smart, Shockor, and DeSautels (1994), Johnston and Boylan (1996) and others. Syntetos and Boylan (2001) provided a modification to correct an identified bias. Studies have compared the bias corrected method with the original without identifying a winner (Eaves & Kingsman, 2004; Syntetos & Boylan, 2005; Teunter & Sani, 2009; and Teunter & Duncan, 2009)

A generalized forecasting method when demand is slow or regular has been suggested, but it potentially introduces more bias than Croston (Teunter & Sani, 2009). Levén and Segerstedt's (2004) proposed methodology introduces a common technique for all demand rates but not for an item with distinct demand rates in different periods. The authors have developed a hybrid technique to adjust for shifts in rates of demand. If demand is not intermittent, a three standard deviation control chart could be constructed assuming that the estimate of the mean demand followed an approximate known distribution.

Croston's Method

See Willemain, et al. (1994) for a concise explanation of Croston's (1972) method. It is not included here to save space. Croston's (1972) recommends small alpha values between 0.1 and 0.2. Since the data sets were designed to have no shifts in the mean and to be consistent with Croston, this work utilizes lower alpha levels.

Syntetos and Boylan Revised Croston Procedure

Syntetos and Boylan (2001) identified a bias in Croston's (1972) method. The bias increases as the value of the smoothing constant increases. It can be minimized by using a small alpha level, but it is still present. Boylan and Syntetos (2005) correct for the bias using Croston's method by multiplying the demand per period by 1−α/2, yielding the following new estimator of mean demand:

$$y_t'' = \left(1 - \frac{\alpha}{2}\right)\frac{z_t''}{p_t''} \qquad (1)$$

When p is the inter demand interval, the bias is expressed as:

$$bias = \left(100\frac{\alpha}{2-\alpha}\right)\left(1 - \frac{1}{p}\right) \qquad (2)$$

Teunter and Sani (2009) advocate that in some cases when only a limited periods have no demand. Syntetos and Boylan (2005) remind us that Croston's assumptions of stationary, iid of demand sizes and intervals, geometrically distributed inter demand intervals and independence of demand sizes and intervals apply to the new estimator.

Confidence Interval for Mean Demand per Period

A moving average would be the ideal estimate if the time series values were independent and identically distributed (iid). A challenge with Croston's method is that a confidence interval would need to be constructed for the ratio of two random variables – demand and time between demand. Syntetos and Boylan (2011) note that assuming independence of the demand size and intervals between demand, that the following relationships hold

$$E = \left(\frac{Z'_t}{p'_t}\right) = E(Z'_t) * E\left[\frac{1}{p'_t}\right] \tag{3}$$

and that

$$E = \left(\frac{Z'_t}{p'_t}\right) \neq E(Z'_t) * \left[\frac{1}{E(p'_t)}\right] \tag{4}$$

In this paper, confidence intervals are constructed as follows.

$$\frac{Z'_t}{p'_t} \pm Z_{\alpha/2}(\widehat{Var}\left(\frac{Z'_t}{p'_t}\right))^{1/2} \tag{5}$$

$$\frac{\left(1-\frac{\alpha}{2}\right)Z'_t}{p'_t - \frac{\alpha}{2}} \pm Z_{\alpha/2}(\widehat{Var}\left(\frac{\left(1-\frac{\alpha}{2}\right)Z'_t}{p'_t - \frac{\alpha}{2}}\right))^{1/2} \tag{6}$$

An approximation to the estimate of the variance supplied by Croston (1972) for the demand estimate per time period is provided by Syntetos and Boylan (2011) and is shown below:

$$V\left(\frac{Z'_t}{p'_t}\right) \approx \left[\frac{\alpha}{2-\alpha}\right]\left[\frac{(p-1)}{p3}\left(\mu^2 + \frac{\alpha}{2-\alpha}\sigma^2\right) + \frac{\sigma^2}{p^2}\right] + \left[\frac{\alpha^4}{1-(1-\alpha)^4}\frac{\mu^2}{p^4}\left(1-\frac{1}{p}\right)\right]\left[9\left(1-\frac{1}{p}\right)p^2 + 1\right] \tag{7}$$

However, they go on to show that the variance for Croston's method can be "safely" approximated as:

$$Var\left(\frac{Z'_t}{p'_t}\right) \approx \left[\frac{\alpha}{2-\alpha}\right]\left[\frac{(p-1)}{p3}\left(\mu^2 + \frac{\alpha}{2-\alpha}\sigma^2\right) + \frac{\sigma^2}{p^2}\right] \tag{8}$$

Furthermore, Syntetos and Boylan (2011) provide the variance for the bias corrected Croston, which they denoted as "SY Croston" and will be adopted here, formulation as:

$$Var\left[\frac{\left(1-\frac{\alpha}{2}\right)Z'_t}{p'_t - \frac{\alpha}{2}}\right] \approx \left[\frac{\alpha(2-\alpha}{4}\right]\left[\frac{\left(p-\frac{\alpha}{2}\right)^2\sigma^2 + p(p-1)\mu^2 + \frac{\alpha}{2-\alpha}p(p-1)\sigma^2}{\left(p-\frac{\alpha}{2}\right)^4}\right] \tag{9}$$

To utilize each of the provided formulations for the variance a standard deviation is required. Determining the standard deviation of the population can be problematic. It would be rare to know the actual population variance. A sample variance is probably more likely to be available.

Control Chart Construction

A 3 standard deviation control was constructed to track the mean demand per period. As long as the mean stays within three standard deviations of the long term average, the series will be considered as "not changing" and "in control". If the mean deviates by more than three standard deviations it will signal that the mean shifted and a new forecasting model should be utilized.

METHODS

Five hundred simulations were conducted for 32 conditions using 3 standard error control charts. The process was then repeated using 3.4 standard error control charts. Four scenarios were simulated for each forecasting methodology. Each scenario represents an item with a given demand between 1.1 periods between demands to 10 periods between demands. The occurrence of demands is assumed to follow a time-dependent Bernoulli process. The first scenario represented items with an average mean time between demands (MTBD) of 1.1, then 2, 5 and 10 periods between demand. The demand was simulated from a population with a normal distribution having a demand of 200 and a standard deviation of 10. However, the occurrence of nonzero demand is assumed to follow a geometric distribution with probability of an occurrence being less than 1. The simulations are repeated for a 3.4 standard deviation control chart based on a t distribution with 20 degrees of freedom. This value produces a lower percentage of time when the control chart signals a problem.

RESULTS

Table 1 illustrates the percent of time that the control chart indicates the process is out of control, when it is actually in control decreases as the mean time between demands increases.

Table 1: Percentage of Observations outside of Control Limits using 3 standard deviations.

		Scenario1	Scenario2	Scenario3	Scenario4
MTBD		1.1	2	5	10
	Estimator				
Alpha = 0.05	**Croston (sample variance)**	3.18	.321	.297	.231
	Croston (pop variance)	3.26	.321	.297	.231
	SY Croston (sample variance)	3.03	.388	.557	.436
	SY Croston (pop variance)	2.96	.394	.555	.436
Alpha = 0.3	**Croston (sample variance)**	19.15	1.91	.804	.857
	Croston (pop variance)	22.40	1.92	.811	.856
	SY Croston (sample variance)	17.75	2.97	3.94	4.13
	SY Croston (pop variance)	20.71	2.98	3.95	4.14

To decrease the out of control signal, the simulation study was repeated with broader control limits. A t distribution with 20 degrees of freedom is approximately 3.4 standard deviations. The value of 3.4 standard deviations is used in the control chart to produce a lower number of out-of-control signals when the system is actually "in control." Table 2 shows that for the "3.4" value, the probability of an out of control signal is now lower than that expected for a traditional control chart when a smoothing value of .05 is used and when the data are truly intermittent (MTBD is at least 2). Using the wider control chart based on 3.4 standard deviations, did achieve the goal of lowering the percent of time that an observation signals "out of control".

Table 2: Percentage of Observations outside of Control Limits using 3.4 standard errors.

		Scenario1	**Scenario2**	**Scenario3**	**Scenario4**
MTBD		1.1	2	5	10
Estimator					
Alpha = 0.05	**Croston (sample variance)**	2.24	.078	.104	.083
	Croston (pop variance)	2.29	.078	.104	.083
	SY Croston (sample variance)	2.07	.122	.208	.183
	SY Croston (pop variance)	2.10	.122	.208	.183
Alpha = 0.3	**Croston (sample variance)**	13.84	1.18	.415	.498
	Croston (pop variance)	17.14	1.19	.416	.498
	SY Croston (sample variance)	12.76	1.81	2.48	2.81
	SY Croston (pop variance)	15.77	1.82	2.49	2.82

DISCUSSION AND CONCLUSIONS

As demand changes managers need guidance when to modify forecasting methodology. The use of control charts is quite common to monitor a process and signal changes in the process. The application of control charts may allow medical professionals to understand when a health related process has changed. This paper addresses these needs. The performance of Croston's method and the bias corrected (SY Croston) methodology are compared. The performance of the models with different smoothing constants is investigated. This paper adds to the increasing body of work related to Croston's method.

REFERENCES

Albers, W. (2011). Risk-Adjusted Control Charts for Health Care Monitoring, *International Journal of Mathematics and Mathematical Sciences*, doi:10.1155/2011/895273.

Altay, N., Litteral, L. A., and Rudisill, F., (2012). Effects of correlation on intermittent demand forecasting and stock control. *International Journal of Production Economics, 135*(1) 275-283.

Boylan, J. E. & Syntetos, A. A., (2007). The accuracy of a modified Croston procedure. *International Journal of Production Economics*, *107*(2), 511-517.

Croston, J. D., (1972). Forecasting and stock control for intermittent demands. *Operational Research Quarterly*, 23(3), 289-303.

Eaves, A. H. C., & Kingsman, B. G. 2004. Forecasting for the ordering and stock-holding of spare parts. *Journal of the Operational Research Society*, 55(4), 431-437.

Herbst, N. R., Huber, N., Kounev, S., & Amrehn, E. (2014). Self-adaptive workload classification and for. for proactive resource provisioning. *Concurrency and Computation*, *26*(12), 2053-2078.

Johnston, F.R. & Boylan, J.E. (1996). Fore. for items with interm. demand, *JORS, 47*, 113-121.

Kadri, F., Harrou, F., Chaabane, S., Sun, Y., & Tahon, C. (2016). Seasonal ARMA-based SPC charts for anomaly detection. *Neurocomputing*, *173*, 2102-2114

Levén, E. & Segerstedt, A., (2004). Inventory control with a modified Croston procedure and Erlang distribution. *International Journal of Production Economics, 90*(3), 361-367.

Ramaekers, K., & Janssens, G. (2014). Optimal policies for demand forecasting and inventory management of goods with intermittent demand.

Syntetos, A. A., & Boylan, J. E. (2001). On the bias of intermittent demand estimates. *International Journal of Production Economics, 71*(1/3), 457-466.

Syntetos, A. A., & Boylan, J. E. (2005). The accuracy of intermittent demand estimates. *International Journal of Forecasting, 21*(2), 303-314.

Syntetos, A. A., & Boylan, J. E. (2011). Intermittent demand: estimation and statistical properties. In *Service Parts Management* (pp. 1-30). Springer London.

Syntetos, A. A., Boylan, J. E. and Croston, J.D (2005). On the categorization of demand patterns. *Journal of the Operational Research Society, 56*, 495-503.

Tan, Y.C., Lee, M. H. and Lam, W. W. W. (2015) "An improved switching rule in variable sampling interval Hotelling's T2 control chart," *Industrial Engineering and Engineering Management (IEEM), IEEE International Conference on*, Singapore, 1412-1416.

Teunter, R. H., & Duncan, L., (2009). Forecasting intermittent demand, a comparative study. *The Journal of the Operational Research Society, 60*(3), p321-329.

Teunter, R.H., & Sani, B., (2009). On the bias of Croston's forecasting method, *European Journal of Operational Research, 194*(1), 177-183.

Teunter, R., Syntetos, A.A., Babai, M.Z., (2010). Determining Order-Up-To Levels under Periodic Review for Compound Binomial (Intermittent) Demand. *EJOR, 203* (3), 619-624.

Wang, Q., Liu, C. S., & Ji, W. Y. (2016). Self-Adjusting ANN Air Pollution Index Forecasting Models Based on Quality Control Charts—A Case Study. *EESED 2015*.

Willemain, T. R., Smart, C. N., & Schwarz, H. F. (2004). A new approach to forecasting intermittent demand for service parts inventories. *Intern. Journal of Forecasting, 20*, 375-387.

Willemain, T. R., Smart, C. N., Shockor, J. H. and DeSautels, P. A., (1994). Forecasting intermittent demand in manufacturing: A comparative evaluation of Croston's method. *International Journal of Forecasting, 10*(4), 529-538.

Xu, Q., Wang, N., & Shi, H. (2012, May). Review of Croston's method for intermittent demand forecasting. In *Fuzzy Systems and Knowledge Discovery (FSKD), 2012* (pp. 1456-1460). IEEE.

Efficacy Beliefs and Customer Collaboration in Online Collaborative Communities: A Relationship Marketing Perspective

Cheng-Chieh Hsiao
Department of Public Relations and Advertising
Shih Hsin University, Taiwan
Email: cchsiao@mail.shu.edu.tw

ABSTRACT

Drawing upon the perspectives of self-efficacy and relationship marketing, this study attempts to examine how efficacy beliefs affect customer collaboration intention in online collaborative communities. Community commitment and community trust serve as key constructs that mediate the relationships between efficacy beliefs and customer collaboration intention. After collecting 476 valid responses from collaborative gaming communities in a globally-leading Massive Multiplayer Online Game (MMOG), the results show that self-relevant and community-relevant efficacy beliefs relate positively to community commitment and community trust. Community commitment and community trust have positive impacts on customer collaboration intention, respectively. Finally, research implications and limitations are also discussed.

KEYWORDS: Customer collaboration, Online collaborative community, Self-efficacy, Collective efficacy, Commitment, Trust

INTRODUCTION

Recently, digital marketing practitioners have emphasized the practice of customer collaboration in online communities, such as Wikipedia, Linux, and Threadless. In these online collaborative communities, crowdsourcing (Brabham, 2013; Howe, 2008) and collective intelligence (Malone, Laubacher, and Dellarocas, 2010; Surowiecki, 2004) are often revitalized through customer participation and collaboration in online activities, such as online learning (Alavi, 1994; Ingram and Hathorn, 2004) and knowledge sharing (Wasko and Faraj, 2004). Therefore, customer collaboration in online collaborative communities becomes significantly influential on the Internet economy (Howe, 2008; Malone et al., 2010).

However, it appears to be difficult to maintain the quality of conjoint outcomes and customers' active participation in online collaborative communities. Successful collaboration in an online collaborative community often depends on the competences of both individual customers and the whole community (Malone et al., 2010; Surowiecki, 2004). According to Bandura (1986, 1997), efficacy beliefs may be classified into self-efficacy and collective efficacy that refer to those beliefs about an individual's and a group's capabilities to perform a task. Both efficacy beliefs are found to influence personal and conjoint performance in several contexts(Feltz and Lirgg, 1998; Schaubroeck, Lam and Xie, 2000). However, little of research has simultaneously examined the consequences of efficacy beliefs in online collaborative communities.

To address these issues, this study attempts to investigate the antecedents of customer collaboration intention in online collaborative communities by drawing upon the perspectives of self-efficacy (Bandura, 1986, 1997) and relationship marketing (Morgan and Hunt, 1994). This study first identifies two types of efficacy beliefs in online collaborative communities: self-relevant and community-relevant efficacy. Then, we develop a conceptual model to examine how efficacy beliefs that a customer perceives influence his or her participation n in an online collaborative community. In the proposed model, community commitment and community trust serve as two key components of relationship quality and mediate the relationships between efficacy beliefs and customer collaboration intention. The proposed model is tested in the context of online gaming communities in a globally-leading Massive Multiplayer Online Game (MMOG), which is characterized by the nature of online collaboration. Our findings will help digital marketing practitioners understand how to improve cusotmer participation and maintain collaboration quality, leading to sustainable advantage of online collaborative communities.

RESEARCH FRAMEWORK AND HYPOTHESES DEVELOPMENT

Our research framework is based on self-efficacy theory and relationship marketing theory. This study argues that self-efficacy theory can be integrated with relationship marketing theory to predict cusotmer collaboration intention in online collaborative communities for two reasons. First, past research suggests that an individual's self-efficacy can generate positive consequences, which will improve his or her performance in organizations (Gist, 1987; Gist and Mitchell, 1992). Second, relationship marketing literature has recognized commitment and trust as intervening roles that mediate between certain antecedents and behavioral outcomes (Morgan and Hunt, 1994). In the model, we propose that self-relevant and community-relevant efficacy beliefs will positively relate to relationship quality (community commitment and community trust), which in turn to improve customer collaboration intention in online collaborative communities. Next, we will develop our hypotheses in detail.

Efficacy Beliefs

According to self-efficacy theory (Bandura, 1977, 1997), efficacy beliefs are classified into self-efficacy and collective efficacy that are recognized to be influenced by different sources of efficacy information (Zaccaro, Blair, Peterson, and Zazanis, 1995). First, self-efficacy is often regarded as a summary of one's judgment toward his or her capabilities to perform a specific task (Gist and Mitchell, 1992). Given the adequate levels of skills and incentives, one's perceived self-efficacy is likely to determine "people's choice of activities, how much effort they will expend, and of how long they will sustain effort in dealing with stressful situations (Bandura, 1977, p. 194)." Furthermore, Bandura (1986, 1997) has also proposed the concept of collective efficacy by extending self-efficacy theory to explain the choice and performance of a group. Collective efficacy is defined as a group's shared belief in its conjoint capabilities to organize and execute the courses of action required to produce given levels of attainments (Bandura, 1986, 1997).

Efficacy Beliefs and Relationship Quality

Berry (1983) suggest that the core of relationship marketing lies in "the attraction, retention, and enhancement of customer relationships" in order to sustain long-term profitability. One important construct that captures the overall nature of relationships between exchange partners is relationship quality. It is generally agreed that commitment and trust are two key components of relationship quality (Morgan and Hunt, 1994). First, commitment is essential for developing successful relational exchange (Gundlach, Achrol, and Mentzer, 1995). Past organizational behavior research has also suggested that an employee's organizational commitment involves his or her strong belief in and acceptance of the organization's goals, willingness to exert considerable effort on behalf of the organization, and definite desire to maintain organizational membership (Porter, Steers, Mowday, and Boulian, 1974). Second, trust is another necessary ingredient for long-term social exchange (Doney and Cannon, 1997; Ganesan, 1994). Past research has indicated that trust encompasses the confidence, reliability, and integrity that one places in his or her exchange partner (Gundlach and Murphy, 1993; Morgan and Hunt, 1994). Trust is also regarded as a type of expectation that reduces the fear that one's exchange partner will act in an opportunistic way (Singh and Sirdeshmukh, 2000).

According to self-efficacy theory (Bandura, 1989), an individual who has a strong belief in his or her capabilities is likely to exert more effort to overcome the challenge. In an online collaborative community, a customer who has a high sense of efficacy is likely to have more opportunities to interact with community members and participate in collaborative activities. He or she tends to obtain numerous valuable resources from successful community activities. The enrichment of the resources is likely to make the player feel socially indebted to others and the community (Gouldner, 1960). Such indebtedness leads to his or her commitment to the community. Thus,

H1. Self-relevant efficacy will relate to community commitment positively.

Self-efficacy theory suggests that community-relevant efficacy represents shared beliefs in capabilities of a social entity (Bandura, 1986, 1997). Thus, a customer who has great confidence in an online collaborative community is likely to feel supported by other members in community activities (Preece, 1999; Rheingold, 1993). Such support can create a sense of community (Blanchard and Markus, 2004), increasing the customer's commitment to the community. Prior research has pointed out the positive relationship between collective efficacy and professional commitment (Ware and Kitsantas, 2007).

H2. Community-relevant efficacy will relate to community commitment positively.

Furthermore, a customer who has strong belief in community members' capabilities may eliminate his or her fear of the failure of community activities. A collective goal can be only achieved when each member feels confident in the whole community. Relationship marketing literature also indicates that shared beliefs about goals, values, behaviors or capabilities can be regarded as an antecedent of trust (Morgan and Hunt, 1994). Therefore,

H3. Community-relevant efficacy will relate to community trust positively.

Relationship Quality and Customer Collaboration Intention

Relationship marketing research suggests that commitment often involves an intention to maintain a valued relationship in the future (Moorman et al., 1992). When a customer is committed to an online collaborative community, he or she tends to feel morally obligated to participate in collaborative activities (Gruen et al., 2000). Thus,

H4. Community commitment will relate to customer collaboration intention positively.

On the other hand, past research has suggested that virtual collaboration with anonymous members in a virtual setting requires a member's beliefs that his or her partners are reliable and integral (Hsiao and Chiou, 2012). When the uncertainty of opportunism is eliminated by community trust in an online collaborative community, a customer is more likely to collaborate with community members. Therefore,

H5. Community trust will relate to customer collaboration intention positively.

The Other Relationship

Trust is regarded as a major determinant of relationship commitment because "mistrust breeds mistrust and such would also serve to decrease commitment in the relationship and shift the transaction to one or more direct short-term exchanges (McDonald, 1981, p. 834)." In an online collaborative community, a customer is less possibly to feel committed to the community unless community trust is already established (Garbarino and Johnson, 1999).

H6. Community trust will relate to community commitment positively.

METHODOLOGY

Data Collection

The research setting in this study is online gaming communities in a globally-leading MMOG. We recruited and invited voluntary participants from three online forums related to the target MMOG to participate in our survey. A total of 476 valid responses were collected. Among these respondents, the average age was 24.03 (SD = 3.95), and 57.98% of them had participated in their current communities for more than six months.

Measures

For most of the construct considered, established scales were used and modified to accommodate the research context. Items for all measures were anchored on 7-point Likert scales (1 = strongly disagree and 7 = strongly agree). The scale of self-relevant efficacy was modified from Bandura (1986) and Hsu et al. (2007). The scale of community-relevant efficacy was measured by three items following Bandura (1997) and Feltz and Lirgg (1998). The construct of community commitment was assessed with four items derived from Gruen et al. (2000) and Mathwick et al. (2008). Three items for community trust were adapted from Chiu et al. (2006) and Hsiao and Chiou (2012). Finally, three self-reported items for customer collaboration intention were developed from our long-term observation and participation in community activities in the target MMOG. The scale was similar to those in past research (Garbarino and Johnson, 1999).

Data Analysis

Following Anderson and Gerbing (1988), confirmatory factor analysis (CFA) was used to assess construct validity in the measurement model. Then, the full structural equation model was estimated to test our hypotheses. All analyses were conducted by using AMOS 5.0 (Arbuckle, 2003).

RESULTS

Confirmatory Factor Analysis

To assess the uni-dimensionality of the scales, we performed a confirmatory factor analysis on five research constructs. The results revealed that the overall fit of the five-factor model was $\chi^2(94) = 371.77$ ($p < 0.01$); CFI = 0.97; NFI = 0.96; SRMR = 0.051. These fit statistics were satisfactory as prior studies have recommended (Bollen, 1989; Hu and Bentler, 1995; McDonald and Marsh, 1990). Thus, our measurement model fit the data well.

Then, we used composite reliability (CR) and average value extracted (AVE) to evaluate internal consistency of constructs. Fornell and Larcker (1981) suggest that the estimates of CR above 0.70 and AVE above 0.50 are considered acceptable. The results showed that the CR and AVE values for all constructs in our research model were higher than the recommended levels, indicating satisfactory internal consistency.

We assessed convergent validity by examining whether the item loadings were significant (Anderson and Gerbing, 1988). The results showed that item loadings listed in the appendix were significant for their hypothesized constructs, supporting satisfactory convergent validity. Finally, we followed Fornell and Larcker's (1981) suggestion to evaluate discriminant validity. The results showed that the square root of AVE was greater than pairwise correlation coefficients for each construct, in supports for discriminant validity of our measures.

Hypothesis Testing

Before testing our hypotheses, we first performed a full structural model. The overall fit of the structural model was $\chi^2(97) = 377.21$ ($p < 0.01$); CFI = 0.97; NFI = 0.96; SRMR = 0.055. The model fit was excellent. The results revealed that there was a significantly positive relationship between self-relevant efficacy and community commitment ($\gamma = 0.11$, $p < 0.01$), in support for H1. As we expected, community-relevant efficacy had positive and significant effects on community commitment ($\gamma = 0.45$, $p < 0.01$) and community trust ($\gamma = 0.57$, $p < 0.01$), supporting H2 and H3. Moreover, the results showed that both community commitment ($\gamma = 0.58$, $p < 0.01$) and community trust ($\gamma = 0.24$, $p < 0.01$) affected customer collaboration intention, respectively. Thus, H4 and H5 received empirical supports. Finally, H6 expected that community trust will relate to community commitment positively. The results showed that community trust was positively related to community commitment ($\gamma = 0.36$, $p < 0.01$), in support for H6.

DISCUSSION AND IMPLICATIONS

Recently, online collaborative communities have met the difficulties in managing virtual interaction and value co-creation among customers. Since the success of customer collaboration in online collaborative communities often involves each member's beliefs about both individual and collective capabilities, this study confirms that a customer's efficacy beliefs may be key determinants of perceived relationship quality in his or her online collaborative communities positively. Specifically, self-relevant efficacy has a positive impact on community commitment, whereas community-relevant efficacy is associated positively with community commitment and community trust. The results also show that a customer's community commitment and community trust are likely to determine his or her collaboration intention in online collaborative communities.

This study contributes to online community literature in several aspects. This study extends current literature by proposing the concept of collective efficacy to explain customer collaboration intention in online collaborative communities. Our simultaneous examination of self-relevant and community-relevant efficacy beliefs is more appropriate for highlighting the nature of crowdsourcing and collective intelligence in online collaborative communities. Next, community-relevant efficacy is similar to cognitive social capital which refers to shared understanding in a social entity. Our findings are contributory greatly for current development of social capital theory by providing additional evidence for the positive relationship between cognitive and relational aspects of social capital in online communities. Finally, although virtual collaboration was applied to numerous online behaviors, past research has put less emphasis on collaborative gaming activities. Thus, our framework will contribute to theoretical advance in online game studies.

This study has several implications for online community managers. First, this study indicates that a customer's self-efficacy is a key determinant of his or her commitment toward a collaborative community. When recruit new members, online collaborative community managers are recommended to assess skills or capabilities of performing community tasks well. The newcomers with high self-efficacy tend to feel committed toward their communities. Second, this study recommends practices that should be implemented to increase a customer's perceptions toward the capabilities of an online collaborative community. Online community managers can establish an achievement-rating system that records the extent to which a collaborative community accomplishes its collective tasks successfully. Finally, online collaborative community managers are suggested to design community-based activities that facilitate members to interact with each other frequently. Frequent interaction in an online collaborative community would deepen a customer's understandings about other members, leading to the customer's greater commitment and trust toward the community.

REFERENCES

References available upon request.

DECISION SCIENCES INSTITUTE

Equilibrium Analysis of an Advertising-Inventory-Pricing Competitive Model

Hani I. Mesak, Louisiana Tech University, Ruston, LA 71272-4460.
Email: mesak@latech.edu
Abdullahel Bari, The University of Texas at Tyler, Tyler, TX 75799.
Email: abari@uttyler.edu
Rob Blackstock, Louisiana Tech University, Ruston, LA 71272-4460.
Email: rblackst@latech.edu

ABSTRACT

Using a market share attraction structure of advertising competition, this research introduces first, a parsimonious inventory-advertising model for which competition is limited to two symmetric firms and obtains its related comparative statics. Following a supermodular game approach, the derived comparative statics remain robust upon considering non-dominant firms competing in an asymmetric oligopoly of N rivals where each firm controls the inventory / advertising decision variables in addition to controlling price. The generalization appears applicable to both non-dominated oligopolies as well as dominated oligopolies. The study also derives closed form solutions for symmetric equilibrium advertising, price and order quantity together with related comparative statics.

KEYWORDS: Advertising, Economic order quantity, Pricing, Comparative statics, Market share attraction models; Supermodular games

INTRODUCTION

Researchers advocate building analytical models that are parsimonious, focusing on the truly important aspects of the problem to permit "what-if" analyses that allow both managers and policy makers to understand how changes in the parameters of their problem might affect their strategies or policies (viz. comparative statics / sensitivity analysis). Researchers also argue that such models should be *robust* in that their comparative statics predictions must hold up to a relaxation of the assumptions ([7], [20]).

Comparative statics, or the study of how the solutions of economic models change as the model parameters and specifications are changed, are important because (1) most of the testable predictions of economic theory are comparative statics predictions, (2) economic equilibrium analysis are often built from comparative statics analyses of the model's components, and (3) many of the insights and results needed by both managers and policy makers are obtained through comparative statics [3].

The functional areas of both marketing and operations represent the key value-adding processes of the modern business enterprise. It is these areas that are influential in specifying what should be produced, how it should be produced, and how to deliver said goods and services to the customers [18]. Thus, this paper begins by developing a model of inventory-advertising competition. As there is consensus that competition is an important phenomenon in today's markets, [24] said competition must be accommodated by using a market share attraction model of advertising competition. Holding the right amount of inventory under different circumstances is essential for achieving sound performance [7].

Whitin [28] was perhaps the first to jointly consider purchasing and marketing decisions by incorporating the effect of price-on-demand within the inventory model. Here the retailer must decide the optimal price and order quantity. The price-dependent demand model was followed by another stream of research to integrate the inventory model with advertising-dependent demand ([9]; [13]; [25]; [27]). While the aforementioned research considered only a single firm, there have been a few studies within a static framework on advertising competition in duopoly / oligopolies ([10]; [15]; [16]; [21]). The above studies, however, do not consider inventory related costs in the modeling effort.

The present study has four main objectives that have not yet been fully addressed. The first objective is to investigate analytically how a firm would adapt optimum order quantity and optimum advertising expenditure in response to changes in any of its own parameters, or competitors' parameters in a symmetric duopoly market. Second, in a truly asymmetric non-dominated oligopolistic market for which every market share is less than 50%, should competitors adjust their order quantities and advertising expenditures in response to changes in market conditions in a manner consistent, or inconsistent, with a symmetric duopoly for which the two competitors share the market equally? The third objective is to compare the normative behaviors of rivals in non-dominated oligopolies and their counterparts related to dominated oligopolies (where one firm has a market share equal to or larger than 50%) in response to changes in model parameters upon the inclusion of the additional variable of price into the analysis. The final objective questions the literature (e.g., [12]) which states that the defensive strategy of non-dominated firms will be to decrease the equilibrium price and quantity of advertising in response to the competitive entry in an oligopoly of fixed market potential. This paper asks, do the results continue to be robust when including in the model the operations variable of order quantity?

The next section of the paper outlines a theoretical model that incorporates advertising and order quantity. The third section derives the comparative statics for a symmetric duopoly. The fourth section reports the results of applying a supermodular games approach to self-comparative statics as a tool for assessing the signs of comparative statics derived for non-dominated asymmetric oligopolies. The fifth section compares the normative behaviors of rivals in response to changes in model parameters for two alternative oligopoly structures in the presence of price. The penultimate section addresses the strategy implications regarding the incumbents' response to new entry. The final section summarizes and concludes the paper. Derivation of key formulas and mathematical proofs of five propositions are reported in an Appendix available upon request.

A MATHEMATICAL MODEL OF INVENTORY-ADVERTISING COMPETITION

This research considers simple one-step competing supply chains in which each supplier (vendor) strives to meet an advertising-dependent demand of potential customers. In doing so, the inventory replenishment process of each supplier of a differentiated product is represented by an economic order quantity (EOQ) model for which its classical assumptions are satisfied (mainly, the demand rate is deterministic and constant, shortages are not allowed, and the order quantity is the same for each order). It is further assumed that any intermediate levels in each chain coordinate their activities fully with their related supplier. Each firm aims at maximizing its profit per unit of time non-cooperatively with other firms.

The model described both in this section and in the one to follow, considers first (as in Little [14] and Mesak [15]) a market share attraction model in a duopoly market, with one advertising spending variable x_j measured in real dollars per unit time for each firm j, where j = 1, 2. Sales of firm *1*, $D_1(x_1, x_2)$, in a market of two competitors is expressed as follows:

$$D_1(x_1,x_2)=\frac{mf(x_1)}{f(x_1)+f(x_2)}=\frac{m\beta_1 x_1^{\delta_1}}{\beta_1 x_1^{\delta_1}+\beta_2 x_2^{\delta_2}}\text{ , and } D_2(x_1,x_2)=m-D_1(x_1,x_2), \quad (1)$$

where *m* is the market potential (considered constant for a mature market) and $f(x_1)$ and $f(x_2)$ are the attraction functions of firms 1 and 2, respectively. The theoretical justification of the advertising-driven market share function associated with $D_j(x_1, x_2)$ given by (1) is discussed in [5]. While some other elaborate forms of $f(x_j)$ can be used, their implications appear to be empirically consistent (see [17]). All rivals are assumed to have concave advertising attraction functions, such that $f'(x_j) > 0$ and $f''(x_j) < 0$ for $x_j > 0$. For all the attraction functions, the measures of advertising effectiveness β's and the shaping parameters δ's are strictly positive parameters, and for a concave attraction function $0 < \delta < 1$. The terms are defined as follows:
P_j = Selling price per unit of firm j
MC_j = Marginal cost per unit of firm j
γ_j = Profit margin per unit sold of firm j: $(P_j - MC_j)$
$C(x_j)$ = Advertising cost function of firm j
Q_j = Order quantity of firm j
C_{oj} = Ordering cost per order of firm j
C_{hj} = Inventory holding cost per unit held per unit time of firm j
F_j = Fixed cost of firm j
m = Market potential (considered constant for a mature market),

Consistent with most empirical industrial organization studies, each firm strives to maximize profit. Based on the above definition of terms, the profit function π_j of firm *j* per unit time is given by

$$\pi_j = \gamma_j D_j(x_1,x_2) - C(x_j) - \frac{Q_j}{2}C_{hj} - \frac{D_j(x_1,x_2)}{Q_j}C_{oj} - F_j, \quad j = 1, 2. \tag{2}$$

It is also assumed that the advertising cost function is convex and of the form $C(x_j) = d_j x_j^{\varepsilon_j}$, where d_j and ϵ_j are positive constants such that $d_j > 0$, and $\epsilon_j \geq 1$ [1] with underlying properties, $C'(x_j) > 0$ and $C''(x_j) \geq 0$, for $x_j > 0$. Defining $\Pi_j = \pi_j / \gamma_j m$, for convenience of analysis, and substituting for $D_j(x_1, x_2)$, j = 1, 2, expression (2) takes the following form:

$$\Pi_1 = \frac{f(x_1)}{f(x_1)+f(x_2)}\left[1 - \frac{C_{o1}}{\gamma_1 Q_1}\right] - \frac{C(x_1)}{\gamma_1 m} - \frac{C_{h1}}{2\gamma_1 m}Q_1 - \frac{F_1}{\gamma_1 m}. \tag{3}$$

$$\Pi_2 = \frac{f(x_2)}{f(x_1)+f(x_2)}\left[1 - \frac{C_{o2}}{\gamma_2 Q_2}\right] - \frac{C(x_2)}{\gamma_2 m} - \frac{C_{h2}}{2\gamma_2 m}Q_2 - \frac{F_2}{\gamma_2 m}. \tag{4}$$

The analysis of this situation is based on the Nash equilibrium solution concept of game theory. Researchers have widely used the Nash equilibrium solution concept in an oligopoly (e.g., [11]; [15]; [21]). The Nash equilibrium solution requires that no single rival unilaterally changes its advertising budget and order quantity given the other rivals' optimal advertising budgets and order quantities. Information on each firm's demand function, cost structure, and decision rules is common knowledge to all firms. The first-order optimality conditions for an interior solution ($x_j^* > 0$ and $Q_j^* > 0$) implies that

$$\frac{\partial \Pi_j}{\partial x_j} = 0, \text{ and } \frac{\partial \Pi_j}{\partial Q_j} = 0, \quad j = 1, 2. \tag{5}$$

Also to ensure that expressions (5) indicate profit maximization, both second-order derivatives $\partial^2\Pi_j / \partial x_j^2$ and $\partial^2\Pi_j / \partial Q_j^2$ must be negative, and $\frac{\partial^2\Pi_j}{\partial x_j^{\,2}}\frac{\partial^2\Pi_j}{\partial Q_j^{\,2}} - \left(\frac{\partial^2\Pi_j}{\partial x_j \partial Q_j}\right)^2$ must be positive for all j (a complete derivation of the first and second order conditions of optimality for firms 1 and 2 are presented in a separate Appendix available upon request). Comparative statics are derived next for a symmetric duopoly.

COMPARATIVE STATICS FOR A SYMMETRIC DUOPOLY

This section provides a theoretical derivation of the impact of changes in each of the shift parameters, namely γ_j, β_j, δ_j, m, d_j, ϵ_j, C_{hj}, C_{oj} for a given rival j on its optimal advertising expenditure x_j^* and optimal order quantity Q_j^* (self-comparative statics), as well as on similar quantities related to the competitors (cross – comparative statics). In a symmetric duopoly, firms (which are highly similar in all economic respects) produce a storable, homogeneous product. These firms compete against each other for the same buyers. Symmetric competition also stipulates that rivals will have the same production and inventory costs, acquire real promotion on the same terms, charge the same fixed price, and face symmetric demand functions [32]. Therefore, all comparable shift parameters are assumed to be equal and firms are assumed to have equal market shares.

Although equations (5) for a symmetric competitive structure could be solved explicitly for x_j^* and Q_j^* in terms of model parameters, several of the self-comparative statics obtained afterwards would have been missing and not all of the cross-comparative statics would have been disclosed. Therefore, the implicit function theory (IFT) (see Bertsekas [6]) is instead used to arrive at expressions for self and cross comparative statics. Because of the curse of dimensionality when the number of decision variables per firm is more than one and when the number of competitors $N \geq 3$, the theoretical analysis is confined, for now, to a duopoly. The generality of the obtained results to a non-dominated asymmetric oligopoly is assessed in the next section.

To study the sensitivity of each x_j^* and Q_j^* (where $j = 1, 2$), to a change in one of the model parameters Θ, equations (5) are partially differentiated with respect to Θ and then equated to zero to obtain:

$$\frac{\partial^2\Pi_1}{\partial x_1^2}\frac{\partial x_1}{\partial\theta}+\frac{\partial^2\Pi_1}{\partial x_1\partial Q_1}\frac{\partial Q_1}{\partial\theta}+\frac{\partial^2\Pi_1}{\partial x_1\partial x_2}\frac{\partial x_2}{\partial\theta}+\frac{\partial^2\Pi_1}{\partial x_1\partial Q_2}\frac{\partial Q_2}{\partial\theta}+\frac{\partial^2\Pi_1}{\partial x_1\partial\theta}=0\ ,$$

$$\frac{\partial^2\Pi_1}{\partial Q_1\partial x_1}\frac{\partial x_1}{\partial\theta}+\frac{\partial^2\Pi_1}{\partial Q_1^2}\frac{\partial Q_1}{\partial\theta}+\frac{\partial^2\Pi_1}{\partial Q_1\partial x_2}\frac{\partial x_2}{\partial\theta}+\frac{\partial^2\Pi_1}{\partial Q_1\partial Q_2}\frac{\partial Q_2}{\partial\theta}+\frac{\partial^2\Pi_1}{\partial Q_1\partial\theta}=0\ ,$$

$$\frac{\partial^2\Pi_2}{\partial x_2\partial x_1}\frac{\partial x_1}{\partial\theta}+\frac{\partial^2\Pi_2}{\partial x_2\partial Q_1}\frac{\partial Q_1}{\partial\theta}+\frac{\partial^2\Pi_2}{\partial x_2^2}\frac{\partial x_2}{\partial\theta}+\frac{\partial^2\Pi_2}{\partial x_2\partial Q_2}\frac{\partial Q_2}{\partial\theta}+\frac{\partial^2\Pi_2}{\partial x_2\partial\theta}=0\ , \text{ and}$$

$$\frac{\partial^2\Pi_2}{\partial Q_2\partial x_1}\frac{\partial x_1}{\partial\theta}+\frac{\partial^2\Pi_2}{\partial Q_2\partial Q_1}\frac{\partial Q_1}{\partial\theta}+\frac{\partial^2\Pi_2}{\partial Q_2\partial x_2}\frac{\partial x_2}{\partial\theta}+\frac{\partial^2\Pi_2}{\partial Q_2^2}\frac{\partial Q_2}{\partial\theta}+\frac{\partial^2\Pi_2}{\partial Q_2\partial\theta}=0\ . \qquad (6)$$

Here, it is also assumed that all second partial derivatives of Π_j with respect to each of the equilibrium values x_j^* and Q_j^* together with each of the *shift* parameters Θ do exist and are continuous. The system of equations (6) can be put in the following matrix form:

$$\begin{bmatrix} \frac{\partial^2\Pi_1}{\partial x_1^2} & \frac{\partial^2\Pi_1}{\partial x_1\partial Q_1} & \frac{\partial^2\Pi_1}{\partial x_1\partial x_2} & \frac{\partial^2\Pi_1}{\partial x_1\partial Q_2} \\ \frac{\partial^2\Pi_1}{\partial Q_1\partial x_1} & \frac{\partial^2\Pi_1}{\partial Q_1^2} & \frac{\partial^2\Pi_1}{\partial Q_1\partial x_2} & \frac{\partial^2\Pi_1}{\partial Q_1\partial Q_2} \\ \frac{\partial^2\Pi_2}{\partial x_2\partial x_1} & \frac{\partial^2\Pi_2}{\partial x_2\partial Q_1} & \frac{\partial^2\Pi_2}{\partial x_2^2} & \frac{\partial^2\Pi_2}{\partial x_2\partial Q_2} \\ \frac{\partial^2\Pi_2}{\partial Q_2\partial x_1} & \frac{\partial^2\Pi_2}{\partial Q_2\partial Q_1} & \frac{\partial^2\Pi_2}{\partial Q_2\partial x_2} & \frac{\partial^2\Pi_2}{\partial Q_2^2} \end{bmatrix} \begin{bmatrix} \frac{\partial x_1}{\partial\theta} \\ \frac{\partial Q_1}{\partial\theta} \\ \frac{\partial x_2}{\partial\theta} \\ \frac{\partial Q_2}{\partial\theta} \end{bmatrix} = -\begin{bmatrix} \frac{\partial^2\Pi_1}{\partial x_1\partial\theta} \\ \frac{\partial^2\Pi_1}{\partial Q_1\partial\theta} \\ \frac{\partial^2\Pi_2}{\partial x_2\partial\theta} \\ \frac{\partial^2\Pi_2}{\partial Q_2\partial\theta} \end{bmatrix}. \quad (7)$$

Designating the 4 x 4 square matrix of the second-order partial derivatives in (7) by matrix ***H***, equations (7) can be rewritten as:

$$\begin{bmatrix} \frac{\partial x_1}{\partial\theta} \\ \frac{\partial Q_1}{\partial\theta} \\ \frac{\partial x_2}{\partial\theta} \\ \frac{\partial Q_2}{\partial\theta} \end{bmatrix} = -\boldsymbol{H}^{-1} \begin{bmatrix} \frac{\partial^2\Pi_1}{\partial x_1\partial\theta} \\ \frac{\partial^2\Pi_1}{\partial Q_1\partial\theta} \\ \frac{\partial^2\Pi_2}{\partial x_2\partial\theta} \\ \frac{\partial^2\Pi_2}{\partial Q_2\partial\theta} \end{bmatrix} \quad (8)$$

The derivations of the elements of matrix ***H*** and all other terms related to expressions (8) are shown in a separate Appendix. The Appendix also shows that matrix ***H*** is nonsingular, so its inverse does exist. Gruca et al. [12] assert that negative semi-definiteness of the square matrix ***H*** is essential in ensuring uniqueness of the Nash equilibrium solution of the system of equations (5). A proof of the negative semi-definiteness of matrix ***H*** is provided in the Appendix. Based on the solution of equations (8) for a symmetric duopoly, the following proposition is introduced with related terms defined below [Proof is found in a separate Appendix].

$$a = \frac{f'}{4f}\frac{C_o}{\gamma Q^2} \text{ (positive term),} \quad (9)$$

$$b = \frac{\left(f''f - f'^2\right)}{4f^2}\left[1 - \frac{C_o}{\gamma Q}\right] - \frac{C''}{\gamma m} \text{ (negative term), and} \quad (10)$$

$$\Delta_1 = -\frac{bC_o}{\gamma Q^3} - a^2 \text{ (positive term).} \quad (11)$$

Proposition 1: *For a symmetric duopoly*

(i) *An increase in the parameters γ, β, or δ of a firm should elicit an increase in the equilibrium advertising and order quantity internally, but cause a decrease in the equilibrium advertising and order quantity of its competitor.*

(ii) *An increase in either of the parameters d or ϵ of a firm should elicit a decrease in the equilibrium advertising and order quantity internally, but cause an increase in the equilibrium advertising and order quantity of its competitor.*

(iii) *An increase in parameter C_h of a firm should elicit a decrease in the equilibrium advertising and order quantity internally, but cause an increase in the equilibrium advertising and order quantity of its competitor.*

(iv) *An increase in parameter C_o of a firm should elicit a decrease in the equilibrium advertising and an increase (decrease) in the equilibrium order quantity if $\Delta_1 - 2a^2 > (<) 0$ internally, but cause an increase in the equilibrium advertising and order quantity of its competitor.*

Part (i) of the above proposition dictates that a firm should favor increasing both its advertising spending and order quantity to enhance profits whereas its competitor would be better off by doing the exact opposite when the above parameters increase. Part (ii) implies that if the parameters associated with the advertising cost function increase, an optimal response for the firm is to reduce its advertising spending and order quantity thus mitigating the impact. However, the competitor should consider this situation as an opportunity to increase its advertising expenditure and order quantity in order to increase profit.
Part (iii) indicates that if the inventory holding cost rate per unit increases, the firm's optimal response should be to decrease its advertising expenditure and order quantity. The firm's competitor, in response, would increase its advertising expenditure and order quantity. If the ordering cost per order of a firm increases, as described in part (iv), the firm should respond by decreasing the advertising expenditure; however the optimal response in the change of order quantity will be dictated by other parameters. The competitor's optimal policy will be to take advantage of the situation by increasing both the advertising expenditure and order quantity. Note that the signs of the comparative statics relating the changes in the marketing parameters (γ, β, δ, d, and ϵ) to changes in optimal advertising are similar to those reported in Mesak [24], although that study does not consider inventory related costs. The remaining comparative statics are unique to the present study. In particular, changes in the above marketing parameters are found to affect the operations decision variable, Q^*. Furthermore, changes in the operations parameters (C_0 and C_h) are found to affect the marketing decision variable, x^*. It is conjectured here that the results depicted in the proposition are generalized to a non-dominated asymmetric oligopoly of N firms for which each firm has a market share less than 50%.
The theoretical findings reported in the above proposition are derived under ideal symmetric conditions that rarely, if ever, materialize in practice. In the next two sections (based in part on Sections 2 and 4 of Mesak et al.[18]), the article will assess the robustness of the theoretical sensitivity results to deviations from ideal conditions through examining the applicability of these results to a practical non-dominated oligopoly setting.

SUPERMODULAR GAMES APPROACH TO SELF-COMPARATVE STATICS

The proposition reported in this section describes the impact of changes in each of the shift parameters (namely γ_j, β_j, δ_j, d_j, ϵ_j, C_{hj}, C_{oj}) for a given firm j on its optimal advertising expenditure x_j^* and optimal order quantity Q_j^* (self-comparative statics) in a non-dominated, asymmetric oligopoly for which the market share of each firm is less than 50%.
Ease of use and flexibility in solving for comparative statics in game-theory problems have made monotone methods popular in the economics literature ([2]; [26]). However, they are still (for all intents and purposes) absent from marketing-operations interface related applications. Therefore, the definition of a supermodular game and its related comparative statics implications are briefly discussed below.
Definition: N firms compete in a smooth supermodular game if the following conditions hold for each firm j and each competitor i:
(C.1) *Differentiability*: The profit equation is twice continuously differentiable with respect to x_j and Q_j.
(C.2) *Complementary Strategies* (of each firm's own strategic variables): $\partial^2\pi_j/\partial x_j \partial Q_j \geq 0$.

(C.3) *Strategic Complements* (for strategic variables between firms):

$$\partial^2\pi_j/\partial x_j\partial x_i \geq 0,\ \partial^2\pi_j/\partial x_j\partial Q_i \geq 0,\ \partial^2\pi_j/\partial Q_j\partial x_i \geq 0 \text{ and } \partial^2\pi_j/\partial Q_j\partial Q_i \geq 0. \quad (12)$$

(C.4) *Complementary Policy Parameter* θ:

$$\partial^2\pi_j/\partial x_j\partial\theta \geq 0 \text{ and } \partial^2\pi_j/\partial Q_j\partial\theta \geq 0. \quad (13)$$

One can think of this as a game of super-complementarity, which implies that there is complementarity among all strategies and a policy parameter. The important thing to notice is that this specification implies increasing marginal returns between all possible pairs of choice variables and the policy parameter. Under these conditions, and assuming a unique Nash equilibrium, the following comparative statics results hold for all firms (Milgrom and Roberts, Theorem 6 and its Corollary [29]):

$$\partial x_j^*/\partial\theta \geq 0;\ \partial Q_j^*/\partial\theta \geq 0. \quad (14)$$

That is, when conditions (C.1) – (C.4) are met, an increase in parameter θ will have a non-negative effect on the Nash advertising budgets and size of the order quantity. It should also be mentioned that when *all* the inequalities in (C.2) – (C.4) are in the opposite direction, the inequalities in (14) are reversed to '≤ 0' (Amir [2]).

Upon employing a supermodular games approach to sensitivity analysis, the obtained self - comparative statics are summarized in Proposition 2 (proven in a separate Appendix).

Proposition 2. *For a non-dominated asymmetric oligopoly*

(i) *An increase in either of the firm's parameters γ, or β should elicit no decrease in the equilibrium advertising nor in the order quantity. Furthermore, an increase in the parameter δ of a firm should elicit no decrease in x^δ nor in the equilibrium order quantity Q.*

(ii) *An increase in either of the parameters d or ε of a firm should elicit no increase in either the equilibrium advertising or the order quantity.*

(iii) *An increase in parameter C_h of a firm should elicit no increase in either the equilibrium advertising or the order quantity.*

(iv) *An increase in parameter C_o of a firm should elicit no increase in equilibrium advertising and elicit no decrease in the equilibrium order quantity.*

The self-comparative statics reported in Proposition 2 for a non-dominated asymmetric oligopoly (market share of each firm is less than 50%) is consistent with those derived for a symmetric duopoly reported in Proposition 1.

The next section attempts to assess the robustness of the theoretical sensitivity results pertaining to optimal advertising and order quantity to a competitive setting that incorporates the additional variable of price. For the related model, the attraction of each firm depends on both advertising x and price P. Self-comparative statics are only derived for two distinct oligopoly structures using a supermodular game approach. Mesak et al. [18] show that in terms of magnitude, a change in a parameter of a rival has a much more significant impact on the equilibrium measures of its own than on those of its competitors.

A MATHEMATICAL MODEL OF INVENTORY-ADVERTISING-PRICING COMPETITION

In section 2 the attraction of firm *j*, A_j, can be put in the form $A_j = f(x_j) = Exp\ (a_j + \delta_j \ln x_j)$, where $\beta_j = Exp(a_j)$. For a multinomial logit market share model (MNL) that also includes price P_j, the attraction function takes on the form $A_j = Exp\ (a_j + \delta_j \ln x_j - c_j P_j)$, $a_j > 0$, $\delta_j > 0$, and $c_j > 0$ (Basuroy and Nguyen [4]), so that expression (2) takes on the following form:

$$\pi_j = m\,(P_j - MC_j - C_{oj}/Q_j)\ Exp\,(a_j + \delta_j \ln x_j - c_j P_j)/(A_j + \Sigma_{i\neq j} A_i) - d_j x_j^{\epsilon j} - Q_j C_{hj}/2 - F_j. \quad (15)$$

The two propositions reported in this section describe the impact of changes in each of; i) the operations parameters (MC_j, C_{oj}, C_{hj}), ii) the advertising cost parameters (d_j, ϵ_j) and iii) the attraction function parameters (a_j, δ_j, c_j) for a given rival j on it's a) optimal advertising expenditure x_j^*, b) optimal price P_j^* and c) optimal order quantity Q_j^* (self-comparative statics) in a non-dominated oligopoly for which the market of each firm is less than 50%, and a dominated asymmetric oligopoly for which one firm has a market share larger than or equals to 50%. Because of the curse of dimensionality (dealing with more than two decision variables per firm and the difficulty in meeting all related conditions when applying a supermodular game approach for comparative statics) and exclusively for Proposition 3 associated with non-dominant rivals, comparative statics are obtained for symmetric firms.

Proposition 3. *For a non-dominated symmetric oligopoly*

i. *An increase in either of the parameters c, d, or* ϵ *of a firm should elicit no increase in internal equilibrium advertising.*

ii. *An increase in the parameter* δ *of a firm should elicit no decrease in internal equilibrium advertising.*

iii. *An increase in either of the parameters MC,* C_o*, or* C_h *of a firm should elicit no decrease in the internal equilibrium price.*

iv. *An increase in the parameter c of a firm should elicit no increase in the internal equilibrium price.*

v. *An increase in the parameter* C_h *of a firm should elicit no increase in the internal equilibrium order quantity.*

vi. *An increase in the parameter* C_o *of a firm should elicit no decrease in the internal equilibrium order quantity.*

Having demonstrated that rivals of a non-dominated oligopoly should adjust their equilibrium advertising and order quantity in response to changes in the parameters MC, (or - γ), δ, d, ϵ, C_o and C_h in a manner consistent with Proposition 1, one may ask: Are the behaviors of rivals in a dominated oligopoly similar to those of a non-dominated oligopoly? The answers to the above question are documented in Proposition 4.

Proposition 4. *For a dominated asymmetric oligopoly*

i. *An increase in either of the parameters MC,* C_o*,* C_h*, d, or* ϵ *of the dominant firm should elicit responses in a manner consistent with the findings of Proposition 3.*

ii. *An increase in the parameter c of the dominant firm should elicit no internal decrease in equilibrium advertising, no internal increase in equilibrium price, nor an internal increase in order quantity.*

iii. *An increase in either of the parameters a, or* δ *of the dominant firm should elicit no internal increase in equilibrium advertising, but elicit no internal decrease in either equilibrium price, or order quantity.*

Propositions 1 through 4 taken together imply that the self-comparative statics related to equilibrium advertising and order quantity for a symmetric duopoly, in the context of the MNL market share model, are generalized to non-dominant firms even upon the incorporation of the additional price variable in the model. However, for a dominated oligopoly, the normative behavior of the dominant firm appears different from the normative behaviors of its non-dominant rivals when it comes to the marketing parameters δ and c associated with the attraction function as well as the operations parameter C_h associated with inventory holding costs as summarized in Table 1.

The next section examines comparative statics related to entry for a symmetric oligopoly in which the marketing variables of advertising and price together with the operations variable of order quantity are all considered.

Table 1: Comparative Statics for Non-dominant and Dominant Firms

	Non-dominant Firm			Dominant Firm		
	x_j^*	P_j^*	Q_j^*	x_j^*	P_j^*	Q_j^*
MC_j	≤ 0	≥ 0	N.O.	≤ 0	≥ 0	≥ 0
C_{oj}	≤ 0	≥ 0	≥ 0	≤ 0	≥ 0	≥ 0
C_{hj}	≥ 0	≥ 0	≤ 0	≥ 0	≤ 0	≤ 0
d_j	≤ 0	N.O.	N.O.	≤ 0	≥ 0	≥ 0
ϵ_j	≤ 0	N.O.	≥ 0	≤ 0	≥ 0	≥ 0
a_j	N.O.	N.O.	N.O.	≤ 0	≥ 0	≥ 0
δ_j	≥ 0	N.O.	N.O.	≤ 0	≥ 0	≥ 0
c_j	≤ 0	≤ 0	N.O.	≥ 0	≤ 0	≤ 0

N.O. stands for "Not Obtained"

COMPARATIVE STATICS RELATED TO ENTRY

In this section, closed form solutions for symmetric equilibrium advertising, price and order quantity are obtained together with related comparative statics with respect to competitive entry. The first order conditions for optimality regarding (15), $\partial\pi_j/\partial x_j = \partial\pi_j/\partial P_j = \partial\pi_j/\partial Q_j = 0$ imply for a symmetric oligopoly that:

$$x^* = (\delta m/ Ncd\epsilon)^{1/\epsilon},\ P^* = N/c(N-1) + MC + (NC_oC_h/2m)^{1/2},\ \text{and}\ Q^* = (2mC_o/N\,C_h)^{1/2} \qquad (16)$$

For (16) to represent a unique symmetric Nash equilibrium, it is shown in the Appendix that the Heissian matrix $\boldsymbol{H}_{3x3}$ of second order partial derivatives of π with respect to x, P and Q is negative semi-definite. Substituting for x^*, P^* and Q^* from (16) into (15) and defining optimal oligopoly profit $\pi_o^* = N\,\pi^*$ produces

$$\pi_o^* = m\,N/c(N-1) - (\delta m/c\epsilon) - (m\,N\,C_oC_h/2)^{1/2} - NF. \qquad (17)$$

Based on (16) and (17), we are in a position to introduce Proposition 5.

Proposition 5. *For a symmetric oligopoly and in the context of the MNL market share model, an increase in the number of competitors N:*

i. Decreases the equilibrium measures x^*, Q^* and π_o^*.

ii. May increase the equilibrium measure P^*.

When it comes to the marketing variable of price, the related result in Proposition 5 (ii) is inconsistent with those reported in Gruca et al. [12], and Basuroy and Nguyen [4]. The above studies consider non-dominated brands in the context of market share attraction models. Further, those studies illustrates falling advertising and price in response to competitive entry. However, they do not incorporate any operations variables in the modeling effort. Proposition 5 (ii) has empirical support. Frank and Salever [8] show that incumbent producers of prescription drugs raise the price after generic entry, while generic incumbents reduce the price after generic entry. There is also support on theoretical grounds for the content of Proposition 5 (ii) based on a symmetric inventory-price model articulated by Min and Chen [19]. The above authors, however, consider C_o and C_h as decision variables in addition to price, and do not incorporate advertising in their competitive model.

CONCLUSIONS, IMPLICATIONS AND DIRECTIONS FOR FUTURE RESEARCH

In short, this research presents a parsimonious inventory-advertising model for which competition is limited to two symmetric firms and derives its comparative statics predictions (Proposition 1). Using a "supermodular games approach", considered a novel application in the operations-marketing interface literature, the above comparative statics are generalized to a non-dominated asymmetric oligopoly of N competing firms, each possessing market shares of less than 50% (Proposition 2). Further generalization for non-dominant firms is materialized when the additional marketing variable of price is incorporated into the attraction function of competing firms (Proposition 3). However, for a dominated oligopoly, the normative behavior of the dominant firm appears different from the normative behaviors of its non-dominant rivals when it comes to changes in the parameters of the attraction function and inventory cost (Proposition 4 and Table 1). The defensive reaction of symmetric incumbents to competitive entry are obtained in Proposition 5. To that end, the main objectives of this study have been achieved.

The main conclusion drawn from the findings is of significant strategic appeal to marketing and production / purchasing managers. Within the context of an MNL market share model, for an oligopolistic market that is not dominated by a single rival (largest market share is less than 50 %), a firm would adjust its advertising spending, order quantity, and price in response to changes in its own shift parameters in a manner consistent with the comparative static properties reported in Propositions 1 and 3. Relaxing the assumption of symmetry would only complicate the analysis without yielding additional insight. However, for a firm that dominates its industry, different courses of action are required for changes related to the parameters of the attraction function and of holding inventory cost. Finally, for non-dominant firms the defensive strategy of decreasing the equilibrium advertising and price in response to competitive entry for a fixed market potential do not necessarily remain implementable upon the inclusion of the operations variable of order quantity in the modeling effort. The studied model offers a framework for further research. Future research would investigate the linkage between our findings and empirical firms' behavior within several industries. In this work we have assumed aggregation of advertising over all media. The current study utilizes a basic EOQ model within a profit maximizing framework, which can later be extended to include taxes and inflation within the model. An interesting area for future research would be to consider different advertising media of various effectiveness and to examine synergy effects among them ([22]). Following the study of Sivakumar [24] for asymmetric competition, the present study can be extended to derive normative defensive strategies in growing markets related to an oligopoly for which one firm dominates the market (its market share is equal to or greater than 50%) while all rivals share the rest of the market equally. In this regard, the dominant firm would have at least one parameter different from the non-dominant competitors. Comparable parameters of non-dominant competitors, however, would be considered to be similar.

REFERENCES

[1] Amaldoss, W., C. He. Product variety, informative advertising, and price competition. Journal of Marketing Research 2010, 47, 146-156.

[2] Amir, R. Supermodularity and complementarity in economics: an elementary survey. Southern Economic Journal 2005, 71 (3), 636-660.

[3] Athey, S., P. Milgram, J. Roberts. Robust comparative statics. Unpublished manuscript 1998. *http://faculty-gsb.stanford.edu/athey/documents/draftmonograph98.pdf*

[4] Basuroy, S., D. Nguyen. Multinomial Logit Market Share Models: Equilibrium characteristics and strategic implications. Management Science 1998, 44 (10), 1396-1408.

[5] Bell, D.E., R.L. Keeney, J.D.C. Little. A market share theorem. Journal of Marketing Research 1975, 12 (May), 136-141.

[6] Bertsekas, D.P. Nonlinear programming, 2nd edition, Athena Scientific, Belmont, MA, 1999.

[7] Coughlan, A.T., Choi, S.C., Chu, W., Ingene, C.A., Moorthy, S., Padmanabhan, V., Raju, J.S., Soberman, D.A., Staelin, R., Z.J. Zhang. Marketing modeling reality and the realities of marketing models. Marketing Letters 2010, 21, 317-333.

[8] Frank, R.G., D.S. Salkever .Generic entry and the pricing of pharmaceuticals. Journal of Economics and Management Strategy 1997, 6, 75-90.

[9] Freeland, J.R. Coordination strategies for production and marketing in a functionally decentralized firm. AIIE Transactions 1980, 12, 126-132.

[10] Friedman, L. Game-theory models in the allocation of advertising expenditures. Operations Research 1958, 6(5), 699-709.

[11] Friedman, J.W. Advertising and oligopolistic equilibrium. Bell Journal of Economics 1983, 14, 464-473

[12] Gruca, T.S., K.R. Kumar, D. Sudharshan. An equilibrium analysis of defensive response to entry using a coupled response function model. Marketing Science 1992, 11, 348-358.

[13] Khouja, M., S.S. Robbins. Linking advertising and quantity decisions in the single-period inventory model. International Journal of Production Economics 2003, 86, 93-105.

[14] Little, J.D.C. Aggregate advertising models: the state of the art. Operations Research 1979, 27, 629-667.

[15] Mesak, H.I. On deriving and validating comparative statics of a symmetric model of advertising competition. Computers & Operations Research 2003, 30, 1791-1806.

[16] Mesak, H.I., J.A. Calloway. A pulsing model of advertising competition: game theoretic approach, part A – Theoretical foundation. European Journal of Operational Research 1995, 86, 231-248.

[17] Mesak, H.I., T.L. Means. Modeling advertising budgeting and allocation decisions using modified multinomial logit market share models. Journal of the Operational Research Society 1998, 49, 1260-1269.

[18] Mesak, H.I., A. Bari, M.S. Luehlfing, F. Han. On modeling the advertising-operations interface under asymmetric competition. European Journal of Operational Research 2015, 240, 278-291.

[19] Min, K.J., Chen, C.K. A competitive inventory model with options to reduce setup and inventory holding costs. Computers& Operations Research 1995, 22 (5), 503-514.

[20] Milgrom, P., J. Roberts. Rationalizability, learning, and equilibrium in games of strategic complementarities. Econometrica 1990, 58 (6), 1255-1277.

[21] Mills, H.D. 1961. A study in promotional competition. F.M. Bass, R.D. Buzzell, M.R. Greene, W. Lazer, E.A. Pessemier, D.L. Shawver, A. Shuchman, C.A. Theodore, G.W. Wilson, eds. Mathematical Models and Methods in Marketing. Richard D. Irwin, Homewood, IL, 271-301.

[22] Naik, P., K. Raman. Understanding the impact of synergy in multimedia communications. Journal of Marketing Research 2003, 40(2), 375-388.

[23] Schmalensee, R. A model of promotional competition in oligopoly. Review of Economic Studies 1976, 43, 42-51.

[24] Sivakumar, K. Manifestation and measurement of asymmetric brand competition. Journal of Business Research 2004, 57, 813-820.

[25] Subramanyam, E.S., S. Kumaraswamy. EOQ formula under varying marketing policies and conditions. AIIE Transactions 1981, 13, 312-314.

[26] Tremblay, C.H., V.J. Tremblay. The neglect of monotone comparative statics methods. Journal of Economic Education 2010, 41 (2), 177-193.

[27] Urban, T.L. Deterministic inventory models incorporating marketing decisions. Computers & Industrial Engineering 1992, 22(1), 85-93.

[28] Whitin, T.M. Inventory control and price theory. Management Science 1955, 2, 61-68.

DECISION SCIENCES INSTITUTE

Evaluating Performance Quality of a Firm's Social Media Activities

Jeen-Su Lim
University of Toledo
Email: jlim@utnet.utoledo.edu

Kee-Sook Lim
University of Toledo
Email: klim2@utnet.utoledo.edu

John Heinrichs
Wayne State University
Email: ai2824@wayne.edu

ABSTRACT

Individual consumers continue to use multiple social media platforms as they share information with their peers, search for information, explore product functionality, and acquire goods and services. Firms must determine how to allocate resources and develop strategies among social media platforms. This requires an understanding of how well a firm's social media platforms are performing to achieve the desired outcomes. This study identifies four dimensions of performance quality and assesses performance quality levels. This study also evaluates the impact of brand origin and industry type on a firm's performance of social media activities.

KEYWORDS: Social Media Platforms, Performance Quality of Social Media Activities, Brand Origin, Industry Type

INTRODUCTION

The use of social media platforms by both consumers and marketers has become prevalent as individuals engage with brands with which they are already familiar. Today, nearly 25% of the world's population use social media platforms whereas in the United States, 42% of adults use multiple social media platform sites (Duggan & Smith, 2013). In fact, using social media platforms can be an effective way for firms to approach significant numbers of potential and current customers. However, in order to gain value with using social media platforms to reach these potentially interested consumers, firms have to do more than just being present on a particular social media platform (Culnan, McHugh, & Zubillaga, 2010).

Hoffman and Fodor (2010) suggest that firms need to specify the motivation to use social media platforms and assess the effectiveness of social media investments at the organization or firm level. Social media has received significant attention from researchers in many disciplines. Previous studies primarily have investigated determinants and consequences of social media adoption and usage at the individual level (Goldenberg, et al., 2009; Lee, Cotte, & Noseworthy, 2010; Trusov, Bodapati, & Bucklin, 2010). These studies also focused on the dynamics and interactions of individual users in social media communities (Dholakia, Bagozzi, & Pearo, 2004;

Kozinets, et al., 2010; Schau, et al., 2009). However, little attention has been given to the adoption of social media platforms at the firm or organization level and evaluation of the social media platform performance quality. Peters, et al. (2013) indicate the importance of shifting our focus from quantity to quality in social media evaluation and calls for research investigating the nature and role of performance quality of social media platforms. Yet there exists limited research investigating the level of social media platform performance quality.
Therefore, the focus of this research is to investigate the role and benefit of social media platform performance quality. To do this, this study first identifies four dimensions of social media platform performance quality. Next, the differences in the level of social media platform performance quality are tested with respect to brand origin and industry type.

LITERATURE REVIEW

Social media platforms have become an important element in the firm's marketing communications process. Social media platforms are permitting firms to engage in individual dialog with consumers without the restrictions of time, place, or medium (Kim & Ko, 2012). Ideally, these individuals are members of other virtual communities and can share their experiences regarding the firm's brands. To begin with, however, the firm must determine which social media platforms to invest and allocate resources. Social media platform performance quality information can help the firm evaluate the success with their engagement within that social media platform.

Performance Quality of Social Media

It is believed that information sharing, trust, and problem solving are accelerated by social capital, increasing the impact and reach of the message (McEvily & Marcus, 2005). Under the context of social media, which is grounded on engagement, sharing, and relationship, if a firm knows how to build up their online users' trust as well as involve them in activities and information sharing, then users are more likely to discuss those brands and talk about them repeatedly thus leading to increased impact and reach.
Social media platforms are connectivity-enabled media that facilitate interaction, co-creation, collaboration, exchange, and publication of information among firms and their networked communities of users (Kim & Ko, 2012; Larson & Watson, 2011). The expanding myriads of social media platforms require the firm to assess the allocation of resources to each platform. To help firms understand with which social media platforms to engage, Kaplan and Haenlein (2010) have categorized social media applications into six groups based on the social media characteristics of media richness and self-disclosure. The six categories are labeled collaborative projects, microblogs and blogs, content communities, social networking sites, virtual game worlds, and virtual social worlds. Given these social media application categories, the firm generates comments and responses from users of these social media platforms at different phases of the consumer's buying cycle to focus on engagement, awareness, and word-of-mouth communication (Hoffman & Fodor, 2010).

Differentiating Factors of Social Media Performance Quality

Previous research studies suggest that the optimal social media strategy varies by user characteristics, firm size, and industry classifications (Aral, Dellarocas, & Godes, 2013; DiStaso & McCorkindale, 2013). One of the primary differentiating factors of social media performance quality is the brand origin of the firm. For firms operating in various locations around the world, it is important to understand how each culture uses social media platforms. Goodrich and de Mooij (2014) report that the local social media platform sites typically generate more traffic than the often cited social media platform of Facebook. Due to the country differences in social media usage, firms originated from various countries may take different social media focus and employ diverse social media portfolio strategies (Berthon et al., 2012; Burton & Soboleva, 2011). These discussions lead to the following hypothesis.

Hypothesis 1: A firm's social media platform performance quality will vary by brand origin.

Another differentiating factor involves the industry classification type of firms. Industrial products firms are currently using social media platform sites to achieve brand objectives such as attracting new customers (Michaelidou, Siamagka, & Christodoulides, 2011). Consumer products firms report that individuals who are engaged with social media platforms are more likely to acquire the brand they engage with. Consumers are also bringing their online experiences with these brands into their own social media platforms rather than solely engaging directly on the firm's various platform sites.

The social media platforms such as Facebook has a location-based recommendation service that can combine local knowledge and word-of-mouth. Consumers can check-in at retail locations and claim special deals offered by the firm. This capability provides retailers with the ability to reach consumers and potentially attract them to a given retail store (Harris & Dennis, 2011). Online retailers are using such capability and are offering interactive features on their social media platform sites to engage consumers with their brand. Further, in the past, researchers have studied the importance of these social motivation initiatives as part of the overall shopping experience. They have reported that social interaction has been identified as an important characteristic for online shopping as social media networking has become a major way in which individuals socialize. Given that shopping can be a popular social activity, it is likely that individuals will combine their shopping and social media networking experiences (Harris & Dennis, 2011). Based on these discussions, the following hypothesis is presented.

Hypothesis 2: A firm's social media platform performance quality of social media activities will vary by industry type.

METHODS

This research focuses on assessing the social media platform performance quality. Social media platform performance quality data were collected and recorded from the firms' social media platform sites. Social media activities that are publicly available on a firm's social media platforms were captured. This study identifies four performance quality dimensions of social media platform. The first two dimensions capture the degree of positivity or negativity of social media mentions regarding a brand or a firm. The third dimension refers to the likelihood that a firm or its brands are being discussed in social media platforms. The fourth dimension is related to the range of influence represented by the size of unique users referencing a firm's brand or the firm. Average values of the performance quality are used as measures of the four dimensions of social media platform performance quality. Brand origin was recorded by determining the country where the firm was headquartered. The industry classification type was determined by the standard industrial classification code and the primary market served by that firm.

RESULTS

Mean values and marginal mean values for the four performance quality dimension measures of social media platform activities show that United States firms and service and retail firms show higher positive average value. Foreign firms and consumer product firms as well as industrial product firms show higher negative average value.

MANOVA Results

Analysis was performed using the two-way two (Brand Origin) by three (Industry Type) MANOVA procedure for the four performance quality dimension measures. The MANOVA tests were used to evaluate the differences in social media platform performance quality between United States and foreign firms as well as among three different industry classifications (consumer products, industrial products, service/retail firms). For the significant main and interaction effect in the MANOVA results, univariate analysis was performed to evaluate which social media platform performance quality dimensions contributes to the significant MANOVA results.

The MANOVA results show a significant brand origin main effect and non-significant two-way interaction effect. For the significant brand origin main effect, univariate analysis was performed to determine which social media platform performance quality contributes to the significant main effect. Univariate brand origin main effect is significant for the three dimension measures of social media platform performance quality. These results provide support for hypothesis 1.

MANOVA results also show that the industry type main effect is significant. For the significant industry type main effect, univariate analysis was performed to determine which social media platform performance quality contributes to this significant main effect. Univariate industry type main effect is significant only for the negativity measure. The negativity dimension shows significant industry differences among the three industry types. A t-test is performed for the negativity dimension to evaluate which pair of the industry types is significantly different. The t-test shows that the difference is significant between consumer product and service/retail firms as well as between industrial product and service/retail firms. The service/retail firms show higher negativity score than consumer and industrial product firms. These results provide support for hypothesis 2.

DISCUSSION AND CONCLUSIONS

This study identifies the importance of understanding performance quality of social media platforms. This paper examines performance quality of social media activities rather than quantity of social media activities. Performance quality measures of social media can be used in evaluating a firm's current social media activities and in determining target levels of social media platform performance quality. Understanding of a firm's social media performance quality can help managers manage social media platforms effectively. The findings show that the brand origin and industry type main effects on social media quality are significant. The results can help firms gain a clearer view of how the industry they operate in uses social media platforms. The performance quality level of social media activities can be used to develop a firm's social media platform strategy. Considering the performance quality level, firms can make appropriate adjustments in developing and managing their social media platforms depending on their current social media activities, strategic goals, and available resources. The findings of this study also provide firms and managers with a tool to measure their social media platform performance quality. Firms can set up standard performance quality goals for their social media activities. Depending on the type of industry in which firms are involved, the target performance quality level of social media activities can be determined.

While this study provides interesting findings, care should be taken in interpreting the results. As the database is created using information from large firms, the results may not apply to small and medium size firms resulting in somewhat limited generalizability. Future research should assess the level of social media performance quality for small and medium size firms.

REFERENCES

References available upon request.

DECISION SCIENCES INSTITUTE
Examining the relationship between external software characteristics and vulnerabilities

Yaman Roumani
Eastern Michigan University
Email: yroumani@emich.edu

Joseph K. Nwankpa
University of Texas Rio Grande Valley
Email: joseph.nwankpa@utrgv.edu

Yazan F. Roumani
Oakland University
Email: roumani@oakland.edu

ABSTRACT

This study examines the relationship between external software characteristics and vulnerabilities. Based on the analysis of 227 vulnerable software products, our results showed that the number of compatible operating systems has a positive effect on vulnerability severity and vulnerability frequency.

KEYWORDS: vulnerability, severity, frequency, software, external characteristics

INTRODUCTION

Software vulnerabilities have been regarded as one of the key reasons for computer security breaches which result in enormous losses (Kirk 2013). With the growth of the software industry and the Internet, the number of vulnerability attacks and the ease with which an attack can be made have increased. Furthermore, since software developers are not always aware of security holes in their code, vulnerabilities will inevitably continue to be discovered after the software is released.

Most of the studies concerning software vulnerabilities have been exploratory in nature, with the majority dedicated to vulnerability detection and prevention and a few devoted to vulnerability predictions. Moreover, there has been a lack of quantitative studies in this area as most vulnerability studies rely on qualitative methods. Despite the existence of few predictive studies (Alhazmi and Malaiya 2005a 2005b 2006; Murtaza et al. 2016; Scandariato et al. 2014; Shin and Williams 2013), some of these studies have been known to have issues with their assumptions (Ozment 2007), while others are not generalizable and do not consider the different characteristics of the software products.

The research undertaken in this study proposes a novel vulnerability prediction model using software characteristics. This study will show that software characteristics can reveal patterns and trends that will offer new insights into the nature of vulnerabilities. The prediction capabilities of the proposed model will be examined to predict the vulnerability severity and vulnerability frequency. The proposed model will be empirically tested using vulnerability data collected from the National Vulnerability Database (NVD). The data analysis of this study will add to the understanding of vulnerability prediction models and will suggest directions for future research in this area. . Based on the analysis, we will be able to make some important research and practical contributions. The results are foreseen to help software companies and IT practitioners in analyzing their own vulnerability risks assessment and implementing any needed changes which can increase their capabilities in providing more secure software products. It is our belief that such prediction capabilities will expand the understanding of vulnerability prediction beyond the existing literature.

This paper is organized as follows. We first review the background literature on vulnerabilities and existing prediction models. We then present the research model. Next, we report an empirical study based on data collected from NVD, followed by a presentation of the data results. We conclude with a discussion of research findings, limitations and implications.

LITERATURE REVIEW

Vulnerabilities

According to Arbaugh et al. (2000), a vulnerability is a "technological flaw in an information technology product that has security or survivability implications". Further studies defined software vulnerability as "a bug, flaw, behavior, output, outcome or event within an application, system, device, or service that could lead to an implicit or explicit failure of confidentiality, integrity, or availability" (Schiffman 2007).

Existing Vulnerability Prediction Models

Existing studies on software security measured security of a system from an operational security perspective (Littlewood et al. 1993). In their paper, Littlewood et al. (1993) analyzed the similarities between security and reliability. It was concluded that the use of effort of the attacker would be a suitable measure of software vulnerabilities. Alves-Foss and Barbosa (1995) proposed Security Vulnerability Index (SVI) to assess the vulnerability of computer systems to common intrusion methods. Based on predefined sets of SVI rules, this model would reveal system vulnerabilities. The SVI model used three factors to calculate SVI value: system characteristics, neglectful acts and malevolent acts. However, one of the drawbacks of SVI was the lack of measure of system factors. Moreover, the SVI model was designed to focus on operating systems only.

The next wave of vulnerability studies focused on predicting vulnerabilities using attack trees, privilege graphs and vulnerability density functions. For example, Dacier et al. (1996) and Ortaelo et al. (1999) proposed to model vulnerabilities using a privilege graph where every node represents user privileges and every edge represents a single vulnerability. The model can be used to construct a variety of ways where the attacker can exploit vulnerabilities and gain user privileges. The privilege graph is then transformed to a Markov chain based on successful attack patterns. Browne et al. (2001) used vulnerability data of Computer Emergency Readiness Team (CERT) to analyze vulnerability incidents trends. The authors concluded that the number of vulnerability incidents which are reported to CERT is related to square root of time. Their proposed model was able to predict the severity of future vulnerability exploitations based on earlier vulnerability reports. Other studies have used vulnerability density analogies. Vulnerability density relies on the number of vulnerabilities found per x lines of code to predict the future number of undiscovered vulnerabilities based on the maturity of the software product. Furthermore, vulnerability density assumes that different software versions are comparable to each other and have static code. Although vulnerability density models have been used to predict vulnerability, however, such models have failed to satisfy major assumptions about their data such as time and effort, operational environment, independence, and static code. Thus, the validity of such models has been questioned (Ozment 2007).

Recent studies on vulnerability prediction used different data mining techniques and mathematical models. Shin and William (2008) performed statistical analysis on nine complexity metrics and showed that complexity metrics can be used to predict vulnerabilities. However, their analysis was limited to JavaScript Engine of Mozilla application framework, thus, the authors concluded that their results may not be generalized to other software products. In their research, Murtaza et al. (2016) mined all vulnerabilities between 2009 and 2014. The authors found that the sequential patterns of vulnerabilities follow a first order Markov property. Moreover, Murtaza et al. (2016) concluded that it is possible to predict the next vulnerability by using the previous vulnerability with a recall of 80% and precision of 90%. However, the study did not take into consideration the different categories or the characteristics of software products.

RESEARCH MODEL

Krusl (1998) classifies software characteristics into internal and external ones. Internal characteristics such as size (lines of code), complexity, coupling…etc. are of interest mostly to software developers and engineers as they are related to the development of software. On the other hand, external characteristics such as compatibility, license, price…etc. are the main properties and features which are relevant to customers and adopters. External software characteristics are always used by customers to evaluate software products in order to make the adoption decision. Furthermore, for customers, external software characteristics are the only measure they can use to evaluate software quality. Based on the relevance of external software characteristics, our proposed model (figure 1) focuses on examining the relationship between such characteristics and vulnerabilities.

For our model, we chose four external software characteristics: software price, software programming language, software source code availability, and software compatibility. Our choice of these four characteristics was based on the availability of information for all software products. Moreover, for our dependent variables, we chose vulnerability severity and vulnerability frequency. Further information about the dependent and independent variables is discussed in the next section.

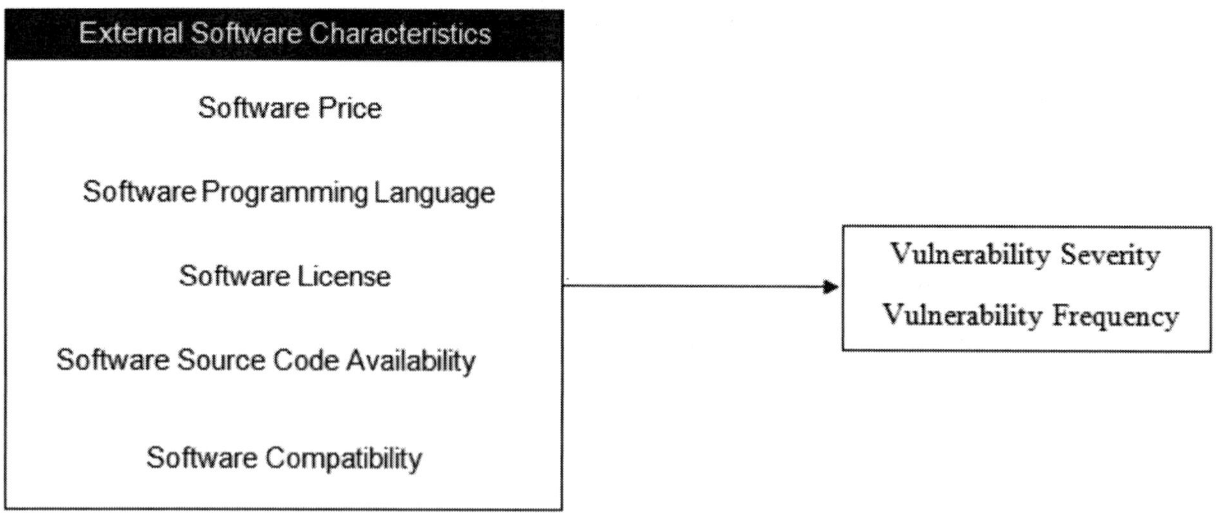

Figure 1: Proposed model

Vulnerability Severity

Vulnerability severity refers to the extent to which an intruder gains unauthorized privilege on various system resources. Oftentimes, vulnerabilities are classified according to their severity levels where each classification is assigned a numerical value. For example, gaining control of the vulnerable host and compromising the entire system is considered critical-level severity vulnerability while being able to collect information about the vulnerable host is considered low-level severity vulnerability.

There have been various tools and measures that were developed to evaluate and measure severity of vulnerabilities. The most accepted measure is the Common Vulnerability Scoring System (CVSS). CVSS is "a universal language to convey vulnerability severity and help determine urgency and priority of response" (Schiffman 2007). It's a universal language and a standard for assessing the severity of vulnerabilities in operating systems and software products (Mell et al. 2007). CVSS offers a way to consistently report on infrastructure vulnerabilities and it solves the issue of multiple, incompatible scoring systems in use today.

CVSS consists of three sets of measures: base measures, temporal measures and environmental measures. Base measures represent the characteristics of a vulnerability which are constant over time and over user environments. Temporal measures, on the other hand, are the characteristics of a vulnerability which change over time but not among user environments. Environmental measures are the characteristics of a vulnerability which are relevant and unique to a particular user's environment. Each set of measures has a different equation that results in a score which in turn is the essence of CVSS metric.

Vulnerability Frequency

The frequency of vulnerability refers to the rate at which vulnerabilities occurs over a unit of time. According to reports by Computer Emergency Readiness Team (CERT), there has been an increase in frequency of vulnerabilities coupled with an increase in speed, automation and sophistication of attacks which makes it more difficult for software vendors and system administrators to keep up to date with security patches and they experience more disruptive security attacks. While frequency of attacks and vulnerability disclosure have received wide interest among researchers, frequency of vulnerabilities remains a lesser explored topic. In this study, we will use vulnerability frequency to measure the number of vulnerability occurrences within a given time period without looking at a specific type or distribution of a vulnerability.

External Software Characteristics

Software Price:

Software price plays an important role in modifying the individual's attitude toward the software in many ways. For instance, research studies which looked at software piracy found that software price to be a significant factor (incentive) which influences the intention to pirate (Gopal and Sanders 2000). In their work, Peace et al. (2003) conducted a survey of 201 respondents and found that software price was among the major reasons for illegally copying software.

Following the same analogy, studies have shown that attackers' attitudes and hackers' motivations for finding vulnerabilities are associated with several factors such as: peer approval, self-esteem, politics, publicity, financial gains, curiosity and sabotage (Shaw et al. 1999). Within the hackers' community, hacking achievements typically help individuals gain higher and more respectable status as it refers to the persons' skills and mastery level. Reaching a higher status is oftentimes associated with noteworthy achievements such as hacking popular software. For those hackers who seek publicity or peer approval, they tend to target software with large user base due to their significant reach. So despite software price, hackers look for vulnerabilities in open source and proprietary software as long as there is a significant user base. Similarly, infamous social networking sites such as Facebook and Myspace are constant targets of vulnerabilities regardless of their service cost. Outside the hacker's community, hackers' incentives tend to vary among political reasons, financial gains, self-esteem and sabotage.

Software Programming Language:

Selecting a suitable programming language is one of the most important decisions which is made during software development cycle. A chosen programming language has direct effect on how software ought to be built and what means must be used to guarantee that the software functions properly and securely. Software programs which are written using an insecure language may cause system dependent errors which are known to be difficult to find and fix (Hoare 1973). For instace, buffer overflows vulnerabilities and other low-level errors are well known issues which caused major problems in C and C++ languages (Cowan 1999).

As of today, there exist numerous programming languages but the topic of security in programming languages has been widely disregarded as it's believed that programming errors and flaws are caused by numerous factors and cannot be easily eliminated. Current approaches to this issue are essentially ad hoc where best programming practices and secure programming techniques are implemented during or after the design stage. Although this approach helps in preventing coding errors and flaws by relying on programmers' skills and experience, it is hard to say with any certainty what vulnerabilities are prevented and to what extent. More importantly, the ad hoc approach does not protect against new and evolving vulnerabilities as it only handles known vulnerabilities and specific coding flaws.

An evolving trend in secure programming has been the use of formal language semantics. Formal language semantics try to reason with and prove security properties of the code. For example, in their paper, Leroy and Rouaix (1998) developed a formal technique to validate a typed functional language to ensure that memory locations always contain appropriate values to avoid buffer overflow vulnerabilities. Although the use of formal language semantics has been advocated (Meseguer and Talcott 1997, Volpano 1997), it has not been adopted as a standard by programmers.

Software Source Code Availability:

Security of open source software (OSS) and closed source software has been a hot topic with many arguments repeatedly presented. Advocates of OSS argue that more reviewers strengthen the security of the software as it eases the process of finding bugs and speeds it up "given enough eyeballs, all bugs are shallow" (Raymond and Young 2000). Opponents of this idea disagree and claim that not all code reviewers and testers have enough skills and experience compared to code reviewers at companies who are more skilled at finding flaws.

The argument is that oftentimes code reviewers and testers need to have further skills other than programming such as cryptography, stenography and networking. Moreover, proponents of closed source software claim that security by obscurity is the main strength of closed source software since it's harder to find vulnerabilities when the code is not accessible. However, proponents of OSS argue that it's possible to gain access to closed source code through publicly available patches and disassembling software (Tevis 2005).

It's important to note that the impact of source code availability on security depends on the open source development model. For instance, the open source cathedral model allows everyone to view the source code, detect flaws/bugs/vulnerabilities and open reports; but they are not permitted to release patches unless they are approved by project owners. OSS projects are typically regulated by project administrators who require some time to review and approve patches. Attackers can take advantage of the availability of source code and published vulnerability reports to exploit them (Payne 2002). However, proponents of OSS argue that vulnerabilities in OSS projects can be fixed faster than those in closed source software because the OSS community is not dependent on a company's schedule to release a patch. Moreover opponents of this idea argue that the lack of incentives in OSS projects can diminish contributors' motivation to fix vulnerabilities.

Despite the continuous debate on OSS security, advocates from both sides agree that having access to the code makes it easier to locate vulnerabilities but they differ about the impact of vulnerabilities on software security. First of all, keeping the source code open provides attackers with easy access to information which might be helpful to successfully exploit the code. Publically available source code gives attackers the ability to search for vulnerabilities and flaws and thus increase the exposure of the system. Second, making the source code publicly available does not guarantee that a qualified person will look at the source and evaluate it. In the bazaar style environment, malicious code such as backdoors may be sneaked into the source by attackers posing as trustful contributors. For instance, in 2003 Linux kernel developers discovered an attempt to include a backdoor in the kernel code (Poulsen 2003). Finally, for many OSS projects there is no selection criterion of programmers based on their skills; project owners tend to accept any help without checking for qualifications or coding skills.

Software Compatibility:

Software producers often create applications to run on a single or a combination of operating systems (OS). From a software viewpoint, maintaining security is the obligation of both the OS and the software program. But since computer hardware such as the CPU, memory and input/output channels are accessible to a software programs only by making calls to the OS, therefore, the OS bears a tremendous burden in achieving system security by allocating, controlling and supervising all system resources.

For the most part, each of today's streamlines OSs has a main weakness. For instance, earlier OSs such as Windows NT, UNIX and Macintosh had a weakness in their access control policies (Krsul 1998). Such OSs did not specify access control policies very clearly which meant that applications that ran by users inherited all the privileges that the access control mechanisms of the OS provided to those users (Wurster 2010). An access control policy requires an OS to give a program or a user the minimum set of access rights necessary to perform a task. In his work, Denning (1983) illustrated the working of an access control policy which typically consists of three entities namely, subjects, objects and access rights matrix. Subjects refer to users or domains whereas objects are files, services, or other resources and access rights matrix specifies different kinds of privileges including read, write and execute which are assigned to subjects over objects. A configuration of the access matrix describes what subjects are authorized to do. Vulnerabilities in OSs tend to rely on weaknesses in configuration of access control matrices to gain access to software applications and system software. This creates a serious problem since vulnerabilities can exploit software applications through the OS, gain access and ultimately take over the system.

Moreover, even with an access control policy in place, consideration must be given to system design. The OSs which are in use today have different architectures and are designed with different kernels without considering security and controlled accessibility as significant design criteria. For instance, a large portion of UNIX and Linux vulnerabilities result from boundary condition errors which are commonly known as buffer overflow (Lee and Davis 2003). These boundary conditions result from a failure to check the bound size of arrays, buffers and strings. Attackers tend to exploit this weakness in UNIX and Linux systems to gain access to system software and software applications. Vulnerabilities in Windows OS on the other hand tend to be evenly divided among exceptional conditions, boundary conditions and access control validations (Lee and Davis 2003). With these types of vulnerabilities root break-ins and execution of arbitrary code are common types of attacks.

METHODOLOGY

Data Collection

In order to obtain data for the dependent variables, we used vulnerability data available in the National Vulnerability Database (NVD) between 2008 and 2014. NVD is considered one of the most reliable and comprehensive vulnerability databases on the web. NVD contains publicly known security vulnerabilities of software and hardware products aggregated from security firms, organizations, forums and advisory groups. Despite the large amount of information in NVD, for the purpose of this study, we collected the following information: the unique name and ID of the vulnerable software, the publication day of the vulnerability and the vulnerability severity score (CVSS). CVSS score was used for vulnerability severity (severity scores ranged from 0 to 10, where 0 refers to least severe vulnerability and 10 is most severe vulnerability). The publication day of the vulnerability was used to calculate vulnerability frequency. To do so, we computed the rate at which vulnerabilities occurred starting from the date of first published vulnerability until the date of the last published one. Vulnerability frequency was determined based on a monthly basis. Given the wide variety and large number of vulnerable software products on NVD, we used SPSS to choose a random sample of 227 software products.

The next step involved data gathering for the independent variables for each vulnerable software product. For each software product, we referred to software vendor's website and publically available information on the web to obtain data regarding the following software characteristics: software price, software programming language, software source code availability, and software compatibility.

Multiple Linear Regression

Multiple linear regression analysis is a mathematical maximization method which predicts the dependent variable based on the association between a dependent variable and two or more independent variables (Ryan 2009). In multiple linear regression, each variable has its own regression coefficient that gives its relative importance in the relationship outcome. According to

Brace et al. (2002), multiple linear regression is appropriate for exploring linear relationships between dependent and independent variables. Also, the dependent variable being predicted should be measured on a continuous scale and the independent variables should be measured on a ratio, interval, ordinal, or nominal scale (expressed using dummy variables). Multiple linear regression analysis involves the creation of a mathematical equation which describes the relationship between the dependent and independent variables (Keller 1997). The prediction of dependent variable (Y) is accomplished by the following equation (Levine et al. 1995):

$$Y = \beta_0 + \beta_1 X_1 + \beta_2 X_2 + \ldots + \beta_i X_i + \varepsilon$$

Where:
Y = the predicted value of Y for observation
X_i = the matrix of covariates
β_0 = Y intercept when all Xi are set to be zero
β_i = the regression coefficient for variable X_i
ε = error term

In order to examine the relationship between vulnerabilities and software characteristics, two regression models were built: a vulnerability severity model and a vulnerability frequency model. Each model included the four independent variables. We also used the proper coding for each independent variable as shown in Table 1 and Table 2. Also, prior to running the analysis, all the required assumptions were tested for each model.

Table 1: Dependent variables

Variable Name	Variable Type	Variable Descriptions & Coding
Vulnerability Severity	Ratio	The average severity level of all vulnerabilities related to a software product.
Vulnerability Frequency	Ratio	The rate at which vulnerabilities occurred over a month starting from the date of first published vulnerability until the date of the last published one.

Table 2: Independent variables

Variable	Variable Type	Variable Description and Coding
Software Price	Interval	This variable considers the price of a single software license
Software Programming Language	Nominal	Indicates the type of programming language used to develop the software. Software programming languages were divided into two groups according to the programming paradigm used. (static language=0, dynamic language=1)
Software Source Code Availability	Nominal	This variable indicates whether software source code is open, closed or mixed. Dummy variables were used in the model.
Software Compatibility	Ratio	Indicates the total number of operating systems which are compatible with the software product.

The multiple linear regression models are shown below:

$$VUL\_SEV = \beta_0 + \beta_1 PRICE + \beta_2 LANGUAGE + \beta_3 SOURCE\_DUMMY1 + \beta_4 SOURCE\_DUMMY2 + \beta_5 COMP + \varepsilon$$

$$VUL\_FRQ = \beta_0 + \beta_1 PRICE + \beta_2 LANGUAGE + \beta_3 SOURCE\_DUMMY1 + \beta_4 SOURCE\_DUMMY2 + \beta_5 COMP + \varepsilon$$

Where:
VUL_SEV = Vulnerability severity
VUL_FRQ = Vulnerability frequency
PRICE = Software Price
LANGUAGE = Software programming language
SOURCE_DUMMY1, SOURCE_DUMMY2 = Software source code availability
COMP = Software compatibility
ε = random error term

RESULTS

Multiple Linear Regression Model: Vulnerability Severity

Table 3 shows that 29.1% of the variance in vulnerability severity is explained by the model. The overall F-test for the model indicates that multiple linear regression is statistically significant at $p < 0.05$.

Table 3: Model summary for vulnerability severity

R Square	Std. Error of the Estimate
.291	1.188

Table 4 evaluated each of the predictor variables individually with respect to the dependent variable. In assessing the effect of the other predictor variables on vulnerability severity, the results showed that software compatibility (number of compatible operating systems) was the only predictor variable that had significant effect on vulnerability severity at a 5% significance level. It's important to note that including and excluding outliers made no difference to the results.

Table 4: Coefficients for the dependent variable: vulnerability severity

	Unstandardized Coefficients		Standardized Coefficients	t	Sig.
	B	Std. Error	Beta		
(Constant)	7.326	.461		13.346	.000*
Software Price	-4.983e-4	.002	-.045	-.035	.284
Software Programming Language	-.245	.567	-.064	-.935	.719
Software Source Code Availability1	.098	.473	.031	.456	.833
Software Source Code Availability2	-.674	.386	-.042	-.834	.453

	Unstandardized Coefficients		Standardized Coefficients		
Software Compatibility	.245	.043	.672	2.092	Sig.004*

* $p < 0.05$

The final multiple linear regression equation for vulnerability severity model is:

$$VUL\_SEV = 7.326 + 0.245\ (COMP)$$

The equation can be described as follows. As the number of compatible operating systems increases by 1, the severity level of a vulnerability increases by 0.245

Multiple Linear Regression Model: Vulnerability Frequency

The model, in Table 5, explained 28.1% of the variance in the dependent variable (vulnerability frequency). The overall F-test for the model indicates that multiple linear regression is statistically significant at $p < 0.05$.

Table 5: Model summary for vulnerability frequency

R Square	Std. Error of the Estimate
.281	1.303

Table 6 evaluated each of the predictor variables individually with respect to the dependent variable. In assessing the effect of the other predictor variables on vulnerability frequency, results showed that software compatibility (number of compatible operating systems) was the only predictor variables that had significant effect on vulnerability frequency at a 5% significant level.

Table 5: Coefficients for the dependent variable: vulnerability frequency

	Unstandardized Coefficients		Standardized Coefficients		
	B	Std. Error	Beta	t	Sig.
(Constant)	.452	.085		6.083	.000*
Software Price	-1.150e-4	.000	-.062	-.752	.842
Software Programming Language	.060	.027	.997	1.593	.393
Public Source Code Availability1	-.055	.049	-.038	-.411	.971
Public Source Code Availability2	-.041	.081	-.098	-.293	.830
Software Compatibility	.072	.043	.232	2.759	.002*

* $p < 0.05$

Multiple linear regression for the vulnerability frequency model produced the following equation:

$$VUL\_FRQ = 0.452 + 0.072(COMP)$$

The equation can be described as follows. As the number of compatible operating systems increases by 1, the frequency of a vulnerability increases by 0.072 per month.

DISCUSSION AND IMPLICATIONS

This paper extends previous research by examining multiple aspects of vulnerability risks including: severity level, and frequency of occurrence. Two novel vulnerability prediction models were proposed and explored for their applicability of using software characteristics to predict vulnerability risks. Both models were found to have significant associations with software characteristics. The vulnerability severity model was fitted to vulnerability data obtained from NVD and the fit was found to be statistically significant. This model observed software compatibility to have significant positive association with vulnerability severity. This result confirms with Krsul (1998) and Wurster (2010) findings that software inherit vulnerabilities from compatible operating systems. The second proposed model was based on vulnerability frequency. The model was fitted to vulnerability frequency data and the fit was found to be statistically significant. This model also observed software compatibility to have a significant positive association with vulnerability frequency.

Our study offers new insights into the area of vulnerability prediction and software security. In this research, the focus was on the external aspects of software products rather than the internal ones. Predicting vulnerabilities based on this approach has not been paid enough attention especially in the software security field. This paper tackles this limitation in research and explores the importance of external software characteristics and their effects on vulnerabilities. A research implication is the discovery of the significant role of software characteristics in predicting vulnerability severity and frequency. More specifically, the results demonstrated that software compatibility (number of compatible operating systems) has significant effect on vulnerability severity and frequency. The other research implication is the creation of two vulnerability prediction models. Such models answered the call of Alhazmi and Malaiya (2006) for the need of more quantitative vulnerability predictive models. Finally, an obvious research implication of the obtained result is the necessity of extending vulnerability risks and software characteristics to encompass other variables in order to improve predictability.

LIMITATIONS

The results presented in this study must be considered in view of certain limitations. First, the data used in the analysis comes from the National Vulnerability Database (NVD). NVD is known as the most reliable vulnerability database but it still suffers from inaccuracies and missing information. In future research, it would be more appropriate to combine NVD with other vulnerability databases such as Open Source Vulnerability database (OSVD) to overcome this limitation. Second, it's important to note that this research analyzed publically reported vulnerabilities without considering unreported/undisclosed data. While this drawback is common among vulnerability research, overcoming this limitation can be achieved through direct contact with software vendors which can be an extension for future research. Third, given the limited information available on software products, the proposed models only considered four external software characteristics. Future research may benefit from considering more software characteristics.

CONCLUSION

This study examined the effects of external software characteristics on vulnerability severity and vulnerability frequency. Our findings offer new insights into the area of vulnerability and software security. The results showed that the number of compatible operating systems has a positive effect on the severity level and frequency of vulnerabilities. Also, this study showed that there is no relationship between each of software price, software programming language, software source availability and vulnerability severity. Similarly, there was no relationship between these characteristics and software frequency. Future research should examine other software characteristics in order to better understand their effect on vulnerabilities.

REFERENCES

Alhazmi, O. H., & Malaiya, Y. K. (2005a). Quantitative vulnerability assessment of systems software. In Proc. annual reliability and maintainability symposium (pp. 615-620).

Alhazmi, O. H., & Malaiya, Y. K. (2005b). Modeling the vulnerability discovery process. In Software Reliability Engineering, 2005. ISSRE 2005. 16th IEEE International Symposium on (pp. 10-pp). IEEE.

Alhazmi, O. H., & Malaiya, Y. K. (2006). Measuring and enhancing prediction capabilities of vulnerability discovery models for Apache and IIS HTTP servers. In Software Reliability Engineering, 2006. ISSRE'06. 17th International Symposium on (pp. 343-352). IEEE.

Arbaugh, W.A., Fithen, W. L. and McHugh, J. (2000), Windows of Vulnerability: A Case Study Analysis, IEEE Computer.

Brown, W. A., and Booch, G. (2002). Reusing Open-Source Software and Practices: The Impact of Open-Source on Commercial Vendors, in C. Gacek (ed.), Software Reuse: Methods, Techniques, and Tools, New York: Springer-Verlag, 123-13.

Browne, H., McHugh, J., Arbaugh, W., and Fithen, W. (2001). A Trend Analysis of Exploitations. IEEE Symposium on Security and Privacy.

Cowan, C., Wagle, P., and Pu, C. (1999). Buffer Overflows: Attacks and Defenses for the Vulnerability of the Decade, DARPA Information Survivability Conference and Expo.

De Ru, W.G., Eloff, J.H.P. (1996), "Risk analysis modelling with the use of fuzzy logic", Computers and Security, Vol. 15 No.3, pp.239-48

Dillman, D. A. (2000). Mail and Internet Surveys: The Tailored Design Method, Wiley, New York.

Dr Dobbs Journal (2009). Open Source Study Reveals High Level of Code Reuse. Retrieved on Jan 25th 2011 at http://www.drdobbs.com/open-source/216401796

Gopal, R., and Sanders, G. (2000). Global software piracy: You can't get blood out of a turnip. Communications of the ACM, 43(9), 83–89.

Hoare, C. A. R. (1974). Hints on Programming Language Design. Computer Systems Reliability: State of the Art Report, Vol. 20, pp. 505-34.

Kirk, J. (2013). Deep cyberattacks cause millions in losses for U.S. banks. Retrieved from http://www.computerworld.com/article/2484007/malware-vulnerabilities/deep-cyberattacks-cause-millions-in-losses-for-u-s--banks.html

Krsul I. V. (1998). Software Vulnerability Analysis. PhD thesis, Purdue University.

Lee, S. C., and Davis, L. B. (2003). Learning from experience: Operating system vulnerability trends. IT Professional, 5(1).

Littlewood, B., Brocklehurst, S., Fenton, N., Mellor, P., Page, S., Wright, D., & Gollmann, D. (1993). Towards operational measures of computer security. Journal of computer security, 2(3), 211-229.

Mell P., Scarfone K., and Romanosky S., "A Complete Guide to the Common Vulnerability Scoring System Version 2.0," Forum of Incident Response and Security Teams, June 2007, http://www.first.org/cvss/cvssEguide.html.

Mercuri, R. T. (2003). Analyzing security costs. Comm. ACM 46(6) 15–18

Murtaza, S. S., Khreich, W., Hamou-Lhadj, A., & Bener, A. (2016). Mining Trends and Patterns of Software Vulnerabilities. Journal of Systems and Software.

Ozment, A. "Improving Vulnerability Discovery Models," Proc. 2007 ACM Workshop on Quality of Protection, ACM Press, 2007, pp. 6-11.

Parrend, P., Frenot, S. (2008). Classification of Component Vulnerabilities in Java Service Oriented Programming (SOP) Platforms. In: CBSE 2008. LNCS, p80-96, Springer Berlin/Heidelberg.

Payne, C. (2002). On the security of open source software. Information Systems Journal, 12(1), 61-78.

Peace, A. G., Galletta, D. F., & Thong, J. Y. L. (2003). Software piracy in the workplace: A model and empirical test. Journal of Management Information Systems, 20, 153E177.

Pham, N. H., Nguyen, T. T., Nguyen, H. A., Wang, X., Nguyen, A. T., and Nguyen, T. N. (2010). Detecting Recurring and Similar Software Vulnerabilities. Proceedings of the 32nd International Conference on Software Engineering (ICSE 2010).

Poulsen, K. (2003). Thwarted Linux backdoor hints at smarter hacks. Retrieved from at: http://www.securityfocus.com/news/7388

Raymond, E.S., and B. Young. (2001). The Cathedral and the Bazaar: Musings on Linux and Open Source by an Accidental Revolutionary. O'Reilly, Sebastopol, CA.

Ryan T. (2009). Modern Regression Methods. New York, NY: Wiley Interscience.

Scandariato, R., Walden, J., Hovsepyan, A., & Joosen, W. (2014). Predicting vulnerable software components via text mining. Software Engineering, IEEE Transactions on, 40(10), 993-1006.

Schiffman, M. (2007), A Complete Guide to the Common Vulnerability Scoring System (CVSS). http://www.first.org/cvss/cvss-guide.html

Schmidt, A.D., Schmidt, H.G., Batyuk, L., Clausen, J.H., Camtepe, S.A., Al-bayrak, S. (2009). Smartphone Malware Evolution Revisited: Android Next Target? In: Proceedings of the 4th International Conference on Malicious and Unwanted Software (MALWARE).

Shaw, D. S.; Post, J. M. and Ruby, K. G. (1999). Inside the minds of the insider, Security Management, 43(12) 34E44.

Shin, Y., & Williams, L. (2013). Can traditional fault prediction models be used for vulnerability prediction?. Empirical Software Engineering, 18(1), 25-59.

Tevis, J. (2005). Automatic Detection of Software Security Vulnerabilities in Executable Program Files. Dissertation submitted to the Department of Computer Science. Auburn University. Auburn, AL.

Wurster, G. (2010). Security Mechanisms and Policy for Mandatory Access Control in Computer Systems. PhD thesis, Carleton University.

DECISION SCIENCES INSTITUTE

Experiential Learning Theory: Evidence from a Study Abroad Program

Satish Nargundkar
Georgia State University
Email: snargundkar@gsu.edu

Milind Shrikhande
Georgia State University
Email: mshrikhande@gsu.edu

ABSTRACT

We propose an integrated model for the design of study abroad programs in RCB, and strategies to measure the effectiveness of such programs. Our integrated design of the study abroad program is based on the Experiential Learning Theory (ELT) proposed in the literature. Effectiveness of the program was measured in terms of cognitive and affective domain learning objectives, using several measures including case analyses, surveys, reflection papers, and team projects. The instructional innovation contained in this integrated approach was successful by all measures. Implications for faculty members involved in designing experiential learning programs, especially study abroad programs, are discussed.

KEYWORDS: Experiential Learning Theory, Study Abroad Programs, Program Design, BEVI Survey, Cognitive and Affective Domains, Instructional Innovation, Integrated Approach

INTRODUCTION

Employers today expect business schools to ensure that students are exposed to some practical "real-world" experience before graduation, so that they are ready to enter the workforce without requiring too much additional training. There is a perceived gap between theory and practice in business education curricula in general. Johnson (2014) identifies a perceived gap in accounting education and practice, while Stringfellow, Ennis, Brennan & Harker (2006) discuss a similar gap between marketing education and practice. Sullivan and Rosin (2008) suggest that the goal of higher education is to provide a link between theory and practice. To achieve this goal, the educational environment needs to create rich connections between the theoretical and experiential curricula (Bass, 2012).

Experiential learning can help bridge the gap between theory and practice. This refers to any approach that helps students in applying their knowledge and conceptual understanding to real-world. This helps students learn to think critically and achieve a higher level of learning. Experiential learning can be achieved either through immersion in a real-world situation, or through a simulation of a real-world problem in a classroom. Simulations in the traditional classroom could include activities such as cases and problem-based studies, projects, or other active learning initiatives (Wurdinger & Carlson, 2010). However, when students are immersed in authentic environments such as internships, field placements, clinical experiences or research projects, the learning becomes significantly more real. Study abroad programs offer a great opportunity for real-world education via immersion in a foreign, unfamiliar culture. It provides a rich source of experiences for students that are difficult, if not impossible to mimic in a classroom.

In order to ensure higher level learning, however, a study abroad program must be designed appropriately, based on sound theoretical foundations. Measuring the effectiveness of such programs through valid instruments is necessary to ensure that the program does not become a glorified vacation (Passarelli and Kolb, 2011). The fundamental question we address is whether higher level learning in both the cognitive and affective domains (Bloom, Englehart, Furst, Hill, & Krathwohl, 1956) can be achieved through a study abroad program that is designed in keeping with the tenets of an underlying theory. We use Kolb's (1984) Experiential Learning Theory (ELT) as the basis for our study abroad program design. Our research is based on one study abroad program that took undergraduate students to India.

The paper is organized into the following sections. In the next section, we briefly describe the basic tenets of ELT, followed by the design of the instructional innovation in our study abroad program to take into account this theory of learning. We then discuss the methodology used to measure student learning, the results achieved, and the discussion and conclusion.

EXPERIENTIAL LEARNING THEORY

Kolb's (1984, p. 41) Experiential Learning Theory (ELT) sees learning as "the process whereby knowledge is created through the transformation of experience. Knowledge results from the combination of grasping and transforming experience". The grasping, or gathering of knowledge, is divided into two related modes, that of concrete experience (CE) and abstract conceptualization (AC), while the transforming of knowledge consists of reflective observation (RO) and active experimentation (AE). According to ELT, the four stages of learning begin with concrete experiences that form the basis for reflections, which allow a person to generalize the learning by forming abstract concepts and models of how the world functions. These concepts can be put to the test by acting upon them in real life. These actions test the concepts and also create new experiences to continue the learning cycle. Figure 1, adapted from Passarelli & Kolb (2011), depicts the learning cycle.

Figure 1: The learning cycle, adapted from Passarelli & Kolb (2011)

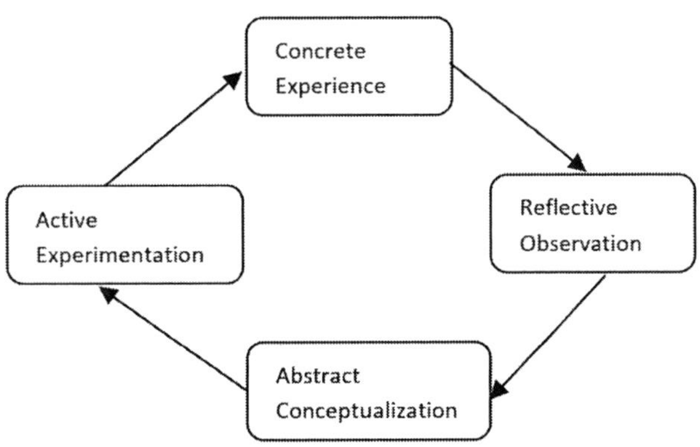

In order to help students go through this learning cycle, the study abroad program must be designed in a holistic way that permits the integration of experiences into meaningful change in the students' perception of the world, as opposed to a shallow, skimming experience that is enjoyed but soon forgotten.

The role of the instructors here is to ensure that the right kind of experiences are made available, time and resources provided for reflection on the experiences, guidance in the formation of abstract concepts, and the setting of boundaries and goals to actively experiment with the newly developed ideas. This requires flexibility on the part of the instructor to function occasionally as the subject matter expert, while at other times stepping back into the role of facilitator or coach. Equally important is the role of a standard setter and evaluator to ensure the quality of experiences delivered to the students as well the expectations regarding the quality of student contributions. Unlike in a traditional classroom, where the instructor is generally the sole provider of knowledge, a study abroad program requires co-ordination between multiple sources of information, such as company executives, faculty members at partner educational institutions in the foreign country, as well as trained tour guides. Further, study abroad programs require the instructors to build relationships with students that go beyond mere exposition of content, to act as catalysts for transformative experiences.

THE INNOVATIVE DESIGN OF OUR STUDY ABROAD PROGRAM

Keeping in mind the elements of ELT, we incorporated specific ideas in our design of the study abroad program. Experiences provided to the students were aligned with tasks that permitted immediate reflection and abstraction, followed by an opportunity for active experimentation, to complete the learning cycle depicted in Figure 1. Several such learning cycles were incorporated into the two-week program. One such cycle, the design thinking workshop, is illustrated here.

Design Thinking Workshop

Students were first given a day long city tour of Hyderabad, India, where they visited several locations of historical and cultural significance (the city tour was organized by the Indian School of Business, Hyderabad). This was their first exposure to India, beyond the airport. During the course of the day, students visited a Hindu temple, an old fort, and an Indian bazaar known for bangles and pearl jewelry, and a museum known for rare collections gathered by a single person from around the world. Besides the obvious learning from these visits, students experienced the chaos, noise, and color of the streets, which was in their words "unlike any we have experienced before". The juxtapositions of modern and ancient, and the rich and the very poor were also evident to them on the streets of Hyderabad in India. This was the concrete experience (CE) phase of the learning cycle. In the evening, they were asked to reflect on what they experienced, and make notes for their reflections paper (RO) that was due at the end of the trip.

The next day, students attended a day-long Design Thinking Workshop (conducted by Mr. Rajib Ghosh and Shipra of DLabs in Hyderabad), which began with an introduction to the concept of design thinking (Brown, 2008). Students were encouraged to think about the needs of the people of India and possible products or services that would help solve some of the problems in that society. Students came up with various ideas for possible products. For instance, having observed that women in India commonly wear ornamental nose rings, one suggestion from students in order to alleviate the effects of air pollution in Indian cities was to wear air filters disguised as nose jewelry (AC).

By the end of the day, students were assigned the task of analyzing consumer personalities by examining the contents of their wallets (an in-class simulation where neighboring students exchanged their wallets and analyzed each other). This was followed by an analysis of the service that a wallet provides, and how the underlying needs that are addressed by the wallet could be better addressed by a redesign of the wallet. Students worked in teams to develop ideas for alternate designs of the wallet to address one specific shortcoming each, such as lack of ease in accessing cards, or a desire among people to have a variety of wallets without buying new ones often. The teams then created a prototype of their new designs using materials like paper, clips, string, tape and scissors (AE). They then presented these ideas to the cohort along with a demonstration of their prototype product.

Through this two-day experience, students went through the entire learning cycle of CE (city tour), RO (reflection in the evening), AC (new way of thinking about the needs of the consumers in this culture), and AE (designing and building a prototype of a new product idea).

Several other learning cycles provided to students included: 1. Company visits followed by related analysis, 2. an active learning session on business negotiations, with instruction on the differences in negotiation methods and norms between the US and India. The students got an opportunity to put this new knowledge to practice the very next day during a visit to a market of Indian handicrafts known for negotiation and bargaining as the expected way of shopping. Thus, the program design repeatedly ensured that students went through the entire learning cycle in a meaningful way, rather than a haphazard collection of activities and sightseeing.

MEASURING THE EFFECTIVENESS OF THE INNOVATION

The following items were used in assessing student learning and transformation as a result of the program.

1. Pre-departure assignments to evaluate baseline cognitive ability.
2. Surveys to measure perceptions of learning and overall satisfaction with the program.
3. BEVI survey to measure changes in attitudes, beliefs, and values about life in general.
4. Evaluation of reflection papers completed individually by students, to evaluate the program objectives in the affective domain, by assessing student perceptions of their entire experience.
5. Evaluation of capstone projects completed by teams. This helped us assess the level of critical thinking as well as student understanding of the new cultural environment.

Pre-departure Assignments

Students worked on some assignments individually to analyze cases of business that entered the Indian market, such as Oreo's ad Fiat, to illustrate two major industry segments – consumer goods and consumer durables. They were given an orientation lecture on the history, political structure, and socio-economic factors pertaining to India. Students were also introduced to the CAGE (cultural, administrative, geographic, and economic) framework to help analyze international business ventures. Students were selected into the program based on their majors (typically Finance and Managerial Sciences) and high GPAs. Twenty two students were selected out of about 50 applicants to the program. They were thus expected to perform well, and we used their case analyses to gauge how well they could apply their understanding of the history and culture of India from classroom experience alone.

Effectiveness Surveys

Effectiveness of a study abroad program can be assessed in two different domains. First, the traditional methods of setting course learning objectives in the cognitive domain, and assessing student performance on assignments, projects and cases, as well as using survey instruments to gauge student perception of their own learning. This was achieved in our program by having them complete a session-by-session feedback form where they rated the effectiveness of each

session on a 5-point Likert scale. Appendix A shows a sample set of questions from the survey. The entire survey has not been included due to its length. However, it is available upon request. All 22 students that went on the trip completed this survey. Averages were computed for each question on the survey, and any open-ended comments were noted. Students were also administered a survey by the University Study Abroad Programs (USAP) office on overall program effectiveness, which included questions on the organization of the trip and the instructor responsiveness throughout the trip, in addition to overall academic quality of the program. Appendix B shows a sample set of questions from the USAP survey.
In addition, individual reflection papers and team projects were evaluated by the instructors to gauge their learning as it related to the cognitive student learning outcomes set out in the syllabus (Garth and Niu, 2010). Sixteen of the 22 students completed this survey. Once again, average scores were computed for each question and comments aggregated.

BEVI Survey

The second, perhaps higher level of learning, that ought to take place in an experiential, immersive program is the changing of attitudes and beliefs about life in general (affective domain), leading to a new world view that can help them adapt better to a changing global environment, as well as the building of relationships with their fellow travelers. The BEVI survey was used to assess these kinds of learning outcomes in the affective domain. The BEVI instrument has been developed and refined by various researchers over several years, and has been validated in many studies (Shealy, 2004; Shealy, 2005). The survey contains 185 questions that represent 17 scales related to beliefs, life events, and values. Some of the scales include, for instance, demographic information, Negative life events, Needs fulfilment, Emotional attunement, and Socio-cultural openness. For a detailed discussion on the BEVI survey, along with a list of the 17 scales and information on the reliability and validity, please see the following website - http://www.thebevi.com/aboutbevi.php#aboutShort. We administered the survey to the students both before and after the trip, in order to measure the changes in the affective domain. We further plan to have the students take the survey one more time, 3-6 months past the trip, to gauge longer-term, transformative changes in their beliefs or values.
Twenty two students went on the study abroad trip. Twenty of them completed the BEVI survey before departure, while 14 of the original 20 completed it post trip. Among the 14, four were dropped from the analysis due to inconsistent answers. The pre/post comparison was done for the 10 valid responses.

Reflection Papers

Students were asked to keep a journal to record the highlights of their daily experiences, and turned in a reflections paper individually at the end of the program. These papers helped us assess some of the affective level learning outcomes. Based on Bloom's (1956) taxonomy, we wanted to gauge whether students went beyond the basic levels of receiving and responding to the higher levels of valuing, articulating and being personally transformed by the experience.

Capstone Projects

Students worked in teams of three on capstone projects at the end of the study abroad trip to create a plan for an existing or new business to enter the Indian market, with an analysis of the financial feasibility and a marketing plan that took the culture into account. The projects helped us gauge their critical thinking ability, as well as how their experience helped them understand the Indian market and consumers beyond their pre-departure understanding from classroom lectures alone.

RESULTS

The results from each of the three surveys are summarized below.

Survey 1: Session-by-session feedback

Feedback on each session conducted during the study abroad program. This included a couple of sessions before departure to India, to provide perspectives on India regarding the political, socio-cultural, and economic climate for business. Some of the survey questions and their results are shown in Appendix A. Table 1 below shows the overall evaluations based on this survey.

Table 1: Overall Evaluation of Various Elements of the Study Abroad Program

OVERALL EVALUATION	AVERAGE SCORE
Quality of academic program	4.96
Quality of lodging (ISB-Hyderabad and ISB-Mohali)	4.91
Quality of Food (ISB-Hyderabad and ISB-Mohali)	4.90
Quality of lodging (ITC Mughal, Agra and The Lalit, New Delhi)	4.95
Quality of Food (ITC Mughal, Agra and The Lalit, New Delhi)	4.95
India study-abroad: Overall experience	5.00

n=22 (100% response rate)

The average score on each of the above 5 elements was over 4.90, indicating a high level of satisfaction among students with the overall experience.
As illustrated earlier, one of the learning cycles involved included a city tour of Hyderabad followed by the design thinking workshop the next day. The average scores for the city tour and the workshop were 4.9 and 4.7 respectively. The high scores reflect the benefits the students perceived from the combination of activities that helped create a richer learning experience. The other example of a learning cycle involving the session on business negotiations received scores of 5.0 and 4.9 respectively.

Survey 2: Evaluation of program directors by study abroad programs office

The results on the key items in this survey by the study abroad office are shown in Table 2.

Table 2: Evaluation of program directors and other aspects of the program

PLEASE RATE YOUR PROGRAM DIRECTORS (FACULTY) ON THE FOLLOWING:	AVERAGE SCORE OUT OF 5.00
Support and guidance provided throughout the program	4.94
Ability to handle emergency situations	4.72
Insight into the host country's culture provided by the directors	4.94
Were the directors available when needed	4.81
Courses you took abroad	5.00
Pre-departure schedule	4.69
Daily Schedule	4.54
Excursions/Travel arrangements	4.94
Living arrangements	5.00

Survey 3: The BEVI survey

The BEVI survey results begin with some demographic information on the sample. Some of the results are shown in Table 3 below.

Table 3: Demographics from BEVI survey	
DIMENSION	DISTRIBUTION
Gender	Females 6, Males 4
Nationality	US Citizens 6, Others 4
Ethnicity	Caucasians 5, Others 5
Religion	Christian 5, Others 5

Several of the BEVI scores are reported in three segments, representing the top 30%, the middle 30%, and the lower 40% in terms of the overall scores on the complete scale. The overall scores represent how well-adjusted people are emotionally in their lives. Interestingly, those who scored in the top third had a family income of only $13,000 per year, the middle third reported $53,000 on average, and the lower 40% reported $70,000 on average. Those in the top 30% of BEVI scores reported three times as many negative life events as those in the bottom 40%. They, however, reported a much higher value for fulfilment of basic needs, indicating that those students with a difficult background in terms of economic hardship and negative events in their life were more resilient than their peers.
As discussed in the description of the BEVI survey earlier, the results of the survey are summarized as scores on various scales, such as *Negative Life Events*, *Self-Certitude*, and *Ecological Resonance*. A comparison of the before trip and after trip scores on the various scales for the three segments shows some interesting changes in the scores of students on these scales after the trip. The direction of changes in scores for this and a few other scales after the trip are shown in Table 4 below:

Table 4: Post trip changes in students on some of the BEVI scales, by segment			
BEVI SCALE	LOWEST 40%	MIDDLE 30%	TOP 30%
Negative Life Events	Increased	Decreased	Unchanged
Identity Diffusion	Increased	Decreased	Decreased
Self-Certitude	Decreased	Decreased	Decreased
Socioemotional Convergence	Decreased	Increased	Increased
Gender Traditionalism	Decreased	Increased	Decreased
Ecological Resonance	Unchanged	Increased	Increased

For instance, *Self-Certitude* scores decreased among all three segments of students. In other words, students' perception of who they were and what life is like became less certain after the trip. This is an interesting but expected finding. When exposed to a new, unfamiliar culture in a developing economy, fundamental assumptions about life get challenged. It is therefore not surprising that students' certainty about their understanding of life went down.
Similarly, *Negative Life Event* scores (perception of negative life events experienced) went up among the lowest 40% (the ones with the lowest scores overall and the highest family income levels), while decreasing among the middle 30%, and remaining unchanged among the top 30% (the ones with the highest scores overall and the lowest family income levels). In other words, students who had already faced challenges in their lives (the top 30%) were not as strongly affected by the exposure to the poverty and challenges faced by the people in India, as students that had not faced similar challenges in their lives (the lowest 40%).

Qualitative Feedback

Besides the quantitative responses to the surveys reported above, students made several comments in writing on the surveys and their reflection papers. We also got feedback verbally, both during the trip itself, as well as during a debriefing meeting within a few weeks of returning from the trip. Since the trip ended on Christmas Eve, the debriefing session was held around the end of January when the next semester was underway.

A few of the comments from the students:

1. *This was a life changing experience that I have recommended to everyone that I can. Overall it was incredible and my only real complaint is that we couldn't stay longer!*

2. *I learned more in 10 days than in a (typical) semester. The last night there I cried because I didn't know why I hadn't taken advantage of these opportunities earlier.*

3. *Truly fantastic program. Would like to see slightly more briefing before meetings/lectures.*

4. *Build more rest days into the program and don't be hesitant to extend the trip beyond Xmas. Few American families would have a problem with postponing Xmas for a trip to India.*

5. *Overall, every professor (GSU included), tour guide, student, etc. were all clearly passionate and genuinely interested in the well-being of our group. Amazing to see such personal behavior in an academic program. Hope to see this program continue, as emerging markets are incredibly important, especially now.*

Excerpts from Reflection Papers

1. *When we arrive in Hyderabad, the first thing that strikes me as we step out of the airport is the constant buzzing in the humid sticky "winter" air. The traffic noise follows us around India and never completely settles, except for the quiet moments we get to spend on the ISB campus. My first encounter of the "perfect chaos" of the Indian traffic happens the very same day when we take a taxicab to the mall. It is a trip to remember – the traffic is fast-paced, appears to have very little structure, and in the absence of rear-view mirrors honking is the only means of communication on the road. Most roads are somewhat underdeveloped, in need of major repair – they are an ongoing concern in India, which is growing too fast and seriously lacks infrastructure to accommodate the high-paced growth of the industries, and distribution of goods and services. It can be a major setback that will put any business venture in jeopardy by causing significant delays in distribution and delivery. However, where one may see only limitations, another may see countless business opportunities. Indeed, India appears to have an unexplored niche for logistics services that will only strengthen as the infrastructure continues to grow.*

2. *It's hard to visit India without any presumptions. Everyone who knew I was going thought that I was going to have some sort of "spiritual awakening." That I would find my inner peace, or my personal god, or any other cliché westerners might attach to an eastern country with such a deep history. This is not to say that people do not experience this in some way when they visit India. As we learned, India is a very large country with 236*

different types of people (as consumer segments for marketing efforts) just in New Delhi. This means a person could have any combination of experiences when visiting. Personally, I saw our visit as a full lifetime in two weeks. There were times when our lives were full from the beauty of it all, and there were times when life hit hard. In this paper, I hope to reflect on my experience with Indian education, business, and culture.

Capstone Projects

Students worked in seven teams of three students each (one team had four students) and turned in projects where they chose a product or service for which they developed a business plan for entering the Indian market. The selection of their products or services alone helped us gauge how the in-country experience deepened their understanding of the needs of the market. We had expected them to write reports on large, branded, multinational firms' products or services. Instead, students' ideas included some of the following:

a. Bariatric oxygen chambers in hospitals for diabetes patients, given the high incidence of diabetes in India and the high rate of long term disability.
b. Wearable air-filters, given the severe air pollution in major Indian cities.
c. A recycling company partnering with a local firm to launch a pilot project in the city of Mumbai.

Students directly tied their product/service ideas to their personal experiences within the country, and quickly identified some of the key needs of people there. Their reports also showed empathy for the problems faced by the people, and their economic limitations.
Overall, the projects demonstrated the level of critical thinking expected of the level of students in the program, but went beyond our expectations in the affective domain. They were able to clearly articulate the unique circumstances of the Indian market, and plan accordingly. Their writing demonstrated the extent to which they had transformed their worldview from a US centric perspective to one that showed awareness of the differences in emerging markets.

DISCUSSION AND IMPLICATIONS

The quantitative results from the basic evaluation surveys clearly indicated that students rated the program highly, both in academic content as well as the overall experience of travel and living arrangements. The BEVI survey results are a little more complex to interpret. First, since the sample size is small in just one travel abroad program, it is hard to generalize the results too much. We see this as a first step, with follow up studies to be conducted with future study abroad programs from our college to various countries. Second, there is some evidence that immediately after a trip, there tends to be a bit of a backlash effect in terms of students attitudes. A trip to a completely foreign culture can be overwhelming, causing students to occasionally "retreat" into more narrow worldviews, contrary to the expectation of expanding horizons. However, around six months after the trip, a third survey can reveal the true long term changes. The third survey will be conducted within the next few months, and may provide additional insights.
A couple of interesting and unequivocal changes in the students as seen on the BEVI include a decrease in Self-certitude scores, and an increase in Ecological resonance. Self-certitude indicates a strong sense of will and a lack of patience with others' difficulties, and disinclination towards deep analysis. A person with a high score would be the kind to say "don't make excuses, think positively and get the job done." A lowering of the score implies an increase in compassion towards others' situation, and greater thought regarding life, and less certainty about one's opinions. Seeing the abject poverty among some of the people in India, as well as a

very different culture could have had this effect on students. This is a positive change that indicates a growth in critical thinking ability as well as emotional maturity. Ecological resonance deals with one's concern for the environment, and the fate of the earth or natural world. An increase in scores here indicates a greater concern for the earth. Once again, experiencing firsthand the level of air and noise pollution in Indian cities, the lack of infrastructure to deal with urban problems adequately by western standards, likely had a positive impact on the students' concern for the environment in general.

While the BEVI report is too detailed to report in full, the above excerpts suffice to indicate that the study abroad program did more than simply create academic, discipline based value. There are clear indications of change in beliefs and values held by the students.

Our evaluation of the students' reflection papers as well as their team based capstone projects also confirmed for us that they were engaged fully in thinking critically about business and culture. Students demonstrated a professional ability in developing business plans with an appropriate entry mode, marketing strategy, financial feasibility, and analysis of the cultural, social, and other issues the business may face. Some of the teams came up with innovative ideas for products/services that further lent credence to the increase in ecological resonance found in the BEVI survey results.

Implications for Faculty conducting study abroad programs

Unlike in a traditional classroom, a study abroad program places a greater burden on the faculty members who conceive of and implement such a program. Careful planning is needed, and thought must be given to how the academic goals will be achieved. Far too many programs are run without a good theoretical underpinning in the design of the activities. Often third party companies organize tours of various countries and take care of travel and living arrangements and company visits. However, there is often no host institution, and the trips can be hit or miss. The company visits and travel are good experiences, but without careful planning, students do not get the opportunity to complete integrated learning cycles as described in the ELT. The reflection, abstraction, and testing phases are often not thought through sufficiently, and the learning can remain incomplete. We believe it is important to design all four activities of the ELT into the program in different ways. To this end, it is beneficial, in our opinion, to have a host institution as a partner in the country you are visiting, to provide a base for academic discussion with local faculty who are experts in doing business in that cultural setting.

This level of planning does place a burden on the faculty doing the planning, especially in the first couple of iterations. A couple of hundred hours were spent by us over a year to plan and implement this study abroad. The planning involves several key aspects:

1. Academic content, including designing the courses, getting them approved in the college, and communicating the content delivery needs to the host institution.
2. Travel arrangements to the host country and travel within that country, including excursions, company visits, and travel between cities as needed. As mentioned before, the mix of academic sessions, city tours, and company visits must be carefully planned, taking into account the learning objectives and learning theory. Travel guides, for example, must be knowledgeable and certified. The guides that accompanied our students to the historical sites, for instance, were certified by the Archaeological Society of India.
3. Attracting and recruiting the right students. This may involve several rounds of talking to various classes to publicize the program, coordinating with the college and university to follow their procedures, interviewing students to ensure that they are motivated enough, and to alleviate any concerns they may have about foreign travel. Putting students in

touch with scholarship opportunities is important. Students also may need help with getting a passport and the appropriate visa to visit the country in question.

4. Making sure students understand expectations for the trip, including emergency procedures, other policies to be followed during travel, as well as a general orientation to the host country prior to departure.
5. Managing the budget and ensuring that the program breaks even. The pricing of the program is a key decision that must be made to ensure that it is low enough to attract enough students and high enough to cover the costs.

Implications beyond study abroad programs

While this paper focused on the design of a study abroad program using ELT, the same idea can be used for experiential learning within a local setting. For instance, a factory visit or a field trip could form the basis for creating the learning cycle espoused by ELT. Making sure that students have time to reflect on the concrete experience, create abstractions, and actively experiment with the learning is the broader implication of this innovation.

CONCLUSION AND FUTURE RESEARCH

Study abroad programs are a rich source of learning for students, and have the potential to be life changing experiences with effective design and implementation. Such programs are one instance of immersive, experiential learning where faculty have an opportunity to build relationships with students that go beyond dissemination of knowledge, and move into a mentoring or coaching role.

How generalizable are the results of this study? This research demonstrated the effectiveness of a program based on ELT in achieving both cognitive and affective goals. We believe that designing a study abroad program using the ELT as a theoretical underpinning and creating a rigorous process to select students will achieve the cognitive goals of helping students think critically. The direction of changes in the affective domain as described by the BEVI results will depend on the backgrounds of the students and the country visited. However, we believe that the experience of a study abroad program will transform students in significant ways.

For future research, collecting data across multiple such programs over multiple years can help us examine specific country effects, as well as permit longitudinal analyses.

APPENDIX A

Session by Session Effectiveness Survey (This is a sample of the questions on the survey). The boldfaced numbers show the average scores received on each question.

Atlanta: November 7th	
Introduction to program (3 hours) Emily Caskey (Travel, GSU expectations), Satish Nargundkar (Geography, languages, arts, Hindi lesson) • Felt rushed, the geography and language session • Especially language, more time for practice needed	1 2 3 4 5 **4.5**
India – History and Political economy (3 hours) Milind Shrikhande (History since ancient times, Political regimes since independence, Societal changes, Financial implications).	1 2 3 4 5 **4.6**

• Enjoyed use of videos and lecture format • Overall lot of information, well structured • Great information for visits later in India	
Atlanta: November 14th	
India – Culture and Management (3 hours) Satish Nargundkar (Modes of Entry (Oreos case), CAGE model, Segmentation/Excel, Process Innovation) • Useful for projects • Overall good practical information	1 2 3 4 5 **4.8**
India – Economy and Growth (3 hours) Milind Shrikhande (India as an economic superpower, International comparison, Growth indicators, Fiat/Tata joint venture case) • Good lecture – important for course objectives • A lot of information – very condensed	1 2 3 4 5 **4.6**
Hyderabad: December 14th	
City Tour: Birla mandir, Salar Jung museum, Charminar, Golconda fort (8 hours) Miss Raiza • All places really beautiful, educating and worth visiting • Could be devoted more than one day • Incredible, eye-opening introduction to India	1 2 3 4 5 **4.9**
Hyderabad: December 15th	
Design Thinking Workshop (8 hours) Rajib Ghosh and Shipra • Fun learning creative ways for emerging markets • Knowledge gained definitely will be applied lot • Speakers were great, thoroughly enjoyed the session!	1 2 3 4 5 **4.7**

Appendix B

University Study Abroad Programs (USAP) office Survey
(This is a sample of the questions on the survey)

1. How satisfied were you with your Program Director's ability to provide guidance and support before & during the program?

2. How satisfied were you with the insight into the host country's culture and/or history that your Program Director provided?

3. Please describe how your Program Director provided insight into the host country's culture and/or history (ex: pre-departure orientation, classroom discussions, cultural excursions, etc):

4. How satisfied were you with the course(s) you took abroad?

5. Please rate each of the following as it applied to your program:
    a. Pre-Departure preparation
    b. Daily schedule
    c. Program-related excursions, visits,tours, activities
    d. Arrangements of group travel
    e. Living arrangements

6. If applicable, how satisfied were you with your Program Director's ability to handle any emergency situations?

REFERENCES

Bass, R. (2012). Disrupting Ourselves: The Problem of Learning in Higher Education, *EDUCAUSE Review*, 47:2, March/April 2012.

Bloom, B., Englehart, M. Furst, E., Hill, W., & Krathwohl, D. (1956). *Taxonomy of educational objectives: The classification of educational goals. Handbook I: Cognitive domain*. New York, Toronto: Longmans, Green.

Boyatzis, R. E., Kolb, D. A., and C. Mainemelis (2000). Experiential Learning Theory: Previous Research and New Directions, in Sternberg, R. J., and L. F. Zhang (Eds.), *Perspectives on Cognitive, Learning and Thinking Styles.* NJ: Lawrence Erlbaum.

Brown, T. (2008). Design Thinking, *Harvard Business Review*, June, pp. 85-92.

Garth, C. and R. Niu (2010). Assessing International Learning: A Mixed Methodological Approach to Assessing Curricular and Extracurricular International Experiences, *The Journal of General Education*, Vol. 59, No. 3, pp. 159-171.

Johnson, R. (2014), Accounting Practitioners Reflect On Faculty Impact: Bridging The Gap Between Theory And Practice, *American Journal of Business Education (AJBE*), 7: 2.

Kolb, D. A. (1984). *Experiential learning: experience as the source of learning and development.* Englewood Cliffs, NJ: Prentice Hall.

Passarelli, A., and D. A. Kolb (2011). Using Experiential Learning Theory to Promote Student Learning and Development in Programs of Education Abroad, WP-11-03, Department of Organizational Behavior, Weatherhead School of Management, Case Western Reserve University. Cleveland, OH 44106-7235.

Shealy, C. N. 2004. A model and method for “making” a combined-integrated psychologist: Equilintegration (EI) Theory, and the Beliefs, Events, and Values Inventory (BEVI). *Journal of Clinical Psychology* 60 (10): 1065-1090.

Shealy, C. N. (2005). Justifying the justification hypothesis: Scientific-humanism, Equilintegration (EI) theory, and the Beliefs, Events, and Values Inventory (BEVI). *Journal of Clinical Psychology*, Vol. 61, No. 1, pp. 81-106.

Stringfellow, L., Ennis, S., Brennan, R., & M. J. Harker, (2006) "Mind the gap: The relevance of marketing education to marketing practice", Marketing Intelligence & Planning, 24:3, pp.245 – 256.

Sullivan, W. M., & Rosen, M. S. (2008). *A New Agenda for Higher Education: Shaping a Life of the Mind for Practice*, San Francisco, CA: Jossey-Bass.

Würdinger, S. D., & Carlson, J. A. (2010). *Teaching for experiential learning: Five approaches*, Toronto, Ontario: Rowman & Littlefield Publishers.

DECISION SCIENCES INSTITUTE

Explorative and Exploitative Use of Smart Tourism Technologies in Travel Planning

C. Derrick Huang*
Florida Atlantic University
dhuang@fau.edu

Jahyun Goo
Florida Atlantic University
jgoo@fau.edu

Kichan Nam
American University of Sharjah
knam@aus.edu

Chul Woo Yoo
Florida Atlantic University
yooc@fau.edu

ABSTRACT

The use of smart tourism technologies, such as travel-related websites, social media, and smartphones, in travel planning has been pervasive and growing. This study examines how travelers use these technologies to enhance travel satisfaction. By adopting the framework of exploration and exploitation, we find that the attributes of smart tourism technologies promote both explorative and exploitative use, while user's security and privacy concerns have a negative impact. Further, explorative use has a strong influence on overall travel experience satisfaction, and exploitative use mainly enhances the transaction satisfaction.

KEYWORDS: Smart Tourism Technologies; Smart Tourism; Travel Planning; Travel Experience; Exploration; Exploitation

INTRODUCTION

Internet and other information technologies have changed consumer behavior. In tourism, these technologies have played a critical role not only for the competiveness of tourism organizations but also for the experience of tourists. Today, the vast majority of travel information search and reservations and payments during the preparation phase of a trip is done over the Internet. A plethora of technology channels and providers, such as traditional destinations' or agencies' web sites, personal blogs, review sites, and social networks, have emerged as smart tourism technologies (STTs), and their impacts have been felt by all participants in travel and tourism, ranging from travel vendors to aggregation providers to information brokers to travelers themselves. Initially, smart tourism technologies have enhanced the efficiency of transaction-oriented functions such as reservation and payment. Although such transaction-related use is still important, travelers increasingly turn to this diverse array of technologies and channels to obtain more accurate, rich, comprehensive, and personalized information from the planning phase of travel to real-time experience [91]. As such, various complex marketing strategies have been developed to assist travelers in making more informed and effective decisions. For instance, the consumers' evaluation scores for hotel performance provided by such sites as tripadvisor.com and booking.com significantly affect travelers' purchasing behavior [5,26].

With such a broad and deep impact of information technologies on travel, it is no wonder that there have been considerable research interests on smart tourism. In particular, a number of studies have been focused on the use of smart tourism technologies during planning phase of travel [e.g., 9,25,77,91,92]. While this stream of research has informed the various types of technologies used in travel and tourism and their attributes, a further examination of the underlying mechanism with which travelers use these STTs can greatly advance our understanding of the role that these technologies play in travel planning activities to achieve satisfaction. In this study, we borrow the powerful framework of exploration and exploitation, first adopted in the context of organizational learning and later extended to information technology use, to inspect the way that smart tourism technologies are used in travel planning. We intend to examine the following research questions: (1) How the attributes of STTs motivate the different use of STTs, and (2) How exploitative and explorative use of STTs influences travel experience satisfaction.

This paper is organized as follows. In the next section, we first review the previous research on smart tourism technologies and their role in travel planning. We then discuss the theory of exploration and exploitation and develop the research model based on this framework. The methodology of the study, as well as the result and analysis, are presented in the ensuing sections. Finally, we discuss the theoretical and practical implication of our research, and offer suggestions for future studies.

LITERATURE REVIEW

Travel Planning and Smart Tourism Technologies

Travel planning and decision making have been the subject of considerable research interests in recent past. Travel planning follows a series of episodes that involve a hierarchical structure of information searches [35,63]. Drawing from several previously proposed models, travel decision-making process can include the following phases: idea formation, searching for information, evaluate alternatives for final decision, and booking [6,36,38,75]. This process model is also consistent with six-stage search process proposed by Kuhlthau [44] and the behavior model of information seeking patterns proposed by Ellis [22]. It is worthwhile to note that travel plans are made in a number of stages, with earlier stages conditioning the later ones. As such, travel planning is not simply sequential; the travel decision process can be iterative with the four phases repeating or even running in parallel for each such decision as destination, itinerary, things to do, and so on [25,57].

STTs play an increasingly important role in all four phases of travel planning. It was predicted as early as the 1990s that the Internet would be accepted as the most important and effective tool to search travel information from the planning phase of travel [11]. Ho et al. [35] propose a conceptual framework of travelers' engagement in tourism information search and planning to understand their online and offline behavior and find prior knowledge and experience as the key basis for online travel information search. Xiang et al. [92] find users' perceived usefulness of the Internet for all categories of travel decisions such as where to visit, what to do, and where to stay has increased from 2007 to 2012. With the advent of new media such as social networks and smartphones, the focus of information search for travel decisions has been gradually shifting from only primary products (flights, lodging, etc.) to information to improve travel experience [17,87,90,92]. It is also noted, however, that travelers are concerned with the possible security or privacy breach with the increasing use of STT [73].

It is generally believed that certain underlying characteristics of STTs drive their higher adoption and usage in travel planning. Xiang et al. [92] posit that the increased popularity of the internet for trip decisions is because the Internet offers higher quality information and richer experience than ever. In the case of social media, the perceived value in travel information search goes up with users' perception of the information reliability and enjoyment [17]. And tourists have found smart phones to be useful in helping them visit more places, have richer experience, and enjoy higher satisfaction with their trips overall [87]. No and Kim [60] further theorize that four attributes of all online tourism information sources—accessibility, information reliability, interaction, and personalization—are key to travel planning (with security and privacy as a potential barrier). But although the factors of STTs leading to their use and usefulness are well studied, the underlying mechanism of how they are used successfully and/or satisfactorily for travel planning has not been examined. For that, we turn to the theory of exploration and exploitation.

Exploration and Exploitation Use

"Exploration of new possibilities" and "exploitation of existing capabilities" have long been recognized as two distinct mechanisms governing the learning and adaptive processes. March [56] points out that exploration refers to concepts as search, experimentation, discovery, and innovation, while exploitation is often associated with terms such as refinement, efficiency, implementation, and execution. Essence of exploration is the development of and experimentation with new alternatives, and exploitation focuses on improving existing resources and processes continuously [48]. Together, activities attributed to exploration and exploitation also constitute the essential course of adoption and use of information technology and systems [14,43].

The concepts of exploration and exploitation are often applied in the context of organizational learning. Recently, the conceptualization of exploration and exploitation has been extended from organizational to individuals learning and decision making. For individuals, exploitation is defined as a behavior that optimizes the performance in the current tasks, while exploration involves a deviation from existing tasks and a quest for alternatives [2]. Many contrasts in characteristics between exploration and exploitation organizational learning, such as slow vs. fast and experimenting vs. refining, also exhibit at the individual level. Burton-Jones and Straub [14] suggest that in information system adoption, exploitation is related to the execution of routines and existing knowledge, whereas exploration involves searching for new and different uses of the systems. In the case of smartphones, it is found that user competence and perceived usefulness are positively correlated with both exploitative and explorative use, while perceived usefulness is significant for exploitative use but not exploration use [43].

For this study, we conceptualize travelers' deployment of STT for trip planning as a combination of exploration and exploitation use. Considering the evolving nature of STTs, this study adopts the conceptual framework of exploration and exploitation in travel planning. We argue that although the use of STTs is involved in every stage of travel planning—idea formation, searching for information, evaluating alternatives for final decision, and booking—individuals interact with STT differently at different travel planning stages, and such differences bring about differentiated consequences. Using STTs to perform the tasks of idea formation and searching for information in the first two phases of the travel decision making process represents explorative use. Such use involves mostly unstructured tasks that require searching, testing, and discovery and takes time to learn and adapt. For instance, finding "potential destinations to visit" and "stores or other places to shop" on the Internet garners moderate but increasing attention by travelers [92]. When successful, such explorative use of STTs would likely enhance the overall experience of travelers. On the other hand, using STTs to complete the tasks of evaluating alternatives and booking of travel products in the last two phases travel planning, which has been well adopted by travelers, represents exploitative use. Xiang et al. [92] find that more than two-thirds of the travelers surveyed in 2007 to 2012 used Internet for searching "information about a particular destination," "hotel prices or places to stay," and "airline fares and schedule/flight time." These activities, involving routine tasks of selecting vendors and aiming at improving transaction efficiency, represent exploitative use of STTs for travel planning. With these two different styles of STT use that travelers engage in during the travel planning process, we present the research model in the next section.

HYPOTHESES/MODEL

Our research model, which examines core antecedents that influence overall travel experience satisfaction with STT use, is presented in Figure 1. Because this study investigates the use of a specific category of information technology (i.e., the STTs), we include the factors that identify the STTs and influence the two different STT uses. Based on the prior literature, key STT attributes and security/privacy concerns are adopted as core antecedents of exploitive and explorative use of STT [60]. In the model, we posit that the former positively promotes the STT use, and the latter rather inhibits the STT use. We also argue that the exploration and exploitation use of STTs contributes to the transaction satisfaction and overall travel experience satisfaction, respectively. Detailed arguments that support these relationships are discussed below.

Figure 1. Research Model

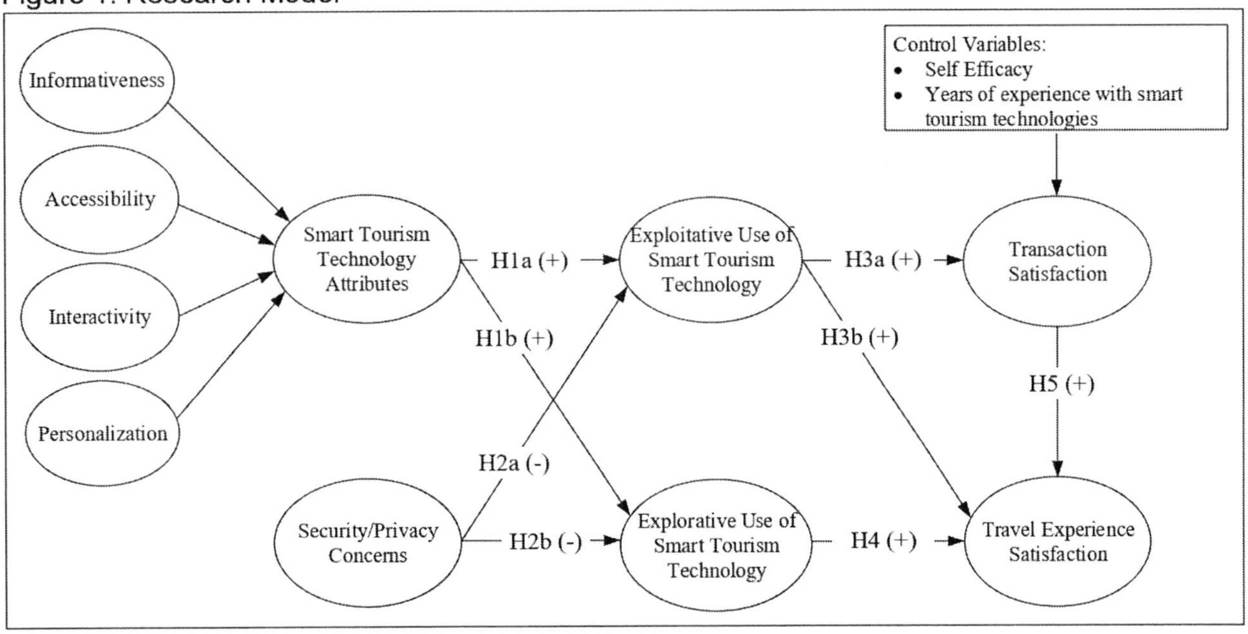

STTs can be identified by four key attributes—informativeness, accessibility, interactivity and personalization—that can enhance the usability and perceived usefulness of the technologies [60]. Informativeness is a combination of the information quality and trust of information as provided by online tourism information sources. Accessibility is the degree to which travelers can easily access and use online tourism information sources. Interactivity facilitates travelers' immediate actions when using STTs via real-time feedback and active communications. And personalization represents the ability of a traveler to obtain specific information to suit his/her personal trip planning needs. In this study, we investigate how these multiple attributes collectively motivate different uses of STTs.

Informativeness is particularly important to exploitative use of STTs: To select and book primary travel products such as air tickets, hotels, and car rentals effectively, travelers need to understand what relevant information to find, where to get the best deals, and how to start a conversation with other travelers on the Internet [91]. Furthermore, the quality and reliability of information have a positive effect on their perceived value [17], resulting in more use for making selection and purchases via e-commerce means [89]. The degree to which travelers can access useful information (accessibility) is associated with usability of STTs [13,47,92], and this perceived ease of use facilitates the search for travel ideas (i.e., explorative use) [43] and enables users to complete transactions easily (i.e., exploitative use). The interactivity of STTs provides more relevant and credible information due to the active participation of users [93], helping users construct initial ideas about travel and enabling efficient travel information search. Besides, travelers are likely to use interactive sites because of the experience of cognitive and affective absorption [86]. Chung and Koo [17] has found that the user enjoyment and absorptive experience from the interactivity of STTs such as social media leads to higher level of perceived value and consequently more usage. Personalization allows for tailor-made services to fit individual traveler's needs and thus increases the perception of service quality [55,60]. In addition, personalized travel planning using STTs allows for complex travel products [89] and increasingly important exploratory activities such as on-the-fly travel decisions [88] . Therefore, we propose the following hypotheses:

H1a *STT attributes are positively associated with the exploitative use of STTs for travel planning.*

H1b *STT attributes are positively associated with the explorative use of STTs for travel planning.*

User's concern for security and privacy is a factor that can impact the use of STTs. The ability to protect user's information and to provide secure transactions is a key evaluation factor for travelers to choose the right website for travel planning [65]. Although security and privacy are no longer a major road block against the use of information technology, they are still listed as the number one reason for not using the Internet for travel planning [92]. For example, concerns of possible security or privacy intrusion can discourage users to use vendor sites or blogs. Such concerns are likely to be more pronounced in the case of exploitative, since much more sensitive information such as personal identification and credit card data is transmitted in the last two stages of travel planning. Therefore, we have the following hypotheses:

H2a *Security and privacy concerns are negatively associated with the exploitative use of STTs for travel planning.*

H2b *Security and privacy concerns are negatively associated with the explorative use of STTs for travel planning.*

As exploitation is generally associated with execution and refinement of routines, the exploitative use of information technologies tends to lead to short-term task performance and efficiency gains [14,49,56]. Exploitative use of STTs in travel planning refers to the evaluation and purchase of travel products, and, as such, the performance gains of such use are due to the incremental improvement over the traditional processes of searching and booking with online and mobile means [35]. Indeed, trip transactions have been a leading application of e-commerce, partially due to such exploitative use of STTs being better and more efficient in accomplishing travelers' planning needs [89]. And travelers have found STTs very useful or essential in selecting destinations or products and completing transactions [92]. When travelers can make better decisions and complete smoother transactions in the last two stages of travel planning, it is likely then that they are more satisfied with the whole trip experience, although the impact may not be as high as transaction satisfaction. Therefore, we propose the following hypotheses:

H3a *Exploitative use of STTs for travel planning is positively related to transaction satisfaction.*

H3b *Exploitative use of STTs for travel planning is positively related to travel experience satisfaction.*

Explorative use of STTs in travel planning focuses on generating trip ideas and searching for relevant information. Although this type of innovative ways of using technologies is not likely to generate process-specific results, there are other benefits to be gained [56,79]. As the use of Internet for searching and booking the primary travel product has reached saturation, travelers increasingly find values in using the Internet to search for secondary products such as museum tickets and shopping detour to enhance the trip experience [91]. Other STTs such as social media and smartphones allow for a richer, deeper, and more interactive research on various aspects of a trip [32,87]; the result of such explorations may include an exotic destination, an off-the-beaten-path tour, or even an on-the-go itinerary, all of which can enhance the overall travel experience in a novel, non-traditional way. Note that since explorative use of STTs does not involve in the e-commerce activities of searching for and booking travel products, it is not likely to directly influence the transaction satisfaction of a traveler. Therefore, we have the following hypothesis:

H4 *Explorative use of STTs for travel planning is positively related to travel experience satisfaction.*

The transactions of making reservations and bookings are part of the overall travel experience. As pointed out in prior literature, service quality leads to a satisfaction of the service, which in turn influences the satisfaction of the overall experience of which the service is a part of [4,59,62] . Therefore, it is perceivable that a better experience in travel transactions would lead to a better experience of the whole trip, and we argue for the following hypothesis:

H5 *Transaction satisfaction is positively related to travel experience satisfaction.*

METHODS

We administered a survey to one of the largest online travel clubs in Korea. To expedite the data collection process, we developed a web survey, which consisted of 9 demographic items, 26 questions with seven point Likert scale, and 18 Boolean type questions. A pilot test with 30 graduate students was performed to ensure that the questions were unambiguous and that there were no technical errors which might impede data collection. After the pilot study, a small number of questions were refined to improve their clarity. Next, with the support of the club administrator, an invitation to participate in the survey was posted as a notice on the general notice section. Two follow-up "reminder" invitations were then posted one week apart. A total of 325 responses were received, of which 319 responses were valid and thus used for the further analysis. This represented a 5.43% response rate. Although this response rate is low, we were satisfied with the results because (1) the average ratio of the traffic in past 30 days to the total number of the registered members to the club was just little over 20%; (2) no financial incentive was offered to the respondents for completing the survey; and (3) the club members surveyed did not know the researchers. The only incentive offered for completing the survey was that the club as a whole would receive a summary project report. The participants were assured that the results would only be reported in an aggregated form to guarantee their anonymity and confidentiality [69].

A summary of the demographic characteristics of 319 responses is provided in Table 1. 72.1% of the respondents in the sample have more than one year of experience in using STTs, and about 98% of the respondents in the sample make one or more trips per year, indicating a good representation of STT user community. Further, the responses were based on a past trip with an average duration of 6.6 days. 39.5% of respondents in the sample spent one or two weeks for planning the trip.

Table 1. Demographic Characteristics of Respondents (N=319)

Characterisitcs		Frequency	Percent
Days of Trip Planning	less than one day	43	13.5%
	2-3 days	97	30.4%
	4-7 days	82	25.7%
	8-14 days	44	13.8%
	15-30 days	30	9.4%
	more than 30 days	23	7.2%
Number of leisure trip per year	never	5	1.6%
	1-2	186	58.3%
	3-4	84	26.3%
	5 or more	44	13.8%
Years of smart tourism technology use	less than 1 year	89	27.9%
	1 years ~ 2 years	82	25.7%
	2 years ~ 3 years	45	14.1%
	More than 3 years	103	32.3%
Education level	Middle school or less	8	2.5%
	High school	41	12.9%
	College/University	164	51.4%
	Graduate school	106	33.2%
Sex	Male	172	53.9%
	Female	147	46.1%
Average duration of the trip chosen for the survey		6.6 days	

All constructs in the survey were measured using multi-item scales. A conscientious effort was made to adapt existing measures validated from prior studies for the latent constructs in this research. Antecedents (i.e., smart tourism technology attributes and security/privacy concerns constructs) to both exploitative and explorative use of STTs was measured with seven-point Likert rating systems, ranging from 1 being strongly disagree to 7 being strongly agree. Following the literature survey studies, on the attributes or properties of online tourism information sources [60,65], we adopted the five most widely used factors: (1) informativeness, (2) accessibility, (3) interactivity, (4) personalization, and (5) security and privacy. While the tourism literature suggests that the first four attributes of STTs would have the positive impact on the tourism overall, the security and privacy issue in the tourism literature is identified as risk or nuisance of online channels. Thus, we drew a line between these two seemingly opposite characteristics of the attributes to bring differential impacts to exploitative and explorative use of STTs.

Seven items were used to capture the breadth and frequency of exploitative use of STTs. These items cover a variety of aspects related to the extent to which the STTs were used for the trip planning experiences including comparison shopping and reservation/payment activities for traditional travel products such as air tickets, lodging, and rental car. These are the activities associated with the last two stages of travel planning (see Section 2.3). Eleven items were used to capture explorative use of STTs, which corresponds to active search and discovery of information in pre-trip travel planning. As such, these measures are to capture a collective use of STTs in the first two stages of travel planning, such as when choosing a destination to visit [27,91] and build expectations for the upcoming trip [31].

Consistent with the research on leisure satisfaction in travel and tourism [cf., 51,59,80], the distinction between instrumental attribute (as being more cognitive-oriented and thus derived from services and activities related to preparation and reservation) and expressive attribute (as being more emotion- or feeling-oriented and thus derived from visual perspective and preference) was maintained in our model of satisfaction. Thus, the differentiation between the travel transaction and the travel experience of satisfaction corresponds to the distinction between instrumental and expressive attributes of satisfaction. Four items for transaction satisfaction and five items for travel experience satisfaction were adopted from Neal et al. [59]. We operationalized both constructs following the method used by Baker and Crompton [4]. Specifically we employed a subjective disconfirmation measure [83] for both transaction and travel experience satisfaction requiring respondents to assess perceptions of satisfaction directly against their desired satisfaction level (defined as the level of satisfaction a traveler desires for the trip) and to record their evaluation with a single score. Instead of using the psychometric measure subject to the criticism of needing to go through the process of subtracting one measurement (expectations) from another measurement (perceptions) in order to compute the actual satisfaction [c.f., 10,20,53,81], we resorted to directly measure a respondent's perception of the level of satisfaction against an expectation standard.

To control for other contextual variables that could also influence the transaction satisfaction, we included the following two control variables in our model: years of experience with smart tourism technologies and self efficacy. Years of experience with STTs was measured in four different levels, while the self efficacy was measured with three items using 7-point Likert scale.

RESULTS

The Partial Least Squares (PLS) method implemented in SmartPLS was chosen to perform a simultaneous evaluation of both the quality of measurement (the measurement model) and hypothesized relationships (the structural model). The PLS technique is appropriate and well-suited for this study because it allows for latent constructs to be modeled with formative indicators in the structural model. The measurement model was assessed through tests of convergent validity, discriminant validity, and reliability. First, exploratory factor analysis (EFA) was performed to check the potential latent factors in the development of measures. We found eight factors that have above 0.7 factor loadings. These results support the unidimensionality of the scales in question. Internal consistency was assessed by using Cronbach's alpha. All constructs employed in this study are higher than 0.75, showing strong reliability [61]. Next, we evaluated convergent validity by testing composite reliability and average variance extracted (AVE) from the measures [40]. Composite reliability values were greater than 0.85, Cronbach's alpha was greater than 0.75, and AVE ranged from 0.65 to 0.89.

These results indicate that the measurement model has high internal consistency and that convergent validity is confirmed [29].

Having validated the measurement modeling, the next step was testing the hypothesized relationships among latent constructs in the structural model. The assessment and estimation of structural model was conducted using SmartPLS [70]. In order to determine the precision of estimation in this particular PLS effort, a bootstrapping procedure with resampling of 200 subsamples was used to determine the statistical significance of the parameter estimates. Based on the results of this procedure, the structural model was assessed examining the magnitude, statistical significance of the path coefficients, and R2 in the structural model. Overall, the results suggest a satisfactory fit of the model to the data. The R2 values of the dependent constructs were 0.46 and 0.22 for travel experience satisfaction and transaction satisfaction, respectively. In addition to evaluating the R^2 value of the endogenous constructs were 0.19 and 0.18 for exploitative use of STT and explorative use of STT, respectively. The results of the PLS analysis are in Figure 2.

Figure 2. Results of the structural model

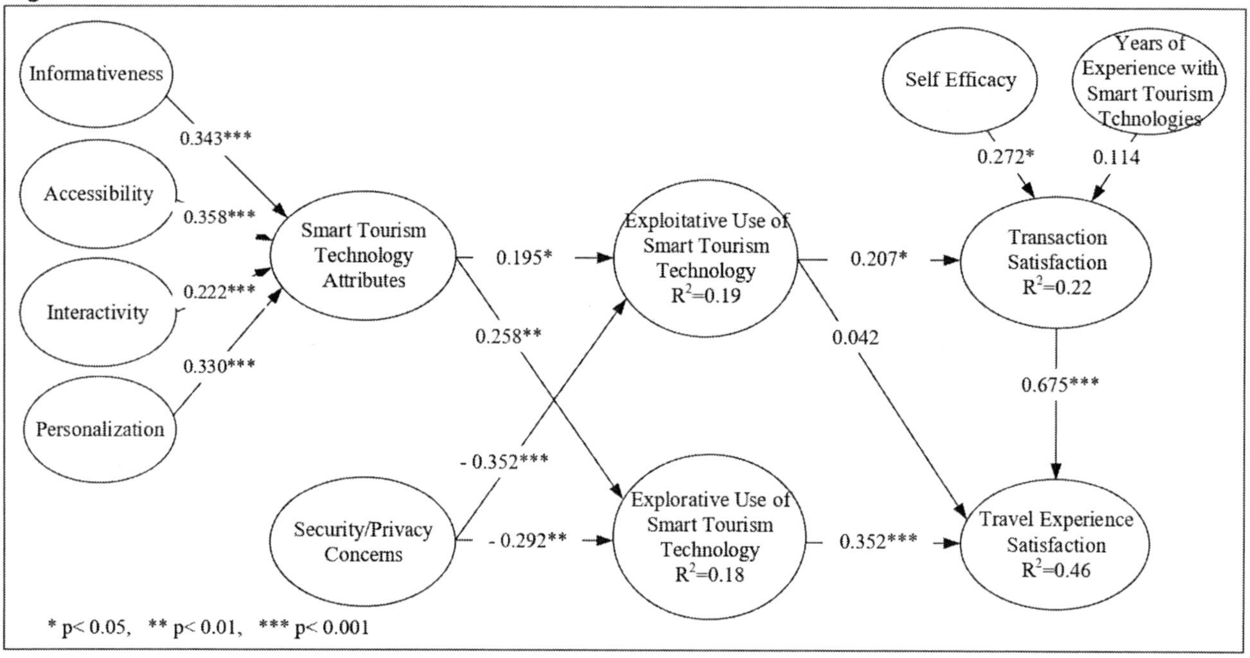

We first note that explorative use of STTs was significantly and positively associated with travel experience satisfaction (β=0.352, p<0.001), supporting H4. The results of exploitative use of STTs were mixed. Exploitative use of STTs was significantly and positively associated with the transaction satisfaction (β=0.207, p<0.05), supporting H3a. However, for travel experience satisfaction, it showed statistically insignificant, albeit a positive association with travel experience satisfaction. Thus H3b was not supported. The possibility of these interesting results is discussed in the next section.

Second, the relationships between both styles of use and their antecedents turned out as expected. Smart tourism technology attributes was significantly and positively associated with both exploitative use (β=0.195, p<0.05) and explorative use (β=0.258, p<0.01) of STT, supporting H1a and H1b, respectively. As hypothesized, the effect of security and privacy concerns on both exploitative and explorative use of STT turned out to be negative and significant, supporting H2a (β= -0.352, p<0.001) and H2b (β= -0.292, p=0.01). These results indicate that multitude properties of STTs have a differential impact on the traveler's consumption style of STTs before and during their trips. Specifically, while STT attributes stimulate the travelers to engage in both explorative and exploitative use, the traveler's concerns of security and privacy with online tourism technologies hinders both styles of STT use. As expected and controlled, self-efficacy showed a significant and positive impact on the transaction satisfaction ($\beta=0.272$, $p<0.05$).

To ensure that our statistical tests above have adequate power, we performed a power analysis to calculate power values for our PLS model using Cohen's [19] power table for multiple regression analysis. As PLS estimates a structural model block by block, we calculated power values block by block [cf., 50]. Because the transaction satisfaction block involves control variables, we took a hierarchical approach to analyze power for incremental explanation of variance, as suggested by Cohen [19]. Thus we conducted nine power analyses. The power values for all these analyses ranged from 0.88 to 0.96 indicating that our sample provides sufficient power at the 0.95 level to detect effects when they are present [19]. As the results are validated, we will discuss the implications of this study in more detail in the next section.

DISCUSSION AND CONCLUSIONS

Given the central role of smart tourism technologies in travel planning, it is important to understand how travelers actually use STTs and the consequences of such usage. We explore the different types of STT use and have revealed several significant and interesting findings. First, our result indicates that explorative use is a strong predictor of travel experience satisfaction ($\beta=0.352$, $p<0.001$). Knowing that such use is employed in the idea formation and information search stages of travel planning, we can interpret this result in two ways. Because finding the right destinations, places to visit, and itinerary is a critical aspect of travel experience, using STTs for this purpose understandably has a great impact on the overall travel satisfaction. Interestingly, we find that exploitative use, an important determinant of transaction satisfaction ($\beta=0.207$, $p<0.05$), only indirectly impacts the overall travel experience through transaction satisfaction. Because the exploitative use of STTs is associated directly with the evaluation of travel products and booking, the last two stages of travel planning, the result of such use is therefore a more efficient and smoother transaction, which in turn contributes to the overall travel experience.

Second, this study explores the role of STT attributes in motivating the exploitative and explorative use of STTs. Although No and Kim [60] identify four factors relevant to the usefulness of STTs, how they actually facilitate STT use by travelers to achieve overall travel experience satisfaction is not known. Our results show that the STT attributes contribute to travelers' adoption of STTs in travel planning, and the influence is stronger on explorative use than on exploitation. This may be explained by the fact that the travelers' exploitation use of STTs is already common and saturated [88], while the exploration use is still emerging and growing [91]; higher level of informativeness, accessibility, interactivity, and personalization can better motivate travelers to experiment with STTs in travel planning in innovative ways such as discovering exotic destinations and finding places to visit on-the-go.

Third, this study shows that security and privacy are still a concern to travelers when using STTs in travel planning. Security and privacy concerns have been examined as a critical factor that hinders online transactions or information disclosure [e.g., 21], but this study points out specifically that these concerns negatively impact both explorative and exploitative use of STTs in all stages of travel planning. It is interesting to note that travelers are concerned with security and privacy even when they explore the online information channels in idea formation and information search, although the negative impacts are not as strong as in the case of exploitative use, which often involves exchange of private information and financial transactions.

As with all research, this study has limitations that must be recognized. A potential limitation concerns the nature of the sample utilized in this analysis. While the sample shows good representation of travelers, these findings can only be generalized to STT users within the sampling frame. Thus, no claim of external validity for this study's findings, particularly in cases of non-leisure travels, can be made. Another limitation is the cross-sectional design employed in this research. Although the results provide strong support for the hypotheses, our model could benefit from a longitudinal research design to provide strong inferences for causality relationships for travel experience from a temporal perspective [30,39]. This is particularly useful because of the fast changing nature of STTs. Future studies can consider designing a longitudinal study to assess the style over time as the combination of available STTs and their attributes evolve.

Despite the limitations described above, our study adds to the stream of literature on smart tourism and smart tourism technologies. The goal of this paper is to identify the mechanism of the actual usage of STTs in travel planning and to understand how the different uses impact the travel experience, and the result shows the close relationships between STT attributes, exploration and exploitation use, and travel satisfaction. Therefore, we believe that this current study contributes to the advancement of our understanding of smart tourism technologies in travel planning, and future extensions to this theme can be expected.

REFERENCES

Will be provided upon request.

DECISION SCIENCE INSTITUTE

Extracting life skills from an introductory Excel programming class

Ben Martz
Shepherd University
bmartz@shepherd.edu

David Manning
Northern Kentucky University
manningd@nku.edu

ABSTRACT

The driver for this paper is the ongoing discussion around skills gaps in the education industry; gaps that suggest what the education industry is teaching does not match up with what employers need or with what students need as life skills. Multiple studies across multiple academic fields document these skill gaps at high school, college, and post college levels. The paper proposes a set of integrated introductory programming concepts based around implicit learning and cognitive science to help address this gap. The authors document how exercises found in an introductory programming class can address the claimed deficits.

KEYWORDS: Problem Solving; Career Skills Gap; Programming Skills; Life Skills

INTRODUCTION

> 'A big gap separates what graduates offer from what most employers need' ~ Doria, et al. 2002

There is much discussion about gaps between the skills the education industry provides students and what skills students need for their jobs and careers. Versions of these gaps have been suggested and data produced at multiple levels: undergraduate, graduate, workforce, etc. Barr and Tagg (1995) define a 'gap' using two areas of concern: the 'espoused theory' and the 'theory in use'.

The gap is more fully exposed when the idea of teaching more real-world concepts, the espoused theory, is compared to what is really going on in schools, the theory in use. For example, a gap exists between what skills students think they need and what skills recruiters are recruiting for. Martz and Landof (2000) found that recruiters rated problem solving skills significantly higher than did students when considering these skills as desirable now, desirable 3 years in the future, and desirable for career advancement. The results showed gaps on multiple skills across all three measures.

LITERATURE REVIEW

There are more suggestions that the gap exists at the undergraduate level. At least two early studies, *Principles for good practice in undergraduate education* (Chickering and Gamson, 1987) and *What research says about improving undergraduate education*

(AAHE, 1996), discuss this concern as they offer suggestions for improving the undergraduate education process. A contemporary study by Educational Testing Service (ETS) (Goodman, et al. 2015), suggests that conditions are not improving, specifically for the US. While concentrating on the 16-34 year old age group, the report found that 'despite having the levels of educational attainment of any previous American generation, these young adults on average demonstrate relatively weak skills [when compared to the same age group form other nations] in literacy, numeracy, and problem solving' (preface). The cause of the rankings (15th of 21, 21 of 21, and 20 of 21) are for other discussions and debates to be argued elsewhere. For the purpose of this paper, the report clearly demonstrates another 'gap' between what is needed and what is being learned.

CIOs have been placing more and more emphasis on the job candidate's knowledge of business fundamentals (Overby, 2006). According to a Forbes magazine survey (2013), top skills that are valued by employers center on '... more about how you think systems through and work within the context of a team...' (Casserly, 2012). Pfeffer and Fong's 2002 analysis of MBA business programs produced a similar concern; an analysis that generated the distress for Doria et al. (2003) to offer the opening quote.

Other studies focus on business oriented and more specifically, information technology jobs and careers. A 2014 report by kdnuggets (a leading website for technology based jobs in business analytics) showed the top five skill-orient phrases most mentioned in job announcements as: team, business, analytics, design, and development (Piateetsky, 2014). Drilling down into information technology 9 of the top 11 IT careers for 2014 listed by *US News and World Report* (Taylor, 2014), include key business areas such as Software Developer, Computer Systems Analyst, Web Developer, Information Security Analyst, Database Administrator, IT Manager, Computer Programmer, Computer Systems Administrator, and Computer Support Specialist.

There are some common threads in the skills being requested. One of the most substantial studies of general skills required for jobs was the 2013 study by the International Data Corporation (IDC), *Skills requirements for tomorrow's best jobs* (Anderson & Gantz, 2013) In this report, IDC analyzed 14.6 million job postings in an effort to identify 1.) jobs with highest growth and wage for 2020 and, 2.) top skills required for these jobs. Their results showed that "The most required skills across all occupations include oral and written communication skills, attention to detail, customer service focus, organizational skills, and problem-solving skills (p. 6)." Three of these; oral and written communication skills, attention to detail, and problem solving skills were evaluated as "cross-functional" or skills being required by more than 50% of the high-growth / high-wage positions reviewed. The concern for a lack of emphasis on these areas is echoed by the Conference Board (Casner-Lotto and Benner, 2006) wherein their survey respondents rated teamwork/collaboration and problem solving skills as "very important" at all three levels of analysis; high school, college, and college graduates. In the more narrow business education area, Topi et al (2010) define critical thinking, problem solving, and creativity as components of the 'foundational knowledge and skills' (p. 21) of an information system professional.

Regardless of level or area, these gaps emerge from the comparison of expectations. Hall and Mirvis (1995) propose that the expectations of the roles played by educating entities and companies hiring graduates have changed. They suggest the change is based on how the typical career is now viewed as self-based versus the long-time, organizational careers of the past. In their view, a career now calls for more "learning how to learn" skills than concentrating on specific skill retraining. One example of a changed expectation posited by Fischer (2013) is the expectation about which institution, the university or the business, is responsible for preparing a new employee.

The purpose of this paper is to indicate how some of the underlying skills found in an introductory programming course are representative of the desirable foundational skills requested; those skills which are applicable in other courses of curriculum, but more importantly, are applicable as candidates for status as 'foundational' (Topi et al. 2010), 'meta-skill' (Hall and Mirvis, 1995), or 'cross-functional' (Anderson & Gantz, 2013). The argument will be supported by examples of foundational skills students are exposed to and practice in a programming course. These foundational skills become primary skills on which more complex skill sets can build. In the end, these complex sets transfer to careers. The overriding proposition is that we are teaching more foundational skills than given credit for and further, we need to show the evidence supporting that claim.

Programming and Problem Solving

At the heart of this proposition is the argument that many of the key skills inherent in programming are problem solving skills. It is programming's proximity to the raw ability of problem solving that makes programming such a strong candidate for foundational career skills. Problem solving skills have been consistently suggested as a foundational, core skill listed across many surveys and reports previously discussed (Casserly, 2012; Anderson & Gantz, 2013; Piateetsky, 2014; Goodman et al., 2015).

In many ways, the programming activity found in introductory programming classes produces implicit learning of problem solving skills. The first way is the problem solving environment of programming. In programming one is constantly charged with going from a problem state to a goal state. A student 'picks up' many skills as they progress through ever increasing problems. Piaget (1929) envisioned implicit learning as a process of assimilation and proposed it as a base learning strategy in early childhood learning. Papert (1980) defined learning as the development of problem solving models by taking skills from one situation and applying them to another situation. This adaptation of skills from situation to situation was termed appropriation. Today, a similar idea is found in the 'transfer' activity found in the Lifelong Learning VALUE Rubric supported by the Association of American Colleges and Universities (AACU) (2015). So, we propose that the basic programming environment produces an environment conducive to and supportive of appropriation of important career skills.

The second skill deals with memory structures. Most people agree with the notion that learning a new fact or skill means it is stored in and can be recalled from long term memory. Many researchers have worked to understand the structures by which memories, and thereby, learning occurs. Schank's (1988) scripts, Thorndyke and Hayes-Roth's (1979) schemata, Sanderland et al. (1983) templates and Roby's (1966) self-enacting response sequences all represent visions of a memory structure that allows the efficient storage and retrieval of facts and information in the brain. Programs themselves act much like these memory structures.

The final factor contributing to the implicit learning of problem solving skills is the actual transference of programming skills to more generic problem solving skills through protocols, metaphors, and analogies. Newell and Simon (1972) created detailed protocols in their General Problem Solver (GPS) model. Minsky (1988) defines a metaphor as 'that which allows us to replace one kind of thought with another'. Schank (1988) is more operational in his definition and suggests a process called analogical mappings. This is where the individual is asked pointedly to compare and contrast the current problem situation with other known problem situations in an effort to gain comparative information to find solutions.

Completing programming problems require the understanding of conceptual 'memory structures' like variables, linked-lists, functions, procedures, etc. The ability to recognize problems and recall and adapt previous solutions to the new problems through analogies operates as a recognized learning process. In the end, the programming environment provides a potentially rich active learning environment for students to learn problem solving skills.

Programming and Problem Solving Topics

If we are you use analogies as the basis for our learning strategy, we must decide on the seminal topics. To help decide what topics to build on, reviewing the proposed curricula from two reference disciplines, Information Systems and Computer Science, generated a listing of topics in introductory programming courses. Table 1 lists selected higher level programming concepts extracted from two curriculum-oriented reports: 1.) the 2013 Computer Science Curriculum Report (ACM/IEEE, 2013); specifically, the Software Development Fundamentals knowledge area; and 2.) the IS 2010 Curriculum Guidelines; specifically, the learning objectives of the suggested application development course (Topi et al., 2010) This extraction seems reasonable as the two teams of authors placed fundamental programming concepts in these course descriptions as indicated in Table 1. The Association for Computing Machinery (ACM) course description defines the topics in the course as 'a prerequisite to the study of most of computer science'. (ACM/IEEE, 2013) and the IS 2010 report provides the following learning objective: 'Students will learn the basic concepts of program design … problem solving, programming logic …' (Topi et al., 2010, p. 56). Using these two curricula areas seems appropriate. While the two disciplines ultimately focus on information technology and programming at different levels, it seems reasonable that there be commonalities in the introductory programming course from both areas.

Table 1: Fundamental Concepts for Introductory Programming Course	
• The role of algorithms in the problem-solving process • Program Decomposition • Basic syntax and semantics of a higher-level language • Variables and primitive data types • Expressions and assignments • Simple I/O including file I/O • Conditional and iterative control structures • Functions and parameter passing • Arrays • Records/structures (heterogeneous aggregates)	• Modular Expressions • Procedures, Functions, SubProcedures • Variables • Literals • Types • Passing parameters • Input/Output (I/O) design • Graphical user interface (GUI) • Conditional logic • Iterative design • Data types (primitive and compound)

• Strings and string processing • Debugging strategies • Documentation and program style • Testing fundamentals and test-case generation	• Arrays • Prototyping • Application integration
Software Development Fundamentals (ACM/IEEE 2013, p167-178)	Application Development Course (Topi et al., 2010, p.56)

Proposed Foundational Learning Programming Concepts

Adopting an appropriation paradigm with a foundation in Piaget's (1929), Papert's (1980), and Schank's (1988) analogous learning models, we created Table 2 to help preview and summarize the rest of this paper. In the leftmost column of Table 2 we list programming areas along with key related items selected from Table 1 that are usually taught in an introductory programming class. The items are the explicit learning activity from the reports mentioned earlier that are guiding curricula in information systems and computer science. We acknowledge that the intensity and level of complexity will differ from discipline to discipline, from program to program, and even from faculty to faculty, but we have provided a detailed programming example for discussion purposes.

The second column of Table 2 is labeled Implicit and identifies example higher level concepts from information systems, computer science, business, and other disciplines that benefit from a student having an understanding of the topic. Essentially, these can be seen as topics which support other, more advanced topics found in an information system or computer science curriculum.

The Appropriation column is used to suggest lifelong skills and possible careers which benefit from the implicit learning of the topic – the concept provides a possible analogy, metaphor, or example of the appropriation of the topic in 'real life'. In this way, this column suggests the 'transfer' skill associated with life skills associated with Lifelong Learning (AACU, 2015). These suggestions are based on a career track matrix in the IS 2010 report (Topi et al, 2010, Figure 6, p. 26), reviews and analysis of the career skill surveys mentioned earlier, and skills found in basic job descriptions. The appropriations are discussed in more detail for each programming topic below.

Table 2: Life Skills from Programming Areas

Explicit Programming Content Area (1)(2)	**Major or Career (Implicit)**	**Life Skills (Appropriation)**
Conditional Processing Variables, conditional statements, Boolean logic, etc.	Business Analyst, Lawyer, Software Engineer, Market Researcher, Insurance Agent, Credit Analyst, Security Officer, Baseball Team Manager, College Basketball Coach.	Tax preparation, Trouble-shooting electrical or mechanical systems, Balancing checkbook, Driving in rush hour traffic, Assembling a kid's toy, Cooking recipes.
Iterative processing Counted loops; conditional loops, searching, sorting, etc.	Quality Assurance Testers, Program Testers, Forensic Accountant, Logistics,	Lawn mowing, Painting a room, Vacuuming a rug,

	Musician, Actuaries, Banker, Assembly line worker, Bus Driver.	Waxing a car, Searching for lost keys, Training for track meet, Exercise routines.
Subroutines Functions, procedures, parameter passing, scope of control, etc.	Accountant, Mechanic, Architect, Mechanical Engineer, Systems Analyst, City Planner, General Manager, Wedding Planner, General Contractor, Nurse or Doctor.	Shopping lists, Planning a holiday meal, Cooking recipes, Doing math problems, Reading blueprints, Preparing taxes (worksheets, schedules, etc.). Reading contracts.
Human Computer Interaction GUI, Modular Design, Application Integration, Program Decomposition, I/O	Web Developer, Artist, Interior Designer, Salesperson, Game Designer, Kitchen Designer, Toymaker.	ATMs, Phone answering machines, Cash registers, Smart thermostats, TV cable box menu, Radio preset buttons.
(1)(Topi et al., 2010; p.56-57); (2) (ACM/IEEE, 2013; p.167-178)		

DETAILED PROGRAMMING EXAMPLES

Area 1: conditional processing - discounted price

Example: "You have the following variables: PURCHASE – the total of purchase by a customer; DISCOUNTED PRICE – the final price a customer pays. Given that the company provides a 10% discount on purchases over $1000, construct the IF – THEN – ELSE statement that provides a 10% of not. Store the result in DISCOUNTED PRICE."

The IF – THEN – ELSE structure is one of the three basic constructs in programming. It has at its base a Boolean condition and two sets of imperative actions. One set of actions is performed if the condition is true and the second set of actions is performed if the condition proves false. The concepts underlying this exercise include Boolean logic (single and compound conditions), conditional behavior, and logic flow. Each of these base concepts grow in complexity as students move from introductory level classes in business and information systems to the expectations of the upper division coursework.

```
If Purchase > 1000 Then
        Discounted_Price = Purchase * .90
Else
        ' no discount applied
        Discounted_Price = Purchase
End If
```

Often a business rule may require two independent conditions have to be true before an action is taken. This adds a level of complexity that can be solved in multiple ways. One way is with a compound condition that checks both situations in a single condition. The second method nests a second IF-THEN-ELSE statement on either the true or the false side of the first IF-THEN-ELSE. By adding a simple three word phrase into the business rule, the logic takes on a higher level of complexity.

Example: 'You have the following variables: PURCHASE – the total of purchase by a customer; DISCOUNTED PRICE – the final price a customer pays; RETURNING – a Boolean variable representing if the customer is a returning customer or a new customer. Given that the company provides a 10% discount *to returning customers* on purchases over $1000, construct the IF – THEN – ELSE statement that provides a 10% of not. Store the result in DISCOUNTED PRICE'.

```
If (Purchase > 1000) AND (Returning = "R") Then
        Discounted_Price = Purchase * .90
Else
        ' no discount applied
        Discounted_Price = Purchase
End If
```

The above situation has two independent conditions where the customer is 'returning' or not (returning customers have an 'R' in the variable), and the purchase price is over $1000 or not. The business rule wishes to reward only those situations where the customer is returning and the purchase is above $1000. The fact that the discount is only applied if both conditions are true allows for the use of the 'AND' compound condition. In essence there is still a binary decision in play – the purchase must be over $1000 and be made by a returning customer to qualify for the discount. Alternately, there is no discount.

However, the business may wish to seek out new customers and provide non-returning customers a 5% discount. At this point there are three potential outcomes (a 10% discount; a 5% discount; and no discount) and since a binary decision can only handle two branches, a second binary decision much be used.

Example: 'You have the following variables: PURCHASE – the total of purchase by a customer; DISCOUNTED PRICE – the final price a customer pays; RETURNING – a Boolean variable representing if the customer is a returning customer or a new customer. Given that on purchases over $1000, the company provides a 10% discount to returning customers and a 5% discount to new customers, construct the NESTED IF statement that provides the appropriate discounted price. Store the result in DISCOUNTED PRICE'.

```
If (Purchase > 1000) Then
      If (Returning = "R")  Then
         Discounted_Price = Purchase * .90
      Else  ' If not returning, then this is a new customer
         Discounted_Price = Purchase * .95
      End if
Else
      ' no discount applied
      Discounted_Price = Purchase
End If
```

In the above example, the three possible outcomes (Over $1000 and New; Over $1000 and Returning; Not over $1000) must be allowed for. This can be done with two IF-THEN-ELSE statements, but one of the outcomes must be nested within the second statement.

The logic in designing which condition operates as the first condition does have some impact on the efficiency or the processing, but not the effectiveness. There are situations where the number of outcomes makes using the basic IF statement unwieldy. The collection of sales tax is just one such case. Here each state has a different rate and therefor a different amount to collect for each purchase amount.

Example: 'You have the following variables: PURCHASE – the total of purchase by a customer; DISCOUNTED PRICE – the final price a customer pays; RETURNING – a Boolean variable representing if the customer is a returning customer or a new customer. STATE CODE – a two character field representing the state for which you need to collect sales taxes (OH, KY, IN). SALES TAX – variable for the calculated sales tax to be collected from the sale. TOTAL PRICE – the total price of the purchase after discount and including sales tax. Given that on purchases over $1000, the company provides a 10% discount to returning customers and a 5% discount to new customers, construct the NESTED IF statement that provides the appropriate discounted price. Store the result in DISCOUNTED PRICE. *On all sales, you should calculate the tax rate based on the STATE CODE and add that tax to the DISCOUNTED PRICE to obtain the TOTAL PRICE*'.

```
If (Purchase > 1000) Then
      If (Returning = "R")  Then
         Discounted_Price = Purchase * .90
      Else  ' If not returning, then this is a new customer
         Discounted_Price = Purchase * .95
      End if
Else
      ' no discount applied
      Discounted_Price = Purchase
End If
Select Case STATE_CODE
      Case is = "OH"
          Sales_tax = Purchase * .0575
      Case is = "KY"
          Sales_tax = Purchase * .06
      Case is = "IN"
          Sales_tax = Purchase * .07
      Case Else
          Msg "error"
End Select
Total_Price = Discounted_Price + Sales_tax
```

The SELECT CASE structure was developed to minimize the coding complexity created by sets of intertwined conditions and IF-THEN-ELSE statements that would be necessary; essentially fifty IF THEN ELSEs for the example here.

Area 2: iterative processing - loops

The iteration construct is one of the major constructs taught in a beginning programming class. Conceptually, a loop is used when you have a set of actions you wish to repeat on a set of data. The set of actions are repeated either 1. A set amount of times – counted loops or 2. Until a condition is met – conditional loops. In our example, we want to determine how much our discounting policy has provided in discounts. Conveniently, we know there were 50 sales made this month. Without the functionality of loops one would have to make 50 copies of the above code and have 50 different names for the purchase variable, making for a long program. Loops usually work in conjunction with a type of storage which could be in computer memory or in a file on a disk. One analogy that is often used is processing a set of files in a file cabinet drawer. One takes out the first file, processes it, and then move to the next file. Loops work the same way. For purposes of our demonstration, we use the READ command to tell the computer to look at the next purchase, returning code, and state code.

Example: 'You have the following variables: <u>COUNTER – a variable used to track the number of records; TOTAL DISCOUNTS – the accumulated total of discounts provided.</u> PURCHASE – the total of purchase by a customer; DISCOUNTED PRICE – the final price a customer pays; RETURNING – a Boolean variable representing if the customer is a returning customer or a new customer. STATE CODE – a two character field representing the state for which you need to collect sales taxes (OH, KY, IN). SALES TAX – variable for the calculated sales tax to be collected from the sale. TOTAL PRICE – the total price of the purchase after discount and including sales tax. Given that on purchases over $1000, the company provides a 10% discount to returning customers and a 5% discount to new customers, construct the NESTED IF statement that provides the appropriate discounted price. Store the result in DISCOUNTED PRICE. On all sales, you should calculate the tax rate based on the STATE CODE and add that tax to the DISCOUNTED PRICE to obtain the TOTAL PRICE. <u>There were 50 sales made this month. Calculate the total of all discounts provided.</u>

```
For Counter = 1 to 50
  Read (Purchase, Returning, State_Code)
  If (Purchase)> 1000) Then
      If (Returning = "R")  Then
         Discounted_Price = Purchase * .90
      Else  ' If not returning, then this is a new customer
         Discounted_Price = Purchase * .95
      End if
  Else
      ' no discount applied
      Discounted_Price = Purchase ]
  End If
  Total_Discounts = Total_Discounts +
                 (Purchase  - Discounted_Price)
  Select Case State_Code
      Case is = "OH"
          Sales_tax = Purchase  * .0575
      Case is = "KY"
          Sales_tax = Purchase * .06
      Case is = "IN"
          Sales_tax = Purchase  * .07
```

```
      Case Else
          Msg "error"
  End Select
  Total_Price = Discounted_Price + Sales_tax
Next Counter
```

As alluded to above, we conveniently knew that there were 50 transactions. This allowed us to use the FOR ... NEXT counted loop. Often we do not know how many times we must execute our look. For this we move to a conditional loop – one that ends when a text condition has been met. In the situation below we have a file of the fifty transactions, one per line, and we will process the transactions while there are still line items left in the file. The operating system manages a Boolean variable EOF as true if there are no more records or false if there are more records. The statement: 'There were 50 sales made this month' is amended to All transactions for the month have been put in a file SALES.DAT with one sale per line.

```
While NOT (EOF)
  Read (Purchase, Returning, State_Code)
...
...
...
Wend
```

The iteration processing here represents a simple example of the concept. More complex instantiations can process very complex situations. For example, loops within loops can produce very efficient and effective searching and sorting algorithms.

Area 3: subroutines - functions

Whether called procedures, subroutines, subprograms, functions, methods, etc., the main ideas communicated in these programming units are around 1. Clustering procedural logic that deals with the same objective or goal; and 2. Designing re-useable, callable code. Extracting one more example from our ongoing program, let's assume that we have found several more programs that must calculate the sales tax on a sales amount and the state in which the sale was made. We can create a function which contains the logic to calculate the appropriate sales tax amount based upon two pieces of information: the amount and the state.

```
Function SalesTax (Amount as single; StCode as string) as single
  Select Case StCode
      Case is = "OH"
          SalesTax = Amount * .0575
      Case is = "KY"
          SalesTax = Amount * .06
      Case is = "IN"
          SalesTax = Amount * .07
      Case Else
          Msg "error"
```

```
  End Select
 End Function
```

This function can then be used in all of the programs where needed to get the sales tax on a sale by letting the function know the amount and the state. One of the teaching opportunities is to point out how the efficiency and effectiveness of the function grows; efficiency based upon the number of times the function is used and effectiveness based upon the number of states coded.

```
Total_Price = Discounted_Price + SalesTax (Purchase, State_Code)
```

Area 4: human computer interaction

The requirement to develop a good, workable, user interface for a computer program finds its ancestry in the study of human factors attributed to originating from WWII (Sanders and McCormick, 1987). Human factors design usually relates to physical machines or hardware and how they are operated by humans.

The discipline of human computer interaction (HCI) emerges from the prolific growth and use of computing in computers but also in (hardware) embedded systems. The evolutions of elevators, cars, ladders, lights, furniture, tools, etc. all fall inside the scope of a human factors or ergonomics discussion. Information technology tools emphasizing human factors would include hardware such as, easy open computer cases, keyboards, mouse, trackballs, video screens, desktops, laptops, tablets, etc. (Hewett et al., 2009). The challenge for the software developers is to take advantage of the new hardware updates.

However, the interaction that occurs between the user and the computer is different; essentially it is a conversation. In this conversation, the user and the computer converse through software using controlled protocols and language - in the general communication sense, not the programming language sense. These conversations are much more complex in that the interactions can become much more dynamic as both the computer and the human may get confused, require clarification, or not comprehend what the other needs or wants. Examples of HCI caused by embedded systems would include such interactions as; setting a VCR clock, touchpad conversation with computer systems on the ATM, cash register, phone, microwave cooking, etc.

How the computer talks to the user is important. For example, the assignment to develop an interactive pizza ordering program (figure 1) can create an active learning environment to; talk about the difference between mutually exclusive choices (radio buttons) and independent binary, cumulative, choices (check boxes) and the corresponding decision logic (IF THEN ELSE; Select Case) necessary to process the choices; appropriately display information; build interactive screen design; describe data validity issues; create unambiguous error message policies; etc.

Example: When the order button is pressed, the program code should identify which ingredients, what size and what type pizza is ordered. Using the costs from the menu below, determine the final cost of the pizza and display the total. You may use your own discretion as to the design of the code's logic (SELECT CASE; Nested IFs; Loops; Subroutines), but you must develop the interface to be a 'friendly' as possible. One example is in Figure 1.

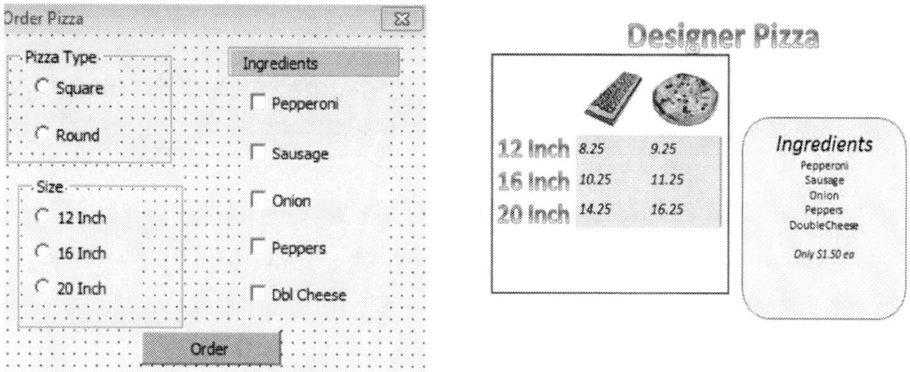

Figure 1: Example of Human Computer Interface

DISCUSSION AND CONCLUSION

Most people immediately see how the basic IF-THEN-ELSE statement applies across many activities. Constructing the appropriate conditional statement and building the imperatives are fundamental to decision making and problem solving. Understanding the nuances between using compound conditions, nested IF statements and SELECT CASE statements also provide core problem solving concepts. For example, these structures can help students later when they are required to design well-structured database searches or develop and apply security rights and authorizations. The logic flow inherent in nested IF statements provide a base foundation for discussions on project management topics. Clearly, the concept of organizing prerequisites and PERT/CPM charts fit well here. Probably the most direct use of the conditional action (IF-THEN-ELSE, NESTED IF, SELECT CASE) and the Boolean logic of compound conditions can be found in the decision making processes of advanced business courses such as Expected Value Tables, Analytics, Project Management, Marketing Research, Business Strategy, etc.

The application of the IF-THEN-ELSE construct permeates the development of life skills. Buying a car, filing taxes, deciding on what to order for lunch all boil down to identifying and understanding consequences if the a condition is true or false. The compound condition with an “AND” has the ability to help limit and refine choices; a car that is blue AND has 4 doors is more precise than a car that is blue OR has four doors.

The thought processes learned while clustering code and processing logic into contained sets of callable code – procedures - can be applied directly to other areas. Two examples would be clustering user requirements to make software development more efficient and the clustering of delivery locations to make delivery logistics more efficient. Those that can design well thought out procedures will probably be able to effectively cluster workflow activities together in project management tasks. When project managers clustering project activities into well-defined subprojects so as to more effectively and efficiently manage the larger project they have implemented the same underlying purpose of procedures, subroutines, functions, and objects with respect to the programming.

Remember, a function is distinguished as a set of code that concentrates on performing a specific role or activity. The inner logic of the subroutine code is not always open to inspection. As with the SalesTax example above, it usually accepts input parameters and provides output results. This characteristic can be found in a multitude of appropriations. One of the more obvious transfers of learning associated with the function (and procedures) is that of black box testing. The issues around testing functions and procedures would apply directly to designing test data for COTS (Customizable off the Shelf). Understanding how to vary input parameters and validate the corresponding output results could be a very valuable skill for accountants as they evaluate the candidates for an Accounting Information System (AIS).

The characteristics of functions and procedures also lend themselves to examples in life skills. One would be the lists one puts together for a day of shopping. One list identifies the stores you plan to visit; grocery, laundry, hardware, etc. and each store has its own list of items (bread, milk, cereal, etc.; pants, shirts, suits, etc.; hammer, hanging hooks, plaster, etc.,) respectively. Viewed in this manner, the store lists are functions called by the main 'to do' list. Each store list has a set of items and activities related to that store. Logically, putting them together makes a day long shopping experience more efficient and effective.

The inclusion of interactive programming in an introductory programming class opens a wide world of possibilities for analogies and metaphors. Everyone has experiences with embedded systems along with complaints and suggestions on how they would do things differently. With the proliferation of smart phones, tablets, car dashboards, etc. the reference disciplines are close to endless. The Association of Computing Machinery (Hewett et al., 2009) recognizes the breadth of HCI as it lists the breadth of supporting disciplines contributing to the discipline of human-computer interaction. These include but are not limited to: cognitive psychology, decision making; programming languages; data visualization; user satisfaction; technology acceptance and use, etc.

The design and implementation of a good, workable, user interface for a computer program becomes a wonderful exercise to educate students on key issues in how humans and computers interact. This activity presents an excellent opportunity to acquaint students with techniques and tools for issues that will later surface in core classes of a IS curriculum such as decision making, writing case analyses, developing user requirements, etc.

The application of the core HCI design principles are applicable life skills. Creating a good conversation means understanding how both sides think. This skill is applicable to many careers and life situations; buying a house, negotiating a contract, etc. One of the more important abilities acquired in this activity would be a higher capacity to better understand why things (embedded systems) don't work. Again, like with all the appropriations mentioned here, this one reverts back to the core problem solving skill mentioned as deficient in all of the skills gaps in the opening.

In conclusion, the paper sets forth the proposition that embedded within the ideas and concepts learned in a programming class hides the introduction to many of the foundational and life skills students need to complete their degrees and to succeed in careers. This suggests one should become a generalist rather than a specialist in the way one presents examples in a programming class. Expressly, the teaching tip is to include many different examples from everyday life within the problems presented for the students to solve. Finding examples from reference disciplines and at multiple levels of difficulty and of association will prove invaluable as students develop their analogies and appropriations. The beginning programming class that acts as the reference course for this paper, has students from many disciplines that are required to take the class; engineers, library science, business, computer science, healthcare, accounting, and math education students just to name a few. All of these students can benefit from a programming class as they "appropriate" and apply the programming concepts to their own discipline. The challenge is to help these students as much as possible by providing them with the proper tools to succeed first in their own chosen careers and then in life as they develop skills of lifelong learners.

REFERENCES

AACU (2015). Association of American Colleges & Universities. Foundations and Skills for Lifelong Learning VALUE Rubric. http://aacu.org/value/rubrics/lifelong-learning accessed March 17, 2015

AAHE (1996). "What Research Says About Improving Undergraduate Education," *AAHE Bulletin*, April 1996.

ACM/IEEE (2013). Computer Science Curricula 2013: Curriculum Guidelines for Undergraduate Degree Programs in Computer Science. Cooperative project of ACM, IEEE, and IEE Computer Society, 2013, http://dx.doi.org/10.1145/2534860

Anderson, C. and Gantz, J.F. (2103). SKILLS REQUIREMENTS FOR TOMORROW'S BEST JOBS Helping Educators Provide Students with Skills and Tools They Need, IDC, October 2013.

Barr, R. B. & Tagg. (1995). "From Teaching to Learning - A New Paradigm for Undergraduate Education," *Change*, Nov/Dec, 13-25, 1995.

Casner-Lotto, J, and Benner, M.W. (2006). Are They Really Ready To Work?. The Conference Board, Inc.,

Casserly, M. (2012). "The 10 Skills That Will Get you Hired in 2013". Forbes. Accessed March 4, 2015. http://www.forbes.com/sites/meghancasserly/2012/12/10/the-10-skills-that-will-get-you-a-job-in-2013/

Chickering, Arthur W. and Gamson. (1987). "Principles for Good Practice in Undergraduate Education," *The Wingspread Journal*, Johnson Foundation, Inc. June.

Doria, J., Rozanski, H.D., and Cohen, E. (2003). What Business Needs from Business Schools, *Strategy+Business*, Fall 2003, Issue 32. Accessed March 14, 2015 http://www.strategy-business.com/article/03305?pg=0

Fischer, K. (2013). A College Degree Sorts Job Applicants, but Employers Wish It Meant More, The Chronicle of Higher Education, vol 59, Iss. 26, March 8, 2013.

Goodman, M.J. Sands, A.M. and Coley, R.J. (2015). America's Skills Challenge. Educational Testing Service, Princeton, New Jersey. January.

Hall, D.T. and Mirvis (1995). The New Career Contract: Developing the Whole Person at Midlife and Beyond, Journal of Vocational Behavior, Vol. 47, Issue 3, pp 269-289.

Hewett; Baecker; Card; Carey; Gasen; Mantei; Perlman; Strong; Verplank. (2009)."ACM SIGCHI Curricula for Human-Computer Interaction". ACM SIGCHI. Retrieved March 6, 2015.

Martz, W. Benjamin, Jr. and Gabrielle Landof. (2000). "Information Systems Careers: A Comparison of Expectations, " *Journal of Computer Information Systems*, Vol. 40, No. 2, Winter 1999-2000, p41.

Minsky, M. (1988). *The Society of the Mind*. Simon and Schuster, 1988.

Newell, A. & Simon, H. (1972). Human Problem Solving. Englewood Cliffs, NJ: Prentice-Hall.

Overby, S. (2006). "How to Hook the Talent You Need," CIO, 2006, pp. 40-54, http://www.cio.com/article/24439/Staffing_How_to_Hook_the_Talent_You_Need, last accessed March 26, 2015.

Papert, S. (1980). *MindStorms*, Basic Books.

Piaget, J. (1929) *The Child's Conception of the World*, New York: Harcourt, Brace & Co, 1929.

Piateetsky, P. (2014). Most Demanded Data Science and Data Mining Skills. Accessed March 3, 2015. http://www.kdnuggets.com/2014/12/data-science-skills-most-demand.html

Roby, Thornton B. (1966). "Self-Enacting Response Sequences," *Psychological Reports,* 19, pp19-31.

Sandelands, L. E., Ashford, S. J., and Dutton, J.E. (1983). "Reconceptualizing the Overjustification Effect: A Template-Matching Approach," *Motivation and Emotion*, Vol. 7, No. 3, 1983

Sanders, M.S. and McCormick, E.J. (1987). *Human Factors in Engineering and Design.* Sixth Edition, New York: McGraw-Hill.

Schank, R. and Abelson, R. (1977). *Scripts, Plans, Goals and Understanding*, Lawrence Erlbaum.

Schank, R. (1988). *The Creative Attitude*, MacMillan.

Taylor, E. (2014). 11 Hottest Tech Jobs of 2014, US News Money, http://money.usnews.com/money/careers/slideshows/11-hottest-tech-jobs-of-2014/2

Topi, H., Valacich, J.S., Wright, R.T., Kaiser, K.M., Nunamaker, J.F., Sipior, J.C., and Vreede, G.J. de. (2008) "Revising the Undergraduate IS Model Curriculum: New Outcome Expectations," Communications of the Association for Information Systems (23:32) 2008, pp 591-602.

Topi, H., Valacich, J.S., Wright, R.T., Kaiser, K.M., Nunamaker, J.F., Sipior, J.C., and Vreede, G.J. de. (2010). "Curriculum Guidelines for Undergraduate Degree Programs in Information Systems," ACM/AIS 2010.

Thorndyke, P. and Hayes-Roth, B. (1979). "The Use of Schemata in the Acquisition and Transfer of Knowledge," *Cognitive Psychology*, Vol. 11, pp82-106.

DECISION SCIENCES INSTITUTE

Factors that influence employees' security policy compliance behavior: an Awareness-Motivation-Capability (AMC) perspective

Xiaofeng Chen
Western Washington University
Email: chenx@wwu.edu

Liqiang Chen
University of Wisconsin-Eau Claire
Email: chenliqi@uwec.edu

ABSTRACT

Information Security Policy (ISP) plays an important role in information security management. Past research investigated various factors from General Deterrence Theory (GDT), Protection and Motivation Theory (PMT), and Rational Choice Theory (RCT). However there is no unifying foundation/framework that can examines all of those factors in a harmonic way so that the research findings can guide the information security practice and research in the employees' ISP compliance management. This study proposes a research model based on the Awareness-Motivation-Capability (AMC) framework to unify the factors to predict employees' ISP compliance intention. We believe that a harmonic approach in managing employees' ISP compliance can create optimal outcomes.

KEYWORDS: Information Security Policy, AMC, Compliance

INTRODUCTION

High profiles of data breach in 2013 and 2014 highlighted the urgency for better data protection in industry. It happened to Home Depot, Target, Citi Bank, JPMorgan, and some other large multi-million dollar companies in the United States in just last several years. It costs $148 million alone for Target to clean up the mess caused by the data breach (Abrams 2014). This estimate may be very conservative since other estimation indicates the cost may top $300 million if all costs are included. The data breach happened at Target in 2013 ushered in a new era of data security. The data breach happened at Target is not because Target didn't have software and hardware measures in place to defend its data. It is because the network credentials was stolen from a third party partner through a malware email attack. It shows again that the weakest link in a security system lies in the human component of the security system (Gonzalez and Sawicka 2002; Misha and Dhillon 2006).

It is a common belief that a security policy is essential to increase the information security level of an organization (Sommestad et al. 2014). Prior research used various theories to study the factors that affect the behaviors of employees' security policy compliance, which include the theory of reasoned action (Bulgurcu et al. 2010), the theory of planned behavior (TPB) (Bulgurcu et al. 2010), protection and motivation theory (PMT) (Herath and Rao 2009; Johnston and Warkentin 2010; Lee et al. 2004; Vance et al. 2012), general deterrence theory (GDT) (D'arcy et al. 2009; Lee et al. 2004; Straub & Nance 1990; Straub & Welke 1998). One aspect that lacks in prior studies is the importance of user awareness of security policy. There is a limited effort in investigating the effect of user awareness of security policy on security compliance. We use the awareness-motivation-capability (AMC) model as the base to build an integrated security compliance model that incorporates constructs from PMT, TPB, and GDT to understand employees' security policy compliance behavior. This framework has implications for both academia and practice. For practitioners, it shows that a systematic approach is needed to make security policy more effective, which includes arousing employee awareness of security policies through management support and building a culture of treating security as critical business practice, motivating employees to comply with the policies through awards and penalties, and increasing employees' capability to comply with the policies by providing necessary education and training. It provides a comprehensive understanding on how security policies should be implemented in organizations. For academia, this study approaches security policy compliance from a new perspective. AMC framework has been used to understand the competitive actions of organizations in strategic research (Chen 1996; Smith et al. 2001). It has yet to be used for interpreting personal actions in MIS research. We believe that the three components that influence an organization's decision to act will also influence a person's decision to act. Those three components can be manifested in a range of variables that are important in interpreting employees' behaviors towards complying with their organization's security policies. It is a systematic attempt to integrate various theories to form a broad view of employees' security policy compliance behavior.

THEORETICAL FOUNDATION AND RESEARCH MDOEL

Awareness-Motivation-Capability framework (AMC)

The organizational literature has identified three drivers that underlie organizational competitive actions: awareness of market conditions, motivation to act, and capability to take action (Chen 1996; Dutton and Jackson 1987; Kiesler and Sproull 1982; Lant et al. 1992). Chen (1996) summarized that awareness is considered a prerequisite for any action or move; with the awareness, an organization will be motivated to act or counter act; and their action will be limited by their capability. In the competitive dynamics research, Chen et al. (2007) suggested that the individual components of the AMC framework are manifested in a range of variables, including action visibility and firm size for awareness, territorial interests in different markets (Gimeno 1999) for motivation, and execution difficulty and information processing (Smith et al. 1991) for capability.

Although AMC has been used to understand competitive actions of organizations, we believe that it is also a good framework for personal actions. Specifically we use this framework to understand employees' action or their intention toward their organization's security policy: comply or not comply. The behavior drivers of AMC framework: awareness, motivation, and capability outlined in the AMC framework will serve as the second-order constructs in this study. We use the three constructs as dimensions to group the other factors that have been studied in prior information security studies. These other factors from various theories are the first-order constructs in this study. We examine the impact of the three behavioral drivers as well as the other factors on employees' intention to comply with their organizations' ISP. This study will build a harmonic model that unifies factors that may have impact on employees' intention to comply with their organizations' ISP. This model provides sound theoretical guidelines for employee ISP compliance programs. Our research model is pictured in Figure 1. In the next section we discuss our research model and hypotheses development.

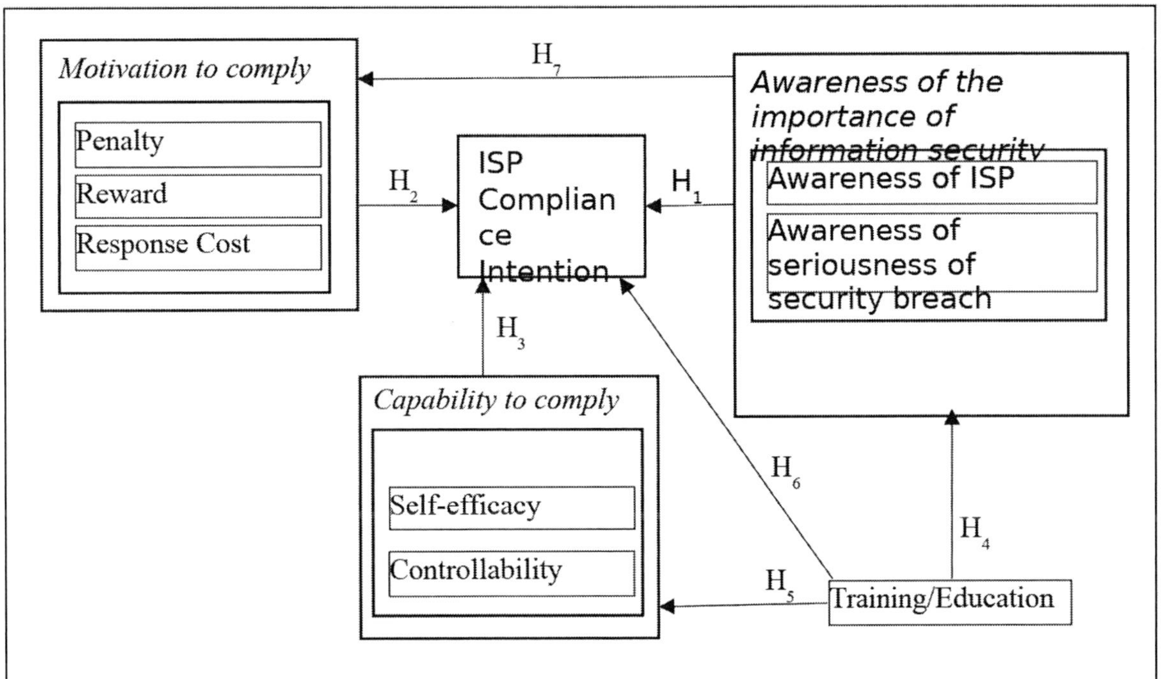

Figure 1: Research Model based on AMC framework

LITERATURE REVIEW AND HYPOTHESIS DEVELOPMENT

Information security has drawn attentions in academia and practice alike due to potential huge economic consequences for organizations. The insiders, referred to the employees in the business context, are recognized as the key component of information security management (Bulgurcu et al. 2010; Hinde 2003; Misha and Dhillon 2006; Theoharidou et al. 2005). The recent trade reports and academic research verify and support the argument. Therefore, human behavior perspective of information security is an important area of information security research and has drawn a great attention from academic researchers. Human behavior in information security management is influenced by information security policy (ISP). ISPs are created in organizations to provide employees with guidelines regarding how to ensure information security when they use information systems to do their work (Whitman et al. 2001; Bulgurcu et al. 2010). We adopt Bulgurcu et al. (2010)'s ISP definition in this study, stating ISP is "a statement of the roles and responsibilities of the employees to safeguard the information and technology resources of their organizations." (Bulgurcu et al. 2010, p. 526). This definition is consistent with many other ISP definitions used in prior research (e.g., D'Arch et al. 2009; Herath and Rao 2009).

One of the research streams in MIS draw on criminological and health belief theories, such as The Theory of Planned Behavior (TPB), Protection Motivation Theory (PMT), Deterrence Theory (DT), and Rational Choice Theory (RCT), to study insiders' compliance behavior toward organizational information security policy (ISP). Factors from different theories were studied separately in some studies or altogether in others without an underline foundation to unify the factors. In this study, we use the AMC framework (Chen et al. 1996) as the unifying foundation to investigate the effect of different factors that underline the behavior drivers and the effect of the behavior drivers on the employees' behavior of security policy compliance.

Effect of awareness on ISP compliance intention

Awareness factor gained a relatively low attention from information security researchers. Bulgurcu et al. (2010) examined the effect of information security awareness (ISA) on employees' attitude toward intention to comply with ISP. Bulgurcu et al. (2010)'s ISA consists of ISP awareness and general information security awareness (GISA). ISP awareness is defined as "an employee's knowledge and understanding of the requirements prescribed in the organization's ISP and the aims of those requirements" and GISA is defined as "an employee's overall knowledge and understanding of potential issues related to information security and their ramifications" (Bulgurcu et al. 2010, p. 532). Siponen and Pahnila (2010) indirectly investigated the awareness of ISP on employees' compliance with ISP via its impact of security visibility. They found that visibly promoting security is an important factor that influences employees' intention to comply with ISP. D'Arcy et al. (2009)'s study found that there is a direct impact of user awareness of security countermeasures on information systems misuse. Lee et al. (2004) conducted an interesting research whose finding are against the belief that information security policy is a key component of information security management. They found that information security policy does not have significant impact on preventing computer abuse, but security awareness does. We argue that the reason for these findings may lie in the employees' awareness of information security policy is low. We tested this assumption in our research. Past studies show the importance of ISP awareness factor. But the construct was not formally theorized in the studies on why it is an important factor for ISP compliance. We argue that according to AMC, awareness factor is an essential component for information security management. Awareness of the importance of an organization's ISP plays an important role in employees' behavior toward ISP compliance. This is one of the theoretical contributions of this study to our knowledge of information security management.

Based on the AMC framework and extant literature, we propose our first set of hypotheses:

H_1: Awareness of the importance of information security has a positive impact on employees' intention to comply with their organization's ISP.

H_{1a}: ISP awareness will positively affect employees' intention to comply with their organization's ISP.

H_{1b}: Awareness of the seriousness of security threats will positively affect employees' intention to comply with their organization's ISP.

Effect of motivation on ISP compliance intention

TPB is a base theory for many ISP compliance or non-compliance studies (e.g., Bulgurcu et al. 2010; D'Arcy et al. 2009; Herath and Rao 2009; Lee et al. 2004; Vance et al. 2012). The theory suggests that attitude, social norms, and behavior controls affect people's intention to perform the actual compliance behavior. Theories based on TPB, such as DT, PMT, and RCT, are used to investigate the antecedents and the antecedents' antecedents (two levels) to employees' attitude and intention to comply or not comply with their organization's ISP.

Although DT as a perspective has been applied to information security research, there is no general formalized definition of the theory (Williams and Hawkins 1986). The theory was applied to the research on the assumption that "individuals are deterred from committing criminal acts only if they perceive legal sanctions as certain, swift, and/or severe" (Williams and Hawkins 1986, p. 545). DT was applied to studies to evaluate penalty factors, such as penalty severity and certainty that may be effective to prevent certain actions from happening, such as non-adherence to security policy (Cheng et al. 2013; D'Arcy et al. 2009; Herath and Rao 2009). The results are inconsistent. Perceived severity of sanctions has been found having direct negative impact on IS misuse intention (D'Arcy et al. 2009; Skinner and Fream 1997; Cheng el al. 2013; Vance et al. 2012); whereas perceived certainty of sanctions has no direct impact on IS misuse (negative measure) intention (Cheng et al. 2013; D'Arch et al. 2009; Hu et al. 2011). In other studies perceived certainty of sanctions has been found having direct impact on ISP compliance (positive measure) (Herath and Rao 2009; Li et al. 2010), but perceived severity of sanction having no (Li et al. 2010). We found that direct impact of perceived severity was mostly found in non-compliance studies, such as misuse or violation (D'Arcy et al. 2009; Skinner and Fream 1997; Cheng el al. 2013); whereas direct impact of perceived certainty was found in compliance studies (Herath and Rao 2009; Li et al. 2010). There is no plausible explanation about the inconsistent results. D'Arcy and Herath (2011) conducted a thorough review and analysis of deterrence theory in the IS security literature. They theorized that the inconsistent results of the effect of DT factors on security behavior may be due to the contingency variables that are not controlled in the studies. These contingency variables may have a moderating effect on the DT variables-to-behavior relationship. The identified two groups of key contingency variables: individual factors and contextual factors. The formal includes self-control, computer self-efficacy, and moral beliefs; the latter includes virtual status and employee position (D'Arcy and Herath 2011). We argue that contingency variables may not only have a moderating effect on the DT variables-to-behavior relationship but also be 'noises' for the relationship. Together all these variables may explain the variances of employees' ISP compliance behavior.

According to PMT (Rogers 1975), people intend to cope with a threat based on the results of two appraisals: threat appraisal and coping appraisal. The motivation to protect themselves from the threat depends on severity of the thread; probability of the occurrence of the threat; the efficacy of the recommended preventive behavior; and sell-efficacy (Rogers 1975; Rogers 1983; Herath and Rao 2009). Motivation can be divided into intrinsic and extrinsic motivation. From the AMC perspective, we believe that the last two factors from PMT are capability factors, not the motivation factors.

RCT argues that an individual's action is determined by balancing the costs and benefits of his options (Bulgurcu et al. 2010). People balance the overall assessment of costs and benefits associated with the outcomes of their actions to determine which actions to take (Paternoster and Pogarsky 2009). We argue that the assessments of costs and benefits can serve as motivations to take actions. Costs can be viewed as motivations to not take actions and benefits can be viewed as motivations to take actions.

We propose that the variables from DT, PMT, and RCT can be grouped into the motivation dimension of the AMC framework. Those variables can be generally placed in the extrinsic motivation category since they are "perceived to be instrumental in achieving valued outcomes that are distinct from the activity itself" (Davis et al. 2992). Extending the application of the AMC framework at the organizational level to the individual level, we theorize that the motivation dimension of the AMC framework determines if a person will take an action or not. After an individual is aware of a potential action, they need to be motivated to take the action. The motivation to take an action can be influenced in the ISP compliance context from three categories of extrinsic factors: rewards, penalty, and cost. The intrinsic factors, which may include enjoyment for an action, may not be in play in this specific context. Both PMT and DT indicate that penalty can deter violations; therefore penalty can be considered as people's motivation to not commit violations outlined in their organization's ISP. Cost may have the same effect as penalty on ISP compliance. Numerous studies have shown that rewards can control behavior (Deci et al. 1999). Accordingly, our second set of hypotheses regarding employees' intention to comply with their organizations' ISP are:

H_2: Motivation has positive impact on employees' intention to comply with their organization's ISP.

H_{2a}: Penalty severity has inversed effect on employees' intention to comply with their organization's ISP.

H_{2b}: Reward has positive effect on employees' intention to comply with their organization's ISP.

H_{2c}: Cost to comply with ISP has negative effect on employees' intention to comply with their organization's ISP

Effect of capability on ISP compliance intention

According to the AMC framework, motivation is not enough for an individual to take an action. The individual has to have the capability to perform certain tasks for the action is actually carried out. In the context of ISP compliance, an employee has to have the capability to follow the policies and perform the tasks. The capability for performing the tasks is influenced by employees' ability to work with computer systems in general and security management (e.g., following the security policy, being about to use various security software) in specific. Several factors outlined in the security research using DT, PMT, and RCT can be placed in this dimension. These factors include self-efficacy with computer systems and employees' perception of controllability over compliance. The self-efficacy is well defined in the security research using PMT (e.g., Herath and Rao 2009). Controllability over compliance measures the employees' perception of support from management over compliance (Dinev and Hu 2007). Our next set of hypotheses are:

H_3: Capability has positive impact on employees' intention to comply with their organization's ISP.

H_{3a}: Self-efficacy with computer systems has positive effect on employees' intention to comply with their organization's ISP.

H_{3b}: Perception of controllability over compliance has positive effect on employees' intention to comply with their organization's ISP.

Security training and education has been found playing important role in security management (e.g., Furnell et al. 2002; Hentea 2005; D'Arcy et al. 2009; Bulgurcu et al. 2010). From the AMC perspective, security training and education can have impact on the awareness and capability dimensions as well as on ISP compliance intention itself. We propose:

H_4: Security training and education program has positive impact on employees' awareness of the importance of information security.

H_5: Security training and education program has positive impact on employees' capability to comply with their organizations' ISP.

H_6: Security training and education program has positive impact on employees' intention to comply with their organizations' ISP.

Effect of awareness of importance of information security on motivation to comply with ISP

The AMC framework proposes the three drivers for actions. However, it does not outline the relationships among the three drivers. There is a lack of empirical studies on the relationships among the three drivers. We argue that to be motivated to take an action, an individual needs to know what the action is concerned about, why it is important to take the action, and what are expected from them. Therefore, the awareness driver of AMC framework should have direct influence on the motivation driver of an action. As a result, we propose in the ISP compliance context:

H_7: Awareness of important of information security has positive impact on employees' motivation to comply with their organizations' ISP.

RESEARCH METHOD

There are two approaches in the research of employee security compliance. One approach is using scenarios to provide a specific security issue (Johnston and Warkentin 2010; Vance et al. 2012) followed by survey to collect information about what factors may affect the behavior of employees' security (compliance) behavior. The other approach is using survey to collect information regarding factors that may influence employees' compliance intention on a generic ISP that is defined as "a statement of the roles and responsibilities of the employees to safeguard the information and technology resources of their organizations." (Bulgurcu et al. 2010, p. 526). The latter is a main approach in the literature of investigating ISP compliance behavior (e.g., D'Arcy et al. 2009; Herath and Rao 2009). We choose to use the second approach in this study. We attempt to examine employees' intention to comply with ISP as defined in a general statement.

There are two techniques to assess a regression structural model: one is the covariance-based SEM as represented by LISREL and the other is component-based (or variance-based) as represented by Partial Least Square (PLS) modeling (Henseler et al. 2009). We will use PLS modeling in this study to investigate the relationships among the factors. PLS requires smaller sample size than covariance-based SEM techniques. In this study there are three second-order constructs, 10 first-order constructs, and over 35 indicators in total. The sample size may needs to be over 700 if we use covariance-based SEM, such as LISREL. Also LISREL may not be able handle the model with this complexity (Chin et al. 2003).

SUMMARY

In this study, we use the AMC framework to build an integrated model that investigates the factors that may influence employees' intention to comply with their organizations' ISP. Past research identified many factors that may affect employees' intention in several different models that do not have a unifying foundation, thus the research findings lack consistency. Also without a unifying foundation, different factors explain employees' compliance behavior from different perspectives. As a result, there is no theoretical consensus about how to implement employee ISP compliance programs and accordingly there is no consistent guidelines for practitioners to follow. By applying the AMC framework in the ISP compliance research, we propose that many factors that may influence employees' compliance with ISP can be grouped into three categories of behavior drivers: awareness, motivation, and capability. The implications of this study are in two folds. In academia, this study for the first time investigates employees' compliance with ISP using the AMC framework. We built a model that uses the three behavior drivers outlined in the AMC framework as the unifying foundation. This unifying foundation re-posits the factors from different theories in the past information security research to understand what affect employees' compliance with their organizations' ISP. This model presents a new perspective in studying employees' ISP compliance. In practice, this study can provide guidelines for managers to design their information security management programs. Managers need to be aware that employees' compliance with their organizations' ISP is critical to secure their organizational information systems and usages. Employees' awareness of the importance of information security and ISP may play an important role in information security management. Other than promoting the importance of information security and ISP by creating awareness programs, managers need to pay attention to help employees to develop capability to comply with their ISPs. Security education and training can help build employees' capability to comply with their organizations' ISP and in turn improve the actual compliance practice. Managing employees' compliance with ISP in information security management is a harmonic process. It cannot be achieved through just one dimension.

Reference:

Abrams, R. "Target puts data breach costs at $148 million, and forecasts profit drop," *New York Times*, extracted at http://www.nytimes.com/2014/08/06/business/target-puts-data-breach-costs-at-148-million.html?_r=0

Bulgurcu, B., Cavusoglu, H, and Benbasat, I "Information security policy compliance: an empirical study of rationality-based beliefs and information security awareness," MIS Quarterly 34(3), 2010, pp. 523-548.

Chaudhuri, S. "Cost of replacing credit cards after Target breach estimated at $200 million," Wall Street Journal, http://www.wsj.com/articles/SB10001424052702304675504579391080333769014.

Chen, M.J. "Competitor analysis and inter-firm rivalry: towards a theoretical integration," Academy of Management Review, 21, 1996, pp. 100-134.

Chen, M.J., Su, K.H., and Tsai, W.P. "Competitive Tension: The Awareness-Motivation-Capability Perspective," *Academy of Management Journal* (50:1), 2007, pp. 101-118.

Cheng, L., Li, Y., Li, W., Holm, E., and Zhai, Q. "Understanding the violation of IS security policy in organizations: an integrated model based on social control and deterrence theory," Computers & Security, 2013, pp. 1-13.

D'arcy, J., Hovav, A., and Galletta, D. "User awareness of security countermeasures and its impact on information systems misuse: a deterrence approach," Information Systems Research 20(1), 2009, pp. 79-98.

Deci, E.L., Koestner, R., and Ryan, R.M. "A meta-analytic review of experiments examining the effects of extrinsic rewards on intrinsic motivation," Psychological Bulletin (125:6), 1999, pp. 627-668.

Dinev, T. and Hu, Q. (2007) "The Centrality of Awareness in the Formation of User Behavioral Intention toward Protective Information Technologies," Journal of the Association for Information Systems 8(7), Article 23.

Dutton, J.E. and Jackson, S.B. "Categorizing strategic issues: links to organizational action," Academy of Management Review 12, 1987, pp. 76-90.

Gimeno, J. "Reciprocal Threats in Multmarket Rivalry: Staking out 'Spheres of Influence' in the U.S. Airline Industry," *Strategic Management Journal* (20:2), 1999, pp. 101-128.

Herath, T. and Rao, H.R. "Protection motivation and deterrence: a framework for security policy compliance in organisations," European Journal of Information Systems 18(2), 2009, pp. 91-109.

Hinde, S. "The law, cybercrime, risk assessment and cyber protection," Computers and Security 22(2), 2003, pp. 90-95.

Hu, Q., Xu, Z. Dinev, T., and Ling, H. "Does deterrence work in reducing information security policy abuse by employees?," Communications of the ACM 54(6), 2011, pp. 54-60.

Johnston, A. and Warkentin, M. "Fear appeals and information security behaviors: an empirical study," MIS Quarterly 34(3), 2010, pp. 549-566.

Kiesler, S. and Sproull, L. "Managerial response to changing environments: perspectives on problem sensing from social cognition," Administrative Science Quarterly 27, 1982, pp.548-570.

Lant, T.K., Milliken, F.J., and Batra, B. "The role of managerial learning and interpretation in strategic persistence and reorientation," Strategic Management Journal 13, 1992, pp. 585-608.

Lee, S.M., Lee, S., and Yoo, S. "An integrative model of computer abuse based on social control and general deterrence theories," Information & Management 41(6), 2004, pp. 707-718.

Misha, S. and Dhillon, G. "Information systems secdurity governance research: a behavioral perspective," 1st Annual Symposium on Information Assurance, 2006.

Paternoster, R. and Pogarsky, G. "Rational choice, agency and thoughtfully reflective decision making: the short and long-term consequences of making good choices," *Journal of Quantitative Criminology* (25:2), 2009, pp. 103-127.

Rogers, R.W. "A protection motivation theory of fear appeals and attitude change," The Journal of Psychology (91), 1975, pp. 93-114.

Rogers, R.W. "Cognitive and physiological processes in fear appeals and attitude change: a revised theory of protected motivation," In Social Psychophysiology: a sourcebook (Cacioppo, J.T. and Petty, R.E., Eds), 1983, pp. 153-176, The Guilford Press, New York.

Siponen, M., Pahnila, S., and Mahmood, M.A. "Compliance with Information Security Policies: An Empirical Investigation", *Computer* 43(2), pp. 64-71, February 2010.

Siponen, M. and Vance, A. "Neutralization: new insights into the problem of employee information systems security policy violations," *MIS Quarterly* 34(3), 2010, p. 487-502.

Smith K. G., Grimm, C. M., Gannon, M. J., Chen, M., Grimm, C. M., Gannon, M. J. "Organizational Information Processing, Competitive Responses, and Performance in the U.S. Domestic Airline Industry," *Academy of Management Journal* (34:1), 1991, pp.60-85.

Smith, K.G., Ferrier, W., and Ndofor, H. "Competitive dynamics research: critique and future directions". In M. Hitt, R. Freeman, & J. Harrison (Eds.). Handbook of Strategic Management, 2001, pp. 315-361. London: Blackwell.

Sommestad, T. Hallberg, J., Lundholm, K., and Bengtsson, J. "Variables influencing information security policy compliance," Information Management & Computer Security 22(1), 2014, pp. 42-75.

Straub, D. and Nance, W.D. "Discovering and disciplining computer abuse in organizations: a field study," MIS Quarterly 14(1), 1990, pp. 45-60.

Straub, D. and Welke, R. "Coping with systems risk: security planning models for management decision making," MIS Quarterly 22(8), 1998, pp. 441-465.

Teodor, S., Hallberg, J., Lundholm, K, and Bengtsson, J. "variables influencing information security policy compliance: a systematic review of quantitative studies," Information Management & Computer Security 22(1), 2014, pp. 42-75.

Theoharidou, M., Kokolakis, S., Karyda, M., and Kiountouzis, E. "The insider threat to information systems and the effectiveness of ISO 17799," Computers & Security 24(6), 2005, pp. 472-484.

Vance, A., Siponen, M., and Pahnila S. "Motivating IS security compliance: insights from habit and protection motivation theory," Information & Management 49, 2012, pp. 190-198.

Vroom, C. and Von Solms, R. "Towards information security behavioral compliance," Computer Security 23(3), 2004, pp. 191-198.

Whitman, M.E., Townsend, A.M., and Aalberts, R.J. "Information systems security and the need for policy," in *Information Security Management – Global Challenges in the Next Millennium*, G. Dhillon, London: Idea Group, 2001, pp. 9-18.

Williams, K.R. and Hawkins, R. "Perceptual research on general deterrence: a critical review," Law & Society Review 20(4), 1986, pp. 545-572.

DECISION SCIENCES INSTITUTE

Financial Data Analytics and Extraction from Security Exchange Commission's (SEC) EDGAR Filings

Richard Green
Texas A&M University - San Antonio
Email: Richard.Green@tamusa.edu

Robert Burdwell
Texas A&M University - San Antonio
Email: Robert.Burdwell@tamusa.edu

Robert Vinaja
Texas A&M University - San Antonio
Email: Robert.Vinaja@tamusa.edu

ABSTRACT

This is a proposal to provide specific industry, business, and financial data to business students and faculty. The data are appropriate for empirical research into issues that involve publicly-owned corporations that are listed on public stock exchanges in the United States. This project involves the development of programs and scripts to make accessing and using the data of the Security Exchange Commission's (SEC) Electronic Data Gathering, Analysis, and Retrieval system (EDGAR) for the purpose of primary empirical academic research.

KEYWORDS: XBRL, EDGAR, Security Exchange Commission, Financial Statement Analysis

INTRODUCTION

This project involves the development of programs and scripts to make accessing and using the data of the Security Exchange Commission's (SEC) Electronic Data Gathering, Analysis, and Retrieval system (EDGAR) for the purpose of primary empirical academic research.
The EDGAR system holds all mandatory filing data for over 9,700 corporate entities. The data are complete from April of 2005 through March 2015. The EDGAR standard taxonomy includes nearly 14,000 terms and can be expanded. This project will start by extracting and analyzing the last five years.
Accessing this data is a daunting task for most would-be researchers due to the sharp learning curve of mastering the details of electronic filing, the extensible business reporting language (XBRL), downloading and parsing the filings.
In fact, the tasks of downloading and parsing of the data are quite straight-forward and can be easily performed by appropriate computer programs. However, at this time, there is NO freely-available, user-friendly set of programs for this purpose.

LITERATURE REVIEW

CRSP - The Center for Research in Security Prices provide a comprehensive database for historical security prices and returns information. Research Data Access CRSP provides data access.

Python- XBRL is a library for parsing XBRL documents, it is a set of scripts that use python to parse XBRL marked-up text. There is also open source python middleware to add XBRL handling to basic python.
Arelle is a project to provide an easy to use open source facility for XBRL. Arelle includes Edgar manual validation. We have downloaded Arelle got the RSS feed to work for all filings. The next step is to export the data to a database. There is also a CVS file of the column headings that can be downloaded. This feature provides a real time saver for the approach to extract the data to MySQL.
Pysec compiles a list of all SEC filings from EDGAR into SQL, downloads them, and parses 50+ key accounting terms from XBRL filings. Pysec is also an open source Python XBRL parser that can extract arbitrary XBRL terms. The "guts" of Pysec were coded by Charles Hoffman, who was one of the originators of XBRL. One of the objectives is to extend this code to extract more than 50 accounting terms. This approach should produce a demo program before the development of the final product.
This approach based on Python scripts does not require loading the data into MySQL or Oracle. One of the potential advantages in that this approach can save a significant amount of disk space and processing time. One of the disadvantages of this approach is that Pysec is a combination of Python scripting (through a version called Django) and Visual Basic. Another limitation is that Pysec does not read XBRL in a zipped folder. Rather, as one of its developers wrote, "...command sec_import_index compiles a list of all SEC filings from EDGAR into SQL, populating the Index model, and will lazily download them as you access them..." EDGAR filings are provided in a zipped file and the ability to search the filings in compressed format would be very efficient. After installing Python and Pysec, one of the required steps is to adjust the settings.py, and modify the DATA_DIR = '/you/directory/to/download/files/to' and set your database. Currently, we had a few issues with the Pysec Phython application. There are a few errors each time pages are run. Thus, even though the program assumes that a copy of the sec filings in XBRL zip files is resident on the local computer, it is parsing them into SQL.
Another approach is to put the data into a MySQL or Oracle Express database, even if only temporarily for processing. Oracle XBRL Extension uses the XML DB feature of Oracle to give solution for collecting, storing, querying, analyzing, and managing XBRL content.
XBRLAnalyst is a financial data platform for Excel that leverages XBRL. XBRLAnalyst allows you to download 20k filings per month for $10 per month. Another alternative is to publish these exports on a web server and then conduct data analysis with Tableau. The same vendor also features a VBA Analyst download and API integration for developers.
Another commercial product by Altova, Raptor XBRL validates the instances against the taxonomy and verifies the formulas and definitions

METHODS AND MODEL

The principal investigator has already developed Python scripts that complete the functions of downloading, saving, and searching the EDGAR data. The next objective is to parse the data once it is downloaded. An additional objective is to make the scripts "user-friendly". A future step is to create an interface to extract these EDGAR filings.
The user interface should allow the user to search for specific companies. Also, the user should be able to search by keywords, then identify the taxonomy items, and use checkboxes to select a specific item from the taxonomy, for instance: depreciation related items. The interface should also provide a search capability to search and navigate the taxonomies.

If the project is installed on the university platform, there will be some small additional demand on the university network servers, as the approximate size of the unzipped database will be

approximately 52 GB. The compressed database with EDGAR files is about 14 GB (about three years' worth of data), and unzipped is 52 GB. The unzipped data will be hosted on MySQL. Since an XBRL element can have a variable number of items, it would be difficult to map directly it to a relational table, because the table with variable columns. The database will be regularly updated by using RSS. The database size will grow over time. At this time, a copy of the proposed database is maintained on a desktop computer which is a 4-core Intel i7 processor and a 600 GB hard disk.
More text about this . . . Figure 1 is a tabular summary of the frequency of work in this stream.

Figure 1: Implementation Model

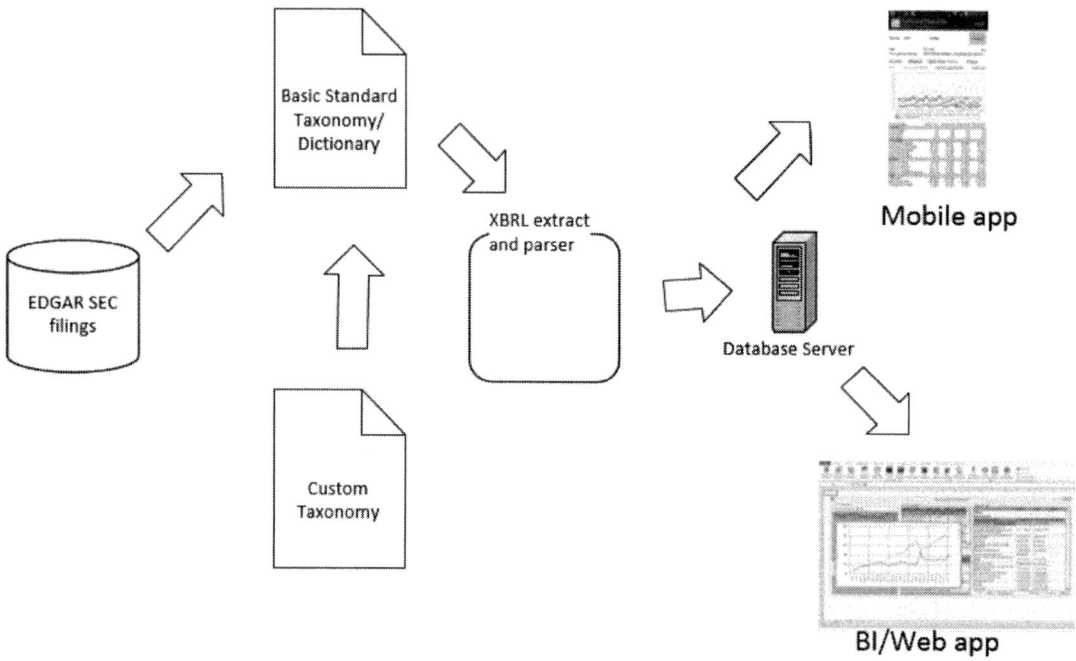

RESULTS

This project plan includes the following steps:

1. Familiarize all participants in the project with XBRL and EDGAR.
2. Select a program for the project from those currently available, including C, C++, Java, and the Perl and Python scripting languages.
3. Develop a description of the desired Graphical User Interface (GUI)
4. Develop a "pseudo-code" (flow chart and scripting) description of the code to be written.
5 Write and test the code.
6. Enlist "Beta" testers from faculty.
7. Debug and address issues from the Beta test phase.
8. Finish and distribute the program to interested faculty and students.

The next step is to develop a mobile app and/or web application to access the data. Use business intelligence analytics software (like Tableau) to create dashboards for comparing financial ratios. Some of these important ratios include asset turnover ratio, inventory turnover ratio, and liquidity ratio. Ratio analysis is used for selecting companies based on industry ratios, evaluating financial strength based on financial statement analysis based on ratios. A sample spreadsheet providing an example of financial statement ratio analysis is provided.

The availability of this application would facilitate research in additional areas such as: analyzing the frequency of errors in XBRL financial documents and the potential impact..

DISCUSSION AND CONCLUSIONS

Benefits of this project include enabling original primary empirical research to be conducted without having to invest tens of thousands of dollars in proprietary database products such as S&P Capital IQ Fundamentals ® from Standard & Poor's Financial Services. Additionally, this project requires no resources that are not already in use in the host university.

This project involves three faculty members but will also involve numerous students, primarily students in computer science. The students, under the direction of faculty, will develop additional programs to make this data easily available to interested users.

Costs of completing this project are minimal. One of the development options requires no software to purchase nor any database to license.

REFERENCES

Bharosa, N., van Wijk, R., Janssen, M., de Winne, N., & Hulstijn, J. (2011). Managing the transformation to standard business reporting: principles and lessons learned from the Netherlands. 12th Annual International Conference on Digital Government Research (dg.o 2011), 151–156. doi:10.1145/2037556.2037578

Borges, F. C. R., & Silva, P. C. da. (2012). A Framework for Processing Business Financial Rules (pp. 47–50). New York, NY, USA: ACM. doi:10.1145/2382636.2382648

Carrillo, E., Chaparro, F., & Santoyo, J. (2008). XBRL and financial information standards: a case success: university-enterprise-government in Universidad Autonoma de Bucaramanga. EATIS '08 Proceedings of the 2008 Euro American Conference on Telematics and Information Systems, 1–3. doi:10.1145/1621087.1621134

Data Access Tools. (n.d.). Retrieved April 8, 2016, from http://www.crsp.com/products/software-access-tools

EDGAR Dashboard. (n.d.). Retrieved April 8, 2016, from https://edgardashboard.xbrlcloud.com/edgar-dashboard/

Fan, W., Geerts, F., Li, J., & Xiong, M. (2011). Discovering Conditional Functional Dependencies. IEEE Trans. Knowl. Data Eng., 23(5), 683–698. Retrieved from http://dl.acm.org/citation.cfm?id=2460396.2460414

Felden, C. (2011). Characteristics of XBRL adoption in Germany. Journal of Management Control, 22(2), 161–186. doi:10.1007/s00187-011-0134-7

Fischer, H., & Mueller, D. (2011). Open Source & XBRL: the Arelle® Project (pp. 29–30). Retrieved from http://eycarat.faculty.ku.edu//myssi/_pdf/4-Fischer -Mueller-Open-source-ArelleProject.pdf

García, R., & Gil, R. (2010). Linking XBRL financial data. In Linking Enterprise Data (pp. 103–125). New York, NY, USA: ACM. doi:10.1007/978-1-4419-7665-9_6

GitHub - Arelle/Arelle: Arelle open source XBRL platform. (n.d.). Retrieved April 8, 2016, from https://github.com/Arelle/Arelle

GitHub - lukerosiak/pysec: Parse XBRL filings from the SEC's EDGAR in Python. (n.d.). Retrieved April 8, 2016, from https://github.com/lukerosiak/pysec

Hoffman, C., & Watson, L. (2009). XBRL For Dummies. For Dummies. Retrieved from https://sourceforge.net/projects/rivetdragonview/

Huang, M., Wang, D., & Wang, K. (2011). Ontology-based Semantic Retrieval of XBRL Data. 2012 Second International Conference on Business Computing and Global Informatization, 0, 363–366. doi:http://doi.ieeecomputersociety.org/10.1109/BCGIn.2011.97

index.html. (n.d.). Retrieved April 8, 2016, from http://www.oracle.com/technetwork/database/database-technologies/xbrl-extension/overview/index.html

Janssen, M., & Tan, Y.-H. (2014). Dynamic Capabilities for Information Sharing: XBRL Enabling Business-to-Government Information Exchange. 2014 47th Hawaii International Conference on System Sciences, 0, 2104–2113. doi:http://doi.ieeecomputersociety.org/10.1109/HICSS.2014.266

Jimei, L., Yuzhou, H., & Meijie, D. (2013). XBRL in the Chinese Financial Ecosystem. IT Professional, 15(6), 36–42. doi:http://doi.ieeecomputersociety.org/10.1109/MITP.2013.59

Kotsiantis, S. B., Kanellopoulos, D., Karioti, V., & Tampakas, V. (2009). An ontology-based portal for credit risk analysis. Computer Science and Information Technology, International Conference on, 0, 165–169. doi:http://doi.ieeecomputersociety.org/10.1109/ICCSIT.2009.5234452

Li, J., Zhao, H., & Du, M. (2012). Analyzing Semantic Heterogeneity in XBRL Taxonomies: An Ontology Perspective. Management of E-Commerce and E-Government, International Conference on, 0, 264–268. doi:http://doi.ieeecomputersociety.org/10.1109/ICMeCG.2012.48

Liu, C., Yao, L. J., Sia, C. L., & Wei, K. K. (2013). The impact of early XBRL adoption on analysts' forecast accuracy - empirical evidence from China. Electronic Markets, 24(1), 47–55. doi:10.1007/s12525-013-0132-8

Madlberger, L., Thöni, A., Wetz, P., Schatten, A., & Tjoa, A. M. (2013). Ontology-based Data Integration for Corporate Sustainability Information Systems. Proceedings of International Conference on Information Integration and Web-Based Applications & Services - IIWAS '13, 353–357. doi:10.1145/2539150.2539208

Pinsker, R., & Li, S. (2008). Costs and benefits of XBRL adoption. Communications of the ACM, 51(3), 47–50. doi:10.1145/1325555.1325565 python-xbrl 1.0.2 : Python Package Index. (n.d.). Retrieved April 8, 2016, from https://pypi.python.org/pypi/python-xbrl/1.0.2

python-xbrl-middleware on PyPI - Libraries. (n.d.). Retrieved April 8, 2016, from https://libraries.io/pypi/python-xbrl-middleware

Rivet Software Dragon View XBRL Viewer download | SourceForge.net. (n.d.). Retrieved April 8, 2016, from https://sourceforge.net/projects/rivetdragonview/

Rosiak, L. (n.d.). OpenGov Voices: PySEC, bringing corporate financial data to the masses. Retrieved April 8, 2016, from https://sunlightfoundation.com/blog/2013/08/02/opengov-voices-pysec-bringing-corporate-financial-data-to-the-masses/

Wang, W., Huang, M., & Wang, Z. (2011). A Storage and Query Mechanism of XBRL Data Based on Native XML Database. 2012 Second International Conference on Business Computing and Global Informatization, 0, 497–500. doi:http://doi.ieeecomputersociety.org/10.1109/BCGIn.2011.131

XBRLAnalyst Delivers Financial Data To Excel | FinDynamics. (n.d.). Retrieved April 8, 2016, from https://findynamics.com/try-xbrlanalyst/

Yingchun, S., & Baohua, T. (2010). Research on the Disclosure Quality of Financial Reporting on the Internet Based on XBRL Technology. 2012 Fourth International Conference on Computational and Information Sciences, 0, 605–608. doi:http://doi.ieeecomputersociety.org/10.1109/ICCIS.2010.153

Zambrano, E., & Samper, J. (2007). XBRL: from common financial vocabularies to intelligent decision making. EATIS '07 Proceedings of the 2007 Euro American Conference on Telematics and Information Systems, 2–5. doi:10.1145/1352694.1352770

Zhu, H., & Wu, H. (2011). Quality of data standards: framework and illustration using XBRL taxonomy and instances. Electronic Markets, 21(2), 129–139. doi:10.1007/s12525-011-0060-4

DECISION SCIENCES INSTITUTE

Firm's Short-term Growth Rate and Earnings Management

Yuanlong He
The College at Brockport, SUNY
Email: yhe@brockport.edu

ABSTRACT

This paper uses performance-matched income increasing discretionary accruals as earnings management measurement and shows a positive association between earnings management and short-term growth rate. Further test suggests there is a positive relationship between earnings management and variance of the growth rate. Since valuation models usually use the growth rate that is derived from analysts' forecast and existing literature suggests that analysts do not fully consider the impact of earnings management indication on the future earnings and growth rate, findings of this paper provide new insights into effect of earnings management on the growth when OJ formula is used.

KEYWORDS: Earnings growth rate, discretionary accruals, earnings management, firm valuation

INTRODUCTION

This paper explores the further understanding of firms' short-term earnings growth rate (as defined by Ohlson and Juettner-Nauroth (2005)). Derived from modern finance valuation theory (PVED) and assuming clean surplus relation, Ohlson and Juettner-Nauroth (2005) states that firm value is determined by next year's expected earnings level (X1), expected short-term earnings growth (g_i) for following periods and long-term growth (γ) (assuming the periods after which the firm reach a steady growth status). In the financial market, analysts usually forecast firms' next period earnings and following period short-term earnings growth, and then based on these forecasted numbers, get the value of the firm and give markets stock pick recommendations. Theoretically, in order to get a proper valuation of a firm's intrinsic value, we need to get a correct intrinsic short-term growth rate(s) to use in the formula. In reality, it is impossible for us to know this intrinsic economic growth rate(s). Rather, in practice, we usually use analysts' forecasted number instead (Easton (2004)). When analysts are capable enough to predict growth rate numbers that are close enough to the intrinsic ones, there is no lost of accuracy in determining the firm's market value by using the model. But when there are systematic errors in over or under prediction of the growth rate when analysts use available information, the predicted value of the firm and inferences from the model will be different from the correct one.

In order to analyze the connection between expected growth rate from analysts' forecasts and intrinsic growth rate from firms' economic performance, first step is to understand several possible factors that may cause the information about the firm's earnings and growth to be distorted. One of the most important ways for the firm to communicate its performance information with the investing public is through accounting reports by using accounting numbers such as earnings, earnings growth, sales, etc. Analysts use information from the reported accounting numbers and other non-financial information to analyze the firm and give their predicted numbers. Since reported numbers have information content for analysts, comparing reported numbers to the intrinsic ones can serve as the link between intrinsic and predicted numbers. First factor that makes reported numbers different from intrinsic ones are errors in recording or reporting accounting numbers and may or may not detected by auditors. Errors not intentionally and undetected may cause the reported numbers different from intrinsic ones and cause the analysts' inference from these incorrect numbers leading to inaccurate predicted growth rate. But since these errors are random, they are not expected to cause systematic errors to the predicted numbers. Second factor that may cause the predicted numbers different from intrinsic ones can be random or non-random errors arise from analysts' estimation, which may be systematic as evidence shows as analysts' optimism. Third factor that makes reported numbers different from intrinsic ones is accounting conservatism. Accounting conservatism can be either defined as in Penman and Zhang (2002) as unconditional conservatism: biased application of historical cost accounting that leads to the value of firms' assets on book lower than market value, or defined as conditional conservatism: asymmetric treatment of good news versus bad news (Basu (1997)). Systematic accounting conservatism will lead to a distorted earnings number and growth rate as reported in GAAP standards comparing to its intrinsic ones. For examples, expensing R&D in current period and recognizing benefits for the later periods will reduce the current reported earnings numbers and increase the future numbers relative to the intrinsic earnings. If analysts cannot take the effect of accounting conservatism on reported numbers into consideration when making prediction based on these reported numbers, then expected numbers would be inevitably be distorted. Last but not least, the widely documented earnings management phenomena can also cause reported numbers be distorted from intrinsic ones and it is the issue this paper intends to address.

The direct effect of earnings management is to cause the reported earnings numbers and earnings growth rate be different from intrinsic ones. But it is not necessary for earnings management to also cause the predicted numbers to be distorted from intrinsic ones. When using the information implied in the reported earnings for prediction, if analysts are capable of anticipating earnings management and their aim is to produce unmanaged numbers, the expected numbers are not distorted and evaluation process is fine. On the other side, if analysts are either incapable of identifying managed part of earnings or they want to minimize the forecast error considering their prediction accuracy and disregard the effect of earnings management, then expected numbers may be distorted from the intrinsic ones through the connection of reported numbers in the middle. Existing literature shows that analysts do not fully incorporate the effect of earnings management in their forecasts and do not fully account for the implications of these forecasts in making their stock recommendations. For example, by using eventual restatement, Ettredge, Shane and Smith (1995) find that analysts only partially discount overstated earnings in revising their earnings expectations. Abarbanell and lehavy (2003a) find that firms with buy (sell) stock recommendations are more (less) engaged in earnings management yet this tendency is not fully incorporated in analysts' earnings forecasts. Hanna and Orpurt (2006) document an association between special items reported on the income statement and analysts' forecast errors, which is consistent with analysts being either unable or unwilling to adjust their forecasts for earning management. A working paper by Givoly, Hayn and Yoder examines whether analysts' earnings forecasts incorporate or exclude the managed earnings component by using restatement group and earnings managed up group. Their finding is that the managed earnings component appears to influence analysts' subsequent earnings forecasts and lead to upward forecast revisions. These evidences suggest that reported distorted numbers by earnings management have an effect on expected numbers and thus on the firms' evaluation. Since the intrinsic earnings growth rate is not available for direct investigation of the distortion effect of earnings management on the growth rate, we have to find an alternative way to study this issue. Investigation of the relationship between reported short-term growth rate and earnings management can serve this purpose since earnings management can be used as a proxy of the degree of distortion effect that is supposed to be. If we find a positive relationship between earnings management and short-term growth rate, we can lead to conclusion that using expected growth rate that is inferred from reported ones will be biased since analysts do not fully compound the effect of earnings management in their projection.

On the one hand, up-ward earnings management directly distorts a firm's reported earnings number and its short-term growth rate, resulting in a distorted and different earnings path from intrinsic one. Up-ward earnings management reports higher growth rate than intrinsic one. On the other hand, there are limitations on the side of GAAP and accounting practices to prohibit manager from optimistically biasing earnings forever. In fact the bias has to be reversed after several periods or even sooner (Barton and Simko (2002)). These two factors together lead to a positive association between earning management and standard deviation of short-term growth rate.

Using a sample of firm-annual observations from 1987 to 2006 from Compustat and IBES analysts forecasts data, this study performs a test on the difference of the firm specific short-term growth rate of those observations that MBE by one-penny verse those observations that Missing expectations by less than one-penny. The results of tests show a weak difference, that is, short-term growth rate of MBE one-penny group is weakly bigger than those of Missing one-penny group.

A second test is done by using samples from same period from Compustat and income increasing performance-matched discretionary accruals as proxy of earnings management. Further, I examine the association between the standard deviation of short-term growth rate of firm's accounting earnings and mean (median) of the income increasing performance-matched discretionary accruals. I find that there are positive correlation between earnings management and short-term growth rate, and between earnings management and the standard deviation of growth rate.

This paper contributes to the literature in several aspects. Firm's short-term growth rate is one of the crucial parts in the fundamental accounting valuation models. It is important to understand possible factors that will affect the short-term growth rate and take them into consideration when forecast earnings or earnings growth rates are used for valuation purpose. Since analysts' forecasts have been shown by prior literature not fully considering the impact of earnings management on the effect of future earnings number and growth rate, analyzing the relationship between earnings management and firms short-term growth rate helps understanding the implication of some factors we needs to consider when using OJ model.

Secondly, this study enhances our understanding of effects of firm's earnings management on distribution of the firm's short-term growth rate. Not only earnings management can distort the firm's earnings path but also its standard deviation. It may be considered as a negative effect of earnings management brings to the firm value.

The remainder of this paper is organized as follows: First, I provide hypotheses development and reviews prior research related to this study. Next section describes research design and empirical proxies. Then I introduce the sample and provide descriptive statistics. The results of testing two hypotheses are presented after that. The last Section provides a brief summary and conclusions.

HYPOTHESES DEVELOPMENT AND PRIOR RESEARCH

Hypotheses development

Under the condition that analysts' forecasts do not fully consider the implication of earnings management effect on the earning and earnings growth, and realized earnings and earnings growth rate have information intent for the forecast purposes, I propose that up-ward earnings management has a positive correlation with the firms short-term growth rate. In order to test if there is a positive relationship between earnings management and firm's reported short-term growth rate, a possible way is to pick a sample with firm observations that reported earnings number is most likely to be managed up and compare these growth rate to those observations that is not likely to be managed up. Existing literature shows meeting or beating expectation by one-penny group (MBE one-penny group) can be a potential candidate for such purpose. Degeorge et al. (1999) exams the distribution of reported earnings numbers and proposes three thresholds for earnings management to achieve. Their paper shows the existence of kinks around these three thresholds and states it is the proof of earnings management. Specifically one of the thresholds is to meet analysts' consensus forecast numbers. They find out that there is a kink just before zero forecast error and an extra pileup of observations at the zero point. Another study about the MBE one-penny group is Burgstahler and Eames (2003) and they provide evidence that both cash flow and discretionary accruals components of earnings are managed upward while forecasts are managed downward for MBE one-penny group. These researches provide justification for focusing on one particular group as proxy for earnings management—meeting or just beating analysts' forecasts by small amount. If earnings management in order to meet or beat expectations leads to distortion of the short-term growth rate, as for MBE one-penny group, we will expect the mean of the short-term growth rate for these firm specific observations be greater than the mean of the short-term growth rate for these same firm's observations when missing expectations by less than one penny.

H1: there is a significant difference in the mean short-term growth rate between these observations when MBE by one-penny and those when missing expectation by one penny for the same firm.

Another way to detect earnings management is by using discretionary accruals. Various accruals models are used in literature as a measurement of the degree of the earnings management. For example, Dechow et al. (1995) evaluates several accrual-based models for detecting earnings management, namely, the Healy Model, the Jones Model, the Modified Jones Model and the Industry Model, and finds out all models are well specified but with lower power to detect earnings management of economically plausible magnitudes. Dechow et al. (2003) further provides three additional modified models based on Jones Model to estimate the discretionary accruals. But discretionary accrual from these models may not be the correct measurement of the level of earnings management due to the mechanical relationship between performances and estimated discretionary accruals. In order to use discretionary accruals as the measurement to test the effect of earnings management on the short-term growth rate, we must separate the effect of firm's performance on the discretionary accruals and make these accruals a real measurement for earnings management. Kothari et al. (2005) uses a performance matched discretionary accruals approach to adjust for the effect of firm's performance on the calculated discretionary accruals from modified Jones model. By matching firms based on ROA, performance-matched discretionary accruals are obtained as the difference of discretionary accruals calculated from modified Jones model between matched pairs. The matching process controls the effect of mechanic relationship between performance and discretionary accruals when discretionary accruals are calculated from those accrual models and can serve as a more accurate measurement for earnings management. In order to test the relationship between realized short-term growth rate and earnings management in this paper, second approach is done by using performance matched discretionary accruals as proxy of earnings management and the correlation between performance matched discretionary accruals and short-term growth rate is investigated. Additionally, following Ashbaugh et al. (2003), I use income-increasing discretionary accruals as proxy of the degree of earnings management since this paper specifically exams the effect of managing earnings up on the firm's short-term growth rate.

H2: there is a positive correlation between performance-matched income increasing discretionary accruals and firm's reported short-term growth rate.

Tests above concern with the effect of earnings management on the level of reported or expected short-term growth rate. Yet another effect of earnings management on reported earnings that can be expected is on the distribution of growth rate. From earnings management hypothesis, a bad firm can manage earnings to mimic good firms as if it is in same line with good firms with respect to current earnings level expectation. But GAAP and accounting practices prohibit manager from optimistically biasing earnings forever. In fact the bias has to be reversed after several periods or even sooner (Barton and Simko (2002)). The effect of this reversion implies a comparably inconstant g_i (low persistence in short term earnings growth) for firms managing earnings for short periods comparing to those by genuine earnings performance. As a result, earnings management implies a different earnings path from the assumed original ones.

H3: higher degree of earnings management as measured by performance-matched discretionary accruals leads to a lower persistence in reported short-term earnings growth rate as measured by standard deviation of g.

<u>Prior research about earnings management</u>

Existing earnings management literature states that firms either manage reported earnings numbers or dampen earnings expectations prior to the earnings announcement in order to meet or beat current analysts' earnings expectations. One school of research in this field focuses on methods of detecting earnings management by using alternative accrual-based models or by examining the distribution of reported earnings numbers and studying the explanation of documented "kink". For example, Dechow et al. (1995) evaluates several accrual-based models for detecting earnings management, namely, the Healy Model, the Jones Model, the Modified Jones Model and the Industry Model, and finds out all models are well specified but with lower power to detect earnings management of economically plausible magnitudes. Dechow et al. (2003) further provides three additional modified models based on Jones Model to estimate the discretionary accruals. Degeorge et al. (1999) exams the distribution of reported earnings numbers and proposes three thresholds for earnings management to achieve. Their paper shows the existence of kinks around these three thresholds and states it is the proof of earnings management. Specifically one of the thresholds is to meet analysts' consensus forecast numbers. They find out that there is a kink just before zero forecast error and an extra pileup of observations at the zero point (MBE one-penny group). Another recent study about the MBE one-penny group is Burgstahler and Eames (2006) and they provide evidence that both cash flow and discretionary accruals components of earnings are managed upward while forecasts are managed downward for MBE one-penny group. These researches provide justification for focusing on one particular group as proxy for earnings management—meeting or just beating analysts' forecasts. Dechow et al. (2003) extends the literature by trying to explain the kink due to boosting of discretionary accruals but with no confirmative answer. Another line of research exams the effect of meeting or beating earnings expectations (or other thresholds) on the stock price and tries to differentiate the group of firms that meet or beat analysts' forecast (MBE) by genuine earnings numbers from other MBE firms by earnings management method. This line of research finds out that there is a market premium awarded to MBE firms upon the meet or beat earnings expectation announcement after controlling the information content of announced earning number or analyst's forecast error (see Lopez and Rees (2001), Kasznik and Mcnichols (2002), and Bartov et al. (2001)). In addition, these researches find out the market seems able to distinguish to a certain degree the firms achieve MBE through genuine earnings performance from those by earnings management.

RESEARCH DESIGN AND EMPIRICAL PROXIES

First part of the empirical test is on the MBE by one-penny VS. Missing by one-penny observations for the same firm. After observations that are MBE by one-penny and Missing by one-penny for a firm are identified, the mean of short-term growth rate of these observations that MBE one-penny and those missing one-penny are separately calculated by using the definition following Ohlson and Juettner-Nauroth (2005). The equation for g calculation is: $g = (X_t+d_{t-1} * r) / X_{t-1} -1$, where X_t is income before extraordinary items for current period (Compustat annual data123), d_{t-1} is the cash dividends last period (Compustat data127), X_{t-1} is income before extraordinary items for last period and r is the risk free rate. For all the firms that both have MBE by one-penny observations and Missing by one-penny observations, an empirical test is done to see whether there is a significant larger growth rate for MBE one-penny than for Missing one-penny observations.

Second part of the empirical test is done by using the income increasing and performance-matched discretionary accruals as the proxies of earnings management. To establish a relationship between earnings management and its effect on the firm's short-term growth rate and the standard deviation of firm's short-term earnings growth rate, I use the income increasing and performance matched discretionary accruals to serve as an indicator of earnings management (Dechow et al. (1995), Dechow et al. (2003), and Kothari et al. (2004), etc). First, discretionary accruals are calculated following Dechow et al. (2003), by using annually observations and by regressions for each year and two-digit SIC group. Following Ashbaugh et al. (2003), I use specific income-increasing discretionary accruals as proxy of the degree of earnings management for following reasons: first, firm specific discretionary accruals are calculated from industry regression and it is the value of residuals from regression. By construction, the mean of the residuals (discretionary accruals) are zero, so using mean of discretionary accruals will not be a good measurement for the degree of earnings management since it mixes the effect of negative discretionary accruals. Second, assuming accrual models are well specified, which numerous researches already testified, income increasing discretionary accruals is the direct effect of trying to management accrual earnings up and naturally serves as the proxy of earnings management. Then I try to match the entire firm observations based on ROA for each year and two-digit SIC group following Kothari et al. (2004). Firms' performance-matched discretionary accruals are calculated as the difference of the matched firms' income increasing discretionary accruals and observations with positive value are kept. On the mean level test, variance of the firms' short-term growth rate is calculated by using the firms' all observations since it measures the distribution of the entire growth rate. I expect there is a positive correlation between income increasing performance-matched discretionary accruals and firm's short-term growth rate. While the mean (median) of the discretionary accruals is calculated by using those observations with income increasing performance-matched discretionary accruals available, I expect there is a positive relationship between average firm-level income increasing performance-matched discretionary accruals and firm's standard deviation of short-term earnings growth (g_i).

I use modified cross-sectional Jones model (Defond and Subramanyam (1998)) to calculate the discretionary accruals. Modified Jones model is specified as below: (estimated for each two-digit SIC-year grouping)

$$\text{Total Accruals} = \alpha + \beta_1 * (\Delta Sales - \Delta Rec) + \beta_2 * PPE + \varepsilon$$

Residuals from the above estimated equations are discretionary accruals. Values of those discretionary accruals that are greater than zero are income increasing discretionary accruals. Matched based on ROA, difference of matched pairs income increasing discretionary accruals serves as proxy of earnings management.

All empirical tests are based on the entire samples from Compustat data from 1987 to 2006. For the first part of test, I perform the univariate test for the difference of the growth rates of specific firm between MBE one-penny and Missing one-penny observations to see if one is significant bigger than the other. As for the second test, besides the univariate test, I perform a multivariate level test by using regression analysis by regressing standard deviation of short-term growth rate on the mean income increasing performance matched discretionary accruals (standard deviation of all firm specific discretionary accruals). To control the size effect, I put mean of firm's total assets (natural log transformed) as independent control variable in the equation. Also prior literature and my test shows there is a significant correlation between growth rate and the standard deviation of the growth rate, so I put the mean of the growth rate as a control variable in my equation. I expect in the regression analysis that the coefficient for the mean of income increasing performance-matched discretionary accruals is positive and significant. Regression models are specified as below:

$$sttd_{g_i} = \beta_0 + \beta_1 * mda_i + \beta_2 * mg_i + \beta 4 * mta_i + \varepsilon_I$$

Where:

$sttd_{g_i}$ = firm i's standard deviation of short-term earnings growth rate
mda_i = firm i's mean(or median) income increasing PM discretionary accruals
mg_i = firm i's mean(or median) short-term earnings growth rate
mta_i = firm i's mean(or median) total assets

SAMPLE AND DESCRIPTIVE STATISTICS

I gather data for calculation of the discretionary accruals and growth rate from Compustat database between 1987 and 2006. Firm observations with fiscal year ended December are chosen. Risk free rate are one-year bond returns from US Treasury and Inflation file from CRSP database. Firms with SICs between 6000 and 6999 are excluded. To control the outlier issue when perform tests, firm-annual with total accruals or any of the independent variables in the extreme 1% tails of their respective distributions are deleted when calculate firms' discretionary accruals, and same control applies to the firms' short-term growth rate. Firm observations with zero or negative book value are deleted from sample.

For the first part of test concerning MBE one-penny VS Missing one-penny, growth rates are calculated from Compustat data according to the formula. As for the analysts' forecast value, following previous literature, I limit observations to those forecasted in 30 days before the releasing of the real earnings number and define the mean earning forecast number for each year as the mean of consensus forecasting numbers. Firm observations of meeting or beating by one-penny sample group are defined as: \$0<=reported quarterly earnings – mean earnings forecast < \$0.015. Firm observations of missing by one-penny group are defined as: \$-0.015<reported quarterly earnings – mean earnings forecast < \$0. There are 89,723 observations with growth rate that are not missing from Compustat and 32,262 observations that are either MBE one-penny or Missing one-penny from IBES database. After merging two database, 5,482 observations that are either MBE one-penny or Missing one-penny and also have short-term growth rate available are left for final test. After taking the mean (or median) of these firm observations' growth rate according to their firm specific growth rate, there are 3,298 observations. Since the final test compares the same firm's MBE one-penny observations' mean (median) growth rate to that of Missing One-penny, the requirement of availability of both MBE one-penny observation and Missing one-penny observation for a firm further reduces the total observation to 710 firms. After control outliers, part one test has a final sample size of 694 firms. Table 1 gives descriptive statistics for the part one test about MBE one-penny VS. Missing one-penny.

Table 1: Descriptive statistics of One-penny group

Number of total observations (firm years)			2,805	Number of total observations (firms)			694
Variables	Mean	Std. Dev	Min	25%	Median	75%	Max
Income before extraordinary items(MM\$)	416.21	1274.55	-17625.00	17.47	83.31	323.08	17853.00
Total assets(MM\$)	14259.75	62301.73	15.57	442.62	1894.58	8236.06	1484101.00
Cash dividends(MM\$)	168.35	540.50	0.00	0.00	0.00	101.26	8375.00
Growth rate (%)	0.10	1.93	-15.63	-0.13	0.15	0.38	21.04

Second empirical test is done by using the income increasing performance matched discretionary accruals. The modified Jones model is estimated for each two-digit SIC-year grouping (SICs between 6000 and 6999 are excluded and at least 10 annual observations are required for each SIC-year grouping). The total number of final observations for the discretionary accruals calculation is 45,824 firm years with 7,412 firms' data for modified Jones model. As for the distribution of the same SIC two-digit group, observations are not equally distributed and the numbers of firm-years range from 10 to 741 with lower quartile of 33, median of 66 and upper quartile of 129. Table 2 reports the descriptive statistic for the discretionary accruals calculation for the entire samples from different discretionary accruals models.

Table 2: Descriptive statistics of accrual model

Number of total observations (firm years)			45,824	Number of total observations (firms)			7,412
Variables	Mean	Std. Dev	Min	25%	Median	75%	Max
Operating cash flow(MM$)	161.55	624.02	-25658.00	0.428	12.313	86.025	25138.00
Income before extraordinary items(MM$)	69.529	368.41	-13355.95	-1.402	4.686	38.126	12436.05
Sales(MM$)	1227.46	3662.01	-6.677	37.296	172.05	782.55	152172.00
Accounts receivable(MM$)	296.32	2436.08	0	5.617	27.936	130.49	287791.00
PPE(MM$)	1188.40	4105.72	0.007	13.848	74.538	487.324	102803.30
Total assets(MM$)	2028.32	9897.96	0.421	49.117	207.186	1021.87	853370.00
Cash dividends(MM$)	31.824	142.753	0.000	-5.308	0.000	6.49	4742.10
Growth rate (%)*	-0.351	27.984	-2241.00	-0.702	0.026	0.449	1600.67
No. of observations in Same SIC two-digit group	113	143	10	33	66	129	741

Descriptive statistics for Growth rate is for 37,961 observations that used to calculate the discretionary accruals by modified Jones model. The outlier treatment is not applied for these two variables at this point. Instead, 1% up-tail and lower-tail deletion is done when calculate the mean discretionary accruals, mean growth rate and mean market to book rations. After delete the outliers, for growth rate, mean is -0.12, median is 0.028, standard deviation is 2.59, lower quartile is -0.67, upper quartile is 0.43, minimum is -19.57 and maximum is 18.95; for mtb, mean is 2.77, median is 1.89, standard deviation is 2.75, lower quartile is 1.18, upper quartile is 3.26, minimum is 0.24 and maximum is 21.51.

Table 3 reports the mean coefficient estimates for the parameters for modified Jones discretionary accruals models. The final column reports the mean explanatory power (adjusted R^2) for the model. Comparing to Dechow et al. (2003), the result of mean coefficient estimates from modified Jones model has the same sign and are all significant.

Table 3: Discretionary Accruals using modified Jones accrual models (1987-2006): Mean coefficient estimation for accrual models based two-digit Sic-year regression (total 349 regressions for Modified model):

	Independent variables		Mean Adj. R^2
Model	Δsales-Δrec	PPE	
Modified	0.017 (3.43)	-0.046 (-13.58)	0.080

Modified Jones model: (estimated for each two-digit SIC-year grouping)

$$\text{Total Accruals} = \alpha + \beta_1 *(\Delta\text{Sales}-\Delta\text{Rec}) + \beta_2 *\text{PPE} + \varepsilon$$

After getting the discretionary accruals for firm observations, observations with positive discretionary accruals are kept as income increasing discretionary accruals. There are total 24,935 observations with income increasing discretionary accruals unevenly distributed in 21

SIC codes. Then match-pair design is performed based on ROA per SIC code and year and performance-matched income increasing discretionary accruals are defined as the difference between the pair's income increasing discretionary accruals. After controlling the outlier issue, there are 12,046 observations with performance-matched income increasing discretionary accruals.

Part three of the empirical test tests the relationship between mean level of discretionary accruals and standard deviation of the growth rate. Mean (median) level of discretionary accruals are calculated as the mean or median of specific firm's performance-matched income-increasing discretionary accruals while the standard deviation of the growth rate is calculated as the firm specific entire period standard deviation of the growth rate. The above 12,046 firm observations leads to 2,616 observations for firms' mean (median) level (as indicated by mean or median of income increasing performance-matched discretionary accruals, and standard deviation of the growth rate of short term earnings, and as a requirement for calculating the standard deviation of short-term growth rate, I require at least 4 observations per firm are available from data.)

EMPIRICAL RESULTS

Test of difference between mean of growth rate as for MBE one-penny vs. Missing one-penny observations (same firm)

From the first hypothesis, MBE one-penny observations have a higher possibility to management earnings up comparing to Missing one-penny observations for the same firm. At mean (median) level, the growth rate for those observations of MBE one-penny group is expected to be greater than that for those of Missing one-penny group. I take the difference of two mean (median) growth rate for the same firm and perform a univariate test to see if the mean value is different from zero. Table 4 presents the results of the test. The mean (median) of the difference of the growth rate (across firms) is positive but t-stat is not significant at 10% level. But since the test is comparing paired numbers from same firm, the non-parametric sign test is more appropriate here. The P-value of 0.0528 from sign test shows that mean (median) of growth rate for MBE one-penny observations is greater than Missing one-penny observations for same company.

Table 4: tests for MBE one-penny Vs. Missing one-penny observations growth rate (694 samples)

	Mean	Student t	P-value of student t	Sign M	P-value of sign M
Mean level	0.060	0.775	0.439	26	0.053
Median level	0.032	0.436	0.663	26	0.053

Test of correlation between short-term growth rate and discretionary accruals

Using income-increasing performance-matched discretionary accruals as the proxy of degree of earnings management, a univariate level correlation test is performed for discretionary accruals and growth rate. For the entire sample, there is no significant correlation found. When I divide the whole sample into 10 tiers according to value of growth rate equally, I find a significant positive correlation from 60%-70%, 70%-80%, 80%-90%, a significant and negative correlation from 20%-30%, 30-40%, while the first two group and middle two and upper tier is not significant. This result is consistent to the earnings management hypothesis and prior literature.

For those firms performed really bad or good, there is no statistically significant earnings management. When firms' growth rate is above zero, there is a positive correlation between earnings management and short-term growth rate. Comparing to the non-performance matched but income increasing discretionary accruals, the difference is the insignificance of upper tier correlation, showing that performance-matched income increasing accruals do controls the mechanical correlation between firms' performance and discretionary accruals when using discretionary accruals models.

Table 5a: Growth rate and performance matched Income Increasing Discretionary Accruals correlations matrix

	0-10%	10-20%	20-30%	30-40%	40-50%	50-60%	60-70%	70-80%	80-90%	90-100%
Mean of g	-3.6234	-1.1709	-0.6627	-0.3114	-0.0612	0.0866	0.2204	0.4252	0.8725	4.0651
Mean of DA	0.0564	0.0572	0.0521	0.0492	0.0404	0.0352	0.0403	0.0481	0.0529	0.0574
Correlation between g and DA	0.0166 (0.5652)	0.0146 (0.6141)	-0.0816 (0.0047)	-0.0770 (0.0077)	-0.0409 (0.1569)	-0.0293 (0.3098)	0.0994 (0.0006)	0.0932 (0.0012)	0.0478 (0.0976)	0.0302 (0.2870)

Total sample size: 12046 observations

Table 5b: Growth rate and not performance matched Income Increasing Discretionary Accruals correlations matrix

	0-10%	10-20%	20-30%	30-40%	40-50%	50-60%	60-70%	70-80%	80-90%	90-100%
Mean of g	-3.5301	-1.0839	-0.5645	-0.2328	-0.0229	0.1049	0.2296	0.4272	0.8707	3.7945
Mean of DA	0.0630	0.0663	0.0573	0.0511	0.0430	0.0399	0.0454	0.0527	0.0605	0.0651
Correlation between g and DA	0.0083 (0.6852)	0.0416 (0.0415)	-0.0270 (0.1865)	-0.0668 (0.0011)	-0.0135 (0.5080)	-0.0086 (0.6744)	0.0481 (0.0184)	0.0647 (0.0015)	0.0413 (0.0430)	0.0465 (0.0241)

Total sample size: 23948 observations

<u>Univariate and regression analyses of correlation between standard deviation of earnings growth rate and mean discretionary accruals (entire samples)</u>

Table 6 presents the univariate correlation results for the discretionary accruals and distribution of growth rate on mean level. We can see that there is a positive correlation between mean (median) of discretionary accruals and firm's standard deviation of the growth rate. The correlation between mean (median) discretionary accruals and standard deviation of the g is 16.25% (13.90%) and is significant at 1% level. The result of this correlation suggests earnings management is positively related to the standard deviation of the growth rate.

Table 6: Correlation Matrix between standard deviation of the firms' short-term growth rate and mean (median) performance-matched income increasing discretionary accruals

	stdd	meanaba	medianaba
stdd	1.000	0.1625 <0.0001	0.139 <0.0001
meanaba		1.000	0.946 <0.0001
medianaba			1.000

I also perform regression analyses of the correlation between these variables on mean level. To control the size effect, I include firms' total asset (natural log transformed) in the regression. Panel A and Panel B is the regression results both for mean or median level of Performance-matched income-increasing discretionary accruals, and the standard deviation of the growth rate. The coefficient of the mean and median level of discretionary accruals is positive and significant at 1% level, which indicates the positive relationship between earnings management and standard deviation of the g. I include in the regression mean of g and mean of total assets as control variables. The negative and significant coefficient for the mean total assets indicates small firms usually have lower persistence in the short-term growth rate.

Table 7: regressions of mean level firm performance-matched income increasing discretionary accruals and standard deviation of growth rate:

Panel A:	Model (firm mean level): $sttd_{g_i} = \beta_0 + \beta_1 * mda_i + \beta_2 * mg_i + \beta_3 * mta_i + \varepsilon_i$			
Intercept	mda	mg	mta	Adj. R^2
1.831 (16.85)***	4.549 (4.92)***	0.072 (3.60)***	-0.086 (-6.06)***	0.04
Panel B:	Model (firm median level): $sttd_{g_i} = \beta_0 + \beta_1 * mda_i + \beta_2 * mg_i + \beta 4 * mta_i + \varepsilon_i$			
Intercept	mda	mg	mta	Adj. R^2
1.939 (18.90)***	3.431 (3.90)***	0.027 (1.16)	-0.095 (-6.75)***	0.04

SUMMY AND CONCLUSIONS

This paper examines the relationship between earnings management and short-term growth rate and tries to explore factors that affect the distribution of short-term growth rate as defined in the valuation model of Ohlson and Juettner-Nauroth (2005). Firm's short-term earnings growth rate is critical in evaluating firm's market value and may be affected by potential earnings management problem. By using MBE one-penny Vs. Missing one-penny observations and performance-matched income-increasing discretionary accruals as proxy for earnings management, I test the hypothesis that earnings management intend to increase reported earnings leads to a higher reported short-term growth rate. Further, I test the hypothesis that higher earnings management leads to a lower persistence in the short-term growth rate. Since prior literature shows that analysts' forecast do not fully consider the impact of earnings management to the future predicted numbers, and reported numbers have an information content for the analysts' prediction, an examination of factors that may affect the distribution of short-term growth rate points out the potential problem when using analysts' forecast as proxy of future expected short-term growth rate when using OJ model.

REFERENCES

Abarbanell, J., & Lehavy, R. (2003). Biased forecasts or biased earnings? The role of reported earnings in explaining apparent bias and over/underreaction in analysts' earnings forecasts. *Journal of Accounting and Economics, 36*(1), 105-146.

Ashbaugh, H., LaFond, R. and Mayhew, B. (2003), "Do non-audit services compromise auditor independence? Further evidence", *The Accounting Review*, Vol. 78 No. 3, pp. 611-39.

Barton, J., & Simko, P. J. (2002). The balance sheet as an earnings management constraint. *The accounting review*, *77*(s-1), 1-27.

Bartov E., D. Givoly, and C. Hayn. 2001. The Rewards to Meeting or Beating Earnings Expectations. *Journal of Accounting and Economics*, 33 (2002) 172-204.

Basu, S. 1977. Investment Performance of Common Stocks in Relation to Their Price-Earnings Ratios: a Test of the Efficient Market Hypothesis. *Journal of Finance*, July, 663-82.

Burgstahler, D. and M. Eames. 2006. Management of Earnings and Analysts' Forecasts to Achieve Zero and Small Positive Earnings Surprises. *Journal of Business Finance & Accounting,* 33(5) & (6), 633-652.

Dechow, P., R. Sloan, and A. Sweeney. 1995. Detecting Earnings Management. *The Accounting Review,* Vol 70, No. 2, pp. 193-225.

Dechow, P., S. Richardson, and I. Tuna. 2003. Why Are Earnings Kinky? An Examination of the Earnings Management Explanation. *Review of Accounting Studies,* 8, 335-384.

Degeorge, F., J. Patel, and R. Zeckhauser. 1999. Earnings Management to Exceed Thresholds. *Journal of Business*, Vol. 72, No. 1.

Easton, P. 2004. PE Ratios, PEG Ratios, and Estimating the Implied Expected Rate of Return on Equity Capital. *The Accounting Review*. Vol. 79, No.1. PP. 73-95

Ettredge, M., Shane, P. B. and Smith, D. B. (1995), Overstated Quarterly Earnings and Analysts' Earnings Forecast Revisions. *Decision Sciences*, 26: 781–799.

Givoly, D., Hayn, C., & Yoder, T. (2008). What do analysts really predict? Inferences from earnings restatements and managed earnings. *SSRN Working Paper Series*.

Hanna& Orpurt. 2006. Analysts' Earnings Forecasts and the Recognition of Nonrecurring Charges. Working Paper

Kasznik, R. and M. McNichols. 2002. Does Meeting Expectations Matter: Evidence from Analyst Revisions and Share Prices. *Journal of Accounting Research*, 40:727-759.

Kothari, S. P., Leone, A. J., & Wasley, C. E. 2005. Performance matched discretionary accruals. *Journal of Accounting and Economics,* Volume 39, Number 1, pp. 23-49

Lopez, T. and L. Rees. 2002. The Effect of Beating and Missing Analyst Forecasts on the Information Content of Unexpected Earnings. *Journal of Accounting, Auditing*, and Finance, 17(spring), pp. 155-184.

Ohlson, J. and B. Juettner-Nauroth. 2005. Expected EPS and EPS Growth as Determinants of Value. *Review of Accounting Studies* 10 (June-September): 349-365.

Penman, S. and Xiao-Jun Zhang (*2002*) Accounting Conservatism, the Quality of Earnings, and Stock Returns. *The Accounting Review:* April 2002, Vol. 77, No. 2, pp. 237-264.

DECISION SCIENCES INSTITUTE

Garment Suppliers' Strategies to Manage Commercial and Social Tensions: An Institutional Logics' Perspective

Marc Mueller
University of St.Gallen
Email: marc.mueller@unisg.ch

Joerg S. Hofstetter
University of St.Gallen
Email: joerg.hofstetter@unisg.ch

Anthony Goerzen
Queen's University
Email: anthony.goerzen@queensu.ca

ABSTRACT

Many scholars suggest that firms decouple standard adoption and compliance. This study focuses on the compromising strategy and presents the conditions under which decoupling and compromising strategies are pursued. The analysis is based on social audit reports of the BSCI for 90 emerging market producers supplying garments to Western buyers.

KEYWORDS: Social issues, Strategy process, Strategic management/operations interface, Operations strategy, International markets

INTRODUCTION

The imposed character of social standards for ensuring acceptable working conditions along with the requirement on inexpensive production relates to the question proposed by Jay (2013): How to react when facing explicitly conflicting demands? We believe institutional theory is an appropriate lens to study this phenomenon. The literature on institutional logics, as a notion of institutional theory, emphasizes the distinguished influence of competing logics on organizations (Thornton & Ocasio, 2008).

A tension exists between commercial and social aspects (Margolis & Walsh, 2003). Appropriate strategies to deal with competing commercial and social logics are decoupling, compromising and combining (Pache & Santos, 2013). Decoupling refers to adopting policies while not implementing them (Meyer & Rowan, 1977). Compromising involves meeting the institutional prescriptions by creating a balance between the goals of the competing institutional logics (Oliver, 1991). Combining concerns the selective coupling of elements of each logic (Pache & Santos, 2013).

We adapt our study to Jay's (2013) call and guide our research by the following question: How do emerging economy suppliers react when confronted with explicitly conflicting demands? The analysis utilizes social audit reports of the Business Social Compliance Initiative (BSCI) for 90 suppliers from Bangladesh, China, India and Turkey in the clothing and textile industries which have completed two full audits between September 2012 and March 2015.

This study offers three major contributions. First, we observe organizations pursuing the compromising strategy which has received little scholarly attention (Pache & Santos, 2013). Second, we find that the strategy selection depends on whether the conflict between the competing institutional logics is salient or not. When the tension between commercial and social demands emerges, garment producers from emerging economies decouple by prioritizing the commercial over the social logic. When growth indicates prosperity on the economic dimension, emerging market suppliers balance the competing demands by reaching the goals of the social logic. Third, we build a bridge between institutional logics and institutional isomorphism as notions of institutional theory. Our results suggest that growing exposure to the social logic through more on-site assessments leads organizations to establish an isomorphic strategic behavior.

THEORETICAL DEVELOPMENT

Strategies to solve conflicts between competing institutional logics are decoupling, compromising and combining (Pache & Santos, 2013). When pursuing a decoupling strategy organizations symbolically accept external demands while not effectively implementing them (Meyer & Rowan, 1977). It follows that decoupling is an appropriate strategy for situations, in which the tensions between competing logics become salient but it can hardly be sustained in the longer run (Pache & Santos, 2013). When following a compromising strategy organizations balance between the goals of the competing institutional logics (Oliver, 1991). According to Pache and Santos (2013), this strategy is less explored than the others. When pursuing a combining strategy organizations build a new organizational identity through combination of logics (Battilana & Dorado, 2010; Jay, 2013).

Decoupling Between the Commercial and the Social Logic

Hypothesis 1: A high performance against the goals of the commercial logic is negatively associated with likelihood to meet the obligations of the social logic, which represents the decoupling strategy.

Compromising Between the Commercial and the Social Logic

Hypothesis 2: The higher the performance improvements against the goals of the commercial logic the greater is the likelihood to meet the obligations of the social logic, which represents the compromising strategy.

The Relationship between the Commercial and the Social Logic Attributed to Exposure

Hypothesis 3: The higher the exposure to the social logic, the more significant is the pattern of choosing a decoupling or compromising strategy to manage the conflicting demands of the commercial and the social logic.

METHODOLOGY

Sample

The BSCI serves as empirical setting for this study. The BSCI (2014) aims to provide its membership companies (i.e., buyers) with a system to improve working conditions in global supply chains (i.e., at the suppliers' sites in risk countries) by offering a code of conduct and an implementation process consisting of recurrent audits and subsequent corrective action plans. According to the BSCI audit methodology, full audits constitute the starting point of the supplier social audit cycle. Therein, the suppliers' compliance is evaluated against the BSCI's code of conduct, which is based on the International Labour Organization (ILO) Conventions, declarations of the United Nations (UN), the Organisation for Economic Co-operation and Development (OECD) and national laws (BSCI, 2009).

Our dependent and independent variables are obtained from social audit reports and such monitoring results are not without criticism. Accordingly, the theoretical sampling of relevant garment suppliers is based on a careful analysis of the audit data and the social issue in question, working hours, is evaluated based on documentation over longer periods of time covering peak and low season. The fashion industry is known to be volatile and we considered suppliers, which doubled or halved sales turnover between two full audits at the most, leaving 90 suppliers for analysis.

Table 1 offers an overview of the sample by outlining the number of producers per country and the percentage of emerging market suppliers meeting the working time requirements as well as the average sales turnover at the time of the latest full audit.

Table 1: Overview of the sample

	Bangladesh	China	India	Turkey
n	12	45	21	12
% of suppliers meeting the working time requirements	75.00	93.33	90.48	41.67
Average sales turnover in EUR	10,382,747	5,557,046	2,364,795	12,953,333

Dependent Variable

The likelihood to meet a social standard's requirements on working time serves as independent variable of this study. It is a dichotomous variable, in which 1 represents an emerging market supplier achieving a 'good' rating in this category and 0 characterizes an emerging market supplier scoring 'non-compliant' or 'improvement needed' on this social issue.

Independent Variables

Sales turnover and sales turnover change are the independent variables of this study, for which we computed z-scores following Bloom et al. (2011). For each independent variable, we subtracted the sample mean and divided by the sample standard deviation as follows:

$$z_i = \frac{X_i - \overline{X}}{\partial_{X_i}} \quad (1)$$

The computation of z-scores allows to set the absolute values into perspective to the entire sample and eases interpretability of the results. A one unit increase in the z-score changes the probability that a garment suppliers fulfils the minimum requirements on working hours by one standard deviation. The analysis builds on the raw data obtained from the social audit reports.

Control Variables

The control variables are country, year of the audit, share of female managers to all managers, share of managers to all workers and auditing company.

RESULTS

Descriptive statistics

The correlations are summarized in table 2.

Table 2: Correlations

	1	2	3	4	5	6	7	8
1 Odds working time requirements	1							
2 Sales turnover z-score	-0.43**	1						
3 Sales turnover change z-score	0.36**	-0.41**	1					
4 Country	-0.26*	0.04	-0.18	1				
5 Audit year	0.13	-0.16	0.22*	0.06	1			
6 Auditor	-0.17	-0.15	-0.04	0.26*	0.12	1		
7 % Female managers/managers	0.24*	-0.01	-0.01	-0.06	0.05	-0.30**	1	
8 % Managers/workforce	0.20	-0.07	0.09	-0.01	0.15	0.12	0.08	1

** $p < 0.01$; * $p < 0.05$.

Hypothesis tests

Table 3 illustrates the results of the logistic regression analysis for the influence of sales turnover z-score and sales turnover change z-score on the probability to fulfill a social standard's requirements on working time, which refer to the hypotheses 1 and 2. Model 1 contains the control variables, of which country ($p < 0.05$) and share of managers to all workers ($p < 0.1$) inhibit a significant influence on the likelihood of a garment producer to meet the working time obligations. Hypotheses 1 and 2 are tested through the models 2 and 3, in which the independent variables are entered individually. Model 2 refers to the cross-sectional analysis, in which the influence of the sales turnover z-score on the probability to live up to a social standard's requirements on working hours is tested. Model 3 assesses the effect of sales turnover change z-score on the odds to meet the working time obligations in a longitudinal model.

In the cross-sectional observation, sales turnover z-score is associated with a negative significant effect on the likelihood to adhere to a social standard's requirements on working hours (Model 2: $b = -1.62$, $p < 0.01$, $\chi^2 = 34.61$). Accordingly, sales turnover is negatively associated with the likelihood to meet the obligations on working time supporting hypothesis 1. In a situation, in which the conflict between the commercial and the social logic becomes salient, the garment producers follow a decoupling strategy by prioritizing commercial over social demands. Amongst the control variables, we record significant influences of the auditing company, the share of female managers to all managers and the share of managers to all workers. The auditing company exercises a significant negative influence ($p < 0.05$) on the likelihood of a garment producer to meet the working time obligations. This supports Short et al.'s (forthcoming) observation that the auditor affects monitoring results. We also observe a positive influence of share of female managers to all managers ($p < 0.1$) on labor practices as suggested by Bloom et al. (2011). The share of managers to all workers ($p < 0.05$) inhibit a significant positive influence on the likelihood to meet the working time obligations.

Table 3: Results of the logistic regression analysis for the likelihood of compliance with working time requirements (H1 & H2)

	Model 1		Model 2		Model 3	
Variables	b	s.e.	b	s.e.	b	s.e.
Control Variables						
Country	-0.79*	0.38	-0.63	0.40	-0.66	0.41
Audit year	1.15	0.79	0.44	0.96	0.81	0.85
Auditor	-0.13	0.09	-0.27*	0.13	-0.17	0.11
% Female managers/managers	2.40	1.58	4.05†	2.09	2.93*	1.71
% Managers/workforce	8.73†	4.79	11.61*	5.61	8.08	5.05
Independent Variables						
Sales turnover z-score			-1.62**	0.58		
Sales turnover change z-score					0.71*	0.32
Constant	1.03	1.83	3.31	2.52	1.94	1.84
n	90		90		90	
χ^2 (df)	17.86** (5)		34.61** (6)		23.75** (6)	

b = Unstandardized regression coefficient; s.e. = Standard error;
** $p < 0.01$; * $p < 0.05$; † $p < 0.1$.

In the longitudinal observation, higher sales turnover change z-score, representing the delta in sales turnover between the last and the second to last social audit, is significantly positive associated with the probability to live up to a social standard's requirements on working hours (Model 3: $b = 0.71$, $p < 0.05$, $\chi^2 = 23.75$). It follows that the higher the growth in sales turnover, the greater is the likelihood to meet the obligations on working time providing support for hypothesis 2. Amongst the control variables, share of female managers to all managers has a significant positive effect ($p < 0.05$) on the likelihood to meet the working time obligations.

While hypothesis 1 illustrates that emerging market suppliers are strongly driven by the commercial logic, particularly in conflict, the behavior adjusts when the conflict eases. Sales turnover growth provides a positive economic outlook, which allows to balance the demands of the competing logics by reaching the obligations of the social logic.

To test hypothesis 3, which states that the higher the exposure to the social logic, the more significant is the pattern of choosing a decoupling or compromising strategy to manage the demands of the commercial and the social logic, we split the sample. On the one hand, the 36 suppliers, which have recently been introduced to the BSCI as indicated by up to two audits, and on the other hand, the 54 suppliers with three and more on-site assessments. All of the 36 suppliers, which have less exposure to the social logic, meet the requirements on working time, implying that the decoupling and compromising strategies cannot be observed for this sub-sample. Table 4 contains the results of the logistic regression analysis for the effect of sales turnover z-score and sales turnover change z-score on the likelihood to meet a social standard's requirements on working hours for the sub-sample of the 56 suppliers with more exposure to the social logic. In the cross-sectional observation, the sales turnover z-score is associated with a negative significant effect on the likelihood to adhere to a social standard's requirements on working hours (Model 4: b = -1.20, $p < 0.05$, $\chi^2 = 22.36$). In the longitudinal observation, higher sales turnover change z-score is significantly positive associated with the probability to live up to the working time obligations (Model 5: b = 0.61, $p < 0.1$, $\chi^2 = 16.98$). In both models, we also observe the positive influence of share of female managers to all managers ($p < 0.1$) on working time requirements. The results support hypothesis 3.

Table 4: Results of the logistic regression analysis for the likelihood of compliance with working time requirements with higher exposure with the social logic (H3)

	Model 4		Model 5	
Variables	b	s.e.	b	s.e.
Control Variables				
Country	-0.54	0.39	-0.47	0.38
Audit year	0.49	1.09	0.93	0.93
Auditor	-0.21	0.13	-0.16	0.12
% Female managers/managers	4.21†	2.31	3.37†	1.96
% Managers/workforce	7.84	6.10	4.03	5.47
Independent Variables				
Sales turnover z-score	-1.20*	0.57		
Sales turnover change z-score			0.61†	0.32
Constant	2.14	2.61	0.71	2.01
n	54		54	
χ^2 (df)	22.36** (6)		16.98** (6)	

b = Unstandardized regression coefficient; s.e. = Standard error;
** $p < 0.01$; * $p < 0.05$; † $p < 0.1$.

DISCUSSION

Emerging market suppliers in the clothing and textile industries face competing demands for low-cost production as part of a commercial logic and compliance with working time requirements attributed to a social logic, which are both imposed by their buyers. This study suggests that after garment producers have gained experience with the emerging social logic, they pursue decoupling and compromising strategies, which are enacted depending on whether the tension between the commercial and social demands are salient or not.

Decoupling to Overcome Salient Tensions between Competing Institutional Demands

Consistent with the predictions, emerging market suppliers in the clothing and textile industries follow a decoupling strategy by prioritizing commercial over social demands when the conflict between the commercial and the social logic becomes salient. In such a situation, the tension between the competing logics constitutes a perfect trade-off, in which the adherence to the prescriptions of one logic does not allow for compliance with the goals of the respective other.

This study complements Bloom et al.'s (2011) and Ortiz-de-Mandojana and Bansal's (forthcoming) non-significant observations for a positive and a negative association between workplace practices and economic performance outcomes. The diverging observations between our and previous investigations can be attributed to dissimilar institutional contexts: emerging markets and developed countries. While the emerging market suppliers in this study operate in an environment characterized by weak regulation allowing for exploitation (Locke et al., 2007), the firms in Bloom et al.'s (2011) and Ortiz-de-Mandojana and Bansal's (forthcoming) investigation are subject to the directives of powerful regulative institutions such as the European Union (EU) and the United States (US) law, which ensure workplace practices at a high and stable level.

Compromising to Ensure Legitimacy of Institutional Referents

As predicted, garment producers follow a compromising strategy when sales turnover growth signals a lessening of pressures on the commercial logic as indicated by an increased likelihood of meeting a social standard's requirements on working hours. This is likely to be attributed to garment producers employing additional workers when customer orders increase, as we find a significant positive correlation between sales turnover growth and workforce growth ($p < 0.05$). We provide empirical evidence for firms pursuing a compromising strategy to manage competing logics, which has received limited scholarly attention (Pache & Santos, 2013).

With Experience Comes Manifestation of the Relationship between the Competing Logics

Supporting the predictions, we observe fundamentally different behaviors to address the institutional logics' conflictive demands for garment producers with more and less exposure to the social logic. The emerging market suppliers with less exposure to the BSCI all comply with social logic's prescriptions while the garment producers with more exposure to the BSCI exhibit consistent strategic behaviors that differs depending on whether the tension between commercial and social demands is salient or not. These findings support the argument that tensions between the competing logics are not always salient allowing for different strategies to be pursued (Smith & Lewis, 2011).

The findings suggest further that strategy variation attributed to competing institutional logics is impermanent because increasing exposure to a new institutional requirement triggers the manifestation of an isomorphic strategic behavior across organizations. Such a process can be described as settlement (Helms et al., 2012).

Limitations and Future Research

Following the decoupling strategy entails to prioritize the commercial over the social logic, and, thus, to infringe the social's logic's prescriptions. While non-compliance with a social standard's requirements can be attributed to audited firms selectively choosing the level of compliance with the standard (Christmann & Taylor, 2006) or to the composition of the auditing team (Short et al., forthcoming) it can also be related to shortcomings inherent to the functioning of the standard which does not comfort the development needs of the audited companies (Reinecke & Ansari, 2015). In line with that, we obtain dissimilar results focusing on a social standard that is designed as an improvement system compared to Jayasinghe (2016) who analyzes a social standard that is designed as a certification. Accordingly, we encourage future research to compare compliance across different social standards, and to investigate how the design of a social standard influences the intensity of tensions between the commercial and social logics.

Our study finds garment manufacturers from emerging economies to enact decoupling and compromising strategies. We could not observe the combining strategy because we focus only on one element of each logic. Thus, we invite scholars to address more elements of the commercial and the social logic to further investigate the combining strategy and its implications for the upholding of labor issues at suppliers' sites in emerging markets.

CONCLUSION

The literature on institutional logics, as a perspective of institutional theory, focuses on the influence of the competing logics on organizations (Thornton & Ocasio, 2008). The commercial and the social logic are characterized by conflictive tensions (Margolis & Walsh, 2003). We approach this tension by studying 90 emerging market suppliers, which are challenged to meet demands for low-cost production as part of a commercial logic and compliance with minimum working time requirements attributed to a social logic, which are both imposed by Western buyers.

The results suggest that emerging market suppliers follow different strategies to cope with the institutional logics' conflicting tensions. When the conflict between commercial and social demands becomes salient, emerging market suppliers embrace the decoupling strategy. When sales turnover growth eases the pressure on the commercial logic, emerging market suppliers follow the compromising strategy by meeting a social standard's working time requirements.

While more work needs to be done to investigate how the design of a social standard can influence the intensity of tensions between the commercial and social logics, as well as the combining strategy and its implications for the upholding of labor issues at suppliers' sites in emerging markets, we have provided a new perspective on competing institutional logics by shedding light on the pursuit of different strategies for (non-) compliance with a social standard's obligations on working time attributed to the conflict between commercial and social demands.

REFERENCES

Battilana, J., & Dorado, S. (2010). Building sustainable hybrid organizations: The case of commercial microfinance organizations. *Academy of Management Journal, 53*, 1419-1440.

Bloom, N., Kretschmer, T., & van Reenen, J. (2011). Are family-friendly workplace practices a valuable firm resource. *Strategic Management Journal, 32*, 343-367.

Business Social Compliance Initiative. (2009). *Code of conduct*. Available at: http://www.bsci-intl.org/resources/code-of-conduct (Accessed: 5 January 2014).

Business Social Compliance Initiative. (2014). *The BSCI approach to good working conditions*. Available at: http://www.bsci-intl.org/about-bsci/bsci-approach/bsci-approach-good-working-conditions (Accessed: 10 December 2014).

Christmann, P., & Taylor, G. (2006). Firm self-regulation through international certifiable standards: Determinants of symbolic versus substantive implementation. *Journal of International Business Studies, 6,* 863-878.

Helms, W. S., Oliver, C., & Webb, K. (2012). Antecedents of settlement on a new institutional practice: Negotiation of the ISO 26000 standard on social responsibility. *Academy of Management Journal, 55*, 1120-1145.

Jay, J. (2013). Navigating paradox as a mechanism of change and innovation in hybrid organizations. *Academy of Management Journal, 56*, 137-159.

Jayasinghe, M. (2016). The operational and signaling benefits of voluntary labor code adoption: Reconceptualizing the scope of human resource management in emerging economies. *Academy of Management Journal, 59*, 658-677.

Locke, R. M., Qin, F., & Brause, A. (2007). Does monitoring improve labor standards? Lessons from Nike. *Industrial and Labor Relations Review, 61*, 3-31.

Margolis, J. D., & Walsh, J. P. (2003). Misery Loves Companies: Rethinking Social Initiatives by Business. *Administrative Science Quarterly, 48*, 268-305.

Meyer, J. W. & Rowan, B. (1977). Institutionalized organizations: Formal structure as myth and ceremony. *American Journal of Sociology, 83*, 340-363.

Oliver, C. (1991). Strategic responses to institutional processes. *Academy of Management Review, 16*, 145-179.

Ortiz-de-Mandojana, N., & Bansal, P. (forthcoming). The long-term benefits of organizational resilience through sustainable business practices. *Strategic Management Journal, forthcoming.*

Pache, A.-C, & Santos, F. (2013). Inside the hybrid organization: Selective coupling as a response to competing institutional logics. *Academy of Management Journal, 56*, 972-1001.

Reinecke, J., & Ansari, S. (2015). When times collide: Temporal brokerage at the intersection of markets and developments. *Academy of Management Journal, 58*, 618-648.

Short, J. L., Toffel, M. W., & Hugill, A. R. (forthcoming). Monitoring global supply chains. *Strategic Management Journal, forthcoming.*

Smith, W. K., & Lewis, M. W. (2011). Toward a theory of paradox: A dynamic equilibrium model of organizing. *Academy of Management Review, 36*, 381-403.

Thornton, P. H., & Ocasio, W. (2008). Institutional logics. In R. Greenwood, C. Oliver, R. Suddaby & K. Sahlin, (Eds.), *The Sage Handbook of Organizational Institutionalism* (pp. 99-129). London: Sage.

(The current version of this work in progress is available from the authors.)

DECISION SCIENCES INSTITUTE

Global growth of service innovation: influence of national culture and organizational structure

Somnath Mukhopadhyay
The University of Texas at El Paso
Email: smukhopadhyay@utep.edu

Kallol Bagchi
The University of Texas at El Paso
Email: kbagchi@utep.edu

Sub Samaddar
Georgia State University
Email: s-samaddar@utep.edu

ABSTRACT

International company's value creation in service related activities grow with its service innovations and its service manager's knowledge of cultures and organizational structures of target markets. This research focuses on the relationships between cultural heterogeneity of the global service market and service innovation growth at country and firm levels. The study links service innovation growth with national culture and four organizational structures – market, family, pyramid, and machine. The article presents analysis based on statistical test results from a sample of forty-three countries and suggests ways of making effective managerial decisions.

KEYWORDS: Service Innovation, Growth, National Culture, Statistical Model, Organizational Structure

INTRODUCTION

The *science of service innovation* promotes the design of new services and enhancement in service delivery systems (Smith-Daniels, 2009). Academicians (Metters & Marucheck, 2007) as well as practitioners (Chesbrough & Spohrer, 2006) call for more research on service innovations instead of focusing on shrinking portion of world economy – the manufacturing sector. In spite of that, there is a lack of emphasis on research on service innovation and growth (Peres et al. 2010).

Song and Song (2009) developed a staged service innovation model that decision makers can use to improve service quality to their customers. Paswan et al. (2009) developed a service innovation typology that helps managers responsible for service innovations. Using a large-sample customer service data set, Froehle (2006) developed a multi-group structural equation model to analyze the interactive influences of customer service representatives and technology on customer satisfaction. Kimes and Thompson (2004) developed a revenue maximizing model for an optimal table-mix in a restaurant. The restaurant implemented the model and obtained increased revenue. Pullman and Gross (2004) explored relationship between different service elements and customers' loyalty which can be strongly mediated by certain types of their emotional behavior. Looney et al. (2008) analyzed social cognitive perspective of service channel preference on online brokerage services. However, it appears that the literature on service growth lacks empirically evident studies on modeling its spread in different countries especially taken into account the variability in their cultural attributes. That is the focus of this study.

Spread of Service Innovation in country's service sector

Building on the works of Peres et al. (2010), diffusion of service innovation can be defined as the process of market penetration of services, which is driven by societal influence. Societal influence can include all of the interdependencies among the various actors including consumers, various decision makers, and market players. According to them a key issue in multinational diffusion is "the mutual influence of diffusion process in various countries," (Peres et al. 2010). Countries differ in their inherent culture and the culture influences decision making of the government, management of organization, and the people who consumes. However, research is scarce in building theories that connect culturally different managerial styles across the globe to improved service innovations and activities at the firm or country levels (Song et al., 2000). Globalization of service and its cross-border growth make it imperative for organizations to target the markets in other nations. The service sector of a nation's economy consists of the *soft parts* of the economy such as insurance, government, tourism, banking, retail, education, and social services, to name a few (Tertiary sector of the economy, 2009). In soft-sector employment, people use time to deploy knowledge assets, collaboration assets, and process-engagement to create productivity (effectiveness), performance improvement potential and sustainability. Typically the output of this time is content (information), service, attention, advice, experiences, and/or discussion (also known as "intangible goods"). As service sector is becoming predominant in most nations, globalization of service and its cross-border growth make it imperative for organizations to target the markets in other nations. Figure 1 shows service per capita for the year 2004 for a few nations. HongKong, Japan and the US are leaders in service per capita spending.

Figure 1: The service per capita of some nations

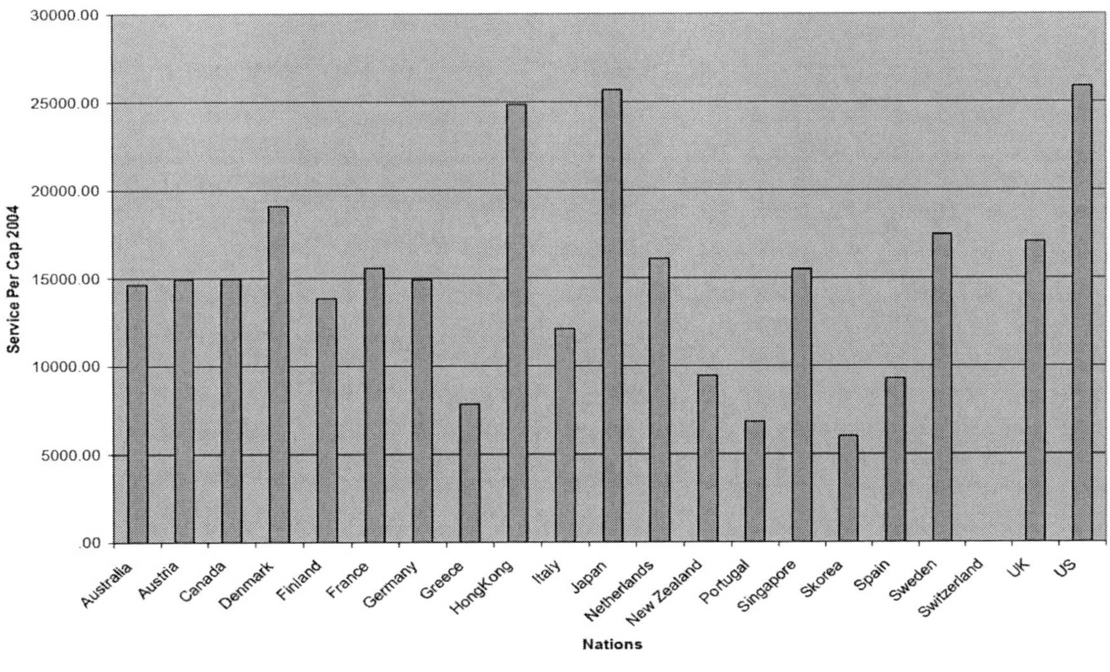

Figure 2 shows the service expenditure in $ per gross domestic product (GDP) per capita in 2004. For most of the nations, service accounted for more than 50% of GDP. It is, therefore, important to find out what causes service growth in various nations.

Figure 2: Service as a percentage of GDP

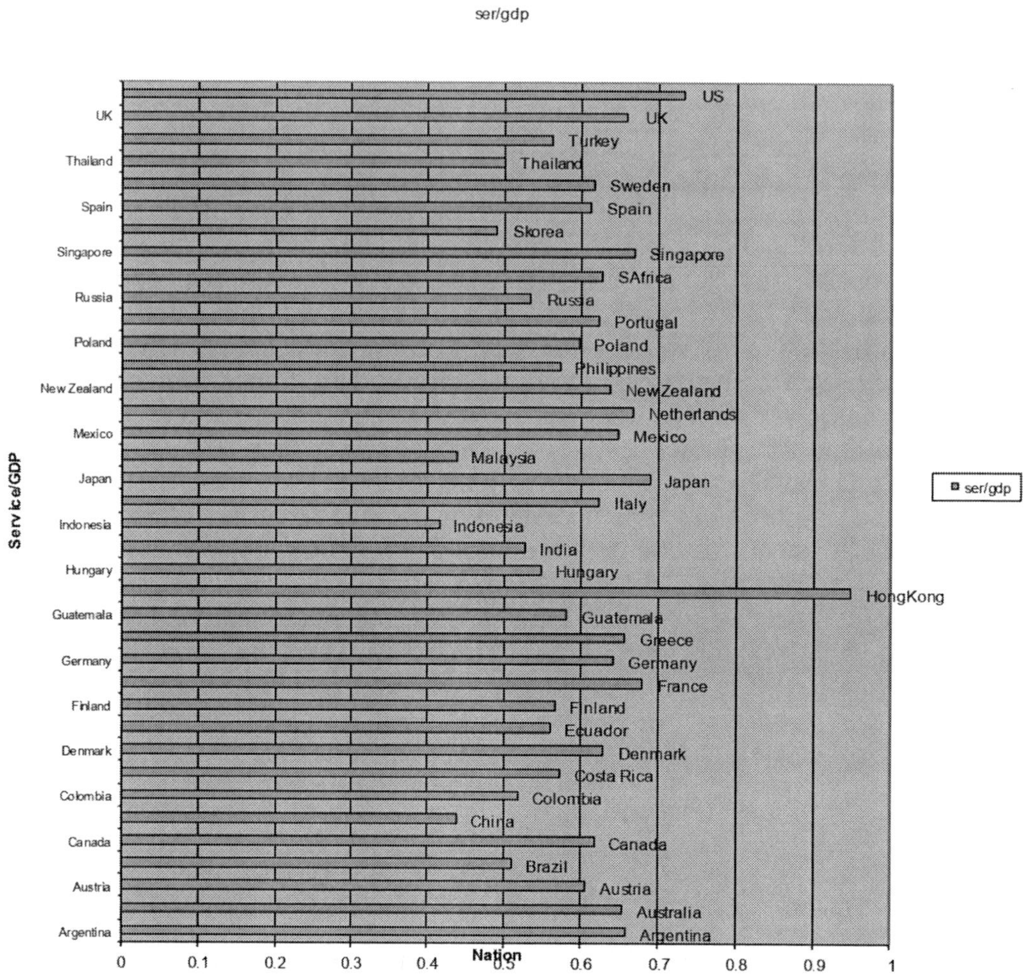

Service growth can partly be attributed to the globalization phenomenon. Research (Stieglitz, 2007; Bhagwati, 2004; Klienschmidt and Cooper, 1988) indicates that organizations that adopt a trans-national and global market focus when developing and commercializing new products in services and technologies generate more global market share and financial gains from their investments. The economic theory of globalization (Hutton and Giddens, 2001) persuasively argues that firms are better off in targeting homogeneous international market.

In terms of service innovation acceptance and growth, the global market is arguably heterogeneous in that it can vary from one nation to the other in its capability of rent generation from innovation spreads. Difference in adoption and innovations across various countries can be one source of this variation. There are at least two theoretical explanations of this variation.

First is from the economic theory-heterogeneity of the economic wellbeing and growths of the nations. The economic wellbeing argument claims that the rich nations will be more rewarding targets than poor nations in terms of global market rent. Economic factors, however, do not provide a fuller understanding of this adoption behavior.

The second reason is that even in the age of globalization, trans-national adoption and diffusion of innovation can be influenced by extra-economic factors (Perks and Wong, 2003). National culture can be one such factor, and a source of the variation of firms' global market returns. The literature, focusing mostly on manufacturing or product innovation, argues that product innovation and growth of trans-national markets for new products can be influenced by national culture (Perks and Wong, 2003). By collecting data from 56 countries on the acceptance rates of PC, cell phones and the Internet based products and services Yeniyurt and Townsend (2003) show that cultural factors plays a significant role in influencing adoption and diffusion of new products at the micro or consumer level. Similar patterns of the influence of culture on phenomenon of trans-national innovation acceptance have started to emerge. For instance, Shivakumar and Nakata (2003) find that cultural factors can impede or facilitate initiation and implementation phases of product innovation. Their study simulated the innovation behavior at the development project levels and analyzed the effect of multicultural development teams.

Organizational and country's cultures drive quality management performance in manufacturing industry (Naor et al., 2008). The same influence is expected in the service industry too. Benedetto, Calantone and Zhang (2003) tested the technology acceptance model by collecting data from 500 firms from a single non-western country, China, and found that influence of culture moderates whether the latest and newest technology will be embraced at the firm level. These early results indicate that the cultural factors influence the spread of innovation. Dhir (2005) points out the role of language in corporate decision making and knowledge creation and innovation. Market growth itself can vary in its effect and conduct across innovation attributes (product or technology or development project) or across unit of analysis (consumer, project teams or firms). From these and other similar studies (Straub, 1994, Samaddar and Kadiyala, 2006), one common thematic pattern emerges that cultural differences can influence the trans-national innovation and its adoption and growth. The global market is heterogeneous from the view point of the potential acceptance of innovation and growth of markets – not only due to economic reasons but also due to cultural differences.

Research Objectives

This research focuses on the relationships between cultural heterogeneity of the global service market and country's service innovation growth. For better economic rent firms should spread their service innovations in target countries by considering together the above economic arguments from previous section and target country's cultural heterogeneity. Managers of the aspiring firms should identify national markets expected to be culturally more receptive to innovations and suitable home for growth for innovation based products or services. Decision making process in identifying nations for potential business spread can start at target nations' cultural factors. We have found that a country's innovation is highly positively correlated with its service activity in our sample.

We used Hofstede's framework (2001) to provide the link between country's growth in service and target country's national cultures. There are other similar theoretical framework linking country's management style and national culture like GLOBE (House et al., 2004). Hofstede's research is, however, pioneer in this area and is widely referenced in the literature. Sondergaard (1994) noted that Hofstede's cultural dimensions provided both a theoretical paradigm as well as data for other studies. Hofstede's work has been replicated and observations are validated (Adler, 1995).

A service consumer's perception of what constitutes a good service is "culture bound" (Stauss and Mang, 1999). Due to increased globalization, factors such as technological and tax-related advantages may gradually be replaced by advantages due to target nation's culture in considering potential market. Understanding the link between target country's cultures and achieving competitive advantage is essential for firms (Riddle, 1986). This research attempts to explore this link.

Specifically, the present paper has three research objectives. First, we build theoretical understanding of how national cultural factors affect the growth of business due to service innovation. To achieve this objective we designed hypotheses and tested them on real data from 43 countries. Service growth at the national level is represented by service value added (World Bank, 2008). Second, this analysis is extended to different service sectors within a nation. Third, contingent upon the results to achieve first research objective, this study offers a classification framework for nations to be targeted for service related business.

HOFSTEDE'S CULTURAL AND ORGANIZATIONAL MODELS AND NATION'S SERVICE GROWTH

Hofstede's Cultural Dimensions

According to Hofstede (2001), culture is formed by the collective mental programming of a group, tribe, minority, or a nation. It can be viewed as the aggregate of individual personality traits (Bagchi, 2003). He classified countries along mainly four dimensions: power distance (PD), uncertainty avoidance (UA), individualism/collectivism (IC), and masculine/feminine (MF). These cultural dimensions are used to rate each of the 53 countries by Hofstede (Hofstede, 2001). These dimensions can be used to delineate leadership types or management practices.

Power Distance (PD)

This measure refers to the extent to which a society accepts the unequal power distribution within or between institutions. A high PD society means that people in that culture more readily accept wider differences in power compared to low PD culture. For example, in some high PD cultures, management decisions will mostly be centralized and hierarchical. In low PD cultures, management decision will be decentralized and more participative.

Uncertainty Avoidance (UA)

This cultural attribute describes the extent to which individuals feel threatened by uncertain and ambiguous situations, and try to avoid them. In a culture with high uncertainty avoidance, mechanisms are created to reinforce and reduce risks. Thus, managers in these nations may have more rigid rules and exhibit less tolerance for uncommon ideas and behaviors. This dimension is related to need for security, dependence on experts, and the application of information. The societal norm in countries with low UA scores includes a tolerance for uncertainty (Bagchi, 2003).

Individualism - Collectivism (IC)

Individualism refers to a loosely coupled social network where people take care of themselves. In contrast, collectivism refers to a tightly coupled social network where the group feeling is very strong. For example, in cultures where IC score is low, employee loyalty is considered more important than efficiency.

Masculine-Feminine (MF)

When the cultural values of human relationships and concern for others are high, the culture is believed to be a *feminine culture*. On the other hand, masculine cultures are believed to be more assertive and material based. A high MF score means the culture is more masculine. Compared to other cultures the US is high in individualism, low in power distance, high in uncertainty avoidance, and high in masculinity.

Culture and Innovation

Technological innovation is an important strategic consideration of many firms. In order to survive in an ever changing and competitive market, firms need to continuously innovate in products and services. Many firms are also considering international research and development (R&D) offshoring in low-cost and high technology nations. We propose that Hofstede's cultural dimensions can explain such innovative service activities.

Low PD societies have more need for more modern industries and service is one of them. Shane, Venkataraman and Macmillan (1995) investigated the role of innovation and PD. They found that in high PD societies, a greater need of approval from hierarchy was needed for innovative activities. So a strict hierarchy can stifle the innovation activities of a firm. High innovative activities such as invention patents are positively associated with low PD (Shane 1992).

Calculated risk taking in innovative activities is a standard way of doing business in many nations. Implementing any innovation involves risks, especially the new ones. Hofstede notes that a weak UA score leads to more basic innovations (Hofstede, 2001, p. 443). Shane et al. (1995) found that in high UA nations, innovators felt more constrained by rules and regulations. They found that innovative activities outside existing organizational norms, rules and procedures were more common in low UA societies. They also observed an association of higher innovation in terms of trademarks granted with low UA values. Thus, a low value of UA is associated with high innovative activities.

Innovative activities in individualistic nations will be greater as individuals have more freedom in work and less need to involve other organizational members (Shane, 1993). Shane, Venkataraman, and, Macmillan (1995) also found that innovative activities outside existing organizational norms in a high IC society is more common. Steenkamp, Hofstede, and, Wedel (1999) and Shane (1992) suggest that a high IC society will exhibit high innovative activities.

Finally, a high masculine society defines success as a status symbol. Any innovation that supports such status symbol will be supported in a society which scores high on the MF dimension.

Innovation and Service

The influence of culture is present not only in the design and quality of many innovative products but also in many innovative services (Hofstede, p. 448, 2001). In developed nations, more opportunities exist among consumers to select from a range of products and services. As De Mooij (2001) observed, culture influences a customer's social needs which in turn is satisfied by use and ownership of innovative products. Two cultural dimensions, UA and MF, for example, are even shown to be unaffected by the influence of personal wealth and are important in influencing many product and service demands (e.g. buying of new car or a new service created by Internet/Web). A high MF society defines success as a status symbol. Any service that can increase the status symbol of a user in a high MF society will be successful. A low UA society stresses the need for purity and expert knowledge (Hofstede, p. 449, 2001).

Innovation in service activity is often a "hidden dimension" which is playing an increasing role in stimulating change and supporting growth in the European economy (Royal Society Report, 2006). For example, the EU average for the share of services in business R&D expenditure had risen to 13% by 2001.

Howells and Tether (2004) persuasively argue that service sector firms are heavily involved with innovations. In particular, service innovation involves softer aspects of innovation such as skills and inter-organizational cooperation practices. Service sector has been a major source of innovation since 1990s. Unlike manufacturing, service firms employ technologies in a major and a creative way. Knowledge intensive business services are innovating and creating newer service products. At the other end of the spectrum routine services such as customer support through telephones are also undergoing rapid innovative structural changes due to technological improvements.

According to Howells and Tether (2004), new service-oriented approaches to innovation have emerged which center around non-technological disembodied innovations that lead to new conceptualization of service innovation. Sustainability of firm, especially in emerging countries, are crucial for investment and growth however, need to be managed carefully because of its complexity (Gunasekaran et al., 2015) Thus we propose that innovative activities and service expenditures of a nation are inextricably and strongly linked. Without any loss of generality, one may consider service expenditures of a nation are strongly related to innovative activities.

From the above discussions, we build four hypotheses:

> *H1-The greater the PD present in a national culture the lower will be the nation's growth of service innovation.*
> *H2- The greater the uncertainty avoidance present in a national culture the lower will be the growth of service innovation.*

H3-The more individualistic a nation's culture is the higher will be the nation's growth of service innovation.
H4-The more masculine a nation's culture is the higher will be the nation's growth of service innovation.

Service Growth and Type of Service Sectors

Within the broad category of "service sector" there is a wide gamut of services. These services vary widely in terms of activities, operating and marketing conditions. For example, transport services involve physical transformation of goods. Information services, engaged in processing of information, involve transformation of information. Financial services involve transformation of financial information while ravel services involve transportation of human beings. We hypothesize:

H5-The influence of cultural dimensions on nation's growth of service innovation is not similar across different service sectors.

Country's Service Growth and Hofstede's Organizational Models

Hofstede (1991) developed several types of organizational models based on his national cultural dimensions. Of the five cultural dimensions he developed, the combination of PD and UA is considered the most important in studying organizations in various national cultures. Organizational structures are decided by who has the power to take decisions (dependent on PD dimension) and what rules and procedures are needed to arrive at a decision (dependent on the UA dimension). The combination of these dimensions yields a four-quadrant framework (based on the combination of low and high values of UA and PD), each of which represents certain profiles of organizations. These four organizational models are: machine, market, pyramid and family. Each quadrant includes countries that share a common degree of national culture dimensions.

Market-like Organization

A *market-like organization* is a combination of small PD and weak UA (Hofstede, 2001). Some examples of nations where these structures are prevalent are the United States, Great Britain, Australia, Canada, and New Zealand. This structure has a preference for decentralized authority and unstructured work flows. This type of organization is usually flexible in its response to problems of production and distribution because of its decentralized nature (Hofstede, 1991). A market-like structure suggests negotiation and a certain type of give-and-take in decision-making situations. Independency and self-interest are perhaps basic social principles (Burcik et al., 2007).

Family-like Organization

A *family-like organization* is derived from a large PD and weak UA (Hofstede, 2001). Some example nations where the structure is common are Slovakia, China, Hong Kong, and Singapore. It consolidates authority autocratically but does not frame business processes with a lot of rules. A family-like organizational structure is paternalistic (materialistic) in its policies and decision-making.

Pyramid-like Organization

A *pyramid-like organization* is made of large PD and strong UA (Hofstede, 2001). Nations where this structure is popular are, for example, France, Czech Republic, Slovenia, Croatia, Serbia, Poland, and Taiwan. It centralizes and focuses authority and prefers structured work flows. A pyramid-like structure of an organization represents a hierarchical organization with a built-in rigidity and reliance on policy to deal with emerging problems. Multiple levels of a bureaucracy slow information exchange and decision-making.

Figure 3: Nation classification by Hofstede's organizational model

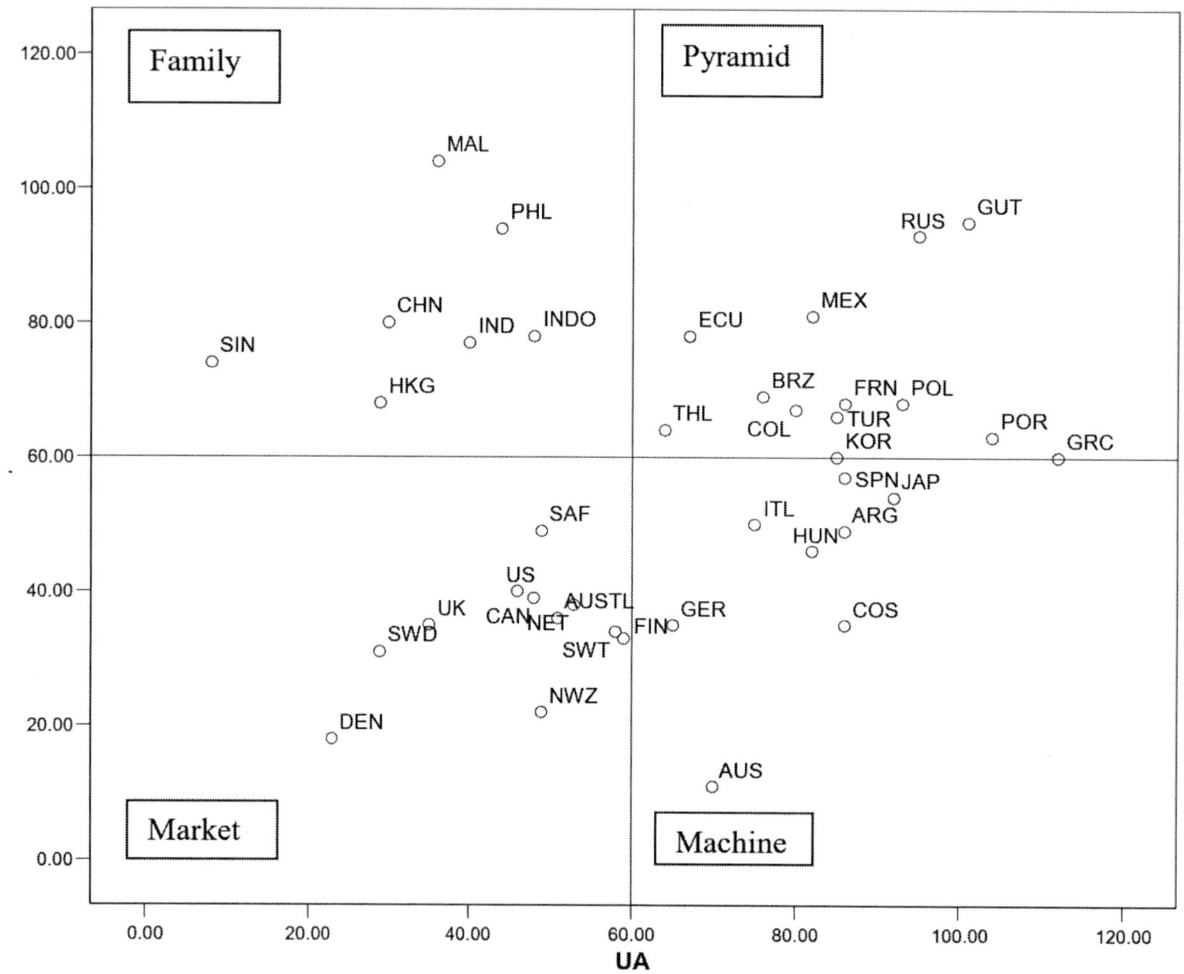

Machine-like Organization

A *machine-like organization* consists of small PD and strong UA (Hofstede, 2001). Some examples nations where this structure is common are Germany, Austria, and Hungary. This type of organizations normally does not centralize authority but usually relies on rules and procedures to structure business processes. A machine-like organizational structure is functionally efficient. Policies and lines-of command are in place to frame decision-making situations. It is an effective bureaucracy. Figure 3 above shows our sample nations in quadrant of organizational structure.

This research also investigates the possibility of differences in the role of organizational structures in service growth in a nation; in particular, we attempt to answer the question - *What organizational structures aid in service growth in a nation?* The above discussion leads to our following hypothesis:

> *H6-The influence of organizational structures on nation's growth of services market is not similar and some structure may be more suitable for growth than others.*

METHODOLOGY AND DATA

Methodology

Kaul and Sengupta (1991) offers an excellent review of modeling methodologies for complex macro-economic systems such as countries and societies. To test hypotheses 1 through 4, we developed a least-squared regression model where the dependent variable is average services value-added per capita (SVA). We found that SVA is highly correlated (0.836) with the innovation variable in our sample. We, therefore, use SVA as a measure for service innovation. The independent variables are nation's PD, UA, IC and MF scores. The regression model is:

$$SVA = b_0+b_1*PD+b_2*UA+b_3*IC+b_4*MF \qquad \text{(model 1)}$$

To test hypothesis 5, we selected four service segments based on availability of data. These segments are: "Computer and communications" or ICT, "Finance and Insurance" or "FinIns", "Transport", and "Travel." The average service activity levels in these 4 sectors are the dependent variables in the regression models:

$$Avg.\ ICT = b02+b_{12}*PD+b_{22}*UA+b_{32}*IC+b_{42}*MF \qquad \text{(model 2)}$$
$$Avg.\ FinIns = b_{03}+b_{13}*PD+b_{23}*UA+b_{33}*IC+b_{43}*MF \qquad \text{(model 3)}$$
$$Avg.Transport = b_{04}+b_{14}*PD+b_{24}*UA+b_{34}*IC+b_{44}*MF \qquad \text{(model 4)}$$
$$Avg.Travel = b_{05}+b_{15}*PD+b_{25}*UA+b_{35}*IC+b_{45}*MF \qquad \text{(model 5)}$$

To test hypothesis 6, we created a 2X2 (PD and UA) typology of nations by using the above independent dimensions for organizational profiles (Hofstede, 1991). We predict what type of country's organizational structure (Pyramid, Family, Market, or Machine) would be more prone to service market growth.

Data

Dependent Variables

To test hypotheses 1 through 4 and hypothesis 6 we computed dependent variable SVA in two steps. First, we calculated net output of services of a nation by subtracting intermediate inputs from total outputs (World Bank, 2008). The net service output number was then divided for a given year by the nation's population for the corresponding year. We obtained the average of these numbers for four years (2000-2004) to get our dependent variable of a nation: SVA.

To test hypothesis 5 we calculated activity levels of service related dependent variables from various service segments - average of Computer, communications and other services (Avg. ICT), the average of Insurance and financial services (Avg. FinIns), the average of Transport services (Avg. Transport), and the average of Travel services (Avg. Travel). These dependent variables are the average of various such services as a percentage of commercial service export for four years 2000-2004.

Independent Variables

As discussed in section 2 earlier, a typology of cultural attributes was created empirically by Hofstede by analyzing data obtained from surveys conducted among individuals in 53 nations in 1968 and 1972. Since all 116,000 respondents were employees of the same firm – IBM, Hofstede was able to hold the influence of corporate culture constant. We used Hofstede's four cultural dimensions - PD, UA, IC, and MF for each nation as the independent variables.

Data Definition

Table 1 shows the data sources and the descriptions of the variable. The study used data from the following 43 nations:

> Argentina, Australia, Austria, Brazil, Canada, China, Colombia, Costa Rica, Denmark, Ecuador, El Salvador, Finland, France, Germany, Greece, Guatemala, Hong Kong, Hungary, India, Indonesia, Iran, Italy, Malaysia, Mexico, Morocco, Netherlands, New Zealand, The Philippines, Poland, Portugal, Russia, South Africa, Singapore, Slovenia, South Korea, Spain, Sweden, Switzerland, Thailand, Turkey, UK , USA and Venezuela.

Both developing and developed nations were part of the set. The developed nations consisted of 47% of the total set. We started with 43 nations and dropped a few countries later from the analysis because of missing data.

Table 1: Data Sources and Their Meanings

Variable	Meaning	Source
SVA	Service Value added (in constant US $ 2000) per capita, averaged over years 2000-2004	World Bank data base (2007)
UA, PD, IC, MF	Hofstede's 4 cultural dimensions	Hofstede (1980, 1991, and 2001)
Innovation	Averaged value of innovation variable for years 1999-2003. The innovation variable value is obtained from a principal component analysis of three innovation variables, No. of patents, No. of R&D workers and no. of research articles published in a given year and averaged over 1999-2003.	World Bank data base (2007)
Avg.Travel, Avg.Transport, Avg.FinIns and Avg.ICT	Corresponding Service sector in % of commercial service exports, averaged over years 2000-2004	World Bank data base (2007)

RESULTS AND ANALYSIS

The OLS regression results are shown in Table 2. The coefficients of all cultural dimensions (except for MF) area significant and in predicted directions. This provides support for hypotheses 1-3, but not for hypothesis 4. The model explains 54% of the variance of SVA in our sample.

Table 2: Culture's Impact on Service Activities.[a]

Model	Variable Name	Unstandardized Coefficients
		B
	Constant	16312.73*** (5240.39)
	PD	-104.03** (50.49)
	UA	-74.19**(32.87)
	IC	93.92** (43.58)
	MF	-47.26 (43.86)
	Dependent Variable:	SVA
Overall Fit	R^2	0.54

[a] We report the unstandardized coefficient, with standard error
in parentheses.
*** p<.01; **p<.05; *p<.10.

To prove hypothesis 5 we selected average service values representing activities in four service sectors: Avg. ICT, Avg. FinIns, Avg. Transport and Avg. Travel. The OLS results are mixed. Results in Table 3 show that only model 2 (please refer to the methodology section earlier) with Avg. ICT as dependent variable has three cultural dimensions significant with expected signs, and Insurance service sector model (model 3 with Avg. FinIns as dependent variable) has one dimension UA significant with expected sign. Transport service sector model with Avg. Transport as dependent variable (model 4) has IC significant with a negative sign. Also Travel services sector model (model 5 Avg. Travel) has MF significant with a positive sign. All models are significant at $p < 0.05$ level. The R^2 values vary from 0.14 to 0.39. Since the models are significant it is clear that cultural factors influence service activities in different service sectors. However, the range of R^2 values proves H5 that the impact is different in different service sectors.

Table 3: Impact of Culture on Various Service Sectors

Model		**2**	**3**	**4**	**5**
	Variable Name	Unstandardized Coefficients	Unstandardized Coefficients	Unstandardized Coefficients	Unstandardized Coefficients
	Constant	**45.67***(11.9)**	3.12(4.15)	**46.34***(11.77)**	**26.55***(7.39)**
	PD	-.06(.12)	-.002(-.04)	-.13(.11)	-.09(.07)
	UA	**-.16**(.08)**	**-.05*(.03)**	-.01(.07)	.01(.05)
	IC	**.18*(.10)**	.05(.04)	**-.19*(.10)**	.01(.06)
	MF	**-.19*(.10)**	.05(.04)	-.10(.09)	**.12*(.06)**
	Dependent Variable:	Avg. ICT	Avg. FinIns	Avg.Transport	Avg.Travel
Overall Fit	R^2	0.39	0.26	0.14	0.18
	N	39	38	38	39

[a] We report the unstandardized coefficient, with standard error in parentheses.

*** p<.01; **p<.05; *p<.10.

To test H6, two dimensional grids of nations based on the organizational model of Hofstede (2001, p. 658) were developed (please refer to Figure 3 previously). The organizational model has four types of organizational structure: market, family, pyramid and machine, based on a 2X2 continuum of UA and PD dimensions (Table 4). Table 5 shows sample PD and UA dimensional values of 43 nations.

Figure 3 previously showed 43 nations in four organizational structures – pyramid, family, machine, and market - based on Hofstede's two cultural dimensions, PD and UA. We clustered each nations PD and UA scores in two groups – high (H) or low (L). We computed average SVA of these four organizational structural groups – PD high-UA high (HH or pyramid structure), PD high-UA low (HL or family structure), PD low-UA high (LH or machine structure), and PD low-UA low (LL or market structure). Table 6 shows the clustering groups of nations, frequency of nations in each cluster and average SVA values Nations which have market types of organizational structures has the highest service related activities.

Table 4: Nation Classification by Organizational Model of Hofstede

Market	**Family**
UA--low, PD—low	UA--low, PD—high
US	Slovakia
UK	China
Australia	Hong Kong
Canada	Singapore
New Zealand	India
Netherlands	Malaysia
Denmark	Indonesia
Sweden	
South Africa	Philippines
Machine	**Pyramid**
UA--high, PD--low	UA--high, PD—high
Austria	France
Germany	Czech
Hungary	Slovenia
Costa Rica	Croatia
Finland	Serbia
Italy	Poland
Switzerland	Taiwan
	Brazil
	Colombia
	Ecuador
	Guatemala
	Greece
	Mexico
	Portugal
	Russia
	South Korea
	Spain
	Thailand
	Turkey

Table 5: The PD and UA Dimensional Values of Nations

COUNTRY_NAME	PD	UA
Argentina	49	86
Australia	36	51
Austria	11	70
Brazil	69	76
Canada	39	48
China	80	30
Colombia	67	80
Costa Rica	35	86
Denmark	18	23
Ecuador	78	67
Finland	33	59
France	68	86
Germany	35	65
Greece	60	112
Guatemala	95	101
HongKong	68	29
Hungary	46	82
India	77	40
Indonesia	78	48
Italy	50	75
Japan	54	92
Malaysia	104	36
Mexico	81	82
Netherlands	38	53
New Zealand	22	49
Philippines	94	44
Poland	68	93
Portugal	63	104
Russia	93	95
SAfrica	49	49
Singapore	74	8
Skorea	60	85
Spain	57	86
Sweden	31	29
Switzerland	34	58
Thailand	64	64
Turkey	66	85
UK	35	35
US	40	46

Table 6 shows statistical significance of differences in average SVA between 6 pairwise combinations of four organizational structures. For example, the first row corresponds to difference in SVA values between countries with pyramid structure and countries with family structures. This pairwise comparison created 6 unique difference-of-means tests. First the equality of variances test (SAS/STAT user guide, V8 pp. 3578-3579) was run to determine if the assumption of equal variance hold true in the subsamples. If the assumption was true then the standard t-test under equality of group variances was performed. If the variance test failed, the approximate t-statistics (Satterthwaite approximation) under the assumption of unequal variances was conducted.

Table 6: Clustering Cultural Group and Their Means

Frequency	Combination	Service average
70	PD high UA High	4166.03
35	PD high UA Low	5718.61
35	PD Low UA High	10813.96
55	PD Low UA Low	15052.58

Table 7 reports statistical tests to determine if the differences of national service levels across the four organizational structures are significant. For example, the first row below the two header rows in Table 7 (a combination "HH-HL" or pyramid versus family) represents the difference of SVA in the two groups - PD is high and UA is high (first group) and PD is high and UA is low (second group). The standardized t-test is reported. Most of the differences are significant, with the exception of pyramid versus family. These results prove hypothesis 6.

Table 7: Statistical Test Results of Difference in Cultural Group Means

Comparison Groups		Difference of means test		Equality of Variance Test		Statistical
Organization	Hofstede	T	Pr > t	F	Pr > F	Significance
Pyramid Vs. Family	HH-HL	-1.27	0.20	4.26	0.00	No
Pyramid vs. Machine	HH-LH	-5.76	0.00	3.58	0.00	Yes
Pyramid vs. Market	HH-LL	-12.08	0.00	2.09	0.00	Yes
Family vs. Market	HL-LL	-6.12	0.00	2.04	0.00	Yes
Family vs. Machine	HL-LH	-2.63	0.01	1.19	0.61	Yes
Market vs. Machine	LL-LH	-2.92	0.00	1.71	0.07	Yes

DISCUSSION AND CONCLUSION

Peres et al. (2010) observed "(R)esearch on the evolution of multi-markets reveals a noteworthy aspect of diffusion that deals with heterogeneity among different social systems in which the same *product* is adopted" (emphasis added). In essence, our study contributes by extending this research to the service sector.

Table 8 summarizes test results. Our results support hypothesis 1-3, but not hypothesis 4. Most of these results are supportive of previous research work. Lynn and Gelb (1996) found e national innovativeness is correlated significantly to low UA (r=-.58**). Steenkamp et al., (1999) found a strong negative association between innovativeness and UA. Finally, Shane et al. (1995) found a high correlation between high IC and granting of invention patents (Shane, 1992). This suggests a high IC society will exhibit high innovative activities. It follows that service innovation is associated with low UA and high IC.

Table 8: Summary of Hypothesis Test Results

Hypothesis	Results
H1. The greater the PD present in a national culture, the lower will be the nation's growth of services market.	Supported
H2. The greater the uncertainty avoidance present in a national culture, the lower will be the nation's growth of services market.	Supported
H3. The more individualistic a nation's culture is, the higher will be the nation's growth of services market.	Supported
H4. The more masculine a nation's culture is, the higher will be the nation's growth of services market.	Not supported
H5: The influence of cultural dimensions on nation's growth of services market is not similar across different service sectors.	Supported
H6: The influence of organizational structures on nation's growth of services market is not similar and some structure may be more suitable for growth than others.	Supported

De Mooij (2001) found that services such as organizing, conferences, exhibitions and trade fairs are strongly correlated with low PD dimension (r=-.69***). Hypothesis 1 is therefore, consistent with that observation: low PD is associated with high service innovation. Steenkamp et al., (1999) found a weaker positive association between innovativeness and MF (at .05 level). A high MF society may be associated with high innovative activities. This suggests an association between a high MF society and high innovative activities and therefore high service expenditures (Hypothesis 4). However, our results do not support hypothesis 4. We recommend further research is needed in this area.

As a country's PD increases, its service innovation decreases. IC is positively related to service innovation in a global sense, whereas, high UA has a negative impact on service innovation as predicted. From the empirical tests we conclude that cultural factors serve to influence trans-national service providers in considering the benefits of taking into account cultural differences between nations in decision makings. In societies measuring lower in power distance, higher in IC and lower in UA, service providers have a greater opportunity to provide trans- national service.

As noted earlier, the results also provide support for hypothesis 5. Results show that ICT service (Avg. ICT) has three cultural dimensions as significant with expected signs, and insurance and financial service sector (Avg. FinIns) has one dimension UA as significant with usual sign. Previous research also supports this conjecture. In travel services which include tourism, high masculine cultures are known to be more likely to report service dissatisfaction (Crotts and Erdmann, 2000) which can result in better services or service innovations.

Finally, our results support hypothesis 6. Previous research shows that the effect of organizational structures on decision making or problem solving is not similar (Hofstede, 1991).

The present research finds that the market type organizational structure may be more suitable than others in service innovation and growth.

Managerial implications and service value creation

From the results it is evident that trans-national service innovation and growth remains unchanged between family and pyramid structures; however it is different for other five pairs of structures. Trans-national service innovation and growth is the highest in market, then in machine, family, and, pyramid structures in that order. Therefore, non-centralized decision making is a key to service innovation and growth. In other words, low PD societies which are based on non-centralized authority are better enablers of service innovation and growth, as market and machine structures indicate.

The results from this paper help shape future research and practice of decision making in trans-national service innovation and growth. Burcik et al., (2007) connected decision making with organizational structure per Hofstede's organizational classification scheme. We discuss decision-making in context of the most relevant organizational structure for service expenditures: The market. The market structure is characterized by non-centralized authority and unstructured workflows. It is flexible in response to problems of production and distribution. It suggests negotiations and certain give-and-take in decision making (Hofstede, 2001). The governance in the market structure is federal in nature and the managerial style is analytical, conceptual and social. Since the market structure is most suitable for service growth, demands of situation, not hierarchy or rules, may help most in service environment to arrive at what decision to make.

From a managerial point of view, the ways to accomplish total interdependence in service sectors should be identified and developed in achieving high relationship quality. The results imply that trans-national service providers from high PD societies should create more relationships with customers so that corporate customer will feel less threatened due to their relative difference in power structure. At the same time, nations with high score on "uncertainty avoidance" have lower service innovation which means that the people involved on these nations feel threatened by ambiguous situations. They should be encouraged to innovate and produce new service and adopt a creative approach. However, further research is required to gain a more complete understanding of ways to enhance symmetric interdependence and reduce interdependence asymmetry in client-service provider relationships.

Present study focuses only on Hofstede's cultural values (Hofstede, 1980; Hofstede, 1991; Hofstede, 2001). Our study does not explain international service differences by other national level factors such as institutional/economic ones. We did not attempt this for two reasons. First, recent literature in economics and finance (Greif, 1994; Landes, 2000; Stulz & Williamson, 2003) demonstrates that culture could be a determinant of economy/institutions. Thus we decided to concentrate on impact of culture on service. Second, additional potentially correlated attributes may introduce multi-collinearilty problem in the data.

Drawing upon past work in the cultural framework developed by Hofstede (1980), we built and tested several hypotheses involving many countries. The study, perhaps the first of its own kind for service sectors, measures cultural value and verifies empirically the influence of national culture in a service sector. The cross-country and sector level analyses suggest that culture is a critical factor in service growth and innovations.

The results of this study should alert service managers to consider cultural dimensions in managing their service related activities in different countries. Managers can create added values to the services they are already providing to a country by getting to know the country's organizational structures. They must bench mark average expected growth in their service activities in the country according to the country's organizational structure. For example, the managers now know that market structure is conducive to service growth. If the managers find out that they are below the benchmarked number, they must act to grow more service related activities. They can expand their market share with more service related innovations in the country. If the country's structure is pyramid then service managers should proceed carefully in investing more in service related activities.

Managers can benefit in targeting new countries as well. If they have the knowledge of new country's cultural framework then they can anticipate the country's organizational structures. For example, if they find that the new country's organizational structure is market type they can then be more aggressive in penetrating the new market. If they are not aggressive enough they can lose potential new businesses to their global competitors.

The knowledge of cultures of new or existing markets for service related businesses adds substantial value in service management. We emphasize that service managers should apply the combined knowledge of country's culture and organizational structures and decide on a suitable plan for service management.

The findings of the study, in particular, support the hypothesis that the degree of uncertainty avoidance, power distance and individualism prevailing in a society affects the nature of service growth, that culture has more pronounced effect on ICT sector of service and that market structure (emanating from low PD and low UA) is most conducive for service growth. The findings have significant implications for service providers in their efforts to maintain relationships with international consumers. From a managerial point of view, the possibility of a cultural difference in customer-provider relationships should be considered carefully while developing international service strategies. To ignore the impacts of cultural differences in a trans-national environment is to run a risk that service practices in one country may prove to be insufficient in another. Finally, in contrast to the assumptions of some variants of the globalization theory, this paper provides support that globalization does not always lead to the borderless world when service growth is considered (Ohmae, 1991; Peres at al. 2010).

REFERENCES

Adler, N. (1995), *International dimensions of organisational behavior (2nd ed.).* Boston, MA: PWS-Kent.

C. Anthony Di Benedetto, & Song, M. (2003). The Relationship between strategic type and firm capabilities in Chinese firms. *International Marketing Review,* Special Issue on Marketing in China, Vol. 2(5), 514-533.

C. Anthony Di Benedetto, Roger J. Calantone, Chun Zhang, (2003) International technology transfer: Model and exploratory study in the People's Republic of China, *International Marketing Review*, Vol. 20(4), 446 – 462

Bagchi, Kallol; Cerveny, Robert; Hart, Paul; and Peterson, Mark, "The Influence of National Culture in Information Technology Product Adoption" (2003).AMCIS 2003 Proceedings.Paper 119

Bhagwati, J. (2004). *In defense of globalization.* Oxford: Oxford University Press.

Burcik,V., Skoun, F., & Skova, R. (2007). Analyzing the effect of culture on curriculum Content: A Research Conception. In C. Eli (Ed.), Information and Beyond, Part 1, *Journal of Issues in Informing Science and Information Technology* 4, 381-393.

Crotts, J. C., & Erdmann, R. (2000). Does national culture influence consumers' evaluation of travel services? A test of Hofstede's model of cross-cultural differences. *Managing Service Quality,* 10(6), 410-419.

Chesbrough, H., & Spohrer, J. (2006). A research manifesto for services science. *Communications of the ACM*, 49(7), 35-40.

De Mooij, M. (2001). The future is predictable for international marketers: Converging incomes lead to diverging consumer behavior. *International Marketing Review*, 17(2), 103-113.

Dhir, K.S. (2005). The Value of Language: Concept, Perspectives, and Policies. *Corporate Communications: An International Journal*, 10 (4), 358-382.

Kimes, C.M. (2006). Service personnel, technology, and their interaction in influencing customer satisfaction, *Decision Sciences*, 37(1), 5-28.

Hofstede, G. (1980). *Culture's consequence: International differences in work-related values.* Beverly Hills, California: Sage.

Hofstede, G. (1991). *Cultures and organizations; Software of the mind.* London: McGraw.

Hofstede, G. (2001).*Culture's Consequences. (2nd ed.).* Thousand Oaks: Sage.

House, R. J., Hanges, P. J., Javidan, M., Dorfman, P. W., & Gupta, V. (eds.) (2004): *Culture, Leadership, and Organizations: The GLOBE Study of 62 Societies.* (Vol. 1). Thousand Oaks, CA: Sage.

Howells, J., & Tether, B. (2004). *Innovation in services: Issues and trends.* Brussels: DG Enterprise.

Hutton,W., & Giddens, A. (eds). (2001). *On the edge. Living with global capitalism*, London: Vintage.

Greif, A. (1994). Cultural beliefs and the organization of society: A historical and theoretical reflection on collectivist and individualist societies. *Journal of Political Economy*, 102(5), 912–950.

Gunasekaran, A., Jabbour, C.J.C., & Jabbour, B.L.S. (2015). Managing Organizations for Sustainable Development in Emerging Countries.

Kaul, T., & Sengupta, J. (1991) Economic Models, Estimation, and Socioeconomic Systems: Essays in Honor of Karl A. Fox, a North-Holland volume in “Contributions to Economic Analysis.”

Kimes, S.E., & Thompson, G.M. (2004). Service personnel, technology, and their interaction in influencing customer satisfaction. *Decision Sciences*, 35(3), 371-392.

Kleinschmidt, E. J., Cooper, R. G. (1988) The Performance Impact of an International Orientation on Product Innovation. European Journal of Marketing, 22(10), 56 – 71.

Landes, D. (2000). Culture makes almost all the difference. In: L.E. Harrison, & S.P.Huntington (Eds.), *Culture matters*, New York, NY: Basic Books.

Looney, C.A., Akbulut, A.Y., & Poston, R.S. (2008). Understanding the determinants of service channel preference in the early stages of adoption: A social cognitive perspective on online brokerage services. *Decision Sciences*, 39(4), 821-857.

Lynn, M., & Gelb, B. (1996). Identifying innovative national markets for technical consumer goods. *International Marketing Review* **13** (1996) (6), pp. 43–57.

Metters, R. (2007), & Marucheck, A. (2007). Service management – academic issues and scholarly reflections from operations management researchers. *Decision Sciences*, 38(2), 195-214.

Naor, M., Goldstein,S.M., Linderman,K.W., & Schroeder, R.G., (2008). The role of culture as driver of quality management and performance: Infrastructure versus core quality practices. *Decision Sciences*, 39(4), 671-702.

Ohmae, K. (1991). *The borderless world: Power and strategy in the interlinked economy.* New York, NY: Harper and Row.

Paswan, A., D'Souza, D., & Zohlfagharian, M.A. (2009). Toward a contextually anchored service innovation typology. *Decision Sciences*, 40(3), 513-540.

Peres, R., Muller, E. & Mahajan, V. (2010) Innovation Diffusion and new product growth model: A critical review and research directions: *International Journal of Research in Marketing*, 27 (2010), 91-106.

Perks, H., & Wong, V. (2003). Guest Editorial: Research in international new product development – current understanding and future imperatives. *International Marketing Review*. 20(4), 344-352.

Pullman, M.E., & Gross, M.A. (2004). Ability of experience design elements to elicit emotions and loyalty behaviors. *Decision Sciences*, 35(3), 571-578.

Riddle, Dorothy I. (1986) Service-led growth. *The role of the service sector in world Development.* New York: Praeger.

Royal Society Report (2006). Hidden Wealth: Science in Service Sector Innovation, available at http://royalsociety.org/page.asp?id=8691.

Samaddar, S., & Kadiyala, S. (2006). Information systems outsourcing: Replicating an existing framework in a different cultural context. *Journal of Operations Management*, 24 (XX), 910-931.

SAS/STAT reference guide at http://www.okstate.edu/sas/v8/saspdf/stat/chap67.pdf

Shane, S. (1992). Why do some societies invent more than others? *Journal of Business Venturing*, 7(1), 29–46.

Shane, S. (1993). Cultural influences on national rates of innovation. *Journal of Business Venturing*, 8(1), 59–73.

Shane, S., Venkataraman, S., & Macmillan, I. (1995). Cultural-differences in innovation championing strategies. *Journal of Management*, 21(5), 931-952.

Shivakumar, S., & Nakata, C. (2003). Designing global new product teams: Optimizing the effects of national culture on new product development. *International Marketing Review,* 20(4), 397-445.

Smith-Daniels, V. (2009). In the issue. *Decision Sciences*, 40(3), 375-380.

Sondergaard, M. (1994). Hofstede's consequences: A study of reviews, citations and replications. *Organisation Studies, 15* (3), 447-456.

Song, X.M., Di Benedetto, C., Song, L. (2000). Pioneering advantage in new service development: A multi-country study of managerial perceptions. *Journal of Product Innovation Management*, 17(5), 378–392.

Song, L.Z., & Song, M. (2009). A staged service innovation model, *Decision Sciences*, 40(3), 571-599.

Stauss, B., & Paul, M. (1999). Culture shocks in inter-cultural service Encounters. *Journal of Services Marketing*, 13(4/5), 329-346.

Steenkamp, J. B., Hofstede, F., & Wedel, M. (1999). A cross-national investigation into the individual and national cultural antecedents of consumer innovativeness. *Journal of Marketing, 63*(2), 55–69.

Straub, D. W. (1994). The effect of culture on IT diffusion: e-mail and fax in Japan and the US. *Information Systems Research*, 5(1), 23-47.

Stiglitz, J. E. (2007). *Making globalization work* (Paperback). New York: W. W. Norton & Company.

Stulz, R.M., & Williamson, R. (2003). Culture, openness, and finance. *Journal of Financial Economics*, 70(3), 313–349.

Tertiary sector of the economy (2009). Available at http://en.wikipedia.org/wiki/Service_Sector)

World Bank, (2008). Available at www.devdata.org.

Yeniyurt, S., & Townsend, J. D. (2003). Does culture explain acceptance of new products in a country? An empirical investigation. *International Marketing Review, 20* (4), 377-396.

DECISION SCIENCES INSTITUTE

Preparing Leaders to Live in a Virtual World: A Template to Enhance Effectiveness of Online Global Supply Simulations

Larry Taube and Doug Parkes
University of North Carolina at Greensboro

Chuck Nemer
The Guru of Biz, LLC

ABSTRACT

We present research examining how teams should be supported in Global Supply Chain Simulations. We utilized three different simulations across multiple courses, and applied a template as the base of our experimentation. We also discuss the process we used to present a uniform experience for all teams across all courses. Student feedback and performances indicate positive student attitudes and team performances.

Keywords: Global Supply Chains, Simulations, Teams, Team Learning

INTRODUCTION

As Rod Tidwell said to Jerry McGuire in the movie by that name – "Show me the money".

This is the message that investors send to the companies they invest in and this is the message that company executives send to their supply chain management professionals in all functions.

In many texts and presentations authors and presenters take a fairly limited view of the scope / reach of Supply Chain Management as a concept. Often we think of things like Manufacturing Planning and Execution, Logistics, etc. depending on the author(s). In this presentation we would like to take a little broader look at the field.

In our constantly changing global economy, the supply chain touches a very diverse set of international customers and suppliers. The extended supply chain encompasses such diverse functions as R&D, Purchasing, Planning, Manufacturing, Marketing & Sales, Finances, Customer Support, Warehousing, Transportation, etc. Supply chain management includes all aspects of the product life cycle – from "cradle to grave". Supply chain management includes both forward logistics (providing products & services to customers) and reverse logistics (returning products, service agreements, recycling, etc.). All of these functions are linked together by Business Processes that are managed and executed in Team Environments – many (if not most) of these Teams are Virtual in nature. This is especially true with large. Multi-national organizations. However, the same fits with local, small businesses as well. Just look around and you will see this is quite true.

Operating in a complex cross-functional environment places special challenges for teams but also makes for an exciting and challenging career for supply chain professionals. If managed effectively, companies can strive for and achieve operational excellence across their own organization and the organization of their business partners (Customers and Suppliers as well.

To this end, Business Leaders must have access to, and be able to use, the processes, systems and tools to attain operational excellence both internally and across organizational boundaries. Then of course, Business Leaders must have effective Functional, Cross-Functional and Cross-Organizational Teams to identify, develop, configure, implement and improve all the processes, systems and tools that are available to them. This is where our Education / Learning processes and programs come in. There are many stakeholders in these venture: Students, Educational Institutions, Companies, Communities, Families, etc.

In the supply chain the basic objective is often presented to Balance Demand and Supply. In any educational venture, the basic objective of each Learning opportunity is to balance the requirements of the Participants and the requirements of all the other Stakeholders. Sometimes this is not so easy.

You may have watched a movie or TV show about some Legal Preceding. You may also have heard it said by the Lawyers reflecting on an examination or cross-examination scenario: "Never ask a question that you don't already know the answer for." The same fits with an Educational Class – especially if you are teaching supply chain management to Graduate Students or Under-Graduate students that are focusing on other disciplines or career tracks. Still, it is a common question that many of us might ask at the beginning of a course or a training program.

From personal experience, occasionally we may have someone say, "I expect to be in a Supply Chain Management role and want to know all I can to be successful." Or, "I am currently in a Supply Chain Management role and I want to improve my knowledge and skills so that I can be more successful and help the company achieve its goals." On the other hand, we must be realistic and instead the real reasons come out: I am here: "Because it is a requirement for graduation. I am here: "Tom improve my chances for advancement." I am here: "Because my boss is forcing me to do this and I will either lose my job or not advance if I don't do it." I am here: "To enhance my Resume."

Then, just to make matters worse we might ask the question: "What do you expect from me / this course?" Now the real truth comes out. You may get some responses like: "an A", "always available and responsive to questions", "fairness", "fun classes" and such. Occasionally someone might say "very good understanding of supply chain principles, concepts and processes." That's the "Requirements of the Participants" side of the balancing act. Now let us look at the other side. Why are folks really in these Learning Adventures? They are in these programs to meet the needs of all the Stakeholders (including the students) - to improve the finances, productivity and asset management of companies (even non-profits), to improve shareholder / stockholder value, and to help manage the long-term future of the organization, its employees and their families.

To that end, Learning is a Shared Responsibility. Students will often come into the classroom on the first day as empty vessels (glasses in the exhibit below). They expect the Professor to just "fill them up" with knowledge that they can take with them. Well, this is true to some extent but surely not all. The Professor, text, learning management system and all the rest definitely contribute to the learning experience but there is much more. In fact, any course is a Team event. The Team consists of the Professor, the student, and the rest of the Class Members. The Professor brings her / his knowledge and experiences and the rest of the Team brings theirs. This in effect expands our Role in the Learning Process believe it or not. We need to channel all of our resources (including those brought by the Students) to provide a full and complete learning experience for everyone (including the Professor).

LITERATURE REVIEW: LINKING SUPPLY CHAIN FUNDAMENTALS TO EDUCATIONAL OBJECTIVES

Our Global Marketplace is comprised of many types of businesses both small and large.

Shareholder or stakeholder value is created when a business can project sustainable growth into its income or profit stream. This is even true for non-profit businesses as they to require funds to meet their stated mission.

Supply chain management encompasses the Flow of products and services from: raw material manufacturers and Intermediate products manufacturers to end product manufacturers, wholesalers, distributors and retailers. These different firms are connected by transportation and storage activities and are integrated through information, planning, and control activities. In this diverse and fast changing environment, firms cannot consider that they are playing in a "Zero Sum Game" where someone wins and someone else loses. Instead, all organizations must focus on improving cost and service levels throughout the chain so that all partners succeed – this is a key learning dimension that must be grasped by any Student at any stage of their life / career.

In order to meet all their sales objectives, global businesses must develop and effectively market new products to meet localized demand. This means that companies must understand the basic needs of their customers and be able to translate those needs into products and services that meet them. A major challenge is to minimize system costs and maximize system service levels while at the same time, speeding time to market and mitigating the inherent presence of uncertainty and risk. This is not an easy thing to accomplish. Educational programs should help students find optimum solutions to real business problems with the understanding that a solution for today may not be optimal for tomorrow. Markets change, businesses change, economies change. Business leaders must understand how to adapt and respond. Educational programs must provide the basis for this understanding.

The global economy has created an expanded requirement for communication, collaboration and partnerships. This represents a special challenge because companies are now dealing with partners across different languages, cultures and time zones. Complex networks of internationally linked suppliers and customers have replaced simple, local interactions between a few suppliers and customers. Supply chain professionals have to somehow manage these complex relationships to meet their financial goals and key requirements of all their stakeholders. This takes Teamwork – most often in Virtual Networks. Current and future business leaders must be given the educational framework to understand the concepts and processes that can deliver operational excellence across functions as well as the understanding of Team dynamics and tools to help Teams communicate and collaborate to achieve company goals.

Taken together, all of these things frame the basic requirements for an innovative educational experience. Virtual Business Simulations can be used as an effective tool to stimulate learning in a creative / collaborative environment. Such programs should provide:

- Conceptual Understanding
- Communication Enhancement
- Challenging Engagement
- Camaraderie / Positive Team Experience

Let's call this the 4 Cs of Success.

We will review the basic design and approach to some different Simulation Tools in the following section. However there are two common threads that run through each of them.

One Thread relates to Team Development. You can pick up any text related to team dynamics and you will likely find the 4 Stages of Team Development: Forming, Storming,

Norming and Performing. In virtual environments the development cycle can be somewhat longer due to the challenges of distance, lack of in-person interaction, scheduling and all the rest. If this is an international team then you have the added dimensions of language and time zones. Well, actually you can have these across borders of the same country in reality. Scheduling presents special challenges to educational teams since students likely have no prior affiliation with each other. Also, usually students will sign up for an on-line learning experience in order to have flexibility to work on things whenever they like. Hum… this can actually lead to some Storming along the way☺. The challenge for the Professor as facilitator is to recognize the challenge and help student teams progress to "Performing" as soon as possible. With that said, students should gain an appreciation for these stages so that they can recognize them in "real life" and have learned strategies for managing each one.

Another Thread relates to the Stages of Organizational Maturity. Again, this type of concept can be found in similar structures in many texts. One structure / format is presented in the following slide which uses an AMR (now Gartner) Text Reference.

Organizations are challenged to move from Functional Silos (every Function for themselves) to a fully collaborative organization that looks for synergies across their own organization as well as the organizations of their key business partners (Customers and Suppliers). Business Simulation Teams can experience this type of dynamic through proper crafting of different simulation "Rounds". We do this by not allowing communication between Team Members in the beginning Round(s) and then encouraging / expecting communication in the later ones. Intra-Team communication is even allowed in the final Round of the Simulation. This provides a reasonable prototype for Inter-company Benchmarking of business processes. The specifics of the approach will be described in following sections below.

PROCESS STEPS TO SETUP AND MANAGE THE LEARNING EXPERIENCE

The following Slide shows the basic steps we use to manage the Business Simulation experience, grading and reporting of results. We use many different templates in the process and are willing to share these upon request. These steps are the same for any of our Business Simulation Learning experiences.

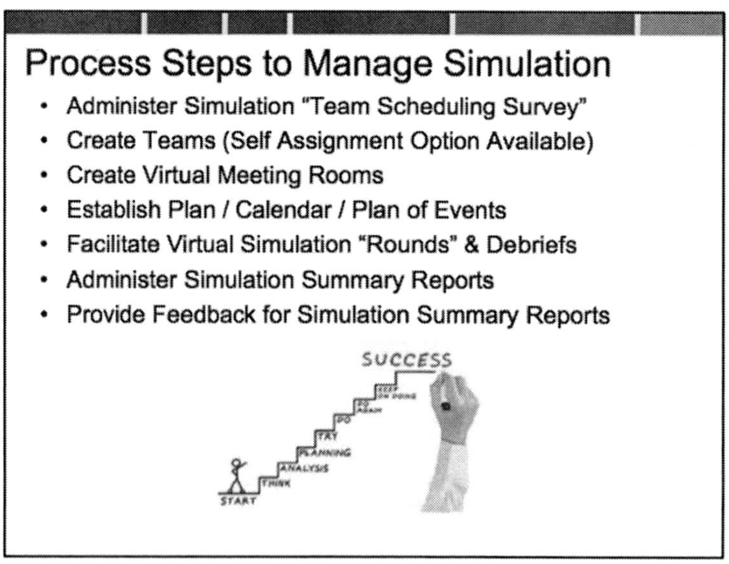

Administer Simulation "Team Scheduling Survey"
All of the Simulations covered here require the active participation of multi-person teams (usually 4 students optimum). With the Root Beer Business Simulation all four Team Members must complete required transactions in the same session for each "Round". With the Fresh Connection (and Cool Connection with its emphasis on Supply Chain Finance) Business Simulation, team members can enter transactions separately as long as this happens between the opening and closing of each "Round". Before each stage / Round, the teams have the opportunity / responsibility to collaboratively plan next steps. Then, after each stage / Round they have to opportunity to collaboratively debrief actions and results. The debrief sessions can be handled in a Professor Facilitated manner – tour preferred approach. Each one of these activities / sessions requires pre-scheduling. All team members must therefore be able to establish common meeting schedules as the very first step.

In fact, schedule availability is a key determinant that we use for Team Member assignment decisions at the very beginning.

A Team Availability Survey was designed to record and analyze the availability of each student in terms of day / time during the week. This is very easy to administer and consolidate input from everyone in the class. The Professor takes this information and assigns people randomly to teams according to common scheduling availability. With that said, students are given the opportunity to self-assign to Teams if they have some preferences – such as experiences from other activities or other reasons. An example of how this is used for scheduling purposes is shown in the following Worksheet. This shows a group of Teams that were created to work on the Fresh Connection Business Simulation. Similar structures have been used for the other simulations as well.

Create Teams (Self Assignment Option Available)
The Professor takes this information and assigns people randomly to teams according to common scheduling availability. With that said, students are given the opportunity to self-assign to Teams if they have some preferences – such as experiences from other activities or other reasons. An example of how this is used for scheduling purposes is shown in the following Worksheet. This shows a group of Teams that were created to work on the Fresh Connection Business Simulation. Similar structures have been used for the other simulations as well.

Create Virtual Meeting Rooms
It seems that students often view / expect on-line courses to be asynchronous in nature – they have assignments to do. They submit the assignments. Professors grade the assignments and they all get an "A+" and then on to graduation☺. Well, maybe this is a little exaggeration but you may get the point. In our on-line courses we try to provide a blended learning experience where there is a combination of asynchronous kids of activities that are augmented with opportunities to inter-personal engagement with other students and the professor. Business Simulations provide a role in this for sure. Virtual Meeting rooms are required to make this happen in an effective way. Now, there are many options here and it is up to the design team to come up with the best approach for each course. We have used two venues – one is Blackboard Collaborate and the other is WebEx. Both are easy to configure and explain to students so that they can then apply utility in Virtual Team Meetings. These meetings are 100% required for running each Simulation. They are also most helpful for planning and debrief sessions during the Semester / Program. Since students need flexibility in scheduling, we create "Open" meeting rooms for each Team as well as an Ad Hoc general meeting room as a kind of Virtual Office. Links to the meeting can also be shared for Guests if this is useful. The following slide shows an example of the Blackboard Collaborate layout. Virtual Sessions can be recorded to support follow-up or

allow non-attending Team Members to review the proceedings.

Establish Plan / Calendar / Plan of Events

You have likely heard of and used a process, we will refer to the Deming Cycle: Plan > Do > Check > Act. It is also referred to under other names as well. In this process you create a Plan. Then you implement the Plan. Then you review key metrics (Check how the Plan worked) and take Action based on the results. These stages actually fit any planning process whatever and we fully employ as a major component of the design with Virtual Simulations in practice. Students must have a clear picture of the journey ahead and we create this in a general planning structure that is then incorporated into the Planning Calendar for the Course Learning Management System. Two Gant Charts are shown below for the Fresh Connect Simulation to illustrate. The first one shows a generic layout and the second one shows some specifics for a recent class. You will see that the Second Planning Worksheet includes specific Milestones for Report Writing. These reports are graded and provided the basis for feedback on Lessons Learned from each stage of the Simulation "Rounds".

Facilitate Virtual Simulation "Rounds" & Debriefs

Once the design is complete the actual simulation Rounds take place. We found that facilitated sessions work well – especially at the beginning. Students will have different levels of ability and experiences with exercises and team activities like this. We usually schedule an introductory meeting with each team and then actively follow the first Simulation Rounds. After that the teams are usually able to work independently of facilitation. In some cases we have weekly follow-up / debrief sessions. This seems quite beneficial. Scheduling is a problem – especially if you are trying to have a joint debrief with multiple teams. However, the recording option is always available to use with students who can't attend in person.

Administer Simulation Summary Reports

While these Business Simulations are done in a Team environment we apply an individual grading approach. Each person is expected to complete one or more Interim Reports and a Final Report that describes their experience and the lessons learned in the process.

We use Microsoft Word Templates to ensure consistency of format. We will be pleased to provide a copy upon request. A copy of the Header Page is shown below which gives insight into major topics that are to be covered in the report. Students are expected to provide detailed narratives and simulation data to support the different sections.

Provide Feedback for Simulation Summary Reports

We looked at the Plan > Do > Check > Act format in relation to the basic design of the Business Simulation process. The same fits with feedback to students on their Learning Experience as reflected in their submitted reports. It is very important for them to receive detailed feedback on each report in order to enhance the learning experience even more. We utilize a standard Template to provide the feedback, which effectively mirrors the structure of the Report Template itself.

The following sections will touch on the overall design for each of the Business Simulation options we have employed. We will provide a general assessment of the links to our course Learning Objectives and also present some advantages and disadvantages of each approach. The intent is not to describe each simulation in detail. If you would like further information on simulation details, then you should contact the supplier directly. We have found our interactions with the professional, technical and customer supply teams of each one quite beneficial.

DESIGN LINKS TO LEARNING OBJECTIVES: THE FRESH AND COOL CONNECTIONS

The Fresh Connection considers Supply Chain Management from a cross-functional business perspective. This actually nicely links in with the overall business process of Sales and Operations Planning. Company leaders must weigh the tradeoffs between decisions made by different functional areas: Purchasing, Sales, Operations and Supply Chain Management. Each of these decisions has financial impact and in this way incorporates the financial perspective as well though there are no traditional financial decisions made in The Fresh Connection. Rather, the system controls the metric calculations and reporting. Of course, each team must be able to understand the financial connections and respond accordingly with future decisions taken.

The following course Learning Objectives are supported through the use of The Fresh Connection business simulation:

- Describe key elements of strategic planning and the alignment of functional strategies to achieve business goals.
- Analyze the principles, and challenges for marketing, sourcing, manufacturing and distribution in a global market.
- Explain the importance of strategic alliances in global sourcing environments.
- Evaluate/justify the mechanisms for measuring performance of global supply chain.
- Analyze approaches and the importance of Team Work in a Virtual environment

These Learning Objectives are supported by the functional decisions that team members make during the course of each Round. A general listing of some that we use in our configuration is presented below. From a design perspective, the simulation is configured to allow simple decisions at the beginning and then add more as teams progress through successive Rounds. In addition, they are not allowed to communicate with each other in the beginning rounds but are allowed / expected to communicate and collaborate during later ones. The intent here is to provide a model for life in a Reactionary / Silo type of Organization to a Collaborative type of Organization. Hopefully the students will see some benefit to the later and will take this with them into real world application.

<u>Typical Purchasing Function Decisions</u>

- Payment Terms (weeks)
- Trade Unit
- Agreed Delivery Reliability (%)
- Delivery Window (hrs.)
- Quality (High, Medium, Low)
- Supplier Development Projects (yes / no)
- VMI with Supplier (yes / no)

<u>Typical Operations Function Decisions</u>

- Raw Material Inspection (yes/no)
- Number of Pallet Locations in Warehouse
- Number of Permanent Employees
- Number of Shifts
- Intake Time (days)
- Capital Equipment Utilized for Operations
- Preventive Maintenance Level
- Breakdown Training Program (yes / no)
- SMED Action (Yes / no)
- Increase Speed (Yes / No)
- Outsource Finished Goods Warehouse (degree)

<u>Typical Sales Function Decisions (By Market Segment)</u>

- Service Level (%)
- Shelf Life (%)
- Order Deadline (cutoff time)
- Trade Unit
- Payment Terms (weeks)
- Promotional Pressure
- Promotion Horizon (long / short)
- VMI Project (yes / no)
- Product Range and Shortage Rules (by Market)
- Forecast Change (By Market)

Typical Supply Chain Function Decisions

- Safety Stock Components (weeks supply) by Product
- Lot Size (weeks supply) by Product
- Frozen Period for Production (weeks)
- Production Interval (days)
- Safety Stock Finished Products (weeks supply)

You can see from the list of decisions above that participants have a fairly broad span of control over many cross- functional areas. All of the decisions have some type of impact on company profitability and asset management effectiveness. The ultimate composite results are measured from a company finance perspective.'

DESIGN LINKS TO LEARNING OBJECTIVES: HBR ROOT BEER GAME

The HBR Root Beer Game considers Supply Chain Management from a cross-supplier distribution network. The cope is fairly limited as it relates to replenishment of finished products throughout the distribution network from Manufacturer through to the final Retailer. Each supply chain partner makes decisions related to the amount of product to purchase or make to support their immediate "customer". Company leaders must weigh the tradeoffs between different ordering strategies. There is a cost of carrying inventory and a cost of stock-out leading to backorders. The team's objective is to minimize the total cost of both throughout the linked supply chain. As with the Fresh Connection, the system controls the metric calculations and reporting. Of course, each team must be able to understand the financial connections and respond accordingly with future decisions taken.

The following course Learning Objectives are supported through the use of The Fresh Connection business simulation:

- Describe key elements of Supply Network planning and the importance of Cross-Functional collaboration to achieve business goals.
- Analyze the principles, concepts and challenges for developing sourcing, manufacturing and distribution strategies in a global market.
- Evaluate/justify the mechanisms for measuring performance of global supply chain.
- Analyze approaches and the importance of Team Work in a Virtual environment

These Learning Objectives are supported by the stock replenishment decisions that team members make during the course of each Round. In our selected Configuration, each simulation Round spans a 35-week planning and execution time horizon. Supply partners enter order quantities for each week and orders must be placed by all team members at the same general time. This is different from the approach in The Fresh Connection. From a design perspective, the simulation is configured to allow customization of the Demand Profile at Retail and some limited selection of planning and delivery lead times and information visibility (see examples in the Slides below). The earlier Rounds are configured to provide a model of an unresponsive supply chain with little information sharing. In later Rounds more information access is given and lead times are shortened. Team members are not allowed to communicate with each other in the beginning rounds but are allowed / expected to communicate and collaborate during later ones. The intent here is to provide a model for life in a Reactionary / Silo type of Organization to a Collaborative type of Organization. Hopefully the students will see some benefit to the later and will take this with them into real world application.

Although the decisions are somewhat limited there is a great deal of learning that can take place as students explore such concepts as: Demand Forecasting, Push vs. Pull distribution strategies, Inter-company communication of demand and supply plans and results, replenishment lot sizing, etc. The decisions made have direct impact on supply chain cost and this is the metric used by teams to check their cumulative success

RESULTS

At the beginning of this paper we brought out the critical question we ask of students "Why are You Here?" We also talked about the need to balance the needs of the students with that of all the other Stakeholders in our learning adventure. To this end we need to provide and active and engaging learning experience for the students that results in their gaining knowledge and skills to be successful in any role the serve in any company / organization they are part of. We have found that addition of Business Simulations to our programs definitely enhances the On-Line Learning experience for both the students and the Professor.

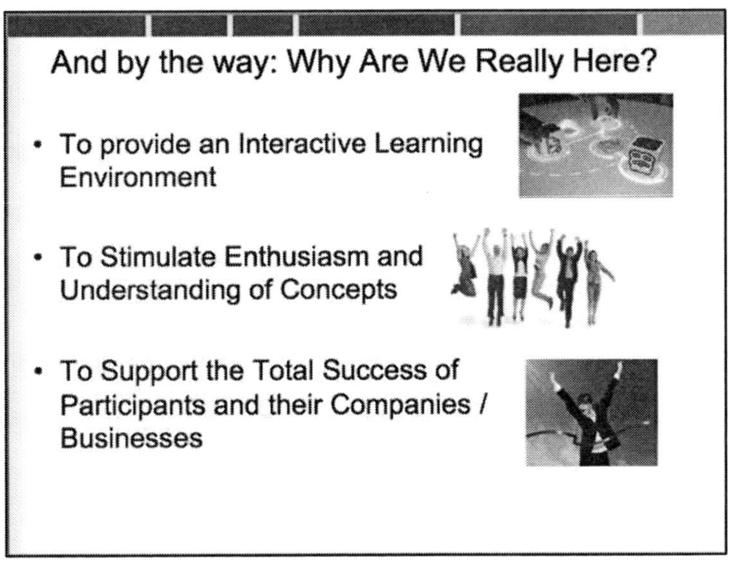

DISCUSSION AND CONCLUSIONS

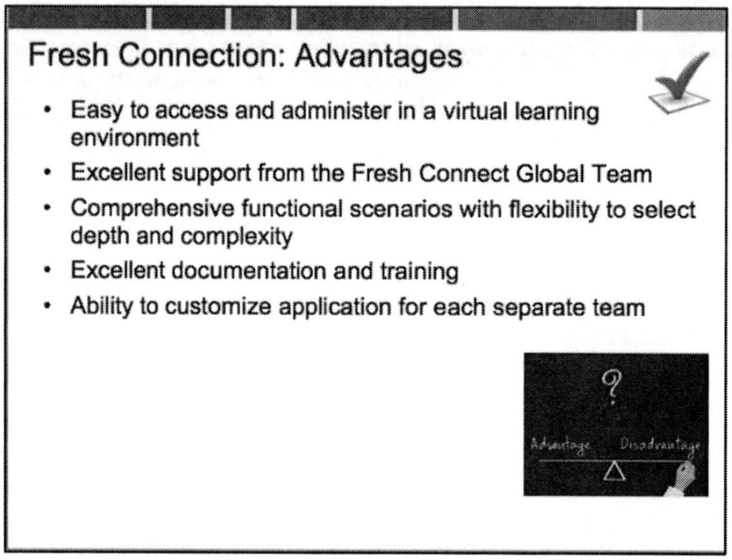

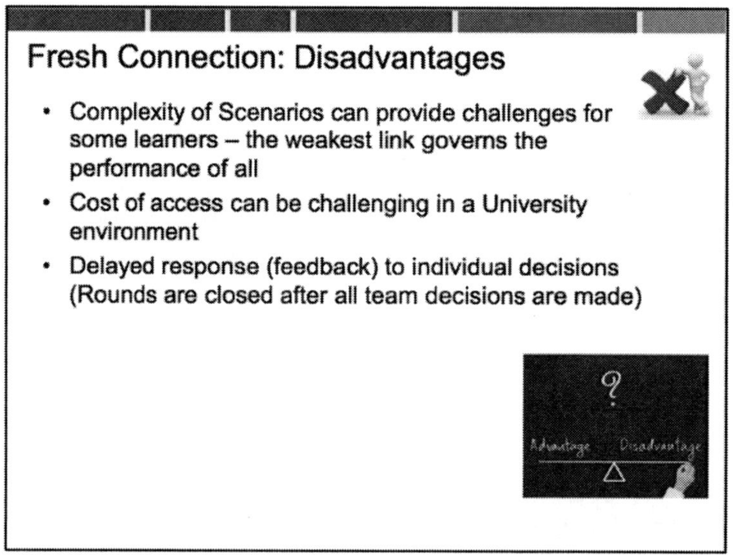

REFERENCES

References available upon request.

DECISION SCIENCES INSTITUTE

Hospital unit understaffing and missed treatments: The moderating effect of teamwork

Ashley Y. Metcalf, Ph.D.
Ohio University
Email: metcalfa@ohio.edu

ABSTRACT

Hospitals throughout the U.S. are facing increasing demand and employee shortages. This capacity issue has led to understaffing in some hospital areas. The current study examines the impact of understaffing in hospital-unit respiratory care and the impact to missed treatment rates. The moderating effect of teamwork is also considered.

KEYWORDS: Healthcare, Staffing, Teamwork, Medical errors, Empirical

INTRODUCTION

Demand for many healthcare frontline workers is expected to increase at above-average rates between the years 2014 – 2024. Demand for registered nurses is expected to increase 16%. Demand for respiratory therapists is expected to increase 12%. Demand for nursing assistants is expected to increase 17% (BLS, 2016). In addition to increasing demand, existing staffing shortages and employee turnover in hospitals has become an increasingly important area of healthcare administration (Aiken, 2011; Jacobson, 2015). Managers within U.S. hospitals are having to deal with chronic understaffing and subsequent impacts to patient care (Jacobson, 2015).

Understaffing of nurses has been associated with higher error rates and poorer quality of care (Lang et al., 2004; Twigg et al., 2015). High demands on frontline employees and lack of staffing to meet those demands can lead to increased error rates (Jacobson, 2015; Twigg et al., 2015) and higher rates of missed treatments. *Missed treatments* are treatments that have been scheduled as part of a patient's care plan but are missed by the frontline employee. In this study, missed treatments are considered a type of medical error.

In addition to staffing concerns, teamwork among frontline employees is particularly important in a hospital environment. Hospitals are very labor-intensive service environments that have to meet the demands of diverse patient needs. Teamwork among hospital caregivers has been shown to increase communication and coordination as well as increase the quality of care to patients. Furthermore, higher levels of teamwork has been shown to decrease medical errors (IOM, 2000; IOM, 2001; Pronovost & Vohr, 2010).

The current study seeks to examine the relationship between teamwork and missed treatments as well as understaffing and missed treatments. In addition, this study investigates if teamwork among frontline employees can be effective at weakening the effects of understaffing on missed treatment rates. So, *does caregiver teamwork moderate the understaffing-missed treatments relationship*?

LITERATURE REVIEW

Literature on Hospital Understaffing

Hospital staffing (and subsequent understaffing) has been of increasing interest, particularly in the nursing literature. Understaffing of nurses has been argued to be a major impediment to providing high-quality care (Aiken et al, 2001; Aiken et al, 2002, Neddleman et al., 2002). In fact, Twigg et al. (2015) found that even after controlling for patient characteristics, understaffing in nurses was associated with higher odds of: infection, pressure injury, pneumonia, deep vein thrombosis, sepsis and gastrointestinal bleed. In addition, the reader should refer to two literature reviews, Lang et al, 2004 and Kane et al, 2007, regarding the impact of nurse staffing on patient outcomes.

Furthermore, hospital understaffing is associated with lower levels of job satisfaction and higher levels of staff burnout (Aiken et al., 2002). This burnout and lack of job satisfactions will only make a staffing situation worse. Understaffing should be actively managed in order to maintain or improve hospital quality of care (Neddleman et al., 2002, Twigg et al., 2015). The current study examines hospital understaffing and the association with missed treatment rates.

Literature on Hospital Teamwork

Teamwork in a healthcare environment is particularly important due to the high labor intensity required for patient care. The lack of teamwork and communication has been shown to increase error rates in hospitals (IOM, 2000; IOM, 2001; Pronovost & Vohr, 2010). The Institute of Medicine (IOM, 2001, 2002) indicated that teamwork can be a valuable mechanism to combat medical errors. Furthermore, recent work in rapid-response teams has indicated these teams have resulted in lower levels of cardiac arrests and lower mortality rates (Berwick et al, 2006; Buist et al, 2002; Chan et al, 2010; DeVita et al, 2004). The current study builds on the idea of staffing teamwork reducing errors and improving quality of care by considering the impact of teamwork on missed treatments. Furthermore, we extend current research to consider if teamwork can dampen the effect of understaffing on missed treatment rates.

HYPOTHESIS DEVELOPMENT AND MODEL

Understaffing is a problem in a labor intensive environments, like health care, where demand for services is increasing. Chronic understaffing of nurses has been shown to be associated with higher hospital-acquired infection rates, higher rates of pneumonia and higher rates of sepsis (Needleman et al., 2002; Twigg et al., 2015). Rogowski et al. (2013) confirmed this trend with NICU nurses, where higher rates of understaffing significantly raised the infection rate for critical infants. In this study, missed treatments are considered a type of medical error. Missed treatments are treatments that are scheduled per the patient's care plan but they are missed by the frontline employee. Therefore, it is expected that higher levels of understaffing will be associated with higher rates of missed treatments.

H1: Higher levels of understaffing are associated with higher missed treatment rates

Training hospital employees for better teamwork skills has been associated with better patient-safety culture, better communications about errors, and staff working together across hospital units (Jones et al., 2013). In addition, nurses with greater teamwork have been shown to have higher levels of job satisfaction, lower burnout, and higher perceived quality of care for their patients (Rafferty et al., 2001). In a recent statement by the American Heart Association, many preventable hospital errors are due to breakdowns in communication, collaboration and teamwork (Wahr et al., 2013). Therefore, in this study, greater levels of teamwork (and its associated communication/collaboration efforts) are expected to lower missed treatment rates for patients.

H2: Higher levels of teamwork within a hospital unit are associated with lower missed treatment rates.

Coordination and information exchange are critical to achieving better patient outcomes (Boyer and Pronovost, 2010; Gittell et al., 2000; Pronovost & Vohr, 2010). Better information exchange is expected to enhance healthcare delivery and reduce medical errors (White et al., 2004). With this in mind, it is expected that coordination and collaboration among frontline employees will create a working environment that will lessen the effects of understaffing on medical errors. In hospital units with high levels of understaffing, the existence of teamwork can help to lessen the impact of the staffing problems on missed treatment rates. Therefore, this study predicts negative moderating (i.e., dampening) effect by teamwork. Figure 1 provides a conceptual model for this study.

H3: Higher levels of teamwork negatively moderate the relationship between understaffing the missed treatments.

Figure 1: Conceptual Model

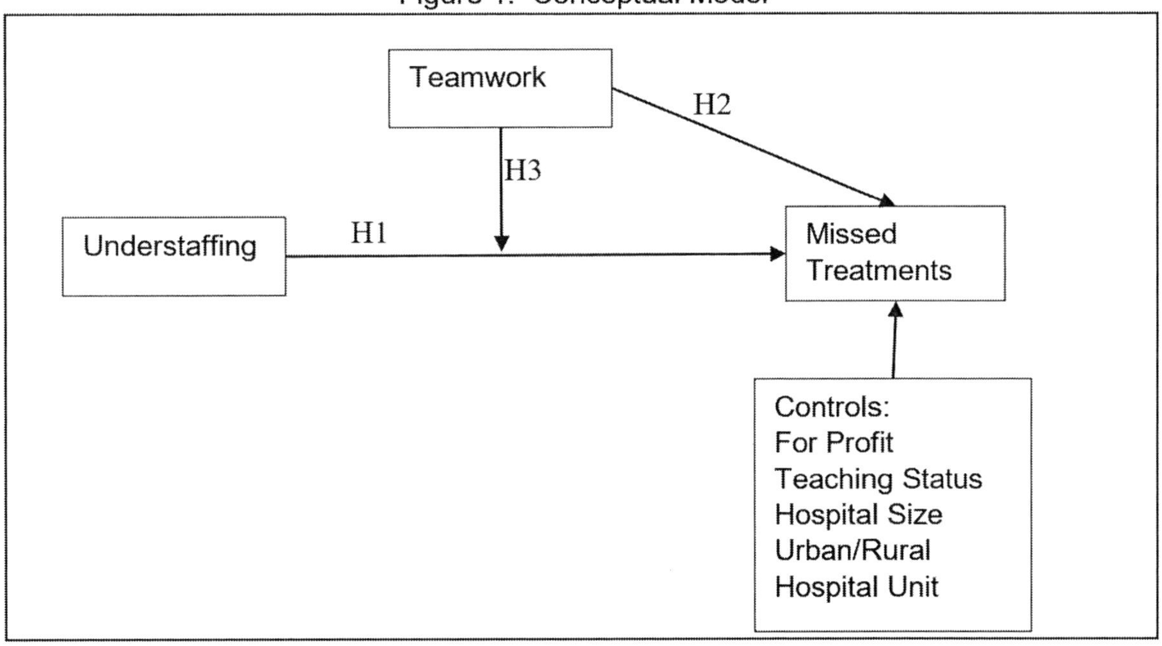

METHODS

Instrument Development

This study was carried out using the field of respiratory care within a set of U.S. non-governmental hospitals. Specifically, we consider four different units within a hospital: Emergency Department (ED), Intensive Care Unit (ICU), Neonatal Intensive Care Unit (NICU) and Adult Inpatient Floors (AI). In each of these units, respiratory therapists are required to provide a variety of care regarding respiratory services. Furthermore, the use of teamwork and the level of staffing (of respiratory therapists) can vary across units in the same hospital. A survey was designed to be completed by the respiratory care manager/supervisor for that particular hospital unit.

Survey questions for *Understaffing* and *Teamwork* were developed by working closely with our industry managers. Both understaffing and teamwork are well understood variables that respiratory care managers are consistently aware. *Understaffing* is the degree to which a hospital unit is under-staffed in respiratory therapists. *Teamwork* is the degree to which the frontline employees (nurses, therapists, etc.) work together to solve problems for patient care.

In order to measure error rates as an outcome measure, a variable was needed that was consistently monitored at the unit-level between hospitals settings. Most variables are aggregated to the hospital-level for government reporting. Other objective data is available at the patient-level (but not necessarily defined by hospital unit). In addition, patient-level data requires significant IRB approvals from each participating hospital because of privacy rights. So, our industry partners and the American Association for Respiratory Care (AARC) were contacted to determine if there were any measures consistently tracked by respiratory care managers at the unit-level within a hospital.

One variable emerged that is known by respiratory care managers across the country (and measured in a consistent way): *missed treatments*. In fact, the AARC maintains a proprietary benchmarking database that tracks missed treatments rates for its participating hospitals. The AARC variable for missed treatments is defined as the percentage of "treatments ordered but not delivered within a given time period" *(AARC, 2016)*. While the full missed treatment database was not available from the AARC, the association provided us with blind (no hospital identifiers) annual numbers for missed treatments. Quartile calculations from the AARC database for missed treatments were used to develop the scale cutoffs which were then used as the survey response options for the missed treatments variable in this study. Details of all survey items are presented in the Appendix.

Hospital control variables such as hospital size (measured as number of beds), profit vs. non-profit, teaching vs. non-teaching, and urban vs. rural were obtained from the American Hospital Association database for our participating hospitals.

Data Collection

The data collection for this study involved several stages, a pre-test, revision, and the main data collection. The proposed research questions in this study are dependent on the practical relevance of the survey questions and the full understanding of the survey items by responding practitioners. Several rounds of instrument pre-testing with industry partners (respiratory care managers/therapists/pulmonologists) were used to ensure the content validity of the survey constructs and question wording. Content validity, defined as the 'adequacy' in which the content in question has been sampled (Nunnally, 1978), is commonly assessed through the evaluation of the survey items by content experts. As such, four academics (professors in operations management) and six practitioners (two respiratory care managers, two pulmonology physicians, and four respiratory therapists) reviewed each of the items included in the survey. If survey items were confusing or unclear, the item was revised and then reviewed again by these experts.

For our main data collection, the survey was distributed online using the Qualtrics software. Respiratory care managers/supervisors were asked to respond to the survey for the specific unit in the hospital (ED, ICU, NICU, or AI) that they managed. In total, usable responses were received from 105 managers/supervisors from 45 different hospitals.

Data Analysis

Multiple regression was used in the STATA 13 software to test the hypotheses. Model 1 tests only the direct effects. Model 2 adds the moderating effect to the model. In addition to the main variables, each model also contains control variables for profit-status (For Profit), teaching status (Teaching), Size, Urban vs. Rural, and hospital unit (ICU, NICU, ED). The dummy variables for hospital unit (ICU, NICU, ED) are interpreted relative to the 'general adult inpatient' units.

RESULTS

Table 1 describes the regression results. Model 1 examines only the direct effects. Hypotheses 1 and 2 are both supported ($p<0.01$). Higher levels of understaffing are associated with significantly higher levels of missed treatments. Greater levels of teamwork within the hospital unit are associated with lower levels of missed treatments.

Model 2 examines the moderating effect of teamwork. Hypothesis 3 is also supported ($p<0.05$). Greater levels of teamwork within a hospital unit dampens the relationship between understaffing and missed treatments.

Control variables for "For Profit", "NICU", and "ED" are significant in both models. So, for-profit hospitals have lower levels of missed treatments. Furthermore, neonatal intensive care units and emergency departments have lower missed treatment rates relative to general adult inpatient units. Finally, teaching status, size of hospital, urban environments, and intensive care units were not significant predictors of missed treatment rates.

Table 1: Regression Results

DV: Missed Treatments	Model 1	Model 2
Understaffing	0.239** (0.095)	0.207* (0.094)
Teamwork (TW)	-0.494** (0.161)	-0.541** (0.159)
UnderstaffingxTW	-	-0.257* (0.118)
For Profit	-0.856* (0.527)	-1.077* (0.527)
Teaching	-0.278 (0.258)	-0.198 (0.256)
Size	0.001 (0.000)	0.000 (0.001)
Urban	-0.712 (0.331)	-0.105 (0.326)
ICU	-0.149 (0.260)	-0.142 (0.255)
NICU	-0.815* (0.397)	-0.966* (0.395)
ED	-0.600* (0.294)	-0.565* (0.289)
*p<0.05, **p<0.01, (standard error)		
N	105	105
R^2	0.27	0.31

DISCUSSION AND CONCLUSIONS

The results show that higher levels of understaffing is associated with higher missed treatment rates. This is consistent with prior literature stating the lack of adequate staffing increases error rates in hospitals (Aiken et al, 2001; Aiken et al, 2002; Jacobson et al., 2015; Lang et al., 2004; Twigg et al., 2015). The results also show that higher levels of teamwork decrease the missed treatment rates. This can be due to the increased levels of communication and collaboration for patient care in a high-teamwork environment.

Furthermore, an interesting finding in this study is the significant moderating effect of teamwork. High levels of teamwork can be used to weaken the effect of understaffing on missed treatments. So, not only does teamwork decrease missed treatments directly, but it also weakens the understaffing effect. This is an interesting effect for managers trying to maintain quality of care. To be clear, this finding is not intended to promote deliberate understaffing of hospital units. However, if a manager is stuck with an understaffed environment, efforts for teamwork and collaboration can help reduce errors and potentially maintain quality of patient care. Managers should consider efforts to increase the level of teamwork which could include initiatives such as teamwork training or work-design to facilitate teamwork and collaboration among frontline caregivers.

Control variables for 'profit status', ED, and NICU were significant in both models. For-profit hospitals have lower missed treatment rates. One explanation of this finding could be due to the focus on profits. Medical errors can be expensive, therefore, for-profit institutions may be more actively managing the prevention of those errors. Furthermore, emergency departments and neonatal intensive care units have lower missed treatment rates compared to the 'general adult inpatient' areas. This can be explained by critical nature of care in these departments and the more active management of fulfilling treatment plans among critical patients.

While this study provides interesting implications for teamwork in an understaffed environment, it is not without limitations. This study asks managers about understaffing but does not use actual staffing ratios. Future studies can use objective data on staffing numbers across hospitals/hospital units and error rates to confirm the findings in this paper. In addition, future work should consider individual factors (i.e., personality traits, burnout, etc.) that can lead to missed treatments. Future work can also consider organizational-level initiatives and cultures that drive missed treatments and other medical errors.

APPENDIX: Survey Items

Hospital Unit

Responses: [1-ICU, 2- NICU, 3-ED, 4-General Adult Inpatient]

1. Which best describes your hospital unit?

Understaffing

Responses: [1-Strongly Disagree, 5-Strongly Agree]

1. This unit is often understaffed in respiratory therapists.

Teamwork

Responses: [1-Strongly Disagree, 5-Strongly Agree]

1. The members of this unit work together as a team for patient care.

Missed Treatments

Responses: [0-0.23%; 0.24%-0.65%; 0.66% - 1.85%; 1.86% - 5%; above 5%]

1. What is your average missed treatments (in this unit)?

REFERENCES

AARC. (2016). AARC Benchmarking System. Missed Treatments: About these metrics. Retrieved April 26, 2016 from: https://c.aarc.org/resources/benchmarking/#

Aiken, L.H., Clarke, S.P., Sloane, D.M., et al. (2001). Nurses' reports on hospital care in five countries. *Health Affairs*, 20(3), 43-53.

Aiken, L.H., Clarke, S.P., Sloane, D.M., Sochalski, J., Silber, J.H. (2002). Hospital Nurse Staffing and Patient Mortality, Nurse Burnout, and Job Dissatisfaction. *JAMA*, 288(16), 1987 – 1993.

Berwick, D.M, Calkins, D.R., McCannon, C.J., Hackbarth, A.D. (2006). The 100,000 Lives Campaign: Setting a Goal and a Deadline for Improving Health Care Quality. *JAMA*, 295(3), 324 – 327.

BLS. (2016). Bureau of Labor Statistics, U.S. Department of Labor, *Occupational Outlook Handbook, 2016-17 Edition*: Registered Nurses, Respiratory Therapists, Nursing Assistants.

Boyer, K.K, & Pronovost, P. (2010). What medicine can teach operations: what operations can teach medicine. *Journal of Operations Management*, 28(5), 367 – 371.

Buist, M.D., Moore, G.E., Bernard, S.A., et al. (2002). Effects of a medical emergency team on reduction of mortality from unexpected cardiac arrests in hospital: preliminary study. *BMJ*, 324, 387 – 390.

Chan, P.S., Jain, R., Nallmothu, B.K., Berg, R.A., Sasson, C. (2010). Rapid Response Teams: A Systematic Review and Meta-analysis. *Arch Internal Medicine,* 170(1), 18-26.

DeVita, M.A., Braithwaite, R.S., Mahidhara, R., et al. (2004). Use of medical emergency team responses to reduce hospital cardiopulmonary arrests. Quality Safety Health Care, 13, 251 – 254.

Gittell, J.H., Fairfield, K.M., Bierbaum, B., Head, W., Jackson, R., Kelly, M. et al. (2000). Impact of relational coordination on quality of care, postoperative pain and functioning, and length of stay: a nine-hospital study of surgical patients. *Med. Care*, 38(8), 807 – 819.

IOM, Institute of Medicine. (2000). *To err is human: Building a safer health system.* Washington, DC: National Academy Press.

IOM, Institute of Medicine. (2001). *Crossing the quality chasm: A new health system for the 21st century.* Washington, DC: National Academy Press.

Jacobson, R. (2015). Widespread Understaffing of Nurses Increases Risk to Patients. *Scientific American* (July 14, 2015). Accessed May 13, 2016 from: http://www.scientificamerican.com/article/widespread-understaffing-of-nurses-increases-risk-to-patients/

Jones, F., Podila, P., Powers, C. (2013). Creating a Culture of Safety in the Emergency Department: The Value of Teamwork Training. *Journal of Nursing Administration*, 43(4), 194 - 200.

Kane, R.L., Shamliyan, T.A., Mueller, C., Duval, S., Wilt, T.J. (2007). The Association of Registered Nurse Staffing Levels and Patient Outcomes: Systematic Review and Meta-Analysis. *Medical Care*, 45(12), 1195 – 1204.

Lang, T.A., Roman, P.S., Hodge, M., Kravitz, R.L., Olson, V. (2004). Nurse-Patient Ratios: A Systematic Review on the Effects of Nurse Staffing on Patient, Nurse Employee, and Hospital Outcomes. *JONA*, 34 (7/8), 326 – 337.

Mekhjian, H.S., Kuman, R.R., Kuehn, L., Bentley, T.D., Teater, P., Thomas, A., Payne, B., Ahmad, A. (2002). Immediate Benefits Realized Following Implementation of Physician Order Entry at an Academic Medical Center. *Journal of the American Medical Informatics Association*, 9(5), 529 – 539.

Meyer, S.M., & Collier, D.A. (2001). An empirical test of the causal relationships in the Baldrige health care pilot criteria. *Journal of Operations Management, 19*(4), 403-425.

Neddleman, J., Buerhaus, P., Mattke, S., Stewart, M., Zelevinsky, K. (2002). Nurse-Staffing Levels and the Quality of Care in Hospitals. *New England Journal of Medicine*, 346(22), p. 1715-1722.

Pronovost, P., & Vohr, E. (2010). *Safe Patients, Smart Hospitals: How One Doctor's Checklist Can Help Us Change Health Care from the Inside Out.* New York, NY: Hudson Street Press.

Rafferty, A., Ball, J., Aiken, L.H. (2001). Are teamwork and professional autonomy compatible, and do they result in improved hospital care? *Quality in Health Care*, 10, 32-37.

Rogowski, J.A., Staiger, D., Patrick, T., Horbar, J., Kenny, M., Lake, E.T. (2013). Nurse Staffing and NICU Infection Rates. *JAMA Pediatrics*, 167(5), p. 444-450.

Twigg, D.E., Gelder, L., & Myers, H. (2015). The impact of understaffed shifts on nurse-sensitive outcomes. *Journal of Advanced Nursing*, 71(7), p. 1564 – 1572.

Wahr, J.A., Prager, R.L., Abernathy, J.H., Martinez, E.A., Salas, E., Seifert, P.C., et al. (2013). Patient Safety in the Cardiac Operating Room: Human Factors and Teamwork. A Scientific Statement from the American Heart Association. *Circulation*, 128, 1139 – 1169.

White, A.A., Wright, S.W., Blanco, R., Lemonds, B., Sisco, J., Bledsoe, S. et al. (2004). Cause-and-effect analysis of risk management files to assess patient care in the emergency department. *Acad. Emerg. Med.*, 11(10), 1035 – 1041.

DECISION SCIENCES INSTITUTE

Impact of New Product Development Flexibility on Performance

Jeen-Su Lim

University of Toledo

Email: jlim@utnet.utoledo.edu

John Heinrichs

Wayne State University

Email: ai2824@wayne.edu

Kee-Sook Lim

University of Toledo

Email: klim2@utnet.utoledo.edu

ABSTRACT

Previous research has recognized the importance of flexibility in the new product development process and its impact on the firm's performance. This study develops and tests empirically a conceptual model that captures the relationships among a firm's new product development flexibility, customer orientation, and market performance. This study also evaluates the moderating effect of innovation strategy on these relationships. The results show that the effect of new product development flexibility on firm performance is contingent upon the type of innovation strategy. Managerial and theoretical implications are discussed.

KEYWORDS: New Product Development, Firm Performance, Market Orientation, Customer Orientation, Innovation Strategy

INTRODUCTION

With increased competition in the global marketplace, firms must achieve flexibility in their new product and service development efforts and become responsive to the changing environment.

In this globalized market, customers have become more empowered due to their ability to obtain increased access to rich online information and access to products and services from a myriad of e-commerce sites. This availability of diverse shopping alternatives and customized product options make global customers less loyal and far less forgiving. As a result of the empowered customer, to successfully compete, firms must be paying continuous attention to customer comments and should monitor the performance of their products and services as well as making rapid adjustments to their product and service offerings to retain and attract customers (Lin & Wu, 2014).

Flexibility in the new product development process can have a significant impact on the value of NPD projects (Kettunen, Grushka-Cockayne, Degraeve, & De Reyck, 2015) such that the more intense or innovative the environment, the greater the value of flexibility. Kettunen, et al. (2015) indicated that the types of flexibility required in NPD include various strategies and decision-making ability that can enable the abandonment of the project development, that can enhance the product development, that can defer the product launch, and that can switch the development strategy to pursue more a more radical innovation.

However, little attention has been given to the contingencies of the NPD flexibility - firm performance relationship. To address these attendant concerns, a conceptual framework is developed to integrate key antecedents and consequences of NPD flexibility. A conceptual model captures the role of NPD flexibility while incorporating customer orientation as an important antecedent. Specifically, the purpose of this study is to examine the relationships among NPD flexibility, customer orientation as an antecedent of NPD flexibility and the consequence of NPD flexibility (i.e., market performance). In addition, this study evaluates the moderating effect of innovation strategy on the relationships among customer orientation, NPD flexibility, and market performance. It should be of interest to marketers and managers because it extends our knowledge of the role and significance of NPD flexibility in the globalized competitive markets.

THEORY DEVELOPMENT AND HYPOTHESES

Part of a firm's survivability strategy is its ability to become innovative and agile by developing a number of innovative product and service technologies and by developing flexibility for introducing, developing, manufacturing, and delivering products and services to target customers.

NPD flexibility can be considered as a specific dynamic capability that enables the firm to quickly and effectively respond to market trends and customer preference changes (Roberts & Grover, 2012). Dynamic capabilities can be interpreted as an extension of the resource-based theory, these specific capabilities should be valuable, difficult to produce, rare and non-substitutable (e.g., Barney, 1991; Day 1994; Piening & Salge, 2015; Wernerfelt, 1984). Further, these capabilities should enable firms to create, deploy and protect the intangible assets that support superior long-run performance of the firm (Teece, 2007).

NPD Flexibility

Previous research studies have demonstrated that the faster a firm is able to develop new products, the greater the probability the firm will outperform its competitors. Therefore, every firm needs to know what factors are important in the new product development process to help them achieve this speed (Tessarolo, 2007) as flexibility can have a significant impact on the

value of NPD projects (Kettunen, Grushka-Cockayne, Degraeve, & De Reyck, 2015). NPD flexibility is achieved by embedding suppliers and customers in the NPD process.
The impact from integrating supply chain members on the new product development process has been very well researched (He, Lai, Sun, & Chen, 2014). Further, as the voice of the customer becomes embedded in the new product development effort, a firm can provide personalized customization products to customers. Thus, customer integration is viewed as a key factor with customer integration being defined as the extent to which customers and firms coordinate mutual decisions. A close relationship between the customers and the firms offers opportunities for improving the accuracy of demand information, which ultimately has the potential to reduce the firm's design and production planning time. As one of the firm's flexible resources, this may significantly affect how quickly the firm can react to new market conditions. Ultimately, the product's success in the market depends not only on the product's performance, but also on the firm's competitors' capability to develop competing products. Thus, the intensity of the market that a firm experiences can become the deciding factor for the pace at which new and improved products are introduced by the firm and its competitors.

Customer Orientation

As noted by Roberts and Grover (2012), the firm needs to be customer-oriented and to have integrated the voice of the customer into the NPD process to be flexible. Customer orientation includes intelligence dissemination that is critical to a firm's ability to sense and respond to market opportunities (Kohli & Jaworski, 1990; Teece, 2007). While customer orientation is focused on a firm's ability to respond to customer needs, NPD flexibility expands beyond just being customer orientated. NPD flexibility requires that a firm possess the capability of designing and developing new products or modifying existing products to serve emerging customer segments. Thus, customer orientation can facilitate the firm in being more flexible by better responding to customer-based opportunities in turbulent markets (Roberts & Grover, 2012; Wang, Zhao, & Voss; 2016).

Moderating Effect of Innovation Strategy

Customer orientation helps firms understand current customers and their expressed needs as well as their latent needs or opportunities (Atuahene-Gima, Slater, & Olson, 2005; Narver, Slater & MacLachlan, 2004). Customer orientation is closely linked to NPD flexibility. In fact, customer orientation has been shown to be a strong link with the success of firms' innovative efforts (Atuahene-Gima, 1996; Kohli & Jaworski, 1990; Slater & Narver, 1994; Zhang & Duan, 2010). Customer orientation can also help non-innovative firms more in achieving NPD flexibility as those firms are less sophisticated in their market-sensing and linking processes and are lacking in the needed innovation capabilities (Kotler & Keller, 2009; Narver, Slater & MacLachlan, 2004; Voola & O'Cass, 2010).
Customer orientation leads to superior performance (Kotler & Keller, 2009). An organization-wide customer orientation has been found to have a positive impact on firm performance and their new products (Jaworski & Kohli, 1993; Moorman, 1995; Narver & Slater, 1990). Also, Kumar et al. (2011) provide evidence indicating that customer orientation has a positive effect on the performance of the firm in both the short run and long run. In addition, research by Zhang and Duan (2010) and Voola and O'Cass (2010) suggest a direct relationship between customer orientation and firm performance.

Zhang and Duan (2010) found slightly stronger direct effect of customer orientation on market performance for non-innovators. Coltman et al. (2008) suggest that customer orientation has a stronger direct effect on responsive criterion such as market performance (e.g., level of repeat business). Thus, non-innovating firms focusing on the immediate effect of satisfying current customer needs (Kumar et al., 2011) can expect that the effect of customer orientation will be stronger on market performance. These discussions lead to the following hypothesis.

Hypothesis 1: The relationship between customer orientation and (a) NPD flexibility and (b) market performance is moderated by a firm's innovation strategy such that the relationship will be stronger for non-innovators than innovators.

The innovation strategy chosen by the firm can help the firm differentiate itself from other firms through innovativeness of their products and services (Bode & Alig, 2011). The innovator strategy pursues the active design and development of the innovation idea. Innovation activities undertaken by the firm focus on the successful implementation of an idea for a product in a certain market (Bode & Alig, 2011). The firm must assess their potential resources and intellectual capital, and then select an appropriate innovation strategy to match their objectives and capabilities. The resource profiles of the firm indicate their ability to respond to market opportunities with the various innovation strategies (Chen, Su, & Tsai, 2007). Each of the innovation strategies evaluated by the firm provides different advantages and has different requirements of the firm.

The type of innovation strategy followed by a firm can drive the relative importance of NPD flexibility and influence the NPD flexibility - firm performance relationship. The chosen innovation strategy can influence the firm's resource allocation and competitive focus of a firm. Innovators must focus on NPD flexibility in addition to innovativeness of products and services to improve their firm's performance. While there is evidence to suggest a direct link between innovativeness and business performance (Hult et al., 2004; Hog & Ha, 2009; Menguc & Auh, 2006; Zhang & Duan, 2010), NPD flexibility is also important for innovators, to improve firm performance. Both becoming innovative and flexible requires high level of attention and resources such that most innovators would expect NPD flexibility has a more positive impact on their firm performance than non-innovators. On the other hand, as non-innovators are focusing on learning and adapting to innovators' product offerings, the ability to identify and respond to environmental changes can be less critical for their market and firm performance. These discussions suggest that the effect of NPD flexibility on firm performance may vary depending on the firm's innovation strategy.

Hypothesis 2: The relationship between NPD flexibility and market performance is moderated by a firm's innovation strategy such that the relationship will be stronger for innovators than non-innovators.

RESEARCH DESIGN

Sample and Data Collection

Data were collected for this study via a mail survey. Top executives of manufacturing firms from two industry groups were selected for this study using a key informant approach. The two industry groups that were selected were from the chemicals and allied products (SIC 28) and industrial and commercial machinery (SIC 35) sectors. A total of 172 useable responses were obtained after the three waves resulting in a response rate of 16.4 percent.

Description of the Measures

Most of the measures were adapted from previous studies. The customer orientation measure was adapted from Kohli and Jaworski (1990). Market performance was measured by using three rating scale items anchored by 5 (to a great extent) and 1 (to a very little extent). These constructs served as the dependent measure; the items were adapted in part from Moorman (1995), Griffin and Page (1993) and Morgan and Strong (2003). Firms are classified into innovator and non-innovators based on the primary innovation strategy pursued by a firm. Out of 172 responding firms, 71 firms were classified into innovators and the remaining 101 firms were classified into non-innovators.

The control variables included in the study are firm size and the respondent's years of working in the present position. A firm's size may have influenced the antecedents of firm performance (Glaister, Dincer, Tatoglu, Demirbag, & Zaim, 2008; Pearce, Freeman, & Robinson, 1987). Firm size was defined as the number of employees in a firm (Im & Workman, 2004; Narver & Slater, 1990) and was used to control for the impact of a firm's resources on the firm's performance (Chandy & Tellis, 2000; Im & Workman, 2004; Lin, Lee, & Hung, 2006; Narver & Slater, 1990). Also included as a control variable was the respondent's number of years in their present position. It was envisioned that "years in the present position" should count for industry experience and how to deal with or how to confront different situations (Zahra & Nielsen, 2002).

RESULTS

Confirmatory Factor Analysis

The measurement properties were assessed in one confirmatory factor analysis (CFA). Confirmatory factor analysis results of the measurement items are presented in Table 1. Table 1 shows means, standard deviations, composite reliabilities, factor loadings, and goodness of fit indices. The fit indices showed that the model resulted in a good fit to the data (χ^2 = 135.17, d.f. = 48, normed fit index (NFI) = .90, comparative fit index (CFI) = .93, root mean square residual (RMSR) = .075).

Table 1: Confirmatory Factor Analysis Results

	Number of Items	Mean	Standard Deviation	Composite Reliabilities (CR)	Lambda Coefficients
Customer Orientation	3	5.54	0.92	0.80	.71 - .78
New Product Development Flexibility	3	3.95	1.09	0.63	.48 - .73
Market Performance	3	4.20	1.65	0.87	.72 - .92
Financial Performance	3	4.70	1.42	0.84	.75 - .84

Note: Fit Indices: χ^2 / d.f. = 135.17 / 48; Normed Fit Index (NFI) = 0.90; Comparative Fit Index (CFI) = 0.93; Root Mean Square Residual (RMSR) = 0.075.

Hypotheses Test

Data were analyzed by path analysis using LISREL 8.8. In testing the path model, the summated scores of the scale items were used as indicators of the construct. Using the multi-group LISREL approach, the path model was estimated for the two innovation strategy type firms. The global fit indices indicate a good fit of the model for the data. The chi-square for the model is 16.00 with 14 degrees of freedom. The normed fit index (NFI) is .91 with goodness of fit index (GFI) of .98. The root mean square residual (RMSR) is .042.

To test whether the path coefficients for the two innovation strategy type firms are significantly different, chi-square difference with one degree of freedom was calculated between the unconstrained model and constrained model with the path coefficient equalities.

The path coefficients from customer orientation to NPD flexibility for the two innovation strategy type firms were compared to test the moderating effect of the type of innovation strategy. The chi-square difference test result showed that the two path coefficients are not significantly different ($\Delta\chi^2 = 0.55$ with 1 d.f., $p > .05$). The path coefficients from customer orientation to NPD flexibility are significant for both innovators and non-innovators with the path coefficient of .49 and .59 respectively. These results do not provide support for the Hypothesis 1a. The chi-square difference for the path from customer orientation to market performance is significant ($\Delta\chi^2 = 5.48$ with 1 d.f., $p < .05$). The path from customer orientation to market performance is positive and significant for the non-innovators ($\beta_{Non\text{-}innovators} = 0.32$, $p < .01$) but not significant for the innovators ($\beta_{Innovators} = -0.08$, $p > .05$). Hypothesis 1b is supported by the results.

The chi-square difference for the path from NPD flexibility to market performance is significant ($\Delta\chi^2 = 4.76$ with 1 d.f., $p < .05$). The path from NPD flexibility to market performance is positive and significant for the innovators ($\beta_{Innovators} = 0.25$, $p < .05$) but not significant for the non-innovators ($\beta_{Non\text{-}innovators} = -0.12$, $p > .05$). These results provide support for Hypothesis 2.

DISCUSSION

This study developed and empirically tested a conceptual model capturing the antecedent and consequence NPD flexibility. The moderating effect of the firm's innovation strategy on the relationships among customer orientation, NPD flexibility, and market performance was also incorporated into the model. The findings provide some insights on the contingency effect of innovation strategy and offer theoretical and managerial implications.

The findings show that the customer orientation-market performance relationship as well as NPD flexibility-market performance relationship are moderated by the type of innovation strategy chosen by the firm. NPD flexibility is positively related to market performance for innovators. However, NPD flexibility is not significantly related to market performance for non-innovators. These results suggest that innovators need to pursue NPD flexibility in addition to innovativeness to be successful in competitive global markets. Being innovative alone is not sufficient for innovative firms to maintain market leadership. For the non-innovators, NPD flexibility is not the type of dynamic capability needed for success as they compete in the global market with other competitive advantages such as cost.

This study also found the significant effect of customer orientation on NPD flexibility for both innovators and non-innovators. Customer orientation as a component of market orientation is a significant antecedent of NPD flexibility. These results provide support for the importance of understanding and sensing customer needs in order to develop the NPD flexibility capability of a firm.

REFERENCES

References available upon request.

DECISION SCIENCES INSTITUTE

Impact of Supply Chain Collaboration on Logistics Performance: Evidence from a Sub-Sahara Africa Nation's petroleum downstream

Benjamin Agyei-Owusu
Kwame Nkrumah University of Science and Technology
Email: bagyei-owusu.ksb@knust.edu.gh

David Asamoah
Kwame Nkrumah University of Science and Technology
Email: dasamoah.ksb@knust.edu.gh

Francis Kofi Andoh-Baidoo
University of Texas Rio Grande Valley
Email: francis.andohbaidoo@utrgv.edu

John Akaribo
Kwame Nkrumah University of Science and Technology
Email: jakaribo@st.knust.edu.gh

ABSTRACT

The need for firms to collaborate effectively with supply chain partners is a subject of interest to researchers. We conduct an extension study to explore the impact of supply chain collaboration on the logistics performance using firms in Ghana's petroleum downstream. The results showed relatively higher levels of external collaboration than internal collaboration among surveyed firms, even though internal collaboration had a stronger impact on a firm's logistics performance. The study also revealed a positive impact of internal collaboration on external collaboration. The study identifies internal collaboration as an important variable deserving great attention by firms in the petroleum downstream.

KEYWORDS: Supply Chain Collaboration, Performance, Sub-Saharan Africa, and Petroleum

INTRODUCTION

The Council of Supply Chain Management Professionals defines supply chain management (SCM) as "the planning and management of all activities involved in sourcing and procurement, conversion, and all logistics management activities. Importantly, it also includes coordination and collaboration with channel partners, which can be suppliers, intermediaries, third party service providers, and customers. In essence, supply chain management integrates supply and demand management within and across companies" (Vitasek, 2010). A core capability of SCM is Supply Chain Collaboration (SCC). SCC is seen as the major driver of effective SCM (Bowersox, 1990; Ellram and Cooper, 1990). Many definitions have been propounded for SCC (Mentzer et al., 2001; Sriram et al., 1992). However, the definition by Simatupang and Sridharan (2002) is the most widely accepted. They define SCC as "two or more independent companies working jointly to plan and execute supply chain operations with greater success than when acting in isolation" (Simatupang and Sridharan, 2002, p.19). Due to intense global competition and recent global trends such as the adoption of outsourcing, today's firms operate in "networked" business environments. Over the past few years, there has been considerable progress in the interconnection among firms in all industry segments (Baldwin, 2012; Trienekens et al., 2012). Most modern supply chains have become extremely complex, global, and with several touch points from raw materials handling to finished goods delivery to customers (Baldwin, 2012; Fawcett et al., 2006). In such interconnected environments, supply chains are expected to show high degrees of flexibility, responsiveness, and collaboration.

SCM does not only involve the effective management and coordination of individuals and organizations involved in the design and execution of activities involved in procuring, manufacturing, and management of logistics, but also includes the integration and coordination of all actors in the supply chain (Naspetti et al., 2009). For competitive advantage to be obtained and sustained, collaboration among members of a supply chain must be achieved (Naspetti et al., 2009). The collaboration includes information sharing, decision synchronization, complementary resource sharing, and aligning other activities with collaborative chain members. This generates competitive advantage for the business organization (Harrison and Now, 2002; Horvath, 2001). Collaboration within organizations and between members of a supply chain is therefore usually associated with organizational benefits.

Studies that empirically explored the effect of SCC on the performance of firms have presented differing results (see Table 1). Some studies point to clear organizational level benefits arising from SCC including access to complementary resources (Park and Song 2004); improving revenue and operational efficiency (Fisher, 1997; Lee et al., 1997); and supply chain cost reductions especially those regarding inter-organization transactions, stock and production (McLaren et al., 2004), and shared risk (Kogut, 1988). Other studies (e.g., Gimenez and Ventura, 2005; Stank et al., 2001) observed no significant performance improvement arising from firms' SCC initiatives. This points to an unclear relationship between SCC and firm performance. SCC efforts also encounter several challenges, resulting in many collaborative efforts becoming unsuccessful or failing to garner the expected level of benefits to stakeholders (Richey et al., 2010). Taken together, these conflicting findings point to the need for more studies to advance our understandings on SCC, in particular the influence of context on SCC initiatives.

Table 1: Varying results from studies on the impact of SCC on performance

Author	Findings
Vickery et al. (2003)	Insignificant direct impact of supply chain Integration on the financial performance of firms.
Gimenez and Ventura (2005)	External Integration stronger than Internal Integration and is motivation for Internal Integration.
Stank et al. (2001)	Indirect impact of External Collaboration on Logistics Service Performance through improved Internal Collaboration. Internal Collaboration occasions External Collaboration.
Germain et al. (2008)	Downstream integration only informs higher logistics performance when organizational performance was high.
Rodrigues et al. (2004)	Cumulative influence of internal and external operations significantly impacts the organization's performance, but individually they do not.
Stock et al. (2000)	Logistics Integration does not always result in performance improvements for firms. Gains accruing from logistics Integration can be obtained only in conjunction with complementary aspects of the organization's supply chain network.
Hakansson and Persson (2004)	The specific network involved plays a role in the level of organizational performance that can be obtained. Gains within one supply chain could well be detrimental in a different supply chain.

In this study, we conduct an extension study and focus on the petroleum and sub-Saharan African contexts that lack SCC studies. Specifically, we study the impact of SCC on firms' logistics performance by considering organizations operating in Ghana's petroleum downstream. The petroleum downstream encompass activities ranging from refinery of crude oil, to storage, transportation, distribution and retailing of petroleum and petroleum products to meet the needs of the Ghanaian economy (Amponsah and Opei, 2014). Due to the expansive nature and scope of the petroleum downstream, as well as some legislations governing the sector, no one firm acts alone in fulfilling end-to-end customer orders. Firms in the petroleum sector must collaborate with other actors within the supply chain to meet the country's energy demands (Greg, 2003). However, despite decades of SCC initiatives in Ghana's petroleum downstream, the supply chain is still fraught with issues of stock-outs, fuel shortages, high operational costs, and other logistics challenges (Amponsah and Opei, 2014; Dasmani, 2014; Ministry of Energy, 2010). In this study, we survey a cross section of firms operating in Ghana's petroleum downstream to explore whether their SCC initiatives have led to improvements in their logistics performance. The current study offers both theoretical and practical contributions. First, we are studying new contexts: sub-Saharan Africa, and the petroleum industry. Results from the study offer new insights into SCC and therefore expands our understanding of SCC initiatives and associated benefits. Second, findings will provide new specific knowledge that organizations operating in the contexts where the study was performed can use to enhance success of SCC initiatives. The results also suggest the need for subsequent studies to take contextual variables into consideration to enhance both their theoretical and practical relevance.

The rest of the paper is organized as follows. A brief review of pertinent literature is presented in the next section, followed by the theoretical background of the study and the research model and hypotheses. Then, we present the methodology leading to the presentation of the results, discussion of the results, and the conclusion.

LITERATURE REVIEW

Supply Chain Collaboration and Performance

Collaboration affords two or more firms to share resources to perform a specific, mutually beneficial undertaking (Pereira and Soares, 2007). In such situations, there is explicit consensus between the parties to leverage combined resources for purposes of delivering sustainable mutual advantages, with emphasis on efficiency throughout the supply chain, profitable areas of growth, and a holistic improvement in performance of the entire chain. In collaboration agreements, each party retains its autonomy but succeeds in gaining new opportunities. A strategic arrangement can for instance enable firms create more effective processes, access new markets and achieve a competitive edge over rivals (Cooke, 1998). With respect to the SCM discipline, the concept of collaboration may be seen as yet being in its infantile stages, having emerged in mid-1990s (VICS, 1998) from the most popular form – Collaboration, Planning, Forecasting and Replenishment (CPFR). It is largely held that before the advent of CPFR, firms practiced more basic types of collaborations such as Vendor Managed Inventory and Continuous Replenishment Programs (Barratt and Oliveira, 2001). More and more manufacturers have concluded that success is impossible without a collaborative pull of resources and skills from partners in the supply chain (Skjoett-Larsen et al., 2003).

Dyer et al. (1998) observed that competitive advantages are achieved in inter-organizational contexts, arguing that arm's-length exchanges, typically characterized by nonspecific investments, limited information sharing and coordination devices, and low interdependence, are incapable of generating profits beyond what strategic collaboration can generate because of their lack of resource and knowledge sharing. They suggest that organizations would have competitive advantages when they move from arm's-length transactions and specialize in collaborative building by investing in relation-specific assets, information sharing, complementary capabilities, as well as instituting control systems that work more effectively. Collaborating firms must be willing to rethink their priorities and move beyond traditional individualistic initiatives. They must be ready and willing to align their goals, strategies, systems, people and processes with key supply chain partners, commit themselves to the collaborative process, establish confidence and industrious communications, share knowledge and information, share risks and rewards, and provide the necessary resources required to support the collaborative effort (Skjoett-Larsen et al., 2003).

Cao and Zhang (2011) in their survey of U.S. manufacturing firms explored the impact of SCC on firm performance from a collaborative advantage paradigm. They found that SCC resulted in both positive collaborative advantage and stronger firm performance. Still in the U.S., Won Lee et al. (2007) studied the effect of supplier linkages, customer linkages, and internal linkages on supply chain performance and observed that supplier linkages positively impacted performance reliability and overall performance, whilst internal linkages positively impacted cost containment performance. The findings of Vereecke and Muylle (2006) also suggest that improving collaboration with both suppliers and customers enabled European firms reap maximum benefits in terms of improvement of performance, whilst collaboration with only one resulted in only minor benefits. The study of Lorentz (2008) explored SCC in an uncertain cross-border context (Finland and Russia) and explored whether it positively impacted supply chain performance. Their findings weakly supported the proposed positive impact of SCC on supply chain performance. Singh and Power (2009) surveyed Australian manufacturing plants in their study and hypothesized that strong customer relationships and strong customer involvement positively impacted firm performance. Their findings supported both hypotheses, although the effect customer relationship on firm performance was greater. Their findings also suggest a strong inter-relationship between collaboration with suppliers and customers. Finally, Stank et al. (2001) explored the impact of internal collaboration and external collaboration on logistics performance using data from firms in North America. Their findings indicated that external collaboration influences increased internal collaboration, which in turn improves service performance.

While the results of prior studies are interesting, the impact of SCC initiatives on performance has not been explored properly with the context of developing countries. Specifically, no study on the subject have originated from Africa. This study exploring the impact of SCC initiatives within the sub-Saharan African context is the first of its kind and provides findings on the impact of SCC on performance that are more specific to the African context.

Overview of Ghana's Petroleum Sub-sector

Ghana has five sedimentary basins that are considered to have prospects for oil and gas: the Tano Basin, Saltpond Basin, Accra/Keta Basin, Cape Three Points Basin which are all off-shore and are fairly well explored; and the Voltaian Basin which is on-shore and is hardly explored (Ministry of Energy, 2010; Owusu and Nyantakyi, 2011). In July 2007, Ghana National Petroleum Corporation (GNPC) and its partners discovered oil in commercial quantities in the Jubilee field in the offshore Tano/Cape Three Points Basin of the Ghanaian continental shelf. Appraisal work conducted on the field has estimated reserves of oil at about 800 million with an upside estimate of 3 billion barrels. The field also has substantial associated natural gas reserves (Ministry of Energy, 2010).Currently, oil production in Ghana occurs at the Saltpond fields and the Jubilee fields. The Saltpond fields is matured and drying up with production in 2014 dropping to 97,300 barrels from 98,289 barrels in 2013. Production in the Jubilee fields on the other hand is on the ascendency rising to 38.7 million barrels in 2014 from 30.4 million barrels in 2013 and 27.4 million in 2012 (Energy Commission, 2015).

The petroleum industry is segmented into upstream, midstream and downstream which covers activities from exploration and production of petroleum through transportation to the marketing of the final products (Ministry of Energy, 2010). The petroleum upstream activities cover mainly petroleum exploration and related operations. Currently, oil production in Ghana occurs at the Saltpond fields and the Jubilee fields. The midstream sector involves all activities between the well-head and the refinery. It includes transportation of oil and gas from the extraction points to refineries onshore and storage of petroleum. Oversight responsibility of the petroleum upstream and midstream is in the hands of the Ghana National Petroleum Corporation, acting on behalf of the Ministry of Energy and Petroleum.

The downstream activities include refinery, processing, storage, transportation, distribution, marketing and sale of petroleum products and natural gas, and trading activities that take place in between. The downstream sector is regulated by the Ghana Petroleum Authority (Amponsah and Opei, 2014). The petroleum downstream fulfils most of the energy needs of the country; the transport needs, and also forms the foundation for many other industries (Greg, 2003). The petroleum products marketed in Ghana are premium gasoline, kerosene, gas oil, residual fuel oil, LPG, and premix. Some of the challenges facing the petroleum downstream include inadequate refining infrastructure, infrastructure for the transportation of petroleum products, storage infrastructure, sales outlets, inefficient distribution of petroleum products, ineffective implementation of petroleum pricing mechanism, and weak institutional and regulatory environment (Ministry of Energy, 2010).

Actors in the Ghana's Petroleum downstream

The Ghana Energy commission indicates that the primary actors in the petroleum downstream sector are the Tema Oil Refinery (TOR), National Petroleum Authority, Bulk Oil Storage and Transportation (BOST) companies, and Oil Marketing Companies (OMCs) (Energy Commission, 2015).

TOR is charged with refining crude oil to address the oil and gas related needs of the country, with the exception of crude oil for power generation. It comprises a Crude Distillation Unit of production capacity of 45,000 barrels per day and a 14,000 barrels per day Residual Fluid Catalytic Cracker unit to process residual fuel oil, a by-product of crude oil processed by the Crude Distillation Unit, into more diesel, gasoline and LPG. Production from TOR has been consistently nose-diving in recent years due to considerable operational challenges, reaching its lowest of about 129,000 tons in 2014 from its average annual peaks of 1.5 million tons in the early to middle of last decade (Energy Commission, 2015). In 2010, TOR produced approximately 70% of the country's needs, but this has dropped to 3% as at 2014. TOR was operating at 3.5% capacity in 2014, further down from 5% capacity in 2013. Meanwhile, based on international standards, 95% capacity utilization is required for refineries to achieve economic viability (Energy Commission, 2015).

The second major actor in Ghana's petroleum downstream is the BOST companies. These companies perform the functions of storage of petroleum products and strategic stocking (Amponsah and Opei, 2014). In Ghana, aside from the facilities for petroleum products storage at TOR, there are also storage facilities at Accra Plains, in Buipe in the Northern Region, near Akosombo in the Eastern Region and at Takoradi in the Western Region (Ministry of Energy, 2010). However, these storage facilities are still considerably limited given the demand in the country. Their locations are far from majority of Ghanaians who demand them. There is therefore the need to have an effective system for transporting and distributing the petroleum products throughout the country.

Thirdly, OMCs and other private firms are also involved in distribution of petroleum products in Ghana usually with Bulk Road Vehicles. They purchase petroleum products from TOR and sell to retailers at a marked-up price. Lastly, the National Petroleum Authority sets and implements pricing policies for petroleum and petroleum products in Ghana. Up till 2001, the Government was the regulator of the prices for petroleum products. This however resulted in debt creation for TOR as the government failed to mark prices up accordingly in 2000 when crude oil prices shot above US$30 per barrel from an initial average price of below US$20 per barrel. Since then, oil prices have risen considerably, with average prices exceeding the $100 mark in 2011 to 2013, but has since dropped to below $50 in 2015 (Arezki and Blanchard, 2015; Bowler, 2015). The considerable fluctuation in oil prices led to the institution of the automatic price adjustment formula. At present, the NPA determines the price margins and based on these, OMCs announce rates indicating a maximum indicative pump prices to the general public (Energy Commission, 2015).

THEORETICAL BACKGROUND

The arguments and hypothesized relationships of this study is founded on the network theory for managing supply chains. Supply chain relationships in the early 1980s were structured around arms-length dealings which are more compatible with the tenets of transaction cost theory (TCT) (Hoyt and Huq, 2000). But, TCT appears to be losing its ability to explicate modern day collaborations based on mutual trust and information sharing found in current day markets (Ghoshal and Moran, 1996). As a result, collaboration based theory is deemed more appropriate. Collaborative relationships founded on trust, thereby reducing transaction related risks under conditions of uncertainty and dynamic change, dominate current supply chain theory (Halldorsson et al., 2007). Collaboration in this period stresses buyer-supplier relationships exhibiting appreciable levels of trust and collaboration not falling to the temptation of discontinuing the collaborative agreements even though a chance to make short-term gains may exist elsewhere. Lamming (1996) presents a theory of SCM arguing the need for collaboration to be long-term and for issues of relationship management to be considered in SCM theory.

The Network perspective posits openness and trust between the parties as a condition for gaining the best possible results from cooperation. Over time, mutual adjustments improve supply chain efficiency and therefore, make them more efficient. Examples of adjustment processes might include an electronic data interchange and B2B connections between the partners for the implementation of a quality control system. By entering into close cooperation with partners who possess complementary competencies, the individual firm is able to utilize resources and skills controlled by other players (Halldorsson et al., 2007). In close and long-term cooperation, the parties are able to establish mutual and strong relations of trust, which may result in the disappearance of cost-consuming, contractual safeguards.

RESEARCH MODEL AND HYPOTHESES

This study adapted the constructs in Stank et al. (2001) developed to explore SCC and logistics performance among firms in North America (Canada, Mexico, and the United States). The original research model has three major constructs: Internal Collaboration, External Collaboration, and Logistics Performance. Internal Collaboration as conceptualized by Stank et al. (2001) refers to the degree of cooperation and teamwork that exists within an organization and among its departments. External Collaboration on the other hand deals with the degree of cooperation and teamwork between the firm and its supply chain partners (Stank et al., 2001). Logistics is viewed as a value-adding supply chain process. Logistics customer value is generally created through effectiveness, efficiency, and/or differentiation (Holcomb, 1994). Logistics Performance as conceptualized by Stank et al. (2001) refers to the measure of how well firms are able to generate logistics customer value. The conceptualization and operationalization of the constructs of the Stank et al. (2001) model was adopted in our study. The original study hypothesized that Internal Collaboration and External Collaboration positively impacted Logistics Performance, and that Internal Collaboration and External Collaboration were positively related.

The research model used in this study as well suggests that both Internal Collaboration and External Collaboration positively impact Logistics Performance. We however varied the relationship between Internal Collaboration and External Collaboration to suit the sub-Saharan African context of this study. Most businesses within the region would only attempt collaborating closely with external entities after they have been able to achieve some level of internal collaboration and have enjoyed benefits of internal collaboration (Chinomona and Pooe, 2013). We therefore hypothesize Internal Collaboration as a precursor for achieving External Collaboration in the sub-Sahara African region. The adapted research model is presented in Figure 1 below.

Figure 1: Research Model and hypotheses

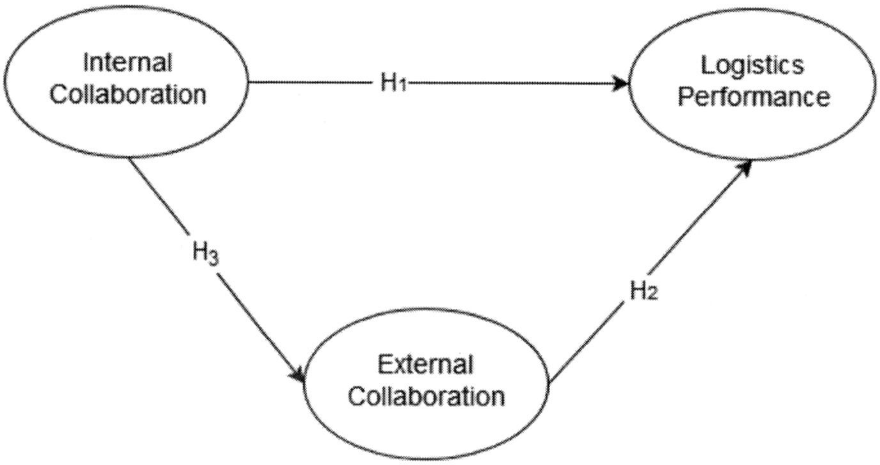

The study proposes that managers who adopt a collaborative perspective to work usually succeed in building esprit de corps across departments or organizations. This usually allows organizations to unite efforts and achieve collective goals of the organization through synergy, in line with the network theory (Stank et al., 2001). Also, trading partners who adopt a collaborative perspective are able to jointly develop long-term demand projections rather than rely upon separate, independently generated forecasts. This results in a better matching between supply and demand (Stank et al., 1999). Both internal collaboration and external collaboration enhance an organization's ability to create logistics value, thereby enabling them to achieve higher logistics performance (Fisher, 1997; Harrison and Now, 2002; Horvath, 2001; Lee et al., 1997). This leads to the following hypotheses:

H_1: Internal Collaboration is positively associated with Logistics Performance
H_2: External Collaboration is positively associated with Logistics Performance

Furthermore, it is proposed that internal collaboration is a necessary condition for realization of external collaboration by organizations in sub-Saharan Africa. A collaborative mechanism should already be in place in-house before firms tackle the relatively more complicated task of collaborating with external firms. The level of internal collaboration is thus an important determinant of the level of external collaboration that can be achieved (Stank et al., 2001). Firms would usually venture out into collaboration with external supply chain partners only after internal collaboration is achieved to a reasonable degree, and has been evidently beneficial. It is perceived that external collaboration results from an extension of successful internal collaboration. This leads to the hypothesis that:

H_3: Internal collaboration is positively associated with External Collaboration.

METHODOLOGY

The present study can be considered an extension (Berthon et al., 2002) of the original Stank et al. (2001) study. An extension study can be described as “a duplication of a target study in which one or more key parameters are altered. Thus, certain parameters are held constant and certain parameters are changed between the target and focal studies” (Berthon et al., 2002, p.419).

The research constructs and research items of Stank et al. (2001) were largely adopted in this study with minor modifications made in order to ensure that they fit the Ghanaian context within which they were to be deployed. In addition, the relationships between the constructs was varied slightly in our study. The adopted research items have the 1995 World Class Logistics Research at Michigan State University as their foundation and had been further refined by Stank et al. (2001) after a pilot survey completed by almost 3,700 respondents in North America, Europe, and the Pacific Rim. This was followed by further refinements through in-depth interviews with 111 top logistics firms to establish a tool for assessing logistical proficiency across a range of integrative and collaborative elements. The Internal Collaboration construct had five measurement items, External Collaboration had six items, and Logistics Performance had six items as well. Details of the research items are presented in Table 2 below.

Table 2: Research Constructs and Research Items

Construct	Acronym	Items
Internal Collaboration	IC1	We maintain an integrated database to facilitate information sharing
	IC2	We effectively share operational information between departments
	IC3	We have adequate ability to share both standardized and customized information internally
	IC4	We provide objective feedback to employees regarding integrated logistics performance.
	IC5	Our compensation, incentive, and reward systems encourage integration
External Collaboration	EC1	We effectively share operational information externally with selected suppliers and/or customers.
	EC2	We have developed performance measures that extend across supply chain relationships.
	EC3	We experience improved performance by integrating operations with supply chain partners.
	EC4	We have supply chain arrangements with suppliers and customers and operate under principles of shared rewards and risks.
	EC5	We have increased operational flexibility through supply chain collaboration.
	EC6	We benchmark best practices/processes and share results with suppliers

Logistics Performance	LP1	Our firm's ability to reduce the time between order receipt and customer delivery to as close to zero as possible.
	LP2	Our firm's ability to meet quoted or anticipated delivery dates and quantities on a consistent basis.
	LP3	Our firm's ability to respond to the needs and wants of key customers.
	LP4	Our firm's ability to provide desired quantities on a consistent basis.
	LP5	Our firm's ability to modify order size, volume or composition during logistics operation.
	LP6	Our firm's ability to accommodate delivery times for specific customers

To test the research model, we conducted a survey of 90 different organizations that operate in Ghana's petroleum downstream, with target respondents being the CEOs of the organizations, heads of logistics or supply chain departments, and other suitably high ranking managers of firms. Twenty actors in Ghana's petroleum downstream were initially identified, notified and surveyed. Snowballing techniques were then used to identify other firms in Ghana who operate in the petroleum downstream. The questionnaires were delivered to managers of the 90 identified firms, and 76 were successfully retrieved, representing a response rate of 84.4%. Only one questionnaire was sent to each responding organization. Respondents were asked to use 5-point Likert scales to indicate the extent to which they agreed to statements measuring internal collaboration, external collaboration, and their logistics performance.

DATA ANALYSES AND RESULTS

Analysis of the model and hypothesized structural paths was performed using SmartPLS version 2.0 (Ringle et al., 2005), a structural equation modelling (SEM) software package (Hair et al., 2012). SEM is a family of statistical procedures that depicts multiple relationships among latent constructs through the use of equations quite similar to multiple regression equations (Hair et al., 2014). Results from the SEM analyses are compared to the results of Stank et al. (2001), and deductions and conclusions are presented.

Estimating the level of Internal and External Collaboration

Based on the responses obtained for the collaboration research items, we estimated the perceived level of internal and external collaboration among firms in Ghana's petroleum downstream. The five measures of internal control, as well as the six measures of external control, were analyzed to provide this information and is presented in Table 3 below. For each research item, the lowest and highest ratings are indicated in the "Min" and "Max" columns respectively, and the mean response for each measure calculated together with its standard deviation (S.D). The higher the mean, the stronger the level of collaboration for that measure as it shows a higher level of "agreement" with the research instruments which were positively framed.

Table 3: Level of Internal and External Collaboration				
	Min	Max	Mean	S.D
Level of Internal Collaboration				
IC1: Integrated database to facilitate information sharing	1	4	3.55	.773
IC2: Share operational information between departments	1	5	3.78	.810
IC3: Share standardized and customized information internally	1	5	3.53	.739
IC4: Objective feedback to employees regarding integrated logistics performance.	2	5	3.67	.681
IC5: Compensation, incentive, and reward systems that encourage integration	1	5	3.76	.764
Average Level of Internal Collaboration			**3.564**	**.753**
Level of External Collaboration				
EC1: Share operational information externally with selected suppliers and/or customers.	1	5	3.67	.719
EC2: Performance measures that extend across supply chain relationships.	1	5	3.57	.869
EC3: Experience improved performance by integrating operations with supply chain partners.	1	5	3.63	.763
EC4: Supply chain arrangements with suppliers and customers and operate under principles of shared rewards and risks.	1	5	3.80	.611
EC5: Increased operational flexibility through supply chain collaboration.	1	5	3.54	.824
EC6: Benchmark best practices/processes and share results with suppliers	2	5	3.83	.719
Average level of External Collaboration			**3.752**	**.751**

The respondents' view on level of collaboration in Ghana's petroleum downstream ranged from a least rating of 3.53 for Item IC3 (our firm possess adequate ability to share both standardized and customized information internally) to a highest rating of 3.83 for Item EC6 (we benchmark best practices/processes and share results with suppliers). The range of the item means was only 0.3 suggesting that respondents viewed the level of collaboration across all measures to be fairly even. Overall, the mean level of internal collaboration was found to be 3.564 which is well above average, whilst the average level of external collaboration was even higher at 3.752. This result indicates respondents perceive both internal collaboration and external collaboration to be high in Ghana's petroleum downstream, but the level of internal collaboration that existed within their firms was lower than the level of external collaboration that existed between them and their supply chain partners. The responses of respondents showed very little variation over items. Also, standard deviation values across items were not significant suggesting a high level of consistency of responses.

Measurement model analyses

The study also sought to explore the impact of both internal collaboration and external collaboration on the logistics performance of the sampled firms. To achieve this objective, partial least squares structural equation modelling (PLS-SEM) techniques were employed to explore the research model presented in Figure 1.

Achieving high validity and reliability of the measurement items is important to make the findings and relationships valid. Validity and reliability of the constructs and measurement items can be confirmed by measuring the average variance extracted (AVE), composite reliability, and Cronbach's Alpha, and ensuring that they meet the acceptable benchmarked standards. The parameter Cronbach alpha measures the correlation among the indicators of a latent variable. A rule of thumb benchmark of 0.7 is used as the acceptance criteria for Cronbach alpha (Chin, 1998). Results presented in Table 4 show that all the Cronbach alpha values for the constructs pass this test. Composite reliability measures the ability of the indicators to explain the variance of their latent variable (Chin, 1998). A rule of thumb benchmark of values of at least 0.7 is used to assess acceptability of unidimensionality of a latent variable. The results in Table 4 show that all latent constructs passed this test. Further, AVE according to Fornell and Larker (1981) measures the amount that a latent variable component captures from its indicators as opposed to the amount due to measurement error. Typically a value greater than 0.5 is recommended (Fornell and Larcker, 1981). AVEs for the all constructs in the research model meet this requirement (see Table 4). Given that the research model passes validity tests, we conclude that the research model is very sound.

Table 4: Attributes of Constructs

Construct	AVE	Composite Reliability	Cronbach's Alpha
External Collaboration	0.6503	0.9027	0.8669
Internal Collaboration	0.7651	0.9071	0.8471
Logistics Performance	0.5718	0.8406	0.7498

We next conducted factor analyses to ensure the measurement items were of adequate quality. There were initial instances of poor loadings for some items (IC1, IC5, EC4, EC5, LP2, and LP6) and these were excluded from the SEM analysis as recommended (Hair et al., 2010). Given the reflective nature of the constructs, removing these items would not adversely affect the constructs or the results (Bollen and Lennox, 1991). Next we tested for discriminant validity. Discriminant validity examines the extent to which a measure correlates with measures of constructs that are different from the construct the measure is intended to assess (Barclay et al., 1995). Discriminant validity is achieved if the AVE for each construct is greater than 0.5 and the square root of the AVE for a construct is greater than the correlation of that construct with other constructs (Fornell and Larcker, 1981). In Table 5, the bold numbers on the diagonals are the square root of the AVEs. Off-diagonal elements are the correlations among constructs. Although the correlation between Internal Collaboration and External Collaboration was high (similarly observed in the original Stank et al. results), all diagonal numbers are greater than the corresponding off-diagonal ones, indicating satisfactory discriminant validity of all the constructs.

Table 5: Test for discriminant validity

	AVE	External Collaboration	Internal Collaboration	Logistics Performance
External Collaboration	0.6503	**0.8064**		
Internal Collaboration	0.7651	0.7911	**0.8747**	
Logistics Performance	0.5718	0.3879	0.4090	**0.7562**

Measuring the impact of SCC on Logistics Performance

PLS provides the magnitude and significance of the hypothesized causal relationships as standardized path coefficients. The parameter estimate of the hypothesized structural path should be statistically significant in the hypothesized direction of the effect (Chin, 1998). The research model of the study showing factor loadings for the research items and path coefficients is shown in Figure 2. R^2 values are shown inside each construct.

Figure 2: Results of hypotheses test

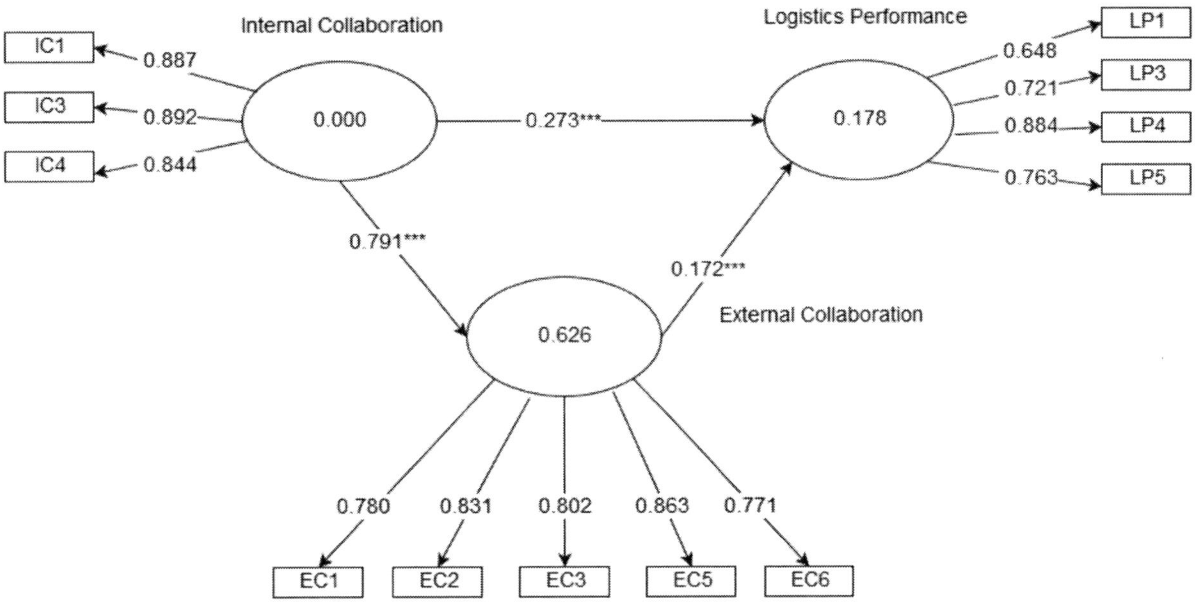

The research sought to ascertain the strength of the relationship between Internal Collaboration and Logistics Performance (H_1) as well as the relationship between External Collaboration and Logistics Performance (H_2) among firms in Ghana's petroleum downstream. The results show that there exists a positive relationship between Internal Collaboration and Logistics Performance, with a path coefficient of 0.273. This relationship was significant at $p < 0.01$, which is a very high level. This agrees with the findings of Stank et al. (2001) who also obtained a strong positive relationship between Internal Collaboration and Logistics Performance. The results of our study also indicated that there existed a positive effect of External Collaboration on Logistics Performance, demonstrated by a path coefficient of 0.172, which was also significant at $p < 0.01$ even though the path coefficient and the t-statistic was slightly lower. This result is different from that of Stank et al. (2001), who did not observe a significant impact of External Collaboration on Logistics Performance. We also sought to ascertain the extent of the effect of Internal Collaboration on External Collaboration (H_3). Results of the SEM analyses reveals a very strong positive impact of Internal Collaboration on External Collaboration, with a path coefficient of 0.791 and the relationship was significant at $p < 0.01$. The results of Stank et al. (2001) study observed a similarly strong positive correlation between the two constructs. All three hypotheses of our study were thus supported. The details of the results of the tests of the hypotheses are summarized in Table 6 below and compared to the results of the Stank et al. (2001).

Table 6: Results of Hypotheses test					
Hs	Hypothesized paths	**Our results**		**Stank et al. (2001)**	
		Effect size	Hypothesis Support	Effect size	Hypothesis Support
H_1	Internal Collaboration → Logistics Performance	0.273 (3.619***)	Supported	0.40 (2.98***)	Supported
H_2	External Collaboration → Logistics Performance	0.172 (2.401**)	Supported	0.01 (0.08)	Not Supported
H_3	Internal Collaboration → External Collaboration	0.791 (35.687***)	Supported		
H_3	Internal Collaboration ↔ External Collaboration			0.79 (9.76***)	Supported

***p < 0.01;

DISCUSSION OF RESULTS

The study suggests that there was high level of internal and external collaboration existing among firms in petroleum downstream of the sub-Saharan African country. It was also revealed that the level of external collaboration among firms was slightly higher than the level of internal collaboration. This result is perhaps not surprising as actors in petroleum downstream typically depend on each other to fulfil customer orders, and as such firms are more likely to focus on improving external collaboration. As noted earlier, no actor in the petroleum downstream performs end-to-end petroleum activities and each typically plays only a small defined role within the petroleum supply chain (Amponsah and Opei, 2014).

Even though the study confirmed positive impacts of both Internal Collaboration and External Collaboration on Logistics Performance, it was revealed that the effect of External Collaboration on Logistics Performance (0.172) was not as strong as the effect of Internal Collaboration on Logistics Performance (0.273). This means that increasing the level of internal collaboration within firms would cause a relatively stronger impact on their logistics performance than increasing the level of collaboration with their external collaboration partners. Actors in the petroleum downstream would therefore stand to gain more by dedicating more resources to improving the level of internal collaboration within their organizations through maintaining integrated databases to facilitate information sharing within the firm, enhancing their ability to share both standardized and customized information internally, and endeavoring to provide objective feedback to employees regarding integrated logistics performance (Stank et al., 2001).

In addition to the positive impact of Internal Collaboration on Logistics Performance, Internal Collaboration was observed to have a strong impact on External Collaboration, suggesting that high levels of internal collaboration achieved by firms should lead to improvements in the level of external collaboration as well. When firms set out to improve the level of internal collaboration, they as well acquire relevant skills, competencies, and gain experiences which serves as a platform for smoother execution of external collaboration initiatives. This further strengthens the case for sub-Saharan African firms focusing efforts on increasing their level of internal collaboration as it has positive impacts on both external collaboration and logistics performance. The differences between the results of this study and that of Stank et al. (2001) do not in any way invalidate the original study, and may have arisen due to the different environmental and contextual factors surrounding the two studies (Asamoah et al., 2015; Asamoah et al., 2016).

CONCLUSION

The study revealed that firms in the Sub-Saharan nation's petroleum downstream focused more on external collaboration compared to internal collaboration even though internal collaboration contributed more to their logistics performance. By way of implication of the study for practice, we call for firms operating within the context of this study to shift focus from concentrating on external collaboration initiatives to focusing more on enhancing internal collaboration. Working towards achieving higher levels of internal collaboration should reflect positively on both external collaboration and logistics performance. Managers of firms in the petroleum downstream and beyond should thus concentrate on developing a culture that fosters effective internal collaboration within their firms.

There are important implications of the study for research. Given the importance that has been attached to the Internal Collaboration construct by the findings of this study, there is the need to more fully explore the dimensions of Internal Collaboration, and to ascertain the antecedents of higher internal collaboration among firms in the petroleum downstream. Also, it would be worth exploring the conditions under which the effects of internal collaboration on external collaboration and logistics performance can be maximized.

The study has few limitations. Even though the study considers the entire petroleum downstream of Ghana, data collection was restricted only to firms physically involved in the moving, storing and sales of petroleum and products. The full petroleum downstream supply chain is conceivably bigger and more complex with banks, financial institutions, government and non-governmental agencies all playing diverse direct and indirect roles. This study has revealed a positive impact of internal collaboration on both external collaboration and logistics performance. Future research would be guided at studying these relationships further and exploring what factors enhance, moderate, and repress the relationships between internal collaboration, external collaboration and logistics performance. Future research should also be directed to exploring how managers can drive the behavioral change necessary to achieve significant internal collaboration within their firms.

REFERENCES

Amponsah, R., and Opei, F. K. (2014). Ghana's downstream petroleum sector: An assessment of key supply chain challenges and prospects for growth. *International Journal of Petroleum and Oil Exploration Research,* 1(1), 1-7.

Arezki, R., and Blanchard, O. (2015). The 2014 oil price slump: Seven key questions. *VOXEU, January,* 13.

Asamoah, D., Andoh-Baidoo, F. K., and Agyei-Owusu, B. (2015). Impact of ERP Implementation on Business Process Outcomes: A Replication of a United States Study in a Sub-Saharan African Nation. *AIS Transactions on Replication Research,* 1(1), 4.

Asamoah, D., Andoh-Baidoo, F., & Agyei-Owusu, B. (2016). Examining the Relationships between Supply Chain Integration, Information Sharing, and Supply Chain Performance: A Replication Study. *AMCIS 2016 Proceedings*

Baldwin, R. E. (2012). Global supply chains: Why they emerged, why they matter, and where they are going.

Barclay, D., Higgins, C., and Thompson, R. (1995). The partial least squares (PLS) approach to causal modeling: personal computer adoption and use as an illustration. *Technology studies,* 2, 285-309.

Barratt, M., and Oliveira, A. (2001). Exploring the experiences of collaborative planning initiatives. *International Journal of Physical Distribution & Logistics Management,* 31(4), 266-289.

Berthon, P., Pitt, L., Ewing, M., and Carr, C. L. (2002). Potential research space in MIS: A framework for envisioning and evaluating research replication, extension, and generation. *Information Systems Research,* 13(4), 416-427.

Bollen, K., and Lennox, R. (1991). Conventional wisdom on measurement: A structural equation perspective. *Psychological bulletin,* 110(2), 305-314.

Bowersox, D. J. (1990). The strategic benefits of logistics alliances. *Harvard Business Review,* 68(4), 36-43.

Bowler, T. (2015). Falling oil prices: Who are the winners and losers. *BBC News, January,* 19.

Cao, M., and Zhang, Q. (2011). Supply chain collaboration: Impact on collaborative advantage and firm performance. *Journal of Operations Management,* 29(3), 163-180.

Chin, W. W. (1998). Commentary: Issues and opinion on structural equation modeling. *MIS Quarterly,* 22(1), vii-xvi.

Chinomona, R., & Pooe, R. I. (2013). The influence of logistics integration on information sharing and business performance: The case of small and medium enterprises in South Africa. *Journal of Transport and Supply Chain Management*, *7*(1), 1-9.

Cooke, J. A. (1998). VMI: very mixed impact? *Logistics Management and Distribution*.
Dasmani, L. (2014). Fuel shortage hits Ghana's capital city *The Africa Report*.

Dyer, J. H., Cho, D. S., and Chu, W. (1998). Strategic supplier segmentation: The next" best practice" in supply chain management. *California Management Review,* 40(2), 57-77.

Ellram, L. M., and Cooper, M. C. (1990). Supply chain management, partnerships, and the shipper-third party relationship. *International Journal of Logistics Management,* 1(2), 1-10.
Energy Commission, G. (2015). 2015 Energy (Supply and Demand) Outlook for Ghana. Accra, Ghana: Ghana Energy Commission.

Fawcett, S. E., Ogden, J. A., Magnan, G. M., and Cooper, M. B. (2006). Organizational commitment and governance for supply chain success. *International Journal of Physical Distribution & Logistics Management,* 36(1), 22-35.

Fisher, M. L. (1997). What is the right supply chain for your product? *Harvard Business Review,* 75(2), 105-106.

Fornell, C., and Larcker, D. F. (1981). Evaluating Structural Equation Models with Unobservable Variables and Measurement Error. *Journal of Marketing Research,* 18(39-50).

Germain, R., Claycombb, C., and Drögec, C. (2008). Supply chain variability, organizational structure, and performance: The moderating effect of demand unpredictability. *Journal of Operations Management,* 26(5), 557–570.

Ghoshal, S., and Moran, P. (1996). Bad for practice: A critique of the transaction cost theory. *Academy of Management Review,* 21, 13–47.

Gimenez, C., and Ventura, E. (2005). Logistics-production, logistics-marketing and external integration – their impact on performance. *International Journal of Operations and Production Management,* 25(1), 20-38.

Greg, L. (2003). Managing the Downstream Oil Supply Chain: A customer-led strategy. *World Energy,* 6(3).

Hair, J. F., Black, W. C., Anderson, R. E., and Tatham, R. L. (2010). *Multivariate data analysis* (Vol. 7). Upper Saddle River, NJ: Prentice Hall.

Hakansson, H., and Persson, G. (2004). Supply chain management: the logic of supply chains and networks. *The International Journal of Logistics Management,* 15(1), 11-26.

Halldorsson, A., Kotzab, H., Mikkola, J. H., and Skjøtt-Larsen, T. (2007). Complementary theories to supply chain management. *Supply Chain Management: An international Journal,* 12(4), 284-296.

Harrison, A., and Now, C. (2002). The role of coherent supply chain strategy and performance management in achieving competitive advantage: an international survey. *Journal of the Operational Research Society,* 53(3), 263-271.

Horvath, L. (2001). Collaboration: the key to value creation in supply chain management. *Supply Chain Management: An International Journal.,* 6(5), 205-207.

Hoyt, J., and Huq, F. (2000). From arms-length to collaborative relationships in the supply chain: An evolutionary process. *International Journal of Physical Distribution & Logistics Management,* 30(9), 750-764.

Kogut, B. (1988). Joint ventures: theoretical and empirical perspectives *Strategetic Management Journal,* 9(4), 319-322.

Lamming, R. (1996). Squaring lean supply with supply chain management. *International Journal of Operations & Production Management,* 16(2), 183-196.
Lee, H. L., Padmanabham, V., and Whang, S. (1997). The bullwhip effect in supply chains. *Sloan Management Review,* 38(3), 93-102.

Lorentz, H. (2008). Collaboration in Finnish-Russian supply chains: Effects on performance and the role of experience. *Baltic Journal of Management,* 3(3), 246-265.
McLaren, T. S., Head, M. M., and Yuan, Y. (2004). *Costs and Benefits in Supply Chain Collaboration* (pp. 258-284).

Mentzer, J. T., Dewitt, W., Keebler, J. S., Min, S., Nix, N. W., Smith, C. D., and Zacharia, Z. G. (2001). Defining supply chain management. *Journal of Business Logistics,* 22(2), 1-25.

Ministry of Energy. (2010). National Petroleum Policy. Ghana: Ministry of Energy

Naspetti, S., Lampkin, N., Nicolas, P., Stolze, M., and Zanoli, R. (2009). Organic supply chain collaboration: a case study in eight EU Countries. *113th EAAE Seminar "A resilient European food industry and food chain in a challenging world", Chania, Crete, Greece.*

Owusu, P., and Nyantakyi, E. (2011). Advances and Challenges of Oıl and Gas Developments in Ghana.

Pereira, C. S., and Soares, A. L. (2007). Improving the quality of collaboration requirements for information management through social networks analysis. *International Journal of Information Management,* 27(2), 86-103.

Richey, R. G., Roath, A. S., Whipple, J. M., and Fawcett, S. E. (2010). Exploring a governance theory of supply chain management: barriers and facilitators to integration. *Journal of Business Logistics,* 31(1), 237-256.

Ringle, C. M., Wende, S., and Will, A. (2005). *SmartPLS 2.0.M3 (beta)*. Hamburg: University of Hamburg.

Rodrigues, A. M., Stank, T. P., and Lynch, D. F. (2004). Linking strategy, structure, process, and performance in integrated logistics. *Journal of Business Logistics,* 25(2), 65-94.

Simatupang, T. M., and Sridharan, R. (2002). The collaborative supply chain. *International Journal of Logistics Management,* 13(1), 15-30.

Singh, P. J., and Power, D. (2009). The nature and effectiveness of collaboration between firms, their customers and suppliers: a supply chain perspective. *Supply Chain Management: An international Journal,* 14(3), 189-200.

Skjoett-Larsen, T., Thernøe, C., and Andresen, C. (2003). Supply chain collaboration: Theoretical perspectives and empirical evidence. *International Journal of Physical Distribution & Logistics Management,* 33(6), 531-549.

Sriram, Ven, Krapfel, R., and Spekman, R. (1992). Antecedents to buyer-seller collaboration: An analysis from the buyer's perspective. *Journal of Business Research,* 25(4), 303-320.

Stank, T. P., Daugherty, P. J., and Autry, C. W. (1999). Collaborative Planning: Supporting Automatic Replenishment Programs. *Supply Chain Management,* 4(2), 75-85.

Stank, T. P., Keller, S. B., and Daugherty, P. J. (2001). Supply chain collaboration and logistical service performance. *Journal of Business Logistics,* 22(1), 29-48.

Stock, G. N., Greis, N. P., and Kasarda, J. D. (2000). Enterprise logistics and supply chain structure: the role of fit. *Journal of Operations Management,* 18(5), 531-547.

Trienekens, J., Wognum, P., Beulens, A. J., and van der Vorst, J. G. (2012). Transparency in complex dynamic food supply chains. *Advanced Engineering Informatics,* 26(1), 55-65.

Vereecke, A., and Muylle, S. (2006). Performance improvement through supply chain collaboration in Europe. *International Journal of Operations & Production Management,* 26(11), 1176-1198.

Vickery, S. K., Jayaram, J., Droge, C., and Calantone, R. (2003). The effects of an integrative supply chain strategy on customer service and financial performance: an analysis of direct versus indirect relationships. *Journal of Operations Management,* 21(5), 523-539.

VICS. (1998). Collaborative Planning Forecasting and Replenishment. Voluntary Guidelines. *www.cpfr.org.*

Vitasek, K. (2010). Supply chain management terms and glossary. *Council of Supply Chain Management Professionals (CSCMP).*

Won Lee, C., Kwon, I.-W. G., and Severance, D. (2007). Relationship between supply chain performance and degree of linkage among supplier, internal integration, and customer. *Supply Chain Management: An international Journal,* 12(6), 444-452.

DECISION SCIENCES INSTITUTE

IMPROVING LEARNING OUTCOMES IN A FLIPPED SPREADSHEET-BASED GRADUATE DECISION MODELING COURSE

Steven P. Coy
Professor of Management
University of Houston-Downtown
coys@uhd.edu

Doug TeDuits
Assistant Professor of Management
University of Houston-Downtown
teduitsd@uhd.edu

James Crawford
Director of Parts and Logistics
Calpine
jay.crawford@calpine.com

ABSTRACT

This paper discusses the challenges related to flipping the classroom in a spreadsheet-based graduate decision modeling course. The purpose of this paper is to extend the conversation on flipped classrooms to the thorny world of teaching spreadsheet decision modeling at the graduate level. After reviewing the literature, we report on our experience in a MBA supply chain management course and a similar master's course for security management executives. Initial course structure, learning outcomes assessment, student feedback, subjective observations, and data-driven course modifications are discussed. Based on our experience, we recommend that instructors provide in-class scaffolding before the classroom activity begins.

KEYWORDS: Flipped classroom, course inversion, spreadsheet decision modeling, continuous improvement, active learning, problem-based learning

INTRODUCTION

This paper discusses our experiences with flipped classrooms in similar graduate decision modeling courses. The bulk of the paper focuses on a graduate supply chain management decision modeling course, which emphasizes computer spreadsheets. After a brief look at the relevant literature, we describe the course structure, report on results of both direct and indirect measures of course efficacy, and discuss changes that we have made to improve learning outcomes and student feedback in subsequent semesters.

In our experience, we have found that student learning outcomes are higher when the course includes a large number of problem-based applications. The use of problem based learning approaches has been studied extensively in the educational literature (see, for example, Hmelo-Silver, 2004), and active learning, in general, has been known to have a positive relationship to higher-order learning for many years (Chickering & Gamson, 1987). Experiential classroom exercises designed to challenge students to apply course concepts are particularly effective (Paul & Mukhopadhyay, 2005). Furthermore, when students work with teammates on these exercises, learning can be even more effective (Trigwell & Sleet, 1990). Learning is enhanced in these cases through synergy and what Topping & Ehly (2001) call "peer-assisted learning." Thus, the combination of problem-based learning with experiential classroom exercises provides a promising approach for improving student learning. Other educational research also emphasizes student-centered classrooms in which students become actively engaged in their own learning and take part in more higher-order tasks (Shea et al., 2012). One way to provide these opportunities during class time is to push the content out of the class and require students to conduct pre-class work.

Given the importance and success of active learning in college classrooms and the coincident rise in popularity of blended (hybrid online) course formats; it is not surprising that interest in flipped classrooms is increasing. In one of the earliest articles on flipped classrooms, Lage, Platt, and Treglia (2000) define course inversion (now commonly known as flipped classroom) as replacing traditional classroom activities (e.g. lectures) with activities that were typically conducted outside of the classroom (e.g., team exercises). Flipped classroom instructional models typically use videos for students to view prior to class, thus preparing them to engage in higher-order interactive activities (Davies et al 2013).

By using a flipped classroom, university faculty have the time to create more in-class student-centered and active learning strategies such as targeted remedial assistance, practice activities, group discussions, small-group problem-solving, group presentations, using group evaluation tools (Zappe, S., Leicht, R. et al 2009 & Khan 2012). In the past 16 years, the growth of online education and blended learning formats have made this process much easier to manage (Sahin, Cavlazoglu & Zeytuncu, 2015).

Even with the increasing popularity of flipped classrooms, it is unlikely that all approaches work well nor that the use of flipped classrooms is appropriate for all courses. For example, research by Kirschner, Sweller, & Clark (2006) suggests that problem-based approaches that rely on "minimum guidance" do not work well because students must have a sufficient foundation in the particular area before they can effectively guide themselves. Hence, it is up to the instructor to design activities that provide the necessary scaffolding to promote learning rather than simply casting their students adrift (for more on scaffolding, see the seminal paper by Wood, Bruner, & Ross, 1976).

Furthermore, according to Davies et al (2013), "Much of the research regarding the specific pedagogical approach of flipping the classroom is only beginning to be published" and Davies points to Lage et al (2000), Moravec et al (2010) and Strayer (2012) in which these approaches are based on "contextually situated learning circumstances." Thus, understanding the costs and the benefits of each approach is essential before integrating these technology-based tools (Bergmann and Sams 2013 & Davies, 2011).

The use of flipped classrooms in introductory spreadsheet courses shows considerable promise as evidenced by a number of studies. Frydenberg (2013), for example, used a student survey to investigate whether the flipped classroom approach in an introductory information systems course was helpful. Students reported that the classroom exercises were motivating and improved their learning. Davies, Dean & Ball (2013) designed an experiment for testing the efficacy of the flipped classroom for teaching spreadsheet analysis in an undergraduate information systems course. They found that the flipped approach led to improved learning outcomes. Evidence of the effectiveness of flipped classrooms in advanced spreadsheet decision modeling courses, however, appears to be scant. In this paper, we contribute to this niche in the flipped classroom literature.

COURSE STRUCTURE

The primary subject course in this study is entitled Decision Modeling for Supply Chain Managers. It is a three-hour graduate course, which is part of the new Supply Chain Management concentration for our MBA and is also required for graduate students seeking a Supply Chain Management certificate. All courses in this concentration are team taught by a faculty member and a corporate partner. The course is hybrid online and meets once per week for two hours and forty-five minutes over an eight-week session.

Learning Objectives (LOs) of the course are shown below. These LOs were developed by Supply Chain Management faculty members in partnership with a large industry panel in order to match curriculum with industry needs.

After completing this course, a student will be able to:

1. Generate forecasts, cost/volume analyses, Monte Carlo simulations, and linear programming models using computer spreadsheets;
2. Analyze real-world business problems in supply chain management and identify the appropriate decision modeling approach;
3. Design effective spreadsheet models to solve complex problems; and
4. Analyze decision model results and related qualitative contextual factors, and recommend specific actions based on this analysis.

The course was divided into eight learning modules. One module was covered each week with online lectures and a team exercise completed in class. With the exception of the introductory module covered in week one, students were expected to complete the assigned reading and practice homework and review all online lecture videos before arriving in class. Each class session was entirely devoted to working on an in-class team exercise. The exercises were designed to be practical applications of the material presented in the reading assignment and online videos. They were intended to reinforce and extend course concepts and skills and build student confidence.

The first module consisted of two team exercises. The first exercise was intended to act as an icebreaker, and the second was used to model how the remaining classes would operate. Since students had already taken classes together over the previous year as part of a graduate cohort, they had developed extensive working relationships with several class members. Consequently, we randomly assigned students to teams to break self-formed groups and to simulate a cross-functional team project in a work environment. We then reshuffled the groups in the fifth week to ensure that students were not saddled with less productive team members for the entire session.

After the introductory session, the remaining class sessions followed a similar pattern. Students completed the various assignments, and reviewed the exercise or case assignment, which was posted online at the beginning of the week. This provided students with an idea of what the requirements of the exercise would be before class, but they were unable to begin the exercise until class started because the data used in the exercise was not revealed until the beginning of the class.

At the beginning of each class, we reviewed the case objectives, and we discussed any concepts or techniques that we believed students would have difficulty with once the exercise began. This review typically took 15-20 minutes to complete, which left students with nearly 2.5 hours to complete the exercise and submit their team's findings.

To simulate real business communication, a team's final work product was submitted in email format with the spreadsheet file included as an attachment. We required students to write emails that were clear, concise and complete. We believe that it is important to teach students how to communicate their analysis and recommendations without resorting to voluminous emails or reports that managers are unlikely to read.

The weekly course modules covered the following topics:

Module 1: Course introduction
Module 2: Excel fundamentals, data visualization, and pivot tables
Module 3: Elementary data analysis and descriptive statistics
Module 4: Regression analysis
Module 5: Time series forecasting
Module 6: Decision making concepts
Module 7: Linear optimization
Module 8: Monte Carlo simulation

DIRECT MEASURES: COURSE ASSESSMENT RESULTS

Students were given an extensive online exam at the end of the course that required them to answer a number of analytical and conceptual questions as well as solve several spreadsheet problems. This exam was worth 40% of the students' grade and was a primary instrument for evaluating individual performance in the course. The exam was also used to evaluate aggregate student performance on the four learning objectives discussed earlier. The results of this assessment are given below.

The assessment results indicate that students struggled on three of the four LOs. Nearly half of the class had significant difficulty generating one or more of the spreadsheet problem types covered in the course (LO1); and about the same proportion of students had significant difficulty with spreadsheet model development (LO3). Most troubling was the class performance on problem recognition (LO2). In this series of questions, students were given a series of problem statements and asked to identify the correct solution approach. Nearly two-thirds of the students were deficient in this area.

INDIRECT MEASURES: STUDENT COURSE EVALUATIONS

At the end of the course, students were asked to complete student course evaluations using a standardized and validated instrument, which contained a number of Likert scale questions and space for written comments. Although the scale questions and student feedback in the course were respectable, three issues emerged from the student comments that caused us some concern. These issues are summarized below.

Table 1: DIRECT MEASURES			
Learning Objective	**Does Not Meet Expectations**	**Meets Expectations**	**Exceeds Expectations**
LO#1. Generate forecasts, cost/volume analyses, Monte Carlo simulations, and linear programming models using computer spreadsheets.	44.9%	28.2%	26.9%
LO#2. Analyze real-world business problems in supply chain management and identify the appropriate decision modeling approach.	62.8%	33.3%	3.8%
LO#3. Design effective spreadsheet models to solve complex problems.	47.1%	35.3%	17.6%
LO#4. Analyze decision model results and related qualitative contextual factors, and recommend specific actions based on this analysis.	34.0%	35.8%	30.2%

1. Groups of four or five students are too large for a linear classroom (rows of computer tables).
2. Several students complained that members of their teams were seemingly unprepared for the class assignments.
3. Students noted that there was a wide degree of Excel skill in their groups, which caused some students to become spectators on the assignment analysis.

The first item was easy enough to fix without changing the pedagogy. But the latter two items confirmed to us that a fully flipped classroom was not entirely effective in this course.

CLASSROOM EXPERIENCE

Although there was certainly room for improvement, many aspects of the course worked well. But since this was a new course in a new MBA concentration using new techniques, we were not surprised to learn that some aspects of the course were not as effective as we had hoped they would be. In this section, we identify some of the aspects of the course that did not work well.

First, we believe the decision to assign groups in week one and then again in week five did not produce the results we expected. Students were very challenged with the amount of course content that they were expected to assimilate each week. Expecting students to successfully process the course material while dealing with the challenges of normalizing a working group, not once but twice, was a bridge too far. Because groups were randomly formed in week one and week five, the chance that all the team members had worked together previously was much less than if the students had selected their groups themselves. The strangers in the groups did not feel the peer pressure to perform in order to support the entire team. Also, because the teams were only together for four weeks, it was often easier for the performers in the first group to tolerate freeloading instead of addressing it because the chance the freeloader would be in their new group was minimal.

We encountered a disparity of MS Excel skills on each team, which depended to a great extent on each student's educational and professional background. We believed that this gap would narrow as the students completed the lectures and more importantly, the homework assignments during the semester. This was not the case. In fact, it was clear that some students who struggled with Excel did not complete all of their out-of-class practice problems and relied, instead, on the stronger members of their teams to carry them through the classroom exercises. This choice did not serve them well during the final exam.

During the setup of each assignment, we attempted to address issues that students would encounter as they attempted to solve the problem. Although some questions were asked during this review, most of the student questions were asked and answered while the teams were working on the assignment. This resulted in the same question often being asked over and over. Furthermore, since this course was team taught by a faculty member and corporate partner, sometimes we would offer students different approaches for resolving specific issues, which could be contradictory. These issues led to frequent class stoppages to answer frequently asked questions or to clarify techniques. We found this process to be an inefficient use of class time.

PROVIDING SCAFFOLDING: A MODEST UNFLIP

In the next semester, one of authors used a similar course structure in a graduate decision modeling course for security executives. Although the context and many of the decision models used in the course were different, the course shared many of the basic characteristics of the supply chain management course: the course was hybrid-online, the course had eight, two hour and forty-five minute scheduled sessions over the semester, and the in-class portion of the course was devoted entirely to spreadsheet exercises. Although this course was not a new offering, it was recently revised.

In general, students in the security management course had less analytical preparation than their MBA counterparts. We found that the majority of the class had poorly defined Excel skills. The disparity between the most prepared and least prepared students was greater than we had observed in the supply chain course. Furthermore, the many tutorials and primers that we provided on the course website were insufficient to bridge the gap. It quickly became apparent that the planned pedagogy did not match well with student skills. As a result, we decided to pivot from a fully-flipped classroom to a partially-flipped classroom. The modified structure included a mini-lecture of about 30 minutes at the beginning of each session. Topics and examples for these mini-lectures were targeted to issues in each area that the instructor had seen students struggle with in the past. This mini-lecture is intended to provide students with the necessary scaffolding to successfully complete the classroom activity.

The modest unflip of the security management course appears to be effective. Although course-level assessment data was not available for this course, final exam performance was satisfactory and student feedback was very favorable. The success of this revision along with our analysis of the indirect and direct measures from the MBA course suggested that similar revisions in the MBA course were warranted. At the time of the writing of this paper, we are currently teaching the supply chain course with the modest unflip. Thus far, this approach has led to improvements in several areas. Although learning outcomes assessment data is not yet available for this course, we believe that there will be substantial improvement.

CONCLUSION

In our experience with the supply chain management course, we identified several areas in which we could improve. Some of these improvements came directly from the student evaluations while others were based on students' performance on the learning objectives. In particular, we found that pushing all of the conceptual content to pre-class work is impractical. Although most students appear to have studied the material, their level of comprehension was inadequate for the task at hand. We have found that a short interactive session at the beginning of the workshop is a particularly useful device for providing the scaffolding that students will need to complete the problem-based activity. This observation is consistent with observations that we cited earlier by Kirschner et al. (2006). Although, in our original model, students were provided videos and practice problems to learn the concepts and tools, this approach is probably closer to the "minimum guidance" identified by Kirschner et al. than we had envisioned. Even so, this does not mean that the flipped format should be discarded. With a modest unflip, we believe that students can benefit from the classroom activity. Therefore, we recommend that instructors who are contemplating designing a flipped classroom for teaching spreadsheet decision modeling should schedule a mini-lecture to review the more important concepts and techniques in class before the activity begins.

REFERENCES

Benware, C. A., & Deci, E. L. (1984). Quality of learning with an active versus passive motivational set. *American Educational Research Journal*, 21(4), 755-765.

Bergmann, J., Overmyer, J., & Wilie, B. (2013). The flipped class: Myths versus reality. The Daily Riff. Retrieved on April 28, 2016 from http://www.thedailyriff.com/articles/the-flipped-class-conversation-689.php.

Bergmann, J., & Sams, A. (2012). Before you flip, consider this. Phi Delta Kappan, 94 (2), 25.

Chickering, A. W., Gamson, Z. F., & Poulsen, S. J. (1987). Seven principles for good practice in undergraduate education. *AAHE bulletin*, *39*(7), 3-7.

Davies, R. (2011). Understanding technology literacy: A framework for evaluating educational technology integration. TechTrends, 55(5), 45–52.

Davies, R. S., Dean, D. L., & Ball, N. (2013). Flipping the classroom and instructional technology integration in a college-level information systems spreadsheet course. *Educational Technology Research and Development*, *61*(4), 563-580.

Davies, R., & West, R. (2013). Technology integration in school settings. In M. Spector, D. Merrill, J. Elen,& M. J. Bishop (Eds.), Handbook of research on educational communications and technology (4th ed.). New York: Taylor & Francis Ltd.

Frydenberg, M. (2013). Flipping excel. *Information Systems Education Journal*, *11*(1), 63.

Hmelo-Silver, C. E. (2004). Problem-based learning: What and how do students learn? *Educational psychology review*, *16*(3), 235-266.

Khan, S. (2012).The one world schoolhouse: Education reimagined. London: Hodder and Stoughton.

Kirschner, P. A., Sweller, J., & Clark, R. E. (2006). Why minimal guidance during instruction does not work: An analysis of the failure of constructivist, discovery, problem-based, experiential, and inquiry-based teaching. *Educational psychologist*, 41(2), 75-86.

Lage, M. J., Platt, G. J., & Treglia, M. (2000). Inverting the classroom: A gateway to creating an inclusive learning environment. *The Journal of Economic Education*, *31*(1), 30-43.

Moravec, M., Williams, A., Aguilar-Roca, N., & O'Dowd, D. K. (2010). Learn before lecture: a strategy that improves learning outcomes in a large introductory biology class. CBE Life Sciences Education, 9, 473–481.

Paul, P., & Mukhopadhyay, K. (2005). Experiential learning in international business education. *Journal of Teaching in International Business*, 16(2), 7-25.

Sahin, A., Cavlazoglu, B., & Zeytuncu, Y. E. (2015). Flipping a college calculus course: a case study. *Journal of Educational Technology & Society*, *18*(3), 142-152.

Shea, P., Hayes, S., Smith, S. U., Vickers, J., Bidjerano, T., Pickett, A et al. (2012). Learning presence: Additional research on a new conceptual element within the Community of Inquiry (CoI) framework. *The Internet and Higher Education*, *15*(2), 89-95.

Strayer, J. F. (2012). How learning in an inverted classroom influences cooperation, innovation and task orientation. Learning Environments Research, 15(2), 171–193.

Topping, K. J., & Ehly, S. W. (2001). Peer assisted learning: A framework for consultation. *Journal of Educational and Psychological Consultation*, *12*(2), 113-132.

Trigwell, K. R., & Sleet, R. J. (1990). Improving the relationship between assessment results and student understanding. *Assessment and Evaluation in Higher Education*, 22, 290-297.

Wood, D., Bruner, J. S., & Ross, G. (1976). The role of tutoring in problem solving. *Journal of Child Psychology and Psychiatry*, *17*(2), 89-100.

Zappe, S., Leicht, R., Messner, J., Litzinger, T., & Lee, H. W. (2009). "Flipping" the classroom to explore active learning in a large undergraduate course. In *American Society for Engineering Education*. American Society for Engineering Education.

DECISION SCIENCES INSTITUTE

"Internet of Things" (IOT)-Enabled Product Monitoring: Insights from Socio-Technical Systems Theory, Affordances Theory, and Structurational Model of Technology

Rebecca Angeles
University of New Brunswick Fredericton
Email: rangeles@unb.ca

ABSTRACT

This qualitative research features case studies of two firms, SteadyServ, a beer inventory management technology solution firm, and Kuehne + Nagel, a global logistics firms offering specialized pharmaceutical goods storage and delivery services. Both firms are using "Internet of Things" (IOT)-enabled sensor solutions in product monitoring. Three theoretical frameworks are applied in the attempt to understand the IT solution deployment experiences of both firms: socio-technical systems theory, affordances theory, and structurational model of technology.

KEYWORDS: Internet of Things (IOT), radio frequency identification (RFID), socio-technical systems theory, affordances theory, and structurational model of technology (Orlikowski), logistics, supply chain management

INTRODUCTION

This research paper featuring two case studies of the firms, SteadyServ, a beer technology solution firm, and Kuehne + Nagel (K+N), a global logistics firm, highlights the use of sensors for "Internet of Things" (IOT) applications, both involving product monitoring. This study also uses these three theoretical frameworks for understanding the information systems implementation experiences of these two firms: socio-technical systems theory, affordances theory, and Orlikowski's structurational model of technology.

Iansiti and Lakhani (2014) articulate the innovative business possibilities enabled by the "Internet of Things" (IOT) or the pervasive deployment of wireless sensors for realizing digitization and connectivity to previously analog tasks, processes, and machine and service operations. In their paper, they focus on how General Electric (GE) has transformed itself from merely manufacturing physical and analog products for business/home appliances, airplane engines for the aviation industry, energy generation infrastructure, lighting, mining, healthcare, transportation, and many more industries, to being a firm that offers services founded on value creation derived from capture, storage, distribution, and analysis of digital data involving various forms of information technology supporting IOT. For instance, GE has a wind farm deal with the global energy giant E.ON. wherein GE offers data analytics services using E.ON.'s extensive operational data to run simulations that suggest solutions for meeting energy demand fluctuations. In the past, GE used to sell physical machines like turbines and related equipment to firms such as E.ON. But today, GE has changed its business model by extracting value from data analytics powered by software assets and charging for these services. GE is an extreme example in terms of a firm that has pushed IOT possibilities to its optimal boundaries. This study of SteadyServ and K+N shows how the use of sensors for product monitoring has given both firms possibilities for offering innovative services to their clients based on data analytics capabilities.

The three theoretical frameworks were chosen because they focus on the interaction between information systems/information technology components and organization in producing the desired outcomes in deploying the specific information systems solution adopted by a firm.

The socio-technical systems theory provides a simple to use framework for analyzing how components of an organizational system (i.e., task, structure, people, and technology) work together.

The affordances theory lens allows researchers to view IT and organizations as entities that exist independently of each other. Yet, IT and organizations can be viewed by researchers as valuable in explaining organization form and function only if it is recognized that they need to be enacted together (Zammuto, 2007). So, although IT and organizations each have their own potentials and constraints, theories such as the affordance theory are needed to understand how they are woven together so that "functional" affordances could emerge. The affordance theory lens admits that a technological object has built-in functionalities, but it needs to be recognized as a "social object" as well. And, as a social object, the technological object influences organizational functioning and performance, which, in turn, cannot be viewed apart from worker expertise, jobs, business processes, and structures (Zammuto, 2007).

Orlikowski's structurational model of technology (1992) recognizes that IT is both the medium and product of human action. Organizational contexts shape human action within organizations. Human agents either reinforce or transform the institutional properties of an organization when using IT.

When taken together, these three theoretical frameworks provide potent tools for generating rich insights that can help us understand how information systems solutions are deployed in firms.

LITERATURE REVIEW

The following section highlights the key concepts, theoretical frameworks, and firm background information used in this study.

Internet of Things (IOT)

"Internet of Things" or IOT is defined as "...a worldwide information infrastructure for the information society in which physical and virtual 'things' were uniquely identified and connected over the wired or wireless internet. These physical and virtual things could include an object or smart device, such as clothes, a watch, a camera, a washer, a building, a bridge, a car, a suite, an animal or even a person...." (Yen, 2015, pp. 2-3). In a global survey of 795 firms, Tata Consultancy Services found that four out of the five firms have already deployed IOT initiatives (Tata Consultancy Services, 2015). The four major areas for IOT application are: (1) product monitoring: tracking products by embedding sensors, software, and other technologies in physical products; (2) premises monitoring: installing sensors, digital cameras, and other devices in firms' business operations sites; (3) customer monitoring: tracking wireless mobile devices carried by customers; (4) supply chain monitoring: installing sensors, digital devices, and cameras in the production and distribution facilities and other points in a firm's supply chain (Tata Consultancy Services, 2015). This study will focus mainly on product monitoring at SteadyServ and Kuehne + Nagel.

Gartner Group projects that there will be 4.9 billion connected devices by 2015, growing to 25 billion connected objects by the end of the decade (Tata Consultancy, 2015). In its global survey of corporate IOT initiatives involving 795 executives in the sample, Tata Consultancy found out the following: (1) About 79 percent of the global firms that responded to the survey already use IOT technologies to track their customers, products, premises, and supply chains; (2) firms that offer higher-priced products will be spending more on IOT in 2015 than those offering lower-priced products; (3) mobile apps have a key role to play in tracking customers and are used by 50 percent of the firms in the sample; (4) in general, IOT adoption is higher in North American and European firms than their counterparts in Asia-Pacific and Latin America; (5) in gaining benefits from IOT, industrial manufacturers are way ahead of the 12 other major global industries represented in the sample; (6) strategic and cultural issues appear to be the biggest constraints in firms in terms of planning for IOT initiatives; and (7) firms that gained the largest revenue increases from their respective IOT initiatives had these attributes: (a) they are more likely to digitally reimagine the businesses ; (b) they were more flexible in altering their business models to suit IOT; (c) they appreciated the breakthrough potential of IOT; (d) they organized themselves to respond rapidly based on performance and customer usage data; (e) they are better at managing internal resistance to IOT internally; (f) they worked on improving the security aspects of IOT technologies they deployed; and (g) they made incremental investments in IOT, ensuring positive returns first, before pouring in larger dollar investments.

Industrial manufacturers appear to be ahead of other industries in gaining benefits from IOT according to the study findings. The following are the typical IOT applications in industrial manufacturing: (1) predictive maintenance of equipment with sensors monitoring parts exceeding thresholds and generating alerts to managers; (2) inventory/asset tracking systems between locations as they move throughout the supply chain; value-added services include tracking ambient storage and delivery conditions such as temperature, pressure, volume, etc.; (3) quality control using sensors, cameras, and lasers to analyze manufacturing processes; (4) smart grid systems for monitoring energy consumption; (5) indoor air quality systems will monitor toxic gas and oxygen levels inside chemical plants to ensure worker safety; temperature monitoring in medical and industrial refrigerators to safeguard "cold chain" temperature-sensitive product items; (6) sensors embedded in foundations of constructed structures will provide load and stress monitoring to ensure building integrity and safety, among others.

The case study method in this research project features product monitoring aspects of the services provided by SteadyServ and Kuehne + Nagel.

Socio-Technical Systems Theory

Building on Leavitt's (1965) socio-technical model, the socio-technical systems (STS) theory as articulated by Bostrom and Heinen (1977) provides a framework for analyzing how components of an organizational system (i.e., task, structure, people, and technology) relate to an information system. Leavitt (1965) identified task, structure, people, and technology as important dimensions of organizations as work systems. The technology dimension of the Leavitt model consists of elements of an information system as an integrated set of software using information technology to transmit, process, and store information (Piccoli, 2008).

The simplicity and elegance of the STS model have been recognized and the framework has been frequently used for studying IS-enabled organizational change (Bostrom et al., 2009; Lyytinen & Newman, 2008; Pitt et al., 2011). Two subsystems constitute the overarching STS system: (1) the tasks and technologies that make up the technical subsystem transform inputs into outputs; and (2) individuals in a work unit, their relationships, reward systems, and authority and work structures make up the social subsystem. Organizational systems are usually faced with targeted goals often instigated by pressure coming from the external environment. The organization's internal environment consisting of both the technical and social subsystems, consequently, need to interact optimally in order to meet organizational goals adopted in response to external pressures. This STS framework has been useful in studying organizational change and in capturing the rich context of factors and interactions involved in deploying information systems in meeting organizational goals. A major missing piece in using the STS theoretical framework, though, is the articulation of how the critical structural, technological, people, and task-based dimensions interact in the process of changing the organization. Thus, this case study's analysis transitions to the use of the "affordances theory" (Gibson, 1976, 1979, 1986) and very specifically, the concept of "functional affordances" (Markus & Silver, 2008). These complementary theoretical lenses will bridge the missing gap and assist in showing how information systems relate to behavioral routines of end workers as manifested in their work practices (Leonardi, 2011) as they try to realize their action goals and values (Markus & Silver, 2008).

Affordances Theory

In understanding the deployment of information technology in organizations, the "affordances" theory has been espoused by a number of academics (Faraj & Azad, 2012; Hutchby, 2001; Leonardi & Barley, 2008; Markus & Silver, 2008; Norman, 1988; Zammuto et al., 2007). Gibson (1997, 1979) first offered the concept of "affordance" in the field of ecological psychology and used it to define the range of possibilities and constraints for action that a material object presents to an actor. Material properties of information systems allow "possibilities for goal-oriented action" or "functional affordances" of that form of technology (Markus & Silver, 2008). Chemero (2008) suggests, though, that affordances have to be perceived by the end user before they can be enacted or actualized. Leonardi (2011) dovetails this idea by suggesting that the end user's ability to perceive the action possibilities proffered by functional affordances depends on the relationships between the form of information system and the end user within the context in which the information system is used. Features of different forms of information technology can be used by human agents or ignored by them, depending on the end purposes they have in mind (Stinchcombe, 1968). Thus, both intended and unintended consequences of information technology are realized through functionalities of material artifacts that "afford" those consequences.

Orlikowski's Structuration Model of Technology

This study applies Orlikowski's "Structurational Model of Technology," (Orlikowski, 1992; Orlikowski & Robey, 1991) to understand how information technology (IT) interacts with organizations. This model draws on Giddens' theory of structuration (Giddens, 1984, 1979, 1976), which proposed the concept of the "duality of structure," "...which refers to the notion that the structure or institutional properties of social systems are created by human action, and then serve to shape future human action...." (Orlikowski & Robey, 1991, p. 147). "...In Giddens' theory, structure is understood to be an abstract property of social systems. Structure is not something concrete, situated in time and space, and it lacks material characteristics. Structure cannot exist apart from the human actors who enact and interpret its dimensions. Structure has only virtual existence. Interestingly, people readily allow their actions to be constrained by these shared abstractions as social structure....The ability of organizational structures to elicit compliance and conformity in the absence of material constraints attests to the power of those socially constructed abstractions....Social structure conditions these social practices by providing the contextual rules and resources that allow human actors to make sense of their own acts and those of other people." (Orlikowski & Robey, 1991, p. 147). Furthermore, Giddens specifies that human interactions are an amalgamation of structures of meaning, power, and moral frameworks enacted in what he calls the "modalities" of these interactions: interpretive schemes, resources, and norms.

"Interpretive schemes...form the core of mutual knowledge whereby an accountable universe of meaning is sustained through and in processes of interaction (Giddens, 1979, p. 83]. Orlikowski & Robey (1991) translate Giddens' concept of "interpretive scheme" within the realm of IT and explain that IT represents reality through a set of concepts of symbols embedded in it by which end users understand their world. Thus, IT is not only a medium for the construction of social reality, but also a means of institutionalizing certain "interpretive schemes" or stocks of knowledge within the organization by standardizing, sharing, and taking them for granted.

Resources are the media through which power is exercised by human actors because it is through these resources that humans can accomplish their objectives and thus, gain "domination" (Orlikowski & Robey, 1991). Therefore, the deployment of IT institutes a certain order of authority, dictating the way work will be performed, and also, resulting in the differential distribution of power in the organization.

Norms are understood as organizational rules that shape "legitimate" behavior. IT is a medium for installing such norms in order to control human behavior in an organization (Orlikowski & Robey, 1991).

Orlikowski incorporates the following components in her framework: first, the human agents, consisting of technology designers, end users, and decision makers; second, the material artifacts that constitute IT itself, and third, the institutional properties of organizations --- structural arrangements, business strategies, ideology, culture, control mechanisms, standard operating procedures, division of labor, expertise, communication patterns, and environmental pressures (Orlikowski, 1992; Orlikowski & Robey, 1991).

The structurational model of technology discusses four critical issues (Orlikowski & Robey, 1991). First, IT is the product of human action, which is responsible for the creation, use, and maintenance of different forms of IT. It is only through the human appropriation of IT that it is able to influence human activity. Second, technology is the medium of human action. Since different forms of IT are used by organizational workers, they mediate organizational work either by facilitating it and in some ways, also constraining it. Third, organizational contexts shape human action within organizations. Human agents are influenced by the institutional properties of their setting which provide the resources, norms, and knowledge they need to work. Furthermore, IT is created and used within certain social and historical circumstances which influence the form and features of this technology. Fourth, human agents either reinforce or transform the institutional properties of an organization when using IT. Weick (1979) characterized technology as "enacted environment" whose construction is determined by an organization's structures of signification, domination, and legitimation. Any change in these three structures indicate the "appropriation" and use of technology.

"Structure of signification" refers to the way the concepts and procedures intrinsic to the knowledge embedded in IT directs the manner in which problems are interpreted and work is conducted in the organization (Orlikowski, 1992). "Structure of domination" refers to IT's ability to control the work of organizational members once it is deployed. "Structure of legitimation" refers to the ability of IT to sanction a particular mode of conducting the work and thus, propagate a set of norms about what is considered legitimate business practice. Orlikowski also incorporates the three modalities of structuration --- interpretive schemes, resources, and norms --- in her application of the structures of signification, domination, and legitimation in the deployment of IT in an organization.

SteadyServ Firm Background

Founded in 2012 in Carmel, Indiana, USA, SteadyServ Technologies developed the SteadyServ iKeg system --- a software as a service (SaaS) based mobile software solution for inventory and order management for the beer industry (Identiv, 2014). This is a breakthrough product/service in that it provides real-time intelligence for beer retail establishments, distributors, and brewers through the use of a smartphone app that runs on IOS or Android devices and also through the use of a web-enabled SaaS portal. This solution also enables synchronization with a beer distributor's order management system to assure beer retailer customers that their inventory can always fill customer demand at any point in time.

Product Monitoring Needs of Draft Beer Industry

Efficient and effective beer management has been an elusive goal in the beer industry for a very long time. This is a major problem in an industry where craft breweries are on the rise and retailers have a wide range of beer brands to choose from to fulfill every increasing end customer expectations at retail outlets like bars, restaurants, and pubs (Intel, 2015). However, in order to offer the best beer mix in a retail outlet, managers need to know how much beer is left on hand in their beer kegs. These assets called kegs are often returned to distributors still containing left over beer, which translates to costly wastage and profit loss for retailers. Traditionally, retail managers relied on old methods like the "first in, first out" mentality to physically lifting kegs to arrive at "guesstimates" of how much beer is left over --- both have led to significant waste of money. A more effective method of tracking beer inventory is needed to alleviate this situation. A sensor-based solution appears to be just what is called for.

Kuehne + Nagel Firm Background

Kuehne + Nagel (K+N) is a based in Switzerland and is a global leader in providing business-to-business sea freight, air freight, overland, and contract logistics services in more than 100 countries (Greengard, 2015). The aerospace, automotive, industrials, high tech, oil and gas, retail, pharmaceutical, and healthcare industries are among the key industries served by K+N. In March 2011, K+N introduced the PharmaChain specialized logistics service for the pharmaceutical and health-care industries. K+N guarantees that its pharma cold chain logistics services follows the best practices guidelines of the World Health Organization (WHO) and that its entire network of facilities is GXP compliant meaning that the firm observes regulations that ensure the delivery of quality high-risk products like pharmaceutical goods and biologics. K+N handles pharma shipments in three categories of facilities: (1) pharma gateways: these have cool zones with temperature ranges of 1-8 and 15-25 degrees Celsius; (2) competence centers: have cooler facilities but do not observe stringent cool zone standards with specific temperature ranges; and (3) pharma branches: do not have special equipment; staff strictly deals with moving goods but are not allowed to physically handle or touch them (Putzger, 2012).

K+N filled a niche in the logistics services marketplace on account of a number of factors. There are multiple stakeholders involved in the shipment of temperature-sensitive pharmaceutical and biologic products. Even for a firm like K+N, delivering logistics services requires coverage of land, air, and water modes of transportation in order to cover the entire world. Traditionally, the pharmaceutical cold chain has been characterized by lack of process visibility leading to serious constraints in the logistics service providers' ability to mitigate shipment delivery problems while the goods are in transit. Limited investment in information technology by different logistics service providers is partly to blame for this lack of visibility. Inadequate equipment performance is also notable --- with more reliable equipment/assets used in logistics found in more developed countries and thus, "breaks" in the cold chain occur in less developed countries where such assets perform less reliably.

Product Monitoring Needs of Pharmaceutical and Life Sciences Industries

Temperature-sensitive products constitute a "cold or cool chain" and the logistics operations of moving them through a physical supply chain are regulated by federal law and guidelines of regulatory agencies. Drug or biotechnical testing laboratories and manufacturers, contract manufacturers and packagers, distribution centers, wholesalers, healthcare facilities, pharmacies, etc., are the usual stakeholders who would be concerned about proper product disposition.

A successful "cold chain" supply chain is one that can deliver products to the customer in usable form. Pharmaceutical drug and biotechnology products must arrive unadulterated and with its efficacy fully intact. Organizations such as the U.S. Food and Drug Administration (U.S./FDA) and the International Conference on Harmonisation of Technical Requirements for Registration of Pharmaceuticals for Human Use (ICH) act as regulatory arbiters and partners in ensuring the arrival of high quality and safe cold chain products.

The pharmaceutical and life sciences industries are faced with two major risks as its physical products traverse its "cold chains": risk of adulterating the products while in transit and storage and the risk of non-compliance with federal regulations, guidelines, and standards. To date, there is no universal standard, guidance, regulator, arbiter, or document with the "final say" on what constitutes a compliant cold chain for a specific geographical area. All affected industries such as the pharmaceutical and life sciences industries currently deal with a multitude of recommendations on how to be compliant from many regulations at different levels, conferences, technical reports, and consultants --- reflecting a totally fragmented regulatory environment for these types of products. Amidst this fragmentation, however, two organizations are preeminent in mandating compliance procedures: the U.S./FDA and ICH.

RESEARCH METHOD

This study uses the case study approach and content analysis in aligning the concepts prescribed by the three theoretical frameworks to the sensor-based systems of SteadyServ and K+N. The case study is an appropriate methodology for understanding complex social phenomena especially for purposes of exploring, describing, and explaining such phenomena (Yin, 1984) and in testing the application of a conceptual framework to a real firm. Also, since there are two firms featured in this study, methodological suggestions from Eisenhardt (1989) and Yin (1984) are used for detecting cross-case patterns, i.e., detecting similarities in the application of the selected theoretical frameworks used in this study to the case facts.

The primary data used was based on the transcription of the conference presentation talk of key executives from SteadyServ and Kuehne + Nagel at the RFID Journal Live! 13th Annual

Conference and Exhibition, on April 15-17, 2015, San Diego, California, USA. The primary speakers from the firms were Steve Hershberger, CEO and Founder of SteadyServ and Terry Sell, the Pharma and Temperature Controlled Airfreight Services, North America, K+N Director. In addition, secondary data sources from academic and trade articles were content analyzed using key concepts in the model. Content analysis was applied to both primary and secondary data. The following are accepted definitions of the content analysis method:

> "Content analysis is any research technique for making inferences by systematically and objectively identifying specified characteristics within text." (Stone & Dunphy, 1966, p. 5).
> "Content analysis is a research technique for making replicable and valid inferences from data to their context." (Krippendorff, 1980, p. 21).
> "Content analysis is a research method that uses a set of procedures to make valid inferences from text." (Weber, 1990, p. 1).

In this study, the concepts used for content analysis were derived from the three theoretical frameworks. This framework forms the "context" of the content analysis method as applied to the sensor systems of SteadyServ and K+N:

> "A context is always someone's construction, the conceptual environment of a text, the situation in which it plays a role. In a content analysis, the context explains what the analyst does with the texts; it could be considered the analyst's best hypothesis for how the texts came to be, what they mean, what they can tell or do. In the course of a content analysis, the context embraces all the knowledge that the analyst applies to given texts, whether in the form of scientific theories, plausibly argued propositions, empirical evidence, grounded intuitions, or knowledge of reading habits.... The context specifies the world in which texts can be related to the analyst's research questions." (Krippendorff, 2004, p. 33).

The secondary data was analyzed within the context provided by the three theoretical, which is considered the "prior theory." "Analytical constructs operationalize what the content analyst knows about the context, specifically the network of correlations that are assumed to explain how available text are connected to the possible answers to the analyst's questions and the conditions under which these correlations could change....analytical constructs ensure that an analysis of given texts models the texts' context of use..." (Krippendorff, 2004, p. 34).

The following key conceptual elements of the content analysis method as stipulated by Krippendorff (2004) were used in this study: (1) body of text selected for the analysis; (2) research question that needed to be addressed; (3) a context of analysis within which interpretations will be made; (4) analytical constructs that operationalize what the analyst knows about the context; and (5) inferences that will be arrived at to address the research question.

STUDY FINDINGS

The following are the study findings for the two firms applying the theoretical frameworks: socio-technical systems theory, affordances theory, and structurational model of technology.

SteadyServ Firm

The following are the findings for applying the three theoretical frameworks to SteadyServ.

Socio-Technical Systems Theory and Affordances Theory/SteadyServ

The concept of "functional affordances" allows us to analyze how end users (i.e., in this case, relevant end users would be beer brewers, distributors, retailers, and others) who subscribe to emerging action goals related to managing and controlling beer inventory within their respective establishments interpret the material properties of an IOT-enabled RFID IT infrastructure system Tables 1 and 2).

Table 1: Conceptual analysis of the functional affordance of beer volume & weight & pressure monitoring at SteadyServ			
Material Properties Of Information Systems	**Use Context**		
	Structure	**People**	**Task**
-Monitoring Features: 1.An iKeg sensor is paired with an RFID tag (tells the sensor what's sitting on top of it). 2.The ikeg sensor sends keg depletion data to the cellular uplink using Verizon wireless network. 3.The cellular uplink transmits encrypted data to the SteadyServ's cloud database and inventory management software, hosted by Amazon.com Inc.'s Web Services. 4.The SteadyServ cloud database analyzes the information for client firm to view on their end users' smartphone, tablet, or pc.	-Entrepreneurial one-man start-up founded by Steve Hershberger in February 2012. -responded to a long-term problem in the beer industry of not being able to manage inventory -innovative solution: IOT-enabled RFID solution in the form of iKeg sensor paired with an RFID tag attached to beer keg -a small, tight firm with a team of 25 people, including engineers in India and a manufacturing team in China	-end user (i.e., beer brewer, pub owner/manager, bartender, or beer retailer) can receive text alerts when a beer keg needs to be replaced -leverage collected beer depletion & consumption data (end users impacted: beer brewers, distributors, retailers) (1) track real-time sales and depletions against goals (2)know the impact of competitive pressure by style, category, size, trending, etc. (3) know the impact of dates, local weather,	+ effective inventory management effect: affordances, if realized, can help beer brewers, distributors, & retailers know accurate inventory needs of their customers, & avoid beer wastage & spoilage + business intelligence effect: affordances, if realized, enable beer brewers, distributors, retailers, & workers "mine" collected beer data and apply

	+ this venture start-up raised $1.5 million, followed by a $5 million Series A round from Elevate Ventures and angel investors. The co-founders are currently in talks about the next round, which Hershberger expects to be in the $4 million to $6 million range. + CEO Hershberger also owns a successful brewery, Flat12 Bierwerks, founded in 2009.	and local events on sales (4) understand the impact of brand and product mix -plot consumption, social & scan data by market: (end users impacted: beer brewers, distributors, retailers) (1)know when, how, and where to allocate staff, marketing and promotional dollars, as well as, focus social activities (2)understand local consumption trends, optimize brands, styles, etc. + beer distributors can easily track which of their customers need additional supply and keep brewers on top of sales trends and quality control	insights for more streamlined beer inventory ordering, promotional campaigns, especially through social media means like tweets or Facebook messages + customer relationship management effect: affordances, if realized, will enable beer brewers, distributors, & retailers identify high-value customers and lengthen, widen, & deepen relationships with these customers + promotional effect: affordances, if realized, will enable beer retailers, establishment owners, & workers create promotional & marketing campaigns that immediately reach high-value individual customers and transmit the latest & most accurate "up-to-the-

			minute" updates on beer inventory on tap

The concept of "functional affordances" in this case study allows us to accomplish the following: (1) identify what relevant functional affordances there are that apply to SteadyServ, analyze how end users (i.e., in this case, relevant end users would be beer brewers, distributors, retailers, SteadyServ workers, and others); (2) understand how these end users who subscribe to emerging action goals related to managing and controlling beer inventory within their respective establishments interpret the material properties of an IOT-enabled RFID IT infrastructure system; and (3) understand the nature of the structure and tasks that end users are working with.

Table 2: Organization-iKeg Solution Affordance: beer volume & weight & pressure monitoring at SteadyServ
1) iKeg Solution Features (material properties of information systems): 1.An iKeg sensor is paired with an RFID tag (tells the sensor what's sitting on top of it). 2.The ikeg sensor sends keg depletion data to the cellular uplink using Verizon wireless network. 3.The cellular uplink transmits encrypted data to the SteadyServ's cloud database and inventory management software, hosted by Amazon.com Inc.'s Web Services. 4.The SteadyServ cloud database analyzes the information for client firm to view on their end users' smartphone, tablet, or PC. **2) Characteristics of Actors** + Bar owners can analyze RFID beer data and apply insights to real-time beer inventory control + Beer distributors that purchase beer data can, in turn, use the beer data showing what retail establishments such as restaurants and bars are ordering, and consequently streamline their beer inventory as well. + Bar workers and managers will be able to do the following with the iKeg system smartphone app: - manage inventory based on real-time keg data and anticipate beer demand better; - discover profitable beer purchases based on regional trends; -track beer shipments; -automate social media messages to valued regular customers and inform them of beer stock levels "up to the latest minute" -and catalog special events.

+ Bar and restaurant and other establishment owners can better manage their beer distributors with the RFID beer inventory data.

+ Bar tenders or managers respond to restore beer inventory levels after receiving text alerts or reading inventory reports on their tablets, laptops, or smartphones.

3) Example of immediate concrete outcomes from data

Steve Hershberger, CEO of SteadyServ, expressed the following: "...The consumer benefits from knowing exactly where their favorite beers are on tap, how much a specific retailer has on hand, how fresh the product is, and which is proving to be the most popular by consumption. For business users, SteadyServ's iQ analytics engine compares performance data in the market as well as integrated unstructured data, such as local weather and social media, and it provides recommendations designed to increase sales, customer loyalty, and product freshness...." (Joshua New, 2015).

Hershberger, in this talk at RFID Journal Live! 2015, shared another insight about the price of beer --- how it becomes inelastic after a period of time. This finding is particularly valuable to beer distributors who sell beer in large quantities:

"So we now have the ability to look at that data and show by product type what's going on in different markets not only today, but looking forward. What is likely to occur. What is likely the mix need to be so that if I'm BW3's I can so I can tell corporately my manager "order this, order this, order this. Raise your price here, lower your price there." Turns out the price of beer is really inelastic to a point. So when you were all out drinking your beers last night and they bring you the pint and they say "well that'll be $5.75." Who says "oh no no no, I'm only paying $5.20 for that beer"? Nobody does that. You just accept it. Would you pay $6? Would you pay $6.25? Probably. Would you pay $14? Depends on the beer. Beer prices are highly elastic to a point and then become highly inelastic. But having the ability to use RFID and IOT technologies allow us to tell with a high degree of accuracy what you need to sell. What the proper mix is. If rebel IPA from Boston beer needs to be on tap. Where it needs to be on tap. And what is it best paired with vs what is it not best paired with? Where do I get halo? Where so I get cannibalization?"

Ryan Kellerman, Director of Beverage Hospitality at A Pots & Pans Production, an Indianapolis-based restaurant management firm, said that he saved time and cut back on "over-ordering" beer at two of the six Scotty's Brewhouses that his firm manages (Boulton, 2014). Prior to using the iKeg solution, Kellerman said that they were wasting about US$2,000 worth of excess draft beer weekly. Now, using the iKeg solution, "...It's helped [Kellerman's firm] control [their] inventory levels tremendously..." so much so that the solution will be deployed in four more brewhouses overseen by his firm. (Boulton, 2014).

Bartenders of two restaurants managed by the Pendleton, Indiana-based CZH Hospitality Group have significantly reduced the amount of beer they waste from just guessing what is left over in the kegs. Carl Bruggemeier, CEO of CZH Hospitality Group, estimates that they sell about US$2,000 worth of beer monthly that would otherwise be wasted without the iKeg solution:
"I consider it paying nothing....It's costing me $70 to garner $1,600 of profits [each month]. It's a

no-brainer." (Cantor, 2014).

4) Goal-directed actions needed to actualize an affordance

-need to know how to use mobile devices
-need to respond to alerts
-need to properly interpret RFID data
-need to ask the "right" questions when performing data mining
-need to act on the insights derived from the data and relate with beer distributors effectively in ensuring desired beer inventory is never out of stock or is immediately replenished
-need to convert real-time data into appealing and timely social media alerts to customers to draw them into the brick-and-mortar establishment --- bar, restaurant, pub, etc.

5) Applicable goals and organizational context

-enable beer brewers, retailers, and distributors to monitor and manage beer inventory more efficiently

-leverage collected depletion & consumption data

+ track real-time sales and depletions against goals
+ know the impact of competitive pressure by style, category, size, trending, etc.
+ know the impact of dates, local weather, and local events on sales
+ understand the impact of brand and product mix

-plot consumption, social & scan data by market

+ know when, how, and where to allocate staff, marketing and promotional dollars, as well as, focus social activities
+ understand local consumption trends, optimize brands, styles, etc.

- (for brewers:) increase efficiencies of marketing campaigns and in-field sales staff, increasing revenue and, market share
- (for beer distributors:) increase acquisition and retention of high performing taps and high value retailers, understanding the optimum beer mix for each retailer, able to cede low value retailers and poor performing taps to competitors
- (for retailers:) increase draft beer revenue, margin and lower waste
-(for retailers:) average retailer ROI exceeds 10X annually

In addition to the basic affordances theory, this study applies the insights of Strong et al. (2014) in extending the affordances theory by articulating affordances in an organizational context and specifying the "actualization" of functional affordances. Strong et al. (2014) posit that the affordance theory has not really clarified how an affordance's potential is actualized, how affordances operate within an organizational context, and how affordances arise as a "bundle" of interrelated affordances.

Strong et al. (2014) articulate how they extended the affordances theory by addressing the following: distinguishing between affordances as potentials for action and their actualization and developing the concept of "organizational affordances."

An "organizational affordance" is one that calls for potential collective actions of its members in the effort to achieve organizational –level immediate outcomes, which should, in turn, support organizational level goals (Strong et al., 2014). The "function" of an "organizational affordance" is expected to be the same across different individuals and different organizational levels. So, for instance, the functionality of the organizational affordance called "temperature, pressure, and volume monitoring of beer" will be the same for all kinds of end users in the roles of beer brewers, distributors, and retailers, bar tenders, restaurant waiters, etc. However, in terms of "structure" of an affordance, what is monitored (i.e., there are different types of beer in many establishments) and the specific purposes for which the beer is monitored in the different retail establishments will be different across all the SteadyServ clientele members. The manner in which the iKeg RFID solution, though, works within the context of the RFID infrastructure and the cloud service support from SteadyServ will be the same across all of the firm's clients.

IT-related affordances are defined by Markus and Silver (2008, p. 622) as "... the possibilities for goal-oriented action afforded to specified user groups by technical objects...." These IT-related affordances are also called "functional affordance" in the context of this study. Zammuto et al. (2007) has a related "take' on this and calls attention to affordances that arise from the interaction of organizational systems and different forms of information technology.

Technology is not viewed as being "static" --- rather, it evolves through time, especially when implemented and used by individuals in an organizational context and "interpret" it during its use (Orlikowski, 2000). Table 2 focuses on the key affordance featured in this case study of SteadyServ: "affordance" of monitoring the temperature, weight, and pressure of beer using RFID sensors.

The authors define actualization of affordances as "...the actions taken by actors as they take advantage of one or more affordances through their use of the technology to achieve immediate concrete outcomes in support of organizational goals...." (Strong et al., 2014, p. 70). In order to move from being an "affordance potential" to being an "actualized affordance," there are certain goal-directed actions required of the relevant end users in the beer industry.

An immediate concrete outcome is a specific expected outcome from the "actualization" of an affordance. In the SteadyServ case study, examples of immediate concrete outcomes are reduction in the amount of beer wasted and reduction in the frequency of reordering imprecise amounts of beer. These concrete outcomes are viewed as useful for realizing overarching organizational goals, which in the case of SteadyServ would include better management of beer inventory and capture of more accurate beer consumption data. These immediate concrete outcomes also serve as an "intermediary" between "actualization" outcomes and a firm's organizational goals (Strong et al., 2014).

Whether or not a specific SteadyServ client achieves its desired organizational level outcomes depends on the consistency, extent, and alignment of the collective actions of the end users in that client firm that interact with the iKeg solution. Strong et al. (2014) further explain that an "affordance" is defined by a set of characteristics related to the nature of an immediate outcome. However, an organization's members may actualize a functional affordance is a variety of ways appropriate to their particular organizational setting. Thus, what we will find is that while different SteadyServ clients will be interacting with the same standardized iKeg solution embedded in an RFID IT infrastructure, what each client chooses to "actualize" in terms of a specific immediate outcome related to having the ability to "monitor the temperature, pressure, and volume of beer" could be different. One client may be interested in monitoring beer strictly to cut down beer wastage. Another client may want to use the monitored beer data primarily for promotional purposes and use social media for informing its highly valued customers at what dates and times to come in for "Happy Hour" consumption of their favorite light beer. Yet another client may want to mine captured beer data to negotiate better beer prices with its top three beer distributors.

Apparently, SteadyServ has achieved a level of success as manifested in the reaching of desired outcomes at beer serving establishments. This is described using the concept of the "immediate concrete outcome" and the accompanying data vignettes in Table 2 illustrate how successful end users have reached certain organizational goals.

Structuration Model of Technology and SteadyServ

The following are the findings of this study concerning the implementation of the SteadyServ keg solution using the theoretical framework of the structuration model of technology by Orlikowski.

Structure of Signification

The SteadyServ iKeg system consists of the following IT infrastructural elements (SteadyServ, 2012; Swedberg, 2013)

(1) Identiv high frequency (HF) 13.56 MHz passive RFID inlay made with NXP semiconductors chip and integrated into a label made by RR Donnelley; this tag is attached to the keg's handle;
(2) SteadyServ's Sensor ring with a built-in RFID reader and weight sensor --- which is used as a platform on which the beer keg sits;
(3) Mobile app enabling end users to manage beer inventory levels from a smartphone; the app is available for both IOS or Android devices;
(4) SteadyServ's gateway installed in every retail outlet like a restaurant, bar, etc. (Swedberg, 2013).

The Uplink/Gateway is a plastic box that contains radio receivers, computer hardware, computer software, and radio transmitters, which is mounted on the wall outside the beer cooler of the retailer's (i.e., bar or restaurant) establishment. Each Uplink/Gateway box has a unique serial number embedded in its Uplink/Gateway software. The Uplink/Gateway boxes have two major functionalities: the Zigbee hardware radio receiver and software stack receives data transmissions from keg sensor/transmitters within range. This Zigbee hardware radio receiver accepts this data, organizes it, and tags the data with information unique to the Uplink/Gateway, including the unit's unique serial number and version number. Keg sensor/transmitter data that has been organized is, then, forwarded to the code division multiple access (CDMA) cell phone gateway.

The CDMA Uplink/Gateway, on the other hand, also is a transmitter/receiver in a box containing radio hardware and software. This box could be designed by a wireless carrier partner such as Verizon Communications (in the U.S.). "This CDMA Uplink/Gateway will then join the wireless carrier's data service by connecting the closest cellphone tower to the on-premise retailer where the Uplink/Gateway has been placed....The Uplink/Gateway relays the data from the Keg Sensor/Transmitter(s) that has been collected by the Zigbee receiver. The

CDMA Uplink/Gateway will communicate with the carrier's network to determine the longitude and latitude of the Gateway and will transmit that data, its software version number, and the data collected by the Zigbee receiver to the SaaS Software." (SteadyServ, 2012).

The beer distributor warehouse receives a number of keg sensor/transmitters, which are installed on the kegs. For instance, the sensor could be mounted at the bottom of the keg. Workers in the distributor warehouse have to make sure that the keg upon which the sensor/transmitter has been attached matches the items listed on the Order Pick List. The Order Pick List could be stored in an SaaS using an electronic data interchange (EDI) connection to the beer distributor's inventory system.

The distributor's warehouse usually uses a paper keg collar, clipped at the keg's top valve, which identifies the contents of the keg. Let's say that for one keg, the warehouse worker sees the label, "Coors Light." The keg sensor/transmitted for this particular keg will, then, transmit its serial number as KS1234 through the uplink Gateway. The computer monitor that shows data coming from the SaaS application will show that the keg sensor is associated to the stockkeeping unit (SKU) for "Coors Light," and confirms that the correct sensor has been attached to the right keg of beer. The Order Pick List will also be shown on the monitor from the SaaS software and this information can help the warehouse worker confirm that the beer keg leaving the distributor warehouse is the right one.

Kegs delivered from SteadyServ to the different retail establishment/customers have sensors/transmitters attached to them. These customers, then, store the kegs in coolers which puts the kegs within radio range of a mesh network that includes the keg sensors/transmitters and the uplink/gateway. Once inside the coolers, the sensors/transmitters of the kegs send data such as the weight parameter (0-20), the sensor/transmitter serial number, the software's version number, among other things. The uplink/gateway, which has its own serial number (e.g., #UG5678) and location longitude and latitude coordinates, collects the data from the sensors/transmitters. The carrier's CDMA cell phone data network, then, transmits this keg data collected by the uplink/gateway (which includes data from the gateway itself) to the SaaS software.

The SaaS software collects this data, which, it then stores in databases in a number of ways. The database supporting the SaaS software has been programmed to correlate the serial number of the sensor/transmitter and the stock keeping unit (SKU) that identifies a beer type and brand. An example can illustrate the way this works. Let us say serial numbers AB0000 to AB5678 are assigned the SKU 998877665544, which points to the product "Heineken" --- a particular beer type and brand. So, "Heineken" is written on the database by the SaaS software when data from sensor/transmitter serial number AB5676 is received, for instance. The same SaaS software has also been programmed to convert weight parameter into a percentage volume of the keg. So, say, using a weight scale of 0-20, a weight measurement of 10 from a specific keg would be converted by the SaaS software into 50% volume.

The location of the kegs in the different retail outlets is also collected by the uplink/gateway and the corresponding coordinates are also determined and recorded. So, for example, let's take the data from keg sensor/transmitter AB5676 with a weight parameter of 10 sent to the SaaS software by uplink/gateway UG1234. The SaaS software converts the data received from the keg of "Heineken" at 4 pm today and indicates that this keg is housed in "Rhum Corner," bar is 30 percent full.

Software with embedded intelligence manage the keg sensors/transmitters and controls the frequency of transmitting data from the sensors/transmitters to the uplink/gateway. This software could be programmed so that, for instance, data will be transmitted only if the weight of the keg changes. Work is underway so that data about the ambient temperature in the cooler and the sensor/transmitter's remaining battery life could be relayed as well.

Once the basic keg volume, date time, and location data are beamed from the Keg Sensor/Transmitter through the Uplink/Gateway into the SaaS software database, a number of actions will now take place that involve acting upon the data gathered.

Institutional customers of SteadyServ can set up their organizational accounts to enable their firm representatives to access their account information. The setup process requires each individual's smartphone number, among other data. All authorized individuals in that firm are allowed to access their account information which should give them insight into the status of their beer inventory and enable them to activate alerts when it is time to replenish the beer. Alerts can be sent using a number of ways: an alert sent as simple SMS text message sent to mobile phones; pop-up push alerts sent to iPhones and Android phones; email messages; recorded voice alerts sent to smartphones, etc. The alerting system uses the individual's smartphone's location based service. Workers get alerts only when they are in an area within the designated longitude and latitude boundaries associated with their workplace as defined in the SaaS database. Workers can choose to receive alerts whether or not they are working during official working hours.

A retail representative can design alerts based on the relative importance of a beer brand and type. So, for instance, if "Molson Canadian" beer is more popular than "Heineken," then, the retail representative can set up the SaaS software in such a way that he/she receives an alert when the system reports a 35 percent remaining volume for "Molson Canadian" beer and 10 percent remaining volume for "Heineken" beer.

Retailers have a number of options for reordering beer once after an alert has been received. First, using an SMS text message, they can contact their beer distributor rep directly. Second, they can send an SMS text message to an SMS gateway designed to transmit electronic data interchange (EDI) transactions to the beer distributor's ordering system. A third party system vendor usually controls this process. Third, they can use the user interface of the software to voice call to the beer distributor's sales rep. Fourth, they can use a reorder app on an iPhone or Android phone that communicates via EDI with the beer distributor's ordering system. Finally, retailers can set their accounts in such a way that automatic reorder messages tailored to the specific demand for a beer type and brand are sent to the beer distributor. So, for example, a rule can be specified in the SaaS software so that "Molson Canada" beer is automatically replenished if the volume falls below the 40 percent level only on Fridays, Saturdays, and Sundays.

Developers of application programming interfaces (APIs) will also have opportunities to write software programs for applications that can access the captured data for a variety of real-time software applications.

Structure of domination

The different elements of the RFID system used for the keg solution represents the "structure of domination" in the way work was conducted because the built-in assumptions, features, and standardized procedures embedded in business processes involved controlled the way inventory was managed in the retailer, distributor, and beer brewer establishments that used the SteadyServ keg solution. RFID system deployment involves complexities related to the physical elements of the working environment. Hershberger articulated the challenges of using RFID technology for the keg solution (Hershberger, 2015): "So it turns out using an IOT device, including RFID, in the coolers is [a] pretty hostile environment. It's pretty hard. So [it] must operate in 32-38 degree temperatures 24 by 7. It must be self-powered by lithium battery, which does not like cold. It must last three years. It must have built materials underneath $100. A full keg actually weighs 170 pounds, which gets dropped off [of] the back of a semi which is

54 inches tall. [A sensor needs to be placed underneath] and the keg could be [stacked too high]. It's a smash force of 2,000 pounds --- so you need to have an IOT device that can withstand 2,000 pounds of smash force. [You also] need to be able to measure [the beer liquid] down to a single pint of beer, which is about eight ounces out of a keg that holds 180 pints. And you need to know exactly when it's going to run out. Meaning I need to know in the next 15 seconds that that keg over there is going to be empty. You need to be able to designate up to 10 different keg sizes and 20 various options....You [also] need to be able to recognize up to 40,000 different types of beers that are commercially available globally. You must be able to use [an] RFID tag to isolate alphanumerically every single keg and never ever have the same number [used] twice. You need to remove the human process with a semi-automated intelligence process. And you need to be able to house the RFID reader and ZigBee transmitter in that device that sits in that horribly complex environment that does not like anything like temperature, power consumption, the whole nine yards..." (Hershberger, 2015).

Social consequences

1) Social structure and social consequences of IT

The focus here is on how IT is implemented, assimilated, and adopted by end users and the resulting outcomes within the social structures that defined the social context of deployment. IT is the medium of human action. Using the structuration perspective, the concept of interpretive schemes, resources, and norms are used to understand how the end users' behavior in the organization is mediated by IT which either facilitates certain outcomes or constrains others. The potential of IOT to provide competitive advantage in the marketplace at this stage has been articulated by Iansiti and Lakhani (2014) and Burkitt (2014). At this stage of the game, perhaps the most significant change emerging as a result of IOT technological possibilities is the attention given to it at the "C suite" level of the firm. A major part of crafting an IOT strategy is determining a new business model for offering IOT-enabled products and services.

In SteadyServ, Hershberger, CEO of SteadyServ articulated their business model, which was to deliver business intelligence-enhanced services to retailers, distributors, and beer brewers (Hershberger, 2015). SteadyServ created a technological solution enabled by IOT to solve supply chain problems associated with beer and tap management. In fact, apps for iPhone and Android smartphones have been developed to facilitate the deployment experience of retailers, distributors, and beer brewers. Without the SteadyServ beer keg solution, there was no instrumentation in place to assist in inventory management in different retail establishments serving beer. Orders and beer replenishment were based on sheer guesses. With increasing competitive pressures in the marketplace, the beer industry had to figure out how to "demand match" beer products with significant micro-trends determined by local tastes, economics, social dynamics, and product seasonality (Hershberger, 2015).

2) Action and social consequences of IT

Retailers using the SteadyServ's iKeg system benefit from the significant improvements in corporate decision making as a result of fine-grained tracking information that give real-time updates on the state of the firm's inventory system. Carl Bruggemeier, CEO of CZH Hospitality, a firm overseeing restaurant and hospitality projects across the US shared this:

"For me, it's all about having near real-time information about all of my draft beer products at my fingertips," Bruggemeier says (Dudley, 2015). "I can get a variety of reports and information on my handheld device. The system allows me to understand my customer's purchasing trends, look at my inventory and compare the information from SteadyServ with the reports I get from my point of sale systems, so that I can verify that I'm getting all the money I should. It has become an invaluable management tool for all the young people that work for me." "The most important thing it has done for us is that we don't run out of the beers our customers wish to purchase," Bruggemeier says. "This makes the customer very happy because previously we might have run out of a very popular and great selling product. There are two outcomes from that – you have an angry customer and you miss out on potential revenue." "We can look at a trend and say 'our customers are telling us they like pale ales' for example," Bruggemeier explains. "We may only have one or two available, but with this information we can go and find others to complement what we already sell. This helps increase customer satisfaction to thereby increase our revenues." "For many years the hospitality industry lagged behind others in the appropriate use of technology, and I think we suffered because of it," he concludes. "I think systems like SteadyServ and the explosion of this kind of technological improvement and availability of data is going to make those that adopt it eminently more powerful in their marketplace and completely responsive to their customers' needs." (Dudley, 2015).

Another significant action SteadyServ undertook was collaborating with Intel Corporation and with the world's best brewers including Heineken, Boston Beer, New Belgium Brewing, Constellation Brands, Molson Coors, and more, in developing the keg IOT-based solution (Hershberger, 2015).

3) Measures of success

Hershberger articulated the different metrics SteadyServ recognized in measuring the success of the keg IOT-based solution (Hershberger, 2015): brewers increased the efficiencies of their marketing campaigns; in-field sales staff increased sales, revenues, and the firm's market share; distributors increased the acquisition and retention of high performing taps and high value retailers; distributors gained a better understanding of the optimum beer mix for each retailer/customer, which, in turn, enabled them to focus on high value customers; retailers increased their draft beer revenue margins and reduce waste; and SteadyServ's return on investment had gone beyond a tenfold increase annually.

Kuehne + Nagel Firm

The following are the findings for applying the three theoretical frameworks to Kuehne + Nagel.

<u>Socio-Technical Systems Theory and Affordances Theory</u>

The concept of "functional affordances" allows us to analyze how end users (i.e., in this case, K+N workers and more specifically, CareTeam members) who subscribe to emerging action goals related to monitoring the temperature of the pharmaceutical and biologic goods shipments under their care headed for various destination points in the world, interpret the material properties of the CartaSense "U sensor-based" IT infrastructure system (Tables 3 and 4).

Table 3: Conceptual analysis of the functional affordance of PharmaChain's temperature monitoring of pharmaceutical products at Kuehne + Nagel

Material Properties Of Information Systems	**Use Context**		
	Structure	**People**	**Task**
-Monitoring Features: 1)CartaSense "U sensors" are attached to and are used to monitor the pharmaceutical products. 2) A communications server uses a web service technology interface to share captured RFID data with external applications. 3)K+N software logs temperature data, times of readings, receipt of measurements, whether the tags were connected to the system at the time of measurement, and reader position, among others, and transfers this data to a database. 4)K+N software also detects temperature deviations from set thresholds and alerts CareTeam to act when exception cases are encountered. 5)PharmaChain system is linked with K+N Login customer portal, which gives all participating firms visibility into all shipment information.	+ K+N has prepared for volatile environment by adapting flexible management structures and processes +K+N business model is both agile and resilient; adaptive management style has been adopted + K+N's "Focus + Excellence" programmed enabled it to develop innovative products and services (i.e., such as PharmaChain) to address needs of specific industry customers + K+N has offered innovative, scalable solutions such as PharmaChain to the pharmaceutical industry and win business contracts from new customers + K+N seeks to use digitization to standardize and automate their services	+ Appropriate end users interpret summary RFID data in the logistics reports generated by the K+N software. + CareTeam members take appropriate remedial action to prevent product spoilage or adulteration when exception cases emerge --- such as when temperature thresholds are exceeded or violated. + CareTeam members perform corrective and preventative action or CAPA and perform root cause analysis whenever there's a problem with the shipment or a deviation from expected standards. + Appropriate end users inform all involved regulatory agencies of the storage and transportation conditions the pharmaceutical product shipments were subjected to from point of origin to final destination.	+ effective pharmaceutical and biologic goods inventory management effect: affordances, if realized, can help shippers such as drug manufacturers where their shipment is at any point in time from the time of departure from origin to arrival at the point of destination + corrective and preventative action effect: affordances, if realized, enable K+N's CareTeam member to undertake effective and appropriate remedial actions to prevent spoilage or wastage of pharmaceutical goods whenever temperature and storage thresholds are violated.

6)PharmaChain system is integrated with Cargo 2000, an airline industry initiative created to ensure compliance with high levels of customer service quality expectations in handling air freight.	+ By 2015, K+N owned 116 logistics facilities and office buildings. K+N also opened its Singapore Logistics Hub and added it to its European logistics center in Leipzig (whose logistics capacity was recently doubled)	+ K+N PharmaChain end users transfer relevant information to the Cargo 2000 system to ensure compliance with airfreight delivery standards. + K+N PharmaChain end users transfer relevant information to the K+N Login system to provide total supply chain visibility to all stakeholders involved in a shipment.	+ information transparency effect: affordances, if realized, will enable appropriate regulatory agencies be apprised about the storage and delivery conditions shipments were subject to --- which is especially important during shipment delays or other problem situations. + effective decision making effect: affordances, if realized, will enable shippers to make sound business decisions on the handling and managing of their shipments whenever exception cases arise in the course of the shipment's journey.

The concept of "functional affordances" in this case study allows us to accomplish the following: (1) identify what relevant functional affordances there are that apply to K+N's PharmaChain, analyze how end users (i.e., in this case, K+N logistics workers in the different logistics centers and hubs and the CareTeam members); (2) understand how these end users who subscribe to emerging action goals related to monitoring the movement and temperature and storage conditions of the pharmaceutical goods interpret the material properties of an IOT-enabled CartaSense IT infrastructure system; and (3) understand the nature of the structure and tasks that end users are working with.

The "function" of an "organizational affordance" is expected to be the same across different individuals and different organizational levels. So, for instance, the functionality of the organizational affordance called "temperature monitoring for pharmaceutical goods" will be the same for all kinds of end users at K+N. However, in terms of "structure" of an affordance, what is monitored (i.e., there are different types pharmaceutical product shipments) and the specific purposes of these products will be different across all K+N clients/shippers. The manner in which PharmaChain, though, works within the context of the U sensor wireless mesh network will work and how this system will interact with K+N Login and K+N Cargo 2000 will be the same for all of the K+N's clients.

Table 3 focuses on the key affordance featured in this case study of K+N: PharmaChain's temperature monitoring of pharmaceutical products at Kuehne + Nagel using CartaSense mesh network of wireless U sensors.

The authors define actualization of affordances as "...the actions taken by actors as they take advantage of one or more affordances through their use of the technology to achieve immediate concrete outcomes in support of organizational goals...." (Strong et al., 2014, p. 70). In order to move from being an "affordance potential" to being an "actualized affordance," there are certain goal-directed actions required of the relevant end users in the logistics industry. Table 4 features goal-directed actions required on the part of K+N workers in item number (4) in order to actualize desired outcomes.

An immediate concrete outcome is a specific expected outcome from the "actualization" of an affordance. In the K+N case study, examples of immediate concrete outcomes are successfully delivering pharmaceutical products as promised, fulfilled guaranteed transit times, adoption of good distribution practice compliance, effectively mitigating problem situations with proactive remedial action, making supply chain visibility information accessible, and promptly informing regulatory agencies involved when needed. These concrete outcomes are viewed as useful for realizing the overarching organizational goal, which in the case of K+N would be guaranteeing high-level customer service quality in the form of timely deliveries wherein pharmaceutical and biologic products remain in a potent and useful state for the sake of the end consumers. These immediate concrete outcomes also serve as an "intermediary" between "actualization" outcomes and a firm's organizational goals (Strong et al., 2014).

Whether or not the K+N logistics worker or CareTeam member achieves its desired organizational level outcomes depends on the consistency, extent, and alignment of the collective actions of these workers with the goals set forth by K+N. Strong et al. (2014) further explain that an "affordance" is defined by a set of characteristics related to the nature of an immediate outcome. However, an organization's members may actualize a functional affordance in a variety of ways appropriate to their particular organizational setting.

Thus, what we will find is that while different K+N logistics workers and CareTeam members will be interacting with the same PharmaChain solution, what each K+N worker chooses to "actualize" in terms of a specific immediate outcome related to having the ability to "monitor the temperature and other ambient conditions surrounding a pharmaceutical shipment" or ensuring timely delivery of a shipment could be different. For instance, a number of CareTeam members could be involved mitigating a situation where a case of a vaccine has been frozen by mistake instead of refrigerated. Freezing has a profound and irreversible impact on a protein-based biologic product, and so, this particular case of vaccine has been compromised. The team members will report the situation to the client/shipper (i.e., a pharmaceutical firm) and agrees to absorb a financial penalty and asks the client to reconsider the disposition of the remaining cases of vaccines in the pallet that were not frozen. In another case, K+N logistics workers in the Singapore distribution center encounters a one-day delay of arrival of 10 pallets of an anti-flu drug from California. They, in turn, communicate with the pharmaceutical firm in California via the K+N Login customer portal and request a remapping of the route for the delivery to the next port of call, which is Hong Kong.

Apparently, K+N has achieved a level of success as manifested in the reaching of desired outcomes. This is described using the concept of the "immediate concrete outcome" and the accompanying data vignettes in Table 4 which illustrate how successful K+N end users have reached certain organizational goals.

Table 4: Organization-PharmaChain Solution Affordance: temperature monitoring of pharmaceutical products at Kuehne + Nagel
1) PharmaChain Solution Features (material properties of information systems): (1)CartaSense "U sensors" are used to monitor the pharmaceutical products. The U sensors are attached to the goods/products whose temperature and location are being monitored. Data from these sensors are transmitted to RFID readers when the shipment arrives at a waypoint or its final destination (Greengard, 2015). These U sensors can monitor temperatures ranging from -35 degrees Celsius to + 65 degrees Celsius with both internal and external probes that support relative humidity within the (0-100%) range. (2) An advanced mesh network connects innumerable wireless U sensors with each other and with a "gateway." (3) The "gateway" connects the mesh network in a specific spot to a central communication server through the use of either a public or private network. (4)Data from all the gateways are gathered real-time by a "communications server," which uses a web service technology interface to share this data with external applications. All U sensor data gathered are, then, transferred to the K+N software which logs temperature data and detects deviation from acceptable thresholds. Other data such as temperature measurements, times of readings, receipt of measurements, whether the tags were connected to the system at the time of measurement, and reader position, among others, are transferred by this software to a database. (5)Technical applications are software products that allow end users to view the data gathered in a usable format. Technical applications may run on any web-enabled device. (6)"Business analytics software" can do further data analysis in order to produce meaningful reports showing things like warehouse mapping, shipment location, temperature thresholds reached, etc. **2) Characteristics of Actors** + Appropriate end users at any point in the K+N supply chain should have the skills to interpret

the logistics reports generated by the K+N software.

+ Upon receipt of alerts, CareTeam members should be able to take appropriate remedial action to prevent product spoilage or adulteration.

+ CareTeam members should be able to perform corrective and preventative action or CAPA and perform root cause analysis whenever there's a problem with the shipment or a deviation from expected standards.

+ Appropriate end users in the K+N PharmaChain supply chain should be able to inform all involved regulatory agencies of the storage and transportation conditions the pharmaceutical product shipments were subjected to from point of origin to final destination.

+ K+N PharmaChain employees should be able to transfer relevant information to the Cargo 2000 system to ensure compliance with airfreight delivery standards.

3) Example of immediate concrete outcomes from data

Terry Sell, Pharma and Temperature Controlled Airfreight Services, K+N, shared the following concerning actual accomplishments achieved by K+N in delivering PharmaChain services:

+ K+N has enabled pharmaceutical supply chain visibility and help clients manage shipments:

"...So in summary, with enabling of the visibility system with our technology provider, we have increased the visibility and control over shipments...."

+ K+N's CareTeam has facilitated proactive remedial action to protect shipments:

"....We have been able to mitigate in-transit issues. We've had active containers meaning they're actively controlled containers mechanically fail. We've been able to catch that, and it is something once we've caught that we have a plan in place to combat that...."

+ K+N has reduced product release time:

" [We have been able to] reduce the product release time, again, so with that pre-clearance, giving them [the clients/shippers] the higher confidence interval that their product is safe, and when they do have their data log or stuff they're pulling off which is reactive, when they do download that information it is going to be exactly what we told them it's going to be, so giving them that confidence, increased confidence that they can begin the downstream pre clearance process...."

+ K+N has helped their clients (shippers) reduce their shipping costs.

+ K+N has been able to fulfill their delivery promises and ensured that products arrive at destination points in a form useful to end customers:

"...So again taking that 14 days [delivery time] down to 5 days. That's very critical for them to get the product to market, and then making sure that the patient, again this always has to come back to the patient, so making sure that the patient gets the product in the right condition at the right time...."

+ K+N has provided their clients timely, complete, and accurate information to enable them to make the right business decisions concerning their shipments:

"...[We have also given]...these companies (i.e., clients) better information and data to support business decisions. So that's, again, we've had a real positive experience with our technology partner CartaSense, we've had a real positive experience with some of our customers who have adapted or have adopted this technology, and we continue to see more and more customers wanting this. So, as they understand what the value is, as they understand what we can give them in terms of information and data, if we're talking about risk mitigation, risk minimization, you know... these are the kind of things that they want to see...."

4) Goal-directed actions needed to actualize an affordance

-need to know the science behind the monitoring of cold-chain pharmaceutical products
-need to interpret data relevant to pharmaceutical cold chain products like temperature, heat, and refrigeration or freezing thresholds, etc.
-need to respond appropriately to exception situations or deviations from standards using corrective and preventative actions to avoid product waste or spoilage
-need to inform regulatory agencies involved in the shipment about conditions the shipment was subjected to, especially in cases of problems or shipment delays
-need to ensure that pharmaceutical products arrive at the end user/consumer destination points in a form that is useful to the consumer
-need to ensure that pharmaceutical products pass all storage and delivery "tests" to ensure that the products arrive in viable form and state

5) Applicable goals and organizational context

-K+N seeks to ensure that pharmaceutical products are safe and effective when they arrive at their client's site
-K+N guarantees transit/delivery time
-K+N guarantees good distribution practice in the course of providing delivery services
-K+N provides appropriate proactive interventions when required
-K+N uses qualified equipment and collaborates with third party providers
-K+N seeks to provide three levels of pharmaceutical cold chain services:
(1)Level 1: services for shipments that do not require special handling and have no particular temperature requirements
(2)Level 2: services for shipments that require specific temperature ranges, but no any special handling procedures
(3)Level 3: services for temperature-sensitive cargo with special handling requirements
-K+N seeks to ensure that their clients/shippers can manage their pharmaceutical goods inventory efficiently and effectively
-K+N has to assist client so that the latter does not get involved in lawsuits filed by their customers
-K+N seeks to help their clients/shippers reduce their shipping costs
-K+N seeks to provide their clients/shippers relevant, accurate, complete, and actionable intelligent information that will enable these clients to make sound business decisions
-K+N seeks to protect their clients by ensuring compliance with all regulatory advisories and

guidelines pertaining to the shipments

Structuration Model of Technology (Orlikowski)

The following are the findings of this study concerning the implementation of K+N's PharmaChain solution for pharmaceutical and life sciences products using the theoretical framework of the structuration model of technology by Orlikowski.

Structure of Signification

K+N's PharmaChain was deployed in March 2011 (Greengard, 2015). The specific elements of K+N's PharmaChain that make up the CartaSense wireless monitoring solution by air and ground shipments are the following (CartaSense, 2015). First, there are the wireless sensors and in the case of K+N, the "U sensors" used to monitor the pharmaceutical products. The U sensors used for the PharmaChain solution can monitor temperatures ranging from -35 degrees Celsius to + 65 degrees Celsius with both internal and external probes that support relative humidity within the (0-100%) range.

An advanced mesh network enables the connection of innumerable wireless U sensors with each other and with a "gateway." Second, the "gateway" connects the mesh network in a specific spot to a central communication server through the use of either a public or private network. Third, data from all the gateways are gathered real-time by a "communications server," which, in turn, uses some kind of web service technology interface in order to share this data with external applications. Fourth, "technical applications" are software products that allow end users to view the data gathered in a usable format. The data gathered can consist of measurements, mesh network architecture data, or other valuable data. Technical applications may run on any web-enabled device. Fifth, "business analytics software" can do further data analysis in order to produce meaningful reports showing things like warehouse mapping, shipment location, temperature thresholds reached, etc.

The U sensors are attached to the goods/products whose temperature and location are being monitored. Data from these sensors are transmitted to RFID readers when the shipment arrives at a waypoint or its final destination (Greengard, 2015).

"U sensors" detect a U sensor gateway within range and starts transmitting data to it. Using some kind of network whether it is a local area network (i.e., Ethernet gateway) or cellular communications network (i.e., general packet radio service or GPRS gateway), the U sensor gateway, in turn, connects with a communications server. The "U sensors" automatically form a dynamic, self-healing mesh network which is resilient even when exposed to rough radio frequency conditions. Resident sensors can also function as "repeaters" for other wireless sensors that cannot sense a U sensor gateway nearby.

All U sensor data gathered are, then, transferred to the K+N software which logs temperature data and detects deviation from acceptable thresholds. Other data such as temperature measurements, times of readings, receipt of measurements, whether the tags were connected to the system at the time of measurement, and reader position, among others, are transferred by this software to a database.

K+N's 24/7/365 CareTeam is alerted via a Web-based shipment tracking system when acceptable temperature thresholds are exceeded, and its members, then, take appropriate remedial action to prevent product spoilage or adulteration. There is also a U sense gateway dashboard that enables K+N workers have supply chain visibility and help manage reader data reception and transmission throughout the journey of the products.

The IT infrastructural elements of this temperature monitoring application are installed in hundreds of points along K+N's global supply chain consisting of warehouses and logistics facilities that oversee the logistics of pharmaceutical and life sciences products of its clients. Chapman, K+N's global pharmaceutical product manager, said, "It's not something every company chooses to use or deploys for all products and situations....It's something that's valuable for critical shipments involving high-value products, and the partnership between our customers and our company is constantly expanding." (Greengard, 2015).

Operational data from the U sensor mesh network is also linked with K+N's Cargo 2000 system to ensure compliance with air freight delivery standards required by this initiative.

Structure of Domination

Moving "cold chain" pharmaceutical products demands thorough scientific knowledge of the product and the nature of the environments where it moves and is stored throughout the delivery journey. A second key requirement is the ability to document data on the operating environments and establishing that they are scientifically sound. Cold chain engineers, packaging engineers, and logistics-related workers should understand these environmental conditions and product parameters better than any inspector. Guidance documents from regulatory agencies spell out valuable criteria for creating tests to ensure the products are protected while in transit and during short-term storage. These tests should accurately represent real-time and real-world shipping environments, primary and secondary shipping containers, transport and storage durations, seasons, and climatic zones. The global supply chain for pharmaceutical products usually include different transportation and several climatic zones, and land, air, and water modes of transportation, each with their accompanying temperature fluctuations.

An information system supporting the documentation needs of the peculiar logistics requirements for pharmaceutical products needs to capture detailed records of stability data, geographical data (including climatic zones), shipping and storage durations at each point in transit, and contingency procedures for delivery delays, out-of-specification conditions, or other unforeseen exception events.

RFID technology should be able to capture all relevant ambient data regarding the pharmaceutical product shipment in order to fulfill regulatory requirements. In the case of K+N, the CartaSense solution offers end-to-end monitoring and alerting abilities using advanced wireless sensor networking (Berkovitch & Leshem, 2014). Vendors need to introduce new paradigms for monitoring assets, providing real-time information, and enabling ad-hoc corrective actions such as increasing or decreasing the air condition temperature set point while in transit, moving the goods from a warm location back to the fridge room, etc.

The quality of the goods is often related to the remaining shelf life of the product, which is often difficult to predict as complete information is usually unavailable on the history of the product environment from the product's creation to its actual arrival time. Also, goods on the same pallets coming from the same manufacturing facility, using the same mode of transportation, can have very different environmental profiles. One pallet in the same shipment may have waited longer on the dock and may have been exposed longer to hotter sunlight, for instance, than other pallets in the same shipment. Adding a wireless sensor to each pallet enables capture of the exact temperature history at each point in transit and the product's shelf life can be more accurately calculated.

Structure of Legitimation for both SteadyServ and Kuehne + Nagel

Standards that govern IOT represent "the structure of legitimation" because they sanction the configuration of the specific elements of the IOT solution used and propagate a set of "norms" about what constitutes a workable IOT solution within different corporate contexts/environments. Observance of IOT standards is important because: (1) standards specify tried and tested solutions which could greatly help a firm deploy IOT solutions under real world conditions; (2) standards require specific IOT solution components provided by vendors and integrators off-the-shelf, thus, helping firms avoid unnecessary development efforts and vendor lock in; and (3) standards enable solutions that are compatible with related business applications.

At this time, there is no central body of standards that can be applied to all possible IOT applications. The use of industrial IOT standards would be relevant specifically for SteadyServ's product monitoring initiative or K+N's temperature monitoring service. The efforts of three specific bodies would have the most impact on the two firms, though.

The first organization is that of the Open Interconnect Consortium (OIC), which is supported by Intel, Samsung Electronics, Hewlett Packard, Lenovo, Dell, among a total of 50 vendor firms. These firms are working to back up open-source standards covering device discovery, communication, data exchange, among other functions. The OIC has developed the source code embodying the consortium's specifications for certified IOT products and released it to developers in 2015 (Lawson, 2014).

The second organization focusing on enterprise IOT is the Industrial Internet Consortium (IIC) consisting of about 100 members including Microsoft, Samsung, Huawei Technologies, General Electric, Cisco Systems, IBM, and Intel (Lawson, 2014). Its approach is different in that rather than developing IOT standards, it intends to work with different standards bodies to coordinate efforts of industries where IOT and older machine-to-machine technologies have been deployed. In so doing, the IIC will define requirements for standards, design reference structures, and create testbeds for these standards.

The third organization is the IEEE (The Institute of Electrical and Electronics Engineers) P2413, which has a working group devoted to organizing the variety of IOT specifications developed by different industry consortia (Lawson, 2014). It will do so by converting information from different IOT platforms into a commonly understood body of data objects.

With the variety of standards bodies emerging, a good predictor of who might prevail is the size, reputation, and momentum of the firms behind them. These are consortia that will more likely gain greater traction and immediate market recognition.

Social consequences

1) Social structure and social consequences of IT

K+N PharmaChain and K+N Login

The supply chain logistics operations of pharmaceutical and life sciences are a complex system of interactions involving multiple parties. Terry Sell from Pharma and Temperature Controlled Airfreight Services – North America, K+N shared this:"[The] current situation is that there are multiple handoffs between different parties. In the freight forwarding world, we don't own [all] assets for the most part. We may have a few trucks here and there, but typically we're not owning our own aircraft. So this is where we have to involve other stakeholders, other providers, and make sure that they are willing to help us in that transit process...."(RFIDJ, Live! Transcript, 2015).

Relationships among K+N clients and trading partners are supported by a Web-enabled value network platform called K+N Login, thus, enabling a digital horizontal social structure supporting integration among these participants. Functioning as a customer portal, K+N Login is a comprehensive supply chain management platform designed to enable K+N clients optimize critical logistics, procurement, and customer service processes; reduce logistics costs; and provide an "up-to-the-minute quick" view of one's inventory in motion using land, sea, and air transportation (K+N, 2015a). This customer portal links shippers, consignees, third-party service providers like warehousing and distribution center owners with K+N, enabling always on real-time communications along a firm's entire supply chain.

Achieving supply chain visibility is a critical feature of a customer portal such as K+N Login. The portal reports and summarizes important supply chain events and generates exception alerts in cases of critical plan changes or expected or actual service interruptions. In the service of shippers, the portal provides information on the location and status of all products shipped worldwide and across all transportation modes, to allow them to manage them down to the purchase order and item level. The portal's event manager releases a notification message to the appropriate end users once a status or key process step has been reached or is about to be reached. The system also generates a confirmation or pre-advice when conditions set by business parameters designed by clients are reached. The portal also has an escalation mechanism that can identify plan changes and potential or actual service disruptions. If an event is overdue, the escalation mechanism will generate alerts to accelerate the response time of the appropriate parties, and thus, the system is assisting these clients in avoiding complaints from their customers and additional costs they may incur due to product delivery delays.

The portal also assists K+N clients in becoming more effective shipment and logistics planners. The portal has tools that consider a variety of cost factors --- such as transport, handling, and inventory --- in determining budgets. Planners can create and streamline operational plans using information on multiple logistics variables. The portal's interactive delivery planning (IDP) features enables on-line planning, and supports delivery planning and business processes for FCL (full container load) and LCL (less than container load) seafreight shipments. Shipping forecasts based on cargo arrivals and departures can be generated. Deliveries can be prioritized base on the need for a particular product. The portal's booking tool enables clients to place bookings more flexibly. Clients may submit shipping instructions and request equipment, advise pick-up addresses, and obtain cargo-readiness dates. Data collected by the portal can also help clients evaluate the performance of their supply chain trading partners and thus, assist them in deciding whether or not to continue their relationships or contracts with these third parties.

K+N Login has SAP Business Objects integrated into it providing portal members with digital reporting tools --- dynamic performance reports/scorecards, volume statistics, freight spend reports, leadtime reports, and fill reports. A built-in portal dashboard presents end users with an overview of logistics activities and order processes in their respective supply chain. Business intelligence tools enable end users to "data mine" collected logistics data for effective planning and decision making.

K+N PharmaChain and Cargo 2000

Because of the complexity involved in logistics operations, this industry is ideal for creating Web-enabled value network electronic environments that can accommodate all necessary entities and participants involved in the process of moving physical goods by land, sea, and air. The PharmaChain solution is integrated with another such Web-enabled environment called "Cargo 2000" (K+N, 2015b). Data captured by PharmaChain is integrated with Cargo 2000.

Terry Sell from Pharma and Temperature Controlled Airfreight Services – North America, K+N, shared this: "...And then we also want to make sure it [PharmaChain] was integrating within our systems. Our visibility system, KN Login, and also it also interacted with the other Cargo 2000 systems which is an industry wide system that gives us information and data so we can match everything up...."

"....We needed to make sure that we had our visibility system in place interacting with industry systems, the Cargo 2000 which gives us data and information, and make sure that that worked with our technology provider with their servers as well so that we could go into the actual monitoring process...." (RFIDJ, Live! Transcript, 2015).

Cargo 2000 is a collaborative initiative of over 35 of the world's leading airlines, forwarders, and third parties involved in air freight services under the auspices of the International Air Transport Association (IATA) (K+N, 2015b). In response to customer demand for high level of service not previously attained in the air freight industry, Cargo 2000 seeks to create shipping process steps and interfaces for the exchange of shipment data among all parties involved and ensure that door-to-door delivery can be planned precisely and monitored using a master operating plan (MOP). Cargo 2000 consists of a three-pronged approach: planning, controlling, and reporting. In the planning step, the MOP involves calculating a shipment cycle based on the process framework, which subsequently creates a route map. This map defines the "latest by" times for the completion of key processes along the transport chain. All firms involved in a shipment collaboratively plan a route map using the standard data interfaces provided by Cargo 2000 which seamlessly combine the route maps of carrier and forwarder.

In the controlling step, the agreed upon route map is issued and the shipment is monitored against this map from origin to destination. The IT systems of both carrier and forwarder are linked to the Cargo 2000 system and are updated when a milestone is completed. Cargo 2000 generates alerts whenever there is a deviation from the route map. This instigates communication between the forwarder/carrier and the shipper/consignee to enable corrective measures to bring the shipment back on schedule. If the delay is considerable and the original plan cannot be followed, then, a new delivery schedule is calculated and the route map adjusted. Exception codes are entered into the Cargo 2000 system to record causes and responsibilities for the shipment delay.

In the reporting step, it is important to establish whether or not the delivery promise was kept and to document reasons when it is not. Cargo 2000 members use standardized procedures and exception codes in reporting their performance. Data submitted by the members are the basis of monthly reports detailing the most frequent causes and responsibilities for shipment delays.

2)Action and social consequences of IT

Moving "cold chain" pharmaceutical products demands thorough scientific knowledge of the product and the nature of the environments where it moves and is stored throughout the delivery journey. A second key requirement is the ability to document data on the operating environments and establishing that they are scientifically sound. Cold chain engineers, packaging engineers, and logistics-related workers should understand these environmental conditions and product parameters better than any inspector. Guidance documents from regulatory agencies spell out valuable criteria for creating tests to ensure the products are protected while in transit and during short-term storage. These tests should accurately represent real-time and real-world shipping environments, primary and secondary shipping containers, transport and storage durations, seasons, and climatic zones. The global supply chain for pharmaceutical products usually include different transportation and several climatic zones, and land, air and water modes of transportation, each with their accompanying temperature fluctuations.

An information system supporting the documentation needs of the peculiar logistics requirements for pharmaceutical products needs to capture detailed records of stability data, geographical data (including climatic zones), shipping and storage durations at each point in transit, and contingency procedures for delivery delays, out-of-specification conditions or other unforeseen exception events.

Unlike the previous section that articulated social structure changes, "action" refers to very specific courses of action afforded by the PharmaChain solution for its end users. Terry Sell of K+N aptly described the existence of PharmaChain as providing K+N workers "proactive" action capabilities: "...A paradigm shift within our company is now we have the ability to act on things...." (RFIDJ, Live! Transcript, 2015).

One important consequence of PharmaChain is K+N's ability to reduce its product release time while in transit by fast-tracking product clearances: "....So if you have data and information that shows that your product is safe and effective, you can start to pre-clear that. You can start to prepare your downstream supply chain. So that's something where you don't have to wait until information is received from a data recording device that was placed on the freight. It's taken off after it has cleared customs, then they give it to the regulatory authorities, they approve it. You can start that process much more rapidly. So that's kind of an added benefit...."(RFIDJ, Live! Transcript, 2015).

Another key action possibility is the ability of K+N logistics workers to take corrective actions when there are deviations in the desired temperature levels of pharmaceutical products while in transit: "....When you're talking about if something does happen in transit, whether as a deviation in temperature on the product, now you can have immediate root cause analysis, and this is where it becomes another critical timing factor because if a deviation occurs, the typical deviation can take anywhere from 7 to 14 days to take and have a full deviation, full CAPA (i.e., corrective and preventive action) process complete. What that means is that is product that is not in the market for sale. So if it's in deviation status or needs to have a CAPA attached to it, ...that item is placed in quarantine or in hold. So if you can speed up that deviation process and take it from 14 days down to 5 days, that has a profound impact, and again, making sure the market can get that product, making sure you can have cash coming in quicker because you're selling that product quicker...." ...."(RFIDJ, Live! Transcript, 2015).

In the case of pharmaceutical products, information tracked on deviations from allowable temperature ranges is very important in deciding on the disposition of the products. When pharmaceutical product shipments run in the millions of dollars, acting expeditiously to save the shipment from wastage of outright disposal is a significant benefit for the shipper client of K+N:

"....But also, when you have a deviation, what's important here, if you have a deviation it doesn't necessarily mean that your product is no good. So if it's frozen, if it's a biologic product, you'll know very quickly that you have to have a disposal process or you're going to bring it back to the origin for disposal. If it's a product that has more stability to it, meaning that it can accept outside of the refrigerated state, 2-8 C maybe to 10 C, then you have what's called time out of range, and you can measure and manage time out of range with this type of system, so you'll know exactly how long it was exposed to temperatures outside of the acceptable range, and then you can make a shelf life calculation…." (RFIDJ, Live! Transcript, 2015).

Another very important entity involved in the logistics process is the regulatory authority like the U.S. Food and Drug Administration (US/FDA). Regulatory agencies need to be apprised about the disposition of the pharmaceutical product shipments that may have been compromised: "…You can give your regulatory authorities, your partner overseas the information so they can make a business based decision. But having that makes it much easier to get these, get these problems cleared up and get it through the CAPA process. You have the ability to mitigate in-transit issues. So again if something is going wrong, if you start to see an alert come out saying hey we're trending too high, well, that's going to be information you can use to make a phone call, so that's how you can be proactive is when you see something happening in real time and it's not correct or doesn't look right, you can make the phone call to make sure things are right. You reduce the product losses. If we know something is not going right, we've got a 24/7 365 team that will sit and monitor these things. They do get push notifications, push alerts, push alarms, so again it is something where that team can help to reduce product loss, and then again, anytime you have information or data, you can help that to drive business decisions…. Are you using the right airlines? Are you using the right process? Can you optimize your packaging? So these are [some things] to consider." (RFIDJ, Live! Transcript, 2015).

Going back to PharmaChain's purpose, which is temperature tracking, mitigating actions can be taken by the appropriate workers --- in the case of K+N, this would be CareTeam members --- if they have the right information at the right time about the disposition of the pharmaceutical product shipments.

Terry Sell once again shared: "So if we look at the outputs this is, again, we're talking about the ambient temperature outside of a packaging system. So it could be a container, it could be a passive palate shipper, insulated shipper with gel packs, but this would be what the actual shipping system is exposed to, and this is the actual product temperature, so you can have a lot of good data from that. GPS. Also make sure you see what's going on from the GPS perspective. What is your trucker doing, what routes is he taking? Is he taking a consistent route? If it's high value do you want him taking a consistent route? Do you want him changing routes? So these are all things we can monitor and start to measure as well. The push notifications, so again, talking about having our 24/7/365 CareTeam. They're getting the alerts, temperature alarm. So what are they going to do about it? How are they going to react upon it? Again, we can build processes based upon that as well. So these are some things that are outputs. So, when we talk about the alerts, not only do we get the alerts and the alarms, we can notate that in the system, so it is something where we can say ok we had an alarm on this sensor, temperature was above the upper threshold for 15 minutes, and then say see details. That's where you can have a corrective measure in there, so when you have a deviation your quality departments at your customers' companies will pull that open, they'll see what the corrective measure was. It gives them information again to make that immediate decision whether or not you know they can close up the CAPA (corrective and preventive action) based upon that. We also talked about how deviations can be measured, the amount of time. So you have the amount of time out of range, you have where it happened. So, these are all things that we can start to measure and monitor and give it information to customers so they can make again business decisions --- so it's very powerful. And, then, importantly is when we talk about the integration of Cargo 2000 feeds. All these three that are codes here, these are Cargo 2000 feeds. And what that does is it gives who had control of that shipment, where was that shipment in the transport process. So, you've got the temperature information here, you get the dates and times here, now you've got the ownership here. So, when you're talking about who was the stakeholder that had a challenge, whether it was on the aircraft, aircraft departed, it arrived here, was there something that went wrong here? This is what is really powerful is when you can start taking all of the data and crunching it together to create really good information and giving that to your customers so that they can see how they can improve their process. What is going right in the process and what is trending wrong? So even if the packaging is successful, the product was safe, we might find something where we're trending wrong. What's going on there? So again it's using data and information and using it in a good format to try and create business decisions and evaluate where your risk is and where your risk could be. Has something changed?" (RFIDJ, Live! Transcript, 2015).

3) Measures of success

K+N's success in providing PharmaChain can be measured in a number of ways. K+N has enabled pharmaceutical supply chain visibility and help clients manage shipments. The firm's notable CareTeam has facilitated proactive remedial action to protect shipments in cases where established temperature thresholds, for instance, were violated or when shipment deliveries were delayed. K+N has also provided their clients timely, complete, and accurate information to enable them to make the right business decisions concerning their shipments, should they have to supplement or override CareTeam decisions. K+N has reduced product release time and accelerated the movement of the pharmaceutical goods through all clearances points. K+N has been able to fulfill their delivery promises and ensured that products arrive at destination points in a form useful to end customers. In the very end, K+N has helped their clients (shippers) reduce their overall shipping costs, while delivering high-quality specialized logistics services.

Terry Sell, Pharma and Temperature Controlled Airfreight Services, K+N shared this:
"So in summary, with the enabled... enabling of the visibility system with our technology provider, we have increased the visibility and control over shipments. We have been able to mitigate in-transit issues. We've had active containers meaning they're actively controlled containers mechanically fail. We've been able to catch that, and it is something once we've caught that we have a plan in place to combat that. So we've found a mitigation strategy for mechanical failure. We're able to help people avoid cost. So are they doing too much? Are they overshooting from a patching perspective, making it too robust? Are we right sizing? So this is where we have to help them to make right business decisions based upon data because in this industry it is based upon scientific rationalization. You can't do it just because you think it's going to be the best way to go. If you can prove it, and you can prove internally to the quality department and the regulatory authorities, that's where you have to be. Reduce the product release time, again, so with that pre-clearance, giving them the higher confidence interval that their product is safe, and when they do have their data log or stuff they're pulling off which is reactive, when they do download that information it is going to be exactly what we told them it's going to be, so giving them that confidence, increased confidence that they can begin the downstream pre clearance process. We talked enough about CAPA, but it is something immediate root cause analysis. So again taking that 14 days down to 5 days. That's very critical for them to get the product to market, and then making sure that the patient, again this always has to come back to the patient, so making sure that the patient gets the product in the right condition at the right time and also giving these companies better information and data to support business decisions. So that's, again, we've had a real positive experience with our technology partner Cart Essence, we've had a real positive experience with some of our

customers who have adapted or have adopted this technology, and we continue to see more and more customers wanting this. So as they understand what the value is, as they understand what we can give them in terms of information and data, if we're talking about risk mitigation, risk minimization, you know... these are the kind of things that they want to see. So with that being said I thought I'd just pass these around very quickly if you'd like to see the actual sensors that go on shipments. And again, nothing... this is not earth shattering technology. It's actually simple technology by design, but it is highly effective, and it's having the entire plan in place with the technology provider on how to deploy this...." (RFIDJ, Live! Transcript, 2015).

CONCLUSIONS

This study features the contextualization of our knowledge around the use and effects of information systems in firms within the specific context of a startup firm offering a beer inventory management solution, SteadyServ, and a global logistics firm specializing in pharmaceutical cold chain shipment deliveries, both using IOT-enabled information systems. This qualititative analysis has woven functional affordances into the relationships among the subsystems of the socio-technical work systems (i.e, iKeg solution in SteadyServ and the PharmaChain solution in K+N). This case study's data is based primarily on transcripts of talks given by key executives from the two firms that have presented in the annual RFID Journal Live! Conference in April 2015 where they described and explained their respective firm's IT system deployment experience. Based on this primary data and secondary data from published sources, evidence is presented for the socio-technical conditions that allow the material properties of information systems to emerge in order to create "functional affordances" needed for IOT/sensor-enabled product monitoring. This research project identifies the appropriation mediators needed in the use of the information systems in order to realize the built-in affordances of these systems (Wheeler & Valacich, 1996). These mediators consist of structure, action goals, user characteristics, and task characteristics required within the context of product monitoring for beer inventory management and temperature control tracking for pharmaceutical goods shipment.

Of great interest here is the deployment of IOT-based technologies because of the potential for creating innovative services that include data analytics capabilities backed up by cloud-based services used to produce actionable information needed for more effective supply chain management operations. Newly emerging innovations like IOT will create options for affordances if researchers could persevere in their understanding of these information systems and the functional affordances arising from their interpretation and use. The two case studies also highlighted the use of information technologies that have very specific use in terms of the needs addressed by the IOT initiative. The Tata Consultancy Group identified the four top areas for IOT applications based on the data the firm obtained from a global sample of firms: premises monitoring, product monitoring, supply chain monitoring, and customer monitoring (Tata Consultancy Report, 2015). The two case studies primarily highlighted product monitoring initiatives by the two firms.

Understanding and awareness of the affordances provided by these IOT-enabled information systems could be useful not only theoretically in terms of analyzing how technical and social subsystems interact and broadening the base of application of the three theoretical frameworks used here. There is a practical benefit as well in terms of gaining insight into creating explicit criteria in selecting hardware and software components from technology vendors, or, more specifically, RFID and sensor vendors, in order to ensure the realization of desired functional affordances.

REFERENCES

References available upon request.

DECISION SCIENCES INSTITUTE

In Search for Impregnable Exchange Relationships with Buyers: Insights for Suppliers

Thomas Clauss
Philipps-University of Marburg
Email: thomas.clauss@wiwi.uni-marburg.de

Chanchai Tangpong
North Dakota State University
Email: charnchai.tangpong@ndsu.edu

ABSTRACT

Economic necessity, relational ties, and emotional connections are important conditions for suppliers to form impregnable exchange relationships (IERs) with buyers. The exploratory investigation through the use of Repertory Grid Technique suggests that helpfulness, friendliness, uniqueness, and flexibility are primacy attributes of suppliers helping them to satisfy those IER conditions, thus enabling them to sustain beneficial relationships with buyers..

KEYWORDS: Buyer-supplier relationships, insights for suppliers, supplier attributes, repertory grid technique

INTRODUCTION

Research on buyer-supplier relationships (BSRs) and supply chains (SCs) has greatly advanced our understanding of various aspects in BSRs and SCs. The extant literature has investigated various types of BSR as well as their behavioral outcomes (Tangpong, Hung, & Li, 2014) and their economic outcomes (Paulraj, Lado, & Chen, 2008). Developed largely from buyer perspective,, this literature has provided managerial prescriptions to buyers and purchasing managers (Tangpong, Michalisin, Traub, & Melcher, 2015). Nevertheless, the BSR and SC literature, with a few exceptions (Kaufman, Wood, & Theyel, 2000) offers limited guidance to suppliers regarding sustaining their exchange relationships with major buyer firms and harnessing such relationships to achieve superior performance.

In this study, we approach the BSR phenomena through a practical research question "*what are the characteristics or attributes of suppliers that enable the suppliers to attain impregnable exchange relationships with major buyers?*" An impregnable exchange relationship (IER) refers to as the exchange relationship that bonds one party with another through its ability to satisfy the exchange partner's multiple needs concurrently (e.g., economic, social, and emotional needs). Therefore, once suppliers form IERs with their major buyers, the buyers would see no needs to seek alternative suppliers. The answer to the research question in this study will largely help suppliers prepare and position themselves for long-term success with buyers.

LITERATURE AND THEORETICAL BACKGROUND

The dynamics in relationships between buyers and suppliers can be viewed from multiple theoretical lenses. In the extant literature, three perspectives, which have been established to offer insights into the BSR and SC dynamics, are (1) strategic perspective, (2) relational exchange, and (3) behavioral operations.

From the strategic perspective, in order to achieve exchange relationships with major buyers that are tenable in the long run, suppliers need to establish relationships that offer the buyers' benefits while increasing their switching costs to other suppliers (Blocker, Houston, & Flint, 2012).The suppliers need to cultivate economic necessity for the buyers, whereby the buyers are greatly dependent on the suppliers. This economic necessity acts as a binding force between the two exchange partners, leading to the buyers' efforts to maintain their exchange relationships with the non-substitutable suppliers (Seabright, Levinthal, & Fichman, 1992). Hence, non-substitutability is the position that any supplier would desire from the strategic perspective.

From the relational exchange perspective, MacNeil (1980) argues that in the course of repeated interactions, firms develop a mutual understanding and build self-enforcing mechanisms such as trust, relational norms or commitment that binds partners together and help significantly reduce transaction costs between them (Morgan & Hunt, 1994). Relational ties requires time to develop in which partners get to know each other and build reliable expectations about the future behaviors of the other (Puranam & Vanneste, 2009). As such, the repeated/frequent buyer-supplier interaction is an important foundation on which suppliers and buyers can cultivate relational ties.

In addition, the behavioral operations perspective (e.g. Gino & Pisano, 2008) suggests that individual behavioral elements such as emotions and feelings provide additional benefits that tie buyers to suppliers. From this perspective, a tight connection with the supplier is also based on the individual preferences of purchasing professionals. The degree of likability in relationships (i.e., the extent to which buyers have formed amicable attitudes toward suppliers) can provides positive emotions, social benefits, and therefore greater personal satisfactions to purchasing managers (Gligor & Autry, 2012). Overall, the likeability of suppliers from which emotional connections with buyers arise can be of significant asset to the suppliers in exchange relationships.

These three perspectives are indeed not mutually exclusive but may coexist in purchasing reality (Blocker et al., 2012). The use of multi-theoretical perspectives to guide research efforts, can potentially yield quite fruitful outcomes in understanding the foundations on which suppliers can develop IERs with buyers. (e.g. Clauß, 2012; Tangpong, Michalisin, & Melcher, 2008). Specifically, we maintain that the true equilibrium in exchange relationships sustainably beneficial to suppliers only occurs when suppliers can concurrently attain (a) economic necessity, (b) relational ties, and (c) emotional connections with buyers. When suppliers have attained only economic necessity with buyers without the support of relational ties and emotional connections, the buyers, although economically dependent on the suppliers, will have motivation to seek ways to reduce such dependence to tip the balance of power in the exchanges. Similarly, even if the suppliers have attained relational ties or emotional connections with buyers, without another cornerstone of economic necessity, the long-term sustainability of their beneficial relationships with buyers is often subject to uncertainty.

We then used the Repertory Grid Technique (RGT) to design and conduct interviews with purchasing managers to tap into what they see in suppliers as critical attributes potentially contributing to their economic necessity, relational ties, and emotional connections in the exchanges. The RGT method used in this study is described in the next section.

METHOD

Repertory Grid Technique and Interview Preparation

To identify the attributes that characterize non-substitutable, repeated/frequent, and well-liked suppliers, we apply the RGT (Kelly, 1955). RGT is a methodological tool that can be used in structured interviews to unveil individuals' perception (e.g. purchasing managers) on attributes of certain subjects of interest (e.g., different types of suppliers).

Identifying such attributes according to the RGT relies on comparison of so-called elements, which are the objects that are investigated in a study (people, situations, suppliers, relationships etc.). For the purpose of our study, the appropriate elements would be the types of suppliers that (a) reflect our research inquiry *a priori* and (b) represent the supplier types that purchasing managers (i.e., our respondents) relate to on a regular basis *a posteriori*. We specify (a) non-substitutable suppliers underlining economic necessity, (b) frequent suppliers forming the context for relational ties, and well-liked suppliers reflecting emotional connections with buyers. In addition, three more supplier types, namely quality suppliers, creative suppliers, and joint-history suppliers, were added to capture most relevant types of suppliers in a typical supplier portfolio. We organized these types of suppliers to create three pairs of contrasting supplier types: non-substitutable vs. substitutable suppliers, frequent vs. infrequent suppliers, and liked vs. disliked suppliers in addition to quality suppliers, creative suppliers, and joint-history suppliers. As a result, each purchasing manager in the RG interview process of this study focused on nine specific suppliers. In total, we involved 24 experienced purchasing managers from German manufacturing firms from various industries in RGT interviews.

Interview Procedure

During the RGT interview interviewees are provided with three elements (i.e. three supplier types) at a time and asked which pair they perceive to be similar to each other but different from the third one. The interviewee was asked to describe the unifying attribute (i.e. construct pole) and the differentiating attribute (i.e. contrast pole) with words or phrases (Kelly, 1955; Wright, 2004). In total, 168 attributes were thus elicited from the 24 interviews in this study. After the elicitation phase, each interviewee rated each of his/her suppliers based on his/her perceptions on supplier attributes (i.e. using a six-point rating scale ranging from 1 (construct pole fully applicable) to 6 (contrast pole fully applicable).

Aggregation of Results

In order to quantitatively analyze RGT data and to characterize the supplier types based on supplier attributes, an aggregation of the 168 identified supplier attributes is necessary. Therefore, two independent coders sorted all attributes (i.e. considering the meaning of the word and phrases for construct as well as contrast pole) iteratively into subgroups until homogeneous attribute groups of similar meanings are built. Thereby, the 168 supplier attributes could be allocated into 23 groups of higher-order supplier attributes. Based on this aggregation, a collective super grid (Wright, 2004) was created by calculating the average rating for each supplier attribute. We then calculated an analysis of variance (ANOVA) with LSD post-hoc procedure to test the significance of the differences of the mean values.

RESULTS

Our RGT analysis revealed 23 supplier attributes that are perceived by purchasing managers in characterizing the nine supplier types. In contrast to substitutable suppliers, the suppliers considered non-substitutable and attaining economic necessity in the buyers' perception are primarily characterized by innovativeness, being organized, uniqueness, competence, flexibility, ease to work with, commitment to the task, conscientiousness, friendliness, and helpfulness. Furthermore, being renowned, friendliness, helpfulness, risk-taking, flexibility, uniqueness, reliability, and ease to work with, are attributes associated with more frequent suppliers who are likely to form relational ties with buyers. Finally, suppliers with which purchasing managers like to work and cultivate emotional connections with, are significantly different from disliked suppliers regarding helpfulness, friendliness, trustworthiness, being renowned, sympathy, competence, uniqueness, being organized, risk-taking, communicative, cooperative, flexibility, innovativeness, commitment to the task, reliability, and conscientiousness.

In sum, we find that only four supplier attributes, (1) helpfulness, (2) friendliness, (3) uniqueness, and (4) flexibility, can potentially cultivate economic necessity, relational ties and emotional connections with buyers concurrently. These attributes supposedly help suppliers form IERs with buyers and are regarded as suppliers' primacy attributes.

DISCUSSION AND CONCLUSION

Our study provides relevant findings for suppliers on how to accomplish IERs with buyers. The four attributes: helpfulness, friendliness, uniqueness and flexibility of suppliers, are the primacy attributes that are shared among the non-substitutable, repeated/frequent, and well-liked suppliers in purchasing managers' perceptions. Our study also reveals theoretical implications that can further enrich the BSR and SC literature. First, this study underlines the importance of using multi-theoretical perspectives to guide research studies in BSRs and SCs. As illustrated in this study, to understand suppliers' attributes contributing to the development of IERs with buyers, it requires the mixture of the strategic perspective, relational exchange, and behavioral operations in guiding the research effort. Second, the findings in this study could also relate to the system dynamics perspective on behavioral operations (e.g. Tangpong et al., 2014). That is, the attributes in forms of friendliness and helpfulness, which are more on personal level, can potentially result in economic necessity and relational ties, which are more on organizational levels, and vice versa, reflecting self-reinforcing mechanisms between the two levels.

From managerial standpoints, this study offers two useful implications. First, the findings of this study underline that helpfulness and friendliness are suppliers' attributes critical to achieving economic necessity, relational ties, and emotional connections with buyers. As such, personality and attitudes of suppliers' decision-making agents toward the buyers' agents, although it may seem subtle, become a salient consideration in suppliers' staffing decisions (Gligor & Autry, 2012). Second, as both personal- (i.e., helpfulness and friendliness) and organizational- (i.e., uniqueness and flexibility) level attributes of suppliers can help them form sustainable and impregnable exchange relationships with buyers, implying different options (i.e., personal vs. organizational approaches) in forming such impregnable relationships with buyers.

REFERENCES

Blocker, C. P., Houston, M. B., & Flint, D. J. (2012). Unpacking what a "relationship" means to commercial buyers: How the relationship metaphor creates tension and obscures experience. *Journal of Consumer Research,* 38 (5), 886-908.

Clauß, T. (2012). The Influence of the Type of Relationship on the Generation of Innovations in Buyer–Supplier Collaborations. *Creativity and Innovation Management,* 21 (4), 388-411.

Gino, F., & Pisano, G. (2008). Toward a theory of behavioral operations. *Manufacturing & Service Operations Management,* 10 (4), 676-691.

Gligor, D. M., & Autry, C. W. (2012). The role of personal relationships in facilitating supply chain communications: A qualitative study. *Journal of Supply Chain Management,* 48 (1), 24-43.

Kaufman, A., Wood, C. H., & Theyel, G. (2000). Collaboration and Technology Linkages: A Strategic Supplier Typology. *Strategic Management Journal,* 21 (6), 649-663.
Kelly, G. (1955). *The psychology of personal constructs.* New York: Norton.

MacNeil, I. R. (1980). *The new social contract: An inquiry into modern contractual relations.* New Haven: Yale University Press.

Morgan, R. M., & Hunt, S. D. (1994). The Commitment-Trust Theory of Relationship Marketing. *The Journal of Marketing,* 58 (3), 20-38.

Paulraj, A., Lado, A. A., & Chen, I. J. (2008). Inter-organizational communication as a relational competency: Antecedents and performance outcomes in collaborative buyer-supplier relationships. *Journal of Operations Management,* 26 (1), 45-64.

Puranam, P., & Vanneste, B. S. (2009). Trust and Governance: Untangling a Tangled Web. *Academy of Management Review,* 34 (1), 11-31.

Seabright, M. A., Levinthal, D. A., & Fichman, M. (1992). Role of individual attachments in the dissolution of interorganizational relationships. *Academy of Management Journal,* 35 (1), 122-160.

Tangpong, C., Hung, K.-T., & Li, J. (2014). Agent-system co-development in supply chain research: Propositions and demonstrative findings. *Journal of Operations Management,* 32 (4), 154-174.

Tangpong, C., Michalisin, M. D., & Melcher, A. J. (2008). Toward a typology of buyer-supplier relationships: A study of the computer industry. *Decision Sciences,* 39 (3), 571-593.

Tangpong, C., Michalisin, M. D., Traub, R. D., & Melcher, A. J. (2015). A review of buyer-supplier relationship typologies: progress, problems, and future directions. *Journal of Business & Industrial Marketing,* 30 (2), 153-170.

Wright, R. P. (2004). Mapping Cognitions to Better Understand Attitudinal and Behavioral Responses in Appraisal Research. *Journal of Organizational Behavior,* 25 (3), 339-374.

DECISION SCIENCES INSTITUTE

Discriminating Rated Leadership in the U.S Presidency from Value Content and Stylistic Variables in State of the Union Addresses: A Data Mining Methodology

Steven Silver
California State University, San Jose.
Email: sds001@calmail.berkeley.edu

ABSTRACT

Data mining methodology is used to study the content of presidential State of the Union messages. Ratings of greatness in leadership from C-Span panels of historians are defined as the dependent variables. The set of independent variables included measures of values, rhetorical style and intellective ability. Results of linear regression models with bootstrapped standard errors indicated a value facet related to self-direction and stylistic variables to significantly discriminate the expert ratings of presidential leadership by historians.

KEYWORDS: Presidential Leadership, Content Analysis, Value Factors, Data Mining.

INTRODUCTION

While the quality of decision-making is likely to have been increased by machine-based advances in AI and decision-support systems, individual leadership in government and corporate sectors remains irreplaceable. Events in the recent decade have directly indicated the strategic importance of leadership or the lack thereof in Washington to the public. The challenge of assessing leadership at the level of the U.S. Presidency, in particular, has attracted a number of investigators. One reason for this is the consummate level of leadership skills that the position demands. A second reason is the range of data on those who have held the position.

The most cited studies of presidential leadership have used ratings of biographical summaries (e.g. Lillienfeld et al 2012; Simonton 1988) or coding of a limited number of prepared speeches (e.g. Emrich, Brower, Feldman and Garland, 2001; Winter 2002) as the basis to discriminate leadership. The present study will use the content of text of State of the Union addresses to discriminate rated leadership in the US Presidency or a set of value, and stylistic variables.

State of the Union addresses are prepared reports delivered to Congress annually. Although these are scripted documents, the general argument in the support of the use of such documents as representative corpuses in the study of presidential leadership has been that presidents have been shown to commonly make changes in texts written by others to ensure they are congruent with their own views and style (Winter 2002)

Among prepared addresses, there are additional reasons to assess content in the running text of *State of the Union Addresses* rather than the more commonly used *Inaugural Addresses*. While *Inaugural Addresses* traditionally set out a broad statement of *goals* for an administration, they are only delivered once in a four year term. In contrast, annual *State of the Union Addresses* are more closely related to accomplishments as well as "visions" and promises. *State of the Union Addresses* can be coded for all 20th and 21st century presidents.

While previous analyses of the content of presidential documents have used human coders to generate levels of study variables, we will introduce a data mining methodology to discriminate presidents on the expert ratings of leadership. Although current capabilities data in mining are best described as "works in progress" in coding the natural language of diverse documents generated by historically significant individuals, they are efficient in coding well-defined and contextualized content.

There are both substantive and methodological objectives to this study. The first objective in this application is to further our understanding of the person component of leadership evidenced in the U.S. presidency. Since this is recognized as a consummate leadership position in the world, contributions to our understanding may have important transfers to the definition of leadership across a range of ranks in government and industry. The second objective of the study to be reported is to advance the methodology that can be applied in content analysis. The computer-based methodology that will be implemented offers the possibility of increased reliability and efficiency of coding large databases from representative content for analyses of leadership. The study can also supplement results of previous studies of motive content (e.g., Winter (2002) since personal and social values are commonly cited organizers of belief systems that remain to be comprehensively assessed across presidents.

LITERATURE REVIEW

A number of investigators have coded *Inaugural Addresses* and/or their own selection of representative speeches by presidents on cognitive style and measures of social motivation (e.g., Suedfeld, Cross and Brcic 2011, Winter 2002). In one of the more rigorously executed and influential studies of presidential leadership, Simonton (1988) had abstracts from standard biographical sources rated on an adjective checklist measure of personality traits and cross-classified traits with measures of leadership "style" abstracted from historians descriptive writings on presidents.

In this and subsequent work, Simonton (e.g. Simonton 2013) recognized that manifested greatness in presidential leadership is a function of both innate abilities and environmentally generated learning. The latter factors roughly labeled as environment enabled opportunity has been emphasized and elaborated in admirable detail by Kernell (1997), Lowi (1986) and Skowronek (1997) among others.

More recently, Lillienfeld, Waldman et al (2012) investigated what they designate as "psychopathic personality traits" that can be adaptive for political leadership. These authors used ratings of biographies by historical experts and student coders with controls for rated intelligence and power motivation. In their result, "fearlessness and interpersonal dominance" were the major traits associated with higher job performance. "Impulsiveness and anti-sociality" were associated with negative job performance.

Although limited to one or two presidents, Suedfeld, Cross and Brcic (2011) found that individual values can be tracked in presidential speeches. Additionally, there is indication that qualities of political leadership that can include values are largely robust across cultures (e.g. Dorfman et al 2012). Ahn and Ettner (2012) have documented the timelessness in leadership related values from analysis of literature across periods that begin in Ancient Greek civilization. Recent application have shown that values can be meaningfully grouped into facets that are combinatorial of the individual values to discriminate "left" and "right" political orientations (Piurko, Schwartz and Davidov 2011) and competitiveness in social dilemmas (Sagiv, Sverdlik and Schwartz 2011). Construct validity for the value facets has been reported in studies that include Piurko et al (2011) and Sagiv et al (2011).

THEORETICAL DEVELOPMENT/MODEL
Defining Factors of Leadership

There are now extensively cited differentiations of the factors of leadership (Bass, 1985; Bass, Avolio, Jung and Berson 2003). While these were initially assessed in questionnaire studies that demonstrated reliability and construct validity (e.g. Rowold and Heinitz, 2007), some measures of the factors have been applied to presidential leadership (e.g. House,

Spangler and Woycke, 1991). The most commonly cited factors have been designated as *transformational, transactional* and *charismatic*. Transformational leaders are considered to emphasize higher motive development and arouse followers' motivation by means of creating and representing an inspiring vision of the future (Bass, 1997). Transactional leadership emphasizes capabilities in getting procedural tasks completed (e.g. congressional approval of appointments and legislation). Charismatic leaders transform the needs, values, preferences and aspirations of followers. These leaders motivate followers to make significant personal sacrifices in the interest of some mission and to become less motivated by self-interest and more motivated to serve the interests of the larger collective (House, Spangler and Woycke, 1991).

Greatness in presidential leadership as rated by historians and political scientists, appears to have principal dependencies on transformational that, in turn these factors would seem to be closely related to values. Accordingly the values will be the predominant independent valuables in the study.

Value Facets in the Study of Presidential Leadership

Although not comprehensively studied in the presidency, background studies of corporate leadership have commonly cited the primacy of values (e.g. Kanter 2011). Values in the comprehensive Schwartz Survey of Values (SVS e.g. Schwartz 1994) have been organized in *facets* that are *constellations of values*. The facets show trade-offs inherent in value systems at higher levels of organization than individual values.

The value facets that will be operationalized in this study are to discriminate presidents on characteristics leadership are *power*, *self-direction*, *benevolence, universalism* and *security.* These are defined in Schwartz's (1994) values in Table 1. In combination, these value facets relate leadership to an open perspective, as in internationalism, belief in change and a willingness to transcend self-oriented motives. These are qualities that historians have recognized in defining dialogues on presidential leadership (e.g. Barber 1992).

Study Variables and Methodology

Dependent variables.

Ratings of Contextualized Leadership. We use the ratings of C-Span historians and related professionals on the leadership of US presidents on ten contexts of leadership as the dependent variable. These include international relations, economic engagement, crisis management and vision in setting an agenda. The dimensionality of ratings on each of sub-dimensions that are defined will be examined in principal component analysis.

C-SPAN Raters of Presidential Leadership

For the year 2000 ratings, C-SPAN's academic advisors used a survey in which participants used a 1 ("not effective") to 10 ("very effective") scale to rate each president on ten qualities of presidential leadership: "Public Persuasion," "Crisis Leadership," "Economic Management," "Moral Authority," "International Relations," "Administrative Skills," "Relations with Congress," "Vision/Setting An Agenda," "Pursued Equal Justice for All," and "Performance Within the Context of His Times."

Surveys were distributed to 147 historians and other professional observers of the presidency. Sixty-five agreed to participate. Participants were guaranteed that individual survey results remain confidential. Summary Ratings Survey responses were tabulated by averaging all responses in a given category for each president. Each of the ten categories was given equal weighting in the total scores. Results of ratings in 2000 were updated in 2009 to include an additional president they generally provide evidence of the stability of the rates.The full set of ratings can be seen at www.c-span.org/presidentialsurvey <http://www.cspan.org/presidentialsurvey>.

Independent variables.

As indicated, measures of personal and social values will be introduced as independent variables hypothesis testing because of the importance they have demonstrated in document analysis and observed behavior and their extensive citations in self-reports on leadership and fundamentals of organizational culture (e.g. Cameron and Quinn 2011).

Facets of *power*, *self-direction*, *benevolence*, *universalism* and *security* as defined by Schwartz (e.g. 1994) and Sagiv, Sverdlik and Schwartz (2011) will be supplemented by a measure of socialized power motivation (i.e. power used for social rather than personal objective, McClelland and Boyatzis, 1982) and measures of rhetorical style. An example of socialized power motivation would be "We must not change the regime for our purposes but for the greater good of the people". McClelland and Boyatzis (1982) have suggested use of power for social objectives to be a quality of leadership. Measures of rhetorical style that are likely to be related to leadership include *abstractness in discourse* and *inclusiveness in referents*. (Emrich, Brower, Feldman and Garland, 2001). It has been suggested by these authors that more accomplished leaders make more extensive use of these qualities in their communications. Updated ratings of presidential intellect (Simonton 2006) as an ability measure supplements the above measures.

Table 1 summarizes definitions of values and rhetorical variables investigated as independent variables. Since numbers of words are likely to relate to the counts of variables that are hypothesized to discriminate presidents on demonstrated leadership, an appropriate control for this independent variables will be included in all analysis.

Table 1: Definition of Coded Values, Motives and Rhetorical Style

Power	authority, dominance, leadership
Self Direction	choosing your own goals, creativity, curiosity, freedom, independence
Universalism	a world at peace, broadmindedness, equality, inner harmony, social justice, unity with nature,
Benevolence	forgiveness, friendship, helpfulness, honesty, loyalty, responsibility
Security	family security, health, national security, reciprocation of favors, sense of belonging, stability of social order,
Negative	Measure of activity inhibition McClelland and Boyatzis (1982); neither, never, no more, not, in contexts of power invocations.
Non-Inclusive	Level of inclusion in referents: he, she, I, it, you vs. we, us, our (Seyranian and Bligh, 2008)
Abstractness vs Concreteness	Use of nouns that have abstract referents as defined in Seyranian and Bligh (2008)
Imagery	Image based and concept based words from Martindale imagery dictionary and Toronto word pool (Emrich, Brower, Feldman and Garland, 2001).

Methodology and Procedures
Designing and Cumulating the Text Corpus for Analysis.

Annual State of the Union addresses for all 20th and 21st century presidents are available through the text of the *Congressional Record* but require recoding into machine-readable documents for the data mining.

Pre-Study Procedures.

Defining Value Facets: Schwartz's definition of individual values and value facets were designed for by this author for self-report ratings. In the SVS survey of values, each value and value facet is given a brief definition and respondents are asked to rate relative importance of the values . In the application of machine coding of values in document content, additional verbal designators were defined to adequately represent usage of an underlying value.

For this, lists of synonyms for each value in the SVS used as independent variables were compiled from *Roget's Thesaurus* (http://www.thesaurus.com/Roget-alpha-index.html) and *Word-net* for the English language (http://wordnet.princeton.edu/). Five synonyms for each value in addition to the SVS definition of the value were defined. Counts of the invocation of defined values in a facet for the document samples of a president were used to define value facet importance.

Power motivation and activity inhibition. Following a similar procedure to the one used in defining value facets definitions, a definition of power motivation and a search of synonyms for the motive as described in the procedures for defining value facets was used to construct indicators the modifier of activity inhibition from McClelland and Boyatzis (1982).

Stylistic Measures of the Rhetoric of Leadership. Modified definition of "imagery" "Abstractness vs. concreteness" and "inclusiveness" in verbal statements by Emrich et al (2001) and Seyranian and Bligh (2008) were included in the independent variables assessed here.

Content Analysis Engines. Versions of *R and SPSS* data mining sub-routines were adapted to the coding of study variables.

RESULTS

Controlling for Lengths of Statements in State of the Union Adresses. When counts of verbal indicators are used as measures of study variables, they generally are increasing with the length of the text that is coded. Methods to adjust counts of variables for total variables, using a constant denominator introduces its own biases. In the present study, the count for each variable was regressed on number of words and the residual was used as a measure of a variable's content. This method allows adjustment for length that can differ across variables.

Model Definition and Testing. To build multivariate regression models of the predictors of leadership given the large number of independent variables relative to the number of presidents, dimensionality of study variables were investigated with principal component analyses (PCA).

To support inference from the small sample size, bootstrapped standard errors[4] were used in independent sample t-tests for the statistical significance of differences across expert rated charismatic leadership. As de Winter (2013) has confirmed, t-tests generally adequate power and Type 1 error rates when applied to small samples under conditions that this study meet.

For the coded value facets listed in Table 1, a three factor solution by the criterion of eigenvalues greater than 1 was found to account for 0.73 of the total variance in the measures. The factors and their weightings are defined in Table 4.

Table 4. Principal Components of Values and Rhetorical Style Variables

	Factor1: Benevolence	Factor 2:Universalism	Factor 3: Self-Direction
Benevolence	0.718		
Abstractness	0.943		
Non-Inclusive	0.835		
Universalism		0.807	
Activity Inhibition		-0.624	
Security		0.765	
Self-direction			0.788
Power			-0.658

Confirmatory PCA indicated that factor scores accounted for .830, .609 and .871, respectively, of the total variance in the items in each of the factor definitions.

The dimensionality in the disaggregated contextual ratings of leadership in the ten sub dimension of C-Span ratings and ability measures of intelligence and openness from Simonton (2006) were also examined in a PCA. A two factor solution by the criterion of eigenvalues greater than 1 was found to account for 0.796 of the total variance in the measures. The factors and their weightings are reported in Table 5. The first factor is a composite measure of overall leadership. The second factor is a measure of intelligence and related abilities that include openness or transparency.

Table 5. Principal components of leadership and ability measures

	Factor 1: Leadership	Factor 2: Intellect
Intellectual brilliance		.696
Openness		.965
Intelligence_IC		.973
Intelligence_IIC		.974
International relation	.767	
Public persuasion	.808	
Crisis leadership	.904	
Economic engagement	.776	
Moral authority	.776	
Administrative skills	.774	

Relations with congress	.887	
Vision in setting an agenda	.830	
Pursued equal justice for all	.527	
Performance with context of the times	.963	

Confirmatory PCA indicated that the factors accounted for .884 and .714, respectively, of the total variance in the items of the factors.

The factorial representation of independent variables was then investigated in regression models with bootstrapped standard errors.

Bootstrapping (e.g. Efron and Tibshirani, 1994) generates smaller standard error estimates for small size samples by resampling methods that build the equivalent of larger sample sizes.

The resampling method that is implemented in this study is as follows.

1.Fit the model and retain the fitted values and the residuals

2.For each pair, (x_i, y_i), in which x_i is the (possibly multivariate) explanatory variable, add a randomly resampled residual, , to the response variable y_i. This creates synthetic response variables where j is selected randomly from the list (1 … n) for every i.

3.Refit the model using the fictitious response variables and retain the quantities of interest (often the parameters, estimated from the synthetic).

4.Repeat steps 2 and 3 a statistically significant number of times.

Regression Model of the Rated Greatness Factor. Results for a regression model of the factors of C-Span rated greatness in leadership indicated that only the self-direction factor was statistically significant (b= 0.537 , t= 2.1 , p=0.5). The intellect factor was in the predicted direction but not statically significant (b= .355, t=1.51, p<.12). Adjusted R^2 for the model was . 302.)

In a detailed review of results for the universalism facet across presidents, it was noted that its invocation is greatest at the times following international treaties and founding of international institutions even when much or most of the background preparation for the events was done in a previous presidency. This observation increases the importance of more extensive controls for environmental variables that include wars and conflicts and the operation of institution in subsequent models of leadership with the defined methodology.

SUMMARY AND DISCUSSION

This study reports initial results from a data mining study of *State of the Union Addresses* for a set of concept-based predictors of presidential leadership. As noted, presidential leadership has been extensively investigated over past decades because its uniqueness and general importance to the well-being of the nation-state and the possible implications of results for high level leadership across government and industrial sectors. The empirical study reported here has used a measure expect rated of leadership as a dependent variable. A set of predictors of rated leadership in value facets, rhetorical style variables and intellective ability have been investigated. *State of Union and Corpuses* across presidents were first adjusted for total number of words in documents since content measures are commonly correlated with total number of words.

For regression model building with a small sample size, principal component analyses of the predictors were first examined. Results for an eigenvalue criterion yielded a three-factor solution. The first factor loaded most highly on the value facet of *benevolence* and the style variables of *non-inclusiveness* and *abstractness*. The second component loaded most highly on the value facets of *universalism* and *security* and power. The third factor loaded most highly on *self-direction* and activity inhibition as negative power.

A principal component analysis of the set of leadership ratings in ten contexts by a C-Span panel of historians and ability indicators that generally relate to intelligence yielded a two-factor solution. The first component was defined to be a combined leadership factor across leadership contexts. The second component was defined to be a measure of intellective ability.

The relationship of the factor extracted from the ten contextualized ratings of presidential leadership by C-Span historians to the principal components of value facet and stylistic variables were then investigated in a regression model. In these results, the factor of self-direction was found to be a significant predictor of the leadership factor derived from the C-Span ratings. An intelligence factor was in a predicted direction but not statistically significant.

Results reported here are preliminary to investigation in more complex modeling value factors in predicting presidential leadership given a small sample size. While the data analysis reported here has focused upon internalized measures of values, motives and stylistic variables in presidents, as predictors of rated leadership, it has been recognized that environments of a presidency have clear influences on evidenced leadership. The extent of this influence relative to internalized orientations of presidents and ways in which both factors interact are a direction for subsequent investigation.

The challenges in analysis that these data pose are not unusual. For example, studies that use clinical histories often face similar challenges since many of the cases occur across different time periods with observations on entities that may or may not have been in the prior time periods.

The understanding of the components of leadership and the predictors of quality in these components from the US presidency as a consummate exercise in leadership retains its potential as an important contributor to the practice of management in both government and industrial sectors. Efficient methodologies including data mining can further our understanding of the combination of internal processes and environmental events that underline greatness in leadership.

References

Ahn, M. and Ettner, L. (2012). Values-based leadership: enduring lessons from the Aeneid. *In Leadership through the Classics* (pp. 3-21). Heidelberg: Springer.
Barber, J. D. (1992). *The Presidential Character* (4th ed.), Englewood Cliffs, NJ: Prentice-Hall.
Bass, B. M. (1985). *Leadership and Performance Beyond Expectations.* New York, Free Press.
Bass, B. M. (1997). Does the transactional–transformational leadership paradigm transcend organizational and national boundaries? *American Psychologist*, *52*(2), 130-139.
Bass, B. M., Avolio, B. J., Jung, D. I. and Berson, Y. (2003). Predicting unit performance by assessing transformational and transactional leadership. *Journal of Applied Psychology, 88*(2), 207-218.
Bilsky, W., Janik, M. and Schwartz, S. (2011). Structural organization of human values-evidence from three rounds of the European Social Survey. *J. Cross-Cultural Psychol.*, *42*, 759-776.
Breiman, L., Friedman, J., Olshen, R. and Stone, C. (1999). *Classification and Regression Trees*. New York, CRC Press.
Budanitsky, A. and Hirst, G. (2006). Evaluating Wordnet-based measures of lexical semantic relatedness. *Computational Linguistics*, *32*(1), 13-47.
Cameron, K. S. and Quinn, R. E. (2011). *Diagnosing and Changing Organizational Culture Based on the Competing Values Framework*. Hoboken, NJ: John Wiley and Sons.
Chen, J., Hsieh, G., Mahmud, J. U. and Nichols, J. (2014, February). Understanding individuals' personal values from social media word use. In *Proceedings of the 17th ACM conference on Computer supported cooperative work and social computing* (pp. 405-414).
C-Span Survey of Presidential Leadership. (2000).
http://www.americanpresidents.org/survey/historians/overall.asp
de Winter, J. (2013). Using the Student's *t*-test with extremely small sample sizes. *Practical Assessment, Research and Evaluation*, 18, 1-12.
Dorfman, P., Javidan, M., Hanges, P., Dastmalchian A. and House R. (2012). GLOBE: A twenty year journey into the intriguing world of culture and leadership. *Journal of World Business,* 47(4), 504-518.
Efron B. and Tibshirani R.J., (1994). *An Introduction to the Bootstrap*, Boca Raton, FL: CRC, Press
Emrich, C. G., Brower, H. H., Feldman, J. M. and Garland, H. (2001). Images in words: Presidential rhetoric, charisma and greatness. *Administrative Science Quarterly*, *46*(3), 527-557.
González, I., Déjean, S., Martin, P. G. and Baccini, A. (2008). CCA: An R package to extend canonical correlation analysis. *Journal of Statistical Software*, *23*(12), 1-14.
House, R. J. and Shamir, B. (1993). Toward the integration of transformational, charismatic and visionary theories. In M. Chemers and R. Ayman (eds), *Leadership: Perspectives and Research Directions*: 81-107. New York: Academic Press.
House, R. J., Spangler, W. D. and Woycke, J. (1991). Personality and charisma in the US presidency: A psychological theory of leader effectiveness. *Administrative Science Quarterly*, 364-396.
Kanter, R. (2011) How great companies think differently. *Harvard Business Review*, Nov. 66-78.
Kernell, Samuel. *Going Public: New Strategies of Presidential Leadership*. Washington, D.C: CQ Press, 1997.
Lilienfeld, S., Waldman, I., Landfield, K., Watts, A., Rubenzer, S. and Faschingbauer, T. (2012). Fearless dominance and the US presidency: Implications of psychopathic personality traits for successful and unsuccessful political leadership. *Journal of Personality and Social Psychology*, *103*, 489-505.
Lowi, Theodore J. *The Personal President: Power Invested, Promise Unfulfilled*. Ithaca: Cornell University Press, 1986
McClelland, D. C. and Boyatzis, R. E. (1982). Leadership motive pattern and long-term success

in management. *Journal of Applied Psychology*, *67*(6), 737-743.
Mosteller, F. and Wallace, D. L. (1963). Inference in an authorship problem: A comparative study of discrimination methods applied to the authorship of the disputed Federalist Papers. *Journal of the American Statistical Association*, *58*(302), 275-309.
Piurko, Y., Schwartz, S. H. and Davidov, E. (2011). Basic personal values and the meaning of left-right political orientations in 20 countries. *Political Psychology*, *32*(4), 537-561.
Rokeach, M., Homant, R. and Penner, L. (1970). A value analysis of the disputed Federalist papers. *Journal of Personality and Social Psychology*, *16*(2), 245-250.
Rowold, J. and Heinitz, K. (2007). Transformational and charismatic leadership: Assessing the convergent, divergent and criterion validity of the MLQ and the CKS. *The Leadership Quarterly*, *18*(2), 121-133.
Sagiv, L., Sverdlik, N. and Schwarz, S. (2011). To compete or to cooperate? Values' impact on perception and action in social dilemma games. *European Journal of Social Psychology*, *41*(1), 64-77.
Schwartz, S. H. (1994). Are there universal aspects in the content and structure of values? *Journal of Social Issues, 50*, 19–45.
Sebastiani, F. (2002). Machine learning in automated text categorization. *ACM (CSUR)*, *34,* 1-47.
Seyranian, V. and Bligh, M. C. (2008). Presidential charismatic leadership: Exploring the rhetoric of social change. *The Leadership Quarterly*, *19*(1), 54-76.
Simonton, DK. (1988). Presidential style: Personality, biography and performance. *Journal of Personality and Social Psychology* 55: 928-36.
Simonton, D. K. (2006). Presidential IQ, openness, intellectual brilliance and leadership: Estimates and correlations for 42 US chief executives. *Political Psychology*, *27*(4), 511-526.
Simonton, D. K. (2013). If innate talent doesn't exist, where do the data disappear. In Kaufman S (Ed.) *The Complexity of Greatness: Beyond Talent or Practice* (pp. 17-26). Oxford: Oxford University Press
Skowronek, Stephen. The Politics Presidents Make: Leadership from John Adams to Bill Clinton. Cambridge, MA: Harvard University Press, 1997.
Suedfeld, P., Cross, R. W. and Brcic, J. (2011). Two years of ups and downs: Barack Obama's patterns of integrative complexity, motive imagery and values. *Political Psychology*, *32*(6), 1007-1033.Taboada, M., Brooke, J., Tofiloski, M., Voll, K. and Stede, M. (2011). Lexicon-based methods for sentiment analysis. *Computational Linguistics*, *37*(2), 267-307.
Winter, D. G. (2002). The motivational determinants of leadership. In R. Riggio, S. Murphy and F. Pirozzolo(Eds.), *Multiple Intelligences and Leadership* (pp. 119-138). Mahwah, NJ: Erlbaum.

DECISION SCIENCES INSTITUTE

Individual Adoption and Use of HR Analytics: Implications of Organizational Adoption

Roslyn Vargas
Nova Southeastern University
Email: roslyn@nova.edu

Yuliya Yurova
Nova Southeastern University
Email: yy21@nova.edu

Cynthia Ruppel
Nova Southeastern University
Email: ruppel@nova.edu

ABSTRACT

High performing organizations are using analytics and evidence-based decision-making. However, human resources (HR) has been slow to adopt this innovation, when the company has adopted analytics and when it has not. This study applies innovation theory, including the Theory of Planned Behavior, to study the adoption and use of HR analytics to identify why the adoption rate may be lagging. Whether or not the company has adopted analytics has an impact on the innovation-decision process and how it moves through the theoretical stages. Attitude was found to be important to HR Analytics adoption and use regardless of company adoption.

KEYWORDS: HR Analytics, Theory of planned behavior, Innovation adoption, Innovation use, Attitudes

DECISION SCIENCES INSTITUTE

Influence of the CEO Characteristics in Mergers and Acquisitions in the Pharmaceutical Industry

Alejandro Sanchez
University of Texas Rio Grande Valley
alejandro.sanchez01@utrgv.edu

Michael A. Abebe
University of Texas Rio Grande Valley
michael.abebe@utrgv.edu

ABSTRACT

It is the purpose of this study to make an analysis of the Mergers and Acquisitions, affected by the CEO characteristics and mediated by the Environmental Munificence. The motive of this paper is the high economic scope of the cross border M&A in the pharmaceutical industry. The characteristics to analyze would be the CEO's tenure, functional background and education. It is being recognized that a long tenure of the CEO is in direct relation to the M&A intensity. A last factor is the CEO education. It appears that there is a positive correlation of the education with the M&A performance.

.

KEYWORDS: Managerial decision making, Firm decisions, Mergers and Acquisitions, CEO characteristics

INTRODUCTION

Poliomyelitis, smallpox, typhoid fever. Those are practically words of the past. But then cancer made its apparition. And then HIV came to hit the society. Sicknesses have changed, but still are sicknesses. And maybe worst, after a cure was found for an illness, another sickness came into the scenario. In one way or another, medical research is a never ending task. That is what the pharmaceutical companies do. Sometimes the cure is far away out of reach for the patients. And the pharmaceutical firms are those that would place the drugs available for the sick. The mission is to find a cure for the sick. And if a pharma company is not operating very well towards this mission, other firm surely would take over. That is when a Merger and Acquisition transaction would take place. Executives in charge of these operations must be extremely careful and skilled to perform successful M&A deals. That is what this study is about.

Taking care of the massive health of people requires high abilities in the pharma companies. There is a long path in regards to investments, research in patients and development, to the final marketing and availability for patients. From the perception of a cure, the research and development, to the testing, clinical trials and approval for market, According to Health Care M&A Information Source, July 2014, the Novartis Corporation acquired the oncology business from the GlaxoSmithKline Corporation for the amount of $16,000 Mill. Yet, this operation was not the only one among these two companies. GlaxoSmithKline plc acquired from the Novartis Corporation the global vaccine business for $5,250 Mill. The proper processing of these two operations would have required a super high amount of skills and knowledge in the CEOs of these firms.

Just by looking at the numbers, asymmetric information could be detrimental for the performance of a company. Keeping with the same source, Actavis plc acquired Forest Laboratories, Inc., for the amount of $25,000 Mill. As we see these figures, it is easier to understand why the Pharmaceutical companies are taking extreme measures into the positioning of their respective CEOs. These positions are highly visible, and any wrong action could end in a damaging M&A operation for the company. Yet, as we see, the companies are switching their business lines and this appears to be in the best convenient mode for them. Therefore, the CEOs still need to operate in the best interest of the companies.

The importance of the analysis of Mergers and Acquisitions cannot be neglected if the number of these operations is continuously increasing. The number of M&A from 1973 to 1979 was 789, compared to 1427 in the 80s, and 2040 in the 90s. These numbers account only to the USA. Also another factor to include is the growing trend to keep the M&A within the own industry. The percentage of M&A from 1973 to 1979 was 29.9% for the own industry, and then growing to 47.8% in the 90s. (Andrade, Mitchell and Stafford, 2014). How can a CEO acquire the talent and then utilize that skill to first recognize the market environment and make an enough out of risk assessment that he or she needs to proceed to a merger or Acquisition?

As we can see in the Figure 1, the total amount spent in M&A in the pharma industry in USA in 2009 was over $140,000 Mill. Data from Levine and Associates, Deals and Deals Makers. In these transactions, the intent to do more research and provide more drugs available for illness is present.

Figure 1

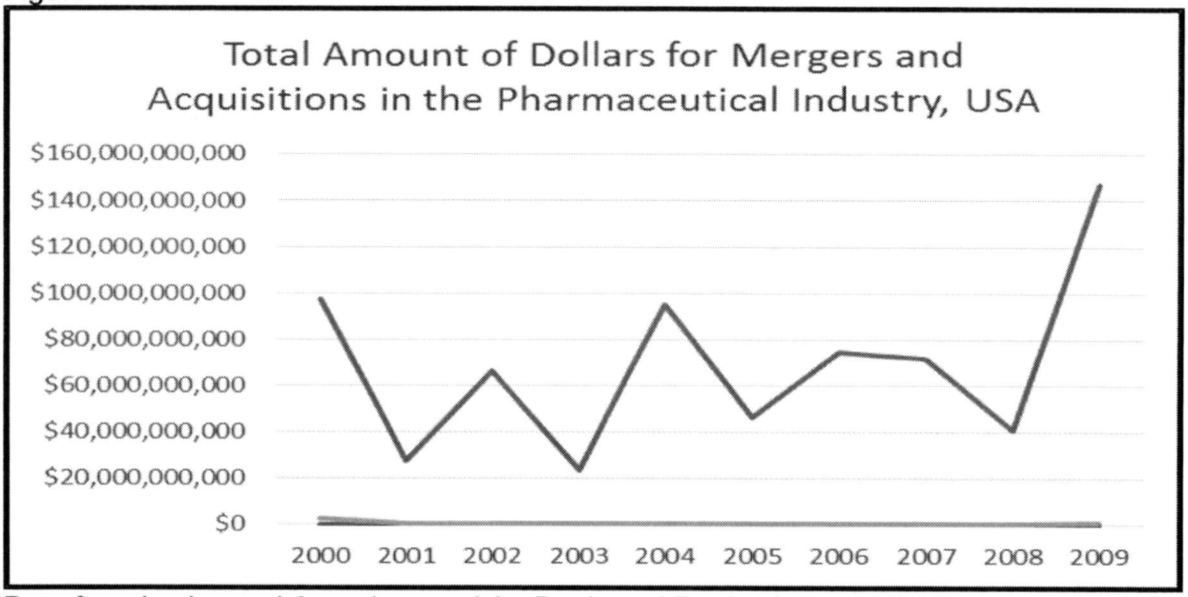

Data from Levine and Associates article. Deals and Deals Makers. A great increase from 2008 to 2009. Source; Health Care M&A Information Source, July 2014.

One aspect that may be worth to analyze is the increase of mergers and acquisitions increase in certain industries and an apparent decrease in other industries. The increase of the operations appears also to be related to a leading research. In the pharmaceutical industry, for example, the leading research is on the cancer, AIDS and Diabetes. In these regards, the authors want to expose the dynamic of the M&A operations in the global industry. By looking at the areas of

M&A, it can be seen that the Multinationals are looking for the trends in the needs of their customers, hence, the social media, real estate, energy and pharmaceutical.

Then, what appears to be an alignment of the Multinational with its own needs is in fact the response of the CEO to the needs of the customers. In other words, the Multinationals are focusing in the combination of maximizing their shareholder value and attaining their customer needs. Pfizer, one of the world pharmaceutical giants, in the brink of a splitting operation, decided to go back and instead manage the Innovative Health and Essential Health businesses. (www.marketwatch.com, 2016, 09/26). Hence, we can say that the M&A process is under a continuous education in the CEOs at the multinational level. Executives are learning what the customer needs and what the Multinational must do.

LITERATURE REVIEW

Upper Echelons Theory

The question of "Why do organizations act as they do?" (Hambrick and Mason, 1984)(p. 193), has opened a wide scope of items to discuss and solve. One of the sides in the answers is the dominance of the coalition on the managers. Yet, the upper echelon theory emphasizes the individual characteristics in the context of the organizational outcomes. Hence, a upper socializing skill in the management may also need to be included. The upper vision may not be exclusive of an individual, but it may be laterally shared. Yet, in order to share information in the management teams, these groups need to have certain characteristics (Nadolska and Barkema, 2013). Thus, they have to be homogeneous.

Also, by looking at the M&A total dollars in the later years in Figure 1, the question of the learning experience by the top management teams appears to have an answer. They learn from past experience, and the trend in the value of the operations is to increase.

Overview of Mergers and Acquisitions

Years ago, it was evident that firms were not taking the right path in regards to where to go when there was a need for merging and acquisition, this statement said because the great number of failed acquisitions, (Barkema and Schjiven, 2008). The trend of the "Merger mania" (Lubatkin, 1983) allured firms to proceed into this process, but the path they took may not be the right, if there was a real need for the merging or Acquisition. However, if the Environmental Munificence is providing support to a competitor, then it is obvious that the Munificence can sustain growth also to the CEO firm. Hence, we can assume with an acceptable degree of confidence that the major corporations in the pharma industry have been learning in how to proceed to the best M&A operations throughout the years, that lately these operations have become more profitable.

Haleblian et al (2009) provided a clear analysis for the beginning of the Acquisition process by listing the value creation and Managerial Self-Interest antecedents. The legitimate desire in the corporate for a market power due to the external competition leads the organization to the M&A. Haleblian mention the cases of the railroad industry and the airline mergers where the final outcome is the raise in stock prices or prices in routes. Even though the prices rose by a factor not disclosed, the "prices on routes serviced by merging firms increased relative to those of a matched sample unaffected by the merger", quoting Kim and Singal, 1993. The service to the customer improved in a greater percentage than the prices.

The CEO functional background may be significant due to the roll playing in the growing number of Mergers and Acquisitions within the same industry. Firms are performing more M&A in the same field of specialty and there is a trend to minimize the out of field M&A. Firms are merging in their area and are diversifying products within their market. The organizational outcomes are being seen as parameters of the knowledge of the main human elements in the Firm, (Hambrick and Mason, 1984). As the merger or acquisition is an outcome of the organizational operation, this action is a product of the CEO performance.

And to continue with this concept analysis, it may become important to explore as an antecedent also Schoenberg (2003), "Individual companies can have a wide range of motives for making an acquisition. These may broadly be classified into three groups: strategic motives, financial motives, and managerial motives", Therefore, assuming the election of a new CEO in a firm, with the Environmental Munificence supporting capability to the competition, this new CEO will see that the firm has one or several combinations of motives for a Merging. The characteristics of the CEO to be able to visualize these needs would have to depend on the tenure, or time in the firm and the functional background. As an additional factor, the gender of the CEO is also included in the analysis.

Need of new content in cross border mergers and acquisitions

According to Lubatkin (1983), following the three FTC classifications, there is not enough evidence to support the synergy association with the size, type and experience of the Firm because the studies that have been performed are more of surveys with Executive opinions instead of actual performance data. Furthermore, the base study of Kitching (1967) has a small sample size that does not support the generalizability of the results.

The Kitching (1967) study appears to open a need for solving the issue of conglomerated mergers. Lubatkin (1983) is proposing an analysis of a large sample of mergers. Hence, the main obstacle in this regards may lie in the fact that conglomerated mergers are not in great numbers that could supply enough statistical information. Furthermore, the suggestion of the use of the Capital Asset Pricing Model inherently implies a merging immobility for the acquiring firms (Lubatkin, 1983) that render available data unfit for the research analysis.

Deepak et al, (1992), found the evidence of a decreased wealth for the bidding firm shareholders when the merging takes place among multiple bidders and conglomerate acquisitions. This finding is in line with the Supply and Demand Law. It is obvious that at more bidders, the final bidding Firm would be the one with the higher proposal, implying a reduction in dividends. This evidence may open the opportunity for an analysis of the Agency Theory in the Mergers and Acquisitions model.

Larsson and Finklestein (1999), findings are clear in the correlation of the synergy realization construct with the Merger Performance. Considering the construct of Synergy, in the analysis they performed, the inclusion of the Combined Potential, Organizational Integration and Employee Resistance; it appears that the concept of Leadership may be a common factor for those three elements in the Synergy construct. This study may have to be performed to cover the need of Leadership in the merger operation. And Leadership may be a rare competence in an environment where for both bidder and target firms; management does not have a full communication across the companies.

Cartwright and Schoenberg (2006), highlights the need for meta-analyses that may study the M&A, making a link of the performance of the models with the human and organizational insights from behavioral studies. Their analysis recognizes that the actual research is not complete nowadays in this field. As an example, Stahl and Voight (2004), p.14, remains with the lack of explanation for a high variance.

A final gap in the research lies in the lack of a deep analysis in the explanation of the high acquisition failure rates. Rostand (1994) reported failure rates of 44-45%, and Kitching (1994) reported 46-50%. As it can be seen, both analyses are congruent in the numbers. The question then could be, to propose a model that would make a good fit for a successful acquisition. One of the obstacles may lie in the repeatability with following acquisitions. Under this gap lies also the fact of the negative average returns. (Agrawal and Jaffe, 2000), (Gregory, 1997). A model with a map analyzing the path taken from the value or values involved in the acquisition may be helpful to clarify the lower returns.

An idea that kept appearing in the search is the relation between the intensity of the mergers and acquisitions and the proper development of the country in the study. Other leading analysis in the merger and Acquisition intensity is the uncertainty. The uncertainty is not necessarily related to the environment munificence. The munificence could be supporting the merged company enough for growth, but the uncertainty can at the same time be a hindrance for a major development in the firm. The last aspect of the analysis is the Executive characteristics as a role in the Merger and Acquisition process. Gosh et al (2014) suggested already the connection between the development of a country and the intensity of the merger and acquisitions. There could be two sides to this section of the analysis: the own development of the country provides the opportunity for the firm to look for the Merger, or the firm see the trend and then look to grow by this means. The munificence of the environment is a factor in the Merger and Acquisition (Sofka and Grimpe, 2010), (Dickson et al, 2013).

Absorptive capacity

The level of the firm to engage in a merger for a target company will be depending also in the absorptive capacity, the slack on resources and the opportunities outside of the firm. As the firm grows, the risk associated with the growth will have a lower cost (Johanson and Vahle, 2009). At this moment, a Small or Medium Size Company (SME) will be looking forward to the growth. And one of the most viable ways of growth is throughout the internationalization. Dickson, Weaver and Vosikys (2013) made an analysis of the external factors leading to the internationalization.

In Figure 2, we can see the increase of transactions from 2013 to 2014.

Figure 2

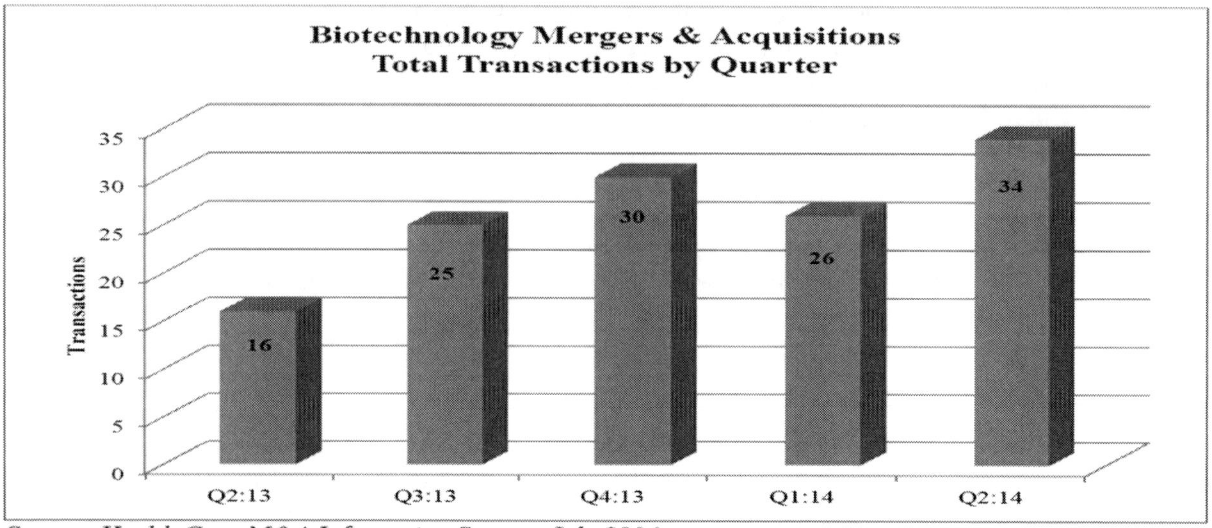

Source: Health Care M&A Information Source, July 2014

Number of M&A in second quarter 2014. Source; Health Care M&A Information Source, July 2014.

A factor to consider is the characteristic of the Firm as a strategic buyer (De Leew, 2009). In The strategic buyer there must be a need for investment, hence, the choice between a new investment and an investment in merging. (Bittlingmayer, 1996). In these conditions, the tenure of the CEO is a key factor for the decision. Even though some research shows that there has been some disastrous results, (Nadolska and Barkema, 2014), if we take a look at the merging and acquisitions in the Pharmaceutical Industry, we can see that these kinds of operations have been mostly successful. Therefore, we must take a look at the CEO characteristics in the field to be able to see what it takes from the CEO to be a good performer. The need of power (Ravenpor, 1993) is not only in the CEO, but it may be an extension on this position of a characteristic of the firm. The firm must always be looking for a balance for the external competition power, because this is a continual force towards the firm. One of the most effective ways to keep back competition is to perform strategic buys or mergers that would close the way for the competition. Therefore, we come to the assumption that the absorptive capacity may also depend in the economic capacity of the firm.

Synergy

Once the CEO and the Board of Directors of the Firm are making the decision for a Merging or Acquisition, it can be useful to turn to the findings of Kitching (1999, p. 91): "The sum of the managerial competence in the parent company plus that of the acquired company fails to equal or exceed the demand of the management tasks found in the newly merged organization", hence, it is critical for the CEO to make an objective assessment of the synergy that can be obtained with the resources togetherness. If the CEO makes the right decision to envision the total managerial competences after the merging, and if these competences are above the necessary, then the merging will be successful. The total amount of Managerial Capabilities must be superior to those required to lead the organization. After this stage, then, begins the learning experience.

Even though there is not enough research in who learns from organizations, (Nadolska and Barkema, 2014), the learning in the firm after the Merging and Acquisition may go far beyond that just the CEO. We can take the example of a manufacturing firm, after the acquisition of a smaller company. The transfer of physical resources and knowledge will necessarily affect the chain command. It is clear that after the operation, the acquiring company will be learning from the top down to the lower management levels from the operation performed. This scope of improved knowledge can be an asset for the CEO to keep on targeting other companies. The Absorptive Capacity (Cohen and Levinthal, 1994) may not necessarily be only in a technological field. This capacity may also include the power of the firm to move when the market conditions change to a more favorable scenario. These changes may include lower taxes, incentives, and labor or raw materials availability.

Role of Environment in Mergers and Acquisitions

The environment plays an engulfing factor around the firm, affecting positively or negatively the performance of the company (Dickson, Weaver and Vosikis, 2013), (Mezias, Park and Choi, 2008). The environment's characteristic is a factor that the CEO only in a few occasions may be able to change, but most of the time, he or she must be forced to act in the conditions dictated by the munificence of the environment. With the solid assumption that the CEO cannot change the environment, therefore, the CEO is the one that must adjust the innovations searching strategies (Sofka and Grimpe, 2010), (Abebe et all, 2011) in order to dig into the environment for opportunities for the firm. Another assumption is that the environment plays the same importance for any firm that stays in touch with the surrounding conditions. The proposition that some companies may not have the same environment effect will not be considered for this analysis. Then, if the environment conditions are equal, hence, the question, why some companies proceed to a merging, or acquisition, or even leave the market, while other firms continue to operate under those conditions?

In order to proceed with the most accurate possible analysis, the economic assumption of "Ceteris Paribus" can be embedded into the inside the firm organizations, Therefore, we will be making the assumption that all CEOs in any company under the influence of the same environment, they all will have the same executive characteristics. From this point, then, the conclusion is that the Environment must have a dynamic behavior. This behavior would have a moving resource capability, giving to the resources certain mobility in the background of the company. However, there are different levels and optics to see the mobility of the environment. In the first scale, we have the munificence at the positive side, and the uncertainty in the other side. Gosh, Bhowmick and Guin (2014) identified two types of levels: the static dimension and the simple-complex dimension. The linkage or explanation of the environment behavior to the executive performance may lie due on the assumption that the characteristics of the environment are not always afloat in the exposed surface of the surrounding factors. Instead, the opportunities may come out and then hide, or the risk and threats may also have a similar behavior. Under this condition, the CEO must have the executive vision well open for the signs of threat or opportunity in the environment. Sometimes those signs may appear in a shadowy pattern and it may be difficult to spot a munificent environment or an uncertain condition.

Executive characteristics in the Mergers and Acquisitions

Overconfidence

It may appear that the overconfidence is a subtle feeling in the CEO, but further research suggests a deeper reason in the executive for this behavior. A quick analysis in some literature will be supporting the fact that the CEO overconfidence is based in the knowledge of facts that are unknown to the rest of the participants or observers in the Merger and Acquisition. Bouwman, Fuller and Nain (2002) found the relation of the stock market with the Mergers and Acquisitions intensity. In their research, the quantity of these operations increased at the higher-valuation market seasons; however, the performance of the acquisitions during high-valuation markets was lower to those acquisitions on lower-valuation markets. Their conclusions are taking us to the finding that CEOs aim to perform more mergers and acquisitions when the target company has a higher value. What is the reason behind this behavior? The cause of the purchase for a higher value may be in the taxing reasons.

Another section of the Bouwman, Fuller and Nain (2002) paper is the Herding behavior, however, The Herding behavior, as per Milbourn, Boot and Thakor, (1999), propose the cause of a desire of an outstanding CEO position, 'involving banks that increase size and scope despite a dissipation of shareholders wealth". In the opposite side, the M&A decision at the acquiring company would hardly depend on the CEO only (Nadolska and Barkema 2014). This decision will usually be on the Top Management. And as we know, in the Top Management Teams, the CEO positions sometimes rotate or are taken from inside the group. So we can make the assumption that the Top Management Teams have CEO characteristics that are similar among the group.

Upper echelons theory

The theory of the tenure of the CEO would give to this position a leader power. This power is supported by the upper echelons theory. Hambrick and Mason, (1984) and Hambrick and Snow, (1977) propose the concept of the field of vision of the CEO, based in that from this position, the CEO may not be able to see in detail everything that is happening in the firm. But the CEO, with the functional background or experience, together with the time in the position, can be able to make an assessment of the Munificence around the firm. The common factor in the decision maker's cognitive base is the knowledge; hence, knowing about the future, alternatives or consequences is the most important skill in the CEOs for the performance in the Firm, when the mergers and acquisitions would be performed.

Tenure

Hambrick and Fukutomi analyzed the CEO tenure time towards the performance in the firm. It appears that the performance follows an inversed U shape, with a sharp higher number of M&A at the middle time of the tenure, then following a decline in performance. Their study is based in previous research by Eitzen and Yetman, (1972).

We see this topic as an interesting approach to analyze how the CEOs steers to the M&A operations. We cannot assume that the CEO performance is related to the pharma company performance in the long period of time, because we have data for 3 years, due to the availability of their tenure years. In order to analyze for more years, the number of CEOs would be more than one for the period of time, or we would have to analyze fewer companies with the longer tenure of the CEOs. Therefore, the 3 years period appears to be a benchmark data for the CEO performance.

THEORY AND HYPOTHESIS DEVELOPMENT:

Model and Propositions

Figure 3

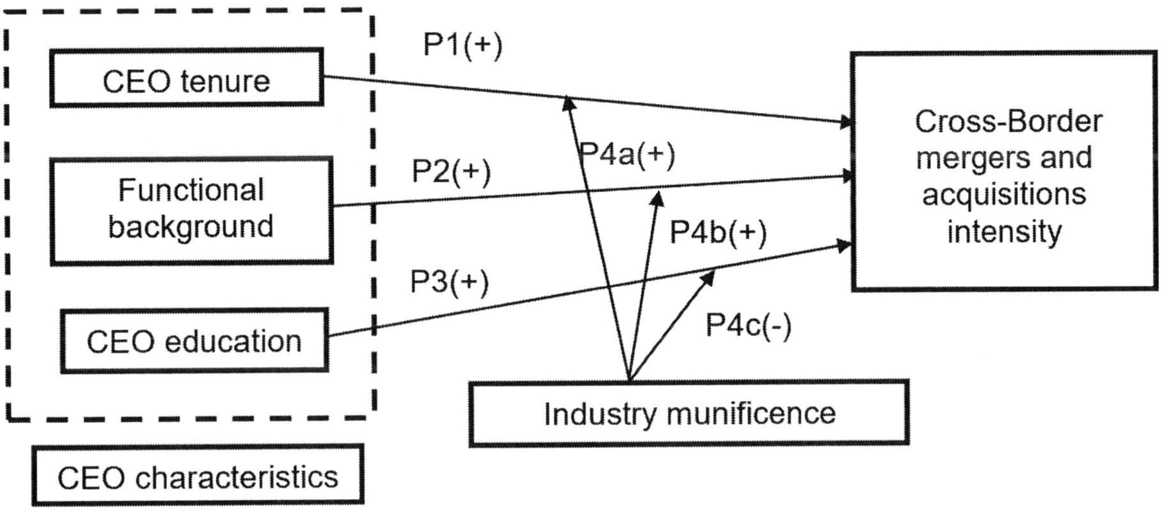

Model and Propositions

Propositions

Proposition 1:

Previous studies (Dikolli, Mayew and Nanda, 2014) found that the CEO tenure is in direct relation with the Firm performance. The CEO earnings are also in an inverse relationship with the CEO turnover. Some findings show that performance from the CEO is positively related whit low to moderate tenure and then the relation becomes negative with greater tenure from the CEO.

P1 (+) Tenure of the CEO will be positively related to the Mergers and Acquisitions Number

Proposition 2. Functional Background.

There are some discrepancies in the studies in regards to the relationship of the background to the intensity of M&A. Some papers argue that the background affects directly the intensity of M&A, while others found that there is no true connectivity of the background to the M&A, however, the significance of some findings that highlight the lack of relation of the educational background with the CEO current performance cannot be neglected. One important skill on the background of the CEOs with a successful performance could be the "leadership and interpersonal skills that are necessary for high –level managerial success" (Gottesman and Morey, 2010, p. 79).

Proposition 2 (+) Functional Background of the CEO will be positively related to the Mergers and Acquisitions number.

The perception of the gender participation in the Merger and acquisition may appear to be downsized or silenced. “The men have their own business language”, (Tienari, 2000), hence, this area may have been underexplored. 20 years after the Glass Ceiling Commission study of the barriers for women and minorities, (Johnson, 2013), the scenario appears to be changing. However, the barriers may not be just vertical, because the apparent obstacles for women to move horizontally to key decision positions. But inside our hypothesis may be an apparent scenario typical to some firms, and that is the effect of the women inside the boards. While the women may not have the leading position, still they may be exerting an authority force behind the board table. Some firms Boards have a more diverse members and the relation of the women to the outcome of M & A will be analyzed in this hypothesis.

Proposition 3

P3 (+) Education of the CEO will be positively related to the Mergers and Acquisitions Number.

P4a (+) The Tenure of the CEO in a more munificent environment will increase the Number of M&A.

Proposition 4

P4b (+) The Functional Background of the CEO will be positively influenced by a more munificent environment to perform a greater intensity of M&A.

P4c (-) The education of the CEO, in a more munificent environment, will be positively related to the intensity of the M&A.

METHODS

Firms Research

For this research, it is being proposed to collect data in Firms that have been performing the most Mergers and Acquisitions from 2010 to 2014 year. The data is being obtained from the Mergent database. We are obtaining a list of 468 firms, however, only the companies with 10 years or more of age will be considered. Also, in the database downloaded, somehow it filtered a couple of firms that may be in the SIC 2834, but with most of the activities in other area, like in the Energy or Petroleum industry. Those companies are not included.

Other data that is also being considered to eliminate firms is the number of employees in 2014. Those with a 0 number of employees on the year 2014 are not being considered. Thus, from 468 firms, after the data filtering, we are obtaining a list of 202 companies in the pharmaceutical industry, with activities in the merging and acquisitions, with employees in 2014 and active in the industry.

Other missing information was in the number of employees in some years, mostly in 2014 and 2015; hence the companies with no employees in those years have to be eliminated. The total amount of companies that did not have the employee’s number was 108. This deduction reduced our sample to 94 companies.

Method

The following factors are in the research:

1. Intensity of the Cross Border Mergers and Acquisitions. Dependent Variable. Number of operations. We are going to use the cross border merging and acquisitions quantity.
2. Tenure of the CEO. Independent Variable. Years
3. Age of the CEO. Independent Variable. Years.
4. Functional Background. Independent Variable.
5. Environment Munificence. Independent Variable. Measured by the percentage increase of the sales from the previous year.

Intensity of the Mergers and Acquisitions

Quantity

The purpose of this research is to gather information in the number of M&A operations that the Firm has performed under the same or late CEO in the position. We are looking to assemble data Cross Border operations from 2012 to 2014. This variable would be giving the first idea of the intensity of M&A.

Number of shares of the Firm before the operation

How many shares the acquiring firm had before the operation. This number would supposedly be lower than after the operation.

Tenure

Time in the position in years

Background.

Education:

Does the CEO has the following schooling?

1. No bachelor
2. Bachelor
3. Master Degree
4. MD or Ph.D.
5. MD and PhD

Some CEOs may only have a bachelor degree and there are some examples were the CEO does not have a bachelor degree.

Munificence

Percentage of sales increase per year. The data obtained were from the years 2012, 2013 and 2014.

RESULTS

The major findings in the research are that the older companies perform the M&A operations more frequently. However, from the major companies, some companies do not engage in these operations so much, or less than the competition, and they obtain higher sales percentage. Therefore, the M&A operations involve a risk that the major companies are facing. However, in return of the risk, the companies are acquiring overseas business units with important research included. Then we could say that the M&A operations are linked to the research, but the risk is more inherent to the research itself. This finding is in line with the risk taking behavior of the CEOs. To expand on this matter, the M&A operations have the risk located in the research and development divisions linked to the movement.

DISCUSSION AND CONCLUSIONS

CEO characteristics

In conclusion, in regards to proposition 1, the low to moderate term in the tenure is being proposed to be in the 3 years, as an average for the 5 years, to 7 years. Within this period, it appears that the performance of the CEO is being positive for the company and that after that period of time, apparently there is a consensus between the company and the CEO that this position must be renewed by other person.

In regards to the functional background, it appears that there is not enough support for the proposition 2 for the direct relation of the functional background to the performance in regards to M&A. This finding appears to be congruent with the answer provided by Warren Buffet if from upper Universities CEOs produce better financial performance. According to Mr. Buffet, the answer is no. Gottesman and Morey (2010), Hymowitz (2006), Wall Street Journal, However, the question is about the background. Yet, in this paper, the background seems to be non-related to the performance of the CEO. Some pharma companies have CEOs from completely different fields. And they still are doing a significantly good performance. Nevertheless, as we see the data and the changes in the CEOs, the notion of a deeper information interchange appears to surge in this environment. A future gap in this field may be the need of more research about the connection of the CEOs with the company. It appears that there is a connection of the good performers CEOs with the best performers companies.

What can be seen from the background analysis may remain inconclusive due to the specific discipline of the pharma industry. The CEOs must have a Medical career included in the background. A mixture of academic research with business acumen and advanced Medicine knowledge are essential tools for CEOs in the pharma industry. The inconclusiveness lies in the possibility of CEOs with other background. This scenario is not very common.

In regards to the education, the results may be different of the Gottesman and Morey (2010) findings. A probably significant addition done in this paper is the advanced education degrees from the CEOs. A substantial aspect arises when the CEOs have a PhD, or even more if they speak different languages. These characteristics are significantly positively correlated to a good performance of the firm, in regards to the M&A operations. Hence, the combination of multilingual skills, MD, and PhD from a related discipline appears to be determinant of a successful performance as CEO. Another characteristic that must be considered is the Law studies in the CEOs. Apparently, the pharma companies are including these CEOs in their boards to be prepared for patent contingencies, very common in this area.

We would suggest for future studies, an interesting detail that appeared in the data. Some pharma companies were going thru the M&A process, simultaneously within. Each company is acquiring a branch of the other company. The acquisitions have been an ongoing research with an already marketed product, or a segment of the company. However, the number of these operations is not great enough to analyze, but the economic amount is high. We do not know how the pharma companies decide to do this type of "castling" movement. Due to the fact that only a few of the best pharma companies are doing these operations, the probable best way to analyze these movements is by the inclusion of other type of companies, doing the same type of operation. This analysis may open the door to how the CEOs in the greater companies operate together for their advantage and the advantage of the customers.

Upper echelons theory

Another conclusion that could be adapted from the important contribution of the Hambrick and Fukutomi (1991) model, (p. 195) is the possible inclusion of the mediating effect of the surrounding boards or groups that the CEO belongs to. This model clarifies the process for the decision making in the CEO. Thus, a possible addition to this model could be the external input for the decision. This external input may not necessarily belong to the environment. In other words, the environment itself for the organization may be affected significantly by the CEO, being more notorious at the change of the CEO.

REFERENCES

Abebe, M. A., Angriawan, A., & Liu, Y. (2010). CEO power and organizational turnaround in declining firms: does environment play a role? *Journal of Leadership & Organizational Studies*, 1548051810385004.

Bebchuk, L. A., Cremers, K. M., & Peyer, U. C. (2011). The CEO pay slice. *Journal of Financial Economics*, *102*(1), 199-221.

Bittlingmayer, G. (1996). Merger as a Form of Investment. *Kyklos*, *49*(2), 127-153.

Bouwman, C. H., Fuller, K., & Nain, A. S. (2009). Market valuation and acquisition quality: Empirical evidence. *Review of Financial Studies*, *22*(2), 633-679.

Castrogiovanni, G. J. (1991). Environmental Munificence; A Theoretical Assessment. *Academy of Management Review*, *16*(3), 542-565.

Deals and Dealmakers. The Health Care M&A Review, Second Quarter, 2014, Vol. 19, No. 2, 2014. Irving Levin Associates Publications and Services.

Dess, G. G., & Beard, D. W. (1984). Dimensions of organizational task environments. *Administrative science quarterly*, 52-73.

Dikolli, S. S., Mayew, W. J., & Nanda, D. (2014). CEO tenure and the performance-turnover relation. *Review of accounting studies*, *19*(1), 281-327.

Ferris, S. P., Jayaraman, N., & Sabherwal, S. (2013). CEO overconfidence and international merger and acquisition activity. *Journal of Financial and Quantitative Analysis*, *48*(01), 137-164.

Fung, S., Jo, H., & Tsai, S. C. (2009). Agency problems in stock market-driven acquisitions. *Review of Accounting and Finance*, *8*(4), 388-430.

Gottesman, A. A., & Morey, M. R. (2010). CEO educational background and firm financial performance. *Journal of Applied Finance (Formerly Financial Practice and Education)*, *20*(2).

Hambrick, D. C., & Fukutomi, G. D. (1991). The seasons of a CEO's tenure. *Academy of management review*, *16*(4), 719-742.

Hambrick, D. C., & Mason, P. A. (1984). Upper echelons: The organization as a reflection of its top managers. *Academy of management review*, *9*(2), 193-206.

Hymowitz, C. (2006, 09, 18). 'Any college will do' Nation's top chief executives find path to the corner office usually starts at State University. Retrieved from: http://www.wsj.com/articles/SB115853818747665842, on Feb 15, 2015.

Kitching, J. (1967). Why do mergers miscarry? *Harvard Business Review*, *45*(6), 84-101.

Malmendier, U., & Tate, G. (2008). Who makes acquisitions? CEO overconfidence and the market's reaction. *Journal of financial Economics*, *89*(1), 20-43.

Nadolska, A., & Barkema, H. G. (2014). Good learners: how top management teams affect the success and frequency of acquisitions. *Strategic Management Journal*, *35*(10), 1483-1507.

Sinkovics, R. R., Zagelmeyer, S., & Kusstatscher, V. (2011). Between merger and syndrome: The intermediary role of emotions in four cross-border M&As. *International Business Review*, *20*(1), 27-47.

Sofka, W., & Grimpe, C. (2010). Specialized search and innovation performance–evidence across Europe. *R&d Management*, *40*(3), 310-323.

Stahl, G. K. (2004). Getting it together: The leadership challenge of mergers and acquisitions. *Leadership in Action*, *24*(5), 3-6.

Tienari, J. (2000). Gender segregation in the making of a merger. *Scandinavian Journal of Management*, *16*(2), 111-144.

DECISION SCIENCES INSTITUTE

Information Exchange Research Opportunities

Sandeep B. Jagani
Central Michigan University
Sandeepkumar.Jagani@CMich.edu

Anand S. Kunnathur, PhD
University of Toledo
Anand.Kunnathur@UToledo.edu

Steven A. Wallace, PhD
University of Toledo
Steve.Wallace@UToledo.edu

ABSTRACT

Building upon the concept of information exchange for business sustainability that gathers, stores and makes available the data related to business processes and products including their basic raw materials, manufacturing processes, the end of life of the product and its potential recycling contributed by organizations through which this product has traveled, we conceptualize how the information from such information exchange will affect traditional methods of doing business and outline research opportunities emerged as a result of interaction of the information exchange and businesses. Further we discuss potential contributions of information exchange towards environmental performance and business sustainability of firms.

KEYWORDS: Information Exchange, Business Sustainability, Environmental Performance, Big data, industrial ecology

INTRODUCTION

Today's economy runs on information. On one hand, companies want to make right investment in right information technologies and systems to manage information that is being generated by themselves internally as well as by sources external to their organizations. Efforts to synthesize this information and utilize it in their organizational setting differ from firm to firm depending on the level of resources and constrain the firm function in (Keller, 1994). But their goal remains to generate stake holder value by making the best use of the information which they have access to. On the other hand, because of rising environmental stewardship goals, companies utilize the information to redesign strategies, products and processes that fit with their environmental objectives. These two objectives are often considered as conflicting. However, when considering the sustainability point view, information can be utilized in such a way that company continues to be environmentally responsible and at the same time keeps growing stakeholder value. To make strategic sustainability decisions, firms need access to accurate external information. Therefore, if there was a centralized data warehouse or an information exchange that gathers, stores and makes available the product lifecycle information associated to business processes and the composition of the products, managers and decision makers across firms will be able to make appropriate sustainability related decisions (Jagani, Wallace, & Kunnathur, 2016). The data gathered by this information exchange are expected to be contributed by various participating organizations through which the product and its components travel during the complete lifecycle. It can make the highest possible contribution to business sustainability goals supply chain or industry wide. This data is not limited to carbon emission or hazardous composition that the product and its components emits during its life cycle but also business processes, manufacturing processes as well as social impact information that each components has made during their journey to the product. This paper outlines various research opportunities during interaction of information exchange and firms who uses it.

The rest of the paper is organized as follows. First, we conduct an extensive literature review to identify the current themes on how information affects traditional methods of doing business. Concurrently, we identify research gaps in the literature and we call for research that bridge these gaps. Next, we identify the overlaps or crossover in business process which information form information exchange creates. Finally, we discuss potential contribution of information exchange towards environmental performance and business sustainability of firms.

LITERATURE REVIEW

Figure 1 is a representation of interaction of Information Exchange (IE) with Business processes. The arrows from information to each of the five critical business processes are the research opportunities which will lead to business sustainability of firms.

Figure 1: Proposed Research Opportunities

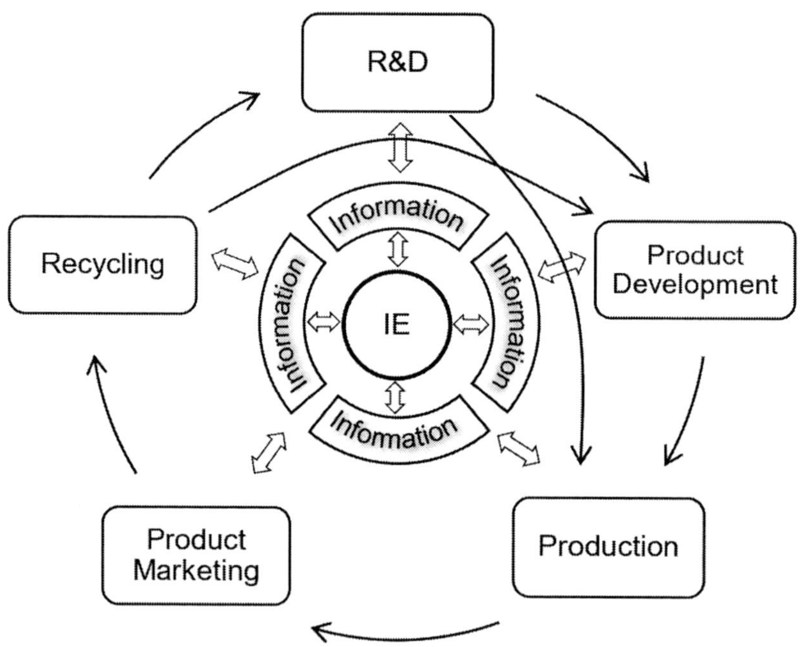

Affecting R&D

A firm' ability to recognize the value of external information and make commercial use of it is critical to its innovative performance (Cohen & Levinthal, 1990). Since, organizational knowledge creation depends crucially upon the information processing capacities of the organization, firms need to carefully manage external information. Zahra and George (2002) argues that it is firms absorptive capacity, based on type of work force, infrastructure and organizational culture, that transforms the available knowledge into innovative ideas. An organization assimilates information about the environment through environmental scanning activities, and this information is communicated to and is shared between functions and departments (Frishammar & Åke Hörte, 2005). Though, it is necessary for this information to be evaluated by door keepers for making key decisions, this information at further stage contributes to the knowledge base of the firm. To our knowledge there is no research that identifies the external information in the terms of ecological data of product and process which a firm gets access to and further relates it to the R&D performance of the firm. Access to the information from information exchange increases the potential of idea generation. This affect R&D by providing environmental, competition as well as technical information and projection to identify suitable choices. The information can be used to develop new materials, new components and new process. This paper calls for research on how external ecological information regarding a product or process that a firm has access will affect R&D activities of the firm.

Affecting Product Development

There is already an adequate research done on relationship of information sharing and new product development (NPD) (Le Dain & Merminod, 2014; Wu, Ming, He, Li, & Li, 2014; Zhou & LI, 2012). When companies integrate internal knowledge for NPD using cross-functional team, it is known as internal integration (Koufteros, Vonderembse, & Jayaram, 2005) or concurrent engineering (Koufteros, Vonderembse, & Doll, 2001). However, companies often use external knowledge from suppliers, market or customers to improve product design. This is known as external integration (Koufteros et al., 2005; Petersen, Handfield, & Ragatz, 2005). Rigby & Zook (2002) with a sample of innovative companies argue that the companies that are concerned about product innovation uses external information to gain competitive advantage. Information on processes of other firms as well as environmental impacts of raw materials, components and processes obtained from the information exchange will provide a completely new external knowledge and consequently offer a different dimension to product design considering the sustainability aspects. This could not only affect the product design step of NPD by choosing right materials that go into the product but also further steps like market projection, competition information, distribution and usage pattern of the product.

Affecting Production of Products (Manufacturing Process)

External integration (Koufteros et al., 2005) is positively associated with manufacturing process improvements (Droge, Jayaram, & Vickery, 2004). On one hand, customers are the driving force behind radical process change (Davenport, 2013). Competition forces companies to increase quality, delivery speed and timeliness of the product. On the other hand, competitors and suppliers provide companies with the information that determines their processes (Avermaete et al., 2004). Information systems plays an important role in transporting the information from the source to the user firm. Tarafdar & Gordon (2007) uses resource based view to demonstrate how information systems affects the success of process innovation in an organization. Firms use IS competencies to enhance their ability to conceive, develop and implement process innovations. Previous researchers have focus on generic information as a source of knowledge that shapes companies process. However, the information from the information exchange is a specific sustainability related information that can be used to make choices about use of types of energy, sustainable practices, education and training of employees and controlling exposure to harmful environmental hazards in a process. Information systems can play a crucial role in reducing energy consumption, and thus CO_2 emissions. Watson, Boudreau, & Chen (2010) explains importance of information in one equation;

Energy + Information < Energy, (Watson et al., 2010, pp. 24)

Affecting Demand

Appropriately designed environmental standards can prompt production of innovative products by firms with lower total cost of a product or increased value (Porter & Van der Linde, 1996). Lowering the cost of products generate higher demand. Additionally, companies can use inputs, viz. raw materials, labor, etc., more efficiently enhancing resource output that makes firms more competitive. Wüstenhagen & Bilharz (2006) outlines the driver being radical growth behind green power demand in Germany during 1973 to 2003. They conclude that growth of green marketing by the company is followed by strong customer demand. Handfield, Walton, Seegers, & Melnyk (1997)'s interviews with environmental managers of five organizations and suggest that in order to be successful for an organization, environmental management strategies must be integrated into all stages of the value chain, which includes all of the processes from product design, procurement, manufacturing and assembly, packaging, logistics, to distribution. If the organization utilizes information from the exchange, they can affect demand by implementing proper education program, green advertisements, enriching products with better features and ultimately reducing carbon footprints. How sustainability information impact product demand yet to be explored.

Affecting Recycling and Reuse

Hischier, Wäger, & Gauglhofer, (2005) compared the environmental impact of waste electrical and electronic equipment recycling with that derived from incineration of all waste and primary production of the raw materials, waste electrical and electronic equipment recycling is considered valuable from an environmental viewpoint. Spath & Weule (1994) identifies need of gathering ecologically relevant product data both for recycling using computer aided information systems. Their conceptual paper calls for systematized approaches using intelligent software for disassembly planning and recycling. Potentially valuable options for the creation of micro-scale recycling markets or assistance with material management are often provided by third parties such as recyclers and logistics providers (Simpson, 2010). Information sharing with wither immediate supply chain partners or distant companies improves the organizational learning and find solutions to problems regarding complex management such as recycling. Information sharing can be facilitated by a common information exchange that can provide firms with alternative disposal and recycling choices, possibility of participation in waste exchanges and thus making a larger industrial ecosystem.

The overlaps created by Information systems

Inundation of information from the IE will bring the business processes closer creating overlapping activates. Firms will see processes that have common activities. Concurrent engineering (Koufteros et al., 2001) is an example from the past that was result of information integration in R&D, new product development and production. As shown in Figure 2, each overlaps will result in new investigation area. Data-driven sustainable R&D, product development and manufacturing tools, best practices, and standards that address cross-industry needs to help develop products and processes that offer not only economically competitive products but also with reduced environmental impact that are socially equitable. Discussion section below highlights the research needs.

Figure 2: Research opportunities from overlaps created by information systems

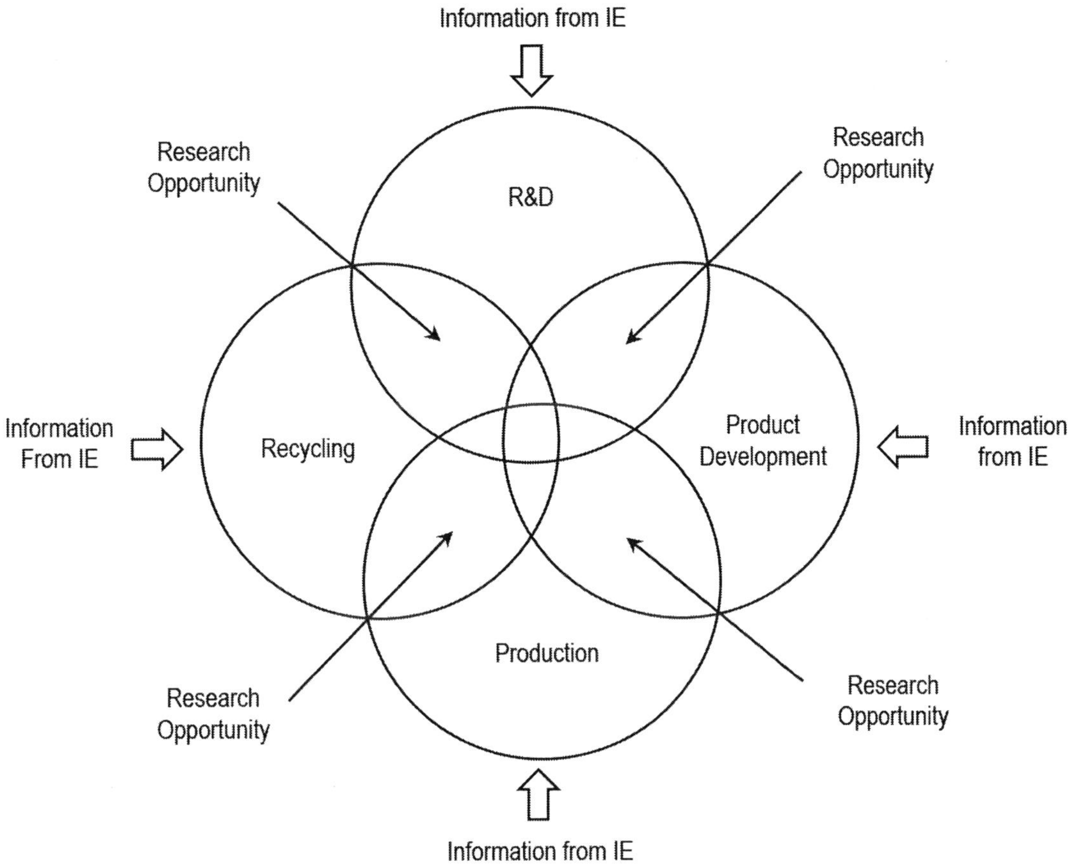

DISCUSSION

Concept of IE is similar to electronic health information exchange (Hersh et al., 2015) which allows doctors, nurses, pharmacists, other health care providers and patients to appropriately access and securely share a patient's vital medical information electronically improving the speed, quality, safety and cost of patient care. IE for sustainability will allow managers of the participating firms to make strategic decision related to sourcing, R&D, production, marketing and recycling of the products based on the information obtained from IE. Information will affect several business processes of firms that aim for business sustainability. For these firms, participation to such IE will be a powerful competitive weapon by adding new IT capabilities (Mata, Fuerst, & Barney, 1995) and attributes that will provide business sustainability.

Investigative research needs to be conducted into the following issues to fill the research gaps mentioned earlier. Several studies and investigation needs to be done to address questions related to the IE and the firms that affect business process. There are obviously overlapping areas as discussed in the previous section. The flow on information to the firm from the IE and to the IE from the firm will enumerate several issues.

As a first priority, detailed exploratory studies need to be done to identify business environments and business processes that can benefit from the aforementioned information based firm centric sustainability vision. Further, based on the findings of these exploratory studies, more focused studies would have to be done to better understand the problems and develop concepts and solutions. Next, case studies, pilot studies, and longitudinal studies need to be done to flesh out and elaborate on the identified issues and concerns which may uncover hidden issues that may require further investigation.

A comprehensive model needs to be developed for selecting the IE information to import, and the effective deployment and use of that information, to inform and/or impact. An effective strategy has to be formulated and implemented for selection of platform that best suits the needs of firms as well as most continent for the handling large amount of data. Infrastructure needed to collect and deploy the IE information has to be thought considering the resource barriers that will be lost as well as erected to stem competitive advantage.

Finally, a study of the openness of the business environment as well as their existing sustainability practices to instigate the willingness of firms to participate in the information exchange has to be done. Modifications and the associated challenges in the firm's business practices that benefit from the IE information in achieving firm sustainability needs also to be studied.

CONCLUSION

It is difficult to make strategic decisions for business sustainability with information from a single entity or even a supply chain. A high level information, from a network of firms and business processes associated with this network of firms needs to be gathered and deployed to make such decisions. Based on the proposal for IE which will act as a repository of data that can be used for business sustainability of the participating firm as well as issues related to IE and firms that are identified by Jagani et al. (2016), this research has recognized various areas that information affects business processes. Ultimately brings processes closer creating overlaps and offering opportunities for research for achieving sustainability. Further, based on the research gaps that we identified from the interaction of information systems and the business process, we suggested new areas for research and issues that need to be addressed by the IE in developing and maintaining IE. We conclude that there is a huge potential contribution of information exchange towards environmental performance and business sustainability of firms.

REFERENCES

Avermaete, T., Viaene, J., Morgan, E. J., Pitts, E., Crawford, N., & Mahon, D. (2004). Determinants of product and process innovation in small food manufacturing firms. *Trends in Food Science & Technology, 15*(10), 474–483.

Cohen, W. M., & Levinthal, D. a. (1990). Absorptive Capacity: A New Perspective on Learning and Innovation. *Administrative Science Quarterly, 35*(1), 128–152. http://doi.org/10.2307/2393553

Davenport, T. H. (2013). *Process innovation: reengineering work through information technology*. Harvard Business Press.

Droge, C., Jayaram, J., & Vickery, S. K. (2004). The effects of internal versus external integration practices on time-based performance and overall firm performance. *Journal of Operations Management, 22*(6), 557–573.

Frishammar, J., & Åke Hörte, S. (2005). Managing external information in manufacturing firms: The impact on innovation performance*. *Journal of Product Innovation Management, 22*(3), 251–266.

Handfield, R. B., Walton, S. V, Seegers, L. K., & Melnyk, S. A. (1997). “Green”value chain practices in the furniture industry. *Journal of Operations Management*, *15*(4), 293–315.

Hersh, W., Totten, A., Eden, K., Devine, B., Gorman, P., Kassakian, S., … McDonagh, M. S. (2015). Health Information Exchange.

Hischier, R., Wäger, P., & Gauglhofer, J. (2005). Does WEEE recycling make sense from an environmental perspective?: The environmental impacts of the Swiss take-back and recycling systems for waste electrical and electronic equipment (WEEE). *Environmental Impact Assessment Review*, *25*(5), 525–539.

Jagani, S. B., Wallace, S. A., & Kunnathur, A. S. (2016). A Research Framework for Business Sustainability using Information Exchange – A Firm Centric Perspective. In *Twenty-second Americas Conference on Information Systems*. San Diego: AMCIS.

Keller, R. T. (1994). Technology-information processing fit and the performance of R&D project groups: A test of contingency theory. *Academy of Management Journal*, *37*(1), 167–179.

Koufteros, X., Vonderembse, M., & Doll, W. (2001). Concurrent engineering and its consequences. *Journal of Operations Management*, *19*, 97–115. http://doi.org/10.1016/S0272-6963(00)00048-6

Koufteros, X., Vonderembse, M., & Jayaram, J. (2005). Internal and external integration for product development: the contingency effects of uncertainty, equivocality, and platform strategy. *Decision Sciences*, *36*(1), 97–133.

Le Dain, M. A., & Merminod, V. (2014). A knowledge sharing framework for black, grey and white box supplier configurations in new product development. *Technovation*, *34*(11), 688–701. Retrieved from 10.1016/j.technovation.2014.09.005

Mata, J. F., Fuerst, W. L., & Barney, J. (1995). Information Technology and Sustained Competitive Advantage: A Resource-Based Analysis. *MIS Quarterly*, *19*(4), 487–505. http://doi.org/10.2307/249630

Petersen, K. J., Handfield, R. B., & Ragatz, G. L. (2005). Supplier integration into new product development: coordinating product, process and supply chain design. *Journal of Operations Management*, *23*(3), 371–388.

Porter, M., & Van der Linde, C. (1996). Green and competitive: ending the stalemate. *Business and the Environment*, 61–77.

Rigby, D., & Zook, C. (2002). Open-market innovation. *Harvard Business Review*, *80*(10), 80–93.

Simpson, D. (2010). Organizational Information Gathering cnd Recycling Performance Outcomes. *Academy of Management Annual Meeting Proceedings*, 1–6. Retrieved from 10.5465/AMBPP.2010.54493642

Spath, D., & Weule, H. (1994). The utilization of hypermedia-based information systems for developing recyclable products and for disassembly planning. *CIRP Annals-Manufacturing Technology*, *43*(1), 153–156.

Tarafdar, M., & Gordon, S. R. (2007). Understanding the influence of information systems competencies on process innovation: A resource-based view. *The Journal of Strategic Information Systems*, *16*(4), 353–392.

Watson, R. T., Boudreau, M.-C., & Chen, A. J. (2010). Information systems and environmentally sustainable development: energy informatics and new directions for the is community. *MIS Quarterly*, *34*(1), 23–38. http://doi.org/Article

Wu, Z. Y., Ming, X. G., He, L. N., Li, M., & Li, X. Z. (2014). Knowledge integration and sharing for complex product development. *International Journal of Production Research*, *52*(21), 6296–6313. Retrieved from 10.1080/00207543.2014.923121

Wüstenhagen, R., & Bilharz, M. (2006). Green energy market development in Germany: effective public policy and emerging customer demand. *Energy Policy*, *34*(13), 1681–1696.

Zahra, S. A., & George, G. (2002). Absorptive Capacity: A Review, Reconceptualization, and

Extension. *Academy of Management Review*, *27*(2), 185–203. http://doi.org/10.5465/AMR.2002.6587995
Zhou, K. Z., & LI, C. B. (2012). How knowledge affects radical innovation: Knowledge base, market knowledge acquisition, and internal knowledge sharing. *Strategic Management Journal*, *33*(9), 1090–1102. Retrieved from 10.1002/smj.1959

DECISION SCIENCES INSTITUTE

Inside the black box of operational capabilities: an evolution from operational practices

Marcia Regina Santiago Scarpin
Fundação Getulio Vargas - FGV-EAESP
Email: mrs.scarpin@gmail.com

Luiz Artur Ledur Brito
Fundação Getulio Vargas - FGV-EAESP
Email: luiz.lbrito@gmail.com

Barbara Bechler Flynn
Kelley School of Business -Indiana University
Fundação Getulio Vargas - FGV-EAESP
Email: bbflynn@iu.edu

ABSTRACT

We investigated the relationship between operational practices and operational capabilities. We conduct a qualitative research, with case studies in four firms, two multinational American firms operating in Brazil and two local Brazilian firms. We collected data through semi-structured interviews with open-ended questions, based on our theoretical review of operational practices and operational capabilities. The interviews were conducted face-to-face. In total, 73 interviews were performed. Our main results were: First, relate the operational practices as an antecedent of operational capabilities. Second, the creation of a typology divided into two constructs: Across-the-Board Capabilities and Standalone Capabilities.

KEYWORDS: Operational practices, Operational capabilities, and Typology.

INTRODUCTION

The conceptual framework of competitive priorities has been predominantly used to define the concept of operational capabilities. The ability of a firm to compete with its direct competitors in quality, delivery, flexibility and cost, has been used to indicate the firm's operational capabilities (*e.g.* Größler & Grübner, 2006; Rosenzweig & Easton, 2010; Wheelwright, 1984). However, the decision what prioritize precedes the development of an operational capability, but it is not the capability itself. Competitive priorities help the firm to do what it wants without wasting resources in lower-priority pursuits (Wheelwright, 1984). For example, a firm's acceptance of a low rate of growth can reflect a decision to retain a set of priorities in which diversification are more highly valued than growth. If diversification is the firm's strategy, operational capabilities such as flexibility, customization, and innovation should be developed to support this strategy.

We also find articles that conceptualize and measure operational capabilities by the result. This is a problematic situation as it creates confusion with the operational performance construct (*e.g.* Cua, McKone, & Schroeder, 2001; Flynn & Flynn, 2004; Schroeder, Bates, &

Junttila, 2002). When operational capabilities are conceived and measured by performance, we get their effect, not the cause. We tend to ignore the path that leads to the result. Illustratively, it's like runners who want to reduce their time without considering the need to change their workout. We would be evaluating the result and not the ways in which time could be reduced. At the organizational level, it is like measuring the quality of the finished product, without evaluating the processes that caused this performance outcome.

Operational capabilities can exhibit equifinality and can be developed through multiple paths. Operational practices can provide an appropriate basis for its beginning (Wu, Melnyk, & Swink, 2012). Since the 90s, operational practices have underpinned many studies in this area. Considered highly standardized and easily imitable procedures, theoretically, according to the Resource Based Theory (RBT) they cannot be sources of sustained competitive advantage. But, effective implementation of "best practices" (Laugen, Acur, Boer, & Frick, 2005, pp. 131) such as total quality management, just-in-time, lean manufacturing, among others, tends to contribute to better performance.

When practices are operationalized in the internal environment of the firm, they can be incorporated as organizational routines, and through the pre-existing tacit knowledge of production, become operational capabilities, thus creating barriers to imitation. However, even with such a logical relationship, most of the operations literature refers to practices but does not mention the concept of operational capabilities (Ahmad & Schroeder, 2003; Dean & Bowen, 1994; Furlan, Vinelli, & Pont, 2011; Hackman & Wageman, 1995; Montabon, Sroufe, & Narasimhan, 2007; Swink, Narasimhan, & Kim, 2005).

One of the recent studies that brought a new approach to the field is Wu et al. (2012), in which the practices are addressed as background to operational capabilities. But despite the merit of promoting debate, and being the first to use a new taxonomy for operational capability, the theoretical argument used by Wu et al. (2012) for developing each capability is fragile and has limited empirical grounding. It uses as a basis the theoretical proposal of Swink and Hegarty (1998), in which one of the main limitations is precisely the lack of specificity of capabilities for the operations area.

In sum, the literature of operations management provides inadequate constitutive definitions of operational capabilities, does not cover the relativization to different contexts, has limited empirical grounding, and does not adequately explores the more extensive empirical literature on operational practices. This study contributes to the debate addressing the following gaps: the lack of a conceptual uniformity of operational capabilities (Flynn & Flynn, 2004; Wu et al., 2010), the lack of empirical studies about the development of operational capabilities in the firm's internal environment (Peng et al., 2008; Schoenherr, Power, Narasimhan, & Samson, 2012; Swink et al., 2005), and the relationship between operational practices and operational capabilities (Wu et al., 2012). Thus, the questions that we intend to investigate are: *what is the relationship between operational practices and operational capabilities? And, what are types of operational capabilities characterized in the firm's internal environment?*

LITERATURE REVIEW

Operational Practices

The benefits of adopting practices such as TQM, JIT, SCM, among others, applied individually are inconsistent, perhaps due to the fact that for the practices to be effective, they need to be associated with other practices over time, in an enabling environment (Benner & Tushman, 2003). Furthermore, the intensive use of operational practices can be antecedents of operational capabilities, which in turn are more rare and difficult to imitate.

Cua et al. (2001) investigated the relationship among TQM, JIT, TPM and operational performance (cost, quality, delivery and flexibility). The main results were that leadership practices, consumer involvement and emphasis on technology had a positive effect on volume flexibility performance. Lee & Kelley (2008) also found that the practices with a high level of learning and improvisation were one of the aspects that helped to develop the dynamic innovation capability. The term "dynamic capability", in this case, is merely semantic, since it is clear that the authors are referring to operational capability.

Benner & Tushman (2003) explained it is necessary for researchers to pay attention to the context in which operational practices are implemented. The industry in which the firm operates influences the type of practices used. For example, firms operating in technologically advanced environments need to develop practices related to radical innovation capability. For those that operate in static environments, the focus should be on the practices that lead to the continuous improvement capability. In general, the successful implementation of operational practices depends on individual characteristics of each firm. Firms need to assess which set of best practices fit with their production process and if they are able to implement them (Shah & Ward, 2003). Powell (1995) argued that tacit aspects linked to the environmental context create a culture where practices affect performance.

Operating practices developed over time can be transformed into an operational capability; this will depend on their level of complexity. Figure 1 of Rondeau, Vonderembse, & Ragu-Nathan (2000) identifies the path between a practice and a competitive capability.

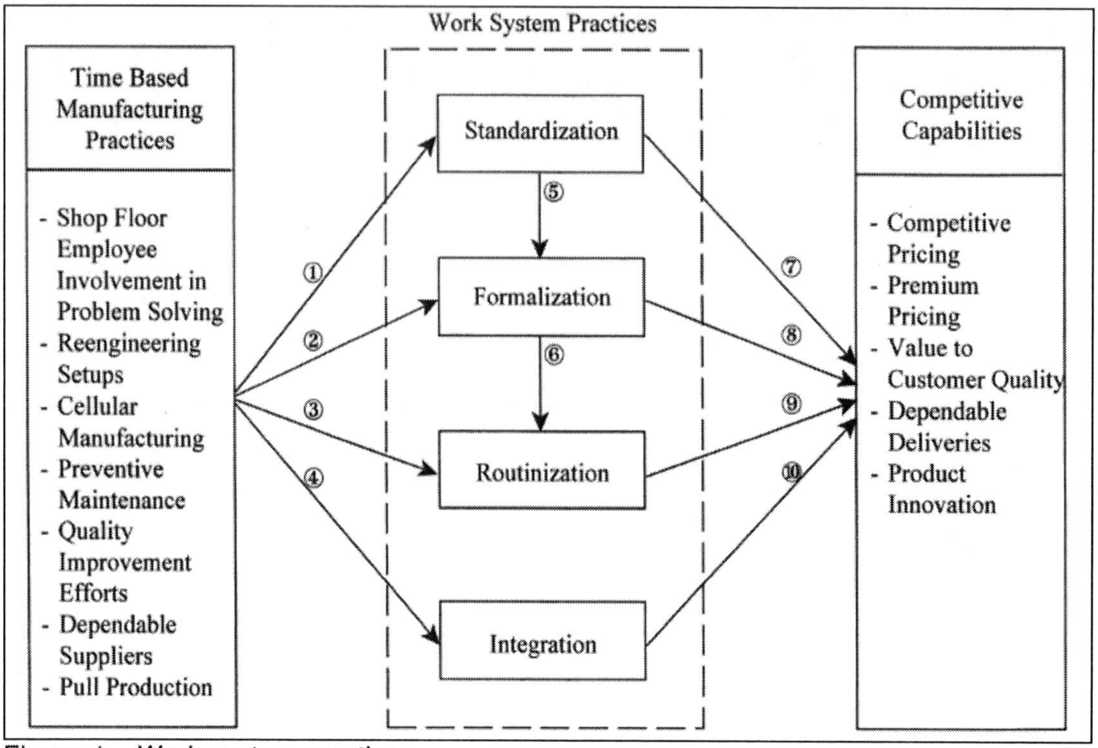

Figure 1 – Work system practices
Source: Rondeau et al. (2000)

Rondeau et al. (2000) observed that firms with standardized routines and integrated operational practices tend to be able to develop competitive capabilities. The study was conducted with 265 firms in the industries of: (1) Furniture and Fixtures; (2) Metals; (3) Industrial; Machinery and Equipment; (4) Transportation and Equipment; and (5) Instruments and Related Products. Each number presented in Figure 1 represents a hypothesis. With the exception of hypotheses three, eight, and nine, the others were confirmed in the study of Rondeau et al. (2000). The main contribution of their study was to show the mechanisms that connect practices and capabilities. Mechanisms pointed out by the authors as most important were standardization and integration. Standardization helps in the development of products and processes, and encourages employee participation in the creation, development and integration of norms that aim to increase customer satisfaction and improve production capacity. Integration, in turn, provides a way for employees to share knowledge, promote learning, and solve problems with cross-functional teams (Rondeau et al., 2000). Although the authors did not work with operational capabilities, this is one of the few studies that separates practices and capabilities, and at the same time shows their relationship.

The distinction between operational practices and operational capabilities is not clear in the literature. Wu et al. (2010) developed a metaphor related to the kitchen of a restaurant to aid in this understanding. For the authors, in a kitchen, resources are all assets, tangible and intangible, such as the stove, utensils and the ability of individuals, which together define the potential of what may or may not be executed in the kitchen, but that separately cannot achieve the ultimate goal. For example, the stove alone does not prepare a food; the chef needs instructions on how to use it along with other resources to complete the dish. The instructions in the kitchen represent operational practices, through standardized processes. Recipes and rules indicate how to combine the resources available for preparation of the dish. The problem with this, however, is that a recipe can be easily copied by competitors' restaurants. But differentiation is not the role of operational practices because they cannot capture less tangible aspects, such as the freshness and quality of ingredients or the chef's experience. The ability to develop dishes that reflect the restaurant's unique history, style and customer preference is the role of capabilities. It will be developed from the skill in food preparation and environment characteristics that are difficult to transfer from one environment to the other, since they involve interactions over time, which translates into a unique specificity of each kitchen. This set of interactions is called a capability (Wu et al., 2010). Sousa & Voss (2002) assert that it is these interaction effects that distinguish successful firms from others, creating inimitable capabilities.

Operational Capabilities

Wheelwright (1984) was the first article to bring the variables, quality, delivery, flexibility, and cost as competitive priorities. For the author, as well as Skinner (1969), firms have to choose a competitive priority and invest in it (even at the expense of other priorities) front of their competitors. This is the principle of trade-off. In contrast to the principle of trade-off, Ferdows and Meyer (1990) developed a model called the sand cone model. This model uses the same variables proposed by Wheelwright (1984). Depending on the complexity of the operational capabilities, they can change or even reinforce each other, becoming cumulative. The sequence begins with quality, goes to delivery, flexibility and ends in cost. Some studies using cumulative capabilities were Kathuria (2000), Corbett & Whybark (2001), Rosenzweig & Roth (2004), Größler & Grübne (2006), Hallgren, Olhager & Schroeder (2011), Liu, Roth & Rabinovich (2011), and Schoenherr, Power, Narasimhan & Samson (2012). In addition to studies that tested the original scale of Wheelwright (1984) and sand cone model (Ferdows & Meyer, 1990), there are those that altered it, including or removing variables (see Noble, 1995; Vickery, Dröge & Markland, 1997; Mapes, Szwejczewski & New, 2000; Flynn & Flynn, 2004; Rusjan, 2005; Peng , Schroeder & Shah, 2008; Avella, Vazquez-Bustelo & Fernandez, 2011).

In the literature review we also found some studies that operationalize the operational capabilities individually. These studies address new operational capabilities, expanding their scope. Some researchers emphasize a unique operational capability, analyzing it deeply in order to understand its role in the value chain. In total were found eight operational capabilities: (1) information systems integration; (2) continuous improvement; (3) innovation; (4) flexibility of processes; (5) mass customization; (6) quality management; (7) supply chain management; and (8) learning. These are described below.

Information System is the capacity to manage a set of tangible assets (e.g. information systems hardware, network infrastructure) and intangible (e.g., software patents, strong vendor relationships) formed from the productive use of information technology (Wade & Hulland, 2004). Continuous improvement is the firm's ability to gradually increase its operational performance (Swink & Hegarty, 1998). Radical innovation creates, improves or implements unique processes that radically improve operational performance (Swink & Hegarty, 1998; Wu et al., 2010, 2012). Flexibility is the operational response capacity of the firm to make changes in its inputs and outputs (Swink & Hegarty, 1998; Wu et al., 2010, 2012). Customization reflects the firm's ability to customize its products to meet the specific needs of its market, producing on a large-scale, for the short-term, and at a cost that is comparable to mass production of non-customized products (Zhang et al., 2003). Quality programs include contextual elements associated with exploratory learning and tacit knowledge and methodological elements related to exploitative learning and explicit knowledge tend to sustain a competitive advantage (Choo, Linderman, & Schroeder, 2007). Supply chain management (SCM) is "defined as a set of three or more entities (organizations or individuals) directly involved in the upstream and downstream flows of products, services, finances, and/or information from a source to a customer" (Mentzer et al., 2001). Miller (1996, pp. 486) described organizational learning as the "acquisition of new knowledge by actors who are capable and have willingness to apply it in their decision making or influencing others in the organization."

Operational Capabilities and Dynamic Capabilities

Operational capabilities are classified as substantives, ordinaries, or zero order capabilities (see Figure 2). These capabilities are a set of abilities and resources that will be used to solve problems, achieve results, or develop new products (Zahra et al., 2006). The term operational capabilities is used by strategy scholars in a different meaning than the one used in this article. It does not focus capabilities related to the Operations Management function, but to all organizational capabilities that are zero order. The Operations Management function can have capabilities of zero and first order.

Dynamic capabilities are first order capabilities. According to Zollo and Winter (2002, pp. 340), they develop "the learned and stable pattern of collective activity through which the organization systematically generates and modifies its operating routines in pursuit of improved effectiveness." Their induce a learning process, helping the creation and development of zero order capabilities (Collis, 1994; Zahra et al., 2006).

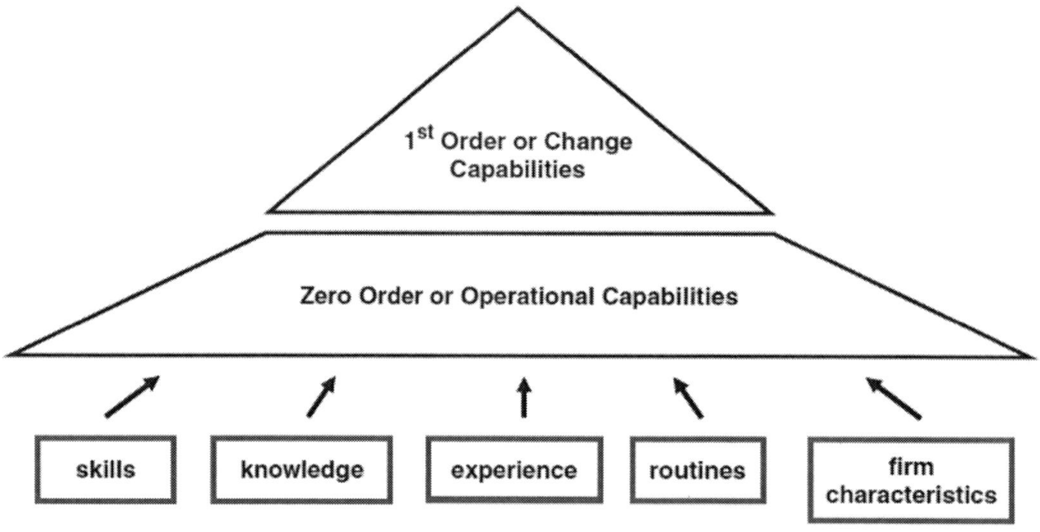

Figure 2 – Winter's capability hierarchy
Source: Hoopes and Madsen (2008)

METHODOLOGY

This multiple case study consists of four cases (Eisenhardt & Graebner, 2007). The use of multiple cases allowed us to understand the patterns that emerged from the data of each case. Cases were based on a variety of evidence, to make them theoretically robust. Each case followed the same research protocol. The main method used was semi-structured interviews in different functions, but technical visits, report analyses, and observations were also conducted. These multiple sources of evidence facilitated the triangulation process (Eisenhardt, 1989). They allowed us to examine the relationship between operational practices and operational capabilities and identify the types of operational capabilities within each case and subsequently cross cases.

Cases

We used theoretical sampling of firms that were recognized by the packaging industry as a reference for best practices and which were known as market leaders. Firms were invited based on their individual characteristics and the strategic sampling plan. To ensure variability, their subsector, size, revenue, time of existence, export, and organizational structure were considered. Two of the cases were multinational and two were local. First, firms were contacted by telephone. A letter of invitation was sent containing a description of the purpose of the research and data collection procedures. After the firm accepted, a first visit for the explanation of the research and an interview were scheduled. Each firm provided a room and a secretary to conduct the interviews. Table 1 shows description of cases.

Table 1 – Description of cases

Cases	Label_Case	Flexi_Case	Paper_Case	Metal_Case
Industry	Packaging	Packaging	Packaging	Packaging
Sector	Adhesives, paints, pigments, varnishes	Flexible Plastic	Paper	Steel
Firm's time	> 60 years	> 60 years	> 125 years	> 60 years
Number of employees	500	800	600	1.000
Number of interviewed	21	18	18	16
Headquarters location	São Paulo/Brazil	Paraná/Brazil	São Paulo/Brazil	São Paulo/Brazil
Exports	Yes	Yes	Yes	Yes
Type of Market	Multinational	Multinational	National	National
Size (revenue > R$300 million	Large	Large	Large	Large
Criteria for selection of firms	BMP (Best Manufacturing Practices)	BMP (Best Manufacturing Practices)	BMP (Best Manufacturing Practices)	BMP (Best Manufacturing Practices)
Criteria for selection of interviewees	Interface production	Interface production	Interface production	Interface production

Development of interview script

Data collection was conducted through semi-structured interviews with open-ended questions, based on our theoretical review (Miles, Huberman, & Saldaña, 2013). The interview script was developed in two phases. In the first phase, an extensive literature review on operational practices and operational capabilities was performed. In the second phase, we conducted a Q-Sort. The questions were intermingled and placed on a form in which respondents classified the questions as TQM, JIT, or SCM. No questions were removed from the interview script, but some adjustments indicated by the respondents were performed. The interview script consists of four sections. First section was directed toward the characterization of the respondents. Second section dealt with the functions related to production, such as Marketing, Sales, and Customer Service etc. The questions were intended to understand the influence of certain activities in the production process. Third section addressed the production process; the interviewees answered questions about their day-to-day activities, and the questions followed a script, which addressed TQM, JIT, and SCM operational practices. The fourth and last section focused on characterization of the firm. A pre-test was conducted.

Interviewees

The interviews were conducted face-to-face, at each of the firms researched. Each participant received the interview script in advance and a statement informing him or her about the necessary conditions for the research. The firms provided one office and a secretary to help in the process. Schedules were made by the secretary. Respondents received an email in advance with basic information about the research.

In total, 73 interviews (65 hours and 22 minutes) were conducted in four different firms. For the first case, 21 interviews were held. For the second case, 18 interviews were held. For the third case, 18 interviews were conducted, and for the fourth case, 16 interviews were conducted. Each interview was approximately 55 minutes (See Table 2, 3, 4, and 5).

Table 2 – Interviews_Label_Case

Case 1					
Date	**Duration in minutes**	**Start time**	**Job Title**	**Equivalent departments**	
10/13/2014	80:41	1:00 PM	1	Manager PTI Brazil	R&D and Continuous Improvement
10/13/2014	79:24	3:00 PM	2	Manager EHS / ELS AS.	R&D and Continuous Improvement
10/14/2014	82:29	8:30 AM	3	Brazil Operations Manager	Production
10/14/2014	51:28	2:00 PM	4	Operations Coordinator	Production
10/14/2014	48:49	1:00 PM	5	Operations Coordinator	Production
10/14/2014	50:19	3:00 AM	6	Project / Processes / Machines Manager	R&D and Continuous Improvement
10/15/2014	75:36	8:30 AM	7	SCM Manager	SCM
10/15/2014	47:50	10:30 PM	8	Finishing Manager	Production
10/15/2014	79:48	1:00 PM	9	HR Manager / Training and Development	Production
10/15/2014	73:38	3:00 PM	10	Quality Manager	Quality
10/29/2014	34:55	8:30 AM	11	Maintenance Coordinator	Maintenance
10/29/2014	50:56	9:30 AM	12	Health and Safety Coordinator	Health and Occupational Safety
10/29/2014	69:22	10:30 AM	13	Purchasing Manager	SCM
10/29/2014	51:17	1:00 PM	14	Sales Coordinator	Marketing and Sales
10/29/2014	34:07	2:00 PM	15	Process Engineer	R&D and Continuous Improvement
10/29/2014	55:44	3:00 PM	16	Logistics Coordinator	SCM
10/30/2014	35:14	8:00 AM	17	Maintenance Supervisor	Maintenance
10/30/2014	48:20	10:00 AM	18	President	Board of Direc tors
10/30/2014	30:12	11:00 AM	19	Maintenance Planner	Maintenance
10/30/2014	24:45	1:00 PM	20	Communications Coordinator	Marketing and Sales
10/30/2014	48:24	2:00 PM	21	Technical Support	Marketing and Sales
Totally	**19 hours, 37 minutes and 05 seconds, with 21 interviewees.**				

Table 3 – Interviews_Flexi_Case

Case 2					
Date	**Duration in minutes**	**Start time**	**Job Title**		**Equivalent departments**
11/25/2015	35:19	8:00 AM	1	Production Supervisor	Production
11/25/2015	35:00	9:45 AM	2	Production Supervisor	Production
11/25/2015	44:39	10:15 AM	3	Production Supervisor 2	Production
11/25/2015	28:14	11:15 AM	4	Production Supervisor	Production
11/25/2015	56:18	1:00 PM	5	Logistics Manager	SCM
11/25/2015	60:00	2:00 PM	6	Production Planning Control	Production
11/25/2015	46:27	3:00 PM	7	S &OP Manager - Logistics	SCM
11/25/2015	48:21	4:00 PM	8	Logistics Supervisor	SCM
11/26/2015	36:30	8:00 AM	9	Industrial Manager	Production
11/26/2015	56:40	9:00 AM	10	Continued Improvement Coordinator	R&D and Continuous Improvement
11/26/2015	55:14	10:00 AM	11	Latin American Coordinator WCOM	R&D and Continuous Improvement
11/26/2015	27:49	11:00 AM	12	Business Manager - Supplies	SCM
11/26/2015	28:04	12:00 AM	13	Paint Production Manager	Production
11/26/2015	57:15	1:00 PM	14	Quality Supervisor	Quality
11/26/2015	40:23	2:00 PM	15	Quality Assurance Manager	Quality
11/26/2015	49:26	3:00 PM	16	Engineering Manager - Maintenance	Maintenance
11/26/2015	45:56	4:00 PM	17	Work Safety Supervisor	Health and Occupational Safety
11/26/2015	35:12	17:35 PM	18	Corporative Director	Board of Directors
Totally	**13 hours 47 minutes 53 seconds, with 18 interviewees.**				

Table 4 – Interviews_Metal_Case

Case 3					
Date	**Duration in minutes**	**Start time**	**Job Title**		**Equivalent departments**
10/07/2015	75:22	2:30 PM	1	Production Planning Control I	Production
10/07/2015	76:26	4:00 PM	2	Production Planning Control II	Production
10/08/2015	42:23	8:10 AM	3	Production Coordinator	Production
10/08/2015	74:24	9:00 AM	4	Quality Coordinator	Quality
10/08/2015	84:39	10:30 AM	5	Production Engineer	Production
10/08/2015	54:08	12:10 PM	6	Maintenance Coordinator	Maintenance
10/08/2015	60:55	2:00 PM	7	Financial Coordinator	SCM
10/08/2015	61:06	3:20 PM	8	Purchasing Manager	SCM
10/08/2015	46:00	4:20 PM	9	Electrical Maintenance Engineer	Maintenance
10/08/2015	59:10	5:20 PM	10	Quality Assistant Manager	Quality
10/20/2015	52:25	10:00 AM	11	Corporative Director	Board of Directors
10/20/2015	66:09	11:15 AM	12	Lithography Manager	Production
10/20/2015	55:24	1:00 PM	13	Logistics Supply Manager	SCM
10/20/2015	61:59	2:00 PM	14	R & D Manager	R&D and Continuous Improvement
10/21/2015	49:54	08:30 AM	15	Assistant Administrative	R&D and Continuous Improvement
10/21/2015	89:25	10:00 AM	16	Coordinator Quality	Quality
10/21/2015	55:14	2:30 PM	17	Sales Manager	Marketing and Sales
10/21/2015	55:49	3:30 PM	18	Commercial Director	Board of Directors
Totally	**18 hours, 49 minutes and 54 seconds, with 18 interviewees.**				

Table 5 – Interviews_Paper_Case

Case 4					
Date	**Duration in minutes**	**Start time**	**Job Title**		**Equivalent departments**
11/03/2015	90:22	9:30 AM	1	Production Supervisor	Production
11/03/2015	52:33	2:00 PM	2	Maintenance Manager	Maintenance
11/03/2015	87:28	3:00 PM	3	Technology and Development Manager	R&D and Continuous Improvement
11/04/2015	54:01	9:00 AM	4	Purchasing Manager	SCM
11/04/2015	37:12	10:00 AM	5	Production Supervisor	Production
11/04/2015	33:01	11:00 AM	6	Industrial Director	Board of Directors
11/04/2015	59:47	2:00 PM	7	Production Manager	Production
11/04/2015	34:19	3:00 PM	8	Export Manager	Marketing and Sales
11/04/2015	30:00	3:30 PM	9	Marketing Analyst	Marketing and Sales
11/04/2015	22:45	4:00 PM	10	Work Safety Coordinator	Health and Occupational Safety
11/05/2015	34:28	4:30 PM	11	Production Planning Control	Production
11/05/2015	43:44	9:00 AM	12	Customer Service	Marketing and Sales
11/05/2015	58:47	10:00 AM	13	Quality Coordinator	Quality
11/05/2015	58:28	11:00 AM	14	Finishing Coordinator	Production
11/05/2015	58:46	2:00 PM	15	Quality Manager	Quality
11/05/2015	32:16	4:00 PM	16	Logistic Coordinator	SCM
Totally	**13 hours, 07 minutes and 57 seconds, with 16 interviewees.**				

In Brazil, a firm is responsible for providing the name of its function and following legal criteria. Each firm has different names for similar functions. To facilitate comparison between cases, we designated the functions by department, as shown in Table 6.

Table 6 – Equivalence of functions by department

Department:	Functions:
Board of Direc tors	President, corporative director, commercial director, director industrial.
Health and Occupational Safety	Health and safety coordinator, work safety supervisor, work safety coordinator.
Maintenance	Maintenance coordinator, supervisor maintenance, planner maintenance, engineering manager – maintenance, electrical maintenance engineer, maintenance manager.
Marketing and Sales	Sales coordinator, communications coordinator, technical support, sales manager, export manager, marketing analyst, customer service.
Production	Brazil operations manager, coordinated operations, finishing manager, HR manager / training and development, production supervisor, production planning control, industrial manager, paint production manager, production coordinator, production engineer, lithography manager, finishing coordinator.
Quality	Quality manager, quality supervisor, quality assurance manager, quality coordinator, quality assistant manager.
R&D and Continuous improvement	Manager PTI Brazil, manager EHS / ELS AS., project / processes / machines manager, processes engineer, continued improvement coordinator, Latin American coordinator WCOM, R&D manager, assistant administrative, technology and development manager.
SCM	SCM manager, purchasing manager, logistics coordinator, logistics manager, S&OP manager – logistics, logistics supervisor, business manager – supplies, financial coordinator, logistics supply manager.

The interviews were conducted in the manufacturing and related departments (see Table 6). Different hierarchical levels were investigated. We conducted interviews with directors, managers, and supervisors, in different departments. All interviews were recorded and transcribed literally, without modifying or removing words. Data analysis was conducted using content analysis (Krippendorff, 2013). Interviews were consolidated in the Table 7.

Table 7 – Consolidated interviews

Departments	Label_Case	Flexi_Case	Metal_Case	Paper_Case	Totally
Board of Directors	1	1	2	1	5
Health and O. Safety	1	1	0	1	3
Maintenance	3	1	2	1	7
Marketing and Sales	3	0	1	3	7
Production	5	7	5	5	22
Quality	1	2	3	2	8
R&D and Continuous Improvement	4	2	2	1	9
SCM	3	4	3	2	12
Total - interviewees	**21**	**18**	**18**	**16**	**73**
Total - hours	**19h, 37m, and 5s**	**13h, 47m, and 53s**	**18h, 49m, and 54s**	**13 h, 07m, and 57s,**	**65h and 22m**

Validate

To validate the constructs, we followed steps suggested by Yin (2010): extensive review of the literature; used multiple sources of evidence in the four cases studied; and use chain of evidence between operational practices and operational capability. To internal validity, we used three techniques: logical model, pattern matching, and rival theories (Miles et al., 2013; Yin, 2010). To external validity, we used multiple cases with different characteristics. Furthermore, to assure reliability, we took into account three steps, stability, replicability, and accuracy. To ensure stability we used the accounting log data. We prepared a spreadsheet with information about interviewees and firms. Replicability was established through the use of the case study protocol, a data base, and an evidence table. To assure accuracy, we conducted a pre-test phase, triangulation of the data coding and, analysis of codes by different researchers. The triangulation of the data coding was done through multiple researchers coding same data.

RESULTS

Within-Case analysis: Label_Case

Label_Case is an American multinational company that uses different types of operational practices exceptionally well. The main operational practices observed in the company were Total Quality Management (TQM), Just in Time (JIT), Supply Chain Management (SCM), Total Productive Maintenance (TPM), Human Resources Management (HRM), Enterprise Lean Manufacturing (ELS), and Environment, Health and Safety (EHS). In general, its practices are integrated. According to the production manager, "practices are not individual; they integrated with each other." This was evident when the firm solved a problem.

Resolution of a problem usually occurs through a plan of action involving several departments and multiple operational practices. According to the manager of the supply chain, "If we have a supply problem, we put everyone in the room and open a joint action plan." Over time, the integration of operational practices not only assists in solving problems; it promotes the development of operational capabilities.

The operational capabilities found in the firm constitute two groups. The first group is called Across-the-Board Capabilities and includes Information Management Capability, Continuous Improvement Capability, and Learning Capability. The term across indicates that the operational capabilities found in this group provide support in developing other operational capabilities belonging to the second group, Standalone Capabilities. The second group is divided into three sub-groups: upstream, operational, and downstream. Upstream refers to Supplier Management Capability. Operational represents the capabilities that are directly related to production, including Operational Efficiency Capability, Innovation Capability, and Flexibility Capability. And finally, downstream we have Customer Support Capability. These capabilities are considered Standalone because they are developed from market demand, with the purpose of adding value for the customer.

Within-Case analysis: Flexi_Case

Flexi_Case is an American multinational firm that produces flexible packaging and uses Best Manufacturing Practices (BMP) in its operations. The main operational practices used by the company are Total Quality Management (TQM), Just in Time (JIT), Supply Chain Management (SCM), Total Productive Maintenance (TPM), Human Resource Management

(HRM), and Environmental, Health, and Safety (EHS). All these practices are integrated into the management system used by Flexi_Case, called World Class Operations Management (WCOM).

WCOM is a set of practices which aims at the continuous improvement of production. It involves the following areas: Autonomous Management; Focused Improvement; Environmental, Health, and Safety; Progressive Quality; Logistics; Planned Maintenance; Product Anticipated Management; and Education and Training. WCOM serves to support production efficiency and develop cost reduction projects.

Cost reduction projects are implemented every four months and involve a set of operational practices. These projects are based on the results of the Flexi_Case's indicators. According to the industrial manager, "We launched the end of 2013 [...] five groups to reduce shears and scraps, [...] that brought an amount of around R$3.000.000.00 cost reduction for 2014." The intensive use of different practices over time can lead to the development of an operational capability.

Operational capabilities found in Flexi_Case constitute two groups, Across-the-Board Capabilities and Standalone Capabilities. Across-the-Board Capabilities constitute: Information Management Capability, Continuous Improvement Capability, and Learning Capability. Standalone Capabilities include: Supplier Capability Management, Operational Efficiency Capability, Innovation Capability, Flexibility Capability, Customization, and Customer Support Capability.

Within-Case analysis: Paper_Case

Paper_Case is a Brazilian firm that produces paper packaging and uses Best Manufacturing Practices (BMP) in their operations. The main operational practices used by the company are Total Quality Management (TQM), Housekeeping (cleaning and organization of the firm), Justin Time (JIT), Supply Chain Management (SCM), and Total Productive Maintenance (TPM). The firm also works with certifications of ISO 9000, ISO 26000, Forest Stewardship Council (FSC), and is beginning to implement Food Safety Management System (FSSC 22000).

Operational practices and certifications are intended to meet customer requests. The food industry is one of the customers with greater requirements. Paper_Case provides packaging for the food industry, and therefore must follow the same standards used in food production. Thus, operational practices are monitored by the firm and audited by external companies and in some cases for audit by customers as well. As the production manager to serve the food industry "you have to have the same level cleaning, organization, and aseptic factories that produce food for children." Although it is clear that Paper_Case has a reactive response to requests from its customers, the implementation of these operational practices favors the development of operational capabilities.

Operational capabilities found in the Paper_Case constitute Across-the-Board Capabilities with Information Management Capability, Continuous Improvement Capability, and Learning Capability, and Standalone Capabilities with Supplier Capability Management, Operational Efficiency Capability, Innovation Capability, Flexibility Capability, Customization Capability, and Customer Support Capability.

Within-Case analysis: Metal_Case

Metal_Case is a Brazilian company that produces metal packaging and uses Best Manufacturing Practices (BMP) in their operations. The main operational practices used by the company are Total Quality Management (TQM), Just in Time (JIT), Supply Chain Management (SCM), Total Productive Maintenance (TPM), Environmental, Health, and Safety (EHS), Development and Implementation of New Machinery and Equipment, and Development of New Processes.

Since 1980, Metal_Case has been investing in operational practices. They are essential for the firm to remain competitive in the market in which it operates the paint industry. The paint market in Brazil is concentrated in three multinationals. This situation creates an aggressive competition from packaging firms that want to sell to these multinationals. Another aspect that affects competition for Metal_Case is its raw material, steel. Steel represents 70% to 80% of the production of metallic packaging, and in Brazil, it is monopolized by Companhia Siderúrgica Nacional (CSN). If Metal_Case is not able to negotiate for better prices, then it needs to invest in its internal resources and its capabilities to generate competitive advantage.

Operational capabilities found in Metal_Case were Across-the-Board Capabilities and Standalone Capabilities. Across-the-Board Capabilities are: Information Management Capability, Continuous Improvement Capability, and Learning Capability. Standalone Capabilities include: Supplier Management Capability, Operational Efficiency Capability, Innovation Capability, Flexibility Capability, and Customer Support Capability.

CROSS-CASE ANALYSIS AND PROPOSITIONS

Theoretical framework has shown that operational practices are not operational capabilities. Operational practices are "standardized procedures that are easy to articulate and well-defined" (Wu et al., 2012, pp. 123). On the other hand, operational capabilities are "firm-specific sets of skills, processes, and routines, developed within the operations management system that are regularly used in solving its problems through configuring its operational resources" (Wu et al., 2010, pp. 726). Embedded in routines and operational processes, operational capabilities need time, management attention, and continuity in the use of operational practices. Differently from operational practices, the operational capabilities cannot be implemented, they emerge gradually over time, based on the experience, unique history of the firm, and problems that decision makers have had to face. The time spent for the development of a capability will depend on just how it is heterogeneous, and the firm's learning ability. Table 8 summarizes the differences between operational practices and operational capabilities.

Table 8 – Differences between operational practices and operational capabilities.

Operational Practices	Operational Capabilities
Generic	Unique
Ready for use	Path dependent development
Standardized	Idiosyncratic
Explicit	Tacit
It involves knowledge	It involves learning
Simple	Complexity

Practices can be important drivers of high performance in today's manufacturing environment, but investments in practices, per se, do not constitute capabilities. The development of a capability consists of practices-performance inter-linked to specific performance gains (Narasimhan et al., 2005). When an operational practice is implemented, over time, this practice ceases to be generic and explicit; it acquires tacit aspects, and becomes unique. Table 9 shows the transition between some operational practices and operational capabilities.

Table 9 – Relationship between operational practices and operational capabilities

Operational Practices:	**Evidence (interviewed)**	**Operational Capabilities**
Kaizen	ELS manager, "In the beginning with 80 employees, we produced 4 million per square meters. After the application of Kaizen, our capacity doubled with the same number of employees."[Label_Case]	Continuous Improvement Capability
Training & Development Plan	R&D manager, "You will always be trained in practice daily, you will receive guidance from someone with a superior position to him. [...]"[Paper_Case]	Learning Capability
Key Performance Indicator (KPI)	Production manager, "from the numbers we can see what happened, look at the report and take actions to combat the problem." [Metal_Case]	Information Management Capability
Supplier Evaluation	Purchasing manager, "by the standard of ISO 9000, we are required to have an evaluation system of our suppliers with active items." [Label_Case]	Supplier Management Capability
Total Quality Management (TQM), Environmental, Health, and Safety (EHS)	Safety manager, "if we have standards for safety as well as TQM [...] we begin to have predictability [...]. It is difficult to measure but it helps in our productivity, low variability, less returns, less claims, and more satisfied customers."[Label_Case]	Operational Efficiency Capability
Development of New Processes	Industrial manager "The guys are four or five years ahead of the market So, we have a center for engineers in the United States just doing it, just helping us, just for us proposing new structures, new projects, and new processes." [Flexi_Case]	Innovation Capability
Flexibility of Delivery	Purchasing manager, "We have flexibility and speed to meet the specific needs of our customers while maintaining a good quality."[Paper_Case]	Flexibility Capability
Process Modularity and Product Modularity	Production manager "Chocolate cookie, you know? Yeah ... The guy sells a cement unit; [...] it will be able to have accuracy, like, 95%. It does not exist in the packaging market The guy will have accuracy in it of 50%, 70%. Normally, the volume is correct." [Flexi_Case]	Customization Capability

Customer Relationship	ELS manager, "We went to a customer to work with them on the setup. Before, the setup was 1 hour and 10 minutes, but after our work, it was down to 30 minutes. We increased their productivity by 30%." [Label_Case]	Customer Support Capability

Kaizen practice is an example of interaction between operational practice and operational capability (see Table 9). Kaizen is a set of practices that allows continuous improvement of manufacturing processes. Employees are trained to lead their own projects. In the case Label_Case, one of the projects involving Kaizen was Quick-Change Tool, also called Single Minute Exchange of Die (SEMED). After the realization of the Kaizen, the firm has reduced setup time, increased the speed of the machines, and implemented best maintenance practices. Implementation of these operational practices, over time, has enabled improvements in the production process, impacting positively on Label_Case's performance. ELS manager said, "Our capacity doubled with the same number of employees."

Operational practices take time to be effective and achieve its final shape. When an operational practice is in fact implemented and is in use, it goes through a process that is path dependent, which caused evolution in it. An operational practice, five years later is not the same practice when it was implemented; several other elements are incorporated into it over time, such as tacit aspects, idiosyncratic decisions, and learning, among others. Its complexity increases as a result of combination of different operational practices interacting with each other.

The same applies to the development of an operational capability. "One swallow does not make a summer". A single operational practice will not be enough to develop an operational capability. Individually they are inconsistent (Benner & Tushman, 2003), but in conjunction with other operational practices, such as Lead Time, JIT, TQM, TPM, among others, they may facilitate the development of operational capabilities. Thus we present the first proposition:

Proposition 1 – Different sets of inter-linked operational practices over time can develop into different operational capabilities in each firm.

However, not all operational capabilities are equal. From the coding of the four cases examined in this study, our results showed that operational capabilities have different functions. Some have the role of increasing the performance of the firm, while others reinforce, modify or reconfigure these first. We summarize them in two major categories: Standalone Capabilities and Across-the-Board Capabilities (see Figure 3).

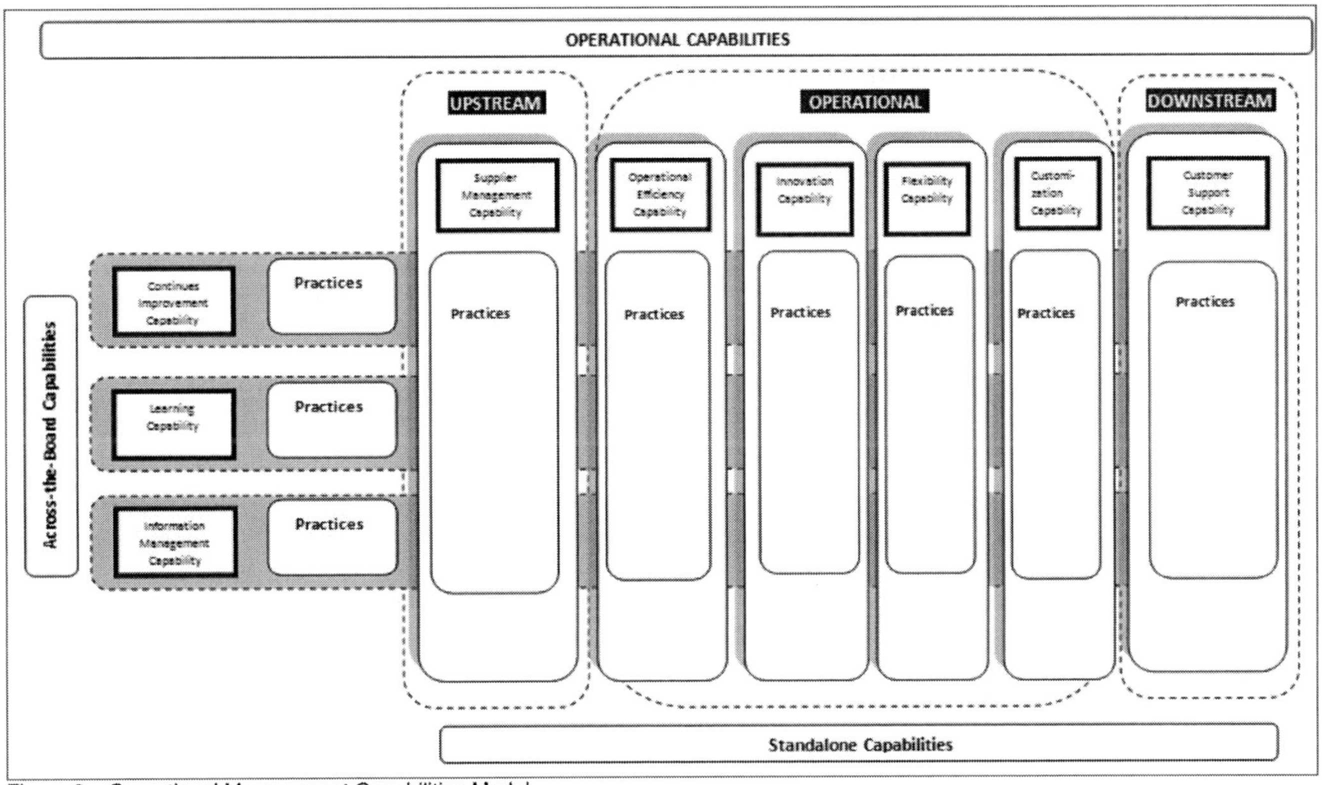

Figure 3 – Operational Management Capabilities Model

Standalone Capabilities are also called, zero order, substantives, ordinaries, or zero order capabilities (Schilke, 2013; Zahra et al., 2006; Zollo & Winter, 2002). All these names, however, are merely semantic; since they have the same meaning with same goal, improve the performance of the firm. They are operational capabilities that reconfigure the organizational resource base (Collis, 1994; Schilke, 2013; Zollo & Winter, 2002). Standalone Capabilities have as purpose to solve problems, achieve results, and develop new products through configuring its operational resources (Wu et al., 2010; Zahra et al., 2006). They are established from the operational function of the firm representing "how you earn your living" (Cepeda & Vera, 2007, pp. 426).

In the four cases analyzed, Label_Case, Flexi_Case, Paper_Case, and Metal Case, we have identified: Supply Management Capability, Operational Efficiency Capability, Innovation Capability, Flexibility Capability, and Customer Support Capability. Customization Capability was found only with Flexi_Case and Paper_Case. Standalone Capabilities may differ among firms; its development depends on the industry in which it operates and the customers they serve. For instance, Paper_Case and Flexi_Case operate in a dynamic market, with constant requests of their clients, in the great majority multinationals. They need to adapt their production process and develop specific capabilities such as flexibility and customization to be able to meet the needs of their customers. On the other hand, Label_Case and Metal_Case operate in a more traditional market, and if on one side, their production processes are more predictable, on the other, they need to focus on Innovation Capabilities and Operational Efficiency Capability to continue as market leaders. However, independent of the type of Standalone Capabilities that the firm presents, its basic characteristic is to achieve specific results of operations; therefore, they have a direct relationship with performance. Considering the context, we formulate the second and third propositions:

Proposition 2 – Standalone Capabilities are operational capabilities adapted to the firm's operational needs and focused on performance.

Proposition 3 –Standalone Capabilities include of Supply Management Capability, Operational Efficiency Capability, Innovation Capability, Flexibility Capability, Customization, and Customer Support Capability.

Across-the-Board Capabilities are first order capabilities; they have direct and indirect influence on the development of new capabilities (Schilke, 2013; Zollo & Winter, 2002). Across-the-Board Capabilities are capability combinations able to reconfigure current operational capabilities, and at the same time to help the development of others (Collis, 1994; Eisenhardt & Martin, 2000; Teece et al., 1997; Zahra et al., 2006). They represent "how you change your operational routines" (Cepeda & Vera, 2007, pp. 426).

When we analyze the interviews for this study, we noticed that some operational capabilities encompassed other capabilities supporting their development. They were called Across-the-Board Capabilities. In total, three of them were found: Continuous Improvement Capability, Learning Capability, and Information Management Capability (see Figure 3).

Across-the-Board Capabilities contribute to the development of Standalone Capabilities. For instance, when the KPIs were classified as belonging to the Information Management Capability, we observe their presence in different Standalone Capabilities. According to the

Flexi_Case production manager "Each department has their own indicators. [...] in the meetings each department talks about their indicators. If the department is with some poor indicator, it needs to open an action plan. The department needs to create a strategy to achieve its target." Decision makers use information to direct or redirect their decisions, and this will affect the shape of other operational capabilities. For example, if the level of service's KPI is below the target, and one of the problems is the lack of flexibility in product delivery, managers will have to find solutions to meet this demand. By measuring the customer service level, indirectly Information Management Capability will influence Flexibility Capability.

Across-the-Board Capabilities are present in different Standalone Capabilities. They have the role of helping develop the Standalone Capabilities. This classification into two different groups allows us to combine variables such that the effects of the interactions between them can be analyzed (Bailey, 1994).

Proposition 4 – Across-the-Board Capabilities influence the development of Standalone Capabilities.

Proposition 5 –Across-the-Board Capabilities include Continuous Improvement Capability, Learning Capability, and Information Management Capability.

Across-the-Board Capabilities are composed of best practice bundles. They are developed over time, using learning mechanism as path dependence (Anand, Ward, Tatikonda, & Schilling, 2009; Eisenhardt & Martin, 2000) and are influenced by the dynamism of the market (Teece et al., 1997). This means that, as well as the Dynamic Capabilities, Across-the-Board Capabilities are capability combinations, able to exploit current operational capabilities, and at the same time support the development of other operational capabilities (Collis, 1994; Eisenhardt & Martin, 2000; Teece et al., 1997; Zahra et al., 2006).

Continuous Improvement Capability in Label Case, Flexi Case, and Metal Case is based on systematic programs of continuous improvement, such as Kaisen, WCOM, and Simplification Project. Employees are instructed on the procedures and steps of each project related to continuous improvement. All projects have similar characteristics; they are focused on problem solving and reduce operational costs. Although Paper_Case does not have a structured program for continuous improvement, it develops actions to improve operational efficiency. Continuous improvement process is related to the firm's learning ability. It is a first order capability that operates on the firm's zero order capabilities, improving them continuously (Collis, 1994; Zollo & Winter, 2002). It is defined as a systematic effort which seeks to find new ways that improve operational process, creating and modifying routines that increase efficiency of the firm (Anand et al., 2009; Zollo & Winter, 2002). When properly implemented, it helps to integrate, adapt, or change its operational processes.

Learning Capability was observed in all four cases, Label Case, Flexi_Case, Paper_Case, and Metal_Case. These firms have operated a long time in the market for at least 60 years or more. They have old and experienced employees that constantly promote both formally and informally learning. Informal learning occurs through the exchange of information between employees, considering firms to have workers together for a long time. Formal learning occurs through meetings, training, action plans for solving the problems, and management tools. The leadership has also been observed as an important mechanism for learning. It allows the exchange of information among employees, promoting learning among them. Learning Capability is a first order capability that helps to develop on the firm's zero order capabilities. It constitutes the firm's systematic methods for modifying operational practices and routines, and can be thought of as 'learning-to-learn' (Collis, 1994; Zollo & Winter, 2002). It is developed over time through the employees' knowledge accumulation. Knowledge happens through cross-functional interaction between areas (Paiva et al., 2008). It needs to be generated, transferred, and learned by employees. According to Eisenhardt & Martin (2000, pp. 1114), "Learning mechanisms guide the evolution of dynamic capabilities." Therefore, coevolution of learning mechanism leads to the dynamic capability (Teece et al., 1997; Winter, 2003; Zollo & Winter, 2002)

Information Management Capability has great influence on the development of Standalone Capabilities. Performance indicators help managers monitor their processes and identify bottlenecks in production. Label_Case and Flexi_Case use a structured methodology to present their indicators. They have panels in different parts of the firm, including the production, with updated data of the indicators and targets. Metal_Case and Paper_Case also have indicators, but they are not presented in a systematic way. Information Management Capability is also a first order capability that supports the changes in the firm's zero order capabilities (Collis, 1994; Zollo & Winter, 2002). The system of information is part of the intricate chain of assets and capabilities (Wade & Hulland, 2004). It generates information that can be transformed into knowledge, benefiting Learning Capability and Continuous Improvement Capability. Dynamic Capabilities as well as the Information Management Capability uses real-time information, such as inventory, sales, and production schedules to reconfigure the resources of the firm. This information helps managers in decision making, in rapid problem solving, and to better understand the production process, adapting it to market changes (Eisenhardt & Martin, 2000).

Proposition 6– Across-the-Board Capabilities are Dynamic Capabilities.

DISCUSSION AND CONCLUSIONS

In this study, we proposed to answer two main questions: 1) what is the relationship between operational practices and operational capabilities? And 2) what are types of operational capabilities characterized in the firm's internal environment?

First, what is the relationship between operational practices and operational capabilities?

Operational capabilities are developed over time through the interaction of operational practices. Operational practices are operational capabilities' antecedents. However, though we know that the development of a capability involves different paths, it is equifinal. We do not ignore the need to use different resources in this process, tangible and intangible, such as leadership and organizational culture. Yet, we believe that operational practices can be a key resource for the development of operational capabilities.

Like Wu et al. (2012), we believe that operational practices are additive. When an operational practice is implemented, other practices can be included to complement it. Over time, they are embedded in the social context of the firm; they develop idiosyncratic aspects and a capability may emerge. We can say that operational capabilities are *idiosyncratic resources developed over time, from inter-linked operational practices, based on the unique history and experiences of the firm, and problems that decision makers have had to face in the day-to-day operations.*

Next, another question to be answered is: 2) what are the types of operational capabilities characterized in the firm's internal environment?

Nine operational capabilities were observed, creating our typology. However, they have been classified into two different constructs. We called the first construct "Standalone Capabilities". They consist of zero order capabilities, and serve to achieve operational results (Wu et al., 2010; Zahra et al., 2006). It is composed of: 1) Customer Support; 2) Innovation; 3) Operational Efficiency; 4) Flexibility; 5) Customization; and 6) Supply Management. The second construct is "called Across-the-Board Capabilities" and provide support in developing other operational capabilities. They can build, change and/or reconfigure Standalone Capabilities (Teece et al., 1997). Across-the-Board Capabilities are considered first order capabilities, and are composed of: Learning, Continuous Improvement, and Information Management (Collis, 1994; Zollo & Winter, 2002). Figure 3 shows the complete typology.

In addition to typology, we have noticed that not all firms have the same operational capabilities. The market in which the firm operates will define the type of operational capabilities necessary for it to compete with its competitors. Even within the firm, operational capabilities can be at different stages of development. Capabilities are not finished resources - they are developed according to the needs of the firm and, therefore, they can be at various levels of maturity. A capability does not last forever; it may cease to exist or be replaced by another that best meets the firm's needs.

The primary theoretical contribution of this study is the creation of an operational capabilities typology based on firms' internal environments. We found two groups of operational capabilities - Standalone Capabilities and Across-the-Board Capabilities. A second contribution is that operational capabilities are not an off-the-shelf resource. They are developed over time through the implementation of operational practices. The relationship between practices and operational capabilities puts forward the idea of operational practices as antecedents of operational capabilities. Moreover, we further differentiated between the constructs of operational practices and operational capabilities and showed the origin of operational capabilities from the internal environment of the firm.

Our model provides a simple but informative tool for managers to gauge progress and determine the impact of improvement efforts on performance. Operational capabilities can be sources of competitive advantage, but the question is how managers can build them in a firm's internal environment. In this study, we have identified operational practices as antecedents of operational capabilities, and we have shown the path that leads to the development of operational capabilities.

This study has some limitations. The first is that we have identified and selected operational practices that were more evident in the interviews, but we know that other practices were left out because they were not mentioned by interviewees or they had not been observed by researchers. The second limitation is that we found evidence, both in literature and case studies, that operational practices are inter-linked; hence when we separate them into categories, we simplify a reality that is actually complex and dynamic. Third, the typology presented here is restricted to the packaging industry located in Brazil. We cannot guarantee that all operational capabilities of this study are found in other industries. However, we do indeed believe that our model of Across-the-Board Capabilities and Standalone Capabilities can be applied in different industries.

For future studies, we suggest that other researchers explore how organizational culture affects the development of operational capabilities. The social context is an important aspect to be considered because it permits a process of mutual learning between the organization and the individuals in it. We also suggest that future research be performed in other industries so that the findings can be compared.

REFERENCES

Ahmad, S., & Schroeder, R. G. (2003). The impact of human resource management practices on operational performance: recognizing country and industry differences. *Journal of Operations Management, 21*(1), 19–43.

Anand, G., Ward, P. T., Tatikonda, M. V., & Schilling, D. a. (2009). Dynamic capabilities through continuous improvement infrastructure. *Journal of Operations Management, 27*(6), 444–461.

Avella, L., Vazquez-bustelo, D., & Fernandez, E. (2011). Cumulative manufacturing capabilities: an extended model and new empirical evidence. *qInternational Journal of Production Research, 49*(3), 707–729.

Bailey, K. D. (1994). *Typologies and taxonomies: an introduction to classification techniques.* California: Sage Publications.

Benner, M. J., & Tushman, M. L. (2003). Exploration, Exploitation and Process Management: the Productivity Dilemma Revisited. *Academy of Management Journal, 28*(2), 238–256.

Brown, K. A., & Mitchell, T. R. (1991). a Comparison of Just-in-Time and Batch Manufacturing: the Role of Performance Obstacles. *Academy of Management Journal, 34*(4), 906–917.

Cepeda, G., & Vera, D. (2007). Dynamic capabilities and operational capabilities: A knowledge management perspective. *Journal of Business Research, 60*(5), 426–437.

Choo, A. S., Linderman, K. W., & Schroeder, R. G. (2007). Method and context perspectives on learning and knowledge creation in quality management. *Journal of Operations Management, 25*(4), 918–931.

Collis, D. J. (1994). Are Note : How Valuable are Organizational Capabilities. *Strategic Management Journal, 15*, 143–152.

Corbett, L. M., & Whybark, D. C. (2001). Searching for the sandcone in the GMRG data. *International Journal of Operations and Production Management, 21*(7), 965–980.

Cua, K. O., McKone, K. E., & Schroeder, R. G. (2001). Relationships between implementation of TQM, JIT, and TPM and manufacturing performance. *Journal of Operations Management, 19*(6), 675–694.

Dean, J. W., & Bowen, D. E. (1994). and Total Quality : Theory Management and Practice Improving Development. *Academy of Management Journal, 19*(3), 392–418.

Eisenhardt, K. M. (1989). Building Theories from Case Study Research. *Academy of Management Review, 14*(4), 532–550.

Eisenhardt, K. M., & Graebner, M. E. (2007). Theory Building from Cases: Opportunities and

Challenges. *Academy of Management Journal, 50*(1), 25–32.
Eisenhardt, K. M., & Martin, J. a. (2000). Dynamic capabilities: what are they? *Strategic Management Journal, 21*, 1105–1121.
Ferdows, K., & Meyer, D. E. (1990). Lasting Improvements in Manufacturing Performance: In Search of a New Theory. *Journal of Operations Management, 9*(2), 168–184.
Flynn, B. B., & Flynn, E. J. (2004). An exploratory study of the nature of cumulative capabilities. *Journal of Operations Management, 22*(5), 439–457.
Flynn, B. B., Schroeder, R. G., & Sakakibara, S. (1994). A framework for quality management research and an associated measurement instrument. *Journal of Operations Management, 11*, 339–366.
Furlan, A., Vinelli, A., & Pont, G. D. (2011). Complementarity and lean manufacturing bundles: an empirical analysis. *International Journal of Operations & Production Management, 31*(8), 835–850.
Größler, A., & Grübner, A. (2006). An empirical model of the relationships between manufacturing capabilities. *International Journal of Operations & Production Management, 26*(5), 458–485.
Hackman, J. R., & Wageman, R. (1995). Total quality management: Empirical, conceptual, and practical issues. *Administrative Science Quarterly, 40*, 309–342.
Hoopes, D. G., & Madsen, T. L. (2008). A capability-based view of competitive heterogeneity. *Industrial and Corporate Change, 17*(3), 393–426.
Kathuria, R. (2000). Competitive priorities and managerial performance: a taxonomy of small manufacturers. *Journal of Operations Management, 18*, 627–641.
Kaynak, H. (2003). The relationship between total quality management practices and
Krippendorff, K. (2013). *Content Analysis: An Introduction to Its Methodology* (3rd ed.). Thousand Oaks, CA: Sage Publications.
Laugen, B. T., Acur, N., Boer, H., & Frick, J. (2005). Best manufacturing practices: What do the best-performing companies do? *International Journal of Operations & Production Management, 25*(2), 131–150.
Lee, H., & Kelley, D. (2008). Building dynamic capabilities for innovation: an exploratory study of key management practices. *R&D Management, 38*(2), 155–168.
Liu, N. (Chris), Roth, A. V., & Rabinovich, E. (2011). Antecedents and consequences of combinative competitive capabilities in manufacturing. *International Journal of Operations & Production Management, 31*(12), 1250–1286. http://doi.org/10.1108/01443571111187448
Mapes, J., Szwejczewski, M., & New, C. (2000). Process variability and its effect on plant performance. *International Journal of Operations & Production Management, 20*(7), 792–808.
Mentzer, J. T., DeWitt, W., Keebler, J. S., Min, S., Nix, N. W., Smith, C. D., & Zacharia, Z. G. (2001). Defining Supply Chain Management. *Journal of Business Logistics, 22*(2), 1–25.
Miles, Matthew B., A., Huberman, M., & Saldaña, J. (2013). *Qualitative data analysis: A methods sourcebook.* Arizona: SAGE Publications.
Miller, D. (1996). Configurations Revisited. *Strategic Management Journal, 17*, 505–512.
Montabon, F., Sroufe, R., & Narasimhan, R. (2007). An examination of corporate reporting, environmental management practices and firm performance. *Journal of Operations Management, 25*(5), 998–1014.
Narasimhan, R., Swink, M., & Kim, S. W. (2005). An exploratory study of manufacturing practice and performance interrelationships: Implications for capability progression. *International Journal of Operations & Production Management, 25*(10), 1013–1033.
Noble, M. a. (1995). Manufacturing Strategy: Testing the Cumulative Model in a Multiple

Country Context. *Decision Sciences, 26*(5), 693–721.
Paiva, E. L., Roth, A. V., & Fensterseifer, J. E. (2008). Organizational knowledge and the manufacturing strategy process: A resource-based view analysis. *Journal of Operations Management, 26*(1), 115–132.
Peng, D. X., Schroeder, R. G., & Shah, R. (2008). Linking routines to operations capabilities: A new perspective. *Journal of Operations Management, 26*(6), 730–748.
Powell, T. C. (1995). Total quality management as competitive advantage: A review and empirical study. *Strategic Management Journal, 16*(October 1993), 15–37.
Rondeau, P. J., Vonderembse, M. A., & Ragu-Nathan, T. S. (2000). Exploring work system practices for time-based manufacturers: their impact on competitive capabilities. *Journal of Operations Management, 18*(5), 509–529.
Rosenzweig, E. D., & Easton, G. S. (2010). Tradeoffs in Manufacturing? A Meta-Analysis and Critique of the Literature. *Production and Operations Management, 19*(2), 127–141.
Rosenzweig, E. D., & Roth, A. V. (2004). Towards a Theory of Competitive Progression : Evidence from High-Tech Manufacturing. *Production and Operations Management, 13*(4), 354–368.
Rusjan, B. (2005). Model for manufacturing strategic decision making. *International Journal of Operations & Production Management, 25*(8), 740–761.
Schilke, O. (2013). On the Contingent Value of Dynamic Capabilities for Competitive Advantage: the Nonlinear Moderating Effect of Environmental Dynamism. *Strategic Management Journal.*
Schoenherr, T., Power, D., Narasimhan, R., & Samson, D. (2012). Competitive Capabilities among Manufacturing Plants in Developing, Emerging, and Industrialized Countries: A Comparative Analysis. *Decision Sciences, 43*(1), 37–72.
Schroeder, R. G., Bates, K. a., & Junttila, M. a. (2002). A resource-based view of manufacturing strategy and the relationship to manufacturing performance. *Strategic Management Journal, 23*(2), 105–117.
Shah, R., & Ward, P. T. (2003). Lean manufacturing : context, practice bundles, and performance. *Journal of Operations Management, 21*, 129–149.
Skinner, W. (1969). Manufacturing - missing link in corporate strategy. *Harvard Business Review., 47*(3), 5-14.
Sousa, R., & Voss, C. A. (2002). Quality management re-visited: A reflective review and agenda for future research. *Journal of Operations Management, 20*(1), 91–109.
Swink, M., & Hegarty, W. H. (1998). Core manufacturing capabilities and their links to product differentiation. *International Journal of Operations & Production Management, 18*(4), 374–396.
Swink, M., Narasimhan, R., & Kim, S. W. (2005). Manufacturing Practices and Strategy Integration: Effects on Cost Efficiency, Flexibility, and Market-Based Performance. *Decision Sciences, 36*(3), 427–457.
Teece, D. J., Pisano, G., & Shuen, A. (1997). Dynamic Capabilities and Strategic Management. *Strategic Management Journal, 18*(7), 509–533.
Vickery, S. K., Dröge, C., & Markland, R. E. (1997). Dimensions of manufacturing strength in the furniture industry. *Journal of Operations Management, 15*, 317–330.
Wade, M., & Hulland, J. (2004). Review: the Resource-Based View and Information Systems Research: Review, Extension, and Suggestions for Future Research1. *MIS Quarterly, 28*(1), 107–142.
Wernerfelt, B. (1984). A Resource-based View of the Firm. *Strategic Management Journal, 5*, 171–180.
Winter, S. G. (2003). Understanding dynamic capabilities. *Strategic Management Journal,*

24(10), 991–995.
Wu, S. J., Melnyk, S. a., & Flynn, B. B. (2010). Operational Capabilities: The Secret Ingredient. *Decision Sciences, 41*(4), 721–754.
Wu, S. J., Melnyk, S. a., & Swink, M. (2012). An empirical investigation of the combinatorial nature of operational practices and operational capabilities: Compensatory or additive? *International Journal of Operations & Production Management, 32*(2), 121–155.
Yin, R. K. (2010). *Estudo de caso: planejamento e métodos* (4th ed.). Porto Alegre: Bookman.
Zahra, S. A., Sapienza, H., & Davidsson. (2006). Entrepreneurship and Dynamic Capabilities: A Review, Model and Research Agenda. *Journal of Management Studies, 43*(4), 917–955.
Zhang, Q., Vonderembse, M. A., & Lim, J. (2003). Manufacturing flexibility: defining and analyzing relationships among competence , capability , and customer satisfaction. *Journal of Operations Management, 21*, 173–191.
Zollo, M., & Winter, S. G. (2002). Deliberate Learning and the Evolution of Dynamic Capabilities. *Organization Science, 13*(3), 339–351.

DECISION SCIENCES INSTITUTE

Institutional Student Retention Initiatives for Accelerated Programs

Amber Lo
Independent Writer
Email: wamberlo@yahoo.com

Jodi Reeves
National University
Email: jreeves@nu.edu

Paul Jenkins
National University
Email: pjenkins@nu.edu

Russell Parkman
National University
Email: rparkman@nu.edu

ABSTRACT

With the increasing availability of higher education programs in an Accelerated Learning (AL) format, student retention in these programs has emerged as a topic that needs to be better understood. This study investigated the applicability of The Institutional Action Model (Tinto, 2012a) to AL students. Empirical data were collected and analyzed statistically. Most of the recommended initiatives from the Institutional Action Model are positively perceived by AL students. They are also willing and capable of using most of them. Institutions can use the results of this research to fine-tune their design of student retention initiatives for AL students.

KEYWORDS: Accelerated learning, Student retention, Retention initiatives

INTRODUCTION

Student retention is an important issue in higher education. Among students who took the ACT college readiness assessment between 2006 and 2012, the first-year dropout rate of those who entered a four-year college was about 12% in 2006 and the same in 2012 (Buddin, 2014). "Retention" is the rate at which a higher education institution retains and graduates students who first enter the institution to work toward a credential, such as the desired undergraduate or graduate degree (Tinto, 2012b). Such a student may transfer to this institution with a part of the credential requirements fulfilled or may start from the beginning of the program. Tinto believes that research should focus on implementable and effective retention policies and initiatives that educational institutions can adopt to enhance student retention rates (Tinto, 2012a). He proposed the Institutional Action Model. The recommended retention initiatives (or "programs") are based on actions that are relatively under the control of the higher education institution.

There has been a call to study retention in specific groups of students. The retention of female students, students of color, online students, and non-traditional students have already been studied. To date, there have not been many studies that are focus on students enrolled in

Accelerated Learning (AL) academic programs. Usually (but not necessarily), students in AL programs share many characteristics of non-traditional undergraduate students, though many are graduate students.

Accelerated Learning (AL) is a form of education that enables students to achieve a desired set of learning outcomes in a shorter period of time in comparison to the conventional learning format (Serdyukov, 2008). The total number of contact hours in a course is the same as that of the conventional format. The total duration of a course is shorter (four to six weeks as opposed to fifteen to sixteen weeks). Within an AL course, the material is taught in longer or more frequent sessions. In AL, courses are compressed and intensive (Serdyukov, 2008). Students are expected to be highly motivated and study independently. Time pressure is inevitable. Since the AL format is gaining popularity among higher education institutions, administrators and faculty in higher education need to understand the persistence factors that are specific to this format, so that proper institutional policies and initiatives should be implemented to enhance student retention in this environment.

AL courses can be delivered on-site or online. An on-site program is an academic program where each of its courses is conducted face-to-face in a physical classroom where the instructor and students are physically present. There is a fixed schedule of class meeting times for face-to-face class sessions in a physical classroom. Because the total length of time for an AL course is compressed, the length of each class period is usually much longer than the usual 60 minute or 90 minute class period in traditional university courses. An online program is an academic program where each of its courses is conducted online via an electronic Learning Management System (LMS). In addition, many such online courses also have a virtual classroom in which an instructor can conduct synchronous and recorded lecture sessions. This virtual classroom performs the same function as a gathering place for the instructor and students to be present at the same time. Conducting such synchronous class sessions is not a necessary condition of an online course. Some AL programs are in a hybrid format which is partly face-to-face and partly online.

This study investigated the applicability of The Institutional Model to students enrolled in AL higher education programs, so as to determine which retention initiatives are suitable for students in these programs. While the topic of student retention has been studied for decades, the retention of students enrolled in AL programs in higher education is a relatively new topic.

LITERATURE REVIEW

This section presents a review of literature that focuses on the retention of students in AL programs. There is also past literature on the retention of adult students and the retention of online students. As the topic of this study is students in AL programs, they are not all adult working students, though the vast majority are. Some may be traditional students and some can be international students who are not allowed to work off-campus. Some AL programs are totally on-site. Therefore, literature about the retention of adult students and online students are not reviewed in the context of this research. While the topic of student retention has been studied for years, the topic of student retention in AL programs has only a short research history. One reason for this is that accelerated higher educational programs did not come on the scene until World War II (Serdyukov, 2008).

The bulk of research on accelerated programs or accelerated learning is on accelerated nursing programs. Stewart, Pope, and Hansen (2010) discussed the use of clinical preceptors to enhance the Accelerated Online Bachelor's to BSN (ACCEL) program in nursing. This paper was not directly related to student retention, but it presented the characteristics of this successful program (a graduation rate of 98.33 percent between October 2004 and October 2006). This nursing program provided an orientation, short online courses, and on-campus intense laboratory and clinical experience sessions. One feature that stood out was its use of the Preceptor Model in which two local experienced nurses acted as the preceptors for a student when the student was performing several hands-on clinical practices. Allen, Van Dyke, and Armstrong (2010) also described a similar accelerated nursing program. Although this work was not directly about retention, it pointed out that hands-on experience was one attribute that makes the program successful. Stuenkel, Nelson, Malloy, and Cohen (2011) discussed the experience of an accelerated BSN program and concludes that offering a stipend to the students to ease their financial burdens contributed to a high retention rate. This study was not based on any formal established theory or model. Rouse and Rooda (2010) reported reasons for attrition from an accelerated baccalaureate nursing program. Among two cohorts of students in the summer of 2006, the attrition rates were 29 percent and 50 percent. The study found that the students were struggling with family issues, the fast pace of the accelerated program, and the difficulty of balancing school, work, and family. Recommendations given included providing a useful orientation to communicate the pace and intensity of the program, asking graduates to share their coping experiences, offering financial advice, and providing information about counseling and stress relief. This investigation was not based on any formally defined theory or model. Driessnack, Mobily, Stineman, Montgomery, Clow, and Eisbach (2011) recommended helping students prioritize knowledge and skills to be learned amidst the vast amount of material covered in a relatively short time frame.

Tatum and Lenel (2012) compared the self-paced teaching method vs. the traditional lecture/discussion method for teaching an accelerated general psychology course. There was no difference between the two when retention was concerned. The theoretical basis of this research was the self-paced learning approach of Keller (1968). This study demonstrated using the self-paced method in an AL course did not affect retention.

THEORETICAL DEVELOPMENT/MODEL

The Institutional Action Model was proposed to analyze student success using factors outside the control of the institution, factors within the control of the institution, and how student success is achieved (Tinto, 2012a). Persistence factors that are individual to each student and, therefore, considered to be outside the control of the institution include those factors in the four boxes outside institutional commitment in Figure 1. They are (a) student's abilities, skills, and level of preparation for higher education, such as academic and social skills, (b) a student's attributes, such as personality, gender, social class, race, and ethnicity, (c) a student's attitudes, values, and knowledge about higher education, such as goals, drive, and motivations, and (d) the external commitments a student has, such as work and family. These factors cannot be easily changed by an institution. This research focused on the conditions that are more under the control of the institution: expectation, support, involvement, and feedback. They are under "Institutional Commitment" in Figure 1. An institution that is committed to student success can design and implement relevant policies, practices, and initiatives to enhance the retention of students by improving these four favorable conditions in the learning environment. Such an environment can enhance the effort that students expend on learning. The more a student learns and succeeds in class after class, the more academic progress a student makes. Such learning and progress contributes to overall student success (Tinto, 2012a).

The first institutional commitment condition for student success is expectation (Tinto, 2012a). Students do best in environments in which clear and consistent expectations are provided. Moreover, students are even more likely to succeed when these clear and consistent expectations are high but still within their capabilities. Expectations can be communicated in concrete ways through orientations as well as formal and informal advising. Receiving useful advising during the entrance time when a student chooses a major or when a student changes majors is particularly important to a student's success.

The second institutional commitment condition for student success is support (Tinto, 2012a). There are three types of support that promote student success: academic, social, and financial. Academic support can be in the form of developmental education courses, tutoring, study groups, and supplemental instruction modules. Social support can be in the form of counseling, mentoring, and ethnic student centers. These centers can provide support for individual students and can act as a safe haven for minority student groups or new students who might feel isolated otherwise. Financial support is mainly in the form of grants and student loans. All such support is most effective when it is relevant to learning, e.g., connected to a particular class a student is taking, and the environment in which learning takes place, e.g., the classroom.

Figure 1: The Institutional Model (Tinto, 2012a)

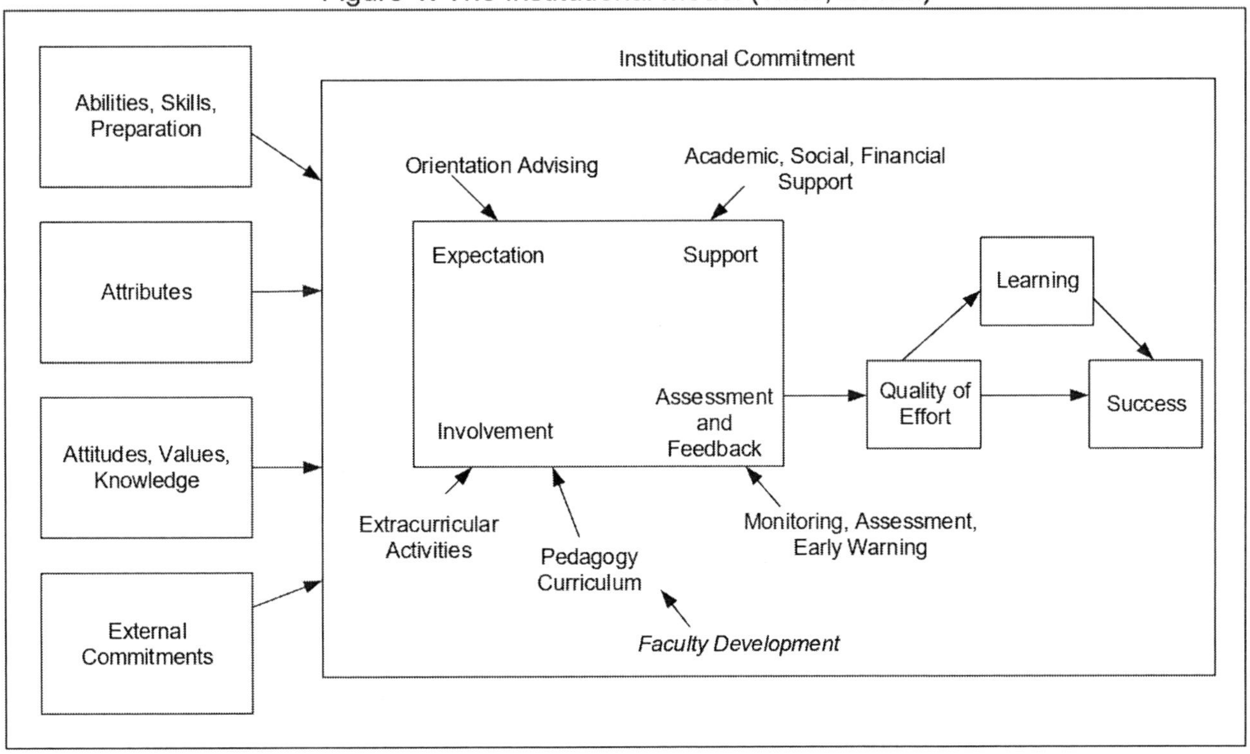

The third institutional commitment condition for student success is assessment and feedback (Tinto, 2012a). Student success is enhanced in an environment in which performance is frequently assessed and the results are provided to faculty, staff, and the students themselves. The monitoring and assessment of student performance and providing of early warning and intervention are actions that an institution can implement.

The fourth institutional commitment condition for student success is involvement (Tinto, 2012a). Involvement is also known as "engagement." Students need to be involved academically and socially for their persistence. Academic involvement can take place in the classroom and can be in the form of building educational communities. In the classroom, there are certain pedagogical strategies that can enhance academic involvement, e.g., collaborative learning, problem-based learning, and project-based learning that require students to work together in teams, service learning that require students to provide service activities to the community and are relevant to classroom learning, and the use of learning communities or cohorts in which the same group of students take the same set of classes throughout and share their experience. The use of appropriate pedagogies for academic involvement should be supported by proper faculty development. Social involvement can be in the form of extracurricular activities.

This research studied various specific institutional retention initiatives derived from the four conditions and general initiatives mentioned in the Institutional Action Model (Tinto, 2012a). Table 1 presents them under each condition. It investigated the perceived usefulness of these initiatives to on-site and online students who are taking AL classes. It also investigated if these students are willing and able to use these retention initiatives. Understanding these issues among this specific group of students can guide higher education institutions in the right direction before they invest resources in creating such initiatives.

Table 1: Institutional Initiatives for the Conditions for Student Success

Condition		Initiative
Expectation	1.	A university-level orientation, which explains the rules and regulations of the institution, the general expectation of all students, and the culture there.
	2.	A program-level orientation, which explains the program-level skills and expectation of student effort.
	3.	Before each course starts, an email from the instructor, which explains the course-level skills and expectation of student effort in this course.
	4.	Setting high and reasonable expectations and holding all students to these expectations fairly.
	5.	A personal career counseling session to help students understand which career paths are suitable for them before enrolling in a program.
	6.	Assigning a personal mentor (either a faculty member or an alumnus/a) who can answer questions about academic issues and career planning.
Support		
Academic Support	7.	A pre-program assessment to determine whether or not a student would need to improve learning skills or take any preparatory courses to succeed in the chosen program.
	8.	Presenting a clear picture of how the knowledge in different courses of the chosen program fits together in an overall picture in the first course.
	9.	In each course in the program, providing a tutor for asking questions.
	10.	In each course in the program, having a study group available.

	11.	In each course in the program, providing relevant supplemental instruction modules, such as pre-recorded video clips, in addition to the normal class components.
Social Support	12.	Giving students the chance to know the faculty and other students in the program or school socially.
	13.	Giving students the chance to know the faculty and students from their own social/ethnic background socially.
Financial Support	14.	Giving access to more grant or scholarship money for the present education.
	15.	Giving access to more student loans for the present education.
Assessment and Feedback	16.	In addition to the exams in each course, giving constant and informal feedback to inform students and the instructor of the students' learning.
	17.	While students are in the program, getting them and their academic advisors informed early about any additional assistance needed to go forward.
	18.	Students maintaining a learning portfolio that documents their own academic accomplishments for reflection and self-assessment purposes.
Involvement	19.	Involving students in class team projects with other equally contributing students during class time.
	20.	Involving students in class team projects with other equally contributing students outside class time.
	21.	Using cohorts to have students taking courses and interacting with the same cohort all the way through the program.
	22.	While students learn the material in a course, giving them the chance to apply the concepts learned (engage in proper problem-based learning).
	23.	Offering opportunities that give students relevant hands-on work experience, such as an internship or a service learning course.
	24.	Offering opportunities that allow students to join and participate in the student chapter of a professional organization in their field of study.
	25.	Offering opportunities for students to join and participate in an institution/school/program level alumni/ae and student online portal.
	26.	Offering opportunities for students to participate in a student-level contest in their field as an extracurricular activity.
	27.	Offering opportunities for students to attend a regular social gathering, such as an annual local BBQ or a quarterly online lecture series with the faculty, alumni/ae, and students in the school.

Research Questions and Hypotheses

Research Question 1: Which of the institutional initiatives recommended in Tinto's Institutional Action Model (2012a) do students taking on-site and online AL courses perceive to be useful for enhancing their persistence? Hypotheses H1 through H54 were for answering this research question.

Research Question 2: Which of the institutional initiatives recommended in Tinto's Institutional Action Model (2012a) are students taking on-site and online AL courses willing and able to use? Hypotheses H55 through H86 were for answering this research question.

For each hypothesis tested, the null version proposes neutrality. The opposite of the null version proposes that students are not neutral (positive or negative). The purpose, achieving students' academic goals, is clearly stated in each question in the questionnaire. All hypotheses are listed in Table 2.

Table 2: The List of Hypotheses	
For Research Question 1: Which of the institutional initiatives recommended in Tinto's Institutional Action Model (2012a) do students taking on-site and online AL courses perceive to be useful for enhancing their persistence?	
Initiatives Concerning Expectation (On-Site Students):	
H1	H1: On-site students are neutral about the perceived usefulness of a university-level orientation (Q1).
H2	H2: On-site students are neutral about the perceived usefulness of a program-level orientation (Q3).
H3	H3: On-site students are neutral about the perceived usefulness of getting an email from the instructor at the beginning of each course to explain the course-level skills and expectation of student effort in this course (Q5).
H4	H4: On-site students are neutral about the perceived usefulness of setting high and reasonable expectations and really holding all students to them fairly (Q6).
H5	H5: On-site students are neutral about the perceived usefulness of having a personal career counseling session to help them understand which career paths are suitable before enrolling in a program (Q7).
H6	H6: On-site students are neutral about the perceived usefulness of being assigned a personal mentor (either a faculty member or an alumnus/a) to answer their questions about academic issues and career planning (Q9).
Initiatives Concerning Expectation (Online Students):	
H7	H7: Online students are neutral about the perceived usefulness of a university-level orientation (Q1).
H8	H8: Online students are neutral about the perceived usefulness of a program-level orientation (Q3).
H9	H9: Online students are neutral about the perceived usefulness of getting an email from the instructor at the beginning of each course to explain the course-level skills and expectation of student effort in this course (Q5).
H10	H10: Online students are neutral about the perceived usefulness of setting high and reasonable expectations and really holding all students to them fairly (Q6).
H11	H11: Online students are neutral about the perceived usefulness of having a personal career counseling session to help them understand which career paths are suitable before enrolling in a program (Q7).
H12	H12: Online students are neutral about the perceived usefulness of being assigned a personal mentor (either a faculty member or an alumnus/a) to answer their questions about academic issues and career planning (Q9).

Initiatives Concerning Academic Support (On-Site Students):	
H13	H13: On-site students are neutral about the perceived usefulness of a pre-program assessment to determine whether or not they need to improve their learning skills or take any preparatory courses to succeed in the program (Q11).
H14	H14: On-site students are neutral about the perceived usefulness of getting a clear picture of how the knowledge in different courses of the program fits together in an overall picture in the first course (Q13).
H15	H15: On-site students are neutral about the perceived usefulness of the availability of a tutor in each course in the program (Q14).
H16	H16: On-site students are neutral about the perceived usefulness of the availability of a student study group in each course (Q16).
H17	H17: On-site students are neutral about the perceived usefulness of the availability of relevant supplemental instruction modules, such as pre-recorded video clips, in addition to the normal class components in each course (Q18).
Initiatives Concerning Academic Support (Online Students):	
H18	H18: Online students are neutral about the perceived usefulness of a pre-program assessment to determine whether or not they need to improve their learning skills or take any preparatory courses to succeed in the program (Q11).
H19	H19: Online students are neutral about the perceived usefulness of getting a clear picture of how the knowledge in different courses of the program fits together in an overall picture in the first course (Q13).
H20	H20: Online students are neutral about the perceived usefulness of the availability of a tutor in each course in the program (Q14).
H21	H21: Online students are neutral about the perceived usefulness of the availability of a student study group in each course (Q16).
H22	H22: Online students are neutral about the perceived usefulness of the availability of relevant supplemental instruction modules, such as pre-recorded video clips, in addition to the normal class components in each course (Q18).
Initiatives Concerning Social Support (On-Site Students):	
H23	H23: On-site students are neutral about the perceived usefulness of having the chance to know the faculty and students in their program or school socially (Q20).
H24	H24: On-site students are neutral about the perceived usefulness of having the chance to know the faculty and students from their own social/ethnic background socially (Q21).
Initiatives Concerning Social Support (Online Students):	
H25	H25: Online students are neutral about the perceived usefulness of having the chance to know the faculty and students in their program or school socially (Q20).
H26	H26: Online students are neutral about the perceived usefulness of having the chance to know the faculty and students from their own social/ethnic background socially (Q21).
Initiatives Concerning Financial Support (On-Site Students):	
H27	H27: On-site students are neutral about the perceived usefulness of having access to more grant or scholarship money for their present education (Q22).
H28	H28: On-site students are neutral about the perceived usefulness of having access to more student loans for their present education (Q23).
Initiatives Concerning Financial Support (Online Students):	
H29	H29: Online students are neutral about the perceived usefulness of having access to more grant or scholarship money for their present education (Q22).

H30	H30: Online students are neutral about the perceived usefulness of having access to more student loans for their present education (Q23).
Initiatives Concerning Assessment and Feedback (On-Site Students):	
H31	H31: On-site students are neutral about the perceived usefulness of receiving constant and informal feedback to inform them and the instructor of their learning in addition to the exams in each course (Q25).
H32	H32: On-site students are neutral about the perceived usefulness of them and their advisors being informed early about any additional assistance needed to go forward while they are in the program (Q26).
H33	H33: On-site students are neutral about the perceived usefulness of maintaining a learning portfolio that documents their own academic accomplishments for reflection and self-assessment purposes (Q27).
Initiatives Concerning Assessment and Feedback (Online Students):	
H34	H34: Online students are neutral about the perceived usefulness of receiving constant and informal feedback to inform them and the instructor of their learning in addition to the exams in each course (Q25).
H35	H35: Online students are neutral about the perceived usefulness of them and their advisors being informed early about any additional assistance needed to go forward while they are in the program (Q26).
H36	H36: Online students are neutral about the perceived usefulness of maintaining a learning portfolio that documents their own academic accomplishments for reflection and self-assessment purposes (Q27).
Initiatives Concerning Involvement (On-Site Students):	
H37	H37: On-site students are neutral about the perceived usefulness of being involved in class team projects with other equally contributing students **during** class time (Q29).
H38	H38: On-site students are neutral about the perceived usefulness of being involved in class team projects with other equally contributing students **outside** class time (Q30).
H39	H39: On-site students are neutral about the perceived usefulness of taking courses and interacting with the same classmates (as a cohort) through the entire program (Q32).
H40	H40: On-site students are neutral about the perceived usefulness of having the chance to apply the concepts they have learned (engage in proper problem-based learning) when they learn the material in a course (Q33).
H41	H41: On-site students are neutral about the perceived usefulness of having the opportunity to take a course that gives them relevant hands-on work experience, such as an internship or a service learning course (Q34).
H42	H42: On-site students are neutral about the perceived usefulness of having the opportunity to join and participate in the student chapter of a professional organization in their field of study (Q36).
H43	H43: On-site students are neutral about the perceived usefulness of having the opportunity to join and participate in a university/school/program level alumni/ae and student online portal (Q38).
H44	H44: On-site students are neutral about the perceived usefulness of having the opportunity to participate in a student-level contest in their field as an extracurricular activity (Q40).
H45	H45: On-site students are neutral about the perceived usefulness of attending regular social gatherings, such as an annual local BBQ or a quarterly online lecture series with the faculty, alumni/ae, and students in the school (Q42).
Initiatives Concerning Involvement (Online Students):	
H46	H46: Online students are neutral about the perceived usefulness of being involved in

	class team projects with other equally contributing students **during** class time (Q29).
H47	H47: Online students are neutral about the perceived usefulness of being involved in class team projects with other equally contributing students **outside** class time (Q30).
H48	H48: Online students are neutral about the perceived usefulness of taking courses and interacting with the same classmates (as a cohort) through the entire program (Q32).
H49	H49: Online students are neutral about the perceived usefulness of having the chance to apply the concepts they have learned (engage in proper problem-based learning) when they learn the material in a course (Q33).
H50	H50: Online students are neutral about the perceived usefulness of having the opportunity to take a course that gives them relevant hands-on work experience, such as an internship or a service learning course (Q34).
H51	H51: Online students are neutral about the perceived usefulness of having the opportunity to join and participate in the student chapter of a professional organization in their field of study (Q36).
H52	H52: Online students are neutral about the perceived usefulness of having the opportunity to join and participate in a university/school/program level alumni/ae and student online portal (Q38).
H53	H53: Online students are neutral about the perceived usefulness of having the opportunity to participate in a student-level contest in their field as an extracurricular activity (Q40).
H54	H54: Online students are neutral about the perceived usefulness of attending regular social gatherings, such as an annual local BBQ or a quarterly online lecture series with the faculty, alumni/ae, and students in the school (Q42).
For Research Question 2: Which of the institutional initiatives recommended in Tinto's Institutional Action Model (2012a) are students taking on-site and online AL courses willing and able to use?	
Initiatives Concerning Expectation (On-Site Students)	
H55	H55: On-site students are neutral about being willing or able to go through a university-level orientation (Q2).
H56	H56: On-site students are neutral about being willing or able to go through a program-level orientation (Q4).
H57	H57: On-site students are neutral about being willing or able to attend a personal career counseling session to help them understand which career paths are suitable for them before enrolling in the program (Q8).
H58	H58: On-site students are neutral about being willing or able to be on a voluntary personal mentor-mentee team (the mentor being either a faculty member or an alumnus/a) for them to ask questions about academic issues and career planning (Q10).
Initiatives Concerning Expectation (Online Students):	
H59	H59: Online students are neutral about being willing or able to go through a university-level orientation (Q2).
H60	H60: Online students are neutral about being willing or able to go through a program-level orientation (Q4).
H61	H61: Online students are neutral about being willing or able to attend a personal career counseling session to help them understand which career paths are suitable for them before enrolling in the program (Q8).
H62	H62: Online students are neutral about being willing or able to be on a voluntary personal mentor-mentee team (the mentor being either a faculty member or an alumnus/a) for them to ask questions about academic issues and career planning

	(Q10).
Initiatives Concerning Academic Support (On-Site Students):	
H63	H63: On-site students are neutral about being willing or able to go through a pre-program assessment to determine whether or not they need to improve their learning skills and any necessary additional preparatory courses before starting the program (Q12).
H64	H64: On-site students are neutral about being willing or able to contact a tutor for help, if needed. (Q15).
H65	H65: On-site students are neutral about being willing or able to join a voluntary student study group. (Q17).
H66	H66: On-site students are neutral about being willing or able to use relevant supplemental instruction modules, such as pre-recorded video clips, in addition to the normal class components, if needed (Q19).
Initiatives Concerning Academic Support (Online Students):	
H67	H67: Online students are neutral about being willing or able to go through a pre-program assessment to determine whether or not they need to improve their learning skills and any necessary additional preparatory courses before starting the program (Q12).
H68	H68: Online students are neutral about being willing or able to contact a tutor for help, if needed. (Q15).
H69	H69: Online students are neutral about being willing or able to join a voluntary student study group. (Q17).
H70	H70: Online students are neutral about being willing or able to use relevant supplemental instruction modules, such as pre-recorded video clips, in addition to the normal class components, if needed (Q19).
Initiatives Concerning Financial Support (On-Site Students):	
H71	H71: On-site students are neutral about being willing or able to take on additional student loans to achieve their academic goal, if needed (Q24).
Initiatives Concerning Financial Support (Online Students):	
H72	H72: Online students are neutral about being willing or able to take on additional student loans to achieve their academic goal, if needed (Q24).
Initiatives Concerning Assessment and Feedback (On-Site Students):	
H73	H73: On-site students are neutral about being willing or able to maintain a learning portfolio that documents their own academic accomplishments for reflection and self-assessment purposes (Q28).
Initiatives Concerning Assessment and Feedback (Online Students):	
H74	H74: Online students are neutral about being willing or able to maintain a learning portfolio that documents their own academic accomplishments for reflection and self-assessment purposes (Q28).
Initiatives Concerning Involvement (On-Site Students):	
H75	H75: Given a choice between (a) working on a class team project with other equally contributing students outside class time and (b) working on a class project by oneself outside class time, on-site students are neutral about (a) and (b) (Q31).
H76	H76: On-site students are neutral about being willing or able to take a course that gives them relevant hands-on work experience, such as an internship or a service learning course (Q35).
H77	H77: On-site students are neutral about being willing or able to join and participate in a student chapter of a professional organization in their field of study (Q37).
H78	H78: On-site students are neutral about being willing or able to join and participate in a

	university/school/program level alumni/ae and student online portal (Q39).
H79	H79: On-site students are neutral about being willing or able to participate in a student-level contest in their field as an extracurricular activity (Q41).
H80	H80: On-site students are neutral about being willing or able to attend a regular social gathering, such as an annual local BBQ or a quarterly online lecture series with the faculty, alumni/ae, and students in their school (Q43).
Initiatives Concerning Involvement (Online Students):	
H81	H81: Given a choice between (a) working on a class team project with other equally contributing students outside the virtual classroom class time and (b) working on a class project by oneself outside the virtual classroom class time, online students are neutral about (a) and (b) (Q31).
H82	H82: Online students are neutral about being willing or able to take a course that gives them relevant hands-on work experience, such as an internship or a service learning course (Q35).
H83	H83: Online students are neutral about being willing or able to join and participate in the student chapter of a professional organization in their field of study (Q37).
H84	H84: Online students are neutral about being willing or able to join and participate in a university/school/program level alumni/ae and student online portal (Q39).
H85	H85: Online students are neutral about being willing or able to participate in a student-level contest in their field as an extracurricular activity (Q41).
H86	H86: Online students are neutral about being willing or able to attend a regular social gathering, such as an annual local BBQ or a quarterly online lecture series with the faculty, alumni/ae, and students in their school (Q43).

METHODS

Instrumentation

The two versions of the questionnaire used were derived directly from Tinto (2012a). One version was offered to on-site students and the other version was offered to online students. For consistency, the questions in both versions were the same with variations on the words "on-site" or "online," as appropriate. For objective questions, the responses were on a five-point Likert scale, with "Strongly Disagree" (1), "Disagree" (2), "Neutral" (3), "Agree" (4), and "Strongly Agree" (5). There were also open-ended questions to allow the subjects to provide more in-depth information. Questions in the questionnaire were divided into different categories that aligned with the conditions of student success in the Institutional Action Model (Tinto, 2012a) and the hypotheses set up. Both versions of the questionnaire are available upon request from the first author.

Research Steps

This research was a quantitative study with a questionnaire survey and statistical analysis. The major steps in the methodology were as follows:

1. Formally defining the research hypotheses based on relevant theoretical model
2. Developing two versions of a questionnaire based on Tinto (2012a), one for students taking an on-site class and one for students taking an online class
3. Obtaining Institutional Review Board (IRB) approval
4. Performing a pre-test on each version of the questionnaire with at least two relevant students, to see if any improvement on the questionnaire is necessary

5. Asking the students (subjects) to voluntarily work on an assignment for bonus points. For this assignment, each subject was given the choice of completing Version A (the questionnaire, on-site or online, as appropriate) and completing Version B (a written assignment about the course learning outcomes of the course he or she was taking)
6. Performing data cleansing and coding based on the answers of the subjects
7. Performing a two-tailed z-test statistical test for each hypothesis to determine whether the null version of each one should be rejected or not.

Subjects

A convenience sample of current AL students were used as subjects in this study. Among this sample, there were two groups of students. The first group was composed of students taking an on-site class. The second group was composed of the students taking an online class.

This study used current students enrolled at a private university ("XYZ University" from here onwards) as subjects. In order to be as comprehensive as possible, at least one on-site class and one online class offered by each college or school of XYZ University were included in data collection. XYZ University is an accredited non-profit university based in California. It offers undergraduate and graduate programs in an accelerated format. In this format, classes are conducted in a one-class-per-month approach. Basically, each 4.5 quarter-unit class is four weeks long. A student, who only takes one class each month, takes classes one by one until all the program requirements are fulfilled. A student can take such a class on-site in a physical classroom or online. An on-site undergraduate class meets ten times during its four-week period (two times a week and two weekends). Each class lasts for 4.5 hours. An online class may still have live lecture sessions via a virtual classroom on the Internet. Similar to a traditional class session in a physical classroom, when a virtual lecture session starts, the instructor and all the students log into the same virtual classroom. Teaching and communication are synchronous via headsets and a shared computer application, such as Microsoft PowerPoint. Usually, such synchronous lecture sessions are offered one to two times a week, as decided by the instructor. Students taking an online course are expected to do a lot of self-learning. Usually, a student takes all the courses on-site or all the courses online. However, for a student who resides in a location where on-site classes are available, this student can take classes in both formats.

RESULTS

Demographics of Subjects

A total of 142 completed questionnaires for on-site classes and 78 questionnaires for online classes were used for data analysis. The respondents who returned these accepted questionnaires will be called "subjects" from here onwards. Student subjects who participated in this survey were both undergraduate and graduate students from various colleges and schools of XYZ University as summarized in Table 3. There was one student who was enrolled in two of the classes. This student did not answer the questionnaire two times.

Table 3: Subject Academic Background

	Undergraduate	Graduate	Total
College of Letter and Sciences (COLS)	On-Site: 8 Online: 3	On-Site: 12 Online: 0	On-Site: 20 Online: 3
School of Business and Management (SOBM)	On-Site: 6 Online: 0	On-Site: 23 Online: 8	On-Site: 29 Online: 8

School of Education (SOE)	On-Site: 1 Online: 0	On-Site: 31 Online: 18	On-Site: 32 Online: 18
School of Engineering and Computing (SOEC)	On-Site: 18 Online: 25	On-Site: 21 Online: 7	On-Site: 39 Online: 32
School of Health and Human Services (SHHS)	On-Site: 1 Online: 4	On-Site: 8 Online: 0	On-Site: 9 Online: 4
School of Professional Studies (SOPS)	On-Site: 0 Online: 11	On-Site: 11 Online: 0	On-Site: 11 Online: 11
School Unknown	On-Site: 2 Online: 2	On-Site: 0 Online: 0	On-Site: 2 Online: 2
Total:	On-Site: 36 Online: 45 Total: 81	On-Site: 106 Online: 33 Total: 139	On-Site: 142 Online: 78 Total 220

As for gender of the subjects, 132 are male, 87 are female, and one subject declined to answer about the gender. 11 of the 220 subjects are 23 years old or under, 104 are between 24 and 33 years old, 65 are between 34 and 43 years old, 39 are 44 years old or over, and the rest declined to answer the question about age. Among the 220 subjects, 197 are domestic students, 19 are international students, and the rest did not answer this question. Among the 220 subjects, 73 are military veterans, 10 are on active military duty, 100 are civilians with no military experience, and the rest declined to answer this question.

Among the 220 subjects, 196 were not enrolled in another course for credit at the same time, 16 were enrolled in another undergraduate course, and 8 enrolled in another graduate course concurrently. Among the 220 subjects, 3 were taking the first course in their programs at the time the questionnaire was answered, 47 had taken 1-4 courses in their programs, 59 had taken 5-10, and 111 had taken more than 10 courses in their respective programs. Among these 220 subjects, 213 had graduation as the major academic goal, 5 were taking courses to eventually transfer to another institution, one was taking courses as needed, not necessary for a degree or for a credential, the rest did not choose any of the above answers. Among the 220 subjects, 206 intended to put in the best effort in every course to learn and to succeed, 7 intended to just put in enough effort to keep themselves in school, 6 intended to put in effort as they felt like it course by course, and one did not choose any of the above answers. Among the 220 subjects, 113 were working full-time regularly for 40 or more hours per week, 10 were working regularly between 35 and 39.99 hours per week, 23 were working regularly between 20 and 34.99 hours per week, 16 were working regularly but fewer than 20 hours per week, 14 were working only whenever a suitable job came up, and 44 were not working at all (unemployed). As for the family responsibilities, among the 220 subjects, 109 of them are responsible for at least 50 percent of taking care of dependents within driving distance, 8 of them are responsible for less than 50 percent of taking care of dependents within driving distance, 92 have no dependents, and the rest did not choose any of the above answers.

Statistical Results

Overall, the research results indicate that, to students who are in an accelerated program, many of the initiatives derived from The Institutional Action Model (Tinto, 2012a) are applicable to both on-site students and online students. On-site students view the usefulness of all initiatives positively except that they are neutral about the usefulness of getting the chance to know the faculty and students from their own social/ethnic background. They are also willing to and capable of using all the initiatives. As for online students, they view the usefulness of most of the initiatives positively. They are neutral about the usefulness of the following: a pre-program assessment to determine the need for learning skills improvement or preparatory courses, being involved in class team projects with other equally contributing students during class time and outside class time, and being involved in a student-level contest in their field. Online students view the usefulness of the following negatively: getting the chance to know the faculty and students from their own social/ethnic background and attending regular social gatherings with faculty, alumni/ae, and students in the school, such as an annual local BBQ party or a quarterly online lecture series. As for their willingness and capability of using the initiatives, online AL students are positive for most of them. However, they are neutral about participating in: a pre-program assessment to determine the need for learning skills improvement or preparatory courses, a study group in each course, a student-level contest in their field, and attending regular social gatherings with faculty, alumni/ae, and students in the school, such as an annual local BBQ party or a quarterly online lecture series. They are negative about choosing a team project outside class time over choosing an individual project outside class time.

Table 4 below is a summary of the findings. Each row corresponds to an initiative. For each initiative, to answer the first research question, a hypothesis was tested for on-site students' perceived usefulness and another hypothesis was tested for online students' perceived usefulness. To answer the second research question, similar, a hypothesis was tested for on-site students' willingness and capability of participation and another one was tested for online students' willingness and capability of participation. A dash denotes that students' voluntary participation in a certain initiative is not applicable and this willingness/capability to participate was not studied. For each hypothesis, a two-tailed z-test with alpha 0.05 (0.025 on each side) was used. The z-score for the null hypothesis to be rejected was 1.96 or higher on the positive side or -1.96 or lower on the negative side. An asterisk next to a z-score denotes that this z-score does not fall into the rejection area, thus, the null hypothesis cannot be rejected.

Table 4: A Complete View of Student Perception and Initiative Participation

		On-Site		Online	
	Expectation	Perception	Participation	Perception	Participation
1.	A university-level orientation, which explains the rules and regulations of the institution, the general expectation of all students, and the culture there.	H1 Positive n: 139 z-score: 6.2276 p-value: 4.7E-10	H55 Positive n: 140 z-score: 8.4838 p-value: 2E-17	H7 Positive n: 78 z-score: 4.2500 p-value: 2.1E-05	H59 Positive n: 78 z-score: 4.0252 p-value: 6E-05
2.	A program-level orientation, which explains the program-level skills and expectation of student effort.	H2 Positive n: 142 z-score: 9.5540 p-value: 1E-21	H56 Positive n: 142 z-score: 10.7309 p-value: 7.3E-27	H8 Positive n: 78 z-score: 6.8565 p-value: 7E-12	H60 Positive n: 77 z-score: 7.0676 p-value: 2E-12
3.	Before each course starts, an email from the instructor, which explains the course-	H3 Positive n: 142	-	H9 Positive n: 78	-

	level skills and expectation of student effort in this course.	z-score: 15.6552 p-value: 3.1E-55		z-score: 16.2021 p-value: 4.9E-59	
4.	Setting high and reasonable expectations and holding all students to these expectations fairly.	H4 Positive n: 142 z-score: 17.7332 p-value: 2.3E-70	-	H10 Positive n: 78 z-score: 11.8515 p-value: 2.1E-32	-
5.	A personal career counseling session to help students understand which career paths are suitable for them before enrolling in a program.	H5 Positive n: 142 z-score: 11.3440 p-value: 7.9E-30	H57 Positive n: 142 z-score: 12.2237 p-value: 2.3E-34	H11 Positive n: 77 z-score: 4.6215 p-value: 4E-06	H61 Positive n: 78 z-score: 6.0764 p-value: 1E-09
6.	Assigning a personal mentor (either a faculty member or an alumnus/a) who can answer questions about academic issues and career planning.	H6 Positive n: 142 z-score: 12.6973 p-value: 6.1E-37	H58 Positive n: 138 z-score: 7.1027 p-value: 1E-12	H12 Positive n: 78 z-score: 9.6732 p-value: 4E-22	H62 Positive n: 73 z-score: 4.8421 p-value: 1E-06
		On-Site		Online	
	Academic Support	Perception	Participation	Perception	Participation
7.	A pre-program assessment to determine whether a student would need to improve learning skills or take any preparatory courses to succeed in the chosen program.	H13 Positive n: 142 z-score: 2.7661 p-value: 0.0057	H63 Positive n: 141 z-score: 3.9607 p-value: 7E-05	H18 Neutral n: 77 z-score: 1.195* p-value: 0.2321	H67 Neutral n: 78 z-score: 1.1778* p-value: 0.2389
8.	Presenting a clear picture of how the knowledge in different courses of the chosen program fits together in an overall picture in the first course.	H14 Positive n: 142 z-score: 11.5578 p-value: 6.7E-31	-	H19 Positive n: 78 z-score: 8.3572 p-value: 6E-17	-

9.	In each course in the program, providing a tutor for asking questions.	H15 Positive n: 141 z-score: 9.7576 p-value: 2E-22	H64 Positive n: 141 z-score: 12.6131 p-value: 1.8E-36	H20 Positive n: 78 z-score: 8.5078 p-value: 2E-17	H68 Positive n: 78 z-score: 11.93303 p-value: 7.96E-33
10.	In each course in the program, having a student study group available.	H16 Positive n: 142 z-score: 8.5133 p-value: 2E-17	H65 Positive n: 141 z-score: 6.6207 p-value: 4E-11	H21 Positive n: 78 z-score: 2.2603 p-value: 0.0238	H69 Neutral n: 78 z-score: 1.2496* p-value: 0.2114
11.	In each course in the program, providing relevant supplemental instruction modules, such as pre-recorded video clips, in addition to the normal class components.	H17 Positive n: 141 z-score: 14.5556 p-value: 5.4E-48	H66 Positive n: 141 z-score: 16.0493 p-value: 5.8E-58	H22 Positive n: 78 z-score: 9.7367 p-value: 2E-22	H70 Positive n: 77 z-score: 11.9934 p-value: 3.8E-33
		On-Site		Online	
	Social Support	Perception	Participation	Perception	Participation
12.	Giving students the chance to know the faculty and other students in the program or school socially.	H23 Positive n: 141 z-score: 7.1992 p-value: 6E-13	-	H25 Positive n: 78 z-score: 2.4470 p-value: 0.01441	-
13.	Giving students the chance to know the faculty and students from their own social/ethnic background socially.	H24 Neutral n: 142 z-score: 0.7895* p-value: 0.4298	-	H26 Negative n: 76 z-score: -3.5416 p-value: 0.0004	-
		On-Site		Online	
	Financial Support	Perception	Participation	Perception	Participation
14.	Giving access to more grant or scholarship money for the present education.	H27 Positive n: 140 z-score:	-	H29 Positive n: 77 z-score:	-

		15.3630 p-value: 2.9E-53		10.9179 p-value: 9.5E-28	
15.	Giving access to more student loans for the present education.	H28 Positive n: 139 z-score: 3.3527 p-value: 0.0008	H71 Positive n: 138 z-score: 2.5393 p-value: 0.0111	H30 Positive n: 77 z-score: 2.3753 p-value: 0.0175	H72 Positive n: 76 z-score: 3.9154 p-value: 9E-05
		On-Site		Online	
	Assessment and Feedback	Perception	Participation	Perception	Participation
16.	In addition to the exams in each course, giving constant and informal feedback to inform students and the instructor of the students' learning.	H31 Positive n: 142 z-score: 22.6393 p-value: 2E-113	-	H34 Positive n: 76 z-score: 10.1101 p-value: 5E-24	-
17.	While students are in the program, getting them and their academic advisors informed early about any additional assistance needed to go forward.	H32 Positive n: 142 z-score: 20.2465 p-value: 3.8E-91	-	H35 Positive n: 77 z-score: 12.8217 p-value: 1.2E-37	-
18.	Students maintaining a learning portfolio that documents their own academic accomplishments for reflection and self-assessment purposes.	H33 Positive n: 142 z-score: 12.6924 p-value: 6.5E-37	H73 Positive n: 139 z-score: 7.4376 p-value: 1E-13	H36 Positive n: 77 z-score: 6.0967 p-value: 1E-09	H74 Positive n: 78 z-score: 5.5048 p-value: 4E-08
		On-Site		Online	
	Involvement	Perception	Participation	Perception	Participation
19.	Involving students in class team projects with other equally contributing students during class time.	H37 Positive n: 142 z-score: 8.3556 p-value: 7E-17	-	H46 Neutral n: 77 z-score: -0.7406* p-value: 0.45894	-

20.	Involving students in class team projects with other equally contributing students outside class time.	H38 Positive n: 142 z-score: 3.7847 p-value: 0.00015	H75 Positive about choosing a team project outside class time over an individual project n: 141 z-score: 2.7057 p-value: 0.0068	H47 Neutral n: 77 z-score: -0.9681* p-value: 0.33299	H81 Negative about choosing a team project outside class time over an individual project n: 77 z-score: -3.4999 p-value: 0.0005
21.	Using cohorts to have students taking courses and interacting with the same cohort all the way through the program.	H39 Positive n: 142 z-score: 12.5591 p-value: 3.5E-36	-	H48 Positive n: 78 z-score: 5.0598 p-value: 4E-07	-
22.	While students learn the material in a course, giving them the chance to apply the concepts learned (engage in proper problem-based learning).	H40 Positive n: 142 z-score: 17.9233 p-value: 7.8E-72	-	H49 Positive n: 77 z-score: 13.9974 p-value: 1.6E-44	-
23.	Offering opportunities that give students relevant hands-on work experience, such as an internship or a service learning course.	H41 Positive n: 141 z-score: 20.5643 p-value: 5.7E-94	H76 Positive n: 142 z-score: 19.2218 p-value: 2.4E-82	H50 Positive n: 78 z-score: 11.0597 p-value: 2E-28	H82 Positive n: 77 z-score: 9.4273 p-value: 4E-21
24.	Offering opportunities that allow students to join and participate in the student chapter of a professional organization in their field of study.	H42 Positive n: 141 z-score: 11.6980 p-value: 1.3E-31	H77 Positive n: 140 z-score: 10.7042 p-value: 9.7E-27	H51 Positive n: 78 z-score: 5.2456 p-value: 2E-07	H83 Positive n: 76 z-score: 4.1279 p-value: 4E-05
25.	Offering opportunities for students to join	H43 Positive	H78 Positive	H52 Positive	H84 Positive

	and participate in an institution/school/program level alumni/ae and student online portal.	n: 142 z-score: 7.5387 p-value: 5E-14	n: 139 z-score: 3.8363 p-value: 0.0001	n: 77 z-score: 2.6345 p-value: 0.0084	n: 77 z-score: 2.4789 p-value: 0.0132
26.	Offering opportunities for students to participate in a student-level contest in their field as an extracurricular activity.	H44 Positive n: 139 z-score: 3.7185 p-value: 0.0002	H79 Positive n: 142 z-score: 3.0869 p-value: 0.002	H53 Neutral n: 76 z-score: -0.9037* p-value: 0.3661	H85 Neutral n: 77 z-score: -1.1452* p-value: 0.25213
27.	Offering opportunities for students to attend a regular social gathering, such as an annual local BBQ or a quarterly online lecture series with the faculty, alumni/ae, and students in the school.	H45 Positive n: 142 z-score: 3.7799 p-value: 0.0002	H80 Positive n: 141 z-score: 4.1017 p-value: 4E-05	H54 Negative n: 77 z-score: -0.2689* p-value: 0.78803	H86 Neutral n: 77 z-score: 0.1717* p-value: 0.8637

DISCUSSION AND CONCLUSIONS

The results of this study point to two theoretical implications. First, all the conditions for student success in the Institutional Action Model (Tinto, 2012a), which are expectation, support (academic, social, and financial), assessment and feedback, and involvement, are more applicable to students in on-site AL programs than to their online counterparts. On-site AL students perceive most of the initiatives positively (except one) and are willing to participate in them. However, as shown in the section above, online AL students are not positive about several of these initiatives. One possible explanation could be the fact that, on-site AL students are closer to students in traditional higher education programs. They still have to attend classes on campus physically and they have more time for the initiatives suggested, especially those under social support and involvement. Online students chose to attend school online and this might mean they have more responsibilities that demand their attention and time. They would like to achieve their academic goals as quickly as possible. Therefore, they are not that positive about pre-assessment, study groups, team projects, team student contests, and social gatherings. We may need a modified version of this model for online AL students. Second, the initiative of giving AL students the chance to socially know the faculty and students from their own social/ethnic background does not apply to either on-site (neutral) or online (negative) students. This initiative under social support needs to be reconsidered.

There are two practical implications for institutions that offer AL programs. First, when students (especially online students) are required to go through a pre-assessment program before they take the first class, it is very important that a positive explanation be given to these new students to let them understand the importance of pre-assessment for their academic success and achievement of their career goals. Second, since online AL students do not prefer some of the initiatives under social support and involvement, institutions have to be careful about giving too many mandatory class team projects. Social events, such as local BBQ parties for faculty and students, might not be as effective among online students as among on-site ones. Providing academic support and letting online AL students work on their own might be more suitable initiatives.

Limitations and Future Research Directions

This study had two limitations. First, the sample used was a convenience sample and not a random sample. Second, data were collected from different class sections of one university and not several different universities that offer AL programs.

There are several future research directions. First, this study can be expanded to use random samples from more than one university that offers AL programs. Further, among these universities chosen, it would even be better if they can be a combination of public and private universities, so as to broaden the scope of such an investigation. Second, a formal qualitative study can be used to study why online students do not prefer initiatives that enhance their involvement, such as joining a voluntary student study group and extracurricular activities, such as a student-level contest and regular local BBQ parties. Doing a formal qualitative study can understand the "why" part of an issue in an in-depth manner. Third, with a more thorough understanding of the suitable initiatives for online AL students, a new version of The Institutional Action Model can be developed for this group of students. Fourth, for each initiative deemed useful by AL students, further studies are needed to determine how they can be designed and executed effectively, so as to be the most useful to AL students. In fact, such further studies can be extended to understand which execution approach is the best for which type of AL students.

Conclusions

This paper has presented an empirical study to verify The Institutional Model by Tinto (2012a). Most of the initiatives derived from this model are deemed to be useful by both on-site and online AL students. One major difference between on-site and online students is the lower perceived usefulness and participation willingness in social activities among online students.

REFERENCES

Allen, P., Van Dyke, Y., & Armstrong, M. L. (2010). "Growing your own" nursing staff with a collaborative accelerated second-degree, web-based program. *The Journal of Continuing Education in Nursing, 41*(3), 118-122.

Buddin, R. (2014). Trends in freshman dropouts and transfers: 2006-2012. ACT Research and Policy. Retrieved November 15, 2014, from http://www.act.org/research/researchers/briefs/2014-14.html

Driessnack, M., Mobily, P., Stineman, A., Montgomery, L. A., Clow, T., & Eisbach, S. (2011, October). We are different: Learning needs of accelerated second-degree nursing students. *Nurse Educator, 36*(5), 214-218.

Keller, F. S. (1968, Spring). Good-bye, teacher .... *Journal of Applied Behavior Analysis, 1*(1) 79-89.

Rouse, S. M. & Rooda, L. A. (2010, November). Factors for attrition in an accelerated baccalaureate nursing program. *Journal of Nursing Education, 49*(6), 359-362.

Serdyukov, P. (2008, March). Accelerated learning: What is it? *Journal of Research in Innovative Teaching, 1*(1), 35-59.

Stewart, S., Pope, D., & Hansen, T. S. (2010, January/February). Clinical preceptors enhance an online accelerated bachelor's degree to BSN program. *Nurse Educator, 35*(1), 37-40.

Stuenkel, D., Nelson, D., Malloy, S., & Cohen, J. (2011, March/April). Challenges, changes, and collaboration: Evaluation of an accelerated BSN program. *Nurse Educator, 36*(2), 70-75.

Tatum, B. C. & Lenel, J. C. (2012, March). A comparison of self-paced and lecture/discussion methods in an accelerated learning format. *Journal of Research in Innovative Teaching, 5*(1), 139-156.

Tinto, V. (2012a). Moving from theory to action: A model of institutional action for student success. In Seidman, A. (ed.). *College student retention* (2nd ed.). NY: Rowan & Littlefield Publishers, Inc.

Tinto, V. (2012b, April). *Completing college: Rethinking institutional action*. Chicago: University of Chicago Press.

DECISION SCIENCES INSTITUTE

Integration of teaching and research: The active-learning and research-led approach in integrating multi-disciplinary concepts in operations management.

Mohan Gopalakrishnan
Supply Chain Management, W. P. Carey School of Business
Arizona State University
USA
mohan@asu.edu

ABSTRACT

In this research, the focus is on integrating teaching and research using the research-led approach where students learn about research findings through active participation in research activities and faculty research interests lead the curriculum content. Using the student active-learning as the center of an experiential activity, the paper presents the experience of enhancing student learning through a product redesign game to understand the interactions between cost goals and information timing. The continuous opportunity to use the game also provided data for further collaborative research that was published in a top-tier research journal. The win-win experience and the lessons learned are shared.

KEYWORDS: Integrating teaching and research, new product development, cost goals, experiential learning, information timing

INTRODUCTION

Recently a faculty-colleague of mine retired from our department after 35+ years of exemplary service. When he spoke during his retirement party he nostalgically recalled how during his initial years, University (business school) wanted him to only focus on teaching and conduct research and dissemination of research in his "personal time". He lamented how times have changed today. This made me reflect on my own experience in linking teaching and research in a progressive manner and that is the focus of this paper. I am not going to discuss about whether we should do it or what are the pitfalls in doing the same. Rather, I will focus on the benefits using literature, and also modern strategies for successfully integrating the two iconic branches of pedagogy. Following this, I will be using a research that was conducted over a 5-year period involving several groups of students as part of an operations course and an accounting course, which provided opportunity for valid data collection using "experimental research" through "experiential learning," and how the analysis of the data led to a collaborative research article published recently in a top-tier accounting journal (Gopalakrishnan, et. al., 2015)

LITERATURE REVIEW

The benefits of integration of teaching and research are non-trivial. First and foremost, it is known that increased knowledge through research certainly improves instructive

competence. Second, it is said that a teacher doing research is more likely to be intellectually alive that generally translates to involvement, and enthusiasm in the classroom. Third, research breeds good intellectual habits and the thorough organizational skills in research tend to influence structure and depth in preparing individual lectures or courses. Finally, students with research teachers have the opportunity to view great minds at work and by virtue of these examples better learn the habits of critical, reflective reason (Altbach and Lewis, 1995). So, if teaching were approached as a scholarly activity, looked at in terms beyond technique, and seen as a phenomenon worthy of study, reflection, and dialogue, then possibilities for integrating teaching and research would open onto new vistas (Weimer, 1997)
The NSF funded Center for the Integration of Research, Teaching, and Learning (CIRTL) formed as a collaborative effort between the University of Wisconsin–Madison, Michigan State University, and Pennsylvania State University, uses three conceptual "pillars" to guide CIRTL's plans, programs, and activities in grooming future faculty who could integrate teaching and research. These include: Teaching-as-Research (TAR), Learning Communities (LC), and Learning through-Diversity (LTD). Specifically, TAR "involves the deliberate, systematic, and reflective use of research methods to develop and implement teaching practices that advance the learning experiences and outcomes of students and teachers"

The framework developed by Griffiths (2004) classifies teaching as: (a) research-led: where students learn about research findings through active participation in research activities where the curriculum content is led by faculty research interests, and information transmission is the main teaching mode; (b) research-oriented: where students learn about research processes; or (c) research-based: where students learn as researchers, and the curriculum is largely designed around inquiry-based activities. In this paper we focus on research-led paradigm to integrate teaching and research.

Furthermore, "active-learning" has been promoted as an excellent strategy for improving student cognition and retention. Active learning is generally defined as any instructional method that engages students in the learning process. In short, active learning requires students to do meaningful learning activities and think about what they are doing (Prince, 2004). Introducing student activity into the traditional lecture, and promoting student engagement through collaborative learning are touted as the corner stones of "active learning." It is also shown that active learning improved learning outcomes relative to individual work across the board (Prince, 2004).

Lastly, the Stanford University center for teaching and learning provides the following four tips for instructors to bring the process as well as the products of research into the classroom (Teaching commons, 2016)
(a) Use of current research perspectives, paradigms, and debates in the classroom to show that knowledge is contested and growing, rather than accepted fact.
(b) Inclusion of recent research results as part of curriculum content.
(c) Introduction of both generic and subject-specific research skills and scholarly activities into course assignments, including literature review, experiment design, peer

review, book review, conference paper presentation, and grant application.
(d) Providing opportunities to let students into your research community in small ways by requiring them to join scholarly email lists or discussion boards, use online conference proceedings as resources for class assignments, or attend departmental talks.

To summarize the literature, three issues relevant to this paper stand out as critical ones for attempting to integrate teaching and research.

(a) The focus of the effort described here is "research-led", where a particular topic is used to provide an experiential-learning opportunity for the students that also serves to provide data/information from an experimental methodology used in answering research questions related to cost specificity and new product development (NPD) process.
(b) The concepts involving cost goals and information handling for NPD are taught using the "active-learning" approach, where students are totally involved in redesigning a product using "Lego" blocks and work in teams to enhance collaborative learning. Later the de-briefing of the game also provides an opportunity to enhance comprehension of the concepts covered as learning objectives for this topic.
(c) Lastly, the whole process follows the one of the tips provided by the teaching and learning center at Stanford University that encourages using the current research perspectives and paradigms to discuss the role of cost goals in NPD. The experiential-learning and the data (class results and its comparison to other data collected) helps shape the debate of conditions where cost goals are effective. Follow-up in executive MBA classes have led to anecdotal evidence that the learning from this course (and the particular topic) has influenced managerial thinking in dealing with cost targets.

Research perspectives

Many firms that compete based on the development of new and innovative products have begun to adopt concurrent new product development (NPD) processes in which product design phases occur in a non-linear and iterative manner. While concurrent NPD processes increase flexibility and reduce time-to-market as compared to traditional sequential processes, concurrency increases task uncertainty since the product design process begins before all important product features and specifications have been established. Such changes can result in costly redesign and rework. Prior research suggests target costing, where product design teams are assigned specific cost goals, is an effective method of controlling costs in sequential NPD. Even so, it unclear whether target costing will improve cost reduction performance when combined with a concurrent NPD process due to increased task uncertainty. We examine experimentally the ability of product design groups to achieve specific or general cost reduction goals under simulated sequential or concurrent NPD. We predict and find that the nature of the NPD process moderates the effect of specific cost reduction goals on actual cost reduction performance. While specific cost goals result in higher reductions in product cost than general cost goals under a sequential NPD process, specific goals are no better than general goals in motivating design groups to reduce product cost under a concurrent NPD process; thus, we demonstrate boundary conditions on the usefulness of target costing as a cost control method (Gopalakrishnan et. al., 2015).

Research-led Teaching:

Both my co-researcher who teaches in the accounting department and me teaching in the supply chain management department collaborated on collecting data using the graduate level managerial accounting, and operations and supply chain management courses to utilize the research-led approach to teaching. We chose target costing as the appropriate teaching module in accounting and new product development as the module in the operations course. We also predominantly chose the classes at the evening MBA and executive MBA courses, since it provided us with students with reasonable amount of work-experience so that they would deal with cost targets in their line of work. Also, these classes were at least 3 hours long, which gave us to the time to implement the experiential learning game and also conduct experiments using the game.

We were careful to avoid the students who overlapped both our courses to minimize duplicity of information. We also chose programs across the country and delivered these modules as guest lectures that gave us the opportunity to engage more students from diverse environments. Students coming to either of the classes were given standard reading material in target costing and the new product development phases (including relevant chapters from the prescribed books in managerial accounting and operations management). In addition, a research article that links the two through NPD metrics was also provided (e.g., Afonso et. al., 2008). Both the introduction of target costing and the NPD processes (sequential versus concurrent) were briefly touched upon from information-theoretic perspectives. For example, "target costing" was introduced as a pricing method used by firms for reducing the overall cost of a product over its entire life-cycle with the help of production, engineering, research and design. Without going over the mechanics at this juncture, students were told that market and other cost information leads to "cost targets." The cost targets could be a fixed one versus a general one (do the best you can). Similarly, for NPD processes they were informed that the information timing differentiated the sequential versus concurrent processes. In the former, all information is generally available for a phase to start its part of the work, while in the latter a phase further down the NPD chain might start with incomplete information and update as new information comes in. Before the start of the experiential learning activity explained next, students do not generally have a well-formed idea of when cost goals would be effective. In other words the following hypothesis that was tested and results published in the research paper is not articulated to them, rather allowing them to uncover through the game and the follow-on discussions.

> *"The nature of the product design process will moderate the relation between cost goal specificity and cost reduction performance; groups assigned a specific cost goal will reduce product cost more than groups assigned a general cost goal under a sequential, but not a concurrent NPD process." (Gopalakrishnan et al., 2015)*

Experiential learning through the Lego game:

The game entails building and costing a truck using the Lego blocks. The finished product is provided in figure 1. Students are assigned to teams in a random fashion (team size was controlled at three). We were able to collect data from hundred plus teams.

Figure 1 Finished Original Truck Design using Lego blocks

Each team was provided with a packet containing the Lego pieces, instruction sheet on how to build the truck and a spreadsheet provided for calculating the cost of the final truck (see figure 2) with instructions on how to do the costing. Once the student-teams finish this activity (that allows them to see how many different parts are used and what is the scope for standardization to reduce cost and improve value), they are given extra Lego parts and an instruction sheet (sample provided as figure 3) to start the redesign activity. At this juncture half the teams are asked to depart to an adjoining room with the other half staying in the same room. The instruction sheets on redesign given to the teams either contain a cost target, such as redesign the truck so that you meet a cost target of "$X" or no cost target, such as redesign the truck so that you can bring down the cost "as much as you can." Also, in the two rooms where student teams now are ready to start their redesign activity, we ensure equal number teams with cost target vs. no cost target. Figure 3 provides the sample instruction sheet with cost target and other quality and design requirements to be met for an accepted re-design. Extra spreadsheets as explained in figure 2 are provided for the teams to keep track of the costs as they redesign.

The two rooms simulate the sequential versus concurrent product development environments. This is implemented as follows. In addition to the truck redesign requirements provided in figure 3, three additional needs from customers (end-customer and governmental regulation) affect the redesign (see figure 4). In the sequential room, all the information is provided in one shot at the beginning of the redesign activity. In the concurrent room these come in a staggered fashion with the student-teams stopped after every 15 minutes and the new requirement provided. A total of 60 minutes is provided to the teams in both the rooms to complete their redesign activity and calculate the cost of their final design.

		ORIGINAL DESIGN			
				Material and Labor	
Plates (Thin)	Beg Inv	End Inv	Qty Used	Cost/Unit	Total Cost
2X2	2			$200	
2X3				$200	
2X4	2			$200	
2X6				$400	
2X8				$500	
2X10	2			$700	
4X4				$400	
4X6	1			$800	
4X10	1			$1,100	
		# of Unique Plates		Subtotal	
Bricks (Thick)					
1X2	13			$200	
1X3	2			$200	
1X4	2			$200	
1X6	1			$400	
1X8	2			$500	
2X2	1			$300	
2X4	4			$500	
2X6				$700	
2X8				$900	
2X10				$1,100	
		# of Unique Bricks		Subtotal	
Special Parts					
Wheels	4		4	$400	$1,600
Axles	2		2	$800	$1,600
Grille	1		1	$500	$500
Windshield	1		1	$800	$800
Steering Wheel	1		1	$400	$400
Roll Bar	1		1	$300	$300
		# of Unique Special Parts	6	Subtotal	$5,200
				TOTAL MAT'L & LABOR	
Overhead Cost					
Number of different parts used				$200	
				TOTAL COST	

Figure 2: Costing spreadsheet

- **If you have any questions please raise your hand.**
- **Your group's objective is to redesign your truck and *achieve a cost target of $16,500.***
- **Your group must also satisfy the following design specifications and quality requirements:**

Design Specifications

1. The redesigned truck must contain all of the special parts (4 wheels, 2 axles, a grill, windshield, steering wheel and roll bar).
2. The truck's components must adhere to the following standards:
   - ✓ The truck's cab must have a roof top.
   - ✓ A light and a roll bar are required and must be placed on top of the cab.
   - ✓ The dimensions of the space inside the cab must not change.
   - ✓ The dimensions of the area behind the driver (back of the cab) must not change.
   - ✓ Doors are required on both sides of the cab.
   - ✓ The dimensions of the engine must not change and it must remain in front of the cab
   - ✓ The dimensions of the truck's bed must not change (the inside of the bed must be 4 x 6 or 24 studs.)
   - ✓ For hauling cargo, the tuck bed must have sides and a tailgate at their current height.
   - ✓ The undercarriage provides legroom for the driver and is required.
   - ✓ The distance between the two axles must not change.
   - ✓ The dimensions of the gas tank must not change.
   - ✓ The dimensions of the front bumper must not change.

Quality Requirements

1. The truck must maintain its integrity during a minor crash test (hitting a wall after traveling 18 inches at a 20% grade).
2. The truck must maintain its integrity while being lifted off the table two times, for five seconds each time.
   - For one lift, the facilitator will only hold on to the cab.
   - For the second lift, the facilitator will only hold on to the truck bed.

Figure 3: Information sheet for truck redesign

First Requirement:

The National Traffic Safety Agency has discovered that this truck becomes a fire hazard when it is hit from behind. Therefore, the gas tank that is located behind the rear axle must be moved.

Second Requirement:

A consumer focus group has found that this truck has insufficient legroom inside the cab. This problem can be corrected by extending the undercarriage to the front axle, thus providing more legroom. The focus group spoke to one driver who got so frustrated he tried to drive with his legs outside the cab.

Third Requirement:

Another consumer focus group recommends two additional changes for this truck. The first recommendation is to remove the indentation from inside the truck bed. Items being hauled in the truck were getting stuck in this sunken area. The second recommendation is to make the truck a four-wheel drive vehicle. This requirement can be met by extending the undercarriage to the rear axle.

Figure 4: Additional customer requirements for truck redesign.

De-briefing and learning

My colleague and I always try and get a graduate student to help us out in administering the game. We also have been present in each other's class during the earlier implementation of the game to understand cross-disciplinary perspectives. Also, during travel (to other institutions) we had a grant that allowed us to travel and team-teach the class in other locations.

Once the game is done and the designs approved, the team bring back their final cost calculations back to the class. They are welcomed by a 2*2 matrix as illustrated in table 1 on the white board or on an overhead screen. The four cells in the matrix provide information on the average costs for the teams falling into that cell. For example, cell 1 is for the teams that were in the room with sequential (up-front) information and had a specific cost target. Similarly, cell 4 is for the teams in room 2 that simulated staggered (concurrent) information and general cost goals.

As a process of learning and discussion, the first is to find out for the teams in each of the rooms what their perception of highest cost-reduction cell. Table 1 tabulates this as an example for one class. As it is evidenced from this table, 60% of the teams that were in the room with sequential information and specific cost goals believed to have the highest cost-reduction, while only 50% of the teams in the room with concurrent information and specific cost goal believed that they had the highest cost reduction. This was due to the fact, that some of the teams could not meet the cost goals in the concurrent information room and they talked about the frustration of time-pressure and constant disruption as they were working on the redesign. Till this point of discussion the teams with general cost goals did not have an idea of the cost target given to the other teams. When the cost target was revealed, there is a sense of surprise and excitement for the teams that beat it in both rooms. However, when the actual cost data averages across the two rooms are revealed (table 2), the excitement turns into debate as to why the ones with lower cost reductions could not improve.

	Cost Goal Type	
NPD Process	***Specific***	***General***
Sequential	1: 60%	2: 40%
Concurrent	3: 50%	4: 50%

Table 1: Class survey on which cell would get the maximum dollars of Cost Reduction by Condition (n = 12)

	Cost Goal Type	
NPD Process	***Specific***	***General***
Sequential	1: $3786	2: $2819
Concurrent	3: $3507	4: $3737

Table 2: Actual Average Dollars of Cost Reduction by Condition (n = 12)

The debate follows the similar path of time pressure, task frustration with disruption (changes in customer requirements), and also the opportunity to use the last design before the change (in the concurrent room) as a benchmark to improve the next change. Hence, table 2 indicates, that if the information handling is sequential (information available upfront as in cases with minimum changes to the existing design—product upgrades) then cost specificity produces a lower cost design. On the other hand, concurrency introduces interesting challenges and opportunities that "do your best" might come out better for breakthrough products. This is clearly demonstrated as cell 1 dominates for sequential and cell 4 surprises for concurrent. At this juncture, the research hypothesis is displayed and the conclusions arrived. Following this depending on the course, either details of the mechanics of target costing or the NPD concurrent design process are discussed. The research paper by Afonso et al., (2008) is also brought up for discussion that ties the target costing approach as an overall framework in NPD to balance critical metrics such as time and cost.

Conclusion

Before the NPD game and subsequent analysis based pedagogy, the content was taught in the traditional way of introducing materials on target costing in managerial accounting and sequential versus concurrent NPD processes in the operations course in an independent manner using text-book based information and once in a while augmented by case studies (e.g., Walton, 1997). Both topics though well received, never created an excitement and did not come out in course evaluations. This integrated, multi-disciplinary effort, really created new enthusiasm for the topics as was evidenced by three critical feedback:

(a) Student comments generally praised the game and also performance in questions related to the topic was improved (case analysis, home work and quizzes).

(b) Increase in the number of working managers who met up with us after class or the course to discuss this specific topic (cost goals) in more detail and in some cases leading to auditing their processes (Gopalakrishnan, et. al., 2007)

(c) The game drew the attention of Boeing Co (Seattle, USA) that was using a different game to train its internal folks on target costing. They verified and validated the game for us, which through the class led to further data collection. This led to a collaborative research that answered the questions on the interactions between cost goals and NPD definitively (Gopalakrishnan, 2015).

(d) Moving forward, the research article becomes the starting point of read for the students. This approach now can be moved from a research-led to a research-based, where additional inquires can be made in a contextual manner differentiating the varying NPD environments (including service-based products). This in turn can lead to more research activities and the cycle continues.

References:

Afonso, P., Nunes, M., Paisana, A., and Braga, A. (2008). "The influence of time-to-market and target costing in the new product development success." *Int. J. Production Economics,* 115, 559–568.

Altbach, P. G., and Lewis, L. S. (1995). "Professorial Attitudes—An International Survey." *Change*, 27 (6), 51–57.

Austin, A. E., Connolly, M. R., and Colbeck, C. L. (2008). "Strategies for Preparing Integrated Faculty: The Center for the Integration of Research, Teaching, and Learning." *New directions for teaching and learning*, 131, 69-81.

Gopalakrishnan, M., Samuels, J. A and Swenson, D. (2007). "TARGET COSTING at a Consumer Products Company." Strategic Finance;, 89, 6; 37-41.

Gopalakrishnan, M., Libby, T., Samuels J. A., and Swenson, D. (2015). "The effect of cost goal specificity and new product development process on cost reduction performance." *Accounting, Organizations and Society,* 42, 1–11

Griffiths, R (2004). "Knowledge production and the research-teaching nexus: the case of the built environment disciplines." *Studies in Higher Education* 29(6), 709-726

Prince, M. (2004). Does active learning work? A review of the research, *Journal of Engineering Education*, 93(3), 223-231.

Teaching commons (2016). "Combining Teaching and Research." Stanford University. https://teachingcommons.stanford.edu/resources/teaching/planning-your-approach/combining-teaching-and-research (downloaded May 15, 2016).

Walton, T (1997). "BLACK & DECKER CORP.: COMPACT POWER--INNOVATION IN THE CORDLESS PROFESSIONAL DRILL AND DRIVER MARKET" Harvard Business School case, Product #: 997003-PDF-ENG

Weimer, M. (1997). "Integration of Teaching and Research: Myth, Reality, and Possibility," *New directions for teaching and learning*, 72, 53-62.

AUTHOR INDEX

Aase, G. 511, 1269
Abebe, M. 825
Abreu, M. 1559
Agarwal, A. 1356
Agyei-Owusu, B. 748
Akaribo, J. 748
Akcam, B. 973
Alikaj, A. 398
Alqahtani, A. 1257
Andoh-Baidoo, F. 748
Angeles, R. 774
Asamoah, D. 748
Assis, N. 1574
Avoaka, P. 1058
Bagchi, K. 698
Bari, A. 587
Bayrak, T. 973
Behara, R. 497
Berenson, M. 1797
Bernardes, E. 1325
Bhadani, A. 21
Blackstock, R. 587
Booker, Q. 1678
Botella, J. 309
Brito, L. 847
Bumblauskas, D. 376, 1479
Burdwell, R. 670
Burke, J. 1325
Chakraborty, S. 54
Chang, I. 480
Changchit, C. 203, 1042
Chavarria, J. 1722
Chen, J. 1346, 1605
Chen, L. 659
Chen, X. 659
Chern, C. 44
Chhabria, R. 1180
Cho, Y. 1627
Choi, S. 1446
Choi, T. 1214
Chou, D. 215
Christodoulidou, N. 1505
Clauss, T. 809
Coy, S. 281, 766
Crawford, J. 766
David, D. 1601
Davies, J. 1013, 1762
DelVecchio, M. 1647
Demiral, E. 1523
Deng, H. 1505
Di Mauro, C. 1083
DiCicco, J. 497
Dickinson, J. 1677, 1751
Dickson, A. 1466
DiRusso, D. 1823
Dole, C. 1722
Dowlatshahi, S. 1688
Escobari, D. 1660
Evans, J. 187
Faisal, M. 293
Feller, A. 343
Flynn, B. 847
Fontem, B. 366
Ford, M. 187
Foroughi, A. 1585
Fortsch, S. 1146
Fratocchi, L. 1083
Frederick, L. 1064
Gao, J. 1823
Gerhart, N. 156
Ghosh, S. 956
Gibson, S. 1574
Giraud-Carrier, F. 1356
Goerzen, A. 689
Goo, J. 632
Gopalakrishnan, M. 343, 896
Graefe-Anderson, R. 366
Graham, R. 81, 1115
Green, R. 670
Gu, Q. 1409
Gudigantala, N. 1559
Gupta, S. 1257
Ha, Q. 1346, 1605
Harrison, J. 1280
Harrison, S. 1013, 1762
He, X. 1206
He, Y. 676
Heinrichs, J. 599, 741
Hofstetter, J. 689, 1689
Hong, P. 1416
Hossain, S. 1138, 1170
Hota, H. 1185
Hou, K. 180
Hsiao, C. 582
Huang, C. 632
Huang, T. 1752
Hung, K. 1622
Huo, B. 1400
Hwang, H. 14, 480
Hwang, J. 524
Hysell, M. 1064
Jagani, S. 839
Jana, R. 1075
Jenkins, P. 874
Jin, Y. 1192
Jitpaiboon, T. 1409
Johnson, D. 223
Johnson, M. 223
Johnson, N. 1064
Joo, S. 931

AUTHOR INDEX

Jothimani, D. 1365
Jung, J. 524
Kaushik, R. 1574
Keane, M. 950
Kersten, G. 537
Khan, H. 551
Kim, D. 1214
Kim, J. 1289
Kim, K. 459
Klaus, T. 203
Knight, R. 497
Kocakulah, M. 1585
Korir, M. 1064
Krehbiel, T. 1806
Krishnamoorthy, M. 341
Kung, L. 44
Kunnathur, A. 839, 1699
Kuo, C. 969
Kuritsyn, G. 1605
Ledwith, A. 136
Lehmberg, D. 1745
Lei, M. 1505
Li, J. 1622
Li, Y. 1532
Li, Z. 969
Liao, Q. 1146
Lien, C. 1
Lim, J. 599, 741
Lim, K. 599, 741
Lin, C. 1699
Lin, E. 14, 480
Lin, L. 180
Lin, S. 1752
Lindsey, M. 576
Lo, A. 874
Lo, L. 1752
Lonkani, R. 1042
Lu, H. 1206
Ludden, P. 136
Lunt, A. 376
Ma, J. 113
Mackelprang, A. 1325
Mai, F. 187
Manning, D. 643
Manyoky, L. 1585
Marsillac, E. 1192
Martz, B. 643
McGrath, M. 1532
Medina, E. 1378
Merhi, M. 505, 1058
Mesak, H. 113, 587
Metcalf, A. 731
Meybodi, M. 251
Meyer, B.C. 168
Michalski, M. 309
Miller, D. 1806
Mohan, S. 343
Morrison, R. 1023, 1660, 1722
Morton, A. 1280
Mueller, M. 689
Mukhopadhyay, S. 698
Mutlu, F. 125
Nam, K. 632
Nandi, S. 435
Narasimhan, R. 309
Nargundkar, S. 618
Nemer, C. 721
Nesterkin, D. 81
Ngamassi, L. 1772
Nguyen, C. 398
Ning, W. 398
Niranjan, T. 95, 341
Nwankpa, J. 604
Oestreich, N. 950
Orzes, G. 1083
Papadopoulos, A. 559, 986
Park, B. 1064
Park, M. 931
Park, S. 459, 459
Parkes, D. 721
Parkman, R. 874
Parsa, P. 97
Patel, S. 505
Pattabhiraman, S. 343
Pavur, R. 576
Peng, H. 44
Penumatsa, L. 1356
Petersen, C. 511, 1269
Pick, J. 907
Pohl, E. 97
Pokharel, S. 125
Porterfield, T. 81
Powless, S. 1128
Qazi, A. 1466
Qin, B. 1416
Quigley, J. 1466
Radhakrishnan, A. 1601
Rahman, S. 1772
Raisinghani, M. 1574
Ramakrishnan, T. 1772
Rao, D. 21
Rao, M. 1180
Ravinder, H. 1797
Re, L. 1280
Rebman, C. 1678
Reeves, J. 874
Ren, L. 124
Rew, D. 267
Rosales, J. 907
Rossetti, M. 97

AUTHOR INDEX

Rothenberger, M. 1505
Roumani, Y. 604, 604
Ruppel, C. 824
Sage, J. 1780
Sage, L. 1780
Saglam, U. 238, 1523
Samaddar, S. 698
Sampet, J. 1042
Sanchez, A. 825
Sankar, C. 1326
Sarkar, A. 907
Sarker, B. 1138, 1170
Sartor, M. 1083
Scarpin, M. 847
Schafer, S. 1128
Schmitt, N. 1280
Sengupta, S. 341
Shankar, R. 21, 1365
Sharma, D. 1075, 1185
Sharma, H. 1075, 1185
Shbool, M. 97
Sheff, P. 1115
Sher, M. 14
Shipley, J. 281
Shipley, M. 281
Shrikhande, M. 618
Silver, S. 814, 1391
Smith, J. 459
Smith, S. 1409
Song, J. 1326
Sonmez, E. 125
Strakos, J. 1540
Su, H. 1797
Sun, S. 1326
Talanker, S. 1239
Taleb, A. 559
Talib, F. 293
Tangpong, C. 809, 1622, 1745
Taube, L. 721
TeDuits, D. 766
Tibbett, H. 366
Ugray, Z. 1318
Uwemi, S. 551
Vahidov, R. 537
Van Vliet, P. 411
Vargas, R. 824
Vinaja, R. 670
Wallace, S. 839
Wang, J. 1823
Wang, P. 1
Wang, Q. 1400
Watson, E. 1289
Welbourne, J. 1722
Welter, C. 1325
Wen, M. 1
Widjaja, A. 1605
Williamson, J. 950
Wu, K. 1
Wu, S. 435
Yadav, S. 1365
Yeh, C. 1
Yildiz, H. 125
Yoo, C. 632
Yoo, S. 931, 1214
Yu, B. 537
Yue, J. 969
Yurova, Y. 824
Zhang, F. 223
Zhang, H. 113
Zhang, M. 1505
Zhang, S. 97
Zhang, Y. 1416
Zhao, X. 1400
Zheng, Y. 1823

Decision Sciences Institute
University of Houston
C.T. Bauer College of Business
334 Melcher Hall, Suite 325
Houston, TX 77204-6021
USA

ISBN 978-1-5108-4273-1

9 781510 842731

CURRAN ASSOCIATES INC.
proceedings.com

47th Decision Sciences Institute Annual Meeting (DSI 2016)

Austin, Texas, USA
19 - 21 November 2016

Volume 2 of 2

DECISION SCIENCES INSTITUTE

47th Decision Sciences Institute Annual Meeting (DSI 2016)

Austin, Texas, USA
19 - 21 November 2016

Volume 2 of 2

ISBN: 978-1-5108-4273-1

Printed from e-media with permission by:

Curran Associates, Inc.
57 Morehouse Lane
Red Hook, NY 12571

Printed by Curran Associates, Inc. (2017)

For permission requests, please contact Decision Sciences Institute
at the address below.

Decision Sciences Institute
University of Houston
C.T. Bauer College of Business
334 Melcher Hall, Suite 325
Houston, TX 77204-6021
USA

Phone: 713-743-4815
Fax: 713-743-8984

info@decisionsciences.org

Additional copies of this publication are available from:

Curran Associates, Inc.
57 Morehouse Lane
Red Hook, NY 12571 USA
Phone: 845-758-0400
Fax: 845-758-2633
Email: curran@proceedings.com
Web: www.proceedings.com

TABLE OF CONTENTS

VOLUME 1

A COMPARATIVE STUDY OF BELIEFS, ATTITUDES, AND BEHAVIOR OF CLICKING TOWARD INTERNET ADVERTISING AMONG RESPONDENTS FROM TAIWAN, AND CANADA 1
P. Wang, M. Wen, K. Wu, C. Yeh, C. Lien

A FRAMEWORK FOR DIABETES SELF-CARE EFFICACY IN EVALUATING PERSONAL HEALTH RECORD 14
E. Lin, H. Hwang, M. Sher

A FRAMEWORK FOR INDEX DEVELOPMENT FOR MEASURING THE PERFORMANCE OF TELECOM OPERATORS: A CONSENSUS-BASED APPROACH 21
A. Bhadani, R. Shankar, D. Rao

A HEURISTIC DATA SAMPLING APPROACH FOR ASSOCIATION RULE CLASSIFICATION UNDER A BIG DATA ENVIRONMENT 44
C. Chern, H. Peng, L. Kung

A LEAN HOSPITAL SUPPLY CHAIN PERSPECTIVE TO IMPROVING PATIENT CARE QUALITY 54
S. Chakraborty

A META-ANALYTICAL VIEW OF NON-TECHNICAL SKILLS FOR BUSINESS AND ENGINEERING STUDENTS 81
T. Porterfield, R. Graham, D. Nesterkin

A MULTI-METHOD INVESTIGATION OF OVERORDERING BEHAVIOR IN SUPPLY CHAINS 95
T.T. Niranjan

A MULTI-OBJECTIVE DECISION MODEL FOR SUPPLY CHAIN COLLABORATION PROGRAMS 97
P. Parsa, M. Shbool, M. Rossetti, S. Zhang, E. Pohl

A NOTE ON MODELING PRODUCT ALLOCATION BETWEEN BRICK-AND-MORTAR AND ONLINE STORES 113
H. Zhang, H. Mesak, J. Ma

A NOTE ON THE SIMPLE TRADING RANGE BREAK-OUT RULE FOR NASDAQ INDEX 124
L. Ren

A SIMULATION MODEL FOR COMPARING THE ROBUSTNESS OF ALTERNATIVE LIQUEFIED NATURAL GAS (LNG) ANNUAL DELIVERY PROGRAMS (ADPS) 125
F. Mutlu, H. Yildiz, E. Sonmez, S. Pokharel

A STUDY OF VIRTUAL PROJECT TEAM TYPES AND THEIR IMPACT ON PROJECT SUCCESS 136
P. Ludden, A. Ledwith

A SYSTEMS THEORY PERSPECTIVE OF DATA ANALYTICS IMPLEMENTATION 156
N. Gerhart

ADDING SPICE TO THE TEACHING OF QUALITY: VARIATION, POKA YOKE, AND A DEFECT COLLECTION 168
B.C. Meyer

AN ECONOMIC PRODUCTION LOT SIZE MODEL IN AN IMPERFECT PRODUCTION SYSTEM WITH A MARKOV PROCESS AND SHORTAGE BACKORDERING 180
K. Hou, L. Lin

AN EMPIRICAL INVESTIGATION OF THE BALDRIGE FRAMEWORK USING APPLICANT SCORING DATA 187
F. Mai, M. Ford, J. Evans

AN EXAMINATION OF CONSUMER ATTITUDES ON ONLINE USER REVIEWS 203
C. Changchit, T. Klaus

AN INNOVATIVE APPROACH TO PROJECT DESIGN OF SOCIAL ENTREPRENEURSHIP 215
D. Chou

AN OPTIMIZATION MODEL FOR DETERMINING BIOREFINERY SIZE AND LOCATION 223
F. Zhang, D. Johnson, M. Johnson

ANALYZING THE EFFICIENCIES OF RENEWABLE ENERGY SOURCES WITH DATA ENVELOPMENT ANALYSIS 238
U. Saglam

APPLYING LEAN MANUFACTURING PRINCIPLES TO NEW PRODUCT DEVELOPMENT 251
M. Meybodi

ARE SERVICE PRODUCTIVITY AND QUALITY IN PERMANENT CONFLICT? (THE EFFECT OF SERVICE INNOVATION AND THE ROLE OF CUSTOMER SATISFACTION) 267
D. Rew

ARTIFICIAL REEF STRUCTURE AND MATERIAL DEPLOYMENT DECISIONS: A BIG DATA ANALYTICS EXERCISE ON PRESENCE AND ABUNDANCE OF REEF FISH 281
S. Coy, M. Shipley, J. Shipley

ASSESSMENT OF TOTAL QUALITY MANAGEMENT IMPLEMENTATION IN INDIAN SERVICE INDUSTRIES 293
F. Talib, M. Faisal

ASYMMETRY, TRUST, INNOVATION, AND PERFORMANCE IN SUPPLY CHAIN MANAGEMENT - A NON-LINEAR APPROACH 309
M. Michalski, J. Botella, R. Narasimhan

BALANCE OR STABILITY: A RE-CONCEPTUALIZATION OF THE KEY ELEMENTS OF SERVICE TRIAD SUSTAINABILITY 341
S. Sengupta, M. Krishnamoorthy, T. Niranjan

BALANCING SERVICE RISK WITH TECHNOLOGY COST FOR WEB-BASED APPLICATIONS USING EMULATION DRIVEN SIMULATION 343
S. Mohan, M. Gopalakrishnan, S. Pattabhiraman, A. Feller

BERMUDAN PUT OPTION PRICING UNDER RISK AVERSION IN BILATERAL GAMMA MODELS 366
B. Fontem, H. Tibbett, R. Graefe-Anderson

BOARD COMPOSITION AND PERSISTENCE ON CAPITAL MARKETS: EMPIRICAL EVIDENCE OF COMPANIES DELISTING FROM THE ASX 376
A. Lunt, D. Bumblauskas

BOWMAN'S PARADOX REVISITED: AN INVESTIGATION OF THREE EAST ASIAN MARKETS 398
C. Nguyen, A. Alikaj, W. Ning

BUILDING EFFECTIVE ONLINE EDUCATION VIDEO LECTURES: RECOMMENDATIONS FROM RESEARCH AND PRACTICE 411
P. Van Vliet

CAN CORPORATE ENTREPRENEURSHIP ATTRIBUTES IN ACQUIRED FIRMS AVOID THEIR ACQUISITION-TURNED-DIVESTITURE FATE? 435
S. Nandi, S. Wu

CONSUMER SELF-CONFIDENCE WITH MOBILE COMMERCE 459
S. Park, S. Park, J. Smith, K. Kim

CONSUMERS' INTENTION TOWARD MOBILE BANKING: FROM PERSPECTIVE OF TRIPARTITE MODEL OF ATTITUDE 480
I. Chang, E. Lin, H. Hwang

CORPORATE SUSTAINABILITY: AN ANALYSIS OF CSR AND CSV 497
R. Behara, R. Knight, J. DiCicco

CRITICAL SUCCESS FACTORS IMPACTING CLOUD-BASED EHR SYSTEMS 505
M. Merhi, S. Patel

CROSS AISLE PLACEMENT IN ORDER PICKING OPERATIONS 511
C. Petersen, G. Aase

CSR AND EMPLOYEE SATISFACTION: MEDIATING ROLE OF MARKETING INNOVATION 524
J. Hwang, J. Jung

DOES NEGOTIATION MATTER FOR BUSINESS RELATIONSHIP? A STUDY OF CREDIBLE INFORMATION DISCLOSURE AND PERCEIVED FAIRNESS 537
B. Yu, R. Vahidov, G. Kersten

E-COMMERCE, CHALLENGES, AND DEVELOPING COUNTRIES 551
S. Uwemi, H. Khan

EFFECT OF INSTITUTIONAL HETEROGENEITY IN PARTNERSHIP CONFIGURATION ON M&A PERFORMANCE 559
A. Papadopoulos, A. Taleb

EFFECTIVENESS OF CONTROL CHARTS FOR INTERMITTENT DEMAND 576
M. Lindsey, R. Pavur

EFFICACY BELIEFS AND CUSTOMER COLLABORATION IN ONLINE COLLABORATIVE COMMUNITIES: A RELATIONSHIP MARKETING PERSPECTIVE 582
C. Hsiao
EQUILIBRIUM ANALYSIS OF AN ADVERTISING-INVENTORY-PRICING COMPETITIVE MODEL 587
H. Mesak, A. Bari, R. Blackstock
EVALUATING PERFORMANCE QUALITY OF A FIRM'S SOCIAL MEDIA ACTIVITIES 599
J. Lim, K. Lim, J. Heinrichs
EXAMINING THE RELATIONSHIP BETWEEN EXTERNAL SOFTWARE CHARACTERISTICS AND VULNERABILITIES 604
Y. Roumani, J. Nwankpa, Y. Roumani
EXPERIENTIAL LEARNING THEORY: EVIDENCE FROM A STUDY ABROAD PROGRAM 618
S. Nargundkar, M. Shrikhande
EXPLORATIVE AND EXPLOITATIVE USE OF SMART TOURISM TECHNOLOGIES IN TRAVEL PLANNING 632
C. Huang, J. Goo, K. Nam, C. Yoo
EXTRACTING LIFE SKILLS FROM AN INTRODUCTORY EXCEL PROGRAMMING CLASS 643
B. Martz, D. Manning
FACTORS THAT INFLUENCE EMPLOYEES' SECURITY POLICY COMPLIANCE BEHAVIOR: AN AWARENESS-MOTIVATION-CAPABILITY (AMC) PERSPECTIVE 659
X. Chen, L. Chen
FINANCIAL DATA ANALYTICS AND EXTRACTION FROM SECURITY EXCHANGE COMMISSION'S (SEC) EDGAR FILLINGS 670
R. Green, R. Burdwell, R. Vinaja
FIRM'S SHORT-TERM GROWTH RATE AND EARNINGS MANAGEMENT 676
Y. He
GARMENT SUPPLIERS' STRATEGIES TO MANAGE COMMERCIAL AND SOCIAL TENSIONS: AN INSTITUTIONAL LOGICS' PERSPECTIVE 689
M. Mueller, J. Hofstetter, A. Goerzen
GLOBAL GROWTH OF SERVICE INNOVATION: INFLUENCE OF NATIONAL CULTURE AND ORGANIZATIONAL STRUCTURE 698
S. Mukhopadhyay, K. Bagchi, S. Samaddar
PREPARING LEADERS TO LIVE IN A VIRTUAL WORLD: A TEMPLATE TO ENHANCE EFFECTIVENESS OF ONLINE GLOBAL SUPPLY SIMULATIONS 721
L. Taube, D. Parkes, C. Nemer
HOSPITAL UNIT UNDERSTAFFING AND MISSED TREATMENTS: THE MODERATING EFFECT OF TEAMWORK 731
A. Metcalf
IMPACT OF NEW PRODUCT DEVELOPMENT FLEXIBILITY ON PERFORMANCE 741
J. Lim, J. Heinrichs, K. Lim
IMPACT OF SUPPLY CHAIN COLLABORATION ON LOGISTICS PERFORMANCE: EVIDENCE FROM A SUB-SAHARA AFRICA NATION'S PETROLEUM DOWNSTREAM 748
B. Agyei-Owusu, D. Asamoah, F. Andoh-Baidoo, J. Akaribo
IMPROVING LEARNING OUTCOMES IN A FLIPPED SPREADSHEET-BASED GRADUATE DECISION MODELING COURSE 766
S. Coy, D. TeDuits, J. Crawford
"INTERNET OF THINGS" (IOT)-ENABLED PRODUCT MONITORING: INSIGHTS FROM SOCIO-TECHNICAL SYSTEMS THEORY, AFFORDANCES THEORY, AND STRUCTURATIONAL MODEL OF TECHNOLOGY 774
R. Angeles
IN SEARCH FOR IMPREGNABLE EXCHANGE RELATIONSHIPS WITH BUYERS: INSIGHTS FOR SUPPLIERS 809
T. Clauss, C. Tangpong
DISCRIMINATING RATED LEADERSHIP IN THE U.S PRESIDENCY FROM VALUE CONTENT AND STYLISTIC VARIABLES IN STATE OF THE UNION ADDRESSES: A DATA MINING METHODOLOGY 814
S. Silver
INDIVIDUAL ADOPTION AND USE OF HR ANALYTICS: IMPLICATIONS OF ORGANIZATIONAL ADOPTION 824
R. Vargas, Y. Yurova, C. Ruppel

INFLUENCE OF THE CEO CHARACTERISTICS IN MERGERS AND ACQUISITIONS IN THE PHARMACEUTICAL INDUSTRY 825
A. Sanchez, M. Abebe
INFORMATION EXCHANGE RESEARCH OPPORTUNITIES 839
S. Jagani, A. Kunnathur, S. Wallace
INSIDE THE BLACK BOX OF OPERATIONAL CAPABILITIES: AN EVOLUTION FROM OPERATIONAL PRACTICES 847
M. Scarpin, L. Brito, B. Flynn
INSTITUTIONAL STUDENT RETENTION INITIATIVES FOR ACCELERATED PROGRAMS 874
A. Lo, J. Reeves, P. Jenkins, R. Parkman
INTEGRATION OF TEACHING AND RESEARCH: THE ACTIVE-LEARNING AND RESEARCH-LED APPROACH IN INTEGRATING MULTI-DISCIPLINARY CONCEPTS IN OPERATIONS MANAGEMENT 896
M. Gopalakrishnan

VOLUME 2

INTERNET USE FOR E-COMMERCE IN US COUNTIES: GEOGRAPHIC PATTERNS AND SOCIO-ECONOMIC INFLUENCES 907
J. Pick, A. Sarkar, J. Rosales
INVENTORY MODELS IN A CLOSED-LOOP SUPPLY CHAIN WITH PRODUCT RETURNS AND REFURBISHMENT 931
S. Yoo, S. Joo, M. Park
INVESTIGATION INTO THE MARRIAGE PENALTY UNDER THE ALTERNATIVE MINIMUM TAX 950
M. Keane, N. Oestreich, J. Williamson
IS SOA REALLY DEAD? 956
S. Ghosh
MAXIMIZATION OF SELLER'S NET REVENUE IN DISCRETE DUTCH AUCTIONS WITH TRANSACTION COST 969
Z. Li, C. Kuo, J. Yue
MEASURING THE IMPACT OF A WEB-BASED BLENDED LEARNING PLATFORM ON STUDENT LEARNING 973
T. Bayrak, B. Akcam
MESSAGES FROM FORTUNE 500 CEOS 986
A. Papadopoulos
METHODOLOGICAL DEVELOPMENTS IN UNDERSTANDING BRAND CREATION AND BRAND IDENTITY – THE CASE OF SEVENS WELLINGTON - AN INTERNATIONAL RECURRING SPORTS EVENT 1013
S. Harrison, J. Davies
MINING FOR THE ENTREPRENEURIAL ELEMENT 1023
R. Morrison
MOBILE BANKING ADOPTION: THAI CONSUMERS' PERSPECTIVE 1042
C. Changchit, R. Lonkani, J. Sampet
MOBILE BANKING RESISTANCE IN IVORY COAST 1058
M. Merhi, P. Avoaka
MODIFYING RESOURCE ALLOCATION FOR TRANSITION OF EMERGENCY DEPARTMENT (ED) VISITS TO URGENT CARE (UC) VISITS 1064
L. Frederick, B. Park, M. Korir, M. Hysell, N. Johnson
MULTI-CRITERIA STOCK PORTFOLIO MANAGEMENT – A DISTANCE FUNCTION APPROACH 1075
D. Sharma, R. Jana, H. Sharma
OFFSHORING AND RESHORING IN THE INTERNATIONALIZATION STRATEGY: A MULTIPLE CASE STUDY APPROACH 1083
C. Di Mauro, L. Fratocchi, G. Orzes, M. Sartor
ON THE JOB TRAINING: A CASE STUDY ON USING CONSULTING EXPERIENCES TO ENHANCE STUDENTS' EMPLOYABILITY 1115
R. Graham, P. Sheff
OPEN SERVICES INNOVATION: IDENTIFYING LINKAGES BETWEEN KNOWLEDGE SOURCING AND FIRM PERFORMANCE 1128
S. Schafer, S. Powless

OPTIMAL LOCATION OF REPAIR STATIONS IN A GARMENTS PRODUCTION LINE 1138
S. Hossain, B. Sarker
ORDERING BLOOD DONATIONS UNDER UNCERTAIN ENVIRONMENT 1146
S. Fortsch, Q. Liao
OVERALL EQUIPMENT EFFECTIVENESS MEASURES OF ENGINEERING PRODUCTION SYSTEMS 1170
S. Hossain, B. Sarker
PERFORMANCE EVALUATION OF A MICRO-IRRIGATION COMPANY USING THE APC MODEL 1180
M. Rao, R. Chhabria
PERFORMANCE OF SUPERVISED ARTIFICIAL NEURAL NETWORKS FOR FOREIGN EXCHANGE RATE PREDICTION 1185
H. Sharma, D. Sharma, H. Hota
POWER AND COLLABORATIVE CLIMATE: BUILDING COMPETITIVE ADVANTAGE THROUGH FLEXIBILITIES 1192
Y. Jin, E. Marsillac
PREVENTING INFERENCE ATTACKS IN ONLINE SOCIAL NETWORKS: A DATA-DRIVEN FRAMEWORK 1206
X. He, H. Lu
PROACTIVE INCENTIVE STRATEGIES FOR QUALITY IMPROVEMENT IN A THREE-STAGE SUPPLY CHAIN 1214
S. Yoo, D. Kim, T. Choi
PROBLEM-SOLVING IS DECISION-MAKING 1239
S. Talanker
RENEWABLE TWO-DIMENSIONAL PRO-RATA WARRANTY ANALYSIS FOR REVERSE SUPPLY CHAIN 1257
A. Alqahtani, S. Gupta
RE-SLOTTING TO REDUCE WAREHOUSE OPERATING EXPENSES 1269
G. Aase, C. Petersen
RETHINKING UNDERGRADUATE BUSINESS CORE CURRICULUM: ONE SCHOOL'S EXPERIENCE OF REDESIGNED CURRICULUM WITH A HOLISTIC APPROACH 1280
A. Morton, J. Harrison, L. Re, N. Schmitt
ROLE OF PERCEIVED PLAYFULNESS/SERIOUSNESS IN LEARNING PROCESS USING BUSINESS SIMULATION GAME 1289
J. Kim, E. Watson
SHOULD BUSINESS ANALYTICS BE TAUGHT TO EVERY UNDERGRADUATE? – WE ARE ALREADY DOING IT 1318
Z. Ugray
SHOULD SUPPLIERS CHOOSE TO BE LEADING INNOVATORS? 1325
A. Mackelprang, E. Bernardes, J. Burke, C. Welter
SITUATION AWARENESS DIFFERENCES ON THE USE OF CLOUD COMPUTING 1326
S. Sun, C. Sankar, J. Song
SOCIAL CAPITAL AND KNOWLEDGE SHARING IN ORGANIZATION: AN INITIAL META-ANALYSIS 1346
Q. Ha, J. Chen
STATUS OF GREEN SUPPLY CHAIN MANAGEMENT ADOPTION IN MIDWEST MANUFACTURING: AN EMPIRICAL STUDY 1356
A. Agarwal, F. Giraud-Carrier, L. Penumatsa
STOCK TRADING DECISIONS USING ENSEMBLE-BASED FORECASTING MODELS 1365
D. Jothimani, R. Shankar, S. Yadav
STRATEGIC GLOBAL WORK-LIFE BALANCE INITIATIVES: THE ROLES OF THE EXPATIRATION CYCLE AND GENDER 1378
E. Medina
SUBJECTIVE WELL-BEING OF CHILDREN OF MIGRANT FAMILIES IN SCHOOLING ALTERNATIVES OF URBAN CHINA 1391
S. Silver
SUBSTITUTES OR COMPLEMENTS? THE IMPACT OF CONTRACTUAL AND RELATIONAL GOVERNANCE ON LOGISTICS INTEGRATION AND OPERATIONAL PERFORMANCE 1400
Q. Wang, B. Huo, X. Zhao
SUCCESS FACTORS FOR A CLASSROOM PROJECT 1409
T. Jitpaiboon, S. Smith, Q. Gu

SUPPLY CHAIN DISRUPTION HANDLING: A DYNAMIC EXTENDED RESOURCE-BASED (DE-RBV) VIEW 1416
B. Qin, P. Hong, Y. Zhang

SUPPLY CHAIN PERFORMANCE ANALYSIS BASED UPON LITTLE'S LAW 1446
S. Choi

SUPPLY CHAIN RISK NETWORK MANAGEMENT (SCRNM): A PARADIGM SHIFT TOWARDS MODELLING SYSTEMIC RISKS AND RISK APPETITE 1466
A. Qazi, A. Dickson, J. Quigley

SUSTAINABLE TOURISM DEVELOPMENT AND SERVICE OPERATIONS MANAGEMENT AT THE MISSOURI STATE PENITENTIARY (MSP) 1479
D. Bumblauskas

THE ANALYSIS OF E-PRODUCT SALES AFFECTED BY ONLINE WORKD-OF-MOUTH AND E-COMMEERCE SERVICE QUALITY BASED ON OBSERVATIONAL LEARNING 1505
M. Lei, M. Zhang, H. Deng, M. Rothenberger, N. Christodoulidou

THE EFFECT OF SOCIAL AND TEMPORAL DISTANCE ON RISK PREFERENCES: AN EXPERIMENTAL INVESTIGATION 1523
E. Demiral, U. Saglam

THE EFFECT OF SOCIAL MEDIA ON PURCHASING BEHAVIOR 1532
M. McGrath, Y. Li

THE EFFECTIVENESS OF INTENTIONAL DESIGN IN AN ONLINE INVENTORY MANAGEMENT CLASS 1540
J. Strakos

THE EFFECTS OF CONSUMER PERCEPTIONS OF ETHICS IN ONLINE GRAY MARKET SOURCING ACTIVITIES ON TRUST AND PURCHASE INTENTION 1559
N. Gudigantala, M. Abreu

THE GLOBAL APTITUDE ASSESSMENT MODEL: A CRITICAL PERSPECTIVE 1574
R. Kaushik, M. Raisinghani, S. Gibson, N. Assis

THE IMPACT OF CHOICE OF COSTING METHOD ON PROJECT/PRODUCT PROFITABILITY 1585
A. Foroughi, M. Kocakulah, L. Manyoky

THE IMPACT OF INTER-ORGANIZATIONAL INFORMATION SYSTEMS ON CAPABILITIES OF BUYER-SUPPLIER DYADS 1601
A. Radhakrishnan, D. David

THE IMPACTS OF SERVICE QUALITY ON CONTINUANCE INTENTION TO USE VIDEO SURVEILLANCE-AS-A-SERVICE 1605
J. Chen, G. Kuritsyn, Q. Ha, A. Widjaja

THE INFLUENCE OF ETHICAL RELATIVISM ON ETHICAL COMPROMISE IN BUSINESS EXCHANGES 1622
J. Li, C. Tangpong, K. Hung

THE INFLUENCE OF MANAGERIAL METACOGNITION ON QUALITY MANAGEMENT PRACTICES AND A FIRM'S SUSTAINABLE COMPETITIVE ADVANTAGES 1627
Y. Cho

THE PRIVATIZATION OF LARGE AND SMALL-SCALE FIRMS AND THEIR DIFFERENTIAL IMPACTS ON THE MACROECONOMY UNDER TRANSITION 1647
M. DelVecchio

THE PROFITABILITY OF US COMMUNITY BANKS: A CROSS-SECTIONAL AND DYNAMIC PANEL ANALYSIS 1660
R. Morrison, D. Escobari

THE RELATIONSHIP BETWEEN OBSERVED AND PUBLISHED MULTIPLE-CHOICE QUESTION DIFFICULTY MAY DEPEND ON WHAT MEANS "RELATED" 1677
J. Dickinson

THE RELATIONSHIP BETWEEN TECHNOSTRESS CREATORS AND ONLINE EDUCATION AMONG STUDENTS 1678
Q. Booker, C. Rebman

THE ROLE OF MARKETING IN REVERSE SUPPLY CHAIN 1688
S. Dowlatshahi

TOWARDS A PROCESS FRAMEWORK FOR SUB-SUPPLIER SUSTAINABILITY MANAGEMENT 1689
J. Hofstetter

TOWARDS A THEORY OF DYNAMIC INFORMATION SECURITY BEHAVIORS 1699
C. Lin, A. Kunnathur

TRAINING BEYOND JOB SKILLS TO ENHANCE PERCEIVED ORGANIZATIONAL SUPPORT AND JOB SATISFACTION IN CENTRAL AMERICAN MAQUILAS 1722
R. Morrison, J. Welbourne, C. Dole, J. Chavarria
TURNAROUND IN LARGE COMPLEX LEGACY ORGANIZATIONS 1745
D. Lehmberg, C. Tangpong
TWO OBSERVATIONS BETWEEN "TRUTH" AND MEH: A COMPLEMENT TO CROSS-TABULATION CHI-SQUARE HYPOTHESIS TESTING 1751
J. Dickinson
UNDERSTANDING THE EFFECT OF FLICKR'S SCREENSHOT ANNOTATIONS ON LEARNING EFFECTIVENESS 1752
T. Huang, S. Lin, L. Lo
UNDERSTANDING THE ORGANIZATIONAL NEEDS OF AN INTERNATIONAL SPORTS EVENT: A SYSTEMS PERSPECTIVE ON SEVENS WELLINGTON - THE WELLINGTON 7S 1762
S. Harrison, J. Davies
USE OF SOCIAL MEDIA IN TEACHING AND ITS IMPACT ON STUDENT LEARNING OUTCOMES 1772
S. Rahman, T. Ramakrishnan, L. Ngamassi
USING A SELF-MANAGED LEARNING CASE IN AN INTERMEDIATE ACCOUNTING I COURSE INCLUDING ETHICS WITH VALUE-ADDED ASSESSMENT 1780
J. Sage, L. Sage
VALIDATING REGRESSION ASSUMPTIONS THROUGH RESIDUAL PLOTS – CAN STUDENTS DO IT? 1797
H. Ravinder, M. Berenson, H. Su
WAS DEMING AGILE? LOOKING AT INFORMATION TECHNOLOGY FRAMEWORKS AND PRACTICES 1806
D. Miller, T. Krehbiel
WECHAT SHOPPING: A STUDY OF COSMETIC PRODUCT SELLING TO COLLEGE STUDENTS IN CHINA 1823
Y. Zheng, J. Wang, D. DiRusso, J. Gao
Author Index

DECISION SCIENCES INSTITUTE

Internet Use for E-Commerce in US Counties: Geographic Patterns and Socio-Economic Influences

James Pick
University of Redlands
Email: james_pick@redlands.edu

Avijit Sarkar
University of Redlands
Email: avijit_sarkar@redlands.edu

Jessica Rosales
University of Redlands
Email: jessica-_rosales@redlands.edu

ABSTRACT

This research examines geographic patterns of internet usage in US counties for engaging in e-commerce and online financial activities. Using the Spatially Aware Technology Utilization Model (SATUM), we posit associations of demographic, economic, employment, and social capital independent variables with five dependent indicators of e-commerce and online financial activities. Spatial bias in regressions is diagnosed and regression findings indicate differing levels of associations of college education, age structure, urban location, and ethnicities for metropolitan, micropolitan, and rural counties. Based upon geographic clustering and regression findings, policies and strategies to remediate the e-commerce digital divide in US counties are recommended.

KEYWORDS: E-Commerce, Internet, Digital Divide, Spatial Autocorrelation, and Policy

INTRODUCTION

In the early 2000's, a report of the Organization for Economic Cooperation and Development (OECD) defined the digital divide as "the gap between individuals, households, businesses and geographic areas at different socio-economic levels with regard both to their opportunities to access information and communication technologies (ICTs) and to their use of the Internet for a wide variety of activities" (OECD, 2001, pp. 5). This definition is revealing, since it refers to the importance of examining both access and use of the internet in relation to the digital divide. Research in mid-2000's (Dewan and Riggins, 2005) contended that most of the digital divide literature focused on first order effects regarding who had access to ICTs. More recently, Weber and Kauffman (2011) have also observed that many studies have aimed at identifying economic, social, and other factors that relate to global ICT access and adoption. In comparison, work that addresses the second order effects of inequality in the ability to use ICTs among those who do have access was relatively sparse. To examine and measure digital divides, nuanced models have been proposed in the literature. An example is the causal and iterative model developed by van Dijk (2005) which posited access to ICT as a four-step, repetitive process comprised of (i) motivation to access, (ii) material access, (iii) skills access, and (iv) usage access. An individual with the appropriate motivation and material access to an ICT, for example the mobile broadband may be skills deficient, or may underutilize broadband access by using it solely for gaming or for any purpose without direct benefit to self or society at large.

In this context, it is interesting to note that at the start of the present decade, reports of the U.S. National Telecommunications and Information Administration (NTIA in US Department of Commerce) tracked internet and broadband adoption at the national and state levels in the United States. An NTIA report (NTIA, 2011) documented rising broadband Internet adoption among Americans along with divide between digital haves and have-nots due to differences in income, education, race and ethnicity, age, employment status, household type, disability status, and motivation factors. However more recent reports not only describe the extent of ICT access, they have started to focus on purpose of usage of ICTs such as the internet (NTIA, 2013) and mobile phones, especially mobile internet (NTIA, 2014). This was portended by Dewan and Riggins (2005) who had observed that understanding ICT usage is an important goal for business and social science researchers since the way consumers use technology has a profound impact on how firms compete globally, how they relate to their customers and business partners, and how they formulate strategies for electronic commerce.

This study examines the use of the internet among US county populations for the purpose of engaging in electronic commerce and related financial activities such as online banking and electronic bill payment. In 2015, total e-commerce sales in US totaled $342 billion, an increase of 14 – 15 % compared to 2014. During the same time, total retail sales increased 1 – 2 %. E-commerce sales in 2015 accounted for 7.3 percent of national retail sales compared to 6.4% in 2014 (US Department of Commerce, 2016). Around the same time, in 2013, over half of American internet users aged 25 years or older relied on the internet for financial services such as online banking (53 percent) and for shopping and other consumer services (52 percent). In fact both of these activities ranked among the top four activities pursued by American internet users, right after internet usage for personal communications (77 percent) and for procuring general information (66 percent) (NTIA, 2013).

Specifically, we examine geographic patterns of adoption and use of the internet for e-commerce purposes in 3,109 counties in the lower 48 states of the United States. Further we examine the influence of demographic, economic, educational, and other social factors on usage of the internet by county populations for engaging in e-commerce and related financial activities. In doing so, we account for the presence of spatial autocorrelation, a common problem that introduces spatial bias in problems in many domains including economic geography as well as adoption and diffusion of information and communications technologies. This is important since the geographic dimension of digital divides, illustrated by the divide in ICT adoption and use by residents in metropolitan areas versus their rural counterparts has been repeatedly documented in NTIA reports (NTIA 2011, 2013, 2014) as well as in a recent report of the White House (The White House, 2015). From a methodological standpoint, diagnosing spatial autocorrelation while examining socio-economic influences on ICT usage is important; in the absence of such diagnosis, the error term of standard OLS models may be spatially autocorrelated thereby overestimating OLS regression findings, as shown by Grubesic (2002) and Gauvin, Granger, and Lothiois (2015).

Our research questions are:

1. Are geographic patterns of internet use for e-commerce and financial activities present for US counties as estimated by spatial autocorrelation?

2. Are US counties significantly clustered in their usage of the internet for e-commerce and financial activities?
3. What are the associations of demographic, economic, educational, and social capital factors with indicators of internet use for e-commerce and financial activities in US counties?
4. How do associations of demographic, economic, educational, and social capital factors with indicators of internet use for e-commerce and financial activities vary in metropolitan, micropolitan, and rural areal sections of the United States?
5. Can regression models of such associations account for the presence of spatial bias?

A unique feature of our study is its focus on internet use for e-commerce at the level of US counties, a standard geography of the US Census. The choice of county as the geographic unit of analysis is justified by the fact that according to the National Association of Counties, US counties are one of America's oldest forms of government dating back to the 1600s. While the structuring of county governments is diverse and basic roles and responsibilities of county governments are partly authorized by the states, counties administer their own economy, education, justice and public safety, healthcare, social services, transportation, and other services that directly impact their residents. In addition, counties are often responsible for implementing an assortment of federal, state and local programs.

Only a handful of prior digital divide studies have examined patterns of internet activity and ICT adoption and diffusion at the level of the US county (The White House 2015; Grubesic, 2002; Khatiwada and Pigg, 2010; Huang, 2006). Since an urban-rural divide is acknowledged to contribute to the digital divide in the US in several studies (NTIA 2011, 2013, 2014; The White House 2015, Pick, Sarkar, and Johnson, 2015a), we examine through subsampling the extent of differences in internet use for e-commerce and socio-economic correlates of such activity in metropolitan, micropolitan, and rural US counties – another unique contribution. According to the US Census Bureau, metropolitan and micropolitan areas both contain core urban areas with a population of at least 50,000 for metropolitan and between 10,000 and 50,000 for micropolitan areas. Each metro- or micropolitan area consists of one or more counties containing the core urban area, as well as any adjacent counties that have a high degree of social and economic integration with the urban core. Rural areas include all territory not included within an urban area. Lastly, among socio-economic correlates, we include an index of social capital; the influence of social capital on technology adoption and use in US households has not been examined until recently (Chen, 2013; Agarwal, Animesh, and Prasad, 2009; Pick et al, 2015a). Examining the association of social capital with internet use for e-commerce and financial activities in US counties is a novelty of this contribution.

The remainder of this paper is organized into sections on literature review of internet use for a variety of purposes in the US, conceptual model of internet use for e-commerce, data and methodology, exploratory analysis of geographical patterns of internet use for e-commerce in US counties, regression findings, policy implications, and conclusions.

LITERATURE REVIEW

In the vast digital divide literature, considerable attention has been paid to address problems and issues pertaining to the access of information and communications technologies (Dewan and Riggins, 2005). As recently argued by Warschauer and Matuchniak (2010), a problem with framing digital inequities as a divide is that, it tends to overplay the "access" aspect of the divide and often ignores the question of "use" of information technology (IT) applications as enabling elements for the purpose of achieving social and possibly economic equity using IT. One may also argue that in the absence of reliable big datasets covering large geographies, such as the United States or of other populous nations, it is difficult for researchers to examine the use of the internet for a variety of purposes.

However, in recent years, there appears to be a shift. At the NTIA's request, the US Census Bureau's July 2011 Current Population Survey (CPS) Computer and Internet Use Supplement included a significant new series of questions regarding online activities of American internet users. This survey of 53,000 households, is a critical and credible source of data about how Americans use the Internet, how they go online, and why some do not. Furthermore, the study by Warschauer and Matuchniak (2010) extensively focused on the use of internet among youth in schools and examined their difference in engagement with various online experiences depending on the type of access, e.g. dial-up versus broadband. In doing so, the authors emphasized the importance of financing youth media programs to tackle inequity in use of technology and the outcomes associated with the use of the internet.

Outside of the realm of education, a handful of studies have examined varied aspects of citizens' electronic engagement with local or federal governments as well as government agencies. Huang (2006, 2007) comprehensively examined e-government adoption by US counties and scrutinized services, functions, and features of county e-government portals. Huang (2006) found that US counties' adoption of e-government is significantly correlated with a county's population, education, household income, and business factors. Counties that adopted e-government were found to be racially diverse.

Huang (2007) reasoned that county populations with higher levels of income, educational attainment, faster population growth, and diverse ethnic structures would demand electronic interaction and possibly services from their local government thus influencing e-government adoption by the local county. Huang (2007) also differentiated e-government diffusion from e-government adoption and found e-government diffusion to be related to population growth, language other than English spoken at home, and economic factors such as home ownership rate, median housing value, and federal funds and grants. Belanger and Carter (2009) posited citizens' demographic attributes as well as their skills (computer experience, internet use, online purchasing, online searching) to be associated with usage of e-government services and found that consistent with previous literature, income, education, age, and frequency of Internet use significantly impact use of e-government services. Since several of these factors are well-known correlates of the digital divide, Belanger and Carter (2009) concluded that the digital divide has a major impact on e-government usage. A subsequent study (Manoharan, 2012) found institutional factors – such as technical capacity of IT employees, website longevity, employee support, organizational size among other factors to be the best predictors of county e-government adoption in the US.

Recently, the study by Roy, Chartier, Crete, and Poulin (2015) conducted large-scale survey of almost 1,600 citizens in outlying, rural areas of Quebec, Canada to understand impediments of citizens in outlying areas to use online government services. Roy et al (2015) found that perceived usefulness, perceived ease of use, perceived risk, and trust determine users' attitudes towards e-government online services. It is interesting to observe that a limited number of studies (Huang 2006, 2007; Manoharan 2012) have been conducted at the level of the US county. Alongside these studies, Roy et al (2015) have acknowledged the role of geography (possible urban-rural divide) in the context of e-government adoption by counties and usage of e-government services by county citizenry.

Interestingly Khatiwada and Pigg (2010) in investigating spatial patterns of internet growth in US counties analogous to Huang (2006, 2007) found market demand to be driving force for internet diffusion. More urban counties with higher levels of educational attainment among its residents, more business establishments, and higher housing value were more likely to have larger presence of internet service providers (ISPs) – an access rather than usage dimension of digital divide. This study is interesting since it explicitly models the role of geography in measuring internet diffusion at the county level, finding that counties with higher number of ISPs were generally surrounded by counties with similar ISP prevalence. Likewise, Gauvin et al (2015) formally considered spatial autocorrelation in order to properly measure the relative impact of age, education, income, gender and geography on the probability of internet usage.

However, no prior work has systematically investigated spatial patterns of internet usage for the purpose of engaging in e-commerce and online financial activities in the United States. Specifically, we examine internet use for electronically purchasing products from well-known retailers, banking online, and paying bills online. Such activities to engage with financial and consumer services are among the most popular uses of the internet by Americans aged 25 years or older in 2011. Using a large sample of 3,109 US counties in the lower 48 states of the US, we examine and characterize geographic hotspots as well as coldspots of internet activity for e-commerce purposes. Further we examine the influence of demographic, economic, educational factors as well as innovation and social capital factors on internet usage for conducting e-commerce and financial activities online by county internet users. In doing so, we explicitly model the presence of spatial bias. These are the unique features of our work.

CONCEPTUAL MODEL

Our conceptual model of internet use in US counties for conducting e-commerce and financial activities is based on the Spatially Aware Technology Utilization Model (SATUM) (Pick and Sarkar, 2016). It posits associations of thirteen demographic, economic, employment, and social capital independent variables with five indicators of internet use for e-commerce dependent variables (Figure 1) based upon antecedent literature. A unique feature of SATUM is its explicit consideration of geographic disparities in internet adoption by combining traditional regression analysis with spatial autocorrelation and geographic clustering analysis. Additionally SATUM works well for varied units of geography such as nations, states, provinces, regions, counties, or zip codes.

The dependent variables included in our conceptual model are (i) banking online in last 12 months, (ii) ordering from Amazon.com in past 12 months, (iii) using internet to make personal purchase in past 30 days, (iv) paying bills online in last 30 days, and (v) ordering from WalMart.com in past 12 months. In 2010, a survey of more than 2,200 internet users aged 18 years and older conducted by the Pew Research Center (Pew, 2010) found purchasing a product online and banking online to be common across generations of users. As stated earlier, a more recent NTIA report (NTIA, 2013) indicated that more than half of all US internet users aged 25 years and older relied on the internet for financial services such as online banking and for shopping and other consumer services. This justifies the inclusion of the five dependent indicators of internet use for e-commerce and financial activities in this study.

Next we present independent variables included in the conceptual model that are posited to be associated with the previously mentioned dependent variables. Associations of independent variables with dependent indicators of internet use for e-commerce are mostly induced from prior literature and are discussed by category as follows:

Demographic influences

A geographic divide has been persistently documented in several reports of the US federal government (The White House, 2015; NTIA 2011, 2013, 2014). One such recent report of the President's Council of Economic Advisors (The White House, 2015) provided evidence of significant disparities in county level rates of home internet adoption in 2013 between large, urban regions such as the Northeastern corridor from Boston to Washington, D.C., the California coastal corridor stretching from the Bay Area to San Diego, and the rural South, the latter dotted by tribal and Indian lands, all homes to large numbers of counties with internet adoption in the lowest quintile among all counties nationwide. An urban-rural divide for internet access has also been reported by Tolbert et al (2007) and Sylvester and McGlynn (2010). Researchers have reasoned that more populous, wealthy urban regions in metropolitan areas with higher levels of educational attainment and higher median home values were more likely to have greater demand for internet services. In mid-2015, almost 66% of internet users aged 15 years or older used the internet for online financial services, online banking, and paying bills in urban areas compared to 54% of their rural peers. For online shopping and obtaining access to general consumer services, the discrepancy was less stark, 70% urban versus 63% for rural users (NTIA, 2016). We posit that percent of urban population is associated with internet utilization for e-commerce and financial activities in US counties.

From a race and ethnic perspective, Whites and Asians have traditionally led other ethnicities in internet use (US Census Bureau, 2014). Recent survey data of US households from the Current Population Survey of the US Census Bureau (NTIA, 2016) indicate that African Americans trailed the US national per capita use (64.6%) of online financial services, banking, and investing by 10%; Asians and Whites surpassed the US average by approximately 14% and 10% respectively. Hispanics were below the US average, faring slightly better than African Americans. The same pattern was largely repeated for using the internet to shop online, make travel reservations, or using other online consumer services. The disparity in internet access due to race and ethnicity has been documented by Agarwal, Animesh, and Prasad (2009), Tolbert et al (2007), and Sylsvester and McGlynn (2010). Given the consensus in prior literature, we posit that race and ethnicity are associated with technology utilization in US counties; for Asians the association is positive, while for Blacks and Hispanics, the association is posited to be negative.

Since elderly people show greater reluctance to adopt new technologies than teenagers (Srinuan and Bohlin, 2011) and age influences on ICT adoption are well-established (Selwyn, 2006; Ono and Zavodny 2007), we include the factors of young dependency ratio and working age population in our conceptual model and posit them to be positively associated with e-commerce dependent variables in our study.

Economic Influences

In 2015, almost 75% of internet users aged 15 years or older with an annual family income of at least $100,000 led those with an annual family income of $25,000 - $49,000 in terms of using online financial services and online banking by almost 15%. For online shopping and using other online consumer services, the gap was higher; 82.6% for those with annual family income exceeding $100,000 compared to 63% for those with an annual family income of $25,000 - $49,000 (NTIA, 2016). In prior digital divide research, economic factors such as income, international trade openness (Baliamoune-Lutz, 2003), and foreign direct investment (Author, 2008), have been widely cited to influence ICT diffusion and utilization. In our model, we posit personal income to be positively associated with e-commerce use of the internet.

In prior research, service sector jobs were also found to increase the likelihood and frequency of internet access by the general population in Tolbert et al (2007). In a study of Chinese provinces (Author, 2013) construction sector expenditures were found to impact the use of personal computers, internet, and fixed phones while not effecting broadband, mobile phones, and web use. Construction costs, specifically installation and maintenance costs were found to be associated with the probability of cell tower location by Buys et al. (2009) for a spatial econometric study of cell phone coverage in sub-Saharan Africa. We argue that in the US, the per capita size of the construction sector will impact the physical and infrastructural aspects of ICT development. Therefore, we posit that services sector and construction sector employment are associated with internet use for e-commerce in US counties.

Innovation, which manifests itself in different forms in the digital divide literature, has often been found to be associated with higher levels of ICT utilization (Quibria et al, 2003). We include professional, scientific, and technical services workforce as an independent indicator for innovation, since this segment of the workforce has been acknowledged be more likely to use ICTs to foster innovation.

Education Influences

In 2015, the disparity between college and high-school graduates in using online financial and banking services was stark; while almost 79% of college graduates used the internet for such services, only 51% of high-school graduates did so. For online shopping, obtaining access to consumer services, and making travel reservations, similar discrepancy exists; high-school graduates (54%) lag college graduates by almost 30% (NTIA, 2016). In prior digital divide literature, there is significant evidence of the influence of education on the adoption of use of ICTs such as the internet. Education correlates such as college graduates per capita (Author, 2005), level of educational attainment (Agarwal, Animesh, and Prasad, 2009; Tolbert et al, 2007; Chen, 2013; Weiner et al, 2013), enrollments in tertiary education and expenditures per student (Andoh-Baidoo, Osatuyi, and Kunene, 2014) have been found to be significantly associated with internet use, broadband access, computer use, and and development of ICT capacity in digital divide studies for the US and other regions of the world. Consequently, we posit that college graduation is associated with ICT availability and use. While income and educational attainment are often highly positively correlated, we include college education as an independent correlate but screen for multi-collinearity in Ordinary Least Squares regressions using the variance inflation factor (VIF). This is discussed in the next section.

In prior work (Pick and Azari, 2008), government spending on education has been found to be associated with adoption and use of PCs, ICT expenditure, and ICT infrastructure quality for a sample of 72 nations. Other studies such as Quibria et al. (2003) have highlighted instances in which government investment in education and private sector support for IT training have been found to be crucial for the development of ICT skills and use. Therefore, we posit that local government education expense is associated with internet use for e-commerce and financial activities among county populations.

Social Capital Influences

Social capital is the scope of ties and linkages in a population through physical and communication means and well as by organizations that foster human collaboration or by bonding between people who possess resources (Putnam, 2001). Social capital was a key factor in a study of the US digital divide for a survey sample of individuals (Chen, 2003), as well as in a two-stage study of the decisions by persons to go online, subject to peer influences (Agarwal et al, 2009). In a state-level study of ICT adoption in the US, social capital was determined to be positively associated with internet access in the household for all 50 states as well as for 42 less urban states (Pick et al, 2015a). In the current study, we posit social capital to enhance internet use for pursuing e-commerce and online financial activities in US counties and use a Putnam-like index (Putnam, 2001) developed by Rupasingha and Goetz (2008).

Our conceptual model of Internet Use for e-commerce and financial activities in US counties is in Figure 1.

Figure 1: Conceptual Model of Internet Use for E-Commerce in US Counties

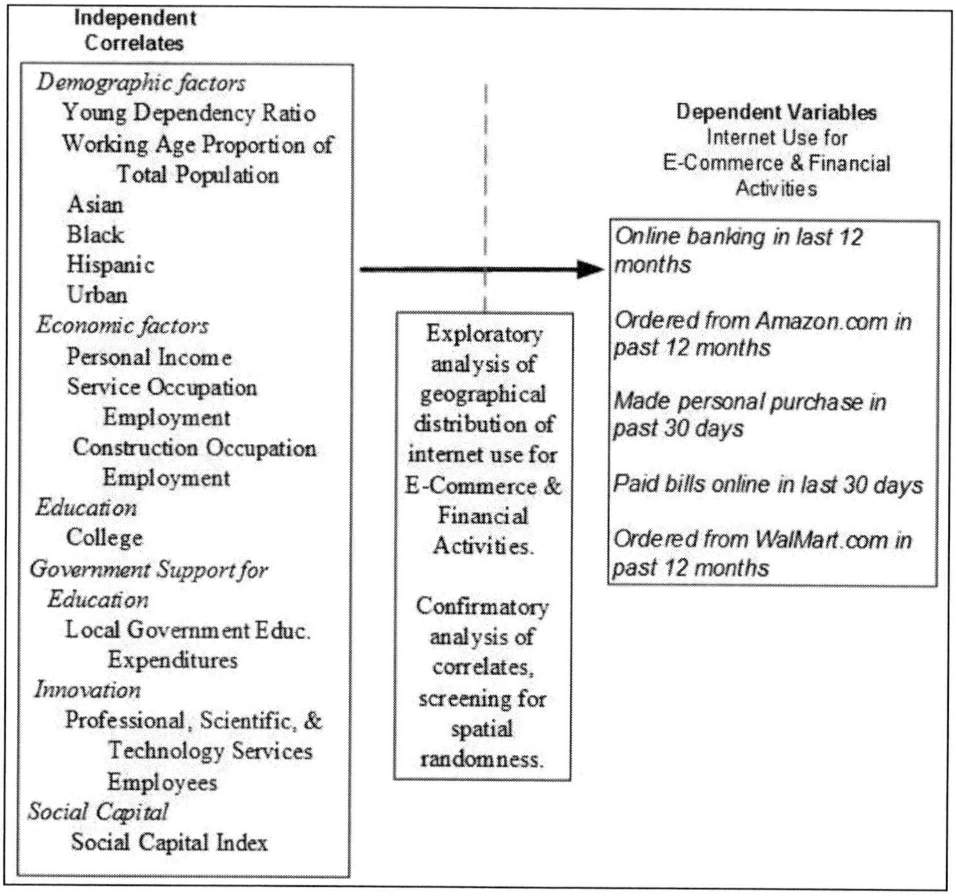

DATA AND METHODOLOGY

Data on five dependent indicators of internet use for e-commerce purposes used in the conceptual model were obtained from Esri/GfK MRI DoubleBase Survey (Esri, 2013). Esri computes estimates of demand for each of these dependent variables in the form of an index; relevant methodology statements can be located at Esri Data, Methodology Statements (2015). Data on the conceptual model's independent variables such as population, income, education, ethnicity, employment, and education expenditure are procured from various US Census sources. For the social capital independent variable, we obtain data on a county-level social capital index from the Pennsylvania State University's Northeast Regional Center for Rural Development (Rupasingha and Goetz, 2008). Data for several independent variables is for the period 2008-12; in contrast, social capital data are from the year 2009 which is the latest year such data are available for from a reliable source. Data for all dependent variables is from the period 2010-12 ensuring time simultaneity. The time-lag between data for dependent versus independent variables is acceptable since independent variables such as income, education, and others are likely to impact internet use for e-commerce after a reasonable lapse in time. Our sample includes data for all 3,109 out of 3,143 county or county equivalents in the lower 48 states of the US as defined by the US Census as of July 2009. Definitions, sources, and descriptive statistics (n = 3,109) of dependent and independent variables are in Table 1.

Table 1: Variables: Definitions, Sources, Descriptive Statistics

Abbreviation	*Name of Dependent Variable*	*Source*	*Year of Data*	*Definition*	*Min*	*Max*	*Mean*	*SD*
BANK12R	Did banking online in last 12 months	BA (esri Business Analyst Data, GfK MRI DoubleBase Survey 2012)	2010-2012	Did banking online in last 12 months (% pop)	0.108	0.514	0.290	0.067
AMZ12R	Ordered from website last 12 mo: amazon.com	BA (esri Business Analyst Data, GfK MRI DoubleBase Survey 2012)	2010-2012	Ordered from website last 12 mo: amazon.com (% pop)	0.056	0.397	0.167	0.052
PURCH30R	Internet last 30 days: made personal purchase	BA (esri Business Analyst Data, GfK MRI DoubleBase Survey 2012)	2010-2012	Internet last 30 days: made personal purchase (% pop)	0.122	0.581	0.296	0.069
BILLS30R	Internet last 30 days: paid bills online	BA (esri Business Analyst Data, GfK MRI DoubleBase Survey 2012)	2010-2012	Internet last 30 days: paid bills online (% pop)	0.125	0.611	0.315	0.082
WALMART12R	Ordered from website last 12 mo: walmart.com	BA (esri Business Analyst Data, GfK MRI DoubleBase Survey 2012)	2010-2012	Ordered from website last 12 mo: walmart.com (% pop)	0.039	0.093	0.074	0.007
Abbreviation	*Name of Independent Variable*	*Source*	*Year of Data*	*Definition*	*Min*	*Max*	*Mean*	*SD*
YOUNGDEPR	Young Dependency Ratio	US Census Bureau, Decennial Census 2010, Summary File 1 (CENDEC10_DP01)	2010	POP 0-19/POP 20-64	0.167	0.884	0.454	0.071
COLLEGER	College Graduates or Higher, Age 18+ (%)	US Census Bureau, American Community Survey 2012, 5-year estimates, Table DP-02	2008-2012	Population Estimate of College Graduates or Higher, Age 18+	0.034	0.537	0.131	0.059
PINCPC12	Personal Income Per Capita	US Dept of Commerce, Bureau of Economic Analysis, CA1-3, Personal Income, Per Capita Income	2012	Personal Income Per Capita ($)	17264.000	116843.000	36523.761	9182.777
WKAGEPOP	Working Age Pop (Pop. 20-64)/Total Pop	CENDEC10_DP01	NA	POP 20-64/Total POP	0.464	0.743	0.579	0.033
SERVICER	Service Occupations (%)	US Census Bureau, American Community Survey (ACS) 2012, 5-year estimates, Table DP-03	2008-2012	Persons 16+ in Service Occupations	0.025	0.211	0.097	0.019
CONSTRUCTR	Construction Industry, Employed Persons 16+ (%)	US Census Bureau, ACS 2012, 5-year estimates, Table DP-03	2008-2012	Construction Industry, Employed Persons 16+	0.000	0.158	0.040	0.014
ASIANR	Asian Population (%)	CENDEC10_DP01	2010	Asian Population	0.000	0.358	0.014	0.023
BLACKR	Black Population (%)	CENDEC10_DP01	2010	Black or African American Population	0.000	0.860	0.096	0.147
HISPANICR	Hispanic/Latino Population (%)	CENDEC10_DP01	2010	Hispanic or Latino Population	0.000	0.957	0.083	0.133
URBAN	Urban Population (%)	CENDEC10_DP01	2010	Urban Population	0.000	1.000	0.780	0.415
LGOVEDEXPR	Local Govt Education Expenditures	National Center for Education Stats	2009	Sum of School District Expenditures divided by total pop for all School	69.573	36664.336	1985.969	1144.669
PSTSVCEMPR	Professional, Scientific, and Tech Services Employees (%)	US Census Bureau, Economic Census 2007	2007	Number of Professional, Scientific, and Technical Services Employees	0.000	1.000	0.621	0.485
FACTORAVE	Transformed Social Capital	Penn State University's Northeast Regional Center for Rural Development (Rupasingha and Goetz, 2008)	2009	Transformed Index of Social Capital	0.000	0.467	0.166	0.042
						n=3,109		

SOURCES	Abbrev	Detailed Reference
US Census Bureau, DEC 2010, Table DP-01	CENDEC10_DP01	US Census Bureau, Decennial Census 2010, Summary File 1
US Census Bureau, ACS 2012, Table DP-02	CENACS12_DP02	US Census Bureau, American Community Survey 2012, 5-year estimates, Table DP-02
US Census Bureau, ACS 2012, Table DP-03	CENACS12_DP03	US Census Bureau, American Community Survey 2012, 5-year estimates, Table DP-03
US Census Bureau, ACS 2012, Table DP-04	CENACS12_DP04	US Census Bureau, American Community Survey 2012, 5-year estimates, Table DP-04
US Census Bureau, ACS 2012, Table DP-05	CENACS12_DP05	US Census Bureau, American Community Survey 2012, 5-year estimates, Table DP-05
Bureau of Economic Analysis, CA1-3	BEA_CA1-3	US Dept of Commerce, Bureau of Economic Analysis, CA1-3, Personal Income, Per Capita Income
Bureau of Economic Analysis, CA04	BEA_CA04	US Dept of Commerce, Bureau of Economic Analysis, CA04, Personal Income Summary
US Census Bureau, Economic Census 2007	CENECON07	US Census Bureau, Economic Census 2007
National Center for Education Statistics, F-33	NCES_F33	US Census Bureau, Governments Division, Local Education Agency (School District) Finance Survey (F-33), National Center for Education Statistics, Common Core of Data
Esri Business Analyst Data	BA	Esri Business Analyst Data, GfK MRI DoubleBase Survey 2012
Rupasingha and Goetz, 2008	---	Pennsylvania State University's Northeast Regional Center for Rural Development

Our methodology is comprised of the following steps: (i) Descriptive statistics are determined for all variables are computed and correlation analysis is used to diagnose multicollinearity among independent variables; (ii) Dependent variables are mapped using a Geographic Information System (Esri's ArcGIS Desktop) (Figure 2) to visualize patterns of internet use for the purpose of engaging in e-commerce. GIS mapping provides important visual cues about spatial distribution of a variable and possible clustering and enables to observe patterns in their data;

(iii) Next K-means cluster analysis is employed using a statistical package (SPSS) to identify groups of counties that are most similar in their adoption and use of the internet for e-commerce. For the purpose of this study, K-means analysis is conducted with K = 6 for the five e-commerce dependent variables. Resultant clusters are mapped and underlying demographic and socio-economic attributes of clusters are examined along with whether clusters conform to state boundaries or boundaries of census metropolitan areas. (iv) E-commerce dependent variables are examined for the presence of spatial autocorrelation using the index Moran's I (Openshaw, 1984). Moran's I is inferential; the null hypothesis is that the values of a variables are randomly distributed across any geography. This is an important precursor to the next step – conducting OLS regression analysis because it enables us to diagnose if the dependent variables exhibit statistically significant patterns of agglomeration of high or low values indicating the presence of spatial bias – a common problem plaguing technology-diffusion datasets. (v) Lastly, we conduct OLS regression analysis to analyze associations of independent variables with e-commerce dependent variables. OLS regressions are performed for each technology dependent variable, in stepwise order, allowing in only those of the nine independent variables with significance levels of equal or less than 0.05. Stepwise entry is appropriate for exploratory investigations of new relationships of factors, as is true presently. All independent variables are tested for the presence of multicollinearity using the Variance Inflation Factor (VIF) using a cutoff value of 5.0. Further diagnostic tests are employed to check if OLS regression assumptions are met using the Joint Wald statistic, Koenker BP statistic, and Jarque-Bera statistic. Spatial distribution of regression residuals is examined for randomness using Moran's I. Model relationships that result in spatially random errors are regarded as valid. When residuals are geographically clustered, we acknowledge the presence of spatial bias in our results. In such instances, regression results have to be treated with caution. More details about the methodology employed in this paper can be found in Pick and Sarkar (2015b).

GEOGRAPHIC PATTERNS

To examine the geographic distribution of e-commerce variables in US counties, each dependent variable is mapped using a Geographic Information System (GIS). The dependent variable maps show that internet use to conduct e-commerce and financial transactions online in US counties do not conform to US state boundaries. The implication is that state-level mapping may show misleading patterns and analyzing correlates of such use at the state level may produce misleading results.

We also employ Moran's I statistic to test the extent of spatial autocorrelation of the dependent variables for all counties is the lower 48 states (n = 3,109), metropolitan counties (n = 1,161), micropolitan counties (n = 637), and rural counties (n = 1,311). It is interesting to observe that all dependent variables are significantly spatially agglomerated at the country level as well as for the metro, and rural samples. However, internet use for e-commerce in micropolitan counties is spatially randomly distributed. This has implications when we conduct OLS regressions to examine the association of independent correlates with the e-commerce dependent variables later in the study. Moran's I values for all 3,109 counties and those in the metro, micro, and rural samples can be found in Tables 3, 4, 5, and 6.

The e-commerce dependent variables were also mapped using the Local Moran's I statistic. This Local Indicators of Spatial Association (LISA)-based method (Khatiwada and Pigg, 2010) yields "hotspots" that are statistically significant clusters of high values (counties that exhibit high use of internet for e-commerce surrounded by similar high use counties) or "coldspots" that are statistically significant clusters of low values. LISA analysis also produces outliers in which a county with high levels of e-commerce and online financial activity is surrounded primarily by counties with low use or vice-versa. For example, LISA analysis shows Lubbock County TX to be a statistically significant high-low outlier for two dependent variables – purchasing from Amazon and online bill payment. Conversely, Benewah County, Idaho as a statistically significant low-high outlier for the dependent variable, shopping from Amazon. Further investigation reveals that Lubbock County TX is home to Texas Tech University, a leading institution of the Texas Tech University System. Benewah, Idaho, located north-northeast of Pullman WA, and Moscow Idaho are home to Washington State University and University of Idaho respectively. We find that most statistically significant outlier counties contain at least one college or university, military reservation or government laboratory – entities that are likely to foster the adoption and use of the internet for e-commerce and online financial activity.

The results of K-Means cluster analysis for e-commerce, shown in Figure 2, identify six clusters, which have been ordered in level of e-commerce from highest (color red) to lowest (grey color). It is quite evident that the higher levels of clusters (1, 2, and 3) correspond to particular major metropolitan areas and surrounding counties. The Northeastern megalopolis is evident stretching from Washington to Boston and up into New Hampshire and Vermont. A similar concentration was also noted for cluster analysis of the three social media variables of Facebook, Twitter, and LinkedIn (Pick, Sarkar, and Rosales, 2015c).

Figure 2: K-means clusters of internet use for E-Commerce in US Counties, 2012

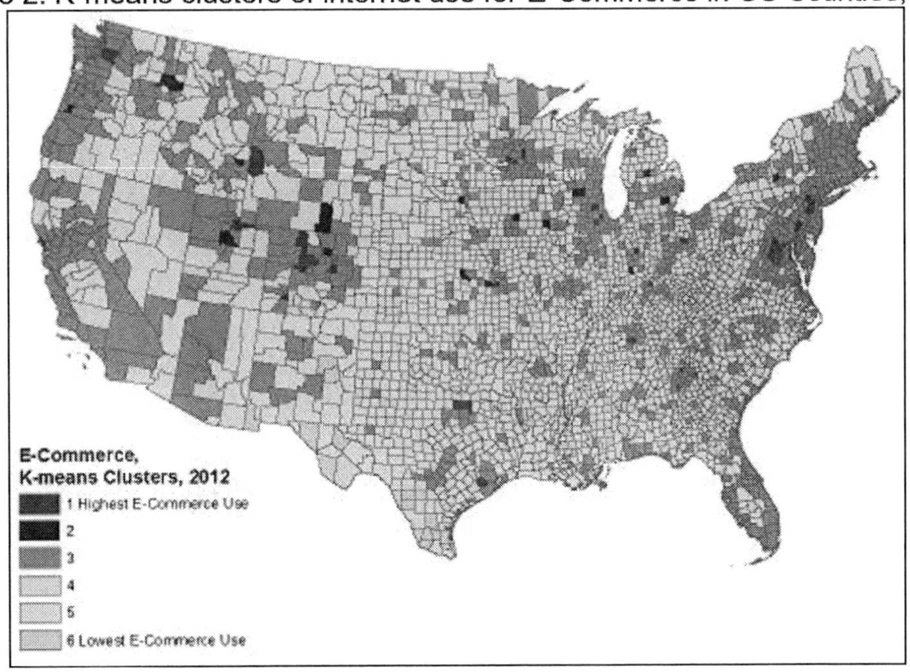

Six other high e-Commerce areas, also noted for social media, are Chicago-Milwaukee major metro areas, Minneapolis-St. Paul, Denver stretching westward to Salt Lake City, San Francisco-San Jose, and Seattle-Portland major metropolitan areas, and Dallas-Fort Worth. Parts of several of these metro areas were also identified by Richard Florida as "high-tech metros" (Florida, 2012 a,b), in particular Boston in the Northeast megalopolis; Boulder, Colorado; San Francisco, and Seattle. A difference in the present research is that broader reaches beyond the major metro boundaries are included and shown to be relevant, for instance the Northeast megalopolis and some counties stretching beyond its traditional boundaries including in New Hampshire and Vermont, and the Rocky Mountain counties in between the Denver and Salt Lake City metros.

California bears some special discussion relative to its e-Commerce patterns. Although only reaching the highest e-Commerce levels for San Francisco, Cluster 3 encompasses 20 large counties that draw a ring around the state's Central Valley, stretching from Napa and Sonoma counties down to San Diego and eastern Riverside counties. This land area of moderately high use is among the largest urban land extents in the nation, only rivalled by the Northeast megalopolis and by the Denver-to-Salt Lake City complex. The explanation of Los Angeles County's lack of inclusion in the highest cluster status is that the County has a quite varied mixture of wealthy and well-educated as well as poor and less-educated communities; therefore, the county's visible strength as an e-Commerce hub and content producer is averaged out by technology-deficient and internet-challenged communities.

The nation's cluster characterizations, given in Table 2 reveal profound differences between the highest and lowest clusters, with ordering from the Amazon website, for instance being about 4 times as intensive in Cluster 1 versus Cluster 6. The e-commerce variable with the least difference across clusters is ordering from the Walmart website which is rather stable across the entire range of clusters only varying only from 7.3 to 7.9 percent use, surprisingly with slightly greater use by the lowest e-commerce Cluster 6 than by Cluster 1. It can be noted on the table also that the cluster continuum is paralleled by educational, income, and urban continua.

Table 2: K-means Clusters of E-Commerce, US Counties, 2012 (Shaded cells show cluster centers)

	Cluster Number						
	1 Highest ICT	2	3	4	5	6 Lowest ICT	Ratio of MAX to MIN
BANK12R	0.454	0.401	0.363	0.316	0.257	0.158	2.87
AMZ12R	0.312	0.306	0.225	0.185	0.139	0.085	3.67
PURCH30R	0.501	0.423	0.371	0.313	0.262	0.172	2.90
BILLS30R	0.524	0.539	0.408	0.332	0.271	0.173	3.04
WALMART12R	0.073	0.077	0.073	0.073	0.074	0.079	0.93
Number of counties	49	21	838	303	1733	165	

REGRESSION RESULTS

The findings from the OLS regressions indicate that the variables significantly influence the adjusted R^2, which signifies the proportion of the variance explained for a given equation. Since R^2 is represents effect size for an OLS regression, the effect size, ranging between 23 and 79 percent, is substantial and confirms the importance of the findings. For this large sample of 3,109 counties, the Jarque-Bera test statistic indicates goodness-of-fit between the regression residuals and the normal distribution (Jarque and Bera, 1980). The Joint Wald Statistic (Wald, 1943), which tests that the parameters associated with a group of independent variables should be included in a model, is consistently positive and significant. The Koenker test statistic, which indicates that the variance of the residuals is not constant, is significant for all the study regressions, but weakens for the metro sample for which 3 out of 5 regressions are insignificant. Overall, this means that for 85 percent of the regressions, equality of residuals' variances is not present across the sample. The failure of the Koenker test (Lyon and Tsai, 1996) may be due to the large size of these samples, ranging from 637 to 3,109, so achieving a model that accounts for variance equality across a much larger set of residuals becomes difficult. It does suggest that models could be formulated with more factors, to try to reduce heteroscedasticity, but that also might create less understandable models.

The OLS findings for the country sample (Table 3) emphasize for e-commerce variables, the importance of college education, age structure, urban location, and the reducing effect of Black and Hispanic ethnicities. College education is the most important factor that relates to online banking, personal purchasing on the Internet, paying bills online on the Internet, and ordering from the Amazon website. By contrast, college education has a strong reducing effect on ordering from the Walmart website. College education is well known for its positive effect on a variety of information technology factors for units of analysis of nations (Baliamoune-Lutz, 2003; Yates et al., 2011) or states/provinces (Pick et al, 2015a).

Table 3: OLS Regression Results (all counties in lower 48 states, n = 3,109)

		Country (All counties in lower 48 states)				
		BANK12R	AMZ12R	PURCH30R	BILLS30R	WALMART12R
Independent Variable	Independent Variable Definition	Did banking online in last 12 months	Ordered from website last 12 mo: amazon.com	Internet Last 30 days: Made personal purchase	Internet Last 30 days: Paid bills online	Ordered from website last 12 mo: walmart.com
YOUNGDEPR	Young Dependency Ratio	0.207***	0.224***		0.307***	0.470***
COLLEGER	College Graduates or Higher, Age 18+	0.674***	0.635***	0.682***	0.671***	-0.372***
PINCPC12	Personal Income Per Capita					0.246***
WKAGEPOP	Working Age Pop (Pop. 20-64)/Total Population	0.184***	0.266***		0.325***	0.283***
SERVICER	Persons 16+ in Service Occupations					
CONSTRUCTR	Persons 16+ in Construction Occupations	0.075***				-0.103***
ASIANR	Asian		0.119***	0.138***		
BLACKR	Black	-0.303***	-0.173***	-0.227***	-0.176***	
HISPANICR	Hispanic	-0.124***	-0.130***	-0.095***		-0.156***
URBAN	Urban	0.189***	0.208***	0.206***	0.205***	-0.125***
LGOVEDEXPR	Local Govt Education Expenditures					
PSTSVCEMPR	Professional, Scientific, and Tech Services Employees					
FACTORAVE	Social Capital					0.212***
OLS Regression Diagnostic Tests						
Joint Wald Statistic		4977.486***	6686.720***	6370.985***	5288.969***	662.016***
Koenker (BP) Statistic		162.252***	148.533***	157.476***	145.238***	353.637***
Jarque-Bera Statistic		64.667***	152.208***	127.460***	195.807***	800.681***
Spatial Autocorrelation of Dep. Var. (Moran's I)		0.564***	0.579***	0.646***	0.512***	0.245***
Spatial Autocorrelation of Regression Residuals (Moran's I)		0.438***	0.402***	0.353***	0.326***	0.158*
Adjusted R^2		0.718***	0.763***	0.750***	0.740***	0.244***
Sample Size		3109	3109	3109	3109	3109
		* significant at 0.05, ** significant at 0.01, *** significant at 0.001				

County age structure relates to e-Commerce usage. In the findings, the young dependency ratio is associated with all dependent variables except personal-purchase. There are similar findings for the associations of working age population. Profound impacts of age structure were present for e-Entertainment in U.S. counties (Pick, Sarkar, and Rosales, 2016), and for effects on information technology variables although there were mixed age structural effects in a study of the prefectures of Japan (Nishida, Pick, and Sarkar, 2014), in particular positive effects of working age population on internet use and mobile telephone subscribers; and positive effects of young dependency ratio on mobile phone expenditures, but inverse effects on broadband subscribers. The present findings imply that counties with greater proportion of younger and working-age population have more e-commerce usage, which can be attributed to the workers' greater familiarity with e-commerce than for non-working adults or retired people.

A somewhat less important influence is the effect of urban location on all e-commerce variables except ordering from Walmart. Urban location has been a consistent positive determinant of ICT usage including in the literature for digital divides in U.S. counties (Chen, 2013), and for social media factors in U.S. counties (Pick et al, 2015c). An explanation is that in the urban setting, the population tends to be more aware of e-Commerce and would generally experience greater variety of e-Commerce services and improved deliveries.

Counties with high proportions of Black and/or Hispanic/Latino population have reduced e-Commerce use, with magnitude of effect similar to that for age structural and urban variables. On the other hand, counties with higher Asian population tend to have increased web-based ordering from Amazon and higher level of personal purchases. This differs from the ethnicity effects on e-Entertainment factors, for which Asian ethnicity was a consistently positive correlate, but Black and Hispanic correlations were largely absent.

Service and construction occupational levels for counties have little influence on e-commerce for the country sample, an instance where overall effects mask underlying strong impacts for the micropolitan and rural subsamples. Social capital, which has been of increasing prominence in digital divide research (Chen, 2013), has positive influence only for ordering from Walmart. This finding is contrary to a prior study that concluded there was a reversed, negative relationship, viz. that Walmart reduces social capital (Carden et al., 2009). Further research would be needed understand why social connections physically present in a county would be associated with purchasing through Walmart e-commerce, i.e. not with purchasing through Amazon's e-Commerce.

The subsample regressions were performed with the same set of dependent and independent variables, excluding the urban variable which is redundant, since the subsampling inherently compares across the metropolitan-micro-rural categories. Regression findings for the metropolitan (metro), micropolitan (micro), and rural subsamples are in Tables 4, 5, and 6.

Without discussing the regression findings in full details, several findings are consistent across the country sample and its metro, micro, and rural subsamples. One such finding is the strong influence of college education for all of the e-commerce variables with the exception of the inverse effect for Walmart. The strong inverse relationships of county proportion Black and proportion Hispanic apply consistently for nearly all of the e-Commerce variables applies across the main sample and subsamples although the Hispanic influence is somewhat weaker for the metro subsample. These ethnic groups in counties are related to reduced e-Commerce usage, regardless of city versus countryside. The robustness of these associations may be tied into culture and lifestyle, possible explanations which need further investigation.

However, independent variables have important differences that vary across the metro-micro-rural continuum. Age structure is very strong for metro counties; moderate for micro counties; and weak for rural ones. For rural, the strongest associations are for both youth and working age population with ordering online from Walmart. One explanation might be the greater presence and visibility of Walmart in rural America, as compared to Amazon. The Walmart company originated in small towns and cities in the rural South, so there is a rural fabric built into the company's culture. Another explanation might be Walmart's strength in distribution of goods across rural America, which reflects the firm's critical core strength in distribution.

Service and construction occupations have limited associations with e-Commerce usage at the metro level, but at the micro level, there is strong associations with e-Commerce for counties with greater presence of service occupation and at the rural level with counties having more construction workforce; again Walmart is distinctive, showing only minor relationship with service or construction occupations.

Table 4: OLS Regression Results (all metropolitan counties in lower 48 states, n = 1,161)

		Metro (All counties in metropolitan statistical areas)				
		BANK12R	AMZ12R	PURCH30R	BILLS30R	WALMART12R
Independent Variable	Independent Variable Definition	Did banking online in last 12 months	Ordered from website last 12 mo: amazon.com	Internet Last 30 days: Made personal purchase	Internet Last 30 days: Paid bills online	Ordered from website last 12 mo: walmart.com
YOUNGDEPR	Young Dependency Ratio	0.364***	0.226***	0.239***	0.379***	0.554***
COLLEGER	College Graduates or Higher, Age 18+	0.747***	0.791***	0.835***	0.737***	
PINCPC12	Personal Income Per Capita					
WKAGEPOP	Working Age Pop (Pop. 20-64)/Total Population	0.229***	0.235***	0.168***	0.335***	0.270***
SERVICER	Persons 16+ in Service Occupations		0.072***		0.110***	
CONSTRUCTR	Persons 16+ in Construction Occupations					
ASIANR	Asian					-0.245***
BLACKR	Black	-0.272***	-0.157***	-0.202***	-0.140***	
HISPANICR	Hispanic	-0.150***		-0.085***		-0.297***
URBAN	Urban	N/A	N/A	N/A	N/A	N/A
LGOVEDEXPR	Local Govt Education Expenditures					
PSTSVCEMPR	Professional, Scientific, and Tech Services Employees					
FACTORAVE	Social Capital					
OLS Regression Diagnostic Tests						
Joint Wald Statistic		1566.858***	2578.872***	2859.118***	2026.713***	313.309***
Koenker (BP) Statistic		5.978	6.947	7.128	20.215***	12.579**
Jarque-Bera Statistic		73.829***	40.924***	15.588***	108.403***	188.736***
Spatial Autocorrelation of Dep. Var. (Moran's I)		0.494***	0.703***	0.782***	0.575***	0.453***
Spatial Autocorrelation of Regression Residuals (Moran's I)		0.658***	0.538***	0.557***	0.558***	0.211**
Adjusted R^2		0.710***	0.783***	0.791***	0.770***	0.280***
Sample Size		1161	1161	1161	1161	1161
		* significant at 0.05, ** significant at 0.01, *** significant at 0.001				

County ethnicities reveal considerable shifts in associations across the metro to rural continuum. Although Black remains inverse in association across the subsamples, Hispanic is weaker for metro than for micro or rural, a phenomenon that is unexplained. The biggest change is for associations with Asian ethnicity in counties. It is fairly weak and positive for the metro subsample; stronger for micro, and very strong for rural. One explanation is that Asian population seeks specialized merchandise and services that are available on the ground in the many ethnic neighborhoods within metro counties, whereas those products and services are less available in micro counties, and may not be physically available in rural counties. Hence the need for online shopping and service platforms expands as counties move from metropolitan to rural.

In the subsamples, social capital continues to be present only for ordering from Walmart and not for the metro subsample. Income is surprisingly weak throughout the regressions, and is mainly a positive factor with ordering from Walmart. Since income and education tend to be highly correlated, the absence of much income effect might be due to education being a stronger factor and displacing income as a factor.

Table 5: OLS Regression Results (all micropolitan counties in lower 48 states, n = 637)

		Micro (All counties in micropolitan statistical areas)				
		BANK12R	AMZ12R	PURCH30R	BILLS30R	WALMART12R
Independent Variable	Independent Variable Definition	Did banking online in last 12 months	Ordered from website last 12 mo: amazon.com	Internet Last 30 days: Made personal purchase	Internet Last 30 days: Paid bills online	Ordered from website last 12 mo: walmart.com
YOUNGDEPR	Young Dependency Ratio	0.253***	0.304***		0.426***	0.537***
COLLEGER	College Graduates or Higher, Age 18+	0.506***	0.523***	0.570***	0.492***	-0.249***
PINCPC12	Personal Income Per Capita					0.148**
WKAGEPOP	Working Age Pop (Pop. 20-64)/Total Population	0.155***	0.302***		0.357***	0.254***
SERVICER	Persons 16+ in Service Occupations	0.137***	0.152***	0.162***	0.175***	
CONSTRUCTR	Persons 16+ in Construction Occupations					-0.252***
ASIANR	Asian	0.153***	0.183***	0.146***	0.220***	
BLACKR	Black	-0.431***	-0.214***	-0.314***	-0.251***	-0.118**
HISPANICR	Hispanic	-0.279***	-0.290***	-0.210***	-0.224***	-0.177***
URBAN	Urban	N/A	N/A	N/A	N/A	N/A
LGOVEDEXPR	Local Govt Education Expenditures					
PSTSVCEEMPR	Professional, Scientific, and Tech Services Employees					
FACTORAVE	Social Capital					0.232***
OLS Regression Diagnostic Tests						
Joint Wald Statistic		1836.020***	1796.956***	1953.261***	1268.341***	143.121***
Koenker (BP) Statistic		26.494***	25.932***	23.395***	39.083***	55.930***
Jarque-Bera Statistic		37.201***	45.765***	19.580***	68.180***	263.755***
Spatial Autocorrelation of Dep. Var. (Moran's I)		0.542	0.321	0.432	0.204	0.066
Spatial Autocorrelation of Regression Residuals (Moran's I)		0.839	0.619	0.302	1.166	-0.011
Adjusted R^2		0.726***	0.706***	0.750***	0.717***	0.232***
Sample Size		637	637	637	637	637
		* significant at 0.05, ** significant at 0.01, *** significant at 0.001				

In summary, regression findings confirm the major variables associated with e-commerce are the county characteristics of college education, age structure, service and construction occupations, ethnicities, and urban-to-rural status. Social capital is limited to its association with ordering from Walmart. For most of the variables, there are substantial differences in strength of association across the metro-micro-urban continuum.

DISCUSSION OF RESULTS: GEOGRAPHIC PATTERNS AND REGRESSIONS

Thematic mapping of the dependent variables reinforces and adds further insights about the patterning and relationships of e-Commerce throughout the country. The extent of web-based ordering from Amazon in the last year (Figure 3) reveals distinctive regions with high and low intensities. The highest intensity areas are the Northeast megalopolis, Chicago-Milwaukee metro areas, an area including Salt Lake City and Denver metros as well as the areas in between, and coastal counties extending from the Seattle metro area down to San Diego, while low concentrations appear in the great Plains, the middle South, and Appalachia. There is a high level of web-based usage of Amazon, with county percent values ranging from 0.6 to 40 percent of population. By contrast, the spatial distribution of Walmart (Figure 4) use by county has nearly entirely the opposite highs and lows, with however, the exception that the Denver to

Salt Lake City metro remains high although Denver is low. Percent usage of Walmart is considerably less than for Amazon, ranging from 0.4 to 0.93 percent.

Table 6: OLS Regression Results (all rural counties in lower 48 states, n = 1,311)

		Rural (All counties in rural areas)				
		BANK12R	AMZ12R	PURCH30R	BILLS30R	WALMART12R
Independent Variable	Independent Variable Definition	Did banking online in last 12 months	Ordered from website last 12 mo: amazon.com	Internet Last 30 days: Made personal purchase	Internet Last 30 days: Paid bills online	Ordered from website last 12 mo: walmart.com
YOUNGDEPR	Young Dependency Ratio				0.164***	0.309***
COLLEGER	College Graduates or Higher, Age 18+	0.412***	0.330***	0.407***	0.339***	-0.430***
PINCPC12	Personal Income Per Capita					0.299***
WKAGEPOP	Working Age Pop (Pop. 20-64)/Total Population				0.126***	0.203***
SERVICER	Persons 16+ in Service Occupations		0.127***		0.128***	
CONSTRUCTR	Persons 16+ in Construction Occupations	0.124***	0.178***	0.148***	0.121***	
ASIANR	Asian	0.221***	0.292***	0.254***	0.275***	-0.106***
BLACKR	Black	-0.438***	-0.187***	-0.367***	-0.341***	
HISPANICR	Hispanic	-0.145***	-0.189***	-0.169***	-0.118***	
URBAN	Urban	N/A	N/A	N/A	N/A	N/A
LGOVEDEXPR	Local Govt Education Expenditures					
PSTSVCEEMPR	Professional, Scientific, and Tech Services Employees					
FACTORAVE	Social Capital					0.286***
OLS Regression Diagnostic Tests						
Joint Wald Statistic		2333.516***	723.997***	1696.859***	955.044***	422.245***
Koenker (BP) Statistic		52.380***	108.431***	94.702***	144.605***	102.893***
Jarque-Bera Statistic		35.806***	161.262***	47.923***	190.902***	102.187***
Spatial Autocorrelation of Dep. Var. (Moran's I)		0.647***	0.506***	0.545***	0.413***	0.364***
Spatial Autocorrelation of Regression Residuals (Moran's I)		0.495***	0.370***	0.345***	0.222**	0.235**
Adjusted R^2		0.650***	0.489***	0.609***	0.525***	0.304***
Sample Size		1311	1311	1311	1311	1311
		* significant at 0.05, ** significant at 0.01, *** significant at 0.001				

Figure 3: US County population (%) that ordered from Amazon.com in past 12 months, 2012

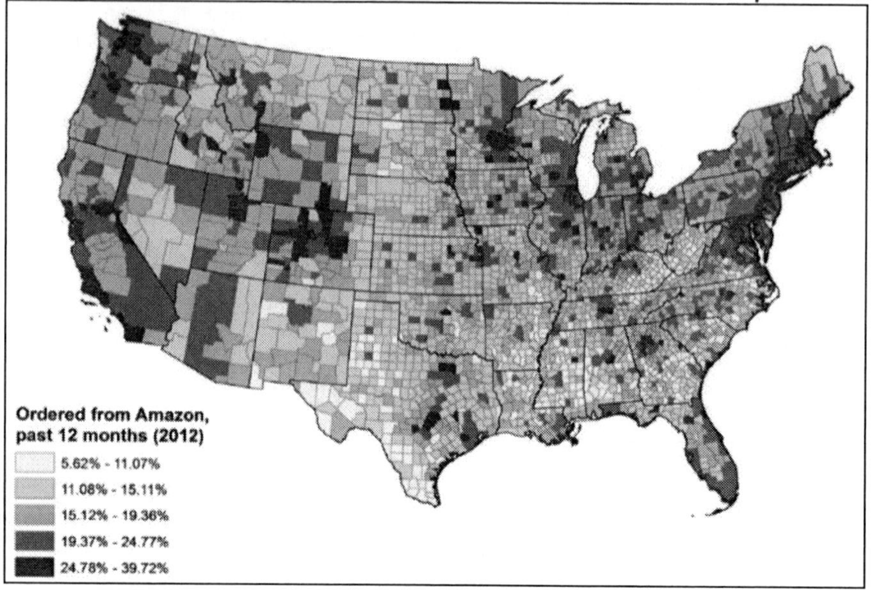

Figure 4: US County population (%) that ordered from WalMart.com in past 12 months, 2012

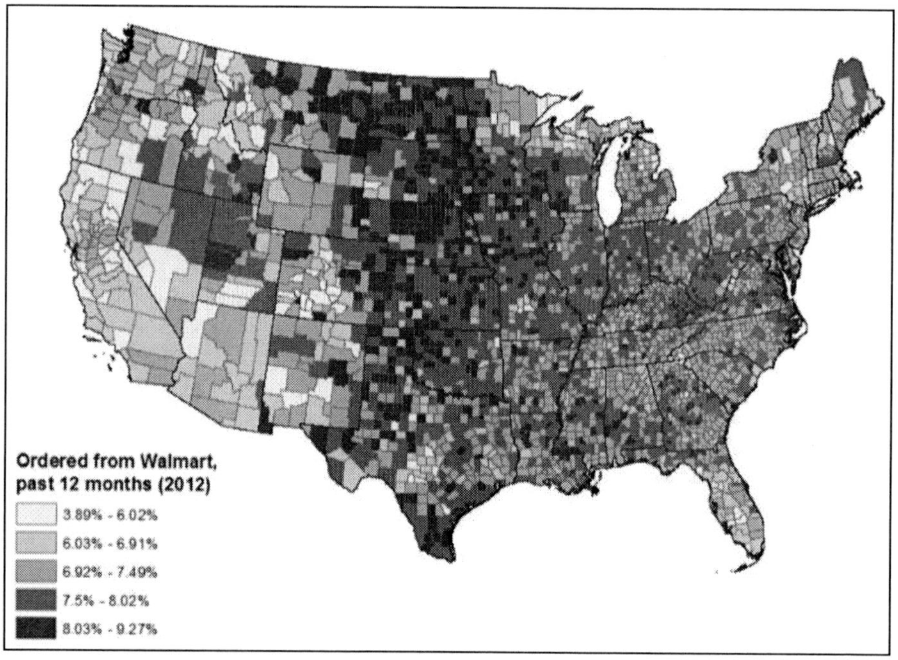

The opposite spatial patterning reinforces largely opposite regression findings between the two major retailers. The results point to Amazon e-Commerce being adopted heavily in urban, educated, and affluent counties, while Walmart e-Commerce is adopted by people in micro and rural areas, who have lower education and are poor. This contrast highlights the practical importance to businesses of spatial mapping in order to understand market areas. A company that is a purveyor of web-based e-Commerce can gain knowledge on the best strategy to expand its marketing coverage, for example to do so in geographic areas of strength for its competitor or emphasize regions of its market dominance. If a firm decides to strengthen market strength in currently weak areas, it would need to critically examine its product and service mix so it could potentially out-compete the present incumbent company. Although the Amazon versus Walmart (Figure 4) maps for e-commerce ordering are of extreme opposites, other firms might be marketing and selling with geographic patterns in between these two giants, and could also benefit strategically by understanding which firm currently dominates in areas the third firm seeks to move into, or other aspects of the geographies.

The geographical cluster differences further inform the key regression findings of the paper. In particular, they show that even though income, education, and urban levels change considerably and in synchrony with each other, they are not the only important determinants of e-commerce usage, but age structure, ethnicity, and occupational shifts also impact e-commerce usage. Hence, a broad set of county dimensions together form the context for use of internet for e-commerce by the citizenry.

POLICY IMPLICATIONS: STRATEGIES FOR BRIDGING E-COMMERCE DIVIDE AMONG US COUNTIES

A county striving to achieve digital transformation and upgrading needs to not only to consider infrastructure, software, and information technology knowledge and skills, but also to think about and plan out how to encourage the best applications and concomitant skills to use the application. How can e-Commerce be utilized beneficially for enhancement of business, government, and the citizenry? Hence the county should consider ways to encourage use of web-based e-Commerce applications to improve the efficiency and productivity, and attain user satisfaction.

E-commerce constitutes a large and rapidly growing transformative phenomenon that is making time-consuming processes of procurement, purchasing, and quality comparisons easier, quicker, and more efficient. Not only does a retail or wholesale company gain greater efficiencies and control, but the citizen can be more informed e-purchasing, can order more quickly and accurately, and can acquire products and services to make the citizen more productive.

The process of encouraging people in a county to undertake this transformation is time-consuming and challenging. It may rest on the government to train and educate purveyors and users of e-Commerce, but responsibility also rests with the companies and other organizations such as nonprofits that provide online e-Commerce services and products. A further point is that this prospective transformation may be thrown off course by low quality of training, greed or negligence in providing faulty products or services, and even malicious intent. However, because of e-Commerce's macro-economic success, we assume overall that encouraging its use is well intentioned and beneficial. The following are recommended policies for stimulating high quality e-commerce use, based on the present study findings. County governments can:

- Provide training programs for citizen users and for small businesses getting started with e-Commerce. Some of the training can take place collaboratively with federal and state agencies. For instance, joint county – U.S. Small Business Administration (SBA) training initiatives can be developed and started.
- Support educational programs that concern e-Commerce by providing grants and/or incentives.
- Consider giving special training, education, and support to the county's e-Commerce-underserved population. The study has identified the e-Commerce-underserved in the county citizenry as being older, Black and Hispanic, of low education, and located in rural

areas. Special training and incentives could be focused on these groups, both for personal skill enhancement in daily life and for career opportunities.

Businesses and non-profit organizations can stimulate e-commerce use in the county by:

- Supporting business training programs to further skills in e-Commerce among employees.
- Modifying hiring practices to encourage hiring of people from the underserved segments of the population.
- Encouraging small businesses to develop and operationalize e-commerce initiatives. This could be done by actively seeking small business suppliers of e-commerce services and/or participating and supporting county or county/federal training programs, such as those of the SBA. Including recognized experts in technology training for small business is motivational.

CONCLUSIONS

E-commerce has grown rapidly in the U.S., yet differentially in various parts of the country. This study posits that SATUM theory applies for e-Commerce at the level of counties in the continental U.S. In testing the theory, data were gathered from government and private sources for the 3,109 counties in the lower 48 states. Spatial autocorrelation and k-means cluster analysis demonstrate that levels of e-Commerce usage are agglomerated – at the high end in metropolitan and megalopolitan complexes, often extending somewhat into counties adjoining the complex. An example is the northeastern megalopolis, which is solidly at high to very high levels of e-commerce and which extends northward into upper New England counties beyond the standard megalopolitan boundary. At the low end are large agglomerations of counties in the prairie states from the Dakotas down to west Texas, in the mid to lower South excluding metro Atlanta and Florida, and in Appalachia.

Regression analysis is applied to estimate five e-Commerce dependent variables, yielding results with strong effect size and identifying for the nation the key county determinants of e-Commerce usage to be higher levels of college education, young age structure, working age population, service and construction occupations, ethnicities, and urban status. These associations are shown to vary somewhat across the metropolitan, micropolitan, and rural subsamples. Although college education remains stable across these categories, service occupations are more prominent for micropolitan counties, whereas construction occupations are distinctive only for rural areas. Age structural effects diminish in importance across the metro to micro to rural range of counties. Ethnic differences indicate consistently inverse effects for counties with higher Hispanic and Black populations, while higher Asian proportion has little effect for metro counties but positive effect for micro and rural counties.

Policy implications include the potential of county government to provide internet services, support training, and give grants and incentives to educational programs in technology and e-Commerce. Counties face a choice to focus these programs on the e-Commerce-underserved citizenry i.e. people who are old, retired, poor, and/or rural, spread the programs evenly across all population segments, or emphasize the population groups most related to e-Commerce. Besides county government, large or medium-sized corporations and some nonprofit organizations can offer further training in ICT and e-Commerce-related skills.

REFERENCES

Agarwal, R., Animesh, A., and Prasad, K. (2009). Social interactions and the 'digital divide': Explaining variations in internet use, *Information Systems Research*, *20*(2), 277-294.

Andoh-Baidoo, F.K., Osatuyi, B., & Kunene, K. (2014). ICT capacity as the investment and use of ICT: Exploring its antecedents in Africa. *Information Technology for Development*, 20(1), 44-59.

Baliamoune-Lutz, M. (2003). An analysis of the determinants and effects of ICT diffusion in developing countries. *Information Technology for Development* 10(3):151-169.

Belanger, F., and Carter, L. (2009). The impact of the digital divide on e-government use, *Communications of the ACM, 52*(4), 132-135.
Carden, A., Courtemanche, C., and Meiners, A. (2009). Does Walmart reduce social capital? *Public Choice* 18:109-136.

Buys, P., Dasgupta, S., Thomas, T., & Wheeler, D. (2009). Determinants of a digital divide in sub-Saharan Africa: A spatial econometric analysis of cell phone coverage. *World Development*, *37*(9), 1494-1505.

Chen, W. (2013). The implications of social capital for the digital divides in America. *The Information Society* 29:13-25.

Dewan, S., and Riggins, F. J. (2005). The Digital Divide: Current and Future Research Directions, *Journal for the Association for Information Systems, 6*(12), 298–336.

Esri Data, Methodology Statements (2015). Methodology Statement: Esri US— Market Potential Database, Retrieved from http://downloads.esri.com/esri_content_doc/dbl/us/J9672_2015_Market_Potential_DB_Methodology_Statement.pdf, May 1, 2016.

Esri. 2013. 2013 US market potential data methodology statement, Retrieved from http://support.esri.com/en/knowledgebase/whitepapers/view/productid/153/metaid/2037, November 1, 2015.

Florida, R. 2012a. *The Rise of the Creative Class*. 10th anniversary edition. New York: Basic Books.

Florida, R. 2012b. America's leading high-tech metros. *The Atlantic*, June 28.

Gauvin, S, Granger, K., and Lorthiois, M. (2015). Analog citizens. *Electronic Commerce Research, 15*, 365-386.

Goetz, S.J., and Swaminathan, H. (2006). Wal-Mart and County-wide Poverty. *Social Science Quarterly, 87*(2), 211-226.

Grubesic, T.H. (2002). Spatial dimensions of internet activity, *Telecommunications Policy, 26*, 363-387.

Huang, Z. (2007). A comprehensive analysis of U.S. counties' e-Government portals: development status and functionalities, *European Journal of Information Systems, 16*, 149-164.

Huang, Z. (2006). E-government practices at local levels: An analysis of U.S. counties' websites, *Issues in Information Systems, 7*(2), 165-170.

Khatiwada, L.K., and Pigg, K.E. (2010). Internet service provision in the U.S. counties: Is spatial pattern a function of demand, American *Behavioral Scientist, 53*(9), 1326-1343.

Jarque, C.M., and Bera, A K. (1980). Efficient tests for normality, homoscedasticity and serial independence of regression residuals. *Economics Letters, 6*(3): 255–259.

Lyon, J.D., and Tsai, C.L. (1996). A comparison of tests for heteroscedasticity. *Statistician, 45*(3), 337-349.

Manoharan, A. (2013). A study of the determinants of county e-government in the United States, The *American Review of Public Administration, 43*(2), 159-178.

Nishida,T., Pick, J., and Sarkar, A. (2014). Japan's prefectural digital divide: A multivariate and spatial analysis. *Telecommunications Policy, 38*: 992–1010.

NTIA. (2016). *Digital Nation Data Explorer*, Retrieved from https://www.ntia.doc.gov/other-publication/2016/digital-nation-data-explorer, May 1, 2016.

NTIA. (2014). *Exploring the digital nation: Embracing the mobile internet*, Washington, DC: National Telecommunications and Information Administration, U.S. Department of Commerce.

NTIA. (2013). *Exploring the digital nation: America's emerging online experience*, Washington, DC: National Telecommunications and Information Administration, U.S. Department of Commerce.

NTIA. (2011). *Exploring the digital nation: Computer and internet usage at home*, Washington, DC: National Telecommunications and Information Administration, U.S. Department of Commerce.

OECD. (2001). *Understanding the digital divide*. Paris, France: Organization for Economic Cooperation and Development.

Ono, H., & Zavodny, M. (2007). Digital inequality: A five country comparison using microdata, *Social Science Research*, 363, 116–139.

Openshaw, S. (1984). *The Modifiable Areal Unit Problem*. Geobooks, Norwich, England.

Pew (2010). Online activities: Activities that are most popular with teens and/or Millennials, Retrieved from http://www.pewinternet.org/2010/12/16/online-activities/, May 1, 2016.

Pick, J., and Sarkar, A. (2016). Theories of the Digital Divide: Critical Comparison. In Proceedings of the 49th *Hawaii International Conference on System Sciences*, IEEE Computer Society. Kauai, HI.

Pick, J., Sarkar, A., and Rosales, J. (2015). A Spatial and Regression Analysis of Social Media in the United States Counties. In Proceedings of the *Pre-Conference Workshop on Locational Analytics and Big Data: Foundations, Emerging Applications and Research, International Conference on Information Systems (ICIS)*. Fort Worth, TX.

Pick, J., Sarkar, A., and Johnson, J. (2015a). United States digital divide: State level analysis of spatial clustering and multivariate determinants of ICT utilization. *Socio-Economic Planning Sciences, 49*: 16-32.

Pick, J., and Sarkar, A. (2015b). *The Global Digital Divides: Explaining Change*. Springer, New York, NY.

Pick, J., & Azari, R. (2008). Global digital divide: Influences of socioeconomic, governmental, and accessibility factors on information technology. *Information Technology for Development*, *14*(2), 95–115.

Putnam, R.D. (2001). Social capital. Measurement and consequences, *Canadian Journal of Policy Research*, *2*, 41-51.

Quibria, M.G., Ahmed, S.N., Tschang, T., and Reyes-Macasaquit, M.-L. (2003). Digital divide: determinants and policies with special reference to Asia. *Journal of Asian Economics*, *13*, 811-825.

Roy, M-C., Chartier, A., Crete, J., and Poulin, D. (2015). Factors influencing e-government use in non-urban areas, *Electronic Commerce Research*, *15*, 349-363.

Rupasingha, A., and Goetz, S.J. (2008). *US County-Level Social Capital Data, 1990-2005.* Penn State University, University Park, PA: The Northeast Regional Center for Rural Development.

Selwyn, N. (2006). Digital division or digital decision? A study of non-users and low-users of computers. *Poetics, 34*(4-5), 273-292.

Srinuan, C., and Bohlin, E. (2011). Understanding the digital divide: A literature survey and ways forward, In Proceedings of *22nd European Regional Conference of the International Telecommunications Society*, Budapest: Innovative ICT Applications - Emerging Regulatory, Economic and Policy Issues.

Sylvester, D.E. and McGlynn, A.J. (2010). The digital divide, political participation, and place, *Social Science-Computer Review, 28*(1), 64-74.

Tolbert, C., Mossberger, K., King, B. and Miller, G. (2007). Are all American women making progress online? African-Americans and Latinas, *Information Technologies and International Development, 4*(2), 61-88.

US Department of Commerce. (2016). *Quarterly retail e-commerce sales.* Retrieved from http://www2.census.gov/retail/releases/historical/ecomm/15q4.pdf, May 1, 2016.

The White House. (2015). *Mapping the digital divide*. Retrieved from https://www.whitehouse.gov/sites/default/files/wh_digital_divide_issue_brief.pdf, November 1, 2015.

Van Dijk, J.A.G.M. (2003). The digital divide as a complex and dynamic phenomenon, *The Information Society, 19*, 315-326.

Wald, A. (1943). Test of statistical hypothesis concerning several parameters when the number of observations is large. *Transactions of the American Mathematical Society*, *54*, 426-482.

Warschauer, M., and Matuchniak, T. (2010). New technology and digital worlds: Analyzing evidence of access, use, and outcomes, *Reviews of Research in Education*, *34*(1), 179-225.

Weber, D.M., and Kauffman, R.J. (2011). What drives global ICT adoption? Analysis and research directions, *Electronic Commerce Research and Applications, 10*(6), 683-701.

Yates, D.J., Gulati, G.J., and Weiss, J.W. (2011). Different paths to broadband access: the impact of governance and polity on broadband diffusion in the developed and developing worlds. In *Proceedings of the 44th Hawaiian International Conference on System Sciences*, IEEE.

DECISION SCIENCES INSTITUTE

Inventory models in a closed-loop supply chain with product returns and refurbishment

Seung Ho Yoo
Sunmoon University
Email: shy1228@sunmoon.ac.kr

Seongpil Joo
Korea University Business School
Email: jsp011@korea.ac.kr

Myung-Sub Park
Korea University Business School
Email: mspark@korea.ac.kr

ABSTRACT

This study investigates a closed-loop supply chain, consisting of a manufacturer responsible for the first-market sales of a new item and a third-party refurbisher responsible for the second-market sales of a refurbished item. We then introduce two different supply chain models with different structures and revealed their distinct characteristics. Specifically, we reveal the effect of the supply chain structure on production lot size, refurbishing lot size, and sales price of a refurbished product, which then jointly affect the overall sales and profit performances. We also suggeste a guideline for the selection of a third-party refurbisher.

KEYWORDS: Inventory, Closed-loop supply chain, Sales return, Refurbishment

INTRODUCTION

In practice, production and inspection systems are often not perfect, so incur not only internal failure costs to internally identify and fix defect problems but also external failures, causing sales returns and reverse logistics flows by passing defects to consumers. In fact, product return is enormous, recorded up to 16% of sales in the catalog retail industry (Peterson and Kumar, 2009) and 11-20% in consumer electronics industry (Douthit et al., 2011), while its main reason is quality dissatisfaction due to defect production. Guide et al. (2006) reported that 20% of returns of HP printers were due to defect problems, and there were 60% of defective returns for Bosch power tools. Thus, to reduce these negative consequences, firms not only invest in prevention and appraisal activities to improve process capability and stability, but also carefully consider disposition of defective items, including product returns. Among various disposition options, such as salvage, recycle, and scrap, any option can be selected. However, it always needs to be profitable since a defective item can preserve technologies and features of a new item, if recovered through a proper value recovery process. Therefore, in this study, we focus on a common value recovery option nowadays, the refurbishment (or remanufacturing) for second-market sales. We investigate the joint decision on inventory (lot sizing) and refurbishing strategies in a closed-loop supply chain with an imperfect manufacturing process and a separate refurbishing process.

A refurbished (or remanufactured) product refers to the product which formerly had a quality problem but has been restored to the condition as functional as new. Refurbishment becomes a common option especially in electronics industry. It helps environment by reducing waste and extending the lifecycle of a product. It can also enhance the profitability since it provides a chance to open up another market segment that would not purchase a new item at full price (Vorasayan and Ryan 2006, Ovchinnikov 2011). However, firms need to carefully consider the possible pitfalls due to channel conflicts. The sales of a refurbished item can negatively affect the first-market sales of a higher-margin new item. Therefore, in this study, we will investigate the optimal decision on the sales price of a refurbished item, which subsequently affect not only the interaction between new and refurbished items but also inventory decisions on both manufacturing and refurbishing processes in a closed-loop supply chain.

In practice, many contemporary firms concentrate on their core processes and outsource others in order to enhance their competitiveness. It leads firms to run their businesses based on a decentralized supply chain system. Therefore, it is practical that we investigate the joint decision on inventory and refurbishing strategies in the context of supply chain management, considering interactions between independent decision makers. Specifically, in this study, we include two key players, a manufacturer responsible for the manufacturing process for the first-market sales of a new item, and a refurbisher handling the refurbishing process for the second-market sales of a refurbished item. Then, we will introduce two different supply chain structures–one integrated and the other decentralized–by considering the integration and separation of manufacturing and refurbishing processes by the manufacturer, the focal company in a supply chain. After building two closed-loop supply chain models with different structures based on the principal-agent paradigm framework, we compare the performances of different supply chain structures and reveal their distinct characteristics. Specifically, we reveal the effect of the supply chain structure on (1) production lot size, (2) refurbishing lot size, and (3) sales price of a refurbished product, which then jointly affect (4) the overall sales and profit performances in a closed-loop supply chain. In addition, we will also suggest a guideline for the selection of a third-party refurbisher by revealing the condition that the decentralized supply chain can outperform the integrated one.

The rest of the paper is organized as follows. In Section 2, the review analysis on the previous literature is presented. Section 3 formulates the basic mathematical models. Section 4 introduces two supply chain models with different structures, and investigates their optimal solutions. Section 5 provides numerous important implications by comparing the performances of models. Then, Section 6 concludes this study along with limitations and future research directions.

LITERATURE REVIEW

Two research streams are directly relevant to the present study: (1) inventory models with imperfect production process, and (2) price decision of a refurbished item.

There have been a vast number of inventory studies considering an imperfect production system since Porteus (1986) and Rosenblatt and Lee (1986). Among them, the present study is in line with the inventory studies of a stable production process, which assumed that the production process yields defective items, following a Bernoulli process and thus generating binomial yields (see Yano and Lee (1995), Grosfeld-Nir and Gerchak (2004), and Khan et al. (2011b) for detailed reviews of relevant studies). While dealing with various relevant issues, the main focus of many studies did not lie in the defect delivery to consumers and subsequent reverse logistics issues, since they implicitly (or sometimes explicitly) assumed that there are no errors in the inspection process, such as Zhang and Gerchak (1990), Cheng (1991), Anily

(1995), Lee et al. (1996), Salameh and Jaber (2000), Tripathy et al. (2003), Leung (2007), Khan et al., (2011a), Ouyang and Chang (2013), and Ullah and Kang (2014). Therefore, most studies concentrated on total cost minimization, while assuming that all defect problems can be internally detected and resolved. There are only a few inventory models with a more practical setting that the defect delivery causes external failures and return-handling issues in a closed-loop supply chain.

Yeh and Chen (2006) investigated an imperfect-quality inventory system with the inspection error and defect delivery to consumers. They incorporated a warranty to resolve the defect delivery problems. Yoo et al. (2009) considered not only the imperfect production process but also Type I and II inspection errors along with subsequent sales returns and multiple disposition options for defects. They investigated the effect of inspection errors and sales returns on the production lot size decision. Then, Yoo et al. (2012b) extended the previous study with Type I and II inspection errors by incorporating joint investment decision on production and inspection reliabilities. They conducted quality cost analyses by identifying four quality cost components, including prevention, appraisal, internal failure and external failure. Yoo et al. (2012a) also extended the previous literature of the imperfect production and inspection system with quality investment by considering continuous improvement under the budget constraint. They revealed that the inspection option change between entire lot screening and no inspection can yield a superior profit performance in a continuous improvement environment. The above studies have dealt with various practical issues relevant to imperfect production and inspection systems by incorporating defect delivery and subsequent sales return issues, but the scope of those studies was limited to a single firm's operational environment. However, nowadays, many firms are struggling to enhance their competitiveness by focusing on their core capabilities while outsourcing many functions to their partners in a supply chain. Therefore, it is more practical that we consider the effect of an imperfect system on a decentralized closed-loop system. In this study, we extend the basic inventory model of Yoo et al. (2012a) with an imperfect production and inspection system into the supply chain perspective by incorporating the interaction between the key players. Specifically, we consider the manufacturer dealing with the manufacturing process for the first-market sales and the third-party refurbisher responsible for the refurbishing process for the second-market sales.

The present study also discovers the pricing issue of a refurbished item. Among various studies relevant to this problem, the present study is directly related to the previous ones considering the market segmentation between new and refurbished items. Vorasayan and Ryan (2006) considered demand substitution between new and refurbished items as in practice, in which the refurbished item competes with the new one based on its lower price. They investigated the pricing decision of a refurbished item similar to the present study. Aras et al. (2011) investigated a joint leasing and refurbishing strategy, with which a manufacturer leases a new item while refurbishing an end-of-lease item. They also considered market segmentation and demand substitution between new and refurbished items. Ovchinnikov (2011) also investigated joint decision on the sales price of a refurbished item and the amount of returns received and refurbished. This study revealed that a firm's pricing strategy is affected by various aspects, including product characteristics, consumer behavior, and cost structure. Similar to the studies above, we consider the pricing decision of a refurbished item, but the present study is different from the previous ones, of which scope is limited to the operational environment of a single firm. We extend the literature by considering a contemporary situation where many firms run their businesses in a decentralized supply chain system. Moreover, note that we introduce this pricing issue of a refurbished item into the research stream of imperfect-quality inventory models. To the best of our knowledge, there are only a few studies incorporating the pricing and lot sizing issues in the context of closed-loop supply chain management.

Overall, the contribution of this study lies in bridging the gap between two research streams: imperfect-quality inventory decision and refurbished item pricing. We extend the literature by developing a comprehensive inventory and pricing model in the context of supply chain management. We provide important implications for the joint management of forward and reverse flows in a supply chain by incorporating the channel conflict issues between new and refurbished items into the inventory decision. In addition, we also reveal the effect of the supply chain structure on the overall performances by considering the process integration and separation.

MATHEMATICAL FORMULATION

Basic Formulation

Figure 1: Inventory flows in the first- and second-market sales processes
(solid line: physical flow of inventory, dotted line: effect on inventory depletion)

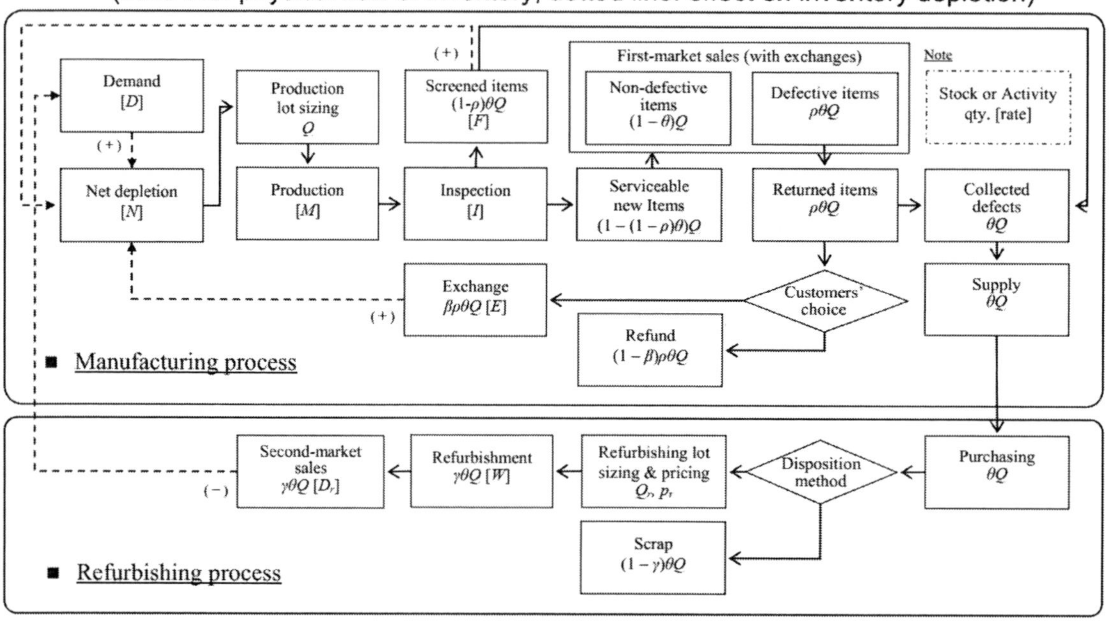

We investigate a closed-loop supply chain consisting of two processes, a manufacturing process for the first-market sales and a refurbishing process for the second-market sales. In this section, we model the profit functions of two processes, and then we will characterize two supply chain models by considering the integration and separation of processes in Section 4. In modeling, we extend the basic inventory model in Yoo et al. (2012a), dealing with imperfect production and inspection processes and subsequent sales return issues. By extending the previous study in a single firm's operational environment, the present study focuses on building a comprehensive supply chain inventory model by incorporating the interaction between supply chain players as in the contemporary supply chain practice. Different from the previous study, we also incorporate the refurbishing issues in order to investigate the channel conflict between the first- and second-market sales of new and refurbished items. Figure 1 illustrates the overall forward and reverse flows in two processes in a closed-loop supply chain. Table 1 summarizes the notation used in this study.

The manufacturing process yields lot size Q of a new item per each cycle T. Both production and inspection systems are imperfect as in practice, which follow the Bernoulli process and generate binomial yields with defective proportion θ and inspection failure proportion ρ, respectively, where $0 \le \theta, \rho \le 1$. Therefore, among θQ of all defective items, only $(1 - \rho)\theta Q$ of defective items are screened by inspection, and $\rho\theta Q$ of unscreened defective items are sold to consumers along with $(1 - \theta)Q$ of non-defective items. Then, consumers detect defects and return them as in practice. Consumers can select a return option among exchange (with its proportion β, $0 \le \beta \le 1$) and refund (with $1 - \beta$), so their respective quantities are $\beta\rho\theta Q$ and $(1 - \beta)\rho\theta Q$ among $\rho\theta Q$ of sales returns.

Table 1: Notation for mathematical models

Q	production lot size (unit, a decision variable)	T_r	refurbishing cycle (time)
Q_r	refurbishing lot size (unit, a decision variable)	N	net depletion rate in production line (unit/unit time)
w	unit wholesale price of a defective item ($/unit, a decision variable)	D	demand rate of a new item in the first market (unit/unit time)
p_r	unit sales price of a refurbished item ($/unit, a decision variable)	D_r	demand rate of a refurbished item in the second market (unit/unit time)
p	unit sales price of a new item ($/unit)	F	screening rate of a defective item (unit/unit time)
u	unit production cost of a new item ($/unit)	E	exchange rate (unit/unit time)
i	unit inspection cost of a new item ($/unit)	M	production rate (unit/unit time)
r	unit return handling cost ($/unit)	M_r	refurbishing rate (unit/unit time)
k	unit refurbishing cost ($/unit)	θ	defective proportion in production line (fraction)
g	unit scrap cost ($/unit)	ρ	inspection failure proportion (fraction)
h	inventory holding cost rate fraction (fraction/unit time)	β	exchange proportion among returns (fraction, $1-\beta$: refund proportion)
H	inventory holding cost rate of a new item ($/unit/unit time)	γ	refurbishing proportion among defects (fraction, $1-\gamma$: scrap proportion)
H_r	inventory holding cost rate of a refurbished item ($/unit/unit time)	Π_i^j	profit of player or process i in Case j
S	setup cost per production run ($/cycle)	i	subscript; M (manufacturer), R (refurbisher), m (manufacturing process), r (refurbishing process)
S_r	setup cost per refurbishing run ($/cycle)	j	superscript; *INT* (an integrated supply chain), *DC* (a decentralized supply chain)
T	production cycle time (time)		

Then, all defective items of θQ (including the screened defects of $(1 - \rho)\theta Q$ and the returned defects of $\rho\theta Q$) are supplied to the refurbishing process. We consider that the refurbishing proportion γ $(0 \le \gamma \le 1)$ is affected by the selling prices of both new and refurbished items p and p_r as follows.

$$\gamma(p_r) = 1 - \frac{p_r}{p}. \tag{1}$$

Not all defects can be refurbished, and only $\gamma\theta Q$ among θQ of defects can be refurbished and sold to consumers in the second market, while $(1 - \gamma)\theta Q$ of remaining defective items are scrapped. We consider that consumers' buying intention for the refurbished item is affected by its price p_r, and the price of a new item p is also considered a reference as in a practical situation. If p_r becomes lower given p, there will be more consumers selecting a refurbished item, i.e., $\partial\gamma/\partial p_r > 0$, but there will be no consumers if $p_r = p$, i.e., $\gamma = 0$.

Then, the second-market sales of a refurbished item can substitute for the first-market sales of a new item as:

$$D = D_0 - D_r, \tag{2}$$

where D_0 is the demand potential in the target segment, D is the first-market sales of a new item and D_r is the second-market sales of a refurbished item, which is directly related to the refurbishing proportion γ in Equation (1). As in Equation (2), we consider a practical situation in many businesses where the consumers' demand consists of two parts, the first- and second-market sales as found in many industries including consumer electronics, apparel and furniture, i.e., $D_0 = D + D_r$.

On the other hand, the manufacturing process yields a lot Q at a production rate M as in the typical EPQ models, and then Q of a new item are depleted at the net inventory depletion rate N in each cycle T, i.e., $T = Q/N$. Note that we consider various sources of inventory depletion as in practice, differently from the traditional EOQ and EPQ models only considering the demand D ($T = Q/D$). As shown in Figure 1 (see the dotted lines), the net depletion rate N consists of the first-market demand rate D in Equation (1), the exchange rate E and the screening rate of defective items by inspection F, i.e., $N = D + E + F$. Considering the relationship $N = Q/T$ from $T = Q/N$ and the respective inventory amount involving each rate, first we obtain the second-market demand D_r as:

$$D_r(p_r) = \gamma\theta Q/T = \gamma\theta N, \tag{3}$$

where γ is in Equation (1).

Similarly, we can also define $F = (1 - \rho)\theta Q/T = (1 - \rho)\theta N$ and $E = \beta\theta Q/T = \beta\theta N$, while $D = D_0 - \gamma\theta N$ from Equations (2) and (3). Then, we obtain the net depletion rate N by solving $N = D + E + F$ with respect to N as follows.

$$N(p_r) = \frac{D_0}{1-((1-\gamma)-(1-\beta)\rho)\theta}, \tag{4}$$

where γ is a function of p_r in Equation (1). In addition, we set the inspection rate I equal to N not to incur unnecessary inventory holding from different rates.

On the other hand, there are two options in the refurbishing process, refurbishment for the second-market sales and scrap as shown in Figure 1. In the refurbishing line, there are two types of items, the item to be refurbished (before refurbishment) and the refurbished item (after refurbishment). The refurbishing line accumulates the refurbished item of refurbishing lot size Q_r at a refurbishing rate M_r, and the refurbished item is depleted at the second-market sales rate D_r in Equation (3) in each refurbishing cycle T_r ($T_r = Q_r/D_r$). Note that the accumulation of the refurbished item means the depletion of the item to be refurbished. Therefore, the item to be refurbished (before refurbishment) is depleted at the refurbishing rate M_r, and it needs to be accumulated at D_r in order to satisfy the second-market demand and avoid unnecessary inventory holding from the rate difference between two types of items. Therefore, note that the inventory holding quantities per unit time are the same between two types of items, while their inventory behaviors are exactly the opposite. The refurbishing cycle T_r is different from the production cycle T, and there are n refurbishing setups in each T, i.e., $n = T/T_r$. Therefore, while there are $\gamma\theta Q$ of items to be refurbished among Q in each cycle T, the refurbishing lot size Q_r decreases as n increases, i.e., $Q_r = \gamma\theta Q/n$. In addition, we suppose that those defects for scrap are disposed instantaneously, so as not to incur unnecessary inventory holding.

Profit Functions

The objective of the manufacturing process is to determine production lot size Q and supply contract offer to the refurbishing process which jointly maximize its profit. Total revenue per cycle of the manufacturing process includes the first-market sales of a new item $p((1-\theta)+\rho\theta)Q$, which also include the exchange request of consumers at no charge ($-p\beta\rho\theta Q$). p is the unit selling price of a new item. We also need to consider the revenue loss from another return option, refund ($-p(1-\beta)\rho\theta Q$). In addition, the manufacturing process also supplies the defective items to the refurbishing process. There exist various contract types in practice, but we only consider the wholesale price contract, the most common contract form due to its simplicity. Therefore, the total transfer payment from the manufacturing process to the refurbishing process is $w\theta Q$, where w is the unit wholesale price of the defective item. In sum, total revenue per cycle of the manufacturing process TR_m can be formulated as follows.

$$\begin{aligned} TR_m &= p((1-\theta)+\rho\theta)Q - p\beta\rho\theta Q - p(1-\beta)\rho\theta Q + w\theta Q \\ &= p(1-\theta)Q + w\theta Q. \end{aligned} \tag{5}$$

On the other hand, there are various sources of cost in the manufacturing process. There is a fixed cost from production setup S in each cycle T. Various variable costs are incurred from relevant activities, including production uQ, inspection iQ, return handling $r\rho\theta Q$, where u, i and r are their respective unit costs. The inventory holding cost in each cycle of the manufacturing process can be defined as $(H/2)(1-N/M)QT$ similar to the traditional EPQ model. H is the inventory holding cost rate of a new item, where $H = hu$ considering the unit cost of a new item incurred in the production line before sales. Therefore, we obtain the total cost per cycle of the manufacturing process TC_m as:

$$TC_m = S + (u + i + r\rho\theta)Q + \frac{H}{2}\left(1-\frac{N}{M}\right)QT, \text{ where } H = hu. \tag{6}$$

By subtracting TC_m in Equation (6) from TR_m in (5) and then dividing it by cycle time T (= Q/N), the total profit per unit time of the manufacturing process Π_m can be defined as a function of Q and w.

$$\Pi_m(Q,w) = [(p(1-\theta)+w\theta)-(u+i+r\rho\theta)]N - \frac{SN}{Q} - \frac{H}{2}\left(1-\frac{N}{M}\right)Q. \tag{7}$$

On the other hand, the refurbishing process needs to determine its refurbishing lot size Q_r and the unit sales price of a refurbished item p_r. The total revenue per each production cycle T of the refurbishing process TR_r is from the sales of a refurbished item to the second market $p_r\gamma\theta Q$ (= np_rQ_r), where p_r is the unit sales price of the refurbished item. The total cost per cycle of the refurbishing process TC_r includes the variable costs from purchasing of defective items $w\theta Q$, refurbishment $k\gamma\theta Q$ and scrap $g(1-\gamma)\theta Q$, where k and g are the unit refurbishing and scrap costs, respectively. There are n (= T/T_r) refurbishing setups per T, so refurbishing setup cost of nS_r is incurred in every production cycle T where S_r is the refurbishing setup cost per setup. In addition, the inventory holding cost of $n(H_r/2)(1-D_r/M_r)Q_rT_r$ is incurred, where D_r is the second-market sales rate of the refurbished item in Equation (3) and M_r is the refurbishing rate. In estimating the inventory holding cost rate in the refurbishing line H_r, we need to consider two types of items in the refurbishing line, the item to be refurbished and the refurbished item. We will deal with different sources of H_r depending on the structure of a closed-loop supply chain in Section 6. Considering all the above, TR_r and TC_r can be defined as:

$$TR_r = p_r\gamma\theta Q, \text{ and} \tag{8}$$

$$TC_r = nS_r + (w + k\gamma + g(1-\gamma))\theta Q + n\frac{H_r}{2}\left(1 - \frac{D_r}{M_r}\right)Q_r T_r . \tag{9}$$

By subtracting TC_r in Equation (8) from TR_r in (9), we obtain the total profit per production cycle of the refurbishing process. Then, dividing it by production cycle time T and also considering $n = T/T_r$ and $T_r = Q_r/D_r$, we obtain the total profit per unit time of the refurbishing process Π_r as a function of Q_r and p_r as follows.

$$\Pi_r(Q_r, p_r) = [p_r\gamma - (w + k\gamma + g(1-\gamma))]\theta N - \frac{S_r D_r}{Q_r} - \frac{H_r}{2}\left(1 - \frac{D_r}{M_r}\right)Q_r , \tag{10}$$

where γ, D_r and N are in Equations (1), (3) and (4) and H_r is the inventory holding cost rate in the refurbishing line, which will be defined differently according to the supply chain case in the next section.

SUPPLY CHAIN MODELS

We consider a typical supply chain situation where the manufacturer has stronger bargaining power over the third-party refurbisher. Therefore, the manufacturer with bargaining power can integrate supply chain processes. The manufacturer also acts as a Stackelberg leader by offering the supply contract of defective items for refurbishment in order to control the refurbisher's action. Then, given the contract offer of the manufacturer, the refurbisher maximizes its own profit.

Case INT: An Integrated Supply Chain

We first consider Case INT involving an integrated supply chain, in which the manufacturer integrates the overall forward and reverse processes including manufacturing and refurbishing. This can be regarded as the ideal scenario since there is no moral hazard and opportunistic behaviors of supply chain players. The supply chain behaves like one entity without double marginalization issue, so we will utilize this ideal Case INT as a benchmark for the decentralized supply chain model. By the integration of manufacturing and refurbishing processes, the manufacturer's profit Π_M^{INT} is the same as that of the entire supply chain, and it does not have to consider the transfer payment between processes.

$$\begin{aligned} \Pi_M^{INT}(Q, Q_r, p_r) &= \Pi^{INT}(Q, Q_r, p_r) \\ &= \Pi_m + \Pi_r \\ &= [(p(1-\theta) + p_r\gamma\theta) - (u + i + r\rho\theta + k\gamma\theta + g(1-\gamma)\theta)]N \\ &\quad - \left[\frac{SN}{Q} + \frac{S_r D_r}{Q_r}\right] - \left[\frac{H}{2}\left(1 - \frac{N}{M}\right)Q + \frac{H_r^{INT}}{2}\left(1 - \frac{D_r}{M_r}\right)Q_r\right] \end{aligned} , \tag{11}$$

where the superscript *INT* denotes Case INT and Π^{INT} denotes the supply chain profit in Case INT. Π_m and Π_r are the profits of manufacturing and refurbishing processes in Equations (7) and (10). Note that in this fully-integrated Case INT, the inventory holding cost rate in the refurbishing line H_r^{INT} needs to include the overall cost components incurred in the forward and reverse supply chain flows. This is since the manufacturer deals with all processes in a supply chain. As already explained in Section 3.1, there are two types of inventory holding in the refurbishing line. For the defective item to be refurbished (before refurbishment), we need to consider the costs incurred in the manufacturing process ($u + i + r\rho$) including returned defective items due to the inspection failure with its proportion ρ. On the other hand, for the refurbished item, we need to add the refurbishing cost k, i.e., ($u + i + r\rho + k$). Therefore, by considering these two types of inventories, while their inventory holding quantities are the same, H_r^{INT} becomes

$$H_r^{INT} = h(2u + 2i + 2r\rho + k). \tag{12}$$

Then, the optimization problem of Case INT can be simply defined as:

$$\text{Maximize} \qquad \Pi_M^{INT}(Q, Q_r, p_r), \tag{13}$$

where Π_M^{INT} (= Π^{INT}) is in Equation (11).

From the first-order necessary conditions of Π_M^{INT}, we obtain the optimal Q^{INT*}, Q_r^{INT*} and p_r^{INT*} as functions of each other.

$$Q^{INT*}(p_r) = \sqrt{\frac{2SN}{H(1-N/M)}}, \tag{14}$$

$$Q_r^{INT*}(p_r) = \sqrt{\frac{2S_rD_r}{H_r^{INT}(1-D_r/M_r)}}, \text{ and} \tag{15}$$

$$p_r^{INT*}(Q,Q_r) = \frac{p(1+\Phi)}{\theta} - \sqrt{\frac{p}{\theta}}\sqrt{\begin{aligned}&(u+i)+r\rho\theta - p(1-\theta)+\frac{S}{Q}-\frac{HQ}{2M}\\&+(1+\Phi)\left[g+\frac{p(1-\theta+\Phi)}{\theta}\right]+(1-\theta+\Phi)\left[\frac{H_r^{INT}Q_r}{2M_r}-\frac{S_r}{Q_r}-k\right]\end{aligned}}, \tag{16}$$

where $\Phi = (1-\beta)\rho\theta$, the sales return proportion for refund, and N and D_r are functions of p_r in Equations (4) and (3). Due to mathematical difficulties involving three decision variables, we do not show the closed-form solutions, but we present the optimal solution based on a numerical example in Section 5. We will utilize the above solution as a benchmark for the decentralized supply chain case.

Case DC: A Decentralized Supply Chain

This section considers Case DC, a decentralized case in a manufacturer-refurbisher dyadic supply chain involving moral hazard. In Case DC, the manufacturer and refurbisher are responsible for their own basic processes, manufacturing and refurbishing, respectively.

Therefore, the manufacturer's profit $\Pi_M^{DC} = \Pi_m$ in Equation (7), and the refurbisher's profit $\Pi_R^{DC} = \Pi_r$ in Equation (10), while the superscript *DC* denotes Case DC. For the inventory holding cost rate in the refurbishing line H_r^{DC} in Case DC, we do not have to consider the cost incurred at the manufacturer's end differently from H_r^{INT} in Equation (12). From the refurbisher's perspective, the cost incurred for the item to be refurbished (before refurbishment) is only w, the wholesale price of a defective item. Then, the unit refurbishing cost k needs to be added for the refurbished item (after refurbishment), i.e., $w + k$. Therefore, by considering two types of inventory holding cost rates similarly in Equation (12), we obtain H_r^{DC} as a function of w.

$$H_r^{DC}(w) = h(2w + k). \tag{17}$$

In Case DC, both manufacturer and refurbisher are only concerned with their own profit maximization as separate economic entities, so Case DC involves the double marginalization problem. The manufacturer, the Stakelberg leader in a supply chain, needs to devise a contract term in order to control the refurbisher's action. Therefore, the problem of Case DC can be characterized as follows.

$$\text{Maximize} \quad \Pi_M^{DC}(Q, w) \tag{18}$$

subject to

$$\Pi_R^{DC}(Q_r, p_r \mid Q, w) \geq \underline{\Pi}_R \tag{19}$$

$$\text{Maximize} \quad \Pi_R^{DC}(Q_r, p_r \mid Q, w). \tag{20}$$

The manufacturer determines the production lot size Q and the wholesale price of defective items for refurbishment w that jointly maximize its own profit in the objective function (18), while satisfying Constraints (19) and (20). Constraint (19) represents the refurbisher's rationality constraint. The refurbisher participates in the contract which guarantees its minimum reservation level $\underline{\Pi}_R$. Constraint (20) is the incentive compatibility constraint of the refurbisher. The refurbisher determines the refurbishing lot size Q_r and the sales price of refurbished item p_r, maximizing its own profit, given the manufacturer's decision on Q and w.

By the backward induction, we first obtain the best response of the refurbisher $p_r^{DC^*}$ and $Q_r^{DC^*}$ as functions of other decision variables from the first-order necessary conditions of Constraint (20).

$$Q_r^{DC^*}(p_r, w) = \sqrt{\frac{2S_r D_r}{H_r^{DC}(1 - D_r / M_r)}}, \text{ and} \tag{21}$$

$$p_r^{DC^*}(Q_r, w) = \frac{p(1+\Phi)}{\theta} - \sqrt{\frac{p}{\theta}}\sqrt{w\theta + (1+\Phi)\left[g + \frac{p(1-\theta+\Phi)}{\theta}\right] + (1-\theta+\Phi)\left[\frac{H_r^{DC}Q_r}{2M_r} - \frac{S_r}{Q_r} - k\right]}, \tag{22}$$

where $\Phi = (1 - \beta)\rho\theta$. H_r^{DC} is a function of w in Equation (17), while D_r is a function of p_r in Equations (3).

Then, by setting $\Pi_R^{DC} = \underline{\Pi}_R$ in Constraint (19), we can characterize the supply contract term w^{DC^*} as:

$$w^{DC*}(Q_r, p_r) = \frac{((p_r - k)\gamma - g(1-\gamma))\theta N - S_r D_r / Q_r - (hk/2)(1 - D_r / M_r)Q_r - \underline{\pi}_R}{\theta N + h(1 - D_r / M_r)Q_r}. \tag{23}$$

Finally, from the first-order necessary condition of (18), we obtain the manufacturer's decision Q^{DC^*}.

$$Q^{DC*}(p_r) = \sqrt{\frac{2SN}{H(1 - N/M)}}, \tag{24}$$

where N is a function of p_r in Equations (4). In the next section, we compare the performance of different supply chain model and suggest a guideline for the supply chain decentralization.

COMPARISON OF SUPPLY CHAIN MODELS

Basic Setting

We show the solutions of Cases INT and DC based on the parameter values as follows. *Example parameters:* unit time = year, D_0 = 10,000 units/year, M = 30,000 units/year, M_r = 20,000 units/year, θ = 0.15, ρ = 0.2, β = 0.5, p = \$800/unit, u = \$500/unit, i = \$50/unit, r = \$100/unit, k = \$100/unit, g = \$50/unit, h = 0.1/unit/year, S = \$100/production cycle, S_r = \$100/refurbishing cycle, and $\underline{\pi}_R$ = \$100,000. By putting the parameter values into the solutions of Cases INT and DC in Equations (14-16) and (21-24) and solving them simultaneously, we obtain the results summarized in Table 2.

Table 2: Optimal solutions under the basic numerical setting (†: decision variable)

	Case INT	Case DC
Manufacturing process		
Production lot size (unit), $Q^{*\dagger}$	261.04	258.00
Wholesale price of a returned item (\$/unit), $w^{*\dagger}$	-	62.34
Net inventory depletion rate (unit/year), N^*	10,865.76	10,703.69
Demand rate of a new item (unit/year), D^*	9,398.88	9,258.69
Production cycle time (day), T^*	8.77	8.80
Refurbishing process		
Refurbishing lot size (unit), $Q_r^{*\dagger}$	31.62	82.78
Unit selling price of a refurbished item (\$/unit), $p_r^{*\dagger}$	504.95	430.63
Inventory cost rate in the refurbishing process (\$/unit/year), H_r^*	124.00	22.47
Refurbishing proportion (fraction), γ^*	0.3688	0.4617
Demand rate of a refurbished item (unit/year), D_r^*	601.12	741.31
Refurbishing cycle time (days), T_r^*	19.20	40.76
Profits		
Supply chain's profit (\$/year), Π^*	1,559,808	1,551,165
Manufacturer's profit (\$/year), Π_M^*	1,559,808	1,451,165
Refurbisher's profit (\$/year), Π_R^*	-	100,000

In Table 2, the decisions in the manufacturing process look very similar between Cases INT and DC, while $Q^{INT^*} > Q^{DC^*}$ and $D^{INT^*} > D^{DC^*}$. However, we can observe that there are significant differences in the decisions of the refurbishing process between Cases INT and DC.

- One main reason is because different supply chain structures induce different decisions on the selling price of the refurbished item p_r^*. In the coordinated Case INT, the manufacturer deals with both new and refurbished items. Therefore, the manufacturer needs to protect the first-market sales of the higher-margin new item by setting p_r^* relatively higher, i.e., $p_r^{INT^*} > p_r^{DC^*}$, and $D^{INT^*} > D^{DC^*}$. On the other hand, it is rational for the third-party refurbisher to facilitate the second-market sales of the refurbished item in Case DC to maximize its own profit, while not considering the overall profit performance of the supply chain, i.e., $\gamma^{DC^*} > \gamma^{INT^*}$ and $D_r^{DC^*} > D_r^{INT^*}$. It is interesting to observe that the opportunistic behavior of the refurbisher lowers the selling price of the refurbished item, while the coordinated supply chain maintains the higher selling price. This is different from a typical view that the decentralized system sets the sales price higher due to moral hazard and double marginalization. In a closed-loop supply chain, we need to carefully consider interaction between new and refurbished items and decision dynamics involving channel conflicts.
- The other differentiating factor is the inventory holding cost rate in the refurbishing line H_r^*. As already shown in Equations (12) and (17), the cost components included in the inventory holding cost are different with respect to the supply chain structure. In Case DC, the contract term w is included, while the manufacturer sets w low in order to control the refurbisher's action in (19) and (23). It allows the third-party refurbisher to maintain the lower inventory holding cost, i.e., $H_r^{DC^*} < H_r^{INT^*}$ in Table 2. Consequently, it results in the overall differences in the refurbishing line operations, i.e., $Q_r^{DC^*} > Q_r^{INT^*}$, and $T_r^{DC^*} > T_r^{INT^*}$.

Overall, the structural difference between Cases INT and DC make these differences explained above, and these allow the third-party refurbisher in Case DC to maintain the better performance in the refurbishing process, including the higher sales performance in the second market but also less refurbishing setups. However, we need to note that the overall profit performance in the coordinated Case INT is superior to the uncoordinated Case DC, i.e., $\Pi^{INT^*} > \Pi^{DC^*}$.

Comparative Static Analysis

We investigate the equilibrium behaviors in Cases INT and DC with respect to environmental changes. We focus on important parameters, while increasing them seven times, *ceteris paribus* as in the basic numerical setting, as: π_R in [40000, 160000], D_0 in [8500, 11500], p in [770, 830], u in [470, 530], k in [70, 130], g in [20, 80], θ in [0.12, 0.18], ρ in [0.11, 0.29], and β in [0.2, 0.8]. Table 3 summarizes the equilibrium behaviors, including the range of each result with the change direction. It reads as follows. For example, in the row Case INT – Q^* and the column u – [470, 530], we can find "253-270(↓)." It indicates that the production lot size of Case INT (Q^{INT^*}) decreases (↓) from the maximum of 270 units to the minimum of 253 units (253-270) as the unit production cost of a new item u increases from \$470/unit to \$530/unit ([470, 530]).

The results in Table 3 can be summarized as follows.

- The relationships shown in Table 2 always hold at all parameter settings. Specifically, Case INT maintains the larger demand requests and lot size in the manufacturing process, i.e., $D^{INT^*} > D^{DC^*}$ and $Q^{INT^*} > Q^{DC^*}$, while Case DC yields those larger in the refurbishing process, i.e., $D_r^{DC^*} > D_r^{INT^*}$, and $Q_r^{DC^*} > Q_r^{INT^*}$. The sales price of the refurbished item sets higher in

Case INT, i.e., $p_r^{INT^*} > p_r^{DC^*}$. The supply chain can be better off when the supply chain is integrated by the manufacturer, i.e., $\Pi^{INT^*} > \Pi^{DC^*}$.

- The changes in $\underline{\pi}_R$, p, u, ρ and β differentiate the equilibrium behaviors of Cases INT and DC (see the superscript † in Table 3), while the behaviors are the same with respect to the changes in D_0, k, g and θ.
- When the refurbisher's bargaing power increases, insisting the higher profit (increasing $\underline{\pi}_R$), the manufacturer needs to decrease the contract term w^{DC^*} in Case DC, while there is no effect in Case INT. Then, it makes $p_r^{DC^*}$ higher and subsequently $D_r^{DC^*}$ less. It is interesting to see that working with the refurbisher with stronger bargaining power lets the overall supply chain be better off, while damaging the manufacturer' profit (increasing Π^{DC^*}, while decreasing $\Pi_M^{DC^*}$ since $\Pi_M^{DC^*} = \Pi^{DC^*} - \Pi_R^{DC^*}$ with $\Pi_R^{DC^*} = \underline{\pi}_R$). An increase of Π^{DC^*} is because a decrease in $D_r^{DC^*}$ allows D^{DC^*} of the new item to increase, which yields the higher margin.
- An increase in the demand base of the first market (increasing D_0) makes room for also increasing D_r^* by decreasing p_r^*, regardless of the supply chain structures. Then, these lead to increases in the lot sizes in both production and refurbishing lines. All supply chain structures benefit from this positive change (increasing Π^{INT^*} and Π^{DC^*}).
- An increase in the sales price of a new item p induces that of a refurbished item p_r^* also to increase in both Cases INT and DC. However, because the relative magnitude of its change is different in each case, the behaviors of D_r^* are different (decreasing $D_r^{INT^*}$, while increasing $D_r^{DC^*}$), while it also induces the differences in the manufacturing process operations between two cases. The supply chain is better off by an increase in p in both Cases INT and DC.
- An increase in the production cost u affects the overall decisions in Case INT since it needs to be considered in estimating the inventory holding costs in both manufacturing and refurbishing lines as shown in Equations (6) and (12). However, the refurbishing line is not affected by u in Case DC as we can see in Equation (17). Therefore, D^{DC^*} is fixed since $D_r^{DC^*}$ is not affected by u in Case DC.
- It is interesting to observe that the equilibrium behaviors of variables are totally opposite with respect to the changes of refurbishing cost k and scarp cost g, while increases in both costs k and g deteriorate Π^* regardless of supply chain structures. Note that refurbishment reduces the losses from scrap, while scrap reduces the opportunity savings from refurbishment. Therefore, an increase in g makes k evaluated relatively less, vice versa.
- As defects increase (increasing θ), p_r^* decreases in both Cases INT and DC because the second-market sales D_r^* need to be facilitated. Then, an increase in D_r^* deteriorates the first-market sales D^*. Overall, an increase in defect production damages supply chain profit Π^*, regardless of supply chain structures.
- An increase in the inspection failure (increasing ρ) damages the supply chain (decreasing Π^*) by raising the sales returns and external failure costs. On the other hand, an increase in the exchange requests (increasing β) can enhance Π^* by reducing the revenue loss from refund (decreasing $1-\beta$). Given the defective production (fixed θ), an increase in ρ induces the smaller Q^* due to a decrease in the net depletion rate in production line N^*, while the larger Q^* is induced by an increase in β and a subsequent increase in N^*.

Overall, it is important not only to embrace an integrate view of the decision structure in a closed-loop supply chain but also to understand different characteristics of various supply chain structures. As we can see above, any environmental change has an influence over the entire supply chain by changing the interaction between supply chain players. Moreover, we need to note again that the supply chain structure can have an important role in differentiating the overall performances of a closed-loop supply chain.

Table 3: Summary of equilibrium behaviors
(Note: min-max(change direction); ↑: increase, ↓: decrease, -: fixed; †: different behaviors between Cases INT and DC)

Increase in:		$\underline{\pi}_R$	D_0	p	u	k	g	θ	ρ	β
Case	Var.	[40000,160000]	[8500,11500]	[770,830]	[470,530]	[70,130]	[20,80]	[0.12,0.18]	[0.11,0.29]	[0.2,0.8]
INT	Q^*	261-261(-)	231-293(↑)	261-261(↑)	253-270(↓)	260-262(↑)	260-262(↓)	258-264(↑)	260-263(↓)	259-263(↑)
	N^*	10866-10866(-)	9236-12495(↑)	10842-10888(↑)	10830-10902(↓)	10835-10897(↑)	10829-10903(↓)	10698-11029(↑)	10784-10949(↓)	10759-10975(↑)
	D^*	9399-9399(-)	7989-10809(↑)	9378-9418(↑)	9368-9430(↓)	9372-9426(↑)	9367-9431(↓)	9242-9543(↓)	9397-9401(↑)	9394-9403(↓)
	Q_r^*	32-32(-)	29-34(↑)	31-32(↓)	32-32(↑)	31-33(↓)	31-32(↑)	27-36(↑)	31-32(↓)	31-32(↑)
	p_r^*	505-505(-)	505-505(↓)	476-534(↑)	489-521(↓)	491-519(↑)	488-522(↓)	495-515(↓)	504-506(↓)	504-506(↑)
	γ^*	0.37-0.37(-)	0.37-0.37(↑)	0.36-0.38(↓)	0.35-0.39(↑)	0.35-0.39(↓)	0.35-0.39(↑)	0.36-0.38(↑)	0.37-0.37(↑)	0.37-0.37(↓)
	D_r^*	601-601(-)	511-691(↑)	582-622(↓)	570-632(↑)	574-628(↓)	569-633(↑)	457-758(↑)	599-603(↓)	597-606(↑)
	Π^*(1k)	1560-1560(-)	1325-1795(↑)	1272-1848(↑)	1234-1887(↓)	1542-1578(↓)	1530-1591(↓)	1354-1759(↓)	1534-1586(↓)	1545-1575(↑)
DC	Q^*	258-258(↑)†	229-289(↑)	258-258(↓)†	251-266(↓)	257-259(↑)	257-259(↓)	255-261(↑)	257-259(↓)	256-260(↑)
	w^*	25-100(↓)	51-71(↑)	55-70(↑)	62-62(-)	49-76(↓)	47-79(↓)	46-74(↑)	62-63(↓)	62-63(↑)
	N^*	10697-10710(↑)†	9100-12308(↑)	10701-10706(↓)†	10704-10704(-)†	10672-10736(↑)	10671-10736(↓)	10555-10856(↑)	10627-10782(↓)	10602-10808(↑)
	D^*	9253-9264(↑)†	7871-10646(↑)	9257-9261(↓)†	9259-9259(-)†	9231-9287(↑)	9231-9287(↓)	9098-9415(↓)	9253-9264(↑)	9251-9266(↓)
	Q_r^*	72-101(↑)†	80-86(↑)	80-86(↓)	83-83(-)†	81-85(↓)	76-91(↑)	79-87(↑)	83-83(↓)	83-83(↑)
	p_r^*	428-434(↑)†	430-432(↓)	416-446(↑)	431-431(-)†	416-446(↑)	416-446(↓)	431-431(↓)	431-431(↑)†	431-431(↓)†
	γ^*	0.46-0.47(↓)†	0.46-0.46(↑)	0.46-0.46(↑)†	0.46-0.46(-)†	0.44-0.48(↓)	0.44-0.48(↑)	0.46-0.46(↑)	0.46-0.46(↓)†	0.46-0.46(↑)†
	D_r^*	736-747(↓)†	629-854(↑)	739-743(↑)†	741-741(-)†	713-769(↓)	713-769(↑)	585-902(↑)	736-747(↓)	734-749(↑)
	Π^*(1k)	1550-1552(↑)†	1318-1785(↑)	1267-1836(↑)	1230-1873(↓)	1534-1569(↓)	1522-1582(↓)	1347-1750(↓)	1526-1577(↓)	1536-1566(↑)

Effect of the Refurbisher's Capability

The results in Tables 2 and 3 demonstrate a typical situation that the integrated supply chain (Case INT) yields a superior profit performance to the decentralized system (Case DC), i.e., $\Pi^{INT^*} > \Pi^{DC^*}$. Note that, however, this is based on the same parameter settings. In a contemporary business environment, we can observe many firms which possess advantages in cost, quality and/or technological expertise by focusing on their core processes while outsourcing others. Therefore, nowadays, many functions and processes are decentralized to the specialized partners possessing their own advantages, and thus we are now running our businesses based on a supply chain. In this section, we consider the third-party refurbisher's possible cost advantages in defect disposition, including refurbishing efficiency and environmental capability, which can be indicated by unit refurbishing cost k and unit scrap cost g. Then, we reveal the conditions under which the decentralized supply chain (Case DC) can achieve the same profit performance as the coordinated supply chain (Case INT), i.e., $\Pi^{DC^*} = \Pi^{INT^*}$.

Table 4: Comparison of decentralized cases, including Cases DC-K and DC-G achieving the coordinated profit performance (†: decision variable)

	Case DC with fixed k and g	Case DC-K with variable k	Case DC-G with variable g
Refurbisher's capability			
Unit refurbishing cost (\$/unit), k	100	85.63†	100
Unit scrap cost (\$/unit), g	50	50	41.46†
Manufacturing process			
Production lot size (unit), $Q^{*\dagger}$	258.00	257.71	258.17
Wholesale price of a returned item (\$/unit), $w^{*\dagger}$	62.34	69.04	66.94
Net inventory depletion rate (unit/year), N^*	10,703.69	10,688.26	10,712.90
Demand rate of a new item (unit/year), D^*	9,258.69	9,245.35	9,266.66
Production cycle time (day), T^*	8.80	8.80	8.80
Refurbishing process			
Refurbishing lot size (unit), $Q_r^{*\dagger}$	82.78	83.73	80.68
Unit selling price of a refurbished item (\$/unit), $p_r^{*\dagger}$	430.63	423.44	434.91
Refurbishing inventory cost rate (\$/unit/year), H_r^*	22.47	22.37	23.39
Refurbishing proportion (fraction), γ^*	0.4617	0.4707	0.4564
Demand rate of a refurbished item (unit/year), D_r^*	741.31	754.65	733.34
Refurbishing cycle time (days), T_r^*	40.76	40.50	40.16
Profits			
Supply chain's profit (\$/year), Π^*	1,551,165	1,559,808	1,559,808
Manufacturer's profit (\$/year), Π_M^*	1,451,165	1,459,808	1,459,808
Refurbisher's profit (\$/year), Π_R^*	100,000	100,000	100,000

We utilize the basic parameter settings in Section 5.1, while letting either k or g a variable (originally k = \$100/unit and g = \$50/unit). Let Cases DC-K and DC-G denote Case DC with variables k and g, respectively. We can find either k or g achieving the coordinated profit performance of Case INT by simultaneously solving Equations (21-24) along with the additional condition $\Pi^{DC^*} = \Pi^{INT^*}$ = \$1,559,808/year in Table 2 (or $\Pi_M^{DC^*} = \Pi^{DC^*} - \Pi_R^{DC^*}$ = \$1,459,808/year with $\Pi_R^{DC^*} = \underline{\pi}_R$ = \$100,000/year). The results are summarized in Table 4. Figures 2(a) and 2(b) also illustrate the behaviors of supply chain profits in Cases DC-K and DC-G with respect to the changes in k and g, respectively, along with Π^{INT^*} in Case INT at fixed k and g for comparison.

Table 4 indicates that the careful assessment of the refurbisher's capability is important to enhance profitability, i.e., $\Pi^{DC\text{-}K^*} = \Pi^{DC\text{-}G^*} > \Pi^{DC^*}$. Specifically, to achieve the coordinated result, i.e., $\Pi^{DC\text{-}K^*} = \Pi^{DC\text{-}G^*} = \Pi^{INT^*}$, the third-party refurbisher needs to be efficient enough to handle the refurbishing activity at unit cost k = \$85.63/unit, or it needs to have environmental capabilities to scrap each defective item at g = \$41.46/unit. More interestingly, Figures 2(a) and 2(b) also indicate that the supply chain can be better off even in the decentralized supply chain structure than in the integrated system. This happens if the manufacturer can sign a contract with the refurbisher which is capable of maintaining either k or g less than each threshold of k = \$85.63/unit (see Figure 2(a)) or g = \$41.46/unit (see Figure 2(b)).

Figure 2: Comparison of supply chain profit Π^* among Cases DC-K, DC-G and INT (×: Case DC-K (Case DC with variable k); ■: Case DC-G (Case DC with variable g); ○: Case INT (at fixed k = \$100/unit and g = \$50/unit)).

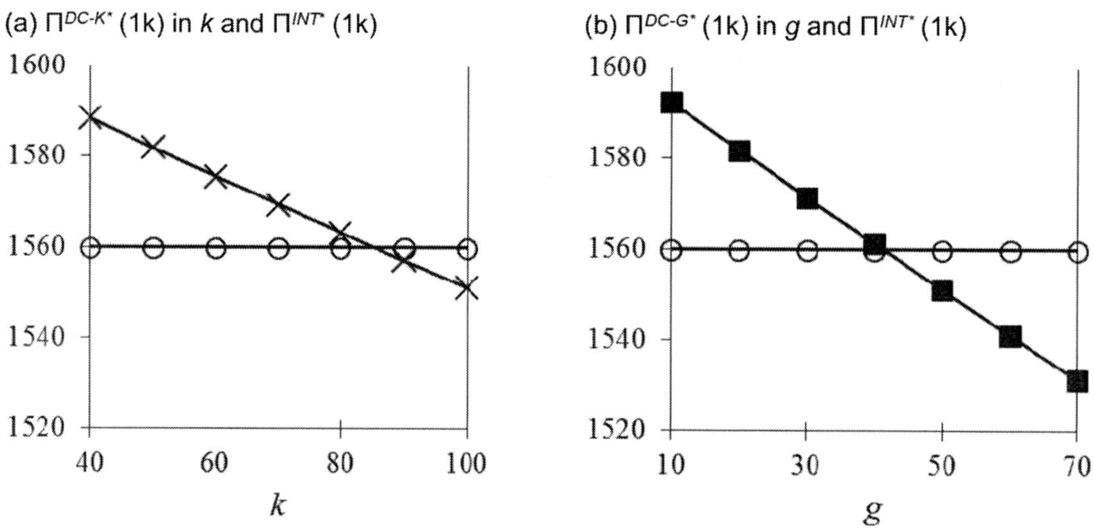

The focal company needs to thoroughly assess core capabilities of supply chain partners from the careful rationalization and selection processes, and it should evaluate possible inefficiencies in a closed-loop supply chain in order to create a synergy in an enabling cooperative environment. It is also imperative for a closed-loop supply chain not only to understand that the reverse process can create a value stream, not a nuisance, but also to have an integrated perspective in order to closely coordinate the forward and reverse flows (Guide and Van Wassenhove 2006).

CONCLUDING REMARKS

This study investigated a closed-loop supply chain, consisting of a manufacturer responsible for the first-market sales of a new item and a third-party refurbisher responsible for the second-market sales of a refurbished item. We then introduced two different supply chain models with different structures, and revealed their distinct characteristics. The implications we obtained through the investigation can be summarized as follows.

First, the demand and production lot size of a new item are yielded larger in the integrated supply chain than in the decentralized one. Second, the sales price of a refurbished item is set lower in the decentralized system. This is since the third-party refurbisher intends to boost up the second-market sales, while the manufacturer needs to protect the first-market sales of the higher-margin new item. It is interesting to observe that the opportunistic behavior of the refurbisher lowers the selling price of the refurbished item, while the coordinated supply chain maintains the higher selling price. This is different from a typical view that the decentralized system sets the sales price higher due to moral hazard and double marginalization. In a closed-loop supply chain, we need to carefully consider interaction between new and refurbished items and decision dynamics involving channel conflicts. Third, the decentralized supply chain maintains the larger lot size and cycle time in the refurbishing line. This is mainly because the cost components included in the inventory holding cost are different with respect to the supply chain structure. The manufacturer sets the wholesale price low in order to control the refurbisher's action. It allows the third-party refurbisher to maintain the lower inventory holding cost. Fourth, when the refurbisher's bargaing power increases, the sales price of the refurbished item increases. It is interesting to see that working with the refurbisher with stronger bargaining power lets the overall supply chain be better off, while damaging the manufacturer' profit. Fifth, an increase in the demand base of the first market makes room for also increasing the second-market sales by decreasing the sales price of the refurbished item, regardless of the supply chain structure. Then, these lead to increases in the lot sizes in both production and refurbishing lines. All supply chain structures benefit from this positive change. On the other hand, an increase in the sales price of the new item induces that of the refurbished item also to increase and lets the supply chain better off, regardless of the supply chain structure. As defects increase, the sales price of the refurbished item decreases in both structures because the second-market sales need to be facilitated, while this change deteriorates the first-market sales. Finally, the careful assessment of the refurbisher's capability is important to enhance profitability and achieve the coordinated result in the decentralized system. The focal company needs to thoroughly assess core capabilities of supply chain partners from the careful rationalization and selection processes, and it should evaluate possible inefficiencies in a closed-loop supply chain in order to create a synergy in an enabling cooperative environment.

We aim to contribute to the body of knowledge and supply chain practices by revealing unique characteristics of different supply chain structures and by providing important implications.

REFERENCES

Anily, S. (1995). Single-machine lot-sizing with uniform yields and rigid demands: Robustness of the optimal solution. *IIE Transactions,* 27(5), 625-633.

Aras, N., Güllü, R., & Yürülmez, S. (2011). Optimal inventory and pricing policies for remanufacturable leased products. *International Journal of Production Economics,* 133(1), 262-271.

Cheng, T. C. E. (1991). An economic order quantity model with demand-dependent unit production cost and imperfect production process. *IIE Transactions,* 23(1), 23-28.

Douthit, D., Flach, M., & Agarwal, V. (2011). Reducing the quantity and cost of product returns in consumer electronics. 2011: Retrieved from http://www.accenture.com/us-en/Pages/insight-reducing-quality-cost-product-returns-consumer-electronics.aspx?c=mc_othrposts_10000034&n=sm_0910, December 5.

Grosfeld-Nir, A., & Gerchak, Y. (2004). Multiple lotsizing in production to order with random yields: review of recent advances. *Annals of Operations Research,* 126(1-4), 43-69.

Guide Jr., V. D. R., & Van Wassenhove, L. N. (2006). Closed-loop supply chains: An introduction to the feature issue (Part 1). *Production and Operations Management,* 15(3), 345-350.

Guide, V. D. R., Jr., Souza, G. C., Van Wassenhove, L. N., & Blackburn, J. D. (2006). Time value of commercial product returns. *Management Science,* 52(8), 1200-1214.

Khan, M., Jaber, M. Y., & Bonney, M. (2011a). All economic order quantity (EOQ) for items with imperfect quality and inspection errors. *International Journal of Production Economics,* 133(1), 113-118.

Khan, M., Jaber, M. Y., Guiffrida, A. L., & Zolfaghari, S. (2011b). A review of the extensions of a modified EOQ model for imperfect quality items. *International Journal of Production Economics,* 132(1), 1-12.

Lee, W. J., Kim, D., Cabot, A. V. (1996). Optimal demand rate, lot sizing and process reliability improvement decisions. *IIE Transactions,* 28(11), 941-952.

Leung, K. F. (2007). A generalized geometric-programming solution to "An economic production quantity model with flexibility and reliability considerations". *European Journal of Operational Research,* 176(1), 240-251.

Ouyang, L. -Y., & Chang, C. -T. (2013). Optimal production lot with imperfect production process under permissible delay in payments and complete backlogging. *International Journal of Production Economics,* 144(2), 610-617.

Ovchinnikov, A. (2011). Revenue and cost management for remanufactured products. *Production and Operations Management,* 20(6) 824-840.

Petersen, A., & Kumar, V. (2009). Get smart about product returns. 2009: Retrieved from http://online.wsj.com/news/articles/SB10001424052970203585004574392464143500106, December 15.

Porteus, E. L. (1986). Optimal lot sizing, process quality improvement and setup cost reduction. *Operations Research,* 34(1), 137-144.

Rosenblatt, M. J., & Lee, H. L. (1986). Economic production cycles with imperfect production processes. *IIE Transactions,* 18(1), 48-55.

Salameh, M. K., & Jaber, M. Y. (2000). Economic production quantity model for items with imperfect quality. *International Journal of Production Economics,* 64(1-3), 59-64.

Tripathy, P. K., Wee, W., & Majhi, P. R. (2003). An EOQ model with process reliability considerations. *Journal of the Operational Research Society,* 54(5), 549-554.

Ullah, M., & Kang, C. W. (2014). Effect of rework, rejects and inspection on lot size with work-in-process inventory. *International Journal of Production Research,* 52(8), 2448-2460.

Vorasayan, J., & Ryan, S. M. (2006). Optimal price and quantity of refurbished products. *Production and Operations Management,* 15(3), 369-383.

Yano, C. A., & Lee, H. L., 1995. Lot sizing with random yields: a review. *Operations Research,* 43(2), 311-334.

Yeh, R. H., & Chen, T., 2006. Optimal lot size and inspection policy for products with warranty. *European Journal of Operational Research,* 174 (2), 766-776.

Yoo, S. H., Kim, D., & Park, M. -S. (2009). Economic production quantity model with imperfect-quality items, two-way imperfect inspection and sales return. *International Journal of Production Economics,* 121(1), 255-265.

Yoo, S. H., Kim, D., & Park, M. -S. (2012a). Inventory models for imperfect production and inspection processes with various inspection options under one-time and continuous improvement investment. *Computers & Operations Research,* 39(9), 2001-2015.

Yoo, S. H., Kim, D., & Park, M. -S. (2012b). Lot sizing and quality investment with quality cost analyses for imperfect production and inspection processes with commercial return. *International Journal of Production Economics,* 140(2), 922-933.

Zhang, X., Gerchak, Y. (1990). Joint lot sizing and inspection policy in an EOQ model with random yield. *IIE Transactions,* 22(1), 41-47.

DECISION SCIENCES INSTITUTE

Investigation into the Marriage Penalty under the Alternative Minimum Tax

Michael S. Keane
San Diego State University
Email: mkeane@mail.sdsu.edu

Nathan Oestreich
San Diego State University
Email: drno@sdsu.edu

James E. Williamson
San Diego State University
Email: james.williamson@sdsu.edu

ABSTRACT

That there is marriage penalty in the federal income tax is well documented. There is also structural penalty in the alternative minimum tax [AMT]. This paper represents an initial investigation of the magnitude of the AMT marriage penalty and how various factors affect it. Calculations of the marriage penalty based on various assumed levels of deductions and AMT adjustments are developed. The AMT does not add significantly to, or reduce, the marriage penalty in the regular tax.

KEYWORDS: Marriage Penalty, Alternative Minimum Tax

INTRODUCTION

The fact that there is marriage penalty in the federal income tax is well documented. The structural penalty was partially removed in the Bush tax cuts and extended by the American Taxpayer Relief Act of 2012, but Congress only adjusted the standard deduction and the tax rate for lower-income taxpayers whose income did not exceed the 25 percent bracket (i.e., income in the 10 percent, 15 percent, and 25 percent brackets). Although the structural penalty has been removed for the vast majority of taxpayers, there are many provisions of the Internal Revenue Code [Code] that can result in a married couple paying more tax than they would as unmarrieds. These include the residence interest limits ($1 million limit for acquisition debt and $100,000 limit for home equity debt are the same for married couples and unmarrieds), actively managed rentals under the passive activity loss limits ($25,000 limit and phase-out beginning at $100,000 is the same for a married couple as it is for unmarrieds), limits and phase-outs for the earned income tax credit, and the $3,000 capital loss deduction limit.

There is structural penalty in the alternative minimum tax [AMT] as well. Structurally, three differences have been identified: (1) the AMT exemption (Revenue Procedure 2015-53, 2015), is $83,800 for a married couple and $53,900 for unmarrieds (two unmarrieds get $107,800, which is $24,000 more than a married couple), (2) the AMT exemption phase out begins at different levels and (3) for marrieds and unmarrieds the 28 percent bracket kicks in at alternative minimum tax base of $$186,300 (Code § 55 and Revenue Procedure 2015-53, 2015)). The AMT is 26% from AMT base of $0 to $$186,300, 28%, over $186,300.

This paper represents an initial investigation of the magnitude of the AMT marriage penalty and how various factors affect it. A spreadsheet has been developed to calculate the marriage penalty based on assumed levels of deductions and AMT adjustments.

OVERVIEW OF AMT, AMT ADJUSTMENTS, AND AMT PREFERENCES

The AMT is imposed in § 55 of the Code. A taxpayer pays the larger of the regular tax or the tentative AMT. The formula for determining the tentative AMT follows:

Regular income tax
Plus or minus AMT Adjustments
Plus AMT preferences
Equals: Alternative minimum taxable income
Minus the AMT exemption
Equals: AMT base
Times: AMT tax rate
Equals: Tentative AMT (net of specified credits)
Minus: Regular income tax
Equals AMT

Detailed descriptions are not provided here, but the following paragraphs include summaries of characteristics.

AMT Adjustments.

Adjustments can be positive or negative. For example, depreciation must be recalculated for AMT generally using slower methods. With respect to a particular asset, the adjustment may be positive in one year and negative in a later year after what is called the turn-around point is passed. For example, for 5-year property, double declining balance is used for regular tax and 150 percent declining balance is used for AMT. No adjustment is made for § 179 write-offs or for additional first-year depreciation (as a result, they are allowed for AMT purposes). Similar rules apply to mining exploration costs and long-term contracts. Similarly, a net operating loss deduction must be calculated using AMT concepts. (Code § 56).

For individual taxpayers, a number of deductions are disallowed or recalculated. One of the ones most significant for large families is that the personal and dependency exemptions are lost. Individuals also lose their deductions for state and local income taxes in total, and they may lose all or part of their deductions for medical expenses and interest.

Another adjustment that can have substantial, even crippling effects in extreme cases, is the adjustment for incentive stock options. There is a positive adjustment in the year of exercise equal to the bargain element (i.e., fair market value – option price). If the stock has appreciated significantly, this can create or increase the AMT in large ways. In the year of sale, the adjustment is reversed (i.e., a negative adjustment in the same amount), but there may not be enough income to absorb this adjustment so there may be no AMT that year.

AMT Preferences.

AMT preferences are always positive. They include the excess of percentage depletion allowed over the taxpayer's basis in the asset and excludable municipal bond interest on specified private development bonds (Code § 57).

AMT Exemptions.

The AMT exemption is a deduction allowed in calculating the AMT base (Code § 55(d)). For 2016, the exemption is $83,800 for married taxpayers and $53,900 for unmarried ones. These amounts are adjusted for inflation (Revenue Procedure 2015 – 53, 2015).

For higher income taxpayers, the exemption is phased out at a rate of 25 percent of AMTI in excess of specified thresholds. For married taxpayers the 2016 threshold is $159,700; for unmarried taxpayers, $119,700 (Revenue Procedure 2015 – 53, 2015).

Since the exemption is phased-out as income increases, the effective rate in the 26 percent bracket is 32.5 percent (26 percent x 1.25); in the 28 percent bracket, 35 percent (28 percent x 1.25).

AMT Tax Rate.

As previously mentioned, the tax rate is 26 percent from AMT base of $0 to $186,300, and 28 percent for base in excess of $186,300. The $186,300 amount is adjusted annually for inflation (Revenue Procedure 2015 – 53, 2015).

EXAMPLES

The first step in an analysis of this nature is to develop scenarios to observe the nature of relationships between the relevant variables. Then further analysis can be undertaken to quantify the relationships and reach conclusions.

Zero Taxable Income

In this scenario, adjusted gross income is set at exactly the sum of the standard deduction and the personal and dependency exemptions. The regular tax is therefore zero. The adjustments necessary for singles to create an AMT equals the exemption amount of $53,600 (2015 amount).

Exemption	$83,400	$53,600	$53,600
AGI	$20,600	$10,300	$10,300
Exemptions	$8,000	$4,000	$4,000
Standard deduction	$12,600	$6,300	$6,300
TI	$0	$0	$0
Adjustments	$107,200	$53,600	$53,600
AMT base	$23,800	$0	$0
Tent. AMT	$6,188		
Marriage penalty	$6,188		

A married couple with exactly the same amount of adjustments will pay AMT of $6,188. This is the marriage penalty, which is caused solely by the difference in AMT exemption amounts.

It is significant that the amount of adjustments to hit AMT is $53,600, and unlikely, but not an impossible amount. If the taxpayer had a business with large deductions and adjustments, she could get there. Another way, that will be developed later, would be to have more dependency exemptions and large itemized deductions for state and local taxes and miscellaneous itemized deductions.

Income of $100,000

This example verifies that the penalty does not change for a couple earning $50,000 each when they still claim personal and dependency exemptions and the standard deduction.

AGI	$100,000	$50,000	$50,000
Exemptions	$8,000	$4,000	$4,000
Standard deduction	$12,600	$6,300	$6,300
TI	$79,400	$39,700	$39,700
Income tax	$11,438	$5,719	$5,719
Adjustments	$71,790	$35,895	$35,895
AMT base	$67,790	$21,995	$21,995
Tent. AMT	$6,188	$0	$0
Marriage penalty	$6,188		

The marriage penalty is still $6,188. Here, however, the adjustments necessary to encounter AMT is only $35,895 each.

Income of $100,000 with Head of Household

A head of household is entitled to a larger standard deduction than other singles ($9,250 versus $6,300). This example, which also increases the exemptions from two to four, investigates whether head of household status has any effect.

AGI	$100,000	$50,000	$50,000
Exemptions	$16,000	$8,000	$8,000
Standard deduction	$12,600	$9,250	$9,250
TI	$71,400	$39,700	$39,700
Income tax	$12,173	$5,719	$5,719
Adjustments	$71,790	$23,000	$35,895
AMT base	$67,790	$9,100	$21,995
Tent. AMT	$6,188	$0	$0
Marriage penalty	$6,188		

The marriage penalty is still $6,188. It is true that the standard deductions will be included in the adjustments, which in this case need to be $23,000 for one and $35,895 for the two individuals, one of whom claims one exemption; the other, three.

Income of $100,000 with Itemized Deductions

This situation adds the complexity when one person claims itemized deductions and the other the standard deduction. If they marry and file jointly, the couple must either itemize or claim the standard deduction. In this case, the couple itemizes on their joint return, and they lose the one standard deduction.

AGI	$100,000	$50,000	$50,000
Exemptions	$16,000	$4,000	$12,000
Itemized/standard			

deduction	$30,000	$28,000	$6,300
TI $54,000 $18,000 $31,700			
Income tax	$7,118	$2,239	$4,294
Adjustments	$82,626	$44,212	$38,414
AMT base	$53,226	$8,612	$16,514
Tent. AMT	$6,721	$0	$0
Marriage penalty	$6,721		

In this particular case, there is a regular tax penalty of $586 ($7,118 - $2,238 - $4,294), and an AMT marriage penalty $6,721. Notice that the joint itemized deductions were only $2,000 more than the one person's itemized deductions. This assumes that the person's itemized deductions were $2,000, and elected to claim the larger standard deduction as an unmarried taxpayer.

Income of $400,000 with Itemized Deductions

Now, we expand the analysis to the point where the 28% AMT tax rate plays a role (i.e., when AMTI exceeds $$186,300). When single, one taxpayer itemizes and files as single; the other, the standard deduction and head of household.

AGI	$400,000	$250,000	$150,000
Exemptions	$0	$8,000	$8,000
Standard/Itemized	$92,331	$92,000	$9,250
TI	$307,669	$150,000	$132,750
Income tax	$76,944	$35,127	$27,563
Adjustments	$43,784	$24,904	$18,880
AMT base	$321,437	$135,105	$106,013
Tent. AMT	$86,276	$35,127	$27,563
Marriage penalty	$23,586		

Here, the marriage penalty rises due to a combination of multiple factors. There is a $16,046 regular tax penalty primarily because of the different tax brackets and the $400,000 AGI results in loss of the exemption deduction and a cut-back of itemized deduction.

Since the AMT is the tentative AMT minus the regular tax, the amount of adjustments for the unmarried to make the tentative AMT and the regular tax equal is determined. If the married couple had exactly that amount of adjustments, the AMT marriage penalty is $25,106, that when added to the regular tax penalty totals $41,152. Some of the factors contributing to this higher penalty are the 28 percent AMT tax bracket on AMT base over $186,300, the difference in AMT exemptions (that now straddles the 28 percent and 26 percent AMT tax brackets), and the phase-out of the AMT exemption. Nearly the entire exemption for married is phased out, while smaller amounts are phased out for unmarrieds.

CONCLUSIONS AND PLANNED FUTURE ANALYSIS

The examples here are the first steps to analyze the marriage penalty in the AMT. The basic penalty caused solely by the differences in AMT exemptions was found to be $6,188. As higher income and different mixes of deductions are introduced, the penalty may increase (and possibly decrease).

Since Congress increased the AMT exemptions and indexed them for inflation, the amount of adjustments and preferences needed for middle-income taxpayers to incur AMT has generally increased. Accordingly, the probability of having to pay the tax has decreased. The possibility is real for some, which increases the complexity of their tax compliance and planning. Policy makers and taxpayers, alike, should be aware of these factors.

In orders of magnitude, the marriage penalty appears to be much less of an issue for the AMT, as compared to the regular tax. Further study will investigate this and other issues for married taxpayers.

For subsequent analysis the calculations will be verified. By the nature of the assumptions that are made, they are essentially close estimates at this point in the analysis.

REFERENCES

Floyd W. Carpenter, Dennis R. Lassila, and Murphy Smith, "The Federal Government's War on Marriage AKA the Marriage Penalty Tax: Unfair to Individuals and Harmful to Society," 16 Journal of Legal, Ethical and Reg. Issues 107 (2013) (cataloging many of the major articles and reports that contain a discussion of the marriage penalty and providing a significant literature review).

Steve Gill, Nathan Oestreich and James Williamson. "The 192 Percent (Really!) Marriage Penalty — Maybe Even More," Tax Notes, April 25, 2016

Internal Revenue Code § 55

Internal Revenue Code § 56

Internal Revenue Code § 57

Revenue Procedure 2015-53, IRB 2015-44 (November 2, 2015)

DECISION SCIENCES INSTITUTE

Is SOA Really Dead?

Suvankar Ghosh
University of Toledo
Suvankar.Ghosh@utoledo.edu

ABSTRACT

Integrating business processes, applications, databases, and systems is a problem that has plagued IT organizations for decades. The Service-Oriented Architecture or SOA, which employs web-based technologies, is the industry's latest attempt to solve the integration problem. Many firms have floundered with implementing SOA which encompasses a complex set of technologies. This has led some industry analysts to send out the word that "SOA is dead". We use the methodology of real options to establish a value for SOA. We conclude that SOA is not dead and is indeed a technology bet that most organizations would find worth making.

KEYWORDS: Managerial decision making, Firm decisions, Value of IT, Real options

INTRODUCTION

Moving to a SOA environment is arguably one of the most important priorities for IT organizations today. SOA holds the key to integrating a firm's many disparate applications, systems, processes, and data – a problem that has bedeviled IT organizations for several decades. SOA envisages a firm's portfolio of applications as essentially comprising services callable over the Internet, and these are referred to as Web Services (Bloomberg & Schmelzer, 2006; Erl, 2006; Krafzig et al., 2005; Marks & Bell, 2006). Business applications expose key functionality and information such as sales tax computation or the state of inventory levels as callable Web Services thereby enabling the reuse of software components and the integration of data and applications across system, organizational, and firm boundaries.

The industry-wide success of any type of software integration technology depends crucially on the industry acceptance of standards underlying the technology. The three main standards underlying Web Services are the Simple Object Access Protocol (SOAP), Web Services Description Language (WSDL), and Universal Description, Discovery and Integration (UDDI) (WSDL Working Group, 2007; UDDI Working Group 2004). SOAP is the messaging protocol governing the exchange of messages between a client and a Web Service; WSDL is the language in which the functionality of Web Services is described to the applications environment; and UDDI is simply the standard for the directory service where these WSDL descriptions are placed and which is queried by applications to determine the services being offered. The SOAP messages are coded in a standard format called XML (SOAP Working Group, 2007). Whereas past efforts in developing integration standards, such as the Distributed Computing Environment (DCE) (DCE Open Group, 1996) and the Common Object Request Broker Architecture (CORBA) (Slama et al., 1999), eventually failed for various reasons such as the lack of agreement between Microsoft and the UNIX vendors which doomed the CORBA standard, SOA and its associated standards are widely embraced by all the key players in the industry.

With all the promise of Web Services, XML, and SOA and the breadth and depth of industry support behind them, a strange thing appears to be happening on the road to the brave new world of SOA. For many organizations, it appears that SOA has been a failure. So much so, the Burton Group, a respected analyst firm, declared “SOA is dead” in early 2009 (Krill, 2009). Anne Thomas Manes, research director at the Burton Group was quoted as saying “Once thought to be the savior of IT, SOA has turned into a great failed experiment – at least for most organizations” (Neubarth 2010). The economic recession of 2007 through 2009 and the overhyping of SOA in the first place of course have played a part in the gloomy sentiment now towards SOA in some quarters. But it is also quite plausible that is there more substance to the disillusionment with SOA beyond those two factors. That the disenchantment with SOA is not merely anecdotal was confirmed in more systematic research by the Gartner Group which indicated that more and more companies are choosing not to invest in SOA (Gartner Press Release, 2008). What is interesting is that amidst this gloom, there is a large and very much pro-SOA camp out there. Evidence of this exists in the growing number of SOA success stories on the SOA.org web site (SOA Industry Case Studies, 2010). IDC, also a respected market research firm, disagrees with the Burton Group stating that SOA is very much alive and has forecast increases in SOA spending worldwide (Nguyen, 2010).

LITERATURE REVIEW

RO Models

An investment project, or a program comprising a series of investments, whose returns are uncertain is exactly the type of investment scenario that is best examined using the lens of real options (RO). SOA would indeed qualify as an investment scenario fraught with uncertainty given the differing views that exist about the benefits of SOA (Gartner Press Release, 2008; Krill, 2009; Neubarth, 2010; Nguyen, 2010; SOA Industry Case Studies, 2010). A variety of RO valuation models have been developed for many types of IT investments. Dos Santos (1991) employs the Black-Scholes (1973) options pricing model (OPM) to an investment in integrated digital services networks (ISDN). Benaroch and Kauffman (2000) apply the Black-Scholes OPM to an investment in electronic banking. Taudes (1998) employs the Geske (1979) compound option to value investment programs involving software upgrades, such as upgrading SAP from R2 to R3. Bardhan et al. (2004) model a multi-stage investment in a series of IT projects made by a firm in the utilities industry. Each stage is modeled as a Black-Scholes option whose options value is deemed to increase the value of the cash flows from the previous stage. Benaroch et al. (2006) offer an alternative approach to valuing multistage investments where the options value of each stage is deemed to reduce the exercise price of the previous stage. Ghosh and Li (2013) develop a new OPM for what they refer to as generalized meta-staged projects. Clearly, there are different types of OPMs that can be developed and employed to view an investment scenario. All models are approximations of reality and Taudes (1998), Bardhan et al. (2004), Benaroch et al. (2006), and Ghosh and Li (2013) actually offer four different OPMs for valuing multistage IT investments from an RO perspective. Although Ghosh and Li (2013) also look at the SOA application, the focus of their research is more on developing an innovative OPM rather than on the SOA application per se.

The main target of this article on the other hand is the value of the SOA technology itself and to address the key question of whether firms should make a bet on SOA or not. Innovation at the level of the OPM itself is certainly useful but an innovative OPM also has the drawback of not being widely adopted. In fact, thus far, Ghosh and Li (2013) is the only article that applies this notion of generalized meta-staged projects. As our focus is more on SOA rather than a new OPM, we use the well-known approach of applying the Geske compound option (1977, 1979) to valuing multi-stage projects. The Geske compound option has been applied in multi-stage investments in the information systems (IS) field as well as in other disciplines and contexts

(Cassimon et al. 2004, Paxson 2007, Jensen and Warren 2001, Perlitz et al. 1999, Taudes 1998). Hence, the Geske compound option approach is a well-known and tried-and-true method for valuing multistage investments. The SOA investment program is multi-stage in that it involves a number of complex technologies, which necessitates a phased deployment.

SOA Technologies

Moving to SOA actually requires implementing several key pieces of technology as shown in Figure 1. The build-out of the SOA infrastructure is therefore best done in phases where in any given phase the organization deploys and absorbs a technology before moving on to the next. The key technology components involved in building the SOA infrastructure include an Enterprise Services Bus (ESB), a directory service (DS), a data transformation service (DTS), a business process management service (BPMS), and adapters (ADPTRS) for adapting existing applications to the Web Services environment (Bloomberg & Schmelzer, 2006; Erl, 2006; Krafzig et al., 2005; Marks & Bell, 2006). These key technologies are further described below:

- The ESB provides the communications infrastructure for transporting files and messages which can be either remote process calls (RPC) or document-oriented messages containing XML documents. The ESB is essentially a distributed message broker (Fiorano ESB, 2009; Progress Software Sonic ESB, 2009). The ESB ensures reliable delivery of the messages and will store them for later delivery if a destination endpoint is temporarily unavailable.

- A UDDI-compliant directory service (DS) maintains information about the various kinds of Web Services that are available in the SOA environment and where they are located. The UDDI server is populated with WSDL descriptions of the available Web Services thus providing external applications with the knowledge of what is available for reuse. New applications can then simply be built as compositions of preexisting Web Services and any new business logic that may need to be created.

- The data transformation service (DTS) provides a general capability for mapping message formats, such as from EDI to XML or from XML to XML (Pervasive ETL, 2007). As the so-called legacy applications deployed years ago employed various proprietary data formats, it is necessary to map these formats to newer XML-based standard formats in order for the legacy information to be consumed by newer applications. Such data mapping is often necessary when messages and documents move across inter-application or inter-organizational boundaries.

- The business process management service (BPMS) enables new applications to be written by simply "orchestrating" existing Web Services. This orchestration could involve invoking a set of existing Web Services in a certain sequence and processing the information returned by these services. The coordinating intelligence which invokes the Web Services and maintains information about the state of the exchanges with these service endpoints is the BPMS. New applications for implementing business processes are simply described to the process manager via an easy-to-use graphical interface, which results in the creation of a script defining the sequence of interactions with the service endpoints for implementing the new business process. A process orchestration engine then simply executes this script. Microsoft BizTalk Server is an example of such a process orchestration product (Microsoft BizTalk Server, 2007).

- Adapters (ADPTRS) take existing applications built in the pre-SOA era, such as an enterprise resource planning (ERP) application, and expose its key functionality in the form of Web Services thereby allowing new integration applications to reuse the business logic embedded in existing applications. As an example, data adapters for an ERP application such as SAP map SAP's proprietary iDoc message format and the ABAP (Advanced Business Applications Programming) interface to standards-compliant XML and Web Service interfaces. While data adapters for major commercial packages can be obtained off-the-shelf from the vendors, the IT organization may have to develop data adapters for applications that were developed in-house. The adapters together constitute an adaptation service.

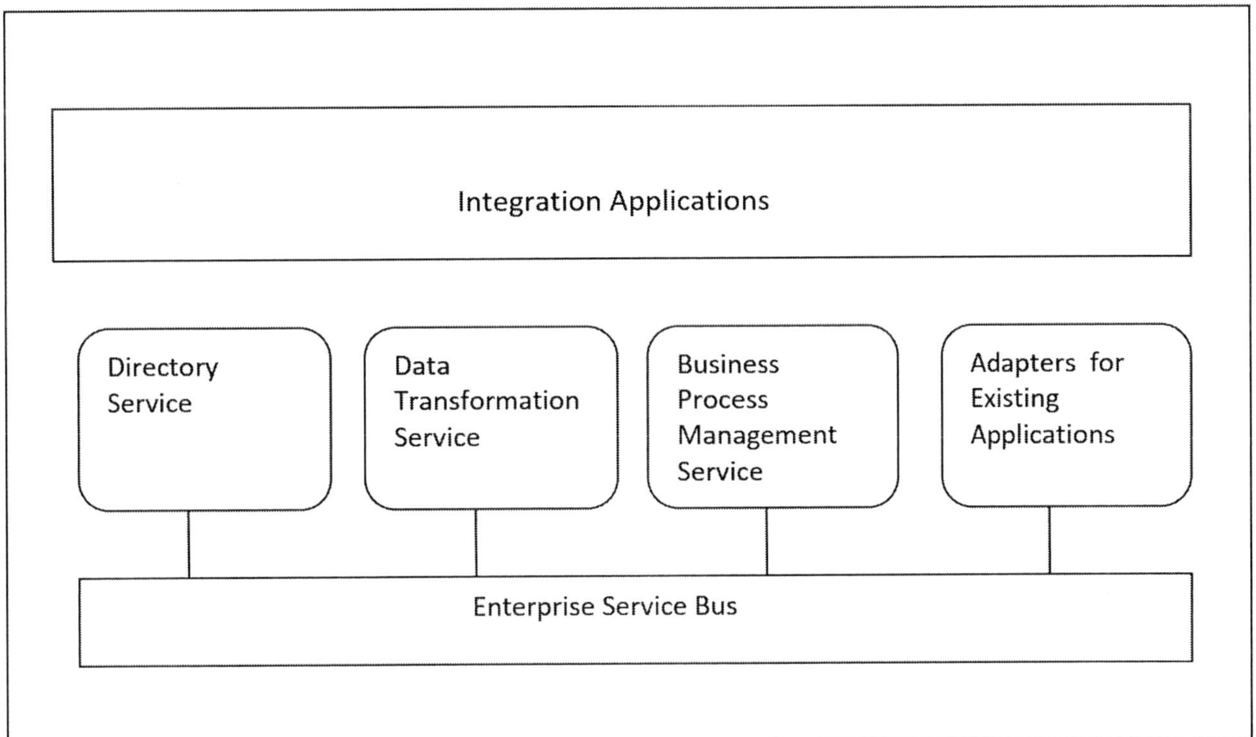

Figure 1: Technologies Comprising SOA

Once the SOA infrastructure has been set up as shown in Figure 1 then newer integration applications can be layered on top of this infrastructure. Each chronological phase in the build-out of the SOA environment refers to the period of time directly after the investment in a major technology component, such as the ESB or the BPMS, has been made and before the decision to invest in the next technology component is made. This phase includes all the activities necessary for the deployment and, more importantly, the absorption of the technology in question by the organization. Such activities include the installation, configuration, testing, and optimization of the technology as well as the training of personnel who will be using, maintaining or enhancing the technology. The complexity of enterprise integration technology ensures that each component of the solution, be it the ESB or the BPM service, takes a certain amount of time to absorb which is not trivial. Consequently, in addition to the cost of the software licenses, a major portion of the cost of the EI solution lies in the services that the firm must purchase from the vendor for the "hand holding" necessary for the effective transfer of knowledge and skills from the vendor to the user.

At the completion of each phase, the firm has the option of making the next investment to continue building the SOA infrastructure or to abandon the investment program. After the SOA infrastructure has been built, the organization can now start to develop new applications leveraging the SOA infrastructure. The cost savings in building new applications leveraging SOA as compositions or orchestrations of Web Services represents the cash flow generating asset resulting from the investment in the SOA infrastructure. At time t_0, if the firm chooses to embark on the build-out of the SOA environment by making the investment to deploy an ESB, which is the foundation of SOA, then there are four investment decisions yet to be made in the future corresponding to the four infrastructure services. As such, if the firm chooses to invest in the ESB, it will then hold a 4-fold compound option on the value of the assets represented by the integration applications. The firm will choose to embark on the SOA build-out program if the value of this 4-fold compound option at t_0 exceeds the cost of the initial investment in the ESB.

THEORETICAL DEVELOPMENT/MODEL

Our model for SOA is based on the well-established Geske compound option model which has been used to model multistage investment programs in many different contexts (Cassimon et al. 2004, Paxson 2007, Jensen and Warren 2001, Perlitz et al. 1999, Taudes 1998). The deployment of each key technology component described in the previous section represents a stage in the build-out of SOA. Geske's original compound option model (Geske, 1977, 1979) was developed for two-stage investment programs where there are two future payments to be made in the program. This can be easily generalized to *n* stages where the n-fold compound option values the option at time origin t_0 to eventually acquire an asset whose present value is V after making *n* payments K_1, K_2, ...K_n at future times t_1, t_2, ...,t_n respectively. The asset is acquired at t_n. These payments are optional and the investor could choose to terminate this sequential investment strategy at any time t_i by not making the payment K_i and thus giving up the possibility to eventually acquire the asset. K_0 is the initial payment made at t_0 to acquire this n-fold compound option. Each stage or phase *i* begins with the investment K_{i-1} made at t_{i-1} and lasts until all the activities pertinent to that phase are complete and the firm can contemplate the decision on the next incremental investment K_i at t_i. The n-th phase ends with the culminating investment K_n. The value of the investment program at any time *t* during phase *i* is the value of an (*n-i*+1)-fold compound option denoted as $C_i(V,t)$ on the underlying asset where V is the value of the asset at *t*, for *i* =1,2,..*n*. The net present value (NPV) of the multistage investment program is then simply $C_1(V,t_0) - K_0$. The value of $C_1(V,t_0)$ is given by (Cassimon et al., 2004):

$$C_1(V,t_0) = VN_n(a_1,a_2,\dots,a_n;A^n) - \sum_{m=1}^{n} K_m e^{-r(t_m-t_0)} N_m\,(b_1,b_2,\dots,b_m;A^m) \tag{1}$$

where

$$a_i = \frac{\ln\left(\frac{V}{V_i^*}\right) + r\tau_i}{\sigma\sqrt{\tau_i}} + \frac{\sigma\sqrt{\tau_i}}{2}$$

$$b_i = \frac{\ln\left(\frac{V}{V_i^*}\right) + r\tau_i}{\sigma\sqrt{\tau_i}} - \frac{\sigma\sqrt{\tau_i}}{2}$$

$$\tau_i = t_i - t_0$$

r = risk-free rate of interest

N_l is the l-variate standard normal distribution whose correlation matrix A^l is given by:

$A^l = (a_{ij})_{i,j=1,..l}\ with\ \{a_{ii} = 1,\ a_{ij} = a_{ji},\ and\ a_{ij} = \sqrt{\frac{\tau_i}{\tau_j}}\ for\ i < j\}$

V_i^* is given by the solution to the equation:

$$C_{i+1}(V_i^*, t_i) = K_i\ for\ i = 1,2,..,n-1 \qquad (2)$$
$$V_n^* = K_n$$

The firm would choose to embark on this investment strategy if $C_1(V, t_0) > K_0$ where K_0 is the initial investment necessary to trigger the multistage investment program.

The NPV obtained from applying an appropriate options pricing model (OPM) such as the Geske compound option model is also referred to in RO literature as the Strategic Net Present Value (SNPV) or the Expanded NPV (Park & Herath, 2007; Trigeorgis, 2005; Trigeorgis & Mason, 1987) where:

$$SNPV = Passive\ NPV + Value\ of Managerial\ Flexibility \qquad (3)$$

Here, the SNPV is simply $C_1(V, t_0) - K_0$. The passive NPV is the NPV obtained from traditional discounted cash flow analysis where the investment strategy is assumed to be fixed *ex ante*. The difference between SNPV and the passive NPV is the value of managerial flexibility, which in this case arises from the abandonment options embedded in this compound option model since management has the ability to abandon the investment program at any of the times t_1 through t_n. We denote as $\bar{V}$ the expected value at t_n of the asset that generates cash flows, acquired when the terminal payment is made at t_n, and μ is the firm's cost of capital for discounting risky cash flows. Then the present value of the embedded abandonment options is given by Equation (4) as:

$$Value\ of\ abandonment\ options = C_1(\bar{V}e^{-\mu\tau_n}, t_0) - \{\bar{V}e^{-\mu\tau_n} - \textstyle\sum_{j=1}^{n} K_j e^{-r\tau_j}\} \qquad (4)$$

where the second term on the right-hand side of Equation (4) is simply the NPV from traditional discounted cash flow analysis.

Recursive Computation of Compound Option Value

The value of the n-fold Geske compound option is found numerically and we used a Mathematica™ program for this purpose. The value of the compound is found recursively. The SOA program represents a 4-fold compound option because after the investment in the ESB which initiates the program, there are four major investments left. These are the deployment of the DS, DTS, BPMS, and ADPTRS. To find the value of this 4-fold compound option, the program first finds the roots of the non-linear equations:

$$C_{i+1}(V_i^*, t_i) = K_i\ for\ i = \{3,2,1\} \qquad (5)$$

which results in the values V_4^*, V_3^*, V_2^* and V_1^*. Also, from Equation (2), we know that $V_4^* = K_4$. The V_i^* values are obtained successively starting from the end of the time horizon and working backwards since the formula for the compound option during any phase i involves the values $V_i^*,. V_{i+1}^*, \ldots V_4^*$.

Parameter Estimation

The assumptions on the cost and the length of time to deploy and absorb the relevant technologies are given in Table 1. We used industry data from IBM for the costs of the various key technology components shown in Table 1. In particular, the IBM WebSphere product line offers all of these components such as the ESB, DTS, and BPMS (IBM Software Online Catalog, 2010). Therefore, we used the IBM WebSphere price list to populate the cost data in the model. The benefits of SOA arise from the reduced cost of building applications since components of an application can be reused as applications are built as a collection of reusable Web Services. We used a value of $1.2M per application resulting from SOA based on benefits data from Ghosh and Li (2013). We assumed that five applications would be built using SOA. The benefits would of course rise as the firm builds more applications using SOA. We were exploring whether SOA could justified based on a moderate number of applications built using SOA such as five.

Table 1: Technology Deployment and Absorption Times and Costs

Technology Component	Length of Time for Deployment and Absorption (months)	Cost ($)	Value
ESB	3	361,000	
Directory Service	3	118,000	
Data Transformation Service	4	206,000	
Business Process Management Service	6	194,000	
Adapters for Existing Applications	8	250,000	
Integration Applications			6,000,000

A key parameter that needs to be estimated is the volatility in the value of the underlying asset as given by the standard deviation σ in the rate of return on the asset. The issue of estimating σ is not specific to the generalized Geske compound option model described in this article and has been extensively discussed in previous IS literature on the application of RO to IT investments (Bardhan et al., 2004; Benaroch, 2002; Benaroch & Kauffman, 1999; Benaroch et al., 2006; Dos Santos, 1991). One general approach is to use historical data on the standard deviation of the rate of return on similar projects to estimate σ. If in-house projects of a similar nature are not available, another possibility suggested by Benaroch and Kauffman (2000) is to look at the risk characteristics of publicly-traded stocks of vendors of IT products and services used in the IT project being invested in. Bardhan et al. (2004) have suggested an approach for the more accurate assessment of the volatility of individual projects belonging to a portfolio of projects based on computing "spreads" in the value of a project depending on different types of scenarios. Clearly, a number of estimation methods for σ have been discussed in IS literature and the Geske OPM described here can simply leverage these methods. We assumed a risk free rate of 2%, a volatility level of 0.6, and a cost of capital of 12%.

RESULTS

Optimal Deployment Sequence

We varied the sequence of deployment of the technology components in the SOA investment program to find the optimal sequence of deploying the SOA components; subject to the constraint that the program begins with the deployment of the ESB followed by the directory service. The ESB is the backbone on which the exchange of Web Service invocations messages occur. Hence, the ESB has to be implemented first before any Web Service can be called. The directory service is also one of the earliest elements to be deployed as it is crucial to the management of the SOA environment. It identifies the Web Services that are available in the SOA environment. But there is flexibility in how the remaining components of SOA are deployed. We varied the sequence of deployment of the remaining components to see which sequence results in the maximum SNPV. It turned out that the deployment sequence of ESB->DS->DTS->BPM->ADPTRS resulted in the maximum value of $3,826,120. This optimal deployment sequence is shown in Figure 2.

A net value of about $4M for building just five applications using the SOA approach provides a powerful case for implementing SOA. As more applications are built using SOA, the benefits would correspondingly rise.

Sensitivity Analysis

We studied the sensitivity of the results to key parameter values by varying volatility σ and the risk-free rate over a range of low, medium, and high values. In the prevailing climate of relatively low interest rates, we set the low end of the range at 1% and the high end at 6% for the risk-free interest rate. While we had chosen a base case volatility of 0.6, we varied volatility from a low of 0.1 to a high of 1.5. This represents a fairly dramatic change in volatility thus encompassing many different scenarios of possible volatility. In our base case, we had used a risk free rate of 2% and a volatility of 0.6.

The results are shown in Table 2. As expected, since the value of a real option rises with increasing volatility and increasing interest rates (Black & Scholes, 1973), the SOA net value as viewed through an RO lens rises correspondingly. Even though the variation in the parameter values was quite dramatic, the SOA SNPV varied in a $3.7M to $4.2M. Essentially SOA brings about $4M of net value in the medium term during which it is assumed that the firm would build five applications leveraging SOA.

Table 2: Sensitivity Analysis of SNPV of SOA

		σ		
		Low 0.1	Medium 0.4	High 1.5
r	Low 1%	$3,661,680	$3,683,710	$4,227,490
	Medium 3%	$3,780,440	$3,791,700	$4,235,660
	High 6%	$3,914,290	$3,918,190	$4,246,950

Value of the Abandonment Options

We also computed the value of the abandonment options by applying traditional or passive NPV analysis to the SOA program. For the base case, using a risk-free interest rate of 2% and a cost of capital of 12%, the passive NPV is:

$$\begin{aligned} Passive\ NPV = {} & 6000000e^{-0.12(2)} - 361000 - 118000e^{-0.02(0.25)} - 206000e^{-0.02(0.5)} \\ & - 194000e^{-0.02(0.8333)} - 250000e^{-0.02(1.3333)} - 200000 = \$3{,}603{,}190 \end{aligned} \quad (7)$$

Hence, the value of managerial flexibility which is the difference between the SNPV and the passive NPV is $222,930. This arises from the value associated with the options that management has to abandon the SOA build-out program at any of the points $t_1, t_2, \ldots, t_4$. The value of these abandonment options is a non-trivial 6% of the total value of the SOA investment program.

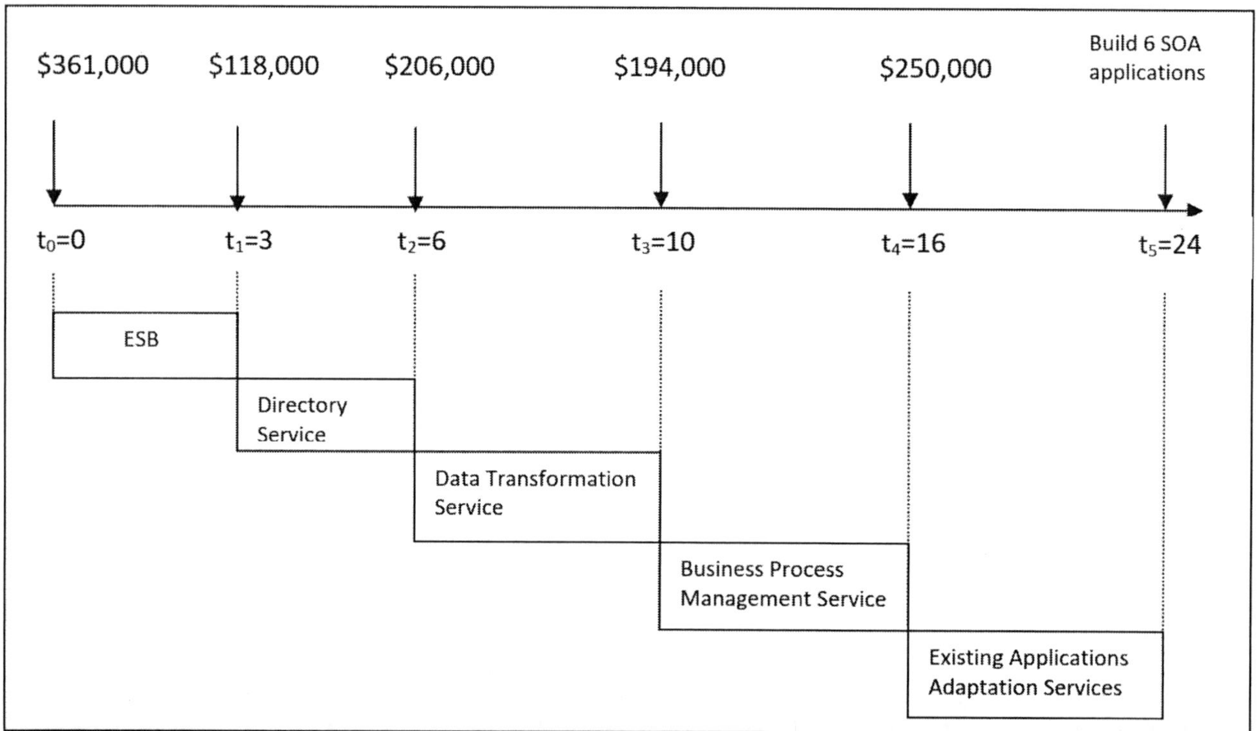

Figure 2: Optimal Deployment Sequence

Discussion of Results

There are two aspects that stand out in the real options analysis of the value of SOA. The first is that the SNPV of the SOA investment program is significant. We found the SNPV from SOA resulting from building just five applications to be around $4M using real-world values of various parameters. This makes a strong case for migrating to SOA. An IT project with a net value of

$4M is a project that any firm, even a major Fortune 500 firm, would find to be an attractive bet. The other aspect that stands out is that the abandonment option actually contributes a non-trivial amount of 6% to the net value of the SOA program. This means that while there is a strong case to be made for embarking on SOA, the firm should not stick to SOA to the bitter end if it turns out that the investment is not returning the value expected of it. A manager implementing SOA would need to explicitly recognize the value of abandonment and manage the program accordingly. A managerial mindfulness of abandonment is actually contrary to how many managers behave, which is why this is a key result which should drive how the SOA program is managed.

IS literature actually shows that managers have the opposite of an abandonment mindfulness. The literature is replete with studies that show that managers are loath to abandon failing IT projects and instead escalate their commitment to such projects (Keil, 1995; Keil et al., 2000; Newman & Sabherwal, 1996; Zmud, 1980). Our study argues from a real options logic that there is a case for embarking on SOA but at the same time the manager needs to shift their mindset from a "stick with the program" mindfulness, which is what the literature shows managers actually do, to an "alertness to abandonment" mindset. We note that recent research does suggest that management indeed gives weight to the real options embedded in an investment strategy (Tiwana et al., 2007). However, this research (Tiwana et al., 2007) speaks to managerial thinking at the point of entry into an investment program, and while it is interesting to note that real options logic does influence the entry, our model for SOA shows that real options logic should drive both the entry and the possible exit from SOA.

CONCLUSION

In this article, we address the key question of what firms should do about SOA. SOA is the key to solving the problem of integrating applications, business processes, databases, and systems that IT organizations have wrestled with for decades. While previous efforts to achieve standards for integration such as CORBA and DCOM failed because of fragmentation of the industry, SOA does appear to have the support from all quarters of the industry. While the vendor support is universal, there have been doubts raised about the value of SOA because some firms have struggled to implement SOA, which has led to calls that "SOA is dead". We show in this article that SOA is far from dead and we encourage firms to make a bet on SOA. We note that while there is a powerful argument to be made for embarking on SOA, firms should not enter into this investment with a "stick to the program at all costs" mindfulness, which is what the literature shows that managers often do. They escalate their commitments to a failing course of action. Managers should instead explicitly recognize that a non-trivial portion of the value of SOA actually comes from the abandonment options embedded in the program.

REFERENCES

Bardhan, I., Bagchi, S., and Sougstad, R. (2004). Prioritizing a portfolio of information technology investment projects. *Journal of Management Information Systems*, 21(2), 33-70.

Benaroch, M. (2002). Managing information technology investment risk: A real options perspective. *Journal of Management Information Systems* 19(2), 43-84.

Benaroch, M., & Kauffman, R.J. (2000). Justifying electronic banking network expansion using real options analysis. *MIS Quarterly*, 24(2), 197-225.

Benaroch, M., Shah, S., & Jeffery, M. (2006). On the valuation of multi-stage information technology investments embedding nested real options. *Journal of Management Information Systems*, 23(1), 239-261.

Black, J., & Scholes, M. (1973). The pricing of options and corporate liabilities. *Journal of Political Economy*, 81(3), 637-654.

Bloomberg, J., & Schmelzer, R. *Service orient or be doomed! – How service orientation will change your business*. Hoboken, NJ: John Wiley and Sons, 2006.

Cassimon, D., Engelen, P.J., Thomassen, L., & Van Wouwe, M. (2004). The valuation of a NDA using a 6-fold compound option. *Research Policy*, 33, 41-51.

DCE Open Group. DCE overview (1996) Available online at <http://www.opengroup.org/dce/info/papers/tog-dce-pd-1296.htm> (accessed on January 22, 2015).

Dos Santos, B. (1991). Justifying investment in new information technologies. *Journal of Management Information Systems*, 7(4), 71-89.

Erl, T. (2006). *Service-oriented architecture (SOA): Concepts, technology, and design*. Upper Saddle Hill River, NJ: Prentice Hall/Pearson Education.

Fiorano ESB (2009). Available online at <http://www.fiorano.com/products/fesb/products_fioranoesb.php> (accessed on April 15, 2009).

Gartner Press Release (2008). Available online at http://www.gartner.com/it/page.jsp?id=790717 (accessed on July 24, 2010).

Geske, R. (1977). The valuation of corporate liabilities as compound options. *Journal of Financial and Quantitative Analysis*, 12, 541-552.

Geske, R. (1979). The valuation of compound options. *Journal of Financial Economics,* 63-81.

Ghosh, S. & Li, X. (2013). A real options model for generalized meta-staged projects – Valuing the migration to SOA. *Information Systems Research*, 24(4), 1011-1027.

IBM Software Online Catalog (2010) Available online at http://www-01.ibm.com/software/info/app/ecatalog/ (retrieved July 4, 2010).

Jensen, K., & Warren, P. (2001). The use of options theory to value research in the service sector. *R&D Management*, 31(2), 173-180.

Keil, M. (1995). Pulling the plug: software project management and the problem of project escalation. *MIS Quarterly*, 19, 421-447.

Keil, M., Mann, J., & Rai, A. (2000). Why software projects escalate: An empirical analysis and test of four theoretical models. *MIS Quarterly*, 24, 631-664.

Krafzig, D., Banke, K., & Slama, D. (2005). *Enterprise SOA – Service oriented architecture best practices*. Upper Saddle Hill River, NJ: Prentice Hall/Pearson Education.

Krill, P. (2009) SOA gets an obituary. InfoWorld <http://www.infoworld.com/article/2675279/applications/soa-gets-an-obituary.html> accessed on May 15, 2016).

Marks, E.A., & Bell, M. (2006). *Service oriented architecture – A planning and implementation guide for business and technology*. Hoboken, NJ: John Wiley and Sons, 2006.

Microsoft BizTalk Server (2007) <http://www.microsoft.com/ biztalk/default.mspx> (accessed on September 23, 2007).

Neubarth, M. 2010. SOA dead or alive? CIO Zone. Available online at <http://www.ciozone.com/index.php/SOA/SOA-Dead-or-Aliveu.html> (accessed on June 24, 2010).

Newman, M., & Sabherwal, R. (1996). Determinants of commitment to information systems development: A longitudinal investigation. *MIS Quarterly* 20, 23-54.

Nguyen, A. (2010). SOA is not dead, says IDC. NetworkWorld. <http://www.networkworld.com/news/2010/032510-soa-is-not-dead-says.html> (accessed on July 23, 2010).

Park, C.S., & Herath, H.S.B. (2000). Exploiting uncertainty – investment opportunities as real options: A new way of thinking in engineering economics. *The Engineering Economist*, 45(1), 1-35.

Paxson, D.A. (2007). Sequential American exchange property options. *Journal of Real Estate Financial Economics*, 34, 135-157.

Perlitz, M., Peske, T., & Schrank, R. (1999). Real options valuation: the new frontier in R&D project evaluation? *R&D Management*, 29(3), 255-269.

Pervasive ETL (2007) <http://ww2.pervasive.com/Integration/ Solutions/ Pages/ETL.aspx> (accessed on October 15, 2007).

Progress Software Sonic ESB (2009) <http://www.sonicsoftware.com/products/ sonic_esb/index.ssp> (accessed on February 14, 2009).

Slama, D., Garbis, J., & Russell, P. (1999) Enterprise CORBA. Upper Saddle River, NJ: Prentice Hall.

SOA Industry Case Studies. 2010. Available online at www.soa-consortium.org/case-study.htm (accessed on May 20, 2010).

SOAP Working Group (2007). SOAP V1.2 specification. Available online at < http://www.w3.org/TR/soap12-part1/#intro> (accessed on February 19, 2009).

Taudes, A. (1998). Software growth options. *Journal of Management Information Systems* 15(1), 165-185.

Taudes, A., Feurstein, M., & Mild, A. (2000). Options analysis of software platform decisions: A case study. *MIS Quarterly*, 24(2), 227-243.

Tiwana, A., Wang, J., Keil, M., & Ahluwalia, P. (2007). The bounded rationality bias in managerial valuation of real options: Theory and evidence from IT projects. *Decision Sciences*, 38(1), 157-181.

Trigeorgis, L. (2005). Making use of real options simple: An overview and applications in flexible/modular decision-making. *The Engineering Economist*, 50, 25-53.

Trigeorgis, L., & Mason, S.P. (1987). Valuing managerial flexibility. *Midland Corporate Financial Journal*, 5(1), 14-21.

UDDI Working Group. (2004). UDDI V3.0.2 specification. Available online at < http://uddi.org/pubs/uddi_v3.htm> (accessed on February 26, 2015).

WSDL Working Group. WSDL 2.0 specification (2007). Available online at < http://www.w3.org/TR/wsdl20-primer/> (accessed on February 27, 2015).

Zmud, R.W. Management of large software efforts. *MIS Quarterly*, 4 (1980), 45-55.

DECISION SCIENCES INSTITUTE

Maximization of Seller's Net Revenue in Discrete Dutch Auctions with Transaction Cost

Full Paper Submission

Zhen Li
Department of Management and Marketing
Middle Tennessee State University, Murfreesboro, TN, USA
E-mail: Zhen.Li@mtsu.edu

Ching-Chung Kuo
Jindal School of Management
University of Texas at Dallas, Richardson, TX, USA
Email: ching-chung.kuo@utdallas.edu

Jinfeng Yue
School of Information Management and Engineering
Shanghai University of Finance and Economics, Shanghai, P.R.China
&
Department of Management and Marketing
Middle Tennessee State University, Murfreesboro, TN, USA
E-mail: Jinfeng.Yue@mtsu.edu

ABSTRACT

This research focuses on the optimal design of discrete Dutch auction to balance the tradeoff between achieving the higher selling price and committing more resources. With consideration of transaction cost incurred by sellers, the objective is to maximize the seller's expected net revenue by determining the optimal number of bid levels and the asking price at each level. The result shows the existence of optimal solutions to the Dutch auction model being considered.

KEYWORDS: Dutch auction; Discrete bid level; Revenue maximization; Transaction cost; Salvage value

INTRODUCTION

In a Dutch auction, the bid price begins at an extremely high value and consecutively decreases according to a predetermined schedule until a bid is made or the reserve price is reached. In the current discrete Dutch auction literature, the expected selling price generally increases with the number of bid levels set. However, the use of more bid levels results in longer duration and higher transaction cost could occur to seller in the longer auctioning process, such as, office administration cost, personnel expenses, storage and maintenance cost. Obviously, there is a tradeoff between achieving the higher selling price and committing more resources. As such, the transaction cast is an important parameter to evaluate the seller's net revenue. In this paper, we consider a more practical objective, which is to maximize the seller's expected net revenue in a discrete Dutch auction by determining the optimal number of bid levels to be set and the asking price at each level.

AUCTION MODEL

We consider a discrete Dutch auction in an independent private value (IPV) setting with symmetric information. Suppose that there are $n \geq 0$ bidders and $m \geq 1$ bid levels $l_1, l_2, ..., l_m$ with $l_1 \leq l_2 \leq ... \leq l_m$. The auctioneer begins with a high asking price l_{m+1} and lowers it to each of $l_m, l_{m-1}, ..., l_2, l_1$ sequentially. The final selling price is l_i if and only if $q \geq 1$ bidders' valuations are in the range $[l_i, l_{i+1})$, no one is willing to pay the higher price l_{i+1} announced previously, and the remaining $n-q$ bidders' valuations are below l_i, $i \in \{1, 2, ..., \mathrm{m}\}$. Suppose that there are $n \geq 0$ bidders and $m \geq 1$ bid levels $l_1, l_2, ..., l_m$ with $l_1 \leq l_2 \leq ... \leq l_m$. The auctioneer begins with a high asking price l_{m+1} and lowers it to each of $l_m, l_{m-1}, ..., l_2, l_1$ sequentially. The final selling price is l_i if and only if $q \geq 1$ bidders' valuations are in the range $[l_i, l_{i+1})$, no one is willing to pay the higher price l_{i+1} announced previously, and the remaining $n-q$ bidders' valuations are below l_i, $i \in \{1, 2, ..., \mathrm{m}\}$. Let *u* be the salvage value, we have $u \leq l_1 \leq l_2 \leq ... \leq l_m$.

As in Li and Kuo (2011, 2013), Cramton et al. (2012), Let each bidder's valuation be drawn from a common uniform distribution $U(0, \bar{v})$, $l_1 = 0$, $l_{m+1} = \bar{v}$, $F(l_1) = 0$ and $F(l_{m+1}) = 1$. Also, let $P(l_i)$ be the probability that the object is sold at l_i, *i* = 1, 2, ..., m, which can be written as

$$\begin{aligned} P(l_i) &= F(l_{i+1})^n - F(l_i)^n \\ &= \left(\frac{l_{i+1}}{\bar{v}}\right)^n - \left(\frac{l_i}{\bar{v}}\right)^n \end{aligned}$$

Let *c* be the transaction cost associated with each bid level. Thus, the seller's expected net revenue, Z_I, can be expressed as the sum of the expected net revenue to auction off the object successfully and the expected net revenue to sell the unsold item in an auction to the strategic shoppers with its salvage value. We have

$$\begin{aligned} Z_\mathrm{I} &= \sum_{i=1}^{m} [l_i - (m+1-i)c] P(l_i) + (u - mc)\left[1 - \sum_{i=1}^{m} P(l_i)\right] \\ &= \sum_{i=1}^{m} l_i \left[\left(\frac{l_{i+1}}{\bar{v}}\right)^n - \left(\frac{l_i}{\bar{v}}\right)^n\right] - c\sum_{i=2}^{m+1}\left(\frac{l_i}{\bar{v}}\right)^n + u\left(\frac{l_1}{\bar{v}}\right)^n \end{aligned}$$

Thus, the discrete Dutch auction in Model I can be formulated as the following NLP:

$$\text{Maximize} \quad Z_{\mathrm{I}} = \sum_{i=1}^{m} l_i \left[\left(\frac{l_{i+1}}{\bar{v}} \right)^n - \left(\frac{l_i}{\bar{v}} \right)^n \right] - c \sum_{i=2}^{m+1} \left(\frac{l_i}{\bar{v}} \right)^n + u \left(\frac{l_1}{\bar{v}} \right)^n$$

$$\text{subject to:} \quad l_{i+1} \geq l_i, \ i = 1, 2, \ldots, \mathrm{m}$$

$$l_1 \geq u$$

$$l_{m+1} = \bar{v}$$

Proposition 1 shows that the objective function is concave, which indicates the existence of optimal solution.

Proposition 1: $Z_{\mathrm{I}} = \sum_{i=1}^{m} l_i \left[\left(\frac{l_{i+1}}{\bar{v}} \right)^n - \left(\frac{l_i}{\bar{v}} \right)^n \right] - c \sum_{i=2}^{m+1} \left(\frac{l_i}{\bar{v}} \right)^n + u \left(\frac{l_1}{\bar{v}} \right)^n$ is concave in $(l_1, l_2, \ldots, l_m)$.

NUMERICAL EXAMPLES AMD ANALYSIS

In this section, we solve a set of problem instances to investigate the impact of the model parameters on the auction outcome. Specifically, it is assumed that the bidder's valuation follows an uniform distribution *U*(0,1), i.e., $\bar{v} = 1$. In addition, let the number of bid levels be $m \in \{1, 2, .., 9\}$, the number of bidders be $n \in \{5, 10, 20, 30, 40, 50\}$, the salvage value be $u \in \{0, 0.1, 0.2, \ldots, 0.8\}$, and the transaction cost per bid level be $c \in \{0.05, 0.1, 0.15, 0.2, .., 0.4\}$. The NLPs based on the various combinations of *m*, *n* (or *λ*), *u* and *c* with $\bar{v} = 1$ are set up and solved by running LINGO.

Table 1 shows the seller's expected net revenues with *u* = 0.1 and *c* = 0.15. The highest Z_{I}^* among all *m* levels for each *n* value is highlighted.

n	$Z^*_{\mathrm{I},\, m=1}$	$Z^*_{\mathrm{I},\, m=2}$	$Z^*_{\mathrm{I},\, m=3}$	$Z^*_{\mathrm{I},\, m=4}$	$Z^*_{\mathrm{I},\, m=5}$	$Z^*_{\mathrm{I},\, m=6}$	$Z^*_{\mathrm{I},\, m=7}$	$Z^*_{\mathrm{I},\, m=8}$	$Z^*_{\mathrm{I},\, m=9}$
5	0.4501	0.4979	0.5061	**0.5069**	0.5068	0.5067	0.5067	0.5067	0.5067
10	0.5749	0.6249	0.6333	0.6346	**0.6348**	0.6348	0.6348	0.6348	0.6348
20	0.6729	0.7130	0.7182	0.7188	**0.7189**	0.7189	0.7189	0.7189	0.7189
30	0.7165	0.7490	0.7524	0.7527	**0.7528**	0.7528	0.7528	0.7528	0.7528
40	0.7417	0.7689	0.7713	**0.7716**	0.7716	0.7716	0.7716	0.7716	0.7716
50	0.7583	0.7818	0.7836	**0.7837**	0.7837	0.7837	0.7837	0.7837	0.7837

Table 1 Z_{I}^* vs. *n* and *m* with $\bar{v}$ = 1, *u* = 0.1 and *c* = 0.15[#].

[#] $Z^*_{\mathrm{I},\, m=a}$ denotes the seller's maximum expected net revenue based on Model I with *α* bid levels.

CONCLUSIONS

This research focuses on the optimal design of discrete Dutch auction with consideration of the transaction cost incurred by sellers. The main objective is to maximize the seller's expected net revenue by determining the optimal number of bid levels and the asking price at each level. Although all of the above results make intuitive sense and have managerial implications, there are several limitations in which the present paper may be extended. For one thing, we assume that the risk-averse bidders will bid based on their valuations. It happen in fast Dutch auctions, and bidders have little time to reevaluate their valuations since the price declines very fast. However, in the case of slow Dutch auctions, bidders may not bid truthfully based on their valuations. We are curious about the impact of the auction speed on the bidder's behavior and the optimal Dutch auction design.

(Proof od propositions is available upon requests from the authors.)

REFERENCES

Cramton, P., Filiz-Ozbay, E., Ozbay, E., Sujarittanonta, P., 2012. Discrete clock auctions: An experimental study. Experimental Economics 15(2), 309 – 322.

Li, Z., Kuo, C.-C., 2011. Revenue-maximizing Dutch auctions with discrete bid levels. European Journal of Operational Research 215(3), 721 – 729.

Li, Z., Kuo, C.-C., 2013. Design of discrete Dutch auctions with an uncertain number of bidders. Annals Operations Research 211(1), 255 – 272.

DECISION SCIENCES INSTITUTE

Measuring the Impact of a Web-Based Blended Learning Platform on Student Learning

Tuncay Bayrak
Western New England University
tbayrak@wne.edu

Bahadir Akcam
Western New England University
bahadir.akcam@wne.edu

ABSTRACT

This study reports on how web-based learning platforms provide opportunities for students to leverage the capabilities of various information and communication technologies to engage in self-directed learning. Because the delivery of course content over such platforms may be a challenge for students, the impact of a blended simulation based learning environment should be studied. The purpose of this study is to measure the impact of a web-based blended learning platform on student learning.

KEYWORDS: Simulation based learning; Computer based training and assessment; Technology-mediated learning; End-user Satisfaction

INTRODUCTION

Various higher education institutions have deploying and implementing web-based learning platforms in blended online learning environments to help students develop positive learning experiences. In addition, since they are committed to improving student access to quality learning materials, more and more higher education institutions are making use of various blended online learning environments to directly support learning and teaching. Although there are numerous web-based options available for training and testing students, they all play an important role in enhancing students' learning experiences. One such tool is MyITLab from Pearson Education that trains and tests essential Microsoft Office skills.

Blended online learning platforms are often employed to enhance student learning experiences, and to provide them with interactive and more engaging learning experiences. However, such tools also allow instructors to create and organize online lessons, enhance classroom teaching, administer and deliver custom quizzes, tests and examinations. Further, they also provide instructors with a computer based assessment platform where they can automatically and quickly track student progress and analyze test results.

Web-based blended learning platforms provide opportunities for students to leverage the capabilities of various information and communication technologies to engage in self-directed learning. Nevertheless, in order for the blended online learning environments to be useful, such factors as user interface specifications, and technical and pedagogical factors should be analyzed. Because the delivery of course content over such platforms may be a challenge for students, the impact of a blended simulation based learning environment should be studied.

The purpose of the study is to develop an instrument to measure the impact of a web-based blended learning platform on student learning. In this study, we propose to customize the original instrument for end-user computing satisfaction by Doll and Torkzadeh (1988) to measure student learning. This study summarizes the key finding from a survey undertaken at a private university located in the Northeast USA.

LITERATURE REVIEW

Identifying the success factors behind the use of computer technologies in organizations has been an important objective of researchers. Some research frameworks such as the Information Systems Success Model (DeLone & McLean, 1992; 2003) focus on the relationship between user attitude, technology, information and net benefits to organization and individuals. Other frameworks such as the Technology Acceptance Model (Davis, 1989; Davis, Bagozzi, & Warshaw, 1989; Doll & Torkzadeh, 1988) specifically focus on user acceptance and satisfaction .

With the increasing role of information technologies in the learning domain, researchers have tried to understand the effectiveness of such technologies in education context. Enhanced classroom, blended learning, and fully online learning are three major forms of e-learning (Garrison & Kanuka, 2004, p. 97). Technologies such as computers, computer networks, projectors, smart boards or handset systems are often employed to enhance classroom activities in enhanced classroom form of e-learning (Draper, Cargill, & Cutts, 2002). Fully online learning such as massive open online courses (MOOCs) does not have in class activities (Rodriguez, 2012). Blended learning represents a learning experience based on a combination of face-to-face learning and online learning. While this categorization of different types of e-learning is useful for distinguishing different uses of technology in education, fully online learning systems advocates have been trying to blend the advantages of in class learning experience with new system features (Byrne, 2014). Our research is based on a blended learning course setting.

Twigg (2003) defines four categories for blended learning: replacement, supplemental, emporium and buffet. In the replacement model, face-to-face class activities are replaced with online activities and class time is reduced. In the supplemental model, online resources are provided as a supplemental source without reducing the class time. Students heavily depend on the online lectures in the emporium model, but they can access a learning resource center to get help. In the buffet model, student can choose among face-to-face and online modules depending on their needs and preferences. Our research setting best fits the supplemental model among these categories. In our research setting, class time was not reduced and instructors used the online resource as a supplemental tool.

In addition to the traditional information systems success research, the education context brought new dimensions related to the dynamics of learning such as learning methods or models. For instance, in their Adaptive Structuration Theory, DeSanctis and Poole (1994) proposes a theoretical model for technology-mediated learning. Gupta and Bostrom (2009) identified learning methods as part of the structural impact. Piccoli et al. (2001) developed a framework for virtual learning environment effectiveness and included learning models as part of the design dimension. Design and human dimensions determine the effectiveness of the virtual learning environment in their study. Bitzer et al. (2012, p. 3) developed a conceptual productivity framework based on Information Success Model (Delone & McLean, 2003), the productivity concept (Grönroos & Ojasalo, 2004), and the learning success theory (Kirkpatrick & Kirkpatrick, 2005).

Despite these research frameworks, Bitzer et al. (2012) indicate that current technology-mediated learning research is not organized around a pivotal theoretical foundation. According to their literature review of 91 peer-reviewed research articles; 56 studies did not have a theoretical foundation and remaining 35 studies cited a theoretical foundation 51 times. Information Systems Success Model (Delone & McLean, 2003) or Technology Acceptance Model (Davis, 1989) were cited only eight times (Bitzer et al., 2012). In their study based on the Information Systems Success Model for e-learning systems, Freezer et al. (2010) report that system quality and information quality indirectly impact the system success, mainly through user satisfaction. In our study, we explore the effectiveness of the technology-mediated learning environment from a pure end-user satisfaction perspective (Doll & Torkzadeh, 1988, 1991). Major constructs of this perspective (content, accuracy, format, ease of use, and timeliness) are also explored.

Information systems (IS) scholars in business schools took the lead in exploring the technology-mediated business education in the early 1990s (Alavi, 1994; Alavi, Wheeler, & Valacich, 1995; Leidner & Jarvenpaa, 1993, 1995), developed frameworks linking technology applications to learning theories (Leidner & Jarvenpaa, 1995), and initially reported promising results (Arbaugh et al., 2009, p. 72). Arbaugh et al. (2009, p. 74) acknowledge the fact that IS scholars actively developed conceptual frameworks, but they were not as active in testing them.

Arbaugh et al. (2009) explored the state of research of online and blended in the business disciplines by examining 182 articles. There is a dramatic increase in volume and quality of research with uneven distribution across business disciplines and reached similar conclusions with Bitzer et al. (2012). They indicated *"the range of untested conceptual frameworks and the lack of discipline-specific theories"* as ample opportunities for scholars in the business field (Arbaugh et al., 2009, p. 71).

Exploring the role of online learning in business education, Rungtusanatham et al. (2004) define four types of online distance education based on content-related, delivery-related, and learning-related issues: Overview Model, Overview Model with Feedback, Technical-Skills Model, and Managerial Learning Model. In our research, students explored content-related, delivery-related and learning-related issues by evaluating factors such as quality of materials, technology ease of use and technology reliability. In terms of four models, Overview Model employs technology like a webcast with limited or not interaction. Overview Model with Feedback introduces feedback capability to the preceding model. Technical-Skills model focuses on the development of competency such as learning a spreadsheet tool as in our research with a feedback capability. Managerial Learning Model addresses more complex topics by focusing on open-ended situations. Our research setting best fits the Managerial Learning Model in terms of students' interaction with the technology to learn a skill, apply it, and test it. But the technology also offers course videos without a feedback capability as in the Overview Model along with the simulation capabilities.

Many introductory information systems courses feature spreadsheet and database applications and simulation based training assessment tools are frequently used in all modes of e-learning. Murphy et al. (2012) indicates that these tools are also effective tools for measuring assurance of learning standards for accredited business schools. Literature on the role of simulation based training and assessment tools in technology-mediated learning frequently referred several tools such as "Skills Assessment Manager" (SAM by Cengage Learning), SimNet (McGraw-Hill), and MyITLab (Pearson) (Hill, 2011). One of the common themes in the literature is the use of these tools in student skill assessment in such courses (Serwatka, 2003) to measure initial skill level of students and to determine exempt status of students for a given course (Tesch, Murphy, & Crable, 2006; Wallace & Clariana, 2005). Such initial assessment is important given the significant misperception of students on their spreadsheet skills at the beginning of such courses (Grant, Malloy, & Murphy, 2009). These tools have more capabilities. For instance, they can simulate a lecture with verbal guidance, provide interactive training with behavioral modeling, offer individual trials without help, and grade the submitted work (Hardin, Looney, & Fuller, 2014, p. 8).

Researchers compared the effectiveness of these tools in different learning forms. Comparing the traditional classroom form to the blended learning form; while some research reported lower attrition rates, lower failure rate, and higher student satisfaction in blended form than in traditional form (Cooper, 2011), other research reported no significant difference between traditional and blended learning forms, despite slightly higher performance (Kakish, Pollacia, & Heinz, 2011) or favorable student rating (Napier, Dekhane, & Smith, 2011) in blended classrooms. Comparing the fully online mode to the blended and traditional classroom modes; one study by Davies, Dean and Ball (2013) reports that blended and traditional form is more effective than the fully online form. Students are frustrated with the simulation's instruction and assessments and they are less likely to take another course in fully online form. Another study (Piccoli et al., 2001) reports some conflicting results that there is no significant difference between fully online and traditional classrooms in terms of performance, but students in the fully online form reported higher computer self-efficiency. Similar to the previous study, participants reported less satisfaction with the learning process in the fully online form.

METHODOLOGY

Research Method and Data Collection

This study was carried out at a private university located in the Northeast USA. The questionnaire was administrated to the entire student population who had enrolled in a required Business Information Systems (BIS) course. The course was required for every student in the College of Business regardless of their majors. The questionnaire was posted on each section's virtual classroom by the instructors at the end of the semester. The survey was administrated after the final grades had been turned in by the instructors so students' decision to participate in the study had no impact on their final grades. Students were informed that they had the right not to participate in the study.

The impact of the interactive learning environment on improving students' essential Microsoft Office skills was measured using a previously validated structured questionnaire adapted from Doll and Torkzadeh (1988), consisting of five subscales: content, accuracy, format, ease of use, and timeliness. Having analyzed the instrument, the authors decided to modify it to incorporate two more measures of overall reliability and satisfaction to capture students' overall satisfaction level with the tool. Once we added the two measures to the survey, we generated 24 items to measure the impact of the tool they used throughout the semester. A number of items in the questionnaire had to be reworded in reference to MyITLab. Overall, 24 items are used to measure and students' perceptions of the tool content, accuracy, format, ease of use, timeliness, reliability and satisfaction. A five-point Likert-type scale was used in the questionnaire where 1=strongly disagree and 5=strongly agree (Appendix A).

Students were informed by their instructors that their participation was voluntary and the confidentiality of their identity in the survey would be maintained. Students were asked to rate the extent to which they agree with each statement in the survey by circling a number from one to five

Sample Profile

The survey of this study was conducted on students who enrolled in a required BIS course. Although the total number of students enrolled in all sections of the same course was 231, responses were obtained from 144 students, for a 62% response rate. Students are first classified based on their gender. As seen in table 1, 70 percent of the students who enrolled in the course are males and the remaining 30 percent are females. Students are also categorized based on the year in which they took the course. 78 percent took the course in their freshmen year and 22 percent took it in their sophomore year. Because it is a required course for every student in the College of Business regardless of their majors, students were also tallied based on their majors. Students' major ranged from Accounting to Exploratory. Table 1 summarizes the data pertaining to students' major, gender, and year.

Table 1: Sample Characteristics

Item	Category	Frequency	Percent	Cumulative percent
Gender	Male	102	70.00	70.00
	Female	42	30.00	100.00
Year	Freshman	112	78.00	78.00
	Sophomore	32	22.00	100.00
Major	Accounting	20	14.00	14.00
	Finance	17	12.00	26.00
	General Business	10	7.00	33.00
	Management and Leadership	17	12.00	45.00
	Marketing /Marketing Comm.	9	6.00	51.00
	Sport Management	28	19.00	70.00
	Exploratory	35	24.00	94.00
	Other	8	6.00	100.00

Internal Consistency, Convergent Validity, and Discriminant Validity

We first computed simple descriptive statistics summaries such as mean and standard deviation about the sample. As seen in Table 2, overall, while item S4 in the satisfaction category attained the lowest mean value, item T2 in the timelines category attained the highest mean value.
The instrument employed in this study was previously validated, however; since we added two more measures to the instrument, we decided to revalidate it. Thus, the instrument was examined to assess its reliability and validity. Because Cronbach's alpha coefficient is considered to provide an unbiased estimate of internal consistency, we first computed the internal consistency reliability values for the entire instrument as well as for each construct using Cronbach's alpha. Cronbach's alpha values in this study range from 0.85 (accuracy) to 0.95 (reliability) (Table 2). The entire instrument attained a Cronbach's alpha value of 0.97. Although the theoretical value of alpha varies from zero to 1, in this study all alpha values are greater than the recommended value of 0.70 (Nunnally and Bernstein, 1994).
The instrument was also assessed using factor analysis, which is often performed to assess variability among observed variables. In this study, we employed principal components as the means of extraction. In order to confirm that independent variables are represented by a particular factor, factor loadings should be greater than 0.70. Factor loadings range from 0.736 (item A1) to 0.976 (items R1 and R2). As reported in table 2, all factor loadings exceed the

recommended threshold value of 0.7 (Nunnally and Bernstein, 1994), which indicates that the instrument used in this study seems to possess good construct validity.

The convergent validity was also assessed. Fornell and Larcker (1981), and Bagozzi and Yi (1988) suggest the average variance extracted (AVE) and individual item reliabilities may be used to assess convergent validity of an instrument. The AVE values range from 0.70 (accuracy) to reliability (0.95). Similarly, item reliabilities range from 0.541 (A1) to 0.951 (R1 and R2). All AVE values are well above the recommended value of 0.5 (Fornell and Larcker 1981), and the item reliability for each item exceeds the commonly used benchmark of 0.5 (Fornell and Larcker 1981), indicating that the revised instrument employed in this study demonstrates a high degree of convergent validity.

Table 2: Factor loading, item reliability, corrected-item-to-total correlation, reliability, AVE

Construct	Item Code (Variable)	Factor Loading	Item Reliability	Item-to-total correlation	Mean	SD	Cronbach's α	AVE
Content	C1	0.855	0.731	0.769	3.71	0.96	0.92	0.76
	C2	0.911	0.830	0.850	3.67	0.95		
	C3	0.873	0.762	0.795	3.56	0.98		
	C4	0.840	0.706	0.753	3.60	1.02		
	C5	0.868	0.754	0.790	3.59	0.96		
Accuracy	A1	0.736	0.541	0.575	3.53	1.12	0.85	0.70
	A2	0.875	0.765	0.751	3.65	1.05		
	A3	0.876	0.768	0.755	3.35	1.16		
	A4	0.857	0.735	0.724	3.75	0.98		
Format	F1	0.890	0.792	0.797	3.76	0.87	0.91	0.80
	F2	0.848	0.719	0.739	3.69	0.98		
	F3	0.936	0.876	0.876	3.75	0.87		
	F4	0.905	0.819	0.822	3.76	0.92		
Ease of Use	E1	0.951	0.905	0.888	3.52	1.15	0.94	0.89
	E2	0.944	0.891	0.872	3.59	1.12		
	E3	0.930	0.865	0.846	3.57	1.13		
Timeliness	T1	0.949	0.901	0.712	3.85	0.91	0.89	0.90
	T2	0.949	0.901	0.671	3.97	0.86		
Reliability	R1	0.976	0.952	0.812	3.55	1.13	0.95	0.95
	R2	0.976	0.952	0.841	3.44	1.23		
Satisfaction	S1	0.911	0.829	0.840	3.45	1.19	0.94	0.85
	S2	0.948	0.899	0.902	3.03	1.22		
	S3	0.951	0.904	0.908	3.06	1.24		
	S4	0.886	0.785	0.804	2.75	1.27		

We also assessed discriminant validity of the instrument to see whether seven constructs are, in fact, unrelated and truly distinct from each other. Discriminant validity can be assessed using the AVE values and the correlations between the constructs. (Fornell and Larcker 1981) suggests that discriminant validity is achieved when the AVE value for a construct is greater than the corresponding squared correlation between two constructs.
To demonstrate discriminant validity we first computed the correlations between the variables. Table 3 summarizes the correlation matrix. As seen in table 3, correlations between constructs range from 0.582 (timeliness-accuracy) to 0.814 (reliability-ease of use).

Table 3: Pair-wise Construct Correlations

Variables	Content	Accuracy	Format	Ease of Use	Timeliness	Reliability	Satisfaction
Content	1.000						
Accuracy	0.687	1.000					
Format	0.695	0.645	1.000				
Ease of Use	0.695	0.744	0.660	1.000			
Timeliness	0.650	0.582	0.601	0.644	1.000		
Reliability	0.654	0.760	0.602	0.814	0.628	1.000	
Satisfaction	0.729	0.759	0.628	0.776	0.622	0.793	1.000

Table 4 summarizes squared correlations among seven factors/variables and the AVE value for each construct. In table 4, off-diagonal elements are the squared correlations between constructs, and diagonal elements are the AVE value for each variable. As seen, the AVE value for each construct is greater than the corresponding squared correlation between the constructs. These numbers demonstrate a high degree of discriminant validity for all seven factors used in this study.

Table 4: Squares of Correlations

Variables	Content	Accuracy	Format	Ease of Use	Timeliness	Reliability	Satisfaction
Content	**0.76**						
Accuracy	0.472	**0.70**					
Format	0.483	0.416	**0.80**				
Ease of Use	0.483	0.554	0.436	**0.89**			
Timeliness	0.423	0.339	0.361	0.415	**0.90**		
Reliability	0.428	0.578	0.362	0.663	0.394	**0.95**	
Satisfaction	0.531	0.576	0.394	0.602	0.387	0.629	**0.85**

ANALYSES AND RESULTS

Having assessed the instrument's validity and reliability through a survey, the impact of a web-based blended learning platform on student learning was further analyzed using a number of factors such as students' gender, major, and the year in which they took the course. All analyses performed in this section were carried out at a significance level of .05.

Since the course in which we employed a web-based learning platform is required for all students regardless of their major, we first assessed students' perception based on the year in which they took the course. While 78 percent took it in their freshmen year, the remaining 22 percent had to take the course in their sophomore year. We ran a t-test to investigate if freshmen and sophomore had significantly different experiences with MyITLab used in this study. As seen in table 5, since the p-value, 0.590, is greater than the level of significance, 0.05, it cannot be concluded that freshmen and sophomore had significantly different satisfaction level and perception of the web-based learning platform employed in this study. Results indicate that the mean values for freshmen and sophomore are not significantly different, allowing us to conclude that the year in which student had to take the course is not an important factor.

Table 5: Freshmen vs. Sophomore: t-test results

	Freshmen	Sophomore	
Construct	Mean	Mean	P-value
Content	3.64	3.58	
Accuracy	3.60	3.48	
Format	3.77	3.63	
Ease of Use	3.57	3.51	0.590
Timeliness	3.90	3.92	
Reliability	3.52	3.41	
Satisfaction	3.09	3.02	
Grand Mean	3.58	3.51	

Students' satisfaction level and perceptions of the tool were also analyzed based on students' major. As seen in table 6, while those who major in Sport Management (MSP) reported the lowest satisfaction level, those who major in Exploratory Business (EXBUS) reported the highest satisfaction level with the web-based learning platform. We ran an ANOVA test to explore if the eight mean values across the various majors were significantly different. Since the F value, 2,46, is greater than the F-critical value, 2.20, we conclude that there is a significant difference among eight mean values, indicating that a student's major does affect his/her satisfaction level with the web-based learning platform (table 6).

Table 6: Students' major and ANOVA test results

	ACT	EXBUS	FIN	GBUS	MLE	MSP	MKT	OTHER			
Construct	Mean	Mean	Mean	Mean	Mean	Mean	Mean	Mean	F	P-value	F critical
Content	3.74	3.80	3.82	3.26	3.54	3.35	3.64	3.73			
Accuracy	3.56	3.79	3.78	3.48	3.43	3.41	3.25	3.53			
Format	4.00	3.84	3.65	3.70	3.51	3.71	3.61	3.59			
Ease of Use	3.85	3.77	3.57	3.43	3.49	3.27	3.22	3.58	2.46	0.03	2.20
Timeliness	4.08	4.04	3.85	3.75	4.03	3.63	3.56	4.31			
Reliability	3.78	3.77	3.53	3.55	3.26	2.98	3.56	3.69			
Satisfaction	3.14	3.41	3.35	2.80	2.93	2.63	3.00	3.06			
Grand Mean	3.73	3.78	3.65	3.42	3.46	3.28	3.41	3.64			

Multiple sections of the same course were offered by six different instructors in the same semester. Although the instructors were of the same gender, we postulated that students taking the same course with different instructors would report different satisfaction level with the tool.

Table 7: ANOVA test results for student satisfaction level and instructors.

	1	2	3	4	5	6			
Construct	Mean	Mean	Mean	Mean	Mean	Mean	F	P-value	F critical
Content	3.79	3.26	3.77	3.72	3.69	3.59			
Accuracy	3.83	3.46	3.75	3.48	3.29	3.52			
Format	3.73	3.63	3.94	3.75	3.65	3.67			
Ease of Use	3.89	2.99	3.69	3.77	3.41	3.66	4.827	0.001	2.477
Timeliness	4.07	3.58	4.15	3.92	3.65	3.92			
Reliability	3.97	3.04	3.64	3.65	3.24	3.53			
Satisfaction	3.62	2.53	3.19	3.25	3.10	3.01			
Grand Mean	3.84	3.21	3.73	3.65	3.43	3.56			

To make a comparison among the students in terms of their satisfaction level, we carried out an ANOVA test. As seen in table 7, while students who took the course with instructor 1 reported the highest satisfaction level, students who took the same course with instructor 2 reported the lowest satisfaction level. Since the p-value, 0.001, is smaller than the level of significance, 0.05, the ANOVA test we carried out suggests that the six mean values are significantly different from one another. Similarly, since the F value, 4.827, is greater than the F critical value, 2.477, it can be concluded that students taking the same course with different instructors experienced significantly different satisfaction level. Hence, instructor is an important factor in determining students' satisfaction level with the tool.

An assumption we made was that students who struggled a lot in the course would report the lowest satisfaction level with the web-based learning tool. However, as seen in table 8, they seem to be the most satisfied student group (mean=3.99). Student who attained a "D" as their final grade reported the lowest satisfaction level. To investigate if the five mean values, as summarized in table 8, are statistically and significantly different, we ran an ANOVA test.

Table 8: Final grade and student satisfaction level.

	A	B	C	D	F			
Construct	Mean	Mean	Mean	Mean	Mean	F	P-value	F critical
Content	3.73	3.58	3.56	3.28	3.60			
Accuracy	3.59	3.55	3.43	3.80	4.13			
Format	3.82	3.71	3.63	3.45	4.00			
Ease of Use	3.58	3.54	3.49	3.53	4.33	3.88	0.0116	2.69
Timeliness	4.02	3.81	3.84	3.80	4.25			
Reliability	3.49	3.47	3.51	3.70	4.00			
Satisfaction	3.01	3.08	3.21	2.85	3.63			
Grand Mean	3.61	3.53	3.52	3.49	3.99			

Since the p-value, 0.0116, is less than the level of significance, and the F value, 3.88, is greater than the F-critical value, we reject our initial assumption and conclude that there is a significant difference among the students in terms of their final grades they attained.

We hypothesized that males would report a higher satisfaction level compared to their female counterparts as computers are perceived as being a male domain. As seen in table 9, it was not the case as both males and females reported the same satisfaction level. To further investigate the data we carried out a t-test. Since the p-value, 0.990 is way greater than the default level of significance, 0.05, it may be concluded that there is no difference between males and females in the course in terms of their satisfaction level (table 9).

Table 9: Gender and satisfaction level.

	Male	Female	
Construct	Mean	Mean	P-value
Content	3.65	3.55	
Accuracy	3.56	3.60	
Format	3.69	3.86	
Ease of Use	3.55	3.59	0.990
Timeliness	3.87	4.00	
Reliability	3.51	3.45	
Satisfaction	3.13	2.92	
Grand Mean	3.57	3.57	

DISCUSSIONS AND CONCLUSION

Although various higher education institutions have been deploying and making use of web-based learning tools to provide their students with better learning experiences, they should be more comprehensively and carefully assessed and analyzed to see whether such tools have negative or positive impact on students' learning and how they affect their learning experiences.

In this study, we made an attempt to redesign a previously designed instrument and validate it through a survey. However, to improve its validity and reliability, this study should be repeated with larger sample sizes. In addition, given that this study was conducted in just one institutions in one semester, there is a need for further research to test the generalizability of our findings.

REFERENCES

Alavi, M. (1994). Computer-mediated collaborative learning: An empirical evaluation. *MIS Quarterly*, 159–174.

Alavi, M., Wheeler, B. C., & Valacich, J. S. (1995). Using IT to reengineer business education: An exploratory investigation of collaborative telelearning. *MIS Quarterly*, 293–312.

Arbaugh, J. B., Godfrey, M. R., Johnson, M., Pollack, B. L., Niendorf, B., & Wresch, W. (2009). Research in online and blended learning in the business disciplines: Key findings and possible future directions. *The Internet and Higher Education*, *12*(2), 71–87.

Bagozzi, R.R., and Yi,Y. (1988). On the evaluation of structured equation models, *Journal of the Academy of Marketing Science*, 16(1), 74-94.

Bitzer, P., Lehmann, K., & Marco Leimeister, J. (2012). A Literature review on indicators for the measurement of technology mediated learning productivity: 2000 to 2011. Retrieved from http://aisel.aisnet.org/amcis2012/proceedings/ISEducation/30/

Byrne, J. A. (2014, March 21). Harvard B-school dips its toe into online education - Fortune Management. Retrieved from http://management.fortune.cnn.com/2014/03/21/harvard-business-online-education/

Cooper, G. (2011). Integrating MyItLab in an introductory computer applications course. In *Proceedings of the World Congress in Computer Science, Computer Engineering and Applied Computing*. Retrieved from http://weblidi.info.unlp.edu.ar/worldcomp2011-mirror/FEC3882.pdf

Davies, R. S., Dean, D. L., & Ball, N. (2013). Flipping the classroom and instructional technology integration in a college-level information systems spreadsheet course. *Educational Technology Research and Development*, *61*(4), 563–580.

Davis, F. D. (1989). Perceived usefulness, perceived ease of use, and user acceptance of information technology. *MIS Quarterly*, *13*(3), 318–340.

Davis, F. D., Bagozzi, R. P., & Warshaw, P. R. (1989). User acceptance of computer technology: a comparison of two theoretical models. *Management Science*, *35*(8), 982–1003.

DeLone, W. H., & McLean, E. R. (1992). Information systems success: the quest for the dependent variable. *Information Systems Research*, *3*(1), 60–95.

Delone, W. H., & McLean, E. R. (2003). The DeLone and McLean model of information systems success: A ten-year update. *Journal of Management Information Systems*, *19*(4), 9–30.

DeSanctis, G., & Poole, M. S. (1994). Capturing the complexity in advanced technology use: adaptive structuration theory. *Organization Science*, *5*(2), 121–121.

Doll, W. J., & Torkzadeh, G. (1988). The measurement of end-user computing satisfaction. *MIS Quarterly*, *12*(2), 259–272.

Doll, W. J., & Torkzadeh, G. (1991). The measurement of end-user computing satisfaction: theoretical and methodological issues. *MIS Quarterly*, *15*(1), 5–10.

Draper, S., Cargill, J., & Cutts, Q. (2002). Electronically enhanced classroom interaction. *Australian Journal of Educational Technology*, *18*(1), 13–23.

Freeze, R. D., Alshare, K. A., Lane, P. L., & Wen, H. J. (2010). IS Success model in e-learning context based on students' perceptions. *Journal of Information Systems Education*, *21*(2).

Garrison, D. R., & Kanuka, H. (2004). Blended learning: Uncovering its transformative potential in higher education. *The Internet and Higher Education*, *7*(2), 95–105.

Grant, D. M., Malloy, A. D., & Murphy, M. C. (2009). A Comparison of student perceptions of their computer skills to their actual abilities. *Journal of Information Technology Education, 8.*

Grönroos, C., & Ojasalo, K. (2004). Service productivity: towards a conceptualization of the transformation of inputs into economic results in services. *Journal of Business Research, 57*(4), 414–423.

Gupta, S., & Bostrom, R. P. (2009). Technology-mediated learning: a comprehensive theoretical model. *Journal of the Association for Information Systems, 10*(9).

Hardin, A. M., Looney, C. A., & Fuller, M. A. (2014). Self-efficacy, learning method appropriation and software skills acquisition in learner-controlled CSSTS environments. *Information Systems Journal, 24*(1), 3–27. http://doi.org/10.1111/isj.12016

Hill, T. G. (2011). Word grader and powerpoint grader. *ACM Inroads, 2*(2), 34–36.

Kakish, K. M., Pollacia, L., & Heinz, a. (2011). Analysis of the effectiveness of traditional versus hybrid student performance for an introductory computing course. Retrieved from http://proc.conisar.org/2011/pdf/1805.pdf

Kirkpatrick, D., & Kirkpatrick, J. (2005). *Transferring learning to behavior: Using the four levels to improve performance*. Berrett-Koehler Publishers.

Leidner, D. E., & Jarvenpaa, S. L. (1993). The information age confronts education: Case studies on electronic classrooms. *Information Systems Research, 4*(1), 24–54.

Leidner, D. E., & Jarvenpaa, S. L. (1995). The use of information technology to enhance management school education: A theoretical view. *MIS Quarterly*, 265–291.

Murphy, M. C., Sharma, A., & Rosso, M. (2012). Measuring assurance of learning goals: effectiveness of computer training and assessment tools. *Information Systems Education Journal, 10*(5), 87.

Napier, N. P., Dekhane, S., & Smith, S. (2011). Transitioning to blended learning: understanding student and faculty perceptions. *Journal of Asynchronous Learning Networks, 15*(1).

Nunnally, J. C., & Bernstein, I. (1994). Psychometry Theory. McGraw Hill, New York.

Piccoli, G., Ahmad, R., & Ives, B. (2001). Web-based virtual learning environments: a research framework and a preliminary assessment of effectiveness in basic IT skills training. *MIS Quarterly*, 25(4), 401. http://doi.org/10.2307/3250989

Rodriguez, C. O. (2012). MOOCs and the AI-stanford like courses: two successful and distinct course formats for massive open online courses. *European Journal of Open, Distance and E-Learning*. Retrieved from http://files.eric.ed.gov/fulltext/EJ982976.pdf.

Rungtusanatham, M., Ellram, L. M., Siferd, S. P., & Salik, S. (2004). Toward a typology of business education in the internet age. *Decision Sciences Journal of Innovative Education, 2*(2), 101–120.

Serwatka, J. A. (2003). Assessment in Online CIS Courses. *Journal of Computer Information Systems, 44*(1).

Tesch, D., Murphy, M., & Crable, E. (2006). Implementation of a basic computer skills assessment mechanism for incoming freshmen. *Information Systems Education Journal*, *4*(13), 3–11.

Twigg, C. A. (2003). Improving learning and reducing costs: New models for online learning. *EDUCAUSE Review*, *38*(5), 28–38.

Wallace, P., & Clariana, R. B. (2005). Perception versus reality–determining business students' computer literacy skills and need for instruction in information concepts and technology. *Journal of Information Technology Education*, *4*.

DECISION SCIENCES INSTITUTE

Messages from Fortune 500 CEOs

Andrew Papadopoulos
Université du Québec à Montréal
Email: papadopoulos.andrew@uqam.ca

ABSTRACT

CEOs are the company's voice to internal and external actors to explain and defend their performance and that of their organization. While many quantitative studies relate the CEO to performance, few have looked at how CEO's use the narrative turn to frame success. We conduct a qualitative analysis using NVivo to discover the themes crafted and Diction to evaluate the semantic features of the text. Our data consists of twenty-six episodes of PBS' CEO Exchange covering 53 CEOs and over 600 pages of transcripts. We propose that CEOs discuss themes evoking notions of surviving, parenting and captaining.

KEYWORDS: CEO, narrative, interviews, qualitative methods, television

INTRODUCTION

The chief executive officer (CEO) is the firm's voice to internal and external stakeholders to bolster their firm's status but also their own. Research has reflected upon this important figure from Charles Barnard's (1938) seminal work on CEO's formal tasks, laying the cornerstones for an explosion of CEO research from both functionalist and interpretative realms. Drawing upon works from a psychological (Resick, Whitman, Weingarden, & Hiller, 2009), attitudinal (Lewin & Stephens, 1994), charisma (Agle, Nagarajan, Sonnenfeld, & Srinivasan, 2006), hubris (Brennan & Conroy, 2013), experiential (Rajagopalan & Datta, 1996), leadership (Farrell et al., 2005), governance (Finkelstein & D Aveni, 1994) and, of course, performance (Haleblian & Finkelstein, 1993) perspectives, among others, researchers across management, finance and strategy, if not all business-related fields, have reflected upon the CEO. However, as much interest exists in the corporate top dog and in spite of extensive research, convergence towards any dominant perspective, given contextual specificities and complex interdependencies (Blettner, Chaddad, & Bettis, 2012; D. C. Hambrick, 2007) has not occurred.

While qualitative approaches have been used to evaluate how leaders use language to discuss their own or their firm's performance (Seyranian & Bligh, 2008), there is a lack of research on the CEO specifically. Moreover, CEOs craft different messages for different audiences (Mäkelä & Laine, 2011), depending on the audience's influence or the event being explained (Leonardi, Neeley, & Gerber, 2012) in an effort to manage their image and status of themselves and their firm through press releases, annual reports, print journalism, television interviews, or speeches. In this exploratory study, we seek to reveal the messages CEOs design through television interviews.

LITERATURE REVIEW: NARRATIVES AND PERFORMANCE

Narratives

We surveyed current research on CEO use of narrative. A Proquest search revealed 166 studies of peer-reviewed scholarly papers (The Boolean search used to conduct the search was: ab(chief executive officer OR ceo) AND all(qualitative or narrat* or story* or senseg* or sensem*). Of those, only 19 deal with the CEO as the object of research directly, with the balance studying the CEO as a member of the top management team or the relationships between and among the CEO, the TMT, chairman, the board or subordinates, or use the CEO to inform about corporate practices. Of the 19, only five use qualitative or narrative analyses of CEO's interviews, letters to shareholders, speeches or discussions. The other 14 mostly deal with remuneration or governance issues with respect to the CEO or with the CEO-attributed rhetoric and rhetorical devices to address privatization, corporate reputation, and changes in leadership, among others

Of the five above, one used DICTION (Larcker & Zakolyukina, 2012) to analyze a large-sample of investor conference calls using econometric techniques. Of the other four, one focuses on one individual CEO (Petit, 2012), another focuses on one firm and their various CEO's over time (Brennan & Conroy, 2013), the third focuses on the visceral attitudes of a CEO as reported by five CEO's and their underlings (Shear, Kakabadse, & Kakabadse, 2013) and the last one looks at a comparison of CEO behavior in subsidiaries from a cross-national perspective (Dörrenbächer & Geppert, 2010).

Moreover, as most approaches have taken a quantitative, positivist approach to the phenomenon, there is an opportunity to confirm, complement or propose alternatives, to the current theoretical underpinnings as many confounding effects and interactions have made advancement in the area using statistical techniques difficult (Blettner et al., 2012) with qualitative research as a possible path to advance the field. First, while there is much about how a CEO positions their firm, their relationships within the firm or how they view various issues related to running a business, there is little research that explores how a CEO speaks about themselves and their role within the firm – a point seminally made by Weick (1995). He suggested that the organization is a system of actions and where information is communicated through various tools for sensemaking and sensegiving purposes. Secondly, there are very few large(r)-sample studies (we did not find any but there might be) of how Fortune 500-type CEO's position themselves and their firm. We, thus, wish to respond to the need for greater research into how business leaders use speech (Brown, Stacey, & Nandhakumar, 2008; Maclean, Harvey, & Chia, 2012; Sonenshein, 2007) and to build upon Maclean et al. (2012) who looked at business elites (not CEOs exclusively), through life-history interviews where success was viewed as a personal, professional or firm-level accomplishment.

Narratives & Audience Messaging

Leaders increasingly realize the importance of narrative in addressing challenges they confront (Denning, 2006; Fleming, 2001). Leaders can use their own personal stories to communicate important messages to others through effective storytelling (Denning, 2006). In the same vein, Rhodes and Brown (2005) insist on the importance of the embodied and lived experience, generally events, that narrative methods allow researchers to reflect upon. Those events are however differently framed for each audience, using different types of language, and sensemaking tools (Gioia & Kumar, 1991; Maclean et al., 2012; Mäkelä & Laine, 2011; Weick, 1995). With respect to context and message, there is a need to understand how intentions are manifested through actions but to understand human conduct, the context of where these actions occur is part and parcel of the analysis (Schültz, 1973, cited by Czarniawska, 1998). With respect to audience, what is said, how it is said, and where it is said all form part of understanding the CEO.

With semi-structured or structured interviews, the interviewer accompanies the interviewee in the sensemaking process (Gabriel, 2000). Media interviews are conversations bound in a point and space in time (Czarniawska-Joerges, 1998). Narratives emerge where a sequence of events are recounted where leaders recount their life story, life experience, organizing processes in a form of a story knitting together random events temporally to construct a meaningful whole (Czarniawska-Joerges, 2008) to constitute an organizational reality where the interview accesses the plurivocal organization (Søderberg, 2006). Narratives serve as connection tools between the person and the social, knit together by "an original state of affairs, an action or an event, and the consequent state of the affairs (Czarniawska-Joerges, 1998). Elites will make sense by legitimating their experience to build or justify successes by presenting stories that claim and maintain self and corporate legitimacy (Maclean et al., 2012).

Performance

The question of performance is a central preoccupation for strategy researchers. The field has approached the issue from primarily an industrial organization (Porter, 1980), resource (Barney, 1991), and leadership (D. C. Hambrick, 2007) perspective – theoretically speaking. While there may be consensus on the importance of performance, different fields have dealt with it differently, leading to a potpourri of measures, including accounting, financial, legitimizing, and social responsibility. Researchers have identified other important firm activities that are considered important precursors of firm performance; including innovation, firm culture, and executive team capabilities, inter alia.

Many studies have also attempted to link CEO leadership to firm performance (e.g. Hambrick, 2007). However, the empirical conundrum for researchers, especially in strategy, is how does the CEO influence performance? Some have ascribed corporate governance mechanisms – structural factors – that limit and facilitate CEO action (Boyd, 1995). Others view the chief executive as human capital – a resource – that brings experience, judgement, knowledge, skills, and expertise to the firm (Chan & Riess, 2004). Some other factors that have been associated with successful CEO leadership are charisma (Agle et al., 2006), emotions (Delgado-García & De La Fuente-Sabaté, 2010), and networks (Geletkanycz, Boyd, & Finklestein, 2001), among others. From a narrative perspective, others have looked at how CEO's use referents, more commonly referred to as benchmarks to frame performance (Short & Palmer, 2008).

The CEO, unlike other executives, has ultimate authority and power over the organization (Finkelstein, 1992), affording them legitimacy in institutional environments. Empirically, the CEO has also been found to generally have greater predictive significance than any other executive Jensen and Zajac (2004). Upper echelon theory has suggested that overall experience and tenure may play significant roles in many aspects of CEO behaviors and outcomes. The experience-tenure relationship has been found to be significant for diversification (Wiersema & Bantel, 1992), resource acquisition (D. C. Hambrick & Fukutomi, 1991), performance Henderson, Miller, and Hambrick (2006), compensation Crumley (2008); (Hill & Phan, 1991), turnover Allgood and Kathleen (2000); (Healy, Lehman, & McDaniel, 1995), entry mode choices (Herrmann & Datta, 2006), and internationalization (Herrmann, 2002), among others.

Executive experience is both a temporal and experiential phenomenon. Temporal experience is related to executive age and firm tenure. While age is a straightforward measure, tenure has been considered from many angles including length of time as a CEO (Boeker, 1997), member of the TMT (Jaw & Lin, 2009), employee of the firm (Wiersema & Bantel, 1992), or working in the same industry D. Hambrick, Geletkanycz, and Fredrickson (1993).. Experiential knowledge has been considered to be diversity in different functional areas or senior management positions, type or length of education, and/or as having international expertise (Herrmann, 2002; Reed & Reed, 1989). We focus on both temporal (age and tenure as CEO) and certain experiential aspects (education and in-firm promotion).

For example, in the context of diversification, firms most likely to diversify had younger top management teams (Wiersema & Bantel, 1992) or CEOs (Herrmann, 2002). Other have found these effects to be curvilinear at the CEO and TMT level as youth initially leads to diversifying attitudes but as retirement age approaches, executives become less likely to expand their product-markets (Jaw & Lin, 2009). Then again others found no relationship (Anderson, Bates, Bizjak, & Lemmon, 2000 & Lemmon, 2000; Cornett, Hovakimian, Palia, & Tehranian, 2003 & Tehranian, 2003). We thus see how experience, both temporal and lived, influence CEO discourse. We explore this opportunity by the following research question: What messages do CEOs of Fortune 500 companies convey in discussing performance?

DATA

CEO Exchange

Our sources of data are from CEO Exchange (Lorentz, 2000-2007), a television program from the US Public Broadcasting Service (PBS). We use over fifty-three unique interview transcripts. There was a total of 78 interviews. We were unable to obtain transcripts for some interviews, especially from the first season. We also excluded other interview of non-corporations (e.g.: Major League Baseball, the National Basketball Association and the Girl Scouts of America). Notwithstanding the missing transcripts, the data source is an appropriate source to capture concrete exchanges and conversations (Czarniawska-Joerges, 1998) - from the television program CEO Exchange (Lorentz, 2000-2007) on the Public Broadcasting Service (PBS). The PBS television program CEO Exchange, ran from February 2000 to summer 2007. See Appendix 1 for a full list of CEOs interviewed. It is a one hour program that interviews two CEOs for about twenty-five minutes each during the one-hour slot. The program positions itself as bringing together, "...the most interesting and innovative CEOs in the world for a lively discussion about themselves, their companies, and their passions in life. (Anonymous, 2007) The interviewer, Jeff Greenfield, is an acclaimed political, media and culture reporter who has worked for a number of different news agencies including CNN (during which time he conducted these interviews for PBS), CBS, and ABC (Anonymous, 2007). As Mr. Greenfield's background is not in business news, he focused on the human side of the CEO (Anonymous, 2007).The program is sponsored by the Society for Human Resource Management (SHRM). Through the sponsorship of the CEO Exchange, SHRM hoped to raise the visibility of the HR profession and highlight the importance of effective human capital strategies.

Each show deals with a specific business theme, including, among others, "Dynamic Leadership in Turbulent Times" from season three and "Happy Customers and Employees: The Recipe for Success" from season four. A full listing of CEOs, their firms, and the individual themes is available from the PBS website (Anonymous, 2007). There were a total of 39 shows produced over the time period with 78 different CEOs being interviewed. The sample for the research covers twenty-six episodes and 53 CEOs, representing over six hundred pages of single-spaced transcribed dialogue.

To identify whether any other studies used an approach where data from a television show is used as content analysis, we used ProQuest and searched for the terms "interview and television" in the abstracts. The results returned 171 peer-reviewed journal articles of which none used a content analysis approach to television show data on CEOs. While there are some marketing studies that have used television shows to explore some theoretical constructs, we are unaware of any research in management or strategy studies that have used a content analysis approach to analyzing data from television. The purpose of this study is to explore how CEO's discuss success to influence and shape 'third party perceptions for their own benefit' (Bowen, Davis, & Matsumoto, 2002).

In a similar approach, other CEO-inspired studies using content analysis have looked at annual reports (McClelland, Liang, & Barker, 2010), magazine articles on generic strategies(Calingo, 1989), CEO representation, including the construction of CEO infamy, in media (Gunther & Grandy, 2009) and newspaper stories (Dong-Jin & Berger, 2004).

Demographic Data

We collected demographic data on the CEO's interviewed from various sources, including regulatory filings (mostly proxy statement), corporate websites, biography.com (the website of the television program of the same name) and other reputable news outlets, including Forbes.com (the business magazine website). This data includes, education history, years CEO, if the CEO was promoted from within or recruited externally, and age, among others.

RESEARCH DESIGN AND METHODOLOGY

Researcher coding

There is a general theme of success being discussed and can analyze the data in a deductive manner to verify existing theory (e.g. upper echelon; stewardship) or to allow categories and relationships to emerge through open coding (Strauss, 1998). There is a question of what analytical approach to use in terms of theory: analytical induction or deduction (Patton, 2002)? While a number of theories postulate on the CEO-performance relationship, we prefer an approach that allows for inductive analysis. Then using the emergent themes, deductive analysis (theory testing) may be useful – an approach suggested by Patton (2002). In our case where we look at how language is used to describe performance, the inter and multidisciplinary nature of theories based in language, leadership, and performance make using a single theoretical framework difficult with respect to achieving a parsimonious view of the phenomenon. We thus seek to unearth patterns and themes through data reduction and sense-making (Patton, 2002).

We used Nvivo, a widely used software tool, to code manually the interviews. Each researcher has gone through each of the interviews and coded independently the transcripts. Omissions and contradictions in coding were resolved through discussion until a consensus was reached. The first round of coding established some emergent themes; a second round of coding refined, parceled or combined concepts in searching for linkages within and across interviews.

Computer-aided text analysis

Diction, our second tool, is a linguistic approach that evaluates specific word frequencies, drawing upon 31 pre-defined dictionaries containing over 10,000 words. These dictionaries search for language that reflect 33 characteristics, including tenacity, aggressiveness, and diversity, among others, leading to five master variable categories (certainty, optimism, realism, activity and commonality) that reflect what the speaker or author is trying to convey. Another set of calculated variables (insistence, variety, embellishment, and complexity) assesses how the speaker tries to convey the message (Short & Palmer, 2008). For example, insistence looks at word repetition while complexity looks at the average number of characters per word. Diction has been used in research assessing presidential speeches (Seyranian & Bligh, 2008) and CEO letters to shareholders (R. J. Craig & Brennan, 2012). See Appendix 3 for more details on how the variables are calculated.

CEO Exchange

We used Diction 7 (Hart & Carroll, 2013), the most recent version of the software, to analyze the transcripts of 53 interviews of CEO Exchange. Recall, that we coded 33 CEO Exchange transcripts using Nvivo. In using 53 interviews, we used the largest sample possible to minimize statistical violations related to small sample sizes. Hair et al. (Hair, Anderson, Tatham, & Black, 1998) suggest 50 observations as a workable minimum to not have normality violations significantly impact results while 30 would be a minimum.

To prepare the data for analysis, we made edits to the original transcripts. First, each transcript generally contained two CEO interviews with questions from the host and the audience, biographical information of the CEOs being interviewed read by the narrator, comments by the CEO's colleagues, an overview of the location of the interview, almost always a business school and various details regarding the transcript, including dates of recording and copyright information. To prepare the document for Diction, we separated each transcript by CEO and removed all text that was not spoken by the CEO leaving only the CEO's words.

Once the 53 documents were prepared in the manner mentioned above, they were loaded as individual documents into Diction. We then applied the standard analysis applying 31 pre-defined terms, four calculated variables and five master variables that are the result of formulas based on the pre-defined terms and calculated variables.

RESULTS

Demographic Data: Who are these CEOs

We present a basic overview of some standard descriptive statistics of our CEO's here below (individual CEO data is in the appendix). Overall, we have a predominantly male cohort (48 vs. 5) that has worked its way up the ranks (only 7 founders), and was promoted to CEO from within the firm (35 insider promotions vs. 18 outside hires). This group has not been educated in America's top schools (only 16 Ivy leaguers) but nearly half (25) have an MBA degree and fewer studied sciences (15). The average age at the time of the interview was about 55.2 years but ranged from as young as 31 to as old as 74 with a standard deviation of about 7.9 years. At the time of the interview, the CEO had been at the helm of the firm for 6.6 years; the range was from as few as 0.5 years to 36.3 years with a standard deviation of about 6.5 years.

We also compiled some post-interview statistics and found that the CEO's interviewed had a shelf life of about 10.8 years, including those that are still leading their firm today (as of March 15, 2014) – only 12 of the 53. The remaining 41 CEOs had various fates. Twenty-one retired on their terms, four sold their shares or were acquired, 11 left for poor performance reasons, and five others left for various reasons, including health, to start other firms or transitioned from CEO to chairman.

CEO Exchange and Nvivo

We proceeded to analyze the interviews by open coding and identified 877 passages covering 53 themes that the CEO's had referred to in their interviews that dealt with success and performance issues, broadly defined, at many different levels, including the individual (CEO or employee), group (team or executives), firm (profit, market share) and stakeholders (shareholders, customers, employees, society).

1. Strategy (16 subthemes and 250 passages e.g. customer treatment, risk taking vision)
2. Employees (9 subthemes/ 106 passages e.g. hiring, remuneration, training)
3. Personal qualities (9 subthemes/252 passages e.g. personality, listening, passions, style) See Appendix 2 for a sample.
4. Experience & life events (9 subthemes/199 passages e.g. academic, professional, family and challenging events)
5. Ethics (7 subthemes/53 passages e.g. safety, social responsibility, philanthropy, sustainability)
6. External perceptions (3 subthemes/17 passages e.g. firm, reputation, CEO image)

We then re-evaluated these themes and passages to see how the CEO's framed these themes and identified three approaches in our preliminary coding of 33 transcripts with respect to performance and success: surviving, parenting and captaining.

Surviving

CEOs point to challenges (crisis, difficulties, and failures) and how they overcame them which in itself is an accomplishment. An interesting pattern emerges; some CEOs turn to non-business failures and juxtapose them to business while others draw upon business related events for comparisons. As we can see in the Bethune quote below, he draws upon his marriage failure to emphasize the importance acknowledging the mistake, learning from it and not making it again.

> Bethune (Continental Airline): There's my first wife, comes to mind. I would think the real issue is not to admit and identify and act on your mistakes. People make mistakes all the time and you ought to step up to it. If you're going the wrong way, say, hey, we screwed up. Let's go back. And I don't know anyone that doesn't make them. I make them all the time.

On the other hand, Bonsignore, below refers to the failure of a merger and recovering from it. While Bethune uses the analogy of a failed marriage, Bonsignore uses metaphors to discuss the failure and recovery. In a similar fashion he speaks of picking yourself up (vs. making a U-turn), he refers to mistakes as tripping on your shoelaces, and getting on with life. They both recognize the importance of acknowledging the mistake, we screwed up and eating humble crow. It is important to mention that some CEOs speak of failures with respect to themselves, using "I" while others refer to us, using "we".

> Bonsignore (Honeywell): We had to eat a lot of humble crow to recover from that (merger). And we've done that. You make a mistake, you pick yourself up and you get on with life. That doesn't mean that anything fundamental to do with this proposition is any less important or any less valuable than it was before we tripped over our shoelaces here.

We see in some other quotes here below, again the usage of metaphors to describe how one does not celebrate failure...by not getting drunk.

> Stemberg (Staples): The ultimate failure is to get fired and I got fired and I think you learn from that. You've also had plenty of business failures. Certainly earlier experiences in Europe were nothing to go out and get drunk about. They were pretty difficult years. People used to joke about our experiences in Europe.

> Stemberg (Staples): They were trying to sell it out from under me and I got into a fight with the principal owners and they told me that I wasn't to be with the company any more. And the next day they came along and said, we have some good news for you.

> Chambers (Cisco): Layoffs is something that I hoped I would never have to do again in my life. You're affecting people who are doing a very good job, and I failed at very few things in life, that I set a personal goal on, and I set a personal goal in never to do layoffs again, and I failed in this one....I think if you change your leadership style when times get tough, your employee team would not understand it. I think as a rule of thumb, you come in as tough as you're ever going to be, day one, and you've got to be very predictable in your style, whether it's with customers, your employees, or others.

Parenting

The role of the parent with respect to a child is multifaceted. A parent will emphasize different roles throughout the life of a child. When a child is a newborn the primary responsibility is to ensure that the parent provides nourishment and safety for the well-being of the child much like a firm, if we use the analogy of a balanced scorecard, must be successful in providing for customer, employees and shareholders. Another role that a parent takes on is that of teacher where he or she must socialize through the transmission of values and appropriate behaviors as well as other more basic life skills, including walking, eating alone, and speaking. This teaching takes place both through mentoring and coaching as well as through incentives and coercion that seek to encourage or discourage certain behaviors. All these parental actions – as the researchers are well versed in from actual experience – are to ensure not only the survival of their offspring but also to set a foundation for success. We find that the CEO's interviewed expressed many of these sentiments.

<u>Teaching</u>

We see with the following interventions that the CEO's wished to transmit to their employees the important cultural aspects of their business with respect to learning, failing and improving. In the case of Donald at Starbucks, he even evokes the term DNA to discuss the transmission of culture.

> Wynn (Wynn Resorts): Speaking of cultures, to show you how different Yahoo is from where we are. In order to teach my employees how to convey luxury and elegance and a feeling of specialness to my guests, I do exactly the opposite of Yahoo. And I spend more money on the staff dining room than I do sometimes on the public one for the public...I want them to feel special and elitist.

Stemberg(Staples): What I would add to that is when people fail, one of the worst things you can do, that if they did their homework and did the best job and then it just doesn't work, the worst thing you can do as a leader is make them a bum. You almost want to make them a hero. They tried to do something new and different. And if the role model in the company and the gossip becomes, you know you try something – that's a good way to get fired, boy that's the death of the company. It would kill a company like ours.

Carly Fiorina (HP): And so one of the changes we've had to make is to get much more focused about what is an acceptable level of performance? And if that performance is not occurring, then we have to act with that employee. We have to coach them to better performance…if not, eventually they will have to be let go.

Donald (Starbucks): We want the new hires to understand what the DNA of our company is. Once they understand what the DNA is, hopefully they're there or they can migrate to that point. What's interesting though is a lot of times if these new employees or partners, don't necessarily understand the culture, can't carry it on, they'll self-select out.

Protecting

With respect to protecting, we found that CEO's were interested in various aspects of protection bet it physical or mental and in some instances more nurturing. The notion of protection touches on many aspects and responds to the protective nature of the CEO with respect to employees and the public where survival, wining and motivation are lynchpins to success.

Bonsignore (Honeywell): But, I think for all of us the public safety is really the first issue here.

Eskew (UPS): We really wanted to get this done early. We didn't want our people and we didn't want our customers to be caught in the middle this time. Our people have been represented by the Teamsters for 80 years. We've only had one nationwide strike. And we really knew that our people didn't want to go through this kind of thing. But we wanted to create a win situation for our customers, our people, for the future generations of UPSers, and for the Teamsters. And we think this contract does that.

McGraw (Mcgraw-Hill): I think being family friendly, as a company and being considerate of a lot of different needs that an employee is going to have means that you're going to have probably more engaged employee base that is going to be more excited about wanting to be with you.

Behaving

One of the more difficult aspects of parenting is how to get a child to do what you want them to do either by direction or by providing incentives and disincentives to encourage or discourage action. In the context of a business environment, these incentives are to align the actions of employees with will of management or shareholders.

Nardelli (Home Depot): Every salaried employee participates in stock options...if you take a store manager, assistant store manager, they are extremely motivated. They take tremendous pride in being a shareholder of Home Depot. And they are as interested in that stock price...

Chambers (Cisco): Keeping the culture is probably the most challenging thing we face. ...you've got to reward people in terms of the culture that you're creating. But it's more important to have them in a nurturing environment that has the right culture. And it's amazing how powerful that is in retaining employees and attracting them...particularly, ones that you want.

Welch (GE): Without question, building in General Electric a meritocracy where it's all about unleashing people: the modern corporation where everyone counts. We grade people on the bottom 10, middle 70 and top 20. and we do it every single year. We do it rigorously. Now people can move from the middle 70 to the top 20, and from the top 20 down to the middle 70. So don't any of you think you're being kind managers, that you're being good people, because you give nice appraisals. That's the cruelest thing you can do to a human being is not let them know where they stand, what they need to do to improve and if they can't improve, ask them to move on as early as possible.

Bethune (Continental): It's a lot easier motivating people when they think and they come to believe that you know them, you like them, you respect them? You can't take these men and women, regardless of what their role is, and take them for granted. You have to appreciate them. When people know that you appreciate them, they work harder for you..and we will compensate and reward employees who look for the best practices from both to create a new culture, and we will punish those who don't.

Providing

A parent is also seen as a provider of food, clothing and shelter to their children. CEO's see themselves and their firms as creating value for their customers, employees, and shareholders by providing what they need be it a products, attentiveness to customer needs, wealth creation for shareholders, benefits for employees or solution to business challenges.

Stemberg (Staples): We want to be close to the customer. When somebody wants to go buy a battery for their Palm or some media storage for their computer media, they want to get it as quickly as they can and get back to going to work. And the more stores we have, the closer we are to you, the better off we are going to be.

Bethune (Continental): The last thing we're going to touch on today is serving the customer. If everybody understands that you have to serve the customer...

Nordstrom(Nordstroms): We want to get our best people on the selling floor. So whether you're in a support role or not, everything we do is about the customer and selling...Customers first, employees second, shareholders third.

> The idea being that if you keep the customers and the employees happy, the results will make the shareholders happy too.

> Nardelii (Home Depot): ... making sure we're doing the right things, to drive volume, to bring value, to create value for our shareholders...

> Donald (Starbucks): We call our employees, partners. They share in the success of the company through bean stock, which are options that we give out each year for the hourly employees. We share our benefit packages. They're the same as our partners at store level. It is all part of taking the success of the company and making sure that everybody has a piece of this. And when we do that, the values are all like-minded. The company will continue to prosper.

The quote below has familial overtones where providing a business solution may not necessarily be good for a person or group of people, child or kids, but is in the best interest of the family.

> Yankowki(Palm): But we sat down with employee groups and sought common answers. They understood the problem we're solving for, bought into it. Sometimes the solution wasn't personally good for them, but they knew that we were working in a direction to make it ultimately good for everyone.

Captaining

Many of the comments presented by the CEO's echoed, at least for us, the notion of a captain at the helm of his ship as a CEO is at the helm of his firm where the leader needs to make decisions as to redirecting and reorienting the strategy of the firm as needed in both difficult and not-so-difficult times. It could be a situation for the captain needs to navigate through a storm, to seek our new opportunities in new lands or to simply stay the course on a destination sailing the seas.

<u>Storms: Hard right or full speed ahead?</u>

In a number of instances CEO's spoke of adjusting courses for the firms when going through difficulties times while others suggest that staying the course and weathering storm may be more appropriate.

> Chambers (Sun): It takes strategy and how and if you need to modify it, to adjust to the new times. You communicate openly and honestly with your employee base, with your customer base. You are realistic about what's causing the problems...are they macroeconomic, in capital spending or is it something you're doing? Does it require focus in different areas during tough times? Yes. You then...determine what your plan of action needs to be.

> Fiorina (HP): [...] are the basic strategies changing? They shouldn't be, just because times get tough if they were the right strategy. Are the basic ways of operating changing? They shouldn't be just because the times are getting tough. Of course, you make different discretionary decisions [...] consolidated 83 divisions into six, with three responsible for developing great products and services, the other three for selling them.

We also see the importance that a CEO gives to staying the course and remaining focused. While in some circumstances, the CEO acknowledges the needs to change course and even chart out new territories – changing strategies – in other instances the CEO argues for an unwavering commitment to the plan.

> Stemberg (Staples): Great execution will beat a great strategy every time. We had a pretty good strategy, but we really focused hard on executing well against that strategy, staying focused and try to remember our customer at all times.

> Semel (Yahoo): ... I was trained to think long term. And I never think quarter by quarter. And I asked my company to never think quarter by quarter. That if we're going to create value, it has to be long term value...we're much smaller than AOL and Microsoft. It's going to be very hard at that point for us to compete. We have no revenue. And we're losing money. That was our first year. And if we follow the strategy that we're talking about, it could take us, I thought, two or three years to see real results...And we have to hang in there and then when we fulfill that strategy...

Seeking Treasures

In other instances, we have seen CEO's speaking about how they wish to improve on their firms or create greater value by seeking out new opportunities in uncharted territories.

> Immelt (GE): We were looking at a lot of our businesses that were making investments in energy efficiency, conservation and greenhouse gas emission reduction. So basically, we, as a management team in 2003 studied the science around global warming...I went in front of the top 30 executives in the company at a quarterly meeting we have, and I said, "hey, guess what team? We're going to drive a big environmental initiative here."

> Gilmartin (Merck): For us, the best way to create shareholder value, and to achieve our growth objectives, is through pursuing our strategy of translating cutting edge science into breakthrough innovations,

The changing and staying the course dichotomies brings to mind the fundamental notion of strategic planning. While strategy may be initially planned, some CEO's will let the eventual course emerge as challenges and unforeseen circumstances – storms – require constant readjustment. In other cases, the CEO sees that strategic plan set in stone that must be held on to no matter what. It is curious to note that both Fiorina at HP and Semel at Yahoo have seen themselves and their firms go through inglorious demises since these interviews.

Diction & CEO Exchange

We prefer to show and discuss what makes CEO's different from the "normalized" speaker; our results indicate that the CEO's as a group demonstrated a number of characteristics that deviated from the normalized values. We include the master variable in parenthesis that contains the pre-defined term as a factor in its determination. For example, High Ambivalence is one of the 31 pre-defined terms (components) and is part of the formula that determines the master variable Certainty. In our discussion, we prefer to focus on how they are trying to communicate, the calculated variables, and what they are trying to convey, the master variables – detailed results are shown in Table 1 below.

Main Variables:

- Low Complexity – calculated variable (CV): 25 individual CEO's below normal range
- Low Certainty – master variable (MV): 28 below

Components:

- High(1) Ambivalence (2) (Certainty): 29 above
- High Self-reference (3) (Certainty): 37 above
- High Tenacity(4) (Certainty): 31 above, 2 below
- High Motion(5) (Activity): 27 above
- Low Familiarity(6) (Realism): 32 below, 1 above

NOTES:

1. The prefix High or Low indicates that the average for the group was either above or below the normal range established by Diction.
2. Words expressing hesitation or uncertainty, implying a speaker's inability or unwillingness to commit to the verbalization being made. Included are hedges (allegedly, perhaps, might), statements of inexactness (almost, approximate, vague, somewhere) and confusion (baffled, puzzling, hesitate). Also included are words of restrained possibility (could, would, he'd) and mystery (dilemma, guess, suppose, seems).
3. All first-person references, including *I, I'd, I'll, I'm, I've, me, mine, my, myself*. Self-references are treated as acts of indexing whereby the locus of action appears to reside in the speaker and not in the world at large thereby implicitly acknowledging the speaker s limited vision.
4. All uses of the verb to be (is, am, will, shall), three definitive verb forms (has, must, do) and their variants, as well as all associated contraction's (he'll, they've, ain't). These verbs connote confidence and totality.
5. Terms connoting human movement (*bustle, job, lurch, leap*), physical processes (*circulate, momentum, revolve, twist),* journeys (*barnstorm, jaunt, wandering, travels*), speed (*lickety-split, nimble, zip, whistle-stop),* and modes of transit (*ride, fly, glide, swim*).
6. Consists of a selected number of words which are the most common words in the English language. Included are common prepositions (*across, over, through*), demonstrative pronouns (*this, that*) and interrogative pronouns (*who, what*), and a variety of particles, conjunctions and connectives (*a, for, so*).

When speaking to a general public audience, CEOs have demonstrated two important characteristics that stand out: complexity and certainty. Complexity is ascertained by the average number of words in a given analyzed file, suggesting an effort for exact phrasing and clear ideas (Hart & Carroll). The low complexity may be explained by a number of reasons. First, given that the television program targets wide audience, the CEO may have chosen to use simpler language to express their sentiment regarding their personal and/or firm successes. Second, the nature of the questions may have dealt with more general and simpler topics than those discussed in other fora leading to similarly less complex responses. Third, as the CEO here is being raised to a certain celebrity status and taken out of the regulatory context of other share-and-stakeholder communications, they may choose to communicate in a more truthful, less convoluted style where their comments will likely have little or no implications for their firms.

Table 1: CEO Exchange Diction Results						
		Diction - Normal Range (vs. Average Value)		**# CEOs (n=51)**		
Terms	**Mean**	**Low**	**High**	**< Low**	**MID**	**> High**
Numerical Terms	10.48	0.30	15.04	0	45	6
Ambivalence	20.58	6.49	19.21	0	22	29
Self-reference	20.62	-1.18	15.10	0	14	37
Tenacity	41.07	23.32	39.76	2	18	31
Accomplishment	13.21	4.96	23.78	0	49	2
Familiarity	113.33	117.87	147.19	32	18	1
Cooperation	2.87	0.36	8.44	1	47	3
Denial	7.30	2.57	10.35	0	41	10
Motion	5.01	0.17	4.35	0	24	27
Insistence (CV)	27.68	9.15	111.15	3	48	0
Variety (CV)	0.50	0.45	0.53	6	33	12
Complexity (CV)	4.31	4.31	4.91	25	26	0
Optimism (MV)	51.40	46.37	52.25	0	34	17
Certainty (MV)	46.14	46.90	51.96	28	23	0
CEO_at_inteview	6.56					
MBA=1	0.49					
Age	55.29					
IvyEd=1	0.29					
Insider=1	0.67					
Science=1	0.29					
MBASCIENCE	0.18					
CEO_duration	10.85					
Stock Performance (n=40)	7.74%					
MV - Master Variable CV - Computed Variable						

All demographic variables used for analysis were based on data as of the interview date. CEO_at_inteview refers to the number of years the CEO was in place at the time of the interview. MBA=1 indicates an MBA or advanced management degree. Age is the age at interview. IvyEd=1 indicates attendance at an Ivey league school. Insider=1 refers to an inside promotion to CEO. Science=1 refers to a science-related education, including engineering. MBASCIENCE refers to a holding an MBA and science degree. CEO_duration is the years that the CEO was in place, including post-interview. Some CEO's are still in place today. Stock Performance (n=40) refers to the price performance of the stock between taking over as CEO and the interview date.

However, when considering the complexity of the CEO-group (n=51), we found that publicly-traded CEO's are likely to be no more or no less cautious in their speech. Finally, we are using transcript data of spoken word in a question and answer format that may have required a more specific Diction application that was more suited to spoken word – spoken text may naturally be less complex than written text.

There is greater research on the role of certainty - language indicating resoluteness, inflexibility, and completeness and a tendency to speak with authority (Hart & Carroll) – with that of performance. In the context of a general interest interview, some have argued that low certainty may suggest deceptive behavior (Craig, Mortensen, & Iyer, 2013).

Demographic aspects

We also investigated if experience, defined temporally and experientially, may shed insight into how CEOs communicate. The table below lays out the correlation analysis of the relationships between eight demographic variables and each of the calculated and master variables. A combined MBA and science degree had an incidence on making insistence lower while variety and realism were amplified, thus not showing a preference for an ordered world but engaging in precise language that leads to tangible and actionable results. While being an inside promotion to CEO led to lower optimism. The possibility here is that these individuals may be less likely to endorse others or advance certain concepts. Is it possible that they had expected this position and thus are not recognizant of others? Could it be that these individuals have been with the firm before and thus already understand how the business works?

Table 2: CEO Exchange Correlations

	CEO Duration	Inside Promotion	MBA	Science Degree	Ivy League Educated	MBA & Science Degree	Stock Price Performance
Computed Variable							
Insistence	-,055	-,161	-,036	-,234	-,184	-,286*	-,260
Embellishment	,028	-,238	-,108	-,051	,221	-,017	,018
Variety	-,019	-,119	-,002	,445**	,110	,280*	,157
Complexity	-,085	-,117	-,014	-,095	-,066	-,115	-,248
Master Variable							
Activity	,039	,065	-,057	-,038	-,099	-,068	-,209
Optimism	-,243	-,277*	-,007	,017	,053	,115	,173
Certainty	,169	,032	-,015	-,264	-,122	-,271	-,120
Realism	-,118	-,039	,203	,180	-,178	,316*	,346*
Commonality	-,249	-,238	,113	-,226	,079	-,179	-,440**

** Correlation significant at 0.01 (bilateral) * Correlation significant at 0.05 (bilateral)
Age and the years that the CEO was in place at the time of the interview were removed for spacing issues. They were uncorrelated with the variables of interest.

DISCUSSION

The researcher-based analysis of the interviewees suggests a CEO who discusses performance from three perspectives: being a survivor, a parent and a captain. This constructed image that the CEO lends to an image where performance is framed as being able to survive and then thrive, to teaching employees how to be not only good but better employees, providing for various stakeholders, managing behaviors, and successfully navigating a firm strategically. From Diction, the CEO Exchange interviews suggest a CEO that engages in self-reference and motion, indicating a locus of action residing with the speaker, disconnected from the external environment, and a condition of movement in speed, transit or processes. These two items suggest a CEO that views himself as the mover and shaker.

Status Enhancement

Why did these CEOs converge on a certain set of messages? Each platform provided to the CEO is an opportunity for the CEO to defend, promote and reinforce their status. Status is a socially constructed basis for a hierarchy based on "unearned ascription of social rank" (Washington & Zajac, 2005) with "an implicit or explicit rank order of individuals or groups with respect to a valued social dimension" (Magee & Galinsky, 2008: 354), based on taken-for-granted beliefs (Berger, Ridgeway, Fisek, & Norman, 1998). While these CEOs may not have the uber-celebrity status of a Donald Trump, they certainly hold status and would be hesitant to do anything that damages their status (Koh, 2010).

CEOs status generates privilege for those at the top: 'star' executives, distort business norms and contribute to skewed distributions of value (Malmendier & Tate, 2009). CEO status may therefore represent an important signal quality (Podolny, 1993) and a tangible basis for decision-making (Podolny, 2005), enabling actors to draw inferences about the firm's unobservable qualities and potential value. Status literature suggests that positive status signals should lead to positive benefits for those who possess it. Our results point to efforts to enhance this signal. More research and reflection is required to better understand and exploit this aspect.

LIMITATIONS & EXTENSIONS

Limitations

There are a number of limitations associated with our study. First, our focus on interviews destined to a general public audience may only capture a small sliver of the platforms available to CEO. Other platforms include analyst conference calls, media interviews, awards and recognitions, and the annual general meeting, among others. Moreover, the CEO may craft different messages for different audiences, using language that may be context-specific. For example, a media interview on CNN may have yielded different results than CEO Exchange as an interview with a financial-market related show on Bloomberg or CNBC.

Second, while Diction provides a convenient tool for textual analysis based on word choice, meaning and intent may not necessarily emerge in the same way as researcher-coded analysis. That is, while the Diction score may suggest ambivalence, a researcher-coded analysis may indeed suggest the opposite. However, the unbiased nature of the Diction tool does counterbalance the risk of researcher bias.

Extensions

There are a number of possible extensions for this paper. First, it would be interesting to look at how CEO's speak about performance in different national contexts. Knowing that firms are embedded in not only their country's institutional context but also their industry's reality, it would be possible to investigate how cultural, regulatory, and normative practices may influence how a

CEO expresses him or herself with respect to performance. Does the CEO of Cemex, a multinational cement supplier, Bimbo, a Mexican-based North American commercial baker, and Pemex, the Mexican national petroleum company, speak the same way of performance as do the CEO's of British Petroleum, Tesco, and the BBC?

Second, given that video data is available, an extension would be to analyze the body language of the CEO's during the interview. This is a promising avenue given the increasing interest and availability of video data – as evidenced by a recent call for papers in Organizational Research Methods allowing for an analysis of for non-verbal cues(Manusov & Trees, 2002).

CONCLUSION

Our research uses novel data from CEO Exchange, a TV show, to study how CEOs use words to reflect on performance. This work in progress found that the CEO may take on many roles when speaking to an audience, including parent and hero, depending on the audience.

APPENDIX

Appendix 1: Selected Quotes to Illustrate Employee Categories

Category	Sub-category	CEO	Representative Comments	Company
Employee	Relations	Carly Fiorina	...the way you treat your employees, do you still treat them with respect and empathy in the tough times as well as in the good times?	Hewlett Packard
Employee	Relations	Tom Stemberg	What I would add to that is when people fail, one of the worst things you can do, that if they did their homework and did the best job and then it just doesn't work, the worst thing you can do as a leader is make them a bum. You almost want to make them a hero.... [...]..you almost want to make them a hero...	Staples
Employee	Relations	Jack Welch	...they will trust you and you'll get to know them. They know what's right. They know what's wrong and give them a voice and you have to believe that, because they see you working.	GE
Employee	Recognition	John Chambers	...birthday breakfasts...once a month on, if you have a birthday in that month, you come and grill the president for an hour and a half. And any topic is fair. Every session, I learn one, two or three things that I did not know going in....	Cisco
Employee	Recognition	Jack Welch	You want them to stretch and try to do something that they didn't think they could do, and then when they do it, they've got a whole different level of self-confidence.	GE

Appendix 2: Diction variable definitions and calculations

Master Variables		
	Definition	**Formula**
Certainty	Language indicating resoluteness, inflexibility, and completeness	[Tenacity + Leveling + Collectives + Insistence] – [Numerical Terms + Ambivalence + Self Reference + Variety]
Optimism	Language endorsing some person, group, concept or event or highlighting their positive entailments.	[Praise + Satisfaction + Inspiration] – [Blame + Hardship + Denial]
Activity	Language featuring movement, change, the implementation of ideas and the avoidance of inertia.	[Aggression + Accomplishment + Communication + Motion] – [Cognitive Terms + Passivity + Embellishment]
Realism	Language describing tangible, immediate, recognizable matters that affect people's everyday lives.	[Familiarity + Spatial Awareness + Temporal Awareness + Present Concern + Human Interest + Concreteness] – [Past Concern + Complexity]
Commonality	Language highlighting the agreed -upon values of a group and rejecting idiosyncratic modes of engagement.	[Centrality + Cooperation + Rapport] – [Diversity + Exclusion + Liberation]

Calculated Variables			
	Assumptions	**Measurement**	**Formula**
Insistence	Repetition of key terms indicates a preference for a limited, ordered world.	A measure of code-restriction. All words occurring three or more times that function as nouns or noun-derived adjectives are identified	[Number of Eligible Words x Sum of their Occurrences] ÷ 10. For small input files, high frequency terms used two or more times are used in the calculation.
Embellishment	Heavy modification slows down a verbal passage by de-emphasizing human and material action	A selective ratio of adjectives to verbs.	Embellishment is calculated according to the following formula: [Praise + Blame +1] ÷ [Present Concern + Past Concern +1].
Variety	A high score indicates a speaker's avoidance of overstatement and a preference for precise, molecular statements.	The ratio of descriptive to functional words	Measure divides the number of different words in a passage by the passage's total words
Complexity	Convoluted phrasings make a text's ideas abstract and its implications unclear.	Word size	Average number of characters-per-word in a given input file.

Appendix 3: Overview of CEOs interviewed

Episode	Interview Date	CEO	Firm	CEO start date	Female	Founder (Y/N)	CEO end date	Years CEO @ Interview	Total Years CEO	How Exit?	Inside Promotion(Y) / Outsider(N)	Age at Interview Date	Education BA FIELD	Education BA School	Education MA Field	Education MA School	Ivy League	MBA
106	2000-09-06	Gordon Bethune	Continental Airlines	nov-1994	N	N	déc-2004	5,85	10,08	Retired	N	59	BS	Abilene Univ.	Advanced Management	Harvard	Yes	Yes
106	2000-09-06	Michael Bonsignore	Honeywell	févr-1993	N	N	juil-2001	7,59	8,41	Replaced (forced)	Y	59	Electrical Engeneering	U.S. Naval Academy	Ocean science	Texas A&M	No	No
202	2000-12-01	Thomas Stemberg	Staples	févr-1986	N	Y	févr-2002	14,83	16,00	Replaced	Y	51	Physical Science	Harvard	MBA	Harvard	Yes	Yes
202	2000-12-01	Carl Yankowski	Palm	déc-1999	N	N	nov-2001	1,00	1,92	Resigned (poor performance)	N	51	Bachelor Science	MIT	Master's undisclosed	MIT	No	No
203	2001-01-24	Scott McNealy	Sun Microsystems	déc-1984	N	Y	avr-2006	16,15	21,33	Resigned (poor performance)	Y	46	Business Administration	Harvard	MBA	Stanford	Yes	Yes
203	2001-01-24	Marc Andreessen	Loudcloud (Netscape previously)	sept-1999	N	Y	juil-2007	2,00	1,50	Resigned (Sold shares)	Y	29	Bachelor Arts/science	Univ. of Illinois			No	No
205	2001-11-04	Carly Fiorina	Hewlett Packard	juil-1999	Y	N	févr-2005	2,35	5,59	Replaced	N	46	Business Administration	Stanford Universit	Ms MIT/MBA Univ. of Maryland		No	Yes
205	2001-11-04	John Chambers	Cisco Systems	janv-1995	N	N	juin-2014	6,84	19,42	in place	Y	51	BA-Law, BS bsiness administration	West Virginia Univ.	MBA	Indiana Univ.	No	Yes
208	2001-09-24	Jack Welch	GE	mars-1981	N	N	sept-2001	20,57	20,50	Retired	Y	65	Chemical engineering	Univ. of Massachusetts	MS -PhD Chemical engineering	Univ. of Illinois	No	No
301	2001-08-01	James Dimon	Bank One corp	mars-2000	N	N	juin-2014	1,42	14,25	in place	Y	46	N/A	Tufts Univ.	MBA	Harvard	Yes	Yes
301	2001-08-01	Raymond Gilmartin	Merck and Company	juin-1994	N	N	mai-2005	7,17	10,92	Retired	N	61	Electrical Engineering	Union college	MBA	Harvard	No	Yes
302	2002-05-03	Charles Lee	Verizon Communications	juin-2000	N	N	mars-2002	1,92	1,75	Resigned (only as co-CEO)	Y(from GTE)	61	Metallurgical Engineering	Cornell Univ.	MBA	Harvard	Yes	Yes
302	2002-05-03	Arthur F. Ryan	Prudential Financial	janv-2000	N	N	janv-2008	2,34	8,00	Retired	Y	60	BA mathematics	Providence college	Honorary PhD	New Jersey Institue of thecnology	No	No
304	2002-07-30	Robert L. Nardelli	The Home Depot	déc-2000	N	N	janv-2007	1,66	6,08	Resigned (poor performance)	N	54	Ba business	Western Illinois Univ.	MBA	Univ. of Louisville	No	Yes
304	2002-07-30	Michael L. Eskew	United Parcel Service	janv-2002	N	N	janv-2008	0,57	6,00	Retired (as CEO only)	Y	45	Industrial Engineering	Purdue Univ.	Advanced Management	Univ. of Pennsylvania (Wharton)	No	Yes
401	2006-01-05	Blake W. Nordstrom	Nordstrom	août-2000	N	N	juin-2014	5,43	13,83	in place	Y	52	Undisclosed Ba	Univ. of Washington			No	No
401	2006-01-05	Jim Donald	Starbucks Coffee Company	mars-2005	N	N	janv-2008	0,85	2,84	Replaced	N	52	BBA	Century Univ.			No	No
403	2005-11-11	Brian L. Roberts	Comcast	nov-2002	N	N	juin-2014	3,03	11,58	in place	Y	46	BS Finance	Univ. of Pennsylvania (Wharton)	Univ. of Arizona		Yes	No
403	2005-11-11	Harold W. (Terry) McGraw III	The McGraw-Hill	déc-1998	N	N	nov-2013	6,95	14,92	Retired	Y	57	BA	Tufts Univ.	MBA	Univ. of Pennsylvania (Wharton)	Yes	Yes
404	2005-12-07	Robert A. (Bob) Eckert	Mattel, Inc.	mai-2000	N	N	déc-2011	5,60	11,58	Retired	N	51	Ba/Bs	Univ. of Arizona	MBA	Northwestern Univ.	No	Yes
404	2005-12-07	Robert A. (Bobby) Kotick	Activision, Inc.	févr-1991	N	N	juin-2014	14,85	23,33	in place	N	42	Drop-out	Drop-out	Univ. of Michigan		No	No
405	2006-02-21	Gary C. Kelly	Southwest Airlines Company	juil-2004	N	N	juin-2014	1,64	9,92	in place	N	51	BBA Accounting	Univ. of Texas at Austin			No	No
405	2006-02-21	William E. (Bill) Greehey	Valero Energy corp	juil-1997	N	N	janv-2006	8,64	8,50	Retired (as CEO only)	Y	69	BBA	St-Mary's Univ.			No	No
406	2006-03-01	Edward J. (Ed) Zander	Motorola, Inc.	janv-2004	N	N	janv-2008	2,16	4,00	Resigned (poor performance)	N	59	Electrical Engineering	Rensselaer Polytechnic	MBA	Boston Univ.	No	Yes
406	2006-03-01	Edward M. (Ed) Liddy	The Allstate corp	janv-1999	N	N	déc-2006	7,16	8,00	Retired (remains chairman)	Y	60	BA	Catholic Universitiy of America	MBA	Georges Washignton Univ.	No	Yes

Episode	Interview Date	CEO	Firm	CEO start date	Female	Founder (Y/N)	CEO end date	Years CEO @ Interview	Total Years CEO	How Exit?	Inside Promotion(Y) / Outsider(N)	Age at Interview Date	Education BA FIELD	Education BA School	Education MA Field	Education MA School	Ivy League	MBA
407	2006-04-12	Kenneth D. (Ken) Lewis	Bank of America corp	avr-2001	N	N	déc-2009	5,03	8,75	Retired	Y	59	BBA	Georgia State Univ.			No	No
407	2006-04-12	Thomas M. (Tom) Ryan	CVS corp	mai-1994	N	N	mai-2011	11,95	17,08	Retired	Y	53	BS (Pharmacy *to be confirmed)	Univ. of Rhode Island	Honorary PhD	Johnson and Wales Univ.	No	No
408	2006-04-10	Bob Wright	NBC Universal, Inc.	sept-1986	N	N	févr-2007	19,61	20,49	Retired	Y	63	LLB - Premed:major psychology,minor history	Univ. of Virginia Law School · College of the Holy Cross			No	No
408	2006-04-10	Doug Morris	Universal Music Group	nov-1995	N	N	juil-2010	10,44	14,75	Resigned (personnal reasons)	N	67	BA Economics	Columbia			Yes	No
409	2006-04-24	Gerard Kleisterlee	Royal Philips Electronics	avr-2001	N	N	mars-2011	5,06	10,00	Retired	Y	59	Electronic Engineering	Technische Universiteit Eindhoven	Advanced Management	Univ. of Pennsylvania (Wharton)	No	Yes
409	2006-04-24	Fred Hassan	Schering-Plough corp	avr-2003	N	N	nov-2009	3,06	6,66	Merger (takeover by Merck)	N	60	Bs Chemical Engineering	Imperial College of Science & Technology	MBA	Harvard	Yes	Yes
	2006-05-02		Bobcats Sports	Was not CEO			mars-2010	NA	NA	Sold his shares								
410	2006-05-02	Robert L. Johnson	BET	janv-1980	N	Y	janv-2000	25,00	25,00	Retired	Y	60	BA	Univ. of Illinois	Master Public Affairs	Princeton	Yes	No
	2006-05-02		RLJ Companies	janv-2006			NA	NA	NA	in place								
410	2006-05-02	J.W. (Bill) Marriott, Jr.	Marriott International, Inc	janv-1970	N	N	mars-2012	36,33	42,25	Retired	Y	74	BS Banking and Finance	Univ. of Utah			No	No
501	2006-11-14	Anne M. Mulcahy	Xerox	août-2001	Y	N	juil-2009	5,29	8,00	Retired	Y	54	BA English and journalism	Marymount College			No	No
501	2006-11-14	Neville Isdell	Coca-cola	juin-2004	N	N	juil-2008	2,45	4,16	Retired	Y	63	BS Social sciences	Univ. of Cape Town	Program Management Development	Harvard	Yes	Yes
502	2006-11-30	Paul S. Otellini	Intel	mai-2005	N	N	mai-2013	1,54	7,99	Retired	Y	56	BA Economics	Univ. of San Francisco	MBA	Berkeley	No	Yes
502	2006-11-30	John W. Thompson	Symantec	avr-1999	N	N	avr-2009	7,67	10,01	Resigned (poor performance)	N	57	BBA	Florida A and M	Management Science	MIT	No	Yes
503	2006-09-26	Clarence Otis, Jr.	Darden Restaurants, Inc.	nov-2004	N	N	juin-2014	1,90	9,58	in place	Y	50	BA Economics Political science	Williams College	Juris Doctor	Stanford	No	No
503	2006-09-26	Mackey J. McDonald	VF corp	janv-1996	N	N	janv-2008	10,74	12,08	Retired	Y	59	BA English	Davidson College	MBA-Marketing	Georgia State Univ.	No	Yes
504	2007-01-30	Brian France	NASCAR, Inc.	sept-2003	N	N	juin-2014	3,38	10,72	in place	Y	44	non-earned	Univ. of Florida			No	No
504	2007-01-30	Gary D. Forsee	Sprint Nextel Corp	mars-2003	N	N	oct-2007	3,91	4,66	Resigned (poor performance)	Y	56	BS Engineering	Univ. of Missouri			No	No
505	2007-02-19	Patricia A. Woertz	Archer Daniels Midland Co.	mai-2006	Y	N	juin-2014	0,80	8,09	in place	N	53	BS Accounting	Univ. of Pennsylvania (Wharton)	Executive Development	Columbia Univ.	Yes	No
505	19-02-2007	Robert W. Lane	Deere & Co	août-2000	N	N	déc-2009	6,55	9,42	Retired	Y	57	BBA	Wheaton College	MBA/Advanced Executive Education	Various	No	Yes
506	2007-02-27	Cathleen P. Black	Hearst Magazines	janv-1995	Y	N	janv-2010	12,16	15,00	Resigned (personnal reasons)	N	62	BA English litterature	Trinty College			No	No
506	2007-02-27	William P. Lauder	Estee Lauder Companies	juil-2004	N	N	juil-2009	2,66	5,08	Resigned (Exit as CEO only)	Y	46	BA/BS	U. of Pennsylvania (Wharton)	MBA	Univ. of Pennsylvania (Wharton)	Yes	Yes
507	2007-03-14	Sir Howard Stringer	Sony corp	juin-2005	N	N	avr-2012	1,78	6,91	Retired	Y	65	BA - Modern History	Oxford	Modern-History	Oxford	No	No
507	2007-03-14	Brad Anderson	Best Buy Co.	juin-2002	N	N	juin-2009	4,78	7,08	Retired	Y	58	AA- BA Sociology	Whardof-Univ. of Denver			No	No
508	2007-03-28	Jeffrey C. Taylor	Eons.com	juil-2006	N	Y	avr-2011	0,74	4,83	Firm Acquired	Y	46	BA	Univ. of massachussets	Executive Education Program	Harvard	No	Yes
	2007-03-28		Monster.com	déc-1996			août-2005	10,32	8,75	Resigned to create Eons.com								

Episode	Interview Date	CEO	Firm	CEO start date	Female	Founder (Y/N)	CEO end date	Years CEO @ Interview	Total Years CEO	How Exit?	Inside Promotion(Y) / Outsider(N)	Age at Interview Date	Education BA FIELD	Education BA School	Education MA Field	Education MA School	Ivy League	MBA
508	2007-03-28	Jeremy Allaire	Brightcove	avr-2004	N	Y	mars-2013	2,99	8,95	Steps Down as CEO only	Y	31	BA Political Science	Macalester College			No	No
509	2007-05-07	Jeffrey R. Immelt	GE	sept-2001	N	N	juin-2014	5,66	12,73	In Place	Y	51	BA/BS Applied Mathematics	Dartmouth College	MBA	Harvard	Yes	Yes
509	2007-05-07	Irene B. Rosenfeld	Kraft	juin-2006	Y	N	juin-2014	0,93	8,00	In Place	N	54	BA Psychology	Cornell	MBA	Cornell	Yes	Yes
510	2007-04-25	Stephen A. Wynn	Wynn	juin-2002	N	Y	juin-2014	4,90	12,00	In Place	Y	65	BA English litterature	Unniversity of Pennsylvania			Yes	No
510	2007-04-25	Terry S. Semel	Yahoo	mai-2001	N	N	juin-2007	5,98	6,16	Resigned (poor performnce)	N	64	BS Accounting	Long Island Univ.			No	No

REFERENCES

Agle, B. R., Nagarajan, N. J., Sonnenfeld, J. A., & Srinivasan, D. (2006). Does CEO charisma matter? An empirical analysis of the relationships among organizational performance, environmental uncertainty, and top management team perceptions of CEO charisma. *Academy of Management Journal, 49*(1), 161-174.

Allgood, S., & Kathleen, A. F. (2000). The effect of CEO tenure on the relation between firm performance and turnover. *The Journal of Financial Research, 23*(3), 373-390.

Anderson, R. C., Bates, T. W., Bizjak, J. M., & Lemmon, M. L. (2000). Corporate governance and firm diversification. *Financial Management, 29*(1), 5-22.

Anonymous. (2007). *PBS: CEO exchange* Retrieved from http://www.pbs.org/wttw/ceoexchange/production.html. February 26, 2013.

Barnard, C. (1938). *The functions of the executive*. Cambridge, MA: Harvard University Press.

Barney, J. B. (1991). Firm resources and sustained competitive advantage. *Journal of Management, 17*(1), 99-120.

Berger, J., Ridgeway, C. L., Fisek, M. H., & Norman, R. Z. (1998). The legitimation and delegitimation of power and prestige orders. *American Sociological Review, 63*(3), 379-405.

Blettner, D. P., Chaddad, F. R., & Bettis, R. A. (2012). The CEO performance effect: Statistical issues and a complex fit perspective. *Strategic Management Journal, 33*(8), 986-999.

Boeker, W. (1997). Strategic change: The influence of managerial characteristics and organizational growth. *Academy of Management Journal, 40*(1), 152-170.

Bowen, R. M., Davis, A. K., & Matsumoto, D. A. (2002). Do conference calls affect analysts' forecasts? *Accounting Review, 77*(2), 285-316.

Boyd, B. K. (1995). CEO duality and firm performance: A contingency model. *Strategic Management Journal, 16*(4), 301-301.

Brennan, N. M., & Conroy, J. P. (2013). Executive hubris: The case of a bank CEO. *Accounting, Auditing & Accountability Journal, 26*(2), 172-195.

Brown, A. D., Stacey, P., & Nandhakumar, J. (2008). Making sense of sensemaking narratives. *Human Relations, 61*(8), 1035-1062.

Calingo, L. M. R. (1989). Environmental determinants of generic competitive strategies: Preliminary evidence from structured content analysis of Fortune and Business Week articles (1983-1984). *Human Relations, 42*(4), 353-353.

Chan, P. S., & Riess, G. (2004). The strategic value of a CEO. *Problems & Perspectives in Management,* (3), 153-162.

Cornett, M. M., Hovakimian, G., Palia, D., & Tehranian, H. (2003). The impact of the manager-shareholder conflict on acquiring bank returns. *Journal of Banking & Finance, 27*(1), 103-131.

Craig, R., Mortensen, T., & Iyer, S. (2013). Exploring top management language for signals of possible deception: The words of satyam's chair Ramalinga Raju. *Journal of Business Ethics, 113*(2), 333-347.

Craig, R. J., & Brennan, N. M. (2012). An exploration of the relationship between language choice in CEO letters to shareholders and corporate reputation. *Accounting Forum, 36*(3), 166-177.

Crumley, C. (2008). A study of the relationship between firm performance and CEO compensation in the U.S. commercial banking industry. *Journal of Applied Management and Entrepreneurship, 13*(2), 26-46.

Czarniawska-Joerges, B. (1998) *A narrative approach to organization studies*. Thousand Oaks, CA: Sage Publications, 87.

Czarniawska-Joerges, B. (2008). *A theory of organizing* Cheltenham, UK: Edward Elgar.

Delgado-García, J. B., & De La Fuente-Sabaté, J. M. (2010). How do CEO emotions matter? Impact of CEO affective traits on strategic and performance conformity in the Spanish banking industry. *Strategic Management Journal, 31*(5), 562-574.

Denning, S. (2006). Effective storytelling: strategic business narrative techniques. *Strategy & Leadership, 34*(1), 42-48.

Dong-Jin, P., & Berger, B. K. (2004). The Presentation of CEOs in the press, 1990-2000: Increasing salience, positive valence, and a focus on competency and personal dimensions of image. *Journal of Public Relations Research, 16*(1), 93-123.

Dörrenbächer, C., & Geppert, M. (2010). Subsidiary staffing and initiative-taking in multinational corporations. *Personnel Review, 39*(5), 600-621.

Farrell, J. B., Flood, P. C., Mac Curtain, S., Hannigan, A., Dawson, J., & West, M. (2005). CEO leadership, top team trust and the combination and exchange of information. *Irish Journal of Management, 26*(1), 22-40.

Finkelstein, S. (1992). Power in top management teams: Dimensions, measurement, and validation. *Academy of Management Journal, 35*(3), 505-538.

Finkelstein, S., & D Aveni, R. A. (1994). CEO duality as a double-edged sword: How boards of directors balance entrenchment avoidance and unity of command. *Academy of Management Journal, 37*(5), 1079-1108.

Fleming, D. (2001). Narrative leadership: Using the power of stories. *Strategy & Leadership, 29*(4), 34-36.

Gabriel, Y. (2000). *Storytelling in organizations: Facts, fictions and fantasies*. Oxford: Oxford University Press.

Geletkanycz, M. A., Boyd, B. K., & Finklestein, S. (2001). The strategic value of CEO external directorate networks: Implications for CEO compensation. *Strategic Management Journal, 22*(9), 889-898.

Gioia, D. A., & Kumar, C. (1991). Sensemaking and sensegiving in strategic change initiation. *Strategic Management Journal, 12*(6), 433-448.

Gunther, M. P., & Grandy, G. (2009). The media's construction of CEO infamy. *Journal of Strategy and Management, 2*(4), 300-328.

Hair, J. F., Anderson, R. E., Tatham, R. L., & Black, W. C. (1998). *Multivariate data analysis* (5th ed.). Upper Saddle River, N.J.: Prentice Hall.

Haleblian, J., & Finkelstein, S. (1993). Top management team size, CEO dominance, and firm performance: The moderating roles of environmental turbulence and discretion. *Academy of Management Journal, 36*(4), 844-863.

Hambrick, D., Geletkanycz, M., & Fredrickson, J. (1993). Top executive commitment to the status quo: Some tests of its determinants. *Strategic Management Journal, 14*(6), 401-418.

Hambrick, D. C. (2007). Upper echelons theory: An update. *Academy of Management Review, 32*(2), 334-343.

Hambrick, D. C., & Fukutomi, G. D. S. (1991). The seasons of a CEO's tenure. *The Academy of Management Review, 16*(4), 719-742.

Hart, R. P., & Carroll, C. (2013). Diction: The text analysis program (Version 7.0). Texas.

Healy, M. C., Lehman, M., & McDaniel, M. A. (1995). Age and voluntary turnover: a quantitative review. *Personnel Psychology, 48*(2), 335-345.

Henderson, A. D., Miller, D., & Hambrick, D. C. (2006). How quickly do CEOs become obsolete? Industry dynamism, CEO tenure and company performance. *Strategic Management Journal, 27*(5), 447-460.

Herrmann, P. (2002). The influence of CEO characteristics on the international diversification of manufacturing firms: An empirical study in the United States. *International Journal of Management, 19*(2), 279-289.

Herrmann, P., & Datta, D. K. (2006). CEO experiences: Effects on the choice of FDI entry mode. *The Journal of Management Studies, 43*(4), 755-778.

Hill, C. W. L., & Phan, P. (1991). CEO tenure as a determinant of CEO pay. *Academy of Management Journal, 34*(3), 707-717.

Jaw, Y.-L., & Lin, W.-T. (2009). Corporate elite characteristics and firm's internationalization: CEO-level and TMT-level roles. *The International Journal of Human Resource Management, 20*(1), 220-233.

Jensen, M., & Zajac, E. J. (2004). Corporate elites and corporate strategy: how demographic preferences and structural position shape the scope of the firm. *Strategic Management Journal, 25*(6), 507-524.

Larcker, D. F., & Zakolyukina, A. A. (2012). Detecting Deceptive Discussions in Conference Calls. *Journal of Accounting Research, 50*(2), 495-540.

Leonardi, P. M., Neeley, T. B., & Gerber, E. M. (2012). How Managers Use Multiple Media: Discrepant Events, Power, and Timing in Redundant Communication. *Organization Science, 23*(1), 98-117.

Lewin, A. Y., & Stephens, C. U. (1994). CEO attitudes as determinants of organization design: An integrated model. *Organization Studies, 15*(2), 183-212.

Lorentz, M. (Writer). (2000-2007) [Television]. In J. A. Anderson (Producer), *CEO Exchange*. Chicago: PBS/WTTW National Productions.

Maclean, M., Harvey, C., & Chia, R. (2012). Sensemaking, storytelling and the legitimization of elite business careers. *Human Relations, 65*(1), 17-40.

Magee, J. C., & Galinsky, A. D. (2008). Social Hierarchy: The self reinforcing nature of power and status. *Academy of Management Annals, 21*(1), 351-398.

Mäkelä, H., & Laine, M. (2011). A CEO with many messages: Comparing the ideological representations provided by different corporate reports. *Accounting Forum, 35*(4), 217-231.

Manusov, V., & Trees, A. R. (2002). 'Are you kidding me?': The role of nonverbal cues in the verbal accounting process. *Journal of Communication, 52*(3), 640-656.

McClelland, P. L., Liang, X., & Barker, V. L., III. (2010). CEO commitment to the status quo: Replication and extension using content analysis. *Journal of Management, 36*(5), 1251-1277.

Patton, M. Q. (2002). *Qualitative evaluation and research methods* (3rd ed.). Beverly Hills, CA: Sage.

Petit, V. (2012). Like a phoenix from the ashes. A Weberian analysis of the charismatic CEO routinization. *European Management Journal, 30*(6), 510-522.

Porter, M. E. (1980). *Competitive strategy*. New York: Free Press.

Rajagopalan, N., & Datta, D. K. (1996). CEO characteristics: Does industry matter? *Academy of Management Journal, 39*(1), 197-215.

Reed, R., & Reed, M. (1989). CEO experience and diversification strategy fit. *The Journal of Management Studies, 26*(3), 251-270.

Resick, C. J., Whitman, D. S., Weingarden, S. M., & Hiller, N. J. (2009). The bright-side and the dark-side of CEO personality: Examining core self-evaluations, narcissism, transformational leadership, and strategic influence. *Journal of Applied Psychology, 94*(6), 1365-1381.

Rhodes, C., & Brown, A. D. (2005). Narrative, organizations and research. *International Journal of Management Reviews, 7*(3), 167-188.

Seyranian, V., & Bligh, M. C. (2008). Presidential charismatic leadership: Exploring the rhetoric of social change. *Leadership Quarterly, 19*(1), 54-76.

Shear, G., Kakabadse, N., & Kakabadse, A. (2013). Visceral behaviours and leadership: a dark side of boardroom life? *The Journal of Management Development, 32*(1), 18-35.

Short, J. C., & Palmer, T. B. (2008). The application of Diction to content analysis research in strategic management. *Organizational Research Methods, 11*(4), 727-752.

Søderberg, A.-M. (2006). Narrative interviewing and narrative analysis in a study of a cross-border merger. *Management International Review, 46*(4), 397-416.

Sonenshein, S. (2007). The role of construction, intuition, and justification in responding to ethical issues at work: The sensemaking-intuition model. *Academy of Management Review, 32*(4), 1022-1040.

Strauss, A. L., & Corbin, J. (1998). *Basics of qualitative research* (2nd ed.). Thousand Oaks, CA: Sage.

Washington, M., & Zajac, E. J. (2005). Status evolution and competition: theory and evidence. *Academy of Management Journal, 48*(2), 282-296.

Weick, K. E. (1995). *Sensemaking in organizations*. Thousand Oaks, CA: Sage Publications, Inc.

Wiersema, M. F., & Bantel, K. A. (1992). Top management team demography and corporate strategic change. *Academy of Management Journal, 35*(1), 91-121.

DECISION SCIENCES INSTITUTE

Methodological Developments in Understanding Brand Creation and Brand Identity – The Case of Sevens Wellington - an International Recurring Sports Event

Sara Harrison
PwC
smlharrison76@gmail.com

John Davies
Victoria University of Wellington
john.davies@vuw.ac.nz

ABSTRACT

This paper demonstrates a multi-methodological approach to understanding brand creation in an international sports event. It describes use of Parent et al.'s model and outlines how Beer's Viable Systems Model provides complementary insights about branding and organizational processes suggesting revision of Parent's model for the Sevens Wellington event.

KEYWORDS: sports events, brand creation/identity, organizational design, systems thinking

INTRODUCTION

The paper reports on one strand of a multi-methodological research project examining the branding process – brand creation and brand identity – within a large international recurring sports event. The paper focuses on the specific case context of the annual two-day *Sevens Wellington* rugby tournament in New Zealand. The Wellington tournament, which has been held in February each year since 2000, is part of what is now known as the *World Rugby Sevens Series*, consisting of ten tournaments in ten countries, played on annual basis.

The *Sevens Wellington* tournament marks round five of the *World Rugby Sevens Series* and over fifteen years has become one of NZ's most popular sporting events. Popular with players and known for its unique 'carnival' atmosphere, the event has traditionally attracted high spectator numbers. Yet in 2014, 2015 and 2016, the event struggled to achieve a 'ticket sellout' as before, and also struggled to meet its sponsorship goals, perhaps amongst other factors, due to a decline in brand strength.

This paper first outlines the development and use of Parent et al's (2012) conceptual framework as a lens to examine branding issues: brand and identity creation for the *Sevens Wellington* event (aka *the Sevens)*. The framework also encompasses organizational variables, and addresses notions and issues related to organizational structure, governance and management. These inter-related organizational and branding issues provide a rationale for adopting a multi-methodological approach to understanding such issues and how they may addressed. Beer's Viable Systems Model (VSM) (1974, 1979, 1981) was considered to provide an alternative and complementary set of perspectives on such matters, and was used alongside Parent et al's 2012 framework to constitute an appropriate multi-methodological approach to both branding and organizational design.

A companion paper (Harrison & Davies, 2016) has demonstrated the wider benefits of the multi-methodological approach (Davies et al, 2004) to understand the inter-relatedness of effective brand creation and underpinning organization-related factors. In this paper, we show how insights from the use of Beer's VSM lead to proposed revision in the Parent et al (2012) model of brand creation.

The paper proceeds with some background on the sport of rugby and Rugby Sevens. Then following a brief overview of relevant literature, it sketches Parent et al's brand creation conceptual model (2012). The paper then provides a parsimonious description of Beer's VSM (1974, 1979, 1981), as a prelude to offering a selective VSM diagnosis and analysis of findings from the brand creation study relevant to the *Sevens* organization. A subsequent section which draws on those findings identifies variables and constructs that beneficially complement Parent et al.'s 2012 model, before proposing revisions to the model that impact its diagnostic potential.

BACKGROUND

The sport of Rugby Union is a sport played globally by men and women, with more than one hundred countries playing in the quadrennial 15-aside Rugby World Cup (RWC) and its qualifying matches. Although the game of Sevens was first played more than one hundred years ago amongst amateur clubs in the United Kingdom, the modern sport played by elite athletes at international level, is relatively new. However, the recent growth is such that in 2016, Rugby Sevens, for men and women, will be part of the Olympic Games in Rio. 15-a-side rugby last featured in the Olympic Games in 1924, when the USA XV won Gold. The *Sevens* tournament in NZ forms part of the *World Series* Olympic Qualifying process.
The responsibility for delivering the *Sevens* tournament had been devolved to the Wellington Rugby Football Union (WRFU, 2014a) by the New Zealand Rugby Union (NZRU), the governing body for rugby union in NZ. The *Sevens* organization is headed by a General Manager, but is, in all respects, a virtual organization. It must deliver the *Sevens* as a tournament event, as an entertainment event, and as a stadium experience. It has an Advisory Board that comprises representatives of the NZRU (2014a, b), WRFU, the Wellington Regional Stadium Trust – as the stadium venue host, and Wellington City Council – as a major sponsor etc.
Sevens is expected to make a significant return on investment to its owners – the NZRU, and its partners – but the seemingly insatiable demand for event tickets that initially sold out in minutes, then hours, then days, no longer exists. The *Sevens* brand had seemingly changed and diminished in strength, and the virtual organization had limited resources, no capital funding base, and no formal governing board to fill a stewardship role to give direction to the organization.

PRIOR and RELATED WORK

Brands and Branding

For detailed coverage of prior work examining the concept of 'brand' and its importance in differentiating a product or service, creating value, and marketing a specific set of features, benefits or experiences, readers are referred to Kotler & Keller (2012), Parent & Séguin (2008), Shank (2009).
With respect to the sports event domain addressed in this paper, we note that recent sports event and management literature has generally focused on the external antecedents that contribute to building sports events brands, such as benefits, 'consumer motives and increasing spectator attendance (Funk et al., 2009). An exception has been the research by Parent and Seguin (2008), who developed a model of brand creation for international large scale one-off sporting events, based on the process of sports events' identity construction previously proposed by Parent and Foreman (2007). Parent et al.(2012) then extended these models for the evaluation of international recurring sports events, and for application in the Northern hemisphere. Unfortunately, there is little research that examines brand creation for sports events in the New Zealand (NZ) context, let alone events so closely associated with the brand

of NZ's national game, rugby.
The wider research, of which this paper represents one strand, sought to address a gap in the literature by examining the inter-relationships between the four referents of Parent et al's (2012) model of brand creation for a recurring international sports event in a NZ context – the *Sevens* rugby tournament. The referents include, but are not limited to: (a) the importance of the LG, (b) the context, (c) the nature of the event, and (d) the induced event experience.
In the following sections we further sketch Parent et al's theoretical framework, focusing on a selective review of the literature relating to concepts of brand knowledge and the referents of Parent et al.'s (2012 model. The findings are then presented, analysed and discussed in the context of Stafford Beer's Viable Systems Model – the VSM (Beer, 1979, 1981; Brocklesby et al., 1995; Davies, 2002). Finally, a revised conceptual model of brand creation for the *Sevens* event is provided along with concluding comments. First, we outline the nature of Parent et al.'s 2012 Model of Brand Creation.

Parent et al's (2012) Model of Brand Creation

The evolution of Parent et al's (2012) model of brand creation is briefly addressed in a companion paper (Harrison & Davies, 2016). Here, we merely sketch the scene for its development. Suffice to say that the branding of recurring international sports events has interest on several counts, for example: temporal - that aspects of branding must be sustained over time for the recurring event, and societal/cultural - that branding can, and perhaps should accommodate the changing international markets and venues. In a sense, there is an international and a local or domestic dimension to branding (Parent et al., 2012).
The 2012 model of event brand creation is depicted in Figure 1, We continue with a sketch of complementary literature relating to the model's referents and their antecedents conceptualized in the model. These referents include the leadership group (LG), the context, the nature of the event, and the induced event experience.

Figure 1. Parent et al.'s 2012 Brand Creation Model
for International Recurring Sports Events

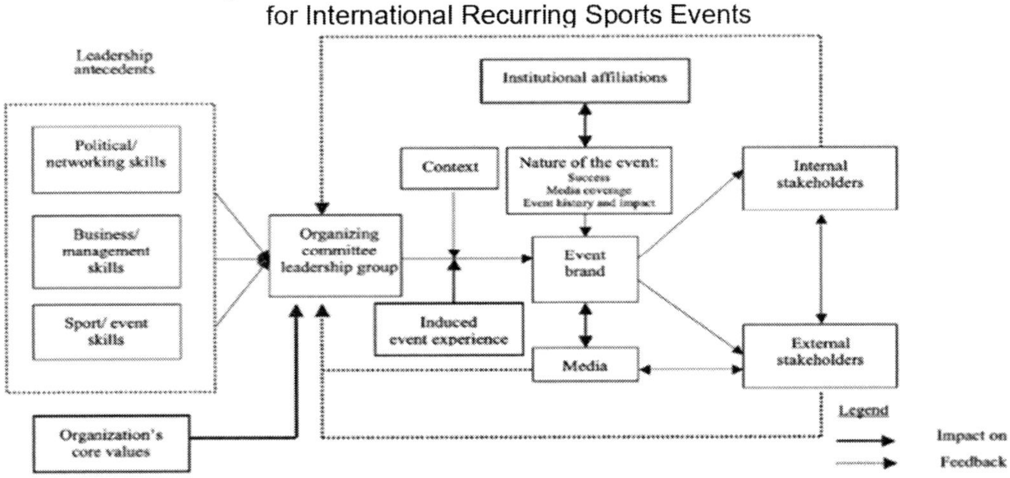

The Leadership Group (LG) - Parent et al. (2012) assert that building a strong brand, and a quality event which satisfies stakeholder needs, requires strong leadership. They have found that effective leadership encompasses a spectrum of skills and attributes: political skills and connections to manage stakeholder relationships; ability to manage a volunteer force; the drive, aptitude and ability to set and maintain high technical standards and a hunger to improve; and also, a leader's or Leadership Group (LG) "commitment and passion for the event, sport and associated and inherent values."

As such the skills and attributes were considered to span political and networking skills, management skills, sports / event skills and values-based actions. Other concepts of particular importance surfaced in the literature have also been embraced, and include stakeholder management (Parent, Olver, & Séguin, 2009; Yukl, 2002), and strategic direction and planning (Mitnzberg & Quinn, 1996).

The Context - The second referent of Parent et al.'s (2012) model encapsulates the context of the event. Whilst a sound strategic direction and planning process represents, in essence, the internal environment that underpins the LG's efforts, and shapes and drives the creation of the brand, Parent et al. (2012) conceptualize the event context as moderating the initial creation of the event by the LG. Having a good understanding of the context of the event is also vitally important, and would include factors such as the sporting and economic environment, the full spectrum of media, technology and culture (Emery, 2010), as well as the local or domestic market environment (Gladden et al., 1998).

The Nature of the Event -The third referent of Parent et al.'s (2012) model is the nature of the event. Factors, here, that act as a catalyst for brand creation include: the standing and recognition of sport in the host region; the presence or absence of a worldwide brand for the sport; and previous event success, media coverage, geographical location, event history and impact. Institutional arrangements and the recurring nature of the event have also been identified to be key factors (Parent & Séguin, 2008; Ross, 2006).

Induced Event Experience - Based on the notion that the strategic construction of the sport brand can only happen after its identity is shaped (Richelieu, 2004), Parent et al. included in their 2012 model an additional referent, '*induced event experience*'. This construct is allied to the evolution of the brand, in as much as evolution represents fine-tuning activities following event execution and debriefing.

Whilst the primary product of the sports industry is the competition that occurs at a sporting event, increasingly, activities - before, during and after the actual competition - are becoming more '*entertainment*' oriented, providing sports consumers with a "diverting or engaging" spectacle or a different kind of ephemeral experience (Shank, 2009, p. 4). In addition, the sporting nature of an event, in itself, is largely associated with, and adds to the spectrum of intangible and subjective features that influence customer patronage decisions.

This preçis of the literature for the wider study has addressed concepts related to brand knowledge; suggested an evolution toward Parent et al.'s (2012) model of brand creation for recurring international sporting events; and summarized the conceptual rationale for the four referents that undergird the model. We also note that the concepts of consumer motives, orientation towards a sports event, and service quality, and then their subsequent effect on behavioural consequences could be appropriately integrated within the context of the '*induced event experience*' referent. It has also been noted that establishing dynamic feedback between the LG referent and '*context*', rather than just a moderating effect, would also have potential to enhance the model.

In summary, restating the importance of understanding, reacting and adapting dynamically to the environment, to context, to stakeholders – spectators, consumers etc; and making appropriate use of communication channels and information for feedback, all pointed towards endorsement of Beer's VSM as a complementary framework for interpretation of the *Sevens* case data (Angen, 2000), As such, Beer's VSM was seen as not only likely to provide a complementary perspective on the *Sevens* organization and Sevens event, but also to offer interpretation and insight about whether important matters surfaced by VSM diagnosis could be accommodated within an enhanced Parent et's 2012 model.

The Viable Systems Model

A detailed description of the theoretical underpinnings of the VSM is not within the scope of this paper, but can be found in Beer (1979, 1981), Brocklesby et al (1995), Brocklesby and Cummings (1996). However, a brief outline of key notions is provided. Beer has conceptualized a viable system as sharing a network of communication channels bonding five complementary sub-systems (Davies, 2013). Beer (1959) suggests that the five sub-systems - identified as also existing in other viable organisms, for example, the brain and body - and the appropriate feedback and information flows that connect those sub-systems, are necessary to facilitate self-adaptive viability. The five sub-systems whose effective systemic functioning and communication links are necessary for organizational viability, are shown in Figure 2.

Figure 2: The VSM – Sub-systems and Systemic Functions

S1 Operations	• autonomous operational units that act out the very identity and purpose of the overall system, doing what the system is designed to do,
Meta-System	• comprising four other sub-systemic functions
S5 Identity	• the creation and promulgation of identity, values, purpose or *raison d'être*, vision, direction and mission, throughout the organization and its wider environment
S4 Intelligence	• strategy development serving the organization's future; focusing on the *future and external* environment
S3 Resourcing	• operational planning, resourcing, formal reporting, regulation, control and audit functions relating to the autonomous units; focusing on the *inside and now* of the organization
S3* Monitoring	• informal monitoring of culture, performance, riskt
S2 Coordination	• effecting overall coordination of autonomous units, ensuring autonomous operational units work in harmony
Environment	• VSM recognition and capture of the environment within the model is necessary to reflect the domain of action for the organization, and to contextualise or ground the internal interactions of the organization

Adapted from Davies (2013) and Brocklesby and Cummings (1996)

Figure 3: Stafford Beer's Viable Systems Model

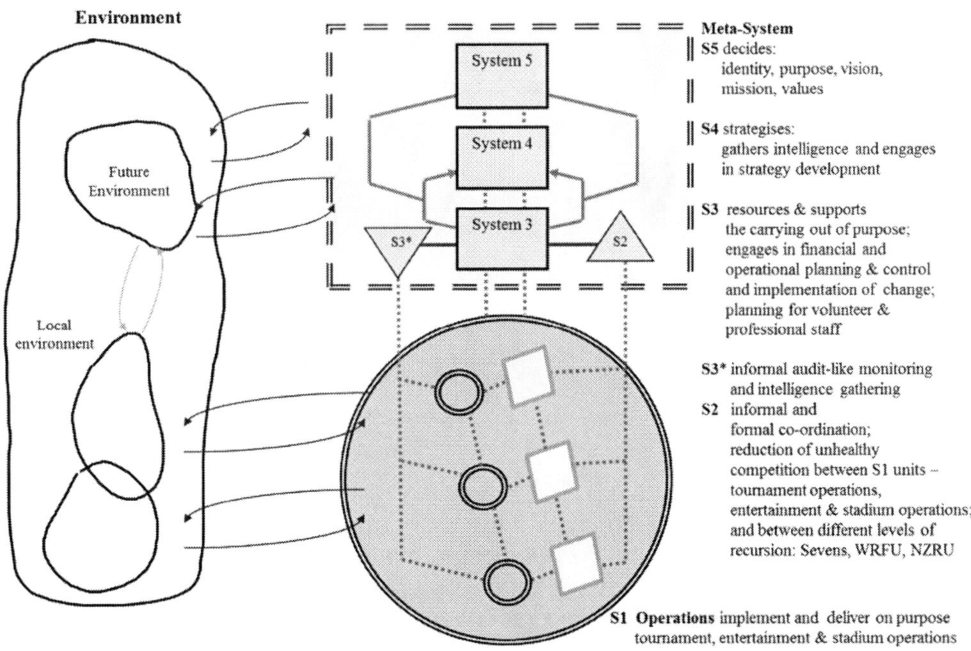

These sub-systems may also be capable of viability. As such, viable systems are *recursive*; that is, viable systems contain embedded viable systems that can be modeled using an identical cybernetic description as the higher (and lower) level systems in the wider systems hierarchy. The *Sevens* organization is presented in Figure 3 as a schematic representation of the VSM. Its cybernetic or systemic strengths are then examined via VSM diagnosis. The VSM framework was used as a lens to provide a systems perspective on key issues that had surfaced in the findings of the wider brand creation study, and that have been identified in the literature.

FINDINGS - THE SEVENS WELLINGTON ORGANIZATION AND THE VSM FRAMEWORK

In conceptualizing and representing the *Sevens* organization as the system of interest – aka the System in Focus (SIF), we note that it is also regarded as a nested S1 unit of the WRFU system, which in turn is embedded as a S1 unit within the NZRU system.
Within the *Sevens* system, and certainly within its own embedded S1 units covering tournament operations, entertainment and stadium operations/experience, it may not be surprising to find *silo effects* in evidence. However, the VSM presentation makes it more readily obvious that considerations of coordination are now seen to encompass elements across different logical levels, *recursion* or *nestedness*, of the overall system; and also between elements at the same level of *recursion* – highlighting, in a different way, not only the complexity of coordination functions, but the difficulty in attending to *silo effects*.

Figure 4: The *Sevens Wellington* System – a Viable System Model and Diagnosis

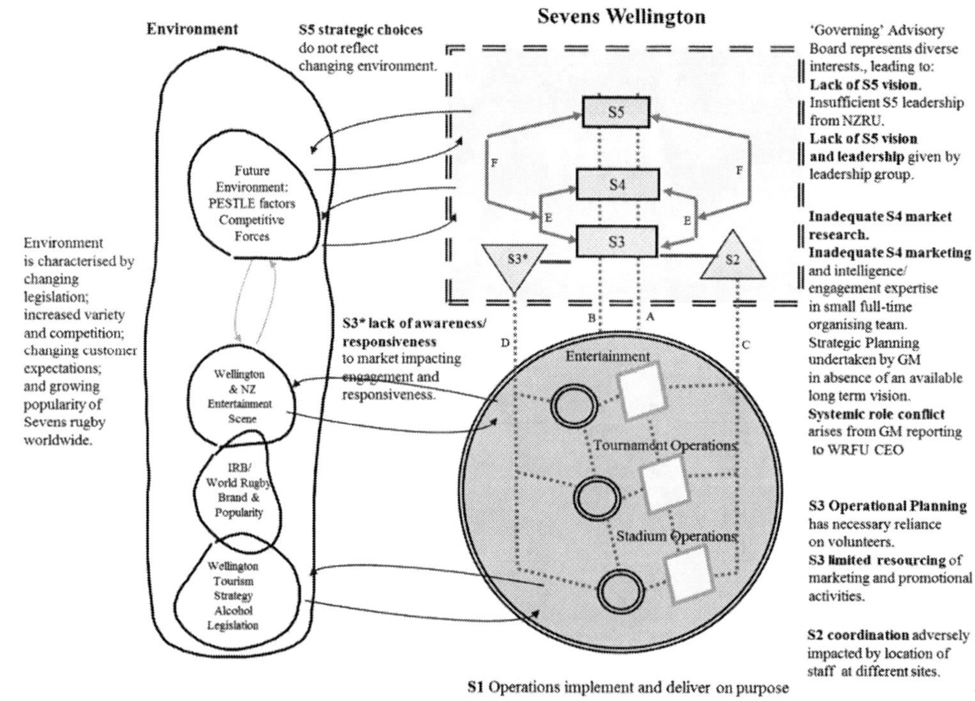

Key issues that had surfaced in the findings of the wider brand creation study, related not only to matters underpinning successful brand development facing the *Sevens* organization, but also to the organization itself, and to environmental forces and factors. As such, elements of Parent et al.'s (2008) model of brand creation were reconceptualized and reinterpreted using the VSM model (see Figure 4), especially to highlight matters that may reflect organizational

effectiveness. These matters include systemic role conflict, systemic overlap in functional duties, and/or systemic gaps or weaknesses matters within the organization or wider system.
As an overview of findings, we note that at the time of the study, there was an absence of S2 and S5 functionality within the wider system relating to the *Sevens* system-in-focus, and its S1 operations. In particular, there was a seeming lack of S2 coordination within the WRFU system, with limitations in the policy framework provided to *Sevens* and less than adequate direction about means of resolving minor incongruencies arising from the sub-optimal local objectives of tournament, stadium and entertainment S1 operations. The S2 systemic weakness associated with the wider WRFU system, has impacted on the *Sevens* event as a S1 sub-system of the WRFU, and on the *Sevens* event as a possible viable system in its own right.
Such matters and other key activities manifesting as the meta-systemic functions are shown as annotations in Figure 4 as illustration of VSM thinking. They are referred to in more detail in the companion paper (Harrison & Davies, 2016).

REVISED CONCEPTUAL MODEL FOR BRAND CREATION AT SEVENS WELLINGTON

In light of the research findings and interpretation of the *Sevens* brand creation 'system' using the VSM framework, a revised conceptual model of brand creation is proposed and presented below (see Figure 5).The key insights portrayed within the revised model reflect a need to distinguish or differentiate the S5 values-creation, vision-making and strategy determination functions, from Parent et al's (2012) all embracing categorization of leadership antecedents; and to identify them explicitly as governance functions. These revisions help make an articulation and dissemination of organizational values, governance and strategic direction, more explicit.

Figure 5. Revised Conceptual Model of Brand Creation for *Sevens*

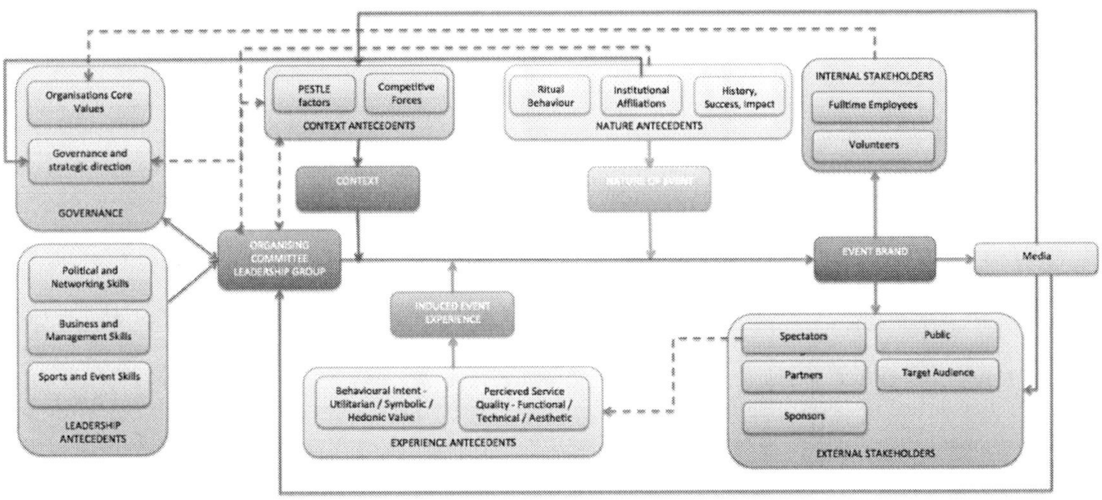

The development of an overarching S5 identity and long-term vision as a governance function, has been separated out, in the revised model. In addition, insights from VSM diagnosis that highlight the importance of the dynamic systemic interplay between strategic and operational planning, scanning and interpreting the external environment, are also incorporated. As such, the S5 function, and especially the notions of creating and disseminating organizational values, effectively provide an organizational context for activities of the LG.
Allied with S5 strategic choice and strategy determination, the S4 strategising and intelligence function - which has a role in identifying long-term strategic trends and factors in the macro environment - is also depicted in the revised model by a new feedback loop with the 'context'

antecedents.
Other erstwhile leadership activities are also reflected in the revised model by their interplay with the LG. In addition, a feedback loop between 'internal stakeholders' and S5 functions has been created to capture not only the essence of S3* informal monitoring and episodic intelligence gathering, but also S2 coordination functions.
The S4 intelligence function is reflected in the revised model mainly within the LG element, but also by the feedback loop with the 'context' and 'nature' antecedents. Being able to proactively identify trends and amend strategic positioning appropriately is a key skill. More localised trends within the environment that capture changes in 'institutional affiliation' and reflect an event's 'history, success and impact', are captured in the model by the '*nature of event*' construct. An additional factor, 'ritual behavior', is proposed as a further refinement to the revised model, given the impact that behavior can have on an event of this nature, in general, and the *Sevens* event, in particular.
Within the local Wellington environment, understanding the target audience is also vitally important. This facet is captured within the revised model by the proposed addition of several antecedents linked to what we may regard as the '*induced event experience*' referent, such as: 'behavioural intent' and 'perceived service quality'. A systemic feedback loop between 'spectators' within the external stakeholder grouping is also suggested to emphasize the importance of information sharing and flow. These communication flows can be conceptualized as part of the S3* monitoring function.
The S4 strategising function reflects activities conducted by the LG and is depicted by the two-directional arrows linking to the S5 governance element. The ability, or *requisite* variety, of the S4 function to manage all such inputs and requirements, to innovate, and also lead structured change, will impact the ultimate creation and success of the event brand.
Within the proposed revised model, the LG also have responsibilities for S3 resourcing, planning and control functions. These include marketing and planning functions in as much as they relate to resourcing the creation of the *Sevens* brand. They also include helping shape the environment for the event; and enabling the effective functioning of S1 units – entertainment, tournament and stadium operations. As depicted within the LG antecedents, there is a grouping of S3-related skillsets which are required in order to create a successful brand, in particular S3 marketing support and S3 commercial/sponsorship management skill-sets.
The interplay between S4 intelligence function, S1 operations, and the environment are reflected in the revised model by the interplay of the 'event brand' and 'internal/external stakeholders' (including media) – which elements have been separated out to provide greater clarity.
External stakeholder attitudes towards the brand may not only include perceptions of service quality held by spectators and sponsors (as stakeholders), but may also be expressed in terms of their behavioural intent. If so, the LG then needs to have access to an effective S3* monitoring system of appropriate *requisite variety*, in order to be able to conduct *ad hoc* market research and surveys, as and when required, to understand how perceptions of the brand may have changed as a result of '*induced event experience*' or as a result of media coverage.
The perceptions of internal stakeholders will also have an impact on the strengthening/weakening and pervasiveness of organizational values, and this is depicted by a new feedback loop in the revised model. The media, as a distinctive stakeholder group, has been separated out, and re-orientated to highlight the impact that media can have on a number of referents.
In summary, the foregoing has attempted to convey how and why the proposed model accommodates and revises Parent et al's (2012) model, especially with respect to its underpinning contextual, LG (governance) and organising committee antecedents.

SUMMARY AND CONCLUSION

This paper has outlined and demonstrated use of Parent et al's (2012) conceptual framework as a lens to examine branding issues: brand and identity creation for the *Sevens Wellington* event. It was noted that the framework also encompasses organizational variables, and addresses matters related to organizational structure, governance and management. These inter-related organizational and branding issues provided a rationale for adopting a multi-methodological approach to understanding such matters and how they may be addressed. Beer's Viable Systems Model – VSM - (1974, 1979, 1981) was considered to provide an alternative and complementary set of perspectives on such matters, and was used alongside Parent et al's 2012 framework to constitute an appropriate multi-methodological approach to examining both branding and organizational design.

The paper reports on a study which was part of a wider project which examined brand issues in large international recurring sports event, and which drew primarily on the brand creation and brand identity model developed by Parent et al (2007, 2008). A companion paper (Harrison & Davies, 2016) has demonstrated the wider benefits of the multi-methodological approach to understand the inter-relatedness of effective brand creation and underpinning organization-related factors. Here, we also demonstrate that the benefits can extend to the use of one methodological framework informing conceptual developments in the other. In this case, we have shown how insights from the use of Beer's VSM lead to proposed revision in the Parent et al (2012) model of brand creation.

In respect of understanding broader branding issues for the *Sevens* event, the findings reported in the companion paper (Harrison & Davies, 2016) indicated the relative importance of several factors – both organizational and brand related - in the management of the *Sevens* brand. In the revised model, for example, the importance of the dynamic interplay between planning/scanning and interpreting the external environment has been made more explicit, and elements from the literature review and key themes from the research findings have also been incorporated.

In summary, the work reported in this paper is part of a wider study that has not only contributed to sport specific event management knowledge that relates to brand creation and brand identity, not only contributed to understanding systemic functions that underpin successful branding processes, and underpin organizational effectiveness, but also to methodological and conceptual developments.

In this respect, we state that the benefits of a multi-methodological approach have been extended beyond use of one model to inform use of another; beyond use of insights from one model to inform insights derived from the other; and to include the conceptual development of one model using insights developed from the other.

REFERENCES

Angen, MJ (2000). Evaluating Interpretive Inquiry: Reviewing the Validity Debate and Opening the Dialogue. *Qualitative health research, 10*(3), 378-395

Beer S. (1959). *Cybernetics and Management*. London: English Universities Press.

Beer S. (1974). *Designing Freedom.* Wiley: Chichester: Wiley.

Beer, S. (1979). *The Heart of the Enterprise*, Wiley, Chichester.

Beer, S. (1981), *Brain of the Firm (2nd Edn)*, Wiley, Chichester.

Brocklesby, John, & Cummings, Stephen. (1996). Designing a Viable Organisation Structure. *Long Range Planning, 29*(1), 49-57.

Brocklesby R. J., Cummings, S. & Davies J. (1995). Demystifying the Viable Systems Model as a Tool in Organisational Analysis. *Asia Pacific Journal of Operations Research,* Vol. 12, No.

1, 65-86.

Davies, J. (2013). Designing Sustainable Sports Organisations - A VSM Approach. In F. Stowell, S. McRobb, R. Lander, R. Ison, J. Holloway, & R. Armson (Eds.), *Systems for Sustainability: People, Organisations, and Environments* (2nd Edn) (Ch. 33, pp. 191-197). London: Springer Science & Business Media. ISBN 0-306-45615-X.

Davies, J., Mabin, V & Cox, J. (2004). The Theory of Constraints and Systems Dynamics: A Suitable Case for Multi-methodology, Proceedings of the *22nd International Conference of the Systems Dynamics S*ociety, Kennedy G *et al* (Eds), Oxford, July 25-29 2004, pp 27.

Davies, J. (2002). Models of Governance - A Viable Systems Perspective, *The Australian Journal of Information Systems*, Vol 9(2), May 2002, 57-66. A

Davies, J. & Mabin, V. (2001). Framing: A Meta-framework for the use of Mixed-Mode Modelling. In M.G. Nicholls, S. Clarke & B. Lehaney (Eds), *Mixed-Mode Modelling: Mixing methodologies for organisational intervention* (pp.63-119), Dordrecht/London: Kluwer Academic Publishers.

Funk, D.C., Filo, K, Beaton, A.A. & Pritchard, M. (2009). Measuring the Motives of Sport Event Attendance: Bridging the Academic-Practitioner Divide to Understanding Behavior. *Sport Marketing Quarterly, 18*(3), 126-138.

Gladden, J.M., Milne, G.R., & Sutton, W.A. (1998). Conceptual framework for assessing brand equity in division 1 college athletics. *Journal of Sport Management, 12*, 1-19.

Harrison, S. & Davies, J. (2016). Understanding the Organisational Needs of an International Sports Event – A Systems Perspective on Sevens Wellington. *Proceedings of the 47th Annual Meeting of Decision Sciences Institute*, , November 19-22 2016,

Kotter, J. P. (2007). Leading Change: Why Transformation Efforts Fail. *Harvard Business Review*(January), 96-103.

Mabin, V., Davies, J. & Cox, J. (2006). Using the Theory of Constraints to Complement Systems Dynamics' Causal Loop Diagrams in Developing Fundamental Solutions, *International Transactions in Operations Research,* Vol 13, 33-57, DOI: 10.1111/j.1475-3995.2006.00532.

NZRU - New Zealand Rugby Union. (2014a). Our Strategic Framework. Retrieved 10 October, 2014, from http://www.nzru.co.nz/about_us/strategic_framework

NZRU - New Zealand Rugby Union. (2014b). Towards 2016 - Empowering Rugby. Retrieved 10 October, 2014, from http://www.nzru.co.nz/about_us/strategic_framework

Parent, Milena M., Eskerud, Line, & Hanstad, Dag Vidar. (2012). Brand creation in international recurring sports events. *Sport Management Review, 15*(2), 145-159. doi: http://dx.doi.org/10.1016/j.smr.2011.08.005

Parent, Milena M., Olver, Denise, & Séguin, Benoit. (2009). Understanding Leadership in Major Sporting Events: The Case of the 2005 World Aquatics Championships. *Sport Management Review, 12*(3), 167-184. doi: http://dx.doi.org/10.1016/j.smr.2009.01.004

Parent, Milena M., & Séguin, Benoit. (2008). Toward a Model of Brand Creation for International Large-Scale Sporting Events: The Impact of Leadership, Context, and Nature of the Event. *Journal of Sport Management, 22*(5), 526-549.

Parent, Milena M., & Foreman, Peter O. (2007). Organizational Image and Identity Management in Large-Scale Sporting Events. *Journal of Sport Management, 21*(1), 15-40.

Richelieu, A. (2004). Building the brand equity of professional sports teams. In B. G. Pitts (Ed.), *Sharing best practices in sports marketing.* Morgantown: WV: Fitness Information Technology.

Ross, S. D. (2006). A conceptual framework for understanding spectator-based brand equity. *Journal of Sport Management, 20*(1), 22-38.

WRFU. (2014a). Wellington Rugby. Retrieved 26 April, 2014, from http://www.wrfu.co.nz/

WRFU. (2014b). Drinking practices of attendees of the Wellington Sevens and Homegrown in 2014. *Wellington Sevens Study.*

DECISION SCIENCES INSTITUTE
Mining for the Entrepreneurial Element

Robert D. Morrison
University of Texas of the Permian Basin
Email: morrison_r@utpb.edu

ABSTRACT

This study reviews the literature on serial and parallel or portfolio entrepreneurship and argues the importance of differentiating between them when conducting research. The entrepreneurial element that researchers seek can only be found deep within the metacognitive processes of parallel entrepreneurs; those who have demonstrated the repeated ability to succeed. Many extant entrepreneurship studies are misleading because they report findings from samples where, based on widely know statistics, most of the entrepreneurs eventually failed or just got lucky once.

KEYWORDS: Entrepreneurship & Strategy, Cognition & Reasoning

INTRODUCTION

Entrepreneurship is often heralded by politicians as being the backbone of the US economy and as a job creator. Aligned with this belief is academia's embrace of entrepreneurship as demonstrated by the dramatic increase in the number of entrepreneurship programs (Inc., 2006) even as academic researchers struggle to clearly define entrepreneurship as a unique discipline (Low, 2001) and understand how entrepreneurs differ cognitively from other economic actors despite some suggestions by learned scholars such as Nobel Laureate Kenneth Arrow (as cited in Sarasvathy, 2000) that the evidence to date has failed to overcome the null hypothesis of no difference. Given the suggested importance of the impact of entrepreneurship on economic growth and employment, one would think that public policy should focus on developing everyone possible into an entrepreneur; however, such a stance ignores the waste that results from the majority of business start-up attempts that result in failure. Indeed, the image of a hard-working visionary achieving incredible success by beating all of the odds is part of the American Dream, but in reality this is part of the entrepreneurial folklore (Brockhaus, 1980) and myths that glorify entrepreneurs (Shane, 2008). In reality entrepreneurial success is a rare occurrence (Short, Ketchen, Shook, & Ireland, 2010). Unfortunately, studies pretty much all agree that most new businesses, as high as 70%, fail (Shane, 2008) and even though some studies have found that as high as 40% of businesses survive at least eight years (Kirchhoff, 1997) this still indicates that most fail. In fact, the data indicate that most businesses in most industries fail (Dumne, Roberts, & Samuelson, 1988) and this has been the norm for decades. In addition, it is rare that a new firm puts well established firms out of business (Audretsch, 1991). Many of those few that do manage to survive do not harvest excessive profits. Studies in the mid-1990s found that two-thirds of owner-operated businesses generated less than $10,000 in annual profits (Audretsch, 1995; Barnett, 1990; Mata & Guimaraes, 1995) and US Federal Reserve Data indicates that the typical profit for owner-managed firms was $39,000 (Audretsch & Mahmood, 1995). The data indicates that most of the self-employed earn less than they could if they were employed by someone else (Hamilton, 2000; Uusitalo, 2001).

The reliance on data collected from all who attempt to start a successful venture has lead researchers to mistakenly generalize that, on average, entrepreneurs are overly optimistic about the opportunities they discover (Shane & Venkataraman, 2000; Ucbasaran, Westhead, Wright, & Flores, 2010). Research argues that this excess of optimism leads to entrepreneurs limiting information searches and enhancing future forecast (Kahneman & Lovallo, 1994; Kaish & Gilad, 1991) and this enhances motivation to the point that entrepreneurs exploit opportunities without conducting sufficient analysis (Busenitz & Barney, 1997). Every success must logically follow a start-up attempt; however, an increase in exploitation of recognized opportunities does not necessarily result in an increase in success rates, failure may increase as well (Shane & Venkataraman, 2000). From this *all who try are certified entrepreneurs* viewpoint it appears that the majority of entrepreneurs blindly pursue opportunities that have odds of success far less appealing than even the least player friendly casino games. Why then, would any rational politician proclaim the economic benefits of entrepreneurship or any learned academic promote entrepreneurship as a career choice? Do college professors, who arguably give advice based on what the research indicates, want most of their students to pick a career where failure is the norm?

The problem lies in how academics classify an individual as an entrepreneur. While the actual definition, as well as the domain, has been the subject of much debate (e.g. Gartner, 1989; McKenzie, Ugbah, & Smothers, 2007; Shane & Venkataraman, 2000; Stevenson & Jarillo, 1990), academic researchers have broadly defined entrepreneurship in such a way that just about anyone can be called an entrepreneur because they recognized something that they perceived as an opportunity and took some steps toward at least evaluating the feasibility of pursuing it. Using this logic it would be possible to classify almost everyone in society as an artist, mathematician, musician, or athlete because at sometime in their life they painted something in a primary school art class, worked math problems in math class, played a musical instrument, or participated in school or playground sports. The problem with the current academic classification of entrepreneurs is that it fails to have some threshold that separates would-be entrepreneurs who mindlessly pursue heartfelt dreams from successful entrepreneurs that really do innovate, create jobs, and contribute to economic expansion. In essence, entrepreneurship researchers have included every basketball player from grade school to the NBA in the population and found statistical support for the hypothesis that basketball players miss most of their shots. In the real world one's career is the thing that they can perform effectively enough to earn a living at; therefore, a real entrepreneur is one who has been sufficiently successful at recognizing opportunities and seeing them through to fruition sufficiently to make a living doing so and create wealth in the long run. Those who tried and failed are simply would-be entrepreneurs just as 200,000 high school basketball stars become something else the day they graduate and find that they do not have a scholarship to college and nobody will pay them to play basketball. Although the study of failure is important, the actions and cognitive processes of would-be entrepreneurs should not be generalized as applying to successful entrepreneurs.

Despite the dismal data on business survival, apparently some people do become successful entrepreneurs. The data indicates that the self-employed are four times more likely to become millionaires than those who work for others (Stanley & Danko, 1996) and the US Federal Reserve Survey of Consumer Finances indicates that 93.3% of business equity in the US in 2007 was held by the top 10% of families in terms of net worth, a number that has remained around the 90% mark for about three decades, and the data also indicates that the top 1% and next 19% also hold a disproportionate percentage of the unincorporated business equity and *other* (commercial, rental, vacation) real estate (Wolff, 2007, 2010). This information provides support for the enthusiasm for entrepreneurship demonstrated by politicians and academicians; membership in the club of business ownership does appear to have its privileges. However, it also underlines the need for researchers to focus more attention on what this small percentage does correctly instead of filling academic journals with pages of studies based on data from populations that is polluted with so much failure. MacMillan (1986) argued the importance of studying repeated entrepreneurial success to really understand entrepreneurship; however, the problem is that observing this rare subset of the business practitioner species in its natural environment is difficult. In fact, most of them live incognito as Stanley and Danko (1996) pointed out.

Arguably, successful entrepreneurs were not overconfident or overoptimistic. They were sufficiently confident and demonstrated an appropriate level of optimism about the opportunity and the adequacy of their skills, knowledge, and experience to be successful. Because a better understanding of people who have founded multiple businesses is crucial for in a free-enterprise economy (Scott & Rosa, 1996) researchers should study habitual entrepreneurs (MacMillan, 1986) because they are more theoretically interesting than those that just got lucky once (McGrath, 1996). Therefore, I concur with Kenneth Arrow, "What is the definition of an entrepreneur? Not only one who succeeds, but one who keeps on succeeding." (Sarasvathy, 2000: 7)

First, this study contributes to the literature by demonstrating the importance of researching entrepreneurial cognition by first separating the successful entrepreneurs from the would-be entrepreneurs and arguing that the findings related to entrepreneurs in the extant literature have been polluted with results from non-entrepreneurs. Second, I provide convincing evidence that researchers should not confuse serial entrepreneurship with serial successes. Third, I suggest that the parallel entrepreneur does not view his or herself as the creator of multiple businesses; but rather that they are "the business" and the multiple legal business entities are simply multiple manifestations of their entrepreneurial abilities. Finally, The most significant contribution is that I introduce the concept of pessimistic falsification as the preliminary internal phase of the metacognition process that occurs in real-life opportunity analysis and precedes the expression of optimism and the positive approach to opportunity reported in empirical studies using surveys and experimentation with business scenarios. I present a framework for viewing the opportunity evaluation process of parallel entrepreneurs where the feasibility evaluation process becomes optimistic only after the experienced entrepreneurial mind has pessimistically scrutinized it in a process similar to Popper's scientific method of falsification where the null hypothesis pre-supposes a high failure rate (Kenneth Arrow as cited in Sarasvathy, 2000).

LITERATURE REVIEW

Opportunity Recognition

Shane and Venkataraman (2000: 218) state that "The field of entrepreneurship involves the study of sources of opportunities; the processes of discovery, evaluation, and exploitation of opportunities; and the set of individuals who discover, evaluated, and exploit them". Opportunity recognition is recognized as an important trait of successful entrepreneurs (Ardichvili, Cardozo, & Ray, 2003). Pattern recognition is a key component of opportunity recognition and the cognitive representations of opportunities of experienced entrepreneurs differ from those of novice entrepreneurs (Baron & Ensley, 2006). Shane and Venkataraman (2000: 221-222) suggest that "two broad categories of factors that influence the probability that particular people will discover particular opportunities: (1) the possession of the prior information necessary to identify an opportunity and (2) the cognitive properties necessary to value it". However, Shepherd and DeTienne (2005) argue that the interaction of prior knowledge and financial reward is complex and may have a moderating effect on opportunity recognition. At any point in time, only some subset of the population will discover a given opportunity (Kirzner,

1973) because asymmetry of beliefs is a precondition for the existence of entrepreneurial opportunities (Hayek, 1945). Novice entrepreneurs envision novelty, technological and industry change; however, experienced entrepreneurs examine pragmatic issues like cash flow and risk. Learning serves as a key driver of the effectiveness of opportunity development (Short et al., 2010). Past experiences develop decision making heuristics that enhance opportunity capture (Bingham, Eisenhardt, & Furr, 2007). Because information about underutilized resources, new technology, unsated demand, and political and regulatory shifts is distributed according to the idiosyncratic life circumstances of each person in the population (Venkataraman, 2007), most novice entrepreneurs have no real concept of what it takes to develop a successful business. This supports the position that entrepreneurs, when nascent or would-be entrepreneurs are included in the definition of the class, are overoptimistic but at the same time it underlines the need to separate successful entrepreneurs from would-be entrepreneurs.

Repeated Entrepreneurial Success

There is considerable heterogeneity among entrepreneurs in the area of opportunity recognition (Gaglio & Katz, 2001; Ucbasaran, Westhead, & Wright, 2009); considering that researcher tend to group would-be entrepreneurs and successful entrepreneurs together in their samples, the variation in business ownership experience may explain this heterogeneity (Baron & Ensley, 2006; Shane & Venkataraman, 2000; Shepherd & DeTienne, 2005; Ucbasaran et al., 2009). The importance of studying individuals who have experienced entrepreneurial success more than once is not a new concept (Alsos & Kolvereid, 1998; Birley & Westhead, 1993; Lamont, 1972; Westhead & Wright, 1998); however, at least at first glance, the finding are mixed. Where Alsos and Kolvereid (1998) found the parallel entrepreneurs had a higher probability of venture implementation than novice and serial founders Birley and Westhead (1993) found no difference in terms of performance between novice, habitual, and serial founders. It is important to note that these findings are not contradictory findings. Alsos and Kolvereid (1998) were examining the new business gestation process from opportunity recognition to implementation whereas Birley and Westhead (1993) were comparing performance in established firms. The fact that the firms in the Birley and Westhead (1993) study had successfully navigated through the start-up process and were operating as ongoing business concerns entails that they had graduated from would-be entrepreneurs status to experienced entrepreneurs. If anything, this supports the importance of controlling for experience when analyzing samples in entrepreneurship research.

It should be noted that the terminology is inconsistent across the entrepreneurship literature. Inexperienced entrepreneurs are often referred to as *novice* or *nascent* entrepreneurs; emphasizing the importance of preserving the title of entrepreneur for those that have demonstrated success I categorize them as would-be entrepreneurs. The terms *repeat* and *habitual* are used to classify individuals that have started up more than one business; however, these terms have been used to describe both those who own multiple businesses concurrently and those who start a new business after exiting or closing an existing business. Individuals that start another business while they are still operating a business that they started or acquired are labeled *parallel* or *portfolio* entrepreneurs. Those who start a business and then move on to start another business are described as *serial* or *sequential* entrepreneurs.

Serial Entrepreneurs

The inspiring concept of the habitual or serial entrepreneur being motivated by the challenge of bringing a recognized opportunity to fruition but disinterested in managing the business once established is discussed in the literature (MacMillan, 1986; McGrath, 1996; Scott & Rosa, 1996) and there are certainly documented examples. But serial entrepreneurship is quite common, maybe as high as one-third of existing business are owned by people who had previously started a business, (Baird & Morrison, 2005; Birley & Westhead, 1993; Kolvereid & Bullvag, 1993) and empirical evidence suggest that there may be additional reasons for the serial entrepreneurship phenomenon. The reason for leaving the first business could range from selling the firm due to the boredom of routine management tasks after the excitement of a business start-up, to termination by management put in place by investors, as was the case of Steve Jobs at Apple and Sandy Lerner at Cisco Systems, to failure of the firm. While it is true that serial entrepreneurs do have entrepreneurial experience, further inquiry is needed to understand if a difference might exist between parallel entrepreneurs and serial entrepreneurs.

Extant literature indicates that examination of both the capabilities and motivations of serial entrepreneurs is necessary. Wright, Robbie, and Ennew (1997b) found that venture capitalists do not uniformly embrace serial entrepreneurs and that care should be taken in assessing experienced entrepreneurs. The same researchers identified three types of serial entrepreneurial behavior namely *venture repeaters*, *organic serials*, and *serial dealmakers*; distinguished by the motivations and the methods used to develop their ventures. Evidence from this study also indicates that the role of active investors varies according to the type of serial entrepreneur and venture (Wright, Robbie, & Ennew, 1997a). Westhead, Ucbasaran, and Wright (2003) suggested than novice and serial entrepreneurs were similar in terms of growth prospects and less likely to express dimensions of entrepreneurial behavior (Westhead, Ucbasaran, & Wright, 2005). Recently, these researchers found that serial entrepreneurs were overly optimistic and less capable of reflecting on failure (Ucbasaran, Westhead, & Wright, 2011). In at least some cases serial entrepreneurs are would-be entrepreneurs that got lucky once (McGrath, 1996).

Studying small owner-operator corporations, under 500 employees, Baird and Morrison (2005) found evidence from bankruptcy filings in one federal district court that serial entrepreneurs use bankruptcy reorganization laws, Chapter 11, to protect their personal credit record while forcing renegotiation of personal guarantees they were initially forced to make with creditors and the IRS during the business start-up. They also found 85% of the businesses in the sample were serial entrepreneurs and were able to determine that 45% had previously started a business that failed. In 70% of the cases the owner-operators started another business, or simply moved operation to another corporation they had previously established, and in 60% of the cases the new business was similar to the one shutdown during or after the Chapter 11 bankruptcy process. Although Chapter 11 is a reorganization process intended to put debt collectors and landlords at bay and keep supplies flowing to preserve the business as a going concern, Baird and Morrison (2005) found that almost all the small corporations in the sample ceased operation. The point of the study was why owner-managers used this legal process if business closure was the apparent plan. They determined that for owner-operators the bankruptcy process was more a delay and renegotiation tactic used as a means of self-employment preservation. Although only a very small portion of small businesses that fail go through the bankruptcy process the fact that the vast majority of owner-operators that used the process could be classified as serial entrepreneurs indicates a need for a better understanding of serial entrepreneurs.

While there are competent entrepreneurs that successfully started a business and leave to start-up subsequent successful businesses (Gompers, Kovner, Lerner, & Scharfstein, 2010), the evidence suggests that not all serial entrepreneurs do it just because they are good at it. This dictates that researchers must take care when generalizing the findings from a sample of serial entrepreneurs as best practices.

Parallel Entrepreneurs

A review of the entrepreneurship literature might lead one to believe that ownership of more than one business at a time is quite rare, Alsos and Kolvereid (1998: 101-102) stated that "It is, however, now becoming widely appreciated that some parallel/portfolio founders own two of more businesses at the same time". Given the data on the concentration of control of business equity in the US Federal Reserve Survey of Consumer Finances it appears that family ownership of multiple companies would have to be very common, at least among the wealthiest families in the US. While research that includes subjects that own multiple businesses appears to be increasing (eg. Ucbasaran, Westhead, & Wright, 2008; Ucbasaran et al., 2009, 2011; Ucbasaran et al., 2010; Westhead et al., 2003, 2005) the majority of this research has focused on comparing portfolio entrepreneurs to novice and serial entrepreneurs with the dependent variable being performance, opportunity recognition, or implementation success.

Although the empirical research on parallel entrepreneurs is limited (Westhead & Wright, 1998), Alsos and Kolvereid (1998) found that parallel entrepreneurs take a less hurried approach and have a higher probability of venture implementation than both novice and serial founders. Westhead et al. (2003) suggested that portfolio entrepreneurs, on average, appear to offer more attractive growth prospects than novice and serial entrepreneurs and portfolio entrepreneurs were more likely to express dimensions of entrepreneurial behavior (Westhead et al., 2005). Ucbasaran et al. (2011) found that while portfolio entrepreneurs are realistic and learn from their failures, serial entrepreneurs were found to be overly optimistic and less capable of reflecting on failure. Parallel entrepreneurs have been found to have easier access to external financing (Lamont, 1972) and this may be due to the accumulation of tacit knowledge (Polanyi, 1983) about business start-up as well as technical and commercial information that can only be gained through personal experience (Star & Bygrave, 1991); both would certainly enhance entrepreneurial intuition (Armstrong & Hird, 2009; Mitchell, Friga, & Mitchell, 2005) and entrepreneurial intentions have been empirically determined to derive from perceptions of feasibility and desirability (Krueger, 1993). Therefore, experience entrepreneurs can be expected to carry out business start-up processes differently from those without experience (Alsos & Kolvereid, 1998) which supports the idea that entrepreneurs think differently (Busenitz & Barney, 1997; Krueger, 1993; Krueger & Brazeal, 1994; Palich & Bagby, 1995). Building on the work of Ericsson and Charness (1994), Krueger (2007) argues that successful entrepreneurs can be characterized by an expert mind-set and experts typically organize or structure the content differently; however, not all successfully make the transition from novice to expert. Therefore, it is vital to the understanding of the entrepreneurial element that we study successful entrepreneurs, those who succeed and keeps on succeeding (Kenneth Arrow as cited in S. D. Sarasvathy, 2000), and parallel entrepreneurs have proven their ability in that respect.

Why Own Multiple Businesses?

Scott and Rosa (1996) suggested that the limits of firm-level analysis have been reached in small business research and urged researchers to focus on the invisibility of real wealth creating activities and the results of multiple ownership. But, why do entrepreneurs who own a successful ongoing concern deflect their time, human capital, and financial resources toward starting or acquiring other businesses? Birley and Westhead (1993) suggest that multiple business ownership results from a growth strategy while Alsos and Kolvereid (1998) add that additional businesses may be a strategy for tax reduction. From a legal perspective, Baird and

Morrison (2005) point out that it is not uncommon for a company, for example a restaurant, to incorporate each location as a unique corporate identity. Each of these explanations has merit and they may in fact be intertwined. However, it should be noted that the tax reduction strategy motivation suggested by Alsos and Kolvereid (1998) in their study in Norway will likely vary from country to country. In the US for example, the profits of wholly owned separate corporations flow-through the parent corporation untaxed, as do the profits from Type S corporations to their shareholders, to accumulate in one entity. This eliminates any advantage gained by having the profits of several entities separate in a stepped income tax system. While individuals and groups of individuals can do business as unincorporated sole-proprietors or unincorporated partnerships, incorporating the business so that it stands as its own corporate person provides some degree of personal protection from legal liability and debt collection in the event of an accident, defective products, or business failure. In the US, the special tax treatment given to Type-S corporations avoids the issue of double taxation of corporate profits as they pass through to shareholders in the form of dividends and the Type-S corporation is the most common The only negatives of incorporating a small enterprise are the minimal initial fees to file a corporation with the Secretary of State in the chosen state, the annual corporate license tax that is usually based on the assets held by the corporation, and the requirement to hold and document annual meetings. According to the IRS (2005) Type S corporations are significant participants in the US economy:

> S corporations are entities whose income and deductions pass through the corporate structure to the shareholders. Since the mid-1980s, the number of S corporations has risen rapidly, growing from 724,749 in 1985 to 3,154,377 in 2002. The growth rate has been even faster among S corporations with more than $10 million in assets. From 1985 to 2002, the number of these larger S corporations grew more than ten-fold, from 2,305 to 26,096....S corporations are now the most common corporate entity. In 2002, the latest year for which data is available, S corporation returns accounted for 59 percent of all corporate returns filed for that tax year. Two million S corporations reported net income of about $248 billion and 1.2 million S corporations reported net losses of about $63 billion.

Some states have added new hybrid forms of doing business that include Limited Liability Companies (LLC), Limited Liability Partnerships (LLP), and Professional Associations (PA) that may be treated for federal tax purposes either as partnerships or Type S corporations. In effect these provide the same legal liability protections while still providing some ownership transfer restrictions that a small company or group of licensed professionals might need in events such as death or exit of an owner.

The purpose for this discussion is that it points out a need to examine the reasons for multiple business ownership, when the criterion is multiple legal operating entities, when identifying parallel entrepreneurs. There are liability and credit reasons that a person who sells auto parts in three locations may want to hold each as three separate corporations, yet they are still operated in practice as the same business. Is this really parallel entrepreneurship? On the other hand, a person who owns a 15 minute oil change company, a restaurant, and an insurance agency might be a more interesting research subject and meet the criteria of repetition of entrepreneurial experience with an entirely new company (Wright et al., 1997b).

The research on multiple business ownership is sparse; however, in a study of 600 small business owners in the UK, Rosa, Carter, and Hamilton (1996) found that 19.6% of men and 8.6% of women owned more than one business. Although not extensively researched, farmers have often pursued multiple ventures simultaneously (Alsos & Carter, 2006; Carter,

1998, 1999, 2001). The extant literature provides little empirical insight into why an individual would want to own multiple businesses but intuitively growth and risk management would be logical explanations. It is likely that there are numerous explanations that are context specific to the individual entrepreneur's situation. For example, individuals who already own a business may inherit an existing business that generates a reliable income stream. Clearly a business owner that recognized the likely decline in business due to changes in market dynamics or technology shifts would be motivated to establish alternative income streams. Then there are likely seasonal issues that come into play also. One can imagine that an owner-operator of a ski rental business would have the need for supplemental income during a significant portion of the year. Beyond these situations, I posit that the initial journey into multiple business ownership is usually the result of an individual having a stable business where reinvestment would not significantly increase the profits because of market saturation. If the second business is successful, then the entrepreneur becomes aware that his or her core competence is the ability to successfully manage a business. Therefore, I propose.

P1: Parallel entrepreneurs do not consider themselves as parallel entrepreneurs. They envision themselves as one multifaceted business entity.

In this stream of inquiry it might also be fruitful to explore issues of locus of control and the entrepreneur's perception of their ability to control outcomes as motivators for investing in additional businesses that they can participate in the management of as opposed to the stocks of publicly traded companies.

UNDERSTANDING THE ENTREPRENEURIAL MIND

Whether or not entrepreneurs differ cognitively from others in society has yet to be settled and the increasing stream of research on entrepreneurial cognition is examining that question from a variety of angles. I suggest, based on personal experience as a successful parallel entrepreneur and interaction with multiple entrepreneurs over a period exceeding three decades, that, in general, entrepreneurs are highly inquisitive individuals that passively evaluated opportunity on a continual basis. This process is a mental exercise similar to a math enthusiast solving Sudoku puzzles. For example, an entrepreneur may be passing through a town and realize that a common fast food restaurant does not exist and evaluate why someone local person has not invested in the franchise and consider the likelihood of success based on population, nearness to a major interstate and other pertinent criteria with no intention of actually pursuing the opportunity. Similarly, when entrepreneurs gather, they conversations discussing business opportunities usually develop. From personal experience, I am also aware that when one owns one or more businesses one is frequently pitched business investment opportunities by others; usually individuals who have a desire and passion but not the capital to pursue their vision.

Proposition 2: The parallel entrepreneur is inquisitive and alert to opportunity by nature and continuously hones those skills by running mental evaluations of potential opportunities, small and large, encountered on a daily or weekly basis

Proposition 3: Only a miniscule portion of the mental evaluations of potential opportunities that the parallel entrepreneur performs mental analyzes on advance to the mental "is the opportunity right for me" evaluation stage that includes limited information gathering and rough calculations.

While just getting lucky once (McGrath, 1996) is likely a somewhat frequent occurrence and could lead to the failure to reject Kenneth Arrow's null hypothesis of no particular set of characteristics that distinguishes individuals in terms of success or failure is interesting, Arrow's suggested definition of entrepreneurs being those who succeed and continue succeeding (as cited in Sarasvathy, 2000) is theoretically more interesting and suggest that he believes that some differences might actually exist. I concur with the position that entrepreneurs do think differently (Busenitz & Barney, 1997; Krueger, 1993; Krueger & Brazeal, 1994; Palich & Bagby, 1995). The high failure rate of business start-ups is a clear indication that success is not given and those who did succeed likely encountered numerous obstacles during the journey. Even if someone did just get lucky once the entrepreneurial experience enhances both general and specific human capital (Chandler, Lyon, & Detienne, 2005); therefore, the experience itself leads to cognitive adaptation that impacts individual self-regulation (Haynie & Shepherd, 2009; Higgins, 1997). Self-regulation is incorporated in the metacognition (Flavell, 1979; Flavell, 1987; Nelson, 1996) process in that "regulation informs the development and generation of new sense-making structures (heuristics) as a function of a changing environment" (Haynie & Shepherd, 2009: 696).

Despite the popular myth that entrepreneurs have a much higher propensity for risk than others in society, the reality is that the risk preference of entrepreneurs is scattered across the risk preference spectrum and may actually be skewed toward risk aversion (Begley & Boyd, 1987; Brockhaus, 1980; Miner & Raju, 2004; Palich & Bagby, 1995; Sarasvathy, Simon, & Lave, 1998; Stewart & Roth, 2001). Masters and Meier (1988), Palich and Bagby (1995), and Norton Jr and Moore (2006) failed to find a difference in risk propensity among entrepreneurs. But entrepreneurs have been found to be more positive about opportunity (Palich & Bagby, 1995) more intuitive (Armstrong & Hird, 2009), more self-confident (Macko & Tyszka, 2009). Macko and Tyszka (2009) did find in an experiment that want-a-be entrepreneurs were more prone to risk and while they did find some evidence of riskier choices among practicing entrepreneurs they underlined the difficulty of simulating real-life situations where actual consequences were involved. The finding that want-a-be entrepreneurs are more prone to risk supports the argument for the need to study experienced entrepreneurs because they approach opportunity and risk differently.

Drawing on Schraw and Dennison (1994), Melot (1998), and Haynie and Shepherd (2009) I argue that successful entrepreneurial experience results in one becoming more metacognitive in the way that they approach opportunity evaluation. The experience of actually starting and running a successful business enlightens one to the complexity of being the decision maker and having everything at risk and greatly enhances ones Entrepreneurial Specific Human Capital (Smith, Matthews, & Schenkel, 2009). As a result they become more intuitive (Armstrong & Hird, 2009) because experience has made them aware that there are multiple ways to formulate a response, so they are more likely to evaluate alternatives before making a decisive move and this explains the findings that parallel entrepreneurs are less hurried (Alsos & Kolvereid, 1998). Furthermore, the experience of actually experiencing the resource scarcity that is the reality for most entrepreneurial start-ups makes parallel entrepreneurs more likely to scan the environment and examine the accessibility of internal and external resources before becoming positive about a potential opportunity.

While I concur that successful entrepreneurs are more self-confident, I argue that they are not over confident about their abilities and the fact that they have had one or more successful ventures provides evidence that they are sufficiently confident about themselves. I suggest that the increased positivity or optimism observed in different studies is a result of instrumentality of the studies and the difficulty simulating the real feeling of potential loss of time, resources, and capital. Based on not less than one dozen real-life collaborations on business opportunity evaluations, I have not witnessed optimism being the initial stance that experienced entrepreneurs take; in fact, the opposite is the norm. Experienced entrepreneurs know that failure is the most likely outcome and take a very pessimistic initial view point. It is only after sufficient eliminations of the reasons that the venture will not succeed that they become excited about the opportunity. However, the nature of the entrepreneurial spirit may inhibit researcher from exhibiting this phenomena. Is it realistic to think that someone like Donald Trump would truly reveal how they analyze a potential business deal? Because entrepreneurs view themselves as "the business" they are very unlikely to express anything but optimism to anyone that does not have "skin in the game" because they know that nobody wants to do business with a failure.

> *Proposition 4: Parallel entrepreneurs take a risk adverse falsification approach to opportunity analysis where the null hypothesis is failure,*

> *Proposition 5: The vast majority of opportunity analysis in the mental exercise stage fail to reject the null hypothesis of failure.*

Is This an Opportunity for Me?

If the potential opportunity passes through the falsification phase because the entrepreneur has found sufficient evidence to reject the null hypothesis of failure this only results in a finding that it is a third person opportunity for someone. The entrepreneur then analyzes personal and associated (i.e. employees, family, network ties) human capital and access to enabling technologies, financial resources, and customer support (Choi & Shepherd, 2004; Haynie, Shepherd, & McMullen, 2009; Ucbasaran et al., 2008, 2009) against requirements of potential opportunity to evaluate if this is a potential opportunity first person opportunity for them (Haynie et al., 2009). Since opportunities are the result of information asymmetries there is always a degree of tacitness and Entrepreneurial Specific Human Capital (ESC) gained through experience and this plays a significant role in understanding the requirements of tacit opportunities (Smith et al., 2009). This ability allows parallel entrepreneurs to reduce uncertainty and dramatically improve their success rates. While would-be entrepreneurs often rush in, parallel entrepreneurs are less hurried and may use an options approach where investments are postponed until key uncertainties are resolved (Alsos & Kolvereid, 1990; McGrath, 1996)

Even if the parallel entrepreneur determines that they have access to the needed skills and resources, the entrepreneur balances the potential income stream against the personal investment of time and capital (Chandler et al., 2005). In the case of persons that have an existing business the decision is moderated by the impact that the new venture may have on the performance of current business operations. However, the moderating effect is likely very context dependent. If the entrepreneur perceives a future downturn in the existing business this would increase the perception of the new venture being beneficial. On the other hand, if the existing business is growing and in need of the entrepreneurs undivided attention the new venture would have to show evidence of extraordinary returns, relative to the existing business, and temporal urgency to warrant the investment of time and resources. Then there could also be instances where a potential opportunity could enhance the performance of an existing business. If the potential opportunity is determined to fit into the parallel entrepreneur's current situation additional resources are invested to do a formal analysis and formulate a business plan. Given that the parallel entrepreneur has an existing business this entails that he or she also has a current income stream and failure of a new venture could impact that income stream as well as result in the loss of hard earned assets. As a result, experienced entrepreneurs are likely to establish a business plan that could be categorized as entrepreneurial fishing where specific parameters are established for the investment of resources and the performance criteria required at each stage of the process. I derive the entrepreneurial fishing term from personal experience with a successful entrepreneur who set detailed guidelines for investing employee time, money, and objectives in the development of new products. He was an avid fisherman and when arriving at a new fishing spot he would clearly state how long the waters would be tested before moving on to other locations.

I also argue that parallel entrepreneurs appreciate the benefit entrepreneurship provides to the economy, the knowledge of an unexploited opportunity may actually be bothersome, and will therefore inform others of opportunities that they find that do not fit into their specific situation. In some instances they may seek a working partner that has the requisite skills but not the capital and enter into a partnership. In other cases they may enlighten someone in their network or a family member to an opportunity that they have validated but do not feel fits into their current situation. If the opportunity is not exploited by others, the entrepreneurwill mentally shelf the information acquired for the event that future circumstances facilitate their ability to pursue the opportunity.

Proposition 5: The parallel entrepreneur balances Entrepreneurial Specific Human Capital, access to resources, skills, and enabling technologies, as well as potential impact on established income streams against the potential income stream of the newly recognized opportunity when determining if the opportunity is "right for me".

Proposition 6: Parallel Entrepreneurs take an options approach on opportunities determined to be "right for me" and invest in formal analysis and planning before pursuing the opportunity.

Proposition 7: Parallel entrepreneurs may seek working partners, inform other entrepreneurs in their network, or inform family members about opportunities that their analysis rejected the null hypotheses for but were found not to be an opportunity for them.

FIGURE 1 Goes About Here

DISCUSSION

This paper has pointed out the importance of truly understanding the entrepreneurial experience of the research subjects. All entrepreneurs are not created equal but the evidence on wealth accumulation strongly suggests that a few are extraordinarily accomplished. Entrepreneurial experience enhances both general and specific human capital (Chandler et al., 2005). Starting a business is difficult and the road to success contains countless landmines and resource destroying detours. As a result of this experience successful entrepreneurs are uniquely aware of the complexity that surrounds any potential business opportunity and tend to first approach opportunities from a pessimistic point of view even though they may not provide outward signs of pessimism. The reason that the extant empirical research on entrepreneurial cognition has failed to capture this important component of the entrepreneurial element that differentiates entrepreneurs from the rest of society is that researchers have incorrectly defined the population of entrepreneurs that are the disequilibrium phenomenon (Sarasvathy, 2000) responsible for driving innovation and economic expansion including would-be entrepreneurs, serial failures, and successful entrepreneurs. Given that failure is the most common entrepreneurial outcome, exceeding 70% by some accounts, the empirical findings of the vast majority of studies are arguably more representative of the entrepreneurially challenged than they are of those who have demonstrated the ability to recognize opportunity and turn it into a sustainable, wealth creating enterprise. This sampling error has resulted in a misrepresentation of the characteristics of entrepreneurs in the academic literature. Entrepreneurship researchers need to follow the suggestion of Kenneth Arrow and define entrepreneurs as those who succeed and keep succeeding if they desire to understand the process of entrepreneurship and discover the entrepreneurial element that is responsible for the job creation and economic expansion.

With entrepreneurship education on the rise in business schools (Inc., 2006) it is imperative that educators understand the true nature of successful entrepreneurial cognition if they wish to instill in students the analytical abilities they need to succeed. The appropriate sample for study is those who have created more than one successful business, yet the empirical research on these successful individuals is grossly inadequate. Unfortunately, entrepreneurs are busy people and that is only amplified for those operating multiple businesses simultaneously. Reflecting on three decades of interaction with dozens of parallel entrepreneurs, I never recall any of them having extra time to participate in research. It is likely that the lack of research on parallel entrepreneurs is due to the difficulty of gaining access; however, this only exacerbates the importance of understanding how they think and underlines the important contribution that such understanding would make to the entrepreneurial literature.

Empirically, I suggest that initial research should likely proceed as semi-structured interviews focusing on past opportunity evaluations of parallel entrepreneurs or asking parallel entrepreneurs to report the opportunities discovered or presented to them in real-life over a period of three to six months and note their thoughts as they evaluate the opportunity. Initially, I can envision the use of content analysis (Barringer, Jones, & Neubaum, 2005) (Chandler & Lyon, 2001) (Gartner, 1990) (Marino, Castaldi, & Dollinger, 1989) and/or Cognitive Mapping (Barr, Stimpert, & Huff, 1992) (Bougon, Weick, & Binkhorst, 1977; Bougon, 1992; Eden, 1992; Eden, Ackermann, & Cropper, 1992; Krueger, 2005; Nadkarni & Barr, 2008; Russell, 1999; Walsh, 1995) as a research tool. However, the difficulty of extracting an internal cognitive process that these individuals likely take for granted should not be underestimated and may require the combination of multiple research methods.

REFERENCES

Alsos, G. A., & Carter, S. (2006). Multiple business ownership in the Norwegian farm sector: Resource transfer and performance consequences. *Journal of Rural Studies, 22*(3), 313-322. doi: 10.1016/j.jrurstud.2005.09.003

Alsos, G. A., & Kolvereid, L. (1998). The Business Gestation Process of Novice, Serial, and Parallel Business Founders. [Article]. *Entrepreneurship: Theory & Practice, 22*(4), 101-114.

Ardichvili, A., Cardozo, R., & Ray, S. (2003). Atheory of entrepreneurial opportunity identification and development. *Journal of Business Venturing, 18*(1), 105-123.

Armstrong, S., & Hird, A. (2009). Cognitive Style and Entrepreneurial Drive of New and Mature Business Owner-Managers. *Journal of Business & Psychology, 24*(4), 419-430. doi: 10.1007/s10869-009-9114-4

Audretsch, D. B. (1991). NEW-FIRM SURVIVAL AND THE TECHNOLOGICAL REGIME. [Article]. *Review of Economics & Statistics, 73*(3), 441.
Audretsch, D. B. (1995). Innovation, Growth and Survival. *International Journal of Industrial Organization, 13*, 441-457.

Audretsch, D. B., & Mahmood, T. (1995). New Firm Survival: New Results Using a Hazaqrd Function. *Review of Economics and Statistics, 77*(1), 97-103.

Baird, D. G., & Morrison, E. R. (2005). Serial Entrepreneurs and Small Business Bankruptcies. *Columbia Law Review, 105*(8), 2310-2368.

Barnett, W. (1990). The Organizational Ecology of a Technological System. *Administrative Science Quarterly, 35*, 31-60.

Baron, R. A., & Ensley, M. D. (2006). Opportunity Recognition as the Detection of Meaningful Patterns: Evidence from Comparisons of Novice and Experienced Entrepreneurs.. *Management Science, 52*(9), 1331-1344.

Barr, P. S., Stimpert, J. L., & Huff, A. S. (1992). Cognitive Change, Strategic Action, and Organizational Renewal. *Strategic Management Journal, 13*, 15-36.

Barringer, B. R., Jones, F. F., & Neubaum, D. O. (2005). A quantitative content analysis of the characteristics of rapid-growth firms and their founders. *Journal of Business Venturing, 20*(5), 663-687. doi: 10.1016/j.jbusvent.2004.03.004

Begley, T. M., & Boyd, D. P. (1987). A Comparison of Entrepreneurs and Managers of Small Business Firms. *Journal of Management, 13*(1), 99-108.

Bingham, C. B., Eisenhardt, K. M., & Furr, N. R. (2007). What makes a process a capability? Heuristics, strategy, and effective capture of opportunities. *Strategic Entrepreneurship Journal, 1*(1-2), 27-47. doi: 10.1002/sej.1

Birley, S., & Westhead, P. (1993). A Comparison of New Businesses Established by "novice" and "habitual" founders in Great Britain. *International Small Business Journal, 12*(1), 38-60.

Bougon, M., Weick, K., & Binkhorst, D. (1977). Cognition in Organizations: An Analysis of the Utrecht Jazz Orchestra. *Administrative Science Quarterly, 22*(4), 606-639.

Bougon, M. G. (1992). Congregate Cognitive Maps: A Unified Dynamic Theory of Organization and Strategy. *Journal of Management Studies, 29*(3), 369-387. doi: 10.1111/j.1467-6486.1992.tb00670.x

Brockhaus, S. R. H. (1980). Risk Taking Propensity of Entrepreneurs. *Academy of Management Journal, 23*(3), 509-520. doi: 10.2307/255515

Busenitz, L. W., & Barney, J. B. (1997). Differences between entrepreneurs and managers in large organizations: Biases and heuristics in. *Journal of Business Venturing, 12*(1), 9.

Carter, S. (1998). The economic potential of portfolio entrepreneurship: Enterprise and employment contributions of multiple business ownership. *Journal of Small Business and Enterprise Development, 5*(4), 297-306.

Carter, S. (1999). Multiple business ownership in the farm sector: assessing the enterprise and employment contributions of farmers in Cambridgeshire. *Journal of Rural Studies, 15*(4), 417-429. doi: 10.1016/s0743-0167(99)00004-2

Carter, S. (2001). Multiple business ownership in the farm sector - Differentiating monoactive, diversified and portfolio enterprises. *International Journal of Entrepreneurial Behaviour & Research, 7*(2), 43-59. doi: 10.1108/13552550110695552

Chandler, G. N., & Lyon, D. W. (2001). Issues of Research Design and Construct Measurement in Entrepreneurship Research: The Past Decade. *Entrepreneurship: Theory & Practice, 25*(4), 101.

Chandler, G. N., Lyon, D. W., & Detienne, D. R. (2005,). *Antecedents and Expolitation Outcomesof Opportunity Identification Processes.*

Choi, Y. R., & Shepherd, D. A. (2004). Entrepreneurs' Decisions to Exploit Opportunities. *Journal of Management, 30*(3), 377-395. doi: 10.1016/j.jm.2003.04.002

Dumne, T., Roberts, M. J., & Samuelson, L. (1988). Patterns of firm entry and exit in U.S. manufacturing industries. *RAND Journal of Economics, 19*(4), 495-515.

Eden, C. (1992). On the Nature of Cognitive Maps. *Journal of Management Studies, 29*(3), 261-265. doi: 10.1111/j.1467-6486.1992.tb00664.x

Eden, C., Ackermann, F., & Cropper, S. (1992). The Analysis of Cause Maps. *Journal of Management Studies, 29*(3), 309-324. doi: 10.1111/j.1467-6486.1992.tb00667.x

Ericsson, K. A., & Charness, N. (1994). Expert Performance. *American Psychologist, 49*(8), 725-747.

Flavell, J. H. (1979). Metacognition and cognitive monitoring: A new area of cognitive–developmental inquiry. *American Psychologist, 34*(10), 906-911. doi: 10.1037/0003-066X.34.10.906

Flavell, J. H. (1987). Speculations about the nature and development of metacognition. In F. E. Weinert & R. H. Kluwe (Eds.), *Metacognition, motivation, and understanding* (pp. 21-29). Hillside, NJ: Erlbaum.

Gaglio, C. M., & Katz, J. A. (2001). The Psychological Basis of Opportunity Identification: Entrepreneurial Alertness. *Small Business Economics, 16*, 95-111.

Gartner, W. B. (1989). "Who Is an Entrepreneur?" Is the Wrong Question. [Article]. *Entrepreneurship: Theory & Practice, 13*(4), 47-68.

Gartner, W. B. (1990). What are we talking about when we talk about entrepreneurship? *Journal of Business Venturing, 5*(1), 15-28. doi: 10.1016/0883-9026(90)90023-m

Gompers, P., Kovner, A., Lerner, J., & Scharfstein, D. (2010). Performance persistence in entrepreneurship. [Article]. *Journal of Financial Economics, 96*(1), 18-32. doi: 10.1016/j.jfineco.2009.11.001
Hamilton, B. (2000). Does Entrepreneurship Pay? An Empirical Analysis of the Returns to Self-Employement. *Journal of Political Economy, 108*(3), 604-631.

Hayek, F. A. (1945). The Use of Knowledge in Society. *American Economic Review, 35*(4), 519.

Haynie, J. M., Shepherd, D. A., & McMullen, J. S. (2009). An Opportunity for Me? The Role of Resources in Opportunity Evaluation Decisions. *Journal of Management Studies, 46*(3), 337-361. doi: 10.1111/j.1467-6486.2009.00824.x

Haynie, M., & Shepherd, D. A. (2009). A Measure of Adaptive Cognition for Entrepreneurship Research. [Article]. *Entrepreneurship: Theory & Practice, 33*(3), 695-714. doi: 10.1111/j.1540-6520.2009.00322.x

Higgins, E. T. (1997). Beyond pleasure and pain. *American Psychologist, 52*(12), 1280-1300. doi: 10.1037/0003-066X.52.12.1280Inc. (2006). Rise of the Entrepreneurial Class. *Inc.* Retrieved from http://www.inc.com/articles/2006/08/schools.html

IRS. (2005). IRS Launches Study of S Corporation Reporting Compliance. *IRS Newswire*. Retrieved from Kahneman, D., & Lovallo, D. (1994). Timid choices and bold forecasts: A cognitive perspective on risk taking. . In R. P. Rumelt, D. E. Schendel & D. Teece (Eds.), *Fundamental issues in strategy: A research agenda* (pp. 71-96). Boston: Ballinger.

Kaish, S., & Gilad, B. (1991). Characteristics of Opportunities Search of Entrepreneurs Versus Executives: Sources, Interests, General Alertness. *Journal of Business Venturing, 6*(1), 45.

Kirchhoff, B. (1997). Entrepreneurship Economics. In W. D. Bygrave (Ed.), *The Portable MBA in Entreprenerusһip*. New York: John Wiley & Sons.

Kirzner, I. (1973). *Competetion and entrepreneurship*. Chicago: University of Chicago Press.

Kolvereid, L., & Bullvag, E. (1993). Novices versus experienced business founders: An exploratory investigation. In S. Birley, I. C. MacMillan & S. Subramony (Eds.), *Entrepreneurship Research: Global Perspectives* (pp. 275-285). Oxford: Pergamon.
Krueger, N. F. (1993). The Impact of Prior Entrepreneurial Exposure on Perceptions of New Venture Feasibility and Desirability. *Entrepreneurship: Theory & Practice, 18*(1), 5-21.

Krueger, N. F. (2005). The Cognitive Psychology of Entrepreneurship Handbook of Entrepreneurship Research. In Z. J. Acs & D. B. Audretsch (Eds.), (Vol. 1, pp. 105-140): Springer US.

Krueger, N. F. (2007). What Lies Beneath? The Experiential Essence of Entrepreneurial Thinking. *Entrepreneurship: Theory & Practice, 31*(1), 123-138. doi: 10.1111/j.1540-6520.2007.00166.x

Krueger, N. F., & Brazeal, D. V. (1994). Entrepreneurial Potential and Potential Entrepreneurs. *Entrepreneurship: Theory & Practice, 18*(3), 91-104.

Lamont, L. (1972). What Entrepreneurs Learn from Experience. *Journal of Small Business Management, 10*(3), 36-41.

Low, M. B. (2001). The Adolescence of Entrepreneurship Research: Specification of Purpose. . *Entrepreneurship: Theory & Practice, 25*(4), 17.

Macko, A., & Tyszka, T. (2009). Entrepreneurship and Risk Taking. *Applied Psychology, 58*(3), 469-487. doi: 10.1111/j.1464-0597.2009.00402.x

MacMillan, I. C. (1986). To Really Learn about Entrepreneurship, Let's Study Habitual Entrepreneurs. . *Journal of Business Venturing, 1*(3), 241.

Marino, K. E., Castaldi, R. M., & Dollinger, M. J. (1989). Content Analysis in Entrepreneurship Research: The Case of Initial Public Offerings. . *Entrepreneurship: Theory & Practice, 14*(1), 51-66.

Masters, R., & Meier, R. (1988). Sex Differences and Risk-Taking Propensity of Entrepreneurs. *Journal of Small Business Management, 26*(1), 31-35.

Mata, P., & Guimaraes, P. (1995). The Survival of New Plants: Start-Up Conditions and Post-Entry Evolution. *International Journal of Industrial Organization, 13*, 459-481.

McGrath, R. G. (1996). *Options and the entrepreneur: Toward a strategic theory of entrepreneurial wealth creation.* Paper presented at the Academy of Management, Cincinnati, OH.

McKenzie, B., Ugbah, S. D., & Smothers, N. (2007). "Who is an Entrepreneur?" Is It Still the Wrong Question? . *Academy of Entrepreneurship Journal, 13*(1), 23-43.

Melot, A.-M. (1998). The relationship between metacognitive knowledge and metacognitive experiences: Acquisition and re-elaboration. *European Journal of Psychology of Education, 13*(1), 75-89. doi: 10.1007/bf03172814

Miner, J. B., & Raju, N. S. (2004). Risk Propensity Differences Between Managers and Entrepreneurs and Between Low- and High-Growth Entrepreneurs: A Reply in a More Conservative Vein. *Journal of Applied Psychology, 89*(1), 3-13. doi: 10.1037/0021-9010.89.1.3

Mitchell, J. R., Friga, P. N., & Mitchell, R. K. (2005). Untangling the Intuition Mess: Intuition as a Construct in Entrepreneurship Research. . *Entrepreneurship: Theory & Practice, 29*(6), 653-679. doi: 10.1111/j.1540-6520.2005.00102.x

Nadkarni, S., & Barr, P. S. (2008). Environmental Context, Managerial Cognition, and Strategic Action: An Integrated View. *Strategic Management Journal, 29*(13), 1395-1427.

Nelson, T. O. (1996). Consciousness and metacognition. *American Psychologist, 51*(2), 102-116. doi: 10.1037/0003-066X.51.2.102

Norton Jr, W. I., & Moore, W. T. (2006). The Influence of Entrepreneurial Risk Assessment on Venture Launch or Growth Decisions. . *Small Business Economics, 26*(3), 215-226. doi: 10.1007/s11187-004-5612-y
Palich, L. E., & Bagby, R. D. (1995). Using cognitive theory to explain entrepreneurial risk-taking: Challenging conventional wisdom. *Journal of Business Venturing, 10*(6), 425-438. doi: 10.1016/0883-9026(95)00082-j

Polanyi, M. (1983). *The Tacit Dimension*. Glouchester, MA: Peter Smith.
Rosa, P., Carter, S., & Hamilton, D. (1996). Gender as a determinant of small business performance: Insights from a British study. *Small Business Economics, 8*(6), 463-478. doi: 10.1007/bf00390031

Russell, R. D. (1999). Developing a Process Model of Intrapreneurial Systems: A Cognitive Mapping Approach. . *Entrepreneurship: Theory & Practice, 23*(3), 65-84.
Sarasvathy, D. K., Simon, H. A., & Lave, L. (1998). Perceiving and managing business risks: differences between entrepreneurs and bankers. *Journal of Economic Behavior & Organization, 33*(2), 207-225. doi: 10.1016/s0167-2681(97)00092-9

Sarasvathy, S. D. (2000). Seminar on Research Perspectives in Entrepreneurship (1997). . *Journal of Business Venturing, 15*(1), 1.

Schraw, G., & Dennison, R. S. (1994). Assessing Metacognitive Awareness. *Contemporary Educational Psychology, 19*(4), 460-475. doi: 10.1006/ceps.1994.1033
Scott, M., & Rosa, P. (1996). Has firm level analysis reached its limits? Time for a rethink?, Editorial, *International Small Business Journal,* p. 81.

Shane, S. (2008). *The Illusions of Entrepreneurship: The Costly Myths That Entrepreneurs, Investors, and Policy Makers Live By.* New Haven, CT: Yale University Press.

Shane, S., & Venkataraman, S. (2000). The Promise of Entrepreneurship as a Field of Research. *Academy of Management Review, 25*(1), 217-226. doi: 10.5465/amr.2000.2791611

Shepherd, D. A., & DeTienne, D. R. (2005). Prior Knowledge, Potential Financial Reward, and Opportunity Identification. . *Entrepreneurship: Theory & Practice, 29*(1), 91-112. doi: 10.1111/j.1540-6520.2005.00071.x

Short, J. C., Ketchen, J. D. J., Shook, C. L., & Ireland, R. D. (2010). The Concept of "Opportunity" in Entrepreneurship Research: Past Accomplishments and Future Challenges. . *Journal of Management, 36*(1), 40-65.

Smith, B. R., Matthews, C. H., & Schenkel, M. T. (2009). Differences in Entrepreneurial Opportunities: The Role of Tacitness and Codification in Opportunity Identification. . *Journal of Small Business Management, 47*(1), 38-57. doi: 10.1111/j.1540-627X.2008.00261.x

Stanley, T., & Danko, W. (1996). *The Millionaire Next Door.* Atlanta: Longstreet.
Star, J. A., & Bygrave, W. D. (1991). The Second Time Arround: The Outcomes, Assets, and Liabilities of Prior Start-up Experience. In S. Birley & S. Subramony (Eds.),

International Perspectives on Entrepreneurship Research (pp. 340-363). Amsterdam: Elsevier Science.

Stevenson, H. H., & Jarillo, J. C. (1990). A Paradign of Entrepreneurship: Entrepreneurial Management. *Strategic Management Journal, 11*(4), 17-27.

Stewart, W. H., Jr., & Roth, P. L. (2001). Risk propensity differences between entrepreneurs and managers: A meta-analytic review. . *Journal of Applied Psychology, 86*(1), 145-153. doi: 10.1037/0021-9010.86.1.145

Ucbasaran, D., Westhead, P., & Wright, M. (2008). Opportunity Identification and Pursuit: Does an Entrepreneur's Human Capital Matter? . *Small Business Economics, 30*(2), 153-173. doi: 10.1007/s11187-006-9020-3

Ucbasaran, D., Westhead, P., & Wright, M. (2009). The extent and nature of opportunity identification by experienced entrepreneurs. . *Journal of Business Venturing, 24*(2), 99-115. doi: 10.1016/j.jbusvent.2008.01.008

Ucbasaran, D., Westhead, P., & Wright, M. (2011). Why Serial Entrepreneurs Don't Learn from Failure. . *Harvard Business Review, 89*(4), 26-26.

Ucbasaran, D., Westhead, P., Wright, M., & Flores, M. (2010). The nature of entrepreneurial experience, business failure and comparative optimism. *Journal of Business Venturing, 25*(6), 541-555. doi: 10.1016/j.jbusvent.2009.04.001

Uusitalo, R. (2001). Homo Entreprenaurus? *Applied Economics, 33*, 1631-1638.

Venkataraman, S. (2007). The distinctive domain of entrepreneurship research: An editor's perspective. In J. Katz & J. Brockhaus (Eds.), *Advances in Entrepreneruship, Firm Emergence, and Growth* (pp. 119-138). Greenwich, CT: JAI Press.

Walsh, J. P. (1995). Managerial and Organizational Cognition: Notes from a Trip Down Memory Lane. *Organization Science, 6*(3), 280-321.

Westhead, P., Ucbasaran, D., & Wright, M. (2003). Differences Between Private Firms Owned by Novice, Serial and Portfolio Entrepreneurs: Implications for Policy Makers and Practitioners. *Regional Studies, 37*(2), 187-200. doi: 10.1080/0034340022000057488

Westhead, P., Ucbasaran, D., & Wright, M. (2005). Decisions, Actions, and Performance: Do Novice, Serial, and Portfolio Entrepreneurs Differ?. *Journal of Small Business Management, 43*(4), 393-417. doi: 10.1111/j.1540-627X.2005.00144.x

Westhead, P., & Wright, M. (1998). Novice, portfolio, and serial founders: are they different? *Journal of Business Venturing, 13*(3), 173-204. doi: 10.1016/s0883-9026(97)90002-1

Wolff, E. N. (2007). *Recent trends in household wealth in the Unitied States: Rising debt and the middle-class squeeze*. Annandale-on-Hudson, NY: Levy Economics Institute of Bard College.

Wolff, E. N. (2010). *Tecent trends in household wealth in the United States: Rising debt and middle-class squeeze - an update to 2007.* Annandale-on-Hudson, NY: Levy Economics Institute of Bard College.
Wright, M., Robbie, K., & Ennew, C. (1997a). Serial Entrepreneurs. *British Journal of Management, 8*(3), 251-268. doi: 10.1111/1467-8551.00064

Wright, M., Robbie, K., & Ennew, C. (1997b). Venture capitalists and serial entrepreneurs. *Journal of Business Venturing, 12*(3), 227-249. doi: 10.1016/s0883-9026(96)06115-0

FIGURE 1

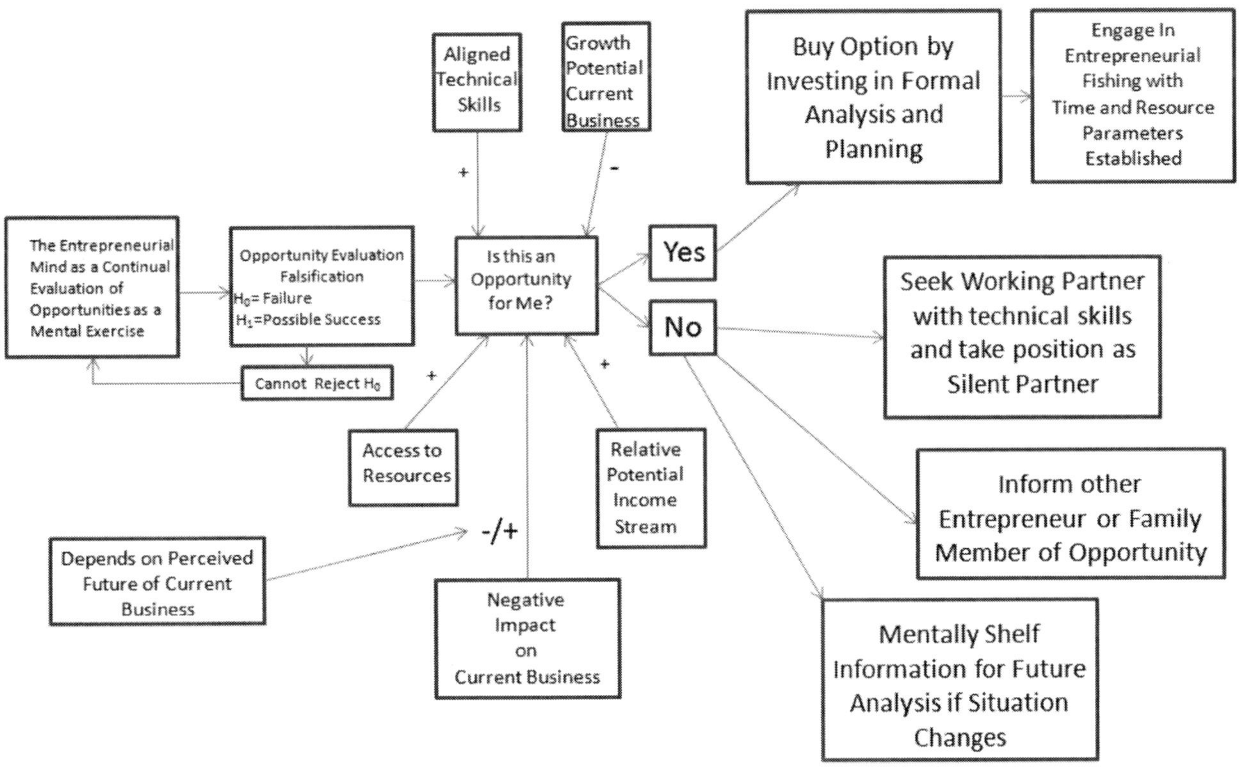

DECISION SCIENCES INSTITUTE

Mobile Banking Adoption: Thai Consumers' Perspective

Chuleeporn Changchit
Texas A&M University-Corpus Christi
Email: chuleeporn.changchit@tamucc.edu

Ravi Lonkani
Chiang Mai University
Email: ravi.l@cmu.ac.th

Jomjai Sampet
Chiang Mai University
Email: jomjai.s@cmu.ac.th

ABSTRACT

With a rapid growth of smart phone users, mobile banking has gained significant importance and the growth of the field is accelerating. To remain competitive, banking services realize the need to run their business to suit the convenience of their customers. However, despite many benefits and popularity of mobile banking, not all consumers are ready to embrace this technology, especially in the developing countries. The objective of this study is to explore determinants of mobile banking adoption in Thailand. The findings reveal factors influencing consumers' attitude toward the usage of mobile banking.

KEYWORDS: Technology Acceptance Model (TAM), Perceived Usefulness, Perceived Ease of Use, Perceived Security, Perceived Privacy, Perceived Trust, Previous Experiences, Technology Competency, Normative Beliefs, Internet Banking, Mobile Banking, Thailand

INTRODUCTION

The rapid expansion of information and communication technologies has had a tremendous impact on all areas of human life (Hanafizadeh et al., 2014). Information technology (IT) has been expanding beyond the traditional organizational boundaries (Zhao et al., 2013). Technology adoption is a complex process influenced by a mix of social, technological, economical, and political factors (Gupta et al., 2014). Emerging technologies often result in new opportunities for businesses and have become one of the major factors that will determine the future success of organizations (Bapna et al., 2014; Bhattacharjee et al., 2006; Holsapple & Singh, 2000).

With the improvement of mobile technologies and devices, mobile banking has been considered as a salient system because of such attributes of mobile technologies as ubiquity, convenience and interactivity (Gu et al., 2009; Turban et al., 2006). To remain competitive in the market, many banks realize the need to run their business to suit the convenience of their customers. Several banks are competing with each other by implementing new and modern electronic system via the Internet connectivity, which is shifting usage from desktops to laptops and mobile devices such as iPhones or iPads (Puschel et al., 2010).

Although Internet technologies and global networking infrastructures have made information sharing much easier and less expensive, the availability of such information systems comes at the expenses of higher risks (Ba et al., 2005). Quite a few customers are still reluctant to adopt this channel of banking services because of their concerns with uncertainty and security (Islam, 2014; Robinson, 2000). A study reported that only 12% of German consumers use their cell phones for banking or shopping (Tanner, 2008).

Many prior studies have been conducted to examine users' behavior to understand how users behave when using mobile banking. For instance, Shaikh, Karjaluoto, & Chinje (2015) examined continuous usage behavior of mobile banking among consumers living in Finland and South Africa. The study found that trust plays a significant role in promoting continuous usage of m-banking. Another study proposed a theoretical model that explains sustained use of mobile banking services (Kang et. al., 2012). The results of the study indicated that perceived usability, channel preference, and perceived value are three major determinants of sustained mobile banking usage.

Even though the literature on the adoption of mobile banking is quite extensive in developed country such as the U.S. (Afshan & Sharif, 2016; Lee et al., 2013; Lin, 2011; Nel & Boshoff, 2014; Staff, 2013), few studies have explored the motivations for mobile banking adoption in a developing countries. In particular, very few studies were conducted to examine the factors impacting the usage of mobile banking in Thailand. Therefore, the objective of this study is to identify factors affecting the adoption of mobile banking in Thailand. We extended the technology acceptance model by integrating new factors for a developing nation. The findings of this study should provide insights for banks to develop strategies and business model of mobile banking to best fit their customers' need.

LITERATURE REVIEW

Rapid advances in mobile technologies and devices have made mobile banking increasingly important in mobile commerce and financial services (Lin, 2011). In recent years, the preference of technology has shifted from a PC to a handheld device, largely due to its portability. A mobile phone and a tablet become an integral part of consumers' lives (Singh et al., 2010). The relatively high prevalence of mobile phone and smartphone use among younger generations, minorities, and those with low levels of income (i.e., groups that are more likely to be unbanked or under-banked) makes mobile phones a potential platform for expanding financial access and inclusion (Federal Reserve Board, 2015).

As with other types of businesses, a mobile phone as a channel provides enormous potential in banking. Mobile banking provides a more convenient means for customers to meet their banking needs with more complete and timely information (Baptista & Oliveira, 2015; Gerrard & Cunningham, 2003). Mobile banking was defined by the Federal Reserve Board (2015) as the use of a mobile phone to access a bank or credit union account, which can be done either by accessing the web page through the web browser on a mobile phone, via text messaging, or by using an application downloaded to a mobile phone. The electronic transaction conducted via mobile devices such as smartphones, is expected to play a larger role in the near future, with more than half a million customers worldwide shopping via mobile devices by 2015 (Deng & Zhang, 2014).

In information system (IS) literature, mobile banking has received ample consideration by both academia and practice (Afshan & Sharif, 2016; Gu et al., 2009; Kim et al., 2009; Luarn & Lin,

2005; Zhou et al., 2010). The extant works in IS have descended their focus on coupling various theoretical models to study intention adoption of mobile banking. For instance, Yu (2014) investigated factors that influence consumers to make a transition from online to mobile banking. The results demonstrated that relative attitude and relative subjective norm positively motivated respondents to switch from Internet to mobile banking while relative perceived behavior control deterred respondents from transitioning. Another study proposed a mobile banking user adoption model based on the Technology Acceptance Model (TAM), integrating social influence, and trust perception to predict the user intention. The findings suggested that perceived usefulness, perceived ease of use, social influence, and trust perception have significant effects on user adoption (Song, 2015). A study by AlSoufi and Ali, (2014) revealed that the intention to adopt mobile banking is not affected by perceived cost and perceived risk.

In addition to the investigation of users' intention on the usage of mobile banking, some studies focused on examining the factors impacting the continuous use of mobile banking. For instances, Kang, Lee, and Lee (2012) develops and empirically tests a theoretical model that explains sustained use of mobile banking services. The results of the study indicated that perceived usability, channel preference, and perceived value were three major determinants of sustained mobile banking use. Another study investigated the invariance of cross-channel cognitive evaluations influencing salient beliefs in mobile banking adoption and continuance-of-use behavior between the users of internet banking and the users of both internet and mobile banking. The results suggested that cross channel evaluations can be both invariant and non-invariant across the two cohorts (Nel & Boshoff, 2014).

Internet and Mobile Banking in Thailand

Banks in Thailand can be classified as the commercial banks, state own banks and Foreign subsidiary banks. Internet in Thailand was dated back to 1987 (Thailand Chapter of Internet Society, 2015). Nowadays, over one third of the population in Thailand has regular access to the Internet (National Statistical Office, 2014). Although there are increasing number of Internet banking in Thailand, not all customers are ready to adopt this channel of banking services (Intana et al., 2013). One study reported that Thai people found security to be insufficient and thus holding them back from adopting Internet banking (Esichaikul & Janecek, 2009). The study also revealed that the lack of customer service was a major reason preventing them from adopting Internet banking as well. Another study also reported trust as a critical factor that led to adoption of using internet banking for Thai banks (Namahoot & Laohavichien, 2015).

With a rapid growth in technology, smart phone applications become popular in this era, with more advanced computing ability and connectivity. In 2014, from 62.3 million of Thai population aged 6 years and over, there were 21.7 (34.9%) millions of Internet users and 48.1 (77.2%) millions of mobile users (National Statistical Office, 2014). It is very obvious that smart phone becomes part of Thai consumers' life. This increasing trend of smart phone users has forced banks in Thailand to offer banking services via a mobile channel. A study conducted in 2014 revealed that sixty-four percent (64%) of Thai consumers used mobile banking apps in Thailand (Statista, 2014). Wonglimpiyarat (2014) investigated the competition and challenges of mobile banking system in Thailand. The study discussed the strategies, SWOT analyses of the mobile banking industry. The results revealed that banks recognized mobile banking as a convenient delivery channel to provide value-added services to the bank customers. The competition forces banks to seek strategic alliances (network collaboration between the banking and ICT industries) to offer innovative solutions in the payment market.

Major bank in Thailand such as Bangkok Bank, Krung Thai Bank, Kasikorn Bank, and Siam Commercial Bank, have developed mobile banking services, but the adoption rate was only 4.5% of the population (Bhatiasevi, 2015). This data indicates the need for more studies to investigate what factors contribute to the low adoption rate compared to other countries. This study is thus aims at identifying factors affecting the adoption of mobile banking in Thailand. The result should provide insight for banks in Thailand on the factors which play a crucial role to the success of mobile banking in Thailand.

THEORETICAL DEVELOPMENT/MODEL

Technology Acceptance Model (TAM) developed by Davis in 1986 is derived from the Theory of Reasoned Action (TRA), developed by Fishbein and Ajzen (1975). TAM was cited in many prior studies as a model to examine factors impacting user acceptance of information systems (Bagozzi, 2007; Davis et al., 1989). The model is successful in predicting about 40% of a system's use (Legris et al., 2003). Lee, Kozar, and Larsen (2003) stated that TAM is considered the most influential and commonly employed theory for describing an individual's acceptance of information systems. A review of prior studies suggested that the Technology Acceptance Model (TAM) was widely used to study users' acceptance of the new technology. Quite a few studies in many countries have widely used TAM to study the use of mobile banking, for example; in Iran by Hanafizadeh, Keating, and Khedmatgozar (2014), in China by Song (2015) and Zhou, Lu, and Wang (2010), in Bahrain by AlSoufi and Ali (2014), in Korea by Gu, Lee, and Suh (2009), in Taiwan by Luarn and Lin (2005), in Portugal by Baptista and Oliveira (2015).

This study has modified the TAM model to include five additional factors: (1) Perceived Privacy (PP), (2) Perceived Security (PS), (3) Previous Experiences, (4) Normative Beliefs (NB), and (5) Technology Competency (TC). The proposed research model is shown in Figure 1 below.

Figure 1: Research model

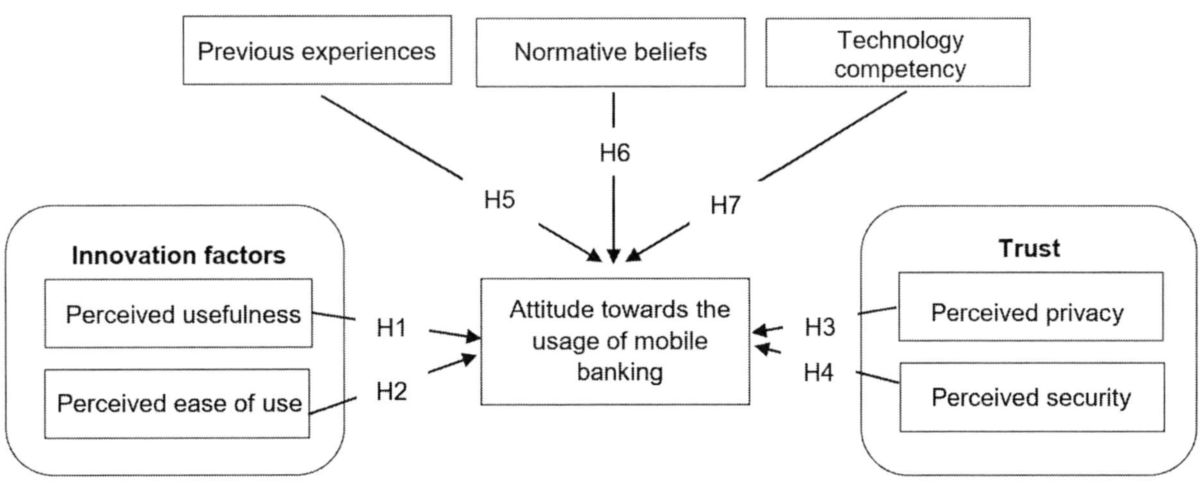

Perceived Usefulness of Mobile Banking

The construct perceived usefulness is defined as the prospective users' subjective probability that using a specific application system will increase his or her job performance within an organizational context (Davis et al., 1989). This factor has a significant effect on usage intention (Agarwal & Prasad 1999; Davis et al., 1989; Venkatesh & Davis, 2000). Perceived usefulness is, thus, predicted to be a positive driver for the attitude towards the usage of mobile banking. Based on these discussions, we propose the following hypothesis:

H1: Perceived usefulness (PU) positively affects the attitude towards the usage of mobile banking in Thailand.

Perceived Ease of Use of Mobile Banking

The construct perceived ease of use is defined as the degree to which the prospective user expects the target system to be free of effort (Davis et al., 1989). This factor plays a crucial role in understanding individual response to information technology (Agarwal & Karahanna, 2000; Chau & Hu, 2001; Hong et al., 2001). Research over the past decade provides evidence of the significant effect perceived ease of use has had on usage intention (Agarwal & Prasad 1999; Venkatesh & Davis, 2000). To prevent the problem of a useful system remaining "under-used", customers do not need to expend significant effort on using mobile banking (Lin, 2011). Based on this discussion, we therefore posit:

H2: Perceived ease of use (PEU) positively affects the attitude towards the usage of mobile banking in Thailand.

Perceived Privacy of Mobile Banking

Invasion of privacy is a situation in which someone tries to find out details about another person's private affairs in a way that is upsetting and often illegal. With mobile banking, invasion of privacy can occur in the form of hacking. With the advance in technology, it allows illegal hackers to access personal records faster and easier than before. It is the responsibility of organization to protect consumers' privacy. The privacy concern becomes a major obstacle to the spread of E-commerce (Islam, 2014). The construct perceived privacy can be defined as the possibility that companies collect data about individuals and use them inappropriately (Jarvenpaa & Todd, 1996; Roca et al., 2009). Zorotheos and Kafeza (2009) stated that a customers' willingness to transact online depended on their perceived privacy control (PPC). Based on this reasoning, it is postulated that:

H3: Perceived privacy (PP) positively affects the attitude towards the usage of mobile banking in Thailand.

Perceived Security of Mobile Banking

Yenisey, Ozok, and Salvendy (2005) defined perceived security in E-commerce as the level of security that users feel while they are shopping online. Flavia´n and Guinalı´u (2006) presented their view of perceived security as a subjective probability with which consumers believe that their personal information (private and monetary) will not be viewed, stored, and manipulated during transit and storage by inappropriate parties in a manner consistent with their confident expectations. Security has been studied and defined in several prior studies. Luarn and Lin (2005) reported that information security was one of the greatest concerns in the adoption of mobile banking. Roca, Garcia, and De la Vega (2009) defined overall perceived security as a threat that created a circumstance, condition, or event with the potential to cause economic hardship to data or network resources in the form of destruction, disclosures, modification of data, denial of service, and/or fraud, waste and abuse. Therefore, it is postulated that:

H4: Perceived security (PS) positively affects the attitude towards the usage of mobile banking in Thailand.

Previous Experiences with Mobile Banking

Research indicates that consumers evaluate their online experiences in terms of perceptions regarding product information, payment, delivery, service, privacy and other such factors (Burke, 2002; Parasuraman & Zinkhan, 2002; Mathwick et al., 2001). Consumers' decision to continue future online transactions depended a lot on whether their past experiences were positive (Shim et al., 2001). The following is the hypothesis for this factor:

H5: Previous experience (PEX) positively affects the attitude towards the usage of mobile banking in Thailand.

Normative Beliefs

Normative beliefs represent the social pressures to perform certain behaviors (Ajzen, 1991). It can also be defined as an individual's perception about the particular behavior, which is influenced by the judgment of significant others such as parents, spouse, friends, teachers, coworkers, and a boss. Hernandez and Mazzon (2007) stated that normative beliefs can be defined as the degree of disagreement among the opinions of key reference groups such as friends, peers or colleagues, superiors, and subordinates in an organizational environment. According to a recent public opinion boom and a widespread use of new technology such as smartphones or tablet devices, people are influenced to adopt technologies used by their relatives and friends. Normative belief becomes an important factor shaping the direction on how to do business. Sprott, Spangenberg, and Fisher (2003) stated that normative beliefs can lead to a socially desirable behavior in a specific situation, thus should be included as a fundamental component of any predictive variables. Based on the foregoing, we propose the following hypothesis:

H6: Normative belief (NB) positively affects the attitude towards the usage of mobile banking in Thailand.

Technology Competency

Technology competency is defined as the extent to which an individual is knowledgeable about and effectively utilizes Information Technology to manage information (Tippins & Sohi, 2003). Typically, consumers with a high level of self-efficacy are more motivated to use technology-based services. Moreover, they have a more positive attitude and intent to use technology-based services than consumers with a low level of technology self-efficacy. Therefore, consumers with a high technology self-efficacy are expected to have positive attitude and behavioral intentions to use mobile banking. High technology competence consumers are likely to perceive that mobile banking is easy to use than low technology competence consumers (Yang, 2010). We, therefore posit:

H7: Technology competency (TC) of subjects positively affects the attitude towards the usage of mobile banking in Thailand.

METHODOLOGY

This study adapted the instrument used in several prior studies as a measurement for the constructs proposed in the research model (Intana et al., 2013; Pikkarainen et al., 2004; Venkatesh & Davis, 2000; Venkatesh et al., 2003; Vijayasarathy, 2004; Wong & Hsu, 2008). The questionnaire consisted of forty-six (46) questions. Thirty-five (35) questions with the five point Likert scale were designed to measure subjects' perceptions on mobile banking. One question (Question# 36) asked "Overall, I prefer to do mobile banking transaction than other forms of banking" as a measurement for subjects' attitude on intention to use mobile banking. Another question (Question# 37) asks "Have you ever used mobile banking?" to measure subjects' actual use of mobile banking. The remaining nine (9) questions were asked to gather some demographic data of the subjects. To validate the clarity of these questions, three professors and three researchers were asked to read through the survey questions. Revisions to the survey were made based on the feedback received.

Four hundred (400) subjects participated in this study. The data were collected from a direct survey administered to student in a northern university in Thailand. Students are deemed as appropriate subjects in this study because they are no doubt the main users of mobile phones and thus become the main target users of mobile banking. In addition, only students who are the current users of mobile banking are included in the data analysis. Of the four hundred (400) subjects, two hundred and fifty-three (253) or 63.25% of them are mobile banking customers. The remaining one hundred forty-seven (147) or 36.75% of subjects have never used mobile banking before and therefore have been disregarded from further analysis. Subjects' demographics are shown in the Table 1 below.

Table 1: Subjects' Demographics (n=253)

	No.	%		No.	%
Gender			**Areas of Study**		
Male	91	35.97	Science and Technology	52	20.55
Female	162	64.03	Health Science	6	2.37
			Social Science	195	77.08
Age					
Below 18	1	0.40	**Monthly Income (in Thai Baht)**		
18 - 34	200	79.05	Below 15,000	172	67.98
35 - 44	50	19.76	15,000 - 30,000	70	27.67
above 44	1	0.40	30,001 - 45,000	7	2.77
No answer	1	0.40	45,001 - 60,000	3	1.19
			Above 60,000	1	0.40
Smartphone					
Yes	248	98.02	**Internet Use per Month**		
No	4	1.58	None	1	0.40
No answer	1	0.40	1 - 5	3	1.19
			6 - 10	7	2.77
			More than 10	242	95.65
Have Internet Package for Smart Phone					
Yes	226	89.33			
No	23	9.09	**Make Purchase via the Internet on a Computer**		
Not applicable	3	1.19	**per Month**		
No answer	1	0.40	None	39	15.42
			1 - 5	194	76.68
			6 - 10	10	3.95

Employment Status					
Yes	98	38.74	More than 10	10	3.95
No	155	61.26			

DATA ANALYSIS AND DISCUSSION

In order to examine the internal consistency of the research instrument, a reliability test was conducted. The test confirms the reliability of the research items with Cronbach's alpha coefficient of 0.946.

The measurement model for the seven constructs was assessed by a confirmatory factor analysis with Varimax rotation in order to test whether the questionnaire items produced the expected number of factors and whether each item was loaded on their appropriated factor. Results from the factor analysis indicates that all items are loaded into six (6) factors. As shown in the Table 2 below, the result from the factor analysis reveals that the ten (10) questionnaire items designed to measure the perceived privacy and perceived security constructs are loaded into the same factor. We, therefore, combined the two factors and labeled it as "Perceived Trust" (PT) factor. The minimum loading factor from the result is at 0.596 which is beyond the minimum acceptance threshold of 0.5 (Field, 2005; Hair et al., 1998: Stevens, 1992). In addition, the factor loading of 0.1633 on item PU 2 was below the suggested threshold, indicating that this item should not be used to measure the PU factor and thus was removed from the data analysis.

The measurement model was further assessed for construct reliability. The composite reliability for all the constructs was above 0.7, conforming to an acceptable threshold suggested by Nunnally and Bernstein (1994). Table 2 below presents the mean, standard deviation, factor loading, and composite reliability of all items assessed in this study.

Table 2: Summary of Measurement Scales

Constructs	M	SD	Factor Loading*	Reliability
Perceive Usefulness				0.758
PU1	4.462	0.809	0.5963	
PU2 (removed)	3.565	1.131	0.1633	
PU3	4.427	0.787	0.7412	
PU4	4.609	0.762	0.7760	
PU5	4.514	0.795	0.7318	
Perceived Ease of Use				0.908
PEU1	3.806	0.890	0.7726	
PEU2	3.972	0.852	0.7702	
PEU3	3.834	0.893	0.7662	
PEU4	4.040	0.835	0.8170	
PEU5	3.957	0.874	0.7168	
Perceived Trust (PP + PS)				0.943
PT1	3.178	1.029	0.8218	
PT2	3.182	1.050	0.8586	
PT3	3.423	1.003	0.7985	

PT4	3.419	1.042	0.7022	
PT5	3.079	1.044	0.7651	
PT6	3.182	0.903	0.7878	
PT7	3.186	0.922	0.8024	
PT8	3.202	0.919	0.7552	
PT9	3.289	0.886	0.6738	
PT10	3.277	0.892	0.8115	
Previous Experiences				0.906
PEX1	3.866	0.885	0.6264	
PEX2	3.917	0.889	0.7429	
PEX3	3.929	0.884	0.7656	
PEX4	4.162	0.808	0.7227	
PEX5	3.704	0.906	0.6174	
Normative Beliefs				0.768
NB1	3.352	0.877	0.6546	
NB2	3.213	0.977	0.5080	
NB3	2.933	1.087	0.7882	
NB4	3.727	1.004	0.5580	
NB5	3.625	1.014	0.6593	
Technology Competency				0.866
TC1	4.202	1.081	0.6617	
TC2	4.403	0.838	0.7712	
TC3	4.174	0.855	0.8715	
TC4	4.273	0.831	0.8118	
TC5	4.111	0.875	0.8298	

* Rotation Method: Varimax with Kaiser Normalization

A multiple regression analysis was conducted to test the seven (7) hypotheses, which hypotheses 3 and 4 were combined into one hypothesis. Our model, therefore, contains six (6) independent variables. The independent variables include perceived usefulness (PU), perceive ease of use (PEU), perceived trust (perceived privacy (PP) and perceived security (PS) were combined into one factor as suggested by the result of factor analysis), previous experience (PEX), normative beliefs (NB), and technology competency (TC). The dependent variable is the attitude toward the usage of mobile banking (ATT). The analysis controls for three subjects' demographics, which are gender, employment status, and areas of study. All control variables are bivariate dummy variables. DGender was coded to the value of 1 for female and 0 for male. DEmploy was coded to the value of 1 for employed and 0 for others. DStudy was coded to the value of 1 if the respondent studies in the field of sciences and 0 for other fields. The regression equation was written as follow:

$$ATT_i = \alpha_0 + \alpha_1 PU_i + \alpha_2 PEU_i + \alpha_3 PT_i + \alpha_4 PEX_i + \alpha_5 NB_i + \alpha_6 TC_i + \alpha_7 DGender_i + \alpha_8 DEmploy_i + \alpha_9 DStudy_i + \varepsilon_i$$

The results from Table 3 show the R^2 and Adjusted R^2 of 54.5% and 52.8% respectively, indicating that the factors investigated are suitable to explain the attitude towards the usage of mobile banking. The F-stat was reported to be at 32.37 and was significant at 1% significant level. This also indicates that the combined factors are able to simultaneously explain the attitude quite well.

Table 3: Relationship between Factors and Attitude towards the Usage of Mobile Banking

Hypotheses	Independent Variables	β	*t*	VIF
H1	Perceive Usefulness	0.115	1.35	1.9048
H2	Perceived Ease of Use	0.436**	5.73	2.0218
H3, H4	Perceived Trust	0.144*	2.18	1.7356
H5	Previous Experiences	0.241**	3.00	2.2844
H6	Normative Beliefs	0.170*	2.45	1.5714
H7	Technology Competency	0.084	1.31	1.3863
	Gender	-0.047	-0.52	1.1795
	Employment Status	0.084	1.00	1.0702
	Area of Study	-0.032	-0.31	1.1162
***n* = 253**				
R-Square	0.545			
Adj R-Square	0.528			
F-stat	32.37***			

* Significant at 5% level, ** Significant at 1% level

Regarding each factor, the results from the multiple regression analysis demonstrates that four out of the six factors are key determinants on whether subjects intend to use mobile banking. These factors are perceived ease of use (PEU; β = 0.436), perceived trust (PT; β =0.144), previous experiences (PEX; β=0.241), and normative beliefs (NB; β=0.170). In contrast, the results show that the factors perceived usefulness (PU; β = 0.115) and the technological competency (TC; β = 0.084) do not significantly affect the attitude toward the usage of mobile banking. The Variance Inflation Factors (VIF) for all factors range between 1.070 and 2.284, which are not greater than 10, indicating that there is no problem of multicollinearity (Hair et al., 2010; Diamantopoulos et al., 2008).

DISCUSSION AND CONCLUSION

In this study, seven (7) factors are predicted to influence the attitude toward the usage of mobile banking were investigated. Besides the two factors (perceived usefulness and perceive ease of use) included in the original TAM model, the modified model proposed to include five additional factors as determinants of attitude toward the usage of mobile banking. These factors are perceived privacy (PP), perceived security (PS), previous experiences (PEX), normative believes (NB), and technology competency (TC). The result from factor analysis suggested that the factors perceived privacy and perceived security should be combined into one factor, and we, thus, label this construct as perceived trust (PT).

The results of this study reveal that four out of six factors examined in the proposed research model play an important role in explaining users' attitudes toward the usage of mobile banking. The first factor is "perceived ease of use". This result supports the TAM findings. Consumers nowadays do not expect to spend a lot of effort in learning how to use technology, thus, they will be more likely to use mobile banking if they believe that it is not difficult to use. The finding suggests that banks should focus on designing the mobile banking features to make it relatively easy to use.

The second factor is "perceived trust". The result in this study reveals that subjects will be more likely to use mobile banking if they can trust that their banking transactions will be kept confidential and secured. It is apparently that they are not willing to transact via a mobile device if the transaction is not considered safe and secured. This finding is consistent with a study conducted by Shaikh et al (2015), which reported that trust was a crucial factor in mobile banking adoption. The result suggests that banks should consider educating their customers about the privacy and security of mobile banking transactions.

The third factor is "previous experiences". The study result points out that subjects will be more likely to use mobile banking if they have a good experience with their previous mobile banking transactions. This result suggests that banks may consider collecting feedback from their mobile banking customers to gain an understanding of their experiences with mobile banking transactions. Their feedback should help banks develop or improve mobile banking features to better serve the expectations of their customers, thereby increasing customers' satisfaction and enhancing their experiences with mobile banking.

The last factor is "normative beliefs". This result points out that subjects' attitude toward the usage of mobile banking can be influenced by their family members, peers, and other social factors. The fact of knowing that someone close to them is using mobile banking makes subjects feel that it is desirable in their lifestyle. The finding suggested that bank could use this strategy to attract more mobile banking customers. For instance, bank managers may consider launching a campaign such as refer-a-friend as a tool to bring in new mobile banking customers.

In contrast to the TAM finding, this study does not find a significant impact of perceive usefulness on subjects' attitude toward the usage of mobile banking. This may due to the fact that Thai consumers are major users of smart phone and thus already realize the benefits of mobile banking. Therefore, the perceived usefulness factor is less important to them than other factors. In addition, banking transactions are usually viewed as high risk activities and thus inhibit them from using mobile banking regardless of their perception on its usefulness. Similar to the perceived usefulness factor, technology competency also does not play an important role in subject's mobile banking adoption. The possible explanation may be because the majority of subjects in this study are ranged between 18-24 years old. This populations usually have a high competency in technology and thus this factor does not reveal to be a significant factor.

As in most empirical studies, there is an inherent limitation in this paper. The sample in this research was limited to subjects in one university. Although only students who are the current users of mobile banking are included in the data analysis, future research should consider expanding demographics to include non-student subjects and users in various countries. A future study may examine these factors in a cross cultural context. In addition, a future study conducted could investigate in more details which feature of mobile banking are deemed necessary or unnecessary to the decision to adopt this technology.

REFERENCES

AlSoufi, A., & Ali, H. (2014). Customers' perception of m-banking adoption in kingdom of Bahrain: An empirical assessment of extended TAM model. *International Journal of Managing Information Technology, 6*(1), 1-13.

Afshan, S., & Sharif, A. (2016). Acceptance of mobile banking framework in Pakistan. *Telematics and Informatics, 33*(2), 370-387.

Agarwal, R., & Karahanna, E. (2000). Time flies when you're having fun: Cognitive absorption and beliefs about information technology usage. *MIS Quarterly, 24*(4), 665–694.

Agarwal, R., & Prasad, J. (1999). Are individual differences germane to the acceptance of information technologies? *Decision Sciences, 30*(2), 361-391.

Ajzen, I. (1991). The theory of planned behavior. *Organizational Behavior and Human Decision Processes, 50*(2), 179-211.

Ba, S., Stallaert, J., Whinston, A. B., & Zhang, H. (2005). Choice of transaction channels: The effects of product characteristics on market evolution. *Journal of Management Information Systems, 21*(4), 173-197.

Bagozzi, R. P. (2007). The legacy of the technology acceptance model and a proposal for a paradigm shift. *Journal of the Association for Information Systems, 8(4),* 244-254.

Bapna, R., Barua, A., & Whinston, A. B. (2014). Special issue: Economics of electronic commerce. *Journal of Management Information Systems, 31*(2), 7-10.

Baptista, G., & Oliveira, T. (2015). Understanding mobile banking: The unified theory of acceptance and use of technology combined with cultural moderators. *Computers in Human Behavior, 50*, 418-430.

Bhatiasevi, V. (2015). An extended UTAUT model to explain the adoption of mobile banking. *Information Development*, 1–16.

Bhattacharjee, S., Gopal, R. D., Lertwachara, K., & Marsden, J. R. (2006). Consumer search and retailer strategies in the presence of online music sharing. *Journal of Management Information Systems, 23*(1), 129-159.

Burke, R. (2002). Technology and the customer interface: What Consumers want the physical and virtual store? *Journal of the Academy of Marketing Science, 30*(4), 411-432.

Chau, P. Y. K., & Hu, P. J. H. (2001). Information technology acceptance by individual professionals: A model comparison approach. *Decision Sciences, 32*(4), 699-719.

Davis, F. D., Bagozzi, R. P., & Warshaw, P. R. (1989). User acceptance of computer technology: A comparison of two theoretical models. *Management Science, 35*(3), 982-1003.

Deng, X., & Zhang, J. (2014). Differentiating the effects of internet usage and wireless usage on business-to-business and business-to-consumer Ecommerce. *Journal of Internet Commerce, 13*(2), 138-157.

Esichaikul, V. & Janecek, P. (2009). A survey of e-banking performance in Thailand. *International Journal of Electronic Finance, 3*(4), 353-373.

Federal Reserve Board. (2015). Consumers and Mobile Financial Services 2015. Retrieved from www.federalreserve.gov/publications/default.htm (accessed December 28, 2015).

Fishbein, M. & Ajzen, I. (1975). *Belief, attitude, intention and behavior: An introduction to theory and research*. Reading, MA: Addison-Wesle.

Flavia´n, C., & Guinalı´u, M. (2006). Consumer trust, perceived security and privacy policy: Three basic elements of loyalty to a web site. *Industrial Management & Data Systems, 106*(5), 601-620.

Gerrard, P., & Cunningham, J. B. (2003). The diffusion of Internet banking among Singapore consumers. *International Journal of Bank Marketing, 21*(1), 16 – 28.

Gu, J. C., Lee, S. C., & Suh, Y. H. (2009). Determinants of behavioral intention to mobile banking. *Expert Systems with Applications, 36*(9), 11605-11616.

Gupta, R., Jain, K., & Mehta, S. J. (2014). Adoption of mobile telephony in rural India: An empirical study. *Decision Sciences, 45(*2), 281-307.

Hanafizadeh, P., Keating, B. W., & Khedmatgozar, H. R. (2014). A systematic review of Internet banking adoption. *Telematics and Informatics, 31*(3), 492–510.

Holsapple, C.W., & Singh, M. (2000). Electronic commerce: From a definitional taxonomy toward a knowledge-management view. *Journal of Organizational Computing and Electronic Commerce, 10*(3), 149-170.

Hernandez, J. M. C., & Mazzon, J. A. (2007). Adoption of internet banking: Proposition and implementation of an integrated methodology approach. *International Journal of Bank Marketing, 25*(2), 72-88.

Hong, W., Thong, J., Wong, W., & Tam, K. Y. (2001). Determinants of user acceptance of digital libraries: An empirical examination of individual differences and system characteristics. *Journal of Management Information Systems, 18*(3), 97-124.

Islam, S. (2014). Systematic literature review: Security challenges of mobile banking and payments system. *International Journal of u- and e- Service, Science and Technology, 7*(6), 107-116.

Intana, M., Chansa-ngavej, C., and Changchit, C. (2013). Factors Encouraging the Internet Banking Adoption in Thailand. *International Journal of Electronic Finance, 7*(3/4), 196-212.

Jarvenpaa, S. L., & Todd, P. A. (1996). Consumer reaction to electronic shopping on the World Wide Web. *International Journal of Electronic Commerce, 1*(2), 59-88.

Kang, H., Lee, M. J., & Lee, J. K. (2012). Are you still with us? A study of the post-adoption determinants of sustained use of mobile-banking services. *Journal of Organizational Computing and Electronic Commerce, 22*(2), 132-159.

Kim, G., Shin, B., & Lee, H. G. (2009). Understanding dynamics between initial trust and usage intentions of mobile banking. *Information Systems Journal, 19*(3), 283-311.

Lee, Y., Kozar, K. A., & Larsen, K. R. T. (2003). The Technology Acceptance Model: Past, Present, and Future. *Communications of the Association for Information Systems, 12*, 752-780.
Lee, H., Zhang, Y., & Chen, K. L. (2013). An investigation of features and security in mobile banking strategy. *Journal of International Technology and Information Management, 22*(4), 23-45.

Legris, P., Ingham, J., & Collerette, P. (2003). Why do people use information technology? A critical review of the technology acceptance model. *Information and Management, 40*(3), 191–204.

Lin, H. F. (2011). An empirical investigation of mobile banking adoption: The effect of innovation attributes and knowledge-based trust. *International Journal of Information Management, 31*(3), 252-260.

Luarn, P., & Lin, H. (2005). Toward an understanding of the behavioral intention to use mobile banking. *Computer in Human Behavior, 21*(6), 873–891.

Mathwick, C., Malhotra, N., & Rigdon, E. (2001). Experiential value: Conceptualization, measurement and application in the catalog and Internet shopping environment. *Journal of Retailing*, *77*(1), 39-56.

Namahoot, K. S., & Laohavichien, T. (2015). An analysis of behavioral intention to use Thai Internet banking with quality management and trust. *Journal of Internet Banking and Commerce, 20*(3), 1-5.

National Statistical Office. (2014). The 2014 household survey on the use of information and communication technology. Retrieved from http://web.nso.go.th/en/survey/ict/data_ict/2014_Full%20Report.pdf, (accessed December 28, 2015).

Nel, J., & Boshoff, C. (2014). An invariance analysis of online-mobile cross-channel evaluations in the banking industry. *Proceedings of the 13th International Conference WWW/Internet*, Porto, Portugal.

Parasuraman, A., & Zinkhan, G. M. (2002). Marketing to and serving customers through the Internet: An overview and research agenda. *Journal of the Academy of Marketing Science, 30*(4), 286-295.

Pikkarainen, T., Pikkarainen, K., Karjaluoto, H., & Pahnila, S. (2004). Consumer acceptance of online banking: An extension of the technology acceptance model. *Internet Research, 14*(3), 224-235.

Puschel, J., Mazzon, J. A., & Hernandez, J. M. C. (2010). Mobile banking: Proposition of an integrated adoption intention framework. *International Journal of Bank Marketing, 28*(5), 389-409.

Robinson, T. (2004). Internet banking: Still not a perfect marriage. *Informationweek,* 17 Apr., 104.

Roca, J. C., Garcia, J. J., & De la Vega, J. J. (2009). The importance of perceived trust, security

and privacy in online trading systems. *Information Management & Computer Security, 17*(2), 96-113.
Shaikh, A. A., Karjaluoto, H., & Chinje, N. B. (2015). Consumers' perceptions of mobile banking continuous usage in Finland and South Africa. *International Journal of Electronic Finance, 8*(2/3/4), 149-168.

Shim, S., Eastlick, M., Lotz, S., & Warrington, P. (2001). An online prepurchase intentions model: The role of intention to search. *Journal of Retailing, 77*(3), 397-216.

Singh, S., Srivastava, V., & Srivastava, R. K. (2010). Customer acceptance of mobile banking: A conceptual framework. *Journal of Management, 7*(1), 55-64.

Song, H. L. (2015). Customer adoption of mobile banking: An integration of TAM with trust and social influence. *Applied Mechanics and Materials, 701-702*, 1323-1327.

Sprott, D. E., Spangenberg, E. R., & Fisher, R. (2003). The importance of normative beliefs to the self-prophecy effect. *Journal of Applied Psychology, 88*(3), 423–431.

Staff, J. (2013). ABA survey: Popularity of mobile banking continues to climb. *The Central New York Business Journal*, 28.

Statista. (2014). Usage of mobile banking apps worldwide in 2014', Retrieved from http://www.statista.com/statistics/468943/usage-of-mobile-banking-apps-worldwide-by-country/ (accessed December 28, 2015).

Tanner, J. C. (2008). Consumers still wary of m-commerce. *Telecom Asia, 19*(7), 8.
Thailand Chapter of Internet Society. (2015). History of the Internet in Thailand. Retrieved from http://www.isoc-th.org/History_ITH.htm (accessed December 28, 2015).

Tippins, M. & Sohi, R. (2003). IT competency and firm performance: Is organizational learning a missing link? *Strategic Management Journal, 24,* 745–761.

Turban, E., King, D., Viehland, D., & Lee, J. (2006). *Electronic commerce 2006: A managerial perspective.* New Jersey: Pearson Education.

Venkatesh, V., & Davis, F. D. (2000). A theoretical extension of the technology acceptance model: Four longitudinal field studies. *Management Science, 46*(2), 186-204.

Venkatesh, V., Morris, M. G., Davis, G. B., & Davis, F. D. (2003). User acceptance of information technology: Toward a unified view. *MIS Quarterly, 27*(3), 425-478.

Vijayasarathy, L. R. (2004). Predicting consumer intentions to use on-line shopping: The case for an augmented technology acceptance model. *Information & Management, 41*(6), 747-762.

Wong, Y. K., & Hsu, C. J. (2008). A confidence-based framework for business to consumer (B2C) mobile commerce adoption. *Personal and Ubiquitous Computing, 12*(1), 77-84.

Wonglimpiyarat, J. (2014). Competition and challenges of mobile banking: A systematic review of major bank models in the Thai banking industry. *Journal of High Technology Management Research, 25*(2), 123-131.

Yang, K. (2010). The effects of technology self-efficacy and innovativeness on consumer mobile data service adoption between American and Korean consumers. *Journal of International Consumer Marketing, 22*(2), 117-127.

Yenisey, M. M., Ozok, A. A., & Salvendy, G. (2005). Perceived security determinants in e-commerce among Turkish university students. *Behaviour & Information Technology, 24*(4), 259 -274.

Yu, C. S. (2014). Consumer switching behavior from online banking to mobile banking. *International Journal of Cyber Society and Education, 7*(1), 1-28.

Zhou, T., Lu, Y., & Wang, B. (2010). Integrating TTF and UTAUT to explain mobile banking user adoption. *Computers in Human Behavior, 26*(4), 760-767.

Zhao X, Xue, L., & Whinston, A. B. (2013). Managing interdependent information security risks: Cyberinsurance, managed security services, and risk pooling arrangements. *Journal of Management Information Systems, 30*(1), 123-152.

Zorotheos, A., & Kafeza, E. (2009). Users' perceptions on privacy and their intention to transact online: A study on Greek internet users. *Direct Marketing: An International Journal, 3*(2), 139-153.

DECISION SCIENCES INSTITUTE

Mobile Banking Resistance in Ivory Coast

Mohammad I. Merhi
Department of Decision Sciences
Judd Leighton School of Business & Economics
Indiana University South Bend
mmerhi@iusb.edu

Paul Avoaka
Department of Decision Sciences
Judd Leighton School of Business & Economics
Indiana University South Bend
mavoaka@iusb.edu

ABSTRACT

This research in-progress aims to investigate the attitudinal and technological factors impacting resistance to mobile banking in Ivory Coast. No research on resistance of mobile banking has been done in Africa in general and specifically in Ivory Coast, which is a country that has a high potential in technological innovations. By conducting this study, we hope to contribute to both practice and academia. We present our set of hypotheses that we aim to test after data collection.

KEYWORDS: Mobile Banking, Ivory Coast, Africa, Technology Resistance, and E-Wallet.

INTRODUCTION

Mobile banking refers to the use of Information Systems (IS) empowering customers to perform a range of financial transactions through Information and Communication Technologies (ICTs) (Anderson, 2010). Financial transactions vary from transfer of money and balance inquiries, to deposits, etc. Generally, mobile banking introduces smarter techniques of doing banking that benefit both the client and the bank. Over the last few years, banks and financial institutions have started to develop and maintain online banking and brokerage to bridge the gap between them and customers. Until now, not all customers are using the mobile banking systems. Customers are still resisting to adopt these systems. This research in progress examines factors impacting mobile banking resistance in Ivory Coast.

Despite the fast growing of electronic market and online banking, mobile banking is still having a hard time grasping the broad users of cellphones. Indeed, this issue is happening in Ivory Coast where we assume that there might be cultural and technological factors that affect mobile banking resistance and adoption. In fact, we claim that the lack of understanding of outcomes, risk, trust, security issues, and the use of another similar method of banking are the main components that challenge mobile banking adoption in Ivory Coast.

Mobile banking in Ivory Coast is characterized mostly by the use of mobile phones associated with a number acting as e-wallet. Ivoirians use mobile banking to perform mostly limited financial transactions such as sending money to someone else and bill pay. This limited use of mobile banking can be caused by many cultural and economical implications that the country is still trying to resolve. Within the last few years, the country demonstrated outstanding growth and success rate in mobile adoption and place itself in the highest world rank. Data from the World Bank showed that Ivory Coast was the fifth country in mobile adoption (World Bank, n. d.). Coupled with these achievements, Ivory Coast is on the road to be an emerging by 2020 and so looking ahead to flourishing sectors capable to boost its economy accordingly according to the Prime minister. However, Ivoirians still resist to use the mobile banking systems that citizens of other countries are using.

LITERATURE REVIEW

Several studies focused on showing factors and advantages of adopting mobile banking as a smarter approach to financial services. Anderson (2010) investigated the creation of consumer value in developing markets through mobile banking. The study revealed that mobile banking is able to accommodate primary banking and electronic transactions services to unbanked consumers in developing markets. Other studies have shown that it drives a technological innovation by allowing customers to do their banking operations with disregard to time or place and in an easy way (Laukkanen, 2007). Using mobile banking facilitates payments and helps to avoid lines and physical presence in a financial institution (Mallat, 2007). In fact, it has the power to harness higher productivity for banks while making user's lives much easier (Malaquias and Hwang, 2015).

Laforet and Li (2005) studied mobile banking in the Chinese market and investigate its capabilities to develop a large-scale Internet economy and found that most online banking users are males (53%) and younger consumers (57%) showed more emphasis in adopting mobile banking rather than elders. Furthermore, the lack of knowledge and perception of outcomes were one the main obstacles to mobile banking adoption in the Chinese market (Laforet and Li, 2005). Luarn and Lin (2005) investigated the factors that drives users' acceptance of mobile banking. By adding three more factors (perceived credibility, perceived financial cost and perceived self-efficacy) to the standard technology acceptance model (TAM) from previous studies, the new model depicted a stronger capability to analyze users' intention to use an information system (Luarn and Lin, 2005). Tan et al (2009) investigated innovative characteristics, benefits and barriers influencing ICT adoption and found that Internet-based ICT adoption provides a low cost yet effective communication tool for customers. However, security continues to be a major barrier. Poon (2008) found that convenience of usage, accessibility, features availability, band management and image, security, privacy, design, content, speed, and fees and charges have a significant impact on e-banking adoption and resistance in Malaysia. Unfortunately and to our best knowledge there is no study that examined the resistance of mobile banking in any country in Africa.

RESEARCH MODEL

To our best knowledge, no research has investigated the resistance of mobile banking in Ivory Coast yet. Thus, in this study we hope to contribute to the body of knowledge by presenting a set of factors that impact the resistance of mobile banking by Ivoirians. Figure 1 presents the mobile banking resistance model. We now present the factors:

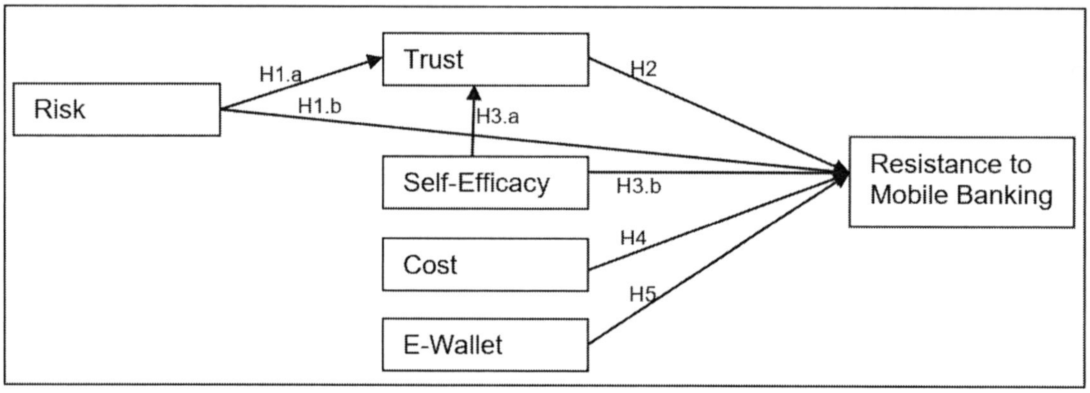

Figure 1. Mobile Banking Resistance Model

Perceived risk

Perceived risk related to security and privacy concerns is associated with using technology in banking. Fraud issues are common in online transactions; users tend to worry about how secure using mobile banking might be the safest way to do their financial transactions. There are also privacy risks and people worry about whether their information are being securely held by the bank or possibly sold to other companies. When someone put his/her information online, he/she can never really know where it goes. Another concept in risk is related to reliability. Reliability expresses the user's trust in the technology to perform accurately the financial transactions. Since an important part of the population in Ivory Coast is so not familiar with the technology, they do not trust it at all. Therefore, we hypothesize that:

H 1.a. Perceived risk negatively impacts trust
H 1.b. Perceived risk positively impacts the resistance of mobile banking

Trust

Trust is the basis for any relationship in the world. In business, trust is very crucial to sustain the liaison between businesses and customers. Studies have shown that trust is one of the key factors that impacts adoption of mobile services (Kim et al., 2009; Koenig-Lewis et al., 2010). Alongside with perceived risk, trust is an important decision making factor for users. Ivoirians do not believe in technology because of their uncertainty about the usefulness, and also how to use it. They have never been exposed to a high-tech environment where everyone sees the input of technology in the growth of the country and also at the personal level. Moreover, only 45% of the population is literate and even within those 45%, a large percentage is not familiar with technology use on a daily basis (National Institute of Statistics). In addition, the urbanization rate is about 50%, which means that half of the population does not live in cities where technology is really helpful and can be fully utilized (National Institute of Statistics). Moreover, the high rate of electronic fraud and cybercrimes in the country has increased the fear of relying on technology for transactions especially financial transactions. Thus, we hypothesize that:

H 2. Trust negatively affects the resistance of mobile banking.

Self-efficacy

Self-efficacy describes the user's self-esteem to use the system or technology (Luarn and Lin, 2005; Merhi, 2016). People are sometimes uncertain or afraid about a new technology; they don't want to feel stupid in front of that technology. Very often, people prefer to avoid embarrassing situations when they feel uncomfortable. . Rather, believing that you can use mobile banking or any new ICT is a big step in the adoption and resistance of that technology. Self-efficacy is simply how an individual believes in herself, how she can master the technology to do tasks. It is expected that higher the perceived self-efficacy leads individuals to trust and not resist using mobile banking. For this reason, we hypothesize:

H 3.a. Self-efficacy positively affects trust.
H 3.b. Self-efficacy negatively affects the resistance of mobile banking.

Cost of Use

Mobile banking usage involves several costs such as device and data. Users are facing a spectrum of unknown cost that generally affects their decision making on adopting mobile banking (Hung et al., 2003; Wu and Wang, 2005). People that are using it need a smartphone with a platform that accepts apps and has a good connectivity to Internet services. In developing countries like Ivory Coast, purchasing a smartphone is not a given for everyone. Indeed, technology devices are not accessible to all of the population. One of the reasons for this is that more than 42% of the population lives below the national poverty line (The World Bank). Moreover, due to high taxes on the retail of technology devices, smartphone are very pricy and retailers do not offer financing options. For this reason, it appears that the cost of use and mobile banking are asymmetrically related (Hanafizadeh et al, 2012). Therefore, we hypothesize that:

H 4. Cost of use positively impacts the resistance of mobile banking.

E-wallet

E-wallet describes the use of mobile phones to perform a certain range of financial transactions such as bill pay or sending money to someone. People use their mobile phone number, which serves as an account to fulfill a task. Credit is put on that account, and people can send money to a family in another city, a friend in a country where the phone carrier is implemented, pay their electric and water bill etc. It is very spread out in the country, and people are doing most of their transactions through this mean. By doing this, they are saving time and do not need services of a bank to manage their day-to-day transactions. In this case, bank accounts seem useless to them and so mobile banking. People prefer to keep their money in cash with them, and whenever they need to do a transaction; they just add credit to their phone number and perform the operation. This procedure constitutes daily routines of several Ivoirians. Banks are totally affected by this factor. Thus, we hypothesize that:

H 5. E-wallet positively impacts the resistance of mobile banking.

PROPOSED METHODOLOGY

Research Method and Measures

The survey methodology is used to assess and investigate the mobile banking resistance model. The population for this study will be Ivoirians. The instrument used for this study will be based on previously validated measures. The majority of the scale items are adopted from the previous literature but adapted to the mobile banking context.

Proposed Analysis Methods

The data collected from the survey instrument will be subjected to various statistical tests. The first analysis tests the data for outliers and normality. After this, construct validity, convergent validity, and discriminant validity will be checked. After confirming the validity of the instrument, Structural Equation Modeling (SEM) will be used to assess and investigate the hypothesized causal paths among the constructs by performing a simultaneous test. This helps to determine if the presented conceptual model had provided an acceptable fit to the empirical data gathered or not.

CONCLUSION

Mobile banking is one of the smartest innovations of our era. The last decades have demonstrated outstanding results and effectiveness in remodeling financial services, and improving people's life. The great benefits of mobile banking cannot be achieved without people adoption to this technology. This research in progress presents a model showing the factors that leads to resistance of mobile banking in Ivory Coast. No study has explored the factors impacting the resistance of mobile banking in Ivory Coast. This study is the first to do so. Studies that examined mobile banking in Africa are scarce. Therefore, we feel that our contribution bridges a significant gap in the literature.

REFERENCES

Anderson, J. (2010). M-banking in developing markets: Competitive and regulatory implications. *Info*, *12*(1), 18-25.

Hanafizadeh, P., Behboudi, M., Ahadi, F., & Ghaderi Varkani, F. (2012). Internet advertising adoption: A structural equation model for Iranian SMEs. *Internet Research*, *22*(4), 499-526.

Hung, S. Y., Ku, C. Y., & Chang, C. M. (2003). Critical factor of WAP services adoption: An empirical study. *Electronic Commerce Research and Applications*, *2*(1), 42-60.

Kim, G., Shin, B., & Lee, H. G. (2009). Understanding dynamics between initial trust and usage intentions of mobile banking, *Information Systems Journal*, 19(3), 283-311.

Koenig-Lewis, N., Palmer, A., & Moll, A. (2010). Predicting young consumers' take up of mobile banking services. *International Journal of Bank Marketing*, *28*(5), 410-432.

Laforet, S. & Li, X. (2005). Consumers' attitudes towards online and mobile banking in China. *International Journal of Bank Marketing*, *23*(5), 362-380.

Laukkanen, T. (2007). Internet vs mobile banking: Comparing customer value perceptions. *Business Process Management Journal*, *13*(6), 788-797.

Luarn, P. & Lin, H. H. (2005). Toward an understanding of the behavioral intention to use mobile banking. *Computers in Human Behavior*, *21*(6), 873-891.

Malaquias, R. F. & Hwang, Y. (2015). Firms' size and use of information and communication technologies Empirical evidence on small businesses in Brazil. *Information Development.*
Mallat, N. (2007). Exploring consumer adoption of mobile payments–A qualitative study. *The Journal of Strategic Information Systems. 16*(4), 413-432.
Merhi, M. I. (2016). Towards a framework for online game adoption. *Computers in Human Behavior. 60*, 253-263.
Poon, W.-C., (2008). Users' adoption of e-banking services: The Malaysian perspective. *Journal of Business and Industrial Marketing. 23*(1), 59-69.
Tan, K.S., Chong, S.C., Lin, B., & Eze, U.C., (2009). Internet-based ICT adoption: Evidence from Malaysian SMEs. *Industrial Management and Data Systems, 109*(2), 224-244.
The World Bank (n.d). Available online at: http://data.worldbank.org/country/cote-divoire.Accessed on January 20, 2016
Wu, J.H. & Wang, S.C. (2005). What drives mobile commerce? An empirical evaluation of the revised technology acceptance model. *Information and Management, 42*(5), 719-729.

DECISION SCIENCES INSTITUTE

Modifying Resource Allocation for Transition of

Emergency Department (ED) Visits to Urgent Care (UC) Visits

Logan Frederick

Illinois State University

Email: ltfrede@ilstu.edu

Borinara Park

Illinois State University

Email: bpark@ilstu.edu

Mercy Korir

Illinois State University

Email: mckorir@ilstu.edu

Michael Hysell

Illinois State University

Email: mkhysel@ilstu.edu

Nicholas Johnson

Illinois State University

Email: najohns@ilstu.edu

ABSTRACT

Hospitals need to ensure patients are utilizing the appropriate level of care. Roughly only a half of the patients seen in an emergency department (ED) have an emergent need to be cared for in an emergency setting. The other half of the ED patients, in fact, could be treated in the urgent care (UC) service. This study utilizes discrete event simulation (DES): 1) to simulate the change in volumes for each service; and 2) to determine how to staff each location to meet appropriate levels of service and financial stewardship. The outcome of the study has to support the hospital administration who wants to reduce the overall staffing costs within the emergency department to make up for the reduced revenue.

KEYWORDS: Discrete Event Modeling, Resource Allocation, System Redesign, Simulation, Decision Making in Health Care

BACKGROUND

Many believe most of the visits to a hospital emergency department(ED) are truly emergent, however only around half of the patients seen in an ED have an emergent need to be cared for in an emergency setting. An ED visit is very expensive due to the cost of providing care and therefore has a high charge to the patient and their insurer. Studies have shown hospitals non-emergent ED usage can range from 12 to 56 percent .[1] Some examples of non-emergent reasons for utilizing the ED would be fever, toothache, and minor lacerations.

Many insurance plans have noticed this trend of non-emergent patients utilizing the high cost emergency services and have decided to make some changes to their payment structure. Some insurance plans will be reducing their payments for non-emergent visits and others will not pay at all. Washington is one of the states denying all forms of payment.

Two of the multiple state funded insurers for the hospital will be reducing payments for non-emergent diagnoses by 82%. The rate will go from a $144 ED rate to a $26 Urgent Care rate, or a difference of $118 per visit. The state funded payers in question account for 66% of the non-urgent patient population or approximately 24 patients per day. This reduction in payment will equate to $1,033,680 in reduced revenue out of a projected $1,261,440. This number will increase if other insurers begin the practice of reducing payment for non-emergent visits. In many of these cases the hospital will never re coup the difference from patients. Due to this change, hospitals need to ensure patients are utilizing the appropriate level of care.

A layperson would believe that the hospital should simply turn away non urgent patients and direct them to an urgent care or their physician's office. However the Emergency Medical Treatment and Labor Act (EMTALA) states *any patient who "comes to the emergency department" requesting "examination or treatment for a medical condition" must be provided with "an appropriate medical screening examination" to determine if he is suffering from an "emergency medical condition". If he is, then the hospital is obligated to either provide him with treatment until he is stable or to transfer him to another hospital in conformance with the statute's directives.*[2] This means a physician must at least see the patient and provide an examination. At this point a patient has registered, seen a nurse, and a physician which is 75% of the process. For efficiency and satisfaction purposes, the physician usually provides treatment.

Many of the non-emergent ED visits could be handled by a lower cost physician office or urgent care type facility. Diagnostic testing is often more expensive within the ED environment than the Urgent Care environment. Hospitals send many specimens through the hospital laboratory at a higher cost vs. Urgent Cares that utilize lower cost point of care testing. The average difference in cost for point of care testing is $17.83 per test, with each non urgent patient averaging 1.4 tests per visit.

The hospital will begin a targeted public awareness campaign to reduce the number of non-emergent patients coming to the ED and redirecting them to a physician office or urgent care. The campaign will focus on education of what types of conditions should be seen in an urgent care. Billboards, flyers, and attending community events will occur across the community over the next few months. Patients who come to the ED with non-emergent conditions will also be educated on the appropriate use of the ED and provided with a flyer about the urgent care.

The anticipated change is a reduction of 3 visits per hour in the ED during urgent care hours, and an increase of 30 to 36 patients per day for the urgent care. By redirecting these non-emergent patients, the ED volume will decrease and the urgent care volume will increase therefore staffing for each site will need to change.

This study utilizes discrete event simulation (DES) by AnyLogic 1) to simulate the change in volumes for each service; and 2) to determine how to staff each location to meet appropriate levels of service and financial stewardship. Hospital administration is hoping to simply transfer staff from the emergency department to the urgent care to maintain their current staffing level expenses as well as looking for ways to reduce the overall staffing costs within the emergency department to make up for the reduced revenue.

CURRENT PROCESS

The hospital simulated for the study is based on a hospital in the Midwest region. The hospital is a level 2 trauma center with 23 ED rooms. The emergency department currently sees around 168 patients per day (7 patients per hour) and the urgent care sees 48 patients per day (4 per hour). The urgent care is not directly connected to the emergency department. The location of the Urgent care is in another building on the same campus as the emergency department.

Figure 1 shows the current operational processes within the urgent care and the emergency department using the discrete simulation blocks. The process shows two separate processes for the ED and the urgent care (UC) facilities. The urgent care process is at the top. The process for the urgent care is rather simple as it mainly has registration, nurse evaluation, and physician evaluation steps. The ED has many more processes, as there are many more options for diagnostic testing. A more complicated patient may need laboratory testing or may need a radiologic exam. Each of these types of tests can have a wide range of timing for completion. For example, a blood sugar could take 3 minutes for completion as compared to a troponin blood test that needs a comparison draw 4 hours later.

Figure 1: Current processes within the urgent care (UC) and emergency department (ED)

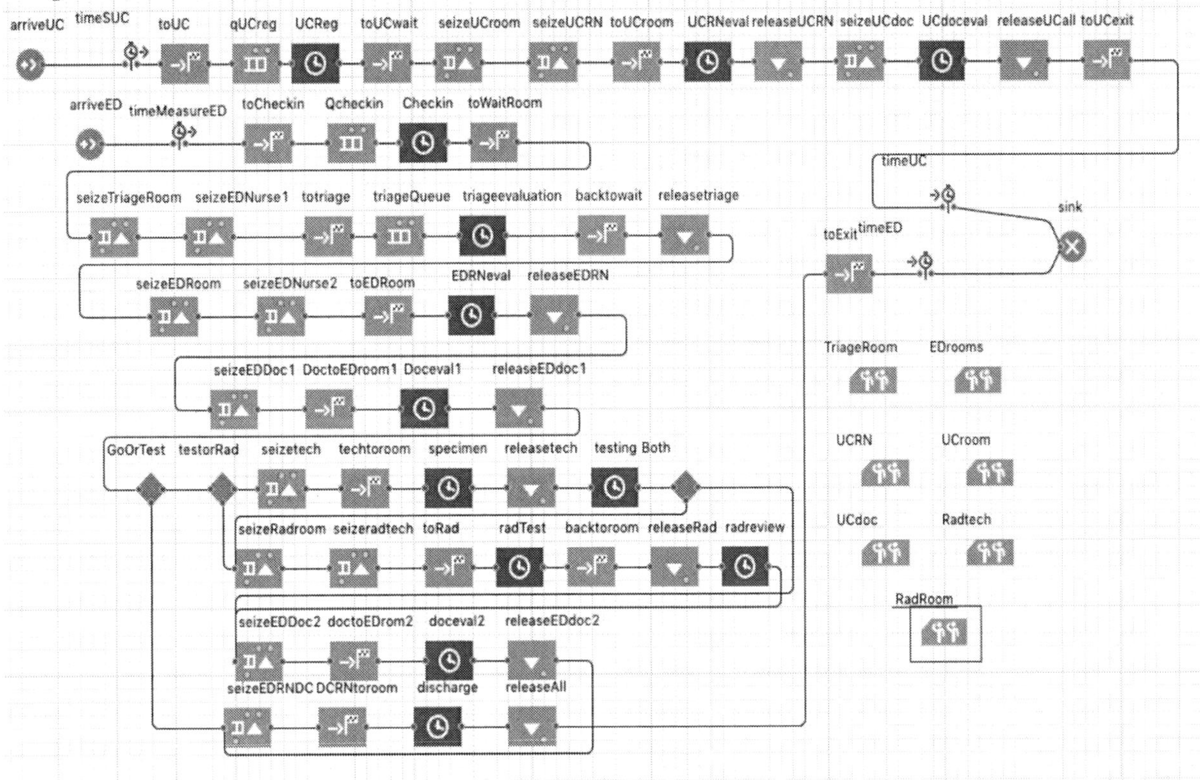

Arrival rates and process times were obtained from time stamped process reports or direct observation by an internal consultant. The ranges of times were entered as triangular distributions within the software to allow for the variation in the length of process steps. Trauma events were not included in the study as they are not frequent enough to quantify.

The ED processes are more complex as it includes a nurse triage step and many more steps for radiology or laboratory testing. The radiology and laboratory testing steps are dependent on the patient's condition, and have quantified percentages in place for probability of the steps.

The DES modeling outcome (Figure 2) shows the current level of service and productivity prior to any volume or staffing changes. The model shows long overall service times (222 minutes) in the emergency department(ED) and shows shorter times (18 minutes) within the urgent care (UC).

Figure 2: Discrete event simulation outcomes on the current level of service and productivity

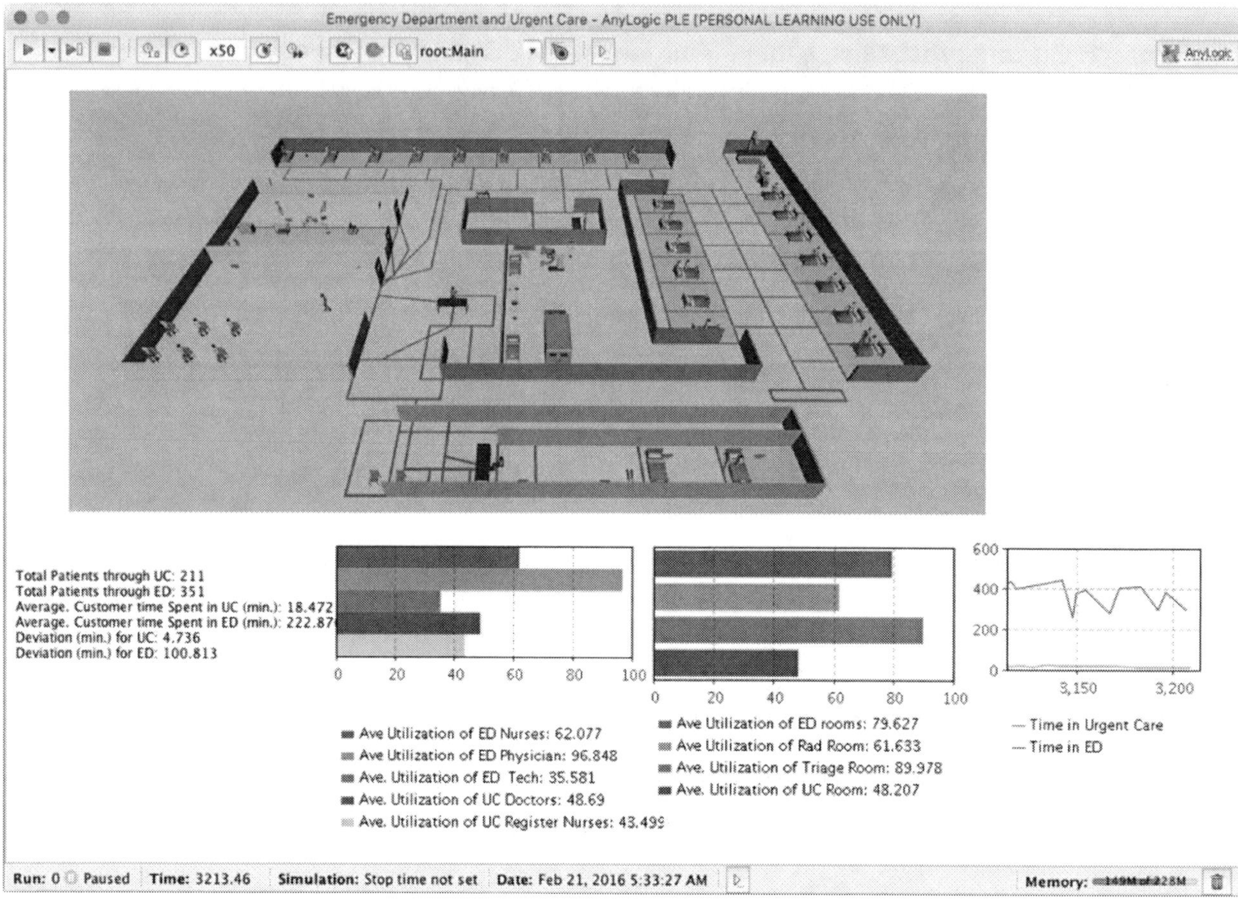

Utilization of staff is good overall in the current process models. ED physicians are currently close to being maxed out at 96%, this is the result of cost cutting measures to only have 2 physicians staffed at a time. Tech and nurse staffing look low, but there are other tertiary duties which do not follow a straight process path and have not been included in the model.

By setting up the current process model we have proven the modeling software can replicate the current service levels within the ED. Proving the model is accurate in the current state was crucial for obtaining the confidence of administration.

CHANGE IN ARRIVAL RATE

As described in the background we will model a shift in the amount of patients arriving at each facility. There will be a shift from 7 ED patients per hour to 4, and the urgent care will go from 4 to 7 patients per hour. The processes and staffing levels will stay the same for the simulation. Figure 3 below shows what happens to length of visit and staffing utilization when this shift occurs.

We need to model out the volume change to show managers what will happen to service times and production levels with the projected volume change. The volume change will have a significant impact on how managers will staff the emergency department and the urgent care. If staffing changes are not changed appropriately, service levels will not be acceptable to patients within the Urgent Care and staffing costs will be too high within the ED. The staffing changes will allow us to recoup the revenue loss created by the state insurance companies.

Results

With the volume change, the model in Fig. 3 is telling us the service length at the urgent care more than doubled up to 39 minutes. The ED time has dropped significantly down to 79 minutes. The standard deviation for the urgent care increased to 20 minutes from 4 minutes with the volume change. If service levels are not significantly better at the urgent care than the emergency room, patients will not choose the urgent care over the emergency department. If the patients still chose the emergency department the project will be unsuccessful, and the revenue loss within the emergency department will be seen.

Figure 3: Discrete event simulation outcomes with changes in the arrival rates

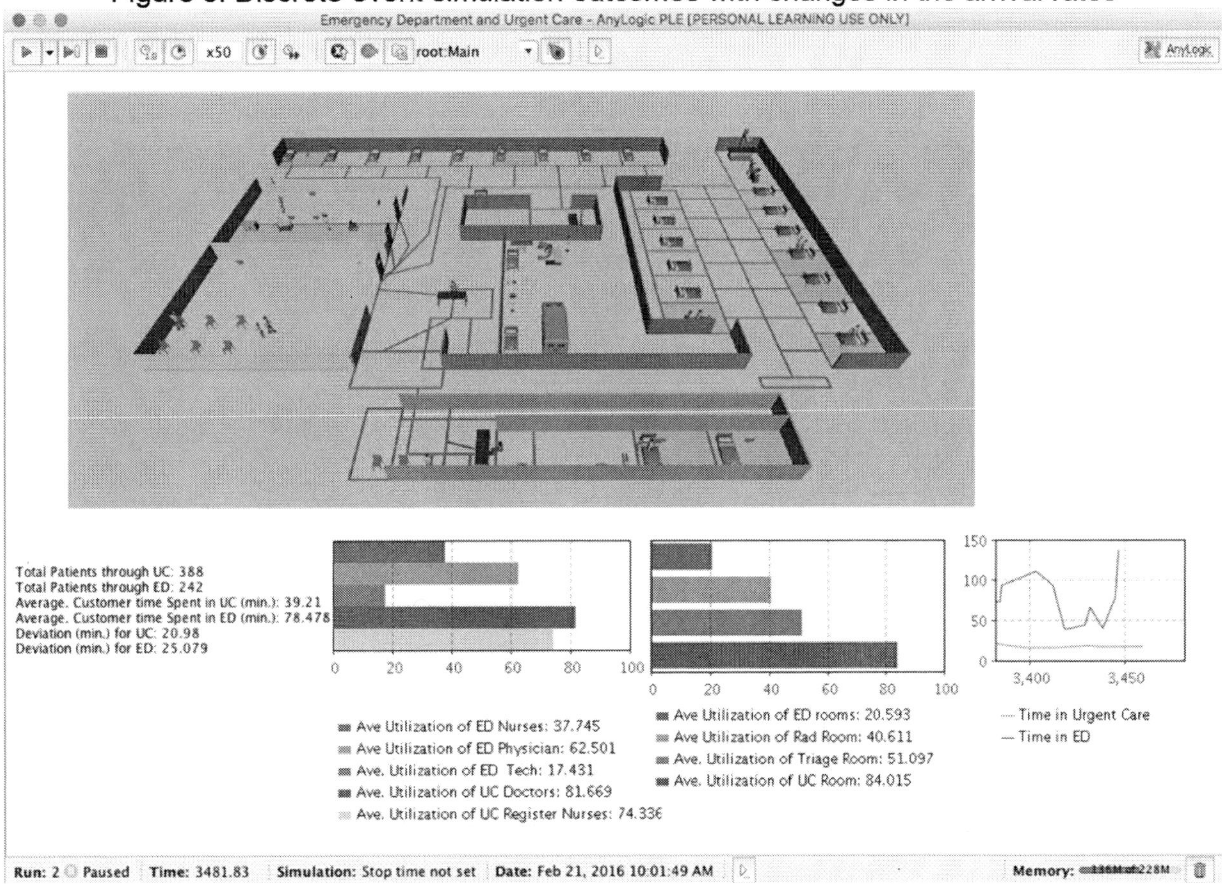

The ED nurse and tech utilization has dropped significantly to 37% and 17% respectively. The room utilization for the urgent care is high(84%) and could be causing some of the increased length of service. The UC doctor and registered nurse utilization is also reaching high levels of utilization(74% and 81%).

The results indicated that we needed to make further changes to staffing and room additions as described in the analytic solution.

RESOURCE (STAFF) ALLOCATION

With the new high utilization of the urgent care and low utilization of the emergency department, staffing needs to be adjusted. Upon review there is a need to reduce a nurse and tech within the emergency department. At the same time we will need to add a nurse and a physician to the urgent care to accompany the new volume. The nurse from the ED was transferred over to the urgent care.

Upon running the model, the urgent care saw no improvements in service times despite adding staff. This was due to a lack of available rooms to utilize. Two rooms were remodeled to become exam rooms and were able to be utilized to see patients. A typical physician office model has a physician and nurse combination working out of 2 rooms per team. Figure 4 shows the statistics from the model with the above changes.

Figure 4: Discrete event simulation outcomes with changes in the resources

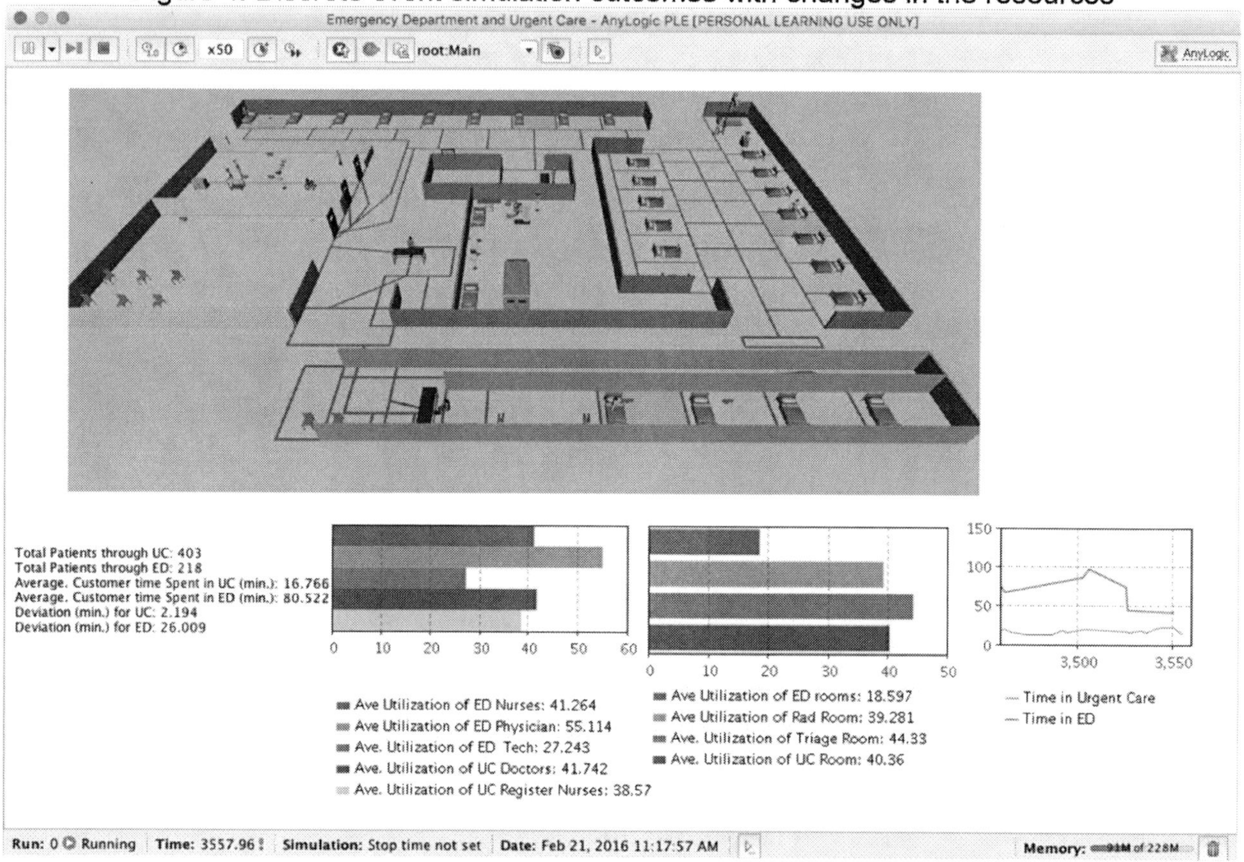

Results

Upon our analytic solution model change we were able to show a reduced length of service in the urgent care (16 min) and maintained a similar level of service within the emergency department (78 min). The overall variability is also reduced in both service locations, especially in the urgent care where we saw the standard deviation drop to 2 minutes. Room utilization was improved to 40% within the urgent care by adding the 2 rooms.

By reducing the ED nurse and tech in the ED, we are still sitting low in overall utilization of ED nurses and techs at 41% and 27% respectively. Without making any physician changes in the

ED, we still see a 55% utilization rate. This tells us, they are still rather busy even with the reduced volume. This is due to the complexity of patients within an ED.

The overall change in expense was the addition of the urgent care physician at a rate of $220,000. This was slightly offset by the reduction of a tech in the ED at a combined cost of $45,000. The change in expense overall would be $175,000 for the hospital.

With the addition of the physician and reduction of ED tech, it now makes the overall change to the budgeted net revenue for the project down even further to $1,208,680.

DISCUSSION

Ideally the hospital had hoped to shift one ED physician over to the urgent care, however upon modeling, the service times increased drastically when only 1 physician was available. The risk of having only 1 physician in the ED was also considered since if a trauma arrived or acuity spiked, the hospital could set themselves up for liability.

There is a potential to reduce 1 more nurse from the ED, but that could come as a shock to the overall culture initially. The culture of nursing is to ensure you have adequate staffing for safe patient care, and a drastic change in staffing could result in low morale and low support of the change. The change could be made but would not happen immediately.

Reducing another nurse could come with a process change of eliminating the triage step. Since there will be less patients coming in, the need for triage should be eliminated as room utilization is no longer an issue. With two nurse reductions and the reduction of another tech, this would add another $185,000 to the staffing reduction bringing the total staffing reduction to $230,000. This has been modeled out to ensure proper productivity and service levels as seen in Figure 5.

Figure 5: Discrete event simulation outcomes with elimination of triage process and tech role

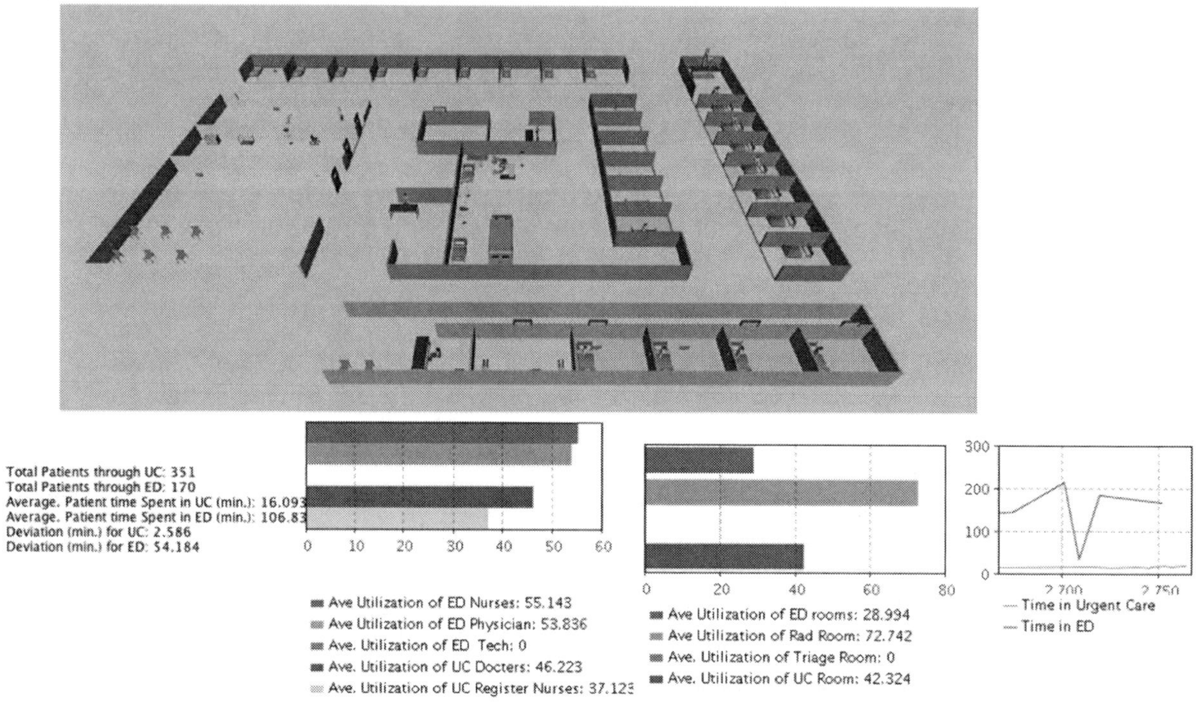

Figure 5 shows the process metrics with the elimination of the triage process and the tech role. With the triage process removed the nurse utilized for that process is now removed. The tech utilization was very low and was only utilized to gather specimens. Nurses could gather specimens and perform many of the tech duties with a lower volume of patients. The nurse productivity is now 55% which will allow for the other tech duties that were not captured by the model. The average service time increased to 106 minutes, but it is still much better than the original of 222 minutes.

There is a potential of underutilization of physicians for the urgent care. There is a strong potential to utilize a mid-level practitioner at a lower cost than a physician, as they will be seeing lower acuity patients within the urgent care setting. A mid-level practitioner purpose is to care for lower acuity cases we are targeting for the urgent care. A mid-level practitioner would only cost $110,000 and could make for an overall reduction in staffing expense for the change to $120,000. This model would allow the hospital to be recoup some of the lost revenue and increase levels of service within the emergency department.

In regards to service times within the ED, there will be a need to reevaluate the overall times when the lower acuity patients are no longer a larger portion of the process. Patients with higher acuity will require longer service and the percentage of patients needing diagnostic testing will increase as well. This can be modeled out at a later time, although it should not affect the proposed staffing reduction.

There is a concern that if we start to see much lower service times within the ED, patients will revert back to utilizing the ED. Volume and service levels will need to be monitored regularly.

CONCLUSIONS

The simulation showed if non urgent patients utilized the urgent care appropriately, it would improve the overall efficiency of the ED. Financially, there will be the ability to reduce staffing by $120,000 by reducing ED staff to recoup some of the loss of revenue by shifting patients from the ED to the Urgent Care.

The reduction of testing costs within the ED vs. the urgent care will reduce $218,667 in costs for the ED. Combining the staffing reductions and testing cost reductions will save the hospital $338,667. While this does not cover the entire loss in revenue from the state insurance policy change, it converts a $1,033,688 loss in revenue to a $695,021 net loss.

One of the biggest unanswered questions will ultimately be if the volume change from the ED to the urgent care will be as large as anticipated. There is a culture change to make and it is unknown what the rate of change will be from the ED volume to urgent care. It will not happen overnight and could take several months to see the level of volume change anticipated. As the transition occurs longer service times will be seen and may become costly to staff.

LIMITATIONS

Since this is a simulation it is not always possible to include trauma scenarios where an ED physician could be utilized for a single patient for a length of time. The process times were entered as a general flow of ED and urgent care patients.

Nursing and tech responsibilities do not always follow a process path and can be variable. There are other metrics that state how many worked hours an ED should have per patient within the ED. Those metrics would be followed as the actual model is in place.

Below are a list of variables that could be accounted for to improve the simulation.
Arrival rates vary across every hour of the day, therefore an average was chosen to run the simulation. Arrival times can vary from 1 patient per hour to 12 patients per hour depending on the hour of day and day of week.

Staffing of physicians, nurses, and techs in the ED is also variable throughout the day. Staffing is currently based on peak times of days. Overnights and early mornings are staffed lightly while mid days and evenings are at full staffing levels.

The ED is open 24 hours, but the urgent care is only open for 10-12 hours of the day. The urgent care is open during the peak hours of the day, but there will be times when non-emergent patients will be seeking care when the urgent care is not open. The ED will be utilized by these patients during this time.

REFERENCES

1 New England Health Institute, A Matter of Urgency: Reducing Emergency Department Overuse 2010, http://www.nehi.net/writable/publication_files/file/nehi_ed_overuse_issue_brief_032610finaledits.pdf

2 CMS 1063-F Medicare Program; Clarifying Policies Related to the Responsibilities of Medicare-Participating Hospitals in Treating Individuals with Emergency Medical Conditions, https://www.cms.gov/Regulations-and-Guidance/Legislation/EMTALA/Downloads/CMS-1063-F.pdf

DECISION SCIENCES INSTITUTE

Multi-criteria Stock Portfolio Management – A Distance Function Approach

Dinesh K. Sharma
University of Maryland Eastern Shore
dksharma@umes.edu

R.K. Jana
Indian Institute of Social Welfare & Business Management
rkjana@iiswbm.edu

Hari Sharma
Virginia State University
hsharma@vsu.edu

ABSTRACT

In this study, we propose a mathematical model for constructing an efficient stock portfolio. It takes into the account maximization of annual return, the minimization of portfolio's risk, and the maximization of dividend. For each objective, the ideal and anti-ideal solutions are calculated separately. The distance function approach is then used to optimally select the portfolio. It minimizes the objective formed by combining the ideal and anti-ideal solutions. To demonstrate the proposed method, a case example is presented based on Dow Jones Industrial Average data. The obtained results have been compared with goal programming techniques considering equal and unequal weights.

KEYWORDS: Portfolio, Multi-criteria Decision Making, Distance Function.

INTRODUCTION

Portfolio management deals with making decisions about creating a mix of investment securities according to the policy that meets the objectives of investment, the allocation of assets for individuals and institutions and balancing the portfolio risk against returns (performance). Thus, portfolio management decisions always require performance measurement which is commonly known as the expected return from the portfolio for a specified level of risk which differs from one investor to another based on the unique goals and circumstances of the investor. The stock markets bounce up and down significantly every week; individual investors clearly should understand the need of a safety net, which is the diversification that prevents the entire portfolio from losing value.

The classic model is the mean-variance optimization model introduced by Markowitz (1952 & 1959). Sharpe (1963) developed a simplified diagonal model for selecting an efficient portfolio. Additionally, the capital asset pricing model (CAPM) was formulated by Sharpe (1964) and Lintner (1965). Markowitz (2008) criticised the relationship explained by Sharpe and Lintner between risk and excess returns, and argued that it is possible to achieve different expected returns from the same risk structure. Markowitz (2008) further emphasized that the mean–variance framework is the cornerstone for assessing the risk of efficient portfolios.

The concept of distance function was proposed by Shephard (1953). Thereafter, different variants of distance function were introduced for solving many business problems (Barros et al., 2011; Färe & Grosskopf, 2000). However, this technique has not been extensively used in the area of portfolio optimization problems to address multi-criteria decision making problems. This motivates us to utilize the distance function concept to solve a multi-criteria stock portfolio optimization problem.

The purpose of the paper is to construct an effective stock portfolio. It is done by utilizing the capability of the distance function approach. This approach ensures the minimization of the difference of the objective value achievable, to the extent possible, from the ideal solution for all the objectives. As a result, for the considered multi-criteria stock portfolio optimization problem, it is possible to select the best combination of stocks.

LITERATURE REVIEW

According to Zelani (1982), distance function is an effective way of solving multi-criteria decision making problems. Romero (1985) established the relationship between the multi-objective programming and distance function approach. The portfolio optimization literature doesn't report much on the application of distance function to solve these problems. A summary of literature review on distance function and portfolio optimization is presented in Table 1.

Table 1: Summary of Literature Review on Distance Function and Portfolio Optimization

YEAR	REFERENCES	JOURNAL
2014	Aouni, Colapinto and Torre	European Journal of Operational Research
2013	Sharma,Jana and Sharma	Journal of Money, Investment and Banking
2011	Barros, Briec and Ratsimbanierana	Journal of Mathematical Finance
2010	Sharma, Sharma and Jana	International Journal of Finance
2009	Sharma, Jana and Sharma	International Research Journal of Finance and Economics
2006	Bilbao-Terol, Perez-Gladish, Arenas-Parra and Rodriguez-Uria	Applied Mathematics and Computation
2000	Färe and Grosskopf	Journal of Productivity Analysis

PORTFOLIO OPTIMIZATION MODEL DEVELOPMENT

In this section, the portfolio optimization model is developed and presented.

Index

s: index for proportion of money invested in security $s \in \{1,2,\cdots,S\}$

Variables and Parameters

X_s = proportion of money invested in a security s

D_s = dividend on stock *s*

R_s^1 = annual rate of return from the security *s* for one year

R_s^3 = annual rate of return from security *s* for the next three years

R_s^5= expected maximum annual rate of return for five years

U_s = maximum proportion of money invested in security *s*

β_s = risk associated with security *s* PE_s = price earnings ratio of security *s*

PE_{max} = maximum price earnings ratio

Model Objectives

(i) **Annual return:** The return from securities must be maximized. Three different investment scenarios have been considered. They are one, three and five year returns. Each of them should be maximized and can be expressed as follows:

(a) One year return objective: $$\max: \sum_{s=1}^{S} R_s^1 X_s \quad (1)$$

(b) Three years return: $$\max: \sum_{s=1}^{S} R_s^3 X_s \quad (2)$$

(c) Five years return: $$\max: \sum_{s=1}^{S} R_s^5 X_s . \quad (3)$$

(ii) **Portfolio's risk:** The systematic risk of a portfolio is denoted by beta and it is measure of the sensitivity of a security's returns to the market returns which is always minimized. The corresponding objective is expressed as:

$$\min: \sum_{s=1}^{S} \beta_s X_s . \quad (4)$$

(iii) **Annual dividend:** The annual dividend income from all the securities must be maximize and the corresponding objective can be expressed as:

$$\max: \sum_{s=1}^{S} D_s X_s . \quad (5)$$

Model Constraints

(i) **P/E ratio constraint**: The sum of the price earnings ratio of each security should be less than or equal to the maximum acceptable limit of thecompany's financial performance. The corresponding constraint can be expressed as:

$$\sum_{s=1}^{S} PE_s X_s \leq PE_{\max} . \quad (6)$$

(ii) **Investment constraint:** The decision maker would like to utilize 100% of his/her fund available for investment and the constraint can be expressed as:

$$\sum_{s=1}^{S} X_s = 1 . \quad (7)$$

(iii) **Diversification constraint:** It is always preferable not to invest too much in a specific security. This reduces the risk of the investment. The diversification constraint can thus be constructed as follows:

$$X_s \leq U_s, \quad s = 1,2,\cdots,S . \quad (8)$$

THE DISTANCE FUNCTION APPROACH

A classical MOP problem can be presented as follows:

$$\min: \{f_1(x), f_2(x), \dots, f_m(x)\} \quad (9)$$

subject to $g_r(x) \leq 0,\ r = 1,2,\dots,R$ (10)

$x \geq 0,$ (11)

where x is vector of n decision variables; $f_i(x)\ (i = 1,2,\dots,m)$ are individual objectives, $and\ g_r(x)\ (r = 1,2,\dots,R)$ are constraint functions.
Let f_i^* be the ideal solution of $f_1(x)$ subject to given set of constraints. Then the auxiliary problem can be formulated as follows (Romero 1985):

$$\min{:}\{\textstyle\sum_{i=1}^{m} w_i\,|f_i^* - f_i(x)|^p\}^{1/p} \quad (12)$$

subject to $g_r(x) \leq 0,\ r = 1,2,\dots,R$ (13)

$x \geq 0.$ (14)

There are different ways of defining the weights w_i. Let f_i^- be the anti-ideal solutions of $f_i(x)$ subject to the given set of constraints. Then according to Hwang and Yoon (1981), the auxiliary problem can be formulated as follows:

$$\min{:}\left\{\sum_{i=1}^{m} \frac{|f_i^* - f_i(x)|^p}{|f_i^* - f_i^-|^p}\right\}^{1/p} \quad (15)$$

subject to $g_r(x) \leq 0,\ r = 1,2,\dots,R\ ;\ x \geq 0.$ (16)

The proposed model is illustrated through a portfolio selection problem considering multiple objectives. A sample of 30 stocks is considered from the Dow Jones Industrial Average and is collected from the online source Yahoo Finance. They are presented in Table 2.

Table 2: Required financial data

Company	Beta	Dividend	Yield	Earnings/ Share	Forward P/E	P/E	Return on Equity	Year 1	Year 3	Year 5
AA	2.17	0.12	0.82%	-1.28	12.56	-13.87	-8.22	58.57%	-24.39%	-11.21%
AXP	2.11	0.72	1.73%	1.53	12.87	27.08	13.78	67.18%	-10.13%	-0.53%
BA	1.28	1.68	2.30%	1.8	16.04	39.03	320.14	87.72%	-5.47%	6.36%
BAC	2.4	0.04	0.22%	0.03	9.02	-62.21	-1.32	100.34%	-26.56%	-13.38%
CAT	1.8	1.68	0.26%	1.41	15.92	44.75	12.07	81.39%	-1.96%	9.97%
CSCO	1.22	0	0.00%	1.04	16.88	24.84	15.5	34.73%	-0.89%	8.55%
CVX	0.63	2.72	3.55%	7.81	154.02	14.64	11.74	19.15%	2.44%	11.37%
DD	1.41	1.64	4.33%	1.92	14.09	19.74	25.17	40.53%	-4.70%	-0.69%
DIS	1.15	0.35	0.99%	1.76	15.52	20.31	9.61	61.25%	1.17%	6.95%
GE	1.59	0.04	2.18%	1.01	14.78	17.8	9.81	47.73%	-17.44%	-9.51%
HD	0.7	0.95	2.92%	1.57	15.06	20.89	14.1	27.06%	-1.83%	0.89%
HPQ	1.02	0.32	0.60%	3.31	10.95	16.04	19.83	48.75%	8.85%	22.06%
IBM	0.76	2.2	1.72%	10.01	10.7	12.88	74.37	26.62%	9.76%	12.63%
INTC	1.18	0.63	2.81%	0.78	12.4	29.14	10.75	45.78%	4.03%	1.30%
JNJ	0.57	1.96	2.98%	4.4	12.3	14.95	26.35	28.62%	3.52%	1.64%
JPM	1.13	0.2	0.44%	2.26	9.45	20.17	5.95	36.11%	-2.72%	7.62%
KFT	0.59	1.16	3.82%	2.03	13.04	14.97	12.54	34.82%	0.49%	2.15%
KO	0.6	1.76	3.18%	2.93	14.91	18.88	30.15	31.89%	4.83%	7.89%
MCD	0.62	2.2	3.26%	4.11	14.11	16.27	33.2	29.53%	15.06%	21.28%
MMM	0.77	2.1	2.50%	4.51	14.75	18.57	28.2	49.37%	3.19%	4.50%
MRK	0.84	1.52	4.03%	5.37	9.56	6.68	33.03	61.41%	-6.18%	6.45%
MSFT	0.97	0.52	1.78%	1.82	13.17	16.07	41.28	47.63%	1.15%	4.70%
PFE	0.7	0.72	4.22%	1.36	7.35	13.81	11.69	33.67%	-8.72%	-4.48%
PG	0.58	1.76	2.78%	4.22	15.65	17.12	16.71	30.91%	1.84%	5.53%
T	0.69	1.68	6.43%	2.12	11.01	12.36	12.65	5.73%	-8.36%	6.59%
TRV	0.65	1.32	2.45%	6.39	9.08	8.42	13.67	34.51%	2.49%	11.20%
UTX	0.98	1.7	2.29%	4.12	14.07	18.17	21.37	54.71%	5.49%	9.87%
VZ	0.64	1.9	6.07%	1.29	12.58	24.38	8.76	7.04%	-1.97%	2.75%
WMT	0.23	1.21	2.19%	3.7	12.67	14.95	21.19	12.71%	7.15%	5.18%
XOM	0.42	1.68	2.49%	3.98	9.4	17.07	17.25	2.94%	-3.56%	5.35%

RESULTS AND ANALYSIS

The following analysis is based on the assumption that the investor will restrict his/her investment proportion to any particular security to 5%. Accordingly, the ideal and anti-ideal solutions for each objective are obtained using LINGO 10.0 and are presented in Table 3.

Table 3: Ideal and anti-ideal solutions

Objective	Ideal Objective Value	Anti-ideal Objective Value
Risk	0.7110	1.2435
Dividend	1.6437	0.8250
Return: 1 year	0.5290	0.2933
Return: 3 year	0.0298	– 0.0589
Return: 5 year	0.0867	0.0103

Three investment scenarios have been considered. They are 1-year, 3-year and 5-year returns. They are presented in the following tables.

Case I: 1-Year return

Table 4a: 1-Year return

X3	X4	X5	X7	X8	X9	X11	X12	X13	X15	X17
0.05	0.02	0.05	0.03	0.05	0.05	0.04	0.05	0.05	0.05	0.05

Table 4b: 1-Year return

X18	X19	X20	X21	X22	X23	X24	X26	X27	X28	X29
0.05	0.05	0.05	0.05	0.05	0.05	0.05	0.05	0.05	0.01	0.05

Table 5: Objective values for 1-Year return

Objective	Compromised Objective Value
Risk	0.8750
Dividend	1.4332
Return: 1 year	0.4344

The minimized objective value is obtained as 0.5678.

Case II: 3-Year return

Table 6a: 3-Year return

X3	X7	X8	X11	X12	X13	X14	X15	X17	X18	X19	X20
0.05	0.03	0.04	0.05	0.05	0.05	0.05	0.05	0.05	0.05	0.05	0.05

Table 6b: 3-Year return

X21	X22	X24	X25	X26	X27	X28	X29	X30
0.05	0.03	0.05	0.05	0.05	0.05	0.05	0.05	0.013

Table 7: Objective values for 3-Year return

Objective	Compromised Objective Value
Risk	0.7573
Dividend	1.5517
Return: 3 year	0.3457

The minimized objective value is obtained as 0.1862.

Case III: 5-Year return

Table 8a: 5-Year return

X3	X7	X8	X11	X12	X13	X15	X16	X17	X18	X19	X20
0.05	0.03	0.03	0.05	0.05	0.05	0.05	0.05	0.05	0.05	0.05	0.05

Table 8b: 5-Year return

X21	X22	X24	X25	X26	X27	X28	X29	X30
0.05	0.04	0.05	0.05	0.05	0.05	0.05	0.05	0.013

Table 9: Objective values for 5-Year return

Objective	Compromised Objective Value
Risk	0.7511
Dividend	1.5243
Return: 5 year	0.3410

The minimized objective value is obtained as 0.2504.

COMPARISON OF RESULTS

The results obtained have been compared with that of the Goal Programming (GP) technique with equal and different priorities (Sharma et al., 2013) and are presented as follows:

Table 10: 1-Year Return using GP and Distance Function

	GP with Equal Priority	GP with Different Priority	Distance Function
Risk	0.7503	0.7971	0.8750
Dividend	1.6023	1.4718	1.4332
1-Year Return	0.3433	0.3999	0.4344

Table 11: 3-Year Return using GP and Distance Function

	GP with Equal Priority	GP with Different Priority	Distance Function
Risk	0.8140	0.7971	0.7573
Dividend	1.3556	1.4718	1.5517
3-Year Return	0.3581	0.3999	0.3457

Table 12: 5-Year Return using GP and Distance Function

	GP with Equal Priority	GP with Different Priority	Distance Function
Risk	0.8283	0.8062	0.7511
Dividend	1.4692	1.4536	1.5243
5-Year Return	0.3753	0.3583	0.3410

The analysis of the results reveals that the proposed model did yield the expected results for the one, three and five year investment. We believed that the risk (beta) and return can be managed better with the proposed model compare to the GP techniques. The above cases are also shown in Figures 1-4.

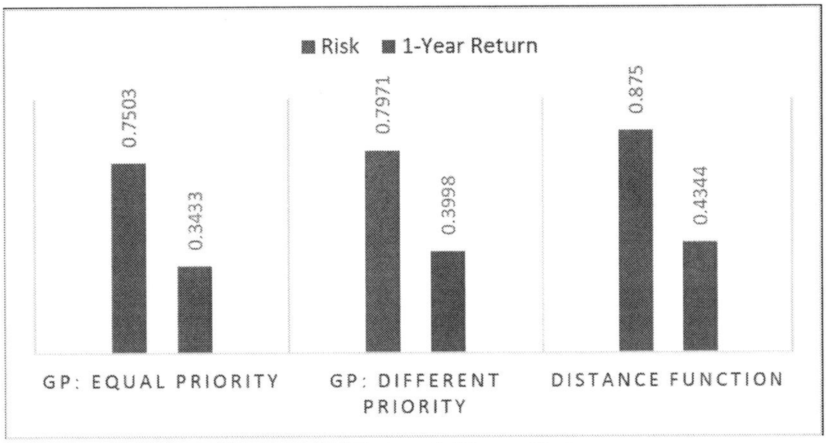

Figure 1: Risk v 1-Year Return

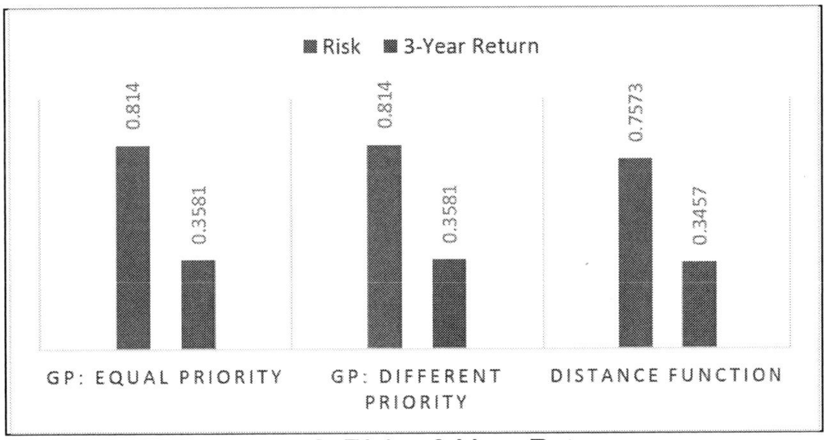

Figure 2: Risk v 3-Year Return

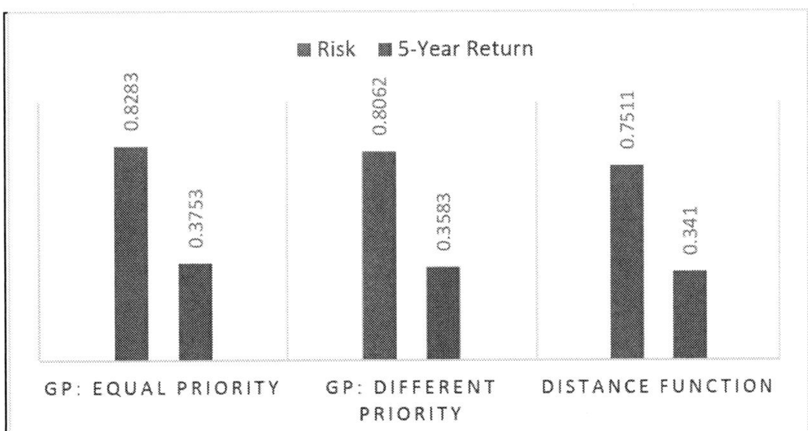

Figure 3: Risk v 5-Year Return

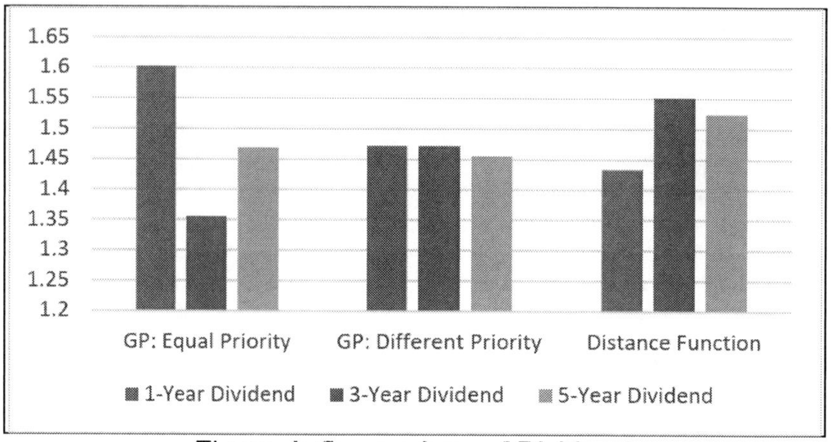

Figure 4: Comparison of Dividend

CONCLUSIONS

This paper proposes a mathematical model of a multi-criteria stock portfolio problem. A distance function based solution technique is then proposed to solve the proposed problem. The proposed model is flexible in nature. It is possible for the decision maker to modify the model. New criteria can be accommodated easily. Therefore, the proposed model can be used as a reference model for any decision maker. The proposed approach is tested with the Dow Jones Industrial Average data. The results obtained have been compared with the GP technique considering equal and unequal weights. It has been observed that the proposed approach provides better results.

REFERENCES

Aouni, B., Colapinto, C., and Torre, D. L. (2014). Financial portfolio management through the goal programming model: Current state-of-the-art. *European Journal of Operational Research* 234 (2014) 536–545.

Barros, C., Briec, W. and Ratsimbanierana, H. (2011). On some class of distance functions for measuring portfolio efficiency. *Journal of Mathematical Finance*, 1, 15-27.

Bilbao-Terol, A., Pérez-Gladish, B., Arenas-Parra, M., and Rodríguez-Uría,M.V. (2006). Fuzzy compromise programming for portfolio selection. *Applied Mathematics and Computation*, 173(1), 251-264.

Chambers, R. G., Chung, Y. H., and Färe, R. (1998). Profit, Directional Distance Functions and Nerlovian Efficiency. *Journal of Optimization Theory and Applications*, 98, 351-364.

(A complete list of references is available upon request)

DECISION SCIENCES INSTITUTE

Offshoring and reshoring in the internationalization strategy: A multiple case study approach

Carmela Di Mauro
University of Catania,
Email: cdimauro@unict.it

Luciano Fratocchi
University of l'Aquila
Email: luciano.fratocchi@univaq.it

Guido Orzes,
University of Udine
Email: guido.orzes@uniud.it

Marco Sartor
University of Udine
Email: sartor1@uniud.it

ABSTRACT

Reshoring and offshoring have been investigated separately by the literature, undermining a deeper comprehension of the firms' international expansion paths. Our paper seeks to fill this gap by: identifying common pattern in offshoring and reshoring initiatives; understanding the interdependencies among offshoring and reshoring motivations; and exploring whether reshoring is a "failure" of the offshoring initiative, or rather an evolution of the firm's strategy. We review literature on offshoring and reshoring motivations and conduct a multiple-case study analysis. This allows us to discuss how the motivations (Why) connect with the How (governance modes), and Where (geographical locations) of offshoring and reshoring.

KEYWORDS: Global Operations, Manufacturing, Reshoring, Offshoring

INTRODUCTION

Since the early 1990s, offshoring has emerged as one of the most widespread strategies adopted by Western companies in order to maintain or to foster their competitive advantage (Contractor et al., 2010). Although offshoring is far from petering out, in the last decade a counter trend has emerged whereby companies that had offshored their production have started bringing production operations back to their home countries or are adopting a regionally-based location strategy (Kinkel, 2012; Ellram et al., 2014).

This phenomenon, known to most with the label "reshoring", was first discovered by the popular press, which built a case out of the fact that some prominent large manufacturers were bringing jobs back to the home country. While at first reshoring seemed to be confined to large companies, there is now solid evidence that it also affects SMEs (Fratocchi et al., 2016). Further, reshoring does not appear to be tied to specific industries, since it spans heterogeneous sectors in terms of knowledge and technology content (Kinkel, 2012; Fratocchi et al., 2015b, 2016).

In the scholarly debate on reshoring the question that has attracted the greatest attention has been "Why do firms reshore?". Motivations for internalization/de-internalization patterns have been defined as always "purposeful and goal oriented" (Benito, 2015), and therefore their investigation represents a key element of firms' international deployment. In addition to responding to "Why" sort of questions, the analysis of motivations provides the basis for understanding which value activities are involved in internationalization, where activities are located, and how they are governed (ibid.).

A wealth of very different reshoring motivations have been proposed in the literature (Fratocchi et al., 2016; Foerstl et al., 2016; Stentoft et al, 2016a; Bals et al, 2016). The very first hypothesis put forward posited that reshoring arises from the correction of managerial errors such as insufficient planning and knowledge of the offshore location (Kinkel & Maloca, 2009). Later, reshoring was acknowledged as the reverse of a fully rational offshoring decision, motivated by contingencies and changes in the offshore or home country environment, such as the rising total costs of ownership in China, or the lower costs of energy in the West (Simchi-Levi et al., 2012; Tate et al., 2014; Martínez-Mora & Merino, 2015). Other scholars have argued that reshoring may follow from the inability of firms to solve complex challenges created by offshore production (Manning, 2014). The heterogeneity of motivations identified by scholars hints to the fact that "multiple" reshoring typologies may be at play (Foerstl et al., 2016), possibly influenced by factors such as the firm's offshoring/internationalization path, the firm's dimension, its strategic focus, and the industry of activity. Finally, other authors have linked reshoring to consumers' pressures on companies, stemming from perceived higher quality of western productions ("made in" effect"; Ancarani et al., 2015; Fratocchi et al., 2016; Grappi et al., 2015; Martínez-Mora & Merino, 2014; Tate et al., 2014; Robinson & Hsieh, 2016) or to the perception of the moral righteousness of producing at home.

With few exceptions, the investigation of the motivations underlying reshoring has mostly been undertaken independently from the analysis of the offshoring that predated them (Gylling et al., 2015). This is in contrast with the idea of Joubioux & Vanpoucke (2016) that "the reshoring decision-making process depends on the offshoring process: i.e., why activities were previously offshored, when and where they were offshored, and to whom these activities were delegated".

The joint analysis of offshoring and reshoring is a missing link that could throw light on long-term internationalization strategies and could help understand when reshoring actually follows from a "failure" of the offshore strategy. Further, from a theoretical standpoint, this disconnection between the analysis of offshoring and reshoring implicitly denies the possibility that reshoring is one of the possible further steps in the internationalization strategy of firms (Fratocchi et al., 2014a, 2015a), and rather depicts it as an "odd" phase when compared to a more "orthodox" linear model of international expansion, as predicted by theoretical approaches such as Internationalization theory (Vernon, 1966) and Internationalization Process Theory (Johanson & Vahne, 1977).

Our paper attempts to fill this gap by pursuing the following goals: first, to identify common pattern (if any) in offshoring and subsequent reshoring initiatives; second, to understand the interdependencies (if any) among offshoring and reshoring motivations; third, to explore whether reshoring is a "failure" of the offshoring initiative, or rather an evolution of the competitive strategy.

Because addressing the above research goals requires detailed historical company information, the case study methodology emerges as the optimal approach. Further, since reshoring is a phenomenon still in the making and only partially investigated, we select the inductive case study methodology with multiple cases (Yin, 2003; Patton, 1990; McCutcheon & Meredith, 1993). We focus on Italian companies operating in labour intensive sectors (footwear, fashion, and travel gear and accessories), and for which the product's country of origin" is likely to represent an important element of customer value ("made in" effect), and therefore a potential motivation for reshoring.

Results allow us developing six propositions encompassing three key aspects of offshoring and reshoring decisions: Why, i.e., the "nature" of offshoring/reshoring motivations; How, i.e., the offshoring and reshoring governance modes; Where, i.e., the geographical location of the offshored and reshored activities. Moreover, results allow qualifying reshoring as a result of strategic change, more than the correction of a managerial error.
The paper is organized as follows. The next section presents the adopted multiple case study methodology. We then analyze the background literature concerning the main offshoring and reshoring motivations and present the framework used to probe the cases for communalities/dissimilarities. In order to answer our research questions, we undertake a within case and a cross case analysis, leading to the formulation of research propositions. Finally, we present some concluding remarks.

METHODOLOGY

Because of the lack of an established theory on reshoring, we employed the inductive case study methodology with multiple cases (Yin, 2003; Patton, 1990; McCutcheon & Meredith, 1993). This approach, being "particularly oriented towards exploration, discovery, and inductive logic" (Patton, 1990), is well suited to the development of data grounded testable theories (Eisenhardt, 1989; Voss et al., 2002). In addition, it fits international business research well, because data are collected from cross-border and cross-cultural settings (Ghauri, 2004; Piekkari & Welch, 2004).
The research protocol adopted consisted of the following steps:
Literature analysis to identify the key motivations involved in offshoring and reshoring initiatives. To this end, we adopted a content-based structured literature review methodology, which ensures objectivity, rigor, and transparency. Structured literature review has been defined as "a systematic, explicit, and reproducible design for identifying, evaluating, and interpreting the existing body of recorded documents" (Fink, 2005: 6). Content-based literature review is a type of structured literature review in which content analysis is employed as a tool for examining the studies (Seuring & Gold, 2012). In particular, we follow the step-based process model for content-based literature review proposed by Seuring & Gold (2012): (1) "material collection"; (2) "category selection"; (3) "material evaluation". Based on the literature review, first we identify elementary reshoring and offshoring motivations, and next we propose a framework of aggregation and interpretation of the motivations identified (see Literature Review section).
Development of a checklist structured into three sections: (1) company and interviewee characteristics (e.g., turnover, number of employees, industry, market, location of the main customers, interviewee role and experience in the company); (2) elements affecting the offshoring decision (e.g., offshore location, year, offshored product/production phase, entry mode, offshoring motivations); (3) elements affecting the reshoring initiative (e.g., year, product/production phase, re-entry mode, supply network of the reshored unit, sales market of the reshored products, reshoring motivations).
Sample selection. The sample selected was composed of four manufacturing companies that offshored and then partly reshored their production. This number of cases is considered acceptable for a multiple case study analysis (Eisenhardt, 1989; Barratt et al., 2011). We included companies operating in labor intensive sectors (fashion, footwear and travel accessories), whose products are also expected to be sensitive to the production location, that is the "made in" effect. This expectation is reinforced by the fact that the four companies are headquartered in Italy, i.e., a country where "made in" is indeed an important competitive factor. Our case firms are also characterized by the status of small and medium enterprises (SMEs). This choice, though reducing the possibility to generalize conclusions to the overall phenomenon of reshoring, avoids possible confounding factors arising from the inclusion in

the sample of large firms (e.g., easier access to finance and global value chains), and therefore adds robustness to our findings. In addition, at least by conventional wisdom, SMEs may be more likely to reshore because of error corrections, since they lack the planning and market forecasting resources of large firms, and are also more likely to have offshored because of "bandwagon" effects (i.e., imitation of competitors). Therefore, the sample chosen may allow drawing interesting conclusions on the relevance of reshoring as "error correction" (Kinkel & Maloca, 2009). The main features of the sampled firms are described in Table 1.

Table 1 – Summary of cases

Company	Sector / product	Revenue (mln €)	Export (%)	Employees	Offshore location	Offshoring year	Reshoring year
Aku	Mountain and outdoor shoes	21.79 (2014)	75%	~330	Romania	1999	2010
Fitwell	Mountain and outdoor shoes	1.85 (2014-2015)	50%	18	Romania	1999	2009
Ska Italia	Zips	3.42 (2014)	40% (25% in China)	~230	China	2000	2010
Roncato	Suitcases and travel accessories	41.80 (2014)	40%	~100	China	1970	2012

Data collection: Structured interviews with the CEOs of the sampled companies using the checklist developed were the first source of data. The checklist was sent to each respondent prior to the interview. Each interview was performed by three members of the research team. The information gathered was supplemented with internal documents (e.g., project plans, reports, market performance, balance sheets) provided by the companies and by external secondary sources (e.g., press reports on the offshoring or reshoring initiatives). Triangulation of multiple sources of evidence provided a stronger substantiation of results (Eisenhardt, 1989). All interviews were recorded and fully transcribed. We created a database for each case consisting of the interview transcripts, field notes, and archival data. We then developed preliminary versions of the case studies reports that were subsequently sent to the company respondents in order to verify the accuracy of the information. As a result of the feedback received, the final versions of the case studies reports were developed.

Within-case and cross-case analysis. Coding and data analysis were conducted manually by three members of the research team to ensure inter-coder reliability (Duriau et al., 2007). An additional researcher was assigned the role of "resident devil's advocate" in order to discuss and resolve any disagreements. Each case was described in terms of the following main macro categories (background of the company, offshoring, reshoring, and present). Sub-categories were then defined for each macro-category. Offshoring and reshoring motivations were classified according to the theory grounded framework presented in the literature review section (see Figure 1 and 2). After the within-case analysis, the cross-case analysis was performed and findings tabulated, to identify common themes and internationalization paths.

Validation of case study results. As suggested by Yin (2003) and Eisenhardt (1989), a number of strategies and actions were adopted to enhance construct validity, internal validity, external validity, and reliability.

LITERATURE REVIEW

In order to define a list of offshoring and reshoring motivations to discuss with companies' respondents, we developed literature reviews of reshoring and offshoring motivations. We followed the step-based process model for content-based literature review proposed by Seuring & Gold (2012): (1) "material collection"; (2) "category selection"; (3) "material evaluation".

Reshoring motivations

In a recent literature review, Fratocchi et al. (2016) identified 33 studies on reshoring. Taking this review as a starting point, we searched for more recent references. In so doing, we initially focused on academic papers belonging to the Elsevier's Scopus dataset and containing the following words in title, keywords and abstract: "reshoring", "re-shoring", "backshoring", "back-shoring", and "back-reshoring". Since the topic is addressed by several disciplines, we decided to perform a keyword search without any reduction in the scope of the journals. We focused our attention only on (1) papers written in English; (2) papers focusing on reshoring of manufacturing activities. This search led to the identification of 30 new papers.

We searched for possible classifications of reshoring motivations adopting an inductive category selection approach. In this respect, we proceeded in two steps: first, we identified elementary reshoring motivations, next we searched for grouping criteria of these elementary motivations. All papers were analyzed and coded. To avoid misinterpretations and improve process reliability (e.g., Denyer & Tranfield, 2009), each paper was independently analysed and elementary motivations were coded by two researchers (researcher triangulation) and in a few cases of disagreement all authors were involved to reach a common conclusion/decision. This coding activity led to 38 elementary reshoring motivations.

Concerning grouping criteria of reshoring motivations, the literature includes both empirically based and theory grounded criteria. The former consist of classifications based on general categories of reshoring motivations (costs, home/host country characteristics, access to skills and knowledge) (Fratocchi et al., 2015a; 2015b; Stentoft et al., 2015; Li et al., 2015). Among theory-based criteria, Ellram et al. (2013) and Ancarani et al. (2015) adopt the dimensions of location advantages from the Eclectic Paradigm (Dunning, 1998). In so doing, both papers indicated that some motivations "cut across all of the categories of factors noted by Dunning (1998)" (Ellram et al., 2013, p. 17). Furthermore, Dunning himself (1998) acknowledged that the motivations defining a specific "raison d'être" evolve over time. More recently, Foerstl et al. (2016) proposed a classification of reshoring and insourcing motivations according to Transaction Cost Economics (TCE) and Organizational Buying Behaviour (OBB) theories. Based on an extensive literature review, the authors found 29 reshoring and insourcing motivations which were classified according to a three level framework. Firstly, two macrocategories were defined (namely "Human and Behavioural Factors" and "Transactional Factors"). Each macrocategory was then divided in two categories ("Bounded rationality" and "Opportunism" vs. "Environmental Uncertainty" and "Asset Specificity") which were finally articulated in eight different subcategories. While we recognize that a firm simultaneously shift from offshore outsourcing to domestic insourcing, we think that location and governance mode are distinct choices and should therefore be analyzed separately (Fratocchi et al., 2014).

Fratocchi et al. (2016) developed a theory-driven classification framework, grounded in both international business and strategic management theories, which distinguishes reshoring motivations based on two variables: the company's strategic goal (i.e., *increasing customer perceived value* vs. *improving cost-efficiency*), and the predominant factors affecting the reshoring decision or "level of analysis" (*internal to the company* vs. *relating to the external environment*). Consistent with theoretical approaches such as the Resource Based View, the authors argue that *customer perceived value* goals may explain a relocation in terms of the firm's need to improve, protect, and maintain the critical attributes driving customer value, such as perceived quality (Eggert & Ulaga, 2002), product innovation (Rivière, 2015; Lindič & Silva, 2011), and customer services (Stringfellow et al., 2008). Hence, this class of relocations occurs when the current location hinders the firm's ability to develop and/or maintain distinctive capabilities (e.g., intellectual property protection; product quality; innovation potential; etc.), to access external knowledge and/or other critical resources, to understand customers' needs and provide effective services. On the contrary, *cost-efficiency* goals explain relocations as the pursuit of lower production costs, for instance stemming from lower unit of labor costs or higher labor productivity, benefits from automation, shorter logistics lead times, fewer inventories, psychic distance, lower monitoring costs, etc. Theoretical approaches such as International Trade Theory and Transaction Cost Theory can be applied to argue that manufacturing reshoring stems from reduced gaps in input costs between the home location and the offshore location, or the high costs of coordinating distant operations and relationships.

With respect to the predominant dynamics, relocations motivated by changes in the *external environment* account for changing characteristics of the business model in the industry the firm operates in, of the home and/or foreign countries, and of the global economy as a whole. In particular, the relative attractiveness of the home and host locations relies on changes in costs and/or endowment of relevant production factors, in institutional factors, in country's strategic assets, in country risk, in barriers to trade and tariffs. On the contrary, the *internal environment* accounts for factors such as a strategic drift of the company, the company's supply chain complexity, innovation orientation, or quest for new valuable resources.

Crossing the two aforementioned dimensions leads to four categories of relocation motivations, i.e., the quadrants of a 2x2 matrix. Hybrid cases (relocations driven simultaneously by internal and external factors or by the quest for customer value and cost reduction) are accounted for explicitly, and are positioned in the sidebars of the matrix.

The framework proposed by Fratocchi et al. (2016) for aggregation of elementary motivations offers numerous advantages: (i) it is theory-based and it encompasses several theoretical approaches used in internal business and international operations management; (ii) it allows interpreting relocation motivations within the realm of firms' purposeful goal-oriented (and sometimes strategic) decisions; (iii) unlike Dunning's "raisons d'etre" of relocations, it explicitly allows for hybrid cases; (iv) unlike Foerstl et al. (2016), it does not mix location and governance mode decisions. Therefore, in the material evaluation phase, in order to ensure construct validity and reliability, all members of the research team positioned elementary motivations within Fratocchi et al.'s (2016) framework separately. Discrepancies (less than 5% of motivations) were solved through a discursive alignment of interpretations.

Figure 1 presents the results of the classification highlighting the 30 motivations proposed by Fratocchi et al. (2016) and the further 8 motivations found in the additional reviewed papers (the total list of motivations and relative references is presented in Appendix A). Motivations cover all the four quadrants, suggesting that reshoring is a very heterogeneous phenomenon, in the sense that it represents a common response to diverse challenges firms may face. Further, the fact that the various motivations belong to all the quadrants, imply the relevance of different theoretical approaches and the usefulness of a holistic approach. For a detailed discussion of motivations, we refer to Fratocchi et al. (2016).

Analyzing reshoring motivations belonging to the most recent contributions, it is interesting to note that several authors have pointed out the relevance of the firm's competitive strategy as a key driver of the reshoring decision. For instance, Grandinetti & Tabacco (2015), Robinson & Hsieh (2016) and Huq et al. (2016) describe cases of companies that revised their global production strategy, and consequently decided to repatriate manufacturing activities earlier offshored. This is consistent with Bals et al. (2016) who retain that in taking reshoring decisions "firms may have more strategic considerations towards global production location and sourcing than in the early stages of the primarily cost-driven offshore" decision. In this respect, reshoring may be conceptualized not as the mere correction of a prior misjudged decision (Gray et al., 2013; Kinkel & Maloca, 2009) but also as a "deliberate strategy" (Mintzberg, 1985) to respond to exogenous or endogenous changes (Mugurusi & de Boer, 2014; Martínez-Mora & Merino, 2014; Fratocchi et al., 2015a; Gylling et al. (2015). Bals et al. (2016) suggest future studies should approach the such two types of reshoring decisions (failure vs. strategy) assuming differentiated perspectives. Among reshoring motivations deriving from very recent contributions, it is worthy of notice the relevance of customers' perceptions of firm's competitive strategy. For instance, Grappi et al (2015) propose that customers' willingness to buy reshored products may motivate companies to relocate production activities in the home country (customer perceived value – external environment quadrant). This is confirmed by case studies regarding companies in the fashion industry, as recently showed by Robinson & Hsieh (2016) analysis of the Burberry case. Finally, attention has been paid also to environmental and social sustainability elements as possible reshoring motivations, stemming from either a deliberate firm's strategy (Ashby, 2016; Robinson & Hsieh, 2016) or environmental legislations in the home country (Sardar et al., 2016).

Figure 1 – Reshoring motivations highlighted in the literature (Adapted from Fratocchi et al., 2016; new motivations are underlined)

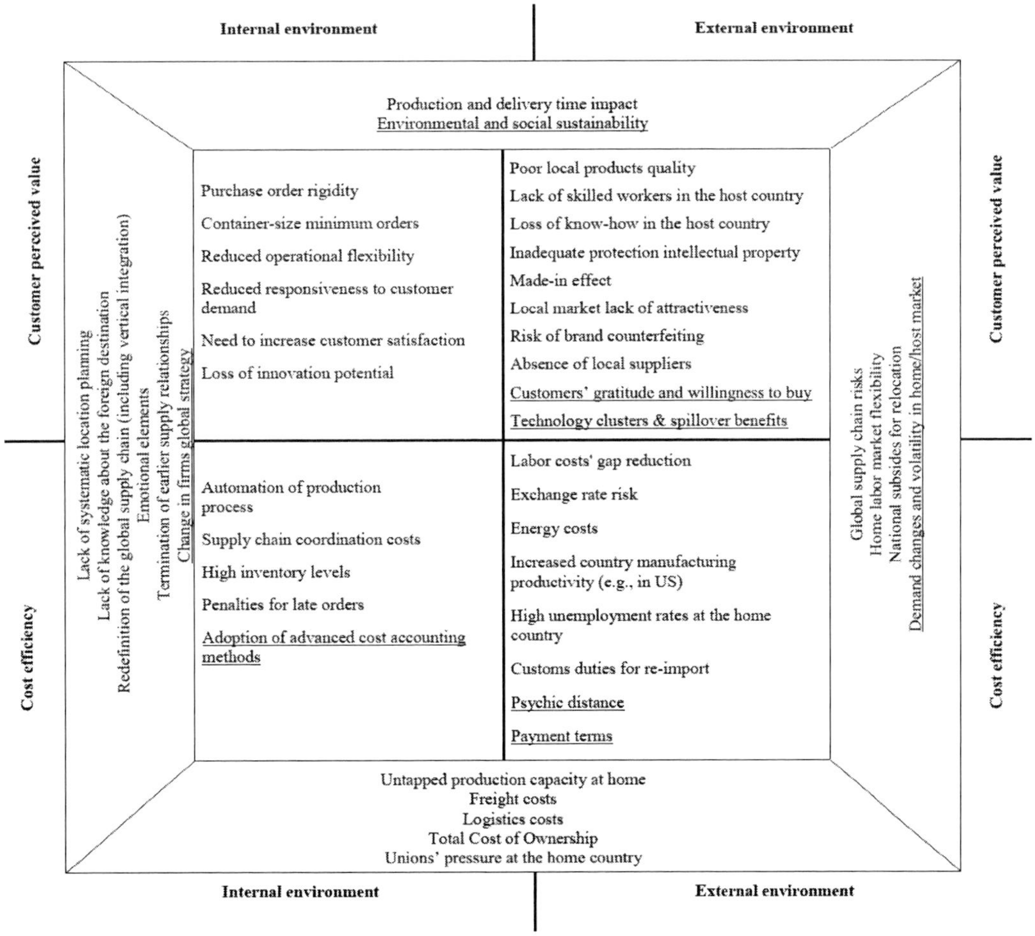

Offshoring motivations

Since offshoring is a multidisciplinary topic, we decided to perform a keyword search without any reduction in the scope of the journals (Seuring & Gold, 2012). The following string was searched in Elsevier's Scopus: (1) ("offshoring" OR "off-shoring") AND ("motivation" OR "driver") referred only to title, keywords and abstract. This allowed us to identify 280 papers on offshoring motivations. We then employed a set of inclusion criteria: (1) peer-reviewed journal papers; (2) papers written in English; (3) papers focusing on offshoring of manufacturing activities; (4) papers highlighting/discussing at least one offshoring motivation based on empirical data. The final list consisted of 35 papers.

We applied the theory-based framework proposed by Fratocchi et al. (2016) as the coding scheme also for literature on offshoring motivations. The classifications of offshoring motivations adopted by the reviewed studies were based on Dunning's (1988) Eclectic Paradigm and therefore share the same limitations of the Dunning-based classification adopted by reshoring studies (see above). We identified 21 offshoring motivations (see Figure 2 and Appendix B). Our motivations are aligned with those recently identified by Mihalache & Mihalache (2015).

The offshoring motivation most frequently cited concerns the *costs and productivity of unskilled labour* in the host country (quadrant cost efficiency – external environment). Several authors (Kinkel & Maloca, 2009; Gylling et al., 2015) rank it as the most important offshoring motivation or one of the most important ones.

Another frequently cited offshoring motivation is the *availability of skilled labour* (quadrant customer perceived value – external environment). Mykhaylenko et al. (2015) argue however that this driver is important but less significant for manufacturing than for service offshoring.

Some authors (e.g. Arlbjørn & Lüthje, 2012; Persaud & Floyd, 2013) emphasise the *quality improvement* (quadrant customer perceived value – external environment). Slepniov et. al. (2013) specify that this improvement originates from the combined effect of some factors available in the host country (e.g. the availability of skilled labour and the local knowledge).

Mohiuddin & Su (2013) quote the *new product development* (quadrant customer perceived value – internal environment) and argue that it is particularly true when the knowledge of the local needs and habits is a requisite for selling abroad. Since this finding is however based on a case study analysis of high tech manufacturing SMEs, future research is needed to understand its validity and generalizability to other contexts (e.g., large firms, low tech firms).

Finally, we found only one motivation in the quadrant cost efficiency – internal environment cited by only one paper focused on SMEs, i.e., the *economies of scale* (Mohiuddin & Su, 2013). This suggests a possible lower relevance of this category of motivations for offshoring decisions.

A cursory look at both reshoring and offshoring motivations (Figure 1 and Figure 2), that there is a significant overlap. The explanation for this is twofold: first, some companies reshore production because the expected offshored benefits were not met in practice ("operational flexibility" for offshoring, "reduced operational flexibility" for reshoring). Second, some strengths of the offshore location in time became the strengths of the homecountry, due the evolving economic and political situation (e.g., "government incentives" for offshoring, "national subsides for relocation" for reshoring). This result suggests that a deep comprehension of the reshoring phenomenon cannot leave aside a joint/comparative analysis of offshoring and reshoring motivations. Such analysis is missing in the present literature. However, a closer look at the matrixes (Figure 1 and Figure 2) also reveals that, despite the offshoring motivations cover all the four quadrants, there is a higher density in the two right quadrants (i.e., cost efficiency – external; value driven – external) when compared to the reshoring ones. This suggests that offshoring tends to be driven predominantly by external dynamics, whereas reshoring by factors internal to the firm. The case analysis will delve into communalities and differences between offshoring and reshoring motivations.

Figure 2 – Offshoring motivations highlighted in the literature

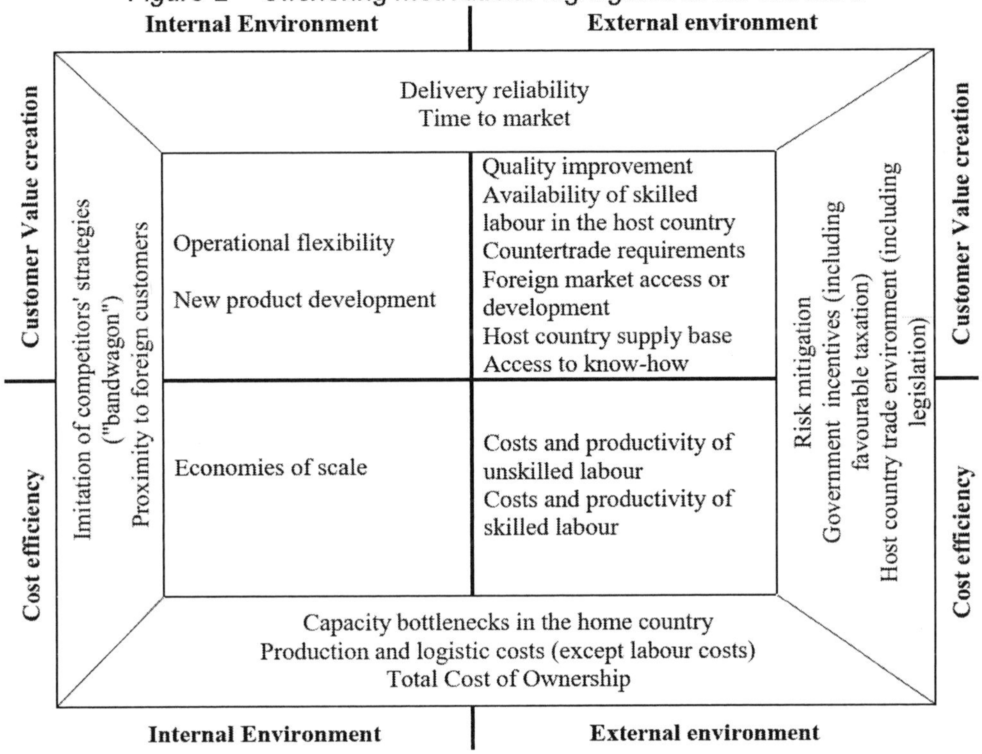

WITHIN CASE ANALYSIS RESULTS

This section presents the results of the within case analysis of the four cases, focusing on the following aspects: company background, offshoring, reshoring, and present situation (i.e., following the implementation of reshoring).
For each case, the motivations for offshoring and reshoring cited by the interviewed CEOs have been classified by the research team using the four quadrant matrixes described in the Literature Review section (see Figure 3-4-5-6). Offshoring and reshoring motivations were further rated by the interviewee as "very relevant", "relevant" or "not relevant". Offshoring and reshoring motivations rated as "Very relevant" by the interviewee are highlighted in bold inside the matrixes.

Aku

Background: Aku is a medium sized company operating in the outdoor and mountain shoe sector. The company evolved from a workshop to the current establishment, which was established in 1991. The headquarter is located in the "mountain shoe" district of Montebelluna in the North-east of Italy.
Offshoring: In the early nineties, due to the growing competition of East-European countries, whose labor costs (both skilled and unskilled) and total costs of ownership were more advantageous than in Western Europe, Aku began approaching Eastern Europe with several (outsourcing and insourcing) offshore arrangements. R&D, quality controls and sourcing of

raw material remained located in Italy. At first, Aku experimented by opening own workshops with the aim to develop a local production culture compatible with the high quality standards required by its market position, and by establishing outsourcing contracts with local producers. Having gained sufficient knowledge of the local production culture, in 1999 Aku opened an own plant in Romania (Cluji Napoca), an offshoring location supported by the availability of skilled manpower. The transfer of operations abroad resulted from the imitation of competitors' strategies, who were too setting up shop in Eastern Europe. In fact, the leading business model of the sector called for cost cutting to face the fierce price competition. The long process of building local knowledge, of adapting to the offshore context, and of developing offshore workers and suppliers, led to quality standards offshore analogous to those at home. As the CEO of Aku puts it: "*In Romania we started from scratch. It was a long story of endurance, but now the quality of product in Romania is analogous to that in Italy*". Hence, offshoring was mainly driven by cost reduction considerations in order to stay apace with competitors (Quadrant 2). However, given that Aku served medium to high segments of the market, the quality of human resources was a key factor in the choice of the offshore location in order to maintain the same quality of the inshore production (Quadrant 1).

At the beginning of the years 2000, Aku also started sourcing light shoes from third parties in the Far East. A small portion of turnover continued to derive from shoes designed and produced in Italy.

Reshoring: Between 2010 and 2011 Aku implemented the reshoring of high segment productions previously carried out in the Romanian plant. Production was repatriated to the historic plant in Italy. High-end sport shoes exhibit a higher technological content, offer greater possibilities of exploiting process automation, and are less dependent on the cost of manpower. According to Aku's CEO, the need to protect the company's knowledge and competencies, the fear of loss of innovation potential, and the need to guarantee proximity of production to R&D and to marketing were the main motivations of the decision to repatriate production. "*A company like ours produces a highly technical product that encompasses also a craftsmanship component. In order to remain globally competitive, we must be able to tell our customer an authentic story and be able to claim that yes, we make the shoes by ourselves, and our knowledge allows us to make the shoes differently from other competitors…*". Currently the "top outdoor end" is entirely designed and produced in Italy, medium-end trekking outdoor are produced and assembled either in Italy or in Romania, while light shoes continue to be outsourced to Asia, given that these low-end segments are more sensitive to price and have a low-technology content. Other key motivations encompass the loss of company's know how because of offshore production, and the need to re-establish roots in the local industrial culture and with the home region, given that the company is historically rooted in its territory. Hence, reshoring motivations are mainly positioned in the upper quadrants of the matrix (Quadrants 1 and 4), given that the need to enhance customer value (through innovation and improved quality of production) explain the reshoring initiative.

Present: Following reshoring turnover has shown a rising trend: from 14 million euro in 2011 to 21.5 in 2014. Currently the "top outdoor end" is entirely designed and produced in Italy, medium-end trekking outdoor are produced and assembled either in Italy or in Romania, while light shoes continue to be outsourced to Asia, given that these low-end segments are more sensitive to price and have a low-technology content.

Figure 3 – Summary of offshoring and reshoring motivations - Aku
(Critical motivations in bold, * *not included in the literature review*)

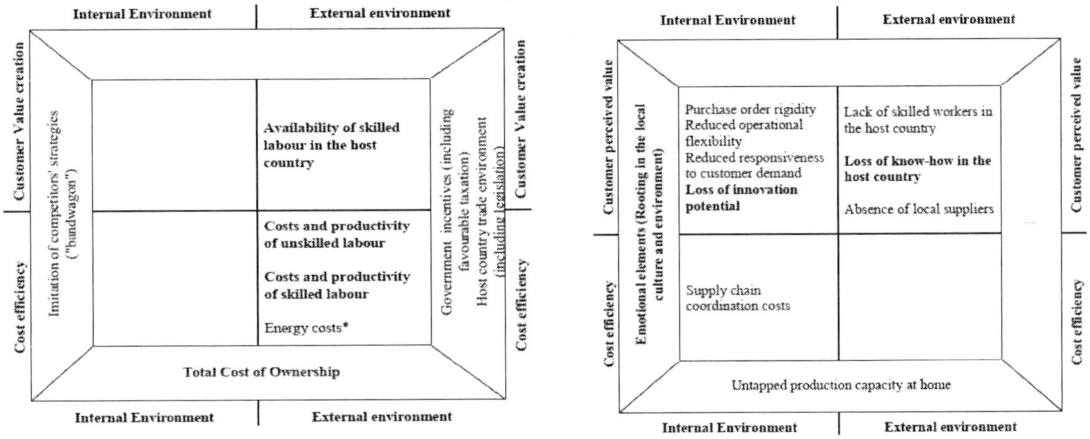

Fitwell

Background: Fitwell is a small company operating in the sector of outdoor and mountain shoes and whose headquarter is located in the shoes district of Montebelluna in North-East Italy. The firm was created in 1979 when Giuliano Grotto founded ONESport, a company specializing in the production of highly technical mountain shoes and quickly acquiring a reputation as producer of boots for Himalayan expeditions. Therefore, the company occupied a niche market characterized by high-reliability and high-quality, also thanks to the local tradition in leather processing techniques. In 1997 ONESport started a collaboration with the French group Lafuma, which bought the brand ONESport the following year. Grotto continued to work for Lafuma as a contract manufacturer producing free climbing shoes - a collaboration that continues up to now. However, Mr Grotto also launched his own new brand, Fitwell, and opened new product niches such as canyoning and freeride. The company adopts an open innovation approach by collaborating with other external entities in developing its new products.

Offshoring: In 1999 Fitwell began outsourcing its production to Eastern Europe, first in Hungary and in the Czech Republic and then in Romania, where there was a tradition for shoe manufacturing. One of the main reasons for outsourcing offshore were pressures from the key customer Lafuma, asking for more competitive costs that could only be achieved by producing in low cost countries (low labor costs and lower TCO), similarly to what was being done by most of the companies in the same sector (imitation of competitors' strategies). The company also benefited from a looser country legislation with respect to labor and contracts with suppliers, and more favorable taxation with respect to Italy. According to Fitwell's CEO: "*I went offshore also because of the politics of globalization. With hindsight, it was a mass mistake. But if 15 years ago I hadn't done it, I wouldn't be here now. There was no other solution*". However, the high quality standards of Fitwell's shoes required a long period of supplier development and training in order to guarantee to customers standards comparable to the Italian ones: "*The cultural approach (to work) in Romania and in Italy are deeply different*". Consistent with the goal to maintain high quality standards, the development function remained in Italy, and so suppliers of raw materials, while production was totally offshored. Therefore, similarly to Aku, Fitwell too was induced to offshore by the need to follow competitors in a race to reduce total costs, and especially costs of labor, given the high labor intensity of its productions.

Reshoring: In 2009 Fitwell partially reshored the Romanian production, deciding to manufacture in Italy all top end shoes (mountain shoes and boots accounting for 40% of turnover) and two out of the three main production stages for medium end shoes. Since all raw materials are produced in Italy, Fitwell can boast today a 100% "made in Italy" product: "*After the global crisis, Italian companies that had offshored lost identity, therefore their strategy has changed to "top of range" products in order to acquire visibility in the market".* Currently only the upper boot for medium range products is manufactured in Romania, given their higher sensitivity to price competition. Romanian contract manufacturers are responsible for high labor intensive production stages, while final high value added phases (e.g., assembling and gluing of the upper shoe) are carried out in Italy. Design and prototyping are outsourced to local companies. The company argues that it would be nearly impossible to reshore production stages now carried out in Romania, because over the years, local competences and know how have dwindled: *"There is a scarcity of specialized manpower and this makes a full scale reshoring impossible".*

Among the reasons for the return to Italy, the strategy to sell Fitwell as a "made in Italy" brand features as prominent, as this helps the company charge a premium price. In addition, the company's need to sustain the brand's identity by improving product quality was a key driver of the decision. The quality differential more than offsets the higher TCO resulting from reshoring. Fitwell's CEO says: "*I am convinced that there is still market space for a small company that can make good shoes*".

Another driver was the loyalty to the home region and sense of belonging to the local territory (emotional elements): "*We came back because we are rooted in the territory, because we are able to manufacture a product but to make it a quality product we must produce it in Italy"* and "*With the concept of made in Italy we have gained as far as quality is concerned, but we have also regained the pride to produce here at home".*

The main motivations of reshoring are the direct consequence of the firm's repositioning of its product offering towards high end segments, and of its becoming a direct provider of end customers rather than being simply a subcontractor of Lafuma. This required investing in quality and branding, in addition to regaining its authenticity as a crafmanship product.

Present: Following reshoring, the company's performance has improved and turnover has risen to the levels before the global economic and financial crisis. Actually the company sales are mainly focused on products sold with its trademark, while contract manufacturing account for less than 20%. Fitwell has opened new niche markets in areas such as canyoning and freeride. The company adopts an open innovation approach by collaborating with other external entities in developing its new products

Figure 4 – Summary of offshoring and reshoring motivations – Fitwell (Critical motivations in bold)

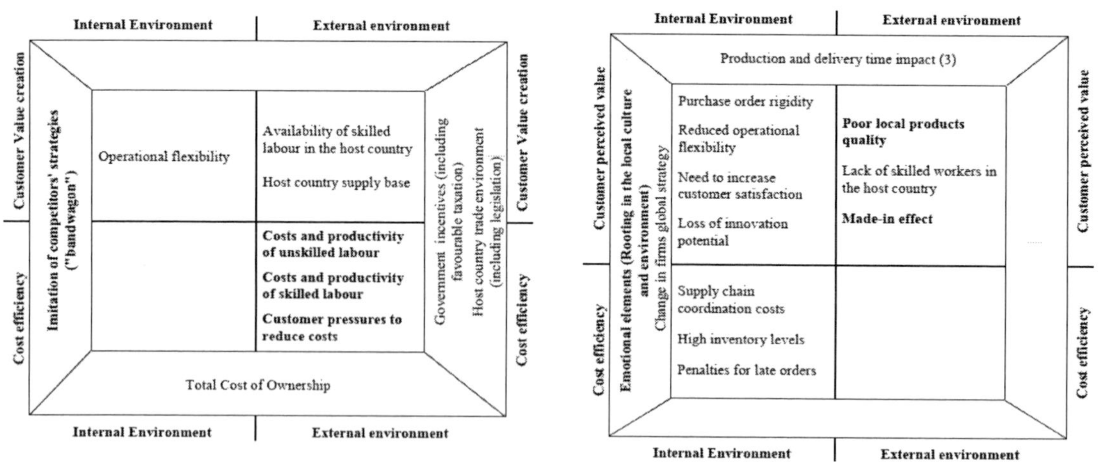

Roncato

Background: Roncato is a medium sized company specialized in suitcases and travel accessories. The heydays of Roncato go back to the '40s when the small craft company began production, while the industrial set up dates back to the '70s. The company boasts a record of innovation in the sector: first to use an assembly line for suitcases, first to develop a trolley, first to build light hard shell suitcases made of polypropylene.
Offshoring: Roncato's offshoring initiatives predate those of many other competitors. The company started relocating production offshore already in the early '70s, by outsourcing the production of soft shell suitcases (approximately 65% of the turnover) to suppliers in South Korea, followed by a further transfer of production to China. Competitive advantage in this segment, in fact, hinged strongly on price, and the Far East undoubtedly offered savings in terms of labor costs and total costs of ownership. In 2000, the creation of a "project and style" department in Italy allowed unifying styling between the Chinese and Italian production lines, whereas beforehand the project and concept differed in the two countries. This change provided the company with the opportunity to maintain its brand characteristics throughout the range of products offered. The advantages of offshore production were further enhanced by the fact that suitcases imported from China into Europe – the main market of Roncato – are subject to low duties.
Reshoring: Starting in 2009 Roncato began the reshoring of high-end productions of hard shell suitcases previously taking place in China. Production was inshored to the historical plant of the company, whereas in China it was outsourced to local producers. Several reasons were at the root of the reshoring decision: the first concerns the strategic repositioning of the brand, which aimed to increase its share in foreign markets building on a "made in Italy" image that commands a premium price. In Roncato CEO's words "*If you want to grow abroad, well it is a different world with respect to Italy where price drives the purchase. Abroad, Italy is seen as an icon of good taste, style, quality, so for foreign buyers a product that is made in Italy not only provides a guarantee of, but also has a greater appeal.*" However, the return of top end productions to Italy was motivated not only by the quest for legitimacy in the eyes of foreign customers but also by the need to be able to improve product quality with respect to offshore production and boost innovation potential. *"We've come back for reasons tied to quality control and know how of production and technological innovation. It is not possible to develop certain (high quality) products in the Far East yet. Control of quality is easier in Italy than in China. Although quality on average has risen in China in the last few years, it is still lower than in Italy".*
Present: Following reshoring, turnover has remained constant and around 40 million euros per year, while employment has risen due to the production lines relocated in Italy.

*Figure 5 – Summary of offshoring and reshoring motivations - Roncato (Critical motivations in bold, * not included in the literature review)*

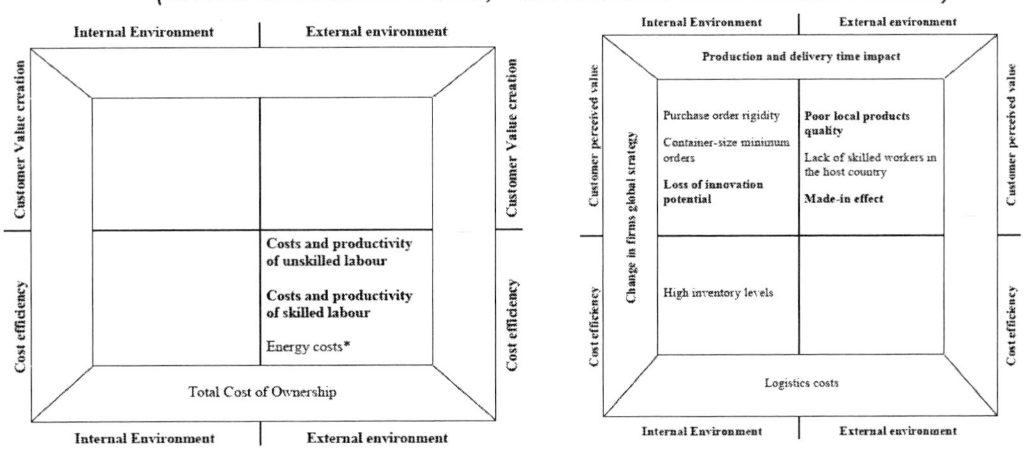

Ska Italia

Background: Ska Italia is a medium sized company which produces zippers for the fashion sector. The company was founded in 1999 out of a previous company in the same sector; since its onset, it has been characterized by a global reach and high efforts innovation. The company's market encompasses two main segments: footwear, fashion and leather requiring a high quality, and generic apparel requiring less stringent quality standards. While competitors on the first segment are located in the West, competitors on the latter are generally located in China.
Offshoring: Ska Italia located its production facilities in China in the area of Canton, while only high value added activities such as R&D remained in Italy. The Chinese location clearly responded to the need to exploit labor cost advantages and a lower total cost of ownership, and to reap the benefits of proximity to customers (apparel and suitcase producers) (access and development of foreign markets). In order to comply with the past Chinese legislation (that prohibited the creation of WFOEs), Ska Italia entered the Chinese market through a joint venture with a local partner. The search for a suitable partner proved to be long, due to the difficulty in finding a medium sized enterprise that could guarantee attention to product quality. The Chinese industrial landscape was in fact characterized predominantly by large companies yielding large volumes. "*Because we were looking for a quality product we did not want to lean on a big partner with respect to which we would be a flea. That would have meant being unable to implement technological and qualitative changes to the Chinese equipment. By partnering with a medium sized company we have managed to achieve a quality level comparable to that obtainable in Europe*". In addition, the company benefited from government incentives for western firms locating in Chinese Special Economic Zones in the form of free granting of land and favorable taxation.
Reshoring: In 2010 the company decided to reshore part of production to Italy by opening up a new plant in the north west (through a joint venture) devoted to the production of high quality zippers for the leather fashion market. New lines were also opened to accommodate the demand from the very top segment of production coming from the fashion and the leather products markets. The rationale for relocating the high end lines back to Italy was many-fold: first, a strategic re-positioning of the company towards the higher segment of the market required a re-organization of production sites. In fact, it was necessary to improve product quality with respect to offshore production: *"There have been improvements in quality that we have been able to undertake in the Italian plant and that were difficult in the Chinese one".* This reason aligns with brand image and the need of Ska Italia's top customers (e.g., Gucci, Ferragamo, Tods) to certify a product fully manufactured in Italy: "*The fashion market demands a made in Italy product, even if sometimes made in Italy is just a cliché rather than a reality".* The Italian plant carries out only specific stages of the production process, while dying and some types of galvanic coatings are outsourced to other Italian producers. The repositioning towards higher segments also required continuous innovation. However, the innovation potential was at risk in the offshore location partially due to inadequate protection of IP in the offshore location: *"We prefer to produce our high tech range in Italy in order to protect our know-how. Taking this knowledge to China would invite the Chinese to take advantage".*
Therefore, the key motivations for reshoring and for offshoring have been those of following customers and complying to customer needs. These included the need to improve operational flexibility and reduce purchase order rigidity, i.e., the possibility of ordering "just in time" small lots, both of which were impossible to achieve through the Chinese plant.
Present: Following reshoring, turnover has remained constant and around 4 million euro per year, while employment has risen due to the production lines relocated in Italy. The new plant is still to produce profits, due to the high initial investment.

*Figure 6 – Summary of offshoring and reshoring motivations – Ska Italia (Critical motivations in bold, * not included in the literature review)*

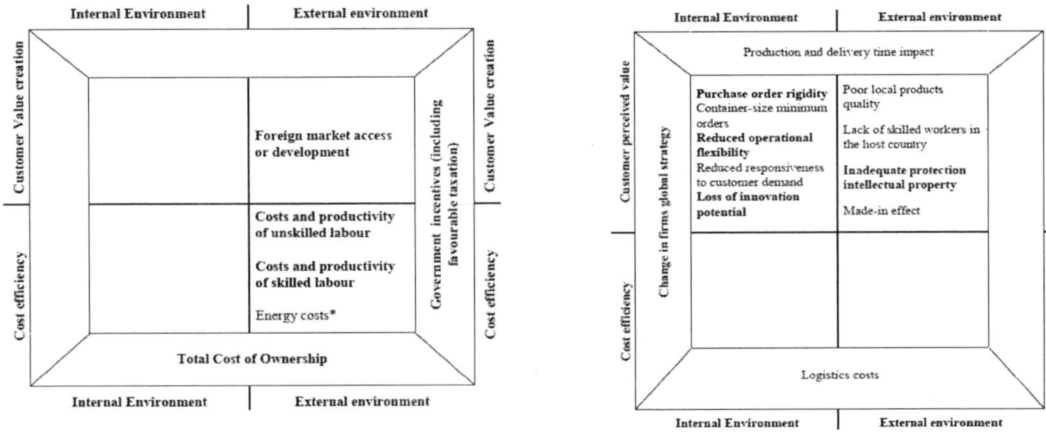

CROSS CASE ANALYSIS RESULTS AND DISCUSSION

Following the within case analysis, a cross case comparison is performed with the aim to identify common patterns in the firms' offshoring and subsequent reshoring initiatives. The cross case analysis is organised around three issues concerning offshoring and reshoring (Why, How, Where). While the "Why" question is directly related to motivations (Mugurusi & De Boer, 2013; Fratocchi et al, 2014a), the other two questions arise because "important issues in companies' internationalization differ systematically across different types of motives" (Benito, 2015). Motives are interconnected with "How" the offshored/reshored activity is organised in terms of governance mode. The "Where" question about the geographical location of the offshored/reshored activities is likely to be tied to the Why question, because relocations that occur for different motives are likely to be related to different places. Based on the cross case analysis, some propositions for future research will be derived.

Why? The "nature" of offshoring/reshoring drivers

The four couples of matrixes reported in the within case analysis section (Figure 3, 4, 5, and 6), highlight that there are indeed common motivations among the four firms, regarding both the type of factors explaining relocation and the "goal" dimension. Our discussion will focus on those motivations considered as very relevant by the companies. With respect to the external/internal environment dimension, all four companies offshored almost exclusively on the base of "external environment" motivations (right-hand side quadrants). This argument seems to be supported by the presence of location strategies either imitating competitors ("bandwagon effect") (Aku and Fitwell) or following customers (Ska). The finding that external dynamics were more relevant than internal factors in offshoring choices can be partially explained by the small/medium size of the four firms, since large and multinational companies are more likely to implement pro-active strategies that influence the external environment (Mariotti et al., 2008).
Turning to the reshoring decision, "internal environment" motivations become more prominent for all firms, especially those regarding innovation potential and logistics (e.g., purchase order rigidity). However, these motivations appear to weight more for the three medium size companies, while Fitwell (the only small one in the sample) is partially affected by them. The lower amount of in-house resources and competences that small firms can generally leverage to accommodate their growth aims (Jarillo, 1989) may explain this finding.

With respect to the "goal" dimension, offshoring is generally driven by "cost-efficiency" motivations (mainly the cost of the labor component; Quadrant 2). While this finding is common to many low technology, labor intensive industries, its interest lies in the fact that it shows that even companies producing goods characterized by a significant "country of origin" effect were not deterred from relocating production in low-cost countries. Though seemingly contradictory, this strategy is generally coherent with the product range analyzed firms offered at the time of offshoring. In particular, at the time of offshoring, Fitwell was mainly a subcontractor (70% of total sales deriving from other companies' trademark products). Further, it never offshored high range products (high-tech mountain boots) sold with its own brand, and for which the "made in" effect was more strongly felt by customers. In a similar vein, Roncato offshored both soft-shell (low range and price sensitive) and polycarbonate hard-shell suitcases (medium to high range). However, it never offshored the production of polypropylene hard-shell suitcases, which are more hi-tech and top of range. Unlike the purely cost-driven offshoring strategies of Fitwell and Roncato, Aku was motivated also by the "availability of skilled human resources in the host country" (Quadrant 1) and Ska by the "foreign market access or development" (Quadrant 1).

When reshoring was undertaken, cost-efficiency goals were never relevant. This is particularly noteworthy since salaries in both offshoring countries involved (Romania and China) have risen considerably in the last few years (UNCTAD, 2015). All companies' implemented reshoring decisions driven by "customer value creation" motivations (upper quadrants). Except for Aku, the "made in Italy" image strongly influenced the decision to reshore. Improving quality by linking production to R&D was relevant for all companies: while the three medium size companies linked to in house R&D, Fitwell leveraged on the network of the Montebelluna district for innovation of materials and styling. Since the quest for innovation and quality concerns high end products, the four firms generally reshored high end segments while lower end products continue to be manufactured offshore. For illustration, Roncato reshored only the manufacturing of hard shell suitcases, in order to improve quality and give visibility to its brand, while it still produces the soft shell ones in China. Similar decisions of partial reshoring were implemented by Aku and Ska. Conversely, low-end segment products with low technology content are never involved in reshoring processes (e.g., Aku's shoes in China and Roncato's soft-shell suitcases).

The case analysis suggests that reshoring follows from a shift in the firms' competitive strategy, from a "cost leadership" strategy to a "differentiation" one (Porter, 1990). On this subject, a very interesting case is that of Fitwell, which reduced the weight of sales as subcontractor from 70% of total revenues (at the time of offshoring) to 20% (after the reshoring implementation), developing an own trademark for high- and medium-end products. More generally, the "made in" effect was a key reshoring driver for Fitwell and Roncato and partly for Ska. The above discussion leads to the formulation of the following propositions that are consistent with extant literature on the role of strategy changes (Grandinetti & Tabacco, 2015; Huq et al, 2016) and the "made in" effect (Martinez- Mora & Merino, 2014; Robinson & Hsieh, 2016) on reshoring decisions.

Proposition 1 – While the predominant motivation for offshoring is cost-reduction, reshoring follows from a strategic shift aimed at increasing the value perceived by the customer.
Proposition 2 – Companies whose product offering included high-end products for which the "made in" effect is relevant, either do not offshore these products (e.g., high-end products for Fitwell) or, if they offshore, they later reshore.

How? An Analysis of Governance Modes

While the four companies differ in the governance mode (outsourcing vs. insourcing) adopted in the offshore location, governance for reshoring is always insourcing. Elaborating on Gray et al. (2013)'s taxonomy of offshoring/reshoring and outsourcing/insourcing yields, analyzed cases' findings may be summarized as in Table 2.
Location and governance have been acknowledged "strategies used to orchestrate the firm's overall value chain" (Mudambi & Venzin, 2010: 1511). However, since "Value creation 'travels' in terms of location and control, [...] firms need to frequently re-evaluate and adapt their offshoring and outsourcing decisions."(p. 1512). Offshoring involves the assessment of which parts of the firm's product offering and which stages of the production process are to be deployed in the offshore location. This requires the evaluation of whether core resources need to be transferred offshore from the inshore location and/or whether core resources are to be sought offshore (Hamel & Prahalad, 1990). In turn, discourse over resources is tightly connected to that of resource control, with increasing emphasis being placed on competences and knowledge intensive production stages (Mudambi, 2008). According to Transaction Cost Economics, the firm should hold close control over processes or stages through which the firm can generate and withhold the highest value and for which there is a risk of opportunistic behavior from third parties (Williamson, 1985).

Table 2 – Offshoring-reshoring options

	Offshore outsourcing	Offshore insourcing
Inshore outsourcing	//	//
Inshore insourcing	Fitwell (medium end segment, Romania) Roncato (high and medium end segments, China)	Aku (high and medium end segments, Romania) Ska (high end segment, China)
Not reshored	Aku (low end segments, Romania) Fitwell (one labour intensive stage of medium end segment production process) Roncato (low end segments, China)	Aku (partially medium end segments, Romania)

Knowledge transfer and resource control preoccupations were certainly at the root of the offshoring governance decisions of some of the case firms. Both Aku and Ska see know-how and continuous innovation as a key source of differentiation and competitive advantage. For these reasons, high value creating activities such as R&D and marketing have always been located in Italy. Further, and consistent with the above, only a small portion of turnover has been outsourced to third parties (10% in the case of Aku and none in the case of Ska).
How does governance link to motives? In the case of Aku, the goal of offshoring of medium and high range products was to cut costs, under the constraint that the offshore location possessed human resources allowing quality standards analogous to those at home. This entailed transferring to Eastern Europe knowledge and competences concerning medium- and high-end segments residing in Italy. The process of building local knowledge and of adapting to the offshore context went through a first attempt at subcontracting in Hungary, soon abandoned and followed by the establishment of an own plant in Romania. In fact, insourcing guaranteed better process control and easier coordination with the production phases that remained in Italy (R&D, quality control, sourcing of leather and other quality goods). On the contrary, the production of light shoes for lower end markets was outsourced to Chinese providers, given that little knowledge transfer was needed for these standardized lower end-segment products. Ska and Aku exhibit very similar patterns of offshoring with respect to quality goals and need for process control. Ska offshored to China since the early start of its activity and established a partnership with a similarly sized local company. The

rationale of the partnership (rather than a subcontracting arrangement) was again to allow adjustment of equipment and of production, processes to Ska's quality requirements, and to ensure control over the company's know-how. In addition, and unlike Aku, Ska was motivated not only by efficiency seeking but also by market seeking in China. In short, these two firms' international expansion leveraged on in-house knowledge but at the same time was constrained by an industry business model that imposed cost cutting. Therefore, outsourcing/insourcing (control) and offshoring to low cost countries (location) can be considered simultaneous and interrelated, with no priority of the one decision over the other (Rugman & Verbeke, 2001).

Offshoring paths link logically with the reshoring decisions. Aku reshored only those productions for which there was a greater need to link production to R&D (i.e., top end shoes) in order to boost the innovation requirements of this segment. For the same reason, insourcing was the governance mode chosen for reshored activities. Low-end productions remained in China, while medium-end products are interchangeably produced in Romania or Italy, given the equivalent quality standards in the two locations. For Ska, the tight control allowed by offshore insourcing led to maintain part of its production offshore and to reshore only the production of high quality zippers for the leather fashion. As in the case of Aku, the repatriation via in house production was important to boost the innovation potential of the company, given that offshoring had entailed a mere transfer of competences to the Chinese partner, and not the integration and acquisition of new knowledge offshore. Though operating in the same sector as Aku (mountain and outdoor shoes), Fitwell's governance strategy offshore was that of outsourcing to Romanian suppliers. At the time of offshoring, Fitwell was mainly a subcontractor of a larger company (LaFuma) that pressed for lower costs. Hence, Fitwell's offshoring initiative was purely efficiency seeking. Offshore outsourcing was certainly motivated by Fitwell's small size and fewer resources with respect to Aku, which made a captive form of offshoring too onerous. The other reason for outsourcing was that Fitwell never offshored the high-end segment, which leveraged on in-house knowledge relating to the production and assembly phases. Given its small size, Fitwell has never had a proper development department, and project, design, and prototyping take place through an open innovation mode. The offshore governance of Roncato's offshoring governance – like Fitwell's – was one of outsourcing, and was too cost driven: the offshoring concerned mainly soft-shell suitcases that, being price sensitive, were uneconomical to manufacture in Western countries. At the same time, Roncato did not leverage any specific knowledge on soft-shell suitcases, since this production was well developed in China with many local producers. Offshoring also included some ranges of hard-shell suitcases that can be classified as medium segment. Roncato maintained R&D and marketing activities in-house in Italy and through time succeeded in making styling homogeneous through its Italian and Chinese production sites.

A parallel can be drawn between Fitwell and Roncato also as far as reshoring is concerned. Fitwell's decision to reshore medium end segments followed the strategic change from subcontractor of other producers to supplier of end customers with an own trademark that planned to appeal to customers based on a "made in Italy" image. Even if Fitwell has no in house R&D, reshoring has taken place through insourcing, in order to leverage on in-house production and assembly competences. Only one low value added, high labor intensive stage of the production process of medium price shoes continues in Romania. For Roncato, while the production of soft-shell suitcases still takes place in China, the need to re-orient the brand towards "made in Italy" has led to the reshoring of medium end, high-technology hard-shell suitcases for which knowledge on materials and design reside in Italy. The insourcing decision follows from the need to establish closer ties with R&D. To conclude, in the cases analysed reshoring always involves very high-end segment products characterized by a high technology content, for which proximity of manufacturing and R&D is important (Aku,

Roncato, Ska). This is true irrespective of the offshore governance mode. The reshoring of medium-end products is more likely when the company has adopted an offshore outsourcing mode and has no strong control on production process that is critical for "made in" sensitive markets (Fitwell in Romania).

As already noted, although the offshore governance modes differ, the four companies all adopted an insourcing mode for reshoring. From a strategic point of view, this reflects the need of these firms, which produce also for medium and high-end markets, to maintain a tight control on own competences. From an operational point of view, insourcing supports the effectiveness of quality controls and of inter-functional coordination between development/R&D and production. This leads to the following proposition already:

Proposition 3 – Irrespective of the governance mode adopted offshore, reshoring of "made in" sensitive products takes place through an insourcing mode.

Where? The impact on firms' supply chains

Offshoring and reshoring strategies implemented by the four companies may be investigated also with respect to the geographical dimension of such decisions. In this respect, two main questions arise:

a) What elements may explain the country where companies offshored?

b) Why companies decided to return in the home country (Italy) and not in a near-to-home one? In other words, why they did not nearshored instead of reshoring?

With respect to the offshoring country, it is worthy noticing that this choice does not correlate with either the timing of offshoring (the three late comers went to China and Romania) or the governance mode (insourcing and outsourcing solutions in both countries). Rather, the industry appears to be the main determinant of the offshore location. Large companies (e.g., Diadora and Lotto) in the mountain boot industry in Italy (and specifically the Montebelluna district) started relocating manufacturing offshore already in the mid '70s. Production was subcontracted to companies in the Far East, following multinationals such as Puma, Adidas and Nike. At the beginning of the nineties, offshoring became an imperative also for SMEs operating in the industry. Following the fall of the Berlin wall in 1989, formerly Eastern Europe countries (and most notably Romania) emerged as both an interesting new market and a low-cost production location (Mutinelli & Piscitello, 1998) for SMEs, especially for simpler tasks like shoe assembling. Consistent with this model, for Fitwell and Aku imitation of competitors' location strategy was a relevant motivation of their location decision.

The offshore location of the case firms is closely tied to the motives for reshoring. In particular, the influence of geographical distance on reshoring motives is suggested by the presence of supply chain management (e.g. Purchase order rigidity and container-size minimum orders) among the key motivations for companies that offshored to China. The fact that these motivations were cited also by Ska, a company that adopted an offshore insourcing governance mode, suggests that the issue concerns transportation and logistics rather than production and supply. While insourcing should have allowed to better size production lots and deliveries to the home market, the geographical distance forced the company to optimize the logistic costs with "full load" shipments. The joint effect of the geographic distance and the insourcing governance mode seems to be at the base of the high relevance assigned by Ska to the "reduced operational flexibility" driver for reshoring. With this respect, it must be noted that, according to Robinson & Hsieh (2016), luxury product manufacturers are induced to reshore since the strategic need to shorten the supply chain and obtain a closer control on it. Accordingly, we formulate the following propositions:

Proposition 4 – Supply chain related reshoring motivations are relevant in the case of geographically distant countries and they mainly concern transport and logistics.

With respect to the alternative reshoring vs. near-shoring (that is, relocation in a near-to-home country), preference for returning to the home country may be mainly explained by the positive "made-in-Italy" effect. As already noted, the "made in" effect was a key reshoring driver for Fitwell and Roncato and partly for Ska. The premium price that this effect commands more than offsets the higher costs of labor with respect to nearby countries, such as Slovenia. This is consistent also with recent case studies of British companies in the fashion industry (Robinson & Hsieh, 2016; Ashby, 2016). In this respect, it is interesting to note that the "made in" effect is considered so relevant that induce companies to reshore in the home country even when production may be placed in another country which benefit from an extremely positive "made in" effect. For instance, Burberry first decided to nearshore its out-sourced production activities to Italian suppliers and then to definitely reshore in UK (Robinson & Hsieh, 2016). Near-shoring is considered a useful alternative only if the specific manufacturing activity or material is not available in the home country (Ashby, 2016). The above discussion leads to the formulation of the following proposition:
Proposition 5 – The positive "made in" effect discourages companies from nearshoring and favours relocation of the entire value chain back to the home country.

Another relevant motivation for repatriating manufacturing activities in Italy is represented, at least for Fitwell and AKU, by their belonging to the Montebelluna mountain shoes district. In other words, the two companies had the possibility to leverage on competences and resources offered by the local environment. In this light, it is worthy of notice that both companies cited the "lack of skilled workers in the host country (Romania)" and the "loss of innovation potential" as relevant motivations for moving back production in Italy. More specifically, the "loss of innovation potential" encompasses both the problem of the co-location between R&D and manufacturing activities and the issue of the interconnection with local business partners. In particular, AKU complained about the costs of identifying suitable local suppliers in Romania as another relevant motivation for reshoring. Finally, an important issue is the "sense of belonging" to the territory (emotional elements) clearly expressed by the founder of Fitwell. This findings are consistent with evidences collected by Belussi (2015) with respect to a sample of Italian industrial districts. We formulate the following proposition:
Proposition 6 – The firm's belonging to an industrial district encourages reshoring to the home country instead of near-shoring due to network effects and for an emotive "sense of belonging".

Discussion

The following discussion aims to summarize the findings from the four case studies by answering the research questions originally set forth:

a) Are there common patterns in offshoring and subsequent reshoring initiatives among firms operating in sectors that are sensitive to the "made in" effect?
b) Do motivations for offshoring link to reshoring motives?
c) Can reshoring be interpreted as a "failure" of the offshoring initiative, or rather as an evolution and adjustment of a sound competitive strategy consistent with the changes in the market environment?

Based on the within and cross case study analysis earlier conducted, the proposed research questions seem intimately interconnected. Therefore, we shall discuss them using a unified perspective. In so doing, we acknowledge Bals et al. (2016) who suggested that future research on reshoring decisions should differentiate between decisions deriving from "deliberate" firm's strategies and those stemming from mistakes and failures. For our sampled firms, reshoring appears as the result of a strategic change (see, in this respect, Mugurusi & de Boer, 2014), more than the correction of an earlier managerial mistake (Kinkel

& Maloca, 2009). More specifically, the decision to (at least partially) repatriate manufacturing activities at home was part of a strategy meant to focus on high- and medium-end products. To this end, it is worth remembering Fitwell's CEO: *"I went offshore also because of the politics of globalization. With hindsight, it was a mass mistake. But if 15 years ago I hadn't done it, I wouldn't be here now. There was no other solution".* In other words, reshoring is not the correction of a mistake made by a single company but the result of a "global suggestion" focused on cost-efficiency. This is consistent with the recent advice of Bals et al. (2016) who retain that offshoring was often purely cost-driven while reshoring is based on a more strategic approach. Therefore, while the strategy of offshoring was fully rational when it took place, changes in the competitive strategy, prompted by the shift of the market towards higher quality products led these firms to re-evaluate their product offering and the manufacturing location of the different product lines. In the jargon of traditional strategic management (Porter, 1980) the firms' competitive strategy shifted from a cost focus to a differentiation strategy. This result it is in line with the latest evidence regarding case studies in the fashion industry (e.g. Robinson & Hsieh, 2016; Ashby, 2016).

Since reshoring was the result of a strategic shift, we found common patterns in offshoring and subsequent reshoring initiatives among the four case studies. More specifically, offshoring was mainly motivated by efficiency-seeking and resource-seeking motives, with the need to follow competitors or the market being the main driver for Aku, Fitwell and Ska. Differently, Roncato, though motivated by labor cost advantages, was rather a first mover. Similarly, in spite of the higher costs of producing in the home country, reshoring took place to improve customer perceived value. This took the form of higher a strengthened "made in" brand, or through effective higher quality and innovation, through more qualified suppliers and tighter links with the company's R&D. This result highlights the existence of a sectoral pattern not only of offshoring but also of reshoring, thus suggesting – as it will be argued below, that reshoring is one ingredient of a broader shift in the competitive strategy of specific industries.

CONCLUSIONS

Contribution to theory

Our paper contributes to Supply Chain Management (SCM) theory in five significant ways. First, we framed and summarized offshoring and reshoring motivations proposed by previous research and highlighted that a full comprehension of the reshoring phenomenon cannot leave aside a comparative analysis of the two phenomena, as recently stated also by Bals et al (2016).

Second, we identified offshoring and reshoring motivations of four manufacturing companies operating in labor intensive sectors. This allowed us to empirically refine the proposed frameworks and to provide the readers with a first estimation of the motivations' importance in the above mentioned sectors.

Third, we shed light on the links between offshoring and reshoring motivations. In short, while there is a tight link between offshoring and reshoring motivations (some of them are the same), cost-driven motivations are more weighty in the case of offshoring, while value-driven motivations are more weighty in case of reshoring.

Fourth, we compared the case study findings and developed six propositions focused on the nature of the offshoring/reshoring motivations and their relationship with governance modes and country characteristics. This represent a relevant theory building effort in a research field mainly characterized by descriptive/exploratory investigations which do not adequately differentiate location and governance mode choices (Fratocchi et al., 2014, 2016; Bals et al., 2016; Stentoft et al., 2016b).

Fifth, we contributed to the debate of reshoring as a "failure" of offshoring initiative, or rather as an evolution /adjustment of a sound competitive strategy consistent with the changes in the market environment. Our study depicts reshoring as a result of a strategic change more than the correction of a managerial error, opening significant research avenues.

Contribution to practice and policy

The findings of our study have also significant managerial implications. Our detailed review and adoption of an integrated framework provides managers with a comprehensive list and classification of offshoring and reshoring motivations (Figure 1 and Figure 2). Moreover, our detailed "within case analysis" offers them some concrete experiences of location changes. Finally, our "cross case analysis" and the following discussion advice managers about the importance of the motivations and the factors affecting them (governance mode and country characteristics). In sum, our study helps managers to take more aware location decision, this way fostering competitiveness (Ellram et al., 2013).
Significant policy guidelines may also be drawn from our study. The comprehension of the offshoring and reshoring motivations and implementation models (including choices regarding in- and out-sourcing alternatives) may help policy makers in the understanding of the ways to limit the de-industrialization in their countries, and how re-attract offshored companies, improving the local GDP and the employment. The message of our study is that a sound policy should involve not only economic incentives, but also no-monetary levers, used ex-ante (i.e., before offshoring) for informing about potential shortcomings of the offshoring choice and ex-post (i.e., after offshoring) for driving the companies back to their home countries.

Limitations and future research

The results of our study should be viewed in light of two major limitations. First, we adopted a multiple case study method and performed qualitative data analyses. Despite several actions were performed by us to enhance validity and reliability of our findings (such as multiple sources of evidence were used; interviews and data analyses were conducted by three members of the research team; a detailed case study protocol was used to guide field research), statistical generalization to a broader population is not allowed.
Second, our sample consisted of four Italian manufacturing SMEs competing in labour intensive sectors. Despite these companies work internationally, caution is needed to extend the results to other countries and industrial contexts. Anyway, Italian is seen as one the most important countries for the reshoring phenomenon (Fratocchi et al, 2015b).
Future case based research may replicate our study in other geographical contexts, industries and on different company sizes. Surveys and/or secondary data quantitative studies could instead be applied to empirically validate our frameworks (Figure 1 and Figure 2), to estimate the relative importance of each offshoring/reshoring driver, as well as to test our propositions.

APPENDIX A: LITERATURE REVIEW ON RESHORING MOTIVATIONS[1]

	Agrawal et al., 2003	Ritter & Sternfels, 2004	Kinkel et al., 2007	Couto et al., 2008	Goel et al., 2008	Ferreira & Prokopets, 2009	Kinkel & Maloca, 2009	Leibl et al., 2009	Shiry et al., 2009	Amighini et al., 2010	Ferreira & Heilala, 2011	Leibl et al., 2011	Powell, 2011	Kinkel, 2012	Simchi-Levi et al., 2012	Sirkin et al., 2012	Tate et al., 2012	**Baldwin & Venables, 2013**	Canham & Hamilton, 2013	Dachs & Kinkel, 2013	**Denning, 2013**	Ellram et al., 2013	Ellram, 2013	Gray et al., 2013	Johnson et al., 2013	Kinkel & Zanker, 2013	McIvor, 2013	Neil, 2013	Nelson, 2013	Regalado, 2013	Arlbjørn & Mikkelsen, 2014	**Bailey & De Propris, 2014a**	**Bailey & De Propris, 2014b**
1	X						X					X		X					X	X		X	X			X					X	X	
2		X						X					X	X		X			X	X						X						X	X
3								X												X							X					X	X
4									X					X	X	X				X				X			X				X	X	
5		X					X							X								X	X								X	X	X
6															X										X							X	
7							X					X		X				X		X				X								X	
8																				X										X			X
9				X			X															X	X									X	
10																								X								X	X
11			X																X	X						X							X
12											X																					X	
13												X																				X	X
14																X																	X
15																			X														
16																																X	
17					X																												X
18																						X	X										X
19										X						X																	X
20						X											X																X
21																						X	X										X
22																													X			X	
23																												X			X		
24							X														X												
25						X																X	X										
26																																X	
27							X																										
28							X																										
29														X																			
30																			X														
31																																	
32																X																	
33						X																											
34																																	
35		X																															
36																																	
37																																	
38																																	
39																																	
40																																	

	Kinkel, 2014	Martinez-Mora & Merino, 2014	Tate et al., 2014	Tate, 2014	Wu & Zhang, 2014	Zhai, 2014	Ancarani et al., 2015	Cowell & Provo, 2015	Fratocchi et al., 2015	Grandinetti & Tabacco, 2015	Grappi et al, 2015	Gylling et al, 2015	Ashby, 2016	Fratocchi et al., 2016	Huq et al., 2016	Joubioux & Vanpoucke, 2016	Lam & Khare, 2016	Robinson & Hsieh, 2016	Srai & Ané, 2016	Uluskan et al, 2016	Zhai et al., 2016	Sardar et al., 2016	Stentoft et al., 2016a	Stentoft et al., 2016b	Total
1	x		x				x	x	x			x		x	x	x	x		x	x	x		x		25
2	x		x	x	x				x					x			x	x	x				x		20
3	x		x	x					x	x				x		x	x	x	x	x			x		17
4	x			x					x					x			x	x	x				x		17
5							x		x	x		x		x			x		x		x		x		17
6		x			x		x	x	x	x		x		x			x		x	x	x		x		16
7	x								x	x		x		x	x		x		x				x		16
8	x		x	x				x	x					x		x	x		x	x			x		14
9	x		x						x					x					x		x		x		12
10			x					x	x					x	x		x		x	x			x		12
11	x								x					x			x		x				x		11
12					x		x		x	x				x			x		x		x		x		11
13			x						x			x		x			x		x	x			x		11
14			x			x	x		x					x					x				x		9
15		x	x				x		x					x				x	x				x		9
16			x	x					x					x			x		x	x			x		9
17									x	x				x			x		x	x					8
18									x	x				x					x				x		8
19									x					x					x					x	7
20									x					x					x						6
21									x					x					x				x		7
22							x		x					x					x				x		7
23			x						x					x					x				x		7
24	x	x	x									x											x		7
25									x					x									x		6
26		x			x							x							x				x		6
27	x								x					x											4
28	x								x					x											4
29	x								x					x											4
30									x					x									x		4
31													x					x	x			x			4
32									x					x											3
33									x					x											3
34										x									x						2
35														x											2
36														x					x						2
37											x														1
38																x									1
39																			x						1
40																			x						1

1	Poor local products quality
2	Labour costs' gap reduction
3	Logistics costs
4	Loss of innovation potential/Vicinity to R&D
5	Production and delivery time impact
6	Total cost of sourcing
7	Supply chain coordination costs
8	Loss of know-how in the host country/IP risks
9	Lack of skilled workers in host country/Availability in home country
10	Global supply chain risks
11	Reduced operational flexibility
12	Reduced responsiveness to customer demand
13	Exchange rate risk
14	National subsides for relocation
15	Made-in effect
16	Energy costs
17	Freight costs
18	Redefinition of the global supply chain (including Vertical integration)
19	Home labour market flexibility (flexicurity)
20	High inventory levels
21	Increased home country productivity
22	Need to increase customer satisfaction
23	Automation of production process
24	**Miscalculation of actual cost/Adoption of new cost accounting methods**
25	Container-size minimum orders
26	**Demand changes at home/host country**
27	Lack of knowledge about the foreign destination
28	Lack of systematic location planning
29	Untapped production capacity at home
30	Emotional elements (e.g. nationalism, patriotism)
31	**Environmental & social sustainability**
32	High unemployment rates at the home country
33	Purchase order rigidity
34	**Change in firm's business strategy (e.g. new business area; focus on core activities)**
35	Penalties for late orders
36	Customs duties for re-import
37	**Customers' gratitude and willingness to buy**
38	**Psychic distance**
39	**Technology clusters & spillover benefits**
40	**Payment terms**

[1] Authors and motivations not included in Fratocchi et al. [2016] are highlighted in bold.

APPENDIX B: LITERATURE REVIEW ON OFFSHORING MOTIVATIONS

Offshoring Drivers	Access to know-how (e.g., knowledge, technology)	Availability of skilled labour in the host country	Capacity bottlenecks in the home country	Costs and productivity of skilled labour	Costs and productivity of unskilled labour	Countertrade requirements	Delivery reliability	Economies of scale	Foreign market access or development	Government incentives (including favourable taxation)	Host country supply base	Host country trade environment (including legislation)	Imitation of competitors' strategies ("bandwagon")	New product development	Operational flexibility	Production and logistic costs (except labour costs) reduction	Proximity to foreign customers	Quality improvement	Risk mitigation	Time to market reduction	Total Cost of Ownership
Nachum & Zaheer, 2005	X								X		X					X	X				X
Bock, 2008					X																
Di Gregorio et al., 2009	X	X			X				X		X				X	X	X				
Driffeld & Chiang, 2009					X																
Guth, 2009	X	X			X											X		X			
Hameri & Hintsa, 2009					X				X							X					
Kinkel & Maloca, 2009			X		X				X	X							X				
Lu & Van Mieghem, 2009					X											X					
Aspelund & Butsko, 2010				X					X				X			X	X				
Fifarek & Veloso, 2010		X																			
Milberg & Winkler, 2010																X					
Mudambi & Venzin, 2010	X																				
Simons & Isely, 2010	X				X																
Temouri et al., 2010	X	X		X	X						X										
Kusaba et al., 2011	X	X					X											X			X
Wang et al., 2011		X			X				X		X		X		X	X			X	X	
Arlbjorn & Luthje, 2012		X			X						X					X	X	X		X	
Cai et al., 2012					X											X					
Jensen & Pedersen, 2012	X	X			X				X						X		X				
Kinkel, 2012	X				X				X	X							X				
Ellram et al., 2013	X	X			X	X			X	X	X					X	X		X		
Fontana & Prencipe, 2013		X							X	X	X						X			X	
Mohiuddin & Su, 2013	X	X			X			X	X		X			X		X					
Persaud & Floyd, 2013	X	X		X			X		X	X			X			X	X	X		X	
Schröder, 2013																					
Slepniov et al., 2013	X	X			X						X					X	X	X			
Ebringa & Kule, 2014					X											X		X	X		
Larsen & Pedersen, 2014	X			X	X															X	
Martínez-Mora & Merino, 2014					X											X					
Szasz & Demeter, 2014					X																
Fragoso-Diaz, 2015					X				X	X	X				X						
Grappi et al, 2015		X							X							X					
Gylling et al., 2015					X						X					X					
Heyman & Tingvall, 2015												X							X		
Mykhaylenko et al., 2015	X	X			X				X		X										

REFERENCES

Ancarani, A., Di Mauro, C., Fratocchi, L., Orzes, G., & Sartor, M. (2015). Prior to reshoring: A duration analysis of foreign manufacturing venture. *International Journal of Production Economics*, 169, 141-155.

Arlbjørn, J. S., & Lüthje, T. (2012). Global operations and their interaction with supply chain performance, *Industrial Management & Data Systems*, 112(7), 1044-1064.

Aspelund, A., & Butsko, V. (2010). Small and Middle-sized enterprises offshoring production: a study of firm decisions and consequences. *Tijdschrift voor Economische en Sociale Geografie*, 101(3), 262-275.

Bailey, D., & De Propris, L. (2014). Manufacturing reshoring and its limits: the UK automotive case. *Cambridge Journal of Regions, Economy and Society*, 7(3), 379-395.

Barratt, M., Choi, T. Y., & Li, M. (2011). Qualitative case studies in operations management: Trends, research outcomes, and future research implications. *Journal of Operations Management*, *29*(4), 329-342.

Benito, G. R. (2015). Why and how motives (still) matter. *The Multinational Business Review*, 23(1), 15-24.

Bock, S. (2012). Supporting offshoring and nearshoring decisions for mass customization manufacturing processes. *European Journal of Operational Research*, 184, 490–508.

Buckley, P. J., & Ghauri, P. N. (2004). Globalisation, economic geography and the strategy of multinational enterprises. *Journal of International Business Studies*, 35(2), 81-98.

Butters, J.K., & Lintner, J. (1945). *Effect of Federal Taxes on Growing Enterprises*, Boston: Harvard University Press.

Cai H., Chen H., & Liu, X. (2012). Offshoring and Employment Structure: Evidence from China. *Journal of Applied Economic Sciences*, 7, 35-47.

Contractor, F. J., Kumar, V., Kundu, S. K., & Pedersen, T. (2010). Reconceptualizing the firm in a world of outsourcing and offshoring: The organizational and geographical relocation of high-value company functions. *Journal of Management Studies*, 47 (8), 1417-1433.

Denyer, D., & Tranfield, D. (2009). Producing a systematic review. In D. A. Buchanan, A. Bryman, (Eds.). *The Sage handbook of organizational research methods*. Thousand Oaks: Sage Publications, 671-689.

Di Gregorio D., Musteen M., & Thomas, D. E. (2009). Offshore outsourcing as a source of international competitiveness for SMEs. *Journal of International Business Studies*, 40, 969-988.

Driffield, N., & Chiang, P. C. M. (2009). The Effects of Offshoring to China: Reallocation, Employment and Productivity in Taiwan. *International Journal of the Economics of Business*, 16 (1), 19-38.

Duriau, V. J., Reger, R. K., & Pfarrer, M. D. (2007). A content analysis of the content analysis literature in organization studies: Research themes, data sources, and methodological refinements. *Organizational research methods*, 10(1), 5-34.

Ebringa, T. O., & Kule, L. (2014). Offshoring for sustainable value management. *Serbian Journal of Management*, 9, 105-119.

Eggert, A., & Ulaga, W. (2002) Customer perceived value: a substitute for satisfaction in business markets? *Journal of Business & industrial marketing*, 17 (2/3), 107-118.

Eisenhardt, K. M. (1989). Building theories from case study research. *Academy of management review*, 14 (4), 532-550.

Ellram, L. M., Tate, W. L., & Petersen, K. J. (2013). Offshoring and reshoring: an update on the manufacturing location decision. *Journal of Supply Chain Management*, 49(2), 14-21.

Fifarek, B. J., & Veloso, F. M. (2010). Offshoring and the global geography of innovation. *Journal of Economic Geography*, 10, 559-578.

Fink, A. (2005). *Conducting Research Literature Reviews: From the Internet to Paper*. London, Sage Publications.

Foerstl, K., Kirchoff, J., & Bals, L. (2016). Reshoring and insourcing: drivers and future research directions. *International Journal of Physical Distribution & Logistics Management*, 46(5).

Fontana, F., & Prencipe, A. (2013). Framing offshoring: antecedents, processes, and outcomes. *International Journal of Innovation and Technology Management*, 10(1).

Fragoso-Diaz, G. (2015). Perceptions of doing business in other countries: a logistic regression analysis of survey results. *International Journal of Supply Chain Management*, 4(4), 52-62.

Fratocchi, L., Di Mauro, C., Barbieri, P., Nassimbeni, G., & Zanoni, A. (2014a). When manufacturing moves back: Concepts and questions. *Journal of Purchasing and Supply Management*, 20(1), 54-59.

Fratocchi, L., Iapadre, L., Ancarani, A., Di Mauro, C., Zanoni, A., & Barbieri, P. (2014b). Manufacturing Reshoring: Threat and opportunity for East Central Europe and Baltic Countries. In A. Zhuplev (Ed.). *Geo-regional competitiveness in Central and Eastern Europe*, The Baltic Countries, and Russia, IGI Global, 83-118.

Fratocchi, L., Ancarani, A., Barbieri, P., Di Mauro, C., Nassimbeni, G., Sartor, M., Vignoli, M., & Zanoni, A. (2015). Manufacturing back-reshoring as a nonlinear internationalization process. In R. van Tulder, A. Verbeke, R. Drogendijk, (Eds). *The future of Global Organizing, Progress in International Business Research (PIBR)*, Emerald, 367-405.

Fratocchi, L., Ancarani, A., Barbieri, P., Di Mauro, C., Nassimbeni, G., Sartor, M., Vignoli M., & Zanoni, A. (2016). Motivations of manufacturing reshoring: an interpretative framework. *International Journal of Physical Distribution & Logistics Management*, 46(2), 98-127.

Grandinetti, R., & Tabacco, R. (2015). A return to spatial proximity: combining global suppliers with local subcontractors. *International Journal of Globalisation and Small Business*, 7(2), 139-161.

Grappi S., Romani S., & Bagozzi, R. P. (2015). Consumer responses to corporate offshoring practices. *Management Decision*, 53(3), 698-712.

Gray, J. V., Skowronsky, K., Esenduran, G., & Rungtudanatham, M. J. (2013). Reshoring Phenomenon: What Supply Chain Academics Ought to Know and Should Do. *Journal of Supply Chain Management,* 49(2), 27-33.

Guth, W. D. (2009). Developing new avenues for growth: Challenges presented by five trends in the global environment. *Journal of International Management*, 15, 251-261.

Gylling, M., Heikkilä, J., Jussila, K., & Saarinen, M. (2015). Making decisions on offshore outsourcing and backshoring: A case study in the bicycle industry. *International Journal of Production Economics*, 162, 92-100.

Hamel, G., & Prahalad, C. K. (1990). Corporate imagination and expeditionary marketing. *Harvard Business Review*, 69(4), 81-92.

Hameri, A. P., & Hintsa, J. (2009). Assessing the drivers of change for cross-border supply chains. *International Journal of Physical Distribution & Logistics Management*, 39(9), 741-76.

Heyman, F., & Tingvall, P. G. (2015). The Dynamics of Offshoring and Institutions. *B.E. Journal of Economic Analysis & Policy*, 15, 1975-2016.

Jensen, P., D., Ø., & Pedersen, T. (2012). Offshoring and international competitiveness: antecedents of offshoring advanced tasks. *Journal of the Academy of Marketing Science*, 40, 313-328

Johanson, J., & Vahlne, J. E. (1977). The internationalization process of the firm-a model of knowledge development and increasing foreign market commitments. *Journal of International Business Studies*, 8(1), 23-32.

Kinkel, S. (2012). Trends in production relocation and backshoring activities. *International Journal of Operations & Production Management*, 32 (6), 696-720.

Kinkel, S., & Maloca, S. (2009). Drivers and antecedents of manufacturing offshoring and backshoring - A German perspective. *Journal of Purchasing & Supply Management*, 15, 54-165.

Kusaba, K., Moser, R., & Rodrigues, A. M. (2011). Low-cost country sourcing competence: A conceptual framework and empirical analysis. *Journal of Supply Chain Management*, 47(4), 73-93.

Larsen, M. M., & Pedersen, T. (2014). Organizational Reconfiguration and Strategic Response: The Case of Offshoring. *Orchestration of the Global Network Organization; Advances in International Management*, 27, 403-432.

Li, D., Crescini, A., Godsell, J., & Karatzas, A. (2015). Right-Shoring: An Empirical Study of the Drivers of Global Supply Network Design. 22nd European Operations Management Association Conference, Neuchâtel, Switzerland.

Lindič, J., & da Silva, C.M. (2011). Value proposition as a catalyst for a customer focused innovation. *Management Decision*, 49(10), 1694-1708.

Lu, L. X., & Van Mieghem, J. A. (2009). Multimarket facility network design with offshoring applications. *Manufacturing & Service Operations Management*, 11 (1), 90-108.

Manning, S. (2014). Mitigate, tolerate or relocate? Offshoring challenges, strategic imperatives and resource constraints. *Journal of World Business*, 49(4), 522-535.

Mariotti, S., Mutinelli M., & Piscitello, L. (2008). The internationalization of production by Italian industrial districts' firms: structural and behavioural determinants. *Regional Studies*, 42(5), 719-735.

Martínez-Mora, C., & Merino, F. (2014). Offshoring in the Spanish footwear industry: A return journey? *Journal of Purchasing & Supply Management*, 20, 225-237.

McCutcheon, D. M., & Meredith, J. R. (1993). Conducting case study research in operations management. *Journal of Operations Management*, 11(3) , 239-256.

Meinlschmidt, J., Foerstl, K., & Kirchoff, J. F. (2016). The role of absorptive and desorptive capacity in sustainable supply management–A longitudinal analysis. *International Journal of Physical Distribution & Logistics Management*, 46(2), 177-211.

Milberg, W., & Winkler, D. (2010). Financialisation and the dynamics of offshoring in the USA. *Cambridge Journal of Economics*, 34, 27-293.

Mintzberg, H., & Waters, J. A. (1985). Of strategies, deliberate and emergent. *Strategic Management Journal*, 6(3), 257-272.

Mohiuddin, M., & Su, Z. (2013). Manufacturing Small and Medium size enterprise's offshore outsourcing and competitive advantage: An exploratory study on Canadian offshoring manufacturing SMEs. *The Journal of Applied Business Research*, 29(4).

Mudambi, R., & Venzin, M. (2010). The Strategic Nexus of Offshoring and Outsourcing Decisions. *Journal of Management Studies*, 47(8), 1510-1533.

Mudambi, R. (2008). Location, control and innovation in knowledge-intensive industries. *Journal of Economic Geography*, 8(5), 699-725.

Mugurusi, G., & de Boer, L. (2013). What follows after the decision to offshore production? A systematic review of the literature. *Strategic Outsourcing: An International Journal*, 6(3), 213-257.

Mugurusi, G., & de Boer, L. (2014). Conceptualising the production offshoring organisation using the viable systems model (VSM). *Strategic Outsourcing: An International Journal*, 7(3), 75-298.

Mutinelli, M., & Piscitello, L. (1998). The Influence of Firm's Size and International Experience on the Ownership Structure of Italian FDI in Manufacturing. *Small Business Economics*, 11(1), 43-56.

Mykhaylenko, A., Motika A., Waehrens B. V., & Slepniov, D. (2015). Accessing offshoring advantages: what and how to offshore. *Strategic Outsourcing: An International Journal*, 8(2/3), 262-283.

Nachum, L., & Zaheer, S. (2005). The persistence of distance? The impact of technology on MNE motivations for foreign investment. *Strategic Management Journal*, 26, 747-767.

Patton, M.Q. (2002). *Qualitative Research & Evaluation Methods*. London: Sage Publications.

Persaud, A., & Floyd, J. (2013). Offshoring and Outsourcing of R&D and Business Activities in Canadian Technology Firms. *Journal of Technology Management & Innovation*, 8 (3).

Piekkari, R., & Welch, C. (2004). Qualitative research methods in international business. In

R. Piekkari, & C. Welch (Eds.). *Handbook of Qualitative Research Methods for International Business*, Edward Elgar Publishing.

Porter, M. E. (1990). The competitive advantage of notions. *Harvard Business Review*, 68(2), 73-93.

Rivière, A. (2015). Vers un modèle de formation de la valeur perçue d'une innovation: le rôle ajeur des bénéfices perçus en amont du processus d'adoption. *Recherche et Applications en Marketing*, 30(1), 5-27.

Rugman, A. M., & Verbeke, A. (2001). Subsidiary-specific advantages in multinational enterprises. *Strategic Management Journal*, 22(3), 237-250.

Schröder, M. (2013). How moral arguments influence economic decisions and organizational legitimacy-the case of offshoring production. *Organization*, 20(4), 551-576.

Seuring, S., & Gold, S. (2012). Conducting content-analysis based literature reviews in supply chain management. *Supply Chain Management: An International Journal*, 17(5), 544-555.

Sharma, R., Lindsay, V., & Everton, N. (2015). Managing institutional differences for international outsourcing success. *Journal of Small Business and Enterprise Development*, 22 (3), 590-607.

Simchi-Levi, D., Peruvankal, J.P., Mulani, N., Read, B., & Ferreira, J. (2012). Is it time to rethink your manufacturing strategy. *Sloan Management Review*, 53(2), 20-22.

Simons, G. P. W., & Isely, P. N. (2010). The effect of offshoring on knowledge flows in the US automobile industry. *Economics of Innovation and New Technology*, 19(6), 553-568.

Slepniov, D., Brazinskas, S., & Wæhrens, B. V. (2013). Nearshoring practices. *Baltic Journal of Management*, 8, 5-26.

Stentoft, J., Olhager, J., Heikkilä, J., & Thoms, L. (2015). Moving manufacturing back: a content-based literature review. 22nd European Operations Management Association Conference, Neuchâtel, Switzerland.

Stringfellow, A., Teagarden, M. B., & Nie, W. (2008). Invisible costs in offshoring services work. *Journal of Operations Management*, 26(2), 164-179.

Szász, L., & Demeter, K. (2015). Business models along supply chain position and servitisation: An empirical investigation of European manufacturers. *Acta Oeconomica*, 65(2), 367-391.

Tate, W. L., Ellram, L. M., Schoenherr, T., & Petersen, K. J. (2014). Global competitive conditions driving the manufacturing location decision. *Business Horizons*, 57, 381-390.

Temouri, Y., Driffield N., L., & Añón Higón, D. (2010). The futures of offshoring FDI in high-tech sectors. *Futures*, 42, 960-970.

Uluskan, M., Joines, J.A., & Godfrey, A. B. (2016). Comprehensive insight into supplier quality and the impact of quality strategies of suppliers on outsourcing decisions. *Supply Chain Management: An International Journal*, 21(1), 92-102.

Vernon, R. (1966). International investment and international trade in the product cycle. *The quarterly journal of economics*, 80(2), 190-207.

Voss, C., Tsikriktsis, N., & Frohlich, M. (2002). Case research in operations management. *International journal of operations & production management*, 22(2), 195-219.

Wang, J., Singh, P. J., Samson, D., & Power, D. (2011). Sourcing from China: experiences of Australian firms. *Supply Chain Management: An International Journal*, 16, 419-427.

Williamson, O. E. (1985). *The economic institutions of capitalism*. New York: The Free Press.

Yin, R. K. (2003). *Case study research: Design and methods*. Thousand Oaks: Sage Publications.

DECISION SCIENCES INSTITUTE

On the Job Training: A Case Study on Using Consulting Experiences to Enhance Students' Employability

Robert Graham
Johns Hopkins University
bgraham@jhu.edu

Pamela H. Sheff
Johns Hopkins University
psheff@jhu.edu

ABSTRACT

One university program piloted and implemented a novel approach to addressing ABET's requirement that students are prepared and meet the engineering community's needs. Graduate students participate in a required, immersive, three-week, team consulting engagement with various non-profit and for-profit organizations. This 1.5-credit course attempts to marry students' development of technical management skills with practical application of non-technical or soft skills, including communication, ethics, strategic analysis, and teamwork, to better positioning them for the work environment's broad and diverse needs. This paper describes the approach, methodology and implementation of the program, as well as data on its success, so other schools can explore implementation.

KEYWORDS: Non-Technical Skills, ABET, Consulting, Management, Curriculum

INTRODUCTION

Employers expect new employees to have not just technical expertise, but also increased dexterity in the non-technical skills that contribute to their ability to provide value on projects. These non-technical skills include communication abilities, ethical understanding and reasoning abilities, analytical skills, leadership and teamwork, along with others. Programs in the U.S. and other countries have attempted a number of approaches toward achieving these goals, with most focused on classroom instruction or discovery, and/or internships. Yet, these attempts often fall short because of their inherent constraints.

A growing chorus of engineering organizations are echoing what they hear from employers, who want graduates who can apply technical and non-technical skills (also referred to as soft skills or behavioral skills) in the work world with equal adeptness. ABET, the American Society of Engineering Education (ASEE), the American Society of Mechanical Engineers (ASME) and the American the National Academy of Engineering

(NAE) are echoing what they hear from employers (Dukhan & Hassif, 2014)."There is nothing soft about cultivating or acquiring these skills, and how critical for success they are for engineers in today's economy" (Palmer et. Al, 2011).

ABET mandates that all engineering programs ensure their students have "an ability to design a system, component, or process to meet desired needs within realistic constraints such as economic, environmental, social, political, ethical, health and safety, manufacturability, and sustainability." Students, according to ABET, require "the broad education necessary to understand the impact of engineering solutions in a global, economic, environmental, and societal context" and that graduates have "knowledge of contemporary issues" (ABET, 2015). Similarly, the American Society of Engineering Educators sees the need for graduating engineers to be better communicators (ASEE, 2014), while the National Society of Professional Engineers advocates for "prowess" among engineers in both technical and non-technical skills (Golden, 2016). But those programs that attempt to integrate non-technical skills into the classroom are not always successful. "Despite the fact that these skills affect personal and organizational outcomes and that universities value curriculum emphasizing interpersonal skills, students often fail to see the benefit" (Halfhill & Nielson, 2007).

To stand out to employers, graduates need a broader mix of technical and non-technical skills. The former are the skills required within a discipline, including specific processes, tools, and techniques (Sukhoo, 2005). Non-technical skills are broadly defined as the competencies necessary to manage one-on-one and one-to-group interactions. Non-technical skills most frequently identified through research (Halfhill, 2007; Law, 2004; Muzio et al, 2007; Pant & Baroudi, 2008; Petter & Randolph, 2009; Stevenson & Starkweather, 2010) include:

- Teamwork
- Leadership
- Decision-making
- Verbal and written skills
- Communication
- Conflict management
- Dealing with ambiguity and change
- Problem-solving
- Giving and receiving constructive feedback

For a finance student, for instance, technical skills might include knowledge and competence in calculating net present value, asset turnover, and assessing the risk of an investment portfolio. Non-technical skills that student might use include presenting the risk in an investment portfolio to senior management and working with colleagues to mitigate risk in that portfolio. Neither of these areas of skills can operate in isolation, a reality that employers are noting in their desire to engage graduates who can perform both well (Porterfield et al, 2015).

(The authors choose to refer to these skills, including communication, project management, leadership, and adapting to change, as non-technical to clearly delineate how they contrast with the technical skills, knowledge and abilities traditionally taught in academic institutions.)

Students, faced with growing costs for their postsecondary education, sense the problem, too. McKinsey, surveying students in nine countries, including the U.S., determined that half of those students are unsure whether their postsecondary education improves the odds of them finding a job. Meanwhile, almost 40 percent of employers asked in the same survey, say they have vacancies in entry-level positions because applicants lack necessary skills for the position (McKinsey, 2012). Ryan Smith, founder and CEO of Qualtrics, wrote in *Fortune*:

> The number one problem I see in academia today is that students are coming out unprepared for the workplace. In other words, they lack on the job training. Universities teach students how to think, but they don't provide real world experience, so people leave school unprepared for the workplace. It's the equivalent of having a pilot graduate from flight school without ever having flown a plane. That's why I believe everyone should graduate from school with the equivalent of 3,000 flight hours so they know how to tackle challenging projects (Smith, 2015).

McKinsey put it more succinctly. "Clearly, employers need to work with education providers so that students learn the skills they need to succeed at work." (McKinsey, 2012).

Engineering programs in the U.S. and other countries have attempted to satisfy this dearth of professional experience by inviting business leaders to lecture, creating simulations and other classroom activities, and supporting real-world extracurricular programs and internships (Galloway, 2007). But these attempts often fail to provide students with realistic situations in which they can identify, engage and improve these non-technical skills in concert with their technical skills. The safety net of the classroom or the inherent role of the mentor in ensuring students stay on track at an internship can greatly erode the students' potential for discovery and learning in these settings. Moreover, while internships may potentially provide vital professional experience, not all students have the opportunity to secure a meaningful internship, and many who do are too often consigned to low-level work.

LITERATURE REVIEW

The most prepared and successful graduates are those who have both technical expertise and non-technical skills. Before focusing on non-technical skills, research first explored the broader concept of competence. To be a successful project manager, several researchers found the needs for greater training and education in non-technical skills (Wateridge, 1997; Wirth, 1992; Pant & Baroudi, 2008). Boyatzis found that competent managers need "an underlying characteristic of a person...including motives, traits, skills, aspects of one's self-image and social role, or body of knowledge which he or she uses" (Boyatzis, 1992). This list of qualities can easily be extrapolated to other fields such as engineering.

Competence has been described as the combination of both job performance and behaviors top performers exhibit. That combination is further enhanced by workers who consider the organization's culture and needs (Cheng et al, 2005). A behavioral competency model for project managers encompassed 12 qualities (Cheng et al, 2005):

- Achievement orientation
- Initiative
- Information seeking
- Focus on client's needs
- Impact and influence
- Directive mess
- Teamwork and cooperation
- Team leadership
- Analytical thinking
- Conceptual thinking
- Self-control
- Flexibility

Subsequent research explored how managers' observations of their technical engineering project management professionals compared to test results for "soft skills quantification" (SSQ) in six areas -- results orientation, interpersonal skills, personal accountability, flexibility, problem-solving, and planning and organization -- resulting in another definition of these non-technical skills (Muzio et al, 2007). Two surveys of more than 200 members of the National Association of Colleges and Employers found that non-technical skills are in greatest demand. "Leadership" and "the ability to work in a team structure," followed by "communication skills" and "problem-solving skills" were the most sought after qualities in new hires (NACE, 2014, 2016). Analyzing the growing library of research on this area, Stevenson determined that "the significance of behavioral competencies in highly technical environments has been amply demonstrated" (Stevenson & Starkweather, 2010).

Employers recognize the need for a mix of technical and non-technical skills. "Often (projects) fail because of a project manager's inability to communicate effectively, work within an organization's culture, motivate the project team, manage stakeholder expectations, understand the business objectives, solve problems effectively, and make clear and knowledgeable decisions" (Belzer, 2001). Employers continue to see employees who cannot accomplish the non-technical aspects of the job. For instance, communication was found to cause 43% of surgical errors (Gawande et al, 2003). Noting that 27% of claims against a health care organization resulted from cognitive and diagnostic errors in the operating room (Wilson, 1999), authors of one study argued, "These findings support the argument that technical skills are necessary, but not sufficient to maintain high levels of performance over time." They further suggest that achieving and maintaining the level of success needed for surgery, "attention needs to be paid to non-technical skills such as team working, leadership, situation awareness, decision making, task management, and communication (Yule et al, 2006). The concern is especially acute in newly hired workers. "Entry level employees might bring knowledge, skills and abilities to the job, but competencies are the result of experience; they are built up over time" (Gokhale, 2005). In 2008, researchers suggested a need to develop training grounds that merge the knowledge of practitioners, seasoned with non-technical skills, with the technical areas best developed in the academia (Berggren & Soderlund, 2008). Put another way, classroom settings are ill-equipped to offer students both the instruction and "seasoning" they need in all of these areas, thus establishing the need for new approaches.

PROGRAM FRAMEWORK

To provide realistic professional seasoning, in 2015 the subject university launched a 1.5 credit required course, entitled The Practice of Consulting. The three-week, immersive course is held during the intersession between spring and fall semesters, after the students have studied business strategy, accounting and finance and professional communications. The objective is to give the entire cohort of graduate engineering students the opportunity to form teams and focus exclusively on the needs of real clients. The school performed a pilot in January 2015, with 27 students participating in team consulting opportunities in Panama, Israel and Baltimore, Maryland. In January 2016, the program was expanded and more formalized, providing 28 students with opportunities to conduct team consulting work with clients in Israel, Honduras, Portugal and Baltimore.

Only students who had successfully completed their first semester in the Master of Science in Engineering Management program, where coursework focused on accounting and finance, innovation and growth strategies and presentation, qualified to participate in this "immersion experience." The course was graded Pass/Fail.

Planning Timeline

Planning for the course begins each year approximately 6–12 months before the students start their work. Course leaders identify potential target employers, including for-profit and not-for-profit organizations, seeking projects, largely related to entrepreneurship and market entry, that can be completed in the necessary time frame and which build on students' fall studies. International projects often require the help of the university's study abroad director to identify and build, since, in addition to the project itself, these "immersions" also seek to provide a strong sense of the host country's business environment and culture.

Working closely with course instructors, organizations chosen to participate in the program develop a one- to two-page explanation of their projects and how they might engage students in the consulting endeavor. In several cases, the consulting engagement involved an existing program that students would refine, extend or support. Early in the MSEM first semester, students receive copies of each summary so they can identify suitable projects.

Program Evolution

In the first year, students simply told program administrators of their interest in a specific opportunity. In year two, students prepared a one-page memorandum in support of the program of their choice, building on a classroom lesson on memo writing. Students submitted these memoranda in late September 2015 for the January 2016 course. Instructors then determined the best mix of students for each project, coordinating students' interests and desires with program logistics. These logistics included the number of students a project could support, travel costs and success in prior courses. Students who undertook overseas opportunities in year two were required to pay a small portion of their travel expense as a means of defraying costs and encouraging a greater commitment to the course. Scholarship funds were available for students needing financial aid to meet this requirement.

Students started their engagement in the first week of January with an overview of the organization, structure, products and services, and goals. The organization and students then discussed goals for the project. These discussions tended to be broader and less defined than the traditional problem/solution approach that these engineering students typically appreciate and favor. Students were forced to identify several important aspects of their project from the onset, including an appropriate team, methods of researching their problem, identification of best solutions, and teamwork within their teams and with their client. In some cases, students attempted to research the solution via secondary sources, rather than explore the range of possibilities that could not be researched in traditional or academic ways. When clients objected to the "academic" solutions, the students realized that they needed to better communicate with their clients and, in the process, practice the very skills that employers seek.

In the first year, the work product – a report, a presentation, accomplishment of a jointly agreed upon goal goal, and/or an reflection on their work – was due during the Spring semester. But for year two, the projects were self-contained within the three-week course period, forcing students to invest heavily in achieving the outcome and overcoming any obstacles in an efficient manner, once again replicating the realities of a work situation.

Unlike nearly every prior academic and work experience, students had to find their way. The traditional problem/solution approach was rarely available because even if a problem was articulated through discussions with the client, students had to determine if the problem the client identified was, in fact, the true problem or if something else actually was the issue. For instance, one group in January 2016 was asked to explore how to expand the effectiveness of endoscopes and were given a possible solution. Their research suggested that the clients' solution would not work as articulated, sending the students out to identify alternative avenues for a solution and communicate this surprising news to the client. This frustrating analytical process is difficult to teach in the classroom, but the immersive consulting project forces students to confront the common workplace reality that the client often cannot recognize the limitations of his or her ideas.

In every case, students working in teams achieved goals providing value to their client. While the effectiveness of these results varied among projects, no organizations expressed dissatisfaction or frustration with the experience, and in most cases, they asked to be considered again for future Practice of Consulting experiences. Two of the organizations that participated in year one participated again in year two.

ASSESSMENT

To assess the success of the program for students, the university conducted a 19-question survey in February 2016. The program attempted to send 27 student participants from 2015 and 28 student participants in 2016 an online survey. (Because some students graduated prior to the issuance of the survey, the appropriate email to reach the students to conduct the online survey was not available.) Exactly 18 students completed the survey. The breakdown of participants includes five students who graduated in Spring 2015, three students who graduated in Fall 2015, four students expected to graduate in Spring 2016 and six students expected to graduate in Fall 2016. Four of the respondents performed their course in the U.S., while the remaining 14 went overseas.

Survey respondents' concentrations within the university's MSEM program included chemical and biomolecular science (2 students), civil (1), computer science (2), communication science (1), environmental systems (1), material sciences (1), mechanical engineering (3), nano/biotech (1), operations research (3), probability and statistics (1) and smart product and device design (2).

Students were asked to evaluate specific aspects of the Practice of Consulting course (Table 1).

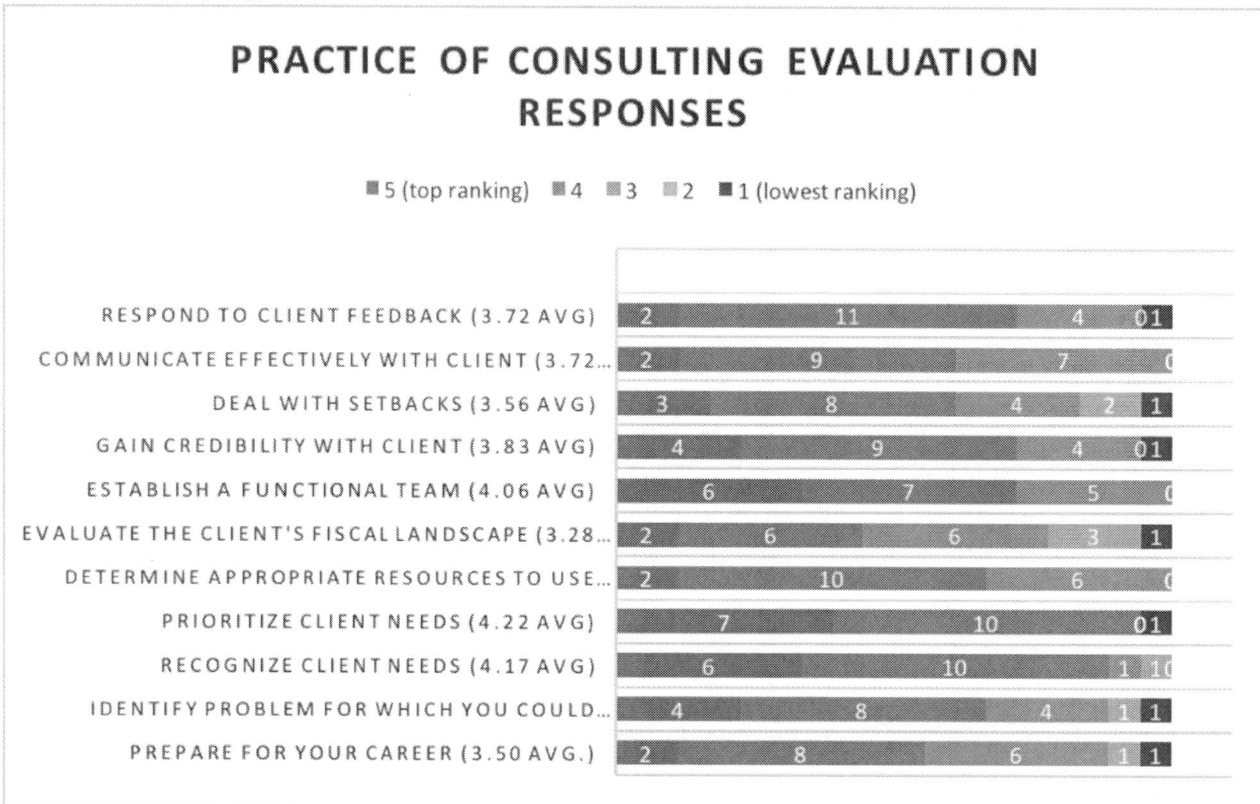

Table 1: Student Reponses to Evaluation

Students also were asked to assess the effectiveness of the course instruction in their first three classes in preparing them for the Art of Consulting course (Table 2).

Given a selection of choices for the prompt, "How would you describe the impact of The Practice of Consulting course? The experience prompted me to:" students responded (when able to select one or more answer):

- Acquire or strengthen a specific skill (6 responses)
- Pursue a field I had not considered before (5 responses)
- Seek a consulting job (2 responses)
- Realize that you preferred more technical engineering (2 responses)
- Another experience to build my story (1 response, written in)

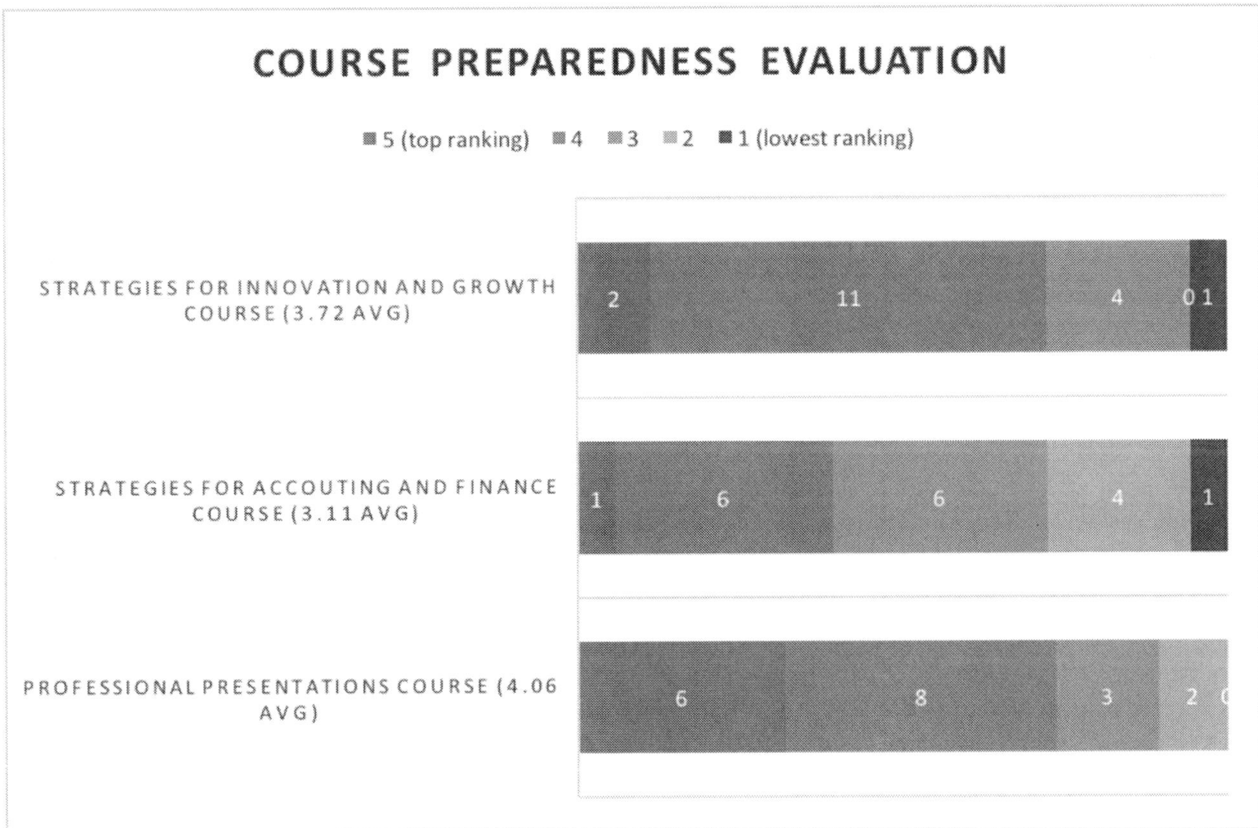

Table 2: Course Preparedness for Practice of Consulting Results

DISCUSSION

The overall results appear favorable. To imitate the real-world nature of the course, students had no clear objectives identified at the beginning of the course, except to accomplish whatever task the client put before them. This vague nature – one engineering students especially find challenging – may contribute to the results shown.

The results suggest several important considerations for this course and others. First, the results may indicate that students may not be aware or able to make a direct connection between what they are learning in the classroom and the non-technical skills employers seek. Given that the subjects of this analysis are engineering students, their recognition of the non-technical skills themselves could vary, as could their ability to assess which ones, if any, were being engaged in specific tasks.

Students provided the best responses to two questions addressing client needs ("recognizing and prioritizing" and "establishing functional teams"). These areas are the easiest to recognize because they are the most concrete. That students found these areas beneficial should come as no surprise. These two areas alone would justify continuing the course, as shifting from the technical aspects of engineering (problem/solution) to the less exact science of determining how to go about a task to meet the needs of a client or employer and to work effectively in teams is of paramount concern and importance in any workplace. Similarly, students' responses to the benefits of a Professional Presentations class on their work bolsters this argument; each team had to deliver a presentation to their client as part of the Practice of Consulting requirements, thus forcing them to apply directly the skills they acquired in the class.

Other results, while still positive, suggest the possibility that the language of the survey instrument or the language used in the classroom is not translating effectively into the workplace situations students face. Additional research on this possibility is warranted.

Surveying students also may be premature, for students may not yet recognize the value of the experience. Being able to provide details about this real-world experience in job interviews could serve to differentiate these students from other graduates. These students would not know or understand this benefit yet, nor would they recognize how using these non-technical skills in the workplace would improve their ability to achieve workplace goals.

CONCLUSION

After two years, this program demonstrates progress toward achieving the goal of greater engagement of students prior to graduation in workplace situations where they can employ both technical and non-technical skills. Using a three-week, immersive approach forces students to act and react to situations at a pace more consistent with what they will face upon graduation. That students often fail to recognize how their instruction has fostered their ability to engage in these real-world situations is worth additional study to determine if students lack an understanding of the specific skills they must employ or if they really do not feel as if their non-technical instruction plays an important role in their preparedness for real workplace situations.

The effectiveness of this Practice of Consulting course in the curriculum of the graduate MSEM program shows promise, as universities continue to seek creative methods for better preparing their students with both technical and non-technical skills employers covet.

REFERENCES

ABET (2015). Criteria for accrediting engineering technology programs. Retrieved March 15, 2016, from http://www.abet.org/wp-content/uploads/2015/10/T001-16-17-ETAC-Criteria-10-16-15.pdf

American Society of Engineering Educators (2014). Fostering 21st century skills in engineering undergraduates. Retrieved March 13, 2016, from https://www.asee.org/file_server/papers/attachment/file/0004/5187/ASEE_2014_Draft_v7.pdf

Belzer, K. (2001). Project management: still more art than science. Retrieved FEbruary 23, 2016 from http://www.pmforum.org/library/papers/2001/ArtthanScience.pdf.

Berggren, C., & Soderlund, J. (2008). Rethinking project management education: social twists and knowledge co-production. *International Journal of Project Management,* 26 (3), 286-295.

Boyatzis, R.E. (1992). The competent manager: a model for effective performance. John Riley and Sons, New York.

Cheng, M., Dainty, A., & Moore, D. (2005). What makes a good project manager? *Human Resource Management Journal*, 15 (1), 25-37.

Dukhan, N., & Hassif, R., (2014). On teaching non-technical skills for the engineers of 2020. QScience Proceedings (World Congress of Engineering Education 2013), 2014, 9.

Galloway, Patricia D. (2007). The 21st century engineer: a proposal for engineering education reform. *Civil Engineering*.

Gawande, A.A., Zinner, M.J., Studdert, D.M., & Brennan, T.A. (2003). Analysis of errors reported by surgeons at three teaching hospitals. *Surgery*, 133, 614–621.

Golden, M. (2016). NSPE advocacy: hard and soft skills. National Society of Professional Engineers. Retrieved March 13, 2016, from http://www.nspe.org/resources/blogs/nspe-blog/nspe-advocacy-hard-and-soft-skills

Gokhale, D. (2005). PM competency mapping. In PMI Global Congress Proceedings, Singapore, February 2005.

Halfhill, T. R., & Nielson, T. M. (2007). Quantifying the "softer side" of management education: an example using teamwork competencies. *Journal of Management Education,* 31(1), 64-80.

Law, S. L., Wong, C. S., & Song, L. J. (2004). The construct and criterion validity of emotional intelligence and its potential utility for management studies. *Journal of Applied Psychology,* 89(3), 483-496.

McKinsey & Company (2012). Education to employment: Designing a system that works. Retrieved September 1, 2015, from http://mckinseyonsociety.com/downloads/reports/Education/Education-to-Employment_FINAL.pdf.

Muzio, E., Fisher, D. J., Thomas, E. R., & Peters, V. (2007). Soft skills quantification (SSQ) for project manager competencies. *Project Management Journal,* 38(2), 30-38.

NACE - National Association of Colleges and Employers. (2014) *Job outlook 2015.* Retrieved November 20, 2014, from https://www.naceweb.org/s11122014/job-outlook-skills-qualities-employers-want.aspx?land-surv-lp-2-spot-joskz-11142014

NACE – National Association of Colleges and Employers (2016). *Job outlook 2017.* Retrieved March 15, 2016, from http://www.naceweb.org/about-us/press/2016/verbal-communication-most-important-candidate-skill.aspx

Palmer, B., Terenzini, P., McKenna, A., Harper, B., & Merson, D. (2011). Design context: where do the engineers of 2020 learn this skill? Proceedings, ASEE Annual Conference and Exposition, Vancouver, BC, Canada, June 26-29, 2011.

Pant, I., & Baroudi, B. (2008). Project management education: the human skills imperative. *International Journal of Project Management,* 26(2), 124-128.

Petter, S., & Randolph, A. B. (2009). Developing soft skills to manage user expectations in IT projects: knowledge reuse among IT project managers. *Project Management Journal,* 40(4), 45-59.

Porterfield, T., Li, X., Johnson, Q., Nesterkin, D., & Graham, R. (2015). Education and assessment of soft skills in business schools: A case study. Decision Sciences Institute 2015 annual meeting, presented November, 22, 2015.

Smith, R. (2015). The best entrepreneurs have this one quality in common. *Fortune*, November 17, 2015. Retrieved March 15, 2016, from http://fortune.com/2015/11/17/best-entrepreneurs-one-common-quality/

Stevenson, D.H. & Starkweather, J. (2010). PM critical competency index: IT execs prefer soft skills. *International Journal of Project Management.* 28(7), 663-671.

Sukhoo, A., Barnard, A., Eloff, M. M., Van der Poll, J. A., & Motah, M. (2005). Accommodating soft skills in software project management. *Issues in Informing Science and Information Technology, 2,* 691–703.

Wateridge, J. (1997). Training for IS/IT project management yes: a way forward. International Journal of Project Management, 15 (5), 283-288.

Wilson, J. (1999). A practical guide to risk management in surgery: developing and planning. Health Care Risk Resources International—Royal College of Surgeons symposium.

Wirth, I. (1992). Project-management education: current issues and future trends. *International Journal of Project Management* 10 (1), 49-54.

Woodruffe, C (1991). Competent by any other name. Personnel Management 12 (3), 38-43.

Yule, S., Flin, R., Paterson-Brown, S., & Maran, N. (2006) Non-technical skills for surgeons in the operating room: A review of the literature. *Surgery*, 139 (2), 140-149.

Decision Sciences Institute

Open Services Innovation: Identifying Linkages between Knowledge Sourcing and Firm Performance

(Full Paper Submission)

Dr. Sarah Schafer
The University of Wisconsin Oshkosh
schafers@uwosh.edu

Dr. Seth Powless
Earlham College
powlese@earlham.edu

ABSTRACT

Few studies exist examining the effects of open services innovation through service-oriented lenses. Using Chesbrough's approach to studying open services innovation, this formative work empirically evaluates firm performance based on combining products and/or processes with services to gain a competitive advantage. Using Knowledge-based firm perspective (KBV), as a conceptual framework, a definition of open services innovation is proposed for this context. Research hypotheses are introduced for potential studies of the three main tenants: diversity of knowledge sourcing, external share, and firm performance. This paper serves as a potential catalyst for further research studies that can promote value to a firm through services foci.

KEYWORDS: Services Innovation, KBV, Knowledge Sourcing

CASE STUDY

In the late 1990's, Apple began what was to become a horizontal product strategy aimed at cross-integration. First emphasizing hardware and software offerings, this integration came to include service offerings through the early and late 2000's. This services integration came to exemplify open services innovation because of the seamless relationships within Apple's product ecosystem. Starting with desktops and laptops, product offerings came to include music devices, mobile computing, tablets, streaming music software, mobile phones, and wearable technologies. Regardless of the specific product line, Apple's services are universal within the Apple ecosystem and as a result, Apple receives a deservedly strong reputation for service. Within this environment lies an open innovation where applications can be developed and shared between computing professionals and end-users. This open services innovation network represents a shared model of open-services, cross-segment governance that the likes of Amazon, Google, and Facebook seek to emulate, often with mixed results.

INTRODUCTION

In today's increasingly fast paced innovative and global environment, services are quickly becoming an integral component to value co-creation. Services represent the majority of value added economic activity in advanced economies. According to the Organization for Economic Cooperation and Development (OECD), services account for approximately 80% of economic activity in the U.S., and over 60% of economic activity in 35 of the top 40 economies internationally (Chesbrough 2011, Mention 2011). At the same time, the breadth of global knowledge for process and product innovations is increasing. This is due in large part to manufacturing industries moving to areas with lower costs which leads to shorter product life spans and commoditization of manufactured goods. Similar to Chesbrough's (2011) thoughts, Mention (2011) states the "internal research and development does not guarantee anymore a sustainable competitive advantage to the firm due to the increased mobility of the knowledge workers and the subsequent inability of the firm to keep control over critical intangible resources," (p. 45). Chesbrough (2011) describes this as an innovation treadmill: those companies that cannot keep up fall off. The system is not sustainable; there is no end and no place to rest, thus posing a major challenge for advanced economies in particular. A key objective to this end is through open service innovation. Whereas, "services-based business models are built around long term customer relationships and recurring revenues. Such business models are the answer to the product-based commodity trap that afflicts so many companies," (Wladawsky-Berger 2011). While traditional business models set in product- and manufacturing-based thinking are based on a closed system that constructs barriers to competition (Chesbrough 2011, Chesbrough and Appleyard 2007), open innovation models exist in a realm where knowledge and technology is exchanged within the wider environment of external organizations (Colombo et al. 2011). By combining these concepts the open services innovation strategy becomes clearer.

In this environment, businesses can rely on platform strategies to bundle their products with services to gain a competitive advantage. An example of using platforms to integrate products and services include Apple's line of products (IPhone, ITouch, IPad) to integrate products with services using open innovation through application development from a variety of sources that are available to customers through their devices. Amazon is another example of a company using a platform approach to integrate open service innovation. The Amazon platform is available to a variety of online sellers to tap into.

As advanced economies become more oriented toward services, products become less important. This leads to businesses having an extrinsic desire to set strategies in service oriented ways. In spite of this shift to a service-oriented focus and its importance, there is little impactful research on service innovation (Chesbrough 2011). Because of this shift coupled with a paucity of research in the field, there is certainly an imperative to further this field through more contemporary research studies (Chesbrough 2011, Love et al. 2011, Van de Vrande 2009).

Set within a framework of knowledge-based theory and further linked to a firm's absorptive capacity, this paper proposes an examination of the effects of firm performance through the use of an open service innovation model. The main idea in open innovation is to exchange knowledge within a wider environment in order to gain a competitive advantage; the main research question explored here is whether firms using an open service innovation strategy in practice have greater overall firm performance than comparable firms that do not. Consequently, the constructs explored here are the *diversity of knowledge sourcing*, *external share*, and *firm performance.* In the last decade there has been an abundance of research on the new paradigm in open innovation, though few empirical studies have been presented in this area. Particularly in services, and results are mixed from those that have. When moving the concept of open innovation toward open service innovation, the few studies in the area have applied open innovation concepts to firms in the business services sector (e.g. Love et al. 2011, Colombo et al. 2011) rather than applying the service model bundle concept suggested by Chesbrough (2011). The research framework in this paper will attempt to extend the generalizability of open innovation into the service realm for any business sector as suggested by current services innovation researchers.

THEORETICAL BACKGROUND

Following Lin (2011) this research is anchored in the knowledge based view (KBV) theory. Some previous studies on open innovation are rooted in the resourced based view (RBV). Due to the nature of open innovation revolving around the exchange of knowledge and the premise that knowledge based view is an outgrowth from RBV (Grant 1997, Scarbrough 1998) thus, embedding this work in KBV is logical. Further adding the dimension of absorptive capacity provides a sound theoretical background for this research.

Kogut and Zander, pioneers in KBV, began the conversation: "the central competitive dimension of what firms know how to do is to create and transfer knowledge efficiently within an organizational context," (1992, p. 384) to add value to the firm. Grant (1997) summarizes the basic assumptions of KBV as paraphrased below;

- Knowledge is seen as the most important "productive resource in terms of its contribution to value added and its strategic significance," (Grant 1997, p. 451);
- Transferability varies between different types of knowledge, mainly between tacit and explicit knowledge;
- Individuals are the creators and receivers of knowledge, various processes and procedures require different breadths and depths of knowledge; and
- Knowledge is subject to economies of scale and scope.

The final assumption is also prevalent in Chesbrough's (2011b) description of the benefits of open service innovation. "KBV theorists suggest that organizational performance ultimately reflects the underlying knowledge-base of the firm," (Scarbrough 1998 p. 192) thus, the organization is viewed as a vehicle for the creation, transformation and application of knowledge (Scarbrough 1998). This in combination with absorptive capacity provides a solid theoretical foundation for this work.

Cohen and Levinthal (1990) discuss the importance of outside sources of knowledge and how external sources are often critical to the innovation process in organizations. They further cite March and Simon's (1958) suggestion that "most innovations result from borrowing rather than invention," (Cohen and Levinthal 1990, p. 128) an observation that "is supported by extensive research on the sources of innovation (e.g., Mueller, 1962; Hamberg, 1963; Myers and Marquis, 1969; Johnston and Gibbons, 1975; von Hippel, 1988)," (Cohen and Levinthal 1990, p. 128). Absorptive capacity is a firm's ability to use prior knowledge to recognize valuable new knowledge, to assimilate that knowledge and apply it in marketable ways (Cohen and Levinthal 1990). In the context of this research, KBV signifies the importance of knowledge as a firm resource while absorptive capacity is the firm's ability or capability of turning that knowledge into profitable ventures. The concept of open innovation builds on this platform.

In defining openness, Chesbrough (2003) states that "open innovation is a paradigm that assumes that firms can and should use external ideas as well as internal ideas, and internal and external paths to market, as firms look to advance their technology," (p. XXIV). This notion is further clarified when Chesbrough et al. (2006) argue that open innovation is "the use of purposive inflows and outflows of knowledge to accelerate internal innovation, and expand the markets for external use of innovation, respectively," (p. 2). Both of these definitions are widely cited for open innovation in the literature (Gassman et al. 2010, Dahlander and Gann 2010, Han et al. 2012, Lichtenthaler 2011, Colombo et al. 2011). Colombo et al. (2011) take these ideas and state them eloquently as such;

[Open innovation] can be described as an emerging innovation management paradigm which suggests that firms should strategically commit themselves to make the most out of their knowledge abundant external environment, with the aim to improve innovation performance

and, ultimately, create economic value. Open Innovation is therefore all about exchanging knowledge and technologies with a wide population of external organizations, such as Universities, clients, competitors, firms from other industries, individuals, NPD [new product development] service providers, suppliers, (p. 167).

Two main areas of open service innovation are discernable from the literature. The first deals with open innovation directly in service sectors (e.g. Love et al. 2011, Colombo et al. 2011) while the second considers open innovation as a platform approach in bundling products with services to gain a competitive advantage (Chesbrough et al. 2011). The few studies in the area have applied open innovation concepts to firms in the business services sector (e.g. Love et al. 2011, Colombo et al. 2011) rather than applying the service model concept as suggested by Chesbrough for any business sector. Chesbrough (2011a) provides four key concepts for open service innovation, summarized as follows;

1. Think of any business as a service in order to gain new growth,
2. Co-create with customers/suppliers/other external organizations,
3. Open innovation specializations with customers/suppliers, and
4. "Effective services innovation requires new business models that profit from internal innovation initiatives and stimulate external innovation activities that add to the value of their own business."

While there is no precise definition in the literature of open service innovation, the key concepts provided by Chesbrough in combination with the above definitions for open innovation provide a working framework: open services innovation is defined here as the evolution of business models to use a service oriented approach to open channels of knowledge exchange in order to propagate any specialized internal or external innovation to bundle products, processes and services that will add value to the firm. Using the Apple horizontal business model, bundling products or processes with services represents an approach that is generalizable to multiple businesses and a wide array of segments.

HYPOTHESIS DEVELOPMENT

Based on the combination of a variety of sources (*i.e.* Neyer et al. 2009, Gumusluoglu and Ilsev 2009, Love et al. 2011, Mention 2011, and Lichtenthaler 2012) the first construct is *diversity of knowledge sourcing* and is defined as the sources of knowledge a firm uses for innovative service ideas. This construct is split into two categories, internal and external. Internal sources are those innovative service ideas that originate within the firm while external sources are those innovative service ideas that originate from outside the firm (*e.g.* suppliers, customers, and partners). Adapting constructs from Love et al. (2011) and applying concepts from Chesbrough and Crowther (2006), the next construct is *external share*. It is defined as the share of new innovative service ideas that originated from external sources. The idea being that firms engaged in a more diverse knowledge portfolio will result in a higher share of applicable innovative service ideas that originated from external sources. Following Love et al. (2011) the *external share* (EX_i) can be derived from an equation similar to the following:

$$EX_i = \beta_0 + \beta_1 IN_i + \beta_2 DS_i + \beta_3 RD_i + \beta_4 EXP_i + \varepsilon_i \quad (1)$$

Where IN_i represents firm characteristics of internal knowledge resources, DS_i is internal design spending, RD_i is internal R&D spending, and EXP_i is the firm's exploratory relationships (the greater the firm's external connectivity the more likely new innovative ideas will be generated from external sources) (Love et al. 2011).

Construct	Construct Definition	Source
Diversity of knowledge sourcing	*Sources of knowledge the firm uses for innovative service ideas.* *Internal* – originates within the firm *External* – originates outside the firm (e.g. suppliers, customers, partners)	Based on a combination of Neyer et al. 2009, Gumusluoglu and Ilsev 2009, Love et al. 2011, Mention 2011, and Lichtenthaler 2012
External Share	*Share of new innovative service ideas from external sources*	Love et al. 2011, and Chesbrough and Crowther 2006
Firm Performance	*Sales growth; profitability; new product success; share of sales attributed to new products; market share; and return on investment (ROI) or internal rate of return (IRR)*	Lin 2011, Love et al. 2011, and Ledwith 2009 (from Langerak et al. 2004, and Slater and Narver 1994)

Table 1.0 – Constructs, definitions, and sources

Pena (2002) argues that knowledge-based firms should mix internal core competencies with external sources because firms that emphasize knowledge diversity have access to a wider range of knowledge bases from these inter-firm relationships (cited by Lin 2011). Expanding on this Lin (2011) suggests that firms with access to diversified knowledge bases can use these internal and external resources to build innovative capabilities. By augmenting the concept of open service innovation – particularly the notion of exchanging knowledge with the external environment – with further sources from the literature the premise is set and hypothesis one is posited as follows;

- H1: Firms with a greater diversity of knowledge sourcing will have a greater number of active service innovations from external sources.

The ultimate goal of a firm is earnings, thus the final construct presented here is *firm performance*. Firms engage in the activities they undertake in order to earn money for their owners and stockholders. According to Lin et al. (2011) the "pursuit of earnings is the primary reason that the companies exist," (p. 337). Any strategy a firm follows is done for the purpose of adding value. As such, knowledge diversity has been recognized as a factor that affects firm performance, however empirical results are inconclusive on the direct relationship between diversity of knowledge and firm performance (i.e. Delios and Beamish 1999) (Lin et al. 2011). This research seeks to test the diversity of knowledge indirectly through the *external share* construct. In related areas, Cohen and Levinthal (1990) argue that increasing technology diversity could improve firm performance. Similarly, results from Gemba and Kodama (2001) show that a diversified technology strategy contributes to firm profitability. Still other studies have reported that an announcement alone of increased R&D expenditures is positively related to an increase in share price (Lin et al. 2011).

- H2: Firms with a greater number of active service innovations from external sources will have higher firm performance.

Figure 1.0 Open Service Innovation Measurement Model

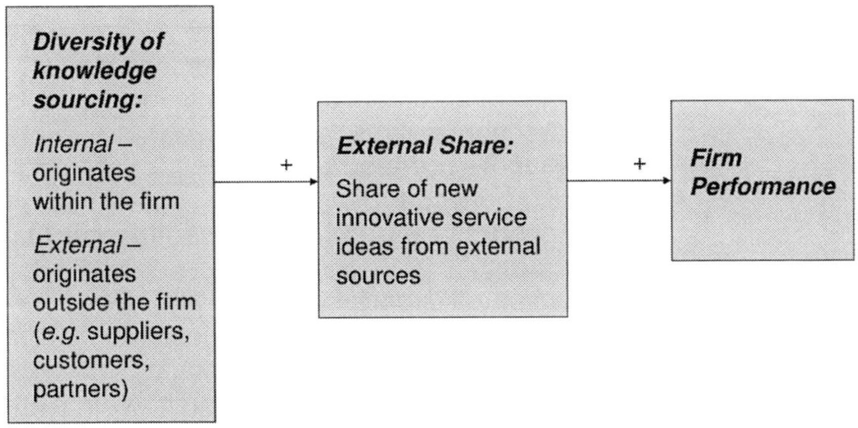

MEASUREMENT ITEMS

To measure the *Diversity of Knowledge Sourcing* and *External Share* constructs a combination of items from the Business Research Development and Innovation Survey (BRDIS) administered by the U.S. Census Bureau and National Science Foundation and items from the U.K. Innovation Index Survey following Love et al. (2011) will be adapted for this research. Disaggregated data from the BRDIS survey is not publicly available thus the items will be formulated into questionnaire format and distributed to a large sample of both service and non-service firms. The first construct is divided into two parts with the intent of isolating innovative service ideas from external sources. A preliminary list of items is presented below (the full list is available in the appendix).

According to Lin (2011) "pursuit of earnings is the primary reason that the companies exist, this measure is considered as one of the most important measures of a firm's performance," (p. 337). Firm performance will be measured by a number of variables to allow for a higher level of understanding of the nature of the relationship between *External Share* and *Firm Performance.* Intended measures include sales growth; profitability; new product success; share of sales attributed to new products; market share; and return on investment (ROI) or internal rate of return (IRR) adapted from the literature (Lin 2011, Love et al. 2011, and Ledwith 2009 [from Langerak et al. 2004, and Slater and Narver 1994]).

Items from UK Innovation Index Survey:
Service ideas from outside the firm (%)
Innovator in service or business model (0/1)
Innovative percentage of sales (% sales)
Diversity of innovation activity (%)
Sales growth (per annum, %age)
Input and process indicators
R&D intensity (% sales)
Design intensity (% sales)
Team working index (%)
Customer interaction index (%)
IP protection index (%)
Firm size (employment)
Firm and market characteristics
Firm age (years)
Single site Firm (% respondents)
Externally owned firm (% respondents)
Exporting firm (% respondents)
Number of competitors (number)
Workforce with degree (% respondents)
Multi-functional working
For sourcing knowledge (% respondents)
For knowledge transformation (% respondents)
For exploiting innovation (% respondents)
Public support
For sourcing knowledge (% respondents)
For knowledge transformation (% respondents)
For exploiting innovation (% respondents)
Exploratory linkages
Customers (% respondents)
Suppliers (% respondents)
Competitors (% respondents)
Consultants (% respondents)
Universities (% respondents)
Public research (% respondents)
Trade associations (% respondents)
Commercial labs (% respondents)
Exploitative linkages
Suppliers (% respondents)
Competitors (% respondents)
Market research companies (% respondents)
Advertising agencies (% respondents)
Professional associations (% respondents)
(From Love et al. 2011)

Items from BRDIS – NSF, U.S. Census
Financial measures of R&D activity
Company R&D expense
- By line of business/business segment
- By type of expense (wages, materials, etc.)
- Outsourced R&D by sector (universities, other companies, etc.)

Similar detail for R&D the company may perform for others under grants, contracts, or other agreements
Measures related to R&D employment
R&D headcount
Measures related to R&D management and strategy
Estimated financial return on R&D
Share of R&D involving science or technology new to the company and/or market
Share of R&D spent on research vs. development
Counts of R&D projects
- Total number of active projects
- Number of projects started in a given year
- Number of projects moved from R&D to production/marketing in a given year

Share of R&D devoted to specific application areas such as health, defense, energy, and transportation
Share of R&D involving specific types of science or technology such as biotechnology, nanotechnology, software, or social sciences
Share of R&D devoted to partnerships, by type or partner organization (academia, government agencies, other companies)
Measures related to intellectual property (IP) and technology transfer
Patent-related data
- Number of patents owned or controlled
- Number of patents applied for and issued in a given year
- Percent of discoveries that the company attempted to patent?

Did the company participate in specific technology transfer activities?
Information about licensing of IP (mainly counts of agreements)
Number of collaborative R&D agreements the company is a party to and who were the partners (universities, suppliers, federal agencies, etc.)

METHODS

While there are multiple approaches to this research study, several steps for the methodology are proposed: first is to demonstrate construct validity. While initially content validity is established through the literature review, convergent and discriminant validity will be assessed after the data collection process. Next, to ensure reliability of the measurement items; the preliminary items will be reviewed with at least one academician and one practitioner to validate the 'borrowed' items for this study. Any adjustments can be made prior to construction of the initial survey. A sample survey will be distributed to a small group of firms for feedback. Because of the nature of this open service innovation study, examining service aspects of all firm types, a final survey will be distributed to a random sample of publicly traded firms from a variety of NAICS codes.

The distribution data set will be generated from an available business data set. Compustat data will be used to obtain additional financial statement data for firm performance variables. The two data sets will be sorted and matched by company name, using only matched records in the final list. Links to the survey will be emailed to respondents as a cost effective and efficient modern means of delivery and data collection. In the meantime, a web-based data collection system will be designed to automatically capture and code respondents' feedback in a database management system (DBMS) for use in the statistical analysis. After a valid time period a follow-up reminder email will be sent urging participation in the survey.

Standard methods will be employed to demonstrate reliability of the dataset and constructs. T-tests for non-response bias will be conducted on early and late responders. Factor analysis and Cronbach's Alpha will be used to assess discriminant and convergent validity respectively. To test the hypotheses an index of the diversity of a firm's knowledge portfolio at a natural breakpoint value will be identified to categorize knowledge diversity of firms between two groups, firms that innovate based on a diverse portfolio of knowledge with external and internal sources and firms that innovate in a more closed system from mainly internal sources. A regression analysis will be performed on the firms with more diverse knowledge sourcing based on the equation presented in section three. Final tests will be performed on firm performance to evaluate if there is a significant difference in firm performance measures between 'closed' system firms and 'open' system firms with high levels of *External Share* knowledge sourcing for innovative services.

EXPECTED RESULTS AND CONTRIBUTIONS

Based on the literature review and concepts that apply to 'openness' in general and to open services innovation in particular, it is expected that firms with a greater diversity of knowledge from internal and external sources will have a higher number of service innovations from external sources. In turn, it is expected that because these firms are utilizing knowledge resources from a wider pool and gaining economies of scale and scope with it that these firms will have higher overall firm performance than firms that do not engage in open service innovation practices.

As a result, findings from this research are expected to contribute to the theoretical value of open service innovation in two ways. First, no other study in the open services innovation area is known to look at all businesses through a service lens and to evaluate the impact of an open service innovation approach by utilizing external knowledge sources to bundle products and/or processes with services to add value to the firm. Second, this is the first known work to propose a clear definition for open service innovation. Should the results stand as expected this proposed research will add credibility to the concept through further generalization of empirical results. Finally, this research is expected to contribute to managerial significance by further explaining the concept of open service innovation in order for managers to put it into practice.

In addition, by providing empirical evidence that firms engaged in this type of strategy will have overall higher performance will help managers understand the importance of putting open service innovation into practice in their firm.

CONCLUSION

There is little argument that platform strategies undertaken by the likes of Apple, Amazon, and Google represent a product-services bundle that allows for a competitive advantage. As advanced economies continue to evolve with more orientation towards services, products become a less important catalyst for innovation unless they have a service component built in to the business model. In spite of this paradigm shift within major business ecosystems, there is little research on the services innovation side of this model. This research provides not just a narrative for the importance of the topic, but allows for additional research to be undertaken that will contribute to the limited existing body of research begun by Chesbrough. This research is not just endemic to consumer technologies, but also to transportation technology with respect to application, 3PL platforms, and both turnkey and design-and-build technologies.

References

Chesbrough, Henry, Open Services Innovation: Rethinking Your Business to Grow and Compete in a New Era (San Francisco: Jossey-Bass, 2011a), Kindle edition.

Chesbrough, H. & Eucher. J. (2011b). Open services innovation: an interview with Henry Chesbrough. Research Technology Management, (Mar-Apr): 12-17.

Chesbrough H. & Appleyard, M. (2007). Open innovation and strategy. *California Management Review*, 50(1): 57-76.

Chesbrough, H. & Crowther, A. (2006). Beyond high tech: early adopters of open innovation in other industries. R&D Management, 36(3): 229-236.

Cohen, W. & Levinthal, D. (1990). Absorptive capacity: a new perspective on learning and innovation. *Administrative Science Quarterly*, 35: 128-152.

Colombo, G., Dell'Era, C. & Frattini, F. (2011). New product development (NPD): service suppliers in open innovation practices: processes and organization for knowledge exchange and integration. *International Journal of Innovation Management*, 15(1): 165-204.

Dahlander, L. & Gann, D. (2010). How open is innovation? *Research Policy*, 39: 699-709.

Delios, A., & Beamish, P. (1999). Geographic scope, product diversification, and the corporate performance of Japanese firms. *Strategic Management Journal,* 20(8): 711–727.

Gassman, O., E. Enkel, & Chesbrough, H. (2010). The future of open innovation. *R&D Management*, 40(3): 213-221.

Gemba, K. & Kodama, F. (2001). Diversification dynamics of the Japanese industry. *Research Policy,* 30(8): 1165–1184.

Grant, R. (1997). The Knowledge-based View of the Firm: Implications for Management Practice. *Long range Planning*, 30(3): 450-454.

Gumusluoglu, L. & Ilsev, A. (2009). Transformational Leadership and Organizational Innovation: The Roles of Internal and External Support for Innovation. *Journal of Production Innovation Management*, 26: 264–277.

Han, W., Oh, W., Im, K., Chang, R., Oh, H. & Pinsonneault, A. (2012). Value cocreation and wealth spillover in open innovation alliances. *MIS Quarterly,* 36(1): 291-315.

Kogut, B. & Zander, U. (1992). Knowledge of the firm, combinative capabilities, and the replication of technology. *Organization Science*, 3(3): 383-397.

Ledwith, A. & O'Dwyer, M. (2009). Market Orientation, NPD Performance, and Organizational Performance in Small Firms. *Journal of Production Innovation Management*, 26: 652–661.

Lichtenthaler, U. (2011). Open innovation: past research, current debates, future directions. *Academy of Management Perspectives*, (Feb):75-93.

Lin, B. (2011). Knowledge Diversity as a Moderator: Inter-firm Relationships, R&D Investment and Absorptive Capacity. *Technology Analysis & Strategic Management,* 23(3): 331-343.

Love, J., Roper, S. & Bryson, J. (2011). Openness, Knowledge, Innovation and Growth in UK Business Services. *Research Policy*, 40: 1438-1452.

Mention, A. (2011). Co-operation and co-opetition as open innovation practices in the service sector: Which influence on innovation novelty? *Technovation*, 31: 44-53.

Neyer, A., Bullinger, A. & Moeslein, K. (2009). Integrating inside and outside innovators: a sociotechnical systems perspective. *R&D Management,* 39(4): 410-419.

Scarbrough, H. (1998). BPR and the Knowledge-based View of the Firm. *Knowledge and process management*, 5(3): 192-200.

Van de Vrande, V., de Jong, J., Vanhaverbeke, W., & de Rochemont, M. (2009). Open innovation in SMEs: Trends, motives and management challenges. *Technovation*, 29: 423–437.

Wladawsky-Berger, I. (2011). Open services innovation. Accessed at: http://blog.irvingwb.com/blog/2011/12/open-services-innovation.html on April 18, 2012.

DECISION SCIENCES INSTITUTE

Optimal Location of Repair Stations in a Garments Production Line

Md Shahriar Jahan Hossain
Louisiana State University
Email: msjhossain1@gmail.com

Bhaba R. Sarker
Louisiana State University
Email: bsarker@lsu.edu

ABSTRACT

In a manufacturing system the defective items detected at the inspection station, are generally scrapped or repaired at regular defect-creating workstation or at a dedicated repair station off the line. In this research a sewing line with an inspection station located at the end, is considered to make decisions concerning these issues. A unit cost function is developed for alternative decisions on each type of defect. To minimize the unit production cost, a fractional mixed integer nonlinear programming (MINLP) problem is formulated and solved optimally. The test problem is reflective of some sewing lines of a readymade garments industry.

KEYWORDS: Rework/repair, Defect, Fractional programming, Optimization, Garments production.

INTRODUCTION

Inspection and repair are two important parts of quality control. In industries quality inspections are done in order to identify nonconformities. Defective items are often sent back to the workstation where the defect occurs. This common repair procedure sometimes reduces line efficiency. At the same time if defective items are repaired at a dedicated repair station it adds a fixed cost for that repair station. On the other hand all defective items are not repairable; some defective items are scrapped incurring waste of material and other related costs. Therefore, it is essential to take an optimal decision on defective items whether they should be scrapped, or repaired at regular on-line workstation(s) or at dedicated off-line repair-station(s) in order to ensure minimum cost of production per unit and optimum number of off-line repair-stations to enhance throughput rate.

According to American Apparel and Footwear Association (AAFA, 2012), apparel and textile industries are the world's third largest industry sector after auto industries, and are good examples of imperfect serial production lines. Due to high labor cost most low-cost garments in America, Australia or European countries are imported from the countries like China, India, Bangladesh or Vietnam where human labor is available with comparatively low cost. Garments quality is a vital factor to capture a new market.

Lot of works have been done to improve the productivity, line efficiency of apparel industries and eventually to reduce the cost of production. Islam et al. (2014) presented a case study for obtaining an optimal layout design in an apparel industry by appropriate line balancing. On the other hand, Bahadir (2011) discussed about assembly line balancing by simulation. Several research are found on optimizing quality inspection and repair for reducing cost of quality or increasing the net profit. Raviv (2013) presented an algorithm for maximizing the expected profit from an unreliable serial production line in which nonconforming items are sent back for repair after going through the inspection stations. None of these study discusses about offline repair facilities for defective items.

Building a suitable framework for taking operational decision on dedicated repair stations still requires extensive research as this involves conflicting objectives. Considering this fact this research focuses in developing a model to minimize the unit cost of production to determine suitable number and location of dedicated off-line repair stations. In order to deal with this objective, following steps are performed in this research:

(a) To determine production cost per unit as a function of cycle time, proportion of defects, fixed and variable cost, which are eventually dependent on the location of off-line repair stations.
(b) To find the optimum number and location of off-line repair station(s) that minimizes the production cost per unit.

The outcomes of this research provide an easily executable framework to determine the requirement of repair facilities for dealing with non-conforming items which are identified at the stage of quality inspection in the sewing line.

PROBLEM DESCRIPTION

Assume a garments production line with *N* sewing stations arranged sequentially to perform a sequence of operations needed to complete a garments product. Each workstation performs different type of operations, completing at least one operation at that station. A product is classified as defective corresponding to the major source (workstation) of defect. An inspection station is located at the end of the line. This inspection station identifies and separates non-conforming items based on the type and origin of the defect(s). Proportion of each type of defective items are estimated from historical experiences. Some workstation may not produce any defects at all and the probability of defect for that workstation is assumed to be zero. If defective items are repaired then number of conforming items increases. Again if the defective items are sent back to the regular on-line sewing station for repair, the regular production may be hampered. The problem thus is to decide whether the defective item should be sent back to original sewing station for repair or there should be a dedicated repair-station so that regular production is not interrupted, or the defective garments should be scrapped. During making this corrective decision, production cost should be kept at a minimum level. The problem described here is a specific situation which can be formulated based on some assumptions:

(a) A balanced garments production line with no parallel workstation is considered.
(b) An inspection station is located at the end of the line with negligible inspection error.
(c) Any particular defective item does not hold multiple types of nonconformity at a time.
(d) Any kind of defects can be repaired and repaired items assumed to be conforming products.
(e) Repair cost is constant for a particular defect repaired at a particular workstation.
(f) Scrapped items are valueless.
(g) There is no space limitation in the shop floor.

MODEL FORMULATION

Before developing the model some notations for system parameters, variables and performance measures are needed to be defined. All notations are defined in the following sub-sections.

System Parameters

C^F = Fixed cost for the sewing line ($/hour), C_k^F = Fixed cost for regular workstation k ($/hour), C_k^f = Fixed cost added for a dedicated off-line repair station for operation k ($/hour), c = Variable cost of sewing a finished item if no item is repaired ($/unit), c_k^d = Variable cost of repairing at dedicated off-line repair station k ($/unit), c_k^r = Variable cost of repairing at regular on-line workstation k ($/unit), N = Total number of workstations, p_k =Proportion of defectives of at workstation k , t_k^P = Processing time of operation at regular workstation k (hours), t_k^R = Repair time of defective item at regular workstation k (hours) and T = Cycle time when no repair work is done (hours).

Intermediate Variables

T_k^R = Total repair time of an item at regular workstation k (hours), T_{eff} = Effective cycle time when repair works are done (hours), and TC = Total cost ($/hour).

Variables and Performance Measures

u = Unit cost ($/unit), x_k = (0,1), the number of dedicated off-line repair stations for operation k and y_k = 0-1 binary variable indicting decision on scrapping (0) or repair (1) for a defect produced at workstation k .

Now, the production cost per unit of good item has to be reduced, which is the prime objective of this research. Thus the optimization problem can be formulated as fractional mixed-integer nonlinear program as written below.

Problem Z_{MINLP}^f

$$Min\ u = \left\{ \left(C^F + \sum_{k=1}^{N} C_k^f x_k \right) T_{eff} + c + \sum_{k=1}^{N} c_k^d p_k x_k + \sum_{k=1}^{N} c_k^r p_k y_k \left(1 - x_k\right) \right\} \Big/ \left(1 - \sum_{k=1}^{N} p_k + \sum_{k=1}^{N} p_k y_k \right) \quad (1)$$

Subject to $(\forall\, k = 1,2,...,N)$

$$x_k - y_k \leq 0 \quad (1a)$$

$$T_{eff} - \left(t_k^P + p_k t_k^R\right) y_k \left(1 - x_k\right) \geq 0 \quad (1b)$$

$$T_{eff} \geq T, x_k \in \{0,1\}, y_k \in \{0,1\} \quad (1c)$$

Problem Z^{f}_{MINLP} is a fractional mixed-integer nonlinear programming problem (MINLP) for which the solution is not immediate. Since the current problem Z^{f}_{MINLP} cannot fit to an existing problem, a series of transformations as amenable to the requirement is done here (Li, 1994; Chang, 2001; Hossain & Sarker, 2016) to achieve the solution goal. After several transformation and letting $w^a = \left[\left(1-\sum_{k=1}^{N} p_k\right)+\sum_{k=1}^{N} p_k y_k\right]^{-1}$, $T_{eff} w^a = w^b$, $x_k w^b = w_k^c$, $x_k w^a = w_k^d$, $y_k w^a = w_k^e$ and $x_k y_k w^a = w_k^f$ Problem Z^{f}_{MINLP} is transformed to a mixed-integer linear programming problem (MILP) as

Problem Z_{MILP}:

$$Min \ \ u = cw^a + C^F w^b + \sum_{k=1}^{N} C_k^f w_k^c + \sum_{k=1}^{N} c_k^d p_k w_k^d + \sum_{k=1}^{N} c_k^r p_k w_k^e - \sum_{k=1}^{N} c_k^r p_k w^f \qquad (2)$$

Subject to $\left(1-\sum_{k=1}^{N} p_k\right) w^a + \sum_{k=1}^{N} p_k w_k^e = 1$ (2a)

and $\forall k = 1,2,...,N$:

$x_k - y_k \le 0$ (2b)

$w^b - t_k w_k^e + t_k w_k^f \ge 0$ (2c)

$Tw^a - w^b \le 0$ (2d)

$w^b + (x_k - 1)M \le w_k^c \le w^b + (1 - x_k)M$ and $0 \le w_k^c \le Mx_k$ (2e)

$w^a + (x_k - 1)M \le w_k^d \le w^a + (1 - x_k)M$ and $0 \le w_k^d \le Mx_k$ (2f)

$w^a + (y_k - 1)M \le w_k^e \le w^a + (1 - y_k)M$ and $0 \le w_k^e \le My_k$ (2g)

$w^a + (x_k + y_k - 2)M \le w_k^f \le w^a + (2 - x_k - y_k)M$, $w_k^f \le Mx_k$ and $0 \le w_k^f \le My_k$ (2h)

$1 \le w^a \le \left(1-\sum_{k=1}^{N} p_k\right)^{-1}$, $w^b \ge T$, $x_k \in \{0,1\}$, $y_k \in \{0,1\}$, (2i)

where M is a very large number. The final version of problem Z_{MILP} has a total of 2+6N variables for N number of workstations, among which x_k, y_k are 0-1 binary integers, and w^a, w^b, w_k^c, w_k^d, w_k^e, w_k^f are positive values. Given $T, C^F, c, C_k^f, c_k^d, c_k^r, p_k, t_k^P$ and t_k^R the problem Z_{MILP} can be solved by a mixed-integer branch and bound method.

A CASE STUDY IN GARMENTS INDUSTRY

The apparel industry is of great importance to the economy in terms of trade, employment, investment and revenue all over the world. On experiencing such an endeavor in a readymade garments (RMG) industry, 5 different 7-workstation sewing lines are considered that manufactures a certain design of branded T-shirts. Separate distinct operations are being done in each of the workstations. The operations follow a sequence as shown in Figure 1.

Figure 1: A branded T-shirt sewing line with 7 different workstations

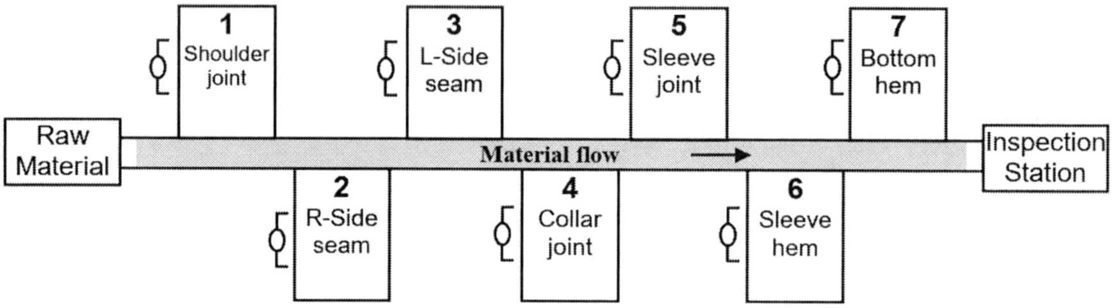

The factory bears a fixed cost of production $100 per hour for a sewing line that includes capital, labor and fixed utility costs. Variable cost of production that includes material and variable utility costs is listed as $3.10 for an item no matter whether the item is defective or not. All other necessary variable costs and fixed costs involved with each workstation (k = 1, 2,...,7) in the first sewing line are estimated from existing data and listed in Table 1. This problem is formulated as Z_{MILP} in order to solve with branch and bound method. For a 7-workstation problem there are 5+15(7) = 110 constraints and 2+6(7) = 44 variables among which 14 variables are 0-1 binary integers. Thus there are 2^{14} = 16,384 nodes to be explored to find the optimum result, which is a big problem indeed to elaborately demonstrate.

Table 1: Fixed and variable costs involved with different operations

W/S k	Operation name	C_k^f ($/hr)	c_k^r ($/unit)	c_k^d ($/unit)	t_k^P (sec/unit)	t_k^R (sec/unit)	Proportion of defects p_k
1	Shoulder Joint	1.70	2.30	0.44	35	20	0.0040
2	R-Side seam	1.50	3.85	1.19	43	125	0.0164
3	L-Side seam	2.20	5.50	1.21	41	100	0.0062
4	Neck Joint	0.80	2.65	0.16	45	35	0.0005
5	Sleeve Joint	4.00	5.10	1.57	44	75	0.0030
6	Sleeve hem	1.80	1.30	0.25	39	10	0.0063
7	Bottom hem	2.20	3.21	1.16	37	60	0.0042

A Three-Station Garments Sewing Line

In order to explain the solution procedure, a 3-workstation garments sewing line is considered with an inspection station located at the end of workstation-3 for demonstrative purposes. Let C^F = $100/hour and c = $3.10/unit. Also, as given in Table 1, C_k^f = {1.70, 1.50, 2.20} dollars/hour, c_k^r = {2.30, 3.85, 5.50} dollars/T-shirt, c_k^d = {0.44, 1.19, 1.21} dollars/T-shirt, t_k^P = {35, 43, 41}/3600 hour/T-shirt, t_k^R = {20, 125, 100}/3600 hour/T-shirt p_k = {0.0040, 0.0164, 0.0062}, and T=43/3600 hour/T-shirt. A branch and bound (B&B) method is applied on this 3-workstation problem and illustrated in Figure 2. A total of 19 nodes were explored. The optimum result is found at node 10 with (x^*, y^*) = {(0,1), (1,1), (0,0)} and the minimum unit cost is $4.37/T-shirt. Here (x_1, y_1) = (0,1) indicates that the defective items produced at first workstation should be repaired at the regular on-line workstation-1. Similarly, (x_2, y_2) = (1,1) indicates that defective items produced at second workstation should be repaired at separate dedicated off-line repair station. Thus the defective items produced at third workstation have to be scrapped.

Figure 2: B&B results for 3-workstation problem

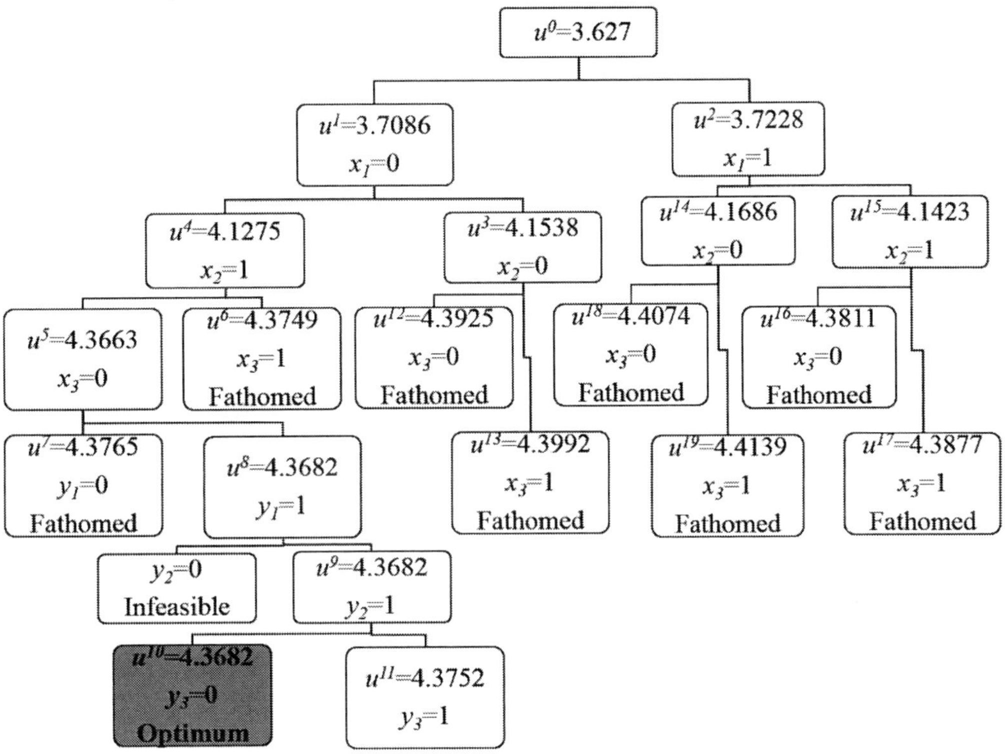

Identical Sewing Lines with Varying Output Quality

Five different identical sewing lines, each with 7 workstations are manufacturing the same T-shirts, but as machine operators are different for different lines, output quality and throughput varies. Though fixed and variable costs as well as production and repair times are assumed to be the same, defect probabilities are not so. Defect probabilities $p_k, \forall k = 1,2,\ldots,7$ at corresponding operations at different sewing lines are listed in Table 2. All other data are the same as shown in Table 1 except p_k.

Results have been summarized in Table 2. Here (*x,y*) in Table 2 indicates the prescribed optimal solutions with number of off-line repair stations, unit production cost and throughput rate for good items in the last three columns, respectively. For sewing lines allowing no offline repair have been analyzed as well. In this case calculations are done by considering very large values for fixed costs of offline repair stations (i.e. $c_k^d \to \infty, \forall k$) in the existing problem setup such that the possibility of selecting a dedicated repair workstation is automatically neglected. The unit cost of production and corresponding throughput rates for good items are calculated from this problem setup (i.e., no offline repair) and noted in the parenthesis in Table 2 along with other optimum results.

Table 2: Decisions made regarding on-line or off-line repair in 5 different sewing lines

Sewing Line		Proportion of defects p_k and decision (x, y)							Number of dedicated repair station	Min. unit Production cost ($/unit)	Throughput Rate for good items (units/hour)
		Workstations									
		1	2	3	4	5	6	7			
1	p_k	0.0040	0.0164	0.0062	0.0005	0.0030	0.0063	0.0042	1	4.4620	79.9689
	(x, y)	(0,1)	**(1,1)**	(0,0)	(0,1)	(0,0)	(0,1)	(0,1)		(4.4880)†	(79.9112)‡
2	p_k	0.0027	0.0011	0.0003	0.0024	0.0012	0.0007	0.0012	0	4.3805	79.8509
	(x, y)	(0,1)	(0,1)	(0,0)	(0,1)	(0,0)	(0,1)	(0,1)		(4.3805)	(79.8509)
3	p_k	0.0060	0.0028	0.0112	0.0159	0.0064	0.0129	0.0017	2	4.4791	83.0450
	(x, y)	(0,1)	(0,1)	**(1,1)**	**(1,1)**	(0,0)	(0,1)	(0,1)		(4.5342)	(79.0228)
4	p_k	0.0031	0.0013	0.0056	0.0030	0.0193	0.0030	0.0098	2	4.5135	83.4057
	(x, y)	(0,1)	(0,1)	(0,0)	**(1,1)**	**(1,1)**	(0,1)	(0,1)		(4.5209)	(79.8138)
5	p_k	0.0008	0.0181	0.0063	0.0072	0.0068	0.0024	0.0155	3	4.5110	92.2509
	(x, y)	(0,1)	**(1,1)**	(0,0)	**(1,1)**	(0,0)	(0,1)	**(1,1)**		(4.5605)	(79.5360)

† Unit production cost if all repairs were done on line. ‡ Throughput rate of good products if all repairs were done on line.

It may be noted that dedicated offline repair workstation provides cost no more than that obtained under no-offline repair policy. This offline repair policy advantageously provide no less throughput rate than that yielded from the online repair system. Though all the system parametric data in Table 1 remains unchanged for this problem except p_k, various optimal results are not the same due to the variation in p_k. For example, there is no dedicated repair station required for sewing lines 2, whereas the number of dedicated off-line repair station required in sewing lines 1, 3, 4 and 5 are 1, 2, 2 and 3 respectively.

CONCLUSION

Deciding, whether the defective items should be repaired on-line at regular workstation(s) or off-line at separate dedicated repair station(s) or should be scrapped instead of repair, is an important concern for making the operational decision in a line production system. This research dealt with locating repair station on or off the production line wherein the inspection is stationed at the end of main line. To describe the implication of the prescribed model a case of T-shirt sewing lines is presented in this article. It is observed that, in general, the optimum unit cost of production is lower and throughput rate for good items is higher for the cases where separate off-line repair station is prescribed. Though the problem investigated pertains to garments industry, this research outcome is beneficial and implementable to many engineering production systems, especially in discrete production systems. Since the garments industry and other engineering industries involve billions of dollars of revenue and sales, a small improvement in those systems will likewise impact the sectors with huge financial benefit to the management and consumers. Considering possibility of detecting nonconformities within the production line, dependent defects and/or the imperfect inspection facilities can be considered for extending the model in future.

References

AAFA (2012). *U.S. Apparel Imports - 2002 – 2011.* American Apparel & Footwear Association, 1601 North Kent Street, Suite 1200, Arlington, VA 22209.

Bahadir, S.K. (2011). Assembly line balancing in garment production by simulation, Chapter 4 in *Assembly Line-Theory and Practice*, edited by Waldemar Grzechca, ISBN: 978-953-307-995-0, published by InTech, Janeza Trdine 9, 51000 Rijeka, Croatia, 67-82.

Chang, C.T. (2001). On the polynomial mixed 0-1 fractional programming problems. *European Journal of Operational Research,* 131 (1), 224-227.

Hossain, M.S.J. & Sarker, B.R. (2016) "Optimal locations of on-line and off-line rework stations in a serial production system," *International Journal of Production Research*, 54(12): pp. 3603-3621.

Islam, M.M., Mohiuddin, H.M., Mehidi, S.H., & Sakib, N. (2014). An optimal layout design in an apparel industry by appropriate line balancing: A case study. *Global Journal of Researches in Engineering*, 14 (5.1), 35-43.

Li, H.L. (1994). A global approach for general 0-1 fractional programming. *European Journal of Operational Research,* 73(3), 590-596.

Raviv, T. (2013). An efficient algorithm for maximizing the expected profit from a serial production line with inspection stations and rework. *OR Spectrum*, 35(3), 609–638.

DECISION SCIENCES INSTITUTE
Ordering Blood Donations Under Uncertain Environment

Sima Fortsch
School of Management
The University of Michigan-Flint
Email: sfortsch@umich.edu

Qunfeng Liao
School of Management
The University of Michigan-Flint
Email: qunliao@umflint.edu

ABSTRACT

Blood is important for hospitals but its demand and supply are uncertain due to seasonality, natural disasters, and available donors, and while perishable, it's a natural resource that cannot be manufactured at the time of need. Our study employs an econometric methodology known as ARMA-in-ARMA-out (AIAO) to practically place orders for donations in this uncertain environment. Instead of economic order quantity (EOQ) and inventory policy changes (not allowed here due to governmental regulations), we show that following our methodology could match supply with demand and increase profits for blood centers without relying on practitioner's experience to place orders.

KEYWORDS: Perishable, Wastage, Shortage, Contribution margin, Inventory turnover

INTRODUCTION

Motivation

The incentive behind our study is the need for *practical* methods to (a) match supply and demand for blood and (b) place just-in-time (JIT) orders to reduce wastage and shortage of this product. We allow placing orders 'exactly' equal to computed values without adjusting quantities based on practitioner experience, which we belive could cause unnecessary variability and thereby contribute to product wastages and shortages. We seek 'practical' approaches because although popular in academic research, the Economic Order Quantity (EOQ) model and changes of inventory policies are not appropriate due to the importance of product and governmental regulations (discussed in upcoming sections). Thus, we must match supply and demand of blood and increased profits for our focused blood center via practical approaches.

Choosing order quantities to satisfy demand while reducing surplus inventory is difficult in general, but it's especially challenging when the product is perishable and surplus inventory could result in product wastage. Having higher than desired product wastage could have a negative impact on a blood center's financial standing, raising operational costs. Similarly, governmental regulations imposed on blood centers demand low product wastage (below 6%)

and sufficient inventory to meet demand during emergencies (Department of Health and Human Services, DHHS, 2011). Therefore, while excess inventory could help blood centers meet demand during emergencies, it is difficult to vent because of the product's rate of perishability. Additionally, recent studies show many doctors prefer using fresh blood (i.e., blood at the beginning of its shelf life) to increase the quality of a patient's care (Abbasi and Hosseinifard, 2014). Hence, an adequate level of inventory is required as under-stocking is risky, negatively influencing patients' lives, while overstocking causes product wastage.

On the supply side, our investigation points out that for the past several decades, blood centers across the world have decreased operational costs and product wastage by lowering inventory due to limited available blood supply. On the demand side, due to the recent increase in demand and price of blood, hospitals have sought to lower demand by using fewer blood packages during surgeries (we were told that for some surgeries blood transfusion is omitted entirely and the patient is treated with steroids injections to speed up his/her recovery instead). Some hospitals have even turned away patients that required considerable blood transfusions during peak demand months. Other hospitals delay non-life-threatening surgeries during high demand cycles. In 2010, for example, some hospitals delayed non-life-threatening surgeries because the demand for blood was higher than anticipated, while the actual supply was lower than projected for the year (DHHS, 2011).

Due to a lack of adequate blood supply, hospitals have been encouraging patients to reach out to social media to supply the blood needed for their surgery. Although delayed surgeries are typically not life threatening, they contribute to increased operational costs at hospitals because they are often high profit margin activities. Nevertheless, despite all efforts from the supply and the demand side, the world-wide problems with adequate blood availability exists because there is a constant rate of increased demand and a continuous rate of decreased supply for blood due to the world-wide aging demographic. Thus, given this problem, we are inspired to examine several ordering methods along with their profit margins to determine how well they allow product availability, high profit margins, and low shortage and wastage rates using one large blood center in the eastern region of the U.S.A.

Challenges for using the existing approaches to lower wastage and increase profitability: Matching supply with demand for blood can be a challenging task due to product perishability (approximately 40 days), limited natural supply source (i.e., cannot be manufactured), the dependency of supply on voluntary donations, and the price of the product (price of blood depends on the hospital's geographic location and the blood center's annual demand rate; the price could reach the price of a laptop computer ($550), a cellphone, or an iPad ($350)). Hence, any amount of excess inventory that might result in wastage is not desirable, as it increases operational costs and the price of blood. Even though most blood centers (not all) are non-profit organizations, achieving lower wastage can reduce operational costs and increase profit margins, which would be directly passed on to the hospitals via product-pricing; thus, the blood center could continue to operate as a non-profit firm more efficiently. Our interview with one of the large hospitals in the region of study indicated that in February of 2011, the hospital had switched suppliers from the Red Cross to other community blood centers due to the price of blood packages promoted by the Red Cross. Hence, we need to achieve profitability by lowering wastage at the focused blood center.

One problem is that although using the EOQ model is popular in the academic realm to allow profitability, this method is not appropriate for blood because in order to maximize profit, this model results in ample shortages that could put patients' lives at risk. An overview of the literature shows several researchers have focused on the EOQ model (e.g., Tajbakhsh et al., 2010), which typically optimizes profit. However, when we examined this model using our empirical data obtained from our focused blood center, we discovered that in order to optimize profit, the EOQ model undertakes a 45% service level, which would be intolerable for hospitals. The shortage cost of this model (Cu, cost of under-stocking) is found to be the price (p) less the fixed and variable costs (c). The problem with this is that the shortage costs don't represent the true costs of not having an adequate inventory of blood. The actual shortage costs of blood for hospitals, which cannot be easily quantified, include the costs of human life, delayed or missed surgeries, transferring patients to another hospital, and complications after surgery, among others. Since these costs are not easily quantifiable, the EOQ model cannot be used for this study. Additionally, our interviews with several blood centers and hospital blood bank representatives showed managers had never used the EOQ model for ordering blood or other products, and were hesitant to practice it.

A search of the literature indicates various inventory models have been studied for perishable products such as blood (discussed in literature review). A recent example, Abbasi and Hosseinifard (2014), used mathematical modeling and simulation to modify the First-in-First-out (FIFO) policy for inventory management applied to blood and platelets for hospital blood banks. The authors divided their FIFO policy into two parts to ensure the freshest inventory is always available. The variable "m" was noted as the shelf life of blood and platelets. The shelf life, m, was then partitioned into two variables m1 and m2, which together equaled m (the total shelf life of the product). The FIFO policy was modified and applied to each stage (m1 and m2) independently. Their inspiring work showed their modified FIFO policy outperforms a simple FIFO policy. However, we found most blood centers use a simple (one-stage) FIFO policy and are not open (or not allowed) to easily modify their inventory policies due to the underlying governmental and medical regulations. Thus, we are required to find methods that significantly reduce product wastages and shortages while increasing the profit margins and allowing the simple FIFO policy (as it's currently in place).

Our practical approach

Instead of the EOQ model and changing inventory policies, we applied practical ordering techniques and the lean principle of accounting budgets to inventory holdings to design a JIT ordering technique (reducing wastages and shortages), which results in increasing profit margins without undesirably changing the operational management of blood. The investigated techniques are listed in the 'Research Methodology' sections. Furthermore, we allowed placing the periodic order quantities to follow an 'automatic process'. The automatic process involves placing the order quantities 'exactly' equal to the computed values each period without any adjustments by the practitioner, which could cause unnecessary variability resulting in higher wastage and shortage of product. Subsequently, we compared the above techniques by monitoring their profit margins, wastage rates, and inventory turnover ratios (to allow availability of fresh inventory).

Research contribution

Our study contributes to the existing literature because not only do we allow ordering methodologies that can be easily implemented in practice, but also we use real-life managerial accounting to seek higher profit margins instead of EOQ. This practice is important in cases that EOQ cannot be implemented. To ensure our contribution to the literature, we examined the work of Schneider and Wallenburg (2013), which summarized 212 quantitative and qualitative published scholarly papers over the duration of 50 years. The authors performed a content analysis to divide the articles into several subdivisions based on the investigations' foci: purchasing and supply management (SCM), logistics, operations management, general management, and miscellaneous. According to their analysis, there were several papers focused on relationship management (i.e., they emphasized the importance of relationship among different departments). Although some studies stressed the relationship between the purchasing department and IT/HR divisions as useful to increase profit, *we found that none of the above studies investigated practical ordering methodology and none of them used real-life accounting practices to increase profit margins*. Similarly, even though we follow the path of Axelsson et al. (2002) and apply sophisticated managerial techniques to develop a modern ordering method for blood, our study is different because the above study analyzes inventory units theoretically, while *we allow continuous budgeting, inventory liquidity, and safety inventory in our decision-making*.

LITERATURE REVIEW

In this study, we focus on the lean or Just-in-Time (JIT) ordering technique to reduce the cost of operations inside the blood center. We acknowledge that this methodology has an impact on the cost of logistics, as orders are placed when needed and might not be combined. Liu et al. (2013), for example, studied a two-echelon supply chain to minimize the cost of logistic service integrators where the demand was assumed to be random and following a normal distribution. In contrast, we will not make any assumption about the demand distribution. Instead, we use real-life data to study the demand pattern and use demand forecasts or previous sales to place orders. Furthermore, Tajbakhsh et al. (2010) used a quantitative method to investigate the EOQ model, which allowed the model to incorporate the supplier's reliability. Although effective and popular, our previous investigation showed the EOQ model is not a practical tool for ordering blood (the reason is mentioned in the Introduction section), and therefore is not included in the current study. The following subsections categorize the literature reviews based on their approaches.

Literature Review of Ordering Methods

Elston and Pickrel (1963) examined the ordering policies for Hospital Blood Bank via simulation in order to reduce wastage. The authors discovered that both inventory and ordering policies significantly affected outdate rates and contributed to a high rate of wastage. They did not, however, consider profitability and practical application to determining order quantities. Somewhat differently, Gélinas et al. (1996) used JIT purchasing and partnership strategies to examine ordering methods. Then, in 2004, Zhang was among the first to use ARMA (Autoregressive Integrated Moving Average) demand in supply chain for manufacturing ordering without consideration to coordinate activities, which resulted in meeting demand without increasing inventory levels. Subsequently, Gaur et al. (2005) and Gilbert and Chatpattananan (2006) also used the ARMA demand process to study ordering models that matched demand patterns. Unlike our study, none of the above studies compared several methods to compute order quantities.

Literature Review for Perishable Products

Focusing on perishable goods and order quantity, Nahmias (1982) reviewed relevant literature for determining ordering policies for fixed-life perishable inventory and inventory subject to continuous exponential decay. The author considered both deterministic and stochastic demand for single and multiple products, and discussed both optimal and suboptimal order policies. In an approximation study, Chiu (1995) created a continuous review perishable inventory model to identify a best ordering policy based on approximations to expected wastage, shortages, and inventory levels. This included introducing an ordering policy under a positive order lead-time to minimize the total expected average cost per unit time. In yet another study, Ravichandran (1995) explored the stochastic process associated with the inventory levels of a continuous review perishable inventory system of (S, s) type. The assumption was that the inventory system followed a homogeneous Poisson process and had a positive lead-time, which derived the stationary distribution of the stochastic process and determined the optimal reorder level. Similarly, Chun (2003) determined the optimal product price for perishable commodities based on the demand rate, buyers' preferences, and length of the sales period. Chun also identified the optimal-order quantity that maximized the seller's total expected profit and proposed a multi-period pricing model. Other related research for inventory management includes a study conducted by Weiss (1980), which considered lost-sales and backlogging continuous review of perishable inventory models, and another study by Adachi et al. (1999), which proposed an inventory model for perishable items using the Markov decision process.

Literature Review of Integrating Managerial Accounting Approach in Supply Chain Studies

According to the literature, several scholars have used managerial accounting for supply chain practices. Buvik (2000), for example, used managerial accounting to document the increased volume of orders and its relationship with improved administrative facilitates and the buyer-seller business relationship. Axelsson et al. (2002) highlighted several management accounting tools for supply chain such as target costing, cost tables, quality-function-price trade-offs, activity-based-costing (ABC) method, and balanced scorecard. Boute et al. (2014 and 2015) explored a time-driven ABC method that estimates activity costs by using productivity measures, and discovered that this method could provide managers with relevant information for supply chain design and planning. Finally, using a survey of managerial accounting, Fayard et al. (2012) found that the resources of internal electronic integration, external electronic integration, internal cost management, and absorptive capacity played a significant role to manage inter-organizational costs.

Deviating from the above literature, we apply the lean principle for estimating practical ordering methodologies and integrate managerial accounting to ensure higher profits. The lean precept allows a company to reduce waste by focusing on ordering just the essential material at the specific time (Kocakülâh et al., 2008). Other authors such as Gélinas et al. (1996) recognized JIT purchasing would result in lead time reduction, inventory level reduction, waste elimination, and quality improvement, however, the above authors didn't include the lean principle of accounting budgets in their investigation, and they didn't study perishable products or a practical approach to ordering methods. Thus, supplementing the above authors, we construct several ordering models to quantify purchasing blood packages as needed. Subsequently, we compare our ordering methods based on their profit margin gain, wastage reduction, ending/average/days of inventory, inventory turnover, and their essential safety inventory to meet demand each month. It's clear that the ordering methodology with lower essential safety inventory is desired, as it meets demand accurately without requiring having a considerable safety inventory that could result in wastage.

DATA

Monthly demand data for blood was obtained from a large blood center in the eastern region of the U.S.A that satisfies blood demand for approximately 200 hospitals. Due to several proprietary agreements between the authors and the blood center, the name of the center cannot be revealed. The obtained time series data includes monthly blood-demand during seven years (2006 through 2012). The study period contains demand disturbances caused by hurricanes Irene (August, 2011) and Sandy (October, 2012). The above disruptions allow us to determine the ordering methodology that is robust during unforeseen events and in an uncertain environment. In addition, 10 hospitals in the same region were visited, and the blood-banking managers were interviewed to gain insight into practical blood procurement practices, as well as their demand patterns. We visited a variety of hospitals (research, large, and small) and represented the combined-demand for all hospitals as one large order for the blood center (Figure 1). Our study focuses on the blood center and we concentrate on placing orders for blood donation following the JIT ordering technique.

RESEARCH METHODOLOGY

Our interviews with hospital blood banking representatives indicated the most popular ordering method in practice was the Order-up-to-Level (OUL) technique, which was often adjusted using the forecasted values realized by 4-period Moving Average (MA) methods. A similar strategy was used in our focused blood center. Therefore, we examined the OUL and MA methods to place orders, as well as two additional ordering methods: 1) placing order quantities equal to the values of demand forecasts obtained by the Box-Jenkins technique and, 2) placing order quantities following previous shipments (not forecasted values) known as the ARMA-in-ARAM-out (AIAO) approach. The AIAO strategy is similar to the Material Requirements Planning (MRP) strategy, but the order quantities are not computed in the same way. We compared the four above methodologies for determining order quantities. Subsequently, we pursued the approach in determining the order quantity that had the lowest wastage rate without increasing shortage of product, while allowing the highest contribution profit margin. We allowed order quantities to be placed equal to the exact computed values (no quantity adjustment was allowed by the practitioner). We believe that adjusting pre-determined order quantities based on practitioner experience could cause unnecessary variability contributing to product wastages and shortages.

Model Setup

For simplicity, a two-stage supply chain is considered that involves manufacturer (blood bank) and retailer (hospital). Figure 1 below shows that we combined all hospitals' blood-orders into one large order (O_H) because our focused blood center recognizes its monthly demand as one large order. Similarly, combining all hospital orders eliminates variability due to the size of each order. In practice, our interview with hospital representatives in the region of our study indicated that large research hospitals and small non-research hospitals have significantly different demand patterns for blood, and thus, they have different sizes for orders. However, we were told that hospitals that are located in geographic proximity often collaborate to fulfill their regular demand when a shortage occurs and to overcome emergency conditions. Therefore, we combine all hospitals' orders and focus merely on ordering methodology between the blood center and the donors (supplier) during each period.

To simplify our practice, we assumed our focused blood center periodically determines order quantities (number of donations) during the last week of each month for the upcoming period when the actual demand for the upcoming period is not yet known. The assumption of placing orders during the last week of each month for the following month's demand was confirmed by interviewing several purchasing managers at various blood centers, including our focused blood center. We were told that due to some emergencies, several orders might be adjusted during the month; however, since generally orders are placed during the last week of each month for the upcoming period, we ignore these special circumstances. Nevertheless, we will show there is no need to adjust orders often when the pre-determined order quantities are obtained using an accurate ordering methodology. Furthermore, due to the high rate of product perishability, we allow the unused blood (or the surplus inventory) to be discarded each month. Although some hospitals can still use one-month-old blood because the shelf life of blood is approximately 40 days, we decided to discard one-month-old blood in order to be conservative in our calculations and to allow having fresh blood available each month. Our personal interviews with several blood doctors indicated the shelf life of blood varies based on the doctor's preference, hospital, and the type of surgery. For example, for high-risk surgeries (or when the patient is very young), some doctors might request fresh blood (no more than two weeks old), while other doctors might not. Hence, we find it's beneficial to allow one-month-old blood to be discarded to always have fresh inventory available.

Figure 1 below shows the general idea used for our study. When hospitals place orders for blood (O_H), the blood center contacts donors (O_t) using several different methods including inviting donors to the blood center, setting a mobile location in public places, going to the donor's residence to get his/her blood, and so on. These different ways to receive a supply of blood are shown in Figure 1 as method 1, 2 … n to reaching donors. In Figure 1, O_t represents the blood center's periodic request for donors (supply), and O_H represent the total monthly demand placed by hospitals (demand). O_t (supply) is assumed to be placed at the end of each period for the upcoming period and O_H (demand) is the actual periodic demand as it occurs. Henceforth, for this investigation, we determine O_t, in a way to match O_H each period.

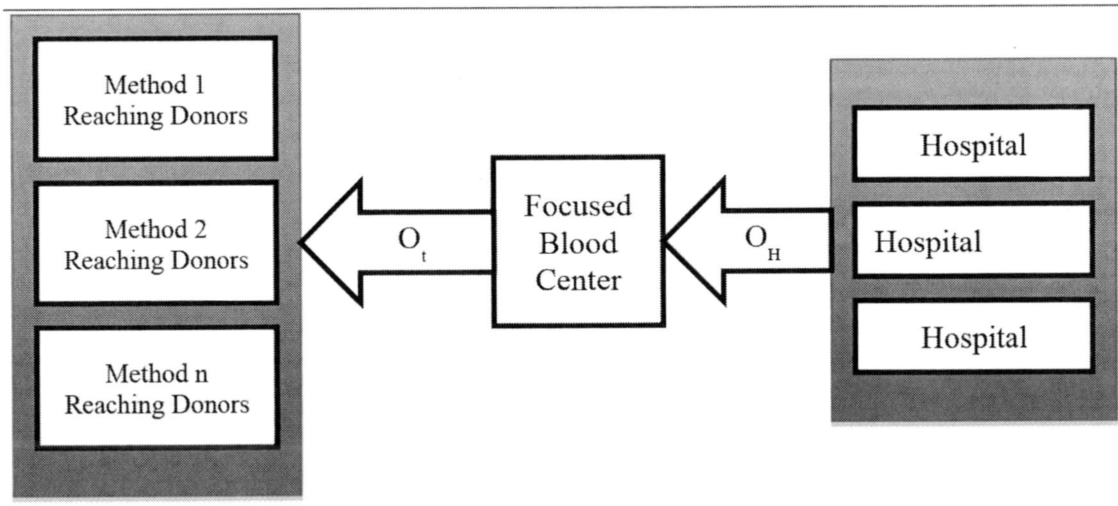

Fig. 1. Supply Chain setting for blood.

To construct orders that match demand pattern, we used the forecasted values of demand and the actual data for previous orders. To construct the contribution margins, we used the actual variable costs and average price for blood in the region of study ($350/package). Our goal is to reduce product wastage and shortage without compromising the hospital's service level and blood center's profitability.

Performance Evaluation

In the year 2011, the U.S. Department of Health and Human Services (DHHS) set the proposed blood wastage rate to ≤ 6% nationwide (DHHS, 2011). According to the DHHS (2011) annual report, blood waste rate in 2011 was approximately 6.4%, which also included a reduction of 15% from the year 2008 and forward. Therefore, we are interested in the method that determines the order quantities that significantly reduces product wastage, keeps high service levels, has higher profit margins, and is robust enough to be used during uncertain environments such as natural disasters.

Constructing Order Quantity

For each period, we placed order quantities using the following techniques.
First, we placed the order quantities based on the values computed by the Order-up-to-Level (OUL) methodology (95% customer service level), which neither follows demand forecasts closely, nor does it follow previous sales, but we found it to be surprisingly popular in practice.

Second, we placed order quantities equal to the computed demand forecasts using two forecasting methodologies: Moving Average (MA) and Box-Jenkins (BXJ). The MA method was used because we found this technique to be popular in practice for both blood centers and hospital blood banks. Although the visited operations used the OUL technique for blood ordering, they often adjusted their order quantities based on the computed values of demand forecasts by the MA method. We investigated the BXJ methodology to signify the effect of the forecasting approaches on waste reduction.

Third, we placed order quantities based on previous sales (not demand forecasts) using the ARMA-in-ARMA-out (AIAO) methodology. ARMA stands for Autoregressive Integrated Moving Average. The AIAO's strategy is similar to the MRP strategy, but the computed order quantities are not the same. This methodology can only be applied when the demand follows an ARMA process; thus, we employed this model after examining our demand data and discovering that our demand represented the ARMA process (Fortsch and Khapalova, 2016). It's worth mentioning that the use of actual data from previous orders to construct upcoming orders has been studied by Zhang (2004), Gaur et al. (2005), and Gilbert and Chatpattananan (2006). The authors proved that once the demand is known to follow an ARMA process, ordering methods using AIAO matched the demand consistently without requiring the practitioner to forecast demand frequently; however, the above authors didn't investigate profitability, and their studies utilized modeling, not real-life data sets. Our study confirms their theoretical models in practical application, as well as allowing us to focus on profitability by using a lean principle of managerial accounting.

To construct the AIAO ordering technique, we follow a methodology suggested by Gaur et al. (2005). These authors mathematically proved that when demand follows ARMA (p, q), the best method to quantify orders should follow ARMA (p, p+q) given in Theorem 1 (Gaur et. al., 2005), where p is the number of autoregressive lags (historical changes in demand) and q is the number of moving average lags (historical changes in moving averages). Examining our demand data shows demand follows ARMA (3, 2) in which the autoregressive lag is 3 (p=3) and the moving average lag is equal to 2 (q=2) (Fortsch and Khapalova, 2016). Thus, the future orders must follow (3, 5) in which p=3 and q=3+2. In the course of constructing the upcoming order quantities, the autoregressive lag (p) represents the number of previous orders we must consider, and the moving average lag (q) represents the number of moving averages of the previous orders we must include in our calculations when determining the order quantities for each period.

It is worth mentioning ordering methods that use demand forecasts to quantify orders such as MA and BXJ place an emphasis on the blood center's ability to forecast demand accurately. Since we place orders for blood donations (supply) at the last week of each month when the actual demand for the upcoming month is not known, monthly forecasted values are used. Therefore, following these methods, the blood centers are required to forecast the demand periodically. When placing orders, we assumed the safety inventory is 5% in order to stay within the industry standard practice (the 5% safety inventory is the nation-wide average because the safety requirement varies alongside state and regional regulations and blood centers' preferences). Afterward, we analyze the *actual* safety inventory required for each methodology to fulfill monthly demand. The superior ordering methodology would be the one that results in the lowest requirement of *actual* safety inventory and the highest contribution profit margin to meet demand each period. Lowest requirement for safety inventory signifies that orders match demand for blood consistently. The following are the monthly order quantities placed using the forecasting approach:

$$MA = quantities\ of\ orders\ are\ based\ on\ 4PMA\ demand\ forecasts \quad (1)$$

$$BXJ = quantities\ of\ orders\ are\ based\ on\ Box\_Jenkins\ forecasts \quad (2)$$

In the AIAO approach, the monthly order quantities are calculated using the ARMA-in-ARMA-out methodology. This method places emphasis on the accuracy of information about previous actual sales (not demand). The simple logic of this approach is that when demand has a specific pattern such as ARMA, periodic demand forecasting is redundant. Gaur et al. (2005) argue that ARMA models resemble real-life settings and carry all information needed to match orders with demands. Therefore, to determine the order quantities, the historical data from the actual shipments can be used directly by fitting previous orders quantities into the ARMA models.

It is worth mentioning a natural assumption of the AIAO technique is previous sales are equal to actual demand (demand = sales), and the patterns of demand (ARMA) stay the same at least for a while. Another assumption of the AIAO technique is that the decision-maker (procurement manager) does not deviate from the theoretical AIAO model when fulfilling orders so that the quantities of the historical sales would precisely represent the quantities of the historical demands. In other words, the shipped order quantities must match the exact order quantities determined by AIAO (cannot be more or less). This assumption may be somewhat unrealistic because the decision-maker may be forced to deviate from the exact order quantities needed each period due to transportation costs, truck loading constraints, holidays, and discount purchasing (Cui et al., 2015). When the shipped order quantities are not equal to the actual demand for each period, the historical order quantity's pattern (or ARMA pattern) can significantly be affected, and this could negatively influence calculations for determining future order quantities. In such cases, the AIAO method might not be appropriate because the order received and the shipped quantities don't match. Nevertheless, several researchers have suggested the importance of using the AIAO methodology, including Zhang (2004), Gilbert and Chatpattananan (2006), and Gaur et al. (2005). As with other scholars, we continue forward and use the AIAO method of quantifying orders regardless of its assumptions. Correspondingly, a similar supposition about matching order quantities with demand each period is used for all ordering models in the literature, including the commonly used EOQ model; thus, this assumption is widely popular among scholars.

Following Theorem 1 of the Gaur et al. (2005) technique, we first examined our demand data and found that the autoregressive lag, p, is 3, and the moving average lag, q, is 2. Therefore, orders were quantified using ARMA (p, p+q) or ARMA (3, 5). Thus, we needed to consider the changes in quantities for three previous shipments and five previous moving averages. AIAO quantifies orders as the following:

$$O_{t+1} = \mu + \rho_1 O_t + \rho_2 O_{t-1} + \rho_3 O_{t-2} + \lambda_1 \varepsilon_{t-1} + \lambda_2 \varepsilon_{t-2} + \lambda_3 \varepsilon_{t-3} + \lambda_4 \varepsilon_{t-4} + \lambda_5 \varepsilon_{t-5} \quad (3)$$

Where ρ_i is the regression coefficient of changes in past shipments quantities, O_{t-i} is the quantity of the orders shipped, t is time interval such that: t is the current period, t-1 is the past period, t-2 is the period before past, etc. λ_i is regression the coefficient of the moving averages for the past shipments, and ε_{t-i} is the value of past period moving averages. Note that ARMA (3, 5) signifies use of the quantities of the three past orders that were shipped, and the five past moving averages of those shipments to quantify the next period's orders (O_{t+1}).

Managerial Accounting Approach

Typically, companies adopt perpetual (continuous inventory) systems to manage their stocks. In a perpetual inventory system, the status of inventory is managed and updated continuously; this is in contrast to a periodic inventory system in which the company determines the quantity of inventory on hand periodically. The difference between the two methods is that the perpetual inventory system provides real time inventory balance information, while the periodic inventory system determines inventory by physical count at the end of each period. The former system, therefore, is more accurate than the latter, and is more appropriate for perishable products.

We compute the cost of goods sold and contribution margins for each ordering method at the end of each period by using the price and cost data obtained from our focused blood center. Furthermore, we compare different ordering methods via contribution margins and inventory turnovers for each ordering technique. Table 1 shows the detailed definitions of the variables used in the study.

Table 1
Definitions of variables

Variable	Definition	Equation
FIFO	Goods are assumed to be used in the order in which they are purchased.	*N/A*
LIFO	The cost of goods sold or issued comes from the most recent purchase.	*N/A*
Moving average method	The cost of inventory is averaged of all similar goods available during the period.	*N/A*
Unadjusted purchase/ Unadjusted order[1]	The predictions of demand using different forecasting techniques.	*UAPUR=Sales+Unadjusted Ending inventory*
Adjusted purchase	The sum of 75% of the current month demand, 25% of the next month demand, and safety inventory.	*Adjusted purchase=75% of the forecasted sales for the current period)+25% of the forecasted sales for the next period+safety inventory*
Safety inventory	Perished or unusable inventory.	*SI=5% of the demand forecast for the current period*

[1] In this paper, we treat order as purchases. We assume that there is no distinguish between order and purchase.

Unadjusted ending inventory	The ending inventory builds up using different ordering methods.	*N/A*
Adjusted ending inventory	The demand for the first week of next month plus the safety inventory.	*AEI=25% * next period order received + 25%* safety inventory of the current period*
Units-used	The sum of the units-sold plus the perished safety inventory.	*Units-used =Beginning inventory units+Units produced-ending inventory units*
Units available for sale	The units available for sale are the units-used minus perished safety inventory.	*Units-used-Safety inventory*
Cost of goods sold	The costs of sold inventory.	*Cost of goods sold =Beginning inventory cost+Cost of goods purchased-Ending inventory cost*
Wastage	Perished blood	*N/A*
Shortage	Unfulfilled orders	*N/A*
Contribution margin	The dollar amount remained from sales revenue after variable expenses have been deducted.	*Contribution Margin =Sales revenue-Cost of goods sold*
Contribution margin ratio	The value of contribution margin scaled by sales revenue.	*Contribution Margin Ratio =Contribution Margin/Sales*
Inventory turnover	The number of times a company's inventory is replaced over one year.	*Inventory Turnover=Sales/ [(Beginning Inventory+Ending Inventory)/2]*
Days sales in inventory	The number of days that a company would need to sell its accumulated inventory.	*Days sales in inventory=365/Inventory Turnover*

<u>Unadjusted/adjusted purchases</u>

In order to analyze the contribution margin for each period as it's done in real-world applications, we define unadjusted purchased quantity as equal to the sum of sales and unadjusted ending inventory. Unadjusted ending inventory is shown in Table 2 (*UAPUR=Sales+Unadjusted Ending Inventory*). However, since it would take at least one week to receive orders, blood centers must place orders during the last week of each month and receive at least 1/4 (one week) of them during the same week in order to have enough supplies to start each period. Therefore, at the start of each month, it is reasonable to assume that blood banks must satisfy the remaining three-weeks' demand of the current period in addition to the first-week's demand of each upcoming month. Nevertheless, the demand for blood fluctuates during each period, and an unadjusted purchase that is merely based on one-month's demand is not appropriate. To overcome this problem, we define the current period adjusted purchase quantity ($APUR_t$) as equal to 75% (3 weeks) of the current monthly allowed purchase ($UAPUR_t$), plus 25% (1 week) of the forthcoming monthly allowed purchase ($UAPUR_{t+1}$), plus the current period of allowed safety inventory (SI_t). *This method is in agreement with real-life accounting practices of industries.* Moreover, using the adjusted purchasing method ($APUR_t$) allows us to consider monthly fluctuations in demand during ordering. This ensures purchased quantities match demand for each period accurately, and decreases product wastage. Hence, we have the following formula for adjusted purchases made during each period: $APUR_t = 0.75 * UAPUR_t + 0.25 * UAPUR_{t+1} + SI_t$ (Table 2).

We also assume excess inventory *older than one month* is discarded because of the rate of perishability of the product. In order to be consistent with industry standards, we allow a safety inventory of 5% for unadjusted purchase (Table 3).

Table 2
Unadjusted purchase emanand adjusted purchase

Panel A: Unadjusted purchase (UAPUR)	
Unadjusted purchase equal to the predictions of demand using different forecasting techniques. It does not consider safety inventory.	
Unadjusted purchase	*UAPUR=Sales+Unadjusted Ending inventory*
Unadjusted purchase using order-up-to-level method	$UAPUR\_OUL_t$= *Calculated by: norminverse (90%, mu, std)*
Unadjusted purchase using moving average method	$UAPUR\_MA_t = SALES_t + UAEI\_MA_t$
Unadjusted purchase using Box-Jenkins method	$UAPUR\_BXJ_t = SALES_t + UAEI\_BXJ_t$
Unadjusted purchase using ARMA-in-ARMA-out method	$UAPUR\_AIAO_t = SALES_t + UAEI\_AIAO_t$
Panel B: Adjusted purchase (APUR)	
Adjusted purchase considers purchase of 75% of the current month demand and 25% of the next month demand and considers safety inventory.	
Adjusted purchase	*Adjusted purchase=75% of the forecasted sales for the current period+25% of the forecasted sales for the next period+safety inventory*
Adjusted purchase using order-up-to-level method	$APUR\_OUL_t = 0.75 * UAPUR\_OUL_t + 0.25 * UAPUR\_OUL_{t+1} + SI\_OUL_t$
Adjusted purchase using moving average method	$APUR\_MA_t = 0.75 * UAPUR\_MA_t + 0.25 * UAPUR\_MA_{t+1} + SI\_MA_t$
Adjusted purchase using Box-Jenkins method	$APUR\_BXJ_t = 0.75 * UAPUR\_BXJ_t + 0.25 * UAPUR\_BXJ_{t+1} + SI\_BXJ_t$
Adjusted purchase using ARMA-in-ARMA-out method	$APUR\_AIAO_t = 0.75 * UAPUR\_AIAO_t + 0.25 * UAPUR\_AIAO_{t+1} + SI\_AIAO_t$

Table 3
Safety inventory

Safety inventory	*SI=5% of the demand forecast for the current period is considered to be safety inventory and assumed to be perished at the end of each period.*
Safety inventory using order-up-to-level method	$SI\_OUL_t = UAPUR\_OUL_t * 0.05$
Safety inventory using moving average method	$SI\_MA_t = UAPUR\_MA_t * 0.05$
Safety inventory using Box-Jenkins method	$SI\_BXJ_t = UAPUR\_BXJ_t * 0.05$
Safety inventory using ARMA-in-ARMA-out method	$SI\_AIAO_t = UAPUR\_AIAO_t * 0.05$

Unadjusted/adjusted Ending Inventory

Table 4 details the method used for estimating excess quantities that have remained in inventory after each period (known as ending inventory). We define adjusted ending inventory (*AEI*) as the observed remaining quantities at the end of each period. At the end of each period, the observed amount of inventory is one week's worth of safety inventory from the current period, which is 25% (or 1/4) of the total safety inventory for the month, plus one-week's worth of (1/4 of) purchase for the next period (25% of unadjusted purchases). The unadjusted purchase is used for calculating the ending inventory because we are interested in the 'upcoming' period's order quantities, and the adjusted purchase would consider the current period. Thus, if we used the adjusted purchases, we would double count the safety inventory. Simply said, the quantities available to fulfill the demand of the ***first week*** for each month is the adjusted ending inventory of the prior month. Thus, the adjusted ending inventory quantities are calculated to be: *AEI=25% * next period orders received + 25%* safety inventory of current period.* This ending inventory is available to satisfy demand at the start of each new month (Table 4).

Table 4
Unadjusted ending inventory and adjusted ending inventory

Panel A: Unadjusted ending inventory (UAEI)	
Unadjusted ending inventory using order-up-to-level method	$UAEI\_OUL_t$ = *ending inventory when hospitals order up to a specific level (having 90% customer service level = 90% of average demand distribution)*
Unadjusted ending inventory using moving average method	$UAEI\_MA_t$ = *ending inventory build up using 4-period moving average to forecast demand.*
Unadjusted ending inventory using Box-Jenkins method	$UAEI\_BXJ_t$ = *ending inventory build up using Box-Jenkins approach to forecast demand.*
Unadjusted ending inventory using ARMA-in-ARMA-out method	$UAEI\_AIAO_t$ = *ending inventory build up using ARMA-in-ARMA-out. This is based on Box Jenkins but it follows the previous shipments (observed sales) instead of forecasted demand (unobserved/estimates of sales) similar to JIT techniques.*
Panel B: Adjusted ending inventory (AEI)	
Adjusted ending inventory	*AEI=25% * next period order received + 25%* safety inventory of current period*
Adjusted ending inventory using order-up-to-level method	$AEI\_OUL_t=0.25*UAPUR\_OUL_{t+1}+0.25*SI\_OUL_t$
Adjusted ending inventory using moving average method	$AEI\_MA_t=0.25*UAPUR\_MA_{t+1}+0.25*SI\_MA_t$
Adjusted ending inventory using Box-Jenkins method	$AEI\_BXJ_t=0.25*UAPUR\_BXJ_{t+1}+0.25*SI\_BXJ_t$
Adjusted ending inventory using ARMA-in-ARMA-out	$AEI\_AIAO_t=0.25*UAPUR\_AIAO_{t+1}+0.25*SI\_AIAO_t$

method	

Units-used and Cost of Goods Sold

To estimate the cost of goods sold for each month, we examine the beginning inventory of each period. Theoretically, the quantity of units-used is equal to the quantity of units-sold when there isn't any product wastage. However, in real-life operations, the units-used are different (higher) from the units-sold because the former consists of both sold items and perished products. Therefore, the quantity of the units-used is equal to the sum of the number of the units-sold, plus the number of perished products. Table 5 summarizes the estimates for the cost of goods sold for each ordering method. We can observe that the cost of goods sold for each period ($COGS_t$) is equal to the costs of beginning inventory units (that is the left over inventory from the previous period, $\$AEI_{t-1}$) plus the cost of purchased units in the current period ($\$APUR_t$) subtracted from cost of ending inventory ($\$AEI_t$). The ending inventory is subtracted because some inventory items are not sold and they would have to be subtracted from the cost of goods-available-for-sale *(GAS)*. Thus, for the cost of goods sold each period, we have the following: $COGS_t = \$AEI_{t-1} + \$APUR_t - \$AEI_t$

Table 5
Inventory equation

Panel A: Units-used	
Units-used	*Beginning inventory units+Units purchased=Units-used+Ending inventory units* ⇒ *Units-used=Beginning inventory units+Units produced-Ending inventory units*
Units-used using order up to level method	$UNITUSED\_OUL_t = AEI\_OUL_{t-1} + APUR\_OUL_t - AEI\_OUL_t$
Units-used using moving average method	$UNITUSED\_MA_t = AEI\_MA_{t-1} + APUR\_MA_t - AEI\_MA_t$
Units-used using Box-Jenkins method	$UNITUSED\_BXJ_t = AEI\_BXJ_{t-1} + APUR\_BXJ_t - AEI\_BXJ_t$
Units-used using ARMA-in-ARMA-out method	$UNITUSED\_AIAO_t = AEI\_AIAO_{t-1} + APUR\_AIAO_t - AEI\_AIAO_t$
Panel B: Units available for sale	
Units available for sale	*Units-used− safety inventory*
Units available for sale using order up to level method	$UNITAVAIL\_OUL_t = UNITUSED\_OUL_t - SI\_OUL_t$
Units available for sale using moving average method	$UNITAVAIL\_MA_t = UNITUSED\_MA_t - SI\_MA_t$
Units available for sale using Box-Jenkins method	$UNITAVAIL\_BXJ_t = UNITUSED\_BXJ_t - SI\_BXJ_t$
Units available for sale using	$UNITAVAIL\_AIAO_t = UNITUSED\_AIAO_t - SI\_AIAO_t$

ARMA-in-ARMA-out method	
Panel C: Cost of goods sold	
Cost of goods sold	*Beginning inventory cost+Cost of goods purchased=Cost of goods sold+Ending inventory cost* $\Rightarrow$ *Cost of goods sold =Beginning inventory cost+Cost of goods purchased-Ending inventory cost*
Cost of goods sold using order up to level method	$COGS\_OUL_t$=$\$AEI\_OUL_{t-1}$+$\$APUR\_OUL_t - \$AEI\_OUL_t$
Cost of goods sold using moving average method	$COGS\_MA_t$=$\$AEI\_MA_{t-1}$+$\$APUR\_MA_t - \$AEI\_MA_t$
Cost of goods sold using Box-Jenkins method	$COGS\_BXJ_t$=$\$AEI\_BXJ_{t-1}$+$\$APUR\_BXJ_t - \$AEI\_BXJ_t$
Cost of goods sold using ARMA-in-ARMA-out method	$COGS\_AIAO_t$=$\$AEI\_AIAO_{t-1}$+$\$APUR\_AIAO_t - \$AEI\_AIAO_t$

Contribution Margin

Contribution margin (CM) is the dollar amount gained from sales revenue after variable expenses have been deducted (Garrison et al., 2014). It is used to cover the organizational fixed expenses and the remaining is profit. It's intuitive that the ordering method with the highest contribution margin would also be the one with the highest net income. We utilize the following equation to estimate the contribution margin:

Contribution Margin=Sales revenue-Cost of goods sold (4)

Contribution Margin Ratio

Contribution margin ratio (CMR) equals to the value of contribution margin scaled by sales revenue. CMR allows firms to estimate the changes in the contribution margin related to changes in the total sales. For example, a CMR of 35% would mean that for each dollar increase in sales, the contribution margin would be increased by 35 cents (or: *$1 sale*CMR of 35%*). The equation is as follows:

Contribution Margin Ratio=Contribution Margin/Sales. (5)

Inventory Turnover

Inventory turnover (IT) shows how many times a company's inventory is replaced over a period of time. It is an efficiency measure that shows the speed at which a company uses its supply of goods over a given time period. It's intuitive that for perishable products, a high rate of inventory turnover is desirable. The following equation is used for IT:

Inventory Turnover =Cost of Goods Sold/[(Cost of Beginning Inventory + Cost of Ending Inventory)/2]

.(6)

Days Sales in Inventory

The days-sales in inventory (DS) simply measures the number of days a company would need to sell its accumulated inventory, and, therefore, it's called the firm's liquidity measure. The liquidity measure is important for organizations to understand the freshness of their product and the number of days needed for the company's inventory to be converted into cash. The following equation is used to measure the liquidity measure:

Days sales in inventory=365/Inventory Turnover. (7)

RESULTS

OUL Method

Our results revealed that estimating upcoming order quantities using the popular Order-up-to-Level (OUL), had the lowest contribution profit margin (43.05%) in comparison to all other methods (Table 6). Furthermore, the days of inventory was 1.06 days and the inventory turns was 346 times per year, which were not significantly different for the BXJ and AIAO methods. On the other hand, Table 7 shows this method resulted in the highest product wastage in comparison to all other methods. During several months, the average product waste for the seven-year period of study was 1,668 packages of blood per month, and during a few months the maximum monthly wastage was 5,225 packages of blood. Although this method had the highest product wastage, it still resulted in stock-outs in several months during the period of study. The average monthly stock-outs was 1,074 units. Thus, although popular in practice, this method does not follow demand, and is not suggested for demand patterns that include monthly fluctuations.

Moving Average Method

Estimating the upcoming order quantities by following the 4-period Moving Average (MA) method resulted the highest inventory turnover rate (354 times per year) and the lowest days of inventory on hand (1.03 days; Table 6). Comparably, this method resulted in the lowest product wastage; however, it had the highest stock-outs in comparison to all other techniques. The average stock-outs for the seven-year period of study was 3,306 units during several months, and the maximum shortage during the study period was 6,560 packages of blood for a few months (Table 7). The contribution profit margin was 45.83%, which was lower than the BXJ and AIAO methods due to high rate of stock-outs for this technique.

BXJ and AIAO Methods

Quantifying upcoming orders using Box-Jenkins techniques of demand forecasting was similar to using the AIAO methodology, which follows the previous shipments (observed sales). The contribution margin for both methods was about 46%, and the inventory turns was 344 times per year for BXJ, and 341 times per year for the AIAO technique. Thus, both methodologies were comparable. On the other hand, since the BXJ method follows demand forecasts instead of the actual (observed) sales, it resulted in product wastage (926 units) during a few months, while the AIAO method did not have any product wastage (Table 7). Even though following the BXJ methodology to quantify upcoming orders had several months that resulted in excess inventory and perished products, during several other months it resulted in shortages of blood. The BXJ technique resulted in average stock-outs of 1,661 units during several months, and the maximum of 4,155 units in a few months during the seven-year study period. The AIAO methodology that had not resulted in any product wastage had the average stock-outs of 1,591 units during several months, and a maximum of 2,235 units.

In conclusion, our results indicate that using the AIAO methodology for quantifying upcoming orders is *slightly* superior for products with monthly fluctuations in demand in comparison to all other techniques studied.

Table 6 Comparison of Inventory Turnover and Profit for different Ordering Methods

Measures	OUL	MA	BXJ	AIAO
CMR	43.05%	45.83%	46.00%	46.02%
Inv_Turns	346/year	354/year	344/year	341/year
Days_Inv	1.06	1.03	1.06	1.07
Demand (solid) Vs. Adjusted Purchases (dotted)	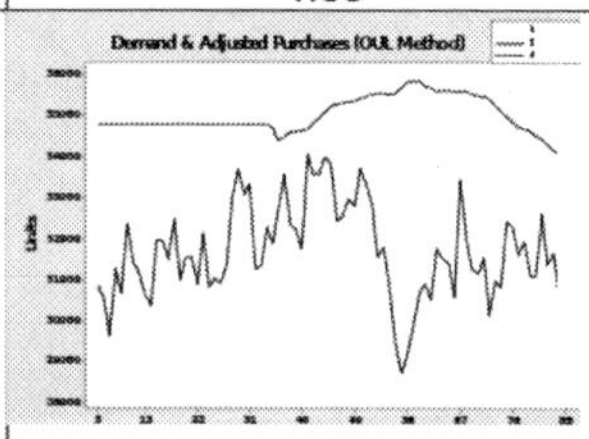		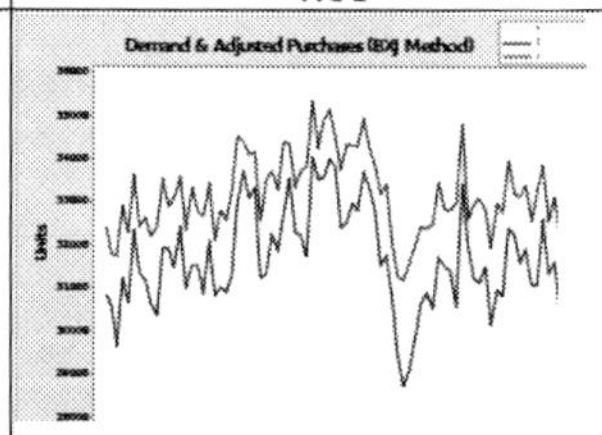	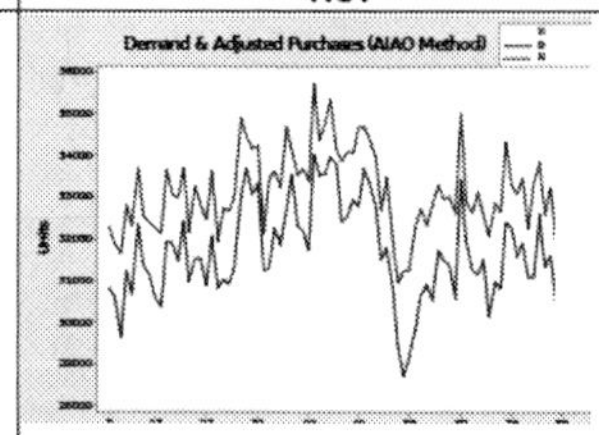
Demand (solid) Vs. Units-used (dotted)	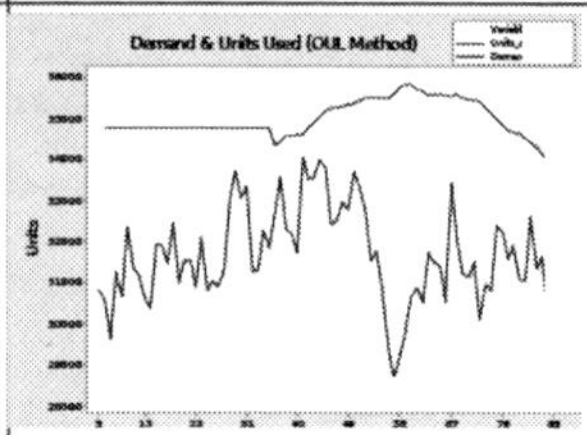	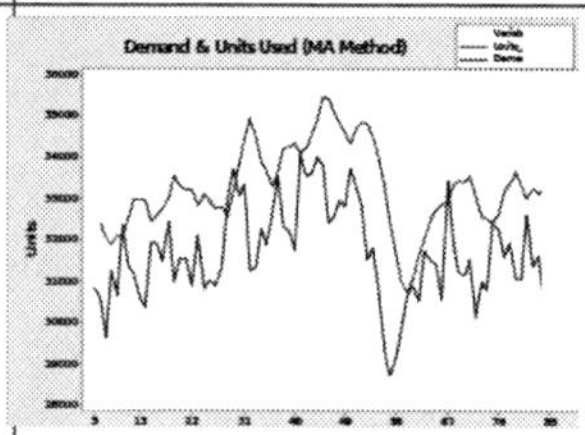	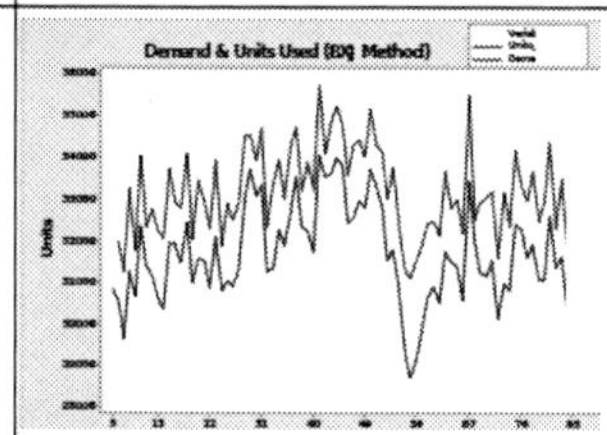	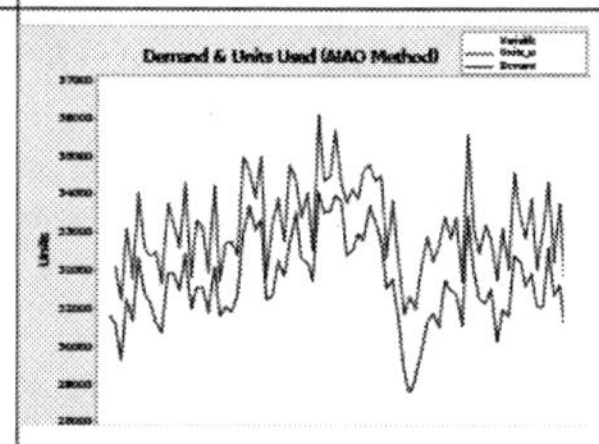
Ending Inventories	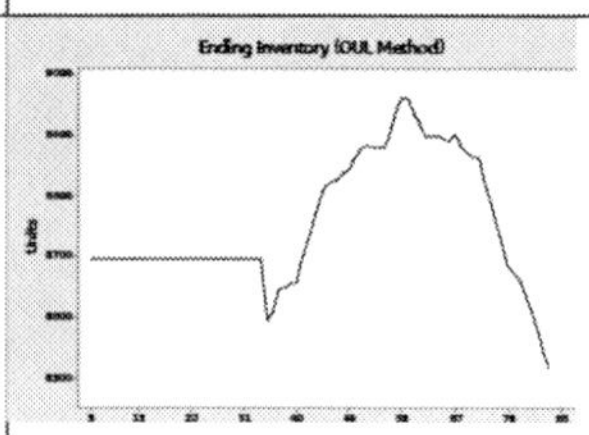	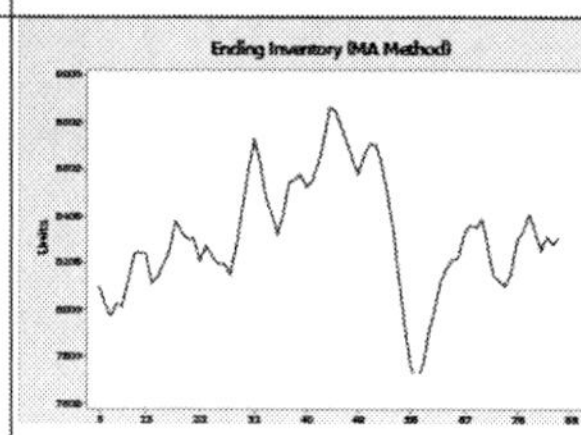	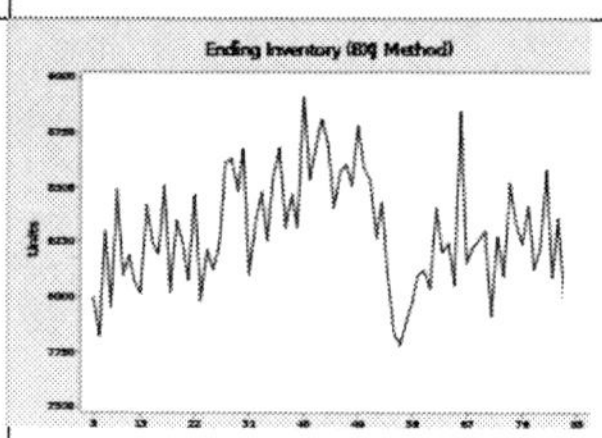	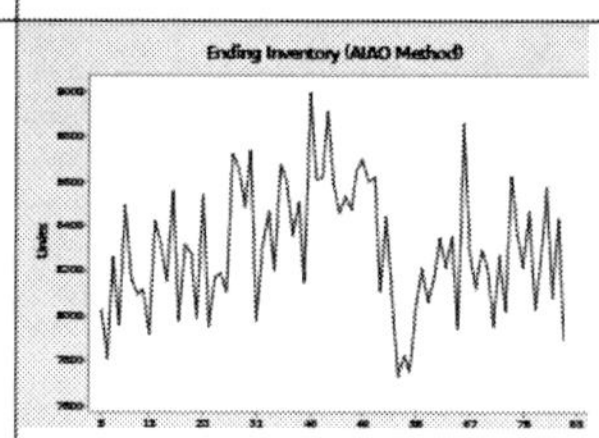

Table 7
Comparison of Wastage/Shortage for different Ordering Methods

Measures	OUL	MA	BXJ	AIAO
	Units (Packages of blood)			
Wastage (+) / Shortage (-)	1,668	-3,306	-1,661	-1,591
Max. Wastage	**5,225**	0	926	0
Max. Shortage	1,074	**6,560**	**4,155**	**2,235**
Wastages (+ numbers) & Shortages (- numbers)	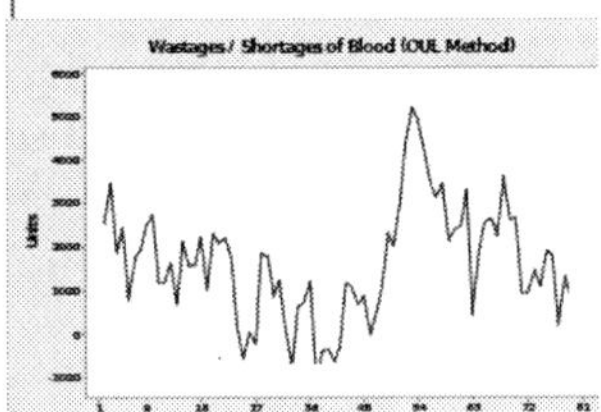	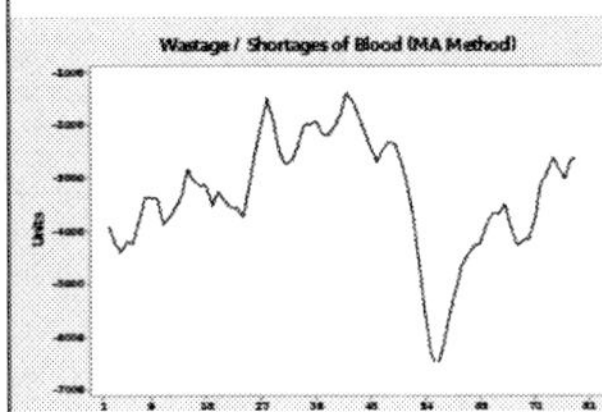	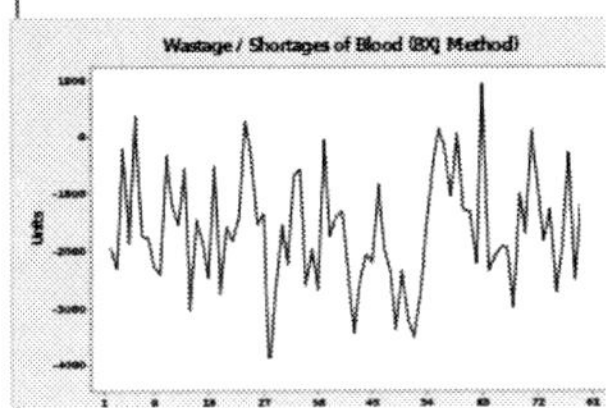	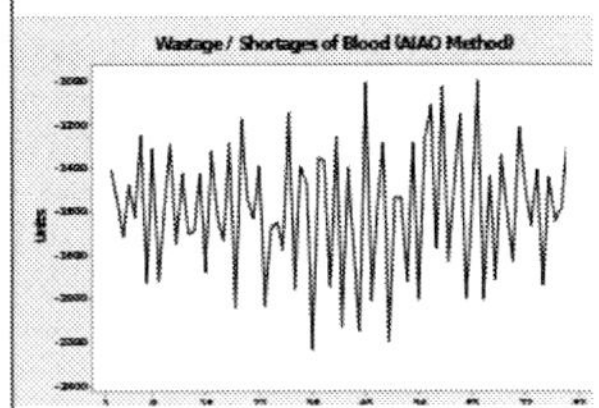

Table 8
Contribution Margin and Inventory Turnover Analyses

Month 6-91	OUL method	MA method	BXJ method	AIAO method
Sales*: (1)	$886,577,340	$885,967,830	$886,577,340	$886,577,340
Cost of goods sold: (2)	$504,869,400	$479,962,360	$478,772,360	$478,577,200
Contribution margin: (3)=(1)-(2)	$381,707,940	$406,005,470	$407,804,980	$408,000,140
Contribution margin ratio: (4)=(3)/(1)	43.05%	45.83%	46.00%	46.02%
Rank	4	3	2	1
Beginning inventory: (5)	$1,478,150	$1,377,170	$1,360,340	$1,365,270
Ending inventory: (6)	$1,441,940	$1,335,180	$1,424,600	$1,440,410
Average inventory: (7)=((5)+(6))/2	$1,460,045	$1,356,175	$1,392,470	$1,402,840
Inventory turnover: (8)=(2)/(7)	345.790	353.909	343.830	341.15
Rank	2***	1**	3	4
Days sales in inventory: (9)=365/(8)	1.056	1.031	1.062	1.070
Rank	2	1	3	4

*The sales revenue is determined as:
(a) demand < units-used: sales=demand*$330;
(b) demand > units-used: sales=units-used*$330.
The units-used is different from units sold because it consists of safety and perished inventories.
**Although MA method results in the freshest inventory, the consequences are many stock-out periods.
***OUL method has the second best for fresh inventory but the contribution margin is the lowest.

CONCLUSION AND MANAGERIAL IMPLICATIONS

In this study, we obtained data from a large blood center located in the eastern region of U.S.A. We investigated a practical technique for determining upcoming order quantities following the JIT principle when the actual demand is not yet known. We analyzed inventory units by allowing continuous budgeting, inventory liquidity, and safety inventory in our decision-making. Due to the importance of the product, the fact that it cannot be manufactured, the dependency of its supply on voluntary donations, and underlying governmental regulations, we sought a practical ordering methodology that resulted in reducing product shortages and wastages. We quantified and compared upcoming orders using four techniques, which included OUL, MA, BXJ, and AIAO. We analyzed each technique by focusing on the product wastage and shortage, contribution profit margins, and inventory turnovers by real-life lean principles of managerial accounting. Prior literature focused on perishable goods theoretically or by simulation models had suggested the use of EOQ model to increase profit, and changing in inventory policies to reduce wastage. However, our interview with the representatives of several blood centers and hospitals blood banks indicated that not only does the EOQ model not match the real-life application in this industry, but also changing inventory practices might not be practical due to governmental regulations and specific medical applications. Therefore, we used the lean principle of the managerial accounting to determine profits to help us choose the technique with higher profit margins.

Our study is unique in combining real-life data and accounting practices, and a practical ordering methodology to determine order quantities. We recommend that decision-makers allows order quantities for requesting donors to be equal to the computed values determined by the AIAO methodology to avoid the unnecessary variability, which in could result product wastage and stock-outs.

REFERENCES

Abbasi, B., Hosseinifard, S. Z., 2014. On the issuing policies for perishable items such as red blood cells and platelets in blood service. Decision Sciences 45, 995-1020.

Adachi, Y., Nose, Y., Kuriyama, S., 1999. Optimal inventory control policy subject to different selling prices of perishable commodities. International Journal of Production Economics 60-61, 389-394.

Axelsson, B., Laage-Hellman, J., Nilsson, U., 2002. Modern management accounting for modern purchasing. European Journal of Purchasing & Supply Management 8, 53-62.

Boute, R., Bruggeman, W., Vereecke, A., 2014. Cost management in the supply chain: an integrated approach-Part 1. Cost Management November/December, 11-15.

Boute, R., Bruggeman, W., Vereecke, A., 2015. Cost management in the supply chain: an integrated approach-Part 1. Cost Management January/February, 40-48.

Buvik, A., 2000. Order frequency and the co-ordination of industrial purchasing relationships. European Journal of Purchasing & Supply Management 6, 95-103.

Chiu, H. N., 1995. An approximation to the continuous review inventory model with perishable items and lead times. European Journal of Operational Research 87, 93-108.

Chun, Y. H., 2003. Optimal pricing and ordering policies for perishable commodities. European Journal of Operational Research 144, 68-82.

Cui R., Allon G., Bassamboo A., Van Mieghem J. A., 2015. Information sharing in supply chains: An empirical and theoretical valuation. Management Science 61, 2803-2824.

Department of Health and Human Services, 2011. National blood collection and utilization survey report. Annual report. http://www.hhs.gov/ash/bloodsafety/2011-nbcus.pdf

Elston R.C., Pickrel J.C., 1963. A statistical approach to ordering and usage policies for a hospital blood bank. Transfusion; 3, 41-47.

Fayard, D., Lee, L. S., Leitch, R. A., Kettinger, W. J., 2012. Effect of internal cost management, information systems integration, and absorptive capacity on inter-organizational cost management. Accounting, Organizations and Society 37, 168-187.

Fortsch, S., Khapalova, E., 2016. Reducing uncertainty in demand for blood. Operations Research for Health Care, Forthcoming.

Garrison, R. H., Noreen, E. W., Brewer, P. C., 2014. Managerial Accounting. McGraw Hill Education.

Gaur, V., Giloni, A., Seshadri, S., 2005. Information sharing in a supply chain under ARMA demand. Management Science, 51, 961-969.

Gélinas, R., Jacob, R., Drolet, J., 1996. Just-in-Time purchasing and the partnership strategy. European Journal of Purchasing & Supply Management 2, 39-45.

Gilbert, K., Chatpattananan, V., 2006. An ARMA supply chain model with a generalized ordering policy. Management Science, 51, 305-310.

Kocakülâh, M. C., Brown, J. F., Thomson, J. W., 2008. Lean manufacturing principles and their application. Cost Management 22, 16-27.

Liu, W., Liu, C., Ge, M., 2013. An order allocation model for the two-echelon logistics service supply chain based on cumulative prospect theory. Journal of Purchasing & Supply Management 19, 39-48.

Nahmias S., 1982. Perishable inventory theory: a review. Operations Research 30, 680-708.

Ravichandran N., 1995. Stochastic analysis of a continuous review perishable inventory system with positive lead time and Poisson demand. European Journal of Operational Research 84, 444-457.

Schneider, L., Wallenburg, C. M., 2013. 50 years of research on organizing the purchasing function: do we need any more? Journal of Purchasing & Supply Management 19, 144-164.

Tajbakhsh, M. M., Lee, C.-G., Zolfaghari, S., 2010. Sole sourcing in EOQ models with Binomial yield. Journal of Purchasing & Supply Management 16, 163-170.

Weiss, H., 1980. Optimal ordering policies for continuous review perishable inventory models. Management Science 42, 1097-1104.

Zhang, X., 2004. Evolution of ARMA demand in supply chain. Manufacturing Service and Operations Management 6, 195-198.

DECISION SCIENCES INSTITUTE

Overall Equipment Effectiveness Measures of Engineering Production Systems

Md Shahriar Jahan Hossain
Louisiana State University
Email: msjhossain1@gmail.com

Bhaba R. Sarker
Louisiana State University
Email: bsarker@lsu.edu

ABSTRACT

Measuring the Overall Equipment Effectiveness (OEE) of an engineering production system is essential for numerous purposes including scheduling, capacity estimation, and budgeting. During last few decades, several performance measurement techniques are developed from the basic OEE structure and are being implemented in different manufacturing industries. These newly developed techniques have some advantages and deficiencies over one another. The objective of this research is to evaluate these performance measurement techniques and their industrial applications. Most of these performance measures evolved from the fundamental concept of OEE. This paper summarizes and compares these techniques from different theoretical and practical perspectives.

KEYWORDS: OEE measures, Review

INTRODUCTION

Industrial equipment are supposed to produce products with a desired capacity, which is not satisfied in many cases. The manufacturing equipment are needed to be kept idle for a variety of reasons, including machine setup, breakdown, maintenance and raw material supply delay. Moreover, due to machine or human errors the production system may not produce 100% quality products. As a result, the equipment and/or a production plants would have an efficiency less than a perfect situation. Gathering a clear idea about the overall efficiency of the equipment is necessary for estimation of production rate, plant capacity, resource allocation, budgeting and scheduling. The overall equipment effectiveness (OEE) is treated as a common measure which is evaluated and used in many industries. However, there are several different approaches for OEE measurements which are termed with different names.

Muchiri and Pintelon (2008) analyzed, how OEE has evolved leading to other tools like total equipment effectiveness performance, production equipment effectiveness, overall factory effectiveness, overall plant effectiveness, and overall asset effectiveness. They discussed two examples of industrial applications of OEE in packaging industry and chemical processing company. On the other hand, Munteanu *et al.* (2010) presented some computing techniques for establishing and improving the OEE measures, which reflect the actual production process in the Romanian automotive industry. Dal *et al.* (2000) presented a practical analysis of operational performance measurement at Airbags International Ltd (AIL), a supplier of airbag safety devices to the automotive industry.

For evaluating the performance of cellular manufacturing systems, Sarker and Li (1998) proposed a new efficiency measure called alternative routing grouping (ARG) efficiency which eliminates some limitations of available grouping measures—grouping efficiency and grouping efficacy; and derived its desirable properties. Besides this, Sarker and Khan (2001) presented a comparison between existing grouping efficiency measures and a new weighted grouping efficiency measure, named "doubly weighted grouping efficiency" measure. The relative performance of this doubly weighted grouping efficiency measure is evaluated by Sarker (2001) with respect to other existing measures.

When several machines operate jointly in a manufacturing line, OEE alone is not sufficient to improve the performance of the system as a whole. Braglia *et al.* (2008) presented a new metric, overall equipment effectiveness of a manufacturing line (OEEML) to overcome this limitation. On the other hand, based on the classical OEE approach of the TPM concept Lanza *et al.* (2013) developed a theoretical measure named as global production effectiveness (GPE), which integrates all aspects of a globally distributed production system and transfers the idea of the overall plant availability to the global production network. Muthiah and Huang (2007) developed an overall throughput effectiveness (OTE) metric based on the idea of comparing actual productivity to maximum attainable productivity. They presented an application of OTE to wafer fab and glass manufacturing industries in order to identify the productivity, bottleneck and opportunities for improvement quantitatively. Later on, Muthiah *et al.* (2008) developed algorithms to automate the factory-level performance monitoring and diagnostics process using OTE. They applied their automated performance diagnostics algorithms in a glass manufacturing industry.

However, Ron and Rooda (2005, 2006) claimed that OEE includes some equipment-independent conditions, which may not be caused by the equipment but by the environment of the equipment. That is why, they defined a new performance measure—equipment effectiveness, *E*, which is related to equipment-dependent states only. This *E* includes only events that are caused by the equipment itself and does not depend upon utilization. They presented an application of this equipment effectiveness measure in a semiconductor industry. Samat *et al.* (2012) proposed a four-phase equipment performance and reliability (EPR) model for measuring maintenance performance based on machine effectiveness. The model is implemented in a semiconductor company.

Wudhikarn (2010) proposed rank-order centroid (ROC) method to identify dissimilarity in weighting each OEE element and thus improved the original OEE. This newly calculating methodology is called as overall weighting equipment effectiveness (WOEE). He presented an application of WOEE in a fiber cement roof manufacturing company. Wudhikarn (2012) also developed another method named as overall equipment and quality cost loss (OEQCL) by adding the loss from cost of quality. This method eliminates some of OEE's weaknesses and expands its scope. Zammori *et al.* (2010) noted that OEE only provides a static representation of a process, and it fails to capture the real variability of its performances. In order to capture the stochastic nature of OEE, they presented an approximated procedure to generate probability density function of OEE. Yuniawan *et al.* (2013) proposed a new procedure to obtain the weights needed for measuring Weighted OEE, by a combined result of simulation and experiment, through the Taguchi method.

The performance measurement techniques and their applications discussed in the above literature survey are summarized in Table 1. Among the surveyed literature it is found that OEE is applied in packaging and chemical processing, automotive as well as (but not limited to) airbags manufacturing industries. Some applications of weighted OEE are found in the fiber cement, waterproofing coatings and crimping manufacturing Lines. On the other hand, some other performance measurement techniques like OAE, OPE, OEEML, and EPR are also reported to be applied in the packaging and chemical processing, automotive, glass and semiconductor manufacturing industries.

Table 1: Production line performance measures and their applications

Reference	Performance measures	Application area
Muchiri and Pintelon (2008)	Overall equipment effectiveness (OEE), Overall asset effectiveness (OAE), Overall plant effectiveness (OPE)	Packaging and chemical processing
Munteanu *et al.* (2010)	Overall equipment effectiveness (OEE)	Romanian automotive
Dal *et al.* (2000)	Overall equipment effectiveness (OEE)	Airbags International Ltd.
Sarker and Li (1998), Sarker and Khan (2001), Sarker (2001)	Doubly weighted grouping efficiency	Cellular manufacturing systems
Braglia *et al.* (2008)	Overall equipment effectiveness of a manufacturing line (OEEML)	Automotive firm—motor basement
Lanza *et al.* (2013)	Global production effectiveness (GPE)	Global manufacturing system
Muthiah and Huang (2007), Muthiah *et al.* (2008)	Overall throughput effectiveness (OTE)	Wafer fab and glass
Ron and Rooda (2005, 2006)	Equipment effectiveness, E	Semiconductor
Samat *et al.* (2012)	Equipment performance and reliability (EPR) model	Semiconductor
Wudhikarn (2010)	Rank-order centroid (ROC) method in overall weighting equipment effectiveness (WOEE)	Fiber cement roof
Wudhikarn (2012)	Overall equipment and quality cost loss (OEQCL)	Fiber cement
Zammori *et al.* (2010)	Generate probability density function of OEE	Waterproofing coatings
Yuniawan *et al.* (2013)	Taguchi method in weighted OEE	Crimping manufacturing Line

The literature survey reveals that same performance measures may be implemented in different type of industries and vice versa. However, a complete summary of the applications and the relationship between different performance measures still need careful attention for extensive research. Thus the objective of this research is to investigate the applications, implications and limitations, in addition to conduct a comparative study among different performance measuring approaches of a manufacturing system, which are evolved from the basic OEE tools. This research is expected to be helpful for the industrial personnel in finding the best way of measuring the overall performance of their production system.

BASIC CONCEPT OF OEE

The concept of OEE was first introduced by Nakajima (1988) as a tool for assessing the success of TPM philosophy. This OEE is based on three main elements which concern with different type of loss. These are, availability rate (A), performance efficiency (P) and quality rate (Q). These elements are determined as A= operating time/ loading time, P = net operating time / operating time and Q = (processed amount – defect amount)/ processed amount. Thus, OEE is the combined effect of these elements, expressed as $OEE = A\,P\,Q$.

Based on this fundamental idea, several other performance measures are evolved and applied in different industrial sectors. Some of those newly developed measures use different weighted factors of A, P and Q, whereas others use monetary factors to evaluate overall effectiveness of the manufacturing plant, line or equipment. The following section discusses these ideas elaborately.

OTHER EFFICIENCY MEASURES

Besides the fundamental idea of OEE, several modified versions of overall effectiveness measures are presented in different articles. Among those ideas, the weighted OEE, stochastic OEE, overall equipment and quality cost loss (OEQCL) are widely applied in engineering production systems.

Weighted OEE

Many researchers disagree with the way of Nakajima (1988) to calculate OEE because of some concrete limitations in the basic OEE. One of the noticeable limitations of traditional OEE is concerned in specifying the weights for each elements (availability, performance and quality) equivalently. Raouf (1994) argued that the characteristics of these elementary loss are totally different. So these should not carry the same weights. He proposed a modified OEE. In his methodology he assigned weights to all the elements using analytical hierarchy process (AHP). In this case, the weighted OEE (termed as PEE) is calculated as

$$PEE = A^{w_1} P^{w_2} Q^{w_3}\,, \tag{1}$$

where weights of A, P and Q are $w_1,\ w_2,\ w_3$ respectively such that $0 \le w_i \le 1$ and $\sum_i^3 w_i = 1$.

Raouf (1994) did not provide clear explanation how to calculate the values for w_i. Wudhikarn (2010) claimed that applying AHP for weight setting is complicated for the decision makers. His proposed methodology was aimed to rectify the weight setting of the weighted OEE's elements. He proposed another alternative simpler weighting method. He used rank-order centroid (ROC) methodology to determine the weights for the weighted OEE method. This technique transforms the swing ranks into the swing weights. The calculating formula of the ROC is defined as

$$w_i = \frac{1}{k}\sum_{j=i}^{k}\frac{1}{r_j}\,, \tag{2}$$

where r_j is the rank of the jth element, k is the total number of the elements, and w_i is the normalized approximate ratio scale weight of the ith element. Now, the weight of each element is specified by using the ROC method as illustrated in the Eq. (2). Thus, the overall weighting equipment effectiveness (WOEE) is calculated as

$$WOEE = w_1 A + w_2 P + w_3 Q \tag{3}$$

Wudikarn (2010) suggested that the machine with lowest OEE should be primarily selected for improving. However, some other research highlighted that the machine with lowest OEE may not have the highest loss while all equal weights for the elements of OEE do not mean the same loss.

Since several researches on OEE improvement faced difficulty when determining the proper weights, Yuniawan *et al.* (2013) proposed a new procedure to cover this drawback. They used simulation and statistical experiments in their research through Taguchi method. Usually Taguchi method is used as an optimization tool but it can statistically measure the relative sensitivity factor of OEE elements caused by different level values. To demonstrate the methodology Yuniawan *et al.* (2013) used a simulation software to obtain the results using Taguchi method. This proposed method was termed as simulation–Taguchi procedure (STP). This technique particularly makes it easier to define performance efficiency since it reflects the maximum capacity of the machine. The simulation consisted of three control factors (availability, performance and quality) using three levels of variations at each of the control factors. All variation levels used triangular random distribution to make it easier to define where the random failure would occur. Each experiment simulation runs 10 replications with each control factor variation parameter level.

Taguchi method usually defines the uncontrollable (noise) factors in an experiment. This method provides signal-to-noise (S/N) ratio calculation in the experiment. The S/N ratio is a measure of the impact of noise factors on performance. The delta (Δ) values are calculated from the differences between maximum and minimum value of S/N ratio for each level of control factors. Finally a simple mathematical equation was used as

$$w_i = \frac{\Delta_i}{\sum_{i=1}^{3} \Delta_i} \tag{4}$$

to obtain the weights. Here Δ_i for i = 1, 2 and 3 are the delta-values for Availability, Performance and Quality respectively. Yuniawan *et al.* (2013) suggested that the same procedures can be used to calculate the weights for the elements in WOEE and PEE as well. It can be objected that STP seems to be difficult to implement. Moreover, obvious and sufficient data are needed to consider while making decisions for the improvement.

The weighted OEE concepts listed above notify that, a concrete direction of choosing a suitable weighted method is not available. Though several researches including Raouf (1994), Wudhikarn (2010) and Yuniawan *et al.* (2013) are reported where weighted method succeeded over the basic OEE concept while implemented in different industrial areas, these weighted OEE measures cannot deal with the stochastic nature of the performance of an equipment or a production plant.

Stochastic OEE

Zammori *et al.* (2011) noticed that deterministic OEE fails to capture the real variability of manufacturing performances. Variability affects work in process and queuing time and makes the time loss uncertain hence creates the possibility of hidden loss. To deal with this stochastic nature of OEE, Zammori *et al.* (2011) proposed an approximated procedure based on the application of the central limit theorem (CLT).

The basic idea of this stochastic OEE is to describe each time loss, T_i by means of a beta distribution. Then CLT is implemented to find the gap between the opening time (*OT*) and the net loading time (*NLT*) which is denoted by G_N and the gap between the *NLT* and the valuable time (*VT*) denoted by G_V. Though both G_N and G_V are independent beta random variables, the CLT assures that both G_N and G_V tend to be normally distributed, with mean and variance given by the following expressions respectively: $G_N \sim N\left(\sum_i \mu_i, \sum_i \sigma_i^2\right)$ and $G_V \sim N\left(\sum_j \mu_j, \sum_j \sigma_j^2\right)$, where i and j denote the number of time loss that belong to G_N and G_V, respectively, and μ, σ denote the mean and standard deviation of that time loss. So, by the definition *NLT* and that of *VT* the normality assumptions are preserved as

$$NLT = (OT - G_N) \sim N\left(OT - \sum_i \mu_i, \sum_i \sigma_i^2\right) \quad (5)$$

$$VT = (NLT - G_V) \sim N\left(OT - \sum_i \mu_i - \sum_j \mu_j, \sum_j \sigma_j^2 + \sum_i \sigma_i^2\right) \quad (6)$$

Now, OEE and its corresponding probability density function (pdf) can be obtained from the ratio of *VT* and *NLT*. As the ratio of two normal random variables does not preserve the normality, Zammori *et al.* (2011) suggested to obtain a standard normal approximation $P(OEE \leq OEE_{critical})$ of the real probability density function of OEE as

$$P(OEE \leq OEE_{critical}) = \Phi_{0,1}\left(\frac{\mu_L - \mu_V}{\sqrt{\sigma_L^2 + \sigma_V^2}}\right) \quad (7)$$

where, μ_L, σ_L are mean and standard deviation of loading time and μ_V, σ_V are mean and standard deviation of valuable time. Zammori *et al.* (2011) also presented a method to decide which corrective action should be deployed first among several potential corrective actions on OEE. To evaluate the potential effects in terms of both efficiency and effectiveness the percentage change in the mean and SD of the OEE is observed by the following expressions,

$$\eta_j = \frac{\hat{\mu}_{OEE_j} - \mu_{OEE_j}}{\mu_{OEE_j}} \text{ and } E_j = \frac{\hat{\sigma}_{OEE_j} - \sigma_{OEE_j}}{\sigma_{OEE_j}}, \quad (8)$$

where η is the efficiency and *E* is the effectiveness of the jth corrective action. $\hat{\mu}_{OEE_j}$ and $\hat{\sigma}_{OEE_j}$ are mean and standard deviation of the new OEE obtained through the intended j^{th} corrective action. To estimate $\hat{\mu}_{OEE_j}$ and $\hat{\sigma}_{OEE_j}$ before the corrective action, a heuristic procedure was suggested which is valid for beta random variables. For doing so, the production engineers were asked to give a pessimistic and a reasonable evaluation of the obtainable reduction of the corresponding time loss. Finally, using the methodology described above, a new pdf of OEE_j was suggested to obtain. Now the easiest way to rank the solutions is to compare OEE_j with a critical value of the OEE and evaluate the probability of each jth corrective action less than the critical OEE. The corrective action is chosen which gives the lowest value of probability.

The proposed approach induces some approximations; thus this approach does not give the exact pdf of OEE. Moreover, it was reported that the method is valid for values of OEE < 90% and when the variability of the equipment internal loss is high. However, this is a good approach indeed, because it allows to identify hidden loss and can estimate the impacts of potential corrective actions in terms of both efficiency and effectiveness.

Alternative to OEE Methods

The overall equipment effectiveness (OEE) and other adapted measures discussed above are not suitable for comparing among dissimilar type of machines those have different capacity and different process parameters such as production capacity, cost of material and quantity of the operator. To eliminate these problems Wudhikarn (2012) proposed a new computing methodology for estimating the quantitative loss in monetary units. This modified method is termed as overall equipment and quality cost loss (*OEQCL*). This method analyzes the loss into three elements of basic OEE approach, but the result is shown in monetary value. In addition to these basic elements, *OEQCL* also adds cost of quality (*COQ*). Thus it becomes

$$OEQCL = AL + PL + QL + COQL, \tag{9}$$

where *AL* is the availability loss, *PL* is the performance loss, *QL* denotes the quality loss and *COQL* denotes the cost of quality loss. These are defined as $AL = OL_A + PCL_A$, where OL_A and PCL_A are respectively denoted for opportunity loss and production cost loss for availability rate element; and $PL = OL_P + PCL_P$, where OL_P and PCL_P are respectively denoted for the opportunity loss and production cost loss for performance efficiency element. On the other hand, the quality loss is expressed as

$$QL = \left(OL_{Q-rej} + DML_{Q-rej} + PCL_{Q-rej}\right) + \left(PCL_{Q-rew} + R_{wk}L_{Q-rew}\right) \tag{10}$$

where, OL_{Q-rej} is the opportunity loss, DML_{Q-rej} is the direct material cost loss and PCL_{Q-rej} is the production cost loss for quality rate sub reject element except direct material cost loss; and PCL_{Q-rew} is the production cost loss for quality rate sub reject element except direct material cost loss and $R_{wk}L_{Q-rew}$ is rework loss. The cost of quality loss is expressed as $COQL = \Sigma CQP_i + \Sigma CQA_i$, where CQA_i is the actual cost of quality for the element i and CQP_i is the cost of quality of element i for production allocating method.

The applications of OEQCL reported by Wudhikarn (2012) shows that in some cases the machine with highest OEQCL also has the highest OEE. In order to implement this method of performance measure, both general cost accounting and cost of quality accounting need to be available completely.

A COMPARATIVE STUDY OF DIFFERENT MEASURES

From the discussion on available performance measures, it can be concluded that the fundamental approach of measuring OEE proposed by Nakajima (1988) considers equal weights to availability (*A*), performance (*P*) and quality (*Q*), which is not practical in many cases. This limitation is overcome by introducing weighted OEE. However, the exponentially weighted OEE method (Raouf, 1994) as well as the linearly weighted OEE method (Wudhikarn, 2010) do not provide a clear explanation how to determine the weights. Weights are mostly subjective in both of these two methods. Whereas, the simulation–Taguchi procedure (Yuniawan *et al.*, 2013) is more practical, because weights are set from statistical experiments. This method requires obvious and sufficient data while being implemented. None of the weighted OEE method can deal with the stochastic nature of OEE. This limitation of the basic and weighted OEE is overcome by the stochastic OEE approach by Zammori (2011), but this method provides an approximated pdf, not exact. On the other hand, Wudhikarn (2012) presented the quantitative loss in terms of monetary units, in his proposed method of performance measure named as, overall equipment and quality cost loss (OEQCL). The general cost accounting and the cost of quality accounting must be completely available for measuring OEQCL of a production system.

Table 2: Comparisons between the existing methods for calculating OEE

SL	Methodology	Author	OEE model	Advantages	Drawbacks
1	Basic OEE	Nakajima (1988)	$OEE = A\,P\,Q$	Fundamental approaches	Each elements are equally weighted.
2	Exponentially weighted OEE (PEE)	Raouf (1994)	† $PEE\|_{AHP} = A^{w_1} P^{w_2} Q^{w_3}$	Added exponential weighted factors	No clear explanation how to determine the weights. Weights are mostly subjective.
3	Overall weighting equipment effectiveness (WOEE)	Wudhikarn (2010)	‡ $WOEE\|_{ROC} = w_1 A + w_2 P + w_3 Q$	Added linear weights	Still cannot explain some case such as lowest OEE machine may not have the highest loss.
4	Simulation–Taguchi procedure (STP)	Yuniawan *et al.* (2013)	Uses simulation and statistical experiments through Taguchi method to obtain the weights.	More practical because weight is set from statistical experiments	Difficult to implement. Obvious and sufficient data have to be available.
5	Stochastic OEE	Zammori (2011)	$P(OEE \le OEE_{critical}) = \Phi_{0,1}\left(\frac{\mu_L - \mu_V}{\sqrt{\sigma_L^2 + \sigma_V^2}}\right)$	Can deal with both efficiency and Effectiveness	Approximated pdf, not exact.
6	Overall equipment and quality cost loss (*OEQCL*)	Wudhikarn (2012)	$OEQCL = AL + PL + QL + COQL$	Quantitative losses presented in terms of monetary unit	General cost accounting and cost of quality accounting must be completely available.

†*Weights* determined by AHP methodology, ‡ *Weights* determined by rank-order centroid (ROC) methodology

CONCLUSION

For numerous reasons the performance of a manufacturing system is required to be measured. The purpose of the performance measure includes scheduling, job sequencing, capacity estimation and budgeting. Overall equipment effectiveness (OEE) is a well-known basic concept of performance measure. Due to some limitations several modifications on OEE are proposed and implemented during last few decades. This research focuses on the evolution of OEE measurement concepts and their applications in engineering production systems. A critical review on different effectiveness measures are presented here along with the advantages and limitations of those measures.

In many manufacturing systems the performance are measured by assigning equal weights to all affecting factors (availability, performance and quality). In those cases a basic OEE measure can be enough to deliver necessary information. However, exponential or linear weights can be assigned to the factors depending on the system behavior. The weights can be obtained by AHP, rank-order centroid methodology or statistical experiments. On the other hand, the stochastic OEE is considered for finding the approximate probability density function of OEE if the parameters or factors are highly probabilistic in nature. If the general cost accounting and the cost of quality accounting are available, an overall equipment and quality cost loss (*OEQCL*) can be evaluated in terms of monetary values. Based on these concluding remarks this survey paper can be treated as a guideline for selecting a suitable performance measurement tool among the existing approaches or developing an appropriate performance measurement technique for a particular type of production system or equipment.

References

Braglia, M., Frosolini, M., & Zammori, F. (2008). Overall equipment effectiveness of a manufacturing line (OEEML). *Journal of Manufacturing Technology Management,* 20(1), 8-29.

Dal, B., Tugwell, P., & Greatbanks, R. (2000). Overall equipment effectiveness as a measure of operational improvement – A practical analysis. *International Journal of Operations and Production Management* 20(12), 1488-1502.

Lanza, G., Stoll, J., Stricker, N., Peters, S., & Lorenz, C. (2013). Measuring Global Production Effectiveness. Forty Sixth CIRP Conference on Manufacturing Systems 2013, *Procedia CIRP,* 7(2013), 31-36.

Muchiri, P., & Pintelon, L. (2008). Performance measurement using overall equipment effectiveness (OEE): literature review and practical application discussion. *International Journal of Production Research*, 46(13), 3517–3535.

Munteanu, D., Gabor, C., Munteanu, I., & Schreiner, A. (2010). Possibilities for Increasing Efficiency of Industrial Equipments. *Bulletin of the Transilvania University of Brasov, Series I: Engineering Sciences,* 3(52), 199-204.

Muthiah, K.M.N., & Huang, S.H. (2007). Overall throughput effectiveness (OTE) metric for factory-level performance monitoring and bottleneck detection. *International Journal of Production Research,* 45(20), 4753-4769.

Muthiah, K.M.N., Huang S.H., & Mahadevan S. (2008). Automating factory performance diagnostics using overall throughput effectiveness (OTE) metric. *International Journal of Advanced Manufacturing Technology,* 36(8), 11–824.

Nakajima, S. (1988). *Introduction to TPM*, Productivity Press, Cambridge, MA.

Raouf, A. (1994). Improving capital productivity through maintenance. *International Journal of Operations and Production Management,* 14(7), 44–52.

Ron, A.J.de., & Rooda, J.E. (2005). Equipment Effectiveness: OEE Revisited. *IEEE Transactions on Semiconductor Manufacturing,* 18(1), 190-196.

Ron, A.J.de., & Rooda, J.E. (2006). OEE and equipment effectiveness: an evaluation. *International Journal of Production Research,* 44(23), 4987-5003.

Samat, H.A., Kamaruddin S., & Azid I.A. (2012). Integration of Overall Equipment Effectiveness (OEE) and Reliability Method for Measuring Machine Effectiveness. *South African Journal of Industrial Engineering,* 23(1), 92-113.

Sarker, B.R. (2001). Measures of Grouping Efficiency in Cellular Manufacturing Systems. *European Journal of Operational Research,* 130(3), 588-611.

Sarker, B.R. and Khan, M. (2001). A comparison of existing grouping efficiency measures and a new weighted grouping efficiency measure. *IIE Transactions* 33(1), 11-27.

Sarker, B.R., & Li, Z. (1998). Measuring matrix -based cell formation with alternative routings. *Journal of the Operational Research Society,* 49(9), 953-965.

Wudhikarn, R. (2010). Overall Weighting Equipment Effectiveness. *Proceedings of the 2010 IEEE IEEM*, 23-27.

Wudhikarn, R. (2012). Improving overall equipment cost loss adding cost of quality. *International Journal of Production Research,* 50(12), 3434-3449.

Yuniawan, D., Ito, T., & Bin, M.E. (2013). Calculation of overall equipment effectiveness weight by Taguchi method with simulation. *Concurrent Engineering,* 21(4), 296-306.

Zammori, F., Braglia, M., & Frosolini, M. (2011). Stochastic overall equipment effectiveness. *International Journal of Production Research,* 49(21), 6469-6490.

DECISION SCIENCES INSTITUTE

Performance Evaluation of a Micro-Irrigation Company Using the APC model

Mohan Rao
Texas A&M University-Corpus Christi
Email: mohan.rao@tamucc.edu

Rishi Chhabria
Texas A&M University-Corpus Christi
Email: Rishi.Chhabria16@gmail.com

ABSTRACT

This article discusses the importance of micro irrigation and focuses on a business in this industry in India. Specifically, the competition it is facing and its efforts to improve its financial performance. To evaluate its performance, a spreadsheet-based application was developed using the APC model. The results are analyzed for possible corrective actions for improvement. This paper would be of interest to researchers and business executives for measuring and evaluating performance in terms of productivity, price recovery and profitability.

KEYWORDS: Decision support systems, Micro irrigation, Multi-factor productivity, Performance measurement, Productivity

INTRODUCTION

With world population growing, there is a need for increased supply of food. Consequently, increased on water resources (De Fraiture et al., 2014). Although more than 70% of the earth is covered with water, less than 1% is accessible for irrigation, drinking and household purposes, which indicates an acute scarcity of water (Whitmee et al., 2015). 83% of this water is used for agriculture. Most of the irrigation uses the surface irrigation or the conventional method of irrigation, which causes a lot of waste due to evaporation, interception and conveyance. Micro irrigation is much more efficient and is gaining popularity. With micro irrigation, the waste of water would be reduced by nearly 56% to 76% (Jagermeyr et al., 2015a). "Drip irrigation is the most efficient method of irrigation, with efficiencies ranging between 90%-95%. The global micro irrigation systems market is one of the fastest growing segments of agriculture industry" (PR Newswire US, 2013).

"Approximately 1.1 billion people in the world live on less than US$1 per day, 800 million of whom are smallholder farmers relying on subsistence agriculture for their livelihood" (Andrezejewski, 2014). India is the second most populous country in the world. The "pressure of survival and the need for additional food are necessitating a rapid expansion of irrigation" in India. Water scarcity is very high making irrigation the largest water consuming sector (Narayanamoorthy, 2009). There is a tremendous opportunity for growth in micro-irrigation in India. A 2012 research study carried out under the partnership of the International Water Management Institute (IWMI) and Sir Ratan Tata Trust (SRTT) found that "only 12.2 percent of potential drip irrigation area and 7.8 percent of potential sprinkler area is covered in the country" (Palanisami and Raman, 2012). That is, about 90% of the potential area is not covered by micro irrigation.

There are more than 150 manufacturers of drip and sprinkler irrigation systems in India. One of the top three companies is Finolex Plasson Industries Pvt. Ltd. Finolex has an ambition to move up from the third place. The focus of this paper is Finolex organization and its performance. Finolex has a joint venture with an Israeli company and is known for its quality products and services. According to Finolex, it has the latest technology (pulse irrigation through pressure-compensated non-drain dripline) with automation. These components are manufactured in India.

The primary focus of this paper is to evaluate the performance of Finolex. Performance measurement is a very broad area with a number of measurement models. They include single factor productivity measures and multi-factor productivity measures (Hannula, 2002; Rao, 2006). Within multi-factor models, there are profit-linked models (Miller and Rao, 1989) that use basic accounting data and provide results in dollars instead of ratios or indexes. One of these models is called the APC model. It "was developed by the American Productivity and Quality Center" (Miller and Rao, 1989). It links productivity to the bottom line profitability. It is used for evaluating the performance of three measures – profitability, productivity and price recovery. Applications of this model have been developed in other industries (Rao, 2006; Rao, 2007; Rao and Phusavat, 2013). This is an appropriate model to measure performance at an organization level.

In this paper a spreadsheet-based performance measurement system is developed using the APC model to evaluate the performance of Finolex. Based on the results and the trend charts, the areas for improvement are identified. This would lead to developing strategies. The remainder of the paper is organized as follows: (a) application development; (b) analysis of results; and (c) summary and conclusion.

APPLICATION DEVELOPMENT

In order to develop the APC application in a spreadsheet, eight quarters (2 years) of data was collected from the organization. A sample data setup for the first two quarters is shown in the Table 1. It is organized into three sections - quantity, price and value - for both inputs and the outputs. The outputs include extrusion, molded items, PVC pipes and other traded items. Inputs are classified into categories such as material, energy, repairs and maintenance, employees, supplies, operating expenses, and sales and distribution. The values (i.e., revenues and expenses) are in lakhs of Indian Rupees (INR). Ten lakhs are equal to one million and 10 million is equal to one crore.

Table 1. Quantities, Prices and Values

	A	B	C	J	K	R	S
1	**Finolex: APC Method for a Multi-period Performance Evaluation (2013-2015)**						
2		QUANTITY		PRICE		VALUE	
3		Period-1	Period-2	Period-1	Period-2	Period-1	Period-2
4		Qty-1	Qty-2	P1	P2	V1	V2
7	PVC Pipes (Mtrs)	1,409,238	636,684	63.40	54.17	89,347,067	34,487,374
8	Other Traded Items (nos)	3,195,033	3,069,526	27.51	28.44	87,891,874	87,290,827
9	**TOTAL PRODUCT**					**638,449,480**	**445,470,124**
10	Polyethylene (kgs)	2,043,602	1,570,500	117.37	113.36	239,856,269	178,029,176
11	PVC Pipes (mtrs)	1,409,238	636,684	65.43	55.07	92,206,173	35,064,400
12	Other Traded Items (nos)	3,195,033	3,069,526	24.11	27.49	77,029,016	84,376,841
13	**Material**					409,091,458	297,470,417
14	Electricity charges (Units consumed in KWH)	1,559,020	1,598,360	8.33	7.92	12,989,309	12,665,942
15	Water charges (Kilo Litres consumed)	1,020	930	126.95	128.83	129,490	119,810
16	**Energy**					13,118,799	12,785,752
17	Buildings (No of buildigs)	2	3	7486.00	11427.67	14,972	34,283
18	Machinery (no of machines)	8	9	448865.50	261174.78	3,590,924	2,350,573
19	Others (Value of Fixed Asset -Rs lakhs)	5,641	5,771	155.69	26.74	878,241	154,331
20	**Repair and Maintenance**					4,484,137	2,539,187
21	Security charges (No of places)	7	7	157554.00	169967.00	1,102,878	1,189,769
22	Communication costs (Total employees on payroll)	637	641	1320.82	1867.40	841,363	1,197,004
23	Printing and stationery (per lak Rs of sales)	6,384	4,455	220.23	122.75	1,406,065	546,809
24	Travelling and conveyance (Total employees on payroll)	637	641	14046.60	9058.33	8,947,687	5,806,392
25	**Supplies**					12,297,993	8,739,974
26	Managers (grade wise employees)	85	86	199335.99	200958.38	16,943,559	17,282,421
27	Staff (grade wise employees)	484	490	42678.96	42999.49	20,656,616	21,069,748
28	Workers (grade wise employees)	68	65	34400.98	34216.97	2,339,267	2,224,103
29	Welfare Expenses (Total employees)	637	641	5557.39	5843.17	3,540,058	3,745,471
30	Contract labor (Number of employees on contract basis)	150	145	49574.19	48491.83	7,436,129	7,031,316
31	Contract labor at branches (Number of employees on contr	74	64	35074.58	32683.84	2,595,519	2,091,766
32	**Employees**					53,511,148	53,444,825
33	Rent (No of offices/godowns)	46	46	33397.15	39941.15	1,536,269	1,837,293
34	Rates and taxes (Production -lakh mtrs)	561	557	3303.83	3128.51	1,853,449	1,742,578
35	Insurance (Value of Fixed Asset - Rs in lakhs)	5,641	5,771	77.37	176.22	436,458	1,016,985
36	Legal and professional fees (number of consultants)	20	20	155677.65	190521.45	3,113,553	3,810,429
37	Miscellaneous expenses (Per lakhs Rs ofSales)	6,384	4,455	203.41	267.93	1,298,695	1,193,541
38	**Operating Expenses**					8,238,424	9,600,826
39	Freight outward (Per lakhs Rs of Sales)	6,384	4,455	3503.38	3141.10	22,367,318	13,992,679
40	Advertisement, publicity and sales promotion (Per lakhs R	6,384	4,455	1171.23	1388.40	7,477,710	6,184,885
41	Sales commission (Per lakhs Rs of Sales)	6,384	4,455	5005.26	1981.53	31,956,026	8,827,137
42	Installation charges(Per lakhs Rs of Sales)	6,384	4,455	393.06	201.66	2,509,510	898,325
43	**Sales and Distribution**					64,310,564	29,903,026
44	Finance costs (Receivables -Rs lakhs)	7,129	5,684	1384.53	2091.72	9,870,301	11,889,326
45	Depreciation (Value of Fixed Asset -Rs lakhs)	5,641	5,771	1899.61	1967.55	10,715,707	11,354,732
46	**Capital**					20,586,008	23,244,058
47	**OVERALL**					**585,638,531**	**437,728,065**
48	**PROFIT/LOSS**					**52,810,950**	**7,742,059**

Once the data is setup, the productivity, price recovery and profitability contributions of each factor and each category are determined. The steps include the following: First, deflated values are calculated by multiplying current period quantities by base-period prices. Second, change ratios are calculated for quantities, prices and values in each period. Third, "performance indexes of productivity, price recovery and profitability are calculated" (Rao, 2006; Rao, 2007) from the change ratios. Finally, the "productivity, price recovery and profitability contributions in dollars are calculated as follows" (Rao and Phusavat, 2013). These contributions from the top level, down to the resource level are plotted so that the trends are easily identified and the problem areas are determined.

ANALYSIS OF RESULTS

The management can begin analyzing the results at the top level. The top-level performance chart is shown in Figure 1. The overall performance chart shows very positive results in price recovery. According to the management, there was a change in state governments where Finolex competes. Those governments relaxed price controls. Finolex also promoted sales in areas with higher margins. These actions have resulted in very positive contributions in price recovery and profitability. The chart also shows that there is a serious problem with productivity. It has been negative through all eight periods although it has an upward trend in recent periods. This upward trend seems to be the effect of investments in automation in recent periods. Overall, this chart indicates that the management at Finolex should be focusing on productivity. In particular, the productivity contributions of the categories and resources should be pinpointed.

Figure 1. Overall Profitability, Productivity and Price Recovery

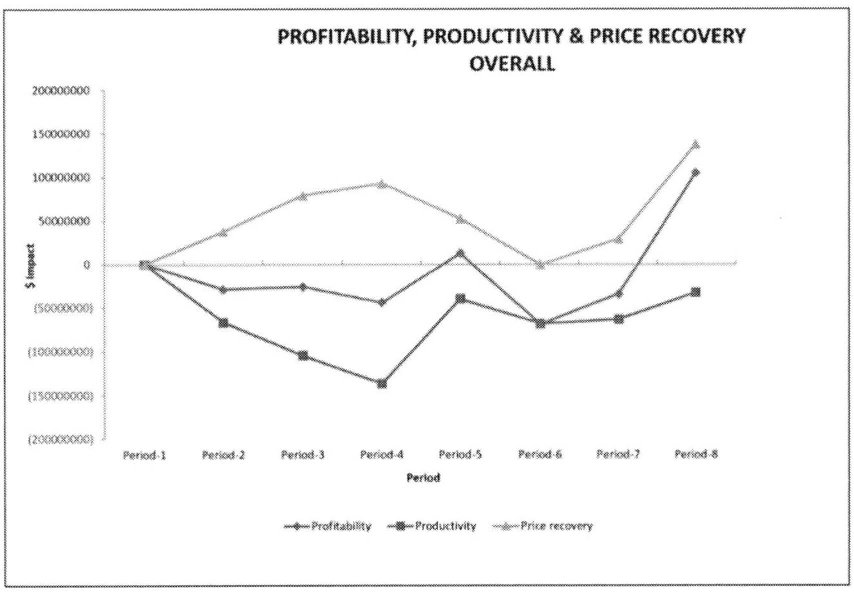

Similar charts for all categories are drawn for visual inspection of trends. Through visual inspection of the category-level charts, it was clear that one Material category stood out from the rest for significant productivity problems.

SUMMARY AND CONCLUSION

Water conservation is very important, and micro irrigation plays an important role. This paper focused on the performance evaluation of a micro-irrigation company using the APC model. A spreadsheet application of the model was developed for this company. Performance charts were drawn and analyzed. Through a top-down approach, it was shown how one could pinpoint the significant problem area in the company.

This paper should be of interest to researchers in the area of micro irrigation, water conservation and in the areas of performance measurement, spreadsheet modeling and decision support systems. Further research includes applications using other models for performance measurement. Further extensions could lead to applications in predictive analytics and prescriptive analytics.

REFERENCES

References available upon request.

DECISION SCIENCES INSTITUTE

Performance of Supervised Artificial Neural Networks for Foreign Exchange Rate Prediction

Hari P. Sharma
Virginia State University
hsharma@vsu.edu

Dinesh K. Sharma
University of Maryland Eastern Shore
dksharma@umes.edu

H.S. Hota
Bilaspur University
proffhota@gmail.com

ABSTRACT

The purpose of this research is to develop Artificial Neural Network (ANN) based models for foreign exchange (FX) rate predictions. Since ANN are capable of recognizing nonlinear patterns by learning patterns of historical data and information. This study focuses on designing and developing models using two ANN techniques: (1) Multi-Layer Perceptron (MLP) with Error Back Propagation Algorithm (EBPA) and (2) Radial Basis Function Neural Network (RBFNN). Both ANN techniques use supervised learning to predict the output. The dataset used for this study are (1) Forex data namely Euro to US Dollar (EUR/USD) and (2) Euro to Japanese Yen (EUR/JPY) with daily and weekly data as three inputs high, low and close along with next day/week close as output. Experimental work is carried out with 10-Fold cross-validation technique and results obtained in the form of Mean Absolute Error (MAE), and Mean Absolute Percentage Error (MAPE) proves that MLP is better than RBFNN for both exchange rate data in case of daily as well as weekly predictions. It has also been observed that ANN models performed better using the closing prices as compared to low or high prices.

KEYWORDS: Foreign Exchange, Artificial Neural Network, Multi-Layer Perceptron, Radial Basis Function Neural Network.

INTRODUCTION

The dynamics of the global foreign exchange market is ever evolving. Therefore, there is a need of continuous improvement in designing and developing models using the latest tools and techniques to capture the trends in foreign exchange (FX) rates. The FX market is also equally lucrative within financial markets (Baillie and McMahon, 1989). Therefore, investors are demanding sophisticated models to make better business decisions and minimize the risk due to fluctuations in exchange rates (Meese and Rogoff, 1983; Kilian and Taylor, 2003; Ni and Yin, 2009). Historically, there have been several forecast models developed using autoregressive coordinated moving average (ARIMA) (Box and Jenkins, 1976), autoregressive restrictive heteroskedasticity (GARCH) (Franses and Ghijsels, 1999) and smooth move autoregressive (STAR) (Sarantis, 2001). However, the models developed using traditional statistical techniques have not yielded satisfactory results during volatile economic conditions. Therefore, researchers are focusing on designing and developing models using the ANN techniques to predict FX rates integrating computational intelligence, signal processing as well as econometrics.

The literature review supports that ANN technique is a promising method for FX rate prediction. However, there are two different types of ANN techniques: supervised and unsupervised. Supervised ANN technique is used widely due to the availability of input as well as output (Target) data. Several authors have demonstrated the use of supervised ANN technique with other intelligent techniques for improved performance of predictive models. The prediction is dependent on training and testing samples. Some authors have used a static partition of training-testing samples which does not reflect the real strength of the predictive model and may be biased for a specific type of pattern. However, k-fold cross validation technique of data mining help designing a robust model by partitioning training and testing samples. This research work focuses on building FX rate prediction model with special emphasis on the selection of suitable input parameters using two ANN techniques: (1) MLP and (2) RBFNN with 10-fold cross validation. The performance of models was tested to validate the results in terms of Absolute Percentage Error (MAPE) and Mean Absolute Error (MAE).

LITERATURE REVIEW

The literature reveals that ANN techniques are better than the conventional statistical methods in predicting non-linear patterns in data (Coats & Faut, 1993; Leonard et al., 1991; Fletcher & Goss, 1993; Salchengerger et al., 1992). Over the past two decades, several mathematical models in finance area have applied ANN to predict trends of foreign exchange rates successfully. Table 1 provides a summary of foreign currency rate models developed by several researchers.

Table 1: Summary of Literature Review

YEAR	REFERENCES	JOURNAL
1998	Zhang & Hu	International Journal of Management Science
1999	Hu et al.	Decision Sciences
2000	Leung et al.	Computers and Operations Research
2001	Davis et al.	International Journal of Intelligent Systems in Accounting
2003	Chun & Kim	Expert Systems with Applications
2004	Chen & Leung	Computers and Operations Research
2007	Panda & Narasimhan	Journal of Policy Modeling
2008	Lean et al.	Neurocomputing
2008	Yu et al.	Neurocomputing
2009	Ni & Yin	Neurocomputing
2013	Sermpinis et al.	European Journal of Operational Research
2013	Georgios et al.	European Journal of Operation Research
2016	Svitlana	Neurocomputing

DATA DESCRIPTION AND PREDICTION METHOD

Data Description

Sample size plays a significant role in designing models to ensure adequate data for learning patterns. Therefore, a large number of samples are necessary to develop exchange rate predictive models. Two foreign exchange rates data (EUR/USD and EUR/JPY) as shown in Table 2, was collected from the website (http://www.oanda.com/currency/historical-rates/) for daily rates from January 1, 2010, to December 31, 2015. The period for the weekly rate was extended from January 1, 1999, to December 31, 2015, to have a larger sample size. A total of 1565 samples for daily and 889 samples for weekly rates was used with three types of inputs: High, Low and Close rates and one output next day/week close rate for developing an exchange rate prediction model. The nonlinear trend of all the three inputs are shown in Figure 1(a) and (b) for exchange rate EUR/USD and EUR/JPY with daily step respectively and in Figure 2(a) and (b) for exchange rate EUR/USD and EUR/JPY with weekly step respectively. It can be observed from these figures that Forex data are highly nonlinear and varies from time to time.

Table 2: Data description of two Forex: EUR/USD and EUR/JPY				
Time Step	Range	Samples	Input	Output
Daily	Jan 1, 2010 to Dec 31, 2015	1565	High, Low, Close	Next Day close
Weekly	Jan 1, 1999 to Dec 31, 2015	889	High, Low, Close	Next Week close

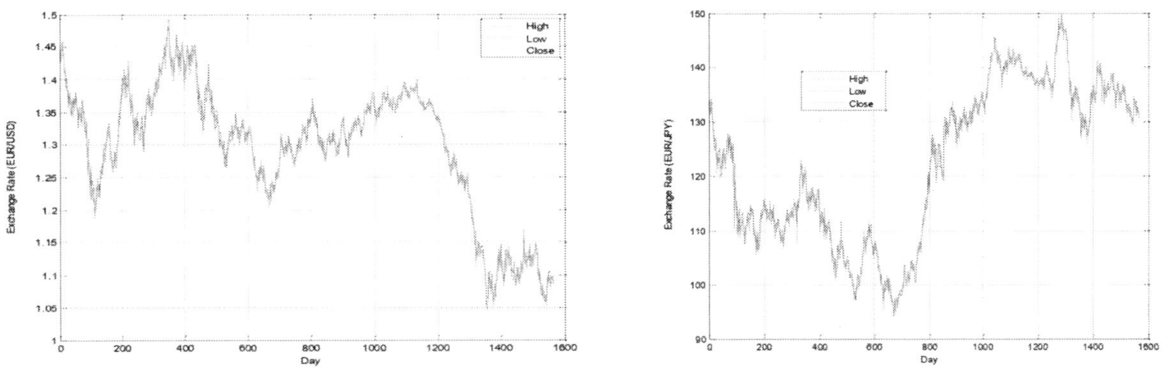

(a) (b)

Figure 1: Trends of Exchange rate (a) EUR/USD (b) EUR/JPY with daily Step.

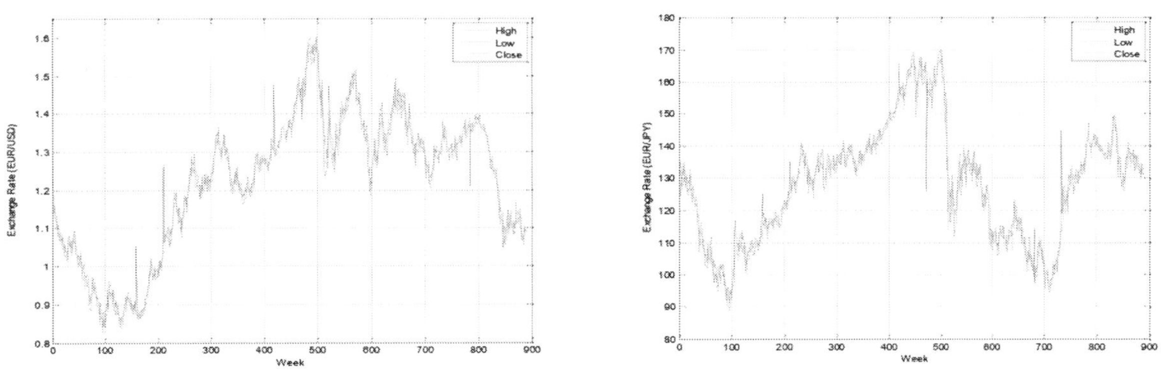

(a) (b)

Figure 2: Trends of Weekly Exchange rate (a) EUR/USD (b) EUR/JPY

Prediction Method

The development of a prediction model for financial data requires techniques like Artificial Neural Network (ANN) because of its capabilities to capture nonlinear nature of data pattern as well as to store a large amount of patterns in the form of weights on its connections. Among several ANN techniques reported in the literature two ANN techniques (Multi-Layer Perceptron (MLP) and Radial Basis Function Neural Network (RBFNN)) are widely used for a nonlinear pattern recognition. Therefore, these techniques are suitable for the development of FX rate prediction model. MLP is a multi-layer neural network with at least one hidden layer along with multiple input and output layers. The number of processing units (Neurons) at input and output layers are equal to the number of elements in input and output vectors respectively. The number of processing units at the hidden layer is decided according to the complexity and level of non-linearity nature of the data (Georgios et al., 2013). MLP is trained with popular Error Back Propagation Algorithm (EBPA) which is calculated based on the gradient descent and maps the input patterns to its corresponding output patterns in a supervised manner by sending back the error signals to adjust weights of the connection. On the other hand, RBFNN also works in a supervised manner with radial basis function as an activation function at the hidden layer. RBFNN generally consists of three layers (Input, hidden and output). The hidden layer of RBFNN differs from MLP because each node represents a cluster of data centered at a particular point within a given radius. Each node in the hidden layer calculates the distance from the input vectors to its own using Euclidian distance formulae (Yu et al., 2008). However, characteristics of input and output layers are very similar in of both type of ANNs.

There are several parameters that influence the performance of both techniques. For example, in MLP, the value of learning rate and the momentum that lies between 0 and 1 may affect the predictive performance of the model as well as avoid the problem of local minima and overfitting. Similarly, in RBFNN, Gaussian function works as an activation function, the value of which depends on the suitable value of its center and width. These parameters may be optimized either using the self-experiment of ANN technique or by any optimization techniques including Particle Swarm Optimization (PSO), Genetic Algorithms (GA) and others. In the proposed research work hidden layer neurons and other parameters as explained above are decided through the experiment. Also, ANN architecture with three neurons in the input layer and one neuron in the output layer is designed.

In order to train and to validate the models popular K-fold cross validation method is used which produces more reliable results since it uses all the parts of the samples as training as well as testing. K-fold is a common technique for estimating the accuracy of prediction models in which entire samples are eventually used for both training and testing. In this method original data is splits into k equal size subsamples out of which k-1 sub-samples are used to train the model, and one subsample is used to validate the trained model, the final result is the average of all the folds. In this research work 10-fold cross validation method is used. In which nine folds are used for training the model while one fold is used for testing the model, and the process is repeated 10 times considering another nine folds as training and one fold as testing.

SIMULATION STUDY

Simulation of the work is carried out with WEKA (http://www.cs.waikato.ac.nz/ml/weka/), which provides many machine learning techniques like a decision tree, ANN, association rule mining, clustering, classification and regression along with data preprocessing tools like K-fold cross-validation, etc. A Graphical User Interface (GUI) feature of WEKA allows a developer to choose machine learning methods by importing data from excel sheet. Exchange rate data explained in the previous section are normalized using simple normalization formulae by dividing each data with a maximum value of data set to produce data ranging from 0 to 1. MLP and RBFNN with 2 to 3 number of input neurons and one output neuron as network topology were used to develop the models, parameters of these two techniques are set as default value. These models are tested using a ten-fold cross-validation and produces average testing results in terms of Mean absolute Error (MAE) and Mean Absolute Percentage Error (MAPE) as shown in Tables 3-6 for different model with different input parameters as High-Low-Close (H-L-C), Low-Close (L-C),

High-Close (H-C) and High-Low (H-L) for both the exchange rate data. Out of two ANN techniques considered in this research work, MLP is performing better than RBFNN. Also, the close value is playing a crucial role in the prediction of FX rate in the combination of High and Low parameters for both FX data. Table 7 entails the consolidated results of EUR/USD FX data. The results reveal that model with L-C and H-C parameters performed equally well (MAPE= 0.621 and 2.917 respectively for MLP and RBFNN) for daily FX data while for weekly FX data model with L-C as input parameters is performing well with MAPE = 1.624 and 6.054 respectively for MLP and RBFNN. On the other hand Table 8 contains EUR/JPY FX results. The results reveal that model with L-C and H-C input parameters is again equal (MAPE= 0.848 and 4.053 for MLP and RBFNN respectively) for daily FX data while it is 2.028 and 5.714 using L-C and 2.217 and 5.737 using H-C respectively for MLP and RBFNN for weekly FX data. Comparative results shown in above tables reveals that close value of is more important than others. A graphical view of comparative prediction results in terms of MAPE for various models with different input parameters is given in Figures 3 (a), (b) and 4 (a), (b) for daily and weekly time step for exchange rate EUR/USD and EUR/JPY respectively. These figures clearly reflect that MLP is performing better than RBFNN for FX data.

Table 3: Experimental results with High, Low and Close (H-L-C) as input

ANN Technique	Time Step	EUR/USD		EUR/JPY	
		MAE	MAPE	MAE	MAPE
MLP	Daily	0.005	0.623	0.007	0.870
	Weekly	0.012	1.643	0.015	2.085
RBFNN	Daily	0.026	3.016	0.033	4.141
	Weekly	0.046	6.273	0.045	5.848

Table 4: Experimental results with Low and Close (L-C)as input

ANN Technique	Time Step	EUR/USD		EUR/JPY	
		MAE	MAPE	MAE	MAPE
MLP	Daily	0.005	0.621	0.006	0.848
	Weekly	0.012	1.624	0.015	2.028
RBFNN	Daily	0.025	2.917	0.032	4.053
	Weekly	0.045	6.054	0.044	5.714

Table 5: Experimental results with High and Close (H-C) as input

ANN Technique	Time Step	EUR/USD		EUR/JPY	
		MAE	MAPE	MAE	MAPE
MLP	Daily	0.005	0.621	0.006	0.848
	Weekly	0.012	1.653	0.016	2.217
RBFNN	Daily	0.025	2.917	0.032	4.053
	Weekly	0.045	6.056	0.044	5.733

Table 6: Experimental results with High and Low (H-L) as input

ANN Technique	Time Step	EUR/USD		EUR/JPY	
		MAE	MAPE	MAE	MAPE
MLP	Daily	0.006	0.700	0.007	0.891
	Weekly	0.012	1.654	0.014	1.979
RBFNN	Daily	0.025	2.923	0.032	4.062
	Weekly	0.045	6.044	0.044	5.737

Table 7: Comparative experimental results with different input parameters for EUR/USD FX

ANN Technique	Time Step	H-L-C	L-C	H-C	H-L
MLP	Daily	0.623	0.621	0.621	0.700
	Weekly	1.643	1.624	1.653	1.654
RBFNN	Daily	3.016	2.917	2.917	2.923
	Weekly	6.273	6.054	6.056	6.062

Table 8: Comparative experimental results with different input parameters for EUR/JPY FX

ANN Technique	Time Step	H-L-C	L-C	H-C	H-L
MLP	Daily	0.870	0.848	0.848	0.891
	Weekly	2.085	2.028	2.217	2.312
RBFNN	Daily	4.141	4.053	4.053	4.062
	Weekly	5.848	5.714	5.733	5.737

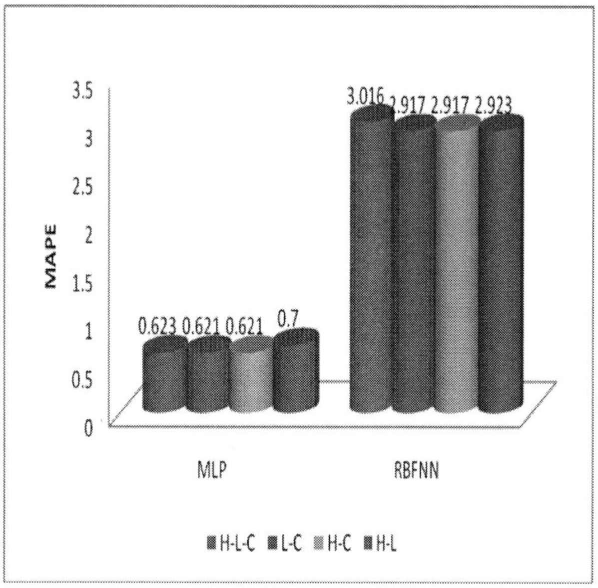

(a)

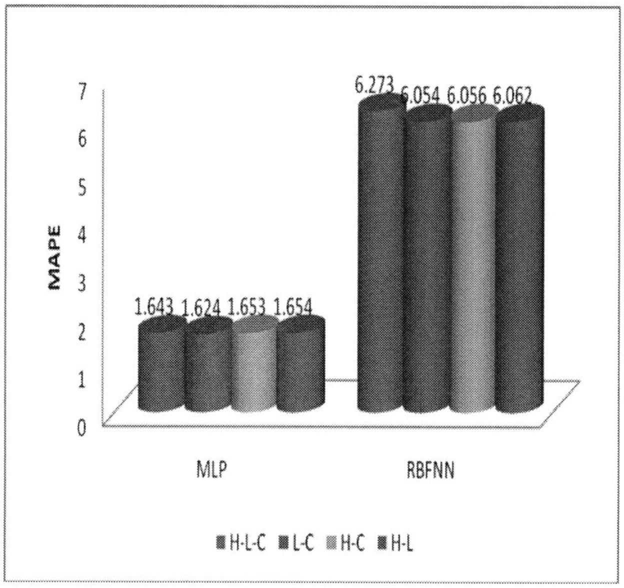

(b)

Figure 3: A comparative graph of MAPE for two ANN techniques for prediction of EUR/USD FX data with various input parameters (a) For daily time step (b) For weekly time step

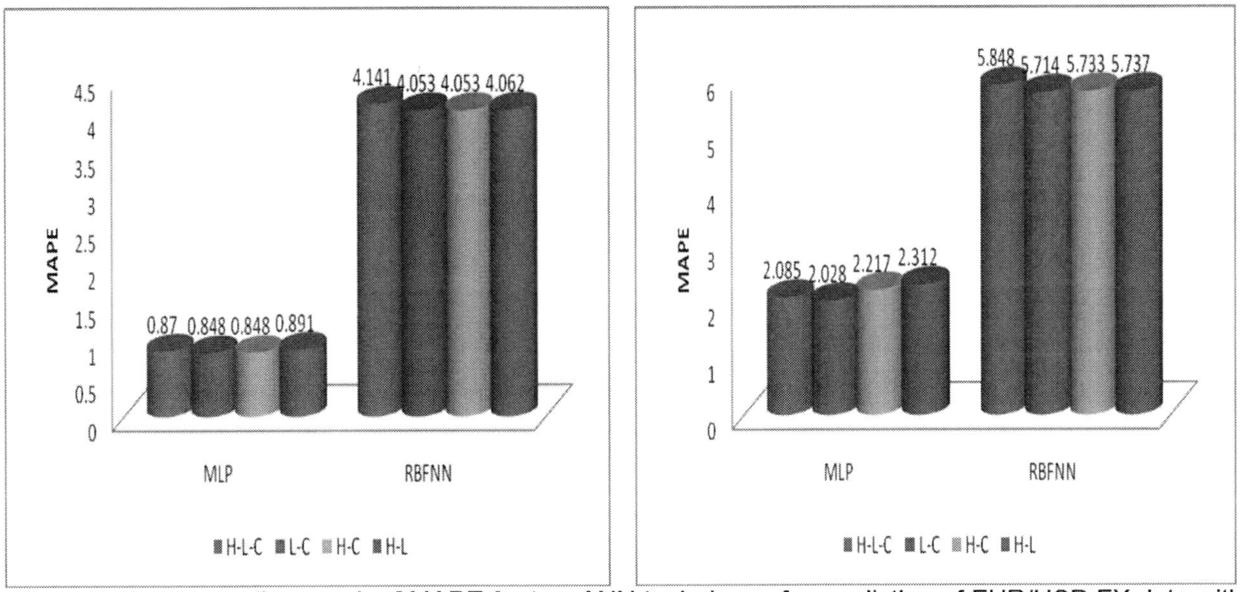

Figure 4: A comparative graph of MAPE for two ANN techniques for prediction of EUR/USD FX data with various input parameters (a) For daily time step (b) For weekly time step

CONCLUSION

Foreign exchange rates prediction is possible with nonlinear models due to nonlinear nature of exchange rates data. ANN techniques are suitable for this type of prediction. Two ANN techniques namely: MLP and RBFNN are used in this research work for predicting two exchange rates EUR/USD and EUR/JPY. Models were trained with default parameters of both the methods with 10-fold cross validation method to obtain more authentic results. The performance of ANN-based models was evaluated regarding MAPE and MAE. It has been observed that MLP outperformed than RBFNN in predicting both exchange rates with daily as well as weekly step with Low and Close as input parameters, It is also noted that models with close as one of the input parameter in the combination of others are performing better than the input parameters without close. This study, as well as previous literature, proves that ANN may be the best choice as an independent model or in a combination of other intelligent techniques for foreign exchange rate prediction. The future scope of extension of this study may include hybridization of the predictive model, feature extraction from exchange rates data and optimization of various parameters of ANN as well as input parameters using evolutionary techniques.

REFERENCES

Baillie, R., & McMahon, P. (1989). *The foreign exchange market: theory and econometric evidence*, Cambridge, UK, 1989.

Bollerslev, T. (1986). Generalized autoregressive conditional heteroskedasticity. *Journal of Econometrics*, 31, 307–327.

Chen, A., & Leung, M.T. (2004). Regression neural network for error correction in foreign exchange forecasting and trading. *Computers and Operations Research*, 31, 1049–1068.

(A complete list of references is available upon request)

DECISION SCIENCES INSTITUTE

Power and collaborative climate: building competitive advantage through flexibilities

Yan Jin
Quinnipiac University
Email: jinyan1999@yahoo.com

Erika Marsillac
Old Dominion University
Email: emarsill@odu.edu

ABSTRACT

In a buyer-supplier relationship (BSR), how is a manufacturer's power related to its collaborative supplier climate and how do these two governance mechanisms simultaneously influence a firm's performance? Evaluating 201 responses from senior manufacturing indicates that power and collaborative climate are positively related. A manufacturing firm's power positively impacts cost and non-cost competitive advantage and is fully mediated by the firm's flexibility. When flexibility exists, a manufacturer's collaborative climate positively influences non-cost advantage and flexibility, with only an indirect impact on cost. This suggests that manufacturing companies need both power and a collaborative climate to sustainably improve overall performance.

KEYWORDS: Supply chain, power, collaborative climate, competitive advantage

1. INTRODUCTION

To cope with increasing changes in competition, manufacturing firms are willing to cooperate with suppliers, manage supplier relationships based on trust and long-term orientation, and communicate more frequently and intensively with suppliers (Cai and Yang, 2008; Singh and Power, 2009; Zhang and Cao, 2011). Despite these adaptations to the traditional buyer-supplier relationship (BSR), the influence of a manufacturing firm's power has been rarely addressed in the literature (Cox, 1999). Simultaneous empirical investigations of the influence of a manufacturing firm's power and a collaborative climate towards its suppliers are even more rare.

Although power and collaborative climate are two different social forces in a buyer-supplier relationship, they are intended to promote desired behaviors in suppliers that favor this manufacturer so that they can co-exist and work together successfully. Power can be used to manage the efficiency of transactions between a manufacturing firm and its suppliers, although the concept of power is a concept that requires opinion alignment and agreement between the dyad. Collaborative climate can foster a long-term BSR so that efficiency is sustainable. This paper contributes to the literature by empirically investigating how these two governance forces work together in a BSR and how they simultaneously influence firm performance. Another contribution of this research is to test the mediating effect of flexibility on the relationships between power and firm performance and between collaborative climate and firm performance, to better explain the importance of flexibility in sustaining a manufacturing firm's competitive advantage.

In the next section, each construct and its interactions are discussed. Following, the research methodology is introduced along with a measurement model. Results of the structural equation model are presented next and the discussion and recommendation for future research are included to conclude.

2. LITERATURE REVIEW AND MODEL DEVELOPMENT

Although power remains a more subjective topic in a BSR, both power and collaboration are important managerial aspects of influencing suppliers' behavior so that the competitive advantages are sustained. We argue that (1) power and collaborative climate do not contradict each other but are positively correlated to each other, (2) they are both positively related to firm performance, and (3) the effects of power and collaborative climate on firm performance are mediated by a manufacturing firm's flexibility. Figures 1a and 1b illustrate these relationships.

*******Insert Figures 1a and 1b about here*******

2.1. A manufacturer's power over its supplier

Power features prominently in buyer-supplier relationships. In this research, power is considered a manufacturing firm's ability to get its suppliers to do what would otherwise not have been done with regard to quality control, product design, process management, material management, and information systems (Gaski, 1988; Lambert and Cooper, 2000; Weber et al., 1991; Wheelwright, 1984). This definition is based on decision areas (e.g., quality control) over which power can be exerted. Some prior research conceptualizes a manufacturer's power over its suppliers based on sources of power (i.e., reward, coercive, legitimate, referent, and expert powers) (Benton and Maloni, 2005; Handley and Benton, 2012; Zhao et al., 2008). Other prior research defines power based on the dependence of other firms on the focal firm (Emery and Marques, 2011; Krajewski et al., 2005) or defines it more generally (Song and Benedetto 2008).

Compared to prior research, the power definition utilized in here has several advantages. As decision areas are aligned with a manufacturing firm's operations structure, this perspective is able to distinguish a manufacturing firm's power over its suppliers from a firm's power over its customers and other downstream channel members. In addition, a power definition based on decision areas lets a manufacturing firm know its strengths and weaknesses in each decision area so that it can identify areas ripe for improvement. It is also easier for a manufacturing firm to exercise its power in a sole decision area than use a single source of power. For example, when a supplier signs a contract with Apple to provide a customized laser (Satariano and Burrows, 2011), the contract is Apple's legitimate source to reward or punish this supplier. The supplier accepts that contract with the intent of expected benefits from collaborating with a valuable global company, which reflects Apple's reference and expert powers. In this case, Apple's power is a combination of all power sources.

2.2. A manufacturer's collaborative climate towards its suppliers

Based on the organizational climate concept (Patterson et al., 2003), the collaborative climate developed by a manufacturing firm shapes the atmosphere of shared norms, beliefs, and attitudes regarding the firm's supplier relationships. Among all aspects of a firm's climate towards its suppliers, trust and long-term orientation most influence relationship performance (Wagner et al., 2010). Trust is a cumulative factor in a quality BSR and is important for a manufacturing firm to maintain long-term relationships (Wagner et. al., 2010). A long-term oriented manufacturing firm is more likely to maintain closer relationships with its suppliers. The closer relationships can result in less opportunistic supplier behavior, which then facilitates a manufacturing firm to cultivate more trust toward its suppliers (Lui and Ngo, 2012).

Of course, trust and long-term orientation do not exist in vacuum. Two major approaches of building trust and developing long-term orientation are through open communication and through prior cooperation with suppliers (Lui & Ngo, 2012; Morgan & Hunt, 1984). Open and timely communication fosters trust by helping resolve conflicts and reaching agreements in a BSR (Morgan & Hunt, 1984). The success of prior cooperation between a manufacturer and its suppliers indicates lower risk in collaborating with the same suppliers in the future. The perception of lower risk facilitates long-term orientation (Lui & Ngo, 2012). Reciprocally, trust and long-term orientation are argued to be able to enhance communication, facilitate information sharing, and foster learning and cooperation between two organizations (Patterson et al., 2003).

2.3. Power and collaborative climate: two sides of a supplier-manufacturer relationship

Power and collaboration are both relational concepts that explain how a manufacturer and suppliers interact in their relationships. From Social Exchange Theory, every relationship has two sides, the symmetrical side that deals with the harmony between two entities in a relationship, and the asymmetrical side that deals with the conflict in a relationship (Baldwin, 1978; Pilbeam, 2013). Based on this theory, power and collaborative climate are two governance mechanisms that a manufacturing firm uses to deal with conflict and promote harmony simultaneously in a manufacturer-supplier relationship. Although there must be alignment between manufacturer and supplier perspectives, particularly with regard to who holds greater power, we argue that it is necessary to manage both power and collaboration in a BSR because they are interdependent and managing either one alone may deteriorate a long-term relationship.

First, power and collaboration complement each other. A manufacturing firm's power comes from suppliers' dependence on some resources owned by the manufacturer or suppliers' expected benefits of working with the manufacturer (Krajewski et al., 2005). Such dependence and expected benefits are sources of power, making suppliers more likely to collaborate with a manufacturing firm. On the other hand, collaboration prevents a manufacturing firm from misusing its power in a buyer-supplier relationship. Exercising power properly is critical to having positive influences of power on suppliers' satisfaction and firm performance (Benton & Meloni, 2005).

Second, either power or collaboration alone cannot build a long-term successful buyer-supplier relationship. A manufacturing firm with diminishing power has less control over suppliers' opportunistic behaviors (Ahmadjian & Lincoln, 2001) and a manufacturing firm without a collaborative supplier orientation may abuse its power over suppliers (Cox, 1999). In either case, the quality of a buyer-supplier relationship will not be sustained and that will hurt firm performance in a long run.

Hypothesis 1: A manufacturing firm's power over its supplier is positively correlated to its collaborative climate towards its suppliers.

2.4. A manufacturing firm's competitive advantage

Competitive advantage indicates the extent to which an organization is able to develop an edge over its competitors (McGinnis & Vallopra, 1999). In this study, two competitive advantages: cost and non-cost (i.e., quality, dependable delivery, and time-to-market) are considered. Cost and the other three measures are separated because they represent two distinct sets of measures (Krause et al., 2007). Cost advantage indicates a manufacturer's ability to maintain profit. Cost means to compete by providing products with the lowest cost. Non-cost competitive advantages reflect a manufacturer's ability to provide a high level of customer service (Shepherd & Gunter, 2005). These customer service focused measures cannot be easily copied by other competitors and thus have sustainable value. Quality means to compete by having products that consistently meet or exceed the customer's expectations. Dependable delivery means to compete by consistently delivering the right product to customers at the right time. Time-to-market means to compete by providing the product faster to customers.

2.5. Direct effects of power and collaborative climate on the firm's competitive advantage

A manufacturer's power with regard to quality control (e.g., inspection) first ensures that suppliers' products meet the manufacturing firm's standard and thus these products will not cause delays and interrupt a manufacturer's operations (Ho et al., 2010). Second, in order to bring a satisfied product to customers, a firm needs suppliers' cooperation in product design related activities (e.g., function) (Vonderembse & Tracey, 1999). Third, a manufacturing firm's ability to get its suppliers to change their processes (e.g., technology capability) determines the extent of alignment between a manufacturing firm and its suppliers (Liker & Choi, 2004). Fourth, the degree to which suppliers would comply with the manufacturer's requests in material management (e.g., storage and retrieval) influences a manufacturing firm's ability to provide speedy and reliable delivery at low cost (Fogarty et al., 1991). Last, suppliers' information systems' adjustments (e.g., network accessibility) as requested by a manufacturing firm, support that manufacturer's inter-firm cooperation (Gunasekaran & Ngai, 2005). As mentioned above, changes in suppliers' quality systems, product management, process, material management, and information systems enhance the manufacturing firm's capabilities to compete on price, quality, delivery, and time-to-market. Therefore, it is hypothesized that:

Hypothesis 2a: A manufacturing firm with a higher level of power over its supplier is more likely have a higher level of cost competitive advantage.

Hypothesis 2b: A manufacturing firm with a higher level of power over its supplier is more likely have a higher level of non-cost competitive advantage.

A climate of trust is able to facilitate information sharing and foster learning between two organizations, contributing greater knowledge and appreciation to a BSR (Corsten & Kumar, 2005). Such openness to a relationship results in greater satisfaction that leads to longer-term successful relationships between a manufacturer and suppliers. With a long-term orientation, a manufacturing firm expects to work closely with its suppliers over a longer period of time. In addition, suppliers could benefit from a BSR with a long-term orientation by having long-term contracts and frequent transactions. The close tie between partners results in a stable relationship and improved performance (Das & Teng, 1998). Open communication allows a manufacturer to become more familiar with suppliers, have a better view of their capabilities, and better predict their behaviors (Morgan & Hunt, 1984). In return, trust and a long-term orientation encourage a manufacturer to communicate with suppliers more frequently and intensively. This reciprocal process commits a manufacturer and its suppliers to their relationships, reduces opportunistic behaviors and eventually improves relationship performance. Prior cooperation combines manufacturer and supplier resources to achieve common goals (Lui & Ngo, 2012). Trust and long-term orientation then foster more cooperation with suppliers in the future, which leads to overall enhanced relationship performance. Given the importance of a manufacturing firm's collaborative company climate on the firm performance, it is hypothesized that:

Hypothesis 3a: A manufacturing firm with a higher level of collaborative climate towards its supplier is more likely have a higher level of cost competitive advantage.

Hypothesis 3b: A manufacturing firm with a higher level of collaborative climate towards its supplier is more likely have a higher level of non-cost competitive advantage.

2.6. A manufacturing firm's flexibility

A manufacturing firm's flexibility improves its adaptability in dynamic environments and the sustainability of its competitive advantages in a supply chain (Narasimhan et al., 2004). In this research, a manufacturing firm's flexibility includes product development (new product introduction and product modification) and production (production volumes and product mixes) flexibilities (Narasimhan et al., 2004; Zhang el al., 2003). Because of these multi-dimensional characteristics, flexibility also needs to be measured by range and mobility (Koste & Malhotra, 1999; Swafford et al., 2006). Range is represented by the number of options offered and the degree of difference among those options offered by a manufacturer. Mobility indicates the responsiveness within the set of products offered, i.e., how quickly and efficiently a switch can be made.

2.7. The mediating effect of a manufacturing firm's flexibility

There are three aspects of a manufacturing firm's flexibility level (Zhang el al., 2003). A high level of flexibility means efficiency in developing new products, modifying existing products, adjusting product varieties and changing production volume. In other words, the manufacturing firm can provide products to its customers at minimal cost. Flexibility also means that the manufacturing firm is able to make prompt changes in product development and production. Thus the firm can introduce products quickly to market, improving the firm's capability to offer a time-to-market that is lower than the industry average. Flexibility indicates that the manufacturing firm is able to maintain the same level of product quality and delivery reliability despite changes in product development and production. Therefore, flexibility ensures the high quality of products and dependable delivery offered by the manufacturing firm.

Power and collaborative climate indicate the different ways a manufacturing firm deals with its suppliers. When a manufacturing firm exerts its power, it explicitly requests that its suppliers make changes in the various decision areas. When a manufacturing firm uses a collaborative climate towards its suppliers, it openly discusses discrepancies, builds cooperation over time, develops trust and posits long-term orientations (Lui & Ngo, 2012; Wagner et. al., 2010). These tactics let suppliers feel confident that if they responsively make the changes requested by the manufacturing firm, they will get more benefits in the long-term and thus are willing to make changes. With changes being made as a result of either a manufacturing firm's power or the firm's collaborative climate, suppliers are better aligned with the manufacturer's operations. With supplier assistance, the manufacturing firm can then respond to customer demand more efficiently and effectively by changing its product development and production, resulting in higher flexibility. Eventually, with increasing flexibility, the firm can better serve customers with low cost, high quality, dependable delivery and quick time-to-market. Giving the relationships mentioned above, it is hypothesized that:

Hypothesis 4a: A manufacturing firm's flexibility mediates the effect of its power over its suppliers on cost advantage and non-cost advantage.

Hypothesis 4b: A manufacturing firm's flexibility mediates the effect of its collaborative climate towards its suppliers on cost advantage and non-cost advantage.

3. RESEARCH DESIGN AND METHODOLOGY

3.1 Measurement Development

Manufacturing firm power items were developed based on power literature (El-Ansary & Stern, 1972; Gaski, 1988; Benton & Maloni, 2005) and literature related to five decision areas (Fogarty et al., 1991; Gunasekaran & Ngai, 2005; Ho et al., 2010; Liker & Choi, 2004; Vonderembse & Tracey, 1999). Power variable items were measured through managerial perceptions using 5-point Likert scales (1 = strongly disagree to 5 = strongly agree) to indicate the extent to which respondents agreed or disagreed with each statement as it applied to their firm's power over suppliers in *quality control* (e.g., inspection of parts shipped to the manufacturing firm), *product design* (e.g., product design capability), *process management* (e.g., process equipment), *material management* (e.g., material verification and tracking methods), and *information systems* (e.g., network accessibility).

A manufacturing firm's collaborative climate items were developed based on BSR literature with trust, long-term orientation, communication and cooperation foci (Lui & Ngo, 2012; Morgan & Hunt, 1994; Patterson et al., 2003; Wagner et al., 2010). Collaborative climate items were measured using 5-point Likert scales to indicate the extent to which respondents agreed or disagreed with statements that a manufacturing firm's external climate facilitated trust, long-term orientation, cooperation, and open communication with their suppliers.

Flexibility items were developed based on flexibility literature (Koste & Malhotra, 1999; Zhang et al., 2003). Flexibility items were measured using 5-point Likert scales regarding a manufacturing firm's flexibility in product development (e.g., introduce new products efficiently) and production (e.g., operate at many high and low production volumes). A firm's competitive advantage items were modified from performance measures used in prior research (e.g., Krause et al., 2007). These items were also measured using 5-point Likert scales regarding a manufacturing firm's capability to compete by offering competitive prices, high quality, dependable delivery, and time-to-market that is lower than the industry average.

After the literature review, a questionnaire was developed and pre-tested to refine content validity through consultations with professionals and practitioners with extensive BSR knowledge. A Q-sort method was applied in a pilot study to assess the preliminary convergent validity and discriminant validity of the instruments (Moore & Benbasat, 1991). Items were revised as needed based on expert feedback, for the large-scale survey.

3.2 Data Collection

The data was collected via an online survey of supply chain professionals in various U.S. manufacturing companies. Respondents took the role of buyers in responding the survey. An initial invitation was sent to each of the potential respondents by email with a link to the online survey website. Two reminder emails were sent out as follow up. Respondents were offered the research results as an incentive for participation and provided with other options (e.g., mail or fax) to answer the survey. 201 usable responses were received, yielding a 3.3% response rate. The response rate (3.3%) of this research is comparable to other research in management literature (e.g., Beltran-Martin et al., 2008), considering a large amount of emails which were likely filtered by security systems, expired due to relocation, and/or the declining response level of top management to email surveys (Baruch & Holtom, 2008; Klassen & Jacobs, 2001).

The external validity of the sample was examined based on the sampling design, its representativeness, and sample size (Short et al., 2002). The study population was collected from three databases of executive contacts, accounting for a large share of the total business and total population of U.S. firms. In addition, the sample covered more than nine manufacturing sectors with a good balance and covered companies of different sizes and different annual sales. For these reasons, the results can be generalized for small, medium, and large companies across a variety of manufacturing industries. Moreover, respondents, including top executives, senior production managers, senior logistics managers, senior purchasing managers, are expected to be knowledgeable of the capabilities of their companies and suppliers, resulting in suitability for this research.

The sample's representativeness was accessed by non-response bias in terms of company size and annual sales. Differences between the 201 respondents[1] and the population[2]

[1] Total number of respondents was 201. However, three respondents didn't provide the company size and annual sale information. Therefore, only 198 were used to calculate the non-respondent bias.

were examined by using Chi-squared tests (Short et al., 2002) among four categories (under 100, 100-249, 250-999, and more than 1000) for company size and five categories (under \$10M, \$10M-\$49M, \$50M-\$99.9M, \$100M-\$499.9M, and more than \$500M) for annual sales. The results (χ^2=2.98, df=3, p>0.25 for company size, and χ^2=1.87, df=4, p>0.5 for annual sales) indicated no significant differences between the sample and the population; thus, response bias is not an issue.

A sample size over 150 or 200 is commonly considered necessary to be able to perform a stable and a rigorous SEM model (Hair et al., 2005). The sample size of 201 useable respondents met this need.

4. MEASUREMENT MODEL RESULTS AND MODEL FIT

To address the issue of common method variance, a single factor model evolving all items is tested (Podsakoff et al. 2003). The model-fit indexes of the model (χ^2= 232.303, df = 377, p = 0.000; RMSEA= 0.161, 90% confidence interval ranging from 0.155 to 0.17; GFI = 0.471; AGFI = 0.389; RMR= 0.117; NFI = 0.327; CFI = 0.31) were far from the acceptable value (Byrne 2001), which indicates that common method variance did not exist.

A manufacturing firm's flexibility was measured by two first-order variables (i.e., product development and production flexibilities). A manufacturing firm's power was measured by five first-order variables (i.e., quality control, product design, process management, material management, and information systems). A manufacturing firm's collaborative climate and non-cost competitive advantage were first-order variables. The cost advantage was a single item measure. Confirmatory factor analyses (CFA) were used to examine the unidimensionality and reliability of nine first-order variables and two second-order variable. The fit indexes of the measurement model indicate the model is acceptable (χ^2=3650.081, df=406; NFI=0.848, CFI=0.940; RMSEA=0.520). All item-to-factor loadings were greater than 0.5 (p<0.001), indicating acceptable scale unidimensionality (Ellis et al., 2010; Shah & Goldstein, 2006). Composite Reliability (CR) values exceeded the 0.7 cutoff for all variables, indicating acceptable reliability (Fornell & Larcker, 1981). AVE values of the seven variables (except non-cost competitive advantage and power) surpassed the 0.5 cutoff. AVEs of two variables were close to cutoff values (0.484 for non-cost competitive advantage and 0.492 for power). The CR values of each variable were greater than its AVE, indicating convergent validity is satisfied (Fornell & Larcker, 1981). Discriminant validity was assessed by comparing the AVE and the MSV for each variable (Fornell & Larcker, 1981). The MSV for each variable was less than the AVE for that variable, which indicated adequate discriminant validity for all variables (Fornell & Larcker, 1981).

After constructs were validated, the hypothesized relationships were tested in a structural model. Weighted scores were calculated for product development and production flexibilities. Composite scores were used as the observed items for a manufacturing firm's flexibility in the structural model. Weighted scores were also calculated for quality control, product design, process management, material management, and information systems of a manufacturer's power regarding its suppliers. Composite scores were used as observed items for a manufacturing firm's power in the structural model. Collaborative climate was a first-order variable and corresponding items were observed items for this variable in the structural model. Non-cost competitive advantage (NCCA) is a formative rather than reflective variable. For this reason, the weighted value of NCCA was used (Bozarth et al., 2009; Cua et al., 2001). The cost

---

[2] One source that provided a mailing list did not disclose information about company size and annual sales. The number of contacts provided by this source is less than 15% of the entire population. Therefore, we calculated the non-respondent bias by comparing the respondents with the population from the other two sources where the company size and annual sales information were available.

advantage is a single item variable and that single item was used in the structural model. Results of the structural model indicated a reasonable model fit (χ^2=1653.516, df=78; CFI=0.970, NFI=0.936; RMSEA=0.064).

5. DISCUSSION

Hypotheses results are summarized in Table 1. Hypothesis 1 evaluated the correlation between power and collaborative climate, and was tested in the mediated model. Results show a significant correlation between the two governance mechanisms with 0.259 of a standardized regression weight and 3.065 of a critical ratio. This suggests that power and collaboration, two very different governing mechanisms developed by the manufacturing firm, are interdependent rather than independent. A direct effect model is used to test Hypotheses 2 and 3. Hypothesis 2 captured the influence of power on competitive advantage. Results suggest that power has a significant direct impact on both cost (standardized coefficient=0.298) and non-cost competitive advantage (standardized coefficient=0.304) in the direct model, thus Hypothesis 2 was supported. Results of Hypothesis 3 show an insignificant effect of collaborative climate on cost or non-cost in the direct model, thus Hypothesis 3 was not supported.

Testing of the mediation effect of flexibility, Hypothesis 4, was conducted through two structural models. A direct effect model was used to test the relationship between a predictor and a dependent variable (power and climate to cost and non-cost in the context of this paper). Since the direct effects of power on cost and non-cost were significant, the mediation effect test for Hypothesis 4a continued with a mediated model. In the mediated model, results suggest that power significantly affects flexibility, which significantly and positively affects cost and non-cost. In addition, direct effects of power on cost and non-cost in the mediated model were not significant. In other words, their direct effects diminished when flexibility (the mediator) is present. Therefore, Hypothesis 4a was supported and flexibility fully mediated the relationship between power and cost and the relationship between power and non-cost. Despite this, the direct effects of climate on cost and non-cost in the direct model were not significant. Therefore the mediation effect test was not continued and there was no mediated effect of flexibility found on either relationship. Hence, Hypothesis 4b was not supported.

A noteworthy finding was that even the direct effect of climate on cost and non-cost in the direct model were not significant, while the indirect effects of climate on cost and non-cost were both positive and significant in the mediated model. In addition, in the mediated model, climate positively and significantly affected the non-cost competitive advantages directly.

*******Insert Table 1 about here*******

6. SUMMARY

Manufacturers are striving to achieve competitive advantage through simultaneous self-improvement initiatives and working with suppliers. Prior BSR research often overlooked power as a governance mechanism in manufacturer-supplier relationships. This research shows that manufacturing firm power and collaborative climate are positively correlated, which means they are not exclusive in a BSR. Furthermore, in the direct model, the firm's power, not collaborative climate, has direct positive impacts on competitive advantage. With flexibility presents, collaborative climate shows significant indirect effects on competitive advantage and significant direct effects on non-cost advantages. Such results also indicate the importance of a balance of power and collaborative climate for manufacturing firms (Ireland & Webb, 2007). Simultaneously managing power and collaborative climate are important to maintain a sustainable BSR, and improve overall competitive advantages.

The results of Hypothesis 4 also indicate the importance of a manufacturing's flexibility on its competitive advantages. With improved flexibility in production and product development, the indirect impacts of power and collaborative climate on cost and non-cost competitive advantages are significant and positive. In fact, in the mediated model, the direct impact of power on non-cost competitive advantage and the direct impact of collaborative climate on cost are negative. Although neither negative impact is significant, without the effect of flexibility, the overall performance worsens.

7. CONCLUSION, LIMITATIONS AND FUTURE RESEARCH

Although this research provides several significant contributions, some limitations need to be addressed in future research. First, this research is a cross-sectional study. Future longitudinal research may provide further insights underlying the relationships between power, the collaborative climate, flexibility and competitive advantages. Since power is a concept requiring mutual agreement between partners, it is possible that the participants had differing views on the power balance in the interaction under analysis, hence power agreement can be examined further. Second, multiple respondents, multiple methods for obtaining measures, and randomizing the item order can be used in future research to moderate mono-respondent problems. The non-random initial sample of US-based supply chain executives of more than nine manufacturing sectors, although representing a good balance and coverage of firms, is a slice of total possible firms and thus could be expanded in future work. Third, future research can improve response rates by using different media for data collection, reaching the intended respondents via state-of-the-art techniques, shortening the questionnaire, and establishing collaborative relationships between researchers and respondents (Dillman et al., 2009). Fourth, because of the low reliability of customer service competitive advantages, a second-order construct might be considered to better represent variables. In addition to these methodological limitations, different research models can be considered. For example, if a manufacturing firm has limited resources to improve its power in one first-order power construct (e.g., quality management), how will the power on quality management and the firm's collaborative climate impact the firm's cost and non-cost competitive advantages?

Overall, this research contributes to the literature by investigating the importance of two governance mechanisms for a BSR and proposes a balanced emphasis on both power and collaborative climate for a manufacturing firm to achieve sustained completive advantages through improving flexibility in product development and production.

REFERENCES

Ahmadjian, C. L., & Lincoln, J. R. (2001). Keiretsu, governance, and learning: Case studies in change from the Japanese automotive industry. *Organization Science*, 12(6), 683-701.

Baldwin, D.A. (1978). Power and Social Exchange. *The American Political Science Review*, 72, 1229-1242.

Baruch, Y. & Holton, B. C. (2008). Survey response rate levels and trends in organizational research. *Human Relations*, 61(8), 1139-1160.

Beltran-Martin, I., Roca-Puig, V., Escrig-Tena, A., & Bou-Llusar, J. C. (2008). Human resources flexibility as a mediating variable between high performance work systems and performance. *Journal of Management*, 34(5), 1009-1044.

Benton, W. C. & Maloni, M. (2005). The influence of power driven buyer/seller relationships on supply chain satisfaction. *Journal of Operations Management*, 23, 1-22.

Bozarth, C. C., D. P. Warsing, B. B. Flynn, & Flynn, E. J. (2009). The Impact of Supply Chain Complexity on Manufacturing Plant Performance. *Journal of Operations Management*, 27, 78–93.

Byrne, B. M. 2001. Structural Equation Modeling with AMOS. Mahwah, NJ: Lawrence Erlbaum.

Cai, S., & Yang, Z. (2008). Development of cooperative norms in the buyer-supplier relationship: the Chinese experience. *Journal of Supply Chain Management*, 44(1), 55-70.

Corsten, D., & Kumar, N. (2005). Do suppliers benefit from collaborative relationships with large retailers? An empirical investigation of efficient consumer response adoption. *Journal of Marketing*, 69(3), 80-94.

Cox, A. (1999). Power, value and supply chain management. *Supply Chain Management: An International Journal*, 4(4), 167-175.

Cua, K. O., K. E. Mckone, & Schroeder, R. G. (2001). Relationships Between Implementation of TQM, JIT, and TPM and Manufacturing Performance. *Journal of Operations Management*, 19, 675–694.

Das, T. K. & Teng, B. S. (1998). Between trust and control: developing confidence in partner cooperation in alliances. *Academy of Management Review*, 23(3), 491-512.

Dillman, D.A., Phelps, G., Tortora, R., Swift, K., Kohrell, J., Berck, J., and Messer, B.L. (2009). Response rate and measurement differences in mixed-mode surveys using mail, telephone, interactive voice response (IVR) and the internet. *Social Science Research*, 38(1), 1–18.

Eliis, S.C., Raymond, M.H., & Shockley, J. (2010). Buyer perceptions of supply disruption risk: A behavioral view and empirical assessment. *Journal of Operations Management*, 28(1), 34-46.

El-Ansary, A. I. & Stern L. W. (1972). Power measurement in the distribution channel. *Journal of Marketing Research*, 9(1), 47-52.

Emery, G. W. & Marques, M. A. (2011). The effect of transaction costs, payment terms and power on the level of raw materials inventories. *Journal of Operations Management*, 29, 236-249.

Fogarty, D. W., Blackstone, J. H. Jr., & Hoffmann, T. R. (1991). *Production and inventory management.* Cincinnati, Ohio: South-Western Pub. Co.

Fornell, C. & Larker, D.F. (1981). Evaluating structural equation models with unobservable variables and measurement error. Journal of Marketing Research, 18, 39-50.

Gaski, J. F. (1988) Distribution channels: a validation study. *International Journal of Physical Distribution and Materials Management*, 18(5), 16-33.

Gunasekaran, A. & Ngai, E. W. T. (2005). Build-to-order supply chain management: a literature review and a framework for development. *Journal of Operations Management*, 23, 423-451.

Hair, J.F., Black, B., Babin, B., Anderson, R.E., & Tatham, R.L. (2005). Multivariate Data Analysis, sixth ed.. *Prentice Hall*, Upper Saddle River, NJ.

Handley, S. M., & Benton, W. C. (2012). The influence of exchange hazards and power on opportunism in outsourcing relationships. *Journal of Operations Management*, 30, 55-68.

Ho, W., Xu, X., & Dey, P. (2010). Multi-criteria decision making approaches for supplier evaluation and selection: a literature review. *European Journal of Operational Research*, 202(1), 16-24.

Ireland, R.D. & Webb, J.W. (2007). A multi-theoretic perspective on trust and power in strategic supply chains. *Journal of Operations Management, 25,* 482-497.

Klassen, R. D., & Jacobs, J. (2001). Experimental comparison of web, electronic and mail survey technologies in operations management. *Journal of Operations Management*, 19, 713-728.

Koste, L.L. & Malhotra, M.K. (1999). A theoretical framework for analyzing the dimensions of manufacturing flexibility. *Journal of Operations Management*, 18,75–93.

Krajewski, L., Wei, J. C., & Tang, L. L. (2005). Responding to schedule changes in build-to-order supply chains. *Journal of Operations Management*, 23, 452-469.

Krause, D.R., Handfield, R.B., & Tyler,B.B. (2007). The relationships between supplier development, commitment, social capital accumulation and performance improvement. *Journal of Operations Management,* 25, 528–545.

Lambert, D. M. & Cooper, M. C. (2000). Issues in supply chain management. *Industrial Marketing Management*, 29(1), 65-83.

Liker, J. K. & Choi, T. Y. (2004). Building deep supplier relationships. *Harvard business review*, December, 106-113.

Liu, S.S. & Ngo, H. (2012). Drivers and outcomes of long-term orientation in cooperative relationships. *British Journal of Management*, 23, 80-95.

McGinnis, M.A. & Vallopra, R.M. (1999). Purchasing and supplier involvement in process improvement: a source of competitive performance. *Journal of Supply Chain Management*, 35(4),42–50.

Moore, G. C. & Benbasat, I. (1991). Development of an instrument to measure the perceptions of adopting an information technology innovation. *Information Systems Research*, 2(3), 192-222.

Morgan, R.M., & Hunt, S.D. (1984). The commitment-trust theory of relationship marketing. *Journal of Marketing*, 58, 20-38.

Narasimhan, R., Talluri, S., & Das, A. (2004). Exploring flexibility and execution competencies of manufacturing firms. *Journal of Operations Management,* 22, 91–106.

Patterson, K.A., Grimm, C.M., & Corsi, T.M. (2003). Adopting new technologies for supply chain management. *Transportation Research Part E*, 39, 95-121.

Pilbeam, C. (2013). Coordinating temporary organizations in international development through social and temporal embeddedness. *International Journal of Project Management*, 31(2), 190-199.

Podsakoff, P. M., S. B. Mackenzie, J. Y. Lee, and N. P. Podsakoff. 2003. Common Method Biases in Behavioral Research: A critical Review of the Literature and Recommended Remedies. Journal of Applied Psychology 88 (5), 879–903.

Satariano, A., & P. Burrows. 2011. Apple's Supply-chain Secret? Hoard lasers. *Business Week*, November 7–November 13, 35–37.

Shah, R. & Goldstein, S.M. (2006). Use of structural equation modeling in operations management research: looking back and forward. *Journal of Operations Management*, 24(2), 148.

Shepherd, C. & Gunter, H. (2005). Measuring supply chain performance: current research and future directions. *Internal Journal of Productivity and Performance Management, 55(3–4), 242–258.*

Short, J. C., Ketchen, D. J., & Palmer, T. B. (2002). The role of sampling in strategic management research on performance: a two-study analysis. *Journal of Management*, 28(3), 363-385.

Singh, P.J. & Power, D. (2009). The nature and effectiveness of collaboration between firms, their customers and suppliers: a supply chain perspective. *Supply Chain Management, An International Journal*, 14(3), 189-200.

Song, M. & Benedetto, C.A.D. (2008). Supplier's involvement and success of radical new product development in new ventures. *Journal of Operations Management*, 26, 1-22.

Swafford, P.M., Ghosh, S., & Murthy, N. (2006). A framework for assessing value chain agility. *International Journal of Operations and Production Management*, 26(2), 118–140.

Vonderembse, M., & Tracey, M. (1999). The impact of supplier selection criteria and supplier involvement on manufacturing performance. *Journal of Supply Chain Management*, 35(3), 33-39.

Wagner, S.M., Eggert, A., & Lindemann, E. (2010). Creating and appropriating value in collaborative relationships. *Journal of Business Research*, 63, 840-848.

Weber, C. A., Current, J. R., & Benton, W.C. (1991). Vendor selection criteria and methods. *European Journal of Operational Research*, 50(1), 2-18.

Wheelwright, S. C. (1984). Manufacturing strategy: defining the missing link. *Strategic Management Journal*, 5, 77-91.

Zhang, Q., & Cao, M. (2011). Supply chain collaboration: impact on collaborative advantage and firm performance. *Journal of Operations Management,* 29, 163-180.

Zhang, Q., Vonderembse, M.A., & Lim, J.S. (2003). Manufacturing flexibility: defining and analyzing relationships among competence, capability, and customer satisfaction. *Journal of Operations Management,* 21(2), 173–191.

Zhao, X., Huo, B., Flynn, B., & Yeung, J. H. Y. (2008). The impact of power and relationship commitment on the integration between manufacturers and customers in a supply chain. *Journal of Operations Management*, 26, 368-388.

FIGURE 1a: Research model - directed model

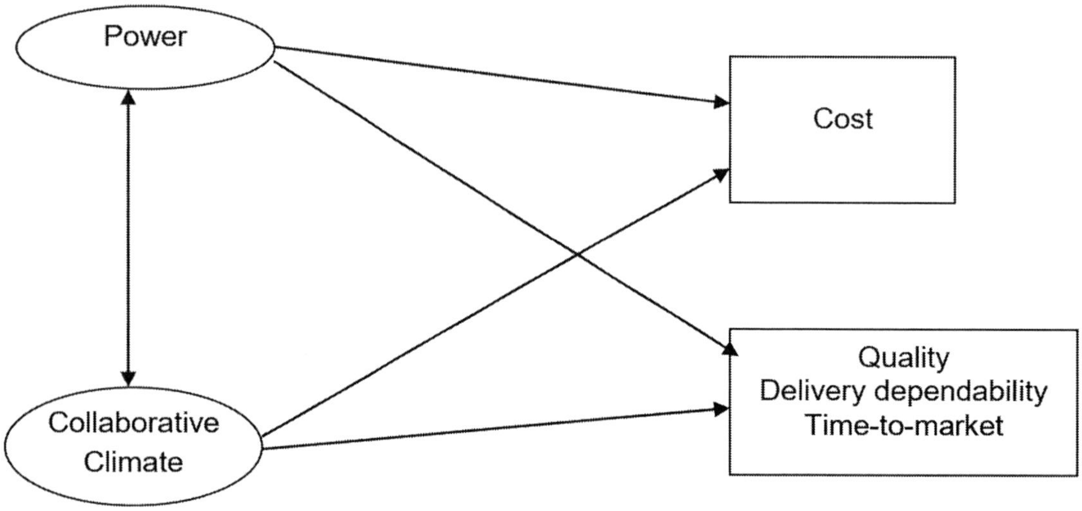

FIGURE 1b: Research model - mediated model

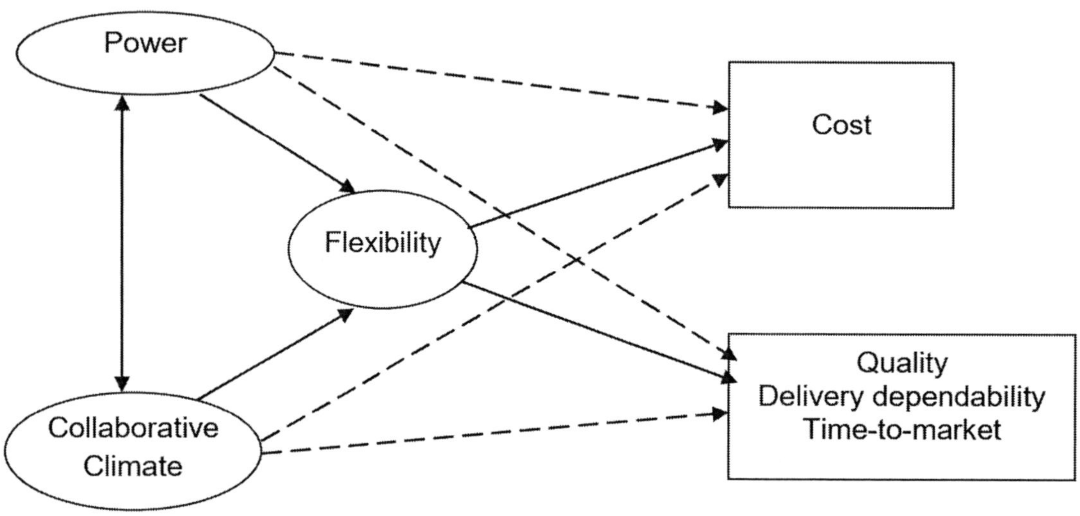

TABLE 1: Results of structural model

	Model used	Support the hypothesis or not?
H1: Power (MP) ←→Climate (MCC)	Mediated model	Yes (p<0.01, standardized coefficient=0.259, critical ratio=3.065)
H2a: Power (MP)→Cost	Direct model	Yes (p<0.01, standardized coefficient=0.298, critical ratio=3.037)
H2b: Power (MP)→ Non-cost (NCCA)	Direct model	Yes (p<0.01, standardized coefficient=0.304, critical ratio=3.141)
H3a: Climate(MCC)→ Cost	Direct model	No (standardized coefficient=-0.168, critical ratio=-1.781)
H3b: Climate(MCC)→ Non-cost (NCCA)	Direct model	No (standardized coefficient=-0.008, critical ratio=-0.092)
H4a: The mediating effect of flexibility for MP→Cost and MP→Non-cost	Direct and mediated model	Yes. Flexibility fully mediated the impacts of power on cost and non-cost. In the direct model, the effects of flexibility on cost and non-cost were significant at p<0.001. In the mediated model, the direct effects of power on cost and non-cost were insignificant while the indirect effects were significant at p<0.05 and p<0.01.
H4b: The mediating effect of flexibility for MCC→Cost and MCC→Non-cost	Direct and mediated model	No (No mediating effect is applicable because in the direct model, the effects of MCC on cost or non-cost were insignificant). However, the indirect effects of MCC on cost and non-cost are both positive and significant at p<0.05 and p<0.01.

DECISION SCIENCES INSTITUTE

Preventing Inference Attacks in Online Social Networks: A Data-Driven Framework

(Full Paper Submission)

Xiaoyun He
Auburn University at Montgomery
xhe@aum.edu

Haibing Lu
Santa Clara University
hlu@scu.edu

ABSTRACT

In recent years, the growth of online social networking sites has been meteoric. With the increasing user involvement, social networks now serve as a repository of all kinds of information. While there have been studies demonstrating private information can be inferred from social networks, few has taken a holistic view on designing mechanisms to prevent the inference attacks. In this study, we present a framework that leverages the data from both social networking service provider and user profiles to proactively find possible inference attacks against users, and suggest minimal modifications to the user profiles to eliminate such attacks.

KEYWORDS: Privacy, inference attacks, online social networks, collaborative approach

INTRODUCTION

Recent years have witnessed unprecedented growth of online social networking sites (OSNs) such as Facebook, LinkedIn, XING, etc. For example, as of December 2015, Facebook reports 1.59 billion monthly active users, with a growth rate as high as 3% per week (Facebook 2015); and LinkedIn boasts over 400 million members in over 200 countries, with a new member joining LinkedIn approximately every second (LinkedIn 2015). The emergence of OSNs has essentially transformed the way people express themselves and establish social connections in the digital era (boyd and Ellison 2007).

Individual users of an online social network can create profiles containing various personal attributes such as age, group affiliation, lists of personal interests, contact information, and so on. Some OSNs offer the ability to create and join groups that share common interests or affiliations, upload live videos, and hold discussions in forums. To alleviate privacy concerns (Barnes 2006), OSNs usually have controls that allow users to choose their own privacy settings, for instance, whether to make your profile public or private, who is allowed to view the profile, contact you, add you to their list of contacts, and so on.

Despite the availability of the privacy setting controls to the users, such controls are not sufficient in enforcing privacy of users (Singh et al. 2009). Indeed, privacy issues arising in

OSNs are of real problem. This has been evidenced by both the media exposure and the studies from the academia (e.g., Dwyer et al. 2007; Gross and Acquisti 2005; Zeller 2006). OSNs users may be vulnerable to various privacy attacks, such as automated user profiling (Balduzzi et al. 2010; Dougnon et al. 2015), identity attacks via user de-anonymization techniques (e.g., Narayanan and Shmatikov 2009; Wondracek et al. 2010), and inference attacks (e.g., He et al. 2006; Lindamood et al. 2009; Zheleva and Getoor 2009), and so on.

In order to prevent some of the above privacy attacks, technical solutions have been proposed in the literature. For instance, several anonymization solutions have been proposed to protect against identity attack in OSNs (e.g., Backstrom et al. 2007; Zou et al. 2009). While a recent study has proposed sanitization techniques that could be used to prevent inference attacks (Heatherly et al. 2013), there lacks a holistic view that can help to enforce privacy requirements or give any assurance on the level of protection in the presence of possible inferences. In this study, we focus on inference attacks, and present a data-driven framework that can be used to alleviate such attacks through the collaboration from both sides of social networks providers and users.

RELATED LITERATURE

Along with the increasing popularity of OSNs, OSNs users encounter growing risks of privacy attacks. Online Social Networking site provides a rich digital forum for social interactions. While some OSNs users are open to sharing and posting personal information, others may not. Often, the privacy risks posed to OSNs users are unexpected and unaware of. The most immediate danger of posting on OSNs is that it may leave a permanent fingerprint of whatever being posted (Rosenblum 2007). With the click of a button, what a user just typed could be instantly disseminated, and stored in countless independent permanent places. Next-minute damage recovering is almost impossible. Worse, the power of a search engine makes it searchable within a few seconds.

Some concrete examples of the privacy risks to OSNs users include stalking, spamming, and the possible damage to their future educational and career opportunities. With the information from a user profile, a potential adversary can determine the likely physical location of the user and thus incur real-world stalking (Gross and Acquisti 2005). In addition, most OSNs, such as Facebook, currently provide the third-party applications with full access to user profile data, which further deteriorate privacy control. For example, a popular Facebook application, Compare Friends, that promised users' privacy in exchange for opinions on their friends later started sell this information (Singh et al. 2009).

Inference Problem

Several studies show that, even OSNs users take advantage of the available privacy setting control to make their profiles or sensitive attributes private (i.e., no one but their friends can see their profile detail), it is still possible to infer private information that a user is not willing to disclose (e.g., He et al. 2006; Heatherly et al. 2013; Lindamood et al. 2009; Zheleva and Getoor 2009). In fact, they demonstrate that a surprisingly large amount of information can be leaked by just exploiting friendship links and/or group affiliations in the real-world online social network data.

In particular, the problem of sensitive attribute inference is to infer the hidden sensitive attribute values of private profiles that are conditioned on the observed sensitive values, links and group memberships in a social network (Zheleva and Getoor 2009). It is assumed that an adversary can apply a probabilistic model for predicting the hidden sensitive values. By combining the given information of a social network in difference ways, the adversary can launch various inference attacks (i.e., attacks without links and groups, attacks using links, attacks using groups, or a mixed of them).

As a simplified example, suppose users have attributes of gender and self-declared political views in a collected Facebook data (Zheleva and Getoor 2009). Assume that user Alice has set her profile as private. From the group information available in Facebook, Alice belongs to four groups: Crochet Mastery, the National Coalition on Health Care, Health Care for America Now, and Hand Embroidery. Based on these public information, the group-based classification model can accurately predict that Alice is female and a liberal. With assumption of 50% private profiles, the attack accuracy for gender attribute reaches at 73.4% by using group-based classification model; and the accuracy is 72.5% by using both links and groups.

The above inference problem does have significant privacy implications. Since fewer users in OSNs hide their friendship links and even if they do, their friendship links can still be constructed through the backlinks from their public profile friends. Group participation information availability is similar - even if a user keeps his / her profile private, his / her participation in a group is displayed on the group's membership list. Currently, most OSNs (e.g., Facebook and MySpace) do not allow users to hide their group membership from public groups.

In addition, privacy attacks to OSNs users may be motivated by the various self-interests of the attackers, such as targeted marketing, insurance screening, email phishing, or political monitoring (Bonneau and Preibusch 2010). These attacks would have negative effects on the credibility and attractiveness of OSNs. Therefore, it is critical for OSNs operators to protect their users against undesired private information digging and inform them of possible privacy breaches. Further, research has shown that simply removing some attribute information or friendship links may not be enough to prevent inference attacks, and thus comprehensive techniques are needed in practice (Heatherly et al. 2013; Lindamood et al. 2009).

PROPOSED FRAMEWORK FOR INFERENCE PREVENTION

As discussed earlier, the various data from different sources including user profiles and postings can be used to initiate inference attacks. On the other hand, some of these data can be leveraged to incorporate privacy protection mechanism into online social network services. Here, we present a data-driven framework addressing the inference problem identified earlier. Figure 1 depicts the framework.

At the service provider side, the online social network data encompasses the profile (personal information, friends list, group memberships, etc.) of all users and their interaction (posts on the walls, status updates, etc.). This data is modeled as a semantic graph and is used to develop a knowledge base consisting of an inference attribution repository and a contradictory information repository.

Figure 1: The Conceptual Framework for Inference Prevention

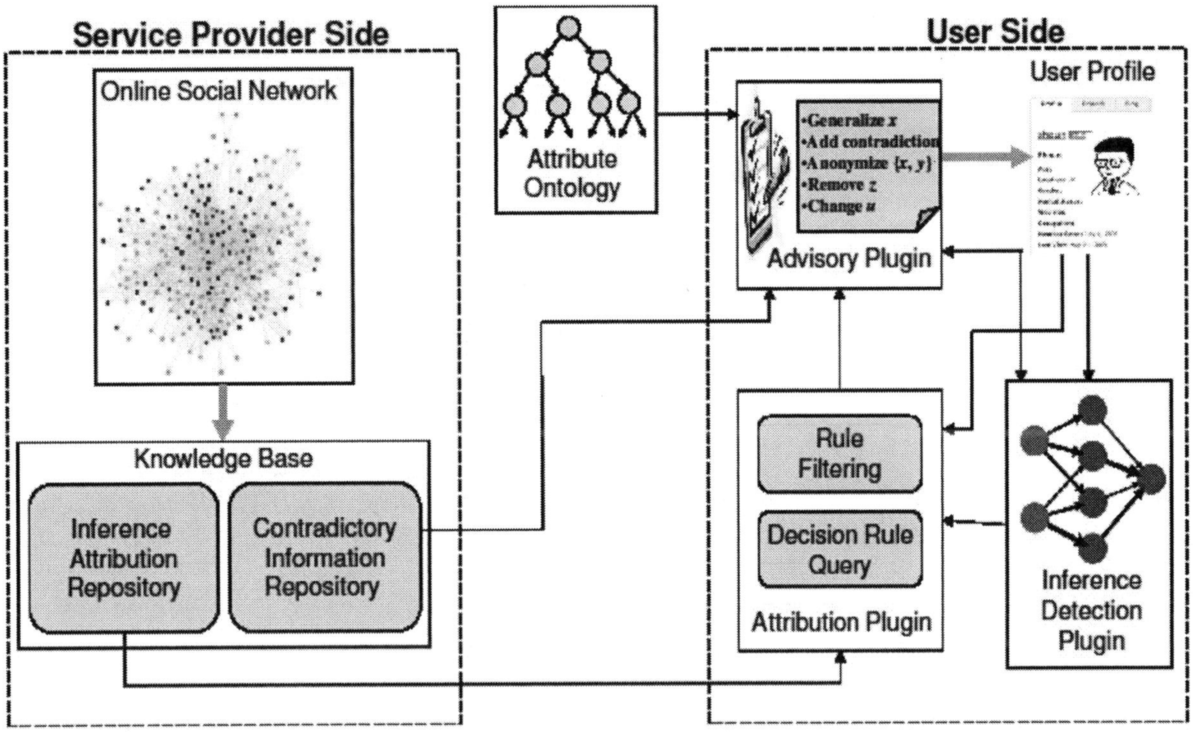

Figure 2: The Flow Chart for Inference Prevention

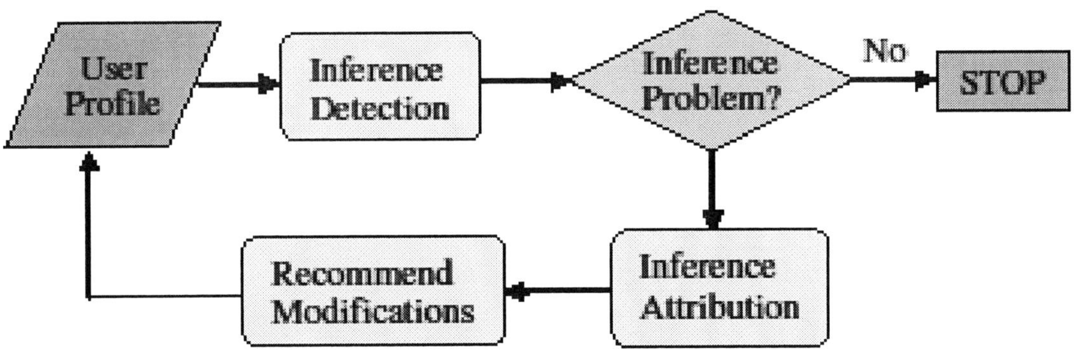

The inference attribution repository is created by applying classification algorithms such as decision tree learners, for example, C4.5 (Quinlan 2014), on the online social network data to discover the attribution rules for sensitive attributes. The contradictory information repository at the service provider site is also a set of rules where the attributes/attribute values in the conditional part of the rule contra-indicate (inversely relate to) the sensitive attribute value.

The service provider also provides a set of plugins including inference detection plugin, attribution plugin, and advisory plugin which can be downloaded by a user and run at his/her site to check any privacy breach or change the profile to avoid such breach. The inference detection plugin is primarily a classifier that given a user profile predicts what sensitive attributes of the user can potentially be leaked. This can be based on any combination of the state of the art inference techniques that have been developed in the literature.

The process flow for inference prevention is shown in Figure 2. This process is initiated by the user whenever the user creates a new online profile or updates an existing profile. This profile is taken as an input to the inference detection plugin running locally at the user site. Based on the privacy preferences of the user, the inference detection plugin detects if the user profile is consistent with the privacy preferences or could possibly leak sensitive attribute values. As a running example, suppose that on January 4, 2010, user Alice has the following attribute values in her profile: Location=`Sunshine State', Group Affiliation = `NewYearBornParty', and Recent Activity = `Just qualified for full driver license'. Since `Sunshine State' implies that she is in Florida, `NewYearBornParty' is a group for people who are born on January 1st, and the age limit for obtaining full driver's license in Florida is 18, thus it can be inferred that Alice's birthdate is January 1, 1992. The inference detection plugin detects the following inference: Location(`Sunshine State') and GroupAffiliation(`NewYearBornParty') and RecentActivity(`Just qualified for full driver license') infers BirthDate(`January 1, 1992').

Once an inference problem is detected, the attribution plugin is activated to determine the source of the problem (i.e., what causes the detected inference). Specifically, the attribution plugin interacts with the inference attribution repository in the knowledge base to identify the possible attribute value(s) contributing to the detected inference problem. Based on the relevant inference rules retrieved from the inference attribution repository, the advisory plugin makes suggestions to the user on what needs to be modified in the profile to break the detected inference.

Note that online social network is a dynamic environment, thus the contents of the knowledge base as well as the inference detection plugin should evolve over time. The OSN service provider needs to keep updating and adding rules to the knowledge base, so that it reflects the most current state of potential inferences. This evolving process may also involve learning from the past experience. The goal is to make it better capture the potential inferences as much as possible.

Functionality Description

We now discuss the detailed functionality of each component of the inference prevention framework and the algorithms employed to support such functionality.

Inference Attribution Repository

The inference attribution repository stores a set of rules for all the attributes that are declared private/sensitive in at least of the user's profile. These rules are derived from the online social network data by applying classification algorithms such as decision tree learners C4.5 for the given set of sensitive attributes. Specifically, for each sensitive attribute, a decision tree can be learned from the data that provides the combination of attribution values leading to the inference of the private data. For example, given a sensitive attribute value y, a standard decision tree generation algorithm C4.5 could potentially come up with an attribution rule that if attribute values x and z are present in the profile or if w and q are present in the profile, y could be inferred.

Contradictory Information Repository

The knowledge base also has a Contradictory Information Repository. This component is used to record inference rules that directly contradict the detected sensitive information. Such contradictory information can also be used to break the detected inferences, since its presence may directly contra-indicate the presence of the inferred information. This can be a very appealing option if the user would like to leave their current profile unchanged but still create the illusion of possessing the contradictory attribute.

The question that then arises is how we can find such contra-indicative information. Such information can actually be derived from the social network data itself, by using a clever trick. The key idea is that we are looking for anti-correlations. To detect these, we thus can reverse or modify the target attribute value in the original data based on which an initial new inference is detected. Then, the same module used for the inference detection (say, decision tree learner) can be run against the newly reversed data. This will give us a new set of inference rules that indicate the given target value. Since we have purposely reversed the original target value, comparing the affecting attribute values in these new rules with those in the initial inference would tell us the contradictory information existing between them.

Inference Detection Plugin

The Inference detection plugin is simply a classifier model made available to users by the service provider to support inference detection. This could be based on any machine learning or data mining technique, or their combination. For example, the service provider could train a neural network based classifier using the online social network data. When the trained model is provided to the user, the user can easily run their profile through the model to identify possible inferences. One requirement of such an approach would be that the underlying models have to be scalable as well as incrementally updatable to incorporate the ever-expanding data accrued in the social network.

Attribution Plugin

The attribution plugin interacts with the knowledge base at the service provider site to determine the possible attributes or attribute values in the user profile that leads to disclosure of sensitive attributes as determined by the inference detection plugin. Specifically, the attribution plugin queries the inference attribution repository for all the rules that includes the given sensitive attribute in the target value or the target value of such rules directly or indirectly influence the conditional part of the rule with the given sensitive attribute in the target value.

Since the attribution repository includes rules created from the entire social network, some of the rules in the query result may not be relevant, as the given user profile may not include the attributes specified in those rules. Therefore, a filtering process is employed to purge out the irrelevant rules.

Advisory Plugin

Advisory plugin is run locally at the user site but it interacts with the contradictory information repository at service provider site, attribute ontology that may be hosted by a third party, and attribution plugin running at user site to suggest possible modifications in the user profile for breaking inference. Some possible modifications can be the following. (1) Generalize attribute values. This option can utilize an attribute ontology for generalization of the relevant attribute values. (2) Perturb attribute values. To break the inference, an attribute value can be distorted. (3) Add contradictory information. Another possibility is to actually introduce new data within the profile that directly contra-indicates the presence of the sensitive value. (4) Remove certain information. Instead of directly adding contradictory information, another possibility is to simply eliminate some of the information causing the inference, thus breaking the linkage. (5) Make some more information private. Instead of making any modifications to the user profile, an alternative is to just make the attributing information itself private. In this fashion, it cannot be used to make the sensitive inferences. Of course, this only applies as long as the newly private made information itself cannot be inferred, thus possibly requiring multiple runs of the inference prevention process. (6) or a combination of all of the above. In certain cases, a single modification of any of the above kinds may not be sufficient to ensure privacy, in which case, we can use a combination of the above to enforce it.

In order to guarantee that the above instrumented modifications have made the user free of inferences, it may be necessary to run inference detection module again. This is due to the possibility of creating new inferences by the modifications.

Ontology

As discussed above, breaking inference may require generalizing some of the attribute values in user profile. For this, the advisory plugin can utilize a relevant ontology which may be provided by a third party, such as VIVO ontology repositories (VIVO 2015) and DAML ontology (DAML 2015). The generalizable attributes in a user profile can be categorized into multiple types based on their semantics and the domains they take their value from. There can be different attribute categories such as address and locations, organizational affiliations, etc. that are generalizable and are commonly used in the online profiles of users. For each category, ontology from appropriate domains needs to be used for attribute value generalization.

Minimization of Modification

In order to break the detected inferences, we may need to modify several attribute values in the user profile. Ideally, we would like to minimize this modification while still breaking the inferences. That is, usability should be enhanced as much as possible while satisfying privacy protection requirement.

Recall that, to determine the inference source for a user, the Attribution plugin may get a set of candidate rules from the knowledge base. Based on these rules, modification suggestions are given. However, among the candidate rules, there may be overlaps on the affecting attribute values. That is, some of the attribute values may appear in multiple candidate rules. Given our rule-based approach, minimizing the modification of user profile is thus equivalent to finding a minimal set of affecting attribute values such that all the candidate rules contains at least one of these attribute values. In other words, we need to find a set of attribute values of the smallest size which would still break all the candidate inferences. This can be solved by finding a minimal set of attribute values.

CONCLUSION AND FUTURE WORK

In this study, we have focused the inference problem arising in the popular online social networking sites. We propose a framework to eliminate the rule-based inference problem by detecting and breaking the inferences that are represented as rules of attributes and / or attribute values. To prevent privacy inferences, user profiles may need to be modified. We briefly show that how this modification can minimized so that usability can be enhanced. We plan to implement and release a privacy plugin for the users of social networking platforms such as Facebook in the future. While our framework protects users from common privacy inferences, background knowledge when added to the user's posts and interactions may still suffice to breach privacy. We plan to examine this issue in the future.

REFERENCES

References available upon request.

DECISION SCIENCES INSTITUTE

Proactive Incentive Strategies for Quality Improvement in a Three-Stage Supply Chain

Seung Ho Yoo
Sunmoon University
Email: shy1228@sunmoon.ac.kr

DaeSoo Kim
Korea University Business School
Email: kimd@korea.ac.kr

Thomas Y. Choi
W. P. Carey School of Business, Arizona State University
Email: thomas.choi@asu.edu

ABSTRACT

This study investigates proactive quality incentive strategies in a three-stage supply chain, consisting of a final assembler, a first-tier supplier (S1) and a second-tier supplier (S2). Five models are introduced by considering different incentive-offering paths among players. We then investigate their distinct characteristics and compare overall performances. A parallel incentive strategy taking a centralized control over S1 and S2 can best enhance the quality, market and profit performances. However, it needs to be carefully adopted since it can deteriorate the final assembler's profit. We provide a guideline for a supply chain to choose the best incentive strategy.

KEYWORDS: Quality improvement, Incentive strategy, Three-stage supply chain, Second-tier supplier, and Principal-agent paradigm

INTRODUCTION

Nowadays, it is commonly observed that a final assembler, such as GM and Toyota, runs its business in a multi-tiered supply chain system, delegating the production of a main component (or a main module) to its direct partner, a first-tier supplier, which also subcontracts the production of a subcomponent (or a sub module) to lower-tier suppliers (second- and/or third-tier suppliers) in the upstream supply chain. In this contemporary manufacturing environment, many firms' performances are significantly affected by the quality performances of lower-tier suppliers. This is more true if we consider a recent outsourcing trend in which many suppliers perform their own research and development (R&D), affecting the performance of a product and hence customer satisfaction and behaviors (Kaya & Özer, 2009). However, it is still not a common practice to proactively control lower tiers, having a direct tie with them. According to Slowick (2013) and Huang et al (2015), approximately 93% of firms work only with their direct partners, delegating the role and responsibility to control lower tiers. It is virtually impossible for many final assemblers to have visibility and proactively control the quality level of lower-tier suppliers. In the next paragraph, we introduce a Boeing case, a typical example of a multi-tiered supply chain situation, suffering from quality problems at lower tiers and reactively responding to them.

On 16 January 2013, the Federal Aviation Administration (FAA) grounded all Boeing 787 Dreamliners worldwide after a Dreamliner caught fire in Boston (D'amato, 2014). The fire was due to electrical failures, especially the internal short circuiting and thermal management problems in the lithium-ion batteries playing a key role in on-board power (D'amato, 2014). Before the grounding, there also had been several other electrical failures worldwide. The series of failures and subsequent grounding seriously tarnished the reputation of both Boeing and airlines, and there were also huge financial losses involved (Williard et al, 2013). Moreover, the situation went worse when the investigation released on March 15 through the National Transportation Safety Board (NTSB). Both the FAA and Boeing failed to identify the root causes of the electrical failures (Williard et al, 2013). The only thing clear was that the fire leading to the grounding was contributed directly by the lithium-ion battery manufactured by a second-tier supplier, GS Yuasa, a Japanese battery cell manufacturer, which was subcontracted by Boeing's first-tier supplier, Thales, a French aerospace technology firm, responsible for the electrical power conversion system (Williard et al, 2013; D'amato, 2014).

In order to drastically reduce the development cost and time for the Dreamliners, Boeing utilized an outsourcing structure similar to an automotive supply chain such as of GM and Toyota, contracting with approximately 50 first-tier suppliers and delegating them complete control of design and production of their pieces (Tang & Zimmerman, 2009). The first-tier suppliers were also fully responsible for controlling their own subcontractors (Tang & Zimmerman, 2009). While outsourcing 70% of the development and production activities, it was virtually impossible for Boeing to have visibility and fully understand the entire processes, especially of the lower tier suppliers (Tang & Zimmerman, 2009). In this tiered system, GS Yuasa produced and tested its battery different from the final design certified for use (Ostrower & Pasztor, 2014). Moreover, Thales' oversight of GS Yuasa did not assure that the manufacturing process of the battery was consistent with industry practices, while Boeing also did not audit GS Yuasa but allowed Thales to perform its own (D'amato, 2014). As a result of a thorough investigation, the NTSB called on Boeing to enhance oversight of its suppliers and entire supply chain (Ostrower & Pasztor, 2014), and Boeing stated that it made progress on enhancing reliability of the battery system by tightening up supplier oversight (Gates, 2015). However, these efforts were too belated and reactive to resolve the problems within a reasonable time period.

Actually, Boeing might have enough chances and time to proactively prevent those problems. As Tang and Zimmerman (2009) pointed out, it could have already recognized not only the limitation of reactive actions but also the importance of proactive control over the lower-tier suppliers when it faced a series of serious delay problems in delivering the Dreamliners to customers in 2008. Not only the incidents due to the lack of proactive control over lower-tier suppliers but also subsequent reactive actions of firms are not of Boeing only but common in practice, especially when a firm operates its business based on a multi-tiered system such as in the automotive industry. For example, Ford recalled SUVs to resolve a fuel system problem that could cause a fire in 2012, incurred by a second-tier supplier using an unapproved manual process to assemble relevant parts (Reuters, 2012). Aston Martin discovered in 2014 that the accelerator pedal arms from a second-tier supplier used counterfeit plastic material, affecting 75 percent of vehicles built between November 2007 and May 2012 (Klayman, 2014). In 2015, Fiat Chrysler recalled 86,000 pickup trucks due to the problems in rear axles from a second-tier supplier, which did not heat-treat those parts properly (Shepardson, 2015). Also in 2015, Toyota needed to find another second-tier supplier after it recalled 12 million vehicles for defective airbag inflators (Shiraki, 2015).

Considering the above, this may be the right time to discover the benefits of proactive control over suppliers in a multi-tiered supply chain system and reveal which type of proactive strategy can better enhance the quality and overall performances of a supply chain. In this study, we consider a three-echelon supply chain, consisting of a final assembler (A), a first-tier supplier (S1) and a second-tier supplier (S2), different from a common practice concentrating only on a dyadic relationship between a buyer and a single supplier. Then, five supply chain models with different incentive strategies are introduced which intend to proactively control the quality performances of suppliers by facilitating their investment in quality, especially considering the second-tier supplier. Note that we do not consider penalty contract schemes which represent reactive actions to correct the quality failures already occurred. The provision of incentives is reasonable in the recent outsourcing trend, in which many subcontractors invest in their own R&D capability and also provide product designs, affecting the performance of a product and subsequently customer satisfaction and demand (Kaya & Özer, 2009). This is different from the traditional role of a supplier which focuses only on meeting the specification the final assembler already determined in order to avoid penalties incurred due to the delivery of defective items. By considering possible incentive-offering paths among three players, combining the individual paths from A to S1, from S1 to S2 and/or from A to S2, we will show various incentive strategies which the final assembler can adopt in a multi-tiered supply chain. Then, we will first answer the following question: What is the condition under which a final assembler can proactively control suppliers by offering an incentive not only to a first-tier supplier but also to a second-tier supplier? Many firms are already aware of the importance the proactive management of lower tiers, but it is still not a common practice. In this study, we introduce proactive incentive strategies and offer a guideline clarifying the conditions under which a final assembler can adopt them. Then, through the comparison of supply chain models, we will answer the next question: Which proactive incentive strategy enhances the overall performances best in a multi-tiered supply chain? There can exist various proactive strategies to control suppliers, and they then will differently affect the overall performances of a supply chain. Especially, it is important to identify which strategy can guarantee the best performance not only to entire supply chain but also to each player. This is since there will be no motivation for the final assembler to adopt an incentive strategy if it helps enhance the profit of the entire supply chain but not its own. Therefore, we will reveal which proactive incentive strategy yields a superior performance in terms of not only the quality performance but also the market and profit performances of the entire supply chain and each player.

LITERATURE REVIEW

Two streams of research are directly relevant to the present study: (1) quality management in a supply chain, (2) supply chain management studies considering the multi-tiered system, beyond a dyadic relationship between a buyer and a supplier.

There have been a number of previous studies relevant to a quality management problem in a supply chain, such as Reyniers and Tapiero (1995), Baiman et al (2000; 2001), Lim (2001), Balachandran and Radhakrishnan (2005), Hwang et al (2006), Zhu et al (2007), Chao et al (2009), Hsieh and Liu (2010), Volodymyr and Christopher (2012). Majority of those studies investigated how a penalty contract based on the information from incoming inspection or/and external failures can control quality problems and minimize total cost. The reason why they adopted a penalty contract as the main option to control a supplier is since they focused on the traditional role of a supplier mainly responsible for the production process, determining the level of conformance quality to design specification the buyer already determined. Therefore, the number of defective items delivered to the buyer or customers is the main concern of those studies, and the penalty contract is a reactive but very appropriate option to control quality failures already occurred.

However, as customer needs become more sophisticated and the competition between supply chains intensifies nowadays, dependency on suppliers which possess expertise in product design becomes higher in practice since it is inefficient and virtually impossible for a final assembler, such as Boeing and Toyota, to command all the relevant capabilities and technologies necessary (Yoo et al, 2015). Therefore, a recent outsourcing trend does not allow suppliers only to focus on conformance quality in production but also requests them to help enhance design quality of a product. Kaya and Özer (2009) and Xie et al (2011) pointed out this trend and investigated product quality mainly determined by a supplier. They focused on the non-contractible aspect of product quality by adopting a buying firm's contract offer based on the wholesale price, even though they considered a situation where not only a buying firm but also consumers can observe quality and their behaviors are also affected. Chen and Deng (2013) also considered a similar situation where customer demand and subsequently buyer's revenue is affected by a supplier's investment and resulting quality. They focused on investigating the effect of the buyer's supplier certification and relevant contract offer, especially under supplier's informational advantage in its quality. In the present study, we focus on the quality aspect which is observable and measurable to both final assembler and customers and their behaviors are also affected similarly to the above studies. Therefore, it is reasonable that we suppose the quality of a supplier is contractible, also considering recent supply chain practices where a final assembler strives to gain clear and complete visibility down through a multi-tiered supply chain. Then, we will reveal how a final assembler can proactively control suppliers' quality and enhance overall performances in a supply chain by facilitating suppliers' quality investment through an incentive offer.

Another research stream directly relevant to our study is supply chain studies dealing with a three-echelon supply chain. They are different from traditional papers focusing on a dyadic relationship between a buyer and a supplier, but they reflect recent issues in a contemporary business environment in which a firm strives to efficiently and effectively manage a multi-tiered supply chain system, similarly to the present one. In this stream, differently from our study, the research interest of a majority of studies has been a joint inventory decision in a three-echelon supply chain, typically in a supplier-manufacturer-retailer supply chain, while also integrating various recent issues, such as coordination through a quantity discount contract (Munson & Rosenblatt, 2001), pricing decision (Corbett & Karmarkar, 2001, Carr & Karmarkar, 2005), closed-loop supply chain design involving used item collection (Savaskan et al, 2004; Savaskan & Van Wassenhove, 2006), multiple suppliers and buyers (Jaber & Goyal, 2008), flexible return policies under demand uncertainty (Ding & Chen, 2008), allocation of cost savings from sharing demand information (Leng & Parlar, 2009), learning-based continuous improvement (Jaber et al, 2010), distribution of imperfect quality items (Sana, 2011), and a facility location problem (Tancrez et al, 2012).

We can recently find several studies dealing with supply chain issues involving the first- and second-tier suppliers similarly to our study. Kayış et al (2013) investigated a manufacturer's problem whether to delegate component procurement to a first-tier supplier or directly control it under information asymmetry about the suppliers' production costs. Huang et al (2015) investigated how a manufacturer can control the second-tier supplier which potentially violates social and environmental standards through either the manufacturer's direct control or delegation to a first-tier supplier. Ang et al (2015) and Bimpikis et al (2015) also similarly studied a manufacturer's sourcing problem involving fist- and second-tier suppliers, while focusing on exploring disruption risk from natural disasters.

However, despite their growing importance, a joint quality management problem in a multi-tiered system has not been studied extensively by academics. There exist only a few relevant studies, such as Dong et al (2013) and Wan et al (2014) which investigated a quality management issue involving both first- and second-tier suppliers. However, the focus of those studies mainly lies in reactively controlling quality failures already occurred through a penalty contract based on the information from incoming inspection and external failures similar to most previous quality management studies dealing with a dyadic relationship between a buyer and a supplier. Our study will introduce various incentive strategies of a final assembler to proactively control quality investment at both first- and second-tier suppliers by considering possible incentive-offering paths among three players. We aim to contribute to the literature by clearly revealing the condition under which the final assembler can adopt each strategy and proactively control suppliers. Moreover, the comparison of proactive incentive strategies will provide an important guideline to practicing managers by clarifying with which strategy the final assembler can enhance overall performances best, including quality, customer demand and profits of entire supply chain and each player.

BASIC FORMULATION

We consider a three-echelon supply chain, consisting of a final assembler, a first-tier supplier (S1) and a second-tier supplier (S2), which is common in the contemporary manufacturing environment. S1 and S2 also have a buyer-supplier relationship like the final assembler and S1. S1 purchases the subcomponent from S2 and supplies the main component to the final assembler after assembling the main and sub components. The supply chain deals with a product such as a vehicle, an electronic device or clothes, so customers' buying intention is mainly affected by the quality and price of a product. The demand is simply defined as follows.

$$D = \alpha - \beta p + \gamma q_1 + \delta q_2, \tag{1}$$

where α is the demand potential, and β, γ and δ are respective coefficients. The sales price of the product p negatively affects D as in many previous studies. To better describe the relationship between product quality and demand, we need the following assumption.

Assumption 1. *The product has a separable architecture with respect to components.*

There can be separable and inseparable architectures in a product as Baiman et al (2001) similarly pointed out. For example, the acceleration performance of a vehicle results jointly from many relevant components, such as an engine, a transmission, a tire and so on. On the other hand, customers also can separately identify and appraise many quality aspects from the vehicle in practice, such as the sound of an audio system, the softness of a leather seat, the performance of a break system and the durability of tires. Among both aspects of product architectures, we focus on the separable architecture in that customers can distinguish the quality of components from the finished product. Therefore, the final assembler has a strong motivation to proactively control suppliers by devising an incentive mechanism which separately evaluates and compensates for the quality level of each supplier.

In Equation (1), the quality levels at S1 and S2, q_1 and q_2, are separately assessed by customers but jointly enhance the demand requests D. We regard each quality level as a single composite measure which combines measurable quality attributes affecting the performance of a product and customer satisfaction and behaviors, similarly as in Karmarkar and Pitbladdo (1997) and Banker et al (1998). For example, quality attributes can be aggregated based on the importance weight of each attribute q_i as in Shi et al (2001) and Kim and Chhajed (2002), i.e., q_1 or $q_2 = \sum w_i q_i$ where the sum of weight $\sum w_i = 1$.

The final assembler purchases the main component from S1 and sells the product assembled to customers. In this study, we suppose that the supply of the product or component is based on the wholesale price contract, which is most basic but one of the most popular contract forms in practice due to its simplicity. Note that we do not focus on the supply contract design but the incentive strategy to enhance quality. The final assembler considers an incentive mechanism to enhance the overall quality of the final product which is jointly determined by quality investment at both S1 and S2. Therefore, the final assembler's profit Π_A is defined as follows.

$$\Pi_A = pD - cD - w_1D - T_{A1} - T_{A2} = \pi_A D - T_{A1} - T_{A2}, \qquad (2)$$

where c is the unit assembly cost, w_1 is the unit wholesale price of the main component paid to S1 and π_A is the marginal profit of the final assembler, i.e., $\pi_A = p - c - w_1 > 0$. T_{A1} and T_{A2} are incentive payments for quality improvement from the final assembler to S1 and S2, respectively. In the next section, we will introduce five different incentive strategies and corresponding supply chain models by considering possible incentive-sharing paths among three players.

On the other hand, S1 supplies the main component to the final assembler by combining its main component and the subcomponent purchased from S2. Both S1 and S2 undertake their own R&D and hence incur the capital investment to enhance the quality levels of their own components. S1 can also consider an incentive mechanism like the final assembler in order to facilitate the quality investment of its direct supplier S2. This is since S1 knows that the quality enhancement at S2 will positively affect the supply of its main component to the final assembler. Therefore, the profits of S1 and S2, Π_1 and Π_2, can be defined as follows.

$$\Pi_1 = w_1D - c_1D - w_2D - \lambda q_1^2 + T_{A1} - T_{12} = \pi_1 D - \lambda q_1^2 + T_{A1} - T_{12}, \text{ and} \qquad (3)$$
$$\Pi_2 = w_2D - c_2D - \eta q_2^2 + T_{A2} + T_{12} = \pi_2 D - \eta q_2^2 + T_{A2} + T_{12}, \qquad (4)$$

where c_1 and c_2 are unit costs of S1 and S2 for component production and w_2 is unit wholesale price of the subcomponent produced at S2. π_1 and π_2 are the marginal profits of S1 and S2, respectively, i.e., $\pi_1 = w_1 - c_1 - w_2 > 0$, and $\pi_2 = w_2 - c_2 > 0$. T_{12} is the quality incentive payment from S1 to S2, differently defined with respect to the supply chain model in the next section. λq_1^2 and ηq_2^2 are capital investments for quality improvement incurred at S1 and S2, respectively, where λ and η are parameters which represent the magnitude of investment. We utilize a quadratic form, increasing and convex in the level of quality, as in many previous studies related to quality investment, such as in Karmarkar and Pitbladdo (1997) and Banker et al (1998).

The main objective of this study is to compare proactive incentive strategies in a three-echelon supply chain, which will subsequently induce different results of quality innovation and overall performances. Therefore, we need to eliminate the effects of other factors, which in turn can distort the comparison result, and hence we add the following assumption.

Assumption 2. *The prices of the final product and components are fixed.*

Assumption 2 indicates a market situation in which a player does not have total control over the prices of items and thus there are no significant price differences between market players. Given this assumption which regards the prices of final product and components, p, w_1 and w_2, as parameters, we will concentrate on revealing the superiority of proactive incentive mechanisms.

In the next section, we introduce five supply chain models with different incentive strategies.

SUPPLY CHAIN MODELS

We consider a three-echelon supply chain, consisting of a final assembler, a first-tier supplier (S1) and a second-tier supplier (S2). Among various types of relationships and power dynamics among players in practice, we focus on a supply chain situation where a buying firm has greater bargaining power, such as in a typical manufacturing supply chain, such as Boeing, GM, Samsung, etc. Therefore, the final assembler is the focal company in the supply chain, leading joint quality innovation by proactively devising incentive strategies for suppliers, while S1 also has power over S2.

We introduce five incentive strategies for a three-echelon supply chain, considering possible incentive-offering paths among three players. They are (1) Case N: a basic case, no incentives (N) for quality improvement, (2) Case S: adopting a sequential incentive mechanism (S) from the final assembler to S1 and then from S1 to S2, (3) Case SI: a sequential incentive mechanism (S) with an additional indirect incentive (I) from the assembler to S1 for subcomponent quality of S2, (4) Case P: a parallel incentive scheme (P) from the assembler to both S1 and S2, forming a triadic relationship between players, and (5) Case PS: combining parallel (P) and sequential (S) incentive mechanisms.

Case N: A Basic Case, No Incentives

The general form of a proactive joint quality management problem with three players can be generalized as follows, based on the principal-agent paradigm.

Problems N, S, SI and PS:

$$\text{Maximize} \quad \Pi_A(T_{A1},\ T_{A2}) \tag{5}$$

$$\text{subject to} \quad \Pi_1(q_1,\ T_{12} \mid T_{A1},\ T_{A2}) > 0 \tag{6}$$

$$\quad \text{Maximize} \quad \Pi_1(q_1,\ T_{12} \mid T_{A1},\ T_{A2}) \tag{7}$$

$$\quad \text{subject to} \quad \Pi_2(q_2 \mid q_1,\ T_{A1},\ T_{A2},\ T_{12}) > 0 \tag{8}$$

$$\quad\quad \text{Maximize} \quad \Pi_2(q_2 \mid q_1,\ T_{A1},\ T_{A2},\ T_{12}) \tag{9}$$

In this three-stage decision problem, the final assembler maximizes its own profit in (5) by determining the quality incentives for S1 and S2, T_{A1} and T_{A2}, but it needs to satisfy S1's constraints in (6) and (7). S1 participates in this joint innovation activity when a positive profit is guaranteed in the individual rationality constraint (6). In the incentive compatibility constraint (7), S1 maximizes its own profit, given the final assembler's decision on T_{A1} and T_{A2}, by determining its best response q_1 and T_{12}, the quality level of the main component and the quality incentive from S1 to S2. S1 also needs to satisfy the constraints of S2 in (8) and (9). S1 also needs to guarantee S2's positive profit in (8), and S2 maximizes its own profit in (9) by determining the quality of subcomponent q_2, given the decisions of the final assembler and S1. We will obtain the solutions of supply chain models based on the above problem framework.

We starts from Case N, the very basic model only with inventory transactions among players as illustrated in Figure 1. There are no incentives for quality improvement among players as in a typical transactional relationship, shown in Equation (10). Therefore, it can be regarded as a reactive strategy, with which the final assembler would correspond to a quality problem after it occurs, not proactively preventing it.

$$T_{A1} = T_{A2} = T_{12} = 0. \tag{10}$$

Figure 1: Case N (A: final assembler, S1: first-tier supplier, S2: second-tier supplier)

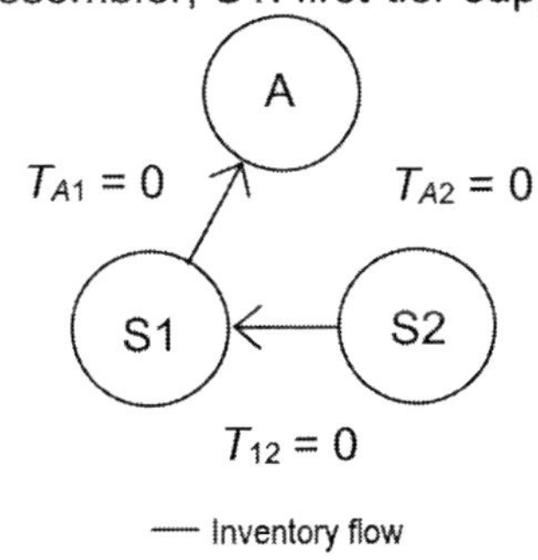

Based on Equation (10) without incentives and Assumption 2 with given p, w_1 and w_2, the final assembler has nothing to control. Therefore, the three-stage decision structure in (5) through (9) reduces to two stages by ignoring (5) and (6). After applying Equation (10) into Equations (2) through (4) and based on the decision structure above, now two-stage, we can obtain the optimal solution by the backward induction like a typical Stackelberg game. We first obtain the best response of S2, $q_2^{N^*}$, from the first-order necessary condition (FONC) of (9) and then the response of S1, $q_1^{N^*}$, from FONC of (7).

$$q_1^{N*} = \frac{\gamma\pi_1}{2\lambda}, \text{ and } q_2^{N*} = \frac{\delta\pi_2}{2\eta}.$$

where $\pi_1 = w_1 - c_1 - w_2 > 0$ and $\pi_2 = w_2 - c_2 > 0$ in Equations (3) and (4).

Applying $q_1^{N^*}$ and $q_2^{N^*}$ above into Equations (1) through (4), we can simply obtain the optimal demand and profits of all players and entire supply chain, i.e., the supply chain profit $\Pi = \Pi_A + \Pi_1 + \Pi_2$. All solutions in this study guarantee the concavity of profit functions by satisfying the second-order sufficient conditions. The solutions of Case N are summarized in Tables 1-3 in Section 4.5.

Case S: A Sequential Incentive Mechanism

Differently from the reactive Case N without quality incentives, we consider a sequential incentive scheme in Case S. This is a common benefit-sharing strategy in practice, in that a buying firm collaborates and shares its collaborative benefit only with its direct supplier. Therefore, as illustrated in Figure 2, the final assembler offers S1 an incentive to proactively control the quality of the main component, and then S1 also offers S2 an incentive for subcomponent quality. The incentives among players are defined as follows.

$$T_{A1} = b_1 q_1,\ T_{A2} = 0, \text{ and } T_{12} = b_2 q_2, \tag{11}$$

where b_1 and b_2 are the marginal incentives of resulting quality, paid from the final assembler to S1 and from S1 to S2, respectively.

Figure 2: Case S

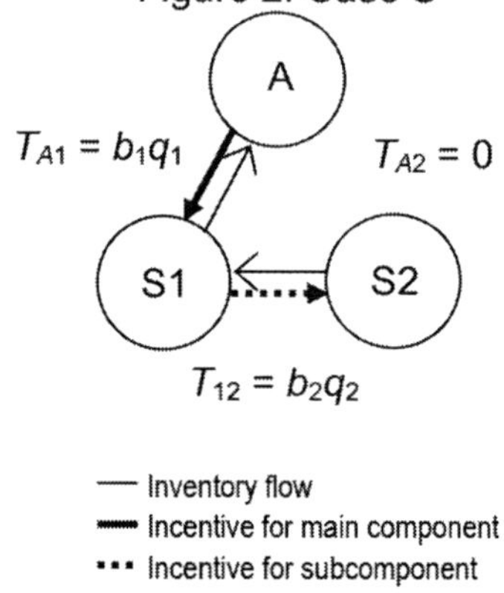

After applying the incentives defined in Equation (11) into the general three-stage optimization problem framework in (5) through (9), we can obtain the solutions by the backward induction. We first obtain the best response of S2 from FONC of (9) as a function of b_2.

$$q_2^{S}(b_2) = \frac{\delta\pi_2 + b_2}{2\eta}.$$

Then, after applying the above $q_2^S(b_2)$ into (7), we can obtain S1's best response by simultaneously solving FONCs of (7).

$$q_1^{S}(b_1) = \frac{\gamma\pi_1 + b}{2\lambda}, \text{ and } b_2^{S*} = \frac{\delta(\pi_1 - \pi_2)}{2}.$$

Next, we obtain the assembler's decision from FONC of (5) after applying the above into (5).

$$b_1^{S*} = \frac{\gamma(\pi_A - \pi_1)}{2},$$

where $\pi_A = p - c - w_1 > 0$ in Equation (2).

Applying b_1^{S*} and b_2^{S*} into $q_1^S(b_1)$ and $q_2^S(b_2)$, we obtain the closed-form solutions of q_1^{S*} and q_2^{S*}. The optimal demand and profits are also easily obtained if we apply b_1^{S*}, b_2^{S*}, q_1^{S*} and q_2^{S*} into Equations (1) through (4). We summarize the solutions of Case S in Tables 1-3 in Section 4.5.

Case SI: A Sequential Incentive Mechanism with an Additional Indirect Incentive for Subcomponent

Collaboration between players in a supply chain is critical to sustain competitive advantage. However, it has been usually between a buying firm and its direct supplier as we describe in Case S. It is still not a common practice that a buying firm has a direct control over its lower-tier suppliers. It is not easy for a buying firm to have enough capability to directly command all suppliers in a multi-tiered supply chain, and it is sometimes restricted by an antitrust law in some countries since it can hinder fair competition between suppliers in lower tiers. However, a final assembler still needs to find a proactive way to control a lower-tier supplier since its quality capability often has a significant impact on the performance of the overall supply chain. Therefore, in Case SI, we introduce an indirect (I) incentive scheme for subcomponent quality in addition to the sequential incentive scheme in Case S. It is from the final assembler to S1 so as to improve S1's incentive control over S2 and subsequently better manage S2's quality investment through S1, as illustrated in Figure 3. The incentives can be defined as follows.

$$T_{A1} = b_1 q_1 + i_1 q_2,\ T_{A2} = 0, \text{ and } T_{12} = b_2 q_2, \tag{12}$$

where i_1 is the marginal indirect incentive for subcomponent quality paid from the final assembler to S1, while direct sequential incentives b_1 and b_2 are the same as in Case S.

Figure 3: Case SI

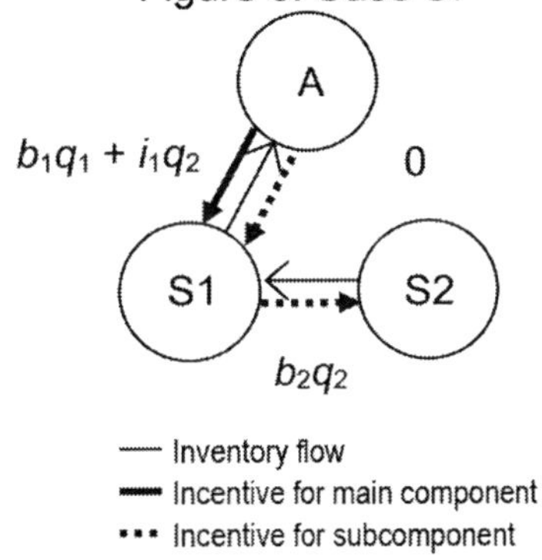

After applying Equation (12) into the general problem defined in (5) through (9) in Section 4.1 and by following the backward induction approach the same as Case S, we obtain the closed-form optimal solutions of Case SI. They are summarized in Tables 1 through 3.

Case P: A Parallel Incentive Mechanism

It has been a common practice that a buying firm concentrates only on controlling its direct supplier as we already stated in Cases S and SI. However, nowadays we can observe contemporary firms which understand the interrelations among players in a multi-tiered supply network as Yan et al (2015) pointed out, such as Honda, Toyota and LG Electronics (LGE). They have tried to establish direct contractual relationships with a lower-tier supplier so as to proactively take better control over quality, especially if S2 potentially exerts a critical impact on the performances of the final assembler and entire supply chain (Yan et al, 2015). In Case P, we adopt this contemporary situation in which the final assembler takes the centralized control over both S1 and S2. The final assembler establishes a direct relationship with S2, bypassing S1, similarly as in the relationship between LGE and Taiwan Semiconductor Manufacturing Company (TSMC), bypassing the first-tier supplier, Qualcomm (Choi & Linton, 2011). Therefore, the sequential relationship between three players changes to a triadic relationship as shown in Figure 4. In this parallel incentive path from the final assembler to both S1 and S2, the incentives among players can be defined as follows.

$$T_{A1} = b_1q_1,\ T_{A2} = b_2q_2, \text{ and } T_{12} = 0. \quad (13)$$

Figure 4: Case P

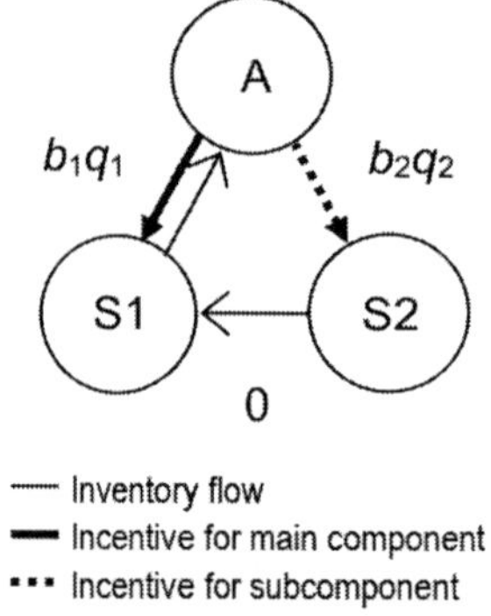

Considering the assembler's centralized control over both S1 and S2 bypassing S1, the three-stage problem structure in (5) through (9) also needs to change to two stages with multiple (two) agents (or followers) like below.

Problem P:

Maximize $\Pi_A(b_1, b_2)$
subject to $\Pi_1(q_1 \mid b_1, b_2) > 0$
Maximize $\Pi_1(q_1 \mid b_1, b_2)$
$\Pi_2(q_2 \mid b_1, b_2) > 0$
Maximize $\Pi_2(q_2 \mid b_1, b_2)$

By following the backward induction similar to former cases but with two agents, we first obtain the best responses of S1 and S2, q_1 and q_2, separately as functions of b_1 and/or b_2. Then, after applying both q_1 and q_2 to the assembler's profit Π_A, we can obtain the final assembler's decision from FONCs of Π_A. The solutions of Case P are summarized in Tables 1-3 in the next section.

Case PS: Combining Both Parallel and Sequential Incentives

Figure 5: Case PS

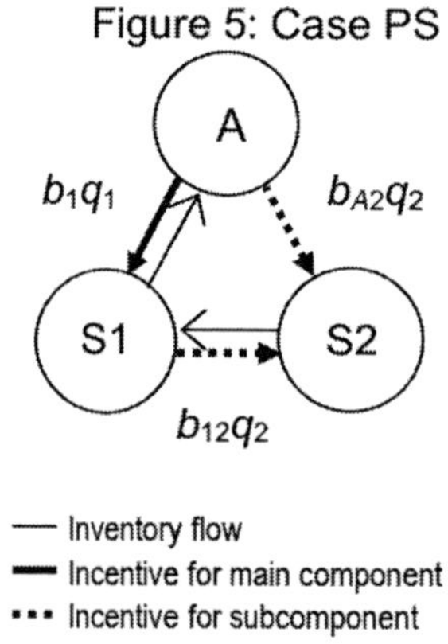

In Case P, we consider a triadic relationship between players involving a parallel incentive path from the assembler to both S1 and S2, while not considering S1's quality incentive for S2. In Case PS, we include all possible incentive paths among players as shown in Figure 5 by combining parallel and sequential incentive schemes in Cases P and S. Therefore, the incentives can be defined in the triadic relationship of Case PS as follows.

$$T_{A1} = b_1 q_1,\ T_{A2} = b_{A2} q_2, \text{ and } T_{12} = b_{12} q_2, \tag{14}$$

where b_{A2} is the quality incentive for subcomponent quality from the assembler to S2 and b_{12} is the incentive from S1 to S2, while S2's total quality incentive is $b_2 = b_{A2} + b_{12}$.

Case PS forms a triadic relationship like Case P, but Case PS maintains the three-stage decision problem described in (5) through (9), accompanying the triple marginalization problem, since it additionally includes the sequential incentive scheme. Applying the incentives in Equation (14), we obtain the closed-form solutions of Case PS, summarized in Tables 1 through 3.

Table 1: Solution summary: Incentives

Case	Incentive		
	b_1^*	b_2^*	i_1^*
N	0	0	N/A
S	$\frac{\gamma(\pi_A-\pi_1)}{2}$	$\frac{\delta(\pi_1-\pi_2)}{2}$	N/A
SI	$\frac{\gamma(\pi_A-\pi_1)}{2}$	$\frac{\delta(\pi_1-\pi_2)}{2}+\frac{\delta(\pi_A-(\pi_1+\pi_2))}{4}$	$\frac{\delta(\pi_A-(\pi_1+\pi_2))}{2}$
P	$\frac{\gamma(\pi_A-\pi_1)}{2}$	$\frac{\delta(\pi_A-\pi_2)}{2}$	N/A
PS	$\frac{\gamma(\pi_A-\pi_1)}{2}$	$\frac{\delta(\pi_1-\pi_2)}{2}+\frac{\delta(\pi_A-(\pi_1+\pi_2))}{4}$	N/A

* $\pi_A = p - c - w_1 > 0$, $\pi_1 = w_1 - c_1 - w_2 > 0$, $\pi_2 = w_2 - c_2 > 0$

* In Case PS, $b_2^{PS*} = b_{A2}^{PS*} + b_{12}^{PS*}$, where $b_{A2}^{PS*} = \delta(\pi_A - (\pi_1 + \pi_2))/2$, and $b_{12}^{PS*} = \delta(\pi_1 - \pi_2)/2 - \delta(\pi_A - (\pi_1 + \pi_2))/4$

Table 2: Solution summary: Quality and demand

Case	Quality		Consumer response
	q_1^*	q_2^*	D^*
N	$\frac{\gamma\pi_1}{2\lambda}$	$\frac{\delta\pi_2}{2\eta}$	$D_0+\frac{\gamma^2\pi_1}{2\lambda}+\frac{\delta^2\pi_2}{2\eta}$
S	$\frac{\gamma(\pi_A+\pi_1)}{4\lambda}$	$\frac{\delta(\pi_1+\pi_2)}{4\eta}$	$D_0+\frac{\gamma^2(\pi_A+\pi_1)}{4\lambda}+\frac{\delta^2(\pi_1+\pi_2)}{4\eta}$
SI	$\frac{\gamma(\pi_A+\pi_1)}{4\lambda}$	$\frac{\delta\pi}{8\eta}$	$D_0+\frac{\gamma^2(\pi_A+\pi_1)}{4\lambda}+\frac{\delta^2\pi}{8\eta}$
P	$\frac{\gamma(\pi_A+\pi_1)}{4\lambda}$	$\frac{\delta(\pi_A+\pi_2)}{4\eta}$	$D_0+\frac{\gamma^2(\pi_A+\pi_1)}{4\lambda}+\frac{\delta^2(\pi_A+\pi_2)}{4\eta}$
PS	$\frac{\gamma(\pi_A+\pi_1)}{4\lambda}$	$\frac{\delta\pi}{8\eta}$	$D_0+\frac{\gamma^2(\pi_A+\pi_1)}{4\lambda}+\frac{\delta^2\pi}{8\eta}$

* $D_0 = \alpha - \beta p$, $\pi_A = p - c - w_1 > 0$, $\pi_1 = w_1 - c_1 - w_2 > 0$, $\pi_2 = w_2 - c_2 > 0$, $\pi = \pi_A + \pi_1 + \pi_2 = p - c - c_1 - c_2 > 0$

Table 3: Solution summary: Profits

Case	Final assembler Π_A^*	S1 Π_1^*	S2 Π_2^*	Supply chain Π^*
N	$D_0\pi_A + \frac{\gamma^2\pi_A\pi_1}{2\lambda} + \frac{\delta^2\pi_A\pi_2}{2\eta}$	$D_0\pi_1 + \frac{\gamma^2\pi_1^2}{4\lambda} + \frac{\delta^2\pi_1\pi_2}{2\eta}$	$D_0\pi_2 + \frac{\gamma^2\pi_1\pi_2}{2\lambda} + \frac{\delta^2\pi_2^2}{4\eta}$	$D_0\pi + \frac{\gamma^2\pi_1(\pi + (\pi_A + \pi_2))}{4\lambda} + \frac{\delta^2\pi_2(\pi + (\pi_A + \pi_1))}{4\eta}$
S	$D_0\pi_A + \frac{\gamma^2(\pi_A + \pi_1)^2}{8\lambda} + \frac{\delta^2(\pi_1 + \pi_2)\pi_A}{4\eta}$	$D_0\pi_1 + \frac{\gamma^2(\pi_A + \pi_1)^2}{16\lambda} + \frac{\delta^2(\pi_1 + \pi_2)^2}{8\eta}$	$D_0\pi_2 + \frac{\gamma^2\pi_2(\pi_A + \pi_1)}{4\lambda} + \frac{\delta^2(\pi_1 + \pi_2)^2}{16\eta}$	$D_0\pi + \frac{\gamma^2(\pi_A + \pi_1)(3\pi + \pi_2)}{16\lambda} + \frac{\delta^2(\pi_1 + \pi_2)(3\pi + \pi_A)}{16\eta}$
SI	$D_0\pi_A + \frac{\gamma^2(\pi_A + \pi_1)^2}{8\lambda} + \frac{\delta^2\pi^2}{16\eta}$	$D_0\pi_1 + \frac{\gamma^2(\pi_A + \pi_1)^2}{16\lambda} + \frac{\delta^2\pi^2}{32\eta}$	$D_0\pi_2 + \frac{\gamma^2\pi_2(\pi_A + \pi_1)}{4\lambda} + \frac{\delta^2\pi^2}{64\eta}$	$D_0\pi + \frac{\gamma^2(\pi_A + \pi_1)(3\pi + \pi_2)}{16\lambda} + \frac{7\delta^2\pi^2}{64\eta}$
P	$D_0\pi_A + \frac{\gamma^2(\pi_A + \pi_1)^2}{8\lambda} + \frac{\delta^2(\pi_A + \pi_2)^2}{8\eta}$	$D_0\pi_1 + \frac{\gamma^2(\pi_A + \pi_1)^2}{16\lambda} + \frac{\delta^2\pi_1(\pi_A + \pi_2)}{4\eta}$	$D_0\pi_2 + \frac{\gamma^2(\pi_A + \pi_1)\pi_2}{4\lambda} + \frac{\delta^2(\pi_A + \pi_2)^2}{16\eta}$	$D_0\pi + \frac{\gamma^2(\pi_A + \pi_1)(3\pi + \pi_2)}{16\lambda} + \frac{\delta^2(\pi_A + \pi_2)(3\pi + \pi_1)}{16\eta}$
PS	$D_0\pi_A + \frac{\gamma^2(\pi_A + \pi_1)^2}{8\lambda} + \frac{\delta^2\pi^2}{16\eta}$	$D_0\pi_1 + \frac{\gamma^2(\pi_A + \pi_1)^2}{16\lambda} + \frac{\delta^2\pi^2}{32\eta}$	$D_0\pi_2 + \frac{\gamma^2\pi_2(\pi_A + \pi_1)}{4\lambda} + \frac{\delta^2\pi^2}{64\eta}$	$D_0\pi + \frac{\gamma^2(\pi_A + \pi_1)(3\pi + \pi_2)}{16\lambda} + \frac{7\delta^2\pi^2}{64\eta}$

* $D_0 = \alpha - \beta p$, $\pi_A = p - c - w_1 > 0$, $\pi_1 = w_1 - c_1 - w_2 > 0$, $\pi_2 = w_2 - c_2 > 0$, $\pi = \pi_A + \pi_1 + \pi_2 = p - c - c_1 - c_2 > 0$

COMPARISON OF INCENTIVE STRATEGIES

In this section, we compare incentive strategies in a three-echelon supply chain and reveal their different characteristics. First, we find the conditions under which the final assembler can adopt the proactive incentive strategies by investigating the results in Table 1.

Proposition 1. *Conditions under which each incentive can exist are as follows.*
(1) b_1^* can exist in all cases when $\pi_A > \pi_1$.
(2) b_2^* exists when $\pi_1 > \pi_2$ in Case S, $\pi_A > \pi_2$ in Case P and $\pi_1 + \pi_2 < \pi_A < 3\pi_1 - \pi_2$ in Case PS. Both b_2^* and i_1^* exist in Case SI when $\pi_1 > \pi_2$ and $\pi_A > \pi_1 + \pi_2$.

Proof. To have $b_1^* > 0$, $b_2^* > 0$, and/or $i_1^* > 0$ in each case from Table 1, we directly obtain the conditions in Proposition 1. □

Figure 6: Conditions under which each incentive strategy exists (A: $\pi_A = \pi_1$, B: $\pi_A = \pi_1 + \pi_2$, C: $\pi_A = 3\pi_1 - \pi_2$, D: $\pi_1 = \pi_2$)

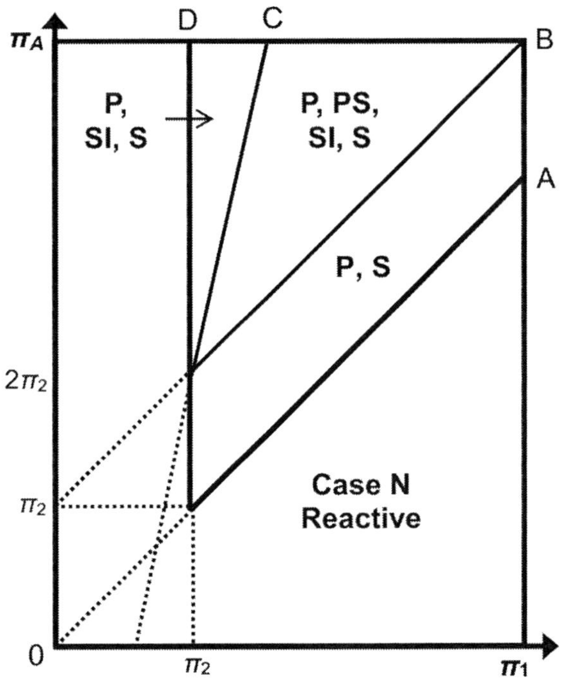

We first need to note that the reason why each player intends to adopt a quality incentive is in order to proactively protect its own business interest and profitability. Observe in Table 1 that each player reflects its own profitability when offering the incentive, i.e., $b_1^* = f(\pi_A)$ in all cases, while $b_2^{S*} = f(\pi_1)$, $b_2^{SI*} = f(\pi_1, \pi_2)$, $b_2^{P*} = f(\pi_A)$ and $b_2^{PS*} = f(\pi_1, \pi_2)$ (see together the incentive-offering paths in Figures 1-5). Therefore, it is straightforward that quality incentives depend on the relative profitability of players, and only a player sufficiently better off than the other has a motivation to proactively control suppliers by offering incentives. That is, as shown in Propositions 1(1) and 1(2), $\pi_A > \pi_1$ to have $b_1^* > 0$, and at least $\pi_1 > \pi_2$ to have $b_2^* > 0$ and/or i_1^* > 0, where the marginal profits of the final assembler, S1, S2 and supply chain are $\pi_A = p - c - w_1 > 0$, $\pi_1 = w_1 - c_1 - w_2 > 0$, $\pi_2 = w_2 - c_2 > 0$ and $\pi = \pi_A + \pi_1 + \pi_2 = p - c - c_1 - c_2 > 0$, respectively, as defined in Equations (2) through (5). If we combine the criteria to have both $b_1^* > 0$ and $b_2^* > 0$ (and also $i_1^* > 0$), the condition areas can be graphically illustrated as in Figure 6, under which the final assembler can proactively utilize each incentive strategy. As shown in Figure 6, each incentive strategy cannot always be adopted. If a buying firm (the final assembler or S1) is not better off than a supplier firm (S1 or S2), i.e., $\pi_A < \pi_1$ or $\pi_1 < \pi_2$, it is a rational decision to reactively respond to quality failures while maintaining only a transactional relationship with suppliers (Case N). Next, we compare the amount of each incentive, which in turn affects the overall performances in a multi-tiered supply chain.

Proposition 2. *Comparing the incentives for S1 and S2 in incentive models, respectively, they are related as:*
(1) $b_1^{S^*} = b_1^{SI^*} = b_1^{P^*} = b_1^{PS^*} > 0$ *if* $\pi_A > \pi_1$. *Otherwise, they do not exist.*
(2) $b_2^{P^*} > b_2^{S^*}$ *without Cases SI and PS if* $\pi_1 < \pi_A < \pi_1 + \pi_2$ *and* $\pi_1 > \pi_2$,
$b_2^{P^*} > b_2^{PS^*} = b_2^{SI^*} > b_2^{S^*}$ *if* $\pi_1 + \pi_2 < \pi_A < 3\pi_1 - \pi_2$, *and*
$b_2^{P^*} > b_2^{SI^*} > b_2^{S^*}$ *without Case PS if* $\pi_A > 3\pi_1 - \pi_2$ *and* $\pi_1 > \pi_2$.
(3) *Comparing Cases SI and S,* $b_2^{SI^*} - b_2^{S^*} = i_1^{SI^*}/2$.

Proof. By directly comparing b_1^* or b_2^* of all incentive models in Table 1, respectively, and considering the conditions to have both b_1^* and $b_2^* > 0$ in Proposition 1, we obtain the results in Proposition 2. □

In the dyadic relationship between the final assembler and S1, the quality incentive for the main component is identical in all cases. There is only a decision whether offering an incentive or not as shown in Proposition 2(1). However, if we expand our view to proactively have a direct control over the lower tier, we can observe that there can be various relationships in the quality incentives for S2 as shown in Proposition 2(2). The results are graphically illustrated in Figure 7. As illustrated in Figure 7(a), when the final assembler forms a triadic relationship in Case P, the largest quality incentive can be offered to S2. This is since the final assembler takes the centralized control over both S1 and S2, and hence the supply chain becomes most efficient by mitigating the multiple marginalization issues (see the two-stage decision structure of Case P shown in Section 4.4). We can also observe that Case P is less restricted in offering the incentive for S2 and hence easier to be adopted than other sequential incentive schemes as we see in Proposition 2(2) and also Figures 6, 7(a) and 7(b). While Case P always offers the largest incentive for S2, we also illustrate the comparison result of sequential incentive schemes without Case P in Figure 7(b) since Case P, directly controlling S2, cannot be considered due to a certain regulation in some practices. We can also interestingly observe that the incentives for S1 and S2 are exactly the same in Cases SI and PS despite their different incentive mechanisms as illustrated in Figures 3 and 5, while Case SI is less restricted to be adopted than Case PS as shown in Figure 7(b). We can also observe that an inefficiency problem occurs in Case SI as pointed out in Proposition 2(3). Note that S1 passes S2 only the half of the final assembler's indirect incentive for subcomponent quality, while it internalizes the other half, i.e., comparing two results with and without indirect incentives of Cases SI and S, $b_2^{SI^*} - b_2^{S^*} = i_1^{SI^*}/2$. Overall, various incentive results, especially for the lower-tier S2, then will differently affect the overall performances. Next, Proposition 3 summarizes the comparison results of quality performances in five supply chain models.

Figure 7: Graphical representation of the case dominating others, in Propositions 2(2), 3(2), 4 and 5(2) (A: $\pi_A = \pi_1$, B: $\pi_A = \pi_1 + \pi_2$, C: $\pi_A = 3\pi_1 - \pi_2$, D: $\pi_1 = \pi_2$)

(a) Including Case P, always dominating (b) Without Case P

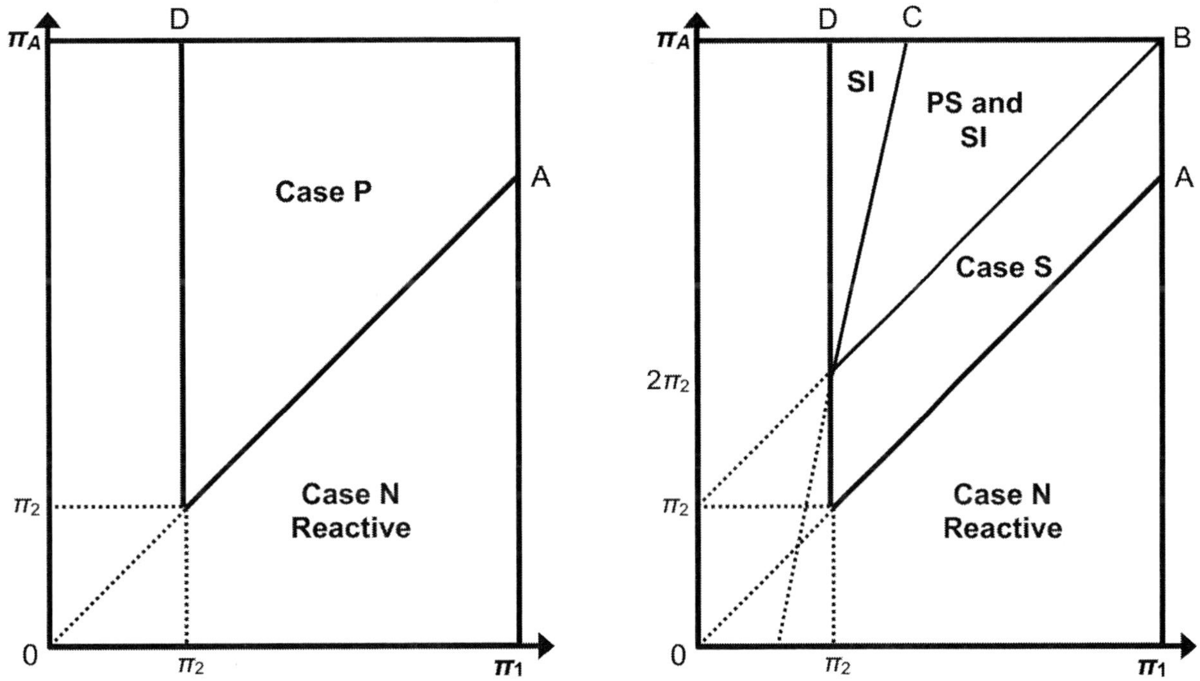

Proposition 3. *The levels of quality at S1 and S2 are related as:*
(1) $q_1^{P^*} = q_1^{PS^*} = q_1^{SI^*} = q_1^{S^*} > q_1^{N^*}$ *if* $\pi_A > \pi_1$.
(2) $q_2^{P^*} > q_2^{S^*} > q_2^{N^*}$ *without Cases SI and PS if* $\pi_1 < \pi_A < \pi_1 + \pi_2$ and $\pi_1 > \pi_2$,
$q_2^{P^*} > q_2^{PS^*} = q_2^{SI^*} > q_2^{S^*} > q_2^{N^*}$ *if* $\pi_1 + \pi_2 < \pi_A < 3\pi_1 - \pi_2$, and
$q_2^{P^*} > q_2^{SI^*} > q_2^{S^*} > q_2^{N^*}$ *without Case PS if* $\pi_A > 3\pi_1 - \pi_2$ and $\pi_1 > \pi_2$.

Proof. By directly comparing q_1^* or q_2^* of all cases in Table 2 and considering the conditions to have both b_1^* and $b_2^* > 0$ in Proposition 1, we obtain the results in Proposition 3. □

We can observe in Propositions 3(1) and 3(2) that all proactive incentive strategies enhance the quality performances at both S1 and S2 than the reactive Case N if they can be adopted, i.e., $q_1^* > q_1^{N^*}$ and $q_2^* > q_2^{N^*}$ for Cases S, SI, P and PS. Because of the same incentive offerings to S1 as shown in Proposition 2(1), the quality levels of the main component at S1 are also induced identical regardless of the incentive strategies as in Proposition 3(1). The quality performances of S2 are also directly determined by the incentives for S2 as shown in Proposition 3(2). Therefore, the case which dominates others can be illustrated the same as Figure 7. As we can see in Proposition 3(2), note that a superior quality result is promised when the final assembler expands its sight and proactively controls the lower-tier supplier S2 as in Case P, PS or SI, i.e., $q_2^{P^*}$, $q_2^{PS^*}$ or $q_2^{SI^*} > q_2^{S^*}$. We cannot expect a higher quality performance when the supply chain player collaborates only with its direct partner as in Case S. Case P always dominates other incentive strategies by proactively forming a triadic relationship and directly controlling both S1 and S2 with the largest incentives as shown in Proposition 3(2) and

Figure 7(a). On the other hand, the indirect incentive in Case SI enhances the quality performance of S2 comparing to Case S, but one needs to remind again that the indirect control accompanies the inefficiency problem as also pointed out in Proposition 2(3). In Case PS, the final assembler directly controls both S1 and S2 like Case P, but a practicing manager needs to note that additionally combining the sequential incentive scheme can rather deteriorate the performance by inducing the marginalization problem.

Proposition 4. *Comparing the demand D^* and supply chain profit Π^*, they are related as follows.*

Case P > S > N without Cases SI and PS if $\pi_1 < \pi_A < \pi_1 + \pi_2$ *and* $\pi_1 > \pi_2$,
Case P > PS = SI > S > N if $\pi_1 + \pi_2 < \pi_A < 3\pi_1 - \pi_2$, *and*
Case P > SI > S > N without Case PS if $\pi_A > 3\pi_1 - \pi_2$ *and* $\pi_1 > \pi_2$.

Proof. By directly comparing D^* or Π^* of all cases in Tables 2 and 3 and considering the conditions in Proposition 1 together, we obtain the results of Proposition 4. □

Because the quality level at S1 is induced the same as shown in Proposition 3(1), the market performance D^* is directly affected by the quality level at S2 shown in Proposition 3(2), and the profit performance of the entire supply chain Π^* is also determined the same. Therefore, Figure 7 can also represent the results of Proposition 4. Case P also guarantees superior market and profit performances of the overall supply chain, while all proactive incentive strategies guarantee the performance enhancement comparing to the reactive strategy (Case N) if they can be adopted. Next, Proposition 5 compares the profit performance of each player.

Proposition 5. *Comparing the profit of each player, we obtain the following properties.*
(1) *For the final assembler's profit Π_A^*, we obtain the following results.*

$\Pi_A^{S*} > \Pi_A^{P*} > \Pi_A^{N*}$ *without Cases SI and PS if* $\pi_1 < \pi_A < \pi_1 + \pi_2$ *and* $\pi_1 > (\pi_A^2 + \pi_2^2)/(2\pi_A)$,
$\Pi_A^{P*} > \Pi_A^{S*} > \Pi_A^{N*}$ *without Cases SI and PS if* $\pi_1 < \pi_A < \pi_1 + \pi_2$ *and* $\pi_2 < \pi_1 < (\pi_A^2 + \pi_2^2)/(2\pi_A)$,
$\Pi_A^{PS*} = \Pi_A^{SI*} > \Pi_A^{S*} > \Pi_A^{P*} > \Pi_A^{N*}$ *if* $\pi_A > \pi_1 + \pi_2$ *and* $\pi_1 > (\pi_A^2 + \pi_2^2)/(2\pi_A)$,
$\Pi_A^{PS*} = \Pi_A^{SI*} > \Pi_A^{P*} > \Pi_A^{S*} > \Pi_A^{N*}$ *if* $\pi_A < (\sqrt{2}+1)\pi_1 - \pi_2$ *and* $\pi_1 < (\pi_A^2 + \pi_2^2)/(2\pi_A)$,
$\Pi_A^{P*} > \Pi_A^{PS*} = \Pi_A^{SI*} > \Pi_A^{S*} > \Pi_A^{N*}$ *if* $\max[\pi_1 + \pi_2, (\sqrt{2}+1)\pi_1 - \pi_2] < \pi_A < 3\pi_1 - \pi_2$, *and*
$\Pi_A^{P*} > \Pi_A^{SI*} > \Pi_A^{S*} > \Pi_A^{N*}$ *without Case PS if* $\pi_A > 3\pi_1 - \pi_2$ *and* $\pi_1 > \pi_2$.

(2) *In terms of the profits of S1 and S2, Π_1^* and Π_2^*, we obtain the following relationships.*

Case P > S > N without Cases SI and PS if $\pi_1 < \pi_A < \pi_1 + \pi_2$ *and* $\pi_1 > \pi_2$,
Case P > PS = SI > S > N if $\pi_1 + \pi_2 < \pi_A < 3\pi_1 - \pi_2$, *and*
Case P > SI > S > N without Case PS if $\pi_A > 3\pi_1 - \pi_2$ *and* $\pi_1 > \pi_2$.

Proof. By directly comparing Π_A^*, Π_1^* or Π_2^* of all cases in Table 3, respectively, and considering the conditions in Proposition 1 together, we obtain the comparison results of Proposition 5. □

Proposition 5(2) indicates that both S1 and S2 are also better off when they are in the triadic relationship under the final assembler's central control in Case P, the same as the result of the entire supply chain in Proposition 4. However, the assembler's profit performance is quite different as shown in Proposition 5(1). The mitigation of multiple marginalization issues in Case P does not always help the final assembler to achieve the superior profit performance as also graphically illustrated in Figure 8. This does mean that Case P cannot always be regarded as a superior alternative even though it not only yields superior quality and market performances but also guarantees the best profit results to S1, S2 and the entire supply chain. The proactive and direct control over all suppliers makes the overall supply chain efficient but imposes a burden to the final assembler by incurring not only additional control issues involving the lower-tier suppliers but also cost issues due to excessive incentive offerings. As the focal company in the supply chain, the final assembler may make a decision to enhance the overall performances of the supply chain and its partners, not considering its own profit but accepting all the burdens. However, it is more rational that the final assembler with the bargaining power does not have any intention to accept its loss. In this situation, the choice of the proactive incentive strategy in the multi-tiered supply chain will follow the results in Proposition 5(1), graphically illustrated in Figure 8, maximizing the final assembler's profitability, rather than the result in Figure 7(a). In order to directly control supply chain partners and mitigate marginalization issues by proactively expanding its view to the lower tier and forming a triadic relationship, the final assembler needs to be sufficiently profitable enough, especially comparing to its direct partner S1 which also has the intention to have the control over the lower-tier supplier S2. That is, π_A needs to be sufficiently larger than π_1 to be in the condition area illustrated in Figure 8 under which Case P guarantees a superior profit to the final assembler. Then, the proactive control over suppliers, especially having a direct tie with the lower tier as in Case P, can be advantageous not only to the entire supply chain but also to the final assembler.

Figure 8: The condition of Π_A^* in each case dominating other cases (A: $\pi_A = \pi_1$, B: $\pi_A = \pi_1 + \pi_2$, C: $\pi_A = 3\pi_1 - \pi_2$, D: $\pi_1 = \pi_2$, E: $\pi_A = (\sqrt{2}+1)\pi_1 - \pi_2$, F: $\pi_1 = (\pi_A^2 + \pi_2^2)/(2\pi_A)$)

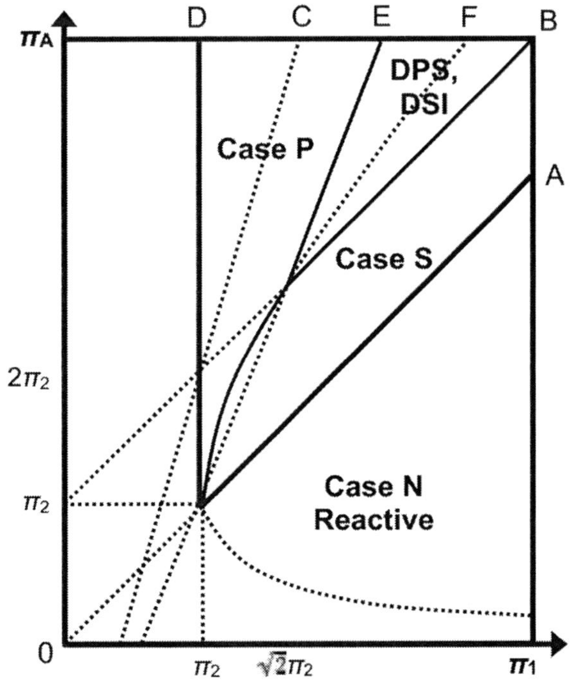

NUMERICAL EXAMPLE

Case FI: Full Integration as a Benchmark

For the numerical example, we add a fully-integrated supply chain model (Case FI) as a benchmark for the former practical cases, decentralized. Case FI can be considered an ideal first-best situation, in which the final assembler can monitor and control all players' actions without incurring cost. By integrating overall processes, the final assembler's profit Π_A^{FI} is the same as the supply chain's profit Π^{FI}, where the superscript FI denotes Case FI.

$$\Pi_A^{FI} = \Pi^{FI} = \Pi_A + \Pi_1 + \Pi_2 = (p - c - c_1 - c_2)D - \lambda q_1^2 - \eta q_2^2 = \pi D - \lambda q_1^2 - \eta q_2^2, \quad (15)$$

where D, Π_A, Π_1 and Π_2 are in Equations (1) through (4). π is the entire supply chain's marginal profit, i.e., $\pi = \pi_A + \pi_1 + \pi_2 = p - c - c_1 - c_2 > 0$.

By simultaneously solving FONCs of the problem (15), we obtain

$$q_1^{FI*} = \frac{\gamma\pi}{2\lambda}, \text{ and } q_2^{FI*} = \frac{\delta\pi}{2\eta}.$$

By applying the above into Equations (1) and (15),

$$D^{FI*} = D_0 + \frac{\gamma^2\pi}{2\lambda} + \frac{\delta^2\pi}{2\eta}, \text{ and } \Pi_A^{FI*} = \Pi^{FI*} = D_0\pi + \frac{\gamma^2\pi^2}{4\lambda} + \frac{\delta^2\pi^2}{4\eta}.$$

The solution of Case FI will be used as the benchmark for practical decentralization cases.

Numerical Example

We introduce a numerical example not only to verify the results of propositions in a practical parameter setting but also to discover important implications more. We set the parameters as follows: $D = \alpha - \beta p + \gamma q_1 + \delta q_2 = 2000 - 10p + 30q_1 + 30q_2$, $\lambda = \eta = 100$, $p = 115$, $w_1 = 60$, $w_2 = 20$, $c = 20$, $c_1 = 20$, $c_2 = 10$. By the parameter setting above, the marginal profits are $\pi_A = p - c - w_1 = 35$, $\pi_1 = w_1 - c_1 - w_2 = 20$, $\pi_2 = w_2 - c_2 = 10$ and $\pi = \pi_A + \pi_1 + \pi_2 = p - c - c_1 - c_2 = 65$. Therefore, we can have the internal solutions in all incentive models (we satisfy the condition area under which Cases P, PS, SI and S can exist in Figure 6). To analyze the profit performance of each incentive contract, we consider the measure introduced in Cachon (2003): the contract efficiency (Π/Π^{FI}), indicating how closely the supply chain profit of each proactive incentive contract approaches the ideal first-best optimum in Case FI. We also additionally consider the profit share of each player ($PS_j = \Pi j/\Pi$). For the final assembler, the focal company in the supply chain, the incentive strategy is attractive if both efficiency and its profit share are high (Cachon, 2003). Table 4 summarizes the solutions.

From the results in Table 4, we can identify several managerial implications below.

- Any proactive incentive strategies provide a supply chain a chance to enhance overall performances as also shown in Propositions 3 through 5. Comparing to reactive no incentive scheme, a reactive strategy (Case N), we can observe that the quality levels at S1 and S2, the demand requests of customers and the profits of the final assembler, S1, S2 and supply chain are all enhanced in any incentive strategies.
- The quality and market performances and the profits of S1, S2 and the entire supply chain are always superior in Case P as also shown in Propositions 3, 4 and 5(2).
- However, we observe that the final assembler's profit is superior not in Case P but in Cases PS and SI, i.e., $\Pi_A^{PS*} = \Pi_A^{SI*} > \Pi_A^{S*} > \Pi_A^{P*} > \Pi_A^{N*}$. This is since the parameter set satisfies the conditions, π_A (= 35) > $\pi_1 + \pi_2$ (= 30) and π_1 (= 20) > $(\pi_A^2 + \pi_2^2)/(2\pi_A)$ (= 18.93) in

Proposition 5(1).

Table 4: Summary of the numerical example (Contract Efficiency, $Eff^i = \Pi^i/\Pi^{FI}$ where i = Case N, S, SI, P or PS; Profit share, $PS_j = \Pi_j/\Pi$ where $j = A$ (the final assembler), 1 (S1) or 2 (S2))

		Benchmark	No Incentive	Incentive Strategies			
		Case FI	Case N	Case S	Case SI	Case P	Case PS
Incentive	b_1	N/A	0	225	225	225	225
	b_2	N/A	0	150	187.5	375	187.5
	i_1	N/A	0	0	75	0	0
Total	T_{A1}	N/A	0	928	1,111	928	928
	T_{12}	N/A	0	338	457	0	274
	T_{A2}	N/A	0	0	0	1,266	183
Quality	q_1	9.750	3.000	4.125	4.125	4.125	4.125
	q_2	9.750	1.500	2.250	2.438	3.375	2.438
Investment	λq_1^2	9,506	900	1,702	1,702	1,702	1,702
	ηq_2^2	9,506	225	506	594	1,139	594
Demand	D	1,435	985	1,041	1,047	1,075	1,047
Profit	Π_A	74,263	34,475	35,516	35,530	35,431	35,530
	Π_1	N/A	18,800	19,714	19,890	20,727	19,890
	Π_2	N/A	9,625	10,244	10,332	10,877	10,332
	Π	74,263	62,900	65,473	65,751	67,034	65,751
Efficiency	Eff	1.0000	0.8470	0.8816	0.8854	0.9027	0.8854
Profit Share	PS_A	1.0000	0.5481	0.5424	0.5404	0.5286	0.5404
	PS_1	N/A	0.2989	0.3011	0.3025	0.3092	0.3025
	PS_2	N/A	0.1530	0.1565	0.1571	0.1623	0.1571

- Proactive incentive strategies also allow a supply chain to become more efficient and approach the ideal profit level of the fully-coordinated Case FI, i.e., Eff^S, Eff^{SI}, Eff^P and Eff^{PS} > Eff^N, while Case P yields the best efficiency of 90.27%, improved by 5.57% from the result of the reactive Case N without any incentive.
- Profit shares of S1 and S2 are also enhanced through proactive incentive strategies, i.e., $PS_1 > PS_1^N$ and $PS_2 > PS_2^N$ in Cases S, SI, P and PS, while Case P guarantees the highest profit shares to both S1 and S2. However, we can observe that proactive strategies deteriorate the final assembler's profit share, i.e., $PS_A < PS_A^N$ in Cases S, SI, P and PS, even though the final assembler's profit itself increases.
- The reactive Case N guarantees the highest profit share to the final assembler. Therefore, it is impossible to initiate joint quality innovation through a proactive incentive strategy if the final assembler, the focal company in a supply chain, only considers its relative share among supply chain's overall profit. The final assembler needs to overcome a myopic view in order to enhance not only the overall performance of the entire supply chain but also its own. .

Overall, it is very important in practice to proactively control suppliers that each supply chain player, especially the focal company, needs to systematically understand the interaction between players in order to have a thorough understanding of performance dynamics in a supply chain.

CONCLUDING REMARKS

This study investigated proactive incentive strategies for quality improvement in a three-stage supply chain, consisting of a final assembler, a first-tier supplier (S1) and a second-tier supplier (S2). Five different supply chain models are introduced by considering different incentive-offering paths among three players. We then investigated their distinct characteristics and compared their overall performances, including quality, market and profit performances. Through investigation and comparison of those models, we found important implications. They can be summarized as follows.

First, only a buying firm sufficiently profitable comparing to a supplier firm can proactively control suppliers by offering incentives. The reason why each player adopts an incentive is in order to proactively protect its own business interest and profitability by controlling its supplier.

Second, when the final assembler forms a triadic relationship by adopting a parallel incentive strategy, offering incentives to both S1 and S2, the largest quality incentive can be offered to S2. This is since the final assembler takes the centralized control over both S1 and S2, and hence the supply chain becomes most efficient by mitigating the multiple marginalization issues.

Third, any proactive incentive strategies, whether parallel or sequential, always provide a supply chain a chance to enhance overall performances. Comparing to reactive no incentive scheme, the quality levels at S1 and S2, the demand requests of customers and the profits of the final assembler, S1, S2 and supply chain are all enhanced in any proactive incentive strategies.

Fourth, the performance of the parallel incentive strategy always dominates other sequential incentive strategies by proactively forming a triadic relationship and directly controlling both S1 and S2 with the largest incentives, in terms of not only quality and market performances but also profit performances at S1, S2 and entire supply chain.

Fifth, however, the parallel incentive strategy cannot always be regarded as a superior alternative in a supply chain. This is since it does not always guarantee the superior profit performance of the final assembler. The proactive and direct control over all suppliers makes the overall supply chain efficient but imposes a burden to the final assembler by incurring not only additional control issues involving the lower-tier suppliers but also cost issues due to excessive incentive offerings. To effectively adopt the parallel incentive strategy, the final assembler needs to be sufficiently profitable enough, especially comparing to its direct partner S1 which also has the intention to have the control over the lower-tier supplier S2.

Sixth, the reactive strategy without incentives guarantees the highest profit share to the final assembler. Therefore, it is impossible to initiate joint quality innovation through a proactive incentive strategy if the final assembler only considers its relative share among supply chain's overall profit. The final assembler needs to overcome a myopic view in order to enhance not only the overall performance of the entire supply chain but also its own. .

We aim to contribute to the body of knowledge and supply chain practices by revealing different characteristics of proactive incentive strategies for quality improvement in a three-stage supply chain and by providing important implications.

REFERENCES

Ang, E., D. Iancu, A., & Swinney, R. (2015). Disruption risk and optimal sourcing in multi-tier supply networks. *Working paper,* Stanford University.

Baiman, S., Fischer, P. E., & Rajan, M. V. (2000). Information, contracting, and quality costs. *Management Science,* 46(6), 776-789.

Baiman, S., Fischer, P. E., & Rajan, M. V. (2001). Performance measurement and design in supply chains. *Management Science,* 47(1), 173-188.

Balachandran, K. R., & Radhakrishnan, S. (2005) Quality implications of warranties in a supply chain. *Management Science,* 51(8), 1266-1277

Banker, R. D., Khosla, I., & Sinha, K. K. (1998). Quality and competition. *Management Science,* 44(9), 1179-1192.

Bimpikis, K., Fearing, D., & Tahbaz-Salehi, A. (2015). Multi-sourcing and miscoordination in supply chain networks. *Working paper,* Stanford University.

Cachon, G. P. (2003). *Supply chain coordination with contracts.* In: Graves, S. C. & De Kok, A. G., editors. *Handbooks in operations research and management science: supply chain management: Design, coordination and operation.* Elsevier Publishing Company.

Carr, S. M., & Karmarkar, U. S. (2005). Competition in multiechelon assembly supply chains. *Management Science,* 51(1), 45-59.

Chao, G. H., Iravani, S. M. R., Savaskan, R. C. (2009). Quality improvement incentives and product recall cost sharing contracts. *Management Science,* 55(7), 1122-1138.

Chen, Y. -J. & Deng, M. (2013). Supplier certification and quality investment in supply chains. *Naval Research Logistics,* 60(3), 175-189.

Choi, T. & Linton, T. (2011). Don't let your supply chain control your business. *Harvard Business Review,* 89(12), 112-117.

Corbett, C. J. & Karmarkar, U. S. (2001). Competition and structure in serial supply chains with deterministic demand. *Management Science,* 47(7), 966-978.

D'amato, P. (2014). Poorly designed battery and unchecked contractors are blamed for 2013 fire aboard 787 Dreamliner. 2015: Retrieved from http://www.dailymail.co.uk/news/article-2860260/Poorly-designed-battery-unchecked-contractors-blamed-fire-aboard-787-Dreamliner-2013.html, December 10.

Ding, D. & Chen J. (2008). Coordinating a three level supply chain with flexible return policies. *Omega,* 36(5), 865-876.

Dong, Y., Xu, K., Xu, Y., & Wan, X. (2013). Quality assurance contracts in a multi-level supply chain. *Working Paper,* The University of Texas at San Antonio, College of Business.

Gates, D. (2015). Boeing 787's problems blamed on outsourcing, lack of oversight. 2015: Retrieved from http://www.seattletimes.com/business/boeing-787rsquos-problems-blamed-on-outsourcing-lack-of-oversight, December 9.

Hsieh, C. -C. & Liu, Y. -T. (2010). Quality investment and inspection policy in a supplier-manufacturer supply chain. *European Journal of Operational Research,* 202(3), 717-729.

Huang, L., Song, J-. S. & Swinney, R. (2015). Managing social responsibility in multi-tier supply chains." *Working Paper.*

Hwang, I. Radhakrishnan, S., & Su, L. (2006). Vendor certification and appraisal: Implications for supplier quality. *Management Science,* 52(10), 1472-1482

Jaber, M. Y. & Goyal, S. K. (2008). Coordinating a three-level supply chain with multiple suppliers, a vendor and multiple buyers. *International Journal of Production Economics,* 116(1), 95-103.

Jaber, M. Y., Bonney, M. & Guiffrida, A. L. (2010). Coordinating a three-level supply chain with learning-based continuous improvement. *International Journal of Production Economics,* 127(1): 27-38.

Karmarkar, U. S. & Pitbladdo, R. C. (1997). Quality, class, and competition. *Management Science,* 43(1), 27-39.

Kaya, M., & Özer, Ö. (2009). Quality risk in outsourcing: Noncontractible product quality and private quality cost information. *Naval Research Logistics,* 56(7), 669-685.

Kayış, E., Erhun, F., & Plambeck, E. L. (2013). Delegation vs. control of component procurement under asymmetric cost information and simple contracts. *Manufacturing & Service Operations Management,* 15(1), 45-56.

Kim, K., & Chhajed, D. (2002). Product design with multiple quality-type attributes. *Management Science,* 48(11): 1502-1511.

Klayman, B. (2014). Aston Martin recalls 17,590 cars due to counterfeit material. 2015: Retrieved from http://www.reuters.com/article/us-autos-astonmartin-recall-idUSBREA141T120140205, December 15.

Leng, M., & Parlar, M. (2009). Allocation of cost savings in a three-level supply chain with demand information sharing: A cooperative-game approach. *Operations Research,* 57(1), 200-213.

Lim, W. S. (2001). Producer-supplier contracts with incomplete information. *Management Science,* 47(5), 709-715.

Munson, C. & Rosenblatt, M. (2001). Coordinating a three-level supply chain with quantity discounts. *IIE Transactions,* 33(5), 371-384.

Ostrower, J., & Pasztor, A. (2014). Air-safety board cites failures before Dreamliner's battery fire. 2015: Retrieved from http://www.wsj.com/articles/faa-boeing-and-gs-yuasa-all-faulted-over-dreamliner-battery-fire-ntsb-says-1417465012, December 8.

Reuters (2012). NHTSA regulators investigating Ford Crown Victoria police cars. 2015: Retrieved from http://www.nydailynews.com/autos/nhtsa-regulators-investigating-ford-crown-victoria-police-cars-steering-control-issue-195-000-vehicles-article-1.1161265, December 13.

Reyniers, D. J., & Tapiero, C. S. (1995). Contract design and the control of quality in a conflictual environment. *European Journal of Operational Research,* 82(2), 373-382.

Sana, S. S. (2011). A production-inventory model of imperfect quality products in a three-layer supply chain. *Decision Support Systems,* 50(2), 539-547.

Savaskan, R. C., Bhattacharya, S., & Van Wassenhove, L. N. (2004). Closed-loop supply chain models with product remanufacturing. *Management Science,* 50 (2), 239-252.

Savaskan, R. C., & Van Wassenhove, L. N. (2006). Reverse channel design: The case of competing retailers. *Management Science,* 52 (1), 1-14.

Shepardson, D. (2015). Fiat Chrysler recalls 180K new pickups, SUVs. 2015: Retrieved from http://www.detroitnews.com/story/business/autos/chrysler/2015/10/27/fiat-chrysler-recalls-new-pickups-suvs/74669032/, December 16.

Shi, L., Ólafsson, S., & Chen, Q. (2001). An optimization framework for product design. *Management Science,* 47(12), 1681-1692.

Shiraki, M. (2015). Toyota to buy 13 million air-bag inflators from Takata rival – sources. 2015: Retrieved from http://www.reuters.com/article/2015/08/21/us-autos-takata-toyota-idUSKCN0QQ03N20150821#vTQX0veMrlw1tWH1.97, December 20.

Slowick, M. (2013). Corporate social responsibility in procurement. 2015: Retrieved from ProcurementLeaders.com, December 5.

Tancrez, J. -S., Lange, J. -C., & Semal, P. (2012). A location-inventory model for large three-level supply chains. *Transportation Research Part E: Logistics and Transportation Review,* 48(2), 485-502.

Tang, C. S., & Zimmerman, J. D. (2009). Managing new product development and supply chain risks: The Boeing 787 case. *Supply Chain Forum: An International Journal,* 10(2), 74-86.

Volodymyr, B., & Christopher, S. T. (2012). Managing opportunistic supplier product adulteration: Deferred payments, inspection, and combined mechanisms. *Manufacturing & Service Operations Management,* 14(2), 301-314.

Wan, X., Xu, K., Dong, Y., & Evers, P. T. (2014). Quality management in a three-level supply chain: The role of methods and costs. *Working Paper,* The University of Texas at San Antonio, College of Business.

Williard, N., He, W., Hendricks, C., Pecht, M. (2013). Lessons learned from the 787 Dreamliner issue on lithium-Ion battery reliability. *Energies,* 6, 4682-4695.

Xie, G., Yue, W., Wang, S., & Lai, K. K. (2011). Quality investment and price decision in a risk-averse supply chain. *European Journal of Operational Research,* 214(2), 403-410.

Yan, T., Choi, T. Y., Kim, Y., & Yang, Y. (2015). A theory of the nexus supplier: A critical supplier from a network perspective. *Journal of Supply Chain Management,* 51(1), 52-66.

Yoo, S. H., Shin, H., & Park, M. -S. (2015). New product development and the effect of supplier involvement. Omega, 51: 107-120.

Zhu, K., Zhang, R. Q., & Tsung, F. (2007). Pushing quality improvement along supply chains. *Management Science,* 53(3), 421-436

DECISION SCIENCES INSTITUTE

Problem-solving is decision-making

Sergei Talanker

Western Galilee College

Email: sergeit@wgalil.ac.il

ABSTRACT

In the following paper I argue that problem-solving and decision-making are just different aspects of the same multi-stage goal-oriented cognitive process. I prove my hypothesis by comparing stage by stage both the decision-making and problem-solving prescribed strategies and the description protocols. If indeed problem-solving and decision-making processes are homological, scientist, studying the same process from different perspectives, might be able to learn from each other and their dialogue may be facilitated through the common vocabulary suggested in this paper.

KEYWORDS: problem-solving, decision-making, naturalistic, algorithm, strategy.

INTRODUCTION

The review of literature reveals that contemporary accounts of the relationship between problem-solving (PS) and decision-making (DM) are contradictory and confusing. In this paper I attempt to clarify the terms and to put them in order.

The thesis that I present in this paper is that PS and DM refer to the same process. I prove my thesis by comparing these processes stage by stage.

Problem-solving is often considered to be based upon application of an algorithm, while decision-making is considered to be based upon experience and intuition. I argue that the division between "algorithmic" and "naturalistic" or experience-based thinking cannot serve as a basis of distinction between problem-solving and decision-making, as problems are often dealt with haphazardly and decisions are often made methodically, and vice versa. In fact, algorithms for problem-solving and decision-making bear striking resemblance. Moreover, I demonstrate that "naturalistic" problem-solving and decision-making patterns, both productive and unproductive, are similar.

The first chapter starts with the various definitions of the term "problem", stemming from the different approaches. Then, the various types of categorizations of problem are presented. Next, the term "solution" is investigated and a "proper" five-stage PS strategy is described, phase by phase. The conditions under which the problems are being properly solved are discussed further. As most problems are not properly solved by people, an account of the different ways in which they cope with unsolved problems is also provided. *Coping* is described as a correlate to the stress that problems cause. A theory of two cognitive systems - rational and experiential - is presented in brief. The distinction between the two systems explains what makes people solve problems properly or hastily, or not at all.

The second chapter starts with the investigation of the concepts of "decision" and "decision conflict" and their relationship to problems. Next, an "optimal" five-stage DM strategy is described and compared to the "proper" PS strategy, stage by stage. Further "sub-optimal" DM patterns are then presented and correlated with coping mechanisms and the functioning of the experiential cognitive system. Next, the context and the conditions that are conducive for using the rational, procedural system is discussed, including when it is preferable and when it is not. Finally, the expert and novice use of the two cognitive systems are discussed.

The paper concludes with a list of suggested definitions of the concepts relating to PS and DM.

LITERATURE REVIEW

Regarding the question of the relationship between problem-solving (PS) and decision-making (DM), no option has been eliminated from the current scholarly discourse. The full range of answers - from "they are the same" to "they have nothing in common" - all have their champions. Some claim that they overlap and argue about where the true division lies. Others claim that one is part of another or the other way around. In numerous articles, PS and DM related terms are interchangeable (Sadler and Zeidler, 2005; Lee and Grace, 2012; Papadouris, 2012).

Cenkseven-Onder and Colakkadioglu (2013) present a survey of different perspectives on the relationship between PS and DM which are still relevant today. The authors note that some researchers argue that problem-solving and decision-making processes share similarities; thus, these concepts must be used together (Adair, 2010; Ivey et al., 1993; Churney, 2001). According to another popular opinion, decision-making and problem-solving are entirely different (Baron and Brown, 1991; Elstein and Schwartz, 2002; Isen, 2001). PS-oriented and DM-oriented researchers perceive these concepts and their interrelation differently. In a series of works dedicated to social PS, D'Zurilla (D'Zurilla and Goldfried, 1971; D'Zurilla and Chang, 1995; Nezu, D'Zurilla and Nezu, 2012) recognizes DM, or selecting the best solution out of many, as one of the five stages of PS. The conflict theory of decision making (Janis and Mann, 1977) sees systematic search for information, careful consideration of all viable alternatives and the unhurried, non-impulsive making of the final decision, in other word, PS, as one of the five DM-patterns.

The task of categorizing the different conceptions of PS and DM is complicated by the variety of domains and contexts in which they appear. In different branches of science, medicine, management, customer services, the classroom, and the social lives of adolescents, different aspects of PS and DM are considered central and marginal. For example, in medicine, PS refers to the ability to formulate and test good hypotheses, while DM refers to the ability to avoid biases (Elstein and Schwartz, 2012). In customer services, PS is considered good if it is creative, diverse, and flexible in categorization, while quality DM is considered good if it is fast, thorough, and efficient (Isen, 2001). In the social lives of adolescents, good decisions are those that one would not regret upon reflection (Baron and Brown, 1991).

The situation is further complicated by researchers relying upon different mind-theories and world-theories. For example, Adair (2010) believes that problems and decision situations are distinct and that decisions create problems. However, he also believes that the mental framework used in PS and DM is similar.

Ohlsson (2012), while criticizing the classical approach to PS (Newel and Simon, 1972), argues that PS involves five distinct cognitive actions: to perceive the problematic situation, retrieve relevant actions, conceptualize the top goal, activate and apply action selection preferences, and assemble a way to evaluate problem states. Theories of these five cognitive functions might be forthcoming from psychological research on perception, memory, intentionality, decision making, and judgment, in which case there is nothing specific to say about them in the context of problem solving. If so, PS is not a proper field of study, and there might not be a distinct theory of PS.

In other words, contemporary conceptualizations of both PS and DM are confusing and contradictory. In this paper I attempt to clarify the terms and the *quid-pro-quos*.

HYPOTHESIS

Among the numerous theses regarding the relationship between PS and DM I support the thesis that states that these concepts refer to the same complex process, compound of distinct stages, each stage demanding different cognitive operations. This process may be defined as any goal-directed sequence of cognitive operations. This definition does not distinguish between a sequence of actions that one *knows* will achieve a goal and a sequence of actions one undertakes when one does *not* immediately know how to reach the goal (Anderson, 1980, quoted by Robertson, 2001).

According to Anderson (1990), PS is a generic term used to cover deciding which action to take. DM also appropriately refers to the same process, but this term emphasizes the evaluation of alternatives, whereas research on PS has traditionally focused on the combinatorial explosion of sequences of action that occur in PS search.

Thus, the hypothesis that I try to defend is one among the others, it is not original or new. The new element that I present in this paper is the systemic approach, considering different approaches to the subject, and the argumentation supporting the hypothesis.

METHODOLOGY

In the numerous items written on the subject, the authors' approach to the conceptualization of DM and PS, including Anderson and others, is usually unquestioned by them. It is either postulated or quoted from another source. In this paper I would like to investigate all the possible conceptualizations of DM and PS, and present an argument in support of the hypothesis stated above.

I will rely on the methodology of conceptual analysis as well as process analysis. Both DM and PS processes are thoroughly described and prescribed in professional literature. There is no need for me to add to add a new protocol or to suggest a new algorithm. I will only compare the existing prescribed and the described DM and PS algorithms and protocols in different contexts.

I will argue that both the prescribed and the described PS and DM processes are homological, stage by stage. In other words, if to each stage of proper PS there is a corresponding optimal DM stage and vice versa, we are prescribing about the same algorithm or strategy. We are talking about the same artificial algorithm or strategy for dealing with problems. If the reasons why people do not solve problems properly and make sub-optimal decisions are the same, if the blunders they make at each stage are the same, DM and PS processes are the same.

Problem-solving is often considered to be based upon application of an algorithm, while decision-making is considered to be based upon experience and intuition. I argue that the division between "algorithmic" and "naturalistic" or experience-based thinking cannot serve as a basis of distinction between problem-solving and decision-making, as problems are often dealt with haphazardly and decisions are often made methodically, and vice versa. In fact, algorithms for problem-solving and decision-making bear striking resemblance and "naturalistic" problem-solving and decision-making patterns, both productive and unproductive, are similar.

PROBLEM SOLVING

What is a "problem"?

According to Anderson (1990), finding a rest room or getting two diet sodas are exemplary problems. In a footnote, Anderson writes that finding a rest room might not seem like much of a problem, but in certain cases (details purposely omitted) it was.

A *problem*, in the broadest sense, is a gap between the given situation and the desired one. Bridging the gap is solving the given problem (Laughlin, 2011; Cenkseven-Onder & Colakkadioglu, 2013). For example: "How much is two plus two?" or "Who was the first president of the United States?" are problems, while "4" and "George Washington" are solutions, in the broad sense, *ad hoc*. This definition is intuitive and simple, but it is not accepted by all experts on the subject. It stems from the classical definition of a problem as the gap between the given and the desirable, which the individual does not immediately know how to bridge (Newel and Simon, 1972). This definition has been accepted by different scholars until this day (Beyth-Marom et al., 1989; Brest and Krieger, 2010; Shoenfeld, 2013). According to this view, the above questions are not problems - for those who know the answers.

This definition of a problem depends on the person solving it. However, it is important to note that finding a solution to a problem does not or should not mean that the problem has ceased to be a problem. For example, a booklet in which I have solved all the problems does not stop being a booklet with problems, either for me or for others. Therefore, we must distinguish between a problem, in the broad sense, and a "real" problem, in relation to an individual who does not know how to solve it immediately.

Dewey's (1910) approach is very close to that of Schonfeld, with one significant difference. In Dewey's terms, a problem is "real" if it arises out of the real life of the one facing it, if it is interesting, and if it is grounded in the social context. Such problems can be called "real life" problems. If this is indeed the case, a number of math problems may be real problems for a student, but may not necessarily represent problems in his life.

This is the primary source of confusion regarding the concept of a problem: if someone does not acknowledge a problem to be a problem, is it still a problem? Well, of course it is. A person may be in denial about having a problem or a problem might not really concern him; nevertheless, it is still a problem.

A problem in itself is timeless and often impersonal. Its "realness", however, relates to the subject facing it. Its "real-lifeness" refers to the subject within a specific time-frame. With a real-life problem, it is a given that unless something changes, life will become worse at a certain point in time. This will happen either because one will no longer be satisfied with the persisting conditions, or because something is threatening to change these conditions for the worse.

What types of problems are there?

In fact, there are many types of problems. According to Robertson (2001), a problem is defined by the following four factors: the given situation, the desired state, the types of actions that can be taken to resolve the problem, and the problem-solving restrictions. Problems can be sorted into category pairs: problems requiring great or little knowledge (domain-specific or generic), well or ill-defined problems (closed or open), semantically rich or poor problems (requiring familiarity with the type of problem or not), problems of insight or problems requiring the application of an algorithm (Robertson, 2001).

Laughlin (2011) defines a problem by its domain, complexity, detail (well or ill-defined), and relationship to other problems.

Each type of problems calls for different sets of skills, knowledge, and *tactics* to solve it. The overall *strategy* for PS is the same for all types of problems. One of the stages of PS strategy, though, is recognizing the type of problem one is facing. Ploya (1957), for example, suggests a four-step strategy (understanding a problem, devising a plan, carrying out the plan, looking back) and numerous tactics for solving mathematical problems.

Newel and Simon (1972) have attempted a titanic challenge of formalizing both the strategy and the tactics of PS at once. Their work proved to be extremely influential; yet in the 1990s, their approach stumbled upon difficulties as it became obvious that the cognitive processes involved in PS are of a distinct and separate nature (Ohlsson, 2012). Research in cognitive psychology, however, has helped classify and order these processes into a sequence of stages.

How do people solve problems?

PS *proper* refers to the rational search for a solution through the application of PS skills and techniques that are designed to maximize the probability of finding the "best" or most adaptive solution for a particular problem (D'Zurilla and Chang, 1995). D'Zurilla's five-phase process of successful social PS can serve as a model for overall PS strategy. It differs from Ploya's model in one particular, but significant, step.

The first phase of PS, *orientation*, involves the formation of a set or an attitude to recognize and accept problematic situations when they occur and to inhibit the tendency to either respond automatically or avoid the problem by doing nothing. In other words, PS starts with a particular mindset: one is oriented towards finding problems. One must first be dissatisfied with the situation in order to be proactive and seek out problems. This is not a natural attitude. PS is by no means a natural process; it just achieves better results than anything else.

In the second phase, one must *formulate* the problem. In the first stage, the question was a matter of recognizing a problem as a problem; in this phase, the question is recognizing the problem type and its parameters. In other words, one must recognize the given situation and the desired outcome(s), as well as what kind of a problem one is dealing with: whether it is domain-specific or generic; open or closed, semantically rich or poor, and whether it is a problem of insight or a problem requiring the application of an algorithm.

During the third phase, one *produces* different courses of action (COA) for solving the problem, based on his understanding of the type of problem he is facing and the heuristic schemes he knows. This is the phase in which the math teacher from Schoenfeld's (2011, 2013) example finds himself when a student suddenly reveals a major misconception or it becomes apparent that the class does not have a good grip on something that the teacher thought they understood. In such a case, the current "game plan" has to be revised on the spot, and replaced with something else. This is the point where the teacher must come up with several good tactics for solving what is now apparent as a specific problem. If the teacher were to follow Ploya's strategy (assuming that it was applicable to our case), he would only need to come up with one good plan and carry it out.

During the fourth phase, called the DM phase by D'Zurilla, one anticipates the possible consequences of each alternative, the value and likelihood of these consequences occurring, and selects the most satisfactory alternative. It is called the DM phase because it involves a rough estimation according to one's intuition and experience. This is the least formal, "managerial" phase. Our math teacher must now make a calculated guess as to which pedagogical tactic has the best chance of dispelling the misconception or tightening the classes' grasp of the subject matter. This would be redundant if the teacher were to follow Ploya's strategy.

The final phase, *verification*, involves trying out the chosen decision. The teacher must implement his tactic and make sure that it works. Of course, if the attempt fails, one has to regress to the previous phase: the teacher must reassess the remaining strategies available to him, pick the one he thinks is the best, and give it a try. After several failed attempts, one might be forced to either give up or regress back to previous phases - perhaps all the way to phase two, or even phase one, if the problem is deemed unsolvable. The idea behind the present strategy is that the time invested in coming up with and weighing different tactics would be returned in the form of the time saved, as the person using this strategy is likely to regress through stages fewer times, compared to the one using Ploya's strategy of testing the first good plan that comes to mind.

Among hybrid PS strategies inspired by both Ploya's concepts and D'Zurilla's scheme one could count TIPS (Newton et al., 2012) and DECIDE (Welch, 1999). Team-Initiated PS (TIPS) begins with establishing the readiness to solve problems. It then divides understand the problem into two steps: understanding the conditions and understanding the reasons. The team is encouraged to hypostatize both the reasons that lead to the problem and come up with different possible solutions to the problem. The solutions are then discussed, and upon the democratically selected solution, action plan is developed and implemented. TIPS turns the PS process into a cycle by adding another step: evaluating and revision. As soon as one problem is solved, environment is scanned for new problems, and the cycle continues as life goes on. Data is collected through all the stages of the cycle.

DECIDE begins with three conceptualization stages: Define a problem, Examine the environment, Create a goal statement. The next step, Invent an intervention plan, includes both brainstorming for multiple hypotheses and identifying an intervention, taking into account the availability of resources. Further, the team Delivers the action plan and then Evaluates it.

What does it take to solve a problem?

According to Schonfeld (2013), one's ability to solve a "real" mathematical problem is determined by four factors: one's knowledge; the use of problem-solving strategies (heuristic strategies); monitoring and self-regulation (aspects of meta-cognition); and, finally, one's beliefs about the domain, problem-solving, and himself.

Another theory, the information capacity, demand and processing model of PS, attributes one's failure to solve a problem to *working memory overload* (Johnstone and El-Banna, 1986). One's cognitive capacity is limited by a number of mental space units he can handle at once, usually 7±2. One's ability to organize information allows him to process bigger amounts of information. Thus, if a problem is represented in one's mind through more units than he can handle at once, he will not be able to solve it. If he knows how to reconceptualize the problems through less units of information, below his working memory limit, he may be able to solve it. The conceptual scheme that helps organize the information also takes chunks of working memory, but it is obviously worth the cognitive space it eats up. The more conceptual schemes one is familiar with, the better his PS chances are, which is consistent with Schoenfeld's second factor.

This model is not without limitations, though. Tsaparlis (1998) examined the limitations of the model and stated the necessary conditions that must be fulfilled in order for the model to be valid. These are as follows: (a) the logical structure of the problem must be simple, (b) the problem has to be nonalgorithmic, (c) the partial steps must be available in the long-term memory and accessible from it,

(d) the students do not employ chunking devices, and (e) no "noise" should be present in the problem statement, "noise" meaning the irrelevant and potentially misleading information that might be included in a problem.

According to a number of studies cited in (Stamovlasis and Tsaparlis, 2012), besides working memory space, other factors such as *logical thinking* and *disembedding ability* (the ability to decontextualize and transfer knowledge), predict success or failure to solve a problem. To sum it up: cognitively developed individual's ability so solve a "real", close, non-algorithmic, domain-specific problem is dependent on his domain knowledge, ability to manipulate his cognitive state and familiarity with conceptual schemes.

The question is: What happens when one does not have the cognitive capacity or the will to solve a problem?

One cannot properly solve all the problems in the world. Most problems do not concern an individual. Some of the problems that do concern him cannot be objectively solved by him, i.e., the conditions cannot be changed from the given to the desirable. In such cases, he must *cope* with the problems subjectively, i.e., accept the given as, if not desirable, then at least acceptable.

According to Lazarus (1966, 1999), coping has to do with the way people manage stressful life conditions. To some extent, stress and coping could be said to be reciprocals of each other. Coping works through two functions: the PS function and the emotional function. Problems lead to stress, but human organisms can only take a limited amount of stress. People have two ways to reduce stress: solve their problems or regulate their emotions related to the stress situation – by either avoiding thinking about the threat or reappraising it – without changing the actual reality of the stressful situation.

For example, when facing a test on American history featuring the question: "Who was the fourth president of the USA?", one may recognize this problem as being semantically simple, closed, domain-specific, and demanding the application of an algorithm. The individual taking the test will come up with a list of possible candidates (Adams, Madison, Jefferson), logically eliminate the wrong answers, and confidently commit to the remaining option. On the other hand, he may give the answer without thinking much, relying upon memory. In such a case, the answer may or may not be correct. While in the first case the problem was solved properly, in the second case it was solved *hastily*. The sooner the problem is solved – the less stress and emotional turmoil one experiences. Another option is not answering the question altogether. If the answer turns out to be wrong, one will need to cope with the ramifications. He may decide that he needs to improve his knowledge, or that he needs to refine his PS technique in history or adapt his PS strategy altogether. Another option is to decide that nothing needs to be done, as the problem is not very important: the question is meaningless; the test is inconsequential; knowledge and education are over-valued. In this case, one is said to be dealing with the problem on a purely emotional level. If one cannot change the outcome, one will change the attitude.

The Two Systems

Numerous authors (Epstein, 2003; Evans and Frankish, 2008; Kahneman, 2011; Evans and Stanovich, 2013) suggest there are two distinct systems operating within our minds: one is rational and the other is experience-based.

In order to take full advantage of this paradigm, its terminology must be further clarified. It should be noted that the word "rational", as used in the rational system, refers to a set of analytical principles and has no implications with respect to the reasonableness of one's behavior, which is an alternative meaning of the word. The experiential system in humans is the same system by which non-human animals adapt to their environments (Epstein, 2003). These systems operate in parallel and are interactive. One does not just solve problems while completely detaching from the emotions. Surveying the thinking patterns of adolescents solving socioscientific problems, Sadler and Zeidler (2005) report that all the adolescents taking part of their study engaged in at least one of the three distinct informal reasoning patterns while problem-solving: rationalistic; emotive; and intuitive.

It is a misconception to identify rational, algorithmic thinking with PS and experience-based, "naturalistic" thinking with DM. As we shall see, people often solve problems by relying on their past experiences and make decisions through the application of algorithms.

By default, our experiential system is activated. One has to suppress his automatic reactions in order for the rational system to take over. This is not like turning on a switch – one has to continuously maintain the rational process, such as proper PS. Otherwise, the experiential system, which is permanently present, will once again take over. Thus, one must continuously monitor oneself throughout the process.

The most important factor to be monitored is one's stress level. If one's stress level is too high, he will "take a shortcut" through the process. If one's stress level falls too low – he will slip into nonchalance. We will further discuss which factors influence stress levels in the coming sections.

How do People not solve Problems?

D'Zurilla's (1971) five-phase process of solving a social problem presumes the potential to either fail or opt out of the process at each phase. One always has an option of acting automatically, either successfully or not. Once again, already in the first phase, facing social or work-related problems, one can either refuse to acknowledge that a problem exists, and either do nothing or act automatically. Acting automatically does not necessarily lead to bad results. Experienced professionals, such as athletes, pilots and even teachers, may act out of instinct - before they have time to cognitively register their actions (Feldon, 2007). They do this in order to avoid *cognitive overload* which happens whenever the total processing demands of external stimuli and internal cognitions exceed available attentional resources (Sweller, 1989). They alleviate their cognitive load by acting automatically. There is a functional dynamic between deliberate (i.e., conscious, rational) and automatic (i.e., non-conscious, experience-based) processing. The mental events available for conscious manipulation and control occur in the working memory, function more slowly, and require more effort than other processes (Feldon, 2007). There is a limit to the capacity of our consciousness, a fact which is vividly evident in novice teachers. The attempt to attend to the needs and behaviors of an entire classroom, while also trying to remember and implement a lesson plan, inundates their available cognitive resources. Therefore, this cognitive overload limits the abilities of novice teachers to effectively adapt to complex classroom dynamics (Doyle, 1986). Expert teachers have no need to consciously address every problem that comes up in the classroom because they automatically rely on their experience. The more problems one can delegate to the automatic cognitive system, the more resources become available to the conscious system. To put it conversely: if one cannot rely on his experience-based automatic behavior, his cognitive abilities will be severely impaired by cognitive overload.

Experts are better than novices primarily at pattern recognition (Fadde, 2009). Where a novice perceives a problem, an expert recognizes a familiar pattern, particularly because he has solved a multitude of similar problems. Now he no longer has to. It is a routine situation for him; he can push the "auto-pilot" button.
The second phase is that of *interpretation*. Textbook problems usually make the job of interpretation easy for the students, but this is not to say that students always understand textbook problems

properly. Tversky and Kahneman's (1974, 1981, 1986) groundbreaking research on decision problems showed that people who possess enough knowledge to solve a decision problem often fail, in most cases, at the phase of reformulating it. This happens because they naturally and automatically settle for the first interpretation that comes to mind, instead of going through the process of solving the problem properly. In Tversky and Kahneman's experiments, the phrasing of the problems was controlled by them, influencing which interpretation was perceived by the subjects first.

During emergency situations, however, there is often no time to solve all the problems by orderly going through the PS stages. Thus, opting out of the PS process may be the right course of action.

Another good way out of a problem was exemplified by Alexander the Great. The Gordian knot could not be untied by any problem-solver, through any algorithm. Alexander opted not to even attempt to untangle the knot, but rather to cut through it.

In the third phase, one may fail because his knowledge or tactical repertoire may not suit the type of problem he faces, or one may skip to phase four or even five, trying to implement the first idea that comes into one's head. When a good idea seems to come to mind, one tends to get swept away in a "eureka" moment. This is sometimes referred to as "opportunistic problem-solving" (Kuo, et al., 2013) or "dodge" (Johnstone and El-Banna, 1986). The proper way to go about PS is, of course, to keep producing ideas before attempting to evaluate them, let alone try them out. There is an old saying, often attributed to the mathematician and the second Chess World Champion, Emanuel Lasker: "If you find a good move, look for a better one". This, however, does not apply to blitz games.

The question is: When should one stop producing ideas and move onto evaluating them? How does one make this decision? "Had we but world enough and time…", it would be prudent to prolong this phase *ad infinitum*,… "But at my back I always hear Time's winged chariot hurrying near". There are three options available: to set a timetable before beginning to produce strategies; to determine, in advance, the number of strategies to be produced; or to move on to the next phase as soon as the first tactic or course of action (COA) comes up. In the latter case, if the COA seems plausible, one tries to implement it immediately. If not, one returns to phase three and repeats the process. The first two options seem to fit the spirit of PS, while the third option is more "naturalistic", and may only be considered proper within certain frameworks to be discussed further. *Brainstorming*, in which ideas are suggested without being immediately judged or critiqued, is not a natural procedure.

In the fourth phase, the process of evaluating the alternative strategies may drag into infinity as well. It is hard to estimate whether a COA will be successful without actually trying it out. Thus, the most natural thing to do is to try and implement the first COA that seems promising.

In the fifth phase, one might fail to implement the COA successfully, because it was flawed, he was not adept at using it, or because he gave up too soon.

B: DECISION MAKING

What is optimal decision-making?

A *decisional conflict* refers to simultaneous opposing tendencies within the individual to accept and reject a given course of action (Janis and Mann, 1977). When there is no conflict, no decision or choice among alternatives needs to be made - one goes on doing what he normally does. On the most basic level, any decision is a choice between doing what one normally does and doing something else. If there is no problem with one's normal routine, then there is no conflict, and no decision needs to be made. One only starts deliberating about changing when there is a problem: a given state is no longer desirable or the existing conditions are threatened.

Whenever a problem arises, one continuously decides whether he wants to follow through with the proper PS process or return to "normal" functioning: doing what nature or experience has taught him to do. Thus, *proper* DM must be similar to proper PS: a series of successive stages through which the decision to change the situation is carried out.

If this hypothesis is correct, one would expect to see rational decision-makers actually solving their problems. In fact, the protocols describing *optimal* DM procedures are very similar to the prescribed PS procedures such as those suggested by D'Zurilla, stage by stage. In other words, people who make good decisions in fact approach decision conflicts by identifying the problems and solving them properly.

Like D'Zurilla, Janis and Mann (1977) describe a five-stage proper DM process. These stages are: appraising the challenge; surveying alternatives; weighing alternatives; deliberating about commitment; and adhering despite negative feedback.

In the first stage, one appraises the challenge. This stage corresponds to D'Zurilla's second phase (problem statement and definition). Janis's protocol refers to situations where a problem is already salient, thus D'Zurilla's first phase (orientation, involving the formation of a set or an attitude to recognize and accept problematic situations when they occur and to inhibit the tendency to either respond automatically or avoid the problem by doing nothing) is presupposed. Being aware of a problem is a pre-condition to successfully dealing with it. In Janus's terms, the right orientation is labeled as vigilance, as opposed to inertia, different types of avoidance, and hyper-vigilance. In other words, one must be able to regard an issue with the appropriate seriousness in order to even begin the process leading to a good decision.

There are, of course, different aspects of the first stage that Janis and Mann emphasize more than D'Zurilla and Nezu. In this stage or phase, according to both approaches, one tries to make sense of the challenge, interpret the information, and categorize it. However, while the PS approach accentuates the wording and the conceptualization of the issue, the DM approach accentuates the assessment of the issue's seriousness or, in other words, whether it is important enough to be taken seriously, and if so, then how seriously. If it is not very important, i.e., no grave consequences are foreseen, one is unlikely to bother making a quality decision about it, and rightfully so.

In the second stage, corresponding to D'Zurilla's third phase, one surveys alternative COAs. Both Janis and D'Zurilla believe that quality coping with a serious issue necessitates producing or finding numerous coping tactics: seeing only one or two options is perceived as lackadaisical.

In the third stage, corresponding to D'Zurilla's fourth phase, one weighs the alternative COAs and decides which one is most likely to be the best. This is the decision stage of the decision-making process. The problem of choosing the COA that is most likely to yield the best results is often referred to as *decision problem*.

In the fourth stage, corresponding to D'Zurilla's fifth and final phase, one implements the decision reached in the previous stage. What is emphasized in DM is the commitment to the decision. In Schoenfeld's paradigmatic example, a teacher, deciding upon a particular course of action which he deems the most appropriate, will probably consider what will happen if it fails. If a teacher asks a student which COA he will choose to solve a problem, the student might hesitate; he most likely would not have hesitated, had he not been asked, but rather allowed to proceed without declaring his COA aloud.

The final stage of DM, adhering despite negative feedback, is not accounted for in PS, because it is considered by D'Zurilla (1971, 2012) to be a separate issue. In DM literature, post-decisional activity received its share of attention, particularly in the context of the Differentiation and Consolidation theory (Svenson, 1992, 1996; Verplaken and Svenson, 1997). According to this theory, the process of DM consists of three major parts: identifying the problem; differentiating among alternatives until there is only a single satisfactory one remains; and manipulating data to bolster the decision made. Svenson's protocol can be refined into an eight-stage protocol (Lee and Grace, 2012), but it would still describe the same process. It has two identification stages, four distinction stages and two consolidation stages. In addition to the previously considered protocols, a "formulating criteria for evaluating options" stage is inserted into this one.

This additional stage deserves special attention. Setting different criteria for weighing the alternative COAs will probably lead to choosing different COAs. In the most important cases, with human lives or large amounts of money on the line, decision problems are solved through application of algorithms that take multiple criteria into account (Olcer and Odabasi, 2005; Yang et al, 2015). These algorithms assign different value to different criteria. Moreover, there is competition among these algorithms as well (Naili et al., 2014). Thus, in order to make the absolutely best decision, one has to decide upon the relevant criteria, their relative weight and the algorithm that would calculate them.

In light of the above, decision problems are well-defined, domain specific, semantically rich problems, requiring application of algorithms. However, in most cases, they are treated as ill-defined, generic problems, stated in general terms and solved relying upon previous experience (Tawfik and Jonassen, 2013). This is how a customer decides which yogurt he should by, but this is not how a large supply chain should.

What is sub-optimal decision-making?

People do not always make optimal decisions. People do not always approach DM vigilantly or in the optimal manner. It is safe to assume that people neither can nor should optimize each of their decisions. Buying a house and selecting a door-knob should not be approached similarly, and normally are not. In a general sense, involvement in an issue, product, or decision is often considered as a motivational factor that affects the cognitive effort that individuals expend on a problem, and on strategies that are used to form a judgement or make a decision (Verplanken and Svenson, 1997; Johnson and Eagly, 1989). The outcome of the decision ought to be worth the mental resources invested in it. Thus, in most cases it is optimal not to optimize the outcome.

According to Herbert Simon (1956), decision-makers are normally oriented towards *satisficing* rather than optimizing the outcome of their decisions. In other words, most decision makers are oriented towards making decisions which are good enough, but not necessarily the best. Since one cannot make all of his decisions optimal, one should try to at least not make outright bad decisions in most cases. Adapting the amount of mental resources one invests in making a decision to the issue's level of seriousness makes a lot of sense. If a teacher makes hundreds of non-trivial decisions a day (Danielson, 2007), he cannot make all of them in an optimal manner. Most of them just have to be good enough not to disrupt the learning process.

According to Janis and Mann, using a satisficing DM strategy does not preclude some or even all of the criteria for vigilant information processing. In other words, one may take a matter seriously and with confidence, and yet decide not to resolve it optimally.

People are generally reluctant to make decisions because DM is very stressful. People seek out different ways to alleviate stress, while the (oh, so long) optimal process of DM means that the stress lingers. For this reason, people tend to resolve issues in a sub-optimal manner. This also explains why people would rather opt out of the prescribed PS procedure. If the levels of stress and mental strain are too high for a person to handle, one will either drop the issue altogether (which ultimately leads to failure and negative consequences) or rush the process and skip stages, reaching sub-optimal (yet, perhaps, satisfactory) results.

How do people cope with problems and conflicts?

Janis and Mann (1977) described 5 distinct patterns of coping with decisional conflicts, which as we have seen, stem from problems. Later, the list of coping patterns was revised to fit the results of empirical research (Mann et al., 1997); yet, the overall division remained intact. If a person pays little or no attention to the problem, either because he fails to notice it or he does not find it serious enough, he will display a pattern of *unconflicted inertia*, or doing nothing new, characterized by low levels of stress, until the problem becomes too serious to ignore. By that time, however, it might be too late to deal with it effectively. The next pattern is *unconflicted change* to another course of action. When a problem seems serious and something needs to be done, varying levels of stress may arise. However, if a new course of action (suggested by someone else or generated spontaneously) promises to suffice to fix the problem, the switch will be made and the levels of stress will diminish. This "repair job" might not necessarily be optimal, but unless the situation changes dramatically, it will not drain mental energy from the decision-maker. If neither non-action nor the new course of action will suffice to fix the problem, one could begin to vigilantly produce new ideas. Alternatively, thinking (perhaps after failing to produce good ideas over a period of time) that he will not be able to produce an idea that will be good enough or that he will not be able to carry them out (perhaps after a few failed attempts), he will fall into one of the patterns of *defensive avoidance*: buck-passing, procrastination, bolstering/rationalization (the latter dropped in 1997). He will avoid investing energy on a project that he has no hope of successfully finishing. His levels of stress will fluctuate from low to high, as he feels the eminence of failure, but is too afraid to think about anything that would remind him of his helplessness and the consequences. *Hyper-vigilance* occurs when one feels that he can find a solution; yet, he does not have enough time to carry out a proper DM process step by step. People are under a lot of stress in such a state, and they tend to rush the process, skipping stages, depending on the level of stress they find themselves under. Being *vigilant* means avoiding all the pit-falls of the other patterns: the temptation to lower the level of stress by ignoring problems or rushing the process, having enough knowledge, believing in one's ability to solve the problem, and having enough meta-cognitive skills to manage one's time and levels of stress.

Vigilancy corresponds to Schoenfeld's four predictors of successful PS: one's knowledge, the use of heuristic strategies, monitoring and self-regulation, and one's beliefs about the domain, problem-solving, and himself. Again, one is vigilant if he can manage his levels of stress, knows enough to come up with good ideas, is familiar with heuristic strategies, and believes in himself.

Does context matter?

As we have seen in the previous chapter, several conditions must be satisfied in order for the proper DM or PS procedure to be followed and effective. One needs knowledge of the subject matter and the heuristic strategies, confidence, some meta-cognitive skills, and plenty of time to resolve complex issues. Following the optimal procedure does not automatically mean success, but it maximizes one's chances. Not following the procedure does not guarantee failure, and under various circumstances it is even preferable.

Klein (1999, 2008, 2009) suggests that "naturalistic", as opposed to "procedural" DM is preferable in numerous situations. In his latest book (2009), he tries to figure out which situations call for which type of DM; yet, he admits that the task is immensely complex. The same can be said of Kahneman's latest opus (2011). There are paradigmatic cases where following a prescribed routine is preferable and there are paradigmatic cases where it is not. Most cases, however, are in the grey areas.

In the context of classroom, social, scientific PS or complex strategic DM, the prescribed protocols are effective. Not following the correct procedures in these contexts when time is abundant is considered ineffective coping, stemming from either negative belief systems or either avoidant or impulsive DM styles (D'Zurilla and Chang, 1995). Coping, or stress-management, has two main functions: problem-focused and emotion-focused (Lazarus, 1999). If one cannot solve a problem, one should at least find a way to save mental energy.

On the other hand, experienced military personnel, pilots (Klein, 2009), athletes, and even teachers (Feldon, 2007, Fadde, 2009) are not advised to use PS or DM procedures in their professional activities, as they work under conditions where time is chronically limited. A lack of time is not naturally conductive to vigilant information processing. Under such conditions, experts are the best decision makers. Experts tend to rely on their vast concrete experience and pattern-recognition, rather than theoretical knowledge and procedures. They excel at problem detecting and problem recognition because etched in their minds are accurate mental models that generate expectancies and alarms when these expectancies have been violated (Klein et al., 2005). They tend to have good intuition about how to proceed in unclear and extreme situations (Klein, 2009).

Different types of people excel in different situations because different situations call for different sets of skills. What fighter pilots rely upon is not what theoretical scientists rely upon. Analysis is no substitute for experience and vice versa.

Decision-making under limited time conditions by experts and novices

A recognition-primed DM model conceived by Klein's think-tank was adopted by the US and Swedish military for its commanders (Ross et al., 2004). It relies on military commanders' experience-based problem detection and recognition. Thus, it is non-applicable for novices. Problem detection and recognition are the first two phases of any PS and DM strategy; however, as I mentioned earlier, experts excel at these two phases, while novices, even if they are well acquainted with the procedures do not do quite as well. The third stage, Klein suggests, should be over as soon as a satisfactory COA is conceived. According to Elstein and Schwartz (2002), expert physicians form hypotheses and their diagnostic plan rapidly, and the quality of their hypotheses is higher than that of novices. This is true of experts in other areas as well. Thus, instead of investing time producing several different tactics, an experienced commander's expertise is trusted to invoke in him a working COA at once. In other words, he makes the decision "naturalistically", rather than rationally. This also saves the trouble of going through phase four, as there are no strategies to compare. Next, the COA is tested and operationalized (details are added) by the staff. Thus, instead of contributing in phase three via brainstorming, the staff only contributes as critics. The roles are reversed. If, in the midst of testing or adding details, a better COA comes up, the two COAs are compared. This means that the process regresses to phase four which, in the case of the ideal scenario, is skipped. Back in phase five, the staff "wargames" the COA to see if the plan would hold up against presumed enemy COAs. If it seems to work well (if not – regression to stage three is eminent), the commander and his staff will commit to the COA and prepare operation orders, based on testing and operationalization.

Thus, a recognition-primed DM procedure is rational in its strategy, but relies upon experience-based decisions. This is not at all unusual. Klein's four-step procedure is structurally similar to Ploya's. In mathematics, just like on the battlefield, experience and intuition matter most. In science, where the big questions are often wide open, breakthroughs may occur from a hunch or the inspiration of a brilliant mind, rather than as a result of thorough research. If one is an expert and his experience and intuition is to be trusted, it makes sense to save valuable time and effort by rushing through stages. Novices and those who do not operate under time pressure conditions should go through the prescribed procedures without skipping stages. Adolescents at schools, like experts in the field, tend to rely upon informal heuristics, but their results are not as good as when they are taught to follow a heuristic strategy (Sadler and Zeidler, 2005; Papadouris, 2012; Lee and Grace, 2012). The suggestion, based on interviews with two students, to teach opportunistic problem-solving to introductory level university students (Kuo et al., 2013), also seems imprudent.

CONCLUSION

I would like to suggest the following nomenclature of terms, relating to PS and DM. Using the common nomenclature should bring the two scientific domains closer together and provide the scientists from both domains with tools to better communicate and understand each other.

Problem is a gap between the given and the desired.

Real problem is a gap which the person facing it does not immediately know how to bridge. It always relates to the person facing the gap.

Real-life problem is a real problem in the social or professional life of the one facing it. The gap in such problems can be stated as dissatisfaction with the given conditions (one would like to graduate, get promoted, etc.) or as a threat to the existing conditions (one would not like to get expelled or fired).

Solution to the problem is that which bridges the gap.

Optimal solution means that there is no better solution to the problem. If two or more solutions are equally good or they cannot be compared, they are each called optimal.

Coping refers to managing life conditions that are stressful. Coping works through two functions: the problem-solving function and the emotional function.

Constructive coping is attempting to deal with a problem through changing the environment.

Emotional coping is attempting to deal with the problem by reappraising it without changing anything in the environment.

Effective solution is any solution that allows one to cope with a problem, either constructively or emotionally.

Sufficient solution is any solution that satisfies the minimal requirements for bridging the gap, but is not necessarily optimal.

Proper solution is the existing optimal solution. Sometimes a problem has no proper solution.

Proper problem-solving process is a five-stage process that gives the one facing a problem the best chances to optimally solve the problem. Trying to solve the problem properly does not guarantee that one finds the proper solution.

Proper decision-making process is a five-stage process, similar to the proper problem-solving process.

Decision refers to a choice between alternative courses of action. Usually, continuing with the current course of action is one of the alternatives. Deciding upon a course of action is a part of the decision-making process.

Decision conflict refers to simultaneous opposing tendencies within the individual to accept and reject a given course of action. It stems from real-life problems. Decision conflict does not stop until the problem is effectively solved. Thus, while going through the stages of the problem-solving process one experiences decision conflict continuously.

Strategy is a conscious, rational approach to PS in general. Proper PS procedure is one of the possible PS strategies.

Course of action or *tactic* is a particular approach to solving a concrete problem or a type of problem.

Decision problem is the problem of choosing the COA that is most likely to yield the best results. They are often problems within larger problems.

Expert is someone who's experiential cognitive system allows for achieving better results than his rational system, particularly in complex situations under time constraints. Experts should not be advised to follow standard procedures under such circumstances. In some contexts, such procedures should be tailored to take advantage of their vast experience.

Rushing through stages occurs when one feels that one will reach a satisfying solution to his problem while saving time and alleviating stress and cognitive load.

Regression through stages occurs when an obstacle interferes with PS at any stage. In such cases, one may suspect that redoing a previous stage could lead to better results.

Experience-based cognitive system is the same system by which human and non-human animals adapt to their environments.

Rational cognitive system is a set of analytical principles and has no implications with respect to the reasonableness of the behavior, which is an alternative meaning of the word. The two systems operate in parallel and are interactive. One does not just solve problems while completely detaching from emotions. It is a misconception to equate rational thinking with problem-solving and the application of experience with decision-making.

References:

Adair, J. (2010). *Decision making and problem solving*. Philadelphia: Kogan Page.
Anderson, J. (1990). *The adaptive character of thought*. Hillsdale, NJ: Lawrence Erlbaum Associates.
Baron, J. and Brown, R. (1991). Toward improved instruction in decision making to adolescents: A conceptual framework and pilot program. In J. Baron and R.V. Brown (Eds.), *Teaching decision making to adolescents* (95-122) Hillsdale, NJ: Lawrence Erlbaum Associates.

Beyth-Marom, R., Fischhoff, B., Jacobs, M., Furby, L. (1989). *Teaching decision making to adolescents: A critical review*. Washington, D.C.: Carnegie Council on Adolescent Development.

Brest, P. and Krieger, L.H. (2010). *Problem solving, decision making, and professional judgment:A guide for lawyers and policymakers*. Oxford: Oxford University Press.

Churney, A.H. (2001). *Promoting children's social and emotional development: A follow up evaluation of an elementary school-based program in social decision-making/social problem-solving*. Dissertation Abstracts International Section A: Humanities and Social Sciences, 62 (1-A): 75.

Danielson, C. (2007). *Enhancing professional practice*. Alexandria, VA: Association for Supervision and Curriculum Development.

D'Zurilla, T. J., and Goldfried, M. R. (1971). Problem solving and behavior modification. *Journal of Abnormal Psychology*, 78, 107-126.

D'Zurilla, T.J. and Chang E.C. (1995). The relations between social problem solving and coping. *Cognitive Therapy and Research*, 19(5), 547-562.

Dewey, J. (1910). *How we think*. Boston: D.C. Heath.

Doyle, W. (1986). Classroom organization and management. In M. C. Wittrock (Ed.), *Handbook of research on teaching* (392–425), New York: Macmillan.

Elstein A.S., Schwartz A. (2002). Clinical problem solving and diagnostic decision making: Selective review of the cognitive literature. *British Medical Journal*, 324, 729–732.

Epstein, S. (2003). Cognitive-experiential self-theory of personality. In Millon, T., &
Lerner, M. J. (Eds), *Comprehensive handbook of psychology (5): Personality and social*

psychology (159-184), Hoboken, NJ: Wiley & Sons.

Evans, J. and Stanovitch, K.E. (2013). Dual-process theories of higher cognition: Advancing the debate. *Perspectives on Psychological Science* 8(3), 223–241.

Evans, J. and Frankish, K. (Eds.) (2009). *In two minds: Dual processes and beyond.* New York: Oxford University Press.

Fadde, P.J. (2009). Expertise-based training: Getting more learners over the bar in less time. *Technology, Instruction, Cognition and Learning*, 7, 171–197.

Feldon, D. (2007). Cognitive load and classroom teaching: The double-edged sword of automaticity. *Educational Psychologist*, 42(3), 123–137.

Frauenknecht, M. and Black, D.R. (2010). Is it social problem solving or decision making? Implications for health education. *American Journal of Health Education*, 41(2), 112-123.

Ivey, A.E., Ivey, M.B., Simek-Morgan, L. (1993). *Counseling and psychotherapy: A multicultural perspective* (3rd ed.), Boston: Allyn and Bacon.

Isen, A.M., (2001). An influence of positive affect on decision making in complex situations: theoretical issues with practical implications. *Journal of Consumer Psychology* 11(2), 75-85.

Janis, I.L., Mann, L. (1977). *Decision making: A psychological analysis of conflict, choice and commitment*. New York: Free Press.

Johnson, B.T. and Eagly, A.H. (1989) Effects of involvement on persuasion: A metaanalysis, *Psychological Bulletin,* 106, 290–314.

Johnstone, A. H., & El-Banna, H. (1986). Capacities, demands and processes—A predictive model for science education. *Education in Chemistry*, 23, 80 – 84.

Kahneman, D. (2011). *Thinking, fast and slow.* New York, NY: Farrar, Straus and Giroux.

Klein, G. (1999) *Sources of power: How people make decisions.* Cambridge, MA: MIT Press.

Klein, G., Pliske, R., Crandall, B. and Woods, D. (2005). Problem detection. *Cognition, Technology and Work*, 7, 14-28.

Klein, G. (2008). Naturalistic decision making. *Human Factors,* 50(3), 456-460.

Klein, G. (2009) *Streetlights and shadows: Searching for the keys to adaptive decision making*, Cambridge, MA: MIT Press.

Kuo, E., Hull, M. M., Gupta, A., and Elby, A. (2013) How students blend conceptual and formal mathematical reasoning in solving physics problems. *Science Education*, 97(1), 32–57.

Laughlin, R.P. (2011). *Group problem solving*. Princeton: Princeton University Press.

Lazarus, R.S. (1966). *Psychological stress and coping process*. New York: McGraw-Hill.

Lazarus, R.S (1999). *Stress and emotion: a new synthesis*. Bristol: Springfield.

Lee, Y.C. and Grace, M. (2012). Students' reasoning and decision making about a socioscientific issue: A cross-context comparison. *Science Education*, 96(5), 787–807.

Mann, L., Burnett, P., Radford, M., & Ford, S. (1997). The Melbourne Decision Making Questionnaire: An instrument for measuring patterns for coping with decisional conflict. *Journal of Behavioral Decision Making*, 10(1), 1-19.

Naili M., Boubetra, A., Tari, A., Bouguezza Y., Achroufene, A. (2014) Brain-inspired method for solving fuzzy multi-criteria decision making problems (BIFMCDM). *Expert Systems with Applications*, 42, 2173–2183.

Newell, A. and Simon, H.A. (1972). *Human problem solving*: Englewood Cliffs, N. J.: Prentice-Hall.

Nezu, Arthur M.; D'Zurilla, Thomas; Nezu, Christine Maguth (2012). *Problem-solving therapy: A treatment manual*. New York: Springer.

Ohlsson, S. (2012). The problems with problem solving: Reflections on the rise, current status, and possible future of a cognitive research paradigm. *The Journal of Problem Solving*, 5(1), 101-128.

Olcer, A.I. and Odabasi, A. Y. (2005) A new fuzzy multiple attributive group decision making methodology and its application to propulsion/maneuvering system selection problem. *European Journal of Operational Research*, 166, 93–114.

Papadouris, N. (2012) Optimization as a reasoning strategy for dealing with socioscientific decision-making situations. *Science Education*, 96(4), 600–630.

Ploya, G. (1957). *How to solve it*. New York: Doubleday.

Robertson, I. S. (2001). *Problem solving*. East Sussex: Psychology Press.

Ross, K. G., Klein, G. A., Thunholm, P., Schmitt, J. F. and Baxter, H. C. (2004). The recognition-primed decision model. *Military Review* (July-August).

Sadler, T.D. and Zeidler, D.L. (2005). Patterns of informal reasoning in the context of socioscientific decision making. *Journal of Research in Science Teaching*, 42 (1), 112–138.

Schoenfeld, A.H. (2011). *How we think: A theory of goal-oriented decision-making and its educational applications*. New York: Routledge.

Schoenfeld, A.H. (2013). Reflections on problem solving theory and practice. *The Mathematics Enthusiast,* 10(1&2), 9-34.

Simon, H. A. (1956). Rational choice and the structure of the environment. *Psychological Review* 63 (2): 129–138.

Stamovlasis, D., & Tsaparlis G. (2012). Applying catastrophe theory to an information-processing model of problem solving in science education. *Science Education*, 96(3), 392–410.

Stanovich, K. E. (2011). *Rationality and the reflective mind*. New York, NY: Oxford University Press.

Svenson, O. (1996). Decision making and the search for fundamental psychological regularities: What can be learned from a process perspective? *Organizational Behaviour and Human Decision Processes*, 65, 252 – 267.

Svenson, O., Salo, I., & Lindholm, T. (2009). Post-decision consolidation and distortion of facts. *Judgment and Decision Making*, 4(5), 397 – 407.

Sweller, J. (1988). Cognitive load during problem solving: Effects on learning. *Cognitive Science,* 12, 257–285.

Tawfik, A. and Jonassen, D. (2013) The effects of successful versus failure-based cases on argumentation while solving decision-making problems. *Education Technology Research and Development*, 61, 385–406.

Tsaparlis, G. (1998). Dimensional analysis and predictive models in problem solving. *International Journal of Science Education*, 20, 335 – 350.

Tverski, A. and Kahneman, D. (1974). Judgment under Uncertainty: Heuristics and Biases. *Science* 185, 1124-1131.

Tverski, A. and Kahneman, D. (1981). The Framing of Decisions and the Psychology of Choice. *Science* 211, 453-458.

Tverski, A. and Kahneman, D. (1986). Rational Choice and the Framing of Decisions. *The Journal of Business*, 59(4), 251-277.

Verplanken, B. and Svenson, O. (1997). Personal involvement in human decision making: conceptualizations and effects on decision processes. In R. Ranyard,W. R. Crozier, & O. Svenson (Eds.), *Decision making: Cognitive models and explanations* (pp. 40 – 57). London: Routledge.

Yang, T., Kuo, Y., Parker, D. & Chen K. H. (2015). A multiple attribute group decision making approach for solving problems with the assessment of preference relations. *Mathematical Problems in Engineering,* 1-10.

DECISION SCIENCES INSTITUTE

Renewable Two-Dimensional Pro-Rata Warranty Analysis for Reverse Supply Chain

Ammar Y. Alqahtani
King Abdulaziz University
Email: aaylqahtani@kau.edu.sa

Surendra M. Gupta
Northeastern University
Email: s.gupta@neu.edu

ABSTRACT

This paper presents an analysis of renewable two-dimensional Pro-Rata Warranty (PRW) policy for an Advanced Remanufacturing-To-Order system for Sensor-embedded products (SEPs). The goal is to predict a warranty period for end-of-life (EOL) components using the sensor information about age and usage of each and every EOL product on hand to meet product, component and recycled material demands while minimizing the cost associated with warranty and maximizing remanufacturer's profit.

KEYWORDS: Reverse Supply Chain, Simulation, Non-Renewable Warranty Policies, Remanufacturing, Sensor-Embedded Products.

INTRODUCTION

Recently, the number of studies dealing with the end-of-life (EOL) stage of a product has gained much attention from researchers (Gungor and Gupta 1999), (Ilgin, and Gupta 2010b). This is due, on one hand, to environmental factors, government regulations and public demands, and on the other hand, to potential economical profits that could be obtained by implementing reverse logistics and product recycling processes. Manufacturers try to cope with consumer awareness towards environmental issues and stricter environmental legislation by setting up facilities that involve the minimization of the amount of waste sent to landfills by recovering materials and components from returned or EOL products (Gungor and Gupta 2002).The chief concern in such product recovery processes is the uncertainty in quantity and quality of recoverable materials, due primarily to the lack of any information about the condition of components before disassembly. The obvious solution is to test each and every component after disassembling them. This, however, can harm the profitability of a remanufacturer depending on testing time and testing costs. Furthermore, if the test shows that the component is non-functional, then all of the allocated time and resources are wasted.

In product recovery, the disassembly process plays an important role since it allows for selective separation of desired parts and materials. EOL products containing missing and/or nonfunctional components increase the uncertainty associated with the disassembly yield. Sensor-embedded products (SEPs) eliminate a majority of uncertainties involved with EOL management by providing life-cycle information (Gupta and Lambert 2008), (Vadde et al. 2008). This includes information about the content of each product and component conditions that enables the estimation of remaining useful life of the components. Once the data about the product is captured, it is possible to make optimal EOL decisions without any preliminary disassembly or inspection operations (Ilgin, and Gupta 2010a, 2010b, 2010c, 2011). After the components are retrieved, the products can be remanufactured.

The quality of a remanufactured product is usually a suspect for consumers. That is, the consumers are unsure if the remanufactured products will render the expected performance. This ambiguity about a remanufactured product could lead the consumer to decide against buying it. With such apprehension held by consumers, remanufacturers often seek market mechanisms that provide assurance about the durability of the products. One strategy that the remanufacturers often use is to offer warranties on their products (Murthy and Blischke 2006).

Product warranties have three key roles. The first role is insurance and protection, allowing consumers to transfer the risk of product failure to sellers (Heal 1977). Next, product warranties can also signal product reliability to customers (Balachander 2001), (Gal-Or 1989), (Soberman 2003), (Spence 1977). Lastly, the sellers use warranties to extract additional profitability (Lutz and Padmanabhan 1995). There are a few articles and books that consider warranty policies for new products' supply chain management (Blischke 1993, 1995, 2011). However, there are not many papers that consider the warranty for the remanufactured products' reverse and closed-loop supply chain management. Base and extended one-dimensional and two-dimensional warranty can be offered for remanufacturing products using Free Replacement Warrantee (FRW) and Pro-Rata Warranty (PRW) policy (Ammar and Gupta 2015a, 2015b, 2015c, 2016a, 2016b, 2016c). The warranty policy and its effect on consumer behavior has been studied by Liao et al. 2015. Yazdia, et al. 2014 proposed a novel mathematical–statistical model where decisions involve pricing of returned used products (cores), the extent of their remanufacturing, selling price and the warranty period for the final remanufactured products to investigate the joint optimization of remanufacturing, pricing and warranty decision-making for end-of-life products. Kuik et al. 2015 presented mathematical models to examine two types of the proposed extended warranty policies for manufacturers to make the comparisons of their possible gained profit of remanufactured products by manufacturers.

SYSTEM DESCRIPTION

The Advanced Remanufacturing-To-Order (ARTO) system deliberated in this study is a product recovery system. A sensor embedded air conditioner (AC) is considered here as an example product. Based on the condition of EOL AC, it goes through a series of recovery operations similar to the one shown in figure 1. Refurbishing and Repairing processes may require reusable components to meet the demand of the product. This requirement satisfies the internal and the external component demand. Both will be satisfied using disassembled components.

EOL ACs arrive at the ARTO system for information retrieval using radio frequency data reader that are stored in the facility's database. Then the ACs go through a six-station disassembly line. Complete disassembly is performed to extract every single component. There are nine components in an AC consisting of, evaporator, control box, blower, air guide, motor, condenser, fan, protector, and compressor. Exponential distributions are used to generate the disassembly times at each station, interarrival times of each component's demand, and interarrival times of EOL AC. All End-Of-Life products (EOLPs) after retrieval of the information are transferred either to station 1 for disassembly or, if EOLP needs only repair for a specific component, to the corresponding station. Two different types of disassembly operations, viz., destructive or nondestructive, are used depending on the component's condition. If the disassembled component is nonfunctional (broken, zero remaining life), then destructive disassembly is used. The unit disassembly cost for a functional component is higher than nonfunctional component. After disassembly, there is no need for component testing due to the availability of information on components' conditions from sensors. It is assumed that the demands and life cycle information for EOLPs are known. It is also assumed that retrieval of information from sensors costs less than actual inspection and testing.

Recovery operations differ for each SEP based on its condition and estimated remaining life. Recovered components are used to meet components and spare parts demands, while recovered products are used for product demands. Also, material demands are met using recycled products and components. Recovered products and components are characterized based on their remaining lifetimes and are placed in different life-bins (e.g. one year, two years, etc.) waiting to be retrieved via a customer demand. Underutilization of any product or component could happen when it is qualified for a higher life-bin and is placed in a lower life bin because the higher life bin is full. Any product, component or material inventory that is greater than the maximum inventory allowed is assumed to be extra and is used for material demand or disposed of.

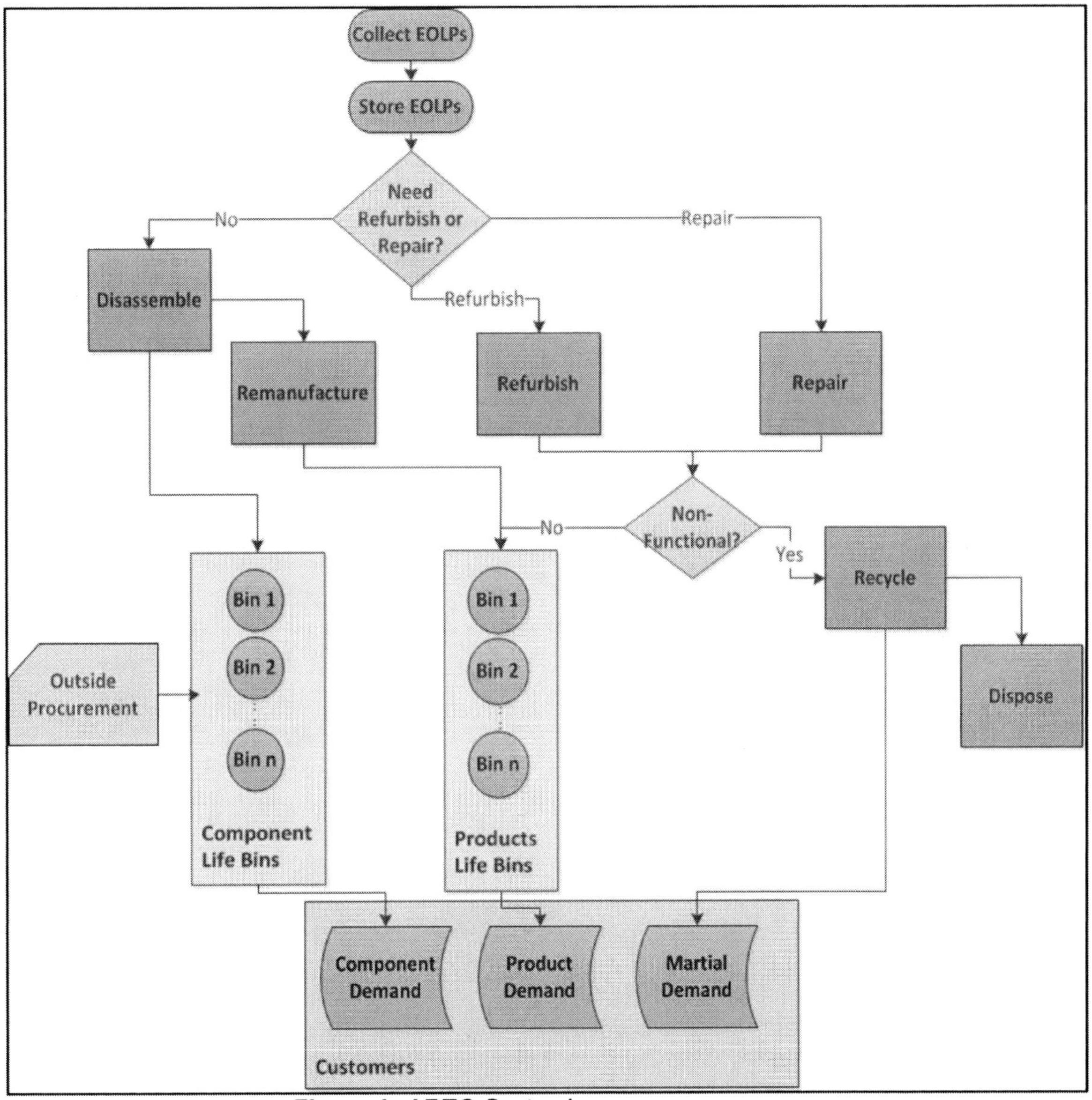

Figure 1: ARTO System's recovery processes

In order to meet the product demand, repair and refurbish options could also be chosen. EOLP may have missing or nonfunctional (broken, zero remaining life) components that need to be replaced or replenished during the repairing or refurbishing process to meet certain remaining life requirement. EOLP may also consist of components having lesser remaining lives than desired, and for that reason might have to be replaced.

TWO-DIMENSIONAL WARRANTY

In a one-dimensional warranty, the policy is valid for an interval called the warranty period, which is defined with respect of a signal variable such as age or usage. Instead, two-dimensional warranties are defined by a region in a two-dimensional plane, typically with one axis representing time or age and the other axis representing the usage. Therefore, many different types of warranties may be defined based on the shape of the warranty coverage region.

Two common possibilities about the region of coverage are shown in figure 2. Figure 2(a), shows the rectangular warranty region with independent limits on time and usage. This region has a tendency to favor the manufacturer because it put bounds on both the maximum time and the maximum usage for the buyer. For a buyer who is a heavy user, the warranty expires before the warranty period W end because usage has reached its maximum limit U. Likewise, for a buyer who is a light user, the warrant expires at time W with total usage below the limit U. In contrast, Figure 2(b) shows the Infinite strips warrant region, the buyer is assured with a minimum time of coverage and a minimum usage. This warranty region is in buyer favor. In this case, a heavy user is covered for a time period W, by which the usage may have exceeded the limit U, and a light user is covered well beyond the time period W, for the policy expires only when the total usage reaches the limit usage U.

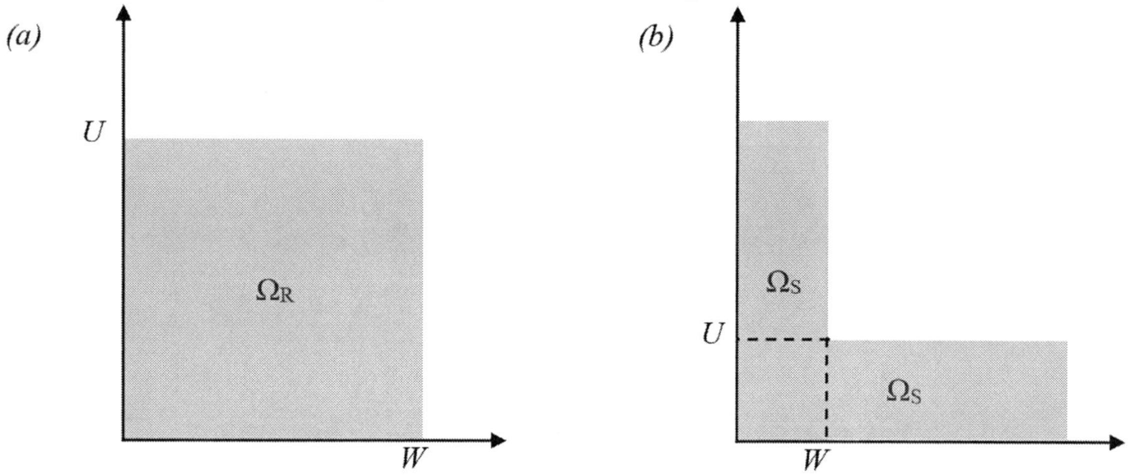

Figure 2: Two-dimensional warranty regions for usage versus time

RENEWING PRO-RATA WARRANTY COST ANALYSIS

In the process of deciding to purchase merchandise, the buyers usually compare features of a product with other competing brands that are selling the same product. In some cases, the competing brands make similar products to each other with similar features such as cost, special characteristics, quality and credibility of the product and even insurance from the provider. In these cases, after sale factors come into effect such as discount, warranty, availability of parts, repairs, and other additional services. These factors are very significant to the buyer in such situation and specially the warranty since it further assures the buyer of the reliability of the product.

A warranty is an agreement that requires the manufacturer to correct any product failures or compensate the buyer for any problems that occurs with the product during the warranty period in relevance to its sale. The objective of the warranty is to promote the products quality and guarantee its performance to assure production for both the manufacturer and the buyer.

There are many different available two-dimensional warrantee policies that most products are sold with. This paper considers the basic Pro-Rata Warrantee (PRW). The basic PRW is when the seller agrees to refund a fraction of the original sales price. The amount refunded depend on the age and usage of the remanufactured item at failure. In the case of unconditional refund, the buyer receives a cash refund and has no obligation to buy a replacement. In the case of conditional refund, the refund is tied to a replacement purchase.

NOMENCLATURE

In renewing policies, the warranty period begins anew with each replacement or repair. While in non-renewing policies, the repaired or replacement item is covered under warranty for the time remaining in the original warranty period. Under renewing PRW policy, a remanufactured product is replaced by a new one if a failure occurs under warranty. The new item comes with a new warranty. Since every failure results in replacement with a new one, the time between failures under warranty are a sequence of independent and identically distributed random variables.

Variables	*Definition*
W	Warranty period;
A	Warranty age limit;
U	Warranty usage limit;
S	Sales price;
C_s	Cost of each replacement;
C_r	Cost of each repair;
L	Remaining Life;
R	Usage rate;
r	Failure rate;
θ	Distribution parameters;
τ_r	Time at which warranty ceases conditional on R = r;
F(|)	Conditional distribution function;
$H(\tilde{\theta}\|r)$	Conditional probability of an item failing under warranty;
N	Number of replacements under warranty;
N_r	Stopping time for the renewal process;
$N(\tilde{\theta}\|r)$	Conditional renewal counting process;
Q	The total refund per item;
Q_r	The total refund per item conditional on R = r;
E[.]	Expected Value;
G(R)	Density function of a random variable r;

PROBLEM FORMULATION

Rectangular Region (Ω_R):

The probability that the remanufactured product fails under warranty is given by:

$$H(\tilde{\theta}|r) = \begin{cases} F(A|r) & if\ r < r_1 \\ F(\tau_r|r) & if\ r \geq r_1 \end{cases} \tag{1}$$

As a result, N_r is distributed according to a geometric distribution function with probability mass function given by:

$$Prob.\{N_r = n\} = H(\tilde{\theta}|r)^{n-1}\,[1 - H(\tilde{\theta}|r)] \tag{2}$$

Hence, the expected value of N_r is given by:

$$E[N_r] = \frac{1}{[1-H(\tilde{\theta}|r)]} \tag{3}$$

The total refund resulting from all replacement remanufactured products is given by:

$$Q_r = \sum_{i=1}^{N_r} R(T_i, rT_i|r) \tag{4}$$

The expected value of Q_r given by:

$$E[Q_r] = E[N_r]\, E[R(T_i, rT_i|r)] \tag{5}$$

The expected warranty cost (i.e. the expected total refund) per unit sale is given by:

$$EC(\tilde{\theta}) = E[Q] = \int_0^{\infty} E[Q_r]\, dG(r) = S\{\int_0^{r_1} [1/(1-F(A|r))\int_0^{K}\left(1-\frac{t_1}{A}\right)\left(1-\frac{rt_1}{U}\right) dF(t_1|r)]\, dG(r)$$
$$+ \int_{r_1}^{\infty}[1/(1-F(\tau_r|r))\int_0^{\tau_r}\left(1-\frac{t_1}{A}\right)\left(1-\frac{rt_1}{U}\right) dF(t_1|r)]\, dG(r)\,\} \tag{6}$$

Infinite strips Region (Ω_S):

Here the approach to obtaining the expected warranty cost per item is similar to that for PRW policy with rectangular region except that *R (t, rt)* is given by

$$R(t,rt) = \begin{cases} \left[1 - Min\left\{\frac{t}{A}, \frac{rt}{U}\right\}\right] S & if\ (t,rt) \in \Omega \\ 0 & if\ (t,rt) \notin \Omega \end{cases} \tag{7}$$

and $H(\tilde{\theta}|r)$ is given by

$$H(\tilde{\theta}|r) = \begin{cases} F(\tau_r|r) & if\ r < r_1 \\ F(A|r) & if\ r \geq r_1 \end{cases} \tag{8}$$

As a result, the expected warranty cost per item, $EC(\tilde{\theta})$ is given by

$$EC(\tilde{\theta}) = S\{\int_0^{r_1} [1/(1-F(\tau_r|r))\int_0^{\tau_r}\left[1 - Min\left(\frac{t}{A}, \frac{rt}{U}\right)\right] dF(t|r)]\, dG(r)$$
$$+ \int_{r_1}^{\infty}[1/(1-F(A|r))\int_0^{k}\left[1 - Min\left(\frac{t}{A}, \frac{rt}{U}\right)\right] dF(t|r)]\, dG(r)\} \tag{9}$$

NUMERICAL EXAMPLE

The example considers renewing Two-dimensional Pro-Rata Warrantee (PRW) policy for the remanufactured AC's components and products with three different remaining lives (1 year, 2 years and 3 years) with three different warranty periods (1 month, 2 months and 3 months) and usage (100 hours, 200 hours and 300 hours). Under this warranty, all failed items are repaired or replaced at no cost to the buyer as long as the failure occurs within the warranty period and usage. The warranty expires when either the age or usage limit is reached. The usage could be tracked and recorded using an embedded sensor. Suppose that there are three set of user population (Light, Medium and Heavy users) with different mean usage rates E(R) as stated in Table 1. The other data used for implementation of the model are shown in Table 2:

Table 1: Users' uniform limits and expected usage rates

Type of Users	*Uniform distribution limits*		*E[R]*
	Lower Rate Limit	*Upper Rate Limit*	
Light (L)	0.10	0.90	0.50
Medium (M)	0.70	1.30	1.00
Heavy (H)	1.10	2.90	2.00

Table 2: Operation costs (disassembly, assembly), sale price and repair cost for AC components

Components	*Cs* = Operation costs ($/unit)	*S* = Sale Price ($/unit)			*Cr* = Repair costs ($/unit)
		L = 1 Year	*L* = 2 Years	*L* = 3 Years	
Evaporator	$4.00	$10	$15	$35	$8.00
Control Box	$4.00	$20	$30	$15	$8.00
Blower	$2.80	$5	$12	$15	$5.60
Air Guide	$1.20	$5	$12	$60	$2.40
Motor	$4.00	$45	$55	$25	$8.00
Condenser	$1.66	$15	$18	$20	$3.32
Fan	$2.34	$15	$18	$20	$4.68
Protector	$0.60	$15	$20	$65	$1.20
Compressor	$3.40	$50	$60	$35	$6.80
AC	$55.00	$180	$240	$310	$85.00

RESULTS

It is assumed that $W = U$; these correspond to warranties of 1 month/100 hours, 2 months/200 hours and 3 months/300 hours. Table 3 and Table 4 give the expected warranty cost for the remanufactured components as a fraction of the sale price (i.e.,$EC(\tilde{\theta})/S$) under rectangular region (Ω_R) and Infinite strips region (Ω_S) PRW warranty for the three cases for W = U = 1, 2 and 3 respectively. Table 5 gives Remanufactured AC expected warranty cost as a fraction of the sales price for Rectangular and Infinite strips Region (Ω_S) PRW. This fraction can be used to predict warranty costs by multiplying the table value by sales price S. Suppose, for example, for the case of rectangular region (Ω_R) that a three years remaining life AC is sold at $310 with a 2 months/200 hours warranty and that on average warranty cost $310(0.0551) = $17.08 or 5.51% of the sale price of the AC for light users and this changes to $310(0. 0667) = $20.68 or 6.67% of the sales price of the AC for medium users and to $310(0.0727) = $22.54 or 7.27% of the sales price for the heavy users. In Infinite strips region (Ω_S) case, the average warranty cost increases to $310(0.5916) = $183.40 or 59.16% of the sales price, $310(0.3501) = $108.53 or 35.01% of the sales price and $310(0. 5574) = $172.79 or 55.74% of the sales price for light, medium and heavy users respectively.

CONCLUSION

The renewing Two-dimensional Pro-Rate warranty (PRW) cost for remanufactured products and components was evaluated in this paper for different periods and usages. The main objective was to introduce the idea of providing a two-dimensional PRW for a remanufactured products and how to predict a warranty period for an end-of-life (EOL) components using the sensor information about the age and usage of each and every EOL components and remanufactured products on hand to meet product, component and recycled material demands while minimizing the cost associated with warranty and maximizing manufacturer's profit. A simulation model was used to optimize the system and predict the warranty period that should be assigned to each and every disassembled component and remanufactured product.

Table 3: AC Components expected warranty cost as a fraction of the sales price for Rectangular Region (Ω_R) PRW

Items	*A* = U	(Expected Warranty Cost)/(Sales Price)			*Items*	*A* = U	Expected Warranty Cost)/(Sales Price)			*Items*	*A* = U	Expected Warranty Cost)/(Sales Price)			Users
		W=1.0	W=2.0	W=3.0			W=1.0	W=2.0	W=3.0			W=1.0	W=2.0	W=3.0	
		0.0261	0.0423	0.0580			0.0243	0.0393	0.0538			0.0252	0.0408	0.0559	Light
	1.00	0.0312	0.0395	0.0436		1.00	0.0289	0.0367	0.0405		1.00	0.0300	0.0381	0.0420	Medium
		0.0314	0.0348	0.0366			0.0292	0.0324	0.0340			0.0302	0.0336	0.0353	Heavy
		0.0290	0.0544	0.0905			0.0270	0.0505	0.0840			0.0280	0.0524	0.0872	Light
Evaporator	2.00	0.0392	0.0659	0.0836	**Air Guide**	2.00	0.0364	0.0612	0.0777	**Condenser**	2.00	0.0378	0.0635	0.0806	Medium
		0.0509	0.0659	0.0730			0.0473	0.0612	0.0679			0.0491	0.0635	0.0704	Heavy
		0.0305	0.0604	0.0896			0.0283	0.0561	0.0832			0.0294	0.0582	0.0863	Light
	3.00	0.0432	0.0831	0.1192		3.00	0.0402	0.0772	0.1107		3.00	0.0417	0.0801	0.1149	Medium
		0.0653	0.1110	0.1340			0.0607	0.1031	0.1245			0.0630	0.1070	0.1292	Heavy
		0.0237	0.0384	0.0525			0.0246	0.0398	0.0545			0.0255	0.0413	0.0566	Light
	1.00	0.0282	0.0358	0.0395		1.00	0.0293	0.0372	0.0410		1.00	0.0304	0.0386	0.0425	Medium
		0.0284	0.0316	0.0332			0.0295	0.0328	0.0344			0.0306	0.0340	0.0357	Heavy
		0.0263	0.0493	0.0820			0.0273	0.0511	0.0851			0.0283	0.0531	0.0883	Light
Control Box	2.00	0.0355	0.0597	0.0758	**Motor**	2.00	0.0369	0.0620	0.0787	**Protector**	2.00	0.0382	0.0643	0.0816	Medium
		0.0462	0.0597	0.0662			0.0479	0.0620	0.0687			0.0497	0.0643	0.0713	Heavy
		0.0276	0.0548	0.0812			0.0287	0.0568	0.0842			0.0297	0.0590	0.0874	Light
	3.00	0.0392	0.0753	0.1080		3.00	0.0406	0.0781	0.1121		3.00	0.0422	0.0811	0.1163	Medium
		0.0592	0.1006	0.1215			0.0614	0.1044	0.1260			0.0637	0.1083	0.1308	Heavy
		0.0240	0.0388	0.0532			0.0249	0.0403	0.0552			0.0258	0.0418	0.0573	Light
	1.00	0.0286	0.0363	0.0400		1.00	0.0297	0.0376	0.0415		1.00	0.0308	0.0391	0.0430	Medium
		0.0288	0.0320	0.0336			0.0299	0.0332	0.0349			0.0310	0.0344	0.0362	Heavy
		0.0266	0.0499	0.0830			0.0276	0.0518	0.0861			0.0287	0.0537	0.0894	Light
Blower	2.00	0.0360	0.0605	0.0768	**Fan**	2.00	0.0373	0.0627	0.0796	**Compressor**	2.00	0.0387	0.0651	0.0826	Medium
		0.0467	0.0605	0.0670			0.0485	0.0627	0.0695			0.0503	0.0651	0.0721	Heavy
		0.0280	0.0554	0.0822			0.0290	0.0575	0.0853			0.0301	0.0597	0.0885	Light
	3.00	0.0397	0.0762	0.1094		3.00	0.0411	0.0791	0.1135		3.00	0.0427	0.0821	0.1177	Medium
		0.0600	0.1019	0.1230			0.0622	0.1057	0.1276			0.0645	0.1097	0.1324	Heavy

Table 4: AC Components expected warranty cost as a fraction of the sales price for Infinite Strips Region (Ω_S) PRW

Items	*A* = U	(Expected Warranty Cost)/(Sales Price)			*Items*	*A* = U	Expected Warranty Cost)/(Sales Price)			*Items*	*A* = U	Expected Warranty Cost)/(Sales Price)			Users
		1.00	2.00	3.00			1.00	2.00	3.00			1.00	2.00	3.00	
		0.0827	0.0944	0.1551			0.1172	0.1338	0.2200			0.1663	0.1897	0.3120	Light
	1.00	0.0516	0.1002	0.2238		1.00	0.0731	0.1421	0.3173		1.00	0.1037	0.2015	0.4500	Medium
		0.0793	0.1740	0.4199			0.1125	0.2468	0.5955			0.1595	0.3499	0.8444	Heavy
		0.1847	0.1847	0.2119			0.2619	0.2619	0.3004			0.3714	0.3714	0.4260	Light
Evaporator	2.00	0.1013	0.1093	0.2238	**Air Guide**	2.00	0.1437	0.1550	0.3173	**Condenser**	2.00	0.2038	0.2198	0.4500	Medium
		0.0895	0.1740	0.4199			0.1270	0.2468	0.5955			0.1800	0.3499	0.8444	Heavy
		0.3109	0.3203	0.3340			0.4408	0.4542	0.4736			0.6250	0.6440	0.6716	Light
	3.00	0.1607	0.1719	0.2244		3.00	0.2278	0.2437	0.3181		3.00	0.3230	0.3456	0.4511	Medium
		0.1267	0.1885	0.4199			0.1797	0.2673	0.5955			0.2548	0.3791	0.8444	Heavy
		0.0929	0.1060	0.1743			0.1317	0.1503	0.2472			0.1868	0.2132	0.3505	Light
	1.00	0.0579	0.1126	0.2514		1.00	0.0821	0.1596	0.3565		1.00	0.1165	0.2264	0.5055	Medium
		0.0891	0.1955	0.4718			0.1264	0.2772	0.6690			0.1792	0.3931	0.9486	Heavy
		0.2075	0.2075	0.2380			0.2942	0.2942	0.3375			0.4172	0.4172	0.4786	Light
Control Box	2.00	0.1138	0.1228	0.2514	**Motor**	2.00	0.1614	0.1741	0.3565	**Protector**	2.00	0.2289	0.2469	0.5055	Medium
		0.1006	0.1955	0.4718			0.1426	0.2772	0.6690			0.2023	0.3931	0.9486	Heavy
		0.3492	0.3598	0.3752			0.4952	0.5102	0.5321			0.7022	0.7235	0.7545	Light
	3.00	0.1805	0.1931	0.2521		3.00	0.2559	0.2738	0.3574		3.00	0.3629	0.3883	0.5068	Medium
		0.1424	0.2118	0.4718			0.2019	0.3003	0.6690			0.2863	0.4259	0.9486	Heavy
		0.1044	0.1191	0.1958			0.1480	0.1689	0.2777			0.2098	0.2395	0.3937	Light
	1.00	0.0651	0.1265	0.2825		1.00	0.0923	0.1794	0.4005		1.00	0.1309	0.2543	0.5679	Medium
		0.1001	0.2196	0.5300			0.1420	0.3115	0.7516			0.2013	0.4416	1.0657	Heavy
		0.2331	0.2331	0.2674			0.3306	0.3306	0.3792			0.4687	0.4687	0.5377	Light
Blower	2.00	0.1279	0.1380	0.2825	**Fan**	2.00	0.1814	0.1956	0.4005	**Compressor**	2.00	0.2572	0.2774	0.5679	Medium
		0.1130	0.2196	0.5300			0.1602	0.3115	0.7516			0.2272	0.4416	1.0657	Heavy
		0.3924	0.4043	0.4216			0.5563	0.5732	0.5978			0.7889	0.8128	0.8476	Light
	3.00	0.2028	0.2170	0.2832		3.00	0.2875	0.3076	0.4015		3.00	0.4077	0.4362	0.5694	Medium
		0.1599	0.2380	0.5300			0.2268	0.3374	0.7516			0.3216	0.4785	1.0657	Heavy

Table 5: Remanufactured AC expected warranty cost as a fraction of the sales price for Rectangular and Infinite strips Region PRW

Components	*A = U*	Expected Warranty Cost)/(Sales Price) for Rectangular Region (Ω_R)			Expected Warranty Cost)/(Sales Price) for Infinite strips Region (Ω_S)			Users
		W=1.0	W=2.0	W=3.0	W=1.0	W=2.0	W=3.0	
AC	1.00	0.0265	0.0428	0.0587	0.2648	0.3023	0.4970	Light
		0.0315	0.0400	0.0441	0.1652	0.3210	0.7168	Medium
		0.0318	0.0353	0.0371	0.2541	0.5574	1.3451	Heavy
	2.00	0.0294	0.0551	0.0916	0.5916	0.5916	0.6787	Light
		0.0397	0.0667	0.0847	0.3246	0.3501	0.7168	Medium
		0.0516	0.0727	0.0839	0.2868	0.5574	1.3451	Heavy
	3.00	0.0309	0.0612	0.0907	0.9957	1.0259	1.0698	Light
		0.0438	0.0841	0.1206	0.5146	0.5506	0.7186	Medium
		0.0661	0.1124	0.1357	0.4059	0.6039	1.3451	Heavy

REFERENCES

Alqahtani, A. Y., & Gupta, S. M. (2016). Non-Renewable Basic Two-Dimensional Warranty Policy Analysis for End-Of-Life Product in Reverse Supply Chain, presented at *Northeast Decision Sciences Institute (NEDSI) Conference*, Alexandria, VA.

Alqahtani, A. Y., & Gupta, S. M. (2015). End-of-Life Product Warranty, *In Proceedings of the Northeast Decision Sciences Institute (NEDSI) Conference*, Cambridge, MA.

Alqahtani, A. Y., & Gupta, S.M. (2015). Extended Warranty Analysis for Remanufactured Products, *In Proceedings of the International Conference on Remanufacturing*, Amsterdam, the Netherlands.

Alqahtani, A. Y., & Gupta, S.M. (2015). Warranty Policy Analysis for End-Of-Life Product in Reverse Supply Chain, *In Proceedings of the Production and Operations Management Society (POMS) 26th annual Conference*, Washington D.C.

Balachander, S. (2001), Warranty signalling and reputation. *Management Science*, 47(9), 1282-1289.

Blischke, W. R., & Murthy, C. N. P. (1994), Warranty cost analysis. Marcel Dekker, New York.

Blischke, W. R., & Murthy, C. N. P. (1996), Product warranty handbook. Marcel Dekker, New York.

Gal-Or, E. (1989), Warranties as a signal of quality. *Canadian Journal of Economics*, 50-61.

Godichaud, M., Pérès, F., Gonzalez, V., Tchangani, A., Crespo, A., & Villeneuve, E. (2011), Integration of warranty as a decision variable in the process of recertification of parts resulting from end-of-life system dismantling. *In Quality and Reliability (ICQR), IEEE International Conference*, 156-160.

Gungor, A., & Gupta, S.M. (1999), Issues in environmentally conscious manufacturing and product recovery: a survey. *Computers and Industrial Engineering*, 36, 811–853.

Gungor, A., & Gupta, S.M. (2002), Disassembly line in product recovery. *International Journal of Production Research*, 40, 2569–2589.

Gupta, S.M., & Lambert, A.J.D. (eds) (2008, Environment conscious manufacturing. CRC Press, Boca Raton.

Heal, G. (1977), Guarantees and risk-sharing. *The Review of Economic Studies*, 549-560.

Ilgin, M. A., & Gupta, S. M. (2010a), Comparison of economic benefits of sensor embedded products and conventional products in a multi-product disassembly line. *Computers and Industrial Engineering*, 59, 748–763.

Ilgin, M. A., & Gupta, S. M. (2010b), Environmentally conscious manufacturing and product recovery (ECMPRO): A review of the state of the art. *Journal of Environmental Management*, 91, 563–591.

Ilgin, M. A., & Gupta, S. M. (2010c), Evaluating the impact of sensor-embedded products on the performance of an air conditioner disassembly line. *The International Journal of Advanced Manufacturing Technology*, 53, 1199–1216.

Ilgin, M. A., & Gupta, S. M. (2011), Performance improvement potential of sensor embedded products in environmental supply chains. *Resources, Conservation and Recycling*, 55, 580–592.

Iskandar, Bermawi P. (1992). Modelling and analysis of two-dimensional warranty policies. PhD Thesis, School of Engineering, The University of Queensland.

Kuik, S. S., Kaihara, T., & Fujii, N. (2015). Stochastic Decision Model of the Remanufactured Product with Warranty. *In Proceedings of the International MultiConference of Engineers and Computer Scientists (Vol. 2).*

Liao, B. F., Li, B. Y., & Cheng, J. S. (2015). A warranty model for remanufactured products. Journal of Industrial and Production Engineering, 32(8), 551-558.

Lutz, N. A., & Padmanabhan, V. (1995), Why do we observe minimal warranties? *Marketing Science*, 14(4), 417-441.

Murthy, D. P., & Blischke, W. R. (2006), Warranty management and product manufacture. Springer, London.

Soberman, D. A. (2003), Simultaneous signaling and screening with warranties. *Journal of Marketing Research*, 40(2), 176-192.

Spence, M. (1977), Consumer misperceptions, product failure and producer liability. *The Review of Economic Studies*, 561-572.

Vadde, S., Kamarthi, S.V., & Gupta, S.M., Zeid, I. (2008), Product life cycle monitoring via embedded sensors. In: Gupta, S.M., Lambert, A.J.D., *Environment conscious manufacturing*. CRC Press, Boca Raton, 91–103.

Yazdian, S. A., & Shahanaghi, K., Makui, A. (2014). Joint optimisation of price, warranty and recovery planning in remanufacturing of used products under linear and non-linear demand, return and cost functions. *International Journal of Systems Science*, 1-21.

DECISION SCIENCES INSTITUTE

Re-slotting to Reduce Warehouse Operating Expenses

Gerald Aase
Northern Illinois University
Email: gaase@niu.edu

Charles Petersen
Northern Illinois University
Email: cpetersen@niu.edu

ABSTRACT

This research examines several class-based re-slotting procedures that re-assigns stock-keeping units (SKUs) in a warehouse secondary storage area to new locations based on the SKU activity. The general notion of re-slotting is to place high activity SKUs in premium locations near the pickup/drop-off points of shipping and receiving. This simulation study compares the performance of three ABC class-based rules for guiding SKU swaps between the front and rear sections. Results are generated using data provided by a large regional distributor located in the Chicagoland area. The simulation results show the class-based re-slotting heuristic provides significant savings in picker travel. While prior research regarding manual warehouse operations has focused on the picking operation, this study introduces a warehouse model that considers both the putaway and picking operations simultaneously.

KEYWORDS: Distribution Warehousing, Re-slotting, Order Picking, Supply Chain

INTRODUCTION

A warehouse, or distribution center (DC), stocks products that are redistributed to various customers including: wholesalers, retailers, and end consumers. The primary warehouse operations are often classified as either inbound or outbound. Receiving and putaway are the main inbound activities, whereas order picking and shipping are considered the main outbound activities. Receiving products, or stock keeping units (SKUs), involves many activities but the primary focus is moving the product off the trucks into the warehouse receiving area. The putaway operation then moves the individual SKUs to the proper location in the warehouse. Once orders are received from customers, order pickers gather the SKUs from the warehouse and deliver them to a designated area for packing and shipping. DCs play a critical role in a supply chain by delivering the right products to the right place at the right time in a cost effective manner.

Today's competitive environment and supply chain integration initiatives have put enormous pressure on warehouse managers to simultaneously increase the throughput rate and lower operating costs of their operations (Frazelle, 2002). Order picking constitutes 50 - 75% of the total operating costs for a typical warehouse (Bozer et al., 2010, Coyle et al., 2003), though it is not clear if this includes the costs for other warehouse operations such as putaway. Nonetheless, these operations are the primary focus for most cost reduction efforts in practice. The use of automation is frequently examined as a means for reducing labor costs associated with picking, but most companies continue using manual order picking due to variability in SKU shape and size, the variability of demand, the seasonality of the products, or the large investment required to automate an order picking system. An abundance of research addresses design and operating issues with an objective to reduce order fulfillment costs. Three broad issues are most prominent: 1) how to pick the SKUs, 2) how to route the pickers in the warehouse and 3) how or where to store the SKUs.

This research explores the third issue more closely based on an inquiry from a pharmaceutical distribution company located in the Chicagoland area. More specifically, this research explores how re-slotting SKUs reduces travel distance, or labor costs, associated with the putaway and order picking operations. Slotting, which involves the assignment of SKUs to specific warehouse locations, is a critical warehouse design decision that is often overlooked after the initial design despite managers and consultants reporting how re-slotting can reduce annual costs by 8-12% (Trebilcock, 2011; Rector, 2012). Published research supports these claims by showing how slotting affects labor costs or operator travel associated with the picking process (Renaud and Ruiz, 2008). However, no research has shown the overall effect of Re-slotting to reduce operator travel for both the putaway and order picking operations. This study will extend the existing research by studying the effect of slotting rules that use information about putaway and picking operations simultaneously. More specifically, this study will explore the effectiveness of various simple heuristic rules used to guide the re-slotting process in a manner that reduces travel distance needed to complete both warehouse operations. Simple re-slotting rules based on the number of times a SKU is putaway and/or picked during the past month are examined using a simulation-based experimental design. We will then conclude the paper by discussing managerial implications for other DCs using manual picking processes.

LITERATURE REVIEW

The push to lower costs and improve customer service through faster response is leading many managers to implement new approaches in their warehouse and distribution facilities. Due to the significant labor costs associated with order picking, this activity has been the topic of much research. The primary focus of most research in this area has been identifying more effective picking, routing or storage policies.

Order Picking: Picking policies determine which SKUs are placed on a pick list and subsequently retrieved from their storage locations by a single picker during a pick tour. Strict-order picking is a common policy where pickers tour the warehouse to pick all line items or SKUs on a single order. This policy is viewed favorably by practitioners because it is easily implemented and order integrity is always maintained. Combining several orders into batches is an alternative policy that has been shown to reduce total picking time significantly (Gibson and Sharp, 1992; Petersen, 2000; De Koster et al., 1999). First-come-first-served (FCFS) batching combines orders as they arrive until the maximum batch size has been reached. Based on results found in the bin-packing literature, it is clear that other heuristics will yield fewer picking tours, which is critical for reducing total travel time across all pick tours. More complex batching techniques that consider both order size and product volumes have been proposed (Ruben et al., 1999), but the logic for these batching methods exceed the capabilities of most warehouse management systems.

Zone picking is another policy that divides the warehouse into zones and allows pickers to retrieve SKUs from within a single zone (Jane, 2000; Petersen, 2000; Petersen, Aase & Heiser, 2004). Some firms have combined batching and zoning into "wave" picking where a picker is responsible for SKUs in their zone. The benefit for these types of policies become apparent as the size of the warehouse increases, but zone picking requires secondary operations to consolidate orders from the different zones. The subject firm designed and implemented a custom zone picking policy to release pick waves that consider delivery routes containing many orders. The simplicity of their policy was easy to implement, has been well received by employees, and has proven quite effective at minimizing pick tours and travel distance.

Routing*:* Routing policies determine the picking sequence of SKUs on the pick list. Using simple heuristics or optimal procedures, the goal of routing policies is to minimize the distance traveled by the picker. Optimal procedures offer the best solution, but they may result in confusing routes (Ratliff and Rosenthal, 1983). Heuristics often yield near-optimal solutions while being easy to use (Petersen and Schmenner, 1999; Hall, 1993). Traversal routing, which is widely used in many warehouses because of its simplicity, provides good results particularly when the pick density per picking aisle is large. When using a traversal policy, pickers must completely traverse the entire aisle once it is entered. A composite heuristic combining traversal and return routes to further reduce picker travel produced near-optimal solutions (Roodbergen and De Koster, 2001). The later approach reflects the routing policy used by the subject firm.

Storage policies: Storage policies, which assign SKUs to storage locations, generally fall into three broad categories. SKUs may be assigned randomly, grouped into classes with similar SKUs that are placed in the same area of the warehouse, or assigned to a location based on demand or volume. Random storage is widely used in many warehouses because it is simple to use, often requires less space than other storage methods, and results in a more level utilization of all picking aisles. Volume-based storage policies assign SKUs with the largest demand to locations near the pick-up/drop-off (p/d) point. Research shows that a within-aisle implementation of volume-based storage significantly reduces travel time (Jarvis and McDowell, 1991; Petersen and Schmenner, 1999). Class-based storage with as few as three storage classes was shown to provide nearly the same savings as volume-based storage in an automated storage and retrieval systems (AS/RS) while requiring less data processing (Hausman et al, 1976; Rosenblatt and Eynan, 1989; Eynan and Rosenblatt, 1994). While research involving automated retrieval systems is rather extensive, most warehouses utilize manual picking methods (Frazelle, 2002).

The effect of class-based storage in a manual picking environment was introduced using a sensitivity analysis (Gibson and Sharp, 1992), but the focus of their research was on batching techniques to reduce picker travel. A comparative study of a manual order picking warehouse revealed that class-based storage reduces picker travel when compared to random storage and offers similar performance as the more complex volume-based storage (Petersen, Aase & Heiser, 2004). Their research showed class-based storage policies are effective across all conditions by changing factor levels in a simulated warehouse environment, but no research documents the benefit by replicating an existing operation. The current research will test these findings using actual data provided by the subject firm.

Current Research Extension: This research offers several extensions that focus on storage policy, which is coined by practitioners as the slotting problem. First, this research examines storage policies by considering the effect on travel distance for both the putaway and order picking activities simultaneously. While published warehouse research frequently considers order picking activities, no research addresses the putaway activity explicitly in a manual warehouse operation. We believe this is a crucial oversight, because the travel distance and time spent performing the putaway and case picking activities are comparable for these operations according to the subject firm. This study will determine the benefit for using information about both activities when assigning SKUs to a location. To accomplish this, the authors will introduce a warehouse model having unique putaway and picking activities that are controlled and measured separately.

A second research extension involves exploring the importance of re-slotting a warehouse on a regular basis as product offerings and demand changes. While consultants and practitioners publish expected labor savings of 8-12% annually, most published research only considers slotting greenfield projects. An adaptive re-slotting approach was proposed using data mining techniques and a binary integer programming technique to assign new products to vacant locations (Chiang, Lin and Chen, 2011). However, the subject firm requested a simple heuristic technique that will help reduce operator travel and hence operating costs. Since their product offering has reasonably stable demand that follows a normal product lifecycle, the subject firm rarely experiences vacant locations. Therefore, the proposed procedures must consider re-organizing the SKUs location assignments. Kee (2003) suggested using ABC analysis for classifying SKUs into storage classes, but no studies exist that document the benefits for using such policies. This research will introduce a simple pairwise exchange heuristic that applies the well-known Pareto concept to assign SKUs to a class based on the putaway and casepick activity.

The goal of this research is to evaluate the performance of a new ABC policy applied to both putaway and casepick operations for the re-slotting process. What portion of the operator time is spent performing the putaway and casepick operations? How much should the subject firm expect to reduce operator travel with a formal re-slotting procedure performed on a regular basis? Will operator travel be less when SKUs are assigned locations based on putaway hits, casepick hits, or a combination of putaway and casepick hits? Are these operations affected more when using forklift-and-pallets that allow operators to turn around within an aisle or when using tugs-and-carts that are pulled in a serpentine manner that traverses complete aisles? The following sections provide a general description of the warehouse operation for the subject firm which we replicate using a simulation model, present the details for our experimental design, and then share results of the simulation study. This paper concludes with a summary of important managerial implications, limitations and opportunities for future research extensions.

WAREHOUSE OPERATION OVERVIEW

This research is motivated by a pharmaceutical distribution center located in the Chicago area that requested assistance for developing a new re-slotting process. In particular, we were asked to 1) determine if re-slotting their secondary storage area will reduce operator travel time for the putaway and casepick operations and 2) to identify best practices for guiding their re-slotting process. This section summarizes key aspects of the subject firm operation including the facility layout and key business operating rules. This section also presents details for the class-based re-slotting heuristic.

Layout and Fulfillment Process Overview: Figure 1 shares the facility layout for the DC examined in this study. While the secondary storage is the primary focus of this research, this image illustrates additional areas that are found within many DC facilities. The two main areas in the DC are dedicated to piece picking and secondary storage. In the piece picking area, individual items on an order are picked and packed in totes corresponding to a single customer order. Piece picking is done using a combination of manual, semi-automatic, and automatic processes. This DC facility is fairly unique since it performs both individual piece picking to provide any piece quantity and a separate operation for case picking full manufacturing cases. Further details of the piece picking processes are omitted since it falls outside the scope of this study. The remainder of this paper will focus on the secondary storage area where the case picking occurs.

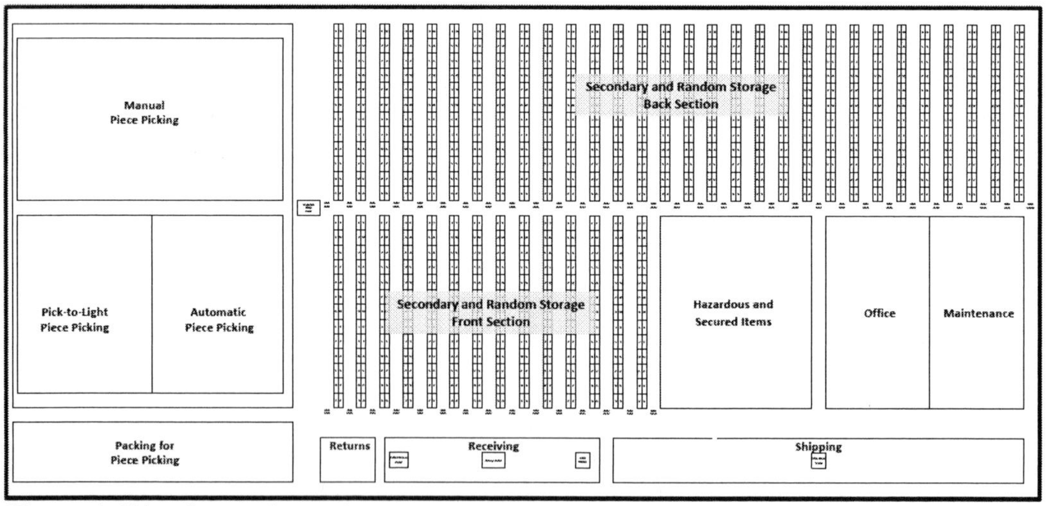

Figure 1: Warehouse Layout

The secondary storage area holds full unopened manufacturing cases for approximately half the active SKUs handled within the DC. The remaining SKUs are stored in flow racks or standard hand stack shelves located in the manual and semi-automatic piece picking areas. SKUs located in secondary storage are packaged in cardboard boxes and picked in full case quantities where each case contained 1-540 pieces. Once a case order is released and picked, it is delivered directly to the shipping area where they are packed and wrapped on a shipping pallet.

Step 1: Figure 2 shares the high-level flowchart for the order fulfillment process. The *Receiving* step handles 5-10 full-truck-loads (FTL) daily from the central DC as well as several FLT and less than truckload (LTL) deliveries from local vendors. The primary focus of the receiving operators is to unload pallets from the trucks and place them in the designated receiving area.

Step 2: *Putaway* largely depends on case quantity and the cubic volume of the cases received for a SKU. Full pallets of a single SKU are putaway using a forklift. SKUs received involving larger case quantities (>=12) are often combined onto a single mixed pallet. The remaining SKUs are arranged on carts assigned to a putaway zone. Tugs are then used to pull 2-4 carts for each putaway tour. The *Putaway* process also depends on whether the putaway zone location is in the *Secondary and Random Storage* areas or one of the *Piece Picking* areas. This research is concerned with re-slotting the secondary storage. Therefore, the *Putaway* process for *Random Storage* and *Piece Picking* areas is considered out of scope for this research. The subject firm turns their inventory approximately once a week on average, therefore this *Case Putaway* operation requires significant time and labor cost each day.

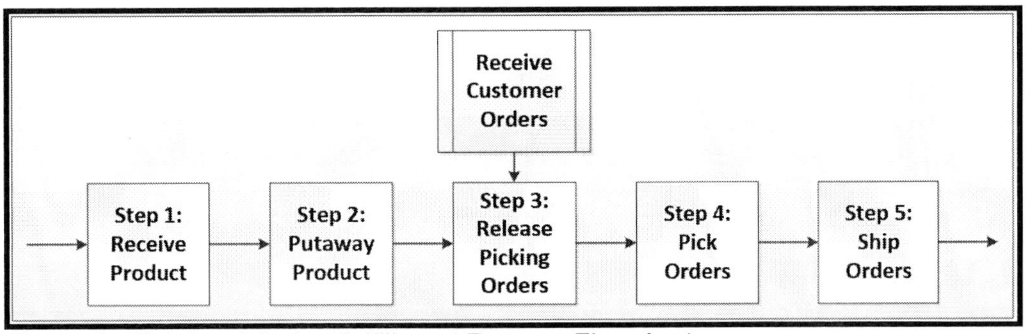

Figure 2: High-level Order Fulfillment Process Flowchart

Step 3: *Releasing Picking Orders* is managed by the warehouse management system (WMS). To establish wave release orders, the WMS system considers all orders placed during the day, the promised delivery time which is generally promised the same day or by the following morning, and the external delivery route. Again, this step is beyond the scope of this research, but the wave designation for every SKU ordered represents a major constraint for their order fulfillment process.

Step 4: *Pick Orders* involves both piece picking and casepicking operations. Full cases are picked by operators from the secondary storage locations using tugs and carts, though a few pallet picks are used for large cubic volume orders sent to other DCs. Once the operators complete their assigned picking tour, the carts are then delivered to drop point in shipping area. Individual piece parts involving partial cases are always picked from one of the three piece picking areas. Again, the travel distance associated with piece picking operations are outside the scope of this research. It is also worth noting that the WMS system may release a customer order into a full casepick order and a second piece pick order. For example, a customer order for 15 bottles of aspirins will likely be released as one case pick order and one piece pick order of three bottles if the full case contains 12 bottles.

The final step of the process, *Ship Orders*, involves both packing and shipping functions. All aspects of this step are outside the scope of this research except the location of the shipping drop point which is relevant to the case picking process when calculating operator travel distances.

Summary of Additional Facility Details and Key Business Rules*:* The following list summarizes information about the warehouse modeled in this research:

- The Secondary and Random Storage Area has 44 picking aisles each containing 12 or 13 bays on a side. There are front and back cross-aisles and a third cross-aisle located approximately halfway back that partitions the area into a front section and a back section (see Figure 1).
- The picking aisles have racks on each side and are wide enough for two-way travel.
- Racks are approximately 25' tall with the secondary storage locations assigned to the lower 7-9'. The remaining space located above the secondary storage is designated as Random pallet storage. Operations associated with random storage are outside the scope of this project.
- The rack design within an aisle is identical for each bay, but the racking design varies between aisles. In general, aisles are designed to handle either 1) full pallets, 2) half pallets with a 2' hand-stack shelf, 3) four hand-stack shelves, or 4) five flow racks.
- Flowracks are 7' deep by spanning across two racks located back-to-back from adjacent aisles. Full cases are loaded into a flow rack from the back side of the flowrack.
- Three pallets are assigned within each bay. Each hand-stack level for a bay has 6 locations and each flow rack level has 8 locations.
- The case capacity of a location depends on the bay configuration and the size of the full manufacturing case for the SKU assigned to the location.
- Each case picking tour begins at the label station located at the right hand side in the receiving area and ends at the drop point located in the middle of shipping.
- Each putaway tour begins and ends at the pickup points located in receiving.
- Case picking is done manually using pallets, mixed pallets or tugs/carts depending on the cubic volume and quantity of cases for each SKU. Case picking is only done from the secondary storage areas. No cases are picked from the piece picking area.
- Secondary storage putaway is done manually using pallets, mixed pallets or tugs depending on the cubic volume and quantity of cases for each SKU.
- Each SKU is assigned to only one secondary storage location, but several adjacent locations may be grouped together as designated as a single location for a SKU.
- Each location is assigned only one SKU.
- There are currently 5 putaway zones assigned to the secondary storage area.
- There are 10 wave releases each night that corresponds to distinct delivery routes. A FTL trailer assigned to each route is located in a unique shipping bay.
- The SKU demands generally follow the 80-20 rule in that a few items account for the majority of the units demanded. The number of SKU 'hits' for both putaway and casepick also follow this principle. A 'hit' is defined as the number of times a location is visited and it also corresponds to an order line item.
- Current practices of the subject firm involve re-slotting SKUs with large annual cubic volumes due to the attention drawn to moving full pallets. They also re-slot the 25-50 SKUs having the highest annual dollar volume for security reasons and SKUs with demands that are rapidly increasing.

SKU Classification Strategy: To operationalize the re-slotting heuristic, SKUs are first assigned to one of four classes using the Pareto 'ABC' concept commonly applied to inventory management practices. For this re-slotting problem, high-activity SKUs during the prior month are assigned to the 'A' class. SKU activity or 'hits' or visits is defined as the number of times a SKU appears as a line item on an order pick list. This also corresponds to the number of times a SKU location is visited during the casepicking operation. This differs from other ABC classifications which commonly use total annual units sold or total annual dollar value for the SKUs. The classification strategy for this research uses 'hits' because the number of location visits has a greater effect on operator travel than the quantity picked. Warehouse managers generally use this measure of 'hits' because subsequent items picked on the same pick tour costs very little.

Similar classifications are generated for three rules which are compared in this research: Casepick hits, Putaway hits and Combined Casepick and Putaway hits. Table 1 summarizes the number of SKUs and Total Hits corresponding to each class for the three rules. For the subject firm of this research, a SKU visited more than 40 times for the casepick operation corresponds to a very high-activity SKU picked 2 or more times per weekday assuming there are approximately 4 weeks or 20 weekdays per month. When applying the concept to the Putaway data, however, high-activity 'A' SKUs correspond to 8 or more hits per month, or about twice weekly. This suggests the putaway operation tends to involve few trips having more cases compared to the casepick operation.

Table 1: SKU Classification Summary

Casepicks				Putaway				Casepicks and Putaway Combined			
Class	Mthly Hits	SKUs	Total Hits	Class	Mthly Hits	SKUs	Total Hits	Class	Mthly Hits	SKUs	Total Hits
A	>40	311	41,997	A	>8	306	3,527	A	>40	373	45,678
B	20-39	298	8,222	B	4-7	1,397	6,825	B	20-39	451	11,428
C	2-19	2,541	15,815	C	2-3	2,193	5,241	C	2-19	4,155	25,738
D	0-1	6,967	719	D	0-1	6,221	2,319	D	0-1	5,138	1,821
	Totals	10,117	66,753		Totals	10,117	17,912		Totals	10,117	84,665

Further analysis of this data reveals the 10,117 SKUs located in Secondary Storage are picked on average 6 times per month, while SKUs are received and putway an average of 2 times per month. This illustrates the subject firm operates a reasonably lean warehouse with excellent inventory turns.

Class Based Re-slotting Heuristic: The proposed heuristic uses a pairwise exchange strategy, where high-activity SKUs located in the back of the warehouse are moved into the Front Section. This is the same logic used by the volume-based and class-based storage policies presented in the current literature where SKUs with the highest demand are located near the pick-up/drop-off (p/d) points. For both the putaway and casepick operations, this entails moving the A, B and C SKUs from the back section to the front section of the *Secondary Storage area.*

Step 1: Prepare Data – acquire data providing the current SKU locations, released casepick orders for the past month, and cases putaway into the secondary storage area for the past month. Confirm the casepick and putaway data is not aggregated across multiple picks or putaways. Determine the activity of each SKU for each operation, and then apply the ABC SKU classification strategies to determine which SKUS are A, B, C or Ds for each of the three rules.

Step 2: Pairwise Exchange – This step involves exchanging a high-activity SKU currently located in the back section with a low-activity SKU located in the front section. On occasion, there may be an open location in front which should be filled with a high-activity SKU currently located in the back section, but this does not happen frequently for the subject firm.

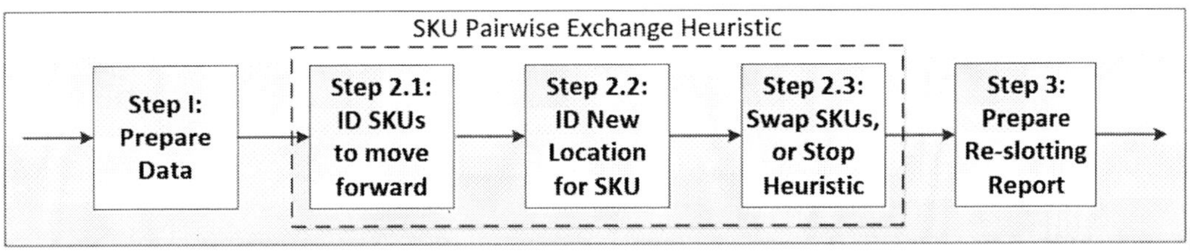

Figure 3: Re-slotting Procedure Flowchart

The pairwise exchange heuristic may be characterized as having three sub-steps as shown in Figure 3. Using the ABC classifications generated during Step 1, Step 2.1 identifies a SKU in the rear section having an 'A' classification or the next highest designation. Step 2.2 then identifies a location having a SKU with a 'D' designation or the lowest possible designation. Substep 2.3 involves the pairwise swap, and it also provides a stopping criteria. As long as the SKU moving forward has a higher ABC designation than the SKU moving back, accept the pairwise exchange and repeat step 2. In other words, a SKU in the back section having a 'C' designation would be swapped with a SKU in the front section having a 'D' designation. However, it won't be swapped with a SKU in the front section having a 'C' designation. The later scenario reflects the stopping criteria where no further attempt is made to identify a pairwise exchange. Step 3 involves preparing a report listing all exchanges identified during Step 2.

EXPERIMENTAL DESIGN

The primary goal of this research is to determine if re-slotting the secondary storage area will reduce operator travel time for both the putaway and casepick operations. An abundance of research has examined many factors affecting travel time for order picking, but no research has explored the importance of the putaway operation. More specifically, this research will explore the following questions:

1. How do the putaway and casepick operations compare with regard to travel distance needed to perform the operations? Exploring this question will indicate the importance of each operation with regard operating costs and hence establish the relative importance of these operations for the subject firm.
2. How much will travel distance be reduced using the pairwise exchange heuristic to re-slot the secondary storage area?
3. Which of the three classification strategies perform best for the putaway and casepick operations?

Simulation Model: To answer these questions, a simulation model was created using structured queries on a SQL Server. The benefits for using this type of model entailed the direct access to actual data from the subject firm including item master data, casepick orders, putaway items and the wave release times for SKUs located in the secondary storage area. The simulation-based study replicated the operations described earlier using actual data for one month. Figure 4 summarizes the experimental design for the simulation study used to answer the three questions identified above. Data for 20 weekdays were used as a basis for the simulation study. Also included in the data set are data for 5 Saturdays which the subject firm operates with a skeleton crew to fulfill same-day emergency orders. The primary performance metric tracked by this study is total operator travel. Results are reported using two explanatory variables. The first variable corresponds to the two operations (putaway and casepicks), whereas the second variable considers the type of equipment used (fork lifts with full pallets, fork lifts with mixed pallets, and tugs/carts. Additional secondary metrics reported include: 1) number of tours, 2) number of aisles visited, and 3) cubic volume.

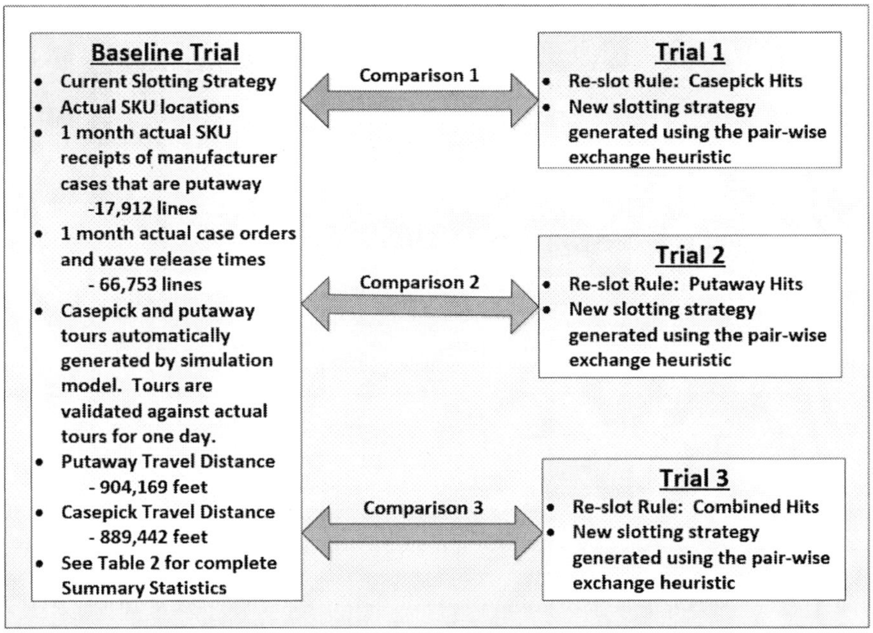

Figure 4: Warehouse Simulation Experimental Design

The simulation study is replicated 4 times, where each trial has a sample size of 25 operating days. The first (baseline) trial uses the current slotting configuration. The remaining three trials involve re-slotting the warehouse using the pairwise exchange heuristic with the three ABC classification rules: casepick hits, putaway hits and combined hits. The only experimental factor for this study is the ABC classification rule, but two explanatory variables are used to provide further insights during the analysis.

Results for the Baseline Trial provide the basis to which the remaining three trials are compared. As summarized in Figure 4, the data set includes 17,912 lines of putaway data and 66,753 lines of casepicking data. Further summary statistics for the Baseline Trial are found in the next section.

RESULTS

Results for the Baseline Trial are shared in Table 2. Comparison of the Combine Total column reveals the travel distance required to complete the putaway and casepick operations are similar for the subject firm: putaway was 904,189 feet and casepick was 889,445 feet. Therefore, it is reasonable to assume managers should consider both operations when re-slotting the secondary storage area.

Casual observation of the Baseline Trail results reveals several additional insights worth noting. The travel distances for the putaway operation are similar ranging from 241,548' for the Mixed Pallet putaways to 367,007' for the Tug/cart putaways. This mix is common for many DCs that use a mix of fork lifts and tugs for this operation. The travel distance for the casepick operation, however, is heavily weighted toward the use of Tugs/carts. This is expected for a pharmaceutical distributor because more of their daily business entails small frequent orders to many customer. Therefore, most of the orders are picked by operators using a tug with 3-4 carts in tow. Mixed pallets are not used for this operation because 98.6% of the casepick orders (65,818 of 66,753) involve fewer than 12 cases. Of the remaining 953 lines, 349 lines involve full pallet picks. Therefore, the subject firm decided to only use tugs/carts when casepick orders do not involve full pallet picks.

Table 2: Baseline Trial Summary Statistics

	Pallet w/ 1 Item		Mixed Pallet		Tug w/ Carts		Combined Total	
Putaway	Lines	393	Lines	1,677	Lines	15,842	Lines	17,912
	Tours	407	Tours	355	Tours	455	Tours	1,217
	Aisles	393	Aisles	776	Aisles	1,171	Aisles	2,340
	Vol. (FT3)	26,707	Vol. (FT3)	9,767	Vol. (FT3)	28,861	Vol. (FT3)	65,335
	Travel (FT)	295,614	Travel (FT)	241,548	Travel (FT)	367,007	Travel (FT)	904,169
CasePick	Lines	290	Lines		Lines	66,463	Lines	66,753
	Tours	349	Tours		Tours	555	Tours	904
	Aisles	290	Aisles		Aisles	2,381	Aisles	2,671
	Vol. (FT3)	20,596	Vol. (FT3)		Vol. (FT3)	57,791	Vol. (FT3)	78,387
	Travel (FT)	258,676	Travel (FT)		Travel (FT)	630,766	Travel (FT)	889,442
Combined Total	Lines	683	Lines	1,677	Lines	82,305	Lines	84,665
	Tours	756	Tours	355	Tours	1,010	Tours	2,121
	Aisles	683	Aisles	776	Aisles	3,552	Aisles	5,011
	Vol. (FT3)	47,303	Vol. (FT3)	9,767	Vol. (FT3)	86,652	Vol. (FT3)	143,722
	Travel (FT)	554,290	Travel (FT)	241,548	Travel (FT)	997,773	Travel (FT)	1,793,611

Results in Table 3 summarize the performance of all trials. Comparison of trial results reveal the Combine Rule, which considers both casepick and putaway hits, performs best with an 18.4% reduction in total travel distance. However, the results for Trials 1 and 2 reveal similar results (15.5% and 14.7%) when using data from either operation alone. These findings are significant since this supports the anecdotal results suggested throughout the business literature indicating a 10-12% improvement is expected.

Further exploration of Table 3 suggests the casepick operation will benefit more than the putaway operation by re-slotting the secondary storage area. When using the combined rule, travel distance to complete the casepick operation is reduced 26.8% whereas the putaway operation improves by 10.0%. This difference is significant, but both represent meaningful savings for any business.

Table 3: Simulation Study Summary Statistics

		Baseline Trial	Trial 1 Casepick Rule		Trial 2 Putaway Rule		Trial 3 Combined Rule	
		Total	Total	% Reduction	Total	% Reduction	Total	% Reduction
Putaway	Tours	1,217	1,209	0.7%	1,212	0.4%	1,211	0.5%
	Aisles	2,340	2,149	8.2%	2,047	12.5%	2,074	11.4%
	Travel (FT)	904,169	849,845	6.0%	815,404	9.8%	813,358	10.0%
CasePick	Tours	904	854	5.5%	864	4.4%	854	5.5%
	Aisles	2,671	1,825	31.7%	2,110	21.0%	1,749	34.5%
	Travel (FT)	889,442	665,757	25.1%	715,217	19.6%	650,629	26.8%
Total	Tours	2,121	2,063	2.7%	2,076	2.1%	2,065	2.6%
	Aisles	5,011	3,974	20.7%	4,157	17.0%	3,823	23.7%
	Travel (FT)	1,793,611	1,515,602	15.5%	1,530,621	14.7%	1,463,987	18.4%

Results in Table 3 also support some intuitive results where the Casepick Rule has a greater effect on the casepick operation (25.1%) when compared to the benefit of using the Putaway rule (19.6%). Similarly, the Putaway Rule has a greater effect on the putaway operation (9.8%) compared to the benefit when using the Casepick Rule (6.0%). Further observation reveals the reduction in travel time is always best when using the Combined Rule, though the differences appear to be statistically insignificant for some circumstances. This dominance reflects the combined effort of the two rules where each rule identifies a unique subset of SKUs that should be moved from the rear section to the front section. By combining the casepick hits and the putaway hits, a small subset of SKUs improve their ABC designation so they are included in the pairwise exchange heuristic.

The results in Table 4 transforms the data from the last row in Table 3 by normalizing the travel distance measures with the number of SKUs moved. Data reveals the Casepick rule results in fewer SKUS moved when compared to the Putaway and Combined rules. This explains the normalized results in the last row which shows the Casepick Rules provides the greatest "bang for the buck." For every 1000 moves, the Casepick Rule resulted in an 8% reduction in travel distance, whereas the Putaway and Combined rules yielded a 4.7-5% reduction in travel distance. This analysis was requested by the subject firm because the estimated they could move approximately 1,000 SKUs on a weekend day using 6 operators.

Table 4: Simulation Results Normalized by Total SKUs Move

	Casepick Rule		Putaway Rule		Combined Rule	
	1,944 SKUs Moved		3,117 SKUs Moved		3,675 SKUs Moved	
	Total	% Reduction	Total	% Reduction	Total	% Reduction
Travel Reduction (ft)	1,515,602	15.5%	1,530,621	14.7%	1,463,987	18.4%
Reduction per 1000 moves	143,009	8.0%	84,373	4.7%	89,694	5.0%

CONCLUDING REMARDS

This study has explored using ABC analysis and a class-based storage strategy to re-slot the secondary storage area of a major pharmaceutical distributor. The results show significant reduction in travel distance for both the putaway and casepick operations. Prior research focused only on the order picking operation for DCs using manual operations. This research has shown additional benefits will be observed by considering SKU activity, or hits, of both operations when re-slotting a warehouse operation. The level of improvement supports the claims made in the business literature. Assuming operator travel accounts for approximately 60% of the putaway and picking operations, managers should expect a labor saving of approximately 11% (60% x 18.4%)

The results of this study naturally have some limitations since they are based on the data for one operation. However, detailed analysis not included in this paper reveal meaningful improvements are expected for the different equipment configurations whether businesses use fork lifts to handle pallets or tugs and carts that traverse the aisles in an orderly manner. These observations certainly suggest more detailed studies are justified to explore the re-slotting problem for various operating environments.

This study clearly shows that the pairwise exchange heuristic was effective for re-slotting the secondary storage area of the subject firm. While these results are not compared to an optimal solution, performance metrics provided by managers of the subject firm suggested they were one of the more efficient DCs for the corporation. Nevertheless, the findings of this initial study suggest further detailed studies are warranted to compare results of class based, volume-based, and optimal re-slotting procedures.

REFERENCES

References available upon request.

DECISION SCIENCES INSTITUTE

Rethinking Undergraduate Business Core Curriculum:
One School's Experience of Redesigned Curriculum with a Holistic Approach

Alysse Morton
Westminster College
amorton@westminstercollege.edu

Jennifer Harrison
jbharrison@westminstercollege.edu

Lauren Lo Re
llore@westminstercollege.edu

Nancy Panos Schmitt
npschmitt@westminstercollege.edu

ABSTRACT

Due to lacking skills, a drastic LE change, and new accreditation, our business school significantly redesigned our undergraduate business school core curriculum. In this paper we discuss the factors leading to the redesign, the components of the redesign, and expound on a critical element of the new curriculum: woven elements.

KEYWORDS: Curriculum redesign, Undergraduate business core, Business quantitative skills, Communication skills, Accreditation requirements

INTRODUCTION

As the world around us changes, we need to adapt our curriculum. Our school's business curriculum was in need of a change due to a variety of factors. With the millennial generation, we found students were lacking in some needed quantitative and communication skills that were necessary to be successful in business. Our liberal education program underwent a drastic makeover such that our previously required courses from liberal education (LE) were no longer going to be offered as a part of the LE program. With innovation in our LE, we need to adapt how we ensure business students get the specific skills they need for business that previously were met from that program. In addition to changes in the LE program, our school is changing accreditation and needed to reevaluate all of our course content to ensure we could meet new and different requirements.

LITERATURE REVIEW

Student Quantitative and Communication Skills Lacking

There are a number of gaps in the skills of business graduates. Research indicates communication skills along with the ability to solve complex problems among the skills that could be better developed in graduates. According to *The Washington Post*, one study found that 40% of college seniors lacked the complex reasoning skills needed in the business world today (Selingo, 2015). A study conducted by the Association of American Colleges and Universities (AACU) found that employers found students weaker in skills such as oral and written communication as well as critical thinking and problem solving than perceived by students (Jaschik, 2015). *The Bloomberg Job Skills Report* identified that communication skills were commonly viewed as the most desired skill from employers that is lacking in students being hired (Levy & Cannon, 2016)

Repetition of Concepts Improves Learning Outcomes

Many researchers (e.g., Ericsson, Krampe, & Clemens, 1993; Baddeley, 2002) argue that variances in the amount of practice account for the majority of performance differences between individuals, resulting from differences in the amount and structure of knowledge stored in long-term memory. When students practice solving problems, they increase their ability to transfer practiced skills to new and more complex problems. This is true in childhood (Glover, Ronning, & Bruning, 1990) and adult years (Li et al., 2008). Practice helps students acquire expertise in subject matter and, therefore, it helps to distinguish novices from experts in given subjects (Ericsson et al., 1993). Cognitive gains from practice often bring about motivation for more learning (Kalchman, Moss, & Case, 2001).

REDESIGNING THE UNDERGRADUATE BUSINESS CORE CURRICULUM

A Drastic Change in Our Liberal Education Program

As our liberal education program adopted a completely new model, the courses were no longer typical. In our old LE program, students were required to take one class from each of seventeen categories. Therefore, as part of the LE program, students could choose to fulfill four of their undergraduate business requirements: College Algebra, Macroeconomics, Statistics, and Ethics. In the new LE program (WCore) students take innovative topics that do not fall into a category like previously offered survey courses. Instead, students need to take two classes in each of three broad categories: Fine Arts & Humanities, Social and Behavioral Sciences, and Science and Math. Students may take courses such as Counting Votes (Science and Math), How We Die in America (Social and Behavioral Sciences), or Vampires: Active Reading, Passive Reading (Fine Arts & Humanities).

Lack of a Specific Math Class in Liberal Education

With no specific math classes as part of the general education curriculum, we needed to rethink the math needs of our students. Although we could require students take a math class such as college algebra as a requirement of the business program, the fact that it wouldn't also count for liberal education credit caused us to think more deeply about the math skills our students actually required. Upon closer inspection, we realized that many of the skills needed for math calculations in business were met earlier in a student's math curriculum. We decided that students would learn better by being introduced to math concepts within a business context. The use of more applied math would allow us to ensure that students better understand the logic behind decisions and the math used to determine those calculations. To tackle the additional math instruction, we added two new courses to the curriculum: Business Fundamentals I, Calculating and Applied Business Math and Modeling.

Changes in Statistics Offerings

As a result of the liberal education changes, the Math department began to rethink what needed to be offered to its students. Of importance to the business school was the Math department's decision to offer two versions of a statistics class. The first course would be called Data and Society and offer statistics more from the view of a consumer of stats rather than a producer of stats. The outcome of this course would be for students to be able to read and understand how statistics are interpreted. The students would see R code as a part of their program but it would be in the context of code already written to complete specific tasks. Although the student would learn about R and the logic of the code, they would not be actually coding the programs. In the alternate class, Introduction to Statistics, students would receive a deeper level of statistics training that would include chi-square and ANOVA analyses. In this course students would learn to code R and write their own programs for analysis. The curriculum redesign committee felt that either of these classes could meet the needs of business students. For students in areas where they would need additional statistics knowledge, students will be advised to take the Introduction to Statistics course. With a new Data Science minor also introduced by an interdisciplinary group, students wishing to pursue this minor would also be encouraged to take the Introduction to Statistics course. Statistics would no longer be a course that counted towards the liberal education requirements, but we felt that the new offerings would work well for our students as a part of our core curriculum.

Ethics Needed in Curriculum

Similar to the math courses from liberal education previously meeting core requirements, we had previously used a Philosophy course to count towards the ethics requirement for our students. Upon closer evaluation, we felt that business ethics should be included more explicitly in our curriculum. We therefore recommended that ethics be introduced as part of the business law class. Within this class we would introduce the students to a framework with which to consider ethical issues. Then, ethics would also be covered, building on the framework developed in the Business Law & Ethics course in five other courses: Financial Accounting, Business Finance, Principles of Management, Principles of Marketing, and Information Technology.

Engaging the World: A New Requirement

As part of the new liberal education program, students are asked to fulfill a requirement that meets the Global Learning Value rubric from the Association of American Colleges & Universities (AAC&U): "a critical analysis of and an engagement with complex, interdependent global systems and legacies (such as natural, physical, social, cultural, economic, and political) and their implications for people's lives and the earth's sustainability." Students will be able to fulfill this requirement by going an international study trip, spending a semester abroad, completing an international internship, or taking a course on campus that is approved for this requirement. We believe that this requirement will help our students better understand global issues, an important piece in today's business world.

Senior Capstone

To help students bring together their learning across the curriculum, a new requirement for each major to have a capstone course was implemented. Previously all students took a strategic management course that acted as a capstone course for most majors. However, we realized with this new senior capstone requirement that it makes sense for each major to identify the best way for their major to experience a capstone.

How to Ensure a Strong Understanding of Concepts

At the same time as the liberal education changes are taking place, our college is seeking AACSB accreditation. Since we needed to re-evaluate the curriculum due to the LE changes, we also wanted to incorporate all elements that would be desired by AACSB. We felt the curriculum was missing some important components. In order to include all of the topics that we believed to be missing from the previous curriculum, we recommended including two new courses in the core curriculum as well as the rearrangement of several courses from their current state. In order to accommodate the new courses as well as limit the credit hours for the undergraduate business core to be no larger than it was previously, we decided as a faculty to change our core courses from 4-credit-hours to 3-credit-hours. The only exception is the Principles of Management course for which course content was adjusted but the credit hours stayed at 4.

Managerial Accounting and Operations Management were added to the curriculum. We removed the operations component from the Principles of Management course and redesigned that course to incorporate the strategy elements previous taught in the capstone course that all students took. As a result of the new senior capstone in the major, we removed the capstone course from our core curriculum and replaced it with an integrative course to be taken at the completion of all other business core courses.

Table 1 contains a brief description of how each of the Standard 9 elements are addressed in the redesign.

Table 1: AACSB Standard 9 Application

General Skill Areas	
Written and oral communication *Addressed by the communication woven skills* **Ethical understanding and reasoning** *Addressed by the Ethics woven element (introduced in Business Law & Ethics and reiterated in Financial Accounting, Principles of Marketing, Principle of Management, Information Technology, and Business Finance)* **Analytical thinking** *Added Applied Business Math & Modeling course and included quantitative woven elements to enhance analytical thinking in terms of math skills* **Information technology** *Include technology as a part of many courses including Business Fundamentals I, Applied Business Math & Modeling, and Information Technology*	**Interpersonal relations and teamwork** *Students in Business Fundamentals I will take a skills assessment to understand how they contribute to a group, various courses will have teamwork components that will use a teamwork rubric introduced in Business Fundamentals I* **Reflective thinking** *Throughout a variety of course students will reflect on their own contribution within the context of society* **Application of knowledge** *As part of the Business Fundamentals II course, students will complete a real-world project that will incorporate all core course content. Additionally, in Business Fundamentals III students will participate in internships in the community. Students will also be required to complete a capstone course as a part of their major that will incorporate synthesis of all ideas as applied to the business world.*

General Business and Management Knowledge Areas	
Economic, political, regulatory, legal, technological, and social contexts of organizations in a global society *Covered in economics courses as well as Principles of Management* **Social responsibility, including sustainability, and ethical behavior and approaches to management** *Covered as part of the Ethics woven element including Business Law and Ethics course* **Financial theories, analysis, reporting, and markets** *Business Finance course will cover these topics* **Systems and processes in organizations, including planning and design, production/operations, supply chains, marketing, and distribution** *Information Technology and Operations Management, two new courses in the core curriculum will cover these items along with Principles of Marketing*	**Group and individual behaviors in organizations and society** *Principles of Management will cover both Strategy and Organizational Behavior topics.* **Information technology and statistics/quantitative methods impacts on business practices to include data creation, data sharing, data analytics, data mining, data reporting, and storage between and across organizations including related ethical issues** *These topics will be covered as part of the Information Technology course as well as the Statistics courses (Data and Society or Introduction to Statistics) and the Applied Business Math and Modeling course. Ethics is a woven element in the Information Technology course*

Creating a Business Fundamentals Series

The new integrative core course is the middle course in a series of courses we call Business Fundamentals. In Business Fundamentals I, students take two 3-credit hour courses that are linked together similar to a learning community. For each course, the same students will be in both sections of the courses: Business Fundamentals I, Communicating and Business Fundamentals I, Calculating. The focus of this initial class is three-fold. The students will be introduced to basic business concepts by forming a company that will have roles and responsibilities. As a company, the students will determine a set of products to sell such that they earn enough money to cover the cost of a service project they will also plan and execute. Throughout the semester, the students will be assigned roles within the company to manage all of the processes. As the students perform the company duties, they will be learning key communication and quantitative skills that will set the foundation for the skills that will be further built upon in their business courses. We refer to these skills as the 'woven' elements' which we believe to be a critical design component of our curriculum redesign. As Business Fundamentals I is the first course students will take in the business program, it will provide a way to determine a starting point for the student skills that we can then assess later in the program. Business Fundamentals II, Integrative Core is a course that students will take once they have completed all of the core business courses. It will be a project-based course that allows the students to pull together their learning and skills from the business core. This course also provides a place where we can administer testing for assessment purposes. We can test on the skill development from their first course. We can also assess the business core knowledge; we use ETS testing for this purpose. Additionally, we can use this course to better prepare students for what is needed when thinking about their internship. The final course is the Business Fundamentals III, Internship. This course will allow students to have hands-on experience in the workplace putting their business core and major knowledge to work. An overview of the curriculum and how it is included in the core is shown in Figure 1.

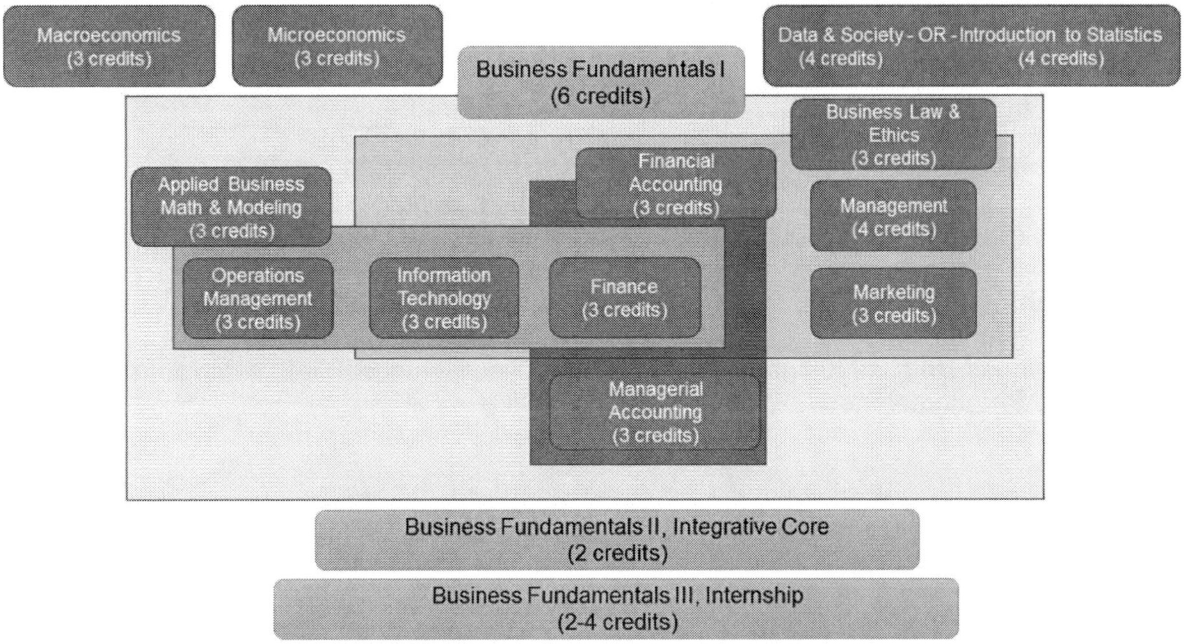

Figure 1: Curriculum Design of Business Undergraduate Core

The Need for Quantitative and Communication Skills

In addition to building the Business Fundamentals series, we also reevaluated the skill needs of the students. Part of this related to the math course as discussed with the liberal education changes, but we also wanted to re-think how quantitative courses in general were offered to the students. To better understand the needs of quantitative skills in the business world, we looked to MBA students who manage positions filled by undergraduates and inquired what skills are most desired. We also surveyed what other peer and aspirant schools were covering in their curriculum, specifically for quantitative skills. We quickly came to the conclusion that students needed to see math in the context of business and they needed to see the skills multiple times throughout the coursework.

Upon further discussion, we determined the following quantitative elements should be 'woven' throughout the curriculum: percentage change, breakeven analysis, markups/margins, time value of money, Excel basic calculations, Excel graphing, graph analysis, solving basic equations. All of these quantitative skills will be introduced to the students in the Business Fundamentals I course. Table 2 shows the distribution of these skills throughout the curriculum. We believe these are the minimum requirements of where the quantitative skills should show up but faculty are encouraged to include these skills whenever possible.

Table 2: Placement of Quantitative 'Woven' Elements in Core Business Classes

Breakeven Analysis Business Fundamentals I Applied Business Math & Modeling Managerial Accounting	**Markups/Margins** Business Fundamentals I Applied Business Math & Modeling Principles of Marketing
Excel Basic Calculations Business Fundamentals I Applied Business Math & Modeling Operations Management	**Percentage Change** Business Fundamentals I Applied Business Math & Modeling Business Finance
Excel Graphing Business Fundamentals I Applied Business Math & Modeling Operations Management	**Solving Basic Equations** Business Fundamentals I Applied Business Math & Modeling Business Finance Operations Management
Graph Analysis Business Fundamentals I Elementary Macroeconomics Elementary Microeconomics	**Time Value of Money** Business Fundamentals I Applied Business Math & Modeling Business Finance

Similar to students needing to build quantitative skills, we also believe students need to see communication elements repetitively to strengthen their skills. After discussing the needs of communication skills, we decided the following communication skills would be 'woven' throughout the curriculum: memo, executive summary, letter, report, blog, standard presentation, pitch presentation. Similar to the quantitative skills, these communication skills will be introduced to the students in Business Fundamentals I.

Table 3: Placement of Communication 'Woven' Elements in Core Business Classes

Blog Business Fundamentals I Principles of Management Operations Management	**Report** Business Fundamentals I Business Finance Principles of Marketing
Executive Summary Business Fundamentals I Managerial Accounting Operations Management	**Standard Presentation** Business Fundamentals I Business Finance Information Technology Principles of Management Principles of Marketing
Letter Business Fundamentals I Business Law & Ethics Business Fundamentals III: Internship	**Pitch Presentation** Business Fundamentals I Business Fundamentals III: Internship Financial Accounting
Memo Business Fundamentals I Applied Business Math & Modeling Principles of Management	

Execution of Design Plan

In order to create these new courses, we received a grant for course development. Faculty applied to be course designers. Each course designer was responsible for developing the course description and learning goals. These were then evaluated by the departments and/or critical stakeholders. The course designers then created a 14-week course topic plan to demonstrate content coverage in terms of breadth and depth of material. This step was also evaluated by the departments and/or critical stakeholders. The final step is for course designers to select the textbook/materials to be used for the course as well as develop a full syllabus to include all of the woven elements, course learning goals, and course content as developed in previous stages. For each course, a minimum requirements has been created to ensure consistency across sections and different professors. To ensure the content is covered as designed, faculty and adjuncts teaching the course will need to complete a form each semester that demonstrates how each of the required elements will be met in the course. These will be evaluated by the course owner who will ensure the standards are being met.

Future Plans

We are interested to see how our new curriculum is evaluated by the students. We are encouraged by the design of the woven elements as well as the assessment points to see how students are developing as they move through our core curriculum. Our curriculum has been designed but not yet implemented. We have designed a process to capture how each course incorporates the assigned woven elements and general knowledge areas. We will be collecting feedback on the experience of using the woven elements after our first semester with the new curriculum. It will be a couple years until the incoming class of 2020 takes the Business Fundamentals II course where they will be assessed on the business content of the curriculum via the ETS exam as well as their quantitative and communication skills as a part of the course. We are excited about the new curriculum and look forward to determining its effectiveness.

REFERENCES

Baddeley, A. D. (2002). Is working memory still working?. *European psychologist*, 7(2), 85.

Ericsson, K. A., Krampe, R. T., & Tesch-Römer, C. (1993). The role of deliberate practice in the acquisition of expert performance. Psychological review, 100(3), 363.

Global Learning VALUE Rubric. (2015). Retrieved March 18, 2016, from https://www.aacu.org/value/rubrics/global-learning

Glover, J. A., Ronning, R. R., & Brunning, R. H. (1990). *Cognitive psychology for teachers.* New York, NY: McMillan.

Jaschik, S. (2015). Well Prepared in Their Own Eyes. *Inside Higher Ed.*

Kalchman, M., Moss, J., & Case, R. (2001). Psychological models for the development of mathematical understanding: Rational numbers and functions. *Cognition and instruction: Twenty-five years of progress*, 1-38.

Levy, F., & Cannon, C. (2016, February 9). The Bloomberg Job Skills Report 2016. Retrieved March 17, 2016, from http://www.bloomberg.com/graphics/2016-job-skills-report/

Li, S.C., Schmiedek, F., Huxhold, O., Röcke, C., Smith, J, & Lindenberger, U. (2008) Working memory plasticity in old age: practice gain, transfer, and maintenance. *Psychology and Aging,* 23 (4), 738

Selingo, J. J. (2015, January 26). Why are so many college students failing to gain job skills before graduation. *The Washington Post.*

DECISION SCIENCES INSTITUTE

Role of Perceived Playfulness/Seriousness in Learning Process Using Business Simulation Game

J.B. Kim
Worcester Polytechnic Institute
Email: jkim3@wpi.edu

Edward Watson
Louisiana State University
Email: ewatson@lsu.edu

ABSTRACT

Largely due to the advances in technology and the familiarity that the younger generation has with digital games, business simulation games have become a more significant part of business education and training. Addressing the dearth of academic investigation in the game-based learning process, this study sheds light on the area by providing a model that examines the role of the perceived seriousness and playfulness associated with the participants' behaviors. From the analysis of empirical data using MBA students, this study reveals how perceived playfulness and perceived seriousness affects the game-based learning process. Based on the analysis of the results, discussions and implications are presented.

KEYWORDS: Business simulation games, Seriousness, Playfulness, Game-based learning process, Motivation, PLS-SEM

INTRODUCTION

Along with rapid advances in IT (Information Technology) development and application, video/digital games have flourished over the past twenty years. While many games are played for entertainment, some games are used for more serious purposes. One type of game that is used for business education and training is referred to as "business simulation games." This study is about the use of business simulation games in the context of business education and training.

We live in the so called "digital age" (Negroponte 1995). From Moore's Law (Moore 1998) we observe how IT advances enable new games to provide an amazing experience to gamers. Meanwhile, so called, "digital generations," who are raised up with IT, highly value the interconnectivity and the decentralization (Kline et al. 2003) that technology allows. Future business education and training needs to be realigned in accordance with the characteristics of new generations. They are not the same as the previous generations. They are exceptionally pragmatic and very visually oriented. They also learn by doing and accept digital as the norm (Hunter 2013). For many of them, the traditional ways of learning are not very effective. Meanwhile, games could be a very effective method of learning because games are familiar, interactive, and engaging. Unfortunately, however, there has been not much attention paid to academic research on games, especially in business education and training settings, so far. We believe this is the right time to address the importance of using games in business education and training from an academic point of view.

"Serious games" have been gaining attention in recent years due to their unique ability to combine entertainment and education (Brandão et al. 2012). Games are known to lead more active engagement of students in the learning process (Mayer et al. 2014; Azadegan et al. 2012; Klabbers 2009; Ben-Zvi 2010; Lainema 2003; Charles et al. 2011). Michael and Chen (2006) suggested serious games can be used for military, educators (primary, secondary, and higher), corporations, non-government organizations (NGOs), artists, and/or basically anyone needs to teach something, pass on a skill, or preach a message. The market for serious games which has grown in recent years dramatically is estimated to range from $2 to $10 billion depending on what areas of serious games (e.g., simulations, and virtual worlds) are included (Reuters, August 23. 2012). Adkins (2013) reported that the projected annual growth rate of revenue of game-based learning and simulation-based learning segment from 2012 to 2017 is 18%. This trend is expected to continue as the newest generation of learners prefer to have multiple streams of information, inductive reasoning, frequent and fast interactions with content, as well as highly-visual literacy skills (Van Eck 2006). They also have characteristics such as exceptional pragmatism, visually oriented, learning by doing, and accepting digital forms of communication and interacting with the world as the norm (Hunter 2013). We observe that serious games will become more and more important for these demanding learners.

Games are also becoming an important part of business education and training. Today's business environment is very complex and dynamic so the traditional linear types of learning methods (e.g., lecture, reading materials) are not enough to make students ready for business practice. Meanwhile, business simulation games can provide students with the opportunity to experience with complex situations that require them to understand multiple business concepts simultaneously. For example, business strategy games require the players to consider various business functions, such as marketing, finance, supply chain at the same time hence the players can be trained for making a better decision based on the diverse perspectives. As Keys (1989) pointed that there are three factors necessary for effective management learning – dissemination of content, opportunities for experience, and feedback, – business simulation games fulfill these three requirements as content is self-discovered, experience is rich, and feedback from simulated reality is more helpful than reality (Lane 1995). Faria and Wellington (2004) identified various advantages of business simulation games to students and teachers. Those perceived advantages include:

- Experiential learning
- Integration of different functional areas
- Theory application
- Demonstration of consequences of decisions
- Teamwork and Involvement
- Interactive/dynamic exercises
- Realistic
- Expose to business competition
- Fun, Interest and motivation

Although business simulation games are an effective way to learn business concepts, there were few academic investigations of the area, especially with regards to the learning process using simulation games in business courses. Among the many elements in the learning process using simulation games, learners' perception would play a significant role. As Miles et al. (1986) suggested, learners' perception toward education using games are important to look into, but there is still a dearth of academic research on this topic. While playfulness in a business simulation game can engage the players more in the game play, which makes the players absorbed and repeatedly play the game, seriousness can call more attention of the players so they would grasp more understanding of the lessons designed in the business simulation game. Although there were a few recent attempts to understand the learning process of individuals using business simulation games (Tao et al., 2009; Lin & Tu, 2012), the results are quite inconsistent and need more clarification.

To address this problem, this study investigates specifically how perceived playfulness and seriousness play roles in the game-based learning process, and how these elements affect participants' game behaviors, namely, game performance and game effort. To achieve this goal, a research model is proposed based on theories related to the constructs of playfulness and seriousness, game process, and learning motivation. Then the proposed research model is tested by empirical data from a survey of MBA students who used a business simulation game as a part of their Operations Management course. By analyzing the results, this study sheds some light on the learning process using simulation games, and provides some insights for business educators as well as business simulation games developers. The remainder of the paper is composed of the theoretical backgrounds related to the study topic, followed by the research model that is tested with empirical data. Then the results from the data analysis, discussions, limitations, and conclusions follow.

THEORETICAL BACKGROUND

In order to build an appropriate research model, it is necessary to address theories relevant to the study such as Game Process Theory, and Self-determination Theory (SDT), and theories related to playfulness and seriousness. Each will be briefly reviewed as follows.

Game Process Theory

Garris et al. (2002) proposed as input-process-outcome game model. They pointed out that learners' motivation is the most significant factor in modeling a game process. By stimulating learner's motivation, instructional games would develop learners self-directed and self-motivated, which ultimately leads them to achieve the desired outcomes. Their model is summarized by mainly three important points. First, the objective of instructional game studies is to design a game incorporating a certain characteristics or features. Second, the process of learning by gaming is described as a game cycle. Specifically the game features initiate a game cycle, in which a user judges the game features. Then based on the user's perception, one takes actions in the game system, which is followed by feedback on the system. After engaging the game through several game cycles, a user would achieve the expected learning outcome. An illustration of this model is presented in Figure 1.

In contrast to the traditional single-trial learning model, Garris et al.'s (2002) provides a model that incorporates multiple trials triggered by game characteristics, which is more common when a game is used as a learning method. In their view, game play involves repeated judgment-behavior-feedback loops, through which game play itself could increase user perceptions toward the game. The incorporation of the game cycle is the hallmark of the model, reflecting the defining characteristic of computer game play. This is consistent with learning theories of Dewey (1938) and Kolb et al. (2000), which emphasize experiential learning approaches.

The closed-loop process in game-based learning is also proposed by other researchers. Simons (1993) stressed that the educational value of simulation comes from repeated trials. He claimed that simulation users try different strategies over time, through which they gradually build understanding of the system. The essence of learning through games is the process in which players formulate and try various hypotheses, then observe the result until they find the hidden relationships among the elements. Through the process, they can experientially learn the subject topics.

Figure 1: Input-Process-Outcome Game Model (Garris et al. 2002)

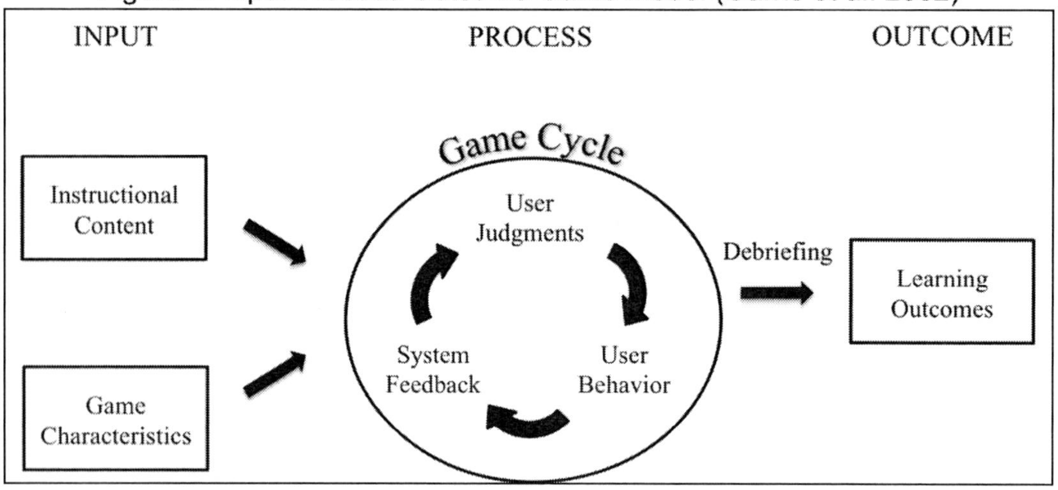

Another instructional game model to be noted is the course performance model suggested by Landers and Callen (2011). They emphasized the properties of instructional games considered for the potential in learning. Accordingly, they proposed a model incorporating indirect determinants that are mediated by direct determinants to affect course performance. The basis of this model was first proposed by Campbell (1990), who tried to explain the determinants of job performance. For example, in his model, conscientiousness (indirect determinant) is mediated by motivation (direct determinant) to influence job performance (outcome). In addition, Kraiger (2003) emphasized two definitive direct determinants of course performance, including learner trainability and motivation. Figure 2 illustrates a model proposed by Landers and Callen (2011) that incorporates indirect determinants mediated by direct determinants to yield learning outcomes in the context of game-based learning.

Figure 2: Course Performance Model (Landers & Callen 2011)

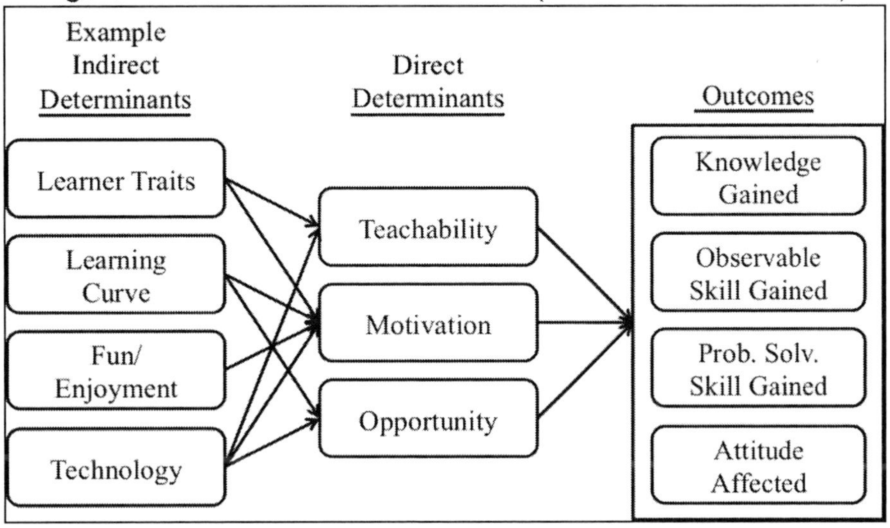

It should be addressed in the model that the indirect determinants are not connected to all the direct determinants. For example, the fun/enjoyment element affects only motivation in the model. This implies that the fun/enjoyment element of the instructional game only stimulates the learner's willingness to play the game, but does not affect the effectiveness of learning subjects. A fun element in a game would encourage a learner to engage with the game longer and, consequently, enhance motivation. Then enhanced motivation would lead to a better understanding of the materials in terms of various aspects of learning outcomes, as the instructional game is aimed for.

Self-determination Theory

Motivation is a significant element in the process of learning. Accordingly, motivation is considered an important part of educational theories. Studies have shown that motivation is positively correlated to academic achievement (Lepper et al. 2005; Harter & Connell 1984; Henderlong & Lepper 1997; Barron & Harackiewicz 2001; Harackiewicz et al. 2002; Schunk et al. 2008). One of the biggest challenges that instructors might encounter is that learners feel learning is boring and unpleasant (Malone & Lepper 1987). Motivating students so they feel excited and engaged to learn is the most effective way to achieve positive learning outcomes.

Deci, Vallerand, and Ryan (1991) highlighted, "the central features of optimal learning are conceptual understanding and the flexible use of knowledge…Correspondingly, the central features of optimal adjustment are feeling good about oneself and acting volitionally to satisfy one's own needs while being attuned to and concerned about the social surrounding (p. 326)." Self-determination theory (SDT; Deci & Ryan 1985; 1991; Ryan 1995; Ryan & Deci 2000) suggests that learning behavior could be motivated by various factors around learners' environments. Accordingly, many research concerned about the factors that promote people's motivation, especially in educational context.

The traditional view claimed that motivation is a unitary phenomenon. However, people may have different degrees of motivation as well as different types of motivation (Ryan & Deci 2000).

Studies of SDT have suggested that there are largely two types of motivation, namely, intrinsic and extrinsic motivation (Deci & Ryan 1985). It is generally accepted that intrinsic motivation is associated with doing something because of inherent interest or enjoyment, whereas extrinsic motivation is associated with doing something by expecting a separable reward (Ryan & Deci 2000).

Ryan and Deci (2000) defined intrinsic motivation as "the doing of an activity for its inherent satisfactions rather than for some separable consequences (p. 56)." An intrinsically motivated person does an activity pursuing fun and/or enjoyment that is innate in the activity. Discovered first by White (1959), the intrinsic motivation phenomenon has been studied to explain human behaviors. Unlike Skinner's (1953) operant theory, which claims all behaviors are motivated by rewards, perspectives from Hull's (1943) learning theory, which asserts all behaviors are motivated by physiological drives, support researchers' effort to find the human's psychological needs satisfied by intrinsically motivated behaviors (Ryan & Deci 2000).

With assumption that intrinsic motivation exists, previous research has shown the conditions that elicit, sustain, and enhance intrinsic motivation as well as those that subdue or diminish it (Ryan & Deci 2000). Cognitive Evaluation Theory (CET), which is a sub-theory of SDT, presented by Deci and Ryan (1985) identifies the factors in social contexts producing variability in intrinsic motivation. In CET, social contexts (e.g. interpersonal events and structures) yielding feeling of competence can increase intrinsic motivation (Ryan & Deci 2000). Thus, conditions such as proper challenge and effective feedback can facilitate intrinsic motivation. Furthermore, CET specifies that a sense of autonomy (also termed as internal perceived locus of causality) accompanied with feeling of competence is important to enhance intrinsic motivation (Ryan & Deci 2000). Simply put, people would have high intrinsic motivation when they feel satisfaction of the need both for competence and autonomy.

On the other hand, extrinsic motivation is defined as "a construct that pertains whenever an activity is done in order to attain some separable outcome (Ryan & Deci 2000, p. 60)." It focuses on the external values expected by doing an activity, in contrast to intrinsic motivation that focuses on the internal values from doing activity itself. SDT suggests that, unlike intrinsic motivation, extrinsic motivation varies based on the degrees of autonomy (Ryan & Deci 2000). For example, a student would study a subject expecting different types of rewards. It could be teacher's praise, or good grades, or even getting a better job in the future. These different rewards are associated with a different degree of autonomy. In SDT, it is termed as the internalization and integration of values and behavioral regulations (Deci & Ryan 1985). Internalization refers to the process of taking in a value or regulation, whereas integration refers to the process of transforming the regulation into their own sense. Based on the degree of internalization and integration, external motivation can be divided into several different forms (Deci & Ryan 1985). As illustrated in Figure 3, the types of motivation are on a continuum of the extent to which the motivation for one's behavior emanates from the sense of self (Ryan & Deci 2000).

Figure 3: Continuum of human motivation (Ryan & Deci 2000)

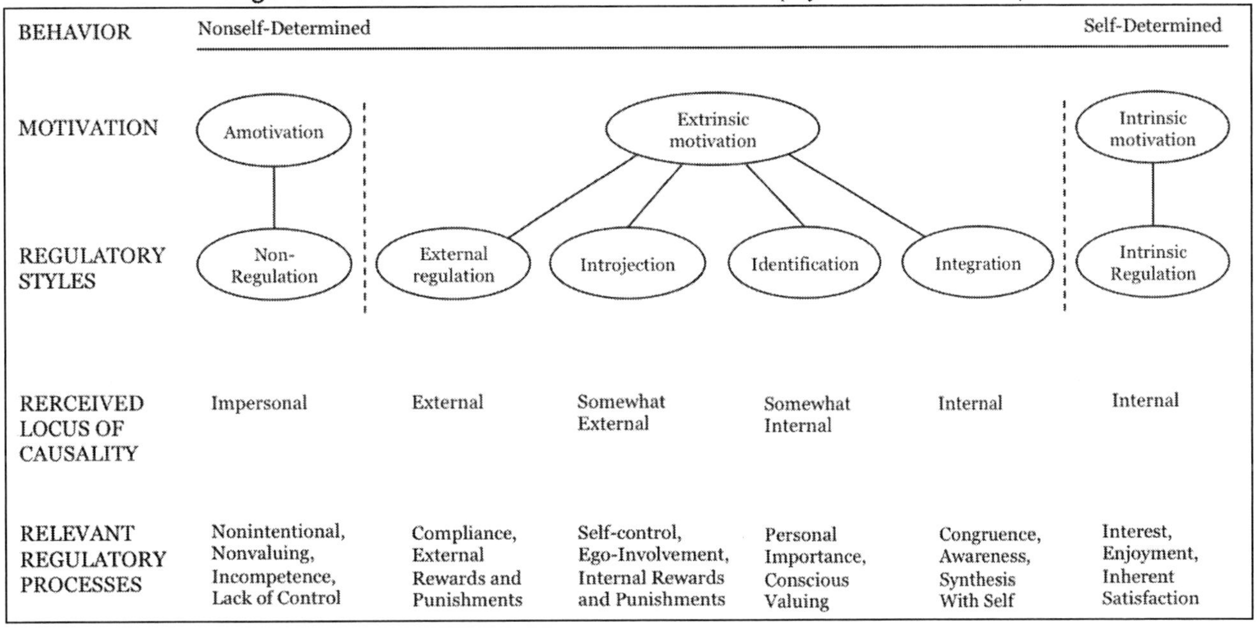

Playfulness and Seriousness

Many business educators use simulation games in their courses because they believe simulation games provide two benefits: student's engagement and learning effectiveness. Business simulation games refer to games that enable students to simulate the real business practices for the purpose of learning business topics by game playing (Tao et al. 2015). Game-based learning contains two simultaneously existing elements, which are playing and learning. By mixing them together, game-based learning uses entertainment, a part of the natural learning process in human development (Bisson & Luckner 1996), to motivate students. Hence, it is not only reasonable but also essential to consider the two elements when we try to understand the game-based learning process.

Seriousness

The concept of seriousness has been considered necessary but often neglected in education (Wilson 1998). If a student doesn't feel serious about school, s/he would lose interest in school and stop paying attention to school activities. Meanwhile, if a student feels serious about school, s/he realizes the importance of school activities, thus puts more efforts into them. With serious attitude, one concentrates, pays attention, and accepts a learner's posture, hence learn (Wilson 1998). It is actually claimed that the students' serious attitudes towards tests could affect their performance (Park 2004; Biggs 1996).

Seriousness is closely related to human's tendency to stick to ideology, or faith to live by (Wilson 1998). When in the serious state of mind, one is said to be "... earnest, committed, wholehearted, sincere, not superficial or pretending (Wilson 1998, p.145)." Seriousness is also closely related to a clear discipline of reason in one's mind to keep monitoring her/his everyday behaviors. Therefore, seriousness promotes one's awareness of situations s/he encounters and efforts to seek the most effective solutions. Ruch (1993) tried to conceptualize the seriousness first in his work on humor. He found that seriousness should be considered as a factor to describe the human mind. Ruch et al. (1996) suggested that there are six facets of the concept of seriousness as Table 1.

Table 1: Elements of seriousness

ELEMENT	DESCRIPTION
Prevalence	"Prevalence of serious states"
Earnest	"A perception of even everyday happenings as important and considering them thoroughly and intensively (rather than treating them superficially)"
Readiness	"The tendency to plan ahead and set long-range goals (and attaining the closest possible harmony with these goals in every action and decision)"
Rationale	"The tendency to prefer activities for which concrete, rational reasons can be produced (thereby considering activities which don't have a specific goal as a waste of time and nonsense)
Sober	"The preference for a sober, object-oriented communication style (for example, saying exactly what one means without exaggeration or ironic/sarcastic undertones)"
Humorless	"Humorless attitude about cheerfulness-related behavior, roles, persons, stimuli, situations, and actions"

There are basically two perspectives of the concept of seriousness. The first view is to consider seriousness as a trait (Ruch et al. 1997). In this view, those who have a high-level trait-seriousness tend to perceive things important and consider thoroughly and intensively. The trait-seriousness is related to one's set of mind to accept her surroundings to the extent of significance. Thus, trait seriousness is represented by one's habitual feelings/actions towards events happening every day.

On the other hand, there are perspectives seeing the seriousness as a state (Ruch et al. 1997). The state generally indicates "affective or cognitive episodes that are experienced in the short run and fluctuate over time (Webster & Martocchio 1992, p. 203)." In this view, seriousness is described as a person's readiness to behave seriously at a moment. Someone who has a high-level state-seriousness is characterized by being "attentive, immersed in deep thought, involved in something perceived as really important, applies a sober or objective perspective or style, is earnest in purpose, and mentally set for levity or amusement (Ruch et al. 1997, p. 478)." This state-seriousness is more closely related to the perceived seriousness towards an event or object. In this sense, this study follows the definition of seriousness as a user's perception to the extent that she thinks about the game in serious aspects.

Playfulness

Play is generally accepted as an inseparable element from games. Indeed, play and games almost always come together, as we refer to game participation as play (Makedon 1984). However, they don't have to be always together. Makedon (1984) suggested that playing and gaming are a necessary but not sufficient condition for each other. Actually we see that some games have a high level of playfulness, whereas others are less playful. It is also possible that some people find high playfulness from a game, while others feel less playful from the same game. Riezler (1941) described a playful attitude as when a player plays within the game itself, regardless of pursuing her/his own goal or a goal set by the rule of the game. Makedon (1984) pointed three important elements of playful game as voluntariness, spontaneity, and intrinsic worthiness.

Although Scholosberg (1947) stated, "the category of playful activity is so loose that it is almost useless for modern psychology (p.215)," several attempts have been made to identify and/or characterize the attributes of playfulness. Dewey (1913) defined playfulness as "the capacity to draw satisfaction from the immediate intellectual development of a topic, irrespective of any ulterior motive (p. 727)." Lieberman (1977) claimed that playfulness could be viewed as a unitary concept. However, she also suggested that there could be multiple dimensions in the concept of playfulness. It is generally accepted that playfulness is a multifaceted construction encompassing factors such as cognitive spontaneity, social spontaneity, physical spontaneity, manifest joy, and sense of humor (Webster & Martocchio 1992; Barnett, 1991; Lieberman, 1977). This study follows this perspective for a relevant theoretical framework. In Table 2, the elements of playfulness are described.

<table>
<tr><th colspan="3">Table 2: Elements of playfulness</th></tr>
<tr><th colspan="2">PLAYFULNESS DIMENSIONS (Lieberman 1977)</th><th>ELEMENTS OF PLAYFULNESS DIMENSIONS (Barnett 1990)</th></tr>
<tr><td colspan="2">Sense of Humor</td><td>Joking, teasing, funny, laughs, clowning</td></tr>
<tr><td colspan="2">Manifest Joy</td><td>Expressing enjoyment, demonstrating exuberance, showing enthusiasm, freely expressing emotion, singing/talking</td></tr>
<tr><td rowspan="3">Spontaneity</td><td>Physical spontaneity</td><td>Coordination b/w movements and activities, physical activeness, active-preferred, frequent runs</td></tr>
<tr><td>Social spontaneity</td><td>Easy response to other's approach, initiating activities, cooperation, leadership role</td></tr>
<tr><td>Cognitive spontaneity</td><td>Inventing own games, using unconventional objects, different character roles, changing activities</td></tr>
</table>

Like seriousness, playfulness can also be viewed from two perspectives, as a trait and a state. In the view of trait-playfulness, playfulness is conceived as relatively stable characteristic of an individual (Lieberman 1977; Moon & Kim 2001). Lieberman (1977) earlier mentioned that playfulness might be accepted not only as part of behavior but also as a personality trait of the individual. Thus, this view emphasizes more on the individual characteristics of personality pursuing enjoyment (Glynn & Webster 1992).

Another view is to see the playfulness as a state of mind. In this view, playfulness is a subjective characteristic of an experience (Ellis 1973), which could be varied based on the context. It is generally accepted that computer-related playfulness as a state has three dimensions: concentration, curiosity, and enjoyment (Moon & Kim 2001). Concentration refers to the process that one's attention is focused on the interactions so she loses self-consciousness, becomes absorbed intensively in the activity (Moon & Kim 2001). Likewise, curiosity is a part of playfulness. When a person's sensory or cognitive curiosity aroused by an activity, she would keep doing an activity (Malone 1981). It is known that people tend to pay more attention to more complex or incongruous things (Berlyne & Lawrence 1964). When children choose their playing object, they are more likely to select toys with novelty and complexity (Ellis & Scholtz 1978). This can be also applied to people's preference of information technology devices. When companies introduce devices with new technology, more attentions and interests are given. The last element of playfulness is enjoyment. People prefer activities that are interesting and fun to one that is boring and uninteresting.

Several studies have previously explored the playfulness in the context of IT usage. Webster and Martocchio's (1992) work is one of the first attempts investigating the playfulness in the context of microcomputer interaction. They depicted that microcomputer playfulness is a situation-specific individual characteristic, which is defined as "an individual's tendency to interact spontaneously, inventively, and imaginatively with microcomputers (p. 202)." Their approach to the playfulness was trait-based. On the other hand, Webster et al. (1993) examined flow in human-computer interaction in which they borrowed many aspects of flow (Csikszentmihalyi 1990), a state-based approach. Yager et al. (1997) examined the several aspect of microcomputer playfulness and found that playfulness is a stable trait. This study adopts Moon and Kim's (2001) definition of perceived playfulness in the context of human-computer interaction as a simulation game user's perception to the extent that s/he thinks about the game in three dimensions, namely, concentration, curiosity, and enjoyment.

In sum, intrinsic/extrinsic motivation and seriousness/playfulness would play a significant role when a person learns something by using serious games. In the next section, a specific research model of this study will be presented based on the theoretical background mentioned above.

RESEARCH MODEL

Based upon the theoretical framework in the previous section, here we suggest a research model that focuses on the relationship among the elements that are relevant to game-based learning.

To begin, seriousness is defined as the extent of readiness to which a person perceives, acts, or communicates seriously regarding an activity (Ruch et al. 1997). In a high state of seriousness a person is very attentive, earnest in purpose, perceives things important, and applies an objective perspective. As mentioned in the previous section, serious mindset of a student would be connected to better learning. With serious attitude, a learner would concentrate, pay attention, and be willing to accept teacher's instruction, which consequently helps her/him learn (Wilson 1998). Indeed, several previous studies have revealed the positive relationship between seriousness and individual performance in the context of learning, professional environments (Park 2004; Biggs 1996; Day & Silverman 1989).

Meanwhile, the relationship between seriousness and task effort and performance would be mediated by extrinsic motivation. As suggested in Landers and Callen's (2001) model, motivation mediates indirect determinant's effects on learning outcomes. Seriousness, one of the potential elements to influence the learning outcome, may increase an individual's motivation, especially extrinsic side, which would ultimately increase the effort and performance. For example, a student who is serious about a school activity (e.g. homework) would pay attention to the benefits s/he could gain by doing the activity, which consequently would evoke her/his extrinsic motivation to keep doing it hard. Hence, seriousness may mediate its relationship with learning effort through extrinsic motivation.

It is generally accepted that high-motivated individuals yield better performance (Ryan 1995; Vallerand 1997). Although the degree of influence of extrinsic motivation on performance is known relatively less than intrinsic motivation (Harlow et al. 1950; Amabile 1979; Deci 1975; Harackiewicz et al 1984; Lepper et al. 1973), especially in regards to the learning process (Deci et al. 1999; Deci & Ryan 1991), several studies shows that extrinsic motivation still plays significant role in learning (Van Etten et al. 1998; Lin et al. 2003). In addition, extrinsic motivation consists of a spectrum of various degrees of internalization. Among them, more internalized motivations, such as integrated regulation, could be closely related to individual's behavior for doing a task well (e.g. high score in game). Hence, extrinsically motivated students may perform well in the simulation game.

On this basis, it is hypothesized as follows:

> H1: Perceived seriousness has a positive effect on extrinsic motivation in the learning process using business simulation games.
>
> H2a: Extrinsic motivation has a positive effect on game effort in the learning process using business simulation games.
>
> H2b: Extrinsic motivation has a positive effect on game performance in the learning process using business simulation games.

Playfulness is defined as a game player's perception that the game would fulfill her/his intrinsic motives, which include concentration, enjoyment, and curiosity. This definition conforms to Moon and Kim's (2001) the definition of perceived playfulness towards World-Wide-Web usage. Also it is connected to the stream of studies that focus on the intrinsic interest, voluntariness, spontaneity of playfulness (Riezler, 1941; Makedon 1984). Playfulness is one of the direct drivers for intrinsic motivation. Given that intrinsic motivation requires an individual's satisfaction of psychological innate needs (Ryan & Deci 2000), playfulness could be a trigger for one's intrinsic motivation toward an activity. For example, young children show characteristics of intrinsic motivation such as activeness, inquisitiveness, curiosity, and playfulness, even without extrinsic rewards (Harter 1978). Without the fun element, a game would hardly attract people to be engaged intrinsically. Reversely, a playful game would easily motivate players to play repeatedly. Hence, playfulness is closely related to intrinsic motivation in a game-based learning process.

While previous literature claimed a significant connection between intrinsic motivation and performance (Tauer & Harackiewicz 2004), the relationship would be mediated by time or efforts spent on the activity (Deci & Ryan 1985; Harackiewicz & Sansone 1991; White 1959). When people are intrinsically motivated, they tend to put great effort on the task, by which they develop better skills and achieve a more favorable performance rating. Thus, in the game-based learning process, intrinsic motivation is related to the efforts that a learner puts in the game, and then the cumulative efforts would be related to the game performance.

On this basis, it is hypothesized as follows:

> H3: Perceived playfulness has a positive effect on intrinsic motivation in the learning process using business simulation games.
>
> H4a: Intrinsic motivation has a positive effect on player's effort in the learning process using business simulation games.
>
> H4b: Player's cumulative effort has a positive effect on player's game performance in the learning process using business simulation games.

It should be noted regarding the relationship between game effort and performance that not everyone who plays multiple runs of the game records a high score. For example, a student may really enjoy a simulation game in a course and play it many times, but s/he might not achieve a high performance rating compared to other students who plays relatively less. One possible explanation of this would be the role of seriousness in the game-based learning process. As mentioned above, seriousness could increase students' attention to learning, which consequently makes her/him prudent to the course materials including the simulation game. Hence, with high seriousness, a student would play game with much carefulness and thoughtfulness when s/he takes an action in the game. Consequently, s/he would reach a desirable score faster than those who are less serious.

On this basis, it is hypothesized as follows:

> H5: Perceived seriousness moderates the effect of game effort on game performance in the game-based learning process.

An overall research model of this study is summarized in Figure 4.

Figure 4. Proposed Research Model

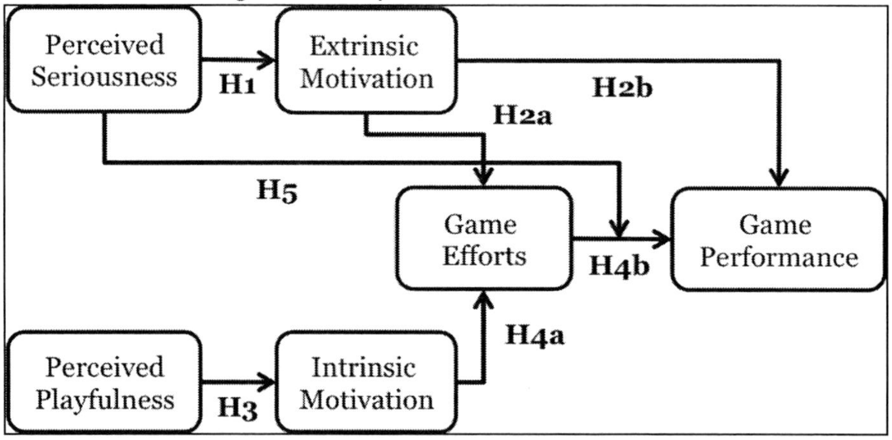

Research Methods

Samples

For quantitative analysis of the proposed model, surveys measuring the constructs in the research model were distributed to 120 MBA students at a Southern public university. The survey respondents enrolled an Operations Management course in three different programs, namely, Full-time, Professional, or Online MBA programs. Regardless of the program formats, in the Operations Management course, students are assigned to play a simulation game related to the project management topic. Before playing the game, students attend an in-class presentation providing game backgrounds, instructions, and game playing tips. Then students can play the game individually and repeatedly as many times as they want by the due date announced (typically in two weeks from the date the simulation game is introduced) outside the class hours. After the due date, students were asked to take the survey on a voluntary basis. For students who participated the survey, a small amount of bonus credits was awarded toward their grades (e.g. depending on the course format, usually worth 0.1 – 0.5% of total course grade). More details about the sample and simulation game are described in Table 3 and Table 4.

Table 3. Classes and Survey Participants

PERIOD	PROGRAM	FORMAT	NUMBER OF STUDENTS ENROLLED	NUMBER OF SURVEY PARTICIPANTS
Spring 2014	Full-time MBA	Traditional face-to-face day classes	48	44
Summer 2014	Online MBA	100% online, no face-to-face meetings	16	15
Fall 2014	Professional MBA	Evening classes (part-time students)	40	35
Spring 2015	Online MBA	100% online, no face-to-face meeting	16	16
Total			120	110

Data Analysis

In the survey, students were asked to answer the questions regarding the perceptions towards the simulation game they played. Among 120 students who were enrolled in this course, 110 responded to the survey. Among them 1 survey was excluded due to the incompleteness, which resulted in a total of 109 survey data observations available. In addition, data for the students' game behaviors, such as game effort and performance, were collected. Game effort was measured by the number of repeated runs played by the students in the simulation game. Then it was converted to a standardized score within each class to control for the effect of the difference among the class settings. Similarly, game performance is measured by the best overall score each student achieved from all of their simulation game results, which was also converted to a standardized score within each class.

Table 4. Game description	
TITLE	NEW PRODUCT RELEASE PROJECT GAME
Topic Area	Project Management
Learning Objectives	Understand how the project management levers (scope, resources, and schedule) improve project outcomes and interact each other project characteristics affect team morale and work quality
Game play	Make weekly decisions as a product development manager to complete a new project development project successfully 3 different scenarios (easy – hard)
Game score	Given at the end of each game play based on four performance dimensions (project scope, schedule, budget, and human resource), Maximum score is 1000
Decisions	Decisions are made individually
Competition	Students can see other students' results
Repeatability	Students can play repeatedly as they want

To analyze the data obtained from the survey, PLS-SEM (Partial Least Squares - Structural Equation Modeling) was used. Being used widely in IS research, PLS-SEM analyzes direct, indirect, and interaction relationship of structural models consisted of constructs measured by multiple items (Venkatesh 2000; Hair et al. 2014). According to Goodhue et al. (2012), 49% of the path analysis studies published in ISR, JMIS, and MISQ from 2006 to 2010 used PLS analysis. The technique has advantages in developing theories especially in exploratory research due to its robustness against measurement and/or sample size (Hair et al. 2010; Gefen et al. 2011; Hair et al. 2014). Given that this study is among the first exploratory attempts to reveal the role of seriousness and playfulness in the simulation game in business education, PLS-SEM is determined to be an appropriate analysis technique. For the statistical analysis purpose, the SmartPLS version 3.2 software was used (Ringle et al. 2015).

In addition, to ensure the validity of the measurement, several steps of the measurement model of the latent constructs, which include examination of factor loadings/weights, reliability of constructs, and discriminant validity were performed. Details of this measurement model are presented in Appendix A.

Analysis Results

The model below depicts the result of the analysis of the proposed game-based learning process model, exploring how seriousness and playfulness works in the learning process through business simulation games. As shown in Figure 5, all the proposed paths except two paths (from extrinsic motivation to game effort and game performance are statistically significant.

DISCUSSIONS

The results of the analysis suggest that the perceived seriousness and playfulness play significant roles in game-based learning processes, especially with business simulation games. Specifically, the two constructs ultimately affect the learners' behaviors in the game, namely, effort and performance. However, the way the two factors affect the game behaviors of learners are different.

Figure 5. PLS-SEM Model Result

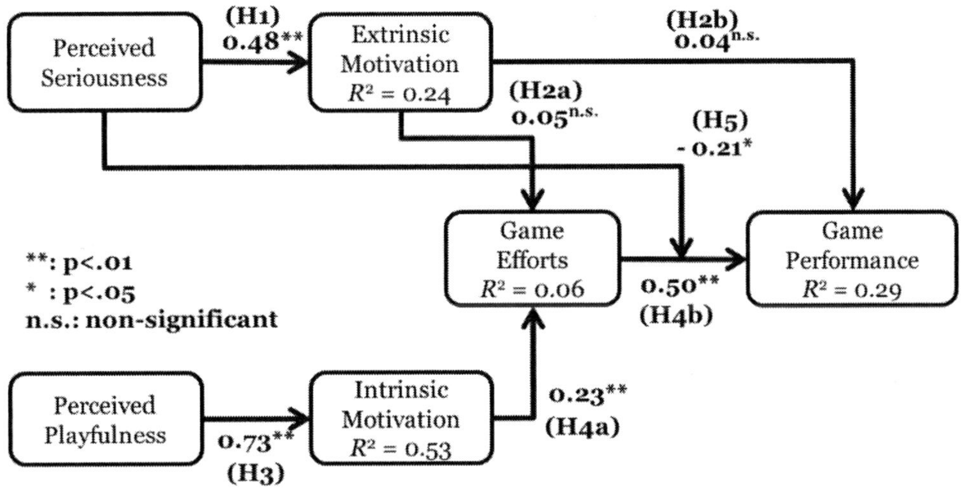

To begin, the effect of the learner's perceived playfulness toward the business simulation game on the game performance is mediated successively by the learner's intrinsic motivation and the game efforts. Hence, H3, H4a, and H4b are supported. This is consistent with the previous literature in motivational theory. Basically individual enjoyment in an activity leads one's intrinsic motivation to repeat the activity multiple times, which eventually increases skill levels and performance (Ryan & Deci 2000). This study is one of the first attempts to apply this relationship to the context of the learning process using business simulation games, thus contributing to the area of game playing for business education and training. By better understanding the relationships among playfulness, motivation, effort, and performance, game designers who develop business simulation games could be more affective in developing instructional games that improve players learning experience. In addition, instructors who intend to use business simulation games effectively in their curriculum can focus on emphasizing the playful element of the game for their students to enhance learning experience.

Meanwhile, the results of the analysis regarding the perceived seriousness raises a couple of cautions in interpretation. First, it is shown that extrinsic motivation directly affects neither the game efforts nor the game performance although the perceived seriousness directly affect extrinsic motivation. This fails to support the hypotheses regarding the effects of extrinsic motivation on the game efforts and the game performance (H2a and H2b), while it supports the hypotheses regarding the effect of the perceived seriousness on extrinsic motivation. This could be explained in an alternative way. Given that extrinsic motivation is more closely related to individual's awareness to the external rewards consequently following an activity, it is important to consider the ultimate goal for learners to pursue by playing the business simulation games. For example, in the Operations Management courses where this study collected data, the MBA students' goal is to learn about the topics related to Operations Management to increase their management skills, and ultimately, to work successfully at the job they desire. The simulation game play is merely one of the many activities in the process that they need to do to achieve the goal. Hence, those who feels high seriousness toward the business simulation game is more likely to have high seriousness toward their course works and future career. Then, they might focus less on the game itself but more on the learning outcomes they could get out of the game. In this sense, they would try to conduct the most cost-effective strategy in their learning process. Learners who have high-seriousness would not spend too much time on playing the game. Instead, they give only a small number of attempts enough to find a relationship underneath and focus more on learning the essential knowledge out of the business simulation game.

It is actually supported by the results of the analysis where the perceived seriousness moderates the relationship between the game efforts and the game performance, which supports H5 in the proposed research model. Shown in Figure 6, there is a disordinal interaction effect with different levels of the seriousness toward the relationship between the game efforts and the game performance. It suggests that a student who perceives high seriousness on the business simulation game would perform well in the game with relatively small efforts. To the contrary, a student who has low seriousness needs to put more effort (i.e. play the game many times) to improve their performance significantly in the game.

Figure 6. Interaction effect of perceived seriousness on game effort – performance

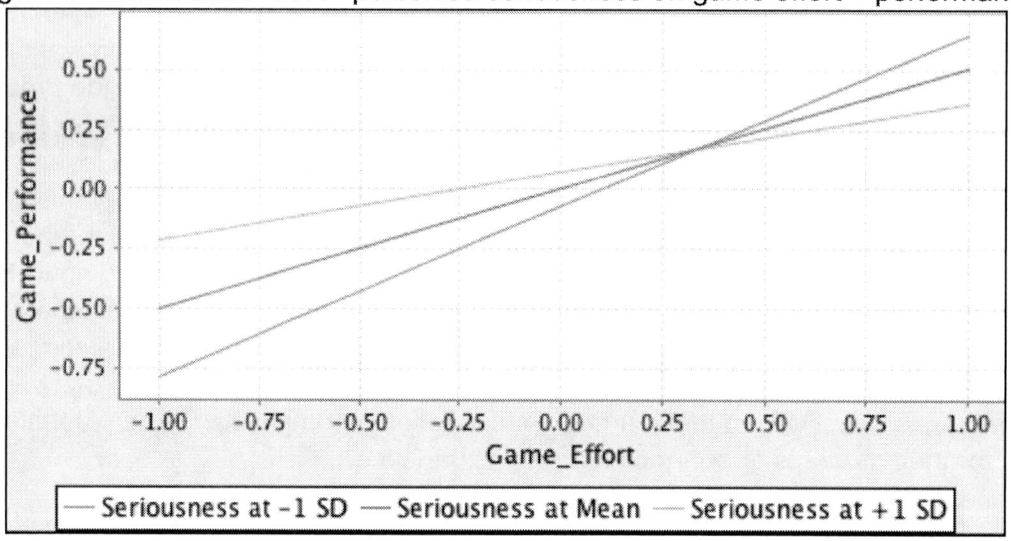

This finding gives a significant implication to the area of business simulation game. Although many previous studies claimed that playfulness is positively related to the performance (Webster & Martocchio 1992; Potosky 2002), few have considered seriousness in the game-based learning process. Moreover, very few could give us a clear explanation why some students learn faster than the others through business simulation games. Many focus on the game-based learning process in which learners experience “trial-and-error” to achieve a certain goal (Higgins 2000; Wideman et al. 2007). However, it is also essential to lead the students to get the goal at a minimum cost (e.g., less playing time). This study reveals that the perceived seriousness could be a key to solve the issue. As Snow et al. (2002) suggested, different styles of introducing simulation games could make difference in students' attitude and performance. By emphasizing and facilitating the seriousness in the game-based learning process, instructors would maximize the efficiency of using simulation games in their course. Likewise, game designers would also apply the principle that emphasizing seriousness in the simulation game would increase the players' learning experience while there still should be playfulness to engage players in the game play. Hence, it is necessary to balance the degree of the seriousness and the playfulness in designing business simulation games to maximize the learning through the games.

LIMITATIONS

This study has limitations with regards to some aspects that should be noted here. First, this study relies on data from a particular business simulation game. Although the game has many common elements with the other business simulation games, and the data were obtained from multiple courses in different formats, the generalizability of the findings could be limited due to the homogeneity of the game used and the topic which the game is about. In addition, as mentioned above, instructional style could affect the students' attitude and performance in game-using learning (Whiteley & Faria 1989; Snow et al. 2002). This study does not capture the difference in instructional styles because all the courses were instructed by the same instructor. Future study might consider including different games and instructional settings to overcome the limitation.

Second, as it is discussed briefly in the previous section, the ultimate goal of using business simulation game in the course is not to make the student get a high score in the game, but to enhance the students' understanding of the course topics and management skills. Although there is close relationship between students' behavior in the simulation game and the learning outcomes (Whiteley & Faria 1989), it is still unclear how the connection works with all things included. By using game performance as the dependent variable, this study fails to investigate the whole process of learning using business simulation game.

Lastly, there might be factors that could influence the perceived seriousness and playfulness of business simulation game. In the future study, it would be worthwhile to include the antecedents of the perceived seriousness and playfulness to understand the whole process of learning through business simulation games.

CONCLUSIONS

With increasing interests and attentions, the area of business simulation game has become a significant part of business education and training. However, there is still a lack of understanding of game-based learning process, especially with regards to the role of perceived seriousness and playfulness. This study sheds light on the area by providing a model of game-based learning process incorporating the perceived seriousness and and playfulness of the players and by analyzing empirical data from the survey of students who enrolled to Operations Management courses in MBA program. From the result of PLS-SEM analysis, it turns out that the perceived playfulness plays a role of antecedent of intrinsic motivation, which affects game efforts and game performance successively. On the other hand, the perceived seriousness affects player's extrinsic motivation as well as moderates the relationship between game efforts and game performance. From this result, it is revealed that the perceived seriousness is important for students to learn more effectively through business simulation game.

The findings of the study give helpful insights to developers who design business simulation games as well as instructors who use business simulation games as a part of their teaching materials. Specifically, developers and instructors can balance the seriousness or playfulness of the game and enhance the effectiveness of the business simulation games depending on the situation and setting. By doing so, they can use different strategies; one might emphasize more on playfulness so students enjoy the game for a substantial amount of time and put more efforts to enhance the learning experience. On the other hand, they can focus more on seriousness so that students might have more attention to the learning itself and complete the tasks in the game in a relatively short time still with good learning outcomes. In either way, providing a balanced approach would be necessary to maximize the effectiveness of game-based learning.

REFERENCES

Adkins, S. (2013). The 2012-2017 Worldwide Game-based Learning and Simulation-based Markets: Key Findings from Recent Ambient Insight Research, *Serious Play Conference 2013.*

Amabile, T. M. (1979). Effects of external evaluation on artistic creativity. *Journal of Personality and Social Psychology*, 37, 221–223.

Azadegan, A., Riedel, J. K. H., & Baalsrud Hauge, J. (2012). Serious Games Adoption in Corporate Training. In M. Ma, M. Oliveira, J. Hauge, H. Duin, & K.-D. Thoben, *Lecture Notes in Computer Science* (Vol. 7528, pp. 74–85–85). Berlin, Heidelberg: Springer Berlin Heidelberg.

Barnett, L. A. (1990). Playfulness: Definition, design, and measurement. *Play & Culture*, 3(4), 319-336.

Barron, K. E., & Harackiewicz, J. M. (2001). Achievement goals and optimal motivation: Testing multiple goal models. *Journal of Personality and Social Psychology*, *80*(5), 706–722.

Ben-Zvi, T. (2010). The efficacy of business simulation games in creating Decision Support Systems: An experimental investigation. *Decision Support Systems*, *49*(1), 61–69.

Berlyne, D. E., II, & Lawrence, G. H. (1964). Effects of Complexity and Incongruity Variables on GSR, Investigatory Behavior, and Verbally Expressed Preference. *The Journal of General Psychology*, *71*(1), 21–45.

Bernard Keys, J. (1989). The Management of Learning Grid for Management Development Revisited. *Journal of Management Development*, *8*(2), 5–12.

Biggs, J. (1996). Western misperceptions of the Confucian-heritage learning culture. *The Chinese Learner: Cultural, Psychological and Contextual Influences*, 45–67.

Bisson, C., & Luckner, J. (1996). Fun in Learning: The Pedagogical Role of Fun in Adventure Education. Perspectives. *Journal of Experiential Education*, *19*(2), 108.

Brandão, J., Ferreira, T., and Carvalho, V. (2012). An Overview on the Use of Serious Games in the Military Industry and Health. In M. Cruz-Cunha (Ed.), *Handbook of Research on Serious Games as Educational, Business and Research Tools* (pp. 182-201). Hershey, PA: Information Science Reference.

Campbell, J.P. (1990) Modeling the performance prediction problem in industrial and organizational psychology. In M.D. Dunnette & L.M. Hough, (eds.) *Handbook of Industrial and Organizational Psychology*, Vol. 1 (2nd ed.), (pp. 687–732). Palo Alto, CA: Consulting Psychologists Press.

Charles, T., Bustard, D., & Black, M. (2011). Experiences of Promoting Student Engagement Through Game-Enhanced Learning. In *link.springer.com.libezp.lib.lsu.edu* (pp. 425–445). London: Springer London.

Chin, W. "The Partial Least Squares Approach to Structural Equation Modeling," in Modern Methods for Business Research, G. A. Marcoulides (ed.), Hillsdale, NJ: Lawrence Erlbaum Associates, Publisher, 1998, pp. 295-336.

Czikszentmihalyi, M. (1990). *Flow: The psychology of optimal experience*. Harper & Row.

Day, D. V., & Silverman, S. B. (1989). Personality and Job Performance: Evidence of Incremental Validity. *Personnel Psychology*, *42*(1), 25–36.

Deci, E. L. (1975). *Intrinsic motivation*. New York: Plenum.

Deci, E. L., & Ryan, R. M. (1985). *Intrinsic Motivation and Self-Determination in Human Behavior*. Springer.

Deci, E. L., & Ryan, R. M. (1991). A motivational approach to self:Integration in personality. In R. Dienstbier (Ed.), Nebraska Symposium on Motivation: Vol. 38. Perspectives on motivation (pp. 237-288). Lincoln: University of Nebraska Press.

Deci, E. L., & Ryan, R. M. (1991). A motivational approach to self: integration in personality. In R. Dienstbier (Ed.), Nebraska symposium on motivation: Vol. 38. *Perspectives on motivation* (pp. 237–288). Lincoln, NE: University of Nebraska Press.

Deci, E. L., Koestner, R., & Ryan, R. M. (1999). A meta-analytic review of experiments examining the effects of extrinsic rewards on intrinsic motivation. *Psychological Bulletin*, 125, 627–668.

Deci, E. L., Vallerand, R. J., Pelletier, L. G., & Ryan, R. M. (1991). Motivation and education: The self-determination perspective. *Educational Psychologist*, *26*(3-4), 325–346.

Dewey, J. (1913). *Interest and effort in education*. Houghton Mifflin.

Dewey, J. (1938). *Experience and Education*. New York: Macmillan.

Ellis, M. J. (1973). *Why people play*. Englewood Cliffs, NJ: Prentice-Hall.

Ellis, M. J., & Scholtz, G. J. L. (1978). *Activity and play of children*. Englewood Cliffs, N.J.: Prentice-Hall.

Faria, A. J., & Wellington, W. J. (2004). A Survey of Simulation Game Users, Former-Users, and Never-Users. *Simulation & Gaming*, *35*(2), 178–207.

Fornell, C., & Larcker, D. F. (1981). Evaluating Structural Equation Models with Unobservable Variables and Measurement Error. *Journal of Marketing Research*, *18*(1), 39–50.

Garris, R., Ahlers, R., & Driskell, J. E. (2002). Games, Motivation, and Learning: A Research and Practice Model. *Simulation & Gaming*, 33(4), 441–467.

Gefen, D., Rigdon, E. E., & Straub, D. (2011). An Update and Extension to SEM Guidelines for Administrative and Social Science Research. *MIS Quarterly*, *35*(2), iii–xiv.

Glynn, M. A., & Webster, J. (1992). The adult playfulness scale: An initial assessment. *Psychological Reports*, *71*(1), 83–103.

Goodhue, D., Lewis, W., & Thompson, R. (2007). Research Note--Statistical Power in Analyzing Interaction Effects: Questioning the Advantage of PLS with Product Indicators. *Information Systems Research*, *18*(2), 211–227.

Hair, J. F., Black, W. C., Babin, B. J., Anderson, R. E., & Tatham, R. L. (2010). Multivariate data analysis (7th ed.). Upper Saddle River, NJ: Pearson Prentice Hall.

Hair, J. F., Jr, Hult, G. T. M., Ringle, C., & Sarstedt, M. (2014). *A Primer on Partial Least Squares Structural Equation Modeling (PLS-SEM)*. Thousand Oaks, CA: SAGE Publications, Inc.

Harackiewicz, J. M., & Sansone, C. (1991). Goals and intrinsic motivation: You can get there from here. *Advances in Motivation and Achievement*, *7*, 21–49.

Harackiewicz, J. M., Barron, K. E., Pintrich, P. R., Elliot, A. J., & Thrash, T. M. (2002). Revision of achievement goal theory: Necessary and illuminating. *Journal of Educational Psychology*, *94*(3), 638–645.

Harackiewicz, J. M., Manderlink, G., & Sansone, C. (1984). Rewarding pinball wizardry: effects of evaluation and cue value on intrinsic interest. *Journal of Personality and Social Psychology*, 47, 287–300.

Harlow, H. F., Harlow, M. V., & Meyer, D. R. (1950). Learning motivated by a manipulation drive. *Journal of Experimental Psychology*, 40, 228–234.

Harter, S. (1978). Effectance motivation reconsidered. Toward a developmental model. *Human development*, *21*(1), 34-64.

Harter, S., & Connell, J.P. (1984). A model on the relationship among children's academic achievement and their self-perceptions of competence, control, and motivational orientations. In J. Nicholls (Ed.), *The development of achievement motivation* (pp. 219-250). Greenwich, CT: JAI Press.

Henderlong, J., & Lepper, M. R. (1997). Conceptions of intelligence and children's motivational orientations: A developmental perspective. In *biennial meeting of the Society for Research in Child Development, Washington, DC.*

Higgins, S. (2000). The logical zoombinis. *Teaching Thinking, 1*(1).

Hull, C. L. (1943). Principles of behavior: an introduction to behavior theory.

Hunter, H. (2013). *Shift: Using Business Simulations and Serious Games*. Createspace Independent Pub.

Klabbers, J. H. (2003). The gaming landscape: a taxonomy for classifying games and simulations. in "LEVEL UP: Digital Games Research Conference" Edited by Marinka Copier and Joost Raessens. p. 54-68, 4-6 November 2003, University of Utrecht, The Netherlands.

Kline, S., Dyer-Witheford, N., and De Peuter, G. (2003). *Digital Play*. McGill-Queen's University Press.

Kolb, D. A., Boyatzis, R. E., & Mainemelis, C. (2000). Experiential learning theory: Previous research and new directions. In R. J. Sternberg & L. F. Zhang (Eds.), *Perspectives on cognitive, learning, and thinking styles* (pp. 227-247). Mahwah, NJ: Lawrence Erlbaum.

Kraiger, K. (2003). Perspectives on Training and Development. In *Handbook of Psychology*. Hoboken, NJ, USA: John Wiley & Sons, Inc.

Lainema, T. (2003). *Enhancing organizational business process perception: Experiences from constructing and applying a dynamic business simulation game*. Turku School of Economics and Business Administration.

Landers, R. N., & Callan, R. C. (2011). Casual Social Games as Serious Games: The Psychology of Gamification in Undergraduate Education and Employee Training. *Serious Games and Edutainment Applications*.

Lane, D. C. (1995). On a resurgence of management simulations and games. *Journal of the Operational Research Society*, 604–625.

Lepper, M. R., Corpus, J. H., & Iyengar, S. S. (2005). Intrinsic and Extrinsic Motivational Orientations in the Classroom: Age Differences and Academic Correlates. *Journal of Educational Psychology*, *97*(2), 184–196.

Lepper, M. R., Greene, D., & Nisbett, R. E. (1973). Undermining children's intrinsic interest with extrinsic reward: a test of the overjustification hypothesis. *Journal of Personality and Social Psychology*, 28, 129–137.

Lieberman, J. N. (1977). *Playfulness: Its Relationship to Imagination and Creativity*. New York, NY: Academic Press.

Lin, Y.-G., McKeachie, W. J., & Kim, Y. C. (2003). College student intrinsic and/or extrinsic motivation and learning. *Learning and Individual Differences*, *13*, 251–258.

Lin, Y.-L., & Tu, Y.-Z. (2012). The values of college students in business simulation game: A means-end chain approach. *Computers & Education*, *58*(4), 1160–1170.

Makedon, A. (1984). Playful Gaming. *Simulation & Gaming*, *15*(1), 25–64.

Malone, T. (1981). Toward a theory of intrinsically motivating instruction. *Cognitive Science*, *5*(4), 333–369.

Malone, T. W., & Lepper, M. R. (1987). Making learning fun: A taxonomy of intrinsic motivations for learning. *Aptitude, Learning, and Instruction*, *3*, 223–253.

Mayer, I., Bekebrede, G., Harteveld, C., Warmelink, H., Zhou, Q., van Ruijven, T., et al. (2014). The research and evaluation of serious games: Toward a comprehensive methodology. *British Journal of Educational Technology*, *45*(3), 502–527.

Michael, D. R., & Chen, S. L. (2005). *Serious Games: Games That Educate, Train, and Inform*. Boston, MA: Thomson Course Technology PTR.

Miles, W. G., Biggs, W. D., & Schubert, J. N. (1986). Student Perceptions of Skill Acquisition through Cases and a General Management Simulation: A Comparison. *Simulation & Gaming*, *17*(1), 7–24.

Moon, J.-W., & Kim, Y.-G. (2001). Extending the TAM for a World-Wide-Web context. *Information & Management*, *38*(4), 217–230.

Moore, G. E. (1998). Cramming more components onto integrated circuits. *Proceedings of the IEEE*, *86*(1), 82–85.

Negroponte, N. (1995). *Being Digital*. New York: Alfred A. Knopf, Inc.

Park, K. (2004). Factors contributing to East Asian students' high achievement: Focusing on East Asian teachers and their teaching. *APEC Educational Reform Summit, 12*.

Potosky, D. (2002). A field study of computer efficacy beliefs as an outcome of training: the role of computer playfulness, computer knowledge, and performance during training. *Computers in Human behavior*, *18*(3), 241-255.

Reuters (2012, August 23). Spend on Serious Games Growing Steadily; Now a Multi-Billion Dollar Industry. *Reuters*. Retrieved from http://www.reuters.com/article/2012/08/23/idUS177583+23-Aug-2012+BW20120823

Riezler, K. (1941). Play and Seriousness. *The Journal of Philosophy*, *38*(19), 505–517.

Ringle, C. M., Wende, S., and Becker, J.-M. 2015. *SmartPLS 3*. Boenningstedt: SmartPLS GmbH, http://www.smartpls.com.

Ruch, W. (1993). Exhilaration and humor. In M. Lewis & J.M. Haviland (Eds.), *The handbook of emotions* (pp. 605-616). New York: Guilford.

Ruch, W., Köhler, G., & Van Thriel, C. (1996). Assessing the" humorous temperament": Construction of the facet and standard trait forms of the State-Trait-Cheerfulness-Inventory-STCI. *Humor*, *9*, 303–340.

Ruch, W., Köhler, G., & Van Thriel, C. (1997). To be in good or bad humour: Construction of the state form of the State-Trait-Cheerfulness-Inventory—STCI. *Personality and Individual Differences*, *22*(4), 477–491.

Ryan, R. M. (1995). Psychological needs and the facilitation of integrative processes. *Journal of Personality*, *63*(3), 397–427.

Ryan, R. M., & Deci, E. L. (2000). Self-determination theory and the facilitation of intrinsic motivation, social development, and well-being. *American Psychologist*, *55*(1), 68.

Schlosberg, H. (1947). The concept of play. *Psychological Review*, *54*(4), 229–231.

Schunk, D. H., Pintrich, P. R., & Meece, J. L. (2008). *Motivation in education: Theory, research, and applications*. Upper Saddle River, NJ: Pearson/Merrill Prentice Hall.

Simons, K. L. (1993). New technologies in simulation games. *System Dynamics Review*, 9(2), 135-152.

Skinner, B. F. (1953). *Science And Human Behavior*. Free Press.

Snow, S. C., Gehlen, F. L., & Green, J. C. (2002). Different Ways to Introduce a Business Simulation: The Effect on Student Performance. *Simulation & Gaming*, *33*(4), 526–532.

Tao, Y.-H., Cheng, C.-J., & Sun, S.-Y. (2009). What influences college students to continue using business simulation games? The Taiwan experience. *Computers & Education*, *53*(3), 929–939.

Tao, Y.-H., Yeh, C. R., & Hung, K. C. (2015). Validating the Learning Cycle Models of Business Simulation Games via Student Perceived Gains in Skills and Knowledge. *Journal of Educational Technology & Society*, *18*(1), 77–90.

Tauer, J. M., & Harackiewicz, J. M. (2004). The Effects of Cooperation and Competition on Intrinsic Motivation and Performance. *Journal of Personality and Social Psychology*, *86*(6), 849–861.

Vallerand, R. J. (1997). Toward a hierarchical model of intrinsic and extrinsic motivation. *Advances in experimental social psychology*, 29, 271-360.

Van Eck, R. (2006). Digital game-based learning: It's not just the digital natives who are restless. *Educause Review*, *41*(2), 16.

Van Etten, S., Pressley, M., Freebern, G., & Echevarria, M. (1998). An interview study of college freshmen's beliefs about their academic motivation. *European Journal of Psychology and Education*, 13, 105–130.

Venkatesh, V. (2000). Determinants of perceived ease of use: Integrating control, intrinsic motivation, and emotion into the technology acceptance model. *Information Systems Research*, *11*(4), 342–365.

Webster, J., & Martocchio, J. J. (1992). Microcomputer Playfulness: Development of a Measure with Workplace Implications. *MIS Quarterly*, *16*(2), 201–226.

Webster, J., Trevino, L. K., & Ryan, L. (1993). The dimensionality and correlates of flow in human-computer interactions. *Computers in Human Behavior*, *9*(4), 411–426.

White, R. W. (1959). Motivation reconsidered: the concept of competence. *Psychological Review*, *66*(5), 297-333.

Whiteley, T. R., & Faria, A. J. (1989). A Study of the Relationship Between Student Final Exam Performance and Simulation Game Participation. *Simulation & Gaming*, *20*(1), 44–64.

Wideman, H. H., Owston, R. D., Brown, C., Kushniruk, A., Ho, F., & Pitts, K. C. (2007). Unpacking the potential of educational gaming: A new tool for gaming research. *Simulation & Gaming*, *38*(1), 10–30.

Wilson, J. (1998). Seriousness and the Foundations of Education. *Educational Theory*, *48*(2), 143–153.

Yager, S. E., Kappelman, L. A., Maples, G. A., & Prybutok, V. R. (1997). Microcomputer playfulness. *SIGMIS Database*, *28*(2), 43–52.

APPENDICES

Appendix A

Table A1. Construct Definitions and Measurement Items

CONSTRUCT NAME	DEFINITION	MEASUREMENT ITEMS [ITEM CODE]
Seriousness	Participant's readiness to perceive, act, or communicate seriously. In a high seriousness state, the individual is attentive, involved in something perceived as really important, applies a sober or objective perspective or style, is earnest in purpose, and not mentally set for levity or amusement (Ruch et al., 1997)	• I am prepared to play the simulation game in earnest. [SR1] • Playing the simulation game is a important thing on my mind. [SR2] (Dropped) • When playing the simulation game, I have a serious mental attitude. [SR3] • When playing the simulation game, I regard my situation objectively and soberly. [SR4] • When playing the simulation game, I am a serious frame of mind. [SR5] • When playing the simulation game, I am in a thoughtful mood. [SR6] (Dropped) • When playing the simulation game, I am not prepared for silliness or nonsense. [SR7] (Dropped) (Revised from Ruch et al., 1994; Ruch et al., 1997)
Playfulness	Participant's perception that the simulation game will fulfill the participant's intrinsic motives, including factors such as concentration, enjoyment, curiosity (Moon & Kim, 2001); Play a game within the game itself (Riezler, 1941); Voluntariness, spontaneity, intrinsic worthiness (Makedon, 1984)	• When playing the simulation game, I do not realize the time elapsed. [PL1] • When playing the simulation game, I am not aware of any noise. [PL2] (Dropped) • When playing the simulation game, I often forget the work I must do. [PL3] (Dropped) • Playing the simulation game gives enjoyment to me. [PL4] • Playing the simulation game gives fun to me. [PL5] (Dropped) • Playing the simulation game keeps me happy. [PL6] (Dropped) • Playing the simulation game stimulates my curiosity. [PL7] • Playing the simulation game leads to my exploration. [PL8] • Playing the simulation game arouses my imagination. [PL9] (Dropped) (Revised from Moon & Kim, 2001)
Extrinsic Motivation	Playing the simulation game to attain the outcome from outside of the simulation game, e.g. grades, higher rank among classmates	• Identified o I think that playing the simulation game will help me better prepare for my job. [EM_ID1] o Playing the simul ation game eventually will enable me to get the better job that I like. [EM_ID2]

	(Ryan & Deci, 2000); Participants' belief that s/he is stimulated to do well in the simulation game seeking for rewards (Guthrie & Wigfield 2000)	o Playing the simulation game will help me make a better choice regarding my job. [EM_ID3] o I believe that playing the simulation game will improve my competence as a worker. [EM_ID4] • Introjected o I play the simulation game to prove to myself that I am capable of completing this course successfully. [EM_IJ1] o I play the simulation game because of the fact that when I succeed in this course I feel important. [EM_IJ2] o I play the simulation game to show myself that I am an intelligent person. [EM_IJ3] (Dropped) o I play the simulation game because I want to show myself that I can succeed in this course. [EM_IJ4] (Dropped) • External regulation o Without playing the simulation game I would not find a better job later on. [EM_RG1] (Dropped) o I play the simulation game in order to obtain a more prestigious job later on. [EM_RG2] o I play the simulation game because I want to have "the good life" later on. [EM_RG3] o I play the simulation game in order to have a better salary later on. [EM_RG4] (Revised from Vallerand et al, 1989)
Intrinsic Motivation	Playing the simulation game for the inherent satisfaction of the simulation game playing itself (Ryan & Deci, 2000); Participants' willingness to participate in the simulation game itself regardless of rewards (Shernoff et al. 2003; Reeve et al. 2004)	• Challenge o I like playing the simulation game because it's a challenge. [IM_CH1] (Dropped) o I like to learn as much as I can from the simulation game. [IM_CH2] o I like to go on to new simulation game that is at a more difficult level. [IM_CH3] o I like complex simulation games because I enjoy trying to figure them out. [IM_CH4] o I like difficult simulation games because I find it more interesting. [IM_CH5] • Curiosity o I ask questions about the simulation game because I want to learn new things. [IM_CU1] o I do extra effort in simulation game because I can learn about things that interest me. [IM_CU2] o I play the simulation game because I am interested in the subject. [IM_CU3] (Dropped)

		○ I play the simulation game really hard because I really like to learn new things. [IM_CU4] • Independent mastery ○ I like to try to figure out how to do well in the simulation game on my own. [IM_MA1] ○ When I don't understand something in the simulation game right away, I like to try to figure it out by myself. [IM_MA2] ○ When I make a mistake in the simulation game, I like to figure out the right answer by myself. [IM_MA3] ○ If I get stuck in the simulation game, I keep trying to figure out the problem on my own. [IM_MA4] ○ I like to play the simulation game without help. [IM_MA5] (Revised from Lepper et al., 2005)
Game Efforts	Participants' behavior to make efforts to the game	• Standardized score based on the number of runs a participants played repeatedly in the simulation game [Game_Effort]
Game Performance	Set of psychological adaptations to the constraints of the simulation game (Ericsson & Lehmann, 1996); Performance that is yielded from more understanding, skills and abilities in simulation game (Salas et al., 2009)	• Standardized score of game result (Best result if multiple runs is applicable) [Game_Performance] (Sheldon et al., 2002; Salas et al., 2009)

Appendix B

First, a confirmatory factor analysis (CFA) was conducted to ensure the constructs used in the research model are tapped correctly by the items. After reviewing the CFA, some items were removed. Then, to examine the adequacy of the measures, loadings and weights of individual items were viewed as following Table A2. Most of the items' loadings are over 0.7, which is desirable, and all are over .5, which is acceptable (Chin 1998).

Table A2. Factor Loadings and Weights

CONSTRUCT	VARIABLE	LOADINGS	WEIGHTS
Seriousness	SR1	0.705	0.260
	SR3	0.885	0.336
	SR4	0.787	0.266
	SR5	0.878	0.353
Playfulness	PL1	0.533	0.167
	PL4	0.886	0.352
	PL7	0.893	0.338
	PL8	0.894	0.332
Extrinsic Motivation	EM_ID1	0.839	0.224
	EM_ID2	0.808	0.176
	EM_ID3	0.850	0.197
	EM_ID4	0.868	0.254
	EM_IJ1	0.570	0.150
	EM_IJ2	0.651	0.162
	EM_RG2	0.620	0.021
	EM_RG3	0.605	0.070
	EM_RG4	0.595	0.060
Intrinsic Motivation	IM_CH2	0.767	0.111
	IM_CH3	0.786	0.128
	IM_CH4	0.786	0.120
	IM_CH5	0.735	0.112
	IM_CU1	0.509	0.071
	IM_CU2	0.684	0.103
	IM_CU4	0.760	0.130
	IM_MA1	0.828	0.124
	IM_MA2	0.834	0.122
	IM_MA3	0.823	0.103
	IM_MA4	0.613	0.066
	IM_MA5	0.754	0.135

Then, composite reliabilities and Cronbachs Alpha were examined to ensure the construct validity. As shown in Table A3, all the variables exceeded the value of 0.80 for composite reliability and 0.70 for Cronbachs Alpha, which indicates the measurements are all reliable.

Table A2. Composite Reliability and Cronbachs Alpha			
CONSTRUCT	NUMBER OF ITEMS	COMPOSITE RELIABILITY	CRONBACHS ALPHA
Seriousness	4	0.889	0.831
Playfulness	4	0.885	0.824
Extrinsic Motivation	9	0.905	0.895
Intrinsic Motivation	12	0.937	0.925
Game Efforts	1	1.000	1.000
Game Efforts	1	1.000	1.000

Lastly, to examine discriminant validity among the constructs, the average variance extracted (AVE) for each construct is reviewed. As shown in the first column of Table A4, all AVEs are above 0.5, which is recommended (Fornell & Larcker 1981). Also, the square root of the AVEs (in bold on the diagonal) are greater than the correlations between the constructs, which ensures the variables are measuring discriminant constructs.

Table A4. Discriminant Validity							
CONSTRUCT	AVE	SERIOUS-NESS	PLAYFUL-NESS	EXTRINSIC MOTIVATION	INTRINSIC MOTIVATION	Game Efforts	Game Perfor-mance
Seriousness	**0.668**	**0.817**					
Playfulness	**0.666**	0.659	**0.816**				
Extrinsic Motivation	**0.520**	0.484	0.648	**0.721**			
Intrinsic Motivation	**0.556**	0.674	0.729	0.582	**0.746**		
Game Efforts	**1.000**	0.144	0.279	0.169	0.233	**1.000**	
Game Performance	**1.000**	0.178	0.177	0.167	0.225	0.485	**1.000**

DECISION SCIENCES INSTITUTE
Should Business Analytics Be Taught to Every Undergraduate? – We are Already Doing It

Zsolt Ugray
Utah State University
Email: Zsolt.Ugray@usu.edu

ABSTRACT

One prediction of a 2011 McKinsey Global Institute study on Big Data is a shortage of "... 1.5 million managers and analysts with the know-how to use the analysis of big data to make effective decisions." While many specialized graduate and undergraduate programs training data analysts with deep analytical skills have been started recently, there is an absence of initiatives to train the projected 1.5 million managers who can apply results of analytics towards effective decision making. I report on our Business School's initiative to require an analytics acumen course for all undergraduate business students to close this gap.

KEYWORDS: Business Analytics, Business Curriculum Development, Course Design, Analytics Instruction

INTRODUCTION

Business Analytics

During the past several years, numerous programs have been created to prepare future employees and entrepreneurs with the skills necessary to utilize business analytics and manage big data. While the number and specifics of the topics and courses included in such programs is not uniform and there is no clear consensus about the content of related curricula, there are clearly observable patterns about what constitutes the knowledge necessary for practitioners of business analytics.

The need for handling and analyzing volumes of data is well supported. The amount of data created, managed and consumed is expected to reach 4 ZB (zettabytes) by 2020 (Gantz & Reinsel, 2012). Handling this vast amount of data with available technology is stretching organizations' abilities (McAfee & Brynjolfsson, 2012). On the one hand, there is continuous pressure to innovate and sustain competitive advantage (Barton & Court, 2012; Bell, 2013). On the other hand, for some organizations, there is the need to stay competitive with early adopters of related technologies (Davenport & Harris, 2010). The need to find, keep, and train business analytics experts, or data scientists, has become an unceasing challenge (Davenport, 2013; Davenport & Patil, 2012; Santaferraro, 2013). It is predicted that by 2018 in the US there will be a shortage of between 140,000 and 190,000 people with deep data science experience and 1.5 million managers with data analytical skills able to convert analytical insights into practice (Manyika et al, 2011).

Business Analytics Education

Academia and industry are focused on addressing the forecasted shortage of 140,000 to 190,000 people with deep data science experience Even with the relatively fast acknowledgement of this gap, the emergence of programs and students graduating do not keep pace with the growing demand for skilled data scientists: in 2010 only 15 full time programs (only 3 them at the undergraduate level) were identified in a review (Wixom et al, 2011). A few years later the number of programs has dramatically increased to 131 full time programs, including 47 at the undergraduate level (Wixom et al, 2014). The increase in interest and demand for business analytics, however, still outpaces the supply of students. Additionally, this recent survey found that prospective employers found university graduates' practical experience and foundational skills lacking.

Very little attention has been paid to the other forecasted shortage: that of 1.5 million managers who will need skills to interpret the results of analytics and convert insights into actions (Manyika et al, 2011). Existing curricular recommendations barely address the general education of business students towards the basic understanding and appreciation of big data and business analytics concepts. Based on the prevalence of large volumes of data in so many fields and areas of business, as well as the recognition of the importance of analytics to effectively compete in those areas (Davenport & Harris, 2010), organizations need people who are conversant in the language of analytics even if they won't become experienced practitioners of data analytics themselves. They ought to understand the basic concepts and capabilities of analytics. They should also be able to identify business problems that can be addressed with analytical tools and – at the other end of the process – they should be able to understand and interpret the results and make actionable recommendations based on them.

My business school was swayed by the argument that it essential to prepare all business students with skills to become data literate and decided to implement a big data analytics acumen course that is part of the required general preparation for all business undergraduate students. Steps of the development of the course, its initial roll out, and first experiences are described below.

COMPETENCY-BASED COURSE DEVELOPMENT

To determine the content for a course that is required by all business undergraduates, a course steering committee was set up. Its goal was to create a course at the sophomore/junior level that is comprehensive, addresses anticipated business needs towards a high level understanding of big data analytics, and suitable for a broad audience. Following (Bowden, 2004), the major steps in competency based development is 1) identifying a common set of skills which are in demand in practice and 2) developing an academic curriculum that empowers students with the corresponding skillset.

The committee relied on several sources of information regarding what is considered essential skills by employers, practitioners, and academic educators (Wilder & Ozgur, 2015; Wixom et al, 2011; Wixom et al, 2014). NCSU (North Carolina State, 2014) maintains a detailed list of graduate programs in analytics. For another good, but less comprehensive list of university program reviews, see the references in (Mamonov et al, 2015).

An often cited understanding of the components of business analytics skillset, based upon (Conway, 2013), is illustrated in Figure 1. Since the target audience is business undergraduates, the need for business domain expertise is only addressed in specific examples. Coverage of applied statistics are dispersed throughout the course and are discussed as necessary for the comprehension of the actual concept, relying on concepts previously covered in the prerequisite Business Statistics course. Technical data management skills are demonstrated and taught throughout the course. Some of the skills are referred to as they are taught in another prerequisite course, Principles of MIS. The limited content that is possible for a single course forced the steering committee to make compromises. As a result, several skills embedded in the three skillset categories are covered only briefly and there is a reliance on synergies with other required business acumen courses.

Figure 1: Business analytics skillset

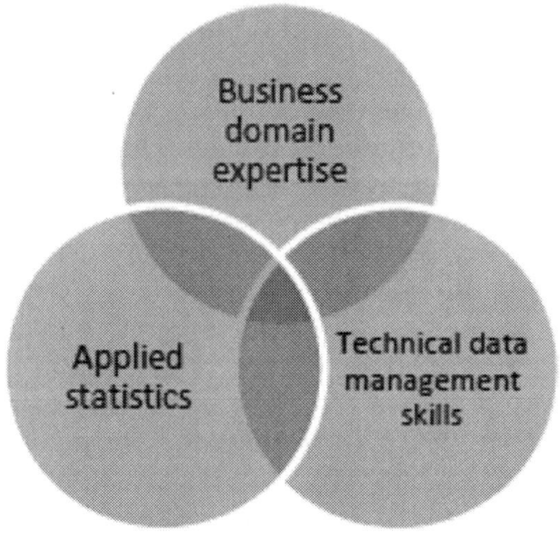

A different perspective of the topics belonging to the business analytics knowledge base is summarized in Wilder & Ozgur (2015). They are discussed as they relate to proposed courses in an undergraduate business analytics curriculum. The proposal is comprised of 5 knowledge domains that include: 1) Project life cycle; 2) Data Management; 3) Analytical techniques; 4) Result deployment and 5) Functional areas (Figure 2.) Components of many of these domains might appear in multiple courses that are more specialized to analytics topics. The list of recommended specialized courses are the following: Data Management; Descriptive Analytics; Data Visualization; Predictive Analytics; Prescriptive Analytics and Data Mining, augmented with an Analytics Practicum and the options for Electives.

Figure 2: Knowledge domains

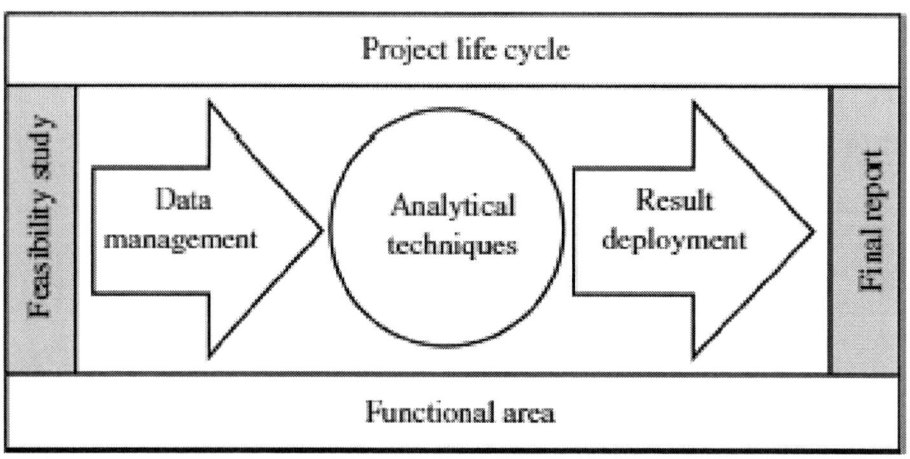

An inescapable decision in business analytics courses is the selection of software tools. While industry and practitioner surveys (Information Week, 2014; KDNuggets, 2015) give a snapshot of the popularity of the available tools they are only one of several factors that play a role in the final decision. There are multiple tools available for all of the tasks and elements of analytics. Data management and retrieval tools, such as SQL and Microsoft Excel / Access are widely available common tools. For data visualization two obvious choices are Tableau (Tableau, 2016) and Power BI by Microsoft (PowerBI,2016). Several of the most widely used Data Mining software platforms, R and Python, require extensive coding (Python, 2016; R, 2016). Others, like KNIME, RapidMiner, and SAS Enterprise Miner allow the user to follow a process oriented view of performing analytics (KNIME, 2016; RapidMiner, 2016; SAS Enterprise Miner, 2016) which has the advantage of a less steep learning curve, making the process of doing analytical work more available to an audience without coding experience.

COURSE CONTENT

Topics

The guiding principles for selecting topics to include into the course content were based on two ideas: 1) to demonstrate the whole process of data analytics 2) to keep the topic coverage relatively simple but rigorous. Steps of the Cross Industry Standard Process for Data Mining (CRSP-DM, 2016; Figure 3.) are often referred in discussion and examples to illustrate not only the individual tasks but also the interrelatedness of tasks and their reliance on each other.

Figure 3. CRISP DM

Accordingly, the following topics are covered in the semester-long course: 1) Data acquisition; 2) Data Cleansing; 3) Data Summarization, 4) Data Visualization; 5) Data Mining. The last topic, Data Mining is covered in the most detail. Besides a general Overview, Prediction, Classification, Validation, Unsupervised, and Supervised Learning are covered with several data mining techniques, such as decision trees, logistic regressions, neural networks, cluster analysis, and association analysis.

Software Tools

The variety of topics require that students gain exposure to several software tools. SQL, Microsoft Excel and Power BI are used in the Data Acquisition module. They were chosen partly because of the prevalence of these tools in practice and partly because students already had exposure to them in an earlier prerequisite course with the exception of Power BI (PowerBI, 2016), which is new to them. Power BI is also used to demonstrate Data Cleansing, Data Summarization and Data Visualization. All of the data mining techniques are introduced in concept at first and then RapidMiner (RapidMiner, 2016) is used to put the concepts to work and analyze relevant data. RapidMiner was chosen for its process oriented view of analytics: it is relatively easy to learn and if one does not want to or need to get into the detailed workings of the algorithms it is a very simple tool to use.
Across the introduction of all of the techniques, every details of the steps of the CRISP-DM framework is emphasized and demonstrated, emphasizing the importance of not only the technical details, but the steps of Business understanding evaluation and Deployment as well.

COURSE DEPLOYMENT

The course was first piloted during the fall semester of 2015 with two instructors and a total of 70 students in 3 sections taught in a lab environment. It was followed by 5 sections taught by 3 instructors in the spring of 2016. Detailed review of student responses and course evaluation are in progress but initial responses from students ranged from great excitement to quiet reservation. It is a course that is definitely stretching the skills and experiences of the typical business undergraduate student. Despite the demands of the course, evaluations were similar to other required business acumen courses and students responded with the typical spread of opinions about how they perceive the usefulness and relevance of topics.
Between the two semesters several minor changes were made to the course that did not affect its original design. Some topics got more time and attention while others were either deemphasized or omitted. The software tools used were upgraded to their latest version with the greatest change of replacing Microsoft's PowerView, PowerQuery and PowerPivot with Power BI which integrates the capabilities of component previously spread across multiple software pieces.
More detailed review of the course, based on instructor evaluations, student course evaluations, and surveys conducted are performed between the semesters of two academic years. At this point no major changes are foreseen.

CONCLUSIONS

With the development and deployment of a new Big Data Analytics course required to be taken by all business undergraduate students our Business School is committed to equipping students with skills that are forecasted to be in great demand for future managers. In contrast to most data analytics program that concentrate on a sequence of several course to prepare students with deep analytical and data science skills, the course presented in this paper is aimed to provide the basic knowledge necessary for understanding the essence of analytics, the way it is used, and the type of results and solutions it provides. Only with these skills will future managers be able to interpret results and put them into practice for improved decision making in organizations.

REFERENCES

Barton, D. & Court, D. (2012). Making Analytics Work for You. *Harvard Business Review*, October, 79-83.

Bowden, J. (2004). Capabilities-driven curriculum design. *Effective learning and teaching in engineering*, 36–47.

Bell, P. (2013). Creating Competitive Advantage Using Big Data. *Ivey Business Journal*, May, 1-5.

Conway, D. (2013). THE DATA SCIENCE VENN DIAGRAM. Retrieved from http://drewconway.com/zia/2013/3/26/the-data-science-venn-diagram

CRISP-DM, (2016). Cross Industry Standard Process for Data Mining (CRISP-DM) https://en.wikipedia.org/wiki/Cross_Industry_Standard_Process_for_Data_Mining

Davenport, T. H. (2013). Keep Up with Your Quants. *Harvard Business Review*, July-August, 120-123.

Davenport, T. H. & Harris, J. G. (2010). *Analytics at Work: Smarter Decisions, Better Results*. Harvard Business School Press.

Davenport, T. H. & Patil, D. J. (2012). Data Scientist: The Sexiest Job of the 21st Century. *Harvard Business Review*, October, 70-76.

Gantz, J. & Reinsel, D. (2012). The Digital Universe in 2020: Big Data, Bigger Digital Shadows, and Biggest Growth in the Far East. *IDC Analyze the Future*, 3, 1-16.

Information Week (2014). 16 Top Big Data Analytics Platforms, Retrieved from: http://www.informationweek.com/big-data/big-data-analytics/16-top-big-data-analytics-platforms/d/d-id/1113609

KDNuggets, (2015). R leads RapidMiner, Python catches up, Big Data tools grow, Spark ignites; Retrieved from: http://www.kdnuggets.com/2015/05/poll-r-rapidminer-python-big-data-spark.html

KNIME (2016). Retrieved from: www.knime.org

Mamonov, S., Misra, R. & Jain, R. (2015). Business Analytics in Practice and in Education: A Competency-based Perspective, *Information Systems Education Journal, 13 (1)* 4-13.

Manyika, J., Chui, M., Brown, B., Bughin, J., Dobbs, R., Roxburgh, C., & Hung-Byers, A. (2011). *Big Data: The Next Frontier for Innovation, Competition, and Productivity*. McKinsey Global Institute, 1-3.

McAfee, A. & Brynjolfsson, E. (2012). Big Data: The Management Revolution. *Harvard Business Review*, October, 61-68.

North Carolina State University (2014). Survey of Graduate Degree Programs in Analytics. Retrieved from: http://analytics.ncsu.edu/?page_idD4184.

PowerBI (2016). Retrieved from: powerbi.microsoft.com

Python (2016). Retrieved from: https://www.python.org/

R (2016): R: The R Project for Statistical Computing. Retrieved from: https://www.r-project.org/

RapidMiner (2016). Retrieved from: www.rapidminer.com

SAS Enterprise Miner (2016). Retrieved from: www.sas.com/en_id/software/analytics/enterprise-miner.html

Santaferraro, J. (2013). Filling the Demand for Data Scientists: A Five-Point Plan, *Business Intelligence Journal, 1), (4)*, 13-18.

Tableau (2016). Retrieved from: www.tebleau.com

Wilder, C. R. & Ozgur, C. O. (2015). Business Analytics Curriculum for Undergraduate Majors. *INFORMS Transactions on Education, 15, (2),* 180-187.

Wixom, B., Ariyachandra, T., Goul, M., Gray, P., Kulkarni, U. & Phillips-Wren, G. (2011). "The Current State of Business Intelligence in Academia: Results from the BI Congress," *Communications of the Association for information Systems, 29,* 300-312.

Wixom, B., Ariyachandra, T., Douglas, D., Goul, M., Gupta, B., Lyer, L., Kulkarni, U., Mooney, J. G., Phillips-Wren, G., & Turetken, O. (2014). "The Current State of Business Intelligence in Academia: The Arrival of Big Data," *Communications of the Association for information Systems, 34,* 1-13.

DECISION SCIENCES INSTITUTE

Should Suppliers Choose to be Leading Innovators?

Alan Mackelprang
Georgia Southern University
Email: amackelprang@gmail.com

Ed Bernardes
West Virginia University
Email: ednilson.bernardes@mail.wvu.edu

Jerry Burke
Georgia Southern University
Email: gburke@georgiasouthern.edu

Chris Welter
Xavier University
Email: welter@xavier.edu

ABSTRACT

Extant research has clearly shown that customers benefit from having more innovative suppliers. However, do suppliers benefit financially from positioning themselves as leading innovators? Utilizing a secondary data based sample of 1039 supplier to customer base observations, we evaluate the extent to which suppliers are able to benefit from positioning themselves as leading (lagging) innovators within their industry. While in general we find that suppliers which employ a leading innovator strategy have higher levels of financial performance, such an effect is not universal. Further, we find that the ability of the supplying firm to leverage their innovative positioning into increased performance is highly contingent upon not only the innovativeness of their own industry, but also the innovativeness of the industries to which they supply. Our results, therefore, suggest that it would be advantageous for suppliers to take a supply chain perspective and strategically incorporate the innovation characteristics of their customers when determining whether or not to be a leading or lagging innovator.

KEYWORDS: strategic positioning; innovation; supply chain; R&D investment; secondary data

DECISION SCIENCES INSTITUTE

Situation Awareness Differences on the Use of Cloud Computing

Shiwei Sun

Auburn University

Email: szs0100@auburn.edu

Chetan Sankar

Auburn University

Email: sankacs@auburn.edu

Jiahe Song

Auburn University

Email: jzs0037@auburn.edu

ABSTRACT

Grounded on the theory of situation awareness, a three-sequential-phase framework was developed. This framework was then used to investigate the situation awareness differences on the use of cloud computing. Using quasi-experimental research design, we executed the study with 33 students. To investigate the situation awareness differences, the students were divided into two groups and assigned to complete the tasks. The repeated measures ANOVA was used to analyze the collected data. The results indicate that the students' situation awareness on the cloud computing use is significantly different as the experimental environment changes. The factors that might cause the differences were explored.

KEYWORDS: Situation awareness theory; Cloud computing; Quasi-experimental research design

INTRODUCTION

A new wave of digital technology associated with the Internet has begun to reconfigure work, employment, and the relations of production in the working environment and beyond. Technologies deriving from the needs of latest years' business strategies and models are considered as new "new" technologies (Howcroft & Taylor, 2014). The wide use of these technologies has changed the working pattern and brings efficiency and convenience to the whole society. Recently, scholars' have put more attention to explore the diffusion of the new "new" technologies.

Cloud computing refers to "the applications delivered as services over the Internet and the hardware and systems software in the data centers that provide those services" (Armbrust et al., 2010, p. 50). It is one of typical new "new" technologies and can be the next wave of IT innovation to change the working pattern (Chou, 2015). For example, with the help of cloud computing, blue-collar workers can collaborate online to complete some complex tasks (Millar, 2008). However, it is not easy for users of cloud computing to comprehensively perceive and acquire the associated expertise and knowledge for their work (Howcroft & Taylor, 2014). Fundamental knowledge about cloud technology is needed for workers.

Information technology (IT) diffusion process has been intensively studied by scholars. Many scholars have investigated the users' situation awareness and use of information technology. For example, Gefen and Straub (1997) explored the gender differences in the perception of information technology. Zhou et al. (2014) investigated students' perceptions of creativity in learning information technology. However, little research has included the situation factors that might influence users' perception and use during their learning process. Given the lack of research on cloud computing learning situation design, we are interested in using the theory of situation awareness to explore how situation awareness differences influence cloud computing knowledge perception outcomes. Situation awareness is convinced as a predominant concern in a variety of domains such as man-computer interactive systems (Kraut, Fussell, & Siegel, 2003). Exploring the situation awareness on the use of cloud computing will help users understand their work. As such, we answer the following research question in this study: *Are there any situation awareness differences on the use of cloud computing?*

To address the research question, a research framework with three-phase design is developed. Following that, we conducted a quasi-experimental design, in which students in introductory level of Management Information Systems (MIS) course are required to learn cloud computing applications knowledge and apply the knowledge to the real situations. Based on the research design, a survey is designed for empirically investigating students' situation awareness on cloud computing use from the two groups in three environments.

The remainder of this article is structured as follows. We first provide a literature review summarizing the cloud computing application use and the theory of situation awareness. Then, we propose a conceptual research framework to adapt to our research setting. Next, we describe the research methodology, followed by an analysis of the collected data. We close with a discussion on the theoretical and practical contributions of the study.

LITERATURE REVIEW

Cloud Computing Use and Its Applications

Cloud computing can be used as a business infrastructure that reduces the need to purchase and maintain expensive computing hardware (Ostermann et al., 2010). Cloud computing originally emerged and quickly developed because of organizations' request for the independence of computing capacity to store and process data. Organizations can gain various benefits by adopting cloud computing practice, including saving cost, improving efficiency, enhancing agility and flexibility, and environmental sustainability (Chou, 2015; Zhang et al., 2010).

There is still not a consensus on the definition of cloud computing. Generally, it is a metaphor of the information technology term that is closely related to utility and consumption of computer resources (Garrison et al., 2012). It was developed in the late 2000s and now is broadly used to provide services over the Internet. Using remote servers and software networks, cloud computing permits various types of information sources to be transferred for real-time processing, which can produce the results without the need to store information on the in-house hardware (Mell & Grance, 2009).

This technology strengthens 'pervasive computing' into "Bring Your Own Devices (BYOD)", such as mobile devices (Howcroft & Taylor, 2014; Venters & Whitley, 2012). Cloud users can get access to cloud computing services through the associated software applications and Web browsers on digital devices. According to Voorsluys et al. (2011), cloud computing providers benefit their users with the following three aspects. The first one is infrastructure as a service (IaaS). It is the service based on physical or virtual machines, such as virtual machines, servers, and network. The second is platform as a service (PaaS). It is the service of computing platform, usually including operating system, database, web server, and a lot of development tools. Last but not least, software as a service (SaaS) is provided to make the clients access to software and databases hardware much more easily.

Cloud computing is widely adopted in various industries and sectors. It also brings a lot of challenges for users because the related knowledge is prerequisite before using. However, if users have to use the advanced technologies to accomplish the tasks, they may face a big challenge (Millar, 2008). There is also an increasing recognition in academics that it is imperative to help users effectively utilize information technology during their work. For instance, using survey data in the automotive industry, Karaali et al. (2011) investigated the factors affecting blue-collar workers' decision of using a web-based learning system.

Situation Awareness Factor in IT Use

The widely accepted definition of situation awareness across domains is "the perception of the elements in the environment within a volume of time and space, the comprehension of their meaning, and the projection of their status in the near future" (Endsley, 1988, p. 97). The task itself, environment (e.g., workload and stress), training, abilities, and other individual factors were identified as the main factors that can influence situation awareness (Endsley, 1995; Roberts, Flin, & Cleland, 2015).

Situation awareness of IT is usually the beginning of IT adoption. Scholars have intensively studied IT diffusion process from users' perception to routine use. Many technology acceptance models and theories have been widely proposed, such as technology acceptance model (TAM) (Davis, 1989), theory of planned behavior (TPB) (Ajzen, 1991), diffusion of innovation theory (DOI) (Rogers, 2003), institutional theory (Scott, 2001; Dacin et al., 2002), theory of acceptance and the use of technology (UTAUT) (Venkatesh et al., 2003), and social cognitive theory (Compeau & Higgins, 1995a, 1995b). For example, Swanson (1988) highlighted user involvement and management commitment for IT implementation. Gefen and Straub (1997) concluded that gender differences greatly influence end users' perceptions of e-mail. Besides gender, other socio-cultural factors, such as national/ethnic differences, influence users' perceptions of information technology (Gefen and Straub, 1997). Zhou et al. (2014) found that students' perceptions of group creativity in learning information technology depend on their domain-related conceptualization and tacit knowledge learning experience.

Straub (2009) summarizes the technology diffusion theories and gave some directions for informal learning. In the study, the author discusses how and why individuals adopt innovations and points out that addressing cognitive, emotional, and contextual concerns could facilitate technology adoption. The author also indicates the research about those concerns would contribute to a better understanding about IT adoption. Other scholars also suggest that the situation can affect individuals' beliefs and emotional response (e.g., Bandura, 1986). Situational or environmental concern had caused more scholars' attention to explore the factors of IT perception and adoption.

Conceptual Framework

From the definition of situation awareness (Endsley, 1988; Endsley, 1995), it can be further broken into three component levels to addressing and assessing team members' operational sense independently. Figure 1 shows the three levels in detail. Level 1 is the perception of elements in an environment within certain time and space. Level 2 is the comprehension of the true meaning of elements. Level 3 is the projection of future status of the elements. The three levels of situation awareness should be considered separately to measure team members' performance.

Based on situation awareness theory and the characteristics of cloud computing use, we designed three research environments (i.e., class knowledge learning, field experiment, and lab data interaction) to investigate students' situation awareness differences. The conceptual framework is shown in Figure 1. The classroom learning is the fundamental learning situation in our design, in which the students can gain basic knowledge on cloud computing and its related equipment. The field work is the context in which the students can perceive cloud computing knowledge and its application as the blue-collar workers' regular working status to locate infrastructure facilities. Lab data interaction provides students opportunity to manipulate recorded data and learn the future use of cloud computing application.

Figure 1: Conceptual framework

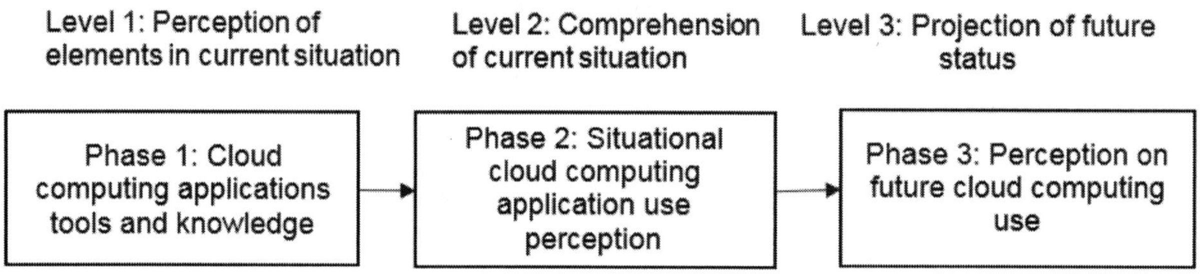

METHODOLOGY

Study Overview

This study was supported by a local company and a research center at a land-grant university in the southeastern US. This company provides technological solutions for the customers to mark their boundaries and infrastructure. The company supplies our research experiment with cloud computing services along with RFID equipment.

The students are recruited in the university. They are all enrolled in an introductory level MIS course. Participation is not mandatory, and extra credits are issued to all the participated one. 33 individuals decide to be involved in this study. Based on the research design, these 33 students were divided into two groups and asked to complete the assigned tasks by three phases. At least one instructor is assigned to each phase. We group three to four students into each team to maintain teamwork and effectively manage all the related tools. Figure 2 demonstrates the tools used in this study.

Figure 2: Cloud computing related application devices used in the experiment

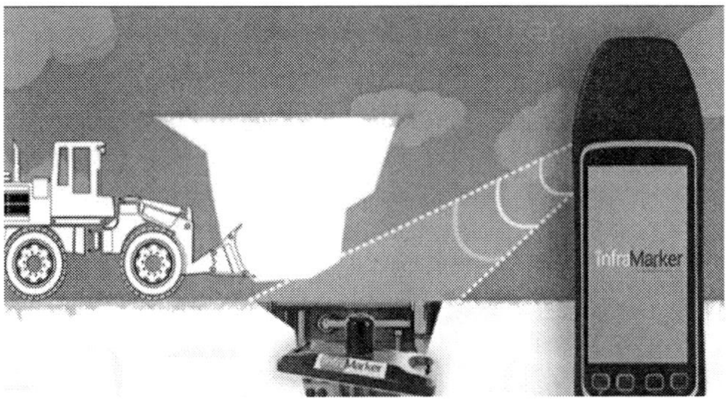

According to the conceptual framework, the three phases are processed in a fixed order because of the incremental learning and perception. The knowledge gained on the cloud computing will be accumulated from one phase to the other. This will match situation awareness theory. Apart from the above design, after the three phases of situation awareness cloud computing, the students also make the presentation, including self-reported knowledge learned during the study, attitudes towards the cloud computing use for blue-collar workers, and the challenge faced during the three phases.

Research Design

Phase 1 Research Design

During phase 1, the participants are expected to learn how to use the equipment and the associated cloud computing software and how to locate infrastructure facilities with these tools. Two instructors present the knowledge that the students needed to understand before the real work in the next phase. Three short videos about the project background, writing to RFID Tags using the mobile App, and basic cloud computing equipment use were shown for the purpose of students' better situation awareness. After the demonstration by the instructors, the students are encouraged to have a closer look at the equipment. At the end of phase 1, students are requested to answer the first round questionnaire based on their situation awareness of learning from both presentation and equipment demonstration. The entire phase 1 is conducted in a classroom.

Phase 2 Research Design

During phase 2, the task was that the participants were separated into two groups to conduct the field work. After phase 1, all the 33 students agree to continue their participation of field operations in phase 2. In this environment, pre-determined utility assets, including Electric, Sewer, and Water, were identified and located. Magnet- and RFID-based markers were buried about 6-12 inches below the ground but directly above the assets.

In order to test the situation awareness differences on the use of cloud computing, we select two out-door locations for our study. One was on campus, in which new version of the equipment was buried and for use. The other field work site was located in another city, in which the equipment was old version bought from the above mentioned local company. In this location, the 48 tags buried in the city had been using for two years. They were buried along the waterline in a subdivision in the city. In both groups, student teams would mimic the role of a utility crew attempting to locate underground infrastructure with RFID technology and cloud computing applications. Correspondingly, the students were separated into two groups. 18 students volunteered to conduct the experiment on campus, while the rest were at another city.

The group located on campus is *Group A* in our experiment, and the other group located outside the campus is *Group B*. Students in both groups are asked to locate buried markers and read (write) information from (to) RFID tags. In both two groups, three or four students are assigned to one team. Each team is given one and a half hours to complete the experiment.
In order to make student teams to perceive a full blue workers' experience of the use of cloud computing application, we let the students read all the tags that are buried and only write a few of them in this phase, although we encourage students to locate as many tags as possible. By doing this, we can eliminate the situation that the same tag is getting overwritten and make sure the students experience fully on cloud computing infrastructure.

Then, the student teams navigate with the Google/ArcGIS maps, identifying the tags using a magnetic locator and read/write to the tag using the Bluetooth reader and Inframarker App. GPS points provide the general location of a buried asset. With the help of GPS information, magnetic locator pinpoints an exact location. In a situation where the same RFID tag is written into multiple times, we can have all the points on the cloud server. However, the RFID tag is only associated with the last write action. Students are requested to fill out the second round questionnaire based on their situation awareness in this phase.

Phase 3 Research Design

In phase 3, the task is that the participants use the data they collected during phase 2 and make data interaction by perceiving the cloud computing for future use. Based on their experiment results in phases 1 and 2, the students have an opportunity to manipulate data in a lab on the computer and understand how the data can be used in the future. The assignments related to the use of cloud computing and infrastructure facilities are given to test the increase of the students' understanding. The work includes exploring cloud computing client's web interface, adjusting GPS points to correct point location errors, exporting data, and importing data into maps.google.com for viewing. Data conversions to cloud computing use are conducted through the whole process. Students are also requested to fill out the third round questionnaire based on their situation awareness during this phase.

Method

Experimental research is best suited to investigate cause-effect relationships (Bhattacherjee, 2012). In this study, we used quasi-experimental research design, which requires treatment manipulation but has high internal and external validity. In our quasi-experimental research design, students who use the new version of cloud computing related equipment are assigned to the treatment group (Group A). The rest student who use the old version of cloud computing related equipment are allocated to the control group (Group B). The sample size 33 also satisfies our quasi-experimental research design and is good for our repeated measure analysis.

To assess subjects' situation awareness effect, a quick questionnaire process by intermittently interrupting a task in the real world is suggested a good means to extract the critical features of the subject's situation awareness (Sætrevik and Eid, 2014). To better serve our research purpose, we designed two open-ended questions as well as eight 5-likert scale questions. The quantitative empirical survey data, and qualitative data from interview texts with instructors and students, and students' presentation slides are analyzed to explore the differences in these two groups. By analyzing the quantitative and qualitative data together, it is good "to explore, describe, explain, predict and influence" (Onwuegbuzie et al., 2009, p 14).

It is hard to operationalize only from situation awareness definition. Based on previous study suggestion (Sætrevik and Eid, 2014), the survey with self-report item method can be used to reflect the extent to which the operators feel they are fully aware of the environment. The main purpose of this study is to measure students' situation awareness on cloud computing use for blue-collar workers' tasks and try to identify the differences in the experiment. Thus, we are not focusing on developing these constructs. The general questions about the students' situation awareness are drawn from previous academic and industry journals. The applicability of all the questions is discussed by the authors. We use a five-point Likert scale to indicate the degree of participants' agreement (ranging from 1= "strongly disagree" to 5= "strongly agree"). For the measurement, we asked participants to indicate their attitude towards the statements. For example, we measure the situation awareness of productivity through the students' attitude towards the statement "*Cloud computing can boost blue-collar workers' productivity*". (See Appendix A)

The questions are all directly used to reflect participants' situation awareness and their attitude towards cloud computing use during their tasks. Based on previous literature on the discussions of benefits and impacts of cloud computing (e.g., Catteddu, 2010; Grossman, 2009; Marston et al., 2011; Sultan, 2010; Venters & Whitley, 2012), we measure the effect of use of cloud computing for blue-collar workers mainly from the following eight aspects: usefulness, productivity, accuracy, complexity, effectiveness, collaboration, flexibility, and reliability. Usefulness is measured by students' situation awareness of the extent to which cloud computing is useful to utility blue-collar workers (e.g., Calheiros et al., 2011). Productivity is assessed by students' situation awareness of the extent to which cloud computing can boost blue-collar workers' productivity (e.g., Brynjolfsson & Hitt, 2003). Accuracy is rated by students' situation awareness of the extent to which cloud computing can increase the accuracy of blue-collar workers' work deliverables (e.g., Zissis & Lekkas, 2012). Complexity is operationalized by students' situation awareness of the extent to which cloud computing can reduce work complexity for blue-collar workers (e.g., A Vouk, 2008). Effectiveness is measured by students' situation awareness of the extent to which cloud computing can make blue-collar workers' work more effective (e.g., Buyya et al., 2009). Collaboration is measured by students' situation awareness of the extent to which cloud computing can help blue-collar workers collaborate online without generating paper-based documents (e.g., T Ograph & Morgens, 2008). Flexibility is represented by students' situation awareness of the extent to which cloud computing can make blue-collar workers' job more flexible (e.g., Foster, 2008). Reliability is delineated by students' situation awareness of the extent to which is measured by students' situation awareness of the extent to which cloud computing can make blue-collar workers' job more reliable (e.g., Armbrust, 2010).

Each participant was encouraged to answer the same questions through the three phases. For a better execution and complete the task within the team, the questionnaires are given to the students by team. Some demographic information is added to the associated response after data collection process. For example, four copies of questionnaires are given to team 1 in Group A immediately after Phase 1. The participants need to provide group number and banner ID on each copy of the questionnaire. This fashion will be used in the 2nd and 3rd rounds of data collection as well. After the three rounds, the researchers put each student's responses together as one piece.

Data Collection

Of the 33 participant, 11 are female (33.33%), and 22 are male (66.67%). 25 are in business related majors (75.76%), and 8 are in engineering related majors (24.24%).

Before conducting the investigation of their situation awareness on cloud computing use, we first ask students to report their cloud computing knowledge level. From their statements, we find that they had little knowledge about cloud computing and its related use to locate infrastructure facilities before conducting this quasi-experiment.

Data Analysis and Results

First, we analyze the correlations among the responses and the variables, such as gender and major. The correlation analysis results indicated that there was no significant relationship among gender, age, major, race/ethnicity, and the students' response towards the attitude to the use of cloud computing during their experiment. Thus, we could rule out the effects of these factors on the situation awareness differences.

Table 1 shows the descriptive analysis results for each question. We can see that the means of *Group A* and *Group B* are both very high in phase 1, which indicates all the respondents hold an active attitude towards the role of cloud computing for blue collar workers' tasks. The situation awareness effect is evident from the results. However, in phases 2 and 3, the students in different situations and learning environments produce different situation awareness outcomes.

Table 1: Descriptive Statistics

	Phase 1				Phase 2				Phase 3			
	Group A		Group B		Group A		Group B		Group A		Group B	
	Mean	Std. Dev.	Mean	Std. Dev.	Mean	Std. Dev.	Mean	Std. Dev.	Mean	Std. Dev.	Mean	Std. Dev.
Q1	4.389	.7775	4.133	.6399	4.611	.5016	3.933	1.033	4.556	.7048	3.714	1.139
Q2	4.222	.8782	4.133	.6399	4.667	.4851	3.867	.9904	4.556	.6157	3.714	1.204
Q3	4.444	.7048	4.067	.7037	4.667	.4851	3.733	1.100	4.556	.6157	3.643	1.008
Q4	4.056	.9984	4.133	.7432	4.444	.6157	3.400	.6325	4.166	.7071	3.357	1.081
Q5	4.444	.9218	4.267	.7037	4.556	.6157	3.667	.8997	4.389	.7775	3.643	1.081
Q6	4.389	.8498	4.466	.7432	4.667	.4851	4.000	.7559	4.389	.6978	3.929	.9169
Q7	4.166	.9236	4.333	.6172	4.611	.5016	3.733	1.033	4.556	.7048	3.571	.9376
Q8	4.389	.9164	4.467	.5164	4.500	.5145	3.600	1.056	4.556	.7048	3.714	1.204

Note: Q1-Q8 were separately used to measure students' situation awareness of cloud computing in the characteristics of usefulness, productivity, accuracy, complexity, effectiveness, collaboration, flexibility, and reliability.

In order to further investigate the differences between the two groups in this quasi-experiment among the three phases, we conduct repeated measures ANOVA analysis to test the differences (See the results in Table 2). The results below in table 2 clearly indicate that there is no significant difference within each phase. However, when we consider the factor of the situation environment for each group, we find that the differences becomes significant.

Table 2: Tests of Within-Subjects Effects

Measure: MEASURE_1

Source		Type III Sum of Squares	df	Mean Square	F	Sig.	Partial Eta Squared	Noncent Parameter	Observed Power[a]
Phase	Sphericity Assumed	.661	2	.331	.896	.414	.028	1.791	.198
	Greenhouse-Geisser	.661	1.900	.348	.896	.409	.028	1.701	.193
	Huynh-Feldt	.661	2.000	.331	.896	.414	.028	1.791	.198
	Lower-bound	.661	1.000	.661	.896	.351	.028	.896	.151
Phase * Group	Sphericity Assumed	3.062	2	1.531	4.149	.020	.118	8.299	.712
	Greenhouse-Geisser	3.062	1.900	1.612	4.149	.022	.118	7.882	.695
	Huynh-Feldt	3.062	2.000	1.531	4.149	.020	.118	8.299	.712
	Lower-bound	3.062	1.000	3.062	4.149	.050	.118	4.149	.506
Error (Phase)	Sphericity Assumed	22.879	62	.369					
	Greenhouse-Geisser	22.879	58.888	.389					
	Huynh-Feldt	22.879	62.000	.369					
	Lower-bound	22.879	31.000	.738					

a. Computed using alpha = .05

We can also find the results from Figure 3. The results show that in phase 1, there is no difference in situation awareness between the two groups. However, as the experimental situation changes in phase 2, the situation awareness difference becomes significantly different. In phase 3, two groups both conducted the learning in the lab, the situation awareness difference is still significant. This might be affected by the knowledge they got in phase 2 because the knowledge they acquired was built on previous step in phase 2.

We find the similar results from the students' self-report open-ended questions. In the survey, the first question is about their situation awareness towards cloud computing use in facilitating blue-collar workers' job. The second question is about their situation awareness of challenges towards cloud computing application use. These results are consistent to the data analysis results. We listed some typical answers from the respondents' responses as evidence.

Figure 3: repeated measures results

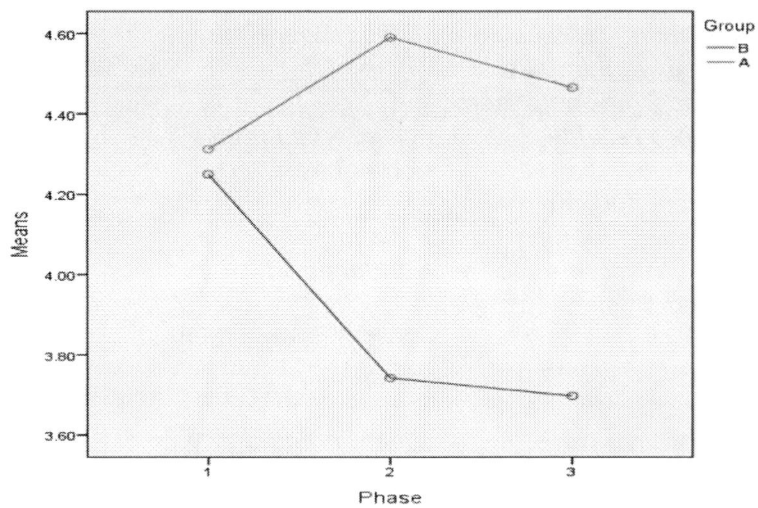

Evidence from open-ended questions

In phase 1, we could find the students hold the same situation awareness attitude. They all have positive attitudes towards cloud computing use in facilitating blue-collar workers' job (See results in Table 3). This is the basic step towards the cloud computing use in classroom.

However, when the study proceeded in phase 2, their attitudes towards cloud computing use in facilitating blue-collar workers' job become significant different. More and more challenges were faced by the students because of hard field work. The students in Group A held more active attitude towards cloud computing use that students in Group B. Students in Group B held the feelings of more and more challenges than those in Group A. We could even noticed that some students doubted the reliability of cloud computing application (See results in Table 4).

In phase 3, the attitudes toward cloud computing use in facilitating blue-collar workers' job is till significantly different. Although all the students in both groups were conducting the learning situation awareness in the same lab, the students in Group B still hold negative attitudes towards cloud computing use (See results in Table 5). Students in Group B produced more complaints on equipment than those in Group A. The results confirmed the finding from the survey data. This might also be because of the close relationship between phases 2 and 3.

Table 3: Selected Answers of Open-Ended Questions in Phase 1			
Situation awareness of attitudes towards cloud computing use in facilitating blue-collar workers' job		Situation awareness of challenges towards cloud computing application usage	
Group A	Group B	Group A	Group B

"If it makes uploading the data easier, there is a sufficient reason to use cloud computing." *"Yes, it would allow for immediate storage of data and possibly for more accurate recording."* *"Cloud computing would be helpful for a collaborative effort in detecting RFID tags and storing data once the tags are logged."* *"Yes, I like the accuracy of the technology."*	*"Yes, it makes locating tags easier and would make underground assets more reliable."* *"Yes, it would make the community much more effective and efficient."* *"Yes, it would be helpful and create effective work."* *"Yes, you could use data collected by anyone else who uses cloud completing access easily."*	*"No, I thought the videos were very helpful."* *"It seemed pretty straightforward."* *"So far: all is understood."* *"No, it seems fairly simple."* *"I did not find any challenges. Pretty easy to use."* *"No."*	*"No."* *"No, I do not find any challenges."* *"Not really. I find myself finding it ok to follow and to understand."* *"No, it's pretty straightforward."*

Table 4: Selected Answers to Open-Ended Questions in Phase 2

Situation awareness of attitudes towards cloud computing use in facilitating blue-collar workers' job		Situation awareness of Challenges towards cloud computing application use	
Group A	Group B	Group A	Group B
"Yes, it really makes things less complicated." *"Yes, it was easy and accurate when locating assets which would be helpful."* *"Yes, because it helps transfer information awhile."* *"Yes, it allows easy and instant access to the information written on tags."*	*"If more reliable technology, it would be helpful."* *"It is a great way to find and locate, but we had a few problems with tagging the magnets."* *"Yes, with updated tech would make it simple."* *"Yes, I can see it being very useful."*	*"No, it was straightforward."* *"We had some difficulty finding a few assets, but we eventually found them by putting the reader/writer closer to the ground."* *"Writing tags and connection issues."* *"The technology was difficult to use at times."*	*"Problems with tagging the magnets."* *"Hard were issues between versions."* *"Yes, we wouldn't find many of the RFID."* *"Yes, having trouble reading tags."*

Table 5: Selected Answers of Open-Ended Questions in Phase 3

Situation awareness of attitudes towards cloud computing use in facilitating blue-collar workers' job		Situation awareness of Challenges towards cloud computing application use	
Group A	Group B	Group A	Group B
"Makes the job easier, as well as makes the data more understandable." *"Cloud helps make jobs for blue-collar workers easier."* *"It makes seeing assets that are buried easier, and can be displayed in a way that's easy to understand."* *"It can help pinpoint locations on google and other websites."* *"It definitely can ease most blue collar work depending on know-how and reliability. Some things didn't happen in the end as they should, which in the real world make things difficult."*	*"To be honest, ours failed but if it worked then it would be awesome."* *"It needs to actually work when locating and editing the tags* *"The idea is really good, as it can be easily accessed and edited, but the actual product does not work."* *"I see the purpose of the technology. However, it is very reliable. "* *"Cloud computing encourages collaboration in data collection for blue-collar jobs. As more collaboration occurs, the more reliable the data becomes."*	*"Very easy phase for our group. No challenge, but enjoyed."* *"No. Phase 3 was very simple and easy to understand."* *"Nope. Simple and efficient."* *"No, though it appears one of our points didn't write to the cloud."* *"Not in phase 3 specifically, but I have security issues with cloud computing in general. For example, it was the apple cloud that all those celebrity pictures leaked from."*	*"The tags wouldn't write. Also, the few that did were not accessible online."* *"Data didn't show up."* *"None of our original points showed up. We had to use another group's login."* *"Yes, our data didn't show up. But the other people's data did."* *"Our only challenge was that our tags in Foley were not recorded to the cloud and we were unable to use our original data."*

DISCUSSIONS

By applying the three-level situation awareness model, we developed a quasi-experimental research design and identifying the situation differences on the use of cloud computing. Based on the repeated measure ANOVA analysis results, we generalize the following aspects. The first one is that students in the same cloud computing use situation can gain the similar situation awareness. The other aspect is that students' situations awareness on cloud computing use changes significantly with the change of environment. The last one is that students' situation awareness is affected by their previous experience.

To further investigate the potential factors that might influence the situation awareness differences, we review the process of the research design. We try to list all the factors in these two experiments (See Table 6) and give the audience a full judgement for the cause of above results. For example, in addition to the change of the experiment location, we can not overlook the training effect either. Different training environments might produce different learning outcomes. The difference might be caused by the training effect. In fact, we used different tutors in phase 2 for students' training. Different tutors are likely to demonstrate the knowledge to the students in different ways. The training approach might be an important factor for producing students' situation awareness. This is because that a better understanding of the knowledge distributed through training can easily lead to a better of situation awareness. We may even posit that students might have very little trouble once they are well trained.

Previous studies have discussed many factors such as gender and age on the situation awareness of information technology use. Our research provides a preliminary understanding of situation awareness difference in information technology diffusion process.

Our study first extends the situation awareness theory in explaining information technology knowledge learning in different experimental environments. Unlike most past studies that use one phase to create a situation to identify situation awareness design, this study is designed with three environments to test learning effects and identifies the differences. The learning outcomes from students' situation awareness results show that the experimental learning effect might be affected by learning situations. This indicates that the situational factor need cause scholars' attention for experimental learning design.

Table 6: Potential Factors That Might Influence Situation Awareness Differences

Factors category	Is it the same between Group A and Group B?		
	Phase 1	Phase 2	Phase 3
Equipment version	Yes. Same version demonstration.	No. Group A used the new version while group B used the old version.	Yes. Same tools used.
Time used	Yes. Same time used.	No. Students in Group B spent more time on average than Group A.	Yes. Same time used.
Task requirement	Yes.	Yes.	Yes.
Environmental distribution	Yes. Same classroom.	No. Group A's field work was conducted on campus and group B's field work was conducted in another city.	Yes. Same lab.
Training and tutors	Yes. Same tutors and training method.	No. Different tutors and training process.	Yes. Same tutors.

Our study provides a better understanding of situation awareness on the use of information technology. Because our research design is based on students' learning context, this can contribute to information systems (IS) education literature. Although the purpose of the study is to find situation awareness differences on the use of cloud computing outcomes, students' learning process has also been investigated. The design can be used for students' learning in introductory level MIS courses in business schools.

The difference may be also caused by the information technology itself. In our study, the students in *Group A* located infrastructure facilities more easily. All the equipment used in this group is the latest. However, the tags used in *Group B* are the old versions. This might affect the reliability of equipment, and, in turn, influences the students' situation awareness of cloud computing use. Thus, the information technology with the best condition can help increase the users' situation awareness.

There are several limitations to this study. First, the generality of the results might be limited. As we just measured the situation awareness differences of cloud computing use to locate infrastructure facilities. The subjects are students in IT related class. Because of surrogate issue and the weakness of quasi-experimental design, the generality of the findings might also be affected. Second, we tested the students' situation awareness with very general questions. These questions were not tested from a pilot study. This may cause the validity bias in methodology. Last, except the version of equipment and field work in different places, we controlled as many factors in our design and discussed all the factors that caused the results. But other potential factors may still exist. For example, some studies suggest that individuals' experiences can influence their situation awareness (e.g., Endsley, 1995). However, it is hard to identify and measure the characteristics that are truly affecting the situation awareness.

Admittedly, the study could not identify all the factors that caused the situation awareness differences. However, it opens up new topics on the situational factors on information technology use in the future. The research design that was conducted could be replicated by controlling other situation factors. We encourage more studies to test the environmental factors in future empirical studies. We provide the following recommendations for future research. First, a lot of other advanced information technologies can be tested. Other situational factors can also be included, which will make a better generality of our research results. Second, in order to better measure the situation awareness on specific information technology use well, we call more studies to develop instruments that can measure and assess situation awareness. Third, besides the three phases design of situation awareness environments presented in this study, other situated research designs are also encouraged.

CONCLUSION

Grounded on the three level situation awareness theory, a conceptual framework with three phases design was proposed to explore the situation awareness outcomes of the use of cloud computing. Specifically, based on the proposed formwork, we executed the research design with two groups of students in three different learning environments (i.e., classroom learning, field work, and lab learning). Following that, the situation awareness differences from the students were discussed by analyzing the survey data. The different learning outcomes were identified by repeated measures ANOVA analysis. The results indicate that situation awareness on cloud computing use is significantly different when the experiment environment changes. The potential factors that might influence this change are discussed. The study findings extend the IT perception literature by taking account of situational factors.

REFERENCE

Ajzen, I. (1991). The Theory of Planned Behavior. *Organizational Behavior and Human Decision Processes, 50*(2), 179-211.

Armbrust, M., Fox, A., Griffith, R., Joseph, A. D., Katz, R., Konwinski, A., & Zaharia, M. (2010). A view of cloud computing. *Communications of the ACM, 53*(4), 50-58.

A Vouk, M. (2008). Cloud computing–issues, research and implementations. CIT. *Journal of Computing and Information Technology, 16*(4), 235-246.

Bandura, A. (1986). *Social foundations of thought and action: A social cognitive theory Englewood Cliffs*, NJ: Prentice Hall.

Bhattacherjee, A. (2012). Social science research: principles, methods, and practices.

Brynjolfsson, E., & Hitt, L. M. (2003). Computing productivity: Firm-level evidence. *Review of economics and statistics, 85*(4), 793-808.

Buyya, R., Yeo, C. S., Venugopal, S., Broberg, J., & Brandic, I. (2009). Cloud computing and emerging IT platforms: Vision, hype, and reality for delivering computing as the 5th utility. *Future Generation computer systems, 25*(6), 599-616.

Calheiros, R. N., Ranjan, R., Beloglazov, A., De Rose, C. A., & Buyya, R. (2011).

CloudSim: a toolkit for modeling and simulation of cloud computing environments and evaluation of resource provisioning algorithms. *Software: Practice and Experience, 41*(1), 23-50.

Catteddu, D. (2010). Cloud Computing: benefits, risks and recommendations for information security. In *Web Application Security* (pp. 17-17). Springer Berlin Heidelberg.

Chou, D. C. (2015). Cloud computing: A value creation model. *Computer Standards & Interfaces, 38*, 72-77.

Compeau, D. R., and Higgins, C. A. (1995a). Application of social cognitive theory to training for computer skills. *Information Systems Research, 6* (2), 118-143.

Compeau, D. R., and Higgins, C. A. (1995b). Computer self-efficacy: development of a measure and initial test. *MIS Quarterly, 19*(2), 189-211.

Dacin, M. T., Goodstein, J., & Scott, W. R. (2002). Institutional theory and institutional change: Introduction to the special research forum. *Academy of Management Journal, 45*(1), 45-56.

Davis, F. D. (1989). Perceived usefulness, perceived ease of use, and user acceptance of information technology. *MIS Quarterly, 13*(3), 319-340.

Endsley, M. R. (1988). Design and evaluation for situation awareness enhancement. In *Proceedings of the Human Factors and Ergonomics Society Annual Meeting* (Vol. 32, No. 2, pp. 97-101). Santa Monica, CA: Human Factors and Ergonomics Society.

Endsley, M. R. (1995). Towards a theory of situation awareness in dynamic systems. *Human Factors, 37*, 32–64.

Foster, I., Zhao, Y., Raicu, I., & Lu, S. (2008, November). Cloud computing and grid computing 360-degree compared. *In Grid Computing Environments Workshop, 2008. GCE'08* (pp. 1-10). IEEE.

Garrison, G., Kim, S., & Wakefield, R. L. (2012). Success factors for deploying cloud computing. *Communications of the ACM, 55*(9), 62-68.

Gefen, D., & Straub, D. W. (1997). Gender differences in the perception and use of e-mail: An extension to the technology acceptance model. *MIS Quarterly*, 389-400.

Grossman, R. L. (2009). The case for cloud computing. *IT professional, 11*(2), 23-27.

Howcroft, D., & Taylor, P. (2014). 'Plus ca change, plus la meme chose?'-researching and theorising the 'new' new technologies. *New Technology, Work and Employment, 29*(1), 1-8.

Marston, S., Li, Z., Bandyopadhyay, S., Zhang, J., & Ghalsasi, A. (2011). Cloud computing—the business perspective. *Decision Support Systems, 51*(1), 176-189.

Mell, P., & Grance, T. (2009). The NIST definition of cloud computing. *National Institute of Standards and Technology, 53*(6), 50.

Miller, M. (2008). *Cloud computing: Web-based applications that change the way you work and collaborate online*. Que publishing.

Ostermann, S., Iosup, A., Yigitbasi, N., Prodan, R., Fahringer, T., & Epema, D. (2010). A performance analysis of EC2 cloud computing services for scientific computing. In *Cloud computing* (pp. 115-131). Springer Berlin Heidelberg.

Onwuegbuzie, A. J., Slate, J. R., Leech, N. L., & Collins, K. M. (2009). Mixed data analysis: Advanced integration techniques. *International Journal of Multiple Research Approaches, 3*(1), 13-33.

Karaali, D., Gumussoy, C. A., & Calisir, F. (2011). Factors affecting the intention to use a web-based learning system among blue-collar workers in the automotive industry. *Computers in Human Behavior, 27*(1), 343-354.

Miller, M. (2008). Cloud computing: Web-based applications that change the way you work and collaborate online. Que publishing.

Roberts, R., Flin, R., & Cleland, J. (2015). Staying in the Zone Offshore Drillers' Situation Awareness. *Human Factors: The Journal of the Human Factors and Ergonomics Society, 57*(4), 573-590.

Rogers, E. M. (2003). *Diffusions of Innovations*. New York: Free Press.

Sætrevik, B., & Eid, J. (2014). The "Similarity Index" as an Indicator of Shared Mental Models and Situation Awareness in Field Studies. *Journal of Cognitive Engineering and Decision Making, 8*(2), 119-136.

Scott,W.R.,(2001), *Institutions and Organizations(2nd ed.)*,Thousand Oaks,CA: Sage.

Straub, E. T. (2009). Understanding technology adoption: Theory and future directions for informal learning. *Review of Educational Research, 79*(2), 625-649.

Sultan, N. (2010). Cloud computing for education: A new dawn?. *International Journal of Information Management, 30*(2), 109-116.

Swanson, E. Burton. *Information System Implementation*. Homewood, IL: Irwin, 1988.

T Ograph, B., & Morgens, Y. R. (2008). Cloud computing. Communications of the ACM, 51(7).

Venkatesh, V., Morris, M. G., Davis, G. B., & Davis, F. D. (2003). User acceptance of information technology: Toward a unified view. *MIS Quarterly, 27*(3), 425-478.

Venters, W., & Whitley, E. A. (2012). A critical review of cloud computing: researching desires and realities. *Journal of Information Technology, 27*(3), 179-197.

Voorsluys, William; Broberg, James; Buyya, Rajkumar (February 2011). "Introduction to Cloud Computing". In R. Buyya, J. Broberg, A.Goscinski. *Cloud Computing: Principles and Paradigms*. New York, USA: Wiley Press. pp. 1–44.

Zhang, Q., Cheng, L., & Boutaba, R. (2010). Cloud computing: state-of-the-art and research challenges. *Journal of internet services and applications, 1*(1), 7-18.

Zhou, C., Chen, H., & Luo, L. (2014). Students' perceptions of creativity in learning Information Technology (IT) in project groups. *Computers in Human Behavior, 41*, 454-463.

Zissis, D., & Lekkas, D. (2012). Addressing cloud computing security issues. *Future Generation computer systems, 28*(3), 583-592.

APPENDIX A: Questionnaire for Each Level of Situation Awareness

Please specify the extent to which you agree with the following statements:	**Strongly Disagree** ←				→ **Strongly Agree**
(1) Cloud computing is useful to utility workers.	1	2	3	4	5
(2) Cloud computing can boost workers' productivity.	1	2	3	4	5
(3) Cloud computing can increase the accuracy of workers' work deliverables.	1	2	3	4	5
(4) Cloud computing can reduce work complexity for workers.	1	2	3	4	5
(5) Cloud computing can make workers' work more effective.	1	2	3	4	5
(6) Cloud computing can help workers collaborate online without generating paper-based documents.	1	2	3	4	5
(7) Computing can make workers' job more flexible.	1	2	3	4	5
(8) Computing can make workers' job more reliable.	1	2	3	4	5

(1) If your job is to use handheld devices to detect RFID tags and record geographic data of the tags for a community, would you be happy to take advantage of could computing for your work? Please explain.

(2) Do you find any challenge(s) during this phase? Is any challenge related to the cloud infrastructure? Please specify.

DECISION SCIENCES INSTITUTE

Social Capital and Knowledge Sharing in Organization: An Initial Meta-analysis

Quang-An Ha
National Cheng Kung University
Email: haquangan@gmail.com

Jeng-Chung Victor Chen
National Cheng Kung University
Email: victor@mail.ncku.edu.tw

ABSTRACT

While organizations recognize the important role of knowledge sharing, the number of studies investigate different factors that foster this behavior also increases. This meta-analysis tries to analyze the relationships between some most popular facets of social capital (trust, social interaction, shared vision) and knowledge sharing under the individual level. The research has once again confirmed the important role of Knowledge sharing to the Performance of the organization. Co-citation analysis of the Social Capital and Knowledge Sharing literatures is carried out to give the reader the picture of the most important studies that had high impacts on this topic.

KEYWORDS: Knowledge Sharing, Social Capital, Meta-analysis, Co-citation Analysis

INTRODUCTION

Knowledge sharing is as an activity through which knowledge is exchanged among people, friends, or members of a family, a community or an organization. To foster those natures of knowledge sharing require an environment that gives opportunities for all process of knowledge. The behavior of sharing knowledge is not only motivated by the individuals but also from the interpersonal relationship among individuals. This phenomenon can be clarified by applying the Social Capital Theory and social capital is also the motivation of behavior to share knowledge in community.

Previous studies see Bourdieu's definition of social capital could be decomposable into two elements: (1) the social relationship that allows individuals to claim access to resources possessed by their associates and (2) the amount and quality of those resources. Organizations have unique advantages for creating knowledge over more open other settings because organizations provide an institutional environment to the develop this capital (Nahapiet & Ghoshal, 1998).

Linking knowledge sharing to the dimension of social capital, previous studies (Nahapiet & Ghoshal, 1998; Wasko & Faraj, 2005) mentioned that the combination and exchange of knowledge is facilitated when properties of structural capital, cognitive capital and relational capital exist. Chiu, Hsu and Wang (2006) integrated the Social Cognitive Theory and the Social Capital Theory to construct a model for investigating the motivations of online community member. This study showed out some facets of social capital such as social interaction ties, trust, identification, shared vision and shared language had influences individuals' knowledge sharing in virtual communities. In addition to Chiu, Hsu and Wang (2006), various studies also used some similar dimensions of social capital (Chang & Chuang, 2011; Nahapiet & Ghoshal, 1998; Wasko & Faraj, 2005) that have the significant impacts on knowledge sharing. Especially, Nahapiet and Ghoshal have a first movement in examining of the role of social capital in the creation of intellectual capital; suggest that social capital should be considered in terms of three clusters: structural, relational, and cognitive. Each of these forms of social capital constitutes an aspect of the social structure and facilitates the combination and exchange of knowledge between individuals within that structure.

Although the relationship between social capital and knowledge sharing have been mentioned separately in previous studies, there is no previous research collecting and clarifying the impact of popular dimensions of social capital on knowledge sharing, which may benefit for researchers and practitioner to have a holistic view of these relationship.

LITERATURE REVIEW

2.1 Knowledge Sharing.

Knowledge sharing simply defined as an activity through which knowledge (i.e. information, skills, or expertise) is exchanged among people, friends, or members of a family, a community. Nonaka & Takeushi (1995) also showed that knowledge sharing occurred through 3 of 4 processes: Socialization – the process of sharing tacit knowledge through shared experiences; Externalization – the process of articulating tacit knowledge into explicit knowledge and Combination – the process of converting explicit knowledge into more complicated and systematic sets of explicit knowledge. Only in Internalization process where explicit knowledge is embodied into tacit knowledge, knowledge sharing doesn't occur.

Knowledge sharing involves a process of communication whereby two or more parties are involved in the transfer of knowledge. Hence, knowledge sharing is also known as a process of communication between two or more participants involving the provision and acquisition of knowledge (Usoro, Sharratt, Tsui, & Shekhar, 2007). Knowledge sharing also refers to the provision of task information and know-how to help others and to collaborate with others to solve problems, develop new ideas, or implement policies or procedures (Cummings, 2004).

2.2 Social Capital

2.2.1 Definition of Social Capital.

Social capital is a broad concept, which refers to the value of connections within and between social networks. In the first systematic analysis of social capital, Bourdieu (1986) defined social capital as the aggregate of the actual or potential resources which are linked to possession of a durable network. Nahapiet and Ghoshal (1998) had expanded this concept as the sum of the assets or resources embedded in the networks of relationships between individuals, communities, networks, or societies. Therefore, social capital is embedded in the relationships between individuals and their connections with their communities (Chang & Chuang, 2011).

So why does social capital work? The answer is simple that "investment in social relations with expected returns", "individuals engage in interactions and networking in order to produce profits" (Lin, 1999, p. 30). Compare to other kind of capital which based on assets, social capital resides in the fabric of relationships between individuals and in individuals' connections with their communities (Putnam, 1995). By the relationship "the embedded resources in social networks will enhance the outcomes of actions" (Lin, p. 31).

Social capital not only exists in the face-to-face environment but also in the virtual setting. Using concept "cyber-networks", Lin (1999) in his research proposed about the emergence of virtual community as a major source of social capital. Many researches also study about the relationship between social capital and knowledge sharing in virtual community (Chiu et al., 2006; Wasko & Faraj, 2005).

2.2.2 Structural Dimension: Social Interaction.

The structural dimension of social capital refers to the ability of individuals in the organization to make connections to others. These connections can help to reduce the amount of time and other efforts to obtain information from inner of organization. Structural dimension focuses on the nature and strength of relationships (Méndez-Durón & García, 2009), determine whether there are social interaction between actors, what the configurations of these interactions are and how network of social interaction could create opportunities for social capital transactions (Adler & Kwon, 2002).

2.2.3 Relational Dimension: Trust and Identification.

Different from structural dimension concerns the properties of the social system and of the network of relations as a whole, relational dimension deals with the nature of the connections between individuals in an organization. The key facets of this dimension are trust, norms, obligations, expectations and identification.

Trust.

Trust can be viewed as "the extent to which a person is confident in, and willing to act on the basis of, the words, actions, and decisions of another" (McAllister, 1995, p. 25) because the value of one member's contributions depends in part on the efforts, contributions, emotional and psychological consequences of others (Stewart & Gosain, 2006). Previous studies on trust suggest that trust is a multidimensional construct that has both cognitive and affective elements (McAllister; Stewart & Gosain, 2006).

Identification.

Identification is the process whereby "individuals see themselves as one with another person or group of people" (Nahapiet & Ghoshal, 1998). Identification is a condition where the interests of individuals merge with the interests of the organization, resulting in the creation of an identity based on those interests (Kankanhalli, Tan, & Wei, 2005). That process also renders the self depersonalized (Bagozzi & Dholakia, 2002). In virtual communities, identification can also refer to an individual's sense of belonging and positive feeling toward that community (Chiu et al., 2006).

2.2.4 Cognitive Dimension: Shared Vision.

Cognitive dimension of social capital concerns the extent to which people in a social network share a common perspective. Those resources that make possible shared interpretations and meanings within virtual community. In this dimension of social capital, share vision is one of the most important variables. Peter Senge (1990) defined shared vision as "... a force in people's hearts, a force of impressive power....At its simplest level, a shared vision is the answer to the question, "What do we want to create?". In organizational setting, shared vision "embodies the collective goals and aspirations of the members of an organization" (Tsai & Ghoshal, 1998, p. 476). Shared vision can be the motivation for all organization to archive the common goal.

2.3. The influence of some facets of Social Capital on Knowledge Sharing

2.3.1. The influence of Social Capital on Knowledge Sharing

The Influence of Social Interaction on Knowledge Sharing.

Social interaction or the connections through contributors who bring their knowledge to the project will improve project success, and that connection through all members, who transfer their knowledge toward their projects also enhance project success (Méndez-Durón & García, 2009). Nahapiet and Ghoshal (1998) showed that network ties influence both access to parties for combining and exchanging knowledge and anticipation of value through such exchange. In virtual community, social interaction ties among members of allow a cost-effective way of accessing a wider range of knowledge sources (Chiu et al., 2006).

- ***H1: Social interaction have a positive impact on Knowledge Sharing***

The Influence of Trust on Knowledge Sharing.

Trust influences the process of knowledge sharing by increasing openness in knowledge transfer, facilitating joint problems solving (Li, 2005). Trust can help reduce relationship risks and when people trust each other, they become more willing to share their resources without worrying that they will be taken advantage of by the other party (Tsai & Ghoshal, 1998). When trust is strong, the effort required for knowledge sharing may not be salient to knowledge contributors because they believe that knowledge shared is not likely to be misused by re-users (Davenport & Prusak, 1998). Trust has been recognized as an important antecedent of knowledge sharing in virtual communities of practice (Usoro et al., 2007).

- **H2: Trust have a positive impact on Knowledge Sharing**

The Influence of Norm on Knowledge Sharing.

Norms are rules or laws to which people must conform or consult when they act (Gregory & Ricky, 2001) and represent the expectations people have of themselves and others.

Rice & Aydin (1991) found that employee reactions to new technology were similar to those of supervisors and employees with whom they frequently communicated. TDifferent management models have mediated the levels and intentions behind knowledge sharing (Lam, 1997). Research by Currie & Suhomlinova's (2006) research addressed institutional regulations and cultural recognition, arguing that both entities hamper the ease withwhich knowledge is shared. The degree to which members are willing to share is proportional to the degree to which organizations expect them to share (Cabrera & Cabrera, 2005).

- ***H3: Trust have a positive impact on Knowledge Sharing***

The Influence of Shared Visions on Knowledge Sharing.

Cognitive dimension of social capital describes how people in social network could share a common perspective or understanding that aspire of the members of an organization to pursuit the collective goal. Sharing the knowledge among people of organization could help them to promote and perform that goal better. Shared vision enhances relative absorptive capacity in knowledge assimilation process and allows firms to engage more into knowledge acquisition (Li, 2005).

H4: Shared Vision have a positive impact on Knowledge Sharing

The Influence of Knowledge Sharing on Performance.

Previous studies showed the empirical evidence proved that knowledge sharing has a positive impact on project performance (Marques, Cardoso, & Zappalá, 2008; McNeish & Mann, 2010; Nelson & Cooprider, 1996).

Knowledge sharing can improve team processes and an improvement in business decision, thus, lead to success and improve performance (McNeish & Mann).

Knowledge sharing is one of the most important factors affecting organizational agility and performance.

H5: Knowledge Sharing have a positive impact on Performance

2.3.2. Conceptual Model

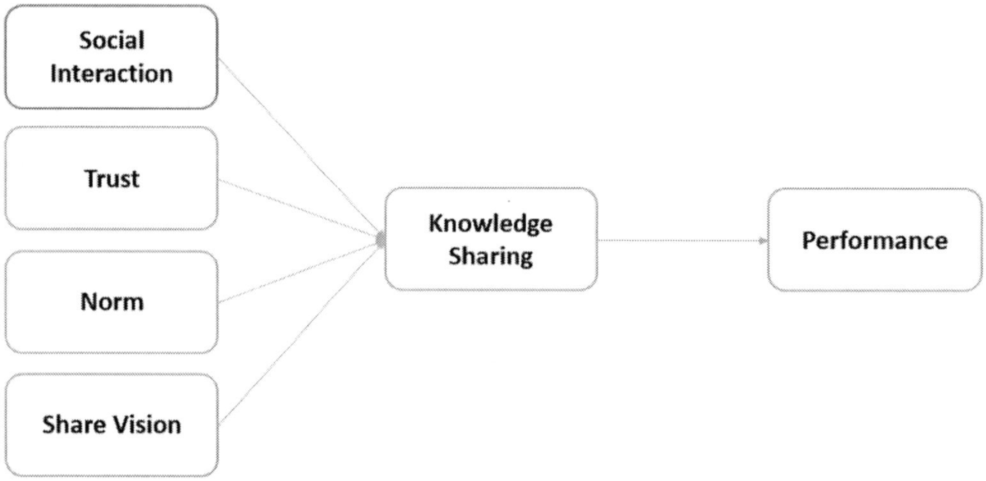

RESEARCH DESIGN AND METHODOLOGY

This study use meta-analysis on published research findings. The samples for this research are empirical studies in all academic journal that we could collect.
We used multiple keywords to search relevant papers such as "knowledge sharing", "social capital", "trust", "social interaction", "knowledge management" from following databases: ScienceDirect Online (SDOL), Business Source Complete [EBSCOhost].
A total of 118 papers were found in the initial search and all studies must be empirical studies which could provide quantitative data. Especially, most of them have the report of correlation between dependents (trust, social interactions, norm, shared visions) and knowledge sharing. The screening resulted in 52 usable relationships. As shown in the tables in the next part, the number of studies that can be used to test our hypotheses varies from 3 to 20.
Methods commonly used in meta-analysis include Hunter and Schmidt (Hunter & Schmidt, 1990), Peterson and Brown (2005) and Borenstein, Hedges, Higgins, and Rothstein (2009).
In this study, we use the Pearson correlation r as the fundamental basis of meta-analysis, and combined Fish Z scores for each construct to test the significance of our hypothesis.
In later part, we used VOSreviewer and Cinetexplorer (van Eck & Waltman, 2014) to draw the images of research in Knowledge Sharing and Social Capital.

RESULTS

4.1. Social interaction and Knowledge Sharing

The relationship between Social interaction of Social capital and Knowledge Sharing is confirmed by 16 studies with the correlations vary from -0.020 to 0.767.

Hypothesis	Number of studies	Model	Correlation	Lower limit	Upper limit	Z value	P value
H1: SI -> KS	16	Fixed	0.492	0.473	0.512	41.119	0.000
		Random	0.457	0.364	0.541	8.647	0.000

Heterogeneity				Tau-squared			
Q	Df	P	I^2	Tau^2	Std	Var	Tau
247.172	15	0.000	93.931	0.047	0.025	0.001	0.218

In the test of Heterogeneity of this analysis, Q-value is significant (247.172^{***}) suggests that the true effect varies from study to study and 93.4% of the relationship is explained by true effect. According to Borenstein et al. (2009), the True Effect Size (fixed) is bigger than 0.5, which means Social Interaction has high effects on Knowledge Sharing. Thus, H1 is supported.

4.2. Trust and Knowledge Sharing

Hypothesis	Number of studies	Model	Correlation	Lower limit	Upper limit	Z value	P value
H2: Trust -> KS	20	Fixed	0.512	0.494	0.530	44.885	0.000
		Random	0.491	0.439	0.540	15.802	0.000

Hypothesis	Number of studies	Heterogeneity				Tau-squared			
		Q	Df	P	I^2	Tau^2	Std	Var	Tau
H2: Trust -> KS	20	117.932	19	0.000	83.889	0.018	0.039	0.000	0.135

The relationship between Trust of Social capital and Knowledge Sharing is confirmed by 20 studies with the correlations vary from 0.139 to 0.670.
In the test of Heterogeneity of this analysis, Q-value is significant (117.932^{***}) suggests that the true effect varies from study to study and 83.9% of the relationship is explained by true effect. According to Borenstein et al. (2009), the True Effect Size (fixed) is bigger than 0.5, which means Trust has high effects on Knowledge Sharing. So we could see that H2 is supported.

4.3. Norm and Knowledge Sharing

The relationship between Norm of Social capital and Knowledge Sharing is confirmed by 03 studies with the correlations vary from 0.459 to 0.734.
In the test of Heterogeneity of this analysis, Q-value is significant (29.971^{***}) suggests that the true effect varies from study to study and 93.327% of the relationship is explained by true effect. Thus, H3 is supported.

Hypothesis	Number of studies	Model	Correlation	Lower limit	Upper limit	Z value	P value
H3: Norm -> KS	03	Fixed	0.562	0.512	0.608	17.754	0.000
		Random	0.571	0.359	0.727	4.648	0.000

Hypothesis	Number of studies	Heterogeneity				Tau-squared			
		Q	Df	P	I^2	Tau^2	Std	Var	Tau
H3: Norm -> KS	03	29.971	2	0.000	93.327	0.055	0.059	0.003	0.234

4.4. Shared Visions and Knowledge Sharing

The relationship between Shared Visions of Social capital and Knowledge Sharing is confirmed by 8 studies with the correlations vary from 0.310 to 0.604.
In the test of Heterogeneity of this analysis, Q-value is significant (54.631^{***}) suggests that the true effect varies from study to study and 87.2% of the relationship is explained by true effect. Therefore, the H4 is supported.

Hypothesis	Number	Model	Correlation	Lower	Upper	Z value	P value

<table>
<tr><th></th><th>of studies</th><th colspan="2"></th><th colspan="2">limit</th><th colspan="2">limit</th><th colspan="2"></th><th></th></tr>
<tr><td rowspan="4">H4: Shared Vision -> KS</td><td rowspan="4">08</td><td>Fixed</td><td colspan="2">0.463</td><td colspan="2">0.431</td><td colspan="2">0.494</td><td>24.680</td><td>0.000</td></tr>
<tr><td>Random</td><td colspan="2">0.484</td><td colspan="2">0.391</td><td colspan="2">0.567</td><td>9.003</td><td>0.000</td></tr>
<tr><td colspan="4">Heterogeneity</td><td colspan="5">Tau-squared</td></tr>
<tr><td>Q</td><td>Df</td><td>P</td><td>I²</td><td>Tau²</td><td>Std</td><td>Var</td><td colspan="2">Tau</td></tr>
<tr><td></td><td></td><td>54.631</td><td>7</td><td>0.000</td><td>87.187</td><td>0.023</td><td>0.016</td><td>0.000</td><td colspan="2">0.153</td></tr>
</table>

4.5. Knowledge Sharing and Team Performance

The relationship between Shared Visions of Social capital and Knowledge Sharing is confirmed by 5 studies with the correlations vary from 0.310 to 0.604.
In the test of Heterogeneity of this analysis, Q-value is significant (90.468^{***}) suggests that the true effect varies from study to study and 95.56% of the relationship is explained by true effect.

<table>
<tr><th>Hypothesis</th><th>Number of studies</th><th>Model</th><th colspan="2">Correlation</th><th colspan="2">Lower limit</th><th colspan="2">Upper limit</th><th>Z value</th><th>P value</th></tr>
<tr><td rowspan="4">H5: KS -> Performance</td><td rowspan="4">05</td><td>Fixed</td><td colspan="2">0.454</td><td colspan="2">0.418</td><td colspan="2">0.488</td><td>21.629</td><td>0.000</td></tr>
<tr><td>Random</td><td colspan="2">0.529</td><td colspan="2">0.354</td><td colspan="2">0.668</td><td>5.272</td><td>0.000</td></tr>
<tr><td colspan="4">Heterogeneity</td><td colspan="5">Tau-squared</td></tr>
<tr><td>Q</td><td>Df</td><td>P</td><td>I²</td><td>Tau²</td><td>Std</td><td>Var</td><td colspan="2">Tau</td></tr>
<tr><td></td><td></td><td>90.468</td><td>4</td><td>0.000</td><td>95.579</td><td>0.059</td><td>0.047</td><td>0.002</td><td colspan="2">0.243</td></tr>
</table>

4.6. Co-citation Analysis

4.6.1. Co-citation Analysis of Knowledge Sharing and Social Capital

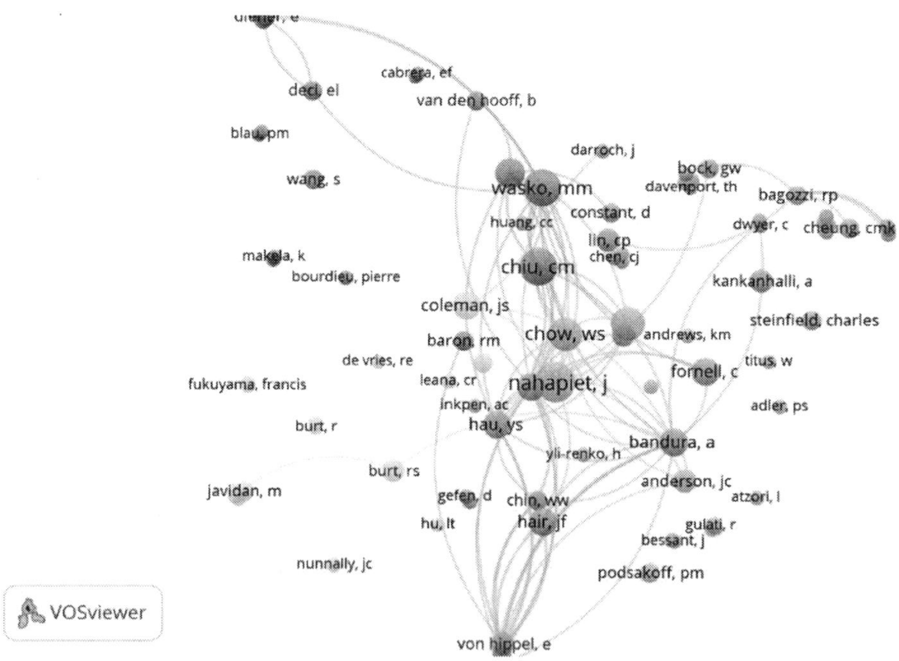

Using the data from 118 studies that mentioned about Social Capital and Knowledge Sharing, we try to figure out the network of co-citation. Each of dot appeared in the figure has at least 3 cocitation, and the cite of dot demonstrate how large of the co-citation of each author.

4.6.2. Knowledge Sharing and Social Capital Term Cluster

Because the number of research related to Knowledge Sharing and Social Capital is limited, we use only the key word “Knowledge Sharing” to find all papers talking about this topic. The terms that related to Knowledge Sharing are extracted from the Abstract of 1034 paper in the same topic after deleting the non-related keywords.

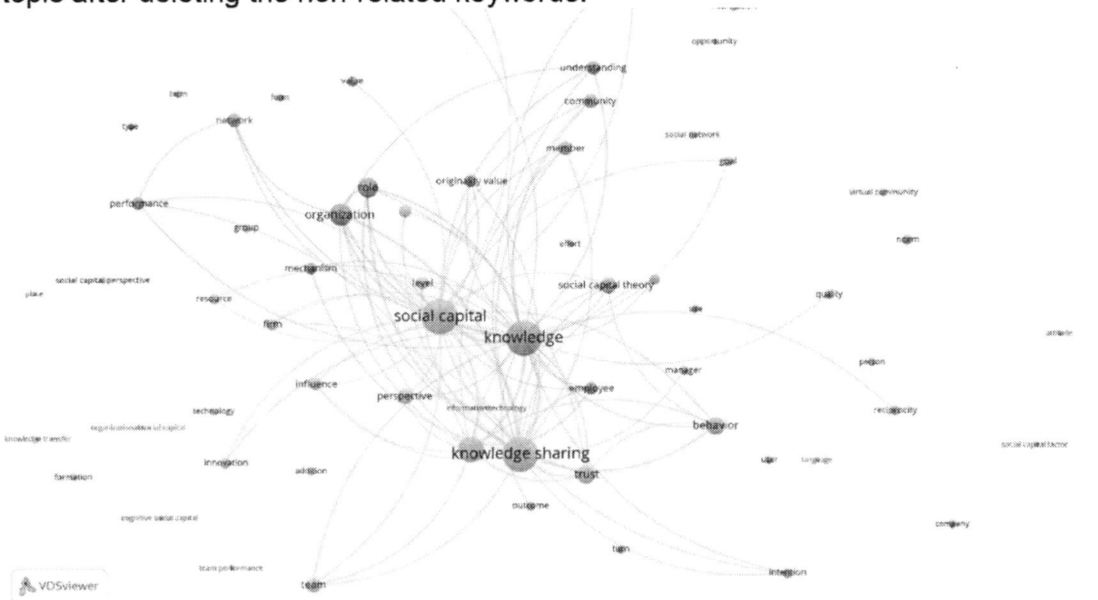

From the result, we could see that these term are classified into 4 clusters that related to 4 major subfields in Knowledge Sharing. We also run the software again to see the trend of keywords. In this analysis, the “originality value” seems to be the recent trend.

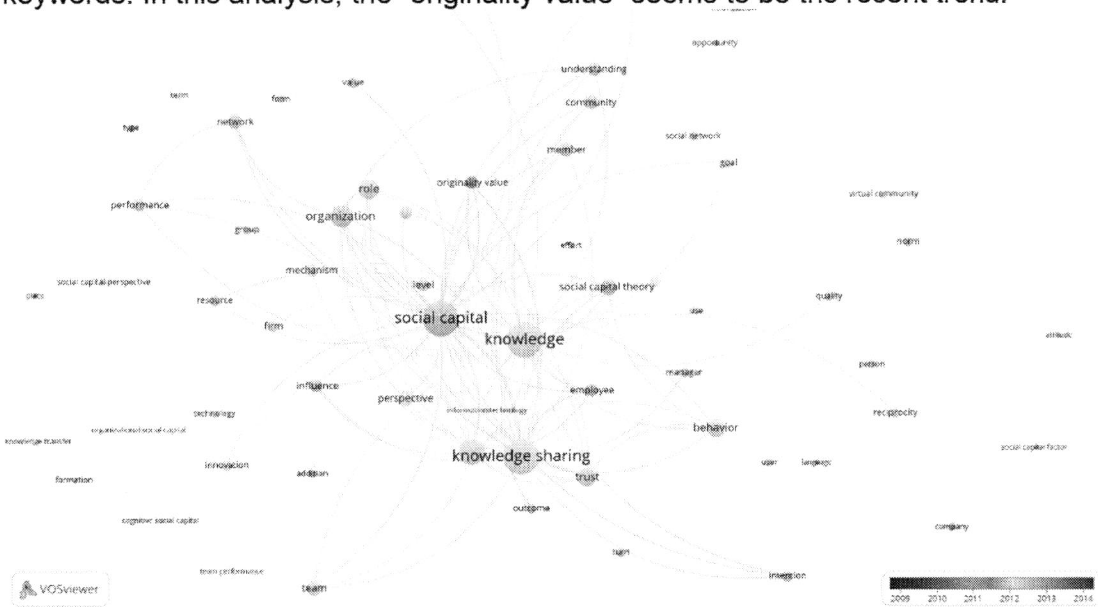

CONCLUSION

The objective of this study is to systematize the literature explaining the relationship between Social Capital and Knowledge Sharing and between Knowledge Sharing and Performance. After reviewing 52 usable relationships, the results of this meta-analysis showed the impacts of Social interactions, Trust, Norm and Shared Vision on Knowledge Sharing in organization. The result of this study also confirm that maintaining the Knowledge sharing behaviors could lead to the better performance of organizations. Thus, this research emphasized the importance of Social Capital in organization and once again urges the leaders of organizations to pay more attention to facets of Social capital to maintain Knowledge sharing behaviors in their organizations.
Our research also faced some limitations. First, the data is taken from variety of studies of different types of organizations that may. Second, the number of available studies to investigate H3 and H5 is still limited, we suggest future research should continue to find more studies from other databases and from newest researches to update this meta-analysis research.

REFERENCES

Adler, P. S., & Kwon, S.-W. (2002). Social capital: Prospects for a new concept. *The Academy of Management Review, 27*(1), 17-40.

Bagozzi, R. P., & Dholakia, U. M. (2002). Intentional social action in virtual communities. *Journal of Interactive Marketing, 16*(2), 2-21.

Borenstein, M., Hedges, L. V., Higgins, J. P. T., & Rothstein, H. (2009). *Introduction to Meta-Analysis*. Chichester: Wiley.

Bourdieu, P. (1986). The forms of capital *Handbook of Theory and Research for the Sociology of Education* (pp. 241-258).

Chang, H. H., & Chuang, S.-S. (2011). Social capital and individual motivations on knowledge sharing: Participant involvement as a moderator. *Information & Management, 48*(1), 9-18-18.

Chiu, C.-M., Hsu, M.-H., & Wang, E. T. G. (2006). Understanding knowledge sharing in virtual communities: An integration of social capital and social cognitive theories. *Decision Support Systems, 42*(3), 1872-1888-1888.

Cummings, J. N. (2004). Work Groups, Structural Diversity, and Knowledge Sharing in a Global Organization. *Management Science, 50*(3), 352-364-364.

Davenport, T. H., & Prusak, L. (1998). *Working knowledge: How organizations manage what they know.* Boston: Harvard Business School Press.

Hunter, J. E., & Schmidt, F. L. (1990). *Methods of Meta-analysis: Correcting Error and Bias in ResearchFindings.*: SAGE Publications.

Kankanhalli, A., Tan, B. C. Y., & Wei, K.-k. (2005). Contributing knowledge to electronic knowledge repositories: An empirical investigation *MIS Quarterly, 29*, 30.

Li, L. (2005). The effects of trust and shared vision on inward knowledge transfer in subsidiaries' intra- and inter-organizational relationships. *International Business Review, 14*(1), 77-95.

Lin, N. (1999). Building a network theory of social capital. *Connections, 22*(1), 28-51.

McAllister, D. J. (1995). Affect- and cognition-based trust as foundations for interpersonal cooperation in organizations. *The Academy of Management Journal, 38*(1), 24-59.

Méndez-Durón, R., & García, C. (2009). Returns from social capital in open source software networks. *Journal of Evolutionary Economics, 19*(2), 277-295.

Nahapiet, J., & Ghoshal, S. (1998). Social capital, intellectual capital, and the organizational advantage. *The Academy of Management Review, 23*(2), 242-266.
Nonaka, & Takeushi. (1995). The knowledge-creating company. *New York.*
Peterson, R. A., & Brown, S. P. (2005). On the Use of Beta Coefficients in Meta-Analysis. *Journal of Applied Psychology, 90*(1), 175-181.
Putnam, R. (1995). Tuning in, tuning out: The strange disappearance of social capital in America. *PS: Political Science and Politics, 28*(4), 664-683.
Senge, P. (1990). *The fifth discipline: The art and practice of the learning organization* (1st ed.): Doubleday/Currency.
Stewart, K. J., & Gosain, S. (2006). The impact of ideology on effectiveness in open source software development teams. *MIS Quarterly, 30*(2), 291.
Tsai, W., & Ghoshal, S. (1998). Social capital and value creation: The role of intrafirm networks. *The Academy of Management Journal, 41*(4), 464-476.
Usoro, A., Sharratt, M. W., Tsui, E., & Shekhar, S. (2007). Trust as an antecedent to knowledge sharing in virtual communities of practice. *Knowledge Management Research & Practice, 5*(3), 199-212.
van Eck, N. J., & Waltman, L. (2014). Visualizing Bibliometric Networks. In Y. Ding, R. Rousseau, & D. Wolfram (Eds.), *Measuring Scholarly Impact: Methods and Practice* (pp. 285-320). Cham: Springer International Publishing.
Wasko, M. M., & Faraj, S. (2005). Why should I share? Examining social capital and knowledge contribution in electronic networks of practice. *MIS Quarterly, 29*(1), 35-57.

DECISION SCIENCES INSTITUTE

Status of Green Supply Chain Management Adoption in Midwest Manufacturing: an Empirical Study

Atul Agarwal
University of Illinois Springfield
Email: aagar3@uis.edu

Francois Giraud-Carrier
University of Illinois Springfield
Email:fgira2@uis.edu

Lakshmi Shilpa Penumatsa
University of Illinois Springfield
Email:lpenu2@uis.edu

ABSTRACT

Companies today are facing increasing regulatory, community, and competitive pressures to consider environmental issues in their quest to pursue profits. They have started looking at Green Supply Chain Management (GSCM) as the new paradigm to reduce the environmental impact of their activities and to produce more environmentally sustainable products and services. The purpose of this study is to understand the extent to which GSCM practices have been implemented in Midwestern manufacturing firms, the driving factors for the implementation and the perceived benefits of GSCM.

KEYWORDS: Green supply chain management, Environmental sustainability, Midwest manufacturing, GSCM adoption

INTRODUCTION

Consumers and regulators are becoming increasingly aware of the impact of industrial activities on the natural environment and the ecosystems that support life. To address pressing environmental concerns, manufacturing and logistics firms are turning to more environmentally friendly supply chain management processes, a practice referred to earlier as GSCM. According to Srivastava (2007), GSCM is defined as "integrating environmental thinking into supply-chain management, including product design, material sourcing and selection, manufacturing processes, delivery of the final product to the consumers as well as end-of-life management of the product after its useful life."

GSCM is an umbrella term for various supply chain management practices, both, within and between firms. Collaboration with external partners is a key supply chain management process. External collaboration can be directed upstream toward suppliers or downstream toward customers. GSCM encourages companies to work with suppliers and customers to address environmental concerns. This approach specially focuses on inter-organizational interactions, where supply chain members share common goals, plan together and collaborate to reduce environmental impacts.

Regarding practices internal to the manufacturer, Srivastava (2007) organizes GSCM practices into four broad categories: (i) Eco-design; (ii) Green manufacturing; (iii) Reverse logistics and network design; and (iv) Waste management. In addition to these four categories, we view environmental management as a key, and often overlooked, dimension of GSCM. We briefly review each of these five categories of practices.

Eco-design

Because much of the environmental impact of a product is determined at the design stage, eco-design consists of designing products and services in such a way as to minimize their environmental footprint over the entire product lifecycle, i.e., from raw materials to production to consumption to disposal at the end of life.

Green Manufacturing

This category includes (i) green purchasing, (ii) reducing material and energy consumption during production, and (iii) recycling and remanufacturing. Green purchasing is the practice of purchasing a product that has a lesser or reduced negative effect or increased positive effect on human health and the environment, when compared with competing products that serve the same purpose (NASPO Green Purchasing 2016). A good practice would be to purchase materials that are either recyclable or reusable, or have already been recycled (Sarkis 2003). Green purchasing affects various dimensions of GSCM, such as, materials used in product design, product design process, supplier process improvement, supplier evaluation and inbound logistic processes (Zhu, Sarkis and Lai 2008). Recycling and remanufacturing allow firms to recover some value from returned or end-of-life products that would otherwise be thrown away.

Reverse Logistics and Network Design

Generally, manufacturing a new product will generate more carbon emissions than reusing an existing asset while recycling can help reduce landfills. In order to recycle or remanufacture products, manufacturers would have to bring their products back to a manufacturing facility which can be achieved through reverse logistics. Reverse logistics can be defined as "the process of planning, implementing, and controlling the efficient, cost effective flow of raw materials, in-process inventory, finished goods and related information from the point of consumption to the point of origin for the purpose of recapturing value or proper disposal" (Rogers and Tibben-Lembke 1998). The network design of a reverse logistics network should enable the transfer of products from a former user to the manufacturer and back to the market again.

Waste Management

A good waste management system should be able to account for all forms of wastes generated across the supply chain. The system should be able to deal with waste minimization, reusing and recycling unavoidable waste, and providing ways to safely dispose of unusable waste and residues. Installing pollution control and prevention technologies can help cut down pollution, which is a wasteful by-product of production. In many cases, manufacturers are required to do so by law. Investing in end-of-pipe pollution control technologies can aid in treating the emissions and waste produced at various stages in the supply chain.

Environmental Management

Environmental Management Systems are strategic management approaches that define how an organization will address its impacts on the natural environment (Darnall et. al, 2008). It is a management system that is implemented from within the organization. According to Lamprecht 1997 Environmental Management Systems consist of an environmental policy, as well as a set of evaluation processes that require the organization to assess its environmental impacts, establish goals, design and implement processes for environmental control, monitor goal attainment, and undergo management review. Popular methodologies include ISO 14000 and Total Quality Environmental Management which reach outside the firm to include both suppliers and customers.

The Midwest region has a long tradition of manufacturing and accounts for 30% of U.S. manufacturing (Midwestern Governors Association 2010). For example, more than 60% of all automobiles and 40% of machinery and primary metals manufactured in the U.S. are built in the Midwest (Midwestern Governors Association 2010). There is a dearth of empirical studies in literature which have examined the degree to which U.S. manufacturers have implemented various GSCM practices and their impact on company performance. The few studies that exist are based on very small sample size and narrowly focused on a particular industry group such as electronics or semi-conductor. In this paper, our purpose is to survey Midwestern manufacturing firms about their level of adoption of GSCM. We survey manufacturing companies in the Midwest to answer the following questions:

1. To what extent do Midwestern manufacturing companies use GSCM practices?
2. What drives the use of GSCM practices by the Midwest manufacturing companies?
3. What are the financial, operational and environmental benefits of GSCM as perceived by the Midwest manufacturing companies?

LITERATURE REVIEW

The first objective of our study is to understand the extent of GSCM adoption by manufacturers in the Midwestern United States. To the best of our knowledge, this research is the first to survey GSCM adoption by U.S. manufacturers especially in the Midwest region, the hot bed of traditional manufacturing in U.S. Studies in other regions and contexts include among others: Zhu, Sarkis and Geng (2005) in China; Holt and Ghobadian (2009) in UK; Zhu et al (2010) in Japan; Zailani et al (2012) in Malaysia; Mitra, and Datta (2014) in India; Böttcher and Müller (2015) in Germany; rekova et al (2014) in Netherlands; de Sousa Jabbour et al (2011) in Brazil; Wu, Ding and Chen (2012) in Taiwan; Lin and Ho (2011) in China; and Large and Thomsen (2011) in Germany.

Our second goal is to understand what motivates or hinders firms to adopt GSCM. Consistent with Corbett and Klassen (2006), we propose that firms adopt GSCM in response to two main forces: (i) Economic forces and (ii) Social forces. We begin our discussion of the literature by considering economic forces.

Economic forces tap into managers' sensitivity to financial rewards and punishments. Naturally, if GSCM practices are good for the business, manufacturers are likely to adopt them, and there are many instances where it is the case. Investment recovery is a good example. It allows the manufacturer to recover through recycling or remanufacturing some value from end-of-life products that would have otherwise been sent to landfills. Network optimization, a GSCM practice falling in the reverse logistics and network design category, is another example. Simchi-Levi (2010) shows that optimization of the supply chain network can reduce transportation costs while lowering the firm's carbon emissions. Redesigning the production process to improve material use can generate large cost savings. GM saved $12 million by implementing reusable containers with its suppliers (McDaniel and Fiksel 2000). Lastly, Porter and van der Linde (1996) discuss several instances in which efforts to reduce pollution have forced the firms to find new ways to produce. Interestingly, the innovations they discuss have generated benefits that more than offset the costs of reducing pollution.

In addition to direct financial gains, GSCM practices can also benefit the firm by improving brand reputation and market value, both of which are important outcomes for managers. In a global survey of 378 senior executives, KPMG found that 41% of respondents cited the desire to enhance brand reputation as a key reason for their involvement in sustainable practices (KPMG 2011). Furthermore, Klassen and McLaughlin (1996) found that financial markets reward firms for environmental excellence and penalize them for environmental mismanagement. Their study illustrates that receiving environmental performance awards was positively associated with financial market valuation while environmental crises negatively impacted market valuation.

In the literature, the relationship between environmental and firm performance has been framed in terms of the resource-based view (RBV) theory. According to RBV, firms that hold valuable and rare resources which are difficult to imitate or for which there is no substitute in the market will enjoy a sustained competitive advantage. Firms rely on natural resources for their operation and survival. Using arguments grounded in RBV theory, Hart (1995) and Hart and Dowell (2010) assert that firms which excel at managing natural resources will outperform competitors. Thus, managers should develop strategies to acquire such capabilities.

Next we turn to social forces and the related framework of institutional theory. Institutional theory describes an "inexorable push toward homogenization" among organizations (DiMaggio and Powell 1983, p. 148), a statement based on the observation that, in stable industries, organizational forms are remarkably similar. Institutional theory advocates that organizations tend to align (or become isomorphic) with their environment. According to DiMaggio and Powell (1983) this happens via the interplay of three mechanisms: coercive, mimetic and normative isomorphism.

Coercive isomorphism denotes the formal and informal pressures exerted on a firm to conform with expectations stemming from the cultural, political and legal environment, for example, the adoption of pollution control equipment in response to government mandates. In the environmental arena, regulation may often be the only way to force firms to curb their pollution (Sterner 2003). Participation in certain markets (e.g., the financial markets) comes with reporting and other stringent requirements. Furthermore, local communities, sometimes with the help of non-government organizations, lobby to keep polluting industries away from them or seek redress from polluters in the aftermath of environmental disasters. Such pressures can be quite immense. For example, settlement of the Deepwater Horizon oil spill in 2010 cost BP $18.7 billion (U.S. Department of Commerce 2015). Henriques and Sardosky (1996) found that a firm's drafting of an environmental plan is positively associated with neighborhood and community pressures. Informal pressures also arise from employees whose morale is positively impacted by the firm's good reputation and practices (Chinander 2001).

Mimetic isomorphism, the second mechanism of homogenization, occurs in response to uncertainty. When managers are unsure about what to do because of technological uncertainty or goal ambiguity, they tend to imitate successful companies. Such a mechanism may be at play in US where companies are investing to reduce their greenhouse gas emissions in spite of considerable uncertainty regarding EPA's ability to implement binding climate change regulations.

Lastly, normative isomorphism as the third mechanism is an outcome of professionalization. It, is the process by which managers in an industry organize themselves to define the conditions and work methods in their industry. The development of industry-sponsored codes of practices, the emergence of industry-wide training programs and the practice of recruiting from the same accredited schools encourage the adoption of homogenous work practices within an industry. The Responsible Care program from the North American chemicals industry is the largest environmental self-regulation program in the world (Iannuzzi 2002). Our GSCM survey instrument addresses all three of these mechanisms.

METHODOLOGY

This empirical study consists of developing a questionnaire and collecting responses from middle to senior level managers in the Midwest manufacturing companies. The questionnaire was divided into three main sections: (1) pressures/drivers for implementing GSCM practices; (2) GSCM practices implemented; (3) performance outcomes. Section 1 on pressures/drivers utilized 18 items which were answered by respondents using a five-point Likert scale. Section 2 on GSCM practices involved items which asked how often companies used 28 different GSCM practices. These items were answered using the five-point Likert scale. Section 3 on performance outcomes used 20 items which asked what happened to the performance in environmental, financial, and operational areas as perceived by each respondent's company. These items again were answered by respondents by using a five-point Likert scale. This survey borrowed many of the question items from Zhu et. al (2007) which focused on studying GSCM adoption within Chinese automotive industry. Additional question items were developed after reviewing relevant research literature (Min & Galle, 1997; Carter & Carter, 1998; Walton, Handfield, & Melnyk, 1998; Carter, Kale, & Grimm, 2000).

The survey was made available to middle to senior level managers at 112 manufacturing companies in the Midwest region. The survey was made available online using www.monkeysurvey.com web site which hosted the survey and the link to complete it was sent to each of the respondent company.

RESULTS AND DISCUSSION

Table 1 shows the four driver factors along as aggregates of pressure items faced by the Midwest manufacturing companies. Surprisingly, we find that pressures related to internal impetus, and not regulatory, are most significant to be faced by Midwest manufacturing companies for implementing GSCM practices. It may be due to the fact that Midwest economy is deeply rooted in manufacturing and the environmental regulations in this region are still evolving and being slowly phased in.

Table 1: Descriptive Statistics on Pressure Factors			
Pressures/Drivers		***Mean***	***Standard Deviation***
DR1	*Regulation*	*3.86*	*1.08*
DR2	*Market*	3.77	1.12
DR3	*Suppliers*	*3.49*	*1.19*
DR4	*Internal Impetus*	*4.06*	*0.99*

The internal impetus factor has the highest mean of 4.06 (4=important; 5=extremely important) among all the four pressure factors. A smaller standard deviation value of 0.99 suggests broader consensus (little variation) among all respondents regarding the importance of this factor as a significant driver for green supply chain initiatives. All the corresponding items within this factor have mean scores above 4.00 with the exception of cost of eco-design/disposal of hazardous material which has a mean of 3.84. It implies that most Midwest manufacturing companies are serious about managing the environmental impact of their manufacturing operations by including environmental concerns in their company's mission statement.

Regulatory pressures with a mean of 3.86 constitute the second most important driver for implementing GSCM practices. Midwest manufacturing companies are facing strong pressures from national, state, and local level environmental regulations with means that are close to 4.00. We also find that the pressure from export countries' environmental regulations is less important than that from domestic environmental regulations. It may be due to environmental regulations within export countries that are not as strict as within United States.

Market related pressure with a mean of 3.77 is the third most important driver for environmental practices among Midwest companies. Pressure coming from environmental requirements of domestic customers as compared to foreign customers is more significant in shaping Midwest manufacturing company's environmental practices. These companies are also feeling significant pressure for establishing a "green" image or footprint. Midwest manufacturing companies do not seem to be facing much direct pressure from their suppliers for green practices. The means for items within this pressure factor ranges from 3.39 to 3.54. It seems that Midwest manufacturing companies are leveraging on their suppliers' capability to deliver environmentally friendly parts/packaging in pursuit of their environmental goals.

Table 2 shows the type and degree to which each of the GSCM practices have been implemented by the Midwest manufacturing companies in response to various underlying pressures identified earlier. The means for all the five practice factors range from 2.82 to 3.73.

Table 2: Descriptive Statistics on GSCM Practice Factors			
Practices		**Mean**	**Standard deviation**
PR1	***Green Purchasing***	***2.82***	***1.45***
PR2	***Cooperation with customers for environmental requirements***	***2.99***	***1.42***
PR3	***Investment Recovery***	***3.59***	***1.28***
PR4	***Eco Design***	***3.48***	***1.43***
PR5	***Internal management***	***3.73***	***1.29***

In general, practice factor means are found to be considerably lower than pressure factor means implying that adoption of GSCM practices has lagged the underlying pressures for environmentally friendly manufacturing. We also find the standard deviation values for GSCM practice items to be higher than those for GSCM pressure items. It suggests that there exists a considerable amount of variance among respondents on the degree to which each company has implemented the GSCM practices.

It seems that the Midwest manufacturing companies have been able to implement GSCM practices related to internal management with a higher degree of success (mean=3.73). Practices such as engaging in environmental compliance and auditing programs, pollution prevention programs, ISO 14000 certification, and environmental management systems all have means reflecting higher levels of implementation. Other internal management practice items such as senior and mid-level management commitment, cross functional cooperation, total quality environmental management, eco-labeling of products, and special training of workers on environmental issues have mean values which imply their adoption to be at the early stages.

Table 2 further shows that GSCM practices related to investment recovery with a mean of 3.59 have the second highest degree of adoption. Mean scores on GSCM practices such as sale of scrap and used materials, recycling of used or defective products, and sale of excess capital equipment are used quite often by the manufacturing companies. GSCM practices related to eco-design are the next most adopted practices with a mean of 3.48. It is noteworthy that the GSCM practice design of process for waste minimization has a very high level of implementation compared to others within the eco-design practice factor. It seems manufacturing companies find it challenging to implement the practice of designing products for reuse, recycle, recovery of material, and component parts (mean=2.96) i.e. products that form a closed loop system. These companies have seen some success in designing products that consume less material and energy as well use less or no hazards component parts.

GSCM practice factors such as green purchasing and cooperation with customers for environmental requirements with means of 2.82 and 2.98 respectively are infrequently implemented by the Midwest manufacturing companies. Table 2 shows that adoption of GSCM practice cooperation with customers in the supply chain for eco-design in terms of seeking their input or inviting them for joint development efforts is the least (mean=2.80). There seems to be at least some cooperation with customers for cleaner production (mean=3.18) and green packaging (mean=3.00). The Midwest manufacturing companies seriously lack implementation of practices related to green purchasing. Barring two GSCM practices within this factor, cooperation with suppliers for environmental objectives and dealing with ISO 14000 certified suppliers, rest of them have mean scores below 3.0. Midwest manufacturing companies need to work closely with suppliers in developing design specifications for environmentally friendly purchase items.

Table 3 relates to the perceived performance outcomes in environmental, financial, and operational areas as a result of GSCM practices implemented by the Midwest manufacturing companies. It is to be noted that the financial performance is examined by considering two distinct dimensions - gains due to cost savings and burden due to increase in costs affiliated with implementing GSCM practices. The study finds environmental performance with a mean of 4.14 (4=slightly improved; 5=greatly improved) to be highest as compared to either operational or financial performance.

Table 3: Descriptive Statistics on GSCM Practice Factors			
Performance		**Mean**	**Standard deviation**
PF1	***Environmental Performance***	***4.14***	***0.86***
PF2	***Financial Gain***	***3.68***	***0.91***
PF3	***Financial Burden***	**3.21**	**0.87**
PF4	***Operational Performance***	***3.67***	***0.85***

It is not surprising that all of the environmental performance items have mean scores above 4.0. GSCM practices at Midwest manufacturing companies have led to significant improvements in reducing waste water and consumption of hazardous or toxic materials, each with a mean of 4.24. Companies have also seen adequate reductions in solid waste and air emissions.

The Midwest manufacturing companies found the financial gain (mean=3.68) to significantly outweigh the financial burden (mean=3.21) that implementation of GSCM practices entailed. Cost savings due to decrease in energy consumption and fines for environmental accidents were most significant. Financial gains also resulted from fee reductions for waste discharge and waste treatment. Gains in operational costs saw least amount of improvement. Further, as a result of implementing GSCM practices, the manufacturing companies experienced significant increase in investment costs (mean=3.49) when compared to other cost areas. The companies did not see much impact in the cost associated with purchasing environmentally friendly materials or environmental training costs.

On the operational performance dimension, the Midwest manufacturing companies saw large improvements in the areas of increased scrap rate and promotion of product quality as a result of GSCM adoption. Companies also felt that GSCM practices have improved capacity utilization, product flexibility (ability to offer product variety), and inventory levels to some extent. Impact of GSCM practices on timely delivery of goods was found to be positive (mean=3.44), but least significant compared to improvements in other operational areas.

CONCLUSION

Our results show some evidence that economic and social forces are pushing the Midwestern manufacturing firms in our sample to adopt GSCM. Both market and regulatory pressures scored high in our survey results. As expected, coercive forces are playing an important role. Interestingly, the source of the strongest pressures comes from within the company. More precisely, it is the commitment to environmental excellence from top management or from headquarters that has the largest impact. Senior managers in the companies we surveyed appear committed to improving the environmental performance of their companies, which suggests that the adoption of GSCM practices may not be a passing fad but rather a transformation of manufacturing and supply chain management practices. The high adoption of ISO 14000 certification suggests the influence of normative forces as well. In the current exploratory study, we have considered regulatory, market and internal forces independently of each other.

Our results also indicate that managers perceive some financial and operational benefits from deploying GSCM. This is also good news for the future of GSCM. For sustainability to be realized, one needs production methods that provide benefits to the firms while preserving scarce environmental resources.

This paper is one of the few research focused on studying the types and degrees of pressures, practices, and performance outcomes faced by Midwest manufacturing companies. Its findings, even though exploratory in nature, add to the continued understanding of environmental issues in the GSCM literature. Future work may include studying environmental responses in other geographic regions by companies within specific manufacturing or service industry.

REFERENCES

References available upon request.

DECISION SCIENCES INSTITUTE

Stock Trading Decisions Using Ensemble-based Forecasting Models

Dhanya Jothimani
Indian Institute of Technology Delhi, India
Email: dhanyajothimani@gmail.com

Ravi Shankar
Indian Institute of Technology Delhi, India
Email: ravi1@dms.iitd.ac.in

Surendra S. Yadav
Indian Institute of Technology Delhi, India
Email: ssyadav@dms.iitd.ac.in

ABSTRACT

In this paper, we propose an ensemble-based forecasting framework for making stock trading decisions. Here, two ensemble models are proposed for predicting the stock index. In first stage, Empirical Mode Decomposition (EMD) and Complete Ensemble Empirical Mode Decomposition with Adaptive Noise (CEEMDAN) are used for decomposing the financial series into various sub-series. In second stage, each series is predicted using a machine learning algorithm, namely, Artificial Neural Network (ANN). Trading rules are defined. The models were tested on Nifty data. Return on investment based on the trading rules of proposed ensemble models was compared with Buy-and-Hold strategy.

KEYWORDS: Financial time series prediction, EMD, CEEMDAN, Trading Rules, Ensemble Models, ANN, Nifty

INTRODUCTION

Stock market attracts investors (naive, well-informed) and spectators alike. Every investor wants to gain profit at minimal risk. However, the complexity of stock market can be attributed to several factors including socio-political events and investors' behavior. This complexity, often, does not enable one to predict the direction of movement of stock prices and determine the timing of trading decision accurately. Hence, prediction of stock prices has gained attention of analysts and academicians from several domains including Finance, Mathematics and Computer Science.

Finance literature deals with two major ways to predict stock price: (i) Fundamental analysis, and (ii) Technical analysis. Fundamental analysis deals with factors like macroeconomic variables and fundamental information such as Price to Earnings (PE) ratio, Earnings Per Share (EPS) and Return on Equity (ROE) (Fischer and Jordan, 1987) to predict the movement of stock price.

Technical analysis analyzes the behavior of past stock price and volume data to predict the future price values. Technical analysis focuses on developing a model that can predict the stock price dynamics accurately. Various statistical and computationally intelligent models have been proposed for forecasting stock prices yet none seems to have captured the complex dynamics of stock market accurately (Atsalakis and Valavanis, 2009; 2013). This led to the concept of ensemble models.

Ensemble models, popular in Machine Learning and Statistics, work on the idea that prediction accuracy can be improved by using multiple predictors than using any of base predictors (Opitz and Maclin, 1999) alone. There are two types of ensemble models: pre-processing and post-processing. Pre-processing deconstructs the dataset into various components and selects a predictor for analyzing each component. Decomposition of time-series is one such preprocessing technique.

In post-processing, the predictors are selected based on data characteristics. For instance, AutoRegressive Integrated Moving Average (ARIMA) are used for modelling stationary and linear data, Generalised AutoRegressive Conditional Heteroskedasticity (GARCH) models for non-linear data and similarly, Artificial Neural Network (ANN) and Support Vector Regression (SVR) for non-stationary and non-linear data.

There are two types of decomposition models: (a) classical model, and (b) non-classical models. Classical model yields three components, namely, trend, seasonal and random. Though widely used, it suffers from few limitations: (i) it works best only with linear data but not with non-linear data, and (b) while aggregating the forecasts of components, it ignores random component leading to loss of information (Theodosiou, 2011). Few signal processing techniques like Discrete Wavelet Transform (DWT) and Empirical Mode Decomposition (EMD) fall under the category of non-classical models and are being used for decomposing time series in time-frequency domain and time domain, respectively (Liu et al, 2012; Lahmiri, 2014; Jothimani et al, 2015; 2016).

EMD was proposed by Huang et al. (1998). It uses Huang-Hilbert Transform (HHT) to decompose non-stationary and non-linear time series into a set of adaptive basis function called Intrinsic Mode Function (IMF). Since it is adaptive, it does not require any *a priori* information. DWT requires prior information regarding scale of decomposition. Despite its advantages of handling non-linear and non-stationary data, DWT suffers from leakage between scales (Crowley, 2010). EMD suffers from limitation of mode-mixing problem (Wu and Huang, 2009; Torres et al, 2011). Mode mixing is defined as either presence of signals of widely different scales in a single IMF or presence of signal of a similar scale in different IMF components. To overcome this limitation, a variation of EMD called Complete Ensemble Empirical Mode Decomposition with Adaptive Noise (CEEMDAN) was introduced (Torres et al, 2011). Similar to EMD, CEEMDAN can be used for data preprocessing.

The paper presents two ensemble forecasting models, namely, ensemble EMD-ANN and ensemble CEEMDAN-ANN models to predict 1-step ahead forecasts for weekly Nifty price index. In first stage, EMD (for EMD-ANN model) and CEEMDAN (for CEEMDAN-ANN) was used to decompose time-series into various components, i.e., Intrinsic Mode Function (IMF) and residue. In second stage, ANN is used to predict each component. The forecasted components are aggregated to obtain the final forecast.

To help the investors to make trading decisions, trading rules are defined and illustrated using forecasts obtained from EMD-ANN and CEEMDAN-ANN models. A comparative analysis was carried out with traditional Buy-and-Hold strategy.

The contributions of the paper are three-fold. Firstly, it demonstrates the use of ensemble model of non-classical decomposition and machine learning algorithm for stock price prediction in Indian stock market. Secondly, it highlights the application of CEEMDAN as a data preprocessing technique. Thirdly, it illustrates the application of ensemble models for making trading decisions.

The paper is organized as follows: Next section discusses the ensemble framework followed by Methodology. Results are discussed followed by presenting few concluding remarks.

ENSEMBLE FRAMEWORK FOR INVESTMENT DECISIONS

The flowchart of the ensemble framework for trading decisions is shown in Figure 1. The detailed steps are as follows:

1. Decompose the original series *F(t)* into various sub-series using EMD and CEEMDAN in case of ensemble EMD-ANN model and CEEMDAN-ANN model, respectively.
2. Forecast each sub-series obtained using Artificial Neural Network (ANN).
3. Aggregate the forecasted sub-series to obtain forecasted series *F'(t)*.
4. Compare the forecasted series *F'(t)* with the original series *F(t)* to calculate error measures, i.e., Root Mean Square Error (RMSE) and Directional Accuracy (DA).
5. Test the forecasting ability of various models, namely, ANN, EMD-ANN and CEEMDAN-ANN using a statistical procedure called Wilcoxon Signed Rank Test (WSRT).
6. Define trading rules for each model and calculate return on investment (ROI).

Empirical Mode Decomposition (EMD)

The steps for decomposing the original time series *F(t)* are detailed below (Huang et al, 1998; 2003):

1. Identify all local minima and local maxima; interpolate them using cubic spline interpolation method to obtain a lower envelope *L(t)* and an upper envelope *U(t)*, respectively.
2. Calculate the mean of lower and upper envelopes using the following formula:

$$M(t) = (L(t) + U(t)) / 2 \tag{1}$$

   Subtract *M(t)* from the original series to obtain a local detail *Z(t)*.

$$Z(t) = F(t) - M(t) \tag{2}$$

3. Repeat Steps 1 and 2 on *Z(t)* till: (a) the value of *M(t)* approaches zero, and (b) the difference between the number of local extrema and zero crossings is at most 1. This process is known as sifting.
   The first IMF obtained component is first intrinsic mode function $IMF_1(t)$ which is nothing but *Z(t)*.

$$IMF_1(t) = Z(t) \tag{3}$$

Figure 1: Flow Chart of Ensemble Framework for Investment Decisions

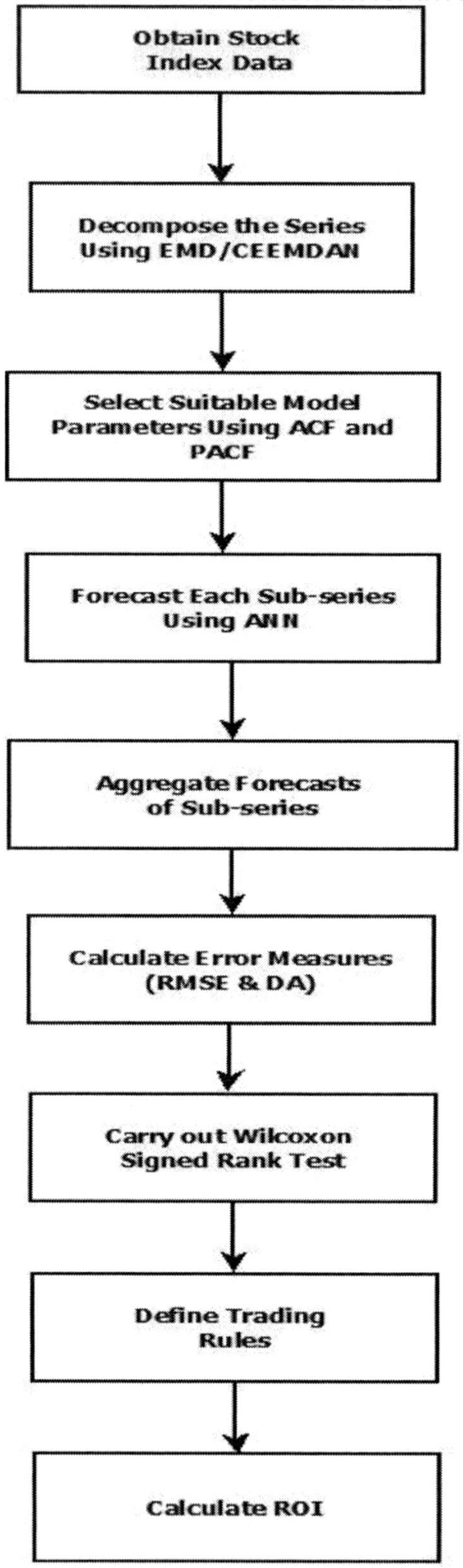

Subtract the details $Z(t)$ from $F(t)$ to obtain residue $R_1(t)$.

$$R_1(t) = F(t) - Z(t) \tag{4}$$

4. Repeat steps 1-3 on $R_1(t)$ to obtain the second IMF $IMF_2(t)$ and the second residue $R_2(t)$. The process is repeated on $R_i(t)$ to obtain $IMF_{i+1}(t)$ and $R_{i+1}(t)$ until $R_{i+1}(t)$ does not have more than two local extrema, where $i=1, 2, \ldots, N-1$.

The original series $F(t)$ is expressed as:

$$X(t) = \sum_{i=1}^{N} IMF_i(t) + R_N(t) \tag{5}$$

Complete Ensemble Empirical Mode Decomposition with Adaptive Noise (CEEMDAN)

Despite the advantages of EMD as an adaptive method to decompose non-linear and non-stationary series, it suffers from a major limitation of mode mixing problem (Wu and Huang, 2009; Torres et al, 2011). Mode mixing is defined as either presence of signals of widely different scales in a single IMF or presence of signal of a similar scale in different IMF components. This affects aliasing of signals in the time-frequency distribution. To overcome this limitation, a variation of EMD known as Complete Ensemble Empirical Mode Decomposition with Adaptive Noise (CEEMDAN) was proposed (Torres et al, 2011).

The detailed procedure of CEEMDAN is as follows:

1. To the original series $F(t)$, add white noise $w^i[t](\sim N(0,1))$ and decompose the combination by I realizations to obtain the first IMF of CEEMDAN using the following formula:

$$\overline{IMF_1}[t] = \frac{1}{I}\sum_{i=1}^{I} IMF_1^i[t] \tag{6}$$

2. Calculate first residue by subtracting first IMF of CEEMDAN from the original series $F(t)$

$$r_1[t] = F(t) - \overline{IMF_1}[t] \tag{7}$$

3. Obtain second mode by decomposing realizations $r_1[t] + \varepsilon_1 E_1(w^i[t])$, $i = 1, 2, \ldots, I$.

$$\overline{IMF_2}[k] = \frac{1}{I}\sum_{i=1}^{I} E_1(r_1[t] + \varepsilon_1 E_1(w^i[t])) \tag{8}$$

$Ej(.)$ is an operator which produces the j-th mode of the signal obtained by EMD.

4. Calculate the kth residue.

$$r_k[t] = r_{k-1}[t] - \overline{IMF_k}[t] \forall \ k=2, \ldots, K \tag{9}$$

5. Calculate I realizations of $r_k[t] + \varepsilon_k E_k(w^i[t])$, $i=1, 2, \ldots, I$ to obtain $(k+1)^{th}$ mode.

$$\overline{IMF_{(k+1)}}[t] = \frac{1}{I}\sum_{i=1}^{I} E_1(r_k[t] + \varepsilon_k E_k(w^i[t])) \tag{10}$$

6. Go to Step 4 for next k.

7. Repeat steps 4 to 6 till it is no longer feasible to decompose the obtained residue. The final residue is defined as:

$$R[t] = F(t) - \sum_{k=1}^{K} \overline{IMF_k} \tag{11}$$

where, K is the total number of modes.

The original series can be expressed as:

$$F(t) = \sum_{k=1}^{K} \overline{IMF}_k + R[t] \tag{12}$$

CEEMDAN provides complete decomposition and exact reconstruction of original data series. It overcomes the mode mixing problem. Similar to EMD, CEEMDAN is adaptive in nature.

METHODOLOGY

National Stock Exchange Fifty Index, commonly known as Nifty, is the benchmark index of Indian stock market. Nifty consists of 50 companies and covers 22 sectors. The original raw data consists of weekly closing prices of Nifty. The dataset covered a period of 8 years ranging from September 2007 to December 2015.

Decomposition of Time Series

The financial time series, i.e., weekly Nifty index, is decomposed using EMD and CEEMDAN for ensemble EMD-ANN and CEEMDAN-ANN models, respectively. Seven relatively stationary IMFs along with residual component were produced in case of both EMD and CEEMDAN, which are shown in Figure 2 and Figure 3, respectively. Now, each sub-series is forecasted using Artificial Neural Network.

Figure 2: Decomposed Signals Obtained Using EMD

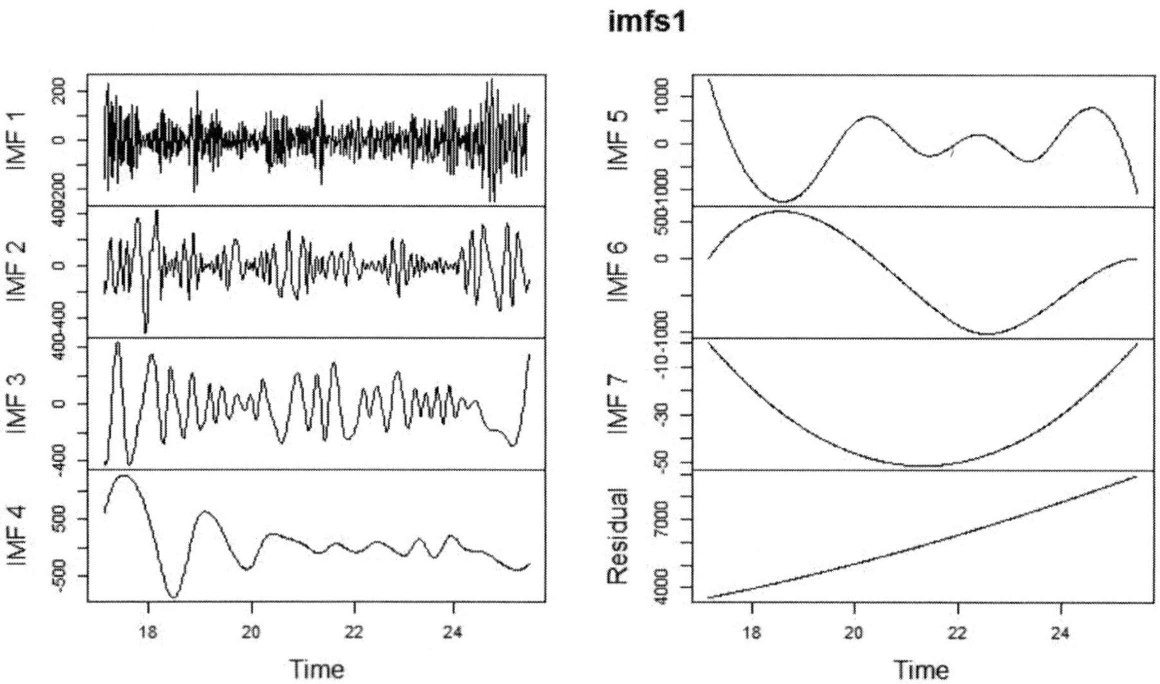

Artificial Neural Network (ANN)

ANN is used for forecasting each sub-series independently, then aggregate the forecasts of sub-series to obtain the final forecasts *F'(t)* of both EMD-ANN and CEEMDAN-ANN models.

Since ANN is a supervised learning algorithm, first 70% of dataset is used for training the network and rest 30% is used to test the validity of the model. A resilient three-layered feed forward network consisting of input layer, hidden layer and output layer is used. Each layer consists of certain number of neurons. Number of neurons in the input layer is determined using the relationship between data and its past values. This relationship is known as lag parameter and is determined using Auto Correlation Function (ACF) and Partial Auto Correlation Function (PACF) plots. The ACF and PACF plots of IMF3 obtained using CEEMDAN are shown in Figure 4. IMF3 at time *t* depends on its past six values since it cuts off at lag 6. Hence, the number of neurons in input layer is six and is expressed as:

$$X(t) = f[X(t-1), X(t-2), X(t-3), X(t-4), X(t-5), X(t-6)] \tag{13}$$

Figure 3: Decomposed Signals Obtained Using CEEMDAN

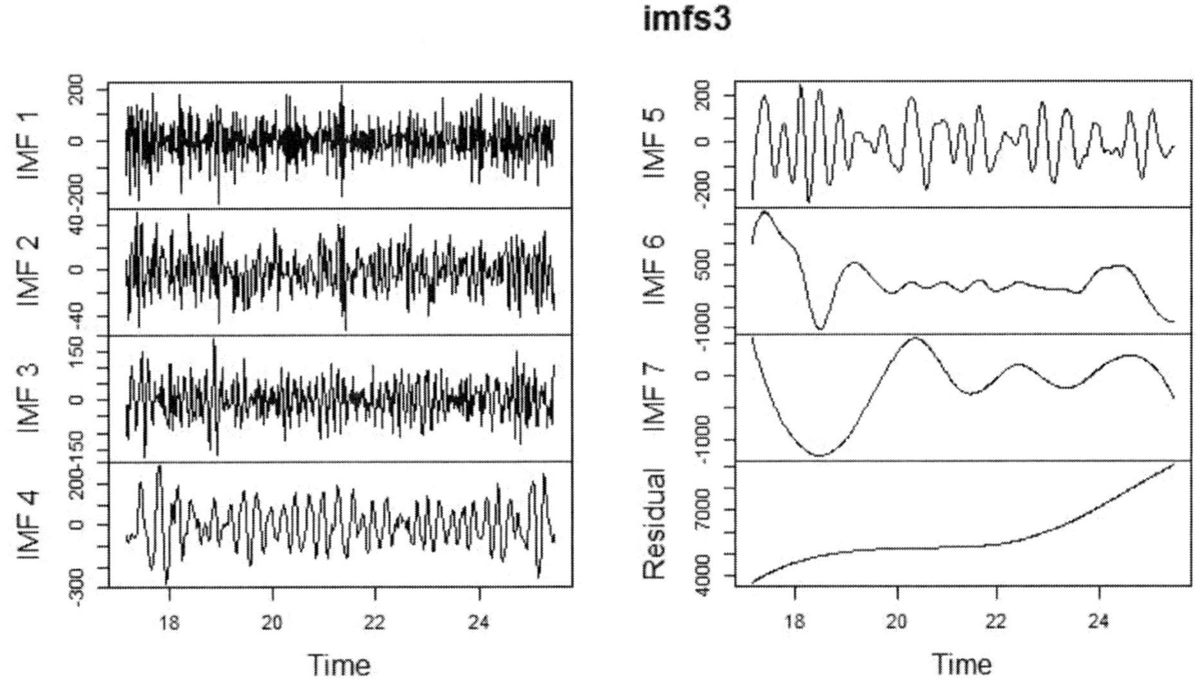

Since it is a regression problem and forecasted value is obtained, hence, the number of neurons in the output layer is one. The number of neurons in the hidden layer is determined iteratively based on the performance of the neural network. Number of neurons in each layer of neural network is shown in Table 1.

Resilient Backpropagation (RBP) algorithm is used for training the model. RBP is preferred over the most commonly preferred back propagation algorithm as it quickens the training process (Liu et al, 2012).

Figure 4: ACF and PACF Plot for IMF_3 Obtained Using CEEMDAN

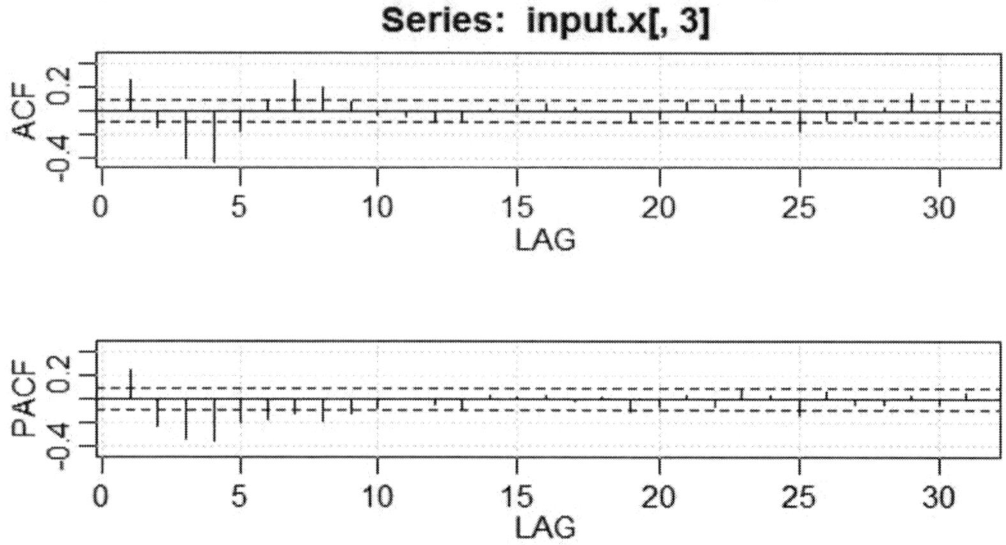

The data is normalized using z scores as a preprocessing step for ANN. It helps to reduce the chances of neural network getting stuck in local optima and fastens the training process (Wu and Lo, 2010).

Similarly, the forecasts are obtained using ANN model without decomposing the data.

Table 1: Number of Neurons for Various IMFs and Residue Obtained Using EMD and CEEMDAN

IMFs	EMD			CEEMDAN		
	Input	Hidden	Output	Input	Hidden	Output
IMF_1	3	8	1	4	9	1
IMF_2	3	9	1	6	10	1
IMF_3	4	10	1	6	8	1
IMF_4	5	8	1	3	10	1
IMF_5	5	10	1	4	9	1
IMF_6	4	11	1	6	10	1
IMF_7	6	10	1	3	8	1
Residue	7	7	1	6	10	1

RESULTS AND DISCUSSION

Performance Measures

The performances of ANN model and both ensemble models are compared using two performance measures, namely, Root Mean Square Error (RMSE) and Directional Accuracy (DA). Error is defined as the difference between the original series and the forecasted series. Square root of mean of errors is known as Root Mean Square Error. Smaller the value of RMSE better are the forecasts. Determining whether the direction of forecasted series is same as the original series is important and is identified using directional accuracy. Higher the DA better are the forecasts. With respect to both performance measures, ensemble CEEMDAN-ANN model is better than remaining two models (Refer Table 2). Performance of EMD-ANN is slightly better than that of ANN model. We validate the results statistically using Wilcoxon Signed Rank Test (WSRT). Figure 5 represents the results of the 1-step ahead forecasts obtained using both EMD-ANN and CEEMDAN-ANN models.

Table 2: Performance Measures		
	RMSE	DA (%)
EMD-ANN	103.37	52.89
CEEMDAN-ANN	50.35	89.00
ANN	165.38	40.00

Figure 5: Forecasts Obtained Using EMD-ANN and CEEMDAN-ANN Models

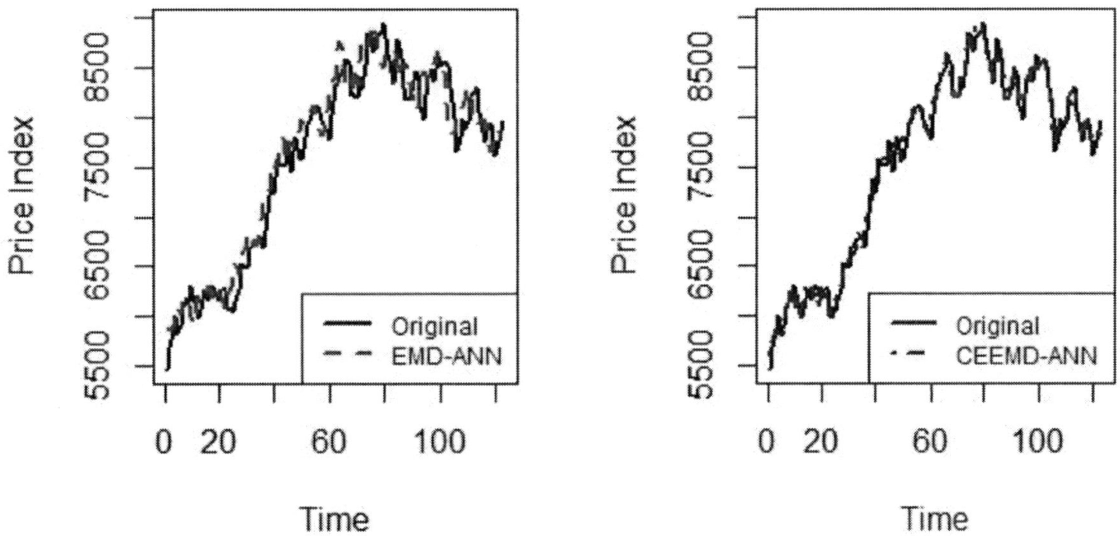

Statistical Validity of Proposed Approach

The predictive capability of the proposed approach should be analyzed and validated statistically. This can be carried out using Wilcoxon Signed Rank Test (WSRT). WSRT is a distribution-free and non-parametric test that analyzes the predictive capability of two models based on their ranks and signs (Diebold and Mariano, 1995; Kao et al, 2013).

Two-tailed WSRT was carried out on RMSE values. Based on the results obtained (Refer Table 3), the null hypothesis of CEEMDAN-ANN and ANN models being same is not accepted since the z statistics value is beyond (-1.96, 1.96) at 99% confidence interval (alpha = 0.01). Similar results were observed in case of comparison between EMD-ANN and ANN models. Hence, it can be concluded that proposed ensemble models outperformed the ANN model.

Table 3: Wilcoxon Signed Rank Test between Hybrid EMD-ANN, Hybrid CEEMDAN-ANN, and ANN models				
	Ensemble EMD-ANN		Ensemble CEEMDAN-ANN	
	Z	Sign	Z	Sign
ANN	-4.188	+	-5.780	+
+: EMD-ANN > ANN, CEEMDAN-ANN > ANN -: EMD-ANN < ANN, CEEMDAN-ANN < ANN =: EMD-ANN = ANN, CEEMDAN-ANN = ANN				

Trading Decision

We can forecast the closing price of Nifty on following week using the proposed model with a reasonable accuracy. Now, using these forecasted values, investors can make their trading decisions. Few trading rules are defined. Here, the trading rules have been defined and illustrated for stock index; the same can be used for making buy/sell decisions for stocks as well.

Let F_k and F'_k be actual and forecasted close price on first trading day in the kth trading week, respectively. Consider a scenario where the close price is expected to rise in the trading week k but it either falls or remains constant. We can use an error index E_k to represent such scenarios and is defined as follows:

$$E_K = \begin{cases} 1 & if \quad F'_k > F_{k-1} \quad and \quad F_k \le F_{k-1} \quad \forall \quad k = 2,3,\ldots,n \\ 0 & otherwise \end{cases} \tag{14}$$

where n is the total number of weeks.

Based on the error index (Hsu, 2014), following three rules are used in this study:

Rule 1: IF (if an investor is not holding any stock on first trading day in the kth week) AND ($F'_{k+1} > F_k$) THEN (s/he is advised to buy the stock on the next trading day in the kth week)

Rule 2: IF (if an investor is holding any stock on first trading day in the kth week) AND ($F'_{k+1} < F_k$) THEN (s/he is advised to sell the stock on the next trading day in the kth week)

Rule 3: IF (the investor is holding any stock on first trading day in the kth trading week) AND ($\sum_{j=0}^{2} E_{k-j} = 3$) THEN (s/he is advised to sell the stock on second trading day in k^{th} trading week)

According to first rule, since the price in the following week is expected to rise, the investor is advised to buy stocks if he does not hold any stock on first day of the trading week. If an investor is holding a stock on the first day of trading week and if the prices are forecasted to fall next week, then according to second rule, the investor is advised to sell his stock on next trading day. According to third rule, investor is advised to sell his held stocks if the forecasts are found to be wrong for three consecutive weeks.

The return on investment (ROI) in each trading strategy is calculated using the following equation:

$$ROI = \prod_{i=1}^{k} \frac{P_{S_i} - P_{B_i}}{P_{B_i}} \tag{15}$$

where, P_{Si} and P_{Bi} represent the selling price and buying price of the ith transaction, respectively.

Here, we assume that the security (stocks or index) can be traded (sold and bought) at the opening price on the next trading day of the week as soon as buying/selling decisions are taken. The transactions based on the trading rules using the results of EMD-ANN model are illustrated in Table 4.

The closing price on August 31, 2015 is 7655.05, which is less than forecasted price of the following week (i.e., 7840.19), hence according to first rule, the investor is advised to buy stocks. On October 12, 2015, it is observed that forecast for next week is 8188.09 which is lower than the current close price (8238.15), hence applying second rule, the investor is advised to sell his stock next day (October 13, 2015) at its opening price (8121.95).

Table 4: Illustration of Trading Rules

Date	Close Price	Forecasted Close Price	Transaction	Transaction Date	E_k	Rule
31-08-2015	7655.05	7840.19	Buy at 7907.95	01-09-2015	1	1
07-09-2015	7789.30	8025.28	-	-	-	0
14-09-2015	7981.90	8036.78	-	-	-	0
21-09-2015	7868.50	8087.50	-	-	-	1
28-09-2015	7950.90	8165.05	-	-	-	0
05-10-2015	8189.70	8295.16	-	-	-	0
12-10-2015	8238.15	8188.09	Sell at 8121.95	13-10-2015	2	0
19-10-2015	8295.45	8036.79	-	-	-	0
26-10-2015	8065.80	7920.82	-	-	-	0
02-11-2015	7954.3	7928.30	-	-	-	0
09-11-2015	7762.25	7977.71	Buy at 7877.60	10-11-2015	1	1
16-11-2015	7856.55	7958.01	-	-	-	0
23-11-2015	7942.70	7809.99	Sell at 7837.00	24-11-2015	2	0
30-11-2015	7781.09	7659.66	-	-	-	0
07-12-2015	7610.45	7773.07	Buy at 7738.50	08-12-2015	1	1
14-12-2015	7761.95	7866.05	-	-	-	0
21-12-2015	7861.05	7847.61	Sell at 7829.40	22-12-2015	2	0

Similarly, since on November 9, 2015, the forecasted close price (7977.71) for next week is higher than current close price (7762.25), the investor is advised to buy stocks according to Rule 1. The process is carried out in the same way for rest of test dataset. Similarly, trading rules are applied for forecasts obtained using ensemble CEEMDAN-ANN model. ROI was calculated for EMD-ANN, CEEMDAN-ANN model and Buy-and-Hold strategy. ROI of CEEMDAN-ANN was 2.8% and 1.5% higher than that of Buy-and-Hold strategy. Trading decisions based on CEEMDAN-ANN model yielded higher ROI than EMD-ANN model. Buy-and-Hold strategy yielded the least returns among all three models.

CONCLUSION

Investment decision making is one of the difficult tasks. The paper presented two ensemble frameworks, namely, EMD-ANN and CEEMDAN-ANN model to predict close price of Nifty index for the following week. Further, trading rules were defined and illustrated to guide the investors with the trading decisions.

Ensemble models used EMD and CEEMDAN to decompose the original time series into various sub-series. Later, each decomposed series was forecasted using ANN for the respective ensemble models. The forecasted sub-series are aggregated to obtain final forecasts.

Performance measures, namely, directional accuracy and RMSE suggest that the performance of ensemble models is better in comparison to traditional ANN model. Further, the results of

WSRT confirm the superiority of predictive capability of ensemble models over traditional ANN model. Trading rules based on forecasts of ensemble models were defined and illustrated so that investors could make trading decisions. Return on investment of ensemble CEEMDAN-ANN model was found to be higher than that of EMD-ANN model and buy-and-hold strategy.

The ensemble forecasting model can be tested for high frequency data and new trading rules can be formulated for the same. A comparative study of model with data from developed and emerging economies would provide useful insights.

APPENDIX

Nomenclature

ACF	Auto Correlation Function
ANN	Artificial Neural Network
ARIMA	AutoRegressive Integrated Moving Average
CEEMDAN	Complete Ensemble Empirical Mode Decomposition with Adaptive Noise
DA	Directional Accuracy
DWT	Discrete Wavelet Transform
EMD	Empirical Mode Decomposition
GARCH	Generalised AutoRegressive Conditional Heteroskedasticity
IMF	Intrinsic Mode Function
PACF	Partial AutoCorrelation Function
RBP	Resilient Back Propagation
RMSE	Root Mean Square Error
ROE	Return On Equity
ROI	Return On Investment
SVR	Support Vector Regression
WSRT	Wilcoxon Signed Rank Test

REFERENCES

Atsalakis G, Valavanis K (2009) Surveying stock market forecasting techniques- Part II: Soft computing methods. *Expert Systems with Applications,* 36(3, Part 2):5932-5941.

Atsalakis G, Valavanis K (2013) Surveying stock market forecasting techniques- Part I: Conventional methods. Zopounidis C, ed., *Computation Optimization in Economics and Finance Research Compendium*, 49 – 104, New York: Nova Science Publishers, Inc.

Crowley P (2010) Long cycles in growth: Explorations using new frequency domain techniques with US data. Bank of Finland Research Discussion Paper No. 6/2010, Retrieved from http://dx.doi.org/http://dx.doi.org/10.2139/ssrn.1573641, February 16.

Diebold FX, Mariano RS (1995) Comparing predictive accuracy. *Journal of Business and Economic Statistics*, 13:253-265.

Fischer D, Jordan R (1987) *Security Analysis and Portfolio Management*, US: Prentice-Hall International.

Hsu CM (2014) An integrated portfolio optimisation procedure based on data envelopment analysis, artificial bee colony algorithm and genetic programming. *International Journal of Systems Science*, 45(12):2645-2664.

Huang N, Shen Z, Long S, Wu M, Shih H, Zheng Q, Yen N, Tung C, Liu H (1998) The empirical mode decomposition and the Hilbert spectrum for nonlinear and non-stationary time series analysis. *Proceedings of the Royal Society of London A: Mathematical, Physical and Engineering Sciences,* 454(1971):903 - 995.

Huang NE, Wu ML, Qu W, Long SR, Shen SSP (2003) Applications of Hilbert Huang Transform to non-stationary financial time series analysis. *Applied Stochastic Models in Business and Industry*, 19(3):245-268.

Jothimani D, Shankar R, Yadav SS (2015) Discrete Wavelet Transform-Based Prediction of Stock Index: A Study on National Stock Exchange Fifty Index, *Journal of Financial Management and Analysis*, 28(2), 35-49.

Jothimani D, Shankar R, Yadav SS (2016) A comparative study of ensemble-based forecasting models for stock index prediction. *MWAIS 2016 Proceedings*, paper 5, Retrieved from http://aisel.aisnet.org/mwais2016/5, May 16.

Kao LJ, Chiu CC, Lu CJ, Chang CH (2013) A hybrid approach by integrating wavelet-based feature extraction with MARS and SVR for stock index forecasting. *Decision Support Systems*, 54(3):1228-1244.

Lahmiri S (2014) Wavelet low- and high-frequency components as features for predicting stock prices with backpropagation neural networks. *Journal of King Saud University - Computer and Information Sciences,* 26(2):218- 227.

Liu H, Chen C, Tian H, Li Y (2012) A hybrid model for wind speed prediction using empirical mode decomposition and artificial neural networks. *Renewable Energy,* 48:545-556.

Opitz D, Maclin R (1999) Popular ensemble methods: An empirical study. *Journal of Artificial Intelligence Research,* 11:169-198.

Theodosiou M (2011) Forecasting monthly and quarterly time series using STL decomposition. *International Journal of Forecasting,* 27(4):1178-1195.

Torres ME, Colominas MA, Schlotthauer G, Flandrin P (2011) A complete ensemble empirical mode decomposition with adaptive noise. *2011 IEEE International Conference on Acoustics, Speech and Signal Processing (ICASSP)*, 4144-4147.

Wu G, Lo S (2010) Effects of data normalization and inherent-factor on decision of optimal coagulant dosage in water treatment by artificial neural network. *Expert Systems with Applications*, 37(7):4974-4983.

Wu Z, Huang NE (2009) Ensemble empirical mode decomposition: A noise-assisted data analysis method. *Advances in Adaptive Data Analysis*, 1(1):1-41.

DECISION SCIENCES INSTITUTE

Strategic Global Work-Life Balance Initiatives: The Roles of the Expatriation Cycle and Gender

Efrain Medina
Texas A&M International University
Laredo, TX 78041
956-263-5659
efrainmedina@dusty.tamiu.edu

ABSTRACT

A considerable body of research has illustrated that work-life balance programs are associated with a number of key employee outcomes. Such results have brought the attention of researchers in understanding how it can influence the success of expatriates. However, there is a gap in literature regarding what type of programs are necessary for the success of female expatriates. The current study contributes to this line of research by identifying some work-life balance programs necessary in each of the stages of the expatriation cycle which can contribute to the success of expatriates, especially female expats.

KEYWORDS: Work-life balance programs, Female expatriates, Expatriation cycle, Work satisfaction, Life satisfaction, Stress level, Performance.

INTRODUCTION

As globalization and technological advancements have rapidly increased over the years, national borders have disappeared. Case in point, the world ratio to trade relative to that of output shows that it has tripled in the last fifty years (World Trade Organization, 2016). As a result, the number of international assignments are becoming critical for the vast majority of organizations that compete on this global scale. Relatedly, international assignments have multiplied for these companies.

Furthermore, there is a need to attain competitive advantage with strategic human resources management. Organizations that compete in the global market have placed high priority on developing and retaining employees with international expertise in terms of their social and human capital (Scullion and Collings, 2006). One survey showed that companies planned to increased international assignments to locations like Japan and Middle East, and that most of these international assignments will be expatriations assignments (Organization Resources Counselors Inc., 2002). Consequently, expatriation has become the main strategic choice to successfully attain competitive advantage in global markets.

Despite these opportunities, there seems to be high failure rate among expatriates that derive from personal and professional factors. One of the reasons behind the high failure rate among expatriates is the lack of preparedness to face the uncertainty of the process including culture shock, lifestyle changes, and lack of support by the organization (Hung-Wen, 2007). This situation has a negative impact for organizations and employees since expatriate failures incur financial, physical, and psychological costs. Failure in an expatriate assignment can cost up to a quarter of a million dollars for the company (Morris and Robie, 2001). Furthermore, crucial talent may leave the organization after the international assignment, taking with them vital knowledge and skills. Moreover, literature regarding expatriation has increased over the years with scholars illustrating different factors that lead to the failure of an expatriation assignment (Hung-Wen, 2007; Tahir and Ismail, 2007, Shortland and Cummins, 2007). One of the most important studies about expatriate failure was conducted by Tung (1982). Unfortunately, dynamic changes over time create a need for updated research. Specifically, there is a literature gap regarding human resources strategies that can be implemented to increase the likelihood of a successful expatriate assignment.

This paper proposes that work-life balance programs, especially those which target the needs of female expatriates may be rewarding intervention. Literature regarding the effects of work-life balance support and its benefits has increased over the years; however, there is a need for studies that focus on how it can influence expatriates' assignment success. Some studies have showed that factors like cultural shock, language barrier, work overload, unrealistic expectations, ineffective cultural training, and lack of support in the repatriation stage can lead to an expatriate's failure (Vallone and Ensher, 2001; Collings et al., 2007; Littrel et al., 2006). Furthermore, lack of work-life balance can lead to role conflict which could be intensified in an unfamiliar environment. Lack of work-life balance support can augment the potential of expatriate failure, especially among women. Male expatriates face several challenges in their international assignments, but such challenges for female expatriates can affect them at a greater level. These woman may well confront specific challenges which include traditional gender roles, home responsibilities, and negative stereotypes. As a result, work-life balance support can have a greater impact toward the success of female expatriates.

This paper argues the importance for organizations to offer work-life balance support as part of the human resource management functional strategy for expatriates, especially female expatriates. Although we contend that work-life balance initiatives benefit both the organization and the employees, we explicitly focus on female expatriates as a result of them facing challenges that affect them at a greater level, which can lead to the assignment's failure. Throughout the paper, we will show some of the challenges that female expatriates face during the four stages of the expatriation cycle: selection, preparation, adjustment, and repatriation. Furthermore, we will discuss some of the work-life balance support that human resources professionals can provide in each of the four stages. The main contributions of the paper are: clarification of challenges faced by female expatriates, and identification of how work-life balance support that increases the probability of an international assignment's success at each stage in the expatriation cycle. See Figure 1 which depicts the conceptual model and expected outcomes for organizations and employees.

For both men and women, work-life balance support can increase the likelihood of success in international assignments. In the survey conducted by Shortland and Cummins (2007), 51 percent of female expatriates thought that work-life balance policies increases performance compared to 17 percent of male expatriates, and 35 percent of the women felt that such policies make a favorable impact in their personal lives compare to only 15 percent of the men.

Figure 1.

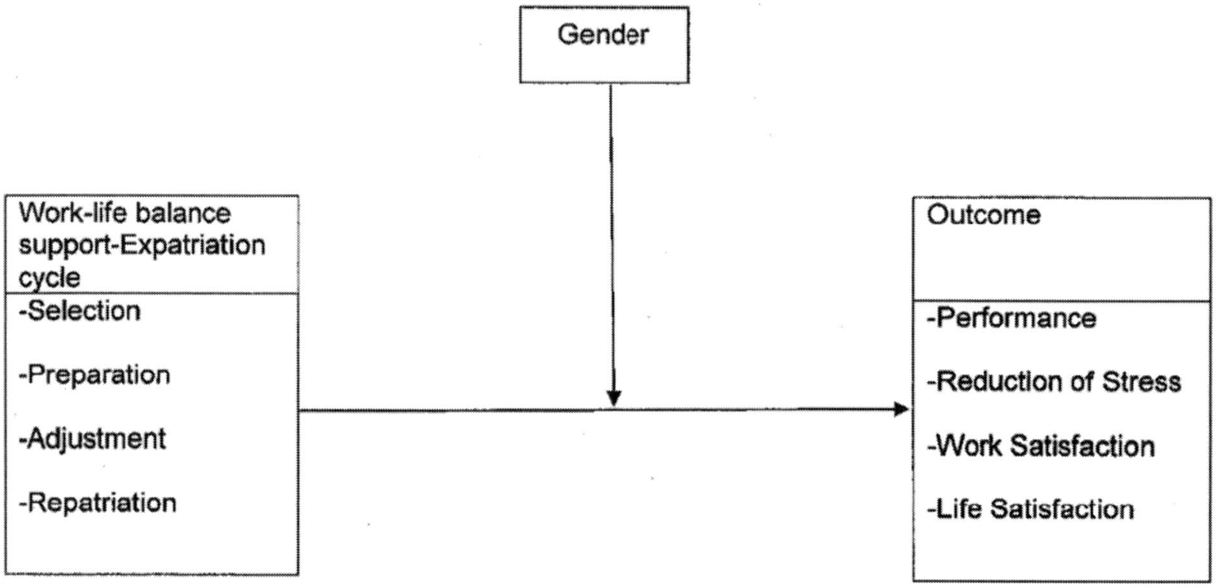

The structure of the paper will proceeds as follows. Section 2 analyzes in detail the concept of work-life balance, reviews literature regarding work-life balance programs and the expatriation cycle, develops the proposition on how work-life balance programs might affect the performance, stress level, work satisfaction, and life satisfaction of a female expatriate. Section 3 contains discussion and conclusion that is drawn from this study.

LITERATURE REVIEW

Work-life balance and benefits

As work-life balance has become important for employees, some organizations have decided to implement supportive policies with the goal of balancing work and life obligations of the employees. These initiatives are mostly voluntary by the organizations, which generally exceed legal requirements (Swody and Powell, 2007). The organizational benefits of offering work-life balance programs for the employees have been noted multiple times by scholars. Such positive outcomes include higher levels of employee engagement and commitment (Casio and Boudreau, 2010). Some studies regarding the benefits of work-life balance have shown significant support toward the implementation of certain policies. Additionally, reinforcement for work-life program attractiveness came from a recent meta-analysis by Butts, Casper, and Yang (2013), which showed that work-life balance has a significant and positive link on key employee outcomes including intention to stay and job satisfaction. It is also possible that the implementation of work-life balance programs can serve to decrease the negative outcomes caused by role conflict, which affects the employees' performance and satisfaction.

Consonant with these benefits of work-life balance support to expatriates can also serve to counteract the negative aspects of an international assignment including culture shock, language barrier, and lack of social support. Typical role expectations of expatriate include longer working hours, constant traveling, and limited time with family (Pascoe, 2005; Fischlmayr and Kollinger, 2010). As a result, work-life balance programs such as flex time, comp time, and paid sick leave can serve to reduce the impact of these international assignment stressors, especially for women expatriates who might face more challenges that their male counterparts. Females in international assignments will entail higher risks than male expatriates as in certain countries they will meet resistance from subordinates, colleagues and clients as certain cultures the issue of gender inequality still remains (Altman and Shortland, 2008). As a result, certain work-life balance programs including flexible time, comp time, and paid-time leave will have a greater effect for female expatriates than males.

Role conflict and female expatriates

When exploring expatriate challenges during the international assignment cycle (see Figure 1), it is important to consider family and work issues, along with the distinctions between them and their interactions. Based on the role conflict theory, female expatriates will most likely have greater challenges than their male counterparts as they will assume more complex roles with the international assignment. The additional roles can create an unbalance between personal and work time that can result in conflict. Focusing most of the time on one role can diminish the quality of another one (Bagger et al., 2008). This equilibrium can be more precarious for women. The study by Harris (2004) explained that female expatriates who often have greater involvement with childcare are more likely to have work-life conflict as a result of adjusting to the new role ushered in with international assignment. Additionally, some studies suggest that expatriate women tend to experience a greater level of work-life conflict in certain countries where gender inequality is still common (Crompton and Lyonette, 2006). Unfortunately, there are few such investigations as expatriate assignments have been traditionally assigned to males. Consequently, many studies are limited to the male expatriate international experience and their experience with their work-life balance.

From the extant literature on the expatriate experience, women expats tend to have a greater involvement in home activities than their male counterparts (Cinamon, 2006). However, these role expectations may be changing as a result of younger generations placing a higher priority on balancing home and work life while lowering their commitment to career development (Sturges and Guest, 2004). Nonetheless, a study by Thanerou (2008) showed that a woman's decision in taking an international assignment tends to have a greater negative effect on family members than if a male takes the same assignment.

Additionally, certain national cultures accept gender inequality which can lead female expatriate to confront an extra layer of discomfort (Altman and Shortland, 2008). As a result, work-life balance support can serve as a greater support for female expatriates than males. Thus, expectation is congruent with the general scholarship on work-life balance. A study by Burnett et al. (2010) suggested that females are more willing to take advantage of work-life balance programs than males especially in the cases where there are higher gender role expectations.

Work-life balance and the expatriation cycle

It is common for expatriates to be recommended for career development. An assignment in a foreign country can create new opportunities as well as challenges for the expatriate. Such international positions can also lead to longer hours of work, employee dissatisfaction, intrusion of personal time, and family conflict. This can lead to the failure of the expatriate's international assignment creating direct and indirect costs for the company. This can also create physical and mental problems for the expatriate in the form of health problems, stress, and low self-esteem (Copeland and Nurell, 2002). There are additional challenges for female expatriates which can increase the likelihood of returning prematurely to the home country, leading to the assignment's failure. Additional challenges include facing gender inequality in some cultures which can create lack of support by coworkers, supervisor, and clients (Altman and Shortland, 2008). As a result, literature regarding the effects of work-life balance support has increased over the years with the main goal of reducing expatriates' failure rate.

Some studies have identified factors that can influence an expatriate failure and the importance of organizational support for expatriate with the intent of preparing them for their international assignment (Shortland and Cummins, 2007; Hung-Wen, 2007; Tahir and Ismail, 2007; Littrell et al, 2006). As females' expatriate assignments have increased over the years, scholars are now exploring the challenges that women expatriate face. Some studies show the additional challenge that women expatriates face compared to males, and the importance of organizational support in the odyssey (Taylor and Napier, 1996; Harris, 2004; Fischlmayr and Killinger, 2010; Makela, Suutari, and Mayerhofer, 2011). Accepting an international assignment will require adapting to a different lifestyle that can disturb the balance between work and personal time. Because of these changes, work-life balance support can minimize such negative effects that result from the differences, which can increase the likelihood of success.

Work-life balance support and selection

Selection of potential candidates for expatriate assignments is the first stage of the expatriation cycle. As there are high costs associated with international assignments, there is a need to optimize the selection process. An increase of female expatriates accepting international assignments has increased over the years, there is still room for progress. The study by Tung (2004) explained that even so there is an increase of females taking international assignments, the number of female participants is still low. Equally important, there is a misconception that female expatriates have lower probabilities of being successful than their male counterparts. This apparent bias creates reluctance to select women for international assignments, and can result in missed opportunities. The study by Tung (2004) asserted that female expatriates are likely to be successful. Because of this opportunity, organizations can implement work-life balance support to encourage gender diversity for international assignments. Organizational support can occur through screening techniques which are gender blind. Instead, selection criteria can favor personal characteristics such as willingness to embrace a different culture and language, emotional maturity, and motivation.

Motivation is also another key issue driving the low number of women accepting international assignments. The study by Collings et al. (2007) explained that the unwillingness of women to take an international assignment can be derived from the potential disruption in their personal lives. This is a barrier that leads qualified women to miss the opportunity for career development. The study by Makela et al. (2011) argued that women are willing to take an expatriation assignment, but family factors discourage them in actually accepting them. This phenomenon is more common for dual-career couples as men that accompany women expatriate may be concerned about their own stalled career development in the foreign country. Male partners are more reluctant to follow in their international assignment as this can result in being unable to acquire a job in the host country and incurring loss of income which can create problems in the relationship (Selmer and Leung, 2003). This stressor can be further amplified since in some countries it is not socially acceptable for men to be unemployed while their female partner supports the family economically.

Work-life balance support is the appropriate answer to solve this dilemma. The type of work-life balance support that would be effective in this situation is to offer the male partner a job in the host country. Literature has showed the importance of the trailing spouse on the success of the expatriate. Offering a position to the partner will increase the willingness to transfer abroad, which can also minimize conflict between work and family role. Interrupting career advancement while being unable to find a job can create loss of self-esteem especially for males which can lead to a higher level of stress and discontent for the male spouse and the family in general (Harvey and Wiese, 1998). As a result, assistance and job support for the male partner can result in greater support for the female expatriate. Consequently, this benefit increases the chances for the project's success. The study by Linehan (2002) showed that ninety-two percent of the female respondents believed an expatriate experiences failure or success would depend on the happiness of their male spouse. Additionally, such support will serve to reduce the negative outcome of role conflict. Based on previous literature, we propose the following:

Proposition 1A: Work-life balance support in the selection stage will have a positive and significant relation for expatriates with the outcomes of performance, reduction of stress, work satisfaction, and life satisfaction.

Proposition 1B: Work-life balance support in the selection stage will have a greater positive and significant relation for female expatriates with the outcomes of performance, reduction of stress, work satisfaction, and life satisfaction.

Work-life balance support and preparation

International assignments can be more challenging than local assignments as it can impose many obstacles for the expatriates. The study by Makela et al. (2011) showed that the three main obstacles for an expatriate are greater responsibilities, a higher level of risk, and cultural differences that can challenge an expatriate's ideals. This can be further intensified for women expatriates as they face more challenges than male expatriates which can increase role conflict. Cultural differences as well as relocation issues are two of the main pre-departure problems that expatriates face which can lead to the failure of the assignment. The study by Foster (2000) showed that employees and employers understand the importance of family inclusion in cross cultural training; hardly any company involved in the study implemented such support.

One of the main challenges that female expatriates face are the differences in culture. Some cultures have prejudice against females in upper positions which can undermine their effectiveness in their new role. Additionally, cultural shock as a result of encountering a different treatment for women as well as the language barrier can result in higher degree of stress, dissatisfaction, helplessness, and family conflict. Consequently, it is a priority for the organization to offer work-life balance support in the form of cross-cultural training to minimize cultural shock which will increase the likelihood of the assignment's success. The study by Littrell et al. (2006) argued that cross cultural training can lower the level of stress as well as providing the necessary skills to cope with cultural shock effects in emotional, psychological, and behavioral areas. There are three types of cross cultural training that an organization can provide: cultural awareness, cultural intelligence and language training.

Cultural awareness training's main goal is to assist expatriates to understand their own culture so they can be able to appreciate the difference with the host country's culture. One of the major incremental challenges is the gender bias in some nations. Because of this problem, it is necessary for cultural awareness training to incorporate the cultural shock of a different treatment towards women. The study by Littrell et al. (2006) argued that cultural awareness training can lead to effective expat adjusting to the new culture as well as decreasing the probability of early returns. This is more salient when women are transferred to countries that are known to have high levels of gender inequality. Some societies follow certain norms and cultural traditions that limit the business decisions of females which creates barriers toward the project's success like in traditional Asian countries (De Cieri and Bardoel, 2009). Understanding the culture before being transferred can influence certain outcomes including level of stress, chances of success, and work and life satisfaction.

The second type of pre-departure training that shows promise for successful adaptation is cultural intelligence training. Cultural intelligence can be defined as an individual's capability to effectively manage relationships with people from diverse cultural backgrounds (Early and Ang, 2003). Literature demonstrating the benefits of cultural intelligence has grown over the years. Cultural intelligence can be classified as a crucial intercultural competency that is necessary for any expatriate that wants to be effective in their international assignment (Ang et al. 2007). This is more relatable to female expatriates as relocation to a traditional country with gender roles expectations can aggravate relationships with the host country's citizens. Cultural intelligence consists of four constructs (motivational, behavioral, meta-cognitive, and cognitive) that can help decrease the effects of cultural shock and increase the likelihood of project success. The study by Rose and Ramalu (2010) showed that cultural intelligence can improve the performance of expatriates as it increases the adaptation capabilities of the employee.

The third type of training which facilitates expatriate adjustment is language training. Language training can provide the means for expatriates to demonstrate their determination in adapting to the host country's culture as well as having more fluent conversations with the natives. The study by Selmer (2006) showed that proficiency in the host country's language has a positive association with interaction adjustment, life adjustment, and work adjustment. If the female expatriate has family members, it is also necessary for them to undertake and complete both cultural awareness and language training. Lack of understanding of the host country's language can create discomfort, stress, negatively impact job performance and engender dissatisfaction among the female expatriate and the family. The study by Bochner (1981) suggested that acquiring a second language can help to respond more effectively to the differences in the host country's culture.

It is crucial for organizations to offer cross-cultural training in the form of cultural awareness, cultural intelligence and language training. Past literature has showed that such support can lead to the success of expatriates especially for females when they are relocated to countries that are known to still have gender bias. Based on extant literature, we propose that:

Proposition 2A: Work-life balance support in the preparation stage will have a positive and significant relationship for expatriates with the outcomes of performance, reduction of stress, work satisfaction, and life satisfaction.

Proposition 2B: Work-life balance support in the preparation stage will have a greater positive and significant relation for female expatriates with the outcomes of performance, reduction of stress, work satisfaction, and life satisfaction.

Work-life balance support and adjustment

A woman expatriates and her family's inability to adjust to their new living and work environment can increase the likelihood of the assignment's failure which can be costly to them and the organization. As a result, organizational support in both work and home life are crucial to succeed in the international assignment. As explained earlier in the paper, international assignments creates different challenges in both living and working environments which are amplified because of gender bias and family responsibilities. Some studies have identified some living and working conditions that require adaptation including accommodations, school arrangements, housing chores, culture, climate, longer working hours, and frequent meetings (Shortland and Cummins, 2007; Makela, Suutari, and Mayerhofer, 2011). Lack of organization support on both working and living environment can result in a female expatriate's dissatisfaction in their working and living role, increased in stress level, and lower performance.

Acculturation of the new living and working environment is one of the main priorities for the female expatriate and her family. The female expatriate and her family will determine the amount of time and level of success to acculturate to the new culture and living environment. Because of the difficult process in adapting to a new lifestyle, it can result in role conflict as their will be unbalance between working and personal time. In order to increase the likelihood of acculturation success, there is a need of work-life balance support in the form of additional cross cultural training in the host country. Female expatriates and her family need to receive further cross cultural training in the form of cultural awareness and language training. Training should be assigned occasionally in the first 3-6 months of the international assignment as it can be consider the most crucial time for the female expatriate and her family.

As explained by Maleka et al. (2011) one of the major reasons for failing the international assignment is the difficulty of the family in adapting to the new culture. Representative of the countries that are locals of the host country should be assigned to assist the female expatriate and her family in time of uncertainty. There will be times in the expatriation process when the female expatriate will deal with difficult situation, and a local consultant can be the best form that the organization can support them. Additional information offered by the consultant regarding culture, norm and values, and language can help speed up the adjustment process. This is more important for female expatriates as some countries still have gender prejudice especially in a working relation between a men and a women. The study by Hutchings and Ratnasari (2006) showed that support from the parent company creates a positive effect to the adjustment factor.

The first weeks for a female expatriate can be regarded as the most difficult in the odyssey. Total concentration at work can mean less time with housing chores which can create family problems. Long hours of work can interfere with family time which can cause stress, dissatisfaction, and an increase of likelihood of the assignment failure. The lack of time for housing responsibilities as well as longer working hours can contribute to job burnout for the female expatriate. The study by Bhanugopan and Fish (2006) argued that one of the problems for expatriates is job burnout which in most occasions occur as a result of role conflict. Because of such issue, it is necessary for offering work-life balance support in the form of home chores assistance and childcare. Fischlmayr and Kollinger (2010) explained that additional support in housing chores which include cleaning, cooking, and child care can increase family time which can decrease work-family tension. This support will depend if the female expatriate has a family; however, we can assume that this type of support will be useful regardless of age and family composition.

Pressures within the family regarding the adjustment in the host country can facilitate the disruption of family equilibrium increasing the likelihood of failing in the international assignment. Those female expatriates that have children tend to focus their attention in different factors that will affect the children's future including educational accommodations. During this stage, it is common for female expatriates to support their children in adjusting to the new school environment as well as facilitating their interaction with children of the host country. Failure to do this can result in dissatisfaction of the children which can disrupt the family's unity. This effect can be amplified depending on the host country's culture. As argued by Harris (2004) in countries with traditional social-cultural norms regarding gender roles, female expatriates will face additional challenges as there will be a negative perception if child related issues are issued to the male partner. The negative effects of this issue can be reduced by the organization supporting the female expatriation in the form of arranging all school-related issues which includes paying for all educational expenses and locating a school that can provide in some form a continuation of the home country's curriculum. The study by Sims and Schraeder (2005) argued that if the company cover all educational expenses of the expatriate's children, it will facilitate the reassimilation process of the home country school system after the international assignment is completed.

The adjustment to a different lifestyle is a difficult process that can determine the failure or success of the international assignment. As a result, it is important for organization to support and enhance the adjustment process of female expatriates. From the information of past studies, we can propose that:

Proposition 3A: Work-life balance support in the adjustment stage will have a positive and significant relationship for expatriates with the outcomes of performance, reduction of stress, work satisfaction, and life satisfaction.

Proposition 3B: Work-life balance support in the adjustment stage will have a greater positive and significant relation for female expatriates with the outcomes of performance, reduction of stress, work satisfaction, and life satisfaction.

Work-life balance support and repatriation

Repatriation is the final stage that a female expatriate needs to endure to finalize their international assignment. Repatriation is an important stage in the expatriation cycle as is the return of employees that have acquired international experience. However, retention of expatriates that have acquired international experience tend to be one of the most difficult challenges for organizations (Scullion and Collings, 2006). A common main uncertainty for expatriates especially females can be expressed in the organization lack of emphasize in explaining what will be their position on the company and advancement opportunities. The study by Taylor and Napier (1996) showed that some of the frustration for female expatriates is the lack of appropriate positions for them, or being assigned positions that tend to use their international skills and knowledge at a minimum level. Such uncertainty about their future can create an expatriate turnover rate up to 30% to 40% after two years of the completion of the international assignments (Stroh, 1995). This is a problem for many companies as they do not develop programs which can create an effective transition for the returning expatriates. The uncertainty of what to expect when they return home can create stress and dissatisfaction in their working and personal roles which can increase the likelihood of failing the international assignment. The study by Lazarova and Caligiuri (2002) argued that the expatriate's perception regarding the level of support by the organization can determine whether the employee will stay or leave upon the repatriation stage of the expatriation cycle. As a result, work-life balance support in the form of clear communication of the position that will be assigned in their return and career development opportunities can create a positive effect in their work and life satisfaction, stress level, and performance in the international assignment.

As the number of female expatriates are increasing every year, there is the need to develop policies that would offer them a position ready for their return. The survey by Fischlmayr and Kollinger (2010) showed that female expatriate tend to be able to have a higher concentration in their international assignment if they know what to expect in their return. Knowing the different opportunities and the position that will be assigned in their return can also be seen as an incentive to succeed in the international assignment. Additionally, losing returning female expatriates can impose a direct and indirect cost for the company. Offering them a secure position when they return to the home country is essential to retain them. There is also a need to communicate the promotional opportunities that will be available when they return home. The study by Bolino (2007) argues that those expatriates that have guaranteed promotion opportunities will rarely leave the organization as there is a higher cost. Successful female expatriates can be consider a competitive advantage for the company as they can share their experience with other employees, and can be consider an inspiration for females to achieve high level positions (Taylor and Napier, 1996). Offering them a secure position as well as promotion opportunities will facilitate the transition to the home country while benefitting the company by retaining personnel with international knowledge and skills.

As international competition increases, there is a need to accumulate personnel with international experience. This type of support can help the female expatriate to focus in adapting to the new culture and lifestyle during the adaptation stage instead of adding pressure of not knowing what to expect in their return. As a result, we can argue that work-life balance support creates positive outcomes for female expatriates. From the information of past studies, we can propose that:

Proposition 4A: Work-life balance support in the repatriation stage will have a positive and significant relationship with expatriates in the outcomes of performance, reduction of stress, work satisfaction, and life satisfaction.

Proposition 4B: Work-life balance support in the repatriation stage will have a greater positive and significant relation for female expatriates with the outcomes of performance, reduction of stress, work satisfaction, and life satisfaction.

DISCUSSION AND CONCLUSIONS

This paper attempts to illustrate the importance of organization support in vital employee and organizational outcomes for all expatriates. The goal of this research was to analyze the importance of offering work-life balance programs in their expatriation cycle, especially for female expatriates. These are compelling topics focusing on the challenges faced by male and especially female expatriates, and their require support from their organizations. Furthermore, the increase of female expatriates during recent years has generated interest for scholars to identify if there are any variances in the type of organization, and their impact on reduction of stress, performance, life and job satisfaction. The insights offered by this study have identified potential contributions to organizational and employee performance and well-being. Still, there are constraints in this preliminary study. First, our propositions are drawn from the literature and need empirical tests. Second, the literature is mostly U.S. based. Thirdly, the study has only addressed challenges faced by heterosexual married couples. Overall, both men and women win and the organization and family too when work-life balance programs are tailored for expat needs, especially for female expats.

REFERENCES

Altman, Y., & Shortland, S. (2008). Women and international assignments: Taking stock—a 25-year review. *Human Resource Management*, *47*(2), 199-216.

Ang, S., Van Dyne, L., Koh, C., Ng, K. Y., Templer, K. J., Tay, C., & Chandrasekar, N. A. (2007). Cultural intelligence: Its measurement and effects on cultural judgment and decision making, cultural adaptation and task performance. *Management and organization review*, *3*(3), 335-371.

Bagger, J., Li, A., & Gutek, B. A. (2008). How much do you value your family and does it matter? The joint effects of family identity salience, family-interference-with-work, and gender. *Human Relations*, *61*(2), 187-211.

Bhanugopan, R., & Fish, A. (2006). An empirical investigation of job burnout among expatriates. *Personnel Review*, *35*(4), 449-468.

Bochner, S. (1981). *The mediating person: Bridges between cultures.* GK Hall & Co.

Bolino, M. C. (2007). Expatriate assignments and intra-organizational career success: Implications for individuals and organizations. *Journal of international business studies*, *38*(5), 819-835.

Burnett, S. B., Gatrell, C. J., Cooper, C. L., & Sparrow, P. (2010). Well-balanced families? A gendered analysis of work-life balance policies and work family practices. *Gender in Management: An International Journal*, *25*(7), 534-549.

Butts, M. M., Casper, W. J., & Yang, T. S. (2013). How important are work–family support policies? A meta-analytic investigation of their effects on employee outcomes. *Journal of Applied Psychology*, *98*(1), 1.

Cascio, W., & Boudreau, J. (2010). *Investing in people: Financial impact of human resource initiatives.* Ft Press.

Cinamon, R. G. (2006). Anticipated work-family conflict: effects of gender, self-efficacy, and family background. *The Career Development Quarterly*, *54*(3), 202-215.

Collings, D. G., Scullion, H., & Morley, M. J. (2007). Changing patterns of global staffing in the multinational enterprise: Challenges to the conventional expatriate assignment and emerging alternatives. *Journal of World Business*, *42*(2), 198-213.

Copeland, A. P., & Norell, S. K. (2002). Spousal adjustment on international assignments: The role of social support. *International Journal of Intercultural Relations*, *26*(3), 255-272.

Crompton, R., & Lyonette, C. (2006). Work-life 'balance'in Europe. *Acta Sociologica*, *49*(4), 379-393.

De Cieri, H., & Bardoel, E. A. (2009). What does 'work–life management'mean in China and Southeast Asia for MNCs?. *Community, Work & Family*, *12*(2), 179-196.

Earley, P. C., & Ang, S. (2003). *Cultural intelligence: Individual interactions across cultures.* Stanford University Press.

Fischlmayr, I. C., & Kollinger, I. (2010). Work-life balance–a neglected issue among Austrian female expatriates. *The International Journal of Human Resource Management*, *21*(4), 455-487.

Forster, N. (2000). Expatriates and the impact of cross-cultural training. *Human Resource Management Journal*, *10*(3), 63-78.

Harris, H. (2004). Global careers: Work-life issues and the adjustment of women international managers. *Journal of Management Development*, *23*(9), 818-832.

Harvey, M., & Wiese, D. (1998). The dual-career couple: female expatriates and male trailing spouses. *Thunderbird International Business Review*, *40*(4), 359-388.

Hung-Wen, L. (2007). Factors that influence expatriate failure: An interview study. *International Journal of Management*, *24*(3), 403.

Hutchings, K., & Wahyuni Ratnasari, S. (2006). Cross-cultural non-work transition stresses: domestic transferees in Indonesia. *Cross Cultural Management: An International Journal*, *13*(2), 114-131.

Lazarova, M., & Caligiuri, P. (2002). Retaining repatriates: The role of organizational support practices. *Journal of world business*, *36*(4), 389-401.

Linehan, M. (2002). Senior female international managers: Empirical evidence from Western Europe. *International Journal of Human Resource Management*, *13*(5), 802-814.

Littrell, L. N., Salas, E., Hess, K. P., Paley, M., & Riedel, S. (2006). Expatriate preparation: A critical analysis of 25 years of cross-cultural training research. *Human Resource Development Review*, *5*(3), 355-388.

Mäkelä, L., Suutari, V., & Mayerhofer, H. (2011). Lives of female expatriates: work-life balance concerns. *Gender in Management: An International Journal*, *26*(4), 256-274.

Morris, M. A., & Robie, C. (2001). A meta-analysis of the effects of cross-cultural training on expatriate performance and adjustment. *International Journal of Training and Development*, *5*(2), 112-125.

Organization Resources Counselors Inc (ORC) (2002), *Worldwide Survey of International Assignment Policies and Practices*, European Edition.

Pascoe, R. (2005). Enriching work and life in the global workplace. *Accounting & tax periodicals*, *48*(4).

Rose, R. C., & Ramalu, S. S. (2010). Expatriate performance in international assignments: The role of cultural intelligence as dynamic intercultural competency. In *International Journal of Business and Management*.

Scullion, H. U. G. H., & Collings, D. G. (2006). Alternative forms of international assignments. *Global Staffing, London: Routledge*, 159-177.

Selmer, J. (2006). Language ability and adjustment: Western expatriates in China. *Thunderbird International Business Review*, *48*(3), 347-368.

Selmer, J., & Leung, A. S. (2003). Provision and adequacy of corporate support to male expatriate spouses: An exploratory study. *Personnel Review*, *32*(1), 9-21.

Shortland, S., & Cummins, S. (2007). Work-life balance: Expatriates reflect the international dimension. *Global Business and Organizational Excellence*, *26*(6), 28-42.

Sims, R. H., & Schraeder, M. (2005). Expatriate compensation: An exploratory review of salient contextual factors and common practices. *Career Development International*, *10*(2), 98-108.

Stroh, L. K. (1995). Predicting turnover among repatriates: can organizations affect retention rates?. *International Journal of Human Resource Management*, *6*(2), 443-456.

Sturges, J., & Guest, D. (2004). Working to live or living to work? Work/life balance early in the career. *Human Resource Management Journal*, *14*(4), 5-20.

Swody, C. A., & Powell, G. N. (2007). Determinants of employee participation in organizations' family-friendly programs: A multi-level approach. *Journal of Business and Psychology*, *22*(2), 111-122.

Tahir, A. H. M., & Ismail, M. (2007). Cross-cultural challenges and adjustment of expatriates: A case study in Malaysia. *Turkish Journal of International Relations*, *6*(3&), 4.

Taylor, S., & Napier, N. (1996). Working in Japan: Lessons from women expatriates. *MIT Sloan Management Review*, *37*(3), 76.

Tharenou, P. (2008). Disruptive decisions to leave home: Gender and family differences in expatriation choices. *Organizational Behavior and Human Decision Processes*, *105*(2), 183-200.

Tung, R. L. (1982). Selection and training procedures of US, European, and Japanese multinationals. *California Management Review*, *25*(1), 57-71.

Tung, R. L. (2004). Female Expatriates:: The Model Global Manager?. *Organizational Dynamics*, *33*(3), 243-253.

World Trade Organization. (2016). Time Series. Retrieved from http://stat.wto.org/StatisticalProgram/WSDBStatProgramYear.aspx?Language=E

DECISION SCIENCES INSTITUTE

Subjective Well-Being of Children of Migrant Families in Schooling Alternatives of Urban China

Steven Silver
California State University, San Jose.
Email: sds001@calmail.berkeley.edu

ABSTRACT

Organizational labor forces in countries that include China, the OECD and U.S. continue to be increasingly composed of workers who migrate across country regions or from other countries. Since their children will enter the next generation of labor forces, it is increasingly relevant to assess the educational experience of these children. Background studies of both children and adults indicate the importance of assessing subjective well-being (SW-B) to overall health and human capital. This study reports results of an initial assessment of SW-B in children of migrant family in an urban center of China across school type, grade and gender differences.

KEYWORDS: Human Capital, Subjective Well Being, Migrant Work Forces, Developing Countries.

INTRODUCTION

In countries including China, the U.S. and OECD, organizational labor forces are increasingly composed of workers who either migrate across regions of the respective country (e.g. rural to urban) or migrate from contiguous or geographically close countries. This is now well recognized as generating high priority welfare issues for migrant workers, their families and society in general. At present, the majority of migrant workers have entered semiskilled or skilled occupations in labor forces. However, the next generation can be anticipated to evidence mobility across a broad range of occupations many of which will be professional due in no small part to educational opportunities in their country of residence. As such, it is increasingly relevant for those who study human capital and productivity in organizational work forces as well as overall well-being to consider the competencies that develop in the education of children of migrant families.

Of course, each country has contextual differences that are important to defining issues and appropriate policy (e.g. Asis 2006 in the Philippines; Liang & Chen 2007 in China; Dreby 2010 in the U.S.), however, China is a case of particular interest because of the large migrations that have occurred in the relatively short period of time since the economic reform in the 1980s. In 2008, it was reported that 225 million individuals migrated from rural agricultural areas to urban areas since 1980 (Lai et al 2014).

In China, the majority of available studies of the educational experience of children of migrant families contrast what are designated as "left behind" children in China's *hukou* system for generating assignment to schools[1] with children who complete a similar curriculum in either rural or urban schools (e.g. Ye & Murray 2005). An important difference between children in the "left behind" category and other children is that they separated from their parents who are migrant workers and live with members of their extended families (e.g., grandparents: *nainai* and *yeye*) and attend school in the initial geographical location of their parents. While the emphasis on contrasts of educational-related outcomes of "left behind" children with other children can be easily understood as a welfare priority, we would suggest that the study of children who now reside with their parents and attend urban schools merits more attention than it has received. Even when children are allowed to reside with migrant families, their educational assignments and experience may commonly differ from those of children of non-migrant workers. Such differences are likely to arise from factors such as differences in the qualities of schools that children of migrant families are assigned to and as a consequence of the general demands in adjustment that migrant families face.

Many children of migrant families are assigned to private schools in their urban areas of residence because the extraordinary number of migrant work families in China has strained the country's educational resources in state schools. Generally private schools in these cases have fewer resources and less well-trained teachers than state schools. As such, there are bases to anticipate that the educational experiences of children of migrant families that reside in urban centers may differ from both those of children of non-migrant families and those of "left-behind" children.

As China advances in its development and social policies (including modifications of the *hukuo* system) there will be increasing numbers of children who live with and attend schools where their parents work relative to "left-behind" children. The results of policy towards such children are likely to have enduring effects on human capital, labor force productivity and growth and development.[2] Since this is early in the academic study of the welfare of children in migrant families who are located and schooled in urban centers of China, this study has an opportunity to give important direction to policy as well as generalizing our understanding of relevant issues in the education and general well-being of children in this category across countries.

As noted by other authors, issues in schooling clearly extend beyond academic achievement (e.g. Berry et al 2006; Chen et al 1997; Coll et al, 1996; Wong 2004). In addition to measures of educational attainment, it is now well recognized in many countries that children's self-reported subjective well-being (SW-B) is a coordinate measure of the quality of educational and socialization experience that has ramifications for psychological functioning in adulthood.

1 The *hukou* system in China uses residency permits to divide Chinese citizens into urban and rural dwellers. A person's *hukou* status determines his or her access to state services. A person with a rural *hukou* status is generally not eligible for state services in urban areas, because *hukou* is primarily inherited from one's parents at the time of birth. Children born in urban areas to parents with rural *hukou* are similarly designated as rural *hukou* holders. As a result, children living in cities with rural *hukou* are not eligible for enrollment in urban public schools even if they were born within the urban district. Montgomery (2014) is among the authors that review the consequencies of this system.

2 For a consideration that can include migrant children's education in these contexts, see Heckman & Yi (2012) andFleisher et al (2010).

LITERATURE REVIEW:

Wen and Lin (2012) studied schooling outcomes of children "left behind" who were enrolled in state schools when one or both parents were rural to urban migrants. In comparison to children of non-migrant parents, "left behind" children were found to be disadvantaged in health behavior and school engagement but not in "perceived satisfaction" with their general life situation. The authors emphasize the importance of family socio-economic status, socializing process and peer and school support to developmental outcome regardless of parents' migrant status. Lai, Liu, Luo et al (2014) examined the academic performance of children in private schools exclusively for migrant children in Beijing and rural public schools in Shaanxi province. They report that although migrant students outperformed rural students initially (possibly because of the skill capabilities of workers who were able to migrate), the gap is increasingly closed because of poorer school resources and lower teacher quality in the private schools they were assigned to in Beijing. Chen, Rubin and Li (1997) studied the relationship between academic achievement and measures of social adjustment across different years. Their results generally support the reciprocal effects between academic achievement and social adjustment proposed by earlier investigators (e.g., Hinshaw (1992). Thus a deficiency or further advantagement in one of the realms is likely to spill over to the other. These and other authors note the low levels of correlation between SES indicators and SWB. In contrast to inference in Wen and Lia (2012), this implies that SES differences independent of resources are unlikely to meaningfully modify 8WB.

STUDY DESIGN: While general differences in academic achievement across state schools and the informal private schools that have been described have been reported in samples that include "left behind" children or urban vs rural locations, we are unable to locate any previous studies of that address SW-B in children of migrant families across school types in their urban locations, school grades and gender. Additionally, available studies have used a global measure of SW-B rather than one that is defined in sub – dimensions of SW-B. Directly, stated the study that will be reported provides an initial assessment of contrasts in the educational experience of children of migrant families that live with their nuclear families and attend schools in the urban setting where their parents work. We study sub-dimensions of SW-B and investigate key intervening variables in the type of school in which they are enrolled, their grade level and gender.

The Multidimensional Students' Life Satisfaction Scale (MSLSS)

A long history has argued for supplementing economic measures of welfare with measures of subjective well-being (refs). In contrast to studies that infer subjective well-being from the absence of psychopathological symptoms, the World Health Organization (e.g., 1964) defined health as a state of complete physical, mental, and social well-being. Pavot, Diener, Colvin, and Sandvik, (1991) defined life satisfaction as a "global evaluation by the person of his or her life". Cowen (1991) elaborated on this perspective in arguing that psychological well-being should be considered on the basis of positive indicators, including indicators like "basic satisfaction with one's self and one's existence or life satisfaction. Life satisfaction that can be measured as SW-B has been differentiated from other well-being constructs such as self-esteem (Terry and Huebner, 1995; Lucas, Diener, and Suh, 1996; Huebner, Gilman, and Laughlin, 1999) and positive affect (Lucas et al., 1996; Huebner, 1991c; Huebner, and Dew, 1996). Although there are now a large number of studies of life satisfaction of adults (Diener, 1994; Veenhoven, 1993 +newer ref), life satisfaction in children has more recently become the focus of empirical work.

Early children's life satisfaction instruments were limited to unidimensional measures of global or general life satisfaction (e.g., Adelman, Taylor, and Nelson, 1989; Dew and Huebner, 1994). The MSLSS was designed to provide a multidimensional profile of children's life satisfaction judgments in specific domains: self, living, school, friends and family

(Huebner 1991a and b). The SW-B measure that we use is a Chinese adaptation of Huebner's Students' Life Satisfaction Scale (MSLSS: e.g., Seligson, Huebner & Valois 2003) that Chen, Rubin and Li (1997) and Chen and Fleischler (2008) have reported construct validity for.

PROCEDURE: Using a Chinese translation of the MSLSS, we examine children's subjective well-being across two types of educational facilities that children of migrant families are enrolled in: privately-run schools limited to children of migrant families and public schools that are also limited to these children. The differences in school type that these children are examined across gender and three grade levels.

For the study, we were given access to state and private schools as major alternatives in school types for children of migrant families in China in one of the major destinations for migrant workers (the Shanghai metropolitan area). In this area as well as other urban centers, assignment to schools is by residential location and space and availability rather than parental background and/or pretesting of children[3]. One of the alternatives is a government run (state) school, a second is a private run school for migrant workers children only[4]. A total of 682 male and female students in U.S. equivalent grades of 3 to 5 in the schools comprise the study sample.

For each school, one of the co-authors initially met with head teachers, informed them of the study intentions and offered each a draft of study questionnaires. Feedback from head teachers was used to modify content and organization where appropriate. Adjusted questionnaire were then given back to the head teachers, and passed to class teachers in different year groups who conducted the survey in class.

RESULTS

Measure Reliability

Sub-scale-reliability was assessed for each of the measured SW-B sub-dimensions with Cronbach's coefficient alpha and item-sum reliability. For self, α = .801, family α = 0.824, school $\alpha = .774$, friends α = .801 and living $\alpha = .738$. Although the sub-dimension reliabilities are lower than for the established instrument, we recognize that the Chinese SLSS is a

3 In Beijing, alternatives in placement include lotteries for placement in different schools as is the practice in many U.S. cities. The majority of urban centers including Shanghai follow the procedure described here.

4 As observed above, common Western differences between the school types are at least questionable in their application to China since the government run schools are thought to be as well or better funded than the type of private school available to children of migrant families. There are two types of private schools in China, one of them is like those in the U.S. They have high tuition and usually provide better educational experiences than public schools. The second type of private school is more like an informal school. Children unable to attend public schools are organized locally, mostly in suburban/rural areas. The resultant schools tend to have limited number of qualified teachers and lower quality teaching facilities. For migrant parents, the best choice for them is to let their children attend a government school. This is difficult for some of them, because of distance and other requirements. While the requirements differ in various districts of Shanghai, parents usually have to provide evidence of stable employment and long-term accommodation that migrant family commonly do not have.

contextualized translation, and consider these levels adequate for an initial study. We further examined the factorial structure of the measures of sub-dimensions in principal components analyses. For sub-dimensions of self, friends and school, a single component accounted for more than two-thirds of the item variances in items. For sub-dimensions of living and family, a single component accounted for more than .50 of the respective item variances.

MANOVA Results

Results were initially analyzed in a multivariate analysis of variance (MANOVA) with the sub-dimensions of the subjective well-being scale measured as dependent variables and type of school (Public vs Private), gender and grade level as independent variables. Main effects of school type and grade were uniformly significant for the multivariate test statistics ((Wilks Lambda: School type ($F=6.344$, $p<.001$), Gender ($F=3.121$, $p<01$), Grade ($F=1.896$, $p<.05$)). In interactions among independent variables in the MANOVA results, only Grade x School type attained statistical significance (Wilks Lambda: $F=1.812$, $p=.05$). Students in grade 5 of public schools had significantly higher scores ($p<.05$) on the combined SW-B measure than any of the other Grade x School type levels. Figure 1 presents the levels of SLSS subscales for each of the independent variables. Univariate analyses of variance for each sub-dimension were then examined.

Figure1: Effects of School Type, Grade Level and Gender one Sub-dimensions of the Children's SW-B Measure.

1(a) School Type

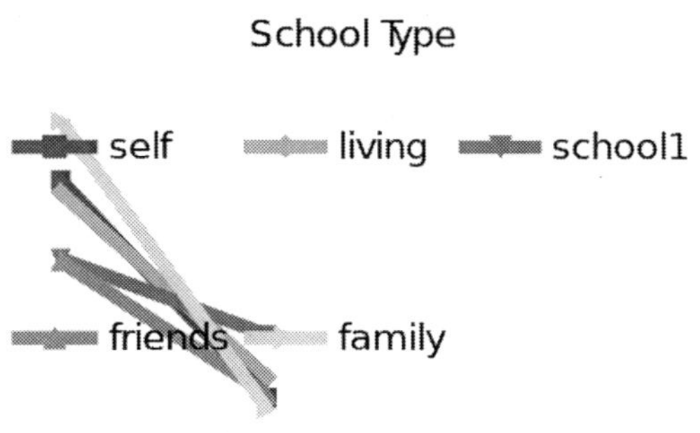

Note 1=State school. 2= Private School

1(b): ***Grade***

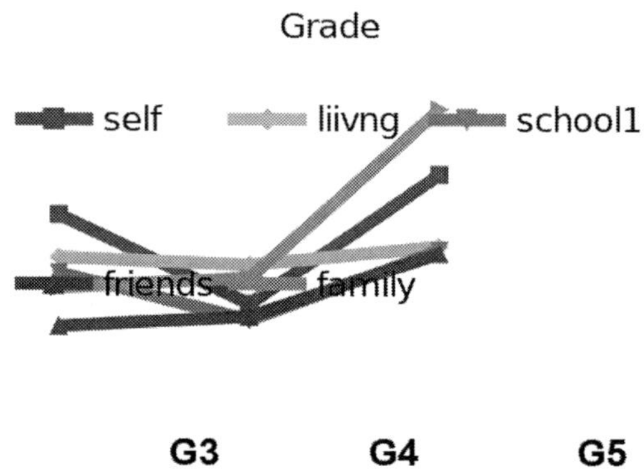

***Note G3= Grade 3 G4 = Grade 4 G5= Grade 5**

1(c): ***Gender***

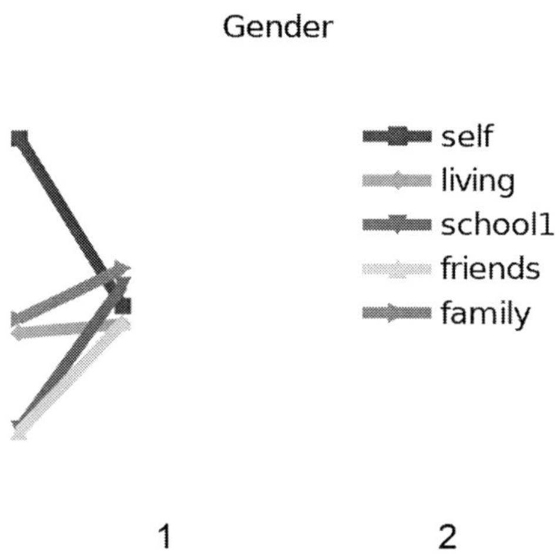

Note: 1= Male and 2= Female

Univariate Results; In results of ANOVAs, each of the sub-dimensions although students in grade 5 had higher scores than students in grades 3 and 4. Effects of school type were statistically significant for family ($F=20.259$, $p<.001$), friends ($F=14.103$, $p<.001$) and self ($F=10.869$, $p<.001$). On all of these sub-dimensions of SW-B, the public school was higher than the private school. Only main effects of grade on family ($F= 6.569$, $p< .001$), attained statistical significance. The grade x school type interaction was significant for family ($F=5.502$, $p<.005$) and friends ($F=4.197$, $p<.02$). The main effect of gender was significant for friends ($F=12.197$, $p<.001$), school ($F=3.609$, $p<.06$) and self ($F=3.847$, $p<.05$). Females were significantly higher than males for friends and school type but significantly lower than males on self.

While corresponding differences between school types have been shown in measures of academic achievement (ref), this is the first time that differences in SW-B as a measure of well-being have been demonstrated across school types. Results for grade show a significant developmental trend that was evidenced for most sub-dimensions of SW-B. The trend indicates an increase from levels of G3 and G4 to the level at G5. The results for grade suggest the possibility of a developmental critical point in the SW-B of children that may merit more attention both conceptually and in policy design. The interaction between school type and grade indicates that while state schools outperform private schools across all grade levels, the differences are most pronounced at the level of grade 5. In gender effects, females are significantly higher than males on the more social dimensions of living, friends and family but lower on the internalized sub-dimension of self.

DISCUSSION

The study that we report is among the few that address children of migrant families that reside with their families in urban locations. Results begin to document factors that affect the level of SW – B of children of migrant families. These results confirm that informal private schools disadvantage children in subjective well-being of as well as in academic achievement. If, as results suggest, grade 5 is a developmental critical point, special attention may be appropriate to developing these dimensions in their educational experiences in grade 4. In the face of the unprecedented worker migrations of the post-Deng period, China has allocated substantial resources to the education of children. Most of the measures of the effects of this investment have been in educational attainment. A wide range of literature that has been reviewed indicates the importance of subjective well-being in children to their functioning as adults. This includes the quality of human capital they bring to labor markets. Results of the study that we report can give direction to policy for the development of SW-B as in both critical points and sub-dimensions that most sensitive to school type and gender differences. Subsequent studies can further inference offered from the results that we report by providing additional evidence of concurrent and predictive validity of the translated SLSS and migrant families and "left behind" children. More generally, the large-scale migrations of workers to urban areas in a number of countries make the study of SW-B of their children a research priority for reasons of their general welfare as well as their contributions in subsequent generations of the labor force.

REFERENCES:

Ahuvia, A. C., & Friedman, D. C. (1998). Income, consumption, and subjective well-being: Toward a composite macromarketing model. *Journal of Macromarketing*, *18*(2), 153-168.

Berry, J. W., Phinney, J. S., Sam, D. L., & Vedder, P. (2006). Immigrant youth: Acculturation, identity, and adaptation. *Applied Psychology*, *55*(3), 303-332.

Chen, X., & French, D. C. (2008). Children's social competence in cultural context. *Annual Review of Psychology*, *59*, 591-616.

Chen, X., Rubin, K. H., & Li, D. (1997). Relation between academic achievement and social adjustment: Evidence from Chinese children. *Developmental Psychology*, *33*(3), 518.

Chen, X.X., Q.H. Huang, S. Rozelle, J.S. Yao & L.X. Zhang (2009) 'Effect of Migration on Children's Academic Performance in Rural China', *Comparative Economic Studies* 51: 323–43

Coll, C. G., Crnic, K., Lamberty, G., Wasik, B. H., Jenkins, R., Garcia, H. V., & McAdoo, H. P. (1996). An integrative model for the study of developmental competencies in minority children. *Child Development*, *67*(5), 1891-1914.

Cowen (1991)

Dittmar, H., Bond, R., Hurst, M., & Kasser, T. (2014). The relationship between materialism and personal well-being: A meta-analysis. *Journal of Personality and Social Psychology*, *107*(5), 879.

Dreby, J. (2010) *Divided by Borders: Mexican Migrants and Their Children*. Berkeley, CA: University of California Press.

Fleisher, B., Li, H., & Zhao, M. Q. (2010). Human capital, economic growth, and regional inequality in China. *Journal of Development Economics*, *92*(2), 215-231.

Hannum, E., M. Wang & J. Adams (2010) 'Rural–Urban Disparities in Access to Primary and Secondary Education under Market Reform', in M.K. Whyte (ed.) *One Country, Two Societies? Rural–Urban Inequality in Contemporary China*, pp. 125–46. Cambridge, MA: Harvard University Press.

Heckman, J. J., & Yi, J. (2012). *Human Capital, Economic growth, and Inequality in China* (No. w18100). National Bureau of Economic Research.

Kahneman, D., & Krueger, A. B. (2006). Developments in the measurement of subjective well-being. *The Journal of Economic Perspectives*, *20*(1), 3-24.

Kooij, D. T., Guest, D. E., Clinton, M., Knight, T., Jansen, P. G., & Dikkers, J. S. (2013). How the impact of HR practices on employee well-being and performance changes with age. *Human Resource Management Journal*, *23*(1), 18-35.

Liang, Z., & Chen, Y. P. (2007). The educational consequences of migration for children in China. *Social science Research*, *36*(1), 28-47.

Lai, F., Liu, C., Luo, R., Zhang, L., Ma, X., Bai, Y., ... & Rozelle, S. (2014). The education of China's migrant children: The missing link in China's education system. *International Journal of Educational Development*, *37*, 68-77.

Mick, D. G., Pettigrew, S., Pechmann, C. C., & Ozanne, J. L. (Eds.). (2012). *Transformative Consumer Research for Personal and Collective Well-being*. London :Routledge.

Montgomery, J. L. (2012). Inheritance of Inequality: Hukou and related Barriers to Compulsory Education for China's Migrant Children, The. *Pacific Rim Legal & Policy Journal*, *21*, 591.

Ru, S. (2006). Problems and Solutions for Child Education for Migrant Rural Worker Families [J]. *Journal of China Agricultural University (Social Sciences Edition)*, *3*, 019.

Seligson, J. L., Huebner, E. S., & Valois, R. F. (2003). Preliminary validation of the brief multidimensional students' life satisfaction scale (BMSLSS). *Social Indicators Research*, *61*(2), 121-145.

Wang, D. (2004). A survey of educational problems among children of migrant workers. *Chinese Population Science*, *4*, 58-64.

Wen, M., & Lin, D. (2012). Child development in rural China: Children left behind by their migrant parents and children of nonmigrant families. *Child Development*, *83*(1), 120-136.

World Health Organization (1964)

Ye, J., & Murray, J. (2005). *Left-behind Children in Rural China: Impact Study of Rural Labor Migration on left-behind children in Mid-West China*. Social Sciences Academic Press.

Zhou, F. (2002). Problems in migrant family education and educational interventions. *Educational Science Research*, *11*, 54-55.

DECISION SCIENCES INSTITUTE

Substitutes or complements? The impact of contractual and relational governance on logistics integration and operational performance

Qianwen Wang
Zhejiang University
Email: qianwen@zju.edu.cn

Baofeng Huo
Zhejiang University
Email: baofeng@zju.edu.cn

Xiande Zhao
China-Europe International Business School (CEIBS)
Email: xiande@ceibs.edu

ABSTRACT

How to safeguard and enhance logistics integration (e.g. information sharing, process coordination) between 3PL users and providers using different governance mechanisms is a crucial issue. Based on transactional cost economics (TCE), this study examined effects of contractual governance (e.g. detailed contract, contract application), relational governance (e.g. trust, relational norm), and their interaction effects on logistics integration, which further leads to operational performance. We conduct a survey to collect data from 247 3PL users in China and tested the conceptual model using the structural equation modeling method.

KEYWORDS: Contractual governance, Relational governance, Logistics integration, 3PL, China

INTRODUCTION

In recently years, more and more firms conduct logistics outsourcing to third-party logistics (3PL) providers, which can help firms to bring higher effectiveness and efficiency. China's 3PL industry is rapidly growing at an annual rate of 20 percent in recent years. In 2014, the total business income of China's 3PL firms is approximately 938 billion yuan, and this number reaches approximately 586 billion yuan at the first half year of 2015. However, most 3PL providers supply limited value-added services to users, such as transportation, distribution and warehousing. Only a small number of them are able to provide advanced logistics services, such as logistics system design and information management (Hong and Liu, 2007). Empirical evidence showed that integrating with supply chain members helps to create competitive advantages, but they more emphasize supplier integration and customer integration (e.g. Flynn et al., 2010), few emphasized logistics integration with 3PL providers (Jayaram and Tan, 2010; Mortensen and Lemoine, 2008; Sheikh and Rana, 2012). Our understanding on what is logistics integration between 3PL users and providers, and what are antecedents or outcomes of logistics integration, are still limited. For examples, how to safeguard and enhance logistics integration with 3PL providers by appropriate governance mechanisms is still under exploration.

According to transaction cost economics (TCE), both contractual and relational governance are important in interfirm relationships (Cannon et al., 2000; Ferguson et al., 2005; Wang et al., 2011; Yu et al., 2006; Zaheer and Venkatraman, 1995). Whether jointly using contractual and relational governance in 3PL relationships is more effective or not remains unclear. There is no consensus about whether they are substitutes (Dyer, 2002; Gulati, 1995), complements (Luo, 2002; Poppo and Zenger, 2002), or no interactions (Cavusgil et al., 2004). Also, we explored how two dimensions of logistics integration (e.g. information sharing, process coordination) improve operational performance.

LITERATURE REVIEW AND RESEARCH HYPOTHESES

Contractual governance and relational governance

Governance is a multidimensional phenomenon that refers to formal and informal rules for a transaction between parties (Griffith and Myers, 2005; Nickerson et al., 2001). According to TCE, firms need to design appropriate governance mechanisms to support transactions (Heide, 1994; Heide and John, 1992). Macneil (1980) developed a typology of "discrete" versus "relational" exchange to respectively represent economic and social relationships. That is, in a buyer-supplier dyad, governance can be realized through contractual or relational governance mechanisms (Heide and John, 1992; Jap and Ganesan, 2000). In this study, we will explore both contractual and relational governance mechanisms.

Detailed contract and contract application are two major contractual governance mechanisms (Faems et al., 2008; Woolthuis et al., 2005; Wuyts and Geyskens, 2005; Zhou and Xu, 2012). Detailed contract is identified "with a large number of clauses that are specified in detail" (Ariño and Reuer, 2005, p.149), and provides a legally bounded framework specifying goals, rights, duties, and responsibilities of each party, formally specifying what is and what is not allowed to behave during the contracting period (Dyer, 2002; Luo, 2002). As a coordination mechanism, detailed contract can entail clauses to safeguard specific assets and ensure the enforceability of a transaction against opportunistic behaviors (Ring and Van de Ven, 1992; Williamson, 1985). Previous studies mainly focus on the initial design element of contractual governance, contract application is also essential because the effectiveness of a contract depends on its application (Antia and Frazier, 2001), including monitoring, assessing or penalizing to prevent unexpected behaviors (Woolthuis et al., 2005).

Relational governance emphasizes soft and "human" elements to coordinate a transaction. Trust and relational norm are two major mechanisms that are widely used in an interfirm relationship (Anderson and Narus, 1990; Arranz and Arroyabe, 2012; Heide and John, 1992; Liu et al., 2009; Luo, 2007). Trust refers to the willingness and confidence to rely on a trading partner, and emphasizes the transaction's cooperative atmosphere (Liu et al., 2009; Monczka et al., 1998; Spekman et al., 1998). It is also a firm's belief that other firms' behaviors will lead to positive outcomes and less unexpected behaviors that may be detrimental to the focal firm (Anderson and Narus, 1990). Relational norm reflects the expectation of attitudes and behaviors in which different parties work cooperatively to achieve mutual goals (Cannon et al., 2000). In particular, it represents a series of mutually oriented behaviors and underlying, flexible and intangible rules, values that are shared by transaction partners. Heide & John (1992) identified three dimensions of relational norm: flexibility, information exchange, and solidarity.

Logistics integration

As Towill (1997) mentioned, all players must think and act as one whole. In this study, based on Bowersox et al. (2002), Flynn et al. (2010), Frohlich and Westbrook (2001) and Romano (2003), we define logistics integration as the degree to which a 3PL user collaboratively manages interfirm logistics processes with its providers to facilitate accurate and timely flows for maximum customer value at low costs and high speed. From the flow perspective, 3PL providers and users need to be connected seamlessly with fully integrated information and material flows. Information sharing and process coordination are two major dimensions of integration (Cai et al., 2010; Liu et al., 2015; Sahin and Robinson, 2002, 2005; Wu et al., 2014). Information sharing implies that partners frequently share important information, such as demand forecast, schedule, and capacity information. Process coordination is more complex than information sharing and implies the synchronization of material flows, such as joint planning (Moharana et al., 2012; Mortensen and Lemoine, 2008; Rabinovich et al., 1999; Samaddar et al., 2006).

Contractual governance and logistics integration

Integration can be viewed as mutual investments to facilitate accurate and timely information and material flows (Vijayasarathy, 2010). A firm's task is to adopt appropriate governance mechanisms to support a transaction. Detailed contract serves as a form of quasi-integration and build a vertical interfirm authority that can subsequently guide both parties' behaviors (Stinchcombe and Heimer, 1985). First, well-articulated clauses narrow the domain in which parties can be opportunistic, such as selling an unauthorized territory and hiding important information; Second, detailed contract specifies of promises, obligations for logistics integration, which aligns partners' incentives and ensures credible information sharing (Cachon and Lariviere, 2001). Also, detailed contract creates a predictable cooperative environment that mitigates exchange hazards and facilitates coordination between parties (Faems et al., 2008). Therefore, we propose:

H1a. Detailed contract is positively related to information sharing.
H1b. Detailed contract is positively related to process coordination.

As contractual governance, detailed contracts and contract application serve distinct functions. (Malhotra and Lumineau, 2011; Mellewigt et al., 2007; Reuer and Arino, 2007). Detailed contract serves as an ex ante coordination mechanism, while contract application is a control mechanism to guarantee the ongoing integration process. Contract application endows 3PL users the legal right to effectively control the transaction, thus information sharing and process coordination can be under the protection of contract application against exchange hazards. Therefore, we propose:

H2a. Contract application is positively related to information sharing.
H2b. Contract application is positively related to process coordination.

Relational governance and logistics integration

Interfirm transactions are typically embedded in social relationships (Heide and John, 1992; Macneil, 1978, 1980). Relational governance mechanisms is effective to nourish cooperation in buyer-supplier dyads with less monitoring and bargaining costs (Barney and Hansen, 1994; Heide and John, 1992; Kim, 2000). When both parties perceive each other as trusted, potential opportunistic behaviors are reduced and cooperative behaviors are promoted (Johnston et al., 2004; Zaheer et al., 1998a, b). Trust ensures a focal firm to be more selective for partners, and ensures their integration are more likely to bring benefits with minimal exchange hazards (Gulati, 1995; Kim et al., 2010; Poppo and Zenger, 2002; Vijayasarathy, 2010). In particular, trust helps firms to gain accurate, comprehensive, and timely information with mutual willingness (Chiles and McMackin, 1996; Lewicki and Bunker, 1995), which leads to improved information sharing between partners. Trust also facilitates coordination activities with mutual willingness and honesty. Therefore, we propose:

H3a. Trust is positively related to information sharing.
H3b. Trust is positively related to process coordination.

Relational norm is based on expectations of mutual interests and prescribes stewardship behaviors to consider both parties' well-being of as a whole (Heide and John, 1992). Logistics integration concerns the joint development of resources and capabilities from a mutual perspective instead of an individual perspective. For 3PL users, relational norm with mutual expectations can help to proactively share important information sharing and coordinate material process with 3PL providers. Therefore, we propose:

H4a. Relational norm is positively related to information sharing.
H4b. Relational norm is positively related to process coordination.

Contractual and relational governance function as complements or substitutes for logistics integration

In a complementary view, firms may simultaneously use several governance mechanisms to take more advantage (Bradach, 1997; Bradach and Eccles, 1989; Weitz and Jap, 1995) because they are constrained in their capacity to contractually foresee and resolve all potential problems. In this way, trust and relational norm can complement them by regulating some aspects that are not explicit in contractual governance (Arranz and Arroyabe, 2012; Macneil, 1978; Poppo and Zenger, 2002). Also, TCE views contractual governance as a legal prerequisite for relational governance by promoting the willingness to engage in a transaction (Roxenhall and Ghauri, 2004), thus trust and relational norm may not exert functions without detailed contract or contract application. Meanwhile, trust or relational norm provide atmosphere or expectations to informally employ contractual governance mechanisms for logistics integration. Thus, logistics integration may be enhanced more by combining contractual and relational governance. Therefore, we propose:

H5a-b. Detailed contract and trust (relational norm) are complements in enhancing logistics integration.
H5c-d. Contract application and trust (relational norm) are complements in enhancing logistics integration.

Nonetheless, contractual and relational governance mechanisms can also function as substitutes from two reasons. First, trust and relational norm essentially embed in a relationship especially in emerging markets, thereby reduce a firm's capacity for detailed contract or contract application. Second, the effective use of detailed contract or contract application may evoke conflicts (Gaski, 1984) and defensive behaviors (Hirschman, 1984; Zand, 1972). Some firms even discourage the use of elaborated contracts because it "indicates a lack of trust and blunts the demands of friendship, turning a cooperative venture into an antagonistic horsetrade"

(Macaulay, 1963, p. 64). Writing contracts may signal distrust, thus narrowing partners' behaviors and disrupting the development of relational governance (Jap and Ganesan, 2000; Pillutla et al., 2003). Therefore, we propose:

H6a-b. Detailed contract and trust (relational norm) are substitutes in enhancing logistics integration.
H6c-d. Contract application and trust (relational norm) are substitutes in enhancing logistics integration.

Logistics integration and operational performance

Operational performance includes cost, quality, delivery and flexibility performance, which indicates several dimensions of a firm's competitive advantages. 3PL Information sharing captures the reciprocal nature of information flows, including both upstream information flows (e.g. orders, demand forecasts, point-of-sales) and downstream information flows (e.g. capacity, delivery schedules, and product), not just information exchange or acquisition. Effective information sharing enhances operational efficiencies by sharing important information and using providers' information systems. For example, Lee et al. (2000) found that information sharing saved supply chain costs by about 23 percent. In contrast, the lack of information sharing and information asymmetry lead to operational inefficiencies. Process coordination between 3PL users and providers reduces the redundancy of inventory, transportation, and order processing, and is the key to attaining flexibility in response to fast-changing environments. Therefore, we propose:

H7a. Information sharing is positively related to operational performance.
H7b. Process coordination is positively related to operational performance.

Information sharing and process coordination play different roles in logistics integration, but some studies focuses on material flows and ignore information flow leads to sub-optimal performance. According to Lee et al. (2000), information sharing about production and delivery schedules improves common forecasts, synchronize production and delivery, which help process coordination to enhance performance. By sharing information about forecast demands with 3PL providers, firms can avoid material flow delays and conflicts, improving the efficiency of process coordination. Patnayakuni et al. (2006) claimed that integrated information flow can facilitate coordination to improve performance. Therefore, we propose:

H7c. Information sharing and process coordination are complements in improving operational performance.

METHODS

Sampling and data collection

To obtain a representative sample, our target samples were randomly selected from manufacturing and service sections of Firm Catalogue of Bohai Sea Economic Area (BSEA) in China. We chose logistics managers or executive managers as key informants who were familiar with their firms' internal and external logistics activities and processes. A total of 1000 questionnaires with the cover letter introducing our research objectives and potential contributions were sent to firms who agreed to take our survey. Finally, 247 usable samples were received and the response rate was 24.7%.

Non-response analyses were tested by comparing the difference between early and late returned samples (Armstrong and Overton, 1977). We divided the sample into two halves based on the date of returned samples, and then compared the two groups on major traits of firms (i.e. firm size, firm ownership) by t-test (Handfield and Bechtel, 2002; Stank et al., 2001).. We also checked potential common method bias using Harman's single-factor test (Podsakoff et al., 2003; Podsakoff and Organ, 1986). Non-response bias and common method bias are not a serious problem in this study.

Measures

For contractual governance, four items of detailed contract that measures the completeness of contract clauses were adapted from Wuyts & Geyskens (2005). Three items of contract application that measures the strictness of contract enforcement ex post were adapted from Antia & Frazier (2001) and Jiang et al. (2013). For relational governance, three items of trust that measures benevolence, honesty and ability of trust were adapted from Kumar et al. (1995) and Tian et al. (2008). Ten items of relational norm that measure flexibility, information exchange, and solidarity were adapted from Heide & John (1992), we averaged the value of three sub-dimensions to get relational norm. Information sharing and process coordination measures are adapted from Narasimhan & Kim (2002) and Morash & Clinton (1998). Operational performance measures were adapted from Devaraj et al. (2007) and Miller & Roth (1994).

Reliability and validity

We used the partial least squares (PLS) method to test the structural equation model. The results were interpreted in two stages, first by an assessment of the measurement model, and second by the structural model. Using approaches of Fornell & Larcker (1981) in a PLS context, we assessed reliability and validity to ensure the appropriateness of the measurement model. Cronbach's alpha and composite reliability were used to assess reliability. Cronbach's alpha ranged from 0.763 to 0.927, and composite reliability ranged from 0.862 to 0.948, both indicating good reliability of our measures.

Convergent validity is the ability of items to convergent together as an expected construct. First, in the measurement model, most of factor loadings were higher than 0.70 with all t-values greater than 2.0. Only one item of operational performance was 0.67 but was still significant at the 0.01 significance level. Second, all values of average variance extracted (AVE) were higher than 0.50, both indicating good convergent validity (Fornell and Larcker, 1981).

The square root of AVE of each construct was greater than correlations between the construct and other constructs, indicating good discriminant validity (Fornell and Larcker, 1981).

*** Formatting Issue - Best Available Paper/Graphic ***

RESULTS

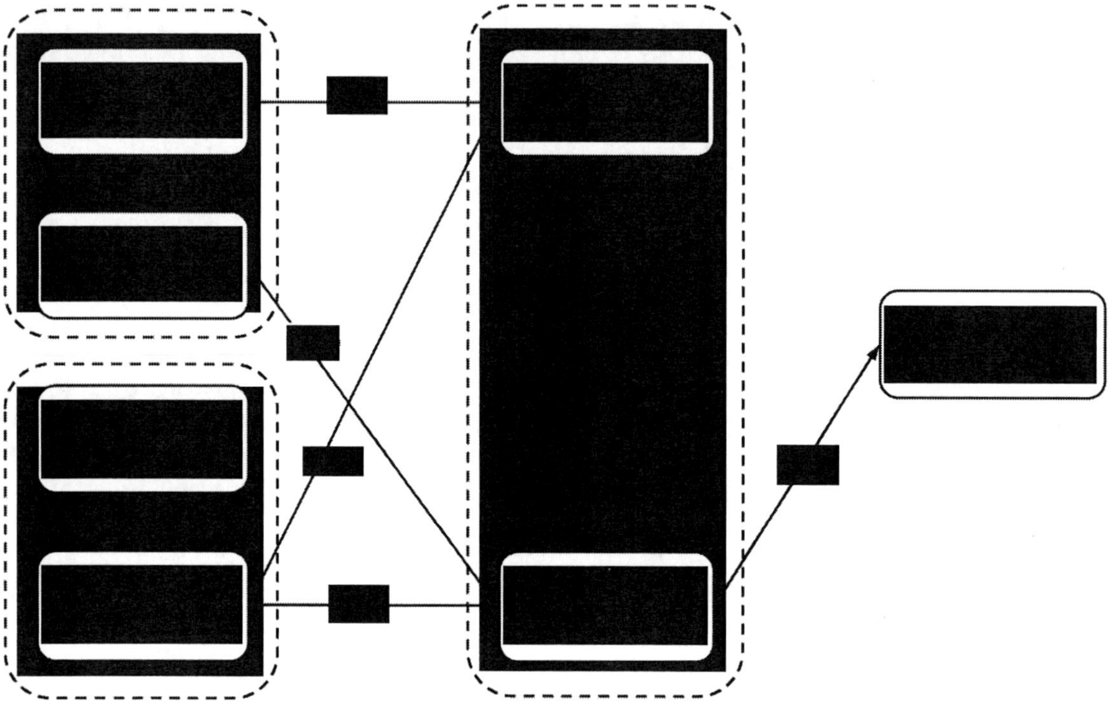

[redacted] [redacted]

[redacted]

DISCUSSION AND CONCLUSIONS

Safeguarding logistics integration using appropriate governance mechanisms

Our results show that both contractual and relational governance enhance logistics integration that further improves operational performance, which extends the "governance-integration" paradigm in supply chain management (Cai et al., 2010; Vijayasarathy, 2010; Wang et al., 2011; Wang et al., 2014; Yeung et al., 2009; Zaheer and Venkatraman, 1995; Zhang and Huo, 2013).

We find four governance mechanisms exert distinct functions in enhancing logistics integration between 3PL users and providers. Firms can contingently take advantage of different governance mechanisms to safeguard logistics integration. For contractual governance, detailed contract and contract application represent coordination and control mechanism, respectively. The results show that detailed contract enhances process coordination, while contract application enhances information sharing. This may be explained that process coordination is more complex and is well-defined in contractual clauses by both 3PL users and providers and is difficult to modify in the transaction, while information sharing is changeable and is enhanced by contract application that emphasizes to control the process. For relational governance, relational norm enhances both information sharing and process coordination between 3PL users and

*** **Formatting Issue - Best Available Paper/Graphic** ***

providers through mutually shared ideas and initiatives, norm and expectations, or even through established common values and cultures. However, surprisingly, trust has no significant effect on both information sharing and process coordination, which are inconsistent with previous studies that demonstrated the positive effect of trust (e.g. Cai et al., 2010; Vijayasarathy, 2010). Two reasons may lead to the surprising result in the unique context of China. First, trust emphasizes the transaction's cooperative atmosphere between transaction parties, but this atmosphere is weak in China without legally contractual protections, which is confirmed by our results that show detailed contract can complement trust. Second, Gargiulo & Ertug (2006) described negative outcomes associated with overly trusted relationships as the "dark side of trust". Trust may lead to unwittingly deactivate monitoring mechanisms, and thus emerge negative results to mitigate positive outcomes, which may lead to the nonsignificant effect of trust on logistics integration.

Furthermore, we find that both complementary and substitutional relationships exist between contractual governance and relational governance mechanisms. First, jointly using detailed contract and trust is more effective in enhancing integration. Detailed contract endows the legitimacy basis for both parties to behave in a certain domain, and to decline negative effects of trust, thus protecting the trusted atmosphere to integrate with each other. Second, compared with other mechanisms, relational norm plays a more important role in enhancing logistic integration. It not only positively influences information sharing and process coordination, but also substitutes detailed contract in enhancing information sharing. Establishing shared norm and values, or even common cultures helps both parties proactively and cooperatively to achieve mutual goals. However, due to the complexity of process coordination, relational norm cannot substitute detailed contract or contract application. Third, trust and contract application substitute with each other in enhancing information sharing. The enforcement of obligations, promises, and expectations are achieved through a relationally-governed exchange because interpersonal and interfirm connections are crucial issues in Chinese firms (Luo, 2000).

Improving operational performance through logistics integration

Differently, an interesting finding shows that information sharing fails to significantly improve operational performance, but complements process coordination in improving operational performance, which indicates that information sharing is insufficient and needs process coordination to exploit its value in improving performance. Our results show that two dimensions of logistics integration exert their different functions. Information sharing plays a fundamental role in logistics integration, while process coordination contains complex transaction mechanisms and transcends organizational boundaries. Process coordination exploits the value of information flows and makes the material flow more fluent across the transaction, and enables 3PL users and providers to engage in complex coordination activities that are traditionally implemented by one party's activities alone (Heide and John, 1990). Thus, it is essential for both 3PL users and providers to focus on both dimensions of logistics integration.

CONTRIBUTIONS, CONCLUSIONS, AND LIMITATIONS

This study makes theoretical contributes in several ways. First, we provide a better understanding of safeguarding logistics integration between 3PL users and providers by simultaneously addressing both contractual (e.g. detailed contract, contract application) and relational governance (e.g. trust, relational norm). We find their different roles in enhancing logistics integration, enriching findings of previous studies. Second, in contrast to popular views, we found that trust has no significant impact on either information sharing or process coordination, while relational norm is more effective on both. This finding makes a significantly unique insight into two relational governance mechanisms. Third, this study provides empirical evidence about how four contractual and relational governance mechanisms individually and jointly influence logistics integration, which further leads to operational performance. Thus, the seemingly paradoxical coexistence of complementary, substitutional, or nonsignificant relationships exists between contractual and relational governance. Fourth, this study identifies two dimensions of logistics integration from the flow perspective: information sharing and process coordination, and empirically examines the relationship between them. We also found the two complement in improving operational performance, enhancing the comprehensiveness and richness of literature.

This study also has some limitations that provide potential directions for future studies. First, we examined four typical governance mechanisms from both contractual and relational perspectives, but other mechanisms may also be important. Second, we collected data from one side of the dyadic relationship, namely, 3PL users. Future studies would design to collect data from both 3PL users and providers. Third, BESA is a region that has the economic and social representativeness of China, such as technology development, market conditions, supply chain management (Zhao et al., 2006), but some idiosyncrasies may be overlooked. Future studies can expand the research scope to other regions for better generalizability.

APPENDIX, TABLES, AND REFERENCES AVAILABLE UPON REQUEST!

DECISION SCIENCES INSTITUTE

Success Factors for a Classroom Project

Thawatchai Jitpaiboon
Ball State University
Email: tjitpaiboon@bsu.edu

Sheila Smith
Ball State University
Email: smariesmith@bsu.edu

Qiannong Gu
Ball State University
Email: qgu@bsu.edu

ABSTRACT

The goal of this survey research is to explore specific classroom project management issues across a wide variety of projects and project management courses to formulate specific project management success factors (practices) that contribute to student team project success. The identified project management success factors might provide guiding principles for both faculty and students as they venture through the project management course. Using the project management success factors, students can learn to follow best practices and faculty also have a complete understanding of students' limitation of learning. The contribution of this study is to attempt to establish recommended project management success factors aiming to guide faculty and students to better prepare while working on the team project.

KEYWORDS: Project Management, Classroom Project, Project Management Success Factors, Students' Project, and Structural Equation Modelling

INTRODUCTION

Team projects are commonplace in project management courses offered at postsecondary institutions for both undergraduate and graduate degrees. Despite the implementation of collaborative learning in higher education, teams still present numerous challenges for faculty and students. The nature of a project management course's content and structure pose an increased challenge for project management educators and teams. Project management teams in an academic environment are highly problematic for faculty and students who face various hurdles during a quest for successful project management knowledge acquisition, and transfer (Langley, 2015). Mir and Pinnington (2014) reported that despite the advancement in project management processes and tools, project success in the workplace has not significantly improved.

The goal of this survey research is to explore specific classroom project management issues across a wide variety of projects and project management courses to formulate specific project management success factors (practices) that contribute to student team project success. The identified project management success factors might provide guiding principles for both faculty and students as they venture through the project management course. Using the project management success factors, students can learn to follow best practices and faculty also have a complete understanding of students' limitation of learning.

LITERATURE REVIEW

Besteiro, de Souza Pinto, and Novaski (2015) conducted an exploratory empirical research on project managers from 28 companies in order to classify critical success factors into 4 driver groups. They proposed 57 variables altogether with 18 for Managerial Abilities group, 19 for Critical Success Factors group, 13 for Monitoring and Control group and 7 for Lessons Learned group. Besteirio, de Souza Pinto, and Novaski (2015) asserted that knowledge management, leadership, and experience help the project to be successful. Anderson et al, (2006) studied the relationship between critical factors and project success and proposed the success factors with three success scales: managerial delivery ability, impacts of the project, and experiences captures. They proposed nine critical success factors including communication, planning approval by stakeholders, formal and well-structured approach, commitment to the project, influence of stakeholders, understanding and accepting the proposal, restrictions, flexibility in the execution, and influence over the processes of the project. The results showed that communication is a significant contribution in order to establish a trusting relationship between the project team members.

In summary, a great deal of literature has addressed various project management success factors in organizational context. Many studies focus on creating the set of success factors (Besteiro, de Souza Pinto, and Novaski, 2015; Fortune et al., 2013; Lundin and Soderholm, 1995; Soderlund, 2002; Carvalho, 2010; Fortune and White, 2006; and Hyvrari , 2006) and others focus on establishing a relationship between the use of the success factors and project performance (Zmud, 1980; Yetton et al., 2000; McFarlan, 1981; Anderson et al, 2006; Martin, Pearson, and Furumo, 2007; Henderson and Lee, 1992; Jiang, Klein, and Means, 2000; Leung, 2001; and Settle-Murphy and Thornton, 1999). However, there has been little research in the success factors done in the classroom level even though academics have suggested that students' project is as complex and difficult as any projects implemented at the organizational level. Since project management study is a social study in which the complexity and difficulty of a project are introduced by human behaviors; thus, creating interesting research gap. The contribution of this study is to attempt to establish recommended project management success factors aiming to guide faculty and students to better prepare while working on the team project.

THEORETICAL DEVELOPMENT/MODEL

Instrument development for the success factors and project performance was carried out in three phases: (1) item generation, (2) online data collection study, and (3) data analysis. An extensive literature review was conducted to identify the domain of constructs and generate the initial measurement items. Next, a questionnaire was developed and delivered to students through online survey online platform called Qualtrics. Third, a data set was collected and analyzed to validate the instrument and test the hypothesized model.

Item generation

Items for each construct were developed based on extensive literature reviews and brain storming with multiple researchers in the project management field. All items are measured on a six-point Likert type scales where 1 = "Strongly Disagree", 2 = "Disagree", 3 = "Somewhat Disagree", 4 = "Somewhat Agree", 5 = "Agree" and 6 = "Strongly Agree. After the rigorous sorting procedures were done, three sub-constructs for the success factors and three sub-constructs for project management performance were emerged. Table 1 lists all items in the initial measurement models for the success factors construct. There are 7 items for Project Management Tools construct, 6 items for Project Management Practices construct, and 6 items for Project Management Support construct.

PROJECT MANAGEMENT SUCCESS FACTORS The following situations describe the extent to which the **project management team is given sufficient project management tools, project management practices, and project management support to carry out a successful project implementation**. Please circle the appropriate number to indicate the extent to which you agree or disagree with each statement as applicable to your project.
PROJECT MANAGEMENT TOOLS **In our organization, we use the project management tools to achieve the following project management activities.**
Communicating among team members (Performance reports)
Sharing information
Making decisions (Decision tree)
Evaluating project progress (Critical path)
Balancing budget (Earned Value Management-EVM)
Informing the evolution of the project (Gantt chart)
Clear detailed task list (Work Break Structure-WBS)
PROJECT MANAGEMENT PRACTICES **In our organization, we identify the following activities as key factors for project success.**
Clear scope definition of project
Establishing goals and deliverables
Commitment of stakeholders, decision-makers, project managers and team members
Clear time requirement
Clear resource and budget requirements
Clear contingency plan
PROJECT MANAGEMENT SUPPORT **In our organization, we receive help from the following supporters.**
Upper management
Business partners
IT personnel
Project managers

Team members
Managerial support for project management processes

Table 1: Items for Project Management Success Factors construct

SURVEY METHODS, DATA COLLECTION, AND SAMPLE CHARACTERISTICS

A cross-sectional self-administered online survey was conducted. The sample frame was obtained from the list of students who either took or has taken the undergraduate level project management course (ISOM300). 111 started the survey, only 94 completed the survey, and 17 questionnaires were empty. Table 2 shows sample demographic information.

1.	**Role in the project team**	
	Project manager	13 %
	Member	48 %
	Team leader	22 %
	Organizer	17 %
2.	**Highest level of education**	
	High school	56 %
	Two-year college	22 %
	Bachelor's degree	28 %
	Master's degree	1 %
	Doctor's degree	0 %
	Other	2 %
3.	**Important skills for the project success**	
	Leadership	68 %
	Responsibility	67 %
	Teamwork	84 %
	Resources	27 %
	Clear goals	66 %
	Communication	81 %
	Reward	15 %
	Punishment	7 %
4.	**Length of project in days**	
	1-5	3 %
	5-10	11 %
	20-30	13 %
	30-50	21 %
	Over 50	52 %
5.	**Number of members in the project team**	
	1	1 %
	2-4	57 %
	5-10	41 %
	Over 10	0 %
6.	**Mode of content delivery**	
	On campus	87 %
	Online	13 %

7.	**Nature of project collaboration**	
	On campus	90 %
	Online	10 %
8.	**Primary use of technology applications**	
	E-mail	88 %
	Word processing	67 %
	Spread sheet	80 %
	Database	30 %
	Programming tools	17 %
	Project management software	44 %
	Social media	22 %
	Cloud space	37 %
	Others	18 %

Table 2: Sample characteristics

Instrument Refinement in Measurement Models – Construct Validity and Reliability

To establish content validity, items for the various constructs were reviewed by three academicians. Based on the feedback from the academicians, ambiguous items were either modified or eliminated. New items were added when necessary. A confirmatory factor analysis (CFA) using structural equation modeling method in Analysis of Moment Structures (AMOS) was conducted to refine the measurement models (Hair, et al., 2006).

The final 94 responses were used for further data analysis. As per the guidelines of Bagozzi (1980), the important properties for a measure to be reliable and valid include content validity, internal consistency of operationalization (unidimensionality and reliability), and construct validity (discriminant and convergent). Content validity was determined through a comprehensive review of the literature, pilot tests, assessment by a panel of practitioners and academics to ensure that measurement items covered the domain of the variable (Nunnally, 1978; Churchill, 1979). Convergent validity criteria require that there be one single latent variable underlying a set of measurement items (Anderson and Gerbing, 1988). The degree of convergent validity is tested through CFA (using SEM) to assess the measurement model properties indicated by the Goodness of Fit Index (GFI) and the Adjusted Goodness of Fit Index (AGFI). The GFI indicates the relative amount of variance and covariance jointly explained by the model. The AGFI differs from the GFI in adjusting for the number of degrees of freedom (Byrne, 1989). Both range from 0 to 1. Values of 0.90 or more are considered a good fit (Hair et al., 1998). The normed fit index (NFI) and comparative fit index (CFI) indicate a relative comparison of the proposed model to the null model. NFI and CFI's values above 0.90 are acceptable (Hu and Bentler, 1999). The next set of fit statistics focus on the root mean square error of approximation (RMSEA). The RMSEA takes into account the error of approximation and is expressed per degree of freedom, thus making the index sensitive to the number of estimated parameters in the model; values less than 0.05 indicate good fit, values up to 0.08 represent reasonable errors of approximation (Browne and Cudeck, 1993), values up to 0.10 indicate mediocre fit, and those greater than 0.10 indicate poor fit (MacCallum et. al., 1996). The original measurement items were tested according to these indices and items contributing to an unacceptable model fit were deleted. Items in *italic* were deleted due to low factor loadings or error term correlations. Cronbach's alpha was also used to assess the reliability of each construct. Values of 0.70 and higher are considered acceptable (Hair et al., 2006). Tables

3 and 4 list the items shown in the final measurement models' result. The results show that all constructs are valid and reliable according to the minimum requirements.

PROJECT MANAGEMENT TOOLS	Final Model Fit
Communicating among team members (Performance reports)	GFI = .98
Sharing information	AGFI = .92
Making decisions (Decision tree)	CFI = .99
Evaluating project progress (Critical path)	NFI = .98
Balancing budget (Earned Value Management-EVM)	RMSEA = .06
Informing the evolution of the project (Gantt chart)	α = .82
Clear detailed task list (Work Break Structure-WBS)	
PROJECT MANAGEMENT PRACTICES	Final Model Fit
Clear scope definition of project	GFI = .99
Establishing goals and deliverables	AGFI = .93
Commitment of stakeholders, decision-makers, project managers and team members	CFI = 1.00
Clear time requirement	NFI = .99
Clear resource and budget requirements	RMSEA = .05
Clear contingency plan	α = .87
PROJECT MANAGEMENT SUPPORT	Final Model Fit
Upper management	GFI = 1.00
Business partners	AGFI = .96
IT personnel	CFI = 1.00
Project managers	NFI = .99
Team members	RMSEA = .00
Managerial support for project management processes	α = .79

Table 3: Model fit indices and reliabilities for Project Management Success Factors

INDIVIDUAL PERFORMANCE	Final Model Fit
Achieve the scope objectives	GFI = 1.00
Meet time requirements	AGFI = 1.00
Manage cost effectively	CFI = 1.00
Sense of accomplishment	NFI = 1.00
Quality of work	RMSEA = .00
	α = .85
PROJECT PERFORMANCE	Final Model Fit

Achieve the scope objectives	GFI = .98
Meet time requirements	AGFI = .89
Manage cost effectively	CFI = .98
Quality of deliverables	NFI = .97
Customer satisfaction.	RMSEA = .11 α = .79
TEAM PERFORMANCE	Final Model Fit
Achieve the scope objectives	
Meet time requirements	GFI = .98
Manage cost effectively	AGFI = .93
Team dynamics	CFI = 1.00
Alignment of project activities (for example, the outcomes from one activity should be tightly matched with the project's objectives)	NFI = .97 RMSEA = .03 α = .82
Balance of obligation.	

Table 4: Model fit indices and reliabilities for Project Management Performance

CONCLUSIONS

The conclusion section of this study is currently not available. The research is still a work-in-progress.

References available upon request

DECISION SCIENCES INSTITUTE

Supply Chain Disruption Handling: A Dynamic Extended Resource-Based (DE-RBV) View

Baohua Qin
University of Toledo, USA
Yanshan University, China
Email: linda_qin2000@yahoo.com

Paul Hong
University of Toledo, USA
Email: Paul.Hong@UToledo.Edu

Yue Zhang
University of Toledo, USA
Email: yue.zhang@utoledo.edu

ABSTRACT

Harsh competition and rapid changing environment have made supply chain risk management a fashionable area of management research. But till now there is no research clearly analyzing the underlying mechanism in supply disruption handling. Drawing upon the Resourced Based View (RBV) including Dynamic Capability Theory, this paper developed Dynamic Extended Resource Based View (DE-RBV) to meet supply risk management requirement. Four different capabilities for supply risk handling are presented, i.e., Preventive Capability, Back-up Capability, Substitute Capability and Warning Capability. A conceptual model is set up which captures the relationships between supply disruption handling capabilities and supply disruption handling performance.

KEYWORDS: Supply chain disruption, Supply risk handling capability, Resource Based View, Dynamic theory

I. INTRODUCTION

On March 17th, 2000, a fire destroyed the production circumstance in Philips's plant in New Mexico, which is a common supplier for both Nokia and Ericsson. As a result, both Ericsson and Nokia suffered serious supply disruption. But Nokia recovered while Ericsson had to exit from cell-phone market. This is a typical case which is well referred by the researchers in supply chain risk management area (Sheffi Y., The Resilient Enterprise: Overcoming Vulnerability for Competitive Advantage, 2005). The reason that Nokia and Ericsson had totally different consequences after the same supply disruption is that the capabilities of the two companies to handle supply risks were different.

Nowadays, the business environment is becoming more and more turbulent and uncertain; organizations are not limited as boundary-conscious entities; many of them are distributed world-wide instead, both physically and virtually. This transition has increased the potential that the disruption may propagate throughout its supply chain network. Globalization, integration and outsourcing, and the continued trend to "lean" have made supply chains more complex and increased the supply chain risks. More and more researchers and practitioners realize the existence of a new risk situation in supply (Juettner, Peck, & Christopher, 2002) (Kajuter, 2003) (Brindley, 2004). Supply chain disruptions have been the most pressing concern facing firms.

Although all companies in a supply chain have to encounter risks in a supply chain to a certain degree, and the supply chain risk may cause great damages to the companies in the supply chain, a MIT study found out most companies haven't thought about managing supply chain risks and vulnerabilities systematically (Sheffi Y., The Resilient Enterprise: Overcoming Vulnerability for Competitive Advantage, 2005). The main reason is that there is no generally consistent understanding about risk management and they lack of operational methods to handle the risks.

1.1 Literature Review

The existing literature about supply chain risk management mainly focused on risk identification, assessment, mitigation and recovery. Most studies have been done by presenting conceptual model via anecdotal evidence, case study, and secondary dataset.

Research on supply chain risk issues mainly covers supply chain vulnerability (Svensson, A conceptual framework for the analysis of vulnerability in supply chains, 2000), business continuity planning (Zsidisin, Melnyk, & Ragatz, 2005), supply chain resilience (Sheffi & Rice Jr, 2005), and supply chain risks (Chopra & Sodhi, 2004) (Hendricks, Singlhal, & Zhang, 2009). (Craighead, Blackhurst, Rungtusanatham, & Handfield, 2007). Christopher (2004) presented some basic rules for creating a resilient supply chain, which includes supply chain understanding, supply base strategy, supply chain collaboration, agility, and creating a supply chain risk management culture (Christopher, Creating resilient supply chains, 2004). Lee presented Triple-A supply chain which has three characters i.e., agility, adaptability and alignment, for the supply chain to give the companies sustainable competitive advantage (Lee H. , 2004).

Regarding supply chain disruptions, there are mainly four research issues in current existing literature:

a) Understanding and perspective on risks. For example, March, et al, presented managerial perspectives on risk and risk taking (March & Shapira, 1987). Paulsson (2007) researched the definitions and understanding of supply chain risk in his dissertation paper (Paulsson, 2007).

b) Identifying the primary drivers and enablers of disruptions and the factors influencing the probability of disruptions (Kilgore, 2003) (Stauffer, 2003) (Craighead, Blackhurst, Rungtusanatham, & Handfield, 2007) (Sheffi Y. , 2005) (Tang, 2006) (Kleindorfer & Saad, 2005). Christopher and Peck (2004) categorized risk into internal to the firm, external to the firm but internal to the supply chain network, and external to the network (Christopher & Peck, Building the Resilient Supply Chain, 2004). Jiang, et al, tries to find the root causes of job dissatisfaction which leads to turnover, which is one of the sources of supply chain risks (Jiang, Baker, & Frazier, 2009).

c) Examining the economic and other consequences of disruptions (Hendricks & Singhal, An empirical analysis of the effect of supply chain disruptions on Long-run stock price performance and risk of the firm, 2005) (Hendricks & Singhal, The effect of supply chain glitches on shareholder value, 2003) (Rice.Jr & Caniato, 2003).

d) Discussing risk management and the process of risk management including risk identification, assessment, practice, strategy, and evaluation. Supply chain strategies and structures that can reduce the possibility and damages of disruptions are also researched (Lee H. , 2004) (Kleindorfer & Saad, 2005) (Sheffi Y. , 2005) (Tomlin, 2006) (Swafford, Ghosh, & Murthy, 2006) (Tang, 2006) (Craighead, Blackhurst, Rungtusanatham, & Handfield, 2007) (Ketchen Jr. & Hult, 2007). Cohen and Kunreuther (Cohen & Kunreuther, 2007) presented a conceptual framework for risk analysis; Neiger, et al., (Neiger, Rotaru, & Churilov, 2009) presented a process engineering methodology for supply chain risk identification; Knemeyer et al developed a process for proactively planning for catastrophic risk events (Knemeyer, Zinn, & Eroglu, 2009). Chopra et al., (Chopra & Sodhi, 2004) pointed two things that managers must do when establishing a supply chain risk management strategy. One is that the whole organization should have a shared understanding of supply chain risk; the second is that general risk-mitigation approaches should be adapted to the circumstances of the company. Using interpretive structural modeling (ISM) method, Faisal et al (2006), did research on the dynamics and relationships between various enablers to mitigate risk in a supply chain. They found trust among supply chain partners, collaborative relationships among supply chain members, information sharing in the supply chain, and knowledge about risks are the enablers which play a key role to counter risks in a supply chain. (Faisal, Banwet, & Shankar, 2006). Braunscheidel et al., (Braunscheidel & Suresh, 2009) did research on the impact of cultural antecedents (market orientation and learning orientation) and three organizational practices (internal integration, external integration and external flexibility) on supply chain agility of a firm which is considered as a risk management initiative.

While extant inquiry is informative, there is no theory provides generally consistent understanding about the underlying mechanism of disruption handling. Although a lot of different strategies and methods to handle supply chain risk are proposed, how those strategies and methods work and why same strategies has different effect for different firm have not been explained.

Hendricks et al. (Hendricks, Singlhal, & Zhang, 2009) empirically test whether operational slack, business diversification, geographic diversification, and vertical relatedness influence the supply chain disruption handling performance. Although Hendricks et al justified the effectiveness of strategies in handling supply chain disruptions, they didn't give the reason why the strategies can affect the level of damages of supply chain disruption. How the strategies work to affect the capabilities of handling supply chain disruption? Why certain companies with the same supply chain strategies have different supply chain disruption handling performance?

Autry and Sanders (Autry & Sanders, 2009) present a framework documenting business continuity planning capabilities. The conceptual framework integrates the technology, processes, and human resources needed to develop supply chain security management capabilities. Technology, processes, and human resources are given as specific categories of dynamic firm capabilities. The categories they proposed are common categories for a firm to do business, and of course those categories will affect risk handling performance, but what risk handling capabilities exactly is, and through what and how those aspects affect risk handling performance, are not analyzed. This weakness will hinder the researchers and practitioners to apply this framework when handling supply chain risk. They cannot explain why one firm suffers more severe supply disruption than another firm with similar capabilities that they presented.

Ponomarov (Ponomarov & Holcomb, Understanding the concept of supply chain resilience, 2009) presented a conceptual framework of the relationship between logistic capabilities and supply chain resilience. In his framework the logistic capabilities includes demand management capabilities, supply management capabilities and information management capabilities. These three capabilities lead to dynamically integrated logistic capabilities. Supply chain resilience includes three steps: event readiness, efficient response and recovery. Again, the capabilities researched here are only common functional capabilities. Ponomarov (2009) introduces "3Cs" core psychological principles of resilience, i.e., control, coherence, and connectedness (Reich, 2006), into supply chain resilience, forming components of capabilities. Although three "Cs" reflects the underlying components of supply chain risk handling capabilities to certain degree, they are too abstract and not operational for supply chain management, because supply chain is quite different with individual human being. In Resilience/ Capability matrix, Ponomarov gives the corresponding aspects and issues of the capabilities corresponding to different stages of supply chain resilience. This is a very good step to make the abstract capabilities more operational. But the issues listed are still isolated; the relationship among the issues and how these issues work to improve resilience are still not clear.

Craighead et al., (Craighead, Blackhurst, Rungtusanatham, & Handfield, 2007) analyze how supply chain design characteristics and mitigation capabilities affect the severity of supply chain disruptions. Craighead et al., present three supply chain structure characteristics including Supply chain density; Supply chain complexity; Node criticality. They also present two supply chain mitigation capabilities including recovery capability and warning capability.

1.2 Importance of This Paper

While extant inquiry is informative, there is a lack of investigations on supply disruption handling capabilities and the underlying mechanism of disruption handling process. How the practices and strategies work for handling risk has not been discovered. This paper provides additional value to this body of knowledge.

The supply risk handling capabilities presented in this paper can help a firm systematically analyze why certain kinds of supply chain practices are good to handle risk in specific situations and find out where capability gaps exist for a firm. The model presented in my paper calls into question whether it is suitable to adopt or fight popular practices such as Lean, Global Sourcing, and Single Sourcing etc., without analyzing the impact of supply risk in a holistic way.

For example, there exist quite different opinions about lean supply chain. Whether lean is good for mitigating supply chain risk or not, different researchers have different opinions because they analyze from different perspectives. The dispute about LEAN's impact on supply risk cannot be understand clearly without the understanding of supply handling capabilities presented in this paper. If we just mention lean without clearly analyzing how 'lean' relates to supply chain capabilities, managers still don't know whether they should be lean and to what level the lean should be when facing specific situations.

The capabilities that I presented can help the managers to decide on using which kind of supply chain practice (for example, Postponement, Component Design, etc) based on their impact on supply risk handing capabilities. My paper gives thorough and extensive analysis of supply disruption handling capability and how they relate to traditional RBV and dynamic capability theory.

II. MAIN CONCEPTS OF THE RESEARCH AREA

To better understand the underlying mechanism of supply chain risk management, it is necessary to make clear the definitions and understanding of the main basic concepts or constructs within this area, i.e., supply chain disruption, supply chain risk, vulnerability, flexibility and resilience. Due to the length limitation of this paper, I just discuss the concepts regarding supply chain disruption.

2.1. Supply Chain Disruption

There exist obviously different understandings about disruption in current literatures (Tang, 2006) (Crandall, 2010) (Fahlen, 1997) (Paulsson, 2007) (Svensson, A conceptual framework of vulnerability in firms' inbound and outbound logistics flows, 2002). I consider disruption as any unwished event, randomly or deliberately, small or big, which leads to deviations from plan and whose consequences are negative. Disruption is an outside event, but the level of disruption is reflected by the effect to the recipient suffered the disruption. Same event might have different impacts on different recipients. Disruption reflects the interaction of the unwished event and the recipient.

Supply chain disruptions are unanticipated events that disrupt the normal flow of materials and goods in a supply chain (Svensson, 2000; Hendricks & Singhal, 2003; Kleindorfer & Saad, 2005) (Craighead, Blackhurst, Rungtusanatham, & Handfield, 2007)

Melnyk et al gives their understanding of supply chain disruption: "the outcome of a process whereby one or more events (to be referred to as the "triggering event") taking place at one point in the supply chain adversely affect the performance of one or more components located elsewhere in the supply chain." (Melnyk, Rodrigues, & Ragatz, 2009)

Melnyk et al, gives a clear description of supply chain disruption, they discussed that supply chain disruption can be viewed as the result of a chain of events. It starts with an event that triggers the disruption, and then transmitted via the supply chain from the source of the event to the firm. As the disruption moves through the chain, the impact is influenced and shaped by the factors such as the location of the disruption in the supply chain, the inventory, buffering polices, ordering, and reactions by the various supply chain partners, the amount of visibility about the disruption, the accessibility of alternative sources of supply, and the lead times. (Melnyk, Rodrigues, & Ragatz, 2009)

In supply chain, disruption source, i.e., the triggering event can be separated into supply side, focal unit or demand side. Supplier Side Supply Chain Disruption (SS-SCD) is the focus of this paper as compared to Customer Side Supply Chain Disruptions (CS-SCD) since it is the most important component for supply chain disruptions. The analysis about the basic constructs suits all kinds of disruption analysis.

A transfer point is a location within a supply chain where a supplier firm hands over what has been ordered to a customer firm in the supply chain (Paulsson, 2007). A successful handing over includes fulfilling the four perfect order objectives: one time delivery, order completeness, order correctness and defect free (Gaudenzi, 2005). Another way is to use four utilities including form utility, possession utility, place utility and time utility to make judgment of whether the conditions of handing over has been satisfied. Handing over failure cannot be avoided. A disruption in supply chain refers to any handing over failure or lack of utilities transferred which leads directly or indirectly to negative consequences for a focal firm. (Paulsson, 2007)

To facilitate estimating the likelihood, based on different relative roles that human beings and random factors play in their cause, disruptions can be divided into three categories: natural disasters, accidents, and intentional attacks (Sheffi Y. , The Resilient Enterprise:Overcoming Vulnerability for Competitive Advantage, 2005) . In my research, I refer disruptions to the result of any unwished event, including the failure of the supply handing over due to the fluctuation of supplier motivation or immorality, rather than just due to outside events.

III. GENERAL RESEARCH FRAMEWORK

A model is "a representation of a system that is constructed to study some aspect of that system or the system as a whole. (Cooper & Emory, 1995)" In this paper, I present an explicative model to improve our understanding of the key concepts and the underlying mechanism of supply risk handling. Based on the clarification of the main constructs of this area above, an overall theoretical model is presented which can reflect the underlying mechanism of supply disruption handling. Fig. 1 is a generalized theoretical model. The model shows the basic mechanism of supply risk management.

Figure 1. Generalized Research Framework

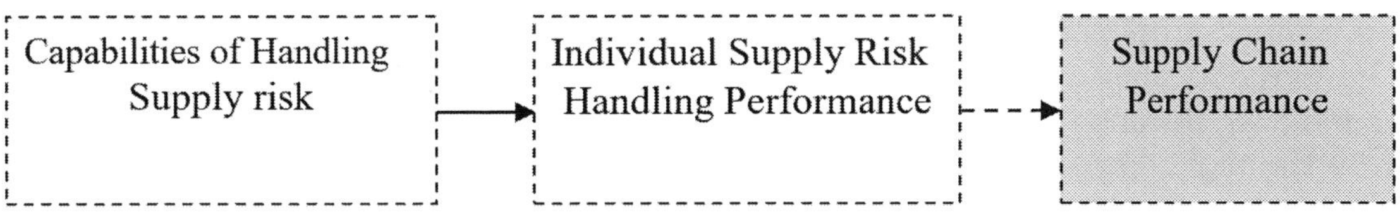

1) Capabilities of handling risk will impact individual supply risk handling performance. Each risk, no matter what kind of, will be handled to certain degree. The result of handling the risk is affected by the capabilities of handling the risk.

2) Individual risk handling performance will affect the supply chain performance. Accumulated risk handling performance affects the overall supply chain performance. We should pay attention to that the relationship between risk handling performance and supply chain performance is not positive linear relationship. Risk handling is a qualifying factor, which means without risk handling, the firm cannot guarantee the competitive advantage or performance of the company if there is any disruptions happened, but more risk handling performance does not necessarily lead to better firm performance. Since the handling of risk is not free, and the disruption may not happen, so sometimes the firm who invests in handling certain disruptions takes more burden of the cost compared with the company who just ignores the disruption without taking any action in the condition that the disruption does not happen in that period. The benefit of invest on risk handling will only show its positive effect when the disruption actually happens, otherwise, when the disruption does not happen, the firm's investment on handling the risk will be the lost compared with other company who took the risk and didn't take any actions. To make it more understandable, let's give further analysis about the difference between making risks handling strategy and other firm strategies.

When we make strategies, we normally make decisions based on "benefit/cost analysis".
For common firm strategies, Benefit= the actually benefit from the firm's strategies.
For risk handling strategies, Benefit= the benefit from avoiding certain disruptions.
Only as the outside threat happens, can the decision maker prove the benefit of handling the risk and justify the cost of taking those actions. For example, if the firm takes action to handle earthquakes, but there is no earthquake happened in that evaluation time period, and if the evaluation criteria are just based on the financial outcome, then the decision maker cannot prove the benefit of the risk handling strategy and cannot justify the investment. The investment of handling disruptions might actually add cost on the firm and lead to disadvantage.
The benefits of other kinds of strategies are consistent with the firm's performance, while the benefit for risk-handling strategies are not so. Without the actually happening of the disruption, they are actually contradicted with each other. So we cannot say that risk-handling performance positively relates to the firm's performance.

Due to the special character of risk handling strategy and practice, one way of solving the conflict between the two "benefits" is to adjust the evaluation criteria of firm's performance based on how much risk it has taken. (Here, risk is from overall risk perspective when making decisions instead of individual risk). Instead of only based on financial outcome during the evaluation time period, the risk taking coefficient should be included.

Firm's performance= Firm's financial performance*(1-Risk-taking Coefficient)

The risk-taking coefficient will decrease if risk-handling performance increases. In this way, the firm's performance might have positive relationship with risk-handling performance. But it is not always the truth because the cost of risk-handling strategy also counts here. Risk-handling performance might decrease risk-taking coefficient, but at the meantime, it might decrease firm's financial performance because of the additional cost of handling the risk. If the cost is too high, it will significantly decrease firm's financial performance, and the cost may not be compensated by the risk-taking coefficient. This sometimes happens when the firm unsuitably invests on a risk-handling strategy which does not provide much benefit to the company.

IV. THEORY DEVELOPMENT—"DE-RBV" FOR RISK MANAGEMENT STRATEGY

4.1. Resource-based theory (RBV)

Resource-based View (RBV) has considered companies as the organization with heterogeneous bundles of resources that are derived internally from tangible and intangible factors including assets, skills and capabilities (Wernerfelt, 1984) (Barney, 1991). There are six major categories of resources, i.e., financial resources, physical resources, human resources, technological resources, reputation, and organizational resources (Grant, The Resource-Based Theory of Competitive Advantage: Implications for Strategy Formulation, Spring 1991). The resources and capabilities that is valuable, rare, inimitable and non-substitutable (VRIN) can provide the basis for sustainable competitive advantage of the company (Barney, 1991) (Peteraf, 1993).

According to Grant (1991), a capability is "the capacity for a team of resources to perform some task or activity." The capabilities of a firm are "what it can do as a result of teams of resources working together." Resources are the source of a firm's capabilities. "For most firms, the most important capabilities are likely to be those which arise from an integration of individual functional capabilities. (Grant, The Resource-Based Theory of Competitive Advantage:

Implications for Strategy Formulation, Spring 1991)" Prahalad and Hamel use the term "core competencies" to describe the central, strategic capabilities, which are "the collective learning in the organization, especially how to coordinate diverse production skills and integrate multiple streams of technology. (Prahalad & Hamel, May/June 1990)" (Grant, The Resource-Based Theory of Competitive Advantage: Implications for Strategy Formulation, Spring 1991) Capabilities can be considered as organizational routines. Capabilities cannot be obtained simply by assembling a group of resources: Capabilities includes complex patterns of coordination among people and other resources. It requires learning through repetition to improve this coordination. Organizational routines are predicable and regular patterns of activity, which consists of a sequence of individual's coordinated actions. In essence, a capability is a routine, or a group of interacting routines. The organization itself is "a huge network of routines." To an organization, routines are like what skills are to the individual. Individual's skills are often carried out without conscious coordination. Organizational routines also involve tacit knowledge. Because capabilities involve interactive resources, they are less mobile than individual resources. Capabilities need to transfer the whole team of resources. Unconscious coordination and tacit knowledge make it difficult to imitate capabilities in a new company. (Grant, The Resource-Based Theory of Competitive Advantage: Implications for Strategy Formulation, Spring 1991)

4.2 Dynamic Capability Theory

'Dynamic capabilities' is defined by Teece (Teece, Pisano, & Shuen, 1997) as "the firm's ability to integrate, build, and reconfigure internal and external competences to address rapidly changing environments." Eisenhardt etc (2000) argue that dynamic capabilities are a set of specific and identifiable processes such as strategic decision making, product development, and alliancing. (Eisenhardt & Martin, Dynamic capabilites: what are they?, 2000) Dynamic capabilities are "the antecedent organizational and strategic routines by which managers alter their resource base—acquire and shed resources, integrate them together, and recombine them—to generate new value-creating strategies (Grant, Toward a knowledge-based theory of the firm, 1996) (Pisano, 1994)" Teece uses 'dynamic capabilities' approach to explain how combinations of competences and resources can be developed, deployed, and protected. Based on this approach, it is important to develop management capabilities, and difficult-to-imitate combinations of organizational, functional and technological skills to effectively coordinate and redeploy internal and external competences (Teece, Pisano, & Shuen, 1997). The term 'dynamic' refers to the capacity to renew competences to achieve congruence with the changing business environment. Timing is critical and the circumstance is difficult to determine here. The term 'capabilities' in 'dynamic capabilities' "emphasizes the key role of strategic management in appropriately adapting, integrating, and reconfiguring internal and external organizational skills, resources, and functional competences to match the requirements of a changing environment." (Teece, Pisano, & Shuen, 1997)

Eisenhardt etc (2000) argued that although dynamic capabilities are idiosyncratic and path dependent, they possess commonalities across firms. In moderately dynamic markets, dynamic capabilities are the traditional conception of routines, while in high-velocity markets they are simple, highly experiential, unstable and fragile processes with unpredictable outcomes (Eisenhardt & Martin, Dynamic capabilites: what are they?, 2000). Since the functionality of dynamic capabilities can be duplicated across firms, their value for competitive advantage lies in the resource configurations that they create, not in the capabilities themselves.
There is some debate regarding the understanding of capabilities. For example, Peng (Peng, 2009), look at capabilities the same as resources. To facilitate the understanding and analyzing

supply chain risks based on RBV (Resource-based theory) and Dynamic capability theory, it is necessary to give a clear understanding of capabilities in this area. My understanding is that the capabilities of handling supply chain risks are different with the capabilities for pursuing competitive advantages. The purpose of supply chain risk handling capabilities is to guarantee the smooth functioning of other capabilities to pursue competitive advantage. So it doesn't matter whether the capabilities can be duplicated or not.

4.3. Extended-RBV

In current integrated world-wide market, almost no company can get sustained competitive advantage without relying on external resources. RBV traditionally downplays external resources as a potential source of competitive advantage on the ground that they are theoretically available to all firms (Barney, 1991). It generally overlooks the joint exploitation of resources through the firm's network relationships. Souter (Souter, 2000) pointed that except for the risks of their own company, risks in other links of their supply chain should also be paid attention to by the company. (Souter, 2000) . Similarly, Christopher et al., also pointed out that company should identify potential sources of the risks "at every significant link along the supply chain. (Faisal, Banwet, & Shankar, 2006)" (Christopher, et al., 2002). Narasimhan emphasized that buying firms must invest in supplier firms in order to develop their capabilities because supplier performance might degrade and it may cause risks to the supply chain (Editorial, Narasimhan, & Talluri, 2009).

From above, we can see that in analyzing supply chain, the narrow perspective of RBV cannot adequately address many issues, especially supply chain risk management. Mathews (Mathews, 2003) gives the term 'Extended RBV' which includes both access to network and internal resources. Network resources may include relation-specific assets, inter-firm routines, complementary resource endowments and effective (network) governance (Dyer & Singh, 1998). Since the purpose of this paper is to handle supply chain disruption instead of getting competitive advantage of the company, the resources that I refer should be generalized to all kind of resources which could help the functioning of the business. Whether they possess the characters of VRIN (valuable, rare, inimitable and non-substitutable) doesn't matter for our topic. This can also avoid the argument and confusion about whether VRIN can be the source of sustained competitive advantage in RBV theory. Another reason is that sometimes it needs the cooperation of the society, government, companies in the whole industry including competitors to handle serious disruptions such as terrorism. So it is not suitable to try to make use of a disruption to get competitive advantage, although sometimes it does work this way.
In a supply chain, when disruption happens, except for actual resources possessed by the company, it is also important to make full use of the potential resources available in the network of the firm to supplement the shortage of the supply.

We can draw great lessons from the Nokia/Ericsson case mentioned earlier regarding supply chain risk management. One is that compared with Ericsson, Nokia has better capability in making use of the resources (both actual and potential) in the supply chain.

When the disruption happened in Philips, Ericsson was not aware of the seriousness and kept on waiting while Nokia took immediate actions, which included the President's visiting Philips to help them to find substitute way to mitigate the shortage of production and trying their best to absorb all the remaining capacity of Philips to support Nokia. When Ericsson realized how serious the situation was, it was too late for them and there was no resource left available for them. To analyze the extended resources more deeply, I describe it with Fig.2:

Figure 2. Illustrated Supply Framework

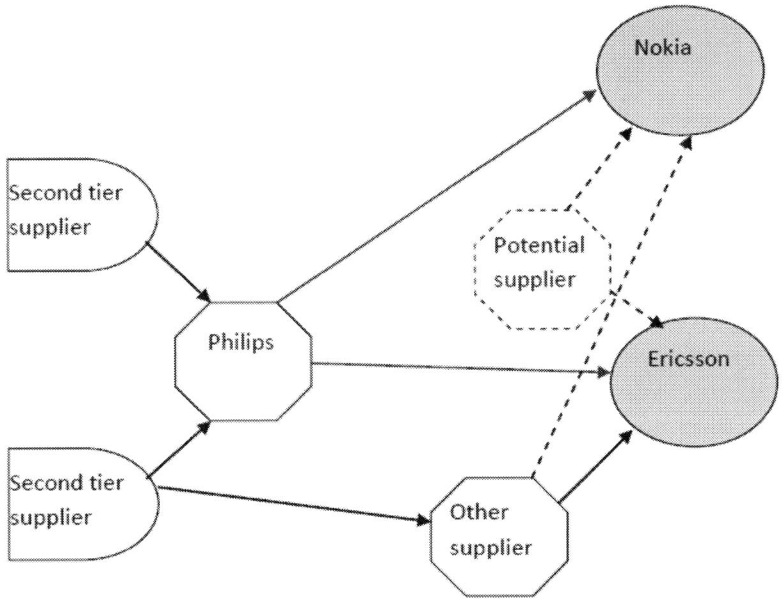

In Fig.2, Philips is the supplier of both Ericsson and Nokia. Ericsson may have another supplier which supplies the same components as Philips does. There might be another potential supplier which currently is not supplier of Ericsson and Nokia, but when disruption happens, the potential supplier's capacity might be used.

Extended Resource perspective allows us to consider the resources in a broader way. First, it does not only consider the resources of the supplier; it also considers the resources of non-supplier whose resources can be utilized when disruption happens. When disruption happens in Philips, it is important for Ericsson to contact potential suppliers and other firms to try to absorb as much capabilities as possible. Secondly, it does not only consider the resources and capabilities in the supplier, i.e., not only consider the reliability of the supplier, it is also important to see whether the capabilities can be fully dedicated to the focal company when disruption happens. For example, if Philips were not the supplier of the same product to Nokia, most of the remaining capability of Philips might have been dedicated to Ericsson when disruption happened to Philips. If this were true, Ericsson wouldn't have suffered so much.

From above, we can see Ericsson was vulnerable to the disruption in the Philips plant not only because it relies on single supplier; but also because there is another major industry player relying on the same supplier (Sheffi Y. , The Resilient Enterprise:Overcoming Vulnerability for Competitive Advantage, 2005). Since I use extended RBV to analyze supply chain disruptions, it is not enough to just evaluate the resources and reliabilities of current or potential suppliers, it is also important to consider how the resources can be available or dedicated to the focused company when disruption happens. This is very important for the recovery or resilience of the focused company.

To think it even more broadly, when evaluate the reliability of first-tier supplier, it might not be enough to just consider the resources and reliability of the second-tier suppliers, it is better to consider how the second-tier suppliers' resources can be dedicated to the first-tier supplier when disruptions happens. Same iterative analysis is with the third and fourth tiers upstream. In summary, the broader the scope of consideration, the better the focused company will be prepared for the disruptions in the supply chain. The environment of the firm can be separated into three levels, i.e., External Environment, Supply Chain Context, and Internal Environment (Brindley, 2004). Extended RBV should consider all the possible resources that the firm can utilize in the entire environment.

4.4. Dynamic Extended RBV (DE-RBV)

RBV holds a relatively static view of resources because of its traditional focus on building barriers (or isolating mechanisms) to prevent competitors from imitating, acquiring or substituting resources. It does not address issues like environment change and supply chain disruptions. Helfat and Petaraf (2003) presented 'Dynamic RBV', which is helpful to analyze supply chain disruptions (Helfat & Peteraf, 2003). From dynamic view, the circumstance of the firm change dynamically; the resources that the firm can utilize (extended resources) also change dynamically. On one hand, it is important for the firm to watch the changes in the supply chain and respond quickly; on the other hand, the firm should actively build up dynamic capabilities to deploy resources to achieve desired goals. Dynamic capabilities enable resources and capabilities to be renewed in congruence with changing environment (Teece, Pisano, & Shuen, 1997).

To meet the requirement of supply chain disruption analysis, this paper presents 'dynamic extended RBV' (DE-RBV), which combines both 'dynamic' and 'extended' perspective on RBV, to analyze the capabilities for handling supply disruptions in the general model. It can help managers to endeavor to handle disruptions in increasingly demanding environments.

4.5. DE-RBV to Risk Management Strategy Analysis: A Practical Framework

Grant presents a practical framework using Resource-based view. The framework that Grant gives is based on two premises: first, the firm's strategy is directed by internal resources and capabilities; second, the primary source of profit for the firm is from resources and capabilities. (Grant, The Resource-Based Theory of Competitive Advantage: Implications for Strategy Formulation, Spring 1991)

To facilitate my explanation, two different perspectives for strategy formulation and analysis are summarized:

- Strategies only from competitive advantage (CA) perspective
- Strategies integrating supply chain risk strategy

There are three different points between the two perspectives:

'Strategies only from CA perspective' neglects the abnormal disruptions which can hinder or even destroy the firm's capability to get competitive advantage. Actually handling supply chain risk should be qualifying factor for pursuing the firm's competitive advantage. Only with the capability to keep the business's continuity can the firm achieve sustained competitive advantage.

Since supply chain risk is integrated into the analysis when establishing strategy of the firm, we cannot perceive internal resources and capabilities as the basic direction for the firm's strategy. Extended RBV should be used here.

Due to the character of dynamic change of supply chain circumstance, dynamic view should be used in the strategy analysis framework.

Based on the difference pointed above, I present my practical framework for risk management strategy analysis based on DE-RBV (see Fig. 3).

Figure 3. DE-RBV Approach to Risk Management Strategy Analysis: A practical framework

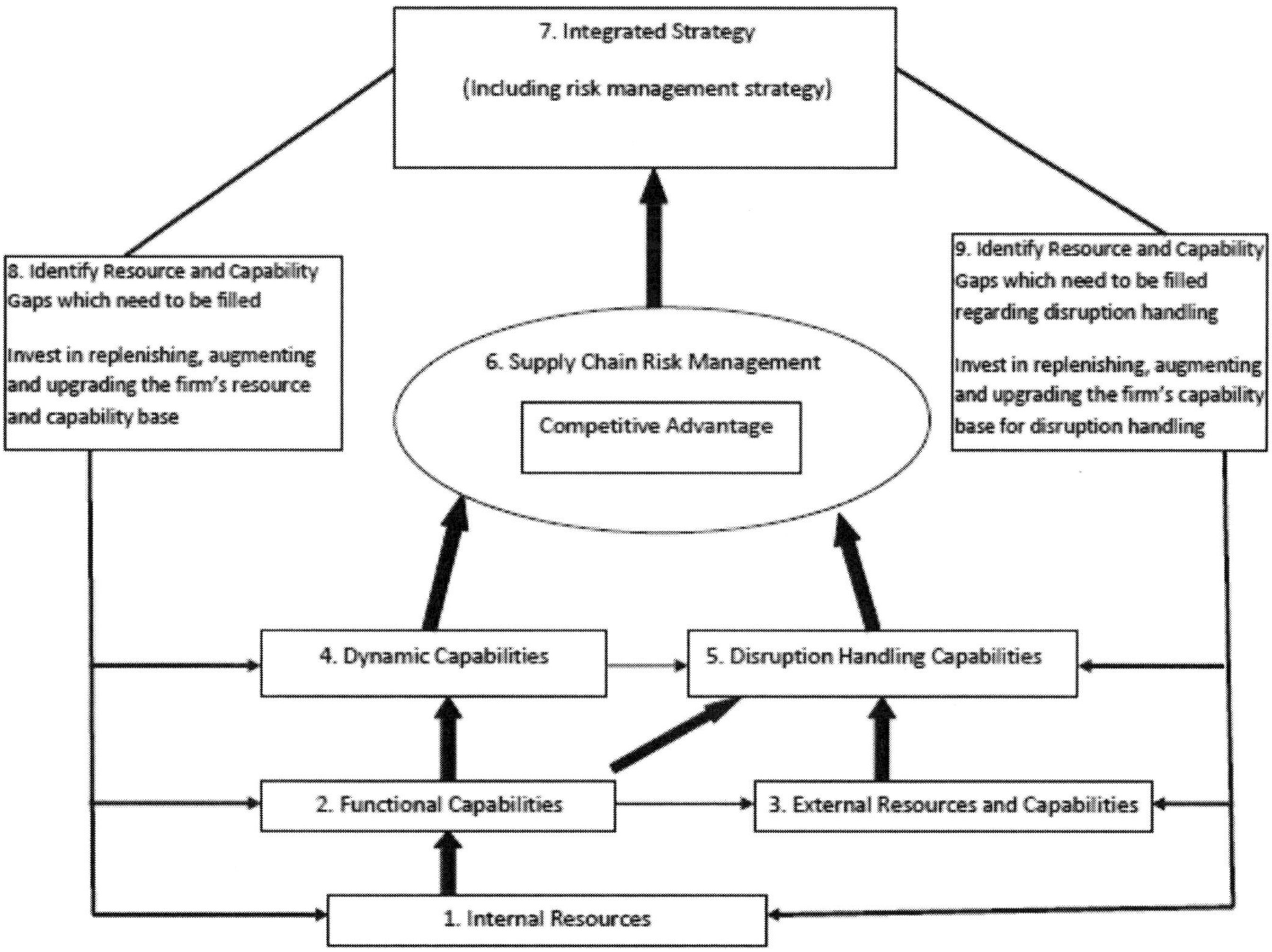

Fig.3 presented in this paper is a framework based on DE-RBV. It is adjusted from Grant's framework based on RBV (Grant, 1991). We can see the stages when doing strategy analysis:

1) Identify and classify the firm's resources. Appraise strengths and weaknesses relative to competitors. Identify opportunities for better utilization of resources.

2) Identify the firm's functional (operational) capabilities. Identify the resources inputs to each capability and the complexity of each capability.

3) Based on the firm's internal resources and capabilities, identify the external resources and capabilities that can be utilized, and the difficulty in the utilization.

4) Based on the firm's functional (operational) capabilities and resources, identify the dynamic capabilities (higher order capabilities) which can reorganize and resemble the composition of the firm's resources and capabilities when situation changes.

5) Based on the firm's dynamic capabilities and resources available, figure out the capabilities to handle supply chain disruptions, which include: Preventive Capability, Back-up Capability, Substitute Capability, and Warning Capability.

6) Based on the firm's dynamic capabilities and disruption handling capabilities, appraise the rent-generating potential of resources and capabilities in terms of: (a) their potential for sustainable competitive advantage, (b) the appropriability of their returns regarding supply chain disruptions handling. Supply chain risk management handling is the base and qualifying factor of the firm's competitive advantage. The investment in handling supply chain risk may not have positive relationship with performance of the company (or competitive advantage) since it is only a qualifying factor. It is not 'the more investment of handling risk, the better the return will be'.

7) Select a strategy which best exploits the firm's resources and capabilities relative to external opportunities and risks. Supply chain risk strategy is an important and necessary part of integral strategy of the company. Without supply chain risk strategy, it is almost impossible for the company to keep sustained competitive advantages.

8) Based on the strategy and the changing situation of the company, identify resource and capability gaps which need to be filled. Then invest in replenishing, augmenting and upgrading the firm's resource and capability base.

9) Based on supply chain risk management strategy and the changing circumstance of the company. Identify resource and capability gaps which need to be filled regarding disruption handling. Then invest in replenishing, augmenting and upgrading the firm's capability base for disruption handling.

Except for the stages described above, there are several points needed to be notified.

- This framework reflects DE-RBV. The extended resource based view is reflected by stage 3. The dynamic view is reflected by: (a) dynamic capabilities in stage 4; (b) after stage 8 and 9, there are arrows coming down, which reflects the perception of changing and reconsidering the resources and capabilities repeatedly and iteratively.

- In stage 6, the competitive advantage is located within the supply chain risk management boundary, which means supply chain risk handling is the qualifying factor and a base to keep competitive advantages. Supply risk is actually disruptions of the resources, so the relationship between supply risk and competitive advantages is as important as the relationship between resources and competitive advantages.

- Supply chain risk strategy is a necessary part of overall strategy. It can be the safeguard of the company to achieve competitive advantages. Based on RBV, business strategy should be viewed as 'a quest for Ricardian rents', which means the "returns to the resources which confer competitive advantage over and above the real costs of these resources" (Grant, The Resource-Based Theory of Competitive Advantage: Implications for Strategy Formulation, Spring 1991).
- Business strategy should be guaranteed by supply chain risk management strategy to make the business continue.

4.6 Hierarchies of Capabilities and 'Supply Chain Risk Management Capability'

Capabilities have different hierarchies. Functional (operational) capabilities are zero-level capabilities, which reflect to what extent the company can make use of its internal resources to keep the business functioning. Dynamic capabilities contrast with ordinary (or operational) capabilities by being concerned with change. As a set of identifiable and specific processes, dynamic capabilities can be perceived as upper order capabilities but it also includes different hierarchies. Some dynamic capabilities are of lower level, while some other dynamic capabilities are of higher level. For example, product development capability is a sort of dynamic capability. Compared with product development, strategic decision making is of higher level dynamic capability because it is based on other dynamic capabilities including product development capability and alliancing capability. Because capabilities are complex, structured and multidimensional (Winter, 2003), dynamic capabilities, as a kind of capability, are also complex. The core idea of dynamic capability is its 'change', i.e., can reorganize and change the use of lower level capabilities and resources.

Supply Chain risk management capability is a kind of capability, but it is a different categorization. It does not classify based on 'routines' or 'processes', but on what the company can do by utilizing the resources and capabilities available. It is consistent with the view that "capability is the capacity for a team of resources to perform some task or activity. (Grant, The Resource-Based Theory of Competitive Advantage: Implications for Strategy Formulation, Spring 1991)" My view of supply chain risk management capability synthesizes resources, the zero-order capabilities and higher-order capabilities, and get a special kind of capabilities, which particularly reflect the capabilities to handle supply chain disruptions. They are different with dynamic capabilities such as product development capability and acquisition capability. Like other dynamic capabilities, supply chain risk management capabilities are also for handling change, especially for handling disruptions that are unexpected changes to the firm. These capabilities are used to guarantee the firm's other capabilities' smooth functioning.

V. SUPPLY DISRUPTION HANDLING CAPABILITIES

Strategy has been defined as an organization matches its internal resources and capabilities with outside opportunities and risks. (Grant, The Resource-Based Theory of Competitive Advantage: Implications for Strategy Formulation, Spring 1991) The resources and capabilities that either belongs to a company or can be handled by a company should be the foundation and starting point when analyzing supply chain risk strategy of the company. 'Supply disruption handling capability' belongs to supply chain risk management capability and particularly refers to the capability to handle supply disruptions. This paper presents the necessary capabilities of handling supply risk including 'Preventive Capability', 'Back-up Capability', 'Substitute Capability' and 'Warning Capability'.

Risk handling is different with common business capabilities. It has to handle the dynamic changing circumstance. Dynamic capabilities help to reorganize and delegate the capabilities and resources of the company when circumstance changes, so better dynamic capabilities can improve supply disruption handling capability. While dynamic capabilities are reflected by the routines and processes in the organization (Grant, 1991), only dynamic capabilities are not enough to handle disruptions in the supply chain since many disruptions' occurrence and pattern are out of expectation. "Ad hoc problem solving (Winter, 2003)" is necessary for risk handling and will affect the function of dynamic capability. I use "Problem Oriented Improvisation" to describe the ad hoc problem solving ability to handle the unforeseen destructed situation without prior preparation or stipulation. The model which reflects this part of relationship is as Fig. 4.

Figure 4. Capabilities of Handling Supply Risk

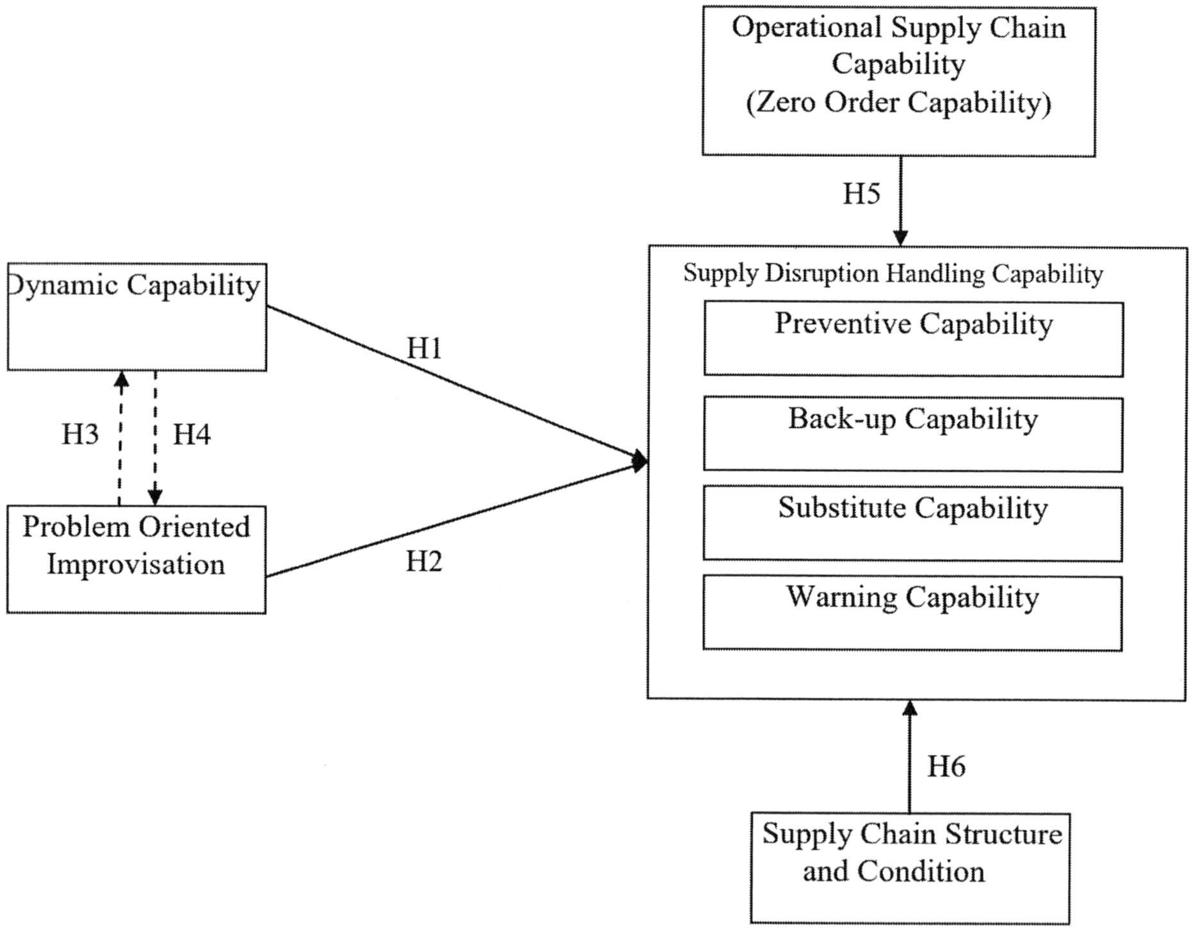

5.1 Preventive Capability

Preventive Capability means to what extent the firm can prevent disruptions before disruptions happen and how much the firm can take actions to mitigate the disruptions. Due to the cost of building up the capability, we cannot say that the more preventive capability the better. The risks and benefits of the preventing certain disruptions have to be balanced to make sure the resources are spent on the capabilities which will give the firm the most benefit.

5.2 Back-up Capability

Back-up Capability means to what extent the firm can use back-up resources to compensate the shortage of the supply. For example, the stocks of the materials, slack in lead times and redundant production capacities belong to 'Back-up Capability'. Back-up Capability actually includes some preventive capability because certain back-up material will actually avoid or mitigate the disruption.

5.3 Substitute Capability

Substitute Capability means when disruption happens, to what extent the firm can use substitute methods to compensate the shortages of the supply. It includes using substitute component, substitute suppliers, changing the design of the product, etc. All the methods which can mitigate the damages of the shortage of the supply after the disruption happens can be considered as substitute capability. Modular Design and Postponement are the ways to increase Substitute Capability. Lean Production can also improve substitute capability. The flexibility caused by lean production can improve substitute capability when disruption happens. The phenomenon that Toyota Company recovered more quickly from the supplier fire disruption than other companies shows Toyota's high substitute capabilities of Lean production and management. This looks like contradictory to the common sense that lean production can increase the supply risk. The reason is that although Lean Production can improve substitute capability it actually reduces Back-up Capability when pursuing cost reduction.

5.4 Warning Capability

Warning Capability means to what extent the firm can foresee or sense the coming disruption in the supply chain. It is based on the experience, knowledge, communication and information systems, and management style of the firm regarding supply disruptions. For example, if the firm has suffered the same kind of disruption many times, it will enhance the sensitivity of the firm, i.e., increase the warning capability. Good information system can improve the communication among different functional departments in the firm and can improve the warning capability. Warning capability also relates to the process of the firm, e.g., lean production has great warning capability due to the process of business. Without much stock and backup component, the problems in the supply and production procedure can be found and pinpoint more easily and quickly.

How decision-makers perceive risk also affect warning capability. Perceived risk affects the strategy and action of the company. Organization culture also affects warning capability.

5.5 Hypotheses in the Model

1) Dynamic capability and supply disruption handling capability

"Dynamic capabilities are the antecedent organizational and strategic routines by which managers alter their resource base—acquire and shed resources, integrate them together, and recombine them—to generate new value-creating strategies (Grant, Toward a knowledge-based theory of the firm, 1996) (Pisano, 1994) (Eisenhardt & Martin, Dynamic capabilites: what are they?, 2000). " Regarding managing supply disruptions, there are also routines and processes for handling supply disruptions. A firm should have processes and procedures in place to reduce uncertainty. The processes and procedures can also provide information, understanding and knowledge needed quickly (Reich, 2006). The routines and processes of handling supply disruptions exist in either explicit or tacit knowledge form, or both of them. The routines and processes are path-dependent, which is formed by the experience of handling the previous supply disruptions. It also can be learned from other companies' experience or knowledge. Dynamic capabilities can improve supply disruption handling capabilities.

Hypothesis 1: Dynamic capabilities positively relate to supply disruption handling capabilities.

2) Problem oriented improvisation and supply disruption handling capabilities

Many times, disruptions happen without enough warning and the firms have to handle while they are not well prepared for. In this situation, dynamic capabilities which are normally reflected by routines and processes are not enough to handle the disruptions. "They may be pushed into 'firefighting' mode, a high-paced, contingent, opportunistic and perhaps creative search for satisfactory alternative behaviors. (Winter, 2003)" Tomlin (2006) separates mitigation tactics and contingency tactics. Mitigation tactics are taken in advance of a disruption, while contingency tactics are response tactics which are adopted only if a disruption happens (Tomlin, 2006). In high-velocity markets, to adapt to changing circumstances, routines have to be unstable processes with unpredictable outcomes. This understanding leads to a richer conception of routines, which not only refer to efficient and robust processes (Nelson & Winter, 1982) but also include more fragile and 'semistructured' processes that are more effective in high-velocity markets (Eisenhardt & Martin, 2000). Winter (Winter, 2003) presented 'ad hoc problem solving' as a possible economically superior substitute for dynamic capability for firms to accomplish change without relying on dynamic capability. Here 'ad hoc problem solving' indicates such change behaviors that do not depend on dynamic capabilities; that are largely non-repetitive; and they are not merely reactive or passive and at least 'intendedly rational'.

Ad hoc problem solving is not routine; especially not highly patterned and not repetitious. It is a response to novel challenges or other relatively unpredictable events from environment. Thus, ad hoc problem solving is a different way to change compared with the exercise of dynamic capabilities (Winter, 2003).

In my model, I use the construct 'problem oriented improvisation' to reflect 'ad hoc problem solving.' I choose this construct because it closely relates to improvisation in organizational theory while 'ad hoc problem solving' has not much clearly related theory to support it. Improvisation is "a just-in-time strategy" (Weick, Substitutes for Strategy, 1987). It deals with the unforeseen event. (Weick, Improvisation as a Minset for Organizational Analysis, September-October 1998)" Improvisation can be done by groups, departments, or firms. It is called 'organizational improvisation' (Moorman & Miner, The Convergence of Planning and Execution: Improvisation in New Product Development, July 1998). 'Organizational improvisation' means the degree to which the composition and execution of an action converge in time (Moorman & Miner, Organizational Improvisation and Organizational Memory, 1998). Improvisation is very important for a firm in a turbulent environment that requires action in a time frame that is shorter than a regular planning cycle. (Moorman & Miner, The Convergence of Planning and Execution: Improvisation in New Product Development, July 1998). Rapid environmental turbulence increases the odds that improvisation provides value. Extensive formal plans in such conditions are not suitable because they are time and resources consuming and the guides that are provided to action are counterproductive because the context changes faster than the planning cycle (Eisenhardt & Tabrizi, Accelerating adaptive processes: Product innovation in the global computer industry, 1995) (Moorman & Miner, The Convergence of Planning and Execution: Improvisation in New Product Development, July 1998). Improvisation often arises when disaster happens. Rather than to utilize unexpected opportunities, improvisation are mainly to overcome obstacles. (Moorman & Miner, The Convergence of Planning and Execution: Improvisation in New Product Development, July 1998)

Regarding supply disruption handling, it is important for the firm to have the competency of improvisation to compensate the lack of formal plan. Scientific professionals saw improvisational activity as tools for flexibility and adaptability (Miner, Bassoff, & Moorman, 2001). Improvisation has been widely used in organizational theory; here I use "problem-oriented improvisation' to refer to the organizational improvisation when handling supply disruptions. When disruption happens, there is not much time for the firm to react, so the more improvisation competency the better the performance of handling supply disruptions. Improvisation can increase the 'supply disruption handling capability.' For example, improvisation can improve 'preventive capability' because when the firm realizes the risk of disruptions, improvisation can make the manager take suitable action quickly which might avoid risk or mitigate the disruption level.

H2(a): 'Problem Oriented Improvisation' positively relates to 'Preventive Capability'.

Improvisation can also improve 'Substitute Capability' of the firm. When supply disruption happens, the firm with good improvisation competence can quickly find substitute ways to compensate the shortage of the supply, which can mitigate the bad effect of the disruptions.

H2(b): 'Problem Oriented Improvisation' positively relates to 'Substitute Capability'.

3) 'Dynamic Capability' and 'Problem Oriented Improvisation'

With the experience of handling supply disruptions, firms can not only build up its capabilities to handle supply risks, but also improve the dynamic capabilities of reorganizing and redistributing the resources. Some improvisation can be retained by firms; some problem-oriented improvisational troubleshooting may be proved to be wrong but the team can still draw a lesson from it for future reference. Firms can routinize the observation of its previous improvisational activities to improve the dynamic capability (Miner, Bassoff, & Moorman, 2001) . This is also a sort of learning-by-doing process. As time goes on, more and more experience from improvisation will be routinized and the dynamic capability will be improved.

H3: More "Problem Oriented Improvisation" will relate to more 'Dynamic Capability".

Dynamic Capability can also improve the improvisational competence. Firms can plan to improvise. Important resources and skills may be required to get the competence of fruitful improvisation. (Moorman & Miner, Organizational Improvisation and Organizational Memory, 1998) (Crossan & Sorrenti, 1997) (Eisenhardt & Tabrizi, Accelerating adaptive processes:

Product innovation in the global computer industry, 1995) The firms with well dynamic capabilities may have better effect when doing improvisation.

H4: More dynamic capability will lead to more 'problem-oriented improvisation'.

Operational Supply Chain Capability and 'Supply Disruption Handling Capability'
Functional supply chain capability (Operational supply chain capability) means the capabilities of the supply chain to perform basic functions of the supply chain, i.e., the capabilities to make materials, money and information flow to go smoothly along the supply chain. I use Functional Supply Chain Capability (Operational supply chain capability) to refer to the accumulated operational capability of the firms in the whole supply chain.

Better functional supply chain capability can improve the capability of the firm to prevent disruptions. It is easier for the firm with better operational capabilities to respond to the changing circumstance quickly. So there might be more odds for the company to avoid disruptions or mitigate the level of disruptions. When disruption happens, it might be easier for the firm to substitute the shortage of the supply to keep business going smoothly. A firm with better operational capability normally is more organized and has efficient communication system and routines, so the firm can be more sensitive to the coming disruptions, i.e., has more warning capability. Based on extended RBV, the resources and capabilities in the supply chain are important for the focused company to handle supply disruptions.

H5: More Operational Supply Chain Capability leads to more 'Supply Disruption Handling Capability'.

5) 'Supply Chain Structure and Condition' and 'Supply Disruption Handling Capability'

Supply chain structure and condition refers to the structure of the supply chain, i.e., whether it is complex, disordered or well organized, the power of the focused company and the relationships with suppliers. A well-organized supply chain structure can be beneficial to the company to handle supply disruptions since it will facilitate the utilization of the resources in the supply chain to handle the disruptions if the supply chain is well-organized.

In the example about Nokia/Ericsson companies, I mentioned that if the company's suppliers' capability is dedicated to another main player in the industry, it will affect the company's capability to overcome risks in the supply chain. In general, the company with more power in the supply chain (supply chain leader) has the capabilities to affect other suppliers' actions, including how much the supplier will dedicate their remaining resources and capabilities to the firm when disruption happens to the supply. The master company of the supply chain has more bargaining power and will set the rules and routines for the supply chain partners. The company with supply chain power may benefit from utilizing the remaining supply chain resources and capabilities to handle supply disruptions.

Good relationship with suppliers will increase the substitute capability and warning capability of the focused company. When disruption happens, good relationship will facilitate the company to communicate with the supplier and dedicate more remaining resources and capabilities to the focused company. Good communication and trust will improve the warning capability of the focused company.

H7 (a): Supply chain structure and condition affect the 'supply disruption handling capability'.

H7 (b): The more power in the supply chain, the more 'supply disruption handling capability' of the focused company.

H7 (c): Better relationship with supplier will increase 'supply disruption handling capability' of the focused company.

V. CONCLUSION AND DISCUSSION

Main contributions of this paper are as below:

- Presents four supply disruption handling capabilities, i.e., preventive capability, warning capability, back-up capability and substitute capability.
- Presents a practical framework to Risk Management Strategy Analysis based on Dynamic Extended Resource Based View (DE-RBV).
- The relationship between supply disruption handling capabilities and supply disruption handling performance is given.

This paper gives thorough and extensive analysis of supply disruption handling capabilities and its relationship with traditional RBV and dynamic capability theory. The supply risk handling capabilities presented in this paper can help a firm systematically analyze why certain kinds of supply chain practices are good to handle risk in specific situations and find out where capability gaps exist for a firm. The model presented in this paper can clearly analyze why and how some popular practices such as Lean, Global Sourcing, and Single Sourcing etc., can affect supply chain risk. Upon the analysis of how the supply chain strategies and practices affect the supply disruption handling capabilities, managers can decide on using which kind of supply chain strategies or practices (e.g., Postponement, Component Design, etc) and to what extent we should utilize them.

The analysis of this paper focuses on the regularities among supply disruption handling methods. A framework of this generality does not explain the details of how a specific supply disruption handling method work in particular circumstances of the company, instead, the framework provides an outline of the main features of supply chain disruption handling, which may guide future research. Based on this, new supply chain risk management methods can be traced, predicted and organized. It will facilitate the judgment and justification of practitioners on supply chain risk management strategies and practices. This framework provides a frame within which subsequent research can examine the specific supply chain risk management method in particular circumstance in greater detail.

The purpose of this paper is to move away some obscurity and conflicts existing in supply chain risk research area and to build up foundation for further research. Based on this general conceptual model, more operational supply risk management methods will be generated and justified.

Although this paper is a good attempt to dig the underlying mechanism of supply chain disruption handling, due to the limitation of this research, the constructs and models presented in this paper need further theoretical and empirical verification and test.

References

Aitken, Childerhouse, Christopher, & Towill. (2005). Designing and Managing Multiple Pipelines. *Journal of Business Logistics , 26* (2).

Autry, C., & Sanders, N. (2009). Supply Chain Security: A Dynamic Capabilities Approach. In G. A. Zsidisin, & B. Ritchie (Eds.), *Supply Chain Risk-A Handbook of Assessment, Management, and Performance* (pp. 307-329). Springer Science+ Business Media, LLC.

Bankoff, G., Frerks, G., & Hilhorst, D. (2004). *Mapping Vulnerability.* Sterling: Earthscan.

Barney, J. B. (2002). *Gaining and Sustaining Competitive Advantage* (Second ed.). New Jersey: Pearson Education, Inc.

Barney, J. (1991). Firm resources and sustained competitive advantage. *Jounral of management , 17* (1), 99-120.

Benjaafar, S. (1994). Models for performance evaluation of flexibility in manufacturing systems. *International Journal of Product Research* , 1383-1402.

Blume, M. (1971). On the assessment of risk. *Journal of Finance , 26* (1), 1-10.

Borge, d. (2001). *The Book of Risk.* New York: John Wiley and Sons Inc.

Braunscheidel, M. J., & Suresh, N. C. (2009). The organizational antecedents of a firm's supply chain agility for risk mitigation and response. *Journal of Operations Management , 27*, 119-140.

Brindley, C. (2004). Supply Chain Risk. In C. Brindley (Ed.). Aldershot, Hampshire, England: Ashgate Publishing Limited.

Buzacott, J., & Mandelbaum, M. (1985). Flexibility and Productivity in Manufacturing Systems. *Proceedings of the IIE Conference* (pp. 404-413). Chicago, IL: Industrial Engineering and Management Press, Atlanta, CA.

Chang, Y., & Makatsoris, H. Supply chian modeling using simulation. *I.J. of simulation , 2* (1), 24-30.

Chopra, S., & Sodhi, M. (2004). Managing risk to avoid supply chain breakdown. *MIT Sloan Management Review , 46* (1), 53-61.

Christopher, M. (2004). Creating resilient supply chains. *Logistics Europe , 18* (11), 14-21.

Christopher, M. (2000). The agile supply chain. *Industrial Marketing Management , 29* (1).

Christopher, M., & Peck, H. (2004). Building the Resilient Supply Chain. *The International Journal of Logistics Management , 15* (2), 1-13.

Christopher, M., McKinnon, A., Sharp, J., Wilding, R., Wilding, R., Peck, H., et al. (2002). *Supply Chain Vulnerability.* Cranfield: Cranfield University.

Cohen, M., & Kunreuther, H. (2007). Operations risk management: overview of Paul Kleindorfer's contributions. *Production and Operations Management , 16* (5), 525-541.

Cooper, D., & Emory, C. (1995). *Business Research Methods* (5th Edition ed.). USA: Richard D. Irwin, INC.

Craighead, C. W., Blackhurst, J., Rungtusanatham, M. J., & Handfield, R. B. (2007). The Severity of Supply Chain Disruptions: Design Characteristics and Mitigation Capabilities. *Decision Sciences , 38* (1), 131-156.

Crandall, R. (2010). Risk Management in Supply Chains:Minimizing disruptions to streamline flow regardless of complexity. *APICS , 20* (1), 30-33.

Crossan, M., & Sorrenti, M. (1997). Making sense of improvisation. In J. Walsh, & A. Huff (Eds.), *Advances in strategic management* (Vol. 14, pp. 155-180). Greenwich, CT: JAI Press.

Dana, J., & Spier, K. (2001). Revenue sharing and vertical control in the video rental industry. *Journal of Industrial Economics , 59*, 223-245.

Deloach, J. (2000). *Enterjprise-wide Risk Management. Arthur Andersen.* London: Financial times, Prentice Hall.

Doll, W. J., & Vonderembse, M. (1991). "The evolution of manufacturing systems: towords the post-industrial enterprise". *Omega , 19* (5), 401-11.

Dyer, J. H., & Singh, H. (1998). The relational view:cooperative strategy and sources of interorganizational competitive advantage. *Academy of Magagement Review , 23* (4), 660-679.

Editorial, Narasimhan, R., & Talluri, S. (2009). Perspectives on risk mangement in supply chains. *Journal of Opertions Management , 27*, 114-118.

Egeland, B., Carlson, E., & Sroufe, L. (1993). Resilience as a process. *Development and Psychopathology , 5*, 517-528.

Eisenhardt, K., & Martin, J. (2000). Dynamic capabilites: what are they? *Strategic Management Journal , 21*, 1105-1121.

Eisenhardt, K., & Tabrizi, B. (1995). Accelerating adaptive processes: Product innovation in the global computer industry. *Administrative Science Quarterly , 40*, 84-110.

Fahlen, K. (1997). *Consequences of disruptions for the efficiency in manufacturing companies: identifying, analysing and handling of disruptions.* Doctoral thesis. Gothenburg University.

Faisal, M. N., Banwet, D., & Shankar, R. (2006). Supply chain risk mitigation: modeling the enablers. *Businiess Process Management Journal , 12* (4), 535-552.

Fisher, M., Hammond, J. H., Obermeyer, W. R., & Raman, A. (1994). Making supply meet demand in an uncertain world. *Harvard Business Review* (May-June), 83-93.

Garrett, S. E. (1986). Strategy First: A Case in FMS Justification. *Proceedings of the Second ORSA/TIMS Conference on Flexible Manufacturing Systems* (pp. 17-13). Ann Arbor, MI: K.E. Stecke and R. Suri (Eds.), Elsevier, Amsterdam, The Netherlands.

Gaudenzi, B. (2005). Managing risks in the supply chain. Powerpoint-presentation. *ISCRiM 5th International Research Seminar on Risk and the Supply Chain*, (pp. 12-13). Cambridge, UK.September.

Gerwin, D. (1989). Manufacturing flexibility in the CAM era. *Business Horizon , Jan/Feb*, 78-84.

Grant, R. (Spring 1991). The Resource-Based Theory of Competitive Advantage: Implications for Strategy Formulation. *California Management Review , 33* (3), 114-135.

Grant, R. (1996). Toward a knowledge-based theory of the firm. *Strategic Management Journal , Summer Special Issue 17*, 109-122.

Graziano, A., & Raulin, M. L. (2000). *Research Methods: A Process of Inquiry.* Needham Heights, MA, USA: Allyn& Bacon.

Grimvall, Jacobsson, & Theeden. (2003). *Risker i tekniska system.* Lund: Studentlitteratur.

Gupta, D., & Buzacott, J. A. (1989). A framework for understanding flexibility of manufacturing systems. *Journal of Manufacturing Systems , 8*, 89-97.

Gupta, Y. P., & Somers, T. M. (1992). The measurement of manufacturing flexibility. *European Journal of Operational Research , 60*, 166-182.

Hair, J. J., Black, W. C., Babin, B. J., Anderson, R. E., & Tatham, R. L. (2006). *Multivariate Data Analysis* (6 ed.). Upper Saddle River, New Jersey, USA: Pearson Education, Inc.,.

Harland, C., Brenchley, R., & Walker, H. (2003). Risk in supply networks. *Journal of Purchasing & Supply Management , 9* (2), 51-62.

Hayes, R. H., & Wheelwright, S. C. (1984). *Restoring our competitive edge: competing through manufacturing.* New York: Wiley.

Helfat, C. E., & Peteraf, M. (2003). The dynamic resource-based view: Capability lifecycles. *Strategic Management Journal , 24*, 997-1010.

Hendricks, K. B., & Singhal, V. R. (2005). An empirical analysis of the effect of supply chain disruptions on Long-run stock price performance and risk of the firm. *Production and Operations Management , 14*, 35-52.

Hendricks, K. B., & Singhal, V. R. (2003). The effect of supply chain glitches on shareholder value. *Journal of Operations Management , 21*, 501-522.

Hendricks, K., Singlhal, V., & Zhang, R. (2009). The effect of operational slack, diversification, and vertical relatedness on the stock market reaction to supply chain disruptions. *Journal of Operations Management , 27* (3), 233-246.

Hubbard, D. (2009). *The Failure of Risk Management: Why It's Broken and How to Fix It.* John Wiley & Sons.

Huber, G. P. (1984). The nature and design of post-industrial organizations. *Management Science , 30* (8), 928-951.

Hult, G. T., Craighead, C. W., & Ketchen Jr., D. J. (August 2010). Risk Uncertainty and Supply Chain Decisions: A Real Options Perspective. *Decision Sciences , 41* (3), 435-458.

Ingalls, R. G. (1998). The value of simulation in modeling supply chains. *the 1998 Winter Simulation conference*, (pp. 1371-1375).

Jiang, B., Baker, R. C., & Frazier, G. V. (2009). An analysis of job dissatisfaction and turnover to reduce global supply chain risk: Evidence from China. *Journal of Operations Management* (27), 169-184.

Jin, Y. (2008). *The influence of power and resources on flexibilities in a supply chain context.* University of Toledo: Dissertation Paper.

Juettner, U., Peck, H., & Christopher, M. (2002). Supply Chain Risk Management: Outlining an agenda for future research'. In Griffiths, Hewitt, & Ireland (Ed.), *LRN2002. Conference Proceedings* (pp. 443-450). The Institute of Logistics and Transport.

Kajuter, P. (2003). Risk Management in Supply Chains. In S. Seuring, M. Muller, M. Coldbach, & U. Schneidewind (Eds.), *Strategy and Organization in Supply Chains* (pp. 321-336). Physica, Heidelberg.

Ketchen Jr., D. J., & Hult, G. T. (2007). Bridging organization theory and supply chain management: The case of best value supply chains. *Journal of Operations Management , 25*, 573-580.

Kilgore, M. (2003). *Mitigating supply chain risks. White Paper.* Atlanta, Georgia: Chainalytics LLC.

Kim, S. W. (2006). The effect of supply chain integration on the alignment between corporate competitive capability and supply chain operational capability. *International Journal of Operations & Production Management , 26* (10), 1084-1107.

Kleindorfer, P. R., & Saad, G. H. (2005). Managing Disruption Risks in Supply Chains. *Production and Operations Management , 14* (1), 53-68.

Kloman, F. (December 2003). Editorial note. *Risk Management Reports , 30* (12), 2.

Knemeyer, M., Zinn, W., & Eroglu, C. (2009). Proactive planning for catastrophic events in suply chains. *Journal of Operations Management , 27*, 141-153.

Knight, F. (1921). *Risk, Uncertainty and Profit.* Boston and New York: Houghton Mifflin Company.

Knight, F. (1921). *Risk, Uncertainty, and Profit.* Boston, MA: Hart, Schaffner & Marx.

Krajewski, L., Wei, J. C., & Tang, L. (2005). Responding to schedule changes in build-to-order supply chains. *Journal of Operations Management , 23*, 452-469.

Lawrence, J., & Pasternack, B. (1998). *Applied Management Science.* John Wiley & Sons, INC.

Lee, H. L., & Whang, S. (2005). Higher supply chain security with lower cost: Lessons from total quality management. *International Journal of Production Economics , 96* (3), 289-300.

Lee, H. (2004). The triple-A supply chain. *Harvard Business Review , 82*, 102-112.

Leeuw, A. D., & Volberda, H. W. (1996). On the concept of flexibility: a dual control perspective. *Omega , 24*, 121-139.

Leonard, M. (2005). *Aon 2005 Political and Economic Risk Map.* London.

Li, S. (2002). *An integrated model for supply chain management practice, performance and competitive advantage.* Toledo: Dissertation paper, University of Toledo.

Mabert, V., & Venkataramanan, M. (1998). Special research focus on supply chain linkages: challenges for design and management in the 21st century. *Decision Sciences , 29* (3), 537-552.

Makhija, M., & Stewart, A. (2002). The Effect of National context on Perceptions of Risk: a Comparison of Planned Versus Free-Market Managers. *Journal of International Business Studies , 33* (4), 737-756.

Manuj, I. a. (2008). Global supply chain risk management. *Journal of Business Logistics* .

Manuj, I., & Mentzer, J. (2008). Global supply chain risk management strategies. *International Journal of Physical Distribution & Logistics Management , 38* (3), 192-223.

March, J. G., & Simon, H. A. (1958). *Organizations.* New York: Wiley.

March, J., & Shapira, Z. (1987). Managerial perspectives on risk and risk taking. *Mgmnt Sci. , 33*, 1404-1418.

March, J., & Sharpira, Z. (1987). Managerial perspectives on Risk and Risk Taking. *Management Science , 33* (11), 1404-1418.

Mathews, J. A. (2003). Comopetitive dynamics and economic learning: an extended resource-based view. *Industrial and Corporate Change , 12* (1), 115-145.

Melnyk, S. A., Rodrigues, A., & Ragatz, G. L. (2009). Using Simulation to Investigate Supply Chain Disruptions. In G. Zsidisin, & B. Ritchie, *Supply Chain Risk: A Handbook of Assessment, Management, and Performance* (pp. 103-121). New York, NY: Springer.

Melnyk, S., Rodrigues, A., & Ragatz, G. L. (2009). Chapter 7: Using Simulation to Investigate Supply Chain Disruptions. In G. A. Zsidisin, & B. Ritchie, *Supply chain risk: a handbook of assessment, management, and performance* (pp. 103-122). New York: Springer Science+Business Media.

Miner, A., Bassoff, P., & Moorman, C. (2001). Organiational Improvisation and Learning: A Field Study. *Administrative Science Quarterly , 46*, 304-337.

Mitchell, V. (. (1995). Organizational risk perception and reduction: a literature review. *British Journal of Management , 6*, 115-33.

Moorman, C., & Miner, A. (1998). Organizational Improvisation and Organizational Memory. *Academy of Management Review , 23* (4), 698-723.

Moorman, C., & Miner, A. S. (July 1998). The Convergence of Planning and Execution: Improvisation in New Product Development. *Journal of Marketing , 62*, 1-20.

Neiger, D., Rotaru, K., & Churilov, L. (2009). Supply chain risk identification with value-focused process engineering. *Journal of Operations Management , 27*, 154-168.

Nelson, R., & Winter, S. (1982). *An Evolutionary Theory of Economic Change.* Cambridge, MA: Belknap Press.

Park, K. (June, 2010). *Dissertation proposal: A resourced-based approach to define and build the resilient supply chain.* University of Toldeo.

Paulsson, U. (2007). *On managing disruption risks in the supply chian--the DRISC model.* Lund, Sweden: KFS i Lund Ab.

Peck, H. (2006). Reconciling supply chain vulneraility, risk and supply chain management. *International Journal of Logistics: Research and Applications , 9* (2), 127-142.

Peng, D. X., Schroeder, R. G., & Shah, R. (2008). Linking routines to operations capabilities: A new perspective. *Journal of Operations Management , 26*, 730-748.

Peng, M. W. (2009). *Global 2010 edition* (2010 ed.). (e. Michele Rhoades, Ed.) Ohio, USA: Jonathan Hulbert.

Persson, F., & Olhager, J. (2002). Performance simulation of supply chain designs. *International journal of production economics , 77*, 231-245.

Peteraf, M. (1993). The cornerstone of competitive advantage. *Strategive Management Journal , 14* (3), 179-191.

Pisano, G. (1994). Knowledge, integration, and the locus of learning: an empirical analysis of process development. *Strategic Management Journal , Winter Special Issue 15*, 85-100.

Ponomarov, S. Y., & Holcomb, M. C. (2009). Building Supply Chain Resilience through Logistics Capabilities. *POMS 20th Annual Conference.* Orlando, Florida U.S.A.

Ponomarov, S. Y., & Holcomb, M. C. (2009). Understanding the concept of supply chain resilience. *The International Journal of Logistics Management , 20* (1), 124-143.

Prahalad, C., & Hamel, G. (May/June 1990). The Core Competence of the Corporation. *Harvard Business Review* , 79-91.

Priem, R. L., & Butler, J. E. (2001). Is the Resource-Based "View" a Useful Perspective for Strategic Management Research? *The Academy of Management Review , 26* (1), 22-40.

Qin, B., Gao, S., & Shen, L. (Nov, 2002). The Systematic Research On the Concepts of “flexibility” in the Domain of Software Engineering. *Proceedings of the 8th Joint International Computer Conference.* Ningbo, China.

Rao, S., & Goldsby, T. J. (2009). Supply chain risks: a review and typology. *The International Journal of Logistics Management , 20* (1), 97-123.

Reich, J. W. (2006). Three psychological principles of resilience in natural disasters. *Disaster Prevention and Management , 15* (5), 793-798.

Rice.Jr, J. B., & Caniato, C. F. (2003). Building a secure and resilient supply network. *Supply chain management review , 7*, 22-30.

Rutter, M. (1993). Resilience: Some conceptual considerations. *Journal of Adolescent Health* , 626-631.

Sethi, A. K., & Sethi, S. P. (1990). Flexibility in Manufacturing: A Survey. *The international Journal of Flexible Manufacturing Systems , 2*, 289-328.

Sheffi, Y. (2005). *The Resilient Enterprise:Overcoming Vulnerability for Competitive Advantage.* Cambridge, MA: MIT Press.

Sheffi, Y. (2005). *The Resilient Enterprise:Overcoming Vulnerability for Competitive Advantage.* MIT Press.

Sheffi, Y., & Rice Jr, J. (2005, Fall). A Supply Chain View of the Resilient Enterprise. *MIT Sloan Mangement Review* , 41-48.

Slack, N. (1983). Flexibility as a manufacturing objective. *International Journal of Operations and Production Management , 3*, 4-13.

Slack, N. (2005). The changing nature of operations flexibility. *International Journal of Operations & Production Management , 25* (12).

Slack, N., & Correa, H. (1992). The flexibilities of push and pull. *International Journal of Operations & Production Management* , *12* (4), 82-92.

Souter, G. (2000). Risks from supply chain also demand attention. *Business Insurance* , *34* (20), 26-28.

Stauffer, D. (2003). Risk: The weak link in your supply chain. *Harvard Business Review* , *81*, 3-5.

Stevenson, M., & Spring, M. (2007). Flexibility from a supply Chain perspective: Definition and review. *International Journal of Operations& Production Management* , *27* (7), 685-731.

Stewart, M., Reid, G., & Mangham, C. (1997). Fostering Children's Resilience. *Journal of Pediatric Nursing* , *12* (1), 21-31.

Svensson, G. (2002). A conceptual framework of vulnerability in firms' inbound and outbound logistics flows. *Int. J. Physical Distrib. Logistics Mgmnt* , *32*, 110-134.

Svensson, G. (2000). A conceptual framework for the analysis of vulnerability in supply chains. *Int. J. Physical Distrib. Logistics Mgmnt* , *30*, 731.

Svensson, G. (2002). A conceptual framework of vulnerability in firms' inbound and outbound logistics flows. *International Journal of Physical Distribution & Logistics Management* , *32* (2).

Swafford, P. M., Ghosh, S., & Murthy, N. (2006). The antecedents of supply chain agility of a firm: Scale development andmodel testing. *Journal of Operations Management* , *24*, 170-188.

Swink, M., & Zsidisin, G. (2006). On the benefits and risks of focused commitment to suppliers. *International Journal of Production Research* , *44* (20), 4223-4240.

Tang, C. S. (2006). Perspectives in supply chain risk management. *International Journal of Production Economics* (103), 451-488.

Tang, C. S. (2006). Robust strategies for mitigating supply chain disruptions. *International Journal of Logistics: Research and Applications* , *9* (1), 33-45.

Teece, D. J., Pisano, G., & Shuen, A. (1997). Dynamic capabilities and strategic management. *Strategic Management Journal* , *18* (7), 509-533.

Terzi, S., & Cavalieri, S. (2004). Simulation in the supply chain context:a survey. *Computers in Industry* , *53*, 3-16.

The Royal Society. (Oct 1992). *Risk Analysis, Perception and Management.* UK: The Royal Society.

Tomlin, B. (2006). On the value of mitigation and contingency strategies for managing supply chain disruption risks. *Management Science* , *52* (5), 639-657.

Upton, D. M. (1994). The management of manufacturing flexibility. *California Management Review , Winter*, 72-89.

Upton, D. M. (1995). What really makes factories flexible? *Harvard business review , July-August*, 74-84.

Valla, J. (1982). The concept of risk in industrial buyer behaviour. *workshop on organisational buyer behaviour December 9-10.* Brussels: European Institute for Advanced Studies in Management.

Vickery, S., Calantone, R., & Droge, C. (1999). Supply chain flexibility: an empirical study. *Journal of Supply Chain Managemetn , 18*, 485-501.

Vickery, S., Droge, C., & Markland, R. (1993). Production Competence and business strategy: do they affect business performance? *Decision Science , 24*, 435-455.

Wang, C. L., & Ahmed, P. k. (2007). Dynamic Capabilities: a review and research agenda. *International Journal of Management Review , 9* (1), 31-51.

Ward, P., McCreery, J., Ritzman, L., & Sharma, D. (1998). Competitive priorities in operations management. *Decision Sciences , 29*, 1035-1046.

Weick, K. (September-October 1998). Improvisation as a Minset for Organizational Analysis. *Organization Science , 9* (5), 543-555.

Weick, K. (1987). Substitutes for Strategy. In D. Teece (Ed.), *The Competitive challenge: Strategies for industrial innovation and renewal: 221-233.* New York: Harper & Row.

Werner, E. (1984). Resilient children. *Young Children* , 68-72.

Wernerfelt, B. (1984). A resource-based view of the firm. *Strategic Management Journal , 5* (2), 171-180.

Williamson, O. E. (1999). Strategy research: governance and competence perspectives. *Strategic Management Journal , 20* (12), 1087-1108.

Winter, S. G. (2003). Understanding Dynamic Capabilities. *Strategic Management Journal , 24*, 991-995.

Wu, D., & Olson, D. (2008). Supply chain risk, simulation, and vendor selection. *International Journal of Production Economics , 114*, 646-655.

Wu, S. J., Melnyk, S. A., & Flynn, B. B. (November 2010). Operational Capabilities: The Secret Ingredient. *Decision Sciences , 41* (4), 721-754.

Zahra, S. A., Sapienza, H. J., & Davidsson, P. (2006). Entrepreneurship and Dynamic Capabilities:A Review, Model and Research Agenda. *Journal of Management Studies , 43* (4), 917-955.

Zelenovic, D. (1982). Flexibility-A Condition for Effective Production Systems. *International Journal of Product Research, IJ Productions , 20* (3), 319-337.

Zhang, Q., Vonderembse, M. A., & Lim, J. S. (2003). Manufacturing flexibility: defining and analyzing relationships among competence, capability, and customer satisfaction. *Journal of Operations Management , 21*, 173-191.

Zhang, Q., Vonderembse, M. A., & Lim, J. S. (2002). Value chain flexibility: a dichotomy of competence and capability. *International Journal of Production Research , 40* (3), 561-583.

Zsidisin, G., Melnyk, S., & Ragatz, G. (2005). An institutional theory perspective of business continuity planning for purchasing and supply management. *International Journal of Production Research , 43*, 3401-3420.

DECISION SCIENCES INSTITUTE
Supply Chain Performance Analysis based upon Little's law

Sangdo (Sam) Choi
Shenandoah University
Email: schoi@su.edu

ABSTRACT

We review Little's Law as a fundament tool to define primary supply chain metrics such as inventory turnover (ITR) and cycle time (or days of supply). Little's Law deals with queueing systems originally, and has applied to operations management. We extend Little's Law to define other asset turnovers. Prior studies show that ITR is negatively correlated with profitability measure. Inventory-related measures affect not only operational efficiency, but also profit margin and liquidity. We suggest that the negative correlation exists because of each firm's stance or supply chain strategy. Using an earns-turns matrix, we propose a framework for supply chain performance analysis. We show empirical results of Dow Jones Indexed firms except financial institutions using the earns-turns matrix. In addition, we analyze supply chain performance of U.S. retail and manufacturing firms.

KEYWORDS: Little's Law, Inventory Turnover, Earns-Turns Matrix, Supply Chain Performance Analysis

TRADITIONAL INVENTORY AND PROFITABILITY MEASURES

Inventory can be measured in four different ways for operations management. First, supply chain professionals measure and analyze physical units to manage inventory. Stock keeping unit is typically used and depends upon shape or material type. For example, ton, cubic-meter, container, or truck unit can be used for physical measures. Supply chain professionals have good understandings about inventory size based on physical units. Secondly, accounting professionals look at dollar amounts to measure and valuate inventory. The two metrics are static measures without respect to company size, or revenue amount. Combining revenue or sales volume with inventory, not only supply chain professionals but also accounting professionals are able to measure how fast inventory moves in the market and how long inventory supplies to the market using a dynamic measure. Inventory turnover (ITR) and days-of-supply (DOS) are the other two inventory-related performance metrics. ITR is defined as the number of times that an inventory cycles during the fiscal year (Blackstone Jr., 2013) as the following:

$$ITR = \frac{Cost\ of\ goods\ sold}{Average\ inventory}. \quad (1)$$

Supply chain professionals tend to use quantity measures rather than dollar values. For example, the traditional economic order quantity (EOQ) model defines ITR as the following:

$$ITR = \frac{Annual\ demand}{Order\ quantity}. \quad (2)$$

ITR under EOQ can be explained as the number of orders to satisfy the annual demand. The denominator of (1), average inventory reflects an inventory trend during a fiscal period, whereas the denominator of (2) is one time order quantity. Typically, beginning and ending balances of the fiscal year are used to compute the average inventory of (1). The numerator of (1), cost of goods sold (CGS) reflects the cumulative sales amount during the same fiscal year that the average inventory is taken into account. The cumulative sales amount during the fiscal year (i.e., flow rate) is valued at the cost, not the price at which revenue is valued. DOS (i.e., flow time) is the reciprocal value of ITR, i.e.,

$$\boldsymbol{DOS} = \frac{1}{ITR}(\boldsymbol{year}) = \frac{12\times Average\ Inventory}{Cost\ of\ goods\ sold}(\boldsymbol{months}) = \frac{365\times Average\ inventory}{Cost\ of\ goods\ sold}(\boldsymbol{days}) \qquad (3)$$

Demeter and Matyusz (2011) emphasize inventory turnover as a visible and concrete marker of world-class performance and also as an indicator of effort to improve value chain processes. The firms should invest less capital in raw material (RM), work-in-process (WIP), or finished goods inventory (FGI) to achieve higher ITR, which can make the firms reduce the amount of working capital to free up loans or invest their funds more profitably.

Inventory account appears on balance sheet showing a financial status as certain date, whereas CGS account appears on income statement showing financial achievement during certain period. Revenue account is the first type of income in the income statement. Gross profit, the difference between revenue and CGS, is the second type of income. CGS consists of all types of costs across primary activities of supply chain such as direct material cost, direct labor cost, and inbound transportation cost. CGS account is a product cost, which means that CGS is inventory cost sold during a period. Period costs are also occurred across supply chain. Marketing and general administration expense is an example of period costs. Operating income is the outcome from both primary and supportive activities across value chain as shown as the following:

$$\boldsymbol{Operating\ income} = \boldsymbol{Sales\ revenue} - \boldsymbol{CGS} - \boldsymbol{SGA} - \boldsymbol{depreciation\ expense}. \qquad (4)$$

Operation income does not involve R&D expense, which is a major part of supply chain activities. Operating income involves depreciation expense, which is non-cash expense. When a retail firm sells the product to a customer, inventory account is credited and decreases in value; CGS account is debited and increases in value. Inventory and CGS accounts are corresponding each other and should be posted at the same time when a sales transaction takes place. Hence, ITR involves inventory trends over the periods and CGS during the periods together. In a similar way, account receivable (AR) account is debited and increases in value; revenue account is credited and increases in value. AR and revenue accounts are also corresponding each other.

We relate inventory-related measures to Little's Law in next sections. The objectives of this paper are to (1) clearly explain analogy of Little's Law to the relationship between ITR and DOS, (2) suggest a new Earns-Turns matrix with ITR and profitability, and (3) analyze Dow-Jones Indexed (DJI) firms and their competitors with the earns-turns matrix. We analyze U.S. retail and manufacturing firms using the earns-turns matrix. ITR is believed to have negative relationship with profitability by researchers in accounting (Gaur et al. 2005). We insist that each firm choose its own position, to focus on either profitability or operational excellence. The Earns-Turns matrix shows that the relationship between profitability and ITR is a matter of choice, not relationship.

This paper is organized as follows. In next section, explains how Little's Law defines inventory turnover and other asset turnovers. The third section provides an earns-turns matrix to analyze supply chain firms. The fourth section shows the supply chain performance analysis of DJI firms using the earns-turns matrix. The fifth section provides the earns-turns matrix analysis of U.S. retail firms. The sixth section provides an earns-turns matrix of U.S. manufacturing firms. The seventh section concludes our discussion.

THE RELATIONSHIP BETWEEN TURNOVER AND DAYS OF SUPPLY BASED ON LITTLE'S LAW

Little's Law applies to supply chain and defines the relationship among the average inventory level, the average flow rate (e.g., CGS), and the average flow time (e.g., DOS). Originally, Little's Law deals with queueing systems, consisting of discrete objects (e.g., customers, patients, job requests), each of which arrives at a rate (e.g., arrival rate) to the system, joins one or more queues, and receives service at a rate (e.g., service rate) and exits from the system at a rate (e.g., leaving rate) (Little 1961, 2011). Little's Law relates the average time spent in the system of objects and the average number of objects in the system via the average rate of arrival to the system. Law 1 establishes the formal statement of Little's Law.

Law 1 (Little 1961) Let W be the average time spent in the system of objects; L, the average number of objects in the system; λ, the average rate of arrival to the system, respectively. Then $L= \lambda W$ holds.

Little's Law has become widely used in not only queuing theory(Stidham Jr. 1974, Whitt 1991), but also operations management (Hopp and Spearman 2000, Cachon and Terwiesch 2004) and computer architecture (Lazowska 1984, Gunther 2010). The three measures are quite different and important measures of effectiveness of system performance, and Little's Law insists that they must obey the "law". Little's Law would not tell the managers how to handle trade-offs or provide innovations to improve their chosen measures, but it lays down a necessary condition. It provides structure for thinking about any operation that can be modeled as a queue and suggests what data might valuable to collect (Little 2011).

Queuing theory takes into account the arrival rate that is endogenous, whereas operations management typically takes into account the leaving rate that is determined by exogenously. The arrival rate, which is endogenous, is a primary input to queuing theory, whereas the leaving rate, determined by exogenously, is a primary input to the operations management. Manufacturing managers target output first. The operations manager decides the arrival to the system to achieve the output target (Little and Graves 2008). Queuing theory and operations management generally use different notations for Little's Law parameters (Hopp and Spearman 2000, Cachon and Terwiesch 2004, Harris 2010, George 2002). Hopp and Spearman (2000) offer alternative words and expanded definition for manufacturing firms: Throughput is the average output of a production process per unit time, work in process as the inventory between the start and the end points of a product routing, and cycle time as the average time from release of a job at the beginning of the routing until it reaches an inventory point at the end of the routing. Cachon and Terwiesch (2004) introduced the following equation:

Corollary 1 (Cachon and Terwiesch 2004) Let I be average inventory, equivalent to L; R average flow rate, equivalent to λ; T average flow time, equivalent to W. The following holds:

$$I = RT. \tag{5}$$

Hence, Little's Law is expressed in a different form such as (5). In other words, $L : \lambda : W = I : R : T$. The inventory, I in (5) is equal to the average inventory during the fiscal year of (1). The average flow rate, R in (5) is equal to the cumulative sales amount during the fiscal year, measured at cost, CGS of (1). R shows how fast the firm sells a product during the fiscal year. The average flow time, T in (5) is the supply time to the market, i.e., DOS, the reciprocal of ITR of (1). T shows how long it takes for the firm to transform inventory to sales. (1) is the retailer version of Little's Law, because transactions between the retailer and the supplier are taken into account. Manufacturer's version of Little's Law involves three types of inventory in the manufacturer: RM, WIP, and FGI. Hence, the total-inventory-day is the sum of RM inventory days, WIP inventory days, and FGI inventory days. Note that $L_k = \lambda_k W_k$ holds for each subsystem k and that $\lambda \neq \lambda_k$ for a manufacturer because flow rates are different across manufacturing stages.

Little's Law applies to AR turnover with I = average AR, R= (net) sales revenue, and T= AR days, the reciprocal value of ART. The meaning of ART is how fast the firm transforms AR into cash. Corollary 2 establishes the definition of ART.

Corollary 2

$$ART = \frac{Net\ revenue}{Average\ AR}, \tag{6}$$

where the average total AR is the average value of beginning and ending balance of the (net) account receivable account.

Little's Law applies to the firm as a whole to compute the asset turnover. The firm takes advantage of all kinds of asset to generate the revenue. Asset turnover involves total assets used and net revenue generated during the fiscal period. Corollary 3 establishes the definition of the asset turnover.

Corollary 3

$$Asset\ turnover = \frac{Net\ revenue}{Average\ total\ asset}, \tag{7}$$

where the average total asset is the average value of beginning and ending balance of the total asset.

The asset turnover measures operational efficiency of the firm as a whole. Turnover ratios provide not only valuable information about operational excellence ands liquidity management, i.e., cash-generating ability of operations and short-term liquidity risk of a firm. A turnover ratio is considered to quantify a global financial performance index and has been tried to see whether it contains information useful in the prediction of future financial problems (Ortin-Angel and Prior 2004).

ITR, an operational efficiency measure, should not be used per se in supply chain performance analysis. ITR can be correlated with other performance measures (e.g., profitability or liquidity) in the firm. If the firm realizes an increase in ITR with a concurrent decrease in profit margin (PM), it does not necessarily indicate an improvement in its capability to manage inventory (Gaur et al 2005). It has been shown that ITR has correlations with other performance measures (e.g., profitability, PM) or industry factors (e.g., firm size, capital intensity), but relations are not consistent across industries or firms. Gaur et al (2005) and Gaur and Kesavan (2009) find that ITR are negatively correlated with gross margin in the retailer industry. Gaur et al (2005) find that investment in capital assets is positively correlated with ITR and that ITR has decreased significantly with time, capital intensity has increased significantly with time. Gaur and Kesavan (2009) find that ITR is positively correlated with firm size, capital intensity, sales ratio, and sales surprise, respectively and that ITR is more sensitive to sales ratio when the firm is experiencing sales decline than when the firm is experiencing sales growth. On contrary, Rumyantsev and Netessine (2007) find that ITR is negatively associated with firm size, arguing that higher inventory level are associated with higher demand uncertainty, longer lead time, higher margins, and lower economies of scale. Gill et al (2010) observe a negative relationship between profitability and average days of AR and a positive relationship between cash cycle and profitability.

AN EARNS-TURNS MATRIX WITH ASSET TURNOVER AND VALUE CHAIN INCOME

The firm mainly seeks for profit, while it should satisfy customers' needs and/or innovate products. Profitability measures have been regarded as the first to-go measure to analyze the firm's performance, how efficient the firm leverages assets to generate earnings. Return on Asset (ROA) and PM are typical measures of profitability (Mottner and Smith 2009). The economic characteristics of each industry affect firm's financial measures such as ROA, PM, and ITR. For example, grocery stores have ROA of 4.03% and food industry ROA of 8.4% on average (Wahlen et al 2008).

Figure 1 Earns vs. Turns matrix with ROA values

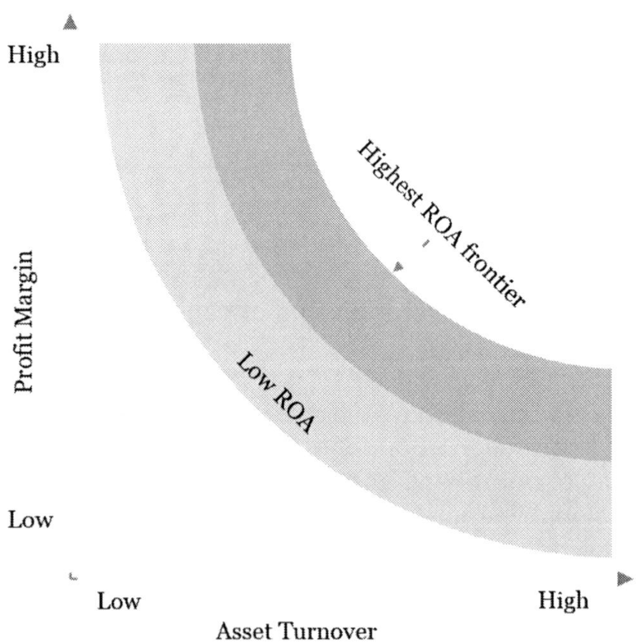

Figure 1 depicts an earns-turns matrix with high (right-upward) or low (left-downward) ROA values. The earns-turns matrix explains what are industry characteristics and how a firm takes a strategic position in the matrix. ROA measure involves not only profitability measure, the former of (8), but also operational efficiency, the latter of (8), by decomposition as follows:

$$\boldsymbol{ROA} = \frac{Earning\ before\ interest\ and\ tax\ (EBIT)}{Average\ asset} = \frac{EBIT}{Net\ sales} \times \frac{Net\ sales}{Average\ asset} \quad (8)$$

Different firms with the same ROA value may locate at different position in Figure 1, or adopt different supply chain strategy. One, located upper-left in Figure 1, may pursue high profit margin with low asset turnover (inefficient asset utilization), whereas the other, located lower-right in Figure 1, may pursue a highly-efficient asset turnover with low profit margin. ROA curves in Figure 1 are convex because the multiplication of profitability measure (e.g., profit margin) and operational efficiency (e.g., asset turnover) is constant.

The elements of ROA are profit margin, which examines firms' earning per sales dollar, and asset turnover, which shows efficiency in using assets to generate sales. PM in ROA involves earing before interests and tax (EBIT) or operating income, whereas profit margin of the income statement is the ratio of gross profit to net sales. Gross profit is from the primary activities cross supply chain. Both primary and supportive activities cross supply chain contribute to generation of revenue. Hence, operating income or EBIT has been used for the profitability measure. EBIT is more comprehensive and defined as follows:

$$\boldsymbol{EBIT = Revenue - CGS - SGA - Depreciation\ expense} \\ \boldsymbol{-other\ expense + nonoperating\ income} \quad (9)$$

Operating income or EBIT does not reflect supply chain costs properly. First, depreciation is non-cash expense, but shows change in book value of an asset. Other expenses and non-operating income do not involve operating activities, but finance or investment activities (e.g., gain or loss from selling equipment). We prescribe value chain income (VCI) as the following:

$$\boldsymbol{Value\ chain\ income = Revenue - CGS - SGA - R\&D} \quad (10)$$

Supply chain costs occur from either primary activities or supportive activities cross value chain. The costs related to primary activities are reflected into the CGS account. Supportive activities are reflected to either the SGA or the R&D account. Depreciation expense is not considered. Value chain margin (VCM) is defined as VCI/Net Sales.

Figure 2 depicts a cost structure of representative DJI firms in each industry and Table 1 shows major DJI firms' cost structure and VCM, expressed in the ratio of costs to net sales. Combining Figure 2 and Table 1, we observe that traditional manufacturing firms (e.g., Alcoa, Applied Material, Boeing, Caterpillar, General Motors, Nucor) and retail firms (e.g., Amazon, Best Buy, Costco Wholesale, Home Depot, Target, Wal-Mart) have low PM because CGS portion is very high and they face with severe competition owing to market maturity. Technology-oriented (e.g., Apple, IBM, Intel, Microsoft, Oracle) and chemical firms (e.g., 3 M, Chevron, Exxon Mobil, Johnson & Johnson, Merck & Co, Pfizer) spend heavily in R&D and are able to keep high PM with entry barrier. Food chain (e.g., McDonald) and consumer goods firms (e.g., Nike, Proctor & Gamble) have better PM than traditional manufacturing firms, but lower PM than tech-firms or pharmaceuticals. Logistics service providers (e.g., FedEx, United Parcel Service) are able to sustain high PM. SGA by logistics service providers is higher than CGS because their primary activities are related to delivery of product and/or service, not transformation (or production) of them.

Among Tech-firms, Advanced Micro Devices is exceptional, because R&D expense is high but VCI margin is small. Advanced Micro Devices is a market follower, whereas Intel is a market leader in semiconductor. Market leaders in such industry generally generate high PM without high R&D expense. Defense industry (e.g., Lockheed Margin, Boeing) or industrial products (e.g., Alcoa, Chevron) spend less in SGA, because they don't need to deal with mass consumers, but government agents across the world or other giant manufacturing and/or service firms. Coca Cola, FedEx, UPS, Nike, McDonald, Verizon, and Apple are famous for high quality product/service, brand loyalty, or innovative top executives.

Figure 2 Cost structure of some Dow Jones Indexed firms

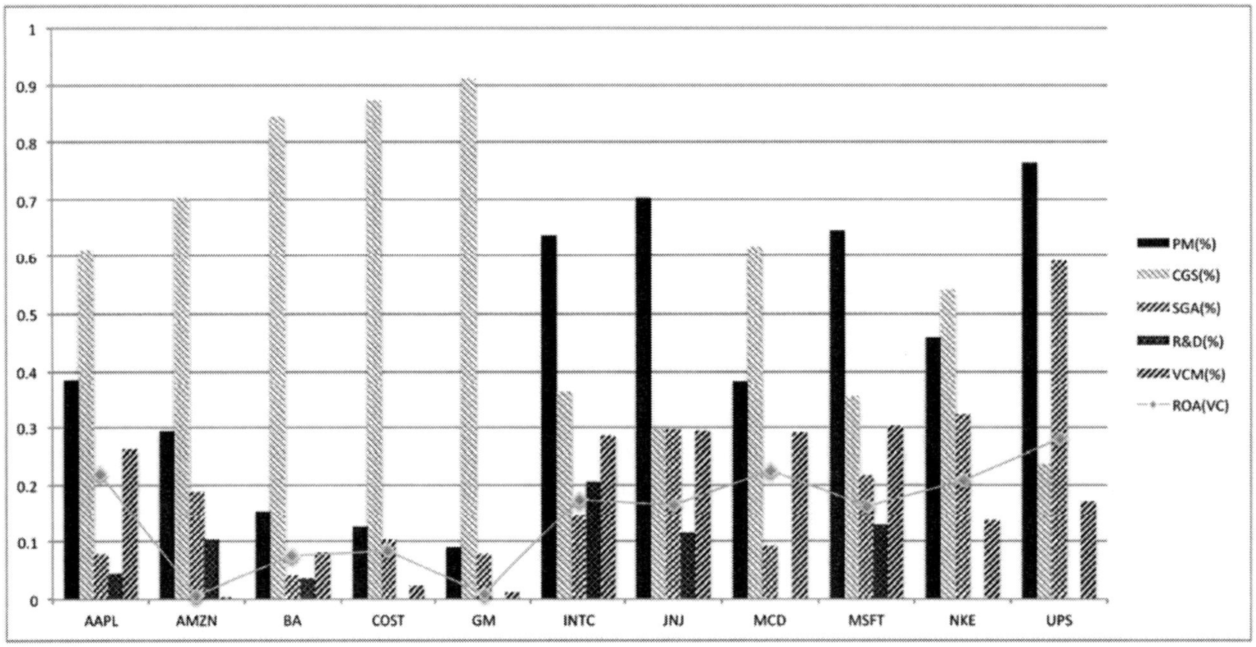

Traditional manufacturing firms and retail firms generate low PM and therefore VCM is scanty. However, Alcoa and Exxon Mobile spend low in SGA and therefore their VCM are fairly good. Amazon and Costco Wholesale have scanty VCM. Amazon aims for growth rather than PM in order to expand market share because online marketplace is so competitive.

Asset turnover divides into finer ratios such as ITR for a closer investigation of the firms' efficiency in managing inventory (Mottner and Smith 2009). It is hard for the firm to operate with high inventory turns while enjoying high PM. For example, Gaur et al (2005) and Gaur and Kesavan (2009) show that ITR are negatively correlated with gross margin in the retailer industry. Two grocery chains may have different strategic position while both of them achieve a similar ROA. One grocery chain generates high PM while operating with low ITR, positioning upper left. The other grocery chain operates very efficiently while generating low PM, position lower right.

The asset productivity varies widely from one manufacturing industry to another (Gupta 1969). For example, Gaur and Kesavan (2009) observe that food retailers have the highest median inventory turns of 10 and that jewelry retailers have the lowest median ITR of 1.54. Grocery store chain has low barriers to entry and exit. Extensive competition arises, which results in a relatively low operating income to sales, or profit margin. ITR is relatively high because grocery stores have to keep agricultural produces fresh. In contrary, pharmaceutical firms should invest considerable amounts in R&D to create new and innovative products. High entry barriers protected by patents or exclusive rights permit them to realize higher PM (Subramanyam 2014)

Table 1 Cost structure, profit margin, and value chain margin of some DJI firms (%)

Firm (Stock symbol code)	Profit margin	CGS	SGA	R&D	VCM	ROA
3 M (MMM)	0.48	0.52	0.20	0.06	0.22	0.22
Abbott Lab (ABT)	0.55	0.45	0.32	0.06	0.16	0.08
Advanced Micro Devices (AMD)	0.33	0.67	0.11	0.20	0.03	0.04
Alcoa (AA)	0.20	0.80	0.04	0.01	0.15	0.10
Amazon (AMZN)	0.29	0.71	0.19	0.10	0.00	0.01
Apple (AAPL)	0.39	0.61	0.08	0.04	0.26	0.22
Applied Materials (AMAT)	0.42	0.58	0.11	0.16	0.16	0.11
Best Buy (BBY)	0.22	0.78	0.19	0.00	0.04	0.10
Boeing (BA)	0.15	0.85	0.04	0.03	0.08	0.08
Caterpillar (CAT)	0.27	0.73	0.10	0.04	0.13	0.08
Coca-Cola (KO)	0.61	0.39	0.38	0.00	0.24	0.12
Costco Wholesale (COST)	0.13	0.87	0.10	0.00	0.02	0.08
Chevron (CVX)	0.36	0.64	0.04	0.01	0.31	0.24
Exxon Mobil (XOM)	0.25	0.75	0.11	0.00	0.13	0.15
FedEx (FDX)	0.64	0.36	0.43	0.00	0.22	0.29
General Electric (GE)	0.40	0.60	0.10	0.00	0.30	0.07
General Motors (GM)	0.09	0.91	0.08	0.00	0.01	0.01
Google (GOOG)	0.62	0.38	0.21	0.15	0.26	0.14
Home Depot (HD)	0.35	0.65	0.20	0.00	0.15	0.30
IBM (IBM)	0.50	0.50	0.23	0.06	0.21	0.16
Intel (INTC)	0.64	0.36	0.15	0.21	0.29	0.17
Johnson & Johnson (JNJ)	0.70	0.30	0.30	0.11	0.29	0.17
Kraft (KRFT)	0.27	0.73	0.16	0.00	0.11	0.09
Lockheed Martin (LMT)	0.12	0.88	0.01	0.00	0.11	0.13
McDonald (MCD)	0.38	0.62	0.09	0.00	0.29	0.22
Merck & Co (MRK)	0.61	0.39	0.26	0.15	0.20	0.08
Microsoft (MSFT)	0.65	0.35	0.22	0.13	0.30	0.16
Nike (NIKE)	0.46	0.54	0.32	0.00	0.14	0.21
Nucor (NUE)	0.09	0.91	0.03	0.00	0.06	0.09
Oracle (ORCL)	0.80	0.20	0.23	0.14	0.43	0.16
Pfizer (PFE)	0.81	0.19	0.28	0.17	0.35	0.10
Proctor & Gamble (PG)	0.50	0.50	0.30	0.00	0.19	0.11
Starbucks (SBX)	0.30	0.70	0.07	0.00	0.23	0.34
Target (TGT)	0.29	0.71	0.20	0.00	0.09	0.16
United Parcel Service (UPS)	0.76	0.24	0.57	0.00	0.17	0.28
Verizon (VZ)	0.61	0.39	0.27	0.00	0.34	0.17
Wal-Mart (WMT)	0.25	0.75	0.19	0.00	0.06	0.13

AN EARNS-TURNS MATRIX ANALYSIS FOR DOW JONES INDEXED FIRMS

We analyze supply chain performance of DJI firms and their competitors in retail and manufacturing industries during 2010 through 2014 using two dimensions of profit margin and asset turnover. To understand industry characteristics, we analyze DJI firms with an earns-turns matrix. Figure 3 depicts the earns-turns analysis for DJI firms except banking or other financial institutions, of which operating activities are not related to supply chain operations. We omit several major firms in order to clearly show the matrix and display firm stock symbol codes, shown in Table 1. Firms generating the highest VCM on each Asset Turnover are the best ROA frontier. Oracle, McDonald, Apple, Fedex, Starbucks, United Parcel Services, Home Depot, Wal Mart, Best Buy, and Costco Wholesale are on the best ROA frontier. Technology-based industries including IT, Chemical, and Pharmaceutical firms are more profitable supply chain, whereas retailers are leaner supply chain pursuing high asset turnover. Traditional manufacturing firms (e.g., General Motors, Advanced Micro Devices, Nucor, Boeing, Caterpillar, Alcoa, Lockheed Martin) are less profitable and less lean than other DJI firms. Technology-based firms generate high VCM with low asset turnover. Microsoft, Google, Cisco which is omitted in Figure 4 and close to Google, Apple, IBM, and Intel which is omitted and close to Johnson & Johnson are IT-related firms. Chemical or pharmaceutical firms are similar to tech-firms. Pfizer, Johnson & Johnson, Merck & Co, Proctor & Gamble, 3 M are examples of chemical or pharmaceutical firms. Retail firms operate efficiently with low VCM. Costco Wholesale, Best Buy, Wal-Mart, Target, Amazon, and Home Depot are representative retailers. Traditional manufacturing firms or industrial goods suppliers have low VCM and operate less efficiently than other industries. Alcoa, General Motor, Advance Micro Device, Nucor, Caterpillar, and Boeing are exemplar traditional manufacturing firms.

Figure 3 Earns vs. Turns matrix of DJI listed firms

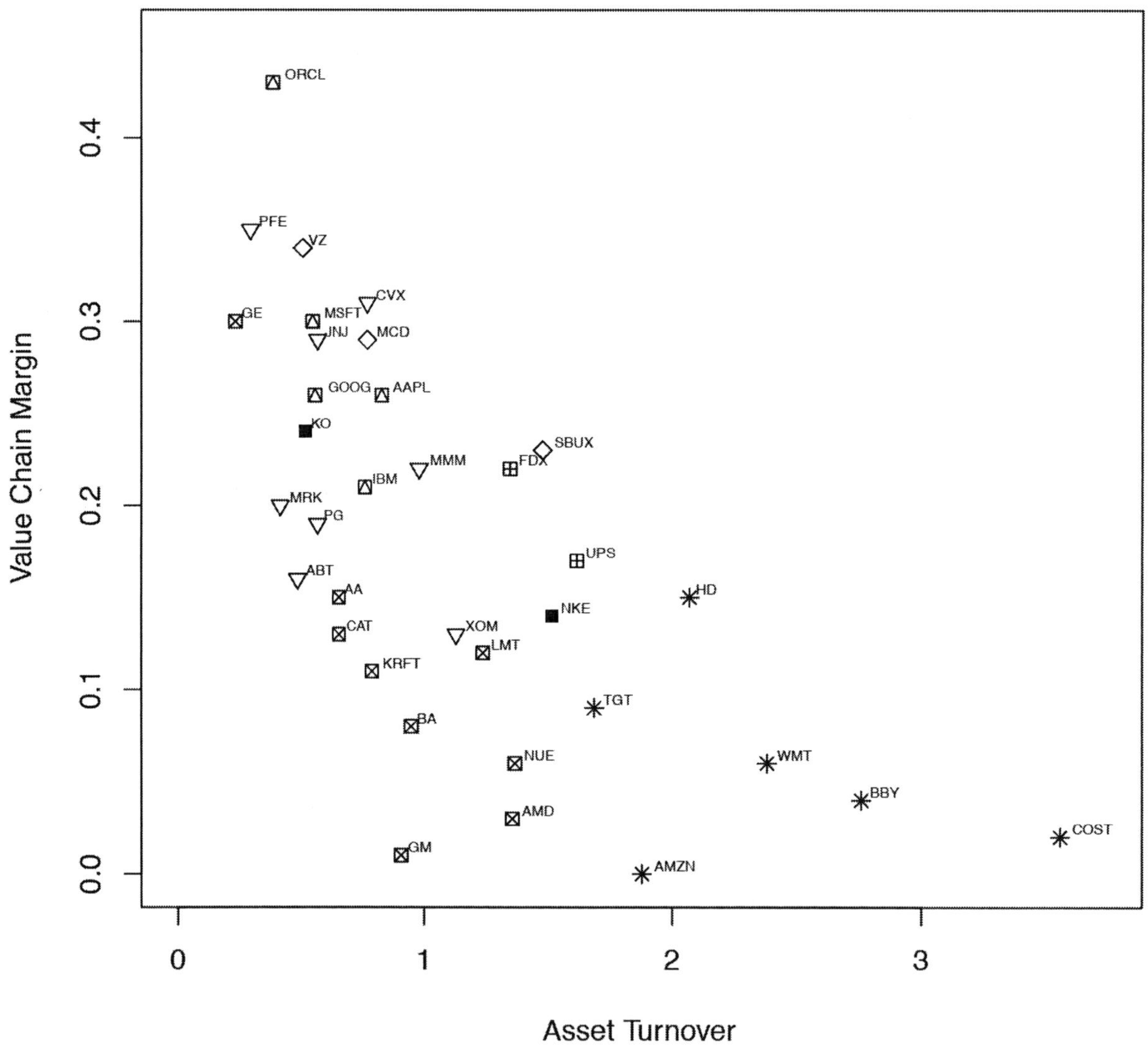

Firms sustaining high PM typically operate with a lower ITR as shown in Figure 3. Firms and industries requiring heavy fixed capacity costs and lengthy conversion (e.g., manufacturing) periods operate under a capacity constraint, therefore a lower asset turnover, while they must generating a relatively high PM (Wahlen et al 2008). For example, primary processing industries (e.g., the metal industry, the chemical industry) usually have a comparatively low fixed asset investment turnover (Gupta 1969). These firms are characterized by formidable entry and oligopolistic market structure. It is also high in R&D oriented and in which the innovation rate and the product obsolescence rate is relatively high (Subramanyam 2014). These firms adopt product differentiation strategy to obtain market power over revenues and profit margin. The differentiation could relate to product capabilities, product service, service, channels of distribution or else (Hall 1980, Porter 1998).

On the contrary, firms operating efficiently generate a relatively low profit margin. For example, the advanced processing industries (e.g., apparel, furniture) tend to have lower fixed asset investment per dollar of sales and, therefore, a higher fixed asset turnover (Gupta 1969). These firms achieve the high asset turnovers by keeping costs as low as possible, for example, minimizing fixed overhead costs, or purchasing in sufficient quantities to realize discounts (Wahlen et al 2008). These firms adopt low-cost leadership. The thrust of the low-cost leadership strategy is to become the lowest-cost producer, enabling the firm to charge the lowest prices and to achieve high sales volumes (Hall 1980, Porter 1998). Such firms can achieve the low-cost position through economies of scale, production efficiencies, outsourcing, or by asset parsimony (Wahlen et al 2008).

Figure 4 Earns vs Turns by firm or product

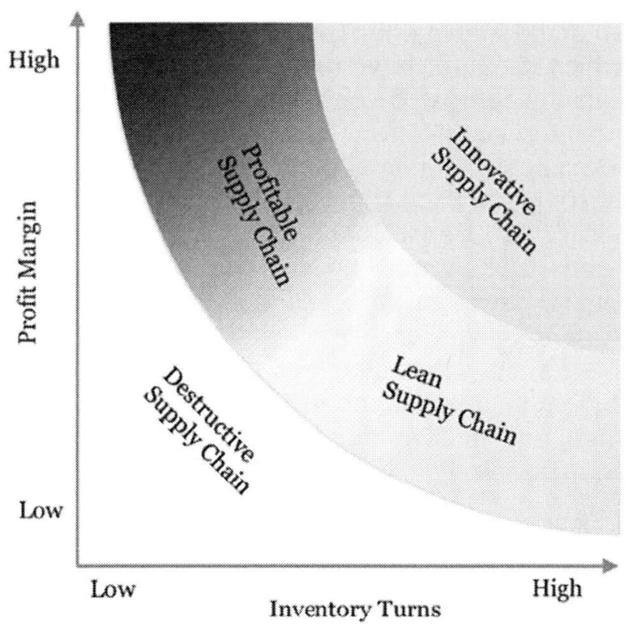

Classifying into two categories (e.g., product differentiation and low-cost leadership) is similar to Fisher (1997)'s work, which classifies products into tow categories (functional and innovative) to provide a framework for choosing a right supply chain of a product. The functional products have the following characteristics: predictable demand pattern, low contribution margin, low product variety, low stock out rate, and so on. The functional products require efficient supply chain in which the firm tries to maintain high average utilization rate, generate high turns and minimize inventory throughout the chain (i.e., high inventory turns), shorten lead time, primarily select for cost and quality. The innovative products are contrary to the functional products, which requiring responsive supply chain firms that can respond quickly to unpredictable demand, deploy excess buffer capacity, primarily select for speed, flexibility and quality. This classification is qualitative and subjective, because it is hard to quantify the characteristics above. For counter example, some chemical firms generate high PM, a key characteristic of innovative product, while their products are functional and inventory turns are not high. Even though chemical products are not innovative, they seem to belong to responsive supply chain category because high PM is guaranteed. Japanese automotive firms adopt just-in-time philosophy (e.g., zero inventory, total quality management) to respond to unpredictable demand and maintain excess capacity, but their PM is relatively low because of market maturity. Japanese automotive firms seem to be efficient supply chain firms, even though their characteristics are close to responsive supply chain.

We classify supply chains into four categories: innovative, profitable, lean, and destructive supply chains as Robeson and Copacino (1994) classifies products into winner, traffic-builder, sleeper, and loser with a quadrant scheme. Robeson and Copacino (1994) simply makes use of profit margin and ITR, not taking into accounts ROA. We involve ROA measure into the earns-turns matrix and use a cursive quadrant. Figure 4 involves ITR and PM, whereas Figures 2 and 3 involve asset turnover and VCM. VCM involves supply chain activities and is related with asset turnover, whereas PM involves inventory (or product sold or delivered) and are related with ITR.

ITR is conceptually connected with profit margin through CGS. Hence, we assocaite ITR with profit margin to analyze supply chains for a product. Responsive (efficient) supply chain by Fisher (1997) is equivalent to profitable (lean) supply chain in our analysis. We name profitable rather than responsive, which seems to have high ITR and is therefore confusing. We name lean instead of efficient, which seems to be cost-focused. We emphasize financial and operational measures rather than qualitative characteristics. Figure 4 depicts four supply chains categories. The innovative supply chain firms can generate high profit margin and operate very efficiently, on or beyond the highest ROA frontier in Figure 4, positioning upper right on the earns-turns matrix in Figure 4. The classification of the profitable and lean supply chains is similar to the one by the generic ROA analysis above in Figure 2 and Fisher (1997). Assuming that firms in the same industry have similar ROA measure (Subramanyam 2014) and that profitability and turnover are negatively correlated with each other (Gaur et al 2005, Gaur and Kesavan 2009), either of two supply chains is most popular. Lastly, the destructive supply chains cannot generate high profit margin and their inventory level is high. Our classification is based on financial measures and involves both operational excellence (cost oriented) and financial measures (revenue oriented).

SUPPLY CHAIN PERFORMANCE ANALYSIS OF U.S. RETAIL FIRMS

In this section, we analyze major U.S. retail firms based upon Figure 5 and Table 2. Figure 5 depicts the earns-turns matrix for major U.S. retailers. Table 2 shows cost structure and VCM, expressed in the ratio of costs to net sales. PM of retail firms in Table 2, involving ITR, shows characteristics of each industry sector and ranges from 0.13 (Costco) to 0.70 (Coach). However, we cannot find any strong correlation between SGA and PM (or CGS). Most of retail firms do not spend high in R&D. Amazon is the only firm that spends 10% or more of net revenue in R&D, referring to Table 1. Hence, Amazon's VCM is almost close to zero. Some firms exploiting high PM (e.g., Coach, Tiffany) spends more SGA and other firms exploiting low profit margin (e.g., Lowe, Blue Nile, Ross Store, Kroger) spends less SGA. VCM ranges from 0.00 (Amazon) to 0.33 (Gap), which is narrower than the range of PM. Majorities of U.S. retail firms have the range of 0.03 and 0.15. Gap and Kohl's exploit more than 0.3 of VCM. Tiffany, Coach, Kirkland, and Buckle exploit around 0.2 of VCM.

Figure 5 Earns vs. Turns matrix of US Retail firms

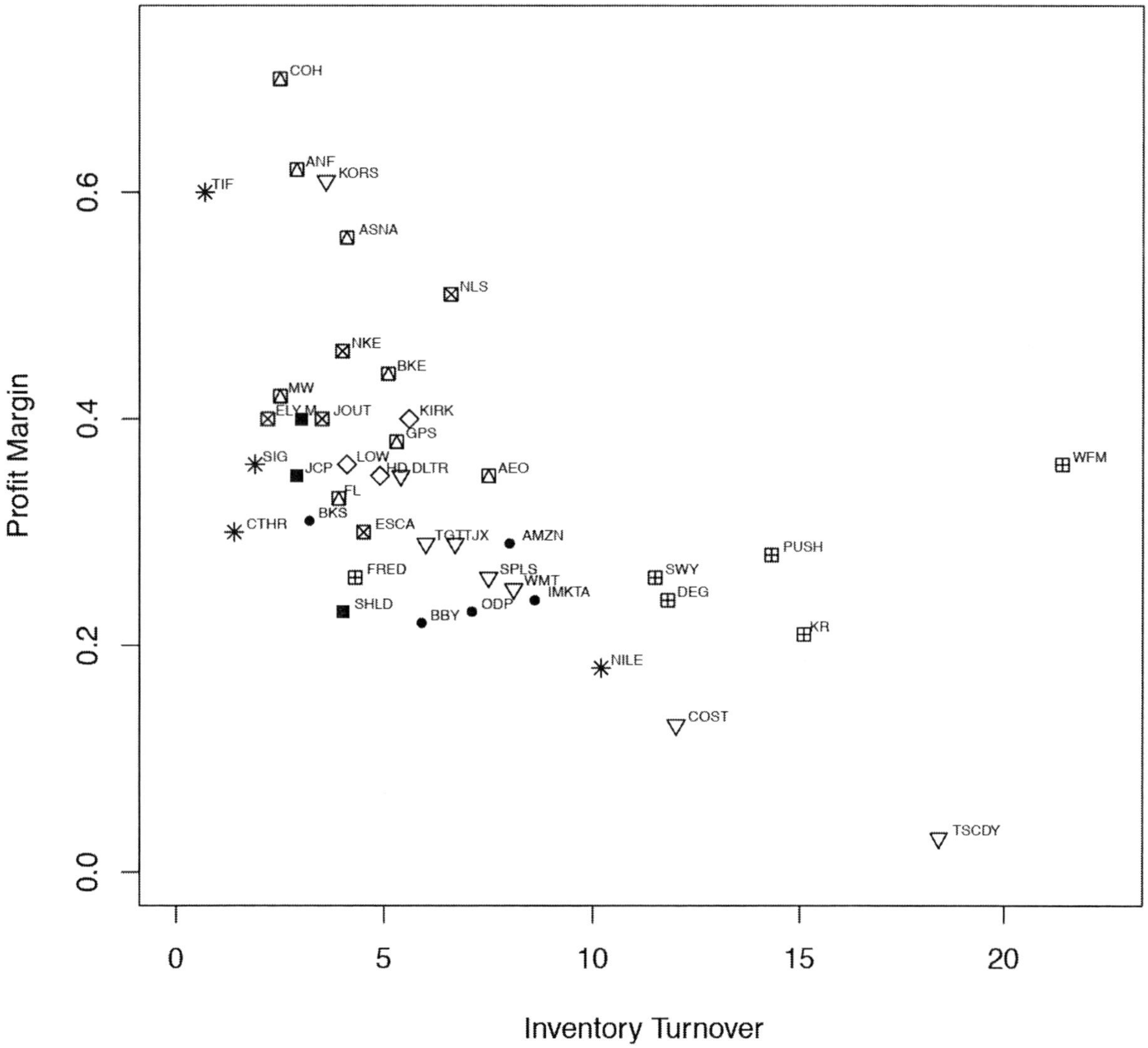

Whole Foods is an innovative supply chain, because its ROA is greater than other retailers, which means by that it generates high profit while operating very efficiently. Whole Foods has been a top grocery chain because of customer satisfaction and loyalty supported by premium product. Grocery chains (e.g., Publix, Kroger, Safeway, Delhaize Group) and discount stores (e.g., Costco Whole, Wal-Mart, Staples, Target, TJ Max, Tesco, denoted by ▽) are lean supply chains, compared to other retailer firms. Grocery chains buy agricultural produces, which have short life cycle, from local farms and have to sell them out in short days. Grocery chains are regional and operate in several states only, not nation-wide. For example, Publix covers Florida, Georgia, Alabama, South Carolina, Tennessee and North Carolina. Wegman, which is not listed in Figure 4, covers New York, New Jersey, Pennsylvania, Virginia, Maryland, and

Massachusetts. PM ranges from 0.21 (Kroger) to 0.36 (Whole Foods), whereas VCM ranges from 0.02 (Safeway) to 0.08 (Publix). Whole Foods exploits high PM, but spends most in SGA among grocery chains. Kroger spends least in SGA and is better off than Whole Foods in VCM. Discount stores are between grocery chains and department stores (e.g., Macy's, JC Penny's), less profitable than department store and less lean than grocery chains. Costco enjoys economy of scale with larger sales volume unit and lower unit price, which makes ITR high. Costco is a membership-based retail firm and shelf-life on display is short.

Table 2 Cost structure, profit margin, and value chain margin of US retail firms

Firm (Stock symbol code)	PM (%)	CGS (%)	SGA (%)	VCM (%)	ITR	ROA
Amazon (AMZN)	0.29	0.71	0.19	0.00	8.0	0.01
Office Depot (ODP)	0.23	0.77	0.22	0.02	7.1	0.04
Barnes & Noble (BKS)	0.31	0.69	0.25	0.05	3.2	0.10
Best Buy (BBY)	0.22	0.78	0.19	0.04	5.9	0.10
Costco Wholesale (COST)	0.13	0.87	0.10	0.02	12.0	0.08
Dollar Tree (DLTR)	0.35	0.65	0.23	0.12	5.4	0.34
Target (TGT)	0.29	0.71	0.20	0.09	6.0	0.16
TJ Maxx (TJX)	0.29	0.71	0.16	0.12	6.7	0.34
Wal-Mart (WMT)	0.25	0.75	0.19	0.06	8.1	0.16
Staples (SPLS)	0.26	0.74	0.21	0.04	7.5	0.09
Big Lots (BIG)	0.39	0.61	0.33	0.07	3.5	0.20
Dollar General (DG)	0.31	0.78	0.19	0.09	4.9	0.16
Family Dollar Stores (FDO)	0.34	0.66	0.29	0.05	4.5	0.14
GameStop (GME)	0.30	0.70	0.22	0.08	5.6	0.19
Ross Stores (ROST)	0.28	0.72	0.15	0.13	6.0	0.35
JC Penney (JCP)	0.35	0.65	0.33	0.02	2.9	0.02
Macy's (M)	0.40	0.60	0.30	0.10	3.0	0.13
Dillard (DDS)	0.37	0.63	0.25	0.12	3.1	0.20
Nordstrom (JWN)	0.38	0.62	0.28	0.10	5.2	0.15
Kohl (KSS)	0.36	0.64	0.23	0.14	3.1	0.18
Michael Kors (KORS)	0.61	0.39	0.29	0.32	3.6	0.57
Home Depot (HD)	0.35	0.65	0.20	0.15	4.9	0.30
Lowe (LOW)	0.36	0.65	0.24	0.11	4.1	0.20
Bed Bath & Beyond (BBBY)	0.39	0.61	0.26	0.13	2.7	0.24
Tiffany (TIF)	0.60	0.40	0.39	0.21	0.7	0.18
Blue Nile (NILE)	0.18	0.82	0.15	0.03	10.2	0.09
Signet Jewelers (SIG)	0.36	0.64	0.30	0.06	1.9	0.07
Publix (PUSH)	0.28	0.72	0.20	0.08	14.3	0.17
Kroger (KR)	0.21	0.79	0.16	0.05	15.1	0.17
Whole Foods (WFM)	0.36	0.64	0.32	0.04	21.4	0.09
Safeway (SWY)	0.26	0.74	0.25	0.02	11.5	0.04
Gap (GPS)	0.38	0.62	0.05	0.33	5.3	0.69
Coach (COH)	0.70	0.30	0.51	0.19	2.5	0.19
Kirkland (KIRK)	0.40	0.60	0.19	0.21	5.6	0.44
Guess (GES)	0.36	0.64	0.31	0.05	4.6	0.07
American Eagle Outfitters (AEO)	0.35	0.65	0.25	0.11	7.5	0.21
Men's Warehouse (MW)	0.42	0.58	0.40	0.02	2.5	0.03
Urban Outfitter (URBN)	0.35	0.65	0.24	0.11	6.4	0.18
Buckle Inc (BKE)	0.44	0.56	0.22	0.22	5.1	0.47
Johnson Outdoors (JOUT)	0.40	0.60	0.32	0.04	3.5	0.06
Nautilus (NLS)	0.51	0.49	0.38	0.11	6.6	0.05
Callaway Golf (ELY)	0.40	0.60	0.33	0.03	2.2	0.05
Foot Locker (FL)	0.33	0.67	0.20	0.13	3.9	0.27

Nike (NKE)	0.46	0.54	0.32	0.14	4.0	0.21
Abercrombie & Fitch (ANF)	0.62	0.38	0.58	0.04	2.9	0.06

Department stores (e.g., Macy's, JC Penny, Kohl's, denoted by ■) are more profitable than discount stores and grocery chains. Home improvement retailers (e.g., Lowe and Home Depot, Kirkland, denoted by ◇) are more profitable than discount stores and grocery chains. PM, CGS, and SGA of department stores are similar, and we conjecture that department store industry would change neither industry infrastructure nor business model for decades.

Apparel retailers (e.g., Coach, Abercrombie & Fitch, Mens Warehouse, Ascena Retail, Buckle, Gap, American Eagle Outfitters, Foot Lockers, denoted by ⍓) are profitable supply chains. Apparel retail firms have strong brand power and subcontract manufacturing offshore while keeping design as a core-competency. Coach is the most profitable supply chain among apparel firms. Sporting or outdoor goods (e.g., Nike, Escalade, denoted by ⊠) can generate similar level of profit margin but operate less efficiently than other apparel retailer firms because of seasonality. Retail firms generally do not spend in R&D, but some sporting or outdoor goods firms (e.g., Johnson Outdoors, Callaway Golf, Nautilus) spend around 3~5% of net sales in R&D. Some apparel firms such as Coach and Men's Warehous spend high in SGA and therefore could not exploit high VCM, compared to high PM.

Among jeweler retailers, denoted by ✱, Tiffany is profitable supply chain, whereas Blue Nile is lean supply chain. Signet Jewelers and Charles & Colvard are middle. Best Buy, a high-tech oriented retailer, has a lower ROA than other retailers. Among book sellers, denoted by ●, Amazon is more lean and generates better return than Barnes & Nobles.

SUPPLY CHAIN PERFORMANCE ANALYSIS OF U.S. MANUFACTURING FIRMS

In this section, we analyze U. S. manufacturing firms using the earns-turns matrix and look into cost structure. Figure 6 depicts the earns-turns matrix for major U.S. manufacturing firms. Profitability seems to have negative correlation with ITR as U.S. retail firms. Some manufacturing firms sustain high profitability while operate efficiently. For some industries (e.g., pharmaceutical, denoted by ⊠, steel, denoted by ●), firms in the same industry are located close each other. For other industries (e.g., beverage, denoted by +, automotive, denoted by ○), homogeneity is weak, i.e., firms in the same industry are spread over a wide area.

Table 3 Cost structure, profit margin, and value chain margin of US pharmaceutical, personal product, and textile firms

Firm (Stock symbol code)	PM (%)	CGS (%)	SGA (%)	VCM (%)	ITR	ROA
Merck & Co (MRK)	0.61	0.39	0.26	0.20	2.8	0.25
Bristol-Myers (BMY)	0.76	0.24	0.30	0.21	2.5	0.33
GlaxoSmithKline (GSK)	0.69	0.31	0.33	0.23	1.7	0.39
Eli Lilly (LLY)	0.75	0.25	0.34	0.17	1.7	0.41
Abbott Lab (ABT)	0.55	0.45	0.32	0.16	3.4	0.26
Novo Nordisk (NVO)	0.83	0.17	0.30	0.39	1.4	1.01
Biogen (BIIB)	0.88	0.12	0.23	0.45	1.6	0.65
Celgene (CELG)	0.95	0.05	0.26	0.37	1.1	0.47
Gilead Sciences (GILD)	0.85	0.15	0.12	0.61	2.5	0.74
Thermo Fisher Scientific (TMO)	0.44	0.56	0.28	0.12	5.6	0.20
Proctor & Gamble (PG)	0.50	0.50	0.30	0.19	6.3	0.28
Colgate-Palmovlive (CL)	0.59	0.41	0.34	0.24	5.1	0.74

Estee Lauder (EL)	0.80	0.20	0.65	0.16	1.8	1.17
Herbalife (HLF)	0.80	0.20	0.69	0.11	2.7	1.64
Kimblerly Clark (KMB)	0.34	0.66	0.19	0.15	6.3	0.39
Clorox (CLX)	0.44	0.56	0.23	0.18	8.3	0.59
Under Armor (UA)	0.49	0.51	0.37	0.12	3.1	0.82
Fossil (FOSL)	0.57	0.43	0.41	0.16	2.6	0.90
Steven Madden (SHOO)	0.35	0.65	0.12	0.24	10.4	0.52

Pharmaceuticals (e.g., Bristol-Myers, Merk & Co, Biogen, Celgene) are the most profitable among manufacturing firms, located in upper-left in Figure 6. Table 3 shows PM, cost structure, VCM, ITR, and ROA of pharmaceuticals and personal products.

Figure 6 Earns-Turns matrix for US manufacturing firms

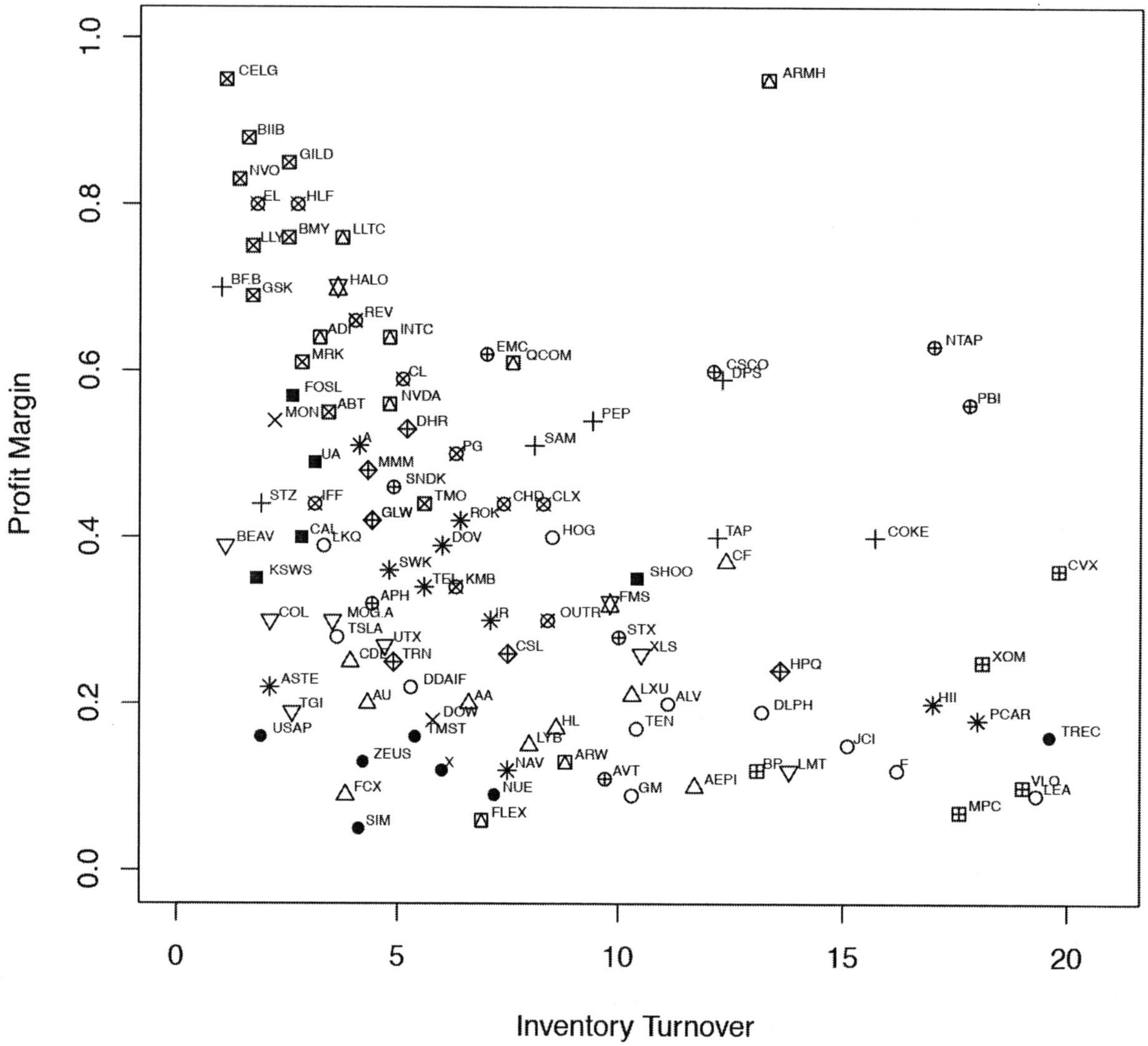

For pharmaceuticals, PM's are high, up to 95%, and VCM's are also high, whereas ITR's are very low. Pharmaceuticals spend more in SGA than other industries, because they do not sell products through resellers but must maintain sales forces having professional knowledge. Thermo Fisher Scientific has the lowest PM and the highest ITR among pharmaceutical, and therefore ROA is close to other firms in pharmaceuticals. Abbott Lab has the second lowest PM and the second highest ITR and ROA is close to other firms as well. Thermo Fisher Scientific and Abbott Lab are lean supply chain among pharmaceuticals. Personal products (e.g., Herbal Life, Estee Lauder, denoted by ⊗ in Figure 6) are generally profitable, less profitable than pharmaceuticals, and less lean than other industries. Herbalife and Estee Lauder generate as good PM, up to 80%, as pharmaceuticals do. Novo Nordisk, Herbalife, and Estee Lauder exploit higher than 1.00 of ROA. Herbalife provides members with premium products. Kimberly Clark maintains low profitability, 34%.

Table 4 shows PM, cost structure, VCM, ITR, and ROA of automotive firms. Automotive firms are generally one of least profitable supply chain because of industry maturity. However, some (e.g., Ford, GM, Delphi, Lear) are lean supply chain and others (e.g., Tesla, LKQ, Harley-Davidson) are less lean supply chain. Car manufacturers and distributers (e.g., Ford, GM) are less profitable than component suppliers (e.g., Delphi, Autolive, Tenneco). Harley-Davidson is a top brand of motorcycle and sustains high profitability. Tesla is famous for electric cars, expensive and premium cars. Harley-Davidson and Tesla are profitable supply chain among automotive firms. However, Tesla lacks of enough inventories to sell and therefore sales speed is not so fast as other traditional automotive firms. In addition, Tesla spends 15% of the revenue in R&D and therefore VCM is negative.

Table 4 Cost structure, profit margin, and value chain margin of US automotive firms

Firm (Stock symbol code)	PM (%)	CGS (%)	SGA (%)	VCM (%)	ITR	ROA
Ford (F)	0.12	0.88	0.10	0.03	16.2	0.09
General Motors (GM)	0.09	0.91	0.08	0.01	10.3	0.08
Harley-Davidson (HOG)	0.40	0.60	0.16	0.22	8.5	0.27
Johnson Controls (JCI)	0.15	0.85	0.08	0.06	15.1	0.21
Lear (LEA)	0.09	0.91	0.03	0.06	19.3	0.18
Delphi (DLPH)	0.19	0.81	0.06	0.12	13.2	0.29
Tenneco (TEN)	0.17	0.83	0.06	0.09	10.4	0.36
LKQ (LKQ)	0.39	0.61	0.28	0.12	3.3	0.53
Tesla Motors (TSLA)	0.28	0.72	0.19	-0.06	3.6	0.21

Table 5 shows PM, cost structure, VCM, ITR, and ROA of technology equipment, industrial equipment, and semiconductor firms. Apple's ITR is 57.9, which is the second highest (McDonald operates with ITR of 145.4) among DJI firms, too high to display in Figure 6 and therefore omitted in Figure 6. However, Apple's asset turnover is 0.83, comparatively low among DJI firms, because it owns and directly operates stores whereas other manufacturing firms sell their products through reseller such as Best Buy. Technical equipment (e.g., Net App, Avnet, Cisco, EMC, Pitney Bowes) and Semiconductors (e.g., Qualcomm, Intel, ARM Holdings, NVIDIA) are generally profitable, less profitable and leaner than pharmaceutical. ITR's are the highest on average because its market is mature and operational excellence must be a competitive edge. ROA of technology equipment providers are close to pharmaceuticals. Technology equipment providers spend more in SGA than other industries as pharmaceuticals do. They also have to maintain sales forces having technical knowledge. Net App, Cisco, ARM Holdings, and Pitney Bowes are innovative supply chain, both profitable and lean, located in upper-right in Figure 6. Each firm of innovative supply chain has its own strength such as tech leadership or patents in new technology.

Table 5 Cost structure, profit margin, and value chain margin of US technology equipment, industrial equipment, and semiconductor firms

Firm (Stock symbol code)	PM (%)	CGS (%)	SGA (%)	VCM (%)	ITR	ROA
Apple (APPL)	0.39	0.61	0.08	0.26	57.9	0.32
Cisco (CSCO)	0.60	0.40	0.24	0.24	12.1	0.27
EMC (EMC)	0.62	0.38	0.33	0.17	7.0	0.33
NetApp (NTAP)	0.63	0.37	0.36	0.12	17.0	0.41
Amphenol (APH)	0.32	0.68	0.12	0.20	4.4	0.26
Pitney Bowes (PBI)	0.56	0.44	0.36	0.17	17.8	0.32
Intel (INTC)	0.64	0.36	0.15	0.29	4.8	0.39
NVIDIA (NVDA)	0.56	0.44	0.10	0.16	4.8	0.36
Qualcomm (QCOM)	0.61	0.39	0.09	0.31	7.6	0.34
Analog Devices (ADI)	0.64	0.36	0.17	0.25	3.2	0.28
Linear Technology (LLTC)	0.76	0.24	0.12	0.46	3.7	0.63
Arrow Electronics (ARW)	0.13	0.87	0.09	0.05	8.8	0.24
Flextronics (FLEX)	0.06	0.94	0.03	0.03	6.9	0.13
Danasher (DHR)	0.53	0.47	0.28	0.18	5.2	0.29
Corning (GLW)	0.42	0.58	0.12	0.21	4.4	0.14
Carlisle Company (CSL)	0.26	0.74	0.12	0.13	7.5	0.23
Trinity Industries (TRN)	0.25	0.75	0.07	0.19	4.9	0.19

Table 6 shows PM, cost structure, VCM, ITR, and ROA of basic materials, steel, machinery equipment and defense firms. Basic materials (e.g., Alcoa, Coeur Mining, Anglo Gold Ashanti, denoted by △) and steel (e.g., Nucor, United States Steel) are the least profitable and ITR's are the second least whereas pharmaceuticals have the lowest ITR. Basic materials and steel are mature (or decline) in product life cycle and squeezed to cut down the price by their customers. Defense (e.g., Triumph Group, United Technology) are one of least profitable and least lean supply chains. Rockwell Automation has low PM but high ITR, therefore sustains good ROA.

Table 6 Cost structure, profit margin, and value chain margin of US basic materials, steel, and machinery equipment, and defense firms

Firm (Stock symbol code)	PM (%)	CGS (%)	SGA (%)	VCM (%)	ITR	ROA
Alcoa (AA)	0.20	0.80	0.04	0.15	6.6	0.13
Coeur Mining (CDE)	0.25	0.75	0.11	0.11	3.9	0.07
Lyondell Basell Industries (LYB)	0.15	0.85	0.02	0.13	8.0	0.26
Green Plains (GPRE)	0.12	0.88	0.03	0.09	13.8	0.22
Anglo Gold Ashanti (AU)	0.20	0.80	0.02	0.16	4.3	0.11
Astec (ASTE)	0.22	0.78	0.15	0.05	2.1	0.28
PACCAR (PCAR)	0.18	0.82	0.03	0.14	18.0	0.16
TE Connectivity (TEL)	0.34	0.66	0.11	0.18	5.6	0.24
Ingersoll-Rand (IR)	0.30	0.70	0.19	0.11	7.1	0.22
Stanley, Black & Decker (SWK)	0.36	0.64	0.23	0.13	4.8	0.25
Navistar (NAV)	0.12	0.88	0.08	0.01	7.5	0.16
Dover (DOV)	0.39	0.61	0.22	0.16	6.0	0.30
Agilent Technologies (A)	0.51	0.49	0.17	0.30	4.1	0.33
Rockwell Automation (ROK)	0.42	0.58	0.23	0.19	6.4	0.46
Lockheed Martin (LMT)	0.61	0.39	0.38	0.24	5.6	0.31
United Technology (UTX)	0.27	0.73	0.10	0.14	4.7	0.20
Rockwell Collins (COL)	0.30	0.70	0.12	0.18	2.1	0.24
Triumph Group (TGI)	0.19	0.81	0.07	0.12	2.6	0.13
Moog (MOG.A)	0.30	0.70	0.14	0.11	3.5	0.25
B/E Aerospace (BEAV)	0.39	0.61	0.13	0.15	1.1	0.23

Table 7 shows PM, cost structure, VCM, ITR, and ROA of beverage, textile and oil/gas firms. Beverage firms (e.g., Dr. Pepper, Pepsico, Coca-Cola Bottling, Brown-Forman, Boston Beer) are generally somewhat profitable supply chain and spread over a wide area. Dr. Pepper, Coca-Cola Bottling, and Molson Coors Brewing are leaner supply chain, whereas Brown-Forman and Constellation Brands are least lean among U.S. retail and manufacturing firms. Beverage firms are spreading cross a wide range in Figure 6, because each brand has different customer segment. Coke has a large customer segment and its ITR is high, whereas Brown Forman has a limited customer segment. Oil and gas firms (e.g., Exxon Mobile, BP, Marathon, Chevron, denoted by ⊞) are less profitable than other industries and leaner supply chain. Oil and gas are daily necessities, which should be supplied every day and could not be expensive. Oil and gas spend very low in SGA, because customers purchase and fill the gas by themselves and sales efforts can be leastly invested. Exxon Mobil spends higher in SGA than other oil and gas firms. Textile firms (e.g., Under Armor, Fossil, denoted by ■) are somewhat profitable and one of least lean supply chains because of demand seasonality. Some textile firms have good brand power and sustain good profitability.

Table 7 Cost structure, profit margin, and value chain margin of US beverage, textile and oil/gas firms

Firm (Stock symbol code)	PM (%)	CGS (%)	SGA (%)	VCM (%)	ITR	ROA
Dr. Pepper Snaple (DPS)	0.59	0.41	0.37	0.22	12.3	0.44
Pepsico (PEP)	0.54	0.46	0.37	0.16	9.4	0.49
Brown-Forman (BF.B)	0.70	0.30	0.30	0.33	1.0	0.53
Boston Beer (SAM)	0.51	0.49	0.35	0.16	8.1	0.89
Under Armour (UA)	0.49	0.51	0.37	0.12	3.1	0.82
Fossile (FOSL)	0.57	0.43	0.41	0.16	2.6	0.90
Steven Madden (SHOO)	0.35	0.65	0.12	0.24	10.4	0.52
Chevron (CVX)	0.36	0.64	0.04	0.31	19.8	0.28
Valero (VLO)	0.10	0.90	0.01	0.10	17.6	0.29
Exxon Mobil (XOM)	0.25	0.75	0.11	0.13	18.1	0.28
BP (BP)	0.12	0.88	0.04	0.07	13.1	0.14

PM has a wide range with the highest 0.95 by Celgene, whereas VCM has narrower range with the highest 0.61 by Gilead Science. Majorities of manufacturing firms exploit VCM between 0.1 and 0.2, relatively higher than U.S. retail firms.

CONCLUSION

Little's Law is a Newton's Law in supply chain management to explain relationships among the inventory, the flow time, and the turnover. Inventory plays an important role in defining turnover, days of supply, and cash-to-cash cycle. We interpret Little's Law in an accounting perspective and apply it to define asset turnovers such as ART and ITR. We analyze DJI listed firms with the earns-turns matrixes and look into U.S. retail and manufacturing firms. Each industry has structural characteristics such as market entry and/or barrier and ROI. Industry structure may affect companies' ROI, but each firm chooses its own supply chain strategy (e.g., profitable supply chain, lean supply chain), which allows to locate at different place in the earns-turns matrix.

For next steps, we collect longitudinal and detail data for each firm to deeply analyze industry characteristic and competitive edges with the earns-turns matrix. We consider the following industries: automotive, retail, and restaurants. Automotive industry has been a symbol of American traditional manufacturing. Competition is severe because German and Japanese makers increase their market shares and new concept car (e.g., electronic car) is emerging. We will analyze automotive firms in U.S. with earns-turns matrix and find a way to compete better. The retail industry has a variety of format such as discount stores, grocery chains, electronic retailers, and online retailers. Firms in a category compete with not only firms in the same industry but also other categories. For example, Amazon competes with not only book-sellers such as Barnes & Nobles, but also other retailers such as eBay and Best Buy. Restaurants have a variety of forms: fast-food restaurants, high-end restaurants, ethnic-oriented restaurants, and so on. Food chains have highest ITR, because they endeavor to provide customers with fresh foods and keep inventories in the form of raw materials, not finished goods.

REFERENCES

Blackstone Jr JH (2013) APICS Dictionary, 14th ed. APICS, Chicago

Cachon GP, Terwiesch C (2004) Matching supply with demand: An introduction to operations management. McGraw-Hill Custom Publishing, New York

Demeter K, Matyusz Z (2011) The impact of lean practices on inventory turnover. International Journal of Production Economics 133:154 – 163

Fisher ML (1997) What is the right supply chain for your product. Harvard Business Review pp 105–116

Gaur V, Kesavan S (2009) The effects of firm size and sales growth rate on inventory turnover performance in the u.s. retail sector. In: Agrawal N, Smith SA (eds) Retail Supply Chain Management, Springer Science + Business Media LLC, pp 25 – 52

Gaur V, Fisher ML, Raman A (2005) An econometric analysis of inventory turnover performance in retail services. Manage- ment Science 51(2):181 – 194

George ML (2002) Lean Six Sigma: Combining Six Sigma quality with lean speed. McGraw-Hill, New York

Gill A, Biger N, Mathur N (2010) The relationship between working capital management and profitability: Evidence from the united states. Business and Economics Journal pp 1 – 9

Gunther N (2010) Analyzing computer system performance with Perl:PDQ. Springer-Verlag, Heidelberg, Germany

Gupta MC (1969) The effect of size, growth, and industry on the financial structure of manufacturing companies. The Journal of Finance 24:517 – 529

Hall WK (1980) Survival strategies in a hostile environment. Harvard Business Review pp 78 – 85

Harris MD (2010) Little's law: The science behind proper staffing. Emergency Physicians Monthly p Feb

Hopp WJ, Spearman ML (2000) Factory physics: Foundations of manufacturing management, 2nd edn. Irwin McGraw Hill, New York

Lazowska ED, Zahorjan J, Graham GS, Sevckik KC (1984) Quantitative system performance: Computer system analysis using queueing network models. Prentice Hall, Englewood Cliffs, NJ

Little JDC (1961) A proof for the queuing formula: L = w. Operations Research 9(3):383 – 387

Little JDC (2011) Little's law as viewed on its 50th anniversary. Operations Research 59(3):536 – 549

Little JDC, Graves SC (2008) Little's law. In: Chhajed D, Lowe TJ (eds) Building intuition: Insights from basic operations management models and principles, Springer Science + Business Media LLC, New York, pp 81 – 100

Mottner S, Smith S (2009) Wal-mart: Supplier performance and market power. Journal of Business Research 62:535 – 541

Ortin-Angel P, Prior D (2004) Accounting turnover ratios and cash conversion cycle. Problems and Perspectives of Manage- ment 1:189–205

Porter ME (1998) Competitive Strategy: Techniques for analyzing industries and competitors. Free Press, New York

Robeson JF, Copacino WC (1994) The logistics handbook, 1st edn. The Free Press, New York

Rumyantsev S, Netessine S (2007) What can be learned from classical inventory models? a cross-industry exploratory investigation. Manufacturing & Service Operations Management 9:409 – 429

Stidham Jr S (1974) A last word on *l* " λ *w*. Operations Research 22(2):417 – 421

Subramanyam KR (2014) Financial statement analysis. McGraw-Hill Education

Wahlen JM, Baginski SP, Bradshaw MT (2008) Financial reporting, financial statement analysis, and valuation: A strategic perspective, 7th edn. Cengage Learning

Whitt W (1991) A review of $l = \lambda w$ and extensions. Queueing Systems 9:235 – 268

DECISION SCIENCES INSTITUTE

Supply Chain Risk Network Management (SCRNM): A Paradigm Shift towards Modelling Systemic Risks and Risk Appetite

Abroon Qazi, Alex Dickson, and John Quigley
University of Strathclyde Business School
Email: {abroon.qazi; alex.dickson; j.quigley}@strath.ac.uk

ABSTRACT

There is a major research gap of developing a supply chain risk management process integrating risk appetite of the decision maker and all stages of the risk management process within an interdependent network of systemic risks. We introduce an iterative process namely Supply Chain Risk Network Management to bridge this gap. We make use of the recently introduced concept of utility indifference curves based risk matrix to capture the risk attitude of the decision maker and demonstrate the application of the proposed process through an illustrative example.

KEYWORDS: Risk appetite, Systemic risks, Supply chain risk network management, Utility indifference curves, Risk matrix

INTRODUCTION

Risk management is a continuous process comprising sequential stages of risk identification, risk analysis, risk evaluation, risk treatment and risk monitoring (SA, 2009). Supply chain risk management (SCRM) deals with managing risks associated with the entire chain involved in transforming the raw material into the finished product that is finally delivered to the customer. Adapting the established risk management framework (SA, 2009), researchers have been proposing various SCRM frameworks (Heckmann et al., 2015, Ho et al., 2015). Besides these frameworks, a number of models and tools have been developed focusing on different stages of the SCRM process (Fahimnia et al., 2015).

Supply chain risks have been generally classified into independent categories like physical, financial, information, relational and innovation (Rao and Goldsby, 2009). The same independent categories of risks are adopted and reflected in the conventional risk matrix based tools used by the practitioners (Norrman and Jansson, 2004). Limited articles in the literature on risk management in general (Ackermann et al., 2014) and SCRM in particular (Badurdeen et al., 2014, Garvey et al., 2015) have focused on the shortcoming of conventional techniques of risk identification and emphasised the need for capturing systemic interactions between risks. Risk assessment/evaluation and risk treatment following the conventional risk identification techniques yield sub-optimal solutions as these techniques fail to account for complex dynamics across the risks and risk sources (Ackermann et al., 2014).

Risk appetite of the decision maker drives the tolerance level with respect to the acceptance of risks. Very few frameworks in SCRM have captured the risk appetite of the decision maker (Knemeyer et al., 2009, Lavastre et al., 2012), however, to the best of the authors' knowledge, no existing study has ever investigated designing a risk management framework within a network setting of interacting risks driven by the risk appetite of the decision maker. Integration of utility indifference curves within the risk matrix has been recently introduced in the literature on risk management that results in discretising the risk matrix into five risk zones: Negligible-no need for further concern; Acceptable-need for monitoring the risks with no investment; Controllable-need for adopting emergency plans; Critical-need for mitigating risks as long as the benefits exceed the costs; and Unacceptable-need for bringing the risks down to the critical level at any cost (Ruan et al., 2015).

Selection of optimal risk mitigation strategies has also gained limited attention both in the literature on risk management in general (Spackova and Straub, 2015) and SCRM in particular (Tuncel and Alpan, 2010, Micheli et al., 2014, Aqlan and Lam, 2015) but the main challenge is to develop these studies further to capture interdependency between risks and to consider the risk appetite of the decision maker as well. The main research question driving our research project is: How can we design a SCRM process integrating the systemic interaction between risks and the risk appetite of the decision maker?

In this study, we aim to contribute to the field of SCRM by introducing a major research gap that has gained limited attention of the researchers. Furthermore, we introduce a new risk management process namely Supply Chain Risk Network Management (SCRNM) and demonstrate why it is important to bridge the identified research gap and to follow our proposed process. We transform the conventional risk matrix in order to make it compatible for assessing interdependent risks in relation to utility indifference curves specific to the decision maker.

LITERATURE REVIEW

We reviewed the articles focusing on the risk management process/framework within the field of SCRM. We also reviewed the existing literature reviews in order to substantiate our findings. Harland et al. (2003) developed a supply network risk management tool and applied it to the electronics sector through conducting four case studies. The main merit of the tool is its exclusive focus on collaborative risk management achieved through engaging the stakeholders across the supply network. Building on the same concept of network wide management of risks, Hallikas et al. (2004) introduced a risk management process integrating different perspectives of supply chain actors and emphasised the need for adopting Systems approach in order to understand the complex dynamics across the network. Systems-oriented SCRM process is also introduced by Oehmen et al. (2009) that captures the interdependency between risks. Advocating the need for adapting the degree of risk management with regard to the contextual factors, Giunipero and Eltantawy (2004) introduced a risk management framework contingent on four determinants: degree of product technology; need for security; importance of the supplier; and purchaser's prior experience with the situation. Supply chain operations reference model (SCOR) has also been modified and considered as an important framework for managing supply chain risks (Sinha et al., 2004, Rotaru et al., 2014). The main limitation of the aforementioned studies and other risk management frameworks proposed by Manuj and Mentzer (2008), Khan et al. (2008) and Tummala and Schoenherr (2011) is their limited focus on capturing the interdependency between risks.

Only two of the selected studies (Knemeyer et al., 2009, Lavastre et al., 2012) considered risk appetite of the decision maker as an important factor and included it in the SCRM framework. Although risk attitude has been considered in the modelling framework of a number of studies as mentioned in the literature review conducted by Heckmann et al. (2015), these articles fail to meet the selection criterion of this study because of their focus on a specific stage of the risk management process. Among the quantitative studies, Tuncel and Alpan (2010) used a timed petri nets framework to model and analyse a supply chain which is subject to various risks. They used Failure Modes and Effects Analysis (FMEA) to identify important risks having higher values of Risk Priority Number (RPN). Elleuch et al. (2014) proposed a comprehensive risk management process integrating the techniques of FMEA, design of experiments, analytical hierarchy process and desirability function approach. Micheli et al. (2014) and Aqlan and Lam (2015) introduced optimisation based techniques for selecting optimal risk mitigation strategies. Although all the mentioned quantitative studies consider interdependency between risks and strategies, critical aspect of modelling interdependency between risks and risk appetite of the decision maker is ignored.

We also reviewed a number of articles focusing on literature reviews and it was surprising to find that only two studies have emphasised the need for modelling interdependency between risks (Colicchia and Strozzi, 2012, Ho et al., 2015). Similarly, despite the fact that existing SCRM frameworks fail to integrate all stages of the risk management process within an interdependent setting of risks and strategies, limited studies have realised the importance of conducting research in this direction. Critical review of the selected articles focusing on the SCRM process/framework and literature reviews reveals an important finding that an integrated risk management framework considering the interdependency between risks and mitigation strategies and risk appetite of the decision maker has neither been explored nor mentioned as a research gap for directing future research. Our study can be considered as an important step towards bridging this major research gap and establishing an agenda for future research.

EXISTING SCRM PROCESS AND CONCEPT OF UTILITY INDIFFERENCE CURVES BASED RISK MATRIX

There is a consensus among researchers that the SCRM process comprises five sequential stages: risk identification; assessment; analysis; treatment; and monitoring (Giannakis and Papadopoulos, 2016) that are analogous to the stages of the standard risk management process (SA, 2009). We present a very simple example to illustrate these stages and identify the main issue with adopting this process in case of interdependent risks. In the risk identification stage, specific risks must be identified. Let us assume that there are five risks namely R1, R2, R3, R4 and R5 that have been identified for a hypothetical supply chain using standard tools of checklists, risk mapping and taxonomies. In the risk assessment stage, each risk is assigned the probability and impact values and in our example, we assign arbitrary values to the risks as shown in Table 1. These risks are subsequently mapped on a risk matrix for the sake of prioritisation (risk analysis) and selecting risk mitigation actions (risk treatment).

Table 1: Risk parameters

Risk	Probability	Impact
R1	0.7	1200
R2	0.4	600
R3	0.1	500
R4	0.5	800
R5	0.9	700

Risk matrix is a two-dimensional plot of risks characterised by the corresponding probability and impact values. For a detailed overview of the history of risk matrix based tools and associated shortcomings, interested readers may refer to the study conducted by Duijm (2015). One of the main limitations of these tools is their lack of capturing risk attitude of the decision maker. Using utility theory, Ruan et al. (2015) introduced a three step process for integrating risk attitude in the risk matrix by: (a) describing risk attitudes of decision makers by utility functions; (b) introducing utility indifference curves and embedding these into the risk matrix; and (c) discretising utility indifference curves.

Firstly, the utility function of the decision maker must be established. In this example, we assume that the decision maker is risk-neutral ($utility\ of\ loss\ [u(l)] = -loss$). The utility indifference curves segregate the entire risk matrix into five regions: unacceptable; critical; controllable; acceptable; and negligible risk zones (Ruan et al., 2015). Therefore, we need a total of four utility indifference curves in order to establish the boundaries of these five regions. On each utility indifference curve, Equations (1) and (2) must hold good for every point *(P)* and a pair of points: P_i and P_j, respectively:

$$p * u(l) + (1 - p) * u(\bar{l}) = constant \tag{1}$$

$$\begin{gathered} p_i * u(l_i) + (1 - p_i) * u(\bar{l}) = p_j * u(l_j) + (1 - p_j) * u(\bar{l}) \\ p_i * \left(u(l_i) - u(\bar{l})\right) = p_j * \left(u(l_j) - u(\bar{l})\right) \end{gathered} \tag{2}$$

where p_i and l_i are the probability and impact values associated with point 'P_i', respectively,
$u(l)$ is the utility value of the loss resulting from realisation of the risk,
$u(\bar{l})$ is the utility value of no loss.

Now, if we consider a point *(P^*)* on each curve having a probability value of 1, the equation for locating other points on the curve is as follows:

$$p * \left(u(l) - u(\bar{l})\right) = u(l^*) - u(\bar{l}) \tag{3}$$

The value of $u(l^*)$ is unique for each curve and influenced by the risk appetite of the decision maker. For a detailed discussion on adopting the process, interested readers may refer to Ruan et al. (2015). In case of a risk-neutral decision maker with $u(\bar{l}) = 0$, Equation (3) is reduced to:

$$p * l = -u(l^*) = constant \tag{4}$$

The five zones representing relative importance of risks are unacceptable (R-I), critical (R-II), controllable (R-III), acceptable (R-IV) and negligible (R-V) as shown in Figure 1. The unacceptable zone also includes the area of the risk matrix beyond the threshold impact (in this case, above the line: Impact=1500). We have assumed that 1500 is the maximum tolerance level of the decision maker beyond which a risk with any probability value must be mitigated. Each risk considered in our example occupies a specific zone. The values of $u(l^*)$ corresponding to the specific points having probability value of 1 on the four curves (Points A, B, C and D) are assumed as -695, -521, -347 and -174, respectively.

As R1 is an unacceptable risk, it must be mitigated at any cost. R5 must be mitigated if the benefit exceeds the cost. We can identify a strategy or combinations of strategies that would either reduce the probability or impact of a risk or a set of risks. It is very easy to conduct the risk treatment as we only need to evaluate the benefits through executing simple arithmetic operations and weigh these against the total cost of implementing strategies. Therefore, we can prioritise risks and select optimal strategies through following a sequential risk management process. During the risk monitoring stage, any new risk(s) and/or changes in the parameters of existing risks must be incorporated in the risk matrix.

Figure 1: Utility indifference curves based risk matrix

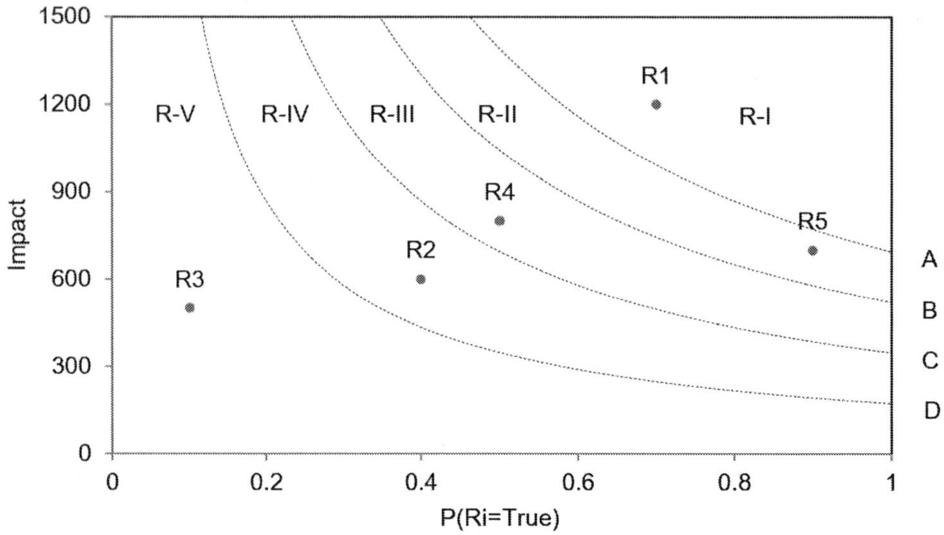

Now let us consider that instead of a set of independent risks, we are dealing with a network of risks where there are interdependencies between risks and a risk might have correlation (positive or negative) with another risk or a set of risks. Similarly, a mitigation strategy can have an association with multiple risks or multiple strategies can influence a single risk. Existing frameworks fail to account for evaluation and treatment of such network of risks. In case of interdependent risks, we need to marginalise the probability values through assigning conditional probability values to the risks. Similarly, the existing risk matrix based tools are not capable of projecting the criticality of interdependent risks. Furthermore, the criterion for conducting cost-benefit analysis for the network of risks and potential strategies taking into account the risk appetite of the decision maker and linking it back to the performance of individual risks on the risk matrix is not established.

PROPOSED PROCESS

We adapt the established risk management framework (SA, 2009) as it is widely used both by the researchers and practitioners (Ahmed et al., 2007). Although the description of terms and concepts used in the framework is controversial (Aven, 2011), our focus is limited to the stages involved in the process. The proposed process is shown as Figure 2. The main contribution of the proposed process is its exclusive focus on the 'systemicity of risks' (Ackermann et al., 2006, Ackermann et al., 2014). Instead of treating risks in silo, we introduce the concept of risk network. The process starts with the specification of context in terms of defining the boundary of the supply chain/network and identifying the stakeholders involved in the risk management process.

Risk network identification is a critical stage where there is a need for bringing a paradigm shift as the existing literature is rife with conventional tools and techniques of identifying risk categories and the concept of developing causal risk paths/risk network has gained limited attention (Badurdeen et al., 2014, Garvey et al., 2015). Besides identifying the risks and risk sources, potential risk mitigation strategies must also be included within the network. Risk network analysis involves determining the (conditional) probability values and loss (utility) values associated with risks and the cost related to implementing potential mitigation strategies. The utility values are driven by the risk appetite of the decision maker. In the risk network evaluation stage, there is a need to explore new risk measures that can be computed easily and are capable of capturing the network wide impact of risks. The measures are also influenced by the risk appetite. In addition to registering the holistic impact of risks within the network setting, there is also a need for visualising the impact of each risk on the network of risks and ensuring that all risks are mitigated to the required level. Therefore, a modified risk matrix capable of evaluating interdependent risks coupled with the mapping of utility indifference curves (Ruan et al., 2015) must be developed and consulted for risk network evaluation.

Figure 2: Supply chain risk network management (SCRNM)

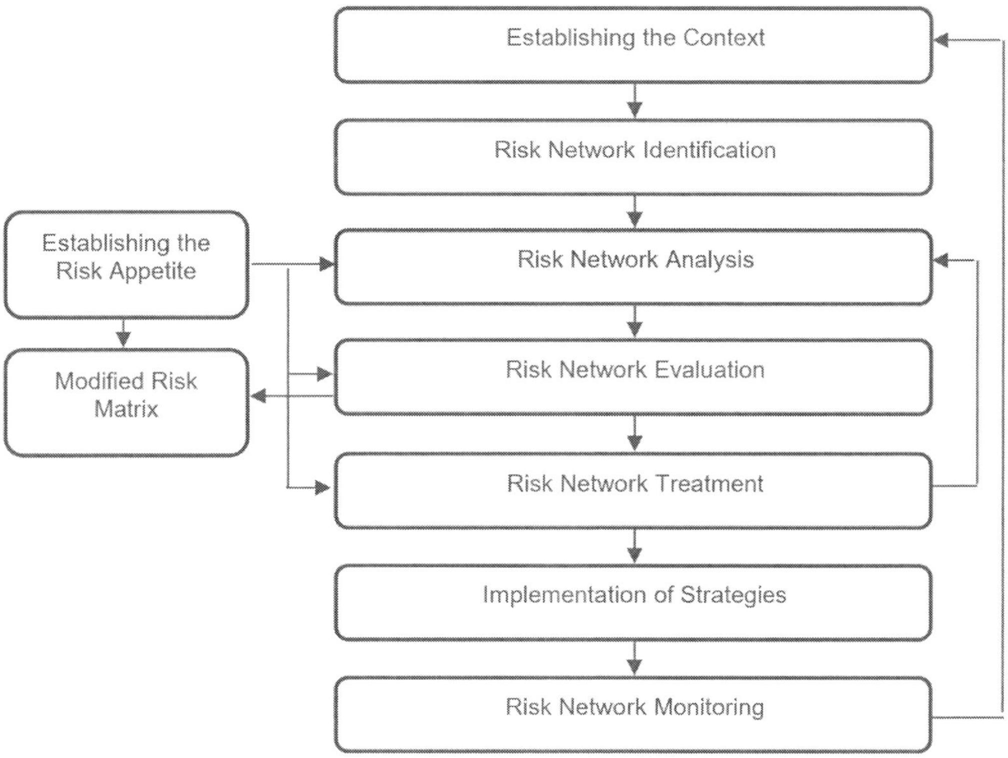

Risk network treatment deals with the evaluation of different combinations of risk mitigation strategies within the network setting. The proposed process flow is in contrast with the one established in extant literature as instead of following a unidirectional flow, it is an iterative process where evaluation of each combination of strategies necessitates re-assessing and re-evaluating the risk network. The iterative process results in the selection of an optimal combination of strategies that not only considers the network wide holistic effect of these strategies but also yields an acceptable configuration of risks mapped on the modified risk matrix. The matrix also helps in identifying critical risks that must be monitored periodically. After determining the optimal combination of strategies, these are implemented and as risk management is a continuous process, there is a need for continuously monitoring risks and updating the risk network on a regular basis.

PROPOSED APPROACH

Based on the efficacy of Bayesian Belief Networks (BBNs) in capturing interdependencies between risks, we consider BBN based modeling of risk network as an effective approach. Such a modeling technique can help managers visualise supply chain risks and take effective mitigation strategies (Qazi et al., 2014, Qazi et al., 2015a). BBNs have already been explored in the literature on risk management (Wu et al., 2015, Ashrafi et al., 2015) and SCRM (Garvey et al., 2015, Nepal and Yadav, 2015, Lockamy, 2014) for modelling and assessing risks. For understanding the mechanics and modelling of BBNs, interested readers may consult Charniak (1991), Jensen and Nielsen (2007), Kjaerulff and Anders (2008), Sigurdsson et al. (2001), Nadkarni and Shenoy (2001) and Nadkarni and Shenoy (2004).

Supply Chain Risk Network

A discrete supply chain risk network $RN = (X, G, P, L, U, C)$ is a six-tuple consisting of [adapted from Qazi et al. (2015c)]:

1. a directed acyclic graph (DAG), $G = (V, E)$, with nodes, V, representing discrete risks and risk sources, X_R, discrete risk mitigation strategies, X_S, loss functions, L, utility functions, U, cost functions, C, and directed links, E, encoding dependence relations,

2. a set of conditional probability distributions, P, containing a distribution, $P(X_{R_i}|X_{pa(R_i)})$, for each risk and risk source, X_{R_i},

3. a set of loss functions, L, containing one loss function, $l(X_{pa(V)})$, for each node v in the subset $V_l \in V$ of loss nodes,

4. a set of utility functions, U, containing one utility function, $u(X_{pa(V)})$, for each node v in the subset $V_u \in V$ of utility nodes,

5. a set of cost functions, C, containing one cost function, $c(X_{pa(V)})$, for each node v in the subset $V_c \in V$ of cost nodes.

Risk network expected loss, $RNEL(X)$, is given by (Qazi et al., 2015b):

$$RNEL(X) = \prod_{X_v \in X_R} P(X_v|X_{pa(v)}) \sum_{w \in V_L} l(X_{pa(w)}) \quad (5)$$

Risk network expected utility for loss, $RNEU(X)$, is given by (Qazi et al., 2015c):

$$RNEU(X) = \prod_{X_v \in X_R} P(X_v|X_{pa(v)}) \sum_{w \in V_L} u(X_{pa(w)}) \quad (6)$$

Risk network expected utility, $RNEU(X, C(X_{s_i}))$ or $RNEU$, is given by:

$$RNEU = f(RNEU(X), C(X_{s_i})) \quad (7)$$

Risk Measure. We make use of a risk measure namely Risk Network Expected Loss Propagation Measure ($RNELPM$) in order to evaluate the relative contribution of each supply chain risk towards the loss propagation across the entire network of risks. $RNELPM$ is the relative contribution of each risk factor to the propagation of loss across the entire network of supply chain risks given the scenario that the specific risk is realised (Qazi et al., 2016).

$$RNELPM_{X_{R_i}} = RNEL\left(X|X_{R_i} = true\right) * P(X_{R_i} = true) \tag{8}$$

Risk Configuration Metric. Risk configuration metric (RCM) represents the preference of the decision maker with regard to the configuration of risks on the modified risk matrix. A pure qualitative metric focusing on the relative number of risks within each risk zone may be represented as follows:

$$RCM_{X_{S_i}} = \frac{n_1 * a_1 + n_2 * a_2 + n_3 * a_3 + n_4 * a_4 + n_5 * a_5}{N} \tag{9}$$

where n_i and a_i represent the number of risks in the risk zone i and the criticality significance of risk zone i on a normalised scale (0-1), respectively,
N is the total number of risks.

However, we consider following risk metric to be appropriate as defined over a range of continuous values and therefore, it will be used in the paper:

$$RCM_{X_{S_i}} = \sum_{X_R} -u\left(RNEL_{X_{S_i}}(X|X_{R_i} = true)\right) * P(X_{R_i})_{X_{S_i}} \tag{10}$$

The normalised risk metric is defined as follows:

$$\overline{RCM}_{X_{S_i}} = 1 - RCM_{X_{S_i}} / max(RCM_{X_S}) \tag{11}$$

where it is assumed that the utility of 'no loss' is 0 and RCM_{X_S} is the entire set of RCM values for all combinations of strategies.

Modelling Process

Following steps must be followed in developing the BBN based risk network of interacting supply chain risks and mitigation strategies:

1. Define the boundaries of the supply network and identify stakeholders.

2. Identify a network of key risks, corresponding risk sources and potential risk mitigation strategies on the basis of input received from each stakeholder through interviews and/or focus group sessions.

3. Refine the qualitative structure of the resulting network involving all stakeholders.

4. Elicit (conditional) probability values, loss (utility) values resulting from risks and cost associated with implementing each potential mitigation strategy and populate the BBN with all values.

5. Run the model corresponding to the risk appetite of the decision maker for assessing and treating risks.

6. Validate the model output involving stakeholders.

Illustrative Example: Demonstration of Key Concepts

In order to demonstrate the key concepts introduced, we present a simple network comprising five risks (Ri) and four potential risk mitigation strategies (Si) as shown in Figure 3. It is assumed that each risk is associated with a loss value of 100 units and each strategy can be implemented at a cost of 30 units. Each risk is considered to have binary states: True (T) or False (F). Similarly, each mitigation strategy is assumed to be in one of the binary states: Yes (Y) or No (N). The (conditional) probability values are shown in Table 2. The shaded cells represent the (conditional) probability values once the corresponding mitigation strategy is selected. It is interesting to consider positive correlation of S1 with R2.

Figure 3: Risk network modelled in GeNIe (GeNIe, 2015)

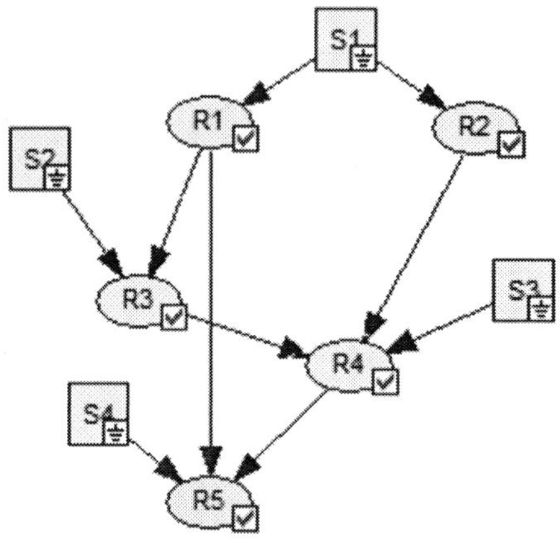

Table 2: (Conditional) probability values [$P(risk = F|parents) = 1 - P(risk = T|parents)$]

Parents								$P(risk = True|parents)$				
R1	*R2*	*R3*	*R4*	*S1*	*S2*	*S3*	*S4*	*R1*	*R2*	*R3*	*R4*	*R5*
				N				0.8				
				Y				0.6				
				N					0.3			
				Y					0.6			
T					N					0.7		
					Y					0.2		
F					N					0.1		
					Y					0.02		
	T	T				N					0.9	
		F									0.5	
	F	T									0.7	
		F									0.1	
	T	T				Y					0.6	
		F									0.3	
	F	T									0.4	
		F									0.01	
T			T				N					0.7
			F									0.5
F			T									0.2
			F									0.1
T			T				Y					0.3
			F									0.1
F			T									0.1
			F									0.03

Risk-Neutral Decision Maker

A risk-neutral decision maker interested in maximising reduction in the risk network expected loss less cost does not account for the relative importance of each risk in terms of its relative position on the modified risk matrix. The decision maker would only select a combination of strategies and make an investment if there is an increase in the reduction of risk network expected loss less cost. Under standard configuration, the risks are evaluated with respect to the existing strategies whereas none of the potential strategies is selected. The relative performance of each combination of strategies is mapped in Figure 4. Each point represents a particular combination of strategies with corresponding cost and risk network expected loss. The solid line represents the threshold where the reduction in risk network expected loss is just equal to the cost of implementing strategies. The points (above) below this line represent all such combinations which are (in)feasible.

The dotted line in black contains the optimal solution (point E) yielding maximum reduction in the network expected loss less cost whereas the dashed line in blue contains the optimal solution (point A) following the criterion of maximising benefit to cost ratio. Although point K is a feasible solution, it is not optimal as it fails to yield a greater reduction in network expected loss less cost relative to that of point E. A red cross represents an optimal solution. The decision maker will select point A if the available budget is less than 60 units but at least 30 units whereas for budget greater than and inclusive of 60 units, point E is the optimal solution.

Figure 4: Identification of optimal combinations of strategies

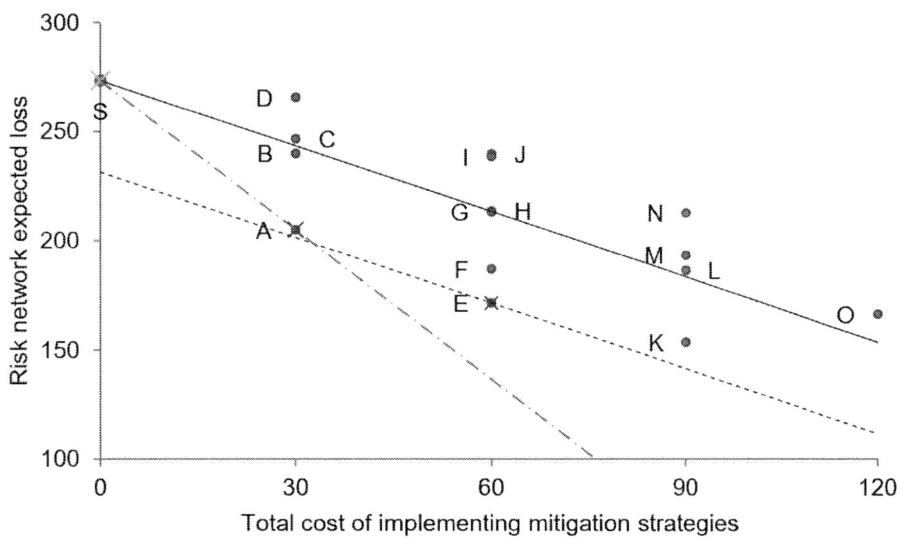

Risk-Averse Decision Maker

In case of a risk-averse decision maker, we assumed the utility function as represented by Equation (12). We also assumed that the upper threshold for the loss value is 500 units. Similarly, the selected $u(l^*)$ values corresponding to the four utility indifference curves are -200, -150, -100 and -50, respectively.

$$u(l) = -(l)^2 \quad (12)$$

Maximising Normalised Risk Configuration Metric subject to Constraints

We mapped the risks corresponding to the standard configuration of network as shown in Figure 5 with all risks located in the unacceptable zone. Next, we evaluated the normalised risk configuration metric for all combinations of strategies as shown in Figure 6. As there are risks located in the unacceptable zone, the constraint of risk network expected loss can be ignored. Therefore, point A is the optimal solution corresponding to the cost of 30 units.

Figure 5: Risk network evaluation under standard configuration (Point S)

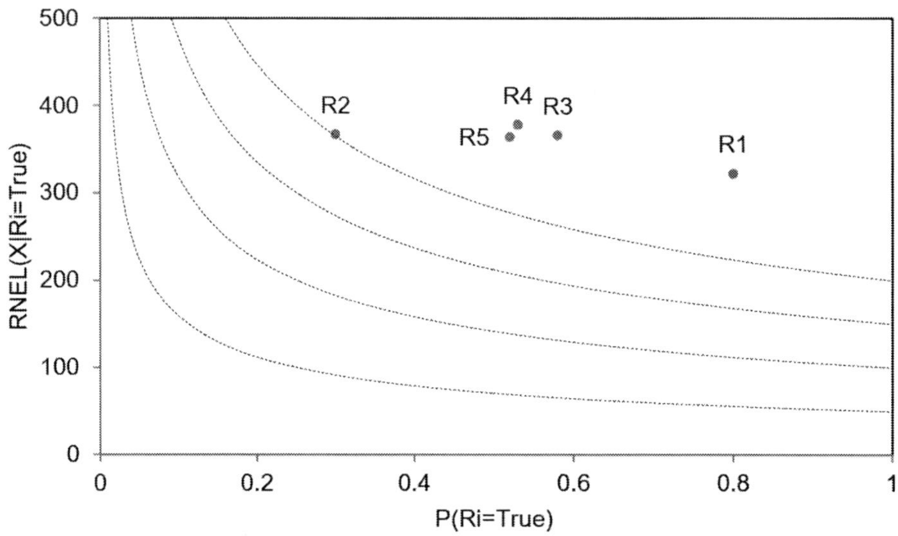

Figure 6: Identification of optimal solutions

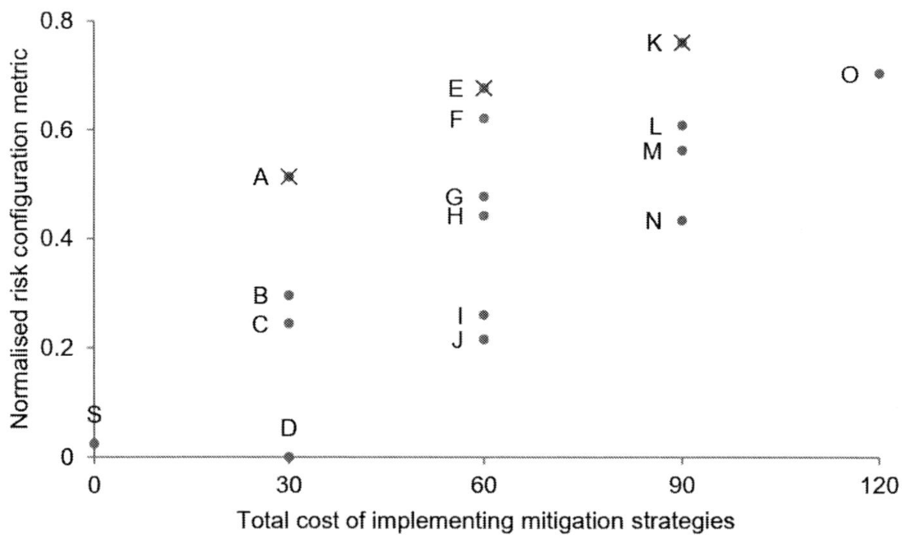

The risk configuration corresponding to point A is shown as Figure 7. As two risks are still in the unacceptable region, we can ignore the constraint of benefit exceeding cost, however, point E yields the best value corresponding to both criteria (maximising $\overline{RCM}$ and minimising '$RNEL + cost$'). The risk configuration relative to point E is shown as Figure 8. There is no risk in the unacceptable region whereas two risks are located in the critical region. Therefore, point K is the only feasible solution as benefit must exceed cost for further investment as shown in Figure 4. As point K yields higher value for $\overline{RCM}$ relative to that of point E, point K is the optimal solution for budget greater than or equal to 90. Point O is not a feasible solution to be considered for optimality. A red coloured cross represents an optimal solution.

Figure 7: Risk network evaluation (point A)

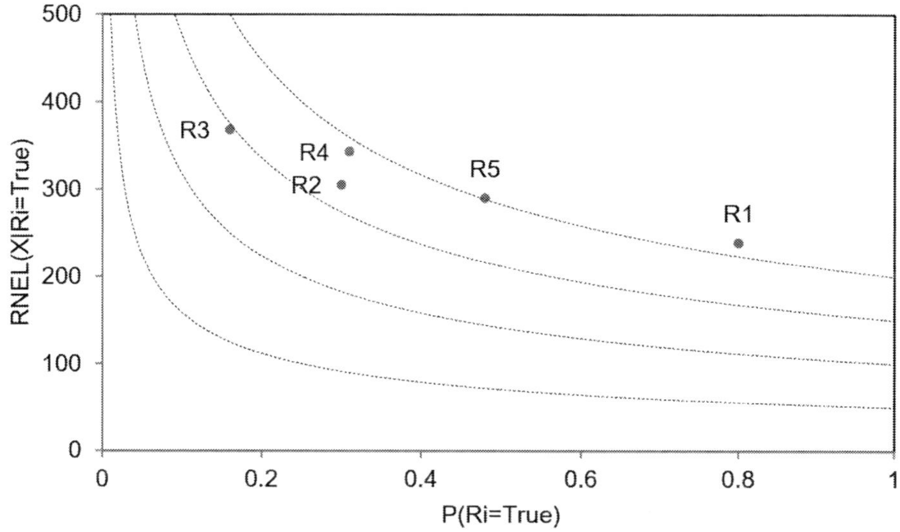

Figure 8: Risk network evaluation (point E)

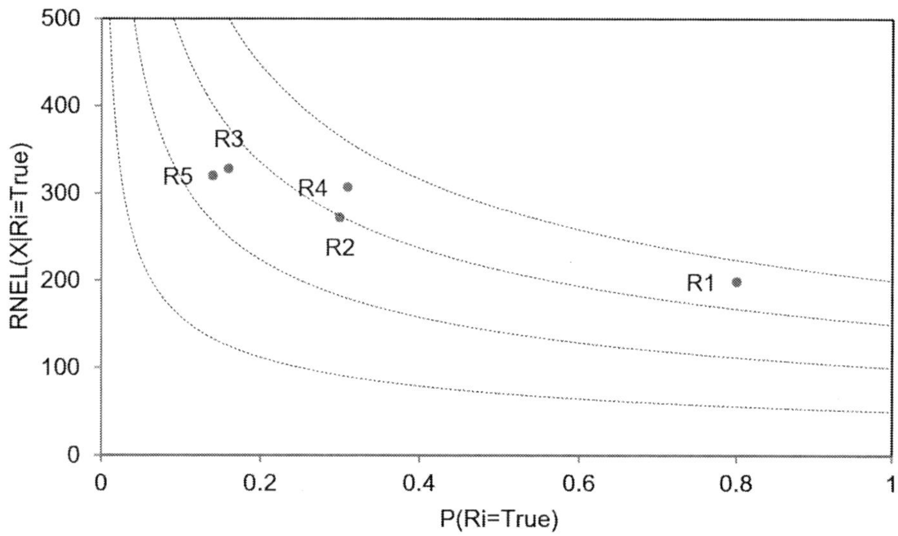

CONCLUSIONS

A number of frameworks and modelling tools have been proposed in the literature on SCRM for identifying, assessing and mitigating risks. These studies have been periodically reviewed for directing future research. Focusing on the theme of risk management process/framework, we selected and critically reviewed quality articles. The hypothesis of our research question was validated that there is no single study focusing on the SCRM process within an integrated framework of interacting risks and the risk appetite of the decision maker. We also reviewed the articles on literature reviews and it was revealed that even these articles have not realised and emphasised the need for conducting research in this direction.

On the basis of our finding, we introduced a new risk management process namely SCRNM. We believe that there is a need for bringing paradigm shift in terms of modelling chains/network of interacting risks and risk sources. Instead of modelling and managing supply chain risks in silo, the researchers must embrace the notion of modelling and managing network of risks and develop effective and efficient tools for practitioners to adopt in real scenarios. There is also a need for exploring tools that integrate all stages of the risk management process instead of focusing on separate stages (Ho et al., 2015). We also introduced an important notion of following an iterative process rather than adopting the conventional unidirectional flow.

There is a need for introducing risk measures that capture the network wide holistic impact of interacting risks. However, optimising the risk network against these measures alone might result in sub-optimal solutions as it is also important to consider the risk appetite of the decision maker. Although expected utility theory provides a standard procedure for decision making under uncertainty, it is not viable to even assess a simple risk network comprising limited number of risks and strategies. Therefore, we introduced the idea of adapting risk matrix for projecting the configuration of interdependent risks. Risk matrix has already been modified for mapping the risk appetite of the decision maker. However, the main limitation is its exclusive application to independent categories of risks. We proposed its adaptation to the context of interdependent risk network.

In order to present a modelling framework for the proposed SCRNM process, we introduced a modelling approach grounded in the framework of BBNs. We made use of an existing risk measure namely $RNELPM$ and introduced a process for managing supply chain risk network with regard to risk-neutral and risk-seeking/risk-averse decision makers. We demonstrated the meaning of key concepts through an illustrative example. The proposed process can help researchers focus on a new stream of research and develop it further. In future, a tool integrating a number of techniques feasible for each stage of the process can be developed and tested in the industry and empirical studies may be conducted for gauging the feasibility of the proposed modelling framework and determining the associated challenges.

REFERENCES

References available upon request.

DECISION SCIENCES INSTITUTE

Sustainable Tourism Development and Service Operations Management at the Missouri State Penitentiary (MSP)

Dan Bumblauskas, Ph.D.
University of Northern Iowa
Email: daniel.bumblauskas@uni.edu

ABSTRACT

The Missouri State Penitentiary is a landmark in Jefferson City, Missouri, and is being utilized for various types of tours, however, the condition and aesthetic appearance of the prison has created concerns. This article documents aspects of dark tourism, service operations management, and sustainable tourism providing recommendations based on research and analytical techniques.

KEYWORDS: Dark Tourism, Service Operations Management, Tourism and Hospitality, Forecasting Application

INTRODUCTION

The Missouri State Penitentiary (MSP and "prison") is a historic landmark in Jefferson City, Missouri. Operated until 2004, this now de-commissioned prison is owned by the State of Missouri and is being utilized for various types of tours by the Jefferson City Convention and Visitors Bureau. The condition and aesthetic appearance of the prison has historically caused some opposition to the prison's previous in-mate and current tour-based operations. While much of the opposition seems to have subsided, some of the environmental and aesthetic concerns include structural stability, hazardous materials, and general appearance to the surrounding businesses and community. Therefore, it is imperative that the city of Jefferson continue to generate revenue to effectively operate, manage, maintain, and upgrade the MSP. This article documents the following:

- a literature review of aesthetic pollution and the dark tourism theoretical construct
- the lease/ownership history and arrangement between the city and state
- the challenges faced to sustainably operate the MSP
- a summary and analysis of the tours offered, visitor data, and revenue data
- an assessment of the MSP compared to benchmarked peer institutions
- conclusions and recommendations for the continued operation of the MSP

For the MSP to have a sustainable facilities and tour operations, additional revenues must be generated to pay for the necessary maintenance items and upgrades to make the prison a world-class tourist destination. Many recommendations are provided to generate additional revenue. Various analytical methods were used to provide recommendations for the MSP management team to consider including:

- Benefits analysis to prioritize the redevelopment projects
- Estimated revenues for offering events such as weddings
- Increasing the operating schedule to offer year round tours

- Offering audio guided tours
- Providing shuttle services from St. Louis and/or Kansas City metro areas
- Offering community days
- Joining or launching a professional association for historical prison tour operators
- Development of office space for state and local government employees
- Increasing the priority to develop on-site lodging facilities

LITERATURE REVIEW

Background and History: The Missouri State Penitentiary

The Missouri State Penitentiary (MSP) is located in downtown Jefferson City, Missouri and has had a major impact on the community economically and as it relates to visual or aesthetic pollution in downtown Jefferson City. Visual and aesthetic pollution have been studied from an ontological perspective (Douglas, 1966; Douglas 2003) and in numerous applications since such as water and beachfront photography (Tudor and Williams, 2003), empirically for an electrical power generation plant (Randall, Ives, and Eastman, 1974), and in general practice (Holden, 2008). Jefferson City is the state capitol of Missouri and is located in the center of Missouri between St. Louis, to the East, and Kansas City, to the West. The left-hand portion of Figure 1 shows an aerial skyline photo of Jefferson City; the MSP is situated just south of this photograph. The right-hand portion of Figure 1 shows an aerial photo of the MSP site (Missouri State Penitentiary Redevelopment Commission, 2002). Figure 2 shows the aerial layout of the prison including the cell blocks, chapel, factory, gas chamber, etc. with the prison grounds circled in red. The surrounding real estate and property have suffered over the years from the aesthetic pollution to the area.

Figure 1: Jefferson City, MO Skyline Photo (MSP located just South of this photo) and MSPRC (Missouri State Penitentiary Redevelopment Commission) Photo Reproduced with Permission

Figure 2: Google Map Photo of MSP (Red Circled Area)

The MSP would be classified as a tourist attraction since it is a historic monument. A wide variety of tours are offered, as detailed in appendix 2, and the role of tour guides at historical sites has been considered by others (Reisinger & Steiner, 2006) as well as creating a typography for the types of tours offered, specifically for wildlife tours (Curtin & Wilkes, 2005). Poria, Butler, & Airey (2003) looked at the impact on tourism visiting religious historical sites and there are some commonalities between their work and that of historical sites such as MSP. The MSP was the first prison west of the Mississippi river and was deemed by Time Magazine as the "bloodiest 47 acres in America," in 1967 (Missouri Department of Economic Development) and housed many famous inmates (e.g., Sonny Liston, 'Pretty Boy' Floyd, etc.) before it closed in 2004. Appendix 1 contains more information on MSP's history. The prison has become a major tourist destination for the state of Missouri. However, there has historically been a faction of residents who have been interested in demolishing the prison because of its condition and aesthetic pollution to the downtown Jefferson City area. One of the primary research questions is whether renovating the prison in Jefferson City to prevent aesthetic pollution to the city would be a worthwhile investment based on forecasted tourist traffic and revenue generating potential.

It is important to note this work builds open prison re-development in terms of cultivating tourism rather than alternative or private management of prisons. Public-private development and re-development activities in Australia (Duffield, 2005), in-mate re-development (Salomone, 2004a; Salomone, 2004b), and the development of new correctional facilities and their impacts (Bonds, 2013) have been documented. It is noteworthy that there is a new prison that was constructed in the surrounding area outside the city center. Theoretically, Lennon & Foley (2000; Cannon-Brookes, 2001; Smith, 2002; Tarlow, 2007) introduced the terminology "dark tourism," which is studied more specifically for prisons by Strange & Kempa (2003) in the context of "dark tourism," for the Alcatraz (California, USA) and Robben Island (South Africa) prison tourist sites. Stone & Shapley (2008) note the need for research related to the demand for dark tourism and Strange & Kempa (2003) note the need for more research on marketing, interviews with prison tour operators, and reviewing visitor expectations as conducted in this research on the MSP. Bumblauskas et al. (2016) describe demand chain management considerations in further detail. Yuill (2004) reviews dark tourism in more detail based on the work of Dunlap (2001) for the Sing Sing Prison (New York, USA) and drawing comparisons to the Pompeii (Italy) natural disaster tourist site.

METHODOLOGY

The theoretical foundation of dark tourism is relatively new (Lennon & Foley, 2000), so research such as this continues to build upon the dark tourism construct. In order to establish the visitor and revenue potential, a comparative analysis was conducted to compare the MSP to other prisons, such as Alcatraz in California. Alcatraz has become a major tourist destination for the San Francisco bay area and each location was visited by the author on multiple occasions. The MSP operated from 1836 to 2004 (Jefferson City Convention and Visitors Bureau) and is 100 years older than Alcatraz. In working with the Jefferson City convention and tourism bureau to investigate the current status of the prison, it was decided that benchmarking other peer institutions would be beneficial. One focus of this research, which includes interviews (n = 6) with numerous entities, was to determine whether there is still interest in demolishing the prison, determining the impact to tourism in the area by reviewing visitor data of the prison, comparing the data to the number of tourists and revenues generated by peer institutions, and forecasting the number of visitors and revenues the MSP could expect for 2016 and beyond. The goal of this analysis was to aid in justifying or refuting whether renovations at the MSP should be conducted to reduce aesthetic pollution by increasing the number of tours to support the needs and safety of guests and visitors.

Another consideration for this study is that the city of Jefferson has been reviewing plans to build a convention center at the MSP site. Some of these preliminary plans have called for the demolition or redevelopment of the prison and residential housing in the surrounding area (KOMU News, 2007; KOMU News, 2010). The primary challenge encountered in conducting this study was locating the data and the information needed from the states of Missouri and those from peer institutions. With the assistance of Diane Gillespie and Steve Picker, Executive Director and Former Executive Director of the Jefferson City Convention and Visitors Bureau, contact information was attained for peer sites and eventually public reports and resources were located which describe the impact on the ambient environment in terms of aesthetic pollution, tourist traffic, and revenues from each prison. The Jefferson City penitentiary has only been offering tours for a short period of time since 2009 (Uhlenbrock, 2009), so learning from the lessons of Alcatraz and others has been extremely beneficial to MSP's operations.

In the case of the MSP, Jefferson City and the state of Missouri must be careful in considering the aesthetic pollution and revenue generation model. As noted by Holden (2008), "Often tourism development is based upon maximizing profits whilst ignoring aesthetic concerns (Holden, 2008)." In this case, the conundrum is that the city of Jefferson must generate revenue to help subsidize the restoration efforts. As such, the prioritization of restoration activities must be accounted for (e.g., a leaking roof was replaced to prevent more extensive damage). The

MSP facility is owned by the state of Missouri which limits the city of Jefferson's ability to fully control operations and make such prioritization decisions at MSP. The city and the state have utilized lease agreements up to 2011 and had been evaluating longer term lease options, which led to a 15 year use agreement with two additional 5 year option agreements (Gillespie, 2016).

The state of Missouri established the Missouri State Penitentiary Redevelopment Commission (MSPRC) to plan for the sustainable operation of the MSP (Missouri State Penitentiary Redevelopment Commission). Figure 3 provides a sample map of one of the redevelopment guidelines issued by the State of Missouri (State of Missouri, Division of Facilities Management, 2006).

Figure 3: State of Missouri MSP Redevelopment District Design Guidelines (State of Missouri, Division of Facilities Management, 2006), Image Reproduced with Permission

The site itself is 137 acres, of which only 5 acres is considered to be the "historic district," portion of the prison. Some of the environmental and aesthetic pollution concerns on the property included:

- Structural stability of buildings
- Hazardous materials such as asbestos and lead-based paints
- Boarded-up entrances and windows
- General maintenance and upkeep such as lawn care and snow removal

The MSPRC Master / Framework Plan (Missouri State Penitentiary Redevelopment Commission, 2002) outlines some of these topics by:

- Ranking the top 10 buildings based on historical value
- Analyzing the condition of each building
- Providing architectural summaries

- Reviewing engineering considerations and challenges
- Initiating environmental investigations such as:
    - Site investigations
    - Hazardous material reviews
    - Environmental assessments

Figure 4 provides a snapshot from the MSPRC Master / Framework Plan conceptual layout for the MSP property.

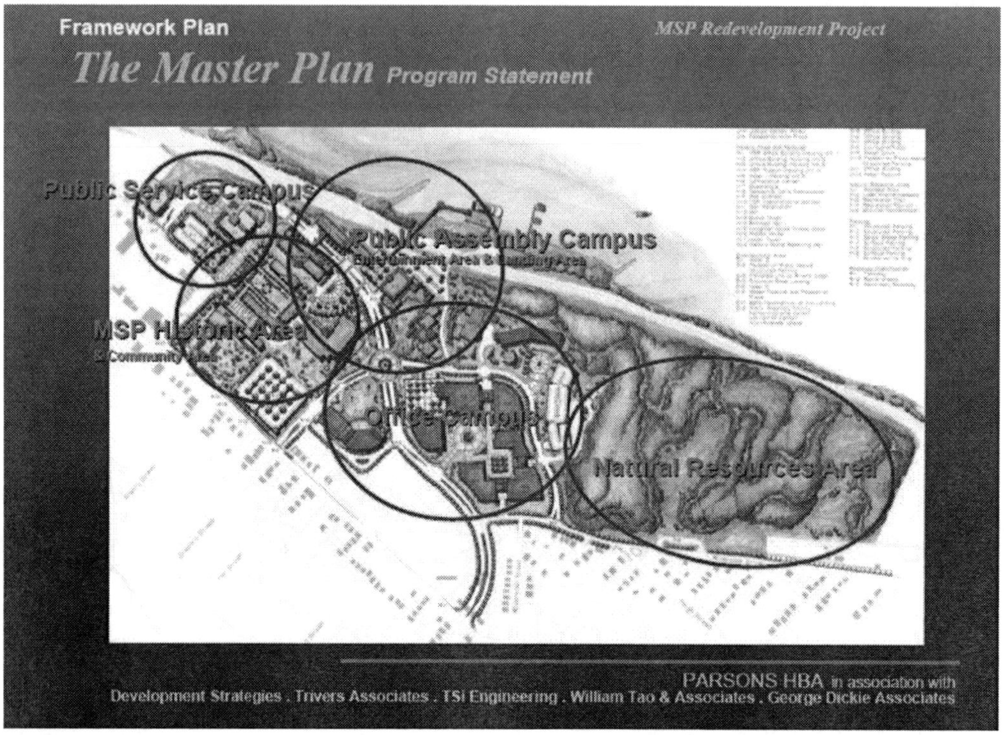

Figure 4: MSPRC Master / Framework Plan (Missouri State Penitentiary Redevelopment Commission, 2002), Image Reproduced with Permission

The MSPRC studied the existing structures and analyzed some of the environmental impact. It is note-worthy that there are minimal hazardous material concerns at the site. Some of the challenges faced by the city of Jefferson in operating the MSP include (Picker, 2011):

- Funding to stabilize the structures (improve aesthetics)
    - E.g., new rooves, windows, etc.
- Redevelopment activities including the historic district and private/public partnerships
- Prioritization of ideas from various organizations such as the city, chamber of commerce, state of Missouri, and the MSPRC
- Staffing MSP during normal business hours (e.g., 9 AM – 5 PM) which seems to be cost prohibitive in terms of salaries, insurance, and utilities (e.g., lighting, trash, electric, water, etc.)

Rather than simply repeating the potential projects that would improve the aesthetic appearance of the MSP as reported by the redevelopment commission, this article focuses on re-development strategies to generate additional revenue to help subsidize the various projects that should be prioritized and undertaken to improve the appearance and safety of the historically significant structures for generations to come. Before a comprehensive sustainability strategy can be deployed for the MSP, the state and city should get the current facilities up to acceptable condition levels. The primary historical revenue generation method is tours. Table 1 shows the various MSP tour options and appendices 2 (2011), 3 (2016) and 4 (2016) include additional details on each tour type.

Table 1: MSP Tour Options (Picker, 2011)

Tour Type	Cost	Description	Other Notes
2-hour history tour	$12/per person	regular tour	
4-hour in-depth tour	$25-35 per person	discover tour	
twilight tour	$17 per person	6-11PM	Visitors are given a lantern to investigate
specialty tour	$17 per person	focus on special events and people	"pretty boy" Floyd MSP escape attempts
ghost tour	$25 per person	unusual occurrences	use activity finding devices in two of housing units and gas chamber
Overnight	$95 per person	Up all night, no sleeping accommodations	'A' Hall and Gas Chamber Access
Group Paranormal	$100 per person	Minimum $1000	Serious searchers for paranormal activity

Tables 2, Figure 5, and Figure 6 show the visitor and revenue data for MSP from 2009 to 2015. MSP experienced a 265 percent increase in the number of visitors and a 323 percent revenue increase from 2009 to 2010. Additional visitor and revenue growth of nearly 50 percent occurred from 2010 to 2011. The average annual visitor growth rate since 2009 to 2016 has been 61 percent and the average annual revenue growth has been 74 percent during that time period. Figure 7 shows the revenue per guest growth over that period which increased from $12.66 (2009) to $17.43 (2015). It is important to note that the projected revenue for 2013 was estimated from the actual revenue per guest from that year. Diane Gillespie (2016) noted that in 2013, MSP was forced to close early in September 2013 due to unexpected repair needs. This early closure impacted the number of visitors as they were not able to offer tours and services during their normal operating period of March 1 to November 30. Projects funded during this repair period included window replacements, mold eradication, and lead-based paint mitigation. In addition, MSP had to cancel 3,000 reservations which impacted local hotels, restaurants, etc. and had economic ripple effects throughout the community (Gillespie, 2016).

Table 2: MSP Visitor and Revenue Data (Picker, S. (2011) and Gillespie, D. (2016), Executive Directors, Jefferson City Convention and Visitors Bureau, 2011)

Year	Visitors	Revenues (Projected)	Revenues (Actual)	Revenue per Guest	Revenues (Projected)
2009	3290	$ 41,650	$ 41,650	$ 12.66	$ 41,650
2010	12000	$176,000	$176,000	$ 14.67	$176,000
2011	17203	$263,000	$263,000	$ 15.29	$263,000
2012	19121	$275,471	$275,471	$ 14.41	$275,471
2013	14581	$288,046	$210,000	$ 14.40	$288,046
2014	22605	$301,409	$301,409	$ 13.33	$301,409
2015	25945	$452,104	$452,104	$ 17.43	$452,104

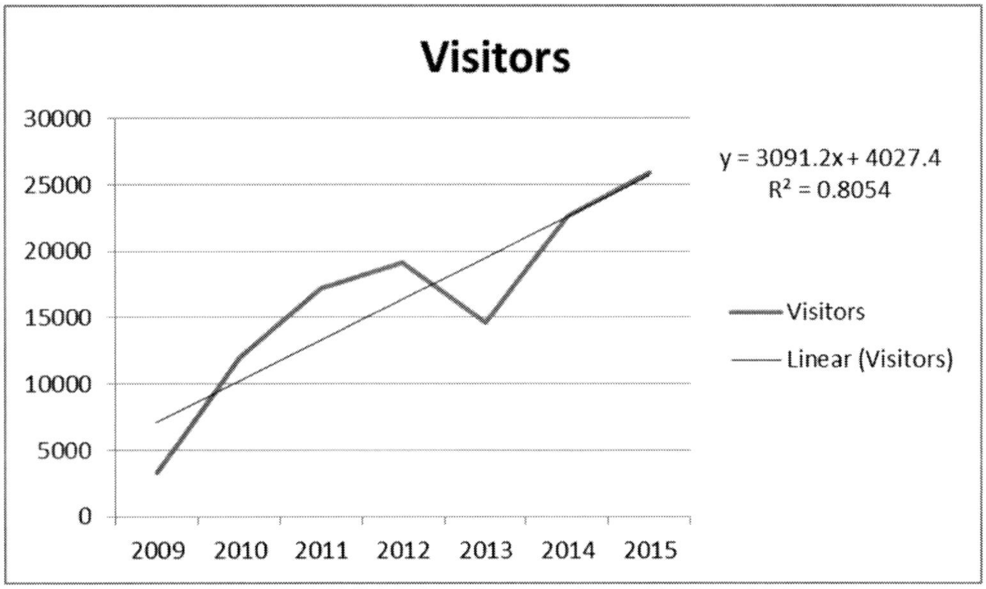

Figure 5: MSP Visitor Counts from 2009 to 2015

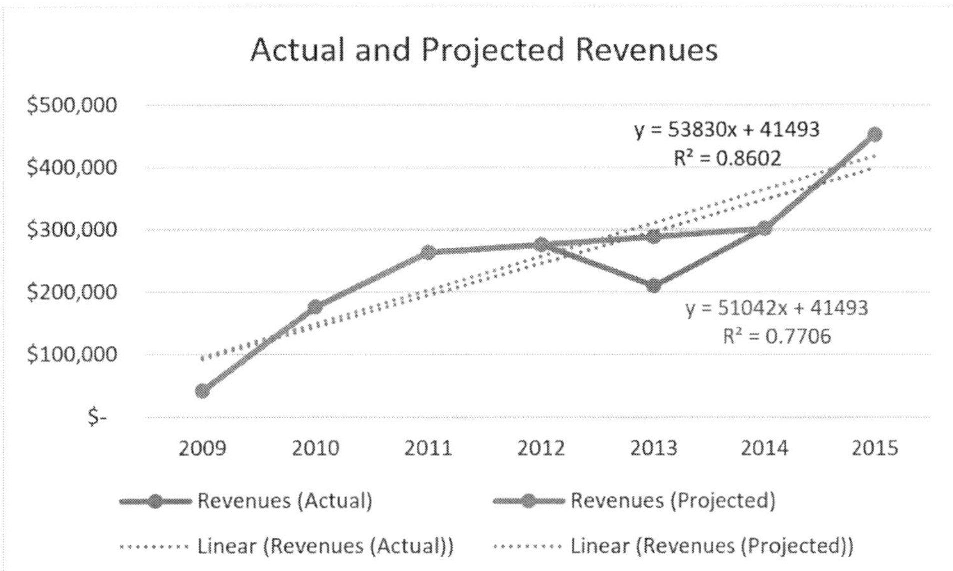

Figure 6: MSP Revenue Growth from 2009 to 2015

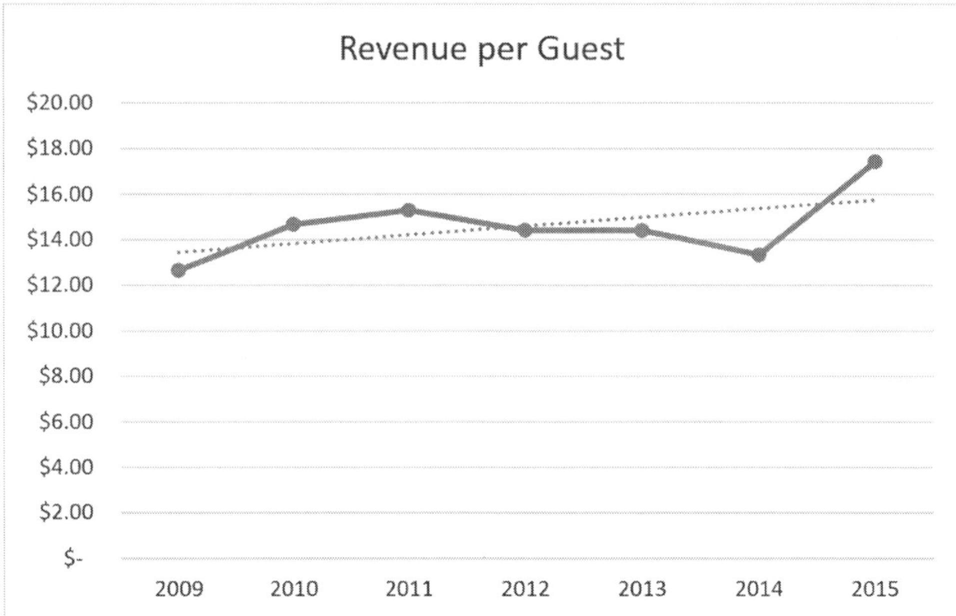

Figure 7: MSP Revenue per Guest from 2009 to 2015

BENCHMARKING

Jefferson City, Missouri's population is approximately 41,297 (City-Data, 2010) and the number of visitors to the prison during the 2011 year, following closure for the season, was 17,203 (Picker, 2011) and at the end of 2015 was 25,945 (Gillespie, 2016). In 2004 when the MSP was opened to the public for the first time 20,000 visitors attended the grand opening event (Cabbage & Bureau, 2011). Alcatraz sees 1.4 million annual visitors (Golden Gate National Parks Conservancy, 2011) with a total population in San Francisco of 808,976 (U.S. Census Bureau and Google Data, 2008). That gives Alcatraz a visitor to resident ratio of 1.73 and MSP's same ratio of 0.42 for 2011 as shown in table 3. Peer prisons include (Picker, 2011):

- The West Virginia Penitentiary (http://www.wvpentours.com/)
    - Moundsville, WV, Population – 9,054
- Ohio State Reformatory (http://www.mrps.org/)
    - Owned by the Mansfield Reformatory Preservation Society
    - Mansfield, OH, Population 49,346
- Eastern State Penitentiary (http://www.easternstate.org/)
    - Philadelphia, PA, Population 1,447,395

Eastern State Penitentiary in Philadelphia is currently attracting in excess of 250,000 visitors annually (Elk, 2011), but has a much smaller visitor-to-resident ratio of 0.17 given the large population of the greater Philadelphia metropolitan area. In addition, the city of Philadelphia also reports 37.4 million visitors annually (Greater Philadelphia Tourism Marketing Corporation, 2011). Other prisons used for comparison in table 3 included Alcatraz in San Francisco, CA. Data was not readily available from each peer institution; however, data for those with available information are shown on Table 3.

Table 3: Prison Comparisons by Population, Visitors per Year and Tourists per Year (2011)

Location	Population	City Visitors per year	Prison Site Tourists per year (ratio)	Source
Jefferson City, MO (MSP)	41,297	N/A	17,203 (0.42)	U.S. Census Picker, Steve
San Francisco, CA (Alcatraz)	808,976	16 M	1.4 M (1.73)	U.S. Census Kiely, Tom Phelps, Nicki California State Parks
Philadelphia, PA (ESP)	1,447,395	37.4 M	250,000 (0.17)	Elk, Sally City of Philadelphia

While perhaps not a direct comparison, Alcatraz has a fascinating history which closely aligns with the MSP. According to Tom Kiely, EVP of Tourism for San Francisco Travel, Alcatraz is used as an instrumental part of the marketing strategy for the San Francisco area. Tom said that "San Francisco received approximately 16M visitors in 2010, generating $8B in revenue for the city, supporting 70K jobs and contributing $500M in tax revenue to the city's general fund. It is our number one industry (Kiely, 2011)." One constraint on Alcatraz is that the U.S. Federal guidelines only allow 3,000 visitors per day during peak portions of the summer which limits the total number of guests allowed to visit the site. Nicki Phelps from the Parks Conservancy suggested that the number of visitors per year could double if it was allowed (Phelps, 2011). In addition, Nicki mentioned that one reoccurring topic that comes up at Alcatraz is development of a casino on site which would not be permissible on federal park land and would distract from the educational objectives of the Alcatraz site. A casino would not be feasible at the MSP either because the casino would need to be on the water as required by the state of Missouri, which could technically be overcome, and because the city of Jefferson has voted against casino development in multiple local elections. The site location for Alcatraz and MSP are both highly desirable with Alcatraz being located in the San Francisco Bay and the MSP located in downtown Jefferson City, situated between the major metro areas of St. Louis and Kansas City, along the Missouri River.

One challenge in attaining information from other peer institutions, e.g., West Virginia Penitentiary and Ohio State Reformatory, is the lack of resources at smaller historical sites and the seasonal closure of the facilities in the winter months. For example, the city of Jefferson and Marshall County (West Virginia Penitentiary) do not have the types of data collection resources which are available to the city of Philadelphia and San Francisco. Most of the facilities close entirely or have limited hours during the winter months. The data from peer institutions illustrates the market potential for the MSP. With hundreds of thousands and millions of visitors touring some of these facilities, there is potential to capture a larger market for prison tours.

FINDINGS AND RESULTS

In order to generate revenue and improve the visual appearance of MSP, the following criteria were considered:

- The constituents and stakeholders that will pressure the prioritization of their agenda(s) for MSP
- Industry trade organizations that share best practices and develop sustainability guidelines
- Marketing and outreach activities
- Forecasting to adequately plan for the visitor growth expected in the coming years

One of the primary decisions to be made is to what extent the prison should be restored and further developed for historical tours and/or commercial use. Because Jefferson City is not "land-locked," and therefore not in need of land to be developed, this has alleviated much of the opposition to MSP continuing to offer tours with a facility in less than ideal aesthetic condition. Appendix 6 provides photographs of the internal cell block conditions and appendix 7 shows the new prison located in a more rural location within the city. It is noteworthy that there is a new $80M federal courthouse directly across the street from the MSP and the city of Jefferson anticipated some complaints about the exterior of the MSP once that facility is fully operational. As such, some of the exterior renovation items were expected to see an increased priority due to political and community pressures. It was also anticipated that redevelopment will add value to the surrounding property values which are primarily residential properties directly bordering the MSP. Many of the residential properties in the area have been abandoned, so there is the potential for indirect aesthetic improvements to surrounding neighborhoods and areas.

One observation about historic prisons in general is that the supply chain support by third parties seems to be more limited than other tourism industries. Many of the prison sites operate independently and the support network in the form of associations is less developed than what is observed in other sectors such as the American Hotel & Lodging Association (http://www.ahla.com/). One organization that does exist is the American Correctional Association (ACA, http://www.aca.org/), which generally seems to cater more to the needs of currently operating correction facilities rather than those licensed to operate historic tours. Special events and outreach activities will remain critical to MSP. For example, items such as the November 2011 airing of MSP on the Sy Fy Network's Ghost Hunters (http://www.syfy.com/ghosthunters/) continue to be a wonderful promotional tool for marketing and advertising the prison.

Forecasting techniques were used to estimate the number of visitors based on the rapid growth rate currently being observed. A linear trend forecast equation for the historical data from 2009 to 2011 yielded a forecast equation of $y = 6956.5 (X) – 3082$ which projected the 2012 ($X = 4$) visitors to be 24,744 ($R^2 = 97.93$ percent); the actual visitor count for 2012 was 19,121 leading to a large deviation. In addition, the 2013 unexpected shutdown event led to a similar large deviation (see table 4). This exemplifies the dangers of linear trend forecasting; despite a high R-square value for the early data, the forecast did not yield very accurate results. Similarly, the projected revenue based on a linear regression forecast was $381,567 for 2012 (actual was $275,471). Fortunately, it was noted in 2011 that this would be an unrealistic growth expectation biased by the large increase from 2009 to 2010, but with a coefficient of determination (R^2) so close to 1 ($R^2 = 98.5$ percent), this was presumed to be a fairly accurate forecast for 2012. Figure 8 shows this data plotted in a graphical format from 2011 and Figure 9 is the updated version through 2015.

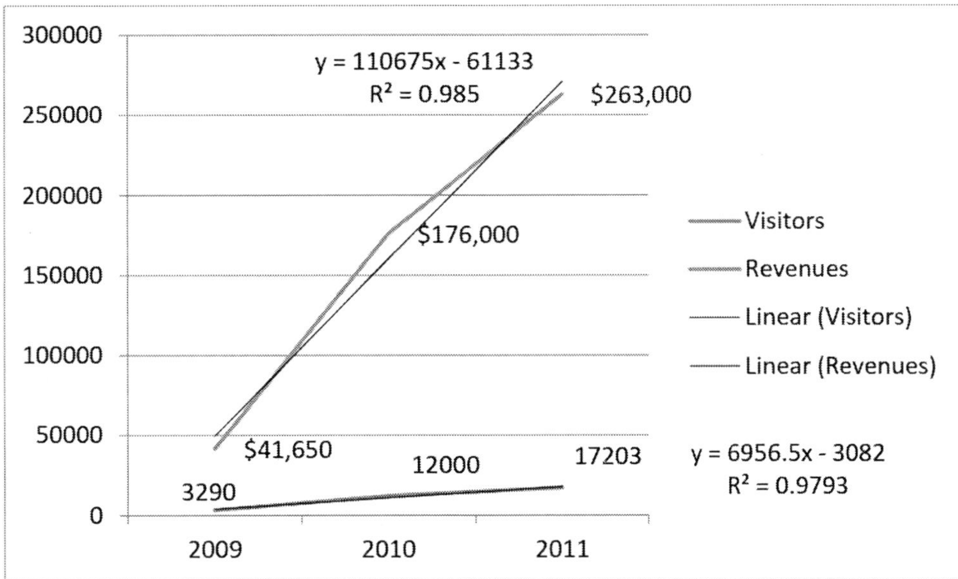

Figure 8: MSP Visitor and Revenue Data with Linear Trend Forecasts (2009 to 2011)

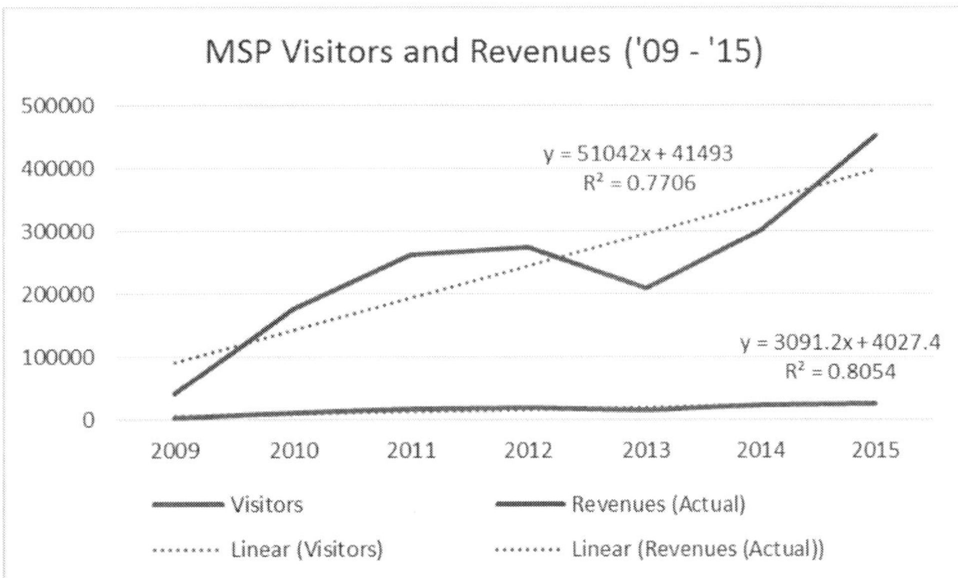

Figure 9: MSP Visitor and Revenue Data with Linear Trend Forecasts (2009 to 2015)

Table 4: Visitor Forecast Accuracy and MAD Error for '09-'11 and '09-'15

Year	Actual	09-'11 Forecast	09-'11 MAD	09-15' Forecast	09-15' MAD
2012	19121	24744	5623	16392.2	2728.8
2013	14581	31700.5	17119.5	19483.4	4902.4
2014	22605	38657	16052	22574.6	30.4
2015	25945	45613.5	19668.5	25665.8	279.2
2016		52570		28757	

Figures 8 & 9 and Table 4 provide a cautionary tale not to put too much weight behind forecasts using limited historical data, even with high R-square values. It also shows how much unexpected events or anomalies, such as the 2013 repair, can 'wreak havoc,' on forecasts. Table 4 shows the dramatic increase in forecast accuracy with more data, the error measured by the MAD decreased from 58,463 visitors to 7,941 visitors over the same time period. The forecast for 28,757 visitors seems to be in line with what should be expected based on more recent annual growth rates.

RECOMMENDATIONS

The recommendations for MSP to increase tourist traffic and revenues are as follows:

- Utilize a benefit analysis to prioritize the redevelopment projects (taxonomy provided)
- Estimate revenues for offering special events, such as weddings
- Increase the operating schedule to offer year round tours
- Offer audio guided tours
- Provide shuttle services from St. Louis and Kansas City (e.g., via Amtrak Line)
- Offer community days
- Join or launch a professional association for historical prison tour operators
- Development of office space for state and local government employees
- Increase the priority to develop on-site lodging facilities

A benefits analysis should be conducted for various scenarios. Here are five sample scenarios or taxonomy for the analysis: (1) complete demolition of the prison; (2) complete restoration of the prison; (3) partial restoration of the prison; (4) construction of a convention center; and (5) construction of a private commercial site integrated with a portion of the existing prison. A weighted-factor method should be used similar to Megan Epler Wood's (2011) example for condominiums vs. hotel development in Belize (Wood, 2011) and those used by Heizer and Render (Heizer & Render, 2010). Some of the specific projects Executive Director Picker and others referenced in State of Missouri reports include:

- Development of offices for state and local government employees (The State of Missouri, Division of Design & Construction, 2002)
- Development of Building No. 5 into a hotel
    - One peer example is the Liberty Hotel in Boston (http://www.libertyhotel.com/) which is the former Charles Street Jail
- Relocating the gas chamber structure closer to the upper yard

- Ensuring that the old powerhouse structure does not have any hazardous materials present
- Building maintenance and upkeep for the historic buildings

Another prospective growth opportunity for MSP is the addition of wedding services. According to the TheKnot.com and as reported by Forbes.com, the average U.S. wedding costs $28,000 with guests often spending over $300 on travel and lodging (Casserly, 2010). The average number of wedding guests that attend a wedding according to a 2011 TheKnot.com survey is 141 (XO Group, Inc. - The Knot, Inc., 2011). Assuming this number of guests would spend $300 each that would amount to over $42,000 per wedding. Assuming that there would be one wedding per weekend in the spring and fall, if we estimate that we would have 26 wedding weekends, this would amount to nearly $1.1M in additional revenue for the convention and visitor's bureau and their partner businesses. Note that not all of the average 141 guests would be spending $300 and that Midwestern weddings often have larger guest lists, e.g., Iowa and Nebraska average over 200 guests per wedding event (XO Group, Inc. - The Knot, Inc., 2011). These figures also do not include a wedding venue charge which is often $300, $500, $1,000, etc. per event. In Missouri, weddings in caves and caverns across the state are very popular and there has been an interest expressed in having wedding ceremonies and receptions at the MSP. There also could be significant implications on regular tours and traffic if weddings become a dominant revenue stream, but this phenomenon is not unprecedented. For example, country clubs that operate banquet facilities and golf courses have shifted in the direction of weddings and special events as well.

It would also be beneficial if MSP were to be open year round, even if the number of tour options and services were to be greatly reduced during the winter months. One opportunity to take advantage of the winter tour season would be to offer audio tours during non-peak times to reduce the necessary staff level while still generating revenue from visitors. One of the issues inherent with this is the requirement to have snow removal (Picker, 2011). Another issue would be having restroom and heated facilities at the site. A final concern is losing some of the value added by having tour guides who have worked with in-mates at the MSP share their stories and experiences. This is also an opportunity to capture some of these stories in an audio format before the tour guides retire. Succession planning must be considered as well for current tour guides and staff.

Another opportunity to entice additional visitors would be to offer a shuttle service from St. Louis and/or Kansas City. This could be accomplished by offering a small tour in St. Louis, perhaps of a local jail, and providing an Amtrak train ticket for a day trip to Jefferson City to tour the MSP. A shuttle bus or van would need to transport guests the short distance from the Amtrak station to the MSP. This would be an expansion to the existing model which brings tours buses with visitors from St. Louis (Cabbage & Bureau, 2011).

Another recommendation is to offer "community days," in which local residents of Jefferson City and the surrounding cities and counties could visit the MSP at a reduced rate or no charge to continue to promote the importance of the penitentiary as a historical landmark and critical tourism location for the city and state. By exposing residents and giving them a firsthand look at the potential of the site, they will begin to feel a stake in the success of the facility. This would also help convey the mission of the prison tour operations to any remaining skeptics that would like to cease operations or re-develop the site. This type of cultural change is critical to sustainable tourism management.

A final recommendation is the establishment of a national or international association of prison tour operators to help bolster marketing efforts and to ensure the establishment of sustainability guidelines for the industry. One of the associations covered in this course is the American Lodging Association (http://www.ahla.com/) and their sustainability guidelines. As operations continue to expand, additional peer benchmarking would be beneficial. One international peer for comparison would be the Kilmainham Gaol in Dublin, Ireland (http://www.heritageireland.ie/en/dublin/kilmainhamgaol/).

CONCLUSION AND FUTURE WORK

In an attempt to generate revenue to improve the infrastructure, an economic development tax referendum was on the local ballot in February 2012 to generate additional funds for upkeep and improvements. The economic development tax plan on the ballot for February 2012 was initiated to provide an invaluable resource in terms of funding to support the redevelopment commission's strategic plans.

The data, marketing collateral & literature and services offered (such as a new museum which opened in 2013) create challenges in when looking to create stable forecast projections for visitors and revenues. Unexpected repairs, such as those observed in 2013, dynamic leasing agreements in the early years of this study, and varying expenses (e.g., labor, insurance, advertising, etc.) all create challenges for the MSP management team. MSP is a non-profit enterprise, so all the proceeds and profits go back into MSP renovations.

There is a great deal of opportunity and excitement surrounding the continued redevelopment, sustainability management practices, and "dark tourism," revenue potential at the MSP. The recommendations provided herein will help generate additional revenue, adequately staff the operation, and continue the pursuit of unanimous community approval to reduce aesthetic pollution from the MSP. Further work includes verifying the actual results to the recommendations provided here post-implementation and tracking the performance of MSP's operations.

APPENDIX 1

MSP History

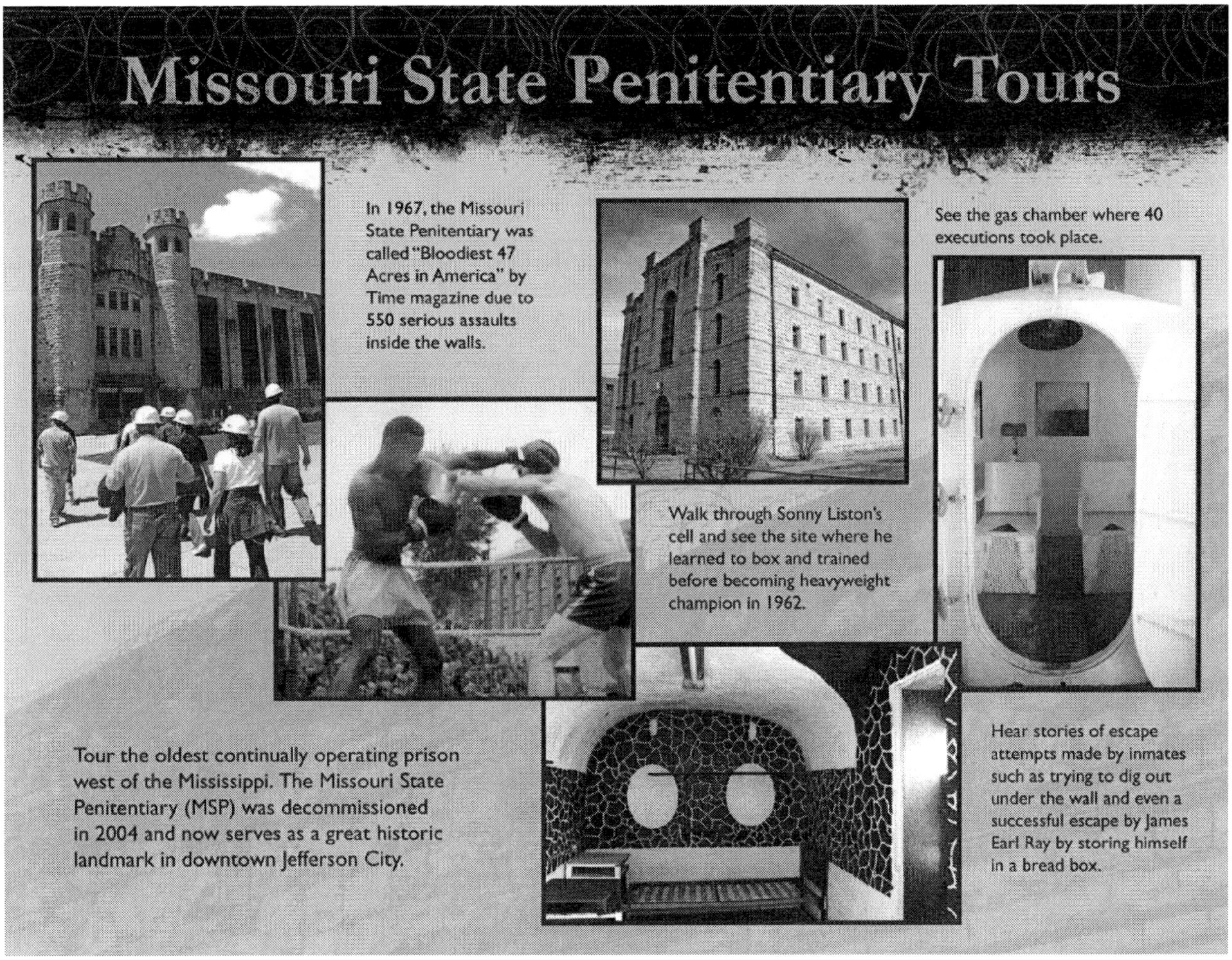

APPENDIX 2

MSP Tour Options (circa 2011)

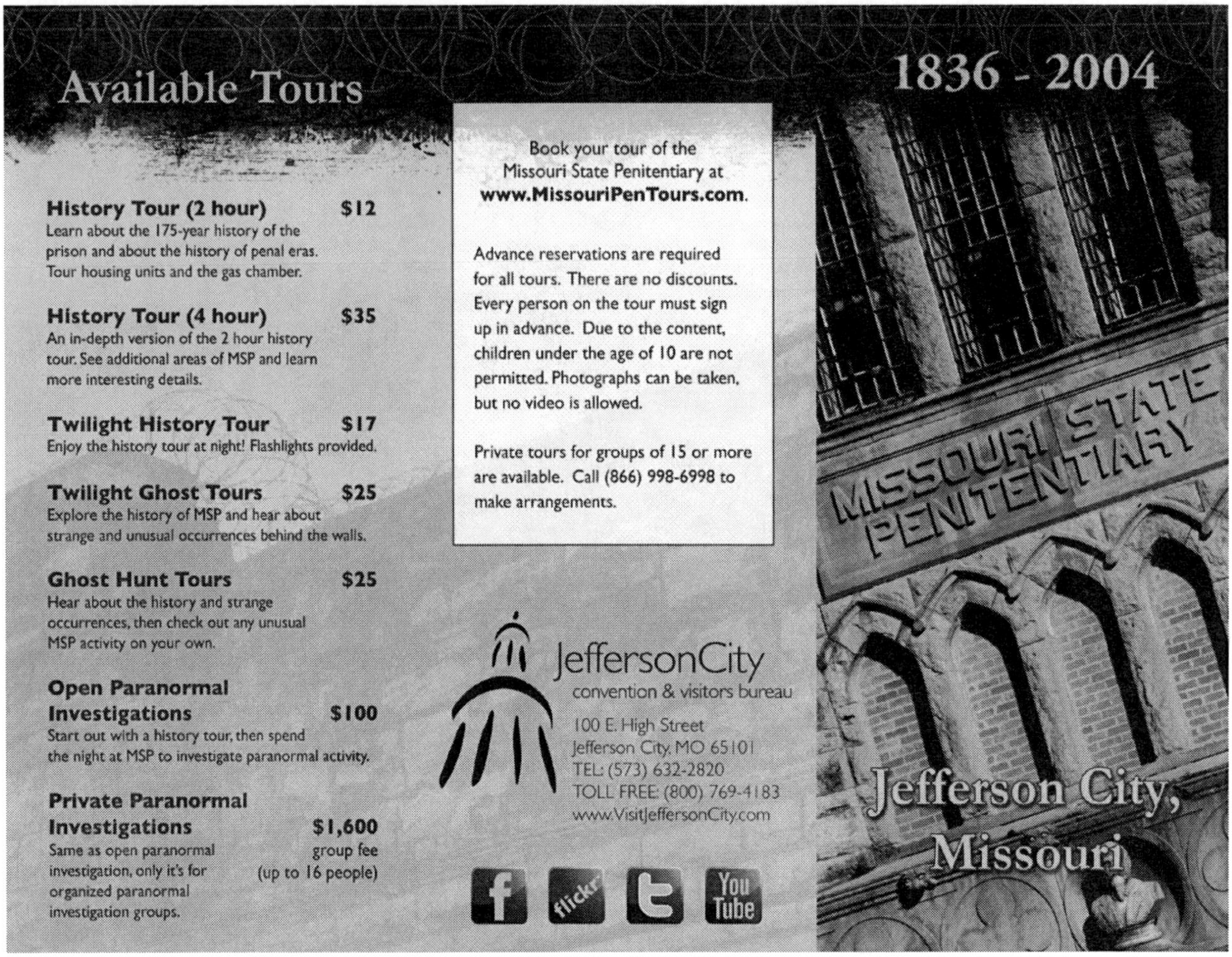

APPENDIX 3

MSP Tri-Fold (circa 2016)

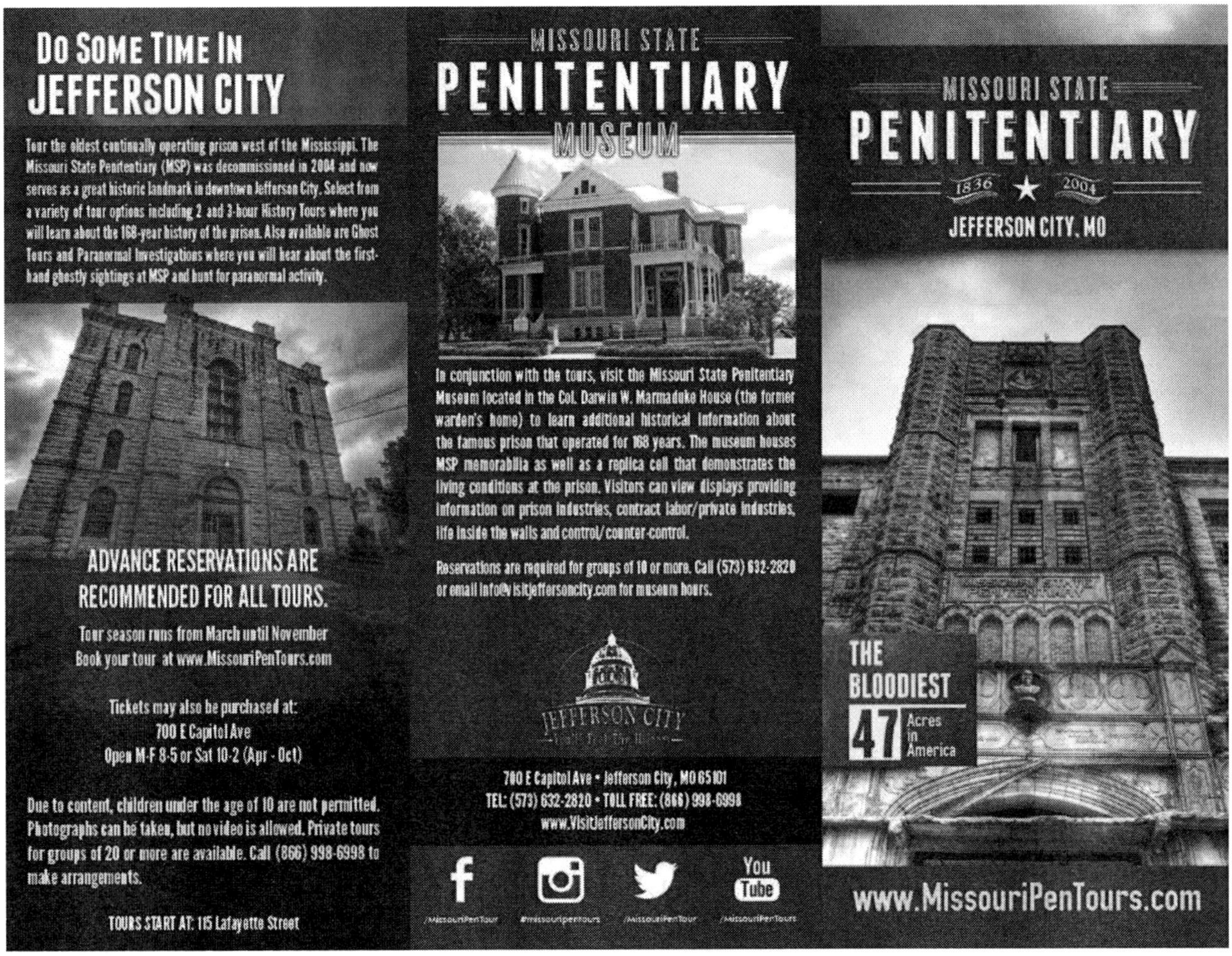

APPENDIX 4

MSP Tri-Fold Tour Options and Pricing (circa 2016)

APPENDIX 5

MSP Cell Block Photos

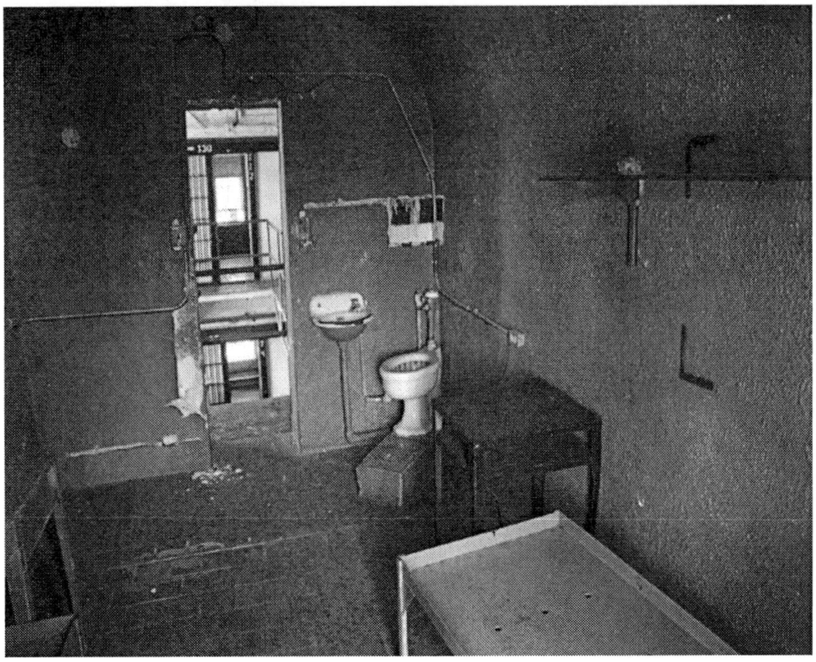

APPENDIX 6

New Prison in Jefferson City, Missouri

REFERENCES

Bonds, A. (2013). Economic development, racialization, and privilege: "Yes in my backyard" prison politics and the reinvention of Madras, Oregon. Annals of the Association of American Geographers, 103(6), 1389-1405.

Bumblauskas, D., Bumblauskas, P., Sapkota, K., Ahsan, M., Misra, P. (2016). Is demand chain management the new supply chain management? Will the demand channel trump the supply channel? Production and Operations Management Society (POMS) 2016 Conference. Orlando, Florida. Available: https://www.pomsmeetings.org/ConfPapers/065/065-0265.pdf.

Cabbage, C., & Bureau, J. C. (Directors). (2011). Missouri State Penitentiary [Motion Picture].

Cannon-Brookes, P. (2001). Dark Tourism: The Attraction of Death and Disaster-By John Lennon and Malcom Foley. Museum Management and Curatorship, 19(2), 221-223.

Casserly, M. (2010, April 22). How Much Should You Spend On A Wedding Gift? Retrieved December 12, 2011, from Forbes.com: http://www.forbes.com/2010/04/22/wedding-gift-shopping-forbes-woman-time-registry.html

City-Data. (2010). City-Data Jefferson City, MO. Retrieved December 12, 2011, from City-Data.com: http://www.city-data.com/housing/houses-Jefferson-City-Missouri.html

Curtin, S., & Wilkes, K. (2005). British wildlife tourism operators: current issues and typologies. Current Issues in Tourism, 8(6), 455-478.

Douglas, M. (1966, 2003). Purity and Danger: An Analysis of the Concepts of Pollution and Taboo. New York: Routledge.

Duffield, C. F. (2005). PPPs in Australia. Public private partnerships: Opportunities and challenges, 5-14.

Dunlap, D. (2001, May 2). Making a Museum Where Thousands Did Their Time. New York Times, Retrieved July 13, 2016, from nytimes.com: http://www.nytimes.com/2001/05/02/arts/02DUNL.html.

Elk, S. (2011, December 2). President and CEO. (name removed for blind peer review, Interviewer) Golden Gate National Parks Conservancy. (2011). Alcatraz. Retrieved December 12, 2011, from Golden Gate National Parks Conservancy: http://www.parksconservancy.org/visit/alcatraz/alcatraz-tours.html

Gillespie, D., & [name removed for blind peer review] (Interviewed 2016, March 24). Executive Director, Jefferson City Convention and Visitors Bureau. (name removed for blind peer review, Interviewer)

Greater Philadelphia Tourism Marketing Corporation. (2011). Research and Publications. Retrieved December 12, 2011, from Philadelphia and the Countryside: http://www.visitphilly.com/research/

Heizer, J., & Render, B. (2010). Operations Management. Upper Saddle River: Prentice Hall, Pearson, Inc.

Holden, A. (2008). Environment and Tourism. New York: Routledge.

Jefferson City Convention and Visitors Bureau. (n.d.). Homepage. Retrieved September 19, 2011, from Homepage: http://visitjeffersoncity.com/

Jefferson City Convention and Visitors Bureau. (n.d.). Missouri State Penitentiary. Retrieved October 12, 2011, from Missouri State Penitentiary History and Timeline: http://www.missouripentours.com/history/timeline.html

Kiely, T. (2011, November and December, 14 and 12 respectively). EVP Tourism, San Francisco Travel. (name removed for blind peer review, Interviewer).

KOMU News. (2007, June 18). KOMU.com. Retrieved September 19, 2011, from Jefferson City Battle: http://www.komu.com/news/jefferson-city-battle/

KOMU News. (2010, October 21). KOMU.com. Retrieved September 19, 2011, from Jefferson City Unveils Plans for Conference Center: http://www.komu.com/news/jefferson-city-unveils-plans-for-conference-center/

Lennon, J. J., & Foley, M. (2000). Dark tourism: The Attraction of Death and Disaster. Cengage Learning EMEA. London and New York, Continuum, ISBN 0-8264-5064-4.

Missouri Department of Economic Development. (n.d.). Missouri State Visitors Bureau. Retrieved October 12, 2011, from Missouri State Penitentiary Tours: www.visitmo.com/missouri-state-penitentiary-tours.aspx

Missouri State Penitentiary Redevelopment Commission. (2002). Master / Framework Plan. Jefferson City: Parsons HBA and the State of Missouri.

Missouri State Penitentiary Redevelopment Commission. (n.d.). Homepage. Retrieved December 12, 2011, from Missouri State Penitentiary Redevelopment Commission: http://oa.mo.gov/fmdc/dc/msp/index.htm

Phelps, N. (2011, December 15). Parks Conservancy. (name removed for blind peer review, Interviewer)

Picker, S., & [name removed for blind peer review] (Interviewed 2011, October 31). Executive Director, Jefferson City Convention and Visitors Bureau. (name removed for blind peer review, Interviewer)

Picker, S., & Fan, J. (Interviewed 2011, November 8). Executive Director, Jefferson City Convention and Visitors Bureau. (name removed for blind peer review, Interviewer)

Poria, Y., Butler, R., & Airey, D. (2003). Tourism, religion and religiosity: A holy mess. Current issues in tourism, 6(4), 40-363.

Randall, A., Ives, B., & Eastman, C. (1974). Bidding games for valuation of aesthetic environmental improvements. Journal of environmental Economics and Management, 1(2), 132-149.

Reisinger, Y., & Steiner, C. (2006). Reconceptualising interpretation: The role of tour guides in authentic tourism. Current Issues in Tourism, 9(6), 481-498.

Salomone, J. (2004a). A low security prison for women: A best practice in Western Australia. In Forum on Corrections Research 16(1), 34-37.

Salomone, J. (2004b). Towards best practice in women's corrections: the Western Australian low security prison for women. Department of Justice, Australia.

Smith, W. W. (2002). Dark Tourism: The Attraction of Death and Disaster-By John Lennon and Malcom Foley. Annals of Tourism Research, 4(29), 1188-1189.

State of Missouri, Division of Facilities Management. (2006). MSP Redevelopment District Design Guidelines. Jefferson City: State of Missouri.
Strange, C., & Kempa, M. (2003). Shades of dark tourism: Alcatraz and Robben Island. Annals of Tourism Research, 30(2), 386-405.

The State of Missouri, Division of Design & Contruction. (2002). Framework Plan For The MSP Redevelopment Project . Jefferson City: MSP Redevelopment Commission.
U.S. Census Bureau and Google Data. (2008, July). Google Public Data. Retrieved December 12, 2011, from Google: http://www.google.com/publicdata/explore?ds=kf7tgg1uo9ude_&met_y=population&idim=county:06075&dl=en&hl=en&q=san+francisco+ca+population

Stone, P., & Sharpley, R. (2008). Consuming dark tourism: A thanatological perspective. Annals of tourism Research, 35(2), 574-595.

Tarlow, P. E. (2007). Dark tourism. Niche Tourism: Contemporary Issues and Trends, Elsevier, Novelli, M. (ed.), 47-59.

Tudor, D. T., & Williams, A. T. (2003). Public perception and opinion of visible beach aesthetic pollution: the utilisation of photography. Journal of Coastal Research, 19(4), 1104-1115.

Uhlenbrock, T. (2009, June 03). Pittsburgh Post Gazette. Retrieved October 12, 2011, from Missouri prison that once held Pretty Boy Floyd and James Earl Ray opens for tours: http://www.post-gazette.com/pg/09154/969555-37.stm

Wood, M. E. (2011, November 10). Responsible Destination Development and Stewardship. Harvard ENVR E-118. Cambridge, MA, USA: Harvard Extension School.

XO Group, Inc. - The Knot, Inc. (2011, March 2). The Knot Unveils 2010 Real Weddings Survey Results (Press Release). Retrieved December 12, 2011, from XO Group, Inc.:

http://www.xogroupinc.com/press-releases-home/2011-press-releases/2011-03-02-2011-real-weddings-survey-results.aspx

Yuill, S. M. (2004). Dark tourism: understanding visitor motivation at sites of death and disaster (Thesis, Texas A&M University).

DECISION SCIENCES INSTITUTE

The Analysis of E-product Sales Affected by Online Word-of-Mouth and E-commerce Service Quality Based on Observational Learning

Ming Lei
Peking University
leiming@gsm.pku.edu.cn

Mingxi Zhang
Peking University
mxzhang@pku.edu.cn

Honghui Deng
University of Nevada Las Vegas
honghui.deng@unlv.edu

Marcus A. Rothenberger
University of Nevada Las Vegas
marcus.rothenberger@unlv.edu

Natasa Christodoulidou
California State University Dominguez Hills
christodoulidou@csudh.edu

ABSTRACT

Information on product sales pages is an important role in consumers' purchase decisions in e-commerce. This paper study two categories of information, online word-of-mouth (WOM) and E-commerce service quality (e-SQ) based on observational learning (OL), by data from the largest B2C platform- Alibaba.com. Our study adopts panel vector auto-regression (PVAR) model to explore the dynamic interactive effects among product sales, WOM and E-SQ OL. We investigate the forecast capability among product sales, online reviews of WOM and OL information about e-SQ through impulse response function analysis and forecast error variance decomposition. The findings are interesting and useful for real e-business.

KEYWORDS: Online word-of-mouth, Online observational learning, E-commerce service quality, Panel vector auto-regression.

INTRODUCTION

Over the last few years, online shopping has become more and more popular, especially for large online shopping mall (such as Amazon.com,Tmall.com). And their reputation and quality assurance are extensively accepted by consumers. Faced with a superb collection of online products, consumers are more likely to rely on the information in product sales page, in order to save time and reduce the risk of purchase (Bikhchandani et al., 1998). Among the tremendous information shown on page, online word-of-mouth (WOM) and online observation learning (OL) are two kinds of vital user-generated information. The extant researches have shown that compared to the traditional marketing activities, the user-generated information is more powerful in the choice behavior on subsequent consumers (Trusov et al., 2009).

In the field of marketing, the social interaction based on opinion or perference is called WOM (Arndt, 1967). And it is named as online WOM if the information is disseminated through network media (Godes et al., 2005). In the field of psychology and economics, the social interaction based on action or behavior is called OL (Bandura, 1977; Bikhchandani et al, 1998). For example, when making choice between two restaurants, customers might be greatly influenced by their friends advice or just simply observate the number of persons who are having meals in each restaurant, even they have own standards and reasons to choose restaurant (Becker, 1991). When this observation is based on metword information, it is named as online OL. The difference between online OL and WOM is mainly reflected in two aspects of information quantity and credibility in the socail interaction. Compared with the latter, the former contains less information (Chen et al., 2011). Bikhchandani (1998) pointed out that online WOM usually includes consumer advice or recommendation (eg. five star review), also the reasons about making a certain evaluation such as describing the use experiences about product. While online OL only reveals the comprehensive results of other consuming behaviors about some product such as appearing on sales ranking list, but does not provide the reasons leading to the result.

In this paper, we will focus on the information of online comments based WOM and E-commerce service quality (e-SQ) based OL. Online comments play an important role in shaping consumers' attitudes and buying behavior which will have influence on the sales of products (such as Chevalier and Mayzlin, 2006). As a special OL information , e-SQ has significant impact on consumers' satisfaction and purchase intention (such as Ho and Lee, 2007). This means that the two types of information have effects on the sales of products both directly and indirectly. So, it is worth to study weather the three elements have dynamic interactions between each other.

In recent years, some scholars have studied the dynamic interaction between the sales of products (or sales) and online WOM. Duan et al.(2008) and Lu et al.(2013) treat the box office and the restaurant income as the research object respectively and fond the dynamic interaction between consumers' offline behavior and online WOM. Different frome this papers, our study based on large B2C electric business platform and reveals the dynamic interaction between online WOM and consumers' noline behaviors. For the empirical model, Some literatures rely on Vecror Auto-Regression (VAR) to analyze the dynamic interaction between online WOM and consumers' behaviors using long time series data of one product (such as stock, new menber registration, constomer value growth) (Luo, 2009; Tirunilla and Tellis, 2012; Trusov et al., 2009; Villanueva, 2008). However, we employ Panel Vector Auto-Regression (PVAR) model explore the topic with panel data of multiple products. For more details, we use the unique empirical data sources of online comment display and measure the positive WOM with the percentage of positive comments label which are derived by text mining of background system. This may provide more detailed information than previous studies such as Sonnier et al.(2011)and Ho-Dac et al.(2013) which regard five and four stars as positive WOM and three stars as negative WOM.

In addition, some scholars have studied the mutual influence on consumer behavior and e-SQ. Finn(2011) reveals the nonlinear effect of e-SQ index on consumer satisfaction. Delone(2003) found that the information quality and consumers satisfaction were positive related. Udo(2010) found that e-SQ not only had a signigicant direct impact on consumer purchase intention but also had a indirect effect through the consumer satisfaction as the intermediate variable. Olrunniwo(2006) pointed out that the electric service manager should adjust operation strategy to improve service quality, which would have a positive influence on consumer purchase intention. Chang(2009) performed an experiment with questionnaire and found that the electric service quality had an effect on consumer loyalty though consumer satisfaction. This literatures have revealed the impact of e-SQ on consumer satisfaction, purchase intention and loyalty, among which few attention have been paid to the direction relation between e-SQ and product sales. This paper focuses on the impact of e-SQ on product sales with the help of the sales data from larg B2C business platform. In additon, we also study the influence of product sales on e-SQ using dynamic model.

Specifically, the topic studied here can be summarized as follows: whether there are long term dynamic interaction between the information of WOM and e-SQ based online OL? Whether product sales have dynamic feedback effect on the information of WOM and e-SQ based online OL? Is it the dynamic cross effect exist between the two kinds of information? Despite answering the three questions, this study will also explore whether the information of product sales, WOM and online OL can predict each other. Specifically, our studies cover two aspects: 1) The moving trends of the three kinds of information variables in the future period if one of them bear a sudden change at present. 2) what extent will an information variable fluctuation contribute to the three kinds of information variables' future multi period fluctuation (or the ability to explain).

DATA DESCRIPTION and RESEARCH STRATEGY

Data

Our data comes from the largest B2C e-commerce platform of China – tmall.com, whose annual sales is one thousand billion RMB in 2012. This paper use notebook data only in empirical study. By the aid of webpage data collection tool, we grab relavant data in the sales page once a week. In order to assure that all of data are obtained in the same moment which can avoid some deviations resulted by data updating in the page due to customers purchase behaviors, we choose to collect data between am 0 and am 6:00 each time. In this period, the customers seldom go to buy on internet and informaiton on product sales page is relatively static. We have obtain data spanning July 15, 2013 to January 13, 2014 (27 weeks). Throughout this period the produts on the shelf was weekly up dataed frequently, that made the panel data extremely unbanlanced. In this study, we only use the data collected from July 29, 2013 to December 9, 2013 (20 weeks) to include more balanced sample data which is required by the PVAR model used [The 20 weeks sample can be interpreted as the data between the 3rd and the 22nd week of the full sample. The main reason for this refinement is that we didn't get the full data of the first two weeks due to inefficiently use of the software. In addition, Tmall revised its sales page design and product classification in the 23rd week, which resulted in a greater changes of the products. So if we extend panel time span, the sample capacity will become much smaller].

Variable Definition

The study contains 3types of variables: product sales, comments based WOM, e-SQ based online OL information (such as:"Description Accordance" and "Refund Rate")。 The logarithm of product sales ($Ln\_wsales_{i,t}$) represent the logarithm of product *i*'s sales at week *t*.

The logarithm of the change of comment volume ($Ln\_volume_{i,t}$) expresses the logarithm of the incremental number of product *i*'s comments in week *t* compared to week *t*-1， unlike most studies use total number of comments (log) measure WOM (such as Chevalier and mayzlin, 2006; Gu et al. 2012). We can explain the relationship between sales and comments more precisely with the help of incremental number of comments (log) because the weekly sales is incremental concept compared to the total sales. The percentage of positive commet tags ($Positive_{i,t}$) means that the proportion of the number of products *i*'s positive comment lags to that of total comment lags up to week *t* [We neglect the negative comments tags in this paper because the positive tags' ratio is highly correlated with the negative ones]. Unlike previous literature who regared five stars (or four stars) as positive comments and one stars (or two stars) as negative ones, this paper use the ratio of positive comment tags to measure the dgree of positive evaluation level. The reason why we choose this variable is that our data comes from Tmall, among which the red ones means positive tags and the green ones says the negative tags [Tmall will analyze each comments by text mining. When the system finds the contents contain a tag, this tag's number will plus 1. Consumers can view the summary information about all the tags in panel called "Cumulative Evaluation" directly]. The text mining technology help Tmall analyze the comments more deeply and provide the consumers with more precise information about the product relative to most B2C platform through out the world, who use just a few "stars" to measure the property of products.

"Description Accordance" ($Depict_{i,t}$) expresses the consistency between product *i*'s description in sellers page and the reality in week *t* and the percentage to average level in the same industry. The calculation rules: (the score of seller's store-the average score of the same industry)/(the highest score of the same industry –the average score of the same industry). "Refund Rate" ($Refund_{i,t}$) means the absolute value of seller's return rate of product *i* in week *t* relative to the average rate of the same industry. The calculation rules: seller store refund rate - the same average refund rate in the same industry(unit: day).

Figure 1 Various Comments Tags about a Notebook in Tmall

As mentioned above, we choose Ln_volume and $Positive$ as proxy for comments based WOM while $Depict$ and $Refund$ as proxy for e-SQ based online OL information.

Statistical Description and Corelation Analysis

Similar to chapter 5, we use the log form of weekly sales and the change of comments [For simplicity, we will describe the logarithm of weekly product sales as "weekly product sales" and the logarithm of the change of comments as "the change of comments"] because product sales comply with the law of diminishing marginal. In general, the product sales will increase rapidly early after the product was shown on the shelves and the increase rate will gradually slow down as time goes by. For the same reason, the change of comments will also agree with the law of diminishing marginal. We also notice that Refund in the data sample have a large skewness and kurtosis [For the original refund data, the skewness is 20.35, kurtosis: 648.52] which comes from the fact that the "refund" speed of few sellers deviate greatly from the mean, even Inconsistent with common sense (such as: "refund" speed is 78.2 days slower than the average). In order to ensure the sample data is a balanced panel, we make all the refund values in the quantile interval of 1%~99%. That means the refund values in the quantile interval of 0-1% will be given the value of quantile at 1% and the values in the quantile interval of 99%~100% will be given the value of quantile at 99% [After the treatment, the skewness of refund is -0.520 and the kurtosis of refund is 2.623]. After the treatment, the descriptive statistics of all variables and correlation are shown in Table 1.

Table 1 The Descriptive Statistics and correlations of all variables

Variables	Mean	Std.	Min	Max	[1]	[2]	[3]	[4]	[5]
[1]Ln_wsales	0.622	1.012	0	6.819	1.000				
[2]Ln_volume	0.438	0.873	0	5.613	**0.879**	1.000			
[3]$Positive$	0.049	0.109	0	0.543	**0.547**	**0.540**	1.000		
[4]$Depict$	0.073	0.138	-0.028	0.448	0.037	0.040	0.029	1.000	
[5]$Refund$	-0.019	1.310	-2.890	2.020	0.063	0.060	0.027	0.072	1.000

Table 1 shows that comments based WOM (Ln_volume and$Positive$) and product sales are highly correlated and Ln_volume has a strong correlation with$Positive$. E-SQ based online OL information (Depict andRefund) is weekly correlated with product sales and the two OL variables also have a small correlation. In addition, WOM variables and online OL information variables are also weekly correlated [For simplicity, comments based WOM and WOM contain the same meaning and e-SQ, OL information, e-SQ based OL].

Methods

The purpose of this paper is to illustrate the dynamic interactions among product sales, comments based WOM and e-SQ based online OL information. The most appropriate method is Panel Vector Autoregression (PVAR) model since it can analyze dynamic interactions among endogenous variables. Time series based Vector Autoregression (VAR) model was proposed by Sims in 1980 and was extented to PVAR model by Holtz-Eakin et al. (1998) and then was developed and extented by Lütkepohl (2007). Now, PVAR have become a useful tool to study variables' dynamic interactions in panel analysis. PVAR model regards all the variables as endogenous variables [Actually, PVAR model can also analyze exogenous variables, but the model is mainly used to study the long-term dynamic interactions among several endogenous variables. So in most cases, exogenous variables are excluded in this model] and each endogenous variable are considered as the function of all the endogenous variables lagged term. This modeling approach reveals the long-term dynamic interactions among all the endogenous variables, the model as shown in equation (1). The model mainly employs the Impulse Response Function (IRF) and forecast Error Variance Decomposition (FEVD) as analysis tools. The former one is used to describe how the current one standard deviation impulse of the error term in one endogenous variable will impact on the trends of its own and other endogenous variables in the future periods. The latter one is used to assess the contribution of each endogenous variable that bear a standardized shock in the current period to the volatility forecasts in the future periods of all the endogenous variables in the system.

$$y_{i,t} = AY_{i,t-n} + Bx_{it} + u_i + f_t + \varepsilon_{it} \tag{1}$$

Where, $y_{i,t} = (Ln_wsales_{i,t}, Ln_volume_{i,t}, Positive_{i,t}, Depict_{i,t}, Refund_{i,t})'$is the vector of endogenous variables, $Y_{i,t-n} = (y'_{i,t-1}, y'_{i,t-2}, \cdots, y'_{i,t-n})'$ is a $1\times5n$ vector [The optimal lag order n of the PVAR model will be determined by the Information Criterion in section 4.2] of all the endogenous variables lagged from 1 period to n periods. A is a $5\times5n$ matrix that consisted by the coefficients to be estimated. x_{it} is exogenous variable. This study do not include exogenous variable and all the variables will be treated as endogenous. u_i is individual effect and it is used to reflect individual differences that cannot be observed directly (such as quality, brand and so on). f_t is time effect and it is used to capture the common shocks of all the individuals at the same time (such as "double 11" promotion). ε_{it} is the error term that subjects to normal distribution.

The rest of the paper will be organized as followed. At first, we will apply System Generalized Method of Moments (SGMM) to estimate the parameters of PVAR model, in which we will clarify which lag term of product sales, comment based WOM and e-SQ based online OL information have significant impact on the current variation of the three kinds of variables. Secondly, we will study the three kinds of variables moving trends in the future periods qualitatively if they suffer one standard deviation shock in the current period using IRF. And then, we will do Granger Causality test for the three variables to verify whether they have significant forecasting power between each other. Finally, we will illustrate how the current fluctuations of the three variables forecast their future variations that are a quantitative perspective evaluation about the forecasting power of one variable's variation on the other's variation, by FEVD. The empirical analysis procedure is shown in Figure 2. Along the procedure, the depth of analysis is increasing and they are logically related to each other [More information in section 3.5 and the first paragraph of section 3.6]. The relationship among the regression results and the three analysis method (IRF, Granger Causality test and FEVD) can be summarized as followed. Generally speaking, if the lag term of variable A have significant impact on variables B, the current shock in A will influence B in the future periods significantly in IRF analysis, A will be the Granger Causality of B in Granger Causality test and the variation of A Have a strong ability to predict the variation of B in FEVD analysis. The empirical results of this paper are consistent with the rules.

Figure 2 the Logic Relationship about Empirical Analysis Procedure of PVAR Model

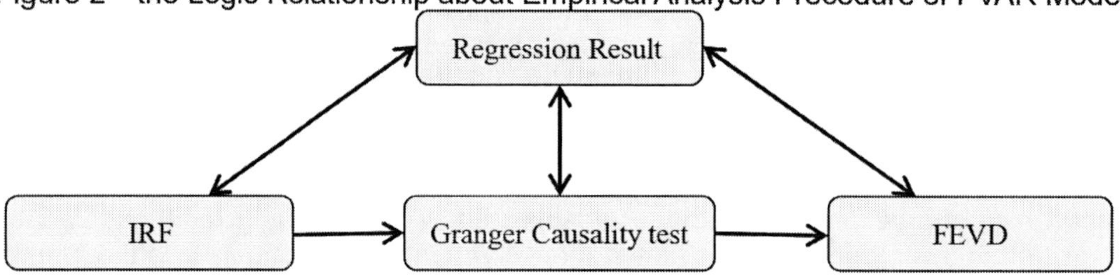

EMPIRICAL RESULTS and ANALYSIS

Stationarity Analysis for Panel Data

Non-stationary time series data means that any past shocks will permanently change the series pattern in the future which may lead to t-test failure and spurious regression (or pseudo related phenomena). Panel data is a sepcial kind of time series data and we need to test the stationary property of all the related variables before regression. In practice, researchers usually use unit root test such as Levin-Lin-Chu test (LLC), Harris-Tzavalis test (HT), Breitung test, Im-Pesaran-Shin test (IPS), Fisher Augmented Dickey-Fuller test (Fisher ADF). The five tests share the same null-hypothesis, that is unit root exists in all the variables of the panel data (non-stationary) [The first four test assume that all the variables in the panel share the same autoregression coefficient while Fisher ADF assumes that each individual has different autoregression coefficient]. The stationary tests for the five key variables in this study are shown in Table 2.

Table 2 the Unit Root Test for all the Variables in PVAR Model

Null-hypothesis	methods	*Ln_wsales*	*Ln_volume*	*Positive*	*Depict*	*Refund*
H_0 : unit	LLC	-22.4738***	-18.2709***	-28.1793***	-14.2187***	-3.8583***
	HT	-44.7098***	-28.0549***	-4.3300***	-2.0007**	-15.7275***

root exist in all the variables	Breitung	-7.6231***	-9.4347***	-3.5587***	-2.1763**	-11.9329***
	IPS	-20.2118***	-16.9324***	-6.4998***	**15.9903**	-12.7599***
	FisherADF	-22.5821***	-22.3656***	-39.1667***	-3.5586***	-26.2894***

（Note: *** p<0.01, ** p<0.05, * p<0.1）

Table 2 shows that nearly [All the test reject the null-hypothesis under 5% significance except that IPS cannot reject the null-hypothesis of "Description Accodance" (Depict). Considering the practical meaning, we don't conduct differential treatment on the variables] all the test reject that the five variables (product sales, the change of comments, positive ratio of tags, "Description Accordance", "Refund Rate") have unit root. That is to say all the variables related to all study is stationary.

Choosing the Lag Order for PVAR Model

We need to determine the optimal lag oreder before parameter estimation and variable forecast using PVAR model. In this study, we will use AIC (Akaike Information Criterion), BIC (Bayesian Information Criterion), HQIC (Hannan-Quinn Information Criterion) to get the optimal lag oreder [Information criterion is used to describe the degree of information loss between a model and the "true model". The smaller one information criterion is, the better the corresponding model is]. The results are shown in Table 3.

Table 3 Information Criterion for PVAR Model

Lag Order	AIC	BIC	HQIC
1	-4.9431	**-3.1921***	-4.3176
2	-5.0634	-3.1798	-4.3886
3	**-5.1741***	-3.1435	**-4.4444***

(Note: * stand for the optimal lag order under different information criterion)

Table 3 indicates that these three kinds of information criterion for the optimal lag order haven't formed a consistent conlusion. There some differences among the three test such as: BIC/HQIC tend to choose simpler model while AIC tends to choose more "plump" model. However, BIC/HQIC is always better than AIC under normal circumstances. In this study we choose one lag order model, which is more concise and ensure the estimation results can be better explained.

Regression Analysis

SGMM estimation method is often used in PVAR model, in which the endogenous variables' lag term is used as instrumental variables for the regression equation. Nervertheless, the conventional method for eliminating time effect and individual effect is Within-Group Mean Difference (or mean difference method). This method will induce SGMM estimation failure as the lag term of endogenous variables will correlated with random error term which will result in instrumental variable failure. In order to overcome this problem, Arellano and Bover (1995) proposed a "forward mean-differencing" method (also known as Helmert process) to eliminate the forward individual mean [Before we use "forward mean-differencing" method, conventional mean-differencing method is used for eliminating the time fixed effect]. In this way, the lag term of endogenous variables and transformed error term are irrelevant from each other. Thus, SGMM estimation can also get effective results [Our analysis method is based on the Stata command pvar, written by Dr. Lian Yujun and Dr. Love. In this study, we modified the command pvar to pvar2 and get the regression results] as shown in Table 4.

Table 4 the estimation results for PVAR model

Current	$Ln\_wsales_{i,t}$	$Ln\_volume_{i,t}$	$Positive_{i,t}$	$Depict_{i,t}$	$Refund_{i,t}$

term / Lag term	Estimateon	T-value	Estimat-eon	T-value	Estimat-eon	T-value	Estimat-eon	T-value	Estimat-eion	T-value
$Ln\_wsales_{i,t-1}$	**0.538***	7.04	**0.207***	4.28	**0.003**	2.12	0.000	0.17	0.024	0.46
$Ln\_volume_{i,t-1}$	**0.259***	5.01	**0.338***	8.84	0.001	1.08	0.000	0.09	-0.050	-1.46
$Positive_{i,t-1}$	**5.918**	2.28	-2.491	-1.51	**0.882***	17.69	0.035	0.48	0.010	0.00
$Depict_{i,t-1}$	**0.854***	2.91	0.075	0.40	0.001	0.08	**0.909***	52.19	0.483	1.20
$Refund_{i,t-1}$	-0.010	-0.97	0.010	1.54	0.000	0.45	0.001	0.76	**0.736***	31.05

(Note: *** p<0.01, ** p<0.05, * p<0.1)

In this paper, we will focus on four kinds of dynamic interactions, which derived from the analysis procedure of Villanueva (2008). The four interactions are summarized as followed. (1) the Reinforcement Effects among product sales, WOM and e-SQ based online OL information. Namely, we will discuss whether the lag terms of the three kinds of variables have impact on their current value. (2) the Direct Effects of WOM and e-SQ based online OL information on product sales. That is to say, we will evaluate the impact of the lag terms of WOM and e-SQ based online OL information variables on sales product. (3) the Feedback Effects of product sales, that is the impact of the lag terms of product sales on the current value of WOM and e-SQ based online OL information variables. (4) the Cross Effects between WOM and e-SQ based online OL information. Namely, we will study how will the lag terms of WOM variables impact e-SQ based online OL information variables and vice versa.

As illustrated in Table 4, we can get the following four conclusions. (1) On the whole, the first order lagged terms of all the variables have significant effect on themselves, which indicates that strengthening effect exist among product sales, WOM and e-SQ based OL information. (2) the first order lagged terms of the change of comments (log) and the percentage of positive tags have positive significant effect on the current state of product sales (log), consistent with most relevant studies such as Chevalier and Mayzlin (2006) [In their study the aggregate comments (lag) corresponds to the change of comments (log) and the percentage of "five star" comments corresponds to the percentage of positive comment tags]. The first order lagged term of "Description Accordance" has significant positive effect on the current state of product sales (log) while the first order lagged term of "Refund Rate" has no significant effect on the current state of product sales (log). This results indicate that whether the description on product sales page comply with the reality has a great influence on the potential purchasing decisions while consumers are not sensitive to the refund speed. This means that the two kinds of WOM variables and "Description Accordance" variable, one of online OL information variables, have a direct effect on product sales while the other variable of online OL information, "Refund Rate", has no direct effect on product sales. (3) The first order lagged term of weekly product sales (log) has significant impact on the current state of the change of comments (log) and the percentage of positive tags [Lu et al. (2013) fond that the first order lagged term of sales had significant effect on the number of comments in restaurant which is consistent with our results] but has no significant effect on the current state of "Description Accordance" and "Refund Rate", which indicate that product sales have feedback effect on WOM and have no effect on e-SQ based online OL information. (4) Neither the first order lagged term of two kinds of WOM variables nor the first order lagged term of e-SQ based online OL information variables have significant impact on the current state of each other. In addition, the first order lagged term of the change of comments (or the percentage of positive tags) has no significant effect on the current state of percentage of positive tags (or the change of comments) and the first order lagged term of "Description Accordance" (or "Refund Rate") has no significant impact on current state of "Refund Rate" (or "Description Accordance"). This means that no cross effect exist not only among WOM variables and e-SQ based online information variables but also between two kinds of variables of WOM (or e-SQ based online information).

IRF Analysis

IRF analysis begins with the error term of one equation in the PVAR system got one standard deviation shock, under the condition that the current and past state of all the other variables unchanged, and then detect the future moving trends of all the endogenous variables [IRF analysis uses Choleski decomposition process, namely orthogonal decomposition is applied to the standard deviation impact of the error term, to generate the IRF, through which all the endogenous variables are required to be ranked by some rules and some hypothesizes about the endogenous relationships are made that the variable ranked near the frond has the effect on the current and lagged term of variables ranked behind it while the latter variable only has impact on the lagged term of the former variables. This means that the front position variable has stronger exogeneity than that ranked later (Liyan Han and Jing Lou, 2010)]. This kind of method can describe the interaction between variables visually. In this study, we applied the Monte Carlo simulation 1000 times and got the IRF diagram as shown in Figure 3 in which the horizontal axis represents the response periods (the unit is week and the maximum periods is 10 weeks) and the vertical axis represents the response of different endogenous variables that react to the impact. In the picture, we also present the 95% confidence interval for the response and the middle line in each small diagram indicates the trend of specific shocks.

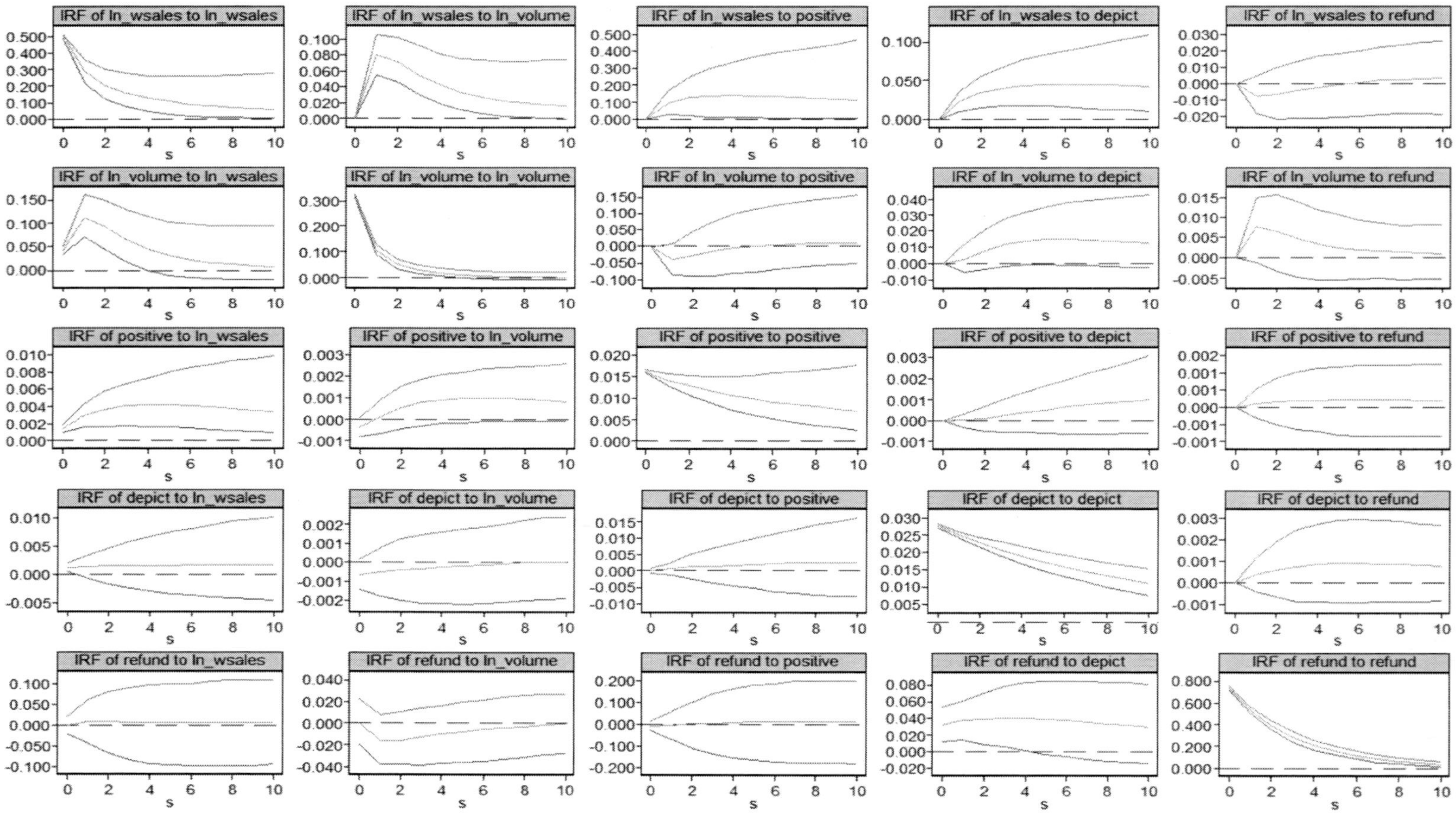

Figure 3 the IRF diagram of product weekly sales, comment based WOM and e-SQ based online OL information

Product weekly sales forecasting has shocks. As illustrated in the first line of Figure 3, as time goes by, the impact that product weekly sales have on itself decreases gradually but with a large value relatively. This means that the prediction of product sales is mainly due to itself. The change of comments has the greatest impact on the prediction of product weekly sales at the first week. The impact gradually decreased to 0 from sixth weeks, which indicates that the impact that the change of comments has on the prediction of product weekly sales weakened gradually with time. The impact that the percentage of positive tags have on the prediction of product weekly sales tends to be stable from the second week and maintains at a high level which means that the positive tags play a very important role in forecasting product sales. The impact that "Description Accordance" online OL information has on product weekly sales increases rapidly from the first four weeks and then slows down but the value is relatively small. The impact of "Refund Rate" is negligible relative to the factors analyzed above.

WOM prediction shocks. As shown in the second and third line of Figure 3, the impacts that the change of comments and the percentage of positive tags have on themselves reach the maximum in the current period and then the former decreases sharply and slows down after three weeks but the later decreases slowly at all the periods. Product weekly sales have the greatest impact on the change of comments at the first week and then the impact decreases gradually and become more flat after six weeks. The impact faced by the percentage of positive tags from product weekly sales increases gradually from the first week to the fourth week and then slowed down after four weeks. The impact that the percentage of positive tags have on the change of comments is negligible. On the contrary, the reverse impact increases gradually from the first week to the fourth week and then become more flat after four weeks with a relative small value. The impact that "Description Accordance" online OL information has on the change of comments resemble that of the percentage of positive tags. The impact that "Refund Rate" online OL information has on the change of comments reaches the maximum at the first week and then gradually decreased to 0. The impact that "Description Accordance" and "Refund Rate" online OL information has on the percentage of positive tags are negligible.

The e-SQ based online OL information shocks. As we can see from the fourth line and the fifth line, the impact that "Description Accordance" and "Refund Rate" have on themselves reach the maximum in the current period and decreased gradually. The impact that "Refund Rate" has on "Description Accordance" increases from the first week to the fourth week gradually and then tends to flat after four weeks while the reverse impact become flat from the first week. Product weekly sales have litter impact on e-SQ based OL information.

Panel Granger Causality Test

The analyses above have verified that the interaction exists among product weekly sales, WOM and e-SQ based online OL information. Nevertheless, the IRF can only describe the moving trends of the variables under the condition that one specific variable get a shock, which didn't reveal the causality relationships among the endogenous variables. At this section, Granger Causality test [Note: Granger Causality relationship is not the true causality relationship, it is a kind of dynamic relationship that reveals the "forecasting power" of one variable to another] is applied to answer this question. The result is shown in Table 5.

Table 5 Granger Causality Test for all the Endogenous Variables in PVAR Model

Granger Dependent Variables	Granger Independent Varables	H_0	χ^2	*P*
Weekly Sales(Log) (*Ln_wsales*)	*Ln_volume*	No	**25.118*****	0.000
	Positive	No	**5.2146****	0.022
	Depict	No	**8.4936*****	0.004
	Refund	No	0.9333	0.334
The change of comments (Log) (*Ln_volume*)	*Ln_wsales*	No	**18.33*****	0.000
	Positive	No	2.2799	0.131
	Depict	No	0.1622	0.687
	Refund	No	2.3768	0.123
The percentage of positive tags (*Positive*)	*Ln_wsales*	No	**4.5136****	0.034
	Ln_volume	No	1.1677	0.280
	Depict	No	0.0069	0.934
	Refund	No	0.1999	0.655
"Description Accordance" (*Depict*)	*Ln_wsales*	No	0.0301	0.862
	Ln_volume	No	0.0085	0.927
	Positive	No	0.2317	0.630
	Refund	No	0.5767	0.448
"Refund Rate" (*Refund*)	*Ln_wsales*	No	0.2143	0.643
	Ln_volume	No	2.1231	0.145
	Positive	No	0.0000	0.996
	Depict	No	1.4377	0.231

(Note: *** $p<0.01$, ** $p<0.05$, * $p<0.1$)

Table 5 shows that the change of comments (log), the percentage of positive tags, "Description Accordance" online OL information are Granger causal for product weekly sales (log). On the contrary, product weekly sales (log) is also Granger causal for the change of comments (log) and the percentage of positive tags but not for the two online OL information variables ("Description Accordance" and "Refund Rate"). In addition, neither the two variables of online WOM nor the two variables of online OL information have Granger Causality with each other and there is also no Granger Causality between WOM and online OL information. The Granger Causality relationships among the three kinds of variables are shown in Figure 4.

Figure 4 reveals that the Granger Causality relationships among the three kinds of variables are consistent with the results of PVAR estimation, i.e. (1)the change of comments (log) and the percentage of positive tags are reciprocal Granger Causality with product weekly sales (log) and in the regression results of PVAR, the first order lagged term of the change of comments (log) (or the percentage of positive tags) has significant impact on the current value of product weekly sales (log) but the converse is not significant. (2) "Description Accordance" online OL information is Granger Causality for product weekly sales but the converse is not, which is consistent with PVAR results that the first order lagged term of "Description Accordance" has significant impact on product weekly sales but the converse is not significant. (3) Granger Causality doesn't exist between WOM and e-SQ based OL information, two kinds of WOM variables, e-SQ based OL information, "Refund Rate" and product weekly sales (log), in which the first order lagged term of one variable also has no significant impact on the other in the results of PVAR.

Figure 4 the Granger Causality Relationships among Product Weekly Sales, Online WOM and E-SQ Based Online OL Information

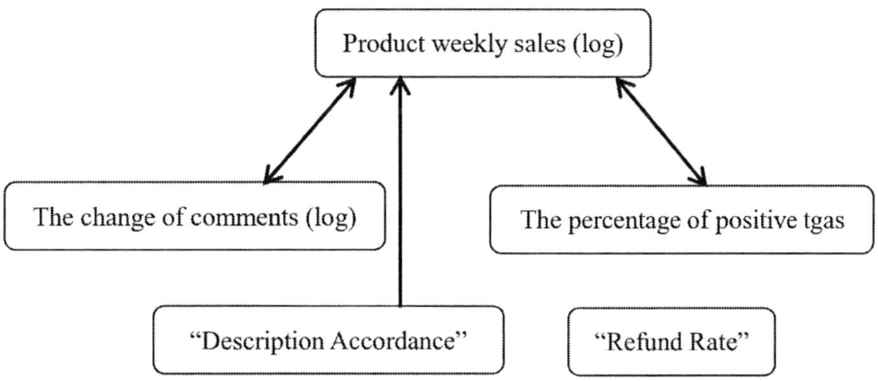

FEVD Analysis

Granger Causality test have revealed the causality relationships among product weekly sales, WOM, e-SQ based online OL information, which can also be interpreted as the "predicting power" of one variable to another. However, this test cannot determine the degree of the "predicting power", namely, cannot reveal the degree of interaction between them. In order to study the interaction between them more precisely, this section will use FEVD to predict the fluctuations of every endogenous variable in future periods and the contribution of one standard deviation shock in current state of all the variables in the system and then evaluate the impact degree of one variable to another. The PVAR(5) system FEVD results are illustrated in table 6. As displayed in Table 6, we can get several conclusions as followed. When predicting product weekly sales, the greatest impact comes from itself in both shot-term and long-term prediction and the impact will decrease gradually from the first period to 20th period (from 100% to 62.9%). The impact of the shock in the change of comments (log) is small and is stable at around 3% in the fifth period. The impact of the shock in "Description Accordance" online OL information will increase slowly from the first period to 20th period but never exceed 4%. The impact of the shock in the percentage of positive tags will increase rapidly (from 0% to 30.6%). The shock in "Refund Rate" online OL information has no contribution to product weekly sales. This results indicate that the change of comments (log) and "Description Accordance" have some contribution to the future fluctuation of product weekly sales but with a week explanation power while the percentage of positive tags are more powerful in predicting the fluctuation of product weekly sales. This implies that the percentage of positive tags is an important reason for product sales and this impact has a long-term effect, such as: 30.6% of the forecasting variance of product weekly sales in the future 20th period can be explained by the percentage of positive tags.

Table 6 the FEVD Results for Each Endogenous Variable in PVAR Model

variables	Periods(week)	Ln_wsales	Ln_volume	$Positive$	$Depict$	$Refund$
	1	**1.000**	0.000	**0.000**	0.000	0.000
	5	**0.830**	0.033	**0.127**	0.010	0.000
Ln_wsales	10	**0.712**	0.030	**0.234**	0.024	0.000
	15	**0.657**	0.028	**0.282**	0.032	0.000
	20	**0.629**	0.027	**0.306**	0.038	0.000
	1	**0.017**	**0.983**	0.000	0.000	0.000
	5	**0.195**	**0.783**	0.019	0.003	0.001
Ln_volume	10	**0.203**	**0.767**	0.019	0.009	0.001
	15	**0.203**	**0.761**	0.022	0.013	0.001
	20	**0.203**	**0.758**	0.024	0.015	0.001
	1	**0.007**	0.000	**0.992**	0.000	0.000
	5	**0.063**	0.002	**0.935**	0.000	0.000
$Positive$	10	**0.097**	0.005	**0.896**	0.002	0.000
	15	**0.111**	0.006	**0.878**	0.005	0.000
	20	**0.117**	0.006	**0.868**	0.009	0.000
	1	0.002	0.001	0.000	**0.997**	0.000
	5	0.004	0.000	0.003	**0.992**	0.001
$Depict$	10	0.007	0.000	0.010	**0.982**	0.001
	15	0.009	0.000	0.018	**0.971**	0.002
	20	0.011	0.000	0.025	**0.961**	0.002
	1	0.000	0.000	0.000	0.002	**0.998**
	5	0.000	0.001	0.000	0.006	**0.992**
$Refund$	10	0.001	0.001	0.001	0.011	**0.986**
	15	0.001	0.001	0.002	0.014	**0.983**
	20	0.001	0.001	0.002	0.015	**0.981**

When forecasting the change of comments (log) (or percentage of positive tags), the largest impact comes from itself and will converge to 75%-77% (or 86%-90%) after 10 periods. Product weekly sales contribute a lot to it and the percentage of contributions maintained at 20.3% around (or 11% around) after 10 periods. "Description Accordance" online OL information have little impact to it and the ratio is 0.9% (or

0.2%) after 10 periods. The contribution of "Refund Rate" online OL information is almost 0. The forecasting power between the change of comments (log) and the percentage of positive tags is also not big. The later can explain 1.9%-2.4% for the future fluctuation of the former and the former can only explain 0.5%-0.6% for the later. This result indicates that the variation in product weekly sales is powerful in explaining the variation of online WOM while the variation in e-SQ based OL information has no explanation ability. In addition, the variations of the two variables in online WOM (the change of comments (log) and the percentage of positive tags) have week explanation ability for each other.

When predicting "Description Accordance" online OL information and "Refund Rate" online OL information, the future variation mostly comes from the shocks in themselves, which contribute 98.2% and 98.6% respectively to the variance forecasting of themselves in the 10th period. Product weekly sales (log) have little explanation ability to them and the ratio is 1.1% and 0 respectively in the 20th period. The contribution of the change of comments (log) is almost 0. The contribution of the percentage of positive tags increases gradually from the first period to the 20th period (from 0 to 2.5%) to the former while is almost 0 to the later. The forecasting power between the two variables of online OL information is also very weak. The later contributes nearly 0 to the former and the former can only explain 1.5% of the future variation for the later. This result indicates that neither the shock in product weekly sales nor the shock in online WOM has explanation power in predicting the future variation of e-SQ based online OL information. The future variation of e-SQ based online OL information variables depend on the shocks in themselves mainly and no strong explanation ability is found from one OL information variable to the other OL information variable.

CONCLUSIONS

This paper applied PVAR model to study the dynamic interaction among product weekly sales, online WOM and e-SQ based online OL information with the help of the largest B2C e-commerce platform in china, Tmall.com, which has rich data in its' sales page. In addition, IRF, Granger Causality test and FEVD were used to analyze the mutual prediction among the three kinds of information. This method can describe the future moving trends of the variables under the current shock in one variable and analyze the forecasting power of the current variation in one variable to the fluctuation of all the variables. The results shows that: (1) Product weekly sales online WOM and e-SQ based online OL information have dynamic effect in themselves, that is their past performance have impact on the current performance significantly. There are dynamic interactions among all the variables in Product sales and online WOM (the change of comments and the percentage of positive tags). Product weekly sales and "Description Accordance" （one of the online OL information variables）only have one directional dynamic effect [The later have siginificant impact on the former while the former do not have siginificant impact on the later] and the other online OL information variable ("Refund Rate") have no dynamic interaction with product weekly sales. (2) Apart from their own impact, the percentage of positive tags has strong explanation ability in prediction the fluctuation of product weekly sales (approaching 30% in the long run). The shock in product weekly sales perform best in explaining the fluctuation of online WOM (in the long run, the explanation ratio is 20 for the fluctuation of the change of comments and the ratio is nearly 12% for the percentage of positive tags). However, the contributions for e-SQ based online OL information variables mainly come from themselves (96% for "Description Accordance" and "98" for "Refund Rate" in the long run).

E-SQ based online OL information. At present, Tmall sellers haven't engaged in improving the level of e-SQ performance according to the sales information especially for the description consistency in products introductions. If sellers present exaggerated or false description, the sales may increase in a short term but it is harmful to the long term revenue for the sellers as "Description Accordance" has a positive dynamic impact on product weekly sales significantly. So sellers should improve the e-SQ according to the sales information and sellers should also address more importance of description consistency.

The comment tags. Because the percentage of positive tags volatility can explain 30% of the fluctuation of product weekly sales, the amount of positive tags will impact the change of product sales greatly. As this reason, Tmall sellers should monitor the number of positive and negative tags timely and raise alarm on the negative comments from consumers. Sellers need respond and explain for the subjective and unfair negative comments to prevent these negative comments from prevailing among consumers. Nevertheless, if the negative comments are due to the defects of the products themselves, sellers should improve the quality of the products from the perspective of revenue and cost and then guide the consumers to write more positive comments on the website page.

REFERENCES

Arndt, J. Role of product-related conversations in the diffusion of a new product [J]. Journal of Marketing Research, 1967, 4(3): 291-295.

Bandura, A. Social Learning Theory [M]. Englewood Cliffs, NJ: Prentice Hall, 1977.

Becker, G. A note on restaurant pricing and other examples of social influences on price [J]. Journal of Political Economy, 1991, 99(5): 1109-1116.

Bikhchandani, S., D. Hirshleifer, I. Welch. A theory of fads, fashion, custom, and cultural change as informational cascades [J]. Journal of Political Economy, 1992, 100(5): 992–1026.

Bikhchandani, S., D. Hirshleifer, I. Welch. Learning from the behavior of others: conformity, fads, and informational cascades [J]. Journal of Economic Perspectives, 1998, 12(3): 151–170.

Chang, H.H., Y. Wang, W. Yang. The impact of e-service quality, customer satisfaction and loyalty on e-marketing: Moderating effect of perceived value [J]. Total Quality Management, 2009, 20(4): 423-443.

Chen, Y., Q. Wang, J. Xie. Online social interactions: a natural experiment on word of mouth versus observational learning [J]. Journal of Marketing Research, 2011, 48(2): 238-254.

Chevalier, J., D. Mayzlin. The effect of word of mouth on sales: online book reviews [J]. Journal of Marketing Research, 2006, 43(3): 345-354.

Delone, W.H. The DeLone and McLean model of information systems success: a ten-year update [J]. Journal of management information systems, 2003, 19(4): 9-30.

Duan, W., B. Gu, A.B. Whinston. Do online reviews matter?—an empirical investigation of panel data [J]. Decision Support Systems, 2008, 45(4): 1007-1016.
Finn, A. Investigating the non-linear effects of e-service quality dimensions on customer satisfaction [J]. Journal of Retailing and Consumer services, 2011, 18(1): 27-37.

Godes, D., D. Mayzlin, Y. Chen, et al. The firm's management of social interactions [J]. Marketing Letters, 2005, 16(3-4): 415-428.

Ho, C.I., Y.L. Lee. The development of an e-travel service quality scale [J]. Tourism Management, 2007, 28(6): 1434-1449.

Ho-Dac, N.N., S.J. Carson, W.L. Moore. The effects of positive and negative online customer reviews: Do brand strength and category maturity [J]. Journal of Marketing. 2013, 77(6): 37-53.

Lu, X., S. Ba, L. Huang, Y. Feng. Promotional marketing of word-of-mouth? Evidence from online restaurant reviews [J]. Information System Research, 2013, 24(3): 596-612.

Luo, X. Quantifying the long-term inpact of negative word of mouth on cash flows and stock prices [J]. Marketing Science, 2009, 28(1): 148-165.

Olorunniwo, F., M.K. Hsu, G.J. Udo. Service quality, customer satisfaction, and behavioral intentions in the service factory [J]. Journal of Services Marketing, 2006, 20(1): 59-72.

Sonnier, G.P., L. McAlister, O.J. Rutz. A dynamic model of the effect of online communications on firm sales [J]. Marketing Science, 2011, 30(4): 702-716.

Tirunillai, S., G.J. Tellis. Does chatter really matter? Dynamics of user-generated content and stock performance [J]. Marketing Science, 2012, 31(2): 198-215.

Trusov, M., R.E. Bucklin, K. Pauwels. Effects of word-of-mouth versus traditional marketing: Findings from an internet social networking site [J]. Journal of Marketing, 2009, 73(5): 90-102.

Udo, G.J., K.K. Bagchi, P.J. Kirs. An assessment of customers'e-service quality perception, satisfaction and intention [J]. International Journal of Information Management, 2010, 30(6): 481-492.

Villanueva, J., S. Yoo, D.M. Hanssens. The impact of marketing-induced versus word-of-mouth customer acquisition on customer equity growth [J]. Journal of Marketing Research, 2008, 45(1): 48-59.

DECISION SCIENCES INSTITUTE

The Effect of Social and Temporal Distance on Risk Preferences: An Experimental Investigation

Elif Ece Demiral
George Mason University
Email: edemiral@gmu.edu

Umit Saglam
East Tennessee State University
Email: saglam@etsu.edu

ABSTRACT

This paper focuses on a pilot study which seeks the effects of two psychological distances, temporal and social distance, on risk preferences. The experimental design is constructed for four treatment groups to find out these effects. This experimental study examines how delayed resolution of risky options influence individual choice and decisions made on behalf of others. The results show that individuals are risk averse for their current and future decisions. However, there is a significant increase in their risk aversion when they are making a decision for the future. These discrepancies in risk preferences occurred due to gender differences.

KEYWORDS: Risk Preferences, Social Distance, Temporal Distance, Gender Differences, Experimental Investigation

INTRODUCTION

Individuals may make more risky decisions on behalf of other people in some situations where the results are not immediately available and there are no immediate consequences as well. Assessing and measuring the risk preferences of individuals over other people's payoff are critical for both economic analysis and policy prescriptions. Previous researches suggest that risk preferences are free parameters and individuals may have different risk attitudes (Kahneman and Tversky, 1979). When we consider risky decisions made on behalf of others, the variation in risk preferences gets even more complicated.

There is a body of research coming from social psychology and economics which shed some light on risk attitudes of individuals when they decide on behalf of others. According to Chakravarty et al. (2011), individuals take more risk than they usually do for themselves, when they make a decision on behalf of others. On the other hand, Reynold et al. (2009) find that individuals make less risky decisions for others than themselves when the reward amount is very small. However, when there is a high reward, they do not find any significant difference in risk preferences between the decisions that are made for self or for others. Stoner (1961), Wallach et al. (1962) and Kogan and Wallach (1964) propose the 'Risky Shift Phenomenon' concept. According to these studies, individuals tend to take more risk than they usually do, when they are in a group. Ertac and Gurdal (2012) focus on the gender difference, and they find that men take more risk than women do, when they make a decision on behalf of a group.

Pollmann et al. (2014) measure how the ex-ante and ex-post accountability affect the risk-taking of an agent. Accountability, in which they let the principal reward the agent based on their content from investment, is reducing the amount of risk taken by the agents.

Researchers also attempted to explain the effect of intertemporal variation in risky behavior. Sagristano et al. (2002) and Savadori and Mittone (2014) suggest that individuals make more risky decisions when they are told that the outcome of the decision will be resolved in a future time.

According to Trobe and Liberman (2003), the construal level theory (CLT), psychological representation of information depends on "psychological distance", that is, on whether the relevant information refers to the near or distant psychological space. CLT is defined under four main dimensions: temporal, social, spatial and hypothetical distance. Thus, one can phrase decisions made on behalf of others as "social distance" and a delayed resolution of a lottery as "temporal distance" according to CLT. CLT also suggests that risk neutrality is more strongly associated with others, who are also construed at a high level, whereas risk seeking and risk avoidance are more strongly associated with the self, which is also construed at a low level. Thus, increase in risky behavior while one decides for other (social distance) can be explained by CLT since individuals generally behave risk averse for their selves.

In this paper, we study the characteristics that affect a person's risk attitudes when she decides on behalf of a stranger and when the outcomes of their decisions are resolved in the future. Specifically, we measure how temporal distance together with social distance would affect the risky decisions made by individuals.

The remainder of this paper is organized as follow: Section 2, provides an experimental design in detail. Section 3, reports the results of four different treatments. We also present our results for gender differences as well. Finally, concluding remarks and a research agenda are discussed in Section 4.

EXPERIMENTAL DESIGN

One way to reveal risk preferences is the multiple price list (MPL) method, which has been used previously and popularized by Holt and Laury (2002) (e.g. Charness et al. 2012). Each subject is presented with a list of 10 decisions between paired gambles which we call lottery A and lottery B. These two lotteries for each decision are displayed in rows. The participant is then asked to choose between two lotteries, either A or B for every decision row. Table 1 illustrates the basic payoff matrix presented to subjects.

Table 1. The Ten Paired-Lottery Choice Decisions

Lottery A				Lottery B				Expected Values		
Chance	Payoff	Chance	Payoff	Chance	Payoff	Chance	Payoff	EV^A	EV^B	Difference
0.1	$20	0.9	$15	0.1	$40	0.9	$1	15.50	4.90	$10.60
0.2	$20	0.8	$15	0.2	$40	0.8	$1	16.00	8.80	$7.20
0.3	$20	0.7	$15	0.3	$40	0.7	$1	16.50	12.70	$3.80
0.4	$20	0.6	$15	0.4	$40	0.6	$1	17.00	16.60	$0.40
0.5	$20	0.5	$15	0.5	$40	0.5	$1	17.50	20.50	-$3.00
0.6	$20	0.4	$15	0.6	$40	0.4	$1	18.00	24.40	-$6.40
0.7	$20	0.3	$15	0.7	$40	0.3	$1	18.50	28.30	-$9.80
0.8	$20	0.2	$15	0.8	$40	0.2	$1	19.00	32.20	-$13.20
0.9	$20	0.1	$15	0.9	$40	0.1	$1	19.50	36.10	-$16.60
1.0	$20	0.0	$15	1.0	$40	0.0	$1	20.00	40.00	-$20.00

The payoffs of each row remain constant, but probability pairs are changed which directly affects the expected value of each lottery. As one moves down in the table, the chances of the higher payoff for each option increase. For example, in the first row lottery A pays $20 with probability 0.1 and pays $15 with probability 0.9, thus the expected value of lottery A is $15.50 ($EV^A$). Although the expected values are not shown to the subjects, they are reported in Table 1. Similarly, the first row pays $40 with probability 0.1 and pays $1 with probability 0.9 for lottery B. Therefore the expected value of lottery B is (EV^B) $4.9. The expected value of lottery A is greater than the expected value of lottery B, and the difference between these two lotteries is equal to $10.60 for the first row. As one moves down, the expected value of both lotteries increase but the raise of lottery B is much faster than then the raise of lottery A. Therefore the expected value of lottery B becomes greater than the expected value of lottery A, for the each row after the fourth one. In fact, for the decision in the tenth row, lottery A pays $20 for sure and lottery B pays $40 for sure. Under the assumption of local non-satiation, the last row is added to test whether subjects understood the instructions. Two subjects who failed to switch to lottery B in the last row are excluded from the data set.In this pilot study, the payoffs were hypothetical and each subject was informed explicitly about this point. Therefore these hypothetical payoffs were not be paid to them. They had also explained that the researchers are interested in what they would do if they actually faced these choices and they were asked to think about their choices carefully.

They had introduced four different decision tasks. The first task required them to make decisions for themselves, where the result of the lotteries will be learned immediately *(Self+Now)*. The second task included making decisions for one's self, where the result of the lottery choice will be learned in three months (Self+Future) (please see Savadori and Mittone, 2014 for an analysis of different temporal distance). The third task asked them to make decision o behalf of a stranger in their university, where the result of the lottery choice will be learned immediately *(Other+Now)*. The fourth and the last asked them to make decisions on behalf of a stranger in their university, where the result of the lottery choice will be learned in three months *(Other+Future)*. To be able to eliminate any possible order effect, the order of the tasks is randomized.

The pilot experiments were run in the United States with pencil and paper and the payoff values were in US Dollars. The payoffs were approximately 10 times the baseline prizes offered in experiments of Holt and Laury (2002) and they were all hypothetical. So one would expect to observe somewhat biased risk preferences through the decision task.

The data was collected from East Tennessee State University, and 35 subjects participated in this study. Gender distribution was very balanced; we had 17 male and 18 female participants. Two of the participants failed to understand the instructions, and they were dropped from the data even though the analysis reported in this paper does not change when we do not drop those subjects as well. The decision sheets were handed out before the start of a class in Business, and only volunteer students participated in the study. After the decision sheets are handed out, the instructions are read aloud. The complete instructions are available in the Appendix. While performing the first task, subjects had no information about the next task. The order of the tasks was randomized to eliminate any possible occurrences of the order effect.

RESULTS

In all of our four treatments, the majority of subjects chose the safe option A in the first rows, when the probability of the higher payoff was small, and then switched to option B without going back to option A. Only 7 out of 35 subjects switched back from B to A at least once. We did not drop the subjects who switched multiple times in the analysis reported in this paper. The results do not change when we exclude those subjects from the data. Even for these subjects who switched back and forth, there is still a clear distinction between clusters of A and B choices. Therefore the total number of "safe" A choices are associated with risk aversion as it is in Holt and Laury (2002) and Chakravarty et al. (2011). Only 2 out of 35 subjects failed to choose lottery B in the very last row. And those subjects are excluded from the analysis since these subjects failed to understand the instructions.

Divergence from Risk Neutrality

We find that individuals are risk averse for their current and future selves which are consistent with the existing literature. However, we realize that there is an increase in subject's risk aversion when they decide about future gambles. Figure 1 shows that the proportion of A choices for each one of the ten decisions. The horizontal axis represents the problem sequence; where the vertical axis represents the fraction of the subjects who chose A from the problem set. The dashed blue line represents the predictions under the assumption of optimum risk neutrality, in which subjects choose A in the first four rows, because the expected value of lottery A is greater than the expected value of lottery B and switch to be in B at the fifth row because the expected value of lottery B is greater than the expected value of lottery A, without switching back. The overall data suggest that subjects are slightly risk lover in *Other+Now* treatment, but this difference is not statistically significant (p>0.1; one-sided two sample proportions test and p>0.1; one-sided Wilcoxon Mann-Whitney U-test).

Figure 1. Lottery Choices

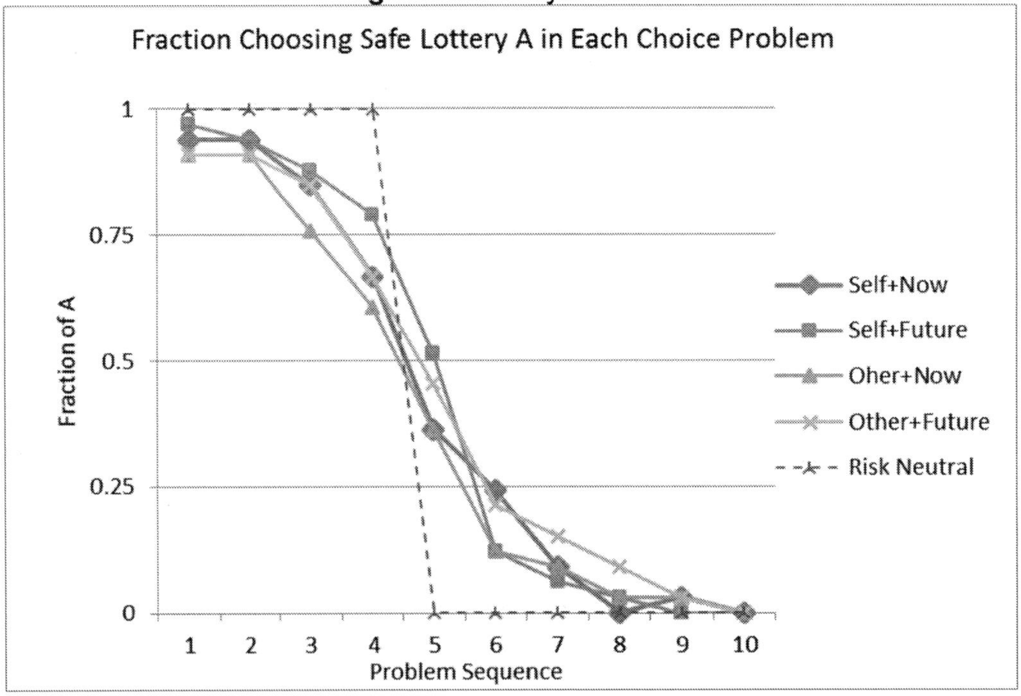

Deciding Over other People's Money: The Effect of Social Distance

When deciding on behalf of a stranger, participants were more risk-taking than they do for themselves when the lottery is played and resolved now. The difference is statistically significant only at the 10 % level (p=0.1; one-sided, two sample proportions test). Table 2 summarizes the total number of "safe" decisions (lottery A) made in each treatment.

Table 2. Total Number of A and B Decisions under Each Treatment

	Self+Now	***Self+Future***	***Oher+Now***	***Other+Future***
A	136	142	126	141
B	194	188	204	189
Total	330	330	330	330

Individuals had the same risk preferences for others in the future as they had for their own future selves (p>0.2; one-sided two sample proportions test and p>0.2; one-sided Wilcoxon Signed Rank Test). Figure 2 shows these trends.

Figure 2.Self-Other Discrepancy

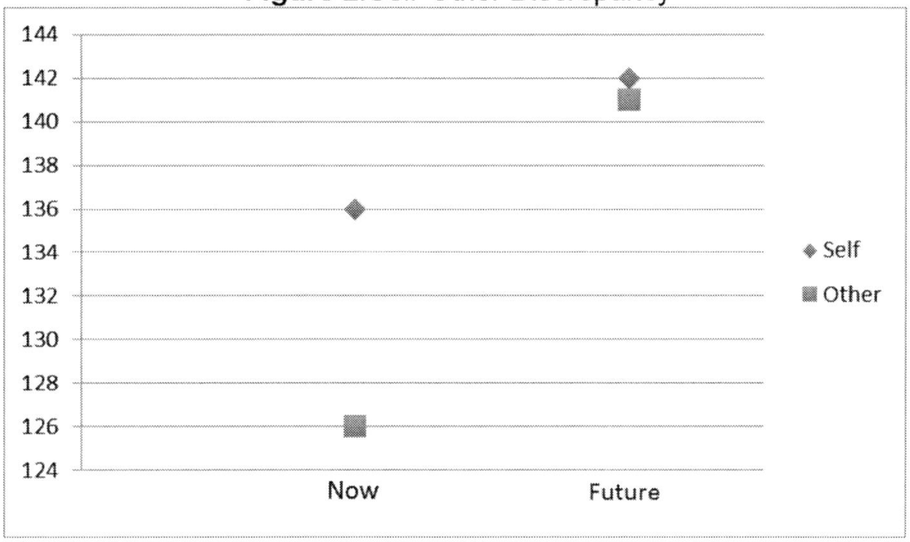

Table 3 reports the risk aversion categories, which depend on the number of safe choices (lottery A) made by each participant (Holt and Laury, 2002). One notable feature of the frequencies in Table 3 is that more than 35 percent of the choice patterns in the *Other+Now* condition involve 3 or less safe choices, which indicates a high level of risk preference when deciding on behalf of other individuals.

When the outcome is resolved in the future: The Effect of Temporal Distance

We observe an increase in risk aversion in both self and other tasks when the lottery is resolved in the future compared to when the lottery is resolved now. Subjects behave more risk averse when they move from *Self+Now* treatment to *Self+Future* treatment. The difference is not statistically significant (p>0.1; one-sided Wilcoxon Signed Rank Test).

However, subjects made more risk averse decisions in *Other+Future* treatment with respect to the *Other+Now* treatment. In addition, the difference between these two treatments is statistically significant (p<0.01; one-sided Wilcoxon Signed Rank Test). In other words, individuals balance the uncertainty of the gamble and the uncertainty of the future more while they decide on behalf of others by making more risk averse decisions.

Table 3. Risk Aversion Classification Based on Lottery Choices					
Number of Safe Choices (A's)	**Risk Preference Classification**	**Proportion of Choice**			
		Self+Now	Self+Future	Oher+Now	Other+Future
0-1	highly risk loving	0.06	0.06	0.09	0.09
2	very risk loving	0.06	0.03	0.12	0.06
3	risk loving	0.21	0.09	0.15	0.12
4	risk neutral	0.30	0.36	0.30	0.21
5	slightly risk averse	0.12	0.33	0.18	0.33
6	risk averse	0.15	0.06	0.06	0.06
7	very risk averse	0.09	0.03	0.06	0.09
8	highly risk averse	0.00	0.03	0.03	0.03
9-10	stay in bed	0.00	0.00	0.00	0.00

Figure 3 shows that individuals tend to behave more risk averse over future decisions in both self and other conditions. However, as reported above, subjects were more responsive to temporal distance when they were deciding over other people's money then they were deciding for their own payoff. Interestingly, a large portion of this 'higher time-discounting for others' is due to the behavior of women.

Figure 3. The Effect of Temporal Distance

Gender Differences in Risk Preferences

Women, in general, responded to different treatments ('Self vs. Other' and 'Now vs. Future') more than men did. A surprising finding is that many of the discrepancies in risk preferences under different treatments were due to women. Table 4 and Table 5 summarize the total number of safe choices that women and men made.

Men, in general, did not change their risk preferences under different treatments. It may be due to gender differences in reaction to a lack of monetary incentives. Men may be reacting more when the payoffs are hypothetical (as it was in our design) and caring less about the task they are performing. This finding, itself, generates another research question: Do men and women react differently to monetary incentives?

Table 4. Total Number of A and B Decisions – Women Only				
	Self+Now	**Self+Future**	**Oher+Now**	**Other+Future**
A	74	82	67	81
B	106	98	113	99
Total	180	180	180	180

Table 5. Total Number of A and B Decisions – Men Only				
	Self+Now	**Self+Future**	**Oher+Now**	**Other+Future**
A	62	60	59	60
B	88	90	91	90
Total	150	150	150	150

Women behaved more risk taking in *Other+Now* treatment than they did in *Self+Now* treatment ($p<0.2$, Wilcoxon Signed Rank Test and $p<0.15$; one-sided two sample proportions test), whereas men did not change their decisions ($p>0.2$; Wilcoxon Signed Rank Test). That means women take more risk on behalf of a stranger when the lottery is resolved immediately. However, women's decisions for themselves and other are the same when the lottery is resolved in 3 months.

Both men and women behaved in the same way, slightly risk averse, in *Other+Future* treatment and in *Self+Future* treatment ($p>0.2$, Wilcoxon Signed Rank Test). That means that the risk preferences both men and women have for future selves and for future others are similar to each other and different from their decisions for present selves and present others. This finding is aligned with the findings of Pronin et al. (2008) in which they report that individuals treat others as they treat their future selves.

DISCUSSION AND CONCLUSIONS

In this study, we explore how social and temporal distances affect risk attitudes of individuals. We find that individuals are risk averse for their current and future decisions. This tendency is consistent with the existing literature as well. However, there is a significant increase in their risk aversion when they are making a decision for the future. In addition, when the subjects are making a decision on behalf of a stranger, they behave slightly risk taking if the lottery is resolved immediately. This finding is consistent with what CLT suggests that social distance is associated with risk neutrality. When the social distance is incorporated with temporal distance, which is the scenario that subjects played the lottery on behalf of a stranger and when the lottery was going to be resolved in 3 months, subjects behaved slightly risk averse. Also, individuals had the same risk preferences for others in the future as they had for their own future selves.

Individuals would have made more risk averse choices when the lottery was resolved in the future. That shows us they discounted the time more for others than for themselves. However the time discounting was in the reverse direction. The subjects made more risk averse decisions for the future, which means balancing the uncertainty of the gamble and the uncertainty of the future.

A surprising result of this study is many of the discrepancies in risk preferences under different treatments were due to women. Women would have taken more risk on behalf of a stranger when the lottery was resolved immediately. However, when the lottery is resolved in the future, their decisions for themselves and the others would be same. In general, men did not differ their risk preferences under different treatments. It may be due to gender differences in reaction to the lack of monetary incentives since our design was based on hypothetical payments. This finding itself poses another research question on gender differences in the effects of hypothetical distance.

This paper is focused on a pilot study which seeks the effects of two psychological distances, temporal and social distance, on risk preferences where there is no monetary incentive. This experiment will be replicated with monetary incentives in the future. Further research will be extended with the measurement of the four main psychological distances as CLT suggests.

REFERENCES

Chakravarty, Sujoy, Glenn W. Harrison, Ernan E. Haruvy, and E. Elisabet Rutström. "Are you risk averse over other people's money?." *Southern Economic Journal* 77, no. 4 (2011): 901-913.

Charness, Gary, Uri Gneezy, and Alex Imas. "Experimental methods: Eliciting risk preferences." *Journal of Economic Behavior & Organization* 87 (2013): 43-51.

Ertac, Seda, and Mehmet Y. Gurdal. "Deciding to decide: Gender, leadership and risk-taking in groups." *Journal of Economic Behavior & Organization* 83, no. 1 (2012): 24-30.

Holt, Charles A., and Susan K. Laury. "Risk aversion and incentive effects."*American economic review* 92, no. 5 (2002): 1644-1655.

Kahneman, Daniel, and Amos Tversky. "Prospect theory: An analysis of decision under risk." *Econometrica: Journal of the Econometric Society* (1979): 263-291.

Kogan, Nathan, and Michael A. Wallach. "Risk Taking: A Study in Cognition and Personality (New York: Holt, Rinehart, and Winston, 1964)." *KoganRisk Taking: A Study in Cognition and Personality1964.*

Leiser, David, Ofer H. Azar, and Liat Hadar. "Psychological construal of economic behavior." *Journal of Economic Psychology* 29, no. 5 (2008): 762-776.

Pollmann, Monique MH, Jan Potters, and Stefan T. Trautmann. "Risk taking by agents: The role of ex-ante and ex-post accountability." *Economics Letters* 123, no. 3 (2014): 387-390.

Pronin, Emily, Christopher Y. Olivola, and Kathleen A. Kennedy. "Doing unto future selves as you would do unto others: Psychological distance and decision making." *Personality and Social Psychology Bulletin* 34, no. 2 (2008): 224-236.

Reynolds, Douglas B., Jacob Joseph, and Reuben Sherwood. "Risky shift versus cautious shift: determining differences in risk taking between private and public management decision-making." *Journal of Business & Economics Research (JBER)* 7, no. 1 (2011).

Sagristano, Michael D., Yaacov Trope, and Nira Liberman. "Time-dependent gambling: odds now, money later." *Journal of Experimental Psychology: General* 131, no. 3 (2002): 364.

Savadori, Lucia, and Luigi Mittone. "Temporal distance reduces the attractiveness of p-bets compared to $-bets." *Journal of Economic Psychology* 46 (2015): 26-38.

Stoner, James Arthur Finch. "A comparison of individual and group decisions involving risk." PhD diss., Massachusetts Institute of Technology, 1961.

Wallach, Michael A., Nathan Kogan, and Daryl J. Bem. "Group influence on individual risk taking." *Journal of abnormal and social psychology* 65, no. 2 (1962): 75-86.

DECISION SCIENCES INSTITUTE

The effect of social media on purchasing behavior

Megan Prock McGrath
Simmons College
mcgratm@simmons.edu

Yulong Li
Simmons College
yulong.li@simmons.edu

ABSTRACT

Social media is a rapidly growing method of both business and personal communication. Increasingly, businesses are recognizing the importance of this growing market, and are adding social media efforts to their marketing campaigns. However, despite the boom in use, marketers still struggle with determining the return on investment (ROI) of social media. The challenge of quantifying ROI has broader implications than purely academic research; last year advertisers worldwide spent $23.68 billion on social networks according to eMarketer.com (2016). In this article we will explore the impact of social media on purchasing behavior as a measure of ROI.

KEYWORDS: social media, ROI, consumer behavior, purchasing behavior, and return on marketing investment

INTRODUCTION

Social media is a rapidly growing method of both business and personal communication. Increasingly, businesses are recognizing the importance of this growing market, and are adding social media efforts to their marketing campaigns. A 2012 survey of 3,800 small and medium sized organizations reported that 85 percent of marketers believe that social media helps small and medium sized organizations generate more awareness of their business and 69 percent of marketers believe social media helps drive consumer traffic (Stelzner, 2012). As Wallace (2012), notes in *Agency Sales* Magazine, "Consumers are already talking, so you might as well join the conversations." Indeed, not only are consumers already engaging on social media, they *expect* companies to be a part of the conversation. One survey indicated that 93 percent of consumers believe that a company should have some kind of social media presence and 85 percent of consumers expect companies and organizations to also interact with customers through social media (Cone 2008).

However, despite the boom in use, marketers still struggle with determining the return on investment (ROI) of social media while print and broadcast media have decades of research quantifying their ROI. The challenge of quantifying ROI has broader implications than purely academic research; last year advertisers worldwide spent $23.68 billion on social networks, a 33.5% increase from 2014 according to eMarketer.com (2016). However, despite companies' increasing focus on social media marketing, many organizations still struggle with understanding how to quantify their efforts. "In spite of the apparent attractiveness of investing in social media advertising, many companies are still challenged by their inability to determine the financial performance of social media activities in terms of financial return on investment (Jobs 2014)." Print and broadcast media has decades of research focused on ROI, however, due to the relatively new nature of the medium; there is still no widely accepted method of measurement for social media. Academic literature to date has tried, with varying degrees of success to create a standard ROI measurement tool. Jobs and Gilfoil (2014), for instance, endorse a reallocation of current advertising spend to social media, with a 30 percent diversion of funds being the recommended starting point. Other academic literature has tried to adapt traditional media ROI measurements to social media, which as Fisher (2009) notes, is a flawed method, "nothing ... has really told me about anything other than new media versions of traditional media campaigns: where to place your ad, sponsored widget or sponsored conversation, and how to judge its effectiveness. How about real social media, finding out how your forum is contributing to your reduction in online support, how customer reviews are affecting sales path, whether your 30 second TV spot crowdsourced in an innovative user generated content (UGC) campaign really made your audience feel engaged?" With so many dollars being spent annually, marketers, CEOs, and shareholders must justify the efforts of social media marketing and be able to accurately and easily define a successful campaign. One way to answer the question currently plaguing the industry and fill a gap in the current literature is to use purchasing behavior as a measure of ROI for social media.

It is clear that while traditional methods of measuring ROI can inform the measurement of ROI in social media, they are not robust enough to capture and analyze the many factors influencing social media. Instead, we must utilize additional theories to successfully define ROI in social media. Purchasing behavior serves as an effective measurement of ROI because, according to Khaniwale, it is one of the greatest predictors of current and future sales.

> *Consumer purchasing behavior "is very important in the marketing field as it forms the basis of marketing strategies. The study of consumer buying behavior facilitates to comprehend the concern such as what the buyers think, what their feelings are, what the reasons behind their decision are, and how they pick among several options…Having an insight into these factors enables marketers to better know and predict not only the demand of their product or service, but also the purchasing motives and purchasing frequency of the product or service. More importantly, if these factors are considered whilst developing new products, it will support in developing products with higher probability of success (*Khaniwale, 2105).

Utilizing purchasing behavior as a measure of ROI is important given its implications in predicting present and future sales, thus impacting an organizations' bottom line.

Last year a McKinsey study (Bughin, 2015) indicated that, "social media recommendations induced an average of 26 percent of purchases across all product," and "in 2014, consumers made 10 percent more purchases on the back of social-media recommendations than they had in 2013." Additionally, in an extensive literature review examining more than 100 articles on consumer online purchasing intentions, Akar and Nasir (2015) noted that social media created a significant positive impact on purchasing behavior. Yet, the authors note, "the study results reveal that while most of the studies focus on the impact of consumer characteristics, and merchant and product characteristics on online purchase intention, the impact of social media is generally underestimated in the literature." Purchasing behavior directly affects sales, and therefore directly impacts a company's bottom line. Understanding the influence of social media on purchasing behavior is imperative to successfully measuring the ROI of a company's social media campaign.

Social media as a method of marketing and communication continues to grow in business, yet social media ROI is a field of research that is still in development and without clear best practices. Purchasing behavior is as a strong measure of ROI in social media because of its power to predict current and future sales. However, existing literature does little to explain or explore social media's impact on consumer purchasing behavior. Utilizing purchasing behavior as a measure of ROI will fill this gap in the literature and offer a useful tool for companies in their marketing and measurement efforts of social media.

In this study we will explore the impact of social media on purchasing behavior as a measure of ROI. In order to do this, we will construct a research model, conduct a survey of social media users, compile and analyze the data, and make recommendations for how companies and organizations can begin to adequately measure social media ROI. The following segments of the article are organized as such, Research Model, Methodology, and Conclusion.

THEORETICAL DEVELOPMENT/MODEL

To successfully measure social media's effect on purchasing behavior we must first define what factors impact ROI in marketing, purchasing behavior, and social media. Although print and broadcast media have decades of research quantifying their ROI, social media, a relatively new channel for marketing, has not benefited from the same level of scholarly study. One reason for this discrepancy in research is that social media as a medium has only existed for a little more than a dozen years, with MySpace.com launching as recently as 2003.

Return on Marketing Investment (ROMI) is defined as revenue generated by a marketing program divided by the cost of the program at a given risk level (Powell, 2002). However, this financial measure is not always a clear metric for many organizations. Fortunately, ROMI is a field of deep research with entire conferences and publications dedicated to measuring it, and a proliferation of metrics have arisen out of the many attempts to create ROMI measurement tools. "In an ARF-Association of National Advertisers survey of senior marketers in 2000, marketers reported a wide range of metrics that were in use in their companies. Some of the measures were quite far removed from sales but had been related to sales in previous analyses, tracking measures such as awareness of the brand or of the advertising, for example. Others were profitability and payout measures that were familiar to finance managers as well as marketers (Cook, 2004)." According to Kitsikeas, Constantine, et al., there are six key measures and impacts of ROI in marketing, as defined below (Katsikeas, Constantine S., et al., 2016).

1. Customer mindset outcomes—customer perceptions and attitudes regarding the firm and its value offering (e.g., brand equity, customer satisfaction);
2. Customer behavior outcomes customer purchase and post purchase behaviors toward the firm and its value offerings (e.g., customer retention, word of mouth);
3. Customer-level performance outcomes—economic outcomes for the firm that concern the behavior of individuals or groups of customers (e.g., customer profitability, CLV);
4. Product market performance outcomes—how the product performs in the marketplace in which it is offered (e.g., unit sales, market share);
5. Accounting performance outcomes—financial outcomes reported in the firm's financial statements and reports (e.g., profitability, return on assets [ROA]); and
6. Financial-market performance outcomes—outcomes reflected in indicators related to stock or debt markets (e.g., total shareholder returns, bond ratings). We use these categories to capture the aspects of marketing performance used in empirical studies.

For the purposes of this paper, these measures provide a helpful framework for examining return on investment in marketing.

In order to run and measure a successful marketing campaign, marketers must first understand consumer behavior; why customers are viewing the company's information and purchasing its products. In fact, consumer behavior models are built on the foundation of these two principles: getting information and product purchasing (Pavlou, Fygenson, 2006). For example, the model of the customer resource life cycle (CRLF) proposed by Ives and Learmonth (1984) centers on three key stages: prepurchase (information gathering), during purchase, and post-purchase. Additionally, Kalakota and Whinston (1997) endorse a three-step model also built upon similar steps: prepurchase interaction (information gathering), purchase, and post-purchase interactions. In each of these models of consumer behavior, purchasing is foundational to successfully understanding consumer behavior. In this paper, we will use purchasing behavior as the lens through which we explore consumer behavior, however, first we must define the factors influencing purchasing behavior. In a 2013 literature review of purchasing behavior research, Shafi compiled the following exhaustive list of all the factors influencing consumer-purchasing behavior (Shafi, 2013):

- Personal factors—occupation, economic situation, personality, lifestyle, etc.
- Social factors—reference groups, family and social roles and status
- Physical factors—atmospherics of the shopping experience
- Marketing mix—mix of the controllable elements of a product's marketing plan
- Environmental factors—factors making up the retail environment
- Cultural factors—established beliefs, values, traditions
- Attitudinal factors—attitude of customer
- Demographic factors—gender, race, age, etc.

As social media use grows, so does its influence on consumer purchasing behavior. Last year a McKinsey study indicated that, "social media recommendations induced an average of 26 percent of purchases across all product," and "in 2014, consumers made 10 percent more purchases on the back of social-media recommendations than they had in 2013 (Bughin, 2015)." Because of this increase in influence, marketers continue to invest in social media channels, however measuring the effectiveness of these efforts plagues the industry. To fully understand the impact of social media on purchasing behavior, we must first understand what factors impact consumer's social media perceptions and interactions. According to Kumar's research, there are a number of variables impacting customer's social media interactions (Kumar, 2016).

- Firm generated social media content—messages posted by the firm
- Customer participation in social media—participation in firm's social media page
- Spending behavior—total dollar amount spent by customer
- Cross buying behavior—total number of distinct categories customer purchased during week
- Customer experience—duration of the relationship of customer with the firm
- Promotion depth index—weighted average of price cuts availed by customer
- Cross-category promotion—proportion of categories bought on promotion by customer
- Time spent on social network—time spent by customers on social networks
- Online social profile—number of online social profiles
- Attitudinal variables—attitude constructs measured by survey instrument
- Demographics—gender, race, age, etc.

When we overlay these three factors, we identify three key intersections, as identified in Figure 1. We can then use these intersections, Customer Perceptions/Attitudinal Factors, Customer Purchase Behavior, and Customer Performance Outcomes/Purchasing Behavior (defined below), as a foundation to examine how social media is affecting consumer purchasing behavior in terms of marketing ROI.

For the purposes of this study, we will explore these intersections, identified as:

- Customer Perceptions/Attitudinal Factors—customer perceptions and attitudes regarding the firm and its value offering (e.g., brand equity, customer satisfaction);
- Customer Purchase Behaviors/Social Factors— Customer behavior outcomes customer purchase and post purchase behaviors toward the firm and its value offerings (e.g., customer retention, word of mouth);
- Customer Performance Outcomes/Purchasing Behavior— Customer-level performance outcomes—economic outcomes for the firm that concern the behavior of individuals or groups of customers (e.g., customer profitability, spending behavior).

Figure 1.

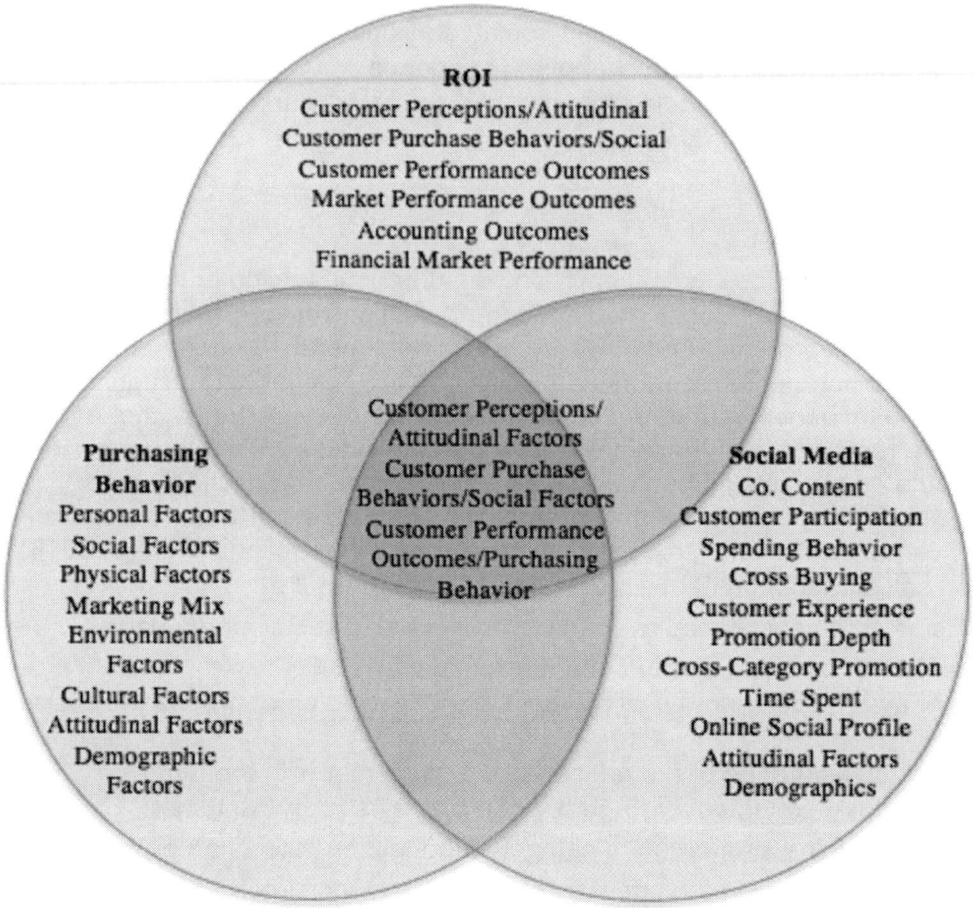

METHODOLOGY

Social media users are a wide and varied audience. Research indicates that social media users with common social characteristics (e.g. age, gender, etc.) tend to behave similarly on social media. Additionally, studies have also demonstrated that social media affects purchasing behaviors differently, depending on the group that is being studied. Market segmentation theory presents an accepted and well-established method to study these behavioral differences. Market segmentation, a concept rooted in economic pricing theory, suggests that marketing efforts are most effective when messages are targeted to discreet audiences, "Grouping together customers with similar product preferences and buying behaviour aids organisations in dealing with market heterogeneity, thereby focusing resources on relatively homogeneous customer segments and thus ensuring an efficient allocation of resources (Venter, 2015)." While 93 percent of consumers expect marketers to be online, consumer market segments have varying degrees of interaction with social media and social media has varying levels of impact on their purchasing behavior. However, according to Canhato, Clark, and Fennemore (2013), market segmentation is still a valid practice in the changing landscape of social media. By allowing customers to self-select into interest groups, social media organically creates market segments. Using these self identified groups, marketers can gather more specific market research and feedback from targeted audiences of consumers.

Because social media allows companies to gain more meaningful insight into customer opinions and encourages customers to self-select into online communities of interest, market segmentation theory provides a helpful lens for examining a companies social media efforts.

Because of the nature of this study, the market segment selected for research must be comprised of both heavy users of social media and customers who engage in online purchasing. Americans over 50, colloquially known as "Baby Boomers" are the ideal market for this research. Boomers are targeted by just 10% of marketing campaigns, however, this market segment actually accounts for half of all consumer spending. Although much research has been focused on the coveted 18-35 year old demographic, Boomers outspend this segment by 2:1 online (Love, 2014). In fact, McClullen (2015) argues that Boomers should be a target for all marketers, "Boomers are prolific online shoppers. According to Nielsen, a third of them shop online and the 50+ segment spends almost $7 billion in ecommerce... Forrester Research found that 72% of adults aged 55-to-63 shop online." Given their online purchasing power, Boomers are a useful segment for study when examining purchasing behavior.

Additionally Boomers are also heavy users of social media. "According to globalwebindex, 70% of online Baby Boomers have a Facebook account. Boomers spend an average of 216 minutes per day on social media. In their use of technology, the youngest Baby Boomers (ages 45-55) are nearly as likely to be online (and to have a home broadband connection) as younger adults (Mander, 2014)." McCullen goes on to point out that Boomers are the fastest growing demographic among social media users, with half actively engaging on social media, "Since 2008, younger Boomers (ages 46-55) usage on social media grew by 150%, which is more rapid than the growth for any other generation. (2015)."

To effectively study the baby boomer market segment, we will conduct both qualitative and quantitative analysis. To begin, we will conduct focus groups comprised of baby boomers that are active social media users. In these focus groups we will ascertain more information on the baby boomer's use of social media, purchasing behaviors, and interactions with online brands. We will ask them about their online behaviors, preferences, social media channels of choice, and spending behaviors. These learnings will then be used to compile a survey instrument that adequately captures the complexity of the interaction between social media and purchasing behavior. Additionally, the focus groups will help us to ascertain the language and knowledge level of the identified population, ensuring that our survey is relatable to the audience. We will then locate our survey population by purchasing lists through marketing services and partnering with local AARP branches to distribute an electronic survey through their social media channels. This mixed methods approach will ultimately enhance the quality of our findings.

Because of their strong purchasing power, propensity to shop online, and heavy social media use, Baby Boomers are an ideal market segment for studying the impact of social media on purchasing behavior. Utilizing market segmentation theory, this article will examine how companies' social media marketing efforts affect baby boomer's purchasing behavior.

CONCLUSION

Purchasing behavior is as a strong measure of ROI in social media because of its power to predict current and future sales. However, existing literature does little to explain or explore social media's impact on consumer purchasing behavior. Utilizing purchasing behavior as a measure of ROI will fill this gap in the literature and offer a useful tool for companies in their marketing and measurement efforts of social media. With the identified framework, we define and explore the factors impacting purchasing behavior in regards to social media. Understanding social media's effect on purchasing behavior will allow marketers to implement successful ROI measurement strategies surrounding social media marketing efforts.

REFERENCES

Akar, Ezgi, and V. Aslihan Nasir. "A Review Of Literature On Consumers' Online Purchase Intentions." *Journal Of Customer Behaviour* 14.3 (2015): 215-233. *Business Source Complete*. Web. 21 Feb. 2016.

Bughin, Jacques. "Getting A Sharper Picture Of Social Media's Influence." *Mckinsey Quarterly* 3 (2015): 8-11. *Business Source Complete*. Web. 21 Feb. 2016.

Canhoto, Ana Isabel, Moira Clark, and Paul Fennemore. "Emerging Segmentation Practices In The Age Of The Social Customer." Journal Of Strategic Marketing 21.5 (2013): 413-428. Business Source Complete. Web. 13 Feb. 2016.

Cone Business. (2008). 2008 business in social media study. Retrieved from http://www.coneinc.com/news/request.php?id=1183

Cook, William A. "ROMI Outlay Brings High Yields To B-To-B Marketers." *B To B* 89.4 (2004): 26. *Business Source Complete*. Web. 25 Mar. 2016.

Cronin, John J. "Teaching ROI Analysis In An Era Of Social Media." *Journal Of Advertising Education* 18.2 (2014): 28-35. *Business Source Complete*. Web. 19 Mar. 2016.

Fisher, Tia. "ROI In Social Media: A Look At The Arguments." Journal Of Database Marketing & Customer Strategy Management 16.3 (2009): 189-195. Business Source Complete. Web. 13 Feb. 2016.

Powell, Guy R. *Return on Marketing Investment: Demand More from Your Marketing and Sales*. 2002. Print.

Ives, Blake, and Gerard P. Learmonth. "The Information System As A Competitive Weapon." *Communications Of The ACM* 27.12 (1984): 1193-1201. *Business Source Complete*. Web. 25 Mar. 2016.

Jobs, Charles G., and David M. Gilfoil. "A Social Media Advertising Adoption Model For Reallocation Of Traditional Advertising Budgets." Academy Of Marketing Studies Journal 18.1 (2014): 235-248. Business Source Complete. Web. 13 Feb. 2016.

Kalakota, Ravi, and Andrew B. Whinston. *Electronic Commerce: A Manager's Guide*. Reading, MA: Addison-Wesley, 1997. Print.

Khaniwale, Manali. "Consumer Buying Behavior." *International Journal of Innovation and Scientific Research* 14.2 (2015): 278-86. Print.

Katsikeas, Constantine S., et al. "Assessing Performance Outcomes In Marketing." *Journal Of Marketing* 80.2 (2016): 1-20. *Business Source Complete*. Web. 19 Mar. 2016.

Kumar, Ashish, et al. "From Social To Sale: The Effects Of Firm-Generated Content In Social Media On Customer Behavior." *Journal Of Marketing* 80.1 (2016): 7-25. Business Source Complete. Web. 27 Feb. 2016.

Love, Robert. "The Smart Money Is on the 50+ Crowd." *AARP.org*. American Assocation of Retired Persons, June-July 2014. Web. 22 Feb. 2016.

Pavlou, Paul A., and Mendel Fygenson. "Understanding And Prediction Electronic Commerce Adoption: An Extension Of The Theory Of Planned Behavior." *MIS Quarterly* 30.1 (2006): 115-143. *Business Source Complete*. Web. 25 Mar. 2016.

Mander, Jason. *Generations: GWI Audience Report Summary Q2 2014*. Rep. GWI Web Index, 2014. Print

McMullen, Tim. "Reasons To Market To Baby Boomers On Social." Promotional Marketing (2015): 1. Business Source Complete. Web. 27 Feb. 2016.

Pick, T. (2013, August 9). 101 vital social media and digital marketing statistics. *Social Media Today*. Retrieved from URL:http://socialmediatoday.com/node/1647801

Shafi, Syed Irfan, and C. Madhavaiah. "The Influence Of Brand Equity On Consumer Buying Behaviour Of Organic Foods In India." *Journal Of Marketing & Communication* 9.2 (2013): 44-51. *Business Source Complete*. Web. 19 Mar. 2016.

Social Network Ad Spending to Hit $23.68 Billion Worldwide in 2015 - EMarketer." *EMarketer*. EMarketer, 15 Apr. 2015. Web. 21 Feb. 2016. <http://www.emarketer.com/Article/Social-Network-Ad-Spending-Hit-2368-Billion-Worldwide-2015/1012357>.

Stelzner, M. (2012, April). How marketers are using social media to grow their businesses. *Social Media Marketing Industry Report*. www.socialmediaexaminer.com/SocialMediaMarketingIndustryReport2012.pdf

Stephen, Andrew T., and Jeff Galak. "The Complementary Roles Of Traditional And Social Media Publicity In Driving Marketing Performance." INSEAD Working Papers Collection 97 (2010): 1-40. Business Source Complete. Web. 13 Feb. 2016.

Venter, Peet, Alex Wright, and Sally Dibb. "Performing Market Segmentation: A Performative Perspective." *Journal Of Marketing Management* 31.1/2 (2015): 62-83. *Business Source Complete*. Web. 21 Feb. 2016.

Wallace, D. (2012). How Small Business can Benefit from Social Media/Networking Sites. *Agency Sale*s Magazine, 42(8), 16-20.

DECISION SCIENCES INSTITUTE

The effectiveness of intentional design in an online inventory management class

Joshua K. Strakos
Baylor University
Email: josh_strakos@baylor.edu

ABSTRACT

Online education is growing fast. Inexperience with online course design may lead instructors and students to doubt its value. I explore the concept of intentional design for online learning. Student attitudes toward online design elements are measured before and after taking an online class. Elements include online review questions and quizzes, problem solving exercises, collaborative online group work, online discussion board participation, and online video lectures. Results show a positive change in student attitudes toward the value of all these. Contributions include linking intentional design to a measurable instructional effectiveness model and providing practical guidance for online course design.

KEYWORDS: Distance learning, Online education, Supply chain management, Instructional design

INTRODUCTION

Online education is growing quickly in the United States. Students taking at least one online course has increased from 1.6 million in 2002 (9.6% of total enrollment) to 21 million in 2011, or 32% of total enrollment (Allen & Seaman, 2013). This rapid and voluminous growth signals a paradigm shift in that online education is no longer an outlier. Instructors can expect to teach an online course sometime in their career – only 13.5% of higher education institutions have no online offerings, and 62.4% offer complete online programs (Allen & Seaman, 2013). Online education is a tool for addressing our social and cultural circumstances; and providing access to education for working adults, geographically separated individuals, and even those such as refugees caught up in political turmoil (Wexler, 2015).

Despite this rapid growth, skepticism abounds amongst faculty. Faculty acceptance of the value and legitimacy of online programs only slightly increased from 27.6% to 30.2% over the same 10 year period during which online enrollment increased 13-fold - with just over a majority of faculty indicating a "neutral" stance on acceptance of the value and legitimacy of online education (Allen & Seaman, 2013). Another study found 48% of professors who had taught online believe online courses are not as good as face to face classes (Benton, 2009). This represents a problem, because academic leaders believe faculty acceptance of online education is critical to the growth of online instruction (Allen & Seaman, 2013).

This growth of online education means that more faculty are teaching online classes – skeptical or not - and the split in online education's growth and its acceptance amongst faculty means that more students will be exposed to faculty who do not believe online education is valuable and legitimate. This may translate into the attitudes of the students and subsequently have a negative impact on the effectiveness of online classes and programs.

Skeptics may be opposed to online education for a number of reasons including risk aversion, resistance to change, or having one bad experience in an online classroom. This mentality, however, is akin to fear of the unknown (Benton, 2009). We are too quick to say as faculty, "in-residence courses are superior to online classes" either because we have not experienced personal success or have we been shown the way to this success (Redpath, 2012).

Skeptics of online education may tend to view the online classroom as a set of limitations which keep them from achieving what they are comfortable and skilled in accomplishing in a face-to-face classroom. This is an implicit recognition of the fundamentally different environment of the online classroom. For example, in a traditional classroom there are standards for class start time, time spent lecturing, and ergonomic factors (all students are learning in the same physical environment at the same time). Interaction between students and other students as well as interactions between students and the instructor are also governed, to an extent, by physical environment, meeting time, and office hours. We sometimes take these factors for granted because they are inherently built into the framework of the in-residence class. An instructor's presence is established with the students (physically) the moment he or she walks into the room. There are boundaries and limits set and defined by walls, class time limits, etc. Accessibility is also addressed almost automatically, as the in-resident student has guaranteed access to the instructor during class times, and most instructors have established office hours outside of class to meet with students.

The other major difference is in the students themselves. Most in-resident students are either full-time or must separate class meeting time from the rest of their schedule. This creates a sense of separation between the classroom learning experience and work, family, and social activities which may influence the amount of time, focus, and effort a student devotes to a class. The fundamental differences discussed above are presented in table 1 below.

Table 1: Fundamental differences between in-residence and online

In Residence	Online
Physical Characteristics of Environment	
Class start time is set	Arbitrary "start" time is up to student
Class length is set	Student consumes material at own pace
Students are in same physical environment	Students' environment varies greatly
Students are physically together	Students are geographically separated
Boundaries set by space and time constraints	No physical boundaries for the classroom
Social Characteristics of Environment	
Students may interact synchronously in class	Students must coordinate synchronous interaction or participate in asynchronous interaction
Instructor presence established during class	Instructor presence must be intentionally planned and executed by instructor
Students guaranteed instructor access in class	Students access to instructor limited to email, phone, or coordinated online meeting times
Students access instructor during office hours	Usually accomplished through email
Student Characteristics	
Full-time or standard set-aside class time	Part-time with full-time jobs
Work and school are separated by space and time	School may be accessed from work
Home and school are separated by space and time	School may be accessed from home

The risk is that instructors identify the differences as threats to the way they know how to conduct a class. Often times, those most averse to online education are those with the little or no experience teaching online (Redpath, 2012). Additionally, delivery method is sometimes confounded with instructional design (Bernard et al., 2009). It takes intentionality on the part of the instructor to establish presence, set boundaries, facilitate communication among students, and guarantee access. I've heard it said that a major drawback of online classrooms is the inability to have meaningful discussion, but the conversation usually stops there without realizing that replication of the in-residence classroom is not the goal of an online course (Brewer & Brewer, 2015). My question is, "what is the purpose and outcome of that discussion?" If the answer is something that can only be accomplished via face to face interaction, then the statement holds. Research suggests that the underlying factors which may be increasing student enjoyment are richer social interactions, feedback, and exchange of information associated with the traditional classroom (Nemanich, Banks, & Vera, 2009). So the instructor should be asking – "how can I achieve these objectives in the online classroom?"

The answer may lie in intentional design. The factors mentioned above may be a built-in part of the traditional face-to-face classroom, however, they are not so in an online classroom. The questions addressed in this research are how to intentionally achieve these same abstract characteristics in the online environment, and how much difference does intentional design make in changing student perceptions of online learning?

This research represents an important theoretical and practical contribution to innovation in online teaching. Theoretically, it connects the concept of learning design to a measurable instructional effectiveness model by showing how intentional design factors can change student satisfaction and attitudes. Practically, it shows how the learning design concept can be easily applied by mainstream educators, which is an area lacking in previous research (Burgos & Griffiths, 2005; Cameron, 2009).

LITERATURE REVIEW AND BACKGROUND

Purpose

The purpose of this study is two-fold. First, it is to reach out to the skeptics of online learning to show that intentional design and treatment of online environmental differences as opportunities (rather than threats) can influence outcomes in terms of student perceptions and attitudes. Second, it is to explore the effectiveness of several intentional design factors, drawn from best practices, which were implemented in an online course. The results show positive changes in student attitude toward each design factor.

Description of students, class, and program

The process described in this paper took place during the design and execution of a fully-online, introductory inventory management class. The class consisted of 12 graduate students, 10 of whom were part of a fully-online Master of Science program. The remaining two students were enrolled in the online course to supplement in-residence programs. The students' majors included Logistics and Operations Research, and all the students had taken classes in their respective programs prior to this class. The 10 online-program students were full-time military officers in operational jobs, where the typical work week consists of 40-60 hours. The full-time officers are also subject to frequent disruptions such as base exercises, temporary duty away from home-station (days to weeks in duration), and long-term deployments (6 months or longer). The 10 online-program students had all taken online courses prior to this course.

Although the methods and techniques described in this research apply to this group of graduate military students, the practical and theoretical implications apply to undergraduate and graduate online education in general. The methods, techniques, and intentionality discussed in this paper bear no unique relationship to either the level or profession of the student, and are generalizable to all online education. These methods are based on intentional design and delivery rather than a specific pedagogical aim toward graduate or undergraduate education.

In this study, I map the Mashaw (2012) model of online instructional effectiveness to several intentional design elements and show how these design elements may be responsible for a change in student attitudes and ultimately increase online instructional effectiveness. It is important for the skeptic to realize just how easily student attitudes and online teaching effectiveness can be affected by a few intentionally designed elements.

What constitutes effectiveness?

The education system is shifting from a process-centered to a learner-centered environment, where learning outcomes and competency-based education are the new standard (Aggarwal & Lynn, 2012; Levine, 2015). Mashaw (2012) discusses the elusiveness of measuring effectiveness as well as the holistic nature of student learning, and states that there is no clear definition of effectiveness. Mashaw develops a model for effectiveness which includes multiple facets of this holistic view, using satisfaction and student self-reporting to capture the concept of effectiveness. This model draws on previous research that shows student satisfaction and attitude are important elements used to measure student success across varying contexts (Alavi, Wheeler, & Valacich, 1995; Arbaugh & Benbunan-Finch, 2006; Graham & Scarborough, 2001). The model also accounts for how perceived learning and satisfaction have been used to study effective techniques in online environments (Eom, Wen, & Ashill, 2006). In these studies, satisfaction is used as a measure of effectiveness.

The overall goal of Mashaw is to show effectiveness as the result of the total synergy of various factors influencing the learning process and to develop a model to capture this holistic measure of effectiveness in a single numerical value. This holistic view of effectiveness is underpinned by the idea that the instructor serves as a mentor to guide and motivate students and to facilitate learning.

Explanation of Effectiveness Model

The model presented by Mashaw includes six constructs and 27 factors forming these constructs. A brief explanation of each of the constructs is provided here. The learning experiences construct captures the extent of learning through factors such as "changes in skill, comprehension, application, attitude, and competencies." The facilitator construct captures how the instructor can create an environment suitable for online learning through clarity, goal communication, inspiration, and encouragement of exploration and discovery. This environment requires an intentionally designed structure in an online course because of the abstract factors and differences listed in table 1. The technology construct focuses on the ability and design of the learning management system (LMS) to facilitate learning and includes factors of usability, dynamic and novel sessions, and modular presentation and flexibility. The interaction and participation construct captures social and environmental factors such as ease of communication, speed of response feedback, and encouragement and motivation of participation. The mentor's inspiration construct captures how the instructor can encourage learning through factors such as activity design, motivation of critical thinking, and individual assistance. Finally, the construct of hindrance and discouragement focuses on removing factors associated with student demotivation. This construct captures the negative effect of pitfalls such as technical frustration, boring content, and lack of guidance. Altogether these constructs characterize the idea of instructional effectiveness as a holistic outcome which is more than the sum of its parts (Mashaw, 2012).

CONCEPT DEVELOPMENT

Design for Effectiveness

The model presented by Mashaw explains what effectiveness is, how it can be conceptualized as a single number, and which factors and constructs have bearing on the overall holistic measure. However, for the online instructor designing a course, and for the skeptic, one needs to answer the question: "How can a course be designed to target effectiveness?"

In the design of a course, the philosophy of continuous improvement should be incorporated (Aggarwal & Lynn, 2012). Best practices in online design should be employed in order to target effectiveness factors (Redpath, 2012). Guides and suggested best practices can be found on many university websites as well as in published studies about online and flipped classrooms. The design elements incorporated here were taken from a synthesis of best practices deemed most applicable to this course (Asef-Vazeri, 2015; Brewer & Brewer, 2015; Hanover Research Council, 2009; Flipped Classroom Field Guide, n.d.; Keengewe & Kidd, 2010). The following section describes how intentional design elements were used in order to try and create presence, usability, interaction, flexibility and accommodation, and understanding and comprehension.

Presence

An online presence was created by using elements which would lend structure to the virtual classroom. These elements included the LMS announcement structure, interaction using online discussion boards, the timeliness of material release, deadlines, scheduling and tempo, and finally instructor availability.

Class announcements were structured to give the course a visual timeline and boundaries, as well as to frequently give feedback to students. In all, 28 announcements were posted over the course of the 10-week quarter. A standard weekly announcement was released at the beginning of each academic week with an emphasis on weekly topics and goals for the week. Additionally, announcements were posted with general feedback on assignments. Explanatory announcements were posted if a number of students had difficulty understanding a particular topic.

Student to student and student to instructor presence was encouraged with the use of discussion boards. Discussion board assignments included peer-feedback. There was also a question and answer forum discussion board where students could post questions (anonymously if desired) to be answered either by other students or by the instructor. The instructor standard for answering questions posted here was within 24-hours, although many of the questions were answered very shortly after students' posting.

Scheduling was intended to create a boundary structure not automatically present in an online classroom. Each class week started at 12:00 AM on Monday morning and ended at 11:59 PM the following Sunday night. Students were informed of this structure up-front and the format was standard throughout the course. Release of course materials for student viewing was done on the Wednesday prior to a class week starting. For example, materials for week three were released to students on Wednesday of week two. This insured that online students (keeping in mind that these are working adults with full-time jobs) were afforded a full two weekends to access reading assignments, online videos, and exercise assignments. This structure dictated the tempo of the course, which was set on a weekly basis by topic. The deadlines, material release, and announcements set clear guidelines and boundaries for student goal "chunks."

Finally, instructor availability was ensured to facilitate the enforcement and feasibility of the temporal structure of the class. The instructor was available via email 24 hours a day, 7 days a week. The service guarantee of a 24-hour or less response time ensured student knew up-front what the expectation was, and could plan accordingly. Although most emails were responded to within a very short period after students' sending them to the instructor. The instructor was also available for live access via telephone or video calling when requested by students. An enhancement to availability could be made by scheduling live office hours via chat, hangout, or other technology-enabled conference space. However, the flexibility afforded by allowing students to schedule independent consultations with the instructor as needed was valuable.

Usability

The usability of the course was of utmost importance in the design phase. Student feedback from previous courses indicated factors such as hard-to-watch video lectures and lack of a friendly user interface. The primary elements used to enhance usability were the video lectures, streamlined and standard course design, and the use of technology (LMS) to deliver this design.

A total of 45 videos were produced in modular format, meaning the videos covered topics in small "chunks" meant to be independent rather than taking a traditional hour long lecture and simply converting it to video format. The design goal was to make all videos 10 minutes or less in length. This goal was adhered to whenever possible, but there were several longer videos with no logical break point for separating them into shorter segments. For example, the working of one example problem took more than 30 minutes. This was a demonstration of a complicated procedure which required step-by-step demonstration. Although much longer than the design-specified goal, this was necessary to convey information to students. Of the 45 videos produced, the average length was 10:06. A majority (62%) of the videos met the goal of 10 minutes or less. Of the videos which exceeded the 10-minute length, the average overrun was 6:47, with only three lasting longer than 20 minutes and only two of those lasting longer than 30 minutes (the longest video was 39:25).

Standardized and streamlined visual and organizational design was used to reduce student fatigue and the learning curve involved with course structure and LMS use (Reisner, 2015). The course was designed and delivered using Blackboard LMS. Once the students were introduced to the material for the first week of class, the course framework did not change. The steps needed to access course content did not change throughout the course. Each class session had a corresponding folder in the course content section of the LMS. In each session's folder, which was on a timed released as described above, was an outline consisting of goals, reading assignments, video lecture assignments, exercise assignments, links and descriptions of discussion board post assignments, and links for turning in assignments via the LMS. All course content was presented from within this framework in one location, so that a student spent minimal time jumping from content area to content area and could focus on the flow of the lesson for the class session. This also built more structure into the course in that the students could visually see the boundaries of each class session within this streamlined LMS framework. The technology used to deliver this LMS experience was accessible to anyone with an internet-capable device and an internet connection. Once enrolled in the LMS class, students were not required to take any additional steps for access to course material.

Interaction

Interaction was a key element of the intentional design process. Both student-instructor and student to student interaction were considered, as these have been linked to a positive effect on student learning (Bernard et al., 2009). Research has also called for design of online education to facilitate more purposeful interaction (Abrami et al., 2011). The main design elements used to ensure an interactive course were service guarantees, use of online discussion boards for peer and instructor feedback, group exercise assignments, and a group project.

Service guarantees come from the service operations management world, and have been incorporated into online or blended courses in the past (Bregman, 2012). The idea is that students will have increased satisfaction with the course due to clear, precise, and well-communicated expectations. Service guarantees are also low-cost to the instructor, force accountability and performance, and add value for students by demonstrating that performance expectations are a two-way street, which in turn generates credibility and trust in the instructor-student relationship.

Peer feedback via the LMS discussion board and assigned group work was used to facilitate meaningful conversation amongst student groups with regard to a class project. Although the outcome of required group work may depend on individual differences (Smith & Kellog, 2015), the intent was to give students the valuable opportunity to learn from one another and incorporate feedback from their peers into the improvement of the project. This was designed to accomplish the purpose of exploiting the experience of the students and enhancing collaboration efforts across groups of students.

Flexibility and accommodation

This course was designed with flexibility and accommodation measures in mind. The challenge was to realize that the student group faced extremely difficult circumstances in some cases. The students were all active duty military officers and 83% of them were only part-time students. Their full-time jobs consisted of 40-60 hour work weeks, temporary duty trips away from home, and even extended deployments of 6 months or longer. Although these were extraordinary challenges which had to be incorporated into the design of the class, the same academic standards had to be applied to all students. The key design element incorporated here was clear expectations and clear communication with the students. More so than with a traditional student group, rates of communication had to be high and follow-up for missed deadlines had to be quick. The key was accommodating students' needs while not relaxing standards.

Understanding and comprehension

The assurance of understanding and material comprehension was essential and foundational. In order to lend to the structure development of the online classroom, frequent assessment of student progress and comprehension were needed. It has been observed in other online classes (K. Schultz, personal communication, December 15, 2015) that students in an online classroom are harder to "bring along" than in-resident students once they have begun to fall behind. To address this need, a quiz was administered at the beginning of each session in order to motivate the students to read and watch the online videos and to assess the students' comprehension of the material at a very basic level. Problem solving exercises were assigned and due on a weekly basis in order to (1) help the students learn and apply the material presented in the reading and lectures and (2) to assess a deeper understanding and an application level of comprehension. The quizzes were scored instantly and feedback was given on the other assignments on a weekly basis. Additionally, active learning exercises using spreadsheet modeling (Strakos, 2016) were successfully used to engage students in learner-centered activities.

Applicability and connection (constructivist design)

In addition to the understanding and knowing levels of comprehension, the course project was designed to facilitate application of concepts and to boost the students' ability to synthesize course knowledge and solve real-world problems by connecting material to business operations. The project was assigned in pieces and feedback was given throughout the quarter. This was intended to encourage the student to work on manageable sections of the project and to guide them in the process of analyzing a real-world inventory problem.

When compared to Mashaw's model of effectiveness, the intentional design mechanisms described above directly map to many of the model's influence factors, as illustrated in table 2 below.

Table 2: Mapping the effectiveness model to course design factors

Construct	Factors	Intentional Design Mechanisms
Learning Experiences	• Understanding and comprehension • Changes in thinking attitude, behavior, or belief • Appreciation for value of learning • Confidence to apply concept • Confidence to handle real-world cases	Quizzes, Problem solving, Project, Feedback structure (peer and instructor), Pre and post class survey
Facilitator Creates online environment of learning	• Identify learning objectives or goals • Modular presentation with clear interconnection • Inspiration to continue • Encourage exploration and discovery	Clear, explicit goals, Modular standardized presentation, Usable timely feedback, challenging problems, project structure, timelines, material release, deadlines, schedule
Technology	• Interface design and usability • Content, organization, and appeal of material • Interactive and dynamic sessions with novelty • Usability of LMS • Flexibility of modules based on control of learner	Streamlined, standardized content presentation, scheduled release, interaction through project and discussion board, instructor flexibility, flexibility inherent with asynchronous structure
Interaction and participation	• Ease of communication (instructor and others) • Reasonable response time to questions; live discussion • Encouragement of participation and motivation for getting involved	Service guarantees, peer feedback, Q&A forum, instructor availability, live feedback sessions
Mentor's Inspiration	• Explanations and presentation methods • Design, challenges, and appropriateness of assignments • Motivation technique for critical thinking • Timely feedback about the student's progress • Assistance at the individual level	Lessons designed to take students from information transfer to application, reading, watching, doing, evaluating others, incorporating feedback, service guarantees, use of LMS grade book, frequent email interaction with individuals, availability for live interaction
Hindrance and discouragement	• Technical frustration and stress • Boring or static content or presentation (lectures) • Dissatisfaction resulting from inflexibility • Discontent from disappointment or unreasonable assignments • Lack of guidance or learning assistance	Standard LMS format, short, creative, and dynamic lecture videos, flexibility based on student needs, peer and instructor help if bogged down on assignment (environment of open questioning), structured to connect goals, timelines, and assignments to LOs and concepts

Proposition: These intentional design mechanisms will improve students' perceptions and satisfaction with the course, therefore improving overall effectiveness.

METHOD AND ANALYSIS

The students were administered a survey about their attitude and perception of online learning and specific learning activities prior to class and at the completion of the class. The questions used to measure student perceptions of the class and specific activities were adapted from Lage, Platt, & Treglia (2000). Students answered these questions on a five point Likert scale and were also given the opportunity to provide qualitative comments to an open-ended question. The Likert scale responses ranged from "strongly disagree" to "strongly agree."

The Likert scale questions were intended to capture student perceptions and attitudes about the online classroom in general as well as specific elements of the course design. The questions were as follows.

Q1: "I am excited about learning in an online classroom."

Q2: "Given the choice, I would prefer to take an in-residence class."

Q3-7: "I am looking forward to:" [stem of question used in the pre-class survey] OR "The following class components were a good use of learning time:" [stem of question used in the post-class survey].

Online review questions / quizzes.
Problem solving exercises.
Collaborative online group work.
Online discussion board participation.
Online video lectures.

Q8: I would rather complete a course project than take a proctored mid-term and final exam.

Q9: Please enter any additional thoughts you may have about taking a distance learning class online (optional).

The results of pre and post-class surveys were compared using a method which has been employed in the assessment of a similar online management science course (Gupta, Mau, & Richardson, 2014). The mean response scores for each question were compared between pre and post-class responses using an independent samples t-test in SPSS. The independent samples test was used because matching data was not collected for a paired samples t-test. The results of this test and a summary of the student's responses to questions one through eight are presented in table 3 below.

Table 3: Results of pre and post-class surveys

	Responses	Strongly Disagree	Disagree	Neutral	Agree	Strongly Agree	Mean	Pre-Post Change
I am excited about learning in an online classroom.	Pre-Class	2	4	6	0	0	2.33	0.50 (ns)
	Post-Class	1	3	5	3	0	2.83	
Given the choice, I would prefer to take an in-residence class.	Pre-Class	0	0	2	3	7	4.42	0.25 (ns)
	Post-Class	0	0	0	4	8	4.67	
I am looking forward to: / The following class components were a good use of learning time:	(The pre and post-class survey questions were identical with the exception of the stem statement as indicated.)							
Online review questions / quizzes.	Pre-Class	1	1	7	3	0	3.00	1.25*
	Post-Class	0	0	0	9	3	4.25	
Problem solving exercises.	Pre-Class	1	2	4	3	2	3.25	1.00*
	Post-Class	0	0	0	9	3	4.25	
Collaborative online group work.	Pre-Class	3	1	4	2	2	2.92	0.33 (ns)
	Post-Class	2	1	4	2	3	3.25	
Online discussion board participation.	Pre-Class	1	1	4	4	2	3.42	0.08 (ns)
	Post-Class	1	2	2	4	3	3.50	
Online video lectures.	Pre-Class	1	2	4	5	0	3.08	1.42*
	Post-Class	0	0	1	4	7	4.50	
I would rather complete a course project than take a proctored mid-term and final exam.	Pre-Class	1	2	1	1	7	3.92	0.17 (ns)
	Post-Class	2	0	0	3	7	4.08	

These results clearly show that students' perceptions of three factors used in the design of the course changed drastically – going from a near-neutral perception of the activity to a positive perception of the value of the activity. These activities, online video lectures, online review questions/quizzes, and problem solving exercises can be mapped to online effectiveness as presented in table 2.

In addition to these statistically significant differences in mean responses, a comparison can be made as to the level of overall agreement or disagreement in the before and after class students as in Gupta, et al. (2014). The results of this before and after comparison of agreement or disagreement are presented in figures 1 through 8 below.

Figure 1: Online classroom attitude

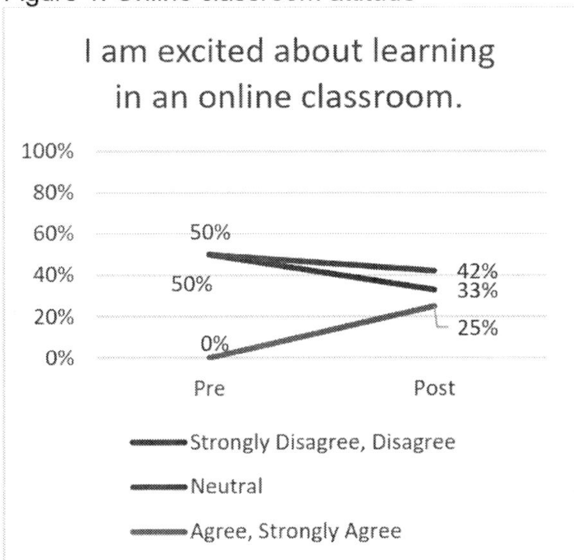

Figure 2: In-residence classroom attitude

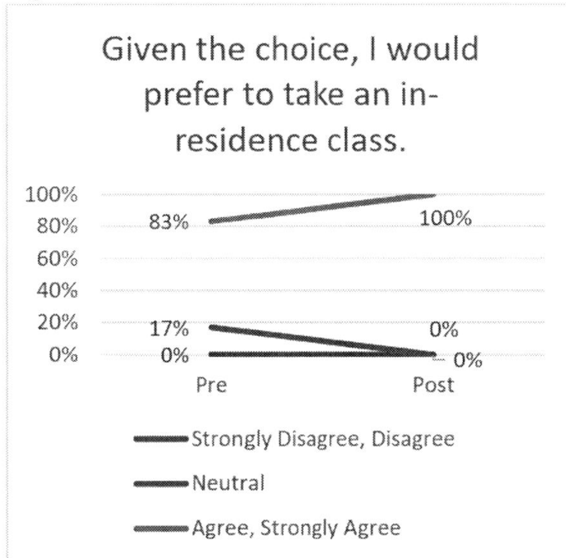

The following questions were asked with a stem of "I am looking forward to:" for pre-class surveys and "The following class components were a good use of learning time:" for post-class surveys.

Figure 3: Review Questions

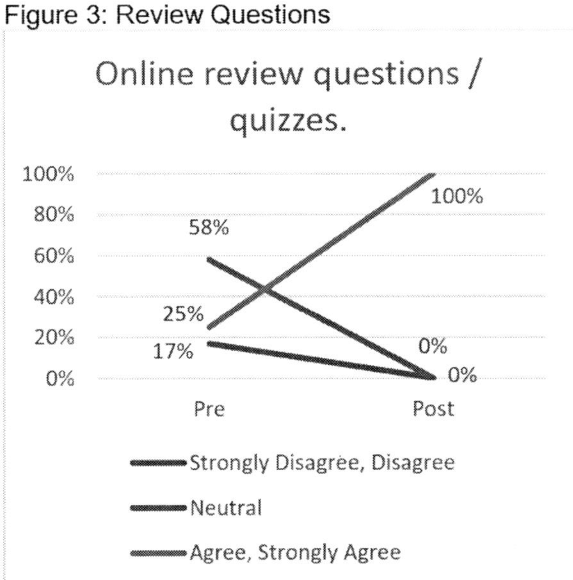

Figure 4: Problem Solving

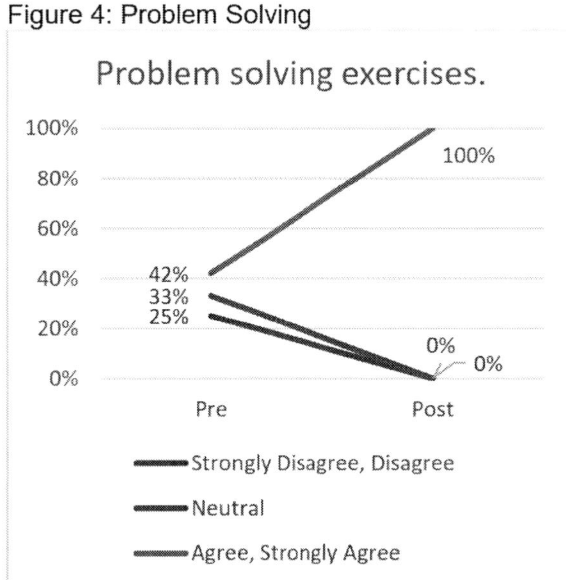

Figure 5: Group Work

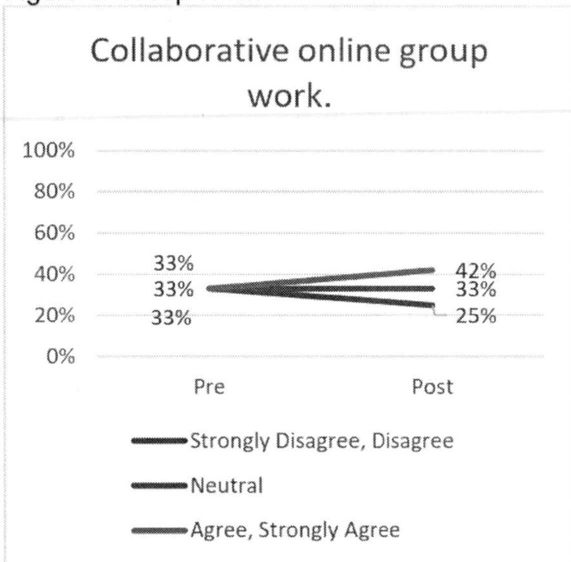

Figure 6: Discussion Boards

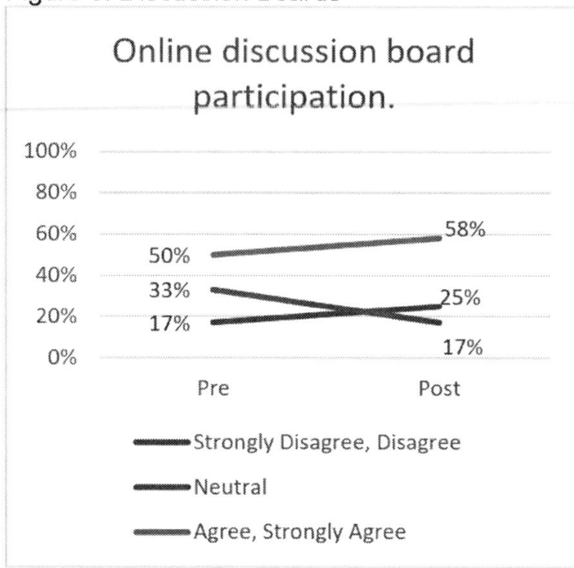

Figure 7: Video Lectures

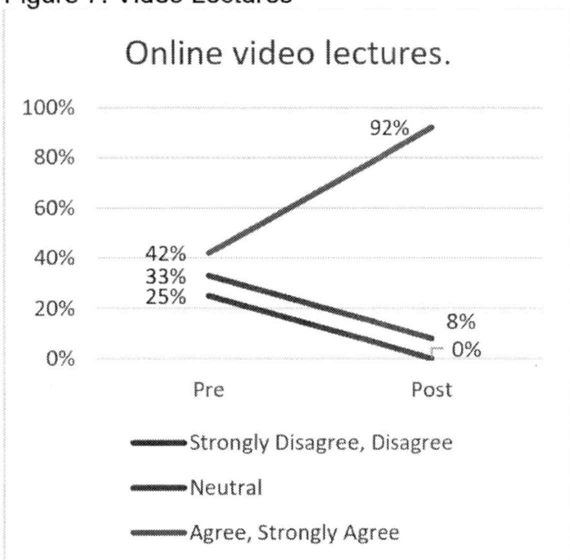

Figure 8: Course Project

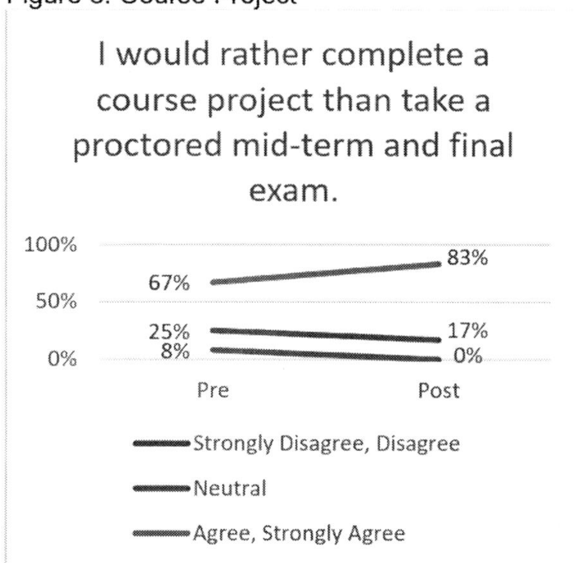

Although not all before and after class responses were statistically significant, figures 1 through 8 show the students had at least some change in attitude toward all the intentional design elements captured by the survey. These results provide evidence that intentionally designed online learning best practices improve students' perception and attitude about the elements of the class. Given that overall effectiveness is characterized as a holistic synergy of design elements, an improved learning experience is likely to be a result.

In addition to the quantitative results of the survey, open-ended comments were collected. It is perhaps these candid comments that capture the best evidence of a change in student attitudes toward the online learning environment and provide support for the effectiveness of the intentional design features incorporated into this class. These comments also provide valuable insight as to why the students' perceptions of the value of the online learning environment in general were skeptical.

Student responses to the open-ended question, “Please enter any additional thoughts you may have about taking a distance learning class online (optional)” are provided below.

Pre-class comments

“I'm not sure how well this DL online collaboration thing is going to work. Already in my group we have completely different time zones to contend with, so there is no live interaction. ... Hopefully it will work out.”

“...I am highly against distance learning...I don't have the time to devote to these online classes that I would like.”

“The most challenging part...is obviously balancing our (sometimes demanding) work schedules with a structured weekly course. ...DL students struggle with being treated like In-res students during previous courses. An example is when we were expected to watch the entire lecture that they sit through when (with some teachers) half of what the class discusses with the professor is chit-chat.”

“Having taken several online courses, both undergraduate and in this program, I have strong reservations about a group project for DL students...several of my classmates who are serving overseas (myself included...) who will have to work out scheduling conflicts due to time zones...on top of balancing a challenging program with families, work, [etc].”

“DL classes through [institution] have been hit or miss so far...the least effective delivery method has been straight recordings of the In-Res lectures...”

Post-class comments

“I really appreciated [the professor] and how he considered what the DL students had been saying about our limited time. His flexibility was refreshing to say the least, and the fact that he was quick to respond to our emails was great...Overall, this was a much better class than we've had in the last several months.”

“Great format...the grading structure is very beneficial to [online]...It still requires you to know the material, but reinforces it more than taking a test when you have to practically apply it.”

“...I am still very against this particular program being in an online setting. I do not feel DL learning is as effective as in-residence.”

“The group project as a DL group was a good thing. We had a goal, a reason to meet each week, and if someone missed out they could make up the next week.”

“Group Homework that is due within the week (especially spreadsheets) is NOT done as a group...it's the first person to get to the session that completes it.”

“The asynchronous format was outstanding! I liked the modular feel of the course content and it allowed us to work the program around our professional/personal lives much more easily! Small group collaboration was fantastic, much better than forced discussion board posting that often isn't very meaningful...”

“The online collaborative group project is not effective. It takes distance students literally days or the entire week to achieve the same level of collaboration that the in-residence students can get face to face in 15 minutes...”

RESULTS

Pre-class Comments indicate a varying, but generally negative attitude toward online learning. As indicated by the pre-class survey, students would overwhelmingly choose to take an in-residence class. Due to this factor, and additional question was added to the post-class survey, which, when combined with the qualitative comments, sheds additional light on the students' overall perception of online learning. This question was intended to gauge if the students would have voluntarily enrolled in the online program, or were attending only because they were selected and enrolled as a part of a professional development program. The question and its results are as follows.

"I wanted to participate in the [institution's] DL Master's program."

Choices and responses: "Yes" - 0 "No" - 4 "I only wanted to attend in-residence" - 8

This reveals a peculiarity of this program which makes changing the attitudes of the students even more difficult than it would be with a group of students enrolled in an online program due completely to their own motivation.

The pre and post-class survey was not designed to measure the entire student experience, but to gather student perceptions of very specific learning activities built into course and to measure general overall changes in attitude toward the online classroom. In general, however, student perceptions of the online classroom improved as a result of taking this course.

Qualitative comments show a definitive change in attitudes toward online learning in general. Although one post-class comment indicated a doubtful and critical attitude of online learning, the overall tone and content of the comments marks a drastic change in attitude, confidence, motivation, and satisfaction with online learning and the intentionally designed elements of this course which were incorporated to improve effectiveness. The online comments concerning group work and discussion board usefulness corroborate the quantitative results.

These results indicate that the most successful elements of this class were the online quizzes, problem solving exercises, and online video lectures. These elements show promise as to the power of simple yet intentional design in improving online learning effectiveness. Overall, the factors created structure by design and presence by incorporating flexibility and ensuring accessibility. Additionally the design facilitated usability, interaction, understanding and comprehension, and applicability and connection.

IMPLICATIONS AND DISCUSSION

In terms of the objectives of this research, which were (1) to explore how intentional design can be incorporated to improve online learning effectiveness and (2) to reach out to skeptics, several conclusions can be drawn. First, from the quantitative and qualitative survey results, we can see that several simple yet specific intentional design factors can change student perceptions.

Second, the results point to how these and other basic applications of best practice can transform the characteristic differences between the online and in-residence classroom from threats to opportunities. When teaching an online class that one has previously taught in-residence, start with a vision and build the course based on best practices. Keep in mind that small changes in design make a big difference in delivery and effectiveness when it comes to the online classroom. Use a step by step approach similar to in-residence course design (Fink, 2013). Ask first, "Where do I want to go?" and then determine the best way to get there.

When considering the limitations of this study, keep in mind that it is conceptual in nature, yet incorporates enough evidence to draw some basic conclusions. It is not a confirmatory study, nor is there a hypothetical model presented. The intent is to contribute conceptual and practical value by linking the intentional design method employed to a model of online learning effectiveness. Additionally, the empirical evidence is from a small sample size and is limited to military students. However, this group of students share many characteristics with all working professionals in terms of part-time study, job and family commitments, and geographic dispersion. The study and its empirical findings are not intended to provide proof, but practical evidence of the value of intentional design.

One of the most difficult aspects of teaching working adults is keeping up with the students as a teacher. The teacher must always seek to add practical value for the student while maintaining academic rigor and meeting course goals. A notable contribution of this research, as discussed by Falconer and Littlejohn (2007) is that the intentional design framework employed here can be shared and reused via the LMS, providing a low-cost, high-value asset for other faculty engaged in online teaching. In the future, research should follow up with determining what the best factors are in online course design. Academically speaking, this future research should look at a cost to outcome ratio of incorporating certain design elements. Additionally, more empirical studies of how specific course design elements are related to specific measures of effectiveness should be conducted. None of the ideas presented here are new in and of themselves. However, the demonstration of their value in a practical setting should motivate and inspire skeptical students and teachers alike. The synergy of intentional design and best practices promises to be of value for the future of online teaching effectiveness.

CONCLUSION

Online education is increasing, so one can either embrace it or try to catch up when eventually faced with teaching in an online program. The consequences of viewing online education as online delivery of in-residence courses can be detrimental for students and their perception of programs as well as to the attitude of the instructor who may experience limited success with this method. For the skeptical online instructor, no one study can remove skepticism. However, studies of this nature should provide a glimmer of hope that effort invested in intentionally designing online courses will pay dividends in student and instructor success. The key to this success is to address fundamental differences between the in-residence and online classroom as opportunities rather than threats.

REFERENCES

Abrami, P. C., Bernard, R. M., Bures, E. M., Borokhovski, E., & Tamim, R. M. (2011). Interaction in distance education and online learning: Using evidence and theory to improve practice. *Journal of Computing in Higher Education*, 23(2-3), 82-103.

Aggarwal, A. K., & Lynn, S. A. (2012). Using continuous improvement to enhance an online course. *Decision Sciences Journal of Innovative Education*, 10(1), 25-48.

Alavi, M., Wheeler, B. C., & Valacich, J. S. (1995). Using IT to reengineer business education: An exploratory investigation of collaborative telelearning. *MIS quarterly*, 293-312.

Allen, I. E., & Seaman, J. (2013). Changing course: Ten years of tracking online education in the United States. *Sloan Consortium*. PO Box 1238, Newburyport, MA 01950.

Arbaugh, J. B., & Benbunan-Finch, R. (2006). An investigation of epistemological and social dimensions of teaching in online learning environments. *Academy of Management Learning & Education*, 5(4), 435-447.

Asef-Vaziri, A. (2015). The flipped classroom of operations management: A not-for-cost-reduction platform. *Decision Sciences Journal of Innovative Education*, 13(1), 71-89.

Benton, T. (2009). Online learning: Reaching out to the skeptics. *Chronicle of Higher Education*. September 18.

Bernard, R. M., Abrami, P. C., Borokhovski, E., Wade, C. A., Tamim, R. M., Surkes, M. A., & Bethel, E. C. (2009). A meta-analysis of three types of interaction treatments in distance education. *Review of Educational Research*, 79(3), 1243-1289.

Bregman, R. L. (2012). 'Eating your own dog food': Applying course concepts in your teaching. *International Journal of Innovation and Learning*, 12(3), 319-331.

Brewer, P.E., & Brewer, E.C. (2015). Pedagogical perspectives for the online education skeptic. *Journal on Excellence in College Teaching*, 26(1), 29-52.

Burgos, D., & Griffiths, D. (2005). "The UNFOLD Project. Understanding and using Learning Design." Educational Cybernetics: Reports.Paper 8. Available at http://digitalcommons.bolton.ac.uk/iec_reports/8

Cameron, L. (2009). *How learning design can illuminate teaching practice*. The Future of Learning Design Conference. Paper 3. December 10. Available at http://ro.uow.edu.au/fld/09/Program/3

Eom, S. B., Wen, H. J., & Ashill, N. (2006). The determinants of students' perceived learning outcomes and satisfaction in university online education: An empirical investigation. *Decision Sciences Journal of Innovative Education*, 4(2), 215-235.

Falconer, I., & Littlejohn, A. (2007). Designing for blended learning, sharing and reuse. *Journal of Further and Higher Education*, 31(1), 41-52.

Fink, L. D. (2013). *Creating significant learning experiences: An integrated approach to designing college courses.* John Wiley & Sons.

Flipped Classroom Field Guide. (n.d.). Available at http://www.cvm.umn.edu/facstaff/prod/groups/cvm/@pub/@cvm/@facstaff/documents/contect/cvm_contect_454476.pdf

Graham, M., & Scarborough, H. (2001). Enhancing the learning environment for distance education students. *Distance Education*, 22(2), 232-244.

Gupta, A., Mau, R. R., & Richardson, T. M. (2014). Assessment of an online management science course. *International Journal of Information and Operations Management Education*, 5(4), 376-402.

Hanover Research Council. (2009). *Best practices in online teaching strategies*. Washington, D.C.. Available at http://uwec.edu/AcadAff/resources/edtech/upload/Best-Practices-in-Online-Teaching-Strategies-Membership.pdf

Keengwe, J., & Kidd, T. T. (2010). Towards best practices in online learning and teaching in higher education. *MERLOT Journal of Online Learning and Teaching*, 6(2), 533-541.

Lage, M. J., Platt, G. J., & Treglia, M. (2000). Inverting the classroom: A gateway to creating an inclusive learning environment. *The Journal of Economic Education*, 31(1), 30-43.

Levine, A. (2015). Time is right for colleges to shift from assembly-line education. *Chronicle of Higher Education*. September 14.

Mashaw, B. (2012). A model for measuring effectiveness of an online course. Decision Sciences Journal of Innovative Education, 10(2), 189-221.

Nemanich, L., Banks, M., & Vera, D. (2009). Enhancing knowledge transfer in classroom versus online settings: The interplay among instructor, student, content, and context. *Decision Sciences Journal of Innovative Education*, 7(1), 123-148.

Redpath, L. (2012). Confronting the bias against on-line learning in management education. *Academy of Management Learning & Education*, 11(1), 125-140.

Reisner, J. (2015). *AFIT EN DL Instructor Orientation* [online course content]. Available at https://afit.blackboard.com

Smith, M. A., & Kellogg, D. L. (2015). Required collaborative work in online courses: A predictive modeling approach. *Decision Sciences Journal of Innovative Education*, 13(4), 563-581.

Strakos, J. K. (2016). Using spreadsheet modeling to teach exchange curves (optimal policy curves) in inventory management. *Decision Sciences Journal of Innovative Education*, 14(1), 51-66.

Wexler, E. (2015). Can online education help refugees earn degrees? *Chronicle of Higher Education Wired Campus Web log.* October 5. Available at http://chronicle.com/blogs/wiredcampus/can-online-education-help-refugees-earn-degrees/57456.

DECISION SCIENCES INSTITUTE

The Effects of Consumer Perceptions of Ethics in Online Gray Market Sourcing Activities on Trust and Purchase Intention

Naveen Gudigantala
University of Portland
gudigant@up.edu

Marcie Abreu
Intel Corporation
marcie.abreu@intel.com

ABSTRACT

Gray market goods are genuine goods that are sourced in an unauthorized manner from a distribution channel. How do consumers judge the ethicality of gray marketer's sourcing practice and what are the implications of such judgments? The results of an experimental study suggest that consumers' ethical judgments of online retailers' sourcing behaviors are guided primarily by inherent rightness (ethical sourcing) or wrongness (gray market sourcing), and secondly by the consequences of such behaviors to consumers. In addition, ethical judgment and perceived consequences for consumers (teleological factors) influenced consumers' purchase intention and trust in online retailers.

KEYWORDS: Ethics in gray markets, Ethics in parallel imports, Hunt-Vitell theory of ethics, Online Ethics, Ethics and Trust, Ethics and Purchase Intention

INTRODUCTION

Gray markets products are genuine goods sold into one market, and then brought (or imported) into another market without the authorization of the intellectual property rights (IPR) owner (Maskus, 2000). This activity is also known as parallel importation (Duhan & Sheffet, 1988). For example, when iPhone 4G was released in the USA, some Apple fans in Hong Kong could not wait for the official launching of iPhone 4G, and some spent in excess of $3,000 to buy a gray market iPhone 4G (Luk, 2010). Unfortunately, gray market goods are not limited to cell phones; a number of tangible and intangible products such as automobiles, heavy construction equipment, watches, cosmetics, prescription drugs, software, broadcast signals, etc. suffer from the gray market activity (Antia, Bergen, & Dutta, 2004). The gray market activity in information technology (IT) industry alone is estimated to be $58 billion, with IT firms suffering losses in profits up to $10 billion (AGMA, 2008). Internet, a global medium which rendered physical barriers irrelevant has fueled the growth of online gray market activities, and efforts by brand owners to contain gray market activities has remained largely fruitless (Bandyopadhyay, 2010).

While there is an increase in online gray market activity, consumers may not always suspect why some genuine goods are sold at lower prices or how online retailers source gray market goods. However, many recent popular press articles are shedding light on gray market activities and educating consumers about the pitfalls of gray market purchases (Herman, 2013; Wolf, 2009). In this context, investigating how consumers form their ethical judgments about online gray market retailers and how such ethical judgments shape their purchase intention and trust becomes an important question and we seek to address this. To guide our investigation, we used Hunt-Vitell theory of ethics (Hunt & Vitell, 2006).

This research has important implications for online retailers sourcing goods from gray markets. The hypotheses developed in the study theorize how consumers form ethical judgments about online gray market activities and how such judgments impact consumers' trust in and purchase intention from an online retailer involved in gray market activities. In addition to learning about consumer behavior in gray market settings, the study also contributes to Hunt-Vitell theory by extending the theory to include the important variable of trust. The paper is structured as following. First, we present background literature on gray markets and consumer ethics. Next we develop hypotheses using Hunt-Vitell theory. In the following sections, we discuss research method, findings, and discussion and conclusion.

LITERATURE REVIEW

Gray Markets

Firms sell their products to end-customers either directly or through a network of authorized partners. Typically, the authorized channel members are provided with substantial discounts as incentives to make profits on the sale of the goods, but are also restricted by agreements to sell the goods only to genuine end-customers. However, when authorized channel members sell the branded goods to unauthorized dealers, gray market goods emerge. These unauthorized dealers typically source branded goods at a discount from authorized sellers and sell them at a price lower than the prevailing market price and make profits in the process. For instance, Hewlett and Packard (HP) alleged Maxicom PC Inc., one of its own authorized channel members, of selling the PC equipment to unauthorized dealers, and reached a settlement to recover more than $4 million offered as pricing discounts (HP, 2008). The difference in prices of the same product in different countries is also a strong incentive for the emergence of gray market activity. In these cases, an unauthorized distributor in country A, where the prices are higher can simply import the products from country B, where the prices are lower, and if the costs of the arbitrage are lower, can make a profit in country A by selling the products at a cheaper rate. For instance, Omega, a Swiss-based watch manufacturing firm is fighting Costco on a copyright infringement case (Morlan, 2010). Omega sells its Swiss-manufactured watches through a global distribution chain. Recognizing that Omega watches are sold at cheaper rates in some countries compared to their US prices, some unknown intermediary purchased the watches and sold them to a New York based company, which in turn imported the watches and sold them to Costco. Neither the New York based company nor Costco was authorized by Omega to sell the watches. Omega alleges that Costco sold the watches for $ 1,299, well below the Omega's U.S. retail price of $ 1,999 (Solomon, 2010).

If gray market activity is not efficiently countered, brand owners face threatening consequences. Gray market sales, on many occasions, dominate the authorized sales. For instance, the sales of gray market personal computers (PC) in India outnumber the authorized PC sales by two to one (Antia et al., 2006). Because a number of gray market goods originally intended for high-end customers appear on low-end stores, the brand reputation suffers. Also, because the gray marketers rarely offer the kind of warranties offered by the authorized dealers, customers face problems with service requests. Overall, gray market activity is proving to be a grave threat to the bottom lines of many multinational companies and many of these companies are not yet ready to face the threat. The risk is particularly severe from Internet-based gray market retailers, because these retailers can buy goods in foreign countries over the Internet and sell them for cheap in the United States. For instance, online gray market pharmacies such as canadadrugs.com, medsforless.com sell gray market prescription drugs to U.S. customers at 10 to 80 percent discount (Bandyopadhyay, 2010). In addition, online gray market exists for goods such as tobacco and consumer electronics (Bandyopadhyay, 2010).

What do customers lose by buying from the online gray market retailers? Consumers face two types of risks: performance and financial risk. After diverting the product from the genuine distribution channels, unauthorized retailers may not stock a product properly. For instance, a prescription drug may not be refrigerated adequately causing them to losing potency and in some cases seriously affecting the patients who may take them (Sudgen, 2009). As for financial risk, many brand owners refuse to honor warranties for gray market products (Gudigantala and Bicen, 2011). Therefore, consumers who purchase big ticket gray market items expose themselves to substantial losses when these products malfunction.

Consumer Ethics

Do ethics matter to consumers? A survey done Creyer (1997) suggests that consumers do really care about ethics and they will reward a firm's ethical behavior by a willingness to pay higher prices for that firm's product. For unethical firms, she found that although consumers may purchase from an unethical firm, they want to pay lower prices. Limbu, Wolf, and Lunsford (2011) used a sample of student respondents to show that non-deception, fulfillment, and security are significant predictors of web site satisfaction, while privacy is related to loyalty. However, Carrigan and Attalla (2001) present a more sobering view of consumer ethics. Using focus group interviews, they found that although consumer awareness is on the rise, this may not result in behavior that favors ethical firms and punishes unethical firms.

In the context of gray markets, the research on consumer ethics is sparse. Liao and Hsieh (2013) examined factors that influence consumers' willingness to purchase gray market smart phones. They found that consumers' attitude towards counterfeit products is positively related to their willingness to purchase gray market phones, whereas perceived risk has a negative relationship with willingness to buy. Their study deems counterfeit products to be gray market goods, while the traditional definition of gray market considers only genuine goods that are diverted from the authorized distribution channels. Zhuang and Tsang (2008) examined ethics involved in gray market activities in a personal selling context in which both buying agents and selling agents exhibited problematic behaviors in exchange. They found that the more the empathy an individual feels for gray market activities, the more inclination that person exhibits to participate in the gray markets. Second, a belief in being punished by their company for indulging in gray market activity had a negative effect in the use of gray market activities. This particular study was conducted in a personal selling context.

In conclusion, although gray market sourcing on part of an online retailer may represent an ethical dilemma for a consumer, very little prior research examined how consumers process such information, how they form judgments about the gray market sourcing practices, and the implications thereof. This study intends to fill such gap. In the next section, we develop hypotheses.

HYPOTHESES

To develop hypotheses for this study, we rely on Hunt-Vitell theory of ethics (Hunt & Vitell, 1986; Hunt & Vitell, 2006). Hunt and Vitell (1986) originally proposed a theory of marketing ethics which is descriptive in nature, and which attempted to describe individual decision-making process for problems that involve ethical content. The scope of this current paper is confined to situations in which consumers are aware of the gray market sourcing of the goods. Therefore, we argue that Hunt-Vitell theory of ethics is a relevant theoretical framework to develop the hypotheses.

Hunt-Vitell theory (1986) addresses is a situation where an individual is faced with a problem perceived to be containing an ethical content. Their theory suggests that once the individual observes this kind of situation, the individual perceives several possible alternatives that might be implemented to resolve the situation. At this point, the individual will invoke two kinds of evaluations: *deontological* and *teleological.* The deontological evaluation concerns the individual evaluation of the inherent rightness or wrongness of the behaviors generated from each alternative. In doing so, an individual compares the behaviors with a set of deontological norms, representing individual's values or rules of behavior. As for norms, they may include general beliefs such as stealing, honesty, cheating, and treating people fairly to issue-specific belief such as deceptive advertising, product safety, sales "kickbacks", confidential of data, etc.

In contrast, teleological evaluation concerns consequences resulting from choosing a certain alternative, and is centered on individual evaluation of how much good versus bad will result from an action. A particular action is ethical if it brings greater positive consequences in relation to the amount of negative consequences (Hunt & Vitell, 2006).

Let us illustrate a simple case to describe how individuals may arrive at deontological and teleological evaluations. Consider the situation: a consumer wants to purchase a laptop from XYZ.com. She comes to know XYZ sourced the laptops in an unauthorized fashion. But the consumer also knows that it is a genuine laptop and XYZ.com sells it for $200 less than anyone on the Internet. When confronted with the question of whether this sourcing behavior is ethical or unethical, a strict deontologist may say it is unethical because the sourcing is unauthorized, while a strict teleologist may say it is ethical because the consumer purchases a genuine laptop for $200 less and therefore benefits her financially.

Hunt-Vitell theory postulates that an individual's ethical judgment is influenced by the individual's deontological evaluation and the individual's teleological evaluation. Applying the theory in the context of gray market sourcing, an individual when aware of the gray market sourcing of an online retailer might use deontological norms (inherent rightness or wrongness of behavior) to judge the online retailer to be unethical. However, changing the context a little bit, if a consumer becomes aware of the gray market sourcing of a product, but if the consumer is offered the product for a price well below the market value, then the consumer might use teleological norm (perceived consequences) to judge the online retailer to be ethical because of the positive consequences accruing to the individual. However, the theory recognizes that some individuals in some cases might act as strict deontologists or teleologists, but they theorize that such situation is unlikely to occur with a majority of individuals (Hunt & Vitell, 1986).

The second major proposition of the Hunt-Vitell theory is that the intention to implement a particular alternative is a function of ethical judgment and teleological evaluation. The proposed relationship between ethical judgment and intention is consistent with the general theories in consumer behavior (Howard & Sheth 1969; Fishbein & Ajzen, 1975). The theory in this context is that ethical judgments influence behavior through intentions. Applying this formulation in the context of gray market sourced products, a consumer may judge an online retailer to be unethical and hence form on an intention not to buy from the website, or vice versa.

The Hunt-Vitell theory also theorizes that ethical judgments may differ from intentions because the teleological evaluation also independently influences intentions. In the context of gray market sourced product, an individual might perceive the sourcing to be unethical and may yet be positively inclined to purchase because of the positive consequence of buying the product at a much cheaper price.

Figure 1: Theoretical Model Used in the Study

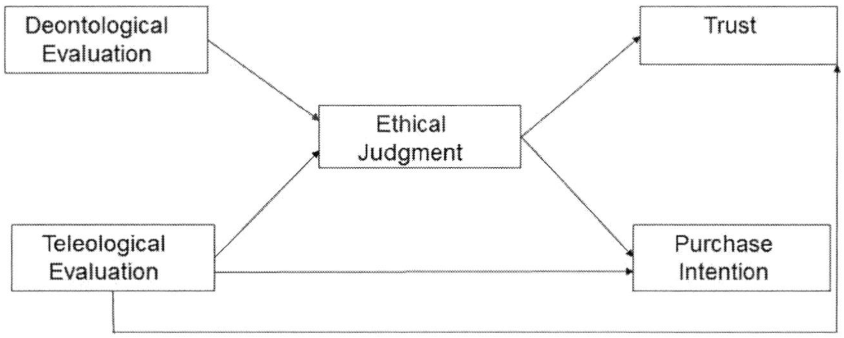

There have been a number of studies that have tested the aforementioned hypotheses, but in contexts other than gray market sourcing. Hunt and Vasquez-Parraga (1993) examined organizational consequences and ethical issues in salesforce supervision. Using an experimental design, they found that managers' intentions to either discipline or reward the behavior of their salespeople were primarily influenced by the inherent rightness or wrongness of the salespeople's behaviors (deontological considerations) and only secondarily by the consequences of salespeople's behaviors on the organization (teleological factors). Vitell, Singhapakdi, and Thomas (2001) examined ethics in the area of consumer purchase behavior in a store by investigating the extent to which consumers rely on ethical norms (deontology) versus perceived consequences of behaviors (teleology). Using three studies, they found that consumers primarily rely on ethical norms and to a lesser degree on perceived consequences in establishing ethical judgments. They also found that there is a significant positive relationship between ethical judgments and behavioral intentions. Mayo and Marks (1990) examined ethics in the context of a marketing research and found that ethical judgments to resolve dilemma in an ethical situation are jointly determined by deontological and teleological evaluations. In addition, they found that the relationship between ethical judgment and intention is weakened when implementation of intention does not include consumer's preferred consequence.

Hence, given the theoretical formulation and prior empirical support, we hypothesize:

H1: Deontological and teleological evaluations significantly influence ethical judgments.
H2: Ethical judgment significantly influences purchase intention.
H3: Teleological evaluation significantly influences purchase intention.

The role of trust in online buyer behavior is well-researched. Hong and Cha (2013) researched the mediating role of trust between perceived risk and purchase intention. Using direct relationships, they found that performance, psychological, financial, and online payment risks have a significant negative influence on purchase intention. Using mediation analysis, they found that trust in an online merchant completely mediates the effect of performance risk, but partially mediates that of the psychological risk. Therefore, trust is an essential element in online buyer behavior and the consumer perceptions of sourcing behavior of online merchants may impact consumer trust in an online retailer. In this study, we postulate that ethical judgment of an online retailer influences trust. This is because consumers find online retailers with authorized sourcing practices to be more dependable and reliable. In addition, we also theorize that any positive consequence (teleological evaluation) may also positively influence trust. Because a consumer is likely to be satisfied when offered a genuine product at a cheaper price. Therefore, we hypothesize:

H4: Ethical judgment significantly influences trust in an online retailer.
H5: Teleological evaluation significantly influences trust in an online retailer.

METHODS

We employed a methodology similar to that of Hunt and Vasquez-Parraga (1993), Vitell et al (2001), in that we used multiple scenarios to test the research hypotheses. We used two factor design (2 X 2 between-subjects design) and manipulated deontological norms (ethical and unethical sourcing by online retailer; unethical sourcing represents gray market goods) and perception of consequences (i.e. lower financial risk (consumers save money) and higher financial risk (consumers may have to pay more or face high financial risk in future)). The scenarios presented to respondents were created in the context of buying a Lenovo laptop from a U.S. based online retailer. We asked the respondent to play the role of potential buyer and evaluate the information provided in the scenario for their decision-making purposes. These scenarios were tested and refined in a pilot study using an undergraduate and graduate sample of twenty-one students.

We conducted the experiment with 114 subjects. The instructions in the questionnaire required respondents to place themselves as a potential buyer in one of the following scenarios. In addition, in scenarios involving gray market sourcing, we asked respondents to consider such information while making their decisions. Once they finished reading the scenario, they answered questions on measures related to perceived financial risk (used for measuring consequences), ethical judgment, purchase intention, and trust. The surveys were done anonymously and the participants were given course credit as motivation to participate in the study. The measures are included in Table 2. The following four scenarios were used:

Table 1: Scenarios Used in the Study

	Deontologically unethical condition (seller sources from gray market)	Deontologically ethical condition (seller sources from authorized distribution channel)
Positive Consequence for Customer (low financial risk)	Scenario 1: ElectronicsForYou.com, a U.S.-based retail e-commerce company recently had an opportunity to import a large number of genuine Lenovo laptops from a wholesaler in China. *The Chinese wholesaler is not authorized by Lenovo to sell to U.S.-based companies.* Normally in the U.S., this laptop is bought at $1100 by ElectronicsForYou.com from authorized U.S. wholesalers and sold at $1200, but ElectronicsForYou.com acquired the laptops for $800 apiece from the Chinese wholesaler in spite of knowing the unauthorized nature of the transaction. ElectronicsForYou.com now sells	Scenario 3: ElectronicsForYou.com, a U.S.-based retail e-commerce company recently had an opportunity to import a large number of genuine Lenovo laptops from a wholesaler in China for only $800 per laptop whereas the U.S-based authorized wholesaler sells the same for $1100. However, the Chinese wholesaler is not authorized by Lenovo to sell to U.S.-based companies. ElectronicsForYou.com decided to decline the purchase offer from the Chinese wholesaler as it is an improper transaction. When Lenovo came to learn about ElectronicsForYou.com's decision, they appreciated the gesture and offered a large

	these genuine Lenovo laptops at $1000 on their website whereas the nearest rival sells the same for $1200. Therefore, a consumer who buys laptop from ElectronicsForYou.com not only gets a genuine Lenovo laptop but also gets it for $200 cheaper than the next best competitor on the Internet.	stock of Lenovo laptops for only $800 per laptop. ElectronicsForYou.com now sells these genuine Lenovo laptops at $1000 on their website whereas the nearest rival sells the same for $1200. Therefore, a consumer who buys laptop from ElectronicsForYou.com not only gets a genuine Lenovo laptop but also gets it for $200 cheaper than the next best competitor on the Internet.
Negative Consequence for Customer (high financial risk)	Scenario 2: ElectronicsForYou.com, a U.S.-based retail e-commerce company recently had an opportunity to import a large number of genuine Lenovo laptops from a wholesaler in China. *The Chinese wholesaler is not authorized by Lenovo to sell to U.S.-based companies.* Normally, this laptop is bought at $1100 from the authorized U.S. wholesaler and sold at $1200, but ElectronicsForYou.com acquired the laptops for $800 apiece from the Chinese wholesaler in spite of knowing the unauthorized nature of the transaction. ElectronicsForYou.com now sells genuine Lenovo laptops at $1000 on their website whereas the nearest rival sells the same for $1200. However, Lenovo discovered this unauthorized transaction through their audits and decided to decline any warranty on this laptop to customers who purchased it on ElectronicsForYou.com. Therefore, a consumer who buys laptop from ElectronicsForYou.com not only gets a genuine Lenovo laptop but also gets it for $200 cheaper than the next best competitor on the Internet. However, once a consumer purchases the laptop, they may run into warranty issues with Lenovo in case of any problems with the laptop in future.	Scenario 4: ElectronicsForYou.com, a U.S.-based retail e-commerce company recently had an opportunity to import a large number of genuine Lenovo laptops from a wholesaler in China for only $800 per laptop whereas the U.S-based authorized wholesaler sells the same for $1100. *However, the Chinese wholesaler is not authorized by Lenovo to sell to U.S.-based companies.* ElectronicsForYou.com decided that it is an improper transaction and declined to purchase from the Chinese wholesaler. However, a local U.S.-based competitor of ElectronicsForYou.com purchased the same laptops from the Chinese wholesaler and sells a large number of them in the market for $1000, whereas ElectronicsForYou.com sells the same for $1200 apiece. Therefore, a consumer who buys laptop from ElectronicsForYou.com gets a genuine Lenovo laptop but pays $200 more than the next best competitor on the Internet.

Table 2: Measures Used in the Study
Ethical Judgment (measured on 1-7 Likert Scale, 1=Very unethical, 7=very ethical) Source: Shelby, D. H., & Vasquez-Parraga, A. Z. (1993) • I feel the sourcing behavior of ElectronicsForYou.com is........ (note: "sourcing" refers to the process used by ElectronicsForYou.com to acquire the laptops to be sold to the end consumers)
Perceived Risk (measured on 1-7 Likert Scale, 1=strongly disagree, 7=strongly agree) Source: Vehagen, Meents, & Tan (2006). (Cronbach alpha: 0.78) • If I were to purchase Lenovo laptop from ElectronicsForYou.com, I would be concerned that the laptop in this website may be more expensive than products in a different place • If I were to purchase Lenovo laptop from ElectronicsForYou.com, I would be concerned that I might be able to buy the same product at a different place at a lower price than in ElectronicsForYou.com • If I were to purchase Lenovo laptop from ElectronicsForYou.com, I may suffer monetary loss due to sales fraud.
Trust (measured on 1-7 Likert Scale, 1=strongly disagree, 7=strongly agree) Source: Hong & Cha (2013). (Cronbach alpha: 0.95) • I believe ElectronicsForYou.com is dependable • I believe ElectronicsForYou.com is reliable

- I believe ElectronicsForYou.com is honest
- I believe ElectronicsForYou.com is trustworthy

Purchase Intention (measured on 1-7 Likert Scale, 1=strongly disagree, 7=strongly agree)
Source: Vehagen, Meents, & Tan (2006). (Cronbach alpha: 0.85)

- If I needed a Lenovo laptop now, I would consider purchasing it from ElectronicsForYou.com
- If I needed a Lenovo laptop in the near future, I would purchase it from ElectronicsForYou.com
- I would recommend ElectronicsForYou.com to a friend

RESULTS

A total of 114 undergraduate and graduate students participated in the experiment among which 61 were male and 53 were female. The average age of participant was 21 years with standard deviation 2 years. The subjects on average had used the Internet to browse products for 11 years (standard deviation 2.5 years) and all the subjects bought something previously from the Internet. The questionnaires containing scenarios were randomly assigned to subjects. A total of 29 subjects worked on scenario#1, 28 worked on scenario#2, 28 worked on scenario#3, and 29 worked on scenario#4.

To ascertain whether or not manipulations worked, we conducted t-tests. We first checked for whether the conditions on deontologically ethical vs. unethical scenarios were perceived by respondents as the way we intended. Scenarios 1 and 2 presented situations in which the online retailers sourced products unethically (Item: "I feel the sourcing behavior of ElectronicsForYou.com is .... unethical (1) .... ethical (7))"; mean=2.65; SD=1.26) and scenarios 3 and 4 presented situations in which products were sourced ethically (mean =5.69; SD=1.53). The t-test showed that the manipulation was successful (t-stat=-11.57, p-value=0.001). Second, we checked for the teleological evaluations. In scenario 2, although the product is cheaper, the customers were told that Lenovo would decline warranty. In scenario 4, the respondents had to pay higher prices. Therefore, scenarios 2 and 4 represented negative consequences in terms of higher perceived financial risk (mean for perceived financial risk = 4.75; SD=1.8). Scenarios 1 and 3 provided situations where in the respondents were able to purchase the laptop considerably cheaper than the nearest rival (mean = 3.4; SD = 1.39). The t-test showed that the manipulation was successful (t-stat=-5.05, p-value=0.001). To measure this, we used the summated scale of the items for perceived risk. Table 3 and Figure 2 summarize the descriptive statistics and trends for the measures used in the study.

Table 3: Summary of Means and Standard Deviations of Constructs in Each Experimental Condition						
Scenario (N =sample)	Deontological Evaluation	Teleological Evaluation	Ethical Judgment Mean (SD)	Perceived Risk Mean (SD)	Purchase Intention Mean (SD)	Trust Mean (SD)
1 (29)	Unethical	Positive (low risk)	2.61 (1.2)	3.68 (1.14)	4.18 (1.55)	2.90 (0.96)
2 (28)	Unethical	Negative (high risk)	2.83 (1.31)	3.98 (1.07)	4.05 (1.40)	2.88 (0.94)
3 (28)	Ethical	Positive (low risk)	5.21 (1.73)	3.67(1.29)	5.29 (1.25)	5.03(1.59)
4 (29)	Ethical	Negative (high risk)	6.14 (1.16)	5.09 (0.64)	4.47 (1.68)	5.67 (1.19)

Figure 2. A Graph of Means of Measures Across the Four Experimental Conditions

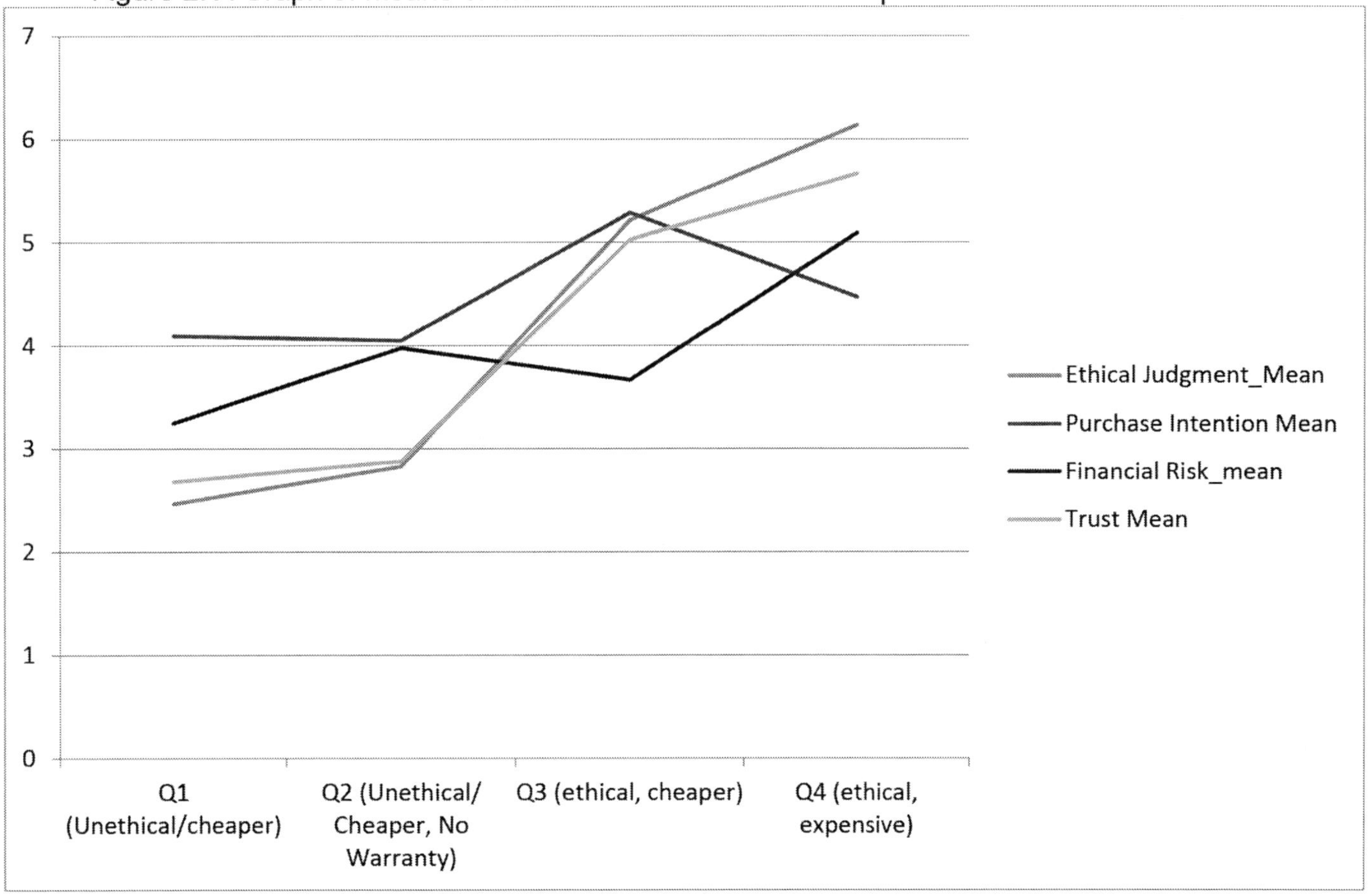

The patterns from the above chart, for the most part, are in expected terms. The means for ethical judgments and trust are higher for ethical sourcing conditions in relation to unethical sourcing conditions. Participants' perceived risk was higher for conditions where they were expected to pay more or when they anticipated issues with warranty. The interesting result can be gleaned from the purchase intention line. The mean for purchase intention is expectedly low and flat for unethical sourcing conditions, but spikes for 'ethical and cheaper' condition, but falls down steeply for 'ethical and expensive' condition.

The results of the multiple regression analyses are provided in table 4 below.

Table 4. Results of Multiple Regression

Dependent Variable	Predictor Variable	Parameter (unstardardized)	Parameter (stardardized)	t-value	p-value	Model R-squared; F-value; significance
Ethical Judgment	Intercept	2.322		10.406	0.0001	0.569 (F=73.37; significance=0.001)
	Deontological Evaluation (dummy variable)	3.035	0.738	11.85	0.0001	
	Teleological Evaluation (dummy variable)	0.643	0.156	2.512	0.013	
Purchase Intention	Intercept	4.593		32.447	0.0001	0.216 (F=10.08; significance=0.001)
	Ethical Judgment	0.355	0.479	5.05	0.001	
	Teleological Evaluation	-0.243	-0.277	-2.91	0.004	
	Ethical Judgment X Teleological Evaluation	-0.074	-0.176	-2.069	0.041	
Trust	Intercept	4.993		9.86	0.001	0.67 (F=75.4; significance=0.001)
	Ethical Judgment	0.849	0.998	6.98	0.001	
	Teleological Evaluation	0.328	0.326	2.48	0.015	
	Ethical Judgment X Teleological Evaluation	-0.05	-0.40	-1.86	0.065	

Multiple regression results show that both deontological evaluations (standardized beta=0.738, p-value =0.001) and teleological evaluations (standardized beta=0.156, p-value=0.013) influenced ethical judgment. However, out of the total 56.9% variation explained, deontological evaluation contributed 54.5% and teleological evaluation contributed only 2.4%. These results are consistent with Hunt-Vitell theory's predictions and support our hypothesis 1.

Purchase intention has been found to be significantly related to ethical judgment (standardized beta=0.479, p-value=0.001), teleological evaluation (standardized beta=-0.277, p-value=0.004), and the interaction effect is also significant (standardized beta=-0.176, p-value=0.041). As seen from the figure 3 below, higher values of ethical judgments are associated with higher values of purchase intention. However, the interaction is significant meaning consumers exhibit higher levels of purchase intention when perceived risk is low compared to when it is high. These results support our hypotheses 2 and 3.

Figure 3. Effects of ethical judgment and teleological evaluation on purchase intention

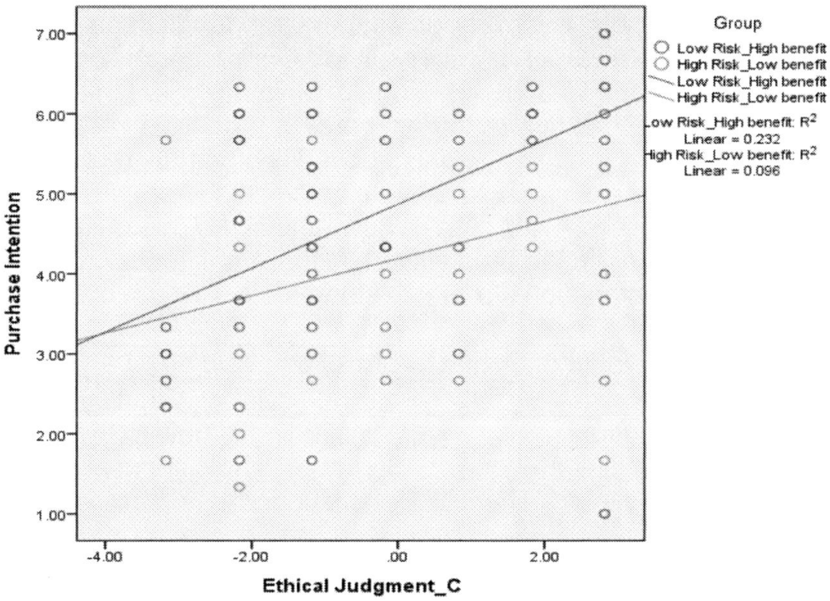

As for hypothesis 4 and 5, we found that trust is influenced not only by ethical judgment (standardized beta=0.99, p-value=0.001) but also by teleological evaluation (perceived risk) (standardized beta=0.326, p-value=0.015), but the interaction effect is insignificant (F=75.4, p-value of model=0.001). We found support for hypotheses 4 and 5. In conclusion, our study found support for all the five hypotheses theorized.

Figure 4. Effects of ethical judgment and teleological evaluation on trust

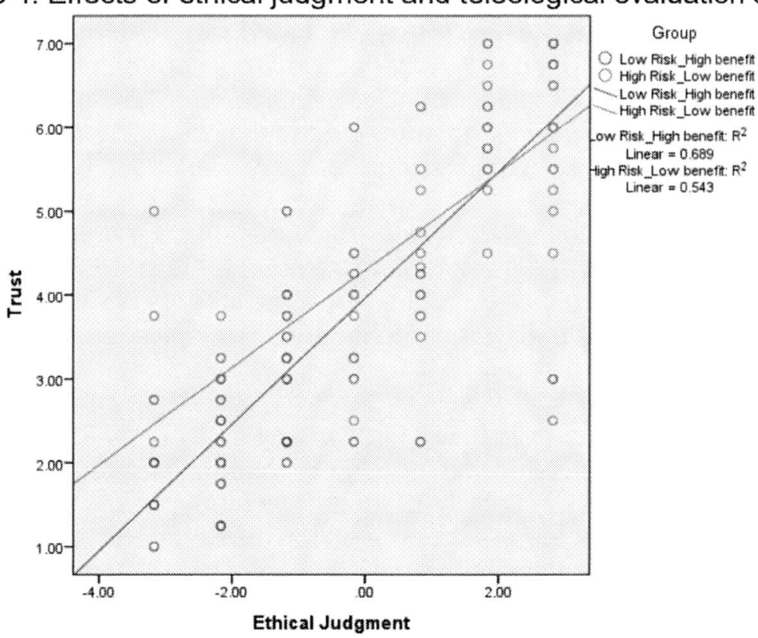

DISCUSSION AND CONCLUSIONS

If consumers know that an online retailer is sourcing genuine goods in an unauthorized fashion, what kinds of implications such awareness will result in? Our research finds that gray market sourcing of products is associated with lower ratings of online retailers in terms of ethical judgments, trust, and purchase intention. Although perceived positive consequences are positively associated with ethical judgments, only about 2% of variation of a total of 57% variation in ethical judgments is explained by such teleological factors; the remaining 55% of variation is attributed to consumers' evaluation of how ethical the online retailers sourcing practices are. All our results confirm the predictions of Hunt-Vitell theory of ethics (2008). The following table provides our contributions from this study.

Table 5: Contributions of this study

Finding	What's new?
1. Ethical judgments about online retailers' sourcing practices are influenced by both deontological and teleological evaluations.	This finding is new to the gray market literature. This finding also confirms Hunt-Vitell theory.
2. Purchase intention of consumers is influenced by both ethical judgments about online retailers and teleological evaluations.	This finding is new to the gray market literature. This finding also confirms Hunt-Vitell theory.
3. Trust in online retailers is influenced by both ethical judgments about online retailers and teleological evaluations.	This finding is new to the gray market literature. This finding is also new to Hunt-Vitell theory.

From table 5, we show that the study makes unique contribution to the literature on ethics involved in gray market sourcing of goods. As far as we are aware of, no prior study on gray market ethics considered a realistic situation faced by consumers and examined the decision-making processes concerning ethical judgments and their implications. Therefore, the first two findings make unique contributions to the literature on gray markets.

The third finding about the relationships between trust and 'ethical judgments and teleological evaluations' is not only unique to the gray market literature, but also to the Hunt-Vitell theory of ethics. Therefore, these relationships extend the Hunt-Vitell theory of ethics by adding trust to their framework and showing that ethical judgments and teleological evaluations significantly influence trust.

The current study is not without its limitations. First, in any study of ethics there is always an element of social desirability associated with consumer responses. We have not measured or controlled for the effects of social desirability. Second, the study makes the assumption that consumers are aware of the sourcing practices of online retailers. This may not be true in a majority of circumstances, although consumer awareness of sourcing activities of firms is generally on the rise (i.e. consumers looking for "green" products). Finally, the current study only included financial risk when conceptualizing teleological evaluations. There may be other types of risks such as performance risks, psychological risks, and online payment risks. Future studies may consider some of these additional risks.

In conclusion, the findings of this study support the predictions of Hunt-Vitell theory. The implications for online retailers engaging in gray market sourcing are clear that the knowledge of these activities negatively influences consumer perceptions of trust and purchase intention. This study also contributes to Hunt-Vitell theory by theorizing how ethical judgments affect trust. This finding extends Hunt-Vitell theory.

ACKNOWLEDGEMENTS

The authors would like to thank the Dundon-Berchtold Institute of Ethics at the University of Portland for supporting this work. We would like to thank Amy Dundon, Jim Berchtold, Dan McGinty, Rev. Mark Poorman, Dr. Tom Greene, and Dr. Mike Eom for their encouragement and support.

REFERENCES

AGMA (2008) "Three Keys to Effectively Addressing the Unauthorized Reseller Market", The Alliance for Gray Market and Counterfeit Abatement, http://www.agmaglobal.org/press_events/FINAL%20Unauthorized%20Market%20Tips%20EMEA%20DRAFT%203-31-08%20doc.pdf (Current May 13, 2016)

Antia, K. D., Bergen, M. E., Dutta, S., & Fisher, R. J. (2006). How does enforcement deter gray market incidence?. *Journal of Marketing*, 70(1), 92-106.

Antia, K.D., M. Bergen., & S. Dutta (2004). "Competing with Gray Markets", *Sloan Management Review*, (46)1, 63-69.

Bandyopadhyay, S. (2010). The internet and gray marketing. *International Business & Economics Research Journal (IBER)*, 9(6), 95-102.

Carrigan, M., & Attalla, A. (2001). The myth of the ethical consumer-do ethics matter in purchase behaviour?. *Journal of consumer marketing*, 18(7), 560-578.

Creyer, E. H. (1997). The influence of firm behavior on purchase intention: do consumers really care about business ethics?. *Journal of consumer Marketing*, 14(6), 421-432.

Duhan, D.F. & Sheffet, M.J. (1988). Gray Markets and the Legal Status of Parallel Importation.

Fishbein, M. & Ajzen, I. (1975). *Belief, Attitude, Intention, and Behavior: An Introduction to Theory and Research*, reading, MA: Addison-Wesley.

Gudigantala, N. & Bicen, P. (2011) "Gray Market for Information Technology (IT) Products: Status, Implications, and Strategies to Address the IT Gray Market Threat," *Communications of the Association for Information Systems*: Vol. 29, Article 10. Available at: http://aisel.aisnet.org/cais/vol29/iss1/10

Herman, M. (2013). "Amazon's Gray Market May Give OEMs a Black Eye", EBN, http://www.ebnonline.com/author.asp?section_id=1098&doc_id=270571 (current May 13, 2016).

Hong, I. B., & Cha, H. S. (2013). The mediating role of consumer trust in an online merchant in predicting purchase intention. *International Journal of Information Management*, *33*(6), 927-939.

HP (2008) "HP Reaches Settlement in Gray Market Case Against Maxicom PC Inc.", Hewlett Packard, http://www.hp.com/hpinfo/newsroom/press/2008/080311a.html (Current May 13, 2016).

Hunt, S. D., & Vitell, S. (1986). A general theory of marketing ethics. *Journal of macromarketing*, *6*(1), 5-16.
Hunt, S. D., & Vitell, S. J. (2006). The general theory of marketing ethics: A revision and three questions. Journal of Macromarketing, 26(2), 143-153. *Journal of Marketing*, 52 (July), 75-83.

Hunt, S. D., & Vasquez-Parraga, A. Z. (1993). Organizational consequences, marketing ethics, and salesforce supervision. *Journal of Marketing Research*, *30*(1), 78-90.

Howard, J.A. & Sheth, J.N. (1969). *The Theory of Buyer Behavior*, New York: Wiley.

Liao, C. H., & Hsieh, I. Y. (2013). Determinants of consumer's willingness to purchase gray-market smartphones. *Journal of business ethics*, *114*(3), 409-424.

Limbu, Y. B., Wolf, M., & Lunsford, D. L. (2011). Consumers' perceptions of online ethics and its effects on satisfaction and loyalty. *Journal of Research in Interactive Marketing*, 5(1), 71-89.

Luk, L. (2010) "IPhone 4 Reaches the Gray Market", Wall Street Journal, http://blogs.wsj.com/chinarealtime/2010/06/30/apples-iphone-4-reaches-the-gray-market/ (current July 10, 2015).

Maskus, K.E. (2000). Parallel imports. *The world economy: Global Trade Policy*, 23, 1269-84.

Mayo, M. A., & Marks, L. J. (1990). An empirical investigation of a general theory of marketing ethics. *Journal of the Academy of Marketing Science*, 18(2), 163-171.

Morlan, K. (2010) "Omega, S.A. v. Costco Wholesale Corporation", More Law Lexapedia, http://www.morelaw.com/verdicts/case.asp?d=37098&n=07-55368&s=CA (Current May 13, 2016)

Shelby, D. H., & Vasquez-Parraga, A. Z. (1993). Organizational consequences, marketing ethics, and salesforce supervision. *Journal of Marketing Research*, 30(1), 78-90.

Solomon, B. (2010) "U.S. Supreme Court to Rule on Costco Copyright Infringement Case", Friends of ORIS, http://www.friendsoforis.com/forum/index.php?showtopic=35856 (Current Aug. 20, 2010).

Sugden, D. R. (2009). Gray Markets: Prevention, Detection, and Litigation. *Oxford University Press*.

Verhagen, T., Meents, S., & Tan, Y. H. (2006). Perceived risk and trust associated with purchasing at electronic marketplaces. *European Journal of Information Systems*, *15*(6), 542-555.

Vitell, S. J., Singhapakdi, A., & Thomas, J. (2001). Consumer ethics: an application and empirical testing of the Hunt-Vitell theory of ethics. *Journal of Consumer marketing*, *18*(2), 153-178.

Wolf. C. (2009). Losing $63 Billion to Gray Market Is Sleuth Obsession, Bloomberg, http://www.bloomberg.com/apps/news?pid=newsarchive&sid=a9CXDajZFhW0 (current May 13, 2016).

Zhuang, G., & Tsang, A. S. (2008). A study on ethically problematic selling methods in China with a broaden concept of gray-marketing. *Journal of Business Ethics*, *79*(1-2), 85-101.

DECISION SCIENCES INSTITUTE`

The Global Aptitude Assessment Model: A Critical Perspective

Rochana Kaushik
Texas A&M University-Commerce
Email: Rochana.Kaushik@tamuc.edu

Mahesh Raisinghani
Texas Woman's University
Email: mraisinghani@twu.edu

Shonda Gibson
Texas A&M University-Commerce
Email: Shonda.Gibson@tamuc.edu

Natalia Assis
Texas A&M University-Commerce
Email: Natalia.Assis@tamuc.edu

ABSTRACT

Educational institutions have been charged and challenged to prepare and produce globally competent graduates. Past research has shown that students are neither formally educated and trained to comprehend the full impact of global interconnectedness, nor to make informed decisions with full knowledge and awareness of the global implications. The Global Competence Aptitude Assessment instrument asserts the ability to capture an individual's capacities of global knowledge, skills, attitudes, and experiences. Employers would like educators to emphasize several key global learning outcomes in an effort to increase graduates' potential to be successful and contributing members of today's global economy.

KEYWORDS: Global competence aptitude assessment, Self-awareness, Open-mindedness, Diversity, attentiveness, Risk taking, Global awareness, Intercultural capabilities, Collaboration across cultures

INTRODUCTION

Many of life's decisions are global in nature. The world has been transformed into an environmentally, politically, socially, and economically connected and interdependent web. Events occurring in one locality are affected, and affect, other locales even though we may not immediately see how the connecting strands tug on each other. Chaos scientists refer to this phenomenon as the "butterfly effect" (Lipman-Blumen, 1996, p. 78). However, most students are not formally educated and trained to comprehend the full impact of global dynamics (issues, trends, processes, and systems) and global interconnectedness, nor to make informed decisions with full knowledge and awareness of the global implications (Olson & Kroeger, 2001).

Varied definitions of global competence have been proposed and discussed in the research, each with a different emphasis, but all centered on some variation describing a body of globally relevant knowledge and awareness and the skills and dispositions required to engage responsibly and effectively in a global environment. Following extensive discussion with representatives from multinational businesses, human resource managers of transnational corporations, senior international educators, United Nations and embassy officials, and intercultural specialists, Hunter (2004) formulated an agreed-upon definition of global competence. According to this diverse panel of experts, a working definition of global competence is: "Having an open mind while actively seeking to understand cultural norms and expectations of others, leveraging this gained knowledge to interact, communicate and work effectively outside one's environment" (Hunter, 2004, p.81). As noted by Hunter, White, and Godbey (2006), this empirically-based description is offered as one plausible definition of global competence that can be customized to fit a specific organization or program.

Although research has revealed slightly different approaches for qualifying the components of global competence, there is notable consistency in the content (Lambert, 1996). Specifically, most operational definitions of global competence center on an individual's level of substantive knowledge, perceptual understanding, and intercultural communication skills. Substantive knowledge includes knowledge of cultures, languages, world history and issues, and human choices (Wilson, 1996). These globally dynamic concepts are typically utilized by individuals as they describe, explain, and possibly predict transnational changes. Perceptual understanding is more difficult to assess and categorize since this component includes an individual's perceptions, emotions, and communication skills. The process an individual incorporates to select, organize, and evaluate the world, as well as understanding others in the world, can be categorized as perceptual understanding (Singer, 1998). Components grouped into intercultural communication skills are those that are drawn upon in an effort to engage effectively with others. Specifically, adaptability, empathy, cross-cultural awareness, intercultural relations, and cultural mediation are skills that are included within intercultural communication (Olson & Kroeger, 2001).

The GCAA model illustrated in figure 1 show the eight identified dimensions that collectively represent global competence: self-awareness, open-mindedness, attentiveness to diversity, risk taking, historical perspective, global awareness and collaboration across cultures.

Figure 1: Global Competence Aptitude Assessment Model

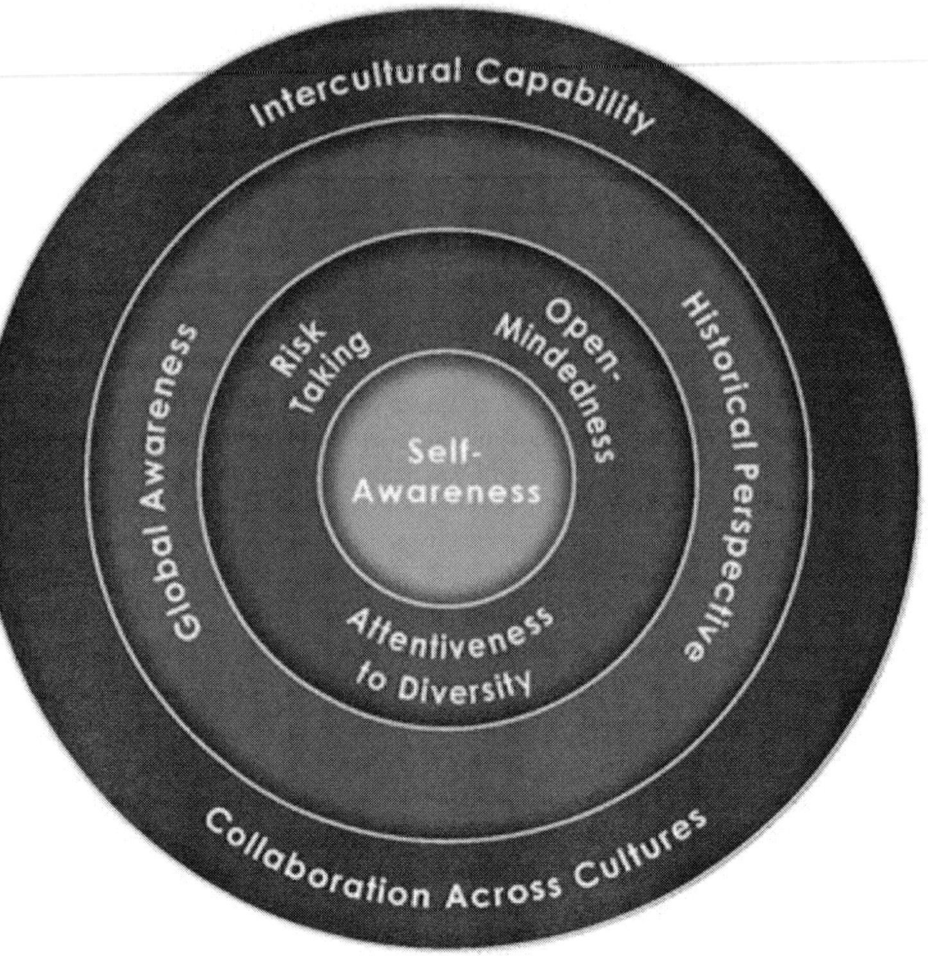

The GCAA provides two overall scores for internal and external readiness and eight component scores to profile global competence. Internal readiness characteristics encompass the personal traits and attitudinal drivers of global competence - self-awareness, open-mindedness, attentiveness to diversity, risk taking. The External Readiness illustrates the knowledge that individual acquires through experiences in life or through education and personal interactions - historical perspective, global awareness, intercultural capabilities and collaboration across cultures. The maximum score for internal and external readiness is 100 each, for a total score of up to 200 points. Individuals who earn high aptitude ratings for both internal (above 80%) and external readiness (above 70%) are considered globally competent (C. Hunter, personal communication, Fall 2013). The instrument is comprised of four distinct sections, each with a different question style. Cross-referencing is utilized throughout the GCAA, whereby each of the eight identified dimensions of global competence is evaluated from a variety of angles, using different styles of questions and varying degrees of difficulty.

LITERATURE REVIEW AND SYNTHESIS

The Global Competence Aptitude Assessment (GCAA) Instrument

Hunter (2004) has defined global competence as "having an open mind while actively seeking to understand cultural norms and expectations of others, and leveraging this gained knowledge to interact, communicate and work effectively in diverse environments." Our increasingly interconnected and interdependent global society requires that individuals demonstrate the ability to fit and function within a global marketplace. Based on over ten years of rigorous research, the Global Competence Aptitude Assessment (GCAA) instrument asserts the ability to capture an individual's capacities of global knowledge, skills, attitudes, and experiences (Hunter, 2006). The instrument also reports on an individual's ability to fit and function within a global environment.

The instrument has been tested in 40 countries on six continents through a series of research studies involving business professionals, government and military, and both students and educators. The GCAA is currently being used in education (students and faculty/staff), business (e.g., L'Oréal), and government and military (e.g., United Nations). Based on past research, ports of instrument use, and the baseline assessments, the GCAA appears to be a reliable and valid instrument capable of measuring constructs related to global competence, including internal and external readiness.

Global Education and Global Competence

Institutions of higher education have arrived at a critical moment in history, a moment in which global challenges and societal need have intersected. Higher education has encountered a new paradigm in which a dynamic and highly interconnected world has called for more globally competent citizens. Global education answers the call for higher education institutions to remain competitive and provide students with the skills and knowledge required to successfully contribute and participate in their chosen fields. Growing connections and interdependency, coupled with increasingly diverse populations and cultures, make global education a necessity (National Education Association, 2010). Institutions of higher education have been challenged to view the goal of producing globally competent graduates as not only a desired outcome, but an institutional imperative (Hudzik, 2011). Along with high school seniors and their families that report a desire to increase global awareness and competence, employers also believe that higher education needs to address global competence (Hart Research Associates, 2010; Lincoln Fellowships Commission, 2004; NACE, 2011). Additionally, scientific topics such as global climate change, pandemics, environmental sustainability, national resource management, international terrorism, and international business command that globally competent teams work together across the world to find solutions to truly global issues and problems (Curie, 2007).

Overall, global competence has been suggested as the critical attribute every student should possess for effective global marketplace engagement and performance. As the world becomes more interconnected, academic organizations are challenged to produce graduates who are prepared, in both practice and knowledge, to embrace and embody a global world view (Bourn & Shiel, 2009; Hicks, 2003; Pike, 2000). A wide variety of research and case studies have shown that students should develop global knowledge, skills, attitudes, and the ability to engage as a citizen of a highly interconnected world.

THEORETICAL DEVELOPMENT/MODEL

Study 1: Baseline Assessment

Methodology

The web-based Global Competence Aptitude Assessment (GCAA) was utilized to directly assess all three Student Learning Outcomes and the overall objective of a university in northeast Texas Quality Enhancement Plan (QEP), which focus efforts in preparing students for an interconnected world. The GCAA was administered to incoming freshman students in a Freshman Success Class, to exiting senior students upon application for graduation, and as a pre-post assessment with students traveling abroad in all programs. These assessments serve as direct measures of student learning in a wide variety of factors that have been shown to impact global competence. The GCAA provides a baseline measure of global competence for incoming students in a pre-assessment format, while the post-assessment measure will reflect student learning over the student's entire undergraduate experience. The summative post-assessment will allow the university to determine if the overall student learning outcomes and objective of the QEP program have been achieved for both the annual and fifth-year reports.

To gather baseline data, for the implementation of its Quality Enhancement Plan (QEP), the university administered the GCAA to a group of students traveling abroad during the summer of 2013 (pre-test n = 28, post-test n = 26) and a control group who did not travel abroad (pre-test n = 35, post-test n = 11). Additional baseline data was gathered from random incoming freshman students (n = 420) in the fall of 2013. The baseline global competence scores revealed areas for improvement, specifically related to the external readiness areas of global awareness (average score 39.9%) and historical perspective (average score 23.1%). The mean average internal readiness scores of 69.8% and external readiness scores of 48.2% indicate overall improvement is needed in an effort to better prepare students for an interconnected world.

The university's QEP seeks to better prepare students for an interconnected world and will strive to improve both internal and external readiness scores to ranges indicative of developing and developed global competence (70 and 80% respectively). Additionally, specific goals have been established for improvement in the critical areas of global knowledge and awareness, where the greatest impact that educators may make is possible. Historical perspective scores in the 50% range, global awareness scores in the 60% range, and overall external readiness scores of 65% demonstrate stretch goals for critically underdeveloped scores revealed in the baseline GCAA results (C. Hunter, personal communication, fall 2013).

The GCAA has been incorporated as one of the class assignments in the Freshman Success Class for all incoming freshman students beginning in the fall of 2014. The assessment will serve as a baseline, offering each student specific areas for improvement along with suggestions on how to improve on these areas; allowing a personalized snapshot of existing competence, with encouragement for continual improvement. Additionally, graduating students will complete the assessment as part of the graduation application process. Utilizing this data from a pre-post group perspective, the university will analyze freshman to graduation gains and will compare results year to year. These analyses will provide both summative and formative measures as evidence of the success of the programs in preparing students for an interconnected world.

Results and Discussion

The following are additional interesting points to highlight from the baseline GCAA assessment results:

- Significantly higher Internal Readiness post-test scores were measured from the study abroad treatment compared with the control group's post-test scores.
- Significantly higher External Readiness post-test scores were measured from the study abroad treatment compared with the control group's post-test scores.
- Generally speaking, students who self-selected the study abroad experience scored higher in almost every pre-test and post-test measure than the students who did not choose to participate in such an experience. This trend was more strongly observed in the External Readiness category. (It should be noted that only one third (⅓) of the control group students participated in the post-test. The GCAA hypothesizes that the more accomplished students were self-motivated and chose to participate again, which raised the group scores substantially in the Historical Perspective dimension.)
- Students who reported travel across continents and/or spent longer durations abroad scored higher in every dimension of global competence than their less-traveled peers.
- Students with greater world language exposure scored higher in all dimensions of global competence (to varying degrees across each) than those with none or more limited language exposure.

All students who completed the GCAA were also asked to review their results report, and then complete a survey about their perspectives regarding the assessment and the results. The students reported their highest and lowest scores, which were recorded in the final GCAA results. Additionally, when asked why they believed their lowest scores were in that particular area, most responded with an answer that reflected a lack of global knowledge, lack of opportunity to encounter global information, or a lack of desire to learn about global dynamics in general. On a positive note, when asked about the potential future use of their individual GCAA results reports, the students indicated (n = 364) they would use it for improving personal knowledge (54%) and for personal improvement (46%). The students reported that the GCAA was of average difficulty (56.4%) or difficult to very difficult (28%). The majority of the students agreed with their individual results, with only 14% disagreeing with portions of the report. After reading the individualized reports, most found the results informative (93%). Interestingly, when asked if all college students should be required to complete the GCAA, less than 16% opposed to its use as an accurate assessment of global competence. Overwhelmingly, the students who completed the GCAA and the survey reported positive experiences and viewed the results as a learning opportunity.

Study 2: Assessment of Validity and Mean Differences Analysis

Purpose

The purpose of the second study was to assess the validity of the GCAA instrument by conducting a correlation analysis, factor analysis, and measure the internal consistency of the data (reliability) using Cronbach's Alpha. Investigation of the significant mean differences in scores (between four colleges and one school) using Analysis of Variance (ANOVA) was also conducted.

Methodology

Correlation analysis, factor analysis and a reliability test was conducted on GCAA data gathered from first time, full-time freshmen students (*n* = 1819) during the fall terms (2014, 2015). Analysis of Variance (ANOVA) was conducted on GCAA data gathered from incoming, first-time, full time freshman students from College of Business (COB) (*n* = 78, 16%), College of Education and Human Services (CED) (*n* = 153, 31%), College of Humanities, College of Social Sciences and Arts (COH) (*n* = 66, 13%), College of Science and Engineering (COS) (*n* = 120, 24%) and School of Agriculture (SOA) (*n* = 77, 16%) in Fall 2015.

Results

The Cronbach's alpha for the ten constructs of the GCAA was α = 0.82 (see Table 1) indicating the instrument was a highly reliable one. As prior research (Hunter, 2006) and studies have shown, the data collected through the study supported that the GCAA is a reliable and valid instruments of measuring the constructs related to global competence.

Table 1: Reliability Statistics

Cronbach's Alpha	Cronbach's Alpha Based on Standardized Items	N of Items
.815	.847	10

Items 1 through 5 were significantly correlated (see Table 2) to one another, while items 5 through 10 were significantly correlated to one another, which correspond to the two components the instrument claimed to have.

Table 2: Correlation Analysis

	Item 1	Item 2	Item 3	Item 4	Item 5	Item 6	Item 7	Item 8	Item 9	Item 10
Item 1	1	.653**	.748**	.833**	.818**	.389**	.211**	.235**	.289**	.329**
Item 2		1	.343**	.391**	.386**	.290**	.135**	.192**	.220**	.247**
Item 3			1	.547**	.459**	.232**	.137**	.136**	.175**	.186**
Item 4				1	.565**	.301**	.139**	.165**	.237**	.282**
Item 5					1	.360**	.223**	.226**	.250**	.284**
Item 6						1	.667**	.661**	.701**	.690**
Item 7							1	.283**	.245**	.228**
Item 8								1	.288**	.276**
Item 9									1	.382**
Item 10										1

Item 1: Internal Readiness Item 2: Self Awareness Item 3: Risk Taking Item 4: Open Mindeness Item 5: Attentiveness to Diversity Item 6: External Readiness Item 7: Historical Perspective Item 8: Global Awareness Item 9: Intercultural Capability Item 10: Collaboration Across Culture

Using ANOVA (see Table 3) to compare college/school differences in the ten constructs of measurement, five showed significant differences across the colleges including: self-awareness, $F(4, 489) = 3.33$, $p = .010$ ($p < .05$); attentiveness to diversity $F(4, 489) = 3.36$, $p = .010$ ($p < .05$); external readiness $F(4, 489) = 6.84$, $p = .000$ ($p < .05$); global awareness $F(4, 489) = 4.86$, $p = .001$ ($p < .05$); and intercultural capability $F(4, 489) = 4.34$, $p = .002$ ($p < .05$).

Table 3: ANOVA

Dependent Variable (Mean Value=M)			Mean Difference	Sig.
Self Awareness	COS (M=70.64)	SOA (M=75.62)	-4.982*	.008
Attentiveness to Diversity	COB (M=66.44)	COH (M=71.67)	-5.231*	.037
	CED (M=66.5)	COH (M=71.67)	-5.013*	.017
External Readiness	COB (M=53.15)	COH (M=58.05)	-4.892*	.045
	CED (M=51.93)	COH (M=58.05)	-6.117*	.001
	CED (M=51.93)	COS (M=57.06)	-5.130*	.001
	CED (M=51.93)	SOA (M=56.66)	-4.734*	.012
Global Awareness	CED (M=41.10)	COH (M=48.27)	-7.168*	.033
	CED (M=41.10)	COS (M=49.00)	-7.895*	.001
	CED (M=41.10)	SOA (M=48.14)	-7.038*	.025
Intercultural Capability	CED (M=63.65)	COH (M=70.44)	-6.792*	.028
	CED (M=63.65)	COS (M=69.53)	-5.878*	.019

Results and Discussion

Study 2 supports the continued use of the GCAA as a reliable and valid instrument. Furthermore, the results assist in the continued implementation and assessment of the influence of the QEP. The results also aid in better understanding students' levels of global competence, specifically between different colleges and schools. This may be particularly important in creation of new programs designed to better prepare students for an interconnected world.

CONCLUSION AND FUTURE RESEARCH DIRECTIONS

Organizations, businesses, groups, and individuals function in a global environment that significantly affects everyday activities. Education is no exception to global influences, often serving as a catalyst for comprehension and adaptation to global trends. Consistently ranked at the top of business, government, and civil society agendas, education is cited as a crucial issue in preparation of individuals to function in an increasingly interconnected world (Schwab, 2007). The forces associated with globalization have influenced the context in which educators operate, have profoundly altered individuals' experiences of education, and have led to a shift in the practice of delivering education. Given the continual restructuring and increasing interconnectedness of the world, the requirements for knowledge and information have changed in terms of structure, function, curriculum, and approach (Cogburn, 1998).

The increasingly interconnected world has brought about continual change, issues, challenges, and opportunities in higher education. In response to the growing need for higher education and increasing demands for global aspects within higher education, many colleges and universities have expanded their missions and presence on a global scale through recruitment of international students, facilitation of faculty collaboration, creation of cooperative degree programs, and study abroad programs (Johnstone, d'Ambrosio, & Yakoboski, 2010). Additionally, college deans such as the University of Pittsburgh's Dr. John T. Delaney (2013) argue that professors must possess strong global awareness if they are to be equipped to help students apply knowledge within an international context and to develop a global perspective.

Higher education has been charged with increasing the level of international and global scholarship and learning, as well as providing students with an international perspective and understanding, specifically in relation to global processes and self-reflection (Tröhler, 2009). The past decade has called upon higher education to create and develop an increasingly global orientation in both pedagogy and curriculum in an effort to provide students with the skills, knowledge, and dispositions to build awareness and engagement with global issues (Mannion, Biesta, Priestley, & Ross, 2011). Educational policymakers suggest embedding global dimensions across the curricula both within and between subject areas.

Future studies would benefit from utilizing the GCAA in order to assist in the measurement and improvement of global competence in other fields besides education. Most employers who hire college graduates expect students to have both a broad range of skills and specific in-depth knowledge in their field upon completion of a college degree (Hart Research Associates, 2010). The American Association of Colleges and Universities (AAC&U) survey of employers recently reported that less than 25% of employers think that two-year and four-year colleges are doing a good job in preparing students for the challenges of the global economy. Specifically, the majority of the respondents argued that both two- and four-year colleges need to make at least some improvements to better prepare students for the global economy.

Future research could probe deeper into the use of the instrument by addressing pre-conditions such as how the instrument may be biased by students who have studied abroad, travelled abroad, and/or are multi-cultural prior to their freshman year when the pre-test data is collected.

A majority of the employers surveyed believe that colleges should place greater emphasis on a variety of global learning outcomes. For example, well over half of the employers called for improvements in students' ability to understand the global context of situations and decisions, global issues and developments and their implications for the future, increased awareness of cultural diversity of the world, and understanding of the role of the United States in the world. Furthermore, 71% of the employers called for improvements to students' ability to collaborate with others in diverse settings and improvements in teamwork skills. When asked to assess the potential value of emerging educational practices, more than half of the employers expect students to take courses that explore big challenges facing society (e.g., environmental sustainability, public health, human rights), to learn about a point of view of non-Westernized societies, to learn about cultural and ethnic diversity, and to complete a project before graduation that demonstrates their knowledge, skills, and experiences related to global issues. Overall, the AAC&U survey shows that employers believe that colleges should be placing more emphasis on several key global learning outcomes in an effort to increase graduates' potential to be successful and contributing members of today's global economy.

REFERENCES

AAC&U. (2007). College learning for the new global century. Report from the National Leadership Council for Liberal Education and Americans' Promise (LEAP). Washington: AAC&U.

Bourn, D., & Shiel, C. (2009). Global perspectives: Aligning agendas? *Environmental Education Research, 15, 661-677.*

Cogburn, D. (1998, October). *Globalization, knowledge, education and training in the information age*. A report prepared for The Congress INFOethics'98, Monaco.

Curie, M. (2007). *Embracing Globalization: Meeting the Challenges to U.S. Scientists and Engineers*. Washington, DC: Sigma XI: The Scientific Research Society.

Gibson, S. A., & Reysen, S. (Submission under review, 2013). Representations of global citizenship in a school environment. *International Journal for Development Education and Global Learning*.

Hart Research Associates. (2010). Raising the bar: Employers' views on college learning in the wake of the economic downturn (AAC&U). Retrieved from http://www.aacu.org/leap/documents/2009_EmployerSurvey.pdf.

Hicks, D. (2003). Thirty years of global education: A reminder of key principles and precedents. *Educational Review*, 55, 265-275. doi: 10.1080/0013191032000118929.

Hudzik, John K. (2011). *Comprehensive internationalization: From concept to action*. Washington, DC: NAFSA: National Association of International Educators.

Hunter, B., White, G. P., & Godbey, G. (2006). What does it mean to be globally competent. *Journal of Studies in International Education,* 10, 267-285.

Hunter, W. D. (2004a). *Knowledge, skills, attitudes, and experiences necessary to become globally competent.* (Doctoral dissertation).

Hunter, W. D. (2004b). Got global competence? *International Educator*, 13(2) 6-12.

Johnstone, D. B., d'Ambrosio, M. B., & Yakoboski, P. J. (2010). *Higher education in a global society*. Northampton, MA: Edward Elgar Publishing

Kaushik, R., Gibson, S., Su, D., & Adkins, T. (2016, April). Assessment of Validity and Mean Differences Analysis of Global Competence Aptitude Assessment (GCAA) Instrument. Presented by R. Kaushik at the Federation Graduate Student Research Symposium, Texas Woman's University, Denton, TX.

Lipman-Blumen, J. (1996). *The connective edge*. San Francisco: Jossey-Bass.

Lambert, R. D. Ed. (1996). Parsing the concept of global competence. In *Educational exchange and global competence*. New York: Council on International Educational Exchange.

Mannion, G., Biesta, G., Priestley, M., & Ross, H. (2011). The global dimension in education and education for global citizenship: Genealogy and critique. *Globalisation, Societies and Education, 9*, 443-456. doi: 10.1080/14767724.2011.605327.

National Education Association (2010) *Global Competence Is a 21st Century Imperative: An NEA Policy Brief.* Washington, D.C.: National Education Association.

Olson, C. L., & Kroeger, K. R. (2001). Global competence and intercultural sensitivity. *Journal of Studies in International Education, 5*, 116-137.

Pike, G. (2000). Global education and national identity: In pursuit of meaning. *Theory and Practice, 39, 67-73.*

Schwab, K. (2007). Proceedings from World Economic Forum. *Global Education Initiative*. Geneva, Switzerland.

Singer, M. R. (1998). *Perceptions and identity in intercultural communication*. Yarmouth, ME: Intercultural Press.

Trohler, D. (2009). Globalizing globalization: The neo-institutional concept of a world culture. *Yearbook Of The National Society For The Study Of Education (Wiley-Blackwell), 108*, 29-48. doi:10.1111/j.1744-7984.2009.01160.x

Wilson, A. H. (1996). The attributes and tasks of global competence. In R. D. Lambert (Ed.), *Educational exchange and global competence.* New York: Council on International Educational Exchange.

Decision Sciences Institute

The Impact of Choice of Costing Method on Project/Product Profitability

Abbas Foroughi
812.465.1667
aforough@usi.edu
Mehmet Kocakulah
812.464.1730
mkocakul@usi.edu
Romain College of Business
University of Southern Indiana
http://www.usi.edu/business/

Lionel Manyoky
Springleaf Financial Services
Evansville IN 47708
800.325.2146

ABSTRACT

Since the 1970s, activity-based costing has enabled companies to identify the true costs of processes and products and to make sound decisions related to the profitability and expense of the products they produce, as well as the effectiveness of their manufacturing and business processes. This paper explores the relative advantages of activity-based costing vs. traditional costing systems. Issues related to the implementation of ABC are discussed. The authors explore a real-life implementation of ABC through analysis of the difference in costs resulting from the use of ABC vs. traditional costing for projects completed by a tower manufacturer.

KEYWORDS: Activity-based costing, traditional cost accounting, and accounting

INTRODUCTION

From the beginning of the industrial revolution until the second half of the 20th century, most manufacturers produced large amounts of a small number of products, with most cost stemming from direct costs such as materials and labor. Traditional cost accounting considered direct materials and direct labor in product cost and only estimated overhead costs, ignoring the increasing role of various types of overhead. As industrial capabilities evolved over the past 75 years, manufacturers were able to produce many types of products, in varying amounts, with each producing a different amount of overhead. Sophisticated machinery for producing customizable products to order and information systems added even more overhead. By the 1970s, information and communication technology made it possible to gather and process more accurate information about the activities that go into producing a product. In 1971, George Staubus' book, Activity Costing and Input-Output Accounting introduced the idea of activity-based costing, which identifies the activities required to produce a product and assigns cost to each product based on the cost of the activities required to produce it (Staubus,1971). The Consortium for Advanced Management –International further refined this new concept and formulated the principles of what is now called activity-based costing (ABC) (Miller, 1995). In the

1990s, Cooper & Kaplin's (1991) *Harvard Business Review* article called for increased use of activity-based cost accounting to identify the true costs of processes and products, so that companies can make sound decisions related to the profitability and expense of the products they produce. ABC has also been strongly advocated in important articles by Kaplan and Bruns (1987), Johnson & Kaplan (1987), Drucker (1999); Drury (2005), Johnson (1990), and Ness & Cucuzza (1995).

ABC was originally conceptualized as an effective costing method for manufacturers, but it has been used by numerous other industries, such as hospitals and related healthcare facilities (Kaplan & Porter, 2001; Gentili, 2014; Dwivedi & Chakraborty, 2015), by the US Postal Service (USPS; Carter, Sedaghat & Williams, 1998), the restaurant and hotel industry (Horgren, 1995; Raab & Mayer, 2007), the life insurance industry (Adams, 1996), universities (Krishnan, 2006; Cox, Downey & Smith, 1999), the accounting profession (Cagwin & Bouwman, 2002), the banking industry (Innes, Mitchell & Sinclair, 2000), the energy sector (Wang et al., 2010; Rof & Capusneanu, 2015), and the food production industry (Faraji, Maghari & Mirsepasi, 2015). Large companies like Chrysler (Ness & Cucuzza, 1995) and United Parcel Service (UPS) have also benefited from using ABC, particularly in the area of supply chain management (Binshan, Collins & Su, 2001). Mahal & Hossain (2015) provide a review of a number of articles about ABC.

This paper explores the relative advantages of activity-based costing vs. traditional costing systems. Issues related to the implementation of ABC are discussed. The authors explore a real-life implementation of ABC through analysis of the difference in costs resulting from the use of ABC vs. traditional costing for projects completed by a tower manufacturer.

LITERATURE REVIEW

Activity-based costing (ABC) assists companies in more accurately costing their products. While traditional costing systems rely on a simple measure for the allocation of overhead, activity-based costing relies on cost pools and cost drivers to assign cost in accordance with overhead usage. The most important component of activity-based costing is the cost driver used (Gilligan, 1990). Cost drivers are the factors that determine the number of activities that will be consumed by a given product. Examples of cost drivers include machine hours, size, complexity, type, and any other product attribute that can determine its cost. This method is utilized in the allocation of overhead expense in managerial accounting. Although researchers differ on the exact steps in ABC costing, it basically calls for the following procedures, which are also illustrated in Figure 1:

1. Determine the activities that go into producing each product and the cost drivers for measuring them.
2. Determine the costs associated with each activity.
3. Determine the percentage of time employees spend on these activities for each product—through interviews, observation, or logs.
4. Calculate activity cost driver rates.

5. Assign costs to products or customers by dividing these activity costs by the output of each activity.

Figure 1: Traditional Product Costing and Activity-Based Product Costing

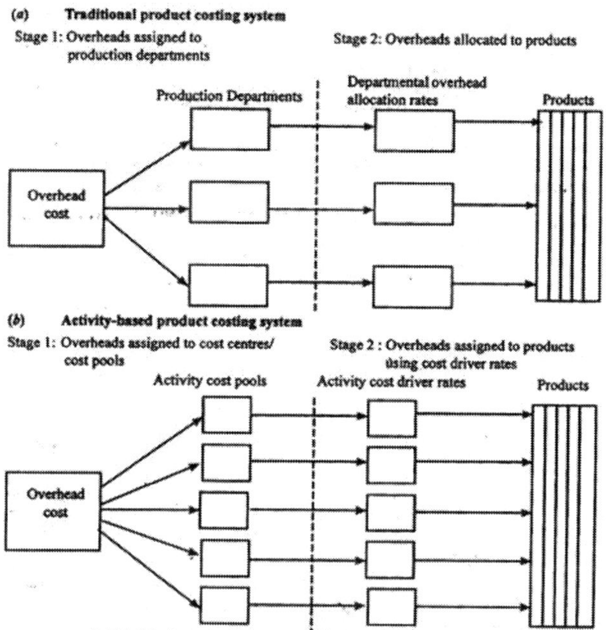

Exhibit 4.6: Comparison of Traditional and Activity-Based Costing Systems

Source: J. Innes and F. Mitchell, *Activity-Based Costing: A Review with Case Studies*, 1990, CIMA,U.K.

Why Use Cost Accounting?

The main purpose of cost accounting (as opposed to financial accounting) in management is to provide data for managers. Managers can use cost data to make decisions that will ultimately improve the company's financial performance. Many of these decisions have to do with which products to advertise for, which to expand, and which to discontinue. Other decisions attempt to improve operations, lower cost, or allow more competitive pricing. Because all of these decisions rely heavily on cost accounting data, having accurate data is essential for a company in order to identify their sources of profit as well as maximize their potential profitability (Hughes & Paulson Gjerde, 2003; Wiersema, 2007).
As product lines have become more complex and markets have become more segmented, companies have developed more products for smaller markets. Sales and profits for these markets are smaller than for the previously massed produced products. This change in the competitive environment has made the need for more accurate costing information even stronger (Stevenson, Barnes & Stevenson, 1996; Cagwin & Bouwman, 2002).

Overhead Allocation Accuracy

Activity-based costing does a better job of allocating overhead expense because it does not group costs that are spread out across many different activities (Arney & Sorice, 1994). Critics of traditional cost accounting systems argue that overhead expenses are being allocated incorrectly, leading to poor management decisions regarding product continuation and pricing. In situations where a competitive bid or cost-plus pricing is required, the actual cost of the product is essential for pricing of a product or service. Decisions based on inaccurate cost data can have a direct impact on the profitability of the company in these situations (Hughes & Paulson Gjerde, 2003; Cooper & Kaplan, 1988).

When indirect cost is a large portion of the overall cost of the product, activity-based costing is superior to traditional costing in providing data for proper pricing decisions (Cheatham & Cheatham, 1996; Škoda, 2009). In past decades, direct labor has been approximately 25-50% of the total cost of a product, but since the 1960s, it has fallen dramatically. The dominant product cost is now indirect cost (Stevenson, Barnes & Stevenson, 1996).

Traditional costing systems tend to use a single rate multiplied by a single factor to determine the overhead allocation for a product, service, or project. This can lead to inaccurate costing, specifically when the incurrence of overhead cost is not proportional to that factor. In a situation where an employee sets up a machine and lets it run while doing other work, using direct labor as the factor for allocating overhead would lead to inaccurate costing. The machine hours, which are typically overhead intensive, are basically ignored, while other activities, assembly for example, are charged high amounts of overhead while using very few resources apart from direct labor. Using a single rate for allocating overhead based on one factor will misallocate overhead because the different operations within a single shop vary widely. Overhead-intensive projects in particular, tend to be underpriced (Wiersema, 2007).

Traditional cost systems have been criticized for over-costing simple products that are produced in large batches as well as products that rely on high usage of the allocation base, but lower usage of other significant factors such as machine hours (Hughes & Paulson Gjerde, 2003). Standard costing systems also tend to show the cost of special or custom products lower than they actually are (Gilligan, 1990). Inaccurate costing can create losses because difficult work will tend to be underpriced. The costing system may not account for special characteristics or special expertise. As these difficult, complex projects are under-bid, the company will win more and more unprofitable work. At the same time, simpler projects will be over-priced and subsequently, less of these more profitable projects will be sought and won by the company. This phenomenon can be concealed by inaccurate or insufficient costing systems, leading to erosion of profit margins and causing damage to the company's financial viability (Wiersema, 2007). When special/difficult projects are priced correctly, there are fewer orders for them, and more orders for standard products. Because special projects require much more support from office staff, a small reduction in the percentage of special orders versus the percentage of standard orders can have a significant impact on the staff resources required for the same level of order activity (Gilligan, 1990).

Representation of Idle Capacity in Total Cost

One issue facing companies is how to deal with idle capacity in product costing. Traditional costing systems tend to distribute the cost of idle capacity across products manufactured, essentially concealing its true cost and artificially inflating product cost. Activity-based costing systems do a better job of separating the cost of idle capacity from the true cost of the manufactured products. Including excess capacity in product cost raises the perceived cost of those products without adding value to them. This increase in costs can influence managers to want to raise the prices of these products to increase profitability. This price increase, in the absence of any product improvement or enhancement, can lower sales, causing an increase in idle capacity. As this new idle capacity is reallocated to even fewer products than before, upward pressure on pricing will continue, driving down sales further. This "death spiral" can be avoided by removing the cost of idle capacity from product costs. To avoid this entirely, some costing systems will only allocate overhead expense to products in proportion to the amount of utilized capacity—excluding idle capacity from product cost. Typical costing system users do not feel that their system sufficiently shows the cost of idle time, but users of activity-based costing systems have indicated that they feel that their systems do a much better job of this when compared to traditional or variable cost systems (Hughes & Paulson Gjerde, 2003). When excluding idle capacity cost from product cost in internal cost accounting, the overall cost stays the same, but the product cost is more accurately represented. This provides a clearer picture of what is making money and what is costing money. Having the idle capacity as an expense directly impacting the bottom line also draws attention to its cost to the company. This could motivate managers to more actively pursue opportunities to utilize excess capacity in order to minimize this cost. When it is distributed among the manufactured products, it is much less obvious and consequently, must less urgent.

Product and Process Improvements through Costing

Aside from showing the cost of products, a cost accounting system can highlight or conceal possible process and product improvements. Traditional cost accounting systems do not provide a basis from which management can improve (Arney & Sorice, 1994). Costing systems that merely show the cost do not show where excess costs may have been incurred. Managers may either conclude that everything is fine, or they may want to make improvements, but feel that they lack the information necessary to make the needed improvements. Managers who feel that their cost systems accurately compute the product cost also feel that these same systems help them reduce costs, measure performance, and enhance revenue (Hughes & Paulson Gjerde, 2003).

Decisions to outsource can be highly influenced by this faulty thinking. Eventually, as more and more operations are outsourced, the margins become razor thin while the production facilities become idle, allocating even more overhead cost to the remaining manufactured products. Survival in this situation is very difficult for a company (Wiersema, 2007). Activity-based costing works the same way management thinks so that improvements can be made using the costing data produced (Arney & Sorice, 1994). The pioneers of ABC specifically designed it to create more accurate information regarding production processes, costs, and product support activities for the purpose of equipping managers to make improvements that will ultimately increase the profitability of the company. Decisions regarding product design, product mix, marketing, and product price all can be better analyzed through accurate product costing data. In other words, the whole point of activity-based costing is to provide management a way to drive continual improvement and ultimately enhance company profitability (Stevenson, Barnes & Stevenson, 1996). ABC can help identify important cost-and-profit enhancement opportunities through the repricing of unprofitable customer relationships, process improvements on the shop floor, lower-cost product designs, and rationalized product variety (Kaplan & Anderson, 2004).

Choosing a Costing System

Without overhead, product costing would be simple. Direct labor and direct materials can be traced directly to products. Overhead is much more difficult to assign correctly and can be a significant portion of product cost. Cost accounting systems (variable, traditional, or activity based) should not be viewed as good or bad, but rather should be chosen based on the appropriateness for the company and the data required (Hughes & Paulson Gjerde, 2003). Traditional costing systems are most appropriate when a company or a shop only makes a single product (Gilligan, 1990). Generally, using a mix of standard costing and ABC will help most companies. Some companies use standard cost systems to allocate direct labor and direct materials and activity-based costing to allocate overhead. Other companies use a standard cost system for financial accounting and activity-based costing for internal accounting. Combining the systems can allow companies to retain the advantages of both systems—

superior control for standard costing and superior overhead allocation for activity-based costing (Cheatham & Cheatham, 1996).

Numerous researchers have outlined internal factors a company should look at closely in determining if it would benefit from implementing ABC. The more of the following factors that exist in the company, the more beneficial it would be to implement ABC (Hicks, 1992; Swenson & Barney, 2001; Škoda, 2009):

1. Direct labor operations have been replaced with automated equipment since the costing system was lastly revised, but overhead is still applied to cost objects based on labor hours.
2. Indirect costs are becoming a much larger percentage of total costs.
3. Only one or a few overhead application rates are in use in the company.
4. The organization finds that one end of its product line is very competitive, while the other is not; but does not understand why.
5. Operations or machinery are used that do not require the same number of operators.
6. Many operations are set up, started, and then run with little or no human intervention.
7. Accounting personnel do not set a priority on determining how to provide relevant information for day-today decision making.

Some caveats remain regarding the implementation of ABC (Bhatti, 2012; Lombardo, 2015; Roztocki & Schultz, 2003). In some cases, high implementation costs result from bringing in experts, a significant amount of time can be involved in gathering relevant information throughout the company, and data flaws can occur while gathering information from various departments. Employees can sometimes resist detailed analysis of their activities (Ness & Cucuzza, 1995). Management must strongly support the decision to implement ABC. The design and implementation of ABC should be the responsibility of a cross-functional team of technicians, including staff from the accounting, finance, IT, marketing, production and engineering departments. Implementing ABC system requires a big budget initially. After implementation, the maintenance of the system is costly, since data concerning numerous activity measures must be collected, checked, and entered into the system on regular basis. ABC system generated data can be misinterpreted and must be used with care when applied in making decisions. Reports generated by ABC system do not conform to Generally Accepted Accounting Principles (GAAP); therefore, an organization using ABC should have two cost systems – ABC for internal use and a traditional system for preparing external reports. Another issue that researchers have found is that some smaller companies, in which expertise lies in only a couple of individuals and there are no formalized business practices, implementation of ABC can be significantly challenging (Cannavacciuolo et al., 2012; Bharara & Lee, 1996; Roztocki et al.,1999; Needy, Bibandi & Gulsen, 2000; Hicks, 1992,1999, 2002).

It is possible to use software like Excel to collect and analyze data for ABC, but companies can receive help in implementing ABC from a number of companies who offer consulting and software. (See Table 1.)

Table 1: ABC Solutions Consulting/Software Companies (Source:Bhatti, 2012; PSC Consulting)

Name of Company/Software	Website
Ignite Technologies	(http://www.ignitetech.com/
SAS ® Activity-Based Management	(www.sas.com
ABC Focus activity based costing software	http://www.cashfocus.com
Activity Based Costing For EXCEL	http://www.mrdashboard.com

Activity Based Costing – Workforce Software	http://www.workforcesoftware.com
SYSPRO Activity Based Costing	http://africa.syspro.com
Activity Based Costing/Management	http://www.business.com
ABC/M systems	http://www.algsoftware.com.au
CostPerform, UK	http://www.costperform.co.uk
ACTIVITY BASED COSTING ANALYSIS	http://www.xjtek.com
Enlighten Software	http://www.enlighten-software.com
Prodacapo ABM	http://www.prodacapo.com/abm
Oracle's Hyperion Profitability & Cost Mngt.	http://www.oracle.com/us/solutions/business-analytics/performance-management/profitability-cost-management/overview/index.html)
proDacapa's Performance Management suite	http://www.abmsystems.com/index.php/solutions-home/prodacapo/pdc-activity-based-costing)
SAP's Profitability & Cost Management	http://go.sap.com/product/financial-mgmt/profitability-cost-mgmt.html
3C Software's Impact:C	http://www.3csoftware.com/
CostPerform	https://www.costperform.com/

METHODOLOGY

The authors studied costing at a medium-sized company that designs, manufactures, installs, and services television and radio broadcast towers throughout the United States and in various parts of the world. The company has other products, but the focus of this paper is the tower division.

There are two basic types of towers—guyed and self-supporting. Guyed towers are typically narrow structures that are supported by a series of wires connected to various points on the tower. Self-supporting towers are towers that stand on their own without the aid of guy wires. Typically, self-supporters are heavier, more expensive towers, but do not require as much land. Guyed towers can be much taller than self-supporting towers, but require a larger piece of land. Both types of towers can be designed to broadcast AM radio, where the tower itself is essentially the antenna.

Both guyed and self-supporting towers can be either weld-together or bolt-together towers. The primary difference is the face size of the towers—the distance from one tower leg to the other. The company's tower manufacturing operation is relatively simple. There are multiple welding stations, cutting stations, a burn table, an angle processing unit, a milling machine and a painting area. Other machines, such as a metal punch, drill presses, and a solid rod bender are present. Most of these machines/stations are labor intensive, requiring an employee to operate the equipment 100% of the time. The angle processing unit is the largest exception to this. The milling machine, the cutting stations, and the burn table also have a portion of operating time that does not require direct labor. A drafting department creates all the required drawings for the manufacturing of the towers.

Because of the highly custom nature of broadcast towers, the company only has a couple standard product lines that are manufactured and inventoried. The majority of the rest of the inventory is raw materials or standard components for custom products. Most products manufactured are done on a per project basis.

The Current Costing System

The company's financial cost accounting system is based entirely on actuals. There is no separate costing system for managerial accounting. As employees work on projects, they scan into the job that they are working on, and scan out when they are done. All direct material is charged directly to the job when it is purchased or pulled from inventory. Aside from error introduced when employees do not scan into and out of projects promptly, there is little to be improved as far as recording the amount of time and materials charged to projects.
There are three main divisions within the company that absorb overhead. Each of these three departments has a certain portion of the overall overhead expense, and from these numbers, each division is given a single burden rate—typically around three (for every dollar of the allocation base approximately $3 of overhead expense is added to the cost). The allocation base for overhead for the entire company is direct labor.

Application of ABC to the Company's Project Costing

Because other divisions within the company use the structural division facilities, it is difficult to estimate the appropriate amount of overhead to be absorbed by these eighteen projects (see Table 3 for project descriptions). For comparison sake, the total amount of overhead absorbed among the projects was held constant across costing systems. The activity based model essentially reallocated the existing overhead more appropriately based on overhead requirements for the activities consumed as opposed to using labor hours.
The Cost Flow Diagram (CFD) for the model indicated that there are four key factors that drive the cost of a tower. These factors are the complexity or level of customization of the tower, the type of tower, the size of the tower, and the cross bracing pattern of the tower.
The complexity or level of customization of a tower can be measured in the number of drawings required for the tower. This is an indication of how much time engineering staff, management staff, and other individuals had to be involved with the project.
The size, type, and cross bracing of the tower can be measured using four factors. The size and type of tower can be measured using number of bolt-together tower sections and number of weld-together tower sections. The number of sections (each is typically 20 feet long) accounts for the height of the tower and the type of sections accounts for the different processes required in manufacturing each section. The cross bracing pattern determines how many welds will be required per section as well as how many angle diagonals will need to be manufactured for a bolt-together section. These can be measured using the number of solid round diagonals for weld-together tower sections and the number of angle diagonals for bolt-together sections.
After researching the operations and overhead cost flow of the company, the approximate cost of each cost driver was determined (See Table 2.) 'Drawing Cost' is the overhead required to produce one tower drawing. While some drawings take longer than others, most towers tend to have a very similar set of drawings, so an average per drawing cost will sufficiently represent the cost of a drawing. 'WT Section Cost' is the overhead expense required to process one weld-together tower section through welding, painting, and milling. 'SR Diagonal Cost' is the overhead cost to measure and cut one solid round diagonal for a weld-together tower section. These solid round diagonals are then welded to the weld-together section tower legs. Once the section is welded, it is processed as a single unit. 'BT Section Cost' is the overhead expense required to process one bolt-together tower section—including welding, painting, and fit-up. 'Angle Diagonal Cost' is the overhead expense required to process one steel angle diagonal.

These are cut to length, punched on each end and in the middle so they have bolt holes, then galvanized and painted.

Table 2: Cost Drivers	
Drawing Cost	$73.94
WT Section Cost	$833.13
SR Diagonal Cost	$5.82
BT Section Cost	$833.13
Angle Diagonal Cost	$6.65

Using these factors for costing, eighteen towers were reviewed. Table 3 shows the projects and their general characteristics.

Table 3: Project Descriptions

Project	Height	Type	Face	Weight
1	445'	Guyed	42"	30,100
2	13'	Self-Supporting Bolt-Together	72"	6,500
3	60'	Guyed	15"	1,300
4	297'	Guyed	36"	10,200
5	346'	Guyed	42"	18,800
6	348'	Guyed	24"	11,900
7	391'	Guyed	24"	11,300
8	199'	AM Guyed	30"	5,800
9	75'	Guyed	48"	5,100
10	296'	AM Guyed	36"	13,600
11	496'	Guyed	36"	25,300
12	862'	Guyed	48"	72,000
13	496'	Guyed	42"	27,000
14	1293'	Guyed Bolt-Together	73"	218,400
15	50'	Self-Supporting Bolt-Together	24"	2,700
16	140'	Self-Supporting	48"	37,900
17	250'	Self-Supporting	Taper	40,000
18	76'	Self-Supporting	36"	4,600

The face size and weight of the towers were not used as cost drivers. This is because these two attributes are accounted for in the both the direct material charged to the job (weight) and in the section processing cost (face size). The difference in the number of welds and amount of time demanded for welding different face size towers is not significant. The only real difference is in the length of the diagonals, only changing the direct materials and leaving the required number of cuts and welds unchanged.

The quantities of activities for each project can be seen below in Table 4. Not all towers have bolt-together sections. Most towers are completely weld-together, but it was still necessary to include separate cost drivers for bolt-together towers because of the differences in the types of activities required in their production.

Table 4: Quantities of Activities for Each Project					
Project	Drawings	WT Sections	SR Diagonals	BT Sections	Angle Diagonals
1	42	23	1,491	0	0
2	23	0	90	2	14
3	36	11	429	0	0
4	40	16	1,013	0	0
5	38	19	1,237	0	0
6	64	21	1,731	0	0
7	52	21	1,845	0	0
8	33	10	670	0	0
9	33	5	283	0	0
10	51	16	1,244	0	0
11	46	26	1,744	0	0
12	68	45	2,906	0	0
13	66	26	1,744	0	0
14	192	5	9,270	45	2,016
15	26	10	330	0	0
16	165	7	189	0	0
17	167	5	270	8	306
18	23	4	404	0	0

Using the costs and quantities for each activity from tables 3 and 4, the overhead allocation can be calculated for each project.

Table 5 shows the amount of overhead that should be allocated for each project based on the quantities and costs of each project.

Table 5: Amount of Overhead for Each Project based on Quantities and Cost of Each						
Project	Drafting OH	WT Section OH	SR Diag. OH	BT Section OH	Ang. Diag. OH	Total OH
1	$3,105.41	$19,162.06	$8,673.80	$0.00	$0	$30,941.26
2	$1,700.58	$0.00	$523.66	$1,666.27	$93	$3,983.55
3	$2,661.78	$9,164.46	$2,496.10	$0.00	$0	$14,322.34
4	$2,957.53	$13,330.13	$5,891.15	$0.00	$0	$22,178.80
5	$2,809.65	$15,829.52	$7,194.47	$0.00	$0	$25,833.65
6	$4,732.05	$17,495.79	$10,071.68	$0.00	$0	$32,299.51
7	$3,844.79	$17,495.79	$10,734.98	$0.00	$0	$32,075.56
8	$2,439.96	$8,331.33	$3,898.34	$0.00	$0	$14,669.63
9	$2,439.96	$4,165.66	$1,646.61	$0.00	$0	$8,252.24
10	$3,770.85	$13,330.13	$7,238.11	$0.00	$0	$24,339.08
11	$3,401.16	$21,661.45	$10,147.32	$0.00	$0	$35,209.93
12	$5,027.80	$37,490.98	$16,908.32	$0.00	$0	$59,427.09
13	$4,879.92	$21,661.45	$10,147.32	$0.00	$0	$36,688.69
14	$14,196.14	$4,165.66	$53,936.72	$37,490.98	$13,399	$123,188.54
15	$1,922.39	$8,331.33	$1,920.08	$0.00	$0	$12,173.80

16	$12,199.81	$5,831.93	$1,099.68	$0.00	$0	$19,131.42
17	$12,347.69	$4,165.66	$1,570.97	$6,665.06	$2,034	$26,783.17
18	$1,700.58	$3,332.53	$2,350.64	$0.00	$0	$7,383.75

Table 6 shows the results of the activity-based costing compared to the current costing estimates.

Table 6: Results of the ABC Costing Compared to Current Costing Estimates

			Original Gross Profit		ABC Gross Profit		
Project	Original Overhead	ABC Overhead	$	%	$	%	Change in Gross Profit
1	$28,764	$30,941	$19,309	14.87%	$17,132	13.20%	-$2,177
2	$6,888	$3,984	$30,129	63.76%	$33,033	69.91%	$2,904
3	$8,476	$14,322	$1,116	6.56%	-$4,730	-27.79%	-$5,846
4	$18,254	$22,179	-$3,869	-8.54%	-$7,794	-17.20%	-$3,925
5	$23,342	$25,834	$5,524	8.48%	$3,032	4.65%	-$2,492
6	$28,107	$32,300	$8,285	10.08%	$4,092	4.98%	-$4,193
7	$18,218	$32,076	$3,617	6.86%	-$10,241	-19.41%	-$13,858
8	$9,094	$14,670	$11,379	23.51%	$5,803	11.99%	-$5,576
9	$8,573	$8,252	$5,593	20.13%	$5,914	21.29%	$321
10	$28,699	$24,339	$14,870	15.18%	$19,230	19.62%	$4,360
11	$29,582	$35,210	-$1,054	-0.86%	-$6,682	-5.47%	-$5,628
12	$64,994	$59,427	$16,143	6.43%	$21,710	8.64%	$5,567
13	$36,372	$36,689	$33,453	23.54%	$33,136	23.32%	-$317
14	$115,320	$123,189	$43,220	8.25%	$35,351	6.75%	-$7,869
15	$9,435	$12,174	-$1,151	-7.58%	-$3,890	-25.61%	-$2,739
16	$46,585	$19,131	$54,344	33.71%	$81,798	50.75%	$27,454
17	$38,556	$26,783	$10,304	9.35%	$22,077	20.02%	$11,773
18	$9,623	$7,384	$26,879	59.40%	$29,118	64.35%	$2,239

Because total sales prices and direct costs do not change regardless of which system is used, they are not shown in Table 6. The differences in overhead calculated as well as the differences in gross profit clearly show the disparity between traditional and activity-based costing systems. Figure 2 shows a visual representation of the original gross margin of the project and the final gross margin as percentages. Direct labor and direct materials were held constant for each project—only the overhead cost was recalculated. This chart shows the difference in perceived profitability of each project. The projects that changed from a positive gross margin to a negative gross margin (projects 3, 4, and 7) are of particular significance.

Figure 2: Original Gross Marin of the Project and Final Gross Margin as Percentages

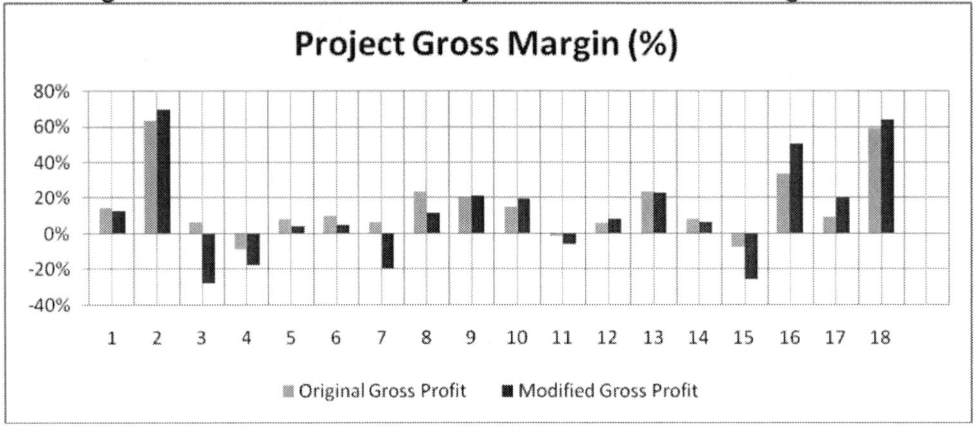

Figure 3 shows the change in gross margin (in dollars) between the two costing methods. The baseline used was the original gross margin, so a small amount indicates very little change between the two costing methods. A large amount, positive or negative, indicates a substantial difference in cost allocation.

Figure 3: Change in Gross Margin (in dollars) between the Two Costing Methods

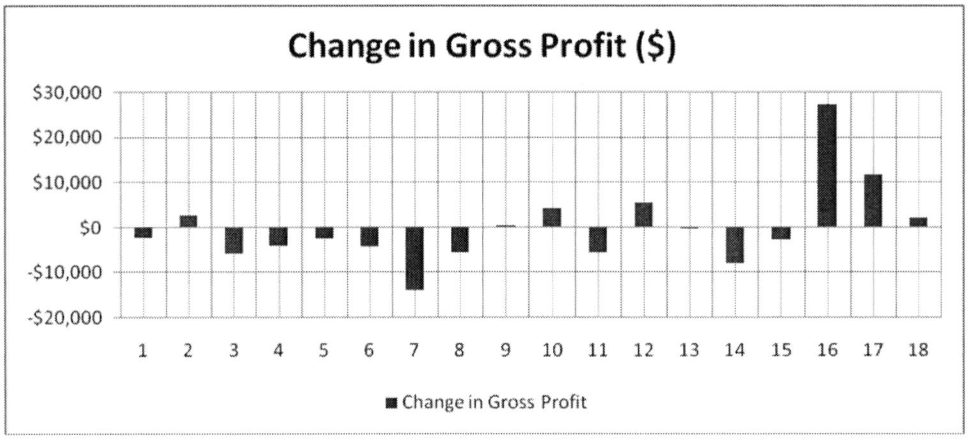

DISCUSSION OF RESULTS AND CONCLUSIONS

As shown in Table 6, significant improvements can be made through the use of an activity-based costing model. Fortunately, much of the company's operations are relatively homogenous—welding, cutting, etc.—and require similar types of labor. This allows their traditional costing system to be relatively accurate on some projects. The large exceptions are the projects that require significant usage of the few machines that can run semi-autonomously, such as the angle processing machine.

The lack of detailed information may still be concealing some valuable data. The company should consider collecting higher quality data before attempting any costing system changes. This will give them a better picture of the current state of their manufacturing operation and identify possible starting points for future improvements in product cost. Collecting higher quality data and performing more data analysis can lay the foundation of a much more effective costing system. This can lead to process, product, and management improvements that ultimately enhance the profitability of the company.

It is very difficult to determine the present capacity of their manufacturing operation without any kind of standard costing figures to compare these numbers to. Currently, the company can only tell what they think a project cost the company, but not what it should have cost. There is no real way to tell if a project took more time than had been estimated or if someone forgot to scan out of the job and was charging hours to it in error.

Using this incomplete data to base important decisions on is problematic to say the least. The seemingly random nature of the results shown in figures 2 and 3 demonstrate that using a costing system based on actuals alone is not sufficient for optimizing operations. Comparing ABC—what the product should have cost based on the operations required to complete it—and the company's current costing—what was charged to a project regardless of the type of work or level of efficiency used in completing it—is not an "apples to apples" comparison.

Understanding the limitations to a costing system is extremely important when attempting to enhance the profitability of your company.

As demonstrated in the discussion section of this paper, accurate costing is critical in effectively managing a manufacturing operation. Furthermore, as shown in the analysis section of this paper, the differences in perceived profitability observed when using different costing systems are significant. Whether or not ABC is the best costing system for the company depends on the cost of implementation, its practicality, and the information obtained through future data collection. A standard costing system combined with a more sophisticated traditional overhead allocation system may be more practical for the company and will still yield accurate enough data where it is not significantly different from ABC. The key is for management to understand the advantages and the limitations of their costing system; basing critical decisions on faulty or incomplete information is more likely to undermine the company's current position than it is to improve it. Companies who adopt activity-based costing will find that it is not only past-focused. It can facilitate future planning by pointing out inefficiencies and waste that lower profits and impact a company's competitiveness (Roztocki, 2001; Škoda, Sláviková, & Lajčin, 2014; Jeyaraj, 2015).

REFERENCES

Adams, M. (1996). Activity-based costing (abc) and the life insurance Industry. *The Service Industries Journal*, 16 (4), 511-526.

Arney, D., & Sorice, R. P. (1994). Activity-based costing: a proactive management tool. *Credit World*, 82(6),17.

Bharara, A. & Lee, C.Y. (1996). Implementation of an activity-based costing system in a small manufacturing company. *International Journal of Production Research*, 34 (4), 1109-1130.

Bhatti, A.T. (2012). www.slideshare.net/ATBHATTI/activity-based-costing-system-15438620, Dec. 1.

Binshan, L., Collins, J. & Su, R.K. (2001). Supply chain costing: an activity-based perspective. *International Journal of Physical Distribution & Logistics Management,* 31, 9-10.

(CAM-I) Consortium for Advanced Management – International, Austin, TX. www.cam-i.org

Cagwin, D. & Bouwman, M.J. (2002). The association between activity-based costing and improvement in financial performance. *Management Accounting Research*, 13(1), 1-39.

Cannavacciuolo, L., Iandoli, L, Ponsiglione, C. & Zollo, G. (2012). An analytical framework based on ahp and activity-based costing to assess the value of competencies in production processes. *International Journal of Production Research*, 50(17),1-12.

Carter, T. L., Sedaghat, A.M. & Williams, T.D. (1998). How abc changed the post office. *Management Accounting*, February, 28-32, 35-36.

Cheatham, C. B. & Cheatham, L. B. (1996). Redesigning cost systems: is standard costing obsolete? *Accounting Horizons*, December, 23-31.

Cooper, R. & Kaplan, R.S. (1988). How cost accounting distorts product costs. *Management Accounting*, 69 (10), 20-27.

Cooper, R. & Kaplan, R. S. (1991). Profit priorities from activity-based costing. *Harvard Business Review*, 69 (3), 130-137.

Cox, K.S., Downey, R. G. & Smith, L.G. (1999). ABCs of higher education: getting back to the basics: an activity-based costing approach to planning and financial decision making. 39th Annual Forum of the Association for Institutional Research, Seattle, WA, May 30-June 3.

Drucker, P. F. (1999). *Management Challenges of the 21st Century*. New York: Harper Business.

Drury, P.F. (2005). *Management Accounting for Business Decisions*, 3rd edition. New Hampshire: Thomson Learning.

Dwivedi, R. & Chakraborty, R. (2015). Activity-based costing model for an engineering department of an indian university. *International Journal of Accounting and Finance*, 5(1), 62-81.

Faraji, T., Maghari, A. & Mirsepasi, N. (2015). A framework for assessing cost management system changes: the case of activity-based costing implementation at food industry. *Management Science Letters*, 5(4), 413-418.

Gentili, A. (2014). Cost accounting for the radiologist. *American Journal of Roentgenology*, 202 (5),1058-1061.

Gilligan, B. P. (1990). Traditional cost accounting needs some adjustments... as easy as abc. *Industrial Engineering*, April, 34-38.

Hicks, D.T. (1992). *Activity-Based Costing for Small and Mid-sized Businesses: an Implementation Guide*. New York: John Wiley & Sons.

Hicks, D.T. (2002). *Activity-based Costing: Making It Work for Small and Mid-sized Companies*, 2nd ed. New York: John Wiley & Sons.

Hicks, D.T. (1999). Yes, abc is for small businesses, too. *Journal of Accountancy*, August 1, 41-44.

Horgren, C.T. (1995). Management accounting: this century and beyond. *Management Accounting Research*, 6, 281-286.

Hughes, S. B. & Paulson Gjerde, K. (2003). Do different cost systems make a difference? *Management Accounting Quarterly,* Fall, 22-30.

Innes, J., Mitchell, F. & Sinclair, D. (2000). Activity-based costing in the u.k.'s largest companies: a comparison of 1994 and 1999 survey results. *Management Accounting Research*, 11, 349–362.

Jeyaraj, S.S. (2015). Activity based costing vs. volume based costing: relevance and applicability. *Journal of International Management*, (4)2, 39-46.

Johnson, H.T. (1990). Activity management: reviewing the past and future of cost management. *Journal of Cost Management*, (3)4, 4-7.

Johnson, H.T. & Kaplan, R.S. (1987). *Relevance Lost: the Rise and Fall of Management Accounting.* Cambridge, MA: Harvard Business School Press.

Kaplan, R.S. & Anderson, S.R. (2004). Time-driven activity-based costing. *Harvard Business Review,* 82 (11), 131-138.

Kaplan, R.S. & Porter, M.E. (2001). How to solve the cost crisis in health care. *Harvard Business Review,* 89 (9), 46-52.

Kaplan, R.S. & Bruns, W. (1987). *Accounting and Management: A Field Study Perspective.* Cambridge, MA: Harvard Business School Press.

Krishnan, A. (2006). An application of activity-based costing in higher learning institution: a local case study. *Contemporary Management Research*, 2(2), 75-90.

Lombardo, C. (2015). Activity based costing advantage and disadvantages. *TheNext Galaxy.com*, June 17. http://thenextgalaxy.com/activity-based-costing-advantages-and-disadvantages-list/

Mahal, I. & Hossain, A. (2015). Activity-based costing (abc)—an effective tool for better management. *Research Journal of Finance and Accounting*, (6)4, 66-73.

Miller, J. A. (1995). *Implementing Activity Based Management in Daily Operations.* Hoboken, NJ: John Wiley & Sons, Inc., 236.

Needy, K.L., Bibanda, B. & Gulsen, M. (2000). A model to develop, assess, and validate an activity-based costing system for small manufacturers. *Engineering Management Journal*, (12)1, 31-38.

Ness, J. A. & Cucuzza, T.G. (1995). Tapping the full potential of abc. *Harvard Business Review,* (73) 4, 130-138.

PCS Consulting: Performance & Cost Systems Software Intelligence & Selection Guidance. http://www.pcsconsulting.com/index.php/services/software.

Raab, C. & Mayer, K. (2007). Menu engineering and activity- based costing - can they work together in a restaurant? *International Journal of Contemporary Hospitality Management*, 19(1), 43-52.

Rof, L.M. & Capusneanu, S. (2015). Increase the performance of companies in the energy sector by implementing the activity-based costing. *International Journal of Academic Research in Accounting, Finance, and Management Sciences*, (5)3, July, 139-148.

Roztocki, N. & Schultz, S.M. (2003). Adoption and implementation of activity-based costing: a web-based survey. *Proceedings of the 12th Annual Industrial Engineering Research Conference (IERC) 2003,* Portland, Oregon, May 18-20.

Roztocki, N., Valenzuela, J.F., Poeter, J.D., Monk, R.M. & Needy, K.L. (1999). A procedure for smooth implementation of activity-based costing in small companies, *Proceedings from the 1999 ASEM National Conference, American Society for Engineering Management*, 279-288.

Roztocki, N. (2001). Activity-based costing for e-business. *Proceedings of PICMET'01*, Vol. 2, Portland, OR- USA, July 29-August 2.

Škoda, M. (2009). The importance of abc models in cost management, *Annals of the University of Petrosani, Economics,* (9)2, 263-274.

Škoda, M., Sláviková, G. & Lajčin, D. (2014). The only correct calculation method in cost management: from activity based costing perspective. *Journal of Business & Management,* (3)3, 8-18.

Staubus, G. J. (1971). *Activity Costing and Input-Output Accounting.* Homewood, IL: Richard D. Irwin, Inc.

Stevenson, T. H., Barnes, F. C. & Stevenson, S. A. (1996). Activity-based costing: beyond the smoke and mirrors. *Review of Business*, Fall, 25-31.

Swenson, D. & Barney, D. (2001). ABC/M: which companies have success? *The Journal of Corporate Accounting and Finance*, March/April, 35–44.

United Parcel Service. Activity-Based Costing at UPS. http://govinfo.library.unt.edu/usps/offices/domestic-finance/usps/pdf/Holsen.pdf

United States Postal Service. Supplying Principles and Practices Manual: 2.5.3 Activity Based Costing. https://about.usps.com/manuals/spp/html/spp2_026.htm

Wang, P., Du, F., Lei, D. & Lin, T. W. (2010). The choice of cost drivers in activity-based costing: application at a chinese oil well cementing company. *International Journal of Management,* 27(2), 367-373.

Wiersema, W. H. (2007). What does this job really cost? *Electrical Apparatus*, June, 48-49.

DECISION SCIENCES INSTITUTE

The Impact of Inter-Organizational Information Systems on Capabilities of Buyer-Supplier Dyads

Abirami Radhakrishnan
Morgan State University
Email: abirami.radhakrishnan@morgan.edu

Dessa David
Morgan State University
Email: dessa.david@morgan.edu

ABSTRACT

Using empirical data from 154 buyer–supplier dyads, we conducted an investigation of direct and indirect effects (through external integration) of IOS usage on capabilities of buyer– supplier dyads. We found that external integration plays a mediating role in the relationship between IOS usage and capabilities of buyer– supplier dyad.

KEYWORDS: Supply chain management, Empirical Methods, MIS / OM Interface

INTRODUCTION

Supply chain integration (SCI) can improve supply chain performance (Srinivasan, Mukherjee, & Gaur, 2011). SCI is comprised of internal integration within a firm and external integration with key supply chain partners (Frohlich & Westbrook, 2001; Schoenherr & Swink, 2012). Firms have gained significant benefits by using various inter-organizational information technology systems (IOS) to collaborate with their supply chain partners (Wang & Wei, 2007; Saeed, Malhotra, & Grover, 2011). IOS is defined as an information system shared by two or more organizations (Cash & Konsynski, 1985).

This study investigates the benefits of IOS enabled external integration at the buyer-supplier dyadic level. Investigating this issue is important because prior researchers have reported inconsistent results.

So, this study addresses the following major research questions:

1. Does IOS usage have a significant direct and indirect (through external integration) impact on capabilities of buyer– supplier dyad?
2. Does external integration with supply chain partners have a significant direct impact on capabilities of buyer– supplier dyad?

We restrict our study to external integration with the largest buyer unit. The largest buyer unit refers to the external customer unit that purchases a major end product in terms of dollar value (adapted from Dong, Carter and Dresner, 2001).

LITERATURE REVIEW

There are two streams of research – the operations management stream and the MIS stream.

The Operations Management Stream

Studies on SCI recognized two types of integration – internal integration within firms and external integration with supply chain partners. Findings are mixed. Several studies showed that integration is beneficial for focal (i.e.) buyer firms (E.g. Frohlich & Westbrook, 2001; Flynn, Huo, & Zhao, 2010; Schoenherr & Swink, 2012; Wiengarten et al., 2014). Some researchers argue that SCI is not an effective strategy for improving performance (E.g. Bask & Juga, 2001, Bagchi et al., 2005; Power, 2005). Some studies found only one firm may realize most or all of the benefits of integration (E.g. Holmberg, 2000; Cousins & Menguc, 2006; Nyaga, Whipple, & Lynch, 2010).

The MIS Stream

IOS systems include EDI, Internet based EDI, supply chain management systems, SRM, CRM, e-procurement systems, open standard IOS and other inter-organizational process automation systems (Croom, 2005; Bagchi et al., 2005; Craighead et al., 2006; Zhu et al., 2006; Magal & Word, 2012; Qrunfleh & Tarafdar, 2014). Prior research points out at assymetrical distribution of benefits from IOS usage in a buyer-supplier dyad (E.g. Kekre & Mukhopadhyay, 1992; Barua & Lee, 1997; Hart & Saunders, 1998; Ghosh & John, 1999; Mukhopadyay and Kekre, 2002).

HYPOTHESES

We have three hypotheses.

H1: There is a direct positive relationship between IOS usage and external integration.
H2: There is a direct positive relationship between external integration with buyer and capabilities of a dyad.
H3: There is a direct positive relationship between IOS usage and capabilities of buyer–supplier dyad.

METHODS

We tested hypotheses with data collected through an internet-based survey that collected information about extent of IOS usage (in a buyer–supplier dyad), external integration with buyer unit and capabilities of buyer–supplier dyad. The constructs were defined, operationalized and measured based on items from the prior research. We used purposive sampling because it was not practical to select buyer-supplier dyads by random probabilistic sampling of supply chain partners. We followed the four-stage method proposed by Dillman (2000) to pretest and pilot test the survey instrument. We received usable data from 154 dyads.

RESULTS

We tested the relationship between constructs using structural equations modeling using EQS 6.2 software. Our results supported hypotheses 1 and 2. We did not find any support for Hypothesis 3.

(For the complete paper, please contact the first author).

REFERENCES

Bagchi, P.K., Ha, B.C., Skjoett-Larsen, T., & Soerensen, L.B. (2005). Supply chain integration: A European survey. *The International Journal of Logistics Management, 16(2)*, 275-294.

Barua, A. & Lee, B. (1997). An economic analysis of the introduction of an electronic data interchange system. *Information Systems Research, 8(4)*, 398-422.

Bask, A.H., & Juga, J. (2001). Semi-integrated supply chains: Towards the new era of supply chain management. *International Journal of Logistics: Research and Applications, 3(1)*, 5-23.

Cash, J., Jr. & Konsynski, B.R. (1985). IS redraws competitive boundaries. *Harvard Business Review, March,* 134-142.

Cousins, P.D., & Menguc, B. (2006). The implications of socialization and integration in supply chain management. *Journal of Operations Management, 24(*5), 604-620.

Craighead, C.W., Patterson, J.W., Roth, P.L., & Segars, A.H. (2006). Enabling the benefits of supply chain management systems: An empirical study of electronic data interchange in manufacturing. *International Journal of Production Research, 44(1)*, 135-157.

Croom, S. (2005). The impact of e-business on supply chain management: An empirical study of key developments. *International Journal of Operations and Production Management, 25(1)*, 55-73.

Dillman, D.A. (2000). *Mail and Internet Surveys: The Tailored Design Method*, second ed. Chichester: John Wiley.

Dong, Y., Carter, C.R., & Dresner, M.E. (2001). JIT purchasing and performance: An exploratory analysis of buyer and supplier perspectives. *Journal of Operations Management, 19(4)*, 471-483.

Flynn, B.B., Huo, B., & Zhao, X. (2010). The impact of supply chain integration on performance: A contingency and configuration approach. *Journal of Operations Management, 28(1)*, 58-71.

Frohlich, M.T., & Westbrook, R. (2001). Arcs of integration: An international study of supply chain strategies. *Journal of Operations Management, 19(2)*, 185–200.

Ghosh, M. & John, G. (1999). Governance value analysis and marketing strategy. *Journal of Marketing, 63*, 131-145.

Hart, C. & Saunders, P. (1997). Power and trust: Critical factors in the adoption and use of EDI. *Organizational Science, 8(1)*, 23-42.

Holmberg, S. (2000). A systems perspective on supply chain measurements. International *Journal of Physical Distribution and Logistics Management, 30(*10), 847-868.

Kekre, S. & Mukhopadhyay, T. (1992). Impact of electronic data interchange technology on quality improvement and inventory reduction programs: A field study. *International Journal of Production Economics, 28(*3*)*, 265-282.

Magal, S.R. & Word, J. (2012). *Integrated business processes with ERP systems*. Jefferson City: Wiley Publications.

Mukhopadhyay, T. & Kekre, S. (2002). Strategic and operational benefits of electronic integration in B2B procurement processes. *Management Science, 48(*10*)*, 1301–1313.

Nyaga, G.N., Whipple, J.M., Lynch, D. F. (2010). Explaining supply chain relationships: Do buyer and supplier perspectives on collaborative relationships differ? *Journal of Operations Management, 28(2)*, 101 – 114.

Power, D. (2005). Supply chain management integration and implementation: A literature review. *Supply Chain Management: An International Journal, 10(4)*, 252-63.

Qrunfleh, S. & Tarafdar, M. (2014). Supply chain information systems strategy: Impacts on supply chain performance and firm performance. *International Journal of Production Economics, 147*, 340-350.

Saeed, K.A., Malhotra, M.K., & Grover, V. (2011). Interorganizational system characteristics and supply chain integration: An Empirical Assessment. *Decision Sciences 42(1)*, 7-41.

Schoenherr, T., & Swink, M. (2012). Revisiting the arcs of integration: Cross validations and extensions. *Journal of Operations Management, 30(*1-2*)*, 99-115.

Srinivasan, M., Mukherjee, D., & Gaur, A. S. (2011). Buyer– supplier partnership quality and supply chain performance: Moderating role of risks, and environmental uncertainty. *European Management Journal, 29*, 260-271.

Wang, E. T. G., & Wei, H. L. (2007). Inter-organizational governance value creation: Coordinating for information visibility and flexibility in supply chain. *Decision Sciences, 38(4)*, 647-674.

Wiengarten, F., Pagell, M., Ahmed, M.U., & Gimenez, C. (2014). Do a country's logistical capabilities moderate the external integration performance relationship? *Journal of Operations Management, 32(*1-2), 51-63.

Zhu, K., Kraemer, K., Gurbaxani, V., & Xu, S. (2006). Migration to open-standard interorganizational systems: Network Effects, switching costs, and path dependency. *MIS Quarterly, 30*, 515-539.

DECISION SCIENCES INSTITUTE

The impacts of Service Quality on Continuance Intention to use Video Surveillance-as-a-Service

Jeng-Chung Victor Chen
National Cheng Kung University
Email: victor@mail.ncku.edu.tw

Grigory Kuritsyn
National Cheng Kung University
Email: ra6007455@mail.ncku.edu.tw

Quang-An Ha
National Cheng Kung University
Email: haquangan@gmail.com

Andree Emmanuel Widjaja
Universitas Pelita Harapan
Email: andree.widjaja@uph.edu

ABSTRACT

Video surveillance is one of the most important components of security. With the development of the Internet and especially cloud computing technologies, customers could use video surveillance service remotely. This research aims to find the major factors that will affect customers' perception of the service quality, and reasons that will drive customers to keep using the service. The result showed that trust to vendors cannot significantly affect the continuance intention, but the reliability, responsiveness, flexibility, and features would be the major players in defining quality, and hence perceived usefulness and continuous intention to use the services.

KEYWORDS: Service quality, Customer satisfaction, Continuance intention, Cloud computing, Video surveillance, VSaaS

1. INTRODUCTION

1.1 Research Background.

Video surveillance is one of the most important elements of any security system which aims to monitor, record, store, and playback the video image for many different purposes such as crime prevention and investigation (city surveillance), industrial use (monitoring manufacturing processes, labor activities, etc.), monitoring traffic and transport safety, retails controlling and security... (Valera & Velastin, 2005). With the development of technologies, video surveillance moved to Local Area Network (LAN) and the Internet toward digitization, networking and intelligentization.

Network video surveillance can be done either in a local area network by a computer or a network video recorder (NVR) with video management software software, or remotely through the Internet by IE browser interface, special client software, or even by mobile devices (Kruegle, 2011) . It still requires a lot of knowledge and expertise for system integrators to establish this kind of system, because they need to be familiar not only with video surveillance equipment and have good installation skills, but also need to be experienced in network mapping, port forwarding and everything that is related with establishing LAN and WAN. It is worth pointing out that network video surveillance has a great scalability and these factors make possible to use it in different size of projects: from household with one and more IP cameras to integrated city surveillance with thousands of cameras used in one project that are connected by LAN, WiFi, 3G, and/or Wimax (Kruegle, 2011). So far there is nothing mentioned about the costs related with installing of IP surveillance, which can also scare away potential customers, especially for household surveillance.

The idea of surveillance in the cloud is not very new, however it still has a few objectives that are needed to be overcome in order to be widely spread among the customers. First objective is network limitations: IP video camera requires a lot of bandwidth in order to deliver desired quality to the customers, and this bandwidth should be sufficient from supplier's side as well as from the consumer side (Zhao, Cui, & Zhang, 2012). Second objective is low awareness of customers: only those who particularly look for the solution of security might be aware of this kind of service.

Surveillance in the cloud could be consider as a version of well-known software model that provides services to the users through the Internet that is called Software-as-a-Service (Cusmano, 2010). This kind of model for IP surveillance in the cloud is called Video Surveillance as a Service (VSaaS) (Limna & Tandayya, 2012; Neal & Rahman, 2012; Zhao et al., 2012). This abbreviation is not widely accepted in the science world; however a lot of manufacturers and some scholars will use exactly the "VSaaS" to describe a network video surveillance system in the cloud. VSaaS provides functions of recording, storing, analyzing and playback in the cloud with help of VMS software preinstalled on the server side. Service providers also offer limited storage capacity for video data, required bandwidth and software maintenance. A user of VSaaS only needs to provide an IP camera and make the right settings so the camera will be able to connect to the service provider server. The video data from a camera will go directly to the VSaaS server, will be stored there until it's overwritten by the latest data or deleted from the server. If a user needs an access to the recorded video data, he/she can use browser or mobile device to connect to the service provider server and retrieve data, playback recorded videos, delete, or export for the further use. There are pros and cons for cloud surveillance that will be very similar as for cloud computing (Armburst et al., 2010; Mather, Kumaraswamy, & Latif, 2009; Mulholland, Pyke, & Fingar, 2010; Neal & Rahman, 2012; Reese, 2009; Zhao et al., 2012). After introduction of video surveillance in the cloud, similar problems and issues as for traditional cloud computing had aroused.

The cloud video surveillance is used by limited amount of people, however, in the year of 2014 it is expected that the world market of VSaaS will grow up to $1 billion, comparing with $500.000 in 2011 (Dale, 2013). Looking at this predicted global trend, it will be very interesting to know if those users have the same points of view and objectives on the cloud computing issues, how they perceive the service quality of VSaaS and what guides them to keep using the service.

This research aims to contribute in two different areas. First, this research hopes to discover the factors that service providers of VSaaS put in prior when describing the service quality. VSaaS factors might be similar with those factors described in the study of Electronic Service Quality (E-S-QUAL) (Parasuraman, Zeithaml, & Malhorta, 2005) and SaaS Service Quality (SaaS-Qual) (Benlian, Koufaris, & Hess, 2011) with some minor adjustment toward security and trust. It also will be very interesting to find out the factors that service providers think should be important for their customers. Second, it might disclose the important consideration that will affect customers' satisfaction and intention to use cloud video surveillance. Knowing the important factors and consideration from both sides, service providers can enhance their service quality and better understand what users expect from their services, they can learn how to increase customers' satisfaction and trigger and strengthen continuance usage intention.

2. LITERATURE REVIEW

2.1 The Software, Platform, Infrastructure (SPI) Framework of Cloud Computing.

Mather et al. (2009) defines cloud computing by 5 attributes: multitenancy (cloud computing model is based on sharing resources at the network level, host level, and application level), massive scalability (the ability to scale systems' bandwidth and storage space), elasticity (ability for users to increase or decrease computer resources as needed, ability to direct resources to other uses if needed) , pay as you go, and self-provisioning of resources (allows users to provision resources by themselves and network resources without intervention of cloud IT personnel). A common model of cloud computing services called "SPI" (software-as-a-service -SaaS, platform-as-a-service - PaaS, and infrastructure-as-a-service - IaaS).

The Software-as-a-Service Model (SaaS).

If in traditional Application Service Providers (ASP) model users buy software online and download it to their hardware, in SaaS model users don't need to buy the software, but rent it in terms of pay-per-use (Mather et al., 2009). Users simply use their browser to access the software without thinking what the operating system is used on the other end, where the software is hosted, or what computer language is used in writing the software (Reese, 2009). Examples of SaaS can be Gmail, Google+, Facebook, etc.

The Platform-as-a-Service Model (PaaS).

In the PaaS model vendors provide an environment for application developers, who develop their applications and provide it through the vendors' platform. Service providers usually develop toolkits that are hosted in the cloud and accessed by users with computer browser, define standards for development, and channels for payment and distribution (Mather et al., 2009). Examples of PaaS can be Windows Azure, Apprenda, Google App Engine, etc.

The Infrastructure-as-a-Service Model (IaaS).

Traditional hosted application model provides an entire infrastructure for customers' applications; sometimes it involves purchasing or leasing a special hardware for the specific application. In the IaaS model vendors also provide the infrastructure, but involving the clouds makes it possible to offer pay-per-use model and to scale the service depending on demand. Vendors can offer either infrastructure or hosting only, or also can offer other services, such as application development, support, and enhancement. IaaS vendors don't give too much details of their hosted servers, for example, computing resources, location, security, backup, and others (Mather et al., 2009). Examples: Amazon Web Services, Rackspace, AppNexus.

2.2 SaaS Service Quality.

The three major reasons why customers stop using SaaS are unfulfilled technical specifications, security problems, and poor quality customer service (Benlian et al., 2011). In the software platform such as SaaS, that is completely dependent on the Internet infrastructure, the issues of data security and service availability are especially vital (Mather et al., 2009). If vendor fail to fulfill customers' expectations about the service, it may have crucial outcome not only for customers, but also for vendors themselves, because SaaS customers have higher bargain power comparing with other software models, and users can switch to another vendors more easily (Choudhary, 2007; Mulholland et al., 2010). All of these put higher responsibility for vendors to offer higher service quality and focus more on quality management. In order to deliver better service quality vendors of SaaS should know toward which aspects they need to allocate the company resources and how users perceive and evaluate the SaaS.

The study of service quality was a very hot topic for the last 30 years. In 1991 (Parasuraman, Berry, & A.Zeithaml, 1991) conducted empirical studies to develop and define service quality (SERVQUAL). They created a multiple-scale instrument to quantify customers' perceptions of companies' service quality, defining service quality as the correspondence to customer needs in the service delivery. The original SERVQUAL instrument defined five service quality elements: Tangibles, Reliability, Responsiveness, Assurance, Empathy.

Service quality model and scale was adopted in many IS studies defining IS service quality from perspectives of IS users or professionals (Kettinger & Lee, 1997; Watson, Pitt, & Kavan, 1998). With the development of the Internet and electronic commerce several adaptations was proposed to the IS service quality measurement to emphasize the difference between customers' evaluation processes for offline and online service quality. It was found out that for researching online service quality the development of more extended scale is required. In the year of 2005 Parasuraman et al. (2005) detailed four broad sets of dimensions that were relevant to electronic services quality perception, those were: efficiency, system availability, fulfillment, and privacy. Later on Swaid and Wigand (2009) developed an e-service quality scale for online retailers with 6 dimensions: website usability, information quality, reliability, responsiveness, assurance, personalization.

Some of the scholars adopted application service provider (ASP) model findings into IS service quality. ASP delivers specified software to clients over the network after that clients install software by themselves. Ma, Pearson, and Tadisina (2005) developed an ASP-Qual model that describes specifics of the model, for instance, they define seven factors of ASP service quality: features, availability, reliability, assurance, empathy conformance, and security. Prior to them, Sigala (2004) developed an ASP service quality model for companies that has ASP-hosted online web stores. She also suggested several factors of ASP service quality: tangibles, reliability, responsiveness, assurance, empathy, trust, business understanding, benefit and risk share, conflict, and commitment.

In the study of Benlian et al. (2011) they examined all existed study on service quality in order to establish a conceptual framework for more precise and in-depth explanation of service quality of SaaS. They believe that ASP scales developed by Sigala (2004) and Ma et al. (2005) would be the closest to SaaS from a conceptual point of view, however these scales "have not being adequately validated with confirmatory factor analysis and nomological validity test" (Benlian et al., p. 90). Benilian et al. also argues that the previous studies on IS service quality disregarded some important factors such as flexibility and security that are the core dimensions of SaaS in books of Mather et al. (2009), Reese (2009), and Mulholland et al. (2010).

SaaS-Qual Factors as a Second-Order Construct.

In the study of Benlian et al. (2011) these six factors of SaaS-Qual were determined as formative second-order latent construct. It means that the six factors are assumed to be a distinct construct capable of verifying independently from others. This independence presumes a formative model in which these six dimensions are not treated as a single underlying whole construct (in their study is SaaS-Qual), but instead the whole construct is seen as formed by the combination of the six underlying construct. In this study the factors of VSaaS quality will be also viewed as second-order construct.

VSaaS as a Version of SaaS.

There are only a few studies that describe video surveillance as a service (VSaaS) (Dale, 2013; Gao, 2013; Limna & Tandayya, 2012; Neal & Rahman, 2012; Zhao et al., 2012). In this study we will use the terms VSaaS and video surveillance in the cloud interchangeably.

Limna and Tandayya (2012) applied software-as-a-service model (SaaS) model on VSaaS, describing its benefits as "the users don't need to have high skills in system configuration and it (SaaS) reduces a usability learning curve" (p.197). They also mentioned that some of the open video surveillance sources are not suitable for the SaaS model, because the design of the system is made according to the software objectives for the enhanced performance. Authors also imply that in order to reduce the cost of services of video surveillance in the cloud, the VSaaS should be developed as SaaS over the Internet.

According to Zhao et al. (2012), the trend of software moving to the cloud cannot be avoided by video surveillance as well, because video surveillance now is no longer analog, but digital, and it also has networking features such as Video Management Software (VMS), Internet Protocol (IP) cameras, and Network Video Recorders (NVR). They claim that "In the Internet age not only the desktop software moves toward online services, but the professional video surveillance also cannot stop the torrent of Internet online services and is gradually converting to this model" (Zhao et al., p. 1336). They also believe that VSaaS will speed up the development of video surveillance industry after implementing the Internet (SaaS) model by improving storage management, writing data capacity, reducing integrated costs, and providing flexible and intelligent analysis.

Gao (2013) in his work explains the basic principles of VSaaS and refers to it as "a pure SaaS solution" (p.296), it does not require costly equipment installed at the client site. He explained that video surveillance in the cloud is transformed to the on-line flowing services that are in easy access for mass-market users.

To have an even better understanding of this fact we can do a review and compare attributes of VSaaS and attributes for cloud computing by Mather et al. (2009) in the Table 2-1:

Table 2-1

Comparison of SaaS and VSaaS Attributes

Attributes by (Mather et al., 2009)	**Attributes definition**	**VSaaS attribute definition(Gao, 2013; Limna & Tandayya, 2012; Zhao et al., 2012)**
Multitenancy	sharing resources at the network level, host level, and application level	all users share the same platform to access to the services
Massive scalability	ability to scale systems' bandwidth and storage space	ability to add as many IP cameras as needed, from household to enterprise level
Elasticity	ability to increase or decrease computer resources as needed, ability to direct resources to other uses if needed	The amount of cameras and storage space can be easily added as the situation requires
Pay as you go	pay only for the time and resources customer use	monthly tariffs per camera, wide choice of additional options
Self-provisioning of resources	allows users to provision resources by themselves and network resources without intervention of cloud IT personnel.	if customers need additional services or devices in the system it can be done quickly and easily by users.

2.3 Continuance Intention.

Continuance intention refers to post-adoption behavior, in the case of IS it is a continued IS usage behavior, the model that was well developed by Bhattacherjee (2001). The big part of this model was borrowed from expectation confirmation theory (ECT) that based on user's psychological motivations which appear after initial adoption. Bhattacherjee model includes concepts such as satisfaction, confirmation, and usefulness as main antecedents of intention of IS continuance intention. Benlian et al. (2011) suggests that in terms of SaaS service quality-related reasons of continuance (discontinuance) intention, the model requires more precise approach to service quality confirmation. They argue that Bhattacherjee (2001) continuance model can present as their nomological framework, where "newly developed measure of SaaS-Qual can stand in for Bhattacherjee's variable of service quality confirmation" (Benlian et al., p. 116). In addition, Benlian et al. assumes that if SaaS-Qual shows adequate nomological validity, "can replace Bhattacherjee's original and rather abstract construct (confirmation), and thus provide a more robust and more highly conceptualized variable within IS continuance model" (Benlian et al., p. 116).

2.4 Perceived Usefulness.

Perceived usefulness is defined by Davis (1989) as "the degree to which a person believes that using a particular system would enhance his or her job performance" (p.320). In the Technology Acceptance Model (TAM) perceived usefulness is an important belief that influences the behavior of IS acceptance among broad range of computer technologies, it captures the instrumentality of IS use; if a system has a high level of perceived usefulness, it means it has a positive use-performance relationship (Davis, 1989; Davis, Bagozzi, & Warshaw, 1989).

The Relationship between Perceived Usefulness and IS Continuance Intention.

In TAM perceived usefulness is defined as a direct predictor of future acceptance intention (Davis, 1989). In the study of Bhattacherjee (2001) he found out that in terms of IS environment perceived usefulness is a significant predictor of user's continuance intention, therefore we hypothesize:

Hypothesis 1: User's perceived usefulness of VSaaS has positive effect on continuance intention of VSaaS.

The Relationship between Perceived Usefulness and Satisfaction.

In the study of Bhattacherjee (2001) they studied the relationship between perceived usefulness and satisfaction, defining the perceived usefulness in this relationship as the most important ex post expectation that influences user's post-acceptance affect, or satisfaction. In the study of SaaS service quality by Benlian et al. (2011) was found that user's perceived usefulness even though is not the main but salient predictor of customer satisfaction, therefore, we hypothesize:

Hypothesis 2: User's perceived usefulness of VSaaS has positive effect on satisfaction with VSaaS.

2.5 Customer Satisfaction.

Customer satisfaction is the most universal and essential concept in marketing, it also the main result of company activity on the market (Patterson, 1993). As was mentioned by Hanan and Karp (1989), the first objective of any business is not to sell, not to supply for customers, but make them satisfied and motivate them to do more business with the company in the future. In the field of information systems studies, the customer satisfaction issue is considered as the key measurement of IS success (DeLone & McLean, 1992). IS professionals have found that customer' satisfaction can be a very reliable criterion for predicting purchase intention, together with system attributes and system quality (Khalifa & Liu, 2003).

The Relationship between Satisfaction and Continuance Intention.

According to the Expectation Confirmation Theory (ECT), user's continuance intention is determined mostly by their satisfaction with prior IS use (Oliver, 1980). The studies of Technology Acceptance Model (TAM) also provide indirect support for the satisfaction-continuance intention relationship (Davis, 1989). In terms of IS continuance intention, in the study of Bhattacherjee (2001) was found that "satisfaction with IS use is the strongest predictor of users' continuance intention" (p.364). Similar results were found in the study of SaaS satisfaction by Benlian et al. (2011), therefore, we hypothesize:

Hypothesis 3: User's satisfaction with VSaaS has positive effect on continuance intention to use VSaaS.

2.6 The Relationship between Service Quality and Perceived Usefulness and Satisfaction.

The Relationship between Service Quality and Perceived Usefulness.

Perceived usefulness is an important factor of customer continuance intention and satisfaction (Bhattacherjee, 2001). As shown in the study of Benlian et al. (2011) service quality has impact on perceived usefulness of SaaS; even though this relationship is not as strong as satisfaction, it still needs to be included in this study. Considering all previous studies we hypothesize:

Hypothesis 4: Service quality of VSaaS has positive effect on perceived usefulness of VSaaS.

The Relationship between Service Quality and Satisfaction.

In the study on SaaS service quality by Benlian et al. (2011) he showed that service quality has a very strong impact on customers' satisfaction. In their study they found that service quality has a larger impact on satisfaction, rather than on perceived usefulness, explaining that the users didn't really have chance to fully experience usefulness of a young SaaS model. Examining the importance of satisfaction, we hypothesize:

Hypothesis 5: Service quality of VSaaS has positive effect on customers' satisfaction with VSaaS.

2.7 Trust.

Trust is claimed to be the main key to understand the relationships between customers and online companies, but the role and significance of trust in the building behavioral intentions toward online service vendors have stayed unclear (Gummerus, Liljander, Pura, & Riel, 2004). Trust is identified as customers' readiness and willingness to rely on service provider, it also minimizes perceived risk of using services (Moorman, Zaltman, & Deshpande, 1992). Users' perception of trust is relied on the competence, benevolence, and integrity of service provider (Mayer, Davis, & Schoorman, 1995). Users' trust evolves through the relationships between customers and service providers as customers accumulate more experience with the providers and find out that their expectation based on promises of service providers are met (Urban, Sultan, & Qualls, 2000).

2.7.1 The Relationship between Service Quality and Trust.

Trust toward service quality was conceptualized in different ways. Parasuraman, Zeithaml, and Berry (1988) defined trust as a dimension of service quality among other factors. In the study of Gummerus et al. (2004) trust is conceptualized as a mediator between service quality dimension and customer satisfaction. In this study they proved that "the conceptualization of trust is an important mediating factor in building customer loyalty in a content-based services context. Trust was found to be the strongest predictor of customer satisfaction, mediating the effect of online quality" (Gummerus et al., p. 182). Therefore, we hypothesize:

Hypothesis 6: VSaaS service quality has positive effect on trust.

2.7.2 The Relationship between Trust and Satisfaction.

Many scholars have studied a relationship between trust and customer satisfaction in the IS field. In the study of Kim, Ferrin, and Rao (2009) is proposed a link between trust and customer satisfaction in terms of examining pre-purchase and post-purchase behavior in online shopping. Another study of customer loyalty in online shopping by Chiu, Lin, Sun, and Hsu (2009) suggests that trust has direct influence on satisfaction. Trust is also seen as critical principal of customer satisfaction in a mobile world context (Lin & Wang, 2006). Considering all studies on trust above, we hypothesize:

Hypothesis 7: Trust has positive effect on satisfaction with VSaaS services.

2.7.3 The Relationship between Trust and Continuance Intention.

According to Liu, Marchewka, Lu, and Yu (2004) trust can determine specific behavioral intention in customers' perception. Malhotra, Sung, and Agarwal (2004) in their study also proved that trusting believes can trigger internet users' behavioral intention, such as continuance intention. Therefore, we hypothesize:

Hypothesis 8: Trust positively related with continuance intention of VSaaS.

3. RESEARCH DESIGN AND METHODOLOGY

3.1 Research Framework.

This study will examine the factors that influence customers' continuance intention toward video surveillance as a service (VSaaS) based on the previous models of SaaS-QUAL (Benlian et al., 2011), and trust as a factor that is influenced by service quality (Gummerus et al., 2004), and which also influence customer satisfaction (Wu, 2013). The conceptual framework of this study is presented in Figure 3-1.

Figure 3-1. Conceptual framework

3.2 Construct Measurements.

This study will use a survey method to collect required data and test developed hypothesis. The measurements of required factors will be taken from previous studies and will be rephrased in order to correspond with the area of video surveillance in the cloud, using 7 point Likert scale from 1 to 7. There will be total of 75 survey questions, excluding demographic questions (please see Appendix 1 for more information):

- 45 items for VSaaS service quality, where 42 items are adopted from the SaaS service quality by Benlian et al. (2011). These factors will be analyzed as second-order construct with a coefficient of each first-order factors to the second-order factors (Benlian et al.);
- 3 items for continuance intention that was adopted from Bhattacherjee (2001) and used in SaaS quality by Benlian et al. (2011);
- 4 items for satisfaction also adopted from Bhattacherjee (2001) and used in studying SaaS quality;
- 4 items for perceived usefulness that is taken from Davis et al. (1989);
- 4 items for trust adopted Wu (2013);

4. RESEARCH RESULTS

This research used a convenient method of online survey for collecting the data for analysis. The data collection was hold from the end of February till the middle of June, 2014. The survey was distributed on the international forums and websites that have any relations with video surveillance in the cloud. Many respondents were contacted directly by the private messages with a request to fill up the survey. Totally, it was 336 responses collected, 5 of them were incomplete that's why we could not use it in the data analysis, what makes the total number of usable responses is 331.

4.1 Descriptive Statistics.

The demographic information of the survey respondents includes: gender (male or female), age (4 groups: 18-29, 30-49, 50-64, and 65 and older), marital status (single, married or in domestic partnership, divorced), region of living (North America, Latin America, Europe, CIS, Asia, Africa, and Australia and Oceania), education (high school, professional college, bachelor degree, master degree, and PhD), respondents' experience with video surveillance and VSaaS services, and application of VSaaS services (home, business, other).

The descriptive information and characteristics of respondents are presented in the table bellows:

Table 4-1
Characteristics of Respondents

Categories (n=331)		**Frequency**	**Percentage**
Gender	Male	263	79.5%
	Female	68	20.5%
Age	18-29	127	38.4%
	30-49	154	46.5%
	50-64	50	15.1%
	65 and above	-	-
Marital Status	Single	113	34.1%
	Married or Domestic Partnership	192	58%
	Widowed	26	7.9%
Region	North America	68	20.5%
	Latin America	51	15.4%
	Europe	154	46.5%
	CIS	30	9.1%
	Asia	28	8.5%
	Africa	-	-
	Australia and Oceania	-	-
Education	High School	13	3.9%
	Professional College	75	22.7%
	Bachelor Degree	114	34.4%
	Master Degree	128	38.7%
	PhD	1	0.3%
Experience with CCTV	Less than 1 year	59	17.5%
	1-2 years	101	30.5%
	3-5 year	98	29.6%
	5 years and more	74	22.4%
Experience with VSaaS	Less than 1 year	136	41.1
	1-2 years	163	49.2
	3-5 year	32	9.7
	5 years and more	-	-
Application of VSaaS	Home	152	45.9%
	Business	162	49%
	Other	17	5.1%

4.2 Confirmatory Factor Analysis.

Confirmatory Factor Analysis (CFA) is a procedure that can imply the estimation and specification of one or more hypothesized model of factors structure. The analysis was conducted by using AMOS software package for SPSS. In the model there are five latent constructs (variables) that are composed with their subsequent multiple items (indicators).

The overall model fit is represented by a few measurements: relative Chi-square (CMIN/DF, should be <5), goodness-of-fit index (GFI, should be >0.9), adjusted goodness-of-fit index (AGFI, >0.9), standardized root mean square residuals (RMR, <0.05), comparative fit index (CFI, should be >0.95), and root mean square error of approximation (RMSEA, <0.08) (Anderson, Babin, Black, Hair, & Tatham, 2006).

Table 4-2
Results of Confirmatory Factory Analysis

Constructs	Items/ Factors	Items reliability			Average Variance Extracted (AVE)
		Standardized factor loading	t-value (C.R)	p-value	
VSaaS Service Quality					
Responsibility	RES_M	0.951	38.598	***	0.904
Reliability	REL_M	0.943	36.959	***	
Flexibility	FL_M	0.950	A	***	
Features	FE_M	0.960	40.629	***	
Satisfaction					
Satisfaction item 1	S1	0.892	A	***	0.743
Satisfaction item 2	S2	0.831	20.031	***	
Trust					
Trust item 1	TR1	0.854	20.792	***	0.742
Trust item 2	TR2	0.875	26.087	***	
Trust item 3	TR3	0.855	A	***	
Perceived Usefulness					
Perceived Usefulness item 1	PU1	0.892	25.583	***	0.802
Perceived Usefulness item 2	PU2	0.904	A	***	
Perceived Usefulness item 3	PU3	0.884	25.021	***	
Perceived Usefulness item 4	PU4	0.902	26.323	***	
Continuance Intention					
Continuance Intention item 1	VSCI1	0.868	A	***	0.760
Continuance Intention item 2	VSCI2	0.875	20.651	***	
Goodness-of-fit measurements of the model (CFA)					
X^2 (p-value)	193.417 (0.000)				
DF	78				
X^2/DF	2.480				
RMR	0.019				
GFI	0.930				
AGFI	0.892				
CFI	0.982				
RMSEA	0.067				

4.3 Structural Equation Modeling.

The CFA shows the good fit of the proposed model, the next step would be to test hypothesis using structural equation modeling in AMOS software. Structural Equation Modeling (SEM) is aimed to verify the overall model and the interrelationships between variables in the study. The same as in CFA, in SEM observed variables are shown by ovals and their indicators are shown by squares in the Figure 4.1:

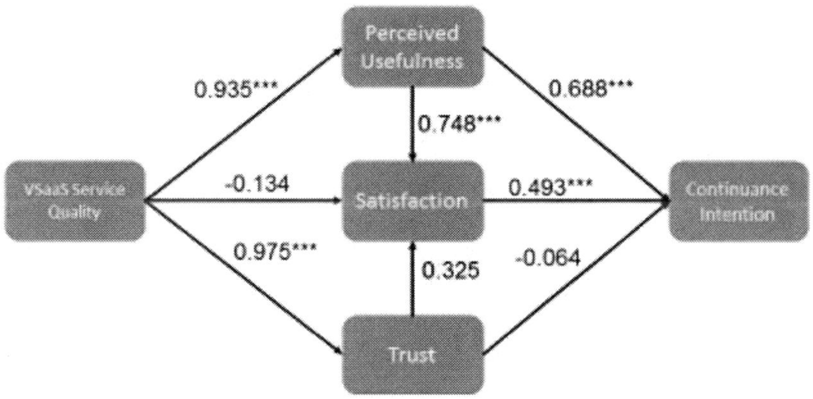

Figure 4-1. Structural equation modeling

In order for the model to have a good fit, the same measurements as in the CFA are used: relative Chi-square (CMIN/DF, should be <5), goodness-of-fit index (GFI, should be >0.9), adjusted goodness-of-fit index (AGFI, >0.9), standardized root mean square residuals (RMR, <0.05), comparative fit index (CFI, should be >0.95), and root mean square error of approximation (RMSEA, <0.08) (Anderson et al., 2006). The results of SEM for this study are presented in the table 4-3:

Table 4-3

Results of Structural Equation Modeling

Path Relationship	Standardized Coefficients	C.R.	p-value	Result
H1: Perceived Usefulness (PU) → Continuance Intention (VSCI)	0.688	5.101	***	Supported
H2: Perceived Usefulness (PU) → Satisfaction (S)	0.748	5.953	***	Supported
H3: Satisfaction (S) → Continuance Intention (VSCI)	0.493	3.269	0.001	Supported
H4: Service Quality (SQ) → Perceived Usefulness (PU)	0.935	25.273	***	Supported
H5: Service Quality (SQ) → Satisfaction (S)	-0.134	-0.391	0.696	Not Supported
H6: Service Quality (SQ) → Trust (TR)	0.975	24.530	***	Supported

Path Relationship	Standardized Coefficients	C.R.	p-value	Result
H7: Trust (TR) → Satisfaction (S)	0.325	1.032	0.302	Not Supported
H8: Trust (TR) → Continuance Intention (VSCI)	-0.064	-0.728	0.467	Not Supported

5. RESEARCH CONCLUSIONS AND SUGGESTIONS

With the development of the Internet, many traditional industries have shifted toward providing services online. It's not only E-commerce, but also online programming, online storage, meeting friends online and so on. Video surveillance wasn't an exception, that's how Video Surveillance as a Service (VSaaS) has appeared. This research is aimed to establish the major factors that can affect service quality of online video surveillance, and also to understand the customers' behavior toward intention to use the service continuously in the future.

Another important unsupported hypothesis of this research that was supported in major works of Parasuraman et al. (1988), and also in the research of SaaS quality of Benlian et al. (2011), is H5 where Service Quality has direct impact on Satisfaction. The reasons that H5 is unsupported can be different: firstly, the construct of service quality was changed in order to have a proper model fit; secondly, biased answers of the respondents; and lastly, the items of service quality that was left (responsiveness, reliability, flexibility, and features) are more likely to affect Perceived Usefulness construct, rather than Satisfaction.

From the results, Service Quality have positive impact on Trust (H6), however Trust do not affect neither Satisfaction (H7) nor Continuance Intention (H8). It shows that Trust is not important factor for people to keep using VSaaS, but it can affect Satisfaction in a very small degree. Hence, the construct Trust can also be eliminated from the further researches.

Another hypothesis that has been supported shows that Service Quality has significant effect on Perceived Usefulness (H4) (it is similar in the study of Benlian et al. (2011) . It means that customers mostly look for useful attributes of the VSaaS, such as those that was left after SEM: Responsiveness, Reliability, Flexibility, and Features. According to the results these four factors of service quality are the most important in evaluating VSaaS quality. At the same time, Perceived Usefulness has a great impact on Satisfaction what makes H2 to be supported also. Hence, to make the customer satisfied, VSaaS providers need to increase Perceived Usefulness of their services based on the factors mentioned above.

The final construct in this research is Continuance Intention (VSCI). According to the results of this research, Perceived Usefulness (in a greater degree) and Satisfaction have positive effect on Continuance intention, what makes H1 and H3 supported. Similar results were achieved in the study about post-acceptance model of IS continuous intentions by Bhattacherjee (2001) and in the study of SaaS quality by Benlian et al. (2011). Hence, according to this research, the major factor of continuance intention for customers to use VSaaS would be Perceived Usefulness, or how useful they think the services are. The managerial implication will be discussed further.

5.2 Research Implications.

5.2.1 Academic Implications.

This research focuses on exploring factors that are important for customers in defining the service quality of the online video surveillance and propose the model of continuance intention to use those services. Although, there are a lot of researches that explore Software-as-a-Service (SaaS) quality models (Benlian et al., 2011; Chou & Chiang, 2013), there are still a limited amount of studies that focus on Video Surveillance-as-a-Service (VSaaS) overall, and service quality or continuance intention of VSaaS in particular, which, as was stated above, is a part of SaaS. Even though these two service models are quite similar, there are still a few major differences that can define the research output. For example, the users of VSaaS are in a very special group of people, who has different concerns about service quality and how they define it. Hopefully, this study can fulfill the gap by understanding not only VSaaS service quality factors, but also by defining the model to study VSaaS quality and continuance intention. Hence, this research may be used as a reference for future studies about online video surveillance.

5.2.2 Managerial Implications.

According to the results of this study, Perceived Usefulness is the major variable that can affect users' Continuance Intention and Satisfaction. In order increase the Perceived Usefulness for customers, the Service Quality should be very high, and the major factors for this are vendor's responsiveness, reliability, flexibility, and features. The higher these four factors, the higher possibility that the customers will keep continuously use the services. These four factors are the major concerns for users when they choose to keep using particular vendor for online video surveillance services.

The findings of the research also contribute to the future marketing strategies for VSaaS vendors and service providers. In their marketing campaigns they would probably need to emphasize more on the possible usefulness of their services. Particularly, it can be responsive customer service (for the factor Responsiveness); it can be accurate, uninterruptable, and punctual service of the vendors (for the factor Reliability); the service should be easily customized, scaled, paying methods should be easily chosen (for the factor Flexibility); vendors of VSaaS should also emphasize on a wide range of functionalities and on a design and appearance of the interface (for the factor Features). Marketers should also define the main customers' segment for their services: whether the main users are mostly CCTV professionals or just home users, male or female, the purpose of the surveillance and so on. Market segments will also define the major characteristics of the marketing campaigns and advertisement.

5.3 Research Limitations.

5.3.1 Sampling.

One of the important parts of this research is a survey that was conducted with the help of online video surveillance users. As the research questions were placed online for a public access there was no chance to control the sampling and choose the right person for filling up the survey. As the most of the respondents (~90%) has less than 2 years' experience with the VSaaS, it might have been affected the results. The applications where the respondents use VSaaS are also different: home users and business users would surely have different perception about the quality of service when they use the online video surveillance. Home users might emphasize more on the beautiful user interface, convenience of the app or the software, flexible ways of paying; when business users would like to have more stable and scalable system.

Countries of origin of the respondents have also affected the results. There were less than 10% of respondents from Asia or CIS countries. And almost 50% of respondents were from Europe. Hence, the country biases are also can seriously affect the results of the study.

5.3.2 Questionnaire Development.

The questions for the survey of this study were written in English. Even though the words that were used to make questions were not very difficult or very special, however, for non-native English speakers it could be hard to fully understand the meaning of all the questions. Also, in the survey there are a few questions that require respondents to have basic vocabulary for video surveillance topic.

Another problem with the questionnaire could be its length. There were too many questions, so that while answering the long survey people's answers become more irrelevant to their real thinking or opinion. If the respondent is not fully involved to the questionnaire then the results can be very biased. However, during the CFA it was shown that some of the items of the survey were useless and can be eliminated in the future studies.

5.4 Future Research Suggestions.

As was stated above, there are not many researches about the VSaaS. This topic is new for the scholars and there are still a lot of chances for future research. First of all, the further research model can be better organized in order to have less constructs and items. The number of survey questions also should be minimized. Future researchers can study business customers and home customers separately, in this case the sampling data would be more homogeneous, and hence the results would be more predictable. The same situation is with country biases: it would be interesting to study the service quality perception and continuance intentions in different regions of the world.

With the fast development of new technologies, the video surveillance is going to be integrated with the “smart house”. It is another interesting field of the research; because in this case a few latest technologies are put together in order to deliver the best experience for the customers. How would users evaluate quality, what reasons will affect their future usage intentions? Those can be the questions for the further research.

References

Anderson, R. E., Babin, B., Black, B., Hair, J. F., & Tatham, R. L. (2006). *Multivariate data analysis*. New Jersey: Prentice-Hall.

Armburst, M., Fox, A., Griffith, R., Joseph, A. D., Katz, R., Konwinski, A., . . . Zaharia, M. (2010). A view of cloud computing. *Communications of the ACM, 53*(4), 50-58.

Benlian, A., Koufaris, M., & Hess, T. (2011). Service quality in Software-as-a-Service: Developing the SaaS-Qual measure and examining its role in usage continuance. *Journal of Management Inormation Systems, 28*(3), 85-126.

Bhattacherjee, A. (2001). Understanding information systems continuance: An expectation-confirmation model. *MIS Quarterly, 25*(3), 351-370.

Chiu, C. M., Lin, H. Y., Sun, S. Y., & Hsu, M. H. (2009). Understanding customers' loyalty towards online shopping: An integration of technology acceptance model and fairness theory. *Behaviour & Information Technology, 28*(4), 347-360.

Chou, S.-W., & Chiang, C.-H. (2013). Understanding the formation of software-as-a-service (SaaS) satisfaction from the perspective of service quality. *Decision Support Systems, 56*, 148-155.

Choudhary, V. (2007). Comparison of software quality under perpetual licensing and software as a service. *Journal of Management Information Systems, 24*(2), 141-165.

Cusmano, M. A. (2010). Cloud computing and SaaS as new computing platforms. *Communications of the ACM, 53*(4), 27-29.

Dale, A. (2013). *Video surveillance as a service (VSaaS) - World - 2013*. Retrieved from Colorado, USA:

Davis, F. D. (1989). Perceived usefulness, perceived ease of use, and user acceptance of information technology. *MIS Quarterly, 13*(3), 319-340.

Davis, F. D., Bagozzi, R. P., & Warshaw, P. R. (1989). User acceptance of computer technology: A comparison of two theoretical models. *MANAGEMENT SCIENCE, 35*(8), 982-1003.

DeLone, W. H., & McLean, E. R. (1992). Information systems success: The quest for the dependent variable. *Information Systems Research, 3*(1), 60-95.

Gao, F. (2013). VSaaS model on DRAGON-Lab. *International Journal of Multimedia and Ubiquitous Engineering, 8*(4), 293-302.

Gummerus, J., Liljander, V., Pura, M., & Riel, A. V. (2004). Customer loyalty to content-based web sites: The case of an online health-care service. *Journal of Service Marketing, 18*(3), 175-186.

Hanan, M., & Karp, P. (1989). *Consumer satisfaction: How to maximize, measure, and market your company's ultimate product*. New York: American Management Association.

Kettinger, W. J., & Lee, C. C. (1997). Pragmatic perspectives on the measurement of information systems service quality. *MIS Quarterly, 21*(2), 223-240.

Khalifa, M., & Liu, V. (2003). Satisfaction with Internet-based services: The role of expectations and desires. *International Journal of Electronic Commerce, 7*(2), 31-50.

Kim, D. J., Ferrin, D. L., & Rao, H. R. (2009). Trust and satisfaction, two stepping stones for succesful e-commerce relationships: A longitudinal exploration. *Information Systems Research, 20*(2), 237-257.

Kruegle, H. (2011). *CCTV surveillance: Video practices and technology*. Burlington: Elsevier Butterworth-Heinemann.

Limna, T., & Tandayya, P. (2012). *Design for a flexible video surveillance as a service.* Paper presented at the 5th International Congress on Image and Signal Processing (CISP), Chongqing, Sichuan, China.

Lin, H. H., & Wang, Y. S. (2006). An examination of the determinants of customer loyalty in mobile commerce contexts. *Information & Management, 43*(3), 271-282.

Liu, C., Marchewka, J., Lu, J., & Yu, C. S. (2004). Beyond concern: A privacy-trust-behavioral intention model of electronic commerce. *Information & Management, 42*(1), 127-142.

Ma, Q., Pearson, J. M., & Tadisina, S. (2005). An exploratory study into factors of service quality for application service providers. *Information & Management, 42*(8), 1067-1080.

Malhotra, N. K., Sung, S. K., & Agarwal, J. (2004). Internet users' iformation privacy concerns (IUIPC): The construct, the scale, and a causal model. *Information Systems Research, 15*(4), 336-355.

Mather, T., Kumaraswamy, S., & Latif, S. (2009). *Cloud security and privacy: An enterprise perspective on risks and compliance*. Sebastopol, CA: O'Reilly Media.

Mayer, R. C., Davis, J. H., & Schoorman, F. D. (1995). An integrative model of organizational trust. *Academy of Management Review, 20*(3), 709-734.

Moorman, C., Zaltman, G., & Deshpande, R. (1992). Relationships between providers and users of market research: The dynamics of trust within and between organizations. *Journal of marketing research, 29*(3), 314-328.

Mulholland, J. A., Pyke, J., & Fingar, P. (2010). *Enterprise cloud computing: A strategy guide for business and technology leaders*. Tampa, FL: Meghan-Kiffer Press.

Neal, D. J., & Rahman, S. (2012). Video surveillance in the cloud? *International Journal on Cryptography and Information Security, 2*(3), 1-19.

Oliver, R. L. (1980). A cognitive model of the antecendents and consequences of satisfaction decisions. *Journal of marketing research, 17*(4), 460-469.

Parasuraman, A., Berry, L. L., & A.Zeithaml, V. (1991). Refineement and reassessment of the SERVQUAL scale. *Journal of Retailing, 67*(4), 420-450.

Parasuraman, A., Zeithaml, V. A., & Berry, L. L. (1988). SERVQUAL: A multiple-item scale for measuring consumer perceptions of service quality. *Journal of Retailing, 64*(1), 12-40.

Parasuraman, A., Zeithaml, V. A., & Malhorta, A. (2005). E-S-QUAL: A multiple-item scale for assessing electronic serice quality. *Journal of Service Research, 7*(3), 213-233.

Patterson, P. G. (1993). Expectations and product performance as determinants of satisfaction for a high-involvement purchase. *Psychology & Marketing, 10*(5), 449-465.

Reese, G. (2009). *Cloud application architecture: Building applications and infrastructure in the cloud*. Sebastopol, CA: O'Reilly Media.

Sigala, M. (2004). The ASP-Qual model: Measuring ASP service quality in Greece. *Managing Service Quality, 14*(1), 103-114.

Swaid, S. I., & Wigand, R. T. (2009). Measuring the quality of e-service: Scale development and initial validation. *Journal of Electronic Commerce Research, 10*(1), 13-28.

Urban, G. L., Sultan, F., & Qualls, W. J. (2000). Placing trust at the center of your Internet strategy. *Sloan Management Review, 42*(1), 39-48.

Valera, M., & Velastin, S. A. (2005). Intelligent distributed surveillance systems: A review. *Vision, Image and Signal Processing, IEE Proceedings, 152*(2), 192-204.

Watson, R. T., Pitt, L. F., & Kavan, C. B. (1998). Measuring information systems service quality: Lessons from two longitudinal case studies. *MIS Quarterly, 22*(1), 61-79.

Wu, I.-L. (2013). The antecedents of customer satisfaction and its link to compliant intentions in online shopping: An integration of justice, technology, and trust. *International Journal of Informatioin Management, 33*(1), 166-176.
Zhao, Z., Cui, X., & Zhang, H. (2012). Cloud storage technology in video surveillance. *Advanced Materials Research, 533*, 1334-1338.

DECISION SCIENCES INSTITUTE

The Influence of Ethical Relativism on Ethical Compromise in Business Exchanges

Jin Li
North Dakota State University
Email: jin.li@ndsu.edu

Chanchai Tangpong
North Dakota State University
Email: charnchai.tangpong@ndsu.edu

Kuo-Ting Hung
Sawyer Business School, Suffolk University
Email: khung@suffolk.edu

ABSTRACT

In this research, we investigated the impact of ethical relativism on ethical compromise likelihood in managerial decision-making. We proposed that ethical relativism is positively related to ethical compromises in business exchanges. Specifically, ethical relativism lets a party in a reciprocal exchange relationship to advocate an ethically questionable or even unacceptable practice requested by the other party in the relationship. We also examined the role of environmental uncertainty as moderating factor in the ethical relativism-ethical compromise relationship. The results of an experiment with business professionals have yielded partial support for our hypotheses.

KEYWORDS: Ethical Relativism, Ethical Compromise, Environmental Uncertainty, and Experiment.

INTRODUCTION

Ethical compromise is a ubiquitous but understudied phenomenon in business exchange relationships. Ethical compromise can be defined as one party's engagement in an ethically unacceptable or questionable practice requested by another party (Tangpong, Li, & Hung, 2016). Decision making agents make ethical compromise for various reasons, one of which is because the norm of reciprocity imposes a sense of moral obligation and a sense of instrumental necessity on the decision-making agents and subordinate them to do so. Since Gouldner's (1960) famous analysis on the norm of reciprocity, researchers in different disciplines such as sociology, psychology, business, and behavioral economics have examined the impacts of the reciprocity norm on the dynamics in various forms of social relationships (e.g., Axelrod & Dion, 1988; Bowen & Jones, 1996; Dahl, Honea, & Manchanda, 2005; Perugini, Gallucci, Presaghi, & Ercolani, 2003). The norm of reciprocity rests upon two fundamental principles: (1) people should help those who have helped them, and (2) people should not harm those who have helped them.

The reciprocity norm is considered a foundation of stakeholder theory (Phillips, 2003; Tangpong & Pesek, 2007), relationship marketing (Dahl et al., 2005; Friedman & Friedman, 1996), and game strategy (Axelrod, 1984; Rappaport & Chammah, 1965). In addition, empirical research has suggested various advantageous effects of the reciprocity norm in business and management contexts. Examples of such advantages include (a) strengthening employee loyalty, commitment, and organizational citizenship behavior (e.g., Deckop et al., 2003; Levinson, 1965; Shore & Wayne, 1993), (b) fostering trust and creating moral community among professionals (Sama & Shoaf, 2008), and (c) reducing opportunism and thus transaction costs in supply chain relationships (Bowen & Jones, 1996; Maitland, Bryson, & Van de Ven, 1985). Therefore, the logic of reciprocity has become a prevalent conceptual framework in analyzing and understanding social relations and exchanges.

While most studies on the norm of reciprocity in the literature have primarily focused on its benevolent effects, research that examines the negative side of this phenomenon has been limited, to our knowledge. Abbink, Irlenbusch, and Renner's (2002), Shang, Chen, and Chen's (2008), and Tangpong, Li, and Hung's (2016) studies are among only few studies that have tapped into the potential dark side of the reciprocity norm in terms of inducing corruption, copyright infringements, and ethical compromise, respectively.

In this study, we want to extend Tangpong et al.'s (2016) study by specifically arguing that ethical relativism is a very important variable that will affect decision makers' ethical compromise likelihood in managerial decision-making. At the same time, we argue that environmental uncertainty plays an important moderating role in the ethical relativism-ethical compromise relationship.

LITERATURE REVIEW AND HYPOTHESIS DEVELOPMENT

Main Effect of Ethical Relativism

In a business exchange relationship, ethical compromise refers to as one party's engagement in an ethically unacceptable or questionable practice requested by another party (Tangpong et al., 2016). Decision making agents make ethical compromise mainly because the norm of reciprocity imposes a sense of moral obligation and a sense of instrumental necessity on the decision-making agents and subordinate them to do so. The norm of reciprocity is a social norm prescribing that individuals should attempt to repay what others have provided them and should not harm those who have helped them (Cialdini, 2006; Gouldner, 1960). This social norm thus plays a major role in stabilizing any social systems (Gouldner, 1960) and is central to human social relationships.

Tangpong et al. (2016) investigated the impact of the reciprocity norm on ethical compromise likelihood in managerial decision-making. They found that the norm of reciprocity compels a party in a reciprocal exchange relationship to advocate ethical compromise and environmental uncertainty and exchange partner's retaliatory power status work as boundary conditions of the reciprocity norm-ethical compromise relationship, in addition to perceived future gain opportunity in the relationships as potential mediating mechanisms of the reciprocity norm-ethical compromise relationship. In this current study we try to examines this issue from a different perspective – ethical relativism.

Ethical relativism argues that morality and ethics are relative to the norms of one's culture and situation. In other words, whether an action is ethical or not depends on the moral norms of the society in which it is practiced or the situation where the decision is made. The same action may be ethical in one society but unethical in another. For people who believes in ethical relativism, there are no universal ethical standards. Research has found that relativistic individuals reject the possibility of formulating and relying on moral principles when making moral judgments, whereas absolutistic individuals believe in and make use of moral absolutes when making judgment (Forsyth, 1980; Rawwas et al.,1995; Schlenker & Forsyth, 1977; Suter et al., 2006).

Based on this line of argument, we propose that ethical relativism can exert influence on decision making agents' ethical compromise likelihood in business exchange relationship. Those who score high on ethical relativism are less like to accept universal ethical rules. Therefore, they are more likely to be affected by the instrumental force of reciprocity norm, thus more prone to making ethical compromise. We therefore propose the following hypothesis:

> *Hypothesis 1: In reciprocal business exchange relationships, decision makers' ethic relativism is positively related to their likelihood of making ethical compromise.*

Moderating effect of environmental uncertainty

Uncertainty has been a key factor that shapes dynamics in managerial decision-making and influences firm behaviors (e.g., Simon, 1957; Thompson, 2003). Arising from rapid changes in technology, markets, and competition (e.g., Kumar, Scheer, & Steenkamp, 1995; Lee, Yeung, & Cheng, 2009), environmental uncertainty, in the context of ethical compromise in business exchanges, is found to be a boundary condition of the reciprocity and ethical compromise relationship (Tangpong et al., 2016). Following this logical thrust, we argue that the main influence of ethical relativism on ethical compromise is moderated by environmental uncertainty. In a fast-changing and uncertain environment, firms are faced with series of challenges ranging from unpredictability of market conditions, changes in customer preferences, technological changes, to various competitive actions from competitors (e.g., Buchko, 1994; Kevin, 1999; Lee et al., 2009). This type of business landscape creates tremendous competitive pressures, and the failure to cope with them can threaten firms' long-term survival (D'Aveni, 1994). For decision makers who uphold ethical relativism, such environmental pressures strengthen their belief of situational ethics and permit them to make ethical compromise. By doing so, they expect to win their partners' trust and form further coalitions and alliances to better cope with such uncertainty. As such, it can be argued that the ethical relativism becomes a greater force exerting influences over decision-making agents of firms to engage in ethical compromises in a highly uncertain business environment. This line of argument suggests Hypothesis 2:

> *Hypothesis 2: Under conditions of high environmental uncertainty, the positive relationship between ethical relativism and ethical compromise in managerial decision making is strengthened.*

EXPERIMENT

To test the proposed hypotheses, we used a scenario-based role-playing experiment as our research methodology. For this experimental research, we used the validated ethical dilemma scenario from Tangpong et al. (2016), which is empirically grounded in a real case of anti-competitive conduct of Microsoft – part of the Sun Microsystems (Sun) versus Microsoft antitrust lawsuit in 2002. The details of the experiment are described as follows.

Participants

Participants in the experiment were 132 experienced business professionals recruited through the alumni association of a university in the East Coast of the U.S. The participant demographics included (a) 66.7% male and 33.3% female, (b) 89.4% Caucasian and 10.6% non-Caucasian, (c) the average age of 47 years, (d) 58.3 working in private sector, 36.4% in public sector, and 5.3% did not mention their sector, and (e) the average management experience of 14.6 years.

Experimental design

In the experiments, we manipulate environmental uncertainty. The participants were randomly assigned into one control group and one experimental group. All participants were asked to read an ethical dilemma scenario developed based on the Microsoft antitrust lawsuit case. As part of the lawsuit, Microsoft was charged with engaging in illegal monopolization and/or monopoly maintenance and with illegally entering into exclusive dealing and exclusionary agreements with Intel. An incident leading up to the charges was that while Sun and Intel were establishing a technology partnership to optimize Sun's operating environment for Intel's processors, Microsoft allegedly intervened in the process by contacting Intel and convincing Intel not to cooperate with Sun, which was a primary competitor of Microsoft at the time. The experimental scenario in this study was based on this incident, in which Company W (a pseudonym name for Intel) is considering a mutually beneficial business relationship with Company X (a pseudonym for Sun). However, the top manager of Company Y (a pseudonym name for Microsoft), an established business partner of Company W, approaches the top manager of Company W and asks him/her not to form the partnership with Company X, which is the main competitor of Company Y. The participants in this experiment assume the role of the top manager at Company W in the scenario. Facing with this dilemma, the participants have to make a yes-no decision whether to comply with the request from Company Y. Given that anti-competitive conducts are considered ethically or even legally questionable, their decision to comply with Company Y's request is thus considered an ethical compromise.

All participants were presented with the same information in the given scenario briefly summarized above. However, those in the experimental group were provided with the manipulation material for environmental uncertainty, while those in the control group were not presented with the manipulation material. Both manipulation checks were successfully performed as the participants in the experimental group indicated that when making the decision, they took the manipulation material regarding environmental uncertainty into consideration to a greater extent than those in the group without that manipulation ($p < 0.001$).

Variables and data coding

The decision likelihood to comply with the ethically questionable request was the dependent variable and was scaled from 1 - 7 (not very likely to very likely to engage in an ethical compromise). The environmental uncertainty manipulation was one of the two independent variables and was coded as 1 and 0 for their presence and absence in the given scenario, respectively. The other independent variable was respondents' ethical relativism, which was measured by a 10-item 7-point Likert scale. These items were developed from previous literature (Forsyth, 1980; Rawwas, Patzer, & Klassen, 1995; Schlenker & Forsyth, 1977; Suter, Kopp, & Hardesty, 2006). Second-order factor scores of these 10 items were used as the composite measure of ethical relativism in the subsequent data analysis. Control variables included ethnicity, gender, age, private sector, and years of management experience. Ethnicity, simply categorized into Caucasian and non-Caucasian, was coded as 1 and 0, respectively.

Male and female were coded as 1 and 0, respectively. Respondents self-reported as being from the private sector was coded as 1, or otherwise coded as 0. Age and years of management experience were kept as continuous variables.

Data analysis and results

The correlation analysis indicated that there was significant correlation between Age and Management Experience (coefficient = 0.766, $p < 0.001$). However, Variance Inflation Factors did not indicate multicollinearity problems among them. Thus, the underlying assumptions of regression analysis were not violated. The results of the regression analysis show that ethical relativism was positively related to the ethical compromise likelihood ($p < 0.05$), thus Hypothesis 1 was supported. The environmental uncertainty, however, was slightly related to the ethical compromise likelihood ($p < 0.1$). The interaction term between the ethical relativism and environmental uncertainty was significant and negatively related to the likelihood of ethical compromise ($p < 0.05$), which was against Hypothesis 2.

DISCUSSION AND CONCLUSION

In this research, we have examined how ethical relativism affects decision-making agents' ethical compromises in business exchanges. We specifically inquired: (1) what is the effect of ethical relativism on ethical compromise likelihood in managerial decision making, and (2) what is the moderating effect of environmental uncertainty on the ethical relativism-ethical compromise relationship. The empirical data from the experiment not only reveal some answers to these questions but also provide directions for further research.

First, there is a significantly positive relationship between ethical relativism and agents' ethical compromise likelihood in reciprocal business exchange in our experiment. Second, ethical relativism interacts with environmental uncertainty in negatively influencing the likelihood of ethical compromise in reciprocal business exchanges, which is against our original hypothesis. This finding is quite counter-intuitive to us. A possible explanation is that ethical relativism may serve as a moral adaptive mechanism that enables individuals to morph their ethical standard to morally justify their action under a specific perceived circumstance (i.e., the target toward which individuals' ethical standard is modified). However, when individuals are less certain about the circumstance as in the case of high uncertainty, such circumstance metaphorically becomes a moving target, which individuals are cognitively less able to adapt their ethical standard toward. As such, they become less decisive in taking actions (i.e., less likely to engage in ethical compromise).

This research has extended the current literature on ethical compromise in two important ways. First, it enriches the currently limited research on ethical compromise by examining the influence of decision makers' ethical relativism on ethical compromise. Second, this research looks at environmental uncertainty as a potential boundary condition that moderates the impact of ethical relativism on ethical compromises in exchange relationships.

REFERENCES

References available upon request.

DECISION SCIENCES INSTITUTE

The Influence of Managerial Metacognition on Quality Management Practices and a Firm's Sustainable Competitive Advantages

Young Sik Cho
Jackson State University
Email: young_sik.cho@jsums.edu

ABSTRACT

The purpose of this study is to explore how managerial metacognition has an influence on a firm's QM practices and their sustainable competitive advantages. A survey method was used to collect a primary data, and a total of 235 viable samples were obtained from senior-level quality managers working in the U.S.-based firms. Structural equation modeling was adopted to test the hypothesized research model of this study. The test results demonstrated that there was a positive synergy effect of metacognition and QM practices on the creation of a firm's sustainable competitive advantages.

KEYWORDS: Metacognition, Quality management, Sustainable competitive advantage, Structural equation modeling, Survey research

INTRODUCTION

Metacognition can generally be defined as a higher-order process reflecting one's awareness and control over the knowledge structure used by people in making an assessment or a decision (Haynie et al., 2010). Specifically, in the context of quality management, a firm's managerial metacognition can be defined as a higher-order psychological mechanism actually possessed by a firm through which it is able to develop a new knowledge structure in order to realize more effective implementation of its lower-order technical mechanisms (i.e., quality management practices) based on a keen understanding of its motivations, assumptions, strengths, and weaknesses (Flavell, 1987; Haynie, 2005; Choo et al., 2007; Haynie and Shepherd, 2009; Haynie et al., 2010). In the literature, it is recognized that quality management (QM) practices and metacognition inherently have the following strong functional similarities. Both mechanisms mainly: (i) focus on process effectiveness (e.g., Berardi-Coletta et al., 1995; Silver, 2004; Kaynak & Hartley, 2008); (ii) emphasize a learning-by-doing approach (e.g., Paris & Winograd, 1990; Hayes et al., 2005); and (iii) pursue continuous improvement by an ongoing knowledge creation process (e.g., Kluwe, 1982; Linderman et al., 2004). Taking these similarities into consideration, it is rationally anticipated that a functional relationship exists between the two mechanisms. However, there is a little insight into the relationship between the "technical mechanism" (i.e., QM practices) and the "psychological mechanism" (i.e., managerial metacognition) (Choo et al., 2007, p. 437) in the operations management literature. In addition, the psychological mechanism has been actively studied for a long time at the higher-order level in many other disciplines such as education (e.g., Schoenfeld, 1987; Borkowski and Muthukrishna, 1992), psychology (e.g., Flavell, 1976; Davidson et al., 1994), entrepreneurship (e.g., Haynie, 2005; Haynie et al, 2012; Cho and Jung, 2014), and international management (e.g., Ang et al., 2007; Kim and Van Dyne, 2012). To date, psychological mechanism-related research in operations management has only been conducted at the cognitive level. However, metacognition is considered as the higher-order process which controls the existing knowledge structure while cognition is regarded as the existing knowledge structure used by people in

making an assessment or a decision. Accordingly, it is anticipated that the functional role of such a higher-order process (i.e., metacognition) on QM practices may be quite different from the role of a lower-order process (i.e., cognition) on them. Thus, this study attempts to explore how a quality manager's higher-order psychological process, metacognition, affects their lower-order technical process, QM practices. Specifically, the following research questions have been examined through this study:
(1) What is the role of managerial metacognition on the effective implementation of QM? In other words, is managerial metacognition related to the effective implementation of QM practices?
(2) If so, how does the synergy of managerial metacognition and QM practices influence the creation of a firm's sustainable competitive advantage?

THEORY AND HYPOTHESES

The Relationship between Metacognition and QM practices

Metacognition is typically illustrated as "thinking about thinking" and "cognition about cognition" (Flavell, 1979, 1987). The study of Haynie et al. (2010) more specifically defined metacognition as "the control that the individual has over their own cognitions as a function of a differing ability to consider alternative cognitive strategies in light of a changing environment" (p.219). Cognition is the knowledge structure used by people in making a decision; whereas, metacognition is a higher-order process controlling over the knowledge structure (Mitchell, Busenitz, Lant, McDougall, Morse, and Smith, 2002; Cho and Jung, 2014). Metacognition is also understood as the process of formulating strategies in order to select from a set of possible cognitive mechanisms (Flavell, 1987; Haynie, 2005; Haynie et al., 2010). Further, many studies indicate that the metacognitive abilities of people can be improved by appropriate training and practices, which is intrinsically different from the intelligence quotient (IQ) of people (Mevarech, 1999; Nietfeld & Schraw, 2002; Schmidt & Ford, 2003; Haynie et al., 2010). Furthermore, in terms of neuroscience, metacognition is known as a function of the prefrontal cortex in human brain which is generally regarded as one of the few distinctions from other primates (Fleming, Weil, Nagy, Dolan, and Rees, 2010; Baird, Smallwood, Gorgolewski, and Margulies, 2013).

Although metacognition can be slightly differently classified into sub-dimensions (Flavell, 1979, 1987; Griffin and Ross, 1991; Nelson, 1996), Hayine and Shepherd (2009) conceptualized metacognition as the following five dimensions: goal orientation, metacognitive knowledge, metacognitive experience, metacognitive strategy (or metacognitive choice), and monitoring. This study basically adopted the Haynie and Shepherd's (2009) "Measure of Adaptive Cognition (MAC)" to measure a managerial metacognition after slightly revising the items to reflect the purpose of this study. Thus, this study employs Haynie and Shepherd's (2009) the original definitions for each metacognition dimension. In the context of metacognition literature, goal orientation can be defined to be "the extent to which the individual interprets environmental variations in light of a wide variety of personal, social, and organizational goals" (Haynie and Shepherd, 2009, p.699). Metacognitive knowledge can be described as "the extent to which the individual relies on what is already known about oneself, other people, tasks, and strategy when engaging in the process of generating multiple decision frameworks focused on interpreting, planning, and implementing goals to manage a changing environment" (Haynie and Shepherd, p.699). Metacognitive experience can be illustrated as "the extent to which the individual relies on idiosyncratic experiences, emotions, and intuitions when engaging in the process of generating multiple decision frameworks focused on interpreting, planning, and implementing goals to manage a changing environment" (p.699). Metacognitive choice (also called as metacognitive strategy) can be conceptualized to be "the extent to which the individual engages in the active process of selecting from multiple decision frameworks the one that best interprets, plans, and implements a response for the purpose of managing a changing environment" (p.700). Finally, metacognitive monitoring can be defined as "seeking and using feedback to reevaluate goal orientation, metacognitive knowledge, metacognitive experience, and metacognitive choice for the purposes of managing a changing environment" (p.700). While the metacognitive mechanism has not yet been examined in operations literature, the metacognition has been actively studied for a long time in many other disciplines such as education (e.g., Schoenfeld, 1987; Borkowski and Muthukrishna, 1992), psychology (e.g., Flavell, 1976; Davidson et al., 1994), entrepreneurship (e.g., Haynie, 2005; Haynie, Shepherd, and Patzelt, 2012; Cho and Jung, 2014) and international management (e.g., Ang, Van Dyne, Koh, Ng, Templer, Tay, and Chandraseka, 2007; Kim and Van Dyne, 2012). Table 1 summarizes the major metacognition-related studies in management literature.

As depicted in Fig. 1, QM practices and metacognition inherently have strong functional similarities. Above all, both QM and metacognition mainly pursue process effectiveness (e.g., Berardi-Coletta et al., 1995; Silver, 2004). Also, both mechanisms heavily rely on a learning-by-doing approach, that is, learning how to perform the activity better by actually doing it (e.g., Paris and Winograd, 1990; Hayes et al., 2005). Besides, both strongly emphasize continuous improvement by an ongoing knowledge creation process (e.g., Kluwe, 1982; Linderman et al., 2004). Taking these similarities into consideration, it is rationally anticipated that a strong positive interaction exists between the two mechanisms. Thus, the following hypothesis is suggested:

Hypothesis 1. Managerial metacognition is positively related to a firm's quality management practices.

Figure 1: A comparison of QM and metacognition

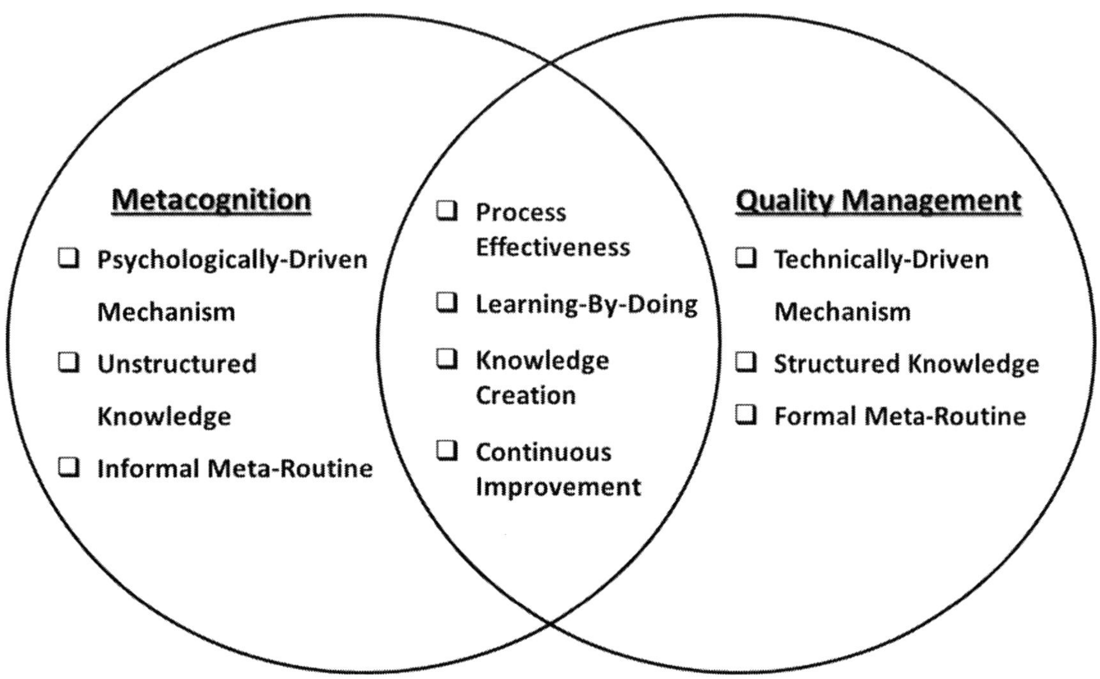

Table 1: Major Metacognition Studies in Management Literature

Study	Purpose	Discipline & Research Type	Sample	Key Finding
Haynie (2005)	To explore how metacognition affects 'cognitive adaptability' in the context of an entrepreneurial task.	Entrepreneurship/ Empirical	Entrepreneurs in the US (N = 73)	Metacognitive awareness relates positively to cognitive adaptability at entrepreneurial tasks; the enhanced cognitive adaptability contributes to improving entrepreneurial task performance.
Ang, Van Dyne, Koh, Ng, Templer, Tay, and Chandraseka (2007)	To explore the relationship between cultural intelligence (CQ) and intercultural effectiveness outcome.	International management/ Empirical	Undergraduate students in the US (N = 235) and Singapore (N = 358); international managers (N = 98); foreign professionals (N = 103)	Metacognitive CQ has a significantly positive effect on both cultural judgment and decision making (CJDM) effectiveness and task performance, while cognitive CQ has a significantly positive effect on CJDM, but not on task performance.
Haynie and Shepherd (2009)	To develop an instrument to assess metacognitive awareness in an entrepreneurial context.	Entrepreneurship/ Empirical	Undergraduate business students in the US (N = 432)	36 measure items were constructed to be used for assessing the five dimensions of metacognitive awareness such as metacognitive experience, knowledge, monitoring, choice, and goal orientation.
Haynie, Shepherd, Mosakowski, and Earley (2010)	To conceptualize a situated metacognitive model of an entrepreneurial mindset.	Entrepreneurship/ Conceptual	Not applicable	The study proposed a metacognitive process model that is able to elucidate how entrepreneurial metacognition affects entrepreneurial task and consequently, entrepreneurial outcome.
Chua, Morris, and Mor (2012)	To investigate how individual variation in terms of cultural metacognition impacts success in intercultural creative collaboration.	Organizational behavior/ Empirical	Middle-level managers (N = 43) and managers attending an executive MBA course in the US (N = 60); university	The study result indicates that individuals with higher metacognitive CQ are more positively associated with intercultural creative collaborations.

			students in the US (N = 236)	
Van Dyne, Ang, Ng, Rockstuhl, Tan, and Koh (2012)	To conceptualize sub-dimensions for each of the four CQ factors.	International management/ Conceptual	Not applicable	The study conceptualized the sub-dimensions of metacognitive CQ as follows: planning, awareness, and checking.
Haynie, Shepherd, and Patzelt (2012)	To explore the role of metacognitive ability and feedback on the cognitive adaptability of naive entrepreneurs.	Entrepreneurship/ Empirical	Undergraduate business students in the US (N = 217)	The study result demonstrates that the benefits of cognitive-based feedback are greater for the naive entrepreneurs with higher metacognitive knowledge.
Kim and Van Dyne (2012)	To examine the relationships between prior intercultural contact, cultural intelligence, and international leadership potential.	International management/ Empirical	Working adults in the US (N = 441); employees (N = 181) and their observers in the US (N = 708)	Cultural intelligence has a mediating effect on the relationship between prior intercultural contact and international leadership potential.
Cho and Jung (2014)	To investigate the relationships between a metacognitive ability, entrepreneurial orientation, and firm performance.	Entrepreneurship/ Empirical	Entrepreneurs in the US (N = 190)	The study has found that an entrepreneurial metacognitive ability is significantly associated with entrepreneurial orientation (EO). Further, the study result demonstrates that EO mediates the effects of entrepreneurial metacognition on entrepreneurial task performance.

The Synergy of Metacognition and QM on a Firm's Sustainable Competitive Advantages

Numerous studies present that the elements of quality management (QM) framework can be clustered by two sub-constructs: human behavior-oriented quality practices and technology-oriented quality practices (Flynn, Schroeder, and Sakakibara, 1995; Anderson, Rungtusanatham, Schroeder, and Devaraj, 1995; Powell, 1995; Dow, Samson, and Ford, 1999; Rahman and Bullock, 2005; Naor, Goldstein, Linderman, and Schroeder, 2008; Jung and Hong, 2008; Gadenne and Sharma 2009; Zu, 2009). For example, quality management (QM) practices such as top management support, employee empowerment, customer focus, supplier relationship are intrinsically classified as the behavioral QM practices. One the other hand, QM practices such as process management, product and service design, strategic planning, quality information are typically clustered as the technical QM. Those studies, as shown in Table 2, also demonstrate that behavioral QM is characterized by features such as human-oriented, intangible, and relationship-driven practices, whereas technical QM can be distinguished by attributes such as mechanical-oriented, tangible, and technology-driven practices (Powell, 1995; Dow et al., 1999; Jun et al., 2006; Naor et al., 2008). Table 3 summarizes the major studies on the relationships between behavioral QM, technical QM, and organizational performance. Ironically most of the studies over the past two decades have maintained that only behavioral-related quality practices (e.g., top management support, employee involvement, supplier involvement, and customer involvement) positively relate to the competitive advantage of a firm, while technical QM practices (e.g., quality information, product design, and process management) do not directly affect the generation of a firm's competitive advantage (Naor et al., 2008; Powell, 1995; Jung and Hong, 2008).

Table 2: A Comparison between Behavioral vs. Technical QM Practices

	Behavioral QM	Technical QM	References
Perspective	Relationship-driven	Technology-driven	Flynn et al., 1995; Anderson, Rungtusanatham, Schroeder, and Devaraj, 1995; Powell, 1995; Dow et al., 1999; Rahman and Bullock, 2005; Jun et al., 2006; Naor et al., 2008; Jung and Hong, 2008; Gadenne and Sharma 2009; Zu, 2009.
Type of Resource	Intangible	Tangible	
Primary Functional Concern	How to do	What to do	
Locus of Managerial Efforts	Leading	Controlling	
Key Practices	Top management support, Employee involvement, Customer involvement, Supplier involvement	Process management, Strategic planning, Product/service design, Quality information	

With respect to QM practices, there is a strong tendency across QM-embedded firms to simply adopt or mimic the most popular QM framework that has been successfully implemented by their leading competitors; this so-called isomorphic nature of QM practices can be explained by institutional theory (Selznick, 1996; Hendricks and Singhal, 1997; Dahlgaard et al., 1998; Jun et al., 2006). However, numerous studies have argued that successful QM implementation is not accomplished equally by every QM-embedded firm (Powell, 1995; Beer, 2003; Jun et al., 2006); for example, one survey study indicated that only approximately one-third of all QM efforts have been successful (Hayes, Pisano, Upton, and Wheelwright, 2005). Therefore, this study presumes that the isomorphism of QM practices acts as one of the primary sources of the failure of QM implementation. Based on this argument, this study postulates that managerial metacognition can help the firm to better understand and control the problems generated through mimicking other firms' QM practices. In turn, these metacognitive findings can help the firm to develop a more effective QM framework in accordance with their operation systems' characteristics, eventually contributing to their sustainable competitive advantages. Namely, it is assumed that there is a positive synergy effect of metacognition and QM practices on the creation of a firm's sustainable competitive advantage. Therefore, the following hypotheses are suggested to explore the relationships:

Hypothesis 2. Managerial metacognition has a positive influence on the relationship between QM practices and a firm's sustainable competitive advantage.

Table 3: Key studies on the relationships between behavioral QM, technical QM, and organizational performance				
Study	**Objective**	**Type & Sample**	**Simplified Model & Results**	**Key Findings**
Powell (1995)	To examine QM as a potential source of sustainable competitive advantage.	Empirical / 54 US-based firms, employing 50 or more workers.	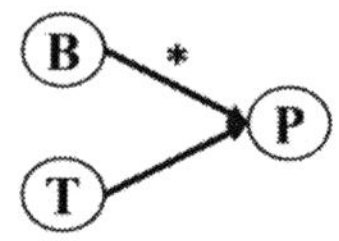	Intangible QM practices such as employee empowerment, executive commitment, and open culture significantly contribute to firm's competitive advantage, while tangible QM techniques such as process improvement, benchmarking, quality training do not generally relate to competitive advantage.
Dow, Samson, and Ford (1999)	To identify the core dimensions of quality management practices and investigate how these practices contribute to superior quality outcomes.	Empirical / 698 manufacturing plants located in Australia and New Zealand.		Only three of the nine quality practice constructs such as employee commitment, shared vision, and customer focus have a significant positive association with superior quality performance.
Jun, Cai, and Shin (2006)	To identify critical elements of QM practices that would contribute to the enhancement of employee satisfaction and loyalty.	Empirical / 407 employees of two Maquiladora-based firms in Mexico.		HR-focused QM practices such as teamwork, employee compensation, and employee empowerment have a significantly positive effect on employee satisfaction. In turn, the reinforced employee satisfaction contributes to a higher level of employee loyalty.
Naor, Goldstein, Linderman, and Schroeder (2008)	To investigate the relationship among organizational culture, infrastructure and core quality practices, and manufacturing	Empirical / 189 manufacturing plants located in six countries including the U.S., Japan,	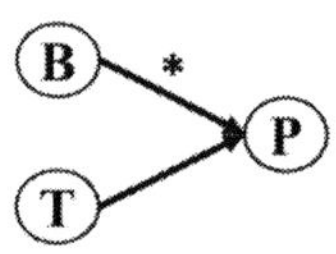	Organizational culture more significantly impacts on infrastructure quality management practices than on core quality management practices, regardless of where the manufacturing plant is located in six countries. Besides, infrastructure quality practices have a positive and significant effect on

	performance.	Sweden, Finland, Germany, and South Korea.		manufacturing performance while core quality practices have no significant effect on it both in the Eastern and the Western countries.
Abdullah, Uli, and Tari (2008)	To examine the impact of soft factors of QM practices on quality improvement and organizational performance.	Empirical / 255 managers of electronics firms located in Malaysia.		Soft QM factors such as management commitment, employee involvement, customer focus, reward, and training are significantly associated with quality improvement. Some soft factors such as management commitment, employee involvement, and customer focus are also significantly associated with organizational performance.
Jung and Hong (2008)	To investigate the relationships among the organizational citizenship behavioral (OCB), soft QM, hard QM, and firm performance.	Empirical / 230 Maquiladora firms located at the border between Texas in the U.S. and Mexico.	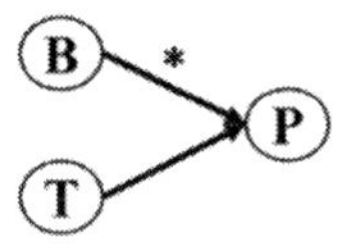	Soft QM factor which consists of leadership, people management, and customer focus shows a strong positive effect on firm performance, while hard QM factor which contains strategic planning, process management, and information analysis does not represent any significant impact on firm performance.

Note: * Significant positive effect; B = behavioral-related quality practices; T = technical-related quality practices; P = performance-related variables.

RESEARCH METHODS

Sample and Data Collection

A survey research method was used to collect a primary data for this study. Initially CEOs was considered as the most ideal target population of this study because CEOs are generally regarded to have a ability to access their organization's comprehensive information and knowledge such as their managerial capabilities, competitive advantages, and firm performances (Miller & Toulouse, 1986; Zahra & Covin, 1993). However, it is a reality that in many cases CEOs are not available for a survey in many cases and moreover, a major part of the survey is directly related to a firm's quality management practices so we extended our target population to Quality Managers as well as senior-level Managers of participating firms. In order to obtain more reliable sample data, we also developed the following criteria for selecting appropriate respondents: (i) Survey respondents must be in an active position in U.S. firms; (ii) Survey respondents must be deeply knowledgeable about their managerial capabilities as well as quality management practices; (iii) Survey respondents must be at least 21 years old to participate; (iv) Survey respondents must be a single respondent of each participating firm; if there is more than one respondent from the same firm, the target respondent will be chosen based on the position in their firm, preferably the highest rank among the respondents.

Survey Procedure

Online survey research was designed to collect a primary sample data for this study, referring to the studies of Dillman, Smyth, and Christian (2008) and Dillman et al. (2014). Survey participants were recruited online through invitation emails. In particular, the email lists of quality managers (N = 2,000) and senior business managers (N = 52,576) were purchased from both Dun & Bradstreet, Inc. and Specialdatabases.com. The target sample size for this study was initially set at 200 respondents and a response rate of the online-based survey was normally expected less than 3%. Hence, after scrutinizing the whole email databases based on the selecting criteria developed in this study, a total of 12,000 email lists were finally prepared for the survey research. This survey study was approved by the Institutional Review Board for Human Subjects Protection (IRB).

Measures

The managerial metacognition-related measure items were adapted from the study of Haynie and Shepherd (2009) but, some items were slightly revised to reflect the purpose of this study, referring to the studies of Haynie (2005) and Haynie et al. (2010). According to the Haynie and Shepherd's (2009) study, the survey was designed to measure the five different metacognitive dimensions such as metacognitive knowledge, metacognitive experience, metacognitive goal-orientation, metacognitive strategy, and metacognitive monitoring. The QM-related measures were developed based on a variety of sources such as Powell (1995), Flynn, Schroeder, and Sakakibara (1995), Samson and Terziovski (1999), Flynn and Saladin (2006), Jun, Cai, and Shin (2006), Naor, Goldstein, Linderman, and Schroeder (2008), Zu (2009), Zu, Robbins, and Fredendall (2010), and Baird, Jia Hu, and Reeve (2011). The resource-based view (RBV) (Barney, 1991) assumes that competing firms within an industry may control different bundles of resources and these resources may not be perfectly mobile across firms so firms' resource differences can be long lasting (Barney and Arikan, 2005). Barney (1991) illustrates four primary features of firm's resource to be sustained competitive advantage (SCA) as follows: valuable, rare, imperfectly imitable, and non-substitutable. Premised on the RBV, Weerawardena (2003) argues that the SCA construct can be operationalized as "whether it is possible for competitors

to duplicate the firm' competitive strategy (Barney, 1991; Grant, 1991) and distinctive capabilities on which advantages have been founded (Grant, 1991; Hall, 1993)" (p.21). However, with respect to a firm's sustainable competitive advantage (SCA), a widely recognized set of measures was not available so we needed to develop most of the measurement scales for this study based on the comprehensive literature review. Accordingly most of items used in this study were newly developed in this study, referring to Barney (1991), McEvily & Chakravarthy (2002), Wiggins & Ruefli (2002), Weerawardena (2003), Barney & Arikan (2005), Barney & Hesterly (2006), and Hitt, Ireland, and Hoskisson (2011).
The survey items were designed to estimate the degree to which the respondents agreed or disagreed with the given statement, based on a seven-point Likert scale, with 1 being strongly disagree and 7 being strongly agree. Before the actual survey, a pilot test was performed with MBA students (N = 24) to increase the reliability of scales. The measurement items and supporting literature are listed in Appendices A, B, and C.

DATA ANALYSIS AND FINDING

Sample Demographics

Email invitations with a web survey link were sent to a total of 12,000 target respondents in over 46 states of the U.S. We administered three rounds of survey invitations and obtained a total of 235 viable samples with a response rate of 1.95%. The χ^2 tests were conducted to examine whether a response bias exists among each round sample; any significant differences (at $p <$ 0.05 level) were not reported between the samples (Zu, 2009). Of the whole sample, about 70% had more than 21 years business history as well as at least 100 employees. Of the sample, 31% was manufacturing firms and 66% was service firms. Of the respondents, 71% were more than 45 years old and 57% were male. A demographic profile of the sample is demonstrated in Table 4. The detailed industrial classifications and SIC codes of participating firms are also summarized in Table 5.

Table 4: Sample Demographics

Category		Count	Proportion (%)
Firm's Age (Length of Time in Business)	Less than 5 years	7	3%
	5 ~ 10 years	16	7%
	11 ~ 20 years	30	13%
	21 ~ 30 years	48	20%
	31 ~ 50 years	46	20%
	51 ~ 100 years	55	23%
	More than 100 years	26	11%
	Missing responses	7	3%
Firm's Size (Number of Employees)	Less than 10 employees	20	9%
	11 ~ 50 employees	34	14%
	51 ~ 100 employees	14	6%
	101 ~ 500 employees	49	21%
	501 ~ 1,000 employees	21	9%
	1,001 ~ 10,000 employees	51	22%
	More than 10,000 employees	39	17%
	Missing responses	7	3%
Industry	Manufacturing	74	31%
	Service	154	66%

	Missing responses	7	3%
Age (Survey Respondents)	Less than 18	0	0%
	18 ~ 29	11	5%
	30 ~ 44	51	22%
	45 ~ 59	124	53%
	More than 59	42	18%
	Missing responses	7	3%
Gender (Survey Respondents)	Female	93	40%
	Male	135	57%
	Missing responses	7	3%

Table 5: Industrial Classification of the Sample

Industrial Classification	Count	Proportion (%)
Agriculture, Forestry & Fishing [01-09][a]	4	2%
Construction [15-17]	10	4%
Apparel & Fabricated Textile Products [23]	2	1%
Papers & Allied Products [26]	0	0%
Printing & Publishing [27]	5	2%
Pharmaceuticals [28]	10	4%
Chemical Products [28]	9	4%
Petroleum Refining [29]	3	1%
Semiconductors & Related Devices [36]	2	1%
Transportation Services [47]	10	4%
Communications Services [48]	8	3%
Wholesale Trade [50-51]	9	4%
Retail Trade [52-59]	12	5%
Financial Services [60-64]	13	6%
Hotels & Other Lodging Places [70]	2	1%
Prepackaged Software [73]	2	1%
Healthcare [80]	23	10%
Legal Services [81]	2	1%
Education [82]	11	5%
Accounting & Business Consulting Services [87]	4	2%
Others	84	36%
Missing responses	10	4%

Note: [a] Two-digit numbers represent the SIC codes.

Reliability of Scales

Reliability is defined as "the stability or consistency of an operational definition," while validity means "the goodness-of-fit between an operational definition and the concept it is purported to measure" (Singleton and Straits, 2010: 146). In other words, a reliable measure may or may not be valid, whereas a valid measure is necessarily reliable (Singleton and Straits, 2010). Thus, we conducted several reliability and validity tests for the measures before testing the hypothesized structural model. First the reliability of scales can be examined by calculating the value of Cronbach's alpha coefficient for each construct (Cronbach, 1951; Nunnally, 1967). The values of Cronbach's alpha for all scales exceeded the acceptable level point of 0.70, ranged from 0.75 for customer involvement to 0.94 for metacognitive strategy (Nunnally and Bernstein, 1994). In addition, Table 6 presents the descriptive statistics and correlations among all variables.

Convergent Validity

Convergent validity refers that all items consisting of a specific construct should share a high proportion of variance in common (Hair et al., 2010). The size of factor loading is considered as a criterion for identifying whether the scale items converge on their assigned latent construct. Thus, the factor loading for each item was computed to examine the convergent validity and the results showed that all items satisfied the suggested threshold of 0.50 factor loading (Hair et al., 2010). In particular, Table 7 shows the test results for the metacognition-related measure items, ranged between 0.84 and 0.93 factor loadings; Table 8 includes the description of each item and the test results of the confirmatory factor analysis (CFA) for the QM-related measures, ranged between 0.75 and 0.95 factor loadings;; Table 9 represents the test results for the items of both SCA and firm performance, ranged between 0.71 and 0.88 factor loadings.

Discriminant Validity

The values of the average variance extracted (AVE) were calculated to investigate the discriminant validity among factors. "Average Variance Extracted refers to the amount of variance that is captured by the latent variable in relation to the amount of variance due to the measurement error in the latent variable (Dillon and Goldstein 1984)" Akgün (2011: 201). The AVE of a value 50 percent or higher indicates discriminant validity among factors (Hair et al., 2010). In this study, the AVE estimate for each factor ranges between 60% for the factor of sustainable competitive advantage and 89% for the factor of supplier involvement, demonstrating that all factors satisfy the adequate level of discriminant validity.

Unidimensionality

Unidimensional measures are described as "a set of measured variables (indicators) can be explained by only one underlying construct" (Hair et al., 2010, p. 674). With respect to the CFA, a comparative fit index (CFI) of above 0.90 suggests statistical evidence of unidimensionality (Bentler, 1992; Al-Hawari, Hartley, and Ward, 2005; Zu, 2009). As shown in Table 10, all the CFI indices for the measurements are higher than 0.90, indicating acceptable unidimensionality..

Table 6: Descriptive Statistics and Correlations

Variable	1	2	3	4	5	6	7	8	9	10	11	12	13	14	15	16	Mean	S.D.
1. Firm's Age[a]																	4.662	1.566
2. Firm's Size[b]	.440**																4.429	1.950
3. Firm's Industry[c]	-.108	-.126															1.675	.469
4. Metacognitive Knowledge	-.078	-.104	-.034														4.842	1.504
5. Metacognitive Experience	-.060	-.034	-.060	.847**													4.774	1.531
6. Metacognitive Goal-Orientation	-.048	.011	-.015	.755**	.769**												4.802	1.626
7. Metacognitive Strategy	-.053	-.055	-.056	.838**	.894**	.794**											4.514	1.611
8. Metacognitive Monitoring	-.024	-.051	-.013	.816**	.856**	.787**	.921**										4.527	1.499
9. Process Management	.048	.061	-.111	.737**	.712**	.652**	.747**	.720**									4.342	1.595
10. Product/Service Design	-.024	.075	-.076	.736**	.719**	.659**	.710**	.719**	.708**								4.491	1.525
11. Quality Information	-.023	.073	-.142*	.704**	.713**	.663**	.736**	.727**	.772**	.726**							4.473	1.658
12. Top Management Support	-.076	-.042	-.069	.725**	.724**	.679**	.745**	.713**	.703**	.674**	.713**						4.702	1.750
13. Employee Involvement	-.079	-.029	-.064	.701**	.697**	.632**	.710**	.687**	.758**	.708**	.744**	.792**					4.200	1.692
14. Customer Involvement	-.059	-.053	-.141*	.668**	.603**	.559**	.587**	.584**	.604**	.598**	.654**	.578**	.554**				5.063	1.441
15. Supplier Involvement	-.056	.066	-.174**	.571**	.571**	.569**	.576**	.564**	.605**	.614**	.634**	.616**	.598**	.652**			4.544	1.559
16. Sustainable Competitive Advantage	-.033	.101	-.124	.627**	.608**	.575**	.610**	.628**	.582**	.667**	.608**	.630**	.623**	.523**	.554**		4.323	1.307

Note: N = 235; Pearson correlation coefficients; ** Correlation is significant at $p < .01$ level (two-tailed); * Correlation is significant at $p < 0.05$ level (2-tailed). [a] The Length of Time in Business; [b] The Number of Employees; [c] "Manufacturing" = 1, "Service" = 2.

Table 7: CFA Test Results of Metacognition Measures

Factors and Underlying Variables	Loading[a]	S.E.[b]	C.R.[c]	AVE[d]
Metacognitive Knowledge (α^e = .801)				
We think of several ways to solve a problem and choose the best one.	.892***	n/a[f]	n/a	.679
We try to use strategies that have worked in the past.	.750***	.054	14.535	(68%)
Metacognitive Experience (α = .899)				
We know what kind of information is most important to consider when faced with a problem.	.909***	n/a	n/a	.816 (82%)
We consciously focus our attention on important business information.	.898***	.045	21.919	
Metacognitive Goal-Orientation (α = .927)				
We often define goals for ourselves.	.928***	n/a	n/a	.865 (87%)
We set specific goals before we begin a task.	.932***	.044	23.350	
Metacognitive Strategy (α = .939)				
We ask ourselves if we have considered all the options when solving a problem.	.934***	n/a	n/a	
We re-evaluate our assumptions when we get confused.	.914***	.037	25.575	.839 (84%)
We ask ourselves if we have learned as much as we could have when we finished the task.	.899***	.040	24.281	
Metacognitive Monitoring (α = .908)				
We stop and go back over information that is not clear.	.928***	n/a	n/a	
We find ourselves analyzing the usefulness of a given strategy while engaged in a given task.	.846***	.043	19.923	.762 (76%)
We find ourselves pausing regularly to check our comprehension of the problem or situation at hand.	.842***	.043	19.758	

Note: N = 235; [a] Standardized factor loading; [b] Standard error; [c] Critical ratio (*t*-value); [d] Average Variance Extracted; [e] Cronbach's alpha; [f] Not applicable (not estimated when loading set to fixed value: i.e., 1.000); *** $p < 0.001$.

Table 8: CFA Test Results of QM Measures				
Factors and Underlying Variables	**Loading[a]**	**S.E.[b]**	**C.R.[c]**	**AVE[d]**
Technical QM Measures				
Process Management (α = .789)				
Clear work or process instructions are given to employees	.834***	n/a	n/a	.654
We make extensive use of statistical techniques to reduce variance in processes	.782***	.070	13.208	(65%)
Product/Service Design (α = .772)				
We thoroughly review new product/service design before the product/service is produced.	.811***	n/a	n/a	.630
We work in teams, with members from a variety of areas (marketing, purchasing, manufacturing, etc.) to introduce new products/services.	.776***	.082	12.080	(63%)
Quality Information (α = .919)				
Information on quality performance is readily available to employees.	.830***	n/a	n/a	
Our quality data (error rates, defect rates, scrap, etc.) are accurate and reliable.	.900***	.060	17.564	.802
Quality data are timely.	.952***	.059	18.962	(80%)
Behavioral QM Measures				
Top Management Support (α^e = .932)				
Our top management provides personal leadership for quality products and quality improvement.	.941***	n/a[f]	n/a	.872
Our top management creates and communicates a vision focused on quality improvement.	.927***	.041	23.868	(87%)
Employee Involvement (α = .840)				
Employees receive quality-related training.	.854***	n/a	n/a	.725
Employees are recognized and rewarded for superior quality improvement.	.849***	.068	15.416	(73%)
Customer Involvement (α = .745)				
Customer complaints are used as a method to initiate improvements in our current processes.	.809***	n/a	n/a	.597
Our customers give us feedback on our quality and delivery performance.	.735***	.081	10.202	(60%)
Supplier Involvement (α = .939)				
We actively engage suppliers in our quality improvement efforts.	.938***	n/a	n/a	.885

We maintain close communication with suppliers about quality considerations and design changes.	.944***	.044	22.256	(89%)

Note: N = 235; [a] Standardized factor loading; [b] Standard error; [c] Critical ratio (*t*-value); [d] Average Variance Extracted; [e] Cronbach's alpha; [f] Not applicable (not estimated when loading set to fixed value: i.e., 1.000); *** $p < 0.001$.

Table 9: CFA Test Results of SCA Measures

Factors and Underlying Variables	Loading[a]	S.E.[b]	C.R.[c]	AVE[d]
Sustainable Competitive Advantage (α = .884)				
My company's resources or capabilities are so VALUABLE that they enable us to exploit opportunities or neutralize threats in our external environment.	.796***	n/a	n/a	
My company has COSTLY-TO-IMITATE resources or capabilities that our competitors cannot easily imitate or develop.	.712***	.077	11.535	.592 (60%)
My company has DIFFICULT-TO-SUBSTITUTE resources or capabilities that cannot be easily substituted by those of our competitors.	.649***	.080	10.329	
My firm has mainly produced ABOVE average market return.	.840***	.069	14.243	
My company has shown PERSISTENT superior business performance to our competitors for a long time.	.832***	.069	14.074	

Note: N = 233 (2 missing values); [a] Standardized factor loading; [b] Standard error; [c] Critical ratio (*t*-value); [d] Average Variance Extracted; [e] Cronbach's alpha; [f] Not applicable (not estimated when loading set to fixed value: i.e., 1.000); *** $p < 0.001$.

Test Results

The structural equation modeling (SEM) analysis was used for testing the hypotheses of this study. First, we assessed the fit of the hypothesized model by several different fit indices such as the normed Chi-square (X^2/d.f.), the comparative fit index (CFI), the root mean square error of approximation (RMSEA), the RMSEA 90% confidence interval, the parsimony normed fit index (PNFI), and the Tucker-Lewis coefficient index (TLI) (Bentler and Bonett, 1980; Mulaik, James, Van Altine, Bennett, Lind, and Stilwell, 1989; Bollen and Long, 1993; Byrne, 1998; Segars and Grover, 1998; Hair et al., 2010). As shown in Table 10, all the goodness-of-fit statistics for measure model met the desirable thresholds for each fit index. Further, all the statistics for the structural model were also within the recommended cutoff criteria.

Table 10: Goodness-of-Fit Statistics of the Hypothesized Research Model

Fit Index	Desirable Threshold	Measure Model	Structural Model
Chi-square (X^2)		973.72	1,051.44
Degree of Freedom (d.f.)		446	448
X^2/d.f.	< 3.00[e]	2.18	2.34
CFI[a]	> 0.90[f]	.93	.92
RMSEA[b]	< 0.08[g]	.07	.07
RMSEA 90% Confidence Interval		.06 ~.07	.07 ~ .08
PNFI[c]	> 0.50[h]	.74	.74
TLI[d]	Close to 1.00[i]	.91	.90

Note: N = 235, [a] Comparative fit index, [b] Root mean square error of approximation, [c] Parsimony normed fit index, [d] Tucker-Lewis coefficient index, [e] Segars and Grover (1998), Hair et al. (2010), [f] Byrne (1998), [g] Bollen and Long (1993), [h] Mulaik, James, Van Altine, Bennett, Lind, and Stilwell (1989), [i] Bentler and Bonett (1980).

The SEM results of the hypothesized model are summarized in Fig. 2 Hypothesis 1 was supported in that managerial metacognition were positively related to both behavioral QM (β = .89, p < .001) and technical QM (β = .92, p < .001) practices. In addition, we developed the competing model (Fig. 3) to scrutinize the authentic effect of metacognition on the relationship between QM practices and a firm's SCAs. The results of the competing model demonstrated that QM practices were not significantly associated with a firm's SCAs. However, the results of the hypothesized model revealed that both behavioral QM (β = .51, p < .001) and technical QM (β = .30, p < .01) had a significantly positive effect on a firm's SCAs. Thus, hypothesis 2 was supported in that managerial metacognition positively influenced on the relationship between QM practices and a firm's SCAs. As a post-hoc study, the direct effect of managerial metacognition on a firm's SCAs was also examined (Fig. 4). The test results showed that metacognition were not directly associated with a firm's SCA (β = -.09, p = -.38). The theoretical and managerial implications of the test results were discussed in the next section.

Figure 2: SEM test results of the hypothesized model

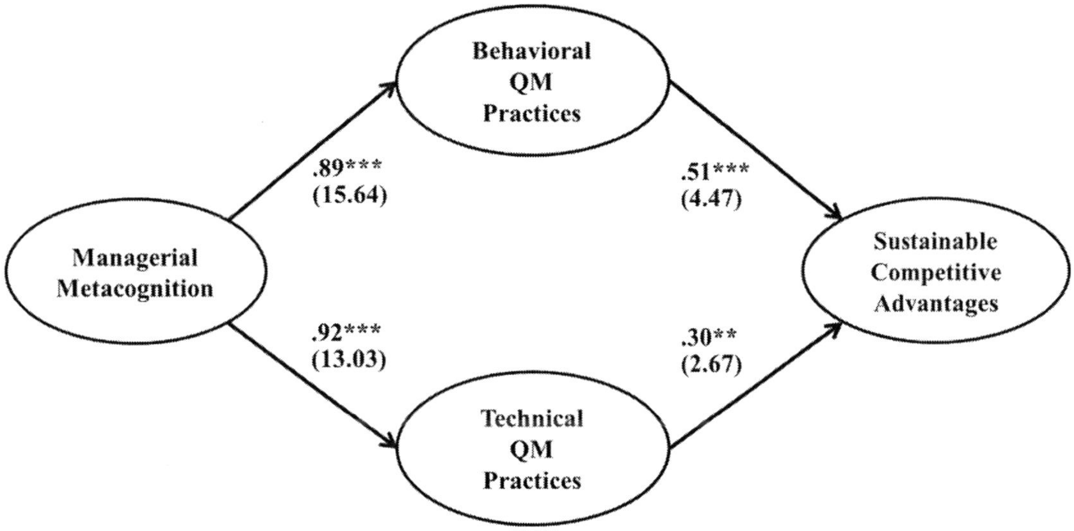

Note: N = 235; standardized path coefficients (β) are reported; the figure in the parenthesis represents the critical ratio (t value); * $p < .05$, ** $p < .01$, *** $p < .001$; X^2/d.f. = 2.347; CFI = .922; RMSEA = .076; TLI = .908; PNFI = .741.

Figure 3: SEM test results of the competing model

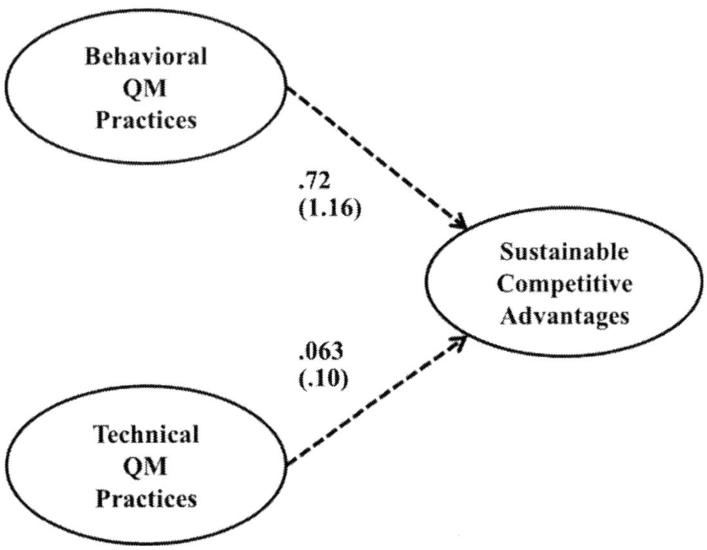

Note: N = 235; standardized path coefficients (β) are reported; the figure in the parenthesis represents the critical ratio (t value); dashed paths are not significant; X^2/d.f. = 2.625; CFI = .934; RMSEA = .083; TLI = .914; PNFI = .685.

Figure 4: The direct effect of managerial metacognition on a firm's SCAs

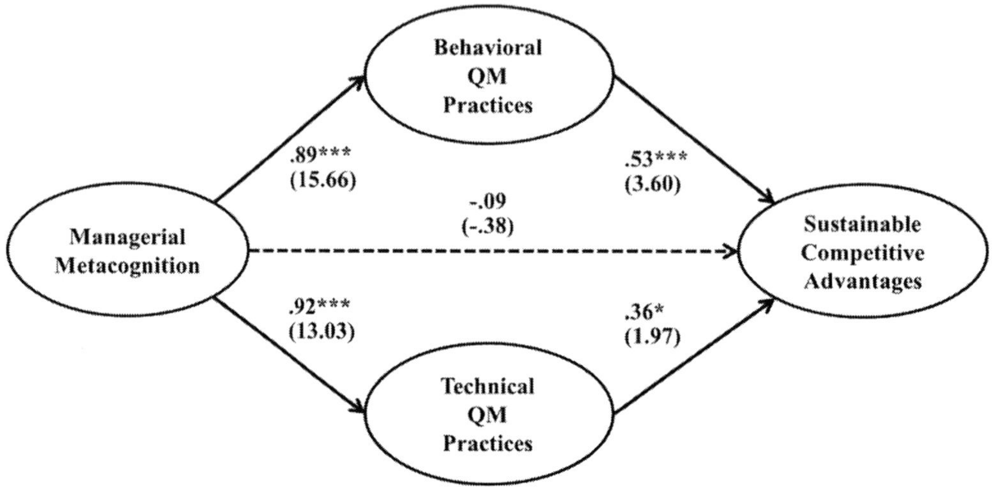

Note: N = 235; standardized path coefficients (β) are reported; the figure in the parenthesisrepresents the critical ratio (t value); dashed paths are not significant; * $p < .05$, ** $p < .01$, *** $p < .001$; X^2/d.f. = 2.352; CFI = .922; RMSEA = .076; TLI = .908; PNFI = .739.

DISCUSSION AND CONCLUSIONS

The study results present that there is a significantly positive association between managerial metacognition and a firm's quality practices, suggesting that better quality practices could eventuate in a firm when they have a higher level metacognitive ability. These findings are basically consistent with the Donaldson's (1987) structural adaptation to regain fit (SARFIT) model, which elucidates that an organizational structure should be continuously adapted to their contingencies for survival. That is, in terms of the contingency theory (Lawrence and Lorsch, 1967; Child, 1972; Donaldson, 1987), the study results imply that a firm's internal contingency factors (i.e., managerial metacognition) can result in the heterogeneous implementation of the firm's QM practices. Consequently, the findings in this study also weaken the 'universal applicability of QM practices' across organizational boundaries, based on institutional theory (Mitki and Shani 1995; Yavas 1995).

In addition, the metacognitive mechanism within organizational activities is typically too ambiguous for competitors to recognize; as a result, the mechanism cannot easily be imitated and substituted by competitors. In fact, the test results demonstrate that there is a positive synergy effect of metacognition and QM practices on the creation of a firm's SCAs. Hence, based on the premise of the resource-based view (Barney, 1991), the results also imply that a managerial metacognition might act as a source of a firm's SCAs.

In summary, this study found that managerial metacognition has a critical role in materializing the positive effect of a firm's QM practices on the creation of their SCAs. Thus, it is expected that the study findings can make some valuable contributions to the QM literature not only by expanding the research scope, but also by providing a new insight into the functional relationship between psychological and technical mechanisms.

REFERENCES

References available upon request.

DECISION SCIENCES INSTITUTE

The Privatization of Large and Small-Scale Firms and Their Differential Impacts on the Macroeconomy Under Transition

Micah DelVecchio
Saginaw Valley State University
Email: mpdelvec@svsu.edu

ABSTRACT

After the fall of the USSR, the process of privatizing state-owned firms was accelerated. Large and small firm sizes entail different frameworks for individual decisions. Privatization of each resulted in differential impacts on economic growth. This is shown using a dynamic panel data model with time lags of privatization measures.

KEYWORDS: International Markets, Market Structure, Property Rights, Socialist Enterprises and Their Transitions, and Models with Panel Data

INTRODUCTION

There isn't much that characterizes a firm better than the size of its employment. This measure of a firm's size is also an accurate indicator of the type of market that the firm is operating within. Very rarely do firms of different sizes operate within the same market. If they did, the market shares would be highly unequal. It's also rare for a large firm to be operating in a market which is not highly concentrated. Likewise, small firms operate in markets that are less concentrated and more competitive. Moreover, these small competitive firms are treated as the most efficient way to allocate goods and services as in a Walrasian general equilibrium. They are also seen as having the greatest incentive to innovate and thus promote long run growth in their pursuit of temporary economic profits. In a free-market system, profit incentives often drive such differentiated market structures leading to varying levels of profit and competition (Curry and George, 1983). In the more competitive markets, the economic profits are only temporary. In the more concentrated markets, profits may be permanent due to a firm's ability to influence market price leading to fewer incentives to innovate.

On the other hand, large firms operating in concentrated markets are not merely profitable due to their abilities to garner market power. Many are often successful due to the efficiency gains coming from economies of scale. Beyond this, and more pertinent to the study at hand, there are both gains due to forward and backward supply linkages à la Coase's "internalization" (Williamson, 1971; Williamson 1981) along with the advantages to innovation as in the classic work of Joseph Schumpeter (Schumpeter, 1942).

In the Coasian "internalization" case of large firms, transaction costs make it so that firms find it profitable to produce a portion of their inputs on their own, or expand into distribution and retail on the side of forward integration. Larger firms then gain efficiency and find it easier to compete. This leads to greater market concentration, but with productivity gains, not losses. In the second case, Schumpeter sees reasons for both greater firm size and concentration to result in higher levels of research, development, and innovation (Archibugi et al, 1995). This is hypothesized due to various reasons: 1) much R&D requires high startup costs, 2) larger firms can diversify their R&D endeavors, 3) larger firms have easier access to finance, and 4) firms with more market power can more easily profit from the new technology through their influence on market price.

Arguments backing the efficiency of small-scale firms are more commonly found in neo-classical (mainstream) economics while the Coasian and Schumpterian theories are considered to be part of the institutionalist field of economics. These two schools of thought motivate an examination of how firm size may affect the economy. If small firms lead to efficiency, then an economy with greater proportions of small business would grow at a faster rate than economies with more large-scale firms present.

A test involving the impact of national-level firm concentration would be limited by the number of countries or regions being examined. The easiest sample to obtain would be purely cross-sectional, as opposed to including a time-varying component as in a panel. Under normal circumstances, using a time component would not give much additional information unless there were drastic changes in the shares of large and small scale firms over time. Without this change, growth rates would simply be higher and stay that way as long as the proportion of small (or large) firms is relatively constant over time. In this everyday case, the variation to study would be between economies, not over time.

However, there are events in which economies undergo radical change. The transition from communism to capitalism is such an instance. The initial proportion of large and small scale firms represent a change which will have a subsequent impact on macroeconomic growth. Ideally, the event to study would be one in which there was a rapid shift from large to small-scale firms (or vice-versa). But even an active anti-trust policy will affect only a small number of firms over a long period of time. So, the transition is a next-best option to study firm size in this way. The firms, both large and small, are newly privatized and the impacts on growth should be seen over time. This allows for both a cross-section and a time component to analyze.

Privatization itself represents institutional change. It involves a radical change in the property rights of the economic decision-makers and thus a radical change in incentives, along with any lingering problems due to incompatibility with old institutions which may stick around. For example, large firms may be privatized, but the financial system may remain largely public. This would create the possibility for easy financing, no matter the risk associated with the loan. For this reason, it is hypothesized that large-scale firms will be more likely to have a negative impact on macroeconomic performance.

This paper proceeds by first looking at the existing literature, including the work done in the vein of economic growth and institutions along with that which examines the post-Soviet transition to capitalism. Theory is then developed and explained in order to motivate the empirical model. The data and estimation strategies are discussed, estimates are presented and then finally the paper offers some conclusions, explanations, and interpretations.

LITERATURE REVIEW

Previous work (North, 1991; North 1997; Williamson, 2000; Acemoglu and Johnson, 2005) focuses on the long-run nature of institutions. It is extremely difficult to conduct a straight-forward comparative static analysis on institutions because of the specific ways in which they determine economic outcomes. Institutions determine the "rules of the game," which anyone can recognize as being extremely important, but changes to the rules occur extremely infrequently and when they do there is usually so much other calamity occurring at the same time that empirical analysis is rendered difficult. Acemoglu, Johnson, and Robinson (2005) address these problems by choosing an extremely long time period over which to analyze the impact of various colonization methods on modern economic growth. The lessons learned from this work have helped elaborate the ways in which institutions work within the economy. The simple yet powerful framework which emerged is coined the "hierarchy of institutions." It is within this framework that we can now use such methods to peer into the short-run operations occurring within the "black box" which represents the precise yet unseen ways in which institutions affect economic outcomes.

The recent work of Falcetti et al. (2006), and Eicher and Schreiber (2010) calls attention to the fact that there are instances where institutional change has a significant and immediate impact on economic growth. These impacts can be thought of as a type of institutional short-run in the sense that they occur as a country transitions to a new state with new initial conditions. While Acemoglu et al. (2005) studied the differential impacts of initial legal and environmental conditions, this paper and Eicher and Schreiber (2010) study the change that occurs on the way to *new* initial conditions, in the sense that new parameters of economic growth are being set. Interestingly, the hierarchy of institutions model can be applied to both the transitional period and the stable period as it includes both long and short-run factors. This fact indicates that what is seen in the short-run may also be indicative of the long-run impact that the new initial conditions will have. While this paper cannot compare the different short-run and long-run institutional impacts coming from a single event or definitively show that long-run gains are or are not the result of short-run pains, the available theory used to explain the results is certainly commensurable with long-run institutional explanations.

This paper uses available data on the differential rates of the privatization of large and small-scale firms during and shortly following the break-up of the Soviet Union. Various estimations show that small-scale firms allow for greater immediate economic growth while large-scale firms are significantly correlated with negative economic growth, even several years after their privatization. The timing and nature of these impacts can be explained by the efficiency of small-scale firms in a competitive market and the lack of competition and efficiency associated with large firms. This evidence lends credence to the importance of competiveness in establishing productivity, as opposed to the notions that large-scale firms could be more important to efficiency and levels of production. Existing literature also examines the institutions of ownership in the transition to capitalism (Eicher and Schreiber, 2010), but this current work breaks the analysis up into firm size. It is by using the differential impacts of small-scale and large-scale privatization to explain the importance of these institutions to growth that this paper makes a unique contribution to the literature.

Literature Review of the Estimation Methods

Estimation of the model poses several problems. The first is that of a dynamic panel model with a lagged dependent variable. As with any panel, it is important to control for the cross-sectional effects by incorporating the unobserved heterogeneity through the use of "within estimation." However, doing this in the presence of a lagged dependent variable will result in biased coefficient estimates (Nickel, 1981). In most circumstances, the inclusion of a lagged dependent variable is handled with a form of GMM estimation which uses all available lags of both the dependent and independent variables (Arellano and Bover, 1995; Blundell and Bond, 1998).

Such models require additional assumptions about the relationship of the independent variables to the unobserved (cross-sectional) effect.

However, in this present work, the data is characterized with more cross-sections than time series, but the cross-sections only amount to the 26 transition economies. This limits the number of instruments which can be used in the GMM estimator and the problem of a "proliferation" of instruments quickly becomes a concern (Roodman, 2009). Thus, in order to ensure unbiased estimation of the coefficients, this paper uses quasi-maximum likelihood following the work of Bhargava and Sargan (1983) and Hsiao, Pesaran, and Tahmiscioglu (2002). The estimation of the dynamic panel is implemented using the recent work of Sebastian Kripfganz (2015), who has made his programs publically available. In this way, the issue of dynamic panel bias, or Nickel bias, is addressed and the model is considered to be identified (excluding other possible sources of endogeneity).

THEORETICAL JUSTIFICATION FOR THE EMPIRCAL MODEL

Traditionally, much of the strength of institutions came from their embeddedness into culture and society (Polanyi, 1957; Williamson, 2000). Acemoglu's theory of the *hierarchy of institutions* seems to draw heavily upon the concept of embeddedness by assuming that economic outcomes will be dependent upon social and political institutions. The hierarchy illustrates this by showing that economic performance is an outcome of economic institutions which are in turn an outcome of political power, itself determined by existing political institutions.

Diagrammatically, Acemoglu represents a simplified and concise version of the theory as seen in Figure 1.

Figure 1: The Hierarchy of Institutions

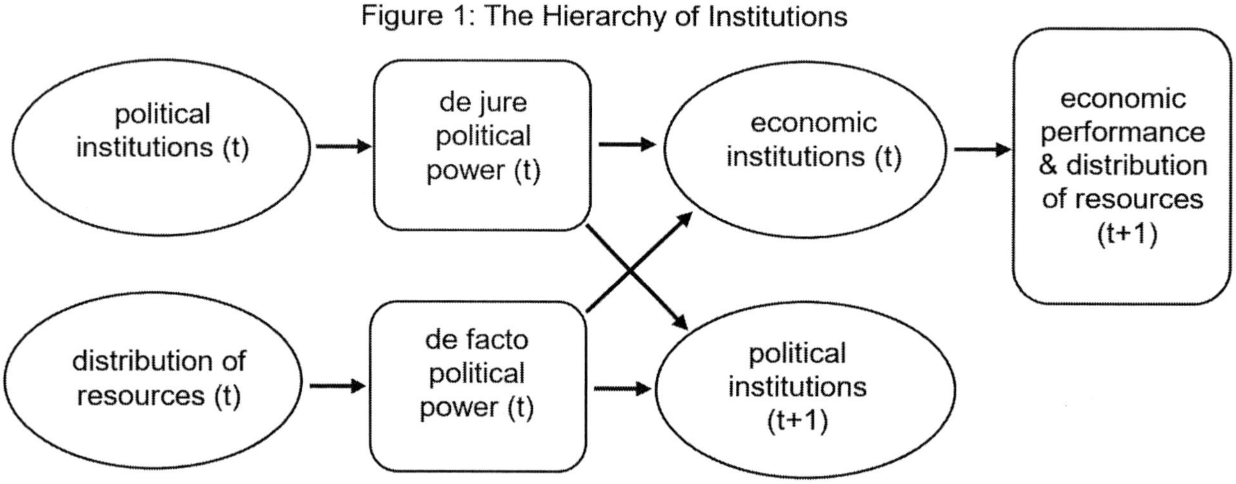

The theory explicitly states from where endogeneity will emerge if one wants to test the relationship between economic institutions and economic outcomes. If there is an omitted variable which comes from the earlier stages of the above system, such a problem could occur. If political institutions and past economic outcomes are omitted from the analysis, it is likely that any measure of economic institutions will be correlated with the error term as the error will have absorbed any unobserved variation due to past political and economic outcomes. These past political and economic outcomes will affect the current economic outcomes through the recursive framework illustrated above, but if omitted, they will be found in the error term thus making identification impossible. In his work, Daron Acemoglu typically uses past measures of political and environmental conditions as instrumental variables in a two-stage OLS setting. Recent advances in dynamic GMM estimation incorporate this method into a more complete and general dynamic setting, as in Eicher and Schreiber (2010) and Falcetti et al. (2006). This paper does not use instruments to incorporate the hierarchy of institutions but instead uses lags of the measures of privatization in the regression model itself.

Daron Acemoglu describes "good institutions" as those that "provide security of property rights and relatively equal access to economic resources to a broad cross-section of society" (Acemoglu et al., 2005). Given the conditions of perfect competition, and the violations which may occur during the transition process, large-scale firms which represent a large share of the market may not be representative of "good institutions" and property rights. They may manage some price control through imperfect competition, construct barriers to entry and obtain easy financing through personal linkages to central banks. The hypothesis here is that large-scale firms will not be conducive to competitive markets and economic growth:

H1: Higher levels of large-scale privatization during the transition process will be associated with lower growth rates.

Conversely, small-scale firms are less complex and are less likely to encounter soft budget constraints. Thus, privatization of small firms should be more likely to be associated with faster economic growth. It's likely these firms will be able to simply take privatized property rights and behave competitively among themselves. Therefore, the second hypothesis that this paper is interested in is given by:

H2: Higher levels of small-scale privatization during the transition process will be associated with higher growth rates.

These hypotheses can be tested using a linear regression model. The particular empirical specification used herein is a dynamic panel model with the following structure:

$$\%\widehat{\Delta GDP}_{i,t} = \beta_0 + \beta_1 \%\Delta GDP_{i,t-1} + \sum_{j=0}^{2} \beta_j Lpriv_{i,t-j} + \sum_{j=0}^{1} \beta_j Spriv_{i,t-j} + controls + \mu_i + \varepsilon_{i,t}$$

Here, $Lpriv_{i,t-j}$ and $Spriv_{i,t-j}$ are the measures of large-scale and small-scale privatization over $t-j$ yearly lags and $\%\Delta GDP_{i,t}$ is the percentage change in real GDP. Also, the μ_i represent the fixed effects due to the i country cross-sections, and could be resolved using only fixed effects estimation, if this was a normal panel. However, given the dynamic and recursive nature of the variables, dynamic panel bias is likely to emerge. Also, the hierarchy of institutions indicates that an estimation of economic growth on economic institutions would omit much of a feedback loop which would be caught up in a correlation between $\varepsilon_{i,t}$ and $\%\Delta GDP_{i,t-1}$, $Lpriv_{i,t-j}$, and $Spriv_{i,t-j}$. Thus, quasi maximum likelihood is used as the preferred method of estimation. Ordinary least squares (OLS) and fixed effects (FE) estimation is used for comparison.

DATA AND INITIAL RESULTS

The data were assembled from various sources and represent 26 transition countries over the period of 1989-2006. What resulted is an unbalanced panel data set with fewer observations from the earlier periods, but with all 26 countries contained in the last year. The main data sources are from the European Bank for Reconstruction and Development (EBRD), The World Bank's World Development Indicators (WDI), The PolityIV Project, and the World Institute for Development Economics Research (WIDER).

The rate of transition among the ex-Soviet economies was quite varied. The EBRD indices are initially on a scale of 1-4 with 0.33 increments. The indices are normalized to a scale of 0-1 for the empirical estimation. In the initial scale, a level of 1 for the large-scale privatization index signifies that less than 25% of the large-scale industries are privatized. A level of 4+ is indicative of 75% or more of the industries being privatized which is comparable to OECD countries. The small-scale privatization index works along the same lines except without specific percentages associated with each level of privatization. Large-scale firms are generally ones with over 500 employees, although in smaller countries they are defined as firms having over 250 employees.

The WDIs provide estimates of real per capita GDP in 2005 international dollars adjusted for PPP. This is then converted into a percent change using logs. Gross fixed capital formation was also from the WDIs and converted into terms of percent change. Inflation came from the EBRD database and represents the annual average. The EBRD small-scale and large-scale privatization indices were normalized to a scale of 0 to 1 so that all the variables have the same scale and changes can be interpreted as, say, a 10% change in privatization. For instance, if the coefficient of one of the indices is 0.50, then a 10% change in that index would result in a 5 percentage point change in GDP, the dependent variable of percent change in per capita real GDP.

Overview of the Measures of Transition

The most essential component of the data comes from the European Bank for Reconstruction and Development (EBRD). These are the EBRD Transition Indicators (EBRD, 2010). In order to test whether privatization has differential impacts on economic growth, these measures of privatization and liberalization are employed. The indicators have been continuously collected and updated since the unofficial start of the transition in 1989. The EBRD produces separate indices for large and small-scale privatization, price liberalization, forex liberalization, and banking liberalization among other measures of institutional change. Jeffrey Sachs (1996) produced some of the first estimates of the EBRD indices' correlations to economic growth and others followed. Havrylyshyn and Rooden (2003) use a cumulative index to explain growth, as does Hernández-Catá (1997). These earlier studies often show a negative relationship between a cumulative EBRD index and the transition-period growth which can be explained by the U-shaped transitional recession and expansion. Because of this U-shaped pattern of growth during the first decade of transition, Popov (2007) uses a cumulative index to divide the relationship into a pre- and post-1996 periods. He shows that before 1996 the relationship is negative among transition countries but turns positive once economies adjust to their new-found economic freedoms. In fact, what Popov illustrates is that the timing in which studies of these kind are conducted is important and will affect the available data and results. Radulescu and Barlow (2002) find that this pattern makes it difficult to find robust results using a cumulative index over the 1991 to 1999 period. This current research appears to be the first to use an annual set of measures to test the impact of institutional change on long-run economic growth by using the separate measures of large and small-scale privatization. Eicher and Schrieber (2010) use a combined index to make inferences. This present work extends those results.

The transition economies included in the sample are given on the next page in Table 1: Transition Economics by Region. The majority of the economies are former Soviet Union economies, while others such as Romania and Poland, had been nominally independent but were clearly with the USSR sphere of influence.

Table 1: Transition Economies by Region

Region	Countries		
Baltic States	Latvia	Lithuania	Estonia
Central and Eastern Europe	Belarus	Bulgaria	Croatia
	Czech Republic	Hungary	Moldova
	Romania	Poland	Russia
	Slovakia	Slovenia	Ukraine
Southeastern Europe and Anatolia	Albania	Bulgaria	Macedonia
	Montenegro	Moldova	Serbia
Caucuses	Armenia	Azerbaijan	Georgia
Central Asia	Kazakhstan	Kyrgyzstan	Tajikistan
	Turkmenistan		

The above economies can be represented by the data over various years following the beginning of the transition from communism to capitalism. The transition began in earnest starting in 1989, but data is not available for all the economies. Due to these constraints, the panel data is unbalanced over the 1989-2006 period of transition.

EMPIRICAL RESULTS

The availability of panel data permits experimentation with different lags in the regression specification. As the data is yearly, and the impact of policy may take years to have an impact on the macroeconomy, it is worth exploring which lags contain significant relationships with the growth in real GDP. These initial trials are given in the following section.

Initial Results

In order to determine *when* the impact of privatization upon per capita real GDP is the strongest, the following regressions were run. The results in Table 2 are more for exploratory purposes and to help choose the number of lags to include, however, the noticeable pattern is one in which lags of the small-scale privatization index soon become insignificant while the large-scale index sees a negative coefficient become more significant with deeper lags up to the 4th lag, which is then insignificant. This indicates that small-scale firms can have an immediate positive impact on growth while large-scale firms reduce the growth rate 2 years later. Such a result may not be all that surprising if large-scale firms take time to become efficient after their initial privatization. Inflation ($Infl_{t-1}$) is used to control for the severe bouts of hyperinflation experienced by the transition economies during this time period. There is a possibility that the hyperinflation was severe enough to have an impact on the real economy and would show up in real GDP despite already having been adjusted for inflation. $GFCF_{t-1}$ is the year-to-year percent change in gross fixed capital formation and is used as a proxy for investment and a control for other sources of economic growth. Time dummies are included, but their coefficient estimates are not presented.

Table 2: Exploratory OLS regressions

	No lags			1 lag			2 lags		
	coeff.	*s.e.*	*p-val*	*coeff.*	*s.e.*	*p-val*	*coeff.*	*s.e.*	*p-val*
$\%\Delta GDP_{t-1}$	0.881	0.025	0.000	0.880	0.026	0.000	0.910	0.026	0.000
$Lpriv_{i,t}$	-0.014	0.011	0.000	0.018	0.015	0.206	0.031	0.015	0.039
$Lpriv_{i,t-1}$	na	na	na	-0.047	0.013	0.000	-0.009	0.016	0.585
$Lpriv_{i,t-2}$	na	na	na	na	na	na	-0.048	0.012	0.000
$Spriv_{i,t}$	0.082	0.011	0.001	0.072	0.015	0.000	0.072	0.016	0.000
$Spriv_{i,t-1}$	na	na	na	0.024	0.001	0.004	0.008	0.019	0.683
$Spriv_{i,t-2}$	na	na	na	na	na	na	0.009	0.015	0.520
$Infl_{i,t-1}$	0.001	0.001	0.001	0.001	0.001	0.004	0.000	0.000	0.030
$GFCF_{i,t-1}$	-0.028	0.014	0.045	-0.027	0.014	0.049	-0.050	0.014	0.000
constant	-0.046	0.006	0.000	-0.047	0.006	0.000	-0.044	0.007	0.000

The EBRD privatization indexes were normalized to a scale of 0-1 for ease of interpretation. In the first regression, with "No lags," the coefficient of $Lpriv_{i,t}$ is -0.014 which indicates that a 10% increase in the level of privatization results in a 0.14 percentage point decline in the growth rate of per capita real GDP. This may seem small, however, the average growth rate in per capita real GDP for the sample is only 1.2% per year. Thus, a 10% increase in large-scale privatization would reduce a 1.2% growth rate to 1.06% which is an 11.6% decline in the growth rate. The coefficients on $Spriv_{i,t}$ can be interpreted the same way. The set of regressions indicate that lags for large scale privatization should go up to 2 years and the lag for small scale privation may go back one year. Inflation seems to have a very small yet significantly negative impact on real GDP. The coefficient on gross fixed capital formation is a bit unexpected. One would expect capital investments to grow the economy, but these economies are in transition and could possibly be still in a condition of over-investment into government-favored areas of production which have been experiencing diminishing returns.

Final Results

In what follows, $GFCF_{i,t-1}$, the change in gross fixed capital formation, has been smoothed by using an HP-filter and then log-differences of the filtered data were computed. The growth in per capita real GDP, $\%\Delta GDP_{t-1}$, has also been filtered and then log-differenced. A Fisher panel unit root test is also run and the null of a unit root is rejected for all variables. In what follows, OLS and fixed effects are reported for comparison, but the quasi-maximum likelihood (QML) estimator is considered to be the consistent and minimum variance estimator among the three. Otherwise, dynamic panel bias won't be accounted for and it's likely a there would be a country-specific effect which would have lasting effects through a feedback effect between the endogenous regressors and the error term even after the fixed effect had been purged by differencing.

Table 3: Main Results

$\%\Delta GDP_t$	OLS	$Fixed\ Effects$	QML
$\%\Delta GDP_{t-1}$	0.9780^{***}	0.9407^{***}	0.9609^{***}
	(0.0238)	(0.0279)	(0.0264)
$Lpriv_t$	0.0236^{**}	0.0237^{*}	0.0376^{**}
	(0.0126)	(0.0149)	(0.0149)
$Lpriv_{t-1}$	−0.0105	−0.0123	0.0014
	(0.0156)	(0.0153)	(0.0165)
$Lpriv_{t-2}$	-0.0381^{***}	-0.0437^{***}	-0.0489^{***}
	(0.0112)	(0.0437)	(0.0117)
$Spriv_t$	0.0430^{***}	0.0634^{***}	0.0472^{***}
	(0.0138)	(0.0150)	(0.0184)
$Spriv_{t-1}$	-0.0240^{*}	−0.0086	0.0018
	(0.0140)	(0.0147)	(0.0167)
$Inflation_{t-1}$	0.0032^{***}	0.0002^{**}	0.0002^{*}
	0.0001	0.0001	0.0001
$GFCF_{t-1}$	-0.0393^{***}	-0.0458^{***}	-0.0730^{***}
	(0.1111)	(0.0129)	(0.0130)
$Constant$	-0.1333^{*}	-0.0215^{*}	-0.0229^{***}
	(0.0058)	(0.01167)	(0.0088)

The quasi maximum likelihood results are preferred and it's easy to see why. The OLS estimate on the lagged value of GDP has an upward bias while the fixed effect estimation, with its dynamic panel bias, is biased downward. The QML estimate of 0.9609 falls between the two, a good sign that it is identifying the statistical relationship.

These results employ some of the most widely used and accepted measures of privatization in a dynamic panel setting, and tell a more complicated story than the one presented by the testable hypotheses. This is due to the fact that while the short-run relationship is unambiguous, the long-run relationship depends on the time period. This gives us the conditional evidence that large-scale privatization is correlated with economic growth in the year of the sale of the public enterprise, but not thereafter. The first year in which large-scale firms are privatized is significantly associated with positive growth and is seen to increase growth by an amount of 0.38% for every 10% increase in privatization. This may be due to the improvement in government balances due to a one-time sale. Privatization is known for having these initial one-time benefits. A possibly more important result is that in the subsequent years of large-firm privatization there is a negative association with economic growth as was hypothesized. One-year lags were also tested, yet the two-year lag is the most significant, indicating that large-scale firms can deteriorate a transition economy over time rather than recover from an initial drop. The amount of the decline in the growth rate more than offsets the initial gains. This would be expected if access to easy capital and poor finance decisions are being made. Such a context is described as a "soft budget constraint" by former Harvard professor, János Kornai (1980). Small-scale firms on-the-other hand, are correlated only with significant and immediate economic growth. There are no lags in which small-scale firm estimations become negative. It simply becomes insignificant in later lags.

In addition to lingering soft budget constraints, there are two other explanations for the results. The first is Blanchard and Kremer's (1997) concept of disorganization in supply chain. In fact, if you assume production linkages and Williamsonian assets-specific investments of large-scale firms are more complex and found on a larger scale, then this explanation may be preferred to one emphasizing the lack of competitiveness in sectors dominated by large industries. It is believed that once the linkages are formed, then the production process will be more organized and associated with positive growth, although if this is true its hasn't occurred yet in this sample. The theory itself supports a notion of laissez faire institutional transition. That is, if you simply leave things alone, eventually capital will be used to its potential and forward and backward linkages between firms will form. No other institutional adjustment is supposed to be required; however, the results may indicate otherwise.

There may be additional complications in using the above theory of asset specificity as an explanation. First-of-all, supply linkages have traditionally been treated as a reason for smaller firms to merge into larger firms - that is to avoid the transaction costs of forming contracts with vendors (Coase, 1950; Williamson, 2000). The fact that smaller firms appear to being doing so well would appear to contradict this incentive to merge (and also explain large firms' negative impact on the economy during transition. That is, these linkages are of smaller importance in general even though the contracting costs are lower in large-scale firms). Secondly, a laissez faire style of privatization and transition isn't what happened. Linkages simple didn't occur on their own. The transition was characterized by the sudden realization that time was needed for the transitional economies to develop an adequate level of competitiveness via laws and regulations (Murrell, 1992). That is, the transition itself was planned and interventionist, which brings us to the second possible explanation of the results: the large scale firms were simply inefficient. This second explanation is simpler and has important implications. The explanation highlights two separate impacts of creating the economic institutions of privatization. These newly privatized firms will have an initial impact on the economy while going through the process of privatization, but once privatized, they will continue to have an impact on the economy long after the change. To see this, a privatized firms needs to be seen for the institution that it is. It isn't a firm but a legal arrangement which has been established by political wrangling. As the economy adjusts to this new legal arrangement, the effects of the new institutions are clear, but this may be the only time that the impact of legal arrangement itself can be recognized. Afterwards it is a type of initial condition, a level-effect, guiding growth at a constrained speed depending upon the quality to the legal arrangement. But, this highlights a unique behavior of institutions in the economy: they are likely the only variable which has an impact whether it is undergoing change. This is especially true of privatization.

CONCLUSION

The results provide evidence that the privatization of large-scale firms (those with typically more than 500 employees) has the result of providing a one-time initial benefit to economic growth followed by an even larger in scale, yet negative impact on economic growth several years later. Small-scale firms are associated with only positive economic growth in the initial period of privatization. It's worth noting that these are changes in growth rates, thus the one-time impacts represent permanent acceleration (or deceleration) of economic growth. That is, the result is higher (or lower) rates of growth which, on average, will remain over the subsequent years. These results come after controlling for inflation and gross fixed capital formation.

Moreover, it's likely small-scale firms are great in number within their respective markets and, in general, large-scale firms are typically less numerous. Therefore, these results may be interpreted as the outcome of transitioning more efficient small-scale firms into efficient markets while transitioning less efficient large-scale firms into less-efficient markets. That is, these results are what you would see if large-scale firms in the sample violated the standard Walrasian general equilibrium assumptions by occupying large shares of their respective markets or if they were associated with institutional problems unique to them, such as disorganized supply chains and soft budget constraints.

At the very least, these results fail to reject such theories of large-scale firm privatization and may be seen as the expected outcome of mainstream economic theory and its views on firm size. As such, this interpretation also calls to attention the routine misapplication of standard economic theory during a process of transition. If large-scale firms are not efficient to begin with, there should be no pressing need or economic justification to privatize them before addressing the poor institutions surrounding them. If efforts to adapt the institutions aren't undertaken, there may be a cost to privatizing large-scale firms which is not found in the privatization of small-scale firms. In contrast, small-scale firms need not be "prepped" for privatization. They may be ready to go on their own without any overhaul in their supply chain and access to finance.

These results and the interpretation of these results extend the development and institutional growth literature in the following ways. First, these results confirm and find additional support for the short-run impact of changing institutions on economic growth as is described in Eicher and Schrieber (2010). Secondly, these results and the interpretation of the results begin to help define Acemoglu's notion of good institutions by testing for and finding significant differences in the impact that firm size has upon economic growth. While the interpretations necessitate further research, the results help open up the black box when it comes to determining the channels through which institutional differences can affect growth.

These results also highlight the fact that privatization itself is not a road to efficient institutions. In fact, privatization may only serve to create extractive institutions should the property be concentrated into large-scale firms. This is simply another type of concentrated power and illustrates a point of tangency between mainstream economic theory and theories of institutional growth. To carry out this line of research, a more detailed examination of market structure and market power during transition should be conducted. The central question coming out of these results asks whether large-scale firms were simply more costly to transition or is the associated fall in real GDP due to true and permanent efficiency losses? The answer to this question would be of concern to all economies and businesses, not only those in transition.

REFERENCES

Acemoglu, Daron, and Simon Johnson. (2005). Unbundling Institutions. *Journal of Political Economy*. 113(5), 949-995.

Acemoglu, Daron, Simon Johnson, and James A. Robinson. (2005). Institutions as the Fundamental Cause of Long-Run Economic Growth. In *Handbook of Economic Growth*, Volume 1A edited by Philippe Aghion and Stephen Durlauf. Oxford, UK: Elsevier.

Archibugi, D., Evangelista, R., & Simonetti, R. (1995). Concentration, Firm Size and Innovation: Evidence from Innovation Costs. *Technovation*. 15(3), 153-163.

Arellano, Manuel and Olympia Bover. (1995). Another Look at the Instrumental Variable Estimation of Error-Components Models. *Journal of Econometrics.* 68 (1), 29–51.

Bhargava, A. and J. D. Sargan (1983). Estimating Dynamic Random Effects Models from Panel Data Covering Short Time Periods. *Econometrica*. 51 (6), 1635-1659.

Blundell, Richard and Stephen Bond. (1998). Initial Conditions and Moment Restrictions in Dynamic Panel Data Models. *Journal of Econometrics.* 87 (1), 115–143.

Curry, Bruce, and Kenneth D. George. (1983). Industrial Concentration: A Survey. *The Journal of Industrial Economics.* 31(3), 203-255.

Eicher, Theo S., and Till Schreiber. (2010). Structural Policies and Growth: Time Series Evidence from a Natural Experiment. *Journal of Development Economics.* 91(1), 169 - 179.

European Bank for Reconstruction and Development. (2010). Annual Report 2005: Annual Review. *EBRD*: London.

Falcetti, Elisabetta, Tatiana Lysenko, and Peter Sanfry. (2006). Reforms and Growth in Transition: Re-Examining the Evidence. *Journal of Comparative Economics*. 34(3), 421-445.

Havrylyshyn, Oleh, and Ron Van Rooden. (2003). Institutions Matter in Transition, but so do Policies. *Comparative Economic Studies*. 45 (1), 2 - 24.

Hernández-Catá, Ernesto. Liberalization and the Behavior of Output during the Transition from Plan to Market. IMF Staff Papers. 44, 198 - 215.

Hsiao, C., M. H. Pesaran, and A. K. Tahmiscioglu (2002). Maximum Likelihood Estimation of Fixed Effects Dynamic Panel Data Models Covering Short Time Periods. *Journal of Econometrics*. 109 (1), 107-150.

Kornai, János, Economics of Shortage: Volumes A and B, North Holland, 1980.

Kripfganz, S. (2015). xtdpdqml: Quasi-Maximum Likelihood Estimation of Linear Dynamic Panel Data Models in Stata.

Marshall, Monty G., Keith Jaggers, and Ted Robert Gurr. (2011). POLITY IV PROJECT: Political Regime Characteristics and Transitions, 1800-2010, Dataset Users' Manual. *Center for Systematic Peace*.

Nickell, Stephen. (1981). Biases in Dynamic Models with Fixed Effects. *Econometrica: Journal of the Econometric Society*. 49(6), 1417–1426

North, Douglass. (1990). *Institutions, Institutional Change and Economic Performance.* New York: Cambridge University Press.

North, Douglass. (1991). Institutions. *Journal of Economic Perspectives.* 5(1): 97-112.

Polanyi, Karl. 1957. The Great Transformation the Political and Economic Origins of Our Time. Boston. Beacon Press.

Roodman, D. (2009). A Note on the Theme of too Many Instruments*. *Oxford Bulletin of Economics and Statistics*. 71(1), 135-158.

Sachs, Jeffrey. (1996). The Transition at Mid-Decade. *The American Economic Review*. 86 (2), 128 - 133.

Schumpeter, J. A. (1942). *Capitalism, Socialism and Democracy*. Routledge. New York.

Subodh, Kandamuthan. (2002). Market Concentration, Firm Size and Innovative Activity: A firm-Level Economic Analysis of Selected Indian Industries Under Economic Liberalization. No. 2002/108. *WIDER Discussion Papers//World Institute for Development Economics (UNU-WIDER)*.

Williamson, Oliver E. (1971). The Vertical Integration of Production: Market Failure Considerations. *The American Economic Review*. 61(2), 112-123.

Williamson, Oliver E. (1981). The Economics of Organization: The Transaction Cost Approach. *American Journal of Sociology*. 87(3), 548-577.

Williamson, Oliver. (2000). The New Institutional Economics: Taking Stock, Looking Ahead. *Journal of Economic Literature*. 38(3), 595-613.

DECISION SCIENCES INSTITUTE

The Profitability of US Community Banks: A Cross-Sectional and Dynamic Panel Analysis

Robert D. Morrison
University of Texas of the Permian Basin
Email: morrison_r@utpb.edu

Diego Escobari
University of Texas Rio Grande Valley
Email: diego.escobari@utrgv.edu
University of Texas Rio Grande Valley

ABSTRACT

This study compares 5,286 community banks operating in rural and metropolitan counties from 2000 through the end of 2013 on the variables attributing to bank profitability using pooled OLS, pooled time-series OLS, and dynamic panels methodologies. Following the SCP and competition-fragility literature one would expect a difference in the variables contributing to profitability. The size of the coefficients indicates that the variables contributing to profitability differ in magnitude when comparing community banks in metropolitan counties to those in rural counties. Both the pooled and time-series OLS models indicate that bank size contributes to profitability more in metropolitan areas.

KEYWORDS: community banking, structure-conduct-performance

INTRODUCTION

The US Banking industry in the US has undergone dramatic changes over the past 30 years as restrictions of both the geographic area of operation and the scope of financial services banks can offer have change dramatically. Until 1911, banks in the US were regulated by the states. Even after federal regulation a two-tiered banking system of both state and federally chartered banks existed and depression era federal regulations limited banks to whatever the state they operated in allowed in terms of geographic areas. The result was a large number of small banks serving communities across the nation. Beyond that, Great Depression era Glass-Steagall Act of 1933, limited the scope financial activities in which commercial banks could participate. Although an in depth discussion is beyond the scope of this paper, those limitations from the 1930s through the 1980s through various court decisions and legislative and regulatory changes. In the 1980s a series of legislative initiatives leading up to the Gramm-Leach-Bliley Act of 1999 eliminated most of the remaining limitations on the geographic scope of banks and restrictions on what services entities in the financial services sector could offer. What followed was a massive progression of acquisitions and mergers as commercial banks, investment banks, and insurance companies combined into comprehensive financial services firms.

In a quest to cover the nation or particular regions of it, publicly traded banks acquired banks across the nation with the vast majority, 87% of branches, being in metropolitan areas. This resulted in a 59% decrease in the number of bank charters and over 80% of all bank assets held by only 107 banks. The remaining 6,356 remaining small banks held only 14% of bank assets. Nonetheless, these small community banks play an important role in the US economy because they continue to provide the vast majority of funding to small businesses and small businesses continue employee the vast majority of people in the US. In addition, more of the US population is migrating to metropolitan areas and that is likely where community banks encounter the greatest competition from the massive nationwide and regional banks. Therefore, it is important to understand how deregulation has changed the competitive environment of community banking.

LITERATURE REVIEW

Structure-Conduct-Performance and Bank Deregulation

Due to the evolution of banking regulation in the US, the restrictions on geographic operating area resulted in most US banks being small banks with tight ties to the communities that operated in. Great Depression era legislation, the Glass-Steagall Act of 1933, also limited the scope of bank activities by prohibiting commercial banks from engaging in investment banking (Calomiris, 2010). The Douglas Amendment in 1956 allowed states to establish the guidelines under which banks from other states could do business; however, the banking industry remained highly regulated and the vast majority of US banks operated in single counties or metropolitan areas with only a few competitors. During this same timeframe, legislative activity in the area of anti-trust made inter-industry data available for researchers to analyze using cross-sectional approaches (e.g., Bain, 1951, 1956). These studies provided insight in to the relationship between competitor concentration in a particular industry, also referred to as the market structure, and profitability. The use of observable industry structure indicators, such as concentration ratios, to measure the degree of competition lead to the development of the structure-conduct-performance paradigm (SCP) (Schmalensee, 1982, 1985, 1989). From one point of view, in highly concentrated markets competitors can collude, implicitly or explicitly, to extract higher profits. In contrast, profits may be the result of efficiencies that result from economies of scale in plant, firm, and advertising efforts.

In the 1980s, there was a movement to enhance competition in the financial services industry. During the legislative process Stephen Friedman (1981), Securities and Exchange Commission Commissioner at the time, commented that in the future only ten large banks would cover the US. Federal Reserve researcher Alton Gilbert (1984) reviewed 45 SCP studies on the banking industry to examine the issues of collusion and efficiencies through achieving economies of scale. He found that the studies on the influence of market structure were highly variable, but did not seem to support that competition concentration leads to collusion in the banking industry and that single small banks do not appear to be more costly to operate than a branch of a large bank. Gilbert (1984) did caution that the studies reviewed did not provide a solid basis to generalize about large banks operating branches across the nation. As the result of a series of legislative actions from the Depository Institutions Deregulation and Monetary Controls Act (DIDMCA) of 1980 to the Gramm-Leach-Bliley Act of 1999, the US financial services industry was deregulated. It turns out that Stephen Friedman was wrong only about the number of banks blanketing the nation, as of 2014 it is 4 instead of 10; JP Morgan Chase, Bank of America, Citi Group, and Wells Fargo. At the end of 2011, only 107 banks held 80% of industry assets and federally insured bank and thrift charters fell from 17,901 in 1985 to 7,353 in 2011. However, despite the industry consolidation and increased competition, locally owned community banks have not disappeared. Despite only holding 14% of total bank assets, they are the most common FDIC insured institution and supply most of the credit to small businesses in the US (FDIC CBS, 2012).

Beyond deregulation, technology has dramatically changed the competitive environment of banking in the last 10 to 15 years. Internet banking has gone from a novel concept to a service that bank customers expect. More recently, smartphones have enabled mobile banking and the ability to take a photo of a check to deposit it combined with mobile electronic payments is quickly making visits to a physical bank a rare event. On the one hand technology can bring cost reductions that lead to greater efficiency; however, the initial capital investment and the need for highly skilled, therefore costly, support staff can put technology implementation out of the reach of small banks. Community banks in large metropolitan areas would arguably have a larger customer base and assets to cover technology implementation and support cost; however, those are the community banks most likely confronting the highest concentration of competition from the large nationwide and regional banks. This is because the large banks have focused on acquisitions in metropolitan areas while avoiding the small rural communities. Therefore, this study compares the factors contributing to community bank profitability on rural versus metropolitan areas.

Determinants of Community Bank Profitability

Studies examining bank profitability have mostly used the SCP paradigm focusing on market concentration and bank efficiency on concentration (e.g., Berger, 1995a; Smirlock, 1985). As discussed previously, the dispute lies in the underlying causation of market power or efficiency through economies of scale. However, regardless of the level of market concentration, community bank profits are related to exogenous economic conditions; however, when faced with favorable economic conditions managerial skill will result in some banks performing better than others (Kupiec & Lee, 2012). Although return on equity (ROE) and return on assets ROA are often used to measure firm profitability, the study of community banks brings an interesting problem because about one-third of small banks are Type-S corporations. Because Type-S corporations act as a pass-through entities that pay no income tax at the corporate level and pass the profits on to shareholders who pay income tax at the individual level, comparing ROA or ROE between Type-S and Type-C banks would be erroneous. Therefore, this study uses pre-tax ROA as a measure of profitability (FDIC variable ptxroa).

Traditionally, banks make profits by operating as financial intermediaries by paying interest on deposits and loaning those funds out at higher rates. As a result, the gross profit from interest comes from the difference in those rates, which is the net interest margin (FDIC variable NIMY). In highly competitive markets to attract depositors banks would offer higher interest rates; however, by the same reasoning, to attract good clients to lend to banks would have to offer attractive loan rates and the net interest margin would be lower in these markets. However, partly due to competition and partly due to deregulation, banks have turned to generating income through non-interest activities that range from fees on services to operations in the forward and futures markets (FDIC variable noniiay). As is the case in any business, operating expenses reduce the gross profits and in banking terminology these are non-interest expenses (FDIC variable nonixay); the more efficient a bank is the lower its relative non-interest expense. Efficiency can come through reaching economy of scale and bank asset size maybe used as a proxy (FDIC variable asset5).

Given that the interest income is the difference in the rates paid on deposits and the interest charged for loans and that higher riskier loans pay higher interest rates, banks can arguably increase profitability by taking on riskier loan portfolios. Because of competition for deposits, there is a lower limit of what a bank can pay and retain sufficient deposits to lend. This is the basis of the charter value or competition-fragility views (Hellmann, Murdock, & Stiglitz, 2000; Keeley, 1990). Because deposit insurance can act as a put option that limits bank shareholder losses to the capital invested, banks may take on more risk and maintain lower capital to asset ratios (CAR). While the literature is not conclusive (Canoy, van Dijk, Lemmen, de Mooij, & Weigand, 2001; Carletti & Hartmann, 2003), Berger (1995b) found that higher CAR was correlated with higher profits. One possible explanation is that higher CAR leads to lower insurance premiums and that results in higher profits. Under either argument CAR is an important factor when it comes to explaining bank profitability (FDIC variable eqv).

MODEL

The data comes from the FDIC quarterly Performance and Conditions Ratios reports. Because this report focuses only on community banks, the data is restricted to those banks that met the definition of community banks in the 2012 FDIC Community Banking Study that reported for the fourth quarter of 2012. The data is from individual banks and excludes bank holding companies. To avoid the issues related to ratios with De Novo banks, institutions that joined the FDIC after January 2, 1998 were not included. A dummy variable indicated whether the bank operated in a rural (0) or metropolitan (1) county. The data contains 296,098 observations from the quarterly FDIC Performance Reports from 5,286 unique community banks operating from 2000 through the end of 2013.

The methodology in this paper follows Goddard, Molyneux, and Wilson (2004). The content of the model is as follows:

$$\Pi_{i,t} = f(\Pi_{i,t-1}\ ,\ s_{i,t},\ o_{i,t}\ ,\ c_{i,t}\ d_{1,i}\ )$$

Where $\Pi i,t$ is the profit of the bank i in year t, as measured by pre-tax return on assets; $s_{i,t}$ is the natural logarithm of total assets average over the preceding five years; $o_{i,t}$ is the off balance sheet or non-interest income; $c_{i,t}$ is CAR; and $d_{1,i} = 1$ for metro and 0 for rural. The inclusion of $s_{i,t}$ captures any relationship between bank size and profitability. Following the SCP literature, a positive sign may indicate that large banks may benefit from economies of scale or scope or they may benefit from brand image. In the alternative, a negative sign may indicate that size results in diseconomies of scale.

Since deregulation began, banks have increased income via non-interest income generated through fees for services and various contingent liabilities such as letters of credit, and other non-traditional banking activities including operations in the forward and futures markets. In competitive markets, non-interest income may play an important role in profitability. CAR is a crude proxy for risk; however, the competition-frailty view argues that less CAR contributes to profitability while the lower deposit insurance premium view argues that higher CAR results in greater profitability. Nonetheless, the goal of this study is not to resolve these differences but to better understand the factors that contribute to bank profitability in community banks operating in rural and metropolitan areas.

The pooled cross-sectional time-series structure of the data set enables the estimation of several variants of the relationship summarized in (1).

Pooled cross-sectional time-series model, estimated using OLS

$$\prod_{i,t} = \alpha_1 + \alpha_2 \prod_{i,t-1} + \alpha\, s_{i,t} + \alpha\, o_{i,t} + \alpha\, c_{i,t} + \alpha\, d_{1,i} + u_{i,t} \quad i = 1, \ldots\ldots N,\ t = 2 \ldots\ldots T \qquad (2)$$

Cross-sectional model, estimated using OLS

$$\prod_{i,t} = \beta_1 + \beta\, s_{i,t} + \beta\, o_{i,t} + \beta\, c_{i,t} + \beta\, d_{1,i} + w_{i,t} \quad i = 1, \ldots\ldots N \qquad (3)$$

Dynamic panel model GMM

$$\prod_{i,t} = \Upsilon_1 + \Upsilon_2 \prod_{i,t-1} + \Upsilon\, s_{i,t} + \Upsilon\, o_{i,t} + \Upsilon\, c_{i,t} + \eta_i + v_{i,t} \quad i = 1, \ldots\ldots N,\ t = 2 \ldots\ldots T \qquad (4)$$

The pooled model, equation (2), is based on the assumption that cross-sectional variation in any independent variable has the same implication for profit variation over time in that variable for an independent bank. During the period from 2000 to 2013, there were major shocks that included a terrorist attack and a banking crisis that resulted in two recessions. Given that banking profits are correlated with economic expansion and recession (Kupiec & Lee, 2012), the use individual bank differences from yearly means of all banks in the sample removes the exogenous effects of the economic cycle; in other words, economy-normalized values. Estimating the equations using both the data as reported and differenced from yearly means for all community banks provides some ability to understand how economic expansion and contraction effects profitability in rural and metropolitan banks differently.

Results

Table 1 reports the summary data on the untransformed dependent and independent variables used in the empirical model. Table 1 reports the summary data for all community banks (observations = 296,098) and for community banks operating in the rural (observations = 160,142) and metropolitan (observations = 135,696) areas.

Table 1
Descriptive Statistics

All Banks							
	roaptx	asset5	noniiay	eqv	nimy	nonixay	observations
mean	1.358655	229266.6	0.809128	10.97072	3.987371	3.065103	296,098
sd	3.483859	428960.3	5.615186	3.809603	0.955995	3.807264	
min	-212.39	1055.25	-23.02	-1.69	-3.24	-0.23	
max	419.01	1.30E+07	1066.4	95.9	72.64	1099.33	
Rural							
mean	1.434388	146835.1	0.691578	11.07118	4.026	2.944052	160,402
sd	1.883635	205449.8	0.86468	3.568647	0.918214	1.136296	
min	-141.32	1055.25	-6.63	-0.62	0	0	
max	53.86	4511235	87.28	81.55	72.64	72.64	

Metro							
mean	1.269134	326706.2	0.94808	10.85198	3.941708	3.208193	135,696
sd	4.719703	578010.3	8.239063	4.072919	0.996888	5.483222	
min	-212.39	2816	-23.02	-1.69	-3.24	-0.23	
max	419.01	1.30E+07	1066.4	95.9	29.02	1099.33	

Pooled OLS Regressions

Tables 2 through 7 report the results of pooled OLS regressions for both the economy-normalized data which is the difference in the individual bank value and the mean for the year of all banks on for that variable.

Table 2. Pooled OLS All Banks Using Non-Economy-Normalized

Source	SS	df	MS
Model	2586444.01	5	517288.802
Residual	1007365.93	296092	3.40220585
Total	3593809.94	296097	12.1372724

Number of obs =	296098
F(5,296092) =	.
Prob > F =	0.0000
R-squared =	0.7197
Adj R-squared =	0.7197
Root MSE =	1.8445

roaptx	Coef.	Std. Err.	t	P>|t|	[95% Conf.	Interval]
lnasset5	-.0525325	.0031807	-16.52	0.000	-.0587665	-.0462985
noniiay	.998067	.0012559	794.68	0.000	.9956054	1.000529
eqv	.0013112	.0009108	1.44	0.150	-.0004738	.0030963
nimy	.8185951	.0036912	221.77	0.000	.8113605	.8258297
nonixay	-1.002629	.0018636	-538.00	0.000	-1.006281	-.998976
_cons	.9590993	.0447775	21.42	0.000	.8713366	1.046862

Table 3. Pooled OLS All Banks Using Economy-Normalized

Source	SS	df	MS
Model	2583750.98	5	516750.195
Residual	878563.155	296092	2.96719653
Total	3462314.13	296097	11.6931753

Number of obs =	296098
F(5,296092) =	.
Prob > F =	0.0000
R-squared =	0.7462
Adj R-squared =	0.7462
Root MSE =	1.7226

droaptx	Coef.	Std. Err.	t	P>|t|	[95% Conf.	Interval]
dlnasset5	-.0428519	.0030309	-14.14	0.000	-.0487924	-.0369113
dnoniiay	.9984751	.0011749	849.87	0.000	.9961724	1.000778
deqv	.0042829	.000853	5.02	0.000	.002611	.0059549
dnimy	.8220789	.0035092	234.26	0.000	.815201	.8289569
dnonixay	-1.003457	.0017441	-575.34	0.000	-1.006876	-1.000039
_cons	-5.41e-06	.0031656	-0.00	0.999	-.0062099	.0061991

Table 4. Pooled OLS Rural Banks Using Non-Economy-Normalized

Source	SS	df	MS		
				Number of obs =	160402
				F(5,160396) =	7987.28
Model	113453.59	5	22690.7181	Prob > F =	0.0000
Residual	455662.024	160396	2.84085653	R-squared =	0.1994
				Adj R-squared =	0.1993
Total	569115.614	160401	3.54808021	Root MSE =	1.6855

roaptx	Coef.	Std. Err.	t	P>|t|	[95% Conf.	Interval]
lnasset5	-.0450983	.0045527	-9.91	0.000	-.0540215	-.0361751
noniiay	1.077926	.0073078	147.50	0.000	1.063603	1.092249
eqv	-.0027492	.0012271	-2.24	0.025	-.0051543	-.0003441
nimy	.9005445	.0056208	160.22	0.000	.8895278	.9115613
nonixay	-1.132732	.0064456	-175.74	0.000	-1.145365	-1.120099
_cons	.9422624	.0623413	15.11	0.000	.8200747	1.06445

Table 5. Pooled OLS Rural Banks Using Economy-Normalized

Source	SS	df	MS		
				Number of obs =	160402
				F(5,160396) =	9984.79
Model	113154.893	5	22630.9786	Prob > F =	0.0000
Residual	363544.699	160396	2.26654467	R-squared =	0.2374
				Adj R-squared =	0.2373
Total	476699.592	160401	2.97192407	Root MSE =	1.5055

droaptx	Coef.	Std. Err.	t	P>|t|	[95% Conf.	Interval]
dlnasset5	-.0447315	.0041818	-10.70	0.000	-.0529277	-.0365354
dnoniiay	1.085784	.0065819	164.97	0.000	1.072884	1.098685
deqv	-.0001967	.0010996	-0.18	0.858	-.0023518	.0019584
dnimy	.9196494	.0051538	178.44	0.000	.909548	.9297508
dnonixay	-1.149914	.0058443	-196.76	0.000	-1.161369	-1.138459
_cons	.0220373	.003977	5.54	0.000	.0142424	.0298321

Table 6. Pooled OLS Metro Banks Using Non-Economy-Normalized

Source	SS	df	MS		
				Number of obs =	135696
				F(5,135690) =	.
Model	2472735.17	5	494547.035	Prob > F =	0.0000
Residual	549951.714	135690	4.05300106	R-squared =	0.8181
				Adj R-squared =	0.8181
Total	3022686.89	135695	22.2755952	Root MSE =	2.0132

roaptx	Coef.	Std. Err.	t	P>|t|	[95% Conf.	Interval]
lnasset5	-.0604381	.0049594	-12.19	0.000	-.0701585	-.0507178
noniiay	.9916712	.0014136	701.54	0.000	.9889007	.9944418
eqv	.0017462	.0013703	1.27	0.203	-.0009395	.004432
nimy	.7977294	.005632	141.64	0.000	.7866908	.8087681
nonixay	-.9910865	.0021221	-467.03	0.000	-.9952458	-.9869273
_cons	1.071039	.0709305	15.10	0.000	.932016	1.210061

Table 7. Pooled OLS Metro Banks Using Economy-Normalized

Source	SS	df	MS		
Model	2470699.04	5	494139.808	Number of obs =	135696
Residual	512765.941	135690	3.77895159	F(5,135690) =	.
				Prob > F =	0.0000
				R-squared =	0.8281
				Adj R-squared =	0.8281
Total	2983464.98	135695	21.9865506	Root MSE =	1.944

droaptx	Coef.	Std. Err.	t	P>|t|	[95% Conf.	Interval]
dlnasset5	-.0412878	.0048799	-8.46	0.000	-.0508524	-.0317232
dnoniiay	.9913288	.0013664	725.51	0.000	.9886507	.9940069
deqv	.0044963	.001328	3.39	0.001	.0018934	.0070992
dnimy	.7958965	.0055364	143.76	0.000	.7850452	.8067478
dnonixay	-.9904214	.0020519	-482.70	0.000	-.994443	-.9863998
_cons	-.0414837	.0055142	-7.52	0.000	-.0522915	-.0306759

From the pooled OLS analysis from both the economy-normalize and non-economy-normalized data the negative coefficient for bank size (asset5) is negative. This provides some support for the position that large banks may encounter diseconomies of scale. Kupiec and Lee (2012) found a curvilinear relationship between size and profitability in community banks where banks as small as $300 million in assets achieved a significant proportion of the gain in profits while banks over $1 billion in assets were less profitable. As expected, the coefficient for non-interest expense is negative in all tables. The fact that CAR (eqv) varies in the level of significance across the different analyses is interesting and need for further investigation. It is noteworthy that there were changes in capital requirements after the 2008 financial crisis.

Pooled Time Series OLS Regressions

Tables 8 through 13 report the results of pooled time-series OLS regressions for both the economy-normalized data which is the difference in the individual bank value and the mean for the year of all banks on for that variable. Because the data is quarterly, the dependent variable, pre-tax ROA, is lagged by 4 observations to capture the profit from one year before.

Table 8. Pooled TS OLS All Banks Using Non-Economy-Normalized

```
Fixed-effects (within) regression               Number of obs      =    264808
Group variable: crossid                         Number of groups   =      5466

R-sq:  within  = 0.1913                         Obs per group: min =        17
       between = 0.9837                                        avg =      48.4
       overall = 0.6838                                        max =        52

                                                F(6,259336)        =  10222.39
corr(u_i, Xb)  = 0.0752                         Prob > F           =    0.0000
```

roaptx	Coef.	Std. Err.	t	P>|t|	[95% Conf.	Interval]
roaptx						
L4.	-.0151202	.001825	-8.28	0.000	-.0186972	-.0115432
lnasset5	-.2956692	.0128646	-22.98	0.000	-.3208835	-.2704548
noniiay	1.016689	.0051139	198.81	0.000	1.006666	1.026713
eqv	.0239564	.0021096	11.36	0.000	.0198216	.0280912
nimy	.8786408	.0068121	128.98	0.000	.8652892	.8919924
nonixay	-1.079463	.0053617	-201.33	0.000	-1.089972	-1.068954
_cons	3.559793	.161227	22.08	0.000	3.243793	3.875794
sigma_u	.5451846					
sigma_e	1.8953757					
rho	.07641415	(fraction of variance due to u_i)				

F test that all u_i=0: F(5465, 259336) = 2.57 Prob > F = 0.0000

Table 9. Pooled TS OLS All Banks Using Economy-Normalized

```
Fixed-effects (within) regression               Number of obs      =    264808
Group variable: crossid                         Number of groups   =      5466

R-sq:  within  = 0.2077                         Obs per group: min =        17
       between = 0.9858                                        avg =      48.4
       overall = 0.7145                                        max =        52

                                                F(6,259336)        =  11331.89
corr(u_i, Xb)  = 0.0764                         Prob > F           =    0.0000
```

droaptx	Coef.	Std. Err.	t	P>|t|	[95% Conf.	Interval]
droaptx						
L4.	-.0014562	.0018147	-0.80	0.422	-.0050131	.0021006
dlnasset5	-.2532024	.0167308	-15.13	0.000	-.2859942	-.2204105
dnoniiay	1.00999	.0047955	210.61	0.000	1.000591	1.01939
deqv	.0263796	.0019936	13.23	0.000	.0224722	.030287
dnimy	.9175164	.0065621	139.82	0.000	.9046549	.930378
dnonixay	-1.076489	.0050965	-211.22	0.000	-1.086478	-1.0665
_cons	-.0057685	.0034263	-1.68	0.092	-.0124839	.0009469
sigma_u	.50932716					
sigma_e	1.7628287					
rho	.07704656	(fraction of variance due to u_i)				

F test that all u_i=0: F(5465, 259336) = 2.74 Prob > F = 0.0000

Table 10. Pooled TS OLS Rural Banks Using Non-Economy-Normalized

```
Fixed-effects (within) regression               Number of obs      =    142943
Group variable: crossid                         Number of groups   =      3106

R-sq:  within  = 0.1137                         Obs per group: min =         1
       between = 0.6879                                        avg =      46.0
       overall = 0.1770                                        max =        52

                                                F(6,139831)        =   2989.01
corr(u_i, Xb)  = -0.1443                        Prob > F           =    0.0000
```

roaptx	Coef.	Std. Err.	t	P>|t|	[95% Conf. Interval]	
roaptx L4.	-.0286746	.0025348	-11.31	0.000	-.0336429	-.0237063
lnasset5	-.2600908	.0179843	-14.46	0.000	-.2953396	-.224842
noniiay	1.177087	.0108638	108.35	0.000	1.155794	1.19838
eqv	.010226	.0029607	3.45	0.001	.0044231	.016029
nimy	.9447741	.009168	103.05	0.000	.9268051	.9627431
nonixay	-1.21727	.0105515	-115.36	0.000	-1.23795	-1.196589
_cons	3.302526	.2191399	15.07	0.000	2.873016	3.732036
sigma_u	.45151986					
sigma_e	1.7541192					
rho	.0621403	(fraction of variance due to u_i)				

F test that all u_i=0: F(3105, 139831) = 2.13 Prob > F = 0.0000

Table 11. Pooled TS OLS Rural Banks Using Economy-Normalized

```
Fixed-effects (within) regression               Number of obs      =    142943
Group variable: crossid                         Number of groups   =      3106

R-sq:  within  = 0.1349                         Obs per group: min =         1
       between = 0.6349                                        avg =      46.0
       overall = 0.1937                                        max =        52

                                                F(6,139831)        =   3633.01
corr(u_i, Xb)  = -0.2824                        Prob > F           =    0.0000
```

droaptx	Coef.	Std. Err.	t	P>|t|	[95% Conf. Interval]	
droaptx L4.	-.0086361	.0025089	-3.44	0.001	-.0135536	-.0037187
dlnasset5	-.4066864	.023388	-17.39	0.000	-.4525265	-.3608462
dnoniiay	1.194264	.0098972	120.67	0.000	1.174866	1.213662
deqv	.0136587	.0026671	5.12	0.000	.0084312	.0188861
dnimy	.9976664	.008516	117.15	0.000	.9809752	1.014358
dnonixay	-1.256684	.0097787	-128.51	0.000	-1.27585	-1.237518
_cons	-.0843095	.0077981	-10.81	0.000	-.0995937	-.0690254
sigma_u	.51602911					
sigma_e	1.5597466					
rho	.09865752	(fraction of variance due to u_i)				

F test that all u_i=0: F(3105, 139831) = 2.39 Prob > F = 0.0000

Table 12. Pooled TS OLS Metro Banks Using Non-Economy-Normalized

```
Fixed-effects (within) regression               Number of obs      =    121865
Group variable: crossid                         Number of groups   =      2652

R-sq:  within  = 0.2468                         Obs per group: min =         1
       between = 0.9868                                        avg =      46.0
       overall = 0.7889                                        max =        52

                                                F(6,119207)        =   6508.77
corr(u_i, Xb)  = 0.2695                         Prob > F           =    0.0000
```

roaptx	Coef.	Std. Err.	t	P>|t|	[95% Conf.	Interval]
roaptx						
L4.	-.0059829	.0026497	-2.26	0.024	-.0111762	-.0007896
lnasset5	-.3870837	.0204479	-18.93	0.000	-.4271612	-.3470063
noniiay	.9792774	.0063348	154.59	0.000	.9668613	.9916934
eqv	.0349243	.0031389	11.13	0.000	.028772	.0410765
nimy	.8714233	.011354	76.75	0.000	.8491697	.8936768
nonixay	-1.054804	.0069426	-151.93	0.000	-1.068411	-1.041196
_cons	4.574221	.2637499	17.34	0.000	4.057276	5.091167
sigma_u	.77265					
sigma_e	2.0447255					
rho	.12494804	(fraction of variance due to u_i)				

```
F test that all u_i=0:     F(2651, 119207) =      2.90         Prob > F = 0.0000
```

Table 13. Pooled TS OLS Metro Banks Using Economy-Normalized

```
Fixed-effects (within) regression               Number of obs      =    121865
Group variable: crossid                         Number of groups   =      2652

R-sq:  within  = 0.2525                         Obs per group: min =         1
       between = 0.9906                                        avg =      46.0
       overall = 0.8054                                        max =        52

                                                F(6,119207)        =   6710.78
corr(u_i, Xb)  = 0.3202                         Prob > F           =    0.0000
```

droaptx	Coef.	Std. Err.	t	P>|t|	[95% Conf.	Interval]
droaptx						
L4.	.0017847	.0026506	0.67	0.501	-.0034105	.0069799
dlnasset5	-.219934	.0270817	-8.12	0.000	-.2730137	-.1668543
dnoniiay	.972894	.0061332	158.63	0.000	.9608731	.9849149
deqv	.0339648	.0030848	11.01	0.000	.0279186	.0400111
dnimy	.9223176	.0113704	81.12	0.000	.9000318	.9446034
dnonixay	-1.039375	.0067974	-152.91	0.000	-1.052698	-1.026053
_cons	.025413	.0107307	2.37	0.018	.004381	.0464449
sigma_u	.67401676					
sigma_e	1.9707322					
rho	.10472332	(fraction of variance due to u_i)				

```
F test that all u_i=0:     F(2651, 119207) =      2.95         Prob > F = 0.0000
```

A review of the time-series OLS indicates that CAR differs from the results in the pooled cross-sectional regressions. In the time-series regressions, CAR (eqv) is positive and significant across all regressions. An interesting result is that lagged pre-tax ROA is negative when significant and is worthy of further investigation although size of the coefficient is relatively small. Otherwise, the signs of the coefficients are the same as in the cross-sectional OLS regressions with size (asset5) and non-interest expense being (nonixay) negative.

Dynamic Panel Estimation

The null hypothesis of the Sargan test that the over-identifying restrictions are valid were rejected for both the non-economy-normalized and economy-normalized panel regressions; therefore, they are not valid. The Arellano-Bond test for zero autocorrelation in first-differenced errors revealed evidence of misspecification for the non-economy-normalized panel regressions. However, there was no evidence of misspecification in the economy-normalized regressions. Despite the results of the Sargan test, the results of the economy-normalized regressions are provided here.

Table 14. Dynamic Panel All Banks Using Economy-Normalized Data

```
Arellano-Bond dynamic panel-data estimation  Number of obs      =    249338
Group variable: crossid                      Number of groups   =      5466
Time variable: timeid
                                             Obs per group:  min =        16
                                                             avg =  45.61617
                                                             max =        51

Number of instruments =    1.5e+03           Wald chi2(9)       =   2444.07
                                             Prob > chi2        =    0.0000
One-step results
                                  (Std. Err. adjusted for clustering on crossid)
```

droaptx	Coef.	Robust Std. Err.	z	P>|z|	[95% Conf.	Interval]
droaptx						
L1.	.3973775	.0441071	9.01	0.000	.3109292	.4838258
L2.	-.0175836	.0152226	-1.16	0.248	-.0474193	.0122521
L3.	-.1011649	.0191132	-5.29	0.000	-.1386261	-.0637036
L4.	.0369237	.0118291	3.12	0.002	.013739	.0601083
dlnasset5	-2.720921	.222671	-12.22	0.000	-3.157348	-2.284494
dnoniiay	.8255317	.051451	16.05	0.000	.7246896	.9263738
deqv	.0777918	.0186109	4.18	0.000	.0413152	.1142685
dnimy	.7787569	.0465123	16.74	0.000	.6875944	.8699194
dnonixay	-.8508638	.068657	-12.39	0.000	-.985429	-.7162986
_cons	.0321022	.0397568	0.81	0.419	-.0458197	.1100241

```
Instruments for differenced equation
        GMM-type: L(2/.).droaptx
        Standard: D.dlnasset5 D.dnoniiay D.deqv D.dnimy D.dnonixay
Instruments for level equation
        Standard: _cons
```

Table 15. Dynamic Panel Rural Banks Using Economy-Normalized

```
Arellano-Bond dynamic panel-data estimation  Number of obs      =    134391
Group variable: crossid                      Number of groups   =      3103
Time variable: timeid
                                             Obs per group:   min =       1
                                                              avg =  43.31002
                                                              max =      51

Number of instruments =    1.5e+03           Wald chi2(9)       =  52572.28
                                             Prob > chi2        =    0.0000
One-step results
```

droaptx	Coef.	Std. Err.	z	P>|z|	[95% Conf.	Interval]
droaptx						
L1.	.4498633	.002912	154.49	0.000	.4441559	.4555707
L2.	-.0310608	.0029281	-10.61	0.000	-.0367997	-.0253219
L3.	-.1364222	.0027547	-49.52	0.000	-.1418214	-.1310231
L4.	.0647087	.002365	27.36	0.000	.0600733	.069344
dlnasset5	-3.173354	.075241	-42.18	0.000	-3.320823	-3.025884
dnoniiay	1.065877	.0126253	84.42	0.000	1.041132	1.090622
deqv	.0288549	.0055402	5.21	0.000	.0179963	.0397135
dnimy	.7833973	.0138901	56.40	0.000	.7561731	.8106214
dnonixay	-1.117461	.0127266	-87.81	0.000	-1.142405	-1.092517
_cons	-.8499601	.0209723	-40.53	0.000	-.891065	-.8088553

```
Instruments for differenced equation
        GMM-type: L(2/.).droaptx
        Standard: D.dlnasset5 D.dnoniiay D.deqv D.dnimy D.dnonixay
Instruments for level equation
        Standard: _cons
```

Table 16. Dynamic Panel Metro Banks Using Economy-Normalized

```
Arellano-Bond dynamic panel-data estimation  Number of obs      =    114947
Group variable: crossid                      Number of groups   =      2652
Time variable: timeid
                                             Obs per group:   min =       1
                                                              avg =  43.34351
                                                              max =      51

Number of instruments =    1.5e+03           Wald chi2(9)       =   1468.22
                                             Prob > chi2        =    0.0000
One-step results
                               (Std. Err. adjusted for clustering on crossid)
```

droaptx	Coef.	Robust Std. Err.	z	P>|z|	[95% Conf.	Interval]
droaptx						
L1.	.3685604	.062088	5.94	0.000	.2468702	.4902506
L2.	-.0129432	.0175742	-0.74	0.461	-.0473881	.0215017
L3.	-.0845967	.0237472	-3.56	0.000	-.1311403	-.038053
L4.	.0199218	.0136042	1.46	0.143	-.0067419	.0465855
dlnasset5	-1.644153	.3033744	-5.42	0.000	-2.238756	-1.04955
dnoniiay	.8151457	.0397175	20.52	0.000	.7373007	.8929906
deqv	.102721	.0309129	3.32	0.001	.0421327	.1633092
dnimy	.9003749	.0895391	10.06	0.000	.7248815	1.075868
dnonixay	-.8179056	.0532217	-15.37	0.000	-.9222183	-.7135929
_cons	.5602436	.1056296	5.30	0.000	.3532133	.7672738

```
Instruments for differenced equation
        GMM-type: L(2/.).droaptx
        Standard: D.dlnasset5 D.dnoniiay D.deqv D.dnimy D.dnonixay
Instruments for level equation
        Standard: _cons
```

Conclusion

The goal of this study is to compare community banks operating in rural and metropolitan counties on the variables attributing to bank profitability using pooled OLS, pooled time-series OLS, and dynamic panels methodologies. Following the SCP and competition-fragility literature and given that community banks operating in metropolitan areas are facing direct competition from massive nationwide and regional banks whereas community banks are not to a great extent, one would expect a difference in the variables contributing to profitability. This study is exploratory in nature in that the purpose is to provide informative insight into areas in need of further research.

Overall, the three methodologies are more alike than different in that the signs of the coefficients are alike across all three methodologies. The size of the coefficients indicates that the variables contributing to profitability differ in magnitude when comparing community banks in metropolitan counties to those in rural counties. Both the pooled and time-series OLS models indicate that bank size contributes to profitability more in metropolitan areas. One could argue that in a rural community with few banks that size is not as important when it comes to attracting and retaining customers. In the results from the dynamic panel analysis, metropolitan banks have a smaller size coefficient than rural banks; however, we must view these results with caution given the results of the Sargan test.

The results across all three methodologies provide some interesting insight into net interest margins, non-interest income, and non-interest expenses. Traditionally, the majority of bank profit comes from the difference in the rate paid for deposits and the rates charged for loans. In both the pooled OLS and pooled time-series OLS models net-interest margins contribute less to profitability in metropolitan banks. This would conform to the competition-fragility argument that competition in the banking sector leads to lower net interest margins. One might expect that banks in metropolitan areas might have more opportunities to profit from non-interest fee income; however, the results from the pooled OLS, pooled time-series OLS, and dynamic panel models indicate that non-interest income contributes less to profitability in metropolitan banks. One possibility might be that metropolitan banks compete with massive nationwide and regional banks and as a result have to compete by offering free or lower cost services whereas the SCP paradigm indicates that small banks in rural communities have a greater ability to collude on fees such as checking, overdraft, letters of credit, and charges for other services. Non-interest expense is negative in all results as expected. The results from the pooled OLS, pooled time-series OLS, and dynamic panel models indicate that non-interest expense has less of an impact on profits in metropolitan banks. Given the higher real estate and labor prices in metropolitan areas one might expect non-interest expense to have more of a negative impact on profits in big cities than small towns. However, it may be possible that efficiencies achieve though economies of scale in metropolitan banks may result in non-interest expenses being less of a factor. In the results from the dynamic panel analysis, metropolitan banks have a larger net interest margin coefficient than rural banks; however, we must view these results with caution given the results of the Sargan test.

Finally, the coefficient for equity was small but positive and significant across all methodologies, except cross-sectional OLS by type, with the coefficient being larger for metropolitan banks. However, future research needs to examine this variable before and after the financial crisis because there were regulatory changes that required increases in CAR after the crisis. It would be interesting to examine the difference in CAR between rural and metropolitan banks prior to the regulatory changes. Given the wide fluctuation in economic conditions over the period of this study all studies were run economy-normalized data where the individual bank numbers for each variable were subtracted for the year mean for all banks. This did not lead to any changes in the signs of coefficients; however, it is noteworthy that only the economy-normalized dataset passed the Arellano-Bond test for zero autocorrelation in first-differenced errors. However, both data samples failed to pass the Sargan test and as a result, one must view the dynamic panel results with caution.

References

Bain, J. S. (1951). Relation of profit rate to industry concentration: American manufacturing, 1936-1940. Quarterly Journal of Economics, 65(3), 293-324.

Bain, J. S. (1956). Barriers to new competition, their character and consequences in manufacturing industries. Cambridge MA: Harvard University Press.

Berger, A. N. (1995a). The profit-structure relationship in banking—Tests of market-power and efficient-structure hypotheses. Journal of Money, Credit & Banking, 27(2), 404-431.

Berger, A. N. (1995b). The relationship between capital and earnings in banking. Journal of Money, Credit & Banking (Ohio State University Press), 27(2), 432-456.

Calomiris, C. W. (2010). The political lessons of Depression-era banking reform. Oxford Review of Economic Policy, 26(3), 540-560. doi: 10.1093/oxrep/grq020

Canoy, M., van Dijk, M., Lemmen, J., de Mooij, R., & Weigand, J. (2001). Competition and stability in banking. The Hague, Netherlands: CBP Netherlands Bureau for Economic Policy Analysis.

Carletti, E., & Hartmann, P. (2003). Competition and stability: What's special about banking? In P. Mizen (Ed.), Monetary History, Exchange Rates and Financial Markets: Essays in honor of Charles Goodhart (Vol. 2). Cheltenham, UK: Edward Elgar.

FDIC CBS. (2012). FDIC Community Banking Study. Washington D.C.: Federal Deposit Insurance Corporation.

Friedman, S. J. (1981). The illusion of intrastate banking. Washington D.C.: Securities and Exchange Commission Retrieved from http://www.sec.gov/news/speech/1981/050581friedman.pdf.

Gilbert, R. A. (1984). Bank market structure and competition. Journal of Money, Credit & Banking, 16(4), 617-645.
Goddard, J., Molyneux, P., & Wilson, J. O. S. (2004). The profitability of european banks: a cross-sectional and dynamic panel analysis. Manchester School (14636786), 72(3), 363-381. doi: 10.1111/j.1467-9957.2004.00397.x

Hellmann, T. F., Murdock, K. C., & Stiglitz, J. E. (2000). Liberalization, moral hazard in banking, and prudential regulation: Are capital requirements enough? American Economic Review, 90(1), 147-165.

Keeley, M. C. (1990). Deposit insurance, risk, and market power in banking. American Economic Review, 60(5), 1183-1200.

Kupiec, P., & Lee, Y. (2012). What factors explain differences in Return on Assets Among Community Banks? Washington D.C.: Federal Deposit Insurance Corporation.

Schmalensee, R. (1982). Product differentiation advantages of pioneering brands. American Economic Review, 72(3), 349.

Schmalensee, R. (1985). Do markets differ much? American Economic Review, 75(3), 341.

Schmalensee, R. (1989). Inter-industry studies of structure and performance. In R. Schmalensee & R. D. Willig (Eds.), Handbook of Industrial Organization (pp. 959-1009). Ansterdam: Elsevier Science Publishers.

Smirlock, M. (1985). Evidence on the (non) Relationship between concentration and profitability in banking. Journal of Money, Credit & Banking, 17(1), 69-83.

DECISION SCIENCES INSTITUTE

The Relationship between Observed and Published Multiple-Choice Question Difficulty may Depend on What Means "Related"

John R. Dickinson
University of Windsor
Email: MExperiences@bell.net

ABSTRACT

The difficulty of a multiple-choice question is its most fundamental property, serving numerous purposes. A commonly available guide to managing item difficulty is in the form of published banks of multiple-choice questions that accompany most introductory texts. The questions are usually classified into three levels of difficulty: Easy, Medium, and Hard. The present study applies and compares two definitions of the extent to which observed difficulty and published difficulty are related. The study finds for the question banks examined that the effectiveness of their classifications does depend on what is defined as "related."

KEYWORDS: Item analysis, item difficulty, multiple-choice questions, *TaxI*, published multiple-choice question taxonomies

Full paper and references available upon request.

DECISION SCIENCES INSTITUTE

The Relationship between Technostress Creators and Online Education among Students

Queen E. Booker
Minnesota State University, Mankato
Email: queen.booker@mnsu.edu

Carl Rebman
University of San Diego
Email: carlr@usd.edu

ABSTRACT

In this study, we examine technology related creators of stress in students taking online classes. We hypothesized that students enrolled in only online courses experience higher technostress than students enrolled in face-to-face only courses. The study involved a convenience sample of students at three regional state universities. The result of the analysis suggests that students enrolled in online only courses do experience higher technostress creators than their face-to-face peers, and that enrollment in online only courses explained 8.1 percent to the variance in the techno creator score.

Keywords: Online education, Technostress, Human-Computer Interaction

INTRODUCTION

Higher education has adopted online education as a component of its mission to provide access to higher education for all. Part of this adoption is driven by perceived student demand to have 24/7 access to course materials so that the student can complete their degree while also addressing other life issues such as work and family. Much of this adoption is the result of the introduction of technology based-learning management systems (LMS). Faculty members are encouraged to use LMS for online instruction and/or supplement the class with additional electronic content and in many cases, offer courses 100% online. For courses that are 100% online students may be expected, for each credit hour, to spend at least 3 hours online. Thus for a 3 credit course, a student could be expected to spend as many as 9 hours per week using some form of technology to successfully complete the course, and more depending on how the instructor grades the course. Prior studies suggest that the use of technology under certain circumstances can induce stress which is also referred to as "technostress."

Stress, broadly defined, is a situation "in which environmental demands, internal demands, or both, tax or exceed the adaptive resources of an individual, social system, or tissue system" (Keller et al, 2012). It is pervasive in today's society, with nearly a third of Americans rating their average stress levels as extreme. Research has shown that stressed people are subject to greater health risks and concomitantly, increased health care costs, as well as productivity losses greater than people with normal stress levels. Highly stressed individuals are at greater risk for multiple health conditions including cardiovascular disease, cancer, diabetes, depression and anxiety, fatigue, obesity, and musculoskeletal pain. (Wolever et al, 2012) Consequences of prolonged stress include adverse psychological and physical health effects, as well as an increased risk of premature mortality (Keller et al, 2012). People who suffer from technostress may also suffer from anxiety which include symptoms like irritability, headaches, nightmares, insomnia, technological rejection, and technological resistance (Tarafdar et al, 2007). The effects of stress on well-being are so well recognized that U.S. Public Health officials have called for a reduction of stress since the 1970s (USPHS, 1979). Thus, if technostress increases stress in online students and a student enrolls in a fully online undergraduate program which could take many years to complete, then it is important that we understand what contributes to the creation of stress in the online learning environment and identify methods to mitigate it. And, as technology is being used a tool for efficient delivery of education, its use will become meaningless without student's continued interest in online education. In fact, a 2014 annual report by the Babson Survey Research Group "Grade Level: Tracking Online Education in the United States" reported online education grew at the slowest rate in more than a decade in Fall 2013. Part of the decline may be to a saturation of the market, or it could be because students are feeling a lack of satisfaction in online education, and part of it may be due experiences of higher levels of stress.

Much of the prior research in technostress has examined the work environment or the general environment, and focuses either on the general population or employees. No current study has examined and measured technostress in students, specifically in the online environment despite its rapid growth. In 2012, the percentage of institutions offering online courses and full programs were 72.9 percent for private for-profit colleges, 48.4 percent of private non-profit, and 70.6 percent of public college (Chin et al, 1997). Despite the slowdown in online education growth, the number of students taking online courses does continue to climb. According to "Grade Level: Tracking Online Education in the United States", an annual report by the Babson Survey Research Group about 5.3 million students took at least one online course in fall 2013, which is approximately 2% of the United States population.

LITERATURE REVIEW

Wang, et al (1995) defines technostress as a "reflection of one's discomposure, fear, tenseness and anxiety when one is learning and using computer technology directly or indirectly that ultimately ends in psychological and emotional repulsion and prevents one from further learning or using computer technology." Technostress is a focus of IS research because researchers and employers are beginning to recognize that stress caused by the use or overuse of technology can lead to lower productivity by employees.

Lazarus' (1966) introduction of the transaction theory of stress from organizational psychology has formed the basis for much of the research and theoretical conceptualization of technostress. He suggests that it is a phenomenon that encapsulates relationships between strain and stress creators. Key aspects of the technostress phenomenon create stress because of information and communications technology use includes but is not limited to techno-overload, techno-complexity, techno-insecurity, techno-uncertainty and techno-invasion. (Ayyagari et al., 2011).

Walz (2012) examined the relationship between technology and stress to learn the stress related issues, to what extent "technostress" affect our personal lives and the consequences of too much technology use. Her results corroborated that the phenomenon known as "technostress" exists. Brod (1984), reported that employees at all levels of the organization experience some level of stress related to the use of information and computer technologies (ICT) at work. Other studies have shown that the type of techno-stress experienced vary and include data smog, multitasking madness, computer hassles, burnout, techno-addiction, and techno-strain (Salanova, et. al 2007; and Brillhart 2004).

Ragu-Nathan et al (2008) describes the different technostress creators as follows:

> "Techno-overload describes situations where information and communication technologies (ICTs) force users to work faster and longer. Techno-invasion describes the invasive effect of ICTs in situations where employees can be reached anytime and feel the need to be constantly connected, thus blurring work-related and personal contexts. Techno-complexity describes situations where the complexity associated with ICTs leads users to feel inadequate with regard to their computer skills and forces them to spend time and effort in learning and understanding ICTs. Techno-insecurity is associated with situations where users feel threatened about losing their jobs, either because of automation from ICTs or to other people who have a better understanding of ICTs. Techno-uncertainty refers to contexts where continuing ICT changes and upgrades unsettle users and create uncertainty so that they must constantly learn and educate themselves about new ICTs."

There have been studies that have examined technostress more specifically for particular groups, such as among librarians, because of rapid introduction of successive computer-based library cataloguing, retrieval and database systems such as LexisNexis (Van Fleet & Wallace, 2001). It showed that the pace of change of library and reference IS were key causes of technostress (Bartlett, 1995; Ennis et al, 2005). The strains were computer use-related anxiety, feelings of isolation and frustration, indifference to needs of library users and negative attitudes towards computer-based information sources (Kupersmith, 1992). Wang et al (2008) reported results from IS use in Chinese organizations found that levels of technostress creators are positively related to power centralization and an organization culture that encourages innovation. It also showed that higher dependence on IS for completion of routine work tasks and lower levels of computer self-efficacy were associated with higher levels of technostress creators (Shu et al ., 2011). Booker et al (2014) explored technostress in students and modified the existing survey to accommodate the learning environment to measure techno-stress in online students. Booker et al also found gender and age contributed to overall technostress in their study.

This study, however, focuses only on techno-creators. This particular focus is to determine if there are differences in experience with techno-creators for online only students as compared to face-to-face students, and to try to understand the external factors that influence the creation of stress for students enrolled in online only courses.

RESEARCH METHODOLOGY

The purpose of this study is to examine if taking online only classes increases technostress in students, specifically the subscale of technostress-creators, and if so, to determine how much of an increase, if that increase is significant, and factors that contribute to that differential. The hypothesis for the study was:

H1: There is no significant difference in techno-stress reported by students enrolled in face-to-face only courses and students enrolled in only online courses.

The instrument used was the subscale from the technostress measure created by Ragu-Nathan et al. (2008), and redesigned specifically for online students by Booker et al (2014). The items developed by Booker et al are shown in Table 1. Techno-stress structure for online students. Only the items for technostress creators are used in this study.

Technostress creators
Techno-overload
TSC_3—I am forced by this technology to work with very tight time schedules.
TSC_4—I am forced to change my study habits to adapt to new technologies.
TSC_5—I have a higher workload because of increased technology complexity.
TCS_6-I have a higher workload because of the online learning environment.
TSC_7-- I have to spend a lot of time everyday reading an overwhelming amount of e-mail messages.
TSC_8-- I have to spend a lot of time everyday reading an overwhelming amount of discussion board messages.
Techno-invasion
TSC_10—I have to sacrifice my vacation and weekend time to keep current on changes to the courses and learning environment.
TSC_11—I feel my personal life is being invaded by this learning environment.
TSC_13—I spend less time with my family due to this technology.*
Techno-complexity
TSC_14—I do not find enough time to study and upgrade my technology skills to meet the needs of the program.
TSC_15—I find new students to this program know more about computer technology than I do.
TSC_16—I often find the learning tools too complex for me to understand and use effectively.
TSC_17—I do not know enough about this technology to complete my courses satisfactorily.
Techno-insecurity
TSC_20—I do not share my knowledge with my peers for fear of being accused of cheating.*
TSC-21-I find younger students in this program know more about computer technology than I do.
TSC-23-I find younger students more easily adapt to changes in the learning environment.
TSC_24—I feel constant threat to my ability to complete the program due to new technologies.
Techno-uncertainty TSC—26 I have to work harder because of delays from hardware, software and network problems.
TSC_27—There are always new developments in the technologies we use in our program.
TSC_28—There are constant changes in computer software in our program.
Technostress inhibitors
Literacy facilitation

TSI_1—Our program encourages knowledge sharing to help deal with new technology.*
TSI_3—Our program provides end-user training before the introduction of new technology.
TSI_4—Our program fosters a good relationship between IT department and students.
TSI_5—Our program provides clear documentation to students on using new technologies.
TSI_6-Our program provides training to new students.
Technical support provision
TSI_7—Our end-user help desk is well staffed by knowledgeable individuals.
TSI_9—Our end-user help desk is responsive to end-user requests.
TSI_10—Our end-user help desk does a good job of answering questions about technology.*
Involvement facilitation TSI_12—Our students are consulted before introduction of new technology.
TSI_13—Our students are involved in technology change and/or implementation.
TSI_14—Our students are encouraged to try out new technologies.

Table 1. Techno-stress structure for online students

All statements were answered using a five-point Likert scale: from 1 ("strongly disagree") to 5 ("strongly agree") with a sixth option of "Not Applicable" or "I do not know" which was coded as 0. The responses were totaled for each usable response to provide a **Total Score**. The responses were divided into two groups – Online Only and Face-to-Face only. The means of the two groups were analyzed using Pearson's t-tests to determine if a significant difference exists between the online only and face-to-face only students. A regression analysis was performed to using Total Score as the dependent variable, and the following independent variables:

- Institution 1 (inst1) – the first of the three regional comprehensive universities to participate in the study; binary variable coded as 1 if the student attended the first of the three universities, 0 if not.
- Institution 2 (inst2) – the second of the three regional comprehensive universities to participate in the study; binary variable coded as 1 if the student attended the second of the three universities, 0 if not.
- White (white) – students who self-identified as white (NOTE: This could include Hispanics, Africans, and other immigrants who self-identify as white as well as international students who self-identify as white); binary variable coded as 1 if the student self-identified as white, 0 if not.
- Gender (gender) – students were allowed to select two options: I self-identify as Male and I do not self-identify as male; binary variable coded as 0 if the student self-identified as Male and 1 if not.
- First Language English (fle) – students whose primary language spoken at home is American English; binary variable coded as 1 if the student selected American English as the primary language spoken, 0 if not.
- Aged 23-30 (23-30) – students who are between the ages of 23 and 30;
- Aged 18-22 (18-22) – students who are between the ages of 18 and 22
- Enrolled Online only (online) – if student reported only taking classes online
- Average Hours worked per week (ahwpw) – number of hours student reported working, on average, per week
- Relationship status (rs) – 1 if the student had a live-in partner, 0 if not

- Family status (fs) – 0 if the student had at least one child, 0 if not
- Average hours per week spent recreationally online (ahpwsro) – number of hours student reported spending, on average, per week not related to completing school work or paid employment
- Junior (jr) – Junior level status of enrollment
- Senior (sr) – Senior level status of enrollment
- Freshman (fr) – Freshman level status of enrollment

The variables Institution 3, Aged over 30 and sophomore were used as control variables.

Data Collection
The data was collected from a convenience sample of students attending three regional comprehensive universities. Students were sent an email describing the nature and purpose of the study asking if they would be interested in participating and if so, to complete a Qualtrics survey. Students were informed that participation was voluntary and that their responses would be confidential to the researchers. A confirmation number was given to students for those instructors who incentivized their students to complete the survey by offering bonus points towards their final grade. All surveys were collected during the last two weeks of Fall 2015 semester. Students were asked demographic questions such as age, gender, ethnicity, primary language, number of hours per week student worked, number of courses enrolled, the number of online courses and the number of hybrid courses, and the number of courses that used any type of technology as part of the class. Students were also asked how much time they spent online for recreational purposes and how many hours per week the student worked. From a population of 37,528 we received 893 responses of which 571 were usable. This resulted in a usable response rate of 1.5%. Gender and Ethnicity demographics are given in Table 2.

Gender/Ethnicity	I Identify as Male	I Do Not Identify as Male	Total
I Identify as White	206	208	414
I Do Not Identify as White	78	79	157
Total	**284**	**287**	571

Table 2. Gender and Ethnicity

Of the sample, 457 spoke English as the first language, 282 were from the first institution, 158 from the second and 131 from the third. 150 of the respondents were seniors, 284 juniors, 73 sophomores and 64 were freshmen. 95 were aged 18-22, 416 were between 23 and 30, and the others were over 30. 227 of the students were enrolled in only face-to-face courses and 344 were enrolled in online only courses.

The descriptive statistics for the overall Total Score and for both groups of students are shown in Table 3. Descriptive Statistics. The average Total Score for the Face-to-Face students was lower than that of the Online students as expected. However, the overall average was closer to the Face-to-Face average than the Online average. The higher variance for the Face-to-Face group also suggest a wider range of responses. This is validated by the range which is 100 for the Face-to-Face students and 59 for the Online students.

.

	Overall	Face-to-Face	Online
Average	48.24	33.54	70.52
Variance	893.4933	776.51	247.32
Maximum	100	100	100
Minimum	0	0	41
Range	100	100	59

Table 3. Descriptive Statistics

T-test Analysis

The t-test between groups was performed on Total Score. The result of the t-test is shown in Table 4. T-test results. As shown in the table, the scores showed a significant difference ($p<0.05$), suggesting there is a significant difference between the technostress creation of Online students and Face-to-Face students.

	Total Score
F	138.11
Sig.	0.00
t	-18.17
df	569.00
Mean Difference	-36.98

Table 4. T-test Results

The t-test result provided support to perform further analysis to understand how much the online only contribute to the difference as well as external variables that might contribute to higher technology related stress. Thus, a regression was conducted using Total Score as the dependent variable and the aforementioned independent variables.

Regression Analysis

A regression analysis was run to ascertain the variable contributions to the overall techno-creator score. The regression statistics are shown in Table 5: Regression Statistics Summary Data. The regression model had an R-square of .46 which indicates that the model explains some but not the majority of the factors that may influence a student's stress related to technology. However, the variables that are used do explain 46% of the score.

Regression Statistics	
Multiple R	0.68
R Square	0.46
Adjusted R Square	0.44
Standard Error	22.30
Observations	571

Table 5. Regression Statistics Summary Data

The variable contributions are shown in Table 7. Regression Model. The significant variables are bolded.

	Coefficients	*Standard Error*	*t Stat*	*P-value*	*Lower 95%*	*Upper 95%*	*Lower 95.0%*	*Upper 95.0%*
Intercept	43.74	5.43	8.05	0.00	33.07	54.41	33.07	54.41
Inst1	-1.06	2.39	-0.44	0.66	-5.76	3.63	-5.76	3.63
Inst2	-2.25	2.66	-0.85	0.40	-7.47	2.97	-7.47	2.97
White	1.19	2.11	0.56	0.57	-2.96	5.34	-2.96	5.34
Gender	3.69	1.89	1.96	0.051	-0.02	7.39	-0.02	7.39
First Language English	**-15.23**	**3.45**	**-4.42**	**0.00**	-22.00	-8.46	-22.00	-8.46
18-22	-4.47	2.49	-1.80	0.07	-9.36	0.41	-9.36	0.41
23-30	5.53	4.28	1.29	0.20	-2.87	13.94	-2.87	13.94
online only	**29.08**	**2.14**	**13.56**	**0.00**	24.87	33.30	24.87	33.30
hours worked	2.01	2.00	1.00	0.32	-1.93	5.94	-1.93	5.94
average hour rec	-0.77	2.66	-0.29	0.77	-5.99	4.46	-5.99	4.46
relationship status	**5.92**	**2.03**	**2.92**	**0.00**	1.94	9.90	1.94	9.90
family status	**5.75**	**2.25**	**2.56**	**0.01**	1.34	10.17	1.34	10.17
Senior	0.43	2.96	0.14	0.89	-5.39	6.24	-5.39	6.24
Junior	3.03	3.21	0.95	0.35	-3.27	9.34	-3.27	9.34
Sophomore	0.11	3.87	0.03	0.98	-7.49	7.70	-7.49	7.70

Table 6. Regression Model

The variables **First Language English, Online Only, Relationship Status and Family Status** all had p-values of less than 0.05. Gender has a p-value of .051. If rounded it would also be significant which is consistent with the Booker et al (2014) results. But because the value is slightly over .05 we did not include it as a significant result for this particular dataset. This is partially due to the coding of Gender as self-identifying as Male or Not Male which is different from coding as Male/Female. Online Only contributes, on average, 29 points towards the techno-creator score. Committed relationships and children increase the score by 6 points each. However, speaking English as the primary language reduces the score by 15 points. English as first language is enough to mitigate the relationship and family status variables but not the online only variable.

DISCUSSION AND CONCLUSION

The purpose of this study was to determine of students in online only courses report higher techno-stress creation than students in face-to-face only. The study was conducted using a convenience sample of students at regional comprehensive institutions. Recall the hypothesis:

H1: There is no significant difference in techno-stress reported by students enrolled in face-to-face only courses and students enrolled in only online courses.

Based on the results of the t-test and the regression model, we reject the hypothesis that there is no significant difference in self-reported technostress creation between students taking online only courses and students taking face-to-face only courses. We can also assume that for this population, age was not a factor in the higher level of techno-stress as was not the academic year in school. Gender could be considered marginally significant with a p-value = 0.051 but it was not highly correlated nor highly significant as a coefficient. First Language English and household variables were highly significant. The results suggest that we can improve online courses and potentially retention as well as reduce stress if we can offer courses in multiple languages. The two factors of relationship status and family status are two factors that cause students to be "place-based" and partially gave rise to the need for online education as a method of improving access to higher education. That these two factors are significant at a p-value of less than 0.05 is important in noting that while the online education environment is providing access, it may also be increasing negative health conditions for the populations that the online system is designed to serve.

The next step for this study is to examine the factors within techno-creation to determine if one or more factors influence the techno-creation score more than others. Additional analysis should be made regarding the number of courses taken online, the course design, and whether or not a faculty are officially trained in and use standards such as Quality Matters and the Online Consortium Pillars. Finally, further analysis should be conducted regarding gender, qualitative versus quantitative, and differences in major programs.

REFERENCES

Ayyagari, R., Grover, V. & Purvis, R., 2011. "Technostress: technological antecedents and implications," *MIS Quarterly*, (35:4), December, pp 831–858

Bartlett, V., 1995. "Technostress and Librarians," *Library Administration and Management*, *9*(4), pp.226-30.

Brillhart, P. E., 2004. "Technostress in the workplace: Managing stress in the electronic workplace,"*Journal of American Academy of Business,* (5:(1/2), September, pp 302–307.

Booker, Q.E., Rebman Jr, C.M. and Kitchens, F.L., 2014. " A model for testing technostress in the online education environment: An exploratory study," *Issues in Information Systems,(15:2),* October, pp. 214-222.

Brod, C., 1984. *Technostress: The Human Cost of the Computer Revolution*. Addison-Wesley, Reading, MA.

Chin, W. W., A. Gopal, W. D. Salisbury, 1997. "Advancing the theory of adaptation structuration: The development of a scale to measure faithfulness of appropriation" *Information. Systems Research,* (8:4), pp 342–367.

Ennis, K. and Library Association eds., 1995. *Guidelines for college libraries: recommendations for performance and resourcing*. Library Association Pub..

Keller, A., Litzelman, K., Wisk, L. E., Maddox, T., Cheng, E. R., Creswell, P. D., & Witt, W. P. (2012). Does the perception that stress affects health matter? the association with health and mortality. *Health Psychology, 31*(5), 677-684. doi:http://dx.doi.org/10.1037/a0026743

Kupersmith, J., 1992. "Technostress and the reference librarian," *Reference Services Review*, (20:2),pp.7-50.

Lazarus, R.S., 1966. Psychological stress and the coping process.

Ragu-Nathan, T. S., Tarafdar, M., Ragu-Nathan, B. S., & Qiang, T., 2008. "The Consequences of Technostress for End Users in Organizations: Conceptual Development and Empirical Validation," *Information Systems Research*, (19:4), 417-433.

Salanova, M., Llorens, S., Cifre, E., & Nogareda, C., 2007. El tecnoestre´s: Concepto, medida y prevencio´n [Technostress: Concept, measurement and prevention]. Nota Te´ cnica de Prevencio´ n, 730. Madrid, Spain: INSHT.

Shu, Q., Tu, Q. and Wang, K., 2011. "The impact of computer self-efficacy and technology dependence on computer-related technostress: A social cognitive theory perspective," *International Journal of Human-Computer Interaction*, (27:10), pp.923-939.

Tarafdar, M., Tu, Q., Ragu-Nathan, B. S., & Ragu-Nathan, T. S., 2007. "The impact of technostress on role stress and productivity," *Journal of Management Information Systems*, (24:1), pp. 301-328.

Van Fleet, C. and Wallace, D.P., 2001. "Virtual Libraries-Real Stress: Change at the Reference Desk," *Advances in Library Administration and Organization*, (18:6).

Walz, K., 2012. "Stress Related Issues Due to Too Much Technology: Effects on Working Professionals" (2012).*MBA Student Scholarship*. Paper 12. http://scholarsarchive.jwu.edu/mba_student/12 accessed [2 march 2016]

Wang, K., Shu, Q., & Tu, Q., 2008. "Technostress under different organizational environments: An empirical investigation," *Computers in Human Behavior*, (24:6) pp. 3002–3013.

Wolever R. Q., Bobinet K. J., McCabe K., Mackenzie E. R., Fekete E., Kusnick C.A., & Baime M. 2012. "Effective and viable mind-body stress reduction in the workplace: a randomized controlled trial," Journal of Occupational Health Psychology. (17:2) pp 246-258.

DECISION SCIENCES INSTITUTE
The Role of Marketing in Reverse Supply Chain

(Full Paper Submission)

Shad Dowlatshahi, Ph.D.
Professor of Operations and Supply Chain
Management (OSCM) and SCM Area Coordinator
Department of Marketing and SCM
Henry W. Bloch School of Management
The University of Missouri-Kansas City
5110 Cherry Street
Kansas City, MO 64110-2499, USA
Phone: (816) 235-2233
Fax: (816) 235-6506
E-mail: shad@umkc.edu

ABSTRACT

The literature review shows that the important interface between reverse logistics and marketing is not properly considered. By using inductive qualitative methodology, this interface is accomplished based on the use of 14 real-life case studies from various industries.

KEYWORDS: Product recovery; Marketing; Reverse supply chain; Case studies; and Marketing-product recovery strategies

DECISION SCIENCES INSTITUTE

Towards a process framework for sub-supplier sustainability management

Joerg S. Hofstetter
University of St.Gallen
Email: joerg.hofstetter@unisg.ch

ABSTRACT

Literature increasingly argues that buying organizations are responsible for the social and environmental practices of organizations further upstream in their supply chain: sub-suppliers, determined by their organizational distance. In such settings, selecting or knowing sub-suppliers, monitoring their performance and influencing them requires different processes versus dealing with direct suppliers. This paper suggests a set of business processes; serving as the basis for future research in managing sub-suppliers.

KEYWORDS: Sub-supplier, sustainable supply chain, supplier management

INTRODUCTION

With continuing outsourcing of value creation to suppliers in many tier levels in the supply chain, an increasing number of sub-suppliers on sub-tier levels contribute important value adding steps to finished goods. This paper follows Grimm et al. (2016), defining sub-suppliers as all indirect upstream suppliers, including traders and service providers but also sub-contractors within the visible horizon (Carter et al., 2015). In essence: sub-suppliers are the suppliers' suppliers, the suppliers' suppliers' suppliers, and so forth. The determining factors for a sub-supplier are contribution of value added in the supply chain, absence of a contractual relationship of the buyer with the sub-supplier, and existence of a direct supplier as a middleman between the buyer and the sub-supplier. The literature also refers to sub-suppliers as upstream suppliers or tier 2 or tier n level suppliers.

Sub-suppliers cause various challenges to buyers' sustainability compliance as buying companies are publicly accused for social and environmental irresponsible practices in their supply chains (Hartmann & Möller, 2015). Chinese supply into the food chain has caused multiple recalls in 2007 (Roth et al., 2008). After the collapse of the Rana Plaza building near Dhaka, Bangladesh on April 24, 2013, most fashion brands and retailers were unable to ensure that none of their garments was produced in one of the affected factories, acting as sub-suppliers in their supply chain (Lund-Thomsen and Lindgreen, 2014).

The scarcity of literature on sub-supplier management (Grimm et al., 2014; Grimm et al., 2016) and the predominantly reactive practices of buying companies to problems caused by sub-suppliers once occurred suggest a limited degree of professionalization of sub-supplier management. Choi and Linton (2011) argued that relying predominantly on direct suppliers, setting the visible horizon to the first tier level, does not adequately account for the risks and opportunities on sub-tier levels.

This paper takes up the conversation arguing that supply chains are in fact supply networks (Mena et al., 2013) and depend on the performance of the various suppliers and sub-suppliers

(Yan et al., 2015). It first describes the characteristics of sub-suppliers versus suppliers and defines sub-supplier management. Based on empirical work, the paper proposes various constellations for buyer/supplier/sub-supplier-relationships, a sub-supplier management framework and sub-supplier management processes, applying the vast literature on supplier management processes to the context of sub-supplier management. Finally, it discusses implications and derives research questions.

CHARACTERISTICS OF SUB-SUPPLIERS

While both suppliers and sub-suppliers, as members of the same supply chain at different tier levels, contribute value-added to the final product or service, the key differentiating factors are the absence of a contractual relationship between the buyer and the sub-supplier as well as the existence of a direct supplier acting as a middleman between the buyer and the sub-supplier (Grimm et al., 2016). Because of this indirect relationship, sub-suppliers often find themselves outside of the buying company's visible horizon (Carter et al., 2015).

The indirect relationship between a buying company and a sub-supplier creates larger distance compared to direct supplier relationships. While buyers may have a history of collaboration with their direct suppliers, providing mutual experience with expectations, decision-making and behavior, their experience with sub-suppliers is often limited to exceptional events like supply disruptions or quality problems. Buying companies know the identity, the location and cultural background of a supplier, yet they usually know little about sub-suppliers as these are often not disclosed by suppliers. On the other hand, sub-suppliers too are little aware of the buyer and its contractual requirements to the supplier (Homburg et al., 2014). Regulation and industry practices limit the degrees of freedom in direct supplier relationships, but hardly cover buyer / supplier / sub-supplier triads.

Power and dependence matter in both buyer / supplier and buyer / sub-supplier relationships (Cox, 2001). While the assessment of power and dependence benefits from transparency about business volumes, sunk cost or specific resources (Pfeffer, & Salancik, 1978), each additional intermediary between a buyer and a sub-supplier makes it more difficult to identify the direct business impact on one another. Still, buyers can be highly dependent on distant sub-suppliers (Yan et al., 2015).

SUB-SUPPLIER MANAGEMENT

Sub-supplier management shall be understood in this paper as the organization and coordination of a buyer's activities to achieve sub-supplier fulfillment of the buyer requirements. This approach recommends buyers to first evaluate the necessity of accessing sub-suppliers and to act accordingly. Buyers might decide any possible form in between not intervening in the supply chain beyond the first tier level at all (leaving governance to the power of the market) to substituting sub-suppliers with own operations.

The literature covers a range of different practices in handling challenges caused by sub-suppliers. These practices are discussed in the context of preventing or solving specific challenges and focus on the buyer. Among the most prominent in operations and supply chain management are buyer strategies to reduce the bullwhip effect (Lee et al., 1997). Researchers deployed multi-echelon inventory models to derive strategies for demand signaling and ordering policies. (Cantor & Katok, 2012). In finance, the hedging of fluctuations of raw material price, currency exchange rate, or labor cost on sub-supplier levels receives continuous attention. Quality management looked at transferring material specifications to sub-suppliers. In supply chain management, scholars have proposed various mapping approaches for supply chains (Ferries, 2009). In sustainability research, a few papers investigate explicitly how buyers influence sub-suppliers, e.g. buyers' sub-supplier management practices to ensure sub-supplier compliance with buyers' corporate sustainability standards (Grimm et al., 2014; 2016), or buyers' capabilities to set up voluntary sustainability initiatives engaging both suppliers and sub-suppliers (Peters et al., 2011.

RESEARCH APPROACH AND CASES

This paper combines analysis of the literature with a field study to derive a grounded process framework for sub-supplier management (Homburg et al., 2014; Eisenhardt, 1989). The research process was started with a definition of the phenomena investigated and followed up by a literature review. This resulted in a first draft for a process framework. A field study was used to explore business practices and experiences. The results of the field study were compared with the draft of the process framework and the literature on the different supplier management and sub-supplier management processes to finalize the process framework presented in the paper.

BUYER / SUPPLIER / SUB-SUPPLIER RELATIONSHIP CONSTELLATIONS

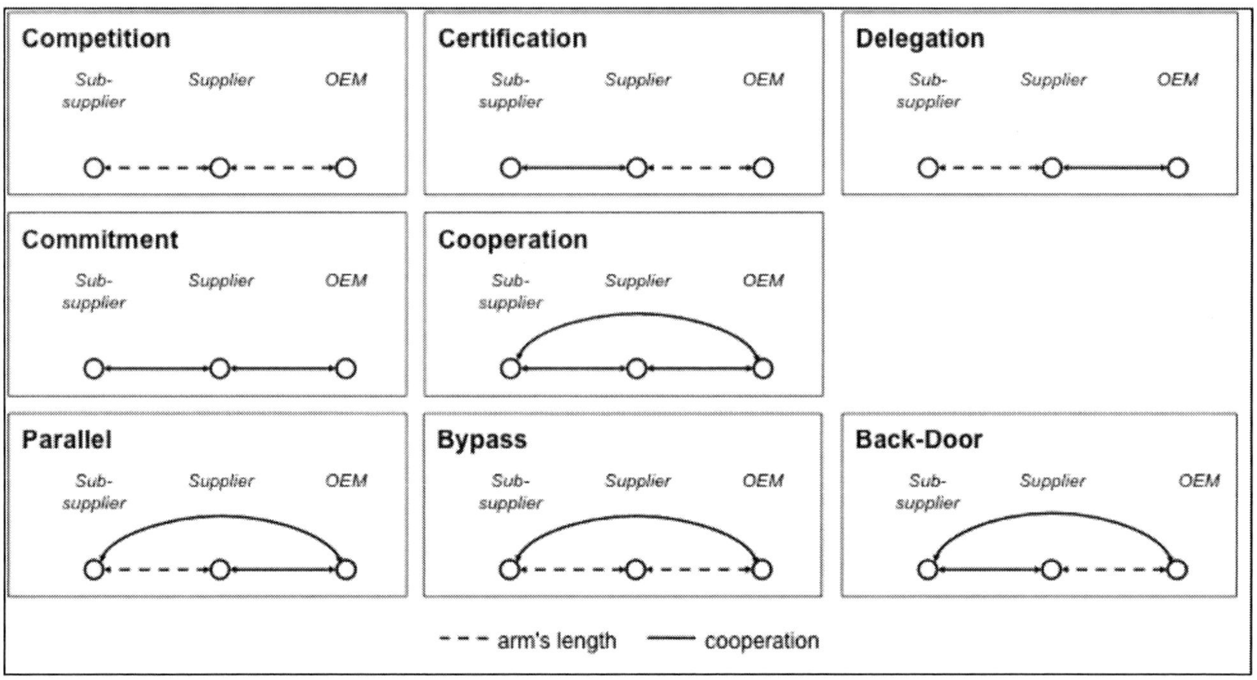

Figure 1: Buyer / supplier / sub-supplier relationship constellations

Collaboration between a buyer and a sub-supplier can take place in different relationship constellations, considering that the buyer or the sub-supplier may collaborate differently with the intermediating supplier. Thus in its most simple form of a chain consisting of the buyer, the (intermediating) supplier and this supplier's supplier, sub-supplier management needs to consider three relationships: the relationship between the buyer and the sub-supplier, the relationship between the buyer and the intermediating supplier, and the relationship between the intermediating supplier and the sub-supplier. The relationships between the buyer and the supplier or between the supplier and the sub-supplier are always direct relationships and may in their extreme form be either arm's length or cooperative, addressing the buyer requirements through open market bargaining or joint resolution (Landeros & Monczka, 1989). The relationship between the buyer and the sub-supplier may either be indirect, with no direct relationship existing at all, or direct and collaborative as there is no sense in establishing a direct relationship for open market bargaining. The eight different constellations for buyer/sub-supplier collaboration are illustrated in figure 1.

SUB-SUPPLIER MANAGEMENT FRAMEWORK

To manage sub-suppliers, buyers have four main options. Each option is associated with specific buyer/sub-supplier relationship constellations. Buyers can manage a sub-supplier (a) jointly with the intermediating supplier, (b) directly without the intermediating supplier, (c) by influencing the sub-supplier's institutional field, or (d) by delegating the full responsibility to the intermediating supplier (figure 2).

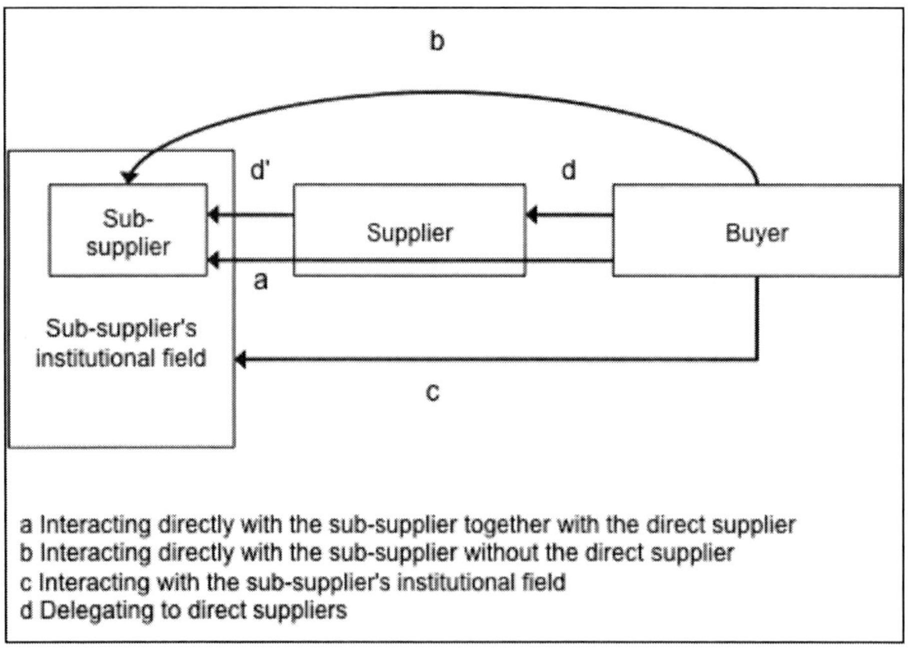

Figure 2: Sub-supplier management framework

Managing the sub-supplier directly together with the direct supplier: The buyer takes the maximum effort to actively engage both with the sub-supplier as well as with the intermediating supplier to develop and implement solutions that are best suited to all concerned members of the chain. This effort intensive approach allows creating win-win-win situations to motivate the concerned organizations to implement the solution and ensures long-term commitment to it. By ensuring the intermediating supplier invests into the sub-supplier, the buyer can safeguard own sub-supplier specific investments. With sub-suppliers delivering directly the intermediating suppliers, fit between the solutions adopted at each partner has high performance impact. Yet, the buyer has limited control over the collaboration between the supplier and the sub-supplier. This approach matches with the constellations cooperation and parallel.

Managing the sub-supplier directly without the intermediate direct supplier: The buyer takes the major effort to actively engage with the sub-supplier. Not including the intermediating supplier increases the danger that the solution developed and implemented with the sub-supplier decreases the supplier's performance or requires changes the supplier objects to implement. This approach of a buyer interacting directly with the supplier of a supplier is likely interpreted by the supplier as hostile act. The higher risk to loosing sub-supplier specific investments by excluding the intermediating supplier requires other safeguards such as the possibility to substitute the supplier without loosing the sub-supplier or a powerful sub-supplier with power over the intermediating supplier. This approach matches with the constellations bypass and back-door.

Influencing the sub-supplier's institutional field: Instead of direct interaction with the sub-supplier, the buyer actively engages in building up institutional pressures driving the sub-supplier to eventually align with the buyer's objectives. Such institutional entrepreneurship approaches (Battilana et al., 2009; Peters et al., 2011) manifest in dedicated organizations such as voluntary sustainability initiatives or in activities such as political lobbying or forming alliances with other stakeholders. That way the buyer does not invest into the sub-supplier but into long-term pressures that motivate the sub-supplier to develop and maintain a desired new practice. Thus, this approach does not match particularly with one of the constellations.

Delegating the management of the sub-supplier to intermediate direct supplier: Instead of directly interacting with the sub-supplier or its institutional field, buyers delegate the sub-supplier management to the intermediating supplier. Traditionally, active management of sub-suppliers (as described above) is treated as an exception, relying solely on market mechanisms and suppliers' own abilities to maintain a solid supply base. This approach matches with the constellations competition, hope, certification, and delegation.

In addition to these four main approaches aiming at changing the behavior of the sub-supplier, more radical approaches to improving the supply chain (from the buyer's perspective) require the buyer to extend own operations upstream into the supply chain. The most radical approach is the insourcing of activities currently performed by the respective supplier or sub-supplier. Instead of integrating the entire part of the chain, buyers may establish a fully controlled competitor to the respective sub-supplier or a fully controlled organization that acts as powerful direct supplier or customer to the sub-supplier. Following Tachizawa and Wong (2014), buyers may fully outsource sub-supplier management activities, conduct them internally, or use a mix of both. For auditing and corrective action it seems common practice that buyers require their suppliers and sub-suppliers to cover the cost by themselves (Hofstetter & Müller, 2014).

SUB-SUPPLIER MANAGEMENT PROCESSES

The literature covers a wide range of supplier management processes, yet only few sub-supplier management processes. Most supplier management processes can be extended to also cover sub-suppliers. Yet, sub-supplier management requires also particular processes. Moeller and colleagues (2006) proposed a structure for supplier management that offers a suitable application for the sub-supplier management context. They differentiate between "out-supplier management", defined as all processes with companies that are not supplying the buyer, "in-supplier management", defined as all processes with contracted suppliers, and "in-supplier dissolution management", defined as all processes with contracted suppliers to end the collaboration. Applied to sub-suppliers, the processes change or evolve as described below. (figure 3).

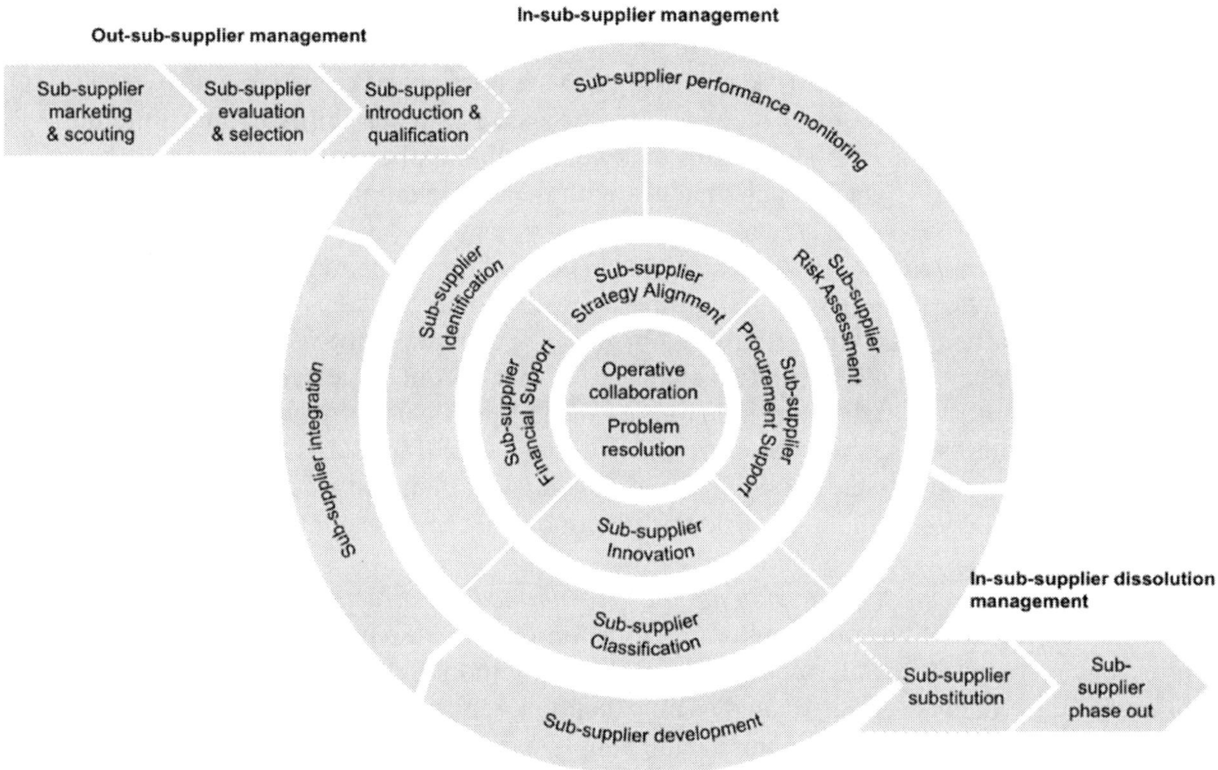

Figure 3: Sub-supplier management processes framework

In-Sub-Supplier Management

In-sub-supplier management refers to all processes that enable the buyer to exert control over existing sub-suppliers. In-sub-supplier management refers to five categories: Sub-supplier relationship management, internal in-sub-supplier management, sub-supplier mutual dependence management, sub-supplier operative collaboration and sub-supplier problem resolution.

In-Sub-Supplier Relationship Management

Sub-supplier relationship management extends the supplier management framework to sub-suppliers, including sub-supplier performance monitoring, development and integration.

Sub-Supplier Performance Monitoring is the process of specifying performance criteria and the measure, collecting performance data from the sub-supplier, comparing actual performance with performance targets, and evaluating identified deviations (Talluri & Sarkis, 2002).

Sub-Supplier Development is the process starting with addressing identified performance gaps with the sub-supplier to establishing lasting changes in sub-supplier practices that enable the sub-supplier to achieve the targeted performance (Krause et al., 2007).

Sub-Supplier Integration is the process of aligning responsibilities, structures and governance between the buyer, the sub-supplier and the intermediate supplier (Flynn et al., 2010).

Internal In-Sub-Supplier Management

Internal in-sub-supplier management processes enable the buyer to manage sub-suppliers. These processes require no interaction with the sub-supplier. They consist of sub-supplier identification, risk assessment, and classification.

Sub-Supplier Identification is the process of identifying the usual supply chains for procured material, defining what makes a supply chain path and a sub-supplier relevant, prioritizing the relevant supply chain paths, investigating the industries involved in these paths, identifying the identity of relevant sub-suppliers, and documenting these relevant sub-supplier, including master data management.

Sub-Supplier Risk Assessment is the process of gathering, analyzing and evaluating data for the identified relevant sub-suppliers and the industries they are part of on the risks they impose on the intermediate supplier, on the buyer and on the entire supply chain (Foerstl et al., 2010).

Sub-Supplier Classification is the process of structuring the large number of sub-suppliers by different criteria on sub-supplier criticality.

In-Sub-Supplier Dependence Management

In-sub-supplier dependence management refers to decisions that establish mutual dependence between the buyer and the sub-supplier, comprising of sub-supplier strategy alignment, innovation, financial support and procurement support.

Sub-Supplier Strategy Alignment is the process of mutually informing about corporate strategy elements and resulting adjustments to the strategy for one another.

Sub-Supplier Innovation refer to the processes of joint research and product development, of spotting or being informed by sub-suppliers about their innovations, and endorsing R&D.

Sub-Supplier Financial Support is the process of supporting a sub-supplier in getting access to investments or financial service at favorable cost.

Sub-Supplier Procurement Support is the process of supporting a sub-supplier in getting better access to material, services or supply conditions.

In-Sub-Supplier Operative Collaboration
In-sub-supplier operative collaboration covers the range of activities on operational level between a buyer, a sub-supplier and the intermediate supplier.

In-Sub-Supplier Problem Resolution
In-sub-supplier problem resolution refers to the processes applied to prevent, resolve, recover and learn from problems relating to availability, price (or cost), quality, counterfeits, legal compliance, environmental issues, social issues, or innovation.

Out-Sub-Supplier Management
Out-sub-supplier management refers to all processes from identifying new sub-suppliers that enable the value creation targeted by the buyer to making them ready for commercial transactions when becoming part of the buyer's supply chain.

Sub-Supplier Marketing and Scouting is the process of attracting companies that are not part of the buyer's supply chain to become part of it as in-sub-suppliers, offering their products or service to the buyer's supplier, and of searching and identifying companies that are not part of the buyer's supply chain and that have great potential to supply products or services to intermediate suppliers fulfilling the buyer's requirements better than the current ones.

Sub-Supplier Evaluation and Selection is the process of collecting reliable information about a potential sub-supplier on multiple criteria defined by the buyer and the decision on how well this company fulfills the requirements, and of prioritizing the investigated out-sub-suppliers upon the evaluation results and the decision on the out-sub-supplier(s) the buyer wants to introduce as new direct suppliers to intermediate suppliers (Chai et al., 2013).

Sub-Supplier Introduction and Qualification is the process starting from suggesting a buyer-selected out-sub-supplier as a new direct supplier to intermediate suppliers to the final decision of an intermediate supplier to contract this sub-supplier (Koh et al., 2012) and of developing the sub-supplier to adopt specified practices and structures and to reliably achieve required performance levels, potentially including qualification screenings, to fit into the operations of the intermediate supplier and buyer's supply chain (Wan et al., 2012).

In-Sub-Supplier Dissolution Management
In-sub-supplier dissolution management refers to the processes for substituting an in-sub-supplier with an alternative sub-supplier and for phasing out this sub-supplier.

Sub-Supplier Switch is the process of replacing an in-sub-supplier currently supplying to an intermediate supplier either by increasing the supply volume of other in-sub-suppliers in a multiple sourcing context or by introducing a new out-supplier (Wagner & Friedl, 2007).

Sub-Supplier Phase-Out is the process of eliminating a sub-supplier from the buyer's supply chain by ending the supply contract.

DISCUSSION AND CONCLUSIONS

Supplier management has received substantial attention in the literature. Supplier management processes have been analyzed on effectiveness and their contingencies. The rather recent extension of buyer attention beyond the direct supplier level to sub-suppliers in multi-tier supply chains calls for an evaluation of these processes in the new context. The indirect relationship between the buyer and the sub-supplier that is mediated by a supplier implies higher distance, different power structures and less degrees of freedom. The definitions and structure suggested by this paper shall provide a framework to investigate sub-supplier management in more detail while still keeping the different sub-supplier management elements in the context of a comprehensive concept.

REFERENCES

Battilana, J., Leca, B., & Boxenbaum, E. (2009). How actors change institutions: towards a theory of institutional entrepreneurship. *Academy of Management Annals*, 3(1), 65-107.

Carter, C. R., Rogers, D. S., & Choi, T. Y. (2015). Toward the Theory of the Supply Chain. *Journal of Supply Chain Management*, 51(2), 89-97.

Chai, J., Liu, J. N., & Ngai, E. W. (2013). Application of decision-making techniques in supplier selection: A systematic review of literature. *Expert Systems with Applications*, 40(10), 3872-3885.

Cox, A. (2001). Understanding buyer and supplier power: a framework for procurement and supply competence. *Journal of Supply Chain Management*, 37(1), 8-15.

Flynn, B. B., Huo, B., & Zhao, X. (2010). The impact of supply chain integration on performance: a contingency and configuration approach. *Journal of Operations Management*, 28(1), 58-71.

Grimm, J. H., Hofstetter, J. S., & Sarkis, J. (2016). Exploring sub-suppliers' compliance with corporate sustainability standards. *Journal of Cleaner Production*, 112, 1971-1984.

Grimm, J. H., Hofstetter, J. S., & Sarkis, J. (2014). Critical factors for sub-supplier management: A sustainable food supply chains perspective. *International Journal of Production Economics*, Vol. 152, 159-173.

Hofstetter, J. S. & Müller, M. (2014). *10 Years of the BSCI - Achievement Study*, Brussels

Homburg, C., Wilczek, H. & Hahn, A. (2014). Looking beyond the horizon: How to approach the customers' customers in business-to-business markets. *Journal of Marketing*, 78 (9), 58-77.

Koh, S. C. L., Gunasekaran, A., & Tseng, C. S. (2012). Cross-tier ripple and indirect effects of directives WEEE and RoHS on greening a supply chain. *International Journal of Production Economics*, 140(1), 305-317.

Krause, D. R., Handfield, R. B., & Tyler, B. B. (2007). The relationships between supplier development, commitment, social capital accumulation and performance improvement. *Journal of Operations Management*, 25(2), 528-545.

Landeros, R., & Monczka, R. M. (1989). Cooperative Buyer/Seller Relationships and a Firm's Competitive Posture. *Journal of Purchasing and Supply Management*, 25(3), 9-18.

Lee, H., Padmanabhan, V., & Whang, S., (1997). Information distortion in a supply chain: the bullwhip effect. *Management Science*, 43 (4), 546–558.

Lund-Thomsen, P., & Lindgreen, A. (2014). Corporate social responsibility in global value chains: where are we now and where are we going?. *Journal of Business Ethics*, 123(1), 11-22.

Mena, C., Humphries, A., & Choi, T. Y. (2013). Toward a Theory of Multi-Tier Supply Chain Management. Journal of Supply Chain Management, 49(2), 58-77.

Moeller, S., Fassnacht, M., & Klose, S. (2006). A framework for supplier relationship management (SRM). *Journal of Business-to-Business Marketing*, 13(4), 69-94.

Peters, N. J., Hofstetter, J. S., & Hoffmann, V. H. (2011). Institutional entrepreneurship capabilities for interorganizational sustainable supply chain strategies. *The International Journal of Logistics Management*, 22(1), 52-86.

Pfeffer, J., & Salancik, G. R. (1978). The external control of organizations: A resource dependence approach. NY: Harper and Row Publishers.

Roth, A. V., Tsay, A. A., Pullman, M. E. & Gray, J. V. (2008). Unraveling the food supply chain: Strategic insights from China and the 2007 recalls. *Journal of Supply Chain Management*, 44(1), 22-39.

Tachizawa, E. M., & Wong, C. Y. (2014). Towards a theory of multi-tier sustainable supply chains: a systematic literature review. *Supply Chain Management: An International Journal*, 19(5/6), 643-663.

Talluri, S., & Sarkis, J. (2002). A model for performance monitoring of suppliers. *International Journal of Production Research*, 40(16), 4257-4269.

Wagner, S. M., & Friedl, G. (2007). Supplier switching decisions. *European Journal of Operational Research*, 183(2), 700-717.

Yan, T., Choi, T. Y., Kim, Y., & Yang, Y. (2015). A theory of the nexus supplier: A critical supplier from a network perspective. *Journal of Supply Chain Management*, 51(1), 52-66.

(The current version of this work in progress is available from the author.)

DECISION SCIENCES INSTITUTE
Towards a Theory of Dynamic Information Security Behaviors

Canchu Lin
Carroll University
Email: clin@carrollu.edu

Anand Kunnathur
University of Toledo
Email: Anand.Kunnathur@utoledo.edu

ABSTRACT

As a theory paper, this study builds a framework that draws on the conceptual gist of organizational sensemaking to show the dynamic nature of information security behavior. It then situates the development of such dynamic information security behaviors in the context of organizational culture and proposes how organizational culture shapes these behaviors.

KEYWORDS: Dynamic information security behavior, Sensemaking, Organizational culture, Information security diagnosing behavior, Information security solving behavior, and Information security performing behavior

INTRODUCTION

A large number of information security incidents that incurred huge financial losses are reportedly due to ignorance, errors, and even deliberate computer abuse behaviors of employees in organizations (Lee & Lee, 2002; Lee et al., 2004; Willison & Warkentin, 2013). Sharing this concern, empirical research has mostly explored individual factors that lead to information security behaviors (ISB) (e.g., see Anderson & Agarwal, 2010; Banerjee, Cronan, & Jones, 1998; Bulgurcu, Cavusoglu, & Benbasat, 2010; Chatterjee, Sarker, & Valacich, 2015; D'Arcy & Herath, 2011; Lee & Kozar, 2005; Vance, Siponen, & Pahnila, 2012; Wright & Marett, 2010). Although ISBs are performed by individual employees, they occur in an organizational setting and therefore take on an organizational identity. Both the materiality and sociality of the organizational context determine individual employees' ISBs and their development patterns. Yet, despite the critical role of the organizational context, a theoretical lens that informs and enables analysis of individual ISBs from an organizational perspective is seriously missing in past and current research.

To fill this research gap, this study attempts to articulate a theory of dynamic information security behaviors (TDISB). Enlightened by the dynamic capabilities perspective (Teece, Pisano, & Shuen, 1997), the TDISB asserts that as tasks, information needs, and technology use in organizations change over time, organizations must develop dynamic capabilities to address the implications on information security that these changes generate. Such dynamic capabilities are mostly performed in their employees' behaviors regarding information security. Thus, viewed from this perspective, ISBs are dynamic in nature. As information security concerns stem from adoption, implementation, and use of technology, which triggers sensemaking (Griffith, 1999), ISBs can be perceived as outcomes of sensemaking. Thus, the TDISB maintains that sensemaking about information security at different phases predicts that different ISBs are required at these different phases of technology use.

Addressing information security in organizations is similar to action-oriented problem solving in some "high-velocity" or "high-hazard", and "high-reliability" situations such as firefighting, manufacturing or computer programming troubleshooting, (Carroll, Rudolph, & Hatakenaka, 2002; Eisenhardt, 1989; Klein, Pliske, Crandall, & Woods, 2005; Repenning & Sterman, 2002; Weick, 1987; 1993), whose characteristics have been examined and well explained from the sensemaking perspective (Rudolph, Morrison, & Carroll, 2009; Weick, 1987). But little has been known about information security sensemaking.

Further, drawing on the research literature of organizational culture, the TDISB explicates how these dynamic ISBs are shaped by organizational culture. The benefit of applying the sensemaking perspective to the study of ISBs stems from its particular strength in analyzing individual behaviors by examining both individual cognition and organizational dynamics. At the individual level, sensemaking involves cognition, which is greatly shaped by organizational culture (Harris, 1994). In this sense, ISBs can be perceived as a site where sensemaking interacts with organizational culture as reinforcing forces. Thus, examining both sensemaking and organizational culture simultaneously holds promise for a deep understanding of the development of ISBs. The importance of organizational culture to the development of ISBs has been highlighted in previous research (e.g., see Da Veiga & Eloff, 2010; Kraemer & Carayon, 2005; Ruighaver, Maynard, & Chang, 2007; Van Niekerk & Von Solms, 2010). Further, organizational culture was sporadically examined as a factor influencing information security policy compliance (e.g., see Hu, Dinev, Hart, & Cooke, 2012). But there has been no theoretical attempt for integrating sensemaking and organizational culture to guide the investigation of ISBs. This study aims to articulate this new approach comprehensively and further develops it as a theoretical framework that constitutes TDISB.

While fulfilling this goal, this study attempts to make the following contributions. First, this study will extend and enhance our understanding of ISBs by conceptualizing some new categories of ISBs. Past research, relying on the deterrence theory, which originated in criminology, mostly focused on exploring negative ISBs and their drivers. Consequently, few ISBs especially positive ones were identified (Posey, Roberts, Lowry, Bennett, & Courtney, 2013). Drawing on the perspective of organizational sensemaking (Weick, 1979, 1995), this study will develop a taxonomy of ISBs based on the characteristics of sensemaking in different phases. The newly developed taxonomy will constitute a rich repertoire of ISBs that represent a heightened and extended understanding of ISBs. Second, this study will provide further insight into the development of ISBs. Past research mostly examined some individual factors that contribute to the development of negative ISBs and information security policy compliance. By nesting sensemaking on information security within the context of organizational culture, this study offers a theoretical framework that helps to examine ISBs from an organizational perspective. Although there are individual differences in ISB, organizational-specific schema shaped by organizational culture would determine the basic character of sensemaking about information security in the workplace and thus common features of individual ISBs. Third, as past research overwhelmingly focused on negative ISBs, an undesirable outcome was that individual employees have not been perceived as being able to positively contribute to information security management in their organizations. In delineating the various ISBs included in the new taxonomy, this study will show that individual employees can be a solution to information security issues (Stanton & Stam, 2006). Thus, this study will help to transform the image of individual employees as possible computer abusers or information security culprit into one of beneficial contributors to information security management.

The rest of the paper is organized as follows. First, we will review the current literature on ISB to provide an overview of major theories used in this area of research and the major findings regarding ISBs. Such a brief review will help us to identify areas of improvement in this field of research and, more importantly, look for directions for future research. We will provide a rationale for why the TDISB that nests sensemaking within organizational culture can help to overcome the limitations of the theoretical approaches currently used in the empirical research. Next, in developing the TDISB, we will draw on Weick's (1979, 1995) theory of organizational sensemaking to analyze information security management in organizations as a process of sensemaking. Analysis of this process of sensemaking will lead to the development of a taxonomy of ISBs. Then, to further the development of TDISB, we will integrate the review of ISB research and a brief review of organizational culture in order to show how organizational culture serves as both a platform and an effective control mechanism for information security management in organizations. Following that, we will focus on showing how different cultures help to promote a variety of ISBs. Lastly, we will discuss contributions of our framework, its possible implications for organizational practice, and future research directions.

INFORMATION SECURITY BEHAVIOR

As employees are deemed as the weakest link in organizations' efforts in addressing information security (Warkentin &Willison, 2009), IS researchers have made efforts to gain a deep understanding of this issue. They examined possible factors that influence employees' ISB and searched for effective means to control ISB. A review of the ISB research literature shows that two major approaches have been developed to the study of ISB. As early studies on ISB mostly used the deterrence theory, the deterrence approach has substantially shaped the research landscape in this area. There are already two literature reviews of the deterrence research on ISB (D'Arcy & Herath, 2011; Siponen, Willison, & Baskerville, 2008). This is enough evidence of the research productivity and also popularity of the deterrence approach. Borrowing the theory from criminology, the deterrence approach researchers applied the concepts of certainty, severity, and celerity of sanctions against illicit behaviors (Gibbs, 1975) in their empirical research. Although behaviors such as misuse or abuse of IS resources were examined, the key concern of the empirical studies of this approach is compliance or noncompliance of organizational information security policies and their antecedents (D'Arcy & Herath, 2011).

Besides the deterrence theory, information security researchers have also utilized behavior theories to examine ISB. These behavior theories have helped us to understand individual employees' cognitive behaviors regarding information security from a social perspective. The approach that represents these empirical studies is hereby named as the social cognitive approach. The social cognitive approach mainly used the theories of ethical/moral behavior (e.g., Banerjee et al. 1998; Culnan & Williams, 2009; Harrington, 1996; Myyry, Siponen, Pahnila, Vartiainen, & Vance, 2009), rational choice (e.g., Bulgurcu et al, 2010; Li, Zhang, & Sarathy, 2010), reasoned action (e.g., Guo, Yuan, Archer, & Connelly, 2011), planned behavior (e.g., Bulgurce et al., 2010; Guo et al., 2011), protection motivation (Ng, Kankanhalli, & Xu, 2009; Herath & Rao, 2009a; Pahnila, Siponen, & Mahmood, 2007), and technology acceptance model (Johnston & Warkentin, 2010; Ng & Rahim, 2005). Similar to the deterrence studies, a large number of empirical studies taking the social cognitive approach treated information security policy compliance as the dependent variable receiving influence from antecedent variables. Such an approach is still popular in recent studies (see, for example, D'Arcy, Herath, & Shoss, 2014; Hu, West, & Smarandescu, 2015; Johnston, Warkentin, & Siponen, 2015, and Vance,

Lowry, & Eggett, 2015). Yet, regrettably, prior research taking those two approaches discovered few ISBs other than policy compliance. More ISBs are yet to be identified.

The social cognitive approach examined antecedents to ISB, including ethics/moral judgment, security-related perceptions (regarding security risk, severity, vulnerability, and susceptibility), coping perceptions (response efficacy, effectiveness and benefits), security-related attitudes and norms, information security awareness, and self-efficacy. These antecedents were examined as predictors of ISB, mostly information security policy compliance. Based on their definitions, these antecedents can be grouped into three categories: ethics and morality, perceptions and attitudes, and knowledge and skills. As a major antecedent, ethics influences an individual's perception of information risk or threat, which then determines his or her behavior toward the risk or threat such as adoption of anti-spyware software (Lee & Kozar, 2005). Similarly, employees with strong moral beliefs are found to be restrained from misuse or abuse behavior (D'Arcy & Herth, 2011). In addition to ethics and moral judgment, perceptions and attitudes are found to be important precursors to ISBs (see, for example, Anderson & Agarwal, 2010; Guo et al. 2011; Johnston & Warkentin, 2010; Ng et al., 2009). Information security related perceptions include those of security risk (see Guo et al., 2011; Wright & Marett, 2010; and Xu, Wang, & Teo, 2005), risk or threat severity, computer or information systems' vulnerability and susceptibility to risks and threats (LaRose, Rifon, & Enbody, 2008; Lee & Larsen, 2009; Ng et al., 2009; Workman, Bommer, & Straub, 2008), possible benefits of coping behavior such as response efficacy (Johnston & Warkentin, 2010; LaRose et al., 2008; Lee & Larsen, 2009; Woon, Tan, & Low, 2005), and security behavior effectiveness (Anderson & Agarwal, 2010; Culnan, Foxman, & Ray, 2008; Ng et al., 2009). These perceptions are positively related to attitude toward security-related behavior (Anderson & Agarwal, 2010), which then leads to security behavior (Guo et al, 2011; Lee & Kozar, 2005). Lastly, knowledge and skills provide employees confidence and expertise needed for positive ISB (Wright & Marett, 2010). Knowledge and skills include information security awareness, more specifically, awareness of risks or threats, and awareness of measures available for coping with risks and threats (Aytes & Connolly, 2004; Bulgurcu at al., 2010; Furnell, 2008; Hu, Hart, & Cooke, 2006; Whitman, 2004), and self-efficacy (Anderson & Agarwal, 2010; Bulgurcu at al., 2010; Lee & Kozar, 2005; Lee & Larsen, 2009; Ng et al., 2009; Woon et al., 2005; Wright & Marett, 2010).

To sum up, the deterrence approach and the social cognitive approach helped to advance our knowledge of negative ISBs and factors influencing information security policy compliance. However, limited progress was made in previous research using those two approaches in extending our understanding to multiple especially positive ISBs. To address this research gap, a different theoretical approach is needed. An ideal theoretical perspective is one that can provide insight into both negative and positive ISBs (Posey et al., 2013) and, more importantly, explain the underpinnings of those behaviors. We argue that the TDISB that integrates sensemaking and organizational culture to provide a systematic examination of ISBs is such an ideal perspective. Our rationale is provided next.

THEORY OF DYNAMIC INFORMATION SECURITY BEHAVIORS

The TDISB provides a new lens for us to examine ISBs by integrating the essentials of sensemaking and organizational culture. Information security management is similar to issues of crisis and safety management in that that they all involve coping with uncertainty and making decisions. Sensemaking and organizational culture have been demonstrably relevant to management of these high-reliability or high-hazard issues (e.g., see Weick, 1987, 1993). However, both have been overlooked in the literature of ISBs.

Sensemaking has been rarely addressed in this thread of literature. But for organizational culture, its role in shaping ISBs was slightly suggested in previous research. Indeed, previous research with the social cognitive approach sporadically showed the impact of organizational culture on the precursors of ISBs. But, organizational culture was mainly examined as one independent variable (in addition to others) (e.g., Bulgurcu et al. 2010; Guo et al. 2011; Herath & Rao, 2009b) or a contingency variable that moderates the relationship between the precursor variables and ISB (e.g., Dinev, Goo, Hu, & Nam, 2009; Hovav & D'Arcy, 2012). Examining organizational culture together with other antecedent factors only aimed to show how organizational culture may contribute to the development of ISB of individuals, but did not reveal any organizational pattern in ISBs. With that approach, our understanding of organizational-level ISBs is still lacking. As their focus was not on organizational culture, previous research did not show the full potential of organizational culture on cultivating and developing different ISBs. Additionally, previous research articulated a view that it is important to develop a specific information security culture in organizations to help to manage information security (see, e.g., Da Veiga & Eloff, 2010; Kraemer & Carayon, 2005; Ruighaver et al., 2007; van Niekerk & von Solms, 2010; Vroom & von Solms, 2004). This view was mostly prescriptive in that it offered culture as a solution to information security problems, but did not explain how culture can play that role. Besides, arguing for establishing an information security culture in organizations deviates from a widely shared view that culture is emergent and complicated, but not imposed (Detert, Schroeder, & Mauriel, 2000). To sum up, previous research, while rarely touched on sensemaking, because of its inadequate design and biased view toward organizational culture, showed us little evidence of organizational culture's role in shaping ISBs.

Yet, both sensemaking and organizational culture are highly relevant to ISBs. Sensemaking links cognition and action (Weick, 1979, 1995) and therefore can explain how individual employees perceive risks and threats to information security by interpreting informational cues and then act to cope with such risks and threats. Similarly, culture is an effective mechanism for behavior control (O'Reilly & Chatman, 1996; Ouchi, 1980; Ray, 1986; Schein, 1985). In this sense, the perspective of organizational culture holds promise for providing insightful explanations for how organizational culture shapes ISBs. Additionally, it can offer insight into the development of multiple such behaviors, as it holds that there is much multiplicity and diversity in organizational culture (Martin, 2002; Van Maanen & Barley, 1984). Overcoming the weaknesses of the deterrence theory and the social cognitive theories, the TDISB can potentially explain how different cultures cultivate and shape different ISBs. Before we show how sensemaking and organizational culture contribute to the development of ISBs, we deem it important to explain how sensemaking and organizational culture are linked together and interactively generate and shape different ISBs. In doing this, we show the gist of the TDISB.

The first main point of this TDISB is that organizational culture facilitates sensemaking, as "shared, relatively coherent interrelated sets of emotionally charged beliefs, values and norms that bind some people together and help them to make sense of their worlds" (Trice & Beyer, 1993, p. 33). Sensemaking refers to a gradual development of a loose agreement among organizational members about how to interpret an event and take action to address it (Orton, 2000). The event is new, unexpected, confusing, and involves a lot of uncertainties (Maitlis & Christianson, 2014). It requires organizational members to use systematic rules to make judgement about causal relationships (Einhorn & Hogarth, 1986). When coping with an event, different organizational members scan different cues of the event, display different beliefs in making judgement, and prefer different actions. Yet over time, these fragmentations among the individual employees are transformed into an organizational consensus, which Weick (1979) termed as “workable version of reality”, which serves as the basis of decision making by organizational members. The final decision culminates the organizational sensemaking process regarding the treatment of that event. The transformational process of integrating individual differences into an organizational agreement and then decision choice is made possible by organizational culture. Organizational culture serves as a “dominant perceptual filter that shapes and biases sensemaking” (Abolafia, 2010, p. 357). When articulating, discussing, and then evaluating various interpretations, preferences, and decision alternatives from individual employees, they draw on beliefs, norms, values, and rules that are supposedly sensible and binding to organizational members (Bowman & Hurry, 1993). Their organizational culture may well be the most readily available source that supplies them with such beliefs, norms, values, and rules. Cultural values such as individualism, hierarchy, egalitarianism, and fatalism provide framing assumptions that influence sensemaking (Malsch, Tremblay, & Gendron, 2012).

Second, the TDISB maintains that organizational culture constitutes a social context for sensemaking. As a macro context or institutional factor, organizational culture serves as three mechanisms – priming (source of social cues), editing (accomplished through social feedback), and triggering (ambiguity and confusion inherent in organizational culture causing interpretations), through which substance of organizational culture such as beliefs, norms, values, and rules is woven into sensemaking (Weber & Glynn, 2006). Further, organizational culture provides the cultural identity for sensemaking by individual employees, which makes their sensemaking as organizational not just individual (Weber & Glynn, 2006). Examples of interactions of sensemaking and organizational culture are already supplied in the literature. For example, the ‘mechanism’ role of institution (culture) enables sensemaking in the context of interorganizational relationships (Vlaar, Van den Bosch, & Volberda, 2006). Similarly, culture’s interaction with sensemaking also occurs in the organizational process of constructing and negotiating compensation policies (Malsch et al., 2012). In the context of ISBs, we will show that sensemaking and organizational culture interact in such a way that sensemaking helps to develop ISBs and then organizational culture facilitates and shapes the development of ISBs by influencing sensemaking.

ORGANIZATIONAL SENSEMAKING AND INFORMATION SECURITY BEHAVIORS

In developing the TDISB, we argue that information security management in organizations is a sensemaking process. Managing information security involves interpretation and choice, a process of sensemaking and decision making, just as many other action-oriented problem solving situations (Rudolph, Morrison, & Carroll, 2009). Technology triggers sensemaking (Griffith, 1999). Organizational members’ social interactions impact how they interact with IT (Agarwal and Prasad, 1998; Moore & Benbasat, 1991; Vaast & Walsham, 2005; Walsham, 1998), leading to social constructions of information security emanated from IT. When a new technology or practice is introduced in an organization, it will trigger much uncertainty, or in Weick’s (1979) term, equivocality. This uncertainty includes unsureness about information security associated with the new technology or practice. What ensues uncertainty or equivocality is sensemaking by organizational members (Weick, 1979; 1995). Organizational members are expected to exhibit multiple behaviors in their information security sensemaking process. Thus, examining this particular sensemaking process helps to reveal possible behaviors of managing information security by organizational members.

Sensemaking is a sequential process and consists of three activities: scanning, interpreting, and responding (Daft & Weick, 1984; Thomas, Clark, & Gioia, 1993). Scanning is about information gathering (Thomas et al., 1993). In this phase of sensemaking, organizational members seek informational cues from their environment to reduce the amount and complexity of information and notice different aspects of a situation such as technology adoption and use. Interpreting refers to the act of making meaning out of ambiguous cues (Porac & Thomas, 2002). In the interpreting phase, organizational members perceive certain issues as relevant or irrelevant to the situation (Barr & Huff, 1997). Lastly, responding is the action based on the interpreting outcomes (Hahn, Preuss, Pinkse, & Figge, 2015). In the responding phase, organizational members seek solutions to address the situation. Although scanning and interpreting are two distinct phases, both involve cognition. In the context of managing information security, organizational members in these two phases of sensemaking tend to behave in a similar manner, i.e., seeking information and making meaning out of it. So, these two phases can be treated as one of perception and understanding. Unlike perception, responding is real action. In the responding phase, managing information security actually involves seeking solutions for information security problems such as risks and threats. From this perspective, we argue that managing information security behaviors in the two phases of scanning and interpreting is similar but very distinct in the phase of responding. As an extension of the sequential view of sensemaking, enactment is regarded as what follows sensemaking (Weick, 1977, 1995). In the enactment phase, organizational members execute their sensemaking outcomes such as decisions. Below, to develop the TDISB, we elaborate three types of ISBs developed in the phases of scanning and interpreting, responding, and enactment.

Information Security Diagnosing Behavior

As technology is equivocal (Weick, 1990), among others, information security implications of technology can trigger intense sensemaking among internal employees. According to Weick (1995), sensemaking is also noticing, gathering facts and opinions. Sensemaking involves individuals' reactions to what they notice in their environment. When involved in technology sensemaking, in the phases of scanning and interpreting, organizational members gather various kinds of information about the technology and its possible impacts from their peers and other social contacts (Fulk, 1993; Gopal & Prasad, 2000). When a technology is just adopted, the uncertainty around it should also involve diverse concerns about information security it may generate. So, at the initial phase of technology implementation, organizational members' sensemaking about the technology may involve finding out the benefits as well as downsides of implementing the technology including possible loopholes in information security that this newly adopted technology may create to the organization. For example, cloud computing provides promises in storing and transferring huge amounts of data. When a technology company decides to adopt it, its employees would throw in numerous questions regarding information security. Specifically, they would identify and discover risks of data breach (Sen & Borle, 2015).

Further, the ongoing nature of organizational sensemaking suggests that employees' discoveries of potential information security issues inherent in the use of this same technology are continuous. They will discover other information security problems which will emerge at subsequent phases of using this same technology. For example, when companies adopted wireless systems, they kept exploring potential security issues and threats of this new adoption until wireless security reached to the level of wired security, but by that time, the wired world may have developed to a level where new security challenges occur, which require addressing different security needs (Katos & Adams, 2005). Similarly, as email is extensively used, large numbers of useless emails may block and slow down email communication. The email spam issue is therefore identified (Caliendo, Clement, Papies, & Scheel-Kopeinig, 2012).

More importantly, employees are motivated to *voice* their concerns and comments regarding information security when they realize that doing that ultimately helps their organization in addressing information security (Hsu, Shih, Hunng, & Lowry, 2015). Thus, to a large extent, internal employees often engage themselves in sensing about technology's possible risks, threats, as well as dangers to information security. Such behaviors aim at discovering potential information security issues and problems, and thus can then be categorized as information security ***diagnosing*** behaviors. ***Information security diagnosing behavior*** is hereby defined as an activity in which employees are engaged in finding out possible risks, dangers, and threats of a technology with regard to information security. One such diagnosing behavior is finding and reporting a potential information-security problem or loophole (Posey et al. 2013).

In line with the social nature of sensemaking, information security diagnosing behaviors pertain to various groups of employees. It may not always be the IT staff of a company that are engaged in such diagnosing behaviors. For example, in a healthcare organization, physicians, nurses, IT professionals, and other groups of employees perceived different information security issues about the same information systems (Vaast, 2007). As non-IT employees ultimately use a newly adopted technology to perform their work duties, they are more likely than IT staff to discover substantial and concrete issues and threats regarding information security.

Information Security Solving Behavior

Although organizational sensemaking is ongoing, it may take on different phases, thus triggering different actions or behaviors (Weick, 1995) toward information security. In the responding phase, organizational members mainly seek methods to solve problems (Hahn et al., 2015). This suggests that even though discovering information security issues and problems is continuous, at a time when such issues and problems have triggered enough organizational awareness, sensemaking may start to move from discovering problems, issues, risks, and threats that the new technology poses to generating solutions to them. For example, for an organization that has suffered from computer crashes caused by malware, the urgent need to stop such crashes may motivate employees to develop anti-malware software (Kim & Kim, 2015).

Accompanying the emerging information security concerns are efforts and motives to search for measures that address the information security concerns. Such measures can be technological as well as behavioral. While IT staff can take a leading role in developing technical measures to address information security concerns inherent in the adoption of a new technology, non-IT employees can make sense of how they can cope with these issues and problems behaviorally (Vaast, 2007). For example, in Vaast's (2007) study, IS professionals reported their continuous development of aggressive tools to detect virus and intrusions from outside, whereas non-IT employees learned to be more sensitive to inquiries about patients' personal information and develop a standard way to reject such inquiries. In the case of implementing cloud computing, while IT professionals may develop technical solutions such as enhancing their IT infrastructure's capability of speedily identifying and alerting about potential hacking activities, non-IT employees may brainstorm about secure ways of sharing sensitive information with their company's external stakeholders, and accumulate their successful experiences and promote them to more employees.

In sensemaking, human agents draw on not only local/organizational but also institutional rules and resources (Weber & Glynn, 2006). Institutions also function to contextualize sensemaking by imposing cognitive constraints on the actors in their sensemaking (Weber & Glynn, 2006;

Weick et al., 2005). To conform to institutional requirements, organizational members may engage themselves in information systems security innovations (Hsu et al., 2012). Besides their own experiences, employees may develop measures to safeguard company information through external learning, an important source of knowledge acquisition (March, 1991). For example, for a company dealing with wireless security issues, employees can turn to Wireless Location Industry Association for more resources, which has developed a set of self-regulation policies for dealing with security implications of wireless systems (Katos & Adams, 2005). Other external learning sites such as professional conferences sponsored and organized by professional organizations helped companies to develop procedures and policies to deal with information security (Hu et al., 2007). Employees' personal as well as professional external networks enable them to learn solutions developed elsewhere. Regardless of the sources, solutions to information security concerns are developed. Thus, behaviors engaged in seeking solutions can be defined as ***information security solving behaviors***. Further examples of such information security exploring behaviors include developing anti-virus software, standard steps in sending and receiving email attachments, and effective anti-phishing methods (Abbasi et al., 2015).

Information Security Performing Behaviors

Finally, the outcome of organizational sensemaking is characterized by the process of enactment (Weick 1995). In Weick's theory of sensemaking, sensemaking and organizing are interconnected and mutually enmeshed (Weick et al., 2005). After numerous communication cycles (Weick, 1979), organizational members will develop a sense about the new phenomenon toward which sensemaking is focused. That newly developed sense will then be saved as an organizational routine that will be used to guide future organizational action toward dealing with such a phenomenon. Weick (1979) named this process as enactment. In the case of sensemaking about information security, when information security issues, problems, and threats have been carefully examined, and reliable measures have been developed to address these issues, problems, and threats, such reliable measures would be saved as organizational procedures or standard practices to deal with information security. In many cases, these procedures and practices would be documented as organizational information security policies to guide action. During the enactment phase, individual behaviors expected from employees would be mostly to follow the prescribed practices and abide by organizational regulations and policies regarding information security. In this sense, ISBs are mostly performing in nature. Thus, such behaviors are defined as ***information security performing behaviors***, which are prescribed in information security policies. For example, once techniques are proposed and developed for ensuring safe and concurrent execution of database transactions (Croker, 1987), they would be covered in organizational information security policies. Employees would be trained to apply those techniques in their work.

TDISB - LINKING ORGANIZATIONAL SENSEMAKING ABOUT INFORMATION SECURITY TO ORGANIZATIONAL CULTURE

Weick's sensemaking theory is a general characterization of the process of organizational sensemaking. Special attention should be paid to sensemaking by diverse groups of organizational members (Maitlis, 2005). As they engage in sensemaking from a variety of organizational positions and subcultures (Dutton & Dukerich, 1991; Gephart, 1993; Weick, 1995), their sensemaking processes unfold in different patterns or forms that lead to different outcomes (Maitlis, 2005). Depending on the sensemaking process characteristics (levels of animation and control) (Maitlis, 2005), organizational sensemaking outcomes in terms of the accounts generated can be unitary and convergent or multiple and divergent (Balogun & Johnson, 2004, 2005). Unity and divergence may very well be manifested in information security sensemaking. The outcome is that shared beliefs and perceptions about information security are developed among organizational members but multiple and different behaviors also emerge among groups of organizational members. This is the role of organizational culture in achieving both centralization and decentralization (Weick, 1987), here in information security management. As organizational culture is about meaning making (Weick, 1987), it cultivates similar and uniformed perceptions and actions toward information security. Thus, common or standard behaviors are developed among organizational members. Yet, organizational culture also enables autonomy in interpretation, improvisation, and different actions (Weick, 1987), thereby leading to multiple but different ISBs.

Organizational culture is complicated. On the one hand, organizational culture represents a common set of beliefs and values shared by organizational members. Such a shared set of beliefs and values indicate that organizational members have reached a consensus on certain core values, which help to unify the whole organization. In this sense, organizational culture plays an important function of integrating various units or departments of an organization. This is the main idea of Martin's (2002) integration perspective on organizational culture. However, the common set of beliefs and values may not be shared equally among individual organizational members, groups, units, and departments in the organization. Further, despite the existence of an integrating organizational culture, subcultures are developed in various units, layers of organizational structure, and interest groups such as unions and management (Saffold, 1988). Development of multiple subcultures appears to be more the rule than an exception in organizations (Van Maanen & Barley, 1984). This differentiation view of organizational culture (Martin, 2002) suggests that organizational culture is not unitary (Saffold, 1988).

Both the integration and differentiation views are implicit in the competing values framework (CVF) of organizational culture (Cameron & Quinn, 2005; Quinn, 1988; Quinn & Rohrbaugh, 1983; Quinn & Spreitzer,1991). Further, the CVF recognizes both the complicated and diverse nature of organizational culture (Denison & Spreitzer, 1991). Moreover, the CVF has been used to enlighten empirical research on the relationship between organizational culture and effectiveness (Denison & Mishra 1995), including effectiveness in organizational control (Hartnell et al., 2011). Because of this, the CVF emerges to be an overarching framework for explaining the possible relationships between organizational culture and behavior control with regard to information security in organizations. The CVF consists of two dimensions---internal vs. external focus, and flexibility and discretion vs. stability and control. Along these two dimensions, four cultures are identified: group, hierarchical, developmental, and rational cultures, although the labels used to describe them differ from study to study. Group culture is an organization or a unit that emphasizes such values as positive working relationships, esprit de corps at work, social support, high morale, growth and development for individual members. Hierarchical culture refers to a place where values of rule control, formalization, efficiency, order, and productivity are highlighted. Developmental culture is one that promotes such values of creativity, exploration, learning, and knowledge generation. Lastly, rational culture is a place where values of customer service, productivity, and competitiveness are highlighted. We draw on the CVF framework to account for culture's role in ISB development.

ROLE OF ORGANIZATIONAL CULTURE IN ISB DEVELOPMENT

Group Culture

Group culture is internally oriented, but it emphasizes flexibility and discretion (Denison & Spreitzer, 1991). Highly endorsed group cultural values include cohesion, open communication, participation, and empowerment (Quinn & Kimberly, 1984). Sharing information, and praising performance are further characteristics of a group culture (O'Reilly, Chatman, & Caldwell, 1991). All these values tend to cultivate positive employee morale (Cameron & Ettington, 1988).

Flexibility and discretion suggest that organizations with a group culture favor measures that are highly adapted to situations with respect to information security. Further, in a group culture, employees feel empowered, and empowerment, compared to directive leadership, more likely stimulates task proficiency, and more importantly, proactivity (Martin, Liao, & Campbell, 2013). In the context of information security in organizations, given the difficulty for a security policy to cover exhaustively all areas of information security, such proactivity from employees is greatly needed, as that means that employees will proactively identify and report security concerns and issues and brainstorm for methods to address them. This helps to promote both information security diagnosing and solving behaviors. For example, in a cooperative cultural context, employees most likely exhibit positive ISBs such as *helping* and *voicing* behaviors (Hsu et al., 2015). Group cultural values also help to create a sense of collective ownership and responsibility among employees (Denison & Mishra, 1995), which are important drivers of uniformity in action towards what is commonly regarded. This suggests that employees in a group culture take it as their own responsibility and obligation to enact what they have already agreed on in information security issues. This will be reflected in uniformity in abiding by information security policies.

Group culture also has the potential in facilitating the antecedents of ISB. Organizationally desired ethics and moral foundations surrounding information security are more likely to be developed and promoted in a group culture than in any of the three other cultures. Such organizationally desired ethics and moral foundations are usually outcomes of employee social interactions facilitated by a group culture. Employees are most likely to identify with and internalize those ethics and moral foundations that they have participated in developing. Further, positive perceptions and attitudes among employees are also more likely to develop in a group culture. For example, voluntary participation, a central feature of group culture, positively links to perceptions and attitudes (Leana, Ahlbrandt, & Murrell, 1992). Empowerment, another main feature of group culture, leads to high level of employee commitment, and citizenship behaviors (Seibert, Wang, & Courtright, 2011; Spreitzer, 2008; Thomas & Velthouse, 1990), which help to cultivate those perceptions and attitudes among employees. Additionally, it can be argued that group culture helps to enhance acquisition of information security related knowledge and skills. From an information processing perspective, employees in a group culture are able to gather and use more information for their work (Turner & Makhija, 2012). An important outcome of active participation is increased practices in decision making, problem solving, and goal setting (Sashkin, 1976), which arguably help to build employees' knowledge and skills including information security awareness knowledge and how-to knowledge. Participation also results in learning through behavioral practice, which leads to skill enhancement (Sashkin, 1976).

The above discussion of how group culture would influence ISBs, especially the review of prior research showing how antecedents contribute to effective ISBs naturally lead to the following propositions:

Proposition 1-a: Group culture promotes information security diagnosing behaviors among employees more than any of the other three cultures.

Proposition 1-b: Group culture promotes information security solving behaviors.

Proposition 1-c: Group culture promotes information security performing behaviors.

Proposition 1-d: Group culture positively contributes to the development of all the three categories of ISB antecedents: ethics and morality, perceptions and attitudes, and knowledge and skills, more than any of the other three cultures.

Hierarchical Culture

Hierarchical culture is internally oriented and has a strong control mechanism in its organizational structure (Denison & Spreitzer, 1991). This culture emphasizes the following values: formal communication, routinization, and consistency (Quinn & Kimberly, 1984). These values stimulate rule compliance, process control, measurement, efficiency, timeliness, and smooth functioning (Hartnell et al., 2011). Employees from a hierarchical culture would be expected to follow rules and their roles would be clearly defined. They would value precise communication, task and process routinization, formalization of work and process, and consistency across units (Quinn & Kimberly, 1984).

In a hierarchical culture, information security policies would prescribe detailed rules, roles, and responsibilities for organizational members to follow, as that culture is rule, and control oriented. Hierarchical culture places priority on process control over human development and so would be more likely to implement technical procedures than to cultivate proactivity in employees to safeguard information security. However, because of formalization, organizations with a hierarchical culture would train their employees regarding their detailed information security policies. When undergoing the training sessions, employees are expected to be taught to have the same moral obligation, perceptions, and attitudes, and same level of knowledge and skills with regard to information security, as consistency and standardization require. Boss, Kirsch, Angermeier, Shingler, and Boss (2009) showed that mandatoriness mediates the relationship between organizational control measures for information security (specification of policies and rules, evaluation, and reward) and employees' ISB (taking precautions). Organizational control measures must be sufficient in hierarchical culture and mandatoriness is clearly communicated to employees.

ISB varies from organization to organization and from context to context. Given the highly contextualized nature, no specific ISB will be recommended as standard behavior. Instead, complying with information security policies will be deemed as a recommended behavior to end users. This is because organizational information security policies are formulated usually tailoring to their specific needs and requirements. In most cases, organizational information security policies define the roles and responsibilities for their employees regarding access to and use of organizational information and technology resources (Bulgurcu et al., 2010). These policies provide detailed descriptions of what employees can and cannot do with respect to accessing and using organizational information and technology resources (Whitman, 2008). The effectiveness of policy compliance by end users depends on how specific the organizational security policy is. This means that the policy's coverage of areas of information security and the corresponding security behaviors must be exhaustive. They have to cover all the areas of information security in the organization. It also means that the organizational policy has to specify each behavior for every area of information security. Specificity not only better informs employees of security behaviors but also enhances their belief that complying with organizational security policies is a must to them (Boss et al., 2009).

With respect to the antecedents of ISBs, hierarchical culture can positively contribute to the development of all the three categories. In a hierarchical culture, given top management's right assessment of the importance of information security to their company, together with their commitment to providing necessary resources, employees are likely to be trained or educated in a top-down manner to be ethically and morally alert to information security, heighten their perceptions and attitudes about information security, and enhance their information security knowledge and skills. In light of the above discussion, we propose the following propositions regarding the concepts of hierarchical culture and ISBs:

Proposition 2-a: Hierarchical culture promotes information security performing behaviors more than any of the other three cultures.

Proposition 2-b: Hierarchical culture positively contributes to the development of information security ethics and morality, perceptions and attitudes, and knowledge and skills.

Developmental Culture

The developmental culture is externally oriented and has a flexible organizational structure (Hartnell et al., 2011). They value growth, stimulation, variety, and autonomy (Quinn & Kimberly, 1984). More importantly, they encourage creativity and exploration. Their external orientation prepares them a sensitivity and keenness to external cues. When a new technology is developed and is demonstrating its potential, externally oriented developmental culture members would capture this new development and exhibit enthusiasm in importing this new technology to their own company. In a similar fashion, once a new method is developed outside their company to address information security issues associated with the new technology, employees with a strong external orientation are highly likely to adopt it. For the same reason, employees from a developmental culture have a strong readiness to interpret external cues occurring in the environment including updated solutions to information security problems. They are quick to take such newly introduced solutions to help to address their internal information security needs. For example, when an information security countermeasure portfolio was developed or updated (Kumar, Park, & Subramaniam, 2008), employees from a developmental culture would be very quick to recommend it to their organizations.

Developmental culture values a flexible organizational structure. When approaching technology, employees from this culture would focus on its technical function in terms of enhancing productivity, as opposed to those from a stability-oriented culture such as hierarchical and rational cultures who may like to explore its social and organizational functions of the technology such as facilitating coordination and control. For example, even though system development methodologies have production, coordination, and organizational control functions, IS developers from a developmental culture perceived them mainly as production technology, ignoring their coordination and organizational functions (Iivari & Huisman, 2007). Benefitted from their external learning inclination (Calantone, Cavusgil, & Zhao, 2002; Rauseo, 2001), employees are capable of seeking new ideas and information available in the external environment, and exploiting its internal resources to develop technical solutions to information security. Thus, employees from a developmental culture are more likely to display information security solving behaviors in coping with information security.

Indeed, among the four competing cultures, developmental culture has the strongest association with innovation (Buschgens, Bausch, & Balkin, 2013). In information security, their innovativeness would be highly likely to be reflected in developing new solutions to information security issues. Likewise, developmental culture cultivates proactiveness among its employees

(Brettel, Chomik, & Flatten, 2015). Their proactiveness would be demonstrated in foreseeing potential risks and threats to information security in technologies and other facilities adopted and used in their companies, and more importantly, in actively seeking measures to address such potential risks and threats. Developmental culture cultivates a risk-taking tendency in employees (Cooper, Edgett, & Kleinschmidt, 2004; McDonald, 2002; Miller & Friesen, 1982). Yet, this risk-taking spirit would be more shown in employees' experimenting with new measures for information security than in operating technology and equipment in their daily routine work processes.

With respect to the antecedents to ISBs, as developmental culture encourages its employees to engage in organizational learning and knowledge developing, it can be expected that they will constantly gain new knowledge and skills to deal with information security issues. Employees from this culture may be less likely to be bonded by moral obligation to try new things even though they may mean risks and threats to information security. And they are less likely to attach too much severity, vulnerability, and susceptibility in their perceptions to the possible risks and threats. However, given their pursuit of innovation and creative solutions to problems, they are more likely to acquire knowledge and skills needed to deal with risks and threats.

Thus, the following propositions can be posited:

Proposition 3-a: Developmental culture positively contributes to information security diagnosing behaviors.

Proposition 3-b: Developmental culture positively contributes to information security solving behaviors.

Proposition 3-c: Among the four cultures, developmental culture contributes to information security solving behaviors the most.

Proposition 3-d: Among the antecedents, developmental culture positively facilitates the knowledge and skill category.

Rational Culture

Similar to developmental culture, rational culture is also externally oriented (Denison & Spreitzer, 1991). Members from a rational culture also tend to develop a keen sensitivity to external cues. Rational culture also emphasizes such values as competitiveness, aggressiveness, productivity, achievement, and competence (Hartnell et al., 2011). When triggered by an external force, this achievement orientation may lead them to be highly concerned with information security. This external force is that their external customers raise such information security concerns about their products or services. To rational culture members, addressing customer needs and enhancing customer satisfaction with their products or services has a highest priority, as this translates into their achievement in the market (Cameron, Quinn, DeGraff, & Thakor, 2006). Because of this, members of a rational culture are sensitive to customers' information security concerns with their products or services. Moreover, they would speedily capture and send these customer feedback back to their companies. Doing this is comparable to identifying possible information security issues and problems inside the organization, i.e., diagnosing behaviors.

Further, rational culture is also positively related to innovativeness, proactiveness, and risk-taking (Brettel et al., 2015), cultural qualities that promote information security solving behaviors. Additionally, rational culture members are mostly result-oriented (Belassi, Kondra, & Tukel, 2007; Jaskyte, 2004). This orientation means an obsessive concern with present or direct results of an effort, which does not encourage exploration, a critical precedent to innovation. But their stability orientation favors a mechanism of organizational control, which is incompatible with innovation. This suggests that employees of a rational culture may not exhibit as many information security solving behaviors as those of a developmental culture.

Rational culture's stability orientation translates into a preference of formal means of organizational control and adherence to existing rules and procedures (Buschgens et al., 2013). This suggests that employees of a rational culture agree with the practice of establishing rules, regulations, and policies to safeguard information security for their organizations. When risks, threats, and dangers of information security are well identified, and corresponding coping measures have been tested effective, employees of a rational culture would like to see them included in their organizational information security policies and regulations and exemplify themselves in abiding by these policies and regulations. Therefore, we can infer that rational culture promotes information security performing behaviors.

For the antecedents of ISBs, rational culture, as developmental culture does, may just promote the category of knowledge and skills. This is because rational culture does not take a strong stance on ethics and morality when it comes to information security. Rational culture, just as developmental culture, is more productivity and efficiency than sociality oriented. It may take a neutral position on ethics and morality. Neither does it encourage ethics and morality nor does it discourage them with respect to information security. As for the perceptions and attitude aspects of the antecedents, rational culture's role is subject to external influences, such as customers. Based on this discussion of rational culture's characteristics, the following propositions can be generated:

Proposition 4-a: Rational culture positively contributes to information security diagnosing behaviors.

Proposition 4-b: Rational culture positively contributes to information security solving behaviors.

Proposition 4-c: Rational culture is more positively related to information security diagnosing behaviors than solving behaviors.

Proposition 4-d: Rational culture positively contributes to information security performing behaviors.

Proposition 4-e: Rational culture positively promotes the knowledge and skills category of the ISB antecedents.

DISCUSSION

The landscape of past research on ISB was dominated by the deterrence approach, which focused its attention on examining negative behaviors such as computer abuse (Willison & Warkentin, 2013). Past research also utilized a number of social cognitive theories, including reasoned action (e.g., see Pahnila, Siponen, & Mahomood, 2007), protection motivation (e.g., see Herath & Rao, 2009; Johnston & Warketin, 2010; Lee & Larsen, 2009), planned behavior (e.g., see Bulgurcu et al., 2010; Herath & Rao, 2009), and moral judgment and ethics (e.g., see Banerjee et al., 1998; Myyry et al., 2009), to explore a series of precursors to ISB but mostly investigated their impact on information security policy compliance only. These two approaches led to an under-exploration of other types of, especially positive ISBs (Posey et al., 2013). To help information security research to navigate out of this impasse, this study proposed the TDISB that integrates sensemaking and organizational culture for studying ISBs. Offering this new theoretical framework, the current study generated significant contributions to ISB research.

The main contribution of this study is that it has extended and advanced our understanding and knowledge of ISBs. Drawing on the organizational sensemaking perspective (Weick, 1979, 1995), this study generated three new categories of ISBs – information security diagnosing behavior, information security solving behavior, and information security performing behavior. Past research explored a number of individual cognitive factors impacting ISB, but treated ISB mostly as a dependent variable. Because of this research design, previous research only shed light on just a few negative ISBs such as computer abuse. A large number of empirical studies conceptualized ISB only as information security policy compliance (e.g., see Bulgurcu et al., 2010; Herath & Rao, 2009; Myyry et al., 2009; Siponen & Vance, 2010; Son, 2011). By offering the three above mentioned categories of ISB, this study adds more specificity and granularity to our knowledge of ISBs. With the development of these three categories of ISB, this study provided benefits to organizations regarding how organizations can assess and influence such ISBs (Stanton, Stam, Mastrangelo, & Jolton, 2005).

Another contribution of this study is that it provided a theoretical lens for examining the organizational role in the development of ISBs. Past research, although occasionally examined organizational efforts such as training (Puhakainen & Siponen, 2010) in improving employees' ISBs, mostly focused on investigating individual factors such as cognition (e.g., see Bulgurcu et al., 2010) and ethics (Siponen & Vance, 2010). Yet, these individual factors are impacted by the organizational context and thus should be examined in this context. By offering the TDISB, this study provides an important direction for researchers to examine ISBs, i.e., to explore the organizational role in the development of these behaviors. This new theoretical framework helps to extend past research by showing how individual cognition (scanning and interpreting) operates in and thereby is constrained and conditioned by the organizational cultural context. This study showed that ISBs are outcomes of sensemaking that is both facilitated and constrained by organizational culture. More importantly, this study advanced our understanding of how culture shapes ISBs in that it offered detailed explanation as to why a same ISB may be positively developed in diverse organizational cultures. For example, the information security diagnosing behavior was shown to emerge in all the four types of culture but was promoted differently in those cultures. Further, incentives, resources, or approaches used in generating the information security solving behavior were shown to be different in, for example, developmental culture and rational culture. Given these benefits, this study helped to overcome limitations in past research that only showed that organizational culture may impact information security policy compliance by individuals.

A third contribution of this study is that it challenged an important underlying assumption of past research especially the deterrence approach. Excessively showing the negative ISBs in past research would help to cultivate a biased view that internal employees constitute a threat to information security. By offering the three categories of ISBs especially the diagnosing and solving behaviors, this study helped to re-image the role of employees as beneficial contributors to information security management in their organizations. It also generated an important implication that employees can be looked as the solution instead of the problem even in the area of information security management (Spears & Barki, 2010).

In addition to the theoretical contributions, this study generated important practical implications for organizations. When making decisions on what approaches to information security control, organizations should assess their cultures first and then adopt approaches that fit their cultures. From the integration and differentiation perspective of organizational culture (Martin, 2002), an organization may have several subcultures existing simultaneously within their organizational boundaries. In this case, adopting an organization wide one-fitting-all information security approach may not be appropriate. Instead, multiple approaches with each fitting its subculture can be adopted. Even in organizations that are overwhelmingly hierarchical in culture, some small participative conclaves can develop among groups or units, which can serve positively their organizations in information security management, as those subcultures would help to promote different but beneficial types of ISBs. For research direction, future research can seek empirical evidence for the theoretical propositions outlined in this study.

REFERENCES

Abbasi, A., Zahedi, F. M., Zeng, D., Chen, Y., Chen, H., & Nunamaker, J. F. 2015. Enhancing predictive analytics for anti-phishing by exploiting website genre information. *Journal of Management Information Systems,* 31(4), 109-157.

Abolafia, M. Y. 2010. Narrative construction as sensemaking: How a central bank thinks. *Organization Studies*, 31, 349–367.

Agarwal, R., & Prasad, J. 1998. A conceptual and operational definition of personal innovativeness in the domain of information technology. *Information Systems Research,* 9(2), 204-215.

Anderson, C., & Agarwal, R. 2010. Practicing safe computing: A multimethod empirical examination of home computer user security behavioral intentions, *MIS Quarterly*, 34(3): 613-643.

Aytes, K., & Connolly, T. 2004. Computer security and risky computing practices: A rational choice perspective. *Journal of Organizational and End User Computing,* 16(3): 22-40.

Balogun, J., & Johnson, G. 2004. Organizational restructuring and middle manager sensemaking. *Academy of Management Journal,* 47, 523-549.

Balogun, J., and Johnson, G. 2005. From intended strategies to unintended outcomes: The impact of change recipient sensemaking. *Organization Studies,* 26, 1573-1601.

Banerjee, D., Cronan, T. P., & Jones, T. W. 1998. Modeling IT ethics: A study in situational ethics. *MIS Quarterly*, 22(1): 31-60.

Barr, P. S., & Huff, A. S. 1997. Seeing isn't believing: Understanding diversity in the timing of strategic response. *Journal of Management Studies,* 34, 337–370.

Belassi,W.,A. Z. Kondra, & O. I. Tukel. 2007. New product development projects: The effect of organizational culture. *Project Management Journal,* 38(4), 12–24.

Boss, S. R., Kirsch, L. J., Angermeier, I., Shingler, R. A., & Boss, R. W. 2009. If someone is watching, I'll do what I'm asked: Mandatoriness, control, and information security. *European Journal of Information Systems,* 18: 151-164.

Bowman, E. H., & Hurry, D. 1993. Strategy through the option lens: An integrated view of resource investments and the incremental choice process. *Academy of Management Review,* 18(4), 760–782.

Brettel, M., Chomik, C., & Flatten, T. C. 2015. How organizational culture influences innovativeness, proactiveness, and risk-taking, fostering entrepreneurial orientation in SMEs. *Journal of Small Business Management,* 53(4), 868-885.

Bulgurcu, B., Cavusoglu, H., & Benbasat, I. 2010. Information security policy compliance: An empirical study of rationality-based beliefs and information security awareness. *MIS Quarterly,* 34(3): 523-548.

Buschgens, T., Bausch, A., & Balkin, D. B. 2013. Organizational culture and innovation: A meta-analytic review. *Journal of Product Innovation Management,* 30(4), 763-781.

Calantone, R. J., Cavusgil, S. T., & Zhao, Y. 2002. Learning orientation, firm innovation capability, and firm performance. *Industrial Marketing Management,* 31, 515–24.

Caliendo, M., Clement, M., Papies, D., & Scheel-Kopeinig, S. 2012. The cost impact of spam filters: Measuring the effect of information system technologies in organizations. *Information Systems Research,* 23, 1068-1080.

Cameron, K. S., & Ettington, D. R. 1988. The conceptual foundations of organizational culture. In J. Smart (Ed.), *Higher education handbook of theory and research:* 356–396. New York, NY: Agathon Press.

Cameron, K. S., & Quinn, R. E. 2005. *Diagnosing and changing organizational culture.* San Francisco, CA: Jossey-Bass.

Cameron, K. S., Quinn, R. E., DeGraff, J., & Thakor, A. V. 2006. *Competing values leadership: Creating value in organizations.* Northampton, MA: Elgar.

Carroll, J. S., Rudolph, J. W., & Hatakenaka, S. 2002. Learning from experience in high-hazard industries. *Research in Organizational Behavior,* 24, 87-137.

Chatterjee, S., Sarker, S., & Valacich, J. 2015. The behavioral roots of information systems security: Exploring key factors related to unethical IT use. *Journal of Management Information Systems,* 31(4), 49-87.

Cooper, R. G., S. J. Edgett, & E. J. Kleinschmidt. 2004. Benchmarking best NPD practices. *Research Technology Management,* 47(1), 31–43.

Croker, L. 1987. Improvements in database concurrency control with locking. *Journal of Management Information Systems,* 4(2), 74-92.

Culnan, M. J., Foxman, E. R., & Ray, A. W. 2008. Why IT executives should help employees secure their home computers. *MIS Quarterly Executive*, 7(1): 49-56.

Culnan, M., & Williams, C. C. 2009. How ethics can enhance organizational privacy: Lessons from the Choice Point and TJX data breaches. *MIS Quarterly,* 33(4): 673-687.

D'Arcy, J., & Herath, T. 2011. A review and analysis of deterrence theory in the IS security literature: Making sense of the disparate findings. *European Journal of Information Systems,* 20: 643-658.

Da Veiga, A., and Eloff, J. H. P. 2010. A framework and assessment instrument for information security culture. *Computers and Security,* 29, 196-207.

Daft, R. L., & Weick, K. E. 1984. Toward a model of organizations as interpretation systems. *Academy of Management Review,* 9, 284–295.

Denison, D. R., & Mishra, A. K. 1995. Toward a theory of organizational culture and effectiveness. *Organization Science,* 6(2): 204-223.

Denison, D. R., & Spreitzer, G. M. 1991. Organizational culture and organizational development: A competing values approach. In R. W. Woodman & W. A. Pasmore (Eds.), *Research in organizational change and development:* 1-21. Greenwich, CT: JAI Press.

Detert, J, Schroeder, R, and Mauriel J. 2000. A framework for linking culture and improvement initiatives in organisations. *Academy of Management Review,* 25, 850–63.

Dinev, T., Goo, J., Hu, Q., & Nam, K. 2009. User behaviour towards protective information technologies: The role of national cultural differences. *Information Systems Journal,* 9(4): 391–412.

Dutton, J. E., & Dukerich, J. M. 1991. Keeping an eye on the mirror: Image and identity in organizational adaptation. *Academy of Management Journal,* 34, 517-554.

Einhorn, H. J., & Hogarth, R. M. 1986. Judging probable cause. *Psychological Bulletin,* 99(1), 3-19.

Eisenhardt, K. M. 1989. Making fast strategic decisions in high-velocity environments. *Academy of Management Journal,* 32, 543-576.

Fulk, J. 1993. Social construction of communication technology. *Academy of Management Journal,* 36(5), 921-950.

Furnell, S. 2008. End-user security culture: A lesson that will never be learnt? *Computer Fraud & Security,* 4: 6-9.

Gephart, R. P. 1993. The textual approach: Risk and blame in disaster sensemaking. *Academy of Management Journal,* 36(6), 1465-1514.

Gibbs, J. P. 1975. *Crime, punishment, and deterrence.* NY: Elsevier.

Gopal, A., & Prasad, P. 2000. Understanding GDSS in symbolic context: Shifting the focus from technology to interaction. *MIS Quarterly,* 24, 509-546.

Griffith, T. L. 199). Technology features as triggers for sensemaking. *Academy of Management Review,* 24(3), 472-488.

Guo, K. H., Yuan, Y., Archer, N. P., Connelly, C. E. 2011. Understanding nonmalicious security violations in the workplace: A composite behavior model. *Journal of Management Information Systems*, 28(2): 203-236.

Hahn, T., Preuss, L., Pinkse, J., & Figge, F. 2015. Cognitive frames in corporate sustainability: Managerial sensemaking with paradoxical and business case frames. *Academy of Management Review,* 4015 (1), 18-42.

Harrington, S. 1996. The effects of codes of ethics and personal denial of responsibility on computer abuse judgments and intentions. *MIS Quarterly,* 20(3): 257-278.

Harris, S. G. 1994. Organizational culture and individual sensemaking: A schema-based perspective. *Organization Science,* 5(3), 309-321.

Hartnell, C. A., Ou, A. Y., & Kinicki, A. 2011. Organizational culture and organizational effectiveness: A meta-analytic investigation of the competing values framework's theoretical suppositions. *Journal of Applied Psychology,* 96(4): 677-694.

Herath, T., & Rao, H. R. 2009a. Protection motivation and deterrence: A framework for security policy compliance in organizations. *European Journal of Information Systems,* 18(2): 106–125.

Herath, T., & Rao, H. R. 2009b. Encouraging information security behaviors in organizations: Role of penalties, pressures and perceived effectiveness. *Decision Support Systems,* 47(2): 154–165.

Hovav, A., & D'Arcy, J. 2012. Appling an extended model of deterrence across cultures: An investigation of information systems misuse in the U.S. and South Korea. *Information & Management,* 49: 99-110.

Hsu, C., Lee, J-N., & Straub, D. W. 2012. Institutional influences on information systems security innovations. *Information Systems Research,* 23(3), 918-939.

Hsu, J. S., Shih, S., Hung, Y. W., & Lowry, P. B. 2015. The role of extra-role behaviors and social controls in information security policy effectiveness. *Information Systems Research,* 26(2), 282-300.

Hu, Q., Dinev, T., Hart, P., & Cooke, D. 2012. Managing employee compliance with information security policies: The critical role of top management and organizational culture. *Decision Sciences,* 43(4): 615-659.

Hu, Q., Hart, P., & Cooke, D. 2006. The role of external influences on organizational information security practices: An institutional perspective. *Proceedings of the 39th Hawaii International Conference on System Sciences.* Los Alamitos, CA: IEEE Computer Society Press.

Hu, Q., Hart, P., & Cooke, D. 2007. The role of external and internal influences on information systems security – A neo-institutional perspective. *Journal of Strategic Information Systems,* 16, 153-172.

Iivari, J., & Huisman, M. 2007. The relationship between organizational culture and the deployment of systems development methodologies. *MIS Quarterly,* 31(1), 35-58.

Jaskyte, K. 2004. Transformational leadership, organizational culture, and innovativeness in nonprofit organizations. *Nonprofit Management and Leadership,* 15(2), 53–68.

Johnston, A. C., & Warkentin, M. 2010. Fear appeals and information security behaviors: An empirical study. *MIS Quarterly,* 34(3): 548-566.

Katos, V., & Adams, C. 2005. Modelling corporate wireless security and privacy. *Journal of Strategic Information Systems,* 14, 307-321.

Kim, S. H., & Kim, B. C. 2014. Differential effects of prior experience on the malware resolution process. *MIS Quarterly,* 38(3), 655-678.

Klein, G., Pliske, R., Crandall, B., & Woods, D. 2005. Problem detection. *Cognition, Technology and Work,* 7, 14-28.

Kraemer, S., & Carayon, P. 2005. Computer and information security culture: Findings from two studies. *Proceedings of the Human Factors and Ergonomics Society 49th Annual Meeting*. Computer Society Press.

Kumar, R. L., Park, S., & Subramaniam, C. 2008. Understanding the value of countermeasure portfolios in information systems security. *Journal of Management Information Systems,* 25(2), 241-279.

LaRose, R., Rifon, N. J., & Enbody, R. 2008. Promoting personal responsibility for Internet safety. *Communications of the ACM,* 51(3): 71-76.

Leana, C., Ahlbrandt, R. S., & Murrell, A. J. 1992. The effects of employee involvement programs on unionized workers' attitudes, perceptions, and preferences in decision making. *Academy of Management Journal,* 35(4): 861-873.

Lee, J., & Y. Lee. 2002. A holistic model of computer abuse within organizations. *Information Management Computer Security,* 10(2): 57–63.

Lee, S. M., Lee, S. G., & Yoo, S. 2004. An integrative model of computer abuse based on social control and general deterrence theories. *Information & Management,* 41(6): 707–718.

Lee, Y., & Kozar, K. A. 2005. Investigating factors affecting the adoption of anti-spyware system. *Communications of the ACM*, 48(8): 72-77.

Lee, Y., & Larsen, K. R. 2009. Threat or coping appraisal: Determinants of SMB executives'decision to adopt anti-malware software. *European Journal of Information Systems,* 18: 177-187.

Li, H., Zhang, J., & Sarathy, R. 2010. Understanding compliance with Internet use policy from the perspective of rational choice theory. *Decision Support Systems,* 48: 635-645.

Maitlis, S. 2005. The social processes of organizational sensemaking. *Academy of Management Journal,* 48(1), 21-49.

Maitlis, S., & Christianson, M. 2014. Sensemaking in organizations: Taking stock and moving forward. *The Academy of Management Annals,* 8(1), 57-125.

Malsch, B., Tremblay, M. S., & Gendron, Y. 2012. Sense-making in compensation committees: A cultural theory perspective. *Organization Studies*, 33, 389–421.

March, J. G. 1991. Exploration and exploitation in organizational learning. *Organization Science,* 2(1), 71-87.

Martin, J. 2002. *Organizational culture: Mapping the terrain*. Thousand Oaks, CA: Sage Publications.

Martin, S., Liao, H., & Campbell, E. M. 2013. Directive versus empowering leadership: A field experiment comparing impacts on task proficiency and proactivity. *Academy of Management Journal,* 56(5): 1372-1395.

McDonald, R. E. 2002. *Knowledge entrepreneurship: Linking organizational learning and innovation*. Ann Arbor, MI: ProQuest Information and Learning.

Miller, D., & P. H. Friesen. 1982. Innovation in conservative and entrepreneurial firms: Two models of strategic momentum. *Strategic Management Journal,* 3, 1–25.

Moore, G. C., and Benbasat, I. 1991. Development of an instrument to measure the perceptions of adopting an information technology innovation. *Information Systems Research,* 2(3), 192-222.

Myyry, L., Siponen, M., Pahnila, S., Vartiainen, T., & Vance A. 2009. What levels of moral reasoning and values explain adherence to information security rules? An empirical study.

Ng, B. Y., Kankanhalli, A., & Xu, Y. 2009. Studying users' computer security behavior: A health belief perspective. *Decision Support Systems*, 46: 815-825.

O'Reilly, C. A., & Chatman, J. A. 1996. Culture as social control: Corporations, cults, and commitment. *Research in Organizational Behavior,* 18: 157-200.

O'Reilly, C. A., Chatman, J., & Caldwell, D. F. 1991. People and organizational culture: A profile comparison approach to assessing person-organization fit. *Academy of Management Journal,* 34(3): 487-516.

Orton, J. D. 2000. Enactment, sensemaking and decision making: Redesign processes in the 1076 reorganization of US Intelligence. *Journal of Management Studies,* 37(2), 213-234.

Ouchi, W. G. 1980. Markets, bureaucracies, and clans. *Administrative Science Quarterly,* 25, 129-141.

Pahnila, S., Siponen, M., & Mahmood, A. 2007. Employees' behavior towards IS security policy compliance. *Proceedings of the 40th Hawaii International Conference on System Sciences*, January 3-6, Los Alamitos, CA: IEEE Computer Society Press.

Porac, J. F., & Thomas, H. 2002. Managing cognition and strategy: Issues, trends and future directions. In A. M. Pettigrew, H. Thomas, & R. Whittington (Eds.), *Handbook of strategy and management:* 165–181. London & Thousand Oaks, CA: Sage.

Posey, C., Roberts, T. L., Lowry, P. B., Bennett, R. J., & Courtney, J. F. 2013. Insiders' protection of organizational information assets: Development of a systematics-based taxonomy and theory of diversity for protection-motivated behaviors. *MIS Quarterly,* 37(4): 1189-1210.

Puhakainen, P., & Siponen, M. 2010. Improving employees' compliance through information security training: An action research study. *MIS Quarterly,* 34(4), 757-778.

Quinn, R. E. 1988. *Beyond rational management*. San Francisco, CA: Jossey-Bass.

Quinn, R. E., & Kimberly, J. R. 1984. Paradox, planning, and perseverance: Guidelines for managerial practice. In J. R. Kimberly & R. E. Quinn (Eds.), *Managing organizational transitions:* 295–313. Homewood, IL: Dow Jones–Irwin.

Quinn, R. E., & Rohrbaugh, J. 1983. A spatial model of effectiveness criteria: Toward a competing values approach to organizational analysis. *Management Science,* 29: 363-377.

Quinn, R. E., & Spreitzer, G. M. 1991. The psychometrics of the competing values culture instrument and an analysis of the impact of organization culture on quality of life. *Research in Organizational Change and Development,* 5: 115-142.

Rauseo, N. A. 2001. *E-Business as a Radical Innovation: The effect of Organizational Capabilities on its Adoption in Brick and Mortar Companies.* Ann Arbor, MI: ProQuest Information and Learning.

Ray, C. A. 1986. Corporate culture: The last frontier of control. *Journal of Management Studies,* 23, 287-297.

Repenning, N. P., & Sterman, J. D. 2002. Capability traps and self-confirming attribution errors in the dynamics of process improvement. *Administrative Science Quarterly,* 47, 265-295.

Rudolph, J. W., Morrison, J. B., & Carroll, J. S. 2009. The dynamics of action-oriented problem solving: Linking interpretation and choice. *Academy of Management Review,* 34(4), 733-756.

Ruighaver, A. B., Maynard, S. B., & Chang, S. 2007. Organizational security culture: Extending the end-user perspective. *Computers & Security,* 26: 56-62.

Saffold, G. S. 1988. Culture traits, strength, and organizational performance: Moving beyond "strong" culture. *Academy of Management Review,* 13(4): 546-558.

Sashkin, M. 1976. Changing toward participative management approaches: A model and methods. *Academy of Management Review,* 1(3): 75-86.

Schein, E. H. 1985. *Organizational culture and leadership.* San Francisco: Jossey-Bass.

Seibert, S. E., Wang, G., & Courtright, S. H. 2011. Antecedents and consequences of psychological and team empowerment in organizations: A meta-analytic review. *Journal of Applied Psychology,* 96: 981-1003.

Sen, R., & Borle, S. 2015. Estimating the contextual risk of data breach: An empirical approach. *Journal of Management Information Systems,* 32(1), 314-341.

Siponen, M., & Vance, A. 2010. Neutralization: New insights into the problem of employee information systems security policy violations. *MIS Quarterly,* 34(3), 487-502.

Siponen, M., Willison, R, & Baskerville, R. 2008. Power and practice in information systems security research. In *Proceedings of the International Conference on Information Systems,* 14-17, Paris, France.

Son, J. 2011. Out of fear or desire? Toward a better understanding of employees' motivation to follow IS security policies. *Information & Management,* 48: 296-302.

Spears, J. L., & Barki, H. 2010. User participation in information systems security risk management. *MIS Quarterly,* 34(3), 503-522.

Spreitzer, G. M. 2008. Taking stock: A review of more than twenty years of research on empowerment at work. In J. Barling & C. L. Cooper (Eds.), *The Sage handbook of organizational behavior:* 73-88. Thousand Oaks, CA: Sage.

Stanton, J. M. and Stam, K. R. 2006. The visible employee. Medford, NJ: Information Today Inc.

Stanton, K. M., Stam, K. R., Mastrangelo, P., & Jolton, J. 2005. Analysis of end user security behaviors. *Computers & Security,* 24, 124-133.

Teece, D. J., Pisano, G., & Shuen, A. (1997). Dynamic capabilities and strategic management. *Strategic Management Journal, 18 (7),* 509-533.

Thomas, J. B., Clark, S. M., and Gioia, D. A. 1993. Strategic sensemaking and organizational performance: Linkages among scanning, interpretation, action and outcomes. *Academy of Management Journal,* 36(2), 239-270.

Thomas, K. W., & Velthouse, B. A. 1990. Cognitive elements of empowerment: An "interpretive" model of intrinsic task motivation. *Academy of Management Review,* 15: 666-681.

Trice, H. M., & Beyer, J. M. 1993. *The cultures of work organizations.* Englewood Cliffs, NJ: Prentice-Hall.

Turner, K. L., & Makhija, M. V. 2012. The role of individuals in the information processing perspective. *Strategic Management Journal,* 33: 661-680.

Vaast, E. 2007. Danger in the eye of the beholders: Social representations of information systems security in healthcare. *Journal of Strategic Information Systems,* 16, 130-152.

Vaast, E., & Walsham, G. 2005. Representations and actions: The transformation of work practices with IT use. *Information and Organization,* 15, 65-89.

Van Maanen, J., & Barley, S. 1984. Occupational communities: Culture and control in Organizations, in B. M. Staw and L. L. Cummings (eds.), *Research in organizational behavior,* pp. 287-365, Greenwich, CT: JAI Press.

Van Niekerk, J. F., & Von Solms, R. 2010. Information security culture: A management perspective. *Computers & Security,* 29: 476-486.

Vance, A., Lowry, P. B., and Eggett, D. 2015. Increasing accountability through user-interface design artifacts: A New approach to addressing the problem of access-policy violations. *MIS Quarterly,* 39(2), 345-366.

Vance, A., Siponen, M., & Pahnila, S. 2012. Motivating IS security compliance: Insights from habit and protection motivation theory. *Information & Management*, 49: 190-198.

Vlaar, P. W., Van den Bosch, F. A., & Volberda, H. W. 2006. Coping with problems of understanding in interorganizational relationships: Using formalization as a means to make sense. *Organization Studies*, 27, 1617–1638.

Vroom, C., and von Solms, R. 2004. Towards information security behavioral compliance. *Computers & Security,* 23, 191-198.

Walsham, G. 1998. IT and changing professional identity: Micro studies and macro theory. *Journal of the American Society for Information Science,* 49(12), 1081- 1089.

Warkentin, M., & Willison, R. 2009. Behavioral and policy issues in information systems security: The inside threat. *European Journal of Information Systems,* 18: 101-105.

Weber, K., and Glynn, M. A. 2006. Making sense with institutions: Context, thought and action in Karl Weick's Theory. *Organization Studies,* 27, 1639-1660.

Weick, K. 1979. *The social psychology of organizing*. Reading, MA: Addison-Wesley.

Weick, K. E. 1987. Organizational culture as a source of high reliability. *California Management Review,* XXIX(2), 112-127.

Weick, K. E. 1990. Technology as equivoque: Sensemaking in new technologies in P. S. Goodman & L. S. Sproull (Eds.), *Technology and organizations* (pp. 1-44). San Francisco: Josey Bass Publishers.

Weick, K. E. 1993. The collapse of sensemaking in organizations: The Mann Gulch disaster. *Administrative Science Quarterly,* 38, 628-652.

Weick, K. E. 1995. *Sensemaking in organizations*. Newbury Park, CA: Sage.

Weick, K. E., Sutcliffe, K. M., and Obstfeld, D. 2005. Organizing and the process of sensemaking. *Organization Science,* 16(4), 409-425.

Whitman, M. E. 2004. In defense of the realm: Understanding threats to information security. *International Journal of Information Management,* 24: 43-57.

Whitman, M. E. 2008. Security policy: From design to maintenance. In D. W. Straub, S. Goodman, & R. L. Baskerville (Eds.), *Information security: Policy, processes, and practices:* 123-151. Armonk, NY: M. E. Sharpe, Inc.

Willison, R., & Warkentin, M. 2013. Beyond D\deterrence: An expanded view of employee computer abuse. *MIS Quarterly,* 37(1), 1-20.

Woon, I. M. Y., Tan, G. W., & Low, R. T. 2005. A protection motivation theory approach to home wireless security. In D. Avison, D. Galletta, & J. I. DeGross (Eds.), *Proceedings of the 26th International Conference on Information Systems*: 367-380. December 11-14, Las Vegas, NV, USA.

Workman, M., Bommer, W., & Straub, D. 2008. Security lapses and the omission of information security measures: An empirical test of the threat control model. *Journal of Computers in Human Behavior*, 24(6): 2799-2816.

Wright, R., T., & Marett, K. 2010. The influence of experiential and dispositional factors in phishing: An empirical investigation of the deceived. *Journal of Management Information Systems*, 27(1): 273-303.

Xu, H., Wang, H., & Teo, H.-H. 2005. Predicting the usage of P2P sharing software: The role of trust and perceived risk. In R.H. Sprague (Ed.), *Proceedings of the 38th Annual Hawaii International Conference on System Sciences*, Los Alamitos, CA: IEEE.

DECISION SCIENCES INSTITUTE

Training Beyond Job Skills to Enhance Perceived Organizational Support and Job Satisfaction in Central American Maquilas

Robert D. Morrison
University of Texas of the Permian Basin
Email: morrison_r@utpb.edu

Jennifer Welbourne
University of Texas Rio Grande Valley
Email: jennifer.welbourne@utrgv.edu

Claudia P. Dole
University of Texas Rio Grande Valley
Email: claudia.dole@utrgv.edu

Juan A. Chavarria
University of Texas Rio Grande Valley
Email: juan.chavarria@utrgv.edu

ABSTRACT

Strategic international human resource management practices must fit the particular cultural idiosyncrasies encountered in the local subsidiary. In the underdeveloped Central America nations education and development opportunities are scarce, therefore; by offering comprehensive training, employers fulfill the implied social contract associated with the type of benevolent paternalism that employees expect.

KEYWORDS: Training, Job Satisfaction, Central America

INTRODUCTION

In recent decades trade liberalization initiatives have increased the level of global competition and manufacturing firms responded by expanding their supply chains globally. Many low skilled assembly operations, such as those found in the apparel industry, shifted to low-wage nations. As the supply chains expanded across national borders not only did organizational complexity increase because of increased geographic distance, but also due to cultural distance between the headquarters' home country and the host countries of the manufacturing facilities. This required many firms to integrate an "I" for the international aspects of their human resource management (HRM→IHRM) or strategic human resource management (SHRM→SIHRM) practices (Schuler, 1992; Schuler, Dowling, & De Cieri, 1993; Wright & McMahan, 1992).

The *culturalist* view (Beechler & Yang, 1994) suggests that a similarity between national or societal-level cultures—as measured by popular categorizations of cultural dimensions or values (e.g., Hofstede, 1980; House, Hanges, Javidan, Dorfman, & Gupta, 2004; Maznevski, Distefano, Gomez, Noorderhaven, & Wu, 1997; Sagiv & Schwartz, 2000; Trompenaars & Hampden-Turner, 1998) —facilitates the transfer of home-country management practices (e.g., Beechler & Yang, 1994; Kogut & Singh, 1988; Newman & Nollen, 1996; Snape, Thompson, Yan, & Redman, 1998) and results in desirable outcomes (England, 1983; Ferris & Wagner, 1985; Lincoln, Olson, & Hanada, 1978). However, empirical research has not always supported this assumption, particularly in the context of the Latin American *maquila* industry. The words *maquila* or *maquiladora* derive from the Spanish verb *maquilar* and are associated with cross-border assembly factories; it originated in Mexico. (see discussion in Paik & Teagarden, 1995; Parra, Fernandez, & Osmond, 1996; Sargent & Matthews, 1998). When investigating Mexican *maquilas*; Paik and Teagarden (1995) found "the highest levels of satisfaction with organization climate, performance appraisal and reward systems were observed in a US-managed maquila as compared to Japanese and Korean counterparts" (p. 579) and they attributed this to differences in international human resource design (IHRM). While investigating workplace values apparel and textile maquilas the Sula Valley metropolitan area in Honduras, Morrison, Chavarria, and Dole (2012) found significantly higher levels of organizational commitment (OC) in production line employees working in North American (US and Canadian) owned factories compared to those working in Chinese and South Korean owned factories. In the Honduras study, the level of OC in North American owned factories was slightly higher, but similar to that found in Honduran owned factories.

These findings are interesting because Chinese, Honduran, Mexican, and South Korean cultures are similar based on Hofstede's (1980) cultural dimensions (see Figure 1.) and quite different from the US and Canadian cultures. Therefore, these results conflict with previous research suggesting that similarity in national culture facilitates the alignment of home country HR management practices with the societal norms and institutions of the host country (Beechler & Yang, 1994; Kogut & Singh, 1988; Newman & Nollen, 1996; Snape et al., 1998) to produce positive outcomes. One potential explanation for these findings is differences in HRM practices.

One aspect of culture that has not been strongly addressed in previous research is the benevolent paternalism that characterizes traditional HRM practices in Mexico and Central America (Diaz-Saenz & Witherspoon, 2000; Martinez, 2003; Osland & Osland, 2005; Paik & Teagarden, 1995). Although there are also paternalistic traditions in Chinese and South Korean cultures (Aycan, 2006; Kim, 1994; Kong, 2009; Lee & Song, 1994; Song & Meek, 1998), there is evidence that the practice of paternalistic leadership may differ from the practices in Latin America. Paik and Teagarden (1995) discuss the "expectations of paternalism" (p. 570) in Mexico and point to comprehensive approaches to human resource development (HRD) like on-site education, birth control, and AIDS awareness training as contributing to performance improvement and reducing turnover.

This study provides a theoretical framework for understanding how firms in this context enhance OC by looking beyond the broad concepts of cultural dimensions to develop strategic human resource management practices that fit the particular cultural idiosyncrasies encountered in the local subsidiary. Specifically, the deeply held expectations of benevolent paternalism in this context lead to an implied social contract wherein employees expect the employer to contribute significantly to their personal development. That development expectation extends beyond job task specific training; therefore, employees value comprehensive human resource development opportunities. The offering of comprehensive training by the employer contributes to the fulfillment of the implied social contract, which provides a perception of organizational support that in turn enhances OC and reduces turnover.

This study contributes to the literature in three ways. First, little research exist in the area of management and HRM in poorer and least developed nations of the world and HRM research in the context of Central America is virtually nonexistent (Osland & Osland, 2005). To the best of my knowledge, no research exists on HRM in the specific context of the maquila industry in Honduras. Second, this study provides theoretical insight into how a firm's implementation of comprehensive human resource development (HRD) better aligns HRM practice with employee expectations of benevolent paternalism, which results in enhanced organizational commitment and related outcomes. Finally, while this study provides practitioners with MNCs operations in Central America with insight on how to improve organizational commitment, it also informs international business practitioners about the need to understand culture at the local level and develop HRM strategies align with the expectations of employees in each specific subsidiary.

Literature Review

The Research Context

The maquila industry provides a unique context for research. The maquila industry began as a cross-border assembly plant arrangement between Mexico and the US with the 1966 Border Industrialization Program (Parra et al., 1996). The 1983 Caribbean Basin Initiative extended the maquila concept to Central America and certain Caribbean island nations (Pastor, 1982; Riding, 1982).

Conceptualizations of National Culture

Geert Hofstede (1980) provided a useful lens for understanding differences in national cultures and firmly established the importance of culture in international business research. Although criticism certainly exists (Dorfman & Howell, 1988; McSweeney, 2002; Oyserman, Coon, & Kemmelmeier, 2002; Robert & Bayacigiller, 1984), with over 54,000 citations, Hofstede's influence on the fields of international business and management is undeniable (Tung & Verbeke, 2010). Despite the criticism of Hofstede's study, "the four cultural dimensions seem to make sense and have been validated in subsequent work" (Thomas, 2002). Nonetheless, culture manifests itself in many forms (Cohen, 2009) and Hofstede's broad conceptualizations of cultural dimensions—Power Distance (PDI), Individualism-Collectivism (IDV), Masculinity-Femininity (MAS), Uncertainty Avoidance (UAI) —leave many things unexplained. For example, there is evidence that constructs of individualism and collectivism is not fully understood and there are different forms of collectivism (e.g., Fiske, 2002; Oyserman et al., 2002; Schwartz, 1990; Triandis, 1995). Collectivism incorporates the concept of close cohesive *in-group* (Triandis, 1995). However, in Latin America individuals orientate the in-group toward family and close friends (Gomez & Sanchez, 2005; Paik & Teagarden, 1995) while in Japan's collectivist culture the work group takes precedence (Lawrence & Yeh, 1994) and HRM systems in China, Japan and South Korea emphasize workplace socialization (Rowley, Benson, & Warner, 2004). The construct of power distance provides another example. Strong hierarchical structures exist in high power-distance cultures and both Asian and Latin American cultures score high in terms of power-distance. However, in the more family oriented Latin American culture employees often skip intermediate supervisors and go directly to the *patrón* (boss) (Davila & Elvira, 2005) whereas evidence indicates that Asian cultures based in Confucian Values such as China, Korea, Japan, and Taiwan tend to value the relational hierarchy. Paik and Teagarden (1995) content that cultural dimensions are broad approximations that "are not sufficiently refined to predict cultural proximity as operationalized in management practices" (p. 573); this reflects the emic (cultural-specific) view (Triandis, 1994) that MNCs need to tailor management practices to the specific local culture (Braun & Warner, 2002).

Figure 1. Comparison of Cultural Dimensions

FIGURE 1
Cultural Dimensions by Country

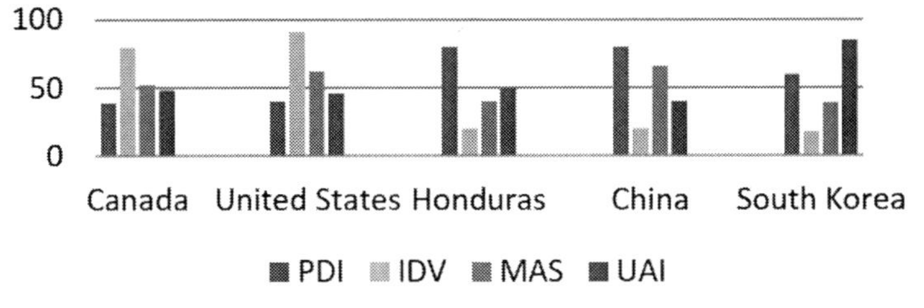

Organizational Commitment

Employee turnover is a major concern in the manufacturing industries because it increases training costs and output decreases because new employees take weeks to become as productive as those who left (e.g., Arthur, 1994; Campion, 1989; Staw, 1980). Although the relationships between OC and workplace measures such as job satisfaction, motivation, performance, and organizational effectiveness are complex, dynamic, and far from being completely understood (Bono & Patton, 2001; Koys, 2001; Ostroff, 1992), empirical research links these constructs to desirable outcomes such as reductions in absenteeism and turnover (e.g., Cotton & Tuttle, 1986; Eisenberger, Stinglhamber, Vandenberghe, Sucharski, & Rhoades, 2002; Meyer, Stanley, Herscovitch, & Topolnytsky, 2002). Therefore, firms can enhance performance by managing in ways that increase commitment (McElroy, 2001).

Conceptually, commitment is an attitude that reflects feelings that include attachment, identification, or loyalty that binds an individual to a course of action or target (Cohen, 2003). Affective commitment, "a strong belief in and acceptance of the organization's goals and values" (Porter, Steers, Mowday, & Boulian, 1974), is the most researched dimension (Fischer & Mansell, 2009). Most studies, 52.4% have used the OCQ instrument developed by Mowday, Steers, and Porter (1979) followed by the three dimension ACS instrument developed by Meyer and Allen (1991) at 30.4%. Based on a meta-analysis including studies that covered 54 countries across nine geographic regions, Meyer et al. (2012) suggest "the fact that the mean scores on the three components of commitment fluctuate around the midpoint across countries provides some evidence for their relevance across countries" (p. 242).

The Relationship between HRM and Commitment

Research has demonstrated the positive link between HRM systems and employee commitment and organizational outcomes (Meyer & Allen, 1997; Mowday, 1998). However, the effect of HRM on OC is neither direct nor unconditional (Meyer & Smith, 2000). In addition, the international context increases the complexity by adding additional factors and there are no clear indications of how a MNC adapts intangibles assets such as HR practice to the local context (Sparrow, Schuler, & Jackson, 1994). Therefore, given the large number of factors in any particular context the study of IHRM is both challenging and important (Bartlett & Ghoshal, 1989; Dowling, 1999; Oddou & Derr, 1999). Nevertheless, a meta-analysis by (Stanley et al., 2007) indicates that the negative correlation between OC and turnover intentions is consistent across nations and empirical research indicates that HRM practices can increase OC (Gaertner & Nollen, 1989; Meyer & Allen, 1997; Ogilvie, 1986).

There is also a positive link between OC and the level of social capital (Clark, 2003). Gomez and Sanchez (2005) suggest that in Latin American social capital is an "informal mechanism that allows MNCs to coordinate and integrate activities, which becomes critical when MNCs are trying to be both locally responsive and cost efficient through globalization" (p. 58). They further advise that in Latin America the form of individual treatment in any HRM practice is very important in the process of building social capital.

There is little agreement about the definition of Human Resource Management (HRM) (Boxall, 1996; Brewster & Mayrhofer, 2012; Goss, 1994; Guest, 1990, 1997; Storey, 1993, 1995, 2007); however, early textbooks (e.g., Fombrun, Tichy, & Devanna, 1984) differentiated it from the mostly administrative tasks associated with personnel management. Generally, Strategic International HRM (SIHRM) can be defined as "human resource management issues, functions, and policies and practices that result from the strategic activities of multinational enterprises and that impact the international concerns and goals of those enterprises" (Schuler et al., 1993). Employees are perceptive of HRM practices (Ogilvie, 1986) and value career oriented practices that include internal promotion, training and development; and employment security (Gaertner & Nollen, 1989).

MNCs encounter the strategic challenge of responding to a variety of national demands while trying to maintain a coherent strategy (Doz & Prahalad, 1986). An ongoing debate exists regarding standardization (convergence) in International HRM (IHRM) practices versus localization of practices to the host context (see discussion in Pudelko & Harzing, 2007; Rosenzweig & Nohria, 1994; Sparrow et al., 1994). While some authors have suggested that best practices exist in IHRM (e.g., Von Glinow, Drost, & Teagarden, 2002) others argue that HRM practices must adapt to the local context (e.g., Bae & Lawler, 2000; Harry & Collings, 2012; Marchington & Grugulis, 2000; Newman & Nollen, 1996). Support for integrative or hybrid approaches also exist (Osland & Osland, 2005; Taylor, Beechler, & Napier, 1996). Adler and Ghadar (1990) suggest that in the context of MNCs, it is not an issue of finding the best international HRM policy, it is an issue of fit between the firms external environment, its overall strategy, and its HRM policy and implementation. Bartlett and Ghoshal (1989) argue that truly transnational organizations maintain a dynamic balance. Given the vast differences in cultures, norms, and institutional requirements that exist in different nations, a MNC would find it difficult to find truly universal policies that fit every situation; therefore, there must be some degree of adaptation to each local context. However, "localization occurs at a slow pace and there are practical, cultural, and strategic factors that impede rapid localization" (Gamble, 2000). As is true with many initiatives, it is relatively easy to formulate localization policies; however, effective localization is not driven from above, it requires an understanding of the host country conditions and the buy-in of both local and expatriate mangers (Fryxell, Butler, & Choi, 2004).

Information gathered from the Honduran Manufacturers Association (Asociación Hondureña de Maquiladores), and the Honduras-Korea Center for Technical Development (Centro de Capacitación Tecnica Honduras Corea) indicates the US, Canadian, and Honduran owned maquilas offer or support employee participation in a broader range of HRD activities. Examples include completion of educational requirements to obtain a diploma for the six year Basic Cycle (Ciclo Basico) of education or high school. A very good example of comprehensive HRD offerings is a US firm that works a four-day-on/four-day-off shift provides cosmetologist training to employees so that they can enhance their income by styling hair or doing manicures on their days off.

HRM in Latin America

Although Latin America is a significant emerging economy, when compared to the emerging economies in Asia and Eastern Europe relatively little management research exists (Nicholls-Nixon, Davila Castilla, Sanchez Garcia, & Rivera Pesquera, 2011). The tensions between the SHRM approach demanded by *global* competition and the *local* approach to HRM that are deeply rooted in Latin American cultural values have received little attention (Davila & Elvira, 2009). In addition, in the area of HRM the existing studies have focused mostly on Mexico or take a multi-country Latin America approach (Von Glinow et al., 2002) and often view all Latin American countries as a relatively homogeneous (see discussion in Davila & Elvira, 2012; Elvira & Davila, 2005; Nicholls-Nixon et al., 2011).

MNCs operating in Latin America struggle to adapt to the local environment because significant differences exist that affect HR practices in different Latin American countries; these include employee benefits and protections institutionalized in local laws; however, despite some country-to-country difference there are similarities; for example, collectivism (Gomez & Sanchez, 2005). However, Latin America collectivism is orientated toward the close cohesive *in-group* (Triandis, 1995) being family and close friends (Davila & Elvira, 2005, 2009; Davila & Elvira, 2012; Gomez & Sanchez, 2005; Martinez, 2003, 2005; Paik & Teagarden, 1995) as opposed to the work group in some other collectivist cultures such as Japan (Lawrence & Yeh, 1994). Citing the expectations of paternalism and the importance of family as some of the challenges faced by management in the Mexican maquila industry, Paik and Teagarden (1995) found that Mexicans did not care what firm they worked for as long as they work for a manager that cared for them. They also related the higher levels of stress reported by Mexican workers in Korean maquilas to the high levels of work ethic, as in *live to work* versus *work to live*, required by those firms. This aligns with Diaz-Saenz and Witherspoon (2000) discussion of how Mexicans view a job as a "means to a single important end: providing a good standard of living for one's family" (p. 159).

Gomez and Sanchez (2005) suggest that in Latin America the role of SHRM is to build social capital as suggested by Snell (1999) and defined by (Nahapiet & Ghoshal, 1998). (Snell, 1999) suggests that the underlying elements of social capital are network ties, interpersonal trust, and shared knowledge. Gomez and Sanchez (2005) argue informal control is even more critical in Latin American countries where formal controls are often ineffective. They also suggest that although HR practices are strongly affected by national dynamics, institutional factors, culture, and local norms" (p. 58), the practices do not have to mirror those local forces perfectly. This provides sufficient flexibility to formulate a hybrid approach that is both culturally sensitive yet still aligned with corporate strategy.

As previously mentioned, research has linked social capital to OC (Clark, 2003). Given the close in-group link to family and close friends, to build social capital in Latin America the HR practices must effectively funnel those family oriented collectivist values toward the organization. Accomplishing this requires that the organization focus on the interpersonal aspect and include the employee's in-group among the beneficiaries (Gomez & Sanchez, 2005). HR departments in Latin American often extend their development activities beyond employees' specific job task to include basic formal education and technical training (Davila & Elvira, 2005; De Forest, 1994) and Paik and Teagarden (1995) found that in-house education and training that included things such as birth control and AIDS awareness enhanced organizational outcomes and reduced turnover. (Gomez & Sanchez, 2005) also discuss the importance of taking a more comprehensive approach to human resources development, "training and development programs can build social capital if they show a genuine, long-term interest/investment orientation in the employee as an individual just as bona fide members of the in-group would" (p. 69) and managers from Mexico and Latin America overwhelmingly believe in training as a reward in addition to the skill building benefits (Drost, Frayne, Lowe, & Geringer, 2002).

Honduras and Central America

There has been little insight into management practices in Central America and it arguably differs from the rest of Latin America in many respects (Osland & Osland, 2005). For example, contemporary Honduras, similar to the other Central American nations, is poly-ethnic. Over 100 years of liberal policies toward foreign investment and immigration created a society made up of indigenous peoples, Europeans (from both Europe and the US), Africans (called Garifunas), Arab-Palestinians (sometimes incorrectly called *Turcos* as in being Turkish), and mixed race combinations referred to as *mestizos* (see discussion in Craft, 1998; Euraque, 1995; González, 1992; Leonard, 2011; Osoi, 2005; Valentine, 1916). Unlike most Spanish speaking Latin American countries, English is spoken as a primary language by many Anglo-European and African descendants that inhabit the Bay Islands and portions of the Atlantic Coast and for decades many children of fruit company local managers attended company schools where English was the language of instruction. Central America also has a long, and somewhat controversial, history with US MNCs (see discussion in Acker, 1988; Chapman, 2007; Laínez & Meza, 1974; Leonard, 2011; Osoi, 2005; Valentine, 1916) that dates back before 1896 when O'Henry coined the term *banana republic* while writing *Cabbages and Kings* (1904) during his lengthy stay in Honduras to avoid his US legal problems. The fruit companies have been a dominating influence in Honduras and the rest of Central America and MNCs play a major role in Latin America's economy. Data from the Economic Commission for Latin America and the Caribbean (CEPAL for its abbreviation in Spanish) indicates that MNCs account for about 50% of registered sales and 40% of exports. Approximately 50% of the Honduran economy links directly to the US (GlobalEdge, n.d.).

Benevolent Paternalism as SHRM in Latin America

Research interest in paternalistic leadership has increased in recent years (Aycan, 2006) and researchers have noted that paternalism is prevalent in Latin American culture and that it traces its origins back to the agrarian culture and the old hacienda (plantation) leadership style (Diaz-Saenz & Witherspoon, 2000; Martinez, 2003, 2005). Analyzing HRM practices in Latin America, (Martinez, 2005) classifies paternalism as a leadership style that perpetuates in contemporary Latin American organizations. Examining the practice in a Mexican textile mill, Boyer (2000) suggest that workers embrace the practice because it is derived from the traditional, gender based family roles embedded in Catholicism which equate the *patron* (boss) as being the caretakers of their workers in a quasi-family manner. As the root word paternal suggests, the concept is much like a parent caring for a child. Reflecting on the hacienda literature from sociology, political science, philosophy, and history, Martinez (2003) describes the practice where plantation owners addressed labor issues by providing housing and food for the worker's entire family, in addition to wages, in exchange for commitment. The benefits often included things like housing and food; however, benefits such as basic education and medical care were common. When hacienda owners built textile mills to expand operations vertically these practices extended into industry (Boyer, 2000).

Like Mexico, Central America was, and largely still is, an agrarian society. New York native Minor Keith went to Costa Rica to build a railroad in the late 1800s. In an interesting series of events, he ended up receiving large plots of land from the Costa Rican government to complete the railroad after the government could not meet its obligations. Keith planted bananas on these lands, created a steamship company, and used the railroad to start what would eventually become the United Fruit Company (see discussion in Acker, 1988; Chapman, 2007). He entered into similar agreements in Colombia, Guatemala, Honduras, and Panama. As he developed these plantations in undeveloped areas along the railroads, he built the housing and infrastructure needed to support the workforce on company lands and the paternalistic leadership style became engrained in *Banana Land* (Ganz, 1950) culture. A paternalistic leader acts as a caring and protective head of the industrial household (Kerfoot & Knights, 1993) by providing benefits or protection to a person independently of his wishes (Kultgen, 1992). Martinez (2005) points out that while some of the scholarly literature labels this *exchange* as paternalism, which Americans may view negatively, Mexicans merely view the exchange as "describing the relationship between the *patrón* (boss) and his employees" (P. 75). Providing an insightful review of the literature, Aycan (2006) states that, "paternalism is a salient and powerful construct that has many faces" (p.462). He argues that "few constructs in the management literature are as intriguing, complex, and controversial.... [it can be]....construed at individual (e.g., paternalistic leadership), organizational (e.g., paternalistic organizational culture and practices), and socio-cultural levels (e.g., paternalism as a cultural dimension)" (p. 445). As Martinez (2005) explains, some Western scholars view paternalism in a negative light and the practice does have its critics. For example, Warren (1999) labels the practice a condescending relationship of master and servant, be it authoritarian or sophisticated paternalism, which holds that only one set of interest should be recognized and the employee must acknowledge that. He describes sophisticated paternalism as consisting of a combination of monetary and non-monetary benefits provided to the employees to circumvent employee driven initiatives such as unionization and collective bargaining.

Pellegrini, Scandura, and Jayaraman (2010) suggest that paternalistic leadership may generalize across cultures. However, they found very different effects in India compared to the US. In India, paternalistic leadership had significant positive effects on both job satisfaction and OC. There was only a positive significant effect on OC in the US and the effect was about half of that seen in India.

Martinez (2005) categorizes the patron-employee relationship as an exchange. Leader-member exchange (LMX) (e.g., Dansereau, Graen, & Haga, 1975; Graen & Uhl-Bien, 1995) and paternalistic leadership are somewhat similar in that they both incorporate the concepts of social exchange (Blau, 1964) and the norm of reciprocity (Gouldner, 1960). The reasoning is that receiving positive beneficial actions creates a sense of indebtedness that the individual can only reduce through reciprocation in a positive beneficial way (Blau, 1964; Eisenberger, Huntington, Hutchison, & Sowa, 1986; Gouldner, 1960; Greenberg & Westcott, 1983). It is noteworthy that these concepts also lie at the core of organizational support theory (Eisenberger, Armeli, Rexwinkel, Lynch, & Rhoades, 2001) discussed in an upcoming section. (Bass, 1985) proposed that LMX might manifest itself in Latin American by way of a paternalistic relationship between leader and subordinate. However, while "LMX clearly incorporates an operationalization of a relationship-based approach to leadership" (Graen & Uhl-Bien, 1995), Pellegrini et al. (2010) argue that "LMX is focused on employee's career development, whereas paternalism is focused on the employee's overall welfare both in work and off-the-job domains" (p. 397).

Paternalism can benefit employers through increased loyalty, commitment, and team cohesion, especially when operating in developing nations (Aycan, 2006), in exchange, the employee receives a perceive sense of security that someone is looking out for them (e.g., Boyer, 2000; Martinez, 2003, 2005). In Latin America "there is a strong concern for a good quality of life for employees" (Briscoe, Schuler, & Tarique, 2012). As in any other culture work plays an important role but the mindset is soundly *work to live* versus *live to work* as a job is seen only as a means of providing a good standard of living for one's family (Diaz-Saenz & Witherspoon, 2000). In general, workers in Latin America expect management to be cognizant of subordinate needs and those needs extent to their families (Diaz-Saenz & Witherspoon, 2000; Greer & Stephens, 1996; Osland, De Franco, & Osland, 1999). This creates an implicit *social contract*—shared beliefs regarding duties and obligations, between employers and their employees—that reflects the involvement of firms in their workers' lives and highlights the fact that employers must provide for both social and economic needs (Diaz-Saenz & Witherspoon, 2000; Elvira & Davila, 2005; Martinez, 2003, 2005). Martinez (2005) suggests that paternalistic practices have adapted to modern competitive pressures; today HRM practices address the paternalistic exchange of benefits, perquisites, reciprocity, and obligations in a somewhat more bureaucratic manner. In the paternalistic leadership style that exists in the modern Latin American economy, HRM functions as an advocate of the employee and its practices center around the employee (Davila & Elvira, 2005, 2009; Martinez, 2003, 2005).

Cheng, Chou, Wu, Huang, and Farh (2004) proposes that there are three types of paternalistic leadership: benevolent leadership, moral leadership, and authoritarian leadership. "Authoritarianism refers to a leader's behavior that asserts absolute authority and control over subordinates and demands unquestionable obedience from subordinates. Benevolence means that the leader's behavior demonstrates individualized, holistic concern for subordinates' personal or familial well-being. Moral leadership can be broadly depicted as a leader's behavior that demonstrates superior personal virtues, self-discipline, and unselfishness" (p. 91). The extant literature on paternalistic leadership in Latin America strongly suggests that it is benevolent in nature and exhibits a somewhat informal organizational hierarchy. For instance, while the power distance dimension is strong in almost every Latin American country; however, within the family-like environment in the Latin American paternal leadership context subordinates workers may feel free to skip their immediate supervisor and speak directly to the general manager about their work or personal problems (Davila & Elvira, 2005). Boyer's (2000) suggestion of alignment with Catholic teachings also provides some evidence of moral leadership underpinnings, at least in the historical context.

In contrast to the less formal paternalistic hierarchy in Latin America, there are indications that Korean (e.g., Kim, 1994; Lee & Song, 1994; Song & Meek, 1998) and Chinese (e.g., Cheng et al., 2004; Farh, Cheng, Chou, & Chu, 2006; Kong, 2009) paternalistic leadership practices take a more authoritarian approach to elicit compliance and instill a sense of obligation. Cheng et al. (2004) point out that in contrast to Western benevolent leadership traditions, in Chinese culture " the *shi-en* behaviours of benevolent leadership are enacted in a situation …[where]…The leader constantly reminds the subordinates who is really in charge in his/her benevolent behaviors" (p. 93). Studies suggest that this traces back to the cultural tradition of Confucianism and Legalism where the father has authority over his children and the whole family and possesses absolute power and legitimacy (e.g., Cheng et al., 2004; Farh et al., 2006). Studying non-Chinese subordinates in 31 overseas branches of a Chinese MNC, Chen and Kao (2009) found that the moral and authoritarian styles of the Chinese paternalistic leadership contributed negatively to psychological health in the workplace as measured by the General Health Questionnaire (Goldberg & Hillier, 1979); the results were different in previous studies using only Chinese subordinates. However, these studies did not include any subsidiaries in Latin America.

The explicit demonstration by the employer of concern for the employee's well-being is an important component of the implied social contract associated with benevolent paternalism. This exchange strongly resemblance resembles the exchange processes incorporated into organizational support theory (Eisenberger et al., 1986).

Perceived Organizational Support

Researcher have proposed perceived organizational support (POS) as an antecedent to OC and numerous studies have found a positive relationship between POS and OC (Bishop, 2005; Eisenberger & Fasolo, 1990; Marique, Stinglhamber, Desmette, Caesens, & De Zanet, 2013; Rhoades & Eisenberger, 2002; Shore & Wayne, 1993). Empirical evidence also supports the view that social exchange processes (Blau, 1964) and the norm of reciprocity (Gouldner, 1960) lie at the core of organizational support theory (Eisenberger et al., 2001). It is noteworthy that these are also associated with paternalism and OC. Organizational support theory holds that employees tend to assign humanlike characteristics to an organization and that employees are more likely to become committed to an organization if they perceive that the organization values their contributions and cares about their well-being (Eisenberger & Fasolo, 1990; Eisenberger et al., 1986). An increase in the employee's POS creates an obligation to care about the organization's welfare and contribute to helping the organization meet its goals. Although conceptually related, POS and OC are theoretically and empirically distinct constructs (Bishop, 2005). Where OC reflects employees' attitude toward the organization, POS reflects employees' perceptions about the organizations attitude toward them (Shore & Tetrick, 1991).

Fulfilling the Implied Social Contract with Comprehensive Training

When it comes to human capital development and education there are substantial differences between the developed and developing nations (e.g., Chimombo, 2005; Ferner & Quintanilla, 1998; Morgan, 1986) and "in Latin America the training and development function is less developed than in other regions" (Briscoe et al., 2012). Although Honduran law states that there are six years of mandatory school attendance, there is virtually no enforcement and outside the metropolitan areas, the average person attends school only two to three years (Murphy-Graham, 2012). Later in life, many of those migrate to the metropolitan areas in search of work. This is a common situation in the least developed nations and it creates significant challenges for employers that must implement world-class manufacturing systems to compete (see discussion in Kaplinsky, 1995; Kaplinsky & Posthuma, 1994; Sargent & Matthews, 1998). Employers must address these constraints by developing the human resources.

Training, formal or informal, is a discretionary organizational investment that employees receive and they can view it as a reward and a form of the organization expressing care about the employee's development (Wayne, Shore, & Liden, 1997). Butler and Teagarden (1993) argue that "the education strategy can result in short-term increased costs, but longer term the benefits of training can contribute to overall effectiveness through development of a more highly skilled workforce" (p.494). In Latin America, managers overwhelmingly indicate that training is a valued reward (Drost et al., 2002) and research indicates that Mexican maquila workers wanted training even if it meant forgoing pay increases (Teagarden, Butler, & von Glinow, 1992). As previously mentioned, evidence suggest that the North American and Honduran owned maquilas offer education and development opportunities that go considerably beyond those required for the performance of work-related tasks, even to the extent that they provide training that enable workers to earn outside income on their days off. This study defines that human resource practice as providing employees with *comprehensive training* opportunities.

Drawing from Adler and Ghadar (1990) and Milliman, Von Glinow, and Nathan (1991), Paik and Teagarden (1995) discuss the role of training as one factor that differentiates between control IHRM design, human relations IHRD, and human resources IHRM design. Specifically, they state that the control design pays little attention to motivating or developing the worker while the human relations design "uses limited training (at best) that focuses on task-specific requirements" (p. 571). However, the human resource design "provides an extensive array of culturally and contextually appropriate benefits; training and development programmes that reduce overall cost and improve quality, and that target developmental and general education needs of workers" (p. 571).

While the expansion of the maquila industry in Honduras by no means eliminated poverty, the impact on poverty reduction was significant and the industry provided improved opportunities for women (Dollar & Kraay, 2002; Hoyos, Bussolo, & Nunez, 2008; Jarmillo & al., 2005; Potoker & Borgman, 2007; Ravallion, 2001). Given that average wages in the maquila industry are significantly higher than those outside the maquila industry, one can argue that the common Honduran line worker generally views training opportunities as a means to enhance their skill set in a way that differentiates them from the millions of other Hondurans that did not complete high school. In a nation where education and training opportunities are limited, a comprehensive skill set enhances job security, and improves the standard of living for them and most importantly their family.

Employees may view comprehensive training, training which goes beyond skills that are job task specific, as more beneficial to their overall personal development (Harel & Tzafrir, 1999; Kalleberg & Moody, 1994; McEnvoy, 1997). Paul and Anantharaman (2004) found that comprehensive training had a positive effect on OC when comparing software firms in India where paternalism is also part of the cultural norm.

PROPOSITIONS

In an underdeveloped nation with limited training and development opportunities, employees may interpret HRM practices that incorporate comprehensive training as a demonstration of management's concern for the individual's wellbeing and as a component toward fulfillment of the implied social contract associated with the benevolent form of paternalism that Martinez (2003, 2005) suggest is the practice in Latin America.

P1: *Hondurans view comprehensive training as fulfillment of the implied social contract*

If the employee feels that the organization has fulfilled their obligations to demonstrate concern and caring for the employee's well-being by providing comprehensive development opportunities, then the employee interpret this as an expression of organizational support.

P2: *Perceived fulfillment of the implied social contract positively enhances the perception of organizational support*

Then the norm of reciprocity (Gouldner, 1960) suggest that if the employee perceives organizational support then the employee will feel an obligation to care about the organization's welfare and contribute to helping the organization meet its goals.

P3: Perceived Organizational Support positively enhances organizational commitment

Finally, a meta-analysis of the empirical research (Stanley et al., 2007) indicates a consistent negative correlation between organizational commitment and turnover intentions across nations.

P4: Increased organizational commitment reduces turnover intentions

Figure 2. Proposed Theoretical Model

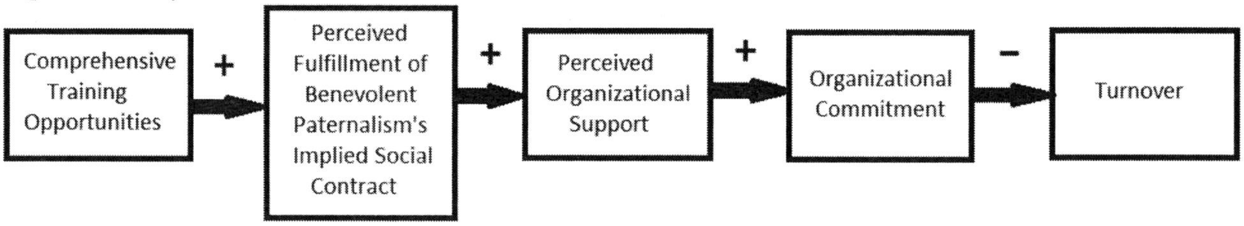

DISCUSSION

This study posits that benevolent paternalism is a deeply embedded trait of Honduran culture. In an impoverished country where over one-third of the workforce is unemployed or underemployed (GlobalEdge, n.d.) and high quality educational opportunities are beyond the reach of the vast majority of the workforce, Hondurans can perceive the comprehensive training provided by employers as an indication of fulfillment of the implicit social contract. Therefore, a SHRM approach that embraces benevolent paternalism and provides development opportunities that extend beyond those required for job specific tasks results in an increase in the perception of organizational support and that enhances OC, leading to improved organizational outcomes. The finding that factories of MNCs from the individualistic and low power-distance cultures of Canada and the US demonstrate higher levels of OC than those operated by MNCs from the collectivist and high power-distance cultures of China and South Korea provide evidence that HRM practices are not necessarily constrained by the headquarters national culture. It is important to understand the not only are there variations in culture both across and within nations, but also, there are considerable differences even within the broad definitions of culture such as individualism-collectivism, power-distance, and even paternalism. To be effective, SHRM policies, and even more importantly the actual practices, must take the particular idiosyncrasies of each subsidiary into account. The desired outcome is a set of human resource practices that support the MNCs strategic goals but do so in a manner that local employees perceive as well aligned with their deeply embedded expectations.

Limitations and Suggestions for Future Research

While the current study examined how HR practices contribute to OC and turnover intentions, it focused solely on the HR practices of comprehensive training. Specifically, this study addressed how Honduran employees can perceive comprehensive training as contributing to the fulfillment of the implied social contract associated with paternalistic leadership. However, it is likely that other HR practices may align with the local culture and contribute to positive outcomes. Another issue that may differentiate Canadian and US factories from Chinese and South Korean factories is the use of local management.

REFERENCES

Acker, A. 1988. *Honduras : The making of a banana republic*. Boston, MA: South End Press.

Adler, N., & Ghadar, F. 1990. Strategic human resource management: a global perspective. In Pieper (Ed.), *Human resource management in international comparison*: 235-260. Berlin: de Gruyter.

Arthur, J. B. 1994. Effects of human resource systems on manufacturing performance and turnover. *Academy of Management Journal*, 37(3): 670-687.

Aycan, Z. 2006. Paternalism:Towards conceptual refinement and operationalization. In U.-c. o. Kim, G. Yang, & K.-k. Hwang (Eds.), *Indigenous and cultural psychology : Understanding people in context*. New York, NY: Springer.

Bae, J., & Lawler, J. J. 2000. Organizational and HRM strategies in Korea: Impact: Impact on Firm Performance in an emerging economy. *Academy of Management Journal*, 43(3): 502-517.

Bartlett, C. A., & Ghoshal, S. 1989. *Managing accross borders: The transnational solution*. Cambridge, MA: Harvard Business School Press.

Bass, B. M. 1985. *Leadership and performance beyond expectations*. New York; London: Free Press ; Collier Macmillan.

Beechler, S., & Yang, J. Z. 1994. The transfer of Japanese-style management to American subsidiaries: contingencies, constraints, and competencies. *Journal of International Business Studies*, 25(3): 467-491.

Bishop, J. W. 2005. A construct validity study of commitment and perceived support variables: A multifoci approach across different team environments. *Group & Organization Management*, 30(2): 153-180.

Blau, P. M. 1964. *Exchange and power in social life*. New York: Wiley.

Bono, J. E., & Patton, G. K. 2001. The job satisfaction – job performance relationship: a qualitative and quantitative review. *Psychological Bulletin*: 376 – 407.

Boxall, P. 1996. The strategic hrm debate and the resource-based view of the firm. *Human Resource Management Journal*, 6(3): 59-75.

Boyer, C. R. 2000. The threads of class at La Virgen: Misrepresentation and identity at a Mexican textile mill, 1918-1935. *The American Historical Review*, 105(5): 1576-1598.

Braun, W., & Warner, M. 2002. The culture-free versus culture-specific management debate. In M. Warner, & P. Joynt (Eds.), *Managing accros cultures: Issues and perspectives*: 13-25. London: Thomson Learning.

Brewster, C., & Mayrhofer, W. 2012. Comparative human resource management: An introduction. In C. Brewster, & W. Mayrhofer (Eds.), *Handbook of research on comparative human resource management*: 1-26. Cheltenham, UK: Edward Elgar Publishing.

Briscoe, D., Schuler, R., & Tarique, I. 2012. *International Human Resource Management, 4th ed*. New York: Routledge.

Butler, M. C., & Teagarden, M. B. 1993. Strategic management of worker health, safety, and environmental issues in Mexico's Maquiladora industry. *Human Resource Management*, 32(4): 479-503.

Campion, M. A. 1989. Ability requirement implications of job design: An interdisciplinary perspectives. *Personnel Psychology*, 42: 1-24.

Chapman, P. 2007. *Bananas : how the United Fruit Company shaped the world*. New York: Canongate.

Chen, H.-Y., & Kao, H. S.-R. 2009. Chinese paternalistic leadership and non-Chinese subordinates' psychological health. *The International Journal of Human Resource Management*, 20(12): 2533-2546.

Cheng, B.-S., Chou, L.-F., Wu, T.-Y., Huang, M.-P., & Farh, J.-L. 2004. Paternalistic leadership and subordinate responses: Establishing a leadership model in Chinese organizations. *Asian Journal of Social Psychology*, 7(1): 89-117.

Chimombo, J. P. G. 2005. Issues in basic education in developing countries: An exploration of policy options for improved delivery. *Journal of International Cooperation in Education*, 8(1): 129-152.

Clark, M. M. 2003. Academics tout 'social capital' as the latest thing in strategic HR. *HR Magazine*, 48(2): 38.

Cohen, A. 2003. *Multiple commitments in the workplace : An integrative approach*. Mahwah, N.J.: Lawrence Erlhaum Associates.

Cohen, A. B. 2009. Many forms of culture. *American Psychologist*, 64(3): 194-204.

Cotton, J. L., & Tuttle, J. M. 1986. Employee turnover: A meta-analysis and review with implications for research. *Academy of Management Review*(4): 55-70.

Craft, L. J. 1998. Ethnicity, oral tradition, and the processed word: Construction of a national identity in Honduras. *Revista Hispanica Moderna*, 51(1): 136-146.

Dansereau, F., Graen, G., & Haga, W. J. 1975. A vertical dyad linkage approach to leadership within formal organizations: A longitudinal investigation of the role making process. *Organizational Behavior and Human Performance*, 13(1): 46-78.

Davila, A., & Elvira, M. M. 2005. Culture and human resource management in Latin America. In M. M. Elvira, & A. Davila (Eds.), *Managing Human Resources in Latin American*: 3-24. London: Routledge.

Davila, A., & Elvira, M. M. 2009. Theoretical approaches to best HRM practices in Latin America. In A. Davila, & M. M. Elvira (Eds.), *Best human resource management practices in Latin America*: 180-188. London: Routledge.

Davila, A., & Elvira, M. M. 2012. Latin American HRM models. In C. Brewster, & W. Mayrhofer (Eds.), *Handbook of research on comparative human resource management*: 478-493. Cheltenham, UK: Edward Elgar Publishing.

De Forest, M. E. 1994. Thinking of a plant in Mexico. *Academy of Management Executive*, 8(1): 33-40.

Diaz-Saenz, H. G., & Witherspoon, P. D. 2000. Psychological contracts in Mexico. In D. M. Rousseau, & R. Schalk (Eds.), *Psychological contracts in employment : cross-national perspectives*. Thousand Oaks, CA: Sage.

Dollar, D., & Kraay, A. 2002. Growth is good for the poor. Washington D.C.: World Bank.

Dorfman, P. W., & Howell, J. P. 1988. Dimensions of national culture and effective leadership patterns: Hofstede revisited. *Advances in international comparative management*, 3(127-150).

Dowling, P. J. 1999. Completing the puzzle: Issues in the development of the field of international human resource management. *Management International Review*, 19(4): 27-43.

Doz, Y., & Prahalad, C. 1986. Controlled variety: A challenge for human resource management in the MNC. *Human Resource Management*, 25(1): 55-71.

Drost, E. A., Frayne, C. A., Lowe, K. B., & Geringer, J. M. 2002. Benchmarking training and development practices: A multi-country comparative analysis. *Human Resource Management*, 41(1): 67-86.

Eisenberger, R., Armeli, S., Rexwinkel, B., Lynch, P. D., & Rhoades, L. 2001. Reciprocation of perceived organizational support. *Journal of Applied Psychology*, 86(1): 42-51.

Eisenberger, R., & Fasolo, P. 1990. Perceived organizational support and employee diligence, commitment, and innovation. *Journal of Applied Psychology*, 75(1): 51.

Eisenberger, R., Huntington, R., Hutchison, S., & Sowa, D. 1986. Perceived organizational support. *Journal of Applied Psychology*, 71(3): 500-507.

Eisenberger, R., Stinglhamber, F., Vandenberghe, C., Sucharski, I. L., & Rhoades, L. 2002. Perceived supervisor support: Contributions to perceived organizational support and employee retention. *Journal of Applied Psychology*, 87(3): 565-573.

Elvira, M. M., & Davila, A. 2005. Emergent directions for human resource management research in Latin America. *The International Journal of Human Resource Management*, 16(12): 2265-2282.

England, G. W. 1983. Japanese and American management: Theory Z and beyond. *Journal of International Business Studies*, 14(2): 131-142.

Euraque, D. A. 1995. Nation formation, Mestizahe and Arab Palestinian immigration to Honduras, 1880-1930s. *Critique: Critical Middle Eastern Studies*, 4(6): 25-37.

Farh, J. L., Cheng, B. S., Chou, L. F., & Chu, X. P. 2006. Authority and benevolence: Employees' responses to paternalistic leadership in China. In A. S. Tsui, Y. Bian, & L. K. Cheng (Eds.), *China's domestic private firms : multidisciplinary perspectives on management and performance*. Armonk, N.Y.: M.E. Sharpe.

Ferner, A., & Quintanilla, J. 1998. Multinationals, national business systems and HRM: the enduring influence of national identity or a process of 'Anglo-Saxonization'. *International Journal of Human Resource Management*, 9(4): 710-731.

Ferris, G. R., & Wagner, J. A. 1985. Quality circles in the United States: A conceptual reevaluation. *The Journal of applied behavioral science*, 21(2): 155-167.

Fischer, R., & Mansell, A. 2009. Commitment across cultures: A meta-analytical approach. *Journal of International Business Studies*, 40(8): 1339-1358.

Fiske, A. P. 2002. Using individualism and collectivism to compare cultures-A critique of the validity and measurement of the constructs: Comment on Oyserman et al.(2002). *Psychological Bulletin*, 128(1): 78-88.

Fombrun, C. J., Tichy, N. M., & Devanna, M. A. 1984. *Strategic human resource management*. New York: Wiley.

Fryxell, G. E., Butler, J., & Choi, A. 2004. Successful localization programs in China: an important element in strategy implementation. *Journal of World Business*, 39(3): 268-282.

Gaertner, K. N., & Nollen, S. D. 1989. Career experiences, perceptions of employment practices, and psychological commitment to the organization. *Human Relations*, 42(11): 975-991.

Gamble, J. E. 2000. Localizing management in foreign-invested enterprises in China: Practical, cultural, and strategic perspectives. *International Journal of Human Resource Management*, 11(5): 883-1004.

Ganz, W. J. 1950. Journey to Banana Land: 21 minutes. New York.

GlobalEdge. n.d. Global edge: Your source for global business knowledge. East Lansing, MI: Michigan State University.

Goldberg, D. P., & Hillier, V. F. 1979. A scaled version of the General Health Questionnaire. *Psychological Medicine*, 9(01): 139-145.

Gomez, C., & Sanchez, J. I. 2005. Managing HR to build social capital in Latin America within MNCs. In M. M. Elvira, & A. Davila (Eds.), *Managing human resourses in Latin America*: 57-74. New York: Routledge.

González, N. L. S. 1992. *Dollar, dove, and eagle : one hundred years of Palestinian migration to Honduras*. Ann Arbor: University of Michigan Press.

Goss, D. 1994. *Principles of human resource management*. London: Routledge.

Gouldner, A. W. 1960. The norm of reciprocity: A preliminary statement. *American Sociological Review*, 25(2): 161-178.

Graen, G. B., & Uhl-Bien, M. 1995. Relationship-based approach to leadership: Development of leader-member exchange (LMX) theory of leadership over 25 years: Applying a multi-level multi-domain perspective. *The Leadership Quarterly*, 6(2): 219-247.

Greenberg, M. S., & Westcott, D. R. 1983. Indebtedness as a mediator of reactions to aid. In J. D. Fisher, A. Nadler, & B. M. DePaulo (Eds.), *New Directions in Helping*, Vol. 1: 85-112. New YorK: Academic Press.

Greer, C. R., & Stephens, G. K. 1996. Employee relations issues for US companies in Mexico. *California Management Review*, 38: 121-145.

Guest, D. E. 1990. Human resource management and the American dream. *Journal of Management Studies*, 27(4): 377-397.

Guest, D. E. 1997. Human resource management and performance: a review and research agenda. *International Journal of Human Resource Management*, 8(3): 263-276.

Harel, G. H., & Tzafrir, S. S. 1999. The effect of human resource management practices on the perceptions of organizational and market performance of the firm. *Human Resource Management*, 38(3): 185-199.

Harry, W., & Collings, D. G. 2012. Localisation: Societies, organisations, and employees. In G. K. Stahl, M. E. Mendenhall, & G. R. Oddou (Eds.), *Readings and cases in international human resource management and organizational behavior*. New York: Routledge.

Hofstede, G. 1980. *Culture's consequences: International differences in work related values*. Beverly Hills, CA: Sage.

House, R. J., Hanges, P. J., Javidan, M., Dorfman, P. W., & Gupta, V. 2004. *Leadership, culture, and organizations: The GLOBE study of 62 societies*. Thousand Oaks, CA: Sage.

Hoyos, R. E., Bussolo, M., & Nunez, O. 2008. Can maquila booms reduce poverty? Washington D.C.: World Bank.

Jarmillo, C. F., & al., e. 2005. DR-CAFTA: Challenges and opportunities for Central America. Washington D.C.: World Bank.

Kalleberg, A. L., & Moody, J. W. 1994. Human resource management and organizational performance. *American Behavioral Scientist*, 37(7): 948-962.

Kaplinsky, R. 1995. Capital intensity in South African manufacturing and unemployment, 1972–1990. *World Development*, 23(2): 179-192.

Kaplinsky, R., & Posthuma, A. 1994. *Easternisation : spread of Japanese management techniques to developing countries*. Ilford: Frank Cass.

Kerfoot, D., & Knights, D. 1993. Management, masculinity and manipulaiont from paternalism to corporate strategy in financial services in Britain. *Journal of management studies*, 30(4): 659-677.

Kim, U. M. 1994. Significance of paternalism and communalism in the occupational welfare system of Korean firms. In U.-c. o. Kim, H. C. Triandis, & H. Han'guk Simni (Eds.), *Individualism and collectivism : theory, method, and applications*: 251-266. Thousand Oaks, Calif.: Sage Publications.

Kogut, B., & Singh, H. 1988. The effect of national culture on the choice of entry mode. *Journal of International Business Studies*, 19(3): 411-432.

Kong, S.-H. 2009. Paternalism revisited: organisational leadership in mainland China. *International Journal of Chinese Culture and Management*, 2(1): 56-72.

Koys, D. J. 2001. The effects of employee satisfaction, organizational citizenship behavior, and turnover on organizational effectiveness: a unit level, longitudinal study. *Personnel Psychology*: 101-114.

Kultgen, J. 1992. Consent and the justification of paternalism. *The Southern Journal of Philosophy*, 30(3): 89-113.
Laínez, V., & Meza, V. 1974. El enclave bananero en la historia de Honduras [The banana enclave in the History of Honduras]. *Anuario de Estudios Centroamericanos*, 1: 187-225.

Lawrence, J. J., & Yeh, R.-s. 1994. The influence of Mexican culture on the use of Japanese manufacturing techniques in Mexico. *Management International Review*: 49-66.

Lee, S. H., & Song, H. K. 1994. The Korean Garment Industry: From Authoritarian Patriarchism to Industrial Paternalism. In E. Bonacich (Ed.), *Global production : The apparel industry in the Pacific Rim*. Philadelphia: Temple University Press.

Leonard, T. M. 2011. *The history of Honduras*. Santa Barbara, Calif.: Greenwood.

Lincoln, J. R., Olson, J., & Hanada, M. 1978. Cultural effects on organizational structure: The case of Japanese firms in the United States. *American Sociological Review*, 43(6): 829-847.

Marchington, M., & Grugulis, I. 2000. 'Best practice' human resource management: perfect opportunity or dangerous illusion? *International Journal of Human Resource Management*, 11(6): 1104-1124.

Marique, G., Stinglhamber, F., Desmette, D., Caesens, G., & De Zanet, F. 2013. The relationship between perceived organizational support and affective commitment: A social identity perspective. *Group & Organization Management*, 38(1): 68-100.

Martinez, P. G. 2003. Paternalism as a positive form of leader subordinate exchange: Evidence from Mexico. *Management Research: The Journal of the Iberoamerican Academy of Management*, 1(3): 227-242.

Martinez, P. G. 2005. Paternalism as a positive form of leadership in the Latin American context: Leader benevolence, decision-making control and human resource management practices. In M. M. Elvira, & A. Davila (Eds.), *Managing Human Resources in Latin America*. New York: Routledge.

Maznevski, M. L., Distefano, J. J., Gomez, C. B., Noorderhaven, N. G., & Wu, P. 1997. The cultural orientations framework and international management research, *Paper presented at the Academy of International Business annual meeting*. Guadalajara, Mexico.

McElroy, J. C. 2001. Managing workplace commitment by putting people first. *Human Resource Management Review*, 11(3): 327-335.

McEnvoy, G. M. 1997. Organizational change and outdoor management education. *Human Resource Management.*, 36(2): 235-250.

McSweeney, B. 2002. Hofstede's model of national cultural differences and their consequences: A triumph of faith = A failure of analysis. *Human Relations*, 55: 89-118.

Meyer, J. P., & Allen, N. J. 1991. A three-component conceptualization of organizational commitment. *Human Resource Management Review*, 1(1): 61-89.

Meyer, J. P., & Allen, N. J. 1997. *Commitment in the workplace : Theory, research, and application*. Thousand Oaks, Calif.: Sage Publications.

Meyer, J. P., & Smith, C. A. 2000. HRM practices and organizational commitment: Test of a mediation model. *Canadian Journal of Administrative Sciences*, 17(4): 319-331.

Meyer, J. P., Stanley, D. J., Herscovitch, L., & Topolnytsky, L. 2002. Affective, continuance, and normative commitment to the organization: A meta-analysis of antecedents, correlates, and consequences. *Journal of Vocational Behavior*, 61(1): 20-52.

Meyer, J. P., Stanley, D. J., Jackson, T. A., McInnis, K. J., Maltin, E. R., & Sheppard, L. 2012. Affective, normative, and continuance commitment levels across cultures: A meta-analysis. *Journal of Vocational Behavior*, 80(2): 225-245.

Milliman, J., Von Glinow, M. A., & Nathan, M. 1991. Organizational life cycles and strategic international human resource management in multinational companies: Implications for congruence theory. *Academy of Management Review*, 16(2): 318-339.

Morgan, P. V. 1986. International human resource management: Fact or fiction. *Personnel Administrator*, 31(9): 43-47.

Morrison, R. D., Chavarria, J. A., & Dole, C. P. 2012. The national culture of firm ownership and work related values in the Honduran maquila industry, *Journal of International Business Studies Paper Development Workshop: Academy of International Business Conference*. Washington, D.C.

Mowday, R. T. 1998. Reflections on the study and relevance of organizational commitment. *Human Resource Management Review*, 8(4): 387-401.

Mowday, R. T., Steers, R. M., & Porter, L. W. 1979. The measurement of organizational commitment. *Journal of Vocational Behavior*, 14: 224-247.

Murphy-Graham, E. 2012. *Opening minds, improving lives: Education and women's empowerment in Honduras*. Nashville: Vanderbilt University Press.

Nahapiet, J., & Ghoshal, S. 1998. Social capital, intellectual capital, and the organizational advantage. *Academy of Management Review*, 23(2): 242-266.

Newman, K. L., & Nollen, S. D. 1996. Culture and congruence: The fit between management practices and national culture. *Journal of International Business Studies*, 27(4): 753-779.

Nicholls-Nixon, C. L., Davila Castilla, J. A., Sanchez Garcia, J., & Rivera Pesquera, M. 2011. Latin America management research: review, synthesis, and extension. *Journal of Management*, 37(4): 1178-1227.

Oddou, G. R., & Derr, C. B. 1999. *Managing internationally : A personal journey*. Orlando, FL: Dryden Press.

Ogilvie, J. R. 1986. The role of human resource management practices in predicting organizational commitment. *Group & Organization Management*, 11(4): 335-359.

Osland, A., & Osland, J. S. 2005. Contextualization and strategic international human resource management approaches: the case of Central America and Panama. *International Journal of Human Resource Management*, 16(12): 2218-2236.

Osland, J. S., De Franco, S., & Osland, A. 1999. Organizational implications of Latin American culture: Lessons for the expatriate manager. *Journal of Management Inquiry*, 8(2): 219-234.

Osoi, G. V. 2005. *Historia de Honduras*. Tegucigalpa, Honduras: Editora Nacional.

Ostroff, C. 1992. A relationship between satisfaction, attitudes, and performance:An organizational level analysis. *Journal of Applied Psychology*, 77(6): 963 – 974.

Oyserman, D., Coon, H. M., & Kemmelmeier, M. 2002. Rethinking individualism and collectivism: Evaluation of theoretical assumptions and meta-analyses. *Psychological Bulletin*, 128: 3-27.

Paik, Y., & Teagarden, M. B. 1995. Strategic international human resource management approaches in the maquiladora industry: a comparison of Japanese, Korean and US firms. *The International Journal of Human Resource Management*, 6(3): 568-587.

Parra, C. A., Fernandez, E. E., & Osmond, C. S. 1996. *Maquiladoras in the New Environment*. Ciudad Juarez, Mexico: Baker & McKenzie.

Pastor, R. 1982. Sinking in the Caribbean Basin. *Roreign Affairs*, 60(5): 1038-1058.

Paul, A. K., & Anantharaman, R. N. 2004. Influence of HRM practices on organizational commitment: A study among software professionals in India. *Human Resource Development Quarterly*, 15(1): 77-88.

Pellegrini, E. K., Scandura, T. A., & Jayaraman, V. 2010. Cross-Cultural generalizability of paternalistic leadership: An expansion of leader-member exchange theory. *Group & Organization Management*, 35(4): 391-420.

Porter, L. W., Steers, R. M., Mowday, R. T., & Boulian, P. V. 1974. Organizational commitment, job satisfaction, and turnover among psychiatric technicians. *Journal of Applied Psychology*, 59(5): 603-609.

Potoker, E., & Borgman, R. H. 2007. The economic impact of the Caribbean Basin Initiative: Has it delivered its promise? *Canadian Journal of Latin American & Caribbean Studies*: 79-119.

Pudelko, M., & Harzing, A. W. 2007. Country-of-origin, localization, or dominance effect? An empirical investigation of HRM practices in foreign subsidiaries. *Human Resource Management*, 46(4): 535-559.

Ravallion, M. 2001. Growth, Inequality, and Poverty. Washington D.C.: World Bank.

Rhoades, L., & Eisenberger, R. 2002. Perceived organizational support: A review of the literature. *Journal of Applied Psychology*, 87(4): 698-714.

Riding, A. 1982. The Central American Quagmire. *Foreign Affairs, America and the World 1982, Special Issue*, 61(3): 641-659.

Robert, K., & Bayacigiller, N. 1984. Cross-national organizational research: The grasp of the blinded men. *Research in Organization Behavior*, 6: 425-476.

Rosenzweig, P. M., & Nohria, N. 1994. Influences on human resource management practices in multinational corporations. *Journal of International Business Studies*, 25(2): 229-251.

Rowley, C., Benson, J., & Warner, M. 2004. Towards an Asian model of human resource management? A comparative analysis of China, Japan and South Korea. *The International Journal of Human Resource Management*, 15(4-5): 917-933.

Sagiv, L., & Schwartz, S. H. 2000. Value priorities and subjective well-being: Direct relations and congruity effects. *European Journal of Social Psychology*, 30(2): 177-198.

Sargent, J., & Matthews, L. 1998. Expatriate reduction and mariachi circles: Trends in MNC human-resource practices in Mexico. *International Studies of Management & Organization*, 28(2): 74-96.

Schuler, R. S. 1992. Strategic human resources management: Linking the people with the strategic needs of the business. *Organizational Dynamics*, 21(1): 18-32.

Schuler, R. S., Dowling, P. J., & De Cieri, H. 1993. An integrative framework of strategic international human resource management. *Journal of Management*, 19(2): 419-459.

Schwartz, S. H. 1990. Individualism-collectivism: Critique and proposed refinements. *Journal of Cross-Cultural Psychology*, 21(2): 139-157.

Shore, L. M., & Tetrick, L. E. 1991. A construct validity study of the survey of perceived organizational support. *Journal of Applied Psychology*, 76(5): 637-643.

Shore, L. M., & Wayne, S. J. 1993. Commitment and employee behavior: Comparison of affective commitment and continuance commitment with perceived organizational support. *Journal of Applied Psychology*, 78: 774-774.

Snape, E., Thompson, D., Yan, F. K.-C., & Redman, T. 1998. Performance appraisal and culture: practice and attitudes in Hong Kong and Great Britain. *International Journal of Human Resource Management*, 9(5): 841-861.

Snell, S. A. 1999. Social capital and strategic HRM: It's who you know. *Human Resource Planning*, 22(1): 62-65.

Song, Y. H., & Meek, C. B. 1998. The impact of culture on the management values and beliefs of Korean firms. 1(1): 33-50.

Sparrow, P., Schuler, R. S., & Jackson, S. E. 1994. Convergence or divergence: Human resource practices and policie of competitive advantage worldwide. *International Journal of Human Resource Management*, 5(2): 267-299.

Stanley, D. J., Meyer, J. P., Jackson, T. A., Maltin, E. R., McInnis, K. J., & Kumsar, Y., et al. 2007. Cross-cultural generalizibility of the three-component model of commitment, *Society for Industrial and Organizational Psychology* New York.

Staw, B. M. 1980. The consequences of turnover. *Journal of Occupational Behaviour*, 1: 253-273.

Storey, J. 1993. The take-up of human resource management by mainstream companies: key lessons from research. *International Journal of Human Resource Management*, 4(3): 529-553.

Storey, J. 1995. *Human resource management : A critical text*. London; New York: Routledge.

Storey, J. 2007. *Human resource management : a critical text*. London: Thomson.

Taylor, S., Beechler, S., & Napier, N. 1996. Toward an integrative model of strategic international human resource management. *Academy of Management Review*, 21(4): 959-985.

Teagarden, M. B., Butler, M. C., & von Glinow, M. A. 1992. Mexico's maquiladora industry: Where strategic human resource management makes a difference. *Organizational Dynamics*, 20(3): 34-47.

Thomas, D. C. 2002. *Essentials of international management : a cross-cultural perspective*. Thousand Oaks, CA: Sage Publications.

Triandis, H. C. 1994. *Culture and social behavior*. New York: McGraw-Hill.

Triandis, H. C. 1995. *Individualism & collectivism*. Boulder: Westview Press.

Trompenaars, F., & Hampden-Turner, C. 1998. *Riding the waves of culture*: McGraw-Hill New York.

Tung, R. L., & Verbeke, A. 2010. Beyond Hofstede and GLOBE: Improving the quality of cross-cultural research. *Journal of International Business Studies*, 41: 1259 – 1274.

Valentine, W. S. 1916. Honduras. *Annals of the American Academy of Political and Social Science*, 68: 185-186.

Von Glinow, M. A., Drost, E. A., & Teagarden, M. B. 2002. Converging on IHRM best practices: Lessons learned from a globally distributed consortium on theory and practice. *Human Resource Management*, 41(1): 123-140.

Warren, R. 1999. Against paternalism in human resource management. *Business Ethics: A European Review*, 8(1): 50-59.

Wayne, S. J., Shore, L. M., & Liden, R. C. 1997. Perceived organizational support and leader-member exchange: A social exchange perspective. *Academy of Management Journal*, 40(1): 82-111.

Wright, P. M., & McMahan, G. C. 1992. Theoretical perspectives for strategic human resource management. *Journal of Management*, 18(2): 295-320.

DECISION SCIENCES INSTITUTE

Turnaround in Large Complex Legacy Organizations

Derek Lehmberg
North Dakota State University
Email: derek.lehmberg@ndsu.edu

Chanchai Tangpong
North Dakota State University
Email: charnchai.tangpong@ndsu.edu

ABSTRACT

Corporate turnaround in the context of large, complex legacy (LCL) organizations appears to be qualitatively different from turnaround in simpler, smaller, and/or newer firms. Although the context is thought to strongly influence turnarounds, the LCL organizational context has yet to be studied specifically. We examine the successful turnaround of IBM, a representative LCL organization. We identify retrenchment and reorientation actions taken, in agreement with existing literature. We also find that IBM undertook repositioning actions, and that cultural change played a major role in successfully implementation. These drivers of success have not been emphasized in the current turnaround research.

KEYWORDS: Corporate Turnaround, Organizational Behavior/Strategic Management, Organizational Change, Strategy Process

INTRODUCTION

In the midst of decline in the years 2004 to 2006, Kodak replaced its CEO, and initiated retrenchment and reorientation efforts (Snyder, 2013). These efforts appear to be consistent with the generally accepted prescriptions of the turnaround literature, which suggests first retrenchment and then reorientation (e.g., Bibeault, 1982; Pearce & Robbins, 1993, 1994). Yet, the company's efforts failed. Kodak declared Chapter 11 bankruptcy in 2012. IBM, on the other hand, was successfully turned around in the mid 1990s, after also facing severe decline. Why was IBM's approach successful while Kodak's was not? The turnaround literature does not yield a ready answer. Although calls have been made for context to be studied more thoroughly in the turnaround literature (e.g., Arogyaswamy, Barker, & Ysai-Ardekani, 1995), turnaround in large complex legacy (LCL) organizations, such as Kodak or IBM, has not been fully examined. In this paper, we explore the case of IBM's successful turnaround under CEO Lou Gerstner. Consistent with common prescriptions in the literature, IBM changed its CEO and pursued retrenchment and reorientation initiatives. Departing from the current emphasis in the turnaround literature, we also find that IBM implemented repositioning strategies, and that cultural change played a critical role in realizing these strategic changes and achieving operational success. This paper contributes to the turnaround literature by highlighting that LCL organizations in decline are a unique turnaround context and by identifying repositioning as a mid-term strategy in turnaround, which may not be necessary for turnaround efforts in typical non-LCL organizational contexts. In addition, this paper identifies the potential moderating effect of cultural change in turnaround attempts of LCL organizations.

RETRENCHMENT, REORIENTATION, AND LCL ORGANIZATIONS AS A TURNAROUND CONTEXT

Corporate turnaround denotes the situation where a firm experiences a performance decline of sufficient magnitude to threaten its ongoing existence (Hofer, 1980; Slatter, 1984), after which it recovers and then sustains a satisfactory level of performance (Arogyaswamy et al., 1995; Barker & Duhaime, 1997). Extant turnaround research has sought to identify drivers of success and failure in turnaround efforts. Two primary turnaround strategies discussed in the literature are retrenchment and reorientation (Arogyaswamy, et al., 1995). Retrenchment, which acts to stem further decline through realizing efficiency improvements (e.g., Pearce & Robbins, 2008), has been argued to be the first step in turnaround (Bibeault, 1982; Hambrick & Schecter, 1983; Pearce & Robbins, 1994; Lohrke et al, 2012; Morrow et al., 2004). Reorientation, on the other hand, aims to return the company to health and improve longer term firm financial performance, and has been characterized as the second stage leading to recovery (Boyne & Meier, 2009; Hofer, 1980; Pearce & Robbins, 1993; Robbins & Pearce, 1992). Despite several decades of research, the literature reports some mixed findings on the impact of retrenchment and reorientation (Castrogiovanni & Bruton, 2000; Filatotchev & Toms, 2006; Trahms, Ndofor, & Sirmon, 2013). Calls have been made to study different contexts which may impact the effectiveness of these strategies (e.g., Arogyaswamy et al, 1995).

We contend that LCL organizations are unique contexts for turnaround efforts. These large entities, incorporate the element of legacy and long history because they have developed and been successful over long periods of time. They tend to have complex organizational structure to handle complex product/service portfolios that have evolved over time (Daft, 2012), and across broad geographies.

The sheer size, complexity, and legacy of the LCL organization may limit the direct impact of leadership change on the turnaround outcomes. Ingrained rituals and practices (e.g., Schein, 2010) may counteract change. Similarly, the context of LCL organizations may also impact the suitability and effectiveness of the established turnaround strategies, and therefore current turnaround literature prescriptions may not apply. Short-term efficiency-based retrenchment strategies may be inadequate to bring the LCL organizations in severe decline back to health, while the size, complexity, and past glory of LCL organizations hinder changes required to successfully implement long-term reorientation strategies in a timely manner. Since LCLs have not been examined in the extant literature, we have a limited understanding regarding: (1) how do declining LCL organizations turn themselves around, and (2) what are key elements critical to LCL organizations' successful turnaround processes? As a step in better understanding turnaround in the context of LCL organizations, we examine IBM's successful turnaround.

CRITICAL ELEMENTS IN SUCCESSFUL TURNAROUND OF IBM

IBM entered into a steep decline in 1991 as sales of mainframe computers, its primary source of revenues and profits, started to fall dramatically. Industry insiders and financial analysts predicted the end of the mainframe computer and the breakup of IBM. The company had grown extremely complex, selling over 25,000 different hardware and software products through 20 different business units (Austin & Nolan, 2000). The company began to retrench, cutting costs and reducing headcount in 1991 and 1992, taking steps towards breaking up the firm, and replacing its CEO in 1993. The new CEO, Louis Gerstner, an outsider with no prior experience in the information technology industry, has been credited with turning the company around. Gerstner's success at turning around the declining IBM was built on key, interrelated actions, including retrenchment, repositioning, and reorientation, as well as cultural change. We will discuss each of these actions and generalize the IBM's successful turnaround process.

Retrenchment

After his arrival in April of 1993, Gerstner's initial approach was to focus on retrenchment. He commented that the challenge was: "...to focus on day-to-day execution, stabilizing the company...." and to avoid discussing future strategies for a period (Gerstner, 2002: 115). Gerstner aimed to quickly reduce costs. In July, IBM announced a $2 billion restructuring charge and "launch [of] a massive program of expense reduction... [including]... reducing our employment by 35,000 people...." (ibid: 101-2). As part of the retrenchment efforts, the company also sold unproductive assets to increase cash, and reduced IT expenses. From 1994 to 1998, cost reduction projects saved the company $9.5 billion.

Repositioning

We consider repositioning to be a mid-term strategy to reposition existing assets and businesses in ways which increase their market relevance and competitiveness. As such, repositioning is about modifying existing strategies and not developing completely new ones. In IBM's case, the mainframe computer was considered outdated, but IBM was able to reposition its mainframe offering to make it more relevant for the changing technological and business environment. The company made some major technological and policy changes in order to reposition its mainframe business. These included making the machines more cost effective by switching to CMOS technology, which was more amenable to large scale production, and a switch from proprietary systems to open systems, which were compatible with those of other producers. Given the strong identification with its historically successful mainframe business and its size, IBM's successful repositioning of its mainframe business was arguably *the* pivotal action that sustained IBM's short- and intermediate-term viability and paved a strong foundation for its longer-term reorientation effort.

Reorientation

IBM's reorientation strategy was a longer-term, complex undertaking involving two important pieces. One of these was the strategy to transform IBM into a service and solution provider. The concept behind this was that IBM's ability to integrate globally and technologically was unmatched by any other firm. Gerstner described this as a bet "to build not just the largest but the most influential services business in the industry" (Gerstner, 2002: 191). The second piece was to reorient the company to become a leader in e-business, and thereby take advantage of the ongoing move towards computing on networks. These decisions, in turn drove subsequent actions such as acquisitions and cultural change efforts needed for the changes to be effective.

Cultural change

Changing IBM's insular culture was "our single most critical and difficult task" in the turnaround (Gerstner, 2000: 171). IBM's culture had developed in the absence of significant competition or external threat. Gerstner began a multiyear ongoing communication effort with consistent emphasis on culture amidst implementation of other actions aimed at changing the culture. He introduced 8 guiding principles, the first of which stated: "The market place is the driving force behind everything we do." This was a strong statement for a company that had become focused primarily on internal politics and procedures. Performance evaluation and compensation were also changed to include variable rewards, pay for performance, and external benchmarking, again marking significant breaks from former practices. Organizational changes, symbolic and functional, played another role in the efforts to influence the company culture. In winter of 1994, the company began to reorganize its sales organization into a group in charge of customer relationships and another of product specialists. The organizational matrix was also reoriented a global basis as Gerstner "[declared] war on the geographic fiefdoms" (Gerstner, 2002: 135).

ANALYSIS

We generalize the key elements in the IBM successful turnaround case into a generic model of turnaround in the context of LCL organizations incorporating leadership change, retrenchment, repositioning, reorientation, and cultural change. Leadership change is an important step in initiating the turnaround process. New leaders who do not have vested interest in the current status quo are more likely to take necessary actions to turn their declining around (Miller, 1991; Ford & Baucus, 1987). Important for LCL turnarounds, Schein (2010) suggests that leaders in mature, established organizations have less direct personal influence on organizational change compared to leaders at earlier stage organizations, and therefore need to rely on more systematic approaches to affect organizational change.

In the turnaround context of LCL organizations, the IBM case provides partial support for the literature's 'first-retrenchment-then-reorientation' (e.g., Bibeault, 1982; Pearce & Robbins, 1993, 1994) prescription, with the addition of repositioning as the intermediary step between retrenchment and reorientation. We contend that this intermediate step is crucial in the LCL context, as suggested by the IBM case. First, retrenchment is needed to mitigate the severity of the decline. With the size and complexity of declining LCL organizations, cost-cutting and pruning down some less profitable product/service lines may not be adequate to fully stop the gravitational momentum of sinking LCL organizations. Some upward movement from profitably repositioning existing core products/services becomes crucial to stabilizing the declining LCL organizations. Once retrenchment and repositioning have successfully paved a stable foundation for the companies, reorientation will have a better chance of being successful. More importantly, repositioning the existing core products/services may act to increase the organization's ability to accept greater levels of change. Repositioning introduces some degree of change but within the existing core products/services, which represent the status quo. This type and degree of change is not only more acceptable to LCL organizations, but also prepares them to accept higher-magnitude changes necessary during the reorientation effort.

Finally, LCL organizations are known for their establishment and legacy, thus often possessing strong organizational culture. A key attribute of strong culture is resistance to change (Schein, 2010). Therefore, parallel efforts to increase the alignment of organizational culture with the firm's goals and competitive context are vital to the turnaround success.

DISCUSSION AND CONCLUSION

This paper contributes to the turnaround literature by examining an exploratory case to better understand how LCL organizations turn themselves around and by identifying key elements critical to the process. Through this exploratory study, we identified repositioning as an important mid-term strategy, which may enable LCL organizations to adjust existing businesses and thereby gain time and momentum for longer-term reorientation strategies. This paper also identified the moderating role of cultural change in turnaround of LCL organizations. IBM's case provides evidence that top management can improve the potential for turnaround by taking actions to promote cultural changes to better align it with the organization's goals.

This research has important implications for top managers of LCL organizations in decline. These managers should place a high priority on identifying and implementing repositioning actions, aimed at improving the situation in the mid-term, and supporting momentum after the benefits of short-term retrenchment actions have been realized. Such momentum may be especially critical because long-term reorientation actions may need extra time to be fully implemented in LCL organizations. Cultural change is another important aspect in LCL turnarounds. The long historical, and embedded nature of LCL organizational culture means long-term, persistent and comprehensive efforts to influence the culture are key to achieving successful cultural change outcomes. Being in crisis may make it easier for top managers to change these aspects of the firm. Managers should not waste these necessary opportunities.

This paper focused primarily on IBM's turnaround. Future research may examine the generalizability to other situations by examining successful turnarounds in LCLs in situations divergent from IBM's. We have made arguments about why the LCL organizational context is unique for turnaround efforts and how it may affect turnaround processes and outcomes. However, we do not clearly and quantitatively state the thresholds dividing LCLs from non-LCLs or perhaps pre-LCLs, which may be a topic for research in the future when our understanding of this area becomes more mature. Additionally, we feel there is an important potential impact of future research on not-for-profit LCL institutions such as academic and government institutions.

REFERENCES

Arogyaswamy, K., Barker, V., & Yasai-Ardekani, M. (1995). Firm turnarounds: An integrative two-stage model. *Journal of Management Studies,* 32(4), 493-525.

Austin, R.D., & Nolan, R.L. (2000). IBM Corporate Turnaround. Harvard Business School Case number 9-600-098.

Barker, V., & Duhaime, I. (1997). Strategic change in the turnaround process: Theory and empirical evidence. *Strategic Management Journal,* 13(1), 15-36.

Bibeault, D. (1982). *Corporate turnaround: How managers turn losers into winners.* New York: McGraw-Hill Book Company.

Boyne, G., & Meier, K. (2009). Environmental change, human resources and organizational turnaround. *Journal of Management Studies,* 45(6), 835-863.

Castrogiovanni, G., & Bruton, G. (2000). Business turnaround processes following acquisitions: Reconsidering the role of retrenchment. *Journal of Business Research,* 48, 25-34.

Daft, R. (2012). *Organization theory and design.* Toronto: Nelson Education.

Filatotchev, I., & Toms, S. (2006). Corporate governance and financial constraints on strategic turnarounds. *Journal of Management Studies,* 43, 407-433.

Ford, J. D., & Baucus, D. A. (1987). Organizational adaptation to performance downturns: An interpretation-based perspective. *Academy of Management Review,* 12, 366-380.

Gerstner Jr., L.V. (2002). *Who says elephants can't dance? Inside IBM's historic turnaround*. Waterville, ME: Thorndike Press.

Hambrick, D., & Schecter, S. (1983). Turnaround strategies for mature industrial-product business units. *Academy of Management Journal,* 26, 231-248.

Hofer, C. (1980). Turnaround strategies. *Journal of Business Strategy,* 1: 19-31.

Lohrke, F., Bedeian, A. & Palmer, T. (2004). The role of top management teams in formulating and implementing turnaround strategies: A review and research agenda. *International Journal of Management Reviews,* 5/6, 63-90.

Miller, D. (1991). Stale in the saddle: CEO tenure and the match between organization and environment. *Management Science,* 37, 34-52.

Morrow, J. L., Johnson, R. A., & Busenitz, L. W. (2004). The effects of cost and asset retrenchment on firm performance: the overlooked role of a firm's competitive environment. *Journal of Management,* 30, 189-208.

Pearce, J., & Robbins, K. (1993). Toward improved theory and research on business turnaround. *Journal of Management*, 19, 613-636.

Pearce, J., & Robbins, K. (1994). Retrenchment remains the foundation of business turnaround. *Strategic Management Journal,* 15, 407-417.

Pearce, J., & Robbins, K. (2008). Strategic transformation as the essential last step in the process of business turnaround. *Business Horizons*, 51, 121-130.

Robbins, K., & Pearce, J. (1992). Turnaround: retrenchment and recovery. *Strategic Management Journal,* 13, 287-309.

Schein, E. H. (2010). *Organizational culture and leadership (Vol. 2)*. John Wiley & Sons.
Slatter, S. (1984). *Corporate recovery.* Harmondsworth, UK: Penguin.

Snyder, P. (2013). *Is this something George Eastman would have done? The decline and fall of Eastman Kodak Company*. Charleston, SC: CreateSpace.

Trahms, C. A., Ndofor, H. A., & Sirmon, D. G. (2013). Organizational decline and turnaround a review and agenda for future research. *Journal of Management*, *39*(5), 1277-1307.

DECISION SCIENCES INSTITUTE

Two Observations Between "Truth" and Meh: A Complement to Cross-tabulation Chi-square Hypothesis Testing

John R. Dickinson
University of Windsor
Email: MExperiences@bell.net

ABSTRACT

Cross-tabulation and its accompanying chi-square statistical hypothesis test is among the most commonly applied types of analysis. Though not without subtle aspects, the basic analysis is straightforward. As with statistical hypothesis testing generally, a p-value is calculated and on that basis the null hypothesis of independence is either rejected or not rejected. The present research demonstrates that the test may be very sensitive to measurement error. Accordingly, an additional perspective is developed with the suggestion that additional descriptive statistics complement the basic test.

KEYWORDS: Cross-tabulation, chi-square, measurement error, statistical significance

Full paper and references available upon request.

DECISION SCIENCES INSTITUTE

Understanding the Effect of Flickr's Screenshot Annotations on Learning Effectiveness

Travis K. Huang
Ling Tung University
Email: travisk.huang@gmail.com

Sheng-Wei Lin
Soochow University
Email: swlin@csim.scu.edu.tw

Louis Yi-Shih Lo
Central Taiwan University of Science and Technology
Email: 106928@ctust.edu.tw

ABSTRACT

As Flickr provides users with a highly interactive photo-sharing environment, this study was performed to make use of Flickr's annotation function to support computer software learning. After users upload their screenshots onto Flickr, they can make three types of annotations—stickers, drawings, and text—to pinpoint the specific portion of the screenshot. Thus, software problems can be described more clearly than with text alone and can be solved with greater certainty. The results, based on data collected from 270 students, indicated that the students' perceived usefulness had a positive influence on online participation, which in turn led to learning effectiveness. These findings are limited to technology-oriented classes.

KEYWORDS: Annotation, perceived usefulness, course difficulty, online participation, learning effectiveness

INTRODUCTION

As e-learning environments have progressed over the past decade, a variety of innovative information technologies and information systems have been developed for educational courses. Social networking sites such as MySpace, Twitter, and Facebook have become enormously successful because of their everyman appeal and have become the most popular platforms for interaction with the world over the Internet. Educators have tended to treat social networking sites as multifunctional platforms for teaching and learning by means of argumentation and discussion (Kalpidou, Costin, & Morris, 2011; Yang & Brown, 2015; Ainin, Naqshbandi, Mogavvemi, & Jaafar, 2015), as students using them have greater opportunities to obtain course materials and interact with their classmates. Hence, teachers and learners alike need to embrace the latest means of interacting with people, course materials, and even data to enhance learning effectiveness.

Improved learning techniques in computer courses is always needed as students sometimes have problems with grasping the material using traditional learning methods. Several social networking sites such as Flickr and Facebook enable users to upload and share photos. Furthermore, they are able to create tags or dialog boxes above the photos. By doing so, people can focus on a specific portion of the photo of interest and interact with friends by leaving comments. This photo-sharing environment can be an innovative method for learners to demonstrate their problems by posting screenshots when they encounter computer software difficulties (Huang, 2015). In particular, Flickr provides its users with a highly interactive photo-sharing environment. After users upload their screenshots onto Flickr, they can make three types of annotations—stickers, drawings, and text—to pinpoint the specific portion of the screenshot by means of the annotation tools, namely photo editor, as shown in Figure 1. Every screenshot is unique and personalized after annotation. As shown in Figure 2, a sticker annotation can be made by drawing a rectangle, locating its position, and adjusting its size. Besides, users can enter text above a screenshot by using text tools, as presented in Figure 3. Hence, software problems can be described more clearly than with text alone and can be solved with greater certainty.

Figure 1: Annotation tools on Flickr

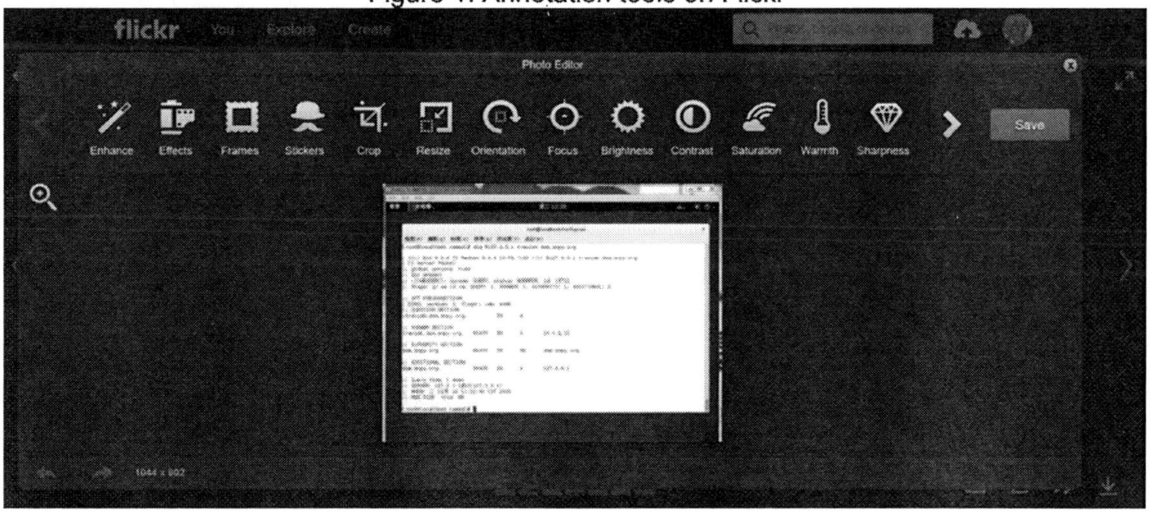

Figure 2: Creating a sticker annotation to a screenshot

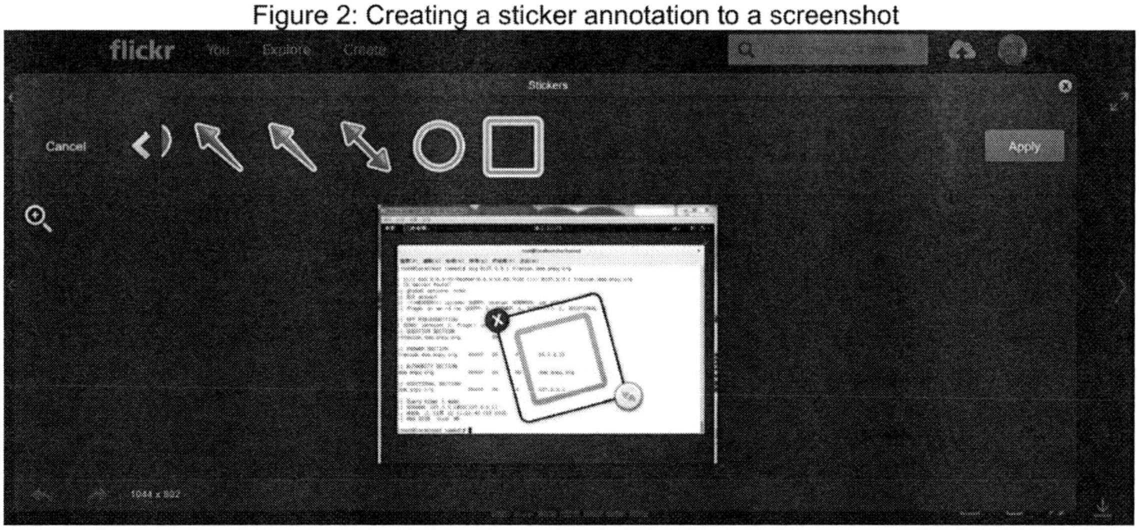

Figure 3: Creating a text annotation to a screenshot

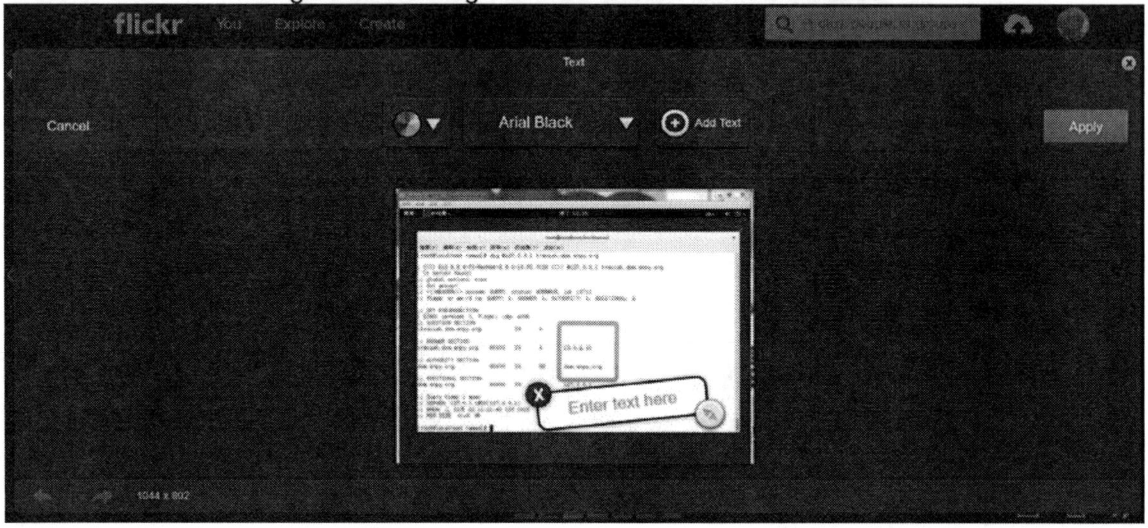

In this study, the course difficulty and the perceived ease of use were used as two critical factors to explain the students' perceived usefulness of new information technologies in the field of e-learning. Hence, this study was performed to answer the following questions: What is the relationship between users' perceived ease of use and the usefulness of Flickr's screenshot annotations for learning computer software? What is the relationship between course difficulty and the usefulness of Flickr's screenshot annotations? What is the relationship between the usefulness of Flickr's screenshot annotations as perceived by users and their learning effectiveness? What is the relationship between the usefulness as perceived by users and online participation? What is the relationship between online participation and learning effectiveness?

LITERATURE REVIEW

Annotations on Flickr

Annotation systems have been developed in recent years to enhance the effectiveness of e-learning. Most systems have focused on text-based annotations, which can be created by highlighting a specific portion of the selected article. For example, Su, Yang, Hwang, and Zhang (2010) developed a personalized annotation management system that was useful for conducting learning tasks. Gao (2013) investigated student participation and interactions when studying an online text with the social annotation tool Diigo. In addition, Chen, Hwang, and Wang (2012) developed a Web 2.0 annotation system, MyNote, for users to leave comments in response to text-based annotations of interest. By doing so, users can read and discuss specific portions of the course materials directly. In fact, text-based annotation is useful for peer critiques (Mendenhall & Johnson, 2010), which can stimulate learners to think through issues and reflect on their own opinions. Thus, learners have more opportunities to elicit deeper learning (Huang, 2015).

This study investigated the interactions that occur between users as they use Flickr's annotations on screenshots to demonstrate their problems. Three types of annotations—stickers, drawings, and text-based annotations—can be used on Flickr. As shown in Figure 1, a software problem is presented by creating annotations on a screenshot with Flickr's photo editor. To clarify the meaning of a specific screenshot, a user can create stickers, draw a rectangle, or create a text-based annotation that includes further explanation. Stickers, drawings, and text-based annotations are all considered screenshot annotations for the purposes of this study.

Flickr's annotation function is very useful for students, especially for computer software learners. When students encounter unpredictable problems, they may not be able to properly describe the problem. Posting screenshots onto Flickr and making annotations can be allow others to help troubleshoot these problems. In short, the Flickr website provides a highly interactive and intuitive environment in which students can depict or comprehend computer software problems with annotations, including stickers, drawings, and text, above a specific screenshot.

Perceived Usefulness

When e-learning systems were introduced to organizations such as industries and universities, they were treated as new information technologies. Many studies have evaluated users' acceptance of e-learning systems by application of the TAM (Davis, Bagozzi, & Warshaw, 1989; Lewis, Agarwal, & Sambamurthy, 2003; Huang, 2015). The TAM adopts the premise that users' ideas about the usefulness and perceived ease of use of a new information technology are the major determinants of their behavioral intentions, and that the perceived ease of use affects the perceived usefulness. In addition, users' behavioral intentions regarding information technology influences their actual usage behavior.

The information technology measured in this study is the use of Flickr's annotations, including stickers, drawing, and text. Because the TAM has successfully explained user acceptance of new information technologies (Venkatesh & Bala, 2008; Dickinger, Arami, & Meyer, 2008), the relationship between users' perceived ease of use and perceived usefulness has been confirmed. As the study intended to identify the antecedents of the users' perceived usefulness of the use of Flickr's annotations, users' perceived ease of use was adopted without question. Hence, the hypothesis based on the fundamental relationship of this TAM was proposed as follows.

Hypothesis 1: The greater users' perceived ease of use, the greater the perceived usefulness of making annotations by using stickers, drawing, and text on Flickr.

Course Difficulty

There are obviously numerous aspects of task difficulty. The aspect that is most relevant to the context of computer software learning is course difficulty, which has been found to have a negative association with learning outcomes and achievement within student groups (Tucker, Jones, Mandy, & Gupta, 2006; Addison, Best, & Warrington, 2006). Although students perceive a higher degree of course difficulty, they spend more time learning the subject by trying to solve the puzzles encountered. This leads to a greater level of academic stress (Tucker, Jones, Mandy, & Gupta, 2006). A high level of difficulty will have a significant effect on students' learning outcomes.

Course difficulty is the degree of difficulty of the subject matter. In this study, the subject matter is computer software, namely, the Linux operating system. A series of tasks about Linux instructions were included in the course. In this study, the course difficulty was defined as the degree of difficulty perceived by the students after they performed a series of tasks. While learning Linux, students often encounter problems of different levels of equivocality and uncertainty. We expect that when students learn computer software with a lower level of difficulty, it is much easier for them to practice software instructions by uploading homework or by troubleshooting for others. In addition, students are more likely to be able to comprehend and solve software problems. Thus, they have more opportunities to interact with others by using stickers, drawing, and text on Flickr. The students should thus demonstrate a higher degree of perceived usefulness, which leads to the following hypothesis.

Hypothesis 2: The lower the level of course difficulty, the greater users' perceived usefulness of making annotations with stickers, drawing, and text on Flickr.

Learning Effectiveness

The perceived effectiveness of an e-learning system should be considered in an assessment of its effectiveness (Bostrom, Olfman, & Sein, 1990). Maki, Maki, Patterson, and Whittaker (2000) also proposed that the degree of satisfaction of an online course and learning achievement are critical for learning effectiveness. In addition, Lowerison, Sclater, Schmid and Abrami (2006) suggested that positive learning experiences include feelings of effective interactions with the instructor and other students and feelings of being in control of one's own learning by means of active participation. In this regard, we included students' perceived satisfaction in our measurement of the effectiveness of the learning experience. When students perceive a higher level of usefulness by making annotations with stickers, drawing, and text on Flickr, they should perceive a higher level of learning effectiveness. The following hypothesis was proposed.

Hypothesis 3: The greater users' perceived usefulness of making annotations with stickers, drawing, and text on Flickr, the greater the learning effectiveness.

Online Participation

Online collaborative environments have also been proven to encourage wider student participation because online discussions encourage more reticent students to participate to a greater extent (Citera, 1998), possibly because online environments provide fewer opportunities for intimidation and less time pressure (Warschauer, 1997). Thus, when students perceive an e-learning environment to have a high level of usefulness, their online participation increases. This study posits that users' perceived usefulness predicts the level of online participation. This concept is captured in the following hypothesis.

Hypothesis 4: The greater users' perceived usefulness of making annotations with stickers, drawing, and text on Flickr, the greater their online participation.

In a computer-supported collaborative learning community, learners' performance is significantly affected by social network properties (Cho, Gay, Davidson, & Ingraffea, 2007), which are a consequence of online participation. Therefore, if users make greater efforts to participate by making annotations with stickers, drawing, and text on Flickr, their learning effectiveness will improve. Based on the foregoing reasoning, the following hypothesis is proposed.

Hypothesis 5: The higher the level of online participation, the greater the learning effectiveness.

The goal of this study was to explain how two factors, perceived ease of use and course difficulty, affect perceived usefulness. In addition to the direct effects of perceived usefulness on learning effectiveness, the indirect effects by means of online participation were also measured. The complete research model is shown in Figure 4.

Figure 4: Conceptual model

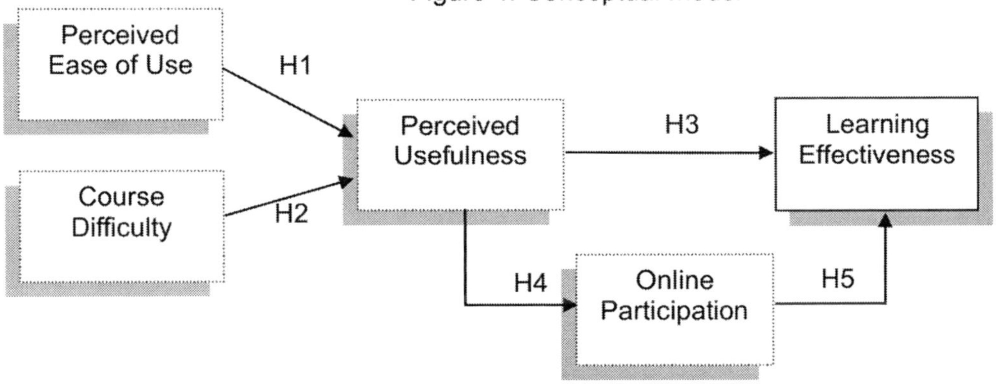

RESEARCH METHOD

Two hundred eighty-three undergraduates majoring in information systems from six sections of the same Linux operating system course were recruited over the course of three semesters. As a major part of the course requirement, the students registered as Flickr members and were required to hand in assignments and to propose questions by means of Flickr. As shown in Figure 5, when homework was assigned, the teacher created a web page on Flickr with images and descriptions.

Figure 5: Assigning homework by posting an image and text comments

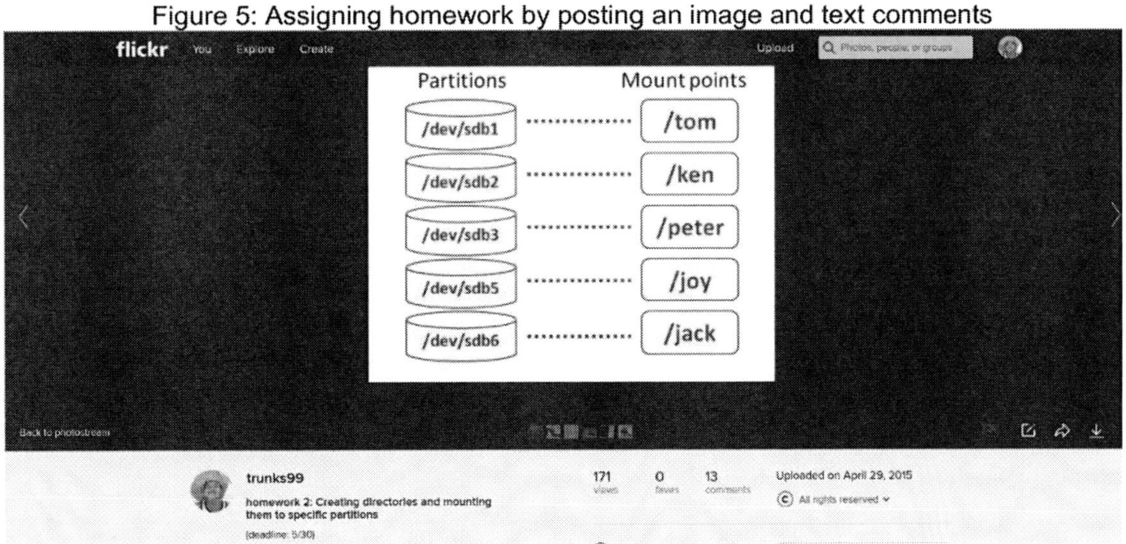

Each homework assignment could be captured in the form of a screenshot. Once the students completed their homework, they uploaded screenshots and posted their Flickr links to the teacher's web space. The students were encouraged to respond to the screenshots posted. Because the students were familiar with social networking media such as Facebook or Flickr they were able to use screenshots and annotations smoothly and fluently.

To investigate the manner in which Flickr's screenshot annotations affect students' learning effectiveness while learning computer software, questionnaires were administered to all 283 students. The students were aware that they were involved in a project but were blinded to the research hypotheses. The questionnaire assessed the perceived ease of use, perceived usefulness, course difficulty, and learning effectiveness after using Flickr's screenshot annotations to upload homework, demonstrate problems, and reply to other students' questions in the context of learning Linux. Two experts codified the students' online participation by evaluating their personal pages and the teacher's web space. The research model shown in Figure 4 was tested, and all of the hypotheses were examined by means of structural equation modeling using the collected data.

The dependent variable was the students' learning effectiveness. The independent variables were the students' perceived ease of use, perceived usefulness, course difficulty, and online participation, which was codified according to the student's usage of Flickr screenshots and annotations. The measurement of each construct is further described as follows.

Perceived Ease of Use and Perceived Usefulness

The items used to measure perceived ease of use and perceived usefulness were adapted from Davis (1993) with modifications. Four items examined perceived ease of use, and three items examined perceived usefulness. The items focused on measuring the students' ease of use and perceptions of usefulness in relation to Flickr's screenshot annotations. The Cronbach's α values for perceived ease of use and perceived usefulness were 0.935 and 0.969, respectively.

Course Difficulty

Addison, Best, and Warrington (2006) developed the Course Experience Questionnaire (CEQ) to measure course difficulty as perceived by students and to evaluate the instructor with 10 items. In this study, four items of interest from this questionnaire were adapted to measure the degree of students' perceived course difficulty. The Cronbach's α value for this four-item measure was 0.937.

Online Participation

The online participation data were codified by two experts from the students' online trials and included the frequency of screenshots and annotations on Flickr. Online participation was evaluated by several indicators, including the number of screenshots posted, the number of annotations created (e.g., stickers, drawings, and text), and the total number of comments posted. These indicators were combined into a single factor, online participation, that assessed the number of objects posted by the students.

Learning Effectiveness

Learning effectiveness was measured by the students' perceived satisfaction with their learning experiences as indicated on a seven-item scale (Lowerison, Sclater, Schmid, & Abrami, 2006). The students were asked to indicate how effectively the Flickr screenshot annotations were used in the course. The last two items were eliminated on the basis of an item-total correlation test. The Cronbach's α value for this five-item measure was 0.888.

RESULTS

Of the 283 students attending the class, 270 completed the questionnaires, giving a response rate of 95.4%. The correlations between the variables were tested using Pearson's correlation coefficient. As shown in Table 1, course difficulty was negatively related to other variables except online participation, whereas online partition was positively related to perceived usefulness and learning effectiveness.

Table 1: Correlations between variables

	1	2	3	4	5
1. Course Difficulty	1				
2. Perceived Ease of Use	-.348**	1			
3. Perceived Usefulness	-.422**	.577**	1		
4. Online Participation	-.060	.140	.156*	1	
5. Learning Effectiveness	-.280**	.413**	.624**	.190**	1

Note. *p< .05. **p<.01.

Structural Model

Using the 270 records, the proposed model was assessed with maximum likelihood estimation using AMOS. Six common model-fit measures were used to assess the model's overall goodness of fit, the ratio of the chi-square value to the degrees of freedom (CMIN/DF), the goodness-of-fit (GFI), the adjusted goodness-of-fit index (AGFI), the comparative fit index (CFI), the root mean square error of approximation (RMSEA), and the normed fit index (NFI). The results indicated that the proposed model (CMIN/DF, 2.18; GFI, 0.91; AGFI, 0.87; CFI, 0.97; RMSEA, 0.07; and NFI, 0.95) had a good fit, because all of the criteria were better than the recommended values (CMIN/DF less than 3, GFI greater than 0.90, AGFI greater than 0.80, CFI greater than 0.95, RMSEA less than 0.80, and NFI greater than 0.90). We therefore used the model to examine our hypotheses.

Figure 7: Standardized path coefficients of the proposed model

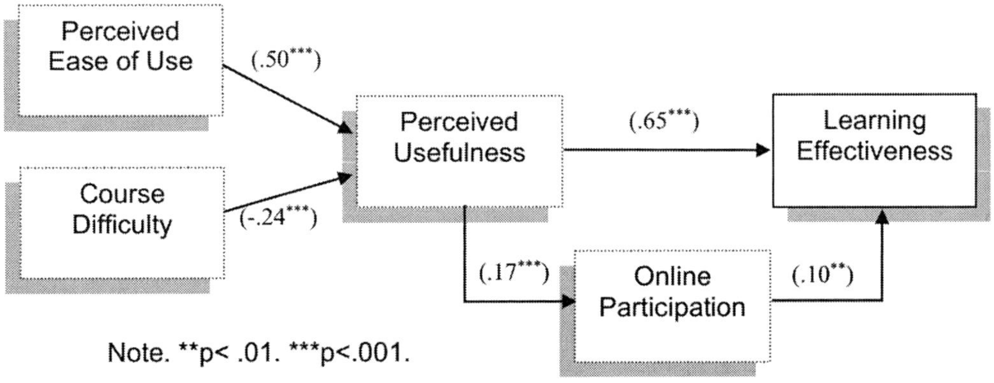

Note. **p< .01. ***p<.001.

As shown in Figure 7, the standardized path coefficient from perceived ease of use to perceived usefulness, which is one of the fundamental TAM relationships, was positive, and the relationship was statistically significant. Hypothesis 1 was thus supported. In addition, the path from course difficulty to perceived usefulness was statistically significant, and the standardized path coefficient was negative, thereby supporting Hypothesis 2. Therefore, perceived ease of use and course difficulty were shown to be antecedents of perceived usefulness.

Both perceived usefulness and online participation were found to have direct positive effects on learning effectiveness, thus confirming Hypotheses 3 and 5. In addition, the relationship between perceived usefulness and online participation was statistically significant, thus confirming Hypothesis 4. We can tell from Hypotheses 3, 4, and 5 that perceived usefulness had both direct and indirect effects on learning effectiveness because of its direct effect on online participation.

Through its direct effects on perceived usefulness, perceived ease of use had a positive indirect effect on learning effectiveness, whereas course difficulty had a negative indirect effect on learning effectiveness. The R^2 value indicates that 46% of the variance in the users' learning effectiveness was explained by their online participation and by perceived usefulness, whereas 39% of the variance in the users' perceived usefulness was explained by perceived ease of use and by course difficulty.

CONCLUSION

During this study, Flickr's screenshot annotations were used to enhance students' learning effectiveness. This method was accompanied by an empirical examination of the effects of course difficulty and online participation, along with factors fundamental to TAM, such as perceived ease of use and perceived usefulness, on learning effectiveness in the context of computer software learning.

As the results show, the students' perceived ease of use and course difficulty were identified as antecedents of perceived usefulness, which had direct and indirect effects on learning effectiveness. The students' perceived usefulness had a positive influence on online participation, which in turn led to learning effectiveness. An important practical implication of our findings is the possibility of improving learning effectiveness in the context of computer software learning by introducing the Flickr platform, which is a great tool for the organization and annotation of information. In fact, Flickr's screenshot annotations can facilitate more practice and cooperative troubleshooting by allowing annotations, including stickers, drawings, and text.

ACKNOWLEDGEMENT

This research was partially funded by the Ministry of Science and Technology, Taiwan, R.O.C., under contract number MOST 103-2410-H-275-006-MY2.

REFERENCES

Addison, W. E., Best, J. & Warrington, J. D. (2006). Students' perceptions of course difficulty and their ratings of the instructor. *College student Journal*, *40*(2), 409-416.

Ainin, S., Naqshbandi, M. M., Mogavvemi, S. & Jaafar, N. I. (2015). Facebook usage, socialization and academic performance. *Computers & Education*, *83*, 64-73.

Bostrom, R. P., Olfman, L., & Sein, M. K. (1990). The importance of learning style in end-user training. *MIS Quarterly*, *14*(1), 101–119.
Chen, Y. C., Hwang, R. H., & Wang, C. Y. (2012). Development and evaluation of a Web 2.0 annotation system as a learning tool in an e-learning environment. *Computers & Education*, *58*, 1094-1105.
Cho, H., Gay, G., Davidson, B., & Ingraffea, A. (2007). Social networks, communication styles, and learning performance in a CSCL community. *Computers & Education*, *49*, 309-329.
Citera, M. (1998). Distributed teamwork: The impact of communication media on influence and decision quality. *Journal of the American Society for Information Science*, *49*(9), 792-800.
Davis, F. D. (1993). User acceptance of information technology: System characteristics, user perceptions and behavioural impacts. *International Journal of Man-Machine Studies*, *38*(3), 475–487.
Davis, F. D., Bagozzi, R. P., & Warshaw, P. R. (1989). User acceptance of computer technology: A comparison of two theoretical models. *Management Science*, *35*(8), 982–1003.
Dickinger, A., Arami, M., & Meyer, D. (2008). The role of perceived enjoyment and social norm in the adoption of technology with network externalities. *European Journal of Information Systems*, *17*, 4–11.
Gao, F. (2013) A case study of using a social annotation tool to support collaboratively learning. *Internet and Higher Education*, *17*, 76-83.
Huang, T. K. (2015). Exploring the antecedents of screenshot-based interactions in the context of advanced computer software learning. *Computers & Education*, *80*, 95-107.
Kalpidou, M., Costin, D., & Morris, J. (2011). The relationship between Facebook and the well-being of undergraduate college students. *Cyberpsychology, Behavior, and Social Networking*, *14*(4), 183-189.
Lewis, W., Agarwal, R., & Sambamurthy, V. (2003). Sources of influence on beliefs about information technology use: An empirical study of knowledge workers. *MIS Quarterly*, *27*(4), 657–678.
Lowerison, G., Sclater, J., Schmid, R. F., & Abrami, P. C. (2006). Student perceived effectiveness of computer technology use in post-secondary classrooms. *Computers & Education*, *47*, 465-489.
Maki, R. H., Maki, W. S., Patterson, M., & Whittaker, P. D. (2000). Evaluation of a web-based introductory psychology course: i learning and satisfaction in on-line versus lecture courses. *Behavior Research Methods of Instruments and Computers*, *32*(2), 230–239.
Mendenhall, A., & Johnson, T. E. (2010). Fostering the development of critical thinking skills, and reading comprehension of undergraduates using a Web 2.0 tool coupled with a learning system. *Interactive Learning Environments*, *18*(3), 263-276.
Su, A. Y. S., Yang, S. J. H., Hwang, W. Y., & Zhang, J. (2010). A Web 2.0-based collaborative annotation system for enhancing knowledge sharing in collaborative learning environments. *Computers & Education*, *55*, 752-766.
Tucker, B., Jones, S., Mandy, A., & Gupta, R. (2006). Physiotherapy students' sources of stress, perceived course difficulty, and paid employment: Comparison between Western Australia and United Kingdom. *Physiotherapy Theory and Practice*, *22*(6), 317-328.
Venkatesh, V., & Bala, H. (2008). Technology acceptance model 3 and a research agenda on interventions. *Decision Science*, *39*(2), 273-315.
Warschauer, M. (1997). Computer-mediated collaborative learning: Theory and practice. *Modern Language Journal*, *8*(4), 470-481.
Yang, C. C., & Brown, B. B. (2015). Factors involved in associations between Facebook use and college adjustment: Social competence, perceived usefulness, and use patterns. *Computers in Human Behavior*, *46*, 245-253.

DECISION SCIENCES INSTITUTE

Understanding the Organizational Needs of an International Sports Event: A Systems Perspective on Sevens Wellington - the Wellington 7s

Sara Harrison
PwC
smlharrison76@gmail.com

John Davies
Victoria University of Wellington
john.davies@vuw.ac.nz

ABSTRACT

This paper seeks to understand the fluctuating fortunes of an annual international sports event over time. In particular, it sheds light on the links between brand creation, organizational effectiveness and organizational variables using the perspective of viable systems thinking first proposed by Stafford Beer.

KEYWORDS: sports events, organizational design, systems thinking, viable systems model

INTRODUCTION

The study reported here was part of a wider multi-methodological research project examining the branding process – brand creation and brand identity – within large international recurring sports events. This paper focuses on the specific case context of the annual two-day *Sevens Wellington* rugby tournament in New Zealand. The Wellington tournament, which has been held in February each year since 2000, is part of what is now known as the *World Rugby Sevens Series*, consisting of ten tournaments in ten countries, played on annual basis.

The *Sevens Wellington* tournament marks round five of the *World Rugby Sevens Series* and over fifteen years has become one of NZ's most popular sporting events. Popular with players and known for its unique 'carnival' atmosphere, the event has traditionally attracted high spectator numbers. Yet in 2014, 2015 and 2016, the event struggled to achieve a 'ticket sellout' as before, and also struggled to meet its sponsorship goals, perhaps amongst other factors, due to a decline in brand strength.

This paper uses findings from the *Sevens Wellington* study to demonstrate the benefits of a multi-methodological approach to understand the inter-relatedness of effective brand creation, and underpinning organization-related factors. Further background on the wider study, and to the sport of rugby and *Sevens* can be found in a companion paper (Harrison & Davies, 2016). The wider study examined brand issues using primarily the model/framework developed by Parent et al. (2012). This framework also, and necessarily, encompasses organizational variables, and addresses notions and issues related to organizational structure, governance and management. These inter-related organizational and branding matters provide a rationale for adopting a multi-methodological approach to understanding the concerns and how they may addressed (Davies et al., 2004; Mabin et al., 2007). As such, the use of Beer's Viable Systems Model (VSM) (1974, 1979, 1981) to provide an alternative and complementary perspective on such organizational matters, was considered to constitute an appropriate multi-methodological approach to both branding and organizational design.

Following a sketch of Parent et al's brand creation model (2012), whose development is described elsewhere (Parent et al, 2007, 2008, 2009), the paper provides an outline of the

VSM (Beer, 1974, 1978, 1979; Brocklesby et al., 1995). It then proceeds with a VSM diagnosis and analysis of findings from the brand creation study relevant to the *Sevens Wellington* organization, whilst a companion paper (Harrison & Davies, 2016) addresses methodological developments in understanding brand creation and brand identity.

RELATED WORK

The research on which this paper is based sought to understand the issue of brand creation and brand identity for the *Sevens Wellington* tournament and aimed to provide qualitative and empirical insights that would influence the continued evolution and strategic management of the brand. The guiding framework for the examination of brand creation was that of Parent et al (2012). The wider research also sought to address a gap in the literature by examining the inter-relationships between the four referents of Parent et al's (2012) model of brand creation for a recurring international sports event in a NZ context – the *Sevens Wellington* rugby tournament. The referents include, but are not limited to: (a) the importance of the LG, (b) the context for the event, (c) the nature of the event, and (d) the induced event experience. The research sets out to explore whether Parent et al's (2012) model can usefully be extended to the Southern hemisphere, specifically to identify and consider factors that may impact brand creation for the *Sevens Wellington* event (hereafter referred to as 'the *Sevens'*.

Figure 1. Parent et al.'s 2012 Brand Creation Model for International Recurring Sports Events

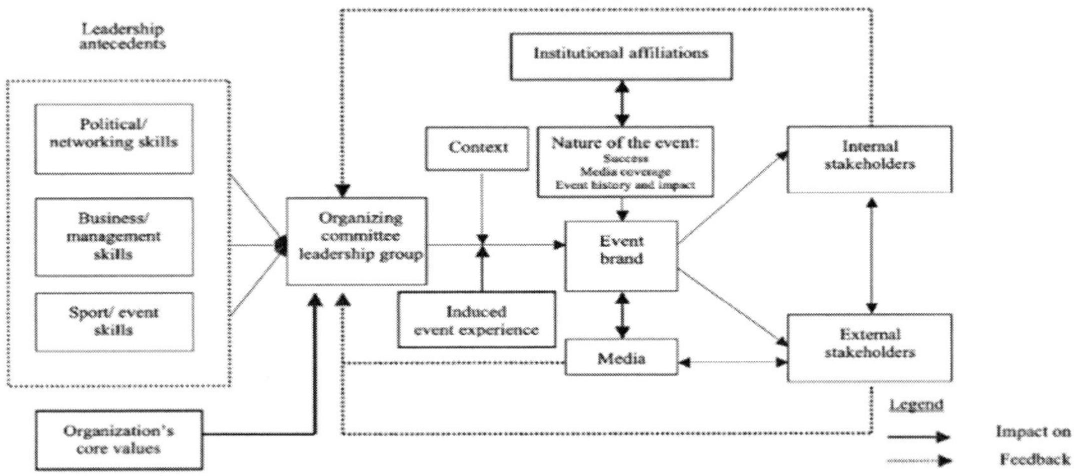

In prior work, extending Aaker's (1992, 2014) generic concepts, Richelieu (2004) identified that sports consumers develop strong emotional attachments to sports events, helping to create a strong brand. Therefore, defining a sports organization's identity is considered to be important aspect in building a brand strategy. Parent & Foreman (2007) later examined the process of organizational identity construction (OIC) in order to better understand how sports event organisers could build their brand more effectively. They proposed that if identity is a core aspect of brand creation, that specific *identity referents* (the central, enduring and distinct elements relating to an organiser's intent and purpose) could become important for brand creation.

Whilst Parent et al. (2012) extended the scope of work on international recurring sports events to the Northern hemisphere, there had been little research that examined brand creation for sports events in the New Zealand (NZ) context, let alone events so closely associated with NZ's national game, rugby. The brand creation study on which this paper is based, sought to address these matters, and similarly to highlight the importance of the same brand equity referents in creating the *Sevens* event brand: in particular, the importance of a Leadership Group (LG) exhibiting political/networking, business/management, and sport/event skills.

Ross (2006) had previously presented a framework for spectator-based brand equity for sports teams. That study surfaced three categories of antecedents to brand equity; those that are organization, market, and experience induced. These categories encompassed ideas put forward by Berry (2000) who not only highlighted the experiential nature of sport in creating memories for spectators, but also how sports brands are in continuous interaction with both spectators/consumers and the organization. These findings, *in toto*, give prominence to the importance of an organization's mission, vision and values in brand creation; and to the concept of 'leadership brand', where employee and organizational values are effectively aligned (Urde, 2003; Ulrich & Smallwood, 2007). These are all factors incorporated within Parent et al.'s (2012) model of brand creation for recurring international sports events.

Drawing on these findings, we suggest that such notions as identity, vision, mission; and their role in understanding, reacting and adapting to the environment, stakeholders etc, all point towards use of Beer's VSM as a complementary framework for understanding the interrelationship of organizational variables with brand creation (Angen, 2000).

The Viable Systems Model

Whilst a detailed description of the theoretical underpinnings of the VSM is not within the scope of this paper, a parsimonious outline is provided. In summary, the VSM embraces the principles of organizational cybernetics in a systems approach to designing complex, adaptable systems that are regarded as organizations (Beer, 1959).

The VSM encompasses five sub-systems - identified as also existing in other viable organisms, the brain and body - and the appropriate feedback and information flows that connect those sub-systems, facilitating self-adaptive viability. These sub-systems may also be capable of viability. As such, viable systems are *recursive*; that is, viable systems contain embedded viable systems that can be modeled using an identical cybernetic description as the higher (and lower) level systems in the wider systems hierarchy.

Beer has conceptualised all viable systems as sharing a network of communication channels bonding these five complementary sub-systems (Davies, 2013). The five sub-systems whose effective systemic functioning and communication links are necessary for organizational viability, are shown in Figure 2.

Figure 2: The VSM – Sub-systems and Systemic Functions

S1 Operations	• autonomous operational units that act out the very identity and purpose of the overall system, doing what the system is designed to do,
Meta-System	• comprising four other sub-systemic functions
S5 Identity	• the creation and promulgation of identity, values, purpose or *raison d'être*, vision, direction and mission, throughout the organization and its wider environment
S4 Intelligence	• strategy development serving the organization's future; focusing on the *future and external* environment
S3 Resourcing	• operational planning, resourcing, formal reporting, regulation, control and audit functions relating to the autonomous units; focusing on the *inside and now* of the organization
S3* Monitoring	• informal monitoring of culture, performance, riskt
S2 Coordination	• effecting overall coordination of autonomous units, ensuring autonomous operational units work in harmony
Environment	• VSM recognition and capture of the environment within the model is necessary to reflect the domain of action for the organization, and to contextualise or ground the internal interactions of the organization

Adapted from Davies (2013) and Brocklesby and Cummings (1996)

The communication links and relationships with each other sub-system, and *the environment,* are depicted graphically in Figure 3. The VSM framework is generally used to help structure thinking about organizational systems, their functioning and activities of interest (for example, branding); the relationships between key elements; the deployment of key resources; and performance and effectiveness. It should be noted that the five inter-related sets of systemic functions are not necessarily role descriptions for individuals or groups contributing to those systemic function; and that the VSM is simply a way of capturing and conveying the interdependence between the sub-systems, their systemic functions and communication links.

Figure 3: Stafford Beer's Viable Systems Model

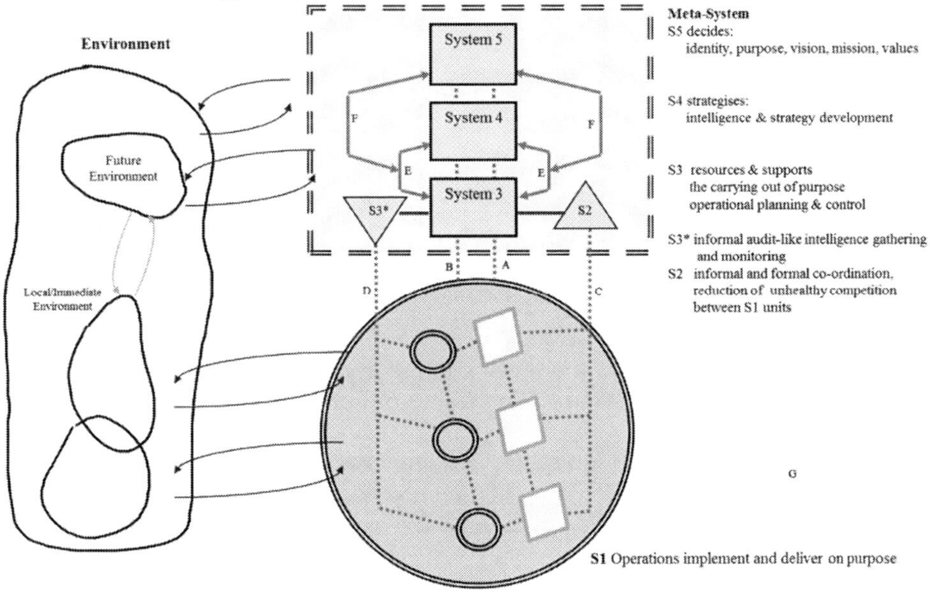

The *Sevens* organization and the VSM Framework

The *Sevens* organization is presented below (Figure 4) as a schematic VSM representation. Its cybernetic or systemic strengths are then presented as a VSM diagnosis. In this initial conceptualization, it should be noted that the *Sevens* organization, the System in Focus (SIF), is also regarded as a nested S1 unit of the WRFU system (2014a), which in turn is embedded as a S1 unit within the NZRU system. Within the *Sevens* system, and certainly within its own embedded S1 units covering tournament operations, entertainment and stadium experience, it may not be surprising to find *silo effects* in evidence. However, the VSM representation makes it more readily obvious that considerations of coordination are now seen to encompass elements across different logical levels of *nestedness*, or *recursion,* of the overall system; and also between elements at the same level of *recursion* – highlighting, in a different way, not only the complexity of coordination functions, but the difficulty in attending to *silo effects.*
Indeed, as mentioned above, key issues that had surfaced in the findings of the wider study, related not only to matters underpinning successful brand development facing the *Sevens* event, the organization, *per se*, but also environmental forces and factors. As such, the various elements contributing to the Parent et al.'s (2012) model have been reconceptualised and reinterpreted using the VSM (Figure 5) to highlight matters that may jeopardize organizational effectiveness. These include, for example, systemic role conflict, systemic overlap in functional responsibilities, and/or systemic gaps or weaknesses within the organization or wider system.

Figure 4: Illustration of NZRU as Set of Nested Organizational Systems

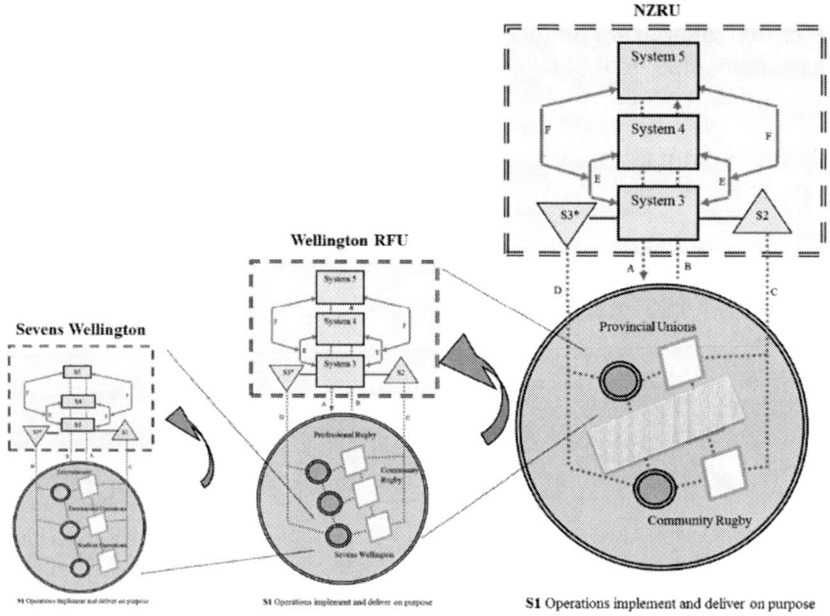

As an overview of findings, we note at the time of the study, there was an absence of S2 and S5 functionality within the wider system relating to the *Sevens* system, and its S1 operations.

Figure 5: VSM Model for *Sevens Wellington* System

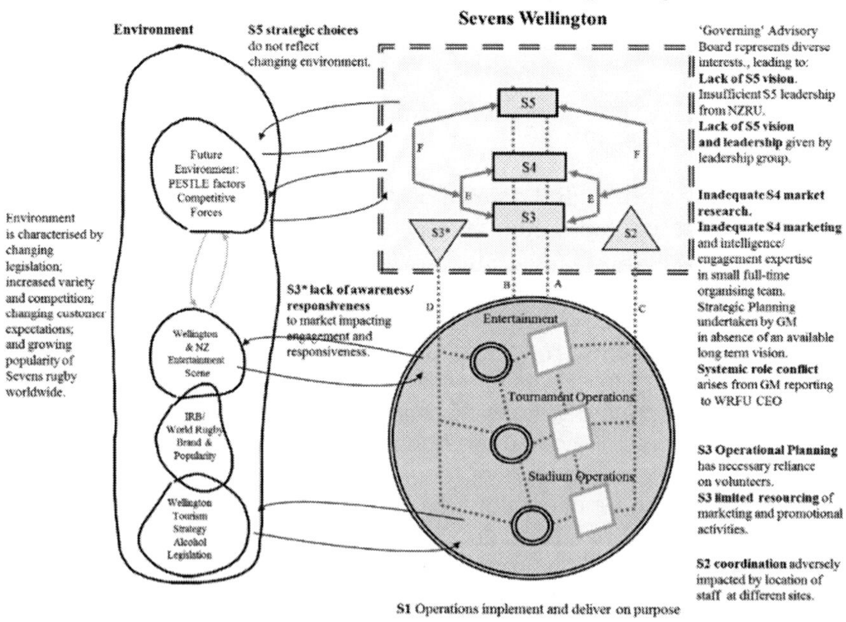

In particular, there was a seeming lack of S2 coordination within the WRFU system, manifest as policy framework limitations adversely impacting *Sevens* organisers; and as less than adequate guidance about managing incompatible sub-optimal local objectives of tournament, stadium and entertainment S1 operations. The S2 weakness within the wider WRFU system has impacted on the *Sevens* as a WRFU S1 sub-system, and on the *Sevens* as a viable system in its own right. Such matters and others manifesting within each systemic function are explored below.

S5 Purpose/Identity/Values/Vision/Mission

The S5 function is responsible for deciding on strategic direction and strategy, the organization's values, vision and mission – and thus for guiding the development of operating and policy decisions within the organization as a whole (See Figure 3). It also has systemic responsibility to project identity, both within the organization and also to the external environment; to balance demands from different parts of the organization. In general, S5 functioning encompasses responsibility for stewardship of the organization, for steering its strategic direction.
One key theme that emerged from the findings of the wider study, could be interpreted as an apparent S5 dysfunction in the *Sevens* organization. This likely stems from a lack of overarching, long-term direction and vision for the *Sevens* tournament within the wider system.
S5 Strategic Framework and Positioning - One of the strategic goals of the NRZU is "two Olympic Gold medals in Rio" - goals that relate specifically to *Sevens* rugby. There are also elements within the overall NZRU strategy that are of specific relevance for *Sevens* rugby. These include increasing commercial revenues generated by *Sevens* to ensure the financial sustainability of the NZRU *Sevens* programme; attracting more people to the game; continuing to enhance traditional international relationships such as those with the global governing body – now known as *World Rugby*; continuing to leverage commercial relationships and global networks to grow its brands; and contributing leadership and expertise to developing the global game in a way that benefits NZ (NZRU, 2014a, b). It is not surprising that perceptions of an apparent emphasis on protecting revenues and profit from the *Sevens* exist. If so, it may be inferred that such other goals and priorities need to be well communicated, if they are to influence *Sevens* S5 thinking.
Indeed, the role that *Sevens* rugby will play (as a S1 of the wider NZRU system) may need to be promoted more widely. In addition, there appears to be an opportunity for a governance structure that promotes a more cohesive role for *Sevens* rugby, in general, and for the *Sevens* tournament which plays such a crucial role in achieving the related strategic goals outlined above.
S5/4/3 Governance Structure - Findings from the brand creation study identified systemic issues associated with the S5 governance role within *Sevens* (Davies, 2002). As stated above, S5 systemic dysfunction can stem directly from a lack of a compelling S5 identity for *Sevens* rugby within the NZRU strategic framework, but it can also be related to other S5 and S3 weaknesses. As the governing body responsible for *Sevens* in New Zealand, the NZRU had gained the hosting rights for the *IRB/World Rugby Sevens Series* event to be held in Wellington and NZ. Although there is a joint 'advisory board' to effect wider S3 resourcing and S2 coordination of the *Sevens*, it appears not to have the status of a governing board, and, as such, is seemingly not charged with carrying out the broader S5 functions usually expected of a governing board.

S4 Strategising/Intelligence

Effective S4 functioning requires thinking about the external environment, both *now* and in the *future*, examining trends and scenarios – and then strategising to provide the S5 governance function with more relevant options for strategic direction. S4 functions also include the responsibility of modelling/understanding the system in its entirety, that is, seeing the organization as a whole related to its both its internal and external environments, and then assessing its resilience in the face of anticipated and unanticipated scenarios and futures, This also contributes to the S4 role of stewardship and securing the future, its long term viability and sustainability

S4 Strategic Planning – Environmental Scanning - As the research findings indicated, the *Sevens* tournament has been faced with several challenging trends, both in the NZ local environment, and globally. Domestic trends include a large shift in perceptions and attitudes around alcohol, and new legislation governing the sale and management of alcohol at events (WRFU, 2014b; AACNZ, 2010). Global trends include spectator and media preferences shifting towards short format sports, and *Sevens*, itself, as a sport is growing in global popularity and significance because of its designation as an Olympic sport. Furthermore, the prevalence of global connectivity and access to digital media via electronic devices will soon change the way people engage with live events and their expectations around how content is delivered. Although the participants in this research generally acknowledged these trends, an under-developed S4 function and lack of S4 resource has limited the strategic response seemingly available to the S5 governance function/board. As a result, the event has been perceived to be 'reacting' to the environment, rather than anticipating the environmental change, and then, in a process of amplification, getting ahead of the competition and becoming a market leader once again.
S4 - Product Life Cycle and Innovation - Other findings of the brand creation study highlighted that the *Sevens* event had reached the 'mature' phase in the product life cycle, perhaps even entering the 'decline' phase. If so, then with increasing pressure from competitors for the sport/entertainment dollar, the *Sevens* organization has need to boost S4 functionality in terms of market intelligence and strategising, and may have to commit more resource to defend the event's market position or to introduce market extension strategies. Indeed, ineffective S4 functioning may compromise the continued success and viability of the *Sevens*. Although the *Sevens* brand, in terms of *Sevens* S5 identity, has evolved organically driven primarily by spectators over time, there had been no underlying change in the product.
S4 Change Leadership - Given changing environmental factors and the need and likelihood of the *Sevens* brand evolving further, a key factor to facilitate change will be an effective S5 function within the wider system enabling strong S5 leadership of S4 strategy in the *Sevens* organization.

S3 Resourcing, Operational Planning and Control

The *Sevens* S3 function can include day-to-day managerial involvement in, and resourcing of S1 units – not just with funds or people, but with policies, guidelines, goals, instruction etc. Effective S3 functioning should also pay attention to, and provide for infrastructure, as well identifying and seeking an optimal balance between the centralization and decentralization of support activities.
S3 Organizational Design and Structure - Within the current *Sevens* organization, the S3 function provides HRM, marketing, sponsorship and communications support that facilitate, but does not deliver S1 operations. As highlighted during the wider research project, there are complex systemic command and control arrangements for staff working on the event, at large. Given the complexity of running a large-scale event which demands success as a sports tournament, as an entertainment extravaganza, and as a stadium experience, there was some evidence that S3 resourcing and support had largely been 'undercooked', especially with respect to the S3 commercial support activities, such as marketing, promotion, sponsorship etc. Resourcing of the *Sevens* organization is placed into context when stating that the GM had been the only person working on the event full-time, although two contracted staff also reported to the GM. A part-time contractor (located in Auckland) was responsible for the sponsorship, commercial and HR functions, whilst a separate WRFU resource was responsible for the communications and PR planning. Positively Wellington Tourism (PWT), the WCC agency, also provided marketing advice and expertise, whilst branding and other creative work was outsourced to an agency. The geographical separation and separate reporting lines can likely lead to S3 dysfunction, if not managed well; and can result in additional complexity; a lack of

responsiveness in decision making; and a lack of cohesiveness or an integrated approach (as borne out in research findings).

Other activities interpreted as systemic weaknesses in the wider research findings, related to 'fan and member engagement' as a potential and untapped S3 resource that could be provided to each of the *Sevens* S1 entertainment, tournament and stadium operations.

S3 Allocation of Human Resources and Volunteers

The findings of the broader study also noted that there had been a high turnover of professional and volunteer personnel within both the WRFU and the *Sevens* organization, indicating the potential for a range of S5 to S1 dysfunctions, as well as the systemic role overload and role conflict that arises from an inadequate S3 resourcing. Some degree of turnover is expected with a high profile event such as the *Sevens* because of its episodic recurring nature, however,the level of turnover was concerning, given resulting losses of S4 intelligence, not only within the *Sevens* organization as an S1 unit, but also within the wider system.

S3 Implementation of Change Management - Given the high profile of the *Sevens* tournament and the S5 reputational risk to the NZRU of the event 'failing', it is vital that the S3 function within *Sevens* is capable of responding to, and implementing change. One goal of effective change management is often to minimise the unintended consequences, distractions and impacts of the change (Davies et al., 2004). For this to occur, systemic roles and responsibilities need to be clear and everyone needs to understand their part in the overarching S5 vision.

S2 Co-ordination

The S2 co-ordination function seeks to ensure that all systems elements work harmoniously together, even accommodating healthy competition. Given the large-scale nature of the event and disparate nature of resources allocated to organizing and delivering the event, effective S2 coordination of resourcing was identified in the findings as being problematic.

The research findings implied that there was inadequate integration of various internal management functions within the *Sevens* organization, especially in relation to S4 strategic planning activities. For example, it was suggested that the external S3 marketing resource, and therefore, relevant marketing information, was not used sufficiently in strategic planning, and neither was the S3 marketing function conducted with awareness of the wider strategic vision. However, it was noted that a *Sevens* S4 working group had been created in 2014 to understand and work with various stakeholder groups, and had been found to improve co-ordination.

S2 Integrated Business Planning - It was suggested that the *Sevens* S4 marketing intelligence function, and S3 use of marketing as resource to the S1 operations, had not been effectively integrated into S4 strategising, or aligned with other systems functions. For example, customer and ticketing data had not been fully exploited to provide effective S4 intelligence, nor analyzed in sufficient appropriate detail to inform future planning, especially in the sponsorship domain.

S1 Operational Elements

S1 operations include those elements that directly interface with the external environment and that enact the identity of the wider system-in-focus, to deliver on the system's purpose, and taking responsibility for implementation of strategy. Whilst the S1 entertainment operation (and subsequent unique carnival atmosphere) has contributed to the success of the event, it had also emerged as a potential weakness, given its unwitting role in the organic development of a *de facto* S5 identity for the event associated with partying and alcohol. This brand imagery has possibly alienated many sponsors and fans. However, the S1 technical delivery of the rugby tournament has traditionally been a strength of the *Sevens*, and has always been rated highly by elite players and *World Rugby* (formerly the IRB), the global governing body.

The *Sevens* organization's relationship with the Stadium as venue owner, and then the relationship between S1 tournament operations, S1 entertainment and S1 stadium operations are areas where potential always exists for improvement. As surfaced in the wider research, trying to effect the 'right S2 balance' between the three S1 units, and coordinating their different goals for overall *Sevens* effectiveness will be critical for future success. The stadium Infrastructure, in particular, is itself a key factor in shaping how spectators are physically segmented, how spectator flow is managed, and therefore whether the S1 stadium experience at the *Sevens* is a success or not.

SUMMARY AND CONCLUSION

The paper reports on a study which was part of a wider project which examined brand issues in a large international recurring sports event, and which drew primarily on the brand creation and brand identity model developed by Parent et al. (2012). The findings of that study were reinterpreted using the lens of Beer's Viable Systems Model (VSM) (1974, 1979, 1981) as an interpretive and diagnostic tool. It was considered that Beer's VSM would provide an alternative and complementary perspective on the organizational notions and issues surfaced by Parent et al.'s model. The harnessing of both frameworks was considered to constitute an appropriate multi-methodological approach to both branding and organizational analysis.

In respect of understanding broader branding issues at *Sevens Wellington*, the research findings indicated the relative importance of several factors –organizational and brand related - in the management of the *Sevens* brand. As such, we note how the primary tournament 'owners', the NZRU and WRFU, could be better informed to determine how best to create additional value through an enhanced understanding, not just of brand creation matters, but of organizational design that facilitates effective systemic functioning appropriate to underpin strategy and brand development. Given the dynamic environment impacting on spectator demand for the *Sevens* event, the wider study sought to provide qualitative and empirical insights that will influence the continued evolution of the *Sevens* brand. This paper considered additional factors that impact brand creation, and utilised Stafford Beer's VSM as an analytical framework to understand the organizational factors that impact the *Sevens* brand creation 'system'.

It was suggested that creating additional capacity for S4 strategic planning, innovation, market research, and S3 marketing and sponsorship functions would enhance *Sevens*' organizational ability to S4 monitor the external environment, engage with the fan base, and to research and prepare sponsorship proposals; and to develop the overall S1 capacity to deliver. The *Sevens* brand could be regarded as mature in as much as demand had already peaked or waned, so better connecting with the fan base and finding the right S2 balance between the S1 rugby operations, and the S1 entertainment offerings, without undermining either, would be crucial. Similarly, boosting S2 coordination efforts to improve aspects of the relationship between the stadium and the tournament, may further enhance S1 operational delivery of the event. Findings also suggest that the strengthening or formalising of existing planning efforts may improve integration across various functional areas, and enhance S4 strategic planning and decision-making. In a related manner, VSM diagnosis suggests that a change in governance structure strengthening links between, say, the *Sevens* organization and the NZRU governance board may result in access to NZRU resources and expertise, and also ensure greater alignment with the overarching NZRU strategy.

In summary, we may conclude that the study has not only contributed to sport specific event management knowledge that relates to brand creation and brand identity, but to the understanding systemic functions that underpin not only successful branding processes, but aspects of organizational design and effectiveness.

REFERENCES

Aaker, David. (2014). The Five Biggest Ideas of the Branding Era. *Marketing News, 48*(7), 22-23.
Aaker, David A. (1992). The Value of Brand Equity. *Journal of Business Strategy, 13*(4), 27.
AACNZ. (2010). Guidelines for Managing Alcohol at Large Events.
Angen, Maureen Jane. (2000). Evaluating Interpretive Inquiry: Reviewing the Validity Debate and Opening the Dialogue. *Qualitative health research, 10*(3), 378-395.
Beer S. (1959). *Cybernetics and Management*. London: English Universities Press.
Beer S. (1974). *Designing Freedom*. Wiley: Chichester: Wiley.
Beer, S. (1979). *The Heart of the Enterprise*, Wiley, Chichester.
Beer, S. (1981), *Brain of the Firm (2nd Edn)*, Wiley, Chichester.
Brocklesby, J, & Cummings, S. (1996). Designing a Viable Organisation Structure. *Long Range Planning, 29*(1), 49-57.
Brocklesby R. J., Cummings, S. & Davies J. (1995). Demystifying the Viable Systems Model as a Tool in Organisational Analysis. *Asia Pacific Journal of Operations Research,* Vol. 12, No. 1, 65-86.
Davies, J. (2013). Designing Sustainable Sports Organisations - A VSM Approach. In F. Stowell, S. McRobb, R. Lander, R. Ison, J. Holloway, & R. Armson (Eds.), *Systems for Sustainability: People, Organisations, and Environments* (2nd Edn) (Ch. 33, pp. 191-197). London: Springer.
Davies, J., Mabin, V & Cox, J. (2004). The Theory of Constraints and Systems Dynamics: A Suitable Case for Multi-methodology, Proceedings of the *22nd International Conference of the Systems Dynamics* Society, Kennedy G *et al* (Eds), Oxford, July 25-29 2004, pp 27.
Davies, J. (2002). Models of Governance - A Viable Systems Perspective, *The Australian Journal of Information Systems*, Vol 9(2), May 2002, 57-66. A
Harrison, S. & Davies, J. (2016). Methodological Developments in Understanding Brand Creation and Brand Identity – The Case of Sevens Wellington - an International Recurring Sports Event. *Proceedings of the 47th Annual Meeting of Decision Sciences Institute*, November 19-22 2016,
Mabin, V., Davies, J. & Cox, J. (2006). Using the Theory of Constraints to Complement Systems Dynamics' Causal Loop Diagrams in Developing Fundamental Solutions, *International Transactions in Operations Research,* Vol 13, 33-57, DOI: 10.1111/j.1475-3995.2006.00532.
NZRU. (2014a). Our Strategic Framework. Retrieved 10 October, 2014, from http://www.nzru.co.nz/about_us/strategic_framework
NZRU. (2014b). Towards 2016 - Empowering Rugby. Retrieved 10 October, 2014, from http://www.nzru.co.nz/about_us/strategic_framework
Parent, M., Eskerud, L, & Hanstad, D.V. (2012). Brand creation in international recurring sports events. *Sport Management Review, 15*(2), 145-159
Parent, MOlver, D, & Séguin, B. (2009). Understanding Leadership in Major Sporting Events: The Case of the 2005 World Aquatics Championships. *Sport Management Review, 12*(3):167-184
Parent, M.M., & Séguin, B. (2008). Toward a Model of Brand Creation for International Large-Scale Sporting Events: The Impact of Leadership, Context, and Nature of the Event. *Journal of Sport Management, 22*(5), 526-549.
Parent, M.M., & Foreman, P.O. (2007). Organizational Image and Identity Management in Large-Scale Sporting Events. *Journal of Sport Management, 21*(1), 15-40.
Richelieu, A. (2004). Building the brand equity of professional sports teams. In B. G. Pitts (Ed.), *Sharing best practices in sports marketing*. Morgantown: WV: Fitness Information Technology.
Ross, S. D. (2006). A conceptual framework for understanding spectator-based brand equity. *Journal of Sport Management, 20*(1), 22-38.
WRFU. (2014a). Wellington Rugby. Retrieved 26 April, 2014, from http://www.wrfu.co.nz/
WRFU. (2014b). Drinking practices of attendees of the Wellington Sevens and Homegrown in 2014. *Wellington Sevens Study*.

DECISION SCIENCES INSTITUTE

Use of Social Media in Teaching and its Impact on Student Learning Outcomes

Shahedur Rahman
Prairie View A&M University
shrahman@pvamu.edu

Thiagarajan Ramakrishnan
Prairie View A&M University
ram@pvamu.edu

Louis Ngamassi
Prairie View A&M University
longamassi@pvamu.edu

ABSTRACT

Social networking sites are transforming the landscape of education and offering new opportunities. Although increasing number of research has investigated the adoption of social media (SM) in teaching, little research has examined the impact of SM use by faculty on learning outcomes. This study examined the impact of SM use on learning outcomes at a Historically Black College and University and found that: 1) perceived usefulness of SM has positive effect on the use of SM in teaching; (2) perceived risk of using SM does not discourage use of SM, and (3) SM use has positive effect on learning outcomes.

KEYWORDS: Social media, Risk, Self-efficacy, Teaching, Learning outcomes

INTRODUCTION

The growth of social media and other Web 2.0 technologies is unprecedented (Lenhart et al., 2010). Social media (SM) is broadly used to describe applications related to collaboration and community (Joosten, 2012; Ngamassi et al., 2014, 2016). SM is also described by other names such as social networking sites (SNSs), blogs, wikis, multimedia platforms, virtual game worlds, and virtual social worlds (Tess, 2013; Ngamassi et al., 2015). SM is generally used on a regular basis by millions of people across the globe for different reasons. A big portion of SM users is made up of youths, most of whom are college students. SM applications such as Facebook, Twitter, MySpace, YouTube, Flickr, Skype, Wiki, blogs have been widely used for information dissemination and gathering, collaborative learning, and online social and professional connections (Cao et al., 2013). Educators are exploring the opportunities of these applications for their learning and teaching value (Elgort et al., 2008). Although the popularity of SM has motivated some faculty to use SM in higher education (Hamid et al., 2015), research shows that SM applications are not extensively used by academicians in teaching. (McCarthy, 2013).

SM applications can enrich student learning experience and improve student learning outcomes (Redecker et al., 2010; Taylor et al., 2012). Learner-centered and SM enriched interactive learning can enhance dynamic faculty–student and student–student interactions. Such interactive learning improves student satisfaction leading to better learning (Redecker et al, 2010) through the use of online social networking technologies. These technologies provide advantages over traditional teaching technology (e.g., lectures, written contents and face-to-face communications) with new opportunities and outlets for creativity (Hamid et al., 2015, Cao et al., 2013).

Although many institutions encourage faculty to adopt SM applications in teaching (Wankel, 2010), many faculty are skeptical about the use of SM in teaching and view SM applications as not conducive to better learning outcomes (Moran et al, 2012). In order to address such skepticism, more research is required to answer if SM use in teaching leads to improved learning outcomes. Therefore, in this study, we examined the factors that influence the use of SM in college teaching and the impact of SM use on student learning outcomes.

RESEARCH MODEL AND HYPOTHESES

Prior studies indicate that the main reason for use of SM in teaching is that SM provides multiple formats, directions and channels of communication, which can improve educational outcomes (Cao et al., 2013). With a view to understanding the use of SM by the teaching faculty, we draw on the literature from technology acceptance, risk, and self-efficacy. Technology adoption theories have been widely used to explain the cause and effect of different factors of SM such as Twitter and blogging as valuable contemporary curriculum content and learning experience (Ajjan & Hartshorne, 2008; Giannakos & Vlamos, 2012; Park, Nam & Cha, 2012). Self-efficacy construct has been used by many information systems (IS) researchers to help explain user behavior with information systems (Claggett & Goodhue, 2011).

Figure 1 gives the conceptual model of our study.

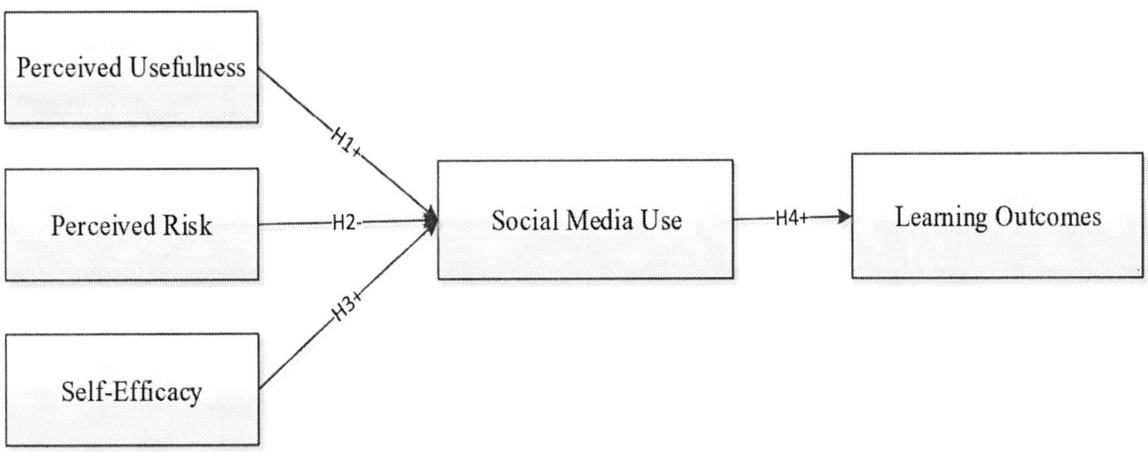

Figure 1: Research Model

Perceived usefulness: Perceived usefulness captures the users' perception regarding the usefulness of specific technology to perform their tasks successfully (Davis, 1986). Prior studies suggest that if the users perceive the technology to be useful in successfully completing their required tasks, they will be more inclined to use the specific technology (Ajjan and Harshone, 2008). SM can enhance interaction between the faculty and the students. SM can help faculty members keep in touch with the students living off-campus as well as with their ex-students. Further, faculty can share data and information that are collected during field study trips with mobile devices and share it with students using SM. This has the potential to make teaching and learning more exciting and real time. Therefore, if the faculty perceive that using SM will enhance their teaching ability, then they will have a positive attitude towards using SM for teaching purposes. Therefore, we hypothesize that:

> ***H1: Perceived usefulness of SM applications has a positive effect on SM use in teaching.***

Perceived Risks*:* Perceived risk examines the users' belief regarding the potential uncertain negative outcome of using a specific technology to complete their tasks (Kim et al., 2014). The users' perceived risk plays an important role in their decisions (Anthony et al., 2006). Some of the risks associated with using SM from a faculty perspective include difficulty of using SM, privacy related issues, time involved, loss of control, and lack of effective assessment tool for evaluating the benefits of SM in teaching and learning (Moran et al., 2012). Such perceived risks and challenges may keep the faculty from moving towards the adoption of SM applications in their classrooms. Thus, we hypothesize that.

> ***H2: Perceived risk of using SM applications has a negative effect on SM use in teaching***

Self-Efficacy: Self-efficacy refers to people's judgments of their readiness to accomplish a certain level of performance (Bandura, 1986). Self-efficacy belief typically determines the effort that someone will invest and how long the effort will persist (Bandura, 1986). In case of SM use, self-efficacy refers to faculty's degree of confidence that they can successfully use SM applications in the classroom. People with high computer self-efficacy set higher goals for themselves and are more persistent in their usage attempts, even in the face of set-backs (Claggett & Goodhue, 2011). Thus, faculty with high self-efficacy may find it easier to adopt and learn using SM in their classrooms. Therefore, we hypothesize that:

> ***H3: Self-efficacy has a positive effect on SM use in teaching.***

SM use: SM use refers to the perception of faculty regarding the use of SM in classroom for teaching purposes. Faculty use different technology and techniques in classroom to ensure that the students learn the materials presented in class. One of the ways faculty can measure the effectiveness of their teaching techniques is through students' learning outcomes. Thus, if the faculty feel that they can improve students' learning outcome through the use of SM, then they are more likely to adopt SM in their classroom settings. Further, prior studies have indicated that the use of SM does have an impact on students' learning outcome (Cao & Hong, 2011). The Institute for Prospective Technological Studies of European Union also reported that students had positive experience using SM applications through content enhancement, creativity experiences, connectivity enrichment, and collaborative engagements (Redecker et al, 2010). Students who expect real-time communication with their instructors can find SM tools such as Tweeting, blogging and virtual interactions very satisfying (Cao & Hong, 2011). Thus, we hypothesize that:

> ***H4: Use of SM in teaching has a positive effect on student learning outcomes.***

RESEARCH METHODOLOGY AND DATA COLLECTION

A survey methodology was used to test our research model. The survey items for measuring the constructs were adapted from previously validated instruments and contextualized in accordance with our research design. The survey items were measured using a five point Likert scale with (1) indicating "strongly disagree" and (5) indicating "strongly agree". A convenient sampling was used to collect data. The survey was administered online using Qualtrics to all the faculty in the College of Business at a Historically Black College and University (HBCU) situated in the Southwest of the United States.

DATA ANALYSIS AND RESULTS

We used partial least square (PLS) techniques to analyze our data. PLS has the ability to handle smaller sample sizes better than other multivariate techniques (Macoulides & Saunders, 2006). We used SmartPLS 2.0 (Ringle, Wende, & Will, 2005) to test our research model. SmartPLS 2.0 provides with measurement model and structural model. The measurement model was used to examine the reliability and the validity of the instrument. The structural model was used to evaluate our hypotheses.

Measurement Model

We examined the average variance extracted (AVE) of the constructs to assess convergent validity. The amount of variance captured by the indicators of the latent construct relative to the amount of variance captured due to the measurement error is provided by AVE (Chin, 1998). The AVE scores for all our constructs were greater than 0.5 (Table 1). This indicates that all our constructs in the model exhibit adequate construct validity (Komiak & Benbasat, 2006; Ramakrishnan et al., 2012).

Table 1: AVE for the Latent Constructs

LATENT CONSTRUCTS	AVE
Perceived Usefulness (PU)	**0.879**
Perceived Risk (PR)	**0.675**
Self-Efficacy (SE)	**0.744**
SM Use (SMU)	**0.713**
Learning Outcome (LO)	**0.968**

We evaluated the discriminant validity by examining the correlation among the latent variables and the square root of the AVEs of those latent variables. For the constructs to exhibit adequate discriminant validity, the correlation among the latent constructs must be lesser than the square root of the AVEs of the latent constructs (Ramakrishnan et al., 2012). Table 2 provides the relationship between the square root of the latent constructs and the correlation among the latent constructs. The correlation among the latent constructs (non-diagonal elements) is lesser than the square root of the AVEs (diagonal elements). This suggests that all the constructs in our model exhibit satisfactory discriminant validity..

Table 2: Square Root of AVEs and Correlation among Latent Constructs

	PU	PR	SE	SMU	LO
PU	**0.93755**				
PR	-0.706	**0.821584**			
SE	0.056	-0.322	**0.862554**		
SMU	0.651	-0.322	0.122	**0.844393**	
LO	0.364	-0.326	0.181	0.357	**0.98387**

The composite reliability of all our constructs was greater than 0.7 (Table 3), indicating adequate reliability.

Table 3: Composite Reliability (CR) for the Latent Constructs	
Perceived Usefulness (PU)	0.978
Perceived Risk (PR)	0.891
Self-Efficacy (SE)	0.744
SM Use (SMU)	0.908
Learning Outcome (LO)	0.995

Structural Model

In PLS, the relationship between the theoretical constructs is represented by the structural model. A recommended 500 random samples were generated using the bootstrapping procedure in SmartPLS (Majchrzak et al., 2005). A one-tailed t-test was used to evaluate the hypotheses as they are unidirectional in nature. The path coefficients, t-values, and their respective p-values for the hypotheses are given in Table 4.

Table 4: Path Coefficients, T-Values, and P-Values for Hypotheses testing

Hypotheses	Path Coefficients	T-Test	Significance
H1	0.91	4.157	0.00***
H2	0.383	1.508	0.07*
H3	0.194	1.058	0.15
H4	0.357	2.249	0.01**

(*p < 0.10 **p < 0.05 ***p < 0.01)

We had R-squares of 0.49 and 0.13 for the SM use and learning outcomes respectively. Thus, 49% of the variance in SM use is explained by our model and 13% of the variance in the learning outcomes is explained by our hypothesized model. Hypothesis H1 examines the relationship between perceived usefulness and SM use in teaching. We found this relationship significant at 0.01 level. Hypothesis H2 looks into the relationship between perceived risk and SM use in teaching. We found this relationship to be significant at 0.10 level but in a different direction than what was hypothesized. Interestingly, we did not find any support for our Hypothesis H3 that looks into the relationship between self-efficacy and SM use in teaching. Hypothesis H4 examines the relationship between SM use and learning outcomes. We found this relationship to be significant also at 0.01 level.

DISCUSSIONS, LIMITATIONS, AND FUTURE DIRECTIONS

The objective of this study was to examine the impact of the use of SM in teaching on learning outcomes at institutions of higher learning. In line with the literature on the factors that influence individuals to adopt new technology (Venkatesh et al., 2003), the results of our study regarding the use of SM indicate that perceived usefulness has positive influence on the intention to use SM in teaching. Thus, if the faculty believe that using SM can enhance their teaching, then they will be inclined to use SM in teaching. We found a significant, but positive relationship between risk perception and the use of SM. This is very interesting. One of the reasons for such a finding may be that the faculty members taking the survey were highly motivated and examined these risks as a challenge that can be overcome. Another reason could be that the faculty members are very familiar with the SM that they use and as such do not consider them risky. Yet another possibility is that there are different dimensions for the perception of risk and we are exploring only one of them. Thus, one of the future directions for this study is to explore in detail the relationship between risk perception and the use of SM in classroom for teaching purpose. The results of our study also indicate a strong relationship between the use of SM and the improved learning outcomes. Thus, the faculty who use SM for teaching do perceive it to be good for the students also and have recorded an improvement in their learning.

Interestingly, however, we did not find any support for the relationship between self-efficacy and the use of SM in teaching even though self-efficacy is important to the intention and the actual use of SM in teaching (Ajjan and Hartshorne, 2008). Thus, rather than directly influencing the use of SM, self-efficacy may be indirectly affecting the behavior intention through some other factors such as perceived usefulness. Therefore, another future direction of this study is to explore more factors that can possibly mediate the relationship between self-efficacy and the use of SM.

Although the data supports the proposed model, the findings of our study must be evaluated in light of its limitations. A convenience sampling methodology was used to conduct this study. All the respondents involved in this study were from the College of Business at an HBCU situated in the Southwest of the United States. Thus, additional study is required to conclude the generalizability of these results. Further, other factors such as privacy, security, experience in using SM, students' perception regarding SM that are relevant to the adoption and use of SM in classroom were not considered in this study. The purpose of this study was to develop and test a model that examines the influence of perceived usefulness, perceived risk, and self-efficacy in the use of SM in teaching. Therefore, future research is required to examine these factors and also to examine additional predictors to improve the scope and explanatory power of our proposed model.

THEORETICAL AND PRACTICAL IMPLICATIONS

This study has got both theoretical and practical implications. From a theoretical perspective, this study adds to the existing research in SM use in teaching. Prior literature on SM in higher education focuses on the adoption of SM applications and its motivators in and out of the classrooms and there are not many empirical studies that examine the utilization of SM in college teaching. (Cao et al., 2013). This study provides a cogent framework to understand the use of SM in college teaching.

This study also has practical implications. This research examines the factors influencing the use of SM by college and university faculty. The results of this study can act as a guideline for college and university administrators to encourage their faculty to use SM in teaching. This study suggests that faculty can be motivated to using SM by convincing them that the use of SM has benefits and leads to improved learning outcomes. In order to motivate the faculty to use SM applications, college and university administrators must create an environment that is conducive to the actual use of SM in teaching leading to improved student learning outcomes.

REFERENCES

Ajjan, H. & Hartshorne, R. (2008). Investigating faculty decisions to adopt Web 2.0 technologies: theory and empirical tests. *The Internet and Higher Education*, *11*(2), 71–80.

Bandura, A. (1986). The explanatory and predictive scope of self-efficacy theory. *Journal of Social and Clinical Psychology*, *4*(3), 359–373.

Cao, Y. & Hong, P. (2011). Antecedents and consequences of social media utilization in college teaching: a proposed model with mixed-methods investigation. *On the Horizon*, *19*(4), 297–306.

Cao, Yingxia, Haya Ajjan, and Paul Haya. 2013. Using social media applications for educational outcomes in college teaching: A structural equation analysis. *British Journal of Educational Technology*, *44*(4), 581-593. doi:doi:10.1111/bjet.12066.

Claggett, Jennifer L. & Goodhue, Dale L. (2011). Have IS Researchers Lost Bandura's Self-Efficacy Concept? A Discussion of the Definition and Measurement of Computer Self-Efficacy. *Proceedings of the 44th Hawaii International Conference* on System Sciences,

Davis, F. (1986), "A technology acceptance model for empirically testing new end-user information systems: theory and results", doctoral dissertation, *Sloan School of Management*, Massachusetts Institute of Technology, Cambridge, MA.

Elgort, I., Smith, A. G., & Toland, J. (2008). Is a wiki an effective platform for group course work? *24*(2), 195-210. Retrieved from http://www.ascilite.org.au/ajet/ajet24/elgort.html

Giannakos, M. N. & Vlamos, P. (2012). Educational webcasts' acceptance: empirical examination and therole of experience. *British Journal of Educational Technology*, *44*, 125–143.

Hamid, Suraya, Waycott, Jenny, Kurnia, Sherah, & Chamg, Shanton (2015), Understanding students' perceptions of the benefits of online social networking use for teaching and learning, *Internet and Higher Education*, *26*, 1-9.

Joosten, T. (2012). *Social media for educators: Strategies and best practices*. Hoboken, NJ, USA: Jossey-Bass.

Komiak, S. Y. X., & Benbasat, I. (2006). The Effects of Personalization and Familiarity on Trust and Adoption of Recommendation Agents. *MIS Quarterly*, *30*(4), 941-960.

Lenhart, A., Purcell, K., Smith, A., & Zickuhr, K. (2010). *Social media & mobile internet use among teens and young adults.* Washington, DC: Pew Internet & American Life Project.

McCarthy, J. (2013). Learning in Facebook: first year tertiary student reflections from 2008 to 2011. *Australasian Journal of Educational Technology*, *29*(3), 337-356.

Moran, M., Seaman, J. & Tinti-Kane, H. (2012). *Blogs, wikis, podcasts and Facebook: how today's higher education faculty use social media*. (Babson Survey Research Group). Boston, MA: Pearson Learning Solutions.

Ngamassi, L., Ramakrishnan, T., and Rahman, S. (2014). Social Media Technology in Disaster Management: Linking Tools to Relief Phases. *In Proceedings of the 2014 DSI Annual Meeting*, Tampa, FL

Ngamassi, L., Ramakrishnan, T., and Rahman, S. (2015). Use of Social Media in Disaster Management. In Z. Ma (Ed.), *Trends and Research in the Decision Sciences* (pp. 25-32). New York, NY: Pearson/FT Press

Ngamassi, L., Ramakrishnan, T., and Rahman, S. (2016). Use of Social Media for Disaster Management: A Prescriptive Framework, *Journal of Organizational and End User Computing, 28*(3), 122-140.

Park, S.Y., Nam, M.-W. & Cha, S.-B. (2012). University students' behavioral intention to use mobile learning: evaluating the technology acceptance model. *British Journal of Educational Technology*, *43*(4), 592–605.

Ramakrishnan, T., Jones, M. C., & Sidorova, A. (2012). Factors Influencing Business Intelligence (BI) Data Collection Strategies: An Empirical Investigation. *Decision Support Systems*, *52*, 486-496.

Redecker, C., Ala-Mutka, K. & Punie, Y. (2010). Learning 2.0—the impact of social media on learning in Europe. Policy brief. *JRC Scientific and Technical Report*. EUR JRC56958 EN.

Taylor, R., King, F. & Nelson, G. (2012). Student learning through social media. *Journal of Sociological Research*, *3*(2), 29–35.

Tess, Paul A. (2013). The role of social media in higher education classes (real and virtual) – A literature review. *Computers in Human Behavior*, *29*, 60-68

Venkatesh, V., Morris, M., Davis, G., and Davis, F. (2003), User Acceptance of Information Technology: Towards a Unified View. *MIS Quarterly*, *27*(3), 425–478.

Wankel, C. (2010). Cutting-edge social media approaches to business education: teaching with Linkedin, Facebook, Twitter, *Second Life, and Blogs (HC)*. Charlotte, NC: IAP.

DECISION SCIENCES INSTITUTE

Using a Self-Managed Learning Case in an Intermediate Accounting I Course Including Ethics with Value-Added Assessment

Judith A. Sage
Boise State University
lloydsage@aol.com

Lloyd G. Sage
Sage & Sage
lloydsage@aol.com

ABSTRACT

An Intermediate Accounting I self-managed learning case including ethics issues was examined. This case incorporated many of the Pathways Commission's Common Body of Knowledge Learning Objectives (2015) and the AICPA Core Competency Framework elements (1999). The effectiveness of this case was determined with a pre/post test [Quiz #3 (pre-test) and Final Exam (post-test)]. There was a significant difference at p = .01. About 6% of the students considered ethics as an important factor in their investment decisions. On a survey the students strongly agreed/agreed (4.56 mean score) that this case increased their understanding of the financial statement analysis topics.

KEYWORDS: Self-Managed Learning, Intermediate Accounting I, Pathways Commission, Ethics

INTRODUCTION

Revision of the university accounting curriculum has been recommended by various committees over several decades. In 2012 the Pathways Commission indicated that accounting educators have responsibilities that encompass both curricular dimension (what we teach) and pedagogical scope (how we teach). In its most recent report, the Pathways Commission (2015) recommended engaging accountants to define a signature pedagogy for learning the accounting common body of knowledge that will support the learning approaches of a diverse student body. According to Apostolou *et. al.*, (2013), there needs to be accounting research to identify the best ways to teach or to learn core professional competencies (e.g., communication skills). This research paper investigated whether a self-managed learning case is a good method of teaching financial statement analysis topics.

In 2012 the Pathways Commission suggested that approaches or learning experiences should be established to assist students in thinking, performing, and making decisions similar to accounting professionals. Earlier, Albrecht and Sack (2000) stated that there is a need to change the delivery method of accounting education. This research study investigated a learning experience that should encourage students to think and make accounting decisions.

Jackson and Durkee (2008) specified that the instructor's role must change from being the presenter of facts to facilitator of active learning to help students acquire the needed professional skills. Teaching techniques that engage students should be an integral part of accounting education (e.g., role playing, real-world case studies, and group activities) according to Helliar (2013). Schulman (2005, pp. 56-57) indicated that one of the characteristics of signature pedagogy involves learning experiences that ensure students are active and interactive. Bandure and Lyons (2012) recommended that instructors should provide different learning approaches (e.g., lecture, problem-solving, or self-managed learning) because students do not all learn using the same technique. The Pathways Commission (2014) recommended that quality education should involve using various teaching methods that permit students to develop the ability to exercise professional judgment in the decision-making process. A self-managed learning financial statement analysis case project (i.e., involving financial data from two corporations in the same industry) for an Intermediate Accounting I course was utilized in our research study.

The AICPA Core Competency Framework for Entry into the Accounting Profession (Framework) (1999) identified a set of essential competencies (encompassing100 elements) for students preparing to enter the accounting profession. These competencies are comparable to the skills set discussed by educators and practitioners in Albrecht and Sack (2000), Canadian Institute of Chartered Accountants [CICA] (2010), the Institute of Management Accountants (1994), Institute of Internal Auditors (1999), and the Accounting Education Change Commission [AECC] (1990). More recently, the Pathways Commission (2015) developed a "Common Body of Knowledge Learning Objectives" for accounting. The self-managed learning case in our research was designed to permit the students in an Intermediate Accounting I course to experience many of the Pathways Commission's learning objectives and about one-half of the AICPA Framework elements.

The Pathways Commission (2015) recommended in their Common Body of Knowledge Learning Objectives that accounting students should be able to interpret financial and nonfinancial data found in external reports (e.g., ratio analysis or trend analysis) for decision making (e.g., investment or credit decisions). Previously, Albrecht and Sack (2000) suggested that accounting courses might focus less on preparation of financial statements and more on analysis. In addition, these authors recommended that an undergraduate accounting curriculum could include the use of accounting information from different industries (e.g., cases or annual reports). In our self-managed learning case project, each team analyzed and presented information from a different industry for decision-making purposes.

Various professional committees have consistently advocated that accounting education should place more emphasis on writing skills, oral skills, and critical thinking skills. The Pathways Commission (2012) indicated that accounting students must possess both technical knowledge and professional skills such as the ability to communicate effectively. In a follow-up report, the Pathways Commission (2014) suggested that quality accounting education should result in students improving their oral and written communication skills. Our self-managed learning case required the students to write, make oral presentations, and utilize critical thinking in making business decisions.

In addition, the International Federation of Accountants (IFAC) identified the essential skills that are needed by individuals desiring to enter the accounting profession in its International Education Standard 3 (IES3), Professional Skills and General Education (2008). The IFAC in IES3 emphasized that interpersonal and communications are necessary skills for accountants entering the profession. Further, the Institute of Chartered Accountants in Australia (ICAA) and Certified Practicing Accountants of Australia (CPA Australia) in their International Accreditation Guidelines for Accounting Degree Programs (ICAA/CPA Australia, 2009) emphasized that cognitive skills (e.g., writing skills and thinking critically) and behavioral skills (e.g., interpersonal skills) are needed by accounting graduates. The self-managed learning case in our research required the students to write, make oral presentations, work in teams, and utilize critical thinking in making business decisions.

The Pathways Commission (2014) denoted that high-quality education encompasses deep learning beyond memorization. The managing partners of the then "Big 8" CPA firms ("Perspectives . . .") (1989) specified that accounting education should emphasize analytical and conceptual thinking instead of rote memorization. Further, students should actively participate in the learning process and not be just passive recipients of information according to the Accounting Education Change Commission [AECC] (1990). Both the Wilkin and Collier (2009) and the Flood and Wilson (2008) studies recommended that accounting programs should deviate from the traditional practice of communicating large amounts of technical knowledge and, instead, facilitate students' understanding of the principles and concepts involved with accounting/business practices. Our self-managed learning case was designed to motivate the students to do some analytical and conceptual thinking and writing.

The Pathways Commission (2012) stated that to be competent an accountant needs not only technical knowledge but also must possess professional skills such as the capability to use knowledge to make reasoned judgments. Also, the Broad Business Perspective Competencies category of the AICPA Core Competency Framework for Entry into the Accounting Profession [Framework] (1999) included strategic/critical thinking as a necessary component for professional success. In addition, Albrecht and Sack (2000) recommended that accounting education delivery methods be altered to allow students to develop critical skills. Further, the Canadian Institute of Chartered Accountants (CICA) in its CA Skills and Competencies (2010) report recommended that students should learn to examine and interpret information and ideas critically. Classroom delivery methods (e.g., self-managed learning cases) should be developed to achieve these goals.

Under the Pathways Commission's Common Body of Knowledge Learning Objectives (2015), accounting students should comprehend how to locate appropriate accounting information for guidance in determining accounting measurement methods. Albrecht and Sack (2000) emphasized the importance of "teaching students how to find answers and how to learn." The ability to locate, obtain, and organize information is one of the skill sets that the AECC (1990) believed that students should possess. Also, the need for entry-level accounting professionals to be able to organize and evaluate information was suggested in the AICPA Framework [Functional Competencies category under Decision Modeling] (1999). Our self-managed learning case required the students to locate, organize, and evaluate financial and nonfinancial information.

The Pathways Commission (2015) suggested that students should be able to interpret not only financial but also nonfinancial data to evaluate operating efficiency and effectiveness. Earlier, Albrecht and Sack (2000) recommended that an undergraduate accounting curriculum should include, among other topics, analysis of accounting information and use of accounting information in making decisions. Also, accounting graduates should be able to analyze the information gathered and form an opinion on the impact of the information in a situation according to the CICA in its CA Skills and Competencies (2010). Our case required the students to analyze company financial/nonfinancial accounting information as a basis for decision making purposes (e.g., the choice of company in which to invest).

The Pathways Commission (2014) specified that high-quality accounting education should prepare students for a lifetime of learning. Previously, Albrecht and Sack (2000) implied that accounting educators need to help students develop their ability-to-learn skills. Further, Gammie and Kirkham (2008) stated that the ability to "learn to learn" is a key competency needed by accountants to adapt to the rapidly changing business environment. The written self-managed-learning financial statement analysis case project in our research study should give the students an opportunity to develop or expand their ability to "learn to learn."

Students should learn to think, do and act as professionals during their educational process according to the Pathways Commission (2015). Prior to this report, Sin, Reid and Jones (2012) advocated that accounting education should help students to develop transferable skills that will help them to make the transition from their present learning environment to the work environment. These transferable skills include report writing and interpersonal skills. Stone and Lightbody (2012) found that interpersonal skills need to encompass both listening and oral communication. Our research involved a self-managed learning case that required the students to not only prepare a written report and make oral presentations, but also to encourage them to learn to listen.

According to Schulman (2005) signature pedagogy should provide learning experiences that hold students accountable for their work (e.g., to clients, peers and faculty). In addition, the AICPA Framework [Personal Competencies category under Professional Demeanor] (1999) indicated that students should objectively respect other's professional assessment or evaluation. Also, Boud *et al.* (2010) suggested that students should learn to make judgments not only about their own work but also the work of others (i.e., peer review) in order to become successful continual learners and future accounting professionals. Our financial statement analysis case project gave the students an opportunity to evaluate their classmates' presentations (i.e., to perform peer review). As a result, the students received feedback/criticism from their peers.

This study contributes to the accounting literature by presenting and analyzing a case that exposes Intermediate Accounting I students to financial and nonfinancial information found in publicly traded company annual reports and/or SEC 10-K reports. This case involved the analysis of two companies within one industry for each team. The case also permitted the students to develop or refine the Pathways Commission's Common Body of Knowledge Learning Objectives (2015) and the AICPA's core competency strategies and techniques (1999) while analyzing, writing, presenting, and evaluating this case project. This study also contributes to the accounting literature by investigating the effects of our self-managed learning exercise. In addition, student opinions of this self-managed learning technique were obtained and analyzed.

THEORY

Learning-to-Learn

Cognitive researchers (Anderson 1970; Gage and Berliner 1984; Ross 1983; and Glaser 1984) have suggested that learning is an active process, which involves several steps. The first step requires the students to be attentive. Secondly, the students must encode the information into their own words in a meaningful manner. Finally, the students must associate the new information with their previously acquired related knowledge.

Johnstone and Biggs (1998) recommended supplementing existing textbook material with real world activities (e.g., realistic case analysis). Our case supplements the textbook material with financial and nonfinancial information from actual corporate annual financial reports and/or SEC 10-K reports. Also, in preparing this outside-of-class case assignment, the students were required to write the financial statement analysis case reports in their own words. Further, this case permitted the students to incorporate many of the Pathways Commission's learning objectives and the AICPA Framework elements encompassing the analysis and evaluation of financial accounting topics. For example, it was necessary for the students to identify the components that needed to be included in the calculation of financial statement ratios.

Writing-to-Learn

The ability of the students to write is important in an accounting career. Communications is an element of the Personal Competencies category of the AICPA Framework (1999). Accounting professionals who are starting their careers should be able to organize and effectively communicate information so that it can be readily understood by the receiving parties.

As suggested by the Pathways Commission (2015), our self-managed learning case assignment gave the students an opportunity to write on financial statement analysis topics. Specifically, the students had two different types of writing exercises (a team report and an individual report) as part of the case requirements.

In summary, the literature suggests that student self-managed learning exercises can enrich the learning process and that writing projects can be utilized as a learning tool. One technique to evaluate students' learning is to use pre- and post-study measurements. According to Angelo and Cross (1993), the purpose of utilizing pre- and post-assessment techniques is to determine whether students have benefited from class discussions and assignments. The pre-test allows the instructor to establish a benchmark of what the students know on the subject matter being investigated before the study technique (case) is utilized. Gordon (1998) has used the pre- and post-assessment technique to evaluate students' knowledge of social responsibility accounting.

In our study Quiz #3, which was administered after discussing the homework problems on financial statement ratio analysis topics (but before the case was assigned), was designated as the pre-test. The Final Exam, which was given after the students completed the case, was considered to be the post-test.

The following hypothesis was used to test the benefit of the self-managed learning technique encompassed in the case:

> H_1: The distribution of scores on the financial statement analysis questions in Quiz #3 (before the self-managed learning exercise) and in the Final Exam (after the self-managed learning exercise) are the same.

Value-Added Assessment

Ennis (1987) stated that attitudes strongly determine the ability to apply intellectual skills (e.g., written communication skills). Stout and Rebele (1996) indicated the need to examine student attitudes toward a classroom teaching method. If students do not have positive attitudes toward a teaching method, desired learning outcomes (e.g., intellectual skills) may not be achieved.

In their study Stone and Shelley (1997) used questionnaires to measure student perceptions of the instructional processes. Ramsay *et al.* (2000) utilized a questionnaire to determine students' preferences for a cooperative learning method. Sawyer *et al.* (2000) administered a survey after the students received their grade and assessment sheet for a case to determine whether the students felt that the case was useful in meeting specified skills. Chu and Libby (2010) utilized a post-assignment questionnaire to evaluate an active learning assignment.

In our research study, students' opinions of the usefulness of the financial statement analysis case project in achieving selected Pathways Commission (2015) learning objectives and AICPA Framework core competencies were measured using a questionnaire (available upon request). Like Sawyer *et al.* (2000), the questionnaire was administered after the students received their case results.

Ethics

In discussing high-quality education, the Pathways Commission (2014) suggested that students should be instilled with a commitment to ethics and integrity. The November 2015 report by the Pathways Commission considered ethics so important that there is an entire section in their Common Body of Knowledge Learning Objectives related to professional values, ethics, and attitudes. Specifically, this Commission believes that students should be able to recognize ethical issues.

The SEC (as mandated by Section 406 of the Sarbanes-Oxley [SOX] Act of 2002) requires a company to disclose whether it has a Code of Ethics. If a company does not have a Code of Ethics, the SEC requires that company to disclose why a Code of Ethics has not been developed. SOX was enacted in response to the downfall of Enron and WorldCom. The purpose of SOX was to restore the general public's confidence in the governance of US corporations.

There are several social theories of corporate governance. One of these theories is the "stockholder theory." Under the stockholder theory a company is responsible only to its stockholders, that is, the employees' actions are focused on maximizing stockholder wealth within the law. Another social theory is "stakeholder theory." The stakeholder theory suggests that a company is responsible to all individuals, groups, etc. that have a stake in the company; not only to stockholders. Navron (2002) identified several basic characteristics of Codes of Ethics. Some of Navron's characteristics include accountability, honesty, integrity, leadership, and responsibility.

Our research study required the students to locate and obtain the Code of Ethics of a company. After reviewing the Code of Ethics, they were to classify the Code as being representative of either the stockholder theory or the stakeholder theory. The students also were required to analyze the Code of Ethics to determine whether Navron's characteristics are encompassed in the Code. Further, the students' individual written reports were analyzed to determine whether they considered the company's Code of Ethics as a factor in their investment decisions.

AICPA Framework

The AICPA Framework (1999) provided a set of needed competencies (100 elements) for all students who are preparing to enter the accounting profession. As discussed previously, the AICPA Framework competencies are classified as functional, personal, and broad business perspective. Our financial statement analysis case incorporated elements of five of the six criteria of the functional competencies category. The specific criteria that were expected to be accomplished with our case were: decision modeling, measurement, reporting, research, and leverage technology to develop and enhance functional competencies.

The AICPA Framework personal competencies category is subdivided into seven criteria (professional demeanor, problem solving and decision making, interaction, leadership, communication, project management, and leverage technology to develop and enhance personal competencies). Our case was designed to permit the students to experience elements of each of these criteria.

In addition, our case exposed the students to six of the seven criteria of the AICPA Framework broad business perspective competencies category. Specifically, the case involved elements of the following criteria: strategic/critical thinking, industry/sector perspective, resource management, legal/regulatory perspective, marketing/client focus, and leverage technology to develop and enhance a broad business perspective.

Our team financial statement analysis case was expected to result in elements of all three categories of the AICPA Framework competencies being integrated into an Intermediate Accounting I course with a minimum of two to three hours of class time. Of course, the amount of class time spent on the project will vary depending on the size of the class.

Pathways Commission – Common Body of Knowledge

The Pathways Commission's Common Body of Knowledge Task Force began by examining the AICPA Competency Framework along with the work of other accounting task forces (e.g., Chartered Professional Accountants Canada, Chartered Accountants Australia, Institute of Management Accountants, and International Accounting Standards Board Education Initiative) to develop learning goals for accounting education (i.e., undergraduate, graduate, and beyond). To concentrate on undergraduate accounting education, a new task force of the Pathways Commission was formed (Knowledge and Pedagogy Task Force). This task force translated the goals of the Common Body of Knowledge Task Force into measurable undergraduate learning objectives.

The learning objectives were categorized into three competency areas (i.e., accounting, broad management, and professional foundational). The accounting competency was divided into six subsections (i.e., external reporting and analysis; planning, analysis and control; taxation compliance and planning; information systems; assurance and internal control; and professional values, ethics, and attitudes). There are five subsections under the professional foundational competencies (i.e., communication; quantitative methods; analytical thinking and problem solving; human relations; and technology). Finally, there are five subsections under the broad management competencies (i.e., leadership; organizational ethics and social responsibility; process management and improvement; governance, risk, management, and compliance; and additional core management competencies). The desired accounting learning objectives have been placed into appropriate subsections of the Pathways Commission's (2015) Common Body of Knowledge Learning Objectives.

One half of the subsections of the accounting competencies have at least one learning objective that the students were exposed to while doing their self-managed learning case. Specifically, all of the learning objectives of the professional values, ethics and attitudes were integrated into the self-managed learning case. For the professional foundational competencies, all of the subsections had at least one learning objective incorporated in the assigned case. At least one half of the learning objectives were expected to be accomplished with this project case for the communication; analytical thinking and problem solving; and human rights subsections. Of the broad management competencies, all except one of the subsections were expected to have at least one learning objective reflected in the case. More than one-half of the learning objectives for the organization, ethics and social responsibility subsection were assimilated into our self-managed learning case.

As mentioned previously, students' opinions of the usefulness of the financial statement analysis case project in accomplishing selected Pathways Commission's learning objectives (2015) and selected AICPA Framework core competencies were measured using a questionnaire. This questionnaire requested the students to indicate their opinions as to whether competencies/learning objectives were achieved in analyzing, writing, presenting, and evaluating their cases.

RESEARCH METHODS

An Intermediate Accounting I class taught by one of the researchers was used in the research experiment. The university utilized in the research is a state university with 96% minority students, which is located in the southwest. The project involved financial statement analysis for the two most recent years of annual reports and/or SEC 10-K reports for two companies within the same industry (e.g., Home Depot and Lowe's) for each team. Each team analyzed a different industry (e.g., hotels, shoe manufacturing, or airlines). An example of the instructions for this case project is found in Exhibit 1.

Industry and Team Selection

The student teams were allowed to select the industry from pairs of companies provided by the instructor. The students formed their own teams consisting of 3-5 students. The researchers have found that students are more motivated to complete this project if at least one of the firms is a regional firm or at least a nationally recognized firm by the students (e.g., Walgreens and CVS). Other than the selection of the industry by the team, the entire case project was prepared outside of class.

Written Reports and Oral Presentations

As can be seen in Exhibit 1, the students were required to prepare a team written report, which included three parts. First, the team was required to calculate liquidity ratios, solvency ratios, and profitability ratios (see Exhibit 1 for the specific ratios) for the two most recent years. Then, the students were to use the financial statement ratio analysis results as the basis for answering a set of questions (see Exhibit 1). For example, "Which company has the more favorable inventory turnover?" Finally, for the most recent year, the team was required to answer another set of questions related to each company's annual and/or SEC 10-K reports. For example, "What are each company's basic and diluted earnings per share?"

In addition, to assure that each student has writing experience in the preparation of this case, each student was required to write a one-page report. This individual report required the students to give their opinions as to the firm they would select for investment purposes. They were expected to support their conclusions based on the team data developed in the first three parts of the case requirements. For the questions on ethical issues, the researchers analyzed the individual reports to determine whether the ethics factors were discussed by the students in support of their investment decisions.

Also, as observed in Exhibit 1, each team was required to present their analysis in an oral presentation (15 to 20 minutes) to their classmates. For the oral presentation, the students were expected to dress as if they were presenting to clients. The other classmates were expected to act in the role of the client and were encouraged to ask questions of the presenting team.

Evaluations

As the Pathways Commission (2012) recommended, the case was designed to promote deep engagement of the students by holding them accountable to the instructor and fellow students through the use of an evaluation form during their oral presentations. Each student's presentation was evaluated as well as the team as a whole.

The evaluation form indicated that the students will be graded (5-1 Likert scale with 5 being the best) based on (1) the content of their segment or topic presented, (2) the organization of their presentations, (3) the use of visual aids during their presentations, and (4) the effectiveness of the delivery of their presentations. These grading characteristics were defined on the evaluation form. For example, the characteristics for effectiveness of the delivery of the individual student's presentation were listed as: (1) Did the presenter's voice enhance the effectiveness of the presentation? (2) Did the presenter maintain good eye contact? and (3) Did the presenter sound natural and professional?

In addition, the evaluation form defined the characteristics on which the teams were evaluated. The team score was based on (1) the content of the team case presented; (2) the organization of the entire team presentation; (3) the coordination of visual aids used by the team; and (4) the cohesiveness of the team presentation.

The instructor evaluated the team and each individual on the team. Also, the non-presenting class members were required to complete the evaluation form. Each classmate and the instructor had equal evaluation weight in determining the student scores for the presentations.

The students were informed to keep the evaluation forms confidential and that only the instructor would compute the presenter's scores. The evaluation form permitted the evaluators to write comments and suggestions for each presenter and for the overall team presentation. The instructor summarized the comments and attached them to the student's individual written report. As the Pathways Commission (2012) suggested, it was expected that the students will benefit from peer evaluation/observation and comments.

When the written reports were returned, each student also received his or her score for the project. The total score for the case was 70 points (team report, 40; individual report, 15; individual presentation, 10; and team presentation, 5).

Testing

Approximately a week following the discussion of the homework problems on the financial statement analysis topics, Quiz #3 was administered. Quiz #3 was given before the students started their self-managed learning exercise (i.e., financial statement analysis case project). In our study Quiz #3 was designated as the pre-test.

About a week after the students made their presentations and completed their team and individual reports, the Final Exam was administered. The Final Exam had questions related to the financial statement analysis topics that were different than those that were given on Quiz #3 but were similar in the level of complexity. The Final Exam was considered as the post-test in our study. The results of Quiz #3 and the Final Exam were used to measure the effect of this self-managed learning exercise technique.

Student Perceptions – Pathways Learning Objectives – AICPA Framework

This study used a questionnaire to measure student perceptions of this self-managed learning technique as Stone and Shelly (1997) did in their research. The questionnaire was utilized to measure the students' opinions of the usefulness of the financial statement analysis case project in accomplishing selected Pathways Commission (2015) learning objectives and the AICPA Framework (1999) core competencies. In addition, the questionnaire was used to ascertain the opinions of the students on the usefulness of the case in understanding the financial statement analysis topics.

Like the Sawyer *et al.* (2000) study, the questionnaire was given after the students received their case results (i.e., their grade and assessment sheet). The questionnaire requested the students to rank (strongly agree = 5, agree = 4, neutral = 3, disagree = 2, or strongly disagree = 1) whether selected AICPA Framework competencies and Pathways Commission learning objectives were accomplished during their case preparation, team presentation, individual presentation, completion of the peer evaluation form, and reviewing peer evaluations. The specific learning objectives and skills evaluated can be observed in Table 2.

RESULTS

The students were tested twice on the financial statement analysis topics. First, Quiz #3 was administered after discussing the homework problems on these topics, but before the case was assigned. Quiz #3 was considered to be the pre-test. The Final Exam was given after the students completed the case. The Final Exam was designated as the post-test. The student quiz and exam results can be observed in Table 1.

TABLE 1
Financial Statement Analysis Case Project Score Results

	Quiz #3 (before the active learning exercise)	Final Exam (after the active learning exercise)
Mean scores	35.53%	76.32%*
Median scores	50%	87.5%
Range	75% - 0%	100% - 25%

*Significant difference Final Exam > Quiz #3 at p =.01

The majority of the students' scores, which related to the financial statement analysis topics, increased or stayed the same after the case was completed. The median score increased from 50% on Quiz #3 to 87.5% on the Final Exam (see Table 1). Also, the mean score increased from 35.53% on Quiz #3 to 76.32% on the Final Exam.

The students' Quiz #3 and Final Exam scores were matched by names. The Wilcoxon signed rank test was utilized to test H_1 (Q3 ≥ FE). Since there was a significant difference (p = .01), H_1 was rejected. The students' exam scores significantly increased as a result of this self-managed learning exercise (see Table 1). Thus, it appears that this type of self-managed learning exercise can be successfully used as a teaching method for financial statement analysis topics in an Intermediate Accounting I course.

Like Sawyer *et al.* (2000), the researchers administered a questionnaire after the students received their grade and assessment sheet for their case. The questionnaire was used to determine whether the students felt that the assigned case was useful in meeting specified Pathways Commission learning objectives and AICPA Framework skills (i.e., value-added assessment). The student questionnaire results can be seen in Table 2.

TABLE 2
AICPA Core Competencies – Student Experiences During Intermediate Accounting I Case Project

Answer the following questions. Please indicate if you believed the items listed below (1 – 56) were accomplished by your team report, individual report, team presentation, individual presentation, and peer evaluation form using the following code **SA** (strongly agree), **A** (Agree), **N** (Neutral), **D** (Disagree), or **SD** (Strongly Disagree). **Note:** *A 5-1 Likert scale was used with 5 being" strongly agree."*

	Mean	Core Competency Skills
		FUNCTIONAL COMPETENCIES
		Decision Modeling – Elements include:
1	4.50	Organizes and evaluates information and alternatives
2	4.50	Links data, knowledge, and insights together for decision-making purposes
		Measurement – Elements include:
3	4.33	Identifies what needs to be measured
4	4.44	Presents the measurement results objectively using applicable standards of disclosure or reporting
5	4.33	Resolves ambiguities when estimates are required
		Reporting – Elements include:
6	4.33	Prepares reports with objectivity, conciseness and clarity
7	4.22	Describes work performed and conclusions reached in a manner that enhances the reports' usefulness
8	4.61	Employs appropriate media in report preparation and presentation
		Research – Elements include:
9	4.06	Identifies relevant information such as industry trends, internal performance history, benchmarks, and best practices
		Leverage Technology to Develop and Enhance Functional Competencies – Elements include:
10	4.39	Accesses appropriate electronic databases to obtain decision-supporting information
		PERSONAL COMPETENCIES
		Professional Demeanor – Elements include:
11	4.28	Evaluates information in a manner free of distortions, personal bias or conflicts of interest
12	4.44	Respects confidentiality
13	4.50	Commits to quality and efficiency
14	4.39	Objectively considers others' professional criticism or evaluation
15	4.61	Adheres to a level of personal appearance appropriate to the environment
		Problem Solving and Decision Making – Elements include:
16	4.39	Makes valid and reliable evaluations of information
17	3.94	Uses experience and comparison in forming opinions
18	4.39	Evaluates the significance of evidence or facts
19	4.17	Seeks consensus where appropriate

20	4.06	Knows when to follow directions, question plans or seek help
		Interaction – Elements include:
21	4.39	Recognizes the value of working within diverse, cross-functional teams
22	4.33	Interacts and cooperates productively and maturely with others
23	4.33	Facilitates free expression and constructive activities of others
24	4.33	Coaches or mentors in appropriate circumstances
25	4.50	Commits to achievement of common goals when working on a team
26	4.33	Recognizes and accommodates the protocols and expectations of teams
		Leadership – Elements include:
27	4.39	Motivates others to achieve excellence
28	4.33	Rallies the support of others to accomplish objectives
29	4.33	Values inputs and points of view of others and responds appropriately
30	4.22	Facilitates development of consensus or compromise as appropriate
31	4.17	Persuades others to a course of action by reasoning or incentive
32	4.22	Practices principles of effective governance
		Communication – Elements include:
33	4.44	Organizes and effectively displays information so that it is meaningful to the receiving party
34	4.11	Expresses information and concepts with conciseness and clarity when writing and speaking
35	4.28	Receives and originates direct and indirect messages as appropriate when listening, reading, writing and speaking
36	4.22	Uses interpersonal skills to facilitate effective interaction
37	4.17	Places information in appropriate context when listening, reading, writing and speaking
38	4.33	Selects appropriate media for dissemination or accumulation of information.
		Project Management – Elements include:
39	4.39	Determines project goals
40	4.28	Prioritizes and delegates as needed
41	4.44	Effectively manages human resources that are committed to the project
42	4.33	Measures project progress
43	4.44	Takes corrective action as needed
44	4.50	Sees projects through to completion or orderly transition
		Leverage Technology to Develop and Enhance Personal Competencies – Elements include:
45	4.67	Exchanges information using appropriate communication technologies such as e-mail and discussion boards
		BROAD BUSINESS PERSPECTIVE COMPETENCIES
		Strategic/Critical Thinking – Elements include:
46	4.22	Identifies strengths, weaknesses, opportunities, and threats associated with a specific scenario, case, or business activity
47	4.28	Transfers knowledge from one situation to another
		Industry/Sector Perspective – Elements include:
48	4.22	Analyzes and prepares strategic information (e.g., market share, customer satisfaction, competitor actions, product innovation, etc.)
49	4.17	Identifies the economic, broad business, and financial risks of the industry/sector
50	4.39	Communicates the financial and nonfinancial performance of an organization's operational processes
		Resource Management – Elements include:
51	3.89	Identifies the effects of market forces on organizations' costs of capital, labor,

		commodities, etc.
		Legal/Regulatory Perspective – Elements include:
52	4.00	Describes the legal and governmental/regulatory environment in which entities operate and the significant costs and benefits of regulation
53	3.94	Recognizes the dynamic nature of political and environmental forces and their implications for organizations and the ways in which they operate.
		Marketing/Client Focus – Elements Include:
54	4.17	Identifies factors that motivate internal and external customers to enter into relationships or continue doing business with an organization
		Leverage Technology to Develop and Enhance a Broad Business Perspective – Elements include:
55	4.72	Search electronic data sources for business and industry information
56	4.50	Uses technology to develop and present strategic information

As mentioned earlier, the questionnaire can also give an indication of the students' belief that certain components of the Pathways Commission's Common Body of Knowledge (2015) were accomplished while analyzing, writing, presenting, and evaluating this case project. Certain questions on the survey relate to the subsections of the Pathways learning objectives. The mean scores of the student rankings (5 = strongly agree) for the Pathways Commission's learning objectives and the AICPA Framework competencies are shown in Table 2. Generally, the students stated that they "strongly agree" or "agree" that the selected learning objectives/core competencies were accomplished by the case (see Table 2). The students' average mean score was 4.39 and the median score was 4.33. The scores ranged from 4.72 to 3.89.

To examine the students' opinions for the external report and analysis subsection, observe the answers in Table 2 to Questions 1, 2, 4, 9, 16, 18, 46, 48, 49, 50, and 51. This was one of the main reasons for this project with most students indicating a 4.2 or higher and a mean score of 4.29. For the planning, analysis, and control subsection, review Questions 3, 7, 13, 16, 18, and 48. Generally, the students believed this subsection was accomplished with all students ranking the project with a score of 4.2 or higher and a mean score of 4.33.

Another purpose of the project was to introduce the students to ethics and social responsibility. Therefore, the researchers were interested in the results of the questions for the professional value, ethics, and attitudes subsection. The pertinent questions for this subsection are Questions 21, 22, 23, 30, 31, 49, 51, 52. 53, and 54. The students believed this project overall improved their knowledge of this subsection with all questions with a ranking of 4.0 or higher except questions 51 and 53 and a mean score of 4.15. The results might improve for this subsection if there were questions on the project requiring the students to review the MD&A section of the company annual reports.

Also, the students' opinions of the project's exposure to all of the subsections of the Pathways professional foundational competencies can be examined in Table 2. Our project was designed to increase student communication skills, which is not normally part of an Intermediate Accounting I course. Thus, the results of the communication subsection are important. The students' evaluation of this subsection is shown in Questions 33, 34, 36, 37, 38, 50, and 56. The majority of the students' scores were 4.2 or higher with a mean score of 4.3.

One of the advantages of the team project is the opportunity for the students to develop better human relations than is normally incorporated in an Intermediate Accounting I course. To view the students' attitudes towards this experience, see Questions 14, 19, 20, 21, 22, 23, 24, 25, 26, 27, 29, 30, 31, and 36. The students' opinion scores were 4.2 or higher for these questions with a mean score of 4.29.

Our project required some use by the students of technology (e.g., locating and downloading their companies' annual reports or SEC reports). A few Questions (8, 33, 38, 50, and 56) show the students' opinions on the project related to the technology subsection. The students indicated that all of their opinion scores were 4.3 or higher with a mean score of 4.44. For the students' opinions of the quantitative methods subsection, review Questions 16, 18, and 55. All of the students' opinion scores for these questions were 4.4 or higher with a mean score of 4.5.

The final Pathways Commission's Common Body of Knowledge competency is the broad management category. Because the project involved teams, it was hoped that the students will have some leadership opportunities. Under this competency the students' opinions of the project associated with the leadership subsection can be seen in Questions 14, 19, 21, 23, 24, 25, 26, 27, 28, 29, 30, 32, 39, 40, 41, and 42. Most of the students' scores for these questions were 4.3 or higher with a mean score of 4.33. The last subsection relates to governance, risk management, and compliance, which was not emphasized in the project. The students' opinions of the impact of the project on this subsection are shown in Questions 32, 52, and 53. The student opinions on these few questions were relatively low with a mean score of 3.9.

As previously discussed, this financial statement analysis case project should facilitate the students in accomplishing elements of all three of the AICPA Framework's broad skills categories (functional competencies, personal competencies, and broad business perspective). Specifically, the researchers expected about one-half of the AICPA Framework's skills to be achieved by the students (see Table 2).

Of the elements that the researchers expected to be accomplished, the students ranked 94.64% as either "strongly agree" or "agree." As shown in Table 2, the fifteen highest elements had a score of 4.44 or higher. As observed in Table 2, there were only three elements that were ranked below 4.00 (Questions 17, 51, and 53). The lower ranking for Question 53 could be explained because not all companies in their annual or SEC 10-K reports discussed how environmental issues affected the way a company operated or was required to operate under regulations. However, the lowest ranked question score of 3.89 (Question 51) still implies that most of the students ranked these elements as either "strongly agree" or "agree."

The questionnaire also requested the students to rank (strongly agree = 5) whether preparing the financial statement analysis case project greatly assisted them in understanding the financial statement analysis topics. The students strongly agreed/agreed (with a ranking of 4.56) that this case project increased their understanding of these topics.

Also, the individual written reports were analyzed to determine whether the students considered the company's Code of Ethics as a factor in their investment decisions. About 6% of the students mentioned ethical considerations as an important factor in their investment decisions.

SUMMARY AND DISCUSSION

The majority of the students received higher scores on the Final Exam related to the financial statement analysis topics after they completed the case than they did on Quiz #3, which reflected only regular class discussion and homework assignments on these topics (see Table

1). There was a significant difference at p = .01 between the mean scores on Quiz #3 (before the case) and on the Final Exam (after the case).

Many specified Pathways Commission (2015) Common Body of Knowledge Learning Objectives and AICPA Framework Core Competencies (1999) were accomplished when the students prepared, presented, and evaluated their cases. On the questionnaire the students ranked 94.64% of the learning objectives/core competencies that the researchers expected to be accomplished as either "strongly agree" or "agree" (see Table 2). Of the expected objectives/elements, 60% of the top fifteen scores (4.44 or higher) were from the personal competencies category. The average mean score for the students was 4.39 and the median score was 4.33. The scores ranged from 4.72 to 3.89.

This case project gave the students an opportunity to incorporate selected Pathways Commission's learning objectives and to experience types of skills recommended by the AICPA Framework (1999) that may not normally be accomplished in a typical Intermediate Accounting I course (e.g., professional foundational/personal competencies). For the selected learning objectives/elements with a score of 4.00 or higher, the professional foundational/personal competencies category had a percentage of expected objectives/elements of 97.14%.

Further, the students indicated that they "strongly agree" or "agree" (rank of 4.56) that this case project increased their understanding of the financial statement analysis topics. Also, about 6% of the students in their individual written reports cited the company's Code of Ethics as a factor in their investment choices.

Also, in the preparation of this case the students were active participants in the learning process as suggested by Schulman (2005) and the AECC (1990). The use of actual company data in this case permitted the students to analyze and interpret financial information as advocated by Albrecht and Sack (2000). Also, as recommended by both the Pathways Commission (2015) and the AECC (1990), the students were required to locate, obtain, and organize/analyze financial and nonfinancial information.

This project can be accomplished using a minimum of two to three hours of class time. In conclusion, it appears that this self-managed learning exercise (case) can be successfully used as a teaching method for financial statement ratio analysis topics in an Intermediate Accounting I course.

EXHIBIT 1
Financial Statement Analysis Case Project Requirements

Note: You will need to download from the company's website each of the company's annual financial statements (that is, the pair of companies that your team selected from the listing provided). Make sure you obtain a complete set of financial statements including accompanying footnotes, not just summary financial statements.

*I. Compute for each company the following ratios for the <u>two most recent years</u> (e.g., 2013 and 2014): Use the definitions of the ratios given in Chapter 5 – Appendix 5A (p. 201) of your textbook. <u>For each ratio, state the formula and show supporting calculations</u>.

Liquidity	**Activity**	**Profitability**	**Coverage**
Current ratio	Receivables turnover	Profit margin on sales	Debt to total assets
Quick ratio	Inventory turnover	Rate of return on assets	Times interest earned
	Asset turnover	Rate of return on common stock equity	

*II. Answer the following questions based on your financial statement ratio analysis results in Part I above. Briefly state underlying reasoning for each of your answers.

1. Which company is in a more liquid position to pay off its current liabilities?
2. Which company has the more favorable accounts receivable turnover trend?
3. Which company has the more favorable inventory turnover trend?
4. Which company has the more favorable asset turnover trend?
5. Which company has the more favorable return on sales trend?
6. Which company has the more favorable return on assets trend?
7. Which company has the more favorable return on common stockholders' equity trend?
8. Which company is in a better position to issue additional long-term debt (e.g., bonds)?
9. From the point of view bondholders, which company is in a better position to pay its interest expense each year?

*III. Answer the following questions based on the information given in each of your company's annual reports and/or SEC Form 10-Ks for the most recent year (e.g., 2014).

1. Based on the income statement for each company, describe "Gains or Losses from Discontinued Operations," if any.
2. What are each company's basic and diluted earnings per share amounts?
3. What inventory methods for each type of inventory does each company use?
4. What depreciation methods are used for each asset category by each company?
5. Describe any contingent liabilities disclosed for each company.
6. Based on the cash flow statement, what is the amount of cash flows for each company from: Operating activities? Investing activities? Financing activities?
7. What new FASB standards have been adopted by each company as indicated in their most recent annual (e.g., 2012) financial statements?
8. Describe any impairment losses disclosed for each company.
9. Which CPA firm audits each company's financial statements? Describe any unusual situation cited in the CPA firm's audit report.
10. Which company is more favorable toward improving/maintaining the environment? Explain.
11. Which company is more concerned about social or community activities? Explain.
12. The SEC (as mandated by Section 406 of the Sarbanes-Oxley Act of 2002) requires the company to disclose whether it has a Code of Ethics. If the company does not have a Code of Ethics, it must disclose why a Code of Ethics has not been developed.
    a. Do each of the companies have a Code of Ethics? **Hint:** Check the SEC Form 10-K Report for each company.
    b. If the company does not have a Code of Ethics, give the company's reason(s) why a Code of Ethics has not been developed.

c. For each company indicate whether its Code of Ethics has the following characteristics: Accountability, Honesty, Integrity, Leadership, and Responsibility.
d. Which of the following theories best characterizes each company's Code of Ethics?
    1. **Stockholder Theory** – Companies are responsible only to stockholders, that is, employees' actions are focused on maximizing stockholder wealth within the law.
    2. **Stakeholder Theory** – Companies are responsible to all individuals, groups, etc. that have a stake in the company; not only to stockholders.

IV. **Individual Written Report** – An individual written report is to be prepared by each student on each team. Overall, in which company would you prefer to invest? Briefly state your reasoning. Limit your reasoning to no more than one page.

V. For the oral presentation each student on each team must participate in making the presentation.

*One set of answers for each team.

REFERENCES

References available upon request.

DECISION SCIENCES INSTITUTE

Validating Regression Assumptions Through Residual Plots – Can Students Do It?

Handanhal Ravinder
Montclair State University
Email: ravinderh@mail.montclair.edu

Mark Berenson
Montclair State University
Email: berensonm@mail.montclair.edu

Haiyan Su
Montclair State University
Email: suh@mail.montclair.edu

ABSTRACT

In linear regression an important part of the procedure is to check for the validity of the four key assumptions. Introductory courses in business statistics take a graphical approach by displaying residual plots of situations where these assumptions are violated. Yet it is not clear that students at this level can assess residual plots well enough to make judgments about the violation of the assumptions. This paper discusses the details of an experiment in progress that addresses this issue using a two-period crossover design. Preliminary results are presented.

KEYWORDS: Regression, Linearity, Homoscedasticity, Scatterplot, Cross-over design

INTRODUCTION

When assessing the assumptions of linearity, independence of error, normality, and equal spread in simple linear regression modeling, students of introductory business statistics are typically presented with an exploratory, graphical approach to the topic of residual analysis (for example, Donnelly, 2015: Anderson, Sweeney & Williams, 2016; Levine, Szabat, & Stephan, 2016). Except for the assumption of independence of error where the Durbin-Watson technique (1951) is presented, no basic text covers any confirmatory approach to any of the other assumptions.

Berenson (2013) however, raises a basic question – are inexperienced undergraduate business students really capable of critically assessing residual plots? If this is not the case, it would be imperative to introduce confirmatory, inferential approaches to supplement the graphical, exploratory approaches currently found in texts and taught in classrooms.

This study is a first step toward answering this question. It focuses on how well students can validate the assumptions of linearity and homoscedasticity through residual plots. The other regression assumptions will be examined in a follow-up study.

LITERATURE REVIEW

Anscombe (1973), in a seminal paper on the graphical approach to residual analysis, clearly demonstrated the importance of data visualization for enhancing an understanding of what a data set is conveying and for assisting in the model-building process in simple linear regression. The scatterplot, however, has been a particular focus of research, given its popularity in the representation of bivariate data, and much work has been done on how well humans assess correlations from scatterplots (Pollock, 1960; Bobko & Karren, 1979; Lauer & Post, 1989; Meyer, Taieb, & Flascher, 2005; Doherty, Anderson, Angott, & Klopfer 2007). Cleveland, Diaconis, & McGill (1982) studied the impact of display factors (such as size of the plotting character, the overall size of the display, the orientation and the size of the point cloud within the frame) on how well subjects were able to assess the underlying correlations. Lauer & Post (1989) demonstrated that density of scatterplots (number of points in the plot) influences the estimation of correlation. Cook and Weisberg (1994) clearly showed why the selected aspect ratio of a scatterplot is essential to its understanding. Berenson (2013), concerned that a graphical residual analysis of the very important homoscedasticity assumption in a regression model may, in itself be insufficient, suggested that such an exploratory approach to residual analysis be supplemented with a confirmatory approach and recommended White's test (1980) for this purpose.

DEVELOPING THE EXPERIMENT

Three treatment variables were selected for this experiment – *aspect ratio*, *plot density*, and *plot characteristic*.

Aspect Ratio: Per Cook and Weisburg (1994), the aspect ratio of a chart is clearly essential to its understanding so aspect ratio became the primary treatment factor in the study. Two levels were selected, (i) the aesthetic 1.61 golden ratio of height to width (or 0.62 height to width in landscape chart format) and (ii) an aspect ratio of twice that value.

Plot Density: Plot density, i.e., the number of plotted points observed in a chart has an impact on how well subjects assess the information in a scatterplot (Lauer & Post, 1989). Again two levels were selected – 20 points per plot versus 60 points per plot.

Plot Characteristic: Plot characteristic has to do with the particular regression assumption that is complied with or violated. There is also the potential for confounding departures from linearity with departures from homoscedasticity. Four types of plot characteristics were selected – one indicating no violation of linearity or homoscedasticity, one possessing indications of significant departure from linearity without evidence of departure of homoscedasticity, one demonstrating significant increases in variability without evidence of departure from linearity, and, lastly, one displaying evidence of significant departure from both linearity and homoscedasticity.

To achieve the desired objective an experiment was then devised to evaluate the percent of correct student assessments to a series of residual plots generated by using the two levels of aspect ratio, with the two levels of plot density and the four types of residual plots nested within each aspect ratio. A two-period crossover design model was employed (Jones & Kenward, 1989; Sheskin, 2011). For each group it was determined that samples of 168 student subjects would be needed to achieve a power of 0.90 to detect a 5 point percent difference (i.e., the effect size) in correct response to the two aspect ratio treatments when testing at the 0.05 level of significance (Pocock, 1983; Fleiss, 1986; Cohen, 1988; Grissom & Kim, 2012).

IRB approval was obtained for the study. Subjects were students (with majors primarily in business) in various introductory undergraduate statistics courses taught by various instructors. They were offered extra credit in their respective statistics classes for their participation in the experiment. The experiment was spread over two semesters. The fall semester constituted group 1 and the spring semester, group 2. Participants were directed to an online survey where they were shown a series of 18 residual plots, 16 that were part of the study and two that were provided for measuring interval validity. Participants were asked to respond to two questions for each residual plot, one focusing on the presence or absence of linearity in the plot and the other on the presence or absence of homoscedasticity in the plot. A randomized sequence of eight residual plots was developed by combining the two levels of plot density with the four levels of plot characteristics. A separate plot used for internal validity was placed in the fifth position. In the fall semester this sequence of nine residual plots was presented to the group 1 subjects with aspect ratio 1 in period 1 followed by aspect ratio 2 in period 2. There was no break between period 1 and period 2. In the spring semester, the group 2 subjects received the same sequence of plots, except that the order of the aspect ratios was switched. The experimental scheme is shown below where "P" is a "study plot" and "*C*" is a control plot.

Group 1: Fall

Period-1 (Aspect Ratio: L)									Period-2 (Aspect Ratio: H)								
P1	P2	P3	P4	*C1*	P5	P6	P7	P8	P9	P10	P11	P12	*C2*	P13	P14	P15	P16

Group 2: Spring

Period-1 (Aspect Ratio: H)									Period-2 (Aspect Ratio: L)								
P9	P10	P11	P12	*C2*	P13	P14	P15	P16	P1	P2	P3	P4	*C1*	P5	P6	P7	P8

The first of the two internal validity residual plots (C1) displayed clearly obvious violations to both assumptions while the other (C2) clearly displayed no violation to either of the assumptions. Students who did not answer each of these four 'obvious' questions correctly were excluded from the study analysis. Either they did not understand the assessment task correctly or did not take the task seriously enough.

INTENDED PRIMARY AND SUPPLEMENTARY RESEARCH QUESTIONS

- *Primary Research Question 1*: How good are students at identifying the different residual plots correctly? This questions pertains to the main purpose of this paper and will have important implications for the teach of introductory business statistics course as well as for textbooks.
- *Primary Research Question 2*: Does a chart's aspect ratio affect visual perception? This research question is expected to shed light on the importance of aspect ratio selection in student ability to correctly graphically assess the linearity and homoscedasticity assumptions through graphic residual analysis.

Given the results of this inferential analysis several additional research questions will need to be addressed:

- *Supplementary Research Question 1:* How good are subjects at identifying the linearity versus the homoscedasticity assumptions in the residual plots?
- *Supplementary Research Question 2:* Controlling for aspect ratio, how does plot density affect perception ability?

- *Supplementary Research Question 3*: Controlling for plot density, how does aspect ratio affect perception ability?
- *Supplementary Research Question 4:* With respect to the various questions is there evidence that subject graphic perception is superior to random guessing?

THE TWO-PERIOD CROSSOVER DESIGN MODEL

A two-period crossover design model was employed in this study. The main advantage to this design is that it is efficient – it uses lots of information through a crossover and is statistically a more powerful design approach than an alternative parallel group model approach which would treat two independent groups separately. The main disadvantage to the two-period crossover design is that the subjects in each group need to be exposed to a sequence of 18 (16 measurable and 2 internal validity control) residual plots and make two responses on each – unfortunately providing more opportunity for boredom or distraction to confound the results than would be had with the alternative parallel group model approach.

Excluding the internal validity control question responses, each student responds twice to each of the residual plots presented – one response involving the student's perception of the presence or absence of pattern (as opposed to random noise) which concerns violation of the linearity assumption and the other response involving the student's perception of the presence or absence of increasing vertical spread which concerns violation of the homoscedasticity assumption.

This two-period crossover design results in 32 binary responses per student subject, each simply scored as correct (1) or incorrect (0). The total number of correct responses to questions pertaining to one of two particular aspect ratios (i.e., the treatment conditions) will then be transformed to percent correct response and reported as a score on a 0 to 100 scale.

The Two-Period Crossover Design

Table 1 presents the data layout for a two-period crossover design. Note that X_{ghi} represents the response by subject *i* in period *h* from group *g*. Here, *g* = 1 (i.e., fall semester) or 2 (i.e., spring semester); *h* = 1 (i.e., the set of charts with low aspect ratio – i.e., approximately the golden ratio – followed by the set of charts with high aspect ratio) or 2 (i.e., the set of charts with high aspect ratio followed by the set of charts with low aspect ratio); and *i* = 1, 2, ..., *n* in group 1 and 1, 2, ..., *m* in group 2. Moreover, note that $T_{g.i} = X_{g1i} + X_{g2i}$; $D_{g.i} = X_{g1i} - X_{g2i}$; and $C_{g.i} = D_{g.i}$ if period 1 or $C_{g.i} = -D_{g.i}$ if period 2.

Table 1. Data Layout for a Two-Period Crossover Design.

Group 1						Group 2					
Subject	Pd.1	Pd. 2	Total	Diff.	Chng.	Subject	Pd. 1	Pd. 2	Total	Diff.	Chng.
1	X_{111}	X_{121}	$T_{1.1}$	$D_{1.1}$	$C_{1.1}$	1	X_{211}	X_{221}	$T_{2.1}$	$D_{2.1}$	$C_{2.1}$
2	X_{112}	X_{122}	$T_{1.2}$	$D_{1.2}$	$C_{1.2}$	2	X_{212}	X_{222}	$T_{2.2}$	$D_{2.2}$	$C_{2.2}$
:	:	:	:	:	:	:	:	:	:	:	:
n	X_{11n}	X_{12n}	$T_{1.n}$	$D_{1.n}$	$C_{1.n}$	*m*	X_{21m}	X_{22m}	$T_{2.m}$	$D_{2.m}$	$C_{2.m}$

Provided that the assumptions of the classical, parametric tests are met, Chassan (1964), Grizzle (1965), and Hills and Armitage (1979) suggested four test procedures to be considered for a two-period crossover design based on the pooled *t*-test statistic. These test procedures are displayed below. On the other hand, under more general conditions, Koch (1972) proposed a corresponding set of four test procedures based on the Mann-Whitney-Wilcoxon rank statistic. Regardless of whether the parametric or distribution-free set of tests is employed, the fourth test procedure is equivalent to what would be used for assessing direct treatment effects in the alternative parallel group design.

The following symbols are used to represent the various effects to be studied:

- λ represents the residual carryover effects of aspect ratio from one period to another and evaluated in Test 1 of a two-period crossover design. If such residual carryover effects are observed, Test 4 must be used in lieu of Test 3 for investigating direct treatment effects.
- π represents the period effects evaluated in Test 2 of a two-period crossover design. If such period effects are observed it would indicate that boredom or lack of concentration likely occurred in period 2 and would require the use of Test 4 instead of Test 3 for investigating direct treatment effects.
- τ represents the direct treatment effect evaluated in Test 3 of a two-period crossover design. A direct treatment effect is the effect that a treatment (here aspect ratio) has during the period it is administered.
- τ|(λ or π) represents the direct treatment effect evaluated in Test 4. Because of carryover or period effects, the second period assessments from each group are discarded and the two period-1 assessments (made under different aspect ratios) are compared.

Four Classical Test Procedures

Each of the four test procedures is based on the pooled *t*-test. In general, let the pooled *t*-test statistic be represented by

$$t_Y = \frac{\overline{Y}_{1..} - \overline{Y}_{2..}}{\sqrt{S^2_{P_Y}\left(\frac{n+m}{nm}\right)}} \text{ where } S^2_{P_Y} = \frac{\sum_{i=1}^{n}(Y_{1.i} - \overline{Y}_{1..})^2 + \sum_{i=1}^{m}(Y_{2.i} - \overline{Y}_{2..})^2}{(n-1)+(m-1)}.$$

Using a level of significance α, the null hypothesis is rejected if $t_Y < t_{(n+m-2);\alpha/2}$ or if $t_Y > t_{(n+m-2);1-(\alpha/2)}$.

Test 1: Testing for Equality of Residual Carryover Effects

For Test 1 the null hypothesis is $H_0 : \lambda_1 = \lambda_2$ and the test statistic is $t_Y = t_\lambda$. Here $\overline{Y}_{1..} = \overline{T}_{1..}$, the mean of the totals of each subject's response to both treatment A and treatment B in group 1, and $\overline{Y}_{2..} = \overline{T}_{2..}$, the mean of the totals of each subject's response to both treatment B and treatment A in group 2. Moreover, $S^2_{P_Y} = S^2_{P_T}$, the pooled variance for these data.

Test 2: Testing for Equality of Period Effects

Assuming $\lambda_1 = \lambda_2$, for Test 2 the null hypothesis is: $H_0 : \pi_1 = \pi_2$ and the test statistic is $t_Y = t_\pi$. Here $\overline{Y}_{1..} = \overline{C}_{1..}$, the mean of the differences or crossover changes between each group 1 subject's response to treatment A in the first period and treatment B in the second period, and $\overline{Y}_{2..} = \overline{C}_{2..}$, the mean of the differences or crossover changes between each group 2 subject's response to treatment A in the second period and treatment B in the first period. Moreover, $S^2_{P_Y} = S^2_{P_C}$, the pooled variance for these data.

Test 3: Testing for Equality of Direct Treatment Effects

Assuming $\lambda_1 = \lambda_2$, for Test 3 the null hypothesis is: $H_0 : \tau_1 = \tau_2$ and the test statistic is $t_Y = t_\tau$. Here $\overline{Y}_{1..} = \overline{D}_{1..}$, the mean of the differences between each group 1 subject's response to treatment A in the first period and treatment B in the second period, and $\overline{Y}_{2..} = \overline{D}_{2..}$, the mean of the differences between each group 2 subject's response to treatment B in the first period and treatment A in the second period. Moreover, $S^2_{P_Y} = S^2_{P_D}$, the pooled variance for these data. (Note that $\overline{D}_1$ here is identical to $\overline{C}_1$ in Test 2).

Test 4: Testing for Equality of Direct Treatment Effects

If $\lambda_1 \neq \lambda_2$ and significant carryover effects are found (or, if $\pi_1 \neq \pi_2$ and significant period effects are found), for Test 4 the null hypothesis is: $H_0 : \tau_1 = \tau_2$ and the test statistic is $t_Y = t_{\tau|\lambda or \pi}$. Here $\overline{Y}_{1..} = \overline{X}_{1.}$, the mean of each group 1 subject's response only to treatment A in the first period, and $\overline{Y}_{2..} = \overline{X}_{2.}$, the mean of each group 2 subject's response only to treatment B in the first period. Moreover, $S^2_{P_Y} = S^2_P$, the pooled variance for these data. Note that this test procedure, making use of only the first period responses in groups 1 and 2, is equivalent to the test for equality of direct treatment effects in a parallel group design.

If the assumption of normality is not met, the distribution-free analogs of each of these tests (Koch, 1972) will be employed.

PRELIMINARY RESULTS

A total of 262 students initially participated in the fall semester. Based on their responses to the four internal validity questions, 185 group 1 students were retained for the study's primary and supplementary analyses while 78 were excluded. Thus, the fall semester student subject participation rate was 70.2 %. Data collection for the spring semester (group 2) is currently in progress.

Ravinder, Berenson, & Su (2016) reported preliminary findings based on a descriptive analysis of the responses from group 1, the fall semester student subjects. The first primary research question was addressed preliminarily and summarized below. The second primary research question, however, is inferentially-based and requires data from both the fall and spring semester student subject groups.

To identify a residual plot correctly, subjects would have to answer both the question on linearity and the question on homoscedasticity correctly. As displayed in Figure 1, subjects in the fall semester had the fewest errors of classification when there were no violations of either kind – linearity or homoscedasticity.

Figure 1: Plot Characteristics and Correct Identification by Student Subjects in Fall Semester.

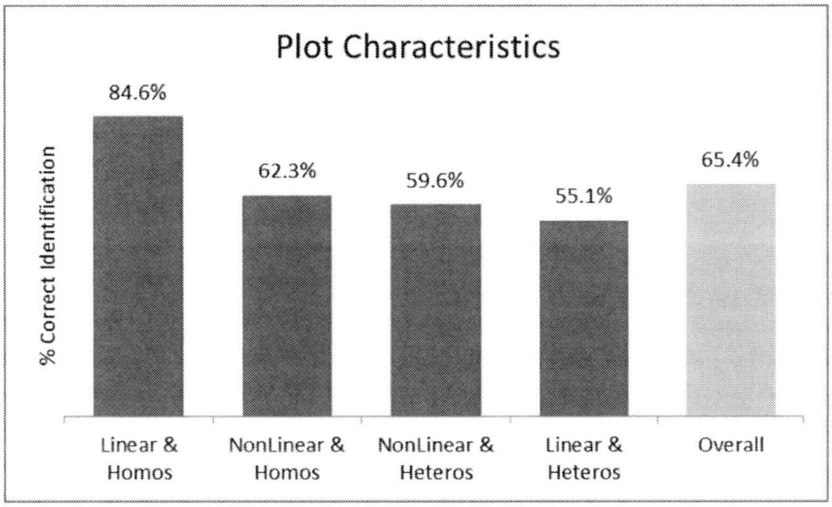

Proper assessments were made 84.6 % of the time. Nevertheless, when there was at least a violation in one of the assumptions, proper identification of the charts were made only between 55.1 % and 62.3 % of the time, calling into question whether textbook and classroom instruction using only graphic residual analysis approaches are sufficient.

Once the data are obtained from group 2 (the spring semester) a similar descriptive analysis will be made individually and then by combining the two groups. The findings here are expected to be an important part of the overall study.

CURRENT STATUS OF RESEARCH

The experiment is in the final stages of obtaining assessments from the spring semester student subjects (group 2). Spring course section enrollments suggest that number of participants should be similar to the fall semester. Having both groups' responses will enable inferential conclusions to be drawn pertaining to the role of aspect ratio as an important factor influencing the ability of students to correctly identify the linearity and homoscedasticity assumptions in residual plots and supplementary analyses will provide important information concerning graphic literacy based on plot density and plot characteristic. Interesting and pedagogically useful results are anticipated.

REFERENCES

Anderson, D.R., Sweeney, D.J., & Williams, T.A. (2016). *Essentials of Modern Business Statistics*, 6th ed. Boston: Cengage Learning.

Anscombe, F. J. (1973). "Graphs in Statistical Analysis," *The American Statistician*, *27*, 17-21.

Berenson, M. (2013). "Using Excel for White's Test – an Important Technique for Evaluating the Equality of Variance Assumption and Model Specification in a Regression Analysis," *Decision Sciences Journal of Innovative Education, 11*(3), 243-262.

Bobko, P., & Karren, R. (1979). The Perception of Pearson Product Moment Correlations from Bivariate Scatterplots. *Personnel Psychology*, *32*, 313-325.

Chassan, J. B. (1964). "On the Analysis of Simple Cross-Overs with Unequal Numbers of Replicates," *Biometrics*, *20*, 206-208.

Cleveland, W.S., Diaconis, P., & McGill, R. (1982). "Variables on Scatterplots Look More Highly Correlated When Scales are Increased," *Science*, *216*, 1138-1141.

Cohen, J. (1988). *Statistical Power Analysis for the Behavioral Sciences.* Hillsdale, NJ: Lawrence Earlbaum Associates.

Cook, R. D., & Weisberg, S. (1994). *An Introduction to Regression Graphics.* NY: Wiley.

Doherty, M.E., Anderson, R.B., Angott, A.M., & Klopfer, D.S. (2007). "The Perception of Scatterplots, "*Perception & Psychophysics*, 69,1261-1272.

Donnelly, R.A. (2015). *Business Statistics*, 2nd ed. Boston: Pearson.

Durbin, J., & Watson, G.S., (1951). "Testing for Serial Correlation in Least Squares Regression (II)," *Biometrika*, *38*, 159-178.

Fleiss, J. L. (1986). *The Design and Analysis of Clinical Experiments.* NY: Wiley.

Grissom, R. J., & Kim, J. J. (2012). *Effect Sizes for Research: Univariate and Multivariate Applications*, 2nd ed. NY: Routledge.

Grizzle, J. E. (1965). "The Two-Period Change-Over Design and Its Use in Clinical Trials," *Biometrics*, *21*, 467-480.

Hills, M., & Armitage, P. (1979). "The Two-Period Cross-Over Clinical Trial," *British Journal of Clinical Pharmacology*, *1*, 7-20.

Jones, B., & Kenward, M.G. (1989). *Design and Analysis of Cross-Over Trials.* London: Chapman & Hall.

Koch, G. G. (1972). "The Use of Nonparametric Methods in the Statistical Analysis of the Two-Period Change-Over Design," *Biometrics*, *28*, 577-584.

Lauer, T.W., & Post G.V. (1989). "Density in Scatterplots and the Estimation of Correlation," *Behaviour & Information Technology*, *8*, 235-244.

Levine, D.M., Szabat, K.A., & Stephan, D.F. (2016). *Business Statistics: A First Course*, 7th ed. Boston: Pearson.

Meyer, J., Taieb, M., & Flascher, I. (2005). "Correlation Estimates as Perceptual Judgments," *Journal of Experimental Psychology, Applied*, *3*,3-20.

Pocock, S. J. (1983). *Clinical Trials: A Practical Approach.* Chichester, England: Wiley.

Pollock, I. (1960). "Identification of Visual Correlational Scatterplots," *Journal of Experimental Psychology*, *59*, 351-360.

Ravinder, H., Berenson, M., & Su, H. (2016). Experimental Assessment of Student Ability to Interpret Regression Diagnostic Plots: Preliminary Results, *Proceedings of the Northeast Decision Sciences Institute 2016 Meeting*, Alexandria, VA.

Sheskin, D. J. (2011). *Handbook of Parametric and Nonparametric Statistical Procedures*, 5th ed. Boca Raton, FL: Chapman & Hall / CRC.

White, H. (1980). "A Heteroscedasticity-Consistent Covariance Matrix Estimator and A Direct Test for Heteroscedasticity," *Econometrica*, *48,* 817-838.

DECISION SCIENCES INSTITUTE

Was Deming Agile? Looking at Information Technology Frameworks and Practices

Dana P. Miller
Miami University
mille704@MiamiOH.edu

Timothy C. Krehbiel
Miami University
krehbitc@MiamiOH.edu

ABSTRACT

This paper attempts to understand the relationship between W. Edwards Deming's quality management philosophy and information technology frameworks and practices, particularly Agile. We contend that the Deming philosophy has contributed to an evolutionary set of information technology frameworks and practices, including IT Service Management (ITSM), Capability Maturity Model Integration (CMMI), Enterprise Architecture (EA), and Agile. We believe that these approaches are often suboptimal due to a lack of understanding the importance of a systems perspective. One approach to a larger systems view is through using Agile within the context of Lean.

KEYWORDS: Quality Management and Systems, Agile, System of Profound Knowledge

INTRODUCTION

Quality management is seen as the evolutionary progression of human organization methods from interchangeable parts, the assembly line, scientific management, and statistical quality control to improve product and service consistency. With increasing intensity since the end of World War II, quality management thought has spread from manufacturing into service sectors such as sales, marketing and customer service and more recently health care, K-12 education, and higher education.

The modern era of quality management associated with manufacturing can be roughly traced from the statistical quality control work of Walter Shewhart at Western Electric in Chicago in the 1920s to the influence of W. Edwards Deming and Joseph Juran on the United States wartime economy in the 1940s and their subsequent influence of the post-war economy of Japan. The rise of quality and manufacturing competitive position in the post-war Japanese economy produced a delayed reaction by US industry in the 1980s to embrace modern quality management. The acceptance of quality management in the United States took on many forms in the 1980s such as Total Quality Management, Six-Sigma and the Malcolm Baldrige National Quality Award. Quality management was further codified in the 90s with the term Lean.

It is perceived the Toyota Production System is possibly the closest an organization has come to implementing and refining Deming's theories (at least in the car production industry). Cynics would say that we tried Deming back in the 80s, we called it Total Quality Management (TQM), and it didn't work. Perhaps Deming's thought is still here but only disguised in Lean and Agile garb and is not recognized as the voice railing against the American style of management in the

80s. Often there is an effort to distance improvement efforts from Deming's ideas since they have been perceived to not work. Perhaps Jack Welch has been viewed to make them work in a small way due to GE's embracement of Six Sigma and the company's share price rise during his tenure? Perhaps the reason Deming's ideas have not worked is that his ideas have never been fully implemented in organizations? Perhaps Deming's ideas did not work is because they are totally revolutionary (but revolutionary without the reign of terror and guillotines and should still have a place in our future)?

To begin our quest for answering the question, "Was Deming Agile?", we searched five databases (Applied Science & Technology Full Text, Business Source Complete, Business Source Complete, and Computers & Applied Science Complete) using the four variants of "Deming" and "Agile" included in a "Title" and "Subject Areas." Fifteen to twenty articles were found when searching on variants of "Agile" and "Total Quality Management." However, direct linkages and in-depth analyses of Deming's work and the Agile movement are not found in the academic literature. Instead, we found an evolution from Deming's work to modern Agile thinking and practices that interweaves through TQM, ITSM, CMMI, EA, the Agile Manifesto, and modern interpretations of Deming's 14 points. Thus the layout for this paper is the progression of thought from Deming's landmark work in the 1980s to the current state of Agile. We conclude with the contention that using Agile and Lean together provides an opportunity to infuse Agile with a systems view currently under-appreciated in the Agile community.

DEMING'S SYSTEM OF PROFOUND KNOWLEDGE

Deming (1982, 1986) challenged current management practices in the 1980s. Table 1 presents his 14 Points for Management that provides the groundwork for his theory of management. (Conklin (2014) provides a contemporary interpretation of Deming's 14 Points). Deming's theory was coined Total Quality Management (TQM) and business, education, military and government organizations jumped on the TQM bandwagon. Deming believed most efforts were superficial and lacked a systems perspective:

> *"Most people imagine the present style of management has always existed, and is a fixture. Actually, it is a modern invention -a prison created by the way in which people interact. This interaction afflicts all aspects of our lives-government, industry, education, healthcare. We have grown up in a climate of competition between people, teams, departments, divisions, students, schools and universities. We have been taught by economists that competition will solve our problems. Actually, competition, we see now, is destructive. It would be better if everybody would work together as a system, with the aim for everybody to win. What we need is cooperation and transformation to a new style of management." (Deming, 1993, p. xi)*

Deming referred to the new style of management as a System of Profound Knowledge (SoPK) which has four parts: (1) Appreciation for a system; (2) knowledge about variation; (3) theory of knowledge; and (4) psychology. To a certain degree, SoPK was a re-packaging of Deming's 14 points.

Those that want to use SoPK to change organizations to be more cooperative and systematic will often feel like the alien Klaatu in the 1951 science fiction film, *The Day the Earth Stood Still* (Blaustein, 1951). Klaatu comes to earth with a message that must be revealed to all the world's leaders simultaneously to warn humans they need to change their competitive and warring ways to avoid total destruction. He is only met with earthly obstacles such as being shot by a soldier upon arrival and that a meeting with the U.S. President in the current political climate is impossible. Klaatu suggests that he be allowed to go among humans to better understand their attitudes and suspicions.

Table 1. Deming's 14 points for management

Deming's 14 Points	Description
1. Constancy of Purpose	Create constancy of purpose toward improvement of product and service, with the aim to become competitive and to stay in business, and to provide jobs.
2. Adopt the New Philosophy	We are in a new economic age. Western management must awaken to the challenge, must learn their responsibilities, and take on leadership for change.
3. Cease Dependence on Mass Inspection	Cease dependence on inspection to achieve quality. Eliminate the need for inspection on a mass basis by building quality into the product in the first place.
4. End the Practice of Awarding Business on the Basis of Price Tag	Instead, minimize total cost. Move toward a single supplier for any one item, on a long-term relationship of loyalty and trust.
5. Improve the System Constantly and Forever	Improve constantly and forever the system of production and service, to improve quality and productivity, and thus constantly decrease costs.
6. Institute Training	Management needs training to learn about the company, all the way from incoming material to customer. A central problem is need for appreciation of variation.
7. Institute Leadership	The aim of supervision should be to help people and machines and gadgets to do a better job. Supervision of management is in need of overhaul, as well as supervision of production workers.
8. Drive Out Fear	Drive out fear, so that everyone may work effectively for the company. No one can put in his best performance unless he feels secure.
9. Break Down Barriers between Departments	People in research, design, sales, and production must work as a team, to foresee problems of production and in use that may be encountered with the product or service.
10. Eliminate Slogans and Exhortations	Eliminate slogans, exhortations, and targets for the work force asking for zero defects and new levels of productivity. Such exhortations only create adversarial relationships, as the bulk of the causes of low quality and low productivity belong to the system and thus lie beyond the power of the work force.
11. Eliminate Numerical Quotas and Management by Objectives (MBO)	The responsibility of supervisors must be changed from sheer numbers to quality, and the job of management is to replace work standards (quotas) by knowledgeable and intelligent leadership. Internal goals set in the management of a company without method, are a burlesque.
12. Remove Barriers that Rob People of Pride of Workmanship	Remove barriers that rob people in management and in engineering of their right to pride of workmanship. This means abolishment of the annual or merit rating and of management by objective.
13. Encourage Education and Self-Improvement	What an organization needs is not just good people; it needs people that are improving with education.
14. Take Action to Accomplish the Transformation	Put everybody in the company to work to accomplish the transformation. The transformation is everybody's job.

POST INDUSTRIAL QUALITY MANAGEMENT AND IT FRAMEWORKS

There appears to be a second era of quality management associated with the post-industrial rise, in the Western world, of the service sector and its associated ubiquity of information technology. Bell (1974) notes that in a post-industrial society more wealth is generated from the services than manufacturing. The post-industrial or post-modern era of quality management can be traced to the early use of mainframe computers in the 1950s in corporations, defense and higher education. The rise of the networked world in the 1990s is a key feature of the post-industrial quality management challenge where there is the capability to link multiple systems that can produce either increased or decreased efficiency with alarming speed.

The quality management concepts of waste reduction and statistical process control seemed more tangible in the manufacturing world and appeared to have little relevance to the highly variable and ephemeral information technology world of computer code and technological expertise. Miller (2014a) argued that a legacy of the military adoption of large mainframe computer systems brought with it a cumbersome, contract driven, requirement traceability laden software development method known as the waterfall model.

Capability Maturity Model Integration (CMMI)

An evolution of the waterfall method was the development of the Capability Maturity Model (CMM) in 1990 by the Software Engineering Institute of Carnegie Mellon University. Jacobs (2006) viewed CMM as the blending of best practices in software development organizations and the philosophy of management gurus like Shewhart, Crosby and Deming. In 2000, the CMM was upgraded to the five-step CMMI, making it applicable to system development as opposed to just software development (Jacobs, 2006). Maturity level 1 is chaos. Maturity levels 2-4 are all about creating the organizational capability to eliminate special-cause variation. Maturity level 5 provides for continuous improvement through the gradual reduction of common cause variation (Anderson, 2012).

Information Technology Infrastructure Library (ITIL) and IT Service Management (ITSM)

The nature of the modern economy had called upon organizations to rely on technical expertise to help make the transition to technology utilization. Very few modern enterprises are not intertwined with IT functions. To combat the high variability of business use of technology a framework called Information Technology Infrastructure Library (ITIL) was developed at the end of the 1980's by the Central Computing and Telecommunications Agency (CCTA), a government agency in Great Britain. The reason for this commissioning was a lack of quality of the IT services procured by the British Government, so that a method had to be found to achieve better quality and simultaneously decrease their costs (Bartlett, 2011).

ITIL originated as a collection of books, each covering a specific practice within the IT industry. Clifford & von Ban (2008), among others, believe ITIL was built around a process model-based view of controlling and managing operations often credited to Deming and his plan-do-check-act (PDCA) cycle. Today, ITIL has developed into a set of practices known as IT Service Management (ITSM) that focuses on aligning IT services with the needs of business. Although ITSM has been adopted as a best practice within some circles of the IT industry worldwide, Meyer (2005) points out several pitfalls including the power of a process manager to dictate how others work, an over-burdening strict protocol to ITSM definitions and processes, and although

ITSM provides a good definition of operational functions it is not a comprehensive definition of everything the organization needs to be successful.

A few anecdotal histories of ITIL/ITSM can be informative to review in consideration of the hermetic nature of technological innovation. Ottenheimer (2012) suggested that the British Military during the 1982 Falklands War had not experienced any major war effort since WWII and their IT had no standards and had difficulty coordinating their efforts. Second, Datamation.com (2004) postulated that the Thatcher Government was looking to outsource IT functions and IBM looked into providing the service and backed away due to lack of standardization and then funds were assigned to the CCTA to develop methods to align IT services with business requirements rather than a focus on technology.

Enterprise Architecture (EA)

There has been tremendous growth in IT infrastructure over the last 50 years and there was no real systematic plan for that growth and the legacy of complexity and confusion persists. This technical legacy is also referred to as technical debt. The emerging discipline of Enterprise Architecture (EA) also provides some hope in trying to use models to explain an organization and it's interactions between strategy, goals, capabilities, process, services and technology. EA can potentially help an organization with strategic decisions by creating a common business language based upon the outcomes of business capabilities.

Often the problem with organizations is that little architecture is done before the organization was created. Miller (2014b) claims that often organizations are never designed, and they are just implemented and evolve into complexity and eventual entropy. Thus, there is a difficulty in IT organizations trying to communicate with the business and concepts such as capability mapping to services (and their associated technology) could potentially help bridge the gap. We contend that Deming's system view can be applied to the practice of EA with the acknowledgement that technology is infused throughout the enterprise.

Agile

The term Agile comes from the Agile Manifesto (see FIGURE 1) which was written at Snowbird Utah in 2001 by a gathering of software developers who were looking at ways to write software better (AgileManifesto.org, 2001). The impetus of the meeting was a reaction to the contract driven requirement delivery of earlier generations of software development often called waterfall. The waterfall model, that limits customer interaction and requirement gathering to the front-end of the software development process, often cumulates in a disappointing unveiling of a new product or service at the back-end. The Agile Way of Working (or Agile) is a collection of principles and practices that supports rapid and flexible response to change.

Agile attempts to bring value to the customer in smaller but more frequent intervals by promoting communication, collaboration, continuous improvement, and reflection within teams of problem solvers. The approach also fosters self-managed teams. Agile accomplishes this by embracing changing requirements, delivering products frequently, using human-centric methods, and engaging the customer in regular collaboration. Agile puts heavy emphasis on articulating goals, facilitating interactions, improving team dynamics, supporting collaboration, and encouraging experimentation and innovation (Smith & Sidky, 2009).

Figure 1: The Agile Manifesto

Manifesto for Agile Software Development

We are uncovering better ways of developing software by doing it and helping others do it.
Through this work we have come to value:

Individuals and interactions over processes and tools
Working software over comprehensive documentation
Customer collaboration over contract negotiation
Responding to change over following a plan

This is, while there is value in the items on
the right, we value the items on the left more.

Kent Beck
Mike Beedle
Arie van Bennekum
Alistair Cockburn
Ward Cunningham
Martin Fowler
James Grenning
Jim Highsmith
Andrew Hunt
Ron Jeffries
Jon Kern
Brian Marick
Robert C. Martin
Steve Mellor
Ken Schwaber
Jeff Sutherland
Dave Thomas

© 20001, the above authors
this declaration may be freely copied in any form,
but only in its entirety through this notice.

Agile is now used widely in software development. However, Dyba & Dingsoyr (2008) and Middleton & Joyce (2010) both noted a lack of hard empirical evidence on the adoption and success of Agile to be extremely weak. A study of nine industry surveys published in 2011 and 2012 on the rates of Agile methods usage found that although the surveys are mostly non-scientific, there are many indicators that Agile is growing and has moved into the mainstream (Stavru, 2014). These indicators include (1) the increasing number of scientific publications and specialized conferences; (2) the significant body of professional literature available; (3) a large number of active professional communities involving Agile; and (4) the increasing number of success stories from large corporations including IBM, Microsoft, SAP, Google, Apple, Cisco Systems, etc. More recently, VerisonOne.com (2014) reported 88% of respondents in a worldwide survey of the software community said their organizations were practicing Agile, and Schur (2015) reported the adoption rate to be 94% and 53% of the adopting organizations indicated that a majority of their Agile projects had been successful. Still, the lack of hard data on both the use and success of Agile is still apparent.

The rising and continued use of Agile corresponds with the dramatic technological changes in our economy. Younger companies and start-ups are in a better position to adopt Agile methods than older organization such as the military, higher education or large corporations which are often siloed in functional areas. A discussion with a colleague who worked many years at Amazon starting in 1997, the year the company became publically traded, said there was no adoption of Agile at the company because they had always been using Agile methods (personal communication, April, 16, 2014). Amazon also views itself as a technology company where there is not a separate department called IT but rather IT is infused in the organization and is there to support the products and services of the company. The likely evolution of IT Departments is that they become commodity brokers of service utilities such as networks email, etc., and more specialized functions will be fused into business units.

Comparing Lean And Agile

Before the software developers met at Snowbird Utah in 2001, Womack, Jones, & Roos (1990) and Liker (2004) analyzed the Toyota Production System and made the term Lean an easy handle to hang on the evolution of industrial processes looking to remove waste and generate value for a customer. In Figure 2 we see that Lean and Agile share many of the same basic ideas and characteristics. Simply put, both Lean and Agile are looking to remove waste from a process that is (supposedly) generating value for a customer.

Figure 2: Lean and agile

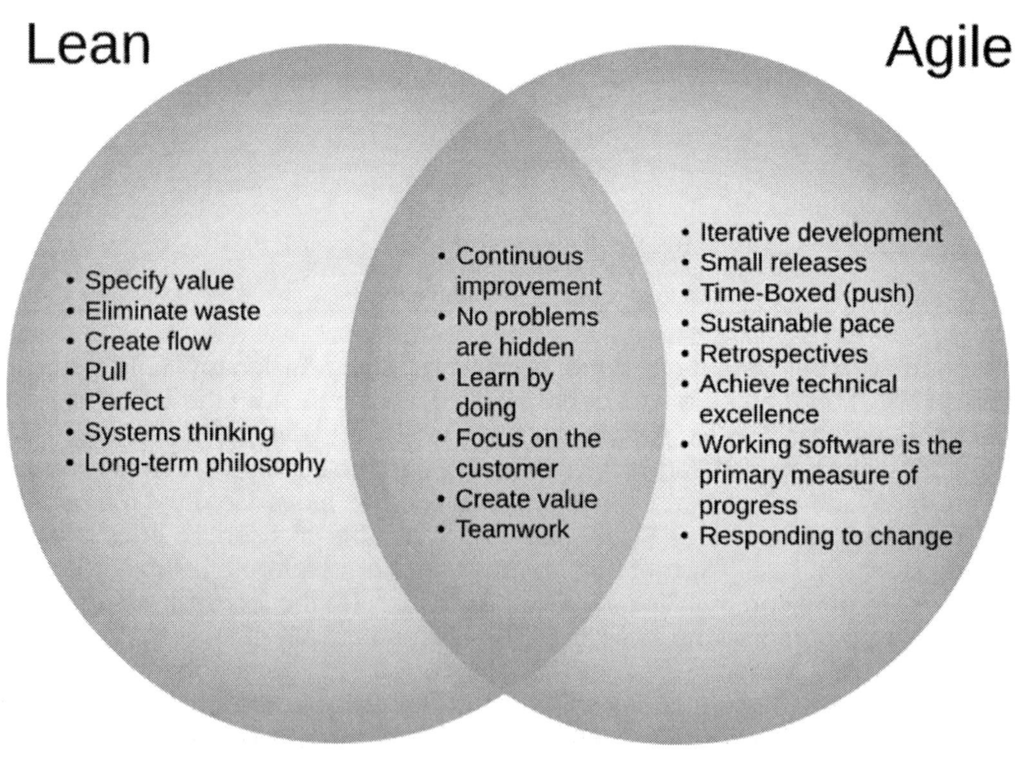

One contrast is Lean requires "pull" and the time-boxed iterations of Agile is basically a "push" system. Second, the systems orientation of Lean, perhaps originating from the early connections between Deming and the Toyota Production System, is not clearly apparent in Agile. Chan (2013) conducted a similar analysis and also concluded that Lean and Agile have much in common but that the principles are not directly aligned. Chan noted the need for Agile to adopt a Lean mindset that focuses on optimizing the entire value stream and not optimizing separate technologies, and refers readers to an article posted by the Lean Enterprise Institute and the following quote:

> *"... lean thinking changes the focus of management from optimizing separate technologies, assets, and vertical departments to optimizing the flow of products and services through entire value streams that flow horizontally across technologies, assets, and departments to customers."* Lean Enterprise Institute (2013)

In other words, Agile suffers from the lack of a systems view of the enterprise.

Anderson (2012) discusses a common conflict software developers have with Lean concepts due to their perception that Lean is associated with process. Developers often view their work as more creative rather than process driven and Agile can be potentially seen as a creative ally but Lean is often viewed as a lumbering process that will stifle creativity. This conflict can be mitigated with a systems view that recognizes innovative effort requires a creative process to design new products and services, and a respect for the innovation also needed to adapt to the long-term philosophy of creating value for the customer.

THE AGILE MANIFESTO AND DEMING'S PHILOSOPHY

As noted earlier, our literature search found no journal articles which explore direct linkages between Agile and the Deming Philosophy. The dearth of publications in refereed outlets, hints at the notion that individuals practicing Agile see little value in the bureaucratic, long process of bringing academic research articles to fruition. However, several books and numerous blogs on Agile do speak directly to Deming's work. Kulak (2011) and Hunter (2012) both hypothesize that while many Agile practitioners have never heard of Deming, a lot of their work is consistent with his philosophy. Smith & Sidkey (2009, p. 244) argue that the concept of ceasing dependence on mass inspection to ensure quality aligns well with Agile thinking and noted that "Building quality into the product sounds clichéd and has been overused by many marketing department. But in an Agile environment, the concept is real and tangible." And, Goodpasture (2015, p.71) writes "Deming focused on eliminating unsatisfactory results before they reached the customer. In Agile parlance, every object must pass its unit, functional, and system test." Yousuf (2009) and Anderson (2012) also noted this alignment with the Agile approach.

In addition to ceasing dependence on mass inspection, Anderson (2012) reported explored relationships between Agile and several other of the 14 Points. Table 2 identifies area of close alignment, particularly in areas of gaining knowledge through education and training, and intrinsically motivating workers by removing fear and barriers to pride of workmanship.
It is illuminating to point out that the mapping exercise in Table 2 is silent to many of the points dealing with leadership and an enterprise-wide systems approach. It is important to note that Deming (1993, p. 91) emphasizes that point #1, constancy of purpose, is all about the aim and purpose of the system, and without it, companies are doomed before they even get started.

Table 2. Mapping Deming's 14 points for management to Agile

Deming's 14 Points	Anderson's Mapping to the Agile Way of Working
1. Constancy of Purpose	Silent
2. Adopt the New Philosophy	Silent
3. Cease Dependence on Mass Inspection	Agile practice of test-first (or test-driven) development.
4. End the Practice of Awarding Business on the Basis of Price Tag	Agile principle of building trust between developers and customers.
5. Improve the System Constantly and Forever	Silent
6. Institute Training	Agile practices such as pair programming encourage on-the-job training.
7. Adopt and Institute Leadership	Silent
8. Drive Out Fear	Agile principle of working at a sustainable pace, along with Agile practices such as using visual management Kanban boards with self-organizing teams help mitigate fear.
9. Break Down Barriers between Departments	Agile practice of organization-spanning roles collaborating with specialist roles.
10. Eliminate Slogans and Exhortations	Silent.
11. Eliminate Numerical Quotas and MBO	Silent.
12. Remove Barriers that Rob People of Pride of Workmanship	Agile practice of short, iterative delivery cycles where everyone on the team gets to see the finished work and demonstrate it to the customer removes barriers to pride in work and help focus everyone on quality.
13. Encourage Education and Self-Improvement	What an organization needs is not just good people; it needs people that are improving with education.
14. Take Action to Accomplish the Transformation	Silent

The implications of this analysis are perhaps best articulated through the four parts of Deming's System of Profound Knowledge (SoPK). Table 3 reflects our conclusion that Agile is strong with respect to Psychology and Theory of Knowledge, moderate with respect to Understanding Variation and weak with respect to Appreciation of a System. Lean thinking could be used to overcome the shortage of a system's view in Agile.

Table 3: System of Profound Knowledge (SoPK) and strength of relationship with Agile

System of Profound Knowledge	Description	Strength of Relationship with Agile
Appreciation for a System	It is important to optimize the *entire* system (a set of activities and processes that work together for the long-term benefit to all stakeholders), not separate components of the system. Optimization of all components separately, rarely leads to optimal system performance. Requires knowledge of Systems Theory.	Weak
Understanding Variation	It is important to understand the variation in a process including the difference between common-cause and special-cause variation. Proper data analysis is required to understand root causes of observed failures and successes. Requires knowledge of Statistics.	Moderate
Theory of Knowledge	It is important to understand that knowledge comes from theory and no number of examples or observations establishes a theory. However, a single observed contradiction to a theory necessitates modification or abandonment of that theory. Requires knowledge of Epistemology.	Strong
Psychology	It is important to understand people and the interactions between people and circumstances, managers and employees, employees and customers. Managers need to learn how to intrinsically motivate their team.	Strong

USING LEAN AND AGILE TOGETHER

Shalloway, Beaver & Trott (2010) and Shalloway (2016) notes that Agile teams often struggle and suggests using Leanban, an approach based on Lean-Thinking that incorporates several agile practices such as Kanban, Scrum, and eXtreme Programming. Further, there is the perception that if a project group (software developers, product designers, etc.) is using an Agile method they don't really need requirements: they can just start building something. But if there are no clear requirements up front, then the output will be unsatisfactory (Hoffmann, 2015; Johnstone, 2015).

One strategy to incorporate a system perspective into the Agile way of working is to use the Lean method to generate basic requirements. Middleton & Joyce (2012) provide examples where Lean and Agile ideas have been fused together, including work done by BBC World-Wide where SPC methods were used to measure Agile software development. Miller (2014b) presented an example where university student change of program forms are still paper and processed differently all over campus. A standardized, electronic workflow process needs to be developed to improve the student change of program processing capability. A Lean method can be used to understand the current state in all areas processing student change of program forms. Once the current state is understood then a future state that serves all areas is developed and forms the basis of requirements for the Agile method to develop the technical solution.

Figure 3 illustrates how Lean and Agile work together. We have used this approach on several projects, and the preliminary assessment of the methodology is positive.

Figure 3: How lean and agile work together

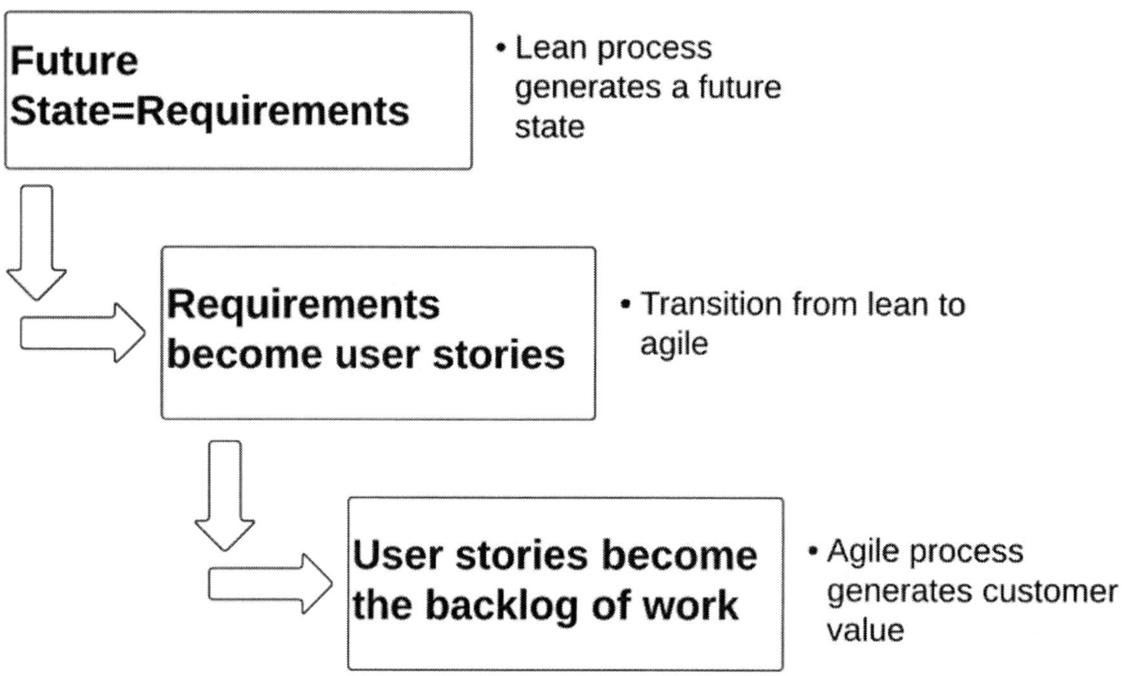

It's The System and Change is Hard

Most improvement efforts that focus only on the use of tools often fail and sputter out. The elusive nature of change and improvement can traced to the culture of the workplace. We can see the thin historical threads of waste removal in the Deming-based quality movement that flows through Lean and Agile, but understanding how these useful tools can be applied to the rapidly changing, technology based, service economy can be challenging. Perhaps there can be progress made if one looks at all the tools and acronyms such as Agile, Lean, CMMI, ITSM, and EA in a holistic manner with a systems perspective. In Figure 4 we illustrate a system's view how Lean and Agile and can become part of a service operation system, from design to the customer. The model illustrates the various components of the system and the intricate interdependence among those components. Optimization of the system requires communication and collaboration. This model can also be used for product development and improvement.

Figure 4: A systems view incorporating Lean and Agile

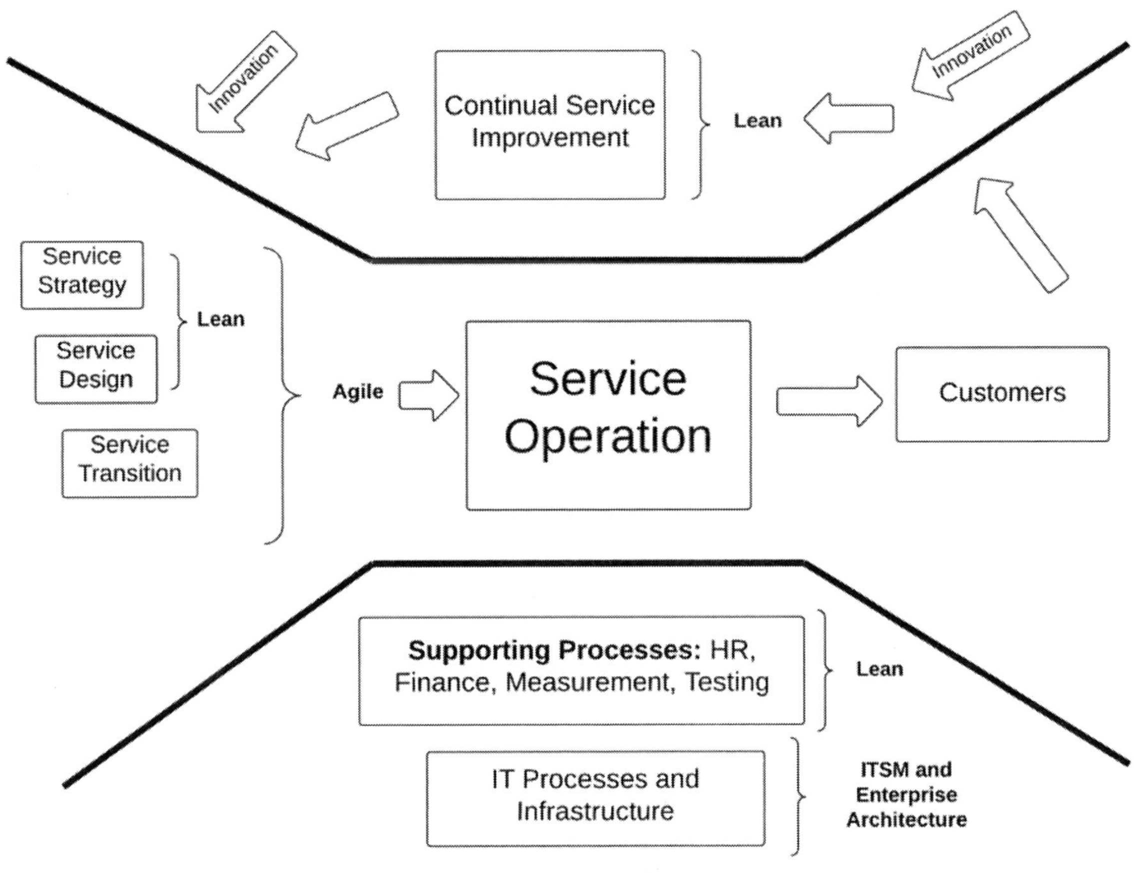

Expertise Silos Generate Fear

Humans progressed into the agrarian era by developing silos to store a surplus of agriculture and we have continued the practice through the industrial and modern technology knowledge age by creating expertise silos. Often there is translation from technical expertise to best practice frameworks expertise but there still tends to be a disconnection between experts and the business areas that provide value to the customer and in the end pay the bills. Much like the siloization of education and higher education in particular, pools of disparate expertise, followed the same pattern into the modern workplace where islands of experts have difficulty understanding one another. The hierarchical nature of organizations attempts to associate expertise with those in power but increasing complexity often does not allow a higher rank to span multiple areas of expertise.

In organizations you have groups of people that view themselves as experts in their areas but in the sum total you don't have an organization aligned with a common aim. You have the production people; IT people; process people; improvement people; Lean people; Agile people; ITSM people; facilities people; marketing people; teaching people, etc. Managing a complex organization without a systems view regarding strategic planning, process, people and technology will lead to overall sub-optimization. Leadership is about creating and managing a system that has an aim, provides value to customers and allows employees to succeed and have pride and joy in work.

Often methods of improvement get attached to the various islands of experts. Agile is only good for software developers. Lean is only good for cutting costs and removing waste in a manufacturing setting or physical service areas such as facilities or food service. ITSM is for the process geeks. We don't need to use Six-Sigma or statistical process control here because we are not making jet engines. Often an improvement effort is started in one silo of an organization and resisted or feared in other parts of the organization meanwhile the whole organization is sub-optimized. The Not-Invented-Here (NIH) phenomenon starts where false pride often drives one part of an enterprise to use a less-than-perfect invention in order to save face by ignoring, boycotting, or otherwise refusing to use or incorporate potentially superior solutions by others. Round and round the misunderstanding goes on in the modern workplace.

Evolving methods and disciplines such as EA and ITSM are being used to attempt to understand organizational complexity and enable improved strategic decisions and also improve IT process stability. Agile has been adopted by organizations to build usable software. Lean and Six Sigma are looked at as tools to improve business process that rely on IT. These tools and methods are used by both product and service organizations often in small, sporadic attempts usually with much implementation confusion as there is generally difficulty by leadership in providing a unified view of the change effort and limiting the long-term value production of the effort. Workers in organizations attempting to change for the better often view the methods of Lean, Six Sigma, Agile, ITSM and EA as separate, transient, non-aligned or even contradictory methods.

The anxiety that runs beneath change efforts is revealed in a conversation with an IT manager who responded negatively to a Lean effort to reduce or avoid costs in their organization. The manager had fear the same amount of budget would not be provided the next year if the Lean efforts were acted upon to identify waste and reduce or avoid costs (personal communication, February, 24, 2015). This view potentially contains a lack of systems perspective, a misunderstanding of Lean or having a biased understanding such as Lean is only for manufacturing and Agile is only for software and the two don't work together?

Another source of organization improvement misalignment is the constant need to label and package ideas that can potentially create change and provide value. Perhaps this need is also driven by the voracious need of easy fixes, marketing, ranking and rating in society? Deming was never a great packager of things. The closest he came was developing the SoPK, which on first appearance, is basically a re-packaging of his 14 points. Understanding and implementing the SoPK requires quite a bit of upfront study and then one needs the environment, courage, capability and long-term view to follow through on the ideas.

To survive into the future, the reliance on experts needs to shift to incorporate holistic systems thinking and experimentation that can contribute to a view of how the organization can provide continually improving products and services. In the fear generating, hierarchical, expert-based, technological worldview the systems thinkers have often found themselves in positions of what Backaitis (2014) calls "courageous despair." They see the larger picture and keep trying to change things but are always going upstream to the prevalent competitive, command and control management systems which tends to view workers as the shifty, X-Types or worse yet turns Y-Types into X-Types!

The Path Forward: An Outside Systems View

To continue with the thread of Deming's thought expressed in the SoPK and the relationship to IT frameworks and practices we can also look through the lens of adult stage of development to develop an outside view (Backaitis, 2014). Individuals acquire a succession of empirically derived world-views through their lifetimes as evidenced by the expert phenomena. Horizontal development contributes to the expert view and vertical development contributes to the outside view that Deming called for that allows the system to understand itself. How does one gain vertical development? Possibly by learning from experiments that translate to experience and contributes to wide learning?

By having more vertical development and understanding the system, people can operate in a way that everyone (management, workers, customers, and suppliers) benefits. The current cultural personality ideal is along the lines of achiever and expert realms and is generally resistant to the outside view. Understanding the system is difficult – typically everyone views the system from his or her own perspective. Understanding the system requires that everyone rise above their individual view to understand the system in the context of the overall goal, what the organization does to achieve this goal, the boundaries and constraints, and to share the sensing and feedback mechanisms.

With an increasing world of volatility, uncertainty, complexity, ambiguity and pervasiveness of connective technologies the need for an outside systems view is needed more than ever. It appears the current culture is not producing the individuals and eventual leaders needed for a change? These larger cultural issues, which need to be addressed, are beyond the scope of this paper but could be the start of a discussion?

The current trend appears to be using Lean, Agile and the other IT frameworks and methods discussed in this paper in a scattered approach to foster process improvement, faster quality software delivery, and organizational understanding. But perhaps these methods can be viewed also as methods to implement SoPK in a small way? Deming, if he were around, would be open to new interpretations of his ideas.

CONCLUSION

Deming was Agile. But being Agile does not mean an individual or organization fully embodies the Deming Philosophy. One of the four principles of Deming's System of Profound Knowledge is Systems Theory, which the Agile movement and current Agile practices have not fully embraced. We believe this lack of systems thinking is often the root cause for the mixed results with Agile initiatives, and that the use of Agile practices within a Lean initiative with a strong systems approach is a valid attempt to overcome that shortcoming.

EPILOGUE

The cultural challenges facing organizations involved in making process improvement progress, providing a systems understanding, reducing fear, and providing employees with pride and joy in work can be seen in the conversation with a friend and former coworker who is a locksmith and has been working in an organization that is 6 years into a Lean implementation (personal communication, December, 27, 2016).

Author: How are things going at work?

Locksmith: Same old sh--t but with new bosses. What was that mind control bulls--t they played on us...5S or something like that?

Author: You mean, "Lean".

Locksmith: Yeah, "Lean". (Shaking his head left-to-right). Yeah, I was on a Lean Project. I worked for a year on a project to figure out how much to charge for a key. We were charging 8 bucks a key and I did all this analysis work and figured we should be charging 14 bucks a key. Then the boss said we should just charge 16 bucks. What a load of crap. I did all this work and he just came in and said charge 16 bucks!

REFERENCES

AgileManifesto.org. (2001), Manifesto for agile software development. Retrieved from http://agilemanifesto.org, March 14, 2016.

Anderson, D. J. (2012). *Lessons in agile management*. Sequim, WA: Blue Hole Press.

Backaitis, N. (2014). The transformation Deming called for: A view through the lens of adult stage development. *Deming Annual Conference*. West Lafayette, IN: The Deming Institute.

Bartlett. R. (2011). Improve Service Delivery with ITIL. *System iNEWS, 386*, December, 13-17.

Bell, D. (1974). *The coming of post-industrial society*. New York: Harper Colophon Books.

Blaustein, J. (Producer), & Wise, R. (Director). (1951). *The day the earth stood still* (Motion Picture). United States: 20th Century Fox.

Chan, K. (2013). Lean vs. agile. Retrieved from http://www.onedesk.com/2013/07/lean-vs-agile/, March 20, 2016.

Clifford, D., & van Bon, J. (2008). *Implementing ISO/IEC 20000 certification: The roadmap. ITSM library*. Amsterdam, The Netherlands: Van Haren Publishing.

Conklin, J. D. (2014). Whole new world: Seasoned quality professionals rethink Deming's 14 points for a new generation. *Quality Progress, 78*(12), December, 52-57.

Datamation.com. (2004). History of ITSM and ITIL. Retrieved from http://forums.datamation.com/showthread.php?32-History-of-ITSM-and-ITIL, March 20, 2016.

Deming, W. E. (1982). *Out of the crisis*. Cambridge, MA: Massachusetts Institute of Technology, Center for Advanced Engineering Study.

Deming, W. E. (1985). Transformation of Western style of management. *Interfaces, 15*(3), May-June, 6-11.

Deming, W. E. (1993). *The new economics: For industry, government, education*. Cambridge, MA: Massachusetts Institute of Technology, Center for Advanced Engineering Study.

Dyba, T., & Dingsoyr (2008). Empirical studies of agile software development: a systematic review. *Information and Software Technology, 50*, 833-859.

Goodpasture, J. C. (2015). *Project management the agile way*. 2nd edition. Plantation, FL: J. Ross Publishing.

Hoffmann, L. (2015). Object lessons. *Communications of the ACM, 58*(3), March, 95-96.

Hunter, J. (2012). How does the Deming management system fit with other management strategies: Interview by Bill Fox, part 2 of 3. Retrieved from http://johnhunter.com/interviews/deming-management-system-fit.htm, March 19, 2016.

Jacobs, D. (2006). *Accelerating Process Improvement Using Agile Techniques*. New York, NY: Auerbach Publications.

Johnstone, J. (2015). Agile quality: Software-development principles create more product value. *Quality Progress, 48*(7), July, 63.

Kulak, D. (2011). What agile software development learned from Deming. Retrieved from http://www.processexcellencenetwork.com/pex-tools-technologies/columns/agile-software-development-learns-from-dr-deming, March 19, 2016.

Lean Enterprise Institute (2013). What is Lean? Retrieved from www.lean.org/whatslean/, March 19, 2016.

Liker, J. K. (2004). *The Toyota way*. New York, NY: McGraw-Hill.

Meyer, D. (2005). Beneath the buzz: ITIL. Retrieved from http://web.archive.org/web/20050404165524/http://www.cio.com/leadership/buzz/column.html?ID=4186, March 19, 2016.

Middleton, P., & Joyce, D. (2012). Lean software management: BBC worldwide case study. *IEEE Transactions on Engineering Management, 59*(1), 20-32.

Miller, D. P. (2014a). Implementing Deming's theories in between process improvement efforts at public universities. *20th Annual International Deming Research Seminar*. New York, NY: The Deming Institute.

Miller, D. P. (2014b). Transforming administrative services through a lean philosophy. *Educause Administrative IT Summit*. Chicago, IL: Educause.

Ottenheimer, D. (2012). This day in history: Falklands war and ITIL. Retrieved from http://www.flyingpenguin.com/?p=17113, March 20, 2016.

Schur, M. (2015). The State of Agile. *PM Network, 29*(9), September, 16-17.

Shalloway, A. (2016). Introducing leanban: The 3rd generation of lean-agile for the team. Retrieved from www.netobjectives.com/blogs/introducing-leanban-3rd-generation-lean-agile-team, March 20, 2016.

Shalloway, A., Beaver, G., & Trott, J. (2010). *Lean-Agile software development: Achieving enterprise agility*. Boston, MA: Pearson Education.

Smith, S., & Sidky, H. (2009). *Becoming agile…in an imperfect world*. Greenwich, CT: Manning Publications Co.

Stavru, S. (2014). Critical examination of recent industrial surveys on agile. *The Journal of Systems and Software, 94*, 87-97.

VerizonOne.com. (2014), 8th Annual State of Agile Survey. Retrieved from http://www.versionone.com/pdf/2013-state-of-agile-survey.pdf, 27, 2015.

Webb, N. J., & Thoen, C. (2010). *The innovation playbook: A revolution in business excellence.* New York, NY: John Wiley and Sons.

Womack, J. P., Jones, D. T., & Roos, D. (1990). *The machine that changed the world*. New York: Rawson Associates.

Yousuf, A. (2009). Agile lessons from a management guru. Retrieved from http://www.infoq.com/articles/deming-and-agile, March 19, 2016.

Decision Sciences Institute

WeChat Shopping: A Study of Cosmetic Product Selling to College Students in China

Yun Zheng
Xinyang Normal University
Email: zhy7208@163.com

Jianfeng Wang
Millersville University of Pennsylvania
Email: jwang@millersville.edu

David DiRusso
Millersville University of Pennsylvania
Email: david.dirusso@millersville.edu

Jianbing Gao
Jinggangshan University
shgaojianbin@126.com

ABSTRACT

This study examines a new form of e-commerce transactions, dubbed W-shopping (WeChat shopping), which occurs through the prolific and growing WeChat social networking application. The research reports the W-shopping experience based on a sample of college students in China. Furthermore, it applies an established model of trust, satisfaction and loyalty to this new form of commerce and is tested using cosmetic product in the WeChat channel. Implications for both theory and practice are discussed.

KEYWORDS: E-commerce; WeChat; Social Media Marketing; Trust; Product Quality; Customer Satisfaction; China

INTRODUCTION

WeChat is a mobile text and voice messaging communication service developed by Tencent in China. It was first released in January 2011 and has exploded in popularity (Wang, 2014). As of January 2015, WeChat has 1.1 billion accounts ("Technode.com) with over 538 million active users ("Tencent.com"), 100 million of which reside outside of China ("Thenextweb.com").

WeChat was primarily a social networking/messaging application, but the company since ventured into e-commerce by integrating buying and selling functionality into it. WeChat-shopping (referred to as "W-shopping" in this paper) is growing rapidly in China. According to a report of W-shopping by World Network ("Weishangshijie.com"), more than 300 million people purchased products via WeChat in 2014. The value of transactions in 2014 was $24.2 billion, which was an increase of 35% compared to 2013.

Whereas "traditional" internet based shopping revolves around e-commerce websites, W-shopping centers around the social network established by WeChat. The products are shared and promoted in a group of people through recommendations by friends. These product messages are then shared amongst friends and the messages themselves spread quickly in a similar fashion as viral marketing messages, although it is all contained within the WeChat app.

This allows WeChat sellers to leverage their circle of friends to help promote and recommend the offer to others, and minimally, the seller can be assured that their message will be seen at least by their circle of friends, but the message often spreads to others.

W-shopping is clearly an important e-commerce trend, as indicated by the 300 million users who have made purchases through WeChat. However, despite the fact that W-shopping is well recognized by practitioners in the field, there have been no academic studies that have investigated this new transaction process. Several key questions are currently unanswered: Does W-shopping share the common shopping process with traditional commerce or e-commerce? Are there any differences between W-shopping and traditional commerce or e-commerce process?

Prior research reveals that product quality, trust and satisfaction are important elements in the buying process. Trust and satisfaction have been established by many scholars as important roles in successful commerce as customers usually do not make purchases from any suspicious sellers (Jarvenpaa et. al., 1999; Urban, 2000), or they won't come back for repeat purchase if they are not satisfied. There is a great deal of literature which addresses the importance of trust and satisfaction in internet shopping (Grabosky 2001; Doney and Cannon 1997), but there is no research exploring the role of trust and satisfaction in W-shopping environment.

Based on our knowledge, this is a very first empirical research addressing the fast growing W-shopping market. We report customers' shopping experience/concerns through WeChat, and intend to uncover the roles of product quality and satisfaction in trust and purchase judgments in W-shopping environment.

LITERATURE REVIEW AND THEORETICAL DEVELOPMENT/MOD

W-shopping is a very efficient shopping channel, and is even faster than traditional e-commerce. It centers around the social network established by WeChat. The products are shared and promoted in a group of people through recommendation by friends. With the forwarding of the message in friend circles, more and more people will be informed of the product within short timeframe. Also, the promotion message through WeChat is certain to be delivered to every contact in friend circles.

In 1965, Buchanan developed club theory through the study of club goods in economics. He argues that there is an "awesome Samuelson gap between the purely private and purely public good". This gap contains goods that are excludable but are shared by more people than typically share a private good by fewer people than typically share a public good. Club is the congregation of people with similar preferences aiming to gain the benefits of scale consumption. Examples of club goods are vehicle, swimming pool, and gold court, etc. In a famous "simulation model", Schelling (1971) shows that a small preference for one's neighbors to be of the same color could lead to total segregation. His theory develops the base for analyzing "people gather in groups" in socio-psychological and political-psychological fields.

In WeChat, there are numerous of clubs based on ties of "alumni", "same origin", "social status", "housewives", etc. The structure is a typical "friend circle". There are at least three people in one club (WeChat group) who know two or more members in another club (WeChat group). Extended in this way, a bigger circle will be formed by the connections of few active members in one club to some active members in other clubs. Circulating in this way, more and more people can be reached. The core function of WeChat is the forwarding of messages. By forwarding a message, one member in a WeChat releases her/his signal of personal characters such as preferences, hobbies, even social status, etc., to all other member receiving messages in the club.

In the internet world, which is overflowing with information, the most scare resource is "attentiveness". The forwarding behavior of WeChat users is an information agent of their character. Through WeChat, the resource of attentiveness is distributed in numerous WeChat groups. Several WeChat users are moving among numerous WeChat groups which consist of members with different characters and preferences. This phenomenon tends to form many stable network clubs which are different in terms of characters and preferences. Hence, the promotion of "right" products is the key for the success of W-shopping. For example, promoting of various sports summer camps in a "children's parents" group may gain more attentions because the products promoted is consistent with the interests or topics of that particular group in WeChat. When the promotion message is not complementary to the main interests of most members in the group, it will be banned, or the message publisher's image or reputation will be damaged. Therefore, it is appropriate to target a specific group of people for particular products such as "low value" and "high quality" items. It is effective for special style differentiation and personalization marketing.

In 2000, Singh and Sirdeshmukh propose a model exploring the roles of trust and agency mechanisms in consumer satisfaction and loyalty judgments, which is shown below in Figure 1. They argue that trust interacts with agency mechanisms in prepurchase stage of transaction, which in turn affects satisfaction and influences loyalty in the postpurchase stage. They declare their model is built on a contingency model of the impact of prepurchase expectations and postpurchase perceptions on satisfaction proposed by Voss et al. (1998), in which quality is included as one component of prepurchase assessment.

Figure 1 Singh and Sirdeshmukh Model of the roles of trust and agency mechanisms in consumer satisfaction and loyalty judgments

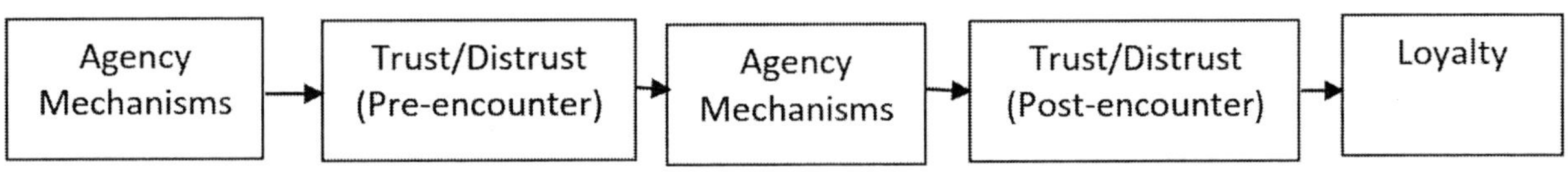

W-shopping is in the early stage of development, and while there is a system to ensure easy payment, there currently exist very few buyer protections such as those found on established e-commerce websites such as Amazon and Taobao. In such an environment, some opportunistic sellers may take the advantage of friend circles in WeChat to sell inferior products as they do not have to fear any institutional safeguards. We believe that product quality is an important element of prepurchase assessment. Thus, we propose a simplified model in W-shopping in Figure 2 built upon the frameworks of Singh and Sirdeshmukh (2000) and Voss et al. (1998). It is argued that perceived product quality influences customer trust, which in turn affects satisfaction leading to consumer purchase in WeChat.

Figure 2 An adaptation of Singh and Sirdeshmukh's model in W-shopping environment

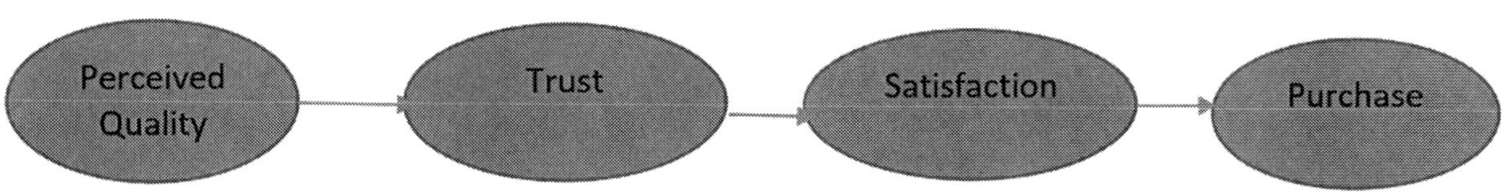

HYPOTHESES DEVELOPMENT

A research framework exploring the role of trust and satisfaction in W-shopping is proposed in Figure 2. Sellers on WeChat should form an environment in which customers feel confident about going through with a transaction. Three elements in the transaction process are perceived product quality, trust and satisfaction.

In an online market environment, buyers cannot meet the seller face to face, so buyers cannot scrutinize the product before making a purchase, and must make payment before receiving the merchandise. Based on social exchange theory (Blau, 1964), trust will not be established until a consumer's expectation is met. High quality product perception or other quality cues such as big brand or quality certification help buyers increase the trust to the seller. Prior studies (Harris and Goode, 2004; Kim, et al., 2004) support the effect of product or service quality on trust. Thus, we propose:

Hypothesis 1: Perceived product quality relates to consumer trust in W-shopping environment.

Trust plays a vital role because consumers may take risks of not knowing the ability and integrity of the seller. Trust also affects the long-term relationship between the buyer and seller through satisfaction. Singh and Sirdeshmukh (2000) argue trust leads to satisfaction, which in turn leads to loyalty. Their model is supported by Chaudhuri and Holbrook's (2001) study on brand loyalty. In W-shopping, the confidence on seller's capability of delivering quality product or service relates to post-purchase satisfaction. Additionally, it has been found that trust can bring buyers with high level of satisfaction on the transaction (Hawes et al., 1989). Thus, we hypothesize:

Hypothesis 2: Consumer trust relates to satisfaction in W-shopping environment.

Using the American Customer Satisfaction Index, Fornell et al.'s (1996) study supports the positive relationship between consumer loyalty and satisfaction. Cristobal et al. (2007) also reveals that customer satisfaction lead to loyalty in e-commerce. Thus, we propose:

Hypothesis 3: Consumer satisfaction relates to purchase in W-shopping environment.

RESEARCH METHODOLOGY AND STATISTICAL ANALYSIS

We employed a "Snowball" sampling procedure. A questionnaire was designed based on several interviews with WeChat marketers. 195 college students were selected as respondents. Data was collected through the distribution of the questionnaire to the members of some college student groups via WeChat. 191 students who live in 12 provinces responded. The results were statistically analyzed by using SPSS software.

We first report the descriptive statistics of consumers' shopping experience on WeChat, followed by the hypotheses testing of the research model.

4.1 Which social networking website college students often use?

Figure 3

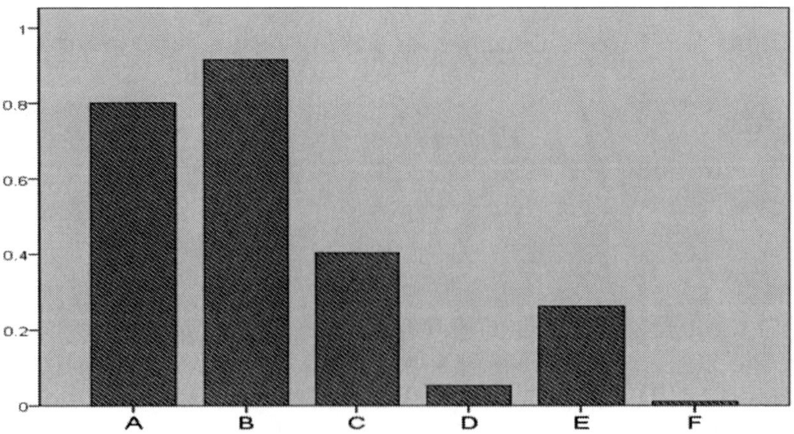

A. WeChat B.QQ C. Micro-Web D. Renren E. PostBlog F. Other

As shown in Figure 3, 91.62% of the students in China, 175 people, use QQ as platform for social networking. WeChat is the second most widely used platform, where 80.1%, or 153 people use it quite frequently. Followed by Micro-web: 40.31% or 77 students use it. 26.18% people use PostBlog. Renren is used by 5.245% students. Only 0.52% or one student chooses "other".

4.2 What are some products college students ever purchased on WeChat?

Figure 4 shows that 76.96% or 145 people ever purchased cosmetics on WeChat while 69.11% bought clothing, followed by 48.17% bought food, and 33.51% for accessories. 12.04% or 23 people purchased other products on WeChat.

Figure 4

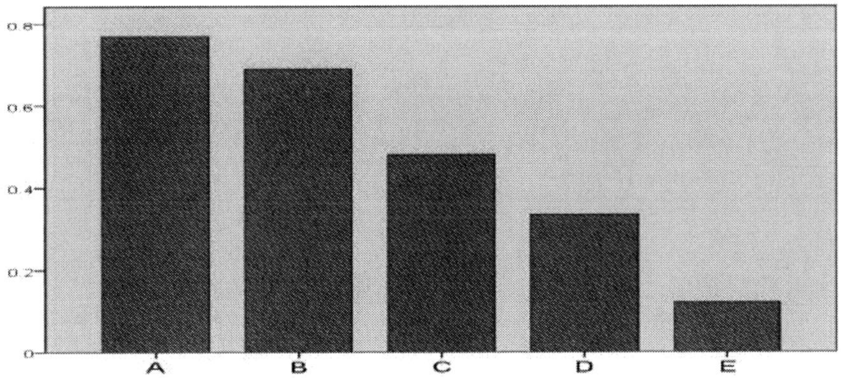

A. Cosmetics B.Clothing C.Food D. Accessories E.Other

4.3 Have you ever purchased above items on WeChat?

Figure 5

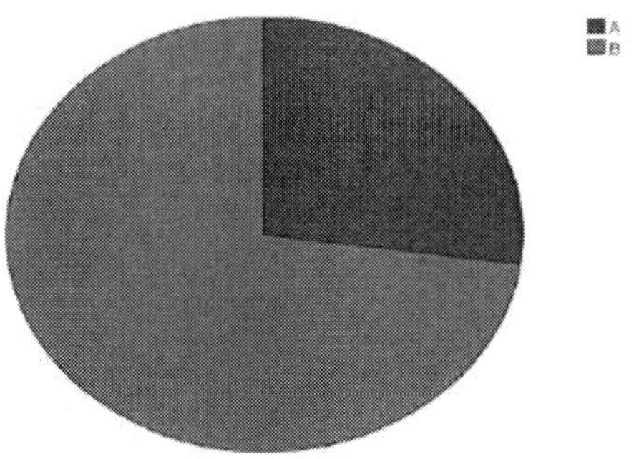

A. Yes B. No

Figure 5 shows 27.2% or 52 people ever purchased above items (cosmetics, clothing, food, or accessories) on WeChat while more than 70% people did not.

4.4 Are you satisfied with the products purchased from WeChat?

The results indicate that among 52 people who have ever purchased products on WeChat, 5.77% or 3 people are satisfied while 44.23% or 23 people are very satisfied. 46.15% chose "neutral". 1.92% are unsatisfied while 1.92% are very unsatisfied.

Table 1

	Frequency	Percent	Cumulative Percent
A.Very Satisfied	3	5.77	5.77
B.Satisfied	23	44.24	50.1
C. Neutral	24	46.15	96.16
D.Not Satisfied	1	1.92	98.08
E.Very Unsatisfied	1	1.92	100.0
Total	52	100.0	

4.5 The reason customers were most unhappy with WeChat experience.

Table 2

	Frequency	Percent	Cumulative Percent
A.Product is completely different from the description provided by the seller	10	19.24	19.24
B.Very expensive	8	15.38	34.62
C.Quality problem of the product	18	34.62	69.24
D.Poor after sales service; Seller does not agree for the return/exchange	8	15.38	84.62
E.Other	8	15.38	100.0
Total	52	100.0	

The results indicate that among 52 people who ever purchased products on WeChat, 19.23% or 10 people report the worst WeChat purchasing experience was caused by the inconsistency between product itself and the description provided by the seller. 15.38% thought they bought the product at a price higher. 34.62% people report quality problem of the products. 15.38% complained poor customer service on W-shopping.

4.6 Have you ever encountered consumer disputes after you purchased a product on WeChat?

Table 3

	Frequency	Percent	Cumulative Percent
A.Encountered	7	13.46	13.46
B.Encountered frequently	7	13.46	26.92
C.Encountered occasionally	10	19.23	46.15
D.Never encountered	28	53.85	100.0
Total	52	100.0	

Among 52 people who ever purchased products on WeChat, 13.46% or 7 people reported that they encountered consumer disputes.13.46% people encountered frequently. 19.23% encountered occasionally. 53.85% or 28 people never encountered consumer disputes on WeChat.

4.7 What method you will take to protect your rights when you encountered disputes on WeChat shopping?

Among 52 people who ever purchased products on WeChat, 67.31% or 35 people choose to negotiate with the seller when they encountered disputes on W-shopping while 15.38% choose to file a complaint, and 9.62% choose to give up their rights.

Table 4

	Frequency	Percent
A. Negotiate with the seller directly	35	67.31
B.File a compaint	8	15.38
C.Give up and keep silence	5	9.62
D.Other	48	7.69

4.8 Which actions did sellers take to compensate you when the products you purchased on WeChat had quality problem or you were not satisfactory?

Table 5

	Frequency	Percent
A.Return or exchange the product within seven days of purchasing	37	71.15
B.Exchange the product with seven days of purchasing, but no return	14	26.92
C.No return or exchange after selling	8	15.38

Among 52 people who ever purchased products on WeChat,71.15% or 37 people report that they wished the seller would agree to return or exchange the product within seven days of purchasing. 26.92% report the seller agreed to return the product within seven days but not for an exchange. 15.38% report the seller chose no return or exchange policy.

4.9 Do customers trust WeChat?

The data shows that 1% or 2% people report they absolutely trust W-shopping. 10.5% report they trust. 63.4% people are neutral. 18.8% people report they do not trust W-shopping while 6.3% report they do not trust W-shopping at all.

Figure 6

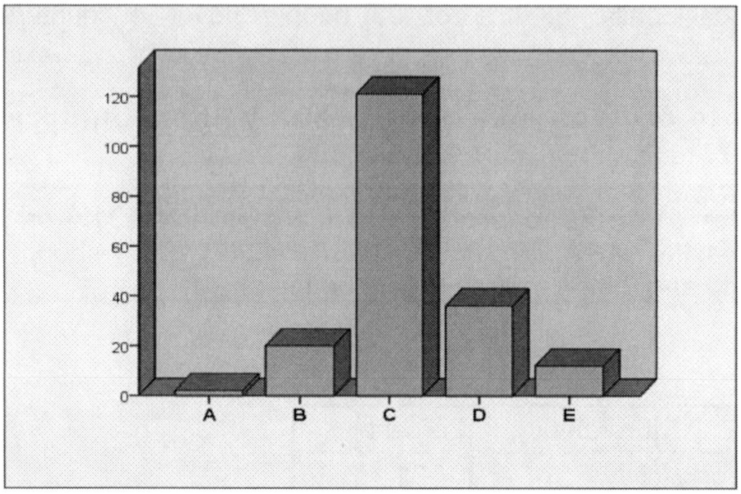

A.Abosolutely trust B.Trut C.Neutral D.Not trust E.Absolutely no trust

4.10 What can enhance customers' trust level on W-shopping?

Table 6

	Frequency	Percent
A.Product certification	126	65.97
B.Invoice	82	42.93
C.Combined with physical store	120	62.83
D.User reviews/comments	76	39.79
E.Other	34	17.8

Table 6 shows that 66% people think product certification can enhance the level of trust toward W-shopping. 42.9% people choose store receipt. 62.8% prefers to buy products via W-shopping from a seller which has physical stores. 39.8% people report they will have more trust on W-shopping if they can find user reviews or comments on the product.

4.11 Consumer acceptability of daily ads on WeChat groups.

Figure 7

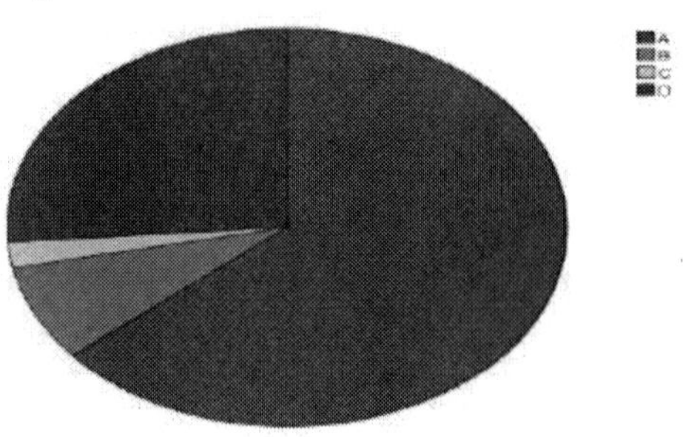

A. 1-3 times B.4-6 times C. more than 7 times D. Unacceptable

Figure 7 shows that 63.9% people can accept 1-3 ads on a We-Chat group. 7.9% think 4-6 ads a day is acceptable. Only 2.1% accept more than 7 ads a day. 26.2% people report that they cannot accept any ads in a We-Chat group.

4.12 What channel college students purchased cosmetics mainly from?

Figure 8

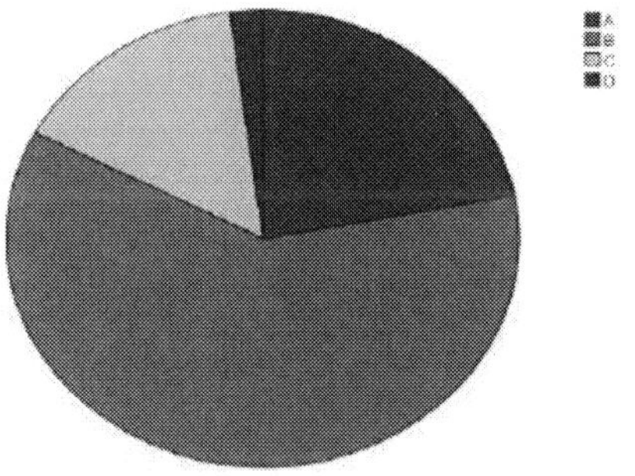

A.Supermarket B.Boutique C.Online Seller D.WeChat Seller

As shown in Figure 8, 22% people report they purchase cosmetics in supermarket. 60.7% people buy in boutiques. 15.2% people choose online sellers while only 2.1% choose WeChat seller to buy cosmetics.

4.13 What do customers think the quality of cosmetic purchased from WeChat?

Figure 9

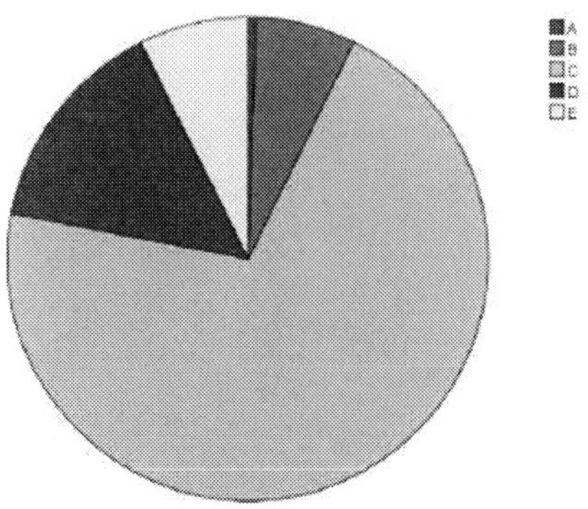

A.Very Good B.Good C.Neutral D.Bad E.Very bad

As shown in Figure 9, 0.5% people think the quality of cosmetics they purchased from We-Chat is very good while 6.8% people think it is good. 70.7% people the quality is normal. 14.7% people report it is not good while 7.3% report very bad.

4.14 What factors may influence your decision of purchasing cosmetics from WeChat?

Figure 10

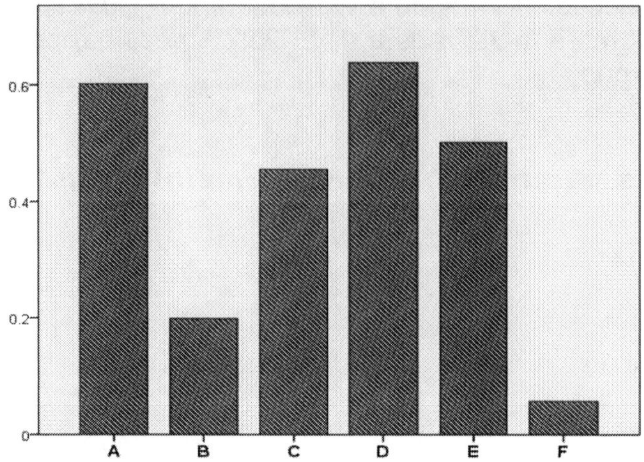

A. Know the seller
B. Seller exhibition of the product
C. Fair price
D. Assurance of product quality
E. Assurance of after sales service
F. Other

Figure 10 shows that 60.2% people think knowing the seller is the main factor that influence their purchasing decision on WeChat. 19.9% people report the product exhibition provided by the seller has impact. Additionally, 45.6% people rated fair price, 63.9% people choose assurance of product quality and 50.3% people think the assurance of after sales service is the main factor.

4.15 What type of promotion program may attract customers in W-shopping?

Figure 11

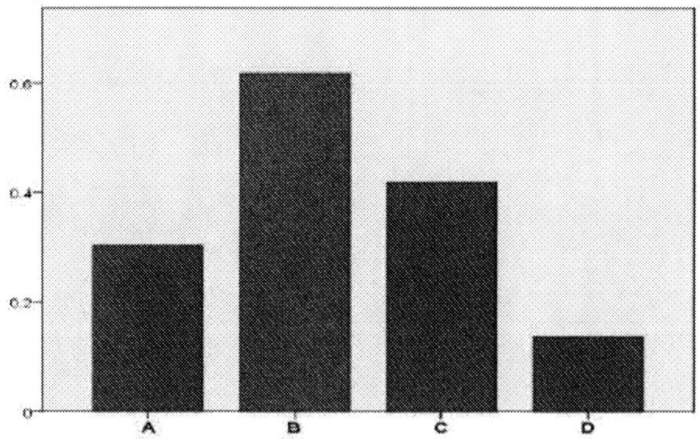

A. Thumb-up discount
B.Forwarding message discount
C.Holiday discount
D.Quantity discount
E.Other

The result shows that more than 30% people think "thumb-up" discount may attract them. 61.8% people are attracted by holiday discount. 41.9% people are interested in quantity discount. 13.6% people choose other ways。

4.16 Hypothesis testing

To test whether perceived quality is related to trust, we use χ^2 test of independence with $\alpha = 0.05$ as criterion for significance. The results show it is statistically significant, χ^2 (16, N=191) = 314.906, $p < .01$ Based on this finding, we can infer consumers are more likely to trust W-shopping when they perceive high quality products on WeChat. Thus, hypothesis 1 is supported.

To test whether trust is related to satisfaction, we use χ^2 test of independence with $\alpha = 0.05$ as criterion for significance. The results show it is statistically significant, χ^2 (20, N=191) = 99.35, $p < .01$. This supports the notion that consumers are more likely to be satisfied with W-shopping when they trust WeChat sellers. Thus, hypothesis 2 is supported.

Finally, to test whether satisfaction is related to customer purchase, we use χ^2 test of independence with $\alpha = 0.05$ as criterion for significance. The results show it is statistically significant, χ^2 (4, N=191) = 87.703, $p < .01$, which indicates that consumers are more likely to purchase on WeChat when they are satisfied with W-shopping. Thus, hypothesis 3 is supported.

CONCLUSIONS AND DISCUSSIONS

This paper reports Chinese college students shopping experience on WeChat. It further examines the roles of perceived product quality and trust in customer satisfaction and purchase judgments in the process of W-shopping. The results support that pre-purchase perceived quality relates to trust, which in turn affects post purchase consumer satisfaction leading to customer loyalty in W-shopping. These results validate Singh and Sirdeshmukh (2000) research model in the new W-shopping environment.

This study also has many practical implications. Even though W-shopping is conducted in a friend circle, it is still critical for sellers to create trust and satisfactory shopping process because some sellers may sell inferior products, sell generic products at higher price, or fail to provide post-purchase customer service. In the early development stage, product quality is a key factor that determines the growth and success of W-shopping in the future. In order for WeChat to grow effectively, it must establish trust between buyers and sellers.

Based on a recent report concerning W-shopping ("Techinasia.com"), issues with quality of products purchase via WeChat commerce are still prevalent. At the moment, it lacks the oversight of a traditional ecommerce platform. As one Sina (one of the largest Chinese online media company) commenter put it: "Taobao has fake products but at least there's platform supervision. On WeChat you just have to trust that [the seller] has a conscience. It's unreliable" ("Uschinahpa.com"). In W-shopping context, perceived product quality is a critical element of prepurchase assessment. In lieu of institutional safeguards (e.g., regulations) sellers can take action themselves to convey trust to the buyer and legitimize the purchasing process through W-shopping. The sellers could exhibit products in a group, provide an official certificate for the product, issue official receipts after purchase, encourage user review/comments, or even combine with brick and mortar store to convince "friends" in the WeChat group to buy. It is also important for sellers to ensure the product quality through offering fair price, and improving after sales services such as offering detailed product return or exchange policies to increase trust which will lead to higher satisfaction and attract repeat buyers.

Interestingly, for those people who ever shopped on WeChat, only 3.84% were either dissatisfied or very dissatisfied with the products as indicated on Table 1. It proves W-shopping channel does have big potential in China. The question of how to promote products on WeChat and attract more people to W-shopping remains critical for the expansion of business.

Asked about the trustworthiness of W-shopping, a quarter respondents report either "not trust" or "absolutely not trust" (Figure 6). Overall trustworthiness of W-shopping remains low in comparison to e-commerce websites. "Product certification", "combination with physical store", "invoice", and "user reviews" are listed as top factors that could enhance the level of W-shopping trust (Table 6).

The results show 63.9% of respondents can accept 1 to 3 WeChat ads on a daily basis, while 26.2% report they do not like ads on WeChat at all (Figure 7). WeChat is a friends circle. The group is formed based on either the connections of people or the common hobbies or topics in life or work. Ads on WeChat should be carefully chosen and designed to meet the common interests of the group, or either the advertiser could be blocked from the group..

Regarding cosmetic products shopping on WeChat, only 2.1% bought from WeChat. A majority customers purchased from either boutiques or supermarkets (Figure 8). It seems cosmetics users want to try the product in person first instead of taking the risk of purchasing online without experiencing it first.

This study reports "product quality", "knowing the seller", "after sales service", and "fair price" are some top factors influencing customers' purchase decision on WeChat. Because all respondents are college students whose purchasing power is limited, low price may become an important factor, however the quality of some products may be affected by the low price. That may be why 22% people who ever bought products on WeChat report quality problem (Figure 9). Since "Know the seller" is one of top factors leading to a purchase, sellers should increase interactions with group members on WeChat.

LIMITATIONS/DIRECTIONS OF FUTURE RESEARCH

To the best of our knowledge, this is the first empirical study in emerging area of W-shopping, and it presents a solid foundation for future research. W-shopping has massive potential in China and beyond. According to Shao's (2015) report, the e-commerce market in China was $198 billion in 2014, and is showing strong growth. Additionally, B2C Internet-shopping was close to $40 billion and 520 million people shopped online while 22.9% of them used cell phone for internet shopping in 2014. Future research could also specifically focus on smaller sellers to determine potentially unknown barriers to entry in this market. Currently only 11% of private WeChat sellers' monthly sales volume is above $16,000 and there are only 3% above $166,000 on average. It is critically important to examine the W-shopping process in order to increase the sales volume of W-shopping among the majority of sellers in the market.

Future studies should also expand beyond college students to determine the generalizeability of the results to other demographics. Additionally, more research is needed to further consider other antecedents of trust, along with risk, perceived benefits, and customer loyalty.

REFERENCES

Blau, P.M. (1964). *Exchange and power in social life*. New York: John Wiley.

Buchanan J. (1965). An economic theory of clubs. *Economica*, 32(125), N.S., pp. 1-14. Reprinted in Robert E. Kuenne, ed. (2000). Readings in Social Welfare, pp. 73-85.

Chaudhuri, A. and Holbrook, M.B. (2001). The chain of effects from brand trust and brand affect to brand performance: the role of brand loyalty. *Journal of Marketing*, 65(2), pp. 81-93

Cristobal, E., Flavian, C. and Guinaliu, M. (2007). Perceived e-service quality (PeSQ): Measurement validation and effects on consumer satisfaction and web site loyalty. *Journal of Service Theory and Practice*, 17(3), pp. 317-340

Doney, P. M. and J. P. Cannon (1997). An examination of the nature of trust in buyer-seller relationships. *Journal of Marketing*, 61, 2, pp.35-51.

Grabosky, P. (2001). *The nature of trust online*. *The Age*, pp.1-12

Fornell, C., Johnson, M.D., Anderson, E.W., Cha, J. and Bryant, B.E. (1996). The American customer satisfaction index: nature, purpose, and findings. *Journal of Marketing*, 60(4), pp. 7-18

Harris, L. C., & Goode, M. M. H. (2004). The four levels of loyalty and the pivotal role of trust: A study of online services dynamics. *Journal of Retailing*, *80*, pp.139-158.

Hawes, J. M, Kenneth, E. M., & Swan, J. E. (1989). Trust earning perceptions of sellers an Buyers. *Journal of Personal Selling and Sales Management,* 9, pp.1-8.

Jarvenpaa, S.L., Tractinsky, N., Saarinen, L., Vitale, M. (1999). Consumer trust in an Internet store: a cross-cultural validation. *Journal of Computer Mediated Communication*, 5 (2)

Kim, H.W., Xu, Y.J. and Koh, J. (2004). A comparison of online trust building factors between potential customers and repeat customers. *Journal of the Association for Information Systems*, 5(10), pp.392-420

Schelling, T.C. (1971). Dynamic Models of Segregation. *Journal of Mathematical Sociology*, 1, 143-186.

Shao, J. (2015). Discussion on WeChat shopping status and future. *Modern Market*, 2015(6).

Singh, J. and Sirdeshmukh, D. (2000). Agency and trust mechanisms in consumer satisfaction and loyalty judgments. *Journal of the Academy of Marketing Science*, 28(1), pp. 150-167

http://www.tencent.com/en-us/content/ir/news/2015/attachments/20150513.pdf (Extracted 8-30-2015)

https://www.techinasia.com/unsafe-product-alert-careful-buy-wechat/ (Extracted 8-30-2015)

http://technode.com/2015/01/22/wechat-reaches-1-1b-registered-accounts-440m-mau/ (Extracted 8-30-2015) http://thenextweb.com/apps/2014/03/19/whatsapp-rival-wechat-is-narrowing-the-gap-as-it-passes-355-million-monthly-active-users/ (Extracted 8-30-2015)

Urban, G.L., Sultan, F., Qualls, W.J. (2000). Placing trust at the center of your Internet strategy. *Sloan Management Review*, 42 (1), pp. 39–48

http://uschinahpa.org/wp-content/uploads/2015/02/China-Updates-Issue-143-2015-5-29.pdf?&session-id=7a9fdc838983f8ec3473f8c5457a1b15 (Extracted 9-1-2015)

Voss, G., Parasuraman, A., and Grewal, D. (1998). The roles of price, performance and expectations in determining satisfaction in service exchanges. *Journal of Marketing*, 62 (October), pp. 46-61

Wang X. (2014). *The changing landscape of china's consumerism.* CP Chandos Publishing, pp.1-12

http://www.weishangshijie.com/hyrd/164.html (Extracted 7-20-2015)

AUTHOR INDEX

Aase, G. 511, 1269
Abebe, M. 825
Abreu, M. 1559
Agarwal, A. 1356
Agyei-Owusu, B. 748
Akaribo, J. 748
Akcam, B. 973
Alikaj, A. 398
Alqahtani, A. 1257
Andoh-Baidoo, F. 748
Angeles, R. 774
Asamoah, D. 748
Assis, N. 1574
Avoaka, P. 1058
Bagchi, K. 698
Bari, A. 587
Bayrak, T. 973
Behara, R. 497
Berenson, M. 1797
Bernardes, E. 1325
Bhadani, A. 21
Blackstock, R. 587
Booker, Q. 1678
Botella, J. 309
Brito, L. 847
Bumblauskas, D. 376, 1479
Burdwell, R. 670
Burke, J. 1325
Chakraborty, S. 54
Chang, I. 480
Changchit, C. 203, 1042
Chavarria, J. 1722
Chen, J. 1346, 1605
Chen, L. 659
Chen, X. 659
Chern, C. 44
Chhabria, R. 1180
Cho, Y. 1627
Choi, S. 1446
Choi, T. 1214
Chou, D. 215
Christodoulidou, N. 1505
Clauss, T. 809
Coy, S. 281, 766
Crawford, J. 766
David, D. 1601
Davies, J. 1013, 1762
DelVecchio, M. 1647
Demiral, E. 1523
Deng, H. 1505
Di Mauro, C. 1083
DiCicco, J. 497
Dickinson, J. 1677, 1751
Dickson, A. 1466
DiRusso, D. 1823
Dole, C. 1722
Dowlatshahi, S. 1688
Escobari, D. 1660
Evans, J. 187
Faisal, M. 293
Feller, A. 343
Flynn, B. 847
Fontem, B. 366
Ford, M. 187
Foroughi, A. 1585
Fortsch, S. 1146
Fratocchi, L. 1083
Frederick, L. 1064
Gao, J. 1823
Gerhart, N. 156
Ghosh, S. 956
Gibson, S. 1574
Giraud-Carrier, F. 1356
Goerzen, A. 689
Goo, J. 632
Gopalakrishnan, M. 343, 896
Graefe-Anderson, R. 366
Graham, R. 81, 1115
Green, R. 670
Gu, Q. 1409
Gudigantala, N. 1559
Gupta, S. 1257
Ha, Q. 1346, 1605
Harrison, J. 1280
Harrison, S. 1013, 1762
He, X. 1206
He, Y. 676
Heinrichs, J. 599, 741
Hofstetter, J. 689, 1689
Hong, P. 1416
Hossain, S. 1138, 1170
Hota, H. 1185
Hou, K. 180
Hsiao, C. 582
Huang, C. 632
Huang, T. 1752
Hung, K. 1622
Huo, B. 1400
Hwang, H. 14, 480
Hwang, J. 524
Hysell, M. 1064
Jagani, S. 839
Jana, R. 1075
Jenkins, P. 874
Jin, Y. 1192
Jitpaiboon, T. 1409
Johnson, D. 223
Johnson, M. 223
Johnson, N. 1064
Joo, S. 931

AUTHOR INDEX

Jothimani, D. 1365
Jung, J. 524
Kaushik, R. 1574
Keane, M. 950
Kersten, G. 537
Khan, H. 551
Kim, D. 1214
Kim, J. 1289
Kim, K. 459
Klaus, T. 203
Knight, R. 497
Kocakulah, M. 1585
Korir, M. 1064
Krehbiel, T. 1806
Krishnamoorthy, M. 341
Kung, L. 44
Kunnathur, A. 839, 1699
Kuo, C. 969
Kuritsyn, G. 1605
Ledwith, A. 136
Lehmberg, D. 1745
Lei, M. 1505
Li, J. 1622
Li, Y. 1532
Li, Z. 969
Liao, Q. 1146
Lien, C. 1
Lim, J. 599, 741
Lim, K. 599, 741
Lin, C. 1699
Lin, E. 14, 480
Lin, L. 180
Lin, S. 1752
Lindsey, M. 576
Lo, A. 874
Lo, L. 1752
Lonkani, R. 1042
Lu, H. 1206
Ludden, P. 136
Lunt, A. 376
Ma, J. 113
Mackelprang, A. 1325
Mai, F. 187
Manning, D. 643
Manyoky, L. 1585
Marsillac, E. 1192
Martz, B. 643
McGrath, M. 1532
Medina, E. 1378
Merhi, M. 505, 1058
Mesak, H. 113, 587
Metcalf, A. 731
Meybodi, M. 251
Meyer, B.C. 168
Michalski, M. 309
Miller, D. 1806
Mohan, S. 343
Morrison, R. 1023, 1660, 1722
Morton, A. 1280
Mueller, M. 689
Mukhopadhyay, S. 698
Mutlu, F. 125
Nam, K. 632
Nandi, S. 435
Narasimhan, R. 309
Nargundkar, S. 618
Nemer, C. 721
Nesterkin, D. 81
Ngamassi, L. 1772
Nguyen, C. 398
Ning, W. 398
Niranjan, T. 95, 341
Nwankpa, J. 604
Oestreich, N. 950
Orzes, G. 1083
Papadopoulos, A. 559, 986
Park, B. 1064
Park, M. 931
Park, S. 459, 459
Parkes, D. 721
Parkman, R. 874
Parsa, P. 97
Patel, S. 505
Pattabhiraman, S. 343
Pavur, R. 576
Peng, H. 44
Penumatsa, L. 1356
Petersen, C. 511, 1269
Pick, J. 907
Pohl, E. 97
Pokharel, S. 125
Porterfield, T. 81
Powless, S. 1128
Qazi, A. 1466
Qin, B. 1416
Quigley, J. 1466
Radhakrishnan, A. 1601
Rahman, S. 1772
Raisinghani, M. 1574
Ramakrishnan, T. 1772
Rao, D. 21
Rao, M. 1180
Ravinder, H. 1797
Re, L. 1280
Rebman, C. 1678
Reeves, J. 874
Ren, L. 124
Rew, D. 267
Rosales, J. 907
Rossetti, M. 97

AUTHOR INDEX

Rothenberger, M. 1505
Roumani, Y. 604, 604
Ruppel, C. 824
Sage, J. 1780
Sage, L. 1780
Saglam, U. 238, 1523
Samaddar, S. 698
Sampet, J. 1042
Sanchez, A. 825
Sankar, C. 1326
Sarkar, A. 907
Sarker, B. 1138, 1170
Sartor, M. 1083
Scarpin, M. 847
Schafer, S. 1128
Schmitt, N. 1280
Sengupta, S. 341
Shankar, R. 21, 1365
Sharma, D. 1075, 1185
Sharma, H. 1075, 1185
Shbool, M. 97
Sheff, P. 1115
Sher, M. 14
Shipley, J. 281
Shipley, M. 281
Shrikhande, M. 618
Silver, S. 814, 1391
Smith, J. 459
Smith, S. 1409
Song, J. 1326
Sonmez, E. 125
Strakos, J. 1540
Su, H. 1797
Sun, S. 1326
Talanker, S. 1239
Taleb, A. 559
Talib, F. 293
Tangpong, C. 809, 1622, 1745
Taube, L. 721
TeDuits, D. 766
Tibbett, H. 366
Ugray, Z. 1318
Uwemi, S. 551
Vahidov, R. 537
Van Vliet, P. 411
Vargas, R. 824
Vinaja, R. 670
Wallace, S. 839
Wang, J. 1823
Wang, P. 1
Wang, Q. 1400
Watson, E. 1289
Welbourne, J. 1722
Welter, C. 1325
Wen, M. 1
Widjaja, A. 1605
Williamson, J. 950
Wu, K. 1
Wu, S. 435
Yadav, S. 1365
Yeh, C. 1
Yildiz, H. 125
Yoo, C. 632
Yoo, S. 931, 1214
Yu, B. 537
Yue, J. 969
Yurova, Y. 824
Zhang, F. 223
Zhang, H. 113
Zhang, M. 1505
Zhang, S. 97
Zhang, Y. 1416
Zhao, X. 1400
Zheng, Y. 1823

Decision Sciences Institute
University of Houston
C.T. Bauer College of Business
334 Melcher Hall, Suite 325
Houston, TX 77204-6021
USA

ISBN 978-1-5108-4273-1

9 781510 842731